Shakespeare Lexicon
and Quotation Dictionary

A COMPLETE DICTIONARY

OF ALL THE ENGLISH WORDS, PHRASES AND CONSTRUCTIONS

IN THE WORKS OF THE POET

BY

ALEXANDER SCHMIDT

THIRD EDITION

REVISED AND ENLARGED

BY

GREGOR SARRAZIN

IN TWO VOLUMES

VOLUME I

A – M

DOVER PUBLICATIONS, INC.
NEW YORK

Abbreviations.

Ado	Much Ado about Nothing.	Lr.	King Lear.
All's or Alls	All's well that ends well.	Lucr.	the Rape of Lucrece.
Ant.	Antony and Cleopatra.	Mcb.	Macbeth.
Arg.	Argument.	Meas.	Measure for Measure.
As	As you like it.	M. Edd.	Modern Editors.
Caes.	Julius Caesar.	Merch.	the Merchant of Venice.
Chor.	Chorus.	Mids.	a Midsummer-night's Dream.
Compl.	A Lover's Complaint.	O. Edd.	Old Editions (i. e. the Folios as well as the Quartos; or the Folios or Quartos alone, if there are no other old editions extant).
Cor.	Coriolanus.		
Cymb.	Cymbeline.		
Ded.	Dedication.		
Epil.	Epilogue.		
Err.	Comedy of Errors.	Oth.	Othello.
F1	the Folio Edition of 1623.	Per.	Pericles.
F2	the Folio Edition of 1632.	Phoen.	the Phoenix and the Turtle.
F3	the Folio Edition of 1663.	Pilgr.	the Passionate Pilgrim.
F4	the Folio Edition of 1685.	Prol.	Prologue.
Ff	all the four Folios, as differing from the existing Quarto Editions.	Qq	the old Quarto Editions, as differing from the Folios.
Gent.	the two Gentlemen of Verona	R2	Richard II.
H4A	First Part of Henry IV.	R3	Richard III.
H4B	Second Part of Henry IV.	Rom.	Romeo und Juliet.
H5	Henry V.	Shr.	the Taming of the Shrew.
H6A	First Part of Henry VI.	Sonn.	Sonnets.
H6B	Second Part of Henry VI.	Tim.	Timon of Athens.
H6C	Third Part of Henry VI.	Tit.	Titus Andronicus.
H8	Henry VIII.	Tp.	Tempest.
Hml.	Hamlet.	Troil.	Troilus and Cressida.
Ind.	Induction.	Tw.	Twelfth Night.
John	King John.	Ven.	Venus and Adonis.
LLL	Love's Labour's Lost.	Wint.	the Winter's Tale.
		Wiv.	the Merry Wives of Windsor

The different Quarto editions are designated in the same manner as in the great Cambridge edition of Messrs. Clark and Wright.

By the initials the unchanged forms and words are meant, as they stand in the respective headings; inflected forms are denoted by their terminations preceded by a dash; f. i. under the article Grow g. means grow, —s grows, —ing growing, etc.

The quotations are from the Globe edition.

Asterisks inserted behind some articles or quotations refer to the Supplement.

Names of Authors quoted in the Supplement indicate, as a rule, editions of Shakespeare's Plays and Poems, or other well-known books connected with Shakespeare, f. i. Wyndham = Shakespeare's Poems by George Wyndham; D. H. Madden = The Diary of Master William Silence by D. H. Madden; S. Lee = A Life of Shakespeare by Sidney Lee.

This Dover edition, first published in 1971, is an unabridged republication of the third revised and enlarged edition as published by Georg Reimer in Berlin in 1902 under the former title *Shakespeare-Lexicon*.

International Standard Book Number: 0-486-22726-X
Library of Congress Catalog Card Number: 70-150407

Manufactured in the United States of America
Dover Publications, Inc.
180 Varick Street
New York, N. Y. 10014

Preface to the First Volume of the First Edition.

The present work, as differing from the existing Shakespearian glossaries, the object of which has been only to explain what has become obsolete and unintelligible in the writings of the poet, is to contain his whole vocabulary and subject the sense and use of every word of it to a careful examination.

As it was not intended to establish a critical standard, but only to furnish some of the necessary materials for criticism, it seemed convenient to lay aside, for the present, the question of the authenticity of the works generally ascribed to Shakespeare, and to consider as genuine all that has been commonly printed together as Shakespeare's, namely the thirty-six plays of the first and second Folios, together with Pericles, and the so called Poems; but to disregard the apocryphal pieces of the latest Folios as well as those which the criticism of still later times has brought into connection with the name of the poet. The stage-directions, too, even those of the earliest editions, have been left unnoticed, as it appeared more than doubtful whether they were written by Shakespeare himself.

In the present unsettled state of textual criticism it could not be decided, whether the Folios or the extant Quartos deserved greater credit. But fortunately the business of a lexicographer was, in this point at least, easier than that of an editor, who must make his choice between different lections, whereas the former may fairly content himself with registering the occurring variations. These have indeed been collated with great care wherever some authority could be attributed to the ancient texts; excluding, of course, those Quartos which the editors of the first Folio meant when speaking of *stolen and surreptitious copies, maimed and deformed by the frauds and stealths of injurious impostors*, namely the Quartos of the Merry Wives and Henry V, the 'First Part of the Contention', the 'True Tragedy, and the earliest impressions of Romeo and Juliet (1597) and of Hamlet (1603). Their variations are, at the best, of the same weight as the conjectures of modern emendators.

The example and reasons of the Cambridge editors have been decisive for adopting the modern orthography, those cases excepted when the different spelling of the old editions was evidently caused by a difference of pronunciation.

As for etymology, which ought to be the groundwork of every general dictionary, its importance seemed subordinate and sometimes even doubtful in ascertaining the sense of words in a particular period, — a period especially in which the genius of the language broke new ways, now and then even with some violence, to supply its increasing wants. Therefore the derivation of words has been neglected on purpose, except when there was no other means of finding out their meaning. Accordingly, in arranging the different significations of one and the same word, a natural and rational rather than an historical order has been observed, as it always seemed the safest way to study and explain the language of Shakespeare by itself, calling in no other help as long as it could be done without. In the definitions themselves as well as in their arrangement there will undoubtedly much be found to object against, but let it at the same time be borne in mind that it is next to impossible to draw everywhere a strict line of demarcation, and that, at any rate, the means of finding the truth for himself have always been placed within the reach of the reader.

Originally a purpose was entertained of making the quotations absolutely complete, even with respect to the most common and constantly recurring parts and forms of speech. As, however, there arose some danger of impairing the utility of the book by hiding momentous questions under cumbrous details, copious use has been made of the signs *f. i.* and *etc.* by way of indicating that sufficient proof, if needed, was offered in every page of the poet.

On the other hand, it was not quite easy to resist the temptation to make this lexicon a general repertory and store-house of Shakespearian lore by collecting and garnering up in it all that the industry of two centuries had done in this branch of literature. But, for once, first thoughts were best. In pursuing too vast a project, the principal design of the work was too likely to have sometimes been lost sight of. Following, therefore, the old maxim that the half is more than the whole, and keeping within the proposed bounds, the task was limited, in whatever reached beyond them, to the smallest possible compass. Obscurities not originating in the peculiar use of words, but in the poet's train of thought, have been considered as quite out of the question and entirely left to the commentators.

Even thus the work would remain extensive enough to make any superfluity a fault. Erroneous opinions and wrong conjectures of modern editors were not admitted, unless they had become too popular to be altogether left unnoticed. Obvious and evident things, that stood in no need of authority, were left to speak for themselves; and only in doubtful cases, or if there had been some particular merit in finding the truth, it seemed unfair not to give every one his due. But after all, truth cannot fare better than to be received as a matter of course.

Foreign and dialectic words and phrases used by Shakespeare will be collected in an appendix to the second volume, for which are also reserved some grammatical remarks designed to prove the justness of several interpretations which would else, perhaps, appear arbitrary and hazardous. They are fewer in number than was at first anticipated, for the excellent Shakespearian Grammar of Mr. Abbott, published in the meantime, together with Sidney Walker's Critical Examination of the Text of Sh., reduced the task to that of a gleaner following in the footsteps of reapers and picking up a few neglected ears.

Of what use the work will be, the event is to prove; — planned it was with a view to make the poet better understood than before; —

to lay a firmer foundation for the criticism of his text; — to furnish reliable materials for English lexicography, which has, since the time of Samuel Johnson, increased in extent rather than in intrinsic value; — to set right, although only one, yet certainly the most prominent landmark in the history of the English language.

While the general reader will look for assistance in the definitions and explanations, scholars and critics will be soonest pleased, if satisfied by the exactness of the quotations. Therefore communications concerning errata will be extremely welcome.

Merely practical considerations prevailed in choosing the English language for the interpretations. No doubt the English of a German will often be found exceptionable and try the indulgence and kindness of the reader. But the author had no greater ambition, — if a lexicographer may be allowed to be ambitious — than to be useful also to born Englishmen.

Koenigsberg in Pr., Febr. 1874.

A. SCHMIDT.

Preface to the Second Volume of the First Edition.

The Appendix of this second volume will contain, besides what has been promised in the preface of the first, a list of the Shakespearian words forming the latter part in compositions, to meet a want not only felt by the author himself on many occasions, but intimated to him by some literary friends. In applying to it, it must always be borne in mind that it pretends to no higher claim than to be a supplement to this dictionary, and has no other object than to complete the quotations of the respective articles, by setting before the reader the whole range of evidence to be found in the works of the poet. For in very many cases the sense of simple words could not be distinctly ascertained except from their compounds. Wherever the boundary line between English and Latin or French composition was hardly discernible, it was thought better to do too much than too little.

One advantage, at least, was gained by the new revision of the whole vocabulary thus instituted. It led to the detection of some words — indexed on the next following leaf — that had been overlooked by the compiler, — a fault which, if nobody else, those at least will be inclined to pardon who ever have been engaged in a similar labour.

The reception the first volume has met with has been, in some respects, beyond the most sanguine expectations. The kind judgments passed on it by the most competent critics were indeed the more gratifying, as they did not, and could not possibly, touch the general design and tendency of the work, but turned on details and the manner of treating particular questions. The justness and soundness of a method cannot be put to a better test than in its bearing on single points at issue. 'Assurance now is made double sure' that much that at first sight, and considered by itself, could not but seem objectionable, will be seen in another light, when in time the peculiar nature and the fundamental law of the whole will be fully perceived.

To make the poet his own interpreter, by discarding all preconceived opinions and subordinating all external means of information to those offered by himself, was throughout the leading principle of the work. What Aristarchus once did for Homer, and Galen for Hippocrates, was yet to be done for Shakespeare. We beg to refer the reader to an extract from Galen's praef. voc. Hippocr. quoted in Professor Lehrs' work 'De Aristarchi studiis Homericis' p. 44: Ὅσα τοίνυν τῶν ὀνομάτων ἐν μὲν τοῖς πάλαι χρόνοις ἦν συνήθη, νυνὶ δ' οὐκέτι ἐστί, τὰ μὲν τοιαῦτα γλώσσας καλοῦσι καὶ ταῦτα ἐξηγησόμενος ἔρχομαι· τὰ δὲ ἄλλα ὅσα ζητήσεως μὲν οὐχ ἥττονος προσδεῖται, συνήθη δέ ἐστιν εἰς τάδε, κατὰ τὰς τῶν συγγραμμάτων αὐτῶν ἐξηγήσεις ἄμεινον ἐπισκοπεῖσθαι. Τίς γὰρ ἡ κρίσις καὶ τί τό θεῖον καὶ τί τὸ ἀρτίως καὶ τίς ἡ ἐπ' ἄκρων εὐεξία καὶ πάνθ' ὅσα τοιαῦτα λόγου παμμήκους εἰς ἐξήγησιν δεῖται, συνήθη δέ ἐστιν οὐδὲν ἧττον ἢ βίος καὶ βραχὺς καὶ τέχνη καὶ μακρὰ καὶ καιρός καὶ ὀξύς· καίτοι καὶ τούτων ἔνια δεῖταὶ τινος ἐξηγήσεως. Ὅθεν ἔμοιγε καὶ θαυμάζειν ἐπῆλθε τῶν ἅπασαν ἐξηγεῖσθαι τὴν Ἱπποκράτους λέξιν ἐπαγγειλαμένων, εἰ μὴ συνίσασιν ὅτι πλείω παραλείπουσιν ὧν διδάρκουσι.

To this Prof. Lehrs observes: Haec omnia primus intellexit in Homero et praestitit Aristarchus. Quare non scripsit glossas, sed in continua poetae interpretatione accuratissime versatus est, in consuetis vocabulis, quorum et ad majorem Homericorum locorum partem plerumque pertinet utilitas et explicatio certior, plus etiam quam in rarioribus et antiquitate obscuratis operae ponens et ne quid praetermittatur verbum verbo reddens. Abjecit illas doctrinae sarcinas, non tam existimans, ex aliis scriptoribus multa ad Homerum illustrandum promi posse quam cavendum esse ne aliorum consuetudine temere ad poetam translata imprudentes in vitia et errores incurramus.

Let us subjoin, for the use of Shakespearian text-emendators, a few more citations from the same work:

Galen (praef. ad L. VI Epid.): πολὺ βέλτιον ἔδοξέ μοι φυλάττοντι τὴν ἀρχαίαν γραφὴν ἀεὶ μὲν σπουδάζειν ἐκείνην ἐξηγεῖσθαι, μὴ δυνηθέντι δέ ποτε τοῦτο πρᾶξαι πιθανὴν τὴν ἐπανόρθωσιν αὐτῆς ποιεῖσθαι.

Quintilian (Instit. orat. IX, 4, 39): Quaedam in veteribus libris reperta mutare imperiti solent et, dum librariorum insectari volunt inscientiam, suam confitentur.

Lehrs (p. 358): Ars critica primum elaborat ut scriptores, quos pauci mss. corruptos exhibent, sine summa offensione legi possint; partim imperfecta ars multa non intelligit inscientia, quae tollit ne quid relinquatur quod absurdum esse putat. Sed gliscentibus studiis, codicibus pluribus paratis, rerum sermonisque scientia vulgata, arte interpretandi exculta, multis obscurioribus locis per variorum tentamina tandem reclusis, in arctiores se fines contrahit, et quo magis primi magistri peccaverunt, eo magis jam ipso contradicendi studio ad fontes suos revertitur.

Koenigsberg Pr., Oct. 1875.

A. S.

Preface to the Second Edition.

This new edition of the Shakespeare Lexicon should properly be called a mere reimpression. The work being stereotyped, there was no scope for comprehensive alterations and improvements. A complete reconstruction that would have answered the many valuable suggestions of other Shakespeare students or even the compiler's own advanced views — especially concerning the comparative authenticity of the Folios and Quartos — was quite out of the question. His task was confined to the correction of misprints and to some small additions for which room could be got by expunging what seemed less important.

But, after all, it is perhaps best as it is. Desirable as it may be to an author entirely to remodel a work of the shortcomings of which he has become painfully aware, there is no denying the fact that such new editions altered and improved into quite new books are, as a rule, an annoyance to the public. Nobody is so rich as not to repine at being obliged to buy the same book three or four times. Indeed, it ought to be a law in the republic of letters that essential changes in books should be separately published in the form of supplements and not worked into the whole so as materially to change its form and character.

Besides, in such a kind of book as this lexicon it is not so much in the opinions of the author that its usefulness consists as in the accuracy with which the necessary materials are brought together to enable those who consult it to form an opinion of their own. And of this the reader may be assured that in the revision of the work no pains have been spared and that the correctness of the quotations will be found all but absolute.

Koenigsberg, Dec. 1885.

A. S.

Preface to the Third Edition.

The text of the third edition, published after the Author's death, had to remain essentially unaltered, for reasons mentioned in the former preface. Only very few slight mistakes in the quotations have been found and corrected, and several short explanations added. Besides, some asterisks were inserted, which refer to the Supplement. A few additions to the Appendix (Quotations from foreign languages and Provincialisms) have been indicated by brackets.

The Supplement contains a compilation of new interpretations of difficult words and phrases, arranged in alphabetical order, selected from different modern annotated editions and other books. As a rule, the opinions of English scholars only have been reproduced, who are the most legitimate commentators of the great English poet. With such interpreters as Murray, Skeat, W. A. Wright, Furnivall, Dowden, Sidney Lee, Ellacombe, D. H. Madden, Wyndham, E. K. Chambers, Herford, Gollancz, Boas, among others, we need scarcely look anywhere else for help. In a few cases, however, some interpretations given by American, Dutch, or German scholars (Furness, Grant White, Hudson, Ch. Allen, Stoffel, Van Dam, Brandl, Max Foerster, W. Franz, Kluge, Koppel, Schroeer, Wetz, and a few others), or some conjectures and explanations of my own have been added.

Sincere thanks are due to Professors Brandl, Foerster, Kluge, Wetz, and to Dr. Vordieck for kind advice and valuable suggestions.

Breslau, Dec. 1901.

Gregor Sarrazin.

A.

A, the first letter of the alphabet: LLL V, 1, 50. 58. Tw. II, 5, 118 sq.

A, a note in music: Shr. III, 1, 74.

A or **An,** indef. art., the two forms differing as at present. *An* for *a: an hair,* Tp. I, 2, 30. *an happy end,* John III, 2, 10. *an hasty-witted body,* Shr. V, 2, 40. *an Hebrew,* Gent. II, 5, 57. *an heretic,* Wiv. IV, 4, 9. Wint. II, 3, 114. John III, 1, 175. H8 III, 2, 102. *an hospital,* LLL V, 2, 881. *an host,* H6B III, 1, 342. Ant. II, 5, 87. *an hostess,* Troil. III, 3, 253. *an household,* H4B IV, 1, 95. *an hundred,* LLL IV, 2, 63. R2 IV, 16. H6B IV, 8, 59. H6C II, 5, 81. H8 V, 1, 172. Cor. V, 5, 114. Caes. II, 2, 77. IV, 3, 175. Hml. II, 2, 383 (Qq. *a hundred*). Lr. I, 1, 135. *an hypocrite,* Meas. V, 41. H4B II, 2, 64. Per. I, 1, 122. *an eunuch,* Tw. I, 2, 56. H6B IV, 2, 175. Cor. III, 2, 114. Tit. II, 3, 128. Ant. II, 5, 5. III, 7, 15. *an humour,* H5 II, 1, 58. *an union,* Mids. III, 2, 210 (Ff *a union*). *an universal,* Troil. I, 3, 121. Caes. I, 1, 49. *an urinal,* Gent. II, 1, 41. *an usurer,* II, 1, 196. *an usurper,* H6B I, 3, 188; cf. Oth. I, 3, 346. Before *one* generally *a; f. i.* Wiv. III, 3, 122. Meas. III, 1, 71. Err. III, 2, 91. IV, 2, 23. Cor. III, 1, 105. Mcb. IV, 3, 101; cf. *Such-a-one.* Twice *such an one:* Mcb. IV, 3, 66. Ant. I, 2, 118. *An* before *w: have an wish,* Per. IV, 4, 2. Of the original indiscriminate use of *an* before consonants as well as vowels a trace is left in the pun of Mrs Quickly: *An fool's head,* Wiv. I, 4, 134.

Superfluous repetition of the ind. art. before adjectives: *a blasting and a scandalous breath,* Meas. V, 122. *a present and a dangerous courtesy,* IV, 2, 171. *a virtuous and a reverend lady,* Err. V, 134. *a dulcet and a heavenly sound,* Shr. Ind. 1, 51. *a common and an outward man,* Alls III, 1, 11. *a maiden and an innocent hand,* John IV, 2, 252. *a mighty and a fearful head,* H4A III, 2, 167. *a slobbery and a dirty farm,* H5 III, 5, 13. *a peaceful and a sweet retire,* IV, 3, 86. *a puissant and a mighty power,* H6B IV, 9, 25. *a weighty and a serious brow,* H8 Prol. 2. *a dismal and a fatal end,* Mcb. III, 5, 21. *a nipping and an eager air,* Hml. I, 4, 2. *a tyrannous and a damned light,* II, 2, 482 (F1 *and damned*). *a malignant and a turbaned Turk,* Oth. V, 2, 352. No less before adjectives placed after their substantives: *a proper stripling and an amorous,* Shr. I, 2, 144. *a goodly portly man and a corpulent,* H4A II, 4, 464. *a goodly dwelling and*

a rich, H4B V, 3, 6. *an honest gentleman, and a courteous, and a kind,* Rom. II, 5, 56. *a very valiant Briton and a good,* Cymb. IV, 2, 369.

As before *hundred* and *thousand* (q. v.) the art. is, though seldom, found before other numerals: *never a one of you,* Tim. V, 1, 96. *not a one of them,* Mcb. III, 4, 131. *a 'leven,* Merch. II, 2, 171 (Q1 *eleven*). *a fourteen,* H4B III, 2, 53. Similarly before *many,* q. v.

Its use after *as, how, so* and *such* is in general conformable to the now prevailing rule (f. i. *so fair a house,* Tp. I, 2, 458. *as good a thing,* V, 169. *how high a pitch,* R2 I, 1, 109), and the passage in H6B IV, 9, 17: *continue still in this so good a mind,* cannot be called an exception; but there are a few instances of its omission: *in so profound abysm,* Sonn. 112, 9. *as good deed,* H4A II, 1, 35 (Ff *as good a deed*). *with as big heart,* Cor. III, 2, 128. It seems to have strayed from its place in the following expressions: *so rare a wondered father,* Tp. IV, 123 (= so rarely wondered a father, i. e. a father endowed with such a rare power of working miracles). *so fair an offered chain,* Err. III, 2, 186. *so new a fashioned robe,* John IV, 2, 27. cf. *such a coloured periwig,* Gent. IV, 4, 196; the phrases *so rare a wonder, such a colour* etc. being treated as simple words, from which adjectives in *ed* might be derived.

Similarly placed between comparatives and their substantives: *with more tame a tongue,* Meas. II, 2, 46; especially when preceded by *no: no better a musician,* Merch. V, 106. *no worse a name,* As I, 3, 126. *with no greater a run,* Shr. IV, 1, 16. *upon no better a ground,* Cor. II, 2, 13. *no worse a place,* Oth. I, 1, 11. *no worse a husband,* Ant. II, 2, 131.

According to custom, the poet says: *once a day, a thousand pound a year* (f. i. Tp. I, 2, 490. Meas. I, 2, 50. II, 1, 127. IV, 2, 158. Err. IV, 1, 21), but also: *once in a month,* Tp. I, 2, 262. *one day in a week,* LLL I, 1, 39.

The art. omitted after *ever* and *never* (f. i. Tp. III, 2, 30. Wiv. III, 5, 94. Err. II, 2, 117. Merch. II, 1, 41), even before the object: *who never yields us kind answer,* Tp. I, 2, 309. *never to speak to lady,* Merch. II, 1, 41. *I never gave you kingdom,* Lr. III, 2, 17; cf. H4A II, 4, 287. H6A III, 2, 134. III, 4, 19. H6C I, 1, 217. Oth. IV, 1, 111 (Qq *a woman*). V, 2, 61. Cymb. IV, 4, 39 etc. Keeping, however, its place, when *never* is but emphatically used for *not: never a woman in Windsor knows more of Anne's mind*, Wiv. I, 4, 135. cf. Meas. IV, 2, 5. Ado II, 1, 336. Merch. II, 2, 166. As III, 3, 107. Shr. I, 1, 240. I, 2, 80. H4A I, 2, 109. II, 1, 19. 31. H4B II, 2, 62. R3 III, 4, 53. H8 Prol. 22. Hml. I, 5, 123. Even in: *there's ne'er a one of you*, Tim. V, 1, 96.

Its omission in the predicate of rare occurrence: *if you be maid or no*, Tp. I, 2, 427. *which would be great impeachment to his age*, Gent. I, 3, 15. *I will return perfect courtier*, Alls I, 1, 221. *as I am true knight*, Tw. II, 3, 54. *he is knight*, III, 4, 257. *I am dog at a catch*, II, 3, 64. *I am courtier cap-a-pe*, Wint. IV, 4, 761. *turn true man*, H4A II, 2, 24. *I must be good angel to thee*, III, 3, 199. *as thou art prince*, 166. *Marcius is chief enemy to the people*, Cor. I, 1, 7. *I'll turn craver*, Per. II, 1, 92. *to be beadle*, 97. cf. H6A V 4, 170. Lr. I, 2, 79.

Often omitted in comparative sentences, and whenever the respective noun expresses the whole class: *stone at rain relenteth*, Ven. 200. *as falcon to the lure away she flies*, 1027. *wilt thou be glass wherein it shall discern authority for sin?* Lucr. 619. *loathsome canker lives in sweetest bud*, Sonn. 35, 4. 22, 12. 55, 4. 85, 6. 7. Meas. II, 1, 269. Mids. I, 1, 184. III, 2, 101. V, 401. As II, 7, 52. 146. 148. IV, 3, 33. Alls IV, 3, 369. Tw. I, 3, 66. III, 1, 131. H6B I, 4, 78. III, 2, 63. H8 I, 1, 158. III, 2, 132. Troil. I, 1, 59. II, 3, 204. III, 2, 200. Tit. II, 3, 302. IV, 2, 172. Caes. V, 2, 5. Hml. I, 3, 76. Lr. II, 4, 270. V, 3, 10. Ant. I, 1, 17. But also in a particular sense: *with coronet of fresh and fragrant flowers*, Mids. IV, 1, 57. *by new act of parliament*, H6C II, 2, 91. *in posture that acts my words*, Cymb. III, 3, 95. In an apposition: *doff this habit, shame to your estate*, Shr. III, 2, 102. Inserted, on the other hand, contrary to the common use: *would he not, a naughty man, let it sleep?* Troil. IV, 2, 34.

Used for *one: he shall not have a Scot of them*, H4A I, 3, 214. *these foils have all a length*, Hml. V, 2, 276. Oftenest in prepositional phrases: *at a birth*, Oth. II, 3, 212. *at a blow*, H6C V, 1, 50. *at a burden*, Err. V, 343. Wint. IV, 4, 267. *at an instant*, Wiv. IV, 4, 4. H4A V, 4, 151. *at a shot*, Hml. V, 2, 377. *at a sitting*, Merch. III, 1, 116. *at a time*, Tp. III, 3, 102. *they are both in a tale*, Ado IV, 2, 33. *in a tune*, As V, 3, 15. *in a word*, Gent. II, 4, 71. Merch. I, 1, 35. Troil. V, 10, 20. *of an age*, Rom. I, 3, 20. *of a bigness*, H4B II, 4, 265. *an two men ride of a horse*, Ado III, 5, 40. *of a mind*, Alls I, 3, 244. *sip on a cup*, Wiv. II, 2, 77. *on a horse*, As V, 3, 16. *on a stalk*, R3 IV, 3, 12. *with a breath*, H8 I, 4, 30. *rosemary and Romeo begin with a letter*, Rom. II, 4, 220.

Inserted before names serving for war-cries: *a Talbot! a Talbot!* H6A I, 1, 128. *a Clifford! a Clifford!* H6B IV, 8, 55. *a Helen, and a woe!* Troil. II, 2, 111. Before names peculiarly used as appellatives: *as I am an honest Puck*, Mids. V, 438. *'tis a noble Lepidus*, Ant. III, 2, 6.

A, a corruption of different particles and formative syllables; 1) being a prefix to many words; cf. *Abase, Abashed, Abed* etc.

2) preceding gerunds (most M. Edd. making use of the hyphen): *go a bat-fowling*, Tp. II, 1, 185. *sat a billing*, Ven. 366. *we'll a birding*, Wiv. III,

3, 247. *goes a birding*, III, 5, 46. 131. *he's a birding*, IV, 2, 8. *lie a bleeding*, Rom. III, 1, 194. *fell a bleeding*, Merch. II, 5, 25. *are a breeding*, LLL I, 1, 97. *a brewing*, Merch. II, 5, 17. *falls a capering*, Merch. I, 2, 66. *a coming*, LLL V, 2, 589. *fall a cursing*, Hml. II, 2, 615. *it was a doing*, Cor. IV, 2, 5; cf. *as long a doing*, R3 III, 6, 7. *fell a doting*, Sonn. 20, 10. *go a ducking*, Ant. III, 7, 65. *a dying*, R2 II, 1, 90. *a feasting*, Wiv. II, 3, 92. *a going*, H8 I, 3, 50. *so long a growing*, R3 II, 4, 19. *was a hanging thee*, Lr. V, 3, 274. *fell a hooting*, LLL IV, 2, 61. *I would have him nine years a killing*, Oth IV, 1, 188. *a making*, Mcb. III, 4, 34. Hml. I, 3, 119. *a chime a mending*, Troil. I, 3, 159. *still a repairing*, LLL III, 193. *a ripening*, H8 III, 2, 357. *a rolling*, V, 3, 104. *set a shaking*, Lucr. 452. *fell a shouting*, Caes. I, 2, 223. *seems a sleeping*, Tim. I, 2, 68. *at gaming, a swearing*, Hml. III, 3, 91 (Ff om.). *she has been too long a talking of*, Ado III, 2, 107. *fell a turning*, Pilgr. 100. 214. *set me a weeping*, H4B II, 4, 301. *comes a wooing*, Shr. III, 1, 35. Oth. III, 3, 71.

3) before substantives; frequently changed to *o', of* and *on*, by M. Edd. Qq and Ff have almost always *five a clock* etc. (f. i. Ado III, 4, 52. H4A I, 2, 139. II, 1, 36.), M. Edd. throughout *o' clock* (cf. *Clock*). The same liberty they have taken with most of the following passages, in which *a* is supported by all or at least by the most authentic old texts:

a) *a* for *of: a mornings*, Ado III, 2, 42. *a days*, H4B II, 4, 251. Tim. IV, 3, 294. *a nights*, Tw. I, 3, 5. Tim. IV, 3, 292. Caes. I, 2, 193. II, 2, 116. *light a love*, Ado III, 4, 47. *cloth a gold*, III, 4, 19. *issue a my body*, Alls I, 3, 27. *out a friends*, 42. *a purifying a the song*, 87. *take leave a the king*, II, 4, 49. *our Isbels a the country and our Isbels a the court*, III, 2, 14. 15. *out a the band*, IV, 3, 227. *no more a that*, IV, 2, 13. *a crow a the same nest*, IV, 3, 319. *a commoner a the camp*, V, 3, 194. *all the spots a the world*, V, 3, 206. *what dish a poison*, Tw. II, 5, 123. *inns a court*, H4B III, 2, 14 (Ff *of*). *John a Gaunt*, R2 I, 3, 76. H4B III, 2, 49. 344 (Ff *of*). *the sweet a the night*, V, 3, 53 (Ff *of*). *be a good cheer*, H5 II, 3, 19. *body a me*, H8 V, 2, 22. *were a my mind*, Troil II, 3, 225 (Q *of*). *loads a gravel*, V, 1, 22. *the sink a the body*, Cor. I, 1, 126; cf. I, 6, 47. II, 3, 79. V, 6, 83. 91. 97. 150. *yond coin a the Capitol*, V, 4, 1. *time out a mind*, Rom. I, 4, 69; cf. *out a door* and *out a doors*, Err. II, 1, 11. H4B II, 4, 229. Cor. I, 3, 120. Hml. II, 1, 99. *the maid is fair, a the youngest for a bride*, Tim. I, 1, 126. *what time a day is it?* 265. *the heels a the ass*, 282 etc.

b) for *on: a Monday*, Hml. II, 2, 406. *a Wednesday*, H4A V, 1, 138. Cor. I, 3, 64. *a Thursday*, H4A II, 4, 74 (Ff *on*). H4B II, 4, 298 (Ff *on*). Rom. III, 4, 20. III, 5, 162. *a Friday*, Troil. I, 1, 78 (Ff *on*). *a Sunday*, Shr. II, 318. *a Sundays*, Hml. IV, 5, 182. *I love a ballad in print a life*, Wint. IV, 4, 264. *a horseback*, H4A II, 3, 104. II, 4, 378. 387. *a my word*, Shr. I, 2, 108. H4B II, 4, 190 (Ff *on*). Cor. I, 3, 62. Rom. I, 1, 1 (Qq *on*). *stand a tiptoe*, H5 IV, 3, 42. *heaved a high*, R3 IV, 4, 86, cf. *look up a height*, Lr. IV, 6, 58. *a my troth*, Cor. I, 3, 63. *a plague a both your houses*, Rom. III, 1, 93. 111. *a pox a drowning*, Oth. I, 3, 366. *a conscience*, Per. IV, 2, 23.

c) for *in: a God's name,* Shr. I, 2, 195. IV, 5, 1. R2 II, 1, 251 (Ff *o'*). III, 3, 146 (Ff *o'*). H6A I, 2, 102. H6B II, 3, 54. IV, 7, 115. H8 II, 1, 78. *a this fashion,* Alls II, 3, 265. Hml. V, 1, 218 (Ff *o'*). *torn a pieces,* H8 V, 4, 80. *I'll see the church a your back,* Shr. V, 1, 5. *kept a coil,* Alls II, 1, 27.

Even this *a* before vowels sometimes changed to *an: set an edge,* Wint. IV, 3, 7. H4A III, 1, 133. *stand an end,* Hml. I, 5, 19. III, 4, 122 (in H6B III, 2, 318 and R3 I, 3, 304 Ff *an end,* Qq *on end*). *an hungry,* Cor. I, 1, 209 (a solecism formed in derision by Coriolanus). *an't = on't,* i. e. of it, Hml. V, 1, 26 (the gravedigger's speech).

A, corrupted from *have* (cf. *God-a-mercy*): *she might a been a grandam,* LLL V, 2, 17. *so would I a done,* Hml. IV, 5, 64 (Ff *ha*).

A, a mutilation of the pronoun *he,* not only in the language of common people (f. i. Ado III, 3, 28. 82. 133. 140. 182. LLL IV, 1, 136. 148. Merch. II, 2, 56. Alls IV, 5, 41. H6B I, 3, 7. IV, 2, 58. 125) but of well-bred persons: *a must keep peace,* Ado II, 3, 201. *a brushes his hat,* III, 2, 41. *a rubs himself with civet,* 50. *is a not approved a villain,* IV, 1, 303. *a shall wear nothing handsome,* V, 4, 104. *whoe'er a was, a showed a mounting mind,* LLL IV, 1, 4. *a killed your sister,* V, 2, 13. *if a have no more man's blood,* 697. *a will make the man mad,* Shr. IV, 5, 35. *a means to cozen somebody,* V, 1, 39. *a will betray us,* Alls IV, 1, 102. *nothing of me, has a?* IV, 3, 129. *a was a botcher's prentice,* 211. *a pops me out,* John I, 68. *an a may catch your hide,* II, 136. *a were as good crack a fusty nut,* Troil. II, 1, 111. *a would have ten shares,* II, 3, 230. *brings a victory in his pocket?* Cor. II, 1, 135. *a shall not tread on me,* V, 3, 127. *as a lies asleep,* Rom. I, 4, 80. *a bears the third part,* Ant. II, 7, 96 etc. Few M. Edd. retain the ancient spelling, most change it to *he.* In many cases even O. Edd. differ, Qq having *a,* Ff *he*: Ado I, 1, 90. II, 1, 17. II, 3, 178. LLL V, 2, 323. 528. 721. H6B II, 2, 75. Rom. V, 1, 38. Hml. II, 1, 58. IV, 5, 185. 190. V, 1, 74 etc. In Alls I, 3, 90 (*one in ten, quoth a!*) *a* seems, at first sight, to be used for *she;* but in fact there is no certain reference to any particular person; cf. *ah! sirrah, quoth a, we shall do nothing but eat,* H4B V, 3, 17. *ho! says a, there's my cap,* Ant. II, 7, 141.

A, a remnant of Anglosaxon suffixes, serving as an expletive void of sense to fill up the metre: *and merrily hent the stile-a,* Wint. IV, 3, 133. *your sad tires in a mile-a,* 135. *my dainty duck, my dear-a,* IV, 4, 324. *of the newest and finest wear-a,* 327. *that doth utter all men's ware-a,* 330. *and a merry heart lives long-a,* H4B V, 3, 50. *down, down, adown-a,* Wiv. I, 4, 44. *you must sing adown, adown, an you call him adown-a,* Hml. IV, 5, 170. *to contract, O the time, for-a my behove, O, methought, there-a was nothing-a meet,* Hml. V, 1, 71 (reading of Qq; Ff *O me thought there was nothing meet*). *leave thy drink and thy whore, and keep in a door,* Lr. I, 4, 138 (M. Edd. *in-a-door*). It is needless to speak of the gibberish of Dr. Caius, who likes to prolong the words by appending an *a,* f. i. Wiv. I, 4, 47. 85 etc.

Aaron, name of the Moor in Tit. II, 1, 12 etc.

Abandon, 1) to leave: *a. the society of this female,* As V, 1, 52. 55. *at your —ed cave,* V, 4, 202. *I have —ed Troy,* Troil. III, 3, 5. *—ed her holy groves,*

Tit. II, 3, 58. *if thou wouldst not reside but where one villain is, then him a.* Tim. V, 1, 114.

2) to desert, to forsake: *left and —ed of his velvet friends,* As II, 1, 50. *—ed from your bed,* Shr. Ind. 2, 117 (forsaken and kept from your bed). *—ed and despised,* H6C I, 1, 188.

3) to give up, to renounce: *he hath —ed his physicians,* Alls I, 1, 15. *so —ed to her sorrow,* Tw. I, 4, 19. *a. all remorse,* Oth. III, 3, 369.

Abase, to lower, to degrade: *a. our sight so low,* H6B I, 2, 15. *a. her eyes on me,* R3 I, 2, 247 (Qq *debase*).

Abashed, made ashamed: *do you with cheeks a. behold our works,* Troil. I, 3, 18.

Abate, (cf. *Bate*) 1) tr. a) to beat down, to overthrow, to humble: *most —d captives,* Cor. III, 3, 132.

b) to weaken, to diminish: *air and water do a. the fire,* Ven. 654. Tp. IV, 56. Mids. III, 2, 432 (*a. thy hours,* = shorten). Merch. V, 198. Shr. Ind. 1, 137. H5 III, 2, 24. Tit. I, 43. Rom. IV, 1, 120. Hml. IV, 7, 116.

c) to blunt, to take off the edge of: *a. the edge of traitors,* R3 V, 5, 35. *from his metal was his party steeled; which once in him —d, all the rest turned on themselves,* H4B I, 1, 117.

d) to reduce in estimation: *I would a. her nothing,* Cymb. I, 4, 73.

e) to deduct, to except: *a. throw at novum,* LLL V, 2, 547.

f) to curtail, with *of: she hath —d me of half my train,* Lr. II, 4, 161.

2) intr. (used by none but Pistol), to decrease: *and fury shall a.* H5 II, 1, 70. IV, 4, 50.

Abatement, 1) diminution, debilitation: Hml. IV, 7, 121 (cf. 116). Lr. I, 4, 64. Cymb. V, 4, 21.

2) lower estimation: *falls into a. and low price,* Tw. I, 1, 13.

Abbess, the governess of a nunnery: Err. V, 117. 133. 156. 166. 280.

Abbey, a convent governed by an abbot or abbess: Err. V, 122. 129. 155. 263. 278. 394. John I, 48. V, 3, 8. H8 IV, 1, 57 (= Westminster A.). IV, 2, 18.

Abbey-gate, the gate of an abbey: Err. V, 165.

Abbey-wall, a wall enclosing an abbey: Gent. V, 1, 9. Err. V, 265. Rom. II, 4, 199.

Abbot, the governor of a monastery: John III, 3, 8. R2 V, 3, 137. V, 6, 19. H8 IV, 2, 18. 20.

Abbreviate, to abridge, to reduce to a smaller form (used only by Holophernes): *neighbour vocatur nebour, neigh —d ne,* LLL V, 1, 26.

A B C, the alphabet, Gent. II, 1, 23 (cf. *Absey-book*).

A-bed, (O. Edd. not hyphened) 1) in bed: As II, 2, 6. Alls V, 3, 228. Tw. II, 3, 1. H5 IV, 3, 64. Cor. III, 1, 261. Rom. III, 4, 7. Mcb. II, 1, 12. Oth. III, 1, 33. IV, 1, 5 (Ff *in bed*). Cymb. III, 3, 33.

2) to bed: *brought a.* = delivered, Tit. IV, 2, 62.

Abel, the second son of Adam slain by Cain: R2 I, 1, 104. H6A I, 3, 40.

Abergany, (O. Edd. *Aburgany,* M. Edd. *Abergavenny*), a name: H8 I, 1, 211. I, 2, 137.

Abet, to assist (in a bad sense), to instigate: Err. II, 2, 172. R2 II, 3, 146.

Abettor, instigator: Lucr. 886.

Abhominable, the correct spelling, in Holophernes' opinion, of *abominable:* LLL V, 1, 26 (quasi inhuman!). cf. *Abominable.*

Abhor, 1) to detest to extremity, to loathe; with an accus.: Ven. 138. Lucr. 195. 349. Sonn. 150, 11. 12. Pilgr. 165. Gent. IV, 3, 17. Wiv. III, 5, 16. Meas. II, 2, 29. Ado II, 3, 101. LLL V, 1, 20. As II, 3, 28. Tw. II, 5, 219. III, 1, 176. John IV, 3, 111. H8 II, 4, 236. Cor. I, 8, 3. Tim. I, 1, 60. IV, 3, 398. V, 4, 75. Oth. I, 1, 6. II, 1, 236. Cymb. V, 5, 40. With an inf.: *what I a. to name,* Meas. III, 1, 102. *my heart —s to hear him named,* Rom. III, 5, 100. Cymb. IV, 2, 357.

Part. *—ed,* adjectively, = detested, abominable: *to act her —ed commands,* Tp. I, 2, 273. *—ed slave,* 351. Meas. II, 4, 183. Alls IV, 3, 28. Wint. II, 1, 43. John IV, 2, 224. Troil. V, 3, 17. Cor. I, 4, 32. V, 3, 148. Tit. II, 3, 98. Rom. V, 3, 104. Tim. IV, 3, 20. 183. V, 1, 63. Mcb. V, 7, 10. Lr. I, 2, 81. V, 3, 210. Cymb. V, 5, 216.

2) to protest against, to refuse as a judge: *I utterly a. you for my judge,* H8 II, 4, 81. Hence in comical imitation of the judicial language: *she that doth call me husband, even my soul doth for a wife a.* Err. III, 2, 164.

3) to fill with horror and loathing: *how —ed my imagination is!* Hml. V, 1, 206 (Qq and M. Edd. *how —ed in my imagination it is!*). *it doth a. me now I speak the word,* Oth. IV, 2, 162.

Abhorring, subst. abomination: *flatter beneath a.* Cor. I, 1, 172. *blow me into a.* Ant. V, 2, 60.

Abhorson, name of the executioner in Meas. IV, 2, 20. IV, 3, 41.

Abide, (used only in the pres. and inf.) 1) intr. a) to stay for a time: *from far where I a.* Sonn. 27, 5. *wherever I a.* 45, 2. Compl. 83. Meas. IV, 2, 26. V, 252. 266. Merch. III, 4, 42. R3 IV, 2, 49. Tim. V, 1, 2. Mcb. III, 1, 140. IV, 2, 73. Ant. II, 2, 250. Cymb. IV, 2, 6. Per. III, 4, 14. Distinguished from *to stay,* as indicating a transient residence: *they cherish it to make it stay there, and yet it will no more but a.* Wint. IV, 3, 99.

b) to remain, not to depart: *sorrow —s and happiness takes his leave,* Ado I, 1, 102. *our separation so —s and flies,* Ant. I, 3, 102. *shall I a. in this dull world?* IV, 15, 60.

c) to continue in a state: *blood untainted still doth red a.* Lucr. 1749. *the king, his brother and yours, a. all three distracted,* Tp. V, 12.

d) to dwell, to be inherent, as a gift or quality: *none* (comfort) *—s with me,* H6B II, 4, 88. *less spirit to curse —s in me,* R3 IV, 4, 197.

e) to stand one's ground, not to flinch or fly: *small lights are soon blown out, huge fires a.* Lucr. 647. *wilt thou not a.?* Troil. V, 6, 30.

2) trans. a) to await (cf. *Stay*): *a. the change of time,* Cymb. II, 4, 4.

b) to endure, to undergo, to suffer: *where thou with patience must my will a.* Lucr. 486. *to a. thy kingly doom,* R2 V, 6, 23. H6C I, 4, 29. II, 5, 75. IV, 3, 58. Cymb. I, 1, 89. Oftener with a negative, = not to bear, not to endure: *a rotten case —s no handling,* H4B IV, 1, 161. *would not a. looking on,* H5 V, 2, 338. Especially after *cannot* and *could not: which good natures could not a. to be with,*

Tp. I, 2, 360. *I cannot a. the smell of hot meat,* Wiv. I, 1. 297. 311. IV, 2, 87. Meas. III, 2, 36. Mids. III, 1, 12. Merch. IV, 1, 54. H4B II, 4, 117. III, 2, 215. H5 II, 3, 35.

c) to meet in combat, to stand, to defy *a. me if thou darest,* Mids. III, 2, 422. *to a. a field,* H4B II, 3, 36. *will a. it with a prince's courage,* Cymb. III, 4, 186.

d) to answer for, to stand the consequences of: *lest thou a. it dear,* Mids. III, 2, 175 (Q1 *aby*). *let no man a. this deed, but we the doers,* Caes. III, 1, 94. *some will dear a. it,* III, 2, 119.

Ability, 1) power to perform: *what poor a. is in me to do him good?* Meas. I, 4, 75. *any thing that my a. may undergo,* Wint. II, 3, 164. V, 1, 143. Troil. III, 2, 92. Hml. V, 2, 384. Plur: *my endeavours filed with my —ies,* H8 III, 2, 171. *your —ies are too infant-like for doing much alone,* Cor. II, 1, 40. *lacks the —ies that Rhodes is dressed in,* Oth. I, 3, 25 (means of resistance). *I will do all my —ies,* III, 3, 2.

2) capacity, skill: *all our —ies, gifts* etc. Troil. I, 3, 179. *he fills it up with great a.* Oth. III, 3, 247.

3) wealth, means, a state of being provided with something: *a. in means,* Ado IV, 1, 201. *out of my lean and low a. I'll lend you something,* Tw. III, 4, 378. H4B I, 3, 45. Quibbling in Alls I, 3, 12.

Abject, adj., mean, despicable: Err. IV, 4. 106. Merch. IV, 1, 92. Shr. Ind. 2, 34. H4B IV, 1, 33. H6A V, 5, 49. H6B II, 4, 11. IV, 1, 105. V, 1, 25. Troil. III, 3, 128. 162. *his eye reviled me as his a. object,* H8 I, 1, 127, i. e. the object of his contempt.

Abject, subst., a castaway: *we are the queen's —s and must obey,* R3 I, 1, 106.*

Abjectly, basely: *he that thinks of me so a.* Tit. III, 3, 4.

Abjure, 1) to renounce upon oath: *this rough magic I here a.* Tp. V, 51. Mids. I, 1, 65. Shr. I, 1, 33. Tw. I, 2, 40. Lr. II, 4, 211.

2) to recant upon oath: *I here a. the taints and blames I laid upon myself.* Mcb. IV, 3, 123.

Able, adj. 1) having the power or means; followed by an inf. expressed or understood: Gent. II, 3, 58. Wiv. I, 1, 54. IV, 5, 111. V, 5, 142. 171. Err. I, 2, 5. Mids. IV, 1, 218. IV, 2, 8. Merch. I, 2, 88. IV, 1, 208. As II, 4, 77. Shr. V, 1, 78. Alls II, 1, 76. II, 3, 49. Wint. II, 3, 117. V, 2, 27. R2 III, 2, 52. H4A I, 2, 102. H4B I, 2, 9. I, 3, 54. H5 III, 7, 85. H6A III, 1, 12. IV, 1, 159. V, 5, 15. 51. H6B I, 3, 220. II, 1, 145 II, 3, 78. IV, 2, 50. 60. IV, 7, 47. V, 1, 101. H6C III, 3, 154. IV, 8, 36. H8 I, 1, 161. I, 2, 31. IV, 1, 62. V, 4, 66. Troil. III, 2, 92. Cor. I, 6, 79. V, 4, 20. Tit. II, 1, 33. Rom. I, 1, 33. V, 3, 223. Tim. III, 2, 54. Per. IV, 6, 3. Comp. *—r,* Caes. IV, 3, 31. Irreg. expr.: *what by sea and land I can be a. to front this present time,* Ant. I, 4, 78.

2) absol. a) vigorous, active: *of as a. body as when he numbered thirty,* Alls IV, 5, 86. *his a. horse,* H4B I, 1, 43. *a weak mind and an a. body,* II, 4, 274. *would it not grieve an a. man to leave so sweet a bedfellow?* H8 II, 2, 142. *a. horses,* Tim. II, 1, 10. *provided I be so a. as now,* Hml. V, 2, 211.

b) skilful, clever: *every hymn that a. spirit affords,* Sonn. 85, 7.

c) competent, sufficient, equal: *as your worth is a.* Meas. I, 1, 9. *be a. for thine enemy rather in power than use,* Alls I, 1, 74. *a. means,* H8 IV, 2, 153.

Able, vb. (cf. Nares' Glossary) to warrant, to answer for: *none does offend, none, I say, none; I'll a. them,* Lr. IV, 6, 172.

Aboard, 1) absol. a) in a ship: Tp. I, 1, 21. Gent. I, 1, 157. Err. IV, 4, 154. Shr. III, 2, 173. Wint. IV, 4, 826. b) into a ship: Gent. II, 3, 36. Err. I, 1, 62. IV, 1, 86. 88. IV, 4, 162. Merch. II, 6, 65. Wint. III, 3, 7. 57. H5 III, 2, 12. 71. Hml. I, 3, 55. IV, 3, 56. Oth. V, 2, 370. Ant. II, 6, 142. Cymb. I, 1, 178. I, 6, 199. Per. IV, 1, 96. 102. Per. V, 1, 5. 9. *to lay knife a.* = to board, to grapple: Rom. II, 4, 214. *laying the prize a.* H6B IV, 1, 25 (= boarding the conquered vessel).

2) with an accus., always replying to the question '*whither'*: *they hurried us a. a bark,* Tp. I, 2, 144. Wint. IV, 4, 790. Ant. II, 6, 82. Per. III, 1, 13. *a. a person* = a. his ship: *I will bring these two moles a. him,* Wint. IV, 4, 868. *I brought the old man and his son a. the prince,* V, 2, 124. *her fortunes brought the maid a. us,* Per. V, 3, 11 (Ff *a. to us*).

Abode, subst., stay, continuance in a place: R3 I, 3, 169. Oth. IV, 2, 231. Ant. I, 2, 182. *your patience for my long a.* Merch. II, 6, 21 (for my being so late). *desire my man's a. where I did leave him,* Cymb. I, 6, 53 (desire him to stay, to remain where etc.). *to make a.* = to dwell, to live: Gent. IV, 3, 23. H6A V, 4, 88. Lr. I, 1, 136. *where is thy a.?* Shr. IV, 5, 38 (πόϑι τοι πόλις;).

Abode, vb. tr. to foreshow, in a bad sense: H6C V, 6, 45. H8 I, 1, 93.

Abodement, omen, in a bad sense: H6C IV, 7, 13.

Abominable, (spelt throughout *abhominable* in F1) detestable, execrable: Tp. II, 2, 163. Wiv. II, 2, 309. Meas. III, 2, 25. LLL V, 1, 27. As IV, 1, 6. H4A II, 4, 508. H4B II, 4, 151. H6A I, 3, 87. H6B IV, 7, 44. H6C I, 4, 133. Troil. V, 4, 3. V, 10, 23. Tit. II, 3, 74. V, 1, 64. Lr. I, 2, 83. Per. IV, 6, 143.

Abominably, detestably: Hml. III, 2, 39.

Abomination, 1) detestableness: *drunken Desire must vomit his receipt, ere he can see his own a.* Lucr. 704.

2) any thing detestable: *incest, that a.* Lucr. 921. *suffer these —s,* 1832. *most large in his —s,* Ant. III, 6, 94. (F1 *abhominations*).

Abortive, adj. 1) born before the due time: *why should I joy in any a. birth?* LLL I, 1, 104.

2) monstrous, unnatural: *allay this thy a. pride,* H6B IV, 1, 60. *if ever he have child, a. be it,* R3 I, 2, 21. I, 3, 228.

Abortive, subst. monstrous birth: *—s, presages and tongues of heaven,* John III, 4, 158.

Abound, 1) to live in wealth and plenty: *never they shall a. as formerly,* H8 I, 1, 83.

2) with *in,* to be copiously stored with: *a. in tears,* Wint. II, 1, 120. *—est in all,* Rom. III, 3, 123. Mcb. IV, 3, 95.

3) to be in great plenty: *diseases do a.* Mids. II, 1, 105. H5 III, 2, 7. IV, 3, 104 (Qq *abundant*). H6B II, 4, 4. H8 III, 2, 195.

About, prepos. 1) round: *clouds a. his golden head,* Lucr. 777. *that self chain a. his neck,* Err. V, 10. 258. *whirl a. the globe,* Tit. V, 2, 49. Tp. III, 2, 147. As III, 2, 191. Shr. I, 2, 141. II, 302. H5 V, 2, 190. H6C V, 1, 108. H8 V, 5, 55. Oth. I, 2, 89. II, 3, 99 etc. *round a.:* Lucr. 1586. Wiv. IV, 4, 31. Meas. III, 1, 125. Ado V, 3, 15. Mids. II, 1, 175. Tit. III, 1, 125.

2) near to a person: *hang no more a. me,* Wiv. II, 2, 17. *he shall not come a. her,* Wint. II, 1, 59. II, 3, 43. *they are all a. his majesty,* John V, 6, 36. *she has nobody to do any thing a. her,* H4B III, 2, 246. *some a. him have wrested his meaning,* IV, 2, 57. H6A III, 1, 38. H6B III, 1, 26. IV, 7, 42. Ant. IV, 15, 48. Cymb. III, 5, 68.

3) carried by, or appendant to, a person: *you have not the book of riddles a. you,* Wiv. I, 1, 209. *you cannot see a white spot a. her,* IV, 5, 116. *his face is the worst thing a. him,* Meas. II, 1, 163. 229. *what privy marks I had a. me,* Err. III, 2, 146. *have you the chain a. you?* IV, 1, 42. *if half thy outward graces had been placed a. thy thoughts,* Ado IV, 1, 103. *the old name is fresh a. me,* H8 IV, 1, 99 (is not yet obsolete with me). *pierce every sense a. thee,* Lr. I, 4, 323. Ado IV, 2, 89. V, 4, 105. Mids. III, 1, 71. As III, 2, 400. Alls II, 3, 214. Wint. IV, 4, 260. H4B I, 2, 208. H5 II, 1, 24. V, 2, 315. R3 I, 3, 244. Lr. II, 4, 42. Cymb. II, 4, 119 etc.

4) anywhere, here or there within a certain locality: *walk a. the town,* Err. I, 2, 22. *where lies thy pain? all a. the breast,* LLL IV, 3, 173. *he is a. the house,* Tw. II, 4, 13 (anywhere in the house). Mids. III, 2, 5. 94. H4A V, 4, 32. H4B III, 2, 329. Caes. II, 2, 24. V, 3, 22. V, 4, 3. Hml. III, 1, 19. *round a.* = throughout: *proclaim it round a. the city,* Meas. V, 514. *look round a. the wicked streets of Rome,* Tit. V, 2, 98. *she throws her eyes a. the painting round,* Lucr. 1499. cf. *I'll lead you a. a round,* Mids. III, 1, 109, i. e. through thick and thin.

5) near in size, quantity, or time: *a. my stature,* Gent. IV, 4, 163. 169. *a. the very hour,* V, 1, 2. Wiv. V, 1, 12. Err. III, 1, 96. LLL I, 1, 238. H4A II, 4, 60. H6C IV, 5, 10. R3 V, 3, 70. 77. H8 IV, 2, 26. Caes. II, 4, 23 etc.

6) in a state of being engaged in, or intent on: *I will tell you what I am a.* Wiv. I, 3, 43. *I am a. no waste,* 46. *the prince is about a piece of iniquity,* Wint. IV, 4, 693. *it is unlawful business I am a.* V, 3, 97. *I was employed in passing to and fro, a. relieving of the sentinels,* H6A I, 1, 70. *look with care a. the town,* Oth. II, 3, 255 (watch all the town carefully). *he is a. it* = he is doing it, Mcb. II, 2, 4. Oth. II, 1, 126. *I will a. it,* Wiv. II, 2, 327 (= I will fall to work). Meas. I, 4, 85. Alls III, 6, 79. *let's a. it,* III, 7, 48. H6A I, 2, 149. H6C IV, 6, 102. *shall we a. it?* H5 III, 7, 167. *a. thy business, Davy,* H4B V, 1, 39. *sound the trumpets, and a. our task,* H6C II, 1, 200. *a. your business straight,* R3 I, 3, 355. *at gaming, swearing, or a. some act that has no relish of salvation,* Hml. III, 3, 91. *a. him, fairies!* Wiv. V, 5, 95 (= at him! take him to task!). *a. it!* Gent. III, 2, 95. 98. Tw. III, 2, 52. R3 IV, 2, 59. Lr. V, 3, 35. Oth. IV, 2, 250. *to go a. sth.* = to get one's self ready for, to be going to do: Merch. II, 4, 25. As I, 1, 180. Alls III, 6, 85. H6A I, 1, 166. H8 I, 1, 131. Cor. III, 2, 98. III, 3, 24. IV, 6, 9. Lr. IV, 4, 24. *I'll roundly go a. her,* Shr. IV, 4, 108 (I'll resolutely try my

fortune with her). *he is very busy a. it,* Ado I, 2, 3. *Mortimer doth stir a. his title,* H4A II, 3, 85. *else shall you not have any hand a. his funeral,* Caes. III, 1, 249. cf. Cor. I, 1, 131. Lr. I, 5, 37.

7) concerning, relating to, with regard to: *we have some secrets to confer a.* Gent. III, 1, 2. *we have lingered a. a match,* Wiv. III, 2, 58. IV, 5, 35. 47. LLL I, 1, 138. Merch. II, 2, 88. V, 147. As II, 7, 172. R2 II, 1, 168. H6A IV, 1, 95. H6C I, 2, 7. H8 III, 2, 406. Cor. V, 2, 74 etc.

8) on account of: *he is mad a. his throwing into the water,* Wiv. IV, 1, 5. *I come a. my brother,* Meas. IV, 1, 48. *you have rated me a. my moneys,* Merch. I, 3, 109. *an old lord rated me in the street a. you,* H4A I, 2, 96. *striking him a. Bardolph,* H4B I, 2, 63. *stop William's wages a. the sack he lost* V, 1, 25. V, 4, 7. H5 II, 3, 38. H6A IV, 1, 91. H6B IV, 1, 31. R3 I, 1, 39. Cor. II, 3, 17.

Transposed: *the house a.* = a. the house, Per. III, Prol. 2 (Gower's speech).

About, adv. 1) round, circularly: *do not turn me a.; my stomach is not constant,* Tp. II, 2, 118. *burn him, and turn him a.* Wiv. V, 5, 105. *he turned me a. with his finger,* Cor. IV, 5, 160.

2) round, on every side: *compass thee a.* Tp. V, 180. *encircle him a.* Wiv. IV, 4, 56. I, 3, 46. John II, 217. H6C IV, 2, 15. R3 I, 4, 59. Hml. I, 5, 71. *round a.: the gentle day, before the wheels of Phoebus, round a. dapples the drowsy east with spots of grey,* Ado V, 3, 26. Troil. V, 7, 5. Tit. IV, 2, 18. Caes. V, 3, 28. Oth. III, 3, 464. *to look a.* = a) to look on all sides, or in different directions: *how it looks a.!* Tp. I, 2, 410. b) to be on the watch: *look a., Davy,* H4B V, 1, 59. *be wary, look a.* Rom. III, 5, 40. *'tis time to look a.* Lr. IV, 7, 93.

3) by a circuitous way: *to wheel three or four miles a.* Cor. I, 6, 20. *his horses go a.* Mcb. III, 3, 11. *my purposes do draw me much a.* Ant. II, 4, 8. Metaphorically. *go not a.* Alls I, 3, 194 (do not shuffle, use no quibbling). *something a., a little from the right,* John I, 170. *why do you go a. to recover the wind of me?* Hml. III, 2, 361. cf. R3 IV, 4, 461.

4) here and there, up and down: *a. he walks,* Lucr. 367. Sonn. 113, 2. Tp. I, 2, 417. Err. V, 187. LLL V, 1, 72. Troil. V, 10, 56 etc. *you might have heard it else proclaimed a.* Shr. IV, 2, 87, i. e. here and there, in divers places.

5) to a certain point, to an appointed or desired place: *I will bring the doctor a. by the fields,* Wiv. II, 3, 81 (i. e. to the appointed place). *brought a. the annual reckoning,* LLL V, 2, 888 (accomplished). *the wind is come a.* Merch. II, 6, 64 (has become favourable). *how a jest shall come a.* Rom. I, 3, 45 (come to pass, be effected). *how these things came a.* Hml. V, 2, 391.

6) upon the point, ready, going: *I was a. to protest,* Ado IV, 1, 286. As II, 3, 21. Alls IV, 5, 73. Wint. II, 1, 65. H4A I, 3, 22. H8 II, 4, 70. Hml. I, 1, 147. II, 1, 50 etc. *what is a. to be?* Cor. III, 1, 189 (= what will become of this?) *to go a.* = to be going, to have in hand, to make it one's task: *his testy master goeth a. to take him,* Ven. 319. *who went a. from this fair throne to heave the owner out,* Lucr. 412. *see how he goes a. to abuse me!* Meas. III, 2, 215. *that thou goest a. to apply a moral medicine to a mortifying mischief,* Ado I, 3, 12. *have gone*

a. to link my friend to a common stale, IV, 1, 65. Mids. IV, 1, 212. Merch. II, 9, 37. Wint. IV, 4, 219. 720. H5 IV, 1, 212. H6B II, 1, 146. *I will go a. with him* (= I will go to work with him, he shall find his match in me) Ado IV, 2, 28. *to set a.* = to prepare, to arrange: *shall we set a. some revels?* Tw. I, 3, 145. *About!* = to work! be not idle! *a., a.; search Windsor castle, elves, within and out,* Wiv. V, 5, 59. *revenge! a.! seek! burn!* Caes. III, 2, 208. *a., my brain!* Hml. II, 2, 617. *and a would a. and a.* H4B III, 2, 302 (he would go on with a vengeance).

Above, adv. 1) in a higher place, overhead; a) in heaven: *by all a., these blenches gave my heart another youth,* Sonn. 110, 6. Tp. I, 1, 71. Wiv. I, 4, 154. Meas. V, 115. Ado V, 2, 27. As III, 2, 3. Alls II, 3, 261. Tw. V, 140. H6A I, 2, 114. V, 4, 39. H6C II, 3, 29. R3 III, 7, 109. Troil. I, 2, 83. III, 2, 165. Tim. IV, 3, 191. Hml. III, 3, 60. Lr. IV, 2, 78.

b) upstairs: *my maid's aunt has a gown a.* Wiv. IV, 2, 78. Err. II, 2, 209. H4A II, 4, 550.

2) besides (when joined to *more* and *over*): *and stand indebted, over and a., in love and service to you,* Merch. IV, 1, 413. *this hath my daughter shown me, and more a., hath his solicitings all given to mine ear,* Hml. II, 2, 126.

Above, prepos. 1) in or to a higher place; a) over: *have not your worship a wart a. your eye?* Wiv. I, 4, 157. *I'll be sure to keep him a. deck,* II, 1, 94. *forty thousand fathom a. water,* Wint. IV, 4, 281. *I'll stay a. the hill,* H6C III, 1, 5. *raise his car a. the border,* IV, 7, 81. *this foul deed shall smell a. the earth,* Caes. III, 1, 274. *though women all a.* (viz the waist) Lr. IV, 6, 127. *all the hairs a. thee,* Cymb. II, 3, 140 (on thy head).

b) overhead: *which like a cherubin a. them hovered,* Compl. 319. *I hear it now a. me,* Tp. I, 2, 407. *the sky that hangs a. our heads,* John II, 397.

c) comparatively higher, in a proper and figurative sense: *sweet a. compare,* Ven. 8. *to write a. a mortal pitch,* Sonn. 86, 6. *lest it should burn a. the bounds of reason,* Gent. II, 7, 23. *soar a. the morning lark,* Shr. Ind. 2, 46. *policy sits a. conscience,* Tim. III, 2, 94. Tp. I, 2, 168. LLL IV, 3, 332. V, 2, 259. 446. Merch. IV, 1, 193. 285. Tw. I, 3, 116. I, 5, 140. II, 5, 156. John V, 6, 38. H6A I, 1, 121. H6B I, 2, 46. II, 1, 6. 12. 15. H6C II, 5, 94. H8 III, 1, 123. Rom. III, 5, 238. Cymb. II, 4, 113. *a. the rest* = above all (which expression is yet unknown to Sh.): Sonn. 91, 6. Gent. IV, 1, 60. Lr. IV, 1, 50.

2) more than: *which shall a. that idle rank remain beyond all date,* Sonn. 122, 3. *one that, a. all other strifes, contended especially to know himself,* Meas. III, 2, 246. *murther I tortured a. the felon,* H6B III, 1, 132. *not a. once,* Hml. II, 2, 455. Merch. III, 4, 76. Troil. I, 2, 111 (viz Paris). Cymb. II, 2, 29. *over and a.* = besides: *over and a. that you have suffered,* Wiv. V, 5, 177.

Abraham, 1) the patriarch: R2 IV, 104. R3 IV, 3, 38. 2) Christian name of Mr. Slender: Wiv. I, 1, 57. 239. 3) *young A. Cupid,* Rom. II, 1, 13, in derision of the eternal boyhood of Cupid, though, in fact, he was at least as old as father Abraham; cf. LLL III, 182 and V, 2, 10. M. Edd., quite preposterously: *young Adam Cupid.*

Abram, = Abraham, in the language of Shylock: Merch. I, 3, 73. 162.

Abreast, in a line, equally advanced, side by side: H5 IV, 6, 17. H6C I, 1, 7. Troil. III, 3, 155.

Abridge, 1) to shorten (used of time): Gent. III, 1, 245. H4B II, 4, 211. Caes. III, 1, 104.

2) With *from*, to cut off from, to curtail of: *to be —d from such a noble rate,* Merch. I, 1, 126.

Abridgement, 1) a summary, short account, abstract: *this brief a. of my will I make,* Lucr. 1198. *then brook a.* H5 V, Chor. 44. *this fierce a. hath to it circumstantial branches,* Cymb. V, 5, 382.

2) that which makes time short, pastime: *what a. have you for this evening?* Mids. V, 39. *look where my a. comes,* Hml. II, 2, 439. (that which is my pastime and makes me be brief. Ff —*s come*).

Abroach; *to set a. =* to cause, in a bad sense: H4B IV, 2, 14. R3 I, 3, 325. Rom. I, 1, 111.

Abroad, 1) at large, in all directions: *the wind will blow these sands a.* Tit. IV, 1, 106.

2) without a certain confine, which may be conceived very differently; a) opposed to one's person: *like fools that in the imagination set the goodly objects which a. they find,* Compl. 137 (= in the world around them). *all my offences that a. you see,* 183 (committed against other people). *his hands a. displayed,* H6B III, 2, 172 (not kept close to the body, but stretched out and displayed). *there's none* (air) *a. so wholesome as that you vent,* Cymb. I, 2, 4 (none without you, out of the precincts of your body). *your means a., you have me, rich,* III, 4, 180 (those besides the resources of your own mind).

b) opposed to any habitation: *this cell is my court: here have I few attendants, and subjects none a.,* Tp. V, 167 (without it, out of it). *how features are a.* III, 1, 52 (out of this island). *to come a. with him,* Merch. III, 3, 10 (to leave the prison-house). *I am glad to see your lordship a.* H4B I, 2, 108. 109 (not confined to your chamber by illness). *rain within doors, and none a.* IV, 5, 9. *if you stir a.* H6C V, 1, 96 (without the fortress). *is he ready to come a.?* H8 III, 2, 83 (to leave his closet). *but to the sport a.* Troil. I, 1, 118 (out of the town). *thy spirit walks a.* Caes. V, 3, 95 (instead of keeping his confines). *no spirit dares stir a.* Hml. I, 1, 161. *no companies a.?* Cymb. IV, 2, 101 (in the neighbourhood of our cell). *what company discover you a.?* 130. *to go a. =* to go out: R2 III, 2, 39. H8 I, 4, 5. Rom. I, 1, 127. III, 1, 2. Caes. III, 2, 256. Lr. I, 2, 186.

c) opposed to one's own country, = in or to foreign countries: Gent. I, 1, 6. Merch. I, 1, 17. Shr. I, 2, 58. Wint. IV, 2, 6. H5 I, 2, 178. H6C III, 3, 70. Tim. III, 5, 47. Mcb. V, 8, 66. Ant. I, 4, 36.

3) here and there, round about in the wide world: *other ventures he has, squandered a.* Merch. I, 3, 22. *so much feared a.* H6A II, 3, 16. *there are cozeners a.* Wint. IV, 4, 257 (= in the world); cf. *as knaves be such a.* Oth. IV, 1, 25. *what news a.?* (= what news in the world?): Meas. III, 2, 87. 234. John IV, 2, 160. V, 6, 16. H4A II, 4, 367. H6C II, 1, 95. R3 I, 1, 134. II, 3, 3. H8 III, 2, 391. Lr. II, 1, 8. *all-telling fame doth noise a.* LLL II, 22. H4B Ind. 29. H6C V, 6, 86. R3 IV, 2, 51. Mcb. V, 1, 79. *why should I carry lies a.?* Wint. IV, 4, 275 (spread them among the people). *it is thought a.* Oth. I, 3, 393. *what should it be that they so shriek*

a.? Rom. V, 3, 190 (so publicly, so within everybody's hearing, instead of "speaking within door", as Iago says in Oth. IV, 2, 144). *and set a. new business for you all,* Tit. I, 192 (to trouble all the people with business that should be the care of one only or a few. F3. 4 *abroach*). *there's villany a.* LLL I, 1, 189 (= on foot). *there's toys a.* John I, 232.

Abrogate, to abolish: LLL IV, 2, 55 (Sir Nathaniel's speech).

Abrook, vb. to brook, to endure: H6B II, 4, 10.

Abrupt, sudden, without notice to prepare the mind for the event: H6A II, 3, 30.

Abruption, breaking off (in speaking): Troil. III, 2, 70.

Abruptly, hastily, without the due forms of preparation: As II, 4, 41.

Absence, 1) the state of not being at a place: Compl. 245. Wiv. III, 3, 117. Meas. I, 1, 19. III, 2, 101. LLL V, 2, 225. Mids. III, 2, 244 Merch. I, 2, 121. III, 4, 4. As II, 4, 85. Tw. I, 5, 4. Wint. I, 2, 12. 194. III, 2, 79. IV, 4, 542. V, 2, 120. John I, 1, 102. R3 III, 4, 25. H4A IV, 1, 73. 76. IV, 4, 16. H5 IV, 1, 302. R3 III, 4, 25. H8 II, 3, 106. Cor. I, 3, 4. 93. III, 2, 95. Tim. IV, 3, 346. Ant. I, 2, 179. IV, 15, 61. Cymb. III, 5, 57. IV, 3, 2. V, 5, 57. Per. I, 2, 112. II, 4, 46. *our substitutes in a.* H4B IV, 4, 6. *in a. of:* Gent. I, 1, 59. Merch. V, 128. R2 II, 1, 219. H5 I, 2, 172. *in the a. of:* Meas. V, 331. Cor. IV, 1, 44.

2) separation from one beloved, and in general the state of being far from a person: *O a., what a torment wouldst thou prove,* Sonn. 39, 9. *nor think the bitterness of a. sour,* 57, 7. *the imprisoned a. of your liberty,* 58, 6. *how like a winter hath my a. been from thee,* 97, 1. *a. seemed my flame to qualify,* 109, 2. Err. I, 1, 45. R2 I, 3, 258. Troil. IV, 5, 289. Caes. IV, 3, 152. Oth. I, 3, 260. III, 4, 179. 182. Cymb. III, 6, 74.

3) Euphemistically, = death: *whose a. is no less material to me than is his father's,* Mcb. III, 1, 135.

4) Used for *absent* by Sir Hugh and Mrs Quickly: Wiv. I, 1, 273. II, 2, 86.

Absent, adj. 1) not present: Meas. III, 1, 209. III, 2, 123. 129. IV, 2, 136. IV, 3, 150. Ado II, 2, 48. Merch. V, 285. As II, 2, 18. III, 1, 3. Alls II, 3, 189. III, 7, 34. Tw. I, 5, 18. Wint. 3, 199. John III, 4, 93. R2 I, 3, 259. H4A IV, 3, 86. V, 1, 49. H6C II, 2, 74. H8 II, 4, 231. Caes. IV, 3, 156. Oth. III, 3, 17. Cymb. III, 4, 109. *the a. time =* time of absence, R2 II, 3, 79; cf. Oth. III, 4, 174. With *from:* Sonn. 41, 2. 89, 9. 98, 1. Alls I, 3, 240. *a. hence,* Merch. V, 120.

2) separated: *they have seemed to be together, though a.* Wint. I, 1, 32. *lovers' a. hours,* Oth. III, 4, 174.

Absent, vb. refl. to keep far, to abstain: *that I should yet a. me from your bed,* Shr. Ind. 2, 125. *a. thee from felicity awhile,* Hml. V, 2, 358.

Absey-book, a primer, which sometimes included a catechism: John I, 196.

Absolute, 1) unconditional, complete, perfect: *no perfection is so a.* Lucr. 853. *he needs will be a. Milan,* Tp. I, 2, 109 (not only in name, or partly, but perfectly). *I have delivered to Lord Angelo my a. power and place here in Vienna,* Meas. I, 3, 13 (without restriction). *pardon a. for yourself,* H4A IV, 3, 50. *upon such large terms and so a.* H4B IV, 1, 186 (unlimited, unconditional). *there the people had more a. power,* Cor. III, 1, 116. Tim. V, 1, 165. Lr. V, 3, 300. *on whom I built an a. trust,* Mcb. I, 4, 14. *I speak not as in a. fear of you,* IV, 3, 38 (in unqualified fear, unallayed by the hope that you may be honest). *my soul hath her content so a.* Oth. II, 1, 193. *I do love her, not out of a. lust, but partly led to diet my revenge,* 301. *by sea he is an a. master,* Ant. II, 2, 166. *made her of lower Syria a. queen,* III, 6, 11 (no more a vassal, but a sovereign). *to you the tribunes he commends his a. commission,* Cymb. III, 7, 10 (with full authority). *not a. madness could so far have raved,* IV, 2, 135.

2) positive, certain, decided, not doubtful: a) of persons: *be a. for death,* Meas. III, 1, 5 (expect it with certainty, be sure to receive no pardon). *you are too a.* Cor. III, 2, 39.**how a. the knave is!* Hml. V, 1, 148. *I am a. 'twas very Cloten,* Cymb. IV, 2, 106. *how a. she's in it,* Per. II, 5, 19. — b) of things: *mark you his a. Shall?* Cor. III, 1, 90. *with an a. 'Sir, not I',* Mcb. III, 6, 40. *I have an a. hope,* Ant. IV, 3, 10.

3) highly accomplished, faultless, perfect: *thou wouldst make an a. courtier,* Wiv. III, 3, 66. *as grave, as just, as a. as Angelo,* Meas. V, 54. *a most a. and excellent horse,* H5 III, 7, 27. *an a. gentleman,* Hml. V, 2, 111. *the a. soldiership you have by land,* Ant. III, 7, 43. *a. Marina,* Per. IV. Prol. 31. Preceded by *most,* it serves as an appellation expressing the highest veneration: *most a. Sir,* Cor. IV, 5, 142. *most a. lord,* Ant. IV, 14, 117. Jestingly: *almost most a. Alexas,* Ant. I, 2, 2.

Absolutely, completely, unconditionally,' without restriction: *this shall a. resolve you,* Meas. IV, 2, 225. *to hear and a. to determine of what conditions we shall stand upon,* H4B IV, 1, 164.

Absolution, remission of sins: Lucr. 354.

Absolve, to remit (a sin), to pardon (a sinner): *the willingest sin I ever yet committed may be —d in English,* H8 III, 1, 50. *—d him with an axe,* III, 2, 264. *to make confession and to be —d,* Rom. III, 5, 233.

Absolver, in *Sin-absolver,* q. v.

Abstain, to refrain from indulgence: Lucr. 130. With *from:* R2 II, 1, 76.

Abstemious, abstinent, temperate: Tp. IV, 53.

Abstinence, the refraining from the gratification of desire: Meas. I, 3, 12. IV, 2, 84. LLL IV, 3, 295. Hml. III, 4, 167.

Abstract, subst. 1) a summary, epitome, abbreviation: *by an a. of success,* Alls IV, 3, 99 (by a successful summary proceeding; cf. *Of*). *this little a. doth contain that large which died in Geffrey,* John II, 101 (Prince Arthur being, as it were, a copy of his father Geffrey in miniature). *brief a. and record of tedious days,* R3 IV, 4, 28. *they are the a. and brief chronicles of the time,* Hml. II, 2, 548 (Ff —s). *a man who is the a. of all faults,* Ant. I, 4, 9 (a microcosm of sinfulness). *I begged his pardon for return, which soon he granted, being an a. 'tween his lust and him,* III, 6, 61 (the shortest way for him and his desires, the readiest opportunity to encom-

pass his wishes; cf. *Between* and *'Tween.* M. Edd. *obstruct,* an unheard of substantive!).

2) a short catalogue, an inventory: *he hath an a. for the remembrance of such places,* Wiv. IV, 2, 63.

Absúrd, (as for the accent, see App. I, 1) contrary to reason, insipid: H6A V, 4, 137. Hml. III, 2, 65. Ant. V, 2, 226. *a fault to nature, to reason most a.* Hml. I, 2, 103.

Absyrtus, Medea's brother, killed and dismembered by her: H6B V, 2, 59.

Abundance, great plenty: Sonn. I, 7. 23, 4. 37, 11. Tp. II, 1, 163. Alls I, 1, 12. John II, 148. H4A II, 1, 63. H4B I, 2, 52. IV, 4, 108. Cor. I, 1, 22. *in a.:* Sonn. 135, 10. Merch. I, 2, 4. Cor. II, 1, 19. Per. I, 4, 36.

Abundant, plentiful: Sonn. 97, 9. R2 I, 3, 257. V, 3, 65. Adverbially: Troil. II, 3, 16.

Abundantly, plentifully: *though a. they lack discretion,* Cor. I, 1, 206.

Abuse, vb. 1) to put to a wrong use, misapply: *why dost thou a. the bounteous largess given thee to give?* Sonn. 4, 5. *their gross painting might be better used where cheeks need blood, in thee it is —d,* 82, 14. LLL II, 227. *if your lass interpretation should a.* Wint. IV, 4, 364 (misinterpret your behaviour).

2) to put to a bad use: *who presently a. it* (their inherited gold) Lucr. 864. 994. 1529. As III, 2, 378. H4B IV, 2, 13. H6B V, 1, 172. Cor. V, 6, 86. Ant. III, 6, 33.

3) to use ill, to maltreat: *for my sake even so doth she a. me,* Sonn. 42, 7. *who cannot a. a body dead?* Lucr. 1267. *he shall not a. Robert Shallow,* Wiv. I, 1, 3. I, 4, 5. Meas. III, 2, 215. Err. V, 199. Mids. II, 2, 134. Shr. V, 1, 111. Tw. IV, 2, 51. 95. R2 II, 3, 137. H5 III, 6, 117. IV, 8, 52. R3 I, 3, 52. H8 I, 3, 28. Lr. II, 2, 156. III, 7, 91. IV, 7, 15. 53. Oth. III, 3, 336. Ant. III, 6, 86.

4) to deface, to disfigure: *thy face is much —d with tears,* Rom. IV, 1, 29. Metaphorically: *a. him to the Moor in the rank garb,* Oth. II, 1, 315 (calumniate him with the Moor as incontinent).

5) to offend, insult: *do not a. my master's bounty by the undoing of yourself,* Ant. V, 2, 43. *you have —d me: 'His meanest garment'!* Cymb. II, 3, 154.

6) to disgrace, dishonour: *my bed shall be —d,* Wiv. II, 2, 306. *this lord, who hath —d me,* Alls V, 3, 299. *shall flight a. your name?* H6A IV, 5, 41. Oth. IV, 2, 14. Per. I, 1, 126.

7) to revile: *hang him, he'll a. us,* Tim. II, 2, 49. *I am of life as honest as you that thus a. me,* Oth. V, 1, 123.

8) to corrupt, to pervert: *to draw forth your noble ancestry from the corruption of —ing time,* R3 III, 7, 199. *wicked dreams a. the curtained sleep,* Mcb. II, 1, 50 (or = deceive?). *charms by which the property of youth and maidhood may be —d,* Oth. I, 1, 174. I, 2, 74. *my sins a. my divination,* Cymb. IV, 2, 351.

9) to deceive: *some enchanted trifle to a. me,* Tp. V, 112. *the prince and Claudio have been mightily —d,* Ado V, 2, 100. As III, 5, 80. IV, 1, 218. Tw. III, 1, 124. V, 22. Wint. II, 1, 141. Cor. III, 1, 58. Tit. II, 3, 87. Hml. II, 2, 632. Lr. IV, 1, 24. IV, 7, 77. V, 1, 11. Oth. IV, 2, 139. Cymb. I, 6, 131. III, 4, 105. 123. *you are —d =* you are mistaken, Cymb. I, 4, 124.

Passages which may be assigned to the 1st as well as the 8th and 9th definitions: *I have heard your royal ear —d,* Meas. V, 139. *she doth a. our ears,* Alls V, 3,295. *dreams a. the curtained sleep,* Mcb. II, 1, 50. *the whole ear of Denmark is rankly —d,* Hml. I, 5, 38. *apt to have his ear —d,* Lr. II, 4, 310. *to a. Othello's ear,* Oth. I, 3, 401. In all these cases the idea of deception is more or less predominant.

Abuse, subst. 1) application to a wrong or bad purpose: *things growing to themselves are growth's a.* Ven. 166. Rom. II, 3, 20. Caes. II, 1, 18.

2) ill treatment: *so him I lose through my unkind a.* Sonn. 134, 12. *rejoice at the a. of Falstaff,* Wiv. V, 3, 8. *why hast thou broken faith with me, knowing how hardly I can brook a.?* H6B V, 1, 92. *I let pass the a. done to my niece,* H6C III, 3, 188. *they'll take no offence at our a.* IV, 1, 13.

3) deception: *this is a strange a.* Meas. V, 205. *is it some a., and no such thing?* Hml. IV, 7, 51. cf. *my strange and self-a. is the initiate fear that wants hard use,* Mcb. III, 4, 142.

4) offence, insult, injury: *to find out this a., whence 'tis derived,* Meas. V, 247. *how the villain would close now after his treasonable —s,* 347. *I shall drive you to confess the wilful a.* H4B II, 4, 339. 340. 343 etc. *answer thy a.* H6B II, 1, 41.

5) corrupt practice or custom: *reason is the bawd to lust's a.* Ven. 792. *do nothing but use their —s in common houses,* Meas. II, 1, 43. *the poor —s of the time want countenance,* H4A I, 2, 174. *cries out upon —s,* IV, 3, 81. *the time's a.* Caes. II, 1, 115 (the present state of things contrary to law and reason).

6) offence, crime: *poor wretches have remorse in poor —s,* Lucr. 269. *this false night's —s,* 1075. 1259. 1315. 1655. *pardon my a.* H6A II, 3, 67. *give him chastisement for this a.* IV, 1, 69. *nor tears nor prayers shall purchase out —s,* Rom. III, 1, 198.

7) fault: *they that level at my —s reckon up their own,* Sonn. 121, 10. *turn their own perfection to a. to seem like him,* H4B II, 3, 27. *it is my nature's plague to spy into —s,* Oth. III, 3, 147.

Abuser, corrupter, depraver: *an a. of the world,* Oth. I, 2, 78; cf. 74.

Abut, to be contiguous, to meet: *whose high upreared and —ing fronts the perilous narrow ocean parts asunder,* H5 Prol. 21. *the leafy shelter that —s against the island's side,* Per. V, 1, 51 (doubtful passage).

Aby, to pay, to atone, to answer: *lest thou a. it dear,* Mids. III, 2, 175. 335 (Ff *abide*).

Abysm, abyss, depth without a visible bottom: Sonn. 112, 9. Tp. I, 2, 50. Ant. III, 13, 147.

Academe, (O. Edd. *Achademe*) academy, school of philosophers: LLL I, 1, 13. IV, 3, 303. 352.

Accent, subst. 1) modulation of the voice in speaking: *you find not the apostraphas, and so miss the a.* LLL IV, 2, 124. *action and a. did they teach him,* V, 2, 99. *well spoken, with good a. and good discretion,* Hml. II, 2, 489.

2) sound of the voice: *a terrible oath, with a swaggering a. sharply twanged off,* Tw. III, 4, 197. *the a. of his tongue affecteth him,* John I, 86. R2 V, 1, 47. R3 IV, 4, 158. Troil. I, 3, 53. Lr. I, 4, 1. *in second a. of his ordnance,* H5 II, 4, 126 (echo).

3) a modification of the voice expressive of sentiments: *till after many —s and delays she utters this,* Lucr. 1719. *prophesying with —s terrible,* Mcb. II, 3, 62. *with timorous a. and dire yell,* Oth. I, 1, 75.

4) pronunciation: *your accent is something finer,* As III, 2, 359. *speaking thick became the —s of the valiant,* H4B II, 3, 25. *neither having the a. of Christians nor the gait of Christians,* Hml. III, 2, 35.

5) word, expression: *those same tongues that give thee so thine own in other —s do this praise confound,* Sonn. 69, 7. *any a. breaking from thy tongue,* John V, 6, 14. *breathe short-winded —s of new broils,* H4A I, 1, 3. *do not take his rougher —s for malicious sounds,* Cor. III, 3, 55. *these new tuners of —s,* Rom. II, 4, 30 (coiners of words).

6) speech, language: *midst the sentence so her a. breaks,* Lucr. 566. *throttle their practised a. in their fears,* Mids. V, 97. *in states unborn and —s yet unknown,* Caes. III, 1, 113. *beguiled you in a plain a.* Lr. II, 2, 117.

Accept, vb. to receive of one's own accord, not to refuse; followed by an accus.: Merch. I, 2, 101 (cf. H6C III, 3, 249). IV, 2, 9. V, 197. Shr. Ind. I, 82. II, 83. 102. Wint. II, 1, 131. R2 II, 3, 162. H4A V, 1, 115. H6A III, 1, 149. III, 3, 82. IV, 1, 120. V, 4, 151. H6B I, 3, 216. V, 1, 15. H6C III, 3, 249. R3 III, 7, 214. 221. IV, 4, 310. Troil. V, 2, 189. Cor. V, 3, 15. V, 4, 62. Tit. I, 222. Tim. I, 1, 156. I, 2, 177. 190. IV, 3, 495. Per. Prol. 12. I, 4, 107. — With *of:* Shr. II, 59. IV, 2, 111. H4A IV, 3, 112. H6A V, 3, 80. Tim. I, 1, 135.

—*ed* = agreeable, welcome: *in most —ed pain,* Troil. III, 3, 30.

Accept, subst. acceptance: *pass our a.* H5 V, 2, 82 (declare our acceptance).*

Acceptable, to be received with content and pleasure: *what a. audit canst thou leave?* Sonn. 4, 12.

Acceptance, free and favourable reception; 1) act. = accepting: *I leave him to your gracious a.* Merch. IV, 1, 165. *poured it to her a.* Wint. IV, 4, 362. H5 I, 1, 83. Cor. II, 3, 9. Oth. III, 3, 470. 2) pass. being accepted: *shall will in others seem right gracious, and in my will no fair a. shine?* Sonn. 135, 8. *makes it assured of a.* Lucr. Ded. 3. *their kind a. weepingly beseeched,* Compl. 207. *for their sake let this a. take,* H5 Epil. 14.

Accéss (áccess in Hml. II, 1, 110), admittance: Gent. III, 2, 60. IV, 2, 4. Shr. II, 98. Tw. I, 4, 16. Wint. V, 2, 119. Rom. II Chor. 9. Mcb. I, 5, 45. With pers. pron.: Shr. I, 2, 269. Cor. V, 2, 85. Hml. II, 1, 110. With *of:* Shr. I, 2, 261. Wint. II, 2, 11. With *to* or *unto:* Gent. III, 1, 109. Meas. II, 2, 19. II, 4, 18. As I, 1, 98. Shr. I, 1, 119. I, 2, 127. Wint. V, 1, 87. H4B IV, 1, 78. H8 III, 2, 17. Cor. V, 2, 85. Hml. II, 1, 110. Oth. III, 1, 38. Per. II, 5, 7.

Accessary, adj. guilty, participating in guilt: *inclined to a. yieldings,* Lucr. 1658. *to both their deaths thou shalt be a.* R3 I, 2, 192.

Accessary, subst. accomplice: *an a. to all sins,* Lucr. 922. *I an a. needs must be to that sweet thief,* Sonn. 35, 13. *I am your a.* Alls II, 1, 35

Accessible, to be arrived at, approachable: *a. is none but Milford way,* Cymb. III, 2, 84.

Accidence, a book containing the rudiments of grammar: Wiv. IV, 1, 16.

Accident, 1) casualty, chance: Sonn. 115, 5. 124, 5. Compl. 247. Tp. I, 2, 178. Meas. IV, 3, 81. Merch. V, 278. Wint. IV, 4, 19. 549. Troil. III, 3, 83. IV, 5, 262. Rom. V, 3, 251. Hml. III, 1, 30. IV, 7, 69. 122. Ant. IV, 14, 84. V, 2, 6. Cymb. V, 5, 76. 278.

2) incident, event: *these happened —s*, Tp. V, 250. *the story of my life and the particular —s gone by*, 305. *this is an a. of hourly proof*, Ado II, 1, 188. Mids. IV, 1, 73. Tw. IV, 3, 11. H4A I, 2, 231. H6A V, 3, 4. Rom. V, 2, 27. Hml. III, 2, 209. Oth. IV, 2, 231. V, 1, 94.

3) mischance, misfortune: *forced by need and a.* Wint. V, 1, 92. *dismay not at this a.* H6A III, 3, 1. *by some unlooked for a. cut off*, R3 I, 3, 214. *this a. is not unlike my dream*, Oth. I, 1, 143. *moving —s*, I, 3, 135. *the shot of a. nor dart of chance*, IV, 1, 278. *all solemn things should answer solemn —s*, Cymb. IV, 2, 192. *with mortal —s opprest*, V, 4, 99.

Accidental, 1) casual, fortuitous: Caes. IV, 3, 146. Hml. V, 2, 393.

2) incidental, occasional: *the doors, the wind, the glove, that did delay him, he takes for a. things of trial*, Lucr. 326 (not inherent to the like undertakings, but occasionally happening). *thy sin's not a., but a trade*, Meas. III, 1, 149.

Accidentally, by accident, fortuitously: Err. V, 361. LLL IV, 2, 143. Cor. IV, 3, 40.

Accite, to cite, to summon: *we will a. our state*, H4B V, 2, 141. *he by the senate is —d home*, Tit. I, 27. Misprinted for *excite*: H4B II, 2, 64.

Acclamation, shouts of applause: Lucr. Arg. 25. Cor. I, 9, 51.

Accommodate, (cf. *Unaccommodated*), to supply with conveniences: *a soldier is better —d* (Qq *a.*) *than with a wife*, H4B III, 2, 72 (where Shallow's and Bardolph's remarks prove that the word was not yet in daily use, but rather affected). *the safer sense will ne'er a. his master thus*, Lr. IV, 6, 81. *—d by the place*, Cymb. V, 3, 32 (favoured).

Accommodation, supply of conveniences, comfort: *all the —s that thou bearest are nursed by baseness*, Meas. III, 1, 14. *with such a. and besort as levels with her breeding*, Oth. I, 3, 239.

Accompany, (the pass. always followed by *with*, never by *by*), to keep company, to attend, not only on a walk or journey: Lucr. Arg. 4. 18. Shr. I, 2, 106. Wint. IV, 2, 53. Tit. I, 333. II, 3, 78. Tim. I, 1, 89. Cor. IV, 3, 41. But also in a state of rest: *joy and fresh days of love a. your hearts*, Mids. V, 30. *how thou art —ed*, H4A II, 4, 440 (in what company thou livest). III, 2, 16. H4B IV, 4, 15. 52. R3 III, 5, 99. H8 IV, 1, 25. Cor. III, 3, 6. Tit. I, 358. Mcb. V, 3, 24.

Accomplice, co-operator, fellow in arms: *success unto our valiant general, and happiness to his —s!* H6A V, 2, 9 (cf. *Complice*).

Accomplish, 1) to make complete, to furnish with what is wanting: *—ed with that we lack*, Merch. III, 4, 61. *—ed with the number of thy hours*, R2 II, 1, 177 (of thy age). *the armourers —ing the knights*, H5 IV Chor. 12. *well —ed*, quite = accomplished, in the modern sense, Gent. IV, 3, 13. *—ed*, absol. = perfect: Compl. 116. Tw. III, 1, 95. Cymb. I, 4, 101. 103.

2) to perform, to fulfil: *with honourable action, such as he hath observed in noble ladies unto their lords, by them —ed*, Shr. Ind. I, 112. *which holy undertaking she —ed*, Alls IV, 3, 60. *all the number of his fair demands shall be —ed*, R2 III, 3, 124. *to a. his projects*, Cor. V, 6, 34. *the vision is —ed*, Cymb. V, 5, 470.

3) to gain, to obtain (cf. *Achieve*): *to a. twenty golden crowns*, H6C III, 2, 152. *what you cannot as you would achieve, you must perforce a. as you may*, Tit. II, 1, 107.

Accomplishment, performance, work: *who this a. so hotly chased*, Lucr. 716. *turning the a. of many years into an hourglass*, H5 Prol. 30.

Accompt, see *Account*.

Accomptant, see *Accountant*.

Accord, subst. 1) harmony of sounds: *gamut I am, the ground of all a.* Shr. III, 1, 73.

2) concord, harmony of minds: *be at a.* As I, 1, 67. *neighbourhood and christian-like a.* H5 V, 2, 381.

3) just correspondence of one thing with another: *how can I grace my talk, wanting a hand to give it that a.?* Tit. V, 2, 18 (Ff *to give it action*).

4) consent: *let your will attend on their —s*, Err. II, 1, 25 (do not desire but what they consent to). *on mine own a.* Wint. II, 3, 63. *with full a. to our demands*, H5 V, 2, 71. *this a. of Hamlet sits smiling to my heart*, Hml. I, 2, 123.

5) assent: *they have galls, good arms, strong joints, true swords, and Jove's a., nothing so full of heart*, Troil. I, 3, 238 (Jove's assent that nothing is so full of heart. M. Edd. *and, Jove's accord!*)*

Accord, vb. to agree: *my consent and fair —ing voice*, Rom. I, 2, 19. Followed by *to*: Gent. I, 3, 90. As V, 4, 139. By *with*: H6B III, 1, 269. H6C III, 2, 77. By an inf.: Compl. 3. H5 II, 2, 86.

Accordant, of the same mind, well inclined: *if he found her a.* Ado I, 2, 14.

According, 1) agreeably, in proportion; with *to*: *and was, a. to his estate, royally entertained*, Lucr. Arg. 14. Gent. I, 2, 8. II, 4, 83. III, 2, 12. IV, 3, 8. Wiv. I, 1, 162. Meas. IV, 3, 83. V, 510. Err. I, 2, 6. Mids. I, 1, 44. I, 2, 3. III, 1, 78. Merch. I, 2, 41. II, 2, 65. IV, 1, 235. As V, 4, 67. 181. Shr. IV, 3, 95. Tw. IV, 3, 31. Wint. III, 3, 30. John V, 2, 118. R2 I, 1, 2. H4A III, 1, 71. H4B V, 5, 73. H5 II, 2, 35. V, 2, 362. H6B II, 4, 95. 99. H6C II, 2, 152. Cor. II, 1, 4. Caes. III, 1, 295. V, 5, 76. Mcb. III, 1, 97. V, 6, 6. Hml. II, 1, 47. II, 2, 552. Cymb II, 3, 63. With *as*: *a. as marriage binds*, As V, 4, 59. *a. as your ladyship desired*, H6A II, 3, 12. H6B III, 2, 12. Caes. I, 2, 261.

2) accordingly, conformably: *and square rest thy life a.* Meas. V, 487.

Accordingly, according to it, conformably: Meas. II, 3, 8. Ado III, 2, 125. John II, 231. H4A I, 3, 3. H6A II, 2, 60. Ant. I, 2, 78. III, 9, 4. Cymb. I, 0, 24. *he is very great in knowledge and a. valiant*, Alls II, 5, 9 (= as valiant).

Accost, to board, to make up to, to address: Tw. I, 3, 52 (not understood by Sir Andrew). III, 2, 23. As for Troil. IV, 5, 59 see *Coast*, vb.*

Account, subst. (in F1 13 times *accompt*, 17 times *account*) 1) reckoning: *tell o'er the sad a. of* *fore-bemoaned moan*, Sonn. 30, 11. *upon remainder of a dear a.* R2 I, 1, 130. H4B I, 1, 167. H5 Prol. 17. H6B IV, 2, 93 *(to cast a.)* R3 V, 3, 11. Rom. I, 5, 120. Tim. II, 2, 142. *a beggarly a. of empty boxes,* Rom. V, 1, 45 (= store).

2) c o m p u t a t i o n: *at your hand the a. of hours to crave,* Sonn. 58, 3 (cf. def. 4). *then in the number let me pass untold, though in thy stores' a. I one must be,* 136, 10. *our compelled sins stand more for number than for a.* Meas. II, 4, 58 (are rather numbered than put to our score; cf. def. 4). *our duty is so rich, so infinite, that we may do it still without a.* LLL V, 2, 200. *in virtues, beauties, livings, friends, exceed a.* Merch. III, 2, 159. Wint. II, 3, 198. H4A III, 2, 176. H6C III, 1, 35. H8 III, 2, 210. Tim. II, 2, 3. Oth. I, 3, 5.

3) e s t i m a t i o n: *no truth of such a.* Sonn. 62, 6. *to stand high in your a.* Merch. III, 2, 157. *when you were in place and in a. nothing so strong and fortunate as I,* H4A V, 1, 37. *his achievements of no less a.* H6A II, 3, 8. *make high a. of you,* R3 III, 2, 71. *no dearer in my a.* Lr. I, 1, 21.

4) e x p l a n a t i o n g i v e n t o a s u p e r i o r, a n-s w e r i n g f o r c o n d u c t (see above Sonn. 58, 3 and Meas. II, 4, 58): *to make an a. of her life to . . . ,* Ado II, 1, 65 (Ff *to make a.*). *to render an a.* IV, 1, 338. *my a. I well may give,* Wint. IV, 3, 21. *when the last a. 'twixt heaven and earth is to be made,* John IV, 2, 216. *I will call him to so strict a.* H4A III, 2, 149. *he shall come to his a.* Cor. IV, 7, 18. *whene'er we come to our a.* 26. *none can call our power to a.* Mcb. V, 1, 43. *sent to my a.* Hml. I, 5, 78.

Account, vb. (never *accompt*), 1) tr. with a double accus., to esteem, to think: *I a. myself highly praised,* Ven. Ded. 3. Lucr. 1245. Meas. III, 2, 203. LLL IV, 1, 25. Merch. IV, 1, 417. Shr. IV, 3, 183. Tw. II, 1, 27. Wint. I, 2, 347. John III, 4, 122. H4A V, 1, 95. H6A II, 4, 120. H6C III, 2, 169. R3 V, 3, 108. Cor. I, 1, 15. 43. Tim. II, 2, 110. Mcb. I, 7, 39. IV, 2, 77. Hml. III, 2, 105. *they a. his head upon the bridge,* R3 III, 2, 72 (i. e. in their opinion his head is already set on London bridge, and consequently in a high position). Cymb. I, 6, 80 (read: *account 's*).

2) intr. with *of*, a) to judge, to estimate: *I a. of them as jewels purchased at an easy price,* Tit. III, 1, 198. *he that otherwise —s of me,* Per. II, 5, 63. b) to make account, to esteem: *I a. of her beauty,* Gent. II, 1, 66.

In Per. Prol. 30 the pass. part. is dissyll.; O. Edd. *account'd,* M. Edd. *account.*

Accountant, (O. Edd. *accountant* and *accomptant*), adj. liable to penalty, punishable, obnoxious to justice: *his offence is so, as it appears a. to the law upon that pain,* Meas. II, 4, 86. *I stand a. for as great a sin,* Oth. II, 1, 302.

Accoutered, fully dressed, fully equipped: *when we are both a. like young men,* Merch. III, 4, 63 (Q1 *apparelled*). *a. as I was, I plunged in,* Caes. I, 2, 105.

Accoutrement, dress, equipage: *not only in the simple office of love, but in all the a., complement and ceremony of it,* Wiv. IV, 2, 5. *point-device in your —s,* As III, 2, 402. *I can change these poor —s,* Shr. III, 2, 121. *in habit and device, exterior form, outward a.* John I, 211.

Accrue, to grow, to be earned: *profits will a.* H5 II, 1, 117 (Pistol's speech).

Accumulate, to heap: *on just proof surmise a.*

Sonn. 117, 10 (add suspicion to what has been plainly proved). *what piles of wealth hath he —d!* H8 III, 2, 107. *on horror's head horrors a.* Oth. III, 3, 370.

Accumulation, amassing, plentiful acquisition: *quick a. of renown,* Ant. III, 1, 19.

Accursed, (trisyll.), cursed, doomed to misery and destruction: *a. tower, a. fatal hand!* H6A I, 4, 76. *thou foul a. minister of hell,* V, 4, 93. *the brat of this a. duke,* H6C I, 3, 4. *their a. line,* 32. *a. and unquiet wrangling days,* R3 II, 4, 55. *O my a. womb,* IV, 1, 54. IV, 4, 138. *my a. sons,* Tit. II, 3, 290. III, 1, 66. *this a. devil,* V, 3, 5. *this a. deed,* 64. Tim. I, 1, 268. *stand aye a. in the calendar,* Mcb. IV, 1, 134. *a. be that tongue,* V, 8, 17.

Accursed (dissyll.) or **Accurst** (cf. *Cursed* and *Curst*), 1) cursed, doomed to misery: *O time most a.* Gent. V, 4, 71. *a. be he that seeks to make them foes,* H6C I, 1, 205. *thou art the cause, and most a. effect,* R3 I, 2, 120. IV, 1, 72. Tit. IV, 2, 79. Rom. IV, 5, 43. Tim. IV, 3, 34. Mcb. III, 6, 49. IV, 3, 107. Cymb. V, 5, 154.

2) unhappy, miserable: *the more am I a.* Ven. 1120. *how a. in being so blest,* Wint. II, 1, 38. *most a. am I to be enjoined to this,* III, 3, 52. *O thoughts of men a.! past and to come seems best, things present worst,* H4B I, 3, 107. H5 IV, 3, 65. H6A V, 2, 18. Tim. IV, 2, 42. Hml. III, 2, 189.

Only twice occurring in prose: *security enough to make fellowships a.* Meas. III, 2, 242. *I am a. to rob in that thief's company,* H4A II, 2, 10 (it is my ill luck to etc.)

Accusation, 1) the act of charging one with a crime or offence: *be you constant in the a.* Ado II, 2, 55. *with public a.* IV, 1, 307. Wint. III, 2, 32. H4A I, 3, 68. H8 III, 1, 54. Cor. III, 1, 127.

2) that which constitutes the charge: *to produce more a.* Wint. II, 3, 117. *read these —s and these grievous crimes,* R2 IV, 223. *roar these —s forth,* H6A III, 1, 40. Cor. I, 1, 46. III, 2, 140. *his a. = a)* the charge brought by him: Meas. II, 4, 157. III, 1, 201. Ado IV, 1, 235. V, 1, 249. H6B I, 3, 206. Ant. III, 6, 23. b) the charge brought against him: *which contradicts my a.* Wint. III, 2, 24. *to his —s he pleaded still not guilty,* H8 II, 1, 12.

Accusative, the objective case in grammar: *what is your a. case?* Wiv. IV, 1, 45.

Accuse, subst., accusation: *York by false a. doth level at my life,* H6B III, 1, 160.

Accuse, vb., to charge with a fault or crime; followed by a simple accus.: Sonn. 117, 1, Meas. IV, 3, 148. IV, 6, 2. V, 140. 160. 305. 309. Ado IV, 1, 179. 217. 234. IV, 2, 40. 50. V, 2, 99. V, 4, 2. Merch. IV, 1, 129. Alls I, 1, 149. V, 3, 289. Wint. I, 1, 17. II, 3, 204. R2 I, 1, 47. V, 2, 13. H4B IV, 5, 166. H6A V, 4, 81. H6B I, 3, 192. III, 1, 103. R3 I, 2, 85. I, 3, 27. I, 4, 139. III, 2, 95. H8 II, 1, 24. II, 4, 122. V, 3, 50. 56. Cor. I, 1, 100. III, 2, 143. V, 6, 5. Tit. V, 1, 130. Tim. IV, 3, 334. Lr. III, 7, 39. Ant. III, 6, 23. Cymb. II, 3, 115. V, 4, 95. Per. IV, 2, 76. *the —ed = the —d* person, R2 I, 1, 17. With *of:* Sonn. 58, 8. 152, 5. Meas. V, 195. Wint. III, 2, 13. H6B I, 3, 180. 185. Cor. I, 1, 92. Hml. III, 1, 124. Ant. III, 5, 10. IV, 6, 19. Cymb. III, 4, 49. *what man is he you are —d of?* Ado IV, 1, 178, in the same sense as: *Polixenes with whom I am —d,* Wint. III, 2, 63. Followed by *in: a. him in his intent towards our wives,* Wiv. II, 1, 180.

—*d in fornication*, Meas. II, 1, 82. *in this which you a. her*, Wint. II, 1, 133 (the prepos. belonging to both pronouns). Peculiar turns of expression: *being —d a crafty murderer*, H6B III, 1, 254. *doth any one a. York for a traitor?* I, 3, 182 (cf. *For*). Absol., at least in appearance: *if thou canst a., or aught intendest to lay unto my charge*, H6A III, 1, 3.

Accuser, one who accuses: Ado IV, 2, 37. R2 I, 1, 17. H6B I, 3, 201. R3 I, 3, 26. H8 II, 1, 104. V, 1, 120. V, 3, 46. Cor. I, 1, 132. Lr. IV, 6, 174. Cymb. III, 2, 2 (O. Edd. *what monsters her accuse*, M. Edd. *what monster's her accuser*).

Accustomed, customary (used of things only): *her a. crossness*, Ado II, 3, 184. *the a. sight of death*, As III, 5, 4. *your a. diligence*, H6A V, 3, 9. *his a. health*, R3 I, 3, 2. *an old a. feast*, Rom. I, 2, 20. *an a. action with her*, Mcb. V, 1, 32.

Ace, a single point on a die: Mids. V, 312 (quibbling with *ass*). Cymb. II, 3, 3.

Acerb, harsh to the taste: *as a. as coloquintida*, Oth. I, 3, 355 (only in Q1, the other O. Edd. *bitter*).

Ache, subst. pain, especially a chronical pain caused by inveterate ills: Meas. III, 1, 130. Ado V, 1, 26. H4B V, 1, 93. Troil. V, 3, 105. Pronounced like the name of the letter H, Ado III, 4, 56, and therefore dissyll. in the plural: Tp. I, 2, 370. Tim. I, 1, 257. V, 1, 202.

Ache, vb. (in O. Edd. *ake*, and rhyming to *brake* and *sake*, Ven. 875. Err. III, 1, 58), to pain, to smart: *whose swelling dugs do a.* Ven. 875. *doth make the wound a.* Lucr. 1116. Tp. III, 3, 2. Err. III, 1, 58. John IV, 1, 41. H8 V, 4, 92. Troil. V, 10, 35. 51. Cor. III, 1, 108. Rom. II, 5, 26. 49. 65. Hml. V, 1, 101. Oth. III, 4, 146. With *at: my wounds a. at you*, Tim. III, 5, 96. *the sense —s at thee*, Oth. IV, 2, 69.

Acheron, the infernal river, supposed by Sh. to be a burning lake: Mids. III, 2, 357. Tit. IV, 3, 44. Mcb. III, 5, 15. (cf. H4B II, 4, 170. H6B I, 4, 42. Lr. III, 6, 8).

Achieve, 1) absol. to make an end, to perform what is intended: *and does a. as soon as draw his sword*, Cor. IV, 7, 23.

2) trans. a) to perform, to execute: *which they shall have no sooner —d but we'll set upon them*, H4A I, 2, 193.

b) to kill, to finish: *bid them a. me*, H5 IV, 3, 91.

c) to gain, to obtain, 1) as the result of exertion: *experience is by industry —d*, Gent. I, 3, 22. Shr. I, 1, 20. 161. 184. 224. I, 2, 268. Alls I, 1, 52. Tw. II, 5, 157. III, 4, 47. V, 378. R2 II, 1, 254. IV, 217. H5 Epil. 7. Cor. I, 9, 33. Tit. II, 1, 80. 106. Ant. III, 1, 20. Per. V, 1, 117. 2) without the notion of exertion: *that sin by him advantage should a.* Sonn. 67, 3. *your fortune —d her mistress*, Merch. III, 2, 210. John IV, 2, 105. H6B V, 2, 46. Oth. II, 1, 61.

Achievement, 1) exploit: *and for a. offer us his ransom*, H5 III, 5, 60. *his —s of no less account*, H6A III, 3, 8. Troil. I, 3, 181. Hml. I, 4, 21.

2) acquisition: *all the soil of the a.* (viz of the crown) *goes with me into the earth*, H4B IV, 5, 190. *a. is command; ungained, beseech*, Troil. I, 2, 319 (when we have obtained what we wished for, we play the masters; if not, the humble suitors). *how my —s mock me*, IV, 2, 71.

Achiever, gainer: *a victory is twice itself when the a. brings home full numbers*, Ado I, 1, 8.

Achilles, the Greek hero: Lucr. 1424. LLL V, 2, 635. Troil. I, 2, 268 (and passim). *like to —' spear*, H6B V, 1, 100 (alluding to Telephus cured by the rust scraped from Achilles' spear, by which he had been wounded).

Achitophel, the counsellor of Absalom, cursed by David: H4B I, 2, 41.

Acknowledge, to appropriate to one's knowledge; 1) to claim acquaintance of: *I may not evermore a. thee, lest my bewailed guilt should do thee shame*, Sonn. 36, 9.

2) to allow the sovereignty or superiority of: *will a. you and Jessica*, Merch. III, 4, 38. *a. the king*, John II, 269. *Christ*, H4A III, 2, 111. Ant. III, 13, 97.

3) to own, to avow, to confess to, the knowledge of a thing or person: Ant. V, 2, 180. Err. V, 322. Wint. I, 2, 401. IV, 4, 430. H5 IV, 1, 225. Rom. III, 5, 195. Lr. I, 1, 10. as a guilt or fault: Wint. III, 2, 62. H4B II, 2, 6. as a truth or right: Ado I, 2, 13. Alls II, 4, 43. to own with gratitude: Lr. IV, 7, 4. — With a double acc.: *this thing of darkness I a. mine*, Tp. V, 276. Tim. I, 2, 130. Lr. I, 1, 216. With an inf.: *a. it to be the hand of heaven*, Alls II, 3, 35. Reflectively: *if the encounter a. itself*, Meas. III, 1, 262, i. e. if the consequences of the meeting be such as to render denying impossible.

Acknowledgment, owning of a benefit received: H5 IV, 8, 124.

Acknown, knowing, acquainted: *be not a. on't*, Oth. III, 3, 319 (do not confess to the knowledge of it).

A-cold, having the sensation of cold: Lr. III, 4, 59. 85. 152.

Aconitum, the poisonous plant Aconitum or wolf's-bane: H4B IV, 4, 48.

Acorn, the fruit of the oak: Tp. I, 2, 464. Mids. II, 1, 31. III, 2, 330. As III, 2, 248.

Acquaint, to make to know, to impart knowledge; with *of: to a. her of it*, Ado III, 1, 40. Wint. II, 2, 48. IV, 4, 423. R3 I, 3, 106 (Qq *with*). Rom. III, 4, 16. Cymb. I, 6, 149. With *with: Brutus —ed the people with the doer*, Lucr. Arg. 23. Tp. II, 2, 41. Wiv. IV, 6, 8. Meas. I, 2, 184. Ado I, 2, 22. LLL V, 1, 122. Merch. I, 2, 110. IV, 1, 154. As I, 1, 128. 138. Alls I, 3, 124. II, 3, 304. Wint. IV, 4, 696. John V, 2, 89. V, 6, 25. R3 III, 5, 65. IV, 4, 329. Tit. II, 1, 122. Mcb. III, 1, 130. Hml. I, 1, 172. Lr. I, 2, 110. I, 5, 2. Ant. III, 6, 58. —*ed with*: Sonn. 20, 3. 88, 5. Gent. IV, 4, 25. Wiv. II, 1, 90. II, 2, 151. 189. III, 1, 68. Meas. II, 1, 214. IV, 1, 51. Err. IV, 3, 91. Merch. IV, 1, 171. As III, 2, 288. IV, 1, 2. Shr. IV, 1, 155. IV, 4, 26. Alls III, 7, 5. IV, 1, 10. V, 3, 106. H4B II, 1, 120. III, 2, 353. R3 IV, 4, 269. H8 V, 1, 170. Troil. II, 3, 122. Tim. III, 3, 38. Caes. II, 1, 256. Oth. III, 3, 99. Per. IV, 6, 210. Followed by a clause: —*ed each other how they loved me*, Wiv. II, 2, 114. *to acquaint his grace you are gone*, Alls III, 6, 84. *a. you that I have received*, H4B IV, 1, 7. *shall be —ed for what you come*, H8 II, 2, 108.

The partic. absol.: *I am as well —ed here as I was in our house*, Meas. IV, 3, 1. *what need she be —ed?* Err. III, 2, 15 (what need she know it?). *be better —ed*, Cymb. I, 4, 132 (i. e. with each other; cf. *Kiss, Know, Love, See* etc.). Once = well known: *that war, or peace, or both at once, may be as things —ed and familiar to us*, H4B V, 2, 139.

Acquaintance, 1) the state of being known to each other, of being acquainted with a thing or person: Sonn. 89, 8. 12. Tp. V, 186. Wiv. I, 1, 255. II, 2, 168. 279. Ado V, 1, 341. Mids. III, 1, 185. 193. 200. As V, 2, 1. 7. Tw. I, 3, 56. V, 91. John V, 6, 13. H4B III, 2, 314. H8 III, 1, 161. Troil. III, 3, 9. Cor. V, 1, 10. Rom. III, 3, 5. Lr. IV, 3, 56. Oth. IV, 2, 192 (Q1 *acquittance*). Cymb. I, 4, 25. Per. IV, 6, 206. *to have a. with*, As I, 3, 50. *to hold my a. with*, Alls II, 3, 240. *to hold a. with the waves*, Tw. I, 2, 16. *to take a.: thou shalt find those children nursed, delivered from thy brain, to take a new a. of thy mind*, Sonn. 77, 12; i. e. thy mind will become anew acquainted with its own thoughts, which had been quite lost from its memory and now seem new to it.

2) a person well known: *what, old a.!* H4A V, 4, 102. Oftener collectively, persons well known, or acquainted with each other: *both stood like old a.* Lucr. 1595. Merch. II, 2, 181. Shr. I, 1, 34. Tw. II, 5, 176. H4A I, 1, 16. H4B III, 2, 38. H8 I, 2, 47. Oth. II, 1, 205.

In the language of Evans = acquainted: Wiv. I, 2, 8.

Acquire, to gain; either by exertion: Alls IV, 3, 80. Troil. II, 3, 201. Hml. III, 2, 8. Ant. III, 1, 15. IV, 15, 28. Or without it: *pomp, the which to leave more bitter than 'tis sweet at first to a.* H8 II, 3, 9.

Acquisition, that which is acquired: Tp. IV, 1, 13.

Acquit, 1) to make full payment for: *till life to death a. my forced offence,* Lucr. 1071, i. e. till life make to death full payment for my offence, till I atone for it by dying; or perhaps: till life, done to death, killed, atone for my offence.

2) to set free, to release from a debt, obligation, or penalty: *I will a. you,* Tw. III, 4, 235. *—ed by a true substantial form,* H4B IV, 1, 173. *if my tongue cannot entreat you to a. me,* V, 5, 133. With *from: may any terms a. me from this chance?* Lucr. 1706. With *of: —ed of grievous penalties,* Merch. IV, 1, 409. V, 138. *God a. them of their practices,* H5 II, 2, 144.

Refl., to clear one's self: *pray God he may a. him of suspicion,* H6B III, 2, 25. *of these supposed evils to a. myself,* R3 I, 2, 77.

3) *to a. one's self well* = to do good work: As I, 1, 134. R3 V, 5, 3.

Partic. *a.* for *—ed:* R3 V, 5, 3; in the sense of delivered, rid of: *I am glad I am so a. of this tinderbox,* Wiv. I, 3, 27.

Acquittance, subst. 1) a writing which is evidence of a discharge: *you can produce —s for such a sum,* LLL II, 161. Cymb. V, 4, 174.

2) acquittal, discharge: *now must your conscience my a. seal,* Hml. IV, 7, 1.

3) payment, retribution: *comforts of sudden respect and a.* Oth. IV, 2, 192 (only in Q1; the rest of O. Edd. *acquaintance*).

Acquittance, vb. to acquit, to clear: *a. me from all the impure blots,* R3 III, 7, 233.

Acre, 1) a ploughed or sowed field within certain limits: *my bosky —s and my unshrubbed down,* Tp. IV, 81. *between the —s of the rye,* As V, 3, 23. *over whose —s walked those blessed feet,* H4A I, 1, 25. *search every a. in the high-grown field,* Lr. IV, 4, 7.

2) a certain quantity of land (160 square rods): *an a. of barren ground,* Tp. I, 1, 70. *ere with spur we heat an a.* Wint. I, 2, 96. *throw millions of —s on us,* Hml. V, 1, 304.

Across, adv. 1) athwart, from side to side; in the phrase *to break one's head or pate a.:* Err. II, 1, 78. Tw. V, 178. Hml. II, 2, 599. In Alls II, 1, 70 it must be remembered that in tilting it was thought disgraceful to break the spear across the body of the adversary, instead of by the push of the point; cf. *Cross* and *Traverse.*

2) folded (of arms): Lucr. 1662. Caes. II, 1, 240.

Across, prep. athwart: *made her flight a. thy father's ground,* Wint. IV, 4, 15.

Act, subst. 1) deed, action: *thy brother was a furtherer in the a.* Tp. V, 73. *the tyrannous and bloody a. is done,* R3 IV, 3, 1 (Qq *deed*). Meas. V, 456. Merch. IV, 1, 19. Alls II, 1, 155. II, 3, 143. III, 7, 7. 46. Tw. IV, 3, 35 (cf. Rom. II, 6, 1). Wint. II, 1, 181. III, 2, 52. John III, 4, 149. IV, 2, 18. IV, 3, 135. R2 IV, 138. H4B Chor. 5. II, 3, 21. IV, 2, 117. H5 I, 2, 231. H6A II, 2, 35. H6B I, 1, 194. III, 2, 118. R3 IV, 4, 280. H8 I, 2, 85. Troil. I, 3, 348. II, 2, 119. III, 3, 131. Cor. I, 2, 5. V, 2, 15. 334. Caes. III, 1, 166. Tit. IV, 1, 64. Rom. III, 3, 110. Mcb. I, 7, 40. IV, 1, 149. Hml. I, 5, 84. III, 3, 91. III, 4, 40. 51. V, 1, 11. V, 2, 392. Lr. II, 4, 114. III, 4, 90. III, 7, 87. IV, 2, 74. Oth. III, 3, 134. IV, 2, 163. V, 2, 190. 203. 211. Ant. I, 2, 148. III, 1, 13 *(make).* IV, 8, 12. V, 1, 22. V, 2, 288. 334. Cymb. II, 1, 66. III, 2, 21. III, 3, 53. III, 4, 94. Per. I, 1, 73. I, 2, 18. V, 1, 140.*Used of cohabitation: *the a. of lust,* Lucr. 1636. *the a. of fornication,* Meas. V, 70. *the a. of sport,* Oth. II, 1, 230. And simply *the a.:* Lucr. 199. 350. 1637. 1704. 1824. Sonn. 152, 3. Meas. II, 3, 26. Troil. III, 2, 90.

2) doing, performing, being active: *age wore us out of a.* Alls I, 2, 30. *all your —s are queens,* Wint. IV, 4, 146. *sets it in a. and use,* H4B IV, 3, 126. *the honour of it does pay the a. of it,* H8 III, 2, 182. *in his particular a. and place,* Hml. I, 3, 26 (i. e. the peculiar line of conduct prescribed to him by his rank. *Ff sect and force*). Alls IV, 3, 55. John III, 3, 57. V, 1, 45. H5 I, 2, 189. H6B V, 3, 10. Troil. III, 2, 96. Cor. I, 9, 19. Tim. V, 1, 26. Ant. II, 2, 46. 149. II, 7, 84. Cymb. V, 3, 29. *to be* or *stand in a.* or *in the a.* = to go forward: Merch. I, 3, 84. Oth. I, 1, 152.

3) agency, operation: *esteem no a. but that of hand,* Troil. I, 3, 199. *distilled almost to jelly with the a. of fear,* Hml. I, 2, 205. *the native a. and figure of my heart,* Oth. I, 1, 62. *poisons which with a little a. upon the blood burn like ...,* III, 3, 328. *our conditions, so differing in their —s,* Ant. II, 2, 116. *apply allayments to their a.* Cymb. I, 5, 22.

4) execution: *the better a. of purposes mistook is to mistake again,* John III, 1, 274. *doing the execution and the a. for which we have assembled them,* H5 II, 2, 17. *give thy thoughts no tongue, nor any unproportioned thought his a.* Hml. I, 3, 60.

5) event: *to the state this heavy a. with heavy heart relate,* Oth. V, 2, 371. *makest thou me a dullard in this a.?* Cymb. V, 5, 265; but cf. def. 6.

6) part of a play: *this dumb play had his acts made plain with tears,* Ven. 359. As II, 7, 143. H4B I, 1, 156. H8 Epil. 3. Mcb. I, 3, 128. Hml. III, 2, 83. V, 2, 346. A play on the word: Tp. II, 1, 252. Tw.

V, 254. Wint. V, 2, 86. John II, 376. R3 II, 2, 39. Mcb. II, 4, 5.

7) decree, law, edict: Meas. I, 2, 174. I, 4, 64. R2 IV, 213. H6C I, 1, 245. 249. II, 2, 91. Cor. I, 1, 85. = the record containing a law or determination: *thyself shalt see the a.* Merch. IV, 1, 314.

Act, vb. 1) absol. to perform the proper functions, to work, to be in action: *we do not a. that often jest,* Wiv. IV, 2, 108 (in a lascivious sense; cf. *Do* and the subst. *Act). the resolute —ing of your blood,* Meas. II, 1, 12. *to a. in safety,* Mcb. III, 1, 54. Hml. V, 1, 12.

2) tr. a) to perform, execute: *I did but a., he's author of thy slander,* Ven. 1006. *to a. her commands,* Tp. I, 2, 273. Wiv. II, 1, 101. Meas. II, 2, 104. Tw. V, 348. John IV, 2, 240. Rom. IV, 1, 120. Caes. II, 1, 63. Mcb. III, 4, 140. IV, 3, 97. Hml. III, 1, 129. III, 4, 108. IV, 5, 125. Lr. II, 1, 20. Oth. I, 1, 172. Per. I, 1, 92.

b) to set to work, to put in action: *here is a hand to hold a sceptre up and with the same to a. controlling laws,* H6B V, 1, 103. *till strange love, grown bold, think true love —ed simple modesty,* Rom. III, 2, 16. *let the world see his nobleness well —ed,* Ant. V, 2, 45.

c) to represent, to perform (as a player): Pilgr. 152. Gent. IV, 4, 174. Wiv. III, 3, 40. Tw. I, 4, 26. Wint. V, 2, 88. H4B IV, 5, 99. H5 Prol. 3. H6C V, 6, 10. H8 I, 2, 195. Troil. I, 3, 158. Cor. II, 2, 100. 149. Rom. IV, 3, 19. Caes. III, 1, 112. Hml. II, 2, 455. Cymb. III, 3, 95. III, 4, 26.

Actaeon, the Theban prince transformed to a stag by Diana: Tit. II, 3, 63. His horns a prototype of cuckoldom: Wiv. II, 1, 122. III, 2, 44.

Action, 1) the state or manner of being active, activity: *the expense of spirit in a waste of shame is lust in a.* Sonn. 129, 2. *the rarer a. is in virtue than in vengeance,* Tp. V, 2, 27. *more reasons for this a. shall I render you,* Meas. I, 3, 48. *strong reasons make strong —s,* John III, 4, 182. *imitate the a. of the tiger,* H5 III, 1, 6. *a gentle business, and becoming the a. of good women,* H8 II, 3, 55. *holding them, in human a. and capacity, of no more soul than camels,* Cor. II, 1, 265. *vice sometimes by a. dignified,* Rom. II, 3, 22. *be what it is, the a. of my life is like it,* Cymb. V, 4, 150. Particularly when activity is attended by exertion: *divide the a. of their bodies from their souls,* H4B I, 1, 195. *the man of a.* II, 4, 406 (the active, 'deed-achieving' man). *they have used their dearest a. in the tented field,* Oth. I, 3, 85. *to lock it* (life) *from a. and adventure,* Cymb. IV, 4, 3. Especially warlike occupation: *in hand and hope of a.* Meas. I, 4, 52. *a., hence borne out, may waste the memory of the former days,* H4B IV, 5, 215. H5 I, 2, 114. IV, 2, 27. Cor. I, 3, 28. IV, 3, 53. Cymb. III, 7, 2. H4B I, 3, 37.

2) exertion, manifestation of vigour, strong exercise: *beauty, whose a. is no stronger than a flower,* Sonn. 65, 4. *motion and long-during a. tires the traveller,* LLL IV, 3, 307. *do not fret yourself too much in the a.* Mids. IV, 1, 14. *a man no mightier than thyself or me in personal a.* Caes. I, 3, 77. *the violence of a. hath made you reek,* Cymb. I, 2, 2. *why hast thou abused ... mine a. and thine own?* III, 4, 107. *they with continual a. are as good as rotten,* Per. IV, 2, 9.

3) the thing done, deed: *his —s show much like to madness,* Meas. IV, 4, 4. As II, 4, 30. IV, 1,

141. Alls IV, 3, 28. Wint. III, 2, 30. 83. John IV, 3, 58. V, 2, 67. H8 IV, 2, 70. Cor. II, 2, 33. Mcb. IV, 2, 3. Oth. I, 2, 98. II, 3, 146 etc.

4) enterprise: *what dangerous a. would I not undergo!* Gent. V, 4, 41. *in what particular a. to try him,* Alls III, 6, 18. Especially a warlike enterprise: *when you went onward on this ended a.* Ado I, 1, 299. John II, 233. III, 4, 14. V, 2, 99. H4A II, 3, 23. 36. III, 3, 2. H4B I, 1, 177. IV, 1, 172. Troil. II, 3, 140. 145. Cor. I, 1, 283. II, 1, 150. IV, 7, 5. Ant. III, 7, 69*etc. Jestingly used of a feat of drinking: H4A II, 4, 23.

5) a fight, in battle as well as in single combat: *how many gentlemen have you lost in this a.?* Ado I, 1, 6. H6B V, 2, 26. Troil. IV, 5, 113.

6) theatrical representation: *we will do it in a. as we will do it before the duke,* Mids. III, 1, 5. *I nill relate, a. may the rest convey,* Per. III Prol. 55. V Prol. 23. Similarly the sight offered to the spectator of a pageant, in contradistinction to a mere recital: *the tract of every thing would by a good discourser lose some life, which —'s self was tongue to,* H8 I, 1, 42.

7) gesticulation, the motions of the body accompanying words spoken or the feelings of the mind: *making such sober a. with his hand,* Lucr. 1403. 1433 (quibbling in 1323). Wiv. I, 3, 50. IV, 5, 121. Meas. IV, 1, 40. LLL V, 2, 99. As IV, 3, 9. Shr. Ind. 1, 110. 132. Tw. I, 5, 311. Wint. IV, 3, 104. John IV, 2, 191. H6B V, 1, 8. R3 I, 3, 66. Troil. I, 3, 149. Cor. III, 2, 76. 122. Tit. III, 2, 40. V, 2, 18. Caes. III, 2, 226. Mcb. V, 1, 32. Hml. I, 2, 84. I, 4, 60. II, 2, 318. III, 2, 19. Oth. I, 1, 61. Ant. III, 12, 35. Cymb. II, 4, 102.

8) a law-suit: *a. of battery,* Meas. II, 1, 187; Tw. IV, 1, 36; Hml. V, 1, 111. *a. of slander,* Meas. II, 1, 190. *I'll bring mine a. on the proudest he,* Shr. III, 2, 236. *upon some a.* Tw. V, 282. *this a. I now go on,* Wint. II, 1, 121. *have you entered the a.?* H4B II, 1, 2. *draw the a.* 162. *four terms or two —s,* V, 1, 90. *though our proper son stood in your a.* Oth. I, 3, 70. *let not a leaner a. rend us,* Ant. II, 2, 19 (a moot-point of less consequence). *make it an a.* Cymb. II, 3, 156.

Trisyll. in the middle of the verse in Oth. II, 3, 146.

Action-taking, resenting an injury by a law-suit, instead of fighting it out like a man of honour: Lr. II, 2, 18.

Actium, the promontory at which the decisive battle between Antony and Octavius was fought: Ant. III, 7, 52 (F1 *Action).*

Active, of an agile and vigorous body (Germ. rüstig): *a decrepit father takes delight to see his a. child do deeds of youth,* Sonn. 37, 2. Ado V, 1, 75. H4B IV, 3, 24. H5 III, 7, 105. H6B IV, 7, 68. In contradistinction to qualities of the mind: *'twixt his mental and his a. parts kingdomed Achilles in commotion rages,* Troil. II, 3, 184. *my speculative and a. instruments,* Oth. I, 3, 271 (Ff *officed).*

Actively, with youthful vigour, briskly (cf. *Activity): since frost itself as a. doth burn as flaming youth,* Hml. III, 4, 87.

Active-valiant, strenuous and brave: H4A V, 1, 90 (in O. Edd. not hyphened).

Activity, fitness for strenuous exertion;

always used in an obscene, or at least ambiguous sense: *doing is a., and he will still be doing,* H5 III, 7, 107 (cf. *Do*). *if she call your a. in question,* Troil. III, 2, 60. *that your a. may defeat and quell the source of all evil,* Tim. IV, 3, 163.

Actor, 1) d o e r: *she revealed the a.* Lucr. Arg. 20. *no outrageous thing from vassal —s can be wiped away,* Lucr. 608. Meas. II, 2, 37. 41. Alls II, 3, 28. Ant. II, 5, 9.

2) s t a g e - p l a y e r: Sonn. 23, 1. Tp. IV, 148. LLL V, 2, 501. Mids. I, 2, 9. 16. III, 1, 82. IV, 2, 43. V, 116. As III, 4, 62. R2 V, 2, 24. H6C II, 3, 28. Troil. Prol. 24. Cor. V, 3, 40. Caes. II, 1, 226. Hml. II, 2, 410. 411. 414. 415. III, 2, 106.

Actual, c o n s i s t i n g i n d o i n g s o m e t h i n g, in contradistinction to thoughts or words: *her walking and other a. performances,* Mcb. V, 1, 13. *in discourse of thought or a. deed,* Oth. IV, 2, 153.

Acture, t h e p e r f o r m i n g o f a r e s p e c t i v e a c t: *with a. they may be, where neither party is nor true nor kind,* Compl. 185 (i. e. such may do the works of love as are void of love; cf. *Activity*).

Acute, h i g h l y r e f i n e d, w i t t y; used only by Armado and Holophernes, and, it should seem, with intended impropriety: *a most a. juvenal,* LLL III, 67. *the gift is good in those in whom it is a.* IV, 2, 73.

Acutely, w i t t i l y; used only by Parolles: *I cannot answer thee a.* Alls I, 1, 221.

Adage, p r o v e r b: H6C I, 4, 126. Mcb. I, 7, 45.

Adallas, name of a Thracian king: Ant. III, 6, 71.

Adam, 1) the progenitor of the human race: Ado II, 1, 66. 259. LLL IV, 2, 40. V, 2, 322. As II, 1, 5. R2 III, 4, 73. H4A II, 4, 106. III, 3, 186. *A. was a gardener,* H6B IV, 2, 142; cf. R2 III, 4, 73 and Hml. V, 1, 35. 42. *the picture of old A.* Err. IV, 3, 13 (meaning the bailiff, because, as the commentators will have it, the buff he wore resembled the native buff of Adam). Used as the symbol of human frailty: H5 I, 1, 29.

2) *Adam Bell,* a famous archer, much celebrated in popular songs and grown proverbial for his skill: Ado I, 1, 261. Therefore substituted for *Abraham,* q. v., by M. Edd. in Rom. II, 1, 13.

3) name of servants: As I, 1, 1. 22 etc. Shr. IV, 1, 139.

Adamant, 1) a s t o n e o f i m p e n e t r a b l e h a r d n e s s: *spurn in pieces posts of a.* H6A I, 4, 52.

2) t h e l o a d s t o n e: *you draw me, you hard-hearted a.* Mids. II, 1, 195. Troil III, 2, 186.

Add, 1) to j o i n t o t h a t w h i c h w a s b e f o r e; followed by a depending clause: *they that a. he's drunk nightly,* Tw. I, 3, 38. II, 2, 7. John III, 1, 153. R2 IV, 18. Troil. II, 3, 141 etc. By an accus.: *—ing one thing to my purpose nothing,* Sonn. 20, 12. 103, 4. LLL II, 252. III, 87. V, 1, 52. Troil. IV, 5, 145. Ant. III, 12, 28 etc. By an acc. and dat.: *rain —ed to a river,* Ven. 71. *to your blessings a. a curse,* Sonn. 84, 13. 85, 10. 135, 11. Pilgr. 206. Meas. II, 4, 72. Ado IV, 1 174. Merch. V, 186. Shr. III, 2, 130. V, 2, 112. Alls III, 7, 35. Tw. V, 83. John II, 347. IV, 2, 13. R2 I, 1, 24. III, 4, 16. H5 III, 6, 142. IV, 8, 88. H6C II, 1, 105. H8 II, 3, 65. Rom. I, 1, 139. Mcb. IV, 1, 33 etc. By a dat. and a clause: *—ing thereto that she would wed me,* LLL V, 2, 446. Wint. II, 1, 67.

2) With *to,* = to i n c r e a s e, to e n r i c h: *the petty streams a. to his flow,* Lucr. 651. *the sea —eth to his store,* Sonn. 135, 10. *death's a great disguiser, and you may a. to it.* Meas. IV, 2, 187. *that art which —s to nature,* Wint. IV, 4, 91. H4B III, 1, 105. H6A I, 1, 103. Troil. II, 2, 106. Tim. III, 1, 54. Caes. II, 1, 267. Lr. I, 4, 292. Similarly *to a. more of a thing to* = to increase the force or quantity of a thing: *to a. a more rejoicing to the prime,* Lucr. 332 (= to increase the rejoicing of the prime). *which to her oratory —s more grace,* 564. *to our perjury to a. more terror,* LLL V, 2, 470. *a. more feathers to our wings,* H5 I, 2, 306. *to a. more measure to your woes,* H6C II, 1, 105. *I need not a. more fuel to your fire,* V, 4, 70. *a. more coals to Cancer,* Troil. II, 3, 206. And without *more: thine eyes have —ed feathers to the learned's wing,* Sonn. 78, 7. *till another Caesar have —ed slaughter to the sword of traitors,* Caes. V, 1, 55. *a. water to the sea,* H6C V, 4, 8. Hence the following peculiarities: *I can a. colours to the chameleon,* H6C III, 2, 191 (i. e. I have more colours than the chameleon; cf. Ven. 398). *the enemy come on refreshed, new —ed,* Caes. IV, 3, 209 (strengthened, reinforced; some M. Edd. *aided*).

3) With *to* = to b e s t o w o n: *she —s honours to his hateful name,* Ven. 994. *their thoughts to thy fair flower a. the rank smell of weeds,* Sonn. 69, 12. *it —s a precious seeing to the eye,* LLL IV, 3, 333. *a. proof unto mine armour with thy prayers,* R2 I, 3, 73. *and to thy worth will a. right worthy gains,* V, 6, 12. *thou wilt but a. increase unto my wrath,* H6B III, 2, 292. *you have —ed worth unto it and lustre,* Tim. I, 2, 154. Cymb. I, 1, 142. *to such proceeding who ever but his approbation —ed,* Per. IV, 3, 26. *Without to: the words would a. more anguish than the wounds,* H6C II, 1, 99 (cf. the German *zufügen*).

4) to m a k e o u t b y a r i t h m e t i c a l a d d i t i o n: *until the goose came out of door and stayed the odds by —ing four,* LLL III, 93; cf. *multiply* in Wint. I, 2, 7.

Adder, a v e n o m o u s s n a k e: Ven. 878. Lucr. 871. Tp. II, 2, 13. Mids. III, 2, 71. 72. 73. Shr. IV, 3, 179. Wint. IV, 4, 268. R2 III, 2, 20. H6C I, 4, 112. R3 I, 2, 19. Tit. II, 3, 35. Tim. IV, 3, 181. Caes. II, 1, 14. Mcb. IV, 1, 16. Hml. III, 4, 203. Lr. V, 1, 57. Cymb. IV, 2, 90. Supposed to be deaf: *my —'s sense to critic and to flatterer stopped are,* Sonn. 112, 10. H6B III, 2, 76. Troil. II, 2, 172.

Addict, vb. refl. to d e v o t e, to d e d i c a t e o n e ' s s e l f: *to a. themselves to sack,* H4B IV, 3, 135. Partic. 1) *—ed* = inclined, devoted: Tw. II, 5, 222. Hml. II, 1, 19. 2) *addict: a.* to vice, Pilgr. 415.

Addiction, i n c l i n a t i o n: *his a. was to courses vain,* H5 I, 1, 54. *to what sport and revels his a. leads him,* Oth. II, 2, 6 (Ff Q1 *addition*).

Addition, 1) t h e s u m m i n g u p o f n u m b e r s: *parcel the sum of my disgraces by a. of his envy,* Ant. V, 2, 164.

2) t h e a c t o f a d d i n g, opposed to diminution: *to thy sweet will making a. thus,* Sonn. 135, 4.

3) t h e t h i n g a d d e d: *and by a. me of thee defeated,* Sonn. 20, 11. *take unmingled thence that drop again, without a.* Err. II, 2, 130. *and this a. more, full thirty thousand marks,* John II, 529. H4A II, 4, 29. Caes. IV, 3, 172. Lr. III, 6, 3. V, 3, 301.

4) a u g m e n t a t i o n, e n h a n c e m e n t: *all aids came for —s,* Compl. 118. *it is no a. to her wit,* Ado II, 3, 242. *titled goddess, and worth it, with a.* Alls IV, 2, 3. *truly to speak, and with no a.* Hml. IV, 4, 17.

5) mark of distinction, denomination, title: *devils' —s, the names of fiends,* Wiv. II, 2, 312. *where great —s swell's, and virtue none,* Alls II, 3, 134. H5 V, 2, 367. Troil. I, 2, 20. II, 3, 258. Cor. I, 9, 66. 72. Mcb. I, 3, 106. III, 1, 100. Hml. I, 4, 20. II, 1, 47. Lr. II, 2, 26. V, 3, 68 (Qq *advancement*). Oth. IV, 1, 105. IV, 2, 163.

6) outward honour: *we will not name desert before his birth, and being born, his a. shall be humble,* Troil. III, 2, 102. *bear hence a great a. earned in thy death,* IV, 5, 141. *the name and all the —s to a king,* Lr. I, 1, 138. *think it no a. nor my wish, to have him see me womaned,* Oth. III, 4, 194.

Addle, in a morbid state; originally applied to eggs, and then to a weak brain: *if you love an a. egg as well as you love an idle head,* Troil. I, 2, 145. *thy head hath been beaten as a. as an egg,* Rom. III, 1, 26.

Address, vb. 1) tr. a) to direct: *toward that shade I might behold —ed the king,* LLL V, 2, 92. *a. your love and might to honour Helen,* Mids. II, 2, 143. *a. thy gait unto her,* Tw. I, 4, 15. *unto your grace I a. the substance of my speech,* H4B IV, 1, 31.

b) to prepare, to make ready: *Duke Frederick —ed a mighty power,* As V, 4, 162. *all imminence that gods and men a. their dangers in,* Troil. V, 10, 14. *in your armours, as you are —ed,* Per. II, 3, 94 (or = dress?). Partic. *—ed* = ready: *—ed to answer his desire,* Lucr. 1606. LLL II, 83. Mids. V, 107. H4B IV, 4, 5. H5 III, 3, 58. Caes. III, 1, 29. Reflectively = to make one's self ready: *I will then a. me to my appointment,* Wiv. III, 5, 135. Merch. II, 9, 19. Alls III, 6, 103. Wint. IV, 4, 53. H6B V, 2, 27. Mcb. II, 2, 24. Hml. I, 2, 216.

2) intr. a) to direct one's speech to: *we first a. towards you,* Lr. I, 1, 193. b) to get ready: *let us a. to tend on Hector's heels,* Troil. IV, 4, 148.

Adhere, to be in accordance: *they do no more a. and keep place together than ...,* Wiv. II, 1, 62. *every thing —s together,* Tw. III, 4, 86. *nor time nor place did then a.* Mcb. I, 7, 52. With *to: a shepherd's daughter, and what to her —s,* Wint. IV, 1, 28 (what is in accordance with her condition). *two men there are not living to whom he more —s,* Hml. II, 2, 21 (to whom his mind is more congenial, who, as v. 12 expresses it, are 'more neighboured to his youth and haviour').

Adieu, farewell; oftener used and in a more familiar way than at present: Ven. 537. Gent. I, 1, 11. 53. III, 1, 50. Wiv. I, 3, 20. II, 1, 139. II, 3, 84. III, 5, 139. IV, 1, 86. V, 3, 6. Meas. I, 4, 90. III, 2, 80. Ado III, 1, 109. III, 3, 100. LLL I, 1, 110. I, 2, 187. II, 213. III, 135. IV, 2, 148. V, 2, 226. 629. Mids. I, 1, 224. I, 2, 112. V, 354. Merch. I, 3, 170. II, 3, 10. II, 7, 76. II, 9, 77. As III, 2, 311. IV, 1, 202. V, 4, 127. Shr. II, 323. IV, 4, 102. Alls IV, 2, 64. Tw. III, 1, 173. IV, 2, 141. Wint. II, 1, 122. IV, 4, 673. John I, 180. III, 1, 326. R2 I, 3, 306. V, 1, 102. H4A V, 4, 99. H5 II, 3, 64. IV, 3, 10. H6A IV, 4, 45. IV, 7, 31. R3 III, 5, 97. IV, 1, 88. 91. V, 3, 102. Troil. I, 2, 303. Cor. II, 3, 87. IV, 1, 20. Rom. II, 2, 136. III, 5, 59. Mcb. II, 4, 37. III, 1, 34. Hml. I, 5, 91. Oth. I, 3, 292. 380. Ant. V, 2, 189. 190. Cymb. I, 1, 108 etc. *to bid a.:* Sonn. 57, 8. LLL V, 2, 241. H6C IV, 8, 29 (cf. *Bid*). Substantively: *twenty —s,* LLL V, 2, 265. Alls II, 1, 53. IV, 3, 101. Troil. IV, 4, 48. Ant. IV, 5, 14.

Adjacent, contiguous: Rom. II, 1, 20. Ant. II, 2, 218.

Adjoin, 1) tr. to join, to tie to: *to whose huge spokes ten thousand lesser things are mortised and —ed,* Hml. III, 3, 20.

2) intr. to be contiguous: *the hills —ing to the city,* Ant. IV, 10, 5.

Adjourn, to defer, to delay: H8 II, 4, 232. Cymb. V, 4, 78.

Adjudge, 1) to adjudicate, to ordain: *to whom the heavens —d an olive branch,* H6C IV, 6, 34. 2) to condemn: *he —d your brother,* Meas. V, 408. With *to: thou art —d to the death,* Err. I, 1, 147. *—d to death,* H6B II, 3, 4. *To* omitted: *to be —d some direful death,* Tit. V, 3, 144.

Adjunct, adj. attending, consequent: *though death be a.* Lucr. 133. *every humour hath his a. pleasure,* Sonn. 91, 5. *though that my death were a. to my act,* John III, 3, 57.

Adjunct, subst. attendant: *to keep an a. to remember thee,* Sonn. 122, 13. *learning is but an a. to ourself,* LLL IV, 3, 314.

Administer, to cause to take: *to keep the oath that we a.* R2 I, 3, 182.

Administration, direction, management: *in the a. of his law,* H4B V, 2, 75.

Admirable, 1) deserving the highest praise, wonderful, delightful: *of a. discourse,* Wiv. II, 2, 234. *a. pleasures,* IV, 4, 80 (Evans' speech). *my a. dexterity,* IV, 5, 120. *brave wars, most a.* Alls II, 1, 26. *the knight's in a. fooling,* Tw. II, 3, 85. *'twill be a.* 186. *an a. conceited fellow,* Wint. IV, 4, 203 (the clown's speech). *O a. youth,* Troil. I, 2, 255. 258. *a.: how this grace speaks his own standing,* Tim. I, 1, 30. *in form and moving how express and a.* Hml. II, 2, 318. *an a. evasion,* Lr. I, 2, 137. *an a. musician,* Oth. IV, 1, 199. *with a. rich words to it,* Cymb. II, 3, 19.

2) to be wondered at: *strange and a.* Mids. V, 27.

Admiral, 1) commander of a fleet: H5 IV, 8, 98. H6C III, 3, 252 (high *a.*). R3 IV, 4, 437.

2) the ship which carries the commander: H4A III, 3, 28. Ant. III, 10, 2.

Admiration, 1) wonder mingled with veneration: *with more than a. he admired her azure veins,* Lucr. 418. Tp. III, 1, 38. H8 V, 5, 43. Cymb. I, 4, 5. IV, 2, 232.

2) wonder, astonishment, emotion excited by any thing strange: *the changes I perceived in the king and Camillo were very notes of a.* Wint. V, 2, 12. *working so grossly in a natural cause, that a. did not whoop at them,* H5 II, 2, 108. IV, 1, 66 (Fluellen's speech). *season your a. for a while,* Hml. I, 2, 192. *struck her into amazement and a.* III, 2, 339. 342. *this a. is much o'the favour of other your new pranks,* Lr. I, 4, 258. *what makes your a.?* Cymb. I, 6, 38. The abstr. for the concr.: *bring in the a.* Alls II, 1, 91.

Admire, 1) to regard with wonder and delight; absol.: Sonn. 59, 14. Wint. V, 3, 41. H4A III, 2, 80. H5 I, 1, 39. Cor. I, 9, 5. With an accus.: Lucr. 392. 418. Sonn. 84, 12. 123, 5. Pilgr. 66. Gent. IV, 2, 43. LLL I, 1, 141. IV, 2, 118. Mids. I, 1, 231. As III, 2, 412. Shr. I, 1, 29. Wint. IV, 4, 625. H4A I, 3, 105. H5 III, 6, 132. H6A II, 2, 39. H6B III, 1, 12. H6C I, 4, 130. Rom. I, 2, 89. Tim. V, 1, 54.

Ant. I, 1, 51. III, 7, 24. Cymb. I, 1, 32. Per. V Prol. 4.

2) to wonder, to be surprised: *wonder not, nor a. not in thy mind,* Tw. III, 4, 165 (letter of Sir Andrew). With *at: these lords at this encounter do so much a.* Tp. V, 154.

Partic. —*d* adjectively: 1) admirable: —*d Miranda!* Tp. III, 1, 37. —*d Octavia,* Ant. II, 2, 121. 2) to be wondered at, strange: *with most* —*d disorder,* Mcb. III, 4, 110.

Admirer, one who admires: H8 I, 1, 3.

Admiringly, with admiration: Alls I, 1, 33. V, 3, 44.

Admission, in *Self-admission,* q. v.

Admit, 1) to suffer to enter: *his ear her prayers* —*s,* Lucr. 558. *and will is* —*ed there,* Sonn. 136, 3. *let her be* —*ed,* Meas. II, 2, 22. Merch. IV, 1, 146. Alls IV, 5, 94. Tw. I, 1, 24. I, 4, 20. H5 II, 2, 156. R3 I, 3, 343. IV, 4, 38. Tim. I, 2, 127. Hml. II, 2, 144. Ant. II, 2, 75. III, 13, 40. With *to:* —*ed to his sight,* Meas. IV, 3, 125. *to your council,* H6B III, 1, 27. Peculiar expressions: *the prince* —*s him,* H4B II, 4, 274 (has intercourse, converses with him). *not petty things* —*ed,* Ant. V, 2, 140 (registered).

2) to allow, to permit; with an accus: Tp. II, 1, 149. Meas. I, 1, 63. Err. I, 1, 15. Tw. I, 2, 45. H4B I, 3, 24. IV, 1, 159. V, 1, 6. V, 2, 24. H5 III, 3, 2. V Chor. 3. Troil. IV, 4, 9. V, 2, 151. Cor. V, 3, 6. V, 6, 20. 69. 96. Hml. III, 1, 108. With dat. and acc.: *a. him entrance,* H8 IV, 2, 107. With an inf.: *they will not a. any good part to intermingle with them,* Ado V, 2, 63.

3) to be for, to declare for, to choose: *whose party do the townsmen yet a.?* John II, 361. *the people do a. you,* Cor. II, 3, 151. *the people will accept whom he* —*s.* Tit. I, 222.

4) to allow, to acknowledge, to grant: *let me not to the marriage of true minds a. impediments,* Sonn. 116, 2. *he* —*s him not for his counsellor,* Wiv. II, 1, 5. *a. no other way to save his life,* Meas. II, 4, 88 (suppose that there were no other way). *hear them speak whose title they a.* John II, 200. *a. me Chorus to this history,* H5 Prol. 32. *we must needs a. the means how things are perfected,* I, 1, 68.

Admittance, permission to enter, reception: *what a.?* LLL II, 80 (what reception did you meet with?). *to give a. to a thought of fear,* H4B IV, 1, 153. *crave a. to your majesty,* H5 II, 4, 66. Tim. I, 2, 122. 134. Hml. II, 2, 51. Cymb. I, 4, 115. II, 3, 73. Peculiar expressions: *any tire of Venetian a.* Wiv. III, 3, 61 (received, in fashion at Venice). *of great a.* II, 2, 235 (admitted to the company and converse of great persons).

Admonish, 1) to exhort, to warn: —*ing that we should dress us fairly for our end,* H5 IV, 1, 9. — 2) to instruct, to guide: *ye choice spirits that a. me,* H6A V, 3, 3 (cf. Epistle to the Hebr. VIII, 5).

Admonishment, 1) warning: *to stop his ears against a.* Troil. V, 3, 2. — 2) instruction, instructive communication: *thy grave* —*s prevail with me,* H6A II, 5, 98.

Admonition, warning: Meas. III, 2, 205. R2 II, 1, 117.

Ado, 1) to do, to deal: *no court, no father nor no more a. with that simple nothing,* Cymb. III, 4, 134. 2) bustle, troublesome business (cf. *to do*

in Hml. II, 2, 369): *let us follow, to see the end of this a.* Shr. V, I, 147. *here's a., to lock up honesty,* Wint. II, 2, 9. *here's such a.* 19. cf. the title of the comedy *Much ado.*

3) more tumult and show of business than the affair is worth: *he makes me no more a. but whips me out of the chamber,* Gent. IV, 4, 31. *show the inside of your purse, and no more a.* Wint. IV, 4, 834. H4A II, 4, 223. H6A III, 2, 101. H6C IV, 5, 27. H8 V, 3, 159. Tit. II, 1, 98 (*this a.*). IV, 3, 102. Rom. III, 4, 23.

4) pains, difficulty: *till they have singled with much a. the cold fault cleanly out,* Ven. 694. *what a. here is to bring you together,* Wiv. IV, 5, 128. Merch. I, 1, 7. Wint. I, 2, 213. R2 V, 5, 74. Lr. IV, 5, 2.

Adon, abbreviation of *Adonis:* Ven. 769. 1070. Pilgr. 76. 120.

Adonis, a youth loved by Venus and killed by a boar: Ven. 3. 68. 179 etc. Sonn. 53, 5. Pilgr. 44. 74 122. 143. Shr. Ind. 2, 52. *thy promises are like — gardens that one day bloomed and fruitful were the next,* H6A I, 6, 6 (perhaps confounded with the garden of King Alcinous, but see Pliny XIX, 19, 1).*

Adoor; out a. = out of door: Err. II, 1, 11. Cor. I, 3, 120. As to *keep in adoor,* Lr. I, 4, 138, see *A.*

Adoors; out a. = out of doors: H4B II, 4, 229. Hml. II, 1, 99. Oth. II, 1, 110 (only in Q1). M. Edd. *out of door* and *doors.*

Adopt, 1) to receive to the place of a child: Oth. I, 3, 191. Joined with *heir: to be* —*ed heir to Frederick,* As I, 2, 246. R2 IV, 109. H6C I, 1, 135. I, 4, 98. II, 2, 88.

2) to receive as one's own what is not so naturally: *a Roman now* —*ed,* Tit. I, 463. *an* —*ed name,* H4A V, 2, 18. *which you a. your policy,* Cor. III, 2, 48. *new* —*ed to our hate,* Lr. I, 1, 206.

Adoptedly, on the ground of adoption; used of a name given in tenderness (cf. *Adoption* and *Adoptious*): *is she your cousin? a.* Meas. I, 4, 47.

Adoption, 1) the taking and treating a stranger as a child of one's own: *a. strives with nature,* Alls I, 3, 151 (adopted children are no less loved than those given by nature). *to work her son into the a. of the crown,* Cymb. V, 5, 56 (into the right of an adopted heir to the crown).

2) the receiving or choosing something as one's own: *stand under the a. of abominable terms,* Wiv. II, 2, 309. *those friends thou hast, and their a. tried,* Hml. I, 3, 62.

Adoptious, not properly belonging, but assumed in tenderness: *pretty, fond, a. christendoms,* Alls I, 1, 188.

Adoration, worship, homage: As V, 2, 102 Tw. V, 5, 274. H5 IV, 1, 262.

Adore, 1) to pay divine honours, to worship: Lucr. 1835. Tp. II, 2, 143. Gent. II, 6, 9. IV, 2, 131. Alls I, 3, 211. Tit. I, 42. II, 1, 61. V, 1, 83. Tim. IV, 3, 35. Lr. I, 4, 312. Cymb. III, 3, 3. Per. II, 4, 11.

2) to love in the highest degree: Lucr. 85. Sonn. 7, 7. Pilgr. 165. LLL V, 2, 673. Tw. II, 1, 48. II, 3, 196. 197. II, 5, 115. R3 I, 2, 177. Ant. III, 2, 8. III, 13, 114. Gent. IV, 4, 204.

Adorer, worshipper: Cymb. I, 4, 74.

Adorn, 1) tr. to deck, to decorate: Lucr. 399.

Wint. I, 2, 392. R2 V, 1, 79. H6A V, 4, 134. R3 I, 2, 258. Tit. I, 388.

2) intr. to put on ornaments: *whose men and dames so jetted and —ed*, Per. I, 4, 26.

Adornings, ornaments: *her gentlewomen tended her i'the eyes, and made their bends a.* Ant. II, 2, 213; i. e. regarded her with such veneration as to reflect beauty on her, to make her more beautiful, by their looks.

Adornment, ornament: Cymb. II, 2, 26. III, 5, 140.

A-doting, in love: fell a. Sonn. 20, 10.

Adowna, burden of a song: Wiv. I, 4, 44; see *A.*

Adramadio, the name given by Costard to Armado: LLL IV, 3, 199.

Adrian, a name: Tp. II, 1, 28. Cor. IV, 3, 2.

Adriana, female name: Err. II, 2, 114. IV, 1, 102. 109.

Adriano, a name: LLL I, 1, 280. IV, 1, 89. V, 1, 9.

Adriatic, adj. concerning the sea east of Italy: *the swelling A. seas,* Shr. I, 2, 74.

Adulation, flattery: H5 IV, 1, 271.

Adulterate, vb. to commit fornication: *she* (viz Fortune) *—s hourly with thine uncle,* John III, 1, 56.

Adulterate, adj. 1) unfaithful to the marriage bed: Lucr. 1645. Err. II, 2, 142. Hml. I, 5, 42.

2) unchaste, lewd: *why should others' false a. eyes give salutation to my sportive blood?* Sonn. 121, 5. *his foul a. heart,* Compl. 175. *the a. Hastings,* R3 IV, 4, 69.

Adulterer, a fornicator (or a man unfaithful to his wife?): Lr. I, 2, 135.

Adulteress, (trisyll.; quadrisyll. in Tit.), a married woman faithless to her husband: Wint. II, 1, 78. 88. II, 3, 4. Tit. II, 3, 109. Lr. II, 4, 134.

Adulterous, unchaste, lewd: *Angelo is an a. thief,* Meas. V, 40 (a secret fornicator). Ant. III, 6, 94.

Adultery, 1) violation of the marriage bed: Meas. II, 1, 82. Wint. III, 2, 15. Cymb. III, 2, 1. V, 4, 33. V, 5, 186.

2) fornication: Lr. IV, 6, 112. Blunderingly used by Mrs Quickly: H5 II, 1, 40.

Advance, vb. 1) tr. a) to bring forward, to make to go on: *your eyes a. straight back to France,* H5 V Chor. 44. *towards which a. the war,* Mcb. V, 4, 21.

b) to lift, to raise: *a. that phraseless hand,* Compl. 225. *the fringed curtains of thine eye a.* Tp. I, 2, 408. *a. their eyelids,* IV, 177. *how he jets under his —d plumes,* Tw. II, 5, 36. *never war a. his bleeding sword,* H5 V, 2, 382. H6A II, 2, 5. R3 I, 2, 40. Troil. IV, 5, 188. Cor. I, 6, 61. II, 1, 178. Tit. II, 1, 125. Rom. II, 3, 5. Used of standards, = to wave: *I must a. the colours of my love,* Wiv. III, 4, 85. *a. your standards,* LLL IV, 3, 367. *these flags of France, that are —d here,* John II, 207. H5 II, 2, 192. H6A I, 6, 1. H6B IV, 1, 98. R3 V, 3, 264, 348. Rom. V, 3, 96.

c) to raise to a higher worth and dignity: *my low-declined honour to a.* Lucr. 1705. *thou art all my art and dost a. as high as learning my rude ignorance,* Sonn. 78, 13. Tp. I, 2, 80. Alls IV, 5, 6. Tw. I, 4, 2. H4B I, 3, 7. IV, 5, 207. H6A III, 1, 31. H8 III, 2, 417. Cor. II, 2, 60. Tit. I, 238. 330. 393. II, 1, 4. IV, 2, 34. 157. Rom. IV, 5, 72. Tim. I, 2, 176. Hml. III, 2, 215. Lr. V, 3, 28. Per. I, 1, 154. IV, 4, 14.

d) to bring to view, to show: *a. their pride*

against that power, Ado III, 1, 10. *every one his love-feat will a. unto his mistress,* LLL V, 2, 123. *you do a. your cunning more and more,* Mids. III, 2, 128.

2) intr. to march forward: Cor. I, 4, 25.

Advancement, promotion to a higher place and dignity: Tp. II, 1, 268. Wint. IV, 4, 867. H4B V, 5, 74. 84. H6A II, 5, 69. R3 I, 3, 75. IV, 4, 241. Hml. III, 2, 62. 354. Lr. II, 4, 203. V, 3, 68 (Ff addition).

Advantage, subst. any favourable condition or circumstance; 1) profit, gain: *that sin by him a. should achieve,* Sonn. 67, 3. *for his a.* Meas. II, 4, 120. IV, 1, 24. Merch. II, 7, 19. Alls I, 1, 17. John II, 206. 577. IV, 2, 60. R2 I, 4, 41. H4A I, 1, 27. III, 1, 109. H5 IV, 1, 190. H6A IV, 6, 44. H6B III, 1, 25. H8 I, 1, 193. Troil. II, 2, 204. Lr. III, 5, 13. *to make a. of* = to profit by: Gent. II, 4, 68. *to take a. of,* in the same sense: Ven. Ded. 3. Wiv. III, 3, 116. John I, 102. II, 297. R2 II, 3, 79. R3 IV, 1, 49. Cor. II, 3, 206. Per. I, 4, 66. *to take a. on:* Ven. 405.

2) condition favourable to success: *refer yourself to this a., first that your stay with him may not be long,* Meas. III, 1, 255. *for a.* Alls I, 1, 215. *she herself, without other a., may lawfully make title,* I, 3, 106. *the plots of best —s,* John II, 40. *I'll use the a. of my power,* R2 III, 3, 42. H4A IV, 3, 2. IV, 4, 28. 78. V, 1, 55. H5 I, 2, 139. H6A I, 4, 12. IV, 4, 19. Troil. V, 2, 130. Cor. IV, 1, 43. Caes. IV, 3, 210. Hml. I, 2, 21. Lr. II, 1, 24. Oth. III, 1, 55. IV, 2, 179. Ant. IV, 11, 4. Cymb. I, 4, 140. IV, 1, 12. V, 2, 11. V, 3, 15.

3) favourable opportunity: *make use of time, let not a. slip,* Ven. 129. *a maid of Dian's this a. found,* Sonn. 153, 2. *all kind of arguments for his a. still did wake and sleep,* Compl. 123 (according as he wanted); cf. *I can change shapes with Proteus for —s,* H6C III, 2, 192 (according as it serves my turn). *the next a. will we take throughly,* Tp. III, 3, 13. Wiv. III, 2, 36. Mids. III, 2, 16. Alls I, 1, 215. John III, 4, 151. V, 7, 62. H4A II, 4, 594. H5 III, 6, 127. H6A II, 5, 129. H6B I, 1, 242. R3 III, 5, 74. V, 3, 92. Troil. III, 3, 2. Mcb. V, 4, 11. Oth. I, 3, 298. II, 1, 248. III, 3, 312.

4) superiority: *I have seen the hungry ocean gain a. on the kingdom of the shore,* Sonn. 64, 6. *a. feeds him fat, while men delay,* H4A III, 2, 180. *having some a. on Octavius,* Caes. V, 3, 6. Ant. IV, 7, 11.

5) interest upon money: *neither lend nor borrow upon a.* Merch. I, 3, 71. *paid back with a.* H4A II, 4, 599. Metaphorically: *with a. means to pay thy love,* John III, 3, 22. *he'll remember with —s what feats he did that day,* H5 IV, 3, 50.

Advantage, vb. 1) to yield profit, to benefit: *our own doth little a.* Tp. I, 1, 34. With an accus: *what may a heavy groan a. thee?* Ven. 950. Gent. III, 2, 42. Meas. III, 1, 265. Tw. IV, 2, 119. H5 IV, 1, 301. Tit. V, 1, 56. Caes. III, 1, 242.

2) to increase by interest: *—ing their love with interest of ten times double gain of happiness,* R3 IV, 4, 323 (M. Edd. *—ing their loan*).

Advantageable, profitable, convenient: H5 V, 2, 88.

Advantageous, useful: *every thing a. to life,* Tp. II, 1, 49. *a. care withdrew me,* Troil. V, 4, 22 (perhaps a care to spy advantages; cf. Alls I, 1, 215)

Adventure, subst. 1) hazard, chance, risk:

to try the fair a. of to-morrow, John V, 5, 22. *at a.* = at random: *spoke at a.* H4B I, 1, 59 (Q *at a venter;* some M. Edd. *at a venture*). *at all —s* = at all hazards, come what may: Err. II, 2, 218. H5 IV, 1, 121. *by hard a.* = unfortunately: As II, 4, 45. *a. of* = risk of: *the a. of her person,* Wint. V, 1, 156.

2) hazardous and striking enterprise: As I, 2, 187. H4A I, 1, 93. I, 2, 169. V, 2, 96. H6A IV, 4, 7. H6C IV, 2, 18. R3 V, 3, 319 (M. Edd. *ventures*). Cymb. III, 1, 82. IV, 4, 3. Per. I, 1, 22. II, 3, 83.

Adventure, vb. 1) to hazard, to risk: *I will not a. my discretion so weakly,* Tp. II, 1, 187. *by —ing both I oft found both,* Merch. I, 1, 143.

2) to run the hazard: *I will a. to be banished myself,* H6B III, 2, 350. *I dare a. to be sent to the Tower,* R3 I, 3, 116.

3) to dare; with an acc.: *Leander would a. it,* Gent. III, 1, 120. *I'll a. the borrow of a week,* Wint. I, 2, 38. *what will you a.?* II, 3, 162. With an inf.: *wouldst a. to mingle faith with him,* Wint. IV, 4, 470. Rom. V, 3, 11. Cymb. I, 6, 172.

4) intr. to try the chance, to run all hazards: *I would a. for such merchandize,* Rom. II, 2, 84. *though peril ... on't, I would a.* Cymb. III, 4, 156. With *on,* = to dare: *then will they a. on the exploit,* H4A I, 2, 192.

Adventurous, daring, bold: H4A I, 3, 191. Tit. V, 3, 112. Hml. II, 2, 333. Per. I, 1, 35. II, 4, 51.

Adventurously, daringly, boldly: H5 IV, 4, 79.

Adversary, 1) opponent, antagonist; in a suit at law: Merch. IV, 1, 4. Shr. I, 2, 278. In single combat: R2 I, 3, 92. H6A V, 5, 33. Lr. V, 3, 123.

2) enemy: Alls III, 6, 28. IV, 1, 17. R2 I, 1, 101. H4A III, 2, 83. V, 5, 31. R3 I, 1, 11. I, 3, 123. III, 1, 182. IV, 4, 4 (Ff *enemies*). V, 3, 112. 166. Cor. IV, 3, 45. Rom. I, 1, 113.

Misapplied by Mrs Quickly: Wiv. II, 3, 98. Fluellen pronounces *athversary:* H5 III, 2, 65. III, 6, 98. 103.

Adverse (as for the accent, see Appendix I, 1) 1) opposed; in a law-suit: *thy a. party is thy advocate,* Sonn. 35, 10. *on the a. side,* Meas. IV, 6, 6. In single combat: *thy a. pernicious enemy,* R2 I, 3, 82.

2) hostile: *to admit no traffic to our a. towns,* Err. I, 1, 15. *though time seem so a.* Alls V, 1, 26. *this a. town,* Tw. V, 87. John II, 57. IV, 2, 172. H6A I, 1, 54. R3 IV, 4, 190. V, 3, 13.

3) contrary to one's wishes: *grow this to what a. issue it can,* Ado II, 2, 52.

Adversely, offensively: *if the drink you give me touch my palate a.* Cor. II, 1, 61.

Adversity, misfortune, calamity: Gent. IV, 1, 12. Err. II, 1, 34. IV, 4, 21. As II, 1, 12. H6A IV, 4, 14. H6C III, 1, 24. Rom. III, 3, 55. Oth. I, 3, 274 (*—ies*). Abstr. pro concr.: *well said, a.!* Troil. V, 1, 14, i. e. mischievous and offensive creature.

Advertise (advértise) 1) to inform: *please it your grace to be —d the duke of York is newly come from Ireland,* H6B IV, 9, 23. H6C II, 1, 116. IV, 5, 9. V, 3, 18. R3 IV, 4, 501. Troil. II, 2, 211.

2) to instruct, to assist with counsel: *I do bend my speech to one that can my part in him a.* Meas. I, 1, 42 (who is able to instruct me about the

part I have to bear to him, or what I have to say to him). *I was then —ing and holy to your business,* V, 388. *he might the king a. whether our daughter were legitimate,* H8 II, 4, 178.

Advertisement, (advértisement) 1) intelligence, information: *this a. is five days old,* H4A III, 2, 172.

2) instruction, advice: *my griefs are louder than a.* Ado V, 1, 32. *that is an a. to a proper maid in Florence, to take heed,* Alls IV, 3, 240. *yet doth he give us bold a.* H4A IV, 1, 36.

Advice, 1) counsel: Lucr. 1409. Compl. 160. Tp. V, 191. Gent. III, 2, 89. 94. Meas. I, 1, 6. IV, 1, 8. V, 113 (*by whose a.*). Alls I, 1, 224. II, 1, 3. Wint. II, 1, 168. IV, 4, 516. H6B I, 2, 72. R3 IV, 2, 3. Troil. I, 3, 388. Tit. I, 228 (*by my a.*). IV, 2, 130. Mcb. III, 1, 21. IV, 2, 66. Hml. II, 1, 67. II, 2, 145. Lr. II, 1, 123. Oth. II, 3, 343. Ant. I, 3, 68. Per. I, 1, 62. *by my a.* = if I may advise you, if you will be ruled by me: *by my a., all humbled on your knees, you shall ask pardon of his majesty,* Tit. I, 472. *by my a. let us impart what we have seen to Hamlet,* Hml. I, 1, 168. Denoting medical advice and attendance: *a. is sporting while infection breeds,* Lucr. 907. *I hope your lordship goes abroad by a.* H4B I, 2, 109. III, 1, 43. Spiritual counsel: *he wants a.* Meas. IV, 2, 154.— O. Edd. confound *advice* and *advise.*

2) deliberate consideration: *so hot a speed with such a. disposed,* John III, 4, 11. *that's not suddenly to be performed, but with a. and silent secrecy,* H6B II, 2, 68. *she will file our engines with a.* Tit. II, 1, 123. Gent. II, 4, 208. Alls III, 4, 19. Tit. IV, 1, 92. Cymb. I, 1, 156. *on a., on more a.* = on reflection, on better consideration: Gent. III, 1, 73. Merch. IV, 2, 6. Shr. I, 1, 117. Tit. I, 379. *upon good a.* R2 I, 3, 233. *after more a.* Meas. V, 469. *with more a.* Gent. II, 4, 207. *on his more a.* H5 II, 2, 43.

Advise, 1) to counsel; absol.: *well hast thou —d,* Gent. I, 3, 34. Shr. I, 1, 41. Per. IV, 3, 51. *to a. one:* Meas. II, 1, 259. III, 1, 260. IV, 6, 3. LLL V, 2, 300. Shr. I, 2, 44. IV, 4, 11. Alls II, 3, 311. Tw. II, 5, 165. Wint. I, 2, 339. 350. H4B I, 2, 153. H8 I, 1, 102. 135. II, 4, 55. Tim. IV, 3, 457. Lr. IV, 5, 29. Oth. II, 3, 332. Cymb. I, 2, 1. II, 3, 13. III, 2, 46. Per. I, 1, 39. *to a. one to sth.: that well might a. him to a caution,* Mcb. III, 6, 44. *I a. you to the best,* Lr. I, 2, 188. *a. the duke to a most festinate preparation,* III, 7, 9. With *for: a. the emperor for his good,* Tit. I, 464 (i. e. concerning his good, his advantage); cf. *you shall a. me in all for Cleopatra,* Ant. V, 2, 137 (concerning the affairs of C.). *to a. a thing: if you a. it,* Meas. IV, 1, 67. *that rock that I a. your shunning,* H8 I, 1, 114. With a double acc.: *this I will a. you,* Shr. IV, 2, 92. Used of spiritual advice: *—d him for the entertainment of death,* Meas. III, 2, 225. *a. him for a better place,* IV, 2, 223. *I am come to a. you,* IV, 3, 55. *friar, a. him,* V, 490.

2) to prevail on by counsel, to persuade, to rule: *let the friar a. you,* Ado IV, 1, 246. *he is —d by aught to change the course,* Lr. V, 1, 2. Particularly in the imperative of the pass., = take my advice, be ruled by me, take heed: Ven. 615. LLL IV, 3, 368. Mids. I, 1, 46. Merch. II, 1, 42. V, 234. Wint. IV, 4, 492. H4A IV, 3, 5. H6B II, 4, 36. H8 I, 1, 139. 145. Oth. I, 2, 55. cf. R3 II, 1, 107.

3) to inform, to instruct: *a. me where I

may have such a ladder, Gent.III, 1, 122. *a. him*, Alls I,1,81 (be his teacher). Hml.IV,7,54. *I hope I need not to a. you further*, III, 5, 27. H8 I, 2, 107. Cor. V, 3, 197. Mcb. III, 1, 129. Lr. I, 3, 23. *are you —d?* Shr. I, 1, 191 (did you hear? do you understand?). H6B II,1,47. *you were —d his flesh was capable of wounds*, H4BI,1,172 (you knew very well, were well aware). *bids you be —d there's nought in France that can be with a nimble galliard won*, H5 I, 2, 251. With *of*, = to inform one of: *—d by good intelligence of this preparation*, H5 II Chor. 12.

4) refl. to consider: *a. you what you say*, Tw. IV, 2, 102. *bid thy master well a. himself*, H5 III, 6, 168. Tit. IV, 2, 129. Lr. II, 1, 29.

5) absol. in the same sense: *lay hand on heart, a.* Rom. III, 5, 192.

Advised, adj. (cf. *Avised*), considerate, deliberate, used of persons as well as things: *the a. head defends itself*, H5 I, 2,179. *the silver livery of a. age*, H6B V, 2, 47. *bade me be a.* R3 II, 1, 107. *when they had sworn to this a. doom*, Lucr. 1849. *by a. respects*, Sonn. 49, 4. *with more a. watch*, Merch. I, 1, 142. *more upon humour than a. respect*, John IV, 2, 214. *with a. purpose*, R2 I, 3, 188. Sometimes = in one's sound senses, not mad: *I am a. what I say*, Err. V, 214. Preceded by *well: mad or well a.?* Err. II, 2, 215. LLL V, 2, 434. John III, 1, 5. R3 I, 3, 318. IV, 4, 518. Tit. IV, 2, 10.

Advisedly, deliberately: Ven. 457. Lucr. 180. 1527. 1816. Merch. V, 253. H4A V, 1, 114.

Advising, subst. advice, counsel: *fasten your ear on my —s*, Meas. III, 1, 203.

Advocate, one who pleads the cause of another: Sonn.35,10. Tp.I,2,477. Err. I, 1, 146. Wint. II, 2, 39. IV, 4, 766. 768. V, 1, 221. R3 I, 3, 87. Cymb. I, 1, 76.

Advocation, pleading: Oth. III, 4, 123.

Aeacides, descendant of Aeacus: Shr. III, 1, 52. cf. H6B I, 4, 65.

Aedile, title of a high officer in ancient Rome, represented by Sh. as a police-officer: Cor. III, 1, 173. 183. 214. 319.

Aegeon, name in Err. I, 1, 141. 158. V, 337. 341.

Aegle (O. Edd. Eagles), a mistress of Theseus': Mids. II, 1, 79.

Aemilia, wife of Aegeon: Err. V, 342. 345. 346.

Aemilius (O. Edd. *Emilius* and *Emillius*), name in Tit. IV, 4, 61. 104. V, 1, 155.

Aeneas, the Trojan hero: Tp. II, 1, 79. H6B V, 2, 62. Troil. I, 1, 111. IV, 1, 2 (and passim). Tit. III, 2, 27. Caes. I, 2, 112. Hml. II, 2, 468. Ant. IV, 14, 53. Cymb. III, 4, 60. Alluded to in Tit. II, 3, 22 and V, 3, 80.

Aenigma, see *Enigma*.

Aeolus, the God of the winds: H6B III, 2, 92.

Aerial (Ff *eriall*, Qq *ayre all*), etherial: *the a. blue*, Oth. II, 1, 39.

Aery, the brood of an eagle: John V, 2, 149. R3 I, 3, 264. 270. *there is an a. of children* Hml. II, 2, 354 (alluding to a company of young actors, chiefly the children of Paul's and the children of the Revels, who at that time were highly applauded).

Aesculapius, the God of physicians: Per. III, 2, 111. Dr. Caius called so in jest: Wiv. II, 3, 29.

Aeson, father of Jason, restored to youth by Medea: Merch. V,14.

Aesop, the fabulist, supposed to have been hunchbacked: H6C V, 5, 25.

Aetna, the volcano in Sicily: Lucr. 1042. Wiv. III, 5, 129. Tit. III, 1, 242.

Afar, at a great distance: *may read the mot a.* Lucr. 830. *chase thee a. behind*, Sonn. 143, 10. *in strands a. remote*, H4A 1, 1, 4. *a. off* = 1) at a great distance: *saw a. off in the orchard this amiable encounter*, Ado III, 3, 160. 2) indirectly: *a kind of tender, made a. off by Sir Hugh*, Wiv. I, 1, 216. *he who shall speak for her is a. off guilty but that he speaks*, Wint. II, 1, 104 (cf. *Far-off*).

Afeard, (Ff *afraid* in LLL V, 2, 582. Merch. I, 2, 47. Troil. IV, 4, 84), afraid, being in fear: Tp. II, 2, 106. III, 2, 142. 144. Wiv. III, 4, 28. Shr. V, 2, 17. Wint. IV, 4, 453. 474. H4A II, 4, 402. Mcb. V, 1, 41. Cymb. IV, 2, 94. *to make a.:* Mids. III, 1, 116. H6A IV, 7, 93. An inf. following: *a. to scratch her foe*, Lucr. 1035. John IV, 2, 135. Caes. II, 2, 67. Mcb. I, 7, 39. Ant. II, 5, 81. III, 3, 1. A clause following: *a. she will do a desperate outrage*, Ado III, 3, 158. Merch. II, 9, 96. Alls V, 3, 153. H5 IV, 1, 148. Rom. II, 2, 139. Hml. V, 2, 310. With *at:* H6B II, 4, 89. With *of*, = 1) fearing: *a. of your four legs*, Tp. II, 2, 62. 148. Mids. III, 1, 28. Shr. V, 2, 19. Mcb. I, 3, 96. 2) anxious about: *to be a. of my deserving*, Merch. II, 7, 29.

Affability, kindness: *her a. and bashful modesty*, Shr. II, 49. *you do not use me with that a.* H5 III, 2, 139. *hide it in smiles and a.* Caes. II, 1, 82.

Affable, kind: *that a. familiar ghost*, Sonn. 86, 9. *an a. and courteous gentleman*, Shr. 1, 2, 98. *with gentle conference, soft and a.* II, 253. *wondrous a. and as bountiful as mines of India*, H4A III, 1, 168. *he was mild and a.* H6B III, 1, 9. *a. wolves, meek bears*, Tim. III, 6, 105.

Affair, any thing that is to be done, or in which a person or community is occupied or concerned: Sonn. 57, 10. 151, 12. Lucr. 45. Gent. II, 4, 119. 185. III, 1, 59. Wiv. II, 1, 114. Meas. III, 1,56. I, 4, 87. III, 1, 159. Ado II, 1, 183. Mids. III, 2, 374. Merch. II, 6, 22. As II, 7, 99. IV, 1, 47. Alls III, 2, 99. H4B II, 3, 2. H6A IV, 1, 181. H6B I, 3, 157. III, 1, 224. 320. H6C IV, 6, 58. R3 I, 3, 122. IV, 4, 398 (Qq *attempt*). H8 V, 1, 13. Troil. I, 3, 247. Cor. V, 2, 88. Caes. III, 1, 135. Mcb. III, 3, 21. Hml. I, 2, 16. 174. III, 2, 321. V, 2,379. Ant. III, 6, 63. IV, 6, 13. Cymb. III, 2, 52 etc.

Affect, subst. inclination: *every man with his —s is born*, LLL I, 1, 152. *to banish their —s with him*, R2 I, 4, 30. *the young —s* Oth. I, 3, 264 (the desires of youth).

Affect, vb. 1) to love: *a lady whom I a.* Gent. III, 1, 82. Wiv. II, 1, 115. IV. 4, 87. Meas. I, 1, 4. 73. Ado I, 1, 298. LLL I, 2, 92. 172. Shr. I, 1, 40. II, 14. Tw. II, 5, 28. H4B IV, 5, 145. H6A V, 5, 57. H6B III, 1, 375. H8 I, 1, 39. II, 3, 29. Troil. II, 2, 59. 60. 195. Tit. I, 1, 28. Tim. I, 2, 30. 221. Lr. I, 1, 1. Cymb. V, 5, 38.

2) to like, to be pleased with; absol. *making peace or war as thou —est*, Ant. 1, 3, 71 (= as thou pleasest). trans.: *I will something a. the letter*, LLL IV, 2, 56 (delight in its iteration, by practising alliteration). *how doth your grace a. their motion?* H6A V, 1, 7. *mock not that I a. the untraded oath*, Troil. IV, 5,178. *not to a. many proposed matches*, Oth.III,3,229.

3) **to aim at:** *—est a sheep-hook,* Wint. IV, 4, 431. *have I —ed wealth or honour?* H6B IV, 7, 104. *to a. the malice and displeasure of the people,* Cor. II, 2, 24. *—s tyrannical power,* III, 3, 1. *—ing one sole throne,* IV, 6, 32. *—ed the fine strains of honour,* V, 3, 149. *stratagem must do that you a.* Tit. II, 1, 105.

4) **to imitate in a constrained manner:** *lest it be rather thought you a. a sorrow than have it,* Alls I, 1, 60. 62. *thou dost a. my manners,* Tim. IV, 3, 199. *a. a saucy roughness,* Lr. II, 2, 102. Partic. *—ing,* absol., = full of affectation, given to false show: *a drawling —ing rogue,* Wiv. II, 1, 145. *lisping —ing fantasticoes,* Rom. II, 4, 29.

5) **to resemble:** *the accent of his tongue —eth him,* John I, 86.

Affectation, artificial show of what is not natural: Wiv. I, 1, 152 (Evans' speech). LLL V, 1, 4 (Qq F1 *affection*). V, 2, 407 (O. Edd. *affection,* though it rhymes to *ostentation*). Hml. II, 2, 464 (Qq *affection*).

Affected, adj. (derived partly from the subst., partly from the verb *affect*) 1) absol. a) **disposed:** *as I find her, so am I a.* Wiv. III, 4, 95. *I am in all a. as your self,* Shr. I, 1, 26. *no marvel, then, though he were ill a.* Lr. II, 1, 100. — b) **assuming an artificial appearance:** *he is too picked, too spruce, too a.* LLL V, 1, 15. — c) **in love:** LLL II, 232.

2) With *to,* = a) **in love with:** *is thine own heart to thine own face a.?* Ven. 157. *I stand a. to her,* Gent. II, 1, 90. — b) **inclined, disposed:** *how stand you a. to his wish?* Gent. I, 3, 60. *that most are a. to these,* LLL III, 26. *how he doth stand a. to our purpose,* R3 III, 1, 171.

Affectedly, lovingly, with tender care: *letters with sleided silk feat and a. enswathed,* Compl. 48.

Affection, 1) bent of mind, disposition: *what warmth is there in your a. towards any of these suitors?* Merch. I, 2, 37. *level at my a.* 41. *the a. of nobleness which nature shows above her breeding,* Wint. V, 2, 40. *there grows in my most ill-composed a. such a stanchless avarice,* Mcb. IV, 3, 77. Chiefly a feeling or natural impulse acting upon, and swaying the mind: *not one .. who my a. put to the smallest teen,* Compl. 192. *by the a. that now guides me most,* Meas. II, 4, 168. *thou hast neither heat, a., limb, nor beauty,* III, 1, 37. *with a. wondrous sensible he wrung Bassanio's hand,* Merch. II, 8, 48. *a., master of passion,* IV, 1, 50 (natural instinct, on which the disposition of the mind depends). *a., thy intention stabs the centre,* Wint. I, 2, 138 (natural propensity, thy power rules the inmost thoughts of men). *with the least a. of a welcome,* H4B V, 5, 173. *if this law of nature be corrupted through a.* Troil. II, 2, 177. *doth a. breed it?* Oth. IV, 3, 99. Plur. *—s* = feelings, passions: *threw my —s in his power,* Compl. 146. *your —s would become tender,* Tp. V, 18. *in the working of your own —s,* Meas. II, 1, 10. *has he —s in him?* III, 1, 108. *war against your own —s,* LLL I, 1, 9. Merch. I, 1, 16. III, 1, 62. V, 87. Shr. IV, 4, 42. Wint. V, 1, 220. John V, 2, 41. H4B IV, 4, 65. H5 IV, 1, 110. Rom. I, 1, 153. II, 5, 12. Caes. II, 1, 20. Oth. II, 1, 245 (Ff *a.*) IV, 3, 101. Ant. I, 5, 12. 17.

2) **love:** *a. is a coal that must be cooled,* Ven.

387. 569. 650. Lucr. 500. 1060. Tp. I, 2, 448. Gent. I, 1, 3. II, 1, 91. Wiv. II, 2, 248. IV, 6, 10. Meas. I, 4, 48. III, 1, 249. Err. V, 51. Ado II, 1, 175. 382. II, 3, 106. 127. 236. III, 1, 42. 55. LLL I, 2, 63. IV, 3, 290. Mids. I, 1, 197. III, 2, 230. Merch. II, 1, 22. As I, 2, 22. IV, 1, 212. 215. Shr. I, 1, 165. III, 1, 76. Alls I, 3, 196. Tw. II, 4, 38. Wint. I, 1, 26. IV, 4, 390. 492. V, 2, 111. H4B IV, 4, 22. V, 5, 17. H6A V, 1, 47. Troil. IV. 4, 6. Cor. V, 3, 24. Rom. II Chor. 2. III, 1, 182. Tim. I, 2, 222. Caes. IV, 3, 205. Hml. I, 3, 100. IV, 7, 19. Lr. I, 1, 223. I, 4, 63. Oth. I, 1, 36. Ant. II, 6, 139. III, 9, 67. III, 13, 7. Cymb. I, 6, 138. With *to: her a. unto Benedick,* Ado V, 4, 90. Shr. IV, 2, 23. H8 III, 2, 35. Lr. I, 2, 94. Personified and masc.: *a. is my captain, and he leadeth,* Lucr. 271. Plural: *made old offences of —s new,* Sonn. 110, 4. *all these trophies of —s hot,* Compl. 218. *fair encounter of two most rare —s,* Tp. III, 1, 75. Err. II, 1, 94. Ado II, 3, 231. As I, 3, 21. H8 III, 1, 129. Oth. I, 3, 112.. Cymb. I, 1, 82. Per. II, 5, 77.

3) **inclination, tendency, wish:** *whatever comes athwart his a.* Ado II, 2, 7. *it is the king's most sweet pleasure and a.* LLL V, 1, 93. *not removes —'s edge in me,* Shr. I, 2, 73. *minister unto the appetite and a. common of the whole body,* Cor. I, 1, 107. *keep you in the rear of your a.* Hml. I, 3, 34. Plur.: *nice —s wavering stood in doubt if best were as it was,* Compl. 97. *my —s are most humble,* Tp. I, 2, 481. *when the rich golden shaft hath killed the flock of all —s else,* Tw. I, 1, 36. *let me wonder at thy —s,* H4A III, 2, 30. *in speech, in gait, in diet, in —s of delight,* H4B II, 3, 29. *in his tomb lie my —s,* V, 2, 124. H5 V, 1, 26. Cor. I, 1, 181. II, 3, 239. Rom. I, 1, 133. Hml. III, 1, 170.

4) **affectation:** *witty without a.* LLL V, 1, 4 (F2.3.4 *affectation*). V, 2, 407 (where the rhyme demands *affectation*). Hml. II, 2, 464 (Ff *affectation*). Used by Evans as a verb: Wiv. I, 1, 234.

Affectionate, loving, fond: Lr. IV, 6, 276.

Affectionately, lovingly, Troil. III, 1, 74.

Affectioned, full of affectation: Tw. II, 3, 160.

Affeered, confirmed, sanctioned: Mcb. IV, 3, 34.*

Affiance, confidence: H5 II, 2, 127. H6B III, 1, 74. Cymb. I, 6, 163.

Affianced, betrothed: *a. to her by oath,* Meas. III, 1, 222. *I am a. this man's wife,* V, 227.

Affined, 1) related, joined by affinity: *then the bold and coward seem all a. and kin,* Troil. I, 3, 25.

2) **bound by any tie:** *be judge yourself whether I in any just term am a. to love the Moor,* Oth. I, 1, 39. *if partially a., or leagued in office, thou dost deliver more or less than truth,* II, 3, 218.

Affinity, relation, or perhaps connexion of any kind: *of great fame in Cyprus and great a.* Oth. III, 1, 49.

Affirm, to say Yes to, to maintain as true: *their own authors a. that the land Salique is in Germany,* H5 I, 2, 43. *I must not blush to a. it,* V, 2, 117. *renege, a.* Lr. II, 2, 84. *I a. it is the woman's part,* Cymb. II, 5, 21.

Affirmation, the act of affirming: *upon warrant of bloody a.* Cymb. I, 4, 63 (of sealing the truth with his blood).

Affirmative, subst. the contrary to a negative: *four negatives make two —s,* Tw. V, 24.

Afflict, to give bodily or mental pain, to distress, to grieve, to mortify: Lucr. 975. Wiv. IV, 2, 233. Meas. III, 1, 11. As III, 5, 33. H6A III, 1, 106. H6B II, 1, 182. H6C I, 4, 38. R3 V, 3, 179. Cor. I, 1, 20. Tit. I, 441. IV, 3, 62. IV, 4, 11. Rom. II, 4, 34. Tim. IV, 3, 337. Hml. II, 1, 106. II, 2, 17. Lr. I, 4, 313. Ant. III, 6, 78. Cymb. IV, 2, 40. Wint. V, 3, 75. *—ed* = distressed, unhappy, wretched: *this —ed fancy,* Compl. 61. *the —ed spirits in the prison here,* Meas. II, 3, 4. *the vile prison of —ed breath,* John III, 4, 19. *he looks much —ed,* H8 II, 2, 63.

Affliction, 1) any painful sensation: *man's nature cannot carry the a. nor the fear,* Lr. III, 2, 49 (the horrors of the thunderstorm).

2) great suffering of the mind, misery: Tp. V, 22. 115. Wiv. V, 5, 178. LLL I, 1, 316. Wint. III, 2, 224. IV, 4, 586. V, 3, 76. H6B III, 2, 301. H8 III, 1, 88. Rom. III, 3, 2. Tim. III, 2, 62. IV, 2, 44. V, 1, 213. Mcb. III, 2, 18. Hml. III, 1, 36. III, 2, 324. IV, 5, 188. Lr. IV, 6, 36. 75. Oth. IV, 2, 48. Cymb. III, 6, 10. V, 4, 108. Abstr. pro concr.: *O fair a.* John III, 4, 36 (= afflicted lady).

Afford, to yield, to grant, to offer; with an accus.: *sometime it* (her grief) *is mad and too much talk —s,* Lucr. 1106. *a. some present speed,* 1305. *every hymn that able spirit —s,* Sonn. 85, 7. 105, 12. Err. III, 1, 24. LLL V, 2, 223. Shr. Ind. 1, 104. V, 2, 13. 14. R2 I, 1, 177. H4A III, 2, 38. H6A III, 1, 148. H6B I, 1, 30. H6C I, 3, 37. III, 2, 147. R3 I, 2, 246. III, 5, 102. IV, 4, 31. V, 3, 80. H8 I, 4, 18. Tit. III, 1, 44. 55. Rom. III, 1, 63. III, 4, 8. IV, 1, 125. V, 1, 73. With a dat. and acc.: *he can a. no praise to thee,* Sonn. 79, 11. *this commendation I can a. her,* Ado I, 1, 176. LLL IV, 1, 39. V, 2, 246. Wint. IV, 4, 16. H6C III, 2, 165. R3 I, 4, 51. Tit. V, 2, 86. Tim. III, 2, 82. IV, 3, 253. Oth. I, 3, 114. *we cannot a. you so* (= you shall not come off so cheap) Alls IV, 1, 53.

Affray, to frighten: Rom. III, 5, 33 (rhyming).

Affright, to terrify; tr.: Lucr. 971. 1138. Mids. V, 142. Wint. III, 3, 37. John IV, 2, 172. H4A I, 3, 104. H5 Prol. 14. H6A I, 4, 43. H6B III, 2, 47. IV, 1, 33. V, 1, 207. H6C IV, 7, 13. R3 I, 3, 227. I, 4, 64. V, 3, 308. Cor. I, 1, 172. Rom. V, 3, 61. Caes. III, 1, 82. Hml. II, 1, 75. Oth. II, 3, 276. V, 2, 100. Per. I, 1, 29. Absol.: *does death a.?* H6B IV, 1, 32.

Affront, subst. *to give the a.* = to face the enemy: Cymb. V, 3, 87.

Affront, vb. to meet, to encounter: *a. his eye,* Wint. V, 1, 75. *—ed with the match and weight of such a winnowed purity in love,* Troil. III, 2, 174. *that he may here a. Ophelia,* Hml. III, 1, 31. *your preparation can a. no less than what you hear of,* Cymb. IV, 3, 29.

Affy, 1) to confide: *I do a. in thy uprightness,* Tit. I, 47.

2) to betroth: *we be —ed,* Shr. IV, 4, 49. *to a. a mighty lord unto the daughter of a worthless king,* H6B IV, 1, 80.

A-field, (O. Edd. not hyphened) in the field: *keep my lambs a.* H6A V, 4, 30. = in the field of battle: Troil. I, 1, 108. III, 1, 147. V, 3, 67.

Afire, on fire, burning: Tp. I, 2, 212. Cor. V, 3, 181. Rom. III, 3, 133. (*o'fire* in Wint. IV, 4, 60).

Afloat, borne by the water, not sinking: Sonn. 80, 9. Caes. IV, 3, 222.

Afoot, 1) on foot: *walked ten mile a.* Ado II, 3, 17. R2 I, 1, 63. H4A II, 2, 13. 27. 38. 50. II, 3, 87. II, 4, 387. H6B V, 2, 8. H6C V, 7, 18. Troil. V, 5, 21.

2) concerning infantry: *of what strength they are a.* Alls IV, 3, 181.

3) in motion and action: *the matter being a.* Meas. IV, 5, 3. *the game is a.* H4A I, 3, 278 (hunted up, started); cf. H5 III, 1, 32. *these rebels now a.* H4B IV, 4, 9. H5 I, 2, 211. Cor. I, 2, 25. Caes. III, 2, 265. Mcb. IV, 3, 185. Hml. III, 2, 83. Lr. IV, 3, 51. *to keep base life a.* Lr. II, 4, 218 (to sustain). *well a.* = in good health: Tit. IV, 2, 29.

Afore, prep. 1) before; of place as well as time: *drive all thy subjects a. thee,* H4A II, 4, 152. *with a muffler a. her eyes,* H5 III, 6, 32. *something's a. it,* Cymb. III, 4, 81. *a fortnight a. Michaelmas,* Wiv. I, 1, 212. *I shall be there a. you,* Lr. I, 5, 5 (Qq *before*).

2) in presence of, in the face of: *here, a. heaven, I ratify this my rich gift,* Tp. IV, 1, 7. *she makes our profession to stink a. the face of the gods,* Per. IV, 6, 145. *a. God!* = by God! R2 II, 1, 200. 238. Rom. II, 4, 170. IV, 2, 31. *a. me!* = by my life, by my soul: *a. me, it is so late,* Rom. III, 4, 34. *a. me, a handsome fellow,* Per. II, 1, 84 (cf *Before* and *Fore*).

Afore, adv. before: *if he have never drunk wine a.* Tp. II, 2, 78 (Stephano speaking).

Afore, conj. before: *I'll forswear keeping house, a. I'll be in these tirrits,* H4B II, 4, 220 (Mrs Quickly's speech).

Aforehand, beforehand, previously: *knowing a. of our merriment,* LLL V, 2, 461.

Aforesaid (used only by Armado, Launcelot and Thersites), mentioned before: LLL I, 1, 277. *as a.* = as I said before: Merch. II, 2, 8. Troil. II, 3, 64.

Afraid, full of fear, in fear: Ven. 898. Pilgr. 274. Wiv. I, 1, 304. IV, 1, 20. Mids. III, 1, 127. III, 2, 321. Tw. III, 1, 142. John IV, 3, 5. H4A II, 4, 406. H6B II, 3, 69. R3 I, 2, 43. I, 4, 65. 111. Troil. IV, 4, 84 (Qq *afeard*). Caes. II, 2, 101. Oth. V, 2, 266. With *of*: Tp. IV, 91. Err. IV, 4, 151. Tw. II, 5, 156. III, 4, 42. John IV, 1, 21. H4A V, 4, 123. H6A I, 1, 26. R3 V, 3, 215. Mcb. V, 3, 59. Hml. II, 2, 359. With an inf. = fearing, not having the courage: *we are less a. to be drowned than thou,* Tp. I, 1, 47. *a. to speak,* LLL V, 2, 582 (Qq *afeard*). *not that I am a. to die,* Alls IV, 3, 271. H6B II, 3, 57. Rom. V, 3, 10. Mcb. II, 2, 51. IV, 3, 165. V, 7, 5. Ant. II, 3, 29. *to be a.,* followed by a depending clause, = to fear, to apprehend: *I am a. he will chastise me,* Tp. V, 262. *I am a. he will have need of washing,* Wiv. III, 3, 193. *I am much a. his mother played false,* Merch. I, 2, 47 (Qq *afeard*). *I am a. his thinkings are below the moon,* H8 III, 2, 133. Ado II, 3, 158. Shr. V, 2, 88. Alls II, 3, 95. Tw. IV, 1, 14. H4A III, 1, 145. V, 4, 126. Mcb. II, 2, 10.

Peculiar expression: *be not of my holy vows a.* Compl. 179, i. e. be not anxious or distrustful about my vows; cf. *Fear,* and *Afeard.*

Afresh, anew: Sonn. 30, 7. Shr. I, 1, 143. Wint. IV, 2, 28. V, 1, 149. R3 I, 2, 56.

Afric, the continent to the south of the Mediterranean: Tp. II, 1, 69. Cor. I, 8, 3. Cymb. I, 1, 167. Adjectively: *parch in A. sun,* Troil. I, 3, 370 (cf. *Britain court, Lethe wharf, Rome gates, Tiber banks* etc.).

Africa, the same: H4B V, 3, 104 (Pistol's speech).

African, subst. inhabitant of Africa: Tp. II, 1, 125.

A-front, in front, directly opposed: H4A II, 4, 222.

After, prep. 1) behind, following, in pursuit of: *Venus' eye which a. him she darts,* Ven. 817. *fly a. summer,* Tp. V, 92. *sent a. thee,* Gent. I, 3, 74. *send a. the duke and appeal to him,* Meas. I, 2, 178. *a. him!* IV, 3, 69. *shut doors a. you,* Merch. II, 5, 53. IV, 1, 396. V, 216. Alls II, 1, 58. R2 V, 6, 52 etc. Implying the notion of desire: *he a. honour hunts, I a. love,* Gent. I, 1, 63. *will they yet look a. thee?* Wiv. II, 2, 146. *is lechery so looked a.?* Meas. I, 2, 148. *inquisitive a. one,* Err. I, 1, 127. *to hearken a. the flesh,* LLL I, 1, 220 (Costard's speech). *hope not a. it,* As III, 5, 45. *look a. him,* Tw. I, 5, 144 (take care of him). H6B III, 1, 219. Mcb. V, 1, 83.

2) under, next to: *a. God, thou set'st me free,* H6C IV, 6, 16.

3) later, posterior to: *a. two days,* Tp. I, 2, 298. III, 2, 93. 148. Gent. II, 1, 30. II, 7, 37. III, 2, 82. 96. Meas. I, 2, 40 etc. *a. all this fooling, I would not have it so,* Meas. I, 2, 71 (i. e. though this fooling may have amused us). *a. well entered soldiers,* Alls II, 1, 6 (quite a Latinism: after having well entered upon our soldiership).

4) according to, conformable to: *imitated a. you,* Sonn. 53, 6. *drawn a. you,* 98, 12. *he does not talk a. the wisest,* Tp. II, 2, 76. *thy complexion shifts to strange effects, a. the moon,* Meas. III, 1, 25. *not made a. this downright way of creation,* III, 2, 112. Ado I, 1, 69. LLL III, 21. IV, 2, 17. Tw. III, 4, 85. Wint. IV, 4, 183. 547. H4B V, 2, 129. H8 I, 3, 14. Troil. III, 2, 209. Cor. II, 3, 234. 238. V, 1, 46. V, 6, 58. Tit. IV, 1, 70. Rom. I, 4, 8. Hml. II, 2, 555. V, 2, 187. Lr. I, 2, 107. Oth. I, 3, 69. Cymb. I, 1, 71. II, 3, 5. IV, 2, 334 etc. Pompey says: *I'll rent the fairest house a. three pence a bay,* Meas. II, 1, 255, i. e. according to, or at, the rate of three pence.

After, adv. 1) behind, following, in pursuit: *and a. bite me,* Tp. II, 2, 10. *and a. do our work,* III, 2, 158. *to post a.* Gent. II, 3, 37. *I must a.* II, 4, 176. *I'll a.* III, 1, 394. V, 2, 51. *follows a.* Wint. IV, 1, 28. H4A I, 3, 126. H6C II, 5, 136. Troil. V, 1, 105. Hml. I, 4, 89. IV, 4, 37 etc. *a., a.!* R2 V, 2, 111. R3 III, 5, 72. Hml. IV, 2, 33.

2) in or at a later time: Lucr. 1522. Wiv. III, 3, 246. Meas. II, 2, 102. V, 168. 513. Ado I, 1, 328. I, 2, 220. R2 III, 1, 44. H6A III, 4, 45 etc. *ever a.* Tp. I, 2, 184. *never a.* Ven. Ded. 5. *shortly a.* Lucr. Arg. 14. *a great time a.* Tp. III, 3, 105. *straight a.* Err. IV, 4, 144 etc.

3) behind: *looking before and a.* Hml. IV, 4, 37.

After, conj. subsequently to the time when: *a. they closed in earnest, they parted in jest,* Gent. II, 5, 13. Wiv. III, 5, 74. Err. V, 261 etc. Followed by a present: *a. my flame lacks oil,* Alls I, 2, 59. *a. he scores,* IV, 3, 253. *A. that,* see *That.*

After, adj.: *an a. fleet,* Oth. I, 3, 35 (a fleet sent after).

After-debts, debts called in at a later time? *He ne'er pays a., take it before,* Alls IV, 3, 255. But probably the hyphen is but a misprint.

After-dinner, the time just after dinner: *an —'s sleep,* Meas. III, 1, 33. *an —'s breath,* Troil. II, 3, 121.

After-enquiry, see *After-inquiry.*

After-eye, vb. to look after: *to a. him,* Cymb. I, 3, 16.

After-hours, later times: R3 IV, 4, 293. Rom. II, 6, 2.

After-inquiry, investigation: Cymb. V, 4, 189.

After-loss, a later loss, a future grief: Sonn. 90, 4.

After-love, future love: Gent. III, 1, 95. R2 V, 3, 35.

After-meeting, later or second meeting: Cor. II, 2, 43.

After-noon, the time from the meridian to the evening: Tp. III, 2, 96. Meas. IV, 2, 125. 133. IV, 3, 87. Err. V, 47. LLL III, 156. 163. IV, 3, 376. V, 1, 95. 98. Merch. I, 2, 93. II, 5, 27. Shr. I, 2, 278. IV, 4, 100. Alls V, 3, 66. John V, 7, 94. H4A III, 3, 224. H4B I, 2, 211. H6A IV, 5, 53. Cor. I, 3, 76. IV, 5, 230. Rom. I, 1, 107. II, 4, 192. 197. Mcb. III, 1, 19. Hml. I, 5, 60. Figuratively: *in the a. of her best days,* R3 III, 7, 186.

After-nourishment, later food: Per. I, 2, 13.

After-supper, the time after supper: Mids. V, 34.*

After-times, succeeding times: H4B IV, 2, 51.

Afterward, in subsequent time: Gent. III, 2, 97. Meas. V, 478. Err. I, 2, 28. Ado V, 4, 122. Merch. II, 1, 41. Alls I, 3, 121. R3 III, 7, 181. Cymb. I, 5, 39.

Afterwards, the same: Sonn. 115, 4. Wiv. I, 1, 147. IV, 2, 91. Meas. IV, 3, 35. Ado III, 2, 25. IV, 1, 3. R2 V, 3, 112. R3 III, 1, 199. Troil. II, 1, 123. IV, 5, 272. Tit. V, 3, 203. Caes. II, 1, 164. Mcb. V, 1, 7. Hml. II, 2, 364. Ant. II, 7, 85. Cymb. III, 1, 80.

After-wrath (not hyphened in O. Edd.) anger breaking out at a later time: Ant. V, 2, 290.

Again, 1) once more, a second time: *they have met a.* Tp. I, 2, 233. *it begins a.* 395. *I ne'er a. shall see her,* II, 1, 111 etc. etc. Absol.: *yet a.!* Tp. I, 1, 41. III, 2, 38. = tell it once more: H4B I, 1, 48. = go once more: Cymb. IV, 3, 1. *as long a.* = twice as long: H6B IV, 3, 7. *once a.* = once more: Ven. 499. Tp. III, 2, 44. IV, 1, 4. Gent. V, 4, 78. 128. Wiv. IV, 4, 14. Meas. V, 270. Err. V, 130. Shr. Ind. 2, 77. John II, 389. IV, 2, 1. V, 4, 2. R2 III, 2, 5. H4A I, 3, 141. III, 1, 37. H5 III, 3, 7. V, 1, 13. H6A III, 2, 19. H6B IV, 4, 14. H6C I, 4, 44. II, 1, 183. 185. IV, 8, 53. H8 I, 4, 107. IV, 1, 1. Troil. II, 2, 2. V, 2, 49. Hml. I, 1, 31 etc.

2) to the previous state; implying not so much repetition of an action as restitution to what was before: *a torment which Sycorax could not a. undo,* Tp. I, 2, 291. *we all were sea-swallowed, though some cast a.* II, 1, 251 etc. Hence = back: *pay a.* Sonn. 79, 8. Err. I, 2, 85. Merch. I, 2, 87. *to give a.*

Tp. V, 168. Meas. II, 1, 107. *bring a.* Meas. IV, 1, 5. As II, 2, 21. *take a.* Gent. II, 1, 124. Err. II, 2, 129. H6C V, 1, 37. *haste you a.* Alls II, 2, 74. *she will speed her foot a.* III, 4, 37. *call the queen a.* Wint. II, 1, 126. Ant. II, 5, 79. *ask a.* John IV, 1, 44. *hie thee a.* Ant. V, 2, 194. *bear a.* Cymb. V, 3, 82. Peculiar expr.: *come a. when you may,* Err. III, 1, 41 (i. e. this time I am not at your service). *nay, come a., good Kate, I am a gentleman,* Shr. II, 217 (go, go, you are mistaken in me). Joined to *back: call her back a.* Gent. I, 2, 51. *I brought him back a.* IV, 4, 57. *go back a.* Err. II, 1, 75. Mids. I, 1, 251. *till Harry's back-return a. to France,* H5 Chor. 41.

3) in return: *who did not whet his teeth at him a.* Ven. 1113. *sitting on a bank, weeping a. the king my father's wreck, this music crept by me,* Tp. I, 2, 390 (while I was answering with tears).* *could not a. reply,* Gent. II, 1, 172. *curse a.* Mids. V, 184. *wooing her until I sweat a.* Merch. III, 2, 205 (in return, in consequence of it). *and I a., in Henry's royal name, give thee her hand,* H6A V, 3, 160. *the winds shall hiss at thee a.* H6B IV, 1, 78. Joined with *back:* Tp. I, 2, 150. cf. H4B III, 2, 187. Troil. IV, 4, 19.

4) in one's turn, on the other hand, on the contrary: *the one is my sovereign, the other a. is my kinsman,* R2 II, 2, 113. *and now a. of him that did not ask, but mock, bestow your sued-for tongues,* Cor. II, 3, 214.

5) moreover, besides, further: *a., if any Syracusian born* etc. Err. I, 1, 19. *and a., sir, shall we sow the headland with wheat?* H4B V, 1, 15. H8 III, 2, 101. Troil. I, 3, 64. Oth. I, 3, 21.

Against (cf. *'Gainst*), prep. 1) towards, to; denoting a direction in general, with or without contrariety; a) made of place: *a. my heart he set his sword,* Lucr. 1640. *the cry did knock a. my very heart,* Tp. I, 2, 9. *she is too bright to be looked a.* Wiv. II, 2, 254. *spurred his horse a. the steep uprising of the hill,* LLL IV, 1, 2. *thou a. the senseless winds shalt grin in vain,* H6B IV, 1, 77. *casts his eye a. the moon,* H8 III, 2, 118. *my duty, as doth a rock a. the chiding flood, should the approach of this wild river break,* 197. *just a. thy heart make thou a hole,* Tit. III, 2, 17. *the leafy shelter that abuts a. the island's side,* Per. V, 1, 51. Hence almost = at, before: *as soon decayed and done as is the dew a. the splendour of the sun,* Lucr. 25. *a. love's fire fear's frost hath dissolution,* 355. *if aught in me worthy perusal stand a. thy sight,* Sonn. 38, 6. *boughs which shake a. the cold,* 73, 3. *make water a. a woman's farthingale,* Gent. IV, 4, 41. *beauty is a witch, a. whose charms faith melteth into blood,* Ado II, 1, 187. *till I break my shins a. it,* As II, 4, 60. *he shall be set a. a brickwall,* Wint. IV, 4, 818. *a. this fire do I shrink up,* John V, 7, 33. *lean thy back a. my arm,* H6A II, 5, 43. *set your knee a. my foot,* III, 1, 169 (kneel down at my feet). *a. the Capitol I met a lion,* Caes. I, 3, 20. *singeing his pate a. the burning zone,* Hml. V, 1, 305. *stood a. my fire,* Lr. IV, 7, 38. cf. Cor. I, 9, 30. Oth. II, 3, 382.

b) used of time, = shortly before, and usually in expectation of: *more clamorous than a parrot a. rain,* As IV, 1, 152. *every one doth so a. a change,* R2 III, 4, 28. *a. ill chances men are ever merry,* H4B IV, 2, 81. *I'll spring up in his tears, an'twere a nettle a. May,* Troil. I, 2, 191. *men shut their doors a. a setting sun,* Tim. I, 2, 150 (quibbling). *to disfurnish*

myself a. such a good time, III, 2, 50. *a. some storm, a silence in the heavens,* Hml. II, 2, 505. *with tristful visage, as a. the doom,* III, 4, 50. As denoting provision and care taken in expectation of an event, = for: *a. this coming end you should prepare,* Sonn. 13, 3. *a. that time do I ensconce me here,* 49, 1. 5. 9. *I must employ you in some business a. our nuptial,* Mids. I, 1, 125. *have toiled their memories a. your nuptial,* V, 75. *I was promised them a. the feast,* Wint. IV, 4, 237. *prepare her a. this wedding-day,* Rom. III, 4, 32. *to prepare him up a. to-morrow,* IV, 2, 46.

c) in a moral sense, = towards, to: *my love and duty a. your sacred person,* H8 II, 4, 41. *it is hypocrisy a. the devil,* Oth. IV, 1, 6.

2) in opposition or repugnance to: Tp. I, 1, 62. I, 2, 158. II, 1, 106. III, 1, 31. III, 3, 75. IV, 141. 202. Gent. I, 2, 43. 111. I, 3, 83. III, 1, 247. III, 2, 26. 41 etc. etc. *the doors are made a. you,* Err. III, 1, 93. IV, 3, 90. Tw. V, 404. Tim. I, 2, 150. Mcb. I, 7, 15. Lr. II, 4, 180. *I'll stop mine ears a. the mermaid's song,* Err. III, 2, 169. Troil. V, 3, 2. Cor. V, 3, 6. *shut his bosom a. our prayers,* Alls III, 1, 9. *a. the blown rose may they stop their nose,* Ant. III, 13, 39. *we must do good a. evil,* Alls II, 5, 53. *let there be weighed your lady's love a. some other maid,* Rom. I, 2, 102. *myself, a. whom I know most faults,* As III, 2, 298 (i. e. against whom I know most faults to object). cf. Cor. III, 1, 10.

Against, conj., in expectation of, and provision for the time when: *a. my love shall be with time's injurious hand crushed . . .* Sonn. 63, 1. *I'll charm his eyes a. she do appear,* Mids. III, 2, 99. *bid the priest be ready to come a. you come,* Shr. IV, 4, 104. *I would be all, a. the worst may happen,* H8 III, 1, 25. *and see them ready a. their mother comes,* Tit. V, 2, 206 (Ff *gainst*). *in the mean time, a. thou shalt awake, shall Romeo by my letters know our drift,* Rom. IV, 1, 113.

Agamemnon, the leader of the Greeks before Troy: H4B II, 4, 237. H5 III, 6, 7. H6C II, 2, 148. Troil. I, 2, 267 (and often).

Agate, a stone of the flint kind, often worn in rings, with little figures cut in it: *his heart, like an a., with your print impress'd,* LLL II, 236. Serving as a symbol of smallness: Ado III, 1, 65. H4B I, 2, 19.

Agate-ring: H4A II, 4, 78.

Agate-stone: Rom. I, 4, 55.

Agazed, furnished, as it were, with gazes, gazing, looking with amazement: *all the whole army stood a. on him,* H6A I, 1, 126.

Age, the period of time assigned to sth., lifetime, duration in general: *peace proclaims olives of endless a.* Sonn. 107, 8. *the stretching of a span buckles in his sum of a.* As III, 2, 140. *an a. of discord,* H6A V, 5, 63. *we shall hardly in our —s see,* Cor. III, 1, 7. *within my a.* (= during my lifetime) IV, 6, 51.

2) a generation of men, a particular period of time, as distinguished from others: *this pattern of the worn-out a.* Lucr. 1350. *the golden a.* Lucr. 60. Tp. II, 1, 168. *the old a.* Sonn. 127, 1. Tw. II, 4, 49. *the a. to come,* Sonn. 17, 7. 32, 10. 101, 12. 104, 13. Wiv. I, 3, 92. IV, 4, 37. Ado V, 2, 80. As III, 2, 240. John I, 213. H4B IV, 4, 46. H6A II, 2, 10. II, 5, 6. R3 III, 1, 73. Hml. III, 2, 26 etc.

Coming near the sense of *century: one poor retiring minute in an a.* Lucr. 962. *some three —s since,* LLL I, 2, 117. *this long a. of three hours,* Mids. V, 33. *how many —s hence,* Caes. III, 1, 111.

3) the period of life, at which a person is arrived: *strong youth in his middle a.* Sonn. 7, 6. *as with a. his body uglier grows,* Tp. IV, 191. *to clothe mine a. with angel-like perfection,* Gentl. II, 4, 66. *all —s,* Meas. II, 2, 5. Wint. IV, 4, 740. *not be many hours of a. more,* R2 V, 1, 57. *sixteen years of a.* Cymb. IV, 2, 199 etc.

4) a stage of life: *his acts being seven —s,* As II, 7, 143.

5) the period when a person is enabled to do certain acts for himself: *he being of a. to govern,* H6B I, 1, 166. *I am of age to keep mine own,* Tit. IV, 2, 104. *to come to a.* = to come to one's majority, H4A I, 3, 253. H6B IV, 2, 153. Rom. I, 3, 56.

6) an advanced period of life: *nor wrong mine a.* (as elder brother) *with this indignity,* Tit. I, 8. *thy prime of manhood daring, thy a. confirm'd, proud, subtle,* R3 IV, 4, 171. Mostly the latter part of life, oldness: Ven. 941. 1148. Lucr. 142. 275. 603. Sonn. 3, 11. 11, 6. 62, 14. 63, 5. 108, 10. 138, 12. Compl. 14. 70. Pilgr. 157. Tp. I, 2, 258. Gentl. I, 3, 15. III, 1, 16. 74. Meas. III, 1, 32. 130. Err. II, 1, 89. V, 329. Ado II, 3, 248. III, 5, 37. LLL IV, 3, 244. Merch. IV, 1, 271. Wint. IV, 4, 78 *(our —s).* H6A II, 5, 1. H8 IV, 2, 67. Tim. III, 5, 80 etc. *Old a.* Lucr. 1759. H5 IV, 3, 44. V, 2, 248.

Abstr. pro concr.: *a., thou hast lost thy labour* (= old man), Wint. IV, 4, 787. *let me embrace thine a.* Tp. V, 121.

Used as a masc.: Sonn. 63, 10.

Aged, old, of things as well as persons: Lucr. 855. Meas. III, 1, 35. Wint. V, 3, 29. R2 II, 1, 72. 2, 74. H6A II, 5, 6. 43. H8 V, 5, 58. Cor. III, 1, 178. Tit. III, 1, 23. 59 (Q2 Ff *noble*). IV, 4, 96. V, 2, 130. Tim. V, 1, 175. V, 3, 8. Lr. IV, 2, 41. IV, 4, 28. Cymb. I, 1, 157. *our a.* = our old men, Tim. V, 1, 179. *a. things,* Lucr. 941. *a. ears,* LLL II, 74. *a. custom,* Cor. II, 3, 176. *to be a. in any kind of course* = to adhere to old customs, Meas. III, 2, 238, cf. Tim. V, 3, 8.

A. cramps = cramps such as old people are wont to suffer, Tp. IV, 261 (cf. Lucr. 855, and *Old*). *my a. eloquence* = the eloquence of my age, Gentl. III, 1, 83. *a. honour* = honour in age, All's I, 3, 216. *a. contusions,* H6B V, 3, 3. *a. night* = night of old age, R3 IV, 4, 16.* *a. wrinkles,* Tit. III, 1, 7. *a. tyranny,* Lr. I, 2, 52. *a. patience,* Per. II, 4, 48.

Agenor, the father of Europa, Shr. I, 1, 173.

Agent, 1) he by whom something is effected: *this entertainment may well become the a.* Wint. I, 2, 114. *night's black —s to their preys do rouse,* Mcb. III, 2, 53.

2) the instrument by whose help something is effected: *being the —s, or base second means,* H4A I, 3, 165. *as the a. of our cardinal, to second all his plot,* H8 III, 2, 59. *thus is the poor a. despised,* Troil. V, 10, 36. cf. H6B III, 2, 115. Cymb. I, 5, 76. Used of the organs of the body: *his other —s aim at like delight,* Ven. 400. Cor. I, 1, 126. Mcb. I, 7, 80.

3) the substitute, deputy: *here is her hand, the a. of her heart,* Gentl. I, 3, 46. *this ungenitured a.* Meas. III, 2, 184. Ado II, 1, 137. John II, 87.

Aggravate, 1) to make greater: *to a. thy store,* Sonn. 146, 10. *I will a. my voice,* Mids. I, 2, 84 (Bottom speaking). 2) to make worse: *I will a. his style,* Wiv. II, 2, 296. *the more to a. the note,* R2 I, 1, 43. Used wrongly by Mrs. Quickly, H4B II, 4, 175.

Aggrieved (Fluellen pronounces *aggriefed*), pained, offended: H5 IV, 7, 170.

Agile, nimble: *his a. arm,* Rom. III, 1, 171.

Agincourt, the battlefield of Henry V: H5 Prol 14. IV Chor. 52. IV, 7, 92.

Agitation, emotion, disturbance: *in this slumbery a.* Mcb. V, 1, 12. — Launcelot uses it for cogitation, Merch. III, 5, 5.

Aglet, tag of a point or lace, pin; sometimes with a head formed into a small figure: *marry him to a puppet or an aglet-baby,* Shr. I, 2, 79, i. e. such a small figure on a pin.

Agnize, to own with pride, to enjoy: *I do a. a natural and prompt alacrity,* Oth. I, 3, 232.

Ago, past, gone, reckoning time from the present: *four days a.* LLL I, 1, 122. As II, 7, 24. Shr. III, 1, 69. IV, 4, 4. Tw. I, 2, 31. I, 5, 282. V, 222 *(but so late a.).* 414. Wint. I, 2, 451. IV, 4, 300. John V, 3, 11. R2 V, 1, 42. H4A I, 1, 26. II, 3, 69. II, 4, 346. H4B II, 4, 93. III, 2, 224. H6C II, 1, 104. R3 V, 3, 279. H8 III, 1, 120. Tit. IV, 2, 23. Rom. I, 5, 42. III, 4, 7. Tim. III, 2, 12. Hml. III, 2, 138. Lr. II, 2, 31. Oth. IV, 1, 86. Cymb. V, 4, 154. *how long is it a.?* H4A II, 4, 360. Cymb. I, 1, 61.

Agone = ago: *long a.* Gentl. III, 1, 85. *an hour a.* Tw. V, 204.

Agony, pangs of death: *charm ache with air, and a. with words,* Ado V, 1, 26. LLL V, 2, 867. H6C V, 5, 39. R3 I, 4, 42. IV, 4, 163. H8 II, 1, 33.

Agood, heartily: *I made her weep a.* Gentl. IV, 4, 170.

Agree, 1) to be in concord: *if music and sweet poetry a.* Pilgr. 103. LLL II, 225. Merch. II, 2, 107. H4A I, 2, 126. H6B IV, 2, 81. Hence to be consistent, to be of one mind, not to differ: *our jarring notes a.* Shr V, 2, 1. *how can these contrarieties a.?* H6A II, 3, 59. Cor. II, 1, 228. Caes. IV, 3, 176. Followed by *with: —ing with the proclamation,* Meas. I, 2, 80. Err. II, 2, 170. Shr. V, 2, 168. Wint. I, 1, 41. H4B V, 5, 139. H6B I, 1, 112. Tit. I, 306. V, 3, 165. Rom. III, 2, 10.

2) to become of one mind, to come to one opinion: *a. whose hand shall go along,* Tit. III, 1, 175. Followed by *upon: ere we can a. upon the first place,* Tim. III, 6, 76. *heard it —d upon that the prince should woo Hero,* Ado I, 3, 64. Transitively in the passive (= to stipulate): *it is thus —d that peaceful truce shall be proclaimed,* H6A V, 4, 116. H6B I, 1, 43. 57. *it stands —d by all voices,* H8 V, 3, 87. *to be —d* = to have come to a compromise: *I am —d,* Shr. I, 1, 147. *conclude and be —d* R2 I, 1, 156. *the traitors are —d,* H5 II Chor. 33. *are you all —d?* H8 V, 3, 91. *thus we are —d,* Ant. II, 6, 57. *are you —d?* Meas. IV, 2, 51. *how —d?* IV, 1, 65. *—d!* (= done!) H6A II, 1, 33. Cor. I, 4, 2. Cymb. I, 4, 182.

3) to yield assent: *unwilling I —d,* Err. I, 1, 61. H6B I, 1, 218. H6C III, 3, 241. H8 Prol. 10 Rom. I, 2, 18. Followed by *to: a. to any covenants,* H6A V, 5, 88. By *with: a. with his demands to the point,* Meas. III, 1, 254.

4) to suit, to be appropriate: *it —s well,* Wiv. I, 1, 20. *drugs fit, and time —ing,* Hml. III, 2, 266. *nothing else with his proud sight —s,* Ven. 288. *his mood with nought —s,* Lucr. 1095. *your appetites do not a. with it,* H5 V, 1, 28.

Agreement, 1) union of mind, consent: *such assurance as shall with either part's a. stand,* Shr. IV, 4, 50.

2) compact, stipulation: *upon a. from us to his liking,* Shr. I, 2, 183, i. e. if he is pleased with what we stipulate. *upon some a.* IV, 4, 33 *upon a.* H4A I, 3, 103.

Agrippa, 1) Menenius A. Cor. I, 1, 52. 2) M. Vipsanius A. Ant. II, 2, 17. 119. IV, 6, 1 and passim.

Aground, on the ground, stranded: *we run ourselves a.* Tp. I, 1, 4.

Ague, cold fits of fever: *burning fevers, —s pale and faint,* Ven. 739. Tp. II, 2, 68. 97. 139. Merch. I, 1, 23. John III, 4, 85. R2 II, 1, 116. H8 I, 1, 4. Troil. III, 3, 232. Caes. II, 2, 113. *The a.* Mcb. V, 5, 4. Plural: Ven. 739. H4A III, 1, 69. IV, 1, 112. Tim. IV, 3, 137.

Aguecheek, name: *Sir Andrew A.* Tw. I, 3, 18. III, 4, 210. 187.

Agued, struck with an ague, chilly: *pale with flight and a. fear,* Cor. I, 4, 38.

Agueface for *Aguecheek:* Tw. I, 3, 46.

Ague-fit, a paroxysm of cold: *this a. of fear,* R2 III, 2, 190.

Ague-proof, able to resist the causes which produce agues: Lr. IV, 6, 107.

Ah, an interjection expressive of various affections, except that of unqualified joy and satisfaction. Mostly an exclamation of mental suffering, of pity, of complaint, of painful surprise: Sonn. 9, 3. 34, 13. 44, 9. 67, 1. 104, 9. 139, 9. Compl. 155. Pilgr. 391. Gentl. II, 1, 5. Err. II, 2, 126. IV, 2, 1. LLL IV, 2, 110. All's III, 4, 18. John III, 3, 54. H6B II, 4, 23. 27. 58. III, 1, 74. 189. III, 3, 5. IV, 4, 41. H6C I, 1, 167. I, 3, 1. V, 2, 5. R3 IV, 4, 9 etc. etc. Sometimes of entreaty and desire: Sonn. 90, 5. Pilgr. 155. Mids. I, 2, 55 etc. Or, on the other hand, of contempt, anger and threat: Pilgr. 56. Tw. II, 5, 41. H6A II, 4, 104. H6B IV, 7, 27. IV, 10, 28. Hml. I, 2, 135 *(ah fie!).* Ant. III, 13, 89. In R3 I, 3, 11. II, 2, 27. 34. 72 Ff *ah,* Qq *oh;* in R2 II, 1, 163 Ff *oh,* Qq *ah.* In Ado III, 5, 26 *(all thy tediousness on me? ah?)* it is the modern *Eh. Ah me!* Rom. V, 1, 10 (as M. Edd. generally write for *Ay me!* which is the usual reading of O. Edd.)

Ah ha! expresses triumph mixed with some contempt: Wiv. II, 2, 158. Tw. III, 4, 104. R3 III, 7, 71. H8 I, 2, 186. Rom. I, 5, 20. Hml. I, 5, 150. Ant. II, 5, 15. In Troil. IV, 2, 82 Qq have *ah ah!* Ff less aptly *ah ha!* In Ado III, 3, 90 Dogberry ejaculates *Ha ah!*

A-height, to the height, up: *look up a.* Lr. IV, 6, 58.

A-high, the same: *one heaved a.* R3 IV, 4, 86.

A-hold, a nautical term: *lay her a.!* Tp. I, 1, 52. evidently purporting an order to keep clear of the land.*

A-hungry, for hungry, used by Slender, Wiv. I, 1, 280, and Sir Andrew, Tw. II, 3, 136; Marcius even says *an hungry,* Cor. I, 1, 209, in imitation of the populace. But cf. St. Mark II, 25.

Aid, subst., assistance of any kind, succour: Sonn. 86, 8. Lucr. 1696. Alls I, 2, 7. Wint. IV, 4, 638. R2 II, 3, 150. H6A I, 1, 143. IV, 4, 23. 29. H6B IV, 5, 7. H6C III, 1, 43. III, 3, 148. 220. R3 V, 3, 173. H8 I, 2, 114. Ant. II, 2, 88. Cymb. V, 4, 43. *for a.* = to seek assistance: H6A IV, 4, 11. H6C III, 1, 28. Tit. IV, 3, 15. *in a.* Ant. V, 2, 27. *the good a.* All's III, 7, 11. *raising of more a.* (= assistants) Err. V, 153. *with a. of soldiers* H6C II, 1, 147. H6B IV, 5, 4. Hml. IV, 1, 33.

A. of one or sth. either = the assistance given by one or sth.: *expecting the a. of Buckingham,* R3 IV, 4, 438. *a lack of Timon's a.* Tim. V, 1, 150. *with the a. of use,* Mcb. I, 3, 146. *by whose a.* Ven. 1190. Tp. V, 40. *keep them from thy a.* Lucr. 912. Sonn. 79, 1. Tp. V, 143. All's I, 3, 242. V, 3, 329. John II, 584. H4A V, 1, 46. H6A I, 2, 82. IV, 3, 12. H6C III, 3, 32. R3 IV, 5, 5. Cor. V, 1, 33. Cymb. V, 4, 43. Per. III, 2, 35. Or the assistance given to one or sth.: *in a. whereof we will raise a mighty sum,* H5 I, 2, 132. *in his poor heart's a.* Lucr. 1784. *be my a.* Tw. I, 2, 53. *they will be at his a.* H6A IV, 4, 41. *flock to their a.* R3 IV, 4, 507. *to our a.* Cor. I, 7, 3. *upon his a.* Mcb. III, 6, 30.

Plural: *surmise of —s incertain,* H4B I, 3, 24. *all —s, themselves made fairer by their place,* Compl. 117, i. e. things serving to set off his person.*

Aid, vb., to assist: *to a. me with thy counsel,* Gentl. II, 4, 185. Wiv. III, 5, 150. All's V, 1, 20. Wint. III, 2, 21. H6A IV, 3, 44. V, 3, 7. H6C II, 5, 76. R3 II, 2, 63. V, 3, 93. Cor. I, 6, 66.

Absolutely: *heaven —ing,* Alls IV, 4, 12. *deny her —ing hand,* R3 I, 3, 96. With an inf.: *—ed to expose the child,* Wint. V, 2, 77.

Aidance, assistance: *when it is barr'd the a. of the tongue,* Ven. 330. *attracts the same for a. 'gainst the enemy,* H6B III, 2, 165.

Aidant, helpful: *be a. and remediate in the good man's distress,* Lr. IV, 4, 17.

Aidless, unassisted: Cor. II, 2, 116.

Aiery, v. *Aery.*

Aigre, sour: *like a. droppings into milk,* Hml. I, 5, 69 (Qq and M. Edd. *eager*).

Ail, to feel ill, to feel pain: *what does she a.?* All's II, 4, 6. *what —est thou?* Wint. III, 3, 83.

Aim, subst. 1) the direction of a missile or of any thing compared with it: *in the a. and very flash of it,* Caes. I, 3, 52. *I will watch the a.* Merch. I, 1, 150. *fly with false a.* All's III, 2, 113. *our safest way is to avoid the a.* Mcb. II, 3, 149.

2) the point, to which the thing thrown is directed, the butt: *mistakes that a.* Ven. 942. *the a. of all is but ...* Lucr. 141. 143. *I miss'd my a.* H6A I, 4, 4. *the Parthian darts lost a.* Ant. IV, 14, 71. *the —s and ends of burning youth,* Meas. I, 3, 5. *the a. of every shot,* R3 IV, 4, 90. Err. III, 2, 63. H4B I, 1, 123. H5 I, 2, 186. H8 V, 3, 118. *her that gave a. to all thy oaths,* Gentl. V, 4, 101, i. e. to whom all thy oaths were addressed. *But, gentle people, give me a. awhile,* Tit. V, 3, 149 (explained by the following *stand all aloof*) = give room and scope to my thoughts.

To cry aim, an expression borrowed from archery, = to encourage the archers by crying out *aim,* when they were about to shoot, and then in a general sense to applaud, to encourage with cheers: *it ill beseems this presence to cry aim to these ill-tuned repetitions,* John II, 196. *to these violent proceedings all my neighbours shall cry a.* Wiv. III, 2, 45. Very dubious in Wiv. II, 3, 93: *cried I a.? said I well?* (Qq Ff *cried game* and *cride-game*), cf. *Game.*

3) the pointing of a missile and of what is similar to it: *end thy ill a. before thy shoot be ended,* Lucr. 579. *the hail of his all-hurting a.* Compl. 310. *a certain a. he took at . . .* Mids. II, 1, 157. *that from the hunter's a. had ta'en a hurt,* As II, 1, 34. H4B III, 2, 285. Troil. I, 3, 15. Hence = intention: *we shall be shorten'd in our a.* Cor. I, 2, 23. *proclaim myself against the level of my a.* All's II, 1, 159.

4) guess, conjecture: *a man may prophesy with a near a.* H4B III, 1, 83. *what you would work me to, I have some a.,* Caes. I, 2, 163. *in these cases, where the a. reports,* Oth. I, 3, 6. Gentl. III, 1, 28. Ado IV, 1, 239.

Aim, vb. 1) to point or direct a weapon; a) absolutely: *here stand we both, and a. we at the best,* H6C III, 1, 8. *I a. a mile beyond the moon,* Tit. IV, 3, 65.

b) trans.: *not where I had —'d them* (my arrows) Hml. IV, 7, 24. figuratively: *some apparent danger —ed at your highness,* R2 I, 1, 14. *it is exceedingly well —ed,* H4A I, 3, 282.

c) intr., followed by *at*: *this bird you —ed at,* Shr. V, 2, 50. figuratively = to endeavour to obtain: *—ing at Silvia,* Gentl. II, 6, 30. *Richmond —s at young Elisabeth,* R3 IV, 3, 40. *the riches of thyself I a. at,* Wiv. III, 4, 18. Ven. 400. H4B I, 1, 124. H6C III, 2, 68. IV, 1, 125. R3 III, 2, 45. H8 III, 1, 138. 2, 448. Cor. I, 1, 267. Oth. III, 3, 223. Followed by the inf.: *the head which princes a. to hit,* H4B I, 1, 149. *I a. to lie with thee,* H6C III, 2, 69.

2) to guess: *thou —est all awry,* H6B II, 4, 58. *if I a. aright,* H6C III, 2, 68. *well —'d of such a young one,* Shr. II, 237. *I —'d so near,* Rom. I, 1, 211. Followed by *at* = to suspect: *that my discovery be not —ed at,* Gentl. III, 1, 45. *—ing at your interior hatred,* R3 I, 3, 65. And = to make conjectures about sth.: *they a. at it,* Hml. IV, 5, 9. *a. better at me by that I now will manifest,* Ado III, 2, 99, i. e. form a better opinion of me.

To aim one, instead of *at one,* rests only upon a conjecture of M. Edd. in Err. III, 2, 66 (O. Edd. *I am thee*).

Air, subst., the element which we breathe: Ven. 64. 654. 1085. Lucr. 778. 1042. 1805. Sonn. 21, 8 (*heaven's a.*) Tp. I, 2, 222. 387. II, 1, 46. IV, 172. 266. V, 21. 102. Gentl. II, 4, 28. IV, 4, 159. Meas. II, 4, 25. LLL I, 1, 236. Wint. V, 3, 78 (= a draught of a., a breath). H6B III, 2, 287. IV, 10, 54 etc. etc. Plural: Hml. I, 4, 41.

Particular characteristics: *the wanton a.* Pilgr. 230 and LLL IV, 3, 104. Rom. II, 6, 19. *the a., a chartered libertine,* H5 I, 1, 48. *as false as a.* Troil. III, 2, 199. *as soft as a.* Ant. V, 2, 314. *A. and water* moist elements, Troil. I, 3, 41; cf. Ven. 654. *A. and fire* finer and quicker elements, in contradistinction to the duller and grosser nature of earth and water: Sonn. 45, 1. H5 III, 7, 22. Ant. V, 2, 292.

Proverbial: *build there, carpenter, the a. is sweet,* Troil. III, 2, 54; cf. H4B V, 3, 9. And figuratively: *who builds his hopes in a. of your good looks,* R3 III, 4, 100.

Sometimes = the open and unconfined air: *bring your music forth into the a.* Merch. V, 53. *bear him out of the air,* Oth. V, 1, 104. *will you walk out of the a.?* Hml. II, 2, 209 (here within the palace). And then = the wide world: *as to be cast forth in the common a.* R2 I, 3, 157. *let it forth to seek the empty, vast and wandering a.* R3 I, 4, 39. *a dedicated beggar to the a.* Tim. IV, 2, 13. *we must all part into this sea of a.* 22. *thou unsubstantial a. that I embrace,* Lr. IV, 1, 7. Hence *to take a.* = to get public: *lest the device take a. and taint,* Tw. III, 4, 145.

Used as the symbol of unsubstantiality: *melted into a.* Tp. IV, 150. *how all the other passions fleet to a.* Merch. III, 2, 108. *she would mock me into a.* Ado III, 1, 75. Troil. III, 3, 225. John II, 387. *feed on the a.* Gentl. II, 1, 179. *eating the a. on promise of supply,* H4B I, 3, 28. *I eat the a.* Hml. III, 2, 99. *charm ache with a.* i. e. with mere words, Ado V, 1, 26.

Air, subst. peculiar look and habits: *seest thou not the a. of the court in these enfoldings?* Wint. IV, 4, 755. *your father's image, his very a.* V, 1, 128. *promising is the very a. o'the time,* Tim V, 1, 25.

Air, subst., a piece of music, played or sung, and chiefly one adapted to words: *a wonderful sweet a., with admirable rich words to it,* Cymb. II, 3, 19. *this music . . . with its sweet a.,* Tp. I, 2, 393. V, 58. Ado II, 3, 60. LLL III, 1, 4. Mids. I, 1, 183 (*your tongue's sweet a.*) *any a. of music,* Merch. V, 76. Plural: Tp. I, 2, 422. III, 2, 145. Tw. II, 4, 5.

Air, vb. 1) to expose to the air, to draw forth: *I beg but leave to a. this jewel; see! and now 'tis up again,* Cymb. II, 4, 96. *died shortly after this world had —'d them,* H8 II, 4, 193. *to a. one's self* = to take fresh air: *thy sea-marge, where thou thyself dost a.* Tp. IV, 70. *to purge melancholy and a. himself,* Wint. IV, 4, 790. *riding forth to a. yourself,* Cymb. I, 1, 110.

2) to lead forth, to lead about: *though I have for the most part been —ed abroad,* Wint. IV, 2, 6.

Air-braving, defying the influence of the air: *a. towers,* H6A IV, 2, 13.

Air-drawn, drawn in air, visionary: *the a. dagger,* Mcb. III, 4, 62.

Airless, wanting fresh air: *a. dungeon,* Caes. I, 3, 94.

Airy, 1) consisting of air: *the a. region,* Rom. II, 2, 21. *Echo's a. tongue,* 163. *you a. toys,* Wiv. V, 5, 46. *your a. wings,* R3 IV, 4, 13. 2) dwelling in the air: *like an a. spirit,* Mids. III, 1, 164. *some a. devil,* John III, 2, 2. 3) wrought by spirits of the air: *this a. charm,* Tp. V, 54. 4) unsubstantial: *a. nothing,* Mids. V, 16. *the a. scale of praise,* Compl. 226. *a. succeeders of intestate joys* (i. e. words) R3 IV, 4, 128. *his a. fame,* Troil. I, 3, 144. *an a. word,* Rom. I, 1, 96. *of so a. and light a quality,* Hml. II, 2, 267.

Ajax, the Greek hero, son of Telamon: Lucr. 1394. 1398. LLL IV, 3, 7 (*as mad as A.*). *Aeacides was A.* Shr. III, 1, 53. *like A. Telamonius, on sheep or oxen could I spend my fury,* H6B V, 1, 26. *the Greeks upon advice did bury A. that slew himself,* Tit. I, 379. *A. is their fool* (i. e. a fool to them) Lr. II, 2, 132. *the seven-fold shield of A.* Ant. IV, 14, 38. Cymb. IV, 2, 252. Troil. I, 2, 14 (and passim). A quibble with *a jakes: your lion, that holds his poll-*

axe sitting on a close-stool, will be given to A. LLL V, 2, 581; and perhaps Troil. II, 1, 70.

Ake, v. *ache.*

Alablaster, (M. Edd. *alabaster*), a kind of gypsum: *ivory in an a. band,* Ven. 363. *her a. skin,* Lucr. 419. *cut in a.* Merch. I, 1, 84. *a. arms,* R3 IV, 3, 11. *smooth as monumental a.* Oth. V, 2, 5.

Alack, interj. expressive of sorrow: Lucr. 1156. Sonn. 65, 9. 103, 1. Pilgr. 133. 239. Tp. I, 2, 151. Meas. IV, 2, 175. IV, 4, 36. LLL II, 186. Mids. II, 2, 153. V, 173. Merch. II, 3, 16. As IV, 3, 52. Wint. IV, 3, 57. John II, 118. III, 1, 305. H4B IV, 2, 14. IV, 5, 229. R3 I, 1, 47. V, 3, 187. Cor. I, 1, 76. Rom. III, 5, 211. Ant. III, 10, 24. Cymb. V, 5, 102 etc. *a. for pity!* Tp. I, 2,132. *a., for mercy!* 436. *a. for woe!* LLL IV, 1, 15. R2 III, 3, 70. *a. the day!* Pilgr. 227. LLL IV, 3, 101. Merch. II, 2, 73. Rom. III, 2, 39. IV, 5, 23. Lr. IV, 6, 185. *a. the heavy day!* R2 III, 3, 8. IV, 257.

Alacrity, cheerful promptitude: *I have not that a. of spirit,* R3 V, 3, 73. Troil. IV, 4, 147. Oth. I, 3, 233. Comically used by Falstaff: *I have a kind of a. in sinking,* Wiv. III, 5, 13.

A-land, 1) on land: Per. II, 1, 31. 2) to land: III, 2, 69.

Alarbus, eldest son of Tamora, Tit. I, 133. 143.

Alarm, subst. (never vb.) 1) a summons to arms, notice of approaching danger: *Jealousy... gives false —s,* Ven. 651. *in a night a.* Troil. I, 3, 171. Hml. II, 2, 532 (Ff *alarum*). III, 4, 120. *is it not an a. to love?* Oth. II, 3, 27 (Ff *alarum*).

2) State of war, hostile attack: *remove your siege from my unyielding heart; to love's —s it will not ope the gate,* Ven. 424. *the reason of this rash a. to know,* Lucr. 473. *their dear causes would to the bleeding and the grim a. excite the mortified man,* Mcb. V, 2, 4. Lastly, disturbance, broil in general: *these home —s,* R2 I, 1, 205.

Alarum, subst., a call to arms, to an attack: *anon their* (the dogs') *loud —s he* (the hare) *doth hear,* Ven. 700. *anon his beating heart, a. striking, gives the hot charge,* Lucr. 433. *sound, sound a.! we will rush on them,* H6A I, 2, 18. I, 4, 99. II, 1, 42. H6B II, 3, 95. V, 2, 3. R3 I, 1, 7. Cor. II, 2, 80. Then a loud noise in general: *to endure her loud —s,* Shr. I, 1, 131. *what new a. is this same?* H5 IV, 6, 35. *strike a., drums!* R3 IV, 4, 148 (sc. to drown the curses of the women). Lastly, combat, contention: *such fierce —s both of hope and fear,* H6A V, 5, 85. In Hml. II, 2, 532 and Oth. II, 3, 27 Qq *alarm,* Ff *alarum.*

Alarum, vb., to call to arms, to the combat: *wither'd murder, —'d by his sentinel, the wolf,* Mcb. II, 1, 53. *he saw my best —'d spirits roused to the encounter,* Lr. II, 1, 55.

Alarum-bell, a bell that gives notice of danger and combat: *ring the a.!* Mcb. II, 3, 79. V, 5, 51.

Alas, interj. expressive of sorrow or pity: Ven. 631. 1075. Lucr. 832. 1624. Sonn. 110, 1. 115, 9. Pilgr. 217. Tp. I, 2, 115. II, 2, 39. III, 1, 15. Gent. II, 2, 21. II, 7, 8: IV, 4, 81. 96. 178. Wiv. I, 4, 37. 120. II, 2, 92. II, 3, 15. III, 3, 55. III, 4, 3. 90. V, 5, 34. Meas. I, 4, 75. 77. II, 1, 6. 279. II, 2, 3. 72. III, 1, 133 etc. etc. *a. the day!* Wiv. III, 5, 39. IV, 2, 70. As III, 2, 231. Tw. II, 1, 25. II, 2, 39. H4B

II, 1, 14. Troil. III, 2, 50. Rom. III, 2, 72. Mcb. II, 4, 23. Oth. III, 4, 158. IV, 2, 124. *a. the heavy day!* Oth. IV, 2, 42. *a. the while!* Merch. II, 1, 31. Frequently joined to *out; v. Out.*

Alate, of late: *methinks you are too much a. i' the frown,* Lr. I, 4, 208 (Ff *of late*).

Alban, (O. Edd. *Albon* and *Albone*), *Saint A.,* name of a saint: *at Saint —'s shrine,* H6B II, 1, 63. *I thank God and S. A.* 108. *S. A. here hath done a miracle,* 131.

Albans, (O. Edd. *Albons* and *Albones;* only in H4B II, 2, 185 Ff *Albans*). *Saint A.,* a town in England: H4A IV, 2, 50. H4B II, 2, 185. H6B I, 2, 57. 83. I, 4, 76. II, 1, 135. V, 2, 68. V, 3, 30. H6C II, 1, 114. 120. II, 2, 103. III, 2, 1. R3 I, 3, 130.

Albany: *the duke of A.* (i. e. Scotland): Lr. I, 1, 2 and passim.

Albeit (in John V, 2, 9 of three, everywhere else of two syllables), although: Wiv. III, 4, 13. Err. V, 217. Merch. I, 3, 62 (Qt *although*). II, 6, 27, As I, 1, 53. I, 2, 274. Tw. III, 3, 31. John V, 2, 9. H4A I, 3, 128 (Ff *although*). V, 1, 102. H4B II, 2, 43. R3 III, 7, 226. IV, 3, 6 (Qq *although*). Troil. III, 2, 142. Oth. V, 2, 349. Cymb. II, 3, 61.

Albion, name of England: H5 III, 5, 14. H6B I, 3, 48. III, 2, 113. H6C III, 7. 49. Lr. III, 2, 91.

Al'ce, for *Alice:* Shr. Ind. 2, 112.

Alchemist, one who practises alchemy: *the sun plays the a., turning the earth to gold,* John III, 1, 78. *you are an a.; make gold of that,* Tim. V, 1, 117.

Alchemy, the art of making gold: *the morning ... gilding pale streams with heavenly a.* Sonn. 33, 4. *your love taught it this a., to make of monsters cherubins,* 114, 4. Caes. I, 3, 159.

Alcibiades, the Athenian general: Tim. I, 1, 250. 2, 74 etc.

Alcides, Hercules: Merch. II, 1, 35. III, 2, 55. Shr. I, 2, 260. John II, 144. H6A IV, 7, 60. Tit. IV, 2, 95. Ant. IV, 12, 44.

Alder-liefest, dearest: H6B I, 1, 28.

Alderman, member of a city corporation: *an —'s thumb-ring,* H4A II, 4, 364. *an agate-stone on the forefinger of an a.* Rom. I, 4, 56. *Aldermen:* R3 III, 7, 66 (Qq *citizens*).

Ale, a liquor made by an infusion of malt and fermentation: *She brews good a. And thereof comes the proverb: Blessing of your heart, you brew good a.* Gentl. III, 1, 304. Mids. II, 1, 50. Shr. Ind. I, 32. 2, 1 (*small a.*). 25 (*sheer a.,* i. e. unmixed a.). 76. Tw. II, 3, 125 (*cakes and a.*). Wint. IV, 3, 8. H4A I, 3, 233. H5 III, 2, 13. IV, 7, 40. H8 V, 4, 11 (*a. and cakes*). *To go to the a.* = to the alehouse, Gentl. II, 5, 61; in allusion perhaps to a Christian festival called so (cf. *Holy-ales*).

Alecto, one of the three Furies: H4B V, 5, 39.

Alehouse, a house where ale is sold: Gentl. II, 5, 9. 56. Ado III, 3, 45. Tw. II, 3, 96. R2 V, 1, 15. H5 III, 2, 12. H6B III, 2, 81. Tit IV, 2, 98. Oth. II, 1, 139. Unchanged in the genit.: H6B V, 2, 67.

Alençon (O. Edd. *Alanson*), a French name: LLL II, 61. 195. H5 III, 5, 42. IV, 7, 161. IV, 8, 101 etc. H6A I, 1, 95. II, 1, 60. III, 2, 65. IV, 1, 173. IV, 4, 27. IV, 6, 14. H6B I, 1, 7. H8 III, 2, 85.

Aleppo, town in Turkish Asia: Mcb. I, 3, 7. Oth. V, 2, 352.

Ale-washed, steeped in ale, dulled by drinking ale: *a. wits,* H5 III, 6, 82.

Alewife, a woman who keeps an alehouse: Shr. Ind. 2, 23. H4B II, 2, 89.

Alexander, 1) the king of Macedon: LLL V, 2, 539. 570. Wint. V, 1, 47. H5 III, 1, 19. IV, 7, 14. 20. Cor. V, 4, 23. Hml. V, 1, 218. 225. 231. — 2) *A. Iden:* H6B IV, 10, 46. V, 1, 74. — 3) Cressida's servant: Troil. I, 2, 45. — 4) son of Antony: Ant. III, 6, 15.

Alexandria, town in Egypt: Ant. I, 4, 3. II, 2, 72. III, 6, 2. III, 13, 168. IV, 8, 30.

Alexandrian, pertaining to Alexandria: *an A. feast,* Ant. II, 7, 102. *our A. revels,* V, 2, 218.

Alexas, attendant on Cleopatra: Ant. I, 2, 1 sq. IV, 6, 12 etc.

Alias, a Latin word = otherwise, else called: *the black prince, alias the devil,* Alls IV, 5, 44. *testy magistrates, a. fools,* Cor. II, 1, 48.

Alice, female name (cf. *Al'ce*): Wiv. I, 1, 211. II, 1, 51. H5 III, 4, 1 sq.

Alien, subst., stranger: *if it be proved against an a. that he seek the life of any citizen,* Merch. IV, 1, 349. *and art almost an a. to the hearts of all the court,* H4A III, 2, 34.

Alien, adj., belonging to others: *every a. pen hath got my use,* Sonn. 78, 3.

Aliena, assumed name of Celia: As I, 3, 130. II, 4, 8. IV, 1, 220. V, 2, 9 etc.

Alight, 1) intr. to descend from horse or carriage: *e'en at hand, —ed by this,* Shr. IV, 1, 120. *there is —ed at your gate a young Venetian,* Merch. II, 9, 86. *newly —ed,* Tim. I, 2, 181 (in all these passages it seems almost = arrived). *bid her a., and her troth plight,* Lr. III, 4, 127.

2) trans.: *a. thy steed,* Ven. 13.

Alike, adv., in the same manner: *since all a. my praises be to one,* Sonn. 105, 3. *Fortune had left to both of us a. what to delight in,* Err. I, 1, 106. LLL IV, 3, 126. Wint. I, 2, 310. V, 4, 457. John II, 331. H8 I, 2, 39. II, 2, 54. Cor. I, 4, 62. IV, 1, 6. Troil. IV, 1, 54. Rom. I, 2, 2. II Chor. 6. Tim. IV, 2, 19. V, 1, 124. Mcb. III, 1, 101. Ant. I, 1, 35. II, 2, 50. 51. III, 13, 34. Cymb. I, 6, 48. III, 2, 37. IV, 1, 13.

Alike, adj. (never preceding the substantive) looking or being like each other, equal: *male twins, all a.* Err. I, 1, 56. *all men are not a.* Ado III, 5, 43. Meas. I, 1, 35. Wint. V, 1, 207. John II, 331. H5 IV, 7, 27. H6A II, 1, 55. H6C V, 6, 4. Cor. I, 3, 25. Tit. I, 174. II, 3, 146. Rom. Prol. 1. Tim. III, 6, 75. Ant. I, 2, 56. Cymb. IV, 2, 5. V, 5, 125.

Alisander, for *Alexander,* in the language of Sir Nathaniel and Costard: LLL V, 2, 567. 572. 575. 578. 583. 587.

Alive, in life, living: Ven. 174. 1009. 1076. Lucr. 1768. Tp. II, 1, 122. 236. II, 2, 25. Gentl. III, 1, 184. V, 4, 66. Meas. IV, 3, 90. V, 472. Merch. II, 2, 75. John IV, 2, 251. H6B III, 2, 64. III, 3, 12. IV, 4, 41. IV, 7, 140. H6C I, 1, 161. I, 3, 33. R3 I, 2, 91. III, 7, 193. IV, 4, 472. Caes. IV, 3, 196 (*now to our work a.*). Lr. V, 1, 59. 62. Ant. IV, 6, 2. Cymb. III, 3, 81. IV, 2, 253 etc.

2) in existence, in the world: *but were some child of yours a. that time,* Sonn. 17, 13. *none else to me, nor I to none a.* 112, 7. *none a. will pity*

me, Pilgr. 400. *there be fools a.* Merch. II, 9, 68. *the cruell'st she a.* Tw. I, 5, 259. *there is scarce truth enough a. to make societies secure,* Meas. III, 2, 240. *I had not left a purse a. in the whole army,* Wint. IV, 4, 631. *the bricks are a. at this day to testify,* H6B IV, 2, 157. Gentl. II, 6, 27. Ado IV, 1, 180. Shr. II, 10. H4A III, 1, 173. H6A I, 4, 85. H6B III, 1, 244. R3 II, 1, 69. Oth. IV, 1, 68.

All, 1) substantively, the whole, opposed to part, every thing: *all lost,* Tp. I, 1, 54. *all is but fortune,* V, 257. Tw. II, 5, 27. *I leave myself, my friends, and a., for love,* Gentl. I, 1, 65. *I have scanted a. wherein I should your great deserts repay,* Sonn. 117, 1. *I shall have gold for all,* H6B I, 2, 107. *my all,* Sonn. 109, 14. *whose all not equals Edward's moiety,* R3 I, 2, 250. *believe not all,* Ant. III, 4, 11. *have my thanks for all,* IV, 14, 140. *and all to all,* Mcb. III, 4, 92*etc. etc. *the one almost as infinite as all, the other blank as nothing,* Troil. IV, 5, 80, i. e. as the universe. *And thou, all they, hast all the all of me,* Sonn. 31, 14 (being to me instead of all deceased friends). *The very all of all is,* LLL V, 1, 115.

In all = everything put down to account: *when but in all I was six thousand strong,* H6A IV, 1, 20. *All in all,* properly every thing in every respect, an expression of mere enforcement for *all: he that can do all in all with her,* H6B II, 4, 51. *he was a man, take him for all in all,* Hml. I, 2, 187 (i. e. consider him with respect to the whole of his qualities). *her love; for that is all in all,* Shr. II, 130. *it hath been all in all his study,* H5 I, 1, 42. *he will do all in all as Hastings doth,* R3 III, 1, 168. *you are all in all in spleen,* Oth. IV, 1, 89. *whom our full senate call all in all sufficient,* 276.

For all = a) once for all: *learn now, for all, I care not for you,* Cymb. II, 3, 111. *for once, for all, and ever,* R2 II, 2, 148. *this is for all* = in short: Hml. I, 3, 131. b) though: *for all you are my man,* Wiv. I, 1, 281. V, 5, 204. Ven. 342. Cymb. V, 4, 209.

At all, a phrase used by way of enforcement, seldom in affirmative sentences, as: *to bear off any weather at all,* Tp. II, 2, 19. *an if this be at all,* V, 117; oftener with a negation either implied: *desist to build at all,* H4B I, 3, 48. *without expense at all,* H6A I, 1, 76; *without more circumstance at all,* Hml. I, 5, 127; or directly expressed: *not at all,* Pilgr. 274. Gentl. II, 4, 96. Meas. IV, 1, 71. IV, 2, 161. Merch. II, 1, 39. Wint. III, 2, 62. V, 1, 20. H8 II, 4, 84. Tit. II, 1, 119. Rom. II, 2, 112. IV, 3, 21. Caes. III, 1, 248. *no time at all:* Sonn. 57, 3. Meas. II, 4, 66. Mids. I, 2, 100. III, 2, 301. Merch. V, 120. All's III, 6, 103. H6C V, 5, 53. Ant. III, 4, 20. *none at all:* LLL IV, 3, 354. As III, 2, 212. H6B I, 4, 52. R3 II, 3, 24. *nothing at all:* Gentl. I, 1, 144. R3 I, 2, 236. *nought at all:* Ven. 911. Err. IV, 1, 91. *this no more dishonours you at all than ...* Cor. III, 2, 58.

All is one, cf. *One.*

And all = and the rest, and every thing else: *Fridays and Saturdays and all,* As IV, 1, 117. *this wins him, liver and all,* Tw. II, 5, 106. *rapier, scabbard and all,* III, 4, 303. *and lose it, life and all,* John III, 4, 144. *words, life and all,* R2 II, 1, 150. *are pluck'd up root and all,* III, 4, 52. *I have entered him and all* H4B II, 1, 11 (Mrs. Quickly). Cor. IV, 2, 27. *leap thou, attire and all, to my heart,* Ant. IV, 8, 14. *bring our crown and all,* V, 2, 232. In the same sense: *that you insult, exult, and all at once, over the wretched,* As III, 5, 36. *did lose his seat and all at once,* H5 I, 1, 36.

This is all = in short: Wint. I, 2, 347.

All but, originally anything except, = scarcely, not even: *Henry's death, my lovely Edward's death, their kingdom's loss, could all but answer for that peevish brat?* R3 I, 3, 194.

All's not offence, Lr. II, 4, 199. cf. Ant. V, 2, 326: *all's not well.*

2) Adjectively and pronominally: a) every, any, any imaginable: *capable of all ill,* Tp. I, 2, 353. *all foison, all abundance,* II, 1, 163. *all happiness bechance to thee,* Gentl. I, 1, 61. *all good,* III, 1, 243. *'gainst all other voice,* Merch. IV, 1, 356. *all bond and privilege of nature break,* Cor. V, 3, 25. *whom with all praise I point at,* II, 2, 94. *all joy befall . . .,* Cymb. III, 5, 9. cf. *all popular rate,* Tp. I, 2, 92. *with all prerogative,* 105. *all strange form,* Compl. 303. *in all desired employment,* LLL IV, 2, 140. Cor. I, 3, 8. III, 1, 129. Caes. III, 1, 246. Lr. II, 4, 107. Mcb. III, 1, 13. *on all cause,* Ant. III, 11, 68. *in all haste,* Wiv. III, 3, 14. *I'll make all speed,* Meas. IV, 3, 109. *with all swift speed,* R2 V, 1, 54. And so even: *without all bail,* Sonn. 74, 2. *without all doubt* (for *any doubt*) H8 IV, 1, 113. *without all remedy,* Mcb. III, 2, 11. Alls II, 3, 173. Cor. III, 1, 144.

b) the whole, without the article before names of towns and countries as well as the words *day* and *night: through all Athens,* Mids I, 2, 5. *in all Venice,* Merch. I, 1, 115. *all Kent,* John V, 1, 30. *all France,* H6A I, 1, 139. H6B IV, 8, 17. *all Europe,* H6A I, 1, 156. I, 6, 15. *all day,* Meas. IV, 1, 20. Mids. II, 1, 66. Merch. I, 1, 117. H6A II, 1, 12. H6B III, 1, 186. *all night,* Meas. IV, 3, 46. LLL I, 1, 44. Shr. IV, 1, 208. John IV, 1, 30. H4A IV, 2, 63. Rom. IV, 4, 10. Caes. II, 1, 88. *all night long,* Hml. I, 1, 160.

The article admissible before *day* and *night: all the day,* Sonn. 43, 2. Wint. IV, 3, 134. *all the night,* Lr. II, 4, 90; indispensable before other words: *all the world,* Tp. I. 2, 69. *all the rest,* I, 2, 226. II, 1, 287. *all the wine* II, 2, 96. *all the kind of the Launces* Gentl. II, 3, 2. *all the difference,* IV, 4, 195. *all the draff,* Wiv. IV, 2, 109. *all the fool* Tw. V, 2, 384. *all the pack of you,* R3 III, 3, 5. etc. etc. Of course, the demonstrative and possessive pronouns serve as well: *all this day,* John III, 1, 18. *all my study,* Tp. I, 2, 74. *all his quality,* I, 2, 193. *in all her trim,* V, 236. *all your part,* Mids. III, 1, 102. *all my flowering youth,* H6A II, 5, 56. *like all your self,* Cor. V, 3, 70. *all his arm,* Hml. II, 1, 88. 95 etc. *all my every part,* Sonn. 62, 2. *You are my all the world,* Sonn. 112, 5. John III, 4, 104.

All the whole, cf. *whole.*

c) only, alone, nothing but: *thou art all my child* = my only child, All's III, 2, 71. *to find a face where all distress is stell'd; many she sees where cares have carved some, but none where all distress and dolour dwell'd,* Lucr. 1444 (nothing but, mere distress). *why write I still all one, ever the same?* Sonn. 76, 5, i. e. always but one thing. *I do smell all horsepiss,* Tp. IV, 199. *all torment, trouble, wonder and amazement inhabits here,* Tp. V, 104. *a gentleman of all temperance,* Meas. III, 2, 251 (a gentleman, the groundwork and sum of whose qualities was temperance). *I was born to speak all mirth and no matter,* Ado II, 1, 343. *he is all mirth,* Ado III, 2, 10. *all to*

make you sport, Mids. I, 3, 114. *vows so born, in their nativity all truth appears,* III, 2, 125. *and not all love to see you, but jealousy . . . ,* Tw. III, 3, 6. *gold, all gold!* Wint. III, 3, 126. *why have my sisters husbands, if they say they love you all?* Lr. I, 1, 102. *I shall never marry like my sisters, to love you all,* 106. *no seconds? all myself?* IV, 6, 198. cf. H4B V, 3, 37.

d) In the plural = every one, the whole number of particulars: *let's all sink,* Tp. I, 1, 67. *all plunged in the foaming brine,* I, 2, 210. *the mariners all under hatches stowed,* 230. *they all have met,* 233. *we all* II, 1, 251 etc. etc.

All of us = we all, Tp. II, 1, 129. V, 212. Wiv. II, 2, 58. R3 II, 2, 101. Caes. II, 1, 212. *all of you:* R2 IV, 237. H6B III, 1, 165. R3 I, 3, 171. *all of them:* Tp. V, 132. Ado V, 1, 44. *all three of them:* Tp. III, 3, 104. *all of yours:* R2 II, 4, 72.

Joined to a substantive without an article: *all hearts i 'the state,* Tp. I, 2, 84. *all corners else of the earth,* I, 2, 491 etc. The article gives it a restrictive sense: *through all the signories,* Tp. I, 2, 71. *fair Milan with all the honours,* 127. *all the devils,* 215. *all the charms of Sycorax,* 339. *all the qualities of the isle,* 337. *I am all the subjects that you have,* 341. *all the infections that . . .* II, 2, 1. *all the blessings of a glad father,* V, 179 etc. etc. Seemingly in a general acceptation: *incensed the seas and shores, yea, all the creatures* (sc. that dwell in them) *against your peace,* Tp. III, 3, 74. *these are the villains that all the travellers* (sc. who have passed through this forest) *do fear so much,* Gentl. IV, 1, 6. Cor. IV, 6, 102.

With a possessive pronoun: *all our reasons,* R3 III, 1, 174. Tp. I, 2, 370. 437. 488. IV, 1, 5 etc. etc.

Used in addressing no more than two persons: *good morrow to you all,* H4B III, 1, 35. *as all you know,* H6B II, 2, 26.

To all our lamentation, Cor. IV, 6, 34, = to the lamentation of us all. *to all our sorrows,* John IV, 2, 102 (cf. *both*).

Best of all: H6C II, 5, 18. *last night of all,* Hml. I, 1, 35 (= the very last night). Caes. I, 1, 65.

From the all that are = from all them that are: Wint. V, 1, 14.

3) Adverbially, a) quite, entirely: *no tongue! all eyes!* Tp. IV, 1, 59. Troil. I, 2, 31. *love is all truth,* Ven. 804. *all tyrant,* 149, 4. *she's all grease,* Err. III, 2, 97. *all adoration,* As V, 2, 102 sq. *all tears,* Hml. I, 2, 149. *he's all the mother's,* R3 III, 1, 156. *all wet,* Ven. 83. *all unpossible,* R2 II, 2, 126. *all dedicated to closeness,* Tp. I, 2, 89. *all wound with adders,* II, 1, 13. *all humbled,* Gentl. I, 2, 59. *all enraged* II, 6, 38. *all armed,* Mids. II, 1, 157. *all with weary task foredone,* V, 381. *all unwarily,* John V, 7, 63. *dashed all to pieces,* Tp. I, 2, 8. Oth. III, 3, 431. *dispossess her all,* Tim. I, 1, 139. *all afire with me,* Tp. I, 2, 212. *all in buff,* Err. IV, 2, 36. *one all of luxury,* Meas. V, 506. *all in post,* H6C V, 5, 84. *all at one side,* Oth. IV, 3, 32. *of all one pain* (quite the same p.) R3 IV, 4, 303. *all alone,* Sonn. 29, 2. 124, 11. As II, 7, 136. Hml. I, 5, 102. Ant. I, 1, 52. *blister you all o'er,* Tp. I, 2, 324. *all as mad as he,* Err. V, 141. *all as soon as I,* John II, 59. V, 2, 170. Cor. I, 9, 44. Lr. IV, 7, 42.

b) serving only to enforce the expression: *all in war with time,* Sonn. 15, 13. *all for want of pruning,* Err. II, 2, 181. *when all aloud the wind doth blow,* LLL V, 2, 931. *what occasion hath all so long detained you*, Shr. III, 2, 105. *all at once*, H5 I, 1, 36. *not all so much for love*, R3 I, 1, 157. *all headlong*, Tit. V, 3, 132. *lay thee all along*, Rom. V, 3, 3. *stand all aloof*, V, 3, 26. *all but now*, Oth. II, 3, 179. *all too timeless*, Lucr. 44. *all too late*, 1686. *all too short*, Sonn. 18, 4. *all too near*, 61, 14. *all too precious*, 86, 2. *all too much*, Gentl. III, 1, 162. *all too wanton*, John III, 3, 36. *all too base*, R2 IV, 1, 28. *all too heavy*, H4B V, 2, 24. *all too dear*, Oth. II, 3, 94. *all too soon*, Cymb. V, 5, 169.

The following passages may be interpreted otherwise: *the marbled mansion all above*, Tim. IV, 3, 191 (= all the marbled mansion above). *down from the waist they are Centaurs, though women all above*, Lr. IV, 6, 127. *things outward do draw the inward quality after them, to suffer all alike*, Ant. III, 13, 34.

c) = although: *thy head, all indirectly, gave direction*, R3 IV, 4, 225. Perhaps also: *his horse is slain, and all on foot he fights* R3 V, 4, 4. But cf. *went all afoot in summer's scalding heat*, H6C V, 7, 18.

d) It is with hesitation that we advance the opinion that, like the German *all* in popular language, it is sometimes used for already: *Methinks I see this hurly all on foot*, John III, 4, 169. *but tell me not, for I have heard it all*, Rom. I, 1, 181. *she could have run and waddled all about*, I, 3, 37.

All-abhorred, H4A V, 1, 16; cf *All* 3 a; or abhorred by all.

All-admiring, H5 I, 1, 39; cf *All* 3 a.

Allay, vb., 1) trans. a) to abate, mitigate, appease: *appetite, which but to-day with feeding is —d*, Sonn. 56, 3. *a. them* (the waters), Tp. I, 2, 2. *—ing both their fury and my passion*, I, 2, 392. *a. thy ecstasy*, Merch. III, 2, 112. *to a. the gust he hath in quarrelling*, Tw. I, 3, 32. *a. this thy abortive pride*, H6B IV, 1, 60. *—'d their swelling griefs*, H6C IV, 8, 42. *a. those tongues*, H8 II, 1, 152. Chiefly of fire and heat: *whose heat hath this condition, that nothing can a.* John III, 1, 342. V, 7, 8. H8 I, 1, 149. And tropically: *a. with some cold drops of modesty thy skipping spirit*, Merch. II, 2, 195. *a cup of hot wine with not a drop of —ing Tiber in't*, Cor. II, 1, 53. *to a. my rages with your colder reasons*, V, 3, 85. b) to weaken, to detract from: *I do not like 'But yet', it does a. the good precedence*, Ant. II, 5, 50.

2) intr. to abate, decrease: *when the rage —s, the rain begins*, H6C I, 4, 146. *the heat of his displeasure . . . would scarcely a.* Lr. I, 2, 179.

Allay, subst., that which abates: *to whose sorrows I might be some a.* Wint. IV, 2, 9.

Allayment, the same: *the like a. could I give my grief*, Troil. IV, 4, 8. *apply —s to their act*, Cymb. I, 5, 22.

All-building, being the ground and foundation of all: *the manacles of the a. law*, Meas. II, 4, 94 (Rowe: *all-holding*; Johnson: *all binding*).

All-changing-word, word or signal of a general change or defection from former opinions and affections: *this commodity, this bawd, this broker, this a.* John II, 582 (M. Edd. *all-changing word*).

All-cheering, cheering, gladdening all: *the a. sun*, Rom. I, 1, 141.

All-disgraced, either completely disgraced, or disgraced with all, despised by all: *her a. friend*, Ant. III, 12, 22.

All-dreaded, feared by all: Cymb. IV, 2, 271.

All-eating, consuming all, destroying every advantage: *an a. shame*. Sonn. 2, 8.

Allegation, assertion: *reprove my a., if you can*, H6B III, 1, 40. *to swear false —s*, 181.

Allege, to produce, to cite: *I can a. no cause*, Sonn. 49, 14. *—d many reasons*, H8 II, 1, 13. *my —d reasons*, II, 4, 225. Troil. II, 2, 168.

Allegiance, fidelity of subjects, loyalty: *to follow with a. a fall'n lord*, Ant. III, 13, 44. *contrary to the faith and a. of a true subject*, Wint. III, 2, 20. Ado III, 3, 5. John III, 1, 175 *(to one)*. R2 II, 1, 108. III, 3, 37. H5 II, 2, 4. H6A V, 5, 3. H6C III, 1, 70. IV, 7, 19. R3 I, 3, 171. H8 I, 2, 62. V, 3, 43. Mcb. I, 1, 28. Hml. IV, 5, 131. *I charge thee on thy a.:* Ado I, 1, 210. 213. Wint. II, 3, 121. H6A III, 1, 86 *(on a. to ourself)*. Lr. I, 1, 170. *to swear a. to one*: John V, 1, 10. H6A V, 4, 169. H6B V, 1, 20. 179. Devotion in general: *pluck a. from men's hearts*, H4A III, 2, 52.

Allegiant, loyal: *I can nothing render but a. thanks*, H8 III, 2, 176.

All-ending, finishing all: *even to the general a. day*, R3 III, 1, 78.

Alley: 1) a shady walk in a garden: Ado I, 2, 10. III, 1, 16. 2) a narrow way in a city: Err. IV, 2, 38. 3) passage in general: *the natural gates and —s of the body*, Hml. I, 5, 67.

All-hail, subst. a term of salutation, expressing a wish of health and happiness: *give the a. to thee*, Cor. V, 3, 139. *greater than both, by the a. hereafter*, Mcb. I, 5, 56. Without the hyphen: Tp. I, 2, 189. LLL V, 2, 158. 339. R2 IV, 169 etc. cf. *Hail*.

All-hail, vb. to cry All hail to: *—ed me*, Mcb. I, 5, 7.

All-hallond eve, the eve of All Saints' day: Meas. II, 1, 130.

All-hallowmas, All Saints' day (1st Nov.): Wiv. I, 1, 211.

All-hallown (Ff *All-hollown*), falling into the time of All Saints' day: *a. summer*, H4A I, 2, 178.*

All-hating, entirely filled with hatred: *in this a. world*, R2 V, 5, 66.

All-hiding, concealing all: *thy black a. cloak*, Lucr. 801.

All-honoured, honoured by all: Ant. II, 6, 16.

All-hurting, never missing: *his a. aim*, Compl. 310.

Alliance, 1) relationship of any kind: Wint. II, 3, 21. H6A II, 5, 53. IV, 1, 62.

2) relationship by marriage: H5 V, 2, 373. H6A V, 5, 42. H6C III, 3, 70. 177. IV, 1, 36. 136.

3) marriage: Ado II, 1, 330. Tw. V, 326. H6C III, 3, 142. R3 IV, 4, 313. 343. Rom. II, 3, 91.

4) league: *let our a. be combined*, Caes. IV, 1, 43.

Alligant. Mrs. Quickly says: *in such a. terms*, Wiv. II, 2, 69; as Intpp. will have it, for *elegant;* but *elegant* is not a Shakespearian word. Perhaps for *allegiant* or *eloquent*.

Alligator, American crocodile: Rom. V, 1, 43.

All-licensed, privileged to do or say anything: *this your a. fool*, Lr. I, 4, 220.

All-obeying, obeyed by all: *from his a. breath I hear the doom of Egypt*, Ant. III, 13, 77. Johnson *all-obeyed*, Anon. *all-swaying*. But cf. *feeling sorrows, a trembling contribution*, etc.

All-oblivious, forgetful of all: *a. enmity*, Sonn. 55, 9 (= enmity of oblivion, hostile oblivion).

Allot, 1) to grant by destiny: *whom favourable stars a. thee for his lovely bed-fellow*, Shr. IV, 5, 41. *thou art —ed to be ta'en by me*, H6A V, 3, 55.

2) to bestow on, to grant in general: *and undeserved reproach to him —ed*, Lucr. 824. *five days we do a. thee*, Lr. I, 1, 176.

Allottery, portion granted: *give me the poor a. my father left me*, As I, 1, 77.

Allow, 1) followed by an accus. a) to grant, to yield, to give: *I would a. him odds*, R2 I, 1, 62. *free speech and fearless I to thee a.*, 123. H4A II, 1, 21. H4B V, 5, 70. H8 III, 1, 151. Rom. II, 3, 86. Tim. III, 3, 41. Hml. I, 2, 38. V, 1, 255 (*she is —ed her virgin rites*). V, 2, 47. Lr. II, 4, 269. Cymb. I, 4, 3. *a. the wind*, All's V, 2, 10 = do not stop it, stand to the leeward of me. *whose roguish madness —s itself to anything*, Lr. III, 7, 105, i. e. allows itself to be employed in anything.

b) to grant, to permit: *if the law would a. it*, Meas II, 1, 239. 240. 241. *the law —s it*, Merch. IV, 1, 303. *the worser was —ed a furred gown*, Meas. III, 2, 8. *being —ed his way*, H8 I, 1, 133. *scholars —ed freely to argue for her*, II, 2, 113. *a. me such exercises*, As I, 1, 76. Tw. I, 5, 210. V, 304. Wint. I, 2, 263. IV, 1, 15. IV, 4, 479. H6C V, 4, 20. Lr. III, 6, 106. V, 3, 233. Cymb. II, 3, 121. — *ing him to monarchize*, R2 III, 2, 164. H4B II, 2, 115. Caes. III, 2, 64. *him in thy course untainted do a.* Sonn. 19, 11.

c) to grant, admit: *who did his words a.* Lucr. 1845. *I well a. the occasion of our arms*, H4B I, 3, 5. *I like them all and do a. them well*, H4B IV, 2, 54.

d) to license: *she is —ed for the day-woman*, LLL I, 2, 136. *an —ed fool*, Tw. I, 5, 101. *you are —ed = an —ed fool*, LLL V, 2, 478.

e) to acknowledge: *so you o'ergreen my bad, my good a.* Sonn. 112, 4. Wiv. II, 2, 236. As I, 1, 49. R2 V, 2, 40. H8 I, 2, 83. II, 4, 4. Troil. III, 2, 98. Cor. III, 3, 45. Oth. I, 3, 224. Cymb. III, 3, 17. *that will a. me very worth his service*, Tw. I, 1, 59 = make me acknowledged.

f) to sanction: *if your sweet sway a. obedience*, Lr. II, 4, 194. — *ed with absolute power*, Tim. V, 1, 165 (trusted, invested by public authority).

2) Followed by *of:* a) to permit: *of this a.* Wint. IV, 1, 29. b) to admit: *ere I will a. of thy wits*, Tw. IV, 2, 63.

3) Absolutely: *her —ing husband*, Wint. I, 2, 185, = conniving.

Allowance, 1) authorisation, permission: *without the king's will or the state's a.* H8 III, 2, 322. *on such regards of safety and a.* Hml. II, 2, 79. *you protect this course, and put it on by your a.* Lr. I, 4, 228. *if this be known to you and your a.* Oth. I, 1, 128. *under the a. of your great aspect*, Lr. II, 2, 112.

2) acknowledgment: *which one must in your a. o'erweigh a whole theatre*, Hml. III, 2, 31. *give him a. for the better man*, Troil. I, 3, 377. *a stirring dwarf we do a. give before a sleeping giant*, II, 3, 146. *syllables of no a. to your bosom's truth*, Cor. III, 2, 57.

his pilot of very expert and approved a. Oth. II, 1, 49 (i. e. of allowed approof, or of acknowledged experience).

All-praised, praised by all: H4A III, 2, 140.

All-seer, he who sees all: R3 V, 1, 20.

All-seeing, seeing all: *a. heaven*, R3 II, 1, 82. *a. sun*, Rom. I, 2, 97.

All-shaking, shaking all: *a. thunder*, Lr. III, 2, 6.

All-shunned, avoided by all: *a. poverty*, Tim. IV, 2, 14.

All-souls' day, the day on which supplications are made for all souls by the Roman church, the 2ᵈ of November: R3 V, 1, 10. 12. 18.

All-telling, divulging everything: *a. fame*, LLL II, 21.

All-the-world, the whole world: *you are my a.* Sonn. 112, 5. John III, 4, 104. O. Edd. without hyphen, cf. *All*.

All-thing, every way: *it had been as a gap in our great feast, and a. unbecoming*, Mcb. III, 1, 13.

All-to, an adverb, meaning 'entirely,' received by some M. Edd. into the text of Sh., but not warranted by O. Edd., which have not the hyphen: *it was not she that call'd him all to nought*, Ven. 993, i. e. that call'd him good for nothing. *The very principals did seem to rend, and all to topple*, Per. III, 2, 17 (i. e. did all seem to topple).

All-too-timeless, Lucr. 44, not hyphened by O. Edd., cf. *timeless*.

Allure, to entice: *to a. his eye*, Pilgr. 48. Tim. IV, 3, 141. Cymb. I, 6, 46. II, 4, 34. Per. V, 1, 46. Absol.: — *ing beauty*, Err. II, 1, 89.

Allurement, enticement, temptation: *take heed of the a. of one Count Rousillon*, All's IV, 3, 241.

Allusion, perhaps used by Holophernes in its old Latin meaning of jesting: *the a. holds in the exchange*, LLL IV, 2, 42. But it may have the modern sense of reference.

All-watched, watched throughout: *the weary and a. night*, H5 IV Chor. 38.

All-worthy, of the highest worth: *O, my a. lord! A. villain!* Cymb. III, 5, 95.

Ally, subst., relation, kinsman: As V, 4, 195. H4A I, 1, 16. R3 I, 3, 330. II, 1, 30. III, 2, 103. V, 1, 15. Rom. III, 1, 114.

Ally, vb., used only in the partic. *allied* = related: Gentl. IV, 1, 49. Meas. III, 2, 109. Tw. II, 3, 104. Wint. I, 2, 339. Rom. III, 5, 182 (Q1 and most M. Edd. *trained*). In a more general sense = joined: *neither allied to eminent assistants*, H8 I, 1, 61.

Allycholly, corrupted from melancholy: Gentl. IV, 2, 27. Wiv. I, 4, 164. cf. *Mallicholie* LLL IV, 3, 14.

Almain, a German: Oth. II, 3, 86.

Almanac, calendar: Err. I, 2, 41 (cf. V, 404). Mids. III, 1, 54. H4B II, 4, 287. Ant. I, 2, 154.

Almighty, omnipotent: Lucr. 568. LLL III, 205. V, 2, 650 (*of lances the a.*). Troil. V, 2, 173. *God Almighty*: H5 II, 4, 77. IV, 1, 3. H6B II, 1, 95.

Almond, fruit of Amygdalus communis: Troil. V, 2, 194.

Almost, for the greatest part, nearly: Lucr. 282. 1413. Sonn. 29, 9. 76, 7. 111, 6. Tp. II, 1, 37. 59. 234. III, 2, 10. IV, 142. Gentl. IV, 2, 139. 4, 148. Wiv. I, 3, 34. II, 1, 88. Meas. I, 2, 113. IV,

2, 109. 226 etc. etc. *you are a. come to part a. a fray,* Ado V, 1, 113 (i. e. what was almost a fray). Following the word which it qualifies: *as like a. to Claudio as himself,* Meas. V, 494. *I swoon a.* Mids. II, 2, 154. cf. *not a.* Err. V, 1, 181. R3 II, 3, 39.* Oth. III, 3, 66. Used emphatically, = even: *more kind than you shall find many, nay a. any,* Tp. III, 3, 34. *or could you think, or do you a. think, although you see,* John IV, 3, 43. *would you imagine, or a. believe,* R3 III, 5, 35. *ere a. Rome should know,* Cor. I, 2, 24.

Alms, subst. sing., what is given in charity: *it were an a. to hang him,* Ado II, 3, 164. *have a present a.* Shr. IV, 3, 5. *hath received an a.* Cor. III, 2, 120. *beg the a.* Meas. III, 1, 35. Seemingly, but not evidently, in the plural: *that by a. doth live,* Lucr. 986. *give a.* Wint. IV, 4, 138. *wherein he puts a. for oblivion,* Troil. III, 3, 146. *I have your a.* Cor. II, 3, 87. *by his own a. empoisoned,* V, 6, 11. *have their a. out of the empress' chest,* Tit. II, 3, 9. *one bred of a.* Cymb. II, 3, 119. — *received you at fortune's a.* Lr. I, 1, 281, literally: on occasion of Fortune's almsgiving, as an alms of Fortune. *And shut myself up in some other course, to Fortune's a.* Oth. III, 4, 122, i. e. and stint myself to the charity of Fortune.

Alms-basket, a basket to receive alms (Troil. III, 3, 145): *they have lived long on the a. of words,* LLL V, 1, 41, i. e. on what they have gathered out of other people's mouths.

Alms-deed, act of charity: *murder is thy a.* H6C V, 5, 79.

Alms-drink, according to Warburton, a phrase amongst good fellows, to signify that liquor of another's share which his companion drinks to ease him; but in the only passage in which it occurs *(they have made him drink a.* Ant. II, 7, 5) it evidently means the leavings.

Alms-house, hospital for the poor: H5 I, 1, 17.

Alms-man, a man who lives upon alms: R2 III, 3, 149.

Aloes, the juice extracted from Aloë vulgaris; a symbol of bitterness: *and sweetens the a. of all forces, shocks, and fears,* Compl. 273.

Aloft, adv., 1) above, opposed to below: *her chamber is a.* Gentl. III, 1, 114. *that you be by her a., while we be busy below,* H6B I, 4, 11. Tit. II, 3, 244.

2) on high: Lucr. 505. Sonn. 78, 6. H6B I, 1, 254. II, 1, 11. V, 1, 204. Tit. II, 1, 2. 13. III, 1, 169. Cymb. V, 5, 471. In Per. IV, 6, 95 O. Edd. *aloft,* M. Edd. *aloof.*

Aloft, prep., above: *now I breathe again a. the flood,* John IV, 2, 139. cf. H6B V, I, 204 (?).

Alone, 1) solitary, without company: *a., it was the subject of my theme, in company I glanced it,* Err. V, 65. Ven. 382. 786. Lucr. 795 *(a. a.).* 1480. Sonn. 4, 9. 29, 2. 36, 4. 66, 14. 105, 13. 131, 8. 141, 8. Pilgr. 130. 297. Gentl. I, 2, 1. II, 1, 21. III, 1, 99. III, 1, 127. IV, 3, 36. V, 4, 4. Wiv. III, 3, 38. Err. III, 1, 96. Ado II, 2, 34. III, 1, 13. LLL IV, 3, 328. Mids. II, 1, 225. 2, 87. Merch. III, 2, 151. As I, 1, 167 *(if ever he go a. again,* i. e. without help). III, 2, 270 etc.

Let alone (originally let be alone) = do not care for: *let them a. awhile, and then open the door,* H4A II, 4, 95. *let her a., and list to me,* III, 3, 110. *let them a.* = do not assist them, H4B II, 3, 41. Hence

= forbear molesting, or meddling with: Tp. IV, 223. 231. Gentl. II, 4, 167. Wiv. IV, 2, 145. Ado III, 3, 48. Mids. III, 2, 332. Merch. III, 3, 19. Tw. IV, 1, 35. Wint. V, 3, 73. R2 V, 3, 86. H4A II, 4, 231. H4B III, 2, 123. H6A I, 2, 44. H8 V, 2, 34. Cor. I, 6, 41. Rom. I, 5, 67. Lr. III, 4, 3. IV, 7, 51. Ant. V, 1, 71. Cymb. V, 5, 305. Then = forbear: *let your epilogue a.* Mids. V, 369. *let thy courtesies a.* All's V, 3, 324. *let't alone,* Shr. IV, 3, 195. *let these threats a.* Troil. IV, 5, 261. H4B II, 1, 169. H8 II, 1, 101. Ant. II, 5, 3. *let alone,* without an object, Tit. IV, 1, 102. Sometimes it is as much as let me do alone: *let me a. with him,* Tw. II, 3, 145. III, 4, 106. 122. 201. Shr. IV, 2, 71. H4A V, 4, 53. H6B IV, 2, 109. H8 I, 4, 34. Cor. I, 2, 27. Tit. I, 449. IV, 3, 114. Rom. IV, 2, 42.

Leave me a. = let me a.: *leave me a. to woo him,* As I, 3, 135 (cf. Cor. I, 2, 27).

2) only, without another: *contenting but the eye a.* Ven. 213. *light a. upon his head,* Lucr. 1480. *thine a.* Sonn. 31, 12. *which thou deservest a.,* 39, 8. 42, 14. 45, 7. 79, 1. 84, 2. 91, 13. Meas. II, 1, 40. Err. II, 1, 107. LLL IV, 1, 34. Cor. I, 6, 76. Ant. III, 13, 154. 11, 38 (= only, but) etc. *All alone:* Sonn. 124, 11. As II, 7, 136. Hml. I, 5, 102. III, 1, 190. *Not alone — but* = not only — but: John I, 210. H8 III, 2, 157. Hml. I, 2, 77. 3, 11. Lr. I, 1, 300.

3) without a parallel: *she is a.* Gentl. II, 4, 167. H8 II, 4, 136 (M. Edd. *thou art, alone*). *that must needs be sport a.* Mids. III, 2, 119. *that it a. is high fantastical,* Tw. I, 1, 15. *I am a. the villain of the earth,* Ant. IV, 6, 30 (par excellence). Perhaps also in: *you all three, the senators a. of this great world,* Ant. II, 6, 9 (cf. *only*).

Along, adv. 1) at one's length: *so soon was she a. as he was down,* Ven. 43. *as he lay a. under an oak,* As II, 1, 30. *stretched a.* III, 2, 253. *lay thee all a.* Rom. V, 3, 3. *that now on Pompey's basis lies a.* Caes. III, 1, 115. *when he lies a.* Cor. V, 6, 57.

2) onward, on; to go, pass, march etc. *along:* Ven. 1093. Gentl. II, 7, 39. V, 4, 162. 168. LLL II, 245. As II, 1, 53. R2 V, 2, 21. H6A IV, 3, 5. H6C V, 1, 76. H8 V, 2, 11 etc. *let's along* = let us go there, Cor. I, 1, 283. Wint. V, 2, 121. *speak the word a.* Caes. IV, 2, 33. *go a. by him* = call at his house, Caes. II, 1, 218. cf. IV, 3, 207 (v. *by*). *I'll go a. by your prescription* (proceed according to your p.) H8 I, 1, 150.

3) together, with one; to go, come etc. *a. with one:* Gentl. II, 4, 88. 176. IV, 3, 39. Wiv. II, 2, 139. IV, 6, 47. V, 1, 25. Meas. IV, 1, 46. 3, 174. Err. V, 236. LLL V, 2, 5. Merch. III, 2, 233. As I, 3, 107. Shr. IV, 5, 51. H4A V, 4, 131. H6B III, 2, 300. H6C II, 5, 134 etc. *along with us to watch,* Hml. I, 1, 26. Separated from *with: with him is Gratiano gone a.,* Merch. II, 8, 2. *else had she with her father ranged a.* As I, 3, 70. Tropically: *your better wisdoms which have freely gone with this affair a.* Hml. I, 2, 16. Without *with: go a.* = come with me, Err. IV, 4, 42. Mids. I, 1, 123. Merch. III, 2, 310. All's III, 2, 98 *(to bear a.* = to take with one). H6C II, 1, 115. III, 2, 123. IV, 5, 25. R3 III, 1, 136. H8 I, 3, 64. Cor. V, 2, 96. II, 3, 157. Rom. I, 1, 201. Caes. IV, 3, 225. Hml. III, 3, 4. Ant. V, 1, 69. Ven. 1093 etc. Without a verb: *a. with me!* Gentl. III, 1, 256. Tit. II, 3, 246.

Along, prep., following the length of: *tra-*

velling a. this coast, LLL V, 2, 557. *the brook that brawls a. this wood,* As II, 1, 32. Troil. V, 8, 22.

Alonso, name of the king in Tp. III, 3, 75. V, 72.

Aloof, at a distance from a person or action, but in close connection with them: *one a. stand sentinel,* Mids. II, 2, 26. *love's not love when it is mingled with regards that stand a. from the entire point,* Lr. I, 1, 243. Chiefly in speaking of persons who are not to be present at, or interfere with, something: *Nerissa and the rest, stand all a.* Merch. III, 2, 42. Tw. I, 4, 12. H6A IV, 4, 21. Tit. V, 3, 151. Rom. V, 3, 1. 26. 282; or who are kept back by caution or fear: *O appetite, from judgment stand a.* Compl. 166. *I stand for sacrifice, the rest a. are the Dardanian wives,* Merch. III, 2, 58. *keep a. from strict arbitrement,* H4A IV, 1, 70. H6A IV, 2, 52. V, 4, 150. H6B I, 1, 227. H6C II, 1, 17. Hml. III. 1, 8. V, 2, 258. Per. IV, 6, 95 (Qq Ff *aloft*). It is, with one exception (Merch. III, 2, 58) always joined with the verbs to stand and to keep.

Aloud, with a raised voice: Ven. 282. 886. Meas. II, 4, 153. Ado II, 1, 108. Tw. II, 5, 94. John III, 4, 70. H5 V, 2, 258. H6B III, 2, 378. R3 I, 4, 50. 54. Troil. I, 3, 259. II, 2, 185. III, 3, 2. Rom. II, 2, 161. III, 1, 169. Mcb. V, 8, 58. Lr. IV, 4, 2. Ant. III, 13, 101. Cymb. I, 6, 26. V, 5, 130.

Of the noise of winds: LLL V, 2, 931. Oth. II, 1, 5. of bells: H6A I, 6, 11. H6B V, 1, 3.

Alphabet, the ABC: Tit. III, 2, 44.

Alphabetical, concerning the letters of the alphabet: *what should that a. position portend?* Tw. II, 5, 130.

Alphonso, name in Gentl. I, 3, 39.

Alps, the mountains in Switzerland: John I, 202. R2 I, 1, 64. Ant. I, 4, 66. *the valleys whose low vassal seat the Alps doth spit and void his rheum upon,* H5 III, 5, 52 (sing.)

Already, opposed to not yet: Lucr. 1589. Sonn. 76, 12. Gentl. I, 1, 72. III, 1, 206. 219. 2, 58. IV, 2, 1. Wiv. II, 3, 9. III, 5, 134. IV, 1, 1. Meas. I, 4, 73. II, 2, 22. 4, 44. III, 1, 270. V, 3, 134. 177. Ado I, 1, 20. II, 3, 5. III, 2, 47. IV, 2, 23. LLL I, 1, 34. IV, 3, 16. V, 2, 683. Mids. III, 2, 384. V, 254. 328. Merch. I, 2, 38. III, 4, 37. V, 146 etc. etc.

Also, likewise, besides; a word of not so frequent occurrence as would be expected, but only in Gentl. III, 2, 25. Wiv. I, 1, 43. III, 1, 9. IV, 4, 67. V, 1, 24. 5, 7. Ado V, 1, 316. III, 3, 35. As II, 2, 9. Tw. I, 2, 39. Wint. IV, 4, 235. H4A II, 4, 440. 459. H4B II, 4, 171. V, 3, 145. H5 I, 2, 77. IV, 1, 80. 6, 10. 7, 28. 39. Tim. III, 6, 2. Caes. II, 1, 329. Hml. V, 2, 402 (Ff *always*). Lr. I, 4, 66.

Altar, the place where sacrifices and prayers are offered: Ven. 103. Compl. 224. Gentl. III, 2, 73. Wiv. IV, 2, 217. All's II, 3, 80. Mids. I, 1, 89. Tw. V, 116. John V, 4, 18. H4A IV, 1, 116. H6A I, 1, 45. H8 IV, 1, 83. Troil. III, 3, 74. IV, 3, 8. Cymb. V, 5, 478. Per. V, 1, 242. 3, 17.

Alter, 1) trans., a) to change: *add to his flow, but a. not his taste,* Lucr. 651. 948. Sonn. 36, 7. 93, 3. 145, 9. Gentl. II, 4, 128. Wiv. II, 1, 52. Tw. II, 5, 112. Wint. I, 1, 37. 2, 384. IV, 4, 586. H4A III, 1, 116. H5 V, 2, 87. H6B III, 1, 5. H6C IV, 3, 31. H8 I, 1, 189. IV, 1, 98. 2, 96. 112. Mcb. I, 5, 73. Lr. IV, 6, 7. Cymb. IV, 2, 365. Per. III, 1, 76. Especially = to make of another mind or humour: *Angelo will not be —ed,*

Meas. III, 2, 220. *there is no power in the tongue of men to a. me,* Merch. IV, 1, 242. Err. II, 2, 7. Ado I, 3, 39. Wint. IV, 4, 475. Cor. V, 4, 9. Oth. III, 4, 125. Per. IV, 6, 112. And = to reverse a law, a judgment: *no power in Venice can a. a decree,* Merch. IV, 1, 219. *but you, sir, —ed that,* Tw. II, 1, 22. John III, 1, 311. R2 III, 2, 214. Followed by *from:* our theme is *—ed from a serious thing,* R2 V, 3, 79. Absol.: *stupid with age and —ing rheums,* Wint. IV, 4, 410.

b) to exchange: *would a. services with thee,* Tw. II, 5, 172.

2) intr., to change: *love is not love, which —s,* Sonn. 116, 3. 11. 115, 8. Ado II, 3, 247. Mids. II, 1, 107. 2, 61. H4B IV, 5, 12 (cf. H8 IV, 2, 96).

Alteration, change: Sonn. 116, 3. Wint. I, 2, 383. IV, 4, 536. H4B III, 1, 52. H6A IV, 1, 54. Cor. IV, 5, 154. Tim. IV, 3, 468. Lr. V, 1, 3. Oth. V, 2, 101.

Althaea, the mother of Meleager: H4B II, 2, 93. H6B I, 1, 234.

Although, notwithstanding, though; followed by the indic. as well as the subjunctive: Sonn. 81, 4. 138, 6. John IV, 2, 83. H6B II, 4, 101. III, 2, 57. R3 III, 2, 123, etc. etc. Sonn. 40, 10. 56, 5. 116, 8. As II, 7, 54. 179. Tw. III, 2, 50. Wint. II, 3, 98. R2 III, 2, 193. H6A V, 5, 38. H6B II, 1, 71. III, 2, 193. H6C IV, 6, 23, etc. etc. *no matter, then, a. my foot did stand . . .* Sonn. 44, 5.

Altitude, height: *nearer to heaven by the a. of a chopine,* Hml. II, 2, 446. *ten masts at each make not the a.* Lr. IV, 6, 53. *he is proud, even to the a. of his virtue,* Cor. I, 1, 40.

Altogether, entirely: *this your request is a. just,* Wint. III, 2, 118. Lucr. 696. Wiv. I, 2, 8. III, 2, 64. As I, 1, 142. 177. Tw. I, 3, 121. R2 III, 4, 13. H4A III, 1, 237. 3, 40. H5 III, 2, 70. R3 I, 3, 156. Hml. III, 2, 42. Oth. I, 3, 25. Joined to the comparative = by far: *much more gentle, and a. more tractable,* Troil. II, 3, 160. Preceded by *not:* Wiv. I, 1, 175. All's IV, 3, 53. 319. Tim. II, 2, 122. Lr. I, 4, 165. II, 4, 234. III, 5, 6. Cymb. I, 4, 51. Sometimes miswritten for *all together.*

Alton. *Lord Verdun of A.,* one of Talbot's titles, H6A IV, 7, 65.

Alway, for always: H4B I, 2, 240. H6C V, 6, 64.

Always, at all times, ever: Ven. 801. Sonn. 76, 9. Pilgr. 329. Tp. II, 1, 175. IV, 174. Gent. II, 4, 31. II, 5, 4. IV, 2, 70. 72. Wiv. IV, 2, 58. V, 5, 122. Meas. I, 1, 26. I, 2, 53. II, 3, 32. IV, 1, 25 (*I am a. bound to you*). Err. I, 1, 64. IV, 3, 32. Ado I, 1, 145. III, 1, 93. III, 3, 64. V, 1, 311. V, 2, 10. LLL IV, 3, 384. V, 2, 495. Merch. III, 5, 4. As I, 2, 57. All's I, 2, 52. IV, 5, 49. Wint. II, 3, 148. R2 II, 1, 20. 221. H4A I, 3, 286. H4B III, 2, 214. 294. H5 V, 2, 165. H6A II, 3, 80. IV, 1, 38. V, 1, 11. H6B IV, 7, 72. H6C II, 2, 47. III, 1, 88. IV, 3, 45. V, 6, 11. R3 III, 1, 48. H8 II, 2, 110. V, 3, 59. Cor. I, 1, 53. III, 3, 8. IV, 5, 193. V, 2, 30. Tim. I, 2, 21. II, 2, 130. III, 1, 33. 36. IV, 3, 237. Caes. I, 2, 212. Mcb. III, 1, 132. Hml. I, 5, 60. Lr. I, 1, 3. 293. Cymb. I, 1, 87. I, 2, 31.

Amaimon (O. Edd. *Amaimon* and *Amamon*), name of a devil: Wiv. II, 2, 311. H4A II, 4, 370.

Amain, with full force; 1) aloud: *cried out a.* H6A I, 1, 128. *cry you all a.* Troil. V, 8, 13.

2) swiftly: *Venus makes a. to him,* Ven. 5. Tp. IV, 1, 74. Err. I, 1, 93. LLL V, 2, 549. H6B III, 1, 282. V, 1, 114. H6C II, 1, 182. II, 3, 56. II, 5, 128. 133. IV, 8, 4. 64. Tit. IV, 4, 65.

Amaze, subst. extreme wonder and admiration: *his face's own margent did quote such —s,* LLL II, 246.

Amaze, vb. 1) to bring into a maze, to make one lose the way: *like a labyrinth to a. his foes,* Ven. 684. *I am —d, methinks, and lose my way among the thorns and dangers of this world,* John IV, 3, 140.

2) to put in confusion, to put in a state where one does not know what to do or to say or to think: *whereat —d . . . in the dark she lay,* Ven. 823. *her earnest eye did make him more —d,* Lucr. 1356. *you are —d; but this shall absolutely resolve you,* Meas. IV, 2, 224. LLL V, 2, 391. Mids. III, 2, 220. 344. Merch. V, 266. As I, 2, 115. Shr. IV, 5, 54. Tw. V, 271. John IV, 2, 137. H6A I, 2, 68. Cymb. IV, 3, 28. *to stand —d:* Wiv. V, 5, 244. Shr. II, 156. Tw. III, 4, 371. John II, 356. Rom. III, 1, 139. Lr. III, 6, 35. Oth. IV, 2, 246. This state may be caused by fear: Ven. 469. 925. Lucr. 446. Wiv. III, 3, 125. V, 3, 18. 19. 20. V, 5, 233. Err. III, 2, 149. Shr. III, 2, 163. John II, 226. R2 I, 3, 81. V, 2, 85. H4A V, 4, 6. H6A IV, 7, 84. R3 V, 3, 341. Caes. III, 1, 96. Mcb. II, 3, 114. V, 1, 86. Hml. I, 2, 235. II, 2, 591. Oth. III, 3, 371. Per. I, 4, 87. Or by the highest admiration: *whose full perfection all the world —s,* Ven. 634. *steals men's eyes and women's souls —th,* Sonn. 20, 8. Or by extreme surprise: Meas. V, 385. Ado II, 3, 118. Alls II, 1, 87. John V, 2, 51. R2 III, 3, 72. H8 III, 2, 373 *(—d at).* Troil. V, 3, 91 *(—d at).* Rom. III, 3, 114. Caes. I, 2, 128.

Amazedly, 1) confusedly: *I shall reply a., half sleep, half waking,* Mids. IV, 1, 151. *I speak a.* Wint. V, 1, 187.

2) in a manner indicating fear or horror: *a. in her sad face he stares,* Lucr. 1591. *why stands Macbeth thus a.?* Mcb. IV, 1, 126.

Amazedness, state of being amazed, extreme surprise, terror: *we two in great a. will fly,* Wiv. IV, 4, 55. *after a little a.* Wint. V, 2, 5.

Amazement, 1) confusion, perplexity, bewilderment: *put not yourself into a. how these things should be,* Meas. IV, 2, 220. *and wild a. hurries up and down the little number of your doubtful friends,* John V, 1, 35. *a. shall drive courage from the state,* Per. I, 2, 26.

2) surprise, astonishment: *all this a. can I qualify,* Ado V, 4, 67. *resolve you for more a.* Wint. V, 3, 87. *they did so to the a. of mine eyes,* Mcb. II, 4, 19. *struck her into a. and admiration,* Hml. III, 2, 339.

3) horror, terror: *no more a.* Tp. I, 2, 14. *I flamed a.* 198. *all torment, trouble, wonder and a. inhabits here,* V, 104. *strike a. to their drowsy spirits,* Troil. II, 2, 210. *distraction, frenzy and a.* V, 3, 85. *a. on thy mother sits,* Hml. III, 4, 112.

Amazon, one of the fabulous race of female warriors: Mids. II, 1, 70. John V, 2, 155. H6A I, 2, 104. H6C IV, 1, 106.

Amazonian, resembling an Amazon: *like an A. trull,* H6C I, 4, 114. *his A. chin,* Cor. II, 2, 95 (beardless).

Ambassador (O. Edd. frequently *embassador*), 1) messenger from a sovereign power: Meas. III, 1, 58. H5 I, 1, 91. 2, 3. II, 4, 31. 65. III Chor. 28. H6A V, 1, 24. 34. 4, 144. H6B I, 1, 45. III, 2, 276.

IV, 8, 7. H6C III, 3, 163. 256. IV, 3, 36. H8 I, 1, 97. 4, 55. II, 4, 172. III, 2, 318. IV, 2, 109. Troil. III, 3, 267. Tit. IV, 4, 100. Hml. II, 2, 40. 51. IV, 6, 10. V, 2, 362. Ant. I, 1, 48. Cymb. II, 3, 59. III, 4, 144. 2) any messenger: LLL III, 53. V, 2, 788. Merch. II, 9, 92.

Amber, a fossil resin: Compl. 37. LLL IV, 3, 87. Resin in general: *thick a. and plum-tree gum,* Hml. II, 2, 201.

Adjectively: Pilgr. 366. LLL IV, 3, 87. Shr. IV, 3, 58. Wint. IV, 4, 224 (placed after the subst. in a popular rhyme).

Amber-coloured: LLL IV, 3, 88.

Ambiguity, uncertainty, obscurity: *till we can clear these —ies,* Rom. V, 3, 216. *out of doubt, and out of question too, and —ies,* H5 V, 1, 48.

Ambiguous, of uncertain signification, obscure: *such a. giving out, to note that you know aught of me,* Hml. I, 5, 178.

Ambition, desire of superiority, of honor and power: Lucr. 68. 411. Tp. I, 2, 105. II, 1, 242. V, 75. Wiv. III, 3, 47. As I, 1, 149. II, 5, 40. All's I, 1, 101. 185. R2 V, 5, 18. H6A II, 4, 112. 5, 123. H6B I, 1, 180. II, 1, 32. 2, 71. III, 1, 143. R3 III, 7, 145. Mcb. II, 4, 28. Hml. II, 2, 258 etc. etc. Plural: *—s, covetings,* Cymb. II, 5, 25. H6B IV, 10, 1 (only F1). Followed by the inf.: *I have no a. to see a goodlier man,* Tp. I, 2, 482. Abstr. pro concr.: *I am still possess'd of those effects for which I did the murder, my crown, mine own a. and my queen.* Hml. III, 3, 55; 'desire' for 'what is desired;' 'my ambition' for 'the object of my ambition.'

Ambitious, desirous of superiority, of honor and power: Lucr. 150. LLL V, 1, 12. Merch. II, 7, 44. III, 2, 152. As IV, 1, 13. All's III, 4, 5. John I, 32. R2 I, 3, 130. H6A I, 3, 29. II, 4, 114. III, 1, 29. H6B I, 2, 18. 3, 112. II, 1, 182. IV, 1, 84. V, 1, 132. H6C II, 2, 19. III, 3, 27. V, 5, 17. Caes. I, 3, 7. Hml. II, 2, 264 etc. Placed after its subst.: *love a.,* John II, 430. Followed by *for: I am a. for a motley coat,* As II, 7, 43. *you are a. for poor knaves' caps,* Cor. II, 1, 76.

Ambitiously, with a desire of superiority: H6B II, 3, 36. Tit. I, 19.

Amble, 1) to move easily and without hard shocks: *my —ing gelding,* Wiv. II, 2, 319. *your wit —s well, it goes easily,* Ado V, 1, 159. As III, 2, 328. 343. 336.*

2) to move affectedly, as in a dance: *the skipping king he —d up and down,* H4A III, 2, 60. *a wanton —ing nymph,* R3 I, 1, 17. *give me a torch: I am not for this —ing,* Rom. I, 4, 11. *you jig, you a., and you lisp,* Hml. III, 1, 151.

Ambuscado, ambush: Rom. I, 4, 84.

Ambush, 1) a covert to surprise the enemy: *lain in a.* Lucr. 233. All's IV, 3, 335. R2 I, 1, 137 *(lay an a.).* H6C IV, 6, 83. Metaphorically: *pass'd by the a. of young days,* Sonn. 70, 9. *who may, in the a. of my name, strike home,* Meas. I, 3, 41.

2) the troops or persons posted in a concealed place: *see the a. of our friends be strong,* Tit. V, 3, 9. *I fear some a.* Cymb. IV, 2, 65.

Amen, term of devotion, = so be it: Tp. II, 2, 98. Wiv. III, 3, 220. Meas. I, 2, 6. II, 2, 157. Ado I, 1, 223. LLL II, 127. IV, 3, 94. As III, 3, 48. Shr. Ind. 2, 100. H5 V, 2, 384. R3 II, 2, 109. III, 7, 241

Troil. II, 3, 37. Rom. III, 5, 229 etc. etc. *happily, a.!* Ant. II, 2, 155. *now, I pray God, a.!* H8 II, 3, 56. At the end of a prayer: Tim. I, 2, 71. In divine service it was the office of the clerk to say A. to what the priest had spoken: Sonn. 85, 6. R2 IV, 173. Ado II, 1, 114. *Amen, amen!* Gentl. V, 1, 8. Mids. II, 2, 62. John II, 287. Rom. II, 6, 3. *I cry a.:* Ado II, 1, 110. R2 I, 3, 102. *I say a.:* Tp. V, 204. Merch. II, 2, 203. III, 1, 22. Shr. II, 322. *Amen to that!* Oth. II, 1, 197. *cry a. to sth.:* Sonn. 85, 6. John III, 1, 181. H5 V, 2, 21. *say a. to sth:* Ado II, 1, 315. R3 I, 3, 21. IV, 4, 197. V, 5, 8. *Amen, amen to that fair prayer say I,* Mids. II, 2, 62. *Marry, amen!* Tw. IV, 2, 109. H8 III, 2, 54. *Marry, and amen!* H4A II, 4, 128. Rom. IV, 5, 14. Substantively: *my a. to it!* H8 III, 2, 45. *God speak this a.* H5 V, 2, 396. *I could cry the a.* H8 V, 1, 24.

Amend, 1) trans. to make better what was wrong, to improve: *weak sights their sickly radiance do a.* Compl. 214. *God a. us! God a.!* LLL IV, 3, 76. Mids. II, 1, 118. V, 214. Tw. I, 5, 48. II, 5, 81. Wint. V, 2, 166. H4A III, 1, 180. III, 3, 27. H4B I, 2, 142. Cymb. II, 3, 35. V, 5, 216. = to cure: *I am ill, but your being by me cannot a. me,* Cymb. IV, 2, 12. cf. II, 3, 35. H4B I, 2, 142. = to repair, to mend: *the case may be —ed,* Rom. IV, 5, 101. *I must excuse what cannot be —ed,* Cor. IV, 7, 12. *it is my shame to be so fond, but it is not in my virtue to a. it,* Oth. I, 3, 321. Lucr. 578. 1614. All's III, 4, 7. R3 III, 7, 115. IV. 4, 291.

2) intrans. to become better from a bad state: *sin that —s is but patched with virtue,* Tw. I, 5, 54. Especially to recover: *the affliction of my mind —s,* Tp. V, 115. *at his touch they presently a.* Mcb. IV, 3, 145.

A-mending, in repairing: *when he speaks, 'tis like a chime a.* Troil. I, 3, 159.

Amendment, change for the better: *I see a good a. of life in thee,* H4A I, 2, 114. Especially recovery: *what likelihood of his a.?* R3 I, 3, 33. Shr. Ind. 2, 131. All's I, 1, 14.

Amends, compensation, atonement: *what shall be thy a. for thy neglect of truth?* Sonn. 101, 1. *I'll kiss each several paper for a.* Gentl. I, 2, 108. *for a. to his posterity,* John II, 6. *Robin shall restore a.* Mids. V, 445. Mostly joined to the verb *to make: your compensation makes a.* Tp. IV, 1, 2. Lucr. 961. Mids. V, 441. H6C V, 1, 100. R3 IV, 4, 295. Mcb. III, 5, 14. Cymb. I, 6, 168. *make a. for sth.:* Gentl. III, 1, 331. *To make a p. a.: make thy love a.* Gentl. IV, 2, 99. Wiv. II, 3, 70. III, 1, 90. 5, 49. Err. II, 2, 54. H6C IV, 7, 2. R3 I, 1, 155. Oth. IV, 1, 255. *I cannot make you what a. I would,* R3 IV, 4, 309. Wrongly for **amendment** = recovery: Shr. Ind. 2, 99.

Amerce, to punish with a pecuniary penalty: *I'll a. you with so strong a fine,* Rom. III, 1, 195.

America, the new Continent: Err. III, 2, 136.

Ames-ace, two aces, the lowest throw at dice: *throw a. for my life,* All's II, 3, 85 (cf. deuce-ace).

Amiable, 1) concerning love, done out of love: *lay an a. siege to the honesty of this Ford's wife,* Wiv. II, 2, 243. *saw afar off in the orchard this a. encounter,* Ado III, 3, 161. 2) lovely, pleasing: *bull Jove, sir, had an a. low,* Ado V, 4, 48. *while I*

thy a. cheeks do coy, Mids. IV, 1, 2. *and in no sense is meet or a.* Shr. V, 2, 141. *O a. lovely death!* John III, 4, 25. *'twould make her a. and subdue my father entirely to her love,* Oth. III, 4, 59.

Amid, in the midst of: *famish them a. their plenty,* Ven. 20. *a. this hurly I intend that all is done in reverend care of her,* Shr. IV, 1, 206.

Amidst, in the midst of: *enthroned and sphered a. the other,* Troil. I, 3, 91.

Amiens: *my Lord of A.* As II, 1, 29.

Amintas, king of Lycaonia, Ant. III, 6, 74 (part of M. Edd. *Amyntas*).

Amiss, adv., originally = astray: *what error drives our eyes and ears a.?* Err. II, 2, 186. Usually = improperly, wrongly, ill: *bear a. the second burden of a former child,* Sonn. 59, 3. *choose a.* Merch. II, 9, 65. *nothing comes a., so money comes withal,* Shr. I, 2, 82. *speed a.* II, 285. *talk'd a. of her,* 293. *that which thou hast sworn to do a. is not a.* John III, 1, 270. *a. employed,* R2 II, 3, 132. *if I have done a.* H6A IV, 1, 27. *gold cannot come a.* H6B I, 2, 92. *take it not a.* (= take it not ill) R3 III, 7, 206. *done aught a.* Tit. V, 3, 129. Caes. I, 2, 273. *a. interpreted,* II, 2, 83. *said or done a.* Oth. II, 3, 201. *such a sight here shows much a.* Hml. V, 2, 413.

Amiss, adj., only used in the predicate, = out of time and order, wrong: *all is a.* Pilgr. 248. *never anything can be a., when simpleness and duty tender it,* Mids. V, 82. *God may finish it when he will, 'tis not a hair a. yet,* H4B I, 2, 27. Tim. II, 2, 217. III, 6, 91. Caes. III, 1, 31. Mcb. II, 3, 102. Ant. II, 2, 19. Contrary to justice: John III, 1, 271.

Negatively: *that shall not be much a.* Meas. III, 1, 200. *'tis not a.* III, 2, 66. *it had not been a.* Ado II, 1, 234. All's IV, 5, 72. Tw. III, 2, 49. H6B IV, 10, 10. V, 1, 76. Tim. V, 1, 14. Oth. IV, 1, 92. Ant. I, 4, 17. Per. IV, 2, 36.

Amiss, subst. 1) wrong, offence: *salving thy a.* Sonn. 35, 7. *urge not my a.* 151, 3. 2) mischief: *to my sick soul each toy seems prologue to some great a.* Hml. IV, 5, 18.

Amity, good understanding, friendship: Mids. IV, 1, 92. Merch. III, 2, 30. III, 4, 3. All's II, 5, 15. Wint. V, 1, 136. John II, 537. III, 1, 105. 231. V, 4, 20. H4B III, 1, 79. IV, 2, 65. H6A III, 1, 68. IV, 1, 62. V, 1, 16. H6C III, 3, 53. 54. R3 I, 3, 281. H8 I, 1, 181. Troil. II, 3, 110. Lr. II, 4, 245 *(hold a.).* Ant. II, 2, 127. II, 6, 130. Plural: Hml. V, 2, 42. Lr. I, 2, 159.

Among (cf. *'mong*), in or into the midst of, in or into the number of: *sometime he runs a. a flock of sheep,* Ven. 685. Lucr. Arg. 7. Sonn. 12, 10. 124, 4. 136, 8. Compl. 190. Gentl. III, 1, 337. IV, 2, 37. Wiv. III, 3, 14. 236. Ado V, 2, 76. LLL III, 197. V, 1, 104. V, 2, 684. Mids. III, 1, 32. III, 2, 67. Merch. I, 2, 120. II, 1, 46. III, 1, 25. III, 2, 182. All's I, 3, 81. IV, 1, 6. Wint. I, 2, 253. V, 2, 132. H4A I, 3, 105. H6A V, 5, 93 etc. etc. Preceded by its substantive: *and mine I pour your ocean all a.* Compl. 256. *go the fools a.* Lr. I, 4, 194.

2) *Among them* = jointly, both together: *you have a. you killed a sweet and innocent lady,* Ado V, 1, 194. *make him hanged a. you,* H4B II, 2, 105. *the man is dead that you and Pistol beat a. you,* V, 4, 19 (Q *amongst*). *a woman lost among ye* (= ruined by you) H8 III, 1, 107. *that will I bestow a. my wife and*

her confederates, Err. IV, 1, 17 (i. e. upon my wife as well as all her confederates). *let his knights have colder looks a. you*, Lr. I, 3, 22 (i. e. from your whole company). *you have a. you many a purchased slave*, Merch. IV, 1, 90, i. e. you possess in common public slaves (cf. *between*).

3) between: *that such immanity and bloody strife should reign a. professors of one faith*, H6A V, 1, 14. Adverbially: *and lusty lads roam here and there so merrily, and ever a. so merrily*, H4B V, 3, 23. (Nares: "To and among was equivalent to here and there. Overbury: She travels to and among." Perhaps corrupted from *ever and anon.* cf. *still an end* for *still and anon*).

Amongst = among (H4B II, 4, 80 Q *among*, Ff *amongst*, H4B V, 4, 19 and R3 II, 1, 53 Qq *amongst*, Ff *among*): Lucr. Arg. 10. As IV, 3, 124. V, 4, 57. Shr. I, 1, 58. I, 2, 266. All's I, 3, 233. Wint. II, 1, 21. R2 IV, 14. H4A I, 1, 82. 3, 47. H6A I, 1, 70. II, 2, 24. III, 1, 182. IV, 1, 138. 7, 83. V, 2, 6. H6C II, 1, 180. V, 6, 58. R3 II, 1, 53. Tit. I, 84. IV, 2, 68. Tim. IV, 2, 23 (*I'll share a. you*) etc. etc.

Amongst them = jointly: *and a. them fell'd him dead*, Lr. IV, 2, 76. — *Nature does require her times of preservation, which perforce I, her frail son, a. my brethren mortal, must give my tendence to*, H8 III, 2, 148, i. e. as well as my brethren.

Amorous, 1) pertaining to love: *his a. spoil*, Compl. 154. *my a. tale*, Ado I, 1, 327. *your a. token*, All's V, 3, 68. *fetter'd in a. chains*, Tit. II, 1, 15. *a. rites*, Rom. III, 2, 8. *their a. sojourn*, Lr. I, 1, 48. *his a. works*, Oth. V, 2, 213.

2) fond, in love: *our fine musician groweth a.* Shr. III, 1, 63. Rom. V, 3, 103. Cymb. V, 5, 195. *a. Phillida*, Mids. II, 1, 68. Merch. II, 8, 9. Shr. I, 2, 144. III, 2, 149. All's III, 5, 72. Troil. V, 5, 4. Ant. II, 1, 33. *unloose his a. fold*, Troil. III, 3, 223. *bent of a. view*, IV, 5, 282. *Phoebus' a. pinches*, Ant. I, 5, 28. *to court an a. lookingglass*, R3 I, 1, 15, i. e. a lookingglass which reflects a face fond of itself.

Followed by *of: a. of their strokes*, Ant. II, 2, 202. by *on: a. on Hero*, Ado II, 1, 161.

Amorously, fondly: *with twisted metal a. impleach'd*, Compl. 205.

Amort, dejected, dispirited: *what, sweeting, all a.?* Shr. IV, 3, 36. *what, all a.?* H6A III, 2, 124.

Amount, vb. (never subst.) to compose in the whole; followed by *to: a. to three ducats*, Err. IV, 1, 30. LLL I, 2, 49. Shr. II, 375. All's IV, 3, 190. H5 III, 2, 33. H6C II, 1, 181. or by *unto:* Err. I, 1, 25. Costard in LLL uses *until* for *to: whereuntil it doth a.* V, 2, 494. 501.

Amphimachus, name of a Greek, Troil. V, 5, 12.

Ample, large, copious, liberal, unrestrained: *this a. third of our fair kingdom*, Lr. I, 1, 82. *an a. tear*, IV, 3, 14. *with a. and brim fulness of his force*, H5 I, 2, 150. *such a. grace and honour*, Meas. I, 1, 24. *in large and a. empery* H5 I, 2, 226. *a. power*, Troil. II, 2, 140. *in very a. virtue of his father*, H4B IV, 1, 163. *a. satisfaction*, Err. V, 252. *my a. hope*, John V, 2, 112. Troil. I, 3, 3. *a. interchange of sweet discourse*, R3 V, 3, 99. *the great dignity ... shall at home be encountered with a shame as a.* All's IV, 3, 82. *at a. view* (= at full and open view) Tw. I, 1, 27. *at a. point* (in full measure) Troil. III, 3, 89. Compar. *ampler: —r strength*, Wint. IV, 4, 414. Superl.

amplest: —st credence, All's I, 2, 11. *with —st entertainment*, Tim. I, 1, 45.

Adverbially: *I know your hostess as a. as myself*, All's III, 5, 46. *how a. you're beloved*, Tim. I, 2, 136.

Amplify, to enlarge: *to a. too much*, Lr. V, 3, 206. *I did a. my judgment.* Cymb. I, 5, 17. to show in the most favourable light, to set off: *deep-brain'd sonnets that did a. each stone's dear nature*, Compl. 209. *his fame ... haply —ied*, Cor. V, 2, 16.

Amply, without restriction, copiously: *can prate as a. and unnecessarily*, Tp. II, 1, 264. *than a. to imbar their crooked titles*, H5 I, 2, 94 (liberally, without reserve). *as a. titled as Achilles*, Troil. II, 3, 203.

Ampthill, place in England, H8 IV, 1, 28.

Amurath, (Ff *Amurah*), name of Turkish sultans: H4B V, 2, 48.

Amyntas, v. *Amintas*.

An, art., v. *a*.

An, conj., in O. Edd. mostly written *and*, but sometimes also *an*, f. i. LLL V, 2, 232. 584. H4A II, 1, 1. H5 IV, 7, 96. H6B V, 1, 72. Caes. IV, 3, 258. M. Edd. have often been too rash in changing *and* to *an*, f. i. Err. IV, 1, 43. Mids. III, 2, 78. H4A I, 3, 125. H5 II, 4, 120. Troil. III, 2, 149. 3, 256. Tit. II, 1, 69 etc.

1) if; followed by the indic. as well as the subj. mood: Err. I, 2, 94. II, 2, 36. III, 1, 39. Ado I, 1, 80. 137. 192. III, 3, 91. LLL II, 248. III, 103. IV, 1, 49. V, 1, 74. Mids. I, 2, 53. 76. IV, 2, 21. Merch. V, 176. H4B I, 1, 13 etc. etc. Of very frequent occurrence in the phrase *an it please you:* Wiv. II, 2, 37. Meas. II, 1, 205. Merch. II, 2, 61. H6B I, 3, 18. *an please you,* H6A V, 4, 10. *an't shall please you,* LLL I, 1, 273. V, 2, 584. Merch. II, 4, 10 (Q1 *if*). H6B I, 3, 190. *an't like you,* Tp. IV, 239. Meas. II, 1, 169. V, 74, etc. etc.

2) if but: *it is best put finger in the eye, an she knew why,* Shr. I, 1, 79. Tp. II, 1, 181. John II, 136.

3) though: *an thou wert a lion, we would do so,* LLL V, 2, 627. Merch. I, 2, 96. H6B IV, 7, 112.

4) In vulgar language = whether: *to spy an I can hear my Thisby's face*, Mids. V, 195. and = as if: *I will roar you an 'twere any nightingale*, Mids. I, 2, 86. H5 II, 3, 11. Troil. I, 2, 139. 189.

An if = if: Tp. II, 2, 120. V, 117. Gentl. I, 1, 75. III, 1, 257. Err. IV, 3, 76. Ado V, 1, 178. LLL I, 1, 50. IV, 1, 137. V, 2, 32. 232. Mids. II, 2, 153. Merch. IV, 1, 445. V, 159. As II, 5, 59. All's II, 1, 74. H6A III, 1, 153. IV, 6, 36. H6B II, 1, 124. 3, 74. H6C I, 1, 137. Oth. III, 4, 83 etc.

What an if = though: *what an if his sorrows have so overwhelm'd his wits*, Tit. IV, 4, 9.

Anatomize (O. Edd. *anathomize*, except Lr. III, 6, 80), to dissect for the purpose of examining the interior structure: *let them a. Regan*, Lr. III, 6, 80. Figuratively = to lay open, to show distinctly: *in her the painter had —d time's ruin*, Lucr. 1450. *should I a. him to thee*, As I, 1, 162. *the wise man's folly is —d*, II, 7, 56. *see his company —d*, All's IV, 3, 37. *my well-known body to a.* H4B Ind. 21. Don Armado writes *annothanize*, and uses it in the sense of to explain: *which to a. in the vulgar*, LLL IV, 1, 69.

Anatomy, 1) skeleton: *a mere a.* Err. V, 238.

that fell a. (Death) John III, 4, 40. Mrs Quickly says *atomy* instead: H4B V, 4, 33. 2) in contempt, = b o d y: *I'll eat the rest of the a.* Tw. III, 2, 67. *in what vile part of this a. does my name lodge?* Rom. III, 3, 106.

Ancestor, progenitor: Ado V, 1, 69. All's IV, 2, 43. V, 3, 196. R2 II, 1, 254. H4A III, 2, 31. V, 2, 11. H4B IV, 4, 61. H5 I, 2, 102. 135. II, 4, 92. R3 III, 7, 119. Cor. II, 3, 253. Tit. I, 84. V, 3, 80. Rom. IV, 3, 41. Caes. I, 2, 112. I, 3, 81. III, 2, 55. Ant. IV, 12, 44. Cymb. III, 1, 17. IV, 2, 48. Per. V, 1, 91. Wrongly for descendant: Wiv. I, 1, 15.

Ancestry, series of progenitors, lineage, noble descent: *by the honour of my a.* Gentl. V, 4, 139. *draw forth your noble a. from the corruption of abusing times,* R3 III, 7, 198. *not propp'd by a.* H8 I, 1, 59. *great nature, like his a., moulded the stuff,* Cymb. V, 4, 48.

Anchises, father of Aeneas: H6B V, 2, 62. Troil. IV, 1, 21. Caes. I, 2, 114.

Anchor, subst., anchorite, hermit: *an —'s cheer in prison be my scope,* Hml. III, 2, 229.

Anchor, subst., iron instrument to hold a ship at rest: *the a. is deep,* Wiv. I, 3, 56 (it is cast out and holds). *to make his a. hold,* Wint. I, 2, 213. *it came home,* 214, i. e. it was dislodged from its bed. *nothing so certain as your —s,* IV, 4, 581. H6C V, 4, 13. 16. R3 I, 4, 26. Tit. IV, 4, 38. *at a.* Per. V Prol. 16.

Anchor, vb., 1) intr. to lie at anchor: H6B IV, 1, 9. Lr. IV, 6, 18. To keep hold in general: *a pair of —ing hooks,* Gentl. III, 1, 118. Figuratively to keep hold of; with *on: my invention —s on Isabel,* Meas. II, 4, 4. *Posthumus — s upon Imogen,* Cymb. V, 5, 393.

2) trans., to place at anchor, and figuratively to fix: *if eyes be —'d in the bay where all men ride,* Sonn. 137, 6. *till that my nails were —'d in thine eyes,* R3 IV, 4, 231. *there would he a. his aspect,* Ant. I, 5, 33.

Anchorage, the anchor and all the necessary tackle for anchoring: *she weigh'd her a.* Tit. I, 73.

Anchovy, a small sea-fish of the genus herring: *—ies,* H4A II, 4, 588. O. Edd. *anchoves.*

Ancient, adj., 1) having happened or existed in former times, and now no more in existence: *the a. Roman honour,* Merch. III, 2, 297. *derived from the a. Capilet,* All's V, 3, 159. *knowledge in the a. wars,* H5 III, 2, 83. *a. writers,* H4A II, 4, 455. *a. ravens' wings,* Lucr. 949.

2) having come down from a time far remote, of long standing: *the a. privilege of Athens,* Mids. I, 1, 41. *the a. saying,* Merch. II, 9, 82. *proverb,* H6B III, 1, 170. *tradition,* H5 V, 1, 74. *a. feast,* Rom. I, 2, 87 (cf. 20: *an old accustomed feast*). *gentry,* H6A II, 4, 93. *gentlemen,* Hml. V, 1, 33. *right,* R3 III, 1, 92. *an a. watchman,* Ado III, 3, 41. *servant,* Shr. I, 2, 47. *a. word of courage,* R3 V, 3, 349. *tale,* John IV, 2, 18. *receptacle,* Rom. IV, 3, 39. *city,* H6B I, 1, 5. *castle,* R2 III, 3, 32. *stones,* R3 IV, 1, 99. *my a. skill,* Meas. IV, 2, 164. *sorrow,* R3 IV, 4, 35. Hence = inveterate: *a. grudge,* Merch. I, 3, 48. *quarrels,* R2 II, 1, 248. Rom. I, 1, 111. *bickerings,* H6B I, 1, 144. *malice,* R2 I, 1, 9. Cor. II, 1, 244. IV, 5, 102. *envy,* IV, 5, 109. *grudge,* Rom. Prol. 3. *his a. knot of dangerous adversaries,* R3 III, 1, 182. On the other hand: *a. love,* Mids. III, 2, 215. Lr. IV, 1, 45. *amities,*

I, 2, 159. Superl.: *ere ancient'st order was,* Wint. IV, 1, 10. — *The a. of war,* Lr. V, 1, 32 (corr.) .

3) former: *call home thy a. thoughts from banishment,* Shr. Ind. 2, 33. *my a. incantations are too weak,* H6A V, 3, 27. *new lamenting a. oversights,* H4B II, 3, 47. *recovered your a. freedom,* H6B IV, 8, 27. *where is your a. courage?* Cor. IV, 1, 3.

4) advanced in years, old: *this a. morsel,* Tp. II, 1, 286. *a very a. smell,* II, 2, 27. *angel,* Shr. IV, 2, 61. *gentleman,* V, 1, 75. Wint. IV, 4, 79. 372. H4A III, 2, 104. H4B II, 4, 91. Tit. III, 1, 17. Rom. I, 1, 99. II, 3, 74. 4, 150. III, 5, 235. Lr. II, 2, 67. Cymb. V, 3, 15.

Ancient, subst. 1) the next in command under the lieutenant: *—s, corporals, lieutenants,* H4A IV, 2, 26. *a. Pistol* H4B II, 4, 74. 89. 120. 164. H5 II, 1, 3. V, 1, 18 (Fluellen pronounces *Aunchient*). Oth. I, 1, 33. 2, 49. 3, 121 and passim. Fluellen says: *an aunchient lieutenant,* H5 III, 6, 13.

2) standard: *an old faced a.,* H4A IV, 2, 34, an old standard mended with a different colour.

Ancientry, old age: *getting wenches with child, wronging the a.,* i. e. the old people, Wint. III, 3, 63. *the wedding mannerly-modest as a measure, full of state and a.* Ado II, 1, 80, i. e. the port and behaviour of old age.*

Ancle, the joint which connects the foot with the leg: Hml. II, 1, 80.

Ancus Marcius, name of the fourth king of Rome, Cor. II, 3, 247.

And, conj., 1) = an; v. *An.*

2) the particle which serves to join clauses and words. Peculiarities of its use: the composed numerals have generally the form '*one and twenty*' etc.: Wint. III, 3, 60. 65. IV, 3, 44. H4A I, 1, 68. II, 2, 17. 4, 206. III, 3, 54. 85. IV, 3, 56. H4B I, 2, 50. 3, 11. H5 I, 2, 57. IV, 8, 111. Troil. I, 2, 171. 255. Tit. I, 79. 195. III, 1, 10. Rom. I, 5, 39. IV, 1, 105. Tim. II, 1, 3. Caes. V, 1, 53. Hml. V, 1, 190. Lr. II, 4, 251. 257. 262. III, 7, 16 etc. etc. But sometimes also *twenty one:* Wint. I, 2, 155. II, 3, 197. IV, 4, 464. V, 1, 126. H4B II, 4, 413. III, 2, 224. H5 I, 2, 61. IV, 8, 88. Cor. II, 1, 170. 171. Tim. III, 2, 43. Caes. III, 2, 248. Mcb. IV, 1, 7. Lr. I, 4, 42 etc. Irregularly: *thirty and six,* H6C III, 3, 96. Troil. Pr. 5. *two hundred fifty,* All's IV, 3, 186. 188 (M. Edd. *and fifty*).

Two and two = by twos, H4A III, 3, 104.

And = and that: *you are abused and by some putter-on,* Wint. II, 1, 141.

Used as a mere expletive in popular songs: *when that I was and a tiny little boy,* Tw. V, 397. *he that has and a little tiny wit,* Lr. III, 2, 74 (Qq *has a little*). *King Stephen was and a worthy peer,* Oth. II, 3, 92 (Q1 and M. Edd. *was a worthy peer*).

Very frequently notions, of which one is subordinate to the other, are joined by *and,* a rhetorical figure called ἓν διὰ δυοῖν by grammarians: *shelves and sands* = sandy shelves, Lucr. 335. *give fear to use and liberty* (to the usual or customary liberty) Meas. I, 4, 62. *with dances and delight* = with delightful dances, Mids. II, 1, 254. *contempt and clamour,* Wint. I, 2, 189. *in the instant of repair and health,* John III, 4, 113. *the tediousness and process of my travel* (= the tedious process) R2 II, 3, 12. *we need your use and counsel,* H4A I, 3, 21. *vouchsafe me hearing and respect,* IV, 3, 31. *the ragged'st hour that time and spite can bring* (= the spite of time, or the spiteful time) H4B I, 1, 151. *the charge and kingly government of this your land*, R3 III, 7, 131. *no more assurance of equal friendship and proceeding* (of an impartial and friendly proceeding) H8 II, 4, 18. *fool and feather*, I, 3, 25. *to keep her constancy in plight and youth* (in youthful plight) Troil. III, 2, 168. *with all my force, pursuit and policy* (with the pursuit of all my force and policy) IV, 1, 18. *time, force and death* = the force of time and death, IV, 2, 107. *through the cranks and offices of man* = the cranking offices, Cor. I, 1, 140. *by interims and conveying gusts*, I, 6, 5. *thy fame and envy* (envious, odious fame) I, 8, 4. *applause and clamour*, I, 9, 64. *the horn and noise o' the monster's*, III, 1, 95. *with the same austerity and garb*, IV, 7, 44. *thy triumphs and return*, Tit. I, 110. *the vigour and the picture of my youth*, IV, 2, 108. *our yoke and sufferance*, Caes. I, 3, 84. *for warnings and portents and evils imminent*, II, 2, 80. *in a general honest thought and common good to all*, V, 5, 72. *our griefs and clamour*, Mcb. I, 7, 78. *your leave and favour*, Hml. I, 2, 51. *in his particular act and place*, I, 3, 26. *by law and heraldry*, I, 1, 87. *reason and sanity*, II, 2, 214. *a combination and a form*, III, 4, 60. *not tomb enough and continent*, IV, 4, 64. *his sables and his weeds*, IV, 7, 81. *respect and fortunes*, Lr. I, 1, 251 (Qq *respects of fortune*). *the image and horror of it*, I, 2, 192. *this milky gentleness and course of yours*, 4, 364. *with every gale and vary*, II, 2, 85. *on the court and guard of safety*, Oth. II, 3, 216. *out of her own love and flattery*, IV, 1, 133. *rather victorious life than death and honour*, Ant. IV, 2, 44. *the flint and hardness of my fault*, IV, 9, 16. *the heaviness and guilt within my bosom*, Cymb. V, 2, 1. Lr. I, 2, 48. 4, 309. IV, 7, 97.

It is the same with adjectives: *thy fair and outward character* (outwardly fair) Tw. I, 2, 51. *with self and vain conceit*, R2 III, 2, 166. *my strange and self abuse*, Mcb. III, 4, 142. *by self and violent hands*, V, 8, 70. *this prostrate and exterior bending*, H4B IV, 5, 149. *the fatal and neglected English* (= fatally neglected) H5 II, 4, 13. *sick and green* (= green-sick), Rom. II, 2, 8. *by free and offer'd light* (freely offered) Tim. V, 1, 48. *his slow and moving finger* (slowly moving) Oth. IV, 2, 56 (Qq *slow unmoving*).

Andiron, ornamental iron at the side of the fireplace: *her —s were two winking Cupids of silver*, Cymb. II, 4, 88.*

Andren, place in France between Guisnes and Ard, probably Arden, H8 I, 1, 7.

Andrew, 1) name of a ship: *my wealthy A.* Merch. I, 1, 27. — 2) *Sir A. Aguecheek*, Tw. I, 3, 18. 46. II, 3, 1 etc.

Andromache, wife of Hector: Troil. I, 2, 6. V, 3, 77.

Andrónici, plur. of *Andronicus:* Tit. II, 3, 189. V, 3, 131 (without article). 176.

Andrónicus, name in Tit. I, 23 etc. etc.

Anele, in *unaneled*, q. v.

An-end = on end: *each particular hair to stand a.* Hml. I, 5, 19. III, 4, 122. cf. *End.*

Anew, 1) another time, afresh: Ven. 60. Sonn. 119, 11. Pilgr. 332. All's I, 1, 4. H4B I, 3, 46. H6B I, 3, 42. Tit. I, 262. Oth. IV, 1, 85.

2) newly, in a new and other manner: *thou art enforced to seek a. some fresher stamp*, Sonn. 82, 7. *and taught it thus a. to greet*, 145, 8.

Angel, 1) messenger of God: Tp. I, 2, 481. Gentl. III, 1, 103. Meas. II, 2, 122. III, 2, 286. LLL V, 2, 103. 297. Mids. III, 1, 132. Merch. II, 7, 56. V, 61. All's III, 2, 129. John IV, 1, 68. H5 I, 1, 28. R3 I, 2, 74 etc. etc. *God's a.* H4A III, 3, 40. *—s of light*, Err. IV, 3, 56. *holy a.* Mcb. III, 6, 45. *heavenly a.* Cymb. II, 2, 50. *good a.* Tp. II, 1, 306. Meas. II, 4, 16. H4A III, 3, 200. H4B II, 4, 362. R3 IV, 1, 93. V, 3, 138. 156. 175. H8 II, 1, 75. III, 2, 442. V, 1, 161. *the better a.* Sonn. 144, 3. *evil a.* Err. IV, 3, 20. LLL I, 2, 178. *ill a.* H4B I, 2, 186. *black a.* Lr. III, 6, 34.

2) genius, demon: *let the a. whom thou still hast served, tell thee*, Mcb. V, 8, 14. *thy a.* Ant. II, 3, 21. *reverence, that a. of the world*, Cymb. IV, 2, 248. *at last I spied an ancient a. coming down*, Shr. IV, 2, 61 (= one coming in good time? cf. John V, 2, 64).*

3) darling: *Brutus was Caesar's a.* Caes. III, 2, 185.*

An a. spake, John V, 2, 64 (Nares: a common phrase of approval of a proposal made by another); it seems rather to mean an unexpected confirmation of what has been said. Perhaps also a quibble is intended, v. the words *purse* and *nobles* v. 61 and 62.

Adjectively: *in a. whiteness*, Ado IV, 1, 163. *that a. knowledge*, LLL I, 1, 113. *my other a. husband*, R3 IV, 1, 69 (which may also mean: my other husband who is now made an angel of heaven).

Angel, a gold coin worth ten shillings (described in Merch. II, 7, 56: *they have in England a coin that bears the figure of an angel stamped in gold*): Wiv. II, 2, 73. Err. IV, 3, 41. John II, 590. III, 3, 8. H4A IV, 2, 6. Quibbles between the two significations: Wiv. I, 3, 60. Ado II, 3, 35. H4A I, 2, 187.

Angelica, christian name of Lady Capulet, Rom. IV, 4, 5.

Angelical, resembling an angel: *fiend a.* Rom. III, 2, 75.

Angel-like, resembling an angel: *a. perfection*, Gentl. II, 4, 66. Adverbially: *how a. he sings!* Cymb. IV, 2, 48.

Angelo, 1) name of the goldsmith in Err. III, 1, 1. IV, 4, 135. 2) of a Venetian commander in Oth. I, 3, 16. 3) of the deputy in Meas. I, 1, 16. 25. 2, 123 and passim.

Anger, subst., emotion of the mind at an injury, choler: Ven. 76. Lucr. 478 *(for a.)* Sonn. 50, 10. Pilgr. 68. Tp. IV, 145. Gentl. IV, 3, 27. Ado I, 1, 251. Mids. II, 1, 104. As I, 3, 42. III, 5, 67. Shr. IV, 1, 175. IV, 3, 77. All's II, 3, 222. Tw. III, 1, 158. Wint. II, 2, 62. H4A I, 1, 107. H5 IV, 7, 40. H6A II, 4, 65. H6C I, 1, 60 *(my heart for a. burns)*. 211. H8 III, 2, 92. Cor. III, 2, 95. Ant. IV, 1, 9 etc. etc.

Anger, vb., to make angry, to provoke: Tp. IV, 169. Gentl. I, 2, 101. 103. Ado II, 1, 146. Tw. II, 5, 11. H4A III, 1, 148. 192. H4B IV, 4, 9. III, 2, 216. Rom. I, 4, 102. II, 1, 22. 23. II, 4, 216. Tim. I, 1, 208. Mcb. III, 6, 15. Lr. IV, 1, 41 *(—ing itself and others,* = giving offence). Oth. II, 1, 153. 274. Ant. II, 6, 21. Cymb. II, 3, 145.

Angerly, adv. angrily: *how a. I taught my brow to frown*, Gentl. I, 2, 62. John IV, 1, 82. Mcb. III, 5, 1.

Angiers, the town of Angers in France, John II, 1, 17. 22 sq.

Angle, subst. 1) corner: *in an odd a. of the isle*, Tp. I, 2, 223. — 2) the instrument to take fish: *give me mine a., we'll to the river*, Ant. II, 5, 10. Figuratively: *the a. that plucks our son thither*, Wint. IV, 2, 52. *thrown out his a. for my proper life*, Hml. V, 2, 66.

Angle, vb., to fish with an angle: *the pleasant'st —ing is to see the fish ...*, Ado III, 1, 26. *I am —ing now*, Wint. I, 2, 180. Ant. II, 5, 16. to a. for sth: *so a. we for Beatrice*, Ado III, 1, 29. Figuratively, to bait, to try to gain: *she did a. for me*, All's V, 3, 212. *the hearts of all that he did a. for*, H4A IV, 3, 84. *to a. for your thoughts*, Troil. III, 2, 162. *one of the prettiest touches of all and that which —d for mine eyes, caught the water though not the fish*, Wint. V, 2, 90.

Angler, a person who angles: Lr. III, 6, 8.

Angry, feeling or showing anger, provoked, properly and tropically: Ven. 70. 283. Lucr. 388. 461. 1421. Sonn. 147, 6. Tp. II, 1, 186. Gentl. II, 1, 164. 4, 23. Wiv. III, 4, 97. V, 5, 213. Meas. II, 2, 120. III, 1, 207. Ado V, 1, 131. 141. Mids. II, 1, 112. III, 2, 323. As IV, 3, 11. Shr. I, 2, 203. II, 210. 250. Wint. III, 2, 147. V, 1, 173. John IV, 2, 268. H5 IV, 7, 58. H6A II, 4, 107. IV, 1, 168. 7, 9. H6B I, 2, 55. III, 1, 15. 2, 125. IV, 2, 134. V, 1, 126. 2, 3. H6C II, 2, 20. R3 I, 2, 74. 242. III, 1, 144. IV, 2, 27. Caes. I, 2, 183. Ant. V, 2, 309 etc. etc. Followed by *at* and *with* (more frequently by the latter) indiscriminately: *I am so a. at these abject terms*, H6B V, 1, 25. *I'm a. at him*, Tim. III, 3, 13. *were he more a. at it* (sc. the commonwealth) Cor. IV, 6, 14. — *be not a. with me*, Ado III, 1, 94. *I should be a. with you*, H5 IV, 1, 217. *be not a. with the child*, R3 II, 4, 36. *art thou a.? what, with me?* Troil. I, 1, 74. *he makes me a. with him*, Ant. III, 13, 141. And on the other hand: *the heavens with that we have in hand are a.* Wint. III, 3, 5. *who therewith a.* H4A I, 3, 40. *a. with my fancy*, Troil. IV, 4, 27.

Trisyllabic in Tim. III, 5, 57: *but who is man that is not a.?*

Angry-chafing (not hyphened by O. Edd.) fretting with rage: Ven. 662.

Anguish, subst., excessive pain, either of body or of mind: *I have stay'd for thee in a., pain and agony*, R3 IV, 4, 163 (Ff. *torment*). *one pain is lessen'd by another's a.* Rom. I, 2, 47. *your other senses grow imperfect by your eyes' a.* Lr. IV, 6, 6. *more fell than a., hunger, or the sea*, Oth. V, 2, 362. — *Is there no play to ease the a. of a torturing hour?* Mids. V, 37. *the words would add more a. than the wounds*, H6C II, 1, 99. *to close the eye of a.* Lr. IV, 4, 15.

Angus, name of a Scottish earl: H4A I, 1, 73.*

An-heires: *Will you go, An-heires?* Wiv. II, 1, 228. Most M. Edd. after Theobald: *mynheers;* others: *on, here; on, hearts; on, heroes; and hear us; cavaleires; eh, sir.*

An-hungry, Cor. I, 1, 209, v. *A.*

A-night, at night: As II, 4, 48. cf. *Night.*

Animal, subst., living creature: Ado IV, 1, 61. As II, 1, 36. 62. Opposed to man: LLL IV, 2, 28. Merch. IV, 1, 132. As I, 1, 16. Including the species of man: Hml. II, 2, 320. Lr. III, 4, 113.

Anjou, a French province: John I, 11. II, 152 and 487 (Ff Angiers). 528. H6A I, 1, 94. V, 3, 95. 147. 154. H6B I, 1, 50. 110. IV, 1, 86.

Ankle, v. *ancle.*

Anna, the confident of Dido: Shr. I, 1, 159.

Annals, relation of events in the order of years: Cor. V, 6, 114.

Anne. 1) Saint A.: Shr. I, 1, 255. Tw. II, 3, 126. — 2) daughter of Roger Earl of March: H6B II, 2, 38. 43. — 3) daughter of Warwick and wife of Prince Edward and King Richard III: R3 I, 2, 9. IV, 2, 53. 3, 39. V, 3, 159. — 4) A. Bullen, afterwards wife of Henry VIII: H8 III, 2, 36. 87. 402. IV, 1, 3. — 5) Anne Page: Wiv. I, 1, 45. 4, 33. II, 1, 168. III, 4, 14. 71 etc.

Annex, to add, to unite to: *and to his robbery had —'d thy breath*, Sonn. 99, 11. *which (heart) whilst it was mine had —'d unto't a million more*, Ant. IV, 14, 17. cf. *Ill-annexed.*

Annexion, addition: *with the —s of fair gems enriched*, Compl. 208.

Annexment, appendage: *each small a., petty consequence, attends the boisterous ruin*, Hml. III, 3, 21.

Annothanize, v. *anatomize.*

Annoy, subst., pain, suffering, grief: *life was death's a.* Ven. 497. *worse than Tantalus' is her a.* 599. *mirth doth search the bottom of a.* Lucr. 1109. *threatening Ilion with a.* 1370. *receivest with pleasure thine a.*, Sonn. 8, 4. *farewell sour a.* H6C V, 7, 45. *rape was root of thine a.* Tit. IV, 1, 49.

2) injury, harm: *good angels guard thee from the boar's a.* R3 V, 3, 156.

Annoy, vb. to molest, to harm, to hurt: *she will not be —'d with suitors*, Shr. I, 1, 189. *one spark of evil that might a. my finger*, H5 II, 2, 102. *thorns that would a. our foot*, H6B III, 1, 67. *without —ing me*, Caes. I, 3, 22. *so far as to a. us all*, II, 1, 160. *what can from Italy a. us*, Cymb. IV, 3, 34.

Annoyance, 1) injury, harm: *doing a. to the treacherous feet*, R2 III, 2, 16. *the herd hath more a. by the breese than by the tiger*, Troil. I, 3, 48. *remove from her the means of all a.* Mcb. V, 1, 84.

2) that which harms or hurts: *a grain, a dust, ... any a. in that precious sense*, John IV, 1, 94. *to souse a. that comes near his nest*, V, 2, 150.

Annual, happening every year, yearly: *a. tribute*, Tp. I, 2, 113. LLL V, 2, 808. H8 II, 3, 64. Hml. II, 2, 73. Per. V Prol. 17.

Anoint (cf. *'noint*), to overspread with a liquid substance: *a. his eyes*, Mids. II, 1, 261. *I'll a. my sword*, Hml. IV, 7, 141. Especially to consecrate by unction: LLL III, 184. V, 2, 523. Wint. I, 2, 358. John III, 1, 136. R2 I, 2, 38. II, 1, 98. II, 3, 96. III, 2, 55. IV, 127. H4A IV, 3, 40. H4B Ind. 32. H6A V, 5, 91. H6C III, 1, 17. 76. 3, 29. R3 IV, 1, 62. 4, 150. V, 3, 124. Mcb. II, 3, 73. Lr. III, 7, 58 (always in the partic. *anointed*).

Anon, soon, presently, immediately after: *a. their loud alarums he doth hear*, Ven. 700. 869. Lucr. 433. Sonn. 33, 5. Pilgr. 79. 122. Tp. II, 2, 89. 147. Wiv. III, 2, 87. 3, 180. IV, 2, 41. 146. Meas. IV, 1, 23. 2, 162. 212. 5, 13. V, 364. Mids. II, 1, 17. III, 2, 18. 356. IV, 1, 183. V, 145. Merch. II, 2, 125. 9, 97. III, 5, 91. As II, 1, 52. Shr. Ind. 1, 130. All's I, 3, 133. IV, 1, 68. H4B III, 4, 187. H5 IV, 1, 26. H6A IV, 7, 19. H6B V, 1, 159. H6C III, 1, 2. R3 I, 4, 168. III, 1, 39. Rom. I, 4, 85. Mcb. V, 5, 34. Hml. V, 1, 309 etc. etc. Used as answer to a call: Rom. II, 2, 137. II, 4, 111. Mcb. II, 3, 22; especially by waiters, instead of the modern *'coming':* H4A II, 1, 5. 4, 29. 36. 41. 49. 58. 63. 72. 97. H4B II, 4, 306.

Used instead of a repeated *sometimes*, *now*, or *then*: *sometime he trots, anon he rears upright*, Ven. 279. *sometime he scuds far off, a. he starts*, 302. *sometimes they do extend their view right on, a. their gazes lend to every place*, Compl. 26. *now proud as an enjoyer and a. doubting the filching age will steal his treasure*, Sonn. 75, 5. *who now hangeth like a jewel in the ear of caelo, and a. falleth like a crab*, LLL IV, 2, 6. *now the ship boring the moon, and a. swallowed*, Wint. III, 3, 94. *then stops again, strikes his breast hard, and a. he casts his eye against the moon*, H8 III, 2, 117.

Ever and a. = e v e r y n o w a n d t h e n: *ever and a. they made a doubt*, LLL V, 2, 102. *a pouncetbox which ever and a. he gave his nose*, H4A I, 3, 38. In the same sense *still and a.: like the watchful minutes to the hour still and a. cheer'd up the heavy time*, John IV, 1, 47 (Corrupted to *still an end*, Gentl. IV, 4, 67).

Till a. = f o r a m o m e n t: Ant. II, 7, 44.

Another, 1) s o m e o r a n y e l s e: *no hope that way is a. way so high a hope*, Tp. II, 1, 241. Gentl. I, 1, 86. Err. I, 1, 113. Wiv. I, 1, 43 etc. etc. *Another while* = at other times, H6B IV, 10, 9. *Remember this a. day*, R3 I, 3, 299 (= one day). LLL IV, 1, 109.

2) s o m e b o d y o r a n y b o d y e l s e: *to choose love by —'s eyes*, Mids. I, 1, 140. Gentl. IV, 4, 23. Wiv. I, 4, 179 etc.

3) d i f f e r e n t: '*tis one thing to be tempted, a. thing to fall*, Meas. II, 1, 18. *I will wed thee in a. key*, Mids. I, 1, 18. III, 2, 388. Tw. III, 1, 119 etc.

4) a n e w, a s e c o n d: *thy sorrow to my sorrow lendeth a. power*, Lucr. 1677. *these blenches gave my heart a. youth*, Sonn. 110, 7. *to scale a. Hero's tower*, Gentl. III, 1, 119. *a. Hero*, Ado V, 4, 62. *I have received from her a. embassy of meeting*, Wiv. III, 5, 131. III, 3, 58. V, 5, 10. *four happy days bring in a. moon*, Mids. I, 1, 3. *enough to purchase such a. island*, H6B III, 3, 3. *you would be a. Penelope*, Cor. I, 3, 92. Ant. V, 2, 77 etc.

5) o n e m o r e: *a. storm brewing*, Tp. II, 1, 19. IV, 1, 244. Gentl. I, 2, 103. II, 1, 135. Wiv. II, 2, 97. Err. II, 2, 64. Wint. IV, 4, 290 etc. *Another time* = once more, Tp. III, 2, 85. *such a. trick*, Tp. IV, 1, 37. Wiv. III, 5, 7. As IV, 1, 40. *such a. proof*, Gentl. I, 1, 97. *be choked with such a. emphasis!* Ant. I, 5, 68.

6) a s e c o n d o f t h e s a m e s o r t o r s e t: *my cousin's a fool, and thou art a.* (= art so too), Ado III, 4, 11. *Leonatus! a banished rascal; and he's a., whatsoever he be*, Cymb. II, 1, 43. *I'll get me one of such a. length*, Gentl. III, 1, 133. *one heat a. expels*, II, 4, 91. *one drunkard loves a.* LLL IV, 3, 50.

It is such a. Nan! = an arch girl, a wicked little Anne! (Germ. auch so eine) Wiv. I, 4, 160. *Benedick was such a.* Ado III, 4, 87. *the prince himself is such a.* H4B II, 4, 275. *you are such a. woman* (Q *such a woman*) Troil. I, 2, 282. *you are such a.* 296. '*tis such a. fitchew*, Oth. IV, 1, 150.

7) = t h e o t h e r: *as you have one eye upon my follies, turn a. into the register of your own*, Wiv. II, 2, 193. *a pair of boots, one buckled, a. laced*, Shr. III, 2, 46. *sometimes her head on one side, some a.* Wint. III, 3, 20. *she had one eye declined, a. elevated*, V, 2, 82. *with one hand on his dagger, a. spread on's breast*, H8 I, 2, 205. Gentl. I, 2, 128. Sonn. 144, 12. Err. V, 425. Ado II, 3, 224. Mids. III, 2, 359. Merch. I, 2, 89. Wint. IV, 4, 176. H4B II, 4, 63. H6C II, 5, 10. Troil. III, 2, 206. Oth. I, 3, 331. Lr. III, 7, 71.

8) *One another*, either separated by other words (as in All's IV, 1, 20. H4B II, 4, 63. V, 1, 86. Troil. III, 2, 206 etc.) or placed together, may as well be used of several persons or things (f. i. John IV, 2, 189. H6A III, 1, 82. Oth. I, 2, 42) as of two: Wiv. I, 1, 257. II, 2, 132. V, 2, 5. 7. Ado III, 2, 80. As V, 2, 39. Tw. III, 4, 214. Wint. V, 2, 13. R2 IV, 185. H6B IV, 7, 139. R3 IV, 3, 10. — *One with another* = pellmell: *he loves . . . both young and old, one with a.* Wiv. II, 1, 118.

Peculiar repetition of the article: *another such a night*, R3 I, 4, 5.

Anselme, name in Rom. I, 2, 68.

Answer, subst., 1) t h a t w h i c h i s s a i d i n r e t u r n, reply: Lucr. 1664. Tp. I, 2, 309. Gentl. I, 1, 81. Wiv. I, 1, 261. Err. II, 2, 13. Lr. IV, 2, 6 etc. etc. Followed by *to*: John II, 44. Merch. I, 3, 11. H6A V, 3, 150. H6B I, 2, 80. IV, 4, 7 etc. Plur.: Mids. III, 2, 287. LLL I, 2, 31. '*His a.*' is ordinarily the answer which he gives, (f. i. Merch. I, 3, 11), but sometimes also the answer which he receives: Merch. II, 7, 72. IV, 1, 52. Tw. I, 5, 282. Cymb. II, 4, 30. *To make a.:* Sonn. 101, 5. Ado III, 3, 50. John II, 121. R2 IV, 20 (*what a. shall I make to this base man?*). H6A V, 3, 150. H6B I, 2, 80. IV, 4, 7, H6C IV, 1, 91. Hml. I, 2, 215. Ant. II, 7, 107.

As an answer may imply a declaration of will and purpose (LLL V, 2, 849. Merch. I, 3, 8 etc.), *to give a. of sth.* is equivalent to *to declare one's meaning about sth.: is not this the day that Hermia should give a. of her choice?* Mids. IV, 1, 141. *I descend to give thee a. of thy just demand*, H6A V, 3, 144.

2) a c c o u n t: *nothing of your a.* Meas. II, 4, 73. *to make your a. before him* III, 2, 165. *thus bound to your a.* Ado V, 1, 233. *let me go no farther to mine a.* 237. *this is not laid to thy a.* Wint. III, 2, 200. *for your days of a.* R2 IV, 159. *he'll call you to so hot an a. of it*, H5 II, 4, 123. *call these foul offenders to their —s*, H6B II, 1, 203. *brought him to his a.*, H8 IV, 2, 14. *follow to the a.* Cor. III, 1, 177. *I know my answer must be made*, Caes. I, 3, 114.

Very near to, and almost coincident with, this signification is that of a t o n e m e n t, r e p a r a t i o n for an offence, punishment: *arrest them to the a. of the law*, H5 II, 2, 143. *render'd to your public laws at heaviest a.* Tim. V, 4, 63. *whose a. would be death*, Cymb. IV, 4, 13.

3) r e t u r n, r e t a l i a t i o n: *Great the slaughter is here made by the Roman; great the a. be Britons must take*, Cymb. V, 3, 79. *in a. of which claim*, H5 I, 2, 249. Especially, as it is explained in Hml. V, 2, 176, the "*opposition of one's person in trial*," in consequence of an offence or a challenge: *it may be his envy is a gentleman of great sort, quite from the a. of his degree*, H5 IV, 7, 142. *and wake him to the a.* Troil. I, 3, 332. *if your lordship would vouchsafe the a.* Hml. V, 2, 176. *he'll not feel wrongs that tie him to an a.* Lr. IV, 2, 14.

In fencing it is the c o m i n g i n or s t r i k i n g i n r e t u r n after having parried or received a hit: *on the a. he pays you as surely*, Tw. III, 4, 305. *if Hamlet give the first or second hit, or quit in a. of the third exchange*, Hml. V, 2, 280.

Answer, vb., 1) to r e p l y; a) absolutely: Gentl. I, 3, 91. II, 2, 13. 7, 89. Meas. I, 2, 18. III, 1,

136. Err. II, 2, 195. V, 89. Ado II, 1, 114. H8 V, 3, 163 etc.

b) *to a. one:* Lucr. 1459. Wiv. IV, 1, 20. Err. I, 2, 77. II, 2, 12. IV, 1, 60. Mids. III, 2, 18. H5 V, 2, 319. H6C III, 3, 66 etc. = to serve one well, to turn one off with a reply: *I am not able to a. the Welsh flannel,* Wiv. V, 5, 172. *I am —ed,* LLL I, 2, 33. *the clerk is —ed,* Ado II, 1, 115. *are you —ed?* Merch. IV, 1, 62. *how a beggar should be —ed,* 440. *an you will not be —ed with reason,* As II, 7, 100. *must she not then be —ed?* (i.e. acquiesce in that answer) Tw. II, 4, 95. *to a. one to sth.: a. me unto this question,* H4A II, 3, 88. *a. me to what I ask you,* Mcb. IV, 1, 60.

c) *to a. to one* = to reply to one: *what canst thou a. to my majesty?* H6B IV, 7, 29. *a. to us,* Cor. III, 3, 61.

d) *to a. sth.* = to reply to sth.: *which heavily he —s with a groan,* Sonn. 50, 11. *I will a. it straight,* Wiv. I, 1, 118. Mids. III, 1, 12. Merch IV, 1, 42. V, 299. H4A I, 3, 66. H6A III, 1, 7. H6B IV, 10, 56. H6C III, 3, 259. Rom. II, 4, 10. Ant. III, 6, 30. *a. me one doubt,* H6C III, 3, 238. Metaphorically = to return: *she —ed my affection,* Wiv. IV, 6, 10. *they cannot a. my distress,* Tit. III, 1, 38. *—ed my steps too loud* (resounded too loud) Cymb. IV, 2, 215.

e) *to a. sth* = to say sth. in answer: *what canst thou a.?* H6B IV, 7, 29. *what —-s Clarence?* H6C IV, 6, 45.

f) *to a. to sth.: a. to this,* Meas. II, 4, 60. Ado IV, 1, 86. All's II, 2, 57. IV, 3, 145. H6C IV, 6, 45. V, 5, 21. Rom. II, 5, 35. = to yield answer on occasion of a peculiar address: *they will not a. to that epithet,* LLL V, 2, 170. *to make you a. truly to your name,* Ado IV, 1, 80. *I a. to that name,* V, 4, 73. *Coriolanus he would not a. to,* Cor. V, 1, 12. Again, to yield answer on occasion of certain questions: *you have —ed to his reputation with the duke and to his valour: what is his honesty?* All's IV, 3, 277. *where we may leisurely each one demand and a. to his part performed,* Wint. V, 3, 153.

2) to reply to one who calls or knocks at the door, to open: *I pray you, a. him,* Meas. I, 4, 14 (cf. v. 8). *knock but at the gate, and he himself will a.* H4B I, 1, 6. Metaphorically: *a. your summons,* Tp. IV, 131. *tapsters —ing every call,* Ven. 849.

3) to agree with, to correspond: *let it a. every strain for strain,* Ado V, 1, 12. *since the heavens have shaped my body so, let hell make crook'd my mind to a. it,* H6C V, 6, 79. *if seconds had —ed him* (= had done like him) Cymb. V, 3, 91. *if thy sweet virtue a. not thy show,* Sonn. 93, 14. *to a. his desire,* Lucr. 1606. Ven. Ded. 7. Tp. I, 2, 190. Meas. III, 1, 253. 2, 269. V, 415. Ado II, 1, 241. 376. Err. III, 1, 20. Troil. I, 3, 15. Oth. I, 3, 278. Cymb. V, 5, 450. Followed by *to: that the place a. to convenience,* Meas. III, 1, 258. *you bear it as —ing to the weight,* Ant. V, 2, 102. *doublet, hat, hose, all that a. to them,* Cymb. III, 4, 173. *if this but a. to my just belief,* Per. V, 1, 239. Absolutely: *I could not a. in that course of honour,* All's V, 3, 98, = act according to her invitation.

4) to satisfy: *our hopes are —ed,* Caes. V, 1, 1. *a. me to-morrow,* Meas. II, 4, 167. As II, 7, 99. Hence = to perform: *to a. other business,* Tp. I, 2, 367. *to a. matters of this consequence,* H5 II, 4, 146. And = to pay: *her audit, though delay'd, —ed must be,*

Sonn. 126, 11. *that praise which Collatine doth owe enchanted Tarquin —s,* Lucr. 83. Err. IV, 1, 82. Wint. V, 3, 8. H4A I, 3, 185. H4B V, 1, 27. H6C II, 6, 55. Cor. V, 6, 67. Ant. III, 12, 33. And intr.: *to bring me down must a. for your raising?* Alls II, 3, 120.

5) To render account: *thou art come to a. a stony adversary,* Merch. IV, 1, 3. H4A II, 4, 565. Cor. III, 1, 162. 325. And hence = to face, to match: *dare as well a. a man,* Ado V, 1, 89. *how we shall a. him,* John V, 7, 60. *all these bold fears I have —ed,* H4B IV, 5, 197. *here I stand to a. thee,* H6C II, 2, 96. *who shall a. him?* Troil. II, 1, 139. *if Hector will to morrow be —ed,* Troil. III, 3, 35 (met in combat). *ready to a. us,* Cor. I, 2, 19. *to a. all the city,* 4, 52. *he will a. the letter's master,* Rom. II, 4, 11. *to a. perils,* Caes. IV, 1, 47. *to a. this extremity of the skies,* Lr. III, 4, 106. V, 3, 152. Ant. III, 13, 27. Irregular construction: *unless you undertake that with me which with as much safety you might a. him,* Tw. III, 4, 273. Absolutely = to be ready for combat: *to a. royally in our defences,* H5 II, 4, 3. *arming to a. in a night alarm,* Troil. I, 3, 171. *while you have throats to a.* Tim. V, 1, 182. *—ing before we do demand of them,* Caes. V, 1, 6 (a quibble). *we will a. on their charge,* 24.

6) not to let slip, to profit by: *a. the time of request,* Alls I, 1, 168. *a. the vantage of his anger,* Cor. II, 3, 267.

7) to render account of: *I shall a. that better to the commonwealth than you ...* Merch. III, 5, 40. Meas. II, 1, 39. IV, 2, 129. *it would scarce be —ed,* Tw. III, 3, 28. Wint. I, 2, 83. H4A III, 3, 198. H6B II, 1, 41. III, 1, 133. IV, 7, 47. Tit. II, 3, 298. Hml. III, 4, 176. Lr. I, 3, 10. Cymb. III, 5, 42. Followed by *for: we that have good wits have much to a. for,* As V, 1, 13. Absolutely = to be responsible: *only thus far you shall a.* Cymb. I, 4, 170.

8) to warrant, to be answerable for: *I'll a. the coinage,* H4A IV, 2, 8. *a. my life my judgment,* Lr. I, 1, 153. 3, 10. II, 2, 154.

9) to atone for: *this shall be —ed,* Wiv. I, 1, 117. *—ing one foul wrong,* Meas. II, 2, 103. III, 2, 188. IV, 3, 172. Err. IV, 3, 31. Tw. III, 3, 33. John IV, 2, 89. H6A I, 3, 52. R3 IV, 2, 96. Caes. III, 2, 85. Ant. V, 2, 178. Followed by *for: if the first had —ed for his deed,* Meas. II, 2, 93. *could all but a. for that peevish brat?* R3 I, 3, 194.

Answerable, 1) correspondent: *it was a violent commencement, and thou shalt see an a. sequestration,* Oth. I, 3, 351. *all things a. to this portion,* Shr. II, 361.

2) responsible: *he shall be a.* H4A II, 4, 571.

Answered, adj. furnished with an answer: *be simple a.* Lr. III, 7, 43 (Qq *answerer*).

Answerer, one who answers: *be simple a., for we know the truth,* Lr. III, 7, 43 (Ff. *answered*).

Ant, emmet: H4A III, 1, 149. Lr. II, 4, 68.

Antenor, name of a Trojan: Troil. I, 2, 206. III, 1, 148. 3, 18 etc.

Antenorides, name of a gate of Troy: Troil. Prol. 17 (Ff. *Antenonidus*).

Anthem, a song performed as part of divine service: H4B I, 2, 213; and then in general a solemn and mournful song: Ven. 839. Phoen. 21. Gentl. III, 1, 240.

Anthonio, v. *Antonio.*

Anthonius, v. *Antonius*.

Anthony, v. *Antony*.

Anthropophagi, man-eaters, cannibals: Oth. I, 3, 144 (seemingly used as a noun proper, and defined by '*Cannibals that each other eat*').

Anthropophaginian, a word used, but, it should seem, not understood by the host in Wiv. IV, 5, 10.

Antiates, inhabitants of Antium: Cor. I, 6, 53. 59. III, 3, 4. V, 6, 80.

Antic (O. Edd. promiscuously *antick* and *antique*, but always accented on the first syllable), adj. 1) belonging to the times, or resembling the manners of antiquity: *show me your image in some a. book*, Sonn. 59, 7. *in him those holy a. hours are seen*, Sonn. 68, 9. 106, 7. *the constant service of the a. world*, As II, 3, 57. *the senators of the a. Rome*, H5 V Chor. 26. *an a. Roman*, Hml. V, 2, 352.

2) ancient: *in this the a. and well noted face of plain old form is much disfigured*, John IV, 2, 21. *the dust on a. time would lie unswept*, Cor. II, 3, 126. *a handkerchief, an a. token*, Oth. V, 2, 216.

3) old and quaintly figured: *stretched metre of an a. song*, Sonn. 17, 12. *I never may believe these a. fables*, Mids. V, 3. *an oak whose a. root peeps out*, As II, 1, 31. *that old and a. song*, Tw. II, 4, 3. *while you perform your a. round*, Mcb. IV, 1, 130. *his a. sword*, Hml. II, 2, 491.

4) odd, fantastic, foolish: *draw no lines there with thine a. pen*, Sonn. 19, 10. *cover'd with an a. face*, Rom. I, 5, 58. *the pox of such a. fantasticoes*, II, 4, 29. *to put an a. disposition on*, Hml. I, 5, 172.

Antic, subst., 1) odd and fantastic appearance: *there appears quick-shifting —s*, Lucr. 459. LLL V, 1, 119 (Armado mistakes the word). 154. *were he the veriest a. in the world*, Shr. Ind. 1, 101.

2) a buffoon, practising odd gesticulations: *drawing of an a.* Ado III, 1, 63. *and there the a. sits*, R2 III, 2, 162. *old father a. the law*, H4A I, 2, 69. *three such —s*, H5 III, 2, 32. *thou a. death*, H6A IV, 7, 18. *like witless —s*, Troil. V, 3, 86.

Antic, vb., to make appear like a buffoon: *the wild disguise hath almost anticked us all*, Ant. II, 7, 132.

Anticipate, to act or come before others: *here art thou in appointment fresh and fair, —ing time*, Troil. IV, 5, 2. *whose footing here —s our thoughts*, Oth. II, 1, 76. Hence = to prevent by acting before: *to a. the ills that were not*, Sonn. 118, 9. *time, thou —st my dread exploits*, Mcb. IV, 1, 144.

Anticipation, the acting before another: *so shall my a. prevent your discovery*, Hml. II, 2, 304.

Antick, v. *antic*.

Anticly, oddly, fantastically: Ado V, 1, 96.

Antidote, medicine: *trust not the physician; his —s are poison*, Tim. IV, 3, 435. *with some a. cleanse the stuff'd bosom*, Mcb. V, 3, 43.

Antigonus, name in Wint. II, 3, 42. III, 3, 27. 98. V, 1, 42 etc.

Antioch, the famous town in Syria: Per. Prol. 17. I, 1, 134, and passim.

Antiochus, name of the king of Antioch: Per. Prol. 17. I, 1, 3, and passim.

Antiopa, an Amazon and daughter of Mars, in love with Theseus: Mids. II, 1, 80.

Antipathy, natural aversion: *no contraries hold more a.* Lr. II, 2, 93.

Antipholus, name of the twin brothers in Err. II, 2, 112. III, 2, 2. 170. IV, 1, 8. 3, 45. V, 13 etc. Plur. *Antipholuses* after the writing of M. Edd.; O. Edd. *Antipholus*, as it is required by the metre: V, 357.

Antipodes, the people living on the opposite side of the globe: Ado II, 1, 273. Mids. III, 2, 55. Merch. V, 127. R2 III, 2, 49. H6C I, 4, 135.

Antiquary, adj. full of old lore: *instructed by the a. times*, Troil. II, 3, 262.

Antique and **Antiquely**, v. *antic* and *anticly*.

Antiquity, 1) old age: *beated and chopp'd with tann'd a.* Sonn. 62, 10. 108, 12. *bald with dry a.* As IV, 3, 106. *hadst thou not the privilege of a.* All's II, 3, 220. *every part about you blasted with a.* H4B I, 2, 208.

2) ancient date, long standing: *bawd is he doubtless, and of a. too*, Meas. III, 2, 72.

3) ancient time: *a. forgot, custom not known*, Hml. IV, 5, 104. In the plur. = remains of ancient times: *to spoil —ies of hammer'd steel*, Lucr. 951.

Antium, town in old Latium and capital of the Volsci: Cor. III, 1, 11. IV, 4, 1 etc.

Antoniad, name of the flag-ship of Antony: Ant. III, 10, 2.

Antonio (in this and the two following names O. Edd. now *th*, now *t*; M. Edd. throughout without an *h*); 1) brother of Prospero: Tp. I, 2, 66. 129. V, 264. 2) father of Proteus in Gentl. II, 4, 54. 3) brother of Leonato in Ado II, 1, 117. 4) father of Petruchio in Shr. I, 2, 54. II, 68. 5) son of the duke of Florence in All's III, 5, 79. 6) the merchant of Venice, passim in Merch. 7) the sea-captain in Tw. II, 1, 16. 35. III, 3, 13 etc.

In O. Edd. the name of the Roman triumvir is repeatedly spelt *Antonio*, which M. Edd. have constantly changed to *Antonius*: Caes. I, 2, 3. 4. 190. I, 3, 37. Ant. II, 2, 7. II, 5, 26.

Antonius, a form frequently introduced into the text by M. Edd. (cf. *Antonio*), used by O. Edd. only in Ant. I, 1, 56. II, 6, 119 (*Marcus Anthonius*); III, 1, 25.

Antony, 1) the Roman triumvir: H5 III, 6, 15. Mcb. III, 1, 57. Caes. I, 2, 29. 204 etc. Ant. I, 1, 19 etc. 2) A. Woodville, brother of Queen Elizabeth in R3 I, 1, 67. 3) A. duke of Brabant: H5 IV, 8, 101. 4) brother of Leonato, else called Antonio: Ado V, 1, 91. 100. 5) A. Dull, the constable in LLL I, 1, 271. 273. 6) a servant in Rom. I, 5, 11.

Antre, cavern: Oth. I, 3, 140.

Anvil, iron block for the use of smiths: John IV, 2, 194. Cor. IV, 5, 116 (*the a. of my sword*).

Any, pron., whoever or whatever it may be; of the same sense and use as now-a-days: *by a. other house or person*, Tp. I, 2, 42. *had I been a. god of power*, 10. II, 1, 161. 2, 19. 72. 108. 177 (*without a. more talking*). III, 3, 34. Gentl. III, 1, 30, etc. In a negative sentence: Tp. I, 2, 31. 352. III, 1, 55 etc. Passing into the sense of every: *tell the clock to a. business*, Tp. II, 1, 289. 2, 32. III, 2, 129. Gentl. III, 1, 11. 134. II, 4, 53. Wiv. IV, 2, 26. Ado III, 3, 169. Mids. I, 2, 73. H4A II, 2, 16 (*a. time* = every moment). R3 I, 4, 145. Ven. 354 etc.

Any thing, in O. Edd. always in two words: Tp. I, 1, 71. 2, 43. Gentl. IV, 1, 42 etc. = everything: *my horse, my ox, my a.* Shr. III, 2, 234. Merch. III, 2, 33. R3 I, 1, 89. Err. V, 144 etc. *shall it be so?*

Any thing (= whatever you please) Wiv. III, 3, 249. *Lord Alexas, sweet Alexas, most any thing Alexas,* Ant. I, 2, 1. *for any thing I know,* H4B V, 5, 146.

Any body also always in two words: Wiv. I, 4, 4. III, 3, 224. Meas. IV, 1, 16 etc. etc.

Any for *anybody: is there a. longs to see ...* As I, 2, 149. *whiles a. speaks that fought with us,* H5 IV, 3, 66. Meas. I, 1, 13. 23. Gentl. V, 4, 4. II, 4, 154. Err. I, 1, 17. II, 2, 211. Lr. I, 4, 246.

Any for anything: *if there be a. of him left, I'll bury it,* Wint. III, 3, 136 (the Clown speaks). *hast a. more of this?* Tp. II, 2, 137.

Joined to the superlative: *as common as a. the most vulgar thing,* Hml. I, 2, 99. *less attemptable than a. the rarest of our ladies,* Cymb. I, 4, 65.

Joined to comparatives of adverbs: *if you trouble him a. more,* Tp. III, 2, 55. *to slander music a. more,* Ado II, 3, 47. Wint. II, 2, 35. IV, 4, 506. R2 III, 2, 208. Troil. II, 1, 129. *You are not to go loose a. longer,* Wiv. IV, 2, 128. Gentl. II, 3, 39. Merch. II, 2, 120. — *shall be a. further afflicted,* Wiv. IV, 2, 233. Cor. I, 1, 1. Caes. I, 2, 45. 167.

Any where (in two words): Wint. III, 3, 68. Rom. II Chor. 12. Mcb. II, 3, 93. Oth. III, 4, 3.

Ap, Welsh particle *(of?):* Rice ap Thomas, R3 IV, 5, 12.

Apace, at a quick pace, fast, quickly: *and homeward runs a.* Ven. 813. Tp. V, 64. Mids. I, 1, 2. As III, 3, 1. Shr. IV, 3, 52. Wint. II, 1, 16. John V, 2, 65. H4A V, 2, 90. H5 IV, 8, 3. R3 II, 4, 13. Rom. II, 4, 233. III, 2, 1. Caes. V, 3, 87. Mcb. III, 3, 6. Lr. IV, 7, 94. Ant. I, 3, 50. IV, 14, 41. V, 2, 325. In speaking of approaching time, almost = soon: *our nuptial hour draws on a.* Mids. I, 1, 2. *Sunday comes a.* Shr. II, 324. *that hour approaches a.* All's IV, 3, 36. *the future comes a.* Tim. II, 2, 157. Of running blood and tears = fast: *I bleed a.* Lr. III, 7, 97. Ant. IV, 7, 6. *each cheek a river downward flow'd a.* Compl. 284. — *To speak a.* = to speak quickly, As III, 2, 208; but also = to speak at random: *you are pleasant, and speak a.* Meas. III, 2, 120. *here they stay'd an hour, and talk'd a.* LLL V, 2, 369.

Apart, 1) separately, by one's self: *stay, stand a.; I know not which is which,* Err. V, 364. *I keep it lonely, a.* Wint. V, 3, 18. *each man a., all single and alone,* Tim. V, 1, 110. *resolve yourselves a.* (= without me), Mcb. III, 1, 137. *Caesar's will? hear it a.* (not in the presence of others) Ant. III, 13, 47. *some nobler token I have kept a.* (not put in the inventory, kept back) Ant. V, 2, 168.

2) at or to a distance from the other company, or from the place in question, off, back: *go a., Adam, and thou shalt hear how he will shake me up,* As I, 1, 29. *to put a. these your attendants* (= to send away) Wint. II, 2, 14. *stand all a.* (= stand back) R2 III, 3, 187. H6B III, 2, 242. R3 IV, 2, 1. Oth. IV, 1, 75. *drew myself a.* Tit. V, 1, 112. *In private will I talk with thee a.* H6A I, 2, 69. *get thee a. and weep,* Caes. III, 1, 282. *to draw a. the body,* Hml. IV, 1, 24. *go but a.* (withdraw with me), Hml. IV, 5, 203. *to draw the Moor a.* Oth. II, 3, 391. *go with me a., I will withdraw,* III, 3, 476. *a. upon our knees* (= let us withdraw and fall on our knees) Cymb. IV, 2, 288.

3) aside: *thy godhead laid a.* As IV, 3, 44. *all*

reverence set a. to him, John III, 1, 159. *lay a. the borrowed glories,* H5 II, 4, 78. *to lay a. their particular functions,* III, 7, 41. *to lay his gay comparisons a.* Ant. 3, 13, 26. *Henry put a.* (made away with) H6B III, 1, 383.

Ape, the animal Simia: Tp. II, 2, 9. IV, 249. Meas. II, 2, 120. Err. II, 2, 200. Ado V, 1, 205. LLL III, 85. 90. 96. IV, 2, 131. H4B II, 2, 77. R3 III, 1, 130. Cor. I, 4, 36. Caes. V, 1, 41. Hml. IV, 2, 19 (Qq *apple). Apes* and *monkeys* are put together with no discernible difference: *on meddling monkey, or on busy a.* Mids. II, 1, 181. *more new-fangled than an a., more giddy in my desires than a monkey,* As IV, 1, 153. —*s and monkeys 'twixt two such shes would ...,* Cymb. I, 6, 39.

Term of reproach: *boys,* —*s, braggarts,* Ado V, 1, 91. *out, you mad-headed a.* H4A II, 3, 80. *this is the a. of form,* LLL V, 2, 325. — *s of idleness,* H4B IV, 5, 123 (= formal, idle apes). Cymb. IV, 2, 194.

Term of endearment: *poor a., how thou sweatest! H6B II, 4, 234. the a. is dead, and I must conjure him,* Rom. II, 1, 16.

Symbol of imitativeness: *Julio Romano would beguile Nature of her custom, so perfectly he is her a.* Wint. V, 2, 108. *O sleep, thou a. of death,* Cymb. II, 2, 31.

To lead apes in hell was the punishment of old maids: Ado II, 1, 43. 49. Shr. II, 34.

A fable now unknown alluded to: *unpeg the basket on the house's top, let the birds fly, and like the famous a., to try conclusions, in the basket creep, and break your own neck down,* Hml. III, 4, 194 (we are perhaps to think of a dove-cote on the top of a house).

Ape-bearer, one who leads about apes: Wint. IV, 3, 101.

Apemantus, name of the Cynic in Tim. I, 1, 62. 181 etc. etc.

Apennines, the mountains of Italy: John I, 202.

A-piece, to the part or share of each: *cost me two shilling a.* Wiv. I, 1, 160. *sixteen businesses, a month's length a.* All's IV, 3, 99. *four bonds of forty pounds a.* H4A III, 3, 117. *an hundred ducats a.* Hml. II, 2, 383.

Apish, like an ape: *proud, fantastical, a., shallow,* As III, 2, 432. *this a. and unmannerly approach,* John V, 2, 131. *with French nods and a. courtesy,* R3 I, 3, 49. *their manners are so a.* Lr. I, 4, 184. Imitative like an ape: *our tardy a. nation,* R2 II, 1, 22.

Apollo, the famous God of ancient Greece: Troil. I, 3, 328. II, 2, 79. Tit. IV, 1, 67. 4, 15. Lr. I, 1, 162. God of music and song: LLL IV, 3, 343. V, 2, 941. Shr. Ind. 2, 37. Troil. III, 3, 305. of art and letters: Per. II, 2, 67. of light and the sun (cf. *Phoebus):* Wint. IV, 4, 30. of prophecy (by the Delphian oracle): Wint. II, 1, 183. 3, 200. III, 1, 14. 2, 117 sq. V, 1, 37. In love with Daphne: Mids. II, 1, 231. Shr. Ind. 2, 61. Troil. I, 1, 101.

Apollodorus, name of the Greek who carried Cleopatra to Caesar, Ant. II, 6, 68.

Apology, excuse: *there needs no such a.* R3 III, 7, 104. LLL V, 1, 142. V, 2, 597. All's II, 4, 51. Rom. I, 4, 2. In Lucr. 31 it is evidently used in the sense of encomium, high praise: *what needeth then —ies be made, to set forth that which is so singular?*

Apoplexed, affected with apoplexy: *but sure, that sense is a.* Hml. III, 4, 73.

Apoplexy, sudden stop of sense and voluntary motion, from an affection of the brains: H4B I, 2, 123. 126. IV, 4, 130. Cor. IV, 5, 239.

Apostle, disciple of Christ: H6B I, 3, 60. R3 V, 3, 216.

Apostropha (O. Edd. *apostrapha*) contraction of a word by omission of a letter: *you find not the —s, and so miss the accent,* LLL IV, 2, 123.

Apothecary, one who sells drugs for medicinal uses: H6B III, 3, 17. Rom. V, 1, 37. 57. V, 3, 119. Lr. IV, 6, 133.

Appal, 1) to strike with extreme fear: *—s her senses and her spirit confounds,* Ven. 882. Troil. IV, 5, 4. V, 5, 15. Mcb. II, 2, 58. III, 4, 60. Hml. II, 2, 590.

2) to abate, destroy (cf. *pall*): *property was thus —ed, that the self was not the same,* Phoen. 37. *methinks, your looks are sad, your cheer —ed,* H6A I, 2, 48.

Apparel (cf. *'parel*), subst., dress: Wiv. III, 3, 78. V, 5, 204. Meas. IV, 2, 46. Ado II, 1, 37. 263. III, 3, 127. 149. Mids. III, 2, 29. IV, 2, 36. Merch. II, 5, 5. As II, 4, 5. III, 2, 243. IV, 1, 88. Shr. Ind. 1, 60. I, 1, 234. II, 317. 354. III, 2, 71. IV, 2, 64. All's IV, 3, 167. Wint. IV, 3, 65. 111. R2 III, 3, 149. V, 2, 66. H4B I, 2, 20. III, 2, 154. 350. H6B IV, 7, 106. Caes. I, 1, 8. Hml. I, 3, 72. Cymb. III, 5, 156. Ornamental dress: *and puts a. on my tatter'd loving,* Sonn. 26, 11.

Apparel, vb., to dress: *I will a. them all in one livery,* H6B IV, 2, 80. *a. thy head,* LLL V, 1, 104 (it is Armado that speaks). *and are —ed thus, like Muscovites,* LLL V, 2, 120. Err. IV, 3, 14. Shr. III, 2, 76. To put in a showy dress: *a. vice like virtue's harbinger,* Err. III, 2, 12. Ado IV, 1, 229. Shr. III, 2, 91. H6A II, 4, 22. Per. I, 1, 12.

Apparent, adj. 1) seeming: *thy strange a. cruelty,* Merch. IV, 1, 21. *it should be put to no a. likelihood of breach,* R3 II, 2, 136. *and is no less a. to the vulgar eye,* Cor. IV, 7, 20. *these a. prodigies,* Caes. II, 1, 198.

2) visible: *by some a. sign let us have knowledge,* H6A II, 1, 3.

3) evident, obvious: *one cannot climb it without a. hazard of his life,* Gentl. III, 1, 116. *is it now a.? Most manifest.* Meas. IV, 2, 144. Wint. I, 2, 270. John IV, 2, 93. R2 I, 1, 13. IV, 124. H4A I, 2, 65. II, 4, 292. H6A IV, 2, 26. 5, 44. R3 II, 2, 130. III, 5, 30. Tit. II, 3, 292. Cymb. II, 4, 56. Caes. II, 1, 198.

4) certain (*heir*): H4A I, 2, 65. = presumptive: H6B I, 1, 152. Per. III Prol. 37. cf. *Heir-apparent.*

Apparent, subst., apparent heir: *as a. to the crown,* H6C II, 2, 64. Figuratively one who has a claim to sth.: *next to thyself, he's a. to my heart,* Wint. I, 2, 177.

Apparently, evidently: *if he should scorn me so a.* Err. IV, 1, 78.

Apparition, significative appearance: *amazed at —s, signs and prodigies,* Ven. 926. *a thousand blushing —s to start into her face,* Ado IV, 1, 161. Especially sight of a spirit or spectre: *fine a.* Tp. I, 2, 317. *this monstrous a.* Caes. IV, 3, 277. Hml. I, 1, 28. I, 2, 211.

Appay, to pay, satisfy: *thou art well appaid*

as well to hear as grant what he hath said, Lucr. 914.

Appeach, to impeach, inform against: *I will a. the villain,* R2 V, 2, 79. 102. Absolutely: *your passions have to the full —ed,* All's I, 3, 197, i. e. informed against you.

Appeal, vb., to refer to a superior judge; absolutely: *or we a. and from thy justice fly,* Cymb. V, 4, 91. Followed by *to*: *to thee my heaved-up hands a.* Lucr. 638. Meas. I, 2, 179. Wint. III, 2, 46. H5 I, 2, 290. II, 2, 78. H6B II, 1, 190. H8 II, 4, 119.

2) to impeach: *if he a. the duke on ancient malice,* R2 I, 1, 9. 27. I, 3, 21.

Hence *appealed*, adjectively, = pertaining to an impeachment: *as for the rest appealed,* R2 I, 1, 142.

Appeal, subst., reference to a superior judge: Lucr. 293. Meas. V, 303. H4B IV, 1, 88. Followed by *to*: H8 II, 4, 234. V, 1, 152.

2) a plea put in before the judge: *my a. says I did strive to prove the constancy and virtue of your love,* Sonn. 117, 13.

4) impeachment: *to make good the boisterous a.* R2 I, 1, 4. IV, 45. 79. Ant. III, 5, 12.

Appellant (Qq ME. *appellant*), impeacher, accuser: R2 I, 1, 34. 3, 4. 52. IV, 104 (*Lords —s*). H6B II, 3, 49. 57.

Appear, 1) to be or become visible: *in each cheek —s a pretty dimple,* Ven. 242. *to make the truth a. where it seems hid,* Meas. V, 66. *graces will a.* Ado II, 1, 129. Ven. 1175. Lucr. 116. 458. 1382. 1434. Sonn. 102, 2. 103, 6. Compl. 93. Wiv. III, 3, 170. Ado I, 2, 22. Mids. I, 1, 185. II, 2, 32. V, 433. Merch. I, 3, 115. III, 2, 297. 4, 3 etc. *Appearing* = visible, H4B IV, 1, 82. *To a. to one* = to be seen by one, to show one's self: *men's faults do seldom to themselves a.* Lucr. 633. *a. to him, as he to me —s, all melting,* Compl. 299. *God's mother deigned to a. to me,* H6A I, 2, 78. Caes. V, 5, 17. *as it may a. unto you* = as you may well perceive, Ado III, 5, 55. Cor. I, 2, 22. Hml. I, 1, 101. Ant. III, 4, 33. *a. it to your mind* = call to mind, Troil. III, 3, 3.

Hence = to be conspicuous: *Aufidius will a. well in these wars,* Cor. IV, 3, 34. *there she —ed indeed,* Ant. II, 2, 193 (perhaps = she was an apparition, like a spirit or goddess).

2) to be or become evident: *it must a. that malice bears down truth,* Merch. IV, 1, 213. R2 I, 1, 26. H4A III, 3, 191. H6A II, 1, 36. H6C III, 3, 146. Hml. IV, 7, 5. Lr. I, 1, 4. With a following noun: *vows so born ... all truth —s,* Mids. III, 2, 125. *that my love may a. plain and free,* Gentl. V, 4, 82. Meas. II, 4, 78. III, 1, 93. Merch. II, 9, 73. IV, 1, 249. H6A II, 4, 20. *he shall a. to the envious a scholar,* Meas. III, 2, 154.

3) to come in sight, to stand in the presence of another: *my saucy bark on your broad main doth wilfully a.* Sonn. 80, 8. *a., and pertly!* Tp. IV, 58. *let her a.* Meas. V, 517. Ado IV, 2, 1. Tw. III, 4, 40. H6A V, 3, 7. Ant. III, 12, 1. *What art thou that darest a. to us* = come before us, Ant. V, 1, 5. *and by and by I shall to thee a.* = come to thee, Mids. III, 1, 89 (Bottom's speech). *to a. this morning to them* = meet them, Troil. V, 3, 69. Cor. I, 5, 21.

4) to seem: Sonn. 31, 7. 53, 11. Tp. I, 2, 497. Gentl. II, 4, 45. Wiv. II, 2, 230. III, 1, 73. Meas. II,

4, 30. III, 1, 213. V, 476. Err. III, 1, 16. IV, 3, 56. Mids. V, 257. H4B II, 1, 125. Caes. III, 1, 165 etc. etc. *This youth* ..... *—s he hath had good ancestors*, Cymb. IV, 2, 47. *How —s the fight?* = how seems the fight to go? Ant. III, 10, 8.

Appeared, adjectively, = apparent, percept-ible, discernible: *your favour is well appeared by your tongue*, Cor. IV, 3, 9 (Hanmer affeer'd; Warburton appeal'd; Jackson apparel'd; Collier ap-proved; Singer appayed).

Appearance, 1) visibleness: *chased your blood out of a.* H5 II, 2, 76. *bearing with frank a. their purposes toward Cyprus,* Oth. I, 3, 38. *there is no a. of fancy in him,* Ado III, 2, 31. *no man should possess him with any a. of fear,* H5 IV, 1, 116.

2) semblance: *had three times slain the a. of the king,* H4B I, 1, 128.

3) personal presence: *if she deny the a. of a naked blind boy in her naked seeing self,* H5 V, 2, 324. H6A V, 3, 8. H8 II, 4, 132. Oth. I, 2, 37 (cf. *not-appearance*).

4) presence, outside: *thy fair a.* Sonn. 46, 8. *you see what a ragged a. it is,* H4B III, 2, 279. *thou hast a grim a.* Cor. IV, 5, 66.

Appearer, one who has a certain appear-ance: *reverend a.* Per. V, 3, 18.

Appease, to put in a state of peace, to calm, to reconcile: *the Eternal's wrath's —d,* Gentl. V, 4, 81. H6B IV, 4, 42. H6C IV, 1, 34. R3 I, 4, 69. Tit. I, 126. Caes. III, 1, 179. Mcb. IV, 3, 17. Cymb. V, 4, 12. 5, 72.

Appellant, writing of Qq for *appealant*, q. v.

Appendix, something appended and con-comitant: *with your a.* (i. e. your bride) Shr. IV, 4, 104.

Apperil, peril, danger: *let me stay at thine a.* Tim. I, 2, 32.

Appertain, to belong to, to become: *all rites that a. unto a burial,* Ado IV, 1, 210. *a congruent epitheton —ing to thy young days,* LLL I, 2, 15. *the —ing rage to such a greeting,* Rom. III, 1, 66. Hence to concern: *I should know no secrets that a. to you,* Caes. II, 1, 282. *what most nearly —s to us both,* Lr. I, 1, 287.

Absolutely = to be incumbent: *ere supper-time must I perform much business —ing,* Tp. III, 1, 96.

Appertaining, subst. that which belongs to a person, external attribute: *the real habi-tude gave life and grace to —s and to ornament,* Compl. 115. *we lay by our —s,* Troil. II, 3, 87 (Ff *appertain-ments*).

Appertainment, the same: Troil. II, 3, 87 (Q *appertainings*).*

Appertinent, adj: belonging, becoming: *as an a. title to your old time,* LLL I, 2, 17. *all the other gifts a. to man are not worth a gooseberry,* H4B I, 2, 194.

Appertinent, subst. = appertainment: *to furnish him with all —s belonging to his honour,* H5 II, 2, 87.

Appetite, 1) desire of food: *to make our —s more keen,* Sonn. 118, 1. 56, 2. 147, 4. Meas. I, 3, 52. Ado II, 3, 247. Merch. II, 6, 9. Tw. I, 5, 98. Wint. II, 3, 16. R2 I, 3, 296. H4B II, 2, 11. H5 V, 1, 27. H8 III, 2, 203. Troil. III, 3, 238. Cor. I, 1, 182. Rom. II, 6, 13. Caes. I, 2, 306. Mcb. III, 4, 38. Lr. I, 1, 120.

Ant. II, 1, 25. Cymb. III, 6, 37. *dry a.* = thirst, Tit. III, 1, 14. This fundamental notion is in most cases retained, when the word indicates desire in general: *that surfeiting the a.* (i. e. the desire of hearing music) *may sicken,* Tw. I, 1, 3. II, 4, 100. Sonn. 110, 10. Troil. I, 3, 120. Cor. I, 1, 107.

2) Sensual desire: Lucr. 546. Wiv. I, 3, 73. Meas. II, 4, 176. Troil. II, 2, 181. Oth. III, 3, 270. Especially carnal lust: Ven. 34. Lucr. 9. Compl. 166. Meas. II, 4, 161. R3 III, 5, 81. Hml. I, 2, 144. Lr. IV, 6, 125. Oth. I, 3, 263. II, 1, 231. Ant. II, 2, 242. Cymb. I, 6, 43.

3) Caprice: *as her a. shall play the god with his weak function,* Oth. II, 3, 353. Will: *dexterity so obeying a.* Troil. V, 5, 27.

Plural *—s:* Sonn. 118, 1. H5 V, 1, 27 (Fluellen). Troil. II, 2, 181. Oth. III, 3, 270. Ant. II, 2, 242.

Applaud, 1) to receive with acclamations, to extol with shouts: *a. the name of Henry with your leader,* H6C IV, 2, 27. *till fields and blows and groans a. our sport,* H4A I, 3, 302. *enter like great triumphers in their —ing gates,* Tim. V, 1, 200. *I would a. thee to the very echo, that should a. again,* Mcb. V, 3, 53. *Caps, hands and tongues a. it to the clouds,* Hml. IV, 5, 107. *that heaven and earth may strike their sounds together, —ing our approach,* Ant. IV, 8, 39.

2) in a weaker sense = to praise, approve: *a. our loves,* Gentl. I, 3, 48. V, 4, 140. H6A II, 2, 36. Tit. I, 164. 321. IV, 2, 30. Mcb. III, 2, 46. Per. II, 5, 58.

Applause, acclamation, shout of appro-bation: *their loud a. and Aves vehement,* Meas. I, 1, 71. Merch. III, 2, 144. H4B I, 3, 91. R3 III, 7, 39. Troil. I, 3, 163. 379. Cor. I, 9, 64. Tit. I, 230. Caes. I, 2, 133 (*—s*).

Praise, approbation in general: *high com-mendation, true a. and love,* As I, 2, 275. Troil. I, 3, 59. II, 3, 211. III, 3, 119. Oth. II, 3, 293.

Apple, 1) the fruit of the apple-tree: Sonn. 93, 13. Tp. II, 1, 91. Merch. I, 3, 102. Shr. I, 1, 139. IV, 2, 101. Tw. I, 5, 167. V, 230. H5 III, 7, 155. H8 V, 4, 64. Lr. I, 5, 16.

2) the *a.* of the eye = eye-ball: *sink in a. of his eye,* Mids. III, 2, 104. *and laugh upon the a. of her eye,* LLL V, 2, 475 (i. e. perhaps: always laugh upon her, though she perhaps look another way?)

Apple-John, a sort of apple which keeps long, but becomes very withered: *I am withered like an old a.* H4A III, 3, 5. H4B II, 4, 2; and in what follows.

Apple-tart, a tart made of apples: *carved like an a.* Shr. IV, 3, 89.

Appliance, cure, medicament: *to tender it and my a.* All's II, 1, 116. *with all —s and means to boot,* H4B III, 1, 29. *that's the a. only which your disease requires,* H8 I, 1, 124. *diseases desperate grown by desperate a. are relieved,* Hml. IV, 3, 10. *who was by good a. recovered,* Per. III, 2, 86. Fi-guratively: *thou art too noble to conserve a life in base —s,* Meas. III, 1, 89, i. e. to preserve thy life by base remedies, by base means.

Application, cure, medicament: *the rest have worn me out with several —s,* All's I, 2, 74.

Apply, 1) trans. a) to make use of: *craft against vice I must a.* Meas. III, 2, 291. Lucr. 531.

LLL V, 2, 77. *to* sth: Compl. 303. Ven. 713. Tw. IV, 1, 13. Especially of medicaments: *to a. a moral medicine to a mortifying mischief*, Ado I, 3, 13. *I never did a. hot liquors in my blood*, As II, 3, 48. *a. to her some remedies*, Wint. III, 2, 153. H6B III, 2, 404. Cor. I, 6, 64. Lr. III, 7, 107. Cymb. I, 5, 21. Figuratively: —*ing fears to hopes, and hopes to fears*, Sonn. 119, 3. *there may be aught —ied which may her suffering ecstasy assuage*, Compl. 68. *what comfort to this great decay may come shall be —ied*, Lr. V, 3, 298.

b) *to put one thing to another: like usury, —ing wet to wet*, Compl. 40.

c) reflectively, *to employ or dedicate one's self: if you a. yourself to our intents*, Ant. V, 2, 126.

d) *to explain*, *moralize on: Nestor shall a. thy latest words*, Troil. I, 3, 32. *how a. you this?* Cor. I, 1, 151. *and these does she a. for warnings and portents*, Caes. II, 2, 80. cf. Ven. 713.

2) intr. a) *to dedicate*, *devote one's self: let your remembrance a. to Banquo*, Mcb. III, 2, 30. cf. Shr. I, 1, 19. b) *to be convenient*, *to agree with: would it a. well to the vehemency of your affection*, Wiv. II, 2, 247.

The preposition *to* omitted: *I'll a. your eye remedy*, Mids. III, 2, 450 (M. Edd. *to your eye*). *Virtue and that part of philosophy will I a.* Shr. I, 1, 19, where Hanmer, against the metre, proposed to read '*to virtue*.' Perhaps = ply, as appay = pay.

Appoint, 1) *to fix*, *to determine*, *to settle: let's a. him a meeting*, Wiv. II, 1, 97. —*ed them contrary places*, II, 1, 216. *the hour she —ed me*, III, 5, 66. III, 1, 95. IV, 4, 15. Meas. III, 1, 223. Mids. I, 1, 177. All's III, 7, 32. H4A I, 2, 190. Tit. IV, 4, 102. *I do a. him store of provender*, Caes. IV, 1, 30. In the passive voice either the person may be subject: *as he was —ed*, Ado III, 3, 171. *shall I be —ed hours*, Shr. I, 1, 103; or the thing: *here is the place —ed for the wrestling*, As I, 2, 154. *let these have a day —ed them*, H6B I, 3, 211. II, 3, 48. 4, 6. *as is —ed us*, H4A III, 1, 86.

Things may be fixed by mutual agreement, and so the word convey the sense of *to concert: as Anne and I had —ed*, Wiv. V, 5, 210. cf. III, 2, 55. IV, 6, 28. V, 1, 15.

2) *to establish by decree: to a. who should attend on him*, H8 I, 1, 74. *he did a. so*, Mcb. II, 3, 58. Hence *to choose*, *to designate*, *nominate* for an office: *being then —ed master of this design*, Tp. I, 2, 162. *to a. some of your council to sit with us*, H5 V, 2, 79. Wiv. I, 4, 124. *if I be —ed for the place*, H6B I, 3, 170. Cymb. III, 5, 10. And = *to order*, *to direct: I'll a. my men to carry the basket*, Wiv. IV, 2, 96. Ado II, 2, 17. Shr. IV, 4, 102. R2 I, 3, 45. H6B II, 4, 77. IV, 7, 45. R3 I, 1, 44. *I am —ed him to murder you*, Wint. I, 2, 412, where *him* is the dativus commodi. *To some retention and —ed guard*, Lr. V, 3, 47 (Ff. only: *to some retention*), i. e. to a guard expressly ordered to keep him.

3) *to furnish*, *to equip* (cf. *at point* s. v. *point*); at least in the participle *appointed: to have you royally —ed*, Wint. IV, 4, 603; in all other instances preceded or followed by *well: you may be armed and —ed well*, Tit. IV, 2, 16. *with well —ed powers*, H4B I, 1, 190. IV, 1, 25. H5 III Chor. 4. H6A IV,

2, 21. H6C II, 1, 113 (cf. *Disappointed*). Singular expression: *to appoint myself in this vexation*, Wint. I, 2, 326, = to dress myself in this vexation (cf. *drest in an opinion, attired in wonder, wrapt in fears* etc.)

Appointment, 1) assignation, stipulation: *I shall be with her by her own a.* Wiv. II, 2, 272. III, 1, 92. Hence = engagement: *I will then address me to my a.* Wiv. III, 5, 135. *to stead up your a.* Meas. III, 1, 261.* *my —s have in them a need*, All's II, 5, 72.

2) direction: *that good fellow follows my a.* H8 II, 2, 134.

3) equipment, furniture: *therefore your best a. make with speed*, Meas. III, 1, 60. *where we'll set forth in best a. all our regiments*, John II, 296. *our fair —s*, R2 III, 3, 53. *by our habits and by every other a.* H4A I, 2, 197. *here art thou in a. fresh and fair*, Troil. IV, 5, 1. *a pirate of very warlike a.* Hml. IV, 6, 16. *where their a. we may best discover*, Ant. IV, 10, 8.

Apprehend, 1) *to take*, *to seize: which I —ed with the aforesaid swain*, LLL I, 1, 276. *in private brabble did we a. him*, Tw. V, 68. 89. *whom we have —ed in the fact*, H6B II, 1, 173. Tim. I, 1, 212. *where we may a. her and the Moor*, Oth. I, 1, 178. Especially *to arrest:* Err. I, 2, 4. Wiv. IV, 5, 119. H5 II, 2, 2. IV, 7, 165. 8, 18. H6C III, 1, 71. Cor. III, 1, 173. Rom. V, 3, 53. 56. Lr. I, 2, 83. II, 1, 110. Oth. I, 2, 77.

2) *to seize by the mind*, *to conceive*, *to form a conception*; a) absolutely: *you a. passing shrewdly*, Ado II, 1, 84 (you have a shrewd way of thinking, of forming ideas). *to a. thus, draws us a profit from all things we see*, Cymb. III, 3, 17. b) followed by an acc.: *a man that —s death no more dreadfully but as a drunken sleep*, Meas. IV, 2, 149. V, 486. *fantasies that a. more than cool reason ever comprehends*, Mids. V, 5. *a. some joy*, 19. *a. nothing but jollity*, Wint. IV, 4, 24. *he —s a world of figures*, H4A I, 3, 209. H4B I, 1, 176. *and —ed here the unknown Ajax*, Troil. III, 3, 124. *a. no fear*, III, 2, 80.

Apprehension, 1) seizure, arrestation: *to question of his a.* H6C III, 2, 122. *that he may be ready for our a.* Lr. III, 5, 20 (i. e. to be apprehended by us).

2) conception, imagination: *the sense of death is most in a.* Meas. III, 1, 78. LLL IV, 2, 69. H4A IV, 1, 66. H6A II, 4, 102. Tim. I, 1, 211. Hml. IV, 1, 11. Oth. III, 3, 139. Followed by *of: the a. of the good gives but the greater feeling to the worse*, R2 I, 3, 300. *he had not a. of roaring terrors*, Cymb. IV, 2, 110.

3) perception: *dark night the ear more quick of a. makes*, Mids. III, 2, 178. *took from you the a. of his present portance*, Cor. II, 3, 232.

4) the faculty of conception or perception: *his evasion cannot outfly our —s*, Troil. II, 3, 124. *if the English had any a., they would run away*, H5 III, 7, 145. *in a. how like a God!* Hml. II, 2, 319. Hence simply for wit: *how long have you professed a.?* Ado III, 4, 68.

Apprehensive, imaginative: *makes it a., quick, forgetive*, H4B IV, 3, 107. Ruled by imaginations and caprices, fantastic: *whose a. senses all but new things disdain*, All's I, 2, 60. *men are flesh and blood, and a.* Caes. III, 1, 67.

Apprentice, v. *Prentice*.

Apprenticehood, state of apprentice, of gaining instruction: *must I not serve a long a. to foreign passages*, R2 I, 3, 271.

Approach, vb., 1) to draw near in time or place: Tp. V, 80. Meas. IV, 1, 58. Merch. II, 9, 88. All's IV, 3, 36. Wint. IV, 4, 52. V, 3, 99. H6A IV, 2, 17. V, 4, 101. Tit. IV, 4, 72. Rom. I, 1, 114. Lr. IV, 7, 93. V, 3, 99. Ant. III, 12, 6. 13, 89. Followed by an accus.: *no woman may a. his silent court*, LLL II, 24. As IV, 3, 110. 120. Tit. I, 13. *the remembrance of her father never —es her heart, but ...* All's I, 1, 57. *when thou dost hear I am as I have been, a. me*, H4B V, 5, 65, i. e. seek my company, access to me. Followed by *to: when he —eth to your presence*, Gentl. V, 4, 32. *—eth boldly to our presence*, H6C III, 3, 44. Joined to *near: a. not near*, Mids. II, 2, 22. *—ing near these eyes*, John IV, 1, 62. *some danger does a. you nearly*, Mcb. IV, 2, 67.

2) to come, arrive: *return'd so soon? rather —ed too late*, Err. I, 2, 43. *they a. sadly and go away merry*, Tim. II, 2, 106. *a fairer former fortune than that which is to a.* Ant. I, 2, 34. *he was expected then, but not —ed*, Cymb. II, 4, 39. cf. Tp. I, 2, 188. IV, 49. 75. Ado I, 1, 95. Meas. V, 405. LLL V, 2, 83. 900. Mids. V, 289. Merch. II, 6, 24. Tw. II, 3, 1. Wint. IV, 4, 213. H4B I, 1, 150. H6A II, 5, 62. Mcb. III, 4, 100. Lr. II, 2, 170. Ant. III, 11, 46. V, 2, 326. *Let him a.* = let him come, let him enter: Wiv. II, 2, 34. LLL V, 2, 512. Mids. V, 107. All's V, 3, 25. Tw. I, 5, 172. John I, 47.

3) to enter, trans.: *if they do a. the city, we shall lose all the sight*, All's III, 5, 1. *she did a. my cabin where I lay*, Wint. III, 3, 23. *like a shepherd, a. the fold and cull the infected forth*, Tim. V, 4, 43 (cf. v. 39). *a. the chamber, and destroy your sight with a new Gorgon*, Mcb. II, 3, 76.

Approach, subst. 1) the act of drawing near: *gives intelligence of Ford's a.* Wiv. III, 5, 86. Mids. III, 2, 381. Wint. I, 2, 422. H5 IV, 1, 90. H6B III, 3, 6. Troil. IV, 1, 43. Mcb. I, 4, 46. Ant. III, 6, 45. = hostile advance, attack: *this apish and unmannerly a.* John V, 2, 131. *England his —es makes as fierce*, H5 II, 4, 9. IV, 2, 36. *should the a. of this wild river break*, H8 III, 2, 198. Tim. V, 1, 167. V, 2, 4. *makes his —es to the port of Rome*, Ant. I, 3, 46. Figuratively: *welcomes the warm a. of sweet desire*, Ven. 386.

2) access: *allowed your a.*, Tw. I, 5, 210. *at the first a. you must kneel*, Tit. IV, 3, 110.

3) arrival, coming: *did look for his a.* Pilgr. 78. *by thy a. thou makest me most unhappy*, Gentl. V, 4, 31. *Navarre had notice of your fair a.* LLL II, 81. *I should be glad of his a.* Merch. I, 2, 142. As II, 7, 8. Wint. V, 1, 89. John II, 216. R2 I, 3, 6. H6A II, 1, 9. Ant. IV, 8, 39. *Mark his first a. before my lady* (= coming, appearing) Tw. II, 5, 217.

Approacher, a person who draws near, a comer: *bid welcome to knaves and all —s*, Tim. IV, 3, 216.

Approbation, 1) approval, assent: *by learned a. of the judges*, H8 I, 2, 71. *the applause and a. the which I give to ...*, Troil. I, 3, 59. *the a. of those*, Cymb. I, 4, 19. *to such proceeding who ever but his a. added*, Per. IV, 3, 26.

2) ratification, attestation: *gives manhood more a. than proof itself*, Tw. III, 4, 198. *nought*

for a. but only seeing, Wint. II, 1, 177. *shall drop their blood in a. of ...*, H5 I, 2, 19. *upon your a.* (to ratify your election) Cor. II, 3, 152. *revoke your sudden a.*, 259. *put my estate on the a. of ...*, Cymb. I, 4, 134.

3) state of being approved: *his worth and credit that's sealed in a.* Meas. V, 245. *coming home, and with most prosperous a.* Cor. II, 1, 114. *give them title, knee and a. with senators on the bench*, Tim. IV, 3, 36.

4) probation, novitiate: *and there receive her a.* Meas. I, 2, 183.

Approof, 1) approval: *either of condemnation or a.* Meas. II, 4, 174.

2) state of being approved: *of very valiant a.* (= of approved valour) All's II, 5, 3. *so in a. lives not his epitaph as in your royal speech*, I, 2, 50, i. e. his epitaph receives by nothing such confirmation and living truth as by your speech. *Prove such a wife as my thoughts make thee, and as my farthest band shall pass on thy a.* Ant. III, 2, 27, i. e. such as, when tried (*a.* = proof), will prove to be beyond anything that I can promise (*band* obj. of *pass*).

Appropriation, probably = acquisition, excellence acquired: *he doth nothing but talk of his horse, and he makes it a great a. to his own good parts, that he can shoe him himself*, Merch. I, 2, 46.

Approve, 1) to like, to be pleased with, to admit the propriety of: *I no way a. his opinion*, Tw. IV, 2, 60. *I muse my mother does not a. me further*, Cor. III, 2, 8. *his scorn I a.* Oth. IV, 3, 52. *I a. your wisdom in the deed*, Ant. V, 2, 149. In a stronger sense = to be fond of: *suffering my friend for my sake to a. her*, Sonn. 42, 8. *that so a. the Moor*, Oth. II, 1, 44. *my love doth so a. him*, IV, 3, 19. And in a weaker sense = to assent to, to give credit: *but the main article I do a. in fearful sense*, Oth. I, 3, 11 (= believe).

2) to experience, to try: *I desperate now a. desire is death*, Sonn. 147, 7. *'tis the curse in love, and still —d*, Gentl. V, 4, 43. *on whose eyes I might a. this flower's force*, Mids. II, 2, 68. *when they have —d their virtues*, Wint. IV, 2, 31. *must a. the common saw*, Lr. II, 2, 167. *I have well —d it*, Oth. II, 3, 317. *a. me, lord*, H4A IV, 1, 9 (= try me, put me to the proof). *Approved* = tried, proved to be so by experiment: *of —d valour*, Ado II, 1, 394. IV, 1, 45. 303. Err. V, 103. Shr. I, 1, 7. 2, 3. All's I, 2, 10. 3, 234. R2 II, 3, 44. H4A I, 1, 54. Tit. V, 1, 1. Oth. I, 3, 77. II, 1, 49.

3) to prove, to justify: *a. it with a text*, Merch. III, 2, 79. *my growth would a. the truth*, H4B I, 2, 180. cf. 214. *which well —s you 're great in fortune*, All's III, 7, 13. *that my sword upon thee shall a.* Tit. II, 1, 35. Mcb. I, 6, 4. Lr. I, 1, 187. II, 4, 186. Oth. II, 3, 64. With a double accus.: *slander doth but a. thy worth the greater*, Sonn. 70, 5. R2 I, 3, 112. H6A V, 5, 69. H6B III, 2, 22. Lr. III, 5, 12. Cymb. IV, 2, 380. V, 5, 245. *I shall not fail to a. the fair conceit the king hath of you*, H8 II, 3, 74, i. e. to justify, to confirm it by showing it to be true. *I am full sorry that he —s the common liar*, Ant. I, 1, 60, i. e. confirms the public slander by his behaviour. *That he may a. our eyes*, Hml. I, 1, 29, i. e. that he may affirm what we have seen. *He that is —d in this offence*, Oth. II, 3, 211, i. e. proved to have com-

mitted this offence. *True swains shall a. their truths by Troilus,* Troil. III, 2, 181, i. e. avouch their faith by comparing themselves to Troilus.

4) to make approved, to commend: *it would not much a. me,* Hml. V, 2, 141. *all that may men a. or men detect,* Per. II, 1, 55.

Approver, he that makes trial: *will make known to their —s they are people such,* Cymb. II, 4, 25.

Appurtenance, that which belongs to sth: *the a. of welcome is fashion and ceremony,* Hml. II, 2, 388.

Apricock, the fruit of prunus Armeniaca: Mids. III, 1, 169. R2 III, 4, 29.

April, the fourth month: Wint. IV, 4, 281. John IV, 2, 120. It is the month of spring and flowers: Sonn. 3, 10. 21, 7. 98, 2. 104, 7. Lucr. 395. Tp. IV, 65. Wiv. III, 2, 69. Merch. II, 9, 93. As IV, 1, 147. Wint. IV, 4, 3. Rom. I, 2, 27. Tim. IV, 3, 41; though a month of inconstant weather, Gentl. I, 3, 85. Compl. 102; and of much rain: Tp. IV, 65. Troil. I, 2, 189 (*he will weep you, an 'twere a man born in April*). Tit. III, 1, 18. Ant. III, 2, 43 (*the A.'s in her eyes*).

Apron, a cloth or piece of leather worn before: H4B II, 2, 190. II, 4, 18. H6B II, 3, 75. IV, 2, 14. Tim. IV, 3, 135. Caes. I, 1, 7. Ant. V, 2, 210. Per. IV, 6, 64.

Apron-man, a man who wears an apron, a mechanic: Cor. IV, 6, 96.

Apt, 1) fit: *in all the play there is not one word a.* Mids. V, 65. LLL I, 2, 19. II, 73. V, 1, 99. Tw. I, 5, 28. John IV, 2, 226. Hml. III, 2, 226. Followed by *for: right a. for this affair,* Tw. I, 4, 35. H4B I, 1, 213. Followed by an infinitive: *—er than thy tongue to tell thy errand,* H4B I, 1, 69. Caes. II, 2, 97.

2) easily impressed, impressionable: *as a. as new-fallen snow takes any dint,* Ven. 354. *she is young and a.* Tim. I, 1, 132 (and may therefore easily be moved to love). *I have a heart as little a. as yours, but yet a brain . . .* Cor. III, 2, 29. *O fatal error, why dost thou show to the a. thoughts of men the things that are not?* Caes. V, 3, 68. *she is of so free, so kind, so a., so blessed a disposition,* Oth. II, 3, 326. *I find thee a.* Hml. I, 5, 31. Thus absolutely = docile: *is she not a.?* H5 V, 2, 312 (= apt to learn).

3) inclined, ready: *youth so a. to pluck a flower,* Pilgr. 240 and LLL IV, 3, 114. *I find an a. remission in myself,* Meas. V, 503 (= a ready pardon, an inclination to pardon). *how a. it is to learn,* Ado I, 1, 294. Shr. II, 166. Tw. III, 1, 138. V, 328. As III, 2, 408. H5 II, 2, 86. H8 II, 4, 122. Rom. III, 1, 34. Caes. III, 1, 160. Lr. II, 4, 309. IV, 2, 65. Oth. II, 1, 175. *So I am a. to do myself wrong* = I am ready, I am about to . . . ., Ado II, 1, 213. As for Tw. V, 135, v. *Aptly.* Apt to that, Rom. III, 1, 44. III, 3, 157. *Apt for depravation,* Troil. V, 2, 131.

4) easily accounted for, natural: *as school-maids change their names by vain though a. affection,* Meas. I, 4, 48. *that she loves him, 'tis a. and of great credit,* Oth. II, 1, 296. *what he found himself was a. and true,* V, 2, 177. *the fit and a. construction of thy name doth import so much,* Cymb. V, 5, 444.

Compar. *apter,* As III, 2, 408 and H4B I, 1, 69. *Aptest,* H4B I, 1, 213.

Aptly, 1) fitly, properly: *leave me, and then the story a. ends,* Ven. 716. *grief and blushes, a. under-*

stood in white and red, Compl. 200. *that part was a. fitted,* Shr. Ind. I, 87. R3 III, 1, 134. Tim. I, 1, 17. *a frock or livery that a. is put on* (i. e. easily, as the frock fits well) Hml. III, 4, 165.

2) willingly, readily: *what's sweet to do, to do will a. find,* Compl. 88, i. e. what is sweet to do, will readily find to do, will readily find business. Tw. III, 4, 212. V, 135 (*apt and willingly* for aptly and willingly). Per. V, 2, 5.

Aptness, 1) fitness, propriety: *in either's a.* Compl. 306 (as either was fit). *be friended with a. of the season* (choose a proper time) Cymb. II, 3, 53.

2) readiness, propensity: *they are in a ripe a. to take all power from the people,* Cor. IV, 3, 23.

Aqua-vitae, ardent spirits: Wiv. II, 2, 318. Err. IV, 1, 89. Tw. II, 5, 215. Wint. IV, 4, 816. Rom. III, 2, 88. IV, 5, 16.

Aquilon, the north wind: Troil. IV, 5, 9.

Aquitaine, part of France: LLL I, 1, 138. II, 8. 136. 140. 146. 149. 160.

Arabia, country in Asia: Tp. III, 3, 22. Merch. II, 7, 42. Cor. IV, 2, 24. Mcb. V, 1, 57. Ant. III, 6, 72.

Arabian, pertaining to Arabia: *on the sole A. tree,* Phoen. 2, i. e. the tree of the Phoenix. *drop tears as fast as the A. trees their medicinal gum,* Oth. V, 2, 350. *O thou A. bird!* (Phoenix) Ant. III, 2, 12. Cymb. I, 6, 17.

Arachne, v. *Ariachne.*

Araise, to raise from the dead: *powerful to a. king Pepin,* All's II, 1, 79.

Arbitrate, to decide, determine: *decides that which long process could not a.* LLL V, 2, 753. John I, 38. R2 I, 1, 50. 200. Mcb. V, 4, 20. The original signification of determination by an umpire still perceptible in Rom. IV, 1, 63.

Arbitrator, umpire; used figuratively: *Out, idle words, weak —s,* Lucr. 1017. *the a. of despairs, just death, kind umpire of men's miseries,* H6A II, 5, 28. *that old common a. Time will one day end it,* Troil. IV, 5, 225.

Arbitrement, 1) decision: *incensed against you even to a mortal a.* Tw. III, 4, 286. *if it come to the a. of swords,* H5 IV, 1, 168. R3 V, 3, 89. Lr. IV, 7, 95. Cymb. I, 4, 52.

2) judicial inquiry: *we of the offering side must keep aloof from strict a.* H4A IV, 1, 70.

Arbour, bower: Ado II, 3, 38. H4B V, 3, 2. Caes. III, 2, 253.

Arc: *Joan of A.* H6A II, 2, 20. V, 4, 49 (O. Edd. *Acre* and *Aire*).

Arch, subst. concave and hollow structure: *as through an a. the violent roaring tide,* Lucr. 1667. *like an a., reverberates the voice,* Troil. III, 3, 120. Cor. V, 4, 50. *the watery a.* (rainbow) Tp. IV, 71. *this vaulted a.* (sc. of heaven) Cymb. I, 6, 33. *let Rome in Tiber melt, and the wide a. of the ranged empire fall,* Ant. I, 1, 33.

Arch, adj. wicked, arrant: *the most a. act of piteous massacre,* R3 IV, 3, 2. *that a. heretic,* John III, 1, 192. *an heretic, an a. one,* H8 III, 2, 102. *a most a. heretic,* V, 1, 45 (cf. *arch-enemy, arch-mock, arch-villain*).

Arch, subst. chief, master: *my worthy a. and patron,* Lr. II, 1, 61.

Archbishop, chief bishop, superintendent of

the suffragans: John III, 1, 143. R2 II, 1, 282. H4A I, 3, 268. III, 2, 119. H4B I, 1, 189. II, 3, 42. IV, 1, 41 etc. H6C IV, 3, 53. H8 III, 2, 74. 402. IV, 1, 24. 86 etc.

Archbishopric, the province over which an archbishop has authority: H8 II, 1, 164.

Arch-deacon, ecclesiastical dignitary who in case of need supplies the bishop's place: H4A III, 1, 72.

Arched, 1) built with an arch: *the gates of monarchs are a. so high,* Cymb. III, 3, 5.

2) bent like an arch: *the right a. beauty of the brow,* Wiv. III, 3, 59. *his a. brows,* All's I, 1, 105.

Archelaus, king of Cappadocia: Ant. III, 6, 69.

Arch-enemy, principal enemy, or wicked enemy? H6C II, 2, 2.

Archer, bowman: Ado II, 1, 401. H6A I, 1, 116. R3 V, 3, 295. 339. Tit. IV, 3, 52. Per. I, 1, 164.

Archery, skill of an archer: *hit with Cupid's a.* Mids. III, 2, 103. *let me see your a.* Tit. IV, 3, 2.

Arch-heretic, v. *Arch.*

Archibald, christian name of Douglas: H4A I, 1, 53.

Architect, figuratively, contriver: *chief a. and plotter of these woes,* Tit. V, 3, 122.

Arch-mock, principal mock: *the fiend's a.* Oth. IV, 1, 71.

Arch-villain, a great and confirmed villain: *an a.* Meas. V, 57. Tim. V, 1, 111.

Arde, place in France: H8 I, 1, 7.

Ardea, town in Latium, besieged by Tarquin: Lucr. Arg. 4. Lucr. 1. 1332.

Arden; *the forest of A.:* As I, 1, 121.*3, 109. II, 4, 15. 16.

Ardent, fiery: *under hot a. zeal,* Tim. III, 3, 33.

Ardour, heat: *the a. of my liver,* Tp. IV, 56. *when the compulsive a. gives the charge,* Hml. III, 4, 86.

Argal, vulgar corruption of the Latin *ergo,* consequently: Hml. V, 1, 13. 21. 55.

Argentine, silvery, silver-hued: *Celestial Dian, goddess a.* Per. V, 1, 251.

Argier, Algier: Tp. I, 2, 261. 265.

Argo, corruption of the Latin *ergo:* H6B IV, 2, 31.

Argosy, large merchantman: Merch. I, 1, 9. 3, 18. III, 1, 105. V, 276. Shr. II, 376. 378. 380. H6C II, 6, 36.

Argue, 1) to reason, to debate, discuss; a) absolutely: *a. like a father,* R2 I, 3, 238. *well have you —d,* IV, 150. H8 II, 2, 113. Cor. I, 1, 225. Caes. V, 1, 48. b) followed by *upon: —ing upon that doubt,* Shr. III, 1, 55. c) followed by an acc.: *we are too open here to a. this,* H8 II, 1, 168. H6A IV, 1, 96.

2) to prove, show: *this heraldry .... argued by beauty's red and virtue's white* (= shown) Lucr. 65. *it —s facility,* LLL IV, 2, 57. H4B IV, 1, 160. H6A II, 5, 7. V, 3, 8. V, 4, 15. H6B III, 3, 30. H6C II, 2, 25. III, 2, 84. R3 III, 7, 40. 174. Rom. II, 3, 33. Tim. V, 1, 30. Hml. V, 1, 11. Oth. III, 4, 38. In H6C with a double accusative.

Argument, 1) reasoning, debate, discussion: *I force not a. a straw,* Lucr. 1021. *all kind of —s and question deep,* Compl. 121. *how did this a. begin?* LLL III, 105. *I'll darkly end the a.* V, 2, 23. V, 1, 19. 2, 84. As I, 2, 50. John I, 36. IV, 2, 54.

H5 III, 2, 104. H6A II, 5, 45 (*in a. upon a case*). Rom. II, 4, 105. Cymb. I, 4, 60. *To hold a.* = to dispute: Pilgr. 30. LLL IV, 3, 61. Ado II, 3, 55. H6A II, 4, 57. *For shape, for bearing, a. and valour* (manner of reasoning or discoursing) Ado III, 1, 96 (O. Edd. *bearing argument,* without a comma).

2) the matter in question, the business in hand: *how can they charitably dispose of anything, when blood is their a.?* H5 IV, 1, 150. *sheathed their swords for lack of a.* H5 III, 1, 21. *I cannot fight upon this a.* Troil. I, 1, 95 (cf. Hml. IV, 4, 54). *all the a. is a cuckold and a whore,* II, 3, 78. *that most may claim this a. for ours,* Mcb. II, 3, 126. *in a. of praise,* All's III, 5, 62; i. e. if praise is the thing required.

3) the theme, the subject: *pour'st into my verse thine own sweet a.* Sonn. 38, 3 (i. e. thou art the theme of my verse). *you and love are still my a.* 76, 10. 79, 5. 100, 8. 103, 3. 105, 9. LLL V, 2, 757. Tw. II, 5, 163. Wint. IV, 1, 29. R2 I, 1, 12. H4B V, 2, 23. H5 III, 2, 85. Troil. II, 3, 104. 105. 106. Tim. III, 3, 20. 5, 23. Lr. I, 1, 218. II, 1, 9. *I should not seek an absent a. of my revenge,* As III, 1, 3 (object). *the rarest a. of wonder,* Alls III, 3, 7. *become the a. of his own scorn,* Ado II, 3, 11; and absolutely: *thou wilt prove a notable a.* Ado I, 1, 258 (= wilt be spoken of, turned into ridicule). *you would not make me such an a.* Mids. III, 2, 242. *it would be a. for a week,* H4A II, 2, 100.

4) that of which a dramatic play treats: *the a. shall be thy running away,* H4A II, 4, 310. H4B IV, 5, 199. Troil. Prol. 25. Hml. III, 2, 149. 242. *there was no money bid for a.* (i. e. for a dramatic subject) Hml. II, 2, 372.

5) contents: *if I would broach the vessels of my love, and try the a. of hearts by borrowing,* Tim. II, 2, 187. cf. the superscr. of Lucr. Arg.

6) cause, reason: *my desires had instance and a. to commend themselves,* Wiv. II, 2, 256. *grounded upon no other a.* As I, 2, 291. *by these —s of fear,* Tw. III, 3, 12. *bloody a.* = cause of bloodshed, 32. H5 IV, 3, 113. H6B III, 1, 241. H6C II, 2, 44. III, 1, 49. R3 I, 1, 148. H8 II, 4, 67. Troil. IV, 5, 26. 27. 29 (a quibble). Hml. IV, 4, 54.

7) a reason offered in proof: *no great a. of her folly,* Ado II, 3, 243. LLL I, 2, 175. Tw. III, 2, 12. H6A II, 4, 59. V, 1, 46. H6B I, 2, 32. Ant. III, 12, 3.

Argus, the keeper of Io, having a hundred eyes: LLL III, 201. Merch. V, 230. Troil. I, 2, 31.

Ariachne, (so O. Edd., and so the verse requires; M. Edd. *Arachne*), for Arachne, the virgin who vied with Minerva in the art of weaving: Troil. V, 2, 152.

Ariadne, the daughter of Minos, forsaken by Theseus: Gentl. IV, 4, 172. Mids. II, 1, 80.

Ariel, the airy spirit in the service of Prospero: Tp. I, 2, 188. 193. 217. 237. 317. 441. 494. III, 3, 84. IV, 1, 33. 49. 164. V, 95 etc.

Aries, the Ram, the first of the twelve signs of the zodiac: Tit. IV, 3, 71.

Aright, rightly, without mistake: *censures falsely what they see a.* Sonn. 148, 4. *never going a.* LLL III, 194. *thou speak'st a.* Mids. II, 1, 42. H6C III, 2, 68. Tit. V, 2, 89. Mcb. IV, 1, 74. Hml. V, 2, 350. Lr. I, 4, 260. IV, 3, 55.

Arion (O. Edd. *Orion*), the singer preserved by the dolphin: Tw. I, 2, 15.

Arise (impf. *arose*, H8 IV, 1, 71. Caes. II, 1, 239. partic. *arose*, Err. V, 388), 1) to mount up, ascend: *the lark arising from sullen earth,* Sonn. 29, 11. *a. forth from the couch of lasting night,* John III, 4, 27. Used of the sun: Ven. 856. Rom. II, 2, 4. Caes. II, 1, 106. Cymb. II, 3, 22.

2) to get up; from a fall: Lr. I, 4, 99. Cymb. IV, 2, 403; from a seat: Tp. I, 2, 169. Ant. III, 11, 46; from table: Caes. II, 1, 239; from kneeling: Tp. V, 181. John I, 162. H6B I, 1, 17. H6C II, 2, 61. R3 I, 2, 185. H8 I, 2, 10. V, 1, 92. Cymb. V, 5, 20. 326; from the ground: Lucr. 1818. Tit. III, 1, 65. Rom. III, 3, 71; from sleep: Meas. IV, 2, 94. Mids. III, 1, 174. V, 333. H6C V, 4, 57. Oth. I, 1, 89. 92. Cymb. II, 3, 29; from death: Sonn. 55, 13; and figuratively: *spotless shall mine innocence a.* H8 III, 2, 301.

3) to be engendered, to begin to exist: *what sorrow may on this a.* Lucr. 186. *and thereupon these errors are arose,* Err. V, 388. H6A IV, 1, 113. 143. *what showers a.* H6C II, 5, 85. H8 IV, 1, 71. Followed by *of:* H5 IV, 7, 186. Followed by *from:* Oth. II, 3, 168.

Aristotle, the famous Greek philosopher: Shr. I, 1, 32. Troil. II, 2, 166.

Arithmetic, the art of computation, of casting accounts: Troil. I, 2, 123. III, 3, 253. Cor. III, 1, 245. Rom. III, 1, 106. Hml. V, 2, 119. Cymb. II, 4, 142.

Arithmetician, one skilled in arithmetic: Oth. I, 1, 19.

Ark, the vessel of Noah: As V, 4, 36.

Arm, the limb from the shoulder to the hand; Sing.: Ven. 31. Err. III, 2, 23. 148. Ado II, 1, 197. As II, 7, 199 (*support him by the a.*). V, 2, 24. H6A II, 1, 17. H6B III, 1, 159 etc. etc. Plur.: Lucr. 517. Pilgr. 148. Tp. II, 1, 119. 2, 35. Wiv. III, 1, 35. V, 5, 58. Meas. III, 1, 85. Mids. IV, 1, 45. All's II, 3, 265. H6A I, 1, 11. 5, 11. II, 3, 63. H6B I, 1, 120 etc. etc. Figuratively: *that Neptune's —s, who clippeth thee about, would bear thee ...,* John V, 2, 34. *knit our powers to the a. of peace,* H4B IV, 1, 177. *the cedar whose —s gave shelter ...,* H6C V, 2, 12. *the a. and burgonet of men,* Ant. I, 5, 23. *beyond mine a.* = without my reach, Wint. II, 3, 5. *—In the owner's —s,* Lucr. 27. *I had him in mine —s,* Meas. V, 198. *lend me an a.* All's I, 2, 73. *holds his wife by the a.* Wint. I, 2, 193. *a. in a.* H6A II, 2, 29. H6B V, 1, 57. *a. to a.* R2 I, 1, 76. *In —s* = in embracements, John III, 1, 103. *To cross or fold or wreathe one's arms,* a sign either of sorrow: Lucr. 793. 1662. Tp. I, 2, 224. Tit. III, 2, 7. Caes. II, 1, 240; or of love: LLL III, 18. 183. IV, 3, 135; or of both: Gentl. II, 1, 19. Double meaning: *this is the very top, the height, the crest, or crest unto the crest, of murder's —s,* John IV, 3, 47. *and dare avow her beauty and her worth in other —s than hers,* Troil. I, 3, 272. Quibble: *so may you lose your —s,* Shr. II, 222. *he was the first that ever bore —s,* Hml. V, 1, 38. John III, 1, 102. 103. *At the —'s end,* As II, 6, 10 = at a little distance: *Hold death awhile at the —'s end* = keep death off awhile. Perhaps a quibble intended in Gentl. V, 4, 57: *I'll woo you like a soldier, at arms' end,* i. e. laying hands on thee for my weapons instead of useless words.

Arm, vb. 1) trans. a) to furnish with weapons of offence or defence: *help to a. me,* R3 V, 3, 78. *I'll go a. myself,* H5 III, 7, 97. *—s her,* Wint. I, 2, 184. Mids. I, 1, 117. John IV, 2, 249. V, 6, 25. R2 V, 3, 48. H6B V, 1, 192. H6C IV, 1, 113. Troil. V, 2, 183. Caes. V, 1, 106. Hml. III, 3, 24 etc. Particularly in the partic. *armed:* Ven. 779. Lucr. 1425 Err. III, 2, 126. Ado V, 4, 128. Mids. II, 1, 157. Shr. IV, 3, 149. John III, 1, 111. R2 III, 2, 25. H6A II, 2, 24. H6B III, 2, 233. H6C I, 1, 38. R3 I, 1, 42. V, 3, 219 etc. Of bees: *—ed in their stings,* H5 I, 2, 193. *—ed tail,* Troil. V, 10, 44.

b) to furnish with anything that will add strength or security: *—ed gauntlets,* John V, 2, 156. *—ed fist,* Troil. II, 3, 212. *—ed heels,* H4B I, 1, 44. H5 IV, 7, 83. *my —ed knees,* Cor. III, 2, 118. *mine —ed neck,* Ant. IV, 8, 14. *their —ed staves in charge,* H4B IV, 1, 120. *the lion's —ed jaws,* H4A III, 2, 102. *the —ed rhinoceros,* Mcb. III, 4, 101. *his brawny sides, with hairy bristles —ed,* Ven. 625.

c) to fit up, to prepare, provide: *even as subtle Sinon, so sober-sad, to me came Tarquin —ed,* Lucr. 1544. *and —ed his long-hid wits,* 1816. *if you are —ed to do as sworn to do,* LLL I, 1, 22. V, 2, 84. *look you a. yourself to fit your fancies to your father's will,* Mids. I, 1, 117. Merch. IV, 1, 11. 264. As IV, 1, 61. Shr. I, 1, 5. *he hath —ed our answer,* All's I, 2, 11 (i. e. has furnished us with a ready and fit answer). *point from point, to the full —ing of the verity,* IV, 3, 72 (so that the truth, as it were, stands proof against contradiction). Wint. I, 2, 184. R2 V, 3, 48. Tit. I, 136. II, 1, 12. Caes. III, 1, 106. Cymb. I, 6, 19. *a. you to the sudden time,* John V, 6, 25. *—ing the minds of infants to exclaims,* Tit. IV, 1, 86. *a. you to this speedy voyage,* Hml. III, 3, 24. *be thou —ed for some unhappy words,* Shr. II, 140. *she is —ed for him,* All's III, 5, 76. *a. thy nobler parts against ...,* John III, 1, 291. H6C IV, 1, 128. Cor. III, 2, 138.

2) intr. to arm one's self, to take arms: *we must not only a. to invade the French,* H5 I, 2, 136. *look you strongly a. to meet him,* II, 4, 49. *a., fight and conquer,* R3 V, 3, 150. *'tis time to a.* 236. Troil. I, 3, 171. III, 1, 150. V, 4, 17. Especially in the imperative: *a., gentlemen, to arms!* H4A V, 2, 42. And twice repeated: *a., wenches, a.!* LLL V, 2, 82. John III, 1, 107. R2 III, 2, 86. H6A II, 1, 38. R3 V, 3, 288. Tit. IV, 4, 62. Mcb. V, 5, 46.

Arm, vb., to take into the arms: *come, a. him,* Cymb. IV, 2, 400.

Armado, fleet: *Spain, who sent whole —s of caracks to be ballast at her nose,* Err. III, 2, 140. *so, by a roaring tempest on the flood a whole a. is scattered,* John III, 4, 2.

Armado or **Armatho,** name of the Spaniard in LLL I, 1, 171. 175. 193. 280 (*Don Adriano de A.*). IV, 1, 89. 100. 2, 94. V, 1, 9. 113. 2, 336.

Armagnac, (O. Edd. *Arminack*), name of a French nobleman: H6A V, 1, 2. 17. 5, 44.

Armenia, country in Asia: Ant. III, 6, 14. 35.

Arm-gaunt, a word not yet satisfactorily explained: *So he nodded, and soberly did mount an a. steed, who neigh'd so high ...,* Ant. I, 5, 48. Johnson: slender as the arm; which is little probable; Warburton: worn by military service; Nicholson: = armor-gloved. There is in Old English another *'gaunt'*, the German *ganz*, signifying whole, healthful, lusty, and *arm-gaunt* may mean completely armed, harnessed, or rather: lusty in arms, full of life and martial spirits.*

Armigero, Wiv. I, 1, 10; v. Latin appendix.

Armipotent: mighty in arms: *the a. Mars,* LLL V, 2, 650. 657. *the a. soldier,* All's IV, 3, 265.

Armour, 1) the habit worn to protect the body in battle: *like unscour'd a.* Meas. I, 2, 171. *clad in a.* H6A I, 5, 3. II, 1, 24. H6C III, 3, 230. IV, 1, 105. *a good a.* Ado II, 3, 17. *a rich a.* H4B IV, 5, 30. Ant. IV, 8, 27. Per. II, 1, 125. *all the complete a.* R3 IV, 4, 189. *the very a. he had on,* Hml. I, 1, 60. *my Lord of York's a.* H6B I, 3, 195. *with burden of our a.* John II, 92. R2 I, 3, 73. H5 V, 2, 143. H6C II, 2, 130. R3 V, 3, 51. Cor. III, 2, 34. Mcb. V, 3, 33. Ant. IV, 4, 1 etc. Plural: *their ―s,* John II, 315. H6C V, 7, 17. Troil. V, 3, 46. Figuratively: *his naked a. of still-slaughtered lust,* Lucr. 188. *if their heads had any intellectual a.* H5 III, 7, 148. *I'll give thee a. to keep off that word,* Rom. III, 3, 54. *put a. on thine ears,* Tim. IV, 3, 123. *with all the strength and a. of the mind,* Hml. III, 3, 12.

2) the whole apparatus of war, offensive as well as defensive arms; *bring away the a. that is there,* R2 II, 2, 107. *our a. all as strong,* H4B IV, 1, 156. *would have a. here out of the Tower,* H6A I, 3, 67. *lands, goods, house, a.* H6B V, 1, 52.

Armourer, 1) manufacturer of weapons: H5 II Chor. 3. IV Chor. 12. H6B II, 3, 50. 58.

2) he who has care of the arms and dresses his master in armour: Troil. I, 2, 6. *thou art the a. of my heart,* Ant. IV, 4, 7.

Armoury, place where instruments of war are deposited: *the town a.* Shr. III, 2, 47. *mine a.* Tit. IV, 1, 113. *his a.* IV, 2, 11.

Arms, 1) weapons: *art with a. contending,* Pilgr. 223. LLL II, 45. *bruised a.* Lucr. 110. 197. *my a.* LLL V, 2, 558. *great in a.* H6A II, 5, 24. *take up a.* H6A III, 2, 70. *rising up in a.* H6B IV, 1, 93. *servant in a. to Henry,* H6A IV, 2, 4. *in a.* = armed, LLL V, 2, 636. John III, 1, 102. R2 III, 2, 202. H6A I, 1, 125. 3, 75. *to arms!* John II, 287. III, 1, 255. H6C I, 2, 28. *to follow a.* = to be a soldier, John II, 31. H6A II, 1, 43. *a man at a.* = an armed knight, H6C V, 4, 42; figuratively: *affection's men at a.* LLL IV, 3, 290. *a man of a.* = a knight, H6A I, 4, 30. *worthy of a.* = hero of war, Troil. IV, 5, 163. *The law of a.* = the law of war, H5 IV, 7, 2; and = the statutes about the use of arms and the forms of duelling: *the law of a. is such that whoso draws a sword, 'tis present death,* H6A III, 4, 38; *I crave the benefit of law of a.* H6A IV, 1, 100 (i. e. of fighting him in duel). Very frequently = war, combat: *calling thee to a.* H6B V, 2, 7. *go not to a. against my uncle,* John III, 1, 308. *the a. are fair, when the intent of bearing them is just,* H4A V, 2, 88. *I see the issue of these a.* R2 II, 3, 152. *most shallowly did you these a. commence,* H4B IV, 2, 118. H6B III, 1, 378. IV, 9, 37. V, 1, 18. *the occasion of our a.* H4B I, 3, 5. IV, 1, 78. *his a. are only to remove from thee the duke of Somerset,* H6B IV, 9, 29. V, 1, 39.

2) Ensigns armorial of a family: H6A I, 1, 80. H6B I, 1, 256. IV, 1, 42. *our officers at a.* R2 I, 1, 204. *a pursuivant at a.* R3 V, 3, 59. Quibbling: Shr. II, 222. Hml. V, 1, 38. Ambiguous: Lucr. 1693. John IV, 3, 47. H6A I, 2, 42.

Army, a body of men armed for war: Lucr. Arg. 5. Lucr. 76. Tp. I, 2, 128. Ado I, 1, 33. II, 1, 254. All's IV, 3, 261. Wint. IV, 4, 631. H5 III, 5, 58. H6A I, 1, 101. 158. II, 5, 88. IV, 3, 2. V, 2, 11. 4, 173. H6B IV, 2, 185. 4, 32. 6, 13. V, 1, 35. H6C I, 1, 6. 2, 64 (vb. in the plural). R3 IV, 3, 50. H8 V, 4, 81. Troil. III, 3, 279. Ant. III.7, 43. Cymb. IV, 4, 31 etc. etc. Figuratively for a great number: *the huge a. of the world's desires,* LLL I, 1, 10. *an a. of good words,* Merch. III, 5, 72.

Aroint, stand off, or be gone, a word of aversion: *a. thee, witch!* Mcb. I, 3, 6. *a. thee, witch, a. thee!* Lr. III, 4, 129.*

Arouse, to awaken: *loud-howling wolves a. the jades,* H6B IV, 1, 3. *―d vengeance sets him new to work,* Hml. II, 2, 510 (O. Edd. *a roused vengeance*).

A-row, in a row, one after another: *beaten the maids a.* Err. V, 170.

Arragon, province of Spain: Ado I, 1, 2. III, 2, 2. Merch. II, 9, 2.

Arraign, to summon before a court of justice: *I'll teach you how you shall a. your conscience,* Meas. II, 3, 21. In general, to accuse: Wint. II, 3, 202. Hml. IV, 5, 93. Lr. III, 6, 22. 48. Oth. III, 4, 152. *accused and ―ed of high treason,* Wint. III, 2, 14. *who can a. me for't?* Lr. V, 3, 159.

Arrant, arch: *a. knave,* Ado III, 5, 35. V, 1, 330. H4B V, 1, 35. 45. V, 4, 1. Hml. I, 5, 124. III, 1, 131. *that a. malmsey-nose knave,* H4B II, 1, 42. *a. counterfeit rascal,* H5 III, 6, 64. *a. traitor,* H5 IV, 8, 10. *a. thief,* Tim. IV, 3, 440. *a. whore,* Lr. II, 4, 52. *a. cowards,* H4A II, 2, 106. Fluellen says even: *as a. a piece of knavery,* H5 IV, 7, 2. *as a. a villain,* 148. *what an a., rascally, beggarly, lousy knave it is,* IV, 8, 36.

Arras, tapestry hangings of rooms, woven with figures: Cymb. II, 2, 26. Serving as a place of concealment: Wiv. III, 3, 97. Ado I, 3, 63. John IV, 1, 2. H4A II, 4, 549. 577. III, 3, 113. Hml. II, 2, 163. III, 3, 28. IV, 1, 9. *Arras counterpoints* = counterpanes of tapestry, Shr. II, 353.

Array, vb. to clothe, dress: *these rebel powers* (the body) *that thee* (the soul) *array,* Sonn. 146, 2. *I drink, I eat, a. myself, and live,* Meas. III, 2, 26. *War, ―ed in flames like to the prince of fiends,* H5 III, 3, 16. *is he ―ed?* Lr. IV, 7, 20.

Array, subst. 1) dress, especially ornamental dress: *the fair sun, when in his fresh a. he cheers the morn,* Ven. 483. *fresh a.* As IV, 3, 144. *your best a.* V, 2, 79. *fine a.* Shr. II, 325. *in all her best a.* Rom. IV, 5, 81. *proud a.* Lr. III, 4, 85. As a vox media: *thou wolf in sheep's a.* H6A I, 3, 55. *mean a.* Shr. IV, 3, 182. Figuratively: *in which a.* (in blood), *brave soldier, doth he lie,* H5 IV, 6, 7. *happiness courts thee in her best a.* Rom. III, 3, 142.

2) order of troops in march and battle: *is marching hitherward in proud a.* H6B IV, 9, 27. *stand we in good a.* H6C V, 1, 62.

Arrearages, remainder of an account: Cymb. II, 4, 13.

Arrest, vb. (cf. *'rest*) 1) to seize, to apprehend a person by virtue of the law: Meas. I, 2, 60. Err. IV, 1, 69. 75. 106. IV, 2, 43. 44. IV, 4, 85. V, 230. Tw. III, 4, 360. H4B II, 1, 9. 48. H5 II, 2, 143. H6B III, 1, 136. V, 1, 136. H8 IV, 2, 13. The cause of the seizure sometimes expressed by the prep. *on: he ―s him on it,* Meas. I, 4, 66; *―ed on a band,* Err.

IV, 2, 49; *I a. thee on capital treason*, Lr. V, 3, 82; more frequently by *of: of capital treason we a. you*, R2 IV, 151. H4B IV, 2, 107. H5 II, 2, 145. H6B III, 1, 97. V, 1, 106. H8 I, 1, 201.

2) to seize a thing for debt: *his horses are —ed for it*, Wiv. V, 5, 119.

3) *I arrest your word* = I take you at your word: Meas. II, 4, 134. LLL II, 160.

Arrest, subst. 1) the taking or apprehending of a person in the way of law: H6B III, 1, 99. Lr. V, 3, 83 (Qq *attaint*). *under an a.* = in prison, Meas. I, 2, 136. Figuratively: Hml. V, 2, 348 (cf. 3).

2) any restraint upon a person binding him to be responsible to the law: *lords you that here are under our a.* R2 IV, 158, i. e. bound to appear in judgment. *He sends out —s on Fortinbras*, Hml. II, 2, 67, i. e. countermandates.

3) stop, stay: *that fell a. without all bail* (sc. death) Sonn. 74, 1 (cf. Hml. V, 2, 348). *served a dumb a. upon his tongue*, Lucr. 1780.

Arrival, the act of coming to a place: *by their secret and sudden a.* Lucr. Arg. 8. *is apprehended for a. here*, Err. I, 2, 4. Shr. IV, 5, 70. Wint. V, 1, 167. R2 I, 3, 8. H6A III, 4, 2.

2) followed by *of*, the reaching, attaining: *if life did ride upon a dial's point, still ending at the a. of an hour*, H4A V, 2, 85.

Arrivance, company coming: *every minute is expectancy of more a.* Oth. II, 1, 42 (Ff. *arrivancy*).

Arrive, 1) intrans. to come to, to reach a place: Tp. I, 2, 292. Err. I, 1, 49. Shr. I, 2, 213. All's II, 1, 82. Wint. II, 3, 196. IV, 4, 633. John II, 51. IV, 2, 115. 160. H5 IV, 8, 131. H6A V, 5, 8. H6C IV, 7, 7. H8 II, 1, 160. Rom. H, 6, 15. Caes. IV, 2, 30. Mcb. V, 8, 35. Hml. V, 2, 388. Oth. II, 1, 58. 89. II, 2, 3. Per. V Prol. 14. With *at*: Lucr. 50. R2 II, 2, 50. With *in*: Tp. I, 2, 171. Shr. IV, 4, 65. With *to*: *I have —d at the last unto the wished haven*, Shr. V, 1, 130. *not —d to pith and puissance*, H5 III Chor. 21. cf. *I have since —d but hither*, Tw. II, 2, 4. With *for*: *—d for fruitful Lombardy*, Shr. I, 1, 3.

To a. at = to obtain: *many so a. at second masters*, Tim. IV, 3, 512.

In general *to arrive* is to reach a place after a previous travel, but sometimes simply = to come: *a savour that may strike the dullest nostril where I a.* (= wherever I come) Wint. I, 2, 422. *where he —s he moves all hearts against us*, Lr. V, 5, 10.

2) trans. to reach: *ere he a. his weary noon-tide prick*, Lucr. 781. *have —d our coast*, H6C V, 3, 8. *—ing a place of potency*, Cor. II, 3, 189. *a. the point proposed*, Caes. I, 2, 110.

Arrogance, presumption: All's II, 1, 198. R3 I, 3, 24. Troil. II, 3, 195. III, 3, 49. Almost = impudence: Shr. IV, 3, 107. H8 III, 2, 278.

Arrogancy, the same: H8 II, 4, 110.

Arrogant, presumptuous: H6A I, 3, 23. H6B III, 2, 205. Tim. IV, 3, 180. Cymb. IV, 2, 127.

Arrow, missile shot with a bow: Ven. 947. Tp. IV, 99. Wiv. V, 5, 248. Ado III, 1, 22. 106. LLL V, 2, 261. Mids. I, 1, 170. III, 2, 101. Merch. I, 1, 148. As III, 5, 31. IV, 3, 4. H4B I, 1, 123. IV, 3, 36. H5 I, 2, 207. R3 V, 3, 339. Rom. I, 1, 215. Hml. III, 1, 58. IV, 7, 21. V, 2, 254. Per. I, 1, 163.

Art, 1) the power of doing something not taught by nature, skill, dexterity: Ven. 291.

Sonn. 53, 7. Meas. I, 2, 189. Mids. I, 1, 192. Shr. III, 1, 66. Wint. IV, 4, 90. V, 3, 68. Mcb. I, 2, 9 etc. etc. *your a. of wooing*, Wiv. II, 2, 244. *the a. to love*, Shr. IV, 2, 8. Opposed to *nature*: Ven. 291. Lucr. 1374. Meas. II, 2, 184. Mids. II, 2, 104. As III, 2, 31. Wint. IV, 4, 90. All's II, 1, 121. H6A V, 3, 192. Rom. II, 4, 94. Caes. IV, 3, 194. Lr. IV, 6, 86.

Sometimes joined with, or synonymous to, practice: *so that the a. and practic part of life must be the mistress to this theoric*, H5 I, 1, 51. *as art and practice have enriched any*, Meas. I, 1, 13. *a practice as full of labour as a wise man's a.* Tw. III, 1, 73. *by the a. of known and feeling sorrows am pregnant to good pity*, Lr. IV, 6, 226 (= experience). *I have as much of this in a. as you, but yet my nature could not bear it so*, Caes. IV, 3, 194 (external skill acquired by labour? Malone explains it by theory, in which he may be right).

Sometimes = magic: Tp. I, 2, 1. 25. 28. 291. 372. II, 1, 297. IV, 1, 41. 120. V, 50. Ep. 14. As V, 2, 67. Wint. V, 3, 110. H4A III, 1, 48. H6A II, 1, 15. H8 III, 1, 12. Oth. I, 2, 79. Perhaps magic may be meant in Sonn. 139, 4: *use power with power and slay me not by a.*

Synonymous to cunning, artifice, craft: *thought characters and words merely but a.* Compl. 174. *his passion, but an a. of craft*, 295.

2) Letters, learning, study: *a. with arms contending*, i. e. a scholar with a soldier, Pilgr. 223. *study his bias leaves and makes his book thine eyes, where all those pleasures live that a. can comprehend*, Pilgr. 62 and LLL IV, 2, 113. *a. made tongue-tied by authority* (science put to silence by power) Sonn. 66, 9. *in them* (thy eyes) *I read such a. as truth and beauty shall together thrive*, Sonn. 14, 10 (= I gather this knowledge). *the liberal —s*, Tp. I, 2, 73. *well fitted in —s* (full of instruction) LLL II, 45. *living a.*, I, 1, 14 (immortal science). *other slow —s entirely keep the brain*, IV, 3, 324. *boys of a.* Wiv. III, 1, 109. All's II, 1, 121. 136. 161. *Padua, nursery of —s*, Shr. I, 1, 2. *had I but followed the —s!* Tw. I, 3, 99. *the commission of thy years and a.* Rom. IV, 1, 64. *those —s they have as I could put into them*, Cymb. V, 5, 338.

Artemidorus, the rhetorician in Caes. II, 3, 10.

Artery, tube conveying the blood from the heart to all parts of the body: *poisons up the nimble spirits in the —ies*, LLL IV, 3, 306. *each petty a. in this body*, Hml. I, 4, 82 (Ff Qq *artire* and *arture*).

Arthur, 1) the fabulous king of Britain: *when A. first in court*, H4B II, 4, 36. *I was then Sir Dagonet in —'s show*, III, 2, 300 (an exhibition of archery by a toxophilite society in London, whose members assumed the names of the knights of the Round Table). *he's in —'s bosom* (for *Abraham's*) H5 II, 3, 10. — 2) *A. Plantagenet*, nephew to king John: John I, 9. II, 2. 153. 156 (*A. of Bretagne*). III, 4, 160 etc. etc. — 3) elder brother of Henry VIII: H8 III, 2, 71.

Article, 1) single clause in a stipulation, particular item in a writing or discourse: *in that last a.* Gentl. III, 1, 366. *this a. yourself must break*, LLL I, 1, 134. 140. Meas. V, 2, 107. R2 IV, 233. 243. H4B IV, 1, 74. 170. 2, 53. H5 V, 2, 78. 94. 97. 360. 374. H6B I, 1, 40. 217. H6C I, 1, 180. III, 3, 135. H8 I, 1, 169. III, 2, 293. 299. 304. Hml.

I, 1, 94. 2, 38. Oth. I, 3, 11. V, 2, 54. Ant. II, 2, 82. 87. Cymb. I, 4, 169. Per. I, 1, 88. *Endures not a. tying him to aught* (= condition) Cor. II, 3, 204. *to every a.* Tp. I, 2, 195. *to the last a.* Oth. III, 3, 22. *to draw my answer from thy —s,* John II, 111 (as from an inventory made by thee). *thou shouldst not alter the a. of thy gentry,* Wiv. II, 1, 53 (= the tenour of thy gentry, thy rank). *I take him to be a soul of great a.,* Hml. V, 2, 122, i. e. of a great item, one who, if virtues should be specified inventorially (cf. v. 118), would have many items in the list.

2) the grammatical article, the word prefixed to substantives: Wiv. IV, 1, 40. 41.

Articulate, 1) intr. to enter into negociations: *the best with whom we may a.* Cor. I, 9, 77. — 2) trans. to draw up in articles, to specify: *these things indeed you have a.,* H4A V, 1, 72 (Ff. *articulated*).

Artificer, artisan: *another lean unwashed a.,* John IV, 2, 201.

Artificial, 1) produced by art, not natural: *makes himself an a. night,* Rom. I, 1, 146. *his a. stone,* Tim. II, 2, 117 (the philosopher's stone). *raise such a. sprites,* Mcb. III, 5, 27. In a bad sense = feigned: *a. tears,* H6C III, 2, 184.

2) artful; a) of persons: *like two a. gods,* Mids. III, 2, 203.*b) of things: *thy prosperous and a. feat,* Per. V, 1, 72.

3) *a. strife,* Tim. I, 1, 37 = the strife, the emulation of art, to vie with nature.

Artillery, cannon, ordnance: John II, 403. H4A I, 1, 57. H6A I, 1, 168. IV, 2, 29. *heaven's a.* Shr. I, 2, 205.

Artist, scholar: *to be relinquished of the —s* (i. e. the learned physicians) All's II, 3, 10. *the a. and unread,* Troil. I, 3, 24. *in framing an a., art hath thus decreed, to make some good, but others to exceed; and you are her labour'd scholar,* Per. II, 3, 15.

Artless, unskilful: *so full of a. jealousy is guilt, it spills itself in fearing to be spilt,* Hml. IV, 5, 19.

Artois, province of France: H6A II, 1, 9.

Arts-man, scholar: LLL V, 1, 85.

Arundel, R2 II, 1, 280 (not in O. Edd., but inserted by M. Edd.)

Arviragus, son of Cymbeline: Cymb. III, 3, 96. V, 5, 359.

As; = in the quality of*; *as a spy,* Tp. I, 2, 455. *as my gift,* IV, 1, 13. *as one relying on your lordship's will,* Gentl. I, 3, 61. *whom she esteemeth as his friend,* III, 2, 37. *I will encounter darkness as a bride,* Meas. III, 1, 84. *I speak not like a dotard nor a fool, as under privilege of age to brag,* Ado V, 1, 60. *if I affect it more than as your honour,* H4B IV, 5, 146. *as loath to depose the child,* R3 III, 7, 208. *we shall acquaint him with it, as needful in our loves,* Hml. I, 1, 173, etc. etc.

Sometimes = like: *true grief is fond and testy as a child,* Lucr. 1094. *these means, as frets upon an instrument, shall tune our heart-strings,* 1140. *when I perceive that men as plants increase,* Sonn. 15, 5. *my bosom as a bed shall lodge thee,* Gentl. I, 2, 114. *no marvel though Demetrius do as a monster fly my presence,* Mids. II, 2, 97. *and sits as one new risen from a dream,* Shr. IV, 1, 189. *which ever as ravenous fishes do a vessel follow,* H8 I, 2, 79. *and hither make as great ambassadors from foreign princes,* I, 4, 55. *he*

sits in his state as a thing made for Alexander, Cor. V, 4, 22. *your face is as a book where men may read Mcb.* I, 5, 63. Caes. I, 2, 128. *the violence of action hath made you reek as a sacrifice,* Cymb. I, 2, 3.

Serving to denote conformity: *as thou say'st,* Tp. I, 2, 62. 219. 271. 420. II, 1, 61. 288, etc. etc. *as 'tis,* I, 2, 310. *as in a dream,* I, 2, 486. *all's hush'd as midnight,* IV, 207. *I know him as myself,* Gentl. II, 4, 62. *if he had been as you, and you as he,* Meas. II, 2, 64. *mad as a buck,* Err. III, 1, 72. *here shall he see gross fools as he,* As II, 5, 58. *dear almost as his life,* All's IV, 4, 6. *humble as the ripest mulberry,* Cor. III, 2, 79. *the humble as the proudest sail,* Sonn. 80, 6. Caes. II, 2, 29. *to have them recompensed as thought on,* Wint. IV, 4, 531. Frequently before *if: as if it had lungs,* Tp. II, 1, 47. Err. IV, 3, 2. Lr. V, 3, 17 etc.

Coward as thou art, R3 I, 4, 286 = that thou art. *unmerciful lady as you are,* Lr. III, 7, 33. cf. Tp. I, 2, 346. Gentl. III, 1, 7. LLL V, 2, 280. H6B I, 3, 86. III, 2, 59. *As you like this, give me the lie another time,* Tp. III, 2, 85 (= according as, if). *as you look to have my pardon, trim it,* V, 292. *as thou lovest thy life, make speed from hence,* Gentl. III, 1, 169. *I conjure thee, as thou believest there is another comfort than this world, that thou ....,* Meas. V, 48. *as you love strokes, so jest with me again,* Err. II, 2, 8. *so befall my soul, as this is false,* V, 209. *as the winds give benefit, let me hear from you,* Hml. I, 3, 2.

Hence used in asseverations and obsecrations: *as I am a man,* Tp. I, 2, 456. IV, 1, 23. Gentl. II, 7, 57. III, 1, 255. Wiv. II, 2, 264. IV, 2, 151. Err. I, 2, 77. Ado IV, 1, 77. V, 1, 85. LLL I, 1, 236. Mids. V, 438. As II, 7, 14. All's IV, 3, 154. V, 3, 113. R2 III, 3, 119. H5 II, 1, 69. R3 IV, 4, 397. H8 III, 2, 221. Lr. IV, 7, 69.

And = in as far as, in as much as: *as I am man, my state is desperate for my master's love; as I am woman, ...* Tw. II, 2, 37. *as thou art but man, I dare; but as thou art prince, I fear thee,* H4A III, 3, 165. *you do repent, as that the sin hath brought you to this shame,* Meas. II, 3, 31.

In a temporal sense = when: *as mine eyes opened, I saw their weapons drawn,* Tp. II, 1, 319. Gentl. V, 2, 38. *I pray you, jest, sir, as you sit at dinner,* Err. I, 2, 62. *peruse this as thou goest,* Merch. II, 4, 39. *you fly them as you swear them lordship,* All's V, 3, 156. *as I was banished, I was banished Hereford,* R2 II, 3, 113. *dogs bark at me as I halt by them,* R3 I, 1, 23. *his lady deceased as he was born,* Cymb. I, 1, 40. *as I slept, methought,* V, 5, 426.

= to wit: *a quest of thoughts, ... as thus: mine eye's due is thy outward part,* Sonn. 46, 13. *as thus: Alexander died, ...* Hml. V, 1, 231. *mad mischances and much misery, as burning fevers, agues pale and faint ....,* Ven. 739. *tired with all these, as, to behold desert a beggar born,* Sonn. 66, 2. *they say, this town is full of cozenage, as nimble jugglers, dark-working sorcerers,* Err. I, 2, 98. *told me what privy marks I had about me, as the mark of my shoulder ....,* III, 2, 147. *but there are other strict observances, as not to see a woman ...,* LLL I, 1, 37. *the seasons' difference, as the icy fang of the winter's wind,* As II, 1, 6. *but when the parties were met themselves, one of them thought but of an If, as 'if you said so, then I said so,'* V, 4, 106. *and of other motions, as promising her marriage,* All's V, 3, 264. *it is stopped with other flattering sounds, as praises of his state,* R2 II, 1, 18. *two Cliffords, as the father and the son,* H6C V, 7, 7. *she had all the royal makings of a queen, as holy oil ....,* H8 IV, 1, 88. *together with the terror of the place, as in a vault ...,* Rom. IV, 3, 39. *for some vicious mole of nature in them, as in their birth ....,* Hml. I, 4, 25.

Correlatively *as ... as, so ... as, such ... as, the same ... as* = in the same degree, of the same quality of which ...: *not so much perdition as an hair,* Tp. I, 2, 30. *so much as makes it light,* Merch. IV, 1, 328. *such senses as we have,* Tp. I, 2, 413. Gentl. IV, 1, 58. Meas. II, 2, 122. *as leaky as an unstanched wench,* Tp. I, 1, 50. 2, 281. 321. 329. 498. II, 1, 68. 238. 2, 63. III, 3, 62. V, 145. 242. 290. *recking as little what betideth me, as much I wish all good befortune you,* Gentl. IV, 3, 40, etc. etc. *to whom as great a charge as little honour he meant to lay upon,* H8 I, 1, 77. *as well at London bridge as at the Tower,* H6A III, 1, 23. *as well my undertakings as your counsels,* Troil. II, 2, 131. *as low as to thy foot doth Cassius fall,* Caes. III, 1, 56 (v. *far, deep* etc.). *as truly as he moves,* Cymb. III, 4, 154. Singular expression: *you that choose not by the view, chance as fair and choose as true,* Merch. III, 2, 133 (i. e. your chance is as fair as your choice is true).

As ... as joining even two adjectives correlatively: *as heavy to me as odious,* Tp. III, 1, 5. *as holy as severe,* Meas. III, 2, 276. *my as fair as noble ladies,* Cor. II, 1, 107. Merch. II, 7, 70. Shr. II, 132. All's IV, 4, 33. Tw. III, 4, 277. Wint. II, 3, 37. R2 V, 3, 20. Troil. IV, 4, 71. Hml. II, 2, 465. Cymb. I, 6, 144. III, 4, 121. Per. II, 5, 66. *not so short as sweet,* R2 V, 3, 117.

As ... as = though, however: *as like him as she is,* Ado I, 1, 116 (= however she may be like him). *as young as I am, I have observed these three swashers,* H5 III, 2, 29. *as cold a night as 'tis,* IV, 1, 119. Ironically: *as honest as I am,* Oth. II, 1, 203.

The correlative sometimes wanting: *this is a strange thing as e'er I looked on,* Tp. V, 289. *a strange one as ever I looked on,* Cor. IV, 5, 21. *an eye of doubt as bid me tell ...,* John IV, 2, 234. *that's worthily as any ear can hear,* Cor. IV, 1, 54. II, 1, 48. Lr. V, 3, 123. 261. Per. III, 2, 62.

A demonstrative pronoun serving as correlative: *those as sleep and think not on their sins,* Wiv. V, 5, 57. *I could not answer in that course of honour as she had made the overture,* All's V, 3, 99. *do me this courteous office as to know of the knight ...,* Tw. III, 4, 278. *that kind of fruit as maids call medlars,* Rom. II, 1, 36. *these hard conditions as this time is like to lay upon us,* Caes. I, 2, 174. *I return those duties back as are right fit,* Lr. I, 1, 99. *those arts they have as I could put into them,* Cymb. V, 5, 338.

As = in the same degree, correlativeness being understood, not expressed: *of as little memory,* Tp. II, 1, 233. *a thousand times as much,* Gentl. II. 1, 121. *three times as much more,* LLL III, 48. *twice as much,* IV, 3, 132. *he's as good at any thing,* As V, 4, 110. Tp. II, 1, 266. V, 23. 169. Gentl. I, 1, 62. III, 1, 142. IV, 2, 2 etc. etc. The indef. art. wanting: *as good deed,* H4A II, 1, 32 (Ff. *as good a deed*).

One *as* wanting: *that's as much to say,* Err. IV,

3, 54 (= as much as to say, cf. Gentl. III, 1, 308 etc.) *I have trusted thee with all the nearest things to my heart, as well my chamber-councils* (= as well as) Wint. I, 2, 236. *which he took fast as 'twas ministered,* Cymb. I, 1, 45. *will continue fast to your affection, still close as sure,* I, 6, 139.

After *so* and *such, as* sometimes for that: *which the conceited painter drew so proud, as heaven, it seem'd, to kiss the turrets bow'd,* Lucr. 1372. *such signs of rage they bear as it seem'd they would debate with angry swords,* 1420. Sonn. 14, 11. 36, 14. 78, 3. 96, 14. Phoen. 25. Gentl. II, 4, 137. LLL II, 174. Mids. III, 2, 359. Shr. Ind. 2, 12. Shr. I, 1, 33. III, 2, 111. IV, 3, 114. All's V, 1, 6. Tw. I, 5, 2. John III, 1, 296. H4A IV, 1, 4. H6A III, 1, 16. V, 1, 43. V, 4, 115. 5, 42. H6B IV, 9, 47. R3 III, 4, 40 (Ff. *that*). III, 7, 161 (Ff. *that*). Troil. III, 2, 104. Tit. II, 3, 103. Hml. II, 1, 95 (Ff. *that*). Oth. I, 1, 73. Ant. V, 2, 20. Even when the subordinate clause has the same subject: *the one so like the other as could not be distinguished,* Err. I, 1, 53. *which harm within itself so heinous is as it makes harmful all,* John III, 1, 41. *I feel such sharp dissension in my breast as I am sick,* H6A V, 5, 86. *such a prince he was as he stood by ...,* H6B II, 4, 45. *hast given unto the house of York such head as thou shalt reign but by their sufferance,* H6C I, 1, 234.

As = so that, the correlative adverb wanting: *we will play our part, as he shall think ...,* Shr. Ind. 1, 70. *and for myself mine own worth do define, as I all other in all worths surmount,* Sonn. 62, 8. *the fixure of her eye has motion in't, as we are mock'd with art,* Wint. V, 3, 68.

As = as if, sometimes with inversion of the subject: *as had she studied to misuse me so,* Shr. II, 160. *as were our England his,* R2 I, 4, 35. *as were a war in expectation,* H5 II, 4, 20. *as had he been incorpsed,* Hml. IV, 7, 88. More frequently with the regular construction: *as they were mad, unto the wood they hie them,* Ven. 323. 357. 473. Compl. 23. Mids. II, 1, 160. III, 2, 258. Shr. I, 2, 157. V, 1, 17. Wint. I, 2, 369. 415. IV, 1, 17. 4, 185. V, 2, 16. 3, 32. H4B IV, 4, 123. H6B I, 1, 103. 187. H6C III, 3, 169. R3 III, 5, 63. H8 I, 1, 10. III, 1, 7. Troil. III, 3, 167. IV, 5, 238. Rom. II, 5, 16. Caes. III, 1, 98. V, 1, 86. Mcb. II, 2, 28. V, 5, 13. Hml. II, 1, 91. IV, 5, 103. Lr. III, 4, 15. V, 3, 201. Ant. I, 2, 103. IV, 1, 1. Cymb. IV, 2, 50. V, 5, 423. Per. Prol. 24. *Like as there were husbandry in war,* Troil. I, 2, 7. *like as it would speak,* Hml. I, 2, 217. *As it were* = in a manner: *as 'twere encouraging the Greeks to fight,* Lucr. 1402. Gentl. IV, 4, 14. Wiv. I, 1, 215. 4, 30. III, 5, 75. Meas. I, 3, 44. II, 1, 94. III, 1, 33. Err. V, 244. LLL IV, 1, 145. 2, 14. 26. V, 1, 15. 121. Merch. I, 1, 11. All's II, 3, 180. Wint. I, 1, 33. IV, 4, 174. H4B V, 5, 21. H6B II, 3, 87. R3 I, 4, 31. III, 1, 77. 173. 4, 91. 5, 93. H8 III, 2, 189. Troil. I, 3, 150. Cor. IV, 4, 15. Caes. II, 1, 283. Tim. I, 1, 10. Hml. I, 2, 10. II, 1, 13. Per. I, 3, 17.

In the same manner before single parts of a sentence: *as fearful of him* (= as if fearful), Ven. 630. *as pitying me,* Sonn. 132, 1. *as stooping to relieve him,* Tp. II, 1, 121. *as by consent,* 203. *as by a thunderstroke,* 204. cf. Ven. 968. 1031. Lucr. 437. 1747. Shr. Ind. 2, 31. H4B II, 1, 141. IV, 5, 158. Troil. I, 1, 35. III, 3, 12. Rom. III, 3, 39. Mcb. II 4, 5.

I speak not as in absolute fear of you, Mcb. IV, 3, 38. Caes. III, 2, 183.

Superfluous: *as for* = for, concerning: *as for you, say what you can,* Meas. II, 4, 169. R2 I, 1, 142. H6B I, 3, 40. 100. 158. IV, 1, 139. 2, 136. H6C I, 3, 4. III, 3, 208. R3 I, 3, 313. H8 V, 1, 33. Tit. III, 1, 198 (cf. *for*).

As yet = yet (v. *yet*). Similarly joined to other expressions of time: *one Lucio as then the messenger,* Meas. V, 74. *as at that time it was the first,* Tp. I, 2, 70. *feels not what he owes, but by reflection, as when his virtues shining upon others heat them,* Troil. III, 3, 100. *that he should hither come as this dire night,* Rom. V, 3, 247. *as this very day was Cassius born,* Caes. V, 1, 72.

As touching = touching: *as touching the hit it,* LLL IV, 1, 123. H5 I, 1, 79. R3 V, 3, 271. Costard even says: *the contempts thereof are as touching me,* LLL I, 1, 191. cf. *as concerning some entertainment,* LLL V, 1, 125. *if you faint, as fearing to do so,* R2 II, 1, 297. *if you suppose as fearing you it shook,* H4A III, 1, 23. *as hating thee, are rising up in arms,* H6B IV, 1, 93. *pale they look with fear, as witnessing the truth on our side,* H6A II, 4, 63. *I told the pursuivant, as too triumphing,* R3 III, 4, 91 (Qq *as 'twere triumphing*). *if he be now returned, as checking at his voyage,* Hml. IV, 7, 63. *but he, as loving his own pride and purposes, evades them,* Oth. I, 1, 12. *our countrymen are gone and fled, as well assured Richard was dead,* R2 II, 4, 17. *I do remain as neuter,* II, 3, 159. *I am as like to call thee so again,* Merch. I, 3, 131. *the tenderness of her nature became as a prey to her grief,* All's IV, 3, 61. *made the days and nights as one,* V, 1, 3.

Redundant before *how: our recountments ... as how I came into that desert place,* As IV, 3, 142. The case is different in Hml. IV, 7, 59: *if it be so — as how should it be so? how otherwise?* The king was going to say: *as it will prove to be,* but altered his expression. cf. *if ever, as that ever may be near,* As III, 5, 28. *when in your motion you are hot and dry, as make your bouts more violent to that end,* Hml. IV, 7, 159.

As treated as a substantive: *and many such-like Ases of great charge,* Hml. V, 2, 43.*

Concerning *like as, when as, where as, while as* v. *like, when, where, while.*

Ascanius, son of Aeneas: H6B III, 2, 116.

Ascapart, a giant vanquished by Bevis of Southampton: H6B II, 3, 93 (not in Ff, but inserted by M. Edd. from the spurious Qq).

Ascaunt, across: *there is a willow grows a. a brook,* Hml. IV, 7, 167 (Ff *aslant*).

Ascend, to mount, climb, 1) trans.: *a. her chamber-window,* Gentl. III, 1, 39. Rom. III, 3, 147. *my chambers,* Wiv. III, 3, 173. *they* (curses) *a. the sky,* R3 I, 3, 287. *a. the brightest heaven of invention,* H5 Prol. 1. *a. the throne,* R2 IV, 111. 113. V, 1, 56. H4B III, 1, 71. *Pantheon,* Tit. I, 333.

2) intr. to rise: *peace a. to heaven,* John II, 86. *it —s me into the brain,* H4B IV, 3, 105. *a., brave Talbot,* H6A II, 1, 28. *the base degrees by which he did a.* Caes. II, 1, 27. *the noble Brutus is —ed,* III, 2, 11. *the dust should have —ed to the roof of heaven,* Ant. III, 6, 49.

Ascension, the act of rising: *his* (the holy eagle's) *a. is more sweet than our blest fields,* Cymb. V, 4, 116 (nearly the ecclesiastical sense of the word).

Ascension-day, holy Thursday: John IV, 2, 151. V, 1, 22. 25.

Ascent, act of rising: *his a. is not by such easy degrees,* Cor. II, 2, 28.

Ascribe, to attribute as to a cause: *which we a. to heaven,* All's I, 1, 232. H5 IV, 8, 113. H6A III, 4, 11. to attribute as a quality: *much attribute he hath, and much the reason why we a. it to him,* Troil. II, 3, 126.

Ash, the Linnaean fraxinus excelsior; used for the lance made of it: *whereagainst my grained a. an hundred times hath broke,* Cor. IV, 5, 114.

A-shaking, to trembling: *sets every joint a.* Lucr. 452.

Ashamed. *To be a.* = 1) to be abashed, to be put to the blush; absolutely: *are you not a.?* Wiv. III, 3, 230. IV, 2, 144. 197. Meas. V, 278. Ado III, 4, 28. LLL IV, 3, 159. Wint. V, 3, 37. H4A I, 3, 118. III, 3, 184. Troil. III, 2, 146. Followed by *of: like stars a. of day,* Ven. 1032. *I am much a. of my exchange,* Merch. II, 6, 35. Ado III, 4, 29. Shr. V, 1, 150. H4A IV, 2, 12. H5 IV, 7, 118. *I am a. on't,* Tim. III, 2, 19. Followed by an infinitive: *art thou a. to kiss?* Ven. 121. Gentl. IV, 2, 111. Merch. II, 3, 17. All's I, 3, 179. John III, 3, 27. H4B II, 1, 88. II, 4, 152. H6A IV, 1, 125. Rom. III, 2, 92. Hml. III, 2, 155. Lr. I, 1, 215. II, 4, 196. Ant. III, 11, 2. Cymb. IV, 4, 40. Followed by a clause: *be thou a. that I have took upon me such an immodest raiment,* Gentl. V, 4, 105. Shr. V, 2, 161. Lr. I, 4, 318. *I am a. I did yield to them,* Caes. II, 2, 106.

2) = disgraced: *you will be a. for ever,* Oth. II, 3, 162 (Qq and most M. Edd. *shamed*).

Asher-house, a farm-house near Hampton-Court, H8 III, 2, 231.

Ashes, 1) the remains of any thing burnt: Sonn. 73, 10. John III, 1, 345. H5 III, 3, 9. H6A III, 1, 190. V, 4, 92. H6B II, 3, 7. Ant. V, 2, 174. *repentant a.* John IV, 1, 111. *mourn in a.* R2 V, 1, 49. *repent in a. and sackcloth,* H4B I, 2, 221. *pale as a.* Rom. III, 2, 55. *the roses in thy cheeks shall fade to paly a.* (= to ashy paleness) Rom. IV, 1, 100.

2) the remains of the human body: H6A I, 6, 24. R3 I, 2, 6. H8 IV, 2, 75. Per. Prol. 2. *of shame's a. shall my fame be bred,* Lucr. 1188. H6A IV, 7, 92. H6C I, 4, 35. H8 V, 5, 42.

Ashford, the birthplace of John Cade: H6B III, 1, 357. IV, 3, 1.

Ashore, 1) on shore, on land: *here shall I die a.* Tp. II, 2, 45.

2) to the shore, to the land: *how came we a.?* Tp. I, 2, 158. II, 2, 129. 133. Wiv. II, 1, 66. Shr. I, 1, 42. 236. H5 III, 3, 27. R3 IV, 4, 439. Oth. II, 1, 83 (reading of Q1). 292. Ant. II, 7, 91. Per. V, 1, 261.

Ash-Wednesday, the first day of Lent: Merch. II, 5, 26.

Ashy, ash-coloured, pale: *anger ashy-pale,* Ven. 76. *dying eyes gleam'd forth their a. lights,* Lucr. 1378. *a. pale,* 1512. *a timely parted ghost, of a. semblance,* H6B III, 2, 162.

Asia, the Continent east of Europe: Err. I, 1, 134. Ado II, 1, 275. H4B II, 4, 178. Ant. I, 2, 105.

Aside, to the side: *hedge a. from the direct*

forthright, Troil. III, 3, 158. *glance a. to new-found methods*, Sonn. 76, 3. *forbear to glance thine eye a.* 139, 6. *he threw his eye a.* As IV, 3, 103. *he trod the water, whose enmity he flung a.* Tp. II, 1, 116. *throwing it a.* Caes. I, 2, 108. *thy brothers beat a. the point*, R3 I, 2, 96. *beats cold death a.* Rom. III, 1, 166. *turn a. and weep for her*, Ant. I, 3, 76. *daff'd the world a. and bid it pass*, H4A IV, 1, 96. *who sees the lurking serpent steps a.* Lucr. 362.

Hence = out of the way: *stand a.:* Gentl. IV, 2, 81. Ado IV, 2, 32. LLL IV, 1, 55. V, 2, 591. Mids. III, 2, 116. As III, 2, 132. Alls V, 3, 270. Shr. V, 1, 63. H4A II, 4, 428. H4B III, 2, 243. 249. H6C III, 3, 110. Caes. II, 1, 312. *step a.* H4A II, 4, 36 (i. e. into a by-room, cf. v. 32). Rom. I, 1, 162. Absolutely: *a., a.!* Wint. IV, 4, 700. Tim. II, 2, 127. Hml. V, 1, 240.

And then = away: *will't please you walk a.?* Meas. IV, 1, 59. Ado III, 2, 73. LLL IV, 3, 212. *stand a.* = go away, Shr. II, 24. *take him a.* Tw. V, 103. *draw a. the curtains*, Merch. II, 7, 1.

To lay a., in speaking of garments, = to take off: *my mourning weeds are laid a.* H6C III, 3, 229. Similarly of other things about a person: *lay a. your stitchery*, Cor. I, 3, 75. *lay a. the sword*, John I, 12. Figuratively: *lay a. the thoughts of Sicilia*, Wint. IV, 2, 58. *and l. aside my blood's royalty*, R2 I, 1, 71. *to lay a. life-harming heaviness*, II, 2, 3. *I lay a. that which grows to me!* H4B I, 2, 100. *pity must be laid a.* H6C II, 2, 10. In the same sense *to cast a.: casting their savageness a.* Wint. II, 3, 188. *which would be worn now, not cast a. so soon*, Mcb. I, 7, 35.

To set a. = to give up, desist from: *our purposed hunting shall be set a.* Mids. IV, 1, 188. *setting all this chat a.* Shr. II, 270. *set this unaccustomed fight a.* H6A III, 1, 93. *all dissembling set a.* H6C III, 3, 119. *Setting aside* = abstractedly from: *setting the attraction of my good parts a.* Wiv. II, 2, 110. *setting a. his high blood's royalty*, R2 I, 1, 58. H4A III, 3, 137. H4B I, 2, 93. 95. H6C IV, 1, 24. Tim. III, 5, 14.

Aside as a preposition: hath rushed a. the law, Rom. III, 3, 26 (cf. *have run by the hideous law*, Meas. I, 4, 63) = has openly evaded the law.

Asinico, (M. Edd. assinego), ass, stupid fellow: *an a. may tutor thee*, Troil. II, 1, 49.

Ask, 1) to inquire; abs.: *that it pleases your good worship to a.* Wiv. I, 4, 145. *let me a.* Meas. I, 4, 21. *why doest thou a. again?* II, 2, 9 etc. A clause following: *thou shouldst rather a. if it were possible*, Ado III, 3, 119. Shr. III, 2, 161. Alls II, 5, 70. John IV, 2, 43 etc. *to a. for* = to enquire after: *the gentleman that you —ed for*, Gent. IV, 2, 32. Err. II, 2, 211. Ado I, 1, 34. LLL III, 168. As III, 2, 235. III, 5, 109. Tw. II, 5, 61. H6A IV, 7, 58. Troil. III, 3, 244. Rom. I, 3, 101. I, 5, 13. III, 1, 101 etc. *to a. of* = to put a question to: *durst not a. of her why ...* Lucr. 1223. *let me a. of these if they ...* H6B V, 1, 109. *and a. 'what news' of me*, Cymb. V, 3, 65. In the language of Evans *to a. of* = to a. for: Wiv. ., 2, 1.

Trans.; the accus. indicating the person questioned: *to a. the spotted princess how she fares*, Lucr. 721. 1594. Sonn. 2, 5. Gent. I, 1, 121. II, 5, 36. Wiv. III, 4, 69. III, 5, 103. IV, 4, 58. Meas. II, 1, 148. II, 2, 137. Ado III, 4, 37. V, 1, 225 etc. *to a. one for* = to put a question to one in order

to be informed about: *—s the weary caitiff for his master*, Ven. 914. As IV, 1, 138. H4B II, 4, 389 etc. *to a. one of*, in the same sense: *why does he a. him of me?* Alls IV, 3, 317. With a double accus., in the same sense: *a. me no reason*, Wiv. II, 1, 4. As V, 2, 38. R2 I, 3, 9. Lr. V, 3, 118 etc. *a. him some questions*, Wiv. IV, 1, 16. Alls I, 1, 123. H6A I, 2, 87 etc. *to a. a. the question*, LLL II, 117 (cf. *Question*).

The accus. indicating the thing inquired after: *the hour that fools should a.* LLL II, 123. *a. my opinion*, Merch. III, 5, 90. *he —ed the way to Chester*, H4B I, 1, 39. *answer that I shall a.* H6B I, 4, 29. *why a. I that?* H6C V, 2, 7.

2) to request, to petition, to beg; absol.: *yet a.* R2 IV, 310. *did not a., but mock*, Cor. II, 3, 215. V, 3, 79. 89. *upon —ing*, Tw. III, 4, 232. *at his —ing*, H8 II, 1, 163. *yet dare I never deny your —ing*, Cor. I, 6, 65. *my offer, not thy —ing*, Hml. I, 2, 46. *to a. for* = to request: *bade me a. for it to-day*, H5 II, 2, 63. *and never —ed for restitution*, H6C III, 1, 118. *to a. of* = to pray: *he —s of you that never used to beg*, Per. II, 1, 66.

Trans.; *to a. a thing* = a) to beg, to express a desire of having, to demand: *a. remission for my folly*, Gent. I, 2, 65. *a. forgiveness*, Meas. IV, 2, 54. Err. IV, 3, 72. Merch. IV, 1, 369. Shr. II, 181. Tw. II, 5, 201. John IV, 2, 63. 64. H6B II, 4, 72. H6C II, 6, 69. 90. III, 1, 44. H8 I, 1, 187. II, 2, 112. Tit. I, 201 etc. b) to require: *that will a. some tears*, Mids. I, 2, 27. *my business —eth haste*, Shr. II, 115. *these great affairs do a. some charge*, R2 II, 1, 159. *the business —eth silent secrecy*, H6B I, 2, 90. *To a. a thing of a person: one boon that I shall a. of you*, Gent. V, 4, 150. Mids. IV, 1, 64. Tw. III, 4, 231. Tit. I, 473. Tim. III, 4, 45. Lr. V, 3, 11. Cymb. V, 5, 97. Per. I, 1, 62 *(nor a. advice of any other thought)* etc. Double accus.: *must a. my child forgiveness*, Tp. V, 198. Meas. III, 1, 173. As IV, 1, 113. Shr. III, 2, 178. Wint. V, 2, 56. John IV, 1, 44. V, 7, 41. Lr. V, 3, 10 etc. *To a. a person for a thing: when I could not a. my father for his advice*, Tp. V, 190. *he —ed me for a thousand marks in gold*, Err. II, 1, 61. *to a. you for my purse*, Tw. III, 4, 369. H4A I, 3, 91. H8 I, 1, 124. Oth. II, 3, 306 etc.

Askance, adv. with a sidelong glance, with a look of indifference or disdain: *taking no notice that she is so nigh, for all a. he holds her in his eye*, Ven. 342. *I have looked on truth a. and strangely*, Sonn. 110, 6. *thou canst not frown, thou canst not look a.* Shr. II, 249.

Askance, vb. to turn aside, to make to look with indifference: *O, how are they wrapped in with infamies, that from their own misdeeds a. their eyes!* Lucr. 637, i. e. who, in consequence of their own misdeeds, look with indifference on the offences of others.

Askaunt, v. *ascaunt.*

Asker, petitioner: *have you ere now denied the a.?* Cor. II, 3, 214.

Aslant, across: *a. a brook*, Hml. IV, 7, 167 (Qq *ascaunt*).

Asleep, 1) in sleep, sleeping: *lying once a.* Sonn. 154, 1. Tp. I, 2, 232. II, 1, 191. 213. 215. 2, 155. III, 2, 68. 122. V, 98. Gentl. III, 1, 25. IV, 2, 136. Ado III, 3, 71. Mids. II, 1, 177. 2, 101. IV, 1, 133. 209. V, 331. Tw. I, 5, 151. H4A I, 3, 221. II,

4, 577. H6A III, 2, 122. H6B I, 1, 249. R3 I, 4, 96. H8 IV, 2, 81. Cor. IV, 5, 2. Hml. III, 3, 89 *(when he is drunk a.).* Oth. IV, 2, 97, etc. *got 'tween a. and wake* (= between a. and awake) Lr. I, 2, 15. Figuratively: *though credit be a.* Wint. V, 2, 67. *their pride and mettle is a.* H4A IV, 3, 22.

2) into sleep: *fall a.* Sonn. 153, 1. H4A III, 3, 112. *laugh me a.* Tp. II, 1, 189. *sing me a.* Mids. II, 2, 7. Tit. V, 3, 163. *rock me a.* H4B II, 4, 211. *lull a.* Cor. III, 2, 115. *to bring her babe a.* Tit. II, 3, 29. *sucks the nurse a.* Ant. V, 2, 313 etc.

Asmath, name of a spirit, H6B I, 4, 27.*

Aspéct, subst. 1) look, glance: *some other mistress hath thy sweet —s,* Err. II, 2, 113. *render'd such a. as cloudy men use to their adversaries,* H4A III, 2, 82. *there would he anchor his a.* Ant. I, 5, 33.

2) look, air, countenance: *whose grim a. sets every joint a shaking.* Lucr. 452. *if you will jest with me, know my a.* Err. II, 2, 32. *declining their rich a. to the hot breath of Spain,* Err. III, 2, 139. *of such vinegar a.* Merch. I, 1, 54. *this a. of mine hath feared the valiant,* II, 1, 8. *what strange effect would they work in mild a.* As IV, 3, 53. *a nuncio of more grave a.* Tw. I, 4, 28. *that close a. of his does show the mood of a much troubled breast,* John IV, 2, 72. *taking note of thy abhorred a.* 224. *thy sad a.* R2 I, 3, 209. *lend the eye a terrible a.* H5 III, 1, 9. *with an a. of iron,* V, 2, 244. *his grim a.* H6A II, 3, 20. *whose ugly and unnatural a.* R3 I, 2, 23. *shamed their a. with store of childish drops,* 155. *'tis his a. of terror,* H8 V, 1, 89. *that smile we would aspire to, that sweet a. of princes,* III, 2, 369. *my young boy hath an a. of intercession,* Cor. V, 3, 32. *put on a most importunate a.* Tim. II, 1, 28. *tears in his eyes, distraction in's a.* Hml. II, 2, 581.

3) view, sight: *ravish doters with a false a.* LLL IV, 3, 260. *our arms, save in a., hath all offence sealed up,* John II, 250. *the dire a. of civil wounds,* R2 I, 3, 127.

4) the peculiar position and influence of a planet: *where mortal stars, as bright as heaven's beauties, with pure —s did him peculiar duties,* Lucr. 14. *till whatsoever star that guides my moving points on me graciously with fair a.* Sonn. 26, 10. *some ill planet reigns: I must be patient till the heavens look with an a. more favourable,* Wint. II, 1, 107. *malevolent to you in all —s,* H4A I, 1, 97. *corrects the ill —s of planets evil,* Troil. I, 3, 92 (Q *influence). under the allowance of your great a.* Lr. II, 2, 112.

Aspen, pertaining to the asp tree: *shake, an 'twere an a. leaf,* H4B II, 4, 117. *tremble like a. leaves,* Tit. II, 4, 45.

Aspersion, a sprinkling of dew or rain: *no sweet a. shall the heavens let fall to make this contract grow,* Tp. IV, 1, 18.

Aspicious, for suspicious, in the language of Dogberry, Ado III, 5, 50.

Aspick, a venomous snake: *swell, bosom, with thy fraught, for 'tis of —s' tongues,* Oth. III, 3, 450. *have I the a. in my lips?* Ant. V, 2, 296. 354. 355.

Aspiration, high desire: *that spirit of his in a. lifts him from the earth,* Troil. IV, 5, 16.

Aspire, 1) followed by *to* = to desire ambitiously: *a. to guide the heavenly car,* Gentl. III, 1, 154. *to a. unto the crown,* H6C I, 1, 53. *that smile*

we would a. to, H8 III, 2, 368. *—d to Solon's happiness,* Tit. I, 177.

2) absolutely, = to rise, to tower; of flames: *love is a spirit all compact of fire, not gross to sink, but light, and will a.* Ven. 150. *the lightless fire which, in pale embers hid, lurks to a.* Lucr. 5. *whose flames a. as thoughts do blow them,* Wiv. V, 5, 101. *the —ing flame of golden sovereignty,* R3 IV, 4, 328. Of mountains: *a cloud in his dim mist the —ing mountains hiding,* Lucr. 548. *digs hills because they do a.* Per. I, 4, 5. *Aspiring* = ambitious: *the —ing French,* H6A V, 4, 99. *Eleanor's —ing humour,* H6B I, 2, 97. John V, 1, 56. R2 V, 2, 9. H6C V, 6, 61.

3) transitively = to ascend, to mount to: *that gallant spirit hath —d the clouds,* Rom. III, 1, 122.

Aspray, see *Osprey.*

A-squint, not in the straight line of vision, perversely: *look'd a.* Lr. V, 3, 72.

Ass, the animal Asinus: Meas. III, 1, 26. Err. IV, 4, 28. 29. Mids. III, 2, 17. 34. IV, 1, 82. 212. Merch. IV, 1, 91. Shr. II, 200. Tw. V, 20 etc. etc. *I will fly, like a dog, the heels o' the a.* Tim. I, 1, 283. *thou borest thy ass on thy back o'er the dirt,* Lr. I, 4, 177 (allusions to well-known fables of Aesop). As a term of reproach, = stupid fellow, dolt: *to make an a. of me,* Mids. III, 1, 124. Wiv. V, 5, 125. Tw. V, 20. *I find the a. in compound with the major part of your syllables,* Cor. II, 1, 64.* Tp. V, 295. Gentl. II, 3, 39. 5, 25. 49. V, 2, 28. Wiv. I, 1, 176. Meas. II, 2, 315. V, 506. Err. II, 1, 14. 2, 201. III, 1, 15. Mids. IV, 1, 27. V, 317 (quibble with *ace). Ado IV, 2, 75. V, 1, 315. LLL V, 2, 628 etc. etc.

Assail, 1) trans. to attack: *—ed by night,* Lucr. 1262. *when violence —s us,* Oth. II, 3, 204. John III, 2, 6. H5 IV, 1, 159. H6A IV, 7, 10. H6B IV, 2, 185. H6C I, 1, 65. Figuratively: *let us a. your ears that are so fortified against our story,* Hml. I, 1, 31. Lucr. 1562. *that fell poison which —eth him,* John V, 7, 9. *—ed with fortune fierce and keen,* Per. V, 3, 88. Especially used of what the poet calls 'an amorous siege:' *beauteous thou art, therefore to be —ed,* Sonn. 41, 6. *either not —ed or victor being charged,* Sonn. 70, 10. *woo her, a. her,* Tw. I, 3, 60. *what lady would you choose to a.* Cymb. I, 4, 136. *I have —ed her with music,* II, 3, 44.

2) absolutely = to make an attack: *to beat —ing death from his weak legions,* H6A IV, 4, 16. *when shame —ed, the red should fence the white,* Lucr. 63. To attempt to seduce: *when they to a. begun,* Compl. 262. *but he —s,* All's I, 1, 126. *the encounter of —ing eyes,* Rom. I, 1, 219.

Assailable, liable to an attack: *they are a.* Mcb. III, 2, 39.

Assailant, attacker: *thy a. is quick,* Tw. III, 4, 245. One who attempts to debauch a woman: *and never stir —s,* As I, 3, 116.

Assassination, murder: *if the a. could trammel up the consequence,* Mcb. I, 7, 2.

Assault, vb. to attack; absol.: *where will you a.?* John II, 408. trans. *to a. thy country,* Cor. V, 3, 123. Lr. II, 2, 156. Oth. V, 2, 258, Metaphorically: *prayer which pierces so that it —s mercy itself,* Tp. Epil. 17.

Assault, subst. attack, onset, storm: *what means death in this rude a.?* R2 V, 5, 106. *they may vex us with shot or with a.* H6A I, 4, 13. *the enemy* doth make a. II, 1, 38. in which a. we lost twelve hundred men, IV, 1, 24. Cor. IV, 5, 180. Mcb. I, 2, 33. Figuratively: I will make a complimental a. upon him, Troil. III, 1, 42. a savageness in unreclaimed blood, of general a. Hml. II, 1, 35 (= incident to all men). Especially an attempt on the chastity of a woman: if, Collatine, thine honour lay in me, from me by strong a. it is bereft, Lucr. 835. Dian no queen of virgins, that would suffer her poor knight surprised, without rescue in the first a. or ransom afterward, All's I, 3, 121. A mere proposal of that kind termed so: the a. that Angelo hath made to you, Meas. III, 1, 188. the a. you have made to her chastity, Cymb. I, 4, 175. All's IV, 2, 51. Cymb. I, 6, 150. III, 2, 8. Used of honourable love: invincible against all —s of affection, Ado II, 3, 120.

Assay, vb. to try, attempt: she hath —ed as much as may be proved, Ven. 608. who ever shunned by precedent the destined ill she must herself a. Compl. 156. a. the power you have, Meas. I, 4, 76. or lose my labour in —ing it, Err. V, 97. if we —ed to steal the clownish fool, As I, 3, 131. to-night let us a. our plot, All's III, 7, 44. the rebels have —ed to win the Tower, H6B IV, 5, 9. I would a. to make thee blush, H6C I, 4, 118. 'twere better not —ed, Hml. IV, 7, 53. come on, a. Oth. II, 1, 121. passion —s to lead the way, II, 3, 207. To a. one, properly to probe, to put one to the proof, is either = to apply to, to accost one with a particular purpose: that he dares in this manner a. me, Wiv. II, 1, 26; bid herself a. him, Meas. I, 2, 186; or to measure swords with one: seeing thou fallest on me so luckily, I will a. thee, H4A V, 4, 34; or to tempt one (followed by to): did you a. him to any pastime? Hml. III, 1, 14.

Assày, subst. (in Sonn. 110, 8 and Lr. I, 2, 47 essay) 1) examination, probation, trial: only he hath made an a. of her virtue, Meas. III, 1, 164. and worse —s proved thee my best of love, Sonn. 110, 8. with windlasses and with —s of bias, Hml. II, 1, 65. he wrote this but as an e. or taste of my virtue, Lr. I, 2, 47. this cannot be, by no a. of reason, Oth. I, 3, 18.

2) attempt, trial: after many accents and delays, untimely breathings, sick and short —s, Lucr. 1720. let us make the a. upon him, Tim. IV, 3, 406. their malady convinces the great a. of art, Mcb. IV, 3, 143. make a. Hml. III, 3, 69. Hostile attempt, attack: galling the gleaned land with hot —s, H5 I, 2, 151. never more to give the a. of arms against your majesty, Hml. II, 2, 71.

Assemblance, semblance, external aspect: care I for the limb, the thewes, the stature, bulk, and big a. of a man? H4B III, 2, 277 (or can it possibly be = the conglomerate? Arrivance is = all that arrives; so assemblance perhaps all that is assembled in a body).

Assemble, 1) trans. to bring or call together: all that are —d in this place, Err. V, 396. H4B IV, 2, 5. for which we have —d them, H5 II, 2, 18. II, 4, 19. V, 2, 64. H6A I, 1, 139. I, 3, 74. R3 III, 7, 84. H8 II, 4, 60. Cor. III, 3, 12. Caes. I, 1, 62. Ant. I, 4, 75. III, 6, 68.

2) intr. (mostly followed by to) to come together: as fast as objects to his beams a. Sonn. 114, 8. to me and to the state of my great grief let kings a. John III, 1, 71. and to the English court a. now, H4B IV, 5, 122. let them a. Cor. II, 3, 225.

Assembly (twice quadrisyllable: Ado V, 4, 34 and Cor. I, 1, 159), a company met together in the same place, whether for amusement or to transact business: Meas. I, 3, 9. Err. V, 60. As V, 4, 159. H4B V, 5, 141. H5 V, 2, 6. H8 I, 4, 67. 87. Cor. I, 1, 159. II, 2, 61. Rom. I, 2, 75. Tim. III, 6, 86. Caes. III, 2, 19. Lr. III, 6, 49. Sometimes = congregation: we have no temple but the wood, no a. but horn-beasts, As III, 3, 50. Ado IV, 2, 57. V, 4, 34. A meeting in arms, for the purpose of rebellion: Is this proceeding just and honourable? Is your a. so? H4B IV, 2, 111 cf. Cor. I, 1, 159.

Assent, subst., agreement: without the king's a. or knowledge you wrought to be a legate, H8 III, 2, 310. by the main a. of all these learned men she was divorced, IV, 1, 31.

Ass-head, head of an ass: you see an a. of your own, Mids. III, 1, 119. Tw. V, 212.

Assign, vb. 1) to allot: like fools that in th' imagination set the goodly objects which abroad they find of lands and mansions, theirs in thought —ed, Compl. 138. in their —ed and native dwelling-place, As II, 1, 63. England from Trent and Severn hitherto is to my part —ed, H4A III, 1, 75. to his conveyance I a. my wife, Oth. I, 3, 286. to Ptolemy he —ed Syria, Ant. III, 6, 15.

2) to appoint: I pray your highness to a. our trial day, R2 I, 1, 151. And with a common inversion: till we a. you to your days of trial, IV, 106 (= till we a. to you your days of trial).

3) to destine: —ed am I to be the English scourge, H6A I, 2, 129. whether I in any just term am —ed to love the Moor, Oth. I, 1, 39 (so Q1; all the other O. Edd. affined).

Assign, subst. appendage (affected expression): six French rapiers and poniards, with their —s, as girdle, hangers, and so, Hml. V, 2, 157. 169.

Assinego, v. Asinico.

Assist, vb. trans., 1) to help: how can they then a. me in the act? Lucr. 350. Tp. I, 1, 15. Gentl. II, 7, 1. Wiv. IV, 5, 92. IV, 6, 3. V, 5, 3. Meas. IV, 2, 11. Ado I, 3, 71. LLL I, 2, 101. 189. Shr. Ind. 1, 92. Shr. I, 1, 163. I, 2, 196. Wint. V, 3, 90. H6C I, 1, 28. 30. Cor. I, 2, 36. Mcb. I, 2, 52. Oth. I, 3, 247. Ant. II, 1, 1. Per. III, 1, 19. Absolutely: a., good friends, Ant. IV, 15, 31.

2) to attend, to join: the king and prince at prayers! let us a. them, Tp. I, 1, 57. midnight, a. our moan, Ado V, 3, 16. yourself, —ed with your honoured friends, bring them to our embracement, Wint. V, 1, 113. Absolutely: Cor. V, 6, 156.

Assistance, 1) help: Sonn. 78, 2. Ado II, 1, 385. LLL V, 1, 123. 127. John III, 1, 158. V, 4, 39. R2 II, 1, 160. H4A IV, 3, 65. H4B I, 3, 21. IV, 5, 194 (by their —s). H6C V, 4, 68. R3 IV, 2, 4. Tim. III, 1, 21. Mcb. III, 1, 124.

2) assistants, associates: affecting one sole throne, without a. Cor. IV, 6, 33 (Hanmer: assistants; cf. LLL V, 1, 127, where O. Edd. inversely have assistants for assistance).

Assistant, subst., helper, associate: her a. or go-between, Wiv. II, 2, 273. to ask those on the banks if they were his —s, R3 IV, 4, 526. allied to eminent —s, H8 I, 1, 62. I'll thy a. be, Rom. II, 3, 90. let me be no a. for a state, but keep a farm and carters, Hml. II, 2, 166 (i. e. no public functionary).

Assistant, adj., helpful: *as the winds give bene-fit and convoy is a.* Hml. I, 3, 3.

Associate, vb. trans., to accompany, to join, attend: *friends should a. friends in grief and woe,* Tit. V, 3, 169. *to a. me,* Rom. V, 2, 6. *a fearful army led by Marcius, —d with* (= by) *Aufidius,* Cor. IV, 6, 76.

Associate, subst., companion: *the bark is ready, and the wind at help, the —s tend,* Hml. IV, 3, 47.

Assuage, to allay, appease: *his fury was —d,* Ven. 318. 334. Lucr. 790. Compl. 69. Cor. V, 2, 83.

Assubjugate, to bring into subjection, to debase: *nor a. his merit, as amply titled as Achilles is, by going to Achilles,* Troil. II, 3, 202.

Assume, 1) to take, to put on: *my very visor began to a. life,* Ado II, 1, 249. *our project's life this shape of sense —s,* Troil. I, 3, 385. *—ing men's infirmities,* Per. Prol. 3. Especially to take a form, an appearance: *I will a. thy part in some disguise,* Ado I, 1, 323. *there is no vice so simple but —s some mark of virtue on his outward parts,* Merch. III, 2, 81. *and these a. but valour's excrement,* 87. *if spirits can a. both form and suit,* Tw. V, 242. *a. the port of Mars,* H5 Prol. 6. *do not a. my likeness,* Tim. IV, 3, 218. *if it a. my noble father's person,* Hml. I, 2, 244. *a. some other horrible form,* I, 4, 72. II, 2, 629. *to a. a semblance that very dogs disdained,* Lr. V, 3, 187. = to take the appearance of: *a. a virtue, if you have it not,* Hml. III, 4, 160. *where reason can revolt without perdition, and loss a. all reason without revolt,* Troil. V, 2, 145. *he it is that hath —d this age,* Cymb. V, 5, 319 (Belarius speaks so, because to Cymbeline he must appear as quite another person).

2) to claim: *I will a. desert,* Merch. II, 9, 51. *like a bold champion, I a. the lists,* Per. I, 1, 61.

Assurance, 1) confidence, certain knowledge: *rather like a dream than an a. that my remembrance warrants,* Tp. I, 2, 45. *my a. bids me search,* Wiv. III, 2, 47. *put your lord into a desperate a. she will none of him,* Tw. II, 2, 8. *a. bless your thoughts!* Tim. II, 2, 189. *I'll make a. double sure,* Mcb. IV, 1, 83. *and from some knowledge and a. offer this office to you,* Lr. III, 1, 41. *For a.* = to make confidence greater: *for more a. that a living prince does now speak to thee,* Tp. V, 108. *for the more better a. tell them that I am not Pyramus,* Mids. III, 1, 21. *for a. let's each one send unto his wife,* Shr. V, 2, 65.

2) that which gives confidence, a) certainty, safety: *jealousy shall be called a.* Ado II, 2, 50. *by this knot thou shalt so surely tie thy now unsured a. to the crown,* John II, 471. *his head's a. is but frail,* R3 IV, 4, 498. *they are sheep and calves which seek out a. in that,* Hml. V, 1, 126. *quite forego the way which promises a., and give up yourself to chance,* Ant. III, 7, 47. cf. *take you a. of her* = make sure of her, Shr. IV, 4, 92. *by an auricular a. have your satisfaction,* Lr. I, 2, 99 (confirmation).

b) a solemn declaration or promise: *give a. to Baptista, as if he were the right Vincentio,* Shr. IV, 2, 69. *give me modest a. if you be the lady of the house,* Tw. I, 5, 192. *plight me the full a. of your faith,* IV, 3, 26. *if you mind to hold your true obedience, give me a.* H6C IV, 1, 141.

c) a certain proof: *to give the world a. of a man,* Hml. III, 4, 62.

d) a legal evidence: *let your father make her the a., she is your own,* Shr. II, 389. 398. *and make a. here of greater sums,* III, 2, 136. *to pass a. of a dower,* IV, 2, 117. *where then do you know best we be affied and such a. ta'en,* IV, 4, 49. *they are busied about a counterfeit a.* IV, 4, 92.

e) surety, warrant: *you should procure him better a. than Bardolph,* H4B I, 2, 36. *having here no judge indifferent, nor no more a. of equal friendship and proceeding,* H8 II, 4, 17.

Assure, 1) to make sure: a) to convince, to persuade: *I know not how I shall a. you further,* All's III, 7, 2. *thy earliness doth me a. thou art uproused by some distemperature,* Rom. II, 3, 39. *a. thyself* = be persuaded: *in his grave a. thyself my love is buried,* Gentl. IV, 2, 115. Tw. I, 2, 9. III, 2, 38. H6B IV, 9, 19. Tit. V, 1, 61. Lr. II, 1, 106. Oth. III, 3, 20. IV, 2, 202. *Assured* or *well assured* = sure, persuaded: Merch. I, 1, 137. I, 3, 29. IV, 1, 315. John II, 534. R2 II, 4, 17. H6B III, 1, 346. III, 2, 349. H6C V, 3, 16. R3 I, 3, 23. II, 1, 37. V, 3, 36. Cor. V, 2, 79. Cymb. I, 5, 81 etc. *stand you so —d,* Shr. I, 2, 156. *remain —d,* Tim. V, 1, 100. *rest —d,* Cor. III, 1, 121. Caes. V, 3, 17. *with —d trust,* Pilgr. 329. *her —d credit* (firm belief) Cymb. I, 6, 159. *—d of* = sure of: *—d of acceptance,* Lucr. Ded. 3. Sonn. 45, 11. Meas. II, 2, 119. All's II, 3, 19. H4B IV, 5, 106. Lr. IV, 7, 56. Irregularly: *this I am —d,* H6A V, 5, 83; cf. *this I do a. myself,* H6B II, 2, 80.

b) to declare solemnly: *I a. you,* Tp. II, 1, 85. 2, 141. Sonn. 111, 13. Wiv. II, 2, 109. Ado IV, 2, 27. LLL IV, 2, 10. V, 1, 99. Mids. I, 2, 14. V, 358. As I, 1, 159. IV, 3, 173. Shr. IV, 3, 191. H4A V, 4, 146. H4B I, 2, 33. V, 3, 70. H6B II, 2, 78. Caes. V, 4, 21 etc. *I'll a. you,* H8 I, 3, 54. IV, 1, 12. *that I a. you,* Troil. V, 1, 45. Lr. II, 1, 106.

2) to make certain and doubtless, to answer for, to warrant: *this shall a. my constant loyalty,* H6C III, 3, 240. *for one sweet look thy help I would a. thee,* Ven. 371. *he of both that can a. my daughter greatest dower,* Shr. II, 345. 347. 381. *I'll a. her of her widowhood,* Shr. II, 124. *Assured* = certain: *thou art —d mine,* Sonn. 92, 2. *incertainties now crown themselves —d,* 107, 7. *faults —d,* 118, 10. John III, 1, 336. H5 IV, 3, 81. H6A I, 2, 82. R3 V, 3, 319. Lr. III, 6, 102. Cymb. I, 6, 73.

3) to affiance: *swore I was —d to her,* Err. III, 2, 145. *when I was first —d,* John II, 535.

Assuredly, surely, certainly: *a. the thing is to be sold,* As II, 4, 96. H6A I, 2, 130. H8 IV, 2, 92. Ant. V, 2, 72.

Assyrian, pertaining to Assyria: *O base A. knight,* H4B V, 3, 105. *the old A. slings,* H5 IV, 7, 65.

Astonish, to confound with some sudden emotion; 1) to strike with admiration: *whose beauty did a. the survey of richest eyes,* All's V, 3, 16. *thou hast —ed me with thy high terms,* H6A I, 2, 93. V, 5, 2. Hml. III, 2, 340 (Qq *stonish*).

2) to amaze, to stun with fear and terror: *stone-still, —ed with this deadly deed,* Lucr. 1730. *neither he nor his compeers my verse —ed,* Sonn. 86, 8. *you have —ed him,* H5 V, 1, 40. *a. these fell-lurking curs,* H6B V, 1, 146. *such dreadful heralds to a. us,* Caes. I, 3, 56.

Astraea, the Goddess of justice: H6A I, 6, 4. Tit. IV, 3, 4.

Astray, out of the right way: *you are a.*
Gentl. I, 1, 109. *lead these rivals so a.* Mids. III, 2,
358.

Astronomer, astrologer, one who professes
to foretell future events by the situation of the stars:
when he performs, —s foretell it, Troil. V, 1, 100.
*learned indeed were that a. that knew the stars as I
his characters; he'ld lay the future open,* Cymb. III,
2, 27.

Astronomical, pertaining to astrology: *how long
have you been a sectary a.?* Lr. I, 2, 165.

Astronomy, astrology, science teaching to
foretell future events by the situation of the stars:
*not from the stars do I my judgment pluck, and yet
methinks I have a.* Sonn. 14, 2.

Asunder, 1) parted, not together: *hearts
remote, yet not a.* Phoen. 29. *could not live a.* H6A
II, 2, 31. *that we two are a.* Cymb. III, 2, 32. *villain
and he be many miles a.* Rom. III, 5, 82. *they whirl
a. and dismember me,* John III, 1, 330. *my chaff and
corn shall fly a.* H8 V, 1, 112. *keep them a.* Wiv. III,
1, 74. H6B I, 4, 54. *part a.* H5 Prol. 22. *pluck them
a.* Hml. V, 1, 287. *will you rent our ancient love a.?*
Mids. III, 2, 215. *from my shoulders crack my arms
a.* H6A I, 5, 11.

2) in two, to pieces: *his woven girths he
breaks a.* Ven. 266. *cut my lace a.* R3 IV, 1, 34 (Qq
in sunder). *cracking ten thousand curbs of more strong
link a.* Cor. I, 1, 73. *hack their bones a.* H6A IV, 7,
47. *to rend his limbs a.* H6B I, 3, 15.

At, prepos. serving to mark a point of place or
time. 1) of place: *at Ardea to my lord,* Lucr. 1332
(cf. *going back to school in Wittenberg,* Hml. I, 2, 113;
but: *depart to Paris to the king,* H6A III, 2, 128). *at
Tunis,* Tp. II, 1, 97. *at Windsor,* Wiv. II, 1, 66. *at
Ephesus,* Err. I, 1, 17. *at Berwick,* H6A II, 1, 83. *at
London,* 179. *at the Tower,* R3 III, 1, 65. *at Exeter,*
IV, 2, 106 etc. etc. Even a country treated as a local
point: *when at Bohemia you take my lord,* Wint. I, 2,
39. — *At the Phoenix,* Err. I, 2, 88. *at your shop,* III,
1, 3. *does he lie at the Garter?* Wiv. II, 1, 187. *at
Master Page's,* III, 2, 86. *at Master Ford's,* IV, 1, 1.
at the Duke Alençon's, LLL II, 61. *at the father's of
a certain pupil of mine,* IV, 2, 159. *at the notary's,*
Merch. I, 3, 173. *at the governor's,* H6A I, 4, 20. *at
my cousin Cressida's,* Troil. III, 2, 1. *at the duke's,*
Oth. I, 2, 44. *at her father's,* I, 3, 241. *meet me at the
North-gate,* Gentl. III, 1, 258. *porter at the gate,* Err.
II, 2, 219. *at the road,* Gentl. I, 1, 53. *at the other hill,*
John III, 298. *at that oak,* Wiv. IV, 4, 42. *at Herne's
oak,* IV, 6, 19. *at the duke's oak,* Mids. I, 2, 113. *whose
throats had hanging at them wallets of flesh,* Tp. III,
3, 45. *at which end of the beam,* II, 1, 130. *at my
mistress' eyes love's brand new fired,* Sonn. 153, 9.
light them at the glow-worm's eyes, Mids. III, 1, 173.
at her father's churlish feet, Gentl. III, 1, 225 (cf.
foot). *close at the heels,* Gentl. III, 1, 325. *out at elbow,*
Meas. II, 1, 61. *out at heels,* Wiv. I, 3, 34. Lr. II, 2,
164. *I am pale at my heart,* Meas. IV, 3, 157. *breathes
at's nostrils,* Tp. II, 2, 65. *foams at mouth,* Troil. V,
5, 36. *overlusty at legs,* Lr. II, 4, 10. *glad at soul,* Oth.
I, 3, 196. *at her window,* Gentl. III, 1, 113. Mids. I,
1, 30. *in at the window,* John I, 171. Caes. I, 2, 320.
shine in at the casement, Mids. III, 1, 59. *thrown in
at the casement,* Lr. I, 2, 64. *my master is come in at
your back-door,* Wiv. III, 3, 24. *soft pity enters at an*

iron gate, Lucr. 595. *saw'st thou him enter at the abbey
here?* Err. V, 278. *true prayers that shall be up at
heaven and enter there,* Meas. II, 2, 152. *enter at a
lady's ear,* H5 V, 2, 100. *fame, late entering at his
heedful ears,* H6C III, 3, 63. *to look out at her lady's
window,* Ado II, 2, 17. *leans me out at her mistress'
window,* Ado III, 3, 156. *talked with you out at your
window,* IV, 1, 85. *talk with a man out at a window,*
IV, 1, 311. *look out at window,* Merch. II, 5, 41. Shr.
V, 1, 32. *it will out at the casement,* As IV, 1, 163. *out
at the keyhole,* 164. *out at the chimney,* 165. *out at
the postern,* Gentl. V, 1, 9. *it would not out at windows
nor at doors,* John V, 7, 29. *see him out at gates,* Cor.
III, 3, 138. *goes out at the portal,* Hml. III, 4, 136. *I
must be brief, lest resolution drop out at mine eyes,*
John IV, 1, 36. *I will fetch thy rim out at thy throat,*
H5 IV, 4, 15. *forth at your eyes your spirits wildly
peep,* Hml. III, 4, 119. — Sometimes other prepositions, as *in* or *on,* would be expected: *feed like oxen
at a stall,* H4A V, 2, 14. *five justices' hands at it,*
Wint. IV, 4, 288 ; but the irregularity may be easily
accounted for. *At land, at sea, at freedom, at liberty,*
v. *land, sea* etc.

Serving to point out a mark aimed at: *love's
golden arrow at him should have fled,* Ven. 947. *shoot
their foam at Simois' banks,* Lucr. 1442. *shoot not at
me,* Sonn. 117, 12. *a stone to throw at his dog,* Wiv.
I, 4, 119. *aiming at Silvia,* Gentl. II, 6, 30. *a certain
aim he took at a fair Vestal,* Mids. II, 1, 158. *to strike
at me,* Wiv. V, 5, 248. *she strikes at the brow,* LLL
IV, 1, 119. *dart thy skill at me,* V, 2, 396. *bore at men's
eyes,* Tim. IV, 3, 116. *bark at a crow,* Ado I, 1, 133.
beat at thy rocky heart, Lucr. 590. *spit at me and
spurn at me,* Err. II, 2, 136. *I shoot thee at the swain,*
LLL III, 66. *reach at the glorious gold,* H6B I, 2, 11
(cf. *reach* and *snatch*). *fling it at thy face,* H6C V, 1,
51. *blow them at the moon,* Hml. III, 4, 209. *throw my
sceptre at the injurious gods,* Ant. IV, 15, 76. *blow at
fire,* Per. I, 4, 4. *uncouple at the hare,* Ven. 674 (to
chase the hare). *that which we run at,* H8 I, 1, 142.
none should come at him, Wint. II, 3, 32. *mow and
chatter at me,* Tp. II, 2, 9. *whet his teeth at him,* Ven.
1113. And thus even: *I am at him upon my knees,*
Ado II, 1, 30 (i. e. bent towards him, anxious to be
heard by him). — *To guess at sth.* v. *guess.*

Serving to mark a point reached: *are you at the
farthest?* Shr. IV, 2, 73. *at farthest* (= at the latest)
Tp. IV, 114. *gape at widest,* Tp. I, 1, 63. *thou hast
me at the worst,* H5 V, 2, 250. *I am at the worst,* Lr.
IV, 1, 27. *almost at fainting under the pleasing punishment,* Err. I, 1, 46. *at least, at last* etc. cf. *least, last,*
etc. Especially in estimations of price and value:
valued at the highest rate, Err. I, 1, 24 (cf. *price, rate*).
I sit at ten pounds a week, Wiv. I, 3, 8. *at a few drops
of womens' rheum he sold the blood and labour of our
great action,* Cor. V, 6, 46. *I do prize it at my love
before the reverend'st throat in Athens* (= worth my
love) Tim. V, 1, 184. *if my love thou hold'st at aught,*
Hml. IV, 3, 60. *what do you esteem it at?* Cymb. I, 4,
85. *buy ladies' flesh at a million a dram,* 147. *thy
speaking of my tongue, and I thine, must be granted
to be much at one* (= of the same value), H5 V, 2,
204. *nothing is at a like goodness still,* Hml. IV, 7,
117.

2) Serving to mark a point of time: *at that time,*
Tp. I, 2, 70. *at which time,* V, 4. *at midnight,* I, 2, 228.

at this hour, IV, 263. *at Hallowmas,* Gentl. II, 1, 27. *at Pentecost,* IV, 4, 163. *at the day of judgment,* Wiv. III, 3, 226. *at eighteen years,* Err. I, 1, 126. *at three years old,* Cymb. I, 1, 58. *at Cain's birth,* LLL IV, 2, 36. *at after supper,* R3 IV, 3, 31 (Ff. *and after supper*). *at the first sight,* Tp. I, 2, 440. *at first dash,* H6A I, 2, 71. *at his departure,* Gentl. IV, 4, 140. *at my depart for France,* H6B I, 1, 2, etc. etc. *men at some time are masters of their fates,* Caes. I, 2, 139 (= there is a time when ...).

Hence = on occasion of: *at the marriage of the king's daughter,* Tp. II, 1, 69. 97. *to sing at a man's funeral,* II, 2, 46. *either at flesh or fish,* Err. III, 1, 22. *lost at a game of tick-tack,* Meas. I, 2, 196. *win a lady at leap-frog,* H5 V, 2, 142. *at fast and loose,* Ant. IV, 12, 28. *at an earthquake,* All's I, 3, 91. *at requiring,* Tp. II, 2, 186. *at pick'd leisure,* V, 247. *at thy request,* III, 2, 128. Gentl. II, 1, 132. *at thy hest,* Tp. IV, 65. *at my command,* V, 48. *arrest him at my suit,* Err. IV, 1, 69. *at your important letters,* V, 138. cf. *pleasure, leisure, control* etc. See also: *at a burden,* Err. V, 343. Wint. IV, 4, 267. *at a birth,* Oth. II, 3, 212. *at a mouthful,* Per. II, 1, 35.

Again = occupied with: *at prayers,* Tp. I, 1, 57. *at play,* V, 185. *at supper,* Gentl. II, 1, 46, etc. etc. *hard at study,* Tp. III, 1, 20. *he thinks he still is at his instrument,* Caes. IV, 3, 293. *at blow and thrust,* Oth. II, 3, 238. *he's at it now,* Wint. III, 3, 109. *they are at it,* V, 5, 36. 7, 10. *O, they are at it,* Cor. I, 4, 21. *a certain convocation of politic worms are e'en at him,* Hml. IV, 3, 22. (*At ebb, at gaze, at a guard, at rest,* v. *ebb* etc.). From this use the following proceeded: *a dog at all things,* Gentl. IV, 4, 14. *I am ill at reckoning,* LLL I, 2, 42. *good at such eruptions,* V, 1, 120. *the very best at a beast* (i. e. to represent a beast), Mids. V, 232. *as good at any thing,* As V, 4, 110. *I am dog at a catch,* Tw. II, 3, 64. *the cur is excellent at faults,* II, 5, 140. *you're powerful at it,* Wint. II, 1, 28. *you are the better at proverbs,* H5 III, 7, 131. *you were ever good at sudden commendations,* H8 V, 3, 122. *I am ill at these numbers,* Hml. II, 2, 120. *more tight at this than thou,* Ant. IV, 4, 15.

As coincidence of time naturally suggests the idea of causality, *at* precedes that which causes any affection: *at his look she flatly falleth down,* Ven. 463. *she trembles at his tale,* 591. *hang their heads at this disdain,* Lucr. 521. *at his own shadow let the thief run mad,* 997. *why quiverest thou at this decree?* 1030. *spread their leaves at the sun's eye,* Sonn. 25, 6. *at a frown they in their glory die,* 25, 8. *they mourners seem at such as . . . ,* 127, 10. *tremble at thy din,* Tp. I, 2, 371. *mount their pricks at my footfall,* II, 2, 12. *do not smile at me,* IV, 9. *to weep at what I am glad of,* III, 1, 74. *my rejoicing at nothing can be more,* III, 1, 94. *at which they prick'd their ears,* IV, 176. *at which my nose is in great indignation,* IV, 199. *admire at this encounter,* V, 154 (cf. *to wonder*). *this passion at his name,* Gentl. I, 2, 16. *'tis love you cavil at,* I, 1, 38. *when you chid at Sir Proteus,* II, 1, 78. *wept herself blind at my parting,* II, 3, 14. *railed at me,* III, 2, 4. *takes exceptions at your person,* V, 2, 3. *shrieked at it,* Wiv. I, 1, 309. *make sport at me,* III, 3, 160. *merry at any thing,* Meas. III, 2, 250. *laugh at it,* LLL IV, 3, 148. *better to weep at joy than to joy at weeping,* Ado I, 1, 28. *grew civil at her song,* Mids. II, 1, 152. *rising*

and cawing at the gun's report, III, 2, 22. *at his sight away his fellows fly,* 24. *I should be mad at it,* Merch. V, 176. *laugh at me, make their pastime at my sorrow,* Wint. II, 3, 24. *hanging the head at Ceres' plenteous load,* H6B I, 2, 2. *the sense aches at thee,* Oth. IV, 2, 69. *which beasts would cough at,* Ant. I, 4, 63. *at whose burden the ocean foams,* II, 6, 20. *courtesy at the censure,* Cymb. III, 3, 55. *took some displeasure at him,* Per. I, 3, 21 (cf. *glad, angry* etc. etc.).

Atalanta, the daughter of Jasius, swift in running and to be won only by one who excelled her: *—'s better part,* As III, 2, 155 (i. e. her beauty and chastity, without her cruelty). *made of —'s heels,* 294.

Ate, the goddess of mischief: *you shall find her the infernal A. in good apparel,* Ado II, 1, 263. *more —s, more —s! stir them on!* LLL V, 2, 694. *an A., stirring him to blood and strife,* John II, 63. *A. by his side come hot from hell,* Caes. III, 1, 271.

Athenian, subst. a native of Athens: Mids. II, 2, 67. III, 2, 36. 41. Tim. I, 1, 183. 192. 2, 35 etc. Lr. III, 4, 185.

Athenian, adj. pertaining to Athens: Mids. I, 1, 12. 162. II, 1, 260. 264. 2, 73. III, 2, 10. 39. IV, 1, 70 etc. Troil. Prol. 6. Tim. passim.

Athens, town of Greece: Mids. I, 1, 41. 119. 159. 205. 2, 5. II, 2, 71. III, 2, 26. 315. IV, 1, 72 etc. Troil. Prol. 3. Tim. I, 1, 39. II, 2, 17. III, 1, 11. 5, 101, etc. Ant. III, 1, 35. 12, 15.

Athol, a Scotch county: *Earl of A.,* H4A I, 1, 72.

Athwart, prep., across, from side to side: *lay his wreathed arms a. his loving bosom,* LLL IV, 3, 135. *heave him a. the sea,* H5 V Chor. 9. *a. men's noses,* Rom. I, 4, 58 (only in the spurious Q1; other O. Edd. *over*). *a. the lane,* Cymb. V, 3, 18. — *A. the heart of his lover,* As III, 4, 45, cf. *across.* Figuratively: *whatsoever comes a. his affection* (= crosses his affection) Ado II, 2, 6.

Athwart, adv., crossly, wrongly: *quite a. goes all decorum,* Meas. I, 3, 30. *all a. there came a post from Wales,* H4A I, 1, 36.

Atlas, (cf. *Demi-Atlas*), the giant supporting the heavens: *thou art no A. for so great a weight,* H6C V, 1, 36.

Atomy, atom, smallest particle of matter: *it is as easy to count —ies,* As III, 2, 245. *eyes who shut their gates on —ies,* III, 5, 13. *a team of little —ies,* Rom. I, 4, 57. Mrs. Quickly uses it instead of *anatomy:* H4B V, 4, 33.

Atone, 1) trans. to reconcile: *since we cannot a. you,* R2 I, 1, 202. *I would do much to a. them,* Oth. IV, 1, 244. *the present need speaks to a. you,* Ant. II, 2, 102. *did a. my countryman and you,* Cymb. I, 4, 42. = to set at peace, to put in accord: *to a. your fears with my more noble meaning,* Tim. V, 4, 58.

2) intr. to agree, to be in concord: *when earthly things made even a. together,* As V, 4, 116. *he and Aufidius can no more a. than violentest contrariety,* Cor. IV, 6, 72.

Atonement, reconciliation: *to make —s between you,* Wiv. I, 1, 33 (Evans' speech). *if we do now make our a. well,* H4B IV, 1, 221. *to make a. betwixt the Duke of Gloster and your brothers,* R3 I, 3, 36.

Atropos, one of the Parcae: H4B II, 4, 213.

Attach, to seize: *every man a. the hand of his fair mistress,* LLL IV, 3, 375. *France hath —ed our*

A   63

merchants' goods at Bourdeaux, H8 I, 1, 95. am myself —ed with weariness, Tp. III, 3, 5. weariness durst
not have —ed one of so high blood, H4B II, 2, 3. may
worthy Troilus be half —ed with that which here his
passion doth express? Troil. V, 2, 161 (i. e. has he a
touch, a feeling of that etc.) — Especially = to arrest: I'll a. you by this officer, Err. IV, 1, 6. 73. that
I should be —ed in Ephesus, IV, 4, 6. Wint V, 1, 182.
R2 II, 3, 156. H6A II, 4, 96. H8 I, 1, 217. I, 2, 210.
Cor. III, 1, 175. Rom. V, 3, 173. Oth. I, 2, 77. The
cause of the arrest adjoined with the prep. of: of capital treason I a. you both, H4B IV, 2, 109 (cf. arrest).

Attachment, arrest, stop: sleep kill those
pretty eyes and give as soft a. to thy senses as infants',
Troil. IV, 2, 5 (cf. arrest, Sonn. 74, 1. Lucr. 1780.
Hml. V, 2, 348).

Attain, to reach, compass, gain; 1) trans.:
ere he a. his easeful western bed, H6C V, 3, 6. but when
he once —s the upmost round, Caes. II, 1, 24. to a. this
hour, V, 5, 42. if opportunity and humblest suit cannot
a. it, Wiv. III, 4, 21. could have —ed the effect of your
own purpose, Meas. II, 1, 13. ere his youth —ed a
beard, Mids. II, 1, 95. Merch. II, 1, 37. R2 II, 3, 64.
H4B IV, 4, 71. H6B I, 4, 74. Cor. I, 1, 269. Cymb.
V, 5, 184.
2) followed by to: till they a. to their abhorred
ends, All's IV, 3, 27. which the gods grant thee to a.
to, Tim. IV, 3, 330. more glory than Octavius shall a.
unto, Caes. V, 5, 38.

Attainder, a staining, soil: stands in a. of
eternal shame, LLL I, 1, 158. have mine honour soiled
with the a. of his slanderous lips, R2 IV, 24. he lived
from all a. of suspect, R3 III, 5, 32. Hence = disgrace: Kildare's a. H8 II, 1, 41.

Attaint, vb., to taint, disgrace: a story of
faults concealed, wherein I am —ed, Sonn. 88, 7. when
time with age doth them a. Pilgr. 344. stand'st not thou
—ed, corrupted, and exempt from ancient gentry? H6A
II, 4, 92. Partic. attaint instead of attainted: you are
a. with faults and perjury, LLL V, 2, 829.
2) to impair, infect: my tender youth was
never yet a. with any passion of inflaming love, H6A
V, 5, 81 (attaint for attainted). cf. Taint, vb. 1.
3) to convict of capital treason: my father
was attached, not —ed, H6A II, 4, 96. I must offend
before I be —ed, H6B II, 4, 59.

Attaint, subst., 1) stain, spot, disgrace: to
him that is as clear from this a. of mine, Lucr. 825.
I will not poison thee with my a. 1072. may'st without
a. o'erlook the dedicated words, Sonn. 82, 2. what
simple thief brags of his own a.? Err. III, 2, 16. there
is no man hath a virtue that he hath not a glimpse of,
or any man an a. but he carries some stain of it, Troil.
I, 2, 26.
2) infection, impairment: the marrow-eating
sickness whose a. disorder breeds, Ven. 741. but freshly
looks and overbears a. with cheerful semblance, H5 IV
Chor. 39.
3) conviction, impeachment: I arrest thee
on capital treason, and in thine a. this gilded serpent,
Lr. V, 3, 83 (Ff. arrest).

Attainture, disgrace: her a. will be Humphrey's
fall, H6B I, 2, 106.

Attask, to reprove, to blame (cf. task): you
are much more —ed for want of wisdom than praised
for harmful mildness, Lr. I, 4, 366 (Ff at task).

Attempt, vb., 1) absolutely = to make an
effort: our doubts are traitors and make us lose the
good we oft might win by fearing to a. Meas. I, 4, 79.
2) trans., a) followed by an accus., α) = to
tempt, to try to win or subdue: he will never
a. us again, Wiv. IV, 2, 226. that neither my coat, integrity, nor persuasion can with ease a. you, Meas. IV,
2, 205. of force I must a. you further, Merch. IV, 1,
421. for him —ing who was selfsubdued, Lr. II, 2, 129.
this man of thine —s her love, Tim. I, 1, 126. cf. how
can that be true love which is falsely —ed? LLL I,
2, 177.
β) to undertake, to endeavour to perform: I'll venge thy death or die renowned by —ing
it, H6C II, 1, 88. never a. any thing on him, H8 III, 2,
17. I have —ed and led your wars, Cor. V, 6, 75. Rom.
II, 2, 68. Caes. V, 3, 40. Oth. III, 4, 22. V, 2, 255.
Cymb. I, 4, 123. Per. V, 1, 175.
b) followed by an inf.: and either not a. to choose,
Merch. II, 1, 39.

Attempt, 1) enterprise, undertaking: I
see what crosses my a. will bring, Lucr. 491. give over
this a. As I, 2, 190. a man may stagger in this a. III,
3, 49. impossible be strange —s to those that weigh
their pains in sense, All's I, 1, 239. I, 3, 260. III, 6,
71. Merch. IV, 1, 350. Tw. III, 2, 31. R3 III, 5, 49.
Cor. V, 3, 146. Tit. III, 1, 50. Oth. IV, 2, 245. Opposed to a performed deed: the a. and not the deed confounds us, Mcb. II, 2, 11. Especially a warlike enterprise: I will not return till my a. so much be glorified,
John V, 2, 111. H4A IV, 1, 61. H4B IV, 1, 15. IV, 2,
45. H6A II, 5, 79. H6C IV, 2, 26. R3 IV, 4, 236 (Ff
success). 398 (Ff affairs). V, 3, 265. Mcb. III, 6, 39.
Oth. I, 3, 29. Figuratively: this a. I am soldier to,
Cymb. III, 4, 186. An attack on the chastity of a woman: the maid will I frame and make fit for his a.
Meas. III, 1, 267. Cymb. I, 4, 126. 128. See also
Lucr. 491.
2) pursuit: such low desires, such poor, such
bare, such lewd, such mean —s, H4A III, 2, 13. one
incorporate to our —s, Caes. I, 3, 136.

Attemptible, (most M.Edd. attemptable), liable
to an attempt, seducible: less a. than any the
rarest of our ladies, Cymb. I, 4, 65.

Attend, 1) absolutely = a) to be ready for
service, to be in waiting: the post —s, and she
delivers it, Lucr. 1333. at the deanery where a priest
—s, Wiv. IV, 6, 31. when the priest —s, Shr. III, 2, 5.
he —eth here hard by, to know your answer, Merch.
IV, 1, 145. All's V, 3, 135. R2 III, 3, 176. H8 V, 2,
19. Tim. I, 1, 7. 114. trip, Audrey! I a., I a. As V, 1,
68 (i. e. I wait on you, I accompany you). she an
—ing star, LLL IV, 3, 231 (i. e. bound to service, subservient to her). this life is nobler than —ing for a
check (i. e. doing service) Cymb. III, 3, 22. we will
fear no poison, which —s in place of greater state,
Cymb. III, 3, 77 (i. e. which is present to do service).
b) = to be attentive, to listen: thou —est
not, Tp. I, 2, 87. shall I tell you a thing? We a. LLL
V, 1, 153. a. and mark, Mids. IV, 1, 98. H4A I, 3,
235. III, 1, 228. H8 I, 1, 158. Cor. I, 9, 4. Rom. II,
2, 167.
2) followed by to = to listen to: mine ears
that to your wanton talk —ed, Ven. 809. we will a. to
neither, John V, 2, 163. your grace —ed to their sugared words, R3 III, 1, 13.

3) followed by *on* or *upon*, a) = to wait o**n**, to serve: *the goddess on whom these airs a.* Tp. I, 2, 422. *we'll both a. upon your ladyship,* Gentl. II, 4, 121. *let your will a. on their accords,* Err. II, 1, 25. Mids. III, 1, 160. Merch. I, 1, 68. As III, 4, 36. Shr. Ind. 2, 35. III, 2, 225. John III, 3, 72; cf. R2 I, 3, 169. H6B V, 1, 80. R3 I, 3, 294. Oth. I, 1, 51. Per. V, 3, 101. *tarry I here, I but a. on death,* Gentl. III, 1, 186 (i. e. I pay my court to death, instead of paying it to Silvia).

b) to wait on, to show respect and duty: *mortal looks adore his beauty still, —ing on his golden pilgrimage,* Sonn. 7, 8. *upon a wooden coffin we a.* H6A I, 1, 19. *will a. on her,* II, 2, 52. *I will a. upon your lordship's leisure,* V, 1, 55. *the solemn feast shall more a. upon the coming space,* All's II, 3, 188 (shall grace the future time).

c) to wait on, to accompany: *sorrow on love hereafter shall a.* Ven. 1136. *fair thoughts and happy hours a. on you!* Merch. III, 4, 41. *to appoint who should a. on him,* H8 I, 1, 75. *all fears —ing on so dire a project,* Troil. II, 2, 134. *a. upon Cominius to these wars,* Cor. I, 1, 241. *let thy wife a. on her,* Oth. I, 3, 297. *I must a. on Caesar,* Ant. V, 2, 206. *—ed on by many a lord and knight,* Per. IV, 4, 11.

4) transitively; a) to regard with attention, to take notice of, to witness: *could not with graceful eyes a. those wars,* Ant. II, 2, 60. Especially to listen to: *will tie the hearers to a. each line,* Lucr. 818. *which speechless woe of his poor she —eth,* 1674. *now a. me,* 1682. *to a. this double voice,* Compl. 3. *too early I —ed a youthful suit,* 78. *dost thou a. me?* Tp. I, 2, 78. 453. Merch. V, 103. Tw. I, 4, 27. H4A I, 3, 210. H6C II, 1, 168. Tit. V, 3, 79. Rom. Prol. 13. Rom. V, 3, 77. Cymb. I, 6, 142. Per. I, 2, 70.

b) to guard, to watch: *I fear I am —ed by some spies,* Gentl. V, 1, 10. *to a. the emperor's person carefully,* Tit. II, 2, 8. *they are in a trunk, —ed by my men,* Cymb. I, 6, 197. *a. my taking* (= are watching to take me, are in wait for me), Lr. II, 3, 5.

c) to take care of: *a. your office,* Wiv. V, 5, 44. Ant. IV, 6, 27. *I must a. his majesty's command,* All's I, 1, 4. *a. his further pleasure,* II, 4, 54. *each hath his place and function to a.* H6C I, 1, 173.

d) to be about, to wait on: *to a. my sons,* Err. I, 1, 58. *I will a. my husband, be his nurse,* V, 98. *to a. the emperor in his royal court,* Gentl. I, 3, 27. *and then I'll presently a. you,* II, 4, 189. Meas. II, 2, 160. III, 1, 160. As I, 2, 177. IV, 1, 184. Lr. I, 1, 35. *I would a. his leisure for a few words,* Mcb. III, 2, 3.

e) to do homage: *he cannot want the best that shall a. his love,* All's I, 1, 82. *a. you here the door of our stern daughter?* Cymb. II, 3, 42.

f) to serve: *let one a. him with a silver basin,* Shr. Ind. 1, 55. *it is the curse of kings to be —ed by slaves,* John IV, 2, 208. *I am most dreadfully —ed,* Hml. II, 2, 276. *who —s us here?* Per. I, 1, 150.

g) to accompany: *if Venus or her son do now a. the queen,* Tp. IV, 88. *I will most willingly a. your ladyship,* Tit. IV, 1, 28. Merch. III, 4, 29. H6C IV, 2, 16. 5, 7. Hml. III, 3, 22. Ant. V, 2, 367. Figuratively: *these lets a. the time,* Lucr. 330. *lingering perdition shall a. you and your ways,* Tp. III, 3, 77. *grace and good disposition a. your ladyship,* Tw. III, 1, 147. John III, 3, 35. IV, 2, 56. H5 IV, 2, 29. H6B II, 3, 38. R3

III, 7, 232. IV, 4, 195. H8 V, 5, 28. Rom. III, 3, 48. Mcb. I, 5, 21.

h) to wait for: *I must a. time's leisure,* Sonn. 44, 12. *one that —s your ladyship's command,* Gentl. IV, 3, 5. *the dinner —s you,* Wiv. I, 1, 279. Meas. IV, 1, 57. Ado V, 4, 36. LLL II, 33. V, 2, 849. Shr. II, 169. All's II, 3, 57. Tw. III, 4, 243. Wint. I, 2, 178. R2 I, 3, 116. H4A IV, 3, 70. H4B I, 1, 3. H6C IV, 6, 82. R3 I, 2, 227. Cor. I, 1, 78. 249. I, 10, 30. Tim. I, 2, 160. III, 4, 37. Mcb. III, 1, 45. V, 4, 15. Hml. V, 2, 205. Lr. II, 1, 127. Oth. III, 3, 281. Ant. III, 10, 32. Cymb. IV, 2, 334. Cor. II, 2, 164. III, 1, 332. 2, 138.

i) to expect: *a. our weightier judgment,* Tim. III, 5, 102.

Attendance, 1) waiting, service: *what, no a.? no regard? no duty?* Shr. IV, 1, 129. *on your a., my lord, here.* Tw. I, 4, 11.

2) presence; act of waiting on one: *wait a. till you hear further from me,* Tim. I, 1, 161 (i. e. do not go away). *To dance a.* = to wait on one without being admitted: *I dance a. here,* R3 III, 7, 56. Followed by *on: I danced a. on his will,* H6B I, 3, 174. *to dance a. on their lordships' pleasures,* H8 V, 2, 31.

Attendant, servant: *here have I few —s,* Tp. V, 166. Err. I, 1, 128. V, 150. Mids. II, 1, 21. As II, 2, 5 (*the ladies, her —s of her chamber*). Shr. Ind. 1, 40. All's I, 3, 258. Wint. II, 2, 14. H6A IV, 2, 10. Caes. IV, 3, 156. Oth. IV, 3, 8. Cymb. II, 4, 124. IV, 2, 132. Followed by *on: lately a. on the Duke of Norfolk,* R3 II, 1, 101. — In Mids. II, 1, 21; Oth. IV, 3, 8; Cymb. IV, 2, 132, it may be also = companion.

Attent, attentive, heedful: *with an a. ear,* Hml. I, 2, 193. Per. III Prol. 11.

Attention, application of the mind to an object: Lucr. 1404. 1610. LLL I, 1, 217. R2 II, 1, 6. H4B I, 2, 142. H8 II, 4, 168. Cymb. V, 5, 117 (*and lend my best a.*).

Attentive, heedful: *be a.* Tp. I, 2, 38. Merch. V, 70. H6C I, 1, 122. Troil. I, 3, 252. Ant. I, 2, 20.

Attentiveness, attention: *how a. wounded his daughter,* Wint. V, 2, 94.

Attest, vb. 1) to certify, testify: *a contract of eternal love, —ed by the holy close of lips,* Tw. V, 161. *a crooked figure may a. in little place a million,* H5 Prol. 16 (i. e. may serve as a certificate for a million). *now a. that those whom you called fathers did beget you,* H5 III, 1, 22 (i. e. certify it by your deeds).

2) to call to witness: *I a. the Gods,* Troil. II, 2, 132.

Attest, subst., testimony: *an esperance so obstinately strong, that doth invert the a. of eyes and ears,* Troil. V, 2, 122 (Ff *test*).

Attire, vb., to dress: *—d in mourning habit,* Lucr. Arg. 19. *finely —d in a robe of white,* Wiv. IV, 4, 72. *I should blush to see you so —d* (so meanly) Wint. IV, 4, 13. *to a. you for our journey,* H6B II, 4, 106. 109. *—d in grave weeds,* Tit. III, 1, 43. *why art thou thus —d?* V, 3, 30. Figuratively: *why art thou thus —d in discontent?* Lucr. 1601. *I am so —d in wonder,* Ado IV, 1, 146 (cf. *wrap* and *enwrap*).

Attire, subst., dress: *in poor and mean a.* As I, 3, 113. *he hath some meaning in his mad a.* Shr. III, 2, 126. Tw. V, 257. H5 V, 2, 61. H6B I, 3, 133.

Caes. I, 1, 53. Mcb. I, 3, 40. Lr. III, 6, 85. Ant. IV, 8, 14. Plural: *I'll show thee some —s*, Ado III, 1, 102. *those —s are best*, Rom. IV, 3, 1. *fetch my best —s*, Ant. V, 2, 228.

Attorney, substitute, proxy: *and will have no a. but myself*, Err. V, 100. *die by a.* As IV, 1, 94. *I, by a., bless thee from thy mother*, R3 V, 3, 83. Especially one who is appointed to transact business for another, advocate, pleader: *the heart's a.* (sc. the tongue) Ven. 335. *as fit as ten groats is for the hand of an a.* All's II, 2, 23. R2 II, 3, 134. H6A V, 3, 166. R3 IV, 4, 127. 413. *his —s general* = those who are appointed by general authority for all his affairs and suits, R2 II, 1, 203. *the king's a.* = what is now called attorney-general: H8 II, 1, 15.

Attorneyed, 1) performed by proxy: *their encounters, though not personal, have been royally a. with interchange of gifts*, Wint. I, 1, 30.

2) employed as an attorney: *I am still a. at your service*, Meas. V, 390.

Attorneyship, the office of a substitute, proxyship: *marriage is a matter of more worth than to be dealt in by a.* H6A V, 5, 56.*

Attract, to draw to, to cause to approach: *who* (sc. the heart) *in the conflict that it holds with death, —s the same* (sc. the blood), H6B III, 2, 165. In a moral sense = to allure, invite: *—s my soul*, Tw. II, 4, 89. *a. more eyes*, H4A I, 2, 238.

Attraction, the power of attracting: *the sun's a thief, and with his great a. robs the vast sea*, Tim. IV, 3, 439. *the a. of my good parts*, Wiv. II, 2, 109. *her sweet harmony and other chosen —s*, Per. V, 1, 46.

Attractive, having the power of attracting: *a. eyes*, Mids. II, 2, 91. *here's metal more a.* Hml. III, 2, 117.

Attribute, subst. 1) essential quality: *his sceptre shows the force of temporal power, the a. to awe and majesty*, Merch. IV, 1, 191. *it is an a. to God himself*, 195. *swear by God's great —s*, All's IV, 2, 25. *could you not find out that by her —s?* Troil. III, 1, 38 (i. e. by the epithets given to her).

2) reputation: *much a. he hath, and much the reason why we ascribe it to him*, Troil. II, 3, 125. *it takes from our achievements the pith and marrow of our a.* Hml. I, 4, 22. *unless you play the pious innocent and for an honest a. cry out: she died by foul play*, Per. IV, 3, 18.

Attribute, vb., to ascribe: *the merit of service is seldom —d to the true and exact performer*, All's III, 6, 64.

Attribution, praise: *such a. should the Douglas have*, H4A IV, 1, 3.

Attributive, ascribing excellent qualities, devoted: *and the will dotes that is a. to what infectiously itself affects, without some image of the affected merit*, Troil. II, 2, 58 (Ff. *inclinable*).

A-twain, in two: *breaking rings a.* Compl. 6. *bite the holy cords a.* Lr. II, 2, 80 (Qq *in twain*). *shore his old thread a.* Oth. V, 2, 206 (only in Q1; the other O. Edd. *in twain*).

Aubrey: *Lord A.* Vere, H6C III, 3, 102.

Auburn, probably = whitish, flaxen: *heads some brown, some black, some a.* Cor. II, 3, 21 (F1 *Abram*). *her hair is a., mine is perfect yellow*, Gentl. IV, 4, 194 (Florio, Ed. 1611: Alburno, a fish called a Blaie

or Bleake. Also the white, the sappe or softest part of any timber subject to worm-eating. Also that whitish colour of women's hair which we call an Alburne or Aburne colour).

Audacious, overbold, impudent: *saucy and a. eloquence*, Mids. V, 103. Wint. II, 3, 42. H4A IV, 3, 45. H6A III, 1, 14. IV, 1, 124. H6B V, 1, 108. Taken not exactly in a bad sense: *your reasons have been a. without impudency*, LLL V, 1, 5 (the learned Sir Nathaniel's speech).

Audaciously, boldly: *durst not ask of her a.* Lucr. 1223. *fear not thou, but speak a.* LLL V, 2, 104.

Audacity, boldness: *it was defect of spirit, life and bold a.* Lucr. 1346. *who would e'er suppose they had such courage and a.?* H6A I, 2, 36. *arm me, a., from head to foot*, Cymb. I, 6, 19.

Audible, 1) so as to be easily heard, loud; adverbially: *the very mercy of the law cries out most a.* Meas. V, 413.

2) capable of hearing, attentive, opposed to deaf: *let me have war; it's spritely walking, a., and full of vent. Peace is a very apoplexy, mulled, deaf, sleepy, insensible*, Cor. IV, 5, 238.

Audience. 1) hearing: *their copious stories oftentimes begun end without a.* (= without being listened to) Ven. 846. *list to your tribunes; a.! peace, I say!* Cor. III, 3, 40. *you yourself have of your a. been most free and bounteous*, Hml. I, 3, 93. *call the noblest to the a.* V, 2, 398. *did gibe my missive out of a.* Ant. II, 2, 74. *the queen of a. nor desire shall fail*, III, 12, 21. *to have a.* = to be heard: LLL V, 1, 140. As V, 4, 157. Tw. I, 4, 18. John V, 2, 119. *to give one a.* = to hear one: As III, 2, 251. John III, 3, 37. IV, 2, 139. H4A I, 3, 211. Caes. III, 2, 2. IV, 2, 47. *lending soft a. to my sweet design*, Compl. 278. *vouchsafe me a.* LLL V, 2, 313. Admittance to a sovereign: H5 I, 1, 92. II, 4, 67. Ant. I, 4, 7. III, 6, 18 (in these two passages absolutely: *to give a.*). *Our a.* = our being heard or admitted, H4B IV, 1, 76 (cf. *your a.* = your hearing, Hml. I, 3, 93). *A second day of a.* = a second court-day: Cor. II, 1, 81.

2) Persons present, witnesses: *dismiss this a.* LLL IV, 3, 209. *'tis meet that some more a. than a mother should o'erhear the speech*, Hml. III, 3, 31. *in this a.* = before these witnesses, V, 2, 251. Especially the spectators in a playhouse: *if any of the a. hiss*, LLL V, 1, 145. *let the a. look to their eyes*, Mids. I, 2, 28. *no a. are able to endure . . .*, H8 V, 4, 65. Figuratively: *the dignity of this act was worth the a. of kings and princes* (= spectatorship) Wint. V, 2, 87. *mutes or a. to this act*, Hml. V, 2, 346.

Audit, final account: *when nature calls thee to be gone, what acceptable a. canst thou leave?* Sonn. 4, 12. *when as thy love hath cast his utmost sum, call'd to that a. by advised respects*, 49, 4. 126, 11. *and how his a. stands who knows save heaven?* Hml. III, 3, 82. *if you will take this a., take this life*, Cymb. V, 4, 27. Account in general: *to steal from spiritual leisure a brief span to keep your earthly a.* H8 III, 2, 141. *I can make my a. up, that all from me do back receive the flour of all, and leave me but the bran*, Cor. I, 1, 148. *to make their a. at your highness' pleasure still to return your own*, Mcb. I, 6, 27. *to your a. comes their distract parcels in combined sums*, Compl. 230.

Auditor, 1) hearer, spectator of a play: *a play toward! I'll be an a.* Mids. III, 1, 81.

2) a person appointed to examine ac-counts: *if you suspect my husbandry or falsehood, call me before the exactest —s,* Tim. II, 2, 165. An officer of the exchequer: H4A II, 1, 63; cf. II, 2, 57.

Auditory, assembly of hearers: *then, noble a., be it known to you,* Tit. V, 3, 96.

Audrey, diminutive of Etheldreda: As III, 3, 1. 2. 98. V, 1, 1. V, 3, 1 etc.

Aufidius, the general of the Volsci: Cor. I, 1, 233 etc. etc. Plural: *six —es,* V, 6, 130.

Auger, a carpenter's tool to bore holes: *your franchises confined into an —'s bore,* Cor. IV, 6, 87.

Auger-hole, hole made by an auger: *here, where our fate, hid in an a., may rush and seize us,* Mcb. II, 3, 128.

Aught, any thing: Lucr. 546. Sonn. 38, 5. 125, 1. Compl. 68. Tp. I, 2, 51. Gentl. III, 2, 47. V, 4, 20. Err. II, 2, 179. 201. Ado V, 1, 292. LLL IV, 3, 354. V, 2, 803. Merch. II, 2, 128. 7, 21. III, 2, 105. V, 183. Tw. V, 111. Wint. I, 2, 395. John II, 511. R2 II, 3, 73. V, 1, 35. H5 IV, 1, 263. H6A I, 5, 37. II, 3, 46. III, 1, 4. H6B IV, 7, 74. R3 I, 2, 100. II, 1, 57. III, 1, 166. Cor. I, 1, 280. II, 3, 205. Troil. II, 2, 52. III, 3, 57. Rom. II, 3, 19. V, 3, 266. Mcb. I, 3, 42. Hml. I, 5, 86. IV, 3, 60. Lr. IV, 6, 49 etc. etc. *I know but of a single part, in a. pertains to the state,* H8 I, 2, 41. *For a. I know* = to my knowledge: All's V, 3, 281. R2 V, 2, 53. Oth. III, 3, 104. Per. II, 5, 78. *for a. thou knowest,* Tit. II, 1, 28. *for a. he knew,* John V, 1, 43. *for a. I see,* Merch. I, 2, 5. Shr. I, 2, 33. H6A I, 4, 68. *for a. that I can tell,* Mids. III, 2, 76. *for a. that I could ever read,* Mids. I, 1, 132.

Augment, vb. trans., to increase: *make something nothing by —ing it,* Lucr. 154. As II, 1, 43. H5 V, 2, 87. H6B III, 1, 169. H6C V, 3, 22. H8 I, 1, 145. Rom. I, 1, 138. Caes. II, 1, 30. Mcb. II, 1, 27. Ant. III, 6, 55.

Augmentation, addition: *more lines than is in the new map with the a. of the Indies,* Tw. III, 2, 85.

Augre, v. *Auger.*

Augur, subst., prophet: *the sad —s mock their own presage,* Sonn. 107, 6. *shrieking harbinger, a. of the fever's end,* Phoen. 7.

Augur, vb., to prophesy: *my —ing hope says it will come to the full,* Ant. II, 1, 10.

Augure (most M. Edd. *augurs*), augur or au-gury? *—s and understood relations have by magot-pies and choughs and rooks brought forth the secret'st man of blood,* Mcb. III, 4, 124.

Augurer, soothsayer in ancient Rome: *the a. tells me,* Cor. II, 1, 1. *the persuasion of his —s,* Caes. II, 1, 200. *the —s, ... plucking the entrails of an offering forth,* II, 2, 37. *swallows have built in Cleopatra's sails their nests: the —s say they know not,* Ant. IV, 12, 4 (O. Edd. *auguries*). *you are too sure an a.* V, 2, 337.

Augury, art of prophesying: *if my a. deceive me not,* Gentl. IV, 4, 73. *we defy a.* Hml. V, 2, 230. *the —ies say,* Ant. IV, 12, 4 (M. Edd. *augurers*).

August, the eighth month of the year: Tp. IV, 134. H6A I, 1, 110.

Augustus, the first Roman emperor: Cymb. II, 4, 11. III, 1, 1 (A. Caesar). 63. V, 5, 82.

Auld, vulgar form for old: *take thine a. cloak about thee,* Oth. II, 3, 99.

Aumerle, son to the Duke of York in R2 I, 3, 1. 64. 4, 1. II, 3, 125 etc

Aunt, a father or mother's sister: Wiv IV, 2, 77. 178. Mids. I, 1, 157. R2 V, 3, 76. 92. 111. 129. H4A III, 1, 196. H6B I, 3, 146. H6C II, 1, 146. R3 II, 2, 62. IV, 4, 283. H8 I, 1, 176. Troil. II, 2, 77. 80. IV, 5, 134. Tit. III, 2, 47. IV, 1, 1. 4. 5. *their a. I am in law* (i. e. by marriage) R3 IV, 1, 24. The name adjoined with *of: her kind a. of Gloster,* R3 IV, 1, 2.

Term for an old gossip: *the wisest a., telling the saddest tale,* Mids. II, 1, 51. for a loose woman: *summer songs for me and my —s, while we lie tumbling in the hay,* Wint. IV, 3, 11.

Aunt-mother, uncertain whether to be called aunt or mother, being both: Hml. II, 2, 394.

Auricular, got by hearing: *and by an a. assurance have your satisfaction,* Lr. I, 2, 99.

Aurora, the Goddess of the morning: Mids. III, 2, 380. Rom. I, 1, 142.

Auspicious, 1) favourable, propitious; always applied to higher powers: *stand a. to the hour,* Lucr. 347. *my zenith doth depend upon a most a. star,* Tp. I, 2, 182. *a. gales,* V, 314. *fortune play upon thy prosperous helm as thy a. mistress,* All's III, 3, 8. *O lady Fortune, stand you a.* Wint. IV, 4, 52. *conjuring the moon to stand a. mistress,* Lr. II, 1, 42.

2) showing joy, happy: *with an a. and a dropping eye,* Hml. I, 2, 11.

Austere, severe, rigid, stern: *this a. insociable life,* LLL V, 2, 809. *with most a. sanctimony,* All's IV, 3, 59. *an a. regard of control,* Tw. II, 5, 73. *of grave and a. quality,* Tim. I, 1, 54.

Austerely, severely: *if I have too a. punished you,* Tp. IV, 1, 1. Singular use: *might'st thou perceive a. in his eye that he did plead in earnest?* Err. IV, 2, 2. This seems to mean: couldst thou perceive, by a very grave and severe expression of his eye, that he was in earnest?

Austereness, strictness, severity: *the a. of my life,* Meas. II, 4, 155.

Austerity, the same: *a. and single life,* Mids. I, 1, 90. *with such a. as 'longeth to a father,* Shr. IV, 4, 7. *with the same a. and garb as he controlled the war,* Cor. IV, 7, 44.

Austria = the duke of Austria: *our cousin A.* All's I, 2, 5. *brave A.* John II, 1. 414. III, 1, 114. III, 2, 3.

Authentic, of acknowledged authority: *a. in your place and person,* Wiv. II, 2, 235. *all the learned and a. fellows,* All's II, 3, 14. *how could ... crowns, sceptres, laurels, but by degree, stand in a. place?* Troil. I, 3, 108. *yet after all comparisons of truth, as truth's a. author to be cited, 'As true as Troilus' shall crown up the verse,* Troil. III, 2, 189.

Author, 1) he or she who first causes or creates any thing: *he's a. of thy slander,* Ven. 1006. *thou* (sc. Lucrece), *the a. of their obloquy,* Lucr. 523. 1244. Ado V, 2, 101. LLL IV, 3, 359. Tw. V, 361. R2 I, 3, 69. H6C IV, 6, 18. H8 II, 1, 139. Cor. V, 3, 36. Hml. IV, 5, 80. *the Gods of Rome forefend I should be a. to dishonour you,* Tit. I, 435. *truth's authentic a.* Troil. III, 2, 189 (he that is the source and prototype of fidelity).

Applied to things, = cause: *you may call the business of the master the a. of the servant's damnation,* H5 IV, 1, 162. *that which is the strength of their amity shall prove the immediate a. of their variance,* Ant. II, 6, 138.

2) writer: *where is any a. in the world,* LLL IV,

3, 312. *politic —s*, Tw. II, 5, 175. *our humble a.* H4B V, 5, 143. *their own —s affirm*, H5 I, 2, 43. *our bending a. hath pursued the story*, H5 Epil. 2. *not in confidence of —'s pen*, Troil. Prol. 24. *at the —'s drift*, Troil. III, 3, 113. Hml. II, 2, 464. Per. Prol. 20.

Authority, 1) legal and official power: *art made tongue-tied by a.* Sonn. 66, 9. *use your a.* Tp. I, 1, 26. *thus can the demi-god A. make us pay*, Meas. I, 2, 124. I, 4, 56. II, 2, 118. 134. IV, 2, 114. IV, 4, 29. Merch. III, 2, 291. IV, 1, 215. Wint. I, 2, 463. II, 1, 53. John II, 113. III, 1, 160. V, 1, 4. H4B IV, 2, 58. V, 2, 82. V, 3, 116. H6A V, 1, 59. V, 4, 135. H6C I, 2, 24 (followed by *over*). H8 II, 4, 4. V, 3, 35. Cor. III, 1, 23. 208. Tim. V, 1, 166. Lr. I, 1, 308. IV, 6, 163. Ant. II, 2, 49. II, 6, 100. III, 6, 33. III, 13, 90. Per. IV, 6, 96. In the plural: a) = legal powers, lodged in different persons: *when two —ies are up, neither supreme*, Cor. III, 1, 109. b) the several attributes of power: *redeliver our —ies there*, Meas. IV, 4, 6. *so it must fall out to him or our —ies*, Cor. II, 1, 260. *soaks up the king's countenance, his rewards, his —ies*, Hml. IV, 2, 17. *would manage those —ies that he hath given away*, Lr. I, 3, 17.

Abstractum pro concreto: *what a. surfeits would relieve us*, Cor. I, 1, 16 (i. e. those in office and power).

2) Power in general: *there is no fettering of a.* Alls II, 3, 252. *he seems to be of great a., and though a. be a stubborn bear …*, Wint. IV, 4, 830. *the power and corrigible a. of this lies in our wills*, Oth. I, 3, 329. cf. John IV, 2, 211. H6A V, 1, 18. 5, 41. H6B III, 1, 316.

3) Justification, countenance, warrant: *thieves for their robbery have a. when judges steal themselves*, Meas. II, 2, 176. *wilt thou be glass wherein it shall discern a. for sin?* Lucr. 620. *words cannot carry a. so weighty*, H8 III, 2, 234. *yea, 'gainst the a. of manners, prayed you to hold your hand more close*, Tim. II, 2, 147. *by his a.* All's IV, 5, 68. Lr. II, 1, 62.

4) that which is claimed in support of opinions or measures: *small have continual plodders ever won save base a. from others' books*, LLL I, 1, 87. *more a., name more*, I, 2, 70. *O, some a. how to proceed*, IV, 3, 287. *my hope, whereto thy speech serves for a.* Tw. I, 2, 20. *bi-fold a.*, Troil. V, 2, 144. *have studied physic, through which art, by turning o'er —ies*, Per. III, 2, 33.

5) dignity, nobleness, majesty: *O, what a. and show of truth can cunning sin cover itself withal!* Ado IV, 1, 36. *that which I would fain call master. What's that? Authority.* Lr. I, 4, 32. *one that, in the a. of her merit, did justly put on the vouch of very malice itself*, Oth. II, 1, 147.

Authórize, 1) to justify: *—ing thy trespass with compare*, Sonn. 35, 6. *his rudeness so with his —d youth did livery falseness in a pride of truth*, Compl. 104.

2) to accredit: *a woman's story at a winter's fire, —d by her grandam*, Mcb. III, 4, 66.

Autolycus, name of the vagabond in Wint. IV, 3, 24. 107 (cf. Hom. Od. XIX, 394).

Autumn, the season between summer and winter: Sonn. 97, 6. 104, 5. Mids. II, 1, 112. Merch. I, 3, 82. Shr. I, 2, 96. H6C V, 7, 3. Troil. I, 2, 139. Lr. IV, 6, 201 (*laying —'s dust*). Ant. V, 2, 87 (O. Edd. *Anthony*).

Auvergne; *Countess of A.*: H6A II, 2, 38 (O. Edd. *Ouergne* and *Auergne*).

Avail, vb., 1) absolutely, = to be of use and advantage: *which to deny concerns more than —s*, Wint. III, 2, 87. *since arms a. not now that Henry's dead*, H6A I, 1, 47.

2) followed by *out of*, = to profit by: *but how out of this can she a.?* Meas. III, 1, 243.

3) transitively, = to benefit, to be profitable to: *it small —s my mood*, Lucr. 1273. *now will it best a. your majesty to cross the seas*, H6A III, 1, 179.

Avail, subst., interest, profit: *as heaven shall work in me for thine a.* All's I, 3, 190. *when better fall, for your —s they fell*, III, 1, 22.

Avarice, covetousness: Mcb. IV, 3, 78. 84.

Avaricious, covetous: Mcb. IV, 3, 58.

Avaunt, exclamation of contempt or of abhorrence, uttered to drive one away: *childish fear, a.!* Lucr. 274. *rogues, hence, a.!* Wiv. I, 3, 90. *a., thou witch!* Err. IV, 3, 80. LLL V, 2, 298. John IV, 3, 77. H4B I, 2, 103. H5 III, 2, 21. H6A V, 4, 21. R3 I, 2, 46. Tit. I, 283. Mcb. III, 4, 93. Lr. III, 6, 68. Oth. III, 3, 335. IV, 1, 271. Ant. IV, 12, 30. Per. IV, 6, 126.

Substantively: *to give her the a.* = to send her packing, H8 III, 3, 10.

Ave, subst., reverential salutation: *their loud applause and —s vehement*, Meas. I, 1, 71.

Ave-Mary, a particular prayer with the Roman Catholics, whose chaplets are divided into a certain number of Ave-Maries and Paternosters: *to number —ies on his beads*, H6B I, 3, 59. *numbering our —ies with our beads*, H6C II, 1, 162.

Avenge, to revenge: *remember to a. me on the French*, H6A I, 4, 94. *shall I not live to be —d on her?* H6B I, 3, 85. *and be —d on cursed Tamora*, Tit. V, 1, 16. *till Caesar's three and thirty wounds be well —d*, Caes. V, 1, 54. Used of divine retribution: *O God! if thou wilt be —d on my misdeeds*, R3 I, 4, 70. *if God will be —d for this deed*, 221 (Qq *revenged*).

Aver, to allege: *—ing notes of chamber-hanging, pictures*, Cymb. V, 5, 203.

Averdupois, v. *Avoirdupois*.

Avert, to turn: *to a. your liking a more worthier way than on a wretch*, Lr. I, 1, 214.

Avised = *advised* (q. v.): *be a. and pass good humours*, Wiv. I, 1, 169 (i. e. yield to reason). *Are you a. o' that?* = how came you by that wisdom? Wiv. I, 4, 106. *art a. o' that?* Meas. II, 2, 132.

Avoid, 1) trans., a) to shun, to endeavour not to meet: *that you might a. him, if you saw him*, Wiv. II, 2, 289. *the fashion of the world is to a. cost*, Ado I, 1, 98. II, 3, 198. V, 1, 270. LLL IV, 3, 264. As II, 5, 35. Tw. III, 4, 338. Wint. I, 2, 433. John I, 215. R2 I, 3, 241. II, 1, 264. H4A V, 5, 13. H4B IV, 5, 209. H5 III, 3, 42. H6C II, 2, 137. II. 6, 66. IV, 6, 28. V, 4, 37. R3 III, 5, 68. III, 7, 151. IV, 4, 218. 410. 411. Caes. I, 2, 200. II, 2, 26. Mcb. II, 3, 149. V, 8, 4. Hml. I, 1, 134. III, 2, 16. III, 4, 150. Lr. I, 1, 126. Cymb. I, 1, 140.

b) to leave, quit: *a. the gallery*, H8 V, 1, 86. *a. the house*, Cor. IV, 5, 25.

c) to get rid of: *what I am I cannot a.* Wiv. III, 5, 152. *I will no longer endure it, though yet I know no wise remedy how to a. it,* As I, 1, 27. *how may I a. the wife I chose?* Troil. II, 2, 65.

d) in pleading, to e v a d e the allegation of the other party by setting up some new matter: *as the matter now stands, he will a. your accusation: he made trial of you only,* Meas. III, 1, 201. *all these you may a. but the Lie Direct, and you may a. that too with an If,* As V, 4, 102.

2) intr. to w i t h d r a w, depart: *let us a.* Wint. I, 2, 462. *here's no place for you; pray you, a.* Cor. IV, 5, 34. Imperatively, = be gone, avaunt: *a.! no more!* Tp. IV, 142. *Satan, a.!* Err. IV, 3, 48. 66. H6B I, 4, 43. Ant. V, 2, 242. Cymb. I, 1, 125.

Avoirdupois (Q Ff *haber-de-pois*), w e i g h t: *the weight of a hair will turn the scales between their a.* H4B II, 4, 277.

Avouch, vb., 1) to a s s e r t, m a i n t a i n: *to make trial of that which every one had before —ed,* Lucr. Arg. 9. *I speak and I a.* Wiv. II, 1, 138. *this —es the shepherd's son,* Wint. V, 2, 69. *if this which he —es does appear,* Mcb. V, 5, 47. *will prove what is —ed there,* Lr. V, 1, 44.

2) opposed to disavow = to o w n, to a c k n o w-l e d g e, to answer for, to make good: *you will think you have made no offence, if the duke a. the justice of your dealing?* Meas. IV, 2, 200. *then my account I well may give, and in the stocks a. it,* Wint. IV, 3, 22. *I'll a. it to his head,* Mids. I, 1, 106. *dare not a. in your deeds any of your words,* H5 V, 1, 77. *a. the thoughts of your heart with the looks of an empress,* H5 V, 2, 253. *what I have said I will a. in presence of the king,* R3 I, 3, 115. *if you'll a. 'twas wisdom Paris went,* Troil. II, 2, 84. *though I could with barefaced power sweep him from my sight and bid my will a. it,* Mcb. III, 1, 120. *is this well spoken? I dare a. it,* Lr. II, 4, 240.

Avouch, subst., a v o w a l, a c k n o w l e d g m e n t: *I might not this believe without the sensible and true a. of mine own eyes,* Hml. I, 1, 57.

Avouchment, used by Fluellen instead of the verb to a v o u c h, H5 IV, 8, 38.

Avow, 1) to m a i n t a i n, to a s s e r t: *of which there is not one, I dare a., but will deserve ...* H8 IV, 2, 142.

2) to m a i n t a i n, to make g o o d: *and dare a. her beauty and her worth in other arms than hers,* Troil. I, 3, 271.

Await, 1) trans., to w a i t f o r, to be in store for: *what fates a. the duke of Suffolk?* H6B I, 4, 35. 67.

2) followed by *for,* = to e x p e c t, to l o o k f o r-ward to: *Posterity, a. for wretched years,* H6A I, 1, 48.

Awake, vb. (impf. and partic. *awaked*). 1) trans. to r o u s e f r o m s l e e p: Tp. II, 1, 318. V, 235. Meas. IV, 2, 159. Merch. V, 110. R3 IV, 1, 85. Hml. I, 1, 152 etc. Metaphorically, to r o u s e f r o m w h a t r e s e m b l e s s l e e p, to put to action: *—d an evil nature,* Tp. I, 2, 93. *and his untimely frenzy thus —eth,* Lucr. 1675. *—s the enrolled penalties,* Meas. I, 2, 170. Ado IV, 1, 199. Mids. I, 1, 13. All's I, 2, 38. Tw. III, 2, 20. V, 47. Wint. III, 2, 114. John V, 4, 43. Troil. I, 3, 251. Ant. I, 3, 61. *it is required you do a. your faith,* Wint. V, 3, 95. *we must a. endeavour for defence,* John II, 81. *my master is —d by great occasion to call upon his own,* Tim. II, 2, 21. *a. your dangerous lenity,*

i. e. begin to be severe, Cor. III, 1, 98. *a. God's gentle-sleeping peace,* R3 I, 3, 288, i. e. stir wars and strife. (cf. *to wake our peace,* R2 I, 3, 132; *we will not wake your patience,* Ado V, 1, 102). *To awake one to sth.: —s my heart to heart's and eye's delight,* Sonn. 47, 14.

2) intrans. a) to c e a s e to s l e e p, to b r e a k from s l e e p: *a., thou Roman dame,* Lucr. 1628. Tp. I, 2, 305. II, 1, 305. 308. IV, 232. Wiv. III, 5, 142. Meas. IV, 3, 32. 34. Mids. II, 2, 82. III, 2, 117. IV, 1, 71. As IV, 3, 133. Shr. I, 1, 183. R2 V, 1, 19. H4B III, 1, 25. H6A I, 1, 78. R3 I, 4, 42. V, 3, 144. Troil. IV, 5, 115 (*a. thee* = a. thou, not = a. thyself). Rom. IV, 1, 106. V, 3, 258 (Q2 *awakening*). Ant. IV, 9, 28. *they have —d,* Mcb. II, 2, 10. *be —d,* Mids. III, 2, 1. H4B V, 5, 55.

b) to be a w a k e, to w a t c h, not to s l e e p: *such as you nourish the cause of his —ing* (i. e. hinder him from sleeping) Wint. II, 3, 36.

Awake, adv., n o t s l e e p i n g, in a state of v i g i l a n c e: *it is my love that keeps mine eye a.* Sonn. 61, 10. Tp. V, 100. 229. Meas. II, 2, 93. Ado II, 3, 18. Mids. III, 2, 69. IV, 1, 198. 203. Wint. IV, 4, 460. H4B V, 5, 55 (Q *awaked*) Troil. I, 3, 255. Tit. II, 2, 17. Caes. II, 1, 88. Cymb. III, 4, 46. V, 4, 127.

Awaken, the same as *to awake;* 1) trans.: *Angelo, belike thinking me remiss in mine office, —s me with this unwonted putting on,* Meas. IV, 2, 119. *ay, mistress bride, hath that —ed you?* Shr. V, 2, 42. *I offered to a. his regard for's private friends,* Cor. V, 1, 23.

2) intr.: *some minute ere the time of her —ing,* Rom. V, 3, 258 (only in Q2; other O. Edd. *awaking*).

Award, to a d j u d g e, to d e c r e e: *the court —s it,* Merch. IV, 1, 300. 303. *lest the supreme king of kings a. either of you to be the other's end,* R3 II, 1, 14. *to a. one sth.: she that makes me sin, —s me pain,* Sonn. 141, 14.

Away, 1) absent, far: *thyself a. art present still with me,* Sonn. 47, 10. *or gluttoning on all, or all a.* 75, 14. *thou a., the very birds are mute,* 97, 12. 98, 13. *if the shepherd be a while a.* Gentl. I, 1, 75. *to discover islands far a.* I, 3, 9. *far from her nest the lapwing cries a.* Err. IV, 2, 27 etc. etc.

2) f r o m a p l a c e: *the sound is going a.* Tp. III, 2, 157. *blow not a word a.* Gentl. I, 2, 118. *to steal a. your daughter,* III, 1, 11. *get thee a.* Err. I, 2, 16. *be all ways a.* Mids. IV, 1, 46. *stand a.* All's V, 2, 17; etc. etc. *that I'll tear a.* = tear off, Gentl. I, 2, 125. *do not tear a. thyself from me,* Err. II, 2, 126.

Joined to different verbs, it implies the idea of spending or destroying by the action: *till thou hast howl'd a. twelve winters,* Tp. I, 2, 296. *I'll weep what is left a.* Err. II, 1, 115. *kissed his hand a.* LLL V, 2, 324. *dream a. the time,* Mids. I, 1, 8. *curse a. a winter's night,* H6B III, 2, 335. *see a. their shilling,* H8 Prol. 12. *Make a.* (cf. *make*) = to make away with, to destroy: *so in thyself thyself art made a.* Ven. 763. *threescore year would make the world a.* Sonn. 11, 8. *To go a.* = to pass: *which shall make it* (the night) *go quick a.* Tp. V, 304.

Away! = begone: Tp. V, 298. Gentl. II, 3, 36. III, 1, 101. IV, 4, 66 etc. etc. *Away with the rest!* Tp. IV, 247 (i. e. take the rest; elsewhere the expression has another sense, cf. *with*). *a. with us to Athens,* Mids. IV, 1, 189. *a. from me!* H6B I, 2, 50. *a. thy hand!* Hml. V, 1, 286 (Qq *hold off*).

She could never a. with me, H4B III, 2, 213 (= she could not bear me, cf. Ben Jonson's Poetaster A. III, Sc. 1).

Redundantly after *whither: whither a.?* Mids. I, 1, 180, = where are you going? Shr. IV, 5, 38. R3 IV, 1, 7. *whither a. so fast?* Gentl. III, 1, 51. LLL IV, 3, 187. R3 II, 3, 1. H8 II, 1, 1.

3) *Come a.* = come here, come to me: Tp. I, 2, 187. Tw. II, 4, 52. Wint. V, 3, 101. H4A II, 1, 24. Mcb. III, 5, 33. Per. II, 1, 17. *To bring a.* = to bring here: Meas. II, 1, 41. R2 II, 2, 107. Tim. V, 4, 68. Lr. II, 2, 146. Per. II, 1, 13. *you must come a. to your father* (= go with me) As I, 2, 60. *to have taken it a.* (= with you) Tw. II, 2, 7. *bring a. thy pack after me*, Wint. IV, 4, 318.

Awe, subst., reverential fear: *wrench a. from fools*, Meas. II, 4, 14. *the attribute to a. and majesty*, Merch. IV, 1, 191. H4B IV, 5, 177. H5 IV, 1, 264. Tim. IV, 1, 17. *to hold one in a.* H6A I, 1, 39. *to keep in a.* Lucr. 245. H6B I, 1, 92. R3 V, 3, 310. Cor. I, 1, 191. Hml. V, 1, 238. Per. Prol. 36. With an objective genitive: *to be in a. of such a thing*, Caes. I, 2, 96. *by my sceptre's a.* R2 I, 1, 118. *stand under one man's a.* Caes. II, 1, 52. The possessive pronoun objectively: *we'll bend it to our a.* H5 I, 2, 224. subjectively: *thy free a. pays homage to us*, Hml. IV, 3, 63.

Awe, vb., to strike with fear and reverence, and hence to keep in complete subjection, to intimidate so as to quell any resistance: *thou* (the horse) *created to be —d by man*, R2 V, 5, 91. *that same eye whose bend doth a. the world*, Caes. I, 2, 123. *pure shame and —d resistance made him fret*, Ven. 69. *I will a. him with my cudgel*, Wiv. II, 2, 291. *shall quips and sentences a. a man from the career of his humour?* Ado II, 3, 250.

Aweary, weary, tired, fatigued: *I am a., give me leave a while*, Rom. II, 5, 25. Followed by *of*, = tired of: *I am a. of this moon*, Mids. V, 255. Merch. I, 2, 2. All's I, 3, 47. IV, 5, 59. H4A III, 2, 88. Troil. IV, 2, 7. Caes. IV, 3, 95. Mcb. V, 5, 49.

Aweless, 1) wanting reverence and fear: *against whose fury and unmatched force the a. lion could not wage the fight*, John I, 266. — 2) inspiring no reverence and fear: *the innocent and a. throne*, R3 II, 4, 52.

Awful, 1) filled with awe: *to pay their a. duty to our presence*, R2 III, 3, 76. *we come within our a. banks again*, H4B IV, 1, 176. Hence = filled with reverence for all that deserves it, conscientious: *thrust from the company of a. men*, Gentl. IV, 1, 46. *a. both in deed and word*, Per. II Prol. 4.

2) inspiring awe: *and a. rule and right supremacy*, Shr. V, 2, 109. *to pluck down justice from your a. bench*, H4B V, 2, 86. *an a. princely sceptre*, H6B V, 1, 98. H6C II, 1, 154.

Awhile (O. Edd. mostly *a while*, sometimes *a-while*, f. i. Tw. I, 4, 12. Wint. IV, 4, 402. John II, 379. H6C II, 3, 5. III, 1, 27. R3 I, 2, 3. IV, 4, 116; rarely in one word: All's II, 3, 283. John II, 416. Rom. I, 3, 8.), some time: *counsel may stop a. what will not stay*, Compl. 159. Gentl. I, 1, 75. II, 4, 80. III, 1, 1. 58. IV, 2, 25. V, 4, 27. Meas. II, 3, 17. 4, 35. III, 1, 160. 180. V, 354. Ado II, 1, 287. IV, 1, 202. 205 etc. etc.

Awkward, 1) perverse, unbecoming: *'tis no sinister nor no a. claim*, H5 II, 4, 85. *with ridiculous and a. action he pageants us*, Troil. I, 3, 149.

2) **adverse**: *by a. wind from England's bank drove back again*, H6B III, 2, 83. *and to the world and a. casualties bound me in servitude*, Per. V, 1, 94.

Awl, an iron instrument of shoemakers: Caes. I, 1, 25.

Awless, v. *aweless*.

A-work, to work, into action (always joined to *set*): *So Lucrece, set a., sad tales doth tell*, Lucr. 1496. *that sets it a.* H4B IV, 3, 124. Troil. V, 10, 38. Hml. II, 2, 510. Lr. III, 5, 8.

Awry, obliquely: *you pluck my foot a.* Shr. IV, 1, 150. *perspectives eyed a. distinguish form*, R2 II, 2, 19. *looking a. upon your lord's departure*, 21. *enterprises ... their currents turn a.* Hml. III, 1, 87 (Ff. *away*). *your crown's a.* Ant. V, 2, 321. Hence = perversely: *thou aimest all a.* H6B II, 4, 58. merely *a.* Cor. III, 1, 305.

Axe, instrument to hew timber, to chop wood, or to kill cattle: *a butcher with an a.* H6B III, 2, 189. *many strokes, though with a little a., hew down the oak*, H6C II, 1, 54. II, 2, 165. V, 2, 11. Tit. III, 1, 185. 186. Tim. V, 1, 214. Metaphorically: *is hacked down and his summer leaves all faded by murder's bloody a.* R2 I, 2, 21. *hew my way out with a bloody a.* H6C III, 2, 181.

Especially the executioner's axe: Meas. IV, 2, 56. IV, 3, 39. Merch. IV, 1, 125. As III, 5, 5. H6B II, 4, 49. H8 II, 1, 61. III, 2, 264. Rom. III, 3, 22. Hml. IV, 5, 218. V, 2, 24. Per. I, 2, 58.

Axle-tree, piece of timber on which the wheel turns: *hear a dry wheel grate on the a.*, H4A III, 1, 132. *strong as the a. on which heaven rides*, Troil. I, 3, 66.

Ay (O. Edd. always *I*) yes: *is not this true? Ay, sir.* Tp. I, 2, 268. II, 1, 44. 67. 94. 101. III, 1, 88. 2, 112. 122. IV, 43. 167. 208. V, 294 etc. etc.

Used to enforce the sense: *every inch of woman in the world, ay, every dram of woman's flesh is false, if she be*, Wint. II, 1, 138. *how you may hurt yourself, ay, utterly grow from the king's acquaintance*, H8 III, 1, 160 etc.

Sometimes = why: *But, for your conscience? Ay, sir; where lies that?* Tp. II, 1, 276. *I would resort to her by night. Ay, but the doors be locked*, Gentl. III, 1, 111. *Ay, but she'll think that it is spoke in hate*, III, 2, 34. *you Banbury cheese! Ay, it is no matter. How now, Mephostophilus! Ay, it is no matter.* Wiv. I, 1, 131. *I understand not what you mean by this. Ay, do, persever, counterfeit sad looks*, Mids. III, 2, 237. *Ay, mistress bride, hath that awakened you?* Shr. V, 2, 42. *Ay, are you thereabouts?* Ant. III, 10, 29 etc. etc.

Ay, interj. (M. Edd. *Ah*): *Ay, alack, how new is husband in my mouth!* John III, 1, 305. Generally coupled with *me*: *Ay me!* Ven. 187. 833. Lucr. 1167. Sonn. 41, 9. Compl. 321. Wiv. I, 4, 68. Err. IV, 4, 111. V, 186. LLL IV, 3, 22. 47. 141. Mids. II, 2, 147. Tw. V, 142. John V, 3, 14. H6B III, 2, 70. 120. 380. R3 II, 4, 49. Tit. III, 1, 64. Rom. I, 1, 167. II, 1, 10. II, 2, 25. III, 2, 36. Caes. II, 4, 39. Hml. III, 4, 51. Ant. III, 6, 76. Cymb. IV, 2, 321. V, 5, 210 etc.

Aye, for ever: *let him that will a. be called, go in to Troy*, Troil. V, 10, 16. *ignomy and shame live a. with thy name*, V, 10, 34. *let this pernicious hour stand a. accursed in the calendar,*

Mcb. IV, 1, 134. *I am come to bid my king and master a. good night*, Lr. V, 3, 235. *a. hopeless to have the courtesy your cradle promised*, Cymb. IV, 4, 27. *the worth that learned charity a. wears*, Per. V, 3, 94. In Per. III, 1, 63 some M. Edd. *aye-remaining lamps* (O. Edd. *ayre*).

Preceded by *for*, in the same sense: *makes antiquity for a. his page*, Sonn. 108, 12. *whiles you to the perpetual wink for a. might put this ancient morsel*, Tp. II, 1, 285. *and I for a. thy footlicker*, IV, 218. *this world is not for a.* Hml. III, 2, 210. Mids. I, 1, 71. 90. III, 2, 387. R2 V, 2, 40. Troil. III, 2, 167. Tim. V, 1, 55. V, 4, 78.

Ayword: *gull him into an a.* Tw. II, 3, 146 (M. Edd. *a nayword*).

Azure, sky-blue, used of the colour of the veins: *her a. veins*, Lucr. 419. *these windows* (sc. eyelids) *white and a. laced with blue of heaven's own tinct*, Cymb. II, 2, 22.

Azured, sky-blue: *'twixt the green sea and the a. vault*, Tp. V, 43. *the a. harebell, like thy veins*, Cymb. IV, 2, 222.

B.

B, 1) the second letter in the alphabet: LLL V, 1, 24. 50. *fair as a text B in a copy-book*, V, 2, 42, i. e. not fair, but black.

2) note in music: Shr. III, 1, 75.

Ba, to cry like a sheep: *will not hear her lamb when it baes*, Ado III, 3, 75. *ba, most silly sheep*, LLL V, 1, 53. *a lamb that baes like a bear*, Cor. II, 1, 12.

Baa, the cry of a sheep: *will make me cry baa*, Gentl. I, 1, 98.

Babble, subst., prattle: *this b. shall not henceforth trouble me*, Gentl. I, 2, 98. *leave thy vain bibble babble*, Tw. IV, 2, 105. *there is no tiddle taddle nor pibble pabble in Pompey's camp*, H5 IV, 1, 71 (Fluellen).

Babble, vb., to prate, to twaddle: *for the watch to b. and to talk*, Ado III, 3, 36. *for school fool, a —ing rhyme*, V, 2, 39. *the —ing gossip of the air*, Tw. I, 5, 292. *vainness, —ing, drunkenness*, III, 4, 389. *our —ing dreams*, R3 V, 3, 308, i. e. blabbing, telling tales. *the —ing echo*, Tit. II, 3, 17. *—ing gossip*, IV, 2, 150. (In H5 II, 3, 17 many M. Edd. *and a babbled of green fields*).*

Babe, generally a little child still at the breast: *a nurse's song ne'er pleased her b. so well*, Ven. 974. Lucr. 814. 1161. Sonn. 22, 12. 143, 3. Gentl. I, 2, 58. Err. I, 1, 73. LLL V, 2, 594. Shr. II, 138. IV, 3, 74. Wint. II, 2, 26. III, 2, 135. John III, 4, 58. H6A I, 1, 49. II, 3, 17. III, 1, 197. III, 3, 47. H6B V, 2, 52. H6C II, 1, 86. V, 7, 29. Tit. II, 3, 29. IV, 2, 67. V, 1, 26. Rom. I, 3, 60. Tim. I, 2, 116. 117. IV, 3, 118. Mcb. I, 7, 21. 55. IV, 1, 30. Hml. III, 3, 71. Lr. I, 3, 19. Ant. V, 2, 48. Cymb. I, 1, 40. Per. I, 4, 42. III Prol. 11. III, 1, 28 etc.

But sometimes children of some growth are called so: *Love is a b.*, Sonn. 115, 13. *holy writ in —s hath judgment shown, when judges have been —s*, All's II, 1, 141 (cf. St. Matthew XI, 25). *those that do teach young —s*, Oth. IV, 2, 111. *at three and two years old, I stole these —s*, Cymb. III, 3, 101. It is used of young Rutland: R3 I, 3, 183; of the sons of Edward IV: R3 II, 2, 84. IV, 1, 99. IV, 3, 9. IV, 4, 9. of the children of Macduff: Mcb. IV, 1, 152. IV, 2, 6.

Baboon (*baboón* in Tim. I, 1, 260; *báboon* in Mcb. IV, 1, 37 and perhaps Per. IV, 6, 189), the animal Cynocephalus: Wiv. II, 2, 9. H4B II, 4, 261. Tim. I, 1, 260. Mcb. IV, 1, 37. Oth. I, 3, 318. Per. IV,

Baby, 1) the same as babe: Meas. I, 3, 30. Ado V, 2, 37. Shr. IV, 3, 67. Wint. II, 1, 6. John V, 2, 56. H6B I, 3, 148. Troil. I, 3, 345. III, 2, 43. Cor. II, 1, 223. III, 2, 115. Tit. V, 3, 185. Hml. I, 3, 105. II, 2, 400. Ant. V, 2, 312. = child in general: H5 III Chor. 20. R3 IV, 1, 103.

2) a doll: *protest me the b. of a girl*, Mcb. III, 4, 106.*

Baby-brow: Mcb. IV, 1, 88.

Baby-daughter: Wint. III, 2, 192.

Babylon, the famous ancient town: *when as I sat in Pabylon*, Wiv. III, 1, 24 (Evans' song). *there dwelt a man in B.*, Tw. II, 3, 84. *the whore of B.* H5 II, 3, 41.

Baccare: *baccare! you are marvellous forward*, Shr. II, 73 (Nares: "a cant word, meaning, go back, used in allusion to a proverbial saying, 'Backare, quoth Mortimer to his sow;' probably made in ridicule of some man who affected a knowledge of Latin without having it." cf. Notes and Queries II, 8, p. 527).

Bacchanals, 1) the revels of Bacchus: *shall we dance now the Egyptian B.*, Ant. II, 7, 110. 2) Bacchants: *the riot of the tipsy B., tearing the Thracian singer*, Mids. V, 48.

Bacchus, the god of wine: LLL IV, 3, 339. Ant. II, 7, 121.

Bachelor, a man unmarried: Meas. IV, 2, 3. Ado I, 1, 201. 248. II, 1, 51. II, 3, 252. Mids. II, 2, 59. Merch. III, 1, 127. As III, 3, 62. All's II, 3, 59. Tw. I, 2, 29. H4A IV, 2, 17. H4B I, 2, 31. H5 V, 2, 230. H6C III, 2, 103. R3 I, 3, 101. Tit. I, 488. Caes. III, 3, 9. 18. In Tp. IV, 67 (*whose shadow the dismissed b. loves*) it signifies a young man looking out for a wife. cf. H4A IV, 2, 17. In Rom. I, 5, 114 the nurse addresses Romeo with the word, so that it should seem to mean a young man in general; but it may mean there a very young knight, a knight bachelor.

Bachelorship, state of a bachelor: H6A V, 4, 13.

Back, subst., 1) the upper, resp. hinder part of the body: Ven. 300. 396. 594. Tp. II, 1, 115. III, 1, 26. V, 91. Wiv. V, 5, 58. Meas. III, 1, 26. LLL I, 2, 75. V, 2, 476. Mids. II, 1, 150. Shr. Ind. 2, 9. R2 I, 2, 51. H6A I, 1, 138. II, 5, 43. H6C III, 2, 157 etc. etc. *making the beast with two —s*, Oth. I, 1,

118. *but the —s of Britons seen*, Cymb. V, 3, 6. *are at our —s* (= are pursuing us) H6C II, 5, 133. *these people at our b.* (= behind us) Caes. IV, 3, 212. *you knew I was at your b.* (= at your elbow, near you) H4B II, 4, 334. *no glory lives behind the b. of such*, Ado III, 1, 110 (they are not praised in their absence). *'tis well you offer it behind her b.* Merch. IV, 1, 293. *being spoke behind your b.*, Rom. IV, 1, 28. *that ever turned their —s to mortal views*, LLL V, 2, 161. *when I turn my b.* Mids. III, 2, 238. As IV, 3, 128. H4B I, 1, 130. Caes. III, 3, 134. Caes. II, 1, 25. Mcb. III, 6, 41. *turn b.* = fly: H4A I, 2, 206. Caes. V, 3, 3.

Properly and figuratively, the part of the body which bears burdens: *more than our —s can bear*, Tit. IV, 3, 48. *his losses that have of late so huddled on his back*, Merch. IV, 1, 28. *a pack of blessings lights upon thy b.* Rom. III, 3, 141. *bearing their own misfortunes on the b. of such as have before endured the like*, R2 V, 5, 29. *I have years on my b. forty eight*, Lr. I, 4, 42. *crack my sinews, break my b.* Tp. III, 1, 26. H6B IV, 8, 30. H6C V, 7, 24. H8 I, 1, 84. Tim. II, 1, 24. *break some gallows' b.* H4B IV, 3, 32.

Used for the whole body, in speaking of clothes: *clothe a b.* Meas. III, 2, 23. *bearing their birthrights proudly on their —s*, John II, 70. *it lies as lightly on the b. of him*, II, 143. *the cloak of night being pluck'd from off their —s*, R2 III, 2, 45. *I bought you a dozen of shirts to your b.* H4A III, 3, 78. *his apparel is built upon his b.* H4B III, 2, 155. *with my armour on my b.* H5 V, 2, 143. *she bears a duke's revenues on her b.*, H6B I, 3, 83. *since you will buckle fortune on my b.* R3 III, 7, 228. *have broke their —s with laying manors on them*, H8 I, 1, 84. *contempt and beggary hangs upon thy b.* Rom. V, 1, 71. *we'll die with harness on our b.* Mcb. V, 5, 52. *who hath had three suits to his b.* Lr. III, 4, 141. *with that suit upon my b.* Cymb. III, 5, 141. Peculiar expressions: *when Gods have hot —s*, Wiv. V, 5, 13, i. e. have carnal desires. *Steel to the very b.*, Tit. IV, 3, 47, i. e. not only in the edge, but also in the back, throughout; the comparison being taken from a knife.

2) the rear of an army: *he leaves his b. unarmed*, H4B I, 3, 79. *other foes may set upon our —s*, H6C V, 1, 61.

3) the outward part of the hand: Caes. I, 2, 221.

4) a support in reserve: *this project should have a b. or second, that might hold, if this should blast in proof*, Hml. IV, 7, 154.

Back, adv., 1) turning or returning from a place or person: Ven. 557. 906. Lucr. Arg. 13. Lucr. 843. 965. 1583. 1670. Sonn. 126, 6. Tp. II, 1, 259. V, 36. Gentl. IV, 4, 57. Wiv. V, 5, 89. Meas. I, 1, 75. II, 2, 143 (*turn b.*) Err. IV, 2, 55. Mids. III, 2, 315 etc. etc. *back again*: Sonn. 45, 11. Tp. I, 2, 150. Gentl. I, 2, 51. Meas. II, 2, 58. Err. II, 1, 75. Mids. I, 1, 251. Merch. I, 1, 151. II, 7, 14. Lr. IV, 2, 91 etc. *urge her to a present answer b.* All's II, 2, 67. *goes to and b.* Ant. I, 4, 46. *b. my ring!* Cymb. II, 4, 118. *give b.* = yield, Gentl. V, 4, 126 (cf. *give*). *to go b.* = to give way, to succumb, get the worst: *goest thou b.? thou shalt go b.*, *I warrant thee*, Ant. V, 2, 155. *make her go b., even to the yielding*, Cymb. I, 4, 115.

2) not coming forward: cf. *to keep, to stand* etc.

Back, vb., 1) to get upon the back of, to

mount: *a colt that's —ed and burthened*, Ven. 419. *I will b. him straight*, H4A II, 3, 74. *Jupiter, upon his eagle —ed*, Cymb. V, 5, 427. Figuratively: *my will is —ed with resolution*, Lucr. 352.

2) to support, to second: *thou —est reproach against long-living laud*, Lucr. 622. *call you that —ing of your friends? a plague upon such —ing!* H4A II, 4, 166. *—ed by the power of Warwick*, H6C I, 1, 52. I, 4, 73. II, 2, 69. IV, 1, 41. 43. R3 I, 2, 236. IV, 3, 47. Tit. II, 3, 54. Rom. I, 1, 40.

3) to adjoin behind: *a garden whose western side is with a vineyard —ed*, Meas. IV, 1, 29.

Backbite, to slander one absent: *they are arrant knaves and will b. No worse than they are backbitten, for they have marvellous foul linen*, H4B V, 1, 36 (Ff. *bitten* for *backbitten*).

Back-door, door on the hind part of a house: Wiv. III, 3, 25. Figuratively: *having found the b. open of the unguarded hearts*, Cymb. V, 3. 45.

Backed, having a back: *b. like a weasel*, Hml. III, 2, 397.

Back-friend. So in Err. IV, 2, 37 the bum-bailiff is called, because he comes from behind to arrest one; and in As III, 2, 167 Rosalind and Touchstone, because they clandestinely overhear Celia's reading of verse (many M. Edd. *how now! back, friends!*)

Back-return, return: *till Harry's b. again to France* H5 V Chor. 41 (*b. again* = repeated return).

Backside, the ground behind: *his steel was in debt, it went o' the b. the town*, Cymb. I, 2, 14 (= round the town. As for the omitted prep. *of*, v. *of* and *side*).

Backsword man, fencer at single-sticks: *I knew him a good b.* H4B III, 2, 70.

Back-trick, a caper backwards in dancing: *I have the b. simply as strong as any man in Illyria*, Tw. I, 3, 131 (perhaps a quibble: the trick of going back in a fight).

Backward, adv. toward the back, back: *b. she pushed him*, Ven. 41. *and b. drew the heavenly moisture*, 541. 1034. LLL V, 1, 50. Merch. II, 2, 103. All's I, 1, 214. 233. I, 2, 48. John V, 5, 3. Troil. I, 3, 128. III, 2, 47. IV, 1, 20. Rom. I, 2, 48. I, 3, 42. 56. Mcb. V, 5, 7. Hml. II, 2, 206. Figuratively = from the wrong end, perversely: *she would spell him b.* Ado III, 1, 61, i. e. she would make vices of his virtues; cf. *backwardly*.

Backward, adj., 1) being in the back: *his b. voice*, Tp. II, 2, 95.

2) turned back: *with a b. look*, Sonn. 59, 5. *restem their b. course*, Oth. I, 3, 38.

3) unwilling, void of zeal: *perish the man whose mind is b. now!* H5 IV, 3, 72.

Backward, subst., what lies behind: *what seest thou else in the dark b. and abysm of time?* Tp. I, 2, 50.

Backwardly, perversely, ill: *does he think so b. of me now, that I'll requite it last?* Tim. III, 3, 18 (cf. *backward*, Ado III, 1, 61).

Backwards, adv., = backward: *fly b.* Cymb. V, 3, 25.

Back-wounding, wounding in the back or from behind: *b. calumny*, Meas. III, 2, 197.

Bacon, hog's flesh pickled: *hang-hog is Latin for b.* Wiv. IV, 1, 50. *a gammon of b.* H4A II, 1, 26. Term for a fat person: *on, —s, on!* H4A II, 2, 95.

Bacon-fed: *b. knaves*, H4A II, 2, 88.

Bad, opposed to good: Sonn. 67,14. 121, 8. 140, 11. 144, 14. Tp. I, 2, 120. Gentl. III, 1, 206. Meas. V, 446. 456. Err. I, 1, 39. V, 67. Merch. III, 1, 46. H6B I, 4, 50. II, 1, 28 etc. etc. Substantively: *O Time, thou tutor both to good and b.* Lucr. 995. *so you o'ergreen my b., my good allow,* Sonn. 112, 4. *creating every b. a perfect best,* 114, 7. *to exchange the b. for better,* Gentl. II, 6, 13. *to make b. good,* Meas. IV, 1, 15. *and good from b. find no partition,* H4B IV, 1, 196. *renders good for b.* R3 I, 2, 69. *make good of b.* Mcb. II, 4, 41. *Thus b. begins and worse remains behind,* Hml. III, 4, 179. *let the time run on to good or b.* Cymb. V, 5, 129.

Badge, subst., mark, cognizance: *to clear this spot by death, at least I give a b. of fame to slander's livery,* Lucr. 1054 (in allusion to the silver badges worn by servants and engraved with the arms of their masters). *heavy tears, —s of either's woe,* Sonn. 44, 14. Tp. V, 267. Ado I, 1, 23. LLL IV, 3, 254. V, 2, 764 (here, as in Tp. V, 267, the strange disguise of the resp. person is meant). Mids. III, 2, 127. Merch. I, 3, 111. R2 V, 2, 33. H4B IV, 3, 113. H5 IV, 7, 106. H6A IV, 1, 105. 177. H6B III, 2, 200. V, 1, 201. 202. Tit. I, 119. II, 1, 89.

Badged, marked as with a badge: *their hands and faces were all b. with blood,* Mcb. II, 3, 107.

Badly, ill: John V, 3, 2 (*how goes the day with us? b., I fear*).

Badness, viciousness: *all men are bad, and in their b. reign,* Sonn. 121, 14. Meas. V, 59. Lr. III, 5, 9. IV, 6, 259.

Baffle, "originally a punishment of infamy, inflicted on recreant knights, one part of which was hanging them up by the heels" (Nares): *an I do not, call me villain and b. me,* H4A I, 2, 113; hence = to use contemptuously in any manner: *I will b. Sir Toby,* Tw. II, 5, 175. *alas, poor fool, how have they —d thee!* V, 377. *I am disgraced, impeached and —d here,* R2 I, 1, 170. *and shall good news be —d?* H4B V, 3, 109.

Bag, sack, pouch: *a b. of flax,* Wiv. V, 5, 159. *put your pipes in your b.* Oth. III, 1, 20. *balmed and entreasured with full —s of spices,* Per. III, 2, 66. *a b. of money,* Wiv. II, 2, 177. *sums in sealed —s,* III, 4, 16. *the b. of gold,* Err. IV, 4, 99. Merch. II, 8, 18. Shr. I, 2, 178. John III, 3, 7. H6B I, 3, 131. Tit. II, 3, 280. Lr. II, 4, 50. Oth. I, 1, 80. Per. III, 2, 41. *With b. and baggage:* As III, 2, 170. Wint. I, 2, 206.

Baggage, 1) the necessaries of an army, only in the phrase "*with bag and b.*": As III, 2, 170. Wint. I, 2, 206.

2) term of contempt for a worthless woman: *you witch, you hag, you b.* Wiv. IV, 2, 194. Err. III, 1, 57. Shr. Ind. 1, 3. Rom. III, 5, 157. 161. Per. IV, 2, 24. IV. 6, 20.

Bagot, a favourite of king Richard II's: R2 I, 4, 23. IV, 1 etc.*

Bagpipe. a musical instrument consisting of a leathern bag and three pipes: Merch. IV, 1, 49. 56. Wint. IV, 4, 183. *the drone of a Lincolnshire b.* H4A I, 2, 86.

Bagpiper, one who plays on a bagpipe: *laugh like parrots at a b.* Merch. I, 1, 53.

Bail, subst., 1) the person or persons who procure the release of a prisoner from custody, by be-

coming surety for his appearance in court: *your good worship will be my b.* Meas. III, 2, 77. *fetch my b.* All's V, 3, 296. *call in my sons to be my b.* H6B V, 1, 111. 120. Tit. II, 3, 295.

2) the security given: *that fell arrest without all b.* Sonn. 74, 2. *I cry b.* Meas. III, 2, 44. *till I give thee b.* Err. IV, 1, 80. *I sent you money to be your b.* V, 382. *I'll put in b.* All's V, 3, 286. *to deny their b.* H6B V, 1, 123.

Bail, vb., to set free from arrest by giving security for appearance in court: *Prison my heart in thy steel bosom's ward, but then my friend's heart let my poor heart b.* Sonn. 133, 10. *you will not b. me?* Meas. III, 2, 85. *let me b. these gentle three,* V, 362. *that* (purse of gold) *shall b. me,* Err. IV, 1, 107. *thou shalt not b. them,* Tit. II, 3, 299. Followed by *from: that blow did b. it* (her soul) *from the deep unrest of that polluted prison,* Lucr. 1725.

Bailiff, subordinate officer of justice: *then a process-server, a b.* Wint. IV, 3, 102.

Bait, subst., meat to allure fish: *she touched no unknown —s, nor feared no hooks,* Lucr. 103. *a swallowed b. on purpose laid to make the taker mad,* Sonn. 129, 7. Pilgr. 53. Ado III, 1, 28. 33 (*to lay a b.*). Merch. I, 1, 101. H4B III, 2, 356. Troil. V, 8, 20 (F1 *bed,* the other Ff *bit,* which is probably the true reading). Cor. IV, 1, 33. Tit. IV, 4, 91. 92. Rom. II Chor. 8. Hml. II, 1, 63. Cymb. III, 4, 59.

Bait, vb., 1) to allure by a bait: *to b. fish,* Merch. III, 1, 55. Metaphorically: *do their gay vestments his affections b.?* Err. II, 1, 94.

2) to make alluring by putting on a bait: *O cunning enemy, that, to catch a saint, with saint dost b. thy hook,* Meas. II, 2, 181. *b. the hook well, this fish will bite,* Ado II, 3, 114. cf. *fine-baited,* Wiv. II, 1, 99.

Bait, vb., 1) to attack with dogs, to set dogs upon: *we'll b. thy bears to death,* H6B V, 1, 148. *have you not set mine honour at the stake and —ed it with all the unmuzzled thoughts that tyrannous heart can think?* Tw. III, 1, 130.

2) to harass in a manner like that of dogs: *Alas, poor Maccabaeus, how hath he been —rd!* LLL V, 2, 634. *to b. me with this foul derision,* Mids. III, 2, 197. *who late hath beat her husband and now —s me,* Wint. II, 3, 92. *my wretchedness doth b. myself,* R2 IV, 238. *—ed with one that wants her wits,* Cor. IV, 2, 43. *—ed with the rabble's curse,* Mcb. V, 8, 29. Caes. IV, 3, 28. In 27 some M. Edd. with F2 *bait,* others with F1, which is undoubtedly in the right, *bay.* In R3 I, 3, 109 Qq: *to be so taunted, scorned and baited at;* Ff: *so baited, scorned and stormed at.*

Bait, vb., of uncertain signification: *ye are lazy knaves, and here ye lie —ing of bombards, when ye should do service,* H8 V, 4, 85 (= to broach?).

Baiting-place, place where bears are baited: H6B V, 1, 150.

Bajazet: *tongue, I must put you into a butter-woman's mouth and buy myself another of Bajazet's mule, if you prattle me into these perils,* All's IV, 1, 46. A passage not yet explained.

Bake, 1) trans., a) to prepare for food by heating in an oven: *and then to be —d with no date in the pie,* Troil. I, 2, 280. *in that paste let their vile heads be —d,* Tit. V, 2, 201. V, 3, 60. *the —d meats,* Rom. IV, 4, 5. Hml. I, 2, 180.

b) to dry and harden, to glue and paste

together: *when the earth is —d with frost,* Tp. I, 2, 256. *if melancholy had —d thy blood,* John III, 3, 43. *—s the elf-locks in foul sluttish hairs,* Rom. I, 4, 90. *—d and impasted with the parching streets,* Hml. II, 2, 481.

2) intr., a) to make bread in an oven: *I wash, wring, brew, b.* Wiv. I, 4, 101. *the heating of the oven, and the —ing,* Troil. I, 1, 24.

b) to be hardened in heat: *fillet of a fenny snake, in the cauldron boil and b.* Mcb. IV, 1, 13.

c) to be produced by hardening, like the crust of a paste: *a most instant tetter —d about, with vile and loathsome crust, all my smooth body,* Hml. I, 5, 71 (Qq and M. Edd. *barked*).

Baked-meats, pastry: *look to the b.* Rom. IV, 4, 5. *the funeral b. did coldly furnish forth the marriage tables,* Hml. I, 2, 180.

Baker, one whose trade is baking: H4A III, 3, 80. *they say the owl was a —'s daughter,* Hml. IV, 5, 42, in allusion to a legend, according to which a baker's daughter, who grudged bread to our Saviour, was transformed into an owl.

Balance, subst., a pair of scales to weigh things: *a mote will turn the b.* Mids. V, 324. Not inflected in the plural: *Are there b. here to weigh the flesh? I have them ready.* Merch. IV, 1, 255 (cf. sense, Mcb. V, 1, 29. Oth. IV, 3, 95. *Antipholus,* Err. V, 357). Metaphorically: *many likelihoods which hung so tottering in the b.* All's I, 3, 130. *to whom I promise a counterpoise, if not to thy estate a b. more replete,* II, 3, 183. *in the b. of great Bolingbroke are all the English peers,* R2 III, 4, 87. H4B IV, 1, 67. Tit. I, 55. Oth. I, 3, 330. — Attribute of justice: Ado V, 1, 212. H4B V, 2, 103.

Balance, vb., to keep in a state of just proportion: *except a sword or sceptre b. it* (my action), H6B V, 1, 9.

Bald, 1) destitute of hair or of natural covering in general: Tp. IV, 238. Err. II, 2, 71. 74. 108. 109. As IV, 3, 106. John III, 1, 324. H4A II, 4, 420. H4B III, 2, 294. H5 V, 2, 169. Cor. II, 3, 21. III, 1, 164.* Tim. IV, 3, 160. Lr. I, 4, 178. *No question asked him by any of the senators, but they stand b. before him,* Cor. IV, 5, 206, i. e. uncovering their heads, they stand in their natural baldness before him.

2) void of reason, unfounded: *'twould be a b. conclusion,* Err. II, 2, 110. *this b. unjointed chat,* H4A I, 3, 65.

Baldpate, a person with a bald head: Meas. V, 329.

Baldpated, destitute of hair: Meas. V, 357.

Baldrick, belt: *hang my bugle in an invisible b* Ado I, 1, 244.

Bale, evil, mischief: *Rome and her rats are at the point of battle; the one side must have b.* Cor. I, 1, 166 (Ff *baile;* Hanmer *bane*).

Baleful, pernicious: *b. sorcery,* H6A II, 1, 15. *our b. enemies,* V, 4, 122. *thou b. messenger,* H6B III, 2, 48. *our b. news,* H6C II, 1, 97. *b. mistletoe,* Tit. II, 3, 95. *that b. burning night,* V, 3, 83. *b. weeds,* Rom. II, 3, 8.

Balk, to neglect, not to care for, to throw to the winds: *make slow pursuit, or altogether b. the prey,* Lucr. 696 (O. Edd. *bauk*).* *b. logic with acquaintance that you have,* Shr. I, 1, 34. *this was looked for at your hand, and this was —ed,* Tw. III, 2, 26.

Balk, to heap, to pile up: *ten thousand bold Scots ... —ed in their own blood did Sir Walter see,* H4A I, 1, 69 *(bathed?).*

Ball, any round body: *—s of quenchless fire,* Lucr. 1554. *two pitch —s for eyes,* LLL III, 199. *a b of wildfire,* H4A III, 3, 45. Particular significations: 1) the round elastic thing to play with: H5 I, 2, 261. 282. II, 4, 131. Per. II, 1, 64. *as swift in motion as a b.* Rom. II, 5, 13. *I'll spurn thine eyes like —s before me,* Ant. II, 5, 64 (quibble). *these —s bound; there's noise in it,* All's II, 3, 314 (= that is well said, that is as it should be). 2) the apple of the eye: Compl. 24. Merch. III, 2, 117; and quibbling in Lucr. 1554. LLL III, 199. H5 V, 2, 17. Ant. II, 5, 64. 3) the globe: *this terrestrial b.* R2 III, 2, 41. *this b. of earth,* H4B Ind. 5. 4) a bullet: *the fatal —s of murdering basilisks,* H5 V, 2, 17. 5) the ensign of sovereignty, the apple or globe: *the sceptre and the b.* H5 IV, 1, 277. Mcb. IV, 1, 121.

Ballad, subst., popular song: *is there not a b. of the king and the beggar?* LLL I, 2, 114. 117. All's I, 3, 64. II, 1, 175. Wint. IV, 4, 186. 188. 262. 263. 610 etc. H4A II, 2, 48. H4B IV, 3, 52. H5 V, 2, 167 (mentioned with contempt: *a rhyme is but a b.*). Song, poem in general: *I will get Peter Quince to write a b. of this dream,* Mids. IV, 1, 221. *a woeful b. made to his mistress' eyebrow,* As II, 7, 148.

Ballad, vb., to make ballads on: *scald rhymers b. us out o' tune,* Ant. V, 2, 216.

Ballad-maker, maker of ballads: *pick out mine eyes with a —'s pen,* Ado I, 1, 254. Wint. V, 2, 27. Cor. IV, 5, 235.

Ballad-monger, term of contempt for a ballad-maker: *I had rather be a kitten and cry mew than one of these same metre —s,* H4A III, 1, 130.

Ballast, to load: *who sent whole armadoes of caracks to be ballast,* Err. III, 2, 141 *(ballast for ballasted). then had my prize been less, and so more equal —ing to thee, Posthumus,* Cymb. III, 6, 78, i. e. my freight would have been more equal in value to thine, I should not have been so much above thee in rank.

Ballow, provincialism for cudgel: *whether your costard or my b. be the harder,* Lr. IV, 6, 247 (Qq *bat*).

Ballow, an unintelligible word in the jargon of Dr. Caius: Wiv. I, 4, 92 (M. Edd. *baille* or *baillez*).

Balm, subst., medicinal ointment: Ven. 27. Lucr. 1466. Wiv. V, 5, 66. R2 I, 1, 172. H6C IV, 8, 41. R3 I, 2, 13. Troil. I, 1, 61. Cor. I, 6, 64 *(—s).* Tim. V, 4, 16. Mcb. II, 2, 39. Lr. I, 1, 218. Ant. V, 2, 314. Serving to anoint kings: R2 III, 2, 55. IV, 207. H4B IV, 5, 115. H5 IV, 1, 277. H6C III, 1, 17.

Balm, vb., 1) to anoint with some thing odoriferous: *b. his foul head in warm distilled waters,* Shr. Ind. 1, 48. *—ed and entreasured with full bags of spices,* Per. III, 2, 65.

2) to anoint with any thing medicinal, to heal: *this rest might yet have —ed thy broken sinews,* Lr. III, 6, 105.

Balmy, 1) full of medicinal power: *with the drops of this most b. time my love looks fresh,* Sonn. 107, 9. *b. slumbers,* Oth. II, 3, 258.

2) fragrant: *b. breath,* Oth. V, 2, 16.

Balsam = balm: *is this the b. that the usuring senate pours into captains' wounds?* Tim. III, 5, 110.

Balsamum, the same: Err. IV, 1, 89.

Balthazar, name of the merchant in Err. III, 1,

19. 22. V, 223; of Don Pedro's attendant in Ado II, 3, 45. 86; of servants in Merch. III, 4, 45. IV, 1, 154. Rom. V, 1, 12.

Ban, subst. 1) curse: *take thou that too, with multiplying —s,* Tim. IV, 1, 34. *with Hecate's b. thrice blasted,* Hml. III, 2, 269. *sometime with lunatic —s, sometime with prayers, enforce their charity,* Lr. II, 3, 19.

2) only in the plural, *bans* (O. Edd. *banes*) = notice of a matrimonial contract proclaimed in the church: *when I shall ask the —s and when be married,* Shr. II, 181. *make feasts, invite friends, and proclaim the —s,* III, 2, 16. *contracted bachelors, such as had been asked twice on the —s,* H4A IV, 2, 18. *I, her husband, contradict your —s,* Lr. V, 3, 87.

Ban, vb., to curse; 1) trans.: *—ing his boisterous and unruly beast,* Ven. 326. Lucr. 1460. H6B II, 4, 25. 2) absolutely: *though she strive to try her strength, and b. and brawl,* Pilgr. 318. *fell —ing hag,* H6A V, 3, 42. H6B III, 2, 319 *(curse and b.).* 333. *upon the —ing shore,* Oth. II, 1, 11 (only in Q1, the rest of O. Edd. *foaming*).

Ban, abbreviation for *Caliban:* Tp. II, 2, 188.

Banbury, name of an English town: *you B. cheese,* Wiv. I, 1, 130 (in allusion to the thinness of Slender, B. cheese being proverbially thin).

Band, subst. 1) tie, bandage: *her arms infold him like a b.* Ven. 225. *ivory in an alablaster b.* 363. *in infant —s crowned king* (i. e. in swaddling clothes) H5 Epil. 9. *the b. that seems to tie their friendship,* Ant. II, 6, 129. Hence = fetters: *release me from my —s,* Tp. Epil. 9. *dissolve the —s of life,* R2 II, 2, 71. *die in —s,* H6C I, 1, 186. And = conjugal ties: *to bind our loves up in a holy b.* Ado III, 1, 114. As V, 4, 136. H6C III, 3, 243. Hml. III, 2, 170.

2) bond, any moral obligation: *now will I charge you in the b. of truth,* All's IV, 2, 56. *according to thy oath and b.,* R2 I, 1, 2. *the end of life cancels all —s,* H4A III, 2, 157. *those lands lost by his father, with all —s of law,* Hml. I, 2, 24 (Ff. *bonds*). *such a wife as my farthest b. shall pass on thy approof,* Ant. III, 2, 26 (v. *approof*). Especially a written obligation to pay a sum, a promissory note: *was he arrested on a b.? not on a b., but on a chain,* Err. IV, 2, 49. The same pun in IV, 3, 32. *'tis nothing but some b. that he is entered into,* R2 V, 2, 65 (Ff. *bond; v.* 67 Qq also *bond*). *he would not take his b. and yours,* H4B I, 2, 37 (Ff. *bond*).

3) a company of persons joined in a common design: *the sergeant of the b.* Err. IV, 3, 30. *our fairy b.* Mids. III, 2, 110. *the gross b. of the unfaithful,* As IV, 1, 199. *we b. of brothers,* H5 IV, 3, 60. *his threatening b. of Typhon's brood,* Tit. IV, 2, 94. Especially a troop of soldiers, an army: *the warlike b. where her beloved Collatinus lies,* Lucr. 255. All's IV, 1, 16. IV, 3, 227. H5 IV Chor. 29. H6B III, 1, 312. 348. H6C II, 2, 68. Tit. V, 2, 113. Tim. IV, 3, 92. Cymb. V, 5, 304. *Bands* = troops: H6A IV, 1, 165. H6C III, 3, 204. Cor. I, 2, 26. I, 6, 53. Ant. III, 12, 25. Cymb. IV, 4, 11.

Band, vb., to unite in troops: *and —ing themselves in contrary parts,* H6A III, 1, 81.

Banditto (O. Edd. *bandetto*), outlaw, robber: *a Roman sworder and b. slave murdered sweet Tully,* H6B IV, 1, 135.

Bandog, a fierce dog kept chained: *the time when screech-owls cry and —s howl,* H6B I, 4, 21.

Bandy, 1) to beat to and fro, as a ball: *my words would b. her to my sweet love, and his to me* (viz, if she were a ball) Rom. II, 5, 14. Figuratively of words, looks, etc.: *well —ied both: a set of wit well played,* LLL V, 2, 29. *to b. word for word and frown for frown,* Shr. V, 2, 172. *I will not b. with thee word for word,* H6C I, 4, 49. *do you b. looks with me?* Lr. I, 4, 92. *to b. hasty words,* II, 4, 178.

2) intrans. to contend, to strive, a) in emulation: *one fit to b. with thy lawless sons, to ruffle in the commonwealth of Rome,* Tit. I, 312. b) in enmity: *I will b. with thee in faction,* As V, 1, 61. *this factious —ing of their favourites,* H6A IV, 1, 190. *the prince expressly hath forbidden —ing in Verona streets,* Rom. III, 1, 92.

Bane, subst., 1) poison: *rats that ravin down their proper b.* Meas. I, 2, 133.

2) destruction, ruin: *though nothing but my body's b. would cure thee,* Ven. 372. *b. to those that for my surety will refuse the boys!* H6B V, 1, 120. *'twill be his death, 'twill be his b.* Troil. IV, 2, 98. *lest Rome herself be b. unto herself,* Tit. V, 3, 73. *I will not be afraid of death and b.* Mcb. V, 3, 59. *two boys ... was the Romans' b.* Cymb. V, 3, 58.

Bane, vb., to poison: *to give ten thousand ducats to have it* (the rat) *—d,* Merch. IV, 1, 46.

Bang, subst., blow: *you'll bear me a b. for that,* Caes. III, 3, 20.

Bang, vb., to beat, thump: *the desperate tempest hath so —ed the Turks,* Oth. II, 1, 21. Figuratively = to strike: *with some excellent jests, firenew from the mint, you should have —ed the youth into dumbness,* Tw. III, 2, 24.

Banish, 1) to condemn to leave the country: Gent. II, 6, 38. III, 1, 217. V, 4, 124. As I, 1, 104. 111. I, 2, 6. 285. II, 1, 28. V, 3, 6. R2 I, 3, 179. H6A IV, 1, 47. H6B II, 3, 42. H6C III, 3, 25. R3 I, 3, 167. Cor. III, 3, 123. Rom. III, 2, 112. Tim. III, 5, 98. 112 etc. etc.

2) to drive away in general: *the plague is —ed by thy breath,* Ven. 510. *b. moan,* Pilgr. 379. Meas. II, 4, 163. V, 64. All's II, 3, 54. John III, 1, 321. H4A I, 3, 181. H6A III, 1, 123. V, 5, 96. H6B I, 2, 18. Oth. V, 2, 78 etc. etc.*

In both significations followed by *from:* Tp. I, 2, 266. Gentl. IV, 1, 47. H4A II, 3, 42. H6B III, 2, 334. Tp. II, 1, 126. Gentl. III, 1, 171. 172. III, 2, 2. Tw. V, 289. H6B V, 1, 167 etc. etc. Or by *hence* or *thence:* Gentl. IV, 1, 23. Shr. Ind. 2, 34. Rom. III, 3, 15. 19, etc.

Followed by a double accus.: *we b. you our territories,* R2 I, 3, 139. *one of our souls ... —ed this frail sepulchre of our flesh,* 196. *b. not him thy Harry's company,* H4A II, 4, 525. *I b. her my bed and company,* H6B II, 1, 197. *—ed fair England's territories,* III, 2, 245. *has —ed me his bed,* H8 III, 1, 119. *and my poor name —ed the kingdom,* IV, 2, 127. *b. him our city,* Cor. III, 3, 101.

His banished years = the years of his banishment, R2 I, 3, 210.

Banisher, he who condemns another to leave his country: *to be full quit of those my --s,* Cor. IV, 5, 89.

Banishment, exile: Lucr. 1855. Gentl. III, 1,

173. As I, 3, 140. Shr. Ind. 2, 33. R2 I, 3, 143. 212.
III, 1, 21. III, 3, 134. H6B II, 3, 12. 14. III, 2, 253.
R3 I, 3, 168. 193. Cor. III, 3, 15. Tit. III, 1, 51. Rom.
III, 2, 131. III, 3, 11. Tim. III, 5, 111. Lr. I, 1, 184
etc. etc.

Banister, servant to Henry of Buckingham, whom
he betrayed: H8 II, 1, 109.

Bank, subst., 1) mound, elevated ground:
sitting on a b. Tp. I, 2, 389. *I upon this b. will rest
my head,* Mids. II, 2, 40. *how sweet the moonlight sleeps
upon this b.* Merch. V, 54. Especially a ridge of earth
set with flowers; a flower-bed: *this primrose b.
whereon we lie,* Ven. 151. *thy —s with pioned and
twilled brims,* Tp. IV, 64. Mids. II, 1, 249. Tw. I, 1, 6.
Wint. IV, 4, 130. R2 III, 4, 105. H6B III, 1, 228.
Cymb. V, 4, 98.

2) the earth **rising on the** side of a
water; a) of a river: Ven. 72. Lucr. 1119. 1437.
John II, 442. H4A I, 3, 98. 106. III, 1, 65. H4B IV,
1, 176.* Troil. III, 2, 10. Caes. I, 1, 50. 63. Cymb. II,
4, 71. Per. II, 4, 24. b) of the sea: Sonn. 56, 11.
H4A III, 1, 45. H6B III, 2, 83. R3 IV, 4, 525 (Qq on
the shore). *were his brain as barren as —s of Libya,*
Troil. I, 3, 328, i. e. the sandy shore.

3) Perhaps = bench (as we speak of a bank of
rowers) in a difficult and much disputed passage in
Mcb. I, 7, 6: *upon this b. and school of time.* All M.
Edd. write: *upon this bank and shoal of time;* but
nowhere else in Sh. the word *bank* occurs in the sense
of sandbank, and *school* is the constant reading of
O. Edd.

Bank, vb. *Have I not heard these islanders shout
out 'Vive le roi!' as I have —ed their towns?* John V,
2, 104; probably the French *aborder:* as I landed on
the banks of their towns.

Bankrupt (O. Edd. often *bankrout*), adj., insolvent: *they prove b. in this poor-rich gain,* Lucr. 140.
a. b. beggar, 711. Sonn. 67, 9. Gentl. I, 4, 42. LLL
I, 1, 27. Mids. III, 2, 85. R2 II, 1, 151. 257. H5 IV,
2, 43. Followed by *of: what a face I have, since it
is b. of his majesty,* R2 IV, 267.

Bankrupt, subst. (O. Edd. mostly *bankrout*),
insolvent trader: *blessed b. that by love so thriveth,*
Ven. 466. Err. IV, 2, 58. Merch. III, 1, 47. IV, 1, 122.
As II, 1, 57. Rom. III, 2, 57. Tim. IV, 1, 8.

Banner, flag, standard: *when his gaudy b.
is displayed,* Lucr. 272. John II, 308. H5 IV, 2, 61.
IV, 8, 87. Cor. III, 1, 8. Tim. V, 4, 30. Mcb. I, 2, 49.
V, 5, 1. Lr. III, 1, 34. IV, 2, 56. Oth. III, 3, 353. Ant.
I, 2, 106. III, 1, 32. Per. V Prol. 19.

Banneret, little flag: *the scarfs and the —s
about thee did manifoldly dissuade me from believing
thee a vessel of too great a burthen,* All's II, 3, 214.

Banns, see Ban.

Banquet, subst., a rich entertainment,
feast: *what b. wert thou to the taste,* Ven. 445. Sonn.
47, 6. Ado II, 1, 178. II, 3, 22. As II, 5, 64. Shr. Ind.
1, 39. H5 I, 1, 56. H8 I, 4, 61. IV, 2, 88. Tit. V, 2,
76. Mcb. I, 4, 56. Ant. I, 2, 11. Joined to *feast: this
is the feast that I have bid ·her to, and this the b. she
shall surfeit on,* Tit. V, 2, 194. *free from our feasts
and —s bloody knives,* Mcb. III, 6, 35.

Sometimes = dessert, a slight refection consisting of fruit and sweetmeats: *my b. is to close our
stomachs up, after our great good cheer,* Shr. V, 2, 9.
we have a trifling foolish b. towards, Rom. I, 5, 124.

ladies, there is an idle b. attends you, Tim. I, 2,
160.

A running banquet, originally a hasty refreshment,
in a lascivious sense: *some of these should find a running b. ere they rested,* H8 I, 4, 12; and for a whipping: *besides the running b. of two beadles,* V, 4, 69.

Banquet, vb., 1) intr., to feast: *the mind shall
b., though the body pine,* LLL I, 1, 25. H6A I, 6, 13.
30. II, 1, 12. Troil. V, 1, 51. Tit. V, 2, 114. Caes.
I, 2, 77.

2) trans. to treat with a feast: *visit his countrymen and b. them,* Shr. I, 1, 202.

Banquo, name in Mcb. I, 2, 34 etc. etc.

Baptise, to christen: *I'll be new —d,* Rom.
II, 2, 50.

Baptism, christening: *washed as pure as sin
with b.* H5 I, 2, 32. H8 V, 3, 162. Oth. II, 3, 349.

Baptista, 1) *B. Minola,* father of Catharine and
Bianca in Shr. I, 1, 85. 2, 97. 118 etc. etc. —

2) female name in Hml. III, 2, 250.

Bar, name of a French nobleman: H5 III, 5, 42.
IV, 8, 103 *(Edward Duke of B.).*

Bar, subst., originally a pole used for hinderance
or obstruction; 1) the rail of a grate: *a secret
grate of iron —s,* H6A I, 4, 10. *I could rend —s of
steel,* 51.

2) the bolt: *each trifle under truest —s to thrust,*
Sonn. 48, 2. *which obloquy set —s before my tongue,*
H6A II, 5, 49.

3) the railing that encloses a place: *unto this
b. and royal interview,* H5 V, 2, 27. Especially the
place where causes of law are tried: *all several sins ...
throng to the b., crying all Guilty,* R3 V, 3, 199. *the
duke came to the b.* H8 II, 1, 12. 31. And other places
of public function: *at which time we will bring the
device to the b. and crown thee for a finder of madmen,*
Tw. III, 4, 154.

4) any thing that separates or confines:
so sweet a b. should sunder such sweet friends, Merch.
III, 2, 119. *life being weary of these worldly —s,* Caes.
I, 3, 96.

5) any impediment: *those —s which stop the
hourly dial,* Lucr. 327. *any cross, any b., any impediment,* Ado II, 2, 4. *the watery kingdom is no b. to stop
the foreign spirits,* Merch. II, 7, 45. *put —s between
the owners and their rights,* III, 2, 19. *having God, her
conscience, and these —s against me,* R3 I, 2, 235.

6) exception against a demand: *other —s he
lays before me,* Wiv. III, 4, 7. *since this b. in law
makes us friends,* Shr. I, 1, 139. *there is no b. to make
against your highness' claim to France,* H5 I, 2, 35.
the founder of this law and female b. I, 2, 42, i. e. this
exception to female succession.

Bar, vb., 1) to shut with a bolt, to shut
in general: *all ports I'll b.* Lr. II, 1, 82. *to b. my
doors,* III, 4, 155. *you b. the door upon your own liberty,*
Hml. III, 2, 351. *which with a yielding latch hath —ed
him from the blessed thing he sought,* Lucr. 340. *things
hid and· —ed from common sense,* LLL I, 1, 57. *To
b. up* = to shut up: *that is stronger made which was
before —ed up with ribs of iron,* Ado IV, 1, 153. *a
jewel in a ten times —ed up chest,* R2 I, 1, 180.

2) to put a stop to, to prevent: *sweet recreation —ed, what doth ensue but melancholy?* Err. V,
78. *I b. confusion,* As V, 4, 131. *merriment, which —s
a thousand harms,* Shr. Ind. 2, 138. *inspired merit so*

by breath is —ed, All's II, 1, 151. *let it be lawful that law b. no wrong*, John III, 1, 186. *b. Harry England*, H5 III, 5, 48. *if you cannot b. his access to the king*, H8 III, 2, 17. *purpose so —ed, it follows, nothing is done to purpose*, Cor. III, 1, 148. *to b. your offence herein*, Cymb. I, 4, 122. *the pangs of —ed affections*, I, 1, 82. *his greatness was no guard to b. heaven's shaft*, Per. II, 4, 15.

3) *to* exclude: *nor have we herein —ed your better wisdoms*, Hml. I, 2, 14. Followed by *from: from his presence I am —ed*, Wint. III, 2, 99. *who should b. me from them?* R3 IV, 1, 22 (Qq *keep*). *we'll b. thee from succession*, Wint. IV, 4, 440. Especially *to* exclude *by express prohibition and exception: a will that bars the title of thy son*, John II, 192. *b. us in our claim*, H5 I, 2, 12. *to b. your highness claiming from the female*, 92. *to b. my master's heirs*, R3 III, 2, 54. *for your claim, I b. it in the interest of my wife*, Lr. V, 3, 85.

Hence = *to* except: *I b. to-night*, Merch. II, 2, 208.

4) *to bar one of sth.* = *to* deprive *one of sth.: —ed of rest*, Ven. 784. *I whom fortune of such triumph —s*, Sonn. 25, 3. *thinking to b. thee of succession*, Cymb. III, 3, 102.

5) *to bar one sth.*, a) = *to* hinder *one from sth.: I will b. no honest man my house*, H4B II, 4, 110. *thou —est us our prayers to the Gods*, Cor. V, 3, 104. *—est me my way in Rome*, Tit. I, 291. 383.

b) = *to* deprive *one of sth.: when the heart is —ed the aidance of the tongue*, Ven. 330. *mine eye my heart thy picture's sight would b.* Sonn. 46, 3. *the lottery of my destiny —s me the right of voluntary choosing*, Merch. II, 1, 16. *—s me the place of a brother*, As I, 1, 20. *heaven and fortune b. me happy hours*, R3 IV, 4, 400.

Barbara (Qq F1 *Barbarie*), female name: Oth. IV, 3, 26. 33.

Barbarian, a native of a rude uncivilized country: *I would they were —s, as they are, though in Rome littered*, Cor. III, 1, 238. *a frail vow betwixt an erring b. and a supersubtle Venetian*, Oth. I, 3, 363.

Adjectively: *thou art bought and sold among those of any wit, like a b. slave*, Troil. II, 1, 52.

Barbarie, see *Barbara.*

Barbarism, manner and quality of a barbarian; either savage cruelty: *b. itself must have pitied him*, R2 V, 2, 36; or rude ignorance and want of good manners: *I have for b. spoke more than for that angel knowledge you can say*, LLL I, 1, 112. *lest b. should a like language use to all degrees*, Wint. II, 1, 84. *the Grecians begin to proclaim b., and policy grows into an ill opinion*, Troil. V, 4, 18.

Barbarous, after the manner of a barbarian; a) savagely cruel: *O b. and bloody spectacle!* H6B IV, 1, 144. IV, 4, 15. Tit. I, 131. 378. II, 3, 118. V, 1, 97. V, 3, 4. Lr. IV, 2, 43. Per. IV, 2, 70.

b) rude: *fit for the mountains and the b. caves where manners ne'er were preached*, Tw. IV, 1, 52. *b. license*, H5 I, 2, 271. *a b. people*, III, 5, 4. *the b. Goths*, Tit. I, 28. *a b. Moor*, II, 3, 78. *the b. Scythian*, Lr. I, 1, 118. *this b. brawl*, Oth. II, 3, 172. *b. and unnatural revolts*, Cymb. IV, 4, 6.

c) ignorant, unlettered: *most b. intimation*, LLL IV, 2, 13. *we will be singuled from the b.* V, 1, 86. *rank me with the b. multitudes*, Merch. II, 9,

33. *to choke his days with b. ignorance*, John IV, 2, 59.

Barbary, 1) the northwestern part of Africa: Merch. III, 2, 272. H4A II, 4, 84. *a B. cockpigeon*, As IV, 1, 151. *a B. hen*, H4B II, 4, 108. *a B. horse*, Hml. V, 2, 155. 168. Oth. I, 1, 112.

2) = Barbary horse: *rode on roan B.* R2 V, 5, 78. *rode he on B.?* 81.

Barbason, name of a demon: Wiv. II, 2, 311. H5 II, 1, 57.

Barbed, armed and harnessed (used only of horses): *his b. steeds*, R2 III, 3, 117. *instead of mounting b. steeds*, R3 I, 1, 10.*

Barber, subst., one whose occupation is to shave and dress hair: *at the —'s*, Ado III, 2, 44. *the —'s man*, 45. *I must to the —'s*, Mids. IV, 1, 25. *like to a censer in a —'s shop*, Shr. IV, 3, 91. H4B I, 2, 29. Hml. II, 2, 521. *like a —'s chair that fits all buttocks*, All's II, 2, 17. *like the forfeits in a —'s shop, as much in mock as mark*, Meas. V, 323 (Nares: 'those shops were places of great resort, for passing away time in an idle manner. By way of enforcing some kind of regularity, and perhaps at least as much to promote drinking, certain laws were usually hung up, the transgression of which was to be punished by specific forfeitures. It is not to be wondered, that laws of that nature were as often laughed at as obeyed').

Barber, vb., to frizzle: *—ed ten times o'er*, Ant. II, 2, 229.

Barber-monger, one who deals much with barbers: *you whoreson cullionly b.* Lr. II, 2, 36.

Bard, singer and soothsayer among the Celts: *a b. of Ireland told me once, I should not live long after I saw Richmond*, R3 IV, 2, 109. Singer in general: *hearts, tongues, figures, scribes, bards, poets, cannot think, speak, cast, write, sing, number his love to Antony*, Ant. III, 2, 16.

Bardolph, 1) *Lord B.:* H4B I, 1, 3. 7. I, 3, 25. 69. IV, 4, 97. — 2) the attendant of Falstaff: Wiv. I, 1, 129. I, 3, 10. III, 5, 1. H4A I, 2, 181 (Qq Ff. *Harvey*). II, 2, 22 54. II, 4, 330 (Qq *Bardoll*), etc. H4B I, 2, 36 etc. H5 II, 1, 2 etc.

Bare, a name: H4B III, 2, 22 (Qq *Barnes*).

Bare, adj., 1) naked, without covering: *on her b. breast*, Lucr. 439. Gentl. IV, 1, 36. III, 1, 272 (a quibble). Merch. IV, 1, 252. As II, 7, 95. III, 3, 61. R2 III, 2, 46. H4B II, 4, 394. Troil. III, 2, 99. Cor. III, 2, 10. Tim. IV, 3, 229. Lr. II, 3, 15. III, 4, 112. III, 7, 59. Oth. IV, 2, 49. With an uncovered head: *how many then should cover that stand b.* Merch. II, 9, 44. Unarmed: *with my b. fists*, H6A I, 4, 36. *b. hands*, Oth. I, 3, 175. Unsheathed: *wear thy rapier b.* Oth. V, 1, 2. In general, unfurnished with what is necessary or comfortable: *what b. excuses makest thou to be gone!* Ven. 188. *like a late sacked island, b. and unpeopled*, Lucr. 1741. *age like winter b.* Pilgr. 160. *b. ruined choirs, where late the sweet birds sang*, Sonn. 73, 4. *the argument all b. is of more worth than ...*, 103, 3. *dwell in this b. island*, Tp. Epil. 8. *that from the seedness the b. fallow brings to teeming foison*, Meas. I, 4, 42. *the sauce to meat is ceremony; meeting were b. without it*, Mcb. III, 4, 37. *left me b. to weather*, Cymb. III, 3, 64; cf. Tim. IV, 3, 265. Threadbare: *it appears by their b. liveries*, Gentl. II, 4, 45. Figuratively: *his right cheek is worn b.* All's IV, 5, 104. *whilst some with cunning gild their* *copper crowns, with truth and plainness I do wear mine b.* Troil. IV, 4, 108. With *of: b. of her branches*, Tit. II, 4, 17.

2) Hence = lean, poor: *duty so great, which wit so poor as mine may make seem b.*, *in wanting words to show it*, Sonn. 26, 6. *b. and rotten policy*, H4A I, 3, 108 (Ff. and M. Edd. *base*). *such poor, such b., such lewd, such mean attempts*, III, 2, 13. *exceeding poor and b.* IV, 2, 75. *lean, sterile and b. land*, H4B IV, 3, 129. *this b. withered trunk*, H4B IV, 5, 230. *art thou so b. and full of wretchedness*, Rom. V, 1, 68. *they* (flatteries) *are too thin and b. to hide offences*, H8 V, 3, 125. Cor. V, 1, 20.* *the b. fortune of that beggar Posthumus*, Cymb. III, 5, 119. = lean, emaciated: *unless you call three fingers on the ribs b.* H4A IV, 2, 80.

3) mere: *uttering b. truth*, Sonn. 69, 4. *they live by your b. words*, Gentl. II, 4, 46. *which is much in a b. Christian*, III, 1, 272 (quibble). *by b. imagination of a feast*, R2 I, 3, 297. Rom. III, 2, 46. Tim. III, 1, 45. Hml. III, 1, 76.

Used substantively: *that termless skin whose b. outbragged the web it seemed to wear*, Compl. 95.

Bare, vb. 1) to strip, to make naked: *have —d my bosom to the thunder-stone*, Caes. I, 3, 49. *that dawning may b. the raven's eye*, Cymb. II, 2, 49 (i. e. open; O. Edd. *bear*).*

2) to shave: *shave the head, and tie the beard, and say it was the desire of the penitent to be so —d before his death*, Meas. IV, 2, 189. *the —ing of my beard*, All's IV, 1, 54.

Barebone, skeleton: *here comes lean Jack, here comes b.* H4A II, 4, 358.

Bareboned, consisting only of bones: *shows me a b. death by time outworn*, Lucr. 1761.

Barefaced, 1) with the face uncovered: *some of your French crowns have no hair at all, and then you will play b.* Mids. I, 2, 100 (quibble). *they bore him b. on the bier*, Hml. IV, 5, 164.

2) undisguised: *though I could with b. power sweep him from my sight*, Mcb. III, 1, 119.

Barefoot, with naked feet: *I must dance b.* Shr. II, 33. All's III, 4, 6. Troil. I, 2, 80. Hml. II, 2, 528. Oth. IV, 3, 39.

Adjectively: *lie tumbling in my b. way*, Tp. II, 2, 11. *a b. brother*, Rom. V, 2, 4.

Barefooted, the same: *would have walked b. to Palestine*, Oth. IV, 3, 39 (only in Q2; the other O. Edd. *barefoot*).

Bare-gnawn, eaten off, eaten lean: *my name is lost, by treason's tooth b. and canker-bit*, Lr. V, 3, 122.

Bare-headed, uncovered: R2 V, 2, 19. H4B II, 4, 388. H6B IV, 1, 54. Lr. III, 2, 60.

Barely, 1) in a state of nakedness: *when you have our roses, you b. leave our thorns to prick ourselves, and mock us with our bareness*, All's IV, 2, 19 (cf. *coldly*, Hml. I, 2, 181; *grossly*, III, 3, 80).

2) merely, only: *shall I not have b. my principal?* Merch. IV, 1, 342. R2 II, 1, 226. Cymb. II, 4, 7.

Bareness, 1) nakedness: *beauty o'ersnowed and b. everywhere*, Sonn. 5, 8. *old December's b.* 97, 4. All's IV, 2, 20.

2) leanness: *for their b., I am sure they never learned that of me*, H4A IV, 2, 77.

Bare-picked, picked to the bone: *for the b. bone of majesty*, John IV, 3, 148.

Bare-ribbed, with bare ribs, like a skeleton: *in his forehead sits a b. death*, John V, 2, 177.

Barful, full of impediments: *a b. strife*, Tw. I, 4, 41.

Bargain, subst., 1) agreement, contract: *so is the b.* As V, 4, 15. *take hands, a b.* Wint. IV, 4, 394. *no —s break that are not this day made*, John III, 1, 93. *to clap this royal b. up of peace*, 235. *I by b. should wear it myself*, H5 IV, 7, 182. *clap hands, and a b.* V, 2, 134. *there's a b. made*, Caes. I, 3, 120. *lest the b. should catch cold and starve*, Cymb. I, 4, 179. A mercantile transaction: *upon what b. do you give it me?* Err. II, 2, 25. *he rails on me, my —s, and my well-won thrift*, Merch. I, 3, 51. III, 1, 59. H4A III, 1, 139. Figuratively, a contract of love: *pure lips, sweet seals in my soft lips imprinted, what —s may I make, still to be sealing?* Ven. 512. Gentl. II, 2, 7. LLL V, 2, 799. Merch. III, 2, 195. Troil. III, 2, 204. Rom. V, 3, 115.

2) the thing stipulated or purchased: *the devil shall have his b.* H4A I, 2, 131. *she was too fond of her most filthy b.* Oth. V, 2, 157.

To sell one a b. = to make one ridiculous, to embarrass one by an unexpected reply: *the boy hath sold him a b.* LLL III, 102. *to sell a b. well is as cunning as fast and loose*, 104.

Bargain, vb., 1) to stipulate: *'tis —ed 'twixt us twain, that she shall still be curst in company*, Shr. II, 307.

2) followed by *for* = to make an agreement about the transfer of sth.: *so worthless peasants b. for their wives*, H6A V, 5, 53. *while his own lands are —ed for and sold*, H6B I, 1, 231. *I have —ed for the joint*, Per. IV, 2, 141.

Barge, a boat for pleasure: H8 I, 3, 63. I, 4, 54. II, 1, 98. Ant. II, 2, 196. 216. Per. V Prol. 20. V, 1, 3.

Bargulus, name of an Illyrian pirate: H6B IV, 1, 108 (Cic. de off. II, 11).*

Bark, subst., ship: Sonn. 80, 7. 116, 7. Tp. I, 2, 144. Err. I, 1, 117. III, 2, 155. IV, 1, 85. 99. IV, 3, 38. Merch. II, 6, 15. Wint. III, 3, 8. V, 2, 73. H6B III, 2, 411. H6C V, 4, 28. R3 III, 7, 162. IV, 4, 233. Troil. Prol. 12. I, 3, 40. Tit. I, 71. Rom. III, 5, 132. V, 3, 118. Tim. IV, 2, 19. V, 1, 53. Caes. V, 1, 67. Mcb. I, 3, 24. Hml. IV, 3, 46. Lr. IV, 6, 18. Oth. II, 1, 48. 189. Per. V Prol. 22. Used as a feminine: Err. IV, 1, 85. Merch. II, 6, 15. Tit. I, 73. Lr. IV, 6, 18; as a neuter: Mcb. I, 3, 24. Tit. I, 71.

Bark, subst., the rind or covering of a tree: Lucr. 1167. Tp. II, 2, 128. As III, 2, 6. 277. 379. Wint. IV, 4, 94. R2 III, 4, 58. H8 I, 2, 96. Tit. V, 1, 138. Ant. I, 4, 66. *Dumain is mine, as sure as b. on tree*, LLL V, 2, 285.

Bark, vb., 1) to peel: *would b. your honour from that trunk you bear, and leave you naked*, Meas. III, 1, 72. *this pine is —ed, that overtopped them all*, Ant. IV, 12, 23.

2) to grow like the bark of a tree: *a most instant tetter —ed about*, Hml. I, 5, 71 (Ff *baked*).

Bark, vb., to cry with the voice of a dog: Ven. 240. Tp. I, 2, 383. Wiv. I, 1, 298. Mids. III, 1, 113. Merch. I, 1, 94. H8 II, 4, 160. Cor. II, 3, 224. Used of a wolf: Ven. 459; of a fox: H6B III,

1, 55. Followed by *at:* Ado I, 1, 132. H6C II, 1, 17. R3 I, 1, 23. Lr. III, 6, 66. IV, 6, 158. Figuratively: *the envious —ing of your saucy tongue against my lord,* H6A III, 4, 33. *that thou —est at him,* Troil. II, 1, 38.

Barkley, M. Edd. *Berkeley,* q. v.

Barkloughly, name of a castle in Wales: R2 III, 2, 1.*

Barky, covered with a bark: *the female ivy so enrings the b. fingers of the elm,* Mids. IV, 1, 49.

Barley, a grain of which malt is made: Tp. IV, 61.

Barley-broth, term of contempt for beer: *can sodden water, a drench for sur-reined jades, their b., decoct their cold blood to such valiant heat?* H5 III, 5, 19.

Barm, yeast: *and sometime make the drink to bear no b.* Mids. II, 1, 38.

Barn, subst., a building for securing the productions of the earth: Tp. IV, 111. Ado III, 4, 49 (quibble). Shr. III, 2, 233. H4A II, 3, 6. Tit. V, 1, 133.

Barn, subst., a little child: Ado III, 4, 49 (quibble). All's I, 3, 28. Wint. III, 3, 70.

Barn, vb., to lay up in a barn: *but like still-pining Tantalus he sits, and useless —s the harvest of his wits,* Lucr. 859.

Barnacle, a kind of goose: Tp. IV, 249.*

Barnardine, name in Meas. IV, 2, 8. 63. 68. 125. 3, 22 etc. V, 472.

Barnardo (M. Edd. *Bernardo*) name in Hml. I, 1, 4 etc.

Barnes, name in H4B III, 2, 22 (Ff. *Bare*).

Barnet, name of an English town: H6C V, 1, 110. V, 3, 20.

Baron, a nobleman next under the viscount: *Earl of Southampton, and B. of Tichfield,* Ven. Dedic. Lucr. Dedic. Merch. I, 2, 72. H6B I, 1, 8. A powerful nobleman in general: H4A IV, 3, 66. H5 III, 5, 46. IV, 8, 94. *four —s of the Cinque-ports,* H8 IV, 1, 48.

Barony, the lordship of a baron: *for a silken point I'll give my b.* H4B I, 1, 54.

Barrabas, the robber set free by Pilate at the request of the Jews: *would any of the stock of B. had been her husband,* Merch. IV, 1, 296.

Barrel, cask, tun: *—s of pitch,* H6A V, 4, 57. *a beer-barrel,* Hml. V, 1, 235.

Barren, 1) sterile: *so b. a land,* Ven. Dedic. 6. Tp. I, 1, 70. I, 2, 338. R2 III, 2, 153 *(the b. earth,* i. e. the earth which serves for a grave) H4B V, 3, 8. Tit. II, 3, 93. *mountains,* Wint. III, 2, 213. H4A I, 3, 89. 159. *winter,* H6B II, 4, 3. *metal,* Merch. I, 3, 135. *women,* Ven. 136. Mids. I, 1, 72. Caes. I, 2, 8. *b. dearth of daughters and of sons,* Ven. 754. Figuratively: *b. skill,* Lucr. 81. *b. rage of death's eternal cold,* Sonn. 13, 12. *rhyme,* 16, 4. *hate,* Tp. IV, 19. *b. practisers, scarce show a harvest of their heavy toil,* LLL IV, 3, 325. *wit,* Err. II, 1, 91. *I am not b. to bring forth complaints,* R3 II, 2, 67. *brain,* Troil. I, 3, 327. *sceptre,* Mcb. III, 1, 62. Followed by *of: trees b. of leaves,* Sonn. 12, 5. *why is my verse so b. of new pride?* 76, 1. *of that kind our rustic garden is b.* Wint. IV, 4, 84. *b. and bereft of friends,* R2 III, 3, 84. *b. of accusations,* Cor. I, 1, 45. *Mine ears, that long time have been b.,* Ant. II, 5, 25, i. e. my ears which have long been, as it were, untilled, unploughed, having heard nothing.

2) dull: *the b. tender of a poet's debt,* Sonn. 83, 4. *b. tasks,* LLL I, 1, 47. *such b. plants are set before us,* IV, 2, 29 (quibble). *the shallowest thickskin of that b. sort,* Mids. III, 2, 13. *now I let go your hand, I am b.,* Tw. I, 3, 84 (quibble). *such a b. rascal,* I, 5, 90. V, 383. *b. ignorance,* R2 I, 3, 168. *such b. pleasures.* H4A III, 2, 14. *some quantity of b. spectators,* Hml. III, 2, 46. *made b. the swelled boast of him that best could speak,* Cymb. V, 5, 162.

Barrenly, without fruit: *let those whom Nature hath not made for store, b. perish,* Sonn. 11, 10.

Barrenness, sterility: *Where Scotland? I found it by the b.* Err. III, 2, 123.

Barren-spirited, dull: *a b. fellow,* Caes. IV, 1, 36.

Barricado, subst., a fortification made in haste, an obstruction: *windows transparent as —es,* Tw. IV, 2, 41. *no b. for a belly,* Wint. I, 2, 204.

Barricado, vb., to fortify: *man is enemy to virginity; how may we b. it against him?* All's I, 1, 124.

Barrow, a small carriage either borne by two men, or supported by one wheel and rolled by a single man: *to be carried in a basket, like a b. of butcher's offal,* Wiv. III, 5, 5.

Barson, a place in England: H4B V, 3, 94.*

Barter, to exchange: *with a baser man of arms they would have —ed me,* H6A I, 4, 31.

Barthol'mew, name of a page: Shr. Ind. I, 105.

Bartholomew, the festival of St. B., the 24th of August: *little tidy B. boar-pig,* H4B II, 4, 250 (roasted pigs being among the chief attractions of Bartholomew fair). *like flies at B. tide,* H5 V, 2, 336.

Basan: *O, that I were upon the hill of B.,* to outroar the horned herd!* Ant. III, 13, 127 (cf. Psalms 22, 12).

Base, subst., 1) the part of a thing on which it stands, the foundation: *laid great —s for eternity,* Sonn. 125, 3. *as doth a galled rock o'erhang and jutty his confounded b.* H5 III, 1, 13. Troil. IV, 2, 109. 5, 212. Tim. I, 1, 64. Caes. III, 2, 192. Hml. I, 4, 71. II, 2, 498.

2) ground, reason: *on b. and ground enough Orsino's enemy,* Tw. V, 78.

Base, subst. 1) (most M. Edd. *bass*). the lowest part in the harmony of a musical composition: *the mean is drowned with your unruly b.* Gentl. I, 2, 96. *'tis now in tune. All but the b.* Shr. III, 1, 46. *means and —s,* Wint. IV, 3, 46. *the very b. string of humility,* H4A II, 4, 6. *b. viol,* Err. IV, 3, 23.

2) *Bases,* plur., 'a kind of embroidered mantle which hung down from the middle to about the knees or lower, worn by knights on horseback' (Nares). It must have consisted of two parts: *Only; my friend, I yet am unprovided of a pair of bases. We'll sure provide: thou shalt have my best gown to make thee a pair,* Per. II, 1, 167.

Base, subst., a rustic game won by the swiftest runner: *to bid the wind a b. he now prepares,* Ven. 303, i. e. to challenge the wind to a race.* *I bid the b. for Proteus,* Gentl. I, 2, 97 (quibble). *lads more like to run the country b. than to commit such slaughter,* Cymb. V, 3, 20.

Base, vb. (M. Edd. *bass*), to sound with a deep voice: *the thunder ... did b. my trespass,* Tp. III, 3, 99.

Base, adj., 1) low in place: *the cedar stoops not to the b. shrub's foot*, Lucr. 664. *lest the b. earth should from her vesture steal a kiss*, Gentl. II, 4, 159. *I do affect the very ground, which is b., where her shoe, which is —r, guided by her foot, which is —st, doth tread*, LLL I, 2, 173. *kisses the b. ground*, IV, 3, 225. *fall to the b. earth from the firmament*, R2 II, 4, 20. *in the b. court he doth attend to speak with you*, III, 3, 176. 180 (i. e. the outer or lower court). *scorning the b. degrees*, Caes. II, 1, 26. In most of the passages it implies also the idea of meanness.

2) of low station, of mean account: *whose —r stars do shut us up in wishes*, All's I, 1, 197. *make conceive a bark of —r kind by bud of nobler race*, Wint. IV, 4, 94. *neighboured by fruit of —r quality*, H5 I, 1, 62. *with a —r man of arms*, H6A I, 4, 30. *b. metal*, Tim. III, 3, 6. *—st metal*, Caes. I, 1, 66. Hml. IV, 1, 26. *unmixed with —r matter*, Hml. I, 5, 104. *our —st beggars are in the poorest thing superfluous*, Lr. II, 4, 267. *'tis the plague of great ones; prerogatived are they less than the b.* Oth. III, 3, 274. *my other elements I give to —r life*, Ant. V, 2, 293.

3) mean, vile: *throwing the b. thong from his bending crest*, Ven. 395. *hiding b. sin in plaits of majesty*, Lucr. 93. *my digression is so vile, so b.* 202. *thou nobly b.* 660. 1000. 1002. Sonn. 33, 5. 34, 3. 74, 12. 94, 11. 141, 6. Gentl. II, 7, 73. III, 1, 157. IV, 1, 29. 73. V, 4, 136. Wiv. I, 3, 23. 97. Meas. III, 1, 89. Ado II, 1, 214. LLL I, 1, 30. 87. I, 2, 51. 61. Mids. I, 1, 232. Merch. II, 7, 50. As II, 3, 32. II, 7, 79. H6A I, 1, 137. IV, 1, 14. IV, 6, 21. R3 III, 3, 180. Cor. I, 1, 161. Tim. IV, 3, 471. Ant. V, 2, 303, etc. etc.

4) of illegitimate birth: *why bastard? wherefore b.?* Lr. I, 2, 6. *why brand they us with base, with baseness? bastardy? base, base?* 10. (cf. the Troublesome reign of King John p. 228: *base to a king = bastard of a king*).

Base-born, of low birth: *contemptuous b. callet as she is*, H6B I, 3, 86. *better ten thousand b. Cades miscarry*, IV, 8, 49. *to let thy tongue detect thy b. heart*, H6C II, 2, 143.

Baseless, without foundation, airy: *like the b. fabric of this vision*, Tp. IV, 151.

Basely, vilely: *they b. fly*, Ven. 894. *b. dignified*, Lucr. 660. *not bought b. with gold*, Lucr. 1068. *the king is not himself, but b. led by flatterers*, R2 II, 1, 241. 253. H4A V, 2, 83. H6A IV, 5, 17. Tit. I, 353. 433. IV, 2, 38. V, 3, 101. Ant. V, 15, 55.

Baseness, 1) low rank: *reflect I not on thy b. court-contempt?* Wint. IV, 4, 758.

2) that which becomes a low station: *some kinds of b. are nobly undergone*, Tp. III, 1, 2. *such b. had never like executor*, 12. *I once did hold it a b. to write fair*, Hml. V, 2, 34.

3) vileness, meanness: *all the accommodations that thou bearest are nursed by b.* Meas. III, 1, 15.* Tw. V, 149. Cor. III, 2, 123. Oth. I, 3, 332. III, 4, 27. Ant. IV, 14, 57. 77. Cymb. I, 1, 142. III, 5, 88. Abstr. pro concr.: *thou unconfinable b.* Wiv. II, 2, 21. *damned b.* Tim. III, 1, 50.

4) illegitimate birth, bastardy: *that forced b. which he hath put upon it*, Wint. II, 3, 78. *why brand they us with base, with b., bastardy?* Lr. I, 2, 10.

Base-string (thus many M. Edd., O. Edd. without hyphen), the string that gives the lowest sound: H4A II, 4, 6.

Base-viol, a stringed instrument for the lowest sounds: Err. IV, 3, 23.

Bashful, shamefaced: *he burns with b. shame*, Ven. 49. *and forth with b. innocence doth hie*, Lucr. 1341. *hence, b. cunning*, Tp. III, 1, 81. *b. sincerity and comely love*, Ado IV, 1, 55. *b. modesty*, Shr. II, 49. *you virtuous ass, you b. fool*, H4B II, 2, 80. *wherefore should you be so b.?* H5 IV, 8, 75 (Fluellen says *pashful*). *and b. Henry deposed*, H6C I, 1, 41. *her b. years*, R3 IV, 4, 326.

Bashfulness, shamefacedness: *no maiden shame, no touch of b.* Mids. III, 2, 286.

Basilisco-like: *knight, knight, good mother, B.* John I, 244 (Nares: "This is in allusion to an old play, entitled Soliman and Perseda, in which a foolish knight, called Basilisco, speaking of his own name, adds, Knight, good fellow, knight, knight. And is answered immediately, Knave, good fellow, knave, knave").

Basilisk, 1) a fabulous serpent, called also *cockatrice* (q. v.) supposed to kill by its look: *make me not sighted like the b.* Wint. I, 2, 388. H5 V, 2, 17. H6B III, 2, 52. 324. H6C III, 2, 187. R3 I, 2, 151. Cymb. II, 4, 107.

2) a kind of ordnance: *of —s, of cannon, culverin*, H4A II, 3, 56.*

Basimecu, term of contempt for a Frenchman: *for giving up of Normandy unto Mounsieur B.*, H6B IV, 7, 31 (baisez mon cul).

Basin, see *Bason*.

Basingstoke, place in England: H4B II, 1, 182.*

Basis, foundation: *the shore that o'er his wave-worn b. bowed*, Tp. II, 1, 120. *build me thy fortunes upon the b. of valour*, Tw. III, 2, 36. *upon this mountain's b.* H5 IV, 2, 30. *Troy, yet upon his b., had been down*, Troil. I, 3, 75. *great tyranny, lay thou thy b. sure*, Mcb. IV, 3, 32.

Pedestal: *that now on Pompey's b. lies along*, Caes. III, 1, 115.

Bask, to warm by exposing to the sun: *who laid him down and —ed him in the sun*, As II, 7, 15.

Basket, a vessel made of twigs or other things interwoven: Wiv. III, 3, 13. 137. 192. III, 5, 5. 99. 104. IV, 2, 33. 94. 121. Hml. III, 4, 193. 195. Ant. V, 2, 343. *Youth in a b.* Wiv. IV, 2, 122, perhaps a proverbial expression, whose sense has not yet been ascertained.

Basket-hilt, the hilt of a sword with a covering like basket-work: *you b. stale juggler*, H4B II, 4, 141, i. e. bully, braggart.*

Bason (M. Edd. *basin*), a vessel to hold water for washing or other uses: Shr. Ind. 1, 55. Shr. II, 350. Tit. V, 2, 184. Tim. III, 1, 7.

Bass, v. *Base*.

Bassanio, friend of Antonio: Merch. I, 1, 57. 69 etc. etc.

Bassianus, brother to the emperor Saturninus: Tit. I, 10 etc. etc.

Basta (from the Italian), enough: *b., content thee, for I have it full*, Shr. I, 1, 203.

Bastard, subst., a sweet Spanish wine: *we shall have all the world drink brown and white b.* Meas. III, 2, 4. *a pint of b.* H4A II, 4, 30. *your brown b. is your only drink*, 82.

Bastard, subst., a person born out of wedlock: *if my dear love were but the child of state, it might for Fortune's b. be unfathered*, Sonn. 124, 2. *—s of his foul adulterate heart*, Compl. 175. *getting a hundred —s*, Meas. III, 2, 125. Ado IV, 1, 190. V, 1, 193. LLL V, 1, 79. As IV, 1, 215. All's II, 3, 100 (*—s to the English*). Wint. II, 3, 73. 139. IV, 4, 83. John I, 207 (*a b. to the time*). H6A I, 1, 93. 2, 47. III, 1, 42. 2, 123. IV, 5, 15. V, 4, 70. R3 IV, 2, 18. Troil. V, 5, 7. Cor. III, 2, 56 (*—s and syllables of no allowance to your bosom's truth*). Caes. V, 4, 2. Lr. I, 2, 6 etc. etc.

Bastard, adj., 1) illegitimately begotten: *this b. graff shall never come to growth*, Lucr. 1062. *this demidevil, — for he's a b. one*, Tp. V, 273. *a b. son of the king's*, H4B II, 4, 307. H6A IV, 6, 20. H6B IV, 1, 136. V, 1, 115. R3 V, 3, 333. Cor. IV, 5, 240.

2) spurious, adulterate: *these b. signs of fair*, Sonn. 68, 3. *beauty slandered with a b. shame*, 127, 4 (i. e. with the shame of spuriousness). *b. virtues*, Gentl. III, 1, 321. *shame hath a b. fame, well managed*, Err. III, 2, 19. *a kind of b. hope*, Merch. III, 5, 8.

Bastardize, to beget out of wedlock: *had the maidenliest star twinkled on my —ing*, Lr. I, 2, 144 (Qq *bastardy*).

Bastardly, adj., = bastard: *thou b. rogue*, H4B II, 1, 55 (Mrs. Quickly's speech).*

Bastardy, illegitimate birth: Lucr. 522. John I, 74. H6B III, 2, 223 (*born in b.*). R3 III, 5, 75. 7, 4. 9. Tit. V, 1, 48 (*his fruit of b. =* his bastard fruit). Caes. II, 1, 138. Lr. I, 2, 10. 144 (Ff. *bastardizing*).

Baste, 1) to sew slightly: *the guards are but slightly —d on neither*, Ado I, 1, 289. *the proud lord that —s his arrogance with his own seam*, Troil. II, 3, 195 (perhaps to be taken in the second signification).

2) to drip fat upon meat on the spit: *the meat wants —ing*, Err. II, 2, 59. *the proud lord that —s his arrogance with his own seam*, Troil. II, 3, 195 (if not to be taken in the first signification).

3) to beat with a stick: *another dry —ing*, Err. II, 2, 64 (quibble).

Bastinado, a sound beating: *I will deal in poison with thee, or in b., or in steel*, As V, 1, 60. *he gives the b. with his tongue*, John II, 463. *gave Amamon the b.* H4A II, 4, 370.

Bat, 1) the animal Vespertilio: Tp. I, 2, 340. V, 91. Mcb. III, 2, 40. IV, 1, 15. Hml. III, 4, 190 (*who, that's but a queen, fair, sober, wise, would from a paddock, from a bat, a gib, such dear concernings hide?*).

2) a heavy stick: *so slides he down upon his grained b.* Compl. 64. *where go you with —s and clubs?* Cor. I, 1, 57. 165. *whether your costard or my b. be the harder*, Lr. IV, 6, 247 (Ff. *ballow*).

Batch, baked bread; metaphorically: *thou crusty b. of nature*, Troil. V, 1, 5.

Bate, subst., quarrel: *breeds no b. with telling of discreet stories*, H4B II, 4, 271.

Bate, vb., (cf. *abate*) 1) trans., a) to beat down, to weaken: *these griefs and losses have so —d me*, Merch. III, 3, 32. *those —d that inherit but the fall of the last monarchy*, All's II, 1, 13.

b) to weaken, diminish: *with —d breath*, Merch. I, 3, 125. *bid the main flood b. his usual height*, IV, 1, 72. *like a —d and retired flood*, John V, 4, 53.

b. thy rage, H5 III, 2, 26. *who —s mine honour shall not know my coin*, Tim. III, 3, 26. Hence = to blunt: *b. his scythe's keen edge*, LLL I, 1, 6 (cf. *unbated* and *bateless*).

c) to deduct, to remit, to except: *thou didst promise to b. me a full year*, Tp. I, 2, 250. *b., I beseech you, widow Dido*, II, 1, 100. *of my instruction hast thou nothing —d*, III, 3, 85. *rather than she will b. one breath of her accustomed crossness*, Ado II, 3, 183. *were this world mine, Demetrius being —d*, Mids. I, 1, 190. *I will not b. thee a scruple*, All's II, 3, 234. *b. me some and I will pay you some*, H4B V, 5, 130. *neither will they b. one jot of ceremony*, Cor. II, 2, 144. *you b. too much of your own merits*, Tim. I, 2, 212. *no leisure —d*, Hml. V, 2, 23. *I cannot be —d one doit of a thousand pieces*, Per. IV, 2, 55. Absolutely: *O let me b.* Cymb. III, 2, 56.

2) intr., a) to fall off: *do I not b.? do I not dwindle?* H4A III, 3, 2. *'tis a hooded valour, and when it appears, it will b.* H5 III, 7, 122 (quibble).

b) to flap the wings, to flutter (a term in falconry): *these kites that b. and beat and will not be obedient*, Shr. IV, 1, 199. *like estridges that with the wind —d*, H4A IV, 1, 99 (O. Edd. *baited*). *a hooded valour, and when it appears, it will b.* H5 III, 7, 122 (quibble). *hood my unmanned blood, —ing in my cheeks*, Rom. III, 2, 14.

Bate-breeding, occasioning quarrels: *this b. spy* (jealousy) Ven. 655. cf. *breed-bate*.

Bateless, not to be blunted: *haply that name of chaste unhappily set this b. edge on his keen appetite*, Lucr. 9.

Bates, name of a soldier in H5 IV, 1, 87.

Bat-fowling, a mode of catching birds at night by means of torches, poles, and sometimes of nets: *you would lift the moon out of her sphere ..... We would so, and then go a b.* Tp. II, 1, 185.*

Bath, 1) ablution: Cor. I, 6, 63. *season slaves for tubs and —s*, Tim. IV, 3, 86 (as a cure of syphilis). Metaphorically: *sleep, ... sore labour's b.* Mcb. II, 2, 38.

2) heat like that in a bath: *and in the height of this b. to be thrown into the Thames*, Wiv. III, 5, 120.

3) watering-place: *grew a seething b., which yet men prove against strange maladies a sovereign cure*, Sonn. 153, 7. 11. 154, 11.

Bathe, 1) trans. to immerse, to wash as in a bath: *the crow may b. his coal-black wings in mire*, Lucr. 1009. *in Lucrece 'bleeding stream he falls and —s the pale fear in his face*, 1775. *these often —d she in her fluxive eyes*, Compl. 50. *when tears our recountments had most kindly —d*, As V, 3, 141. *—d thy growing with our heated bloods*, H6C II, 2, 169. *—d in maiden blood*, Tit. II, 3, 232. *b. their hands in it*, Caes. II, 2, 79. *b. our hands in Caesar's blood*, III, 1, 106. *b. my dying honour in the blood*, Ant. IV, 2, 6. *had I this cheek to b. my lips upon*, Cymb. I, 6, 100.

2) intr., to be in a bath, to be immersed in a fluid as in a bath: *she —s in water, yet her fire must burn*, Ven. 94. *to b. in fiery floods*, Meas. III, 1, 122. *eagles having lately —d*, H4A IV, 1, 99. *in which so many smiling Romans —d*, Caes. II, 2, 86. *to b. in reeking wounds*, Mcb. I, 2, 39. *chaste Dian —ing*, Cymb. II, 4, 82.

Batlet, a small bat to beat linen when taken

out of the buck: *I remember the kissing of her b.* As
II, 4, 49.

Battalia (thus Ff; Qq **battalion**), host, army:
our b. trebles that account, R3 V, 3, 11. *when sorrows
come, they come not single spies, but in —s,* Hml. IV,
5, 79.

Battalion, v. *Battalia.*

Batten, to grow fat: *b. on cold bits,* Cor. IV,
5, 35. *could you on this fair mountain leave to feed,
and b. on this moor?* Hml. III, 4, 67.

Batter, to beat with successive blows,
and hence to bruise, to shake, to demolish: *his —ed
shield,* Ven. 104. *rude ram, to b. such an ivory wall,*
Lucr. 464. 723. 1171. *with a log b. his skull,* Tp. III,
2, 98. *these haughty words of hers have —ed me like
cannon-shot,* H6A III, 3, 79. *the ram that —s down
the wall,* Troil. I, 3, 206. *Achilles in commotion rages
and —s down himself,* II, 3, 186. *his —ed shield,*
Tit. IV, 1, 128. *the ram to b. the fortress of it,* Ant.
III, 2, 30. *the thunderer whose bolt —s all rebelling
coasts,* Cymb. V, 4, 96. Absol., to make attacks
in the manner of a ram: *the wreckful siege of
—ing days,* Sonn. 65, 6. *so you would leave —ing,*
Err. II, 2, 36 (i. e. beating). *their —ing cannon,* John
II, 382. Followed by *at: the tyrant has not —ed at
their peace?* Mcb. IV, 3, 178.

Battery, 1) the act of battering, assault:
where a heart is hard they make no b. Ven. 426. *as
they did b. to the spheres intend,* Compl. 23. *to leave
the b. that you make 'gainst mine,* 277. *this union shall
do more than b. can to our gates,* John II, 446. *if I
begin the b. once again,* H5 III, 3, 7. *where is best
place to make our b. next,* H6A I, 4, 65. *her sighs will
make a b. in his breast,* H6C III, 1, 37. *talks like a
knell, and his hum is a b.* Cor. V, 4, 22. *make b. to
our ears with the loud music,* Ant. II, 7, 115. *cannot
keep the b. from my heart,* IV, 14, 39. *her judgment,
which else an easy b. might lay flat,* Cymb. I, 4, 22.
make raging b. upon shores of flint, Per. IV, 4, 43.
make a b. through his deafened parts, V, 1, 47.

2) unlawful beating of another: *I'll have
mine action of b. on thee,* Meas. I, 1, 188. *I'll have
an action of b. against him,* Tw. IV, 1, 36. *and will
not tell him of his action of b.* Hml. V, 1, 111.

Battle, subst., 1) fight, encounter between
opposite armies: Ven. 99. Lucr. 145. 1438. Mids.
V, 44. Shr. I, 2, 206 (*pitched b.*). H6A I, 1, 129. 4.
78. IV, 1, 19 (*at the b. of Patay*). H6B IV, 2, 188.
V, 2, 49. etc. etc. Never used of a sea-fight, but placed
in contradistinction to it: *provoke not b., till we have
done at sea,* Ant. III, 8, 3. — *To give one b.* H6A V,
2, 13. Cor. I, 6, 11. *to strike a b.* H5 II, 4, 54. *to
fight —s,* H6A I, 1, 31. *to bid one b.* H4A V, 2, 31.
H6C I, 2, 71. III, 3, 235. V, 1, 63. 77. 111. *arise
my knights o' the b.* Cymb. V, 5, 20 (created knights
on the field of battle).

2) a single fight: *I say and will in b. prove,*
R2 I, 1, 92. *this feast of b. with mine enemy,* I, 3, 92.
a maiden b. (= an unbloody combat) Troil. IV, 5,
87. Any other combat: *give b. to the lioness,* As
IV, 3, 131. *his cocks do win the b. still of mine,* Ant.
II, 3, 36.

3) an army prepared for or engaged in fight:
like heralds 'twixt two dreadful —s set, John IV, 2,
78. H4A IV, 1, 129. H4B III, 2, 165. IV, 1, 179.
H5 IV Chor. 9. IV, 2, 54. H6A IV, 7, 13. H6C I, 1,

15. II, 1, 121. II, 2, 72. V, 4, 66. R3 I, 3, 130. V,
3, 24. 88. 138. 292. Troil. III, 2, 29. Ant. III, 9, 2.
squares of b. H5 IV, 2, 28.

4) division of an army: *our main —'s front,*
H6C I, 1, 8. *the French are bravely in their —s set,*
H5 IV, 3, 69. *their —s are at hand,* Caes. V, 1, 4.
set our —s on, V, 3, 108. *lead our first b.* Mcb. V, 6, 4.

5) an array similar to an army drawn up: *on
his bow-back he hath a b. set of bristly pikes,* Ven. 619.

Battle, vb. intr. to contend in fight: *lions
war and b. for their dens,* H6C II, 5, 74.

Battle-axe, axe used in fight: *reared aloft
the bloody b.* Tit. III, 1, 169.

Battlement, a wall raised on a building
with embrasures; only used in the plural: John
II, 374. R2 III, 3, 52. Rom. IV, 1, 78. Caes. I, 1, 43.
Mcb. I, 2, 23. I, 5, 41. Hml. V, 2, 281. Oth. II, 1, 6.

Batty, like a bat: *till o'er their brows death-
counterfeiting sleep with leaden legs and b. wings doth
creep,* Mids. III, 2, 365.

Bauble, a trifle, a useless plaything: *a
paltry cap, a custard-coffin, a b., a silken pie,* Shr.
IV, 3, 82. *off with that b.* V, 2, 122. *an idiot holds his
b. for a god,* Tit. V, 1, 79. *his shipping, poor ignorant
—s,* Cymb. III, 1, 27. Cassio calls Bianca so: *thither
comes the b. and falls me about my neck,* Oth. IV, 1,
139; and Pisanio the letter of Leonato: *senseless b.,
art thou a feodary for this act?* Cymb. III, 2, 20.

In a restricted sense, = the fool's club: *I
would give his wife my b., to do her service,* All's IV,
5, 32. *like a great natural that runs lolling up and
down to hide his b. in a hole,* Rom. II, 4, 97; (in both
passages with a hidden obscenity).

Used adjectively = insignificant, contemptible: *the sea being smooth, how many shallow b.
boats dare sail upon her patient breast,* Troil. I, 3, 35.

Baubling, insignificant, contemptible:
a b. vessel was he captain of, Tw. V, 57.

Bavin, brushwood, light and combustible
matter: *shallow jesters and rash b. wits, soon kindled
and soon burnt,* H4A III, 2, 61.

Bawble and **Bawbling** s. *Bauble, baubling.*

Bawcock, a term of endearment, synonymous to
chuck, but always masc.: *how now, my b.! how dost
thou, chuck?* Tw. III, 4, 125.* *that's my b.* Wint. I, 2,
121. *good b., bate thy rage; use lenity, sweet chuck,*
H5 III, 2, 26. *the king's a b. and a heart of gold,* IV, 1, 44.

Bawd, procurer or procuress; 1) masc.:
Meas. II, 1, 231. 237. 248. III, 2, 20. IV, 2, 15. As
III, 2, 85. H5 III, 6, 65. V, 1, 90. Troil. I, 2, 307.
V, 10, 37. Tim. II, 2, 62. 89. Lr. II, 2, 21. Per. IV, 6,
42. 2) fem.: Meas. III, 2, 63. 208. Wint. II, 3, 68.
Rom. II, 4, 136.* Tim. IV, 3, 114. 134. Oth. IV, 2, 20.
Per. V Prol. 11. 3) of uncertain gender: Meas. II,
1, 76 (*a —'s house*). H4A I, 2, 9. Lr. III, 2, 90. Fi-
guratively: *O strange excuse, when reason is the b.
to lust's abuse!* Ven. 792. Lucr. 623. 768. 886. Meas.
III, 1, 150. John II, 582. III, 1, 59. R2 V, 3, 67. Hml.
III, 1, 113. —*

Bawd-born, born as a bawd, a bawd from
birth: *bawd is he doubtless, and of antiquity too; b.*
Meas. III, 2, 72.

Bawdry, 1) obscenity, unchaste lan-
guage: *the prettiest love-songs for maids, so without
b.* Wint. IV, 4, 194. *he's for a jig or a tale of b.*
Hml. II, 2, 522.

2) unchastity: *we must be married, or we must live in b.* As III, 3, 99 (rhyming to *Audrey*).

Bawdy, unchaste: *if b. talk offend you,* Meas. IV, 3, 188. *a b. planet,* Wint. I, 2, 201. *a b. song,* H4A III, 3, 15. *to hear a merry b. play,* H8 Prol. 14. *every false drop in her b. veins,* Troil. IV, 1, 69. *the b. hand of the dial is now upon the prick of noon,* Rom. II, 4, 118. *bloody b. villain,* Hml. II, 2, 608. *the b. wind that kisses all it meets,* Oth. IV, 2, 78.

Bawdy-house, house of prostitution: H4A III, 3, 19. 114 *(this house is turned b.; they pick pockets).* 179. H4B II, 4, 157. H5 II, 1, 37. Per. IV, 5, 7.

Bawl, to cry with vehemence: *you —ing blasphemous dog,* Tp. I, 1, 43.*those that b. out the ruins of thy linen,* H4B II, 2, 27.

Bay, subst., 1) an arm of the sea, extending into the land: *my affection hath an unknown bottom, like the b. of Portugal,* As IV, 1, 211. *in such a desperate b. of death,* R3 IV, 4, 232.

2) port: *anchored in the b. where all men ride,* Sonn. 137, 6. *if any Syracusian born come to the b. of Ephesus,* Err. I, 1, 20. *you sent me to the b. for a bark,* IV, 1, 99. *who put unluckily into this b.* V, 125. *the scarfed bark puts from her native b.* Merch. II, 6, 15. *Port le Blanc, a b. in Brittany,* R2 II, 1, 277. *from the Athenian b. put forth toward Phrygia,* Troil. Prol. 6. *returns with precious lading to the b.* Tit. I, 72. *that he may bless this b. with his tall ship,* Oth. II, 1, 79. *go to the b. and disembark my coffers,* II, 1, 210.

Bay, subst., laurel: *my dish of chastity with rosemary and —s,* Per. IV, 6, 160.

Bay, subst., division in the architectural arrangement of a building, marked by any leading feature, most commonly by the single windows or other openings: *if this law hold in Vienna ten year, I'll rent the fairest house in it after three pence a b.* Meas. II, 1, 255.*

Bay, subst., 1) barking: *uncouple here and let us make a b. and wake the emperor and his lovely bride,* Tit. II, 2, 3.

2) the state of a chase, when the game is driven to extremity and turns against its pursuers: *she hears the hounds are at a b.* Ven. 877.*'tis thought your deer does hold you at a b.* Shr. V, 2, 56. *to rouse his wrongs and chase them to the b.* R2 II, 3, 128. *turn on the bloody hounds and make the cowards stand aloof at b.* H6A IV, 2, 52.

3) the state of being in the power of another: *Ah, that I had my lady at this b., to kiss and clip me till I run away!* Pilgr. 155. *I would we had a thousand Roman dames at such a b., by turn to serve our lust,* Tit. IV, 2, 42.

Bay, adj., brown; used of horses: *I'ld give b. curtal and his furniture,* All's II, 3, 65. *a b. courser,* Tim. I, 2, 217. *to ride on a b. trotting-horse,* Lr. III, 4, 57.

Bay, vb., 1) to bark, a) intr.: *what moves Ajax thus to b. at him?* Troil. II, 3, 98. *we are at the stake, and —ed about with many enemies,* Caes. IV, 1, 49.

b) trans., = to bark at: *I had rather be a dog and b. the moon,* Caes. IV, 3, 27. *set the dogs of the street to b. me,* Cymb. V, 5, 223.

2) to chase, to drive to bay: *they —ed the bear with hounds of Sparta,* Mids. IV, 1, 118. *the*

French and Welsh *—ing him at the heels,* H4B I, 3, 80. *here wast thou —ed, brave hart,* Caes. III, 1, 204.

Baynard's Castle, the residence of Richard III at the time of his usurpation: R3 III, 5, 98. 105.

Bayonne, town in France: H8 II, 4, 172.

Bay-tree, laurel: *the —s in our country are all withered,* R2 II, 4, 8.

Bay-window, a window forming a recess in the room and projecting outwards from the wall: *it hath —s transparent as barricadoes,* Tw. IV, 2, 40.

Be. As what is regular and conformable to the present use of the word may be found in every page of the poet, we shall only point out what is of rarer occurrence or has now grown obsolete.

I) Anomalies of the conjugation: 1) *Is* instead of *are: Ill deeds is doubled with an evil word,* Err. III, 2, 20 (F2,3,4 and M. Edd. *are*). *when his disguise and he is parted,* All's III, 6, 113. *his brother is reputed one of the best that is,* IV, 3, 323. *or is your gold and silver ewes and rams?* Merch. I, 3, 96. *more lines than is in the new map,* Tw. III, 2, 84. *that's the wavering commons,* R2 II, 2, 129. *is all things well?* H6B III, 2, 11. cf. *is all things ready?* R3 III, 4, 4 (Ff. *are*). *he's inclined as is the ravenous wolves,* H6B III, 1, 78 (M. Edd. either *are,* or *wolf*). *hands, to do Rome service, is but vain,* Tit. III, 1, 80 (M. Edd. *are*). *what manners is in this?* Rom. V, 3, 214.

Especially after numerals, when a sum made up of several things is considered as a whole: *what is ten hundred touches unto thee?* Ven. 519. *is twenty hundred kisses such a trouble?* 522. *forty ducats is too much to lose,* Err. IV, 3, 97. *and so to study, three years is but short,* LLL I, 1, 181. *how many inches is in one mile?* V, 2, 188. *fifteen wives is nothing,* Merch. II, 2, 170. *what is six winters?* R2 I, 3, 260. *eight yards of uneven ground is threescore and ten miles afoot with me,* H4A II, 2, 27. *from nine till twelve is three long hours,* Rom. II, 5, 11. Caes. I, 3, 155.

And after *here, there, where: here's more of us,* Tp. V, 216. *for thy three thousand ducats here is six,* Merch. IV, 1, 84. *here's eight that must take hands,* As V, 4, 134. *here's flowers for you,* Wint. IV, 4, 103. *here's but two and fifty hairs,* Troil. I, 2, 171. *here's many else,* Cor. I, 9, 49. *thou thinkest there is no more such shapes as he,* Tp. I, 2, 478. *there's but five upon this isle,* III, 2, 6. *there's many have committed it,* Meas. II, 2, 89. *there's other of our friends will great us here,* IV, 5, 12. *there's none but witches do inhabit here,* Err. III, 2, 161. *there's two tongues,* Ado V, 1, 171. *there is three,* LLL V, 2, 231. *there is five in the first show,* V, 2, 543. *there is two or three lords and ladies more married,* Mids. IV, 2, 16. *there is two hard things,* III, 1, 48. *there's letters from my mother,* All's II, 3, 293. *there's four or five,* III, 5, 98. *there is no woman's sides can bide ...,* Tw. II, 4, 96. *there's expenses for thee,* III, 1, 49. *there is three carters,* Wint. IV, 4, 331. *there's few or none do know me,* John IV, 3, 3. *is there not wars?* H4B I, 2, 85. *there's five to one,* H5 IV, 3, 4. *there's two of you; the devil make a third!* H6B III, 2, 303. *for living murmurers there's places of rebuke,* H8 II, 2, 132. *there is more pangs and fears,* III, 2, 368. *there's some of ye,* V, 3, 144. *there is a thousand Hectors in the field,* Troil. V, 5, 19. *there is forty ducats,* Rom. V, 1, 59. *there is tears for his love,* Caes. III, 2, 29. *there's wondrous things spoke of him,* Cor. II, 1, 152. *there's daggers in men's smiles*, Mcb. II, 3, 146. *there's letters sealed*, Hml. III, 4, 202. *there's tricks in the world*, IV, 5, 5. *there is no mo such Caesars*, Cymb. III, 1, 36. *there is no more such masters*, IV, 2, 371. *where is the thousand marks thou hadst of me?* Err. I, 2, 81. II, 1, 65. *where's the Bastard's braves?* H6A III, 2, 123.

2) *be* instead of *is*: *Good night, good rest. Ah! neither be my share!* Pilgr. 181. *I hope it be not so*, Wiv. II, 1, 113. Especially after *to think*: *That is the chain which you had of me. I think it be*. Err. V, 379. *I think he be angry indeed*, Ado IV, 2, 141. *I think he be transformed into a beast*, As II, 7, 1. *I think this Talbot be a fiend of hell*, H6A II, 1, 46. *that, I think, be young Petrucio*, Rom. I, 5, 133. *I think it be no other*, Hml. I, 1, 108. *I think the king be touched at very heart*, Cymb. I, 1, 10. cf. Caes. I, 1, 66.

3) *be* instead of *are*: *by our ears our hearts oft tainted be*, Lucr. 38. *thy love is of more delight than hawks or horses be*, Sonn. 91, 11. *since all alike my songs and praises be to one*, 105, 3. *thine eyes have put on black and loving mourners be*, 132, 3. *and in our faults by lies we flattered be*, 138, 14. *when their deaths be near*, 140, 7. *mad slanderers by mad ears believed be*, 140, 12. *there be that can rule Naples as well as he*, Tp. II, 1, 262. *these be fine things*, II, 2, 121. *there be some sports*, III, 1, 1. *these be brave spirits*, V, 261. *say if they be true*, V, 268. *be they of much import?* Gentl. III, 1, 55. *but the doors be locked*, 111. *be there bears in the town?* Wiv. I, 1, 298. *very rogues, now they be out of service*, II, 1, 182. *here be my keys*, III, 3, 172. *hence shall we see what our seemers be*, Meas. I, 3, 54. *here be many of her old customers*, IV, 3, 3. *Interjections? Why, some be of laughing*, Ado IV, 1, 23. *these be the stops that hinder study quite*, LLL I, 1, 70. *the cowslips tall her pensioners be*, Mids. II, 1, 10. *those be rubies*, 12. *what fools these mortals be!* III, 2, 115. *the ground whereon these sleepers be*, IV, 1, 91. *there be land-rats and water-rats*, Merch. I, 3, 23. *there be fools alive*, II, 9, 68. *these be the Christian husbands*, IV, 1, 295. *there be some women*, As III, 5, 124. *impossible be strange attempts to those*, All's I, 1, 239. *be these sad signs confirmers of thy words?* John III, 1, 24. *where be your powers?* V, 7, 75. *minding true things by what their mockeries be*, H5 IV Chor. 53. *his fears be of the same relish as ours are*, IV, 1, 114. *be these the wretches that we played at dice for?* IV, 5, 8. *where be these warders?* H6A I, 3, 3. *wake when others be asleep*, H6B I, 1, 249. *here they be that dare and will disturb thee*, IV, 8, 6. *where be thy brothers?* R3 IV, 4, 92. *help you that be noble*, Cor. III, 1, 228. *such men as he be never at heart's ease*, Caes. I, 2, 208. *where be the sacred vials?* Ant. I, 3, 63.

4) *thou beest* (or *be'st*) = *thou be*, after *if*: *if thou beest Stephano touch me*, Tp. II, 2, 104. 107. *speak once in thy life, if thou beest a good moon-calf*, III, 2, 25. *if thou beest a man, show thyself in thy likeness*, 137. *if thou beest Prospero, give us particulars*, V, 134. *speak, if thou beest the man*, Err. V, 341. 344. *if thou beest rated by thy estimation, thou dost deserve enough*, Merch. II, 7, 26. *if that thou beest found … thou diest for it*, As I, 3, 45. *if thou beest not damned for this, the devil himself will have no shepherds*, III, 2, 88. *if thou beest not an ass, I am a youth of fourteen*, All's II, 3, 106. *if thou beest yet a fresh uncropped flower, choose thou thy husband*, V, 3, 327. *if thou beest*

capable of things serious, thou must know …, Wint. IV, 4, 791. *if ever thou beest mine, I get thee with scambling*, H5 V, 2, 216. *if thou here beest found, the world shall not be ransom for thy life*, H6B III, 2, 295. *if thou beest death, I'll give thee England's treasure*, III, 3, 2. *if thou beest not immortal, look about you*, Caes. II, 3, 7. *if that thou beest a Roman, take it forth*, IV, 3, 103. *if thou beest as poor as he, thou art poor enough*, Lr. I, 4, 22 (Qq *be*). *if thou beest valiant, list me*, Oth. II, 1, 216. *disprove this villain, if thou beest a man*, V, 2, 172.

After *whether*: *whether thou beest he or no, I not know*, Tp. V, 111. Beginning the sentence, the conjunction being omitted: *beest thou sad or merry, the violence of either thee becomes*, Ant. I, 5, 59.

5) *Being* often a dissyllable, f. i. Ven. 18. Lucr. 260. Tp. I, 2, 79. 91. IV, 1, 68. Gentl. II, 4, 93. III, 1, 57. 249. 2, 45 etc. etc. But as often, at least, monosyllabic: Ven. 24. 29. 1033. 1068. Tp. I, 2, 72. 74. 76. 97. 121. 353. 438. III, 3, 58. V, 28. Gentl. I, 1, 158. II, 7, 26. V, 3, 7 etc. etc. (cf. *carrying*, Hml. I, 4, 31. *borrowing*, I, 3, 77. *doing*, Mcb. I, 4, 23. *giving*, Cor. V, 6, 54. *growing*, H8 I, 2, 116. *laying*, Lr. IV, 6, 201. Ant. II, 2, 55. *lying*, Caes. IV, 3, 201. *playing*, Ant. II, 5, 11. *seeing*, Shr. Ind. 2, 134. Shr. III, 2, 182. H6C I, 1, 218. 247. Hml. III, 1, 33. Oth. I, 3, 203. *throwing*, I, 1, 52. *tying*, Cor. II, 3, 205).

6) *I were* = *I was*, but only in conditional and subordinate clauses: *if ever I were traitor, my name be blotted from the book of life*, R2 I, 3, 201. *I am a rogue, if I were not at half-sword with a dozen of them*, H4A II, 4, 182. *if I did think, sir, I were well awake*, Tp. V, 229. *shouldst thou but hear I were licentious*, Err. II, 2, 133.

7) *thou wert* = *thou wast*: *for a woman wert thou first created*, Sonn. 20, 9. *I grant thou wert not married to my Muse*, 82, 1. *thou truly fair wert truly sympathized*, 82, 11. *thou wert immured*, LLL III, 125. *behaviour, what wert thou till this madman showed thee?* V, 2, 337. *thou wert born a fool*, Wint. II, 1, 174. *hearing thou wert dead*, R2 III, 2, 73. *I heard thee say that thou wert cause of Gloster's death*, IV, 37. *I was a poor groom when thou wert king*, V, 5, 73. *thou hast lost much honour that thou wert not with me in this action*, H4A II, 4, 22. *thou wert taken with the manner*, 346. *why didst thou tell me that thou wert a king?* V, 3, 24. *how wert thou handled, being prisoner?* H6A I, 4, 24. *yet tellest thou not how thou wert entertained*, 38. *why didst thou say, of late thou wert despised?* II, 5, 42. *when thou wert regent for our sovereign*, H6B I, 1, 197. *since thou wert king, the commonwealth hath run to wreck*, I, 3, 126. *where wert thou born?* II, 1, 82. *no less beloved than when thou wert protector to thy king*, II, 3, 27. *whom thou wert sworn to cherish and defend*, R3 I, 4, 213 (Ff. *wast*). *she was dead ere thou wert born*, II, 4, 33 (Ff. *wast*). *thou wert not wont to be so dull*, IV, 2, 17 (Ff. *wast*). *a dream of what thou wert*, IV, 4, 88 (Ff. *wast*). *having no more but thought of what thou wert*, 107. *when wert thou wont to walk alone?* Tit. I, 339. *wert thou thus surprised?* IV, 1, 51. *Othello, that wert once so good*, Oth. V, 2, 291.

8) *he were* = *he was*: *his giving-out were of an infinite distance from …*, Meas. I, 4, 54 (M. Edd. *givings-out*). *so great fear of my name 'mongst them were spread*, H6A I, 4, 50 (M. Edd. *was*). *Adonis'*

garden that one day bloomed and fruitful were the next, I, 6, 7 (M. Edd. gardens). and they it were that ravished our sister, Tit. V, 3, 99. this most constant wife, who even now were clipped about with this most tender air, Cymb. V, 5, 451. After if: ne'er repent it, if it were done so, Gentl. IV, 1, 30. if there were a sympathy in choice, war, death ... did lay siege to it, Mids. I, 1, 141. most true, if ever truth were pregnant by circumstance, Wint. V, 2, 33. if the deed were ill, be you contented to have a son ...., H4B V, 2, 83. if ever·any grudge were lodged between us, R3 II, 1, 65. if ever Bassianus were gracious in the eyes of royal Rome, Tit. I, 11. if to fight for king and commonweal were piety in thine, it is in these, 115. Caes. III, 2, 84. Again: one would think it were Mistress Overdone's own house, Meas. IV, 3, 3. I could say she were worse, Ado III, 2, 113. if we did think his contemplation were above the earth, H8 III, 2, 131. I should think here were a fairy, Cymb. III, 6, 42.

9) they was = they were: which of the two was daughter of the duke, that here was at the wrestling? As I, 2, 282. their states was sure, R3 III, 2, 86 (Ff. and M. Edd. were). thy temples should be planted with horns as was Actaeon's, Tit. II, 3, 63. there was more than one; ay, more there was, IV, 1, 38. used to say extremities was the trier of spirits, Cor. IV, 1, 4 (F2,3,4 and M. Edd. extremity). All these seeming irregularities, which have been regarded by the ignorant as so many blemishes, must be considered in connexion with the original forms of English conjugation, which, indeed, in Shakespeare's time began to become obsolete.

10) been = are: he, doing so, put forth to seas, where, when men been, there's seldom ease, Per. I Prol. 28. In Per. II, 3, 82 been may be taken as the participle. In Cymb. II, 3, 27 the O. Edd. have: with every thing that pretty is; which some M. Edd. have, for the sake of the rhyme, changed to pretty bin.

II) Remarkable use. 1) as a principal verb; a) = to exist: thou nursest all and murtherest all that are, Lucr. 929. that which is has been before, Sonn. 59, 1. tongues to be (= to come, future) 81, 11. ages yet to be, 101, 12. truth may seem, but cannot be, Phoen. 62. an if this be at all, Tp. V, 117. such names and men as these which never were, Shr. Ind. 2, 98. that that is is, Tw. IV, 2, 17. from the all that are, Wint. V, 1, 14. for those that were, it is not square to take on those that are, revenges, Tim. V, 4, 36. the purposes I bear, which are or cease, as you shall give the advice, Ant. I, 3, 67. the most precious diamond that is, Cymb. I, 4, 81. which must not yet be but by self-danger, III, 4, 148. Mcb. I, 3, 141.

Being = life, existence: tongues to be your being shall rehearse, Sonn. 81, 11. my health and happy being at your court, Gentl. III, 1, 57. Pisa gave me my being, Shr. I, 1, 11. if the cause were not in b. Wint. II, 3, 3. would I had no being, H8 II, 3, 102. best state, contentless, hath a distracted and most wretched being, Tim. IV, 3, 246. whose star-like nobleness gave life and influence to their whole being, V, 1, 67. there's none but he whose being I do fear, Mcb. III, 1, 55. (But cf. and that thy being some say of breeding breathes, Lr. V, 3, 143; Ff. and M. Edd. tongue). every minute of his being thrusts against my nearest of life, 117. end his being, Hml. II, 1, 96. I fetch my life and being from men of royal siege, Oth.

I, 2, 21. my being in Egypt (= my kind of life in E.) Ant. II, 2, 35. he quit being, Cymb. I, 1, 38. to shift his being, I, 5, 54. all the villains past, in being, to come, V, 5, 212. the womb that their first being bred, Per. I, 1, 107. from whence we had our being and our birth, I, 2, 114.

b) to be to one = to belong to one: I was then advertising and holy to your business, Meas. V, 387. your hand and heart should be more to me than any, H8 III, 2, 189. half all Cominius' honours are to Marcius, Cor. I, 1, 277. whilst this machine is to him, Hml. II, 2, 124. to thine and Albany's issue be this perpetual, Lr. I, 1, 68.

c) to be = to be the case: it is not that I bear thee love, As III, 5, 93. O absence, what a torment wouldst thou prove, were it not thy sour leisure gave sweet leave to entertain the time with thoughts of love, Sonn. 39, 10. were it not that my fellow-schoolmaster doth watch Bianca's steps, Shr. III, 2, 140. were it not that I have bad dreams, Hml. II, 2, 262. were't not that we stand up against them all, Ant. II, 1, 44. cf. Cor. III, 2, 48. Lr. IV, 6, 144.

Being that = while: being that I flow in grief, Ado IV, 1, 251. you loiter here too long, being you are to take soldiers up, H4B II, 1, 199.

d) = to happen, to come to pass: where was this? Hml. I, 2, 212. (what is, my lord? III, 2, 127, is an elliptical question, viz = what is a fair thought?). an 'twere to me, I should be mad at it, Merch. V, 176. If it will not be, Ado II, 1, 208; and Will't not be? John III, 1, 298, are expressions of impatience, like the German: wird's bald?

e) Let be = no matter: no longer shall you gaze on it, lest your fancy may think anon it moves. Let be, let be. Wint. V, 3, 61. since no man has aught of what he leaves, what is't to leave betimes? Let be. Hml. V, 2, 235 (Ff. om.) 'twill be naught: but let it be; bring me to Antony, Ant. III, 5, 24. what's this for? Ah, let be, IV, 4, 6. Caes. I, 3, 80. let it be so; thy truth then be thy dower, Lr. I, 1, 110. let it be so; yet have I left a daughter, I, 4, 327. Hence the following passage receives its proper light: they were ratified as he cried 'Thus let be,' H8 I, 1, 171 (the expression being characteristic of the carelessness with which Wolsey hurried his business). — Quite different is the sense of Ado V, 1, 207: but soft you, let me be; i. e. let me alone; no more joking! — Be it so = no matter: Ant. III, 12, 10. cf. Cor. V, 2, 12.

f) As will, shall etc. are used instead of will go, shall go etc., so is for is or has gone: towards Florence is he? All's III, 2, 71.

g) Followed by an infinitive, = to be busied: he hath been all this day to look you, As II, 5, 34. I have been to seek you, Oth. V, 1, 81. courtesies which I will be ever to pay and yet pay still, Cymb. I, 4, 39. I'll fit you, and not be all day neither, All's II, 1, 94.

h) = to be written: if you have writ your annals true, 'tis there, that ..., Cor. V, 6, 114.

2) Peculiarities of its use as an auxiliary verb.

a) Such phrases as 'that is brave, that is well' are common enough, but the following expressions: this was well counterfeited, As IV, 3, 167; 'tis well blown, lads, Ant. IV, 4, 25, and: this is fought indeed! IV, 7, 4; well moused, Lion, Mids. V, 274; well flown, bird, Lr. IV, 6, 92, may deserve notice.

b) be it his pleasure, All's III, 1, 16, = let him

do at his pleasure, I care not. *be 't so: declare thine office,* Ant. III, 12, 10, = what of that?

c) *be it possible,* Shr. III, 2, 127 = if it be possible (cf. *if*), and thus also *be it so* = if it be so; if: *be it so she will not marry with Demetrius, I beg the ancient privilege of Athens,* Mids. I, 1, 39. *be it that she survive me,* Shr. II, 125.

d) *how is it with you?* either = how do you do? Tw. III, 4, 97. Cor. I, 6, 33. V, 6, 10. Oth. III, 4, 33; or = how stands the case with you? *How is it with her? doth she not think me an old murderer?* Rom. III, 3, 93. cf. *so is it not with me as with that Muse stirred by a painted beauty,* Sonn. 21, 1. *'tis so with me,* Meas. I, 1, 82. *were he my kinsman, it should be thus with him: he must die to-morrow,* Meas. II, 2, 82. *it is not so with him that all things knows,* All's II, 1, 152. *it had been so with us, had we been there,* Hml. IV, 1, 13.

e) *am I but three inches?* (sc. high) Shr. IV, 1, 29. cf. *if she say I am not fourteen pence on the score,* Shr. Ind. 2, 24. *to outlive the age I am,* Per. V, 1, 15.

f) Verbs neuter often conjugated with *to be,* instead of *to have: this gentleman is happily arrived, my mind presumes, for his own good and ours,* Shr. I, 2, 213. *Cardinal Campeius is arrived, and lately,* H8 II, 1, 160. *miracles are ceased,* H5 I, 1, 67. *what he feared is chanced,* H4B I, 1, 87. *how every thing is chanced,* Caes. V, 4, 32. *the deep of night is crept upon our talk,* IV, 3, 226. *the Volsces are entered in the Roman territories,* Cor. IV, 6, 40. *sith I am entered in this cause so far,* Oth. III, 3, 411. *that fallen am I in dark uneven way,* Mids. III, 2, 417. *his highness is fallen into this apoplexy,* H4B I, 2, 122. *they are gone a contrary way,* All's III, 5, 8. *though he be grown so desperate to be honest,* H8 III, 1, 86. *our sister's man is certainly miscarried,* Lr. V, 1, 5. *they were stolen unto this wood,* Mids. II, 1, 191. *Worcester is stolen away to-night,* H4A II, 4, 392. *Campeius is stolen away to Rome,* H8 III, 2, 57. *whither are they vanished?* Mcb. I, 3, 80. *his lordship is walked forth into the orchard,* H4B I, 1, 4 etc. etc.

But the use of *is* instead of *has* in transitive verbs must be considered as an inadvertence in writing, the rather as the other forms of the two verbs, in which there is no consonance, are never thus confounded: *the king by this is set him down to sleep,* H6C IV, 3, 2.* *what late misfortune is befallen king Henry,* IV, 4, 3. *my life is run his compass,* Caes. V, 3, 25. *he is entered his radiant roof,* Cymb. V, 4, 120.

Beach, strand: Merch. IV, 1, 71. H5 V Chor. 9. Cor. V, 3, 58. Lr. IV, 6, 17. Cymb. I, 6, 36.

Beached, formed by a flat strand: *in the b. margent of the sea,* Mids. II, 1, 85. *upon the b. verge of the salt shore,* Tim. V, 1, 219.

Beachy = beached: *the b. girdle of the ocean,* H4B III, 1, 50.

Beacon, 1) a signal by a lighted fire: H4B IV, 3, 117. H6A III, 2, 29. Per. I, 4, 87. Figuratively: Troil. II, 2, 16.

2) lighthouse: *approach, thou b. to this under globe,* Lr. II, 2, 170.

Bead, 1) any small globular body: *with amber bracelets,* —s (= pearls) *and all this knavery,* Shr. IV, 3, 58. *these crystal* —s (i. e. tears) John II, 171. —s *of sweat,* H4A II, 3, 61. —s *of sorrow* (tears) Caes. III, 1, 284.

2) any thing extremely small: *you b., you acorn,* Mids. III, 2, 330. Hence name of a fairy: Wiv. V, 5, 53 (Ff. *Bede*).

3) *Beads* = rosary: Err. II, 2, 190. R2 III, 3, 147. H6B I, 1, 27. I, 3, 59. H6C II, 1, 162. R3 III, 7, 93.

Beaded, of the form of a bead: *b. jet,* Compl. 37 (O. Edd. *bedded*).

Beadle, public whipper: H6B II, 1, 136. 140. 148. H8 V, 4, 69. Lr. IV, 6, 164. Per. II, 1, 97. Figuratively: LLL III, 177. John II, 188. H5 IV, 1, 178.

Beadsman, a man hired by another to pray for him (cf. H5 IV, 1, 315): *I will be thy b.* Gentl. I, 1, 18. *thy very beadsmen learn to bend their bows against thy state,* R2 III, 2, 116.

Beagle, a small sort of dog; used of persons who follow another as dogs do their master: *she's a b., true-bred,* Tw. II, 3, 195. *get thee away and take thy* —s *with thee,* Tim. IV, 3, 174.

Beak, 1) the sharp and crooked bill of a bird of prey: Ven. 56. Lucr. 508. H6B III, 2, 193. Cymb. V, 4, 118.

2) bill in general: *turn their halcyon* —s *with every gale,* Lr. II, 2, 84.

3) the forecastle of a ship: *now on the b., now in the waist, the deck, in every cabin, I flamed amazement,* Tp. I, 2, 196.

Be-all: *that but this blow might be the b. and the end-all here,* Mcb. I, 7, 5; i. e. that with this blow all were done and finished, no consequences ensuing of it.

Beam, subst., 1) a long piece of timber: *the king your moth did see, but I a b. do find in each of three,* LLL IV, 3, 162. *a rush will be a b. to hang thee on,* John IV, 3, 129.

2) that part of a loom on which weavers wind the warp: *I fear not Goliath with a weaver's b.* Wiv. V, 1, 24.

3) anything of great length and weight, as f. i. a heavy lance: *stands colossus-like, waving his b.* Troil. V, 5, 9.

4) the part of the balance at the ends of which the scales are suspended: *which end of the b. should bow,* Tp. II, 1, 131. *we shall weigh thee to the b.* All's II, 3, 162. *in justice' equal scales, whose b. stands sure,* H6B II, 1, 205. *till our scale turn the b.* Hml. IV, 5, 157.

5) ray of light; emitted from the sun: Err. II, 2, 31. III, 2, 56. Mids. III, 2, 392. All's V, 3, 34. R2 I, 3, 146. H6A V, 3, 63. V, 4, 87. H6B III, 1, 223. 353. H6C V, 3, 12. R3 I, 3, 268. Rom. II, 5, 5. Tim. V, 1, 226. Lr. II, 2, 171. Cymb. IV, 4, 42. V, 5, 472. or from the moon: Mids. II, 1, 162. V, 277. Rom. I, 4, 62. or from the eye: Ven. 487. Lucr. 1090. Sonn. 114, 8. Wiv. I, 3, 68. H8 IV, 2, 89. Cor. III, 2, 5.* from a candle: Merch. V, 90. from a bright sword: H6A I, 1, 10. *cloudy death o'ershades his* —s *of life,* H6C II, 6, 62 (cf. R3 I, 3, 268).

Bean, a kind of pulse, faba vulgaris: H4A II, 1, 9.

Bean-fed, nourished with beans: *a fat and b. horse,* Mids. II, 1, 45.

Bear, vb.; Impf. *bore* (f. i. Sonn. 127, 2. Compl. 300. Tp. I, 2, 141. 145. II, 1, 266. Meas. I, 4, 51. Gentl. III, 1, 167. Err. V, 343. LLL IV, 3, 17. As IV,

2, 17. Tw. II, 1, 30 etc.), sometimes *bare:* Err. II, 1, 73. H6A I, 2, 139. H6B IV, 10, 83. V, 2, 64. Rom. V, 2, 13. In H4A I, 3, 42 and R3 II, 1, 89 Ff. *bare,* Qq *bore;* in Wint. I, 2, 309 O. Edd. *bear,* M. Edd. *bare.* Partic. *borne* (M. Edd. *born* in the sense of *natus*), f. i. Ven. 202. Lucr. 2. Sonn. 12, 8. 36, 4. 68, 3. Wiv. II, 1, 134. Meas. IV, 1, 48. IV, 2, 114. 147. 183 etc. etc.; once *bore:* Hml. V, 1, 205, but only in Qq, not in Ff.

I. trans. 1) to support or carry (a load), to convey: *borne by the trustless wings of false desire,* Lucr. 2. *no bearing yoke they knew,* 409. *borne on the bier,* Sonn. 12, 8. *the beast that —s me,* Sonn. 50, 5. Tp. II, 2, 180. III, 1, 24. IV, 251. Gentl. I, 2, 120. II, 4, 159. III, 1, 129. Err. II, 1, 73. V, 143. Mids. III, 2, 315. As III, 2, 176. 179. All's III, 3, 5. H4A I, 3, 42. H6A I, 2, 139. H6B V, 2, 64. R3 III, 1, 128. Hml. IV, 5, 164. V, 1, 205. Ant. III, 7, 9 etc. *To b. up* = to support, sustain: *my sinews, b. me stiffly up,* Hml. I, 5, 95. As we say: to bear the expense of sth., so Sh.: *what penny hath Rome borne, to underprop this action?* John V, 2, 97.

2) to carry, to bring, to deliver: *I'll b. him no more sticks,* Tp. II, 2, 167. *b. it* (the money) *to the Centaur,* Err. I, 2, 9. *b. it with you,* IV, 1, 41. *and his head borne to Angelo,* Meas. IV, 2, 183. *never to England shall he b. his life,* H6A IV, 4, 38. Figuratively: *he —s his thoughts above his falcon's pitch,* H6B II, 1, 12. *b. his hopes 'bove wisdom,* Mcb. III, 5, 30. Especially = to convey, to deliver, in speaking of letters and what is like them: *for —ing the letter,* Gentl. I, 1, 125. III, 1, 53. Wiv. I, 3, 80. II, 1, 134. Meas. IV, 3, 98. As III, 5, 135. Tw. IV, 2, 120. Rom. V, 2, 13. *there's the money, b. it straight,* Err. IV, 2, 63. *a sonnet,* LLL IV, 3, 17. *b. true intelligence betwixt the armies,* H4A V, 5, 9. *b. her this jewel,* H6A V, 1, 47. *an order,* R3 II, 1, 88. 89. *—ing the king's will from his mouth expressly,* H8 III, 2, 235.

3) to conduct, to bring, in speaking of persons: *they bore us some leagues to sea,* Tp. I, 2, 145. *b. me to prison,* Meas. I, 2, 121. *that we may b. him hence,* Err. V, 158. 160. *b. me unto his creditor,* IV, 4, 123. *go b. him hence,* 133. *b. them to my house,* V, 35. *let Diomedes b. him and bring as Cressid hither,* Troil. III, 3, 30. Wint. I, 2, 436. H4A V, 5, 14. H5 II, 2, 181. H6B III, 1, 212. 213. IV, 7, 64. H6C II, 1, 115. IV, 8, 53. V, 5, 4. 68. 69. Cor. III, 1, 213. Passively: *he is borne about invisible,* = he moves about, Err. V, 187.

4) to endure, to suffer: *b. an everduring blame,* Lucr. 224. *they that lose half with greater patience b. it,* 1158. *so shall those blots by me be borne alone,* Sonn. 36, 4. *will b. all wrong,* 88, 14. Meas. II, 3, 20. *hence hath offence his quick celerity, when it is borne in high authority,* IV, 2, 114. Wiv. IV, 5, 112. Err. I, 1, 47. 142. I, 2, 86. III, 1, 16. V, 89. Ado III, 2, 132. LLL V, 2, 813. *b. this, b. all,* As IV, 3, 14. *it is but weakness to b. the matter thus,* Wint. II, 3, 2. V, 1, 137. H5 III, 6, 134 *(the losses we have borne).* H6B IV, 1, 130. R3 I, 3, 103. *never —ing like labour,* Cor. I, 1, 103.

To bear off = to go through, to stand sth.: *here's neither bush nor shrub, to b. off any weather at all,* Tp. II, 2, 18.*

To b. sth. hard or *hardly* = to be vexed at: *who —s hard his brother's death,* H4A I, 3, 270. *have*

aught committed that is hardly borne by any, R3 II, 1, 57.

To b. a p. hard = to owe one a grudge: *Caesar doth b. me hard, but he loves Brutus,* Caes. I, 2, 317. *Ligarius doth b. Caesar hard,* II, 1, 215. *if you b. me hard,* III, 1, 157.*

5) to be pregnant with: *b. amiss the second burden of a former child,* Sonn. 59, 3. *the autumn —ing the wanton burden of the prime, like widowed wombs after their lords' decease,* 97, 7. Hence = to produce (as a fruit), to bring forth (as a child): *to b. their fruits of duty,* R2 III, 4, 62. *good wombs have borne bad sons,* Tp. I, 2, 120. *that bore thee two sons,* Err. V, 343. *your father's wife did after wedlock b. him,* John I, 217. *the curse of her that bare thee,* H6B IV, 10, 83. *would I had never borne thee son,* H6C I, 1, 217. *the infant that is born to-night,* R3 II, 1, 71. *the queen that bore thee,* Mcb. IV, 3, 109. *it were better my mother had not borne me,* Hml. III, 1, 126. *she that bore you,* Cymb. I, 6, 127.

Partic. *born* (O. Edd. always *borne*): Sonn. 123, 7. Tp. I, 1, 35. I, 2, 260. IV, 188. Wiv. II, 2, 40. Meas. II, 1, 202. II, 2, 97. III, 1, 196. III, 2, 100. Err. I, 1, 17. 37. LLL IV, 3, 217. Mids. II, 2, 123. H6A IV, 7, 40. Hml. I, 4, 15 etc. etc. *a beggar born,* Sonn. 66, 2. *a gentleman born,* Wiv. I, 1, 9. 287. Wint. V, 2, 141—150. *a Bohemian born,* Meas. IV, 2, 134. *any Syracusian born,* Err. I, 1, 19. *being younger born,* John I, 71. *Geffrey was thy elder brother born,* II, 104. *our youngest born,* Lr. II, 4, 216. Figuratively: *vows so born,* Mids. III, 2, 124. *I can tell thee where that saying was born,* Tw. I, 5, 10. *temptations have since then been born to us,* Wint. I, 2, 77. *this act so evilly born,* John III, 4, 149 (perhaps = carried on, executed). Followed by *of: born of thee,* Sonn. 78, 10. *conscience is born of love,* 151, 2. *what stuff 'tis made of, whereof it is born,* Merch. I, 1, 4. *conceived of spleen and born of madness,* As IV, 1, 217. *this man was born of woman,* Tim. IV, 3, 501. *On* instead of *of: 'tis a monster begot upon itself, born on itself,* Oth. III, 4, 162. Used substantively: *that is honour's scorn, which challenges itself as honour's born,* All's II, 3, 141.

6) to be charged with, to administer, to manage: *she —s the purse,* Wiv. I, 3, 75. *he who the sword of heaven will b.* Meas. III, 2, 275. *you would b. some sway,* Err. II, 1, 28. *to b. a charge,* All's III, 3, 5. *all the sceptres and those that b. them,* Wint. V, 1, 147. *think you I b. the shears of destiny?* John IV, 2, 91. *to b. the inventory of thy shirts,* H4B II, 2, 19. *b. the balance and the sword,* V, 2, 103. 114. *where every horse —s his commanding rein,* R3 II, 2, 128. cf. *the hard rein which both of them have borne against the old kind king,* Lr. III, 1, 27. *the part of business which I b. i' the state,* H8 III, 2, 146. *b. the great sway of his affairs,* Troil. II, 2, 35. *O, if he had borne the business!* Cor. I, 1, 274. *the rest shall b. the business in some other fight,* I, 6, 82. *I wish you had borne the action of yourself,* IV, 7, 15. *a forerunner, which —s that office,* Tim. I, 2, 125. *not b. the knife myself,* Mcb. I, 7, 16. *hath borne his faculties so meek,* 17. *to b. a part in this injury,* Lr. V, 1, 86 (Ff. *to be a party*). *bore the commission of my place and person,* Lr. V, 3, 64. *a charge we b. in the war,* Ant. III, 7, 17.

7) to carry on, to administer, to exe-

cute: *the conference was sadly borne*, Ado II, 3, 229. *we'll direct her how 'tis best to b. it*, All's III, 7, 20. *the manner how this action hath been borne*, H4B IV, 4, 88. *this act so evilly borne*, John III, 4, 149 (some M. Edd. *born*). *so may a thousand actions be all well borne without defeat*, H5 I, 2, 212. *he —s all things fairly*, Cor. IV, 7, 21. *how plainly I have borne this business*, V, 3, 4. *b. it as our Roman actors do*, Caes. II, 1, 226. *things have been strangely borne*, Mcb. III, 6, 3. *he hath borne all things well*, 17. *being in, b. it* (a quarrel) *that the opposed may beware of thee*, Hml. I, 3, 67. *to b. all smooth and even*, IV, 3, 7. *To bear up* = to arrange, to devise: *'tis well borne up*, Meas. IV, 1, 48.

To b. a part, Lucr. 1135. 1327. Shr. I, 1, 199. Wint. IV, 4, 298. 670 etc. (cf. *part*). *And with deep groans the diapason b.*, Lucr. 1132. *and, sweet sprites, the burthen b.* Tp. I, 2, 381. *the holding every man shall b.* Ant. II, 7, 117 (O. Edd. *beat*).

Under this head the following phrases, too, may be registered: *to bear one company*, Gentl. IV, 3, 34. Shr. IV, 3, 49. H6A II, 2, 53. H6C I, 3, 6. R3 II, 3, 47. H8 I, 1, 212 etc. (cf. *company*). *to b. witness*, Tp. III, 1, 68. Err. IV, 4, 80. Ado II, 3, 240. Ant. IV, 9, 5 etc. (cf. *witness*). *to b. evidence*, R3 I, 4, 67 (Ff. *give*).

8) to manage, to wield, to direct: *b. thine eyes straight*, Sonn. 140, 14. *thus must thou thy body b.* LLL V, 2, 100. *b. your body more seeming*, As V, 4, 72. *thus I bore my point*, H4A II, 4, 216. *mark how he —s his course*, H4A III, 1, 108. *you b. too stubborn and too strange a hand over your friend*, Caes. I, 2, 35 (cf. *to b. a hard rein*, Lr. III, 1, 27).

9) to be marked with, to show: *which like a waxen image 'gainst the fire, —s no impression of the thing it was*, Gentl. II, 4, 202. *the expressure that it —s, green let it be*, Wiv. V, 5, 71. *—ing the badge of faith*, Mids. III, 2, 127. *who this inscription —s*, Merch. II, 7, 4. *nor brass nor stone nor parchment —s not one* (example) Wint. I, 2, 360. *he doth b. some signs of me*, II, 1, 57. *—s so shrewd a maim*, H6B II, 3, 41. *the wounds his body —s*, Cor. III, 3, 50. IV, 2, 28. *must b. my beating to his grave*, V, 6, 109. Cf. *such signs of rage they b.* Lucr. 1419. *b. a fair presence* (i. e. observe a decent carriage) Err. III, 2, 13. *with the same haviour that your passion —s*, Tw. III, 4, 226. *the quarrel will b. no colour for the thing it is*, Caes. II, 1, 29. *b. welcome in your eye, your hand, your tongue*, Mcb. I, 5, 65. Cor. II, 3, 134.

Hence: *to b. a shape, a face* etc.: *when your sweet issue your sweet form should b.* Sonn. 13, 8. *would bark your honour from that trunk you b.* Meas. III, 1, 72. *what figure of us think you he will bear?* I, 1, 17. *b. the shape of man*, Merch. III, 2, 277. *my man Tranio, —ing my port*, Shr. III, 1, 36. *he did b. my countenance*, V, 1, 129. *thou —est thy father's face*, All's I, 2, 19. *whose form thou —est*, John I, 160. *b. the name and port of gentlemen*, H6B IV, 1, 19. *a woman's face*, H6C I, 4, 140. *his image,* V, 5, 54. *a woman's face*, Tit. II, 3, 136.

10) = to wear: *before these bastard signs of fair were borne*, Sonn. 68, 3. *if he have wit enough to keep himself warm, let him b. it for a difference* ... Ado I, 1, 69. *the city-woman —s the cost of princes on unworthy shoulders*, As II, 7, 75. *thy father's father wore it, and thy father bore it*, IV, 2, 17. *b. arms*,

John II, 346. *himself had borne the crown*, R2 III, 4, 65. *you b. a many* (stars) *superfluously*, H5 III, 7, 79. *she —s a duke's revenues on her back*, H6A I, 3, 83. *this monument of the victory will I b.*, H6B IV, 3, 12. *I will b. upon my target three suns*, H6C II, 1, 39. Cymb. V, 2, 6. Ant. IV, 6, 7 *(b. the olive)*.

11) to carry, to win: *His word might b. my wealth at any time*, Err. V, 8. *I'll b. it all myself*, Shr. V, 2, 79. *let me but b. your love*, *I'll b. your cares*, H4B V, 2, 58. *as your horse —s your praises*, H5 III, 7, 82. *his honesty rewards him in itself, it must not b. my daughter*, Tim. I, 1, 131. *b. the palm alone*, Caes. I, 2, 131. *you'll b. me a bang for that*, III, 3, 20. *so may he with more facile question b. it* (= conquer), Oth. I, 3, 23. *To b. it* = to carry the prize: *he ne'er had borne it out of Coventry*, H4B IV, 1, 135. *a should not b. it so, a should eat swords first: shall pride carry it?* Troil. II, 3, 227. *To b. away* = to win: *did b. the maid away*, Pilgr. 224. (But: *they have borne life away*, H5 IV, 1, 181, = they came safely off).-

12) to contain: *often reading what contents it —s*, Compl. 19. *more feet than the verses would b.* As III, 2, 175. *what else more serious importeth thee to know, this* (letter) *—s*, Ant. I, 2, 125. *his letters b. his mind, not I*, H4A IV, 1, 20.

13) to have inherently, to have within, to harbour: *his tender heir might b. his memory*, Sonn. 1, 4. *in the suffering pangs it* (love) *bears*, Compl. 272. *that's a brave god and —s celestial liquor*, Tp. II, 2, 122. *all the accommodations that thou —est are nursed by baseness*, Meas. III, 1, 14.

To bear love: Sonn. 10, 1. 152, 4. Tp. I, 2, 141. Gentl. III, 1, 167. Wiv. IV, 6, 9. As III, 5, 93. Epil. 13. Shr. I, 1, 111. IV, 4, 29. Wint. III, 2, 229. IV, 4, 528. H4A III, 3, 3. H6C II, 1, 158. R3 III, 4, 65. Oth. V, 2, 40. *To bear good will*: Gentl. IV, 3, 15. *the reverent care I b. unto my lord*, H6B III, 1, 34. *the great respect they b. to beauty*, H8 I, 4, 69. *zeal and obedience he still bore your grace*, III, 1, 63. *b. some charity to my wit*, Oth. IV, 1, 124. *To bear hate*: Mids. III, 2, 190. Merch. IV, 1, 61. Tit. V, 1, 3. *hatred*, Rom. II, 3, 53. *the ancient grudge I b. him*, Merch. I, 3, 48. *for no ill will I b. you*, As III, 5, 71. *the law I b. no malice*, H8 II, 1, 62. *To b. a purpose: to know the purposes I b.* Ant. I, 3, 67. *so mortal a purpose as then each bore*, Cymb. I, 4, 44. *you b. a graver purpose, I hope*, 151. *To b. a mind* = to be of a disposition: *had thy mother borne so hard a mind*, Ven. 202. *beasts b. gentle minds*, Lucr. 1148. 1540. Tp. II, 1, 266. Gentl. V, 3, 13. Tw. II, 1, 30. H4B III, 2, 251. 257. H6B I, 2, 62. III, 1, 24. H8 II, 3, 57. — *These nobles should such stomachs b.* H6A I, 3, 90. *with such dispositions as he —s*, Lr. I, 1, 309. *b. free and patient thoughts*, IV, 6, 80. *To b. a hard opinion of his truth*, Gentl. II, 7, 81. *b. a good opinion of my knowledge*, As V, 2, 60. *that opinion which every noble Roman —s of you*, Caes. II, 1, 93. *to clear her from that suspicion which the world might b. her*, Lucr. 1321. — *To b. in mind* = to remember: Ant. III, 3, 32.

14) to be endowed with, to own, to have: *our drops this difference bore*, Compl. 300. *she —s some breadth*, Err. III, 2, 114. *instances which shall b. no less likelihood*, Ado II, 2, 42. *a heavy heart —s not an humble tongue*, LLL V, 2, 747. *make the drink to b. no barm*, Mids. II, 1, 38. *no metal can b.*

half the keenness, Merch. IV, 1, 125. *when what is comely envenoms him that —s it*, As II, 3, 15. *it —s an angry tenour*, IV, 3, 11. *true servants that b. eyes to see*, Wint. I, 2, 309. *the common praise it —s*, III, 1, 3. *where they should b. their faces*, IV, 4, 246. *will b. no credit*, V, 1, 179. *that those veins did verily b. blood*, V, 3, 65. *some sins do b. their privilege on earth*, John I, 261. *b. possession of our person*, II, 366. *that —s a frosty sound*, H4A IV, 1, 128. *the speech of peace that —s such grace*, H4B IV, 1, 48. *between two blades, which —s the better temper*, H6A II, 4, 13. *b. that proportion to my flesh and blood*, H6B I, 1, 233. *to b. so low a sail*, H6C V, 1, 52. *with the dearest blood your bodies b.* V, 1, 69. *b. a weighty and a serious brow*, H8 Prol. 2. *their practices must b. the same proportion*, V, 1, 130. *through the sight I b. in things*, Troil. III, 3, 4. *the beauty that is borne here in the face, the bearer knows not*, 103. *your liberties and the charters that you b.* Cor. II, 3, 188. *thy face —s a command in it*, IV, 5, 67. *there's the privilege your beauty —s*, Tit. IV, 2, 116. *I b. a brain*, Rom. I, 3, 29. *b. fire enough to kindle cowards*, Caes. II, 1, 120. *every drop of blood that every Roman —s, and nobly —s*, 137. *to think that Caesar —s such rebel blood*, III, 1, 40. *that every nice offence should b. his comment*, IV, 3, 8. *under heavy judgment —s that life*, Mcb. 1, 3, 110. *the heart I b.* V, 3, 9. *I b. a charmed life*, V, 8, 12. *that it us befitted to b. our hearts in grief*, Hml. I, 2, 3. *whose grief —s such an emphasis*, V, 1, 278. *b. a wary eye*, V, 2, 290. *doth b. an excellency*, Oth. II, 1, 65 (reading of the Qq). *that the probation b. no hinge nor loop*, III, 3, 365. *b. no life*, IV, 2, 58. *b. hateful memory*, Ant. IV, 9, 9. *I'll show the virtue I have borne in arms*, Per. II, 1, 151. Concerning Meas. IV, 4, 29 *(bears of a credent bulk)* v. *Of.*

Particularly: *to b. a name*, Sonn. 127, 2. Meas. III, 1, 39. John I, 160. H6B IV, 1, 19. Tit. III, 1, 249. *to b. the name* = to have the first name, to be the first in estimation: H6A IV, 4, 9. *he —s the title of a king*, H6B II, 2, 140. *b. the addition nobly ever*, Cor. I, 9, 65.

15) *to b. one in hand* = to abuse one with false pretences or appearances: *the duke bore many gentlemen in hand and hope of action*, Meas. I, 4, 51. *b. her in hand until they come to take hands*, Ado IV, 1, 305. *she —s me fair in hand*, Shr. IV, 2, 3. *to b. a gentleman in hand, and then stand upon security*, H4B I, 2, 42. *how you were borne in hand, how crossed*, Mcb. III, 1, 81. *that so his age and impotence was falsely borne in hand*, Hml. II, 2, 67. *whom she bore in hand to love with such integrity*, Cymb. V, 5, 43.

16) *to b. down* = to overturn, to overwhelm, to crush (cf. III, 5): *malice —s down truth*, Merch. IV, 1, 214. *—s down all before him*, H4B I, 1, 11. *to b. me down with braves*, Tit. II, 1, 30. *a woman that —s all down with her brain*, Cymb. II, 1, 59.

17) *to b. out* = a) to stand, to get the better of: *love alter not with his* (time's) *brief hours and weeks, but —s it out even to the edge of doom*, Sonn. 116, 12. *it is impossible they* (the Turkish fleet) *b. it out*, Oth. II, 1, 19. *let summer b. it out*, i. e. get the better of it, make it supportable, Tw. I, 5, 21. b) to support or defend to the last, to countenance: *I hope your warrant will b. out the*

deed, John IV, 1, 6. *if I cannot b. out a knave against an honest man*, H4B V, 1, 53.

II. Reflectively: *to bear one's self* = to behave: *old woes, not infant sorrows, b. them mild*, Lucr. 1096. *how I may b. me here*, Tp. I, 2, 425. Meas. I, 3, 47 (O. Edd. only *bear*, not *bear me*). IV, 2, 147. Ado I, 1, 13. II, 3, 233. III, 1, 13. LLL V, 2, 744. Shr. Ind. I, 110. R2 V, 2, 50. H4A I, 3, 285. V, 4, 36. H4B V, 1, 74. H5 II, 2, 3. H6B I, 1, 184. III, 1, 6. H6C II, 1, 13. IV, 3, 45. H8 II, 1, 30. Cor. IV, 7, 8. Rom. I, 5, 68. Tim. III, 5, 65. Hml. I, 5, 170. *he —s him on the place's privilege*, i. e. he shapes his conduct to the liberty the place affords him, he presumes on the privilege of the place, H6A II, 4, 86. The original signification may be perceived in H6A II, 4, 14: *between two horses, which doth b. him best*, i. e. which has the best carriage (cf. I, 8). — Hence the subst. *bearing*, q. v., and a striking instance of the use of the partic. *borne*: *if he were proud, or covetous of praise, or surly borne*, Troil. II, 3, 249, i. e. of a surly behaviour.

III. Intrans. and absolutely. 1) to support loads: *I had my load before, now press'd with —ing*, Ven. 430. *your mistress —s well*, H5 III, 7, 48.

2) to endure, to suffer, to be patient: *tempt us not to b. above our power*, John V, 6, 38. *—ing fellowship* (i. e. fellowship in suffering) Lr. III, 6, 114. *you must b.* (= have patience, be indulgent) H4B V, 3, 31. *O God, seest thou this, and —est so long?* H6B II, 1, 154. *we'll b., with your lordship*, Tim. I, 1, 177.

Especially *to bear with one or sth.* = to be indulgent towards one: *with foul offenders thou perforce must b.* Lucr. 612. Tp. IV, 5, 199. Gentl. I, 1, 127. LLL V, 2, 417. As II, 4, 9. John IV, 2, 137. H4B II, 4, 63. H6A IV, 1, 129. R3 I, 3, 28. III, 1, 127. 128. IV, 4, 61. Cor. II, 1, 65. Caes. III, 2, 110. IV, 3, 119. 135. 255. Hml. III, 4, 2. Lr. IV, 7, 83.

3) to be fruitful: *happy plants are made to b.* Ven. 165. *to grow there and to b.* All's I, 2, 55. *the —ing earth*, Ven. 267. *—ing boughs*, R2 III, 4, 64.

4) to behave: *instruct me how I may formally in person bear like a true friar*, Meas. I, 3, 47 (M. Edd. *bear me*).

5) to take one's course, to sail, to drive: *which* (rock) *being violently borne upon*, Err. I, 1, 103. *and then she —s away*, IV, 1, 87. *a Turkish fleet, and —ing up to Cyprus*, Oth. I, 3, 8. *therefore b. up, and board 'em*, Tp. III, 2, 3.*

To bear back = to press back in a throng: *here one being thronged —s back*, Lucr. 1417. *stand back; room; b. back*, Caes. III, 2, 172 (hence the trans. use of *to bear down*).

6) to be situated with respect to another place: *my father's house —s more toward the market-place*, Shr. V, 1, 10.

7) *to bear up* = to stand firm: *an undergoing stomach, to b. up against what should ensue*, Tp. I, 2, 158. *so long as nature will b. up with this exercise*, Wint. III, 2, 241.

Bear, subst., 1) a beast of prey, of the genus *Ursus*: Ven. 884. Pilgr. 394 (M. Edd. *beasts*). Tp. I, 2, 289. Wiv. I, 1, 298. 304. Err. III, 2, 159. Ado III, 2, 80. Mids. II, 1, 180. II, 2, 30. 94. III, 1, 112. IV, 1, 118. V, 22. Tw. II, 5, 11. H4A I, 2, 83 *(as melancholy as a lugged b.)*. H6B V, 1, 144 *(my two* *brave —s*, i. e. the Nevils, who had a bear for their cognizance, cf. v. 203). H6C II, 1, 15. Troil. V, 7, 19. Caes. II, 1, 205 (betrayed with glasses). Ant. IV, 14, 3 etc. etc.

2) a **constellation**: *seems to cast water on the burning b. and quench the guards of the ever-fixed pole,* Oth. II, 1, 14.

Bear-baiting, the sport of baiting bears with dogs: Tw. I, 3, 98. II, 5, 9. Wint. IV, 3, 109.

Beard, the hair that grows in the face: Lucr. 1405. Tp. V, 16. Gentl. IV, 1, 9. *a great round b.* Wiv. I, 4, 20. *a little yellow b., a Cain-coloured b.* 23. Meas. IV, 2, 188. 3, 76. Err. V, 171. Ado II, 1, 32. 277. III, 2, 49. V, 1, 15. LLL V, 2, 834. Mids. I, 2, 50. 92. *your straw-colour b., your orange-tawny b., your purple-in-grain b., or your French-crown-colour b., your perfect yellow,* 95. IV, 2, 36. Merch. I, 3, 118. II, 2, 99. III, 2, 85. As I, 2, 76. II, 7, 155 *(b. of formal cut).* III, 2, 218. 394. 396. Shr. III, 2, 177. Wint. IV, 4, 728 *(will make him scratch his b.).* H4B V, 3, 37. H5 III, 2, 75. H6A I, 3, 47. H6B III, 2, 175 etc. etc. *beard to beard,* Cor. I, 10, 11 and Mcb. V, 5, 6. Witches had beards: Wiv. IV, 2, 204. Mcb. I, 3, 46.

Figuratively the **prickles on the ears of corn:** *with white and bristly b.* Sonn. 12, 8. *the green corn hath rotted ere his youth attained a b.* Mids. II, 1, 95.

Beard, vb., **to face, to set at defiance:** *no man so potent breathes upon the ground but I will b. him,* H4A IV, 1, 12. *do what thou darest; I b. thee to thy face. What! am I dared and —ed to my face?* H6A I, 3, 44. 45. *brave thee! ay, and b. thee too,* H6B IV, 10, 40. Used in jest by Hamlet: *thy face is valanced since I saw thee last: comest thou to b. me in Denmark?* Hml. II, 2, 443.

Bearded, adj., having a beard: *b. like the pard,* As II, 7, 150. H4B V, 1, 71. Oth. IV, 1, 67.

Beardless, wanting a beard: John V, 1, 69. H4A III, 2, 67.

Bearer, 1) one who carries a burden: *my dull b.* (i. e. the horse) Sonn. 51, 2.

2) one who conveys and delivers a letter or a message: LLL IV, 1, 55. Hml. I, 2, 35 (Ff. *for bearing*). V, 2, 46.

3) **sufferer**: *when crouching marrow in the b. strong cries of itself No more,* Tim. V, 4, 9.

4) **wearer, owner:** *O majesty, when thou dost pinch thy b., thou dost sit like a rich armour,* H4B IV, 5, 29. *thou (the crown) hast eat thy b. up,* 165. *though it* (pomp) *be temporal, yet if fortune divorce it from the b.* H8 II, 3, 15. *the beauty that is borne here in the face the b. knows not,* Troil. III, 3, 104.

Bear-herd, (this is the Shakespearian form of the word, cf. Shr. Ind. 2, 21 and H4B I, 2, 192; the other passages have *berrord, berard* and *bearard,* but never *bear-ward,* as some M. Edd. choose to write), bear-leader: Ado II, 1, 43. Shr. Ind. 2, 21. H4B I, 2, 192. H6B V, 1, 149. 210.

Bearing, subst., 1) manner of moving, port: *quick b. and dexterity,* Lucr. 1389. *I know him by his b.* Ado II, 1, 166. III, 1, 96.

2) behaviour: *a man of good repute, carriage, b. and estimation,* LLL I, 1, 272. *we shall see your b.* Merch. II, 2, 207. Tw. IV, 3, 19. Wint. IV, 4, 569. H4B V, 1, 84. H5 IV, 7, 185. H6B V, 2, 20. Cor. II, 3, 257.

Bearing-cloth, the mantle or cloth in which a child was carried to the font: Wint. III, 3, 119. H6A I, 3, 42.

Bear-like, like a bear: Mcb. V, 7, 2.

Bearn, spelling of some M. Edd. for *barn* (= little child) q. v.

Bear-ward, see *Bear-herd.*

Bear-whelp, whelp of a bear: *an unlicked b.* H6C III, 2, 161. Tit. IV, 1, 96.

Beast, animal in a restrictive sense, land-animal, quadruped (though Evans calls the louse so, Wiv. I, 1, 21); opposed to fishes and birds: *the —s, the fishes and the winged fowls,* Err. II, 1, 18; to birds: *—s did leap, and birds did sing,* Pilgr. 377. *a fault done first in the form of a b., and then in the semblance of a fowl,* Wiv. V, 5, 10. *a bird of my tongue is better than a b. of yours,* Ado I, 1, 141. *when —s most graze, birds best peck,* LLL I, 1, 238. *throw her forth to —s and birds of prey,* Tit. V, 3, 198. *why birds and —s from quality and kind,* Caes. I, 3, 64. Opposed to man: *that in some respects makes a b. a man, in some other a man a b.* Wiv. V, 5, 5. Meas. III, 2, 3. Err. II, 2, 81. III, 2, 87. V, 84. Merch. I, 2, 96. As II, 7, 1. IV, 3, 49. Shr. IV, 1, 25. Wint. IV, 4, 27. Tim. IV, 3, 323. Mcb. I, 7, 47. Lr. II, 4, 270 etc. A play on the word: *any strange b. there makes a man,* Tp. II, 2, 32.

In general it is only large and powerful animals that are called so, as the lion: Gentl. V, 4, 34. Mids. V, 140. 230. As IV. 3, 118. H5 IV, 3, 94. the tiger: Hml. II, 2, 472. the boar: Ven. 999. the griffin (gripe): Lucr. 545. the lion, bear and elephant: Troil. I, 2, 20. the bull: Wiv. V, 5, 5. Ado V, 4, 47; cf. Caes. II, 2, 40. the horse: Ven. 326. Sonn. 50, 5. H5 III, 7, 21. H6B V, 2, 12. *thou owest the worm no silk, the b. no hide, the sheep no wool, the cat no perfume,* Lr. III, 4, 109. *vast confusion waits, as doth a raven on a sickfallen b.* John IV, 3, 153. It is but indirectly that it refers to a sheep: LLL II, 222. Hence often = **savage animal**: *since men prove —s, let —s bear gentle minds,* Lucr. 1148. *—s shall tremble at thy din,* Tp. I, 2, 371. *heavens keep him from these —s!* II, 1, 324. *leave thee to the mercy of wild —s,* Mids. II, 1, 228. 2, 95. H6C II, 2, 12. *no b. so fierce but knows some touch of pity,* R3 I, 2, 71.

As, in contradistinction to man (see above, and Cymb. V, 3, 27) and even to horse (H5 III, 7, 26) it is a term of contempt, it, of course, serves as such when applied to men, which is done even in the noblest language: *the b. Caliban,* Tp. IV, 140. *what a b. am I to slack it!* Wiv. III, 4, 115. *O you b.! O faithless coward,* Meas. III, 1, 136. *ere this rude b. will profit,* III, 2, 34. *O monstrous b.! how like a swine he lies!* Shr. Ind. 1, 34. *a king of —s,* R2 V, 1, 35. *thou art a b. to say otherwise,* H4A III, 3, 140. *wilt thou not, b., abide?* Troil. V, 6, 30. *what a b. was I to chide at him!* Rom. III, 2, 95. *what a wicked b. was I to disfurnish myself against such a good time,* Tim. III, 2, 49. *that incestuous, that adulterate b.* Hml. I, 5, 42.

To make the b. with two backs, Oth. I, 1, 117, the French *faire la bête à deux dos*

Beast-like, brutal, savage: *her life was b. and devoid of pity,* Tit. V, 3, 199 (Qq *beastly*).

Beastliness, brutality, coarseness: *that bolting-hutch of b.* H4A II, 4, 496.

Beastly, adj., like a beast: *we have seen nothing; we are b., subtle as the fox for prey* etc. Cymb. III, 3, 40. cf. Wiv. V, 5, 10. Tim. IV, 3, 329. Hence = brutal, inhuman: *not to relent, is b., savage, devilish,* R3 I, 4, 265. *at the murderer's horse's tail, in b. sort, dragged through the field,* Troil. V, 10, 5. *O barbarous, b. villains!* Tit. V, 1, 97. *her life was b. and devoid of pity,* V, 3, 199 Ff. *beast-like).*

Oftenest = coarse, bestial: *so that in the —iest sense you are Pompey the Great,* Meas. II, 1, 229. *their abominable and b. touches.* III, 2, 25. Err. III, 2, 88. H4A I, 1, 44. H4B I, 3, 95. Cor. II, 1, 105. Tit. II, 3, 182. Tim. III, 5, 71. V, 1, 177. Lr. II, 2, 75. Cymb. I, 6, 153.

Adverbially: *how b. she doth court him,* Shr. IV, 2, 34. *he stabbed me in mine own house, and that most b.* H4B II, 1, 16 *what I would have spoke, was b. dumbed by him,* Ant. I, 5, 50. *will give you that like beasts which you shun b.* Cymb. V, 3, 27.

Beat, vb., impf. *beat:* Lucr. 489. Tp. III, 2, 119. IV, 175. Wiv. IV, 2, 212. V, 1, 21. Err. III, 1, 7. Shr. IV, 1, 79. H4B I, 1, 109. H6A IV, 6, 14. H6B III, 2, 102. R3 I, 2, 96. Troil III, 3, 213. Participle *beaten:* Lucr. 175. 1563. Wiv. I, 1, 114. IV, 5, 96. 115. Err. II, 1, 76. II, 2, 40. 48. V, 1, 170. Ado V, 1, 124. V, 4, 104. 111. Merch. II, 1, 35. Shr. Ind. 2, 87. Shr. IV, 1, 3. John III, 4, 6. V, 2, 166. H4B Ind. 25. H6B III, 1, 191. III, 2, 317. R3 V, 3, 334. H8 I, 3, 44. V, 5, 32. Troil. II, 1, 105. Rom. III, 1, 25. Caes. I, 3, 93. Mcb. V, 6, 8. Hml. II, 2, 277. Lr. I, 5, 46. IV, 6, 292. Oth. II, 3, 380. Ant. I, 4, 57. II, 2, 197. III, 1, 33. IV, 7, 11. Cymb. III, 1, 26. V, 5, 344 etc. Partic. *beat:* Wint. I, 2, 33. II, 3, 91. Troil. II, 1, 76. V, 5, 7. Cor. I, 6, 40. I, 10, 8. II, 3, 224. IV, 5, 127. Tit. IV, 4, 71. Caes. V, 5, 23. Ant. IV, 8, 1. 19. Partic. *beated:* Sonn. 62, 10 (Malone *bated,* Steevens *blasted,* Collier *beaten).*

I. trans. 1) to treat or punish with blows, to inflict blows upon: *I could find in my heart to b. him,* Tp. II, 2, 160. III, 2, 93. 119. Wiv. I, 1, 114. IV, 2, 89. 212. IV, 5, 96. 115 *(b. black and blue).* V, 1, 21. Meas. I, 3, 30. Err. II, 1, 74. II, 2, 40. 48. III, 1, 7. IV, 4, 33. V, 1, 170. Ado II, 1, 147. 207. V, 4, 111. Mids. II, 1, 204. Wint. II, 3, 91. R2 III, 3, 141. H6B III, 1, 171. R3 V, 3, 334. Troil. II, 1, 105. Cor. II, 3, 224. Rom. III, 1, 25. Lr. I, 5, 46. Oth. II, 3, 380 etc. *I saw him b. the surges under him,* Tp. II, 1, 114 (cf. Caes. I, 2, 107). *—ing his kind embracements with her heels,* Ven. 312 (cf. *heel* and *scorn). beaten with brains,* Ado V, 4, 104 (i. e. mocked). *I have bobbed his brain* (i. e. mocked him) *more than he has beaten my bones,* Troil. II, 1, 76. *b. not the bones of the buried,* LLL V, 2, 667.

2) to conquer at play or in fight: *are we not beaten?* John III, 4, 6. V, 2, 167. *so is Alcides beaten by his page,* Merch. II, 1, 35. *beaten a long time out of play,* H8 I, 3, 44. *five times I have fought with thee, so often hast thou beat me,* Cor. I, 10, 8. IV, 5, 127. Mcb. V, 6, 8 (or = treat with blows?). Ant. II, 3, 27. 38. III, 1, 33. IV, 7, 11. Cymb. III, 1, 26.

3) to turn some way, to drive, either by blows, or by other means; a) by blows: *and be new beaten home,* Err. II, 1, 76. *I will b. this method in your sconce,* II, 2, 34. *beaten out of door,* Shr. Ind. 2, 87.

I'll beat thee out of thy kingdom with a dagger of lath, H4A II, 4, 150. b) to drive by arms or else by superior force: *—ing reason back,* Ven. 557. *honest fear doth too too oft betake him to retire, beaten away by brainsick rude desire,* Lucr. 175. 278. *patience is quite beaten from her breast,* 1563. *Pompey, I shall b. you to your tent,* Meas. II, 1, 262. *self-harming jealousy! fie, b. it hence,* Err. II, 1, 102. *b. away those blushes,* Ado IV, 1, 163 (Ff. *bear). we are high-proof melancholy and would fain have it beaten away,* V, 1, 124. *your kindred shuns your house, as beaten hence by your strange lunacy,* Shr. Ind. 2, 31. *he's beat from his best ward,* Wint. I, 2, 33. *—s his peace to heaven,* John II, 88. *b. them hence!* H6A I, 3, 54. *to b. assailing death from his weak legions,* IV, 4, 16. *thus is the shepherd beaten from thy side,* H6B III, 1, 191. *when from thy shore the tempest b. us back,* III, 2, 102. *b. away the busy meddling fiend,* III, 3, 21. *unresolved to b. them back,* R3 IV, 4, 436. *to b. this from his brains,* H8 III, 2, 217. *we'll b. them to their wives,* Cor. I, 4, 41. *they had beat you to your trenches,* I, 6, 40. *have beat us to the pit,* Caes. V, 5, 23. *when thou wast beaten from Modena,* Ant. I, 4, 57. *from Actium b. the approaching Caesar,* III, 7, 53. *to b. me out of Egypt,* IV, 1, 2. *we'll b. 'em into bench-holes,* IV, 7, 9. *we have beat him to his camp,* IV, 8, 1. *we have beat them to their beds,* IV, 8, 19.

4) to strike; in different forms of expression: *as reproof and reason b. it* (my will) *dead,* Lucr. 489. *thy brothers b. aside the point,* R3 I, 2, 96. *the bell then —ing one,* Hml. I, 1, 39. *b. your breast,* R3 II, 2, 3. *and —s her heart,* Hml. IV, 5, 5. *sparkle like the beaten flint,* H6B III, 2, 317. Very often to beat *down* = to strike down: *to b. usurping down,* John II, 119. *hath beaten down young Hotspur and his troops,* H4B Ind. 25. *whose swift wrath b. down the never-daunted Percy,* I, 1, 109. *b. down Alençon,* H6A IV, 6, 14. *b. down Edward's guard,* H6C IV, 2, 23. *to b. down these rebels here at home,* R3 IV, 4, 532. *b. down our foes,* Troil. II, 2, 201. *Ajax bravely b. him down,* III, 3, 213. *Polydamas hath beat down Menon,* V, 5, 7.

5) to knock, to batter: *I'll b. the door,* Wiv. I, 1, 73 (Evans' speech). *if I b. the door down,* Err. III, 1, 59. *as he would b. down the gate,* Shr. V, 1, 17. *will you b. down the door?* Troil. IV, 2, 44. *the golden bullet —s it* (the castle) *down,* Pilgr. 328. *shall we b. the stones about thine ears?* H6C V, 1, 108. *— they shall b. out my brains with billets,* Meas. IV, 3, 58. *on the ragged stones b. forth our brains,* Tit. V, 3, 133. *b. out his brains,* Tim. IV, 1, 15. — What means: *b. Cut's saddle,* H4A II, 1, 6? (clean it by knocking?)

6) to drive to and fro, to shake, to lash (in speaking of the wind and what is like it): *an idle plume, which the air —s for vain,* Meas. II, 4, 12. *when we shall hear the rain and wind b. dark December,* Cymb. III, 3, 37. *shake like a field of beaten corn,* H8 V, 5, 32. *grass beat down with storms,* Tit. IV, 4, 71. *— with what loud applause didst thou b. heaven,* H4B I, 3, 92. *the lark whose notes do b. the vaulty heaven,* Rom. III, 5, 21.

7) to hammer, to forge: *walls of beaten brass,* Caes. I, 3, 93. *the poop was beaten gold,* Ant. II, 2, 197. A technical word of tawers: *beated and chopped with tanned antiquity,* Sonn. 62, 10.*

8) to mark with tracks by frequent walking: *in the beaten way of friendship,* Hml. II, 2, 277.

9) to strike, to play on (a drum): *then I b. my tabor,* Tp. IV, 175. *your drums, being beaten, will cry out,* John V, 2, 166. *b. loud the tabourines,* Troil. IV, 5, 275. *b. thou the drum,* Cor. V, 6, 151. Tim. IV, 3, 96. Lr. II, 4, 119. IV, 6, 292. — In Ant. II, 7, 117: *the holding every man shall b. as loud as his strong sides can volley,* M. Edd. *bear.*

10) to treat rudely or ignominiously: *beaten for loyalty excited me to treason,* Cymb. V, 5, 344.

II. absol. and intrans.; 1) to strike, to knock: *by —ing on her breast,* Lucr. 759. *the bell then —ing one,* Hml. I, 1, 39. *b. at this gate,* Lr. I, 4, 293.

2) to rush with violence, to dash: *all which together, like a troubled ocean, b. at thy rocking heart,* Lucr. 590. *the tide of pomp that —s upon the high shore of this world,* H5 IV, 1, 282.

3) to bate, to flutter: *these kites that bate and b.* Shr. IV, 1, 199.

4) to move with pulsation, to throb: *his —ing heart,* Lucr. 433. *my boding heart pants, —s,* Ven. 647. *ere your pulse twice b.* Tp. V, 103. 114. *no woman's sides can bide the—ing of so strong a passion,* Tw. II, 4, 97. *when living blood doth in these temples b.* John II, 108. R2 III, 3, 140. H4B II, 4, 26. R3 IV, 1, 35. Troil. III, 2, 38. Tit. III, 2, 20. *my head —s as it would fall in twenty pieces,* Rom. II, 5, 50. — Hence transitively = to shake by throbbing: *may feel her heart —ing her bulk,* Lucr. 467.

5) to hammer, to ponder: *do not infest your mind with —ing on the strangeness of this business,* Tp. V, 246. *thine eyes and thoughts b. on a crown,* H6B II, 1, 20. *whereon his brains still —ing,* Hml. III, 1, 182. Hence absolutely = to be troubled by thoughts: *to still my —ing mind,* Tp. IV, 163. And in speaking of things, = to engross the mind: *for still 'tis —ing in my mind,* Tp. I, 2, 176. *the tempest in my mind doth from my senses take all feeling else save what —s there,* Lr. III, 4, 14.

Beating, subst., receiving blows, a cudgelling: Err. II, 1, 79. Wint. IV, 3, 29. 62. Cor. V, 6, 109.

Beatrice, female name in Ado, passim; of three syllables: III, 1, 2. 15. 46. 50. V, 4, 72. 88. of two syllables: III, 1, 21. 24. 29. 37. 43.

Beaufort (O. Edd. *Beauford*), *Henry B.,* bishop of Winchester and afterwards cardinal: H6A I, 3, 60. III, 1, 127. H6B I, 1, 88. 3, 71. II, 2, 71. II, 4, 53 etc.

Beaumond; *Lord of B.:* R2 II, 2, 54.

Beaumont, French name: H5 III, 5, 44. IV, 8, 105.

Beauteous, very fair, handsome, (of things and persons): Ven. 365. 862. 1107. Lucr. 18. Sonn. 4, 5. 10, 7. 27, 12. 34, 1. 41, 6. 54, 1. 13. 84, 13. 104, 5. Compl. 99. Tp. V, 183. Gentl. V, 2, 12. LLL II, 41. IV, 1, 61. IV, 2, 136. V, 2, 41. Mids. I, 1, 104. V, 131. Merch. III, 2, 98. Shr. I, 2, 86. 255. IV, 2, 41. Tw. I, 2, 48. John IV, 2, 15. IV, 3, 137. R2 V, 1, 13. H6A V, 5, 2. H6B I, 1, 21. R3 IV, 4, 315. 405. V, 3, 321. Tit. IV, 2, 72. Rom. I, 2, 68. II, 2, 122. Mcb. II, 4, 15. Hml. IV, 5, 21. Ant. II, 6, 17 (*b. freedom*).

Beauteous-evil, beautiful and bad at the same time: Tw. III, 4, 403.

Beautied, cf. *Beauty,* vb.

Beautiful, = beauteous: Sonn. 106, 3. Compl. 211. Gentl. II, 1, 73. IV, 4, 185. LLL IV, 1, 63. Mids.

III, 1, 151. Merch. II, 3, 11. Shr. Ind. 2, 64. I, 2, 120. IV, 3, 178. Tw. II, 1, 27. III, 1, 157. H6A V, 3, 78. Rom. III, 2, 75. Tim. I, 2, 153. Cymb. V, 5, 63.

Beautify, to render beautiful: *to blush and b. the cheek again,* H6B III, 2, 167. *to b. thy triumphs,* Tit. I, 110. *this unbound lover, to b. him, only lacks a cover,* Rom. I, 3, 88. *what this fourteen years no razor touched, I'll b.* Per. V, 3, 76. Reflectively: *each in her sleep themselves so b.* Lucr. 404, i. e. are beautiful. Partic. *—ied: seeing you are —ied with goodly shape,* Gentl. IV, 1, 55. Adjectively: *the most —ied Ophelia; that's an ill phrase, a vile phrase; —ied is a vile phrase,* Hml. II, 2, 110 (= beautiful).

Beauty, subst. 1) assemblage of graces to please the eye and mind: Ven. 70. 119. Sonn. 54, 1. Tp. I, 2, 415. III, 2, 107. Gentl. I, 3, 86. II, 1, 59. III, 1, 78. III, 2, 73. IV, 2, 9. 45. Meas. II, 4, 80. III, 1, 37. 186. Wiv. II, 1, 2. III, 3, 59 etc. etc. Plural: *those whose —ies make them cruel,* Sonn 131, 2. *sympathy in years, manners and beauties,* Oth. II, 1, 233 (as relating to two persons). Concretely = the several parts and qualities which constitute the beauty of a person or thing: *mortal stars, as bright as heaven's —ies,* Lucr. 13. *one that composed your —ies,* Mids. I, 1, 48. *I might in virtues, —ies,... exceed account,* Merch. III, 2, 158. *your good —ies,* Hml. III, 1, 39. In the singular also = that which makes beautiful, the ornament: *the b. of the world,* Hml. II, 2, 319.—*

Used as a feminine: *b. herself is black,* Sonn. 132, 13. *b. (may) brag, but 'tis not she,* Phoen. 63. *b. doth b. lack, if that she learn not of her eye to look,* LLL IV, 3, 251.

2) a beautiful person: LLL V, 2, 158. Merch. III, 2, 99 (?). Tw. I, 5, 182. 186. H6A V, 3, 46. Rom. I, 1, 234. 2, 89. Collectively: *there will be the b. of this kingdom,* H8 I, 3, 54.

Beauty, vb., to embellish, to adorn: *the harlot's cheek, beautied with plastering art,* Hml. III, 1, 51, which participle may, perhaps, more properly be considered as an adjective, = furnished with beauty.

Beauty-waning, declining in beauty: *a b. and distressed widow,* R3 III, 7, 185.

Beaver, 1) the visor of the helmet: *their armed staves in charge, their —s down,* H4B IV, 1, 120. *and faintly through a rusty b. peeps,* H5 IV, 2, 44. *I'll hide my silver beard in a gold b.* Troil. I, 3, 296. *he wore his b. up,* Hml. I, 2, 230.

2) the helmet: *I saw young Harry, with his b. on,* H4A IV, 1, 104. *I cleft his b.,* H6C I, 1, 12. *is my b. easier than it was?* R3 V, 3, 50.

Becalm, to keep from motion by intercepting the wind: *must be be-leed and calmed by debitor and creditor,* Oth. I, 1, 30 (the prefix *be* belonging to both verbs. However, the simple verb *to calm* is found in the same sense H6B IV, 9, 33).

Because, by cause, on account; 1) followed by *of: this swain, b. of his great limb or joint, shall pass Pompey the Great,* LLL V, 1, 135. *they dare not fight with me, b. of the queen my mother,* Cymb. II, 1, 21.

2) followed by *that: b. that I familiarly sometimes do use you for my fool, your sauciness will jest upon my love,* Err. II, 2, 26. Mids. II, 1, 21. As I, 3, 117. John V, 2, 96. R3 III, 1, 130. Cor. III, 2, 52.

3) without *that,* in the same sense: Ven. 378. 885. 1094. Lucr. 35. Sonn. 42, 6. 101, 9. 102, 14. Pilgr.

106. Gentl. I, 2, 24. II, 1, 61. 76. II, 4, 173. II, 5, 60. III, 1, 147. 156. 345. III, 2, 57. IV, 1, 59. IV, 2, 28. IV, 4, 84. 100. 182. Wiv. IV, 1, 25. V, 1, 24 etc. etc. 4) preceded by *for*, in the same sense: *not for b. your brows are blacker*, Wint. II, 1, 7. *and why rail I on this commodity? but for b. he hath not woo'd me yet*, John II, 588. *and for b. the world is populous, I cannot do it*, R2 V, 5, 3.

Bechance, to befall, to happen to; without and with *to: let there b. him pitiful mischances*, Lucr. 976. *what hath —d them*, H6C I, 4, 6. *all happiness b. to thee in Milan!* Gentl. I, 1, 61. Absolutely: *such a thing —d would make me sad*, Merch. I, 1, 38.

Beck, subst., significant nod, as a sign of command: *thy b. might from the bidding of the gods command me*, Ant. III, 11, 60. *serving of —s and jutting-out of bums*, Tim. I, 2, 237 (i. e. servile attention to becks). *At a person's b.* = at command: *being at your b.* Sonn. 58, 5. *ready at thy b.* Shr. Ind. 2, 36. *they have troops of soldiers at their b.* H6C I, 1, 68. *with more offences at my b. than I have thoughts to put them in*, Hml. III, 1, 127.

Beck, vb., to beckon, to call by a nod, to command: *when gold and silver —s me to come on*, John III, 3, 13. *whose eye —ed forth my wars and called them home*, Ant. IV, 12, 26.

Beckon, to make a sign: *he —s with his hand and smiles on me*, H6A I, 4, 92. *this hill, with one man —ed from the rest below*, Tim. I, 1, 74 (i. e. called forth with a wink). *it —s you to go away with it*, Hml. I, 4, 58. *Iago —s me*, Oth. IV, 1, 134. *To b. sth.* = to command sth. by a sign: *Mars, —ing with fiery truncheon my retire*, Troil. V, 3, 53.

Become, vb., to come to be, to grow, to get: (Impf. *became*, partic. *become*: conjugated with the auxiliary verb *to be*): *make the young old, the old b. a child*, Ven. 1152. Lucr. 1479. Sonn. 120, 13. Tp. V, 206. Gentl. II, 1, 144. II, 5, 43. Wiv. I, 3, 83. Meas. III, 1, 120. 136. Err. I, 1, 50. Ado II, 3, 11. Mids. II, 2, 120. Merch. I, 2, 88. II, 2, 156. II, 3, 21. IV, 1, 387. H6A IV, 1, 65. V, 4, 128 etc. The predicate an adjective: *your affections would b. tender*, Tp. V, 19. Gentl. IV, 4, 161. Meas. III, 1, 35. Err. I, 1, 126. Merch. V, 226. H6B III, 1, 7. R3 I, 2, 221 etc. The pred. a participle: *the rod —s more mocked than feared*, Meas. I, 3, 27. *for the which Antonio shall be bound. Antonio shall b. bound*, Merch. I, 3, 6.

Followed by *as: the tenderness of her nature became as a prey to her grief*, All's IV, 3, 61. *thy blessed youth —s as aged*, Meas. III, 1, 35. Troil. III, 3, 11; cf. *As.*

Followed by *of: is of a king b. a banished man*, H6C III, 3, 25. *what shall b. of those in the city?* Meas. I, 2, 100. *what then became of them I cannot tell*, Err. V, 354. Ado IV, 1, 211. Tw. II, 2, 37. John III, 1, 35. R2 II, 1, 251. H6B I, 4, 32. H8 II, 1, 2. Troil. V, 4, 35. Ant. IV, 4, 29

Seemingly = to come, to get, in the following passages: *I cannot joy, until I be resolved where our right valiant father is become*, H6C II, 1, 10. *where is Warwick then become?* IV, 4, 25, which cannot be as much as: *what has become of Warwick.* Cf.: *and here, to do you service, am become as new into the world*, Troil. III, 3, 11 (unless *into* be = *unto*).

Become, vb.; impf. *became*: Compl. 111. Gentl. III, 1, 227. H4A V, 2, 61. H4B II, 3, 25. Partic. *be-*

comed: Rom. IV, 2, 26. Ant. III, 7, 26. Cymb. V, 5, 406. cf. *misbecomed:* LLL V, 2, 778.

1) to be suitable, to accord with: *to shun this blot, she would not blot the letter with words, till action might b. them better*, Lucr. 1323. *yet so they mourn, —ing of their woe* (cf. *Of*), *that every tongue says beauty should look so*, Sonn. 127, 13. *the dozen white louses do b. an old coat well*, Wiv. I, 1, 19. *your falsehood shall b. you well to worship shadows*, Gentl. IV, 2, 130 (= if you worship shadows). *her hands whose whiteness so became them as if but now they waxed pale for woe*, Gentl. III, 1, 227. *the night's dead silence will well b. such sweet-complaining grievance*, III, 2, 86; cf. *soft stillness and the night b. the touches of sweet harmony*, Merch. V, 57. *the right arched beauty of the brow that —s the shiptire. A plain kerchief; my brows b. nothing else*, Wiv. III, 3, 60—63. *do not these fair yokes b. the forest better than the town?* V, 5, 112. *the night is dark; light and spirits will b. it well*, V, 2, 14. *beauty's crest —s the heavens well*, LLL IV, 3, 256. *I am not tall enough to b. the function well*, Tw. IV, 2, 8. *I speak amazedly; and it —s my marvel and my message*, Wint. V, 1, 187. *speaking thick became the accents of the valiant*, H4B II, 3, 25. *inter their bodies as —s their births*, R3 V, 5, 15. *how the wheel —s it!* Hml. IV, 5, 172. *observe how Antony —s his flaw*, Ant. III, 12, 34, i. e. accommodates himself to his misfortune.

2) to fit, to suit: *it would b. me as well*, Tp. III, 1, 28. *not the morning sun better —s the grey cheeks of the east*, Sonn. 132, 6. Meas. II, 2, 62. Ven. 968. *to be merry best —s you*, Ado II, 1, 346. *doth not my wit b. me rarely?* III, 4, 70. *nothing —s him ill*, LLL II, 46. *it would ill b. me*, IV, 2, 31. *if his own life answer the straitness of his proceeding, it shall b. him well*, Meas. III, 2, 270. *parts that b. thee happily enough*, Merch. II, 2, 191. *such fair ostents of love as shall conveniently b. you there*, II, 8, 45. *mercy —s the throned monarch better than his crown*, IV, 1, 188. *it —s me well enough*, Tw. I, 3, 106. *no more than well —s so good a quarrel*, H6B II, 1, 27. *a good rebuke, which might have well —d the best of men*, Ant. III, 7, 27.

3) without a determinative adverb, = to set off, to grace, to be decent: *that cap of yours —s you not*, Shr. V, 2, 121. *as those two eyes b. that heavenly face*, IV, 5, 32. *O thou, whose wounds b. hard-favoured death*, H6A IV, 7, 23. *the wounds b. him*, Cor. II, 1, 135. *vilest things b. themselves in her*, Ant. II, 2, 244 (lend themselves a grace, are graceful). cf. Gentl. II, 7, 47. Wiv. I, 1, 241. Mids. II, 2, 59. As I, 1, 76. 84. III, 4, 3. III, 5, 114. Epil. 11. H4A V, 2, 61. H6A III, 2, 54. V, 3, 177. H6C II, 2, 85.

Very frequently used of persons, in the sense of to adorn, to grace: *she will b. thy bed*, Tp. III, 2, 112. *b. disloyalty* Err. III, 2, 11 (= give disloyalty a grace). *though it be pity to see such a sight, it well —s the ground*, As III, 2, 256. *did ever Dian so b. a grove as Kate this chamber?* Shr. II, 260. *glister like the god of war, when he intendeth to b. the field*, John V, 1, 55. *if I b. not a cart as well as another man*, H4A II, 4, 545. *God and his angels guard your sacred throne, and may you long b. it*, H5 I, 2, 8. *yon island carrions ill-favouredly b. the morning field*, IV, 2, 40. *royal fruit, which will well b. the seat of majesty*, R3 III, 7, 169. *how bravely thou —st thy bed, fresh lily,*

Cymb. II, 2, 15. *he would have well — d this place,* V, 5, 406.

Sometimes the subject and object ought to change places: *and controversy hence a question takes, whether the horse by him became his deed, or he his manage by the well-doing steed,* Compl. 111. *well did he b. that lion's robe,* John II, 141. *that head of thine doth not b. a crown,* H6B V, 1, 96. *youth no less —s the light and careless livery that it wears,* Hml. IV, 7, 79. *sorrow would be a rarity most beloved, if all could so b. it,* Lr. IV, 3, 26. *how this Herculean Roman does b. the carriage of his chafe,* Ant. I, 3, 84.

4) without an object, = to be proper, to be decorous: *set this diamond safe in golden palaces, as it —s,* H6A V, 3, 170. *let us give him burial, as —s,* Tit. I, 347. *Becoming =* decent, graceful: *within the limit of b. mirth,* LLL II, 67. *I never saw a vessel of like sorrow so filled, and so becoming,* Wint. III, 3, 22 (made unintelligible by M. Edd. setting a comma after *sorrow). Becomed,* in the same sense: *gave him what b. love I might,* Rom. IV, 2, 26.

Becoming, subst., grace: *whence hast thou this b. of things ill, that, in my mind, thy worst all best exceeds?* Sonn. 150, 5. *my —s kill me, when they do not eye well to you,* Ant. I, 3, 96.

Bed, subst., 1) an article of furniture to sleep on: Ven. 108. 397. Lucr. 975. Tp. III, 2, 112. Gentl. I, 2, 114. II, 1, 87. Meas. I, 2, 150. II, 4, 102. III, 1, 375 etc. etc. *the b. of Ware* (an enormous bed, still preserved) Tw. III, 2, 51. *to make the b.* Wiv. I, 4, 102. Shr. IV, 1, 203. *to keep one's b.* H4A IV, 1, 21. *on his b. of death,* All's II, 1, 107. *upon his death's b.* Wiv. I, 1, 53. *go to thy cold b. and warm thee,* Shr. Ind. I, 10. Lr. III, 4, 48. *when I came unto my beds,* Tw. V, 410 (the plural serving to indicate the unsettled life of a vagabond?). *a bed v. A - bed. in b.:* Err. V, 63. All's V, 3, 110. Rom. II, 3, 42. IV, 1, 93. Cymb. II, 4, 57. *to b.:* Gentl. IV, 2, 94. Wiv. II, 2, 124. Err. IV, 3, 32. Ado III, 3, 96. Mids. V, 371. Tw. II, 3, 7. 8. 9. 207. III, 4, 31 etc. etc. *brought to b.* = delivered: Tit. IV, 2, 62. 153; followed by *of:* Wint. IV, 4, 266. *brought to b.* = laid to b.: Per. III Prol. 9. *I knew of their going to b.* (= of their sexual commerce) All's V, 3, 264. *whom I can lay to b. for ever,* Tp. II, 1, 284 (= put to eternal sleep).

Bed as the symbol of matrimony: *robbed others' beds' revenues of their rents,* Sonn. 142, 8. Tp. IV, 1, 21. Wiv. II, 2, 306. Err. II, 1, 108. II, 2, 147. III, 2, 17. 43. V, 163. Ado III, 1, 45 (*as fortunate a b.*). Mids. II, 1, 73. All's II, 3, 97. H6C II, 2, 154 etc. *my b. and company,* Mids. II, 1, 62. H6B II, 1, 197. *board and b.* Mids. V, 31. As V, 4, 148. *table and b.* H6C I, 1, 248.

Couch in general: *find you out a b.* Mids. II, 2, 39. 64. III, 2, 429. Symbol of a settled lodging: *raiment, b. and food,* Lr. II, 4, 158.

Figuratively any place in which something is couched: *those sleeping stones ... by this time from their fixed —s of lime had been dishabited,* John II, 219. *from their dark —s once more leap her eyes,* Ven. 1050. *thunder shall not so awake the —s of eels,* Per. IV, 2, 155. Frequently = death-bed, grave, sepulchre: *in that oozy b. where my son lies,* Tp. V, 151. *his paved b.* Meas. V, 440. *wormy —s,* Mids. III, 2, 384. *they died in honour's lofty b.* Tit. III, 1, 11. *this b. of death,* Rom. V, 3, 28. — *O my accursed womb, the*

b. of death! R3 IV, 1, 54, i. e. the birth-place of death.

2) bank of earth: *—s of roses,* Wiv. III, 1, 19. *primrose —s,* Mids. I, 1, 215. *this flowery b.* IV, 1, 1. *—s of flowers,* Tw. I, 1, 40. *lily —s,* Troil. III, 2, 13.

Bed, vb., 1) to take to bed, to cohabit with: *woo her, wed her and b. her,* Shr. I, 1, 149. *I will not b. her,* All's II, 3, 287. 290. *I have wedded her, not —ed her,* III, 2, 23.

2) to lay as in a bed: *therefore my son in the ooze is —ed,* Tp. III, 3, 100. *a thousand favours of amber, crystal, and of —ed jet,* Compl. 37 (i. e. put in a setting; most M. Edd. *beaded*).

3) to lay flat: *your —ed hair starts up,* Hml. III, 4, 121.

Bedabble, to sprinkle: *—d with the dew,* Mids. III, 2, 443 (cf. *Dew-bedabbled*).

Bedash, to bespatter, to wet: *had wet their cheeks, like trees —ed with rain,* R3 I, 2, 164.

Bedaub, to besmear, to soil: *all — ed in blood,* Rom. III, 2, 55.

Bedazzle, to dazzle, to make dim by too much light: *—d with the sun,* Shr. IV, 5, 46.

Bedchamber, sleeping apartment: Ven. 784. R3 I, 2, 111. H8 III, 2, 77. Tit. IV, 1, 108. Cymb. I, 6, 196. II, 4, 66. *makes him of his b.* I, 1, 42 (i. e. his page).

Bedclothes, blankets and coverlets for beds: All's IV, 3, 287.

Bede, name of a fairy: Wiv. V, 5, 53 (cf. *Bead*).

Bedeck, to adorn, to grace: *such —ing ornaments of praise,* LLL II, 79. *in that true use which should b. thy shape, thy love, thy wit,* Rom. III, 3, 125.

Bedew, to moisten as with dew: *b. her grass with blood,* R2 III, 3, 99. *the tears that should b. my hearse,* H4B IV, 5, 114. *your laments, wherewith you now b. King Henry's hearse,* H6A I, 1, 104.

Bedfellow, one who sleeps in the same bed: Tp. II, 2, 42. Ado IV, 1, 149. 151. Merch. V. 233. 284. Shr. IV, 5, 41. H4B III, 2, 6. IV, 5, 22. H5 II, 2, 8. R3 IV, 4, 385 (Qq *playfellows*). H8 II, 2, 143. Cor. II, 2, 69. Ant. I, 2, 51 (*go, you wild b.*). Cymb. IV, 2, 295. Per. Prol. 33.

Bedford. *John Duke of Bedford,* brother to Henry V: H5 IV, 1, 3. IV, 3, 8. 53. H6A I, 1, 99. I, 4, 27 (Ff. *Earl of B.*). III, 2, 87. H6B I, 1, 83 etc.

Bed-hangings, curtains: H4B II, 1, 158.

Bedim, to darken: *—ed the noontide sun,* Tp. V, 41.

Bedlam, 1) a hospital for lunatics: *to B. with him!* H6B V, 1, 131. *Tom o' B.* (the usual name of a sort of vagabond beggars), Lr. I, 2, 148. Adjectively: *B. beggars,* Lr. II, 3, 14 (q. v.).

2) a lunatic: *B., have done!* John II, 183. *get the B. to lead him,* Lr. III, 7, 103. Adjectively: *art thou b.?* H5 V, 1, 20 (Pistol's speech). *the b. brainsick duchess,* H6B III, 1, 51. *a b. and ambitious humour,* H6B V, 1, 132.

Bedmate, bedfellow: Troil. IV, 1, 5 (fem.).

Bed-presser: *this b., this horseback - breaker,* H4A II, 4, 268, i. e. this heavy, lazy and dissolute fellow.

Bedrench, to moisten: *such crimson tempest should b. the green lap of King Richard's land,* R2 III, 3, 46.

Bedrid, confined to the bed: LLL I, 1, 139.

Wint. IV, 4, 412. Hml. I, 2, 29. *afflict him in his bed with b. groans*, Lucr. 975.

Bed-right, that which married people may claim from each other; matrimonial duty: *no b. shall be paid till Hymen's torch be lighted*, Tp. IV, 96 (some M. Edd. *bed-rite*).

Bed-room, room for lying: *then by your side no b. me deny*, Mids. II, 2, 51.

Bed-swerver, one who is false to the marriage-bed: *she's a b.* Wint. II, 1, 93.

Bed-time, the usual hour of going to rest: Err. I, 2, 28. Mids. V, 34. H4A V, 1, 125

Bed-vow, marriage-vow: Sonn. 152, 3.

Bedward, toward bed: *tapers burned to b.* Cor. I, 6, 32 (the two parts of the word *toward* enclosing, instead of preceding, the substantive; cf. *Parisward*).

Bedwork, work done in bed, that is without toil: *they call this b., mappery, closet-war*, Troil. I, 3, 205.

Bee, the insect Apis mellifica: Lucr. 836. 840. 1769. Tp. I, 2, 330. V, 88. Gentl. I, 2, 107. H4B IV, 5, 75. 78. H5 I, 2, 187. H6A I, 5, 23. H6B III, 2, 125 (*bees that want their leader*). IV, 2, 89. Tit. V, 1, 14 (*led by their master*). Caes. V, 1, 34 (*Hybla —s*). Cymb. III, 2, 36. Of feminine gender: *when the b. doth leave her comb in the dead carrion*, H4B IV, 4, 79. *rob the b. of her honey*, Per. II, 1, 51. Quibble between *be* and *bee*, Shr. II, 207.

Beef, 1) the animal Bos taurus; only in the plural: *flesh of muttons, beefes or goats*, Merch. I, 3, 168. *now has he land and beeves*, H4B III, 2, 353.

2) the flesh of oxen prepared for food: Meas. III, 2, 59. Shr. Ind. 2, 8. IV, 3, 23. 26. 28. 30. Tw. I, 3, 90. H5 III, 7, 161. H6B IV, 10, 61. cf. *bull-beeves*, H6A I, 2, 9. An obscene meaning seems hidden in Meas. III, 2, 59 and Shr. IV, 3, 28. Prince Henry calls Falstaff his *sweet b.*, H4A III, 3, 199.

Beef-witted, with no more wit than an ox: Troil. II, 1, 14 (cf. also Tw. I, 3, 90).

Beehive, case in which bees are kept: H6B IV, 1, 109.

Beer, liquor made of malt and hops; *double b.:* H6B II, 3, 65. *small b.:* H4B II, 2, 8. 13. H6B IV, 2, 73. Oth. II, 1, 161.

Beer-barrel, barrel for holding beer: Hml. V, 1, 235.

Beesom, v. *bisson.*

Beetle, subst., 1) insect of the genus Coleoptera: Tp. I, 2, 340. Meas. III, 1, 79. Mids. II, 2, 22. Mcb. III, 2, 42. Lr. IV, 6, 14. Ant. III, 2, 20. Cymb. III, 3, 20.

2) rammer: *if I do, fillip me with a three-man b.* H4B I, 2, 255 (a rammer so heavy that it requires three men to manage it).

Beetle, vb., to jut, to hang over: *the summit of the cliff that —s o'er his base into the sea*, Hml. I, 4, 71.

Beetle-brows, prominent brows: *here are the b.* (sc. a mask) *shall blush for me*, Rom. I, 4, 32.

Beetle-headed, having a head like a rammer, stupid: *a whoreson b. flap-eared knave!* Shr. IV, 1, 160.

Befall. Impf. *befell:* Meas. III, 1, 227. As IV, 3, 103. H6C III, 1, 10. Partic. *befallen:* Lucr. 1599. Err. I, 1, 124. H4B I, 1, 177. H6C II, 1, 106. IV, 4,

3. R3 I, 4, 16. Hml. IV, 3, 11. Oth. II, 4, 304. V, 2, 307.

1) trans. to happen to: *what uncouth ill event hath thee befallen*, Lucr. 1599. *more blessed hap did ne'er b. our state*, H6A I, 6, 10. Meas. I, 1, 59. Mids. I, 1, 63. Tw. III, 3, 8. III, 4, 371. H6B I, 4, 37. H6C III, 1, 10. IV, 1, 76. IV, 4, 3 (*is befallen* instead of *has befallen;* cf. *Be*). IV, 6, 95. R3 I, 4, 16. Ant. II, 2, 42.

Frequently used optatively: *so b. my soul as this is false!* Err. V, 208. *many years of happy days b. my gracious sovereign!* R2 I, 1, 20. H6A II, 5, 115. Cymb. III, 5, 9. *now fair b. your mask!* LLL II, 124. *whom fair b. in heaven*, R2 II, 1, 129. *now fair b. thee and thy noble house*, R3 I, 3, 282. This latter phrase serving also as a congratulation: *now fair b. thee, good Petruchio! the wager thou hast won*, Shr. V, 2, 111. *now fair b. you! he deserved his death*, R3 III, 5, 47.

2) intr. to happen: *those things do best please me that b. preposterously*, Mids. III, 2, 121. V, 156. As IV, 3, 103. H4B I, 1, 177. H6C II, 1, 106. Caes. V, 1, 97. Hml. IV, 3, 11. Oth. II, 3, 304. V, 2, 307. *b. what fortune will*, Tit. V, 3, 3. *b. what will b.* LLL V, 2, 880. *b. what may b.* H6B III, 2, 402. Tit. V, 1, 57. Followed by *to: mark how heavily this befell to the poor gentlewoman*, Meas. III, 1, 227. *and more such days as these to us b.* H6B V, 3, 33. Followed by *of: dilate at full what hath befallen of them and thee till now*, Err. I, 1, 124.

Befit, 1) to suit: *any business that we say —s the hour*, Tp. II, 1, 290. V, 165. *how that name —s my composition!* R2 II, 1, 73. H6C V, 7, 44. *blind as his love and best —s the dark*, Rom. II, 1, 32. Absolutely: *it well —s you should be of the peace*, H4B III, 2, 98.

2) to become: *those petty wrongs thy beauty and thy youth full well —s*, Sonn. 41, 3. *you may conceal her, as best —s her wounded reputation*, Ado IV, 1, 243. H6C III, 2, 2. Hml. I, 2, 2. Ant. II, 2, 97. Per. I, 1, 120. II, 3, 66.

Before, I. Preposition, opposed to behind and after, locally and temporally: *I drink the air b. me*, Tp. V, 102. *I had rather go b. you*, Wiv. 3, 2, 5. *other bars he lays b. me*, Wiv. III, 4, 7. *was carried with more speed b. the wind*, Err. I, 1, 110. *let's go hand in hand, not one b. another*, V, 425. *b. the palace gate*, Tit. IV, 2, 35. *I see b. me*, Cymb. III, 2, 80 (not what is behind or to the right and left). *are you crept b. us?* Gentl. IV, 2, 18. *b. their time*, V, 1, 15. *b. his death*, Meas. IV, 2, 189. *an hour b. his entering*, IV, 4, 10. *if thou seest her b. me*, Wiv. I, 4, 168. *thy vices bud b. thy spring*, Lucr. 604. *b. the judgment*, Err. IV, 2, 40. *go b. me*, Merch. II, 5, 38 etc. etc.

In the same sense in some cases where modern usage would prefer other prepositions: *kneel down b. him*, Meas. II, 2, 44. *thrice bowed b. me*, Wint. III, 3, 24. *fall b. his feet*, John V, 4, 13. *bow my knee b. his majesty*, R2 I, 3, 47. Caes. II, 1, 320. Ant. II, 3, 3. *lets fall his sword b. your highness' feet*, H6A III, 4, 9.

Thou runnest b. me (= from me), Mids. III, 2, 423. *who quickly fell b. him* (= by his hands), As IV, 3, 132. *better to fall b. the lion than the wolf*, Tw. III, 1, 140. *our enemies shall fall b. us*, H6B IV, 2, 37. *the king b. the Douglas' rage stooped his anointed head*

H4B Ind. 31. *down goes all b. him,* H5 III Chor. 34. *to mow 'em down b. me,* H8 V, 4, 23. *the ground shrinks b. his treading,* Cor. V, 4, 20. cf. II, 2, 109.

Frequently = in presence of: *I'll speak it b. the best lord,* Wiv. III, 3, 53. *know you b. whom you are?* As I, 1, 45. *what colour for my visitation shall I hold up b. him?* Wint. IV, 4, 567. *stepped forth b. the king,* H4A V, 2, 46. *let's beat him b. his whore,* H4B II, 4, 280. *b. this royal view,* H5 V, 2, 32. *what say't thou, man, b. dead Henry's corse?* H6A I, 1, 62. *thus bold b. thy sovereign,* H6C II, 2, 86. *dally not b. your king,* R3 II, 1, 12. *your appeal to us there make b. them,* H8 V, 1, 153. *makes vow b. his uncle,* Hml. II, 2, 70. *before your ladyship she puts her tongue a little in her heart,* Oth. II, 1, 106. *were cast away b. us,* Per. II, 1, 19. — Sometimes noting power and authority: *take her hand b. this friar,* Ado V, 4, 57. *b. this holy friar, I am your husband,* 58. *she will not here b. your grace consent,* Mids. I, 1, 39. *I was b. Master Tisick the deputy,* H4B II, 4, 92. *thou wilt answer this b. the pope,* H6A I, 3, 52. *we'll hear more of your matter b. the king,* H6B I, 3, 39. — In like manner = to the presence of: *bid come b. us Angelo,* Meas. I, 1, 16. *he must b. the deputy,* III, 2, 35. 38. *he shall bring you b. the duke,* IV, 3, 147. Lr. II, 1, 33.

Before heaven = in the face or sight of heaven: *whom I detest b. heaven and your honour,* Meas. II, 1, 69. *plays such fantastic tricks b. heaven,* II, 2, 121. *I confess b. high heaven and you,* All's I, 3, 198.

Hence, *before God* = by God: *b. God! and in my mind, very wise,* Ado II, 3, 192 (Ff. *fore*). *b. God, Hal, if Percy be alive, thou get'st not my pistol,* H4A V, 3, 51. *b. God, I am exceeding weary,* H4B II, 2, 1. *b. God, Kate, I cannot look greenly,* H5 V, 2, 148. *b. the gods, I am ashamed on't,* Tim. III, 2, 19. 54. *b. my god, I might not this believe,* Hml. I, 1, 56. — And in consequence of this use, *before me* = by my soul: *b. me, she's a good wench,* Tw. II, 3, 194. *b. me! look where she comes,* Oth. IV, 1, 149 (cf. *afore* and *fore*).

Before = preferably to: *b. you I love your son,* All's I, 3, 149. *to wear our mortal state to come with her b. the primest creature,* H8 II, 4, 229. *whose false oaths prevailed b. my perfect honour,* Cymb. III, 3, 67. *loved b. me,* IV, 2, 29. — To go *b.* one = to be better than, to excel one: *if she went b. others I have seen,* Cymb. I, 4, 78. *if that thy gentry go b. that lout,* V, 2, 8 (cf. the quibble in Wiv. III, 2, 5). — Used after the verb *to prefer: this b. all the world do I prefer,* Tit. IV, 2, 109. *prefer a noble life b. a long,* Cor. III, 1, 153 (cf. *prefer*).

Placed after its substantive: *submissive fall his princely feet b.* LLL IV, 1, 92.

II. Adverb, 1) in a local sense, a) in front, on the fore part: *near-legged b.* Shr. III, 2, 57. *had he his hurts b.?* Mcb. V, 8, 46.

b) in advance: *go b.* Lucr. 1302. Gentl. II, 4, 186. Wiv. II, 2, 175. V, 4, 3. Err. I, 1, 96. Ado IV, 2, 68. Merch. I, 2, 146. II, 5, 40 etc. *I come b. to tell you,* Wiv. III, 3, 122. Merch. II, 9, 87. V, 117. *get thee b. to Coventry,* H4A IV, 2, 1. *haste b.,* John III, 3, 6. *I am sent with broom b.,* Mids. V, 396. *whose love to you, though words come hindmost, holds his rank b.* Sonn. 85, 12. *thou art so far b., that swiftest wing of recompense is slow to overtake thee,* Mcb. I, 4, 16. *I'll away b.* H6C II, 5, 136. *away b.* John V, 6, 43. *b., and greet his grace,* H4B IV, 1, 228. *b., and apace,*

Rom. II, 4, 232 (Qt and some M. Edd. *go b.*). *God before* = God being our leader: H5 I, 2, 307. III, 6, 165. *the better foot b.* = with the utmost speed: John IV, 2, 170. Tit. II, 3, 192.

2) in a temporal sense = a) in time preceding, previously: *that which every one had b. avouched,* Lucr. Arg. 9. *the night b.* Lucr. 15. *poorer than b.* 693. Sonn. 30, 12. 40, 2. 115, 1. 123, 8. Tp. I, 2, 219. II, 1, 74. 273. II, 2, 23. III, 2, 48. V, 194. Gentl. IV, 2, 55. IV, 4, 25. Wiv. III, 3, 9. IV, 5, 62. Meas. IV, 2, 121. Mids. II, 1, 167. H6A I, 2, 67. H6B II, 4, 72. Tim. III, 2, 52. Hml. II, 2, 75. Cymb. IV, 2, 191. V, 3, 47 etc. *the days b.* = former times, H4B IV, 1, 100. Sometimes = already before: *I had my load b., now pressed with hearing,* Ven. 430. *that is stronger made which was b. barred up with ribs of iron,* Ado IV, 1, 153. *we were Christians enow b.* Merch. III, 5, 24. *many likelihoods informed me of this b.* All's I, 3, 129. *you said so much b., and yet you fled,* H6C II, 2, 106. — *Once b.* = ere this: *once b. he won it of me,* Ado II, 1, 289.

b) in advance, beforehand: *weeping b. what she saw must come,* Err. I, 1, 72. *told our intents b.* LLL V, 2, 467. *he that made us with such large discourse, looking b. and after,* Hml. IV, 4, 37 (= forward and back; originally in a local sense, but figuratively applied to time; cf. *before, a joy proposed; behind, a dream,* Sonn. 129, 12.).

c) earlier: *when the butt is out, we will drink water, not a drop b.* Tp. III, 2, 2. *you might have come b.* Err. III, 1, 63.

III. Conjunction, 1) earlier than, ere: *the wind is hushed b. it raineth,* Ven. 458. *b. Noah was a sailor,* Tw. III, 2, 16. *b. we met or that a stroke was given,* H6A IV, 1, 22. Ven. 416. Sonn. 40, 4. 68, 3. Tp. I, 2, 39. IV, 15. 44. Meas. II, 1, 177. Err. I, 1, 64. II, 2, 67 etc. etc. *my absence was not six months old, b. herself had made provision for her following me,* Err. I, 1, 46. *I'll not be long b. I call upon thee,* Wint. III, 3, 8.

In speaking of future things, it is followed by the subjunctive mood: *end thy ill aim b. thy shoot be ended,* Lucr. 579. *let there be some more test made of my metal, b. so noble and so great a figure be stamped upon it,* Meas. I, 1, 50. *b. the time be out,* Tp. I, 2, 246. *kneel to the duke, b. he pass the abbey,* Err. V, 129. *I pardon thee thy life b. thou ask it,* Merch. IV, 1, 369. *I must away to-day, b. night come,* Shr. III, 2, 192. *assured loss b. the match be played,* John III, 1, 336. *wilt needs invest thee with mine honours, b. thy hour be ripe,* H4B IV, 5, 97. *which I could with a ready guess declare, b. the Frenchman speak a word of it,* H5 I, 1, 97. *how canst thou tell who will deny thy suit, b. thou make a trial of her love?* H6A V, 3, 76. *I must offend b. I be attainted,* H6B II, 4, 59. *we shall have more wars b. it be long,* H6C IV, 6, 91. *will you hence, b. the tag return?* Cor. III, 1, 248. cf. *b. the time that Romeo come,* Rom. IV, 3, 31.

Followed by *shall*: Tp. III, 1, 22. Merch. III, 2, 303. Ant. IV, 8, 3. Followed by *will*: John II, 345. H6A III, 2, 43. R3 III, 2, 44. Cor. V, 2, 7.

2) rather than: *he'ld yield them up, b. his sister should her body stoop to such abhorred pollution,* Meas. II, 4, 182. *treble that, b. a friend shall lose a hair,* Merch. III, 2, 303. *take my body, soul and all, b. that England give the French the foil,* H6A V, 3, 23. *France*

should have torn and rent my very heart, b. I would have yielded to this league, H6B I, 1, 127. *I'll have this crown of mine cut from my shoulders, b. I'll see the crown so foul misplaced,* R3 III, 2, 44 (Qq *ere I will see*).

Before that = before: *a little time b. that Edward sick'd and died,* H4B IV, 4, 127. *b. that England give the French the foil,* H6A V, 3, 23.

Before-breach, a breach committed in former times: *punished for b. of the king's laws,* H5 IV, 1, 179.

Beforehand, in anticipation: *I see what crosses my attempt will bring,... all this b. counsel comprehends,* Lucr. 494. *O let us pay the time but needful woe, since it hath been b. with our griefs,* John V, 7, 111, i. e. since the state of things has anticipated our griefs, has, forestalling them, engrossed all our care and attention. cf. *Forehand.*

Before-time, before this, formerly: *I have b. seen him thus,* Cor. I, 6, 24.

Befortune, to betide: *all good b. you,* Gentl. IV, 3, 41.

Befriend, to be kind to, to favour; in speaking of persons: *if thou please, thou mayst b. me so much as to think I come one way of the Plantagenets,* John V, 6, 10. cf. Tim. III, 2, 64. *God b. us, as our cause is just,* H4A V, 1, 120. *if in his death the Gods have us —ed, great Troy is ours,* Troil. V, 9, 9. *O happy man, they have —ed thee* (in banishing thee), Tit. III, 1, 52. *I shall beseech him to b. himself,* Caes. II, 4, 30. — In speaking of things, = to benefit, to be fortunate for: *that you were once unkind, —s me now,* Sonn. 120, 1. *my rest and negligence —s thee now,* Troil. V, 6, 17. *O earth, I will b. thee more with rain* (of tears) *than youthful April,* Tit. III, 1, 16.

Beg, 1) trans., to ask with humility, to seek by petition (the object never indicating the person applied to, but only the thing requested): *'tis but a kiss I b.* Ven. 96. *I'll b. her love,* Lucr. 241. Compl. 42. Gentl. V, 4, 24. Meas. II, 4, 69. V, 379. LLL V, 2, 207. Mids. I, 1, 41. II, 1, 120. 208. III, 2, 375. IV, 1, 63. 160. Merch. V, 164. 180. As III, 5, 6. John V, 7, 42. R2 I, 1, 140. IV, 302. V, 2, 113. H4A IV, 3, 62. H6A IV, 5, 32. H6B II, 4, 92. H6C III, 2, 63. R3 I, 2, 179. Troil. III, 2, 145. Caes. III, 1, 57. 261. Hml. IV, 7, 106. Ant. II, 1, 6 etc. to ask something in the quality of a mendicant: *beg my food,* As II, 3, 31. — *a race or two of ginger, but that I may b.* Wint. IV, 3, 51 (probably = that they may give me into the bargain). *you cannot b. us, sir, I can assure you,* LLL V, 2, 490 (i. e. cannot prove us to be idiots, and apply, as the writ *de idiota inquirendo* prescribed, to be our guardian). cf. *fool-begged.*

To beg sth. of one: that love I begged for you he —ed of me, Err. IV, 2, 12. *b. the alms of palsied eld,* Meas. III, 1, 35. Merch. IV, 1, 363. V, 221. H6C III, 2, 27. R3 II, 1, 39. Troil. IV, 5, 47. Cor. II, 3, 123. Rom. III, 3, 152. Hml. III, 4, 172. Lr. I, 4, 121. Per. II, 1, 142 etc. Similarly: *I begged the empire at thy hands,* Tit. I, 307.

2) intr., a) *to b. of one: bound to b. of my lord general,* Cor. I, 9, 80. *to b. of thee, it is my more dishonour than thou of them,* III, 2, 124. *I b. of you to know me,* Tim. IV, 3, 494. *he —ed of me to steal it,* Oth. V, 2, 229.

b) *to b. for sth.: —ed for that which thou unasked shalt have,* Ven. 102. *b. for grace in vain,* Tit. I, 455. V, 2, 180. *I b. for justice,* Rom. III, 1, 185. *would now be glad of bread, and b. for it,* Per. I, 4, 41.

c) *to b. of one for sth.: b. of her for remedy,* Mids. III, 2, 109.

d) followed by a clause: *b. that thou mayst have leave to hang thyself,* Merch. IV, 1, 364. *we b. that you do change this purpose,* Wint. II, 3, 149. *I b. that you'll vouchsafe ... Lr. II, 4, 157. I should have —ed I might have been employed,* H6A IV, 1, 72. Caes. II, 2, 82.

e) absolutely: *how I would make him fawn and b.* LLL V, 2, 62. *being so great, I have no need to b.* R2 IV, 309. *as you would b., were you in my distress,* R3 I, 4, 273. 274. *thou keepest the stroke between thy —ing and my meditation,* IV, 2, 118. *why, b. then,* Troil. IV, 5, 48. *he asks of you, that never used to b.* Per. II, 1, 66. = to gather alms: *b. thou or borrow,* Err. I, 1, 154. *I shall b. with it from door to door,* IV, 4, 40. As I, 1, 80. As Epil. 11. H4A V, 3, 39. H4B I, 2, 84. Rom. III, 5, 194. Lr. IV, 1, 33.

Beget. Impf. *begot:* Gentl. III, 1, 294. Meas. V, 517. As I, 1, 61. Tit. V, 1, 87. Partic. ordinarily *begot,* f. i. Ven. 168. Meas. III, 2, 116. LLL IV, 2, 70. V, 2, 869. Merch. III, 2, 65. As IV, 1, 216. V, 4, 177. John I, 75. 175 etc. sometimes *begotten:* All's III, 2, 61. Wint. III, 2, 135. H6A II, 5, 72. V, 4, 37 (cf. *misbegotten, true-begotten, first-begotten*).

1) to procreate; as a father: *thou wast begot,* Ven. 168. *who begot thee?* Gentl. III, 1, 294. *I did b. her,* H6A V, 4, 11. Meas. III, 2, 116. LLL IV, 2, 70. Merch. III, 2, 65. As I, 1, 61. Wint. III, 2, 135. John I, 75. 175. H4A II, 4, 250. H5 III, 1, 23. H6A V, 5, 74. R3 V, 3, 157. Tit. V, 1, 32. Lr. I, 1, 98. Cymb. V, 5, 331 etc. *the issue was not his begot,* R3 III, 5, 90. Followed by *of: my trust, like a good parent, did b. of him a falsehood,* Tp. I, 2, 94. *whose influence is begot of that loose grace,* LLL V, 2, 869. *that was begot of thought,* As IV, 1, 216. *a child begotten of thy body,* All's III, 2, 61. *no heir begotten of his body,* H6A II, 5, 72. *begotten of a shepherd swain,* V, 4, 37. *beget mine issue of your blood,* R3 IV, 4, 297. *begot of nothing but vain fantasy,* Rom. I, 4, 98. Followed by *on: I begot him on the empress,* Tit. V, 1, 87. *begot upon itself,* Oth. III, 4, 162. cf. *I will b. mine issue of your blood upon your daughter,* R3 IV, 4, 297.

2) to produce: *gold that's put to use more gold —s,* Ven. 768. *—s him hate,* Lucr. 1005. Gentl. III, 1, 97. LLL II, 69. As V, 4, 177. Shr. I, 1, 45 (*friends*). Wint. V, 1, 133. R2 II, 2, 36. V, 3, 56. H6A III, 3, 87. H6C II, 5, 63. 91. R3 IV, 3, 26. Lr. II, 1, 35.

3) to get: *whom he begot with child,* Meas. V, 517. *you must acquire and b. a temperance,* Hml. III, 2, 8.

Beggar, subst., 1) mendicant, masc. and fem.: Tp. II, 2, 34. Gentl. II, 1, 26. Meas. III, 2, 133. 194. Err. IV, 4, 39. Ado III, 4, 30. IV, 1, 134. LLL I, 2, 115. IV, 1, 67. Merch. IV, 1, 440. As III, 3, 85. As Epil. 10. All's V, 3, 335. R3 I, 4, 274. etc. etc. *some she beggar,* Tim. IV, 3, 273. *—s mounted run their horse to death,* H6C I, 4, 127. *a ballad of the king and the b.* LLL I, 2, 115. cf. IV, 1, 67 and R2 V, 3, 80 (v. *Cophetua*). Followed by *of: a b., brother? of my kind uncle,* R3 III, 1, 112.

2) a person extremely poor and mean: Lucr. 216. 711. 985. Sonn. 66, 2. Meas. IV, 3, 13. Merch. III, 1, 48. H6C II, 2, 154. R3 I, 2, 42 etc. etc.

Beggar, vb. 1) to reduce to beggary: *lean, rent and —ed by the strumpet wind,* Merch. II, 6, 19. *big Mars seems bankrupt in their —ed host,* H5 IV, 2, 43. *it* (conscience) *—s any man that keeps it,* R3 I, 4, 145. *bowed you to the grave and —ed yours for ever,* Mcb. III, 1, 91. Metaphorically: *b. the estimation which you prized richer than sea and land,* Troil. II, 2, 91. *it —ed all description,* Ant. II, 2, 203.

2) followed by *of,* = to deprive, to make destitute of: *now nature bankrupt is, —ed of blood,* Sonn. 67, 10. *necessity, of matter —ed, will nothing stick our person to arraign,* Hml. IV, 5, 92.

Beggar-fear, fear becoming a beggar: *with pale b. impeach my height,* R2 I, 1, 189.

Beggarly, adj. 1) becoming a beggar: *b. thanks,* As II, 5, 29. *a b. denier,* R3 I, 2, 252.

2) extremely poor and mean: Shr. IV, 1, 140. H4A IV, 2, 75. H5 IV, 8, 36. V, 1, 5. H8 II, 3, 83. Rom. V, 1, 45. Lr. II, 2, 16. Oth. IV, 2, 158.

Beggar-maid: Rom. II, 1, 14.

Beggar-man: Lr. IV, 1, 31.

Beggar-woman: H6B IV, 2, 151.

Beggary, state of extreme indigence: Meas. III, 2, 99. Mids. V, 53. John II, 596. H4B IV, 1, 35. H6B IV, 1, 101. IV, 2, 58 *(b. is valiant).* R3 IV, 3, 53. Rom. V, 1, 71. Ant. I, 1, 15. Cymb. I, 6, 115 *(the b. of his change,* = contemptible meanness). II, 3, 124. V, 5, 10.

Begin. Impf. *began,* f. i. Ven. 175. 367. Lucr. 1439. 1471. 1696. Pilgr. 144 etc. etc. *begun* only when required by the rhyme: Ven. 462. Lucr. 374. Compl. 12. 262. Tw. V, 414. R2 I, 1, 158. Rom. I, 2, 98. Hml. III, 2, 220 (in Caes. V, 1, 114: *that work the Ides of March begun, the Ides of March is* = on the Ides of March). — Partic. *begun:* Ven. 845. Lucr. 26. Tp. I, 2, 34. Meas. II, 4, 159 etc. etc. (in H5 V, 1, 75 O. Edd. *begun,* M. Edd. *begun*).

1) trans. to commence; followed by an accus.: *their copious stories oftentimes begun end without audience,* Ven. 845. Lucr. 26. *the strumpet that began this stir,* Lucr. 1471. 1612. Merch. III, 2, 71. As V, 3, 27. 4, 177. H5 III, 3, 7. John III, 1, 94. H6A III, 1, 75. Caes. V, 1, 114. Mcb. I, 2, 33. III, 2, 55. Oth. II, 3, 178. Ant. IV, 14, 106 etc. etc. *I will, out of thine own confession, learn to b. thy health,* Meas. I, 2, 39, i. e. drink to thee, but not after thee, in order not to be infected with thy disease. cf. Sonn. 114, 14 (*to begin to one,* or *to begin a health* = to drink to one). *he* (Caesar) *did b. that place,* R3 III, 1, 70, = laid its foundation, began its erection. Similarly: *would she b. a sect* (= found a sect) Wint. V, 1, 107. *you might b. an impudent nation* (= become the founder, the progenitor of ..) All's IV, 3, 363. *love is begun by time, and time qualifies the spark and fire of it,* Hml. IV, 7, 112. *an ancient tradition, begun upon an honourable occasion,* H5 V, 1, 75 (= caused, occasioned). *time had not scythed all that youth begun,* Compl. 12. *which, out of use and staled by other men, b. his fashion,* Caes. IV, 1, 39. Followed by an infinitive preceded by *to: to tie the rider she —s to prove,* Ven. 40. 175. 554. Lucr. 342. 374. 1439. 1639. 1696. Compl. 262. Pilgr. 144. Tp. I, 2, 34. II, 1, 29. IV, 219. V, 67. 80. Gentl. I, 1, 10. II, 4, 208. V, 1, 1 etc. etc.

2) absol.; a) opposed to end, = to make a commencement: *where she ends she doth anew b.* Ven. 60. *once more the engine of her thoughts began,* 367. 462. *twice she doth begin ere once she speaks,* Lucr. 567. 1303. 1598. *if it be poisoned, 'tis the lesser sin that mine eye loves it and doth first b.* Sonn. 114, 14 (cf. Meas. I, 2, 39). Tp. I, 2, 395. Gentl. II, 4, 32. V, 4, 113. Meas. II, 4, 159. Err. V, 356. LLL V, 1, 46. V, 2, 903. Mids. III, 1, 76. R2 I, 1, 158. H6A II, 2, 22. Troil. Prol. 28. Troil. IV, 5, 93. Rom. II, 4, 220. Hml. III, 2, 220.

b) to take rise: *then —s a journey in my head,* Sonn. 27, 3. *there are pretty orders —ing,* Meas. II, 1, 249. *how did this argument b.?* LLL III, 105. *and there —s my sadness,* As I, 1, 5. *and there —s new matter,* IV, 1, 81. *a great while ago the world begun,* Tw. V, 414. *the report of her is extended more than can be thought to b. from such a cottage,* Wint. IV, 2, 50. *let it rest where it began at first,* H6A IV, 1, 121. *there —s confusion,* 194. *then began the tempest,* R3 I, 4, 44. *since first the world begun,* Rom. I, 2, 98. *a curse b. at very root on's heart,* Cor. II, 1, 202. *as the world were now but to b.* Hml. IV, 5, 103. *when it appears to you where this —s,* Ant. III, 4, 33. *then began a stop,* Cymb. V, 3, 39.

Beginner, author: *where are the vile —s of this fray?* Rom. III, 1, 146. *a sin in war, damned in the first —s,* Cymb. V, 3, 37.

Beginning, subst., commencement: *sweet b., but unsavoury end,* Ven. 1138. *this pamphlet, without b.* Lucr. Dedic. 1. Tp. II, 1, 158. Wiv. I, 1, 254 *(in the b.).* Mids. V, 111. As I, 2, 119. John I, 5. H4A IV, 2, 85. H4B III, 1, 85. H5 IV, 1, 91. Cor. III, 1, 329. Tit. V, 3, 202. Caes. IV, 3, 234. Oth. II, 3, 185. Cymb. III, 4, 182.

2) enterprise: *to hinder our —s,* H5 II, 2, 187.

Begnaw, to gnaw, corrode: *begnawn with the bots,* Shr. III, 2, 55. *the worm of conscience still b. thy soul,* R3 I, 3, 222.

Begone (v. *Go*) away: As III, 3, 105. Ant. III, 13, 152. IV, 12, 17.

Begrime, to soil: *—d with sweat, and smeared all with dust,* Lucr. 1381. *her name is now —d and black as mine own face,* Oth. III, 3, 387.

Beguile, 1) to deceive, to cheat; absol.: *the better to b.* Hml. I, 3, 131. trans.: *the top o'erstrawed with sweets that shall the truest sight b.* Ven. 1144. *it —d attention, charmed the sight,* Lucr. 1404. *to mock the subtle, in themselves —d,* 957. *thou dost b. the world, unbless some mother,* Sonn. 3, 4. 59, 2. Compl. 170. Pilgr. 402. Gentl. V, 4, 64. Wiv. I, 3, 95. Meas. IV, 2, 164. Mids. I, 1, 239. II, 1, 45. Shr. Ind. 2, 57. Shr. I, 2, 138. III, 1, 37. All's IV, 3, 333. V, 3, 306. Tw. V, 142. 143. John III, 1, 99. R2 IV, 1, 281. H5 IV, 1, 171. H6A I, 2, 65. H6B III, 1, 226. Rom. III, 2, 132. IV, 5, 55. Tim. IV, 3, 331. Mcb. I, 5, 64. Lr. II, 2, 117. IV, 6, 63. V, 3, 154. Oth. IV, 1, 98. Ant. III, 7, 78. V, 2, 326.

Followed by *of,* = to cheat one of sth.: *—d him of a chain,* Wiv. IV, 5, 33. 38. *you owe me money, and now you pick a quarrel to b. me of it,* H4A III, 3, 77. *whoe'er he be that in this foul proceeding hath thus —d your daughter of herself and you of her,* Oth. I, 3, 66. Sometimes = to rob one of sth.: *light seeking light doth light of light b.* LLL I, 1, 77. *would b. Nature of her custom, so perfectly he is her ape,* Wint. V, 2, 107. *b. them of commendation,* H4A III, 1, 189. *where injury of chance rudely —s our lips of all rejoindure,* Troil. IV, 4, 37. *so let the Turk of Cyprus* *us b.* Oth. I, 3, 210. In a good sense, = to take or draw from one in a pleasing manner: *and often did b. her of her tears, when I did speak...,* Oth. I, 3, 156.

Followed by *to,* = to betray: *—d me to the very heart of loss,* Ant. IV, 12, 29.

2) to deceive pleasingly, to drive away by an agreeable delusion: *how shall we b. the lazy time?* Mids. V, 40. 374. *to b. two hours in a sleep,* All's IV, 1, 25. Tw. III, 3, 41. R2 II, 3, 11. Hml. III, 2, 236. *take choice of all my library, and so b. thy sorrow,* Tit. IV, 1, 35. *I am not merry, but I do b. the thing I am, by seeming otherwise,* Oth. II, 1, 123. *so —d with outward honesty, but yet defiled with inward vice,* Lucr. 1544, i. e. the thing he was being made away with, as it were, by the appearance of honesty. But may be the word must be taken here as an adjective, in the sense: armed with guile, able to deceive.

Behalf. 1) use, purpose: *in that b.* (viz to know his pleasure) *we single you as our solicitor,* LLL II, 27. *the sands that run in the clock's b.* Cymb. III, 2, 75, i. e. which, by their running, do the service of a clock.

2) affair, cause: *the sonnet you writ to Diana in b. of the count Rousillon* (viz to warn her from his practices), All's IV, 3, 355. *my meaning in it was very honest in the b. of the maid,* 247. *in right and true b. of thy deceased brother Geffrey's son,* John I, 7. *that men of your nobility and power did gage them both in an unjust b.* H4A I, 3, 173. *In b. of* = in the name of: *demanded my prisoners in your majesty's b.* H4A I, 3, 48. *in our king's b. I am commanded to kiss your hand,* H6C III, 3, 59. *in the duke's b. I'll give my voice,* R3 III, 4, 20. *which in my lord's b. I come to entreat your honour to supply,* Tim. III, 1, 17.

3) cause, interest: *cannot insinuate with you in the b. of a good play,* As Epil. 9. *to speak in the b. of my daughter,* All's IV, 5, 76. *a true gentleman may swear it in the b. of his friend,* Wint. V, 2, 176. *I have much to say in the b. of that Falstaff,* H4A II, 4, 532. *rob in the b. of charity,* Troil. V, 3, 22. *the emperor's coming in b. of France,* H5 V Chor. 38. *even in thy b. I'll thank myself,* H4A V, 4, 97. *bearing the king in my b. along,* H6C II, 1, 115. *you shall give me leave to play the broker in mine own b.* IV, 1, 63. *you in our b. go levy men,* 130. *shall your city call us lord, in that b. which we have challenged it?* John II, 264 (viz in the interest of Arthur).

Hence *in b. of* = in favour of: *let me have thy voice in my b.* Wiv. I, 4, 168. Mids. III, 2, 331. Merch. I, 3, 74. All's IV, 4, 28. John II, 8. H6A II, 4, 130. H6B III, 2, 208. IV, 1, 63. R3 IV, 1, 51 (only in Ff.). IV, 4, 357. V, 3, 122. Troil. III, 3, 16. Cor. IV, 2, 3. V, 2, 25. Rom. III, 1, 116. Tim. I, 2, 97 (*in your own b.*). Lr. IV, 2, 20 (*in your own b.*). Oth. III, 3, 2. *whisper him in your behalfs,* Wint. IV, 4, 827 (Autolycus' speech).

On b. of, in the same sense: *this shall on her b. change slander to remorse,* Ado IV, 1, 212. *to whet your gentle thoughts on his b.* Tw. III, 1, 117 (or is it, in these two passages, = concerning him?) *mustering in his clouds on our b. armies of pestilence,* R2 III, 3, 86. *to engross up glorious deeds on my b.* H4A III, 2, 148. *that you on my b. would pluck a flower,* H6A II, 4, 129. *I have moved my lord on his b.* Oth. III, 4, 19 (Qq *in*).

Behave, 1) reflectively, = to conduct one's self, with respect to external deportment: *thou —dst thyself as if thou hadst been in thine own slaughter-house,* H6B IV, 3, 5. — 2) intr., in the same sense: *how have I then —d, that he might...,* Oth. IV, 2, 108. — 3) the partic. *behaved* = having a behaviour: *and gather by him, as he is behaved, if it be the affliction of his love or no,* Hml. III, 1, 35.

In Tim. III, 5, 22 O. Edd. have: *with such sober and passion unnoted he did behoove his anger;* which has by M. Edd. been changed to *behave,* and interpreted in the sense of to govern, to manage.

Behaviour, external carriage and deportment, as it is expressive of sentiments and disposition: *her sad b. feeds his vulture folly,* Lucr. 556. *he lends thee virtue and he stole that word from thy b.* Sonn. 79, 10. *for thy face and thy b.* Gentl. IV, 4, 72. *the hardest voice of her b., to be Englished rightly, is "I am Sir John Falstaff's,"* Wiv. I, 3, 52. II, 1, 23. LLL V, 1, 13. *b., what wert thou till this madman showed thee?* V, 2, 337 (= good manners). Merch. I, 2, 81. II, 2, 196. *those that are good manners at the court are as ridiculous in the country as the b. of the country is most mockable at the court,* As III, 2, 48. Shr. Ind. 1, 95. Shr. I, 1, 71. I, 2, 169. II, 50. III, 2, 13. Tw. I, 2, 47. *practising b. to his own shadow,* Tw. II, 5, 20. III, 4, 203. H4A I, 2, 232. H8 IV, 2, 103. Cor. II, 3, 45. Hml. III, 2, 338. Ant. II, 6, 77. Remarkable passage: *thus, after greeting, speaks the king of France in my b. to the majesty, the borrowed majesty of England here,* John I, 3, i. e. in the tone and character which I here assume.

The plural *behaviours* = gestures, manners, external appearance: *I will teach the children their —s,* Wiv. IV, 4, 66. *a fool when he dedicates his —s to love,* Ado II, 3, 9. *whom she hath in all outward —s seemed ever to abhor,* II, 3, 100. *all his —s did make their retire to the court of his eye,* LLL II, 234. *thine eyes see it so grossly shown in thy —s,* All's I, 3, 184. *inferior eyes, that borrow their —s from the great,* John V, 1, 51. *which give some soil perhaps to my —s,* Caes. I, 2, 42. *poor Cassio's smiles, gestures and light —s,* Oth. IV, 1, 103 (Qq *behaviour*).

Sometimes coming near the sense of moral conduct: *what cause hath my b. given to your displeasure?* H8 II, 4, 20. *if you should lead her into a fool's paradise, as they say, it were a very gross kind of b., as they say,* Rom. II, 4, 177 (the nurse's speech). *to make inquire of his b.* Hml. II, 1, 5. *when we are sick in fortune, often the surfeit of our own b.* Lr. I, 2, 130.

Behead, to execute by cutting off the head: Meas. V, 462. Err. V, 127. H6A II, 5, 91. H6B IV, 7, 26. 102. R3 III, 2, 93. Tit. V, 3, 100.

Behest, commandment: *or kings be breakers of their own —s,* Lucr. 852. *opposition to you and your —s,* Rom. IV, 2, 19. *let us with care perform his great b.* Cymb. V, 4, 122.

Behind. I. Adverb, 1) on the back part, in the back: *the scalps of many, almost hid b.* Lucr. 1413. *himself, b., was left unseen,* 1425. *and break it in your face, so he break it* (his wind) *not b.* Err. III, 1, 76. *an two men ride of a horse, one must ride b.* Ado III, 5, 41. *a coward which hoxes honesty b.* Wint. I, 2, 244. *he, being in the vaward, placed b. on purpose,* H6A I, 1, 132. *come from b. I, 2, 66. lag b.* III, 3, 34. *Casca, like a cur, b. struck Caesar on *the neck*, Caes. V, 1, 43. *tripped me b.* Lr. II, 2, 126. *as we take hares, b.* Ant. IV, 7, 13. *look b.* = look back, Oth. II, 1, 158. Applied to time: *before, a joy proposed, b. a dream* (= when past) Sonn. 129, 12. *my grief lies onward, and my joy b.* 50, 14.

2) following another, preceded or outstripped by another: *I thy babe chase thee afar b.* Sonn. 143, 10. *so shall I no whit be b. in duty,* Shr. I, 2, 175.

3) remaining after the departure of another: *thou shalt live in this fair world b.* Hml. III, 2, 185. *to leave b.:* Lucr. 734. Sonn. 9, 6. Tp. III, 3, 41. IV, 156. Mids. III, 2, 319. R2 II, 3, 97. H6C II, 2, 49. R3 IV, 4, 496. *to stay b.:* John V, 7, 70. Ant. III, 7, 20.

4) not yet happened, or not yet produced to view, future: *there's more b. that is more gratulate,* Meas. V, 535. *where we'll show what's yet b.* 545. *two lads that thought there was no more b. but such a day to-morrow as to day,* Wint. I, 2, 63. *Glamis, and thane of Cawdor; the greatest is b.* Mcb. I, 3, 117. *bad begins and worse remains b.* Hml. III, 4, 179.

II. Preposition, 1) on the back part, at the back of: *the lion walked along b. some hedge,* Ven. 1094. *b. the arras,* Wiv. III, 3, 97. *they threw me off from b. one of them,* IV, 5, 69. Err. IV, 3, 19. V, 122. Ado I, 3, 63. Mids. IV, 1, 53. V, 397. Merch. II, 8, 47. As II, 1, 30. H4A III, 3, 112. H4B V, 5, 10. R3 I, 4, 275. *to come b. folks,* H6B IV, 7, 89 (= to attack them from behind). *no glory lives b. the back of such,* Ado III, 1, 110 (i. e. they are ill spoken of in their absence). *it will be of more price, being spoke b. your back, than to your face,* Rom. IV, 1, 28.

2) left at a distance, coming after: *she will outstrip all praise and make it halt b. her,* Tp. IV, 11. Gentl. II, 4, 71. Merch. III, 2, 130. *or come one minute b. your hour,* As IV, 1, 195. *a month b. the gest prefixed for his parting,* Wint. I, 2, 41.

3) remaining after the departure of: *and left b. him Richard,* H6B II, 2, 19. *and leave me here in wretchedness b. ye,* H8 IV, 2, 84. *she would have died to stay b. her* (= not to accompany her) As I, 1, 115. Troil. I, 1, 83. *I'll lean upon one crutch and fight with t'other, ere stay b. this business,* Cor. I, 1, 247.

Behind-door-work, what is made behind the door: Wint. III, 3, 76.

Behindhand, being in arrear: *these thy offices are as interpreters of my b. slackness,* Wint. V, 1, 151.

Behold, impf. and partic. *beheld;* 1) trans. a) to see: *b. two Adons dead!* Ven. 1070. *when he beheld his shadow,* 1099. 1129. Lucr. 416. 447. 451. 746. 800. 1115. Sonn. 106, 13. Tp. I, 2, 491. V, 18. 106. 236. Gentl. II, 4, 209. V, 4, 101. Wiv. IV, 2, 125. Meas. I, 2, 45. Err. IV, 4, 108. V, 330. LLL I, 1, 247. IV, 3, 36. Mids. I, 1, 209. Merch. II, 7, 68. H5 IV Chor. 42. 46. H6A II, 2, 10. 42. R3 II, 4, 56. Cor. III, 1, 21. Ant. III, 3, 8, etc. etc. *beheld the king my father wrecked,* Tp. I, 2, 435. *to b. desert a beggar born,* Sonn. 66, 2. *I might b. addrest the king and his companions,* LLL V, 2, 92. —*s her bleed,* Lucr. 1732. *can the son's eye b. his father bleed?* Tit. V, 3, 65. *To b. and to see* joined: *you saw the mistress, I beheld the maid,* Merch. III, 2, 200. *prithee, see there! behold, look, lo!* Mcb. III, 4, 69. *b. and see,* Ant. I, 1, 13.

b) to regard, to look on: *who* (viz the sun) *doth the world so gloriously b. that cedar-tops and hills seem burnished gold,* Ven. 857. *that eye which looks on her confounds his wits; that eye which him —s ...* Lucr. 291. *will you go with us to b. it* (= to be spectators of it) Wiv. II, 1, 214. cf. Err. V, 128. Meas. I, 3, 43. Mids. I, 1, 10. H6A I, 4, 96. Troil. III, 3, 91. IV, 5, 236. V, 2, 69. Oth. V, 1, 108. *all his virtues, not virtuously of his own part beheld, do in our eyes begin to lose their gloss,* Troil. II, 3, 127, i. e. his virtues, not regarded by himself as it becomes a virtuous man, but with pride and arrogance.

2) absol. to see: *what dost thou to mine eyes, that they b., and see not what they see?* Sonn. 137, 2. *come down, b. no more,* Caes. V, 3, 33. *I can b. no longer,* Ant. III, 10, 1. *a mother should not sell him an hour from her —ing,* Cor. I, 3, 10 (= from her sight). Very remarkable, though unnoticed by the commentators, is the following passage: *I am wild in my beholding* = I look wild, Per. V, 1, 224. cf. Lucr. 1590.

Beholden, v. *Beholding.*

Beholder, spectator, witness: As I, 2, 139. Wint. V, 2, 18. H6A I, 4, 46. R3 IV, 4, 68. Troil. Prol. 26. = he who looks on sth.: *was this the face that like the sun did make —s wink?* R2 IV, 284.

Beholding (most M. Edd. *beholden*) obliged: *she is b. to you,* Gentl. IV, 4, 178. *a justice of peace sometimes may be b. to his friend for a man,* Wiv. I, 1, 283. Meas. IV, 3, 166. Merch. I, 3, 106. As IV, 1, 60. Shr. I, 2, 274. II, 78. John I, 239. R2 IV, 160. H4A II, 1, 98. R3 II, 1, 129. III, 1, 107. H8 I, 4, 41. IV, 1, 21. V, 3, 157. V, 5, 71. Tit. I, 396. V, 3, 33. Caes. III, 2, 70. 72. Per. II, 5, 25.

Behoof, advantage, benefit: *to be forbod the sweets that seem so good, for fear of harms that preach in our b.* Compl. 165. *this tongue hath parleyed unto foreign kings for your b.* H6B IV, 7, 83.

Behoof-ful, v. *behooveful.*

Behoove or **Behove,** subst. = behoof, in an old song, Hml. V, 1, 71.

Behoove or **Behove,** vb., 1) to be advantageous to: *if you know aught which does b. my knowledge thereof to be informed,* Wint. I, 2, 395. *there are cozeners abroad; therefore it —s men to be wary,* IV, 4, 257. — 2) to become: *while these do labour for their own preferment, —s it us to labour for the realm,* H6B I, 1, 182. *you do not understand yourself so clearly as it —s my daughter and your honour,* Hml. I, 3, 97. *which —s me keep at utterance,* Cymb. III, 1, 73. In Tim. III, 5, 22: *with such sober and unnoted passion he did b. his anger, ere 'twas spent, as if he had but proved an argument,* M. Edd. have changed the word to *behave,* but cf. *to become* Lr. IV, 3, 26 and Ant. I, 3, 84.

Behooveful or **Behoveful** (Qq *behoofeful*) fitting, becoming: Rom. IV, 3, 8.

Behowl, to howl at: *the wolf —s the moon,* Mids. V, 379 (O. Edd. *beholds*).

Being, subst. v. *Be.*

Bel, the God of the Chaldaeans: *like god —'s priests in the old church-window,* Ado III, 3, 144.

Belarius, name in Cymb. III, 3, 106. V, 5, 317. 333. 455.

Belch, name in Tw. I, 3, 47.

Belch, vb., 1) absol. to vomit: *the —ing whale,* Troil. V, 5, 23. Per. III, 1, 63. *'tis a good constraint* *of fortune it* (the sea) *—es upon us,* Per. III, 2, 55. *thy food is such as hath been —ed on by infected lungs,* IV, 6, 179.

2) trans. to vomit forth: *my panting bulk which almost burst to b. it in the sea,* R3 I, 4, 41. *when they are full, they b. us,* Oth. III, 4, 106. *the bitterness of it I now b. from my heart,* Cymb. III, 5, 137. *— to belch up,* in the same sense: Tp. III, 3, 56.

Beldam or **Beldame,** 1) grandmother: *to show the b. daughters of her daughter,* Lucr. 953. *shapes her sorrow to the —'s* (Hecuba's) *woes,* 1458. *the old b. earth,* H4A III, 1, 32.

2) term of contempt for an old woman: *old men and —s in the streets do prophesy upon it,* John IV, 2, 185. *b., I think we watched you at an inch,* H6B I, 4, 45. *—s as you are,* Mcb. III, 5, 2.

Belee, to place on the lee, or in a position unfavorable to the wind: *—d and calmed by debitor and creditor,* Oth. I, 1, 30.

Belfry, that part of the steeple where the bell is hung: Per. II, 1, 41.

Belgia, Belgium: Err. III, 2, 142. H6C IV, 8, 1.

Belie, to tell lies about, to misrepresent: *I think my love as rare as any she —d with false compare,* Sonn. 130, 14. *that I may not be so, nor thou —d,* 140, 13. *my cousin is —d,* Ado IV, 1, 148. V, 1, 42. 67. 222. 274. All's IV, 3, 299. Tw. I, 4, 30. John III, 4, 44. R2 II, 2, 77. H4A I, 3, 113. H4B I, 1, 98. Oth. IV, 1, 36. V, 2, 133. Cymb. III, 4, 38. V, 2, 2.

Belied, adj., full of lies: *she concludes the picture was b.* Lucr. 1533.

Belief, 1) credit given: Wiv. V, 5, 132. As V, 2, 63. John III, 1, 31. Mcb. I, 3, 74. IV, 3, 184. Hml. I, 1, 24. Ant. III, 7, 76. Per. IV, 4, 23. *to be in the b.* Tw. III, 4, 149. *b. of it,* Oth. I, 1, 144. *his b. in her renown,* Cymb. V, 5, 202.

2) opinion: *holds b. that, being brought into the open air, it would allay ....,* John V, 7, 6. *she's in a wrong b.* H6A II, 3, 31. *if this but answer to my just b.* Per. V, 1, 239.

Believe, 1) absol. to have faith: *how strange it seems, not to b., and yet too credulous,* Ven. 986. *—ing souls,* H6B II, 1, 66. *give their money out of hope they may b.* H8 Prol. 8. *so I b.* (= I b. it), Gentl. III, 2, 16. cf. Meas. IV, 1, 12. Followed by *in: his blessings and his curses touch me alike, they're breath I not b. in,* H8 II, 2, 54.

2) trans., a) to give credit to; the object either denoting the person or thing on whose authority one relies, or the thing taken to be true: *α) I do well b. your highness,* Tp. II, 1, 172. *would they b. me?* III, 3, 28. Sonn. 17, 1. 138, 2. Compl. 262. Wiv. II, 1, 148. Meas. I, 2, 19. II, 4, 172. IV, 1, 12. Err. V, 306. Mids. III, 2, 347. H6B IV, 8, 22 etc. etc. *he —s himself,* Tw. III, 4, 408 (thinks to be true what he says). *To be —d:* Sonn. 140, 12. Meas. II, 4, 149. V, 31. R3 IV, 4, 372. Mcb. V, 8, 19. *Believe me,* sometimes = truly, indeed: *b. me, it carries a brave form,* Tp. I, 2, 410. *do you not perceive the jest? No, b. me,* Gentl. II, 1, 161. Shr. III, 2, 116. Tw. I, 4, 8. Wint. IV, 4, 203. H6C IV, 5, 22. H8 IV, 1, 37.

β) I'll b. both, Tp. III, 3, 24. *I do b. it,* IV, 11. *will not let you b. things certain,* V, 125. Wiv. II, 1,

129. Meas. II, 2, 58. II, 4, 55. III, 2, 162. Ado III, 1, 116. Mids. V, 2. R3 I, 3, 25. Tit. V, 1, 71. *Bevis was —d,* H8 I, 1, 38. *b. so much in him that he is young,* Hml. I, 3, 124 etc. etc. *b. this of me,* All's II, 5, 47. = to b. in sth.: *thou —st no god,* Tit. V, 1, 71. *let pity not be —d,* Lr. IV, 3, 31. Followed by a clause: *now I shall b. that there are unicorns,* Tp. III, 3, 21. 44. Mids. III, 2, 52. Err. III, 2, 21. As V, 2, 64. R3 III, 5, 35 etc. *do not b. but I shall do thee mischief,* = b. that I shall do etc., Mids. II, 1, 236. *I'll not b. but they ascend the sky,* R3 I, 3, 287. *could not b. but that I was in hell,* I, 4, 62.

b) to think, to be of opinion: *the silly boy, believing she is dead, claps her pale cheek,* Ven. 467. *never b. that it could so preposterously be stained,* Sonn. 109, 9. *he did b. he was indeed the duke,* Tp. I, 2, 102. *b. not that the dribbling dart of love can pierce a complete bosom,* Meas. I, 3, 2. I, 4, 39. II, 1, 9. III, 2, 27. 139. LLL I, 1, 160. Mids. III, 1, 15. As II, 2, 15. Tw. I, 3, 91. R3 III, 2, 39. Caes. I, 3, 31. Oth. III, 3, 40 etc. *I do make myself b. that you may do ...,* Meas. III, 1, 205.

Belike, as it seems, it should seem, I suppose: *b. it hath some burden then,* Gentl. I, 2, 85. *b. then you are in love,* II, 1, 85. *she is dead b.?* IV, 4, 80. *b. she thinks that Proteus hath forsook her,* IV, 4, 151. Wiv. III, 1, 53. Meas. IV, 2, 118. V, 126. 131. Err. IV, 1, 25. IV, 3, 91. LLL II, 52. IV, 1, 137. Mids. I, 1, 130. Shr. Ind. 1, 75. Shr. I, 1, 104. II, 16. IV, 3, 103. All's IV, 5, 106. Tw. III, 3, 29. III, 4, 268. R2 III, 3, 30. H4B II, 2, 11. H5 III, 7, 55. H6A III, 2, 62. H6B III, 2, 186. H6C I, 1, 51. II, 1, 148. IV, 1, 96. 106. 118. IV, 3, 7. V, 1, 14. R3 I, 1, 49. I, 3, 65. Tit. IV, 2, 50. Caes. III, 2, 275. Hml. III, 2, 149. 305. Lr. IV, 5, 20. Oth. V, 2, 317. Ant. I, 2, 35. IV, 3, 5.

Followed by *that: b. that now she hath enfranchised them,* Gentl. II, 4, 90.

Bell, a hollow body of metal for making sounds; used on the steeples of churches for different kinds of service: *bells set on ringing,* Lucr. 1493. Err. IV, 2, 53. Ado V, 2, 81. John II, 312. H6A I, 6, 11. H6C V, 1, 3. Tit. V, 3, 197. *the clock hath strucken twelve upon the b.* Err. I, 2, 45. *the Windsor b. hath struck twelve,* Wiv. V, 5, 1. *the b. then beating one,* Hml. I, 1, 38. *till the b. have told eleven,* Oth. II, 2, 11. *the midnight b.* John III, 3, 37. Ant. III, 13, 185. *awake the citizens with the b.* Oth. I, 1, 90. *where —s have knolled to church,* As II, 7, 114. 121. *the sacring b.* H8 III, 2, 295. *the —s of Saint Bennet,* Tw. V, 42. *b. and burial,* Hml. V, 1, 257. *a heavy-hanging b.* Lucr. 1493. *the surly sullen b.* Sonn. 71, 2. H4B I, 1, 102. Rom. IV, 5, 86. *curfew b.* Rom. IV, 4, 4. *funeral b.* H6C II, 5, 117. Rom. V, 3, 206. *a warning b.* H6A IV, 2, 39. *the alarum b.* Mcb. II, 3, 79. H4B III, 1, 17. See besides R2 V, 5, 57. H4B IV, 2, 5. Per. II, 1, 38. 45. *b., book and candle shall not drive me back,* John III, 3, 12 ("in the solemn form of excommunication the bell was tolled, the book of offices for the purpose used, and three candles extinguished with certain ceremonies." Nares). Used in houses: Mcb. II, 1, 32. 62. II, 3, 79. 85. Oth. II, 3, 175. The chiming of —s a delightful music: *matched in mouth like —s,* Mids. IV, 1, 128. *you are —s in your parlours,* Oth. II, 1, 111. *like sweet —s jangled,* Hml. III, 1, 166. — *Ding dong bell* the burden of a song: Tp. I, 2, 404. Merch. III, 2, 71. *he hath a heart as sound as a b.* Ado III, 2, 13 (in allusion to the proverb: *as the fool thinketh, the bell clinketh*). Put on the necks of some animals: *falcon's —s,* Lucr. 511. As III, 3, 81. H6C I, 1, 47. *my wether's b.* Pilgr. 272. Worn by Morisco dancers, H6B III, 1, 366.

2) the cup of a flower: *a cowslip's b.* Tp. V, 89.

Bellario, name in Merch. III, 4, 50. IV, 1, 105. 119. 143. 167. V, 268.

Bell-man, a kind of watchman, part of whose office was to bless the sleepers: *the owl, the fatal b., which gives the sternest good-night,* Mcb. II, 2, 3.

Bellona, the Goddess of war: Mcb. I, 2, 54. not named, but alluded to in H4A IV, 1, 114.

Bellow, vb., to roar; used of bulls: Merch. V, 73. Wint. IV, 4, 28. of bulls and lions: Tp. II, 1, 311. of men: Hml. III, 2, 36. Lr. V, 3, 212 (*—ed out*). *the croaking raven doth b. for revenge,* Hml. III, 2, 265.

Bellows, instrument used to blow the fire: Ant. I, 1, 9. Per. I, 2, 39.

Bellows-mender: Mids. I, 2, 44. IV, 1, 207.

Bell-wether, a wether which leads the flock, with a bell on his neck: *a jealous rotten b.* Wiv. III, 5, 111. *to be bawd to a b.* As III, 2, 85.

Belly, the part of the body from the breast to the thighs: Ven. 594. Wiv. I, 3, 69. II, 1, 66. III, 5, 23. 37. V, 5, 149. Meas. IV, 3, 160. LLL V, 2, 683. 698. Merch. III, 5, 42. As II, 7, 154. III, 2, 215. Shr. IV, 1, 8. Wint. I, 2, 204. H4A II, 4, 499. III, 3, 57. IV, 2, 23. H4B I, 2, 165. IV, 3, 23. H6C II, 3, 20. Cor. I, 1, 100. Tim. I, 1, 210. Lr. III, 6, 33 etc. etc.

Belly, vb., to make like a round belly, to swell: *your breath of full consent —ied his sails,* Troil. II, 2, 74. cf. *Big-bellied, Great-bellied.*

Belly-doublet, the doublet covering the belly; jestingly used for the belly itself: *with your arms crossed on your thin b.* LLL III, 1, 19 (O. Edd. *thinbellies doublet* and *thinbellie doublet*). *turned away the fat knight with the great b.* H5 IV, 7, 51.

Bellyful, as much as satisfies the appetite: *rumble thy b.* Lr. III, 2, 14. *hath his b. of fighting,* Cymb. II, 1, 23.

Belly-pinched, pinched with hunger, starved: *the b. wolf,* Lr. III, 1, 13.

Belman, name of a dog: Shr. Ind. I, 22.

Belmont, name of the country-seat of Portia in Merch. I, 1, 161. 171. II, 2, 188. IV, 1, 457. V, 17.

Belock, to enclose: *this is the hand which, with a vowed contract, was fast —ed in thine,* Meas. V, 210 (cf. *Lock*).

Belong, 1) to be the property of: *to thee I so b.* Sonn. 88, 13. *a better state to me —s than that which on thy humour doth depend,* 92, 7. *the broken bosoms that to me b.* Compl. 254. LLL II, 224. V, 2, 381. Tw. V, 9. R2 III, 4, 93. H4B IV, 5, 233. H4A V, 5, 26. H6A III, 1, 165. H6B III, 2, 140. H8 I, 1, 39. Rom. III, 2, 103. Tim. I, 2, 95. Ant. I, 3, 78.

2) to be the quality or business of: *to hear with eyes —s to love's fine wit,* Sonn. 23, 14. *to you it doth b. yourself to pardon,* 58, 11. *we know what —s to a watch,* Ado III, 3, 40. *there is no need of any such redress, or if there were, it not —s to you,* H4B IV, 1, 98. *and know the office that —s to such,* H6A III, 1, 55.

3) to be due: *to things of sale a seller's praise —s,* LLL IV, 3, 240. *thy beauty sounded, yet not so deeply as to thee —s,* Shr. II, 194. *all appertinents —ing to his honour,* H5 II, 2, 88. *disdaining duty that to us —s,* H6B III, 1, 17. *here is more —s to her,* Tit. II, 3, 122. *the duty which to a mother's part —s,* Cor. V, 3, 168. *no blame —s to thee,* Tim. II, 2, 231. *knows what —s to reason,* III, 1, 38. *a solemn earnestness, more than indeed —ed to such a trifle,* Oth. V, 2, 228.

4) to make part of: *we know what —s to a frippery,* Tp. IV, 224. *all things that b. to house and house-keeping,* Shr. II, 357. *this thorn doth to our rose of youth rightly b.* All's I, 3, 136. *I b. to the larder,* H8 V, 4, 4. *my noble steed with all his trim —ing,* Cor. I, 9, 62. *any other part —ing to a man,* Rom. II, 2, 42.

5) to be appendant to, connected with: *such danger to resistance did b.* Lucr. 1265. *here it is, and all that —s to it,* All's II, 2, 38. *I am proof against that title and what shame else —s to it,* Wint. IV, 4, 873. *an if there be no great offence —s to it, give your friend some touch of your late business,* H8 V, 1, 12. *and showed what necessity —ed to it,* Tim. III, 2, 15. *wilt thou hear more? all that —s to this,* Cymb. V, 5, 147.

Belonging, subst., that which belongs to one: *thyself and thy —s are not thine own so proper as to waste thyself upon thy virtues,* Meas. I, 1, 30, i. e. whatever is in thee, thy endowments: Cor. I, 9, 62?

Beloved, loved: *her b. Collatinus,* Lucr. 256. *happy I that love and am b.* Sonn. 25, 13. 89, 10. *my b.* 105, 2. Gentl. I, 3, 57. V, 4, 44. 45. Err. V, 6. Merch. III, 2, 181. As IV, 1, 82. Shr. I, 2, 3. V, 1, 26. Tw. II, 4, 20. II, 5, 101 (*the unknown b.*). Wint. IV, 4, 503 (*this my fair b.*). H4A I, 3, 267. H6B II, 3, 26. H6C III, 2, 163. IV, 8, 17. V, 1, 103. H8 II, 1, 92. Troil. I, 2, 314 (*that she b.*). IV, 5, 292. Cor. III, 1, 315. V, 2, 99 (*this man was my b.* = my friend). Tit. IV, 2, 47. Rom. II Chor. 5. 12. Tim. I, 1, 85 (*her late b.*). I, 2, 136. III, 6, 85. Hml. III, 2, 186. Lr. I, 1, 140. I, 2, 57 (*the b. of your brother*). II, 4, 135. IV, 3, 25. V, 3, 239. Oth. I, 2, 12. Ant. I, 1, 16. I, 2, 22. Cymb. IV, 2, 384. Per. V, 1, 30.

Followed by *of* (never *by*): *thou art b. of many,* Sonn. 10, 3. 150, 14. Mids. I, 1, 104. As I, 1, 116. 174. Shr. I, 2, 176. Wint. III, 2, 4. H6B I, 2, 44. Cor. III, 2, 133. Caes. II, 1, 156. Ant. I, 4, 37.

Beloving, loving: *you shall be more b. than beloved,* Ant. I, 2, 22.

Below, adv., in a lower place, relatively to something higher: *clapping their proud tails to the ground b.* Ven. 923. *coucheth the fowl b. with his wings' shade,* Lucr. 507. *keep b.* (in the cabin) Tp. I, 1, 12. *night kept chained b.* (in hell) IV, 31. *there's one master Brook b.* (downstairs) Wiv. II, 2, 151. H4B II, 4, 74. H6B I, 4, 11. R3 IV, 4, 86. 301. Troil. I, 3, 4. 130. Tit. II, 3, 244. IV, 3, 43. V, 2, 3. Rom. III, 5, 55 (reading of the spurious Q1 and M. Edd. The other O. Edd. *so low*). Tim. I, 1, 74. IV, 3, 17. Caes. V, 1, 108. Hml. II, 2, 507. III, 3, 97. Lr. II, 4, 58. IV, 6, 69. Ant. IV, 15, 13.

Below, prepos., beneath, lower than: *his thinkings are b. the moon,* H8 III, 2, 134. *b. thy sister's orb* (the moon), Tim. IV, 3, 2. *all the abhorred births b. crisp heaven,* 183. *b. the beam of sight,* Cor. III, 2, 5. *fell b. his stem,* II, 2, 111. *b. their cobbled* shoes, I, 1, 200. *to the dust b. thy foot,* Lr. V, 3, 137. *place your hands b. your husband's foot,* Shr. V, 2, 177. *pluck stout men's pillows from b. their heads,* Tim. IV, 3, 32. *buckled b. fair knighthood's bending knee,* Wiv. V, 5, 76. *one yard b. their mines,* Hml. III, 4, 208. *zephyrs blowing b. the violet,* Cymb. IV, 2, 172. *shall I always keep b. stairs,* Ado V, 2, 10. *a league b. the city,* Meas. IV, 3, 103. *a place b. the first,* Cor. I, 1, 270. *who were b. him,* All's I, 2, 41. *from b. the duke to beneath your constable,* II, 2, 32.

Belt, cincture, girdle: Pilgr. 365. H4B I, 2, 158. Mcb. V, 2, 16.

Belzebub, the prince of devils: Tw. V, 291. H5 IV, 7, 145. Mcb. II, 3, 4.

Bemad, to madden: *—ing sorrow,* Lr. III, 1, 38.

Bemeet, to meet: *our very loving sister, well bemet!* Lr. V, 1, 20.

Bemete, to measure: *I shall so b. thee with thy yard,* Shr. IV, 3, 113.

Bemoan, to bewail: *was ever father so —ed his son?* H6C II, 5, 110 (cf. *Fore-bemoaned*).

Bemock, to treat with mockery: *b. the modest moon,* Cor. I, 1, 261.

Followed by *at: wound the loud winds, or with bemocked at stabs kill the still-closing waters,* Tp. III, 3, 63.

Bemoil, to bemire, to bedraggle: *in how miry a place, how she was —ed,* Shr. IV, 1, 77.

Bemonster, to make like a monster: *b. not thy feature,* Lr. IV, 2, 63.

Bench, subst. 1) a long seat: Tw. I, 5, 158. H4A I, 2, 4. Rom. II, 4, 37. Caes. III, 2, 263.

2) the seat of judges, of senators: *to pluck down justice from your awful b.* H4B V, 2, 86. *pluck the grave wrinkled senate from the b.* Tim. IV, 1, 5. *senators on the b.* IV, 3, 37.

3) the senate itself: *a graver b. than ever frowned in Greece,* Cor. III, 1, 106. *their obedience fails to the greater b.* 167.

Bench, vb., 1) intr., to sit on a seat of justice, to be judge: *b. by his side,* Lr. III, 6, 40. — 2) trans. to seat on a bench, to raise to authority: *whom I from meaner form have —ed and reared to worship,* Wint. I, 2, 314.

Bencher, member of a court or council, senator: *a perfecter giber for the table than a necessary b. in the Capitol,* Cor. II, 1, 92.

Bench-hole, the hole of a privy: *we'll beat 'em into —s,* Ant. IV, 7, 9.

Bend, subst., look: *that same eye whose b. doth awe the world,* Caes. I, 2, 123. *tended her i' the eyes and made their —s* (viz the bends of their eyes) *adornings,* Ant. II, 2, 213 (cf. *adorning*). v. *Bent.*

Bend, vb., impf. *bended:* Cor. II, 1, 281 and Hml. II, 1, 100; *bent:* H6C V, 2, 22 and Per. II, 5, 48. Partic. *bended:* Gentl. III, 1, 229. R2 V, 3, 98. H5 V Chor. 18. H6B I, 1, 10. Ant. II, 5, 12. *bent:* Ven. 618. Sonn. 90, 2. 143, 6. Pilgr. 68. 311. 417. John II, 37. H4B II, 4, 55. Lr. I, 1, 145 etc. etc.

I. trans. 1) to crook, to inflect: *he —s her fingers,* Ven. 476. *my —ed hook,* Ant. II, 5, 12. *his bruised helmet and his —ed sword,* H5 V Chor. 18 (i.e. bent out of shape). cf. *to come off the breach with his pike bent bravely,* H4B II, 4, 55. Hence *to b. the bow* = to make the bow ready for shooting: Lucr. 580. R2 III, 2, 116. Lr. I, 1, 145.

2) used of other instruments of war, = to direct, to turn, to point: *our cannon shall be bent against the brows of this resisting town,* John II, 37. *to b. the fatal instruments of war against his brother,* H6C V, 1, 87. *the which* (falchion) *thou once didst b. against her breast,* R3 I, 2, 95. *—ing his sword to his great master* (= against his master) Lr. IV, 2, 74. cf. *than midday sun fierce bent against their faces,* H6A I, 1, 14. *the revenging gods 'gainst parricides did all their thunders,* Lr. II, 1, 48. Metaphorically: *b. not all the harm upon yourself,* Ado V, 1, 39. *my revenges were high bent upon him,* All's V, 3, 10. *b. your sharpest deeds of malice on this town,* John II, 379. *——ing all my loving thoughts on thee,* Sonn. 88, 10. *we b. to that the working of the heart,* LLL IV, 1, 33. *b. thoughts and wits to achieve her,* Shr. I, 1, 148. *for the which myself and them b. their best studies,* John IV, 2, 51. *bent all offices to honour her,* Per. II, 5, 48. — *homeward did they b. their course,* Err. I, 1, 118. *towards Coventry b. we our course,* H6C IV, 8, 58. R3 IV, 5, 14 (Ff *power* instead of *course*). *these three lead on this preparation whither 'tis bent,* Cor. I, 2, 16. *—ing their expedition toward Philippi,* Caes. IV, 3, 170. — *I do b. my speech to one,* Meas. I, 1, 41. *to our own selves b. we our needful talk,* Troil. IV, 4, 141. *my sanctity will to my sense b. no licentious ear,* Per. V, 3, 30. — Chiefly used of the eyes: *the eyes of men are idly bent on him,* R2 V, 2, 25. *why dost thou b. thine eyes upon the earth?* H4A III, 3, 45. *no gaze such as is bent on sun-like majesty,* III, 2, 79. *why such unplausive eyes are bent on him,* Troil. III, 3, 43. *—ed their light on me,* Hml. II, 1, 100. *b. your eye on vacancy,* III, 4, 117. *now b., now turn the office and devotion of their view upon a tawny front,* Ant. I, 1, 4. — Similarly of the brows (= to knit): *why do you b. such solemn brows on me?* John IV, 2, 90. *or b. one wrinkle on my sovereign's face,* R2 II, 1, 170. *how the ugly wench doth b. her brows,* H6A V, 3, 34. *bent his brow,* H6C V, 2, 22. *though her frowning brows be bent,* Pilgr. 311.

The partic. *bent* = inclined, prone, intent: *like to a mortal butcher bent to kill,* Ven. 618. *the world is bent my deeds to cross,* Sonn. 90, 2. *bent to follow that which flies,* 143, 6. *you all are bent to set against me,* Mids. III, 2, 145. *bent to hear,* John II, 422. *bent to dim his glory,* R2 III, 3, 65. *bent to know the worst,* Mcb. III, 4, 134. *my best spirits are bent to prove upon thy heart . . . . ,* Lr. V, 3, 139. — *not to anger bent,* Pilgr. 68. *if to women he be bent,* 417. *all his mind is bent to holiness,* H6B I, 3, 58. *bent to meditation,* R3 III, 7, 62. *bent to the spoil,* Tit. IV, 4, 64. *their mind is bent against Caesar,* Caes. II, 3, 6. *and madly bent on us, chased us away,* Err. V, 152. *every thing is bent for England,* Hml. IV, 3, 47. *a sort of naughty persons, lewdly bent,* H6B II, 1, 167. *how Thaliard came full bent with sin,* Per. II Prol. 23, i. e. fully intent upon sin.

Reflectively: *you . . . towards York shall b. you,* H4A V, 5, 36, i. e. direct yourselves, take your way. *we beseech you, b. you to remain here,* Hml. I, 2, 115, i. e. be inclined.

To bend up = to strain (like a bow): *b. up every spirit to his full height,* H5 III, 1, 16. *b. up each corporal agent to this terrible feat,* Mcb. I, 7, 79.

3) to bow: *—ed knees,* Gentl. III, 1, 229. *b. my limbs* R2 IV, 165 (Ff *knee*). *I b. my knee,* V, 3, 97. 98

H6A V, 1, 61. H6B I, 1, 10. V, 1, 173 (*b. thy knee to me*). H6C II, 3, 33. V, 1, 22. *must b. his body,* Caes. I, 2, 117. *b. the dukedom to most ignoble stooping,* Tp. I, 2, 114. *we'll b. it to our awe,* H5 I, 2, 224. —*ing down his corrigible neck,* Ant. IV, 14, 73. *except she b. her humour,* Cymb. I, 5, 81.

II. intrans. 1) to be crooked: *his —ing crest* (of a horse) Ven. 395. *his —ing sickle,* Sonn. 116, 10. *his crest that prouder than blue Iris —s,* Troil. I, 3, 380.

2) to bow, to bow down, properly and figuratively: *—ing twigs,* R2 III, 4, 32. *whose boughs did b. with fruit,* Cymb. III, 3, 61. *a cliff whose high and —ing head* ..., Lr. IV, 1, 76. *and —ing forward struck his heels* ... H4B I, 1, 44. *—ing knee,* Wiv. V, 5, 76. *my —ing down,* Meas. III, 1, 144. *I would b. under any weight,* Ado V, 1, 286 (= submit to). *b. low,* Merch. I, 3, 124. cf. R2 III, 3, 73. H4B IV, 5, 149. H5 IV, 1, 272. H6C III, 1, 18. Troil. III, 3, 71. Cor. III, 2, 119. Caes. III, 1, 45. Lr. III, 6, 116. Followed by *to: the nobles —ed as to Jove's statue,* Cor. II, 1, 281. *most humbly —ing to your state,* Oth. I, 3, 236. *Bending* = courteous: *as —ing angels,* Troil. I, 3, 236; or = submissive: *the —ing peers that flattered thee,* R3 IV, 4, 95. *our —ing author,* H5 Epil. 2 (or = bowed down by his too heavy load?).

3) to take one's course, to turn: *thither we b. again,* All's III, 2, 57. *who for Bohemia b.* Wint. V, 1, 165. Figuratively, = to tend: *my thoughts and wishes b. again toward France,* Hml. I, 2, 55. *always —ing towards their project,* Tp. IV, 174. *or —s with the remover to remove,* Sonn. 116, 4.

Beneath. 1) Adv., below: *it droppeth as the gentle rain from heaven upon the place b.* Merch. IV, 1, 186. *that next (is disdained) by him b.* Troil. I, 3, 131. *hears it roar b.* Hml. I, 4, 78. *b. is all the fiends,'* Lr. IV, 6, 129. Adjectively: *this b. world,* Tim. I, 1, 44 (cf. *Under*).

2) Prepos. lower than, below, under: *b. the sky,* Wint. I, 2, 180. *b. the moon,* Lr. IV, 6, 26. *the dust b. thy foot,* V, 3, 137 (Ff *below*). *whose heads grow b. their shoulders,* Oth. I, 3, 145. *sinks b. the yoke,* Mcb. IV, 3, 39. *from below your duke to b. your constable,* All's II, 2, 32. *damned b. all depth in hell,* Oth. V, 2, 137. *so far b. your breeding,* Tw. V, 331. *flatter b. abhorring,* Cor. I, 1, 172. *it smites me b. the fall I have,* Ant. V, 2, 172. *not b. him in fortunes,* Cymb. IV, 1, 11.

Benedicite, ecclesiastical salutation: Meas. II, 3, 39. Rom. II, 3, 31 (v. Appendix).

Benedick, name in Ado I, 1, 35 and passim. O. Edd. once *Benedict:* I, 1, 89.

Benediction, blessing: Wint. IV, 4, 614. Mcb. IV, 3, 156. Lr. IV, 3, 45. IV, 7, 58. Cymb. V, 5, 350. *thou out of heaven's b. comest to the warm sun,* Lr. II, 2, 168 (modification of the proverb: *out of God's blessing into the warm sun*).

Benedictus; *Carduus B.,* the blessed thistle, a medicinal herb: Ado III, 4, 74. 77.

Benefactor, he who confers benefits: Tim. III, 6, 79. Used blunderingly by Elbow in Meas. II, 1, 50.

Benefice, an ecclesiastical living: *then dreams he of another b.* Rom. I, 4, 81.

Beneficial, 1) beneficent: *to seek thy life by b. help,* Err. I, 1, 152 (the help given thee by some

benefactors among thy friends). *take up the rays of the b. sun,* H8 I, 1, 56. — 2) advantageous, profitable: *these b. news,* Oth. II, 2, 7.

Benefit, subst., 1) something good done to one, an act of kindness: *throwing him into the water will do him a b.* Wiv. III, 3, 195. *do a poor wronged lady a merited b.* Meas. III, 1, 207. 268. As I, 2, 36. II, 7, 186. *give me now a little b., out of those many registered in promise,* Troil. III, 3, 14. *we are born to do —s,* Tim. I, 2, 106. *then is death a b.* Caes. III, 1, 103. Cor. I, 1, 156. Lr. I, 4, 308. IV, 6, 61. Oth. I, 3, 314. *but to know so must be my b.* III, 4, 119.

The original signification yet discernible, though approaching to that of advantage in general, in the following instances: *O b. of ill!* Sonn. 119, 9. *Debarred the b. of rest,* Sonn. 28, 2. *omitting the sweet b. of time to clothe mine age with angel-like perfection,* Gentl. II, 4, 65. *by the b. of his light,* Err. I, 1, 91. *yet have I the b. of my senses as well as your ladyship,* Tw. V, 313. H6A IV, 1, 100. R3 III, 1, 48. Mcb. V, 1, 11. *as the winds give b.* Hml. I, 3, 2. *with the next b. of the wind,* Cymb. IV, 2, 342. IV, 4, 42.

2) as a term of law, = a bestowal of property or rights upon one: *accept the title thou usurpest, of b. proceeding from our king,* H6A V, 4, 152. *take to your royal self this proffered b. of dignity,* R3 III, 7, 196.

3) advantage, profit: *is likewise your own b.* Meas. III, 1, 157. *of whom I hope to make much b.* Err. I, 2, 25. *that would have done the time more b.* Wint. V, 1, 22. V, 2, 119. R2 II, 3, 14. *for their country's b.* H6A V, 4, 106. *I'll lop a member off and give it you in earnest of a further b.* V, 3, 16. H6B I, 3, 101. R3 IV, 4, 36. Cor. V, 5, 96. V, 3, 142. V, 6, 67. Tim. IV, 3, 526. *receive the b. of his dying,* Caes. III, 2, 47. Ant. V, 2, 128. — *for the b. of silence* = for the sake of silence, Meas. V, 190.

4) *benefits* = natural advantages, endowments, accomplishments: *disable all the —s of your own country,* As IV, 1, 34. *when these so noble —s shall prove not well disposed,* H8 I, 2, 115.

Benefit, vb., 1) trans. a) to do good to: *a man, a prince, by him so —ed,* Lr. IV, 2, 45. b) to advantage, to be of use to: *what course I mean to hold shall nothing b. your knowledge,* Wint. IV, 4, 514.

2) intr. to profit: *but b. no further than vainly longing,* H8 I, 2, 80.

Benet, to snare: *benetted round with villanies,* Hml. V, 2, 29.

Benevolence, a tax, nominally a gratuity: *blanks, —s,* R2 II, 1, 250.* — Evans uses the word in a rather vague sense: *to do my b.to make atonements,* Wiv. I, 1, 33, i. e. to do a good and pious work.

Bénign, kind: *a better prince and b. lord,* Per. II Prol. 3 (accent on the first syll.).

Benison, blessing: *God's b. go with you,* Mcb. II, 4, 40. Lr. I, 1, 268. IV, 6, 229. Per. II Prol. 10.

Bennet, = Benedick. 1) *the bells of Saint B. may put you in mind: one, two, three,* Tw. V, 42.* — 2) *Sir B. Seely,* R2 V, 6, 14.

Bent, subst., 1) tension, straining (properly an expression of archery, but used tropically of mental dispositions): *her affections have their full b.* Ado II, 3, 232. *thy affection cannot hold the b.* Tw. II, 4, 38. *and here give up ourselves, in the full b. to lay our* *service freely at your feet*, Hml. II, 2, 30. *they fool me to the top of my b.* III, 2, 401. *and every thing at b. for England*, IV, 3, 47 (Qq and M. Edd. *is bent*).

2) tendency, a leaning or bias of the mind, inclination, disposition: *two of them have the very b. of honour*, Ado IV, 1, 188. *to your own —s dispose you*, Wint. I, 2, 179. *to set his sense on the attentive b.* Troil. I, 3, 252. *if that thy b. of love be honourable*, Rom. II, 2, 143. *I can give his humour the true b.* Caes. II, 1, 210.

3) cast of the eye, look (cf. *Bend*): *that met them in their* (the eyes') *b.* H5 V, 2, 16. *gives all gaze and b. of amorous view on the fair Cressid*, Troil. IV, 5, 282. *they wear their faces to the b. of the king's look*, Cymb. I, 1, 13. — Similarly of the forehead: *eternity was in our lips and eyes, bliss in our brows' b.* Ant. I, 3, 36.

Bentii, name in All's IV, 3, 188.

Bentivolii, name in Shr. I, 1, 13.

Benumb, to make torpid, to deprive of sensation and action: *of partial indulgence to their —ed wills*, Troil. II, 2, 179.

Benvolio, name in Rom. I, 1, 74. II, 4, 71 etc.

Bepaint, do dye: *whose frothy mouth, —ed all with red*, Ven. 901. *else would a maiden blush b. my cheek*, Rom. II, 2, 86.

Bepray = pray: LLL V, 2, 702 (Ff Q2 *pray*).

Bequeath, to leave by will: Lucr. 534. 1181. 1184. Pilgr. 142. As I, 1, 2. All's I, 1, 44. I, 3, 105. IV, 2, 43 (*—ed down from many ancestors*). John I, 109. R2 III, 2, 149. Troil. V, 10, 57. Caes. III, 2, 141. Per. I, 1, 50. II, 1, 130.

2) in a wider sense, = to leave, to yield, to bestow upon: *her contrite sighs unto the clouds —ed her winged sprite*, Lucr. 1727. *my horns I b. your husbands*, Wiv. V, 5, 30. *and yours of Helena to me b.* Mids. III, 2, 166. *his crown —ing to his banished brother*, As V, 4, 169. *you to your former honour I b.*, 192. *b. to death your numbness*, Wint. V, 3, 102. *b. thy land to him and follow me*, John I, 149. *to whom I do b. my faithful services*, V, 7, 104. *a sister I b. you*, Ant. II, 2, 152.

Bequest, legacy: *Nature's b. gives nothing but doth lend*, Sonn. 4, 3.

Berattle, to cry down: *and so b. the common stages*, Hml. II, 2, 357.

Bereave, impf. *bereft:* H6B III, 2, 41. R3 I, 2, 138. partic. *bereaved:* H6C II, 5, 68 and Lr. IV, 4, 9; *bereft:* Ven. 381. 439. Lucr. 835. Sonn. 5, 11. Tp. III, 3, 76 etc. etc.

1) *to b. one of sth.* = to deprive, to strip one of: *thee of thy son they have bereft*, Tp. III, 3, 76. Merch. III, 2, 177. Shr. V, 2, 143. R2 II, 1, 237. III, 3, 84. H6A V, 3, 195. H6B III, 2, 269. H6C II, 5, 68. 93. R3 I, 2, 138. Troil. III, 2, 57. 59. Cor. III, 1, 158. Tit. II, 3, 282. Tim. V, 4, 70. Ant. V, 2, 130. Per. II, 1, 9. IV, 1, 32.

2) *to b. one sth.*, in the same sense, used only in the passive form; the subject being either the person deprived or the thing taken away: *'tis your fault I am bereft him so*, Ven. 381. *say that the sense of feeling were bereft me*, 439. *all your interest in those territories is utterly bereft you*, H6C III, 1, 85. *the rites for which I love him are bereft me*, Oth. I, 3, 258.

3) *to b. sth. from one: from me by strong assault it is bereft*, Lucr. 835.

4) *to b. sth.* = to take from, to impair, to spoil: *the sun —s our sight*, Lucr. 373. *beauty's effect with beauty were bereft*, Sonn. 5, 11. *which* (beauty) *the hot tyrant* (lust) *stains and soon —s*, Ven. 797. *if thou live to see like right bereft*, Err. II, 1, 40. *whose dismal tune bereft my vital powers*, H6B III, 2, 41. *I think his understanding is bereft*, H6C II, 6, 60. *in the restoring his bereaved sense*, Lr. IV, 4, 9.

Bergamo, town in Italy: Shr. V, 1, 81.

Bergomask: *a B. dance*, Mids. V, 360. 368. Nares: "a rustic dance, framed in imitation of the people of Bergamasco, a province in the state of Venice, who are ridiculed as being more clownish in their manners and dialect than any other people in Italy. All the Italian buffoons imitate them."

Berhyme, to make rhymes upon: As III, 2, 186. Rom. II, 4, 43.

Berkeley (O. Edd. now *Barkley*, now *Berkley*); 1) name of a place: R2 II, 2, 119. II, 3, 1. 33. H4A I, 3, 249. 2) name of persons; a) *Lord B.*, R2 II, 3, 55. 68. b) attendant of Lady Anne in R3 I, 2, 222.

Berlady, v. *Lady*.

Bermoothes, the Bermudas: *to fetch dew from the still vexed B.*, Tp. I, 2, 229.

Bernardo, name in Hml. I, 1, 4 sq. O. E. *Barnardo*.

Berown (the later Ff and M. Edd. *Biron*, but the name has always the accent on the last syllable, and rhymes to *moon*, IV, 3, 232), name in LLL I, 1, 15. 53. 100. 110. II, 66. 215. IV, 1, 53. 106. IV, 3, 123. 145. 284. V, 2, 34. 60. 133. 272. 283. 457. 851 etc.* cf. *Melun*.

Berrord, v. *Bearherd*.

Berry, small fruit: Ven. 460. 604. 1104. Tp. I, 2, 334. II, 2, 164. Mids. III, 2, 211. H5 I, 1, 61. Tit. IV, 2, 177. Tim. IV, 3, 425. Ant. I, 4, 64. Per. V Prol. 6.

Berry, French name: H5 II, 4, 4. III, 5, 41.

Bertram, name in All's I, 1, 83 and passim.

Berwick (O. Edd. *Barwick*), town in England: H6B II, 1, 83. 159. H6C II, 5, 128.

Bescreen, to shelter, to conceal: *thou that thus —ed in night so stumblest on my counsel*, Rom. II, 2, 52.

Beseech (impf. *beseeched*, Hml. III, 1, 22. partic. *beseeched*, Compl. 207), to entreat, to ask; 1) with an accus. denoting the person applied to: *I heartily b. thee*, Ven. 404. Tp. II, 1, 100. III, 1, 34. III, 2, 72. III, 3, 106. Gentl. II, 4, 100. V, 4, 149. Wiv. I, 1, 72. I, 4, 79. III, 2, 80. Meas. II, 1, 126. II, 2, 35. II, 4, 39. IV, 3, 60. IV, 4, 17. V, 520. Err. V, 251. Ado III, 3, 100. V, 1, 315. LLL I, 1, 232. IV, 2, 94. IV, 3, 193. V, 1, 103. 155. Mids. III, 1, 194. Merch. IV, 1, 243. H6B I, 3, 198. H6C II, 3, 38. R3 I, 1, 84. I, 2, 218. I, 3, 25. H8 IV, 2, 135. Caes. II, 4, 30. Hml. III, 1, 22 etc. etc. *I shall b. your highness*, All's II, 3, 113. *I b. your grace that I may know the worst*, Mids. I, 1, 62. *I b. you a word*, LLL II, 197. Very often without the pronoun I: *b. you*, Tp. I, 2, 473. II, 1, 1. Wint. I, 1, 11. II, 1, 112. 116. Cor. III, 1, 149. Cymb. I, 1, 153. III, 5, 38 etc. cf. *I*.

2) *to b. one of sth.:* *I humbly do b. you of your pardon*, Oth. III, 3, 212.

3) *to b. something: their kind acceptance weepingly beseeched*, Compl. 207. *I b. your worship's pardon*, Mids. III, 1, 183. *I b. your society*, LLL IV, 2, 166. *b.*

listening, Shr. IV, 1, 68. *I b. your pardon,* Lr. I, 4, 90. *b. your patience,* Cymb. I, 1, 153.

4) absolutely: *have patience, I b.* Err. IV, 2, 16. *I earnestly b.* Ant. II, 2, 23. *O, no, no. Yes, I b.* Cymb. I, 6, 200.

Beseech, subst., e n t r e a t y: *achievement is command; ungained, b.* Troil. I, 2, 319.

Beseecher, o n e w h o e n t r e a t s: Sonn. 135, 13.

Beseek for b e s e e c h: H4B II, 4, 175 (Mrs. Quickly's speech).

Beseem, to b e c o m e: *sad pause and deep regard b. the sage,* Lucr. 277. Sonn. 132, 10. Gentl. II, 7, 43. III, 1, 66. Err. V, 110. LLL II, 108. Shr. IV, 5, 65. John II, 196. R2 III, 3, 7. IV, 116. H6A III, 1, 19. IV, 1, 31. IV, 7, 86. H6C III, 3, 122. IV, 7, 84. Rom. I, 1, 100.

Beseeming, subst. s e e m i n g, a p p e a r a n c e: *I am the soldier that did company these three in poor b.* Cymb. V, 5, 409.

Beset, used only as a participle, 1) e n c l o s e d so as to p r e v e n t e s c a p i n g: *the thicket is b., he cannot scape,* Gentl. V, 3, 11.

2) p r e s s e d h a r d, i n d i s t r e s s: *tell her she is dreadfully b.* Lucr. 444. *now, daughter Silvia, you are hard b.* Gentl. II, 4, 49. *O God defend me! how am I b.!* Ado IV, 1, 78. *I was b. with shame and courtesy,* Merch. V, 217. *we are b. with thieves,* Shr. III, 2, 238. *drew to defend him when he was b.* Tw. V, 88.

Beshrew, vb. (O. Edd. sometimes *beshrow*); once used in the infinitive: *she will b. me much,* Rom. V, 2, 26; generally only in the first person of the present, and with one exception *(I b. all shrews,* LLL V, 2, 46) without the pronoun *I.*

Originally a mild, indeed very mild, form of imprecation, = w o e t o: *b. that heart that makes my heart to groan,* Sonn. 133, 1. *b. his hand, I scarce could understand it,* Err. II, 1, 49. *b. my hand, if it should give your age such cause of fear,* Ado V, 1, 55. Mids. II, 2, 54. Tw. IV, 1, 62. Wint. II, 2, 30. John V, 5, 14. R2 III, 2, 204. H5 V, 2, 241. H6B III, 1, 184. Troil. IV, 2, 12. Rom. II, 5, 52. III, 5, 229. Hml. II, 1, 113. Oth. IV, 3, 78. III, 4, 150.

Sometimes it is so far from implying **a curse** as to be uttered coaxingly, nay even with some tenderness: *b. your heart, fair daughter, you do draw my spirits from me,* H4B II, 3, 45. *if thou wantest any thing and wilt not call, b. thy heart,* V, 3, 59. *come, come, b. your heart, you'll never be good,* Troil. IV, 2, 29. *b. him for it! how comes this trick upon him?* Oth. IV, 2, 128. *b. your eyes, they have o'erlooked me,* Merch. III, 2, 14.

The phrases *b. me, b. my heart,* used as forms of simple asseveration (= indeed): *b. me, the knight is in admirable fooling,* Tw. II, 3, 85. *b. me, I would* (be a queen) H8 II, 3, 24. *b. my very heart, I think you are happy in this second match,* Rom. III, 5, 223. The following clause frequently preceded by *but: b. me, but you have a quick wit,* Gentl. I, 1, 132. *b. me, sir, but if he make this good, he is as worthy for an empress' love,* II, 4, 75. *b. my heart, but I pity the man,* Mids. V, 295. *b. me, but I love her heartily,* Merch. II, 6, 52. John V, 4, 49. H6C I, 4, 150.

Beside, I. Adv. 1) to the side: *sometimes falls an orient drop b.* Ven. 981.

2) m o r e o v e r, to b o o t: *the argument all bare*

is of more worth than when it hath my added praise b. Sonn. 103, 4. *b., she hath prosperous art ...,* Meas. I, 2, 189. Shr. IV, 5, 66. John I, 137. H6A III, 1, 24. IV, 1, 25. 143. V, 1, 15. V, 5, 46. Cor. II, 3, 254. Caes. IV, 3, 213. Ant. II, 5, 71.

3) else: *if I had self-applied love to myself and to no love b.* Compl. 77. *and one day in a week to touch no food and but one meal on every day b.* LLL I, 1, 40 (= on every other day). *when she* (nature) *did starve the general world b. and prodigally gave them* (graces) *all to you,* II, 11. *we pray with heart and soul and all b.* R2 V, 3, 104. *his insolence is more intolerable than all the princes in the land b.* H6B I, 1, 176. *to frustrate both his oath and what b. may make against the house of Lancaster,* H6C II, 1, 175. *your charms and every thing b.* Mcb. III, 5, 19. *save him, and spare no blood b.* Cymb. V, 5, 92.

II. Prepos. 1) b y t h e s i d e o f: *at the Saint Francis here b. the port,* All's III, 5, 39. *some* (hair) *hanging her pale cheek b.* Compl. 32. *foes that strike b. us* (= strike the air) Mcb. V, 7, 29.

2) o u t o f: *very many have been b. their wit,* Ado V, 1, 128. *to put him quite b. his patience,* H4A III, 1, 179 (only in Q2; the other O. Edd. *besides*). *b. themselves with fear,* Caes. III, 1, 180.

3) a b s t r a c t e d l y f r o m: *b. the charge, the shame, the imprisonment, you have ...* Err. V, 18. LLL IV, 2, 48. H6A III, 4, 8. H6B I, 3, 71. H8 Prol. 19. *over and b.* Shr. I, 2, 149.

Besides. I. Adv. 1) m o r e o v e r: *b., his soul's fair temple is defaced,* Lucr. 719. 845. 1317. Gentl. III, 1, 64. 86. 233. 245. V, 2, 41. Wiv. III, 1, 67. IV, 6, 55. Meas. I, 2, 78. IV, 2, 101. IV, 6, 5. V, 185. Err. IV, 1, 35. V, 259. Merch. II, 1, 15. II, 8, 10. III, 2, 275. As II, 4, 83. III, 2, 60. III, 4, 33. III, 5, 74. Tw. I, 5, 46. John V, 4, 41. H6A III, 3, 60. R3 III, 2, 12. V, 3, 12. Cymb. I, 5, 25.

2) else: *you are so strongly in my purpose bred that all the world b. methinks are dead,* Sonn. 112, 14. *all parts b.* H4A III, 1, 188. *wert thou the son of Jupiter and no more but what thou art b.* Cymb. II, 3, 131.

II. Prepos. 1) b y t h e s i d e o f: *b. the groves, the skies, the fountains, every region near seemed all one mutual cry,* Mids. IV, 1, 120 (unless it be here = over and above).

2) o u t o f: *who with his fear is put b. his part,* Sonn. 23, 2. *I am an ass, I am a woman's man and b. myself. What woman's man? and how b. thyself? Marry, sir, b. myself, I am due to a woman,* Err. III, 2, 78. *how fell you b. your five wits?* Tw. IV, 2, 92. H4A III, 1, 179 (Q2 *beside,* q. v.). *quite b. the government of patience,* Cymb. II, 4, 149.

3) a b s t r a c t e d l y f r o m, o v e r a n d a b o v e: *nor can imagination form a shape, b. yourself, to like of,* Tp. III, 1, 57. *b. your cheer, you shall have sport,* Wiv. III, 2, 81. 4, 7. IV, 2, 13. Err. IV, 3, 88. V, 359. Merch. II, 9, 90. As I, 1, 17. Wint. IV, 4, 828. R2 III, 4, 88. Tim. II, 1, 2. Mcb. I, 3, 122. Lr. III, 1, 1. Ant. III, 13, 118.

Besides that, heading a sentence, = n o t t a k i n g i n t o a c c o u n t t h a t: *b. that they are fair with their feeding, they are taught their manage,* As I, 1, 12. Tw. I, 3, 31. I, 5, 184.

Besiege, vb. 1) to l a y s i e g e t o, to surround with armed forces: *to b. Ardea,* Lucr. Arg. 4. Lucr.

1. John II, 489. H5 III, 2, 115 (Macmorris pronounces *beseeched*). H6A I, 1, 157. I, 4, 1. H6B I, 3, 175. H6C I, 2, 50. = to make an assault upon: *the famished English faintly b. us one hour in a month*, H6A I, 2, 8. Metaphorically: *when forty winters shall b. thy brow and dig deep trenches in thy beauty's field*, Sonn. 2, 1. *and long upon these terms I held my city, till thus he gan b. me*, Compl. 177. *he rather means to lodge you in the field, like one that comes here to b. his court*, LLL II, 86.

2) to beset, to harass: *all frailties that b. all kinds of blood*, Sonn. 109, 10. *the fire and cracks of sulphurous roaring the most mighty Neptune seem to b.* Tp. I, 2, 205. —*d with melancholy*, LLL I, 1, 233. *the malady that doth my life b.* All's II, 1, 10. *the women so b. us*, H8 V, 4, 35.

Beslubber, to daub, to smear: *to make them (our noses) bleed, and then to b. our garments with it*, H4A II, 4, 341.

Besmear, to daub, to soil: Sonn. 55, 4. Merch. V, 219. Tw. V, 55. John III, 1, 236. H8 I, 2, 124. Caes. III, 1, 107 (= to dye).

Besmirch, to soil: H5 IV, 3, 110. Hml. I, 3, 15.

Besom, broom: H6B IV, 7, 34.

Besonian, v. *Bezonian*.

Besort, vb., to suit, to be in accordance with: *such men as may b. your age*, Lr. I, 4, 272.

Besort, subst., suitableness, convenience: *with such accommodation and b. as levels with her breeding*, Oth. I, 3, 239 (*accommodation and besort = besorting, or convenient, accommodation*).

Besotted, infatuated: *you speak like one b. on your sweet delights*, Troil. II, 2, 143.

Bespeak. Impf. *bespoke*: Err. III, 2, 176. V, 233. H6A IV, 6, 21. *bespake*: Tw. V, 192. R2 V, 2, 20. Partic. *bespoke*: H4A I, 2, 144. Lr. V, 3, 89.

1) to speak to: *I bespake you fair and hurt you not*, Tw. V, 192. *bespake them thus: I thank you, countrymen*, R2 V, 2, 20. H6A IV, 6, 21. Hml. II, 2, 140. *then fairly I bespoke the officer to go in person with me to my house*, Err. V, 233.

2) to order or engage against a future time: *I bespoke it not*, Err. III, 2, 176. IV, 3, 62. IV, 4, 139. Merch. III, 1, 131. Shr. IV, 3, 63. Tw. III, 3, 40. H4A I, 2, 144. *my lady is bespoke*, Lr. V, 3, 89 (= engaged).

Bespice, to season with spices: *mightst b. a cup*, Wint. I, 2, 316 (= poison).

Bespot, in *blood-bespotted*.

Bess, diminutive of *Elisabeth*: H6C V, 7, 15.

Bessy, the same: *come o'er the bourn, B., to me*, Lr. III, 6, 27 (*mad Tom and mad Bess* being usually companions).

Best, adj., superl. of *good*: *I am the b. of them that speak this speech*, Tp. I, 2, 429. 430. *my b. way is ...*, II, 2, 39. 164. V, 58. 221. Gentl. I, 2, 21. III, 2, 31. Meas. IV, 2, 76. Mids. I, 1, 170 etc. etc. *make your b. haste*, Wint. III, 3, 10. *let your b. love draw to that point* (= greatest), Ant. III, 4, 21. *full many a lady I have eyed with b. regard*, Tp. III, 1, 40.

Sometimes = good: *how is't with you, b. brother?* Wint. I, 2, 148. *my b. Camillo*, IV, 2, 61. *see, our b. elders*, Cor. I, 1, 230.

Sometimes added in courtesy, without a distinct sense: *I come to answer thy b. pleasure*, Tp. I, 2, 190. *at your b. command*, John I, 197. *therefore to our b. mercy give yourselves*, H5 III, 3, 3. *which for your b.*

ends you adopt, Cor. III, 2, 47. *dignities which vacant lie for thy b. use and wearing*, Tim. V, 1, 146. *at your b. leisure*, Caes. III, 1, 5.

It is best, followed by a clause: *'tis b. we stand upon our guard*, Tp. II, 1, 321. Meas. III, 1, 151. Rom. III, 5, 219. *counting b. to be with you alone*, Sonn. 75, 7. Elliptically: *b. you stop your ears*, Shr. IV, 3, 76. Followed by the infinitive without *to: it is b. put finger in the eye*, Shr. I, 1, 78. Elliptically: *b. sing it to the tune of Light o' love*, Gentl. I, 2, 83. *b. beware my sting*, Shr. II, 211. *b. first go see your lodging*, Tw. III, 3, 20. *b. not wake him*, H8 I, 1, 121. *b. play with Mardian*, Ant. II, 5, 4. *b. draw my sword*, Cymb. III, 6, 25. *To* before the infinitive: *b. to take them up*, Gentl. I, 2, 134. — Cf. *'twere b. pound you*, Gentl. I, 1, 109. *'twere b. he speak*, Caes. III, 2, 73.

Oftener personally: *be quick, thou'rt b.* Tp. I, 2, 366. *you're best consider*, Cymb. III, 2, 79. Especially, when joined with *were*, either without or with *to* before the infinitive: *you were best stick her*, Gentl. I, 1, 108. Wiv. III, 3, 165. LLL V, 2, 171. As I, 1, 154. Shr. V, 1, 15. 106. All's II, 3, 267. Wint. V, 2, 143. Lr. I, 4, 109. Oth. I, 2, 30. Cymb. III, 6, 19. *whither were I b. to send him?* Gentl. I, 3, 24. Mids. I, 2, 2. 93. Merch. II, 8, 33. V, 177. Tw. III, 4, 12. H6A V, 3, 83. H6B V, 1, 196. R3 I, 1, 100 (Qq *he do it*). IV, 4, 337. With the clause preceding: *make your excuse wisely, you were b.* Tw. I, 5, 34. H6B II, 1, 189. Caes. III, 3, 13. Oth. V, 2, 161.

B. substantively used; = the b. man: *my name be yoked with his that did betray the b.* (viz the Redeemer), Wint. I, 2, 419. = persons of highest quality: *I'll make the b. in Glostershire know on't*, Wiv. V, 5, 190. *send us to Rome the b.* Cor. I, 9, 77. = the b. thing: *the b. is, she hath no teeth to bite*, Gentl. III, 1, 348. Meas. IV, 3, 167. *feast with the b.*, Shr. V, 2, 8 (= feast on the best things in my house; cf. *With*). *good as the b.*, Tim. V, 1, 24 (= it cannot be better). *what is b., that b. I wish in thee*, Sonn. 37, 13. *all my b. is dressing old words new*, 76, 11. *all these I better in one general b.* 91, 8. *b. is b., if never intermixed*, 101, 8. *in the blazon of sweet beauty's b.* 106, 5. *creating every bad a perfect b.* 114, 7. *all my b. doth worship thy defect*, 149, 11. *thy worst all b. exceeds*, 150, 8. *you are created of every creature's b.* Tp. III, 1, 48. *invert what b. is boded me to mischief*, 71. *the b. is past*, III, 3, 51. *thou, b. of dearest*, Sonn. 48, 7. *b. of my flesh*, Cor. V, 3, 42. *Best of* = best: *thy b. of rest is sleep*, Meas. III, 1, 17. *worse essays proved thee my b. of love*, Sonn. 110, 8. *b. of comfort*, Ant. III, 6, 89. Inversely: *I have bred her in qualities of the b.*, Tim. I, 1, 125 (= in the best qualities).

One's best = what is in one's power: *do thy b. to pluck this serpent from my breast*, Mids. II, 2, 145. Tw. I, 4, 40. Wint. II, 1, 27. H4A V, 2, 93. H5 II, 2, 19. Troil. I, 3, 274. *All one's b.*, in the same sense: *I have spoken for you all my b.* Oth. III, 4, 127. *I shall in all my b. obey you*, Hml. I, 2, 120. — *Let us make the b. of it*, Cor. V, 6, 148 = let us not take it too grievously, put a good face on it. *I'll none of it: hence! make your b. of it*, Shr. IV, 3, 100, probably = do with it as you please.

To have the b. = to carry the day, H6C V, 3, 20. — *I advise you to the b.* Lr. I, 2, 188 = to what is best for you. — *I hope all's for the b.* (= all is well) H6C III, 3, 170. *I thought all for the b.* = I

meant well, Rom. III, 1, 109. *we did for the b.* = we
meant well, Cor. IV, 6, 144. — *Aim we at the b.* H6C
III, 1, 8 (= to the best of our powers). *the sport is
at the b.* (= at the most advantageous turn of fortune)
Rom. I, 5, 121. *you take us even at the b.* Tim. I, 2,
157 (= at best advantage). *how fare you? Ever at
the b., hearing well of your lordship,* III, 6, 29. (= as
well as possible). *take up this mangled matter at the
b.* Oth. I, 3, 173. — *In the best* = in any case:
*was this a lover, or a lecher whether? bad in the b.,
but excellent in neither,* Pilgr. 102. *murder most foul,
as in the b. it is, but this most foul,* Hml. I, 5, 27. —
The best = best: *the b. persuaded of himself,* Tw. II,
3, 162. *how likest thou this picture? the b., for the
innocence,* Tim. I, 1, 199.

Best, adv. Lucr. 1111. Sonn. 43, 1. Tp. I, 2, 286.
Gentl. I, 2, 102. III, 1, 93. 128. Meas. II, 2, 74 etc. etc.
to love b. Ven. 77. Sonn. 115, 10. Gentl. I, 2, 28.
Wiv. IV, 4, 87 etc. *b. alarumed,* Lr. II, 1, 55.

Best, a name: H6B IV, 2, 23.

Bestain, to spot: *we will not line his thin —ed
cloak with our pure honours,* John IV, 3, 24.

Best-conditioned, of the best cast of mind:
Merch. III, 2, 295.

Bested (O. Edd. *bestead*): *I never saw a fellow
worse b.,* H6B II, 3, 56, i. e. in a worse plight; cf.
Stead.

Best-esteemed, most respected: *my b. acquaintance,* Merch. II, 2, 181.

Bestial, becoming a beast: *his b. appetite,*
R3 III, 5, 81. Hml. IV, 4, 40. Oth. II, 3, 264.

Bestilled, reading of Ff. in Hml. I, 2, 204; Qq
and M. Edd. *distilled;* but cf. *bestraught* = distraught,
and *distain* = bestain.

Bestir, to stir, 1) trans. to put in motion, to
agitate: *thy spirit hath so —ed thee in thy sleep,* H4A
II, 3, 60. *you have so —ed your valour,* Lr. II, 2, 58.
— 2) intr.: Tp. I, 1, 4 (the ship-master's speech).

Best-moving, best persuading: *we single
you as our b. fair solicitor,* LLL II, 29.

Bestow, 1) to stow, to lodge, to place:
*some good conceit of thine in thy soul's thought will b.
it,* Sonn. 26, 8 (= will treasure it up in thy heart).
b. your luggage where you found it, Tp. V, 299. *how
should I b. him?* Wiv. IV, 2, 48. *the devil take one
party and his dam the other! and so they shall be both
—ed,* IV, 5, 109. *in what place you have —ed my money,* Err. I, 2, 78. Merch. II, 2, 179. H6A III, 2, 88.
Caes. I, 3, 151. Mcb. III, 1, 30. Hml. II, 2, 547. III, 4,
176. IV, 3, 12. Lr. II, 4, 292. IV, 6, 293. *I will b.
you where you shall have time to speak your bosom
freely,* Oth. III, 1, 57 (i. e. conduct you to a place).
Reflectively: *can you tell where he —s himself?* Mcb.
III, 6, 24 (= where he lives at present). *her father
and myself will so b. ourselves ...,* Hml. III, 1, 33. 44
(= place, hide ourselves). *b. yourself with speed,* H5
IV, 3, 68 (= repair to your post). — In speaking of
a marriageable girl, it passes into the sense of to
marry: *not to b. my youngest daughter before I have
a husband for the elder,* Shr. I, 1, 50. *to have her so
—ed,* IV, 4, 35.

2) to employ: *that* (rope) *will I b. among my
wife and her confederates,* Err. IV, 1, 16. *'tis labour
well —ed,* Wiv. II, 1, 248. *labour ill —ed,* Ado III, 2,
103. *in heedfullest reservation to b. them,* Alls I, 3,
231. *what pains I have —ed,* H4B IV, 2, 74. *whose

life were ill —ed ... where Helen is the subject? Troil.
II, 2, 159. *good deeds evilly —ed,* Tim. IV, 3, 467.
Absolutely: *all my powers do their —ing lose,* Troil.
III, 2, 39, i. e their functions.

Hence = to spend, to lay out: *labouring in
moe pleasures to b. them* (the estates of others) *than
the true gouty landlord which doth owe them,* Compl.
139. *how little is the cost I have —ed in purchasing
the semblance of my soul,* Merch. III, 4, 19. *I would
I had —ed that time in the tongues,* Tw. I, 3, 97. *I
would have —ed the thousand pound,* H4B V, 5, 12.
I will b. a breakfast to make you friends, H5 II, 1, 12.
b. it at your pleasure, Ant. V, 2, 182. *wilt thou b. thy
time with me?* Caes. V, 5, 61.

Reflectively, = to deport one's self: *how
and which way I may b. myself to be regarded in her
eye,* Gentl. III, 1, 87. *the boy —s himself like a ripe
sister,* As IV, 3, 87. *tell me how you would b. yourself,*
John III, 1, 225. *see Falstaff b. himself in his true
colours,* H4B II, 2, 186.

3) to grant, to give, to afford; a) absolutely: *this young parcel of bachelors stand at my —ing,*
All's II, 3, 59. *though he were unsatisfied in getting,
yet in —ing he was most princely,* H8 IV, 2, 56. —
b) followed by an accus.: *the kiss I gave you is —ed
in vain,* Ven. 771. *that fresh blood which youngly thou
—est,* Sonn. 11, 3. *that sad breath his spongy lungs
—ed* Compl. 326. *favours which they did b.* LLL V,
2, 125. Gentl. II, 4, 72. As I, 2, 35. Shr. II, 100. All's
II, 1, 203. III, 7, 12. Tw. I, 5, 200. Cor. I, 1, 129.
Tim. I, 1, 145. — c) followed by a dative and an
accus.: *b. her funeral,* Tit. IV, 2, 163. *b. your needful
counsel to our business,* Lr. II, 1, 128. — d) mostly
followed by on: *I must b. upon the eyes of this young
couple some vanity of mine art,* Tp. IV, 40. *b. thy smiles
on equal mates,* Gentl. III, 1, 158. *to b. her on Thurio,*
III, 1, 13. 162. Wiv. II, 2, 202 (*—ed much on her,* =
spent much to win her). Err. II, 2, 80. III, 1, 117.
Ado I, 1, 10. II, 1, 237. II, 3, 175. III, 5, 26. LLL V,
2, 670. Merch. II, 2, 145. V, 101. As V, 4, 7. Tw. II,
4, 86. III, 2, 8. H5 IV, 1, 313. H6B IV, 7, 76. H6C
IV, 1, 56. H8 II, 1, 163. II, 4, 14. III, 1, 182. III, 2,
159. Troil. V, 2, 25. Tit. I, 219. Hml. IV, 1, 4 (*b. this
place on us a little while*). Lr. I, 1, 166. Oth. II, 1, 102.
145. IV, 1, 13. Ant. III, 13, 84. Per. II, 5, 77. IV, 4,
41. *—ed her on her own lamentation,* Meas. III, 1, 237,
i. e. left her to her lamentation. — e) followed by
of (as *of* and *on* are throughout confounded by the
old writers): *to b. it all of your worship,* Ado III, 5,
24 (Dogberry's speech). *I will b. some precepts of
this virgin,* All's III, 5, 103. *what b. of him?* Tw. III,
4, 2. *of him b. your sued-for tongues,* Cor. II, 3, 215.

Bestraught, distracted: *I am not b.,* Shr. Ind.
2, 26 (Sly's speech).

Best-regarded, of highest rank and estimation: Merch. II, 1, 10.

Bestrew, to scatter over, to strow: Tp.
IV, 1, 20. Shr. Ind. I, 56 (part. *bestrewed*). 2, 42.

Bestride, (impf. and partic. *bestrid*) 1) to step
on or over: *b. the rock; the tide will wash you off,*
H6C V, 4, 31. *when I first my wedded mistress saw
b. my threshold,* Cor. IV, 5, 124.

2) to stride over with the legs extended
across, like the Colossus of Rhodes: *b. the narrow
world like a Colossus,* Caes. I, 2, 135. *his legs bestrid
the ocean,* Ant. V, 2, 82. cf. H4A V, 1, 123.

3) **to mount** as a rider: *that horse that thou so often hast bestrid,* R2 V, 5, 79. *when I b. him, I soar,* H5 III, 7, 15. H6C II, 1, 183. Cymb. IV, 4, 38. *when he —s the lazy-pacing clouds,* Rom. II, 2, 31. *a lover may b. the gossamer,* II, 6, 18.

4) **to defend** one fallen in battle: *when I bestrid thee in the wars,* Err. V, 192. H4A V, 1, 122 (a quibble). H6B V, 3, 9. Cor. II, 2, 96. Figuratively: *he doth b. a bleeding land,* H4B I, 1, 207. *like good men b. our down-fallen birthdom,* Mcb. IV, 3, 4.

Bestrow, see *Bestrew.*

Best-tempered, of hardest metal: *the b. courage,* H4B I, 1, 115.

Bet, vb., to lay a wager: *I won of you at —ing,* H5 II, 1, 99. 111. Transitively: *—ed much money on his head,* H4B III, 2, 50.

Bet, subst., wager: Hml. V, 2, 170.

Betake (impf. and partic. *betook:* LLL I, 1, 237. Per. I, 3, 35), refl. vb., to compose one's self, to prepare, to think of, to enter on; always followed by *to: every one to rest themselves b.* Lucr. 125. 174. Per. II, 3, 115. *whenas himself to singing he —s,* Pilgr. 114. *betook myself to walk,* LLL I, 1, 237. *b. thee to thy faith,* All's IV, 1, 83. *that defence thou hast, b. thee to it,* Tw. III, 4, 240. 252. *b. thee to nothing but despair,* Wint. III, 2, 210. *b. me to my heels,* H6B IV, 8, 67. *every man b. him to his legs,* Rom. I, 4, 34. *hath betook himself to travels,* Per. I, 3, 35.

Beteem, to grant, to allow: *rain, which I could well b. them from the tempest of my eyes,* Mids. I, 1, 131. *so loving to my mother that he might not b. the winds of heaven visit her face too roughly,* Hml. I, 2, 141 (Qq beteeme, Ff. beteene).

Bethink (impf. and partic. *bethought*). I. to think, to consider: *trifles unwitnessed with eye or ear thy coward heart with false —ing grieves,* Ven. 1024. *bade him b. how nice the quarrel was,* Rom. III, 1, 158. — Followed by an accus., = to think of: *while we b. a means,* H6C III, 3, 39. *well bethought,* Hml. I, 3, 90. Per. V, 1, 44.

II. used reflectively, 1) = to think, usually followed by *of,* and once by *on: b. you of some conveyance,* Wiv. III, 3, 135. *and not b. me straight of dangerous rocks,* Merch. I, 1, 31. *b. thee of thy birth,* Shr. Ind. 2, 32. *b. you of the young prince your son,* R3 II, 2, 96. *b. thee on her virtues,* H6A V, 3, 191. — Followed by a clause: *I b. me what a weary way ...* R2 II, 3, 8. — *It may be I shall otherwise b. me,* Caes. IV, 3, 251.

2) **to consider:** *good my lord, b. you,* Meas. II, 2, 87. 144. *that I may be assured, I will b. me,* Merch. I, 3, 31. John III, 1, 204. Rom. III, 5, 197. Per. I, 2, 83. Followed by *of: 'twas bravely done, if you b. you of it,* Ado V, 1, 279. *he hath better bethought him of his quarrel,* Tw. III, 4, 327.

3) **to recollect:** *and now do I b. me,* Mids. IV, 1, 155. Tw. V, 356. *b. thee once again, and in thy thought o'errun my former time,* H6C I, 4, 44. *as I b. me,* 101. *b. yourself wherein you may have offended him,* Lr. I, 2, 174. Followed by *of: I have bethought me of another fault,* Meas. V, 461. *if you b. yourself of any crime,* Oth. V, 2, 25.

Bethought, adj., having a thought; meaning: *and am b. to take the basest and most poorest shape,* Lr. II, 3, 6.

Bethump, to cuff: *I was never so —ed with words,* John II, 466.

Betide, partic. *betid:* Tp. I, 2, 31. R2 V, 1, 42. Cymb. IV, 3, 40. 1) intr. to happen, to come to pass: *what news else —th here,* Gentl. I, 1, 59. *tales of woeful ages long ago betid,* R2 V, 1, 42. *a salve for any sore that may b.* H6C IV, 6, 88. Followed by *to: there is not so much perdition as an hair betid to any,* Tp. I, 2, 31. *and so b. to me as well I tender you,* R3 II, 4, 71. *what is betid to Cloten,* Cymb. IV, 3, 40. Followed by *of* (= to become): *if he were dead, what would b. of me?* R3 I, 3, 6.

2) trans., to happen to, to befall: *what —th me,* Gentl. IV, 3, 40. *woe b. thee,* Tit. IV, 2, 56. *more health and happiness b. my liege,* R2 III, 2, 91. H6B I, 4, 69. R3 I, 2, 17. 112.

Betime, vb., to betide, to chance: *no time shall be omitted that will b. and may by us be fitted,* LLL IV, 3, 382 (O. Edd. and many M. Edd. *be time*).

Betime, adv., 1) soon, before it is too late: *put up thy sword b.* John IV, 3, 98. H6B III, 1, 285. 2) early: *all in the morning b.* Hml. IV, 5, 49. Ant. IV, 4, 20.

Betimes, the same, 1) soon, before it becomes too late: *let me say amen b., lest the devil cross my prayer,* Merch. III, 1, 22. Wint. I, 2, 297. H6B III, 1, 297. H6C IV, 8, 62. V, 4, 45. Troil. II, 2, 106. Caes. II, 1, 116. IV, 3, 308. Mcb. IV, 3, 162. Cymb. V, 2, 17.

2) early, at an early hour: *is hanged b. in the morning,* Meas. IV, 3, 49. IV, 4, 18. V, 101. Tw. II, 3, 2. R2 II, 1, 36. H4A II, 4, 600. R3 III, 1, 199. Mcb. III, 4, 133. Hml. V, 2, 235. Oth. I, 3, 383. II, 3, 335. Ant. IV, 4, 27.

Betoken, to foreshow, to signify: *a red morn, that ever yet —ed wreck to the seaman,* Ven. 453. *this doth b. the corse they follow did with desperate hand fordo its own life,* Hml. V, 1, 242.

Betoss, to toss, to agitate: *my —ed soul did not attend him,* Rom. V, 3, 76.

Betray, 1) to deceive: *would yet again b. the fore-betrayed,* Compl. 328. *do not b. me, sir; I fear you love Mistress Page,* Wiv. III, 3, 82. *we'll b. him finely,* V, 3, 22. 24. *not you to me, but I —ed by you,* LLL IV, 3, 176. *by oppressing and —ing me,* Tim. IV, 3, 510. *win us with honest trifles, to b. us in deepest consequence,* Mcb. I, 3, 125. *she must die, else she'll b. more men,* Oth. V, 2, 6. *never was there queen so mightily —ed,* Ant. I, 3, 25. — Absolutely: *wear them, b. with them* (false hairs) Tim. IV, 3, 146. Per. IV, 3, 47.

Especially = to entrap, to ensnare: *lain in ambush to b. my life,* Lucr. 233. *why hath thy servant, Opportunity, —ed the hours thou gavest me to repose?* 933. *how many lambs might the stern wolf b., if like a lamb he could his looks translate,* Sonn. 96, 9. *the letter that I dropped to b. him,* Tw. III, 2, 83. *that thou —edst Polixenes,* Wint. III, 2, 186. *have all limed bushes to b. thy wings,* H6B II, 4, 54. *wouldst thou b. me?* R3 I, 1, 102. *to lay a complot to b. thy foes,* Tit. V, 2, 147. *unicorns may be —ed with trees,* Caes. II, 1, 204. *I will b. tawny-finned fishes,* Ant. II, 5, 11. *who are in this relieved, but not —ed,* V, 2, 41. *the shes of Italy should not b. mine interest and his honour,* Cymb. I, 3, 29.

Sometimes almost = to seduce: *can it be that modesty may more b. our sense than woman's lightness?*

Meas. II, 2, 169. *these b. nice wenches, that would be —ed without these*, LLL III, 23. *some jay of Italy hath —ed him*, Cymb. III, 4, 52.

2) to deliver by fraud into the power of enemies: *to b. you*, All's III, 6, 32. *to b. the Florentine*, IV, 3, 326. Wint. I, 2, 419. V, 1, 193. H4A I, 3, 81. H5 III, 6, 143. H6A III, 2, 82. H6B IV, 4, 58. IV, 10, 28. 34. H6C IV, 4, 8. H8 II, 1, 110. III, 1, 67. Cor. V, 6, 92. Tit. IV, 2, 106. Oth. V, 2, 77. Ant. IV, 12, 10. 24. IV, 14, 26. Cymb. III, 4, 87. Followed by *to: those thine eyes b. thee unto mine*, Lucr. 483. *are we —ed thus to thy overview?* LLL IV, 3, 175. *would not b. the devil to his fellow*, Mcb. IV, 3, 128. cf. All's IV, 1, 102. H6A I, 1, 144. Lr. III, 4, 98.

3) to deliver, to expose: *when he himself himself confounds, —s to slanderous tongues and wretched days*, Lucr. 160. *thou —ing me, I do b. my nobler part to my gross body's treason*, Sonn. 151, 5. *to b. him to another punishment*, Wiv. III, 3, 208. *she did b. me to my own reproof*, Err. V, 90. *to b. a she-lamb to a ram*, As III, 2, 85. *b. themselves to every modern censure*, IV, 1, 6. *he his honour —s to slander*, Wint. II, 3, 85. *doth b. to loss the conquest*, H6A IV, 3, 49. *—ed to fortune*, IV, 4, 39. *by thy guile —ed to death*, R3 V, 3, 133. *to b. you to sorrow*, H8 III, 1, 56.

4) to reveal what should be kept secret: *I do b. myself with blushing*, LLL I, 2, 138. *how sometimes nature will b. its folly*, Wint. I, 2, 151. *that e'er thy tongue hath so —ed thine act*, Ant. II, 7, 84. Tit. IV, 2, 117. 149.

Betrim, to deck, to adorn: *which spongy April at thy hest —s*, Tp. IV, 65.

Betroth, to affiance: *—ed her to County Paris*, Rom. V, 3, 238. *—s himself to unquietness*, Ado I, 3, 49. Generally in the partic. *—ed: to whom I am —ed*, Gentl. IV, 2, 111. Mids. IV, 1, 177. Tw. V, 270. H6A V, 5, 26. R3 III, 7, 181. *we are —ed*, Gentl. II, 4, 179. *—ed lovers*, H5 II, 4, 108. Tit. I, 406. *his old —ed*, Meas. III, 2, 293. Tit. I, 286.

Better, adj., compar. of good: Sonn. 59, 11. Tp. I, 2, 496. II, 1, 281. Gentl. I, 1, 159. II, 1, 145. III, 1, 276. 385. Wiv. I, 1, 121. II, 2, 172. Meas. II, 4, 77. Err. III, 1, 29. IV, 2, 25. Merch. I, 2, 96. V, 96. As III, 2, 155 etc. etc. *the b. foot before* = with all speed: John IV, 2, 170. Tit. II, 3, 192. *still b. and worse*, Hml. III, 2, 261. *'tis b. using France than trusting France*, H6C IV, 1, 42. *b. it were a brother died at once*, Meas. II, 4, 106. Elliptically: *b. forbear* (= it is b. to forbear) Gentl. II, 7, 14. *b. have none than plural faith*, V, 4, 51. *b. three hours too soon than a minute too late*, Wiv. II, 2, 327. *b. shame than murder*, IV, 2, 45. H6B IV, 8, 49. H6C IV, 5, 26. H8 II, 3, 12. Mcb. III, 2, 19. Ant. III, 4, 23. *— he had b. starve than but once think*, H8 V, 3, 132. *he were b.*, in the same sense: *you were b. speak first*, As IV, 1, 73. *she were b. love a dream*, Tw. II, 2, 27. John IV, 3, 95. H4B I, 2, 102. Troil. I, 3, 370 (Q *it were b.*). Hml. II, 2, 550. The infinitive preceded by *to: I were b. to be married of him*, As III, 3, 92. *I were b. to be eaten to death*, H4B I, 2, 245. *— thou hadst been b. have been born a dog*, Oth. III, 3, 362. *thou wert b. thou hadst struck thy mother*, H4B V, 4, 11 (Doll's speech). *— The b.* = better: *it shall be the b. for you*, Meas. II, 1, 233. *how much the b. to fall before the lion*, Tw. III, 1, 139. *you are the b. at proverbs*, H5 III, 7, 131. *— The b. part* = the greater part: *how*

thy *worth with manners may I sing, when thou art all the b. part of me?* Sonn. 39, 2. *am b. than thy dear self's b. part*, Err. II, 2, 125. *were I not the b. part made of mercy*, As III, 1, 2 (but III, 2, 155 in its original sense). cf. *she will but disease our b. mirth*, Cor. I, 3, 117, i. e. our mirth which would be greater without her company. *— More b.* cf. *More.*

Better, adv., compar. of well: Tp. IV, 197. Gentl. V, 2, 18. V, 4, 3. Meas I, 3, 7. II, 1, 268. Ado III, 1, 116. Mids. III, 2, 35 etc. etc. *he could never come b.* (= more welcome) Wint. IV, 4, 187. *makes me the b. to confer with you*, Gentl. III, 2, 19.

Better worth = more worth: *his health was never b. worth than now*, H4A IV, 1, 27. *the very train of her worst wearing gown was b. worth than all my father's lands*, H6B I, 3, 89. *— To dare b.* = to dare rather: *dares b. be damned than to do it*, All's III, 6, 96. *Surrey durst b. have burnt that tongue than said so*, H8 III, 2, 253. *— It can be no b.* = it must, alas! have been so, Meas. V, 189.

Better, subst., 1) = something better: *seldom comes the b.* R3 II, 3, 4. *exchange the bad for b.* Gentl. II, 6, 13. *b. is by evil still made b.* Sonn. 119, 10. *did you ever hear b.* LLL IV, 1, 97. *I never looked for b. at his hands*, R3 III, 5, 50. *who seeks for b. of thee*, Tim. IV, 3, 24. 267. Cor. II, 1, 255. *— get the b. of them* = to vanquish them, Caes. II, 1, 326.

2) superior, one to whom precedence is due, either on account of higher qualities (as in H6B I, 3, 113: *my b. in the field;* cf. Shr. IV, 3, 75 R3 I, 2, 140. Troil. V, 2, 33) or of higher rank: *the courtesy of nations allows you my b.* As I, 1, 50. II, 4. 68. *under the degree of my —s*, Tw. I, 3, 125. John I, 156. H4B IV, 3, 71. H6B I, 3, 112. 114. V, 1, 119. H6C V, 5, 36. Tim. I, 2, 12. Hml. III, 4, 32. Lr. I, 4, 277. III, 6, 109. — (*When better fall*, All's III, 1, 22. *they'll fill a pit as well as b.* H4A IV, 2, 73. This substantive use the word has in common with all other adjectives).

Better, verb., 1) to improve: *dedicated to closeness and the —ing of my mind*, Tp. I, 2, 90. *he is furnished with my opinion, which, —ed with his own learning, comes with him*, Merch. IV, 1, 158. *his lands and goods, which I have —ed rather than decreased*, Shr. II, 119. *we will b. it in Pisa*, IV, 4, 71. *—ing thy loss makes the bad causer worse*, R3 IV, 4, 122 (i. e. magnifying). *but since he is —ed, we have therefore odds*, Hml. V, 2, 274 (= since he has perfected himself in his art). *striving to b., oft we mar what's well*, Lr. I, 4, 369. The following passages lead over to the second signification: *being red, she loves him best, and being white, her best is —ed with a more delight*, Ven. 78. *now counting best to be with you alone, then —ed that the world may see my pleasure*, Sonn. 75, 8. *all these I b. in one general best*, 91, 8.

2) to surpass: *he hath —ed expectation*, Ado I, 1, 16. *I will b. the instruction*, Merch. III, 1, 76. *what you do still —s what is done*, Wint. IV, 4, 136. *each day still b. other's happiness*, R2 I, 1, 22. *you are like to do such business. Not unlike, each way, to b. yours*, Cor. III, 1, 49. *they do b. thee*, Per. IV, 6, 172.

Bettering, subst., improvement, progress: *compare them (my verses) with the b. of the time*, Sonn. 32, 5.

Better-spoken, "speaking in better phrase and matter": Lr. IV, 6, 10; cf. 7.

Betumble, to disorder by tossing: *from her —d couch she starteth*, Lucr. 1037.

Between, prepos., 1) in the intermediate space (locally as well as temporally): *I lie b. that sun and thee*, Ven. 194. *b. ten and eleven*, Wiv. II,2, 86. Lucr. 390. Pilgr. 92. Wiv. I, 4, 27. III, 5, 47. Meas. I, 2, 29. III, 1, 223. Err. III, 2, 132. Mids. II, 1, 156. V, 34. 176. 208. *speak b. the change of man and boy*, Merch. III, 4, 66 etc. etc. Implying hinderance: *the locks b. her chamber and his will*, Lucr. 302. *to have no screen b. this part he played and him he played it for*, Tp. I, 2, 107 (i. e. wishing to play it for himself). *b. my soul's desire and me is Clarence*, H6C III, 2, 128. *come b. us*, Rom. II, 4, 71 (= assist me). *stood b. much heat and him*, Hml. III, 4, 3. *step b. her and her fighting soul*, 113. *come not b. the dragon and his wrath*, Lr. I, 1, 124. *to come b. our sentence and our power*, 173 (= to cross).

2) noting comparison or distinction: *tossed b. desire and dread*, Lucr. 171. *weighed b. loathness and obedience*, Tp. II, 1, 130. *made compare b. our statures*, Mids. III, 2, 291. H6A II, 4, 10. Ant. I, 2, 143 etc.

3) noting intercourse: *what a war of looks was then b. them*, Ven. 355. *heaven rain grace on that with breeds b. them*, Tp. III, 1, 76. Lucr. 405. Phoen. 33. Gentl. III, 2, 23. Wiv. I, 1, 34. 57. 102. II, 1, 208. III, 2, 25. Meas. III, 1, 162. IV, 1, 42. Ado I, 1, 64. LLL II, 41. V, 1, 102. Merch. I, 3, 84. II, 2, 159. III, 2, 321. All's III, 2, 36. *what is b. you?* Hml. I, 3, 98. I, 5, 139. *he may come and go b. you*, Wiv. II, 2, 130. All's V, 3, 259. Oth. III, 3, 100. Ant. III, 4, 25.

4) noting partnership: *lest b. them both it should be killed*, Lucr. 74 (= by them). *he was begot b. two stockfishes*, Meas. III, 2, 116. *I have some marks of yours upon my pate, some of my mistress' marks upon my shoulders, but not a thousand marks b. you both*, Err. I, 2, 84. *b. you I shall have a holy head*, II, 1, 80. *b. them they will kill the conjurer*, V, 177. *a Bergomask dance b. two of our company*, Mids. V, 361. *that b. you and the women the play may please*, As Epil. 17. *shall not thou and I b. them*, H5 V, 2, 220 (i. e. under the colours of S. D. and S. G.). *b. us we can kill a fly*, Tit. III, 2, 77. *he shall fall b. us*, Oth. IV, 2, 245. *I crave our composition may be written and sealed b. us*, Ant. II, 6, 60. *the unlawful issue that their lust hath made b. them*, III, 6, 8.

Between, adv., in the same sense: *these shrugs, when you have said 'she's goodly' come b., ere you can say 'she's honest'*, Wint. II, 1, 75. *as you had slept b.* IV, 1, 17. *the river hath thrice flowed, no ebb b.* H4B IV, 4, 125. *no impediment b.* Cor. II, 3, 236. *a more unhappy lady ne'er stood b.* Ant. III, 4, 13. *come you b., and save poor me*, Per. IV, 1, 90. *else he never would compare b.* R2 II, 1, 185. *gone b. and b.* Troil. I, 1, 72. cf. *Goer-between, Broker-between*.

Between, subst., interval: *there is nothing in the b. but getting wenches with child*, Wint. III, 3, 62 (the shepherd's speech).

Betwixt, prepos., of the same use as between (in R3 Qq usually *betwixt*, Ff. *between*).

1) *b. twelve and one*, Ado IV, 1, 85. *each soil b. that Holmedon and this seat of ours*, H4A I, 1, 65. As I, 1, 52. H4A I, 3, 45. III, 3, 49. IV, 2, 44. R3 III, 7, 48. Ant. III, 2, 29 etc. Idea of hinderance: *I will stand b. you and danger*, Wint. II, 2, 66. *set bounds*

b. their love and me, R3 IV, 1, 21. *thou keepest the stroke b. thy begging and my meditation*, IV, 2, 119.

2) *just the difference b. the constant red and mingled damask*, As III, 5, 123. All's I, 3, 116. Wint. I, 1, 4. II, 1, 87. H4A III, 1, 220. R3 I, 4, 82 etc.

3) *b. mine eye and heart a league is took*, Sonn. 47, 1. Meas. V, 218. Ado I, 1, 62. Mids. I, 1, 84. As IV, 3, 141. Wint. I, 1, 25. R2 I, 1, 50. III, 1, 12. V, 1, 73. H4A V, 5, 10. H6A I, 1, 106. III, 1, 139.189. IV, 1, 96. 131. V, 4, 99. R3 I, 1, 73. I, 3, 37. H8 I, 1, 180 etc.

4) *share the advice b. you*, All's II, 1, 3. *things known b. us three*, Wint. IV, 4, 571. *b. ourselves let us decide it then*, H6A IV, 1, 119.

Bevel, crooked: *I may be straight, though they themselves be b.*, Sonn. 121, 11.

Beverage, drink: *wholesome b.* Wint. I, 2, 346.

Bevis, a fabulous knight in the time of William the Conqueror: H8 I, 1, 38. (In H6B II, 3, 93 the spurious Qq add: *as B. of Southampton fell upon Ascapart*).

Bevy, troop, flock: *none here in all this noble b. has brought with her one care abroad*, H8 I, 4, 4. *he and many more of the same b. that I know the drossy age dotes on*, Hml. V, 2, 197 (Qq *breed*).

Bewail, to lament: Mids. IV, 1, 61. H6B III, 1, 217. H8 III, 2, 255. Cor. V, 6, 154. *Bewailed*, adjectively, = lamentable: *lest my —ed guilt should do thee shame*, Sonn. 36, 10.

Beware, vb. (only used in the imperative and infinitive), to take heed: 1) absolutely: *shake off slumber and b.* Tp. II, 1, 304. R2 V, 3, 39. H6C V, 6, 84. Troil. III, 3, 228. Tit. II, 1, 69. IV, 1, 96. Infinitive: *hadst thou but bid b.* Ven. 943.

2) followed by an accus.: *b. the rope's end*, Err. IV, 4, 45. Merch. III, 3, 7. As IV, 1, 200. H4A II, 4, 299. Caes. I, 2, 18. Mcb. IV, 1, 71. Lr. III, 4, 146. III, 6, 9. Infinitive: *best b. my sting*, Shr. II, 211. *bids you b. the Ides of March*, Caes. I, 2, 19.

3) followed by *of*: *b. of being captives*, All's II, 1, 21. *b. of them*, III, 5, 19. R3 I, 3, 292. Caes. II, 3, 1. Hml. I, 3, 65. Oth. III, 3, 165. Infinitive: *you would keep from my heels and b. of an ass*, Err. III, 1, 18. Cor. IV, 6, 54. Hml. I, 3, 67.

4) followed by a clause: *b. you lose it not*, H8 III, 1, 172.

In one passage it has the sense: to take care of, to guard: *priest, b. your beard; I mean to tug it*, H6A I, 3, 47.

Bewaste, in *time-bewasted*, q. v.

Beweep, 1) to weep over: Sonn. 29, 2. R3 I, 3, 328. I, 4, 251 (Ff. *he bewept my fortune*; Qq *when I parted with him*). II, 2, 49. Tim. V, 1, 161. Lr. I, 4, 324.

2) to bedew with tears: *sweet flowers, which bewept to the grave did go with true-love showers*, Hml. IV, 5, 38.

Bewet, to wet, to moisten. Partic. *bewet*: *his napkin, with his true tears all bewet*, Tit. III, 1, 146.

Bewhore, to call whore: *my lord hath so —d her*, Oth. IV, 2, 115.

Bewitch, to charm by witchcraft: Ven. 777. Lucr. 173. Compl. 131. Mids. I, 1, 27. Tw. III, 4, 113. H4A II, 2, 18. H6A III, 3, 58. H6B I, 1, 157. H6C III, 3, 112. R3 III, 4, 70. Rom. II Chor. 6. Tit. V, 3, 85. Per. II, 5, 49.

Bewitchment, power of charming: *I will counterfeit the b. of some popular man,* Cor. II, 3, 108.

Bewray, to discover: *longing to hear the hateful foe — ed,* Lucr. 1698. *to hear her secrets so —ed,* Pilgr. 352. H6A IV, 1, 107. H6C I, 1, 211. III, 3, 97. Tit. II, 4, 3. V, 1, 28. Cor. V, 3, 95. Lr. II, 1, 109. III, 6, 118.

Beyond, prepos., 1) on the other side of: *in the pool b. your cell,* Tp. IV, 182. *as I came b. Eton,* Wiv. IV, 5, 68. H4A III, 1, 76. H5 I, 2, 63. III, 6, 180. H6B I, 3, 128. R3 IV, 2, 48.

2) farther than: *b. all date,* Sonn. 122, 4. *she that dwells ten leagues b. man's life,* Tp. II, 1, 247. *is quite b. mine arm,* Wint. II, 3, 5. *my grief stretches itself b. the hour of death,* H4B IV, 4, 57. *I aim a mile b. the moon,* Tit. IV, 3, 65. *far b. my depth* (to swim) H8 III, 2, 361.

Various metaphorical use: *an earnest inviting, which many my near occasions did urge me to put off; but he hath conjured me b. them,* Tim. III, 6, 13 (past them, out of them). *you look b. him* = you construe him amiss, H4B IV, 4, 67. cf. *to cast b. ourselves in our opinions,* Hml. II, 1, 115. *the king hath gone b. me* = has disappointed, overreached me, H8 III, 2, 409. *if it be so far b. his health* = if he is so ill, Tim. III, 4, 75. *that wound, b. their feeling, to the quick,* Tit. IV, 2, 28, i. e. though their rude insensibility may not feel it.

Mostly = surpassing, above: *extremes b. extremity,* Lucr. 969. *our escape is much b. our loss,* Tp. II, 1, 3. *b. all credit,* II, 1, 59. III, 1, 72. V, 207. Wiv. IV, 2, 186. Err. V, 201. Ado I, 1, 14. Shr. I, 2, 90. Wint. I, 2, 144. II, 3, 198. IV, 2, 45. John IV, 3, 117. H4A I, 3, 200. H4B I, 3, 59. H6C II, 5, 51. H8 III, 1, 135. Troil. II, 3, 254. Cor. II, 2, 93. III, 1, 245. Caes. II, 2, 25. Mcb. V, 1, 65. Hml. I, 4, 56. Lr. I, 1, 58. Ant. III, 6, 87. III, 7, 76. Cymb. III, 3, 86. 4, 8. IV, 1, 12. V, 5, 165. I, 6, 80.

Beyond, adv.: *ambition cannot pierce a wink b.* (= farther), Tp. II, 1, 242. *mine is beyond beyond,* Cymb. III, 2, 58, i. e. surpasses all that is surpassing.

Bezonian, base fellow: H4B V, 3, 118. H6B IV, 1, 134.*

Bianca, female name: Shr. I, 1, 75 and passim. Oth. III, 4, 170 and passim.

Bias, subst. that which draws to a particular direction, preponderant tendency: *study his b. leaves and makes his book thine eyes,* Pilgr. 61 and LLL IV, 2, 113. *nature to her b. drew in that,* Tw. V, 267. *commodity, the b. of the world,* John II, 574. *this vile-drawing b., this sway of motion,* 577. 581. *the father falls from b. of nature,* Lr. I, 2, 120. — A weight on one side of a bowl which turns it a certain way: *thus the bowl should run, and not unluckily against the b.,* Shr. IV, 5, 25. *my fortune runs against the b.* R2 III, 4, 5.* — In a bad sense, that which is from the straight line, indirect ways, shifts: *and thus do we with windlasses and with assays of b., by indirections find directions out,* Hml. II, 1, 65.

Adjectively: *thy sphered b. cheek,* Troil. IV, 5, 8 (Intpp.: swelled as the bowl on the biassed side).

Bias, adv., out of a straight line, awry: *every action whereof we have record, trial did draw b. and thwart,* Troil. I, 3, 15.

Bias-drawing, subst., a turn awry: *faith and*

---

troth, strained purely from all hollow b. Troil. IV, 5, 169.

Bibble-babble, idle talk: Tw. IV, 2, 105. H5 IV, 1, 71 (Fluellen says *pibble pabble*).

Bickering, quarrel: *we shall begin our ancient —s,* H6B I, 1, 144.

Bid (Impf. *bid* and *bade; bid:* Ven. 946. Lucr. 1268. Meas. I, 3, 37. Err. IV, 3, 120. Mids. IV, 1, 200. As IV, 3, 7. Shr. I, 2, 30. II, 179. IV, 3, 94, etc. etc. *bade:* Pilgr. 182. 204. Tp. I, 2, 194. 219. Gentl. II, 1, 9. II, 6, 6. IV, 4, 50. Wiv. II, 2, 104. Shr. I, 2, 37. All's II, 1, 111. V, 3, 84 etc. etc. — Partic. once *bidden:* Ado III, 3, 32 (Verges' speech); everywhere else *bid:* Ven. 943. Sonn. 57, 8. Meas. V, 78. Ado V, 1, 155. Merch. II, 5, 11. As I, 2, 63. All's IV, 2, 53. John IV, 2, 63. R2 I, 3, 238. H6B II, 4, 85. R3 IV, 3, 39. Tit. I, 338. V, 2, 193. Caes. IV, 1, 35. Hml. II, 2, 372. Oth. I, 3, 15. Per. I, 3, 5).

1) to invite: *to b. you come in to dinner,* Ado II, 3, 256. *b. the Jew to sup to-night with ...,* Merch. II, 4, 17. *I am not bid to wait upon this bride,* Tit. I, 338. — Followed by a simple accus.: *b. your friends,* As V, 2, 79. *provide the feast and b. the guests,* Shr. II, 318. *b. all my friends again,* Tim. III, 4, 111. Followed by *to* before a noun: *he hath bid me to a calf's head,* Ado V, 1, 155. *my eye to the painted banquet —s my heart,* Sonn. 47, 6. *I am bid forth to supper,* Merch. II, 5, 11. *b. the duke to the nuptial,* As V, 2, 47. *they b. us to the English dancing-schools,* H5 III, 5, 32. *the feast that I have bid her to,* Tit. V, 2, 193. *kill them and b. me to them,* Tim. I, 2, 85. *thou —est me to my loss,* Cymb. III, 5, 165.

2) to offer: *there was no money bid for argument,* Hml. II, 2, 372. *I b. for you as I'ld buy,* Cymb. III, 6, 71. — *b. them battle,* H4A V, 2, 31. H6C I, 2, 71. III, 3, 235. V, 1, 63. 77. *to b. the wind a base,* Ven. 303. *I b. the base for Proteus,* Gentl. I, 2, 97 (cf. *Banns*).

3) to wish: *to b. adieu:* Sonn. 57, 8. LLL V, 2, 241. H6C IV, 8, 29. *farewell:* Wiv. III, 3, 127. R2 II, 2, 8. H6B II, 4, 85. R3 I, 2, 223. III, 5, 71. Rom. II, 3, 34. Mcb. I, 2, 21. *good morrow:* Shr. III, 2, 124. R3 III, 4, 52. *good night:* Ven. 534. Pilgr. 182. Ado III, 3, 156. John V, 5, 6. R3 IV, 3, 39. *welcome:* Tp. V, 110. Wiv. I, 1, 201. Err. III, 1, 68. Ado I, 1, 155. Merch. I, 2, 140. III, 2, 225. As V, 4, 40. H6A IV, 3, 40. Cymb. I, 6, 30 etc. *b. God speed him well,* R2 I, 4, 32.

4) to order, to command; a) followed by a simple accus.: *I'll be bid by thee,* All's IV, 2, 53. *if honour b. me on,* H4A IV, 3, 10. *b. them all home,* Cor. IV, 2, 1. 5. —

b) followed by a simple infinitive: *hadst thou but bid beware,* Ven. 943. *the messenger who —s beware,* Cor. IV, 6, 54. *the lady bade take away the fool,* Tw. I, 5, 57. *time —s be gone,* H4B I, 3, 110. *wisdom —s fear,* Lr. II, 4, 310. *Hector bade ask,* Troil. IV, 5, 71. with *to:* R2 II, 2, 115. — Hence passively: *we b. this be done,* Meas. I, 3, 37. *what he —s be done,* Cor. V, 4, 23.

c) followed by an accus. and infin. without *to:* *they b. thee crop a weed,* Ven. 946. Lucr. 434. 1268. 1292. Compl. 46. Tp. I, 2, 37. IV, 72. Gentl. II, 1, 9. II, 6, 6. III, 1, 258. IV, 2, 10. IV, 4, 39. Wiv. II, 2, 104. III, 2, 47. III, 5, 51. IV, 2, 112. Meas. I, 1, 16. 186. I, 3, 37. IV, 5, 9. V, 29. Err. II, 1, 35. II, 2,

189. III, 1, 30. IV, 1, 37. IV, 3, 20. V, 166 etc. etc. Passively: *he must be bid go forth,* Caes. IV, 1, 35. *so was I bid report,* Oth. I, 3, 15. — Sometimes the infin. supplied from what precedes or follows: *hast thou performed the tempest that I bade thee,* Tp. I, 2, 194. *as thou badest me*, *in troops I have dispersed them,* 219. II, 2, 7. III, 2, 9. Gentl. IV, 4, 50. Ado III, 3, 32. Merch. II, 5, 53. H8 V, 1, 157. Ant. IV, 14, 82.

d) followed by an accus. and an infin. preceded by *to: that which I would discover the law of friendship —s me to conceal,* Gentl. III, 1, 5. Mostly in the passive: *you were not bid to speak,* Meas. V, 78. *I was bid to come,* As I, 2, 63. *being bid to ask,* Per. I, 3, 5.

e) followed by a clause: *obedience —s I should not b. again,* R2 I, 1, 163. *b. him a should not think of God,* H5 II, 3, 21. *b. thy mistress, when my drink is ready, she strike upon the bell,* Mcb. II, 1, 31. The passage in All's V, 3, 84 is an anacoluthon.

Bidding, subst., command: *to thy strong b. task Ariel,* Tp. I, 2, 192. Merch. II, 5, 9. All's II, 5, 93. Wint. II, 1, 125. II, 3, 168. 207. H5 III, 7, 30. Cor. V, 4, 24. Tit. IV, 4, 107. Caes. V, 3, 87. Oth. IV, 3, 15. Ant. I, 4, 34 (plur.). III, 11, 60. III, 13, 87. Cymb. III, 4, 67. 73. Per. V, 1, 248. *at a person's b.:* All's II, 1, 18. 67. Tim. I, 1, 278. Lr. IV, 6, 104. *at our great b.* Mcb. III, 4, 129.

Biddy, a call to allure chickens: *ay, b., come with me,* Tw. III, 4, 128.

Bide (the same as *abide,* q. v.); impf. *bid,* R3 IV, 4, 304. 1) intr. to stay, to remain, to dwell: *some* (hairs) *in her threaden fillet still did b.* Compl. 33. *that to close prison he commanded her, with many bitter threats of —ing there,* Gentl. III, 1, 236. cf. Tit. II, 3, 284. Mids. III, 2, 186. Tit. V, 2, 137. Mcb. III, 4, 26. Ant. IV, 14, 131. Cymb. III, 4, 131. 138. *the gold —s gold that others touch,* Err. II, 1, 110. *in whose cold blood no spark of honour —s,* H6C I, 1, 184. *to b. upon't, thou art not honest,* Wint. I, 2, 242 (= to say it once more).

2) trans., a) to endure, to bear: *and patience b. each check,* Sonn. 58, 7. 139, 8. LLL I, 1, 115. Tw. II, 4, 97. 127. R3 IV, 4, 304. Lr. III, 4, 29.

b) to undergo, to meet: *I'll b. your proof,* Tw. I, 5, 71. *b. the touch,* H4A IV, 4, 10. *b. the mortal fortune of the field,* H6C II, 2, 83. *b. the encounter of assailing eyes,* Rom. I, 1, 219.

Biding, subst. abode: *blows these pitchy vapours from their b.* Lucr. 550. *I'll lead you to some b.* Lr. IV, 6, 228.

Bier, a frame of wood to convey dead bodies to the grave: Sonn. 12, 8. R2 V, 6, 52. Rom. III, 2, 60. IV, 1, 110. Hml. IV, 5, 164. Cymb. IV, 2, 22.

Bifold, twofold, double: Troil. V, 2, 144 (dubious; O. Edd. *by-fould* and *by foul*).

Big, 1) large; used of any dimension: *how to name the —er light, and how the less,* Tp. I, 2, 335. *the more it seeks to hide itself, the —er bulk it shows,* III, 1, 81. *a dog as b. as ten of yours,* Gentl. IV, 4, 62. *there is no woman's gown b. enough for him,* Wiv. IV, 2, 72. *this —er key,* Meas. IV, 1, 31. *if it* (the apparel) *be too b. for your thief,* IV, 2, 48. *he is not so b. as the end of his club,* LLL V, 1, 138. *let me have a —er* (cap) Shr. IV, 3, 68. *b. round tears,* As II, 1, 38. *no woman's heart so b. to hold so much,* Tw. II, 4, 99. *the husband is the —er* (fool), III, 1, 40. *although the sheet were b. enough for the bed of Ware,* III, 2, 50.

whose (the crown's) *compass is no —er than thy head,* R2 II, 1, 101. *the spoons will be the —er,* H8 V, 4, 40. *a carbuncle entire, as b. as thou art,* Cor. I, 4, 55. *I'll run away till I am —er,* V, 3, 128. *he seems no —er than his head,* Lr. IV, 6, 16. *a bump as b. as a young cockerel's stone,* Rom. I, 3, 53. *no —er than an agate-stone,* I, 4, 55. *another stain, as b. as hell can hold,* Cymb. II, 4, 140. *a court no —er than this cave,* III, 6, 83. *with —est tears o'ershowered,* Per. IV, 4, 26.

2) bulky, thick: *he is too b. to go in there,* Wiv. III, 3, 142. IV, 2, 80. *she is too b. for me to compass,* Err. IV, 1, 111. *nay, —er; women grow by men,* Rom. I, 3, 95. With the idea of corresponding strength: *his leg is too b. for Hector's,* LLL V, 2, 644. *the centre is not b. enough to bear a schoolboy's top,* Wint. II, 1, 102. *with hearts in their bellies no —er than pins' heads,* H4A IV, 2, 23. *care I for the limb, the thewes, the stature, bulk, and b. assemblance of a man?* H4B III, 2, 277. *an arm as b. as thine,* Cymb. IV, 2, 77.

3) pregnant: *let her sport herself with that she's b. with,* Wint. II, 1, 61. *b. of this gentleman,* Cymb. I, 1, 39. *autumn, b. with rich increase,* Sonn. 97, 6. *the b. year, swoln with some other grief, is thought with child,* H4B Ind. 13. Tropically: *his eye being b. with tears,* Merch. II, 8, 46. *how b. imagination moves in this lip,* Tim. I, 1, 32 (which may be also: a mighty, powerful imagination). *thy heart is b., get thee apart and weep,* Caes. III, 1, 282, i. e. full, fraught with grief. cf. *b. discontent,* Compl. 56.

4) swelled, inflated, haughty: *my mind hath been as b. as one of yours,* Shr. V, 2, 170. *wear the surplice of humility over the black gown of a b. heart,* All's I, 3, 99. *their rhymes, full of protest, of oath and b. compare,* Troil. III, 2, 182. *thy words are —er,* Cymb. IV, 2, 78. *A b. look is an angry and threatening look: shall lessen this b. look,* H8 I, 1, 119. Oftener *to look big: look not b., nor stamp,* Shr. III, 2, 230. *if you had but looked b. and spit at him, he'ld have run,* Wint. IV, 3, 113. *if that the devil and mischance look b. upon our affairs,* H4A IV, 1, 58. cf. *to look with forehead bold and b. enough upon the power of the king,* H4B I, 3, 8. — *A b. heart =* a stout heart: *I mock at death with as b. heart,* Cor. III, 2, 128. *a heart as b.* Cymb. IV, 2, 77. Hence in general = stout, manly, powerfully active: *b. Mars seems bankrupt in their beggared host,* H5 IV, 2, 43. *the b. wars, that make ambition virtue,* Oth. III, 3, 349. *A b. voice =* a loud and manly voice: *his b. manly voice, turning again toward childish treble,* As II, 7, 161. *boys with women's voices strive to speak b.* R2 III, 2, 114. Hence in general = loud: *whilst I was b. in clamour,* Lr. V, 3, 208.

Costard and Fluellen use the word instead of Great. *Pompey the B.* and *Alexander the B.* LLL V, 2, 553. H5 IV, 7, 14.

Bigamy, the marrying a widow: R3 III, 7, 189 (which was prohibited by a canon of the council of Lyons, A. D. 1274).

Big-bellied, big as if with child: *to see the sails conceive and grow b. with the wanton wind,* Mids. II, 1, 129. cf. *Belly,* vb.

Big-boned, having large bones: *no b. men framed of the Cyclops' size,* Tit. IV, 3, 46.

Biggen, nightcap: *as he whose brow with homely b. bound snores out the watch of night,* H4B IV, 5, 27.

Bigness, thickness: *their legs are both of a b.* H4B ll, 4, 265 (= of the same b.; cf. *A*).

Bigot, a name; *Lord B.*: John IV, 2, 162. 3, 103.*

Big-swoln, greatly swelled: *the sea, threatening the welkin with his b. face,* Tit. III, 1, 224. ready to burst: *my b. heart,* H6C ll, 2, 111.

Bilberry, whortleberry: *pinch the maids as blue as b.* Wiv. V, 5, 49.

Bilbo, 1) a Spanish blade, a blade in general: *to be compassed, like a good b., in the circumference of a peck,* Wiv. III, 5, 112. *I combat challenge of this latten b.* I, 1, 165.

2) *Bilboes,* a kind of fetters annexed to bars of iron, used at sea for mutinous sailors: *I lay worse than the mutines in the b.* Hml. V, 2, 6.

Bile (M. Edd. *boil*), inflamed tumor: Troil. II, 1, 2. Cor. I, 4, 31. Lr. II, 4, 226.

Bill, subst., the mouth of a bird: Ven. 1102. Mids. III, 1, 129. Cymb. IV, 2, 225. Used for the mouth, with allusion to the sense of the verb *to bill*: Wint. I, 2, 183.

Bill, subst., "a kind of pike or halbert, formerly carried by the English infantry, and afterwards the usual weapon of watchmen" (Nares): Ado III, 3, 44. R2 III, 2, 118. Rom. I, 1, 80. Tim. III, 4, 90 (a quibble). Play upon the word: *a goodly commodity, being taken up of these men's —s,* Ado III, 3, 191. *when shall we go to Cheapside and take up commodities upon our —s?* H6B IV, 7, 135. *Brown bill,* a particular sort of halbert for the use of war: H6B IV, 10, 13. Lr. IV, 6, 92.

Bill, subst., 1) any written paper, note, billet: *with —s on their necks 'Be it known etc.,'* As I, 2, 131 (erroneously taken by some commentators in the sense of halbert). *error i' the bill,* Shr. IV, 3, 146. 152 (what v. 130 had been *'note'*). *give these —s unto the legions on the other side,* Caes. V, 2, 1.

2) an order drawn on a person, directing him to pay money to another person: *in any b., warrant, quittance, or obligation,* Wiv. I, 1, 10. *I have —s for money by exchange from Florence,* Shr. IV, 2, 89.

3) a reckoning (cf. *tavern-bill*): *why then preferred you not your sums and —s,* Tim. III, 4, 49. 90.

4) a list, specification: *I'll draw a b. of properties,* Mids. I, 2, 108. *receive particular addition, from the b. that writes them all alike,* Mcb. III, 1, 100.

5) a public advertisement, placard: *he set up his —s here in Messina and challenged Cupid at the flight,* Ado I, 1, 39.* *by proscription and —s of outlawry,* Caes. IV, 3, 173.

6) a draft of a law, presented to the parliament, but not yet enacted: *I'll exhibit a bill in the parliament for the putting down of men,* Wiv. II, 1, 29. *that self b. is urged,* H5 I, 1, 1. cf. 19. 70.

Bill, vb., to join bills: *two silver doves that sit a —ing,* Ven. 366. *as pigeons b.* As III, 3, 82. Troil. III, 2, 60 (where a quibble seems to be intended).

Billet, subst., a small log of wood: *they shall beat out my brains with —s,* Meas. IV, 3, 58.

Billet, vb., to direct by a ticket where to lodge; to quarter: *the centurions and their charges, distinctly —ed, already in the entertainment,* Cor. IV, 3, 48. *go where thou art —ed,* Oth. II, 3, 386.

Billiards, game played on a table with balls: Ant. II, 5, 3.

Billingsgate, place in England: H4B II, 1, 182 (Ff and M. Edd. *Basingstoke*).

Billow, great wave: Tp. III, 3, 96. H4B III, 1, 22. H5 III Chor. 15. R3 I, 4, 20. H8 III, 1, 10. Caes. V, 1, 67. Oth. II, 1, 12. Per. III Prol. 45. III, 1, 46. III, 2, 58.

Bind (impf. and partic. *bound,* but *bounden* in As I, 2, 298 and John III, 3, 29), 1) to fasten or restrain by a tie: *he will not in her arms be bound,* Ven. 226. Lucr. 1501. *they must be bound,* Err. IV, 4, 97. 109. V, 145. Ado IV, 2, 67. V, 1, 233. Tit. II, 126. Rom. I, 2, 55 etc. Absolutely: *fast b., fast find,* Merch. II, 5, 54. Followed by *to: those fair arms which bound him to her breast,* Ven. 812. Err. I, 1, 82. John IV, 1, 4. H6A I, 1, 22. Tit. II, 1, 16 etc. *To b. in* = to confine: *cribbed, confined, bound in to doubts and fears,* Mcb. III, 4, 24. *to b. up* = to paralyze, to restrain: *my spirits are all bound up,* Tp. I, 2, 486. *when poisoned hours had bound me up from mine own knowledge,* Ant. II, 2, 90.

2) to tie, to confine with any ligature: *they that reap must sheaf and b.* As III, 2, 113. *the packet is not come where that and other specialties are bound,* LLL II, 165. *I'll b. it* (the wounded leg) *with my shirt,* Oth. V, 1, 73. *let me but b. it* (your forehead) *hard,* III, 3, 286. *bound with victorious wreaths,* R3 I, 1, 5. *bound with triumphant garlands,* IV, 4, 333. *his brows bound with oak,* Cor. I, 3, 16. *bound with laurel boughs,* Tit. I, 74. Used of books (= to put in a cover): *I'll have them fairly bound,* Shr. I, 2, 147. Rom. III, 2, 84.

To bind up, in the same sense: *having bound up the threatening twigs,* Meas. I, 3, 24. *to b. him up a rod,* Ado II, 1, 226 (Ff *to b. him a rod*). *to b. our loves up in a holy band,* III, 1, 114. *b. up those tresses,* John III, 4, 61. 68. *b. up your dangling apricocks,* R2 III, 4, 29. — *bound up his wound,* As IV, 3, 151. R3 V, 3, 177. And figuratively: *b. up the petty difference,* Ant. II, 1, 48. — *to see his work so noble vilely bound up,* Wint. IV, 4, 22.

To b. in = to enclose, surround: *bound in with the triumphant sea,* R2 II, 1, 61. 63. *a hoop of gold to b. thy brothers in,* H4B IV, 4, 43. *a costly jewel, bound in with diamonds,* H6B III, 2, 107.

3) to knit: *b. this knot of amity,* H6A V, 1, 16.

4) to oblige, to engage; a) to engage by a legal tie, to pawn, to pledge, to mortgage: *he learned but surety-like to write for me under that bond that him as fast doth b.* Sonn. 134, 8. *in surety of the which one part of Aquitaine is bound to us,* LLL II, 136. *for the which Antonio shall be bound,* Merch. I, 3, 5. 6. 10. V, 137. *bound to himself! what doth he with a bond that he is bound to?* R2 V, 2, 67. *Montague is bound as well as I,* Rom. I, 2, 1.

To b. to one = to engage in the service of one: *my duty is bound to your lordship,* Lucr. Ded. 5. *bound to her imposition,* Lucr. 1697. *how much in duty I am bound to both,* H6A II, 1, 37. *so shall you b. me to your highness' service,* H6C III, 2, 43. *the fragments of her faith are bound to Diomed,* Troil. V, 2, 160. *nature, to thy law my services are bound,* Lr. I, 2, 2. *he's bound unto Octavia,* Ant. II, 5, 58. *time hath rooted out my parentage and to the world and awkward casualties bound me in servitude,* Per. V, 1, 95. The partic. without *to: bound servants, steal!* Tim. IV, 1, 10. *with all bound humbleness,* All's II, 1, 117.

b) to engage, to tie by any other obligation, especially a moral one: *to b. him to remember my good will*, Gentl. IV, 4, 103. *to b. me, or undo me*, Ado IV, 4, 20. *it most of all these reasons —eth us, in our opinions she should be preferred*, H6A V, 5, 60. *your lordship ever binds him*, Tim. I, 1, 104. *in which I b., on pain of punishment, the world to weet we stand up peerless*, Ant. I, 1, 38. Absolutely: *marriage —s*, As V, 4, 59. Very frequent is the partic. *bound* = obliged: *bound by my charity and blest order, I come*, Meas. II, 3, 3; *I am bound by oath*, R3 IV, 1, 28. mostly followed by *to* and an infin.: *by law of nature thou art bound to breed*, Ven. 171. Sonn. 58, 4. Meas. IV, 3, 100. Err. V, 305. LLL IV, 1, 56. Merch. IV, 1, 65. Shr. V, 2, 164. John III, 1, 65. Lr. III, 7, 8. Ant. II, 6, 124. Cymb. I, 6, 81 etc. *I will be bound to pay it*, Merch. IV, 1, 211. *I dare be bound again, that your lord will never more break faith*, V, 251. *I dare be bound he's true*, Cymb. IV, 3, 18. *how can we for our country pray, whereto* (viz to pray for our country) *we are bound, together with thy victory, whereto we are bound?* Cor. V, 3, 108. — Followed by *to* and a noun: *to plainness honour is bound*, Lr. I, 1, 150. — Followed by *against: how much I could despise this man, but that I am bound in charity against it*, H8 III, 2, 298.

Bound to one = obliged to one, owing him gratitude: *so shall I evermore be bound to thee*, Wiv. IV, 6, 54. Meas. IV, 1, 25. LLL I, 2, 156. Merch. IV, 1, 407. V, 135. Wint. IV, 4, 575. H4B III, 2, 181. H6A II, 4, 128. H8 I, 2, 112. III, 2, 165. V, 3, 114 *(bound to heaven in daily thanks)*. Cor. 3, 159. Rom. IV, 2, 32 etc. *Bound to one for sth.*: As I, 1, 16. Tw. III, 4, 297. Oth. I, 3, 182. — *Bounden:* As I, 2, 298 and John III, 3, 29. For *bound* = prepared, ready (as perhaps also in Meas. III, 2, 167. John II, 522. H6C II, 4, 3. Hml. I, 5, 6. Lr. III, 7, 11. Cymb. I, 6, 81) see the article *Bound*.

Biondello, name in Shr. I, 1, 42. 213 etc.

Birch, the tree betula: *the threatening twigs of b.* Meas. I, 3, 24.

Bird, 1) a feathered flying animal: Ven. 67. 455. 532. 1101. Lucr. 88. 457. 871. 1107. 1121. Sonn. 73, 4. 97, 12. 113, 6. Pilgr. 282. 377. Wiv. III, 1, 18. Ado II, 1, 230. LLL I, 1, 103. V, 2, 933. Mids. III, 1, 138. V, 401. Merch. III, 1, 32. As II, 5, 4. H6B II, 1, 8 etc. etc. *birds of prey*, Meas. II, 1, 2. *enticing —s* = decoy-birds, H6B I, 3, 92. *b. of night* = owl, Caes. I, 3, 26. *the Arabian b.* (Phoenix) Cymb. I, 6, 17. *the rod and b. of peace* (i. e. the dove) H8 IV, 1, 89. *I heard a b. so sing*, H4B V, 5, 113. Allusion to the proverb *'tis a bad b. that fouls its own nest'*, As IV, 1, 208; to the proverb *'birds of a feather flock together'*: H6C II, 1, 170. III, 3, 161.

2) the young of any fowl: *as that ungentle gull, the cuckoo's b., useth the sparrow*, H4A V, 1, 60. *if thou be that princely eagle's b.* H6C II, 2, 91. *ravens foster forlorn children, the whilst their own —s famish in their nests*, Tit. II, 3, 154.

3) used as a term of endearment: *this was well done, my b.* Tp. IV, 184. *am I your b.? I mean to shift my bush*, Shr. V, 2, 46. *I would I were thy b.* Rom. II, 2, 183. *come, b., come*, Hml. I, 5, 116. *the b. is dead that we have made so much on*, Cymb. IV, 2, 197.

Bird-bolt, a short arrow with a broad flat end, used to kill birds without piercing: Ado I, 1, 42. LLL IV, 3, 25. Tw. I, 5, 100.

Birding, bird-shooting: *we'll a b. together*, Wiv. III, 3, 247. III, 5, 46. 131. IV, 2, 8.

Birding-piece, a gun to shoot birds with, fowling-piece: Wiv. IV, 2, 59.

Birdlime, a glutinous substance to catch birds: *my invention comes from my pate as b. does from frize*, Oth. II, 1, 127.

Birnam, name of a forest in Scotland: Mcb. IV, 1, 93. V, 2, 5. V, 3, 60 etc.*

Biron, name, see *Berowne*.

Birth, 1) the act of coming into life: *truer stars did govern Proteus' b.*, Gentl. II, 7, 74. Wiv. V, 5, 87. LLL IV, 2, 36. V, 2, 521. Wint. IV, 4, 80. H6C V, 6, 44. Troil. IV, 4, 40 etc. Plur. *births:* Wint. V, 1, 118. R3 IV, 4, 215 (Ff *birth*).

2) the act of bringing forth: *two children at one b.* H6B IV, 2, 147. *both at a b.* Oth. II, 3, 212. *a grievous burthen was thy b. to me*, R3 IV, 4, 167. *am I a mother to the b. of three?* Cymb. V, 5, 369.

3) that which is born: *a dearer b. than this his love had brought*, Sonn. 32, 11. Tp. II, 1, 230. Ado IV, 1, 215. LLL I, 1, 104 etc. Plur. *births:* H4B IV, 4, 122. H5 V, 2, 35.

4) extraction, descent: *some glory in their b.* Sonn. 91, 1. 37, 5. 76, 8. Gentl. I, 3, 33. V, 2, 22. Wiv. III, 4, 4. Ado II, 1, 172. Merch. II, 7, 32. As I, 1, 10. Shr. Ind. 2, 20. H6A I, 2, 72. II, 4, 28. II, 5, 73. III, 1, 95. III, 3, 61. V, 1, 59. H6B IV, 2, 152. V, 1, 119. R3 III, 7, 120. V, 5, 15 (—s) etc. *a match of b.* = a high-born match, John II, 430.

Birth-child, a child adopted on account of its being born within a certain domain: *Thetis' b.* Per. IV, 4, 41.

Birth-day, the day on which a person was born: Caes. V, 1, 71. Ant. III, 13, 185. Per. II, 1, 114.

Birthdom, that which belongs to one by birth, especially the mother-country: *let us rather hold fast the mortal sword and like good men bestride our down-fallen b.* Mcb. IV, 3, 4.

Birth-hour, the hour in which one is born: *worse than a slavish wipe or —'s blot*, Lucr. 537.

Birth-place, the place where one is born: Cor. IV, 4, 23.

Birthright, a privilege to which one is entitled by birth: *his b. to the crown*, H6B II, 2, 62. *to lose his b.* H6C I, 1, 219. II, 2, 35. *bearing their —s on their backs*, John II, 70 (i. e. their patrimonies). *thy goodness share with thy b.* All's I, 1, 73, i. e. thy goodness may partake of thy inheritance, may be as great as the nobleness of thy birth.

Birth-strangled, strangled in being born: Mcb. IV, 1, 30.

Biscuit, hard dry bread baked for sea-voyages: *as dry as the remainder b. after a voyage*, As II, 7, 39. *as a sailor breaks a b.* Troil. II, 1, 43.

Bishop, spiritual governor of a diocese: R2 IV, 101. H4A III, 2, 104. H6A III, 1, 53. 76. 78. 131. IV, 1, 1 *(Lord B.).* V, 1, 60. H6B I, 1, 8. IV, 4, 9. R3 III, 5, 100. IV, 4, 503. H8 II, 4, 172. III, 2, 312 etc. = archbishop: H4B I, 1, 200. III, 1, 95. IV, 2, 15 *(lord b.)*. H6C IV, 4, 11. IV, 5, 5.

Bisson, purblind: *your b. conspectuities*, Cor. II, 1, 70 (O. Edd. *beesom*). *threatening the flames with b. rheum*, Hml. II, 2, 529 (i. e. blinding tears). In Cor.

III, 1, 131 O. Edd. *bosom multiplied*, some M. Edd. *bisson multitude.*

Bit, 1) the iron part of a bridle which is put in the mouth of the horse: *the iron b. he crusheth 'tween his teeth*, Ven. 269. Meas. I, 3, 20. Shr. III, 2, 57. H5 IV, 2, 49. H8 V, 3, 23.

2) morsel: LLL I, 1, 26. As II, 7, 133. Troil. V, 2, 159. V, 8, 20 (Q *bait*, F1 *bed*). Cor. IV, 5, 36. Tim. II, 2, 174.

Bitch, female dog: Wiv. III, 5, 11. *the son and heir of a mongrel b.* Lr. II, 2, 24.

Bitch-wolf, female wolf: *thou —'s son*, Troil. II, 1, 11.

Bite, vb. (partic. *bit*: H4A II, 1, 19. Rom. I, 1, 157. Lr. I, 4, 236. IV, 7, 37. *bitten*: H8 V, 4, 64, and in *fly-bitten* and *weather-bitten*, q. v. Of the impf. no instance).

1) to seize or crush with the teeth; a) absolutely: *she hath no teeth to b.* Gentl. III, 1, 349. *this fish will b.* Ado II, 3, 114. I, 3, 37. R2 I, 3, 303. H5 V, 1, 46. H6B V, 1, 152. H6C V, 6, 77. R3 I, 3, 290. Lr. III, 6, 70. Ant. V, 2, 247.

b) trans.: *he stamps and —s the poor flies*, Ven. 316. Tp. II, 2, 10. III, 2, 38. Ado III, 2, 80. H4A II, 1, 19. Troil V, 7, 19. Lr. III, 6, 18. IV, 7, 37. Ant. II, 5, 80. *whereof the ewe not —s*, Tp. V, 38. *to b. off*, Lr. I, 4, 236. *atwain*, II, 2, 80. *Bit and bitten* = injured by biting, gnawn: *the bud bit with an envious worm*, Rom. I, 1, 157. *bitten apples*, H8 V, 4, 64. — *To b. one's tongue* = to b. off one's tongue: *shall we b. our tongues*, Tit. III, 1, 131; and then = to be silent: *so York must sit and fret and b. his tongue*, H6B I, 1, 230. *view this face, and b. thy tongue, that slanders him with cowardice*, H6C I, 4, 47. — *To b. the lip*, a sign of commotion: *—s his lip with a politic regard*, Troil. III, 3, 254. *he —s his lip and starts*, H8 III, 2, 113. Particularly of anger: *thou canst not frown, nor b. the lip, as angry wenches will*, Shr. II, 250. R3 IV, 2, 27 (Ff. *gnaws*). Cor. V, 1, 48. — *I will b. my thumb at them*, Rom. I, 1, 48—58 (i. e. "defy them by putting the thumb-nail into the mouth, and with a jerk from the upper teeth make it to knack." Cotgrave). — *To b. one by the ear*, an expression of endearment: Rom. II, 4, 81. — *To b. the law by the nose* = to mock the law: Meas. III, 1, 109.

2) figuratively used, a) absol.; of the weather: *the winter's wind, when it —s and blows upon my body*, As II, 1, 8. II, 7, 185. H6B III, 2, 337. H6C IV, 8, 61. Hml. I, 4, 1. of a cutting sword: *I have a sword and it shall b.* Wiv. II, 1, 136. R2 I, 3, 303. Lr. V, 3, 276. *Biting* = bitter: *a —ing jest*, R3 II, 4, 30. = sharp, severe: *most —ing laws*, Meas. I, 3, 19. *—ing statutes*, H6B IV, 7, 19. = grieving, mortifying: *a —ing affliction*, Wiv. V, 5, 178. *a —ing error*, Ado IV, 1, 172. *to b. at sth.* = to inveigh against sth.: Troil. II, 2, 33 (quibble).

b) trans., = to nip: *a frost that —s the first-born infants of the spring*, LLL I, 1, 101. Shr. V, 2, 139. H4B I, 3, 41. = to cut: *my dagger muzzled, lest it should b. its master*, Wint. I, 2, 157. Troil. V, 2, 171. = to grieve, to pain: *their guilt now 'gins to b. the spirits*, Tp. III, 3, 106. R2 I, 3, 292. = to hurt, to injure: *thou camest to b. the world*, H6C V, 6, 54. *exceeding mad, in love too, but he would b. none*, H8 I, 4, 29. *dare b. the best*, V, 3, 45

(the image in most of the last passages being taken from a dog). cf. *Fly-bitten.*

Bitter, having an acrid taste, like wormwood: *b. wormwood*, Lucr. 893. *sauces*, Sonn. 118, 6. *pills*, Gentl. II, 4, 149. *physic*, Meas. IV, 6, 8. *gall*, LLL V, 2, 237. Rom. I, 5, 94. *taste*, H4B IV, 5, 79. *sweeting*, Rom. II, 4, 83. Metaphorically used of any thing disagreeable, painful, mortifying or injurious: *a b. deputy*, Meas. IV, 2, 81. *a b. fool*, Lr. I, 4, 150. *your b. foe*, Mids. III, 2, 44. *the base, though b. disposition of Beatrice*, Ado II, 1, 215. *no bitterness that I will b. think*, Sonn. 111, 11. *consecrate commotion's b. edge*, H4B IV, 1, 93. *thou b. sky*, As II, 7, 184. *sweet and b. fancy*, IV, 3, 102. *read in the b. letter*, Oth. I, 3, 68. *b. business*, Hml. III, 2, 409. *b. words*, Lucr. 1460. As III, 5, 69. Shr. II, 28. *terms*, H5 IV, 8, 44. Tit. II, 3, 110. *names*, R3 I, 3, 236. *breath*, Mids. III, 2, 44. *taunts*, H6C II, 6, 66. *scoffs*, R3 I, 3, 104. *threats*, Gentl. III, 1, 236. *invective*, Lucr. Arg. 24. *wrong*, Mids. III, 2, 361. *jest*, LLL IV, 3, 174. *injuries*, H6A II, 5, 124. *a b. thing*, As V, 2, 48. *b. shame*, John III, 4, 110. *the b. bread of banishment*, R2 III, 1, 21. *b. fasts*, Gentl. II, 4, 131. *the b. sentence*, R3 I, 4, 191. *consequence*, IV, 2, 15. *b., black and tragical*, IV, 4, 7. *—est enmity*, Cor. IV, 4, 18 etc. etc. Followed by *to: you are too b. to your country-woman*, Troil. IV, 1, 67. *makes the world b. to the best of our times*, Lr. I, 2, 49. *to make this b. to thee*, Oth. I, 1, 104. Followed by *with: do not be so b. with me*, Mids. III, 2, 306. As III, 5, 138.

Adverbially: *'tis b. cold*, Hml. I, 1, 8.

Substantively: *to talk their —est*, Wint. III, 2, 217.

Bitterly, adv., 1) in a manner expressing poignant grief: *wept b.* Gentl. IV, 4, 176. *cried b.* Rom. I, 3, 54. — 2) with acrimony: *speak b.* Meas. V, 36. R3 III, 7, 142. 192. IV, 4, 180. H8 I, 2, 24. — 3) sharply: *the north-east wind blew b. against our faces*, R2 I, 4, 7. — 4) calamitously: *some consequence yet hanging in the stars shall b. begin his fearful date*, Rom. I, 4, 108.

Bitterness, 1) vexation, grief: *the b. of absence*, Sonn. 57, 7. *no b. that I will bitter think*, 111, 11. *joy could not show itself modest enough without a badge of b.* Ado I, 1, 23. John III, 4, 111. Oth. I, 1, 163.

2) acrimony: *say not so in b.* As III, 5, 3. *contempt nor b. were in his pride or sharpness*, All's I, 2, 36. *you do measure the heat of our livers with the b. of your galls*, H4B I, 2, 198. R3 I, 3, 179. Tit. IV, 4, 12. Cymb. III, 5, 137.

Bitter-searching, thrilling: *b. terms*, H6B III, 2, 311 (Ff. without the hyphen).

Bitumed, pitched with bitumen: Per. III, 1, 72. III, 2, 56 (O. Edd. *bottomed*).

Blab, 1) absol. = to tell what ought to be kept secret: *these blue-veined violets whereon we lean never can b.* Ven. 126. *when my tongue —s, then let mine eyes not see*, Tw. I, 2, 63. H6B IV, 1, 1. Troil. III, 2, 132. Oth. IV, 1, 29.

2) trans.: *Beaufort's red sparkling eyes b. his heart's malice*, H6B III, 1, 154. Tit. III, 1, 83.

Black, adj. (Compar. *blacker*: As IV, 3, 35. Wint. II, 1, 8. III, 2, 173. Oth. V, 2, 131. Per. I, 1, 135. Superl. *blackest*: Lucr. 354. Gentl. III, 1, 285. Hml. IV, 5, 131. Oth. II, 3, 357). 1) of the colour of night: Lucr. 1454. Sonn. 127, 9. Gentl. III, 1, 287.

Wiv. V, 5, 20. 41. Meas. II, 4, 79. LLL V, 2, 266. 844. Mids. II, 2, 22. III, 1, 128. III, 2, 357. V, 171. Wint. II, 1, 8. R2 IV, 95. H6C II, 1, 161. Rom. I, 1, 237 etc. etc. *The B. Prince*, All's IV, 5, 44 (a quibble). R2 II, 3, 101. H5 I, 2, 105. II, 4, 56. IV, 7, 97. H6B II, 2, 11. *b. chaos*, Ven. 1020. *b. cloud*, Tp. II, 2, 20. *b. storm*, H6B III, 1, 349. *b. vesper's pageants*, Ant. IV, 14, 8. *beaten b. and blue*, Wiv. IV, 5, 115. *pinch us b. and blue*, Err. II, 2, 194. *we will fool him b. and blue*, Tw. II, 5, 12.

2) of a dark complexion; often opposed to *fair: I have sworn thee fair and thought thee bright, who art as b. as hell*, Sonn. 147, 14. cf. 127, 1. 131, 12. Gentl. V, 2, 10. Ado III, 1, 63. LLL IV, 3, 253. 261. Rom. I, 1, 237. Oth. I, 3, 291. II, 1, 130 etc. Proverb: *b. men are pearls in beauteous ladies' eyes*, Gentl. V, 2, 12. Synonymous to ugly: *though ne'er so b., say they have angels' faces*, Gentl. III, 1, 103. *the air hath starved the roses in her cheeks and pinched the lily-tincture of her face, that now she is become as b. as I*, IV, 4, 161. cf. Ant. I, 5, 28. *all the pictures fairest lined are but b. to Rosalind*, As III, 2, 98. LLL IV, 3, 247. H6A I, 2, 84.

3) Figuratively, = evil, wicked, horrible, dismal: *so b. a deed*, Lucr. 226. Wint. III, 2, 173. R2 IV, 131. *—est sin*, Lucr. 354. Oth. II, 3, 357. *b. lust*, Lucr. 654. *words —er in their effect than in their countenance*, As IV, 3, 35. *actions —er than the night*, Per. I, 1, 135. *thoughts b.* Hml. III, 2, 266. *b. scandal*, R3 III, 7, 231. *b. envy*, H8 II, 1, 85. *my b. and deep desires*, Mcb. I, 4, 51. *vengeance*, Oth. III, 3, 447. *b. Nemesis*, H6A IV, 7, 78. *the —est devil*, Hml. IV, 5, 131. Oth. V, 2, 131. *b. Macbeth*, Mcb. IV, 3, 52. *you secret, b. and midnight hags*, IV, 1, 48. *hell's b. intelligencer*, R3 IV, 4, 71. *b. magician*, I, 2, 34. *holy seems the quarrel upon your grace's part, b. and fearful on the opposer*, All's III, 1, 5. *thou'rt damned as b. —, nay, nothing is so b.*, John IV, 3, 121. *it will be a b. matter for the king that led them to it*, H5 IV, 1, 151. *he had a b. mouth that said other of him*, H8 I, 3, 58. *this b. strife*, Rom. III, 1, 183. *as b. defiance as heart can think*, Troil. IV, 1, 12. *in our b. sentence and proscription*, Caes. IV, 1, 17. *reward not hospitality with such b. payment*, Lucr. 576. *the —est news*, Gentl. III, 1, 285. *b. tidings*, R2 III, 4, 71. *that b. name, Edward black prince of Wales*, H5 II, 4, 56. *that b. word death*, Rom. III, 3, 27. *b. despair*, H6B III, 3, 23. R3 II, 2, 36. *a b. day*, R3 V, 3, 280. Rom. IV, 5, 53. *b. funeral*, IV, 5, 85. *b. stage for tragedies*, Lucr. 766. *bitter, b. and tragical*, R3 IV, 4, 7. *b. and portentous must this humour prove*, Rom. I, 1, 147. *die under their* (my curses') *b. weight*, John III, 1, 297.

Adverbially: *looked b. upon me*, Lr. II, 4, 162.

Black, subst., black colour: *clad in mourning b.* Lucr. 1585. *in the old age b. was not counted fair*, Sonn. 127, 1. *thy b. is fairest in my judgment's place*, Sonn. 131, 12. *have put on b.* 132, 3. *in b. mourn I*, Pilgr. 263. *b. is the badge of hell*, LLL IV, 3, 254. *in b. my lady's brows are decked*, 258. 261. *put on sullen b.* R2 V, 6, 48. *hung be the heavens with b.* H6A I, 1, 1. *we mourn in b.* 17. *all in b.* Rom. III, 2, 11. *suits of solemn b.* Hml. I, 2, 78. *let the devil wear b.* III, 2, 137. *— which is not under white and b.* (= not written down) Ado V, 1, 314. *though the truth of it stands off as gross as b. and white*, H5 II, 2, 104. — Plur. *blacks* = black stuffs or clothes: *were they false as o'erdyed*

blacks, Wint. I, 2, 132, i. e. black things dyed over with another colour.

Blackamoor, negress: *I care not an she were a b.* Troil. I, 1, 80.

Blackberry, the berry of the bramble: *shall the blessed sun of heaven prove a micher and eat —ies?* H4A II, 4, 450. Used to denote a thing of little worth: *if reasons were as plentiful as —ies*, H4A II, 4, 265. *is not proved worth a b.* Troil. V, 4, 13.

Blackbrowed, blackfaced: *b. night*, Mids. III, 2, 387. Rom. III, 2, 20.

Black-cornered, hiding things in dark corners: *when the day serves, before b. night, find what thou wantest by free and offered light*, Tim. V, 1, 47.

Blackfaced, having a black face, gloomy: *b. night*, Ven. 773. *cloud*, Lucr. 547. *storms*, 1518. *b. Clifford*, R3 I, 2, 159.

Blackfriars, name of a quarter of London: H8 II, 2, 139.

Blackheath, a heath near London: H5 V Chor. 16.

Blackmere: *Lord Strange of B.* (one of Talbot's titles), H6A IV, 7, 65.

Black-monday, Easter-Monday: Merch. II, 5, 25.

Blackness, 1) black colour: *the raven chides b.* Troil. II, 3, 221. *a white that shall her b. fit*, Oth. II, 1, 134. *night's b.* Ant. I, 4, 13.

2) wickedness: *to keep his bed of b. unlaid ope*, Per. I, 2, 89.

Black-oppressing, harassing with dark thoughts: LLL I, 1, 234 (O. Edd. without the hyphen).

Bladder, the bag in the body which serves as the receptacle of the urine: *—s full of imposthume*, Troil. V, 1, 24. Taken out and inflated with air, it serves for several purposes: *blows a man up like a b.* H4A II, 4, 366. *swim on —s*, H8 III, 2, 359. *—s and musty seeds*, Rom. V, 1, 86.

Blade, 1) the green shoot of corn before it grows to seed; used as an emblem of youth: *done in the b. of youth*, All's V, 3, 6 (M. Edd. *blaze*, on account of the following simile).

2) the cutting part of a weapon: *you break jests as braggarts do their —s*, Ado V, 1, 190. H6A II, 4, 13. H6C I, 3, 50. Rom. I, 4, 84. Mcb. II, 1, 46. V, 8, 11. Used for the whole sword: *he shakes aloft his Roman b.* Lucr. 505. Mids. V, 147. 351. R3 I, 4, 211. Rom. I, 1, 85.

3) a fencer: *a very good b.! a very tall man!* Rom. II, 4, 31 (expressions ridiculed by Mercutio)

Bladed, having blades: *decking with liquid pearl the b. grass*, Mids. I, 1, 211. *though b. corn be lodged and trees blown down*, Mcb. IV, 1, 55.*

Blain, a botch: *itches, —s, sow all the Athenian bosoms*, Tim. IV, 1, 28.

Blame, subst., 1) reprehension, disapprobation: *whose crime will bear an ever-during b.* Lucr. 224. *not that devoured, but that which doth devour, is worthy b.* Lucr. 1257. Pilgr. 301. Err. III, 1, 45 H6C V, 5, 54. R3 IV, 1, 25. Cor. V, 3, 90. V, 5, 147. Hml. IV, 7, 67. Lr. II, 4, 147. Oth. I, 3, 177. Cymb. V, 3, 3. *shall render you no b.* All's V, 1, 32. *he hath much worthy b. laid upon him*, All's IV, 3, 7. *his absence lays b. upon his promise*, Mcb. III, 4, 44. *lay not your b. on me*, Oth. IV, 2, 46.

2) that which deserves disapprobation, crime, sin: *blotting it with b.* Ven. 796. *authority for sin, warrant for b.* Lucr. 620. *vast sin-concealing chaos, nurse of b.* 767. 1343. Sonn. 129, 3. H6A IV, 5, 47. R3 V, 1, 29. Plural: *my high-repented* —*s,* All's V, 3, 36. *the taints and* —*s I laid upon myself,* Mcb. IV, 3, 124. = fault: *'tis his own b.* Lr. II, 4, 293. *to lay the b. upon her own despair,* V, 3, 254.

Blame, vb., to censure, to find fault with: Ven. 53. Sonn. 40, 6. 58, 14. 70, 1. 103, 5. Tp. III, 3, 4. Wiv. V, 5, 16. Mids. V, 364. As V, 2, 109. All's II, 1, 88. H6A II, 1, 57. IV, 1, 178. H6B I, 1, 220. H6C II, 1, 157. IV, 1, 101. IV, 6, 30. R3 I, 2, 44. Cymb. IV, 2, 197 etc. *but yet be* —*d,* Sonn. 40, 7. *this was not to be* —*d,* All's III, 6, 54. But usually *to blame* in the passive sense, = blameable: *those proud lords to b. make weak-made women tenants to their shame,* Lucr. 1259. *death is not to b.* Ven. 992. Lucr. 1278. Err. IV, 1, 47. LLL I, 2, 108. Merch. III, 5, 23. V, 166. Shr. IV, 3, 48. All's V, 3, 129. H4B II, 4, 390. R3 II, 2, 13. H8 IV, 2, 101. Rom. III, 5, 170. Caes. II, 2, 119. Hml. III, 1, 46. Oth. III, 3, 211. Cymb. III, 5, 51 *(made me to b. in memory).* Always of persons, except Lr. I, 2, 44: *the contents are to b.* Hml. V, 2, 331: *the king is to b.,* = the king is in fault. (O. Edd. sometimes *too blame,* f. i. Ven. 992. Err. IV, 1, 47. Merch. V, 166. Lr. I, 2, 44. Caes. II, 2, 119. Cymb. III, 5, 51. cf. *wilful-blame*).*

Blameful, reprehensible, guilty: *with bloody b. blade,* Mids. V, 147. *her b. bed,* H6B III, 2, 212. *as b. as ...,* R3 I, 2, 119.

Blameless, not meriting censure, guiltless: *so far b. proves my enterprise,* Mids. III, 2, 350. *Hermione is chaste, Polixeness b.* Wint. III, 2, 134.

Blanc: *Port le B.,* a bay in Brittany, R2 II, 1, 277.

Blanch, 1) *Lady B.,* niece to king John: John II, 64. 423. III, 4, 142 etc. — 2) name of a dog: Lr. III, 6, 66.

Blanch, vb., to make pale: *when mine* (cheek) *is* —*ed with fear,* Mcb. III, 4, 116.

Blank, subst., 1) a paper unwritten: *what thy memory cannot contain commit to these waste —s,* Sonn. 77, 10. *what's her history?* a b. Tw. II, 4, 113. *his thoughts, would they were* —*s, rather than filled with me,* III, 1, 115.

2) a lot by which nothing is gained: *it is lots to* —*s* (= it is very probable) Cor. V, 2, 10.

3) a white paper given to the agents of the crown, which they were to fill up as they pleased, to authorize their demands: *new exactions, as* —*s, benevolences,* R2 II, 1, 250.

4) the white mark in the centre of a butt, the aim: *out of the b. and level of my brain,* Wint. II, 3, 5. *a b. of danger,* Troil. III, 3, 231. *as level as the cannon to his b.* Hml. IV, 1, 42. *let me still remain the true b. of thine eye,* Lr. I, 1, 161. *stood within the b. of his displeasure,* Oth. III, 4, 128.

Blank, adj. 1) white, unwritten: *with b. space for different names,* Wiv. II, 1, 77. *our substitutes shall have b. charters,* R2 I, 4, 48.

2) void of anything, empty, of no contents: *in the extremity of great and little, valour and pride excel themselves in Hector, the one almost as infinite as all, the other b. as nothing,* Troil. IV, 5, 81.

3) without rhyme: *in the even road of a b.*

verse, Ado V, 2, 34. *an you talk in b. verse,* As IV, 1, 32. *the b. verse shall halt for it,* Hml. II, 2, 339.

Blank, vb., = to blanch, to make pale: *each opposite that* —*s the face of joy,* Hml. III, 2, 230.

Blanket, subst., 1) cover for the bed: H4B II, 4, 241. Hml. II, 2, 532. Lr. III, 4, 67. Cymb. III, 1, 44.

2) curtain: *nor heaven peep through the b. of the dark,* Mcb. I, 5, 54. cf. Cymb. III, 1, 44.

Blanket, vb., to cover with a blanket: *b. my loins,* Lr. II, 3, 10.

Blaspheme, 1) trans. to speak with impious irreverence of: *you do b. the good in mocking me,* Meas. I, 4, 38. —*ing God,* H6B III, 2, 372. *does b. his breed,* Mcb. IV, 3, 108.

2) absol. to utter blasphemy: *you b. in this,* John III, 1, 161. *liver of* —*ing Jew,* Mcb. IV, 1, 26.

Blasphemous, impiously irreverent: *you bawling, b., incharitable dog,* Tp. I, 1, 43.

Blasphemy, impious and irreverent language about what ought to be held sacred: *that in the captain's but a choleric word, which in the soldier is flat b.* Meas. II, 2, 131. *I would speak b ere bid you fly,* H6B V, 2, 85. — Abstr. pro concreto: *now, b., that swearest grace o'erboard, not an oath on shore?* Tp. V, 218 (= blasphemous fellow).

Blast, subst., 1) cold and violent gust of wind: *unruly* —*s wait on the tender spring,* Lucr. 869. 1335. Wint. IV, 4, 111. 376. R3 I, 3, 259. Mcb. I, 7, 22. Lr. III, 1, 8. IV, 1, 9. Oth. II, 1, 6. symbol of destruction: *airs from heaven or* —*s from hell,* Hml. I, 4, 41. —*s and fogs upon thee!* Lr. I, 4, 321. *virtue preserved from fell destruction's b.* Per. V, 3, 89.

2) the blowing of a wind instrument: *when the b. of war blows in our ears,* H5 III, 1, 5. *let the general trumpet blow his b.* H6B V, 2, 43. Cor. I, 4, 12. *for one b. of thy minikin mouth,* Lr. III, 6, 45.

Blast, vb., 1) trans., a) to blight, to make to wither: *bud and be* —*ed in a breathing while,* Ven. 1142. *he* —*s the tree,* Wiv. IV, 4, 32. H6B III, 1, 89. H6C IV, 4, 23. V, 7, 21. R3 III, 4, 71. Tim. IV, 3, 538. Mcb. I, 3, 77. Hml. III, 1, 168. III, 4, 65. Lr. II, 4, 170 (Ff. *blister*). = to strike with any pernicious influence: *the injury of many a* —*ing hour,* Compl. 72. *a* —*ing and a scandalous breath,* Meas. V, 122. *every part about you* —*ed with antiquity,* H4B I, 2, 208. *I'll cross it, though it b. me,* Hml. I, 1, 127. *with Hecate's ban thrice* —*ed,* III, 2, 269. *to see it mine eyes are* —*ed,* Ant. III, 10, 4. *you were half* —*ed ere I knew you,* III, 13, 105 (half withered). *when he shall find our paragon to all reports thus* —*ed,* Per. IV, 1, 36.

b) to split, to burst: *with brazen din b. you the city's ear,* Ant. IV, 8, 36.

2) intr., a) to be blighted, to wither: *thy hasty spring still* —*s, and ne'er grows old,* Lucr. 49. —*ing in the bud,* Gentl. I, 1, 48.

b) to burst: *this project should have a back or second, that might hold, if this should b. in proof,* Hml. IV, 7, 155.

Blastment, blast, pernicious influence of the wind and weather: *in the morn and liquid dew of youth contagious* —*s are most imminent,* Hml. I, 3, 42.

Blaze, subst., flaring flame; always used figuratively: *in the b. of youth,* All's V, 3, 6 (O. Edd. *blade*). *his rash fierce b. of riot cannot last,* R2 II, 1,

33. *in his b. of wrath,* Troil. IV, 5, 105. *their b. shall darken him for ever,* Cor. II, 1, 274. *the main b. of it is past,* IV, 3, 20. *these —s, giving more light than heat, you must not take for fire,* Hml. I, 3, 117.

Blaze, vb., 1) intr. to burn with a bright flame: *two red fires in both their faces —d,* Lucr. 1353. *as it —d, they threw on him great pails of ...,* Err. V, 172. *one every —ing star,* All's I, 3, 91 (i. e. every comet; cf. Caes. II, 2, 30). H6C II, 1, 36. V, 4, 71. Tim. II, 2, 170. Hml. IV, 7, 191. The following passages lead over to the second signification: *red cheeks and fiery eyes b. forth her wrong,* Ven. 219. *the heavens themselves b. forth the death of princes,* Caes. II, 2, 31.

2) trans. to make public: *till we can find a time to b. your marriage,* Rom. III, 3, 151 (cf. *Emblaze*).

Blazon, subst., 1) coat of arms: *each fair instalment, coat and several crest, with loyal b., evermore be blest,* Wiv. V, 5, 68. *thy tongue, thy face ... give thee five-fold b.,* Tw. I, 5, 312.*

2) interpretation, explanation: *I think your b. to be true,* Ado II, 1, 307.

3) publication, proclamation: *but this eternal b.* (i. e. publication of eternal things) *must not be to ears of flesh and blood,* Hml. I, 5, 21. Originally = trumpeting forth: *in the b. of sweet beauty's best,* Sonn. 106, 5.

Blazon, vb., 1) to trumpet forth, to praise: *if the measure of thy joy be heaped like mine and that thy skill be more to b. it,* Rom. II, 6, 26. *excels the quirks of —ing pens,* Oth. II, 1, 63. to proclaim in general: *libelling against the senate, and —ing our injustice every where,* Tit. IV, 4, 18. *O thou goddess, thou divine Nature, how thyself thou —est in these two princely boys,* Cymb. IV, 2, 170.

2) to interpret, to explain: *each several stone, with wit well —ed, smiled or made some moan,* Compl. 217.

Bleach, to whiten (used of linen), 1) trans.: *maidens b. their summer smocks,* LLL V, 2, 916. — 2) intr. *what honest clothes you send forth to —ing,* Wiv. IV, 2, 126. *the white sheet —ing on the hedge,* Wint. IV, 3, 5.

Bleak, 1) cold, chill: *thou liest in the b. air,* As II, 6, 16. *to make his b. winds kiss my parched lips,* John V, 7, 40. Tim. IV, 3, 222. Lr. II, 4, 303 (Ff high).

2) exposed to the cold, open to the cold wind: *our lodgings, standing b. upon the sea,* Per. III, 2, 14.

3) pale with frost, chilled: *look b. in the cold wind,* All's I, 1, 115.

Blear, vb., to make (the eyes) watery: *the Dardanian wives, with —ed visages, come forth ...,* Merch. III, 2, 59. Hence = to dim: *while counterfeit supposes —ed thine eye,* Shr. V, 1, 120. *the —ed sights are spectacled to see him,* Cor. II, 1, 221.

Bleat, subst., cry of a calf: Ado V, 4, 51.

Bleat, vb., to cry as a sheep: Merch. IV, 1, 74. Wint. I, 2, 68. IV, 4, 29. as a calf: Ado III, 3, 76. LLL V, 2, 255.

Bleed (impf. *bled,* Cor. I, 9, 48. partic. *bled,* As IV, 3, 149. Cor. V, 1, 11) 1) intr. to lose blood, to run with blood: Ven. 924. 1056. Lucr. 1449. 1551. 1732. 1824. Merch. III, 1, 67. As IV, 3, 149. Shr. Ind. 2, 60. John II, 86. R2 I, 1, 194. H4A II,

4, 341. IV, 1, 115. V, 4, 2. 137. H4B IV, 4, 2. H6A II, 4, 50. 52. H6B III, 2, 188. R3 I, 2, 56. 234. IV, 4, 272. Troil. V, 3, 82. Tit. I, 34. V, 3, 65. Rom. III, 1, 194 *(lie a —ing).* V, 3, 175. Tim. I, 2, 80. Caes. II, 1, 171. Mcb. II, 2, 55. IV, 3, 31. Hml. V, 2, 315. Ant. V, 2, 341 etc. *to b. to death,* Merch. IV, 1, 258. Troil. II, 3, 80. Oth. V, 1, 45. *to b. away,* John V, 4, 24. *my nose fell a —ing* (a sign that something of consequence was to happen) Merch. II, 5, 25. *bleeding stream* = stream of blood, Lucr. 1774. *bleeding* frequently = bloody: *on the —ing ground,* John II, 304. *—ing war,* R2 III, 3, 94. *that never war advance his —ing sword,* H5 V, 2, 383. *unscarred of —ing slaughter,* R3 IV, 4, 209. *the —ing business they have done,* Caes. III, 1, 168. *their dear causes would to the —ing and the grim alarm excite the mortified man,* Mcb. V, 2, 4. — *Dismiss the controversy —ing,* Cor. II, 1, 86, i. e. without having, as it were, dressed and cured it.

Figuratively: *the heart —s,* to denote a pain or sorrow touching the core of the heart: *the thought of it doth make my faint heart b.* Ven. 669. *will not my tongue be mute, my frail joints shake, ... my false heart b.?* Lucr. 228. Pilgr. 267. Tp. I, 2, 63. Wint. III, 2, 52. H6B IV, 1, 85. *now all these hearts ... with —ing groans they pine,* Compl. 275. *my heart —s inwardly that my father is so sick,* H4B II, 2, 51. cf. *I b. inwardly for my lord,* Tim. I, 2, 211. *the testimonies whereof lie —ing in me,* Cymb. III, 4, 23.

To b. = to be let blood, figuratively: *this is no month to b.* R2 I, 1, 157. *have brought ourselves into a burning fever, and we must b. for it,* H4B IV, 1, 57.

2) trans., to shed like blood: *she did, I would fain say, b. tears,* Wint. V, 2, 96. *the drops that we have bled together,* Cor. V, 1, 11.

Blemish, subst., anything that disfigures, spot, stain: *on their garments not a b.* Tp. I, 2, 218. *speaking thick, which nature made his b.* H4B II, 3, 24. Mostly in a moral sense: *the b. that will never be forgot,* Lucr. 536. *he spied in her some b.* 1358. Meas. V, 108. Tw. III, 4, 401. Wint. I, 2, 341. Plural: Wint. V, 1, 8. Ant. II, 3, 5. III, 13, 32.

Blemish, vb., to injure or impair the beauty of, to disfigure: *beauty —ed once 's for ever lost,* Pilgr. 179. *you should not b. it* (your beauty) R3 I, 2, 128. *I shall give thee thy deserving, and b. Caesar's triumph,* Ant. IV, 12, 33. In a moral sense, = to stain, to dishonour: *in this —ed fort,* Lucr. 1175. *a gross and foolish sire —ed his gracious dam,* Wint. III, 2, 199. R2 II, 1, 293. R3 III, 7, 122. IV, 4, 370. Ant. I, 4, 23.

Blench, subst., inconstancy, aberration: *these —es gave my heart another youth,* Sonn. 110, 7.

Blench, vb., to start: *if he but b., I know my course,* Hml. II, 2, 626. *patience herself doth lesser b. at sufferance than I do,* Troil. I, 1, 28 (v. *less* and *lesser*). Hence = to fly off, to be inconstant: *hold you ever to our special drift, though sometimes you do b. from this to that,* Meas. IV, 5, 5. *could man so b.?* Wint. I, 2, 333. *there can be no evasion to b. from this and to stand firm by honour,* Troil. II, 2, 68.

Blend (partic. *blended,* Troil. IV, 5, 86 and Cor. III, 1, 103; *blent,* Merch. III, 2, 183 and Tw. I, 5, 257) 1) to mix: Merch. III, 2, 183. Tw. I, 5, 257. Troil. IV, 5, 86. Cor. III, 1, 103.

2) intr. to mingle: *the heaven-hued sapphire*

and the opal b. with objects manifold, Compl. 215 (according to Walker, *blend* is here a participle, = blent).

Bless (impf. and partic. monosyllabic and dissyllabic without any difference). 1) **to wish happiness to, to pronounce a benediction upon:** Tp. IV, 104. Gentl. III, 1, 146. Wiv. V, 5, 68. Meas. V, 137. Mids. V, 407. 411. IV, 1, 95. H6A I, 1, 28. H6B II, 1, 35. R3 I, 4, 242 etc. *God b. your house*, Wiv. I, 1, 74. II, 2, 53. *God b. the king*, LLL IV, 3, 189. *O Lord b. me*, H6B II, 3, 77 (= stand by me!). *Saint Denis b. this happy stratagem*, H6A III, 2, 18. *Jesu b. him*, H6B I, 3, 6. *Jesus b. us* (= preserve us!) H4A II, 2, 86. H6C V, 6, 75. *a paramour is, God b. us, a thing of naught*, Mids. IV, 2, 14. *she for a woman, God b. us*, V, 327. *God b. my ladies! are they all in love?* LLL II, 77. *God b. me from a challenge* (= preserve me from) Ado V, 1, 145. *God b. the prince from all the pack of you*, R3 III, 3, 5 (Qq *keep*). *heaven b. thee from a tutor*, Troil. II, 3, 32. *heavens b. my lord from fell Aufidius*, Cor. I, 3, 48. And without the word *God* or *heaven*: *b. our poor virginity from underminers*, All's I, 1, 131. *b. me from marrying a usurer*, Wint. IV, 4, 271. *b. thee from whirlwinds*, Lr. III, 4, 60. *b. thee from the foul fiend*, IV, 1, 60.

Similarly: *God b. the mark* (cf. God save the mark, v. *mark*), an exclamation used in the sense of 'saving your reverence': *the Jew my master, who, God b. the mark, is a kind of devil*, Merch. II, 2, 25. *and I, God b. the mark, his Moorship's ancient*, Oth. I, 1, 33. *God* omitted: *he had not been there — b. the mark — a pissing while*, Gentl. IV, 4, 20.

God likewise omitted in other cases: *b. you, sir*, Wiv. II, 2, 160. II, 3, 18. III, 5, 61. Meas. III, 2, 12. 81. Mids. III, 1, 121. All's II, 4, 14. *b. you with such grace as ...*, Shr. IV, 2, 44. *b. my soul*, Wiv. II, 1, 11. 16. Lr. III, 4, 60 (Ff *bliss*).

2) **to praise, to glorify:** *God be blest*, Shr. IV, 5, 18. *—ed be the great Apollo*, Wint. III, 2, 138.

3) **to consecrate, to make happy in consequence, to turn to advantage:** *the dedicated words which writers use of their fair subject, —ing every book*, Sonn. 82, 4. *naming thy name —es an ill report*, 95, 8. *it* (mercy) *—eth him that gives and him that takes*, Merch. IV, 1, 287. *what damned error, but some sober brow will b. it and approve it with a text*, III, 2, 79. *likely in time to b. a regal throne*, H6C IV, 6, 74. *if not to b. us and the land*, R3 III, 7, 192. *some spirit put this paper in the packet, to b. your eye withal*, H8 III, 2, 130. *you b. me, Gods*, Cor. IV, 5, 141. — Followed by *with*: *never did he b. my youth with his*, Ven. 1119. *would not b. our Europe with your daughter*, Tp. II, 1, 124. *the grace that with such grace hath blest them*, Gentl. III, 1, 146. *he will b. that cross with other beating*, Err. II, 1, 79. *they did not b. us with one happy word*, LLL V, 2, 370. Mids. II, 1, 102. Wint. V, 1, 33. 174. H6A I, 2, 86. H6C IV, 2, 23. R3 I, 3, 9. V, 3, 321. H8 II, 4, 36. Oth. II, 1, 79. Ant. I, 2, 161.

To b. one's self = to esteem one's self happy: *if I can cross him any way, I b. myself every way*, Ado I, 3, 70. *now b. thyself: thou mettest with things dying, I with things new-born*, Wint. III, 3, 116. *you would b. you to hear what he said*, H4B II, 4, 103.

The partic. *blest* or *blessed* a) = **happy, fortunate:** *that love-sick love by pleading may be blest*, Ven. 328. *—ed bankrupt that by love so thriveth*, 466.

this —ed league to kill, Lncr. 383. *means more —ed than my barren rhyme*, Sonn. 16, 4. 43, 9. 52, 1. 56, 12. *it* (my heart) *hath thought itself so —ed never*, 119, 6. *that —ed wood*, 128, 2. *what foul play had we that we came from thence? or —ed was 't we did?* Tp. I, 2, 61. IV, 86. V, 202. Gentl. V, 4, 117. Wiv. II, 2, 279. III, 3, 48. Meas. III, 1, 34. Mids. II, 2, 91. IV, 1, 79. Merch. I, 3, 90. II, 1, 46. As III, 3, 59. Shr. IV, 2, 45. Wint. II, 1, 36. IV, 4, 858. John III, 1, 251. H6A I, 6, 10. Cor. II, 2, 62. Ant. II, 2, 248. Cymb. I, 6, 159. V, 4, 121. *with a —ed and unvexed retire*, John II, 253. *barred him from the —ed thing he sought*, Lucr. 340, i. e. blest with beauty; cf. *and you in every —ed shape we know*, Sonn. 53, 12.

b) **full of blessings, bestowing health and prosperity:** *with fair —ed beams*, Mids. III, 2, 392. *such force and —ed power*, IV, 1, 79. *it is twice blest; it blesseth him that gives and him that takes*, Merch. IV, 1, 186. *the blest infusions that dwell in vegetives*, Per. III, 2, 35. *the blessed sun*, Shr. IV, 5, 18. H4A I, 2, 10. II, 4, 449. Tim. IV, 3, 1. *moon*, Rom. II, 2, 107. Ant. IV, 9, 7.

c) **blissful; holy:** *I'll rest, as after much turmoil a —ed soul doth in Elysium*, Gentl. II, 7, 38. *God's —ed will*, Wiv. I, 1, 273. *bound by my charity and my blest order*, Meas. II, 3, 3. *O you —ed ministers above*, V, 115. *some —ed power deliver us*, Err. IV, 3, 44. Merch. V, 220. H6A III, 3, 15. R3 III, 1, 42. H8 IV, 2, 30. Rom. II, 3, 53. *she's full of most —ed condition*, Oth. II, 1, 255. *so free, so kind, so apt, so —ed a disposition*, II, 3, 326. *when you are desirous to be blest, I'll blessing beg of you*, Hml. III, 4, 171, i. e. when you return to virtue.

Blessed-fair, happy as well as beautiful: *what's so b. that fears no blot?* Sonn. 92, 13 (O. Edd. without the hyphen).

Blessedly, 1) **fortunately:** *b. holp hither*, Tp. I, 2, 63. 2) **holily:** *the time was b. lost*, H5 IV, 1, 191.

Blessedness, 1) **happiness:** *and found the b. of being little*, H8 IV, 2, 66. — 2) **the favor of God,** the state of being blessed by God: *so shall she leave her b. to one*, H8 V, 5, 44. — 3) **holiness, sanctity:** *lives and dies in single b.* Mids. I, 1, 78.

Blessing, 1) **benediction:** Tp. V, 179. Gentl. II, 3, 27. Wiv. I, 1, 76. Merch. I, 3, 91. II, 2, 83. 89. All's I, 3, 27. H6A V, 4, 25. R3 I, 2, 69. II, 2, 106 etc. etc. *b. on one:* Tp. IV, 109. 117. Wiv. II, 2, 112. All's II, 3, 97. H8 II, 1, 90. Mcb. IV, 2, 26. *blessing of your heart, you brew good ale*, Gentl. III, 1, 306. cf. Wiv. IV, 1, 13; H4B II, 4, 329 (Ff. *on*) and *Of. on his b.* = as he wished to have his b., As I, 1, 4. H6A IV, 5, 36. *sleeps in —s*, H8 III, 2, 398. *did the third a b.* Lr. I, 4, 115. *when thou dost ask me b.* Lr. V, 3, 10. *I'll b. beg of you*, Hml. III, 4, 172.

2) **the state of being blessed, divine grace:** *b. against this cruelty fight on thy side*, Wint. II, 3, 189. *I had most need of b., and Amen stuck in my throat*, Mcb. II, 2, 32.

3) **means of happiness, gift, benefit:** *you to your beauteous —s add a curse*, Sonn. 84, 13. *a b. that he bestows on beasts*, Err. II, 2, 80. *what b. brings it?* Ado I, 3, 8. II, 1, 30. Merch. III, 2, 114. III, 5, 80. All's I, 3, 28. Wint. III, 2, 108. H6B I, 1, 22. H8 II, 3, 30. Rom. III, 4, 141. Cymb. III, 5, 167 *and steal immortal b. from her lips*, Rom. III, 3, 37.

Blind, adj., 1) destitute of the sense of seeing; properly and figuratively: Lucr. 378. 758. Sonn. 27, 8. 113, 3. 136, 2. 148, 13. Tp. IV, 90. 194. Gentl. II, 1, 76. II, 3, 14. II, 4, 93. 212. IV, 4, 4. Wiv. III, 5, 11. Ado II, 1, 205. LLL IV, 3, 224. 334. Mids. I, 1, 235. Merch. II, 1, 36. II, 6, 36. Tw. V, 236 (*the b. waves,* i. e. the regardless w.). H6B III, 2, 112 (*b. and dusky spectacles*). R3 I, 4, 259 (*to thy own soul so b.,* = so regardless of ...). Cor. V, 6, 118 (*his b. fortune*). H5 III, 3, 34 etc.

2) dark, obscure: *folded up in b. concealing night,* Lucr. 675. *b. forgetfulness,* R3 III, 7, 129 (Ff. *dark*). *the b. cave of eternal night,* V, 3, 62.

Blind, vb. to deprive of sight: to dazzle: *his eyes began to wink, being —ed with a greater light,* Lucr. 375. *—ing tears,* R2 II, 2, 16. *such a sight will b. a father's eye,* Tit. II, 4, 53. LLL I, 1, 76. 83. IV, 3, 228. R2 IV, 245. H6A I, 1, 10. H6B III, 3, 14. Lr. II, 4, 167. *a blinded god* = a blindfolded god, Gentl. IV, 4, 201.

Blindfold, adj., = blind: *b. fury,* Ven. 554. *death,* R2 I, 3, 224.

Blindly, regardlessly: *the brother b. shed the brother's blood,* R3 V, 5, 24.

Blindman: *now you strike like the b.,* Ado II, 1, 205. *it will glimmer through a —'s eye,* H6A II, 4, 24 (M. Edd. in two words). In Merch. V, 112 and Lr. II, 4, 71 O. Edd. also in two words).

Blindness, want of sight: Gentl. IV, 2, 47. H5 V, 2, 344. Cymb. V, 4, 197. *muffle your false love with some show of b.,* Err. III, 2, 8, i. e. with some blinding show.

Blindworm, slow-worm: Mids. II, 2, 11. *—'s sting,* Mcb. IV, 1, 16.

Blink, to twinkle with the eye: *the portrait of a —ing idiot,* Merch. II, 9, 54. *adoptious christendoms, that —ing Cupid gossips,* All's I, 1, 189. to steal an amorous look: *show me thy chink, to b. through with mine eye,* Mids. V, 178.

Bliss, subst., the highest degree of happiness, absolute felicity: Lucr. 389. Sonn. 129, 11. Err. I, 1, 119. Mids. III, 2, 144. V, 181. Merch. II, 9, 67. III, 2, 137. Shr. V, 1, 131. H6A V, 5, 64. H6B III, 3, 27. H6C I, 2, 31. III, 3, 182. IV, 6, 70. Tit. III, 1, 149. 273. Rom. I, 1, 228. V, 3, 124. Lr. IV, 7, 46. Oth. III, 3, 167. V, 2, 250. Ant. I, 3, 36. *Bliss be upon you,* an ecclesiastical salutation: Meas. III, 2, 228. Rom. V, 3, 124.

Blister, subst., a pustule, an ulcer: *a b. on his sweet tongue!* LLL V, 2, 335. *which oft the angry Mab with —s plagues,* Rom. I, 4, 75. *for each true word a b.* Tim. V, 1, 135. *takes off the rose from the fair forehead of an innocent love and sets a b. there,* Hml. III, 4, 44.

Blister, vb., 1) trans. to cover with blisters: *a southwest blow on ye and b. you all o'er,* Tp. I, 2, 324. *a gentlewoman who, falling in the flaws of her own youth, hath —ed her report,* Meas. II, 3, 12. *—ed be thy tongue for such a wish,* Rom. III, 2, 90. *this tyrant whose sole name —s our tongues,* Mcb. IV, 3, 12. In Lr. II, 4, 170 Ff *to fall and b.,* Qq *to fall and blast her pride.*

2) intr. to rise in blisters: *if I prove honeymouthed, let my tongue b.* Wint. II, 2, 33.

Blistered: *the faith they have in tennis, and tall stockings, short b. breeches, and those types of travel,* H8 I, 3, 31, probably = garnished with puffs.

Blithe, gay, mirthful: *be you b. and bonny,* Ado II, 3, 69. H5 II, 3, 4. Tit. IV, 4, 111. *so buxom, b. and full of face,* Per. Prol. 23. *crickets sing at the oven's mouth, e'er the —er for their drouth,* Per. III Prol. 8.

Blithild: *descended of B., which was daughter to king Clothair,* H5 I, 2, 67.

Bloat = bloated, swollen; introduced into the text but by conjecture: *let the b. king tempt you again to bed,* Hml. III, 4, 182; Qq *blowt,* Ff *blunt.*

Block, a piece of timber, rather thick than long; 1) the wood on which criminals are beheaded: Meas. II, 4, 181. IV, 2, 55. IV, 3, 39. 69. V, 419. H4B IV, 2, 122. H6B IV, 1, 125. R3 III, 4, 108. V, 1, 28.

2) the wood on which hats are formed: *he wears his faith but as the fashion of his hat; it ever changes with the next b.* Ado I, 1, 77. Hence the form and fashion of a hat: *this' a good b.,* Lr. IV, 6, 187.

3) a stupid or insensible fellow: *what a b. art thou that thou canst not (understand me)?* Gentl. II, 5, 27. *thy conceit will draw in more than the common —s,* Wint. I, 2, 225. *how thou stirrest, thou b.* Per. III, 2, 90. — Transitional: *past the endurance of a b.* Ado II, 1, 247. *if silent, why, a b. moved with none (wind)* III, 1, 67. *that which here stands up, is but a quintain, a mere lifeless b.* As I, 2, 263. *what tongueless —s were they!* R3 III, 7, 42. *you —s, you stones, you worse than senseless things,* Caes. I, 1, 40.

4) something to obstruct the passage: *who like a b. hath denied my access to thee,* Cor. V, 2, 85.

Blockhead, a head like a wooden block: *your wit will not so soon out as another man's will; 'tis strongly wedged up in a b.,* Cor. II, 3, 31.

Blockish, clumsy, stupid: *b. Ajax,* Troil. I, 3, 375.

Blois, French town: H6A IV, 3, 45.

Blomer: *Sir William B.* H8 I, 2, 190 (O. Edd. *Blumer*).

Blood, the fluid which circulates through the arteries and veins: Gentl. II, 4, 28. Wiv. IV, 4, 33. Meas. I, 3, 52. II, 4, 20. Err. II, 2, 143. V, 193. Ado IV, 1, 38. Tw. III, 2, 66. III, 4, 22. IV, 1, 47. H4A II, 3, 47. H5 IV, 4, 68. H6A I, 5, 6 etc. etc. Plural *bloods:* Err. I, 1, 9. Merch. III, 1, 43. All's II, 3, 125. Wint. I, 2, 109. R2 III, 3, 107. H6C II, 2, 169. R3 III, 3, 14. 21. IV, 4, 50 (in these three last passages Ff *blood*). Troil. IV, 1, 15. Tim. IV, 3, 539. Per. I, 2, 113. — *to let a p. b.:* LLL II, 186. R2 I, 1, 153. R3 III, 1, 183. Troil. II, 3, 222. Caes. III, 1, 152. Cymb. IV, 2, 168. — *flesh and b.:* Tp. V, 74. 114. Ado V, 1, 34. LLL I, 1, 186. IV, 3, 214. Merch. II, 2, 98. III, 1, 37. 40. Shr. Ind. 2, 130. All's I, 3, 38. Tw. V, 36. Wint. IV, 4, 705. H6B I, 1, 233. Hml. I, 5, 22. Lr. II, 4, 224. III, 4, 150. *no hand of b. and bone,* R2 III, 3, 79. *my breath and b.!* Lr. II, 4, 104. — *man of b.* (= murderer), Mcb. III, 4, 126. *o'er shoes in b.* Mids. III, 2, 48. cf. Mcb. III, 4, 136. — *a drop of blood* (= a trifle): *a rush, a hair, a drop of b., a pin,* Err. IV, 3, 73. — Figuratively: *the subtle b. of the grape,* Tim. IV, 3, 432.

In blood, a term of the chase, = in a state of perfect health and vigour: *the deer was, as you know, sanguis, in b.* LLL IV, 2, 4. *if we be English deer, be then in b.; not rascal-like to fall down with a pinch, but rather, moody-mad and desperate stags, turn on the bloody hounds,* H6A IV, 2, 48. *thou rascal, that art worst in b. to run, leadest first to win some vantage,* Cor. I, 1, 163. *but when they shall see his crest up again, and the man in b., they will out of their burrows,* IV, 5, 225.

Serving to denote relation and consanguinity: *such a warped slip of wilderness ne'er issued from his b.* Meas. III, 1, 143. *you are my eldest brother, and in the gentle condition of b. you should so know me,* As I, 1, 48. *had it been the brother of my b.* Tw. V, 217. *farewell, my b.* R2 I, 3, 57. *he is not Talbot's b.* H6A IV, 5, 16. *b. against b., self against self,* R3 II, 4, 62. *near in b.* Mcb. II, 3, 146. cf. *that b. which owed the breadth of all this isle,* John IV, 2, 99. Caes. I, 1, 56.

Hence, emphatically, = noble birth, high extraction: *a gentleman of b.* Gentl. III, 1, 121. H5 IV, 8, 95. *it (love) was different in b.* Mids. I, 1, 135. *to be restored to my b.* H6A II, 5, 128. III, 1, 159. *a prince of b., a son of Priam,* Troil. III, 3, 26.

Symbol of the fleshly nature of man: *all frailties that besiege all kinds of b.* Sonn. 109, 10. *my sportive b.* 121, 6. *nor gives it satisfaction to our b.* Compl. 162. *the strongest oaths are straw to the fire i' the b.* Tp. IV, 53. *the resolute acting of your b.* Meas. II, 1, 12. *b., thou still art b.* II, 4, 15. 178. V, 477. *beauty is a witch against whose charms faith melteth into b.* Ado II, 1, 187. II, 3, 170. IV, 1, 60. LLL IV, 3, 96. V, 2, 73. Mids. I, 1, 68. 74. Merch. I, 2, 20. All's III, 7, 21. As V, 4, 59. Troil. II, 3, 33. cf. Lr. III, 5, 24.

Hence = disposition, temper: *it better fits my b. to be disdained of all,* Ado I, 3, 30. *runs not this speech like iron through your b.?* V, 1, 252. *fetching mad bounds, which is the hot condition of their b.* Merch. V, 74. *when you perceive his b. inclined to mirth,* H4B IV, 4, 38. *my b. begins to flatter me that thou dost (love me)* H5 V, 2, 239. *strange, unusual b., when man's worst sin is, he does too much good,* Tim. IV, 2, 38. *blood and judgment,* Hml. III, 2, 74. *the b. and baseness of our natures,* Oth. I, 3, 332. *our bloods no more obey the heavens than our courtiers still seem as does the king's (sc. blood)* Cymb. I, 1, 1. Emphatically, = high temper, mettle: *thy Fates open their hands; let thy b. and spirits embrace them,* Tw. II, 5, 159. *though sometimes it show greatness, courage, b.* H4A III, 1, 181. *his vow made to my father, while his b. was poor,* IV, 3, 76. *can lift your b. up with persuasion,* V, 2, 79. *our —s are now in calm,* Troil. IV, 1, 15. Or = passion, anger: *thou heatest my b.* LLL I, 2, 32. V, 2, 697. *to let these hands obey my b.* Lr. IV, 2, 64. Caes. IV, 3, 115.

2) a young man: *young —s look for a time of rest,* Caes. IV, 3, 262. *all the hot —s between fourteen and five and twenty,* Ado III, 3, 141. Especially = a man of mettle, a spirited fellow: *sweet —s,* LLL V, 2, 714. *as many and as well-born —s,* John II, 278. *what cannoneer begot this lusty b.?* 461. *the breed of noble —s,* Caes. I, 2, 151.

Blood-bespotted, spotted with blood: H6B V, 1, 117.

Blood-boltered, having the hair clotted with blood: Mcb. IV, 1, 123.

Blood-consuming, preying on the blood: *b. sighs,* H6B III, 2, 61.

Blood-drinking; 1) preying on the blood: *b. sighs,* H6B III, 2, 63. 2) bloodthirsty: *my b. hate,* H6A II, 4, 108. 3) soaked with blood: *in this detested, dark, b. pit,* Tit. II, 3, 224.

Bloodhound, a fierce hound that follows by the scent of blood: *come, you starved b.* H4B V, 4, 31.

Bloodied, made bloody, bloody: *to breathe his b. horse,* H4B I, 1, 38. *how his sword is b.* Troil. I, 2, 253.

Bloodily, in a bloody manner: *how b. the sun begins to peer,* H4A V, 1, 1. *the gashes that b. did yawn upon his face,* H5 IV, 6, 14. *how they at Pomfret b. were butchered,* R3 III, 4, 92. *that thou so many princes so b. hast struck,* Hml. V, 2, 378.

Bloodless, 1) void of blood, pale: *b. fear,* Ven. 891. *at last he takes her by the b. hand,* Lucr. 1597. *in b. white and the encrimsoned mood,* Compl. 201. *meagre, pale and b.* H6B III, 2, 162. *thou b. remnant of that royal blood,* R3 I, 2, 7. *pale and b. emulation,* Troil. I, 3, 134. *struck pale and b.* Tit. III, 1, 258.

2) without shedding blood: *with b. stroke my heart doth gore,* Tw. II, 5, 117.

Blood-sacrifice, sacrifice of the blood: *cannot my body nor b. entreat you to your wonted furtherance?* H6A V, 3, 20.

Bloodshed, shedding of blood, slaughter: John IV, 3, 55. H4B IV, 5, 195.

Bloodshedding, the same: H6B IV, 7, 108.

Bloodstained, stained, coloured with blood: *Severn's flood ... b. with these valiant combatants,* H4A I, 3, 107. *this unhallowed and b. hole,* Tit. II, 3, 210. *thy b. face,* V, 3, 154 (O. Edd. *blood-slain*).

Blood-sucker, 1) the vampire: *pernicious b. of sleeping men,* H6B III, 2, 226. 2) murderer: *a knot you are of damned —s,* R3 III, 3, 6.

Blood-sucking, preying on the blood: *b. sighs,* H6C IV, 4, 22.

Bloodthirsty, desirous to shed blood: H6A II, 3, 34.

Bloody, (comp. *bloodier,* Mcb. V, 8, 7, superl. *bloodiest,* John IV, 3, 47) 1) stained with blood: *here friend by friend in b. channel lies,* Lucr. 1487. Sonn. 50, 9. Mids. V, 144. As IV, 3, 94. 139 etc. etc.

2) consisting of blood: *b. drops,* As III, 5, 7. *lust is but a b. fire,* Wiv. V, 5, 99 (i. e. a fire of or in the blood). *to break within the b. house of life,* John IV, 2, 210 (rather to be explained by a prolepsis).

3) attended with bloodshed: *b. death,* Lucr. 430. *in b. fight,* Pilgr. 280. Tp. I, 2, 142. Meas. II, 4, 181. John III, 4, 148. H4B V, 4, 14. H5 II, 4, 51. H6A I, 1, 156. II, 2, 18 etc. *the bloodiest shame =* the most shameful bloodshed, John IV, 3, 47. *in such b. distance,* Mcb. III, 1, 116.

4) bloodthirsty, cruel: *the boar, that b. beast,* Ven. 999. Lucr. 1648. Sonn. 16, 2. 129, 3. Tp. IV, 220. Merch. III, 3, 34. IV, 1, 138. Tw. III, 4, 243. As II, 3, 37. John IV, 1, 74. H6A II, 5, 100. IV, 2, 8. 51. V, 4, 62. H6B III, 1, 128. H6C V, 5, 61. R3 IV, 3, 6. Mcb. IV, 1, 79. V, 8, 7. Oth. V, 2, 44.

5) blood-red: *unwind your b. flag,* H5 I, 2, 101. *set up the b. flag,* Cor. II, 1, 84. Caes. V, 1, 14.

Bloody-faced, of bloody appearance: *in*

a theme so b. as this (sc. war against the king): H4B I, 3, 22.

Bloody-hunting, pursuing with blood-thirstiness: *Herod's b. slaughtermen*, H5 III, 3, 41.

Bloody-minded, bloodthirsty: H6B IV, 1, 36. H6C II, 6, 33.

Bloody-sceptred, governed with a sceptre stained with blood: *O nation miserable, with an untitled tyrant b.* Mcb. IV, 3, 104.

Bloom, subst., 1) blossom: *shall have no sun to ripe the b. that promiseth a mighty fruit*, John II, 473. 2) state of youth and growing vigour: *his May of youth and b. of lustihood*, Ado V, 1, 76.

Bloom, vb., to flower, to put forth blossoms: *Adonis' gardens that one day —ed and fruitful were the next*, H6A I, 6, 7.

Blossom, subst., the flower of a plant: Pilgr. 229 and LLL IV, 3, 103. Tp. V, 94. LLL V, 2, 812. As II, 3, 64. H6A II, 4, 47 (a rose). 75. H6B III, 1, 89. Figuratively, a hopeful child: *b., speed thee well*, Wint. III, 3, 46. *O that this good b. could be kept from cankers*, H4B II, 2, 101. *there died my Icarus, my b.* H6A IV, 7, 16. *whose rarest havings made the —s dote*, Compl. 235, i. e. those who were full of youth and rare promise (cf. R2 V, 2, 46). Ironically: *you are a beauteous b.* Tit. IV, 2, 72. *In the —s =* in the prime: *already appearing in the —s of their fortune*, Wint. V, 2, 135. *cut off even in the —s of my sin*, Hml. I, 5, 76.

Blossom, vb., to put forth blossoms: H8 III, 2, 353. Oth. II, 3, 383. *—ing time*, Meas. I, 4, 41. *melt their sweets on —ing Caesar*, Ant. IV, 12, 23.

Blot, subst., 1) a spot or stain on paper: *nature, drawing of an antick, made a foul b.* Ado III, 1, 64. *with inky —s and rotten parchment bonds*, R2 II, 1, 64.

2) anything disfiguring: *worse than a slavish wipe or birth-hour's b.* Lucr. 537. *the —s of Nature's hand*, Mids. V, 416. *full of unpleasing —s*, John III, 1, 45.

Especially in a moral sense, = stain, disgrace, reproach: Lucr. 1322. Sonn. 36, 3. 92, 13. 95, 11. Gentl. V, 4, 108. Err. II, 2, 142. John II, 114. R2 IV, 325. V, 3, 66. H4A I, 3, 162. H5 II, 2, 138. H6A II, 4, 116. H6B IV, 1, 40. R3 III, 7, 234. Tit. II, 3, 183. Lr. I, 1, 230. *time hath set a b. upon my pride*, R2 III, 2, 81. *marked with a b., damned in the book of heaven*, IV, 236.

Blot, vb., 1) to spot with ink: *she would not b. the letter with words*, Lucr. 1322. *here are a few of the unpleasantest words that ever —ed paper*, Merch. III, 2, 255.

2) to stain; a) properly: *like misty vapours when they b. the sky*, Ven. 184. *when clouds do b. the heaven*, Sonn. 28, 10. b) figuratively: *—ing it* (beauty) *with blame*, Ven. 796. *before you b. with your uncleanness that which is divine*, Lucr. 192. *b. with hell-born sin such saint-like forms*, 1519. *who can b. that name with any just reproach?* Ado IV, 1, 81. *a good mother that —s thy father*, John II, 132. Absolutely: *praise too short doth b.*, LLL IV, 3, 241.

3) to obliterate with ink; and hence to efface, to erase, to destroy: *to b. old books and alter their contents*, Lucr. 948. *what wit sets down is —ed straight with will*, 1299. *my name be —ed from the book of life*, R2 I, 3, 202. H6B I, 1, 100. *it —s*

thy beauty, Shr. V, 2, 139. *forth of my heart those charms, thine eyes, are —ed*, Oth. V, 1, 35. *To b. out*, in the same sense: *Hero itself can b. out Hero's virtue*, Ado IV, 1, 83. *to b. out me, and put his own son in*, H6C II, 2, 92. *as shall to thee b. out what wrongs were theirs and write in thee the figures of their love*, Tim. V, 1, 156.

Blow, subst., violent application of the hand, fist, or an offensive weapon: Tp. III, 2, 72. Err. II, 1, 53. II, 2, 37. 160. III, 1, 13. 56. Tw. II, 5, 75. R2 II, 1, 254. III, 2, 189. H5 IV, 8, 15. H6A I, 3, 69. III, 4, 40. IV, 6, 19. H6B II, 3, 93. H6C I, 1, 12. I, 4, 50. II, 1, 86. II, 5, 81. R3 IV, 4, 516. Cor. II, 1, 268. Caes. V, 1, 27 etc. etc.; used even of a dagger: Lucr. 1725. 1823. *to fight a b.* H6B I, 3, 220 (Peter's speech). *to strike a b.* H6B IV, 7, 84. *chop this hand off at a b.* H6C V, 1, 50. *fall to —s*, H6B II, 3, 81. *were at —s*, Ant. II, 6, 44. *I found them at b. and thrust*, Oth. II, 3, 238.

Figuratively, any injury or infliction of pain: *how many bear such shameful —s*, Lucr. 832. *falls under the b. of thralled discontent*, Sonn. 124, 7. *what a b. was there given!* Tp. II, 1, 180. LLL V, 2, 291. *that gives not half so great a b. to hear as will a chestnut in a farmer's fire*, Shr. I, 2, 209. *how I took the b.* Troil. I, 2, 294.

Hence = punishment: *meet the b. of justice*, Meas. II, 2, 30. *that keeps you from the b. of the law*, Tw. III, 4, 169. *though full of our displeasure, yet we free thee from the dead b. of it*, Wint. IV, 4, 445.

Blow, vb., to flower, to bloom (partic. *blown;* of the impf. no instance): *eaten by the canker ere it b.* Gentl. I, 1, 46. LLL V, 2, 293. Mids. II, 1, 249. Per. III, 2, 95. *to b. up*, Troil. I, 3, 317. *Blown =* in full blossom: *as chaste as is the bud ere it be blown*, Ado IV, 1, 59. *roses blown*, LLL V, 2, 297. *blown youth*, Hml. III, 1, 167. *with all his crimes broad blown, as flush as May*, III, 3, 81. *against the blown rose they stop their nose that kneeled unto the buds*, Ant. III, 13, 39 (= the rose that has done blossoming?)

Blow, vb. (impf. *blew:* John V, 1, 17. R2 I, 4, 7. H4B V, 3, 89. H8 V, 3, 113. partic. *blown:* Ven. 778. 826. 1071. Lucr. 647. 1330. Ado III, 1, 66. LLL V, 2, 409. Wint. IV, 4, 820. H4A IV, 2, 53. H4B Ind. 16 etc. etc. *blowed:* H5 III, 2, 96, in Macmorris' speech, and Oth. III, 3, 182, in the reading of the Ff.).

1) to move as air; a) intr.: *b., till thou burst thy wind*, Tp. I, 1, 8. Err. III, 2, 153. IV, 1, 91. LLL V, 2, 931. As II, 7, 174. Wint. III, 3, 154. IV, 4, 552. R2 I, 4, 7. H6C II, 5, 55. III, 1, 86. 87. Rom. III, 2, 64. Cymb. IV, 2, 172. followed by *on:* Tp. I, 2, 323. As II, 1, 8. II, 7, 49. followed by *at: to b. at fire*, Per. I, 4, 4.

b) trans., *α*) to drive a current of air upon: *thou —est the fire*, Lucr. 884. *sorrow ebbs, being blown with wind of words*, 1330. *air thy cheeks may b.* Pilgr. 235 and LLL IV, 3, 109. *as thoughts b. them*, Wiv. V, 5, 102. *a vane blown with all winds*, Ado III, 1, 66. *—ing the fire*, Shr. IV, 1, 9. *would b. you through and through*, Wint. IV, 4, 112. *you have blown this coal*, H8 II, 4, 79. *ye blew the fire*, V, 3, 113. *the very ports they b.* Mcb. I, 3, 15. *do but b. them to their trial, the bubbles are out*, Hml. V, 2, 201. *to blow one's nails:* LLL V, 2, 923 and H6C II, 5, 3; an expression also used to denote patient endurance: *we may b. our nails together and fast it fairly out*, Shr. I, 1, 109.

β) to drive by a current of air: *the wind would b. it off*, Ven. 1089. *—s the smoke into his face*, Lucr. 312. 550. *till it b. up rain*, 1788. *blow not a word away*, Gentl. I, 2, 118. *blown round about the pendent world*, Meas. III, 1, 125. *would b. me to an ague*, Merch. I, 1, 23. 168. Shr. I, 2, 49. All's I, 1, 134. Wint. V, 3, 50. John III, 4, 128. V, 1, 17. V, 2, 50. H4B I, 1, 80. V, 3, 90. H5 III, 6, 161. H6B III, 1, 350. IV, 8, 57. H6C I, 4, 145. II, 5, 86. III, 1, 84. 85. V, 3, 11. V, 4, 3. Cor. V, 2, 80. Hml. II, 2, 599. Oth. III, 3, 445. Per. I, 2, 39.

γ) to put in some state by a current of air or breath: *to fan and b. them dry*, Ven. 52. *their light blown out*, 826. *small lights are soon blown out*, Lucr. 647. Shr. II, 136. John IV, 1, 110. V, 2, 86. Cor. V, 2, 48.

2) to breathe, to pant, to puff; a) intr.: *sweating and —ing and looking wildly*, Wiv. III, 3, 94. — b) trans.: *my sighs are blown away, my salt tears gone*, Ven. 1071. *from lips new-waxen pale begins to b. the grief away that stops his answer so*, Lucr. 1663 (i. e. begins to speak). *titles blown from adulation*, H5 IV, 1, 271. *that breath fame —s*, Troil. I, 3, 244. *the devotion which cold lips b. to their deities*, IV, 4, 29. *when I shall turn the business of my soul to such exsufflicate and blown surmises*, Oth. III, 3, 182, i. e. perhaps = puffed out, empty; see sense 3.

3) to inflate, to swell: *how imagination —s him*, Tw. II, 5, 48. *it —s a man up like a bladder*, H4A II, 4, 366. *blown Jack*, IV, 2, 53. *ne'er through an arch so hurried the blown tide*, Cor. V, 4, 50. *blown ambition*, Lr. IV, 4, 27. *this —s my heart*, Ant. IV, 6, 34 (makes it full to bursting). *a vent of blood and something blown*, V, 2, 352. *our blown sails*, Per. V, 1, 256.

4) to sound a wind-instrument, to produce the sound of a wind-instrument: a) trans.: *from mine ear the tempting tune is blown*, Ven. 778. *to b. a horn before her*, John I, 219. *a pipe blown by surmises*, H4B Ind. 16. *let the general trumpet b. his blast*, H6B V, 2, 43. *b. thy blast*, Cor. 1, 4, 12. *'tis well blown*, Ant. IV, 4, 25.

b) intr.: *when the blast of war —s in our ears*, H5 III, 1, 5. *trumpet, b. loud*, Troil. I, 3, 256. IV, 5, 11. 275.

c) having as object that which is the effect of the sound: *the loud trumpet —ing them together*, H4B IV, 1, 122.

5) to throw up into the air: *the cannon, when it has blown his ranks into the air*, Oth. III, 4, 135. *he stands there like a mortar-piece to b. us*, H8 V, 4, 48. *and b. them at the moon*, Hml. III, 4, 209. To b. up, in the same sense: *will undermine you and b. you up*, All's I, 1, 130. H5 III, 2, 68. 96. *my heart will be blown up by the root*, Troil. IV, 4, 56 (a quibble).

6) to foul, to sully with ordure, applied to flies: *to suffer the flesh-fly b. my mouth*, Tp. III, 1, 63. *with flies blown to death*, Wint. IV, 4, 820. *let the water-flies b. me into abhorring*, Ant. V, 2, 60. Also, to deposit eggs: *summerflies that quicken even with —ing*, Oth. IV, 2, 67. *these summerflies have blown me full of maggot ostentation*, LLL V, 2, 409.

Blower-up, one who blows sth. up by the force of gunpowder: *bless our poor virginity from underminers and blowers-up!* All's I, 1, 132.

Blowse, a ruddy fat-faced wench: Tit. IV, 2, 72.

Blubber, to weep so as to wet the mouth and cheeks: *—ing and weeping, weeping and —ing*, Rom. III, 3, 87. In H4B II, 4, 421 it is used only in a stage-direction.

Blue, adj., one of the seven original colours: Wiv. V, 5, 74. LLL V, 2, 904. Wint. II, 1, 13. 15. Shr. III, 2, 69. Tim. IV, 3, 181. *Blue the colour of the dress of servants:* Shr. IV, 1, 93. H6A I, 3, 47. *to pinch or beat black and blue:* Wiv. V, 5, 115. Err. II, 2, 194. Tw. II, 5, 12. *blue alone: pinch the maids as b. as bilberry*, Wiv. V, 5, 49. The rainbow called *blue:* Lucr. 1587 (cf. All's I, 3, 157). Tp. IV, 80. Troil. I, 3, 180. Light amidst darkness called *blue: the lights burn b.; it is now dead midnight*, R3 V, 3, 180. *the cross b. lightning*, Caes. I, 3, 50. Mountains: *the skyish head of b. Olympus*, Hml. V, 1, 277. *or b. promontory with trees upon't*, Ant. IV, 14, 5. Veins shining through the skin: *her two b. windows* (viz. the eyelids) *faintly she up-heaveth*, Ven. 482. *b. veins*, Lucr. 440 (cf. Sonn. 99, 3). *her b. blood changed to black in every vein*, 1454. *and here my bluest veins to kiss*, Ant. II, 5, 29. cf. Cymb. II, 2, 23. — The black circle round the eyes caused by much weeping or sorrow: *round about her tear-distained eye b. circles streamed*, Lucr. 1587. *a lean cheek, a b. eye and sunken*, As III, 2, 393.

Blue, subst.: *her breasts, like ivory globes circled with b.* Lucr. 407. *the aerial b.* Oth. II, 1, 39. *the enclosed lights, now canopied under these windows, white and azure laced with b. of heaven's own tinct*, Cymb. II, 2, 23. — Name of a certain flower (corn-flower?): *the yellows, the blues, the purple violets*, Per. IV, 1, 15.

Blue-bottle, a fly with a large blue belly: *you b. rogue*, H4B V, 4, 22 (Ff. *blue-bottled*), an allusion to the blue dress of the beadles.

Blue-cap, a name given to the Scotch from their blue bonnets: H4A II, 4, 392.

Blue-eyed, having a blueness, a black circle about the eyes (cf. As III, 2, 393): *this b. hag*, Tp. I, 2, 269.*

Blue-veined, having blue veins: *b. violets*, Ven. 125.

Bluish, blue in a small degree: *b. tinsel*, Ado III, 4, 22.

Blumer, see *Blomer.*

Blunt, adj., 1) having a thick edge, not sharp: *thy (love's) edge should —er be than appetite*, Sonn. 56, 2. *as b. as the fencers' foils*, Ado V, 2, 13. R3 IV, 4, 226. Troil. I, 3, 316.

2) dull in understanding: *b. Thurio*, Gentl. II, 6, 41. *of so easy and so plain a stop that the b. monster with uncounted heads can play upon it*, H4B Ind. 18. Err. IV, 2, 21.

3) rough, regardless, harsh: *no gentle chase, but the b. boar, rough bear, or lion proud*, Ven. 884. *a sharp wit matched with too b. a will: whose edge hath power to cut, whose will still wills it should none spare that come within his power*, LLL II, 49. *with hasty Germans and b. Hollanders*, H6C IV, 8, 2. *that Clarence is so harsh, so b., unnatural, to bend the fatal instruments of war against his brother*, V, 1, 86. *I have too long borne your b. upbraidings*, R3 I, 3, 104.

4) plain, unceremonious: *a good b. fellow*, John I, 71. *I judge by his blunt bearing he will keep his word*, H5 IV, 7, 185. *a plain b. man*, Caes. III, 2, 222. (Shr. II, 45 and III, 2, 13?)

5) clumsy, awkward: *this is too curious-good,*

this b. and ill, Lucr. 1300. 1504. Sonn. 103, 7. Ado III, 5, 12 (in Dogberry's speech). Merch. II, 7, 8. Shr. II, 45. III, 2, 13. H6B IV, 1, 67. H6C III, 2, 83. Caes. I, 2, 299.*Hml. III, 4, 182 (Qq *blowt*, M. Edd. *bloat*). Cymb. V, 5, 325.

Blunt, vb., to dull the edge of, to repress, weaken, impair: *devouring time, b. thou the lion's paws,* Sonn. 19, 1. *—ing the fine point of seldom pleasure,* 52, 4. *b. the sharpest intents,* 115, 7. *by —ing us to make our wits more keen,* Compl. 161. *b. his natural edge,* Meas. I, 4, 60. Err. II, 1, 93. H4A III, 2, 77. H4B IV, 4, 27. V, 2, 87. Mcb. IV, 3, 229. Hml. III, 4, 111.

Blunt, name: 1) *the heads of Oxford, Salisbury, B. and Kent,* R2 V, 6, 8. 2) *Sir Walter B.,* H4A I, 1, 63. III, 2, 162. IV, 3, 32. V, 3, 20. H4B I, 1, 16 (*both the —s*). 3) H4B IV, 3, 81. 4) *Sir James B.* R3 IV, 5, 11. V, 3, 30 etc.

Bluntly, unceremoniously, impolitely: *no more but plain and b. 'to the king,'* H6A IV, 1, 51. *good news or bad, that thou comest in so b.?* R3 IV, 3, 45. *deliver a plain message b.,* Lr. I, 4, 36.

Bluntness, unceremoniousness, rude plainness: *who, having been praised for b.,* doth *affect a saucy roughness,* Lr. II, 2, 102.

Blunt-witted, rude and stupid: H6B III, 2, 210.

Blur, subst., a blot, a stain: Lucr. 222.

Blur, vb., to stain, to disfigure: *thy issue —'d with nameless bastardy,* Lucr. 522. *never yet did base dishonour b. our name,* H6B IV, 1, 39. *such an act that —s the grace and blush of modesty,* Hml. III, 4, 41. *time hath nothing —'d those lines of favour which then he wore,* Cymb. IV, 2, 104.

Blurt, vb., followed by *at* = to pish at, to hold in contempt: *whilst ours was —ed at,* Per. IV, 3, 34.

Blush, vb., to redden in the face: Ven. 33. Lucr. 54. 479. 792. 1344. Sonn. 67, 10. 99, 9. Pilgr. 130. 351. Gentl. V, 4, 104. 165. Ado IV, 1, 35. 161. LLL I, 2, 106. 138. IV, 3, 129. 131. Merch. II, 6, 38. As I, 1, 163. II, 7, 119. All's II, 3, 76. V, 3, 140. Wint. III, 2, 32. IV, 4, 12. John IV, 1, 113. V, 2, 153. R2 III, 2, 51. H4A II, 4, 344. V, 2, 62. H4B II, 2, 81. H5 V, 2, 117. H6A II, 4, 66. IV, 1, 93. H6B III, 1, 98. III, 2, 167. H6C I, 4, 46. 118. V, 1, 99. R3 I, 2, 57. I, 4, 141. H8 II, 3, 42. Troil. I, 2, 180. III, 2, 108. Tit. III, 1, 15. Rom. III, 3, 39. Lr. I, 1, 10. Ant. I, 1, 30. III, 11, 12. V, 2, 149. Per. I, 1, 135 etc. *—ing red,* Lucr. 1511. *the —ing morrow,* 1082. cf. John V, 5, 2. R2 III, 3, 63. *the —ing rose,* Ven. 590. *his —ing honours* (i. e. blossoms) H8 III, 2, 354. *to b. like a black dog* (= to have a brazen face) Tit. V, 1, 122. Followed by *at:* Lucr. 1750. Sonn. 128, 8. Compl. 307. John IV, 3, 76. H5 I, 2, 299. H6B II, 4, 48. Cor. V, 6, 99. Oth. I, 3, 96. Followed by *on: —ing on her* (= —ing in looking at her) Lucr. 1339.

With an accus. indicating the effect; = to express by blushes: *I'll b. you thanks,* Wint. IV, 4, 595.

Blush, subst., red colour suffusing the cheeks: Ven. 558. Ado IV, 1, 43. As I, 2, 31. H6C III, 3, 97. Troil. I, 3, 228. Rom. II, 2, 86. Tim. IV, 3, 386. Hml. III, 4, 41. 82. Plur. *— es:* Lucr. 55. Compl. 200. 304. Meas. II, 4, 162. Ado IV, 1, 163. All's II, 3, 75. IV, 3, 373. Wint. IV, 4, 67. H5 V, 2. 253.

Bluster, vb., used only in the partic. *blustering* = boisterous, tempestuous: *stormy —ing weather,* Lucr. 115. *make fair weather in your —ing land,* John V, 1, 21. *a tempest and a —ing day,* H4A V, 1, 6. *early in —ing morn,* Per. V, 3, 22.

Bluster, subst., boisterous tempest: *threaten present —s,* Wint. III, 3, 4. *in the b. of thy wrath,* Tim. V, 4, 41.

Blusterer, a boisterous fellow: *a reverend man,... sometime a b. that the ruffle knew of court, of city,* Compl. 58.

Blusterous, tempestuous: *a more b. birth had never babe,* Per. III, 1, 28.

Boar, the male swine: Ven. 410. 588. 589. 641. 884. 1115. Pilgr. 126. Mids. II, 2, 31. Shr. I, 2, 203. H4B II, 2, 159. R3 III, 2, 11. 28. 75. III, 4, 84. IV, 5, 2. V, 2, 7. V, 3, 156. Tit. IV, 2, 138. Tim. V, 1, 168. Ant. II, 2, 183. IV, 13, 2. Cymb. II, 5, 16.

Board, subst. (cf. *aboard*). 1) a piece of timber sawed thin: *ships are but —s,* Merch. I, 3, 22.

2) table: *fed from my trencher, kneeled down at the b.* H6B IV, 1, 57. *I would have left it on the b.* Cymb. III, 6, 51. *at b.* Err. III, 2, 18. V, 64. *b. and bed:* Mids. V, 31. As V, 4, 148. Oth. III, 3, 24.

3) an authorized assembly: *the honourable b. of council,* H8 I, 1, 79.

Board, vb., 1) to enter (a ship) by force: *I —ed the king's ship,* Tp. I, 2, 196. Wiv. II, 1, 93. Tw. V, 65. H6B IV, 9, 33. Hml. IV, 6, 18. Oth. I, 2, 50. Figuratively, = to accost, to address, to woo: *he would never have —ed me in this fury,* Wiv. II, 1, 92. *I am sure he is in the fleet: I would he had —ed me,* Ado II, 1, 149. LLL II, 218. Shr. I, 2, 95. All's V, 3, 211. Tw. I, 3, 60. Hml. II, 2, 170. *bear up and b. 'em* (= drink), Tp. III, 2, 3.

2) to furnish with food: *we cannot lodge and b. a dozen or fourteen gentlewomen,* H5 II, 1, 35.

Boarish, appertaining to a boar: *b. fangs,* Lr. III, 7, 58.

Boar-pig, a young boar: *Bartholomew b.* H4B II, 4, 251.

Boar-spear, a spear used in hunting boars: As I, 3, 120. R3 III, 2, 74.

Boast, vb., to brag, to make an ostentatious display of sth.; 1) absolutely: *why should proud summer b.,* LLL I, 1, 102. *our —ing enemy,* H6A III, 2, 103. Troil. IV, 5, 290. Cor. II, 1, 23. Mcb. IV, 1, 153. Oth. I, 2, 20. Cymb. V, 5, 18. *upon my death the French can little b., in yours they will,* H6A IV, 5, 24.

Followed by a superfluous *it: nor should that nation b. it so with us,* H6A III, 3, 23.

2) followed by a clause, or by an infinitive: *he shall not b. that thou art ...,* Lucr. 1063. *thou shalt not b. that I do change,* Sonn. 123, 1. *she may b. she hath beheld the man,* H6A II, 2, 42. *to b. how I do love thee,* Sonn. 26, 13. *the patience that you so oft have —ed to retain,* Lr. III, 6, 62. III, 7, 19.

3) followed by *of: of public honour and proud titles b.,* Sonn. 25, 2. 86, 11. 91, 12. Gentl. II, 4, 111. John III, 1, 53. R2 I, 1, 52. I, 3, 273. H4A I, 1, 77. H5 IV, 8, 120. H6A IV, 1, 44. H6C I, 4, 159. Cymb. II, 3, 85.

4) followed by an accusative denoting the effect: *when beauty —ed blushes* (= showed ostentatiously) Lucr. 55. *do not smile at me that I b. her off,* Tp. IV, 9, i. e. cry her up for your acceptance. *What canst*

thou b. of things long since, or any thing ensuing? Ven. 1077 (here *what* may be interpreted otherwise; cf. *What*).

5) reflectively: —*s himself to have a worthy feeding,* Wint. IV, 4, 168. *every present time doth b. itself above a better gone,* V, 1, 96. *now b. thee, death,* Ant. V, 2, 318.

Boast, subst., expression of ostentation or pride: *my b. is true,* Compl. 246. Mids. I, 1, 103. As IV, 3, 91. Oth. V, 2, 264. Cymb. II, 3, 116. V, 5, 162. Per. IV, 6, 195. *my resolution shall be thy b.* Lucr. 1193. *I could make as true a b. as that,* H5 III, 7, 66. *when every thing doth make a gleeful b.* Tit. II, 3, 11, i. e. shows its joy exultingly. Followed by *of: his b. of Lucrece' sovereignty,* Lucr. 36. *make no b. of it,* Ado III, 3, 20. As II, 5, 38. Followed by an infin.: *cannot make b. to have,* Troil. III, 3, 98.

Boastful, vaunting: *steed threatens steed, in high and b. neighs piercing the night's dull ear,* H5 IV Chor. 10.

Boat, a small vessel: Sonn. 80, 11. Tp. I, 2, 146 (O. Edd. *butt*). Gentl. II, 3, 60. Err. I, 1, 77. Tw. I, 2, 11. H6A IV, 6, 33. R3 IV, 4, 524. Troil. I, 3, 35. 42. II, 3, 277. Cor. IV, 1, 6. Lr. III, 6, 28. Oth. II, 3, 65. Ant. II, 7, 136. Cymb. II, 4, 72. III, 1, 21. IV, 3, 46. Per. III, 1, 13.

Boatswain, an officer on board a ship: Tp. I, 1, 1. 10. 13. II, 2, 48. V, 99. Per. IV, 1, 64.

Bob, vb., 1) to move in a short, jerking manner: *when she drinks, against her lips I b.* Mids. II, 1, 49.

2) to drub, to thump: *beaten, —ed and thumped,* R3 V, 3, 334. *I have —ed his brain more than he has beat my bones,* Troil. II, 1, 76.

3) to get cunningly: *gold and jewels that I —ed from him, as gifts to Desdemona,* Oth. V, 1, 16. *you shall not b. us out of our melody,* Troil. III, 1, 75.

Bob, subst., a rap, a dry wipe: *he that a fool doth very wisely hit doth very foolishly, although he smart, not to seem senseless of the b.* As II, 7, 55.

Bobtail, with a tail cut short: *b. tike or trundle-tail,* Lr. III, 6, 73.

Bocchus (O. Edd. *Bochus*): *B. the king of Libya,* Ant. III, 6, 69.

Bode, 1) absol. to be ominous; in a bad sense: *my —ing heart pants, beats, and takes no rest,* Ven. 647. —*ing screech-owls,* H6B III, 2, 327. *I would croak like a raven, I would b., I would b.* Troil. V, 2, 191. *the raven o'er the infected house, —ing to all,* Oth. IV, 1, 22.

2) trans., to portend, to foreshow (in a good as well as a bad sense): *I pray God his bad voice b. no mischief,* Ado II, 3, 83. *he brushes his hat o'mornings; what should that b.?* Ado III, 2, 42. Shr. V, 2, 107. 108. H6B I, 2, 31. III, 2, 85. H6C II, 1, 39. Tit. II, 3, 195. Rom. I, 4, 91. Oth. IV, 3, 59. V, 2, 246. *to b. sth. to one: invert what best is —d me to mischief,* Tp. III, 1, 71. *this —s some strange eruption to our state,* Hml. I, 1, 69.

Bodement, presage: *this foolish girl makes all these —s,* Troil. V, 3, 80. *sweet —s!* Mcb. IV, 1, 96.

Bodge, evidently = to budge (cf. H4A II, 4, 388. Cor. I, 6, 44, and *budger*), to yield, to give way: *with this, we charged again: but, out, alas! we —d again,* H6C I, 4, 19.

Bodied, having a body: *ill faced, worse b.* Err. IV, 2, 20.

Bodiless, incorporeal, unsubstantial: *this b. creation ecstasy is very cunning in,* Hml. III, 4, 138.

Bodily, adj., 1) concerning the body: *in b. health,* H4B II, 2, 111. *some b. wound,* Oth. II, 3, 267. *the dearest b. part of your mistress,* Cymb. I, 4, 162.

2) not only thought, but real: *what* (counsels) *ever have been thought on in this state, that could be brought to b. act ere Rome had circumvention?* Cor. I, 2, 5.

Bodkin, a sharp instrument to make holes by piercing: *what is this? a cittern-head; the head of a b.* LLL V, 2, 615. *betwixt the firmament and it you cannot thrust a —'s point,* Wint. III, 3, 87. *when he himself might his quietus make with a bare b.* Hml. III, 1, 76. In Hml. II, 2, 554 Qq *God's bodkin,* Ff. *bodykins.*

Body, subst., 1) the frame of an animal: *though nothing but my —'s bane would cure thee,* Ven. 372. Lucr. 1266. Tp. IV, 191. V, 109. Gentl. V, 4, 134. Wiv. II, 2, 145. II, 3, 40. Meas. II, 4, 54. III, 1, 188. V, 97. 210. Err. I, 2, 100. II, 2, 134. III, 2, 118. IV, 3, 9. LLL V, 2, 100. Merch. I, 3, 152. III, 2, 267. All's IV, 5, 86. H6B III, 2, 34. Tit. II, 4, 17. Oth. IV, 1, 217 etc. etc. *of his own b. he was ill* (= he himself was given to fleshly sin) H8 IV, 2, 43. *till I have issue of my b.* All's I, 3, 27. R3 IV, 4, 57. *a child begotten of thy b.* All's III, 2, 61. H6A II, 5, 72. *first-fruits of my b.* Wint. III, 2, 98. — *squires of the night's b.* H4A I, 2, 28. — *God's b.!* H4A II, 1, 29 (om. Ff.). *b. o' me, where is it?* H8 V, 2, 22.*— Used as masc. and fem. according to the gender of the person: Sonn. 151, 7. Tit. II, 4, 17.

2) corpse: H6A II, 2, 4. IV, 7, 57. H6B IV, 1, 145. Hml. IV, 2, 28.*IV, 3, 1. V, 2, 411 etc. etc.

3) shape in general: *thy captain is even such a b.* Ant. IV, 14, 13.

4) person: *unworthy b. as I am,* Gentl. I, 2, 18. *the damned'st b.* Meas. III, 1, 96. *an eminent b.* IV, 4, 25. V, 210. *a reverent b.* Err. III, 2, 91. *my little b. is aweary of this great world,* Merch. I, 2, 1. *a b. would think,* As IV, 3, 166. *an hastywitted b.* Shr. V, 2, 40. *mock your workings in a second b.* H4B V, 2, 90. *I commit my b. to your mercies,* V, 5, 130. *and have our —ies slaughtered,* H6A III, 1, 101. *to attach the —ies of the duke's confessor etc.* H8 I, 1, 217. *any mortal b.* Tit. II, 3, 103. *to keep those many —ies safe,* Hml. III, 3, 9. cf. *anybody, somebody* and *nobody.* — *to come under one —'s hand,* Wiv. I, 4, 105.

5) the main part, the bulk: *the b. of your discourse is sometime guarded with fragments,* Ado I, 1, 287. *they would bind me here unto the b. of a dismal yew,* Tit. II, 3, 107, i. e. to the trunk. Hence = anything that constitutes the essential and vital part of sth.: *thus most invectively he pierceth through the b. of the country, city, court, yea, and of this our life,* As II, 1, 59. *I will through and through cleanse the foul b. of the infected world,* II, 7, 60. *you perceive the b. of our kingdom how foul it is,* H4B III, 1, 38. *to show the very age and b. of the time his form and pressure,* Hml. III, 2, 26. With a play upon the word: *such a deed as from the b. of contraction plucks the very soul,* III, 4, 46.

6) the whole of a collective mass: *never*

such a power was levied in the b. of a land, John IV, 2, 112. *in the b. of this fleshly land,* 245. *the voice and yielding of that b. whereof he is the head* (i. e. the state) Hml. I, 3, 23. *the charters that you bear in the b. of the weal,* Cor. II, 3, 189. *whether that the b. public be a horse whereon the governor doth ride,* Meas. I, 2, 163. *the public b.* Tim. V, 1, 148. *the common b.* (= the people), Cor. II, 2, 57. Ant. I, 4, 44. Per. III, 3, 21.

= armed force, army: *we are a b. strong enough to equal with the king,* H4B I, 3, 66.

Body, vb., to shape, to invest with a body: *as imagination —ies forth the form of things unknown,* Mids. V, 14.

Body-curer, a physician for the body: *soul-curer and b.,* Wiv. III, 1, 100.

Bodykins, a scurrilous exclamation: Wiv. II, 3, 46. *God's b.* Hml. II, 2, 554 (Qq *bodkin*).

Bog, quagmire: Tp. II, 2, 2. Err. III, 2, 121. Mids. III, 1, 110. H5 III, 7, 61. Lr. III, 4, 54.

Boggle, to start off, to swerve, to be inconsistent: *you b. shrewdly, every feather starts you,* All's V, 3, 232.

Boggler, a swerver, inconstant woman: *you have been a b. ever,* Ant. III, 13, 110.

Bohemia, name of a German country: Wint. I, 1, 2. I, 2, 39 *(at B.).* III, 3, 2 etc. = king of B.: I, 1, 24. I, 2, 230. 334. IV, 4, 599 etc.

Bohemian, adj. pertaining to Bohemia: *here's a B. Tartar,* Wiv. IV, 5, 21. subst.: *a B. born,* Meas. IV, 2, 134.

Bohun, name: *now, poor Edward B.* H8 II, 1, 103.

Boil, subst., see *Bile.*

Boil, vb. 1) intr. to swell with heat; properly and figuratively: *her blood doth b.* Ven. 555. *thy brains, now useless, b. within thy skull,* Tp. V, 60. *where I have seen corruption b. and bubble,* Meas. V, 320. *his —ing bloody breast,* Mids. V, 148. *—ing choler,* H6A V, 4, 120. *b. thou first i' the charmed pot,* Mcb. IV, 1, 9. *b. and bake,* 13. *b. and bubble,* 19.

2) trans. to steep or cook in heated water: *let me be —ed to death with melancholy,* Tw. II, 5, 3. *what flaying? —ing?* Wint. III, 2, 177. *these —ed brains of nineteen and two and twenty,* III, 3, 64. *choice doth b., as 'twere from forth us all, a man distilled out of our virtues,* Troil. I, 3, 349 (as in a retort). *he might have —ed and eaten him too,* Cor. IV, 5, 201 (M. Edd. *broiled*). *such —ed stuff,* Cymb. I, 6, 125 (i. e. come out of the powdering-tub).

Boisterous, the very contrary to *gentle*; wild, intractable, rudely violent, noisy and tumultuous: *his b. and unruly beast,* Ven. 326. *with a base and b. sword,* As II, 3, 32. *'tis a b. and a cruel style,* IV, 3, 31. *feeling what small things are b. there* (in the eye) John IV, 1, 95. *to make good the b. late appeal,* R2 I, 1, 4. *roused up with b. untuned drums,* I, 3, 134. *the harsh and b. tongue of war,* H4B IV, 1, 49. *an honour snatched with b. hand,* IV, 5, 192. *O b. Clifford, thou hast slain the flower of Europe,* H6C II, 1, 70. *the waters swell before a b. storm,* R3 II, 3, 44. *it* (love) *is too rough, too rude, too b.* Rom. I, 4, 26. *the bleak air, thy b. chamberlain,* Tim. IV, 3, 222. *each small annexment attends the b. ruin,* Hml. III, 3, 22. *this more stubborn and b. expedition,* Oth. I, 3, 228.

Boisterously, with rude violence: *a sceptre snatched with an unruly hand must be as b. maintained as gained,* John III, 4, 136.

Boisterous-rough, rudely violent: *what need you be so b.?* John IV, 1, 76 (O. Edd. without hyphen).

Bold, adj., 1) of high courage, daring; in a good sense: *b. Hector,* Lucr. 1430. *b. Leander,* Gentl. III, 1, 120. Ven. 401. Lucr. 1559. Pilgr. 163. Tp. II, 1, 117. As I, 2, 184. Meas. III, 1, 215. H6B IV, 4, 60. H6C IV, 8, 10 etc. etc. *ring'd about with b. adversity,* H6A IV, 4, 14. — Used of an imposing external appearance: *b. oxlips,* Wint. IV, 4, 125. *who's that that bears the sceptre? Marquess Dorset. A b. brave gentleman,* H8 IV, 1, 40.

2) impudent: *men can cover crimes with b. stern looks,* Lucr. 1252. *as bad as those that vulgars give —est titles,* Wint. II, 1, 94. *these —er vices,* III, 2, 56. John IV, 3, 76. R2 V, 3, 59. H6A IV, 1, 103. H6B III, 2, 238. H6C II, 2, 85. H8 V, 3, 84. Lr. I, 4, 263. IV, 6, 235. Oth. I, 1, 129 etc. *make his b. waves tremble,* Tp. I, 2, 205. *the b. winds speechless,* Hml. II, 2, 507.

3) not timorous, confident: *defect of spirit, life, and b. audacity,* Lucr. 1346. *which makes me the —er to chide you,* Gentl. II, 1, 89. *be b., I pray you,* Wiv. V, 4, 2. *let me be b.; I do arrest your words,* Meas. II, 4, 133. *making the b. wag by their praises —er,* LLL V, 2, 108. Mids. I, 1, 59. Merch. II, 2, 190. 211. II, 7, 70. All's IV, 5, 97. H6A III, 1, 63. H6B I, 1, 29. Troil. I, 3, 192. *To be so b.* = to take the liberty: *if your maid may be so b., she would request ...,* Lucr. 1282. *to say they err I dare not be so b.* Sonn. 131, 7. *I'll be so b. to break the seal,* Gentl. III, 1, 139. *I'll be so b. as stay,* Wiv. IV, 5, 13. *let me be so b. as ask you,* Shr. I, 2, 251. *may I be so b. to know the cause of your coming?* Shr. II, 88. H5 III, 2, 152. V, 1, 12. H6A II, 1, 78. Tit. IV, 3, 90. *To be b., in the same sense: may I be b. to think these spirits?* Tp. IV, 119. *I dare be b. with our discourse to make your grace to smile,* Gentl. V, 4, 162. Wiv. IV, 5, 54. Shr. I, 2, 219. II, 51. All's III, 6, 84. H4A III, 2, 134. H6A II, 3, 25. H6B I, 3, 96. H8 II, 1, 72. IV, 1, 13. Cor. II, 1, 106. Tim. II, 2, 208. — Sometimes = confident: *be b. to play, our play is not in sight,* Ven. 124 (= play confidently). *therefore to give them from me was I b.* Sonn. 122, 11. *then be b. to say Bassanio's dead,* Merch. III, 2, 187. *that may you be b. to say,* Tw. I, 5, 12. *To make so b. and to make b., in the same sense: I'll make so b. to call,* Mcb. II, 3, 56. *making so b. to unseal their grand commission,* Hml. V, 2, 16. *I make b. to press upon you,* Wiv. II, 2, 162. *you made b. to carry into Flanders the great seal,* H8 III, 2, 318. Oth. III, 1, 35. Cymb. I, 6, 197. *To be b., or to make b. with* = to make free with: *I will first make b. with your money,* Wiv. II, 2, 262. *I will only be b. with Benedick for his company,* Ado III, 2, 8. *if I cut my finger, I shall make b. with you,* Mids. III, 1, 187. *I will be b. with time and your attention,* H8 II, 4, 168. *that* (one of your nine lives) *I mean to make b. withal,* Rom. III, 1, 81. *(to be b. with one* = towards one: Shr. I, 2, 104. Oth. III, 3, 228). In a similar sense: *we are too b. upon your rest,* Caes. II, 1, 86.

4) confident, trusting: *be b. you do so grow in my requital,* All's V, 1, 5. *I am b. her honour will remain hers,* Cymb. II, 4, 2. *my hopes, not surfeited to death, stand in b. cure,* Oth. II, 1, 51. Followed

by *of: b. of your worthiness, we single you ...*, LLL II, 28. Followed by *in: be b. in us*, Tit. V, 1, 13. *he is b. in his defence*, Lr. V, 3, 115. — *To make b.* = to confide: *which I'll make b. your highness cannot deny*, Cymb. V, 5, 89.

Bold, vb., to embolden, encourage: *it toucheth us, as France invades our land, not —s the king*, Lr. V, 1, 26.

Bold-beating, apparently = browbeating: *your b. oaths*, Wiv. II, 2, 28.

Bolden, to embolden, encourage: *art thou thus — ed by thy distress*, As II, 7, 91. *but am —ed under your promised pardon*, H8 I, 2, 55.

Bold-faced, of a courageous and confident look: *and like a b. suitor 'gins to woo him*, Ven. 6. *b. victory*, H6A IV, 6, 12.

Boldly, 1) courageously: Meas. V, 299. R2 I, 1, 145. II, 1, 233. IV, 133. H4A V, 1, 40. H6B V, 1, 86. H6C III, 3, 44. R3 V, 3, 269. H8 III, 1, 39. V, 3, 56. Caes. II, 1, 172. Ant. III, 13, 47.

2) confidently: *thus far I will b. publish her*, Tw. II, 1, 30. *we may b. spend upon the hope of what is to come in*, H4A IV, 1, 54. Wint. I, 2, 74.

Boldness, 1) courage: *if wit flow from it as b. from my bosom*, Wint. II, 2, 53. John V, 1, 56. Troil. III, 2, 121.

2) freedom from timidity, assurance: *whilst my poor lips at the wood's b. by thee blushing stand*, Sonn. 128, 8. *you call honorable b. impudent sauciness*, H4B II, 1, 134. Shr. II, 89. Tw. V, 73. Wint. III, 2, 219. H8 V, 1, 161.

3) confidence: *in the b. of my cunning*, Meas. IV, 2, 165 (= confidence in my cunning). cf. *Bold* sub 4.

4) impudence: *a strumpet's b.* All's II, 1, 174. III, 2, 79. Tw. III, 4, 41. Wint. I, 2, 184. R3 I, 2, 42. Cymb. I, 6, 18.

Bolin, bowline: *slack the —s there*, Per. III, 1, 43.

Bolingbroke (O. Edd. mostly *Bullingbroke*). 1) *Henry B.*, afterwards King Henry IV: R2 I, 1, 124 etc. etc. H4A I, 3, 137. III, 1, 64 etc. H6A II, 5, 83. H6B II, 2, 21. — 2) *Roger B.*, the conjurer: H6B I, 2, 76.

Bollen, swollen: *here one being thronged bears back, all b. and red*, Lucr. 1417 (O. Edd. *boln*). Some M. Edd. in Merch. IV, 1, 57 *a b. bagpipe*; O. Edd. *woollen*.

Bolster, subst., cushion (to support the head?): *here I'll fling the pillow, there the b.*, Shr. IV, 1, 204.

Bolster, vb., to make a bolster, by lying one under the other: *damn them then, if ever mortal eyes do see them b. more than their own*, Oth. III, 3, 399.

Bolt, subst., 1) a sort of arrow with a round bob at the end of it: *I'll make a shaft or a b. on't*, Wiv. III, 4, 24 (i. e. I will take the risk, whatever may come of it). *a fool's b. is soon shot*, H5 III, 7, 132. cf. As V, 4, 67.

2) any arrow: *the b. of Cupid*, Mids. II, 1, 165. *'twas but a b. of nothing, shot at nothing*, Cymb. IV, 2, 300.

3) thunderbolt: *rifted Jove's stout oak with his own b.* Tp. V, 46. *thy sharp and sulphurous b.* Meas. II, 2, 115. Cor. V, 3, 152. Cymb. V, 4, 95.

4) bar of a door: *with massy staples and cor-*

responsive and fulfilling —s, Troil. Prol. 18. *to oppose the b. against my coming in*, Lr. II, 4, 179.

5) iron to fasten chains, and hence *bolts* = chains, fetters: *lay —s enough upon him!* Meas. V, 350. *—s and shackles!* Tw. II, 5, 62. *give me the penitent instrument to pick that b., then free for ever*, Cymb. V, 4, 10. *no —s for the dead*, 205.

Bolt, vb., 1) to fetter: *which shackles accidents and —s up change*, Ant. V, 2, 6.

2) to sift: *the fanned snow that's —ed by the northern blasts*, Wint. IV, 4, 375. *so finely —ed didst thou seem*, H5 II, 2, 137. *you must tarry the —ing*, Troil. I, 1, 18. *ill schooled in —ed language*, Cor. III, 1, 322.

Bolter, sieve: H4A III, 3, 81.

Boltered, in *blood-boltered*, q. v.

Bolting-hutch, wooden receptacle for bolted flour: *that b. of beastliness*, H4A II, 4, 495.

Bombard, a large leathern vessel to carry liquors: *yond same black cloud looks like a foul b. that would shed his liquor*, Tp. II, 2, 21. *that huge b. of sack*, H4A II, 4, 497. *here ye lie baiting of —s, when ye should do service*, H8 V, 4, 85.

Bombast, subst., cotton used to stuff out garments: *my sweet creature of b.* H4A II, 4, 359. Metaphorically = fustian: *with a b. circumstance horribly stuffed with epithets of war*, Oth. I, 1, 13. Double sense: *rated them ... as b. and as lining to the time*, LLL V, 2, 791.

Bona; *the lady B.:* H6B II, 6, 90. III, 3, 56 etc. R3 III, 7, 182.

Bona-roba, a handsome girl (in the cant of swaggerers): *we knew where the —s were and had the best of them*, H4B III, 2, 26. *she was then a b.; doth she hold her own well?* 217 (Florio's Dictionary: 'Buonarobba, as we say good stuff, that is, a good wholesome plumcheeked wench.' Cowley, Essay on Greatness: 'I would neither wish that my mistress nor my fortune should be a bona-roba; but as Lucretius says, Parvula, pumilio, χαρίτων ἴα, tota merum sal.')

Bond, 1) ligament: *I tore them* (the hairs) *from their —s*, John III, 4, 70. 74. *with a b. of air ... knit all the Greekish ears to his tongue*, Troil. I, 3, 66. Plural *bonds* = cords or chains with which one is bound: *gnawing with my teeth my —s asunder*, Err. V, 249. 339. *to grace in captive —s his chariot wheels*, Caes. I, 1, 39. Cymb. V, 4, 28 (a quibble). V, 5, 402. cf. *— s of death*, I, 1, 117.

Especially a moral tie: *whereto all —s do tie me*, Sonn. 117, 4. *everlasting b. of fellowship*, Mids. I, 1, 85 (i. e. marriage). *a weak b. holds you*, III, 2, 268. *the natural b. of sisters*, As I, 2, 288. V, 4, 148. Tw. V, 159. Wint. IV, 4, 584. R2 IV, 76. H6A IV, 7, 20. H8 III, 2, 188. Troil. V, 2, 154. 156. Cor. V, 3, 25. Caes. II, 1, 124. Lr. I, 2, 118. II, 1, 49. II, 4, 181.

2) obligation, duty: *vow, b. nor space, in thee hath neither sting, knot, nor confine*, Compl. 264. *you make my —s still greater*, Meas. V, 8. *my love* (as a mother) *hath in't a b.* All's I, 3, 194. *within the b. of marriage, is it excepted I should know no secrets?* Caes. II, 1, 280. *'tis a b. in men*, Tim. I, 1, 144. *breathing like sanctified and pious —s the better to beguile*, Hml. I, 3, 130.* *I love your majesty according to my b.* Lr. I, 1, 95. *I knew it for my b.* Ant. I, 4, 84. *every good servant does not all commands: no b. but to do*

just ones, Cymb. V, 1, 7. *he could not but think her b. of chastity quite cracked*, V, 5, 207. Followed by *to: my b. to wedlock*, H8 II, 4, 40.

3) a deed or obligation to pay a sum or perform a contract: *sealed false —s of love*, Sonn. 142, 7. *he learned but surety-like to write for me under that b.* 134, 8. *his words are —s*, Gentl. II, 7, 75. *I am here entered in b. for you*, Err. IV, 4, 128 (a quibble). Mids. III, 2, 267. Merch. I, 3, 28. 69. 146 *(single b.)*. 160. II, 6, 6. II, 8, 41. III, 1, 50. III, 2, 285. 319. III, 3, 4. IV, 1, 37. 249 etc. Tw. III, 1, 25. R2 II, 1, 64. V, 2, 65 (Qq *band*). H4A III, 3, 117. Tim. I, 2, 66. II, 1, 34. Hml. I, 2, 24 (Qq *bands*). Cymb. III, 2, 37. *(to enter a b.* Err. IV, 4, 128 and R2 V, 2, 65; *to cancel a b.* R3 IV, 4, 77. Mcb. III, 2, 49. Cymb. V, 4, 28). It may come near the sense of pawn or pledge: *I'll make assurance double sure and take a b. of fate*, Mcb. IV, 1, 84; and that of debt: *I will discharge my b.* Err. IV, 1, 13. Followed by *to: my b. to the Jew is forfeit*, Merch. III, 2, 319.

4) claim given by such a deed, ownership: *for what they have not that which they possess they scatter and unloose it from their b.* Lucr. 136. *my —s in thee are all determinate*, Sonn. 87, 4. *cancel his b. of life*, R3 IV, 4, 77. *cancel and tear to pieces that great b. which keeps me pale*, Mcb. III, 2, 49 (i. e. Banquo's life).

Bondage, 1) want of freedom, a) captivity: *and true to b.* (the hair tied up in a fillet) *would not break from thence*, Compl. 34. *I will pray, to increase your b.* Meas. III, 2, 79. *would you not suppose your b. happy, to be made a queen?* H6A V, 3, 111. R2 I, 3, 89. Cymb. III, 3, 44. V, 4, 3.

b) servitude: *he held such petty b. in disdain*, Ven. 394. *the harmony of their tongues hath into b. brought my too diligent ear*, Tp. III, 1, 41. *b. is hoarse, and may not speak aloud*, Rom. II, 2, 161. Tp. III, 1, 89. As V, 1, 59. All's II, 3, 239. III, 5, 67. Wint. IV, 4, 235. Caes. I, 3, 90. V, 5, 54. Lr. I, 2, 52. Oth. I, 1, 46. Cymb. I, 6, 73. Double meaning: *let his arms alone; they were born for b.* Cymb. V, 5, 306.

2) obligation, tie of duty: *the vows of women of no more bondage be to where they are made, than they are to their virtues*, Cymb. II, 4, 111.

Bondmaid, female slave: Shr. II, 2.

Bondman, serf, slave: Err. V, 141. 287. Merch. I, 3, 124. H6B I, 3, 130. Tit. IV, 1, 109. Caes. I, 3, 101. 113. III, 2, 32. IV, 3, 44. 96. V, 1, 42. V, 3, 56. Ant. III, 13, 149.

For a quibble's sake, = a man bound with cords: Err. V, 288.

Bond-slave, the same: Tw. II, 5, 208. R2 II, 1, 114. Oth. I, 2, 99.

Bone, 1) the solid part of the body: *tires with her beak on feathers, flesh and b.* Ven. 56. *so did this horse excel a common one, in shape, in courage, colour, pace and b.* 294. *no hand of blood and b.* R2 III, 3, 79. *nerve and b. of Greece*, Troil. I, 3, 55. *vigour of b.* III, 3, 172. *here lies thy heart, thy sinews and thy b.* V, 8, 12. *that you may live only in b.* Tim. III, 5, 105. *a ring of posied gold and b.* Compl. 45. *whale's b.* LLL V, 2, 332. *cricket's b.* Rom. I, 4, 63.

2) a piece of bone, and what is made of it: *a death's head with a b. in his mouth*, Merch. I, 2, 56. IV, 1, 112. John IV, 3, 148. H6C III, 2, 125. Troil.

I, 3, 392. Tim. IV, 3, 535. Mcb. V, 3, 32 etc. *thy —s are hollow*, Meas. I, 2, 56. *thy —s are marrowless*, Mcb. III, 4, 94. *— by these ten —s!* H6B I, 3, 193 (i. e. the ten fingers). *weave their thread with —s*, Tw. II, 4, 46 (i. e. a sort of bobbins, made of bone or ivory). *let's have the tongs and the —s*, Mids. IV, 1, 32 (a musical instrument now unknown).

3) *Bones* a) = skeleton: *thy* (death's) *detestable —s*, John III, 4, 29. *goodman Death, goodman —s*, H4B V, 4, 32. cf. *the bone face on a flask* (a death's head?) LLL V, 2, 619.

b) used for the whole body, = limbs:[*] *fill all thy —s with aches*, Tp. I, 2, 370. *of his —s are coral made*, 397. *my old —s ache*, III, 3, 2. *will never out of my bones*, V, 284. *guiltless labour, when it lies starkly in the traveller's —s*, Meas. IV, 2, 70. *my —s bear witness*, Err. IV, 4, 80. *virtue's steely —s look bleak i'the cold wind*, All's I, 1, 114. *have broke their sleep with thoughts, their brains with care, their —s with industry*, H4B IV, 5, 70. *yon island carrions, desperate of their — s*, H5 IV, 2, 39. *bid them achieve me and then sell my —s*, IV, 3, 91. *hack their —s asunder*, H6A IV, 7, 47. *I have bobbed his brain more than he hath beat my —s*, Troil. II, 1, 76. *aching —s*, V, 10, 35. 51. *an ache in my —s*, V, 3, 106. *how my —s ache*, Rom. II, 5, 26. *I feel't upon my —s*, Tim. III, 6, 130. *if thou canst mutine in a matron's —s*, Hml. III, 4, 83. *— Unintelligible: O their —s, their —s!* Rom. II, 4, 37 (perhaps = I should like to beat them. Most M. Edd. *their bons*).

c) the remains of the dead: *shall curse my —s*, Lucr. 209. *when death my —s with dust shall cover*, Sonn. 32, 2. Ado V, 1, 294. V, 3, 22. All's II, 3, 148. Tw. II, 4, 63. Wint. IV, 2, 6. John II, 41. H5 IV, 3, 98. R3 I, 4, 33. H8 III, 2, 397. Rom. IV, 1, 82. Oth. IV, 2, 136 etc. *beat not the — s of the buried*, LLL V, 2, 667 (cf. Troil. II, 1, 76).

Bone-ache, pain in the bones (lues venerea?): Troil. II, 3, 20. V, 1, 26.

Bone-face, a death's head? *the carved b. on a flask*, LLL V, 2, 619 (O. and M. Edd. *carved-bone face*).

Boneless, without teeth: *plucked my nipple from his b. gums*, Mcb. I, 7, 57.

Bonfire, a fire made as an expression of public joy: Wint. V, 2, 24. H6A I, 1, 153. I, 6, 12. H6B V, 1, 3. Mcb. II, 3, 22. Oth. II, 2, 5.

Bonfire-light: H4A III, 3, 47.

Bonjour, morning salutation: *with horn and hound we'll give your grace b.* Tit. I, 494. cf. Appendix.

Bonnet, subst. covering for the head; worn by men: Ven. 339 (351 *hat*). 1081. 1087. Merch. I, 2, 81. As III, 2, 398. R2 I, 4, 31. H5 IV, 1, 224. Cor. III, 2, 73. Hml. V, 2, 95.

Bonnet, vb., to take off the bonnet, to show courtesy: *those who, having been supple and courteous to the people, bonneted, without any further deed to have them at all, into their estimation and report*, Cor. II, 2, 30, i. e. who obtained the good opinion of the people by taking off their caps, by mere courtesies, without any other merit to gain it (*them*, sc. their estimation and report). cf. *Off-cap*.

Bonny, 1) blithe, cheerful: *be you blithe and b.* Ado II, 3, 69. *b. Kate*, Shr. II, 187. III, 2, 229. *b. sweet Robin*, Hml. IV, 5, 187. *a cherry lip, a b. eye*, R3 I, 1, 94.

2) stout, strong: *made a prey for carrion kites and crows even of the b. beast he loved so well,* H6B V, 2, 12. *the b. prizer of the humorous duke,* As II, 3, 8 (most M. Edd. *bony*).

Bonville; *Lord B.,* H6C IV, 1, 57.

Bony, stout, strong: *the b. prizer of the humorous duke,* As II, 3, 8 (O. Edd. *bonny*).

Book, subst., 1) a volume to read or write in: Sonn. 23, 9. Tp. I, 2, 166. III, 2, 97. V, 57. Gentl. I, 1, 20. Ado II, 3, 3. LLL I, 1, 74. 87. IV, 2, 25. Merch. IV, 1, 157. Shr. I, 2, 148. II, 101 etc. etc. *the bloody b. of law you shall yourself read,* Oth. I, 3, 67. *my b. of songs and sonnets,* Wiv. I, 1, 206 (probably the Songs and Sonnets of Lord Surrey, printed in 1556). *the b. of riddles,* Wiv. I, 1, 209. *—s for good manners,* As V, 4, 95. *a b. of prayer,* R3 III, 7, 98. *we quarrel in print, by the b.,* As V, 4, 95 (alluding to Vincentio Saviolo's treatise on Honour and Honorable Quarrels). *fights by the b. of arithmetic,* Rom. III, 1, 106. *you kiss by the b.* I, 5, 112. *without b.* = by memory: Tw. I, 3, 28. II, 3, 161. Troil. II, 1, 19. Rom. I, 2, 62.

Emphatically, the bible: *I'll be sworn on a b.* Wiv. I, 4, 156. Meas. II, 1, 162. Merch. II, 2, 168. *I'll be sworn upon all the —s in England,* H4A II, 4, 56. *who can give an oath? where is a b.?* LLL IV, 3, 250. *God's b.* H6B II, 3, 4. *here, kiss the b.* (i. e. the bottle), Tp. II, 2, 135. 146. — *Bell, b. and candle,* John III, 3, 12, i. e. the b. of offices, cf. *bell.*

Sometimes, = account-book: *his land is put to their —s,* Tim. I, 2, 206. *keep thy pen from lenders' —s,* Lr. III, 4, 101. *such gain the cap of him that makes 'em fine, but keeps his b. uncrossed,* Cymb. III, 3, 26. *your neck is pen, b. and counters,* V, 4, 173. cf. *thou thinkest me as far in the devil's b. as thou and Falstaff,* H4B II, 2, 49. *damned in the b. of heaven,* R2 IV, 236.

B. of memory = day-book, memorandum-book: *I'll note you in my b. of memory,* H6A II, 4, 101. *blotting your names from —s of memory,* H6B I, 1, 100, i. e. from historical record. Without the apposition, in the same sense: *I have been the b. of his good acts,* Cor. V, 2, 15. *enrolled in Jove's own b.* III, 1, 293. *mark him and write his speeches in their —s,* Caes. I, 2, 126. *shall live within the b. and volume of my brain,* Hml. I, 5, 103. *who has a b. of all that monarchs do,* Per. I, 1, 94. Hence, *to be in —s* = to be in favour: *the gentleman is not in your —s,* Ado I, 1, 79. *a herald, Kate? O put me in thy —s,* Shr. II, 223.

Figuratively: *this precious b. of love, this unbound lover, to beautify him, only lacks a cover,* Rom. I, 3, 87. *was ever b. containing such vile matter so fairly bound?* III, 2, 83. *was this fair paper, this most goodly b., made to write whore upon?* Oth. IV, 2, 71. *in this b. of beauty* (sc. Bianca) John II, 485. cf. *princes are the glass, the school, the b., where subjects' eyes do learn, do read, do look,* Lucr. 615. *poor women's faces are their own faults' —s,* 1253. LLL IV, 3, 103. Mids. II, 2, 122. H4B II, 3, 31. R3 III, 5, 27. Troil. IV, 5, 239. Mcb. I, 5, 63. Per. I, 1, 15. — *And now I will unclasp a secret b. and read you,* H4A I, 3, 188. *that one might read the b. of fate,* H4B III, 1, 45. *unclasped to thee the b. even of my secret soul,* Tw. I, 4, 14. Hence the following phrases: *is from the b. of honour razed quite,* Sonn. 25, 11. *and my name put in*

the b. of virtue, Wint. IV, 3, 131. *my name be blotted from the b. of life,* R2 I, 3, 202. *that you should seal this lawless bloody b. of forged rebellion with a seal divine,* H4B IV, 1, 91. *one writ with me in sour misfortune's b.* Rom. V, 3, 82.

Serving to denote copious language: *and tire the hearer with a b. of words,* Ado I, 1, 309. *a whole b. full of these carpet-mongers,* V, 2, 32.

2) any writing or paper: *by that time will our b. be drawn* (sc. the articles of agreement) H4A III, 1, 224. 270. *a b.? O rare one!* Cymb. V, 4, 133, sc. a paper containing the oracle of Jupiter.

3) study, learning: *I'll to my b.* Tp. III, 1, 94. *keep a good student from his b.* Wiv. III, 1, 38. *my son profits nothing in the world at his b.* IV, 1, 15. *which with experimental seal doth warrant the tenour of my b.* Ado IV, 1, 169. *makes his b. thine eyes,* LLL IV, 2, 113. *in that vow we have forsworn our —s,* IV, 3, 319. *finds tongues in trees, —s in the running brooks,* As II, 1, 16. *and fitter is my study and my —s than wanton dalliance with a paramour,* H6A V, 1, 22. *my b. preferred me to the king,* H6B IV, 7, 77. *what, at your b. so hard?* H6C V, 6, 1. *a beggar's b. outworths a noble's blood,* H8 I, 1, 122.

Book, vb., to register in a book: *b. both my wilfulness and errors down,* Sonn. 117, 9. *let it be —ed with the rest of this day's deeds,* H4B IV, 3, 50. *that we may wander o'er this bloody field to b. our dead, and then to bury them,* H5 IV, 7, 76 (M. Edd. *look*).

Bookful, reading of some M. Edd. in Ado V, 2, 32; O. Edd. *a whole book full of …*

Bookish, given to books, more acquainted with books than with men and things: *whose b. rule hath pulled fair England down,* H6B I, 1, 259. *the b. theoric,* Oth. I, 1, 24. = lettered: *though I am not b., yet I can read waiting-gentlewoman in the scape,* Wint. III, 3, 73 (the shepherd's speech).

Bookman, studious man, scholar: LLL II, 227. IV, 2, 35.

Bookmate, fellow-student: *the prince and his —s,* LLL IV, 1, 102.

Book-oath, oath made on the Bible: *I put thee now to thy b.* H4B II, 1, 111.

Boon, a favour begged or granted: *a smaller b. than this I cannot beg,* Gentl. V, 4, 24. *to grant one b.* 150. R2 IV, 302. *you will take exceptions to my b.* (i. e. to the b. which I'll ask) H6C III, 2, 46. R3 I, 2, 219. II, 1, 95. Tit. II, 3, 289. *my b. I make it that you know me not,* Lr. IV, 7, 10. Oth. III, 3, 76. Cymb. V, 5, 97. 135. Per. V, 3. 20.

Boor, peasant: *what wouldst thou have, b.?* Wiv. IV, 5, 1. *let boors and franklins say it, I'll swear it,* Wint. V, 2, 173.

Boorish, rustic, vulgar: *the society, which in the b. is company,* As V, 1, 53.

Boot, subst., covering for the foot and leg; particularly worn by horsemen: Gentl. V, 2, 6. Shr. III, 2, 45. 213. IV, 1, 147. All's II, 5, 39. III, 2, 6. Tw. I, 3, 12. R2 V, 2, 77. H4A II, 1, 91 (quibble). III, 1, 68. H4B II, 4, 270. V, 3, 136. Lr. IV, 6, 177. Used by fishermen: Wiv. IV, 5, 101. *over —s in love,* Gentl. I, 1, 25. *give me not the —s,* Gentl. I, 1, 27, = do not make a laughing-stock of me (allusion to the torture of the boots?).

Boot, subst., 1) booty: *make her their —s,* H4A

II, 1, 91 (a quibble). *make b. upon the summer's velvet buds,* H5 I, 2, 194. *and thou make b. of this,* H6B IV, 1, 13.

2) profit, advantage: *give him no breath, but now make b. of his distraction,* Ant. IV, 1, 9. *vail your stomachs, for it is no b.* (= it is of no avail), Shr. V, 2, 176. *talk no more of flight, it is no b.* H6A IV, 6, 52. *there is no b.* R2 I, 1, 164.

3) something given into the bargain: *there's some b.* Wint. IV, 4, 651. 690. *young York he is but b.* R3 IV, 4, 65. *I'll give you b.* Troil. IV, 5, 40. *with b.* Meas. II, 4, 11 and Lr. V, 3, 301. *to b.* = into the bargain: *thou hast thy will, and Will to b.* Sonn. 135, 2. H4A III, 2, 97. H4B III, 1, 29. Troil. I, 2, 260. Mcb. IV, 3, 37. Lr. IV, 6, 230. Cymb. I, 5, 69. II, 3, 35. IV, 2, 314.

Grace to b., Wint. I, 2, 80, evidently means: God help us! God be gracious to us! And so, too, perhaps: *Saint George to b.* R3 V, 3, 301.

Boot, subst., to put on boots: *b., b., master Shallow,* H4B V, 3, 140.

Boot, vb., 1) to avail: *it —s not to complain,* R2 III, 4, 18. *it —s not to resist,* H6C IV, 3, 59. Transitively: *it —s thee not,* Gentl. I, 1, 28. *it shall scarce b. me to say Not guilty,* Wint. III, 2, 26. R2 I, 3, 174. H6C I, 4, 125. Tit. V, 3, 18. Per. I, 2, 20.

2) to present into the bargain: *I will b. thee with what gift beside thy modesty can beg,* Ant. II, 5, 71.

Boot-hose, spatterdashes: *a kersey b. on the other,* Shr. III, 2, 68.

Bootless, adj., unavailing, useless: *leave this idle theme, this b. chat,* Ven. 422. Sonn. 29, 3. Tp. I, 2, 35. LLL V, 2, 64. Mids. II, 1, 233. Merch. III, 3, 20. H4A I, 1, 29. H6C I, 4, 20. II, 3, 12. II, 6, 23. 70. R3 III, 4, 104. H8 II, 4, 61. Tit. III, 1, 75. Lr. V, 3, 294. Oth. I, 3, 209. Per. V, 1, 33.

Bootless, adv.: Mids. II, 1, 37. H5 III, 3, 24. Tit. III, 1, 36. Caes. III, 1, 75. Quibbling: *I sent him b. home,* H4A III, 1, 67 (without boots, and without advantage).

Booty, spoil taken from an enemy: H4A I, 2, 184. H6C I, 4, 63. Tit. II, 3, 49. *Fortune drops —ies in my mouth,* Wint. IV, 4, 863.

Bopeep, a play of children, consisting in looking out and drawing back, for the purpose of frightening each other: *that such a king should play b.* Lr. I, 4, 193.

Borachio, name in Ado I, 3, 43. IV, 2, 12. V, 1, 215.

Border, subst., confine: *when the morning sun shall raise his car above the b. of this horizon,* H6C IV, 7, 81. *the —s maritime lack blood,* Ant. I, 4, 51.

Border, vb., to confine, to limit: *that nature, which contemns its origin, cannot be —ed certain in itself,* Lr. IV, 2, 33.

Borderer, one who dwells on a border: *to defend our inland from the pilfering —s,* H5 I, 2, 142.

Bore, subst., a hole: *confined into an auger's b.* Cor. IV, 6, 87. *fill the —s of hearing* (i. e. the ears) Cymb. III, 2, 59. = the caliber: *yet are they (my words) much too light for the b. of the matter,* Hml. IV, 6, 26.

Bore, vb., 1) trans. to perforate: *this whole earth may be —d,* Mids. III, 2, 53. *now the ship —ing*

the moon with her main mast, Wint. III, 3, 93. Figuratively = to overreach, to trip up: *at this instant he —s me with some trick,* H8 I, 1, 128.

2) absol. *and with a little pin —s through his castle-wall,* R2 III, 2, 170. *those milk-paps that through the window-bars b. at men's eyes,* Tim. IV, 3, 116.

Boreas, the north wind: Troil. I, 3, 38.

Born, see *Bear.*

Borough, a town with a corporation: Shr. Ind. 1, 13. H4A IV, 3, 69. H6C II, 1, 195.

Borrow, subst., the borrowing, taking as a loan: *yet of your royal presence I'll adventure the b. of a week,* Wint. I, 2, 39.

Borrow, vb., 1) to take upon credit (opposed to lend: Ven. 961. Lucr. 1083. 1498. Merch. I, 3, 62). a) absolutely: *'tis much to b.* Ven. 411. 961. *beg thou or b.* Err. I, 1, 154. *neither lend nor b.* Merch. I, 3, 62. 70. *—ing only lingers it out,* H4B I, 2, 265. *shut his bosom against our —ing prayers,* All's III, 1, 9 (i. e. that he might lend us his assistance). Tim. II, 2, 187. *—ing dulls the edge of husbandry,* Hml. I, 3, 77. Followed by *of: good day, of night now b.* Pilgr. 209. *the sun —s of the moon,* Troil. V, 1, 101. Tim. II, 2, 105. III, 6, 17. 84. IV, 3, 69. Oth. I, 3, 215.

b) trans.; followed by a simple accus.: *all fair eyes that light will b.* Lucr. 1083. 1498. *go b. me a crow,* Err. III, 1, 80. *—s money in God's name,* Ado V, 1, 319 (i. e. is a beggar). *his —ed purse,* Merch. II, 5, 51. *b. me Gargantua's mouth,* As III, 2, 238. H4A III, 3, 20. H4B II, 1, 103. Rom. I, 4, 17. Tim. III, 2, 13. III, 6, 111. Hml. III, 2, 167. Ant. II, 2, 103. With *of: articles are —ed of the pronoun,* Wiv. IV, 1, 41. *we'll b. place of him,* Meas. V, 367. Merch. I, 2, 86. Shr. I, 1, 107. All's III, 7, 11. R2 III, 4, 23. H4B V, 5, 13. Cymb. II, 1, 5. Tim. III, 6, 22. With *from: as if from thence they —ed all their shine,* Ven. 488. *from whom each shining star doth b. the beauteous influence,* 861. Gentl. II, 4, 38. John V, 1, 51. Cymb. III, 4, 174.

2) to receive, to take (cf. the passages above: Lucr. 1083. Wiv. IV, 1, 41. Meas. V, 367. Merch. I, 2, 86): *that to his —ed bed he make retire,* Lucr. 573. *which —ed from this holy fire of Love a dateless lively heat,* Sonn. 153, 5. *I bepray you, let me b. my arms again,* LLL V, 2, 702. *youth is bought more oft than begged or —ed,* Tw. III, 4, 3 (i. e. received as a present). *any drop thou —edst from thy mother,* Troil. IV, 5, 133.

3) to assume, to adopt: *you b. not that face of seeming sorrow, it is sure your own,* H4B V, 2, 28. *if but as well I other accents b.* Lr. I, 4, 1. *Borrowed* = assumed, usurped, not real: *a —ed title hast thou bought too dear,* H4A V, 3, 23. *lay apart the —ed glories,* H5 II, 4, 79. *why do you dress me in —ed robes?* Mcb. I, 3, 109. And hence = adulterated, counterfeited, false: *those —ed tears that Sinon sheds,* Lucr. 1549. *fairing the foul with art's false —ed face,* Sonn. 127, 6. *all that —ed motion seeming owed,* Compl. 327. *the —ed veil of modesty,* Wiv. III, 2, 42. *in these my —ed flaunts,* Wint. IV, 4, 23. *the —ed majesty of England here,* John I, 4. *his feathers are but —ed,* H6B III, 1, 75. *in this —ed likeness of shrunk death,* Rom. IV, 1, 104. *take her from her —ed grave,* V, 3, 248. *this —ed passion stands for true old woe,* Per. IV, 4, 24.

Borrower, one who borrows: *the answer is as ready as a —'s cap*, H4B II, 2, 125 (O. Edd. *borrowed*). *I must become a b. of the night for a dark hour*, Mcb. III, 1, 27. *neither a b. nor a lender be*, Hml. I, 3, 75.

Bosky, woody: *my b. acres and my unshrubbed down*, Tp. IV, 81. *you b. hill*, H4A V, 1, 2 (O. Edd. *busky*).

Bosom, subst., that part of the body which contains the heart: *from his soft b. never to remove*, Ven. 81. *within my b. my boding heart pants*, 646. LLL IV, 3, 136. Mids II, 2, 105. Merch. IV, 1, 245. 252. As V, 4, 121. Shr. Ind. I, 119. All's IV, 1, 84. Tw. III, 1, 132. H4A III, 3, 174. R3 IV, 4, 234. V, 1, 24. V, 2, 10. Mcb. V, 1, 61 etc. Also, the folds of the dress covering the breast: *what seal is that, that hangs without thy b.?* R2 V, 2, 56. cf. *and says, within her b. it* (the flower) *shall dwell*, Ven. 1173. *my b. as a bed shall lodge thee* (the letter), Gentl. I, 2, 114. *my herald thoughts in thy pure b. rest them*, III, 1, 144. *thy letters shall be delivered even in the milk-white b. of thy love*, 250. *in her excellent white b. these* etc. Hml. II, 2, 113 ("It should be mentioned that women anciently had a pocket in the fore part of their stays, in which they not only carried love-letters and love-tokens, but even their money and materials for needlework." Nares).

In a moral sense, 1) the place of tender affections and favor: *and in her b. I'll unclasp my heart*, Ado I, 1, 325. *and in his b. spend my latter gasp*, H6A II, 5, 38. *so I might live one hour in your sweet b.* R3 I, 2, 124 (Qq *rest* instead of *live*). *the sons of Edward sleep in Abraham's b.* IV, 3, 38. *sweet peace conduct his soul to the b. of good old Abraham*, R2 IV, 103. cf. *he's in Arthur's b.* H5 II, 3, 10. *will sometimes divide me from your b.* Ant. II, 3, 2. *to pluck the common b. on his side*, Lr. V, 3, 49.

2) the receptacle of secrets: *to lock it in the wards of covert b.* Meas. V, 10. *emptying our —s of their counsel sweet*, Mids. I, 1, 216. *you shall secretly into the b. creep of that prelate*, H4A I, 3, 266. *thou and my b. henceforth shall be twain*, Rom. III, 5, 240. *thy b. shall partake the secrets of my soul*, Caes. II, 1, 305. *I am in their —s*, V, 1, 7. *you are of her b.* Lr. IV, 5, 26.

3) the seat of desires, of passions, of inmost thoughts and wishes: *go to your b.; knock there, and ask your heart*, Meas. II, 2, 136. *how shall this b. multiplied digest the senate's courtesy?* Cor. III, 1, 131 (some M. Edd. *bisson multitude*; but cf. H4B I, 3, 98. Lr. V, 3, 49). And then = desires, inmost thoughts: *you shall have your b. on this wretch*, Meas. IV, 3, 139. *you have your father's b. there*, Wint. IV, 4, 574. *to speak your b. freely*, Oth. III, 1, 58.

4) scarcely distinguishable from *heart*: *they whose guilt within their —s lie*, Lucr. 1342. *no love toward others in that b. sits*, Sonn. 9, 13. 24, 7. 31, 1. 120, 12. 133, 9. *the broken —s*, Compl. 254. Tp. II, 1, 278. Gentl. V, 4, 68. Meas. I, 3, 3. Mids. I, 1, 27. II, 2, 42. 49. 50. *brassy —s*, Merch. IV, 1, 31. *flinty b.* All's IV, 4, 7. *harder —s*, Wint. I, 2, 153. *hollow —s* H5 II Chor. 21. All's I, 3, 131. III, 1, 8. Tw. I, 5, 241. II, 1, 40. III, 1, 170. Wint. I, 2, 113. 238. II, 2, 53. John IV, 1, 32. H6A IV, 3, 48. H6B III, 3, 23. V, 2, 35. *my —'s lord sits lightly in his throne*,

Rom. V, 1, 3 (i. e. the genius who rules my affections). Mcb. II, 1, 28. IV, 3, 2. Lr. II, 1, 128. Oth. IV, 2, 14 etc. — Adjectively, = dearest: *the b. lover of my lord*, Merch. III, 4, 17. *no more that thane of Cawdor shall deceive our b. interest*, Mcb. I, 2, 64.*

Applied to things, 1) the surface: *when I strike my foot upon the b. of the ground*, John IV, 1, 3. *to march so many miles upon her peaceful b.* R2 II, 3, 93. III, 2, 19. 147. Tim. I, 1, 66. *the bounded waters should lift their —s higher than the shores*, Troil. I, 3, 112. *sails upon the b. of the air*, Rom. II, 2, 32. *wooes the frozen b. of the north*, I, 4, 101.

2) the enclosure: *to whose flint b. my condemned lord is doomed a prisoner*, R2 V, 1, 3.

3) the depth, the interior, the inmost recesses: *through night's black b.* Lucr. 788. *shines through the transparent b. of the deep*, LLL IV, 3, 31. *send destruction into this city's b.* John II, 410. *the gaudy day is crept into the b. of the sea*, H6B IV, 1, 2. R3 I, 1, 4. *one drop of blood drawn from thy country's b.* H6A III, 3, 54. Somewhat strangely: *this respite shook the b. of my conscience*, H8 II, 4, 182 (some M. Edd. from Holinshed: *bottom*).

Bosom, vb., to inclose in the heart, to harbour carefully: *b. up my counsel, you'll find it wholesome*, H8 I, 1, 112.

Bosomed, adj., intimate: *you have been conjunct and b. with her*, Lr. V, 1, 13.

Boss, to emboss, to stud: *Turkey cushions —ed with pearl*, Shr. II, 355.

Bosworth, place in England: *in B. field*, R3 V, 3, 1.

Botch, subst. patch: *to leave no rubs nor —es in the work*, Mcb. III, 1, 133.

Botch, vb., to patch: *'tis not well mended so, it is but —ed*, Tim. IV, 3, 285. *To b. up* = to piece up unskilfully: *how many fruitless pranks this ruffian hath —ed up*, Tw. IV, 1, 60 (= has brought about on the most frivolous occasion). *devils that suggest by treasons do b. and bungle up damnation with patches, colours*, H5 II, 2, 115. *they aim at it, and b. the words up fit to their own thoughts*, Hml. IV, 5, 10.

Botcher, mender of old clothes: All's IV, 3, 211. Tw. I, 5, 51. Cor. II, 1, 98.

Botchy, full of botches; 1) patched, bungled; 2) ulcerous: *if he hath biles,... and those biles did run, did not the general run then? were not that a b. core?* Troil. II, 1, 6 (where evidently a quibble is intended).

Both, the one and the other: *b. find each other*, Sonn. 42, 11. *thy registers and thee I b. defy*, 123, 9. Tp. I, 2, 450. IV, 1, 22. V, 149. Gentl. I, 1, 138. II, 4, 121. II, 5, 20. Wiv. IV, 6, 16. Meas. III, 1, 231. III, 2, 33. IV, 2, 184. Err. I, 1, 56. V, 169 etc. etc. Relating to two parts of a sentence: *what foul play had we,... or blessed was't we did? Both, both, my girl*, Tp. I, 2, 61. *now I will believe that there are unicorns, that in Arabia there is one phoenix....; I'll believe b.* III, 3, 24. *I received no gold, but I confess that we were locked out. Thou speakest false in b.* Err. IV, 4, 103. *as I am his kinsman and his subject; strong b. against the deed*, Mcb. I, 7, 14.

Joined to a substantive: *on b. sides*, Shr. I, 1, 110. *on b. sides the leaf*, LLL V, 2, 8. *there is expectance here from b. the sides*, Troil. IV, 5, 146. *b. the proofs are extant*, Wiv. V, 5, 126. *b. the Blunts*,

H4B I, 1, 16. *b. the Sicils and Jerusalem*, H6C I, 4, 122. *b. these letters*, Wiv. IV, 4, 3. *b. your poets*, Sonn. 83, 14. *b. our inventions*, Shr. I, 1, 195 etc. Peculiar use: *were you b. our mothers*, All's I, 3, 169 (= the mother of us both). *b. our remedies within thy help and holy physic lies*, Rom. II, 3, 51 (the remedy for us both). *to b. your honours*, Hml. III, 1, 42. cf. III, 2, 92. *having proceeded but by b. your wills*, Cymb. II, 4, 56. *but clay and clay differs in dignity whose dust is b. alike*, IV, 2, 5 (= the dust of both of which). cf. *for b. our sakes*, Shr. V, 2, 15. *b. your pardons*, Wint. V, 3, 147. *b. their deaths*, R3 I, 3, 192 (cf. *to all our sorrows*, John IV, 2, 102).

Joined to pronouns: *by us b.* Tp. I, 2, 241. 323. II, 1, 306. Gentl. V, 2, 37. Wiv. I, 3, 77. 80. Meas. V, 4. Mids. II, 2, 41 etc. *b. they*, R3 IV, 4, 65 etc. Followed by *of: b. of us*, Err. I, 1, 106. Ado V, 1, 46. H6B III, 2, 182. H6C III, 3, 161. Lr. III, 1, 27. *thy weal and woe are b. of them extremes*, Ven. 987. *you b. of you*, Err. V, 291.

Joined to *twain: I love b. twain*, Sonn. 42, 11. *I remit b. twain*, LLL V, 2, 459.

Used for *two: he may come and go between you b.* Wiv. II, 2, 130. *in b. my eyes he doubly sees himself, in each eye one*, Merch. V, 244. cf. *b. the Sicils*, H6C I, 4, 122. *b. the Blunts*, H4B I, 1, 16. Cor. III, 1, 111.— Used of more than two persons: *let not this wasp outlive, us b. to sting*, Tit. II, 3, 132, i. e. both you and us.

Both ... and = as well as: *tutor b. to good and bad*, Lucr. 995. 1036. Sonn. 44, 7. 117, 9. Compl. 21. Tp. I, 2, 83. 392. V, 71. Wiv. II, 1, 117. Meas. I, 1. 41. I, 3, 45. II, 4, 176. V, 477. Err. I, 1, 14. II, 2, 199. III, 1, 44. IV, 1, 46. IV, 3, 86. Ado IV, 1, 200. Merch. III, 5, 18. Wint. III, 2, 69. R2 III, 3, 141. H5 V, 2, 53. H6A V, 5, 85. H6C I, 1, 87. R3 II, 3, 22. III, 1, 129. H8 IV, 2, 39. Ant. III, 6, 80 etc. Two adjectives thus joined: *both a present and a dangerous courtesy*, Meas. IV, 2, 171. Two verbs: *he b. pleases men and angers them*, Ado II, 1, 146. *I b. may and will*, LLL V, 2, 714. *which b. thy duty owes and our power claims*, All's II, 3, 168. — Used of more than two things: *b. favour, savour, hue and qualities*, Ven. 747. *she was b. pantler, butler, cook*, Wint. IV, 4, 56. *b. he and they and you*, H4A V, 1, 107. — The conjunction *and* omitted: *b. in time, form of the thing, each word made true and good*, Hml. I, 2, 209. *since now we will divest us b. of rule, interest of territory, cares of state*, Lr. I, 1, 50. Wint. IV, 4, 56.

Both-sides, double-tongued, double-hearted: *damnable b. rogue*, All's IV, 3, 251.

Bots, small worms found in the entrails of horses: *begnawn with the b.* Shr. III, 2, 56. *to give poor jades the b.* H4A II, 1, 11. Used as an execration: *b. on it*, Per. II, 1, 124.

Bottle, 1) a small vessel to put liquor in: Tp. II, 2, 77. 97. 125. 127. 130. 156. 180. III, 2, 73. 87. IV, 208. 213. Wiv. II, 2, 319. Meas. III, 2, 182. As III, 2, 211. H4A IV, 2, 2. 6. H4B I, 2, 237. H5 III, 6, 82. H6C II, 5, 48 (*leather b.*). Oth. II, 3, 152 (*a twiggen b.*). *hang me in a b. like a cat and shoot at me*, Ado I, 1, 259 ("It appears that cats were enclosed, with a quantity of soot, in wooden bottles suspended on a line, and that he who could beat out the bottom of the bottle as he ran under it, and yet escape its contents, was the hero of the sport." Dyce). — Used as a masculine: Tp. II, 2, 180.

2) *b. of hay* = truss of hay: Mids. IV, 1, 37.

Bottle-ale, bottled ale: *the Myrmidons are no b. houses*, Tw. II, 3, 29. *you b. rascal*, H4B II, 4, 140.

Bottled, big-bellied: *that b. spider*, R3 I, 3, 242. IV, 4, 81.

Bottom, name in Mids. I, 2, 18. 22. III, 1, 8. IV, 1, 221. IV, 2, 1 etc.

Bottom, subst., 1) the lowest part of any cavity: *the b. poison, and the top o'erstrawed with sweets*, Ven. 1143. *ebbing men most often do so near the b. run*, Tp. II, 1, 227. Wiv. III, 5, 13. As IV, 1, 211. H4A I, 3, 203. H5 I, 2, 164. H4B V, 3, 57. R3 I, 4, 28. 32. Troil. III, 3, 198. Rom. III, 5, 56. Cymb. II, 2, 39. Figuratively: *it concerns me to look into the b. of my place*, Meas. I, 1, 79 (i. e. to know it throughout). *it shall be called Bottom's dream, because it hath no b.* Mids. IV, 1, 222. *now I see the b. of your purpose*, All's III, 7, 29. *I do see the b. of Justice Shallow*, H4B III, 2, 324. *you are too shallow, to sound the b. of the after times*, IV, 2, 51. Troil. III, 3, 312. Cor. IV, 5, 209. Tit. III, 1, 217. Rom. III, 5, 199. Mcb. IV, 3, 60. Cymb. IV, 2, 204. Per. V, 1, 166. *when your lordship sees the b. of his success in it*, All's III, 6, 38 (i. e. when you see the whole stretch and issue of his enterprise). *therein should we read the very b. and the soul of hope*, H4A IV, 1, 50 (we should try our fortune, as it were, to the lees, and there were nothing left to hope). *we then should see the b. of all our fortunes*, H6B V, 2, 78. — *Now to the b. dost thou search my wound*, Tit. II, 3, 262, i. e. thou touchest upon my deepest grief. cf. *mirth doth search the b. of annoy*, Lucr. 1109. *the tent that searches to the b. of the worst*, Troil. II, 2, 17. *mine ear, therein false struck, can take no greater wound, nor tent to b. that*, Cymb. III, 4, 118.

2) a ship: *my ventures are not in one b. trusted*, Merch. I, 1, 42. *with the most noble b. of our fleet*, Tw. V, 60. John II, 73. H5 III Chor. 12.

3) a low ground, a valley: *west of this place, down in the neighbour b.* As IV, 3, 79. *to rob me of so rich a b.* H4A III, 1, 105.

4) a ball of thread: *beat me to death with a b. of brown thread*, Shr. IV, 3, 138.

Bottom, vb., to wind, to twist thread: *as you unwind her love from him, you must provide to b. it on me*, Gentl. III, 2, 53.

Bottom-grass, grass growing in a deep valley, rich pasture: *sweet b. and high delightful plain*, Ven. 236.

Bottomless, 1) fathomless: *O, deeper sin than b. conceit can comprehend*, Lucr. 701. Tit. III, 1, 218. — 2) having no bottom: *or rather b., that as fast as you pour affection in, it runs out*, As IV, 1, 213.

Bouciqualt, name in H5 III, 5, 45. IV, 8, 82.

Bough, branch: Ven. 37. Sonn. 73, 3. 102, 11. Tp. V, 94. As II, 7, 111. III, 2, 143. IV, 3, 105. Wint. V, 3, 133. R2 III, 4, 64. H5 III, 2, 20. Tit. I, 74 (*bound with laurel —s*). Tim. IV, 3, 265. Mcb. V, 4, 4. Hml. IV, 7, 173. Cymb. III, 3, 61.

Boult, name in Per. IV, 2, 1 etc.

Bounce, vb., 1) to make a sudden leap with some noise: *he, spying her, —d in*, Pilgr. 83. *when I saw the porpus how he —d and tumbled*, Per. II, 1, 26.

2) to be noisy, to bully, to swagger: *the —ing Amazon*, Mids. II, 1, 70 (or is it = stout, plump?)

Bounce, interj., slap, bang: *b. would a' say*, H4B III, 2, 304. *he speaks plain cannon fire and smoke and b.* John II, 462.

Bound, vb., 1) intr. to spring, to leap, to rebound: *he leaps, he neighs, he —s*, Ven. 265. Lucr. 1669. H4A II, 3, 52. H5 III, 7, 13. Troil. I, 3, 41. Rom. I, 4, 21. *these balls b.* All's II, 3, 314. *grief —eth where it falls*, R2 I, 2, 58.

2) trans. to make to leap: *if I might buffet for my love, or b. my horse for her favours*, H5 V, 2, 146.

Bound, vb., to confine, to limit: *a gentle flood, who, being stopped, the —ing banks o'erflows*, Lucr. 1119. *the —ed waters*, Troil. I, 3, 111. *whose veins b. richer blood than lady Blanch?* John II, 431. *how are we parked and —ed in a pale*, H6A IV, 2, 45. *I could be —ed in a nutshell*, Hml. II, 2, 260. — Followed by *to: to whose high will we b. our calm contents*, R2 V, 2, 38 (or impf. of *to bind?*). *To bound in*, in the same sense: *glorify the banks that b. them in*, John II, 442. *this sinister* (cheek) *—s in my father's* (blood) Troil. IV, 5, 129.

Bound, subst. 1) leap: *what rounds, what — s, what course, what stop he makes*, Compl. 109. *fetching mad —s*, Merch. V, 73. All's III, 3, 299. Quibbling: *soar with them above a common b.* Rom. I, 4, 18.

2) limit, boundary: *the sea hath —s*, Ven. 389. Err. II, 1, 17. *a confidence sans b.* Tp. I, 2, 97. *above the —s of reason*, Gentl. II, 7, 23. *past the —s of patience*, Mids. III, 2, 65. H4A I, 3, 200. *leap all civil —s*, Tw. I, 4, 21. *beyond the b. of honour*, Wint. III, 2, 52. *the —s of modesty*, Rom. IV, 2, 27. *above a common b.* I, 4, 18 (quibble). *the very utmost b. of all our fortunes*, H4A IV, 1, 51. *no end, no limit, measure, b.* Rom. III, 2, 125. — Used of the enclosing banks of a river: John II, 444. III, 1, 23. V, 4, 55. Tit. III, 1, 71. Tim. I, 1, 25.

= inclosure, precinct, district: *bourn, b. of land, tilth, vineyard, none*, Tp. II, 1, 152: *roaming clean through the —s of Asia*, Err. I, 1, 134. *—s of feed*, As II, 4, 83. *the cottage and the —s that the old carlot once was master of*, III, 5, 107. *all the fertile land within that b.* H4A III, 1, 77. *a kingdom for it was too small a b.* V, 4, 90. *forth the —s of France*, H6A I, 2, 54. *in your city's —s*, Tim. V, 4, 61.

= barrier, hinderance: *hath he set —s betwixt their love and me?* R3 IV, 1, 21. *revenge should have no —s*, Hml. IV, 7, 129.

Bound, adj., 1) ready, prepared: *that she is b. in honour still to do what you in wisdom still vouchsafe to say*, John II, 522. *I am b. to hear*, Hml. I, 5, 6. *both b. to revenge*, H6C II, 4, 3. *like a man to double business b.* Hml. III, 3, 41. *we are b. to the like*, Lr. III, 7, 11. cf. *Bind* p. 114.

2) destined or intending to go; usually followed by *to: I am b. to Persia*, Err. IV, 1, 3. *b. to sea*, 33. Merch. I, 3, 18. Shr. IV, 5, 55. All's III, 5, 37. 98. Tw. II, 1, 43. III, 1, 85. Wint. IV, 4, 736. John I, 150. Cor. III, 1, 54. Cymb. III, 6, 59. *you would answer very well to a whipping, if you were but b. to it*, All's II, 2, 58 (= destined to undergo it). Followed by *for: b. for Naples*, Tp. I, 2, 235. Hml. IV, 6, 10. Cymb. III, 6, 62. *the proud full sail of his*

great verse, b. for the prize of all too precious you, Sonn. 86, 2. Joined to *whither* and *thither: whither are you b.?* All's III, 5, 36. Tw. II, 1, 10. Wint. IV, 4, 677. 736. Cymb. III, 6, 58. *are you b. thither?* Troil. I, 1, 118.

Technical use: *all the voyage of their life is b. in shallows and in miseries*, Caes. IV, 3, 221 (= delayed, stopped; cf. the naval term *port-bound*).

Bounden, bound, obliged: *I rest much b. to you*, As I, 2, 298. *I am much b. to your majesty*, John III, 3, 29.

Boundless, unconfined, unbridled: *thy b. flood*, Lucr. 653. *b. sea*, Sonn. 65, 1. *b. tongue*, Wint. II, 3, 91. *beyond the infinite and b. reach of mercy*, John IV, 3, 117. *the desire is b.* Troil. III, 2, 89. *as b. as the sea*, Rom. II, 2, 133. *b. theft in limited professions*, Tim. IV, 3, 430. *b. intemperance*, Mcb. IV, 3, 66. *b. happiness*, Per. I, 1, 24.

Bounteous, 1) liberal, munificent: Tp. IV, 60. 103. Meas. V, 448. R3 II, 2, 93. H8 I, 3, 55. II, 1, 52. Tim. IV, 3, 167. 423. Mcb. III, 1, 98. Oth. III, 3, 7. Per. IV, 4, 17. *have of your audience been most free and b.* Hml. I, 3, 93. *to be free and b. to her mind*, Oth. I, 3, 266.

2) liberally bestowed, rich: *b. largess*, Sonn. 4, 6. *b. gift*, 11, 12.

Freely, but very intelligibly used in the following passages: *we'll share a b. time in different pleasures*, Tim. I, 1, 263. *doors that were ne'er acquainted with their wards many a b. year*, III, 3, 39. *I greet thy love, not with vain thanks, but with acceptance b.* Oth. III, 3, 470, (i. e. with full and unreserved acceptance, as it becomes a friend). *let's to-night be b. at our meal*, Ant. IV, 2, 10 (let us not be niggardly).

Bounteously, liberally: *I'll pay thee b.* Tw. I, 2, 52.

Bountiful, 1) liberal: *if that one be prodigal, b. they will him call*, Pilgr. 412. *b. Fortune*, Tp. I, 2, 178. As I, 2, 37. H4A III, 1, 168. Tim. III, 1, 11. 42.

2) of rich contents, full of meaning: *that's a b. answer that fits all questions*, All's II, 2, 15.

Used adverbially: *and give it b. to the desirers*, Cor. II, 3, 109.

Bountifully, plenteously: *commend me b. to his lordship*, Tim. III, 2, 58 (be not niggardly in commendations).

Bounty, 1) liberality, munificence: *which bounteous gift thou shouldst in b. cherish*, Sonn. 11, 12. 53, 11. Gentl. I, 1, 152. III, 1, 65. Wiv. I, 3, 77. Merch. III, 4, 9. Tw. V, 47. Wint. IV, 4, 365. R2 II, 3, 67. H5 II, 2, 92. H6B V, 1, 81. R3 III, 7, 17. H8 III, 2, 184. Troil. IV, 5, 102. Rom. II, 2, 133. Tim. I, 1, 6. 285. I, 2, 215. Mcb. IV, 3, 93. Lr. I, 1, 53. IV, 6, 229. Cymb. I, 6, 78. V, 5, 98 etc.

2) a liberal gift: *monarchs' hands that let not b. fall where want cries*, Compl. 41. *all thy treasure, with his b. overplus*, Ant. IV, 6, 22. *—ies*, Tim. I, 2, 129. III, 2, 85. H8 III, 2, 160.

3) hearty disposition to do one good, active benevolence: *the king who had even tuned his b. to sing happiness to him*, All's IV, 3, 12. *derive a liberty from heartiness, from b., fertile bosom*, Wint. I, 2, 113. *I thank thee, king, for thy great b., that not only givest me cause to wail, but teachest me the way ...*, R2 IV, 300. *to you this honorable b. shall belong*, H4A V, 5, 26. *as Hector's leisure and your —ies shall concur*

together, Troil. IV, 5, 273. *the less they deserve, the more merit is in your b.* Hml. II, 2, 558. *do not abuse my master's b. by the undoing of yourself,* Ant. V, 2, 43. *I'll pay your —ies,* Per. II, 1, 149.

Bourbon; 1) *Duke of B.:* H5 III, 5, 41. IV, 5, 12. IV, 8, 82. 2) *Lord B., our high admiral,* H6C III, 3, 252.

Bourdeaux, town in France: *Richard of B.,* R2 V, 6, 33 (i. e. Richard II). *B. stuff,* H4B II, 4, 69. H6A IV, 2, 1. IV, 3, 4. 8. 22. H8 I, 1, 96.

Bourn, 1) l i m i t, c o n f i n e, b o u n d a r y: *b., bound of land, tilth, vineyard, none,* Tp. II, 1, 152. *one that fixes no b. 'twixt his and mine,* Wint. I, 2, 134. *like a b., a pale, a shore,* Troil. II, 3, 260. *the undiscovered country from whose b. no traveller returns,* Hml. III, 1, 79. *from the dread summit of this chalky b.* Lr. IV, 6, 57. *I'll set a b. how far to be beloved,* Ant. I, 1, 16. *from b. to b., region to region,* Per. IV, 4, 4.

2) b r o o k: *come o'er the b., Bessy, to me,* Lr. III, 6, 27.

'Bout, prepos., = a b o u t, q. v.: Tp. I, 2, 220. Wiv. IV, 6, 42. Cor. II, 1, 225. Cymb. IV, 2, 283.

Bout, subst., a t u r n, a p a s s (in fencing): *the gentleman will, for his honour's sake, have one b. with you,* Tw. III, 4, 337. *make your —s more violent,* Hml. IV, 7, 159. *I'll play this b. first,* V, 2, 295. Menacingly: *I'll have a b. with thee,* H6A I, 5, 4. III, 2, 56. Used of dancing: *ladies .... will have a b. with you,* Rom. I, 5, 19 (only in the spurious Q1; the rest of O. Edd. *walk about).*

'Bove, prepos., = a b o v e, q. v.: Tp. II, 1, 118. Tim. III, 3, 1. Mcb. III, 5, 31. Lr. III, 1, 6.

Bow, subst. 1) i n s t r u m e n t t o s h o o t a r r o w s: Ven. 581. Lucr. 580. LLL IV, 1, 24. 111. Mids. I, 1, 169. II, 1, 159. III, 2, 101. As IV, 3, 4. Troil. I, 3, 355. III, 1, 126. Rom. I, 4, 5. Hml. IV, 7, 23. Per. V, 1, 249. *To bend a b.:* Mids. I, 1, 9. R2 III, 2, 116. *draw your b.* Shr. V, 2, 47. Lr. IV, 6, 88. *a' drew a good b.* H4B III, 2, 48. *the b. is bent and drawn,* Lr. I, 1, 145.

2) r a i n b o w: *thy blue b.* Tp. IV, 80. *heavenly b.* 86.

3) y o k e: *as the ox hath his b.* As III, 3, 80.

Bow, vb., 1) trans. a) t o b e n d: *a three-pence —ed would hire me,* H8 II, 3, 36. *you're a young foolish sapling and must be —ed as I would have you,* Per. IV, 2, 94. *and —ed her hand to teach her fingering,* Shr. II, 151,

b) t o i n c l i n e, t o b e n d d o w n: *she —s her head, the new-sprung flower to smell,* Ven. 1171. *—s his vassal head,* LLL IV, 3, 224. *—ed his eminent top to their low ranks,* All's I, 2, 43. *feathers which b. the head,* IV, 5, 112. *—ing his head against the steepy mount to climb his happiness,* Tim. I, 1, 75. *to the ground their knees they b.* Lucr. 1846. *—ed my knee unto this king of smiles,* H4A I, 3, 245. *b. my knee before his majesty,* R2 I, 3, 47. *b. a knee to man,* H6B V, 1, 110. *should b. his knee,* H6C II, 2, 87. *knees humbly —ed,* Rom. III, 1, 161. Cymb. V, 5, 19. *and b. this feeble ruin* (my mutilated body) *to the earth,* Tit. III, 1, 208. *whose heavy hand hath —ed you to the grave,* Mcb. III, 1, 89. *this gate ... —s you to a morning's holy office,* Cymb. III, 3, 3. *necessity so —ed the state,* H4B III, 1, 73.

Reflectively: *b. themselves when he did sing,* H8

III, 1, 5. *—ed her to the people,* IV, 1, 85. *my thoughts ... b. them to your gracious leave,* Hml. I, 2, 56.

c) t o c r u s h, t o s t r a i n: *he —ed his nature,* Cor. V, 6, 25. *that you should fashion, wrest or b. your reading,* H5 I, 2, 14.

d) t o e x p r e s s b y b e n d i n g d o w n: *my knee shall b. my prayers to them,* Ant. II, 3, 3.

2) intr., a) t o b e n d, t o s t o o p: *her voice is stopt, her joints forget to b.* Ven. 1061. *heaven, it seemed, to kiss the turrets —ed,* Lucr. 1372. *the shore that o'er his wave-worn basis —ed,* Tp. II, 1, 120. *which end of the beam should b.* 131. *plants with goodly burthen —ing,* IV, 113. *my legs, like loaden branches, b. to the earth,* H8 IV, 2, 2. *my knees, who —ed but in my stirrup,* Cor. III, 2, 119. *to b. in the hams,* Rom. II, 4, 57. *the flame o' the taper —s toward her,* Cymb. II, 2, 20.

= t o b e n d i n t o k e n o f s u b m i s s i o n: *to insinuate, flatter, b.* R2 IV, 165. *why hath thy knee forgot to b.?* H6B V, 1, 161. R3 I, 3, 161. Cor. V, 3, 29. Caes. V, 1, 42. Followed by *to: b. to a new-crowned monarch,* Merch. III, 2, 49. *to thee like osiers —ed,* Pilgr. 60 and LLL IV, 2, 112. John III, 1, 74. H6B IV, 1, 125. H6C I, 4, 94. Lr. I, 1, 150. Followed by *before: thrice —ed before me,* Wint. III, 3, 24. *the gods that Romans b. before,* Caes. II, 1, 320.

b) t o s t o o p, t o s i n k u n d e r p r e s s u r e: *whose sinewy neck in battle ne'er did b.* Ven. 99. *join with the spite of fortune, make me b.* Sonn. 90, 3. *needs must I under my transgression b.* 120, 3. *like an ass whose back with ingots —s,* Meas. III, 1, 26. *which in weight to re-answer, his pettiness would b. under,* H5 III, 6, 137. *if I b., they'll say it was for fear,* H6A IV, 5, 29. *—s unto the grave with mickle age,* H6B V, 1, 174. *who sensibly outdares his senseless sword, and when it —s, stands up,* Cor. I, 4, 54. *that which makes me bend makes the king b.* Lr. III, 6, 116.

c) t o a c c o m m o d a t e o n e's s e l f: *to crush this a little, it would b. to me,* Tw. II, 5, 153; cf. H5 I, 2, 14.

Bow-back, a r c h e d, c r o o k e d b a c k: *on his* (the boar's) *b.* Ven. 619.

Bow-boy, the boy with the bow, viz C u p i d: Rom. II, 4, 16.

Bow-case, c a s e f o r a b o w: H4A II, 4, 273.

Bowels, 1) the e n t r a i l s: *whose b. suddenly burst out,* John V, 6, 30. V, 7, 31. H4A V, 3, 36. H5 II, 1, 54. R3 I, 4, 212. Caes. V, 3, 42. Tropically: *gnaws the b. of the commonwealth,* H6A III, 1, 73. *tearing his country's b. out,* Cor. V, 3, 103. Considered as the seat of pity, tenderness, and of sensibility in general: *and bids you, in the b. of the lord, deliver up the crown,* H5 II, 4, 102. *there is no lady of more softer b.* Troil. II, 2, 11. *my b. cannot hide her woes,* Tit. III, 1, 231. *thou thing of no b. thou,* Troil. II, 1, 54.

2) that which is one's own flesh and blood, c h i l d r e n: *thine own b., which do call thee sire, the mere effusion of thy proper loins, do curse the gout ... for ending thee no sooner,* Meas. III, 1, 29.

3) the i n n e r p a r t o f a n y t h i n g: *the cannons have their b. full of wrath,* John II, 210. *out of the b. of the harmless earth,* H4A I, 3, 61. *rushed into the b. of the battle,* H6A I, 1, 129. *rushing in the b. of the French,* IV, 7, 42. *into the fatal b. of the deep,* R3 III, 4, 103. *into the b. of the land,* V, 2, 3. *pouring war*

into the b. of ungrateful Rome, Cor. IV, 5, 136. *when some envious surge will in his brinish b. swallow him*, Tit. III, 1, 97.

Bower, subst., an arbour, a shady recess amidst trees and flowers: Ado III, 1, 7. Mids. III, 1, 202. III, 2, 7. IV, 1, 66. Tw. I, 1, 41. H4A III, 1, 210. Cor. III, 2, 92. = a pleasant habitation: *sweet beauty hath no name, no holy b.* Sonn. 127, 7.

Bower, vb., to enclose, to lodge in a delightful manner: *b. the spirit of a fiend in mortal paradise of such sweet flesh*, Rom. III, 2, 81.

Bowget, reading of O. Edd. Wint. IV, 3, 20; rhyming to *avouch it;* M. Edd. *budget.*

Bow-hand, the hand which draws the bow, or which holds the bow? Doubtless the latter. *Wide o' the b.*, LLL IV, 1, 135, i. e. far from the mark.

Bowl, subst., 1) a vessel to drink in, rather wide than deep: LLL V, 2, 935. R3 V, 3, 63. 72. H8 I, 4, 39. Caes. IV, 3, 142. 158. Ant. III, 13, 184. *a gossip's b.* Mids. II, 1, 47.*Rom. III, 5, 175. *standing b.* (i. e. a bowl resting on a foot) Per. II, 3, 65; cf. Stage-direction in H8 V, 5.

2) ball of wood used for play: Cor. V, 2, 20. Cymb. II, 1, 8. *thus the b. should run*, Shr. IV, 5, 24. *at —s*, R2 III, 4, 3. Cymb. II, 1, 54.

Bowl, vb. (rhyming to *owl:* LLL IV, 1, 140), 1) trans., to roll as a bowl: *b. the round nave down the hill of heaven*, Hml. II, 2, 518. b) to pelt with any thing rolled: *—ed to death with turnips*, Wiv. III, 4, 91.

2) intr. a) to play at bowls: *challenge her to b.* LLL IV, 1, 140. b) to move like a bowl: *if it* (the dance of the satyrs) *be not too rough for some that know little but —ing*, Wint. IV, 4, 338.*

Bowler, player at bowls: *a very good b.* LLL V, 2, 587.

Bowline, see *Bolin.*

Bowsprit (O. Edd. *bore-sprit*), a large boom projecting over the stem of a ship: Tp. I, 2, 200.

Bow-string, string of a bow: *he hath twice or thrice cut Cupid's b.* Ado III, 2, 11. *hold or cut —s*, Mids. I, 2, 114, = come what come may. Capell: 'When a party was made at butts, assurance of meeting was given in the words of that phrase; the sense of the person using them being, that he would hold or keep promise, or they might cut his bowstrings.' (?)

Bow-wow, a cry imitative of the barking of dogs: Tp. I, 2, 382. 383.

Box, subst., 1) a case to hold some thing: Wiv. I, 4, 47. All's II, 3, 296. Wint. IV, 4, 782. Troil. V, 1, 12. 29 (*thou damnable b. of envy*). Rom. V, 1, 45. Tim. III, 1, 16. Hml. V, 1, 120. Cymb. III, 4, 191. V, 5, 241. Per. III, 2, 81.

2) *b. on or of the ear* = blow on the side of the face: *I will take thee a b. on the ear*, H5 IV, 1, 231. *a b. of the ear*, Merch. I, 2, 86. H4B I, 2, 218 (*give*). *if he took you a b. o' the ear*, Meas. II, 1, 189. H6B IV, 7, 91. *to take him a b. a th' ear*, H5 IV, 7, 133. 181.

Box-tree, a shrub, buxus sempervirens: *get ye all three into the b.* Tw. II, 5, 18.

Boy, a male child, a lad: Tp. III, 3, 43. IV, 90. 101. Wiv. II, 2, 132. IV, 1, 11 etc. etc. Used as a word of contempt for young men: Ado V, 1, 83. 187. Cor. V, 6, 101. 104. 117 etc. Familiar term in address-

ing, or speaking of, grown persons: *then to sea, —s*, Tp. II, 2, 56. Gentl. II, 1, 54. 85. III, 1, 188. 395. Wiv. I, 3, 62. III, 1, 109. Shr. IV, 1, 43 etc. Often = page, young servant: *if thou seest my b.* Gentl. III, 1, 257. *I keep but three men and a b.* Wiv. I, 1, 285. Shr. IV, 4, 8. H5 III, 2, 30. R3 IV, 2, 32. *'mong —s, grooms and lackeys*, H8 V, 2, 18. H4B II, 4, 268 etc. *the hangman —s*, Gentl. IV, 4, 60. *a postmaster's b.* Wiv. V, 5, 199. — *Your town is troubled with unruly —s*, Err. III, 1, 62, (allusion to the *angry* or *roaring boys*, a set of young bucks who delighted to commit outrages and get into quarrels). *I shall see some squeaking Cleopatra-boy my greatness*, Ant. V, 2, 220, i. e. I shall see some boy, performing the part of Cleopatra, as my highness. cf. As. F1 *Cleopatra Boy;* F2.3 *squeaking-Cleopatra-boy.*

Boyet, name in LLL II, 13. 20. 161. IV, 1, 55. V, 2, 79. 81. 174 etc. Rhyming to *debt:* V, 2, 334.

Boyish, pertaining to a boy· *from my b. days*, Oth. I, 3, 132. childish: *b. troops*, John V, 2, 133.

Boy-queller, boy-killer (cf. *man-queller*): Troil. V, 5, 45.

Boys: *Sir Rowland de B.* As I, 1, 60. I, 2, 235.

Brabant, dukedom in the Low-Countries: LLL II, 114. H5 II, 4, 5. III, 5, 42. IV, 8, 101.

Brabantio, name in Oth. I, 1, 79. 106. I, 2, 55. I, 3, 47. 172.

Brabble, subst., quarrel, broil: *in private b. did we apprehend him*, Tw. V, 68. *this petty b. will undo us all*, Tit. II, 1, 62. (*If we leave our pribbles and prabbles*, Wiv. I, 1, 56. *pribbles and prabbles*, V, 5, 169. *leave your prabbles*, IV, 1, 52. *keep you out of prawls and prabbles*, H5 IV, 8, 69. All this in the Welsh dialect of Evans and Fluellen).

Brabbler, quarreller, noisy fellow: *we hold our time too precious to be spent with such a b.* John V, 2, 162. — Name of a yelping dog: *he will spend his mouth, and promise, like B. the hound*, Troil. V, 1, 99.

Brace, subst., 1) couple: *my b. of lords*, Tp. V, 126. *a b. of words*, LLL V, 2, 524. *of tongues*, John IV, 1, 98. *of draymen*, R2 I, 4, 32. *of greyhounds*, H6C II, 5, 129. *of courtezans*, R3 III, 7, 74. *of warlike brothers*, Troil. IV, 5, 175. *of testy magistrates*, Cor. II, 1, 46. *of the best of them*, III, 1, 244. *of kinsmen*, Rom. V, 3, 295. *of harlots*, Tim. IV, 3, 79. *of Cyprus gallants*, Oth. II, 3, 31. *of unprizable estimations*, Cymb. I, 4, 99. — Without a genitive: *here comes a b.* Cor. II, 3, 67. — Not inflected in the plural: *two b. of greyhounds*, Tim. I, 2, 195.

2) armour: *it hath been a shield twixt me and death';* — *and pointed to this b.* Per. II, 1, 133 (cf. *vantbrace*). Figuratively: *it* (Cyprus) *stands not in such warlike b.* Oth. I, 3, 24 (= state of defence).

Brace, vb., to strain up, to prepare: *a drum is ready —d that shall reverberate as loud as thine*, John V, 2, 169.

Bracelet, ornament for the wrist: *—s of thy hair*, Mids. I, 1, 33. *amber —s*, Shr. IV, 3, 58. *bugle b.* Wint. IV, 4, 224. 611. Cymb. V, 5, 204. 416.

Brach, a kind of scenting-dogs: *b. Merriman, the poor cur is emboss'd; and couple Clowder with the deep-mouthed b.* Shr. Ind. I, 17 (there is certainly a corruption in one place). *hound or spaniel, b. or lym*, Lr. III, 6, 72. Also = bitch: *I had rather hear Lady, my b., howl in Irish*, H4A III, 1, 240. *truth's a* *dog must to kennel; he must be whipped out, when the lady brach may stand by the fire and stink,* Lr. I, 4, 125. In Troil. II, 1, 126 M. Edd. *brach,* O. Edd. *brooch.*

Bracy, name: *Sir John B.* H4A II, 4, 367.

Brag, vb., 1) intransitively; to b o a s t: *when virtue —ed, beauty would blush for shame,* Lucr. 54. Phoen. 63. LLL V, 2, 683. Merch. III, 4, 69. 77. John III, 1, 122. V, 1, 50. H4B II, 4, 247. V, 3, 124. H5 III, 6, 160. V, 1, 6. V, 2, 144. Oth. II, 1, 225. Having *of* before the thing boasted: *b. not of thy might,* Ven. 113. Wiv. III, 3, 212. Err. III, 2, 16. Mcb. II, 3, 101. Lr. V, 3, 280. Having *to* before the person to whom the boast is made: *art thou —ing to the stars,* Mids. III, 2, 407. *you have heard him b. to you he will,* Tw. III, 4, 348. *to b. unto them, 'thus I did,'* Cor. II, 2, 151. Followed by a clause: *nor shall Death b. thou wanderest in his shade,* Sonn. 18, 11. Gentl. IV, 1, 69. Ado V, 1, 60.

In two passages it is evidently used in a good sense, = to talk with pride, to be justly proud: *Verona —s of him to be a virtuous youth,* Rom. I, 5, 69. *conceit, more rich in matter than in words, —s of his substance, not of ornament,* II, 6, 31.

2) transitively: *your —ed progeny,* Cor. I, 8, 12. *he —s his service,* Cymb. V, 3, 93.

Brag, subst., b o a s t: *Caesar's thrasonical b. of 'I came, saw, and overcame,'* As V, 2, 34. H5 III, 7, 83. Troil. IV, 5, 257. Tit. I, 306. Cymb. III, 1, 23. V, 5, 176.

Braggardism, boastfulness: Gentl. II, 4, 164.

Braggart, boaster: Ado V, 1, 91. 189. LLL V, 2, 545. Merch. III, 2, 261. All's IV, 3, 370. 372. H5 II, 1, 64. Cor. V, 6, 119. Rom. III, 1, 105. Tim. IV, 3, 161. Mcb. IV, 3, 231. Lr. II, 2, 133.

Bragless, unboasted: *if it be so, yet b. let it be,* Troil. V, 9, 5.

Braid, adj. deceitful: *since Frenchmen are so b., marry that will, I live and die a maid,* All's IV, 2, 73.

Braid, vb., 1) to w e a v e, i n t e r l a c e: *his —ed hanging mane,* Ven. 271. *slackly —ed in loose negligence,* Compl. 35.

2) to reproach: *'twould b. yourself too near for me to tell it,* Per. I, 1, 93.

Brain, subst., the s o f t m a s s i n c l o s e d i n t h e s k u l l; used, with one restriction, indiscriminately in the singular and plural: *have I laid my b. in the sun and dried it?* Wiv. V, 5, 143. *to sear me to the b.* R3 IV, 1, 61 (Ff —s). *our —'s flow* (i. e. our tears) Tim. V, 4, 76. *yet ha' we a b. that nourishes our nerves,* Ant. IV, 8, 21. *his —s are forfeit to the next tile that falls,* All's IV, 3, 216. *I'll never believe a madman till I see his —s,* Tw. IV, 2, 126. *make a quagmire of your mingled —s,* H6A I, 4, 109. *I am cut to the —s,* Lr. IV, 6, 197 etc.

The plural alone used in the phrases *to beat out, to dash out, to knock out a person's brains:* Meas. IV, 3, 58. As IV, 1, 98. All's III, 2, 16. Wint. II, 3, 139. H6A III, 1, 83. Troil. II, 1, 111. III, 3, 304. Tit. V, 3, 133. Rom. IV, 3, 54. Tim. I, 1, 193. IV, 1, 15. Oth. IV, 2, 236. Cymb. IV, 2, 115. cf. *when the —s were out, the man would die,* Mcb. III, 4, 79.

Considered as the organ of thought; a) in the singular: *a drunken b.* Ven. 910. *her troubled b.* 1040. 1068. Lucr. 460. Sonn. 77, 11. 86, 3. 108, 1. Tp.

IV, 159. Wiv. I, 1, 44. IV, 2, 166. Ado II, 3, 250. V, 4, 87. LLL I, 1, 166. IV, 3, 324. V, 2, 857. Merch. I, 2, 19. As II, 7, 38. IV, 3, 4. Tw. I, 5, 63. 92. Wint. II, 3, 6. IV, 4, 701. John V, 7, 2. R2 V, 5, 6. H4B IV, 3, 105. H6B I, 2, 99. III, 1, 339. H8 III, 2, 113. Rom. I, 3, 29 (cf. *bear*). Hml. III, 2, 237 etc. — b) in the plural: Tp. V, 59. Wiv. III, 2, 30. III, 5, 7. IV, 2, 231. Tw. I, 3, 44. I, 5, 122. Wint. I, 2, 145. H4B III, 1, 19. Oth. II, 3, 35. The plural, of course, used with reference to several persons: *how are our —s beguiled,* Sonn. 59, 2. Wiv. III, 1, 122. Mids. V, 4. Wint. III, 3, 64. But also the singular: *women's gentle b. could not drop forth such giant-rude invention,* As IV, 3, 33. *—s* treated as a sing.: All's III, 2, 16. Hml. III, 1, 182. Lr. I, 5, 8.

Liver, b. and heart, these sovereign thrones, Tw. I, 1, 37. *to you, the liver, heart and b. of Britain,* Cymb. V, 5, 14.

To be beaten with —s = to be mocked· Ado V, 4, 104. *there has been much throwing about of —s,* Hml. II, 2, 376, i. e. much satirical controversy.

A dry b. = a dull brain, a brain incapable of thinking: As II, 7, 38. Troil. I, 3, 329. cf. *have I laid my b. in the sun and dried it?* Wiv. V, 5, 143. *O heat, dry up my —s,* Hml. IV, 5, 154. *to sear me to the b.* R3 IV, 1, 61 (= to deprive me of thought). cf. *Dry.* Falstaff's reasoning in H4B IV, 3, 105 rests on quite another physiological theory.

A hot b., Wint. IV, 4, 701 = an inventive fancy; cf. *such seething —s, such shaping fantasies,* Mids. V, 4. *a false creation proceeding from the heat-oppressed b.* Mcb. II, 1, 39. — *Boiled —s,* Wint. III, 3, 64 = hot-headed fellows.

Brain, vb., 1) to k i l l by b e a t i n g o u t t h e b r a i n s: *there thou mayst b. him,* Tp. III, 2, 96. *I could b. him with his lady's fan,* H4A II, 3, 24. Figuratively, = to d e f e a t: *that —ed my purpose,* Meas. V, 401.

2) to conceive in the brain, to u n d e r s t a n d: *such stuff as madmen tongue and b. not,* Cymb. V, 4, 147.

Brained, adj., endowed with a brain: *if the other two be b. like us, the state totters,* Tp. III, 2, 7.

Brainford (M. Edd. *Brentford*), place in England: Wiv. IV, 2, 78. 88. 100. 179. IV, 5, 28. 120.

Brainish, brainsick: *and in this b. apprehension kills the unseen good old man,* Hml. IV, 1, 11.

Brainless, stupid: *the dull b. Ajax,* Troil. I, 3, 381.

Brain-pan, skull: H6B IV, 10, 13.

Brain-sick, mad: *b. rude desire,* Lucr. 175. H6A IV, 1, 111. H6B III, 1, 51. V, 1, 163. Troil. II, 2, 122. Tit. V, 2, 71.

Brainsickly, madly: *you do unbend your noble strength, to think so b. of things,* Mcb. II, 2, 46.

Brake, thicket: *round rising hillocks, —s obscure and rough,* Ven. 237. *hasting to feed her fawn hid in some b.* 876. *kennelled in a b.* 913. Pilgr. 126. Mids. II, 1, 227. III, 1, 4. 77. 110. III, 2, 15. H6C III, 1, 1. *the rough b. that virtue must go through,* H8 I, 2, 75. — *Some run from brakes of Ice, and answer none, and some condemned for a fault alone,* Meas. II, 1, 39, a passage, as it seems, hopelessly corrupt. Some M. Edd. write *breaks of ice,* others *brakes of vice.* So much is certain, that the idea hidden in the words *brakes of Ice* must be antithetical to *a fault alone.*

Brakenbury, name in R3 I, 1, 88. 105. I, 4, 66 (Ff. *ah keeper, keeper*). V, 5, 14 *(Sir Robert B.)*

Bramble, blackberry bush, and in general a rough prickly shrub: *the thorny —s and embracing bushes*, Ven. 629. *hangs odes upon hawthorns and elegies on —s*, As III, 2, 380.

Bran, the husks separated from the flour by bolting: *to dine and sup with water and b.* Meas. IV, 3, 160. *fast a week with b. and water*, LLL I, 1, 303. *chaff and b.* Troil. I, 2, 262. *leave me but the b.* Cor. I, 1, 149. *meal and b. together he throws*, III, 1, 322. *nature hath meal and b.* Cymb. IV, 2, 27.

Branch, subst., a shoot of a tree: As IV, 2, 5.*Wint. IV, 4, 115. R2 III, 4, 63. H6A II, 5, 12. H6C IV, 6, 34. V, 2, 14. H8 IV, 2, 2. V, 5, 54. Per. II, 2, 43. V Prol. 6. Figuratively, = arm: *made thy body bare of her two —es*, Tit. II, 4, 18. Particularly used as a simile for children and descendants: *the —es of another root are rotted*, Lucr. 823. *lopped the b.* H6C II, 6, 47. *why grow the —es now the root is withered?* R3 II, 2, 41. cf. R2 I, 2, 13. 15. Cymb. V, 4, 141. V, 5, 454. Hence: *my low and humble name to propagate with any b. or image of thy state*, All's II, 1, 201. *as a b. and member of this royalty*, H5 V, 2, 5. *that from his loins no hopeful b. may spring*, H6C III, 2, 126.

= part, article, particular: *it is a b. and parcel of mine oath*, Err. V, 106. *that violates the smallest b. herein*, LLL I, 1, 21. *in every lineament, b., shape, and form*, Ado V, 1, 14. *the Sisters Three and such —es of learning*, Merch. II, 2, 66. *not to break peace, or any b. of it*, H4B IV, 1, 85. *an act hath three —es*, Hml. V, 1, 12. *this fierce abridgement hath to it circumstantial —es*, Cymb. V, 5, 383. Used, with special propriety, of the ramification of a pedigree: *he sends you this most memorable line, in every b. truly demonstrative*, H5 II, 4, 89.

Branch, vb., to shoot out: *there rooted betwixt them then such an affection, which cannot choose but b. now*, Wint. I, 1, 27.

Branched, adorned with needlework representing flowers and twigs: *in my b. velvet gown*, Tw. II, 5, 54.

Branchless, destitute, bare: *if I lose my honour, I lose myself: better I were not yours than yours so b.* Ant. III, 4, 24.

Brand, subst., 1) a burning piece of wood: Err. V, 171. Mids. V, 382. R2 V, 1, 46. H6B I, 1, 234. Cor. IV, 6, 115. Caes. III, 2, 260. III, 3, 41. Lr. V, 3, 22.

2) Cupid's torch: *Cupid laid by his b. and fell asleep*, Sonn. 153, 1. 9. *his heart-inflaming b.* 154, 2. *two winking Cupids, nicely depending on their —s*, Cymb. II, 4, 91.*

3) mark of infamy, stigma: *my name receives a b.* Sonn. 111, 5. Wint. II, 1, 71. Cor. III, 1, 304.

Brand, vb., to stigmatize: Lucr. 1091. R3 IV, 4, 141 (Qq. *where should be graven*). H8 III, 1, 128. Hml. IV, 5, 118. Lr. I, 2, 9. Ant. IV, 14, 76.

Brandish, to shake, to flourish: *never b. more revengeful steel*, R2 IV, 50. *if I b. any thing but a bottle*, H4B I, 2, 236. *b. your crystal tresses in the sky*, H6A I, 1, 3. *his —ed sword*, 10. IV, 7, 6. Mcb. I, 2, 17. V, 7, 13.

Brandon. *Sir William B.*: R3 V, 3, 22. 27. V, 5, 14.

Brass, an alloy of copper and zinc: *pewter and b.* Shr. II, 358. *b. cannon*, H5 III, 1, 11. *b., cur! offerest me b.?* IV, 4, 19. *trumpet, send thy b. voice* ..., Troil. I, 3, 257. *a leaf of b.* Tit. IV, 1, 102. Serving for tablets to write on, and hence a symbol of imperishable memory: *with characters of b.* Meas. V, 11. *since nor b. nor stone nor parchment bears not one* (example), Wint. I, 2, 360. *live in b.* H5 IV, 3, 97. H8 IV, 2, 45. *hold up high in b.* Troil. I, 3, 64. Emblem of hardness and strength: *and b. eternal slave to mortal rage*, Sonn. 64, 4. 65, 1. 107, 14. *as if this flesh were b. impregnable*, R2 III, 2, 168. *walls of beaten b.* Caes. I, 3, 93. *bind them in b.* Per. III, 1, 3. — Denoting insensibility and obduracy: *unless my nerves were b. or hammered steel*, Sonn. 120, 4. *can any face of b. hold longer out*, LLL V, 2, 395.

Brassy, hard as brass, pitiless: *b. bosoms and rough hearts of flint*, Merch. IV, 1, 31.

Brat, term of contempt for a child: Err. IV, 4, 39. Wint. II, 3, 92. 163. III, 2, 88. H6A V, 4, 84. H6C I, 3, 4. V, 5, 27. R3 I, 3, 194. III, 5, 107. Cor. IV, 6, 93. Tit. V, 1, 28. Cymb. II, 3, 124.

Brave, adj., 1) valiant: *hast thou kill'd him sleeping? O b. touch!* Mids. III, 2, 70. *b. conquerors*, LLL I, 1, 8. V, 2, 671. Merch. II, 2, 12. All's II, 1, 16. H6A II, 1, 28. III, 2, 101. 134. IV, 3, 34. H6B IV, 8, 21. H6C IV, 1, 96. V, 7, 8. Tit. I, 25. Mcb. I, 2, 5. 16. Cymb. I, 1, 166 etc. etc.

2) becoming (in speaking of things), gallant (of persons), such as one ought to be: *I'll devise thee b. punishments for him*, Ado V, 4, 130. *wear my dagger with the —r grace*, Merch. III, 4, 65. *what a noble combat hast thou fought between compulsion and a b. respect!* John V, 2, 44. *I have thrown a b. defiance in King Henry's teeth*, H4A V, 2, 43. *this is most b. that I must, like a whore, unpack my heart with words*, Hml. II, 2, 611. *what's b., what's noble, let's do it*, Ant. IV, 15, 86. *their b. hope, bold Hector*, Lucr. 1430. *my b. spirit!* Tp. I, 2, 206. *the Duke of Milan and his b. son*, 438. *his more —r daughter*, 439. *you are gentlemen of b. mettle*, II, 1, 182. *O b. monster, lead the way*, II, 2, 192. *b. Master Shooty, the great traveller*, Meas. IV, 3, 18. *this is a b. fellow*, Wint. IV, 4, 202. *the society of your b. father*, V, 1, 136. *I'll be a b. judge*, H4A I, 2, 73. *that's my b. boy*, Cor. V, 3, 76. *b. lords*, Tit. IV, 2, 136. *my b. Egyptians*, Ant. III, 13, 164. *—st at the last, she levelled at our purposes*, V, 2, 338.

3) fine, splendid, beautiful: *see the b. day sunk in hideous night*, Sonn. 12, 2. *wear their b. state out of memory*, 15, 8. *youth like summer b., age like winter bare*, Pilgr. 160. *a b. vessel*, Tp. I, 2, 6. *it carries a b. form*, 411. *that's a b. god and bears celestial liquor*, II, 2, 122. *he were a b. monster indeed, if they were set in his tail*, III, 2, 12. *he has b. utensils, which, when he hath a house, he'll deck withal*, 104. *so b. a lass*, 111. 113. *this will prove a b. kingdom to me*, 153. *O b. new world*, V, 183. *these be b. spirits*, 261. *full merrily hath this b. manage, this career, been run*, LLL V, 2, 482. *O that's a b. man! he writes b. verses* etc. As III, 4, 43. *b. attendants*, Shr. Ind. I, 40. *a —r choice of dauntless spirits did never float* ..., John I, 72. *a —r place in my heart's love hath no man than yourself*, H4A IV, 1, 7. *b. death, when princes die with us*, V, 2, 87. *when shall we go to Cheapside? marry, presently. O b.!* H6B IV, 7, 137. cf.

138. *welcome to this b. town of York,* H6C II, 2, 1. *their b. pavilions,* Troil. Prol. 15. *is not that a b. man?* I, 2, 202. *this b. o'erhanging firmament,* Hml. II, 2, 312. *this is a b. night to cool a courtezan,* Lr. III, 2, 79. *from this most —st vessel of the world struck the main-top,* Cymb. IV, 2, 319.

Brave, vb., 1) to display bravery, to carry a threatening appearance: *have fought with equal fortune and continue a —ing war,* All's I, 2, 3. *art come in —ing arms,* R2 II, 3, 112. 143. Followed by a superfluous *it: Lucius and I'll go b. it at the court,* Tit. IV, 1, 122.

Mostly transitive, = to defy, to oppose, to bully: *so rich a thing, —ing compare,* Lucr. 40. *to b. him* (time) *when he takes thee hence,* Sonn. 12, 14. *b. not me,* Shr. IV, 3, 126. *—d in mine own house,* 111. *that faced and —d me in this manner so,* V, 1, 124. *my state is —d with ranks of foreign powers,* John IV, 2, 243. *darest thou b. a nobleman,* IV, 3, 87. *to b. me,* H4B II, 4, 232. *how I am —d and must perforce endure it,* H6A II, 4, 115. *b. death by speaking,* IV, 7, 25. *thou wilt b. me with these saucy terms?* H6B IV, 10, 38. Tit. II, 3, 126. IV, 2, 36. 137. Caes. IV, 3, 96. Oth. V, 2, 326. Ant. IV, 4, 5.

2) to make fine and splendid: *thou* (viz the tailor) *hast —d many men,* Shr. IV, 3, 125. *he should have —d the east an hour ago,* R3 V, 3, 279.

It must be left undecided, in which of these two significations the following passages are to be understood: *shall a beardless boy ... b. our fields,* John V, 1, 70; and: *when traitors b. the field,* R3 IV, 3, 57. One acceptation is supported by the analogous use of the verb *to become* (q. v. sub 3; cf. besides: *the foe vaunts in the field,* R3 V, 3, 288); the other by a similar expression in H5 IV, 2, 36: *our approach shall so much dare the field that England shall couch down in fear and yield.* It must, however, be borne in mind that in this latter passage the word *dare* is used with peculiar propriety, being a technical term of falconry.

Brave, subst., display of valour, defiance, threatening: *I will not bear these —s of thine,* Shr. III, 1, 15. *there end thy b. and turn thy face in peace,* John V, 2, 159. *where's the Bastard's —s, and Charles his gleeks?* H6A III, 2, 123. *this b. shall oft make thee to hide thy head,* Troil. IV, 4, 139. *to bear me down with —s,* Tit. II, 1, 30.

Bravely, 1) valiantly: *he b. broached his boiling bloody breast,* Mids. V, 148. *he's b. taken here,* All's III, 5, 55. *full b. hast thou fleshed thy maiden sword,* H4A V, 4, 133. H4B II, 4, 54. H5 III, 6, 77. R3 V, 3, 312. Troil. III, 3, 213. Cor. V, 3, 117. Mcb. V, 7, 26. Lr. IV, 6, 202. Cymb. V, 4, 72.

2) in a becoming manner, so as to excite the cry: *'well done! bravo!': b. the figure of this harpy hast thou performed,* Tp. III, 3, 83. *tight and yare and b. rigged,* V, 224. *was't well done? b., my diligence,* V, 241. *'twas b. done,* Ado V, 1, 279. *swears brave oaths and breaks them b.* As III, 4, 45. *and revel it as b. as the best,* Shr. IV, 3, 54. *steal away b.* All's II, 1, 29. *away, and leave her b.* II, 3, 216. *b., coragio!* II, 5, 97 (= well done!). *b. confessed and lamented by the king,* Wint. V, 2, 93. *O b. came we off,* John V, 5, 4. *the French are b. in their battles set,* H5 IV, 3, 69. *she takes upon her b. at first dash,* H6A I, 2, 71. *Pucelle hath b. played her part,* III, 3,

88. *when I have been dry and b. marching,* H6B IV, 10, 15. *see you do it b.* Tit. IV, 3, 113. *here we may see most b.* Troil. I, 2, 198. *now thou diest as b. as Titinius,* Caes. V, 4, 10. *do b., horse!* Ant. I, 5, 22. *how b. thou becomest thy bed,* Cymb. II, 2, 15. *a piece of work so b. done,* II, 4, 73.

The passages sub 1. may, indeed, all be taken in the same sense.

Bravery, 1) display of valour, ostentation, bravado: *come down with fearful b.* Caes. V, 1, 10. *the b. of his grief did put me into a towering passion,* Hml. V, 2, 79.

2) act of defiance, state of defiance: *upon malicious b. dost thou come to start my quiet,* Oth. I, 1, 100 (Ff *knavery*). *the natural b. of your isle,* Cymb. III, 1, 18.

3) splendor, finery: *hiding thy* (the sun's) *b.* Sonn. 34, 4. *where youth, and cost, and witless b. keeps,* Meas. I, 3, 10. *his b. is not of my cost,* As II, 7, 80. *with scarfs and fans and double change of b.* Shr. IV, 3, 57.

Brawl, vb., 1) to be at discord: *whose advice hath often stilled my —ing discontent,* Meas. IV, 1, 9. *his divisions, as the times do b., are in three heads,* H4B I, 3, 70. *O —ing love! O loving hate!* Rom. I, 1, 182.

2) to quarrel: *though she strive to try her strength, and ban and b.* Pilgr. 318. Err. IV, 1, 51. LLL III, 1, 10. Shr. I, 2, 188. IV, 1, 209. IV, 3, 10. R3 I, 3, 324.*

3) to be clamorous, to be loud: *what a —ing dost thou keep,* H4A II, 2, 6. *what are you —ing here,* H4B II, 1, 71. In a somewhat milder sense: *the brook that —s along this wood,* As II, 1, 32. — *To b. down* = to throw down by peals of cannon: *till their soul-fearing clamours have —ed down the flinty ribs of this contemptuous city,* John II, 383.

Brawl, subst. 1) a row, squabble: *but he is a devil in private b.* (= single combat, duel), Tw. III, 4, 259. *be gone, good ancient: this will grow to a b. anon,* H4B II, 4, 187. *we shall much disgrace with four or five most vile and ragged foils, right ill disposed in b. ridiculous, the name of Agincourt,* H5 IV Chor. 51. *none basely slain in —s,* Tit. I, 353. *three civil —s, bred of an airy word,* Rom. I, 1, 96 (Ff *broils*). *if we meet, we shall not scape a b.* III, 1, 3. 148. 194. *put by this barbarous b.* Oth. II, 3, 172. 256.

2) quarrel, altercation: *his sports were hindered by thy —s,* Err. V, 77. *with thy —s thou hast disturbed our sport,* Mids. II, 1, 87. Tw. V, 364. H5 IV, 8, 69. H6A II, 4, 124. Tit. IV, 3, 93.

3) a French dance: LLL III, 9.

Brawler, in *Night-brawler,* q. v.

Brawn, 1) a fleshy mass: *the b. buttock,* All's II, 2, 19. *that damned b. shall play Dame Mortimer,* H4A II, 4, 123.* *Harry Monmouth's b., the hulk Sir John,* H4B I, 1, 19.

2) the musculous arm: *and in my vantbrace put this withered b.,* Troil. I, 3, 297. *to hew thy target from thy b.* Cor. IV, 5, 126. *the —s of Hercules,* Cymb. IV, 2, 311.

Brawny, fleshy, musculous: *his* (the bear's) *b. sides,* Ven. 625.

Bray, subst., the sound of a trumpet:

with harsh-resounding trumpets' dreadful b. R2 I, 3, 135.

Bray, vb., **to sound like a trumpet:** *—ing trumpets and loud churlish drums,* John III, 1, 303. *when every room hath blazed with lights and —ed with minstrelsy,* Tim. II, 2, 170. *the kettle-drum and trumpet thus b. out the triumph of his pledge,* Hml. I, 4, 11.

Braze, to **harden:** *if damned custom have not —d it (your heart) so that it is proof . . .,* Hml. III, 4, 37. *I have so often blushed to acknowledge him, that now I am —d to it,* Lr. I, 1, 11.

Brazen, made of brass: *lived registered upon our b. tombs,* LLL I, 1, 2. *with his (the bell's) iron tongue and b. mouth,* John III, 3, 38. *a b. canstick,* H4A III, 1, 131. *b. images,* H6B I, 3, 63. *b. cannon,* Hml. I, 1, 73. *b. trumpet,* R2 III, 3, 33 and Troil. IV, 5, 7; and hence: *trumpeters, with b. din blast you the city's ear,* Ant. IV, 8, 36.

Figuratively, = extremely strong, impregnable: *loosed them (the winds) forth their b. caves,* H6B III, 2, 89. *that thy b. gates of heaven may ope,* H6C II, 3, 40. *wert thou environed with a b. wall,* II, 4, 4.

Brazen-face, impudent person: Wiv. IV, 2, 141.

Brazen-faced, impudent: Lr. II, 2, 30.

Brazier, artisan who works in brass: *he should be a b. by his face,* H8 V, 4, 42.

Breach, 1) the space between the several parts of a solid body parted by violence: *she crops the stalk, and in the b. appears green dropping sap,* Ven. 1175. *patches set upon a little b.* John IV, 2, 32. Figuratively, = a wound, a hurt: *makes more gashes where no b. should be,* Ven. 1066. *a b. that craves a quick expedient stop,* H6B III, 1, 288. *where this b. now in our fortunes made may readily be stopped,* V, 2, 82. *the very b. whereout Hector's great spirit flew,* Troil. IV, 5, 245. *his gashed stabs looked like a b. in nature,* Mcb. II, 3, 119. *cure this great b. in his abused nature,* Lr. IV, 7, 15 (some of these passages may as well be taken in the second signification).

2) a gap in a fortification: *to make the b. and enter this sweet city,* Lucr. 469. *with the b. yourselves made,* All's I, 1, 136. *to come off the b. with his pike bent,* H4B II, 4, 55. *pouring like the tide into a b.* H5 I, 2, 149. *once more unto the b.* III, 1, 1. III, 2, 1. 22. 116. III, 6, 76. H6A II, 1, 74. III, 2, 2. Rom. I, 4, 84. Oth. I, 3, 136.

3) the rupture, difference: *yet there is no great b.* H8 IV, 1, 106. *there's fallen between him and my lord an unkind b.* Oth. IV, 1, 238. *nuptial —es* (= divorces) Lr. I, 2, 162 (only in Qq).

4) infraction, violation: *the impious b. of holy wedlock vow,* Lucr. 809. *two oaths' b.* Sonn. 152, 5. *your b. of promise,* Err. IV, 1, 49. *b. of honour,* LLL II, 170. *of laws,* H5 IV, 1, 179. H6B II, 4, 66. *it (the compact) should be put to no apparent likelihood of b.* R3 II, 2, 136. *our b. of duty,* H8 II, 2, 69. *of the peace,* I, 1, 94. *of custom,* Hml. I, 4, 16. Cymb. IV, 2, 10. *of faith,* Cymb. III, 4, 27.

5) the breaking of waves, the surf: *took me from the b. of the sea,* Tw. II, 1, 23.

Bread, 1) food made of corn: *an honest maid as ever broke b.* Wiv. I, 4, 161. *I love not the humour of b. and cheese,* II, 1, 140. Meas. I, 3, 53. III, 2, 195 (*brown b.*). Ado III, 5, 42 (*an honest soul, as ever broke b.*). As III, 4, 15 (*the touch of holy b.*).*

R2 III, 2, 175. V, 5, 85. H4A II, 4, 590. 592. H4B II, 4, 258. H5 V, 1, 9. H6A III, 2, 41. Cor. I, 1, 25. Tim. I, 2, 48. Lr. V, 3, 94. Per. I, 4, 41. 95. *God's b.! it makes me mad,* Rom. III, 5, 177.

2) food in general: *work for b.* Mids. III, 2, 10. *eating the bitter b. of banishment,* R2 III, 1, 21. *full of b.* Hml. III, 3, 80 (cf. Ezekiel 16, 49). *buys b. and clothes,* Oth. IV, 1, 96.

Bread-chipper, one who chips bread: H4B II, 4, 342; cf. 258.

Breadth, 1) the extent from side to side: *the length and b.* Ado V, 1, 11. Hml. V, 1, 119. *requital to a hair's b.* Wiv. IV, 2, 4. *she bears some b.* Err. III, 2, 114. *as broad as it hath b.* Ant. II, 7, 48.

2) wideness, extent, distance in general: *if there be b. enough in the world, I will hold a long distance,* All's III, 2, 26. *that blood which owed the b. of all this isle,* John IV, 2, 99. *the spacious b. of this division* (wider than the sky and earth) Troil. V, 2, 150. *he will repent the b. of his great voyage,* Per. IV, 1, 37.

Break, vb., impf. *brake:* Ven. 469. Err. V, 48. H4A I, 1, 48. R3 III, 7, 41. Usually *broke:* Wiv. I, 1, 125. I, 4, 161. Err. V, 149. Ado III, 5, 42. LLL III, 118. As I, 2, 135. II, 4, 47. Tw. V, 188 etc. etc. Partic. *broke* (never adjectively before a noun), f. i. Sonn. 143, 2. 152, 3. Pilgr. 32. 41. Tp. III, 1, 37. IV, 99. Wiv. I, 1, 115. Meas. II, 4, 126. V, 218. Err. I, 2, 50. V, 169. Ado II, 1, 310. V, 1, 139. LLL V, 2, 440 etc. Or *broken:* Lucr. 1758. Sonn. 61, 3. Compl. 254. Pilgr. 40. 172. Gentl. II, 5, 19. II, 6, 11. Ado II, 3, 245. LLL III, 71. As I, 1, 134. I, 2, 150.* II, 1, 57. III, 5, 102. IV, 3, 155 etc. etc.

I) trans. 1) to rend apart, to crack: *—eth his rein,* Ven. 264. *his girths,* 266. *broken glass,* Lucr. 1758. Pilgr. 172. *—ing rings a-twain,* Compl. 6. *—ing their contents* (i. e. tearing the papers), 56. *b. her virgin-knot,* Tp. IV, 1, 15. *has broke his arrows,* 99. *I'll b. my staff,* V, 54. *the seal,* Gentl. III, 1, 139. *broke bread,* Wiv. I, 4, 161 and Ado III, 5, 42. Meas. II, 4, 126. Err. II, 2, 140. IV, 3, 31. Ado V, 1, 139. 189. As I, 2, 135. II, 4, 47. III, 5, 102. Shr. I, 2, 267 (*b. the ice*). II, 149. III, 2, 48. Wint. III, 2, 130. R2 II, 2, 59. II, 3, 27. H4A II, 4, 238. H6B I, 2, 26. 28. IV, 1, 42. H6C V, 4, 4. R3 V, 3, 341. Cor. I, 1, 210 etc. *to b. one's back* = to strain or dislocate it with too heavy a burden: Tp. III, 1, 26. H6B IV, 8, 30. H8 I, 1, 84. *she broke her brow* = bruised her forehead, Rom. I, 3, 38. *to b. the head* = to crack the skin of the head, so that the blood comes: Wiv. I, 1, 125. Tw. V, 178. 188. H4A III, 1, 242. H4B II, 1, 97. III, 2, 33. H5 III, 2, 42. *to b. the pate:* Err. II, 1, 78. II, 2, 220. III, 1, 74. All's II, 1, 68. *the sconce:* Err. I, 2, 79. *the costard:* LLL III, 71. *broken limb,* As I, 1, 134. I, 2, 150. H4B IV, 1, 222. Tit. V, 3, 72. *b. your necks,* H6A V, 4, 91. *b. my shin,* LLL III, 118. Rom. I, 2, 53. *we b. the sinews of our plot,* Tw. II, 5, 83. — *To b. a lance* = to enter the lists: H6A III, 2, 50.

Metaphorically: *to b. the heart* = to kill with grief: Lucr. 1239. Compl. 254 (*the broken bosoms*). Cor. I, 1, 215. Lr. III, 4, 4 etc. = to die: *they will b. their hearts but they will effect,* Wiv. II, 2, 323. *almost broke my heart with extreme laughter,* Tit. V, 1, 113. — *My charms I'll b.,* Tp. V, 31 (expression taken from the magic wand). *her sobs do her intendments b.* Ven. 222.

the unity had not been broken, R3 IV, 4, 380. cf. H4B IV, 5, 69.

2) **to shatter in pieces, to batter down:** *our windows are broke down in every street,* H6A III, 1, 84. *hunger broke stone walls,* Cor. I, 1, 210. 4, 16. *the doors are broke,* Hml. IV, 5, 111. = **to disperse,** in speaking of a misty vapour: Pilgr. 40.

3) **to burst through, to open by violence:** *her brother's ghost his crazed bed would b.* Meas. V, 440. *he —s the pale,* Err. II, 1, 100. *to b. his grave,* Wint. V, 1, 42. *how has the ass broke the wall,* Tim. IV, 3, 354. *the mad mothers with their howls do b. the clouds,* H5 III, 3, 40. Used of an army: *all our ranks are broke,* H5 IV, 5, 6. H6C II, 3, 10. *the army broken,* Cymb. V, 3, 5. — Joined with *ope* and *up: —s ope her locked-up eyes,* Lucr. 446. *broke open my lodge,* Wiv. I, 1, 115. Err. III, 1, 73. Cor. III, 1, 138. *b. up the seals,* Wint. III, 2, 132. *b. up the gates,* H6A I, 3, 13. *ghosts b. up their graves,* H6B I, 4, 22. *b. up this* (sc. a letter), Merch. II. 4, 10. *To b. up,* in the sense of *to carve: Boyet, you can carve; b. up this capon* (sc. a letter), LLL IV, 1, 56 (cf. the French *poulet* = love-letter).

4) **to open, to make a disclosure of:** *b. thy mind to me,* H5 V, 2, 265. *we shall meet, and b. our minds at large,* H6A I, 3, 81. *b. a word with you,* Err. III, 1, 75. *b. this enterprise to me,* Mcb. I, 7, 48. *b. the cause of our expedience to the queen,* Ant. I, 2, 184. *the —ing of so great a thing,* V, 1, 14. — As in Shr. I, 2, 267, *to break the ice* is = **to open the matter, to pave the way,** so in Wiv. III, 4, 22 *b. their talk* = open their conversation (cf. Troil. III, 3, 215).

5) **to interrupt:** *b. the parle,* Tit. V, 3, 19. *you have now a broken banquet,* H8 I, 4, 61 (with a double sense). *you have broke it,* Troil. III, 1, 53. *a tearing groan did b. the name of Antony,* Ant. IV, 14, 31 (cut it in two). *to b. a person's sleep* = to keep one waking, and to be waking: *my slumbers should be broken,* Sonn. 61, 3. *have broken their sleep with thoughts,* H4B IV, 5, 69. Cor. IV, 4, 19. *b. not your sleeps for that,* Hml. IV, 7, 30 (don't be uneasy).

To b. off = **to discontinue, to leave off, to cut short:** *brake off his late intent,* Ven. 469. *b. off thy song,* Meas. IV, 1, 7. *which was broke off,* V, 218. *b. off your conference,* John II, 150. *b. the story off,* R2 V, 2, 2. *brake off our business,* H4A I, 1, 48. H5 I, 1, 90. H6C II, 2, 110. R3 III, 1, 177. *with patience calm the storm, while we bethink a means to b. it off,* H6C III, 3, 39, i. e. to make it cease.

To b. up = **to dismiss, to adjourn:** *like a school broke up,* H4B IV, 2, 104. *b. up the court,* H8 II, 4, 240. *b. up the senate till another time,* Caes. II, 2, 98. *b. we our watch up,* Hml. I, 1, 168.

6) **to violate, to infringe, not to keep:** *b. an article,* LLL I, 1, 134. *your bidding,* All's II, 5, 93. *a compact,* H6A V, 4, 164. *custom,* Merch. I, 3, 65. *his day,* Merch. I, 3, 165. *faith,* Merch. V, 253. *honesty,* Wint. I, 2, 288. John V, 2, 8. H6C IV, 4, 30. R3 IV, 4, 386. *to b. one's fast,* a) = **to eat meat in the time of fasting:** John I, 235; b) = **to breakfast:** Gentl. II, 4, 141. Err. I, 2, 50. H6C II, 2, 127. *a hest,* Tp. III, 1, 37. *hours,* Gentl. V, 1, 4. *a law,* R3 I, 4, 205. 215. *an oath,* Sonn. 152, 6. Gentl. IV, 4, 135. LLL I, 1, 66. V, 2, 355. 440. R2 IV, 214. H6C I, 2, 16. I, 4, 100. II, 2, 89. III, 1, 79. *the peace,* Ado II, 3, 202. H6A I, 3, 58. *the possession of a royal bed,*

R2 III, 1, 15. *promise,* As IV, 3, 155. *sanctuary,* R3 III, 1, 47. *seasons,* R3 I, 4, 76. *time,* All's II, 1, 190. R2 V, 5, 43. *troth,* LLL I, 1, 66. V, 2, 350. *truth,* Sonn. 41, 12. *vows,* Sonn. 152, 3. Pilgr. 32. 41. 42. Gentl. II, 6, 11. Mids. I, 1, 175. Ant. I, 3, 31 *(those mouth-made vows, which b. themselves in swearing).* *one's word,* Err. III, 1, 76. H4B II, 3, 10.

The person, to whom a vow or promise is not kept, adjoined with the prepos. *to:* all *oaths that are broke to me,* R2 IV, 214; or with the prepos. *with: —ing faith with Julia,* Gentl. IV, 2, 11. *make him with fair Aegle b. his faith,* Mids. II, 1, 79. *b. an oath with thee,* Merch. V, 248. *to b. promise with him,* Tw. II, 3, 137. *hath with Talbot broke his word,* H6A IV, 6, 2. *hast thou broken faith with me,* H6B V, 1, 91. *b. an oath with him,* R3 IV, 4, 378 (Qq *by him*). And without an object: *I would not b. with her,* Wiv. III, 2, 57, i. e. I would not b. my word to her. cf. Merch. I, 3, 137.

7) **to crush, to weaken, to impair:** *an old man, broken with the storms of state,* H8 IV, 2, 21. *I shall b. my wind* = be out of breath, H4A II, 2, 13. *pursy insolence shall b. his wind with fear and horrid flight,* Tim. V, 4, 12. *floods of tears will drown my oratory, and b. my very utterance,* Tit. V, 3, 91. *is not your voice broken?* H4B I, 2, 206. *a broken voice* (i. e. trembling with emotion) Hml. II, 2, 582. *and kissing speaks, with lustful language broken,* Ven. 47, i. e. trembling with lustful desire.

Hence = **to tame, to make docile:** *thou canst not b. her to the lute,* Shr. II, 148. *thou wantest —ing,* Err. III, 1, 77.

8) *to b. a jest* = **to crack a joke:** *you b. jests as braggarts do their blades,* Ado V, 1, 189. *to b. a jest upon the company,* Shr. IV, 5, 72. *—s scurrile jests,* Troil. I, 3, 148. And similarly: *he'll but b. a comparison or two on me,* Ado II, 1, 152. *I may have some odd quirks and remnants of wit broken on me,* II, 3, 245.

9) **Peculiar uses:** *a poor earl's daughter is unequal odds, and therefore may be broke without offence,* H6A V, 5, 35, = broken with; the omission of *with* being perhaps caused by the following *without. Hell itself —s out contagion to this world,* Hml. III, 2, 407, = vomits forth, quite like the German *ausbrechen;* but Ff. and M. Edd. have *breathes out. So he b. it* (his word) *not behind,* Err. III, 1, 76 (= break wind). *Break any breaking here,* Err. III, 1, 74.

10) The partic. *broken* in different significations easily explained by what precedes: *a broken mouth* = a mouth with gaps in its teeth, All's II, 3, 66. *broken meats* = meats half eaten, remnants of victuals: Lr. II, 2, 15. cf. *a broken banquet,* H8 I, 4, 61. *broken tears,* Troil. IV, 4, 50, i. e. tears breaking forth. *I make a broken delivery of the business,* Wint. V, 2, 10, i. e. a fragmentary report, having many gaps in it. *In broken English,* H5 V, 2, 264. 265; in a language consisting only half of English. *Broken music* = music on stringed instruments ("the term originating probably from harps, lutes, and such other stringed instruments as were played without a bow, not having the capability to sustain a long note to its full duration of time." Chappell): *this broken music in his sides,* As I, 2, 150. *your answer in broken music,* H5 V, 2, 263. *here is good broken music,* Troil. III, 1, 52.

II) **intrans. 1) to part in two, to burst,**

to open: *the berry —s before it staineth*, Ven. 460. *have a care the honeybag b. not*, Mids. IV, 1, 16. *if one (point) b.* Tw. I, 5, 26. *my girdle b.* H4A III, 3, 171. *b. thou in pieces*, H6A V, 4, 92. *like a glass did b. in the rinsing*, H8 I, 1, 167. *my high-blown pride broke under me* (like a bladder) III, 2, 362. *whereagainst my grained ash an hundred times hath broke*, Cor. IV, 5, 114. *the impostume that inward —s*, Hml. IV, 4, 28; cf. *and when it —s, I fear will issue thence the foul corruption* etc. John IV, 2, 80. *the army —ing, my husband hies him home*, All's IV, 4, 11, i. e. disbanding.

Used of the heart and heart-strings: Ven. 336. Lucr. 1716. Compl. 275. Shr. IV, 3, 78. Wint. III, 2, 175. R2 II, I, 228. H6B III, 2, 320. H6C II, 5, 78. R3 IV, 4, 365. Tit. III, 1, 60. Rom. III, 2, 57. Absolutely: *O b., o b.!* Ant. V, 2, 313.

Flaky darkness —s within the east, R3 V, 3, 86, = dissolves, disperses. And hence, in the same sense, applied to the contrary: *the day*, or *the morning —s*, John V, 4, 32. H5 IV, 1, 88. H6B II, 2, 1. Rom. III, 5, 40. Caes. II, 1, 101. Oth. III, 1, 34.

2) **to burst, to discharge itself**: *his passion is so ripe, it needs must b.* John IV, 2, 79. *b. into extremity of rage*, Err. V, 48. *b. into some merry passion*, Shr. Ind. 1, 97. *to b. into this dangerous argument*, John IV, 2, 54. *sin gathering head will b. into corruption*, R2 V, 1, 59. *to b. into this woman's mood*, H4A I, 3, 237. *broke into a general prophecy*, H8 I, 1, 91. *do not b. into these deep extremes*, Tit. III, 1, 216. *from ancient grudge broke to new mutiny*, Rom. I Chor. 3. To b. forth: *his malice 'gainst the lady will suddenly b. forth*, As I, 2, 295. *diseased nature —s forth in strange eruptions*, H4A III, 1, 27. *—ing forth in riots*, Lr. I, 4, 222. *your letters did withhold our —ing forth*, Ant. III, 6, 79. To b. out: *b. out into tears*, Ado I, 1, 24. *such —ing out of mirth*, LLL V, 1, 121. *b. out into a second course of mischief*, H5 IV, 3, 106. *into a flame*, H6A III, 1, 191. *into terms of rage*, H6C I, 1, 265. *lest the new healed wound of malice should b. out*, R3 II, 2, 125. *you will b. out*, Troil. V, 2, 51. *b. out to bitterest enmity*, Cor. IV, 4, 17. *mature for the violent —ing out*, IV, 3, 27. *—s out to savage madness*, Oth. IV, 1, 56. *might b. out and swear*, Cymb. IV, 2, 140. Hence = to take rise: *such a deal of wonder is broken out within this hour*, Wint. V, 2, 26. *lest parties b. out*, Cor. III, 1, 315. *this will b. out to all our sorrows*, John IV, 2, 101 (turn to our sorrow).

3) **to force one's way**: *to break in*, Err. III, 1, 80. 98. H6A I, 1, 119. II, 1, 71. H6B III, 2, 278. H6C I, 1, 8. 29. *b. into his son-in-law's house*, H6B IV, 7, 117. IV, 10, 35. *b. within the bloody house of life*, John IV, 2, 210. *broke out to acquaint you with this evil*, John V, 6, 24. *life looks through and will b. out*, H4B IV, 4, 120. *—s like a fire out of his keeper's arms*, H4B I, 1, 142. *within this mile b. forth a hundred springs*, Tim. IV, 3, 421. *break loose*, Err. V, 169. Mids. III, 2, 258. H4B I, 1, 10. *I must from this enchanting queen b. off*, Ant. I, 2, 132. *one of her feathered creatures broke away*, Sonn. 143, 2. *I will not b. away*, Err. IV, 4, 1. *b. among the press*, H8 V, 4, 88. *love —s through*, Ven. 576. *through the floodgates —s the silver rain*, 959. Sonn. 34, 5. Shr. IV, 3, 175. H4A I, 2, 226. H6B IV, 8, 24. Rom. II, 2, 2. *he —eth from the sweet embrace*, Ven. 811. 874. *on what occasion b. those tears from thee?* Lucr. 1270.

would not b. from thence, Compl. 34. Err. V, 149. As II, 4, 40. R2 II, 1, 281. H6A I, 4, 44. H6C II, 1, 75. R3 I, 4, 9. *tears which b. from me perforce*, Lr. I, 4, 320. *wherefore —s that sigh from the inward of thee?* Cymb. III, 4, 5. And without the idea of violence, = to escape, to come from, to quit: *anon did this b. from her*, Wint. III, 3, 27. *any accent —ing from thy tongue*, John V, 6, 14. *you have broken from his liking*, Wint. V, 1, 212 (have acted against his will).

4) **to fall to pieces, to lose strength or validity**: *all bond and privilege of nature, b.!* Cor. V, 3, 25. *no bargains b. that are not this day made*, John III, 1, 93. *midst the sentence so her accent —s, that twice she doth begin ere once she speaks*, Lucr. 566 (The passage in Ant. V, 1, 14 may be taken in this sense as well as in that of opening, communicating).

Especially = to become bankrupt: *he cannot choose but b.* Merch. III, 1, 120. *broken bankrupt*, As II, 1, 57. R2 II, 1, 257. H4B V, 5, 128. Rom. III, 2, 57. Tim. IV, 2, 5. V, 1, 10. Cymb. V, 4, 19.

5) **to fall out**: *are they broken?* Gentl. II, 5, 19. *it cannot be the Volsces dare b. with us*, Cor. IV, 6, 48. With a quibble: *the broken rancour of your high-swoln hearts, but lately splintered....*, R3 II, 2, 117.

6) **to open, to make a disclosure**; with *to* or *with* before the person, and *of* or *about* before the thing: *then after to her father will I b.* Ado I, 1, 328. *now will we b. with him*, Gentl. I, 3, 44. *I will b. with her*, Ado I, 1, 311. *I have broke with her father*, II, 1, 310. *have broken with the king*, H8 V, 1, 47. *let us not b. with him*, Caes. II, 1, 150. *I am to b. with thee of some affairs*, Gentl. III, 1, 59. *and instantly b. with you of it*, Ado I, 2, 16. *I faintly broke with thee of Arthur's death*, John IV, 2, 227. *b. with your wives of your departure*, H4A III, 1, 144. *to b. with him about it*, Ado II, 1, 162. *to b. with him about Beatrice*, III, 2, 76.

7) **to spread by dashing**, as waves: *their* (the waves') *ranks began to b. upon the galled shore*, Lucr. 1440. *the —ing gulf*, Err. II, 2, 128. *on the —ing seas*, R2 III, 2, 3.

8) **to b. off** = to discontinue to speak: *do not b. off so*, Err. I, 1, 97. Mids. V, 98. John IV, 2, 235. H6B II, 2, 77. III, 1, 325. R3 III, 7, 41. Caes. II, 1, 116. Hml. I, 1, 40. Lr. V, 2, 262.

Break, subst: *the b. of day* = the dawn: *ere the b. of day*, Lucr. 1280. *at b. of day*, Sonn. 29, 11. Meas. IV, 1, 3. Mids. III, 2, 446. V, 408. 429. Merch. III, 2, 51 (*in b. of day*). V, 29. Rom. III, 3, 168. Per. III, 1, 77.

Breaker, transgressor: *—s of their own behests*, Lucr. 852. *a b. of proverbs*, H4A I, 2, 132. *of the law*, H6A I, 3, 80.

Breakfast, subst., the first meal in the day: Tp. V, 164. Gentl. III, 1, 329. V, 4, 34. Wiv. III, 3, 246. H4A II, 4, 116. III, 3, 193. H5 II, 1, 12. III, 7, 156. H6B I, 4, 79. R3 IV, 4, 176. H8 III, 2, 202. Tim. I, 2, 78. IV, 3, 336. Ant. II, 2, 184. Per. IV, 6, 131.

Break-neck, a dangerous business: *to do't or no, is to me a b.* Wint. I, 2, 363.

Break-promise, a person who breaks his promise: *will think you the most pathetical b.* As IV, 1, 196.

Break-vow, a person who breaks his vows: *that daily b., he that wins of all*, John II, 569.

Breast, subst., 1) the part of the body between the neck and belly, in men and beasts: broad *b.* Ven. 296. *his back, his b.* 396. 648. 1182. Lucr. 439. 1122. Pilgr. 382. Sonn. 153, 10. Tp. III, 3, 47. LLL IV, 3, 173. 185. Mids. II, 2, 146. Merch. IV, 1, 252. H6A I, 5, 10. III, 3, 87. Cor. II, 2, 126 etc. etc. *tugging to be victors, b. to b.* H6C II, 5, 11. Tropically: *dare sail upon her* (the sea's) *patient b.* Troil. I, 3, 36. *the lightning seemed to open the b. of heaven,* Caes. I, 3, 51. *conjure from the b. of peace such bold hostility,* H4A IV, 3, 43.

2) the dugs of women: *her —s, like ivory globes,* Lucr. 407. Sonn. 130, 3. Cor. I, 3, 43. Mcb. I, 5, 48. *when thou sucked'st her b.* H6A V, 4, 28. Tim. IV, 3, 178.

3) the heart: *lest the deceiving harmony should run into the quiet closure of my b.* Ven. 782. *or tyrant folly lurk in gentle —s,* Lucr. 851. *dumb presagers of my speaking b.* Sonn. 23, 10. 109, 4. *to physic your cold b.* Compl. 259. Tp. I, 2, 288. Gentl. V, 4, 7. *if my b. had not been made of faith,* Err. III, 2, 150. *kisses the base ground with obedient b.* LLL IV, 3, 225. *stirs good thoughts in any b. of strong authority,* John II, 113. IV, 2, 73. *what his b. forges, that his tongue must vent,* Cor. III, 1, 258. *O my b., thy hope ends here,* Mcb. IV, 3, 113. 197.

4) musical voice: *the fool has an excellent b.* Tw. II, 3, 20.

Breast, vb., to stem: *and —ed the surge,* Tp. II, 1, 116. *the huge bottoms, —ing the lofty surge,* H5 III Chor. 13.

Breast-deep, as high as the breast: *set him b. in earth,* Tit. V, 3, 179.

Breastplate, armour for the breast: *what stronger b. than a heart untainted!* H6B III, 2, 232.

Breath, 1) the air inhaled and ejected: Ven. 189. 444. 474. 929. Lucr. 400. 1666. Sonn. 130, 8. Pilgr. 37. Tp. I, 2, 326. Gentl. II, 3, 32. III, 1, 327. Err. III, 2, 135. *as* Epil. 20. LLL V, 2, 267. Cor. I, 1, 61 etc. The following passages may serve to explain some of the following significations: *life's but b.* Per. I, 1, 46. *a b. thou* (life) *art,* Meas. III, 1, 8. cf. Merch. III, 2, 298. All's IV, 3, 62. *then others for the b. of words respect,* Sonn. 85, 13. *my vow was b.* Pilgr. 37. *scarce think their words are natural b.* Tp. V, 157. *gentle b. of yours my sails must fill,* Tp. Epil. 11. *as there comes light from heaven and words from b.* Meas. V, 225. *the sweet b. of flattery conquers strife,* Err. III, 2, 28. *with bated b. and whispering humbleness,* Merch. I, 3, 125. *so am I driven by b. of her renown,* H6A V, 5, 7. *words of so sweet b. composed,* Hml. III, 1, 98.

2) a single respiration: *it is a life in death, that laughs and weeps, and all but with a b.* Ven. 414. *he would kiss you twenty with a b.* H8 I, 4, 30.

Hence = a very short time: *one minute, nay, one quiet b. of rest,* John III, 4, 134. *allowing him a b., a little scene, to monarchize,* R2 III, 2, 164. *a night is but small b. and little pause to answer matters of this consequence,* H5 II, 4, 145. *give me some b., some little pause,* R3 IV, 2, 24.

3) the state or power of breathing freely, opposed to a state of exhaustion: *how hast thou lost thy b.* Err. IV, 2, 30. *that no man might draw short b. to-day but I and Harry Monmouth,* H4A V, 2, 49. *pause, and take thy b.* H6A IV, 6, 4. *stops he now for b.?* R3 IV, 2, 45. *take thy b.* Troil. IV, 5, 192. *give me b.* Tim. II, 2, 33. *drink to Hamlet's better b.* Hml. V, 2, 282.

almost *dead for b.* Mcb. I, 5, 37.* *keep yourselves in b.* Troil. V, 7, 3. *I am scarce in b.* Lr. II, 2, 57. *out of b.* Err. IV, 1, 57. Mids. II, 2, 88. Tw. III, 4, 152. Ant. III, 10, 25.

4) a gentle exercise, causing a quicker respiration: *he hopes it is no other but for your health and your digestion sake an after-dinner's b.* Troil. II, 3, 121. *either* (fight) *to the uttermost, or else a b.* IV, 5, 92.

5) life: *to make more vent for passage of her b.* Lucr. 1040. *made me stop my b.* 1180. *bids him possess his b.* 1777. *you still shall live where b. most breathes,* Sonn. 81, 14. *the b. thou givest and takest,* Phoen. 19. *they'll suck our b.* Err. II, 2, 194. *the endeavour of this present b.* LLL I, 1, 5. *fly away, b.* Tw. II, 4, 54. *when your first queen's again in b.* Wint. V, 1, 83. *in the vile prison of afflicted b.* John III, 4, 19. *fearing dying pays death servile b.* R2 III, 2, 185. *ere thou yield thy b.* H6A IV, 7, 24. *pledges the b. of him in a divided draught,* Tim. I, 2, 49. *pay his b. to time,* Mcb. IV, 1, 99 etc. *My b. and blood!* Lr. II, 4, 104. cf. John IV, 2, 246.

6) words, language: *permit a blasting and a scandalous b. to fall on him,* Meas. V, 122. *that with thy b. hast killed my child,* Ado V, 1, 272. *charge their b. against us,* LLL V, 2, 88. *in the converse of b.* 745. *lay b. so bitter on your bitter foe,* Mids. III, 2, 44. 168. *commends and courteous b.* Merch. II, 9, 90. John II, 148. III, 1, 148. R2 I, 3, 215. III, 3, 33. IV, 128. Troil. I, 3, 244. Rom. III, 1, 161. Lr. I, 1, 61. Oth. IV, 2, 5 etc. *beg their stinking —s* (= voices) Cor. II, 1, 252. Used of singing: *uttering such dulcet and harmonious b.* Mids. II, 1, 151. *so sweet a b. to sing,* Tw. II, 3, 21. — Of the sound of trumpets: *make all our trumpets speak, give them all b.* Mcb. V, 6, 4.

7) a thing without substance, a trifle: *a dream, a b., a froth of fleeting joy,* Lucr. 212. *a dream of what thou wert, a b., a bubble,* R3 IV, 4, 88. *rather than she will bate one b. of her accustomed crossness,* Ado II, 3, 184. cf. *as b. thou art,* Meas. III, 1, 8.

8) the free air in motion: *their* (the damps') *exhaled unwholesome —s make sick the life of purity,* Lucr. 779. *when summer's b. their masked buds discloses,* Sonn. 54, 8. *wished himself the heaven's b.* Pilgr. 234. John IV, 1, 110. V, 4, 33. Mcb. I, 6, 5. Per. I, 1, 99 etc.

Breathe, 1) to respire, to draw in and throw out the air: *panting he lies and —th in her face,* Ven. 62. *so long as men can b. and eyes can see,* Sonn. 18, 13. *while Stephano —s at's nostrils,* Tp. II, 2, 65. *no sighs but of my —ing,* Merch. III, 1, 100. *to b. upon my love,* Gentl. V, 4, 131.

Transitively: *his breath —th life in her,* Ven. 474. *b. life into a stone,* All's II, 1, 76. *I b. free breath,* LLL V, 2, 732. *b. infection,* H6A III, 2, 287. *b. foul contagious darkness,* IV, 1, 7. *here could I b. my soul into the air,* H6B III, 2, 391. *b. sighs,* Tw. II, 2, 40. H6B III, 2, 345. *that I may b. my last in wholesome counsel,* R2 II, 1, 1 (double sense). *—d his latest gasp,* H6C II, 1, 108. *Montague hath —d his last,* V, 2, 40. breathless *b. forth power,* Ant. II, 2, 237. The object denoting the result: *with our sighs we'll b. the welkin dim,* Tit. III, 1, 212.

2) to make a single respiration: *before you can b. twice,* Tp. IV, 45. *I have not —d almost since I did see it,* Err. V, 181. *whilst we b., take time to do him dead,* H6C I, 4, 108.

3) to take breath, to rest from action:

three times they —*d*, H4A I, 3, 110. *when you b. in your watering*, II, 4, 17. *b. a while, and then to it again*, 275. *give me leave to b. awhile*, V, 3, 46. *we b. too long*, V, 4, 15 (= we tarry too long; cf. *breathing*). *stay and b. awhile*, 47. *give the house of Lancaster leave to b.* H6CI, 2, 13. *I lay me down a little while to b.* II, 3, 2. *now b. we*, 6, 31. *b. you, my friends*, Cor. I, 6, 1. Transitively, = to let take breath: *to b. his bloodied horse*, H4B I, 1, 38.

4) to take exercise: *sick for* —*ing and exploit*, All's I, 2, 17. *'tis the* —*ing time of day with me*, Hml. V, 2, 181 (the time of taking a walk). *here is a lady that wants* —*ing too* (i. e. dancing) Per. II, 3, 101. Reflectively: *thou wast created for men to b. themselves upon thee*, All's II, 3, 271. — The participle *breathed* (= the French *mis en haleine*) = in full career, in the full display of strength: *I am not yet well breathed*, As I, 2, 230. *as swift as breathed stags*, Shr. Ind. 2, 50 (cf. the adj. *breathed*).

5) to blow, to pass as air: *when winds b. sweet*, Compl. 103. *the air* —*s upon us here most sweetly*, Tp. I, 1, 46. IV, 173. Tw. I, 1, 6. Rom. IV, 3, 34. Hml. IV, 7, 67. Cymb. I, 3, 36. *how ugly night comes* — *ing at his heels*, Troil. V, 8, 6. *a warmth* —*s out of her*, Per. III, 2, 94. Transitively: *hell itself* —*s out contagion*, Hml. III, 2, 407 (Qq *breaks*).

6) to live: *how can my Muse want subject to invent, while thou dost b.* Sonn. 38, 2. *where breath most* —*s*, 81, 14 (quibble). *when he* —*d, he was a man*, LLL V, 2, 668. *here let us b.* Shr. I, 1, 8. John II, 419. III, 2, 4. V, 4, 36. H6A V, 4, 127. IV, 2, 31. H6B I, 2, 21. R3 I, 1, 21. 161. I, 2, 140. III, 7, 25. Ant. III, 12, 14 etc. *do I not b. a man*, H6C III, 1, 82. cf. *the plainest creature that* —*d upon this earth a Christian*, R3 III, 5, 26. Double sense: *and mercy then will b. within your lips like man new made*, Meas. II, 2, 78 (to live and to speak).

7) to speak, to utter; a) trans.: *b. it in mine ear*, Gentl. III, 1, 239. —*d a secret vow*, Merch. III, 4, 27. *O hear me b. my life*, Wint. IV, 4, 371. *let the church b. her curse on* ..., John III, 1, 256. *we* —*d our counsel*, IV, 2, 36. —*ing to his breathless excellence the incense of a vow*, IV, 3, 66. *by all the blood that ever fury* —*d*, V, 2, 127. V, 7, 65. R2 I, 1, 173. I, 3, 153. 173. 257. II, 1, 8. III, 4, 82. R3 I, 3, 286. Rom. I, 1, 117. Tim. III, 5, 59. Hml. II, 1, 31. Lr. V, 3, 143. Oth. IV, 1, 281. *To b. forth: thus* —*s she forth her spite*, Lucr. 762. —*ed forth the sound that said 'I hate,'* Sonn. 145, 2. *To b. out: what he* —*s out his breath drinks up again*, Lucr. 1666. *my soul the faithfullest offerings hath* —*d out*, Tw. V, 117. *b. out invectives*, H6C I, 4, 43. IV, 1, 112.

b) intrans.: *speak, b., discuss*, Wiv. IV, 5, 2. *this* —*ing courtesy*, Merch. V, 141 (= courteous words). *to give* —*ing to my purpose*, Ant. I, 3, 14. *the youth you b. of*, Hml. II, 1, 44. cf. Tw. I, 1, 6 and see *Sound*.

Breathed, adj., endowed with breath: *a man so b. that certain he would fight from morn till night*, LLL V, 2, 659. *would you not deem it b.?* Wint. V, 3, 64. *b. as it were to an untirable and continuate goodness*, Tim. I, 1, 10. *that need to be revived and b. in me*, H4B IV, 1, 114. *I will be treble-sinewed, hearted, b.* Ant. III, 13, 178 (cf. *breathe* 4.).

Breather, 1) one who lives: *when all the* —*s of this world are dead*, Sonn. 81, 12. *I will chide no*

b. in the world, As III, 2, 297. *she shows a body rather than a life, a statue than a b.* Ant. III, 3, 24.

2) one who utters sth.: *no particular scandal once can touch, but it confounds the b.* Meas. IV, 4, 31.

Breathing, subst. (cf. *to breathe*) stop, delay: *till after many accents and delays, untimely* —*s, sick and short assays*, Lucr. 1720. *you shake the head at so long a b.* Ado II, 1, 377.

Breathing-while, time sufficient for drawing breath, a very short time: *bud and be blasted in a b.* Ven. 1142. *cannot be quiet scarce a b.* R3 I, 3, 60.

Breathless, 1) being out of breath: Ven. 541. Mids. II, 1, 37. H4A I, 3, 32. Tim. V, 4, 10. Caes. I, 3, 2. Lr. II, 4, 31. Ant. II, 2, 237.

2) lifeless: *here b. lies the king*, H4A V, 3, 16. V, 4, 137. John IV, 3, 66. R2 V, 6, 31. H6B III, 2, 132.

Brecknock, place in Wales: R3 IV, 2, 126.

Breech, the garment worn by men over the lower part of the body; once not inflected: *that you might ne'er have stolen the b. from Lancaster*, H6C V, 5, 24 (i. e. usurped the authority of your husband). *Breeches:* Gentl. II, 7, 49. Shr. III, 2, 44. John III, 1, 201. H8 I, 3, 31. Lr. I, 4, 190. Oth. II, 3, 93. *though in his place most master wear no* —*es*, H6B I, 3, 149 (have not the authority due to the husband).

Breech, vb., 1) to cover as with breeches, to sheathe: *their daggers unmannerly* —*ed with gore*, Mcb. II, 3, 122.

2) to flog: *if you forget your quies, your quaes, and your quods, you must be preeches*, Wiv. IV, 1, 81 (Evans means to say *breeched*). *I am no* —*ing scholar in the schools*, Shr. III, 1, 18 (i. e. no schoolboy liable to a flogging).

Breed, vb. (impf. and partic. *bred*), I) trans., 1) to beget; properly and figuratively (= to produce, to cause): *which bred more beauty in his angry eyes*, Ven. 70. *thing like a man, but of no woman bred*, 214. 167. 444. 742. 753. Lucr. 411. 490. 499. 690. 872. 1188. 1837. *to b. another thee*, Sonn. 6, 7. 108. 13. 111, 4. Gentl. V, 4, 1. Ado III, 1, 11. LLL I, 2, 106. Merch. III, 2, 63. 96. All's I, 1, 154. I, 3, 151. Tw. III, 4, 207. Wint. V, 1, 12 *(the sweetest companion that e'er man bred his hopes out of)*. John I, 124 *(this calf bred from his cow)*. H4A I, 1, 11. H4B IV, 2, 74 *(to b. this present peace)*. H6A I, 2, 30 (O. Edd. *breed*, M. Edd. *bred)*. III, 3, 11. IV, 1, 193. V, 5, 4. H6B I, 3, 210. H6C II, 2, 121 *(the wound that bred this meeting)*. 164. III, 3, 68. R3 I, 4, 110. IV, 4, 424. H8 I, 1, 182. Tit. II, 3, 146 *(every mother* —*s not sons alike)*. V, 3, 62. Rom. I, 1, 96. Caes. V, 3, 101. Mcb. III, 4, 30. Oth. III, 4, 73 *(the worms that did b. the silk)*. Ant. II, 7, 29. Cymb. IV, 2, 35. — Reflectively: *that policy may b. itself so out of circumstance*, Oth. III, 3, 16 (may find origin and food in accidents).

Well bred = of good extraction: *a gentleman well bred and of good name*, H4B I, 1, 26. *true bred* = genuine: V, 3, 71. *my hounds are bred out of the Spartan kind*, Mids. IV, 1, 124. *she is not bred so dull but she can learn*, Merch. III, 2, 164 (so stupid by nature). *the dainties that are bred in a book*, LLL IV, 2, 25 (Nathaniel's speech). *Bred out* = degenerated: *our mettle is bred out*, H5 III, 5, 29. *the strain of man's bred out into baboon and monkey*, Tim. I, 1, 259.

2) to bring up: *a Bohemian born, but here*

nursed up and bred, Meas. IV, 2, 135. Merch. II, 1, 3. As I, 1, 4. 11. 114. II, 7, 96. IV, 1, 179. Tw. I, 2, 22. Lr. I, 1, 98. Cymb. I, 1, 42. 145. Often = to k e e p, to f e e d: *his horses are bred better*, As I, 1, 11. *a servant that he bred*, Lr. IV, 2, 73. *one bred of alms and fostered with cold dishes*, Cymb. II, 3, 119. *must I be unfolded with one that I have bred?* Ant. V, 2, 171. *which may both b. thee and still rest thine*, Wint. III, 3, 48 (furnish thee with the means of education). *you are so strongly in my purpose bred that all the world besides methinks are dead*, Sonn. 112, 13 (so kept and harboured in my thoughts).

II) intr., 1) to b e g e t children, to p a i r, to be fruitful: *by law of nature thou art bound to b.* Ven. 171. *a —ing jennet*, 260. *my ewes b. not*, Pilgr. 246. *the spring is near when green geese are a breeding*, LLL I, 1, 97. *would not a pair of these have bred?* Tw. III, 1, 55. *desire to b. by me*, Wint. IV, 4, 103. *O blessed —ing sun*, Tim. IV, 3, 1. *the earth feeds and —s by a composture*, IV, 3, 444. Used of money bringing interest: *I make it b. as fast*, Merch. I, 3, 97. Figuratively: *'tis such sense, that my sense —s with it*, Meas. II, 2, 142 (i. e. many thoughts are awakened by it in me). *there is no measure in the occasion that —s, therefore the sadness is without limit*, Ado I, 3, 4.

2) to be p r o d u c e d, to h a v e b i r t h: *here never shines the sun, here nothing —s unless the nightly owl or fatal raven*, Tit. II, 3, 96. *where they most b. and haunt, the air is delicate*, Mcb. I, 6, 9. Tropically, = to g r o w, to a r i s e, to develop itself: *advice is sporting while infection —s*, Lucr. 907. *heavens rain grace on that which —s between them*, Tp. III, 1, 76. *thereof the raging fire of fever bred*, Err. V, 75. *what may chance or b. upon our absence*, Wint. I, 2, 12. *what is —ing that changeth thus his manners*, 374. *what better matter —s for you*, John III, 4, 170. *so will this base and envious discord b.* H6A III, 1, 194. *see what —s about her heart*, Lr. III, 6, 81. *much is —ing*, Ant. I, 2, 199.

Breed, subst. 1) o f f s p r i n g: *nothing 'gainst time's scythe can make defence save b.* Sonn. 12, 14. Figuratively, = i n t e r e s t: *when did friendship take a b. of barren metal of his friend?* Merch. I, 3, 135.

2) r a c e: *twice fifteen thousand hearts of England's b.* John II, 275. *this happy b. of men*, R2 II, 1, 45. *royal kings, feared by their b.* 52. (horses) *of the best b. in the north*, H8 II, 2, 4. *Rome, thou hast lost the b. of noble bloods*, Caes. I, 2, 151. *O worthiness of nature! b. of greatness!* Cymb. IV, 2, 25. In H6A I, 2, 30 M. Edd. *bred*.

Hence = f a m i l y, e x t r a c t i o n: *blaspheme his b.* Mcb. IV, 3, 108.

3) s o r t, k i n d: *are these the b. of wits so wondered at?* LLL V, 2, 266. *this courtesy is not of the right b.* Hml. III, 2, 327. *he and many more of the same b. that I know the drossy age dotes on*, V, 2, 197 (Ff. *bevy*).

Breed-bate, (cf. *bate*) one w h o c a u s e s q u a rr e l s: *no tell-tale nor no b.* Wiv. I, 4, 12.

Breeder, 1) one w h o b e g e t s: *when the work of generation was between these woolly —s in the act*, Merch. I, 3, 84. *why wouldst thou be a b. of sinners?* Hml. III, 1, 123. Perhaps in the following passage also: *as loathsome as a toad amongst the fairest —s*

of our clime, Tit. IV, 2, 68; but this may be = people who are of the fairest breed or race.

2) f e m a l e: *the fair b. that is standing by* (sc. a mare), Ven. 282. *the unbacked b.* 320. *you love the b. better than the male*, H6C II, 1, 42.

3) a u t h o r: *time is the nurse and b. of all good*, Gentl. III, 1, 243. *the b. of my sorrow*, H6C III, 3, 43. *hath been b. of these dire events*, Tit. V, 3, 178.

Breeding, 1) the b r i n g i n g up, n u r t u r e: *she had her b. at my father's charge*, All's II, 3, 121 (cf. II, 2, 2). Lr. I, 1, 9. *let us swear that you are worth your b.* H5 III, 1, 28. *did these bones cost no more the b. but to play at loggats with 'em?* Hml. V, 1, 100. *who deserved so long a b. as his white beard came to*, Cymb. V, 3, 17 (= who deserved to live so long as to breed his long white beard).

2) e d u c a t i o n: *you are a gentleman of excellent b.* Wiv. II, 2, 234. Merch. II, 7, 33. As III, 2, 31. III, 3, 85. Tw. III, 4, 204. V, 331. Wint. IV, 4, 591 (741?). V, 2, 41. H4B II, 2, 39. H8 IV, 2, 134. Lr. III, 1, 40. V, 3, 143. Oth. I, 3, 240. Cymb. IV, 4, 26. Hence = g o o d m a n n e r s: *'tis my b. that gives me this bold show of courtesy*, Oth. II, 1, 99. And = k n o w l e d g e, i n s t r u c t i o n: *my b. was as your highness knows*, Cymb. V, 5, 339.

3) in the language of low people, as it seems, = d e s c e n t, e x t r a c t i o n: *of what having, b.* Wint. IV, 4, 741. *honest gentleman, I know not your b.* H4B V, 3, 111.

Breese, g a d f l y: *the herd hath more annoyance by the b. than by the tiger*, Troil. I, 3, 48. *the b. upon her, like a cow in June*, Ant. III, 10, 14.

Breff = b r i e f, in the language of Captain Jamy, H5 III, 2, 126.

Brentford, see *Brainford*.

Bretagne (O. Edd. *Britaine* and *Brittaine*), a province of France: John II, 156. 301 etc. R2 II, 1, 285. H5 II, 4, 4. H6B I, 1, 7. R3 V, 3, 324.

Breton (O. Edd. *Britaine* and *Brittaine*), native of Bretagne: R3 IV, 3, 40. IV, 4, 523. V, 3, 317. 333.

Brevity, s h o r t n e s s: *imitate the honourabe Romans in b.* H4B II, 2, 135. *the rude b. and discharge of one* (sigh), Troil. IV, 4, 43. *b. is the soul of wit*, Hml. II, 2, 90.

Brew, to m a k e b e e r; absolutely: *I wash, wring, b., bake etc.* Wiv. I, 4, 101. Transitively: *she —s good ale*, Gentl. III, 1, 304. *the proverb 'Blessing of your heart, you b. good ale,'* 306. Comically used of sack: *go b. me a pottle of sack*, Wiv. III, 5, 29. Figuratively, = to c o n t r i v e, to p r e p a r e, to t e m p e r: *that sunshine —ed a shower for him*, H6C II, 2, 156. *if I could temporize with my affection, or b. it to a weak and colder palate*, Troil. IV, 4, 7. *she drinks no other drink but tears, —ed with her sorrow, meshed upon her cheeks*, Tit. III, 2, 38. *our tears are not yet —ed*, Mcb. II, 3, 130. The gerund or participle in a neuter sense: *another storm —ing*, Tp. II, 2, 19. *there is some ill a —ing towards my rest*, Merch. II, 5, 17.

Brewage, d r i n k b r e w e d: *I'll no pullet-sperm in my b.* Wiv. III, 5, 33.

Brewer, one w h o m a k e s b e e r: *a —'s horse*, H4A III, 3, 10. *he that gibbets on the —'s bucket*, H4B III, 2, 282. *—s mar their malt with water*, Lr. III, 2, 82.

Brew-house, b r e w e r y: Wiv. III, 3, 10.

Briareus, the fabulous giant with a hundred hands: *a gouty B.* Troil. I, 2, 30.

Bribe, subst., a present made to corrupt a person: H6B III, 1, 104. 109. H6C III, 2, 155. Cor. I, 9, 38. Caes. IV, 3, 3. 24. In Wiv. V, 5, 27 O. Edd. *brib'd buck,* M. Edd. *bribe buck; cf. bribed.*

Bribe, vb., to win, to seduce: *therefore hath she —d the Destinies to cross the workmanship of Nature,* Ven. 733. *mark how I'll b. you,* Meas. II, 2, 145. John II, 171. Tim. I, 2, 244.

Bribed, adj. made a bribe: *divide me like a b. buck,* Wiv. V, 5, 27 (cf. *deformed, disdained, enforced, stained* etc. in an active sense).*

Briber, that which wins, prevails with a p.: *his service done were a sufficient b. for his life,* Tim. III, 5, 61.

Brick, burned clay for the use of builders: *a garden circummured with b.* Meas. IV, 1, 28. *the —s,* H6B IV, 2, 157. *a b. wall,* IV, 10, 7. Wint. IV, 4, 818.

Bricklayer, mason: H6B IV, 2, 43. 153.

Bridal, nuptial festival: *such observancy as fits the b.* Oth. III, 4, 150.

Adjectively: *b. bed,* John II, 491. Rom. III, 5, 202. V, 3, 12. *b. chamber,* Shr. IV, 1, 181. *b. day,* H6C II, 2, 155. *b. dinner,* Shr. III, 2, 221. *b. flowers,* Rom. IV, 5, 89.

Bride, subst. a woman newly married or about to be married: Meas. III, 1, 84. As V, 4, 184. Shr. II, 398. III, 2, 94. 153 etc. V, 2, 42. All's II, 5, 28. John III, 1, 209. H6A V, 3, 152. H6B I, 1, 252. H6C III, 3, 207. 225. IV, 1, 7 etc. Tit. I, 319 etc. Rom. I, 2, 11. III, 5, 116. IV, 5, 3. 33. Tim. I, 1, 123. Oth. II, 3, 180. Per. I, 1, 6. III Prol. 9.

Bride, vb.; *to b. it* = to play the bride: *shall sweet Bianca practise how to b. it?* Shr. III, 2, 253.

Bride-bed, marriage-bed: Mids. V, 410. Hml. V, 1, 268.

Bridegroom, a man newly married or about to be married: Merch. III, 2, 52. As V, 4, 184. Shr. III, 2, 5. 153. 248 etc. H4A I, 3, 34. Troil. IV, 4, 147. Rom. III, 5, 146. IV, 1, 107. IV, 4, 27. V, 3, 235. Mcb. I, 2, 54. Lr. IV, 6, 202. Ant. IV, 14, 100.

Bridge, 1) a building raised over water for the convenience of passage: Ado I, 1, 318. H4A IV, 3, 70. H5 III, 6, 2. 4. 14. 93. 100. H6A I, 4, 67. H6B IV, 4, 49 (*London b.*). IV, 5, 3. R3 III, 2, 72. Lr. III, 4, 58.

2) the bony part of the nose: *down with the nose, down with it flat; take the b. quite away of him that* ....*,* Tim. IV, 3, 157.

Bridgenorth, place in England: H4A III, 2, 175. 178.

Bridget, female name: Wiv. II, 2, 11. Meas. III, 2, 83. Err. III, 1, 31.

Bridle, subst., rein: Ven. 37. Err. II, 1, 13. Shr. IV, 1, 83.

Bridle, vb., 1) to govern, to restrain: Err. II, 1, 14. H6B I, 1, 200. IV, 7, 112 H6C IV, 4, 19.

2) to put a bridle on: *mine was not —d,* H5 III, 7, 54.

Brief, adj. (compar. *briefer,* Shr. III, 1, 67; superl. *briefest,* Ant. IV, 15, 91), short (but never used of space, not even in H8 III, 2, 140 and Mcb. V, 5, 23): *this b. abridgement of my will I make,* Lucr. 1198. *my woes are tedious, though my words are b.* 1309. *nor can I fortune to b. minutes tell,* Sonn. 14, 5. *b. hours,* 116, 11. *our dates are b.* 123, 5. *a little b.*

authority, Meas. II, 2, 118. *makes beauty b. in goodness,* III, 1, 186. *stay,* IV, 1, 45. *time,* Ado II, 1, 375. *b. as the lightning,* Mids. I, 1, 145. *a tedious b. scene,* V, 56. *with all b. and plain conveniency,* Merch. IV, 1, 82. *life,* As III, 2, 137. *to teach you gamut in a —er sort,* Shr. III, 1, 67. *a thousand businesses are b. in hand,* John IV, 3, 158 (must be speedily dispatched). *b. mortality,* H5 I, 2, 28. *a b. span* (sc. of time), H8 III, 2, 140. *night,* Troil. IV, 2, 11. *farewell,* Cor. IV, 1, 1. *sounds,* Rom. III, 2, 51. *out, out, b. candle* (i. e. life) Mcb. V, 5, 23. *when I came back — for this was b. — I found them close together,* Oth. II, 3, 237. *postures beyond b. nature,* Cymb. V, 5, 165. *the —est end,* Ant. IV, 15, 91. *this b. world,* Tim. IV, 3, 253.

To be b. = 1) to spend little time in sth.: *we must be b.* Wiv. III, 3, 8. John IV, 1, 35. R3 IV, 3, 57. Troil. IV, 5, 237. Lr. V, 3, 245. 2) to use few words: *I hope she will be b.* Mids. V, 323. *to be b.* Merch. II, 2, 140. Tw. III, 4, 174. R2 III, 3, 10. R3 I, 4, 90. Hml. II, 2, 92. *be b.:* Wiv. II, 2, 81. Meas. V, 26. Ado IV, 1, 1. R3 II, 2, 43. IV, 2, 20. *be curst and b.* Tw. III, 2, 46. Followed by *with: I will be b. with you,* Wiv. II, 2, 187. R2 III, 3, 12. 13. — Without *be: b., short, quick,* Wiv. IV, 5, 2. *b., I pray you,* Ado III, 5, 5.

That's the breff and the long, H5 III, 2, 126 (captain Jamy's speech). *that is the brief and the tedious of it,* All's II, 3, 34.

In b. = in few words: *desires to know in b. the grounds and motives,* Compl. 63. *open the matter in b.* Gentl. I, 1, 135. Err. I, 1, 29. H6C IV, 1, 89. *In b.,* absolutely, = in short: *in b., to set the needless process by,* Meas. V, 92. Ado V, 4, 105. As IV, 3, 143. Shr. I, 1, 40. 216. IV, 3, 156. John II, 72. 267. R3 V, 3, 87. Rom. I, 3, 73. Hml. II, 2, 68. Lr. IV, 3, 24. *In very b.* Merch. II, 2, 146.

Brief = in brief, in short: *b., I recovered him,* As IV, 3, 151. John V, 6, 18. Per. III Prol. 39.

Used adverbially: *it were a grief, so b. to part with you,* Rom. III, 3, 174.

Brief, subst., 1) a letter: *bear this sealed b. with winged haste to the lord marshal,* H4A IV, 4, 1.

2) any short writing, a note, a summary, abstract: *I will make a prief of it in my note-book,* Wiv. I, 1, 146 (Evans' speech). *there is a b. how many sports are ripe,* Mids. V, 42. *the hand of time shall draw this b. into as huge a volume,* John II, 103. *this is the b. of money, plate and jewels, I am possessed of,* Ant. V, 2, 138.

3) a short account: *she told me in a sweet verbal b., it did concern your highness,* All's V, 3, 137.

Unintelligible passage: *whose ceremony shall seem expedient on the now born* (or *borne?*) *b.,* All's II, 3, 186 (some intpp.: contract, licence of marriage). Perhaps simply the letter is meant, dispatched by the countess to Helen in II, 2, 66, which the king may have got notice of during his conversation with Bertram.

Briefly, 1) in few words, concisely: *show me b. how,* Ado II, 2, 11. As III, 2, 53. John II, 52. H4B IV, 1, 54. H5 V, 2, 73. Cor. III, 1, 285. Rom. I, 3, 96. Caes. III, 3, 11. 17. 26. 27. Lr. IV, 6, 233.

2) in short: *b., I do mean to make love to Ford's wife,* Wiv. I, 3, 47. II, 2, 208. Ado V, 1, 250. Mcb. II, 3, 139.

3) lately: *'tis not a mile; b. we heard their drums,* Cor. I, 6, 16.

4) quickly: *b. die their joys that place them on the truth of girls and boys,* Cymb. V, 5, 106. *and time that is so b. spent with your fine fancies quaintly eche,* Per. III Prol. 12. Sometimes = without hesitation, without further ceremony: *go put on thy defences. B., sir,* Ant. IV, 4, 10. *therefore b. yield her, for she must overboard,* Per. III, 1, 53.

Briefness, 1) shortness, tartness: *I hope the b. of your answer made the speediness of your return,* Cymb. II, 4, 30.

2) quickness: *b. and fortune, work!* Lr. II, 1, 20. *in feathered b. sails are filled,* Per. V, 2, 15.

Brier, a prickly plant, a wild species of the rose: *each envious b. his weary legs doth scratch,* Ven. 705. Tp. IV, 180. Err. II, 2, 180. Mids. II, 1, 3. III, 1, 110. III, 2, 29. 443. V, 401. As I, 3, 12. All's IV, 4, 32. Wint. IV, 4, 436. Cor. III, 3, 51. Tit. II, 3, 199. Tim. IV, 3, 422. *of colour like the red rose on triumphant b.* Mids. III, 1, 96. *from off this b. pluck a white rose with me,* H6A II, 4, 30 (= rose-bush).

Bright, shining, luminous, clear, splendid: *the b. sun,* Ven. 485. H8 V, 5, 51. *the b. track of his fiery car,* R3 V, 3, 20. R2 III, 3, 67. *moon,* LLL V, 2, 205. *star,* Ven. 815. 862. Lucr. 13. Mids. III, 2, 60. All's I, 1, 97. H6A I, 1, 56. I, 2, 144. *beams,* All's V, 3, 34. R3 I, 3, 268. *day,* Lucr. 1518. H6B II, 4, 1. Caes. II, 1, 14. Ant. V, 2, 193. *heaven,* H5 Prol. 2. *eye,* Ven. 140. Lucr. 1213. Sonn. 1, 5. 20, 5. 43, 4. Mids. II, 2, 92. R2 III, 3, 69. *weapons* or *swords,* Lucr. 1432. John IV, 3, 79. R2 III, 2, 111. Oth. I, 2, 59. *glass,* Pilgr. 87. *pearl,* 133. *gold,* Merch. V, 59. Tim. IV, 3, 383. *metal,* H4A I, 2, 236. *hair,* R3 I, 4, 53. Troil. IV, 2, 113. *made Lud's town with rejoicing fires b.* Cymb. III, 1, 32 etc. — *b. Phoebus,* Wint. IV, 4, 124. *Apollo,* LLL IV, 3, 343. *Diana,* Per. III, 3, 28. *angels are b.* Mcb. IV, 3, 22. cf. Rom. II, 2, 26 and H8 IV, 2, 88.

Hence = of splendid beauty: *thy b. beauty,* Lucr. 490. *I tell the day, to please him thou art b.* Sonn. 28, 9. 147, 13. Pilgr. 87. *she is too b. to be looked against,* Wiv. II, 2, 254. *so quick b. things come to confusion,* Mids. I, 1, 149. III, 2, 60. *since her time are colliers counted b.* LLL IV, 3, 267. *thou wilt show more b. and seem more virtuous when she is gone,* As I, 3, 83. *I will be b., and shine in pearl and gold,* Tit. II, 1, 19.

And = illustrious, glorious: *wisdom wishes to appear most b. when it doth tax itself,* Meas. II, 4, 78. *Troy had been b. with fame and not with fire,* Lucr. 1491. *b. fame,* H6A IV, 6, 45. *honour,* H4A I, 3, 202. Troil. III, 3, 151

Likewise = cheerful, gay: *be b. and jovial,* Mcb. III, 2, 28. *my fancy, more b. in zeal than the devotion which cold lips blow to their deities,* Troil. IV, 4, 28 (but here the simile may be a burning flame).

Used adverbially: *she reflects so b.* Lucr. 376. *shine b.* Sonn. 55, 3. 65, 14. LLL IV, 3, 30. Mids. V, 278. Merch. V, 1. Shr. IV, 5, 2. 4. 5. Wint. V, 1, 95. H5 V, 2, 172. *burn b.* H6B V, 1, 3. Tit. I, 324. Rom. I, 5, 46.

Bright-burning: *b. Troy,* Tit. III, 1, 69.

Brighten, to make bright or illustrious: *for yours* (sc. honour), *the God of heaven b. it!* H4B II, 3, 17.

Brightly, with a clear light: *shines b.* Merch. V, 94. Tit. IV, 2, 90.

Brightness, clear light, splendor: *swear that b. doth not grace the day,* Sonn. 150, 4. *in her*

(fortune's) *ray and b.* Troil. I, 3, 47. *the b. of her cheek would shame those stars,* Rom. II, 2, 19.

Bright-shining: *b. day,* H6C V, 3, 3.

Brightsome, only in the spurious True Tragedy 20, 49.

Brim, edge, rim: *on the brook's green b.* Pilgr. 80. *thy banks with pioned and twilled —s,* Tp. IV, 64. *bring me but to the very b. of it* (the cliff) Lr. IV, 1, 78. *his bonnet, under whose b.* Ven. 1088. *to make the coming hour o'erflow with joy and pleasure drown the b.* All's II, 4, 48. *will fill thy wishes to the b.* Ant. III, 13, 18. *a cup stored unto the b.* Per. II, 3, 50. (*b. fulness,* v. *brimfulness*).

Brimful, full to the top: *our legions are b.* Caes. IV, 3, 215. Followed by *of: b. of sorrow,* Tp. V, 14. *his eye b. of tears,* H4B III, 1, 67. *b. of fear,* Oth. II, 3, 214.

Brimfulness: *with ample and b. of his force,* H5 I, 2, 150 (O. and M. Edd. in two words).

Brimstone, sulphur: *to put fire in your heart, and b. in your liver,* Tw. III, 2, 22. *Fire and b.!* (used as an execration): Tw. II, 5, 56. Oth. IV, 1, 245.

Brinded, spotted: *thrice the b. cat hath mewed,* Mcb. IV, 1, 1.

Brine, 1) salt water: *he shall drink nought but b.* Tp. III, 2, 74. *whipped with wire, and stewed in b.* Ant. II, 5, 65.

2) the sea: *plunged in the foaming b.* Tp. I, 2, 211. *an the b. and cloudy billow kiss the moon,* Per. III, 1, 45.

3) used of tears: *showers of silver b.* Lucr. 796. *the b. that seasoned woe had pelleted in tears,* Compl. 17. *'tis the best b. a maiden can season her praise in,* All's I, 1, 55. *eye-offending b.* Tw. I, 1, 30. *what a deal of b.,* Rom. II, 3, 69.

Brine-pit, a salt spring: *the fresh springs, —s,* Tp. I, 2, 338. *and made a b. with our bitter tears,* Tit. III, 1, 129.

Bring (impf. and partic. *brought*). 1) to fetch, to lead from another place to where a p. is: *Fortune hath mine enemies brought to this shore,* Tp. I, 2, 180. *was hither brought with child,* 269. II, 1, 134. II, 2, 74. III, 3, 48. IV, 37. V, 188. 240 etc. etc. *being so hard to me that brought your mind* (= delivered your message) Gentl. I, 1, 147. *to b. word,* Err. IV, 3, 37. Merch. I, 2, 138 etc. (cf. *word*). And then *to b.* alone in the sense of to tell, to inform: *who —s back to him,* Hml. V, 2, 204. *b. me how he takes my death,* Ant. IV, 13, 10.

Under the same head the following passages must be registered: *you rub the sore, when you should b. the plaster,* Tp. II, 1, 139. *cursed hours which forced marriage would have brought upon her,* Wiv. V, 5, 243. *whereas he from John of Gaunt doth b. his pedigree* (= derive), H6A II, 5, 77. *be brought against me at my trial-day,* H6B III, 1, 114. cf. *this complaint we b.* All's V, 3, 163. *I'll b. mine action on the proudest he,* Shr. III, 2, 236 (cf. *action*). *she shall b. him that which he not dreams of* (sc. as a dower) Wint. IV, 4, 179.

2) to conduct, to lead, to accompany: *let me b. thee where crabs grow,* Tp. II, 2, 171. *canst thou b. me to the party?* III, 2, 67. *the prize I'll b. thee to,* IV, 205. *and thither will I b. thee,* Gentl. I, 1, 55. *till the last step have brought me to my love,* II, 7, 36. *give leave that we may b. you something on the way,* Meas. I, 1, 62. cf. *shall I b. thee on the way?* Wint. IV, 3, 122. *I'll b. you thither, my lord,* Ado III, 2, 3.

the rank of osiers —s you to the place, As IV, 3, 81. *let me b. thee to Staines*, H5 II, 3, 2. *b. me but out at gate*, Cor. IV, 1, 47. Caes. I, 3, 1. *b. him away*, Oth. V, 2, 337 (Ff. *without him*). *the —ing home of bell and burial*, (i. e. the solemn interment) Hml. V, 1, 256.

Figuratively: *b. truth to light*, Lucr. 940. *being from the feeling of her own grief brought by deep surmise of others' detriment*, 1578. *I'll b. thee to the present business*, Tp. I, 2, 136. *hath into bondage brought my too diligent ear*, III, 1, 42. *the sin hath brought you to this shame*, Meas. II, 3, 31. *he would never b. them to light*, III, 2, 188. *to b. thee to the gallows*, Merch. IV, 1, 400. *till I have brought him to his wits again*, Err. V, 96. *thou —est me out of tune*, As III, 2, 262. *you b. me out* (= put me out) 265. *and b. you from a wild Kate to a Kate conformable*, Shr. II, 279. *now we are undone and brought to nothing*, V, 1, 45. *to which title age cannot b. thee*, All's II, 3, 209. *b. his particulars to a total* (= sum up the items) Troil. I, 2, 124.

3) *to prevail on, to cause, to make*: *b. her to try with main-course*, Tp. I, 1, 38 (Story: '*b. her to. Try with maincourse;*' *to b.* to being a term of navigation, = to check the course of a ship). *he that —s any man to answer it that breaks his band*, Err. IV, 3, 31. *the mightiest space in fortune nature —s to join like likes*, All's I, 1, 237. *he was brought to this by a vain prophecy*, H8 I, 2, 146. *in which you brought the king to be your servant*, III, 2, 315. *you b. me to do, and then you flout me too*, Troil. IV, 2, 27. *we should b. ourselves to be monstrous members*, Cor. II, 3, 13. *I cannot b. my tongue to such a pace*, 56. *and to such wondrous doing brought his horse*, Hml. IV, 7, 87. *I will b. thee to hear*, Lr. I, 2, 184. *I could as well be brought to knee his throne*, II, 4, 216. *which brought them to be lamented*, Ant. V, 2, 366. *b. it to that*, II, 5, 33, = make it mean that.

To bring to pass = to do, to effect: *we do not know what's brought to pass under the profession of fortune-telling*, Wiv. IV, 2, 183. *a thing not in his power to b. to pass*, Merch. I, 3, 93 (cf. *pass*).

To b. asleep = to lull to sleep: *a nurse's song of lullaby to b. her babe asleep*, Tit. II, 3, 29. *brought a bed* or *to bed* = delivered· Tit. IV, 2, 62. 154.

4) *to give birth*: *a dearer birth than this his love had brought*, Sonn. 32, 11. *to b. false generations*, Wint. II, 1, 148. *brought thee to this world*, Cor. V, 3, 125 (cf. *b. forth*).

The use of the word in connexion with certain adverbs is easily explained by what precedes:

To b. about = to accomplish by a rotation: *until the twelve celestial signs have brought about the annual reckoning*, LLL V, 2, 808. *the yearly course that —s this day about*, John III, 1, 81. *ere the six years can change their moons and b. their times about*, R2 I, 3, 220. *how many hours b. about the day*, H6C II, 5, 27.

To b. down = to lower, to humble, to reduce: *—s down the rate of usance*, Merch. I, 3, 45. *to b. me down must answer for your raising*, All's II, 3, 119. *b. down rose-cheeked youth to the tub-fast*, Tim. IV, 3, 86. *brought them down again*, Per. IV, 2, 17.

To b. forth, 1) to give birth to: *she had not brought forth thee*, Ven. 203. *green plants b. not forth their dye*, Pilgr. 284. *b. forth more islands*, Tp. II, 1, 93. 162. III, 2, 113. Wint. II, 3, 65. R2 II, 2, 64. H5 V, 2, 48. H6C V, 6, 50. R3 II, 2, 67. Cor. V, 3, 126. Caes. II, 1,

14. Mcb. I, 7, 72. Ant. I, 2, 113. Per. V, 1, 105. And in general, = to produce: *b. forth eternal numbers*, Sonn. 38, 11. 72, 13. 103, 1. Tp. V, 170. H4B I, 1, 178. — 2) to bring to light: *to b. forth this discovery*, All's V, 3, 151. *have brought forth the secret'st man of blood*, Mcb. III, 4, 125. — 3) to speak, to utter: *if that the praised himself b. the praise forth*, Troil. I, 3, 242. — 4) to produce on the stage: *on this unworthy scaffold to b. forth so great an object*, H5 Prol. 10. *Antony shall be brought drunken forth*, Ant. V, 2, 219.

To b. forward = to make to stand forth: *Northumberland arrested him at York and brought him forward to his answer*, H8 IV, 2, 13.

To b. in, 1) to bear or carry from without to within a certain precinct: *—ing wood in*, Tp. II, 2, 16. *a foolish knight that you brought in here*, Tw. I, 3, 16. *to b. you in again* (sc. into your place of lieutenant) Oth. III, 1, 53. III, 3, 74. *Fortune —s in some boats that are not steered* (= into the port) Cymb. IV, 3, 46. Especially used of things wanted and required: *look you b. me in the names of some six*, Meas. II, 1, 286. *if I b. in your Rosalind*, As V, 4, 6. *brought in matter that should feed this fire*, John V, 2, 85. *shall b. this prize in very easily*, H4B III, 1, 101. *such a mighty sum as never did the clergy at one time b. in*, H5 I, 2, 135. *proclaimed reward to him that —s the traitor in*, R3 IV, 4, 518. — 2) to bring to a person's assistance: *to thy sensual fault I b. in sense*, Sonn. 35, 9. *your own wisdom —s in the champion Honour on my part*, All's IV, 2, 50. *had York and Somerset brought rescue in*, H6A IV, 7, 33. — 3) to produce, to lay before a p.: *every tongue —s in a several tale*, R3 V, 3, 194. *at many times I brought in my accounts*, Tim. II, 2, 142. *b. in the evidence*, Lr. III, 6, 37. — 4) to bring about, to introduce: *four happy days b. in another moon*, Mids. I, 1, 2. *the whirligig of time —s in his revenges*, Tw. V, 385. *I witness to the times that brought them in*, Wint. IV, 1, 12. *didst b. in wonder to wait on treason*, H5 II, 2, 109. *b. in cloudy night*, Rom. III, 2, 4.

To b. low = to b. down, to weaken, to reduce to misery: *horses journey-bated and brought low*, H4A IV, 3, 26. *we are not brought so low but we can kill a fly*, Tit. III, 2, 76. *brought low by his own heart*, Tim. IV, 2, 37 (cf. *low*).

To b. off = to clear, to procure to be acquitted: *I know a way ... will b. me off again*, H8 III, 2, 220.

To b. on = to induce: *when we would b. him on to some confession*, Hml. III, 1, 9. = to cause to come: *it is love's spring, and these* (tears) *the showers to b. it on*, Ant. III, 2, 44.

To b. out = to b. forth; a) to beget: *let it* (thy womb) *no more b. out ingrateful man*, Tim. IV, 3, 188. b) to produce: *if I make not this cheat b. out another*, Wint. IV, 3, 129. c) to bring to light: *the time will b. it out*, Lr. V, 3, 163. d) to show, to name: *b. him out that is but woman's son can trace me in the tedious ways of art*, H4A III, 1, 47.

To b. up = 1) to cause to advance near: *b. up the brown bills*, Lr. IV, 6, 91. 2) to move, to dispose: *b. him up to liking*, Wint. IV, 4, 544. 3) to feed, to entertain, to educate: *one that I brought up of a puppy*, Gentl. IV, 4, 3. *those ... I brought up to attend my sons*, Err. I, 1, 58. Ado I, 1, 241. Shr. I, 1, 14. I, 2, 87. H6B IV, 2, 113. Tit. V, 1, 84. Hml. II, 2, 11. Per. IV, 2, 14. *I have brought him up ever since he was three years old*, Shr. V, 1, 85. *heaven hath brought me up to be your daughter's dower*, All's IV, 4, 19 (perhaps = made me come here). cf. *bringing-up*.

To b. under = to overcome, to subdue: *not the least of all these maladies but in one minute's fight — s beauty under*, Ven. 746.

Finally, *to be with a p. to bring* = to give him a sound lesson, to bring him to reason, to overcome him; with a lascivious sense, when spoken to women. *To be with a p.*, without that apposition, is an ambiguous expression, as it may mean 'to join' in a friendly sense as well as to fight, to combat (cf. *With*). The addition of *to bring* gives it expressly the latter signification: *I ll be with you, niece, by and by. To bring, uncle? Ay, a token from Troilus*. Troil. I, 2, 305.

Bringer, he who brings, or that which brings: *b. of that joy*, Mids. V, 20. *the first b. of unwelcome news*, H4B I, 1, 100. *safed the b.* Ant. IV, 6, 26.

Bringing-forth, achievement: *let him be but testimonied in his own bringings-forth, and he shall appear to the envious a scholar, a statesman and a soldier*, Meas. III, 2, 153.

Bringing-up, education: *a good b.* Gentl. IV, 4, 74. Shr. I, 1, 99. *a plague on my b.*, H4A II, 4, 547.

Brinish, having the taste of salt; used of tears: *the b. pearl* (i. e. tears) Lucr. 1213. Compl. 284. *her b. tears*, H6C III, 1, 41. of the sea: *when some envious surge will in his b. bowels swallow him*, Tit. III, 1, 97.

Brink, edge, margin: *I have no strength to pluck thee to the b.*, Tit. II, 3, 241. *you surprise me to the very b. of tears*, Tim. V, 1, 159.

Brise, see *breese*.

Brisk, 1) nimble, sprightly: *these most b. and giddy-paced times*, Tw. II, 4, 6. *cheerly, boys, be b. awhile*, Rom. I, 5, 16.

2) smart, trim: *to see him shine so b. and smell so sweet*, H4A I, 3, 54.

3) full of fire, spirituous: *a cup of wine that's b. and fine*, H4B V, 3, 48.

Brisky, the same, in the scurrile poetry of Flute: *most b. juvenal*, Mids. III, 1, 97.

Bristle, subst., the stiff hair of swine: Ven. 625. Tw. I, 5, 3.

Bristle, vb., to erect as the swine does its hair: *boar with —d hair*, Mids. II, 2, 31. *doth dogged war b. his angry crest*, John IV, 3, 149. *b. up the crest of youth*, H4A I, 1, 98. *b. thy courage up*, H5 II, 3, 5 (Pistol's speech). *with his Amazonian chin he drove the —d lips before him*, Cor. II, 2, 96 (= bearded).

Bristly, thick set with bristles: *b. pikes* (sc. the bristles of the boar) Ven. 620. *sheaves borne on the bier with white and b. beard*, Sonn. 12, 8.

Bristol (O. Edd. *Bristow*, except R2 II, 2, 135), town in England: R2 II, 2, 135. II, 3, 164. III, 2, 142. H4A I, 3, 271. H6B III, 1, 328.

Britain, the country of the English: LLL IV, 1, 126. *—'s isle* H6B I, 3, 47. H8 I, 1, 21. Cymb. I, 4, 1. 179. I, 6, 113. II, 4, 19. 45. V, 1, 20 etc. *in the B. court*, Cymb. II, 4, 37 (cf. *on Lethe warf, Tiber banks, Rome gates, Afric sun*). Ancient orthography makes no distinction between *Britain, Bretagne* and *Briton*, q. v.

Britany, 1) Bretagne: R2 II, 1, 278 (O. Edd.

Britaine, as in 285). H6C II, 6, 97. IV, 6, 97. R3 IV, 4, 529 (O. Edd. *Brittaine*).

2) Britain: Cymb. I, 4, 77.

British, belonging to Britain: Lr. III, 4, 189. IV, 4, 21. IV, 6, 256. Cymb. III, 5, 65. V, 5, 480.

Briton (O. Edd. *Britain*), native of Britain: Cymb. I, 4, 28. I, 6, 67. III, 1, 33. III, 5, 20. IV, 2, 369 etc. Adjectively: *the B. reveller*, I, 6, 61. *a B. peasant*, V, 1, 24.

Brittle, fragile: *as glass is, b.* Pilgr. 87. 172. R2 IV, 287. 288. *b. life*, H4A V, 4, 78. *glass*, R3 IV, 2, 62.

Broach, vb., 1) to spit: *bringing rebellion —ed on his sword*, H5 V Chor. 32. *I'll b. the tadpole on my rapier's point*, Tit. IV, 2, 85.

2) to tap: *if I would b. the vessels of my love*, Tim. II, 2, 186. *he bravely —ed his boiling bloody breast*, Mids. V, 148.

3) to let out, to shed: *this blow should b. thy dearest blood*, H6A III, 4, 40. H6B IV, 10, 40. H6C II, 3, 16.

4) to set abroach (q. v.), to set loose, to begin: *I will continue that I —ed in jest*, Shr. I, 2, 84. *a portent of —ed mischief to the unborn times*, H4A V, 1, 21. *what hath —ed this tumult but thy pride?* H6C II, 2, 159. *that for her love such quarrels may be —ed*, Tit. II, 1, 67. *the business she hath —ed in the state*, Ant. I, 2, 178. 180.

Followed by *to*, = to give the first hint or impulse: *whether ever I did b. this business to your majesty*, H8 II, 4, 149.

Broad, 1) wide, extended from side to side: *b. breast*, Ven. 296. *buttock*, 298. AdoI, 1, 318. All's IV, 7, 57. H6A I, 3, 36. Troil. I, 3, 27. Rom. II, 4, 88. Ant. II, 7, 48.

2) vast, extensive: *b. main*, Sonn. 80, 8. *till by b. spreading it disperse to nought*, H6A I, 2, 135. *the world is b. and wide*, Rom. III, 3, 16. Tropically: *those honours deep and b. wherewith your majesty loads our house*, Mcb. I, 6, 17.

3) puffed with pride: *in full as proud a place as b. Achilles*, Troil. I, 3, 190.

4) plain, evident: *proves thee far and wide a b. goose*, Rom. II, 4, 91 (Ff. *abroad*).

5) free, unrestrained: *as b. and general as the casing air*, Mcb. III, 4, 23. *from b. words ... Macduff lives in disgrace*, III, 6, 21. *his pranks have been too b. to bear with*, Hml. III, 4, 2.

Used adverbially: *b. awake* = wide awake, Tit. II, 2, 17 (Ff. only *awake*). *with all his crimes b. blown* (= full-blown), Hml. III, 3, 81. *who can speak —er than he that has no house*, Tim. III, 4, 64 (= more freely).

Broad-fronted, having a large forehead: *b. Caesar*, Ant. I, 5, 29.

Broadside, discharge of all the guns on one side of a ship: *fear we —s?* H4B II, 4, 196.

Broad-spreading, spreading widely: *his b. leaves*, R2 III, 4, 50.

Brocas (O. Edd. *Broccas*), name in R2 V, 6, 14.

Brock, badger; used as a term of reproach: *marry, hang thee, b.* Tw. II, 5, 114.

Brogue, wooden shoe: Cymb. IV, 2, 214.

Broil, subst., 1) tumult, noisy quarrel, contention: *leave this peevish b.* H6A III, 1, 92. *in this civil b.* H6B IV, 8, 46. *stop, or all will fall in b.*

B																																											149

Cor. III, 1, 33. *when wasteful war shall statues overturn, and —s root out the work of masonry*, Sonn. 55, 6. *civil —s*, H6A I, 1, 53. *take delight in —s*, III, 1, 111. IV, 1, 185. H6C V, 5, 1. R3 II, 4, 60. Rom. I, 1, 96 (Qq. *brawls*). Lr. V, 1, 30.

2) war, combat, battle: *new —s to be commenced in strands afar remote*, H4A I, 1, 3. *the tidings of this b. brake off our business*, I, 1, 47. *moved with remorse of these outrageous —s*, H6A V, 4, 97. *the vaunt and firstlings of those —s*, Troil. Prol. 27. *their soldier, and being bred in —s*, Cor. III, 2, 81. *say to the king the knowledge of the b. as thou didst leave it*, Mcb. I, 2, 6. *feats of b. and battle*, Oth. I, 3, 87.

Broil, vb., 1) trans. to cook over coals: Shr. IV, 3, 20. Cor. IV, 5, 201 (Ff. *boiled*).

2) intr. to suffer extreme heat, to sweat: *where have you been —ing?* H8 IV, 1, 56. In the following passage: *that will physic the great Myrmidon, who —s in loud applause*, Troil. I, 3, 379, it may mean 'who basks in the sunshine of applause, even to broiling,' or: 'who is basted with applause as meat with fat.'

Broke, to do the business of a procurer: *and —s with all that can in such a suit corrupt ...*, All's III, 5, 74; or that of a pawnbroker: *redeem from —ing pawn the blemished crown*, R2 II, 1, 293.

Brokenly, in a broken and incorrect language: *to hear you confess it b.* H5 V, 2, 106.

Broker, agent, negotiator: *they say 'a crafty knave does need no b.*,' H6B I, 2, 100. Especially a procurer, a go-between: *vows were ever —s to defiling*, Compl. 173. *a goodly b.* Gentl. I, 2, 41. (commodity) *that sly devil, that b.* John II, 568. *this bawd, this b.* 582. *to play the b.* H6C IV, 1, 63. hence, *b., lackey*, Troil. V, 10, 33 (some M. Edd. *broker-lackey*). *his vows are —s*, Hml. I, 3, 127.

Broker-between, procurer: Troil. III, 2, 211.

Brooch, subst., a jewel worn in the hat or elsewhere: LLL V, 2, 620. Wint. IV, 4, 610. H4B II, 4, 53. *just like the b. and the tooth-pick, which wear not now*, All's I, 1, 171.

Figuratively, = ornament: *love to Richard is a strange b. in this all-hating world*, R2 V, 5, 66. *he is the b. indeed and gem of all the nation*, Hml. IV, 7, 94. In Troil. II, 1, 126 (*I will hold my peace when Achilles' b. bids me, shall I?*) most M. Edd. write *brach;* but the sense of the old text may be: shall I hold my peace when any of Achilles' appurtenances bids me, f. i. his brooch, which you resemble indeed in serving to set him off?

Brooch, vb., to adorn as with a brooch: *not the imperious show of Caesar ever shall be —ed with me*, Ant. IV, 15, 25.

Brood, subst., the hatch, the young birds hatched at once: *doves will peck in safeguard of their b.* H6C II, 2, 18. Cor. V, 3, 162. Used of men: *bring forth brave b.* Tp. III, 2, 113. *a b. of traitors*, H6B V, 1, 141. *Typhon's b.* Tit. IV, 2, 94. Tropically: *all that b.* (of vices) *to kill*, Lucr. 627. *make the earth devour her own b.* Sonn. 19, 2. *the hatch and b. of time*, H4B III, 1, 86. — *To sit on b.* = to ponder: *there's something in his soul, o'er which his melancholy sits on b.* Hml. III, 1, 173.

Brood, vb., to sit as on eggs: *and birds sit — ing in the snow*, LLL V, 2, 933.

Brooded, adj., furnished with brood, having a brood to guard: *in despite of b. watchful day, I*

would into thy bosom pour my thoughts, John III, 3, 52, i. e. the day that is on its guard like a hen attending her chickens.

Brook, assumed name in Wiv. (Ff. *Broom*): II, 1, 224. II, 2, 150. 157. III, 5, 58. V, 5, 114 etc. etc. Quibble in II, 2, 157.

Brook, subst., small natural stream of water: Ven. 162. 1099. Pilgr. 43. 75. Tp. IV, 128. V, 33. Wiv. II, 2, 157. Mids. II, 1, 84. Merch. II, 7, 47. V, 96. As II, 1, 16. 32. 42. III, 2, 305. Shr. Ind. 2, 52. H6B III, 1, 53. H6C IV, 8, 54. Tim. IV, 3, 225. Hml. IV, 7, 167. *Flying at the b.*, H6B II, 1, 1 = hawking at water-fowl.

Brook, vb., to bear, to endure: *a woeful hostess —s not merry guests*, Lucr. 1125. *to b. this patiently*, Gentl. V, 3, 4. *my business cannot b. this dalliance*, Err. IV, 1, 59. LLL IV, 2, 34. Shr. I, 1, 117. John III, 1, 36. H4A IV, 1, 62. V, 4, 66. 74. 78. H5 V Chor. 44. H6B I, 1, 170. IV, 9, 45. V, 1, 92. H6C I, 1, 5. III, 2, 18. V, 6, 27. R3 III, 7, 162. IV, 4, 158. Tit. II, 1, 77. Tim. III, 5, 117. *to b. well* = to put up with: *b. such disgrace well*, As I, 1, 140. *ill: how ill we b. his treason*, H6A IV, 1, 74. *in that you b. it ill, it makes him worse*, R3 I, 3, 3. Coming near the sense of to like: *this shadowy desert I better b. than flourishing peopled towns*, Gentl. V, 4, 3. *how —s your grace the air?* R2 III, 2, 2. *whom Henry ne'er could b.* H6A I, 3, 24. *how hath your lordship —ed imprisonment?* R3 I, 1, 125.

Followed by a clause: *if they can b. I bow a knee to man*, H6B V, 1, 110. By an infinitive: *b. to be commanded*, Cor. I, 1, 266. *would have —ed the eternal devil to keep his state in Rome*, Caes. I, 2, 159.

Broom, besom: *I am sent with b. before*, Mids. V, 396.

Broom, name assumed by Ford, according to Ff.; Qq. *Brook*, q. v.

Broom-grove: *thy —s, whose shadow the dismissed bachelor loves, being lass-lorn*, Tp. IV, 66; certainly not groves or woods of genista, which would be non-sense, but perhaps woods overgrown with genista, pathless woods.

Broomstaff, handle of a broom: *at length they came to the b. to me*, H8 V, 4, 57 (this seems to mean: they came within a broomstaff's length of me).

Broth (cf. *barley-broth, hell-broth, snow-broth*) liquor in which flesh is boiled: *my wind cooling my b.* Merch. I, 1, 22. *sauced our —s*, Cymb. IV, 2, 50.

Brothel, house appropriated to the purposes of prostitution: Tim. IV, 1, 13. Hml. II, 1, 61. Lr. I, 4, 266. III, 4, 99. Per. V Prol. 1.

Brothel-house, the same: Ado I, 1, 256.

Brother (plural indiscriminately *brothers* and *brethren*) 1) one born of the same father and mother: Pilgr. 104. Tp. I, 1, 66. I, 2, 66. 67. 75. 92. 118. 122. 127 etc. etc. Plur. *brothers:* Gentl. IV, 4, 4. Wiv. IV, 2, 52. H4B IV, 4, 43. V, 2, 46. H5 IV, 1, 24. IV, 3, 60. H6C III, 2, 109. 116. IV, 1, 58. V, 4, 35. R3 I, 2, 96. Tit. I, 287. I, 3, 100. Tim. IV, 3, 3. Ant. II, 2, 150. Cymb. IV, 2, 3. Plur. *brethren:* Ado II, 1, 67. H4B IV, 4, 26. H6C I, 3, 25. Troil. II, 2, 190. Tit. I, 89. 104. 146. 160. 348. 357. V, 1, 104.

B. = half-brother: R3 V, 3, 95.

2) = brother in law: Err. II, 2, 154. III, 2, 25. As V, 2, 20. Shr. V, 2, 6. H4A I, 3, 156. R3 I, 3, 62.

IV, 4, 316. Caes. II, 1, 70. IV, 2, 37. 39. Lr. IV, 5, 1. *are the —s parted?* Ant. III, 2, 1.

3) term of endearment for friends: Wint. I, 2, 4. H5 IV Chor. 34. IV, 1, 87. H8 V, 4, 66 *(—s). sworn b.* Ado I, 1, 73. Wint. IV, 4, 607. H4A II, 4, 7. H4B III, 2, 345 (cf. *swear). they shook hands and swore —s,* As V, 4, 107. *my sworn b., the people,* Cor. II, 3, 102. cf. *my b. general, the commonwealth,* H4B IV, 1, 94.

4) fellow-creature: *thisguiltwould seem death-worthy in thy b.* Lucr. 635. *we cannot weigh our b. with ourself,* Meas. II, 2, 126. *would call their —s fools,* Merch. I, 1, 99. *amongst my brethren mortal,* H8 III, 2, 148.

5) associate, colleague: *my b. Angelo,* Meas. III, 2, 219. *my b. justice,* 267. *thy b. cardinals,* H8 III, 2, 257. *you a b. of us* (i. e. a peer), V, 1, 107. *good b.* Tim. III, 4, 7. *I hold you but a subject of this war, not as a b.* Lr. V, 3, 62. cf. 67. Plural *brothers: my co-mates and —s in exile,* As II, 1, 1. *him* (the mayor) *and all his —s,* H6C IV, 7, 34. *here come our —s,* Tim. V, 2, 13. *any of my —s of the state,* Oth. I, 2, 96. *Brethren: my friends and brethren in these great affairs,* H4B IV, 1, 6. *t.te mayor and all his brethren,* H5 V Chor. 25. R3 III, 7, 44. H8 V, 5, 71. *brethren and sisters of the hold-door trade,* Troil. V, 10, 52. *some certain of your brethren,* Cor. II, 3, 59. Especially kings calling each other *brothers:* Wint. IV, 2, 26. V, 1, 141. V, 3, 5. John II, 547. III, 1, 161. H5 I, 2, 122. II, 4, 75. V, 2, 2.

6) a member of a religious order: *a b. of your order,* Meas. I, 3, 44. *I am a b. of gracious order,* III, 2, 231. *a barefoot b.* Rom. V, 2, 5. Synonymous to friar: Meas. III, 2, 14.

Followed by *of: b. of Gloster,* H6C IV, 5, 16. R3 I, 3, 62. *of England,* John II, 547. III, 1, 161 (cf. *of*).

Brethren trisyllabic: Tit. I, 89. 348. 357.

Brotherhood, 1) quality and love of a brother: *finds b. in thee no sharper spur?* R2 I, 2, 9. H5 II, 1, 114. H6C IV, 1, 55. R3 I, 1, 111. II, 1, 108.

2) association, corporation: *degrees in schools and —s in cities,* Troil. I, 3, 104. Religious order: *by my b.!* Rom. V, 2, 17.

Brother-in-law, brother of a man's wife: R2 V, 3, 137. H4A I, 3, 80. Father of a man's daughter-in-law: Wint. IV, 4, 720.

Brother-like, adj. becoming a brother: *this is b.* H6C V, 1, 105.

Brother-love, brotherly affection: H8 V, 3, 173.

Brotherly, adv., as becomes a brother: *I speak but b. of him,* As I, 1, 162. *to use your brothers b.* H6C IV, 3, 38. *I love thee b.* Cymb. IV, 2, 158.

Brow, 1) the arch of hair over the eye: *the right arched beauty of the b.* Wiv. III, 3, 60. *to sit and draw his arched —s,* All's I, 1, 105. *his louring —s o'erwhelming his fair sight,* Ven. 183. 490. Ado III, 5, 14. LLL III, 198. As III, 5, 46. Wint. II, 1, 8. *even here, between the chaste unsmirched b. of my true mother,* Hml. IV, 5, 119. *To bend one's brow or brows* (= to frown): Lucr. 709. Pilgr. 311. John IV, 2, 90. H6A V, 3, 34. H6C V, 2, 22. *bliss in our brows' bent,* Ant. I, 3, 36 (= in our look: cf. *bent). a b. unbent,* Lucr. 1509. *To knit one's brow or brows:* H6B I, 2, 3. II.!, 1, 15. H6C II, 2, 20. III, 2, 82. *unknit*

that threatening b. Shr. V, 2, 136. *smoothed —s,* H6A III, 1, 124. The word passes by almost imperceptible degrees into the following signification.

2) the forehead; the singular and plural forms used indiscriminately: *she kissed his b., his cheek, his chin,* Ven. 59. 339. Sonn. 33, 10. Gentl. I, 2, 62. Err. II, 2, 138. LLL IV, 3, 185. V, 2, 392 *(hold his —s, he'll swoon).* As III, 3, 62. Wint. I, 2, 149. Tw. V, 249. R3 IV, 1, 60. Rom. I, 3, 38 etc. *put my eye-balls in thy* (death's) *vaulty —s,* John III, 4, 30. *who hast not in thy —s an eye discerning thine honour,* Lr. IV, 2, 52. Figuratively: *our cannon shall be bent against the —s of this resisting town,* John II, 38 (i. e. the walls). *on the b. o'the sea stand ranks of people,* Oth. II, 1, 53 (i. e. on the shore).

3) the whole countenance: *thou canst not see one wrinkle in my b.* Ven. 139. *to cloak offences with a cunning b.* Lucr. 749. *to mask their —s and hide their infamy,* 794. *the light will show, charactered in my b., the story of sweet chastity's decay,* 807. *O carve not with thy hours my love's fair b.* Sonn. 19, 9. *time delves the parallels in beauty's b.* 60, 10. *there is written in your b. honesty and constancy,* Meas. IV, 2, 163. *speak you this with a sad b.* Ado I, 1, 185. *if in black my lady's —s are decked,* LLL IV, 3, 258. *where fair is not, praise cannot mend the b.* IV, 1, 17. *till o'er their —s ... sleep .. doth creep,* Mids. III, 2, 364. *sees Helen's beauty in a b. of Egypt,* V, 11. *what damned error, but some sober b. will bless it,* Merch. III, 2, 78. *speak, sad b. and true maid,* As III, 2, 227. *by the stern b.* IV, 3, 9. *the wrinkles in my —s,* H6C V, 2, 19. *'tis but the pale reflex of Cynthia's b.* Rom. III, 5, 20. Figuratively: *outface the b. of bragging horror,* John V, 1, 50. *here walk I in the black b. of night,* V, 6, 17.

Sometimes = aspect, appearance: *by this face, this seeming b. of justice, did he win the hearts of all,* H4A IV, 3, 83. *like a gallant in the b. of youth,* H6B V, 3, 4. *though all things foul would wear the —s of grace,* Mcb. IV, 3, 23. *to be contracted in one b. of woe,* Hml. I, 2, 4 (cf. *a b. of much distraction,* Wint. I, 2, 149).

Brow-bound, crowned: *b. with the oak,* Cor. II, 2, 102.

Brown, adj. of a dusky colour: *b. bread,* Meas. III, 2, 194. *b. and white bastard,* III, 2, 4. H4A II, 4, 82. *b. furze,* Tp. I, 1, 71. *paper,* Meas. IV,3,5.* *thread,* Shr. IV, 3, 138. *hair,* Wiv. I, 1, 48. Ado III,4, 14 *(—er).* As III, 4, 9 *(—er).* Ant. III, 3. 35. III, 11, 14. *heads,* Cor. II, 3, 20. *she is too b.* Ado I, 1, 174. *—er than her brother,* As IV, 3, 89. *as b. as hazelnuts,* Shr. II, 256. *the b. wench,* H8 III, 2, 295. *a b. favour,* Troil. I, 2, 101—105. — *a b. bill* (cf. *bill)* H6B IV, 10, 13. Lr. IV, 6, 92 (a kind of halbert, whose name is of uncertain origin).

Substantively: *though grey do something mingle with our younger b.* Ant. IV, 8, 20.

Brownist, adherent to a sect founded in the reign of Queen Elisabeth by Robert Brown: *I had as lief be a B. as a politician,* Tw. III, 2, 34.

Browny, somewhat brown: *his b. locks,* Compl. 85.

Browze, to nibble: *—ing of ivy,* Wint. III, 3, 69 (cf. *of). the barks of trees thou —dst,* Ant. I, 4, 66. Intr.: *there is cold meat i' the cave; we'll b. on that,* Cymb. III, 6, 38.

Bruise, vb., 1) to hurt by a contusion: *I throw thy name against the —ing stones*, Gentl. I, 2, 111. *I —d my shin*, Wiv. I, 1, 294. *falling from a hill, he was so —d*, H4A V, 5, 21. Applied to defensive arms, = to dint: *—d arms*, Lucr. 110. R3 I, 1, 6. *his —d helmet*, H5 V Chor. 18. *—d pieces*, Ant. IV, 14, 42. The same sense in the following passages: *we thought not good to b. an injury till it were fully ripe*, H5 III, 6, 129 (to open an ulcer by squeezing it). *Palamedes sore hurt and —d*, Troil. V, 5, 14. *they yet glance by and scarcely b.* Lr. V, 3, 148 (though it seems here to be = to hurt, to wound in general).

2) to crush, to grind, to destroy: *let us be keen and rather cut a little than fall and b. to death*, Meas. II, 1, 6. *a wretched soul, —d with adversity*, Err. II, 1, 34. *b. me with scorn*, LLL V, 2, 397. *b. her flowerets with the armed hoofs of hostile paces*, H4A I, 1, 8. *leads ancient lords to bloody battles and to —ing arms*, III, 2, 105. *—d underneath the yoke of tyranny*, R3 V, 2, 2. *put in their hands thy —ing irons of wrath*, V, 3, 110. *his contempt shall not be —ing to you, when he hath power to crush*, Cor. II, 3, 210. *the law shall b. him*, Tim. III, 5, 4. *that the —d heart was pierced through the ear*, Oth. I, 3, 219.

Bruise, subst., hurt, contusion: *with grey hairs and b. of many days*, Ado V, 1, 65. *that feel the —s of the days before*, H4B IV, 1, 100. Hurt in general: *the sovereignest thing was parmaceti for an inward b.* H4A I, 3, 58.

Bruit, subst., rumor: H6C IV, 7, 64. Troil. V, 9, 4. Tim. V, 1, 196.

Bruit, vb., to announce with noise: *by this great clatter one of greatest note seems —ed*, Mcb. V, 7, 22. *the king's rouse the heavens shall b. again*, Hml. I, 2, 127.

Hence = to report, to noise abroad: *his death being —ed once*, H4B I, 1, 114. *thou art no less than fame hath —ed*, H6A II, 3, 68.

Brundusium, town in ancient Italy: Ant. III, 7, 22.

Brunt, heat of an onset, violent shock: *in the b. of seventeen battles*, Cor. II, 2, 104.

Brush, subst., the act of stripping off: *have with one winter's b. fell from their boughs and left me open, bare for every storm*, Tim. IV, 3, 264. Hence, as synonymous to *bruise*, = hurt, injury: *forgets aged contusions and all b. of time*, H6B V, 3, 3. *tempt not yet the —es of the war*, Troil. V, 3, 34.

Brush, vb., 1) to rub with a brush: *—es his hat*, Ado III, 2, 41. *their blue coats —ed*, Shr. IV, 1, 94.

2) to strip off: *as wicked dew as e'er my mother —ed with raven's feather from unwholesome fen*, Tp. I, 2, 321.

Brute, adj., bestial, brutal: *it was a b. part of him*, Hml. III, 2, 110.

Brutish, bestial: *wouldst gabble like a thing most b.* Tp. I, 2, 357. *as sensual as the b. sting itself*, As II, 7, 66. *b. wrath*, R3 II, 1, 118. *O judgment, thou art fled to b. beasts*, Caes. III, 2, 110. *unnatural, detested, b. villain*, Lr. I, 2, 82.

Brutus: 1) the elder B., Lucr. Arg. 18. Lucr. 1734. 1807. H5 II, 4, 37. Cor. I, 1, 220. III, 1, 187. Tit. IV, 1, 91. Caes. I, 2, 159. I, 3, 146.

2) the younger B.: Merch. I, 1, 166. H6B IV, 1, 136. Caes. I, 2, 32 etc. Hml. III, 2, 109. Ant. II, 6, 13. III, 2, 56. III, 11, 38.

3) Decius (Decimus) B.: Caes. I, 3, 148 etc.

Bubble, subst., small bladder of water: *the b. reputation*, As II, 7, 152. *like —s in a late-disturbed stream*, H4A II, 3, 62. *a dream of what thou wert, a breath, a b.* R3 IV, 4, 88. *the earth hath —s, as the water has*, Mcb. I, 3, 79. *do but blow them to their trial, the —s are out*, Hml. V, 2, 202.

Hence = cheat, humbug: *if your lordship find him not a hilding, hold me no more in your respect. On my life, my lord, a b.* All's III, 6, 5.

Bubble, vb., to rise in bubbles: *(her blood) —ing from her breast*, Lucr. 1737. *where I have seen corruption boil and b.* Meas. V, 320. *a —ing fountain*, Tit. II, 4, 23. Mcb. IV, 1, 11. 19. 21. 26.

Bubukle, a corrupt word, formed by captain Fluellen half of *carbuncle*, half of *bubo*, probably meaning a red pimple: *his face is all—s*, H5 III, 6, 108.

Buck, 1) the male of the fallow deer: Wiv. V, 5, 27. Troil. III, 1, 127. Symbol of cuckoldom: Wiv. III, 3, 167. Err. III, 1, 72. *a b. of the first head*, LLL IV, 2, 10 (Return from Parnassus, 1606: 'a buck of the first year, a fawn; the second year, a pricket; the third year, a sorrel; the fourth year, a soare; the fifth, a buck of the first head; the sixth year, a complete buck').

2) linen in washing: *she washes —s here at home*, H6B IV, 2, 51 (= she is a laundress).

Buck-basket, a basket for linen to be washed: Wiv. III, 3, 2. III, 5, 88. 90. 145. V, 5, 117.

Bucket, vessel to draw water out of a well: John V, 2, 139. R2 IV, 185. H4B V, 1, 23. *the brewer's b.* H4B III, 2, 283.

Bucking, washing: *throw foul linen upon him, as if it were going to b.* Wiv. III, 3, 140.

Buckingham, 1) county of England: H6C IV, 8, 14. 2) *Duke Humphrey of B.*, a) H6B I, 1, 69. 172. I, 3, 72. 116. I, 4, 58. II, 1, 165. IV, 8, 20. V, 1, 15 etc. H6C I, 1, 10. b) *Henry Duke of B.* R3 I, 3, 17 etc. etc. H8 II, 1, 107. alluded to: I, 2, 195. c) the son of the latter: H8 I, 1, 115. 199 etc. III, 2, 256.

Buckle, subst., instrument of metal to fasten parts of dress: Troil. III, 1, 163. Ant. I, 1, 8.

Buckle, vb., 1) to fasten with a buckle: Wiv. V, 5, 76. Shr. III, 2, 46. John II, 564. R3 III, 7, 228. V, 3, 211. Troil. V, 3, 46. Ant. IV, 4, 11. *he that —s him in my belt*, H4B I, 2, 158. *he cannot b. his distempered cause within the belt of rule*, Mcb. V, 2, 15. Hence to b. *in* = to confine: *the stretching of a span —s in his sum of age*, As III, 2, 140. *b. in a waist most fathomless with spans and inches*, Troil. II, 2, 30.

2) intr. (probably from the phrase: *to turn the buckle behind*) to join in close fight: *in single combat thou shalt b. with me*, H6A I, 2, 95. *all our general force might with a sally of the very town be —d with*, IV, 4, 5. *hell too strong for me to b. with*, V, 3, 28. *I will not bandy with thee word for word, but b. with thee blows twice two for one*, H6C I, 4, 50.

3) to bow: *whose fever-weakened joints, like strengthless hinges, b. under life*, H4B I, 1, 141.

Buckler, shield: H4A II, 4, 186 (cf. *sword-and-buckler*). *I give thee the —s* (= I yield thee the victory) Ado V, 2, 17.

Buckler, vb., to shield, to defend: *I'll b. thee against a million*, Shr. III, 2, 241. *the guilt of murder —s thee*, H6B III, 2, 216. *b. falsehood with a pedigree*, H6C III, 3, 99.

Bucklersbury, a street of London chiefly inhabited by druggists: *smell like B.* Wiv. III, 3, 79.

Buckram, coarse linen stiffened with glue: H4A I, 2, 201. II, 4, 213. 217. 227. 228. 236. 243. *thou say, thou serge, nay, thou b. lord*, H6B IV, 7, 28.

Buck-washing, laundry: Wiv. III, 3, 166.

Bud, subst., 1) unexpanded flower: Ven. 416. Lucr. 848. Sonn. 1, 11. 18, 3. 35, 4. 54, 8. 99, 7. Pilgr. 132. Gentl. I, 1, 42. 45. 48. Ado IV, 1, 59. LLL V, 2, 295. Mids. I, 1, 185. II, 1, 110. II, 2, 3. IV, 1, 58. 78. Shr. V, 2, 140. Tw. II, 4, 114. John III, 4, 82. H4B I, 3, 39. H5 I, 2, 194. H6B III, 1, 89. Rom. I, 1, 158. I, 2, 29. II, 2, 121. Ant. III, 13, 40. Cymb. I, 3, 37. Per. V Prol. 6.

2) the shoot of a plant: *make conceive a bark of baser kind by b. of nobler race*, Wint. IV, 4, 95.

Bud, vb., to put forth buds or gems: Ven. 1142. Lucr. 604. Sonn. 95, 3. Pilgr. 171. Shr. IV, 5, 37 (*young —ing virgin*). H4A V, 4, 72. *which is —ed out*, H8 I, 1, 94 (= has come to light).

Budge, (O. Edd. *bouge, boudge*) to stir: *they cannot b. till your release*, Tp. V, 11. *sit you down, you shall not b.* Hml. III, 4, 18.

Mostly = to give way, to flinch, to flee: *my conscience says: Launcelot, b. not. B., says the fiend. B. not, says my conscience*, Merch. II, 2, 20. *I'll not b. an inch*, Shr. Ind. 1, 14. *afoot he will not b. a foot*, H4A II, 4, 388. H6A I, 3, 38. *hence we will not b.* H6C V, 4, 66. *they did b. from rascals worse than they*, Cor. I, 6, 44. *I will not b. for no man's pleasure*, Rom. III, 1, 58. *must I b.? must I observe you?* Caes. IV, 3, 44 (i. e. must your caprices make me quail?)

Budger, one who gives way: *let the first b. die the other's slave*, Cor. I, 8, 5.

Budget, subst. leathern bag: *and bear the sow-skin b.* Wint. IV, 3, 20 (rhyming to *avouch it*; O. Edd. *bowget*).

Budget, part of the interjection *mum-budget*, enjoining secrecy: *I come to her and cry 'mum'; she cries 'budget'*, Wiv. V, 2, 7. 10. V, 5, 210.

Buff, leather prepared from the skin of the buffalo; used for the dress of sergeants and catchpoles: *a fellow all in b.* Err. IV, 2, 36. *he's in a suit of b. which 'rested him*, 45. *is not a b. jerkin a most sweet robe of durance?* H4A I, 2, 48. 52.

Buffet, subst., blow: *I could divide myself and go to —s*, H4A II, 3, 35. *the blows and —s of the world*, Mcb. III, 1, 109. *fortune's —s and rewards*, Hml. III, 2, 72. *stand the b. with knaves*, Ant. I, 4, 20.

Buffet, vb., 1) absol., to beat, to box: *not a word of his but —s better than a fist of France*, John II, 465. *this civil —ing*, H4A II, 4, 397. *if I might b. for my love*, H5 V, 2, 146.

2) trans. to beat: *—s himself on the forehead*, Wiv. IV, 2, 25. *did b. thee*, Err. II, 2, 160. *we did b. it* (the torrent) *with lusty sinews*, Caes. I, 2, 107 (cf. *beat*, Tp. II, 1, 114).

Bug, bugbear: *fear boys with —s*, Shr. I, 2, 211. *the b. which you would fright me with*, Wint. III, 2, 93. *Warwick was a b. that feared us all*, H6C V, 2, 2.

such —s and goblins, Hml. V, 2, 22. *are grown the mortal —s o' the field*, Cymb. V, 3, 51.

Bugbear, frightful object, walking spectre: *would he not let it sleep? a b. take him!* Troil. IV, 2, 34.

Bugle, 1) hunting horn: Ado I, 1, 243.

2) bead of black glass: *b. bracelet*, Wint. IV, 4, 224. *your b. eyeballs*, As III, 5, 47.

Build, (impf. *built*, R3 III, 1, 73. Mcb. I, 4, 13. Per. Prol. 18. *builded*, Compl. 152. partic. *built*, Sonn. 119, 11. 123, 2. Gentl. III, 1, 15. Wiv. II, 2, 224. R2 II, 1, 43 etc. *builded*, Sonn. 124, 5. Ant. III, 2, 30);

1) to frame, to erect, to construct; a) absol.: *when we mean to b., we first survey the plot*, H4B I, 3, 41. 48. *b. there, carpenter*, Troil. III, 2, 53. Tim. IV, 3, 533. Hml. V, 1, 46. Frequently used of birds making their nests: *sparrows must not b. in his house-eaves*, Meas. III, 2, 186. Merch. II, 9, 29. Wint. IV, 3, 23. R3 I, 3, 264. Ant. II, 6, 28 (cf. IV, 12, 3). Figuratively: *shall love in —ing grow so ruinous?* Err. III, 2, 4. (*as the cement of our love, to keep it —ed*, Ant. III, 2, 30. cf. Sonn. 119, 11. 124, 5). *if I mistake in those foundations which I b. upon*, Wint. II, 1, 101. *an habitation giddy and unsure hath he that —eth on the vulgar heart*, H4B I, 3, 90. *a pretty plot, well chosen to b. upon*, H6B I, 4, 59.

b) trans.: *experience for me many bulwarks —ed*, Compl. 152. *her chamber is built so shelving*, Gentl. III, 1, 115. Wiv. II, 2, 224. R2 II, 1, 43. H4B I, 3, 59. H5 I, 2, 198. IV, 1, 317. H6B IV, 7, 41. R3 III, 1, 69. 73. Tit. IV, 1, 59. Hml. III, 2, 141. Lr. III, 2, 90. *in* (= on; cf. *in*) *thy shoulder do I b. my seat* (= throne), H6C II, 6, 100. *b. nests*, Ant. IV, 12, 3. *b. his statue*, Per. II Prol. 14. *his apparel is built upon his back*, H4B III, 2, 155 (i. e. hangs upon him as on a rack). Similarly: *this jewel holds his —ing on my arm*, Per. II, 1, 162, = still hangs on my arm. *To b. up: thy pyramids built up with newer might*, Sonn. 123, 2. *this Antioch Antiochus the Great built up*, Per. Prol. 18. Figuratively: *'tis only fortune thou disdainest in her, the which I can b. up*, All's II, 3, 125.

The tropical use extends very far: *ruined love, when it is built anew*, Sonn. 119, 11. *it* (my love) *was —ed far from accident*, 124, 5. *who —s his hopes in air of your good looks*, R3 III, 4, 100; cf. Troil. IV, 5, 109. *to b. his fortune*, Tim. I, 1, 143; cf. Tw. III, 2, 35. *nor b. yourself a trouble out of his scattering and unsure observance*, Oth. III, 3, 150; cf. H4B IV, 1, 110. *from this moment I b. on thee a better opinion*, Oth. IV, 2, 208. *hath built Lord Cerimon such strong renown as time shall ne'er decay*, Per. III, 2, 47. *will it serve for any model to b. mischief on?* Ado I, 3, 48. *on that ground I'll b. a holy descant*, R3 III, 7, 49 (Ff *make*). *b. their evils on the graves of great men*, H8 II, 1, 67. *on whom I built an absolute trust*, Mcb. I, 4, 13.

2) to trust, rely: *to b. upon a foolish woman's promise*, Wiv. III, 5, 42. *if on my credit you dare b. so far to make your speed to Dover*, Lr. III, 1, 35 (cf. above: Wint. II, 1, 101. H4B I, 3, 90).

Building, subst. 1) construction, frame: *I am a worthless boat, he of tall b.* Sonn. 80, 12.

2) edifice: Lucr. 944. Gentl. V, 4, 9. Err. I, 2, 13. H6B I, 3, 133. Tit. V, 1, 23. Tim. III, 4, 65. Mcb. II, 3, 74. Cymb. IV, 2, 355. Per. II, 4, 36. Figuratively: *the strong base and b. of my love*, Troil. IV,

2, 109. *the —s of my fancy*, Cor. II, 1, 216. Lr. IV, 2, 85.

Bulk, 1) trunk, body: *her heart ... beating her b.* Lucr. 467. *smothered it within my panting b.* R3 I, 4, 40. *to shatter all his b. and end his being,* Hml. II, 1, 95.

2) Especially largeness of the body, great size: *all the more it seeks to hide itself, the bigger b. it shows,* Tp. III, 1, 81. *my authority bears of a credent b.,* Meas. IV, 4, 29 (i. e. great credit). *she is spread of late into a goodly b.* Wint. II, 1, 20. *grew by our feeding to so great a b.* H4A V, 1, 62. *care I for the limb, the thewes, the stature, b. and big assemblance of a man?* H4B III, 2, 277. *that such a keech can with his very b. take up the rays of the beneficial sun,* H8 I, 1, 55. *though the great b. Achilles be thy guard,* Troil. IV, 4, 130. *cannot cover the monstrous b. of this ingratitude with any size of words,* Tim. V, 1, 68. *grow in thews and b.* Hml. I, 3, 12. *who with half the b. o'the world played as I pleased,* Ant. III, 11, 64. Used of ships: *for shallow draught and b. unprizable,* Tw. V, 58. *shallow boats ... with those of nobler b.* Troil. I, 3, 37. *light boats sail swift, though greater —s draw deep,* ll, 3, 277 (Q and M. Edd. *hulks*).

3) a part of a building jutting out: *stalls,* *—s, windows,* Cor. II, 1, 226. *stand behind this b.* Oth. V, 1, 1.*

Bull, the male of black-cattle: Tp. II, 1, 312. III, 3, 45. Wiv. V, 5, 3. Ado I, 1, 263—265. V, 1, 184. V, 4, 43. 48. Mids. II, 1, 180. IV, 1, 127. Wint. IV, 4, 28. H4A II, 4, 271. IV, 1, 103. H4B II, 2, 172. 192. H6C II, 5, 126. Troil. V, 1, 60. V, 7, 10. 12. Tit. V, 1, 31.
= Taurus, one of the twelve signs of the zodiac: Tit. IV, 3, 71.

Bull-bearing, bearing a bull: *b. Milo,* Troil. II, 3, 258.

Bull-beeves, beef: *they want their porridge and their fat b.* H6A I, 2, 9.

Bull-calf, male calf: H4A II, 4, 287. Name of one of Falstaff's recruits: H4B III, 2, 183 etc.

Bullen, family name of the second wife of Henry VIII: *Sir Thomas —'s daughter,* H8 I, 4, 92. *Anne B.* III, 2, 36. 87. 88. (*this candle burns not clear,* III, 2, 96. 'There may be a play intended on the word *Bullen,* which is said to have been an ancient provincial name for a candle.' Staunton).

Bullet, ball to load guns: Ven. 461. Pilgr. 328. LLL III, 65. V, 2, 261. John II, 227. 412. H4B II, 4, 124. 127. IV, 3, 36. H5 IV, 3, 105. H6A IV, 7, 79. *quips and sentences and these paper —s of the brain,* Ado II, 3, 249.

Bullock, castrated bull, ox: *so they sell —s,* Ado II, 1, 202. *a good yoke of —s,* H4B III, 2, 42.

Bully, a brisk, dashing fellow: *discard, b. Hercules, cashier,* Wiv. I, 3, 6. *said I well, b. Hector?* 11. *my hand, b.; thou shalt have egress and regress,* II, 1, 225. *bless thee, b. doctor,* II, 3, 18. 29 etc. *b. knight,* IV, 5, 17. *what sayest thou, b. Bottom?* Mids. III, 1, 8.* *O sweet b. Bottom!* IV, 2, 19. *I love the lovely b.* H5 IV, 1, 48.

Bully-monster (cf. *bully*): Tp. V, 258.

Bully-rook, apparently the same as *bully:* Wiv. I, 3, 2. II, 1, 200. 207. 213.

Bulwark, bastion, fortification: Compl. 152. John II, 27. H5 IV, 1, 173. H6A I, 4, 67. II,

1, 27. III, 2, 17. R3 V, 3, 242. *it is proof and b. against sense,* Hml. III, 4, 38.

Bum, subst., buttocks: Meas. II, 1, 228. Mids. II, 1, 53. Tim. I, 2, 237.

2) name in Meas. II, 1, 227.

Bum-baily, a subordinate officer employed in arrests: Tw. III, 4, 194 (most M. Edd. *bum-bailiff*).

Bumbard, see *Bombard.*

Bump, protuberance: *upon its brow a b. as big as a young cockerel's stone,* Rom. I, 3, 53.

Bunch, 1) a cluster: *vines with clustering —es,* Tp. IV, 112. *b. of grapes,* Meas. II, 1, 133 (name of a room).

2) number of things tied together: *a b. of radish,* H4A II, 4, 205. *—es of keys,* H4B I, 2, 44.

Bunch-backed (Q2 sq. and most M. Edd. *hunch-backed*) crook-backed: R3 I, 3, 246. IV, 4, 81.

Bung, a low term for a sharper: *away, you cutpurse rascal! you filthy b., away!* H4B II, 4, 138.

Bung-hole, the hole at which a barrel is filled: Hml. V, 1, 226.

Bungle, to make or mend clumsily; with up: *botch and b. up damnation with patches,* H5 II, 2, 115.

Bunting, the bird Emberiza miliaria: *I took this lark for a b.* All's II, 5, 7.

Buoy, subst., floating mark on the water: Lr. IV, 6, 19.

Buoy, vb. to lift up: *the sea, with such a storm, would have —ed up ... the stars,* Lr. III, 7, 60.

Bur, see *Burr.*

Burden or **Burthen** (in O. Edd. more frequently *burthen*), subst., 1) load: Lucr. 735. Sonn. 23, 8. Tp. I, 2, 156. IV, 113. Merch. IV, 1, 95. As II, 7, 167. III, 2, 341. Wint. I, 2, 3. II, 3, 206. John II, 92. 145. R2 I, 3, 200. H4B V, 2, 55. H5 I, 2, 201. H6B III, 1, 298. IV, 8, 30. H6C II, 1, 81. R3 III, 7, 229. IV, 4, 113. H8 II, 3, 43. III, 2, 384. Rom. I, 4, 22. Tim. IV, 3, 145. Hml. III, 1, 54. Ant. II, 6, 20.

2) the quantity a vessel will carry: *a vessel of too great a b.* All's II, 3, 216. Figuratively: *matter needless, of importless b.* Troil. I, 3, 71.

3) birth: *bear amiss the second b. of a former child,* Sonn. 59, 4. *delivered of such a b.* Err. I, 1, 56. *bore thee at a b. two fair sons,* V, 343. 402. *brought to bed of twenty money-bags at a b.* Wint. IV, 4, 267. John III, 1, 90. R3 IV, 4, 167. H8 V, 1, 70. Per. V, 3, 47.

4) undersong: *and sweet sprites the b. bear,* Tp. I, 2, 381. *I would sing my song without a b.* As III, 2, 261. *such delicate —s of dildos and fadings,* Wint. IV, 4, 195. cf. *wealth is b. of my wooing dance,* Shr. I, 2, 68.

Plays on the word: *choosing so strong a prop to support so weak a b.* Ven. Dedic. 2 (load and birth). Sonn. 97, 7. Tp. IV, 113. R3 IV, 4, 167. — *Heavy! belike it hath some b. then,* Gentl. I, 2, 85 (load and undersong). Ado III, 4, 45.

Burden or **Burthen,** vb., 1) to load; a) absol. *overborne with —ing grief,* H6A II, 5, 10. b) trans.: *the colt that's backed and —ed being young,* Ven. 419. *wild mass —s every bough,* Sonn. 102, 11. Shr. II, 203. H6B III, 2, 320. Rom. I, 4, 23. Followed by *with: b. our remembrance with a heaviness,* Tp. V, 199. Err. I, 1, 108. II, 1, 36.

2) to charge: *this is false he —s me withal,* Err. V, 209. 268.

Burdened, adj., made a burden, burdensome: *now thy proud neck bears half my b. yoke,* R3 IV, 4, 111.

Burdenous (O. Edd. *burthenous*), heavy: *b. taxations,* R2 II, 1, 260.

Burden-wise (O. Edd. *burthen-wise*), as an undersong: *for b. I'll hum on Tarquin still, while thou on Tereus descant'st better skill,* Lucr. 1133.

Bur-dock, see *Burr-dock.*

Burgher, freeman of a borough: *a wise b. put in for them,* Meas. I, 2, 103. *like signiors and rich —s on the flood,* Merch. I, 1, 10. *native —s of this desert city,* As II, 1, 23.

Burglary, used wrongly by Dogberry: Ado IV, 2, 52.

Burgomaster, chief magistrate of a city: *with nobility and tranquillity, —s and great oneyers,* H4A II, 1, 84. In Rom. I, 4, 56 the spurious Q1 *burgomaster,* the rest of O. Edd. *alderman.*

Burgonet, a close-fitting helmet: H6B V, 1, 200. 204. 208. *the demi-Atlas of this earth, the arm and b. of men,* Ant. I, 5, 24.

Burgundy (O. Edd. mostly *Burgonie*); 1) country between France and Germany: H5 III, 5, 42. IV, 8, 102. V, 2, 7. 68. H6A III, 2, 42. III, 3, 36 etc. H6C II, 1, 143. IV, 6, 79. IV, 7, 6. R3 I, 4, 10. Lr. I, 1, 35. 261 *(waterish B.)* etc.

2) = duke of B.: H6A II, 1, 8. III, 2, 77. 101. III, 3, 37 *(the B.).* H6C IV, 6, 90. Lr. I, 1, 46 etc.

Burial, 1) interment: Ado IV, 1, 210. Mids. III, 2, 383. R2 V, 5, 119. H6A II, 5, 121. R3 I, 4, 288. Tit. I, 84. Rom. IV, 5, 87 *(b. feast).* Caes. III, 1, 275. V, 5, 77. Hml. IV, 5, 213 *(Qq funeral).* V, 1, 2. 5. 28. 257. *To give a p. b.:* H6A IV, 7, 86. Tit. I, 347. V, 3, 192. Per. II, 4, 12. Followed by *of* = the act of burying: *nor would we deign him b. of his men,* Mcb. I, 2, 60.

2) = grave: *vailing her high-top lower than her ribs to kiss her b.* Merch. I, 1, 29.

Burier, he who, or that which buries: *darkness be the b. of the dead,* H4B I, 1, 160.

Burly-boned, bulky: *or cut not out the b. clown in chines of beef,* H6B IV, 10, 60.

Burn (impf. and partic. *burned* and *burnt*); trans. 1) to consume with fire: *to b. the guiltless casket,* Lucr. 1057. Sonn. 19, 4. Tp. III, 2, 103. Gentl. III, 1, 155. Ado IV, 1, 165. Mids. I, 1, 173. As II, 3, 23. H6A V, 4, 33. H6B I, 1, 234. II, 3, 7. IV, 6, 17. IV, 7, 16 etc. etc. Tropically: *that a maiden heart hath —ed,* As IV, 3, 41. *to b. daylight* = to lose time: Wiv. II, 1, 54 and Rom. I, 4, 43. Similarly: *to b. this night with torches,* Ant. IV, 2, 41. *To b. up* = to consume entirely by fire: Tp. III, 1, 17. John III, 1, 340. V, 3, 14. H6C II, 1, 84. Oth. IV, 2, 75 (cf. Tim. IV, 3, 141). *To b. out.* a) = to put out, to drive out, to destroy by fire: *b. out mine eyes,* John IV, 1, 39. 59. *ye blaze to b. them out* (like a wood) H6C V, 4, 71. *one fire —s out another's —ing,* Rom. I, 2, 46. *tears,... b. out the sense and virtue of mine eye,* Hml. IV, 5, 155. b) to have done burning, to extinguish: *fair torch, b. out thy light,* Lucr. 190. *dying coals burnt out in tedious nights,* 1379. *she —ed out love as soon as straw out-burneth,* Pilgr. 98. *you are as a candle, the better part —t out,* H4B I, 2, 178. *night's candles are —ed out,* Rom. III, 5, 9 (cf. R2 II, 1, 34. Lr. IV, 6, 40 and *out*).

2) to injure by fire or heat: *b. him with their tapers,* Wiv. IV, 4, 62. V, 5, 105. *the sun doth b. my face,* Ven. 186. *we have —t our cheeks,* Ant. II, 7, 129 (inflamed them by drinking). = to scorch (of meat): *the pig is —ed,* Err. II, 1, 66. = to brand: *being burnt in the hand for stealing of sheep,* H6B IV, 2, 67. = to infect with syphilis: *light wenches will b.* Err. IV, 3, 58. *she is in hell already and —s poor souls,* H4B II, 4, 366. *a —ing devil take them,* Troil. V, 2, 196. *b. him up,* Tim. IV, 3, 141. *no heretics —ed but wenches' suitors,* Lr. III, 2, 84. cf. the quibble in Gentl. II, 5, 56.

3) to prepare by fire: *b. some sack,* Tw. II, 3, 206.* *burnt sack,* Wiv. II, 1, 223. III, 1, 112.

II) Reflectively, *to b. one's self* = to be consumed with fire; properly and figuratively: *mine ears that to your wanton talk attended, do b. themselves for having so offended,* Ven. 810. *though he b. himself in love,* Gentl. II, 5, 56. *take heed lest by your heat you b. yourselves,* H6B V, 1, 160. *violent fires soon b. out themselves,* R2 II, 1, 34. *my snuff and loathed part of nature should b. itself out,* Lr. IV, 6, 40.

III) Intrans., 1) to be on fire, to flame: *Titan, with —ing eye,* Ven. 178. *an oven that is stopped, —eth more hotly,* Ven. 332. *Troy that —s so long,* Lucr. 1468. 1474. Sonn. 115, 4. Tp. I, 2, 199. III, 1, 18. Gentl. I, 2, 30. II, 7, 23. Meas. V, 295. Err. III, 2, 100. IV, 3, 57. John V, 2, 53. H6A I, 4, 96. III, 2, 28. H6B I, 4, 42. III, 2, 118. V, 1, 3. R3 V, 3, 180. Tit. V, 3, 83 etc. etc.

Metaphorically, to be inflamed with passions and affections: *he —s with bashful shame,* Ven. 49. *the maiden —ing of his cheek,* 50. *—ing blushes,* Compl. 304. *—ing fevers,* Ven. 739. *they b. in indignation,* John IV, 2, 103. *—s with revenging fire,* H6B IV, 1, 97. *my heart for anger —s,* H6C I, 1, 60. *revenges b. in them,* Mcb. V, 2, 3. Especially used of amorous desire: *my flesh is soft and plump, my marrow —ing,* Ven. 142. *his drumming heart cheers up his —ing eye,* Lucr. 435. *sighs that —ing lungs did raise,* Compl. 228. *when he most —ed in heart-wished luxury,* 314. *she —ed with love,* Pilgr. 97. *liver —ing hot,* Wiv. II, 1, 121. *—ing youth,* Meas. I, 3, 6. LLL V, 2, 73. Wint. IV, 4, 35. H6A I, 2, 108. Hml. I, 3, 116. III, 4, 87.

2) to flame, to shine, to blaze: *the lamp that —s by night,* Ven. 755. *two lamps, —t out,* 1128. (sun and moon) *that b. by day and night,* Tp. I, 2, 336. Merch. V, 89. Hml. I, 1, 38. *tapers —ed to bedward,* Cor. I, 6, 32. *the barge —ed on the water,* Ant. II, 2, 197. *here —s my candle out,* H6C II, 6, 1.

3) to be spoiled, or consumed by fire: *the capon —s,* Err. I, 2, 44. II, 1, 63. *condemned to b.* H6A V, 4, 1. Figuratively: *thus have I shunned the fire for fear of —ing,* Gentl. I, 3, 78.

Burnet, the plant Sanguisorba officinalis: H5 V, 2, 49.

Burning-glass, a glass which collects the rays of the sun and produces intense heat: Wiv. I, 3, 74.

Burnish, vb., used only in the partic. *burnished* = bright, shining: *cedar-tops and hills seem —ed gold,* Ven. 858. *the shadowed livery of the —ed sun,* Merch. II, 1, 2. *like a —ed throne,* Ant. II, 2, 196.

Burr, the rough head of the burdock: *I am a kind of b., I shall stick,* Meas. IV, 3, 189. Mids. III,

2, 260. As I, 3, 13. 17, H5 V, 2, 52. Troil. III, 2,119.

Burr-dock, the plant Arctium Lappa; introduced into the text by conjecture only in Lr. IV, 4, 4; Qq *hor-docks,* Ff. *hardocks.* Some M. Edd. *hoardocks, harlocks* etc.

Burrow, hole made in the ground by conies: *they will out of their —s, like conies after rain,* Cor. IV, 5, 226.

Burst, subst., sudden breaking forth, peal, explosion; used of sounds only: *a hollow b. of bellowing,* Tp. II, 1, 311. *the b. and the ear-deafening voice of the oracle,* Wint. III, 1, 8. *the instant b. of clamour that she made,* Hml. II, 2, 538. *—s of horrid thunder,* Lr. III, 2, 46. *the snatches in his voice, and b. of speaking,* Cymb. IV, 2, 106 (his broken and exploding manner of speaking).

Burst, vb., 1) trans. to break: *blow till thou b. thy wind,* Tp. I, 1, 9 (cf. *break*). *the glasses you have b.* Shr. Ind. 1, 8. *a headstall of sheep's leather which hath been often b.* Shr. III, 2, 60. *how her bridle was b.* IV, 1, 83. *he b. his head,* H4B III, 2,347. *make him b. his lead and rise from death,* H6A I, 1, 64. *open the gates, or we'll b. them open,* I, 3, 28. *my breast I'll b. with straining of my courage,* I, 5, 10. *why thy canonized bones have b. their cerements,* Hml. I, 4, 48. *bellowed out as he'ld b. heaven,* Lr. V, 3, 213. *your heart is b.* Oth. I, 1, 87. *hath b. the buckles on his breast,* Ant. I, 1, 7. *endured a sea that almost b. the deck,* Per. IV, 1, 57.

2) intr. to break, to crack: *stretch his leathern coat almost to —ing,* As II, 1, 38. *my panting bulk which almost b.* R3 I, 4, 41. *would thou wouldst b.* Tim. IV, 3, 373. *let me not b. in ignorance* (sc. with impatience) Hml. I, 4, 46; cf. 48. Especially used of the heart: *if my heart were great, 'twould b. at this,* All's IV, 3, 367. H4B II, 4, 410. H6C V, 5, 59. Caes. III, 2, 190. Lr. V, 3, 182. 199. *To b. out* = to break forth: *whose bowels suddenly b. out,* John V, 6, 30. *had the passions of thy heart b. out,* H6A IV, 1, 183.

Burthen, Burthenous and **Burthen-wise,** see *Burden* etc.

Burton, town in England: H4A III, 1, 96.

Burton-heath, apparently = Burton-on-theheath, a village on the borders of Warwickshire and Oxfordshire: Shr. Ind. 2, 19.*

Bury, town in England: John IV, 3, 114. H6B II, 4, 71. III, 2, 240.

Bury, vb., to deposit in a grave: *he might be —ied in a tomb so simple,* Ven. 244. Sonn. 31, 4. 9. 64, 2. Phoen. 64. Gentl. II, 1, 24. IV, 2, 108. Err. V, 50. Ado III, 2, 70. V, 1, 69. V, 2, 105. Mids. V, 355. Merch. III, 1, 6. As I, 2, 124. H6A I, 4, 87. III, 2, 83. H6B IV, 1, 143. H6C III, 2, 129. R3 II, 1, 90. IV, 3, 28. Hml. V, 1, 1 etc. etc. *b. it* (my staff) *certain fathoms in the earth,* Tp. V, 55. cf. Tit. II, 3, 2. *her —ing grave,* Rom. II, 3, 10. *Buried* = dead: *beat not the bones of the —ed,* LLL V, 2, 667. *by the —ed hand of warlike Gaunt,* R2 III, 3, 109. *within this coffin I present thy —ed fear,* R2 V, 6, 31. *with my child my joys are —ed,* Rom. IV, 5, 64. *the majesty of —ed Denmark,* Hml. I, 1, 48. Tropically: *a swallowing grave, seeming to b. that posterity,* Ven. 758. *—ing in Lucrece' wound his folly's show,* Lucr. 1810. *in thine own bud —est thy content,* Sonn. 1, 11. *in themselves their pride lies —ed,* 25, 7. *in his grave my love is —ed,* Gentl. IV, 2, 115. *must be —ed*

but as an intent that perished by the way, Meas. V, 457. *words seemed —ed in my sorrow's grave,* R2 I, 4, 15. *in your bride you b. brotherhood,* H6C IV, 1, 55. *in the deep bosom of the ocean —ed,* R3 I, 1, 4. *b. all thy fear in my devices,* Tit. IV, 4, 112. *do with their death b. their parents' strife,* Rom. Prol. 8. *in this I b. all unkindness,* Caes. IV, 3, 159. *his familiars to his —ed fortunes,* Tim. IV, 2, 10. *till the flies and gnats of Nile have —ed them for prey,* Ant. III, 13, 167 (= eaten them up). Frequently = to conceal *—ed this sigh in wrinkle of a smile,* Troil. I, 1, 38. *half their faces —ed in their cloaks,* Caes. II, 1, 74. *our youths and wildness shall no whit appear, but all be —ed in its gravity,* 149. *in dumb silence will I bury mine* (news) Gentl. III, 1, 207. *take the sacrament to b. mine intents,* R2 IV, 329. *this breast hath —ed thoughts,* Caes. I, 2, 49. *she rendered life, thy name so —ed in her,* Ant. IV, 14, 34.

Burying, subst., burial: *give her b.* Per. III, 2, 72.

Burying-place, churchyard: *be henceforth a b. to all that do dwell in this house,* H6B IV, 10, 68.

Bush, thick shrub: *the thorny brambles and embracing —es,* Ven. 629. 871. Lucr. 973. Tp. II, 2, 18. 145. LLL IV, 1, 7. IV, 3, 137. Mids. II, 1, 3. III, 1, 61. 110. III, 2, 406. 408. V, 22. 136. As IV, 3, 114. Tit. II, 3, 12. Tim. IV, 3, 423. Lr. II, 4, 305. Cymb. IV, 2, 292. *the thief doth fear each b. an officer,* H6C V, 6, 12; cf. Lucr. 973 and Mids. V, 22. *be married under a b. like a beggar,* As III, 3, 85. *good wine needs no b.* As Epil. 4. 6 (alluding to the bush of ivy which was usually hung out at vintners' doors). *birds never limed no secret —es fear,* Lucr. 88. *am I your bird? I mean to shift my b.* Shr. V, 2, 46. *myself have limed a b. for her,* H6B I, 3, 91. *limed —es to betray thy wings,* II, 4, 54. *limed in a b.* H6C V, 6, 13. *I have a fine hawk for the b.* Wiv. III, 3, 248.

Bushel, measure containing eight gallons: *two grains of wheat hid in two —s of chaff,* Merch. I, 1, 117.

Bushy, name in R2 I, 4, 23. 53. III, 1, 2 etc.*

Busily, actively, earnestly: *who are b. in arms,* H4A V, 5, 38. *how b. she turns the leaves,* Tit. IV, 1, 45.

Business. Plur. *businesses:* All's I, 1, 220. III, 7, 5. IV, 3, 98. Wint. IV, 2, 15. John IV, 3, 158. Lr. II, 1, 129 (Qq *business*). 1) employment, occupation: *full of careful b. are his looks,* R2 II, 2, 75. *when I shall turn the b. of my soul to such ... surmises,* Oth. III, 3, 181. But to both passages the second sense also is applicable.

2) that in which one is occupied, which engages his care and attention: *and then I'll bring thee to the present b. which now's upon us,* Tp. I, 2, 136. *there's other b. for thee,* 315. 367. III, 1, 96. Wiv. III, 5, 64. Meas. I, 4, 8. 70. III, 1, 48. III, 2, 151. V, 318. 388. Err. I, 2, 29. II, 1, 11. IV, 1, 35. 59. Ado II, 1, 195. Mids. III, 2, 395. Merch. I, 1, 63. II, 2, 213. II, 8, 39. III, 2, 325. As II, 3, 55. All's I, 1, 220. II, 3, 114. IV, 3, 98. V, 2, 36. Wint. IV, 2, 15. John IV, 3, 158. R3 I, 3, 355. III, 1, 186. H8 I, 1, 99 *(carry).* IV, 1, 4 *('tis all my b.).* Caes. IV, 1, 22. Lr. II, 1, 129. Ant. III, 7, 54 etc. etc. *to do b.:* Tp. I, 2, 255. Hml. III, 2, 409. *do my b.* Gentl. IV, 4, 70. *you have done your b.* Shr. IV, 2, 110. *we'll pass the b. privately,* IV, 4, 57. *come from the See in*

special b. from his holiness, Meas. III, 2, 233. *employ you in some b.* Mids. I, 1, 124. *the daughter of the king of France, on serious b., importunes personal conference*, LLL II, 31. *nor ever more upon this b. my appearance make*, H8 II, 4, 132. *raise you .. on b.* Caes. IV, 3, 248. *he might at some great b. fail you*, All's III, 6, 16. *brake off our b. for the Holy Land*, H4A I, 1, 48. *that's my b. to you*, Tp. III, 3, 69. *my b. is but to the court*, All's II, 2, 4. *I have b. to my lord*, Troil. III, 1, 63. *on b. to my brother Cassius*, Caes. IV, 3, 248.

3) affair, concern, cause, matter of question, things: *set a mark so bloody on the b.* Tp. I, 2, 142. *this is no mortal b., nor no sound that the earth owes*, 406. *this swift b. I must uneasy make*, 450. *more widows of this —' making*, II, 1, 133. *they'll tell the clock to any b. that we say befits the hour*, II, 1, 289. *there is in this b. more than nature was ever conduct of*, V, 243. *beating on the strangeness of this b.* 247. *to have hearing of this b.* Meas. III, 1, 211. *when you have a b. for yourself, pray heaven you then be perfect*, V, 81. *prejudicates the b.* All's I, 2, 8. *in so just a b. shut his bosom*, III, 1, 8. *nothing acquainted with these —es* (quite = matters) III, 7, 5. *lower messes perchance are to this b. purblind*, Wint. I, 2, 228. *your followers I will whisper to the b.* 437 (cf. Tp. II, 1, 289). *you smell this b. with a sense as cold*, II, 1, 151. *those that think it is unlawful b.* V, 3, 96. *what is the b.?* (= what is the matter?) III, 2, 143; cf. Mcb. II, 3, 86 and Oth. I, 3, 13. *sweat in this b. and maintain this war*, John V, 2, 102. *to look into this b. thoroughly*, H6B II, 1, 202. *to look on the b. present*, H8 I, 1, 206. *debate this b.* II, 4, 52. *the Lord increase this b.* III, 2, 161. *speak to the b.* V, 3, 1. *our b. is not unknown to the senate*, Cor. I, 1, 58. *stay behind this b.* (sc. the war) 247. *had he died in the b., how then?* I, 3, 20. *you are like to do such b.* III, 1, 48. *he has betrayed your b.* V, 6, 92. *the bleeding b. they have done*, Caes. III, 1, 168. *all our service were poor and single b.* Mcb. I, 6, 16. *now could I drink hot blood and do such bitter b.* Hml. III, 2, 409. *I do serve you in this b.* Lr. I, 2, 194. *let him command ... what bloody b. ever*, Oth. III, 3, 469. *you do mistake your b.* Ant. II, 2, 45 etc. Often trisyll., f. i. R2 II, 1, 217. R3 II, 2, 144. Caes. IV, 1, 22.

Busiless, see *Busyless*.

Buskined, dressed in buskins or half-boots: *the bouncing Amazon, your b. mistress*, Mids. II, 1, 71.

Busky, H4A V, 1, 2; see *Bosky*.

Buss, subst., kiss: *thou dost give me flattering — es*, H4B I, 4, 291.

Buss, vb., to kiss: *and b. thee as thy wife*, John III, 4, 35. *yond towers whose wanton tops do b. the clouds*, Troil. IV, 5, 220. *thy knee —ing the stones*, Cor. III, 2, 75 (cf. *Ear-bussing*).

Bustle, vb., to stir, to be active: *leave the world for me to b. in*, R3 I, 1, 152. *come, b., b., caparison my horse*, V, 3, 289. *I heard a —ing rumour*, Caes. II, 4, 18, i. e. a noise caused by a great stir and commotion of people.

Busy, adj., 1) employed with earnestness, active; used of persons and things: Ven. 383. Lucr. 1790. Sonn. 143, 6. Tp. III, 1, 15 (corr. pass.). Ado I, 2, 3 (*he is very b. about it*). 29. III, 5, 6. As III, 4, 62. Shr. V, 1, 15. V, 2, 81. H4B V, 2, 76. H5 IV Prol. 13. H6B I, 4, 11. III, 1, 339. R3 I, 3, 145.

V, 3, 18. H8 II, 2, 81. Troil. IV, 2, 8. Rom. IV, 3, 6. Caes. II, 1, 232. Oth. IV, 1, 241 (*he's b. in the paper*).

2) in a bad sense, = officious, prying, meddling: *on meddling monkey or on b. ape*, Mids. II, 1, 181. *the b. meddling fiend*, H6B III, 3, 21. *thou findest to be too b. is some danger*, Hml. III, 4, 33. *too b. in my fears*, Oth. III, 3, 253. *some b. and insinuating rogue*, IV, 2, 131.

Busy, vb., to employ, to keep engaged: *idle words, b. yourselves in skill-contending schools*, Lucr. 1018. *they are —ied about a counterfeit assurance*, Shr. IV, 4, 91. *to b. giddy minds with foreign quarrels*, H4B IV, 5, 214. *—ied in his majesty*, H5 I, 2, 197. *—ied with a morris-dance*, II, 4, 25. *—ied about decrees*, Cor. I, 6, 34. *do you b. yourself about that?* Lr. I, 2, 155 (Ff. *with that*).

Busyless, Theobald's emendation, approved by most M. Edd., in Tp. III, 1, 15 (O. Edd. *most busie lest, when I do it*), but entirely to be rejected. Singer's conjecture: '*most busiest, when I do it,*' is somewhat less improbable, but then it should be at least: '*when I am doing them.*' Perhaps the poet wrote: *most busy rest, when I do it* (= when I make or take it; cf. Tw. V, 136 and see the art. *do*).

But, except: *b. in them it were a wonder*, Phoen. 32. *all b. mariners plunged in the foaming brine*, Tp. I, 2, 210. *I'll die on him that says so b. yourself*, Gentl. II, 4, 114. *if all aim b. this be levelled false*, Ado IV, 1, 239. *what she should shame to know herself b. with her most vile principal*, Wint. II, 1, 92. *b. on this day let seamen fear no wreck*, John III, 1, 92. *my honour is at pawn, and b. my going nothing can redeem it*, H4B II, 3, 8. *I think a' be* (one of the greatest men) *b. goodman Puff*, V, 3, 93. *the greatest man in England b. the king*, H6B II, 2, 82 etc. etc.

Hence *all but* (which is at present = almost) = anything except, but not, not however: *could all b. answer for that peevish brat*, R3 I, 3, 194. *of his content, all b. in that*, Cymb. III, 2, 35.

After negations: *be subject to no sight b. thine and mine*, Tp. I, 2, 302. III, 1, 55. III, 2, 74. III, 3, 81. Gentl. I, 1, 131. I, 3, 56. IV, 1, 43. Meas. I, 1, 37. I, 4, 11. Err. I, 1, 53. III, 1, 25 etc. After negative comparatives = than: *apprehends death no more dreadfully b. as a drunken sleep*, Meas. IV, 2, 150. *these poor informal women are no more b. instruments of some more mightier member*, V, 237. *they would have no more discretion b. to hang us*, Mids. I, 2, 83. *thou knowest no less b. all*, Tw. I, 4, 13 (*no sooner ... but*, see soon).

It has the same sense, when it may be rendered by otherwise than: *I have done nothing b. in care of thee*, Tp. I, 2, 16. *I should sin to think b. nobly of my grandmother*, 119. *ambition cannot pierce a wink beyond b. doubt discovery there*, II, 1, 243. *yond same cloud cannot choose b. fall by pailfuls*, II, 2, 24 (cf. choose). *'tis a thing impossible I should love thee but as a property*, Wiv. III, 4, 10. *nature never lends .... b. she determines ....*, Meas. I, 1, 39. *will they ever b. in vizards show their faces?* LLL V, 2, 271. *how speed you with my daughter? how b. well?* Shr. II, 284. *I never read b. England's kings have had large sums of gold and dowries with their wives*, H6B I, 1, 128. *he would miss it rather than carry it b. by the suit of the gentry*, Cor. II, 1, 254. *aged custom, but by your voices, will not so permit me*, II, 3, 177. After *cannot: it cannot be b. thou hast murdered him*, Mids. III, 2, 56. H6B III, 2, 177. *our soul cannot b. yield you forth to public thanks*, Meas. V, 7. *it cannot b. turn him into a notable contempt*, Tw. II, 5, 223 etc.

= unless, if not; followed by the indicative: *and, b. he's something stained with grief, thou mightst call him a goodly person*, Tp. I, 2, 414 (= if he were not). *and b. infirmity hath something seized his wished ability, he had himself ....,* Meas. V, 1, 141. *ne'er may I look on day, b. she tells to your highness simple truth*, Err. V, 211. *I here do give thee that with all my heart which, b. thou hast already, with all my heart I would keep from thee*, Oth. I, 3, 194. *death will seize her, but your comfort makes the rescue*, Ant. III, 11, 48. *and, b. she spoke it dying, I would not believe her*, Cymb. V, 5, 41. Other instances: *I am much deceived b. I remember the style*, LLL IV, 1, 98. *can you not hate me, b. you must join in souls to mock me too?* Mids. III, 2, 150 (cf. *since brass, nor stone ... but sad mortality o'ersways their power*, Sonn. 65, 2. *a man cannot steal, b. it accuseth him*, R3 I, 4, 139). *I'll die for't b. some woman had the ring*, Merch. V, 208. *I would be sorry, b. the fool should be as oft with your master as with my mistress*, Tw. III, 1, 45 (cf. *beshrew*). Followed by the subjunctive: *and b. thou love me, let them find me here*, Rom. II, 2, 76 (as the case is only supposititious). cf. *b. I be deceived, our fine musician groweth amorous*, Shr. III, 1, 62. *b. I be deceived, Signior Baptista may remember me*, IV, 4, 2. Followed by a participle: *but being charged, we will be still by land*, Ant. IV, 11, 1 (= if we are not charged). By a gerund: *that which, but by being so retired, o'erprized all popular rate*, Tp. I, 2, 91.

Still oftener *but that*, in the same sense: *the sky would pour down stinking pitch, b. that the sea dashes the fire out*, Tp. I, 2, 4. *had come along with me, but that his mistress did hold his eyes locked*, Gentl. II, 4, 88. *welcome, Mercade, b. that thou interruptest our merriment*, LLL V, 2, 725. *b. that it would be double-dealing, I would you could make it another*, Tw. V, 32. cf. Tp. II, 2, 162. Meas. I, 2, 103. II, 2, 31. III, 1, 190. IV, 4, 26. Wiv. III, 5, 15. IV, 5, 120. Err. IV, 1, 3. LLL V, 2, 381. As I, 2, 259. Wint. IV, 4, 10. H6A I, 2, 24. IV, 1, 71. H6B III, 2, 216. V, 2, 84. H6C I, 4, 84. R3 III, 2, 83. IV, 4, 229. Hml. I, 5, 13. Cymb. III, 6, 41. V, 5, 46 etc. etc.

Similarly = that not: *who sees his true love in her naked bed ...., but his other agents aim at like delight?* Ven. 399, = nobody can see her .... without his senses aiming etc. And thus always after negative sentences: *never any with so full soul, b. some defect in her did quarrel with the noblest grace*, Tp. III, 1, 44. *what lets b. one may enter at her window?* Gentl. III, 1, 113 (cf. *let*). *he had not been here a pissing while, b. all the chamber smelt him*, IV, 4, 21. *fear not b. that she will love you*, III, 2, 1. *wise! why, no question, b. he was*, Meas. III, 2, 146. *there had she not been long b. she became a joyful mother*, Err. I, 1, 50. *it could never be b. I should know her*, II, 2, 204. *I am not yet so low b. that my nails can reach unto thine eyes*, Mids. III, 2, 298. *I never saw b. Humphrey did bear him like a noble gentleman*, H6B I, 1, 183. With some predilection after the verbs of thinking: *they think not b. that every eye can see the same disgrace*, Lucr. 750 (= they think that every eye can see etc.) *I do not*

think b. Desdemona's honest, Oth. III, 3, 225. *do not believe b. I shall do thee mischief*, Mids. II, 1, 236 (= be sure that I shall etc.) *your uncle must not know b. you are dead*, John IV, 1, 128. *my master knows not b. I am gone hence*, Rom. V, 3, 132. *there is no reason b. I shall be blind*, Gentl. II, 4, 212 (= there is every reason that etc.). *let it not be doubted b. he'll come*, Wiv. IV, 4, 43 (= that); cf. Err. III, 1, 92. Shr. II, 333. H4A II, 2, 14 (see *doubt*). Similarly after *to deny*, negatively used, = that: *it must not be denied b. I am a plain-dealing villain*, Ado I, 3, 33. *I neither can nor will deny b. that I know them*, All's V, 3, 167.

Likewise = who not, that not; after negations: *no fisher b. the ungrown fry forbears*, Ven. 526. *what wax so frozen b. dissolves with tempering*, 565. *not the least of all these maladies b. in one minute's fight brings beauty under*, 746. *no object b. her passion's strength renews*, 1103. *not a soul b. felt a fever*, Tp. I, 2, 209. *not a holiday fool there b. would give a piece of silver*, II, 2, 30. *not an eye that sees you b. is a physician*, Gentl. II, 1, 42. *nobody b. has his fault*, Wiv. I, 4, 15. *there's nothing under heaven's eye b. hath his bound*, Err. II, 1, 17. *there's not a man I meet b. doth salute me*, IV, 3, 1. *not the worst b. jumps twelve foot*, Wint. IV, 4, 347. *not the least of these b. can do more in England than the king*, H6B I, 3, 74. *who finds the heifer dead ... but will suspect...*, III, 2, 190. *no man b. prophesied revenge for it*, R3 I, 3, 186. *which of you b. is four Volsces?* Cor. I, 6, 78. — Sometimes the personal pronoun added: *there's not a hair on's head b. 'tis a Valentine*, Gentl. III, 1, 192. *not a man b. he hath the wit*, Err. II, 2, 88. — *But = that not*, the relative pronoun being the object: *what could he see b. mightily he noted?* Lucr. 414. *nor gates of steel so strong b. time decays*, Sonn. 65, 8. *what should it be that he respects in her b. I can make respective in myself?* Gentl. IV, 4, 200. *what is in Silvia's face, b. I may spy more fresh in Julia's?* V, 4, 114. *what towns of any moment b. we have?* H6A I, 2, 5. *no meed b. he repays sevenfold*, Tim. I, 1, 288. *no jutty, frieze, b. this bird hath made his pendent bed*, Mcb. I, 6, 7.

= if not: *it shall go hard b. I'll prove it*, Gentl. I, 1, 86. *what they think in their hearts they may effect, b. they will break their hearts b. they will effect*, Wiv. II, 2, 323. *who knows yet b. from this lady may proceed a gem*, H8 II, 3, 78. cf. Meas. V, 314. Shr. II, 15.

But for = were it not for, without: these mine eyes, b. for thy piteous lips, no more had seen, Ven. 504. *a woman, happy b. for me*, Err. I, 1, 38. *wise, b. for loving me*, Ado II, 3, 241 (except in loving me). cf. Lucr. 1420. Gentl. II, 1, 113. Err. IV, 4, 158. V, 20. LLL IV, 3, 233. Merch. V, 250. All's II, 4, 8. Wint. IV, 4, 447. John II, 216. H4A I, 3, 63. III, 1, 203. III, 3, 41. H4B IV, 3, 103. IV, 5, 139. H5 IV, 1, 295. H6B II, 2, 41. IV, 10, 12. R3 V, 3, 330. Troil. I, 3, 77. Rom. III, 4, 6. Tim. IV, 3, 95. Ant. II, 2, 221. Cymb. III, 6, 32. Per. IV, 6, 127. Cor. IV, 5, 57.

B. = only: *would I might b. ever see that man*, Tp. I, 2, 169. *did us b. loving wrong*, 151. *having seen b. him and Caliban*, 479. 489. II, 1, 65. 224. III, 2, 101. III, 3, 102. Gentl. I, 1, 34. I, 2, 29 etc. etc. *you b. waste your words*, Meas. II, 2, 72. *I say, b. mark his gesture*, Oth. IV, 1, 88. *he who shall speak for her is afar off guilty b. that he speaks*, Wint. II, 1, 105. *consume away in rust, b. for containing fire to harm*

mine eye, John IV, 1, 66. — *b. now* may be = **n o t
e a r l i e r t h a n n o w**: *begin these wood-birds b. to
couple now?* Mids. IV, 1, 145; or = **even at this
instant**: *whose whiteness so became them, as if b.
now they waxed pale for woe*, Gentl. III, 1, 228. *and
even now, b. now, this house, these servants .... are
yours*, Merch. III, 2, 171. But usually it is = **j u s t
n o w**, speaking of things very lately happened: *b.
now her cheek was pale*, Ven. 347. *b. now I lived*, 497.
Gentl. I, 1, 71. Merch. III, 2, 169. John V, 7, 66. R3
I, 3, 31 etc. *b. even now*, Merch. I, 1, 35. *even b. now*,
Lr. I, 1, 217 (cf. *even*). Similarly: *the catch you taught
me b. erewhile*, Tp. III, 2, 127. *she leaps that was b.
late forlorn*, Ven. 1026. *b. seven years since*, Err. V,
320. — *But* superfluously joined to *only*: *my lord
your son had only b. the corpse ... to fight*, H4B I, 1,
192. *I intend b. only to surprise him*, H6C IV, 2, 25. *he
only lived b. till he was a man*, Mcb. V, 8, 40 (cf. *only*).

Lastly and most commonly, as a particle of objection, = **h o w e v e r, n e v e r t h e l e s s**: Tp. I, 1, 72.
I, 2, 34. 48. 52. 63. 216. 238. 358 etc. etc. After
negations: Tp. I, 2, 142. 183. 219. 356 etc. etc. *But
that*, in the same sense: *could not take truce with the
unruly spleen of Tybalt, b. that he tilts at Mercutio's
breast*, Rom. III, 1, 163. *Not only ... but:* Tp. I, 2, 99.
210 etc. (cf. *only*). *But yet*, see *yet*. — *Were you a
woman, I should woo hard b. be your groom*, Cymb.
III, 6, 70 (= I should not desist from wooing, till
I had succeeded **in** becoming your groom? or = I
should woo hard to be etc.?). Irregularities: *if they
march along unfought withal, b. I will sell my dukedom*,
H5 III, 5, 12. *whenever Buckingham doth turn his hate
on you or yours, but with all duteous love doth cherish
you and yours, God punish me*, R3 II, 1, 33.

But, subst. see *Butt*.

Butcher, subst., one that kills animals for the
table: Ven. 618. Wiv. III, 5, 5. LLL V, 2, 255. H4B
II, 1, 101. H5 V, 2, 147. H6B III, 1, 210. III, 2, 189.
195. IV, 2, 27. IV, 3, 1. IV, 7, 58. H8 I, 1, 120. Caes.
II, 1, 166. Cymb. III, 4, 99. Tropically, one who delights in slaughter, a murderer; absolutely or followed
by *of:* *tyrants, —s, murderers*, As III, 5, 14. *b. of an
innocent child*, John IV, 2, 259. R2 I, 2, 3. 48. H6C
II, 2, 95. V, 5, 61. 63. 77. V, 6, 9. Cor. I, 9, 88. IV,
6, 95. Rom. II, 4, 24 *(b. of a silk button)*. Caes. III,
1, 255. Mcb. V, 8, 69. Followed by *to: b. to the sire*,
R3 V, 5, 26.

Butcher, vb., to slay, to slaughter: *teaching stern murder how to b. thee*, R2 I, 2, 32. H4A I,
1, 42. R3 I, 2, 67. I, 3, 276. III, 4, 92. IV, 4, 393.
V, 3, 122. Tit. IV, 4, 55.

Butcherly, adj., savage, murderous: *what
stratagems, how fell, how b.* H6C II, 5, 89.

Butcher-sire, one who kills his child: *or b. that
reaves his son of life*, Ven. 766 (O. Edd. without
the hyphen).

Butchery, 1) slaughter-house: *this house is
but a b.* As II, 3, 27.

2) slaughter: H4A I, 1, 13. R3 I, 2, 54. 100.
IV, 3, 5.

Butler, 1) a servant employed in furnishing the
table: Tp. V, 277. Wint. IV, 4, 56.

2) name of a servant: H4A II, 3, 70. 75.

Butt, subst. 1) a **c a s k** containing two hogsheads: *a rotten carcass of a b.* Tp. I, 2, 146 (most
M. Edd. *boat*).* *I escaped upon a b. of sack*, II, 2, 126.

137. III, 2, 1. *you ruinous b.* Troil. V, 1, 32 (why
that epithet?).

2) **m a r k, aim**: *as an aim or b.* H5 I, 2, 186.
I am your b., and must abide your shot, H6C I, 4, 29.

3) **g o a l, b o u n d**: *here is my journey's end, here
is my b.* Oth. V, 2, 267.

4) a thrust given by a horned animal, or rather
the part of the body with which it is given, viz the
horned head: *an hasty-witted body would say your
head and b. were head and horn*, Shr. V, 2, 41.

Butt, vb., to **s t r i k e w i t h t h e h e a d** like a
horned animal: *look how you b. yourself in these sharp
mocks! will you give horns?* LLL V, 2, 251. *they b.
together well*, Shr. V, 2, 39. *the beast with many heads
—s me away*, Cor. IV, 1, 2.

Butt-end, the largest or blunt end: *that
is the b. of a mother's blessing*, R3 II, 2, 110.

Butter, subst. oily substance obtained from cream
by churning: Wiv. II, 2, 317. III, 5, 118. V, 5, 148.
H4A I, 2, 23. II, 1, 65. II, 4, 134. 560. IV, 2, 67.

Butter, vb., to smear with butter; to cook
with butter: *I'll have my brains ta'en out and —ed*,
Wiv. III, 5, 8. *—ed his hay*, Lr. II, 4, 127. *eat no
fish of fortune's —ing*, All's V, 2, 9.

Butterfly, insect of the genus papilio: Mids.
III, 1, 175. Troil. III, 3, 78. Cor. I, 3, 66. IV, 6, 94.
V, 4, 12. Lr. V, 3, 13.

Butter-woman, a woman that sells butter: *it
is the right butter-women's rank to market*, As III, 2,
103. *tongue, I must put you into a —'s mouth*, All's
IV, 1, 45.

Buttery, a room where provisions are laid up:
take them to the b. and give them friendly welcome, Shr.
Ind. 1, 102.

Buttery-bar, the same: *bring your hand to the
b. and let it drink*, Tw. I, 3, 74.

Buttock, the hindmost part of the body, the
backside: *broad b.* Ven. 298. *his melting b.* 315. *a
barber's chair that fits all —s, the pin-b., the quatch-
b., the brawn-b., or any b.* All's II, 2, 17. *one that
converses more with the b. of the night than with the
forehead of the morning*, Cor. II, 1, 56* — Plur. *—s*
in the same sense: *in what part of her body stands
Ireland? in her —s*, Err. III, 2, 120.

Button, subst., 1) a catch to fasten the dress:
a silk b. Rom. II, 4, 24. *undo this b.* Lr. V, 3, 309.
he will carry 't; 'tis in his —s, Wiv. III, 2, 71; Germ.:
er hat es in der Tasche (or = bachelors' buttons?)

2) a knob on a cap: *on fortune's cap we are
not the very b.* Hml. II, 2, 233..

3) bud: *the canker galls the infants of the spring
too oft before their —s be disclosed*, Hml. I, 3, 40.

Button, vb., to fasten with buttons; with
up: *one whose hard heart is —ed up with steel*, Err.
IV, 2, 34.

Button-hole, the loop in which a button
is caught: *let me take you a b. lower*, LLL V, 2,
706, perhaps = let me speak without ceremony.

Buttress, wall standing out and built to support
another wall: Mcb. I, 6, 7.

Butts, name in H8 V, 2, 10. 20. 33.

Butt-shaft, arrow: *Cupid's b.* LLL I, 2, 181.
*the very pin of his heart cleft with the blind bow-boy's
b.* Rom. II, 4, 16 (Nares: a kind of arrow used for
shooting at butts; formed without a barb, so as to
be easily extracted).

Buxom, lively, fresh, brisk: *of b. valour,* H5 III, 6, 27 (Pistol's speech). *a female heir, so b., blithe, and full of face,* Per. Prol. 23.

Buy, in the phrase *God buy you,* a contraction from *God be with you,* in the sense of the modern good-bye (M. Edd. generally *be with you*): As III, 2, 273. IV, 1, 31. V, 3, 41. Tw. IV, 2, 108. H5 IV, 3, 6. V, 1, 70. H6A III, 2, 73. Troil. III, 3, 294. Hml. II, 1, 69. II, 2, 575 (Qq *God buy to you*). IV, 4, 30. IV, 5, 200. Oth. I, 3, 189 (here Ff., certainly with good reason, *God be with you*). III, 3, 375.

Buy, vb. (impf. and partic. *bought*) to acquire by paying a price; absolutely: *to sell myself I can be well contented, so thou wilt b. and pay,* Ven. 514. *I will never b. and sell out of this word,* LLL III, 143. *I will b. with you, sell with you,* Merch. I, 3, 36. *I'ld have you b. and sell so,* Wint. IV, 4, 138. *before he'll b. again,* H6A III, 2, 43. *things created to b. and sell with groats,* Cor. III, 2, 10. *I bid for you as I do b.* Cymb. III, 6, 71 (as I pay indeed; M. Edd. *as I'ld b.*) etc. *To b.* of one: Wint. IV, 4, 230.

Transitively: *they b. their help,* Lucr. 913. 1067. Tp. V, 265. Wiv. II, 2, 206. IV, 4, 73. V, 5, 246. Meas. III, 2, 2. Err. I, 1, 58. IV, 1, 16. 88. IV, 3, 6. 8. Ado I, 1, 181. LLL II, 243. IV, 3, 386. V, 2, 224. 226. Merch. II, 2, 179. IV, 1, 93. As II, 4, 72. 88 etc. etc. *would all my wealth would b. this for a lie,* Cor. IV, 6, 161. *To b. a p. sth.:* Wiv. IV, 4, 69. All's IV, 1, 45 (*b. myself another*). Mcb. IV, 2, 40. *To b. sth. from a p.:* Ven. 517. Mcb. I, 7, 32. *To b. sth. of a p.:* Mids. II, 1, 122. All's IV, 1, 45. H6B III, 3, 18. Cor. I, 4, 5. Hml. IV, 7, 142. Lr. I, 1, 162. Oth. I, 3, 61. *To b. and sell =* to make a bargain of: *the cardinal does b. and sell his* (the king's) *honour as he pleases,* H8 I, 1, 192, cf. Mcb. IV, 2, 41. *bought and sold =* betrayed: *it would make a man mad as a buck, to be so bought and sold,* Err. III, 1, 72. *you are bought and sold,* John V, 4, 10. *from bought and sold lord Talbot,* H6A IV, 4, 13. *thy master is bought and sold,* R3 V, 3, 305. *thou art bought and sold among those of any wit,* Troil. II, 1, 51. *To b. out =* to redeem: *not being able to b. out his life,* Err. I, 2, 5. *dreading the curse that money may b. out,* John III, 1, 164. *they have bought out their services,* H4A IV, 2, 24. 35 (= bought themselves off from service). *an honour in him which —s out his fault,* Tim. III, 5, 17. *oft 'tis seen the wicked prize itself —s out the law,* Hml. III, 3, 60 (= quits the penalty).

To b. sometimes (cf. *to purchase*) = to acquire, to procure, to gain: *who —s a minute's mirth to wail a week?* Lucr. 213. *b. terms divine in selling hours of dross,* Sonn. 146, 11. *to be in love, where scorn is bought with groans,* Gentl. I, 1, 29. *a folly bought with wit,* 34. *to b. you a better husband,* Meas. V, 430. *the endeavour of this present breath may b. that honour,* LLL I, 1, 5. *the goose that you bought,* III, 110 (cf. 102). *with that I will go b. my fortunes,* As I, 1, 79. *blood hath bought blood and blows have answered blows,* John II, 329. *which* (his merit) *—s a place next to the king,* H8 I, 1, 65 etc. *till honour be bought up,* All's II, 1, 32 (till there is no honour left to be gained). *I have bought golden opinions from all sorts of people,* Mcb. I, 7, 32.

Very frequently it might be exchanged with *to pay* or *to pay for;* f. i. *beauty is bought by judgment of the eye,* LLL II, 15 (i. e. beauty is paid, its price

is fixed by the judgment of the purchaser). *can the world b. such a jewel?* Ado I, 1, 183. *thou and thy brother both shall b. this treason even with the dearest blood your bodies bear,* H6C V, 1, 68. *I never do him wrong, but he does b. my injuries,* Cymb. I, 1, 105 (he pays for them, as if they were benefits). *I bid for you, as I do b.* III, 6, 71. cf. *overbuy.* — This is especially the case in the phrase *to buy dear: you shall b. this sport as dear as all the metal in your shop will answer,* Err. IV, 1, 81. *you shall b. this dear,* Mids. III, 2, 426. *the lord of Stafford dear to-day hath bought thy likeness,* H4A V, 3, 7. *bought his climbing very dear,* H6B II, 1, 100. *who would not b. thee dear?* V, 1, 5. *and yet the end of all is bought thus dear, the breath is gone, and the sore eyes see clear,* Per. I, 1, 98.

Buyer, purchaser: Wint. IV, 4, 614. Hml. V, 1, 113.

Buzz, an interjection, or rather a sibilant sound to command silence: *the actors are come hither, my lord. B., b.* Hml. II, 2, 412.*

Buzz, subst., whisper: *on every dream, each b., each fancy,* Lr. I, 4, 348.

Buzz, vb., 1) to hum: *among the —ing pleased multitude,* Merch. III, 2, 182. *should be, should b.* Shr. II, 207 (quibble between *be* and *bee*). *—ing night-flies,* H4B III, 1, 11. H6C II, 6, 95. H8 III, 2, 55. Tit. III, 2, 64. Caes. V, 1, 37. Transitively: *and b. lamenting doings in the air,* Tit. III, 2, 62.

2) to whisper: *did you not of late days hear a —ing of a separation,* H8 II, 1, 148. *however these disturbers of our peace b. in the people's ears,* Tit. IV, 4, 7. Transitively: *where doth the world thrust forth a vanity that is not quickly —ed into his ears?* R2 II, 1, 26. *and b. these conjurations in her brain,* H6B I, 2, 99. *I will b. abroad such prophecies,* H6C V, 6, 86.

Buzzard, a mean kind of hawk: *O slow-winged turtle! shall a b. take thee?* Shr. II, 208. *while kites and —s prey at liberty,* R3 I, 1, 133. — In Shr. II, 207 and 209 probably = a buzzing insect, a beetle or a fly.

Buzzer, a whisperer, tale-bearer: *wants not —s to infect his ear with pestilent speeches of his father's death,* Hml. IV, 5, 90.

By, vb., = *aby,* a blundering correction of M. Edd. for *buy* in Mids. III, 2, 426 (cf. Err. IV, 1, 81. H4A V, 3, 7. H6B II, 1, 100. H6C V, 1, 68. Per. I, 1, 98).

By, prepos., close to, at the side of, with: *by Venus' side,* Ven. 180. *by her side,* 1165. *and by my side wear steel,* Wiv. I, 3, 84. *close by the Thames side,* III, 3, 16. *in a rock by the sea-side,* Tp. II, 2, 138. *dost thou wear thy wit by thy side,* Ado V, 1, 126. *sitting by a brook,* Pilgr. 43. 75. Shr. Ind. 2, 52. *by fountain clear,* Mids. II, 1, 29. *by a country fire,* Wiv. V, 5, 256. H4B II, 1, 95. *when icicles hang by the wall,* LLL V, 2, 922. *picture-like to hang by the wall,* Cor. I, 3, 12. Cymb. III, 4, 54. *lying by the violet in the sun,* Meas. II, 2, 166. *I live by the church,* Tw. III, 1, 3. 5. 7. *I dwell by the Capitol,* Caes. III, 3, 27. *to lie discoloured by this place of peace,* Rom. V, 3, 143. *in a bloody field by Shrewsbury,* H4B Ind. 24. *who ran away by Gad's hill,* II, 4, 333. *in the field by Tewksbury,* R3 I, 4, 56. II, 1, 111 (Ff. *at*). Used before persons: *here friend by friend in bloody channel lies,* Lucr. 1487. *except I be by Silvia,* Gentl. III, 1, 178. *you must walk by us on our other hand,* Meas. V,

17. *kneel by me*, 442. *stand by me*, Err. V, 185. *to sleep by hate*, Mids. IV, 1, 150. *as many as could well live one by another*, Merch. III, 5, 25. *she bid me stay by her a week*, Shr. II, 179. *'twas a commodity lay fretting by you*, 330. *stay you by this gentleman*, Tw. III, 4, 282. *an I were now by this rascal*, H4A II, 3, 24. *watch here by the king*, H4B IV, 5, 20. *that you be by her aloft*, H6B I, 4, 10. *if thou be found by me*, III, 2, 387. *to die by thee*, 400. *stay by me*, H6C I, 1, 31. *stay and lodge by me this night*, 32. *will you stand by us*, IV, 1, 145 (cf. *to stand by honour*, Troil. II, 2, 68. *you stayed well by't*, Ant. II, 2, 179; see *stand* and *stay*). *the goodliest woman that ever lay by man*, H8 IV, 1, 70. *an he had stayed by him*, Cor. II, 1, 143. *let them have cushions by you*, III, 1, 101. *here by Caesar*, Caes. III, 1, 162. *she shall be buried by her Antony*, Ant. V, 2, 361. *your being by me cannot amend me*, Cymb. IV, 2, 11.

Hence, denoting motion, = along the side of, past: *to seize the souls that wander by him*, Lucr. 882. *this music crept by me upon the waters*, Tp. I, 2, 391. *go on, out at the postern by the abbey-wall*, Gentl. V, 1, 9. *I love to walk by the Counter-gate*, Wiv. III, 3, 85. *to walk by this Herne's oak*, IV, 4, 40. *have for long run by the hideous law as mice by lions*, Meas. I, 4, 63. *as they fly by them*, Merch. I, 1, 14. *stray about by holy crosses*, V, 31. *jumps along by him*, As II, 1, 53. *creep like shadows by him*, Wint. II, 3, 34. *that gentleman that rode by Travers*, H4B I, 1, 55. *as I halt by them*, R3 I, 1, 23. *to come by him where he stands*, Cor. 2, 3, 46. 52. *came they not by you?* Mcb. IV, 1, 137. *goes slow and stately by them*, Hml. 1, 2, 202. — Hence used to indicate the stages of a way: *and so by many winding nooks he strays*, Gentl. II, 7, 31. *I will bring the doctor about by the fields*, Wiv. II, 3, 81. *he can come no other way but by this hedge-corner*, All's IV, 1, 2. *sent me over by Berkeley*, R2 II, 3, 33. *go along by him*, Caes. II, 1, 218 (i. e. call at his house in going home). *the enemy marching along by them*, IV, 3, 207.

By the way, 1) = on the way: Meas. V, 458. Err. V, 235. Mids. IV, 1, 204. Merch. III, 2, 231. 2) = by the by: Shr. IV, 2, 115 (cf. *way*).

The notion of *beside* also perceptible in the following phrases: *day by day*, = every day, Sonn. 75, 13. 117, 4. Tp. V, 163. All's III, 1, 18. Tit. V, 2, 58. *drop by drop*, Wiv. IV, 5, 100. *joint by joint*, Meas. V, 314. Troil. IV, 5, 233. Rom. V, 3, 35. *limb by limb*, Troil. IV, 5, 238. *man by man*, Mids. I, 2, 3. *man by man, boy by boy, servant by servant*, H4A III, 3, 65. *night by night*, H6B III, 1, 111. Rom. I, 4, 70. *name by name*, Troil. IV, 5, 160. *one by one*, Ven. 518. Compl. 38. Wint. V, 1, 13. H6B I, 3, 102. Caes. II, 1, 112. *piece by piece*, H4A V, 3, 27. *point by point*, H6C II, 5, 24. H8 I, 2, 7. Per. V, 1, 227. *step by step*, Tp. III, 3, 78. *wave by wave*, Tit. III, 1, 95.

No less in the phrase *'by one's self'* = alone, without company: *the king's son have I landed by himself*, Tp. I, 2, 221. *withdraw into a chamber by yourselves*, Ado V, 4, 11. *practise by myself*, Shr. I, 1, 83. *court her by herself*, I, 2, 137. *we'll have this song out by ourselves*, Wint. IV, 4, 315. *let him have a table by himself*, Tim. I, 2, 30. *Britain is a world by itself*, Cymb. III, 1, 13.

Likewise in the phrase *'to come by sth.'* (originally = to come beside, to come up with, and then to

obtain, to get possession of sth.): Tp. II, 1, 292. Gentl. III, 1, 125. V, 4, 96. Ado II, 1, 338. LLL III, 43. Merch. I, 1, 3. I, 2, 9 (cf. *come*).

The idea of 'way, direction' still discernible in cases, where it seems to denote simple locality: *by land*, Tp. V, 220. Ant. II, 6, 90. *by water*, II, 6, 89. *by sea and land*, Shr. V, 2, 149. *by flood and field*, Oth. I, 3, 135. *by east*, LLL I, 1, 248. *by east, west, north and south*, V, 2, 566. *by the west*, Mids. II, 1, 158. *by south and east*, H4A III, 1, 75. The idea of way, direction, acting together with that of instrumentality: *she takes him by the hand*, Ven. 361. 1124. *hanging by his neck*, 593. *catch her by the neck*, 872. cf. Lucr. 253. Tp. II, 2, 108. Wiv. I, 1, 308. IV, 6, 44. V, 5, 155. Meas. I, 3, 29. III, 1, 109. IV, 1, 55. V, 343. Ado V, 1, 90. 318. LLL IV, 1, 114. As I, 2, 224. II, 7, 199. IV, 3, 163. Tw. I, 3, 70. H6C V, 4, 69. Oth. III, 3, 423. *By the hand* = at hand, near: *till we had his assistance by the hand*, H4B I, 3, 21.

Local presence leading over to the idea of time: *by moonshine*, Tp. V, 37. *by moonlight*, Mids. I, 1, 30. *run from her by her own light*, Err. III, 2, 99. *by his light did all the chivalry of England move*, H4B II, 3, 19. *I may read by them* (the exhalations) Caes. II, 1, 45. *by that music let us all embrace*, H4A V, 2, 99. Hence: *by day*, Gentl. III, 1, 109. H6B I, 1, 26. *by night*, Gentl. III, 1, 110. III, 2, 83. H6B I, 1, 26. *by day and night*, Tp. I, 2, 336. *by night and day*, Err. IV, 2, 60 (see *day* and *night*). And in general = at a certain point of time, but always meaning: when it has come, or will come to that time: *by the next moon prepare to die*, Mids. I, 1, 83. *to con them by to-morrow night*, I, 2, 103. *by day's approach look to be visited*, III, 2, 430. *meet me all by break of day*, V, 429. cf. Ado V, 1, 261. V, 4, 13. Merch. II, 6, 59. Shr. IV, 3, 190. All's I, 3, 255. III, 6, 82. John II, 219. R2 I, 3, 194. H4A II, 4, 564. Lr. V, 3, 114. Oth. IV, 1, 225. *by seven o'clock*, Gentl. III, 1, 226. Meas. II, 1, 34. IV, 2, 67. 124. Merch. II, 2, 122. As IV, 1, 184. H4A I, 2, 139. H5 III, 7, 168. Troil. III, 3, 296. *by the second hour*, R3 V, 3, 31. Troil. II, 1, 134. Caes. II, 1, 213. *By this* = by this time: *by this the love-sick queen began to sweat*, Ven. 175 (= when it had come to this). 697. 877. 973. 1165. Lucr. 1079. 1268. 1772. Wiv. IV, 1, 3. V, 5, 185. Err. III, 1, 115. V, 118. Ado I, 1, 3. III, 2, 79. Shr. IV, 1, 120. All's V, 3, 134. H6C IV, 3, V, 1, 3. V, 5, 90. Troil. V, 2, 183. Tit. III, 1, 109. IV, 3, 66. Caes. I, 3, 125. Lr. IV, 6, 45.

As it is used, like *with*, to denote nearness or company, so also to indicate the person subject to an activity: *I would thou hadst done so by Claudio*, Meas. V, 473 (= with Claudio, or rather in the case of Claudio). *though my mocks come home by me, I will now be merry*, LLL V, 2, 637. *I would they would forget me, like the virtues which our divines lose by 'em*, Cor. II, 3, 64. *so disguise shall, by the disguised, pay with falsehood false exacting*, Meas. III, 2, 294: i. e. disguise shall be allowed to pay with falsehood the demands of one who is himself a disguised hypocrite. (cf. the modern use of *to deal*; see also *to set* in such phrases as *to set little by sth.*, Gentl. I, 2, 82). — Thus, after the verbs of speaking and thinking, *by* sometimes comes to be = *of*: *virtuous in any thing that I do know by her*, Ado V, 1, 312 (originally = with her, in her, about her). *that 'many' may be meant* by the fool multitude, Merch. II, 9, 26. *how say you by the French lord?* I, 2, 58. *I would not have him know so much by me*, LLL IV, 3, 150. *thus I conceive by him*, Shr. V, 2, 22 (a quibble). *by him and by this woman here what know you?* All's V, 3, 237. *speak the truth by her*, Gentl. II, 4, 151. *but by bad courses may be understood that their events can never fall out good*, R2 II, 1, 213. *how think you by that?* H6B II, 1, 16. *how say you by this change?* Oth. I, 3, 17. *to speak ... not by your own instruction, nor by the matter which your heart prompts you*, Cor. III, 2, 54.

Nearly related to the idea of a way is that of a means or instrument: *by your art*, Tp. I, 2, 1. *by foul play*, 62. *by telling of it*, 100. *by providence divine*, 159. 180. 204. 275. 497. II, 2, 38. III, 2, 49. V, 40 etc. etc. *they live by your bare words*, Gentl. II, 4, 46. *I live by food*, As II, 7, 14. Frequently after *to appear*, *to know*, *to mean*, and similar words: *I can* (remember); *by what? by any other house or person?* Tp. I, 2, 42. *I know it by thy trembling*, II, 2, 83. *I know her by her gait*, IV, 102. *it appears by their bare liveries*, Gentl. II, 4, 45. IV, 2, 89. *what mean you by that saying?* V, 4, 167. Wiv. III, 1, 73. III, 5, 12. V, 2, 7. 16. V, 5, 208. *I thought by your readiness in the office...*, Meas. II, 1, 275. V, 330. 499. *gather the sequel by that went before*, Err. I, 1, 96 (cf. H6A II, 3, 69). *I guess it stood in her chin, by the salt rheum*, III, 2, 131. IV, 4, 96. LLL II, 229. *to choose love by another's eyes*, Mids. I, 1, 140. *the mazed world, by their increase, now knows not which is which*, II, 1, 114. 264. III, 2, 236. 349. V, 257. As IV, 3, 8. H6A III, 1, 124. *you seem to understand me, by each at once her chappy fingers laying upon her skinny lips*, Mcb. I, 3, 44. — After the verbs of measuring: *that* (thy mind) *they measure by thy deeds;* Sonn. 69, 10. *He would have weighed thy brother by himself*, Meas. V, 111. *I measure him by my own spirit*, Ado II, 3, 149. *we measure them by weary steps*, LLL V, 2, 194. — Peculiar expressions: *she is dead, and by strange manner*, Caes. IV, 3, 189. *his solicitings, as they fell out by time, by means and place*, Hml. II, 2, 127. *to part by the teeth the unowed interest of proud-swelling state*, John IV, 3, 146. *either send the chain or send me by some token*, Err. IV, 1, 56 (i. e. so that I may prove the legitimacy of my commission by a token). *say, by this token, I desire his company*, Meas. IV, 3, 144. *go, by this token*, R3 IV, 2, 80. — *By heart, by leave, patience, pardon*, see the resp. words.

To the same source must be traced its use in denoting the sum of difference between things: *too much by one*, Gentl. V, 4, 52. *ere the ships could meet by twice five leagues*, Err. I, 1, 101. *one* (child) *too much by thee*, Ado IV, 1, 131. *too long by half a mile*, LLL V, 2, 54. 760. Mids. V, 63. Tw. V, 139. Wint. IV, 4, 724. V, 3, 29. H4A III, 2, 73. H8 I, 2, 208. Cor. III, 1, 103. Hml. II, 2, 466. Similarly: *by many a year before*, H8 II, 4, 49. *not to come near our person by ten mile*, H4B V, 5, 69. — *By how much .... by so much* = the more, the more: *by how much defence is better than no skill, by so much is a horn more precious than to want*, As III, 3, 62. *by how much unexpected, by so much we must awake endeavour*, John II, 80. *and so much less of shame in me remains, by how much of me their reproach contains*, Compl. 189. *you are the better at proverbs, by how much a fool's bolt is soon shot*, H5 III, 7, 131. *by how much she stri-*

ves to do him good, she shall undo her credit with the Moor, Oth. II, 3, 364. *by so much is the wonder in extremes*, H6C III, 2, 115 (= the more).

Equally, in expressing the measure, by which an action is regulated, especially the stages of a successive action: *make him by inch-meal a disease*, Tp. II, 2, 3. *which you shall find by every syllable a faithful verity*, Meas. IV, 3, 131. *sell by gross*, LLL V, 2, 319. *loves her by the foot; he may not by the yard*, 674. *'tis purchased by the weight*, Merch. III, 2, 89. *utters it by great swarths*, Tw. II, 3, 162. *buy maidenheads by the hundreds*, H4A II, 4, 398. *by the dozens*, H8 V, 4, 33. *by ones, by twos, and by threes*, Cor. II, 3, 47. *he's to make his requests by particulars*, 48. *will bear the knave by the volume*, III, 3, 33. *they'll give him death by inches*, V, 4, 42. *peruse him by items*, Cymb. I, 4, 7. *I will believe you by the syllable*, Per. V, 1, 169. Similarly: *compound with him by the year*, Meas. IV, 2, 25. *two thousand ducats by the year*, Shr. II, 371. *a thousand pounds by the year*, H5 I, 1, 19. *O that I knew he were but in by the week*, LLL V, 2, 61. *what expense by the hour seems to flow from him*, H8 III, 2, 108. *how Diomed, a whole week by days, did haunt you*, Troil. IV, 1, 9. *for quick accumulation of renown, which he achieved by the minute*, Ant. III, 1, 20, i. e. every minute; cf. *should by the minute feed on life and lingering by inches waste you*, Cymb. V, 5, 51. Strangely, but intelligibly: *this was but as a fly by an eagle*, Ant. II, 2, 186, i. e. as a fly for every one to feed on in a company of eagles.

Serving also to denote the instrumentality of persons: *and do pronounce by me*, Tp. III, 3, 76. *send him by your two men to Datchet-mead*, Wiv. III, 3, 141. *she sent for you by Dromio home to dinner*, Err. II, 2, 156. *ourselves we do remember by you*, V, 292 (by seeing you bound). *I see by you I am a sweet-faced youth*, 418. *or else by him my love deny*, As IV, 3, 62. *send for your daughter by your servant here*, Shr. IV, 4, 58. *I sent to her by this same coxcomb tokens and letters*, All's III, 6, 122. *you'll nothing to my lord by me?* Tw. III, 1, 148. *Bohemia greets you by me*, Wint. V, 1, 181. *the king by me requests your presence*, John IV, 3, 22. *send him word by me*, V, 3, 7. *the countess by me entreats*, H6A II, 2, 40. *the commons send you word by me*, H6B III, 2, 243. *by her he had two children*, IV, 2, 147. *send to her by the man that slew her brothers a pair of bleeding hearts*, R3 IV, 4, 271. H8 IV, 2, 117. Tit. I, 181. IV, 2, 10. *and by him do my duties to the senate*, Oth. III, 2, 2. *forborne the getting of a lawful race, and by a gem of women*, Ant. III, 13, 108. *she soon shall know of us, by some of ours*, V, 1, 57. *the Roman emperor's letters, sent by a consul to me*, Cymb. IV, 2, 385. Similarly: *but we do learn by those*, Meas. I, 4, 53 (= we are informed). *this you might have heard of here by me or by some other*, Cymb. II, 4, 77. *had his titles by Tenantius whom he served with glory*, I, 1, 31. cf. *this island's mine by Sycorax my mother*, Tp. I, 2, 331. *by her I claim the kingdom*, H6B II, 2, 47. *by my mother I derived am from Lionel Duke of Clarence*, H6A II, 5, 74. *you are damned both by father and mother*, Merch. III, 5, 18. so (virtuous uncles) *hath this both by the father and mother*, R3 II, 3, 22. *better it were they all came by the father, or by the father there were none at all*, 23. cf. *by the mother's side*, John I, 163. Ant. II, 2, 120 (see *side*).

The idea of instrumentality prevails also in the

phrase *'by the name of'*: *call us by our names,* Err. II,
2, 168. IV, 3, 3. *I have wooed Margaret by the name
of Hero,* Ado III, 3, 155. *by that name as oft as Lancaster doth speak of you, his cheek looks pale,* H4A
III, 1, 8. *crowned by the name of Henry the Fourth,*
H6B II, 2, 23. *that which we call a rose by any other
name would smell as sweet,* Rom. II, 2, 44. *this diamond he greets your wife withal by the name of most
kind hostess,* Mcb. II, 1, 16. Hence the following expression: *if thou takest up the princess by that forced
baseness which he has put upon't,* Wint. II, 3, 78 (i. e.
as if she were a bastard, which name he falsely gives
her).

It is the same after the verbs *to conjure* and *to
swear;* and in adjurations without a verb preceding:
she conjures him by high almighty Jove, Lucr. 568.
swear by this bottle, Tp. II, 2, 125. *I charge you by
the law,* Merch. IV, 1, 138. *to break an oath by him,*
R3 IV, 4, 381. *by all above,* Sonn. 110, 6. Tp. II, 2,
127. 148. III, 1, 53. III, 2, 17. 56. III, 3, 1. IV, 226.
Gentl. I, 2, 41. II, 5, 1. III, 1, 166. IV, 1, 36. IV, 2,
100. V, 4, 139. Wiv. I, 1, 88. 156. 161. 168. 173.
II, 1, 14 *(by me)* etc. etc.

The idea of instrumentality passing into that of
causality: *the remembrance of my former love is by a
newer object quite forgotten,* Gentl. II, 4, 195. *by his
master's command,* IV, 2, 79. *as school-maids change
their names by vain, though apt affection,* Meas. I, 4,
48. *I do it ... from Lord Angelo by special charge,*
I, 2, 123. *he would not, but by gift of my chaste body,
release my brother,* V, 97. *might have ta'en revenge,
by so receiving a dishonoured life,* IV, 4, 34. *howsoever
it seems not in him, by some large jests he will make,*
Ado II, 3, 205. *challenge me by these deserts,* LLL V,
2, 815. *feared by their breed and famous by their birth,*
R2 II, 1, 52. *boiling choler ... by sight of these our
enemies,* H6A V, 4, 122. *whereby his suit was granted,*
H8 I, 1, 186. *and by those* (ways of honour) *claim
their greatness, not by blood,* V, 5, 39. *all good seeming,
by thy revolt, shall be thought put on for villany,* Cymb.
III, 4, 57.

And hence = **according to**: *men will kiss even
by their own direction,* Ven. 216. *that posterity which
by the rights of time thou needs must have,* 759. *by
consent,* Tp. II, 1, 203. *of a better nature than he
appears by speech,* I, 2, 497. *and by your own report
a linguist,* Gentl. IV, 1, 56. *which served me as fit by
all men's judgments,* IV, 4, 167. *goes to them by his
note,* Wiv. IV, 2, 64. *I durst have denied that ... by
what rule?* Err. II, 2, 69. *there is no more sailing by
the star,* Ado III, 4, 58. *that she were a maid by these
exterior shows,* IV, 1, 41. *call forth your actors by the
scroll,* Mids. I, 2, 16. *choose by show,* Merch. II, 9, 26.
what should his sufferance be by Christian example,
III, 1, 73. *an hour by his dial,* As II, 7, 33. *we quarrel
in print, by the book,* V, 4, 94 (Rom. I, 5, 112). *the
property by what it is should go, not by the title,* All's
II, 3, 137. *that the great figure of a council frames by
self-unable motion,* III, 1, 13. *an it be not four by the
day,* H4A II, 1, 1. *fought a long hour by Shrewsbury
clock,* V, 4, 151. *I stay too long by thee,* H4B IV, 5,
94 (i. e. in thy opinion). *Talbot means no goodness
by his looks,* H6A III, 2, 72. *censure me by what you
were,* V, 5, 97. *so that, by this, you would not have him
die,* H6B III, 1, 243. *I will go by thy direction,* R3
II, 2, 153. *by the book he should have braved the east*

an hour ago, V, 3, 278. *I'll go along by your prescription,* H8 I, 1, 151. *to speak ... not by your own instruction,* Cor. III, 2, 53. *a catalogue of all the voices set
down by the poll,* III, 3, 10. *things of like value differing in the owners are prized by their masters,* Tim. I,
1, 171 (according to the worth of their masters). *a
recompense more fruitful than their offence can weigh
down by the dram,* V, 1, 154. *by the rule of that philosophy by which I did blame Cato,* Caes. V, 1, 101. *by
the clock 'tis day,* Mcb. II, 4, 6. *by the verities on thee
made good, may they not be my oracles as well?* III, 1,
8. *I will make questions and by them answer,* Oth. III,
4, 17. *that ebb and flow by the moon,* Lr. V, 3, 19.
those that make their looks by his, Ant. I, 5, 56. *by
him this creature is no such thing,* III, 3, 43 (according
to his account). *by all likelihood,* Cymb. I, 4, 54.
having proceeded but by both your wills, II, 4, 56. *there's
no going but by their consent,* Per. IV, 6, 208.

Lastly, nine times out of ten, denoting the agent
of something done: *cheated of our lives by drunkards,*
Tp. I, 1, 59. I, 2, 241. 270. 319 etc. etc.

By, adv., 1) **near; present**: *in a cool well by,*
Sonn. 154, 9. *I stole into a neighbour thicket by,* LLL
V, 2, 94. *go with me into the chantry by,* Tw. IV, 3,
24. *though we upon this mountain's basis by took stand,*
H5 IV, 2, 30. *the bleeding witness of her hatred by,*
R3 I, 2, 234. *close by,* Tp. I, 2, 216. *fast by,* H6B III,
2, 189. *hard by,* Wiv. III, 3, 10. IV, 2, 40. Merch.
IV, 1, 145. As III, 5, 75. Lr. III, 2, 61. *to be by,* Ven.
1101. Lucr. 1318. Tp. III, 1, 34. Gentl. III, 1, 175.
Err. III, 2, 56. Mids. III, 2, 108. Merch. IV, 1, 289.
V, 95. As I, 2, 174. Wint. V, 2, 3. John III, 1, 119.
R2 II, 1, 211. H6C V, 5, 55. Rom. I, 1, 112. *have by
some surgeon,* Merch. IV, 1, 257. *a copse that neighbours by,* Ven. 259. *thy lustre thickens when he shines
by,* Ant. II, 3, 28. *to sit by,* Tp. III, 1, 28. *to stand by,*
Ven. 282. Meas. V, 138. Merch. III, 2, 189. Shr. IV,
2, 5. H6B II, 4, 45. R3 I, 2, 128.

2) **aside, off**: *he throws that shallow habit by,*
Lucr. 1814. *go by, Jeronimy,* Shr. Ind. 1, 9. *let them
lay by their helmets,* R2 I, 3, 119. *hung their heads
and then lay by,* H8 III, 1, 11 (= lay down, were
smoothed). *offence's gilded hand may shove by justice,*
Hml. III, 3, 58. *set it by awhile,* V, 2, 295. *I will walk
by,* Oth. V, 2, 30. *stand by* = stand back: Ado IV,
1, 24. Shr. I, 2, 143. John IV, 3, 94. H6B II, 1, 72.
Ant. III, 11, 41 (cf. *stand*).

3) **after verbs of motion,** = **near, up**: *came
tripping by,* Sonn. 154, 4. *then came wandering by a
shadow like an angel,* R3 I, 4, 52.

4) **passing, past**: *there will come a Christian
by,* Merch. II, 5, 42. *as I came by,* R2 II, 2, 94. *who
was't came by?* Mcb. IV, 1, 140. *to go by* a) = to pass:
the particular accidents gone by, Tp. V, 305. *the time
goes by,* Tw. III, 4, 398. Wint. V, 3, 31. H5 IV, 3, 57.
Troil. I, 2, 184. Lr. I, 2, 168. Ant. III, 12, 6. b) =
to pass unnoticed: *lets go by the actor,* Meas. II, 2,
41 (i. e. leaves him unpunished). *the first's for me;
let her go by,* Shr. I, 2, 256 (= let her alone). *lets go
by the important acting of your dread command,* Hml.
III, 4, 107. *lets go by no vantages,* Cymb. II, 3, 50
(cf. *go*).

5) **by and by** = **presently**: Ven. 347. Lucr.
1292. Sonn. 73, 7. 75, 10. Tp. II, 1, 13. II, 2, 181.
III, 2, 156. Gentl. I, 3, 87. IV, 2, 103. Wiv. IV, 1, 7.
Meas. III, 1, 155. IV, 2, 73. Err. V, 351. LLL V, 2,

96. Mids. III, 1, 89. IV, 1, 185. As IV, 3, 139. Tw. III, 4, 192. IV, 2, 77. Wint. IV, 4, 518. R2 V, 5, 36. H4A I, 2, 42. V, 4, 109. H5 II, 2, 2. H6B I, 3, 2. II, 1, 142. Troil. I, 2, 304. Cor. II, 2, 119. V, 3, 202. Tit. III, 1, 202. Rom. II, 2, 151. III, 1, 175. III, 3, 76. Caes. II, 1, 305. IV, 3, 247. Hml. III, 2, 400. Oth. II, 1, 291. V, 2, 91. Ant. III, 11, 24 etc.

By-dependance, accessory circumstance: *and all the other —s from chance to chance,* Cymb. V, 5, 390 (some M. Edd. *by-dependancies*).

By-drinkings, drinkings between meals: H4A III, 3, 84.

By-gone, past, former: *this satisfaction the*

b. day proclaimed, Wint. I, 2, 32. *thy b. fooleries were but spices of it,* III, 2, 185.

By-past, of former times: *forced examples ... to put the b. perils in her way,* Compl. 158.

By-path, by-way, indirect means: *—s and indirect crooked ways,* H4B IV, 5, 185.

By-peep, to look aside: *then —ing in an eye base and unlustrous,* Cymb. I, 6, 108.

By-room, adjoining chamber: H4A II, 4, 32.

By-word, proverb: *made us —s to our enemies,* H6C I, 1, 42.

Byzantium, ancient name of Constantinople: Tim. III, 5, 60.

C.

C, the third letter of the alphabet: Tw. II, 5, 96. a note in music: Shr. III, 1, 76.

Cabbage, plant called in botany b r a s s i c a: *good worts! good c.,* Wiv. I, 1, 124.

Cabin, subst., 1) small room, small inclosed place: *let him* (the boar) *keep his loathsome c.,* Ven. 637. *she bade good night that kept my rest away, and daff'd me to a c. hanged with care,* Pilgr. 183. *make me a willow c. at your gate,* Tw. I, 5, 287. Figuratively: *her eyes are fled into the deep dark —s of her head,* Ven. 1038.

2) apartment in a ship: Tp. I, 1, 15. 18 *(to c.).* 28. I, 2, 197. Wint. III, 3, 24. R3 I, 4, 12. Hml. V, 2, 12. Ant. II, 7, 137.

Cabin, vb., 1) to lodge: *and c. in a cave,* Tit. IV, 2, 179. 2) to confine: *I am —ed, cribbed, confined, bound in to saucy doubts and fears,* Mcb. III, 4, 24.

Cabinet, close habitation (= cabin): *the lark from his moist c. mounts up on high,* Ven. 854. *they* (the veins) *mustering to the quiet c.* (the heart) Lucr. 442.

Cable, subst., strong rope or chain to which the anchor is fastened: Tp. I, 1, 34. H6C V, 4, 4. Oth. I, 3, 343. Ant. II, 7, 77. *what restraint and grievance the law will give him c.* (to put upon you) Oth. I, 2, 17 = will give him scope.

Cacaliban, corruption of *Caliban:* Tp. II, 2, 188.

Cackle, vb. to cry as a goose: Merch. V, 105. Lr. II, 2, 90.

Cacodemon, evil spirit: R3 I, 3, 144.

Caddis, worsted riband: *inkles, —es, cambrics,* Wint. IV, 4, 208. *caddis-garter,* H4A II, 4, 79 ('Garters were then worn in sight, and therefore to wear a coarse, cheap sort, was reproachful.' Nares).

Cade, 1) a small barrel: *stealing a c. of herrings,* H6B IV, 2, 36.

2) name in H6B: *John C. of Ashford,* III, 1, 357. IV, 2, 5. 33. IV, 8, 49 etc. etc.

Cadence, the flow of verses: *the golden c. of poesy,* LLL IV, 2, 126.

Cadent, continually falling: *with c. tears fret channels in her cheeks,* Lr. I, 4, 307.

Cadmus, the brother of Europa and founder of Thebes: Mids. IV, 1, 117.

Caduceus, Mercury's rod: *and Mercury, lose all the serpentine craft of thy c.* Troil. II, 3, 14.

Cadwal, name in Cymb. III, 3, 95. III, 6, 29. IV, 2, 188 etc.

Cadwallader, as it seems, = W a l e s, perhaps so called from the last of its British kings: H5 V, 1, 29 (Pistol's speech).

Caelius (O. Edd. *Celius*), name in Ant. III, 7, 74.

Caesar, 1) name; a) *Julius C.:* Meas. II, 1, 263. III, 2, 47. LLL V, 2, 618. As V, 2, 34. All's III, 6, 56. R2 V, 1, 2. H4B I, 1, 23. II, 4, 180. H6A I, 1, 56. I, 2, 139. H6B IV, 1, 137. IV, 7, 65. H6C V, 5, 53. R3 III, 1, 69. Caes. I, 1, 35 etc. Hml. III, 2, 108. V, 1, 236. Ant. I, 5, 29. III, 2, 54. Cymb. II, 4, 21. III, 1, 2 etc.

b) *Octavius Caesar:* Caes. III, 1, 276. V, 1, 24. 54 etc. Mcb. III, 1, 57. Ant. I, 1, 21 etc. Cymb. III, 1, 1 *(Augustus C.).* V, 5, 460 etc.

2) = emperor: Wiv. I, 3, 9. H5 V Chor. 28. H6C III, 1, 18 *(no bending knee will call thee C. now).* R3 IV, 4, 336 *(she shall be sole victress, —'s C.).* Tit. I, 10. Caes. III, 2, 257 *(here was a C.!).* Ant. V, 2, 8.

Caesarion, son of Cleopatra: Ant. III, 6, 6. III, 13, 162.

Cage, 1) an enclosure to keep birds in: Ado I, 3, 36. As III, 2, 389. Tit. III, 1, 84. Lr. V, 3, 9. Cymb. III, 3, 42.

2) a prison for petty malefactors: *his father had never a house but the c.* H6B IV, 2, 56.

3) wicker-work, basket: *I must up-fill this osier c. of ours with baleful weeds,* Rom. II, 3, 7.

Caged, 1) confined in a cage: *c. nightingales,* Shr. Ind. 2, 38. 2) like a cage or prison: *she would the c. cloister fly,* Compl. 249.

Cain, the first son of Adam and murderer of Abel: LLL IV, 2, 36. John III, 4, 79. R2 V, 6, 43. H4B I, 1, 157. H6A I, 3, 39. Hml. V, 1, 85.

Cain-coloured, of the colour of Cain's hair, reddish: *a C. beard,* Wiv. I, 4, 23.

Caitiff, subst., wretch, slave; masc. and fem.: *I* (Helena) *am the c. that do hold him to it,* All's III, 2, 117. *for queen, a very c. crowned with care,* R3 IV, 4, 100. *alas, poor c.* (Bianca) Oth. IV, 1, 109. *she finds a hound and asks the weary c. for his master,* Ven. 914. Used as a term of reproach: Meas. II, 1,

182. 193. V, 53. Tim. IV, 3, 235. V, 4, 71. Lr. II, 1, 64 (Ff. *coward*). III, 2, 55. Oth. V, 2, 318.

Used adjectively: *this pernicious c. deputy,* Meas. V, 88. *a c. recreant to my cousin Hereford,* R2 I, 2, 53. *a c. wretch,* Rom. V, 1, 52.

Caius, 1) Roman name: *C. Marcius,* Cor. I, 1, 7 etc. etc. Tit. IV, 3, 56. V, 2, 151. *C. Cassius,* Caes. II, 1, 162. 166. III, 1, 186. *C. Ligarius,* II, 1, 215. *C. Marcellus,* Ant. II, 6, 117. *C. Lucius,* Cymb. II, 3, 60. II, 4, 11 etc. assumed name of Kent, Lr. V, 3, 283.

2) name of the French doctor in Wiv. I, 2, 2. I, 4, 3 etc. etc.

Cake, subst., composition of flour, butter, sugar etc. baked into a small mass: *your c. there is warm within,* Err. III, 1, 71. *dried —s,* H4B II, 4, 159. Troil. I, 1, 15. 24. *old —s of roses,* Rom. V, 1, 47. *—s and ale,* Tw. II, 3, 124. *ale and —s,* H8 V, 4, 11. *our cake is dough on both sides* (= our plans are utterly hopeless) Shr. I, 1, 110; cf. *my c. is dough,* V, 1, 145.

Caked, coagulated, clotted: *their blood is c., 'tis cold, it seldom flows,* Tim. II, 2, 225.

Calaber, uncertain geographical name; it is certainly not Calabria: *the Dukes of Orleans, C., Bretagne and Alençon,* H6B I, 1, 7.

Calais (O. Edd. *Callice*), French town: John III, 3, 73. R2 I, 1, 126. IV, 13. 82. H5 III, 2, 48. III, 3, 56. III, 6, 150. IV, 8, 130. V Chor. 7. H6A IV, 1, 9. 170. H6C I, 1, 238.

Calamity, 1) great misfortune: *too well I feel the different plague of each c.* John III, 4, 60. *sticking together in c.* 67. *so armed to bear the tidings of c.* R2 III, 2, 105. *we must find an evident c., though we had our wish,* Cor. V, 3, 112. *thou art wedded to c.* Rom. III, 3, 3. *his wits are drowned and lost in his —ies,* Tim. IV, 3, 89.

2) misery: *there is no true cuckold but c.* Tw. I, 5, 57. *and free my country from c.* H6A I, 2, 81. *why should c. be full of words?* R3 IV, 4, 126. *you are transported by c.* Cor. I, 1, 77. *makes c. of so long life,* Hml. III, 1, 69.

Calchas, Trojan priest and father of Cressida: Troil. III, 3, 31. IV, 1, 37 etc.

Calculate, to compute future events: *why old men fool and children c.* Caes. I, 3, 65. Transitively, = to compute for prophetical purposes: *a cunning man did c. my birth,* H6B IV, 1, 34.

Caldron, see *Cauldron.*

Calendar, 1) almanac: Err. V, 404 (cf. I, 2, 41). Mids. III, 1, 54. John III, 1, 86. R3 V, 3, 276. Caes. II, 1, 42. Mcb. IV, 1, 134. Per. II, 1, 58.

2) note-book, record: *the care I have had to even your content, I wish might be found in the c. of my past endeavours,* All's I, 3, 4. *he is the card or c. of gentry,* Hml. V, 2, 114.

Calf (the genitive case in O. Edd. *calves*), 1) the young of the cow: Ado III, 3, 76. V, 1, 156 (*he hath bid me to a calves head*). V, 4, 50. LLL V, 1, 25. V, 2, 247. 248. 252. Wint. I, 2, 124. John I, 124. H6B III, 1, 210. IV, 2, 29. Troil. III, 2, 200. Tit. V, 1, 32. Hml. III, 2, 111. V, 1, 125. *calves' guts,* Cymb. II, 3, 34. *he that goes in the calves skin,* Err. IV, 3, 18 (cf. *buff*). *hang a calves skin on those recreant limbs,* John III, 1, 129. 131. 133.* *is not parchment made of sheep-skins? ay, and of calves skins too,* Hml. V, 1, 124.

2) the fleshy part of the leg behind: *his leg is too big for Hector's. More c.,*certain.* LLL V, 2, 645.

Calf-like, resembling calves: *c. they my lowing followed,* Tp. IV, 179.

Caliban, name in Tp. I, 2, 284. 308 etc. etc.

Calipolis, a character in the bombastic tragedy 'the Battle of Alcazar': H4B II, 4, 193.

Caliver, a kind of musket: H4A IV, 2, 21. H4B III, 2, 289. 292.

Calked, see *Caulked.*

Call, vb., I) to name: *thou might'st c. him a goodly person,* Tp. I, 2, 415. 417. III, 1, 51. III, 2, 104. V, 130. 175 etc. etc. *for mine, if I may c. offence,* Per. I, 2, 92. *they c. themselves saltiers,* Wint. IV, 4, 334. *c. you yourself Aeneas?* Troil. I, 3, 245. *called* = by name: Tp. I, 2, 66. Err. V, 342. Mids. II, 1, 34. H6A V, 3, 53 etc. *what do you c. your knight's name?* Wiv. III, 2, 21. *what may I c. your name?* Shr. II, 67. *know not now what name to call myself,* R2 IV, 259. *that thou hadst —ed me all these bitter names,* R3 I, 3, 236. *though thou —est thyself a hotter name than any is in hell,* Mcb. V, 7, 6. *if thy name be —ed Luce,* Err. III, 1, 53. *is not your name, sir, —ed Antipholus?* V, 286. *my name is —ed Vincentio,* Shr. IV, 5, 55. *my name is Pistol —ed,* H5 IV, 1, 62. — *what do ye c. there?* All's II, 3, 25. *good master What-ye-call't* (= Thingumbob) As III, 3, 74. — *how far is 't —ed to Forres?* Mcb. I, 3, 39.

II) to pronounce a name: *doth thy other mouth c. me?* Tp. II, 2, 101. *you were best to c. them generally,* Mids. I, 2, 2. *answer as I call you,* 18. *I c. thee not,* R3 I, 3, 234. *c. forth your actors,* Mids. I, 2, 15.

III) to order or tell a p. to come, to summon: *spirits which I have from their confines —ed,* Tp. IV, 121. *—ed forth the mutinous winds,* V, 42. 147. Gentl. I, 2, 51. II, 1, 9. II, 3, 62. Wiv. II, 2, 156. Meas. I, 1, 15. Err. I, 2, 29. IV, 3, 7. IV, 4, 149 etc. *a Greek invocation, to c. fools into a circle,* As II, 5, 61. *this your —ing back,* Oth. IV, 2, 45. *the next parliament, —ed for the truce of Winchester and Gloster,* H6A II, 4, 118. *to c. a present court of parliament,* H6B V, 3, 25. *our prerogative —s not your counsels, but our natural goodness imparts this,* Wint. II, 1, 164. *call not your stocks,* Lr. II, 2, 135. *to call to life,* H6A IV, 7, 81. *to c. to mind* = to recollect: Lucr. 1366. Gentl. III, 1, 6. H6A III, 3, 68. H8 II, 4, 34. *c. all your senses to you,* Wiv. III, 3, 125. *desire her call her wisdom to her,* Lr. IV, 5, 35. *will their good thoughts c. from him,* Ant. III, 6, 21. *thralled discontent, whereto the inviting time our fashion —s,* Sonn. 124, 8. *c. not me to justify the wrong,* 139, 1. *she —ed the saints to surety that she would never put it from her finger,* All's V, 3, 108. *you shall be —ed to no more payments,* Cymb. V, 4, 160. *to c. young Claudio to a reckoning,* Ado V, 4, 9. *I will c. him to so strict account,* H4A III, 2, 149. *to c. in question* (cf. *question*) = to consider: As V, 2, 6. Rom. I, 1, 235. Caes. IV, 3, 165. or = to doubt of: Tw. I, 4, 6. Sometimes *to c.* = to appoint, to designate, to choose: *is my lord of Winchester installed and —ed unto a cardinal's degree?* H6A V, 1, 29. *to be —ed into a huge sphere,* Ant. II, 7, 16. *are you —ed forth from out a world of men to slay the innocent?* R3 I, 4, 186 (Ff. *drawn*). — *To c.* = to awake: *if thou canst awake by four o'the clock, I prithee c. me,* Cymb. II, 2, 7.

To c. back usually = to summon to return, f. i. Gentl. I, 2, 51; but also = to call to mind: *she in thee —s back the lovely April of her prime,* Sonn. 3, 10; and = to revoke: *to c. back her appeal she intends unto his holiness,* H8 II, 4, 234.

To c. in = to invite to enter, f. i. Wiv. II, 2, 156; but also = to summon to appear: *c. in my sons to be my bail,* H6B V, 1, 111; = to make to return from pursuit: *call in the powers,* H4B IV, 3, 28. = to revoke, to resume what is in other hands: *if you c. in the letters patent that he hath,* R2 II, 1, 202.

To c. up = 1) to awake from sleep: *where once thou —'dst me up at midnight to fetch dew from . . . ,* Tp. I, 2, 228. *he is —ed up,* Meas. IV, 2, 94. *the unfolding star —s up the shepherd,* IV, 4, 219. *an there be any matter of weight chances, c. up me,* Ado III, 3, 91. 178. *we'll c. up the gentlemen,* H4A II, 1, 50. *c. up Lord Stanley,* R3 V, 3, 290. Oth. I, 1, 142. 176. — 2) to rouse, to raise in any way: *which you might, as cause had —ed you up, have held him to,* Cor. II, 3, 202. *we'll c. up our wisest friends,* Hml. IV, 1, 38.

IV) to utter a loud sound or cry for a certain purpose: *do not approach till thou dost hear me c.* Tp. IV, 50. *and will to-morrow with his trumpet c. to rouse a Grecian,* Troil. I, 3, 277. Lr. V, 3, 99. *I see him stamp thus and c. thus: come on, you cowards,* Cor. I, 3, 35. *to mourn thy crosses, with thy daughter's, c. and give them repetition to the life,* Per. V, 1, 246. Especially to attract notice on a purposed visit: *who —s?* Gentl. IV, 3, 4. *go knock and c.* Wiv. IV, 5, 9. 17. *who's that which —s?* Meas. I, 4, 6. *who —s?* Merch. V, 46. *this is the house; please it you that I c.?* Shr. IV, 4, 1. *I were best not c., I dare not c.* Cymb. III, 6, 19. *before I entered here, I —ed,* 47 etc. etc. Hence = to make a visit or a stop at a place: *this is the hour that Silvia entreated me to c.* Gentl. IV, 3, 2. *who —ed here of late?* Meas. IV, 2, 77. *to-day, as I came by, I —ed there,* R2 II, 2, 94. Followed by *at: c. at Flavius' house,* Meas. IV, 5, 6. *to c. at all the ale-houses,* Ado III, 3, 44. Transitively, = to seek, to come for: *I'll c. you at your house,* Meas. IV, 4, 18. *we'll c. thee at the cubiculo,* Tw. III, 2, 56.

To c. to a p. = 1) to cry to, to tell to come: *the keeper of the prison, c. to him,* Wint. II, 2, 1. 2) to apply to a p. for assistance: *if any power pities wretched tears, c. that I c.* Tit. III, 1, 210. *I'll tell you true, I'll c. to you,* Tim. I, 2, 223.

To c. for = to ask for, to demand: *your father —s for you,* Gentl. I, 3, 88. *the advantage of the time prompts me aloud to c. for recompense,* Troil. III, 3, 3. Err. III, 1, 34. Shr. III, 2, 172. John II, 39. H4A I, 2, 57. H6A I, 3, 84. V, 3, 66. R3 I, 3, 320. H8 V, 2, 7. Tit. III, 1, 205. Rom. IV, 4, 2. Ant. IV, 5, 7 etc.

To c. upon = 1) to invoke: *he that —s on thee* (as his Muse) Sonn. 38, 11. *whilst I alone did c. upon thy aid,* 79, 1. *forgot upon your dearest love to c., whereto all bonds do tie me,* 117, 3. *and c. upon my soul within the house.* Tw. I, 5, 288. *it is my soul that —s upon my name,* Rom. II, 2, 165. — 2) to cry out for, to apply to: *the undeserver may sleep, when the man of action is —ed on,* H4B II, 4, 407. *nor —ed upon for high feats done to the crown,* H8 I, 1, 60. *who is it in the press that —s on me?* Caes. I, 2, 15. *who —s on Hamlet?* Hml. IV, 2, 3. *thou —est on him that hates thee,* Lr. III, 7, 88. In a less emphatical sense:

I am bound to c. upon you (viz. for your evidence); *and I pray you, your name?* Meas. III, 2, 167. *speak not till we c. upon you,* V, 287. Caes. II, 2, 122. — 3) to demand, to claim: *a very serious business —s on him,* All's II, 4, 41. *your own business —s on you,* Merch. I, 1, 63. Hence = to solicit payment: *what need I be so forward with him* (viz death) *that —s not on me?* H4A V, 1, 130. *my master is awaked by great occasion to c. upon his own,* Tim. II, 2, 22. — 4) to come to speak to, to meet: *at that place c. upon me,* Meas. III, 1, 278. *may be I will c. upon you anon,* IV, 1, 23. *there have I made my promise to c. upon him,* 36. *look to thy bark: I'll not be long before I c. upon thee,* Wint. III, 3, 9. — 5) to visit: *to c. upon him,* Troil. II, 3, 119. *remember that you c. on me to-day,* Caes. II, 2, 122. *to c. timely on him,* Mcb. II, 3, 51. *I'll c. upon you ere you go to bed,* Hml. III, 3, 34. And in a moral sense: *full surfeits and the dryness of his bones c. on him for 't,* Ant. I, 4, 28.

To c. out = to cry loudly or instantly: *sometimes you would c. out for Cicely,* Shr. Ind. 2, 91. *a joy past joy —s out on me,* Rom. III, 3, 173 (= asks for, invites me instantly).

Call, subst. 1) summons: *tapsters answering every c.* Ven. 849. *to come at traitors' —s,* R2 III, 3, 181. *why he appears upon this c. of the trumpet,* Lr. V, 3, 119.

2) an instrument to call or entice birds: *another way I have to man my haggard, to make her come and know her keeper's c.* Shr. IV, 1, 197 (perhaps to be taken in the first signification). *they would be as a c. to train ten thousand English to their side,* John III, 4, 174.

Calling, subst., 1) appellation: *I am more proud to be Sir Rowland's son, and would not change that c.* As I, 2, 245.

2) vocation, profession: *you have paid the prisoner the very debt of your c.* Meas. III, 2, 265. Ado IV, 1, 170. As III, 3, 108. H6A III, 1, 32. H8 II, 4, 108. V, 3, 69. Per. IV, 2, 43 (except in the last passage, always used of the ecclesiastical profession).

Callot or **Callat** or **Callet,** a woman of bad character, a trull: *a c. of boundless tongue,* Wint. II, 3, 90. *contemptuous base-born c. as she is,* H6B I, 3, 86. *to make this shameless c. know herself,* H6C II, 2, 145. *a beggar in his drink could not have laid such terms upon his c.* Oth. IV, 2, 121.

Calm, adj., quiet, serene, not stormy: *seas,* Tp. V, 314. Err. I, 1, 92. Cor. IV, 1, 6. *be c., good wind,* Gentl. I, 2, 118. *in the —est night,* H4B III, 1, 28. Figuratively, = tranquil, undisturbed by passion or troubles: *an humble gait, c. looks,* Lucr. 1508. *what dangerous action would I not undergo for one c. look,* Gentl. V, 4, 42. *c. words,* John II, 229. *to whose high will we bound our c. contents,* R2 V, 2, 38. *the cankers of a c. world and a long peace,* H4A IV, 2, 32. *the bloody-minded queen that led c. Henry, as doth a sail, fill'd with a fretting gust, command an argosy,* H6C II, 6, 34. *be c.* Cor. III, 1, 37. 57. *c. submission,* Rom. III, 1, 76. *that drop of blood that's c.,* Hml. IV, 5, 117. *as c. as virtue,* Cymb. V, 5, 174. Adverbially: *how c. and gentle I proceeded,* Ant. V, 1, 75.

Calm, subst., serenity, stillness, tranquillity: *a soul as even as a c.* H8 III, 1, 166. *the unity and married c. of states,* Troil. I, 3, 100. *our bloods* *are now in c.* IV, 1, 15. *a sudden c.* Rom. III, 5, 136. *if after every tempest come such —s,* Oth. II, 1, 187 (Qq *calmness*). Mrs. Quickly confounds *calm* with *qualm,* and Falstaff improves upon it: *sick of a c.; yea, good faith. So is all her sect; an they be once in a c., they are sick,* H4B II, 4, 40—42.

Calm, vb. 1) to appease: *c. the fury of this flaw,* H6B III, 1, 354. *c. the storm,* H6C III, 3, 38. *this tempest,* Tit. IV, 2, 160. *seas,* Per. II, 1, 138. Tropically: *to c. contending kings,* Lucr. 939. *we'll c. the Duke of Norfolk,* R2 I, 1, 159. *their mutiny,* H6B III, 2, 128. *his contumelious spirit,* 204. *soon —ed,* Troil. IV, 5, 99. *to c. my thoughts,* Tit. I, 46. *these fits,* II, 1, 134. *c. thee,* IV, 1, 83. IV, 4, 29. *his rage,* Hml. IV, 7, 193.

2) to becalm, to keep from motion by intercepting the wind: *a ship that, having scaped a tempest, is straightway —ed and boarded with a pirate,* H6B IV, 9, 33 (F1 *calme*). *beleed and —ed,* Oth. I, 1, 30 (here the prefix *be* may belong to both verbs).

3) intr. to become serene: *her cloudy looks will c. ere night,* Pilgr. 312.

Calmly, quietly, tranquilly: *and c. run on in obedience,* John V, 4, 56. *c., I do beseech you,* Cor. III, 3, 31. Hml. IV, 5, 116.

Calmness, stillness of the sea: *if after every tempest come such c.* Oth. II, 1, 187 (Ff. *calms*). Freedom from passion, mildness: *defend yourself by c. or by absence,* Cor. III, 2, 95.

Calphurnia (most M. Edd. *Calpurnia*), the wife of Caesar: Caes. I, 2, 1 etc.

Calumniate, to slander: *envious and —ing time,* Troil. III, 3, 174. *as if those organs had deceptious functions, created only to c.* V, 2, 124.

Calumnious, slanderous: All's I, 3, 61. H8 V, 1, 113. Hml. I, 3, 38.

Calumny, slander: Meas. II, 4, 159. III, 2, 197. Wint. II, 1, 72. 73. Hml. III, 1, 141.

Calve, vb., to bring forth (used as of a cow): *not Romans, though —d i' the porch o' the Capitol,* Cor. III, 1, 240.

Calydon: *the prince of C.* H6B I, 1, 235, i. e. Meleager, whose life depended on a brand kept by his mother Althaea and was destroyed by her throwing it into the fire.

Cam, see *Kam.*

Cambio, name in Shr. II, 83. 86. IV, 4, 74 etc.

Camblet, see *Chamblet.*

Cambria, ancient name of the western part of England: Cymb. III, 2, 44. V, 5, 17.

Cambric, fine white linen: Wint. IV, 4, 208. Cor. I, 3, 95. Per. IV Prol. 24.

Cambridge: *Richard Earl of C.,* H5 II Chor. 23. II, 2, 13 etc. H6A II, 5, 54. 84. H6B II, 2, 45.

Cambyses, king of ancient Persia: *I will do it in king C. vein,* H4A II, 4, 425 (allusion to Thomas Preston's "Lamentable Tragedy, mixed full of pleasant mirth, containing the life of Cambyses king of Persia").

Camel, the animal Camelus: R2 V, 5, 16. Troil. I, 2, 271. II, 1, 58. Cor. II, 1, 267. Hml. III, 2, 394. 395. Term of reproach for a blunt, heavy fellow.

Cameleon, see *Chameleon.*

Camelot, place in Somersetshire, where great numbers of geese were bred: *goose, if I had you upon*

Sarum plain, I'ld drive ye cackling home to C., Lr. II, 2, 90.

Camillo, name in Wint. I, 1, 1. 2, 209 etc.

Camlet, see *Chamblet.*

Camomile, the plant Matricaria Chamomilla: *though the c. the more it is trodden on the faster it grows,* H4A II, 4, 441.

Camp, subst., the resting-place of an army: Lucr. Arg. 13. 18. All's IV, 1, 93. IV, 3, 200. 219. V, 3, 188. 194. H4A IV, 1, 30. H4B I, 1, 113. H5 II, 1, 117. III, 6, 81. IV Chor. 4. IV, 1, 25. 72. 303. IV, 4, 80. Troil. II, 3, 20. Cor. I, 7, 7. I, 9, 61. Tit. IV, 1, 64. IV, 2, 180. Tim. V, 1, 183. Caes. V, 3, 105. Oth. III, 3, 345. Ant. IV, 5, 8. IV, 8, 1.

Camp, vb. 1) intr. to pitch a camp, to fix tents: *sent him forth from courtly friends, with —ing foes to live,* All's III, 4, 14.

2) to lodge, to harbour, to serve as a camp for: *had our great palace the capacity to c. this host,* Ant. IV, 8, 33.

Campeius: *Cardinal C.* H8 II, 1, 160. II, 2, 97. III, 2, 56.*

Can, subst., a drinking vessel: *I hate it as an unfilled c.* Tw. II, 3, 7.

Can, vb., to be able, to have power (2. pers. *can* for *canst* in H4A II, 2, 34: *list if thou can hear the tread of travellers;* Q1 and most M. Edd. *canst*).

Absolutely: *they c. well on horseback* (= they are skilful horsemen). Hml. IV, 7, 85 (Ff *ran*). *she never could away with me,* H4B III, 2, 213 (cf. *away*). *I can no more,* H6B III, 2, 120. 365. H8 IV, 2, 173. Hml. V, 2, 331. Ant. IV, 15, 59 (= my strength fails me).

Followed by an accusative: *the priest in surplice white, that defunctive music can,* Phoen. 14 (knows, is skilled in). *the strongest suggestion our worser genius can,* Tp. IV, 1, 27. *all I can is nothing to her,* Gentl. II, 4, 165. *for what, alas, can these my single arms?* Troil. II, 2, 135. *come what sorrow can, it cannot countervail the exchange of joy,* Rom. II, 6, 3 (but here *what* may not be object, but subject of *can*). *what can man's wisdom in the restoring his bereaved sense?* Lr. IV, 4, 8 (Q1 *wisdom do*). *and on it said a century of prayers, such as I can, twice o'er,* Cymb. IV, 2, 392 (= know).

Regularly followed by an infinitive: Tp. I, 1, 23. I, 2, 38. 40. 41. 173. 186 etc. etc. *cannot,* Tp. I, 1, 26. II, 1, 242. III, 1, 92 etc. etc. *could,* Tp. I, 2, 360. 439. II, 1, 265 etc. etc. *I can tell you* = I dare say: *this will shake your shaking, I can tell you, and that soundly,* Tp. II, 2, 88. *cannot but* = must necessarily: Meas. V, 7. Ant. III, 4, 6 etc. *no more my fortune can but curse the cause,* H6A IV, 3, 43. *can't no other but, I your daughter, he must be my brother?* All's I, 3, 171, i. e. is there no other way but, when I am your daughter, he must be my brother?

Used in the sense of *may: what is't thou canst demand?* Tp. I, 2, 245. *here can I sit alone, unseen of any,* Gentl. V, 4, 4. *grow this to what adverse issue it can, I will put it in practice,* Ado II, 2, 53. *say what thou canst, I'll go along with thee,* As I, 3, 107. *but this I will not do, do how I can,* II, 3, 35. *I will not stir from this place, do what they can,* Mids. III, 1, 125. *do what you can, yours will not be entreated,* Shr. V, 2, 89. *look how we can, or sad or merrily, interpretation will misquote our looks,* H4A V, 2, 12. *where each man thinks all is writ he speken can*, Per. II Prol. 12. *the hand could pluck her back that shoved her on*, Ant. I, 2, 131 (= would like to). *yes, something you can deny for your own safety*, II, 6, 95. *if we fail, we then can do't at land*, III, 7, 53. Lr. II, 4, 249.

Can, old orthography for *gan* (or = did?): *through the velvet leaves the wind, all unseen, can passage find*, LLL IV, 3, 106 (Pilgr. 232 *gan*). *and every one with claps can sound: our heir apparent is a king!* Per. III Prol. 36.

Canakin, little can: Oth. II, 3, 71. 72.

Canary, subst. 1) wine from the Canary islands, sweet sack: *drink c. with him*, Wiv. III, 2, 89 (quibble in 90). *a cup of c.* Tw. I, 3, 85. 88. *you have drunk too much —ies*, H4B II, 4, 29 (Mrs. Quickly's speech).

2) a quick and lively dance: *breathe life into a stone, quicken a rock, and make you dance c. with spritely fire and motion*, All's II, 1, 77. cf. the quibble in Wiv. III, 2, 89 — 91.

What Mrs. Quickly means by the word in Wiv. II, 2, 61 and 64, it is not easy to say; most Intpp. suspect *quandary*, but this word is unknown to Sh.

Canary, vb., to dance: *to jig off a tune at the tongue's end, c. to it with your feet*, LLL III, 12.

Cancel, vb., to annul, destroy: *an expired date, —ed ere well begun*, Lucr. 26. *—ed my fortunes*, 934. *through her wounds doth fly life's lasting date from —ed destiny*, 1729. *weep afresh love's long since —ed woe*, Sonn. 30, 7. *c. all grudge*, Gentl. V, 4, 143. *the end of life —s all bands*, H4A III, 2, 157. *—ing your fame*, H6B I, 1, 99. *his statutes —ed*, H6C V, 4, 79. *c. his bond of life*, R3 IV, 4, 77. *our —ed love*, Rom. III, 3, 98. *the power to c. his captivity*, Caes. I, 3, 102. *c. and tear to pieces that great bond*, Mcb. III, 2, 49. *c. these cold bonds*, Cymb. V, 4, 28.

Cancel, subst., destruction: *we might proceed to c. of your days*, Per. I, 1, 113 (Qq *counsel of*; Ff *cancel off*; it may very well be the verb enforced by the adverb *off*).

Cancer, the sign of the summer solstice: *add more coals to C. when he burns*, Troil. II, 3, 206.

Candidatus, Roman name of a suitor for a high office, so called from his white gown: *be c. then and put it on*, Tit. I, 185.

Candle, a taper, a light: Wiv. V, 5, 106. LLL IV, 3, 269. Mids. V, 253. Merch. II, 9, 79. V, 90. 92. Shr. IV, 5, 14. Tw. IV, 2, 87. John III, 3, 12 (*bell, book and c.*; see *book*). H4A II, 1, 49. H4B I, 2, 177. 179. II, 4, 267. H8 III, 2, 96. Lr. I, 4, 237. *must I hold a c. to my shames?* Merch. II, 6, 41. *seek him with c.* As III, 1, 6. *I see no more in you than without c. may go dark to bed*, III, 5, 39. *those gold —s fixed in heaven's air*, Sonn. 21, 12. *by these blessed —s of the night*, Merch. V, 220. *night's —s are burnt out*, Rom. III, 5, 9. Mcb. II, 1, 5. — Used as a symbol of life: *here burns my c. out*, H6C II, 6, 1. *out, out, brief c.* Mcb. V, 5, 23.

Candle-case, a case to keep candles in: *a pair of boots that have been —s*, Shr. III, 2, 45.

Candle-holder, he who holds the candle, and is an assistant, but not a partaker of the pleasure of others: *I'll be a c. and look on*, Rom. I, 4, 38.*

Candle-mine, inexhaustible magazine of tallow: H4B II, 4, 326.

Candlestick, instrument to hold candles: H4A III, 1, 131 (Qq *canstick*). H5 IV, 2, 45.

Candle-waster, one who wastes candles by sitting up all night, probably not a reveller, as some have supposed, but a nocturnal student; a bookworm: *patch grief with proverbs, make misfortune drunk with —s*, Ado V, 1, 18; i. e. drown grief with the wise saws of pedants and book-worms.

Candy, the isle of Candia: Tw. V, 64.

Candy, vb., 1) to sugar: *let the —ied tongue lick absurd pomp*, Hml. III, 2, 65.*

2) to congeal: *twenty consciences, that stand 'twixt me and Milan, —ied be they and melt ere they molest*, Tp. II, 1, 279. *the cold brook, —ied with ice*, Tim. IV, 3, 226 (cf. *discandy*). — Originally: to make white (with sugar or hoar-frost).

Candy, confectionery; used adjectively: *what a c. deal of courtesy*, H4A I, 3, 251.

Canidius, name in Ant. III, 7, 20. 27. 58. 80. IV, 6, 16.

Canker, subst., 1) a worm that preys upon blossoms: *this c. that eats up love's tender spring*, Ven. 656. *loathsome c. lives in sweetest bud*, Sonn. 35, 4. *c. vice the sweetest buds doth love*, 70, 7. *like a c. in the fragrant rose*, 95, 2. *a vengeful c. eat him up to death*, 99, 12. *grief that's beauty's c.* Tp. I, 2, 415. *in the sweetest bud the eating c. dwells*, Gentl. I, 1, 43. *kill —s in the musk-rose buds*, Mids. II, 2, 3. *the —s of a calm world and a long peace*, H4A IV, 2, 32. *that this good blossom could be kept from —s*, H4B II, 2, 102. *hath not thy rose a c.?* H6A II, 4, 68. 71. *full soon the c. death eats up that plant*, Rom. II, 3, 30. *the c. galls the infants of the spring*, Hml. I, 3, 39. *to let this c. of our nature come in further evil*, V, 2, 69.

2) a corroding evil: *and heal the inveterate c. of one wound by making many*, John V, 2, 14. *banish the c. of ambitious thoughts*, H6B I, 2, 18. *the c. gnaw thy heart*, Tim. IV, 3, 49.

3) the dog-rose: *I had rather be a c. in a hedge than a rose in his grace*, Ado I, 3, 28. *to put down Richard, that sweet lovely rose, and plant this thorn, this c. Bolingbroke*, H4A I, 3, 176. cf. *canker-bloom*.

Canker, vb., 1) to eat, to corrode: *foul —ing rust the hidden treasure frets*, Ven. 767. *old partizans —ed with peace*, Rom. I, 1, 102. 2) to grow corrupt, to become venomous: *as with age his body uglier grows, so his mind —s*, Tp. IV, 192.

Cankered, adjectively, = infected, polluted, evil: *for this they have engrossed and piled up the c. heaps of strange-achieved gold*, H4B IV, 5, 72. *I will fight against my c. country*, Cor. IV, 5, 97. Implying the idea of malignancy, = venomous, wicked: *a c. grandam's will*, John II, 194. *this ingrate and c. Bolingbroke*, H4A I, 3, 137. *your c. hate*, Rom. I, 1, 102.

Canker-bit, worm-eaten: *my name is lost, by treason's tooth bare-gnawn and c.* Lr. V, 3, 122.

Canker-bloom, the wild rose: *the —s have full as deep a dye as the perfumed tincture of the roses*, Sonn. 54, 5.*

Canker-blossom, a blossom eaten by a canker; or the same as *canker-bloom: O me! you juggler! you c.! you thief of love!* Mids. III, 2, 282.

Canker-sorrow (perhaps better without the hyphen) grief preying like a worm: *but now will c. eat my bud*, John III, 4, 82.

Cannibal, anthropophagite: H6C I, 4, 152. V, 5, 61. Oth. I, 3, 143. Pistol confounds it with *Hannibal:* H4B II, 4, 180.

Cannibally, in the manner of a cannibal: *c. given,* Cor. IV, 5, 200.

Cannon, great gun for battery: Lucr. 1043. Wiv. III, 2, 33. LLL III, 65. As II, 7, 53. H5 III, 1, 11. H6C V, 2, 44 (cf. H5 II, 4, 124. Qq and M. Edd. *clamour*). Rom. V, 1, 65. Hml. I, 2, 126. IV, 1, 42. Oth. III, 4, 134. — Plur. *cannons: the —s have their bowels full of wrath,* John II, 210. *unless we sweep 'em from the door with —s,* H8 V, 4, 13. *as —s overcharged with double cracks,* Mcb. I, 2, 37. (let) *the —s to the heavens* (speak) Hml. V, 2, 288. — Plur. *cannon: the thunder of my c.* John I, 26. *our c. shall be bent ...,* II, 37. *their battering c. charged to the mouths,* 382. *of basiliks, of c., culverin,* H4A II, 3, 56. *the nimble gunner with linstock now the devilish c. touches, and down goes all before them,* H5 III Chor. 33. *such daily cast of brazen c.* Hml. I, 1, 73. *if we could carry c. by our sides,* V, 2, 166 (Qq *a cannon*). — Uncertain: *our cannons malice vainly shall be spent,* John II, 251.

Cannon-bullet, Tw. I, 5, 100.

Cannoneer, the engineer who manages the cannon: John II, 461. Hml. V, 2, 287.

Cannon-fire, John II, 462.

Cannon-shot, a discharge of cannon: *these haughty words have battered me like roaring c.* H6A III, 3, 79.

Canon, rule, law: *contrary to thy established proclaimed edict and continent c.* LLL I, 1, 263. *selflove, which is the most inhibited sin in the c.* All's I, 1, 158. *the c. of the law* (sc. of the divine law) *is laid on him,* John II, 180. *against the hospitable c.* Cor. I, 10, 26. *'twas from the c.* III, 1, 90.*religious —s, civil laws are cruel,* Tim. IV, 3, 60. *or that the Everlasting had not fixed his c. 'gainst self-slaughter,* Hml. I, 2, 132.

Canonize, to make a saint of, to receive into the number of saints: *—d and worshipped as a saint,* John III, 1, 177. IV, 52. H6B I, 3, 63. Hml. I, 4, 47.* = to glorify in general: *and fame in time to come c. us,* Troil. II, 2, 202.

Canopy, subst., 1) a covering of state over a throne, or borne over the head in processions: *were't aught to me I bore the c.* Sonn. 125, 1.*a rich embroidered c.* H6C II, 5, 44.

2) a covering over a bed: *costly apparel, tents and —ies,* Shr. II, 354. *—ies of costly state,* H4B III, 1, 13. *thy c. is dust and stones,* Rom. V, 3, 13. *their shadows seem a c. most fatal, under which our army lies,* Caes. V, 1, 88. Figuratively, = the firmament: *where dwellest thou? Under the c. Where's that? In the city of kites and crows,* Cor. IV, 5, 41. *this most excellent c., the air, this brave o'erhanging firmament,* Hml. II, 2, 311.

Canopy, vb., to cover as with a canopy: *trees ... which erst from heat did c. the herd,* Sonn. 12, 6. *her eyes had sheathed their light, and —ied in darkness sweetly lay,* Lucr. 398. *the enclosed lights* (viz the eyes) *now —ied under these windows,* Cymb. II, 2, 21. *love-thoughts lie rich when —ied with bowers,* Tw. I, 1, 41.

Canstick = candlestick: H4A III, 1, 131 (Ff *candlestick*).

Canterbury, English town, seat of the primate: John III, 1, 144. R2 II, 1, 282. H4A I, 2, 140. H5 I, 2, 1. H8 II, 4, 218. III, 2, 402. IV, 1, 25. 86 etc. = archbishop of C.*: *stand up, good C.,* H8 V, 1, 114.

Cantherize, to raise blisters as with cantharides: *for each true word a blister! and each false be as a —ing to the root o'the tongue,* Tim. V, 1, 136 (M. Edd. *cauterizing*).

Cantle, piece: *and cuts me from the best of all my land a huge half-moon, a monstrous c. out,* H4A III, 1, 100 (Qq *scantle*). *the greater c. of the world is lost with very ignorance,* Ant. III, 10, 6.

Canton, song: *write loyal —s of contemned love,* Tw. I, 5, 289.

Canvas, subst., coarse linen, commonly used for sails: *your white c. doublet will sully,* H4A II, 4, 84.

Canvas-climber, a sailor that goes aloft to handle sails: *washes off a c.* Per. IV, 1, 62.

Canvass, vb., to shake and toss as in a canvas; to take to task: *I'll c. thee in thy broad cardinal's hat,* H6A I, 3, 36. *I will toss the rogue in a blanket. An thou dost, I'll c. thee between a pair of sheets,* H4B II, 4, 243.

Canzonet, little song: LLL IV, 2, 124 (Holophernes' speech).

Cap, subst., a garment to cover the head; worn as well by women (Ado III, 4, 72. LLL II, 209. Shr. IV, 3, 55. 63. V, 2, 121. All's I, 1, 170. H4B II, 4, 298. Oth. IV, 3, 74) as by men: *not one man but he will wear his c. with suspicion,* Ado I, 1, 200 (on account of the horns hidden under it). *fling up his c.* H6B IV, 8, 15. *he that throws not up his c. for joy,* H6C II, 1, 196. *hurled up their —s,* R3 III, 7, 35. *they threw their —s,* Cor. I, 1, 216. *take my c., Jupiter,* II, 1, 115. *—s, hands and tongues applaud it,* Hml. IV, 5, 107. *they cast their —s up and carouse together,* Ant. IV, 12, 12. *there's my c.* (viz. thrown into the air) II, 7, 141. *our masters may throw their —s at their money,* Tim. III, 4, 102 (= they may whistle for it). *— worn in the c. of a tooth-drawer,* LLL V, 2, 622. *you should wear it in your c.* Shr. III, 4, 72. *thou art fitter to be worn in my c.* H4B I, 2, 17. *do not you wear your dagger in your c.* H5 IV, 1, 57. *this* (glove) *will I also wear in my c.* 229. *wear it for an honour in thy c.* IV, 8, 63. *good men's lives expire before the flowers in their —s,* Mcb. IV, 3, 172. *wore gloves in my c.* Lr. III, 4, 88. Figuratively: *they wear themselves in the c. of the time,* All's II, 1, 55 (= are the ornaments of the age). *a very riband in the c. of youth,* Hml. IV, 7, 79. *— put off's c.* All's II, 2, 10. *as ready as a borrower's c.* H4B II, 2, 125. *the c. plays in the right hand,* Tim. II, 1, 18. *I have ever held my c. off to thy fortunes,* Ant. II, 7, 63. *came in with c. and knee,* H4A IV, 3, 68 (i. e. with bare heads and bows). *ambitious for poor knaves' —s and legs,* Cor. II, 1, 77. *c. and knee slaves,* Tim. III, 6, 107. *such gain the c. of him,* Cymb. III, 3, 25.* — *a c. of flowers,* Pilgr. 363 (not Sh.'s poem). *a baby's c.* Shr. IV, 3, 67 etc.

Cap = cardinal's hat: *he'll make his c. coequal with the crown,* H6A V, 1, 33. *let his grace go forward, and dare us with his c. like larks,* H8 III, 2, 282.

Figuratively = the top: *thou art the c. of all the fools alive,* Tim. IV, 3, 363 (with an allusion, perhaps, to the fool's cap). cf. *on fortune's c. we are not the very button,* Hml. II, 2, 233.

Cap, vb., to cover as with a cap, to top: *I will c. that proverb with 'There is flattery in friendship,'* H5 III, 7, 124. cf. *Offcap.*

Capability, ability, mental power: *gave us*

not that c. and god-like reason to fust in us unused, Hml. IV, 4, 38.

Capable, I) absol. 1) capacious: *a c. and wide revenge,* Oth. III, 3, 459.

2) impressible, receptive: *lean but upon a rush, the cicatrice and c. impressure thy palm some moment keeps,* As III, 5, 23. *his form and cause conjoined, preaching to stones, would make them c.* Hml. III, 4, 127.

3) able, well gifted: *if their daughters be c., I will put it to them,* LLL IV, 2, 82 (a quibble). *bold, quick, ingenious, forward, c.* R3 III, 1, 155. *his horse is the more c. creature,* Troil. III, 3, 310.

II) followed by *of,* 1) susceptible: *which any print of goodness wilt not take, being c. of all ill,* Tp. I, 2, 353. *heart too c. of every line and trick of his sweet favour,* All's I, 1, 106. *so thou wilt be c. of a courtier's counsel,* 223. *if thou beest c. of things serious,* Wint. IV, 4, 791. *urge them while their souls are c. of this ambition,* John II, 476. *I am sick and c. of fears,* III, 1, 12. *his flesh was c. of wounds and scars,* H4B I, 1, 172. *c. of our flesh,* H8 V, 3, 11 (subject to the temptations of our fleshly nature). *c. of nothing but inexplicable dumb-shows and noise,* Hml. III, 2, 13.

2) able, qualified to have or possess: *and of my land ... I'll work the means to make thee c.* Lr. II, 1, 87.

Capacity, 1) power of containing, extent: *thy c. receiveth as the sea,* Tw. I, 1, 10. *which gifts ... the c. of your soft cheveril conscience would receive,* H8 II, 3, 31. *had our great palace the c. to camp this host,* Ant. IV, 8, 32.

2) ability: *God comfort thy c.* LLL IV, 2, 44. *your c. is of that nature that to your huge store wise things seem foolish,* V, 2, 376. *this is evident to any formal c.* Tw. II, 5, 128. *of good c. and breeding,* III, 4, 204. *you that are old consider not the —ies of us that are young,* H4B I, 2, 197 (the first and second significations joined: what youth is able to do, and what it is able to hold or contain). *too subtle-potent ... for the c. of my ruder powers,* Troil. III, 2, 26. *holding them, in human action and c., of no more soul than camels,* Cor. II, 1, 265. *to my c. =* in my opinion, Mids. V, 105. — Sir Hugh uses the word for *capable,* Wiv. I, 1, 223.

Cap-a-pe, from head to foot: *I am courtier c.* Wint. IV, 4, 761. *armed at point exactly, c.* Hml. I, 2, 200.

Caparison, subst., horse-cloth: *rich —s or trapping gay,* Ven. 286. *here is the steed, we the c.* Cor. I, 9, 12. Autolycus calls so his rags: *with die and drab I purchased this c.* Wint. IV, 3, 27.

Caparison, vb., to cover with a horse-cloth: *c. my horse,* R3 V, 3, 289. Jestingly of human dress: *—ed like a man,* As III, 2, 205. *—ed like the horse,* Shr. III, 2, 67.

Cape, 1) headland: *will trench him here and on this north side win this c. of land,* H4A III, 1, 113. *what from the c. can you discern at sea?* Oth. II, 1, 1.

2) the part of a garment hanging from the neck behind: *with a small compassed c.* Shr. IV, 3, 140.*lace for your c.* Wint. IV, 4, 323.

Capel, abbreviation for *Capulet:* Rom. V, 1, 18. V, 3, 127.

Caper, subst., 1) a leap, a spring, in dancing or mirth: *we that are true lovers run into strange —s,*

As II, 4, 55. *I can cut a c.* Tw. I, 3, 129. *he offered to cut a c. at the proclamation,* Per. IV, 2, 116.

2) the unexpanded flower of the caper-bush, used for pickling: *I can cut a c. And I can cut the mutton to 't,* Tw. I, 3, 129 (quibble).

3) name in Meas. IV, 3, 10.

Caper, vb., to leap, to jump: Tp. V, 238. Wiv. III, 2, 68. LLL V, 2, 113. Merch. I, 2, 66. Tw. I, 3, 150. H4A III, 2, 63 (only in Q1; the other O. Edd. *carping*). H4B I, 2, 216. H6B III, 1, 365. R3 I, 1, 12.

Capet: *Hugh C.,* the ancestor of the French kings: H5 I, 2, 69. 78. 87.

Caphis, name of a servant in Tim. II, 1, 13.

Capilet: 1) *Diana C.,* name in All's V, 3, 147. 159. 2) name of a horse in Tw. III, 4, 315.

Capital, adj. 1) chief, principal: *military title c.* H4A III, 2, 110. *she is our c. demand,* H5 V, 2, 96. *so c. a calf,* Hml. III, 2, 111.

2) punishable by loss of life: *in such c. kind,* Cor. III, 3, 81. *so c. in nature,* Hml. IV, 7, 7. *c. crimes,* H5 II, 2, 56. *offences,* Wint. IV, 4, 823. Per. II, 4, 5. *treason,* R2 IV, 151. H4B IV, 2, 109. H6B V, 1, 107. Mcb. I, 3, 115. Lr. V, 3, 83.

3) mortal, pernicious: *to poor we thine enmity 's most c.* Cor. V, 3, 104.

Capite: *in c. =* holding immediately of the king: *men shall hold of me in c.* H6B IV, 7, 131.

Capitol, the castle of ancient Rome: Lucr. 1835. Cor. I, 1, 49. IV, 2, 39 etc. Tit. I, 12. 41. 77. Caes. I, 1, 68. I, 2, 187. I, 3, 20. II, 1, 111. III, 2, 41 etc. Hml. III, 2, 109. Ant. II, 6, 18. Cymb. I, 6, 106.

Capitulate, to make an agreement, to draw up articles, to treat: *c. against us and are up,* H4A III, 2, 120. *or c. again with Rome's mechanics,* Cor. V, 3, 82.

Capocchia, see Appendix.

Capon, castrated cock: Gentl. IV, 4, 10. Err. I, 2, 44. As II, 7, 154. H4A I, 2, 8. 129. II, 4, 502. 585. Hml. III, 2, 100. Used as a term of reproach: Err. III, 1, 32. Ado V, 1, 156. Cymb. II, 1, 25 (perhaps *= cap on;* i. e. with a coxcomb). Quibbling, like the French *poulet,* for a love-letter: *Boyet, you can carve; break up this c.* LLL IV, 1, 56.

Cappadocia, country in Asia Minor: Ant. III, 6, 70.

Capriccio (O. Edd. *caprichio*) fancy, caprice: *will this c. hold in thee?* All's II, 3, 310.

Capricious, of uncertain meaning: *I am here with thee and thy goats, as the most c. poet, honest Ovid, was among the Goths,* As III, 3, 8. Evidently an allusion to the Latin *capra* (goat), and a quibble between goats and Goths. The word may mean what it does to-day. Perhaps *=* goatish.

Captain, 1) leader, commander in general: *c. of our fairy band,* Mids. III, 2, 110. *the c. of his horse,* All's IV, 3, 327. *being c. of the watch to-night,* H6A II, 1, 61. *a wise stout c.* (viz. the mayor of York) H6C IV, 7, 30. *=* leader of a troop of robbers: Gentl. IV, 1, 65. V, 3, 2. 10. 12.

2) the commander of a ship: Meas. I, 2, 13. Tw. I, 2, 47. V, 3. 72. 261. H6B IV, 1, 107.

3) leader of a company: All's II, 1, 38. II, 5, 34. IV, 1, 8. H4A IV, 2, 4. H4B II, 4, 149. 387. III, 2, 66. H6A II, 2, 59. V, 3, 128. R3 V, 3, 30. 40. 44. Cor. V, 2, 57. Hml. IV, 4, 1. V, 2, 406. Lr. V, 3,

26. Oth. III, 3, 59. Ant. III, 13, 184. Cymb. IV, 2, 344 etc.

4) chief commander: *his c. Christ*, R2 IV, 99. *great Mars, the c. of us all,* Troil. IV, 5, 198. *like soldiers, when their c. once doth yield,* Ven. 893. *affection is my c., and he leadeth,* Lucr. 271. 298. *his —'s heart,* Ant. I, 1, 6. *who does in the wars more than his c. can, becomes his —'s c.* III, 1, 21. *thy grand c. Antony,* III, 1, 9. *the ass more c. than the lion,* Tim. III, 5, 49. cf. Meas. II, 2, 130. H6A III, 2, 71. III, 4, 16. IV, 1, 32. IV, 2, 3. IV, 4, 17. Cor. V, 2, 55. Tit. V, 3, 94. Ant. IV, 14, 90 etc. Used in the vocative: H6A V, 3, 97. Tim. I, 2, 74. III, 5, 6. Oth. I, 2, 53. Figuratively: *he is the courageous c. of complements,* Rom. II, 4, 20 (cf. *king*). Used of women: *a phoenix, c. and an enemy,* All's I, 1, 182 (i. e. a mistress of his heart). *where's c. Margaret?* H6C II, 6, 75. *our great —'s c.* Oth. II, 1, 74 (cf. Ant. III, 1, 21).

5) the general as the instrument and substitute of a higher power: *the figure of God's majesty, his c., steward,* R2 IV, 126. *O thou, whose c. I account myself,* R3 V, 3, 108.

6) in familiar language, a term of endearment, nearly = stripling, spark: *come, c., we must be neat,* Wint. I, 2, 122. *how now, c., what do you in this wise company?* Tim. II, 2, 76.

7) adjectively used, = predominant, overruling: *therefore are feasts so solemn and so rare, since, seldom coming, in the long year set, like stones of worth they thinly placed are, or c. jewels in the carcanet,* Sonn. 52, 8. *captive good attending c. ill,* 66, 12.

Captain-general, commander in chief: Troil. III, 3, 279.

Captainship, quality of a general: *and of our Athens to take the c.* Tim. V, 1, 164. *the itch of his affection should not then have nicked his c.* Ant. III, 13, 8.

Captious, probably = capacious: *yet in this c. and intenible sieve I still pour in the waters of my love,* All's I, 3, 208.

Captivate, vb., 1) to keep in prison: *restrained, —d, bound,* LLL III, 126 (Armado's speech). — 2) to subdue, to bring into bondage: *to triumph upon their woes whom fortune —s,* H6C I, 4, 115. — 3) to bind in love, to charm: *to c. the eye,* Ven. 281.

Captivate, adj. or partic., captive, prisoner: *and sent our sons and husbands c.* H6A II, 3, 42. *women have been c. ere now,* V, 3, 107.

Captive, subst., 1) prisoner: R2 I, 3, 88. H6A I, 1, 22. H6C II, 1, 127. Tit. IV, 2, 34. Caes. III, 2, 93. Lr. V, 3, 41. Cymb. V, 5, 73. 385. *c. bonds,* Caes. I, 1, 39. *a c. chariot,* H5 III, 5, 54. *my c. state,* H6C IV, 6, 3 (in these three passages seemingly an adj., but really a subst.)

2) one ensnared by beauty: *yet hath he been my c. and my slave,* Ven. 101. *beware of being —s before you serve,* All's II, 1, 21.

3) one vanquished and subdued: *the coward c. vanquished doth yield,* Lucr. 75. *the conclusion is victory: on whose side? the king's. The c. is enriched: on whose side? the beggar's,* LLL IV, 1, 76. *deliver you as most abated —s to some nation that won you without blows,* Cor. III, 3, 132.

Captive, adj., 1) taken prisoner, in the state of a prisoner: *this c. scold,* H6C V, 5, 29. *held c.* Troil. II, 2, 77.

2) captivated, gained by some excellence: *whose words all ears took c.* All's V, 3, 17. *my woman's heart grossly grew c. to his honey words,* R3 IV, 1, 80.

3) vanquished, subdued: *a c. victor that hath lost in gain,* Lucr. 730. *c. good attending captain ill,* Sonn. 66, 12. *when many times the c. Grecian falls, you bid them rise and live,* Troil. V, 3, 40. Followed by *to: c. to thee and to thy Roman yoke,* Tit. I, 111. *or friends with Caesar, or not c. to him,* Ant. II, 5, 44 (= subject).

Captived, taken prisoner (or perhaps = defeated?): *and all our princes c. by the hand of that black name, Edward,* H5 II, 4, 55.

Captivity, 1) state of being a prisoner: H6B II, 2, 42. H6C IV, 5, 13. Mcb. I, 2, 5.

2) state of being vanquished, defeat: *triumphant death, smeared with c., young Talbot's valour makes me smile at thee,* H6A IV, 7, 3.*

3) servitude, slavery: *so every bondman in his own hand bears the power to cancel his c.* Caes. I, 3, 102. *had they ... given to c. me and my utmost hopes,* Oth. IV, 2, 51.

Capucius, name in H8 IV, 2, 110.

Capulet, name in Rom. I, 1, 81 etc. etc. *the —s,* III, 1, 2. 38.

Car, subst. 1) the chariot of Phoebus: Sonn. 7, 9. Gentl. III, 1, 154. Mids. I, 2, 37. H6C I, 4, 33. II, 6, 13. IV, 7, 80. R3 V, 3, 20. Ant. IV, 8, 29. Cymb. V, 5, 191.

2) any vehicle of dignity: *triumphant c.* H6A I, 1, 22. *thy* (Revenge's) *c.* Tit. V, 2, 53.

3) = cart? *though our silence be drawn from us with —s,* Tw. II, 5, 71 (F2.3.4 *cares;* Hanmer *by the ears;* Johnson *with carts* etc.). In our copy of the Staunton Folio the word certainly looks more like *ears* than *cars.* cf. *Ear.*

Car, name in H8: *John de la C.* I, 1, 218. I, 2, 162. *John C.* II, 1, 20.

Carack, see *Carrack.*

Carat (Ff *charect* and *charract*); 1) the weight used by goldsmiths: *how much your chain weighs to the utmost c., the fineness of the gold, and chargeful fashion,* Err. IV, 1, 28. 2) the weight that expresses the fineness of gold: *other gold less fine in c.* H4B IV, 5, 162.

Caraways, comfits made with cumin seeds: *a dish of c.* H4B V, 3, 3, or a sort of apples?

Carbonado, subst. meat cut across to be broiled: *let him make a c. of me,* H4A V, 3, 61. *scotched him and notched him like a c.* Cor. IV, 5, 199.*

Carbonado, vb., to cut or hack like a carbonado: *it is your —ed face,* All's IV, 5, 107. *eat adders' heads and toads —ed,* Wint. IV, 4, 268. *I'll so c. your shanks,* Lr. II, 2, 41.

Carbuncle, 1) a precious stone of deep red colour: Err. III, 2, 138. Cor. I, 4, 55. Hml. II, 2, 485. *had it been a c. of Phoebus' wheel,* Cymb. V, 5, 189.

2) a gangrenous ulcer: *a plague-sore, an embossed c.* Lr. II, 4, 227.

Carbuncled, set with carbuncles: *c. like holy Phoebus' car,* Ant. IV, 8, 28.

Carcanet, collar of jewels: *captain jewels in the c.* Sonn. 52, 8. *to see the making of her c.* Err III, 1, 4.

Carcass, a dead body, when spoken of with disgust: *give his c. to my hounds,* Mids. III, 2, 64. *the rotten c. of old Death,* John II, 456. *—es of unburied men,* Cor. III, 3, 122. *a c. fit for hounds,* Caes. II, 1, 174. Despicably used of living bodies: *his body is a passable c.* Cymb. I, 2, 11. *would have given their honours to have saved their —es,* V, 3, 67. Figuratively, the decaying remains of any thing, **the ruins:** *the c. of a beauty spent and done,* Compl. 11. *a rotten c. of a butt,* Tp. I, 2, 146. *the —es of many a tall ship,* Merch. III, 1, 6.

Card, subst., 1) a paper painted with figures, used in games: *I have faced it with a c. of ten,* Shr. II, 407. *have I not here the best —s for the game,* John V, 2, 105. *as sure a c. as ever won the set,* Tit. V, 1, 100. *she has packed —s with Caesar,* Ant. IV, 14, 19.

2) the face of a sea-compass: *the very ports they blow, all the quarters that they know in the shipman's c.* Mcb. I, 3, 17. Figuratively: *we must speak by the c.* (i. e. with the utmost preciseness) Hml. V, 1, 149. *he is the c. or calendar of gentry,* V, 2, 114 (cf. *map*).

3) *a cooling card* = that which dashes hopes: *there all is marred; there lies a cooling c.* H6A V, 3, 84 (perhaps not the same word, but derived from *Carduus benedictus*).

Card, vb., to mix, to debase by mixing: *—ed his state, mingled his royalty with capering fools,* H4A III, 2, 62.

Cardecue, (M. Edd. *quart d'écu*), a quarter of a French crown, fifteen pence: *for a c. he will sell the fee-simple of his salvation,* All's IV, 3, 311. *there's a c. for you,* V, 2, 35.

Carder, one who cards wool: *the clothiers have put off the spinsters, —s, fullers,* H8 I, 2, 33.

Cardinal, subst., a member of the college by which and out of which the pope is elected: John III, 1, 138. 181. III, 4, 76. V, 7, 82 etc. H6A I, 3, 19. 36. 49. V, 1, 29. H6B I, 1, 174. I, 2, 27. I, 3, 64 etc. R3 III, 1, 32. H8 I, 1, 51. II, 1, 160. II, 2, 106. III, 2, 257 etc. etc.

Cardinal, adj., chief, principal: *holy men I thought ye, upon my soul, two reverend c. virtues; but c. sins and hollow hearts I fear ye,* H8 III, 1, 103 (with a quibbling allusion to the dignity of the addressed persons).

Cardinally, for *carnally,* in the language of Elbow: *a woman c. given,* Meas. II, 1, 81.

Card-maker, one who makes cards for combing wool or flax: Shr. Ind. 2, 20.

Carduus Benedictus, the herb blessed thistle, used as a medicament: Ado III, 4, 73.

Care, subst., 1) grief, sorrow: *deep-drenched in a sea of c.* Lucr. 1100. *in her (Hecuba) the painter had anatomized ... grim —'s reign,* 1451. *her lively colour killed with deadly —s,* 1593. *winter, which being full of c. makes summer's welcome thrice more wished,* Sonn. 56, 13. *c. killed a cat,* Ado V, 1, 133. *dull with c. and melancholy,* Err. I, 2, 20. *knows not my feeble key of untuned —s,* V, 310. *undone and forfeited to —s for ever,* All's II, 3, 284. *c. is an enemy to life,* Tw. I, 3, 3. *Nestor-like aged in an age of c.* H6A II, 5, 6. *nor grieve that Rouen is so recovered; c. is no cure,* III, 3, 3. *so —s and joys abound as seasons fleet,* H6B II, 4, 4. *while heart is drowned in —s,* H6C III, 3, 14 etc.

2) anxious concern, solicitude: *save thieves and —s and troubled minds that wake,* Lucr. 126. *to whose (his soul's) weak ruins muster troops of —s,* 720. *carrier of grisly c.* 926. *age is full of c.* Pilgr. 158. *it (my heart) keeps on the windy side of c.* Ado II, 1, 327. *they lose it that do buy it with much c.* Merch. I, 1, 75. *you are withered; 'tis with —s,* Shr. II, 240. *brings a thousand-fold more c. to keep,* H6C II, 2, 52 etc. — *To take no c.* = to be unconcerned: *take you no c.* H6A I, 4, 21. *take no c. who chafes, who frets,* Mcb. IV, 1, 90. *take thou no c.* Ant. V, 2, 269.

3) watchful regard and attention: *all my mind, my thought, my busy c. is how to get my palfrey from the mare,* Ven. 383. *with what c. he cranks and crosses,* 681. *her whose busy c. is bent to follow,* Sonn. 143, 6. *I have used thee with human c.* Tp. I, 2, 346. *I thank thee for thine honest c.* Gentl. III, 1, 22. *fixing our eyes on whom our c. was fixed,* Err. I, 1, 85. *thanks, provost, for thy c. and secrecy,* Meas. V, 536. *effect it with some c.* Mids. II, 1, 265. *my chief c. is to come fairly off ...* Merch. I, 1, 127. *I am content, in a good father's c., to have him matched,* Shr. IV, 4, 31. *be wary in thy studious c.* H6A II, 5, 97. *the reverent c. I bear unto my lord,* H6B III, 1, 34. *make the rabble call our —s fears,* Cor. III, 1, 137 etc. *Past cure I am, now reason is past c.* (= pays no more attention to me) Sonn. 147, 9. *past cure is still past c.* LLL V, 2, 28. *past hope, past c., past help,* Rom. IV, 1, 45 (the spurious Q1 and most M. Edd. *cure*). cf. H6A III, 3, 3. — *Be't not in thy c.* = be unconcerned about it: Tim. III, 4, 117. *so much for my peculiar c.* = as regards myself, Cymb. V, 5, 83. — Followed by *of: I have done nothing but in c. of thee,* Tp. I, 2, 16. *in so profound abysm I throw all c. of others' voices,* Sonn. 112, 9. *the great c. of goods,* Err. I, 1, 43. *in c. of your most royal person,* H6C III, 2, 254. *for this c. of Tamora,* Tit. IV, 2, 170. Per. I, 2, 28. — Followed by an infinitive: *is wandered forth in c. to seek me out,* Err. II, 2, 3. — Used for the object of attention: *thou best of dearest and mine only c.* Sonn. 48, 7. *speak, thy father's c.* H6A IV, 6, 26.

To have c. = to be attentive, to do one's office: *good boatswain, have c.* Tp. I, 1, 10. *To have a c.,* in the same sense: *good cousin, have a c. this busy time,* Ado I, 2, 28. Followed by *of,* = to pay attention to: *let some of my people have a special c. of him,* Tw. III, 4, 69. *my lady prays you to have a c. of him,* 103. *to have a reverent care of your health,* H4B I, 2, 113. *have a c. of thyself,* II, 4, 410. *I must have a c. of you,* Per. IV, 1, 50. cf. *the care you have of us,* H6B III, 1, 66. *of whom you seem to have so tender c.* H6C IV, 6, 66. *most charitable c. have the patricians of you,* Cor. I, 1, 67. *hast thou no c. of me?* Ant. IV, 15, 60. *the horses with all the c. I had, I saw well chosen,* H8 II, 2, 2. — Followed by an infinitive, = to be intent or bent on: *it seems he hath great c. to please his wife,* Err. II, 1, 56. *the c. I have had to even your content,* All's I, 3, 3. *I have more c. to stay than will to go,* Rom. III, 5, 23.

To have a c. = to take heed, in the language of low people: *have a c. of your entertainments,* Wiv. IV, 5, 77. *have a c. that your bills be not stolen,* Ado III, 3, 43. *have a c. the honey-bag break not,* Mids. IV, 1, 15.

To keep a c. = to care for, to be interested

in: *if of life you keep a c.* Tp. II, 1, 303. *To make a c.*, in the same sense: *if you make a c. of happy holding her*, Wint. IV, 4, 366. *keep good quarter and good c. to-night*, John V, 5, 20 (= be on your guard).

To take some c. = to take pains: *we will take some c.* LLL V, 2, 511. *he took some c. to get her cunning schoolmasters*, Shr. I, 1, 191. cf. *that we have taken no c. to your best courses*, Per. IV, 1, 39 (*to* = for, tending to). *of your own state take c.* Wint. IV, 4, 459 (mind your own state). *I have ta'en too little c. of this*, Lr. III, 4, 33 (I have paid too little attention to this). *let no man take c. for himself*, Tp. V, 257 (= let no man be attentive to his own interests).

Care, vb., to take care, to be solicitous: *one that —s for thee, and for thy maintenance commits his body to painful labour*, Shr. V, 2, 147. *who c. for you like fathers*, Cor. I, 1, 79. *those that c. to keep your royal person from treason's secret knife*, H6B III, 1, 173. *c. no more to clothe and eat*, Cymb. IV, 2, 266. *what was first but fear what might be done, grows elder now and —s it be not done*, Per. I, 2, 15.

Mostly used negatively, to express indifference: *I c. not* = it is all one to me, Gentl. II, 1, 123. *and said she —d not*, Ado V, 1, 176. *and then I c. not*, Merch. III, 3, 36. Shr. II, 241. *I know not, nor I greatly c. not.* R2 V, 2, 48. *that Timon —s not*, Tim. V, 1, 174. 180 etc. *I would not c. a pin*, LLL IV, 3, 19.

Followed by *for: what —s he now for curb or pricking spur?* Ven. 285. *now Nature —s not for thy* (death's) *mortal vigour*, 953. Tp. I, 1, 17. II, 2, 51. Gentl. III, 1, 311. 345. IV, 4, 87. V, 4, 132. Wiv. III, 4, 27. Ado V, 4, 103. LLL V, 2, 27. As II, 4, 2. 90. III, 5, 111. Tw. III, 1, 31. Wint. V, 1, 46. H6B III, 2, 359. Tim. V, 1, 181. Oth. V, 2, 165 etc. — Affirmatively, in this sense, only in contradistinction to negative assertions: *thou art a merry fellow and —st for nothing. Not so, sir, I do c. for something, but I do not c. for you*, Tw. III, 1, 32. *I c. not for thee. If I had thee in Lipsbury pinfold, I would make thee c. for me*, Lr. II, 2, 10. *when thou hadst no need to c. for her frowning*, I, 4, 211.

Followed by an infinitive: *to hear music the general does not greatly c.* Oth. III, 1, 18. *I do not greatly c. to be deceived*, Ant. V, 2, 14. Followed by *though: I c. not though he burn himself in love*, Gentl. II, 5, 55. By an *and if: I c. not an she were a black-a-moor*, Troil. I, 1, 79. *I c. not if I have*, As V, 2, 85 (H4B I, 2, 142). Followed by an interrogative clause: *what c. I who calls me ill or well*, Sonn. 112, 3. *he —s not what he puts into the press*, Wiv. II, 1, 79. *get me some repast, I c. not what*, Shr. IV, 3, 16. *when I lose thee again, I c. not*, All's III, 3, 217. *he —d not who knew it*, H5 III, 7, 117. *I c. not which, or Somerset or York, all's one to me*, H6B I, 3, 104. *I c. not whither*, II, 4, 92. *neither to c. whether they love or hate him*, Cor. II, 2, 14. 18. A very remarkable passage: *I seek not to wax great by others' waning, or gather wealth, I c. not with what envy*, H6B IV, 10, 23 (= indifferently).

Indifference may be a softened expression of dislike: *I c. not to get slips of them*, Wint. IV, 4, 84 (= I should not like); as well as of a wish: *I c. not if I do become your physician*, H4B I, 2, 142 (= I should like).

Care-crazed, broken, worn away with care: R3 III, 7, 184.

Career, 1) the ground on which a race is run: *shall quips and sentences awe a man from the c. of his humour?* Ado II, 3, 250. *I shall meet your wit in the c.* V, 1, 135. *and so conclusions passed the —s* (O. Edd. *careires*) Wiv. I, 1, 184 ('Bardolph means to say: and so in the end he reeled about like a horse passing a c. To pass a c.* was a technical term.' Malone).

2) race: *full merrily hath this brave manage, this c., been run*, LLL V, 2, 482. *stopping the c. of laughing with a sigh*, Wint. I, 2, 286. *if misfortune miss the first c.* R2 I, 2, 49.* *when down the hill he holds his fierce c.* H5 III, 3, 23. *he passes some humours and —s*, II, 1, 132 (Pistol's speech).*

Careful, 1) full of cares, subject to anxiety, sorrow, or want: *c. hours have written strange defeatures in my face*, Err. V, 298. *full of c. business are his looks*, R2 II, 2, 75. *let us our lives, our souls, our debts, our c. wives .... lay on the king*, H5 IV, 1, 248 (cf. 145: *their wives left poor behind them*). *by Him that raised me to this c. height*, R3 I, 3, 83. Probably also in the following passage: *I am not tall enough to become the function well, nor lean enough to be thought a good student; but to be said an honest man and a good housekeeper goes as fairly as to say a c. man and a great scholar*, Tw. IV, 2, 11 (i. e. a great scholar, but oppressed with want and lean with fasting).

2) attentive, provident: *how c. was I ... each trifle under truest bars to thrust*, Sonn. 48, 1. *as a c. housewife runs to catch ...,* 143, 1. Tp. I, 2, 174. Err. I, 1, 79 (*for*). Wint. IV, 4, 702. H4B II, 4, 348. R3 II, 2, 96. V, 3, 54. H8 I, 2, 130. Tit. IV, 3, 21. V, 1, 77. V, 3, 21. Rom. III, 5, 108. Lr. III, 3, 21. Ant. IV, 3, 7. Per. III Prol. 16. III, 1, 81. *under the covering of a c. night, who seemed my good protector*, Per. I, 2, 81 (the night being treated here as a reasonable being). Strange expression: *till time beget some c. remedy*, Tit. IV, 3, 30; perhaps a corrupt passage (v. *carefully* in v. 28); we should substitute *cureful*, if this were a Shakespearian word.

With a negation: *the eagle suffers little birds to sing and is not c. what they mean thereby*, Tit. IV, 4, 84 (= does not care).

Carefully, heedfully, attentively: *to inquire c. about a schoolmaster*, Shr. I, 2, 166. R2 V, 5, 80. H5 II, 4, 2. Tit. II, 2, 8. IV, 3, 28. Hml. I, 1, 6. Lr. I, 2, 125. Oth. V, 1, 99.

Careires, see *Career*.

Careless, 1) free from cares or anxiety: *c. infancy*, Wiv. V, 5, 56. *with such a c. force and forceless care*, Troil. V, 5, 40. *youth no less becomes the light and c. livery*, Hml. IV, 7, 80.

2) heedless, regardless: *c. lust stirs up a desperate courage*, Ven. 556. *a c. herd jumps along by him*, As II, 1, 52. *every thing about you demonstrating a c. desolation*, III, 2, 400. *too c. patient as thou art*, R2 II, 1, 97. *what my grandsire got my c. father fondly gave away*, H6C II, 2, 38. *c. heirs*, Per. III, 2, 28. — Followed by *of: a c. hand of pride*, Compl. 30. *c. of thy sorrowing*, Pilgr. 398. Meas. IV, 2, 150. Shr. IV, 2, 79. H4B IV, 4, 29. H6C IV, 6, 86. Tit. I, 86.

3) in a passive sense, = not cared for, indifferent: *to throw away the dearest thing he owed, as 'twere a c. trifle*, Mcb. I, 4, 11. *or I will throw thee from my care for ever into the staggers and the c. lapse of youth and ignorance*, All's II, 3, 170.

Carelessly, 1) without care or concern: *and fleet the time* c. As I, 1, 124.

2) heedlessly, negligently: *thy brother being c. encamped,* H6C IV, 2, 14. *it may be thought we held him c.* Rom. III, 4, 25. *wear them* (*his wrongs*) *like his raiment c.* Tim. III, 5, 33. *if Caesar c. but nod on him,* Caes. I, 2, 118.

Carelessness, unconcernedness, indifference: *and out of his noble c. lets them plainly see it,* Cor. II, 2, 16.

Care-tuned, tuned by cares, in the key of sorrow: *more health and happiness betide my liege than can my c. tongue deliver him,* R2 III, 2, 92.

Carl, peasant: *or could this c., a very drudge of nature's, have subdued me?* Cymb. V, 2, 4.

Carlisle, English town: *the bishop of C.* R2 III, 3, 30. *here is C. living,* V, 6, 22. 24.

Carlot, peasant: *the cottage and the bounds that the old c. once was master of,* As III, 5, 108.

Carman, a man whose employment it is to drive a cart: Meas. II, 1, 269. H4B III, 2, 341.

Carnal, 1) eating flesh: *that this c. cur preys on the issue of his mother's body,* R3 IV, 4, 56.*

2) fleshly, sensual: *c., bloody and unnatural acts,* Hml. V, 2, 392. *our c. stings,* Oth. I, 3, 335.

Carnally, in a carnal manner: *know you this woman? c., she says,* Meas. V, 214; cf. *cardinally,* II, 1, 81.

Carnarvonshire, county in Wales: H8 II, 3, 48.

Carnation, 1) flesh colour: *a' could never abide c.* H5 II, 3, 35. *c. ribbon,* LLL III, 146.

2) flower of the genus of dianthus: *our —s and streaked gillyvors,* Wint. IV, 4, 82.

Carol, subst. 1) song of devotion: *no night is now with hymn or c. blest,* Mids. II, 1, 102. — 2) any song: *this c. they began that hour,* As V, 3, 27.

Carouse, subst., a hearty drink, a full cup at a draught to the health of a person, a toast: *quaff —s to our mistress' health,* Shr. I, 2, 277. *drink —s to the next day's fate,* Ant. IV, 8, 34.

Carouse, vb., to drink hard: *having all day —d and banqueted,* H6A II, 1, 12. *we were —ing to the second cock,* Mcb. II, 3, 26. *c. together like friends long lost,* Ant. IV, 12, 12. Transitively: *that blood ... hast thou tapped out and drunkenly —d,* R2 II, 1, 127. cf. Oth. II, 3, 55. Followed by *to,* = to drink, to empty a cup to the health of a person, to toast: *as if he had been aboard, — ing to his mates,* Shr. III, 2, 173. *c. full measure to her maidenhead,* 227. *the queen —s to thy fortune,* Hml. V, 2, 300. *Roderigo .... to Desdemona hath to-night —d potations pottle-deep,* Oth. II, 3, 55.

Carp, subst., a species of cyprinus: All's V, 2, 24. Hml. II, 1, 63.

Carp, vb., to cavil, to find fault, to mock: *such —ing is not commendable,* Ado III, 1, 71. *—ing fools,* H4A III, 2, 63 (Q1 *capering*). *envious —ing tongue,* H6A IV, 1, 90. *—ing censures,* R3 III, 5, 68. *do hourly c. and quarrel,* Lr. I, 4, 222. — Followed by *at: our motion will be mocked or —ed at,* H8 I, 2, 86.

Carpenter, one who works in timber: Ado I, 1, 187. H6A V, 3, 90. Caes. I, 1, 6. Hml. V, 1, 48. *build there, c.; the air is sweet,* Troil. III, 2, 53.

Carper, caviller, censurer: *shame not these woods by putting on the cunning of a c.* Tim. IV, 3, 209.

Carpet, a covering for floors or tables: *be ... the —s laid, and every thing in order?* Shr. IV, 1, 52. *upon the grassy c. of this plain,* R2 III, 3, 50. *the purple violets and marigolds shall as a c. hang upon thy grave,* Per. IV, 1, 17. *he is knight, dubbed with unhatched rapier and on c. consideration,* Tw. III, 4, 258 (i. e. dubbed not in the field, for military prowess, but in consideration of service done on the carpet, i. e. in peace).

Carpet-monger, one who is at home on carpets and in ladies' bowers: Ado V, 2, 32.

Carrack, a large ship of burden, a galleon: Err. III, 2, 140. Oth. I, 2, 50.

Carranto, see *Coranto.*

Carriage, 1) the act of carrying or conveying, transportation: *lest, being missed, I be suspected of your c. from the court,* Cymb. III, 4, 190.

2) that which is carried or borne, the load: *time goes upright with his c.* Tp. V, 3. *easing me of the c.* Wiv. II, 2, 179.

3) that which carries or bears, a vehicle: *for many —s he hath dispatched to the sea-side,* John V, 7, 90. Likewise the frame on which cannon rests: *behold the ordnance on their —s,* H5 III Chor. 26. Tropically: *sometimes her levelled eyes their c. ride, as they did battery to the spheres intend,* Compl. 22 (cf. v. 281: *his eyes he did dismount*). In the affected language of the time = the hanger of a sword: *three of the —s are very dear to fancy; most delicate —s. What call you the —s? The —s are the hangers. The phrase would be more german to the matter, if we could carry cannon by our sides,* Hml. V, 2, 158—169.

4) the power of bearing: *he was a man of good c., great c., for he carried the town-gates on his back,* LLL I, 2, 74. *making them women of good c.* Rom. I, 4, 94 (both times a quibble).

5) bearing, deportment: *teach sin the c. of a holy saint,* Err. III, 2, 14. *fashion a c. to rob love from any,* Ado I, 3, 31. LLL I, 1, 272. I, 2, 72. V, 2, 306. Tw. III, 4, 81. H4A II, 4, 466. H4B V, 1, 84. H8 III, 1, 161. IV, 2, 145. Rom. I, 4, 94 (quibbling). Tim. III, 2, 88. *how this Herculean Roman does become the c. of his chafe,* Ant. I, 3, 85.

6) management: *the violent c. of it will clear or end the business,* Wint. III, 1, 17. *as if the passage and whole c. of this action rode on his tide,* Troil. II, 3, 140.

7) import, tenour: *by the same covenant and c. of the article designed his* (moiety) *fell to Hamlet,* Hml. I, 1, 94.

Carrier, 1) one whose trade is to carry goods for others: H4A II, 1, 36. 46.

2) one who conveys or brings sth.: *misshapen Time ... c. of grisly care,* Lucr. 926. So understood by the clown in Tit. IV, 3, 86.

3) messenger: *this punk is one of Cupid's —s,* Wiv. II, 2, 141. *what says Jupiter? ... art not thou the c.?* Tit. IV, 3, 86.

Carrion, 1) corrupted flesh: Meas. II, 2, 167. H4B IV, 4, 80. Hml. II, 2, 182. *c. kites,* H6B V, 2, 11 (kites feeding on c.). *c. flies,* Rom. III, 3, 35. *this foul deed shall smell above the earth with c. men,* Caes. III, 1, 275.

2) a skeleton: *a c. Death, within whose empty eye ...,* Merch. II, 7, 63. *and be a c. monster like thyself* (Death), John III, 4, 33.

174 **C**

3) term of contempt for **flesh**: *out upon it, old c.!
rebels it at these years?* Merch. III, 1, 38. *why I rather
choose to have a weight of c. flesh,* IV, 1, 41.

4) term of contempt for **persons**: *that foolish
c., Mistress Quickly,* Wiv. III, 3, 205. *yon island —s
... ill-favouredly become the morning field,* H5 IV, 2,
39. *for every scruple of her* (Helen's) *contaminated c.
weight,* Troil. IV, 1, 71. *out, you green-sickness c.! out,
you baggage,* Rom. III, 5, 157. *old feeble – s,* Caes. II,
1, 130.

Carry, 1) to **convey**, to **bear**: *he will c. this
island home in his pocket,* Tp. II, 1, 90. *I'll c. it to
the pile,* III, 1, 25. *c. this,* IV, 253. *c. the wine in,* Wiv.
I, 1, 195. cf. Ven. 582. Wiv. III, 3, 14. LLL I, 2, 74.
IV, 3, 34. Merch. IV, 1, 9. As I V, 1, 55. John III, 1,
201. H4A II, 4, 285. H6A I, 3, 65. H8 III, 2, 319. V,
1, 131. *before him he —ies noise, and behind him he
leaves tears,* Cor. II, 1, 175. *he could not c. his honours
even,* IV, 7, 37. *that kiss I —ed from thee,* V, 3, 47. Mcb.
II, 2, 49. — Used of winds and waves: *was —ied
towards Corinth,* Err. I, 1, 88. *was —ied with more
speed before the wind,* 110. *with shame ... he was
—ied from off our coast,* Cymb. III, 1, 25. *To c. coals*
= to put up with an affront: H5 III, 2, 50. Rom. I,
1, 1. cf. *to c. crotchets,* IV, 5, 120.

Frequently implying the idea of violence, = to
drag or **fetch away**: *when that fell arrest without
all bail* (viz Death) *shall c. me away,* Sonn. 74, 2.
—ied to prison, Meas. I, 2, 61. *to c. him to execution,*
IV, 2, 159. *his valour cannot c. his discretion, and the
fox —ies the goose,* Mids. V, 237. *c. this mad knave
to the gaol,* Shr. V, 1, 95. *carries poor souls to hell,*
Err. IV, 2, 40. *thou art violently —ied away from grace,*
H4A II, 4, 491. *c. Sir John to the Fleet,* H4B V, 5,
97. *he shall not c. him* (as a prisoner) Troil. V, 6, 24.
Tropically: *what is it —ies you away?* H4A II, 3, 78.

2) to **bear sth., in order to deliver it to another**:
to c. a letter, Lucr. 1294. Gentl. I, 1, 112. 154. IV, 4,
106. Wiv. III, 2, 32. LLL III, 50. *she can fetch and
c. Why, a horse can do no more: nay, a horse cannot
fetch, but only c.* Gentl. III, 1, 274. *here is the head,
I'll c. it myself,* Meas. IV, 3, 106. *To carry sth. to
a p.:* *which he must c. for a present to his lady,* Gentl.
IV, 2, 79. IV, 4, 49. *I must c. her word,* Wiv. III, 5,
48. *he hath —ied notice to Escalus,* Meas. IV, 3, 134.
Used without propriety by Evans: *can you c. your
good will to the maid?* Wiv. I, 1, 238. 244.

3) to **bear away as a prize, to gain**: *that
kiss I —ied from thee,* Cor. V, 3, 47. *he would miss
it* (the consulship) *rather than c. it but by the suit of
the gentry,* II, 1, 254. *shall c. half my love with him,*
Lr. I, 1, 103. Hence = to **conquer**: *resolved to c.
her,* All's III, 7, 19. *think you he'll c. Rome?* Cor. IV,
7, 27. *when he had —ied Rome,* V, 6, 43. *To carry
it* = to do, to have the better, to carry the victory:
he will c. it, Wiv. III, 2, 70. LLL III, 141. All's IV, 1,
30. 42. Troil. II, 3, 3. 228. 229. Cor. II, 2, 4. II, 3,
42. Tim. III, 5, 48. Oth. I, 1, 67. *To carry it away,*
in the same sense: Rom. III, 1, 77. Hml. II, 2, 377.

4) to **bear, to push on to a certain distance**: *and —ied you a forehand shaft a fourteen
and fourteen and a half,* H4B III, 2, 52. *this speed of
Caesar's —ies beyond belief,* Ant. III, 7, 76.

5) to **manage, to execute**: *if you think well
to c. this,* Meas. III, 1, 267. *let there be the same net
spread for her, and that must your daughter and her*

gentlewomen c. Ado II, 3, 223. *this well —ied shall
on her behalf change slander to remorse,* IV, 1, 212.
this sport, well —ied, shall be chronicled, Mids. III, 2,
240. *we may c. it thus,* Tw. III, 4, 150. *all this business
our reverend cardinal —ied,* H8 I, 1, 100. *he'll c. it so
to make the sceptre his,* I, 2, 134. *c. it so as I have set
it down,* Lr. V, 3, 37. With **on**: *—ies on the stream
of his dispose without observance or respect of any,*
Troil. II, 3, 174. With **out**: *hardly shall I c. out my
side,* Lr. V, 1, 61 (= win, make out my game). —
With **through**: *my good intent may c. through itself to
that full issue,* Lr. I, 4, 3.

6) to **convey, to import**: *words cannot c.
authority so weighty,* H8 III, 2, 233. *speaks things in
doubt, that c. but half sense,* Hml. IV, 5, 7.

7) to **lead up, to bring**: *a mighty strength
they c.* Ant. II, 1, 17. *and c. back to Sicily much tall
youth,* II, 6, 7.

8) to **bear, to sustain**, without the idea of
motion: *the stocks c. him,* All's IV, 3, 122. *man's nature
cannot c. the affliction,* Lr. III, 2, 48. *she that —ies
up the train,* H8 IV, 1, 51. *I will c. no crotchets,* Rom.
IV, 5, 120. Used of weapons, = to **wear**: *c. armour,*
H6A II, 1, 24. *forbidden late to c. any weapon,* III,
1, 79.

9) to **bear, to be with child of**: *repent
you of the sin you c.* Meas. II, 3, 19.

10) to **bear, to have in or on**: *it —ies a
brave form,* Tp. I, 2, 411. *the second, silver, which this
promise —ies,* Merch. II, 7, 6. *where an unclean mind
—ies virtuous qualities,* All's I, 1, 48. *my imagination
—ies no favour in it but Bertram s,* 94. *a bear-whelp
that —ies no impression like the dam,* H6C III, 2, 162.
he —ies some stain of it, Troil. I, 2, 26. *let's to the
Capitol, and c. with us ears and eyes for the time, but
hearts for the event,* Cor. II, 1, 285. *the noblest mind
he —ies that ever governed man,* Tim. I, 1, 291. *that
—ies anger as the flint bears fire,* Caes. IV, 3, 111.
—ing the stamp of one defect, Hml. I, 4, 31. *if our
father c. authority with such dispositions,* Lr. I, 1, 308.

11) Reflectively, = to **bear one's self, to
behave**: *how does he c. himself,* All's IV, 3, 120.
*and like her true nobility, she has —ied herself towards
me,* H8 II, 4, 143. — *To c. one's self through* = to be
borne out, to succeed without failing, see sub 5, and
Lr. I, 4, 3.

Carry-tale, tale-bearer: *this c., dissentious
jealousy,* Ven. 657. *some c.* LLL V, 2, 463.

Cart, subst. 1) a **carriage on two wheels**
used by husbandmen: *then to c. with Rosalind,* As III,
2, 114. *provide some —s and bring away the armour,*
R2 II, 2, 106. *may not an ass know when the c. draws
the horse?* Lr. I, 4, 244. *I cannot draw a c.* V, 3, 38.

2) the **vehicle in which criminals are carried to**
execution: *if I become not a c. as well as another man,*
H4A II, 4, 546.

3) the **car or chariot of Phoebus**: *Phoebus' c.*
Hml. III, 2, 165.

Cart, vb., to **expose in a cart, by way of**
punishment: *leave shall you have to court her ... to c.
her rather: she's too rough for me,* Shr. I, 1, 55.

Carter, a man whose trade is to drive a cart:
Wint. IV, 4, 331. R3 II, 1, 121. Hml. II, 2, 167.

Carthage, the town of Queen Dido: Tp. II, 1,
82. 83. 84. 85. Mids. I, 1, 173. Merch. V, 12. Shr.
I, 1, 159.

Carve, 1) to cut, to hew: *Macbeth ... with his brandished steel ... —d out his passage,* Mcb. I, 2, 19.

2) to cut meat at table: *a calf's head and a capon, the which if I do not c. most curiously, say my knife is naught,* Ado V, 1, 157. *to c. a capon,* H4A II, 4, 502. *let's c. him as a dish fit for the gods,* Caes. II, 1, 173. Absolutely: *Boyet, you can c.* LLL IV, 1, 55. *—d to thee,* Err. II, 2, 120. Hence = to show great courtesy and affability: *she discourses, she —s,* Wiv. I, 3, 49. *a' can c. too and lisp,* LLL V, 2, 323 (quibble in IV, 1, 55). cf. Dyce's Glossary. Followed by *for,* = to indulge, to do at a person's pleasure: *he may not, as unvalued persons do, c. for himself,* Hml. I, 3, 20. *he that stirs next to c. for his own rage holds his soul light,* Oth. II, 3, 173.

3) to engrave: *c. on every tree the fair, the chaste and unexpressive she,* As III, 2, 9. 182. 379. Tit. V, 1, 139. *where cares have —d some* (distress) Lucr. 1445. *hard misfortune, —d in it* (the face) *with tears,* 1713. *c. not my love's fair brow,* Sonn. 19, 9.

4) to shape by cutting: *she* (nature) *—d thee for her seal,* Sonn. 11, 13. *a pair of —d saints,* R2 III, 3, 152. *a head fantastically —d upon it,* H4B III, 2, 335. *c. out dials,* H6C II, 5, 24. And in general, to form, to fashion: *—ing the fashion of a new doublet,* Ado II, 3, 18. *—d like an apple-tart,* Shr. IV, 3, 89.

Carved-bone, of carved bone: *the c. face on a flask,* LLL V, 2, 619 (so O. and M. Edd.; perhaps it ought to be: *carved bone-face*).

Carver, 1) sculptor: *so much the more our —'s excellence,* Wint. V, 3, 30.

2) In the passage of R2 II, 3, 144: *be his own c. and cut out his way,* there is a combination of various significations: one who provides for himself; one who indulges his passions; and one who cuts his way.

Casca, name in Caes. I, 2, 179 etc. etc.

Case, subst., 1) contingency, possible event: *I would not spare my brother in this c.* Err. IV, 1, 77. Mids. I, 1, 45. 63 etc. *in any c.* Wiv. II, 2, 131. Mids. IV, 2, 40. Shr. IV, 4, 6. John I, 147. H4A V, 2, 25 etc. *If case* = in case, if it happen: *if c. some one of you would fly from us,* H6C V, 4, 34 (cf. *chance*).

2) state of things, situation, circumstances: *the wind wars with his torch to make him stay, and blows the smoke of it into his face, extinguishing his conduct in this c.* Lucr. 313. *feeble desire like to a bankrupt beggar wails his c.* 711. *my c. is past the help of law,* 1022. *our c. is miserable,* Tp. I, 1, 35. 58. II, 1, 290. Wiv. IV, 1, 64. Meas. IV, 2, 178. Err. I, 1, 128. IV, 2, 5. Ado IV, 1, 203. LLL IV, 3, 131. V, 2, 273 (*in lamentable —s*). As Epil. 7. Shr. IV, 2, 45. H6A II, 1, 72. H6B I, 3, 218 (*I cannot fight; pity my c.*). III, 1, 217. Rom. IV, 5, 99. Mcb. I, 7, 7. Lr. IV, 6, 150. Oth. I, 3, 6 etc. — *She hath been in good c.* = in good circumstances, H4B II, 1, 115. *To be in c.* = to be able: *I am in c. to justle a constable,* Tp. III, 2, 29.

3) question of law, cause, question in general: *eternal love in love's fresh c. weighs not the dust and injury of age,* Sonn. 108, 9. *he is 'rested on the c.* Err. IV, 2, 42. *'tis a plain c.* IV, 3, 22. *dare no man answer in a c. of truth?* H6A II, 4, 2. *for the truth and plainness of the c.* 46. *in argument upon a*

c. II, 5, 46. *to be mine own attorney in this c.* V, 3, 166. *that in this c. of justice my accusers may stand forth,* H8 V, 3, 46. *his quillets, his —s, his tenures.* Hml. V, 1, 108. *when every c. in law is right,* Lr. III, 2, 85. *idiots in this c. of favour would be wisely definite,* Cymb. I, 6, 42 (in this question about beauty). *I will make one of her women lawyer to me, for I yet not understand the c. myself,* II, 3, 80.

4) variation of nouns in declension: *accusative c.* Wiv. IV, 1, 46. *vocative c.* 53. *genitive c.* 59. *—s,* 72.

Case, subst., 1) that which incloses and covers a thing, a box, a sheath: Err. IV, 3, 23. Ado I, 1, 184. II, 1, 98. H4A V, 3, 54. H4B III, 2, 351. Rom. IV, 5, 100. Tim. I, 2, 103. Lr. I, 5, 34. Jestingly for a mask: LLL V, 2, 387. Rom. I, 4, 29. cf. Ado II, 1, 98. Metaphorically, a) ornaments, dress: *accomplished in himself, not in his c.* Compl. 116. *O place, o form, how often dost thou with thy c., thy habit, wrench awe from fools,* Meas. II, 4, 13. *I have —s of buckram, to immask our garments,* H4A I, 2, 201. — b) the body as the cover of the soul: *what wilt thou be when time hath sowed a grizzle on thy c.?* Tw. V, 168. *heart, crack thy frail c.* Ant. IV, 14, 41. *this c. of that huge spirit now is cold,* IV, 15, 89. Perhaps = the skin: *though my c. be a pitiful one, I hope I shall not be flayed out of it,* Wint. IV, 4, 844.* — c) the eyelids, and the sockets of the eyes: *her eyelids, —s to those heavenly jewels,* Per. III, 2, 99. *they seemed almost, with staring on one another, to tear the —s of their eyes,* Wint. V, 2, 14. *Read. What, with the c. of eyes?* Lr. IV, 6, 147. cf. 150.

2) a certain quantity contained in a cover, perhaps a pair: *I have not a c. of lives,* H5 III, 2, 5 (but there may be meant a cover, a strong box, to secure life from hurts).

Case, vb., 1) to put in a case, to cover: *you must c. me in leather,* Err. II, 1, 85. *like a cunning instrument —d up,* R2 I, 3, 163. Hence = to mask: *c. ye, c. ye; on with your vizards,* H4A II, 2, 55. *with faces fit for masks, or rather fairer than those for preservation —d,* Cymb. V, 3, 22. — Used of the eyelids inclosing the eyes: *her eyes as jewellike and —d as richly.* Per. V, 1, 112. (cf. *Discase* and *Uncase* = undress).

Metaphorically, = to surround, to cover: *as broad and general as the —ing air,* Mcb. III, 4, 23. And = to hide: *if thou wouldst not entomb thyself alive and c. thy reputation in thy tent,* Troil. III, 3, 187. *thou mayst hold a serpent by the tongue, a —d lion by the mortal paw,* John III, 1, 259, i. e. a lion hid in his cave (M. Edd. *chafed!*).

2) to skin, to flay: *we'll make you some sport with the fox ere we c. him,* All's III, 6, 111.

Casement, part of a window, made to turn and open on hinges: Wiv. I, 4, 2. Mids. III, 1, 57. 59. Merch. II, 5, 31. 34. As IV, 1, 163. All's II, 3, 225. V, 3, 93. 230. R2 V, 2, 14. Lr. I, 2, 65. Cymb. II, 4, 34.

Cash, ready money: *I shall have my noble? In c. most justly paid,* H5 II, 1, 120.

Cashier, vb., to discard from service: *c., let them wag, trot, trot,* Wiv. I, 3, 6. *what does his —ed worship mutter?* Tim. III, 4, 60. *when he's old, —ed,* Oth. I, 1, 48. *thou, by that small hurt, hast —ed Cassio,* II, 3, 381. — In the slang of Bardolph it seems to mean: to ease a person of his cash: *and being fap, sir, was, as they say, —ed,* Wiv. I, 1, 184.

'Casion, = occasion, in the provincial dialect used by Edgar: Lr. IV, 6, 240.

Cask, box or small chest for jewels: *a jewel, locked into the wofullest c.* H6B III, 2, 409.

Casket, subst. the same: Lucr. 1057. Merch. I, 2, 100. 105. 115. II, 1, 23. II, 6, 33. II, 7, 2. 15. II, 9, 4. 11. 12. III, 2, 39. 203. John V, 1, 40. Tim. I, 2, 164. Per. I, 1, 77. III, 1, 67.

Casket, vb., to put in a casket: *I have writ my letters, —ed my treasure,* All's II, 5, 26.

Casque, head-piece, helmet: R2 I, 3, 81. H5 Prol. 13. Troil. V, 2, 170. Cor. IV, 7, 43 (*from the c. to the cushion,* i. e. from military to civil authority).

Cassado: *Gregory de C.,* H8 III, 2, 321 (so O. Edd. after Hall and Holinshed; some M. Edd. *Cassalis*).

Cassandra, daughter of Priam, a prophetess: Troil. I, 1, 47. I, 2, 159. II, 2, 100. V, 3, 30 etc.

Cassibelan, king of Britain in the time of Julius Caesar: Cymb. I, 1, 30. III, 1, 5. 30. 41.

Cassio, name in Oth. I, 1, 20 etc. etc.

Cassius, friend and brother-in-law of Brutus: Caes. I, 2, 30 etc. etc. Ant. II, 6, 15. III, 11, 37.

Cassock, military cloak: *dare not shake the snow from off their —s,* All's IV, 3, 192.

Cast, vb., (impf. and partic. *cast; casted* only in H5 IV, 1, 23). 1) to throw: *a ladder made of cords, to c. up, with a pair of hooks,* Gentl. III, 1, 118. *from thence* (the Tarpeian rock) *into destruction c. him,* Cor. III, 1, 214. *will all headlong cast us* (= ourselves) *down,* Tit. V, 3, 132. *spit, and throw stones, c. mire upon me,* Cymb. V, 5, 222. *—ing their savageness aside,* Wint. II, 3, 188. *not c. aside so soon,* Mcb. I, 7, 35. *c. by their grave beseeming ornaments,* Rom. I, 1, 100. *a noble spirit ever —s such doubts, as false coin, from it,* H8 III, 1, 170. *his dignity and duty both c. off,* Wint. V, 1, 183. *c. off his chains of bondage,* R2 I, 3, 89. *none but fools do wear it; c. it off,* Rom. II, 2, 9. *the shape which thou dost think I have c. off for ever,* Lr. I, 4, 332. *To cast into my teeth,* Caes. IV, 3, 99 (= to upbraid me). *they c. their caps up,* Ant. IV, 12, 12; and in the same sense without *up: when you c. your greasy caps,* Cor. IV, 6, 130.

2) to drop, to let fall: *when you c. out the anchor,* Wint. I, 2, 214. *c. your nets,* Tit. IV, 3, 7.

3) to throw, to pour: *fire, fire; c. on no water,* Shr. IV, 1, 21. *seems to c. water on the burning bear,* Oth. II, 1, 14. Figuratively: *c. your good counsels upon his passion,* Wint. IV, 4, 506.

4) to throw to the ground: *though he took up my legs sometime, yet I made a shift to c. him,* Mcb. II, 3, 46 (a quibble). Figuratively: *for thee, oppressed king, I am c. down* (= depressed) Lr. V, 3, 5.

5) to raise, to form by throwing up earth: *the blind mole —s copped hills towards heaven,* Per. I, 1, 100. *throws down one mountain to c. up a higher,* I, 4, 6.

6) to throw off, to shed: *he hath bought a pair of c. lips of Diana,* As III, 4, 16. *c. thy humble slough,* Tw. II, 5, 161. *with —ed slough and fresh legerity,* H5 IV, 1, 23. *your colt's tooth is not c. yet,* H8 I, 3, 48.

7) to drive away: *be c. from possibility of all,* H6A V, 4, 146. *to be exiled, and thrown from Leonati seat, and c. from her his dearest one,* Cymb. V, 4, 60.

8) to throw out, to eject; used of the sea: *we all were sea-swallowed, though some c. again,* Tp. II, 1, 251. *since I was c. ashore,* Tp. II, 2, 129. *the sea hath c. me upon your coast,* Per. II, 1, 60. Hence = to vomit: *his filth within being c., he would appear a pond as deep as hell,* Meas. III, 1, 93. *I made a shift to c. him,* Mcb. II, 3, 46 (quibble). *what a drunken knave was the sea to c. thee in our way,* Per. II, 1, 62. With *up: did the sea c. it up?* Per. III, 2, 57. *thou, beastly feeder, art so full of him, that thou provokest thyself to c. him up,* H4B I, 3, 96. *their villany goes against my weak stomach, and therefore I must c. it up,* H5 III, 2, 57. *the sepulchre hath oped his jaws, to c. thee up again,* Hml. I, 4, 51. *till he* (the whale) *c. bells, steeple etc. up again,* Per. II, 1, 46. With *out: the city c. her people out upon her,* Ant. II, 2, 218.

To cast the gorge = to be about to vomit: *she whom the spital-house and ulcerous sores would c. the gorge at,* Tim. IV, 3, 40.

9) to direct, to turn: *to c. thy wandering eyes on every stale,* Shr. III, 1, 90. *there was —ing up of eyes,* Wint. V, 2, 51. *to whom do lions c. their gentle looks?* H6C II, 2, 11. *he —s his eye against the moon,* H8 III, 2, 117. *c. her fair eyes to heaven,* IV, 1, 84. *whose bright faces c. thousand beams upon me,* IV, 2, 89. *c. his eyes upon me,* V, 2, 12. *to c. one's eyes so low,* Lr. IV, 6, 12.

10) to throw away as worthless; with *forth: the —ing forth to crows thy baby-daughter,* Wint. III, 2, 192. *to be c. forth in the common air,* R2 I, 3, 157. With *off* = 1) to discard, to disinherit: *the prince will in the perfectness of time c. off his followers,* H4B IV, 4, 75. *with what poor judgment he hath now c. her off,* Lr. I, 1, 294. 2) to ruin: *dead, forsook, c. off,* John V, 7, 35. *are we undone? c. off? nothing remaining?* Tim. IV, 2, 2. With *out: thy brat hath been c. out,* Wint. III, 2, 88. Mostly with *away* = 1) to throw away, to waste or lavish: *if you thought your love not c. away,* Gentl. I, 2, 26. *I would be loath to c. away my speech,* Tw. I, 5, 184. *hast thou yet more blood to c. away?* John II, 334. *let us c. away nothing,* Troil. IV, 4, 22. *he is gone, he is gone, and we c. away moan,* Hml. IV, 5, 198. *be't lawful I take up what's c. away,* Lr. I, 1, 256. Followed by *on: will you c. away your child on a fool?* Wiv. III, 4, 100. *thy words are too precious to be c. away upon curs,* As I, 3, 5. *I will not c. away my physic but on those that are sick,* III, 2, 376. *to c. away honesty upon a foul slut,* 3, 35. — 2) to let perish: *the poor wench is c. away,* LLL V, 2, 682. *'tis but one c. away,* As IV, 1, 189. *do not c. away an honest man for a villain's accusation,* H6B I, 3, 205. *win straying souls with modesty again; c. none away,* H8 V, 3, 65. *c. me not away,* Rom. III, 5, 200. *thou hast c. away thyself, being like thyself,* Tim. IV, 3, 220. *it were pity to c. them* (women) *away for nothing,* Ant. I, 2, 142. — 3) to shipwreck: *if he thrive, and I* (like a boat) *be c. away,* Sonn. 80, 13. *hath an argosy c. away,* Merch. III, 1, 105. *c. away and sunk on Goodwin Sands,* John V, 5, 13. *c. away before us even now,* Per. II, 1, 19.

11) to dismiss: *the state cannot with safety c. him,* Oth. I, 1, 150. *our general c. us thus early for the love of his Desdemona,* II, 3, 14. *you are but now c. in his mood,* 273. *whereon it came that I was c.* V, 2, 327.

12) to bestow, to confer, to impart; fol-

lowed by *on: the government I c. upon my brother,* Tp. 1, 2, 75. *wouldst thou have me c. my love on him?* Gentl. I, 2, 25. *my fortunes having c. me on your niece,* Tw. II, 5, 78. *which I doubt not but our Rome will c. upon thee,* Cor. II, 1, 218. *c. your election on him,* II, 3, 237. *the ingratitude that Rome c. on my noble father,* Ant. II, 6, 23.

13) to turn, to place, to put in a state: *why hast thou c. into eternal sleeping those eyes,* Ven. 951. *since you to non-regardance c. my faith,* Tw. V, 124. *Clarence whom I have c. in darkness,* R3 I, 3, 327 (Qq *laid*). *c. in prison,* Cymb. III, 2, 38. Reflectively: *and put on fear, and c. yourself in wonder,* Caes. I, 3, 60.

14) to throw, as dice or lots: *however God or fortune c. my lot,* R2 I, 3, 85.

15) to compute, to calculate: *when as thy love hath c. his utmost sum,* Sonn. 49, 3. *you c. the event of war and summed the account of chance,* H4B I, 1, 166. *let it be c. and paid,* V, 1, 21. *he can write and read and c. accompt,* H6B IV, 2, 93. *to c. beyond ourselves in our opinions,* Hml. II, 1, 115 (= to be mistaken). *I know not what counts harsh fortune —s upon my face,* Ant. II, 6, 55. *think, speak, c., write, sing, number his love,* III, 2, 17. *To cast the water* = to inspect the urine as a diagnostic: *c. the water of my land,* Mcb. V, 3, 50.

Cast, subst., 1) a throw of dice: *to set all at one c.* H4A IV, 1, 47. *I have set my life upon a c.* R3 V, 4, 9.

2) the forming in a mold: *such daily c. of brazen cannon,* Hml. I. 1, 73.

3) tinge, coloring: *the native hue of resolution is sicklied o'er with the pale c. of thought,* Hml. III, 1, 85.

Castalion-King-Urinal, a nonsensical title which the host gives to Dr. Caius in Wiv. II, 3, 34. To make out sense, Hanmer proposed *Cardalion,* Capell *Castillian.* cf. *to cast the water* in Mcb. V, 3, 50.

Castaway, a ruined person: *he thence departs a heavy convertite; she there remains a hopeless c.* Lucr. 744. *and call us wretches, orphans, —s,* R3 II, 2, 6. *and she whom mighty kingdoms court'sy to, like a forlorn and desperate c., do shameful execution on herself,* Tit. V, 3, 75. *that ever I should call thee c.!* Ant. III, 6, 40.

Castigate, to chasten: *if thou didst put this sour-cold habit on to c. thy pride, 'twere well,* Tim. IV, 3, 240.

Castigation, chastening, maceration: *this hand of yours requires a sequester from liberty, fasting and prayer, much c.* Oth. III, 4, 41.

Castle, a strong house, fortified against assault: Pilgr. 327. Wiv. III, 3, 232 (*Windsor C.*). IV, 5, 7 (*there's his chamber, his house, his c.*). V, 5, 60. John V, 1, 31 (*Dover C.*). R2 II, 2, 135 (*Bristol C.*). II, 3, 53. III, 2, 1 (*Barkloughly C.*). III, 3, 20. H5 IV, 7, 91. H6A II, 2, 41. III, 1, 47. H6B I, 4, 38. V, 2, 68. H6C I, 1, 206. R3 IV, 2, 107. Mcb. IV, 1, 56. Oth. II, 1, 203 etc. etc. *My old lad of the c.* H4A I, 2, 48 ('a familiar appellation, equivalent to *old buck*. Gabriel Harvey tells us of *old lads of the castle,* with their rapping babble; roaring boys.' Nares). Used as the emblem of security: *we steal as in a c., cocksure,* H4A II, 1, 95. *stand fast and wear a c. on thy head,* Troil. V, 2, 187.

In Tit. III, 1, 170 (*which of your hands hath not defended Rome, and reared aloft the bloody battleaxe, writing destruction on the enemy's c.?*) the word has unnecessarily been interpreted in the sense of casque, helmet. Marcus says: each hand of yours has been employed in defending Rome and in assailing and destroying the strongholds of enemies.

Castle-ditch: Wiv. V, 2, 1.

Castle-wall: H6A V, 3, 129.

Casual, accidental: Hml. V, 2, 393. Cymb. I, 4, 100.

Casually, accidentally: *search for a jewel that too c. hath left mine arm,* Cymb. II, 3, 146 (i. e. by an accident to which it ought not to have been exposed, and which is a reproach to me).

Casualty, accident: *builds in the weather on the outward wall, even in the force and road of c.* Merch. II, 9, 30. *turned her to foreign —ies,* Lr. IV, 3, 46. *and to the world and awkward —ies bound me in servitude,* Per. V, 1, 94.

Cat, 1) the domestic animal of the genus Felis: Lucr. 554. Tp. II, 1, 288. Gentl. III, 3, 8. Mids. II, 2, 30. III, 2, 260. Merch. IV, 1, 48. 55. As III, 2, 109. All's IV, 3, 267. H4A IV, 2, 65. H5 I, 2, 172. Rom. II, 4, 19 (*prince of —s;* cf. *Tybalt*). III, 1, 80 etc. etc. Used as a term of reproach: All's IV, 3, 295. 307. V, 2, 20. Troil. V, 1, 67. Cor. IV, 2, 34 (Collier *curs,* Staunton *bats*). — *Here is that which will give language to you, c.* Tp. II, 2, 86 (alluding to an old proverb, that good liquor will make a cat speak). *a part to tear a c. in,* Mids. I, 2, 32. *care killed a c.* Ado V, 1, 133 (though it has nine lives, Rom. III, 1, 81). *as melancholy as a gib c.* H4A I, 2, 83. *the c. is gray,* Lr. III, 6, 47. *she shall have no more eyes to see withal than a c.* Shr. I, 2, 116. *the c. will mew,* Hml. V, 1, 315. *like the poor c. in the adage,* Mcb. I, 7, 45 ('the cat loves fish, but dares not wet her feet'). *hang me in a bottle like a c. and shoot at me,* Ado I, 1, 259.

2) = the civet-cat: *civet is the very uncleanly flux of a c.* As III, 2, 70. *thou owest the c. no perfume,* Lr. III, 4, 109.

Cataian, a Chinese; used as a term of reproach: *I will not believe such a C., though the priest o' the town commended him for a true man,* Wiv. II, 1, 148. *my lady's a C., we are politicians,* Tw. II, 3, 80.

Catalogue, a list, register: All's I, 3, 149. Cor. III, 3, 8. Mcb. III, 1, 92. Cymb. I, 4, 5. cf. *catelog,* Gentl. III, 1, 273.

Cataplasm, a salve: *no c. so rare, collected from all simples that have virtue, can save the thing from death,* Hml. IV, 7, 144.

Cataract, mighty fall of water, a waterspout: *you —s and hurricanoes, spout till you have drenched our steeples,* Lr. III, 2, 2.

Catarrh, defluxion of humours: *the rotten diseases of the south, the guts-griping, ruptures, —s,* Troil. V, 1, 22.

Catastrophe, 1) that which produces the final event of a dramatic piece: *the c. is a nuptial,* LLL IV, 1, 77. *and pat he comes like the c. of the old comedy,* Lr. I, 2, 146.

2) conclusion, end: *this his good melancholy oft began, on the c. and heel of pastime, when it was out,* All's I, 2, 57.

Falstaff uses it for the backside: *I'll tickle your c.* H4B II, 1, 66.

Catch, subst., 1) the act of catching, or the thing caught: *no doubt but he hath got a quiet c.* Shr. II, 333. *Hector shall have a great c., if he knock out either of your brains,* Troil. II, 1, 110.

2) a song sung in succession: Tp. III, 2, 126. 135. Tw. II, 3, 18. 60. 64. 97.*

Catch, vb. (Impf. *caught:* LLL V, 2, 421. Merch. I, 1, 3. Wint. III, 1, 4. V, 2, 90. H4B III, 2, 194. Per. IV, 1, 88. *catched:* Cor. I, 3, 68. Partic. *caught:* Ven. 547. Wiv. III, 3, 45. Ado I, 1, 87. III, 1, 104. LLL V, 2, 69. As II, 7, 68 etc. *catched:* LLL V, 2, 69. All's I, 3, 176. Rom. IV, 5, 48).

1) to seize, to take, to capture, whether by pursuit or by stratagem; absolutely: *which (greyhound) runs himself and —es for his master,* Shr. V, 2, 53. *some dogs will c. well,* Tw. II, 3, 65. Transitively: *jealous of —ing,* Ven. 321 (i. e. fearing to be caught). *now quick desire hath caught the yielding prey,* 547. *the dove sleeps fast that this night-owl will c.* Lucr. 360. Sonn. 143, 1. 11. *for stale to c. these thieves,* Tp. IV, 187. *to c. a saint, with saints dost bait thy hook,* Meas. II, 2, 180. Wiv. III, 3, 45. LLL V, 2, 69. Ado III, 1, 104. Shr. II, 204. All's III, 6, 115. Wint. V, 2, 90. H4A III, 3, 43. H6B III, 3, 16. H6C V, 6, 17. Troil. IV, 4, 106. Cor. I, 3, 68. Hml. I, 3, 115. Oth. IV, 1, 46. Ant. II, 5, 15. V, 2, 350 etc. etc. Figuratively: *if the assassination could ... c. with his surcease success,* Mcb. I, 7, 3.

2) to snatch: *thy wit is as quick as the greyhound's mouth, it —es,* Ado V, 2, 12. *c. this casket,* Merch. II, 6, 33.

3) to seize with the eye or by thought, to perceive: *nor his own vision holds what it doth c.* Sonn. 113, 8. *he had the dialect and different skill —ing all passions in his craft of will,* Compl. 126. *his eye begets occasion for his wit; for every object that the one doth c. the other turns to a mirthmoving jest,* LLL II, 70. *my fear hath —ed your fondness,* All's I, 3, 176. *has caught me in his eye,* Tim. IV, 3, 476. *Cleopatra, —ing but the least noise of this, dies instantly,* Ant. I, 2, 144 (cf. Ado V, 2, 12).

Intr., followed by *at,* = to guess: *you may be pleased to c. at mine intent by what did here befal me,* Ant. II, 2, 41.

4) to lay hold, to take: *the bushes in the way some c. her by the neck,* Ven. 872. *if I can c. him once upon the hip,* Merch. I, 3, 47. *to c. the strong fellow by the leg,* As I, 2, 223. *ready to c. each other by the throat,* R3 I, 3, 189. *till I have caught her once more in mine arms,* Hml. V, 1, 273. *I'll c. thine eyes,* Ant. V, 2, 156.

Followed by *at* (= to stretch out the hand for): *saucy lictors will c. at us, like strumpets,* Ant. V, 2, 215. And transitively in a similar sense: *that makes him gasp and stare and c. the air,* H6B III, 2, 371 (= gasp for breath).

5) Sometimes, indeed, scarcely differing from to take: *and cruel death hath —ed it from my side,* Rom. IV, 5, 48. *and am right glad to c. this good occasion,* H8 V, 1, 110. *thy nature is too full o'the milk of human kindness, to c. the nearest way,* Mcb. I, 5, 19. *consumption c. thee!* Tim. IV, 3, 201. *perdition c. my soul,* Oth. III, 3, 90. — With *up: a blanket, in the alarum of fear caught up,* Hml. II, 2, 532.

6) to overtake: *cries to c. her,* Sonn. 143, 6. *sail so expeditious that shall c. your royal fleet far off,*

Tp. V, 315. *the mild hind makes speed to c. the tiger,* Mids. II, 1, 233. *that our swift-winged souls may c. the king's,* R3 II, 2, 44. — Nearly = to find, to surprise: *an a' may c. your hide and you alone,* John II, 136.

7) to attract, to charm: *I shall report, for most it caught me, the celestial habits,* Wint. III, 1, 4. *beauty and honour in her are so mingled that they have caught the king,* H8 II, 3, 77. *things in motion sooner c. the eye than what not stirs,* Troil. III, 3, 183.

8) to get possession of, to attain: *if thou c. thy hope,* Sonn. 143, 11. *have is have, however men do c.* John I, 173. *torment myself to c. the English crown,* H6C III, 2, 179. *thinkest thou to c. my life so pleasantly,* Troil. IV, 5, 249. cf. Wiv. III, 3, 45.

9) to get, to receive: *from yielders all things c.* Mids. III, 2, 30. *our very petticoats will c. them* (burrs) As I, 3, 15. *fight closer, or you'll c. a blow,* H6C III, 2, 23. *to c. my death,* Rom. II, 5, 53. *a noble nature may c. a wrench,* Tim. II, 2, 218. *you caught hurt in parting two that fought,* Per. IV, 1, 88.

Very often used of diseases: *he is sooner caught than the pestilence,* Ado I, 1, 87. 89. *how I caught it,* Merch. I, 1, 3. *all the evils that thou hast caught,* As II, 7, 68. *so quickly may one c. the plague,* Tw. I, 5, 314. *would send them back the plague, could I but c. it for them,* Tim. V, 1, 141. *to c. cold:* Gentl. I, 2, 136. Err. III, 1, 37. Ado III, 4, 66. Shr. IV, 1, 46. H4B III, 2, 194. Troil. IV, 2, 15. Lr. I, 4, 113. Cymb. I, 4, 180. With *of* before the person, by whom one is infected: *they have the plague, and caught it of your eyes,* LLL V, 2, 421. *it is caught of you,* Wint. I, 2, 386. *we c. of you,* H4B II, 4, 49. *wise bearing or ignorant carriage is caught, as men take diseases, one of another,* V, 1, 85.

Hence, without *of,* = to receive by contagion or infection: *my ear should c. your voice* etc. Mids. I, 1, 188. *to c. them* (the measles) Cor. III, 1, 80. Tim. IV, 3, 358.

Catching = contagious: *sickness is —ing,* Mids. I, 1, 186. H4A IV, 1, 30. H8 I, 3, 37. Cor. III, 1, 310. Caes. III, 1, 283.

Catcher, in *Gull-catcher,* q. v.

Catechise, to try by questions: *what kind of —ing call you this?* Ado IV, 1, 79. *I must c. you for it,* Tw. I, 5, 68. *I suck my teeth and c. my picked man of countries,* John I, 192. Explained in its original sense (to instruct by questions and appropriate answers): *I will c. the world for him, that is, make questions, and by them answer,* Oth. III, 4, 16.

Catechism, 1) instruction concerning religion, by means of questions and answers: *to say ay and no to these particulars is more than to answer in a c.* As III, 2, 241.

2) an elementary book in the form of questions and answers: *honour is a mere scutcheon: and so ends my c.* H4A V, 1, 144.

Cate-log for *catalogue:* Gentl. III, 1, 273 (Launce's speech).

Cater, vb. to provide food: *he that provi-dently —s for the sparrow,* As II, 3, 44.

Cater-cousin, quatre-cousin, remote relation, misapplied by Gobbo to persons who peaceably feed together: *his master and he are scarce —s,* Merch. II, 2, 139.*

Caterpillar, the larva of the butterfly: Ven.

798. R2 II, 3, 166. III, 4, 47. H4A II, 2, 88. H6B III, 1, 90. IV, 4, 37. Per. V, 1, 60.

Caterwauling, see *Catterwauling.*

Cates, delicious food, dainties: *though my c. be mean, take them in good part,* Err. III, 1, 28. *dainties are all c.* Shr. II, 190. *I had rather live with cheese and garlic than feed on c.* H4A III, 1, 163. *and see what c. you have,* H6A II, 3, 79. *these c. resist me, she but thought upon,* Per. II, 3, 29.

Catesby, name in R3 I, 3, 322. III, 1, 157 etc.

Cathedral, adj. pertaining to the seat of a bishop: *in the c. church of Westminster,* H6B I, 2, 37.

Catlike, adj., resembling a cat: *couching with c. watch,* As IV, 3, 116.

Catling, catgut: *unless the fiddler Apollo get his sinews to make —s on,* Troil. III, 3, 306. Name of a musician: Rom. IV, 5, 132.

Cato, ancient Roman, celebrated for his virtue: Merch. I, 1, 166. Cor. I, 4, 57 (O. Edd. *Calues*). Caes. II, 1, 295. V, 1, 101. His son: Caes. V, 3, 107. V, 4, 4. 8.

Cat-o'-mountain, wild cat: *and more pinch-spotted make them than pard or c.* Tp. IV, 262. *your c. looks,* Wiv. II, 2, 27.

Catterwauling, cry of cats, dissonant howling: *what a c. do you keep here!* Tw. II, 3, 76. *what a c. dost thou keep!* Tit. IV, 2, 57.

Cattle, domestic beasts: *a reverend man that grazed his c. nigh,* Compl. 57. *he blasts the tree and takes the c.* Wiv. IV, 4, 32. *to bring the ewes and the rams together and to offer to get your living by the copulation of c.* As III, 2, 85. *boys and women are for the most part c. of this colour,* 435. *make poor men's c. break their necks,* Tit. V, 1, 132.

Caucasus, chain of mountains between Europe and Asia: *by thinking on the frosty C.* R2 I, 3, 295. *Prometheus tied to C.* Tit. II, 1, 17.

Caudle, subst., a warm drink, a cordial for the stomach: *where lies thy pain? a c., ho!* LLL IV, 3, 174. *ye shall have a hempen c. then and the help of hatchet,* H6B IV, 7, 95 (Ff in both passages *candle*).

Caudle, vb., to serve as a caudle, to refresh: *will the cold brook, candied with ice, c. thy morning taste, to cure thy o'ernight's surfeit?* Tim. IV, 3, 226.

Cauf, the modern pronunciation of *calf,* blamed by Holofernes: LLL V, 1, 25.

Cauldron, boiler, large kettle: Mcb. IV, 1, 4. 11. 13. 21. 34. 36. 41.

Caulked, having the seams stopped with oakum: *a chest c. and bitumed ready,* Per. III, 1, 72. *how close 'tis c. and bitumed,* III, 2, 56.

Cause, subst., 1) that which produces an effect, or is the motive of an action: *where is no c. of fear,* Ven. 1153. *since why to love I can allege no c.* Sonn. 49, 14. *I weep for thee, and yet no c. I have,* Pilgr. 137. *the c. of all my moan,* 295. *who hath c. to wet the grief on't,* Tp. II, 1, 127. *I have cursed them without c.* V, 179. II, 1, 1. Gentl. IV, 4, 152. Wiv. II, 1, 108. III, 3, 108. IV, 2, 138. Meas. II, 1, 121. 142. III, 2, 140. V, 181. Err. I, 1, 29. III, 1, 91. LLL IV, 3, 218. Mids. III, 1, 82. Tw. III, 1, 166. H6C III, 2, 142. Hml. V, 2, 394. Ant. IV, 15, 5 etc. etc. *a breaking c. of heavenly oaths,* LLL V, 2, 355 (= a cause of breaking oaths). *they can be meek that have no other c.* Err. II, 1, 33 (= no cause to be otherwise). *though sometimes you do blench from this to that, as c. doth minister,*

Meas. IV, 5, 6; cf. *the rest shall bear the business in some other fight, as c. will be obeyed,* Cor. I, 6, 83.* *it is the c., it is the c., my soul,* Oth. V, 2, 1. *O madness of discourse, that c. sets up with and against itself,* Troil. V, 2, 143. *for what c.* Err. I, 1, 31. *for that cause* (that thou mightst be my prisoner) *I trained thee to my house,* H6A II, 3, 35 (= for that purpose). *he feels himself distracted, but from what c., he will by no means speak,* Hml. III, 1, 6. *upon what c.* Err. V, 123. R3 I, 1, 46. Per. I, 3, 20. *upon especial c.* H6A IV, 1, 55. *on special c.* Lr. IV, 6, 219. *will forget with the least c. these his new honours,* Cor. II, 1, 245. *much more c. = with much more c.,* H5 V Chor. 34. *Why* before the subordinate clause omitted: *as well appeareth by the c. you come,* R2 I, 1, 26. H6A II, 5, 54. H6B I, 3, 68.

Referring to persons, = author: *if the c. were not in being, part o' the c., she the adulteress,* Wint. II, 3, 3. *thou wert c. of noble Gloster's death,* R2 IV, 37. *I was c. your highness came to England,* H6B I, 3, 68. *thou art the c. and most accursed effect,* R3 I, 2, 120. *God pardon them that are the c. of it,* I, 3, 315.

The first and second c. will not serve my turn, LLL I, 2, 184. *the quarrel was upon the seventh c.* As V, 4, 52. 69. *a gentleman of the first house, of the first and second c.* Rom. II, 4, 26 (allusions to terms in the art of duelling, fashionable in the poet's time, and especially to the book of Vincentio Saviola 'Of honour and honourable quarrels').

2) that which a person, a party or nation pursues, interest, ground or principle of action: *give your c. to heaven,* Meas. IV, 3, 129. 145. *such temperate order in so fierce a c.* John III, 4, 12. *I must withdraw and weep upon the spot of this enforced c.* V, 2, 30. *breed a kind of question in our c.* H4A IV, 1, 68. *justice … whose rightful c. prevails,* H6B II, 1, 205. *I cheered them up with justice of our c.* H6C II, 1, 133. Hml. V, 2, 350. Ant. I, 2, 143. Cymb. V, 4, 71 etc.

3) any subject of question and debate: *made me acquainted with a weighty c. of love between your daughter and himself,* Shr. IV, 4, 26. *your manner of wrenching the true c. the false way,* H4B II, 1, 121. *what counsel give you in this weighty c.?* H6B III, 1, 289. *the chief c. concerns his grace of Canterbury,* H8 V, 3, 3. Especially a suit or action in court: *being judge in love, she cannot right her c.* Ven. 220. *and leave you to the hearing of the c.* Meas. II, 1, 141. II, 2, 1. V, 167. 302. Merch. IV, 1, 155. 173. Tw. V, 363. H6B IV, 7, 93. II, 1, 204. H8 V, 3, 121 etc.

4) matter, question, affair in general: *the c. craves haste,* Lucr. 1295. *the extreme parts of time extremely forms all —s to the purpose of his speed,* LLL V, 2, 751. *turn him to any c. of policy, the Gordian knot of it he will unloose,* H5 I, 1, 45. *now to our French —s,* II, 2, 60. *give me hearing in a c.* H6A V, 3, 106. *I'll acquaint our duteous citizens with all your just proceedings in this c.* (the execution of Hastings) R3 III, 5, 66 (Ff *case*). *leave us to cure this c.* Cor. III, 1, 235. II, 3, 202. *come, the c.* Caes. V, 1, 48 (= to the purpose?). *what was thy c.? adultery?* Lr. IV, 6, 111. *sith I am entered in this c. so far,* Oth. III, 3, 411. — Strange expression: *hearing your high majesty is touched with that malignant c. wherein the honour of my dear father's gift stands chief in power,* All's II, 1, 114.

Cause, vb., to be the author or cause of: —*d his death,* R2 I, 2, 38. R3 II, 2, 19. —*d our swifter composition,* Cor. III, 1, 2. Ant. V, 2, 34. Troil. IV, 4, 4 etc. Followed by an infinitive with or without *to,* = to occasion, to make; 1) with *to: he had* —*d his own father-in-law to be murdered,* Lucr. Arg. 1. *destiny the never-surfeited sea hath* —*d to belch up you,* Tp. III, 3, 56. Meas. III, 2, 21. Mids. III, 2, 117. (Merch. II, 2, 141.). H5 IV, 7, 9. H6B IV, 7, 39. H6C II, 2, 91. H8 III, 2, 324. Oth. II, 1, 281. Cymb. V, 5, 219. — 2) without *to: these news would c. him once more yield the ghost,* H6A I, 1, 67. *c. the musicians play me that sad note,* H8 IV, 2, 78. *that letter I* —*d you write,* 128.

Cause = because: *therefore called so, c. they take vengeance of such kind of men,* Tit. V, 2, 63. *from broad words and c. he failed his presence at the tyrant's feast, I hear Macduff lives in disgrace,* Mcb. III, 6, 21.

Causeless, adj., having no cause: *she tells them 'tis a c. fantasy,* Ven. 897 (groundless). *they say miracles are past; and we have our philosophical persons, to make modern and familiar, things supernatural and c.* All's II, 3, 3 (inexplicable).

Causeless, adv., without cause: *you, with the rest, c. have laid disgraces on my head,* H6B III, 1, 162. *made me down to throw my books and fly, c. perhaps,* Tit. IV, 1, 26.

Causer, he who or that which causes: *love's denying, faith's defying, heart's renying, c. of this,* Pilgr. 252. *and study too, the c. of your vow,* LLL IV, 3, 311. *is not the c. of the timeless deaths of these Plantagenets as blameful as the executioner?* R3 I, 2, 117. *bettering thy loss makes the bad c. worse,* IV, 4, 122.

Cautel, deceit, falseness: *in him a plenitude of subtle matter, applied to* —*s, all strange forms receives,* Compl. 303. *perhaps he loves you now, and now no soil nor c. doth besmirch the virtue of his will,* Hml. I, 3, 15.

Cautelous, false, deceitful: *your son will or exceed the common or be caught with c. baits and practice,* Cor. IV, 1, 33. *swear priests and cowards and men c.* Caes. II, 1, 129 (who are not to be trusted).

Cauterize, to burn with hot iron: a word introduced into our texts by M. Edd. in Tim. V, 1, 136; O. Edd. *cantherizing,* q. v.

Caution, subst. 1) warning: *with c. that the Florentine will move us for speedy aid,* All's I, 2, 6. *many mazed considerings did throng and pressed in with this c.* H8 II, 4, 186. *my c. was more pertinent than the rebuke you give it,* Cor. II, 2, 67. *for thy good c. thanks,* Mcb. IV, 1, 73. *so 'tis put on me, and that in way of c.* Hml. I, 3, 95. *I have this present evening from my sister been well informed of them, and with such* —*s, that if they come, I'll not be there,* Lr. II, 1, 104. 2) provident care: *that well might advise him to a c., to hold what distance his wisdom can provide,* Mcb. III, 6, 44.

Cavaleiro or **Cavalero,** a gallant, a man of fashion: *C. Slender,* Wiv. II, 3, 77. *I'll drink to Master Bardolph, and to all the* —*s about London,* H4B V, 3, 62.

Cavaleiro-justice: Wiv. II, 1, 201. 206.

Cavalery = 1) cavaleiro: *help c. Cobweb to scratch,* Mids. IV, 1, 25 (Bottom's speech).

2) order or company of cavaliers: *she'll disfurnish us of all our c.* Per. IV, 6, 12 (Q1 *caualereea;* the other O. Edd. *caualeres* and *cavaleers;* M. Edd. *cavaliers*).

Cavalier, sprightly military man: *who is he ... that will not follow these culled and choice-drawn* —*s to France?* H5 III Chor. 24. As to Per. IV, 6, 12, cf. *cavalery.*

Cave, subst., 1) cavern, habitation in the earth: Ven. 830. Gentl. V, 3, 12. Meas. I, 3, 22. As II, 7, 197. IV, 3, 146. V, 4, 202. Tw. IV, 1, 52. H5 II, 4, 124. Tit. II, 3, 24. IV, 2, 179. Rom. III, 2, 74. Tim. V, 1, 122. 129. V, 2, 10. Lr. III, 2, 45. Ant. V, 2, 356. Cymb. III, 3, 38. III, 6, 83 etc. *grim c. of death* (viz night) Lucr. 769. *fall into the blind c. of eternal night,* R3 V, 3, 62. *lean-faced Envy in her loathsome c.* H6B III, 2, 315. *which way shall I find Revenge's c.?* Tit. III, 1, 271. (cf. *cave-keeping,* and *cell*). *cursed the gentle gusts and he that loosed them from their brazen* —*s,* H6B III, 2, 89. *the c. where Echo lies,* Rom. II, 2, 162.

2) any hollow place: *these lovely* —*s, these round enchanting pits* (viz dimples) Ven. 247. *as the snail shrinks backward in his shelly c.* 1034.

Cave, vb., to dwell in a cave: *that such as we c. here,* Cymb. IV, 2, 138 (cf. *to cabin, house*).

Cave-keeper, a person who lives in a cave: Cymb. IV, 2, 298.

Cave-keeping, dwelling in a cave: *in men, as in a rough-grown grove, remain c. evils that obscurely sleep,* Lucr. 1250, i. e. secret vices and passions; cf. *cave* in H6B III, 2, 315 and Tit. III, 1, 271.

Cavern, a deep recess under the earth: *which blood, like sacrificing Abel's, cries, even from the tongueless* —*s of the earth, to me,* R2 I, 1, 105. *O, then by day where wilt thou find a c. dark enough to mask thy monstrous visage?* Caes. II, 1, 80.

Caviary (M. Edd. *caviare*), the roe of the sturgeon: *the play pleased not the million; 'twas c. to the general,* Hml. II, 2, 457.

Cavil, vb., 1) to quarrel, to find fault: *you do not well in obstinacy to c. in the course of this contract,* H6A V, 4, 156. *let's fight it out and not stand* —*ing thus,* H6C I, 1, 117. *in the way of bargain I'll c. on the ninth part of a hair,* H4A III, 1, 140. Followed by *at* or *with: 'tis love you c. at,* Gentl. I, 1, 38. *in vain I c. with mine infamy,* Lucr. 1025. *thus* —*s she with every thing she sees,* 1093.

2) to raise frivolous objections: *you c., widow; I did mean, my queen,* H6C III, 2, 99.

Cavil, subst., frivolous objection: *that's but a c.; he is old, I young,* Shr. II, 392.

Caw, to cry as a chough: *choughs rising and* —*ing at the gun's report,* Mids. III, 2, 22.

Cawdor, name in Mcb. I, 2, 53 etc.

Cease, vb., 1) trans., to discontinue, to make an end of: —*ing their clamorous cry,* Ven. 693. *when he hath* —*d his ill-resounding noise,* 919. *O time, c. thou thy course,* Lucr. 1765. *here c. more questions,* Tp. I, 2, 184. *c. thy counsel,* Ado V, 1, 3. *heaven c. this idle humour in your honour,* Shr. Ind. 2, 14. *may c. their hatred,* H5 V, 2, 380. *c. these jars,* H6A I, 1, 44. *c. our hot pursuit,* II, 2, 3. *c. these execrations,* H6B III, 2, 305. *particularities and petty sounds to c.* V, 2, 45. *to c. this civil war,* H6C I, 1, 197. Tit. III, 1, 136. Rom. II, 2, 152. Tim. II, 2, 3.

42. Hml. V, 2, 374. Lr. I, 1, 196. Cymb. V, 5, 255. Per. II, 1, 1. — Passively: *importune him for my moneys; be not —d with slight denial, nor then silenced...,* Tim. II, 1, 16. Followed by an infinitive: *c. to persuade,* Gentl. I, 1, 1. *to lament,* III, 1, 241. *which never —th to enlarge itself,* H6A I, 2, 134. H6B III, 1, 351. III, 2, 205. IV, 4, 3. H6C IV, 8, 50. Rom. II, 2, 119. Lr. I, 1, 114. Cymb. IV, 4, 31.

2) intr. a) to leave off, to stop: *at which time you said our work should c.* Tp. V, 5. *so your affection would c.* Gentl. II, 1, 92. *c., no more,* Wint. II, 1, 150. H6B III, 2, 339. Cor. III, 3, 20. Rom. V, 3, 249. Cymb. V, 5, 484. Per. III, 1, 77. V, 1, 146. *miracles are —d,* H5 I, 1, 67.

b) to come to an end, to perish: *and both (my life and honour) shall c. without your remedy,* All's V, 3, 164. *if all were minded so, the times should c.* Sonn. 11, 7. *things at the worst will c.* Mcb. IV, 2, 24. *that things might change or c.* Lr. III, 1, 7. *and machination —s,* V, 1, 46 (in V, 3, 264 perhaps subst.). *which (my purposes) are or c., as you shall give the advice,* Ant. I, 3, 67.

c) to desist: *she —d in heavy satisfaction,* All's V, 3, 99. *that ambitious Constance would not c. till she had kindled France,* John I, 32. *why c. you* (desist from fighting) *till you are so* (lords of the field) Cor. I, 6, 48. *if he were putting to my house the brand, I have not the face to say 'beseech you, c.,'* IV, 6, 117.

Cease, subst. extinction: *the c. of majesty dies not alone,* Hml. III, 3, 15. *is this the promised end? or image of that horror? Fall, and c.!* Lr. V, 3, 264 (perhaps verb). In Hml. Qq *cesse.*

Ceaseless, endless, everlasting: *thou c. lackey to eternity* (viz time) Lucr. 967.

Cedar, the tree cedrus: Lucr. 664. Tp. V, 48. LLL IV, 3, 89. H6B V, 1, 205. H6C V, 2, 11. R3 I, 3, 264. H8 V, 5, 54. Cor. V, 3, 60. Tit. IV, 3, 45. Cymb. V, 4, 141. V, 5, 453. 457.

Cedar-top: Ven. 858.

Cedius, name in Troil. V, 5, 11.

Celebrate, to perform solemnly: *a contract of true love to c.* Tp. IV, 84. 132. Wint. V, 1, 204. Per. V, 3, 80. *more than my dancing soul doth c. this feast of battle,* R2 I, 3, 91. H6A I, 6, 14. Mcb. II, 1, 51. Hml. I, 1, 159. *and c. our drink,* Ant. II, 7, 111.

Celebration, solemn performance (always used of nuptials): Tp. IV, 29. Tw. IV, 3, 30. Wint. IV, 4, 50. H8 IV, 1, 10. Oth. II, 2, 7.

Celerity, swiftness: *hence hath offence his quick c.* Meas. IV, 2, 113 (= its rapid spreading? or its alacrity?). *the swift c. of his death,* V, 399. *motion of no less c. than that of thought,* H5 III Chor. 2. *with great speed of judgment, ay, with c.* Troil. I, 3, 330. *she hath such a c. in dying,* Ant. I, 2, 149. *c. is never more admired than by the negligent,* III, 7, 24.

Celestial, heavenly: *I'll sigh c. breath,* Ven. 189. *with ugly rack on his* (the morning's) *c. face,* Sonn. 33, 6. Pilgr. 69 and LLL IV, 2, 121. Tp. II, 2, 122. Gentl. II, 6, 10. 34. Wiv. III, 1, 109. LLL V, 2, 807. Mids. III, 2, 227. Wint. III, 1, 4. H5 I, 1, 31. H6A V, 4, 40. V, 5, 65. H8 IV, 2, 80. Hml. I, 5, 56. II, 2, 109. Cymb. V, 4, 114. Per. I, 1, 21. V, 1, 251.

Celia, name in As I, 2, 3. I, 3, 69. 130.

Celius (M. Edd. *Caelius*) name in Ant. III, 7, 74.

Cell, small and close habitation, espe-cially of a religious person: Tp. I, 2, 20. 39. 347. IV, 161. 182. 195. V, 84. 291 etc. Gentl. IV, 3, 43. V, 1, 3. V, 2, 42. Rom. II, 2, 189. II, 4, 193. II, 5, 70. 79. III, 2, 141. III, 5, 232 etc. *in thy* (Opportunity's) *shady c., where none may spy him, sits Sin,* Lucr. 881. *sweet c. of virtue and nobility* (a grave) Tit. I, 1, 93. *proud death, what feast is toward in thine eternal c.* Hml. V, 2, 376. *arise, black vengeance, from thy hollow c.* Oth. III, 3, 447 (Ff *the hollow hell*). *unto us it is a c. of ignorance,* Cymb. III, 3, 33. cf. *Cave.*

Cellar, room under ground, used as a repository of provisions: *my c. is in a rock,* Tp. II, 2, 137.

Cellarage, the same: *you hear this fellow in the c.* Hml. I, 5, 151.

Cément, subst. any substance which makes two bodies cohere: *as broken glass no c. can redress,* Pilgr. 178. *your temples burned in their c.* Cor. IV, 6, 85. *the piece of virtue which is set betwixt us as the c. of our love,* Ant. III, 2, 29.

Cément, vb. to unite closely: *how the fear of us may c. their divisions,* Ant. II, 1, 48.

Censer, a fire-pan in which perfumes were burned to sweeten the atmosphere; such had, of course, their lids perforated, and sometimes adorned with figures: *here's snip and nip and cut and slish and slash, like to a c. in a barber's shop,* Shr. IV, 3, 91. *you thin man in a c.* H4B IV, 4, 21.

Censor, a high officer of ancient Rome: Cor. II, 3, 252.

Censorinus, surname of the elder Cato; by conjecture only in our texts: Cor. II, 3, 251 (O. Edd. *and nobly named, so twice being Censor was his great ancestor*).

Censure, subst., 1) judgment, opinion: *betray themselves to every modern c. worse than drunkards,* As IV, 1, 7. *how blest am I in my just c., in my true opinion,* Wint. II, 1, 37. *to give their c. of these rare reports,* H6A II, 3, 10. *the king is old enough to give his c.* H6B I, 3, 120. *to give your —s in this weighty business,* R3 II, 2, 144. *no discerner durst wag his tongue in c.* H8 I, 1, 33. *giddy c. will then cry out: 'O, if he had borne the business'!* Cor. I, 1, 272. *let our just —s attend the true event,* Mcb. V, 4, 14. *take each man's c., but reserve thy judgment,* Hml. I, 3, 69. *their virtues else ... shall in the general c. take corruption,* I, 4, 35. *the c. of the which one must o'erweigh a whole theatre of others,* III, 2, 30. *we will both our judgments join in c. of his seeming,* 92 (Ff *to censure*). *your name is great in mouths of wisest c.* Oth. II, 3, 193. *I may not breathe my c.* IV, 1, 281. *in our c.* Per. II, 3, 34.

2) judicial sentence, condemnation: *to suffer lawful c. for such faults,* Cor. III, 3, 46. *or endure your heaviest c.* V, 6, 143. *to you remains the c. of this hellish villain,* Oth. V, 2, 368.

3) blame: *no might nor greatness in mortality can c. scape,* Meas. III, 2, 197. *beware my c. and keep your promise,* As IV, 1, 200. *to avoid the carping —s of the world,* R3 III, 5, 68. *forgetting your late c. both of his truth and him,* H8 III, 1, 64. *the fault would not scape c.* Lr. I, 4, 229. *must court'sy at the c.* Cymb. III, 3, 55. *fear not slander, c. rash,* IV, 2, 272.

Censure, vb., 1) to judge, to estimate: *how the world will c. me for choosing so strong a prop ...,* Ven. Dedic. 2. *where is my judgment fled, that —s falsely what they* (my eyes) *see aright?* Sonn. 148, 4. *I hear how I am —d: they say I will bear* *myself proudly*, Ado II, 3, 233. *whose equality by our best eyes cannot be —d*, John II, 328. *c. me by what you were, not what you are*, H6A V, 5, 97. *say you consent and c. well the deed*, H6B III, 1, 275 (=approve). *do you know how you are —d here in the city?* Cor. II, 1, 25. *c. me in your wisdom*, Caes. III, 2, 16. *how I may be —d, something fears me to think of*, Lr. III, 5, 3. Absolutely: *the shouting varletry of —ing Rome*, Ant. V, 2, 57. Followed by *on: that I should c. thus on lovely gentlemen*, Gentl. I, 2, 19. Followed by *of: to c. of his seeming*, Hml. III, 2, 92 (Qq *in c.*).

2) to sentence: *has —d him already; and the provost hath a warrant for his execution*, Meas. I, 4, 72. *erred in this point which now you c. him*, II, 1, 15. *when I, that c. him, do so offend*, 29. *until their greater pleasures first be known that are to c. them*, Lr. V, 3, 3.

Censurer, he that passes a judgment: *we must not stint our necessary actions in the fear to cope malicious —s*, H8 I, 2, 78.

Centaur, fancied monster of ancient mythology, half man and half horse: Mids. V, 44. Tit. V, 2, 204. Lr. IV, 6, 126.

Name of an inn: Err, I, 2, 9. 104. II, 2, 2. 9. IV, 4, 153. V, 410.

Centre (or *Center*), the middle point: *many lines close in the dial's c.* H5 I, 2, 210. *the marketplace, the middle c. of this cursed town*, H6A II, 2, 6. *in the c. of this isle*, R3 V, 2, 11. *pierce the inmost c. of the earth*, Tit. IV, 3, 12. *as true as earth to the c.* Troil. III, 2, 187. *the strong base and building of my love is as the very c. of the earth, drawing all things to it*, IV, 2, 110. Absolutely, = the middle point of the earth: *the moon may through the c. creep and so displease her brother's noontide*, Mids. III, 2, 54. *I will find where truth is hid, though it were hid indeed within the c.* Hml. II, 2, 159. = the earth, as the supposed centre of the world: *the c. is not big enough to bear a school-boy's top*, Wint. II, 1, 102. *the heavens themselves, the planets and this c. observe degree*, Troil. I, 3, 85.

Figuratively, the soul, opposed to the body: *poor soul, the c. of my sinful earth*, Sonn. 146, 1. *affection, thy intention stabs the c.* Wint. I, 2, 138. *happy he whose cloak and c. can hold out this tempest*, John IV, 3, 155 (M. Edd. *cincture*). *turn back, dull earth, and find thy c. out*, Rom. II, 1, 2.

Centurion, a Roman military officer who commanded a century: Cor. IV, 3, 47.

Century, 1) a hundred: *said a c. of prayers*, Cymb. IV, 2, 391.

2) a company of about a hundred men: Cor. I, 7, 3. Lr. IV, 4, 6.

Cephalus, a hero of ancient fable, loved by Aurora, and married to Procris, whom he unintentionally killed; alluded to Mids. III, 2, 389; corrupted by Bottom to *Shafalus:* V, 200.

Cerberus, the hell-hound of ancient fable: LLL V, 2, 593. H4B II, 4, 182. Troil. II, 1, 37. Tit. II, 4, 51.

Cerecloth, waxed linen; serving as a shroud for dead bodies: *it* (lead) *were too gross to rib her c. in the obscure grave*, Merch. II, 7, 51.

Cerements, the same: *why thy canonized bones, hearsed in death, have burst their c.* Hml. I, 4, 48.

Ceremonial, adj., pertaining to a ceremony: *the priest attends to speak the c. rites of marriage*, Shr. III, 2, 6.

Ceremonious, 1) full of solemn ceremony, solemn: *O, the sacrifice! how c., solemn and unearthly it was!* Wint. III, 1, 7.

2) according to the customary forms of civility: *then let us take a c. leave and loving farewell of our friends*, R2 I, 3, 50. *throw away respect, tradition, form and c. duty*, III, 2, 173. *the fearful time cuts off the c. vows of love*, R3 V, 3, 98. *not entertained with that c. affection as you were wont*, Lr. I, 4, 63.

3) observant of forms: *you are too c. and traditional*, R3 III, 1, 45. *this Troyan scorns us, or the men of Troy are c. courtiers*, Troil. I, 3, 234.

Ceremoniously, according to the forms of civility, duly: *and c. let us prepare some welcome for the mistress of the house*, Merch. V, 37.

Ceremony, 1) external form, outward rite: *before all sanctimonious —ies may be ministered*, Tp. IV, 16. *after many —ies done, he calls for wine*, Shr. III, 2, 171. *the people must have their voices, neither will they bate one jot of c.* Cor. II, 2, 145. *leave no c. out*, Caes. I, 2, 11. *Caesar shall have all true rites and lawful —ies*, III, 1, 241. *what c. else?* Hml. V, 1, 246. Fluellen speaks of the *—ies of the wars*, H5 IV, 1, 73. Used of the customary forms of civility: *use a more spacious c. to the noble lords*, All's II, 1, 51. *I am so fraught with curious business that I leave out c.* Wint. IV, 4, 526. *c. was but devised at first to set a gloss on faint deeds, hollow welcomes*, Tim. I, 2, 15. *when love begins to sicken and decay, it useth an enforced c.* Caes. IV, 2, 21. *the sauce to meat is c.* Mcb. III, 4, 36. *the appurtenance of welcome is fashion and c.* Hml. II, 2, 389. Used of the external duties of love: *so I, for fear of trust, forget to say the perfect c. of love's rite*, Sonn. 23, 6. *in all the accoutrement, complement and c. of it* (love) Wiv. IV, 2, 6. — Applied to the outward forms of state: *no c. that to great ones longs, not the king's crown* etc. Meas. II, 2, 59. *his* (the king's) *—ies laid by, in his nakedness he appears but a man*, H5 IV, 1, 109. *what have kings, that privates have not too, save c., save general c.* 256; cf. 257. 261. 269. 283. 295. *what, no more c.?* Ant. III, 13, 38.

2) any thing or observance held sacred: *to urge the thing held as a c.* Merch. V, 206. *and hast a thing within thee called conscience, with twenty popish tricks and —ies*, Tit. V, 1, 76. Used of festal ornaments hung on Caesar's images: *disrobe the images, if you do find them decked with —ies*, Caes. I, 1, 70 (cf. I, 2, 289). Of signs, prodigies and the like superstitions: *quite from the main opinion he held once of fantasy, of dreams and —ies*, Caes. II, 1, 197. *I never stood on —ies, but now they fright me*, II, 2, 13.*

3) ritual and solemn performance of a sacred act: *to give our hearts united c.* Wiv. IV, 6, 51 (i. e. the solemn celebration of our union or marriage). *not sorting with a nuptial c.* Mids. V, 55. *this contract, whose c. shall seem expedient*, All's II, 3, 185. *all the c. of this compact sealed in my function*, Tw. V, 163. *all's now done, but the c. of bringing back the prisoner*, H8 I, 1, 4. *you saw the c.?* IV, 1, 60.

Ceres, the goddess of agriculture: Tp. IV, 60. 75. 117. 167. H6B I, 2, 2.

Cerimon, name in Per. III, 2, 47. V, 3, 59 etc.

Cern, vb., = concern: *what —s it you if I wear pearl and gold?* Shr. V, 1, 77 (F2 etc. *concerns*).

Certain, adj. (compar. *certainer:* Ado V, 4, 62), 1) undoubted, undeniable: *her c. sorrow writ*

uncertainly, Lucr. 1311. *that's most c.* Tp. III, 2, 64.
will not let you believe things c. V, 125. 158. Gentl. II,
1, 37. Wiv. III, 3, 120. Meas. III, 2, 117. Err. II, 2,
96. Ado I, 1, 126. V, 4, 62. Mids. I, 1, 92. Merch. III,
1, 29. V, 287. Tim. III, 4, 47. Ant. III, 6, 97 etc. etc.
*until our fears, resolved, be by some c. king purged and
deposed*, John II, 372 (i. e. a king about whose right
there can be no doubt). *For certain* = certainly: H8
V, 2, 13. Caes. IV, 3, 189. Mcb. V, 2, 8. 14.

2) reliable: *these are c. signs to know faithful
friend from flattering foe*, Pilgr. 429. *thou* (life) *art
not c., for thy complexion shifts to strange effects after
the moon*, Meas. III, 1, 23. *nothing so c. as your anchors*,
Wint. IV, 4, 581. *there is no c. life achieved by others'
death*, John IV, 2, 105. *for the c. knowledge of that
truth*, I, 61. *believe my words, for they are c. and
unfallible*, H6A I, 2, 59. *a c. knowledge*, Troil. IV, 1,
41. *that's a c. text*, Rom. IV, 1, 21.

3) stated, fixed: *a c. aim he took at a fair
vestal*, Mids. II, 1, 157. *and c. stars shot madly from
their spheres*, 153 (cf. *and little stars shot from their
fixed places*, Lucr. 1525). *so can I give no reason,
nor I will not, more than a lodged hate and a c. loathing
I bear Antonio*, Merch. IV, 1, 60. *you shall run a c.
course*, Lr. I, 2, 89. *that nature, which contemns its
origin, cannot be bordered c. in itself*, IV, 2, 33. Perhaps
in the following passage also: *why, fearing of time's
tyranny, might I not then say 'Now I love you best',
when I was c. o'er incertainty, crowning the present,
doubting of the rest?* Sonn. 115, 11.

Hence = settled, fixed, unavoidable: *and
now this pale swan in her watery nest begins the sad
dirge of her c. ending*, Lucr. 1612. *I will not consent
to die this day, that's c.* Meas. IV, 3, 59. *rich she shall
be, that's c.* Ado II, 3, 32. *I will live so long as I may,
that's the c. of it*, H5 II, 1, 16. *death is c. to all*, H4B
III, 2, 41 etc.

4) sure, assured, having no doubts: *be
c., nothing truer*, Mids. III, 2, 280. *be c. what you do*,
Wint. II, 1, 127. *art thou c. this is true?* Cor. V, 4, 47.
to make me c. it is done, Cymb. III, 4, 31. Followed
by *of*: *of this I am not c.* All's IV, 3, 304. *c. of his
fate*, Oth. III, 3, 168. *I am c. on't*, Ant. II, 2, 57.

5) particular, some: *as a c. father says*, LLL
IV, 2, 153. *a c. pupil of mine*, 159. H4A I, 3, 33.
H6A IV, 1, 95. Hml. I, 5, 10 etc. Plural: *bury it c.
fathoms in the earth*, Tp. V, 55. *for c. words he spake
against your grace*, Meas. V, 129. Err. I, 2, 24. V, 232.
Wint. IV, 4, 236. Merch. I, 3, 85. H4A IV, 3, 19. H5
I, 2, 47. Cor. V, 6, 93. Hml. III, 1, 16. *we wait for c.
money*, Tim. III, 4, 46 etc. Followed by *of*: *to hunt the
boar with c. of his friends*, Ven. 588. *I would send
for c. of my creditors*, Meas. I, 2, 136. *Some certain* =
some, or a certain: *till some c. shot be paid*, Gentl.
II, 5, 6. *some c. treason*, LLL IV, 3, 190. *some c. snatch*,
Tit. II, 1, 95. Plural: *some c. special honours*, LLL V,
1, 112. *to reform some c. edicts*, H4A IV, 3, 79. *his
true titles to some c. dukedoms*, H5 I, 1, 87. I, 2, 247.
some c. dregs of conscience, R3 I, 4, 124. *some c.
jewels*, Per. III, 4, 1. Followed by *of*: *I have moved
already some c. of the noblest-minded Romans*, Caes.
I, 3, 122. *some c. of your brethren*, Cor. II, 3, 59.

Certain, adv., certainly: *I'll
send him c. word of my success*, Meas. I, 4, 89. *'tis c.
so*, Ado II, 1, 181. *c., said she, a wise gentleman*, V,
1, 166. *his leg is too big for Hector's; more calf, c.*

LLL V, 2, 645. *a man so breathed that c. he would
fight*, 659. *this beauteous lady Thisby is c.* Mids. V,
131 (oxytone, and rhyming to *plain*). *Lorenzo, c.*
Merch. II, 6, 29. *most c. you do usurp yourself*, Tw. I,
5, 199. II, 3, 66. Wint. I, 2, 362. IV, 4, 578. John I,
59. H4B IV, 4, 130. H8 II, 4, 71. Caes. IV, 3, 189.
Ant. IV, 5, 11. Cor. II, 1, 123.

Certainly, surely: Tp. I, 2, 41. 428. Wiv. IV,
2, 16. Ado II, 1, 265. III, 1, 57. Merch. II, 2, 1. 28.
III, 1, 129. As III, 4, 22. IV, 1, 140. Wint. I, 2, 391.
IV, 3, 94. John III, 4, 118. H4A IV, 1, 40. H5 II, 1, 20.
III, 6, 55. IV, 3, 82. V, 1, 47. H8 II, 1, 39. Troil. III,
1, 66. Cor. II, 3, 167. Lr. V, 1, 5. Oth. III, 4, 133.
Ant. II, 7, 39. Per. III, 2, 78. — *C. resolved* = firmly,
steadfastly resolved: *and therefore are we c. resolved*,
H6A V, 1, 37.

Certainty, 1) indubitableness: *not a resemblance, but a c.* Meas. IV, 2, 203. *for more c.* Merch.
II, 6, 26. Wint. V, 2, 42. Cymb. IV, 4, 27.

2) that which cannot be doubted: *we here
receive it a c.* All's I, 2, 5. *he is furnished with no —ies*,
H4B I, 1, 31. *I speak from —ies*, Cor. I, 2, 31. *if you
desire to know the c. of your dear father's death*, Hml.
IV, 5, 140. *—ies either are past remedies*, Cymb. I,
6, 96.

3) assurance: *upon thy c. and confidence what
darest thou venture?* All's II, 1, 172. *encourage myself
in my c.* III, 6, 81.

Certes (dissyllabic in Tp. and Err., monosyll.
in H8 and Oth.), certainly: *for c. these are people
of the island*, Tp. III, 3, 30. *c., she did*, Err. IV, 4, 78.
LLL IV, 2, 169. H8 I, 1, 48. Oth. I, 1, 16.

Certificate, subst., instruction, direction,
certain information: '*Sir John Falstaff, knight,
to the son of the king, nearest his father, Harry Prince
of Wales, greeting.*' *Why, this is a c.* H4B II, 2, 132.

Certify, 1) to convince: *Antonio —ied the
Duke they were not with Bassanio in his ship*, Merch.
II, 8, 10. *I go to c. her, Talbot's here*, H6A II, 3, 32.

2) to inform: *what infamy will there arise, when
foreign princes shall be —ied that for a toy King
Henry's peers destroyed themselves*, H6A IV, 1, 144.
*I'll to the king and c. his grace that thus I have resigned
my charge to you*, R3 I, 4, 97 (Ff *signify to him*). *then
—ies your lordship that this night he dreamt ...*, III,
2, 10 (Qq *sends you word*).

Cesario, assumed name of Viola: Tw. I, 4, 2.
10. II, 4, 2 etc. etc.

Cess, *Out of all cess* = excessively, immoderately: *poor jade, is wrung in the withers out of
all c.* H4A II, 1, 8 (the carrier's speech).

Cesse = to cease: *which better than the first,
O dear heaven bless! Or ere they meet, in me, O nature,
c.!* All's V, 3, 72 (the later Ff *cease*). Cf. *Cease*, subst.

Chace, a term of tennis-play (cf. Dyce's Glossary p. 75), used by the poet with some latitude, =
a match played at tennis: *he hath made a match with
such a wrangler that all the courts of France will be
disturbed with —s*, H5 I, 2, 266.

Chafe, subst., fret, passion, fury: *how this
Herculean Roman does become the carriage of his c.*
Ant. I, 3, 85.

Chafe, vb., 1) trans. a) to heat, to warm:
he —s her lips, Ven. 477. *fain would I go to c. his
paly lips with twenty thousand kisses*, H6B III, 2, 141.

b) to inflame, to make furious: *her inter-*

cession —d him so, Gentl. III, 1, 233. *I c. you, if I tarry*, Shr. II, 243. Partic. *chafed: have I not heard the sea puffed up with winds rage like an angry boar chafed with sweat?* Shr. I, 2, 203 (the sweat of the boar being compared with the foam of the sea). *a —d bull*, H6C II, 5, 126. *are you —d?* H8 I, 1, 123. *lion*, III, 2, 206. *their high blood —d*, Troil. Prol. 2. *being once —d*, Cor. III, 3, 27. *the —d boar*, Tit. IV, 2, 138.

2) refl.: *do not c. thee, cousin*, Troil. IV, 5, 260.

3) intr., to fret, to fume, to rage: *he will c. at the doctor's marrying my daughter*, Wiv. V, 3, 9. *Paris so —d*, Troil. I, 2, 181. *take no care who —s, who frets*, Mcb. IV, 1, 91. Used of the sea: *I would you did but see how it —s, how it rages*, Wint. III, 3, 89. *the murmuring surge that on the unnumbered idle pebbles —s*, Lr. IV, 6, 21. Of a swollen river: *the troubled Tiber — ing with her shores*, Caes. I, 2, 101. And so, perhaps, we ought to read also in Tim. I, 1, 25: *our gentle flame provokes itself and like the current flies each bound it chafes with. What have you here?* (*chafes* as a dissyllable. O. Edd. *chases. What* etc. M. Edd. *chafes. What* etc.)

Chaff, the husks of corn separated by thrashing: Merch. I, 1, 117. Wint. IV, 4, 630. H4B IV, 1, 195. Cor. V, 1, 26. 31. Figuratively: *how much honour picked from the c. and ruin of the times*, Merch. II, 9, 48. *where my c. and corn shall fly asunder*, H8 V, 1, 111. *asses, fools, dolts! c. and bran!* Troil. I, 2, 262.

Chaffless, without chaff: *the gods made you, unlike all others, c.* Cymb. I, 6, 178.

Chain, subst., a series of links or rings connected; used as an ornament: Wiv. IV, 5, 34. 38. Err. II, 1, 106. III, 1, 115. III, 2, 171. V, 1, 10 etc. Ado II, 1, 197. LLL V, 2, 56. As III, 2, 191. Tw. II, 3, 129.* H4B II, 4, 52. Serving to bind and restrain: Tp. V, 233. Wiv. I, 1, 308. IV, 4, 33. V, 1, 6. R2 I, 3, 89. H6B V, 1, 145. H6C V, 7, 11. *hung up in —s*, H6C I, 3, 28. Ant. V, 2, 62. *keys that hung in —s*, Wint. IV, 4, 624. *a thrifty shoeing-horn in a c.* Troil. V, 1, 62. *his speech was like a tangled c.* Mids. V, 125. — Metaphorically: *leading him prisoner in a red-rose c.* Ven. 110. *fettered in amorous —s*, Tit. II, 1, 15. *in —s of magic*, Oth. I, 2, 65.

Chain, vb., to bind with a chain; properly and figuratively: Lucr. 900. Tp. IV, 31. Err. IV, 1, 26. H6A II, 3, 39. Rom. IV, 1, 80. Ant. IV, 8, 14 (*c. mine armed neck* = embrace me). *to c. up and restrain the poor*, Cor. I, 1, 87 (to fetter them completely). — Followed by *to: affection —s thy tender days to the sweet glances of thy honoured love*, Gentl. I, 1, 3. *—ed to the ragged staff*, H6B V, 1, 203. *c. my soul to thine*, H6C II, 3, 34.

Chair, 1) a movable seat: John IV, 1, 5. R2 I, 3, 120. H4A II, 4, 415. H8 IV, 2, 3. Lr. III, 7, 34. 67. *a barber's c. that fits all buttocks*, All's II, 2, 17. *sitting in a lower c.* Meas II, 1, 132 (one designed for the ease of sick people). *sit and pant in your great —s of ease*, Tim. V, 4, 11. Symbol of the repose becoming old age: *run a tilt at death within a c.* H6A III, 2, 51. *when sapless age ... should bring thy father to his drooping c.* IV, 5, 5.

2) a seat of public authority: *the several —s of order*, Wiv. V, 5, 65 (in St. George's chapel at Windsor). *his dukedom and his c. with me is left*, H6C II, 1, 90. *for c. and dukedom, throne and kingdom say*, 93. *sat down in a rich c. of state*, H8 IV, 1, 67

(a raised chair, with a canopy over it). *behold that c. stand empty*, V, 3, 10. *the —s of justice*, Cor. III, 3, 34. *power, unto itself most commendable, hath not a tomb so evident as a c. to extol what it hath done*, IV, 7, 52 (i. e. self-applause is most fatal in public functions).* *the praetor's c.* Caes. I, 3, 143. *let him go up into the public c.* III, 2, 68 (the Roman rostra). Frequently = the throne: *dost thou so hunger for mine empty c.?* H4B IV, 5, 95. H6B I, 2, 38. H6C I, 1, 51. 168. I, 4, 97. II, 6, 20. V, 5, 19. R3 IV, 4, 470. V, 3, 251. Ant. III, 6, 4.

3) a sedan: Oth. V, 1, 82. 96.

Chair-days, the time of repose, the evening of life: *in thy reverence and thy c., thus to die in ruffian battle*, H6B V, 2, 48.

Chalice, cup: Wiv. III, 5, 29. Mcb. I, 7, 11. Hml. IV, 7, 161.

Chaliced, having a cup: *c. flowers*, Cymb. II, 3, 24.

Chalk, vb., to mark, to trace out: *it is you that have —ed forth the way which brought us hither*, Tp. V, 203. *not propped by ancestry, whose grace —s successors their way*, H8 I, 1, 60.

Chalky, consisting of chalk: *c. cliffs* (of England) Err. III, 2, 129. H6B III, 2, 101. *this c. bourn*, Lr. IV, 6, 57.

Challenge, subst. 1) claim: *of benefit proceeding from our king, and not of any c. of desert*, H6A V, 4, 153.

2) an exception made in law against a person: *and make my c. you shall not be my judge*, H8 II, 4, 77 (but perhaps here also = claim).

3) summons to single combat: Wiv. I, 4, 114. Ado I, 1, 41. V, 1, 145. V, 2, 57. LLL V, 2, 713. Tw. II, 3, 140. III, 2, 43. III, 4, 157. 209. H4A V, 2, 53. Troil. I, 3, 272. III, 3, 35. Rom. II, 4, 8. Lr. IV, 6, 141. Ant. IV, 1, 6.

Challenge, vb. 1) to claim as due: *that we our largest bounty may extend where nature doth with merit c.* Lr. I, 1, 54. *so much duty as my mother showed to you ..., so much I c. that I may profess due to the Moor*, Oth. I, 3, 188. Followed by an accus.: *c. me by these deserts*, LLL V, 2, 815. *shall your city call us lord, in that behalf which we have —d it?* John II, 264. *I am a subject, and I c. law*, R2 II, 3, 134. *I will c. it* (my glove) H5 IV, 1, 233. IV, 7, 132. IV, 8, 9. *all her perfections c. sovereignty*, H6C III, 2, 86. *I c. nothing but my dukedom*, IV, 7, 23. *these graces c. grace*, IV, 8, 48. *dares not c. it*, Troil V, 2, 94. *he dares ne'er come back to c. you*, Rom. III, 5, 216. *his worthiness doth c. much respect*, Oth. II, 1, 213. — With *of: I combat c. of this latten bilbo*, Wiv. I, 1, 165. *subjects may c. nothing of their sovereigns*, H6C IV, 6, 6. *these white flakes had —d pity of them*, Lr. IV, 7, 31. With *from: but beauty from Venus' doves doth c. that fair field*, Lucr. 58.

2) to urge as a right: *when she shall c. this, you will reject her*, LLL V, 2, 438. *that is honour's scorn, which —s itself as honour's born and is not like the sire*, All's II, 3, 141.

3) to call to a contest: *when these suns ... by their heralds —d the noble spirits to arms*, H8 I, 1, 34. Especially to single combat: *—d Cupid at the flight*, Ado I, 1, 40. 42. *I will c. him*, V, 1, 335. *c. thee to trial of a man*, V, 1, 66. 200. LLL IV, 1, 140. V, 2, 696. 699. Tw. III, 2, 36. III, 4, 313. As I, 2,

178. H4A V, 2, 47. H6C IV, 7, 75. *to c. him the field*, Tw. II, 3, 136 (most M. Edd. *to the field;* perhaps *to field,* cf. Rom. III, 1, 61).

4) **to accuse:** *dishonoured thus and —d of wrongs*, Tit. I, 340. *who may I rather c. for unkindness than pity for mischance*, Mcb. III, 4, 42.

Challenger, 1) **claimant:** *he bids you then resign your crown and kingdom indirectly held from him the native and true c.* H5 II, 4, 95. *whose worth stood c. on mount of all the age for her perfections*, Hml. IV, 7, 28. cf. also R2 V, 3, 19.

2) **one who defies or calls to a single combat:** As I, 2, 170. 175. 180. IV, 3, 32.

Cham, khan, the sovereign prince of Tartary: *fetch you a hair off the great —'s beard*, Ado II, 1, 277.

Chamber, 1) **lodging-room:** Lucr. 302. 1626. Gentl. II, 4, 184. II, 7, 83. III, 1, 114. IV, 2, 122. IV, 4, 21. 91. Wiv. III, 3, 173. 225. Ado II, 2, 18. V, 4, 11. Mids. III, 1, 50. V, 424. Tw. I, 1, 29. H6A II, 5, 19. H6B III, 2, 132 etc. etc. *my —s are honourable*, Wiv. IV, 5, 23. *shall that victorious hand be feebled here, that in your —s gave you chastisement*, John V, 2, 147. *the days are near at hand that —s will be safe*, Mcb. V, 4, 2. *a lady's c.* Wint. IV, 4, 225. R3 I, 1, 12. *great c.* = saloon: Wiv. I, 1, 157. Mids. III, 1, 58. Rom. I, 5, 14. *is the banquet ready in the privy c.?* H8 I, 4, 99. *step into the c.* Wiv. IV, 2, 11. 176 (= closet).

To be of a person's c. = to attend on, to be chamberlain of a person: *the ladies, her attendants of her c.* As II, 2, 5. *those sleepy two of his own c.* Mcb. I, 7, 76. *those of his c., as it seemed, have done't,* II, 3, 106. *you are of our c., and our mind partakes her private actions to your secrecy*, Per. I, 1, 153.

2) translation of the title *camera regis* given to London: *welcome to London, to your c.* R3 III, 1, 1.

3) **a small piece of ordnance:** *to venture upon the charged —s bravely*, H4B II, 4, 57.

Chamber, vb., see *Chambered.*

Chamber-council (or rather *chamber-counsel*), private thought or care, opposed to public business: *I have trusted thee with all the nearest things to my heart, as well my —s, wherein priest-like thou hast cleansed my bosom*, Wint. I, 2, 237.

Chamber-door: H5 IV, 5, 14. H6A II, 1, 42. H8 V, 3, 140 *(wait at c.).* Hml. IV, 5, 53. Lr. II, 4, 119.

Chambered, lodging, harboured: *even in the best blood c. in his bosom*, R2 I, 1, 149.

Chamberer, a man conversant with the arts of peace, opposed to a soldier; the same as carpet-monger, q. v.: *have not those soft parts of conversation that —s have*, Oth. III, 3, 265.

Chamber-hanging, tapestry: *averring notes of c., pictures*, Cymb. V, 5, 204.

Chamberlain, 1) the officer charged with the direction and management of the private apartments of the king: R3 I, 1, 77. 123. I, 3, 38. III, 2, 114. H8 I, 4, 56. 72. 90. II, 2, 13. 62. Mcb. I, 7, 63. *thinkest that the bleak air, thy boisterous c., will put thy shirt on warm*, Tim. IV, 3, 222.

2) a servant who has the care of the chambers in an inn: H4A II, 1, 52.

Chamber-lie, urine: H4A II, 1, 23.

Chamber-maid, a woman who has the care of the chambers: Tw. I, 3, 54. Rom. V, 3, 109. Lr. IV, 1, 65.

Chamber-pot, a vessel used in bed-rooms: Cor. II, 1, 85.

Chamber-window, window of a chamber: Gentl. II, 6, 34. III, 1, 39. III, 2, 83. Ado II, 2, 18. 43. II, 3, 3. 89. III, 2, 116. III, 3, 156. IV, 1, 92. All's IV, 2, 54.

Chamblet (M.Edd. *camlet* or *camblet*), camelot: *you i' the c., get up o' the rail*, H8 V, 4, 93.

Chameleon, an animal of the genus Lacerta or lizard: *the c. Love can feed on the air*, Gentl. II, 1, 178. *do you change colour? Give him leave; he is a kind of c.* II, 4, 26. *I can add colours to the c.* H6C III, 2, 191. *of the —'s dish: I eat the air*, Hml. III, 2, 98.

Champ, name in Cymb. IV, 2, 377.

Chámpaign or **Chámpain,** subst., open country: *with shadowy forests and with —s riched,* Lr. I, 1, 65. *daylight and c. discovers not more*, Tw. II, 5, 173 (O. Edd. *champian*).

Chámpaign, adj., open, level: *their smoothness, like a goodly c. plain, lays open all the little worms that creep*, Lucr. 1247.

Champaigne, a province of France: H6A I, 1, 60.

Champian, see *Champaign* subst.

Champion, subst., 1) a man who undertakes a cause in single combat: *her c. mounted for the hot encounter*, Ven. 596. *the —s are prepared*, R2 I, 3, 5. *demand of yonder c.* 7. *I can produce a c. that will prove ...*, Lr. V, 1, 43. *like a bold c. I assume the lists*, Per. I, 1, 61.

2) he who fights for a person or a cause: *brings in the c. Honour on my part*, All's IV, 2, 50. *thou Fortune's c.*, John III, 1, 118. *be c. of our church*, III, 1, 255. 267. *God, the widows' c. and defence*, R2 I, 2, 43. *his new-come c., virtuous Joan d'Arc*, H6A II, 2, 20. *his —s are the prophets and apostles*, H6B I, 3, 60. *now will I be Edward's c.* H6C IV, 7, 68.

3) **hero, bold warrior:** *a stouter c. never handled sword*, H6A III, 4, 19. *the most complete c. that ever I heard*, H6B IV, 10, 59. *renowned for hardy and undoubted —s*, H6C V, 7, 6. *Rome's best c.*, Tit. I, 65. 151.

Champion, vb., to challenge, to oppose in combat: *come fate into the list, and c. me to the utterance*, Mcb. III, 1, 72.

Chance, subst., 1) **fortune, be it good or ill:** *every fair from fair sometime declines, by c. or nature's changing course untrimmed*, Sonn. 18, 8. *they say there is divinity in odd numbers, either in nativity, c., or death*, Wiv. V, 1, 4. *made a push at c. and sufferance*, Ado V, 1, 38. *he never did fall off, but by the c. of war*, H4A I, 3, 95. *now good or bad, 'tis but the c. of war*, Troil. Prol. 31. *in the reproof of c. lies the true proof of men*, Troil. I, 3, 33. *injury of c. puts back leave-taking*, IV, 4, 35. *common —s common men could bear*, Cor. IV, 1, 5. *woe to her c.* Tit. IV, 2, 78. *if c. will have me king, why, c. may crown me, without my stir*, Mcb. I, 3, 143. *the shot of accident, nor dart of c.* Oth. IV, 1, 278. *what injuries you did us, we shall remember as things but chance by c.* Ant. V, 2, 120. *I shall show the cinders of my spirits through the ashes of my c.*, 174. *I'll yet follow the wounded c. of Antony*, III, 10, 36. — Used in the sense of good luck: *if it be thy c. to kill me*, Tw. III, 4, 177. *and, now it is my c. to find thee out, must I behold thy death?* H6A V, 4, 4. *if I might in entreaties find success, as seld I have the c.* Troil. IV, 5, 150. *to fail in the disposing of those —s which* *he was lord of,* Cor. IV, 7, 40. *thy dowerless daughter, thrown to my c.* Lr. I, 1, 259. *she lives! if it be so, it is a c. which doth redeem all sorrows,* V, 3, 266. *my better cunning faints under his c.* Ant. II, 3, 35 (= good luck at play; cf. Wiv. V, 1, 4). *this was strange c.: a narrow lane, an old man, and two boys,* Cymb. V, 3, 51.

2) **eventuality, possibility of good or bad success:** *you must take your c.* Merch. II, 1, 38. *take you my land, I'll take my c.* John I, 151. *come on, and take the c. of anger,* Lr. III, 7, 79. *wilt take thy c. with me?* Cymb. IV, 2, 382. *bring me unto my c.* Merch. II, 1, 43. *to comfort you with c.,* assure yourself ..., Tw. I, 2, 8. *summed the account of c.* H4B I, 1, 167. *I would set my life on any c., to mend it or be rid on't,* Mcb. III, 1, 113. *and the c. of goodness be like our warranted quarrel,* IV, 3, 136. *think what a c. thou changest on,* Cymb. I, 5, 68. *so am I that have this golden c. and know not why,* V, 4, 132. — *Main chance* = principal eventuality, the probable course of things: *the which observed, a man may prophesy of the main c. of things as yet not come to life,* H4B III, 1, 83. *main c. you meant, but I meant Maine,* H6B I, 1, 212.

3) **accident:** *both stood like old acquaintance in a trance, met far from home, wondering each other's c.* Lucr. 1596 (i. e. wondering at the accident which brought them to see each other). *not of this country, though my c. is now to use it for my time,* Meas. III, 2, 230. *where c. may nurse or end it,* Wint. II, 3, 183. *to be the slaves of c.* IV, 4, 551. *how —'s mocks and changes fill the cup of alteration,* H4B III, 1, 51 (M. Edd. *how chances mock*). *an act that very c. doth throw upon him,* Troil. III, 3, 131. *a wild exposure to each c.* Cor. IV, 1, 36. *by some c. shall grow dear friends,* IV, 4, 20. *secure from worldly —s and mishaps,* Tit. I, 152. *By c.* = by accident: *but by c. nothing of what is writ,* Meas. IV, 2, 218. *since you are strangers and come here by c.* LLL V, 2, 218. 557. Shr. I, 2, 182. Wint. IV, 4, 733. John III, 4, 63. R2 I, 4, 8. Troil. IV, 2, 73. Cor. V, 3, 180. Hml. IV, 7, 162. A quibble perhaps intended in John I, 169: *by c. but not by truth* (= by good luck, but not by honesty).

4) **event:** *may any terms acquit me from this c.* Lucr. 1706. *against ill —s men are ever merry,* H4B IV, 2, 81. *what c. is this that suddenly hath cross'd us?* H6A I, 4, 72. *how will the country for these woeful —s misthink the king?* H6C II, 5, 107. *what an unkind hour is guilty of this lamentable c.?* Rom. V, 3, 146. *had I but died an hour before this c.,* Mcb. II, 3, 96. *you that look pale and tremble at this c.* Hml. V, 2, 345. *I spake of most disastrous —s,* Oth. I, 3, 134. *we grieve at —s here,* Cymb. IV, 3, 35. *from c. to c.* V, 5, 391.

Chance, vb., 1) to be guided by fortune, to come by fortune: *you that choose not by the view, c. as fair and choose as true,* Merch. III, 2, 133. *by what strange accident I —d on this letter,* V, 279. *Marina thus the brothel scapes and —s into an honest house,* Per. V Prol. 1.

2) to happen: *but it —s the stealth of our most mutual entertainment with character too gross is writ on Juliet,* Meas. I, 2, 157. *if it c. the one of us do fail,* H6A II, 1, 31.

Followed by *to,* in the sense of **perhaps, perchance:** *lest the base earth should from her vesture c. to steal a kiss,* Gentl. II, 4, 160. *wherein if he c. to fail, he hath sentenced himself,* Meas. III, 2, 271. Shr.

Ind. 1, 52. Shr. IV, 1, 209. V, 1, 3. Wint. I, 1, 1. H6C III, 2, 24. V, 5, 65. H8 I, 4, 26. V, 1, 146. Cor. I, 2, 34. II, 1, 82. III, 3, 22. Rom. I, 5, 86. Lr. II, 4, 248. Cymb. IV, 2, 332. Followed by the infinitive without *to: I may c. have some odd quirks and remnants of wit broken on me,* Ado II, 3, 244. *it may c. cost some of us our lives,* H4B II, 1, 12. *you may c. burn your lips,* Troil. I, 1, 26 (Ff *to burn*).

3) **to come to pass, to occur:** *an there be any matter of weight —s,* Ado III, 3, 91. *what may c. or breed upon our absence,* Wint. I, 2, 11. *that what he feared is —d,* H4B I, 1, 87. *omit all the occurrences, whatever —d,* H5 V Chor. 40. *read with thee sad stories, —d in the times of old,* Tit. III, 2, 83. *every good hap that —s here,* Rom. III, 3, 171. *bring us to him, and c. it as it may,* Tim. V, 1, 129. *tell us what hath —d to-day,* Caes. I, 2, 216. III, 1, 287. *bring us word how every thing is —d,* V, 4, 32. *how —s it they travel?* Hml. II, 2, 343. *a more unhappy lady, if this division c., ne'er stood between,* Ant. III, 4, 13. *this —d to-night,* Per. III, 2, 77. Followed by an inf.: *that shall be the day that Hotspur and your Harry c. to meet,* H4A III, 2, 141.

How chance = **how chances it:** *how c. you went not with Master Slender?* Wiv. V, 5, 230. *how c. thou art returned so soon?* Err. I, 2, 42. *how c. the roses there do fade so fast?* Mids. I, 1, 129. *how c. Moonshine is gone?* V, 318. *how c. thou art not with the prince?* H4B IV, 4, 20. *how c. the prophet could not ...,* R3 IV, 2, 102. *how c. my brother Troilus went not?* Troil. III, 1, 151. *how c. the king comes with so small a train?* Lr. II, 4, 64.

Chancellor, 1) the keeper of the great seal: H6C I, 1, 238. H8 III, 2, 394.

2) **secretary:** *one Gilbert Peck, his c.* H8 I, 1, 219 (Ff *counsellor*). II, 1, 20.

Chandler, one who makes or sells candles: *would have bought me lights as good cheap at the dearest —'s in Europe,* H4A III, 3, 52.

Change, subst., **alteration, variation:** *why are you grown so rude? what c. is this?* Mids. III, 2, 262. *the —s I perceived in the king,* Wint. V, 2, 11. H4B IV, 5, 151. H5 I, 1, 37. H6B V, 1, 101. H6C IV, 4, 1. R3 III, 5, 81. Cor. III, 1, 27. Tim. I, 1, 84. IV, 3, 66. Caes. IV, 2, 7. Ant. II, 6, 54 etc. *nine —s of the watery star* (the moon) Wint. I, 2, 1. *the —s of the moon,* Oth. III, 3, 178. — *speak between the c. of man and boy,* Merch. III, 4, 66. *she hath not seen the c. of fourteen years,* Rom. I, 2, 9. — *double c. of bravery* (i. e. a double set of attire) Shr. IV, 3, 57. *c. of honours* = new honours, Cor. II, 1, 214 *(chance?)* Used of vicissitudes of fortune: *to take your c. upon you,* As I, 3, 104 (F2 etc. *charge*). *chance's mocks and —s fill the cup of alteration,* H4B III, 1, 52. *that he his high authority abused and did deserve his c.* (i. e. his deposition) Ant. III, 6, 34. *the miserable c. now at my end,* IV, 15, 51. *which* (sc. death) *shackles accidents and bolts up c.* V, 2, 6. — Used of innovations and revolutions in the state: *here's a c. indeed in the commonwealth,* Meas. I, 2, 107. *shall revolt from him and kiss the lips of unacquainted c.,* John III, 4, 166. *fresh expectation troubled not the land with any longed for c.* IV, 2, 8. *lean-looked prophets whisper fearful c.* R2 II, 4, 11. *every one doth so against a c.* III, 4, 28. *comets importing c. of times and states,* H6A I, 1, 2. *before the times of c., still is it so,* R3 II, 3, 41. *frights, —s, horrors,* Troil. I, 3, 98. *it is prodigious:*

there will come some c. V, 1, 101. *love the fundamental part of state more than you doubt the* c. *on't,* Cor. III, 1, 152. *quietness would purge by any desperate* c. Ant. I, 3, 54. — Euphemism for changing humour, caprice: *you see how full of —s his age is,* Lr. I, 1, 291. cf. *ambitions, covetings,* c. *of prides,* Cymb. II, 5, 25. For inconstancy and fickleness: *a woman's gentle heart, but not acquainted with shifting* c., Sonn. 20, 4. *to set a form upon desired* c. 89, 6. *therefore in that* (thy eye) *I cannot know thy* c. 93, 6. *that* c. *is the spite,* Gentl. IV, 2, 69 (a quibble). *not I pronounce the beggary of his* c. Cymb. I, 6, 115.

2) variation in music and poetry: *why is my verse so barren of new pride, so far from variation or quick* c. Sonn. 76, 2. *and in this* c. *is my invention spent,* 105, 11. *what fine* c. *is in the music!* Gentl. IV, 2, 68.

3) a tour in dancing: *in our measure do but vouchsafe one* c. LLL V, 2, 209.

4) exchange: *maintained the* c. *of words with...,* Ado IV, 1, 185. *he that I gave it to in* c. H5 IV, 8, 30. *give us a prince of blood in* c. *of him,* Troil. III, 3, 27. *it is but* c., *for Octavius is overthrown by Brutus,* Caes. V, 3, 51.

Change, vb., I) trans. 1) to alter: *if all these petty ills shall* c. *thy good,* Lucr. 656. *to* c. *their kinds,* 1147. c. *decrees of kings,* Sonn. 115, 6. *the fashion of the time is —d,* Gentl. III, 1, 86. Wiv. III, 5, 69. Meas. I, 2, 110. I, 3, 54. I, 4, 47. V, 389. Err. I, 2, 99. II, 2, 154. V, 297. Mids. II, 1, 230. Merch. I, 1, 76. As II, 1, 18 etc. *to* c. *colour:* Gentl. II, 4, 23. As III, 2, 192. Wint. V, 2, 98. R3 III, 5, 1. *nor* c. *my countenance,* H6B III, 1, 99. *to* c. *one's mind:* Gentl. III, 2, 59. V, 4, 109. Ado III, 2, 119. *my mind is —d,* R3 IV, 4, 456. c. *thy thought, that I may* c. *my mind,* Sonn. 10, 9. *you must* c. *this purpose, or I my life,* Wint. IV, 4, 39. — Used reflectively: *all things* c. *them to the contrary,* Rom. IV, 5, 90. — Sometimes = to transform: *new created the creatures that were mine, or —d them,* Tp. I, 2, 82. *O Bottom, thou art —d,* Mids. III, 1, 117. *as if with Circe she would* c. *my shape,* H6A V, 3, 36. *O that I knew this husband which must* c. *his horns with garlands,* Ant. I, 2, 5 (= make of another appearance; most M. Edd. *charge*). cf. Cor. V, 3, 152, where likewise M. Edd. *charge.* — = to make to be of another mind or disposition: *nor I to none alive, that my steeled sense or —es right or wrong,* Sonn. 112, 8. *to* c. *this currish Jew,* Merch. IV, 1, 292. *I am —d: I'll go sell all my land,* Oth. I, 3, 388.

Followed by *to: the state government was —d from kings to consuls,* Lucr. Arg. 26. *her blue blood —d to black,* Lucr. 1454. *to* c. *your day of youth to sullied night,* Sonn. 15, 12. *sorrow —d to solace,* Pilgr. 203. c. *you to a milder form,* Gentl. V, 4, 56. Err. II, 2, 201. Ado IV, 1, 213. H6A V, 3, 36. H6B III, 1, 332. R3 I, 1, 7. Caes. I, 3, 66. Followed by *into: Tranio is —d into Lucentio,* Shr. I, 1, 242. *their thimbles into armed gauntlets* c. John V, 2, 156.

2) to put one thing in the place of another: *to* c. *habits,* LLL V, 2, 542. *'tis a good shilling, or I will* c. *it,* H5 IV, 8, 77. *ere the six years can* c. *their moons,* R2 I, 3, 220.

3) to exchange: *they have —d eyes,* Tp. I, 2, 441. c. *your favours,* LLL V, 2, 134. 137. 468. *the spring, the summer, autumn ...* c. *their wonted liveries,*

Mids. II, 1, 112. *would not* c. *that calling to be adopted heir to Frederick,* As I, 2, 245. *wilt thou* c. *fathers?* I, 3, 93. *as we* c. *our courtesies,* All's III, 2, 100. *the lark and toad* c. *eyes,* Rom. III, 5, 31. — Having *with* before the person with whom the exchange is made: *I scorn to* c. *my state with kings,* Sonn. 29, 14. *—ing place with that which goes before,* 60, 3. 128, 9. Meas. V, 339. LLL V, 2, 238. R2 III, 2, 189. H4A I, 3, 101. H5 III, 7, 12. Hml. I, 2, 163. Oth. I, 3, 317. — Having *for* before the person or thing received in exchange: *my gravity could I* c. *for an idle plume,* Meas. II, 4, 11. Err. III, 1, 47. LLL V, 2, 844. Mids. II, 2, 114. As III, 2, 301. Shr. III, 1, 81. Wint. I, 2, 68. H6A I, 1, 151. H6B I, 1, 219. Troil. IV, 2, 96. Oth. II, 1, 156. IV, 3, 98.

II) intr. to be altered: *by chance or nature's —ing course untrimmed,* Sonn. 18, 8. *the sky —s when they are wives,* As IV, 1, 149. *I hope my holy humour will* c. R3 I, 4, 121. *their minds may* c. Caes. II, 2, 96. *that things might* c. *or cease,* Lr. III, 1, 7 (= suffer a complete revolution). *the Moor already —s with my poison,* Oth. III, 3, 325. Used of the moon: Tp. II, 1, 184. LLL V, 2, 212. 214. Mids. V, 256. Shr. IV, 5, 20. H5 V, 2, 173. Rom. II, 2, 110.

= to be inconstant: *no, time, thou shalt not boast that I do* c. Sonn. 123, 1. *his - ing thoughts,* Gentl. IV, 4, 124. *it* (his faith) *ever —s,* Ado I, 1, 76. *if my passion* c. *not shortly,* 221. *Hortensio will be quit with thee by —ing* (= by loving another) Shr. III, 1, 92. *wind-changing Warwick now can* c. *no more,* H6C V, 1, 57. *shallow —ing woman,* R3 IV, 4, 431. *go, wind, to wind, there turn and* c. *together,* Troil. V, 3, 110. *give that —ing piece to him,* Tit. I, 309. *think what a chance thou —st on,* Cymb. I, 5, 68.

= to change colour or countenance: *he —s more and more,* Ado V, 1, 140. *his eye is hollow, and he —s much,* H4B IV, 5, 6. *how they* c.*! their cheeks are paper,* H5 II, 2, 73. *he smiles, and Caesar doth not* c. Caes. III, 1, 24. *thou —d and self-covered thing, bemonster not thy feature,* Lr. IV, 2, 62. c. *you, madam?* Cymb. I, 6, 12.

Followed by *to: faith itself to hollow falsehood* c. John III, 1, 95. *our solemn hymns to sullen dirges* c. Rom. IV, 5, 88. Followed by *into: he —d almost into another man,* All's IV, 3, 5. Followed by *for: she must* c. *for youth,* Oth. I, 3, 356. *thou holdest a place for which the pained'st fiend of hell would not in reputation* c. Per. IV, 6, 174.

Changeable, 1) varying in colour: *the tailor make thy doublet of* c. *taffeta, for thy mind is a very opal,* Tw. II, 4, 76.*

2) inconstant: c., *longing and liking, proud etc.* As III, 2, 431. *report is* c. Lr. IV, 7, 92. *these Moors are* c. *in their wills,* Oth. I, 3, 352.

Changeful, inconstant, uncertain: *presuming on their* c. *potency,* Troil. IV, 4, 99.

Changeling, 1) inconstant person, waverer: *fickle —s and poor discontents,* H4A V, 1, 76. *his nature in that's no* c. (= has not changed, is still the same) Cor. IV, 7, 11.

2) a child left or taken by the fairies in the place of another: *she never had so sweet a* c. Mids. II, 1, 23. *a little* c. *boy,* 120. *her* c. *child,* IV, 1, 64. *this is some* c. Wint. III, 3, 122. *she's a* c. IV, 4, 705. Used of a letter substituted for another: *placed it safely, the* c. *never known,* Hml. V, 2, 53.

Channel, subst., 1) the bed of running waters: *you nymphs, called Naiads, leave your crisp —s*, Tp. IV, 130. *shall leave his native c. and o'erswell thy shores*, John II, 337. H4A III, 1, 103. Cor. III, 1, 97. Caes. I, 1, 64. Figuratively: *the crystal tide that in the sweet c. of her bosom dropt*, Ven. 958. *here friend by friend in bloody c. lies*, Lucr. 1487. *each cheek a river ...; O, how the c. to the stream gave grace*, Compl. 285. *fret —s in her cheek*, Lr. I, 4, 307.

2) a gutter, kennel: *throw the quean in the c.* H4B II, 1, 52. 53. *as if a c. should be called the sea*, H6C II, 2, 141.

3) the narrow sea between Britain and France: *waft me safely cross the C.* H6B IV, 1, 114.

Channel, vb., to furrow: *no more shall trenching war c. her fields*, H4A I, 1, 7.

Chanson, song: *the first row of the pious c. will show you more*, Hml. II, 2, 438 (Ff *Pons Chanson* & *Pans Chânson*).

Chant, vb., to sing: *the free maids do use to c. it*, Tw. II, 4, 47. *the lark that tirra lirra —s*, Wint. IV, 3, 9. *the birds c. melody on every bush*, Tit. II, 3, 12. *she —ed snatches of old tunes*, Hml. IV, 7, 178. Followed by a superfluous *it*: *she hears them* (his hounds and horn) *c. it lustily*, Ven. 869. — Having *to* before the thing addressed or celebrated in song: *—ing faint hymns to the cold fruitless moon*, Mids. I, 1, 73. *he so —s to the sleeve-hand*, Wint. IV, 4, 211. *he —s a doleful hymn to his own death*, John V, 7, 22.

Chanticleer, the cock: *I hear the strain of strutting c.* Tp. I, 2, 385. *my lungs began to crow like c.* As II, 7, 30.

Chantry, a private chapel: Tw. IV, 3, 24. H5 IV, 1, 318.

Chaos, the confused matter supposed to have existed before the creation: *and, beauty dead, black c. comes again*, Ven. 1020. *vast sin-concealing c.* (sc. the night), Lucr. 767. *to disproportion me in every part, like to a c. or an unlicked bear-whelp*, H6C III, 2, 161. *this c., when degree is suffocate*, Troil. I, 3, 125. *mis-shapen c. of well-seeming forms*, Rom. I, 1, 185. *when I love thee not, c. is come again*, Oth. III, 3, 92.

Chap, see *Chaps*.

Chape, the metal part at the end of a scabbard: *had the whole theoric of war in the knot of his scarf, and the practice in the c. of his dagger*, All's IV, 3, 164.

Chapel, a little church: Ado V, 4, 71. Merch. I, 2, 14. As III, 3, 67. Wint. III, 2, 240. V, 3, 86. John II, 538. H8 III, 2, 406. Hml. IV, 1, 37. IV, 2, 8. Cymb. II, 2, 33.

Chapeless, without a chape: *an old rusty sword, with a broken hilt and c.* Shr. III, 2, 48.

Chapfallen, with a shrunk jaw: *not one* (gibe) *now, to mock your own grinning? quite c.?* Hml. V, 1, 212. cf. *Crestfallen*.

Chaplain, an ecclesiastic who performs service in a chapel: *the c. of the Tower*, R3 IV, 3, 29. H8 V, 3, 16. Also one that officiates in domestic worship: H6C I, 3, 3. H8 I, 2, 162. 166.

Chapless, without a jaw: *yellow c. skulls*, Rom. IV, 1, 83. Hml. V, 1, 97.

Chaplet, garland: *on old Hiems' thin and icy crown an odorous c. of sweet summer buds*, Mids. II, 1, 110.

Chapman, 1) buyer: *you do as chapmen do, dispraise the thing that you desire to buy*, Troil. IV, 1, 75. — 2) seller: *beauty is bought by judgment of the eye, not uttered by base sale of chapmen's tongues*, LLL II, 16.

Chapped or **Chapt**, writing of M. Edd. in H4B III, 2, 294; O. Edd. *chopt*, q. v.

Chaps, never used in the sing.; 1) the jaws, the mouth: *open your c. again*, Tp. II, 2, 89. *now doth Death line his dead c. with steel*, John II, 352. *I'll thrust my knife in your mouldy c.* H4B II, 4, 139. *before his c. be stained with crimson blood*, H6B III, 1, 259. *he unseamed him from the nave to the c.* Mcb. I, 2, 22. *then, world, thou hast a pair of c., no more*, Ant. III, 5, 14.

2) wrinkles: *my frosty signs and c. of age*, Tit. V, 3, 77. In Lucr. 1452 M. Edd., according to Q7, *chaps;* all the other Qq *chops*, q. v.

Chapter, a division of a book: *where lies your text? in Orsino's bosom. In what c. of his bosom?* Tw. I, 5, 242.

Char, see *Chare*.

Cháract, distinctive mark: *even so may Angelo, in all his dressings, —s, titles, forms, be an arch-villain*, Meas. V, 56.

Cháracter, subst. (only in R3 III, 1, 81 charácter); 1) writing, letter or figure used in writing: *since mind at first in c. was done*, Sonn. 59, 8 (= since thought was first expressed in writing). Sonn. 85, 3* (an unintelligible passage). *which on it had conceited —s*, Compl. 16. *thought —s and words merely but art*, 174. *there is a kind of c. in thy life, that to the observer doth thy history fully unfold*, Meas. I, 1, 28. *our most mutual entertainment with c. too gross is writ on Juliet*, I, 2, 159. *when it deserves, with —s of brass, a forted residence 'gainst the tooth of time*, V, 11. *there lie, and there thy c.* Wint. III, 3, 47 (i. e. the writing concerning Perdita's name). *written down old with all the —s of age*, H4B I, 2, 203. *razing the —s of your renown*, H6B I, 1, 101. *without —s fame lives long*, R3 III, 1, 81. *even as substance, whose grossness little —s sum up*, Troil. I, 3, 325. *in —s as red as Mars his heart inflamed with Venus*, V, 2, 164. *the c. I'll take with wax*, Tim. V, 3, 6. *he cut our roots in —s*, Cymb. IV, 2, 49 (= letters). *Apollo, perfect me in the —s*, Per. III, 2, 67.

= handwriting: *you know the c.* Meas. IV, 2, 208. *this is not my writing, though much like the c.* Tw. V, 354. *the letters of Antigonus, which they know to be his c.* Wint. V, 2, 38. *know you the hand? 'tis Hamlet's c.* Hml. IV, 7, 53. Lr. I, 2, 66. II, 1, 74. Cymb. III, 2, 28. Per. III, 4, 3.

2) Figuratively, outward marks bespeaking inward qualities: *a mind that suits with this thy fair and outward c.* Tw. I, 2, 51. *what harm can your bisson conspectuities glean out of this c.* (sc. my face)? Cor. II, 1, 71. *I paint him in the c.* (= such as he appears), V, 4, 28.

Character, vb. (accented on the first or second syll.), to write, to inscribe: *what's in the brain that ink may c.* Sonn. 108, 1. *thy gift, thy tables, are within my brain full —ed with lasting memory*, 122, 2. *in their barks my thoughts I'll c.* As III, 2, 6. — *the light will show, —ed in my brow, the story of sweet chastity's decay*, Lucr. 807. *the table wherein all my thoughts are visibly —ed and engraved*, Gentl. II, 7, 4.

show me one scar —ed on thy skin, H6B III, 1, 300. *these few precepts in thy memory see thou c.* Hml. 1, 3, 59.

Charácterless, unrecorded: *and mighty states c. are grated to dusty nothing*, Troil. III, 2, 195.

Charáctery, writing: *fairies use flowers for their c.* Wiv. V, 5, 77. *all my engagements I will construe to thee, all the c. of my sad brows*, Caes. II, 1, 308.

Charbon, name: *young C. the puritan*, All's I, 3, 55 (perhaps = Firebrand).*

Chare, task-work, job, drudgery: *as the maid that milks and does the meanest —s*, Ant. IV, 15, 75. *when thou hast done this c., I'll give thee leave to play till doomsday*, V, 2, 231.

Charge, subst., 1) load, burden: *'tis a great c. to come under one body's hand*, Wiv. I, 4, 104. *you embrace your c. too willingly*, Ado I, 1, 103. *my stay to you a c. and trouble*, Wint. I, 2, 26.

2) luggage: *they have great c.* H4A II, 1, 51. *one that hath abundance of c. too*, 64.

3) weight: *I have about me many parcels of c.* Wint. IV, 4, 261. *the letter was not nice, but full of c., of dear import*, Rom. V, 2, 18. *many such like Ases of great c.* Hml. V, 2, 43 (a quibble).

4) accusation: *beside the c., the shame, imprisonment*, Err. V, 18. *you may season it in the c.* Hml. II, 1, 28. *we need not put new matter to his c.* Cor. III, 3, 76. Oftener *to lay sth. to c.*: Ado V, 1, 228. As III, 2, 370. John I, 256. R2 I, 1, 84. H6A III, 1, 4. H6B III, 1, 134. R3 I, 3, 326. Lr. I, 2, 139 (Ff. *on the c.*); cf. *lay*. — Singular expression: *might we lay the old proverb to your c., so like you, 'tis the worse*, Wint. II, 3, 96 (= apply to you).

5) expense, cost: *shall worms, inheritors of this excess, eat up thy c.?* Sonn. 146, 8. *bear his c. of wooing*, Shr. I, 2, 216. *the c. and thanking shall be for me*, All's III, 5, 101. *is't not I that undergo this c.?* John V, 2, 100. *this expedition's c.* I, 49. R2 II, 1, 159. H4A I, 1, 35. H6A V, 5, 92. H8 I, 1, 77. Troil. IV, 1, 57. Cor. V, 6, 68.* Caes. IV, 1, 9. Hml. IV, 4, 47. Lr. II, 4, 242. Ant. III, 7, 17 (here it may also be = command). — Plural *charges: for costs and —s in transporting her*, H6B I, 1, 134. *the —s of the action*, Cor. V, 6, 79. *At the c. of: thou must be hanged at the state's c.* Merch. IV, 1, 367. All's II, 3, 121. H4A I, 3, 79. Lr. I, 1, 10. *I will be at —s for a looking-glass*, R3 I, 2, 256 (make some expense). *Of a person's charge: sent over of the king of England's own proper cost and —s*, H6B I, 1, 61. *On a person's c.: have by some surgeon on your c.* Merch. IV, 1, 257.

6) a person or thing entrusted to the care of another: *how darest thou trust so great a c. from thine own custody?* Err. I, 2, 61. *tell me how thou hast disposed thy c.* 73. *patience, even for this c.* Per. III, 1, 27 (the new-born child). *where is the gold I gave in c. to thee?* Err. I, 2, 70. *how now, my c.! Now, my sweet guardian*, Troil. V, 2, 6 (a quibble from which it is evident that it had also the sense of pupil, ward).

7) commission, order, office: *Ariel, thy c. exactly is performed*, Tp. I, 2, 237. V, 317. Wiv. III, 3, 7. Meas. I, 2, 123. IV, 2, 106. Ado III, 3, 7. 25. All's III, 3, 4. Wint. V, 1, 162. John IV, 2, 75. R2 IV, 152. H4B I, 2, 72. IV, 2, 99. H5 III, 6, 114. H6A IV, 5, 42. II, 1, 62. H6B III, 1, 321. H6C III, 3, 258.

IV, 6, 86. V, 4, 20. R3 III, 7, 131. H8 I, 4, 20. Troil. IV, 4, 128. *on c.* = at command, IV, 4, 135. — *To give in c.* = to command: *in the same fashion as you gave in c.* Tp. V, 8. H6A II, 3, 1. H6C IV, 1, 32. R3 I, 1, 85. IV, 3, 25. Passively: *so am I given in c.* H6B II, 4, 80. *To have in c.* = to be commanded: *as by your majesty I had in c.* H6B I, 1, 2.

= a military post or command: *I'll procure this fat rogue a c. of foot*, H4A II, 4, 597. III, 3, 208. 210. V, 1, 118. H5 IV, 3, 6. R3 V, 3, 25. 53. Ant. III, 7, 17. IV, 4, 19. Hence = the troops under a person's command: *my whole c. consists of ancients* etc. H4A IV, 2, 25. *the centurions and their —s*, Cor. IV, 3, 48. *bid our commanders lead their —s off*, Caes. IV, 2, 48.[1]

8) the order or signal of attack: *his beating heart, alarum striking, gives the hot c.* Lucr. 434. *and upon this c. cry 'God for Harry'*, H5 III, 1, 33.

9) the attack itself: *we have heard the —s of our friends*, Cor. I, 6, 6. *we will answer on their c.* Caes. V, 1, 24. *when the compulsive ardour gives the c.* Hml. III, 4, 86. *their armed staves in c.* H4B IV, 1, 120, i. e. couched, prepared for the onset.

Charge, vb., 1) to load, to burden: *or nicely c. your understanding soul with opening titles miscreate*, H5 I, 2, 15. *his soul shall stand sore —d*, 283. *things unluckily c. my fantasy*, Caes. III, 3, 2. *the heart is sorely —d*, Mcb. V, 1, 60. *if sleep c. nature*, Cymb. III, 4, 44. Hence = to put to expense: *not to c. you*, Wiv. II, 2, 171.

2) to commission: *that I beat him and —d him with a thousand marks*, Err. III, 1, 8. *my lady —d my duty in this business*, Lr. IV, 5, 18 (but here perhaps = commanded).

3) to accuse: *my heart doth c. the watch*, Pilgr. 194. *in this the madman justly —th them*, Err. V, 213. Meas. V, 200. All's V, 3, 167. H8 I, 2, 174. Cor. III, 3, 1. 42. Oth. IV, 2, 186. *you c. me that I have blown this coal*, H8 II, 4, 93. *we c. you that you have contrived ...*, Cor. III, 3, 63. Having *with* before the thing imputed: *when thou shalt c. me with so black a deed*, Lucr. 226. *and —s him with such a time ...*, Meas. V, 197 (= with having committed his offence at such a time). *she was —d with nothing but what was true*, Ado V, 1, 104. All's IV, 2, 34. H4A II, 4, 566. III, 2, 21. H8 V, 1, 147. Ant. II, 2, 83.

4) to enjoin, to order: *your physicians have expressly —d that I should ...* Shr. Ind. 2, 123. Usually followed by an accus. indicating the person commanded: *nature hath —d me that I hoard them not*, Compl. 220. *I c. thee that thou attend me*, Tp. I, 2, 452. IV, 259. As III, 2, 149. H6B III, 2, 256. IV, 6, 2. IV, 7, 132. R3 I, 4, 194. *we c. you, stand!* Ado III, 3, 176. *I c. thee, do so*, IV, 1, 77. V, 2, 39. Mids. II, 2, 85. Shr. Ind. 1, 16. H4B V, 4, 18. H6B IV, 1, 114. H6C V, 5, 81. Rom. III, 1, 145. *—ing the groom to hie*, Lucr. 1334. *my master —d me to deliver a ring*, Gentl. V, 4, 88. Ado I, 1, 210. Err. IV, 1, 70. As I, 1, 3. 71. IV, 3, 72. Tw. II, 1, 15. H6A I, 3, 76. IV, 1, 135. — The infinitive following without *to: c. Agrippa plant those in the van*, Ant. IV, 6, 8. The thing ordered in the accus.: *the king hath straitly —d the contrary*, R3 IV, 1, 17. *my lady —d my duty in this business*, Lr. IV, 5, 18 (but this may be explained otherwise).

5) to adjure, to entreat instantly: *Satan,*

avoid! I c. thee, tempt me not, Err. IV, 3, 48. IV, 4, 57. *I c. you, on your souls, to utter it*, Ado IV, 1, 14. *I c. you by the law, proceed to judgement*, Merch. IV, 1, 238. *I c. thee, be not thou more grieved than I am*, As I, 3, 94. *now will I c. you in the band of truth, remain there but an hour*, All's IV, 2, 56. *I c. thee, fling away ambition*, H8 III, 2, 441. *they —d him even as those should do that had deserved his hate*, Cor. IV, 6, 112. *speak, I c. you*, Mcb. I, 3, 78. *by what more dear a better proposer could c. you withal*, Hml. II, 2, 297.

6) to call to account, to challenge: *and c. us there upon intergatories*, Merch. V, 298. *to c. me to an answer*, John III, 1, 151.

7) to attack: *c.! and give no foot of ground*, H6C I, 4, 15. *mend and c. home*, Cor. I, 4, 38. *whoever —s on his forward breast*, All's III, 2, 116. *to c. in with our horse upon our own wings*, III, 6, 52. *will c. on us*, H5 IV, 3, 70. *c. upon our foes*, H6C II, 1, 184. Transitively: *either not assailed or victor being —d*, Sonn. 70, 10. *you c. him too coldly*, Wint. I, 2, 30. H6C I, 1, 8. Troil. III, 2, 29. Cor. I, 6, 4. Lr. II, 1, 53. Ant. IV, 11, 1.

8) to prepare for an attack, to load: *their battering cannon —d to the mouths*, John II, 382. H4B II, 4, 57. 121. III, 2, 280. Cor. V, 3, 152 (O. Edd. *change*). — Figuratively: *I shall meet your wit in the career, an you c. it against me*, Ado V, 1, 136. *what are they that c. their breath against us?* LLL V, 2, 88.

Chargeful, expensive: *the fineness of the gold and c. fashion*, Err. IV, 1, 29.

Charge-house, certainly a school-house, but uncertain of what kind: *do you not educate youth at the c. on the top of the mountain?* LLL V, 1, 87 (Armado's speech!).

Chariness, nicety, scrupulousness: *I will consent to act any villany against him, that may not sully the c. of our honesty*, Wiv. II, 1, 102.

Charing-cross, place in England: H4A II, 1, 27.

Chariot, 1) a carriage of state, especially a triumphal car: *their mistress (viz Venus) in her light c. quickly is conveyed*, Ven. 1192. *in a captive c. bring him our prisoner*, H5 III, 5, 54. *my sword, my c. and my prisoners*, Tit. I, 249. *horse and —s let us have*, II, 2, 18. *her* (Queen Mab's) *c. is an empty hazel-nut*, Rom. I, 4, 67. *and when you saw his c. but appear*, Caes. I, 1, 48. *shall set thee on triumphant —s*, Ant. III, 1, 10. *follow his c.* IV, 12, 35. *seated in a c.* Per. II, 4, 7.

2) a car formerly used in war: *it fits us therefore ripely our —s and our horsemen be in readiness*, Cymb. III, 5, 23.

Chariot-wheel: H6B II, 4, 13. Tit. V, 2, 47. Caes. I, 1, 39.

Charitable, full of charity, benevolent, ready or fit to relieve distress: *c. deeds*, Lucr. 908. *let him have all c. preparation*, Meas. III, 2, 222. *a c. duty*, Err. V, 107. *with c. hand*, Ado IV, 1, 133. *born under a c. star*, All's I, 1, 205. *a c. office*, Wint. IV, 3, 80. *a just and c. war*, John II, 36. *license*, H5 IV, 7, 74. *deeds*, R3 I, 2, 35. *care*, Cor. I, 1, 67. *murderer*, Tit. II, 3, 178. *deed*, III, 2, 70. *wish*, IV, 2, 43. *title*, Tim. I, 2, 94. *men*, III, 2, 82. *intents*, Hml. I, 4, 42. *prayers*, V, 1, 253. *bill*, Cymb. IV, 2, 225.

Charitably, benevolently, with Christian love: *how can they c. dispose of any thing, when blood is their argument?* H5 IV, 1, 149.

Charity, that disposition of heart which inclines men to think favourably of their fellow-men, and to do them good: Compl. 70. Tp. I, 2, 162. Gentl. II, 5, 60. Meas. II, 3, 3. II, 4, 63. 66. 68. IV, 3, 53. LLL IV, 3, 127. 364. Merch. I, 2, 85. IV, 1, 261. Shr. IV, 1, 214. IV, 3, 6. Wint. III, 3, 113. John II, 565. R2 III, 1, 5. H4B IV, 4, 32. H5 IV, 8, 129. H6B III, 1, 144. H6C V, 5, 76. R3 I, 2, 68. I, 3, 274. 277. II, 1, 49. II, 2, 108. H8 I, 2, 143. II, 4, 86. III, 1, 109. III, 2, 298. IV, 2, 33. Troil. III, 3, 173. V, 3, 22. Cor. V, 6, 12. Tit. V, 1, 89. Tim. I, 2, 229. IV, 3, 534. Lr. II, 3, 20. III, 3, 17. III, 4, 61 (*ao*). V, 3, 166. Oth. IV, 1, 124. Cymb. II, 3, 114. IV, 2, 169. V, 4, 170. Per. I, 2, 100. III, 2, 44. 75. III, 5, 14. V, 3, 94. *your —ies*, Wint. II, 1, 113. *fie! c., for shame, speak not in spite*, H6B V, 1, 213. *for c., be not so curst*, R3 I, 2, 48. *for shame, if not for c.* I, 3, 273. H8 II, 1, 79. IV, 2, 23. *of c., what kin are you to me?* Tw. V, 237.* — Synonymous to *piety: the bastard Faulconbridge is now in England, ransacking the church, offending c.* John III, 4, 173.

Name of a female saint: *by Gis and by Saint C.*, Hml. IV, 5, 58.

Charlemain (trisyllabic), 1) Charlemagne: All's II, 1, 80. — 2) Carloman, son of Lewis of Germany: H5 I, 2, 75 (Sh., adopting Holinshed's mistake, calls him Charlemagne's grandson, being his great-grandson).

Charles, 1) Charlemagne: *Charles the Great, having subdued the Saxons*, H5 I, 2, 46. 61. 71. 77. 84. — 2) C. duke of Lorraine, dispossessed by Hugh Capet: H5 I, 2, 70. — 3) the French king C. the sixth: H6B I, 1, 41. 44. — 4) the dauphin, afterwards Charles VII: H6A I, 1, 92. II, 1, 48. III, 2, 123 etc. — 5) C. duke of Orleans: H5 IV, 8, 81. — 6) C. Delabreth, high constable of France: H5 III, 5, 40. IV, 8, 97. — 7) the emperor Charles V: H8 I, 1, 176. — 8) C. duke of Suffolk: H8 V, 1, 56. 59. 72. 78. — 9) the father of the king of Navarre: LLL II, 163. — 10) C. the wrestler: As I, 1, 95 etc. I, 2, 134 etc. II, 2, 14. — 11) *Charles' wain*, popular name of the Great Bear: H4A II, 1, 2.

Charm, subst., 1) magic power, means of a magic influence: *honest fear, bewitched with lust's foul c.* Lucr. 173. *who, with a c. joined to their suffered labour, I have left asleep*, Tp. I, 2, 231. 339. III, 3, 88. IV, 95. V, 2. 17. 31. 54. Tp. Epil. 1. Wiv. II, 2, 107. Meas. IV, 1, 14. Ado II, 1, 187. III, 2, 72. Mids. II, 1, 183. R3 I, 3, 215. III, 4, 64. Cor. I, 5, 22. Mcb. I, 3, 37. V, 8, 13 etc. — *Charm* and *spell* placed together as two different things: *she works by —s, by spells, by the figure*, Wiv. IV, 2, 185. *never harm, nor spell nor c.* Mids. II, 2, 17. *unchain your spirits now with spelling —s*, H6A V, 3, 31 (*charming spells*, V, 3, 2). *your vessels and your spells provide, your —s and every thing beside*, Mcb. III, 5, 19 (cf. *spell*).

Charm, abstr. pro concr., = charmer: *when I am revenged upon my c., I have done all*, Ant. IV, 12, 16. *O this false soul of Egypt, this grave c.* 25 (v. 30 *spell*).

2) that which irresistibly gains the affections: *'even thus, quoth she, the warlike God unlaced me', as if the boy should use like loving —s*, Pilgr. 150. *bewitched by the c. of looks*, Rom. II Chor. 6. *whose age has —s in it, to pluck the common bosom on his side*, Lr. V, 3, 48. *all the —s of love soften thy*

waned lip, Ant. II, 1, 20. *forth of my heart those —s, thine eyes, are blotted*, Oth. V, 1, 35.

Charm, vb., 1) intr. to work with magic power: *—ing spells*, H6A V, 3, 2. *nor witch hath power to c.* Hml. I, 1, 163. *ere I could give him that parting kiss which I had set betwixt two —ing words,* Cymb. I, 3, 35.*more —ing with their own nobleness,* V, 3, 32.

2) trans. a) to affect by magic power: *I'll c. his eyes against she do appear*, Mids. III, 2, 99. 376. *—ing your blood with pleasing heaviness*, H4A III, 1, 218. *whose dangerous eyes may well be —-ed asleep*, H4B IV, 2, 39. *—ing the narrow seas to give you gentle pass,* H5 II Chor. 38. *this siren, that will c. Rome's Saturnine,* Tit. II, 1, 23. *has almost —ed me from my profession,* Tim. IV, 3, 454. *I'll c. the air to give a sound,* Mcb. IV, 1, 129. *no witchcraft c. thee,* Cymb. IV, 2, 277.

Special significations: to fortify, to make invulnerable by spells: *I bear a —ed life*, Mcb. V, 8, 12. *I, in mine own woe —ed, could not find death,* Cymb. V, 3, 68. — To force to obey: *And for my sake, when I might c. thee so, for she that was thy Lucrece, now attend me,* Lucr. 1681. *and upon my knees I c. you, by all vows of love, that you unfold to me …*, Caes. II, 1, 271. — To produce, to call forth: *music such as —eth sleep*, Mids. IV, 1, 88. *'tis your graces that from my mutest conscience to my tongue —s this report out,* Cymb. I, 6, 117. — To appease, to make silent: *c. ache with air and agony with words,* Ado V, 1, 26. *I will c. him first to keep his tongue,* Shr. I, 1, 214. *to tame a shrew and c. her chattering tongue,* IV, 2, 58. *it shall c. thy riotous tongue,* H6B IV, 1, 64. *I will c. your tongue,* H6C V, 5, 31. *c. your tongue,* Oth. V, 2, 183.

b) to fascinate, to subdue the affections (but there is always some trace of the primary signification): *it beguiled attention, —ed the sight,* Lucr. 1404. *not one … my leisures ever —ed,* Compl. 193. *my parts had power to c. a sacred nun,* 260. *I —ed their ears,* Tp. IV, 178. *Fortune forbid my outside have not —d her,* Tw. II, 2, 19.

Charmed, adj. endowed with a charm: *threw my affections in his c. power,* Compl. 146. *boil thou first in the c. pot,* Mcb. IV, 1, 9.

Charmer, sorceress: Oth. III, 4, 57.

Charmian, female name in Ant. I, 3, 15. 71. I, 5, 1 etc. etc.

Charmingly, in an enchanting manner, delightfully: *this is a most majestic vision, and harmonious c.* Tp. IV, 119.*

Charneco, a sort of wine, probably coming from Portugal: H6B III, 3, 63.*

Charnel-house, a place where the bones of the dead are reposited: Rom. IV, 1, 81. Mcb. III, 4, 71.

Charolois, name of a French nobleman: H5 III, 5, 45.

Charon, the ferryman of Tartarus: Troil. III, 2, 11. Spoken of, though not named: R3 I, 4, 46.

Charter, subst. 1) recorded right, and in general right, privilege: *be where you list, your c. is so strong that you yourself may privilege your time to what you will,* Sonn. 58, 9. *thou art too dear for my possessing, … the c. of thy worth gives thee releasing,* 87, 3. *if you deny it, let the danger light upon your c. and your city's freedom,* Merch. IV, 1,

39. *I must have liberty, as large a c. as the wind, to blow on whom I please,* As II, 7, 48. *you need but plead your honourable privilege; … of that I have made a bold c.* All's IV, 5, 97. *take from Time his —s and his customary rights,* R2 II, 1, 196. *taking him from thence, you break no privilege nor c. there,* R3 III, 1, 54. *my mother, who has a c. to extol her blood,* Cor. I, 9, 14. *ever spake against your liberties and the —s that you bear i' the body of the weal,* II, 3, 188. *let me find a c. in your voice, to assist my simpleness,* Oth. I, 3, 246.

2) *blank c.* = carte blanche: *our substitutes shall have blank —s, whereto, when they shall know what men are rich, they shall subscribe them for large sums of gold,* R2 I, 4, 48.

Chartered, privileged: *the air, a c. libertine,* H5 I, 1, 48 (cf. As II, 7, 48).

Chartreux, name of a religious order: *a monk of the C.* H8 I, 1, 221. *a C. friar,* I, 2, 148.

Chary, nice, heedful: *bearing thy heart, which I will keep so c. as tender nurse her babe,* Sonn. 22, 11. *the —iest maid is prodigal enough, if she unmask her beauty to the moon,* Hml. I, 3, 36.

Charybdis, the vortex in the straits of Sicilia: *when I shun Scylla, your father, I fall into C., your mother,* Merch. III, 5, 19.

Chase, subst., 1) hunting: Ven. 3. 696. 883. Oth. II, 3, 369. *this is the c.* Wint. III, 3, 57 (commonly explained as meaning the hunted beast).

2) a ground well stored with game: *at the lodge upon the north-side of this pleasant c.* Tit. II, 3, 255.

3) pursuit in general: *I am out of breath in this fond c.* Mids. II, 2, 88. As II, 1, 40. *seek thee out some other c.* H6B V, 2, 14; cf. H6C II, 4, 12. R3 III, 2, 30. Figuratively: *you see this c. is hotly followed,* H5 II, 4, 68.* *by this kind of c. I should hate him,* As I, 3, 33 (= by this way of following up the argument). *To hold the c.* = to pursue: Mids. II, 1, 231. *To hold in c.,* in the same sense: Lucr. 1736. Sonn. 143, 5. John I, 223. Cor. I, 6, 19. *To give c.:* Hml. IV, 6, 16. *To have in c.:* Gentl. V, 4, 15. *I did send a ring in c. of you* (= after you), Tw. III, 1, 124. *in the c. of this fair couple,* Wint. V, 1, 189.

4) course, race: *if thy wits run the wildgoose c.* Rom. II, 4, 75. *the barren, touched in this holy c.* Caes. I, 2, 8.

Chase, vb., 1) to hunt: *the roe that's tired with —ing,* Ven. 561. *unless it be a boar, and then I c. it,* 410. Wiv. V, 5, 252.

2) to pursue; absol.: *all swoln with —ing, down Adonis sits* (earlier Qq *chafing*) Ven. 325. Transit.: *who this accomplishment so hotly —d,* Lucr. 716. Sonn. 143, 10. Tp. V, 35. Merch. II, 6, 13. H4A I, 1, 24. H6A I, 5, 3. Tim. I, 1, 25 (M. Edd. *chafes*). Cymb. III, 3, 42. V, 3, 48. *to c. injustice with revengeful arms,* Lucr. 1693. *though Fortune should c. us with our father,* Wint. V, 1, 217. *to rouse his wrongs and c. them to the bay,* R2 II, 3, 128. *to c. us to our graves,* R3 IV, 4, 54.

3) to drive away: *their rising senses begin to c. the ignorant fumes,* Tp. V, 67. Followed by *from:* Lucr. 1834. Gentl. II, 4, 134. All's III, 2, 106. John III, 4, 83. R2 II, 1, 118. H5 V, 2, 38. H6A I, 2, 115. H6C I, 1, 90. *—d your blood out of appearance,* H5 II, 2, 75. *c. hence,* H6A I, 3, 55. H6B III, 1, 144. *c. away,* Err. V, 153. H6B III, 2, 44.

Chase, subst., see *Chace.*

Chaser, pursuer: *then began a stop i' the c., a retire,* Cymb. V, 3, 40.

Chaste, pure, undefiled, continent: Lucr. 7. 322. 682 *(—st).* 840. 1836. Sonn. 154, 3. Phoen. 4. Tp. IV, 66. Wiv. II, 1, 83. V, 5, 89. Meas. II, 4, 184. V, 97. Ado IV, 1, 59. LLL V, 2, 252. Mids. II, 1, 162. Merch. I, 2, 117. As III, 2, 3. 10. Shr. II, 263. All's IV, 3, 18. Wint. III, 2, 35. 133. IV, 4, 33. H4A I, 2, 32. H6A V, 4, 51. V, 5, 20. H8 IV, 2, 132. 170. Troil. I, 3, 299. Cor. V, 3, 65. Tit. II, 1, 108. IV, 1, 90. Rom. I, 1, 223. Hml. III, 1, 140. Oth. IV, 1, 47. 73. V, 2, 2. 249. Cymb. II, 4, 82. II, 5, 13 etc.

Chastely, in a chaste manner: All's I, 3, 218. III, 7, 34. Cor. V, 2, 28.

Chástise, 1) to punish severely: Tp. V, 263. John II, 117. V, 2, 84. R2 II, 3, 104. H6A I, 5, 12. R3 IV, 4, 331. Troil. V, 5, 4. Tit. I, 32. Ant. V, 2, 54. 2) to reprimand, to set to rights: *that I may c. with the valour of my tongue all that impedes thee from the golden round,* Mcb. I, 5, 26.

Chástisement, severe punishment, correction: Meas. V, 257. John V, 2, 147. R2 I, 1, 106. IV, 22. H4B IV, 1, 217. H6A IV, 1, 69. R3 V, 3, 113. Caes. IV, 3, 16.

Chastity, purity of the body: Ven. 751. Lucr. Arg. 7. Lucr. 692. 808. Compl. 297. 315. Pilgr. 50. Phoen. 61. Gentl. IV, 3, 21. Meas. II, 4, 185. V, 410. Ado IV, 1, 96 *(there is not c. enough in language).* Mids. III, 1, 205. As III, 4, 18. Shr. II, 298. All's IV, 2, 46. H6B V, 1, 186. Tit. II, 3, 44. 124. V, 2, 177. Rom. I, 1, 216. Oth. V, 2, 276. Ant. I, 2, 47. Cymb. I, 4, 176. II, 2, 14. V, 5, 179. 207. Per. IV, 6, 130. 160.

Chat, subst., prate, in a good as well as bad sense: *leave this bootless c.* Ven. 422. *palmers' c. makes short their pilgrimage,* Lucr. 791. Tp. II, 1, 266. LLL IV, 3, 284. Shr. II, 270. H4A I, 3, 65. III, 1, 63. *To have some c.:* Shr. II, 163. H6C III, 2, 109. *let's hold more c.,* LLL V, 2, 228.

Chat, vb., to prate: Err. II, 2, 27. Shr. III, 2, 123. V, 2, 11. Rom. IV, 4, 26. Transitively: *your prattling nurse into a rapture lets her baby cry while she —s him,* Cor. II, 1, 224 *(cf. speak),* = of him.

Chatham: *the clerk of C.,* H6B IV, 2, 92 ('a nonentity in history.' Douce).

Chatillon (O. Edd. *Chatillion*), French name: John I, 1. 30. II, 46. 51. 53. H5 III, 5, 43. IV, 8, 98.

Chattels, movable goods: *she is my goods, my c.* Shr. III, 2, 232. H5 II, 3, 50. H8 III, 2, 343 (so M. Edd., following Holinshed; O. Edd. *castles*).

Chatter, vb., 1) to utter inarticulate sounds, resembling human speech: *apes that mow and c. at me,* Tp. II, 2, 9. *—ing pies,* H6C V, 6, 48. *apes and monkeys would c. this way,* Cymb. I, 6, 40. — Hence of a restless tongue: *to tame a shrew and charm her —ing tongue,* Shr. IV, 2, 58. 2) to make a noise by collision of the teeth: *when the wind came to make me c.* Lr. IV, 6, 103.

Chaudron, entrails: *add thereto a tiger's c.* Mcb. IV, 1, 33.

Che, *I* (Somersetshire dialect): Lr. IV, 6, 239. 246.

Cheap, adj., bearing a low price in market: *then must your brother die. And 'twere the —er way,* Meas. II, 4, 105. *let what is dear in Sicily be c.* Wint.

I, 2, 175. R2 V, 5, 68 *(—est).* H4B V, 3, 20. H6B I, 1, 222. Cor. II, 1, 100. IV, 5, 249. V, 1, 17. V, 6, 47. Per. IV, 2, 65. IV, 6, 131.

Hence, = of small value: *the goodness that is c. in beauty makes beauty brief in goodness,* Meas. III, 1, 185. *so stale and c. to vulgar company,* H4A III, 2, 41. *man's life's as c. as beast's,* Lr. II, 4, 270.

Cheap, adv. sold *c. what is most dear,* Sonn. 110, 3. *I hold your dainties c.* Err. III, 1, 21. *h. their manhoods c.* H5 IV, 3, 66 (cf. *Hold*). *buy land now as c. as ...,* H4A II, 4, 394. *would have bought me lights as good c. at the dearest chandler's,* III, 3, 51 (the word being originally a subst., = bargain).

Cheapen, to offer to buy, to chaffer, to bid for: *virtuous, or I'll never c. her,* Ado II, 3, 33. *she would make a puritan of the devil, if he should c. a kiss of her,* Per. IV, 6, 10.

Cheaply, at a low price: *so great a day as this is c. bought,* Mcb. V, 8, 37.

Cheapside, quarter of London: H6B IV, 2, 74. IV, 7, 134.

Cheat, vb., to deceive, to swindle; 1) absol.: *you base, rascally, —ing, lack-linen mate,* H4B II, 4, 133. — 2) transit.: *I hope you do not mean to c. me so,* Err. IV, 3, 79. *how to c. the devil,* LLL IV, 3, 288. With *of,* = to swindle out of sth.: Tp. I, 1, 59. III, 2, 49. John II, 572. R3 I, 1, 19.

Cheat, subst., deceit, swindling: *my revenue is the silly c.* Wint. IV, 3, 28 (= the harmless fraud, not attended by bloodshed). 129.

Cheater, 1) swindler: Sonn. 151, 3. Err. I, 2, 101. H4B II, 4, 152. Tit. V, 1, 111. *a tame c.* (evidently a cant phrase; cf. Fletcher's Fair Maid of the Inn IV, 2, and '*the silly cheat*' in Wint. IV, 3, 28) H4B II, 4, 106, i. e. a man who uses false dice and other tricks, but is harmless else. 2) = escheator, an officer of the exchequer, employed to exact forfeitures: *I will be c. to them both, and they shall be exchequers to me,* Wiv. I, 3, 77. The same quibble is, perhaps, intended in H4B II, 4, 111.

Check, subst., 1) stop, hinderance: *shall a beardless boy ... brave our fields ... and find no c.?* John V, 1, 73. *—s and disasters grow in the veins of actions,* Troil. I, 3, 5. *and posts ... sans c. to good and bad,* 94. 2) rebuke, reproof: *patience bide each c.* Sonn. 58, 7. *against all —s, rebukes and manners,* Wiv. III, 4, 84. As IV, 1, 169. *so devote to Aristotle's —s as Ovid be an outcast,* Shr. I, 1, 32 (i. e. Aristotle's austere morals). *rebellion shall lose his sway, meeting the c. of such another day,* H4A V, 5, 42. H4B IV, 3, 34. Tim. II, 2, 149. Lr. I, 3, 20. Oth. I, 1, 149. III, 3, 67. IV, 3, 20. Ant. IV, 4, 31. Cymb. III, 3, 22.

Check, vb., 1) trans. a) to bridle, to restrain: *had doting Priam —ed his son's desire,* Lucr. 1490. *to c. the tears in Collatinus' eyes,* 1817. *if I can c. my erring love, I will,* Gentl. II, 4, 213. *in this spleen ridiculous appears, to c. their folly, passion's solemn tears,* LLL V, 2, 118. *c. thy contempt,* All's II, 3, 164. *hadst thou ne'er given consent that Phaethon should c. thy fiery steeds,* H6C II, 6, 12. *nor c. my courage for what they can give,* Cor. III, 3, 92. *c. this hideous rashness,* Lr. I, 1, 152. Followed by *from: hardly can I c. my eyes from tears,* H6C I, 4, 151.

b) to stint, to repress: *sap —ed with frost,*

Sonn. 5, 7. *men as plants increase, cheered and —ed even by the self-same sky,* 15, 6. *none so small advantage shall step forth to c. his reign, but they will cherish it,* John III, 4, 152. *great tyranny! goodness dare not c. thee,* Mcb. IV, 3, 33. *I am desperate of my fortunes if they c. me here,* Oth. II, 3, 338.

c) to treat as a bondman: *thy bastard shall be king, that thou mayst be a queen and c. the world,* John II, 123.* *this earth affords no joy to me, but to command, to c., to o'erbear such as are of better person than my self,* H6C III, 2, 166.

d) to rebuke, to chide: *if thy soul c. thee that I come so near,* Sonn. 136, 1. *be —ed for silence, but never taxed for speech,* All's I, 1, 76. *to c. time broke in a disordered string,* R2 V, 5, 46 (Ff *hear*). *I have —ed him for it,* H4B I, 2, 220. *—ed and rated by Northumberland,* III, 1, 68. *next time I'll keep my dreams unto myself, and not be —ed,* H6B I, 2, 54. *he cannot swear, but it* (conscience) *—s him,* R3 I, 4, 140. *then I —ed my friends,* III, 7, 150. *—ed like a bondman,* Caes. IV, 3, 97. *the good king his master will c. him for it,* Lr. II, 2, 149.

2) intr., to start, to be startled: *if he be now returned, as —ing at his voyage, and that he means no more to undertake it,* Hml. IV, 7, 64.* Applied to a hawk stopping at the sight of a game not seen before: *with what wing the staniel —s at it,* Tw. II, 5, 125. *and, like the haggard, c. at every feather,* III, 1, 71. — cf. *Half-checked.*

Checker, to variegate in the manner of a chess-board: *a purple flower sprung up, —ed with white,* Ven. 1168. *the snake... with shining —ed slough,* H6B III, 1, 229. *the green leaves ... make a —ed shadow on the ground,* Tit. II, 3, 15. *—ing the eastern clouds with streaks of light,* Rom. II, 3, 2.

Cheek, the side of the face below the eye: Ven. 45. 185. Lucr. 386. Tp. II, 1, 229. Gentl. IV, 4, 159. Err. I, 2, 46. II, 1, 90. LLL V, 2, 465. Mids. V, 339. As III, 2, 153 etc. etc. *c. by jole* = close: *I'll go with thee, c. by jole,* Mids. III, 2, 338. *— here by the —s I'll drag thee up and down,* H6A I, 3, 51 (= by the beard?). Figuratively: *to save unscratched your city's threatened —s,* John II, 225. *not the morning sun of heaven better becomes the grey —s of the east,* Sonn. 132, 6. *the sea, mounting to the welkin's c.* Tp. I, 2, 4. *tears the cloudy —s of heaven,* R2 III, 3, 57. *to tear with thunder the wide —s o'the air,* Cor. V, 3, 151. *she hangs upon the c. of night like a rich jewel,* Rom. I, 5, 47.

Cheek-roses, blooming cheeks: Meas. I, 4, 16. cf. Gentl. IV, 4, 159. Mids. I, 1, 129.

Cheer, subst., 1) cheerfulness, high spirits: *if they sing, 'tis with so dull a c.,* Sonn. 97, 13. *their c. is the greater that I am subdued,* Ado I, 3, 74. *I have not that alacrity of spirit, nor c. of mind,* R3 V, 3, 74. *ne'er let my heart know merry c.* Tit. II, 3, 188. *receive what c. you may,* Mcb. IV, 3, 239. *you are so sick of late, so far from c.* Hml. III, 2, 174. *my royal lord, you do not give the c.,* Mcb. III, 4, 33 (i. e. the merry disposition which should attend a feast). *to remain here in the c. and comfort of our eye,* Hml. I, 2, 116 (under the genial influence of our eye). *that lived, that loved, that liked, that looked with c.* Mids. V, 299 (Pyramus' speech).

Good c.! = courage! be of good heart! Merch. IV, 1, 111. Caes. III, 1, 89. Ant. IV, 15, 83. *Be of good*

c.: Merch. III, 5, 6. As IV, 3, 164. H5 II, 3, 19. R3 IV, 1, 38 (Qq *have comfort*). H8 V, 1, 143. Ant. V, 2, 21. *have a better c.:* All's III, 2, 67. *What c.?* = how is it with you? Tp. I, 1, 2. Mids. I, 1, 122. Shr. IV, 3, 37. Wint. I, 2, 148. Tim. III, 6, 44. Cymb. III, 4, 41.

2) countenance, aspect, as expressive of disposition: *she securely gives good c. and reverend welcome to her princely guest,* Lucr. 89. *whereat she smiled with so sweet a c.* 264. *all fancy-sick she is and pale of c.* Mids. III, 2, 96. *bid your friends welcome, show a merry c.* Merch. III, 2, 314. *your looks are sad, your c. appalled,* H6A I, 2, 48. *chance of war hath wrought this change of c.* Tit. I, 264.

3) food, entertainment: *I have good c. at home,* Wiv. III, 2, 53. 81. *pray God our c. may answer my good will,* Err. III, 1, 19. *small c.,* 26. *better c.* 29. *here is neither c. nor welcome,* 66. *good c.* V, 392. Ado V, 1, 153. *here is c. enough,* Shr. Ind. 2, 103. *wedding c.* III, 2, 188. *one mess is like to be your c.* IV, 4, 70. *some c. is toward,* V, 1, 14. *our great good c.* V, 2, 10. *make good c.* H4B V, 3, 18. *poor c.* Tit. V, 3, 28. *our wedding c.* Rom. IV, 5, 87. *royal c.* Tim. III, 6, 56. *an anchor's c.* Hml. III, 2, 229.* *better c.* Cymb. III, 6, 67. In R2 I, 2, 70 Q1 *c.,* the other O. Edd. *hear.*

Cheer, vb., 1) trans. a) to make cheerful, to comfort, to encourage: *to c. the ploughman with increaseful crops,* Lucr. 958. Pilgr. 394. Err. III, 2, 26. H4B IV, 2, 9. H6A I, 4, 90. V, 2, 1. H6C I, 4, 77. II, 2, 4. 5. 78. V, 4, 65. R3 I, 3, 5. II, 2, 114. V, 3, 174. Troil. V, 3, 92. Tit. I, 457. IV, 4, 88. Rom. II, 3, 25. Ant. III, 6, 81. Cymb. III, 5, 67. *this push will c. me ever, or disseat me now* (Dyce *chair*; but there is no verb *to chair* in Sh.) Mcb. V, 3, 21. *be —ed,* Ant. V, 2, 184. *c. yon stranger, bid her welcome,* Merch. III, 2, 240. *c. your neighbours,* H8 I, 4, 41 (amuse them by sprightly conversation). — Used of the influence of the sun: *he —s the morn,* Ven. 484. *—ed and checked even by the self-same sky,* Sonn. 15, 6. *all the world is —ed by the sun,* R3 I, 2, 129. *ere the sun advance his burning eye, the day to c.* Rom. II, 3, 6. *To c. up,* in the same sense: *—ing up her senses,* Ven. 896. *his drumming heart —s up his burning eye,* Lucr. 435. *—ed up the heavy time,* John IV, 1, 47. H5 IV, 6, 20. H6A I, 5, 16. H6C I, 1, 6. II, 1, 133. II, 2, 56. R3 V, 3, 71. Mcb. IV, 1, 127. Used reflectively: *c. thyself a little,* As II, 6, 5. *c. up yourself,* H4B IV, 4, 113.

b) to encourage, to incite: *and here's the heart that —s these hands to execute the like upon thyself,* H6C II, 4, 9. *and all the madness is, he —s them up too,* Tim. I, 2, 43. III, 5, 114.

c) to salute with sounds of joy: *a cry more tuneable was never holla'd to, nor —ed with horn,* Mids. IV, 1, 130.

2) intr. to be in a state or disposition, to fare: *how —est thou, Jessica?* Merch. III, 5, 75 (Qq *farest*).

Cheerer, giver of joy: *her vine, the merry c. of the heart,* H5 V, 2, 41.

Cheerful, 1) in good spirits, full of joyful animation: Tp. IV, 147. V, 250. Wiv. V, 5, 179. As I, 3, 96. John IV, 2, 2. R2 II, 2, 4. H4A II, 4, 465. H5 IV Chor. 40. H6B I, 1, 36. R3 III, 7, 39 (Qq *loving*). V, 3, 121. Rom. V, 1, 5. Ant. III, 2, 44. Cymb. IV, 2, 402. Per. IV, 1, 40 (mostly in the phrase '*be cheerful*').

2) gladdening, animating, genial: *this had been c. after victory,* H4B IV, 2, 88. *O c. colours! see where Oxford comes,* H6C V, 1, 58. *the snake lies rolled in the c. sun,* Tit. II, 3, 13.

Cheerfully, 1) with good spirits, gladly: Shr. IV, 3, 38. H5 IV, 1, 204. H6A IV, 1, 167. R3 I, 3, 34. III, 4, 50. V, 3, 269. Hml. III, 2, 133. IV, 5, 109.

2) in a comforting and encouraging manner: *thou speakest c.* H5 IV, 1, 34.

Cheerless, comfortless: *all's c., dark and deadly,* Lr. V, 3, 290.

Cheerly, adv., cheerfully, briskly, gladly: *thou lookest c.* As II, 6, 14. *lusty, young, and c. drawing breath,* R2 I, 3, 66. *c. to sea,* H5 II, 2, 192. *but c. seek how to redress their harms,* H6C V, 4, 2. *in God's name, c. on,* R3 V, 2, 14. *look c.* Tim. II, 2, 223. *Cheerly!* Tp. I, 1, 6. 29. As II, 6, 19. H4A V, 4, 44. Rom. I, 5, 16. 90.

Cheese, the curd of milk, coagulated and pressed: Wiv. I, 1, 130 *(Banbury c.).* I, 2, 13. II, 1, 140. II, 2, 318. V, 5, 86. All's I, 1, 154. H4A III, 1, 162. Troil. II, 3, 44. V, 4, 12 *(that stale old mouse-eaten dry c., Nestor).* *toast c.* H5 II, 1, 9. *toasted c.:* Wiv. V, 5, 147. H6B IV, 7, 14. Lr. IV, 6, 90.

Cheese-paring, the pared rind of cheese: H4B III, 2, 332.

Chequer, see *Checker.*

Chequin, zechin, an Italian gold coin: Per. IV, 2, 28.

Cherish, 1) to hold dear, to embrace with affection, to harbour in the heart: *which bounteous gift thou shouldst in bounty c.* Sonn. 11, 12. *there's no virtue whipped out of the court; they c. it to make it stay there,* Wint. IV, 3, 97. *thy voluntary oath lives in this bosom, dearly —ed,* John III, 3, 24. *thou hast a better place in his affection than all thy brothers; c. it, my boy,* H4B IV, 4, 23. *hath taught us how to c. such high deeds even in the bosom of our adversaries,* H4A V, 5, 30. *whom thou wert sworn to c. and defend,* R3 I, 4, 213. *doth c. you and yours,* II, 1, 34.

Hence, to treat with tenderness, to give warmth, ease, or comfort to: *as Priam him did c., so did I Tarquin,* Lucr. 1546. *should have been —ed by her child-like duty,* Gentl. III, 1, 75. *he that —es my flesh and blood loves my flesh and blood,* All's I, 3, 51. *look to thy servants, c. thy guests,* H4A III, 3, 194. *the fox, who, ne'er so tame, so —ed and locked up,* V, 2, 10. *the better —ed, still the nearer death,* 15. *(the snake) —ed in your breasts,* H6B III, 1, 344. *must gently be preserved, —ed and kept,* R3 II, 2, 119. *c. those hearts that hate thee,* H8 III, 2, 444. *I should kill thee with much —ing,* Rom. II, 2, 184. *better might we have loved without this mean, if this be not —ed,* Ant. III, 2, 33.

2) to treat in a manner to encourage growth, to foster, to nurse up: *to dry the old oak's sap and c. springs,* Lucr. 950. *what doth c. weeds but gentle air?* H6C II, 6, 21. *if thou dost love fair Hero, c. it,* Ado I, 1, 310. *killing that love which thou hast vowed to c.* Rom. III, 3, 129.

Hence = to promote, to support: *how you the purpose c. whiles thus you mock it,* Tp. II, 1, 224. *though you and all the rest so grossly led this juggling witchcraft with revenue c.* John III, 1, 169. *none so small advantage shall step forth to check his reign, but*

they will c. it, III, 4, 152. *you that do abet him in this kind, c. rebellion and are rebels all,* R2 II, 3, 147. *swaying more upon our part than —ing the exhibiters against us,* H5 I, 1, 74. *and as we may, c. Duke Humphrey's deeds,* H6B I, 1, 203. *c. factions,* Tim. III, 5, 73.

3) to comfort, to encourage: *I leave to be, if I be not by her fair influence fostered, illumined, —ed, kept alive,* Gentl. III, 1, 184. *repair me with thy presence, Silvia; thou gentle nymph, c. thy forlorn swain,* V, 4, 12. *our crimes would despair, if they were not —ed by our virtues,* All's IV, 3, 86.

Cherisher, one who treats with tenderness: *he that comforts my wife is the c. of my flesh and blood,* All's I, 3, 50.

Cherry, the fruit of Prunus Cerasus: Ven. 1103. Mids. III, 2, 209. John II, 162. Per. V Prol. 8. *as like you as c. is to c.* H8 V, 1, 171. *thy lips, those kissing —ies,* Mids. III, 2, 140. *c. lips,* V, 192. R3 I, 1, 94. *c. nose,* Mids. V, 338.

Cherry-pit: *'tis not for gravity to play at c. with Satan,* Tw. III, 4, 129 (a game consisting in pitching cherry-stones into a small hole).

Cherry-stone, used to denote a trifle: *a rush, a hair, a drop of blood, a pin, a nut, a c.* Err. IV, 3, 74.

Chertsey, name of a monastery within some miles of London: R3 I, 2, 29. 215. 226.*

Cherub, a celestial spirit, next in order to the seraphim: *So (sc. good) is it, if thou knewest our purposes. I see a c. that sees them,* Hml. IV, 3, 50.

Cherubin, the same: *such —s,* Sonn. 114, 6. *like a c.* Compl. 319. Tp. I, 2, 152. Merch. V, 62. H8 I, 1, 23. Troil. III, 2, 74. Tim. IV, 3, 63. Mcb. I, 7, 22. Oth. IV, 2, 63. Cymb. II, 4, 88.

Chesnut, 1) fruit of the Castanea Vesca: Shr. I, 2, 210. Mcb. I, 3, 4.

2) the brown colour of it: *your c. was ever the only colour,* As III, 4, 12.

Chest, 1) a box of wood or other materials: Sonn. 48, 9 (quibble). 52, 9. 65, 10 *(Time's c. =* the coffin, the grave). Wiv. IV, 2, 62. Merch. I, 2, 33. II, 9, 23. Shr. II, 353. John V, 2, 141. R2 I, 1, 180. H6B IV, 7, 105. Cor. II, 1, 144. Tit. II, 3, 9. Ant. IV, 5, 10. Per. III, 1, 71. III, 2, 50.

2) the thorax: *the large Achilles ... from his deep c. laughs out a loud applause,* Troil. I, 3, 163. *come, stretch thy c.* IV, 5, 10. Hence = breast: *where it may find some purer c. to close so pure a mind,* Lucr. 761.

Chester, English town: H4B I, 1, 39.

Chetas, one of the gates of Troy: Troil. Prol. 16.

Chevalier, knight: John II, 287. H6A IV, 3, 14.

Cheveril (Fr. *cuir de chevreuil*) roebuck-leather; symbol of flexibility: *a sentence is but a c. glove to a good wit: how quickly the wrong side may be turned outward!* Tw. III, 1, 13. *which gifts ... the capacity of your soft c. conscience would receive, if you might please to stretch it,* H8 II, 3, 32. *here's a wit of c., that stretches from an inch narrow to an ell broad,* Rom. II, 4, 87.

Chew, to grind with the teeth: *the veriest varlet that ever —ed with a tooth,* H4A II, 2, 26. *foul with —ed grass,* H5 IV, 2, 50. Figuratively: *heaven in my mouth, as if I did but only c. his name,* Meas. II, 4, 5. *—ing the food of sweet and bitter fancy,* As

IV, 3, 102. *capital crimes, —ed, swallowed and digested,* H5 II, 2, 56.

Hence = t o r u m i n a t e, to p o n d e r: *c. upon this,* Caes. I, 2, 171.

Chewet or **Chuet**, a k i n d o f pie, made of minced meat: *peace, c., peace!* H4A V, 1, 29. Some take it here in the sense of c h o u g h, Fr. *chouette,* without, however, assigning an authority for this use.

Chick, the y o u n g of fowls; a word of tenderness: *my Ariel, c., that is thy charge,* Tp. V, 316. cf. *March-chick.*

Chicken, the y o u n g o f f o w l s: H6B III, 1, 249. 251. Troil. I, 2, 147. Tim. II, 2, 72. Mcb. IV, 3, 218. Cymb. V, 3, 42.

Chide (impf. *chid:* Lucr. 1528. Gentl. I, 2, 52. 60. II, 1, 78 etc. partic. *chid:* Err. IV, 1, 50. Mids. III, 2, 200. 312. H4A II, 4, 410. H6B III, 1, 175. H6C II, 5, 17. Tim. I, 1, 176. Oth. IV, 2, 113. Ant. I, 4, 30. *chidden:* Gentl. II, 1, 12; and always so, when preceding a substantive: Troil. II, 2, 45. Caes. I, 2, 184. Oth. II, 1, 12).

1) trans. to r e b u k e, to s c o l d at: *thus —s she Death,* Ven. 932. *but c. rough winter that the flower hath killed,* Lucr. 1255. 1528. Sonn. 8, 7. 41, 10. 57, 5. 99, 1. 145, 6. Tp. I, 2, 476. Gentl. I, 2, 52. II, 1, 12. 89. Err. IV, 1, 50. Mids. III, 2, 200. 218. As II, 7, 64. III, 2, 297. IV, 1, 36. IV, 3, 54. Shr. I, 1, 164. Tw. III, 3, 3. Wint. V, 3, 24. R2 III, 2, 188. H4A II, 4, 410. V, 2, 63. H5 I, 2, 308. IV Chor. 20. H6B III, 1, 175. H6C III, 2, 138. V, 4, 24. R3 II, 2, 35. Troil. I, 2, 6. II, 2, 45. II, 3, 221. III, 2, 114. V, 3, 39. Cor. III, 2, 132. Rom. II, 3, 81. II, 6, 2. Tim. I, 1, 176. Caes. I, 2, 184. II, 1, 177. Mcb. III, 1, 57. Hml. III, 4, 107. Lr. I, 3, 1. II, 4, 228. Oth. IV, 2, 113. Ant. I, 4, 30. *intend to c. myself,* Gentl. IV, 2, 103. *I chid Lucetta hence,* I, 2, 60. *he hath chid me hence,* Mids. III, 2, 312. All's III, 7, 42. John IV, 1, 87. H6C II, 5, 17. *c. him hither,* H4B IV, 5, 63. Singular expression: *a thing like death to c. away this shame,* Rom. IV, 1, 74. Coming near the sense of t o c u r s e: *he runs and —s his vanished, loathed delight,* Lucr. 742. *—s the dice in honourable terms,* LLL V, 2, 326. *the one* (his unkindness) *he —s to hell,* Wint. IV, 4, 564.

Figuratively, = to be n o i s y a b o u t: *the sea that —s the banks of England,* H4A III, 1, 45. *the chidden billow seems to pelt the clouds,* Oth. II, 1, 12 (Qq *chiding*). = to resound, to p r o c l a i m a l o u d: *caves and womby vaultages of France shall c. your trespass and return your mock in second accent of his ordinance,* H5 II, 4, 125.

2) intr. to s c o l d, to q u a r r e l; a) absol.: *he 'gins to c., but soon she stops his lips,* Ven. 46. Lucr. 484. Gentl. III, 1, 98. Wiv. V, 3, 11. Mids. II, 1, 145. III, 2, 45. As III, 5, 64. 65. IV, 3, 64. Shr. I, 2, 95. 227. Wint. V, 3, 26. H6B I, 2, 41. III, 1, 182. Caes. IV, 3, 123. Oth. II, 1, 108. III, 3, 301. IV, 2, 114. Ant. I, 1, 49. IV, 1, 1.

b) Followed by *at: when you chid at Sir Proteus for going ungartered,* Gentl. II, 1, 78. Ado IV, 1, 130. LLL IV, 3, 132. As III, 5, 129. Wint. IV, 4, 6. Rom. III, 2, 95.

c) Followed by *with: for my sake do you with Fortune c.* Sonn. 111, 1. Oth. IV, 2, 167. Cymb. V, 4, 32.

Figuratively, = to resound, to be n o i s y:

never did I hear such gallant —ing, Mids. IV, 1, 120. *churlish —ing of the winter's wind,* As II, 1, 7. *as doth a rock against the —ing flood,* H8 III, 2, 197. *and with an accent tuned in self-same key retorts to —ing fortune* (i. e. to the tempest), Troil. I, 3, 54. *thou hast as —ing a nativity as fire, air, water, earth, and heaven can make,* Per. III, 1, 32.

Chider, one who clamors and quarrels: Shr. I, 2, 228.

Chief, adj. 1) p r i n c i p a l: *the field's c. flower,* Ven. 8. *thy c. desire,* Sonn. 10, 8. Gentl. III, 1, 340. LLL IV, 1, 51. Mids. I, 2, 30. Merch. I, 1, 127. H4A III, 2, 109. H6A I, 4, 6. III, 1, 130. IV, 1, 146. H8 V, 3, 3. 118. Cor. I, 1, 8. Tit. V, 3, 122. Tim. IV, 2, 44. Mcb. II, 2, 40. III, 1, 11. Hml. I, 1, 106. IV, 4, 34. Ant. II, 6, 10. IV, 12, 27. Per. IV, 3, 5. *my lord c. justice,* H4B V, 2, 1. V, 3, 144. V, '5, 48. Used in the predicate: *every present sorrow seemeth c.* Ven. 970. *stands c. in power,* All's II, 1, 115. *I was the c. that raised him to the crown, and I'll be c. to bring him down again,* H6C III, 3, 262. *my friends, of whom he's c.* Cor. V, 2, 18. *that she hath thee, is of my wailing c.* Sonn. 42, 3. Corrupted passage: *are of a most select and generous c. in that,* Hml. I, 3, 74 (Ff. *cheff*). — *both for myself and them, but, c. of all, your safety,* John IV, 2, 49. Superl. *chiefest: employ your —est thoughts to courtship,* Merch. II, 8, 43. John II, 39. H6A I, 1, 177. II, 2, 12. H6B III, 2, 324. H6C IV, 3, 11. IV, 5, 3. R3 V, 3, 300. Troil. I, 2, 292. Cor. II, 2, 88. V, 6, 150. Tit. V, 2, 125. Mcb. III, 5, 33. Hml. I, 2, 117. Per. Prol. 18.

In chief = principally: *but in c. for that her reputation was disvalued,* Meas. V, 220. *unto your grace do I in c. address the substance of my speech,* H4B IV, 1, 31.

2) e x c e l l e n t, m o s t i m p o r t a n t: *the c. perfections of that lovely dame,* H6A V, 5, 12. *but, with the first of all your c. affairs, let me entreat,* H6C IV, 6, 58.

3) m a i n, g r e a t e s t p a r t of: *all France with their c. assembled strength,* H6A I, 1, 139. *that his c. followers lodge in towns about him,* H6C IV, 3, 13.

Chief, subst., c o m m a n d e r, c a p t a i n: *farewell, great c.* Ant. IV, 14, 93.

Chief-justice, see *Chief.*

Chiefly, p r i n c i p a l l y: Ven. 568. Pilgr. 113. 324. Tp. III, 1, 35. V, 14. Gentl. IV, 4, 72. Ado III, 3, 168. All's II, 1, 108. H4A II, 4, 445. H6C IV, 6, 17. Rom. V, 3, 30. Tim. I, 2, 95. Hml. II, 2, 467. Ant. II, 2, 33. Cymb. I, 5, 72.

Child (Plur. *children;* trisyll. in Err. V, 360 and Tit. II, 3, 115. Perhaps also Mcb. IV, 3, 177), 1) i n f a n t: Lucr. 431. Gentl. III, 1, 124. Wiv. II, 2, 133. IV, 4, 64. Err. I, 1, 84. Ado III, 2, 7. Hml. II, 2, 404 etc. etc. Term of reproach: *come, recreant; come, thou c., I'll whip thee with a rod,* Mids. III, 2, 409. Used of a female child, in opposition to a male: *a boy or a c.* Wint. III, 3, 71. *With c.* = pregnant: Tp. I, 2, 269. Meas. I, 2, 160. II, 3, 12. LLL IV, 3, 90. John III, 1, 89. H6A V, 4, 62. Per. III Prol. 40. *great with c.* Meas. II, 1, 91. *with c. by* a p.: Meas. I, 2, 92. I, 4, 45. Merch. III, 5, 42. H4B Ind. 14. *with c. of:* R3 III, 5, 86. *To get a woman with c.:* Meas. I, 2, 74. I, 4, 29. IV, 3, 180. All's IV, 3, 213. V, 3, 302. Wint. III, 3, 62. *To go with c.:* H4B V, 4, 10. R3 III, 5, 86.

2) male or female descendant in the first degree: Tp. I, 1, 65. I, 2, 348. III, 3, 72. V, 198. Gentl. III, 1, 70. Wiv. III, 4, 76. 100. Meas. I, 3, 25. Merch. III, 5, 2 etc. etc. *now you speak like a good c. and a true gentleman,* Hml. IV, 5, 148. *your children's children,* R3 V, 3, 262. *lest child, child's children, cry against you woe,* R2 IV, 148. *left you wife and child,* Mcb. IV, 3, 26. Figuratively: *if my dear love were but the c. of state,* Sonn. 124, 1. *this c. of fancy* (sc. Armado) LLL I, 1, 171. *this same c. of honour and renown,* H4A III, 2, 139. *the great c. of honour, Cardinal Wolsey,* H8 IV, 2, 6. *this noble passion, c. of integrity,* Mcb. IV, 3, 115. *be a c. o'the time,* Ant. II, 7, 106 (= accommodate yourself to circumstances).

3) a young knight: *C. Rowland to the dark tower came,* Lr. III, 4, 187 (scrap of an old song).

Child-bed, the state of a woman in labour: Wint. III, 2, 104. Per. III, 1, 57. V, 3, 5.

Child-changed, changed to a child: *the untuned and jarring senses, O, wind up of this c. father,* Lr. IV, 7, 17 (a father whom I now have to nurse as if he were my child).*

Childed, having children: *he c. as I fathered,* Lr. III, 6, 117.

Childeric, Merovingian king, deposed by Pepin, H5 I, 2, 65 (it should be *Chilperic*).

Childhood, 1) the time in which men are children: Mids. IV, 1, 173. Rom. III, 3, 95 (*the c. of our joy*). Mcb. II, 2, 54 ('*tis the eye of c. that fears a painted devil*). *in their —s,* Wint. I, 1, 25. *c. innocence,* Mids. III, 2, 202. *c. proof,* Merch. I, 1, 144.

2) the relation to parents: *thou better knowest the offices of nature, bond of c.,* Lr. II, 4, 181.

Childing, bringing forth children, fruitful: *the spring, the summer, the c. autumn, angry winter, change their wonted liveries,* Mids. II, 1, 112.

Childish, pertaining to, or becoming a child; always in a bad sense: Ven. 898. Lucr. 274. 1825. As II, 7, 162. Wint. IV, 4, 413. H6B I, 1, 245. H6C V, 4, 38. R3 I, 2, 155. H8 V, 3, 25. Cor. II, 3, 183. Rom. I, 1, 217.

Childish-foolish, foolish like a child: R3 I, 3, 142.

Childishness, qualities of a child: *perhaps thy c. will move him more than can our reasons,* Cor. V, 3, 157. In a bad sense: As II, 7, 165. Ant. I, 3, 58.

Child-killer, murderer of a child: H6C II, 2, 112.

Childlike, becoming a child: *cherished by her c. duty,* Gentl. III, 1, 75. *a c. office,* Lr. II, 1, 108.

Childness, humour of a child: *and with his varying c. cures in me thoughts that would thick my blood,* Wint. I, 2, 170.

Chill = I will (Somersetshire dialect): Lr. IV, 6, 239. 247.

Chill, adj., cold, stiff and shivering with cold: *cold modesty, hot wrath, both fire from hence and c. extincture hath,* Compl. 294. *the many will be too c. and tender,* All's IV, 5, 56. *my veins are c.* Per. II, 1, 77.

Chilling, the same: *a c. sweat o'erruns my trembling joints,* Tit. II, 3, 212.

Chime, harmony of sounds: *hell only danceth at so harsh a c.* Per. I, 1, 85. Especially of a set of bells: *we have heard the —s at midnight,* H4B III, 2,

228. *when he speaks, 'tis like a c. a-mending,* Troil. I, 3, 159.

Chimney, 1) the structure of brick which conveys the smoke: Wiv. IV, 2, 57. As IV, 1, 166. H4A II, 1, 3. H6B IV, 2, 156. H6C V, 6, 47. Mcb. II, 3, 60.

2) the fireplace: Wiv. V, 5, 47. H4A II, 1, 22. Cymb. II, 4, 80.

Chimney-piece, ornamental part of a fireplace: *and the c. chaste Dian bathing,* Cymb. II, 4, 81.

Chimney-sweeper, one whose trade is to clean chimneys: LLL IV, 3, 266. Cymb. IV, 2, 263.

Chimney-top, the small turret above the roof in which the chimney ends: Caes. I, 1, 44 (in H6C V, 6, 47 *chimney's top*).

Chin, the part of the face below the mouth: Ven. 59. 85 (*upon this promise did he raise his c.*). Lucr. 420. 472. Compl. 92. Tp. II, 1, 249. IV, 183. Err. III, 2, 131. Mids. II, 1, 109 (some M. Edd. *thin*). Merch. II, 2, 100. III, 2, 84. As I, 2, 76. III, 2, 217. 223. Tw. I, 5, 267. III, 1, 54. Wint. II, 3, 101. H4A I, 3, 34. H4B I, 2, 23. 207. 271. H5 III Chor. 22. III, 4, 37. Troil. I, 2, 150 etc. Cor. II, 2, 95. Lr. III, 7, 38. 76.

China, porcelaine: *they are not C. dishes, but very good dishes,* Meas. II, 1, 97.

Chine, 1) the spine: *and like to mose in the c.* Shr. III, 2, 51.

2) a piece of the spine, cut for cooking: *or cut out the burly-boned clown in —s of beef,* H6B IV, 10, 61. *let me ne'er hope to see a c. again,* H8 V, 4, 26.

Chink, subst., 1) fissure: *talk trough the c. of a wall,* Mids III, 1, 66. V, 134. 159. 178. 194.

2) Plur. *chinks*, in popular language, = clinking money: *he that can lay hold of her shall have the —s,* Rom. I, 5, 119.

Chioppine, see *Chopine*.

Chip, subst., small piece of wood; used of the keys of the piano: *those dancing —s, o'er whom thy fingers walk with gentle gait,* Sonn. 128, 10.

Chip, vb., to cut into small pieces: *a' would ha' —ed bread well,* H4B II, 4, 258 (cf. *bread-chipper,* 342). *that noseless, handless, hacked and —ed, come to him,* Troil. V, 5, 34.

Chiron, name in Tit. II, 1, 26 etc.

Chirp, to utter the sounds of small birds: *thinks he that the —ing of a wren, by crying comfort from a hollow breast, can chase away the first-conceived sound?* H6B III, 2, 42.

Chirrah, says Armado for *sirrah:* LLL V, 1, 35.

Chirurgeonly, in the manner of a surgeon: Tp. II, 1, 140.

Chisel, instrument with which stone is pared away: *what fine c. could ever yet cut breath,* Wint. V, 3, 78.

Chitopher, name in All's IV, 3, 187.

Chivalrous, becoming a knight: *c. design of knightly trial,* R2 I, 1, 81.

Chivalry, 1) knighthood, deeds and qualities of a knight: *glorious by his manly c.* Lucr. 109. *we shall see justice design the victor's c.* R2 I, 1, 203. *Christian service and true c.* II, 1, 54. *a truant to c.* H4A V, 1, 94. *we kept together in our c.* H5 IV, 6, 19. *the son of c.* H6A IV, 6, 29. *the flower of Europe for* *his c.* H6C II, 1, 71. *the prince of c.* Troil. I, 2, 249. *his fair worth and single c.* IV, 4, 150. *i' the vein of c.* V, 3, 32. *his device, a wreath of c.* Per. II, 2, 29.

2) the body or order of knights: *by his light did all the c. of England move,* H4B II, 3, 20. *when all her c. hath been in France,* H5 I, 2, 157.

Choice, 1) the act of choosing, election: *but then woos best when most his c. is froward,* Ven. 570. *with a leavened and prepared c.* Meas. I, 1, 52. Mids. I, 1, 69. 139. 141. 239. IV, 1, 141. Merch. II, 1, 13. II, 9, 15. 49. Shr. I, 1, 138 *(there's small c. in rotten apples).* III, 1, 17. All's I, 3, 151. II, 3, 84. V, 3, 45. Wint. IV, 4, 319. 426. H6A V, 3, 125. Troil. I, 3, 348. Cor. II, 3, 105. Tit. I, 17. 318. 321. Rom. I, 2, 18. Hml. I, 3, 20. 22. III, 2, 68. Oth. I, 3, 358. II, 1, 238. Per. II, 5, 18. *Of a person's c.* = chosen by a p.: *you have here, lady, and of your c., these reverend fathers,* H8 II, 4, 58. *five tribunes, of their own c.* Cor. I, 1, 220. *At your c.* = as you please: Cor. I, 9, 36. III, 2, 123. Lr. II, 4, 220. *To make c.* = to choose, to select: *now make your c.* Merch. II, 7, 3. III, 2, 43. H8 I, 4, 86. *make the c. of thy own time,* All's II, 1, 206. *make c.* II, 3, 78. *make c. of either's moiety,* Lr. I, 1, 7. *rather makes c. of loss,* Ant. III, 1, 23. *make c. of which your highness will see first,* Mids. V, 43. *make c. of whom your wisest friends you will,* Hml. IV, 5, 204. *made a worthy c.* H6C IV, 1, 3. *made a simple c.* Rom. II, 5, 38. *to make some meaner c.* Tit. II, 1, 73. *To take c.* = to choose at pleasure: *had I a sister were a grace, or a daughter a goddess, he should take his c.* Troil. I, 2, 258. *take your c. of those that best can aid your action,* Cor. I, 6, 65. *come, and take c. of all my library,* Tit. IV, 1, 34.

2) power of choosing, judgment: *sense to ecstasy was ne'er so thralled but it reserved some quantity of c., to serve in such a difference,* Hml. III, 4, 75.

3) the person or thing chosen: *this is my father's c.* Wiv. III, 4, 31. *your c. is not so rich in worth as beauty,* Wint. V, 1, 214. H4B I, 3, 87. H6A V, 1, 26. H6C IV, 1, 9. Tit. IV, 2, 78.

4) sufficient number to choose among: *ability in means and c. of friends,* Ado IV, 1, 201.

5) the best part, select assemblage: *a braver c. of dauntless spirits,* John II, 72. *so full-replete with c. of all delights,* H6A V, 5, 17. *this ring he holds in most rich c.* All's III, 7, 26 (= holds it in highest estimation). *men of c.* H4B I, 3, 11. Lr, I, 4, 285.

Choice, adj., 1) chosen, appointed: *wishing me to permit my chaplain a c. hour to hear from him a matter of some moment,* H8 I, 2, 162.

2) select, excellent: *a most singular and c. epithet,* LLL V, 1, 17. *the c. love of Gremio,* Shr. I, 2, 236. *ye c. spirits,* H6A V, 3, 3. *the c. and master spirits of this age,* Caes. III, 1, 163. *in c. Italian,* Hml. III, 2, 274. *most c., forsaken,* Lr. I, 1, 254. — Superl. *choicest: the —st music of the kingdom,* H8 IV, 1, 91.

Choice-drawn, selected with care: *these culled and c. cavaliers,* H5 III Prol. 24.

Choicely, not indiscriminately, but with nice regard to preference: *a band of men, collected c., from each county some,* H6B III, 1, 313.

Choir, 1) a band of singers in divine service: *her heavy anthem still concludes in woe, and still the c. of echoes answer so,* Ven. 840 (cf. 834). *the c. sung the 'Te Deum',* H8 IV, 1, 90.

2) the part of the church where the choristers are placed: *upon those boughs which shake against the cold, bare ruined —s, where late the sweet birds sang,* Sonn. 73, 4.

3) the part of a church eastward of the nave, separated from it, usually, by a screen of open work: *having brought the queen to a prepared place in the c.* H8 IV, 1, 64.

Choke, to suffocate: *impatience —s her pleading tongue,* Ven. 217. *—d with a piece of toasted cheese,* Wiv. V, 5, 147. R2 II, 1, 37. H6A II, 5, 123. III, 2, 46. V, 4, 120. Troil. I, 3, 126. Tit. V, 3, 175. Tim. I, 2, 38. Caes. I, 2, 249. Ant. I, 5, 68. *as corn o'ergrown by weeds, so heedful fear is almost —d by unresisted lust,* Lucr. 282. *they 'll o'ergrow the garden and c. the herbs,* H6B III, 1, 33. cf. R2 III, 4, 44. *leaving their earthly parts to c. your clime,* H5 IV, 3, 102 (= to poison the air). *fearful scouring doth c. the air with dust,* Tim. V, 2, 16.

Hence = to oppress, to make away with, to kill: *else imputation might reproach your life and c. your good to come,* Meas. V, 427. *that's the way to c. a gibing spirit,* LLL V, 2, 868. Ado II, 3, 264. Shr. II, 378. John IV, 2, 58. H4B I, 1, 184. H6A II, 4, 112. H6B III, 1, 143. H8 I, 2, 4. Cor. IV, 7, 49. Rom. I, 1, 200. Caes. III, 1, 269. Mcb. I, 2, 9. Oth. V, 2, 55. Cymb. III, 5, 77. — Reflectively: *when to my good lord I prove untrue, I'll c. myself,* Cymb. I, 5, 87.

To c. up, in the same sense: *where none will sweat but for promotion, and having that, do c. their service up even with the having,* As II, 3, 61. *our garden is full of weeds, her fairest flowers —d up,* R2 III, 4, 44.

Choler, 1) anger: Wiv. II, 3, 89. III, 1, 11. LLL II, 206. Shr. IV, 1, 175. H4A I, 3, 129. H4B II, 4, 176. H5 IV, 7, 38. 188. H6A IV, 1, 168. V, 4, 120. H6B I, 3, 155. V, 1, 23. H8 I, 1, 130. II, 1, 34. Cor. II, 3, 206. III, 1, 83. III, 3, 25. Rom. I, 5, 91. Tim. IV, 3, 372. Caes. IV, 3, 39. Lr. I, 2, 23. Oth. II, 1, 279. — Quibbling with *collar:* H4A II, 4, 356. Rom. I, 1, 4.

2) bile: *let's purge this c. without letting blood,* R2 I, 1, 153. Hml. III, 2, 315 (a quibble in both passages). cf. 319.

Choleric, 1) irascible: Err. II, 2, 63. Shr. IV, 1, 177. Lr. I, 1, 302.

2) angry: *a c. word,* Meas. II, 2, 130. *before you were so c.* Err. II, 2, 68. Caes. IV, 3, 43. Per. IV, 6, 177. Followed by *with: are you so c. with Eleanor,* H6B I, 2, 51.

3) making irascible: *too c. a meat,* Shr. IV, 3, 19. 22 (cf. Err. II, 2, 63. Shr. IV, 1, 175. 177).

Cholic, a pain in the bowels: *the teeming earth is with a kind of c. pinched,* H4A III, 1, 29. *pinched with the c.* Cor. II, 1, 83. Singular expression: *blow, villain, till thy sphered bias cheek outswell the c. of puffed Aquilon,* Troil. IV, 5, 9 (partly explained by H4A III, 1, 29—31; cf. Ven. 1046).

Choose (impf. *chose:* Sonn. 95, 10. Tp. V, 190. Gentl. III, 1, 17 etc. partic. *chosen:* Meas. II, 1, 283. Ado III, 3, 6. Merch. I, 2, 35. As IV, 1, 198 etc. *chose:* Pilgr. 299. LLL I, 1, 170. Cor. II, 3, 163. 222. Caes. II, 1, 314. Oth. I, 1, 17, —and, used adjectively, LLL V, 1, 98).

1) to make choice, to elect; a) absol.: *press never thou to c. anew,* Pilgr. 332. *if we c. by the horns,* LLL IV, 1, 116. Merch. I, 2, 99. II, 1, 16. II, 7, 35. III, 2, 132. H6A V, 5, 50. H6C IV, 1, 61.

b) trans. **to make choice of, to select:** —*ing so strong a prop to support so weak a burden,* Ven. Dedic. 2. *when as thine eye hath chose the dame,* Pilgr. 299. Tp. V, 190. Meas. II, 1, 283. Err. IV, 3, 96. Ado V, 1, 136. 281. Mids. I, 1, 140. Merch. I, 2, 34. 35. 99. II, 7, 5. II, 9, 11. As IV, 1, 198. Shr. II, 305. Wint. V, 1, 65. R2 II, 1, 29. H6B I, 4, 59. H6C III, 3, 115. IV, 6, 31. H8 II, 2, 2. Troil. II, 2, 67. Cor. II, 3, 163. 222. III, 1, 169. Tit. I, 23. 190. Hml. IV, 5, 106. Oth. I, 1, 17. III, 3, 189. Ant. I, 2, 62. III, 4, 37. Cymb. I, 1, 139. I, 4, 136 etc. *rather what he cannot change than what he* —*s,* Ant. I, 4, 15 (= what he likes, pleases).

Chosen = select, choice: *a guard of chosen shot,* H6A I, 4, 53. *chosen soldiers,* H6C III, 3, 204. *to rank our chosen truth with such a show,* H8 Prol. 18. *this chosen infant,* H8 V, 5, 49. *other chosen attractions,* Per. V, 1, 46. *Chose,* in the same sense: *the word is well culled, chose,* LLL V, 1, 98 (Holofernes' speech). — *Chosen* = destined by Providence: *chosen from above, to work exceeding miracles,* H6A V, 4, 39. — Quite adjectively: *she's the chosen of Signior Hortensio,* Shr. I, 2, 237 (elected bride).

To c. a p. sth.: *to c. me a husband,* Merch. I, 2, 23. *c. himself a wife,* Wint. IV, 4, 418.

Followed by a double accus.: *Langton, chosen archbishop of Canterbury,* John III, 1, 143. *would c. him pope,* H6B I, 3, 65. *Thomas More is chosen Lord chancellor,* H8 III, 2, 393.

Followed by *for: being chosen for the prince's watch,* Ado III, 3, 6. *I chose Camillo for the minister,* Wint. III, 2, 160. *I c. Clarence for protector,* H6C IV, 6, 37. *c. Caesar for their king,* Caes. I, 2, 80.

Followed by *as: whom right and wrong have chose as umpire,* LLL I, 1, 170.

To c. out: which for their habitation chose out thee, Sonn. 95, 10. *c. out some secret place,* R2 V, 6, 25. *what a time have you chose out,* Caes. II, 1, 314. — *To c. forth: which out of a great deal of old iron I chose forth,* H6A I, 2, 101.

I rather c. = I like better: *I rather chose to cross my friend ... than heap on your head ...,* Gentl. III, 1, 17. *why I rather c. to have a weight of carrion flesh than to receive ...,* Merch. IV, 1, 40. *I rather c. to wrong the dead ... than I will wrong such honourable men,* Caes. III, 2, 130.

I cannot c. (with or without *but*) = I must necessarily: *she cannot c. but love,* Ven. 79. *that cannot c. but amaze him,* Wiv. V, 3, 18. *thou canst not c. but know,* Tw. II, 5, 188. *she cannot c. but be old,* H4B III, 2, 221. *Aufidius will appear well in these wars* (i. e. play a brave part): *.. he cannot c.* Cor. IV, 3, 39. cf. Sonn. 64, 13. Tp. I, 2, 186. II, 2, 24. Gentl. IV, 4, 82. Merch. III, 1, 120. Shr. Ind. I, 42. All's I, 1, 158. I, 3, 220. Wint. I, 1, 26. H4A I, 3, 279. III, 1, 148. V, 2, 45. R3 IV, 4, 289. Rom. I, 3, 50. Hml. IV, 5, 68. Lr. I, 4, 18. Cymb. I, 6, 71.

2) To do at one's pleasure: *if you will not have me, c.* Merch. I, 2, 51. *I hope I may c.* Shr. V, 1, 48. *thou wrongest thyself, if thou shouldst strive to c.* All's II, 3, 153. — *I shall not c.* = I must: *you shall not c., sir, come!* Wiv. I, 1, 316. *you shall not c. but drink,* Shr. V, 1, 12. *thou shalt not c. but go,* Tw. IV, 1, 61. *he should not c. but give them to his master,* Tit. IV, 3, 74. *he shall not c. but fall,* Hml. IV, 7, 66.

3) to make a difference, to distinguish: *I think there is not half a kiss to c. who loves another best,* Wint. IV, 4, 175 (the shepherd's speech).

Chooser, one that chooses: *so far forth as herself might be her c.* Wiv. IV, 6, 11.

Chop, vb., 1) to do any thing with a quick motion, to pop: *and then we will c. him in the malmsey-butt,* R3 I, 4, 160 (Ff *throw*). 277 (Ff *drown*).

2) to mince: *I will c. her into messes,* Oth. IV, 1, 211. — *Chopped* = rent and split with toil or age: *beated and chopt with tanned antiquity,* Sonn. 62, 10. *her pretty chopt hands,* As II, 4, 50. *give me always a little, lean, old, chopt, bald shot,* H4B III, 2, 294 (M. Edd. *chapt*). *clapped their chopt hands,* Caes. I, 2, 246 (M. Edd. *chapt*). — *Chopping* = mincing, affected: *the chopping French we do not understand,* R2 V, 3, 124 (according to Wright = changing one meaning for another).

To c. away or *off* = to cut off: *c. away that factious pate of his,* H6B V, 1, 135. *his head to be* —*ed off,* Meas. I, 2, 70. H5 IV, 1, 142. H6C II, 6, 82. V, 1, 50. R3 III, 1, 193. Tit. III, 1, 72. 153.

Chop, subst. fissure, crack: *her cheeks with* —*s and wrinkles were disguised,* Lucr. 1452 (M. Edd. *chaps*). cf. *Chaps.*

Chopine, a kind of high shoe, worn by ladies: *your ladyship is nearer to heaven than when I saw you last, by the altitude of a c.* Hml. II, 2, 447.

Chop-logic, a reasoner, sophist: *how now, c., what is this?* Rom. III, 5, 150.

Choppy, full of clefts: *each at once her c. finger laying upon her skinny lips,* Mcb. I, 3, 44 (some M. Edd. *chappy*).

Chops, a person resembling a piece of meat: H4A I, 2, 151.* H4B II, 4, 235.

Chord, string of a musical instrument: *that would fret the string, the master c. on's heart,* H8 III, 2, 106 (O. and M. Edd. *cord;* perhaps = fibre).

Chorus, interpreter in a dumb show or other play: *whereupon it made this threne to the phoenix and the dove, as c. to their tragic scene,* Phoen. 52, *for the which supply, admit me c. to this history,* H5 Prol. 32. *this is one Lucianus, nephew to the king.* *You are as good as a c., my lord,* Hml. III, 2, 255.

Chorus-like, like an interpreter in a dumb show: *and all this dumb play had his acts made plain with tears, which, c., her eyes did rain,* Ven. 360.

Chough, the bird Corvus monedula: *I myself could make a c. of as deep chat,* Tp. II, 1, 266. *russet-pated* —*s,* Mids. III, 2, 21. —*s' language, gabble enough,* All's IV, 1, 22. *scared my* —*s from the chaff,* Wint. IV, 4, 630. *magot-pies and* —*s and rooks,* Mcb. III, 4, 125. *'tis a c.* Hml. V, 2, 89.* *the crows and* —*s that wing the midway air,* Lr. IV, 6, 13.

Chrisom (corrupted to *Christom* by Mrs. Quickly), a white vesture put upon the child after baptism: *a' made a finer end and went away an it had been any c. child,* H5 II, 3, 12. In the bills of mortality such children as died within the month of birth were called *chrisoms.*

Christ, the Saviour: R2 IV, 93. 99. 170. H4A I, 1, 19. III, 2, 111. H5 IV, 1, 65. H6A I, 2, 106. H6B V, 1, 214. R3 I, 4, 195. Corrupted to *Chrish* by Captain Macmorris in H5 III, 2; see Appendix.

Christen, vb., to baptize: Merch. IV, 1, 398. As III, 2, 284. R3 I, 1, 50. Tit. IV, 2, 70 (*c. it with thy dagger's point*).

Christen = Christian: *there's ne'er a king c. could be better bit*, H4A II, 1, 19 (Ff *in Christendom*). *and can call them all by their c. names*, II, 4, 8 (Ff om.).

Christendom, 1) the whole of the regions inhabited by Christians: *the lyingest knave in C.*, Shr. Ind. 2, 26. II, 188. John II, 75. H4A I, 2, 109. II, 1, 19 (Qq *christen*). III, 1, 164. H6A II, 4, 89. H6B II, 1, 126. H6C III, 2, 83. R3 III, 4, 53. H8 III, 2, 67. *all the kings of C.* John III, 1, 162. *the states of C.* H6A V, 4, 96. *committing freely your scruple to the voice of C.* H8 II, 2, 88. *C. shall ever speak his virtue*, H8 IV, 2, 63. *an older and a better soldier none that C. gives out*, Mcb. IV, 3, 192.
2) Christianity: *by my c.* John IV, 1, 16. *their clothes are after such a pagan cut too, that, sure, they 've worn out C.* H8 I, 3, 15.
3) Christian name, appellation: *with a world of pretty, fond, adoptious —s, that blinking Cupid gossips*, All's I, 1, 188.

Christening, subst., baptizing: H8 V, 4, 10. 38. 78. 87.

Christian, subst., a professor of the religion of Christ: Gentl. II, 5, 58. 61. III, 1, 272. Wiv. I, 1, 103. Meas. II, 1, 56. Err. I, 2, 77. Merch. I, 3, 43. 162. 179. II, 3, 11. II, 4, 19. II, 5, 15. II, 8, 16. III, 1, 66. III, 5, 22. IV, 1, 387. As IV, 3, 33. Tw. I, 3, 89. III, 2, 75. R2 IV, 83. H4A V, 5, 9. H4B II, 2, 76. R3 III, 5, 26. H8 II, 1, 64. V, 3, 180. Hml. III, 2, 35. Oth. IV, 2, 83 etc.

Christian, adj. professing the religion of Christ; becoming one who professes it; pertaining to Christianity: Wiv. III, 1, 96. IV, 1, 73. Merch. II, 5, 33. II, 8, 16. III, 1, 52. III, 3, 16. Shr. III, 2, 72. All's IV, 4, 2. John V, 2, 37. R2 II, 1, 54. IV, 93. 130. H4B IV, 2, 115. H5 I, 2, 241. H6A IV, 2, 30. V, 1, 9. V, 3, 172. H6B IV, 7, 44. R3 I, 4, 4. III, 7, 96. 116. IV, 4, 408. H8 II, 2, 93. 131. III, 1, 99. III, 2, 244. IV, 2, 156. Hml. IV, 5, 200. V, 1, 1. Oth. I, 1, 30. II, 3, 172 etc.

Christian-like, 1) adj. becoming a Christian: *with a most C. fear*, Ado II, 3, 199. *C. accord*, H5 V, 2, 381. *a C. conclusion*, R3 I, 3, 316.
2) adv. *he most C. laments his death*, H6B III, 2, 58.

Christmas, the festival celebrated in memory of the birth of Christ: *at C.* LLL I, 1, 105. *to dash it like a C. comedy*, V, 2, 462. *a C. gambold or a tumbling-trick*, Shr. Ind. 2, 140.

Christom, see *Chrisom*.

Christopher, name: Shr. Ind. 2, 19. R3 IV, 5, 1*

Christophero, the same: Shr. Ind. 2, 5. 75

Chronicle, subst., historical account of events in order of time: Sonn. 106, 1. Tp. V, 163. Shr. Ind. 1, 4. H4A I, 3, 171. V, 2, 58. H4B IV, 4, 126. H5 I, 2, 163. IV, 7, 98. H8 I, 2, 74. Troil. II, 3, 166. IV, 5, 202. Cor. V, 3, 145. Hml. II, 2, 549. Ant. III, 13, 175.

Chronicle, vb., to record, to register: *should not be —d for wise*, Gentl. I, 1, 41. *this sport, well carried, shall be —d*, Mids. III, 2, 240. *this deed is —d in hell*, R2 V, 5, 117. *to suckle fools and c. small beer*, Oth. II, 1, 161.

Chronicler, writer of a chronicle: *and the foolish —s of that age found it was Hero of Sestos*, As IV, 1, 105 (some M. Edd. *coroners*). *I wish ... but such an honest c. as Griffith*, H8 IV, 2, 72.

Chrysolite, a precious stone, of a green colour: Oth. V, 2, 145.

Chuck (= *chicken*), a term of endearment: LLL V, 1, 117. V, 2, 667. Tw. III, 4, 126. H5 III, 2, 26. Mcb. III, 2, 45. Oth. III, 4, 49. IV, 2, 24. Ant. IV, 4, 2.

Chud = I would (Somersetshire dialect): Lr. IV, 6, 243.

Chuet, see *Chewet*.

Chuff, a dull fellow who is well off, but does not know how to enjoy his wealth: *are ye undone? no, ye fat —s; I would your store were here!* H4A II, 2, 94 (cf. Nares' and Dyce's Glossaries).

Church, 1) a building consecrated to Christian worship: Wiv. V, 5, 196. Merch. I, 2, 14. Shr. III, 2, 181. IV, 4, 88. V, 1, 5. V, 1, 42. Tw. III, 1, 3. III, 2, 81. H4A V, 1, 73. III, 3, 9. H4B II, 4, 250. Mcb. IV, 1, 53. Hml. III, 2, 141. IV, 7, 127. V, 1, 55 etc. *I can see a c. by daylight*, Ado II, 1, 86. *parish c.* As II, 7, 52. *cathedral c.* H6B I, 2, 37.
2) a community regulated by certain ecclesiastical institutions, and represented by the body of the clergy: *I am of the c.* (i. e. a clergyman), Wiv. I, 1, 32. *why thou against the c. so wilfully dost spurn*, John III, 1, 141. 255. III, 4, 172. H5 I, 1, 10. H6A I, 1, 32. 33. III, 1, 46. H6B I, 1, 186. *Ephesians of the old c.* H4B II, 2, 164. Used as a fem: H8 V, 3, 117; cf. John III, 1, 141. 255. Without the article: *dignities of c.* H6A I, 3, 50. *till holy c. incorporate two in one*, Rom. II, 6, 37.
3) divine service; used without the article: *at c.* Wiv. IV, 6, 49. *to c.*: Merch. I, 1, 29. As II, 7, 114. 121. III, 3, 86. Tw. I, 3, 136. H6A I, 1, 42. Rom. IV, 5, 81. *To the c. and from the c.*, seemingly = to c. and from c.: Shr. III, 2, 151. IV, 4, 94. — Used, especially, of the marriage-ceremony: *when mean you to go to c.?* Ado II, 1, 371 (= to be married). *are come to fetch you to c.* III, 4, 102. *first go with me to c. and call me wife*, Merch. III, 2, 305. *'tis time we were at c.* Shr. III, 2, 113. *to put on better ere he go to c.* 128. *hie you to c.* Rom. II, 5, 74. *get thee to c. o' Thursday, or never after look me in the face*, III, 5, 162. *we'll to c. to-morrow*, IV, 2, 37.

Church-bench, seat in the porch of a church: *let us go sit here upon the c. till two*, Ado III, 3, 95.

Church-door: Rom. III, 1, 100.

Church-like, becoming a clergyman: *whose c. humours fits not for a crown*, H6B I, 1, 247.

Churchman, an ecclesiastic: Wiv. II, 3, 49. 57. Tw. III, 1, 4. H6A I, 1, 33. 40. III, 1, 111. H6B I, 3, 72. II, 1, 25. 182. R3 III, 7, 48. H8 I, 3, 55. I, 4, 88. III, 1, 117. V, 3, 63.

Church-way, the way leading to the church: *every one lets forth his sprite, in the c. paths to glide*, Mids. V, 389.

Church-window: Ado III, 3, 144.

Churchyard, cemetery: Mids. III, 2, 382. Wint. II, 1, 30. John III, 3, 40. H6A I, 2, 100. Cor. III, 3, 51. Rom. V, 3, 5. 11. 36. 172. 182. 186. Hml. III, 2, 407.

Churl, 1) peasant, rude and ill-bred fellow: *when that c. Death with his bones with dust shall cover*, Sonn. 32, 2. *good meat is common; that every c. affords*, Err. III, 1, 24. *c., upon thy eyes I throw all the power this charm doth owe*, Mids. II, 2, 78. Wint. IV, 4, 443. H6B III, 2, 213. Tim. I, 2, 26. Cymb. III,

6, 65. Femininely: *Lavinia, though you left me like a c.* Tit. I, 486.

2) niggard, miser: *and, tender c., makest waste in niggarding,* Sonn. I, 12 (cf. *beauteous niggard,* 4, 5). *then, —s, their thoughts, although their eyes were kind, to thy fair flower add the rank smell of weeds,* 69, 11. *O c.! drunk all, and left no friendly drop to help me after,* Rom. V, 3, 163.

Churlish, 1) rough, rude, brutal: *scorning his c. drum and ensign red,* Ven. 107. cf. John II, 76 and III, 1, 303. *ill-nurtured, crooked, c., hard in voice,* Ven. 134. *with javelin's point a c. swine to gore,* 616. *those* (tears) *at her father's c. feet she tendered,* Gentl. III, 1, 225. *the icy fang and c. chiding of the winter's wind,* As II, 1, 7. cf. *c. winter's tyranny,* H4B I, 3, 62. *he disabled my judgment: this is called the reply c.* As V, 4, 81. 98. *this c. messenger,* Tw. II, 2, 24. *unknit this c. knot of all-abhorred war,* H4A V, 1, 16. *a good soft pillow were better than a c. turf in France,* H5 IV, 1, 15. *this c. superscription,* H6A IV, 1, 53. *c. as the bear,* Troil. I, 2, 21. *c priest,* Hml. V, 1, 263.

2) niggardly: *my master is of c. disposition and little recks to find the way to heaven by doing deeds of hospitality,* As II, 4, 80. *nothing do I see in you, though c. thoughts themselves should be your judge, that I can find should merit any hate,* John II, 519.

Churlishly, rudely: *how c. I chid Lucetta hence,* Gentl. I, 2, 60.

Churn, to agitate cream for making butter: *and bootless make the breathless housewife c.* Mids. II, 1, 37.

Chus, name of a Jew in Merch. III, 2, 287.

Cicatrice, scar: All's II, 1, 43. Cor. II, 1, 164. Hml. IV, 3, 62. Meaning a slight mark or impression: *lean but upon a rush, the c. and capable impressure thy palm some moment keeps,* As III, 5, 23.

Cicely, name of female servants: Err. III, 1, 31. Shr. Ind. 2, 91.

Cicero, the Roman orator (cf. *Tully*): Caes. I, 2, 185. 281. I, 3, 4. II, 1, 141. IV, 3, 178.

Ciceter (most M. Edd. *Cicester*), Cirencester: *our town of C. in Glostershire,* R2 V, 6, 3.

'Cide (O. Edd. *side*) = decide: *to c. this title is impanneled a quest of thoughts,* Sonn. 46, 9.

Cilicia, country in Asia Minor: Ant. III, 6, 16.

Cimber; 1) Metellus C.: Caes. I, 3, 134. II, 1, 96 etc. 2) Publius C.: III, 1, 53. 57. 72.

Cimmerian; so the Moor is called in Tit. II, 3, 72, from the phrase '*Cimmerian darkness;*' or = Scythian?

Cincture, blundering conjecture of M. Edd. for centre (q. v.) in John IV, 3, 155.

Cinders, 1) ashes: *beauty, truth and rarity here enclosed in c. lie,* Phoen. 55. *sorrow concealed doth burn the heart to c.* Tit. II, 4, 37. *I should make very forges of my cheeks, that would to c. burn up modesty,* Oth. IV, 2, 75.

2) embers: *I shall show the c. of my spirits through the ashes of my chance,* Ant. V, 2, 173. — Falstaff ludicrously calls the stars so: *if you do not all show like gilt twopences to me, and I in the clear sky of fame o'ershine you as much as the full moon doth the c. of the element, which show like pins' heads to her,* H4B IV, 3, 58.

Cinna, 1) the conspirator: Caes. I, 3, 132. II, 1, 96 etc. 2) the poet: III, 3, 29 etc.

Cinque-pace (O. Edd. *Cinque-pace* and *Sink-a-pace*), a dance, 'the steps of which were regulated by the number five' (Nares): *wooing, wedding, and repenting, is as a Scotch jig, a measure, and a c.; ... and then comes repentance and, with his bad legs, falls into the c. faster and faster, till he sink into his grave,* Ado II, 1, 77. *I would not so much as make water but in a c.* Tw. I, 3, 139.

Cinque-ports, five English havens lying towards France: Hastings, Romney, Hythe, Dover, and Sandwich; to which afterwards Winchelsea and Rye have been added. Being under obligation to furnish ships in war at their own expense, they enjoyed, in return, particular privileges, as that of sending two members to parliament, called *barons of the C.:* H8 IV, 1, 49.

Cinque-spotted, having five spots: *a mole c., like the crimson drops i'the bottom of a cowslip,* Cymb. II, 2, 38.

Cipher, subst., the arithmetical mark, which, standing by itself, expresses nothing: *mine were the very c. of a function,* Meas. II, 2, 39. *a most fine figure! to prove you a c.* LLL I, 2, 59. *there I shall see mine own figure. Which I take to be either a fool or a c.* As III, 2, 308. *like a c., yet standing in rich place, I multiply ...,* Wint. I, 2, 6. *let us, —s to this great accompt, on your imaginary forces work,* H5 Prol. 17.

Cipher, vb., = to decipher: *some loathsome dash the herald will contrive, to c. me how fondly I did dote,* Lucr. 207. *the illiterate, that know not how to c. what is writ in learned books,* 811. *the face of either —ed either's heart,* 1396.

Circe, the sorceress in the Odyssey who changed men to beasts: Err. V, 270. H6A V, 3, 35.

Circle, subst., 1) the round, the ring: *round about her tear-distained eye blue —s streamed,* Lucr. 1587. *glory is like a c. in the water,* H6A I, 2, 133. 136. *the wheel is come full c.* Lr. V, 3, 174 (Qq *circled*). = the ring drawn by magicians: *a Greek invocation, to call fools into a c.* As II, 5, 62. And with a quibble: *if you would conjure in her, you must make a c.* H5 V, 2, 320. *to raise a spirit in his mistress' c.* Rom. II, 1, 24.

2) diadem: *thus have I yielded up into your hand the c. of my glory,* John V, 1, 2. *and of thee craves the c. of the Ptolemies,* Ant. III, 12, 18.

3) compass, circuit: *a great magician, obscured in the c. of this forest,* As V, 4, 34. *to whip this dwarfish war from out the c. of his territories,* John V, 2, 136.

Circle, vb., to enclose, to surround: *her breasts, like ivory globes —d with blue,* Lucr. 407. *the crimson blood —s her body in on every side,* 1739. *until thy head be —d with the same* (sc. the diadem), H6B I, 2, 10. *modest Dian —d with her nymphs,* H6C IV, 8, 21. *the imperial metal —ing now thy brow,* R3 IV, 4, 382. *her two branches* (viz her arms) *whose —ing shadows kings have sought to sleep in,* Tit. II, 4, 19. *you heavy people, c. me about,* III, 1, 277. — *the maid with swelling drops gan wet her —d eyne,* Lucr. 1229 (round eyes? or eyes surrounded with black circles?)

Circled, adj. round: *the moon that monthly changes in her c. orb,* Rom. II, 2, 110. cf. Lucr. 1229 (?).

Circuit, 1) circle (= diadem): *the golden c. on my head,* H6B III, 1, 352. *how sweet a thing it is to wear a crown, within whose c. is Elysium,* H6C I, 2, 30.

2) **enclosed space:** *since I have hemmed thee here within the c. of this ivory pale,* Ven. 230. *(sweet tomb that in thy c. dost contain the perfect model of eternity,* Rom. V, 3, 12; reading of the spurious Q1).

Circumcised, having the prepuce cut off: Oth. V, 2, 355.

Circumference, periphery: *to be compassed, like a good bilbo, in the c. of a peck,* Wiv. III, 5, 113. *his horns are invisible within the c.* Mids. V, 247. *though all these English were harboured in their rude c.* John II, 262.

Circummured, walled round: *a garden c. with brick,* Meas. IV, 1, 28.

Circumscribe, to restrain: *from where he —d with his sword, and brought to yoke, the enemies of Rome,* Tit. I, 68. *and therefore must his choice be —d unto the voice and yielding of that body whereof he is the head,* Hml. I, 3, 22.

Circumscription, restraint, confinement: *I would not my unhoused free condition put into c. and confine,* Oth. I, 2, 27.

Circumspect, cautious: H6B I, 1, 157. R3 IV, 2, 31.

Circumstance, 1) condition, state of things: *so (sc. a fool) by your c., I fear you'll prove,* Gentl. I, 1, 37 (a quibble). *you speak like a green girl, unsifted in such perilous c.* Hml. I, 3, 102. *but in our c. and course of thought 'tis heavy with him,* III, 3, 83.

2) something attending and affecting a fact or case (indiscriminately used in the singular and plur.): *assailed by night with —s strong of present death,* Lucr. 1262. *what is the quality of mine offence, being constrained with dreadful c.* 1703. *swerve not from the smallest article of it, neither in time, matter, nor other c.* Meas. IV, 2, 108. *no incredulous or unsafe c.* Tw. III, 4, 89. *do not embrace me till each c. of place, time, fortune, do cohere,* V, 258. *all other —s made up to the deed,* Wint. II, 1, 178. *the c. considered ...,* H4A I, 3, 70. *if your grace mark every c., you have great reason to do Richard right,* H6A III, 1, 153. *all —s well considered,* R3 III, 7, 176. *one scene in it comes near the c. which I have told thee ...,* Hml. III, 2, 81. *all quality, pride, pomp and c. of glorious war,* Oth. III, 3, 354.

Especially, facts from which a certain presumption arises, which give evidence of some truth (cf. above: Lucr. 1262. 1703. Tw. III, 4, 89. Wint. II, 1, 178): *most true, if ever truth were pregnant by c.* Wint. V, 2, 34. *if —s lead me, I will find where truth is hid,* Hml. II, 2, 157. *and can you by no drift of c. get from him why he puts on this confusion?* Hml. III, 1, 1 (Qq conference). *imputation and strong —s which lead directly to the door of truth,* Oth. III, 3, 406.

3) occurrence, accident: *he that loves himself hath not essentially but by c. the name of valour,* H6B V, 2, 39. *the pretence whereof being by —s partly laid open,* Wint. III, 2, 18. *that policy ... may breed itself so out of c.* Oth. III, 3, 16 (Ff —s).

4) particulars, detail: *if pleased themselves, others, they think, delight in such-like c.* Ven. 844 (= in such a detailed account). *it must with c. be spoken by one whom she esteemeth as his friend,* Gentl. III, 2, 36. *with c. and oaths so to deny this chain,* Err. V, 16. *in all these —s I'll instruct you,* Shr. IV, 2, 119. *I know nothing of the c. more,* Tw. III, 4, 287.

the interruption of their churlish drums cuts off more c. John II, 77. *the c. I'll tell you more at large,* H6A I, 1, 109. *tell us here the c.* H6B II, 1, 74. *to give me leave, by c., but to acquit myself,* R3 I, 2, 77. cf. 80. *who, in his c., expressly proves that no man is the lord of any thing,* Troil. III, 3, 114. *and tell them both the circumstance of all,* Tit. IV, 2, 156. *say either, and I'll stay the c.* Rom. II, 5, 36. *the true ground of all these piteous woes we cannot without c. descry,* Rom. V, 3, 181 (= without further particulars). *you do remember all the c.* Hml. V, 2, 2. *my —s must first induce you to believe,* Cymb. II, 4, 61. — Used for a detailed proof, a deduction from point to point: *so, by your c., you call me fool,* Gentl. I, 1, 36. *that I can deny by a c.* 84.

5) ceremony, phrases: *and —s shortened, the lady is disloyal,* Ado III, 2, 105.* *to wind about my love with c.* Merch. I, 1, 154. *the lie with c.* As V, 4, 100 (= given indirectly, with some phrases). *to leave frivolous —s, tell Signior Lucentio ...,* Shr. V, 1, 28. *his approach, so out of c. and sudden,* Wint. V, 1, 90 (= without ceremony). *what means this passionate discourse, this peroration with such c.?* H6B I, 1, 105. *and so, without more c. at all, I hold it fit that we shake hands and part,* Hml. I, 5, 127. *evades them with a bombast c. horribly stuffed with epithets of war,* Oth. I, 1, 13.

Circumstanced: *I must be c.* Oth. III, 4, 201, = I must submit to circumstances.

Circumstantial, 1) consisting of particulars: *this fierce abridgement hath to it c. branches, which distinction should be rich in,* Cymb. V, 5, 383. — 2) indirect, involved in phrases: *the lie c.* As V, 4, 85. 90, = the lie with circumstance, 100.

Circumvent, to overreach, to foil: *it might be the pate of a politician, one that would c. God,* Hml. V, 1, 88.

Circumvention, foiling or disappointing by superior cunning: *which (wit) is so abundant scarce, it will not in c. deliver a fly from a spider, without drawing their massy irons and cutting the web,* Troil. II, 3, 17. *what ever have been thought on in this state, that could be brought to bodily act ere Rome had c.?* Cor. I, 2, 6.*

Cistern, a receptacle of water: *like ivory conduits coral —s filling,* Lucr. 1234. *or keep it as a c. for foul toads to knot and gender in,* Oth. IV, 2, 62. *so half my Egypt were submerged and made a c. for scaled snakes,* Ant. II, 5, 95. Tropically: *your wives, your daughters, your matrons and your maids, could not fill up the c. of my lust,* Mcb. IV, 3, 63.

Citadel, a small fortress in or near a city: All's IV, 1, 61. Oth. II, 1, 94. 211. 292. III, 3, 59. V, 1, 126. Ant. IV, 14, 4.

Cital, mention: *he made a blushing c. of himself,* H4A V, 2, 62.

Cite, 1) to summon: *to which she was often —d by them, but appeared not,* H8 IV, 1, 29.

2) to call up, to invite, to urge: *the morning rise doth c. each moving sense from idle rest,* Pilgr. 195. *for Valentine, I need not c. him to it,* Gentl. II, 4, 85. *had I not been —d so by them, yet did I purpose as they do entreat,* H6B III, 2, 281. *it —s us to the field,* H6C II, 1, 34.

3) to quote: *the devil can c. Scripture for his purpose,* Merch. I, 3, 99. *as truth's authentic author to be —d,* Troil. III, 2, 188.

4) to mention, to recount: *we c. our faults, that they may hold excused our lawless lives*, Gentl. IV, 1, 53. *whose aged honour —s a virtuous youth*, All's I, 3, 216 (cf. *speak* and *bespeak*). *the peace, whose want gives growth to the imperfections which you have —d*, H5 V, 2, 70. *I do digress too much, —ing my worthless praise*, Tit. V, 3, 117. With *up : thou shalt have thy trespass —d up in rhymes*, Lucr. 524. *thence we looked toward England, and —d up a thousand fearful times*, R3 I, 4, 14.

Citizen, freeman of a city; townsman: Lucr. 465. Meas. IV, 6, 13. Err. V, 142. Merch. IV, 1, 351. As II, 1, 55. Shr. I, 1, 10. IV, 2, 95. John II, 231. 362. 536. H4A III, 1, 261. H5 I, 2, 199. V Chor. 24. H6A I, 3, 62. I, 6, 12. II, 3, 41. H6B IV, 4, 50. H6C IV, 8, 19. R3 III, 5, 65. III, 7, 1 etc. H8 IV, 1, 7. Cor. I, 1, 15 etc. Tit. I, 164. IV, 4, 79. Rom. I, 1, 99. III, 1, 138. Caes. I, 2, 321. III, 2, 246. Oth. I, 1, 90. Ant. V, 1, 17.

Used adjectively, = cockney-bred, effeminate: *but not so c. a wanton as to seem to die ere sick*, Cymb. IV, 2, 8.

Cittern, guitar: *what is this? a c. head*, LLL V, 2, 614 ('the cittern had usually a head grotesquely carved at the extremity of the neck and finger-board.' Nares).

City, a corporate town: Lucr. 1369. 1554. Gentl. III, 2, 91. Meas. I, 1, 11. I, 2, 101. II, 1, 243. IV, 3, 103. V, 514. Err. I, 2, 31. V, 4. 323. Ado III, 5, 29. Mids. I, 2, 106. II, 1, 215. Merch. III, 3, 30. IV, 1, 39. As II, 1, 23. II, 7, 74. H5 V Chor. 19. H6A I, 4, 11. 68. H6B I, 1, 121. IV, 4, 47. IV, 5, 6. Ant. IV, 14, 59 etc. Joined to *town: razeth your —ies and subverts your towns*, H6A II, 3, 65. *see the —ies and the towns defaced*, III, 3, 45. *twelve —ies and seven walled towns of strength*, III, 4, 7. *turned out of all towns and —ies*, R3 I, 4, 146. — Joined to other words: *sometime a blusterer, that the ruffle knew of court, of c.* Compl. 59. *he pierceth through the body of the country, c., court*, As II, 1, 59. *met him in boroughs, —ies, villages*, H4A IV, 3, 69. — Denoting the body of the citizens: *the c. favours them*, H6C I, 1, 67. *to rage the c. turn, that him and his they in his palace burn*, Per. V, 3, 97. — Used as a fem.: *the c. cast her people out upon her*, Ant. II, 2, 218. — Followed by *of: the c. of London*, H6A III, 1, 77. Followed by the name without *of: in the famous ancient c. Tours*, H6B I, 1, 5. I, 3, 53. *their c. Corioli*, Cor. I, 3, 111. *your c. Rome*, Cor. V, 6, 93. — *Make not a c. feast of it, to let the meat cool ere we can agree upon the first place*, Tim. III, 6, 75.

Figuratively, for female innocence guarded against assaults: *to make the breach and enter this sweet c.* Lucr. 469. *and long upon these terms I held my c.* Compl. 176. *in blowing him down again, you lose your c.* All's I, 1, 137.

City-gate: Gentl. III, 1, 252. H6A III, 2, 1. IV, 2, 5. H6C V, 1, 21.

City-mill: Cor. I, 10, 31.

City-woman, wife or daughter of a citizen: *the c. bears the cost of princes*, As II, 7, 75.

Civet, a perfume from the civet-cat: Ado III, 2, 50. As III, 2, 66. 69. Lr. IV, 6, 132. Alluded to in Lr. III, 4, 109.

Civil, 1) relating to the community of the citizens of a state: *religious canons. c. laws are*

cruel, Tim. IV, 3, 60. *c. war* = intestine war: Sonn. 35, 12. LLL II, 226. John III, 1, 264. H5 V, 2, 243. H6C I, 1, 197. II, 5, 77. *c. arms* (= arms borne in civil war): R2 III, 3, 102. *swords:* H4B V, 5, 112. Ant. I, 3, 45. *c. blood makes c. hands unclean*, Rom. Prol. 4. *c. blows*, H4B IV, 5, 134. *brawls*, Rom. I, 1, 96. *broils*, H6A I, 1, 53. H6B IV, 8, 46. *buffeting*, H4A II, 4, 397. *butchery*, H4A I, 1, 13. *dissension*, H6A III, 1, 72. *enmity*, H6C IV, 6, 98. *strife*, Ven. 764. Caes. I, 3, 11. III, 1, 263. *tumult*, John IV, 2, 247. *c. wounds* (i. e. wounds made in civil war): R2 I, 3, 128. R3 V, 5, 40. Tit. V, 3, 87.

2) reduced to order and law, well-governed, peaceful: *they are reformed, c., full of good*, Gentl. V, 4, 156. *whose see is by a c. peace maintained*, H4B IV, 1, 42. *the c. citizens kneading up the honey*, H5 I, 2, 199. *bringing them to c. discipline*, H6B I, 1, 195. *the round world should have shook lions into c. streets*, Ant. V, 1, 16.

3) decent, well-mannered, polite: *shook off my sober guards and c. fears*, Compl. 298. *in honest, c., godly company*, Wiv. I, 1, 187. *a c. modest wife*, II, 2, 101. *the rude sea grew c.*, Mids. II, 1, 152. *if you were c. and knew courtesy*, III, 2, 147. *a c. doctor*, Merch. V, 210.* *tongues I'll hang on every tree, that shall c. sayings show*, As III, 2, 136. *leap all c. bounds*, Tw. I, 4, 21. *where is Malvolio? he is sad and c.* III, 4, 5. *receive those that are c.* H4B II, 4, 97. *this honest, virtuous, c. gentlewoman*, 328. *Kent is termed the —est place of all this isle*, H6B IV, 7, 66. *come, c. night, thou sober-suited matron*, Rom. III, 2, 10. *the mere form of c. and humane seeming*, Oth. II, 1, 243. *you were wont be c.*, II, 3, 190. *many a c. monster*, IV, 1, 65. *who's here? if any thing that's c., speak; if savage ...*, Cymb. III, 6, 23. — *C. as an orange*; Ado II, 1, 304 (a quibble: *civil* and *Seville*). — Superl. *civilest*, H6B IV, 7, 66.

Civility, good breeding, decorum, politeness: *any madness I ever yet beheld seemed but tameness, c. and patience*, Wiv. IV, 2, 28. *use all the observance of c.* Merch. II, 2, 204. *that in c. thou seemest so empty*, As II, 7, 93. 96. *from the sense of all c.* Oth. I, 1, 132. Cymb. IV, 2, 179.

Civilly, with decorum: *I have savage cause; and to proclaim it c., were like a haltered neck ...*, Ant. III, 13, 129.

Clack-dish, a wooden dish or box ('carried by beggars; it had a movable cover, which they clacked to attract notice.' Nares): *his use was to put a ducat in her c.* Meas. III, 2, 135.

Clad, clothed, drest: *c. in mourning black*, Lucr. 1585. *in that dimension grossly c.* Tw. V, 244. *c. in arms*, R2 I, 3, 12. *a woman c. in armour*, H6A I, 5, 3. *the morn, in russet mantle c.* Hml. I, 1, 166.

Claim, subst., demand of a supposed right, pretension: Err. III, 2, 64. John II, 280. V, 2, 101. H5 I, 2, 12. 87. II, 4, 85. 110. H6B II, 2, 7. III, 1, 375. H6C II, 2, 162. Lr. V, 3, 84. *your c. to France*, H5 I, 2, 36. *To lay c. to sth.:* Lucr. 1794. Err. III, 2, 84. 85. 89. 144. As V, 1, 7. John I, 9. 72. R2 II, 3, 135. H6B II, 2, 40. H6C I, 1, 152. *To make c.:* John III, 4, 143. H5 I, 2, 68. 96. H6C IV, 7, 59.

Claim, vb., to challenge, to demand as a right: Lucr. 1715. Gentl. V, 4, 135. Err. III, 2, 82. IV, 1, 110. Merch. III, 2, 139. IV, 1, 231. All's II, 3, 168. II, 4, 43. III, 2, 75. John I, 91. V, 2, 94.

H4A V, 1, 44. H5 I, 2, 256. H6A V, 4, 167. H6B I, 1, 239. 242. II, 2, 35. 47. V, 1, 1. H6C I, 1, 49. IV, 7, 46. R3 III, 1, 50. IV, 2, 91. IV, 4, 469. H8 IV, 1, 15. V, 5, 39. Troil. IV, 5, 51. Cor. II, 3, 194. III, 2, 83. Mcb. II, 3, 126. Hml. V, 2, 401. Ant. II, 2, 130. *To c. a promise* = to remind a person of a promise: *I c. the promise for her heavenly picture*, Gentl. IV, 4, 92. *I'll c. that promise at your highness' hands*, R3 III, 1, 197. With *from: virtue —s from beauty beauty's red*, Lucr. 59. With *of: —s marriage of me*, Err. IV, 4, 159. John I, 122. II, 153. R3 III, 1, 194.

Absolutely: *to bar your highness — ing from the female*, H5 I, 2, 92. 104. H6C I, 2, 19.

Clamber, to climb: *c. not you up to the casements then*, Merch. II, 5, 31. *—ing the walls to eye him*, Cor. II, 1, 226. *on the pendent boughs her coronet weeds —ing to hang*, Hml. IV, 7, 174.

Clamorous, vociferous, loud: *ceasing their c. cry* (i. e. their loud barking) Ven. 693. *more c. than a parrot against rain*, As IV, 1, 151. *be c. and leap all civil bounds*, Tw. I, 4, 21. *the herds were strangely c. to the frighted fields*, H4A III, 1, 40. *are you not ashamed with this immodest c. outrage to trouble and disturb the king and us?* H6A IV, 1, 126. *that I am thus encountered with c. demands of date-broke bonds*, Tim. II, 2, 37. *whom I will beat into c. whining*, Lr. II, 2, 25. Denoting, perhaps, the sound of wailing (cf. *clamour*): *the c. owl that nightly hoots and wonders ...*, Mids. II, 2, 6. *the sound that tells what hour it is are c. groans*, R2 V, 5, 56.

Used of other sounds than the human voice: *with the c. report of war* (viz drums and trumpets) *thus I will drown your exclamations*, R3 IV, 4, 152. *those c. harbingers of blood and death* (viz trumpets), Mcb. V, 6, 10. *kissed her lips with such a c. smack that at the parting all the church did echo*, Shr. III, 2, 180.

Clamour, subst., outcry, vociferation: *the venom —s of a jealous woman*, Err. V, 69. *I'll rail and brawl and with the c. keep her still awake*, Shr. IV, 1, 210. *contempt and c. will be my knell*, Wint. I, 2, 189. *the bitter c. of two eager tongues*, R2 I, 1, 49. *what tumultuous c. have we here?* H6B III, 2, 239. *with all the applause and c. of the host*, Cor. I, 9, 64. *we'll bring him to his house with shouts and —s*, Caes. III, 2, 58. *whilst I can vent c. from my throat*, Lr. I, 1, 168. *lest by his c. the town might fall in fright*, Oth. II, 3, 231.

Frequently = loud wailing: *he pens her piteous —s in her head*, Lucr. 681. *'my daughter' and 'my wife' with —s filled the air*, 1804. *often shrieking undistinguished woe, in —s of all size, both high and low*, Compl. 21. *sickly ears, deafed with the —s of their own dear groans*, LLL V, 2, 874. *add to my —s*, Troil. II, 2, 106. *we shall make our griefs and c. roar upon his death*, Mcb. I, 7, 78. *the instant burst of c. that she made*, Hml. II, 2, 538. *she shook the holy water from her heavenly eyes, and c. moistened*, Lr. IV, 3, 33. *whilst I was big in c.* V, 3, 208.

Used of other sounds; of bells: *an hour in c.* Ado V, 2, 84. Of cannon: *their soul-fearing —s*, John II, 383. Of the thunder: *the immortal Jove's dread —s*, Oth. III, 3, 356. Of drums and trumpets: *braying trumpets and loud churlish drums, —s of hell*, John III, 1, 304. *start an echo with the c. of thy drum*, V, 2, 168. Of tempests: *hanging them* (the billows) *with deafening c. in the clouds*, H4B III, 1, 24. *not the dreadful spout which shipmen do the hurricano call, shall dizzy with more c. Neptune's ear*, Troil. V, 2, 174. Of the noise of a chase, a battle etc.: *a savage c.* Wint. III, 3, 56. *peace, you ungracious —s! peace, rude sounds!* Troil. I, 1, 92. *and more he spoke, which sounded like a c. in a vault, that mought not be distinguished*, H6C V, 2, 44 (Ff *cannon*).

Clamour, vb., to cry, to wail: *the obscure bird —ed the livelong night*, Mcb. II, 3, 65.

Strange expression: *'tis well they are whispering: c. your tongues, and not a word more*, Wint. IV, 4, 250.* Nares: 'An expression taken from bell-ringing; it is now contracted to *clam*, and in that form is common among ringers. The bells are said to be *clammed*, when, after a course of rounds or changes, they are all pulled off at once, and give a general crash or clam, by which the peal is concluded.' Dyce: 'Mr. Hunter observes that the same phrase occurs in Taylor the Waterpoet's Sir Gregory Nonsense: *Cease friendly cutting throats, c. the promulgation of your tongues'*. And Mr. Arrowsmith explains *clamour* to mean curb, restrain, considering it as equivalent to *chaumbre* or *chammer* (Fr. chommer), and cites the following passages from Udall's translation of the Apophthegms of Erasmus: '*For Critias menaced and threatened him, that unless he chaumbred his tongue in season* etc. and: *from no sort of men in the world did he refrain or chaumbre the taunting of his tongue.*' — It ought, after all, to be taken into account that in our passage it is the Clown that is speaking. If not a misprint, as Gifford supposed, it may be a misapplication of the word for 'charm.'

Clang, the sound of a trumpet: *loud 'larums, neighing steeds, and trumpets' c.* Shr. I, 2, 207.

Clangor, the same: *in the very pangs of death he cried, like to a dismal c. heard from far*, H6C II, 3, 18. cf. *Trumpet-clangor*.

Clap, vb., A. trans. 1) to strike with a quick motion, without hurting, to tap, to pat: *—s her pale cheek, till —ing makes it red*, Ven. 468. *this hand hath made him proud with —ing him*, R2 V, 5, 86. To c. a person on the shoulder was a sign of approbation and applause: LLL V, 2, 107. Ado I, 1, 261. Troil. III, 3, 139. cf. *it may be said of him that Cupid hath —ed him o'the shoulder, but I'll warrant him heart-whole*, As IV, 1, 48. *To c. one's hands* = to strike the hands together by way of applause: H6B I, 1, 160. Troil. II, 2, 87. Caes. I, 2, 246. Hence *to c.* = to applaud: *if the people did not c. him and hiss him*, Caes. I, 2, 261. *are —ed for it*, Hml. II, 2, 356.

To c. hands = to pledge one's faith by joining hands: *and so c. hands, and a bargain*, H5 V, 2, 133. Hence: *and c. thyself my love*, Wint. I, 2, 104 (= promise to marry me by putting thy hand in mine).

2) to do anything with a quick motion, to put, to thrust: *—ing their proud tails to the ground below*, Ven. 923. *hath —ed his tail between his legs*, H6B V, 1, 154. *—s me his sword upon the table*, Rom. III, 1, 6 (= strikes with his sword upon the table). *we were dead of sleep, and all —ed under hatches*, Tp. V, 231. *boys c. their female joints in stiff unwieldy arms*, R2 III, 2, 114. *a pennyworth of sugar, —ed into my hand by an underskinker*, H4A II, 4, 25. *the very thought of this fair company —ed wings to me*, H8 I, 4, 9. *the new proclamation that's —ed upon the court-gate*, H8 I, 3, 17 (= posted up unexpectedly). *but*

(he will) *return with an invention and c. upon you two or three probable lies,* All's III, 6, 106. *this Commodity ...,* —*ed on the outward eye of fickle France, hath drawn him from his own determined aid,* John II, 583. *and on your heads* (I'll) *c. round fines for neglect,* H8 V, 4, 84.

To c. on = to put on, to set hastily: *c. on more sails; pursue,* Wiv. II, 2, 142. *Antony* —*s on his seawing, and like a doting mallard flies after her,* Ant. III, 10, 20.

To c. to = to shut hastily: *hostess, c. to the doors,* H4A II, 4, 305. *who, upon the sudden,* —*ed to their gates,* Cor. I, 4, 51.

To c. up = a) to shut up: *let them be* —*ed up close,* H6B I, 4, 53. *I wish I could be made so many men, and all of you* —*ed up together in an Antony,* Ant. IV, 2, 17. — b) to make up by joining hands, to accomplish hastily: *was ever match* —*ed up so suddenly?* Shr. II, 327. *no longer than we well could wash our hands* (sc. of blood) *to c. this royal bargain up of peace,* John III, 1, 235 (cf. above: *to c. hands*).

B. intr., 1) to applaud: *when their ladies bid them c.* H8 Epil. 14. — 2) to hit quickly and without effort: *a' would have* —*ed i' the clout at twelve score,* H4A II, 2, 51. — 3) to enter upon, to begin with alacrity and briskness: *I would desire you to c. into your prayers,* Meas. IV, 3, 43. *c. us into Light o' love,* Ado III, 4, 44. *shall we c. into it* (a song) *roundly?* As V, 3, 11.

Clap, subst., 1) striking together of hands to express applause: *whose shouts and* —*s outvoice the deep-mouthed sea,* H5 V, Chor. 11. *every one with* —*s can sound 'Our heir apparent is a king,'* Per. III Prol. 36.

2) *At a c.* = at a blow: *fifty of my followers at a c.* Lr. I, 4, 316.

Clapper, the tongue of a bell: *he hath a heart as sound as a bell, and his tongue is the c.* Ado III, 2, 13. See, besides, *Shoulder-clapper.*

Clapper-claw, to drub, to thrash: *he will c. thee tightly,* Wiv. II, 3, 67; cf. 69. 71. *now they are* —*ing one another; I'll go look on,* Troil. V, 4, 1.

Clare, name of a female saint: *the votarists of Saint C.* Meas. I, 4, 5.

Clarence, 1) Lionel Duke of C., son of Edward III: H6A II, 4, 83. II, 5, 75. H6B II, 2, 13. IV, 2, 145. IV, 4, 29. — 2) Thomas of C., son of Henry IV: H4B IV, 4, 16 etc. H5 V, 2, 84. — 3) George of C., son of Richard of York and brother to Edward IV and Richard III: H6C II, 6, 104. III, 3, 208 etc. R3 I, 1, 34 etc. etc.

Gen. *Clarence'*: H6B IV, 2, 145. IV, 4, 29. R3 I, 4, 191. II, 1, 136. III, 1, 144. IV, 2, 55.

Claret wine, French wine of a pale red colour: H6B IV, 6, 4.

Claribel, daughter of king Alonso in Tp. II, 1, 70. 245. 258. V, 209.

Clasp, subst., 1) a catch to hold something together: *with coral* —*s and amber studs,* Pilgr. 366 (not Shakespearean). *that book in many's eyes doth share the glory, that in gold* —*s locks in the golden story,* Rom. I, 3, 92.

2) embrace: *the gross* —*s of a lascivious Moor,* Oth. I, 1, 127.

Clasp, vb., 1) trans., a) to fasten together, to shut: *though forfeiters you* (seals of wax) *cast*

in prison, yet you c. young Cupid's tables, Cymb. III, 2, 39.

b) to join: *we'll c. hands,* Per. II, 4, 57.

c) to embrace: *a slave, whom Fortune's tender arm with favour never* —*ed,* Tim. IV, 3, 251. *I am glad to c. thee,* Troil. IV, 5, 204.

2) intr., to cling: *and* —*ing to the mast, endured a sea that almost burst the deck,* Per. IV, 1, 56.

Clasping, subst., embrace: *your untimely* —*s with your child,* Per. I, 1, 128.

Clatter, subst. rattling noise of arms: *by this great c., one of greatest note seems bruited,* Mcb. V, 7, 21.

Claudio, name: 1) Meas. I, 2, 64. 117. 128 etc. etc. 2) Ado I, 1, 11. 85. 211 etc. etc. 3) Hml. IV, 7, 40. 4) Caes. IV, 3, 242. 244. 290. 291. (M. Edd. *Claudius*).

Claudius, see *Claudio* 4.

Clause, inference, conclusion: *do not extort thy reasons from this c., for that I woo, thou therefore hast no cause,* Tw. III, 1, 165.

Claw, subst., the foot of an animal armed with sharp nails: Lucr. 543. LLL IV, 2, 65. Mids. IV, 2, 42. As V, 2, 26.

Claw, vb., to scratch in a pleasing manner: *look, whether the withered elder hath not his poll* —*ed like a parrot,* H4B II, 4, 282. *if a talent be a claw, look how he* —*s him with a talent,* LLL IV, 2, 66. Figuratively, = to smooth, to humour: *laugh when I am merry and c. no man in his humour,* Ado I, 3, 18. — Used blunderingly: *but age hath* —*ed me in his clutch,* Hml. V, 1, 80 (Ff *caught*).

Clay, earth, dust: *temper c. with blood of Englishmen,* H6B III, 1, 311. *and cast you* (viz the eyes) *with the waters that you lose to temper c.* Lr. I, 4, 326. Considered as that to which man must return after death: *kings' misdeeds cannot be hid in c.* Lucr. 609. *when I perhaps compounded am with c.* Sonn. 71, 10. *this was now a king, and now is c.* John V, 7, 69. *the dead with charity enclosed in c.* H5 IV, 8, 129. *a pit of c. for to be made for such a guest,* Hml. V, 1, 104. *imperious Caesar, dead and turned to c.* 236. — Considered as the stuff of which man and mortal things are made: *that sweet breath which was embounded in this beauteous c.* John IV, 3, 137. *men are but gilded loam or painted c.* R2 I, 1, 179. *this foolish-compounded c., man,* H4B I, 2, 8. *this lump of c.* H6A II, 5, 14. *kingdoms are c.* Ant. I, 1, 35. *c. and c. differs in dignity,* Cymb. IV, 2, 4.

Clay-brained, having a brain of clay, stupid: H4A II, 4, 251, cf. *clodpole* and Oth. V, 2, 164.

Clean, adj., free from dirt or any stain: Gentl. III, 1, 278. Err. III, 2, 105. Ado IV, 1, 143. Mids. IV, 2, 40. As III, 2, 443. All's IV, 3, 166. H4B IV, 1, 201. Cor. II, 3, 67. Tim. IV, 3, 364. Mcb. V, 1, 49. Followed by *of: c. of such filth,* H6B IV, 7, 34.

Clean, adv., quite, entirely: *c. starved for a look,* Sonn. 75, 10. *roaming c. through the bounds of Asia,* Err. I, 1, 134. *disfigured c.* R2 III, 1, 10. *though not c. past your youth,* H4B I, 2, 110. *domestic broils c. overblown,* R3 II, 4, 61. *renouncing c. the faith they have in tennis,* H8 I, 3, 29. *this is c. kam,* Cor. III, 1, 304. *c. consumed,* Tit. I, 129. *c. from the purpose,* Caes. I, 3, 35. *wash this blood c. from my hand,* Mcb. II, 2, 61. *it is c. out of the way,* Oth. I, 3, 366. *ere c. it o'erthrow nature,* Cymb. III, 6, 20.

Cleanly, adj., careful to avoid filth: *the —iest shift is to kiss,* As IV, 1, 77 (instead of spitting, as orators do).* *not neat, but c.* Wint. I, 2, 123. *wherein neat and c., but to carve a capon?* H4A II, 4, 502.

Cleanly, adv., 1) in a clean manner, without stain: *and live c. as a nobleman should do,* H4A V, 4, 169. — 2) quite, entirely: *ceasing their clamorous cry till they have singled with much ado the cold fault c. out,* Ven. 694. *hast not thou full often struck a doe, and borne her c. by the keeper's nose?* Tit. II, 1, 94 (= in the very face of the keeper).

Cleanly-coined (not hyphened in O. Edd.) forged in a neat manner, so as to have a good and spotless appearance: *fold my fault in c. excuses,* Lucr. 1073.

Cleanse, to make clean, to purify: *c. the foul body of the infected world,* As II, 7, 60. *priestlike thou hast —d my bosom,* Wint. I, 2, 238. *—ing them from tears,* R2 V, 5, 54. *c. the stuffed bosom of that perilous stuff,* Mcb. V, 3, 44.

Clean-timbered, neatly framed, free from any fault of the body: *Hector was not so c.* LLL V, 2, 642.

Clear, adj., 1) bright, transparent, pellucid: *those round c. pearls* (viz tears) *of his,* Lucr. 1553. *c. wells spring not,* Pilgr. 281. *by fountain c.* Mids. II, 1, 29. Troil. III, 3, 314.

2) apparent, evident: *what he will make up full c.* Meas. V, 157. *such c. lights of favour,* Tw. V, 344. *c. excuse,* H4A III, 2, 19. *it* (the truth) *is so c., so shining and evident,* H6A II, 4, 23. *proofs as c. as founts in July,* H8 I, 1, 154. *'tis c., they'll say 'tis naught,* H8 Epil. 4.

3) sounding distinctly: *crack my c. voice with sobs,* Troil. IV, 2, 114.

4) perspicacious: *the c. eye's moiety and the dear heart's part,* Sonn. 46, 12. *mine eye's c. eye, my dear heart's dearer heart,* Err. III, 2, 62. Applied to the mind: *the ignorant fumes that mantle their —er reason,* Tp. V, 68. *when you shall come to —er knowledge,* Wint. II, 1, 97. *something hath puddled his c. spirit,* Oth. III, 4, 143. *in our own filth drop our c. judgements,* Ant. III, 13, 113. *by her own most c. remembrance,* Per. V, 3, 12. cf. Troil. III, 3, 314.

5) bright, shining, luminous: *O thou c. God* (sc. the sun) *and patron of all light,* Ven. 860. *form happy show to the c. day with thy much —er light,* Sonn. 43, 7. *it is almost c. dawn,* Meas. IV, 2, 226. *in the c. sky of fame,* H4B IV, 3, 56. *those c. rays which she infused on me,* H6A I, 2, 85. *darkening my c. sun,* H8 I, 1, 226.

6) beautiful, magnificent, glorious: *to praise the c. unmatched red and white,* Lucr. 11 (double meaning: bright and chaste). *not making worse what nature made so c.* Sonn. 84, 10. *that c. honour were purchased by the merit of the wearer,* Merch. II, 9, 42. *you c. heavens!* Tim. IV, 3, 27. *think that the —est gods have preserved thee,* Lr. IV, 6, 73 (opposed to 'some fiend').

7) spotless, irreproachable: *in his c. bed might have reposed still,* Lucr. 382. *I cannot project mine own cause so well to make it c.* Ant. V, 2, 122. *lest my life be cropped to keep you c.* Per. I, 1, 141. Hence = pure, innocent: *a c. life ensuing,* Tp. III, 3, 82. *if you know yourself c., I am glad of it,* Wiv. III, 3, 123. *your mind is the —er, and your vir-*

tues the fairer, Troil. II, 3, 163. *he should the sooner pay his debts and make a c. way to the gods,* Tim. III, 4, 77 (or = free, open, unencumbered?). *you cannot make gross sins look c.* III, 5, 38. *Duncan hath been so c. in his great office,* Mcb. I, 7, 18. *keep my bosom franchised and allegiance c.* II, 1, 28. *persever in that c. way thou goest,* Per. IV, 6, 113. Followed by *from: c. from this attaint of mine,* Lucr. 825. *my remembrance is c. from any image of offence,* Tw. III, 4, 249. *I am c. from treason to my sovereign,* H6B III, 1, 102. *I am c. from this misdeed of Edward's,* H6C III, 3, 183.

8) serene, cheerful: *you, the murderer, look as bright. as c., as yonder Venus,* Mids. III, 2, 60. *say that she frown; I'll say she looks as c. as morning roses newly washed with dew,* Shr. II, 173. *with a countenance as c. as friendship wears at feasts, keep with Bohemia,* Wint. I, 2, 343.

9) free, rid, off from: *the villanies of man will set him c.* Tim. III, 3, 31. (*a c. way,* III, 4, 77, = free, unencumbered?). *were I from Dunsinane away and c.* Mcb. V, 3, 61. Followed by *of: to get c. of all the debts I owe,* Merch. I, 1, 134. *let me be c. of thee,* Tw. IV, 1, 4. *they got c. of our ship,* Hml. IV, 6, 19.

Clear, adv. 1) bright; joined to *burn: my most full flame should afterwards burn —er,* Sonn. 115, 4. *burn, bonfires, c. and bright,* H6B V, 1, 3. *this candle burns not c.* H8 III, 2, 96.

2) plainly, manifestly, distinctly: *as c. as is the summer's sun ... all appear to hold in right and title of the female,* H5 I, 2, 86. (I see) *c. as day,* H6B II, 1, 107. *understand more c.* Troil. IV, 5, 165. *the sore eyes see c.* Per. I, 1, 99.

3) serenely: *only look up c.; to alter favour ever is to fear,* Mcb. I, 5, 72.

Clear, vb., 1) trans. a) to make bright, to cleanse: *the poisoned fountain —s itself again,* Lucr. 1707. *c. thy crystals,* H5 II, 3, 56. *that will c. your sight,* Err. III, 2, 57. *c. up that cloudy countenance,* Tit. I, 263. *the sun not yet thy sighs from heaven —s,* Rom. II, 3, 73 (= clears heaven from thy sighs).

b) to free from obscurity or ambiguity: *my letters shall c. that doubt,* Wint. IV, 4, 633. *till we can c. these ambiguities,* Rom. V, 3, 217. *all other doubts, by time let them be —ed,* Cymb. IV, 3, 45.

c) to bring to an issue, to settle an affair: *this wrestler shall c. all,* As I, 1, 178. *the violent carriage of it will c. or end the business,* Wint. III, 1, 18.

d) to free from any thing obnoxious: *see the coast —ed,* H6A I, 3, 89. *when he was poor, imprisoned, I —ed him with five talents,* Tim. II, 2, 235.

e) to pay, to cancel: *all debts are —ed between you and I,* Merch. III, 2, 321. *the imposition —ed hereditary ours,* Wint. I, 2, 74.*

f) to rid; followed by *of: and will by twos and threes at several posterns c. them o' the city,* Wint. I, 2, 439. *till the ship be —ed of the dead,* Per. III, 1, 49.

g) to justify, to absolve: *the blackest sin is —ed with absolution,* Lucr. 354. *to c. this spot by death,* 1053. *the body's stain her mind untainted —s,* 1710. *he in time may come to c. himself,* Meas. V, 150. *these lords can c. me in it,* Wint. II, 3, 143. *and thus far c. him,* H8 II, 4, 167. *I shall c. myself,* V, 3, 65. Followed by *from: to c. her from that suspicion,* Lucr. 1320. *why shall not I* (clear myself) *from this com-*

pelled stain? 1708. *thy father's charge shall c. thee from that stain*, H6A IV, 5, 42. *you will c. yourself from all suspect*, H6B III, 1, 140. — *s her from all blame*, Lr. II, 4, 147. — Followed by *of: let us be —ed of being tyrannous*, Wint. III, 2, 5. *a little water —s us of this deed*, Mcb. II, 2, 67.

2) intr. to become bright: *till heaven —s*, Sonn. 148, 12. *so foul a sky —s not without a storm*, John IV, 2, 108.

Clearly, 1) plainly, with clear discernment: *if she can make me know this c.* All's V, 3, 316. *you do not understand yourself so c.* Hml. I, 3, 96.

2) quite: *a most extracting frenzy of mine own from my remembrance c. banished his*, Tw. V, 289. *how much King John hath lost in this which he accounts so c. won*, John III, 4, 122.

3) stainlessly: *and wound our tottering colours c. up, last in the field, and almost lords of it,* John V, 5, 7.*

Clearness, 1) brightness, purity: *we make foul the c. of our deservings, when of ourselves we publish them*, All's I, 3, 6. Abstr. pro concr.: *and in the fountain shall we gaze so long till the fresh taste be taken from that c.*, Tit. III, 1, 128.

2) freedom from suspicion, spotlessness: *always thought that I require a c.* Mcb. III, 1, 133.

Clear-shining, bright: *in a pale c. day*, H6C II, 1, 28.

Clear-stories, only by conjecture in our texts in Tw. IV, 2, 41: *it hath bay windows transparent as barricadoes, and the c. towards the south north are as lustrous as ebony.* F1 has *cleer stores*, the other Ff *clear stones*, which may be right. *Clear-stories* are, according to some, upper rows of windows, as in halls and churches; according to others, windows without a transom or cross-piece in the middle of them. A word of uncertain meaning and, at any rate, unknown to Shakespeare.

Cleave, to stick, to hold to; followed by *to: my tongue c. to my roof*, R2 V, 3, 31. *thy son's blood —ing to my blade*, H6C I, 3, 50. Figuratively, a) to fit, to sit well on: *new honours, like our strange garments, c. not to their mould*, Mcb. I, 3, 145. b) to adhere closely, to stick to, to abide by: *thy thoughts I c. to*, Tp. IV, 165. *and c. to no revenge but Lucius,'* Tit. V, 2, 136. *if you shall c. to my consent, it shall make honour for you*, Mcb. II, 1, 25.

Cleave (Impf. *cleft*: Wint. III, 2, 197. H6C I, 1, 12. *clove*: Lr. I, 4, 175. Partic. *cleft*: Compl. 293. Gentl. V, 4, 103. Ado II, 1, 261. Tw. V, 230. H6B IV, 10, 13. Rom. II, 4, 16. Hml. III, 4, 156. *cloven* — always joined to a subst. —: Tp. I, 2, 277. II, 2, 13. LLL V, 2, 655. Troil. I, 2, 132. Cor. I, 4, 21).

1) trans. to split, to rive: *thy false dart mistakes that aim and —s an infant's heart*, Ven. 942. cf. Gentl. V, 4, 103. LLL IV, 1, 138. Rom. II, 4, 16. *to c. a heart in twain*, Meas. III, 1, 63. Wint. III, 2, 197. Hml. III, 4, 156. *have cleft his club to make fire*, Ado II, 1, 261. *an apple, cleft in two*, Tw. V, 230. *my brain-pan had been cleft*, H6B IV, 10, 13. H6C I, 1, 12. Tim. III, 4, 91. *when thou clovest thy crown in the middle*, Lr. I, 4, 175. *O cleft effect!* Compl. 293 (double, different). *and c. the general ear with horrid speech*, Hml. II, 2, 589 (= tear). *a cloven pine*, Tp. I, 2, 277. *cloven tongues*, II, 2, 13. *cloven lemon*, LLL V, 2, 655. *cloven chin*, Troil. I, 2, 132. *cloven army*, Cor. I, 4, 21.

2) intr. to part asunder, to crack: *unless our good city c. in the midst and perish*, Cor. III, 2, 28. *as if the world should c.* Ant. III, 4, 31. *O c., my sides!* IV, 14, 39.

Clef (O. Edd. *Cliff*) a key in music: *D sol re, one c., two notes have I*, Shr. III, 1, 77. *any man may sing her, if he can take her c.* Troil. V, 2, 11 (Ff *life*).

Clemency, disposition to treat with kindness: *stooping to your c.* Hml. III, 2, 160.

Clement, adj, disposed to kindness, mild: *you are more c. than vile man*, Cymb. V, 4, 18.

Clement, name: 1) —*'s inn*, H4B III, 2, 15. 223. 299. 331. 2) *C. Perkes*, V, 1, 42.

Cleomenes, name in Wint. II, 1, 184. II, 3, 195. III, 2, 126. V, 1, 112.

Cleon, name in Per. III, 1, 79. III, 3, 1 etc.

Cléopátra, the famous queen of Egypt: As III, 2, 154. Rom. II, 4, 44. Cymb. II, 4, 70. Ant. I, 1, 43 etc. etc.

Clepe, to call: *she —s him king of graves*, Ven. 995. *he —th a calf cauf*, LLL V, 1, 24. *are clept all by the name of dogs*, Mcb. III, 1, 94. *they c. us drunkards*, Hml. I, 4, 19. (In Mcb. and Hml. O. Edd. *clipt* and *clip*; cf. the quibble in LLL V, 2, 603).

Clergy, the body of ecclesiastics: H5 I, 1, 80. I, 2, 134. H6B I, 3, 131. H8 IV, 2, 44.

Clergyman, ecclesiastic: John IV, 2, 141. R2 III, 3, 28. IV, 324. R3 III, 7, 95.

Clerk, 1) scholar: *great —s have purposed to greet me with premeditated welcomes*, Mids. V, 93. *large gifts have I bestowed on learned —s*, H6B IV, 7, 76. *all the —s, I mean the learned ones*, H8 II, 2, 92. *deep —s she dumbs*, Per. V Prol. 5.

2) the reader of responses in church service: *and like unlettered c. still cry Amen*, Sonn. 85, 6. *answer, c.* Ado II, 1, 114. 115. *am I both priest and c.? well then, Amen*, R2 IV, 173. *take the priest, c., and some witnesses*, Shr. IV, 4, 94.

3) a subordinate officer employed as a writer: *c., draw a deed of gift*, Merch. IV, 1, 394. *the judge's c.* V, 143. 163. 181. 234. 237. 261. 281. 305. *the c. of Chatham*, H6B IV, 2, 92.

4) *St. Nicholas' —s* (= highwaymen) H4A II, 1, 68; cf. *Nicholas*.

Clerklike, scholar-like: *c. experienced*, Wint. I, 2, 392.

Clerkly, adj., learned: *thou art c.* Wiv. IV, 5, 58 (the host's speech).

Clerkly, adv. 1) with great penmanship: *'tis very c. done*, Gentl. II, 1, 115. — 2) scholarlike, adroitly: *hath he not twit our sovereign lady here with ignominious words, though c. couched*, H6B III, 1, 179.

Clew, see *Clue*.

Client, 1) one who applies to a lawyer or counsellor for advice in a question of law: Ven. 336. Lucr. 1020. Meas. I, 2, 110. Used adjectively: *windy attorneys to their c. woes*, R3 IV, 4, 127 (Ff. *clients*).

2) customer: *when she should do for —s her fitment, she has me her quirks*, Per. IV, 6, 6 (the bawd's speech).

Cliff, 1) a steep bank: Err. III, 2, 129. H6B III, 2, 101. Lr. IV, 1, 76. IV, 6, 67. Hml. 1, 4, 70.

2) = *Clef*, q. v.

Clifford, name; 1) the elder C.: H4B IV, 8, 20.

55. C. of Cumberland, V, 2, 1 etc. H6C I, 1, 7. 2) the younger: H6C I, 1, 55 etc. R3 I, 2, 159.

Clifton, name in H4A V, 4, 46. 58.*

Climate, subst. the condition of a place with respect to the temperature of the air: *it is the quality of the c.* Tp. II, 1, 200. *leave it to the favour of the c.* Wint. II, 3, 179. *the c. is delicate*, III, 1, 1. *is not their c. foggy, raw and dull*, H5 III, 5, 16. *though he in a fertile c. dwell*, Oth. I, 1, 70.

Hence = region, country: *that in a Christian c. souls refined should show …*, R2 IV, 130. *they are portentous things unto the c. that they point upon*, Caes. I, 3, 32. And almost = sky, heavens: *by this hand, that sways the earth this c. overlooks*, John II, 344.

Climate, vb., to reside in a country of a particular temperature: *the blessed gods purge all infection from our air whilst you do c. here*, Wint. V, 1, 170.

Climature, region: *unto our —s and countrymen*, Hml. I, 1, 125.

Climb (impf. and partic *climbed*), 1) intr. a) to creep up by little and little, and with effort: *c. o'er the house*, LLL I, 1, 109. H5 III Chor. 8. *bought his —ing very dear*, H6B II, 1, 100. 103. *—ed into his garden*, IV, 10, 8. *unto their nest*, H6C II, 2, 31. *unto crowns*, IV, 7, 62. Tit. II, 3, 242. *To c. up: —ed up to walls*, Caes. I, 1, 43. *you do c. up it now*, Lr. IV, 6, 2 (Qq *c. it up*).

b) to rise: *be it as the style shall give us cause to c. in the merriness*, LLL I, 1, 202. *—ing fire*, H6A IV, 2, 11. *man and birds are fain of —ing high*, H6B II, 1, 8. *that by a pace goes backward, with a purpose it hath to c.* Troil. I, 3, 129. *things at the worst will cease, or else c. upward to what they were before*, Mcb. IV, 2, 24. *down, thou —ing sorrow*, Lr. II, 4, 57. *let our crooked smokes c. to their nostrils*, Cymb. V, 5, 477.

2) trans. a) to ascend creepingly and with effort: *—ed the steep-up heavenly hill*, Sonn. 7, 5. *—ing trees*, LLL IV, 3, 341. As V, 2, 42. H6B II, 1, 98. IV, 10, 37. H8 I, 1, 131. Tit. I, 327. II, 1, 1. unto 2, 22. Rom. II, 2, 63. Oth. II, 1, 189. Cymb. III, 3, 47.

b) to reach creepingly and with effort: *to c. his wonted height*, Lucr. 775. *c. her window*, Gentl. II, 4, 181. II, 6, 34. *her chamber*, III, 1, 115. *c. a bird's nest*, Rom. II, 5, 76. *to c. his happiness*, Tim. I, 1, 76.

Climber-upward, one who climbs up: Caes. II, 1, 23. cf. *Canvas-climber*.

Clime, 1) climate: *pestilence hangs in our air, and thou art flying to a fresher c.* R2 I, 3, 285. *the north, where shivering cold and sickness pines the c.* V, 1, 77. *leaving their earthly parts to choke your c.* H5 IV, 3, 102.

2) region, country: *the best-regarded virgins of our c.* Merch. II, 1, 10. *back again unto my native c.* H6B II, 2, 84. *the fairest breeders of our c.* Tit. IV, 2, 68. *matches of her own c.* Oth. III, 3, 230. *to use one language in each several c. where our scenes seem to live*, Per. IV, 4, 6.

Cling, 1) intr. to adhere closely, to twine round: *how they clung in their embracement*, H8 I, 1, 9. *two spent swimmers, that do c. together and choke their art*, Mcb. I, 2, 8.

2) trans. to shrink or shrivel up: *upon the next tree shalt thou hang alive, till famine c. thee*, Mcb. V, 5, 40.

Clink, subst., sharp ringing sound: *I heard the c. and fall of swords*, Oth. II, 3, 234.

Clink, vb. to ring, to jingle: *a long lease for the —ing of pewter*, H4A II, 4, 51. *let me the canakin c.* Oth. II, 3, 71.

Clinquant, glittering, shining: *the French, all c., all in gold, like heathen gods*, H8 I, 1, 19.

Clip, 1) to cut with shears: *Judas Maccabaeus clipt is plain Judas*, LLL V, 2, 603. *this ornament … will I c. to form*, Per. V, 3, 74. Hence = to curtail, diminish: *nor more nor —ed, but so*, Lr. IV, 7, 6.

2) to embrace, surround: *to c. Elysium, and to lack her joy*, Ven. 600. *she —ed Adonis in her arms*, Pilgr. 148. 156. Wint. V, 2, 59. Cor. I, 6, 29. IV, 5, 115. Ant. IV, 8, 8. Cymb. V, 5, 451. *Neptune's arms who —eth thee about*, John V, 2, 34. *—ed in with the sea*, H4A III, 1, 44. *no grave shall c. in it a pair so famous*, Ant. V, 2, 362. *you elements that c. us round about*, Oth. III, 3, 464. *his meanest garment, that ever hath but —ed his body*, Cymb. II, 3, 139. Dubious passage: *who with their drowsy, slow and flagging wings c. dead men's graves*, H6B IV, 1, 6 (Ff. *cleap*).*

3) see *Clepe*.

Clipper, one who cuts off the edges of coin: *it is no English treason to cut French crowns, and to-morrow the king himself will be a c.* H5 IV, 1, 246.

Clip-winged, having curtailed wings: *a c. griffin*, H4A III, 1, 152.

Clitus, 1) the friend of Alexander: H5 IV, 7, 41. 48 (O. Edd. *Clytus*). 2) servant to Brutus: Caes. V, 5, 4 etc.

Cloak, subst., the outer garment with which the rest are covered: Sonn. 34, 2. Gentl. III, 1, 130. 131 etc. Wiv. I, 3, 18. Ado III, 3, 126. Shr. I, 1, 212. V, 1, 69. John IV, 3, 24. 155. H4B I, 2, 34. II, 4, 395. V, 1, 95. H5 IV, 1, 24. H6B II, 1, 109. 115. R3 II, 3, 32. H8 IV, 1, 73. Tim. II, 1, 15. III, 1, 14. Caes. I, 2, 215. II, 1, 74. Hml. I, 2, 77. Oth. II, 3, 99. Cade calls so the caparison of a horse: H6B IV, 7, 55. — Figuratively: *the c. of night*, Lucr. 801. R2 III, 2, 45. Rom. II, 2, 75.

Cloak, vb., to cover: *to c. offences with a cunning brow*, Lucr. 749.

Cloak-bag, portmanteau: Cymb. III, 4, 172. *that stuffed c. of guts*, H4A II, 4, 497.

Clock, subst. the instrument which tells the hour by a stroke upon a bell: *when I do count the c.* Sonn. 12, 1. 57, 6. *tell the c.* Tp. II, 1, 289. *the c. gives me my cue*, Wiv. III, 2, 46. Err. I, 2, 45. IV, 2, 54. LLL V, 2, 914. Merch. II, 6, 4. As III, 2, 319. All's I, 2, 39. Tw. III, 1, 141. R2 V, 5, 50. H4A I, 2, 8. V, 4, 152. H5 IV Chor. 15. H6A I, 2, 42. R3 V, 3, 276. Caes. II, 1, 192. Mcb. II, 1, 2. II, 4, 6. Cymb. III, 2, 75. V, 5, 153. *to weep 'twixt c. and c.* Cymb. III, 4, 44. *his Jack o' the c.* R2 V, 5, 60 (cf. *Jack*). *like a German c., still a repairing*, LLL III, 192 (clocks were a German invention, and their original machinery very cumbrous).

By four of the c. Meas. IV, 2, 124. *by five of the c.* Merch. II, 2, 123. *about three of the c.* H4B I, 2, 210. *'twill be two of the c.* V, 5, 3 (Q *two a c.*). *by eleven of the c.* Troil. III, 3, 297 (Ff. *eleven a c.*). *'Tis not yet ten o' the c.* Oth. II, 3, 14 (Qq *ten a c.*). *by four o' the c.* Cymb. II, 2, 6. *Four of c.* Merch. II, 4, 8 (Q1 *four a c.*) *eleven o' c.* Wiv. II, 2, 324.

Everywhere else O. Edd. have *a clock*, not *o' clock*:

it hath struck ten a c. Wiv. V, 2, 12. *'tis one a c.* V, 5, 78. Err. II, 1, 3. IV, 1, 10. Ado III, 4, 52. Merch. II, 6, 63. As II, 7, 22. IV, 3, 2. Shr. IV, 3, 189. Rom. IV, 4, 4. *What is't a c.?* As III, 2, 317. R3 III, 2, 4. V, 3, 47. Caes. II, 2, 114. II, 4, 22. *What's a c.?* Meas. II, 1, 290. H4A II, 1, 36. H6B II 4, 5. R3 IV, 2, 112. *By seven a c.* Gentl. III, 1, 126. As IV, 1, 185. *At five a c.* Err. I, 2, 26. Merch. II, 5, 25. *At* omitted: *let him be sent for to-morrow eight a c.* Wiv. III, 3, 210 (F2 *by eight a c.*). *provide your block and your axe to-morrow four a c.* Meas. IV, 2, 56. *what a c. to-morrow shall I send to thee?* Rom. II, 2, 168 (Q1 and M. Edd. *at what a c.*).

Dr. Caius asks: *vat is de c.?* Wiv. II, 3, 3.

Clock, vb., see *Cluck.*

Clock-setter, one who regulates the clock: *old time the c.* John III, 1, 324.

Clod, a lump of earth: *this sensible warm motion to become a kneaded c.* Meas. III, 1, 121. *to make an account of her life to a c. of wayward marl,* Ado II, 1, 65. *but a c. and module of confounded royalty,* John V, 7, 57.

Cloddy, consisting of clods, earthy: *(the sun) turning the meagre c. earth to glittering gold,* John III, 1, 80.

Clodpole (cf. *Clotpole*), blockhead: Tw. III, 4, 208.

Clog, subst., any thing hung upon an animal to hinder motion; encumbrance: *enfranchised with a c.* (like a dog) Ado I, 3, 35. *here comes my c.* All's II, 5, 58. *stealing away from his father with his c. at his heels,* Wint. IV, 4, 695. *with c. of conscience,* R2 V, 6, 20. *to hang —s on them,* Oth. I, 3, 198.

Clog, vb., to load with any thing that encumbers: *so much blood as will c. the foot of a flea,* Tw. III, 2, 66. *the —ing burthen of a guilty soul,* R2 I, 3, 200. *—s me with this answer,* Mcb. III, 6, 43. *traitors ensteeped to c. the guiltless keel,* Oth. II, 1, 70 (Ff *enclog*).

Cloister, subst., monastery: Compl. 249. Gentl. I, 3, 2. Meas. I, 2, 182. Mids. I, 1, 71. All's IV, 3, 280.

Cloister, vb., to confine in a monastery: *and c. thee in some religious house,* R2 V, 1, 23. = to shut up: *and therefore still in night would —ed be,* Lucr. 1085.

Cloistered, adj., concerning cloisters, confined to the precincts of a cloister: *ere the bat hath flown his c. flight,* Mcb. III, 2, 41.

Cloistress, a nun: Tw. I, 1, 28.

Close, subst. 1) enclosure: *a tree, which grows here in my c.* Tim. V, 1, 208.

2) conclusion, end: *the setting sun, and music at the c.* R2 II, 1, 12.*

3) union: *attested by the holy c. of lips,* Tw. V, 4, 161. *let me be blest to make this happy c.* Gentl. V, 4, 117. *keep in one consent, congreeing in a full and natural c., like music,* H5 I, 2, 182.

4) hostile meeting, grapple, fighting hand to hand: *meet in the intestine shock and furious c. of civil butchery,* H4A I, 1, 13.

Close, adj., 1) shut fast, so as to have no opening, tight: *the curtains being c.* Lucr. 367. *c. prison,* Gentl. III, 1, 235. *near to her c. and consecrated bower,* Mids. III, 2, 7. *for all the sun sees or the c. earth wombs,* Wint. IV, 4, 501. *in this c. walk,*

H6B II, 2, 3. *spread thy c. curtain, love-performing night,* Rom. III, 2, 5. cf. *the c. night doth play the runaway,* Merch. II, 6, 47. *c. prisoner,* Oth. V, 2, 335 (kept in c. prison). *keep the door c.* H8 V, 4, 30. *hold c. thy lips,* H6C II, 2, 118. *hold your hand more c.* Tim. II, 2, 148 (cf. *Close* adv.).

2) secret: *this is c. dealing,* H6B II, 4, 73. *another secret c. intent,* R3 I, 1, 158. *a c. exploit of death,* IV, 2, 35. *your c. fire,* Tim. IV, 3, 142. *this must be known; which being kept c. ...* Hml. II, 1, 118. Subjectively: *show your wisdom in your c. patience,* Meas. IV, 3, 123. *that c. aspect of his,* John IV, 2, 72. *no lady —r,* H4A II, 3, 113. *the c. enacts and counsels of the heart,* Tit. IV, 2, 118. *to himself so secret and so c.* Rom. I, 1, 155. *the c. contriver of all harms,* Mcb. III, 5, 7. *c. delations,* Oth. III, 3, 123. *still c. as sure,* Cymb. I, 6, 139. *c. villain,* III, 5, 86.

Close, adv. 1) in strict confinement: *I will take order for her keeping c.* R3 IV, 2, 53. *the son of Clarence have I pent up c.* IV, 3, 36. *let them be clapped up c.* H6B I, 4, 53. *keep c. within your chamber,* Hml. IV, 7, 130. Cymb. III, 5, 46. *c. pent-up guilts,* Lr. III, 2, 57.

Hence, *to keep c.* = to keep, to guard carefully, to save economically: *what there is else, keep c.; we'll read it at more advantage,* H4A II, 4, 593. *keep it c.* Wint. III, 3, 128. *let housewifery appear: keep c.* H5 II, 3, 65 (Pistol's speech). Perhaps quibbling: *fire that's —st kept, burns most of all,* Gentl. I, 2, 30.

2) so as not to stir, still, pent up, as it were, in one's self: *the English, in the suburbs c. intrenched,* H6A I, 4, 9 (cf. Gentl. I, 2, 30). Especially, when joined to *stand: stand thee c. under this penthouse,* Ado III, 3, 110. *stand c.* Mids. III, 2, 41. H4A II, 2, 3. 79. 103. H6B I, 3, 1. *stand you thus c. to steal the bishop's deer?* H6C IV, 5, 17. *let's stand c. and behold him,* H8 II, 1, 55. *stand c., the queen is coming,* IV, 1, 36. Caes. I, 3, 131. Mcb. V, 1, 24. Ant. IV, 9, 6. *you great fellow, stand c. up,* H8 V, 4, 92 (i. e. stand upon your feet and do not stir, do not throw your arms about). Absolutely: *c., in the name of jesting,* Tw. II, 5, 23 (= keep still, do not betray yourselves by any noise or motion).

3) secretly: *an onion, which in a napkin being c. conveyed,* Shr. Ind. I, 127 (cf. Lr. III, 2, 57).

4) very near, in contact: *c. by,* Tp. I, 2, 216. *c. by the Thames side,* Wiv. III, 3, 16. *c. by the ground,* Ado III, 1, 25. *to lie c. by his honest bones,* Wint. IV, 4, 467. *c. by the battle,* Cymb. V, 3, 14. *c. at the heels,* Gentl. III, 1, 325. *lay thine ear c. to the ground,* H4A II, 2, 34. Rom. V, 3, 4. *now sit we c. about this taper,* Caes. IV, 3, 164. *thou visible god, that solderest c. impossibilities,* Tim. IV, 3, 388. *to follow c.* Meas. I, 4, 67. H4A II, 4, 241. Rom. III, 1, 40. Hml. IV, 5, 74. *wait c.* H4B I, 2, 65. *c. fighting,* Rom. I, 1, 114. *fight —r, or you'll catch a blow,* H6C III, 2, 23.

Hence = so as to shut entirely: *stop c. their mouths,* Tit. V, 2, 165. *to seel her father's eyes up c. as oak,* Oth. III, 3, 210. *draw the curtain c.* H6B III, 3, 32. H8 V, 2, 34.

Close, vb., I) trans. 1) to shut; used of eyes only: Ven. 1127. LLL V, 2, 90. All's V, 3, 118. H6A III, 3, 48. H6C I, 3, 11. II, 3, 31. Lr. IV, 4, 15. *To c. up,* likewise of eyes: Lucr. 163. LLL V, 2, 825. H6B III, 2, 395. III, 3, 32. R3 I, 3, 225. Tit. III, 1, 263.

To c. up = to shut up, to fill up: *my banquet is to c. our stomachs up,* Shr. V, 2, 9. *c. the wall up with our English dead,* H5 III, 1, 2. *with busy hammers* —*ing rivets up,* IV Chor. 13. *to c. the day up, Hector's life is done,* Troil. V, 8, 8.

2) to join: *c. your hands, and your lips too,* John II, 533. *do thou but c. our hands with holy words,* Rom. II, 6, 6.

3) to enclose: *some purer chest to c. so pure a mind,* Lucr. 761. *my father and Lavinia shall be* —*d in our household's monument,* Tit. V, 3, 194. *a despised life* —*d in my breast,* Rom. I, 4, 110. —*d in a dead man's tomb,* V, 2, 30. *the gift which bounteous nature hath in him* —*d,* Mcb. III, 1, 99. *To c. in,* in the same sense: *whilst this muddy vesture of decay doth grossly c. it in,* Merch. V, 65. *c. in pollution,* Tw. I, 2, 49. — *To c. up: that this my body might in the ground be* —*d up in rest,* H6C II, 1, 76.

II) intr. 1) to be shut: *these eyes shall never c.* H6C I, 1, 24. *downy windows, c.* Ant. V, 2, 319. *the marble pavement* —*s,* Cymb. V, 4, 120.

2) to join: *many lines c. in the dial's centre,* H5 I, 2, 210. *she* (the scotched snake) *will c. and be herself,* Mcb. III, 2, 14.

3) to join in fight, to grapple, to fight hand to hand: *in the* —*ing of some glorious day,* H4A III, 2, 133. *if I can c. with him, I care not for his thrust,* H4B II, 1, 20.

4) to come to an agreement: *after they* —*d in earnest, they parted very fairly in jest,* Gentl. II, 5, 13 (quibbling). *an 'twere dark, you'ld c. sooner,* Troil. III, 2, 51. Followed by *with: c. with him, give him gold,* Wint. IV, 4, 830. *better than to c. in terms of friendship with thine enemies,* Caes. III, 1, 202. *he* —*s with you in this consequence,* Hml. II, 1, 45. Hence = to humour, to tamper with: *wrong this virtuous gentlewoman to c. with us,* H4B II, 4, 354. *this* —*ing with him fits his lunacy,* Tit. V, 2, 70. And absolutely, in the same sense: *how the villain would c. now, after his treasonable abuses,* Meas. V, 346 (= make his peace, make reparation. Blundering M. Edd. *gloze*).

Closely, 1) nearly, with little space intervening: *follow Fluellen c. at the heels,* H5 IV, 7, 179.

2) in narrow confinement: *mewed up c.* Shr. I, 1, 188. R3 I, 1, 38.

3) secretly, under hand, so as not to be seen: *I have been c. shrouded in this bush,* LLL IV, 3, 137. *c. to conceal what we impart,* H4 I, 1, 159. *go c. in with me,* John IV, 1, 133. *meaning to keep her c. at my cell,* Rom. V, 3, 255. *we have c. sent for Hamlet hither,* Hml. III, 1, 29 (i. e. in such a manner that he shall not be aware of our intention).

Closeness, recluseness: *all dedicated to c. and the bettering of my mind,* Tp. I, 2, 90.

Close-stool, the chief utensil of a privy: LLL V, 2, 580. All's V, 2, 18.

Closet, 1) any room for privacy: Wiv. I, 4, 39. 66. 70. John IV, 2, 267. H5 V, 2, 211. H6B II, 4, 24. R3 II, 1, 133. Tit. III, 2, 82. Rom. IV, 2, 33. Caes. II, 1, 35. Hml. II, 1, 77 (Ff *chamber*). III, 2, 344. III, 3, 27. IV, 1, 35. Lr. I, 2, 65. Cymb. I, 5, 84. Per. III, 2, 81. Tropically: *my mind ... still pure doth in her poisoned c. yet endure,* Lucr. 1659. *my heart ... a c. never pierced with crystal eyes,* Sonn. 46, 6.

2) a repositary in the side of a room: *I found it in his c.; 'tis his will,* Caes. III, 2, 134. *unlock her c., take forth paper,* Mcb. V, 1, 6. *I have locked the letter in my c.* Lr. III, 3, 12. *a c. lock and key of villanous secrets,* Oth. IV, 2, 22.

Close-tongued, keeping silence, not communicative: *c. treason,* Lucr. 770.

Closet-war, war carried on not with arms, but with feats performed in the closet: Troil. I, 3, 205.

Closure, 1) enclosure: *into the quiet c. of my breast,* Ven. 782. Sonn. 48, 11. *within the guilty c. of thy walls,* R3 III, 3, 11.

2) conclusion, end: *on the ragged stones beat forth our brains, and make a mutual c. of our house,* Tit. V, 3, 134.

Cloten, name in Cymb. III, 4, 136 etc.

Cloth, 1) any thing woven for dress or covering: *c. of gold,* Ado III, 4, 19. Ant. II, 2, 204. *scanting a little c.* H5 II, 4, 48. *c. of any colour,* Cor. III, 1, 253. *a livery, a squire's c.* Cymb. II, 3, 128. *the c. of honour* (= the canopy) H8 IV, 1, 48. *shrouded in c. of state,* Per. III, 2, 65. *Painted c.* (i. e. a species of hangings for rooms, made of canvas painted in oil, with various devices and mottos): Lucr. 245. LLL V, 2, 579. As III, 2, 291. H4A IV, 2, 28. *painted cloths,* Troil. V, 10, 47.

2) handkerchief: *this c. thou dippedst in blood of my sweet boy,* H6C I, 4, 157. *bloody c., I'll keep thee,* Cymb. V, 1, 1. *the fire and cloths,* Per. III, 2, 87.

3) Plur. *clothes,* a) dress: Meas. V, 264. Shr. I, 1, 129. III, 2, 115. 119. All's II, 5, 48. IV, 1, 57. V, 2, 4. Tw. I, 3, 11. Wint. V, 2, 141. H8 I, 3, 14. Cor. IV, 5, 157. Rom. IV, 5, 12. Tim. II, 2, 114. Hml. IV, 5, 52. IV, 7, 176. Lr. IV, 6, 168. Oth IV, 1, 96 (Ff *cloth*). Cymb. III, 5, 147. IV, 2, 81. Per. IV, 2, 52.

b) linen: *take up these clothes,* Wiv. III, 3, 155. *foul c.* III, 5, 101. 108. 115. IV, 2, 126. 145. 148. *conveyed to bed, wrapped in sweet c.* Shr. Ind. 1, 38. *lay more c. on his feet,* H5 II, 3, 24 (cf. *Bedclothes*). *Swathing clothes* = wrappers for an infant: H4A III, 2, 112. Cymb. I, 1, 59.

Clothair, French king of the Merovingian dynasty: H5 I, 2, 67.

Clotharius, the same: H8 I, 3, 10.

Clothe, to cover with dress: *to c. a back,* Meas. III, 2, 23. *to feed and c. thee,* Hml. III, 2, 64. *to c. you as becomes you,* Shr. IV, 2, 120. —*d like a bride,* Per. I, 1, 6. Followed by *in: began to c. his wit in state and pride,* Lucr. 1809. —*ing me in these grave ornaments,* H6A V, 1, 54. *c. me in a forced content,* Oth. III, 4, 120 (cf. *Dress*). *in steel,* Per. II, 1, 160. Followed by *with: to c. mine age with angel-like perfection,* Gentl. II, 4, 66. *I c. my naked villany with old odd ends,* R3 I, 3, 336. Absolutely: *care no more to c. and eat,* Cymb. IV, 2, 266 (= to wear or provide clothes).

Clothier, a maker of cloth: H6B IV, 2, 5. H8 I, 2, 31. *draw me a* —*'s yard,* Lr. IV, 6, 88 ('an arrow the length of a clothier's yard.' Dyce).

Clotpole or **Clotpoll** (cf. *Clodpole*), blockhead: *I will see you hanged like* —*s,* Troil. II, 1, 128 (why are clotpoles hanged?). *call the c. back,* Lr. I, 4, 51. Denoting, in its original sense, the head: *I have sent Cloten's c. down the stream,* Cymb. IV, 2, 184.

Cloud, subst., visible collection of vapours

in the upper air; properly and figuratively: Ven.533. 820. 972. Lucr. 371. 547. 777. 1727. Sonn. 28, 10. 33, 5. 34, 3. Tp. I, 2, 192. II, 2, 20. III, 2, 150. IV, 93. Gentl. I, 3, 87. LLL V, 2, 204. 758. Mids. III, 2, 379. IV, 1, 193. John II, 252. R2 III, 1, 20. H4B IV, 5, 99. H5 III, 3, 31. 40. H6B II, 1, 15. II, 4, 1. R3 I, 3, 196. II, 3, 32. H8 V, 5, 45. Rom. I, 1, 139. III, 1, 122. III, 5, 198. Tim. III, 4, 42. Hml. IV, 5, 89. Ant. IV, 14, 2 etc. *Will Caesar weep? he has a c. in's face. He were the worse for that, were he a horse,* Ant. III, 2, 51 (a dark spot between the eyes of a horse, which was regarded as a blemish, was called *a cloud*).

Cloud, vb., 1) trans. to overspread with clouds, to darken: Lucr. 1007. LLL V, 2, 203. R2 III, 2, 68. H6C II, 3, 7. IV, 1, 74. Per. I, 1, 74. *to hear my sovereign mistress —ed so,* Wint. I, 2, 280 (= darkened, stained).

2) intr. to become dark with clouds: *had not his* (eyes) *—ed with his brow's repine,* Ven. 490. *the scene begins to c.* LLL V, 2, 731.

Cloud-capped, having a summit rising to the clouds: *c. towers,* Tp. IV, 152.

Cloud-eclipsed, darkened by clouds: *why her two suns were c. so,* Lucr. 1224.

Cloud-kissing, rising to the clouds: *c. Ilion,* Lucr. 1370.

Cloudiness, the state of being overcast with clouds: Ado V, 4, 42.

Cloudy, overcast with clouds; properly and figuratively: *so do thy lips make modest Dian c. and forlorn,* Ven. 725. *no c. show of stormy weather,* Lucr. 115. *c. Lucrece,* 1084. *c. looks,* Pilgr. 312. *when you are c.* Tp. II, 1, 142. *the c. cheeks of heaven,* R2 III, 3, 57. *c. men,* H4A III, 2, 83. *c. brow,* H6B III, 1, 155. *death,* H6C II, 6, 62. *wrath,* R3 I, 3, 268. *princes,* II, 2, 112. Tit. I, 263. II, 3, 33. Rom. III, 2, 4. Mcb. III, 6, 41. Per. III, 1, 46 (*c. billow*).

Clout, 1) piece of cloth or linen: *or madly think a babe of —s were he,* John III, 4, 58. *gavest the duke a c. steeped in …* R3 I, 3, 177. *she looks as pale as any c.* Rom. II, 4, 218. *a c. upon that head where late the diadem stood,* Hml. II, 2, 529. *with —s about their heads,* Ant. IV, 7, 6 (or is it here = a cuff? (cf. *Swathing-clouts* and *Dishclout*).

2) the marked centre of the butts: *he'll ne'er hit the c.* LLL IV, 1, 136. *clapped i' the c.* H4B III, 2, 51. *i' the c.!* Lr IV, 6, 92.

Clouted, fortified with nails, or, according to others, patched: *spare not but such as go in c. shoon,* H6B IV, 2, 195. *and put my c. brogues from off my feet, whose rudeness answered my steps too loud,* Cymb. IV, 2, 214.

Clove, an aromatic spice, the flower-bud of the clove-tree: LLL V, 2, 654.

Clover, the plant trifolium: H5 V, 2, 49.

Clowder, name of a dog: Shr. Ind. I, 18.

Clown, 1) a rustic, churl: *a swain! a most simple c.!* LLL IV, 1, 142. *the c. bore it, the fool sent it,* IV, 3, 17. 18. As II, 4, 66. V, 1, 12. 52. 56. Wint. IV, 4, 616. H6B IV, 10, 60.

2) buffoon, jester: As II, 2, 8. Hml. II, 2, 336. III, 2, 43 (= fool, 49).

Clownish, funny, full of jokes: *if we assay'd to steal the c. fool out of your father's court,* As I, 3, 132.

Cloy, vb., 1) to satiate, to glut, to surfeit: *and yet not c. thy lips with loathed satiety,* Ven. 19. *—ed with much, he pineth still for more,* Lucr. 98. *c. the hungry edge of appetite,* R2 I, 3, 296. H4B V, 5, 143. H5 II, 2, 9. H6A II, 5, 105. R3 IV, 4, 62. Tit. III, 2, 55. Ant. II, 2, 241. Cymb. I, 6, 47. IV, 4, 19.

2) to stroke with a claw: *his royal bird prunes the immortal wing and —s his beak,* Cymb. V, 4, 118.

Cloyless, preventing satiety: *with c. sauce,* Ant. II, 1, 25.

Cloyment, surfeit: Tw. II, 4, 102.

Club, a heavy stick: *Hercules' c.* Ado II, 1, 262. III, 3, 147. LLL I, 2, 182. V, 1, 139. V, 2, 593. Ant. IV, 12, 46. *a Grecian c.* As IV, 1, 98. *bats and —s* Cor. I, 1, 57. 165. Rom. IV, 3, 54. — In any public affray, the cry was *Clubs! Clubs!* by way of calling for persons with clubs to part the combatants (Nares): As V, 2, 44. H6A I, 3, 84. H8 V, 4, 53. Tit. II, 1, 37. Rom. I, 1, 80.

Cluck, vb. to call with the voice of a hen conducting her chickens: *when she, poor hen, hath —ed thee to the wars,* Cor. V, 3, 163 (O. Edd. *clock'd,* which may have been Sh.'s orthography).

Clue or **Clew,** a ball of thread: *you have wound a goodly c.* All's I, 3, 188.

Cluster, subst. a number (properly of bees) gathered into a close body; swarm, crowd: *gave way unto your —s,* Cor. IV, 6, 122. *here come the —s,* 128.

Cluster, vb., to grow in bunches: *—ing filberts,* Tp. II, 2, 175. *vines with —ing bunches,* IV, 112. Used of a throng: *to start into the —ing battle of the French,* H6A IV, 7, 13.

Clutch, subst., clenched fist, grasping hand: *hath clawed me in his c.* Hml. V, 1, 80 (the clown's song).

Clutch, vb. 1) to clench: *putting the hand in the pocket and extracting it —ed,* Meas. III, 2, 50. *not that I have the power to c. my hand, when his fair angels would salute my palm,* John II, 589.

2) to grasp: *in thy hands —ed as many millions,* Cor. III, 3, 71.*come, let me c. thee,* Mcb. II, 1, 34.

Clyster-pipe, a tube used for injections: Oth. II, 1, 178.

Clytus, see *Clitus.*

Cneius: *C. Pompey,* Ant. III, 13, 118.

Coach, a close carriage: Wiv. II, 2, 66. LLL IV, 3, 34. 155. Merch. III, 4, 82. Tit. II, 1, 7. Hml. IV, 5, 71.

Coach-fellow, a horse drawing in the same carriage with another: *you and your c. Nym,* Wiv. II, 2, 7.

Coach-maker, one whose occupation is to make coaches: Rom. I, 4, 69.

Coact, to act together, to play together as on a stage: *but if I tell how these two did c., shall I not lie in publishing a truth?* Troil. V, 2, 118.

Coactive, acting in concurrence: *with what's unreal thou* (affection) *c. art,* Wint. I, 2, 141.

Coagulate, congealed, curdled: *c. gore,* Hml. II, 2, 484.

Coal, the residue of burned wood, ignited or charred: Ven. 35. 338. 387. Lucr. 47. 1379. Merch. III, 5, 28. Wint. V, 1, 68. John IV, 1, 109.

V, 2, 83. H5 III, 6, 110. H6B V, 2, 36. H6C II, 1, 83. H8 II, 4, 79. 94. Troil. II, 3, 206. Cor. I, 1, 177. IV, 6, 137. V, 1, 17. Per. III Prol. 5. *To carry —s* = to pocket insults: H5 III, 2, 50. Rom. I, 1, 2.

Coal-black, black as a coal: Ven. 533. Lucr. 1009. R2 V, 1, 49. H6B II, 1, 112. H6C V, 1, 54. Tit. III, 2, 78. IV, 2, 99. V, 1, 32.

Coarse, unrefined, base: *of what c. metal ye are moulded,* H8 III, 2, 239.

Coarsely, basely, rudely: *there is a gentleman that serves the count reports but c. of her,* All's III, 5, 60.

Coast, subst., the sea-shore: LLL V, 2, 557. Merch. I, 1, 168. Wint. IV, 4, 280. R2 III, 3, 4. H6A I, 3, 89 (*see the c. cleared;* proverbial phrase). H6B I, 2, 93. III, 2, 113. IV, 8, 52. H6C III, 3, 205. V, 3, 8. R3 IV, 4, 433. Cymb. III, 1, 26. IV, 2, 205. IV, 3, 25. V, 4, 96. Per. II Prol. 34. II, 1, 60. III, 1, 73. V Prol. 15. V, 3, 19.

Coast, vb., to steer, to sail not by the direct way, but in sight of the coast, and as it were gropingly: *anon she hears them chant it lustily, and all in haste she —eth to the cry,* Ven. 870. *and, —ing homeward, came to Ephesus,* Err. I, 1, 135. *the king in this perceives him, how he —s and hedges his own way,* H8 III, 2, 38. *these encounterers that give a —ing welcome ere it comes,* Troil. IV, 5, 59 (i. e. who make the first step to meet the hesitating approach of a suitor). Some M. Edd. *accosting.**

Coat, 1) the upper garment: Meas. IV, 2, 204. Ado III, 2, 7. Mids. II, 1, 11. II, 2, 5. As I, 3, 16*(used of a female garment). II, 1, 37. II, 7, 43. Shr. IV, 1, 135. IV, 3, 55. Wint. I, 2, 157. IV, 3, 71. R2 I, 4, 61. H4B III, 2, 311. H5 II, 4, 38. 47. IV Prol. 26. IV, 3, 118. H8 Prol. 16. III, 2, 276. Oth. V, 1, 25. *an herald's c.* (= a tabard) H4A IV, 2, 49. *blue coats* (the dress of common servingmen): Shr. IV, 1, 94. H6A I, 3, 47. *tawny —s* (the dress of the retainers of an ecclesiastical dignitary): H6A I, 3, 47. 56. III, 1, 74. *c.* = the vesture as indicative of rank: *she was sought by spirits of richest c.* Compl. 236. — Proverbial expressions: *there's a hole made in your best c.* Wiv. III, 4, 144. *if I find a hole in his c.* H5 III, 6, 89. *I would not be in some of your —s,* Tw. IV, 1, 33. *when they have lined their —s,* Oth. I, 1, 53.

2) armour: R2 I, 3, 75. H4A IV, 1, 100. V, 3, 25. H6A I, 1, 85. H6B IV, 2, 65. H6C II, 1, 160. Per. II, 1, 142.

3) coat of arms: Lucr. 205. Wiv. I, 1, 17. 18. 20. 29 (quibbling). V, 5, 67. R2 III, 1, 24. H6A I, 1, 81. I, 5, 28. *—s in heraldry,* Mids. III, 2, 213. *thou shalt wear it* (the blood) *as a herald's c.* H6B IV, 10, 75.

Cobble, to mend, to botch (shoes): Cor. I, 1, 200. Caes. I, 1, 22.

Cobbler, mender of shoes: Caes. I, 1, 11. 23.*

Cobham: 1) *Rainold Lord C.,* R2 II, 1, 279. 2) *Eleanor C.,* H6B II, 3, 1. 3) *Lord C.,* H6C I, 2, 40. 56.

Cobloaf, a crusty uneven loaf ('with a round top to it'. Halliwell): Troil. II, 1, 41.

Cobweb, 1) the net of a spider: Merch. III, 2, 123. Shr. IV, 1, 48.

2) name of a fairy: Mids. III, 1, 165. 184. 186. IV, 1, 8. 10.

Cock, 1) the male of the hen: Pilgr. 338. Tp. II, 1, 30. Gentl. II, 1, 28. Shr. II, 227. H5 IV Chor. 15. R3 V, 3, 209. Hml. I, 1, 147. 150. 157. I,

2, 218. Ant. II, 3, 36. Cymb. II, 1, 24. 25. 26. *ere the first c. crow,* Mids. II, 1, 267. H4A II, 1, 20. Lr. III, 4, 121. *the second c.* Rom. IV, 4, 3. Mcb. II, 3, 27. — Figuratively: As II, 7, 90.

2) the male of other birds: *the ousel c.* Mids. III, 1, 128. *I have no pheasant, c. nor hen,* Wint. IV, 4, 770. = woodcock, Wint. IV, 3, 36.

3) the weathercock: Lr. III, 2, 3.

4) the part of the lock of a gun which strikes fire: *Pistol's c. is up,* H5 II, 1, 55.

5) a spout to let out liquor: *I have retired me to a wasteful c., and set mine eyes at flow,* Tim. II, 2, 171 (the eyes shedding tears being themselves the wasteful cock).*

6) cockboat: *yond tall anchoring bark diminished to her c.* Lr. IV, 6, 19.

Cock, a corruption or rather disguise of the name of God: *by C.* Hml. IV, 5, 61. *—'s passion,* Shr. IV, 1, 121 (cf. *Cox*). *by c. and pie,* Wiv. I, 1, 316. H4B V, 1, 1.

Cock-a-diddle-dow, imitation of the crowing of cocks: Tp. I, 2, 386.

Cock-a-hoop: *you will set c.! you'll be the man!* Rom. I, 5, 83; evidently = you will pick a quarrel, you will play the bully; perhaps with allusion to the custom of making cocks fight within a broad hoop, to prevent their quitting each other; cf. *Inhooped.* (Coles: *To be cock-a-hoop,* Ampullari, insolesco, cristas erigere). Not hyphened in O. Edd., at least not in F1.*

Cockatrice (or *Basilisk,* q. v.) an imaginary creature, supposed to be produced from a cock's egg and to have so deadly an eye as to kill by its very look: Lucr. 540 (Gen. —'). Tw. III, 4, 215. R3 IV, 1, 55. Rom. III, 2, 47.

Cocker, to pamper: *a beardless boy, a —ed silken wanton,* John V, 1, 70.

Cockerel, a young cock: Tp. II, 1, 31. Rom. I, 3, 53.

Cockle, an obnoxious weed, supposed by some to be the Agrostemma githago of Linnaeus, by others the Lolium temulentum or darnel: *sowed c. reaped no corn,* LLL IV, 3, 383. *the c. of rebellion, which we ourselves have ploughed for, sowed and scattered,* Cor. III, 1, 70.

Cockle, a muscle-shell: *'tis a c. or a walnut-shell,* Shr. IV, 3, 66. *sail seas in —s,* Per. IV, 4, 2. *his c. hat and staff,* Hml. IV, 5, 25 (the badge of pilgrims bound for places of devotion beyond sea).

Cockled, enclosed in a shell: *the tender horns of c. snails,* LLL IV, 3, 338.

Cockney, as it seems, a person who knows only the life and manners of the town, and is consequently well acquainted with affected phrases, but a stranger to what every child else knows: *this great lubber, the world, will prove a c.* Tw. IV, 1, 15. *cry to it, as the c. did to the eels when she put 'em i' the paste alive,* Lr. II, 4, 123.*

Cock-pigeon, male pigeon: As IV, 1, 151.

Cockpit, an area where cocks fight, and hence the pit in theatres: H5 Prol. 11.

Cockrel, see *Cockerel.*

Cockshut time, the time when the cockshut, that is a large net employed to catch wood-cocks, used to be spread; or the time when cocks and hens go to roost; the evening twilight: R3 V, 3, 70.*

Cock-sure, quite secure: H4A II, 1, 95.

Cocytus (O. Edd. *Ocitus*), a river in the Tartarus of the ancients: Tit. II, 3, 236.

Cod, 1) the codfish: *she that in wisdom never was so frail to change the —'s head for the salmon's tail,* Oth. II, 1, 156.

2) a husk containing the seeds of a plant: *I remember the wooing of a peascod instead of her, from whom I took two —s and, giving her them again, said with weeping tears 'Wear these for my sake.'* As II, 4, 53 (= peas? Evidently a quibble is intended, —s signifying also the testicles).

Codding, lecherous, lustful: *that c. spirit had they from their mother,* Tit. V, 1, 99.

Codling, an unripe apple: *or a c. when 'tis almost an apple,* Tw. 1, 5, 167.

Codpiece, a part of the male dress, very indelicately conspicuous in the poet's time: Gentl. II, 7, 53. Meas. III, 2, 122. Ado III, 3, 146. LLL III, 186. Lr. III, 2, 27. 40. Serving to stick pins on: Gentl. II, 7, 56; or to carry the purse in: Wint. IV, 4, 623.

Co-equal, of the same rank, equal: *he'll make his cap c. with the crown,* H6A V, 1, 33.

Cœur-de-lion (O. Edd. *Cordelion*), the Lionhearted, surname of Richard I: John I, 54. 85. 136. 253. II, 12. H6A III, 2, 83.

Coffe, writing of O. Edd. for *cough* in Mids. II, 1, 54 (cf. *Loffe*).

Coffer, subst., 1) a chest of money: Wiv. II, 2, 286. 306. III, 3, 225. IV, 2, 62. Meas. I, 2, 155. Merch. IV, 1, 354. Shr. II, 352. R2 I, 4, 43. 61. H4A I, 3, 85. H4B I, 3, 74. H5 I, 1, 18. II, 2, 168. Tim. I, 2, 199. Caes. III, 2, 94. Cymb. I, 6, 123.

2) a chest or trunk for other uses: H6A I, 6, 25 (*the rich-jewelled c. of Darius*). Oth. II, 1, 210. Per. III, 4, 2 (III, 1, 68 O. Edd. *coffin*).

3) treasure, ready money: *hold, there's half my c.* Tw. III, 4, 381.

Coffer, vb., to lay up in a coffer: *the aged man that —s up his gold,* Lucr. 855.

Coffer-lid, cover; used of the eyelids: *the —s that close his eyes,* Ven. 1127.

Coffin, subst. 1) the chest in which a dead body is buried: Merch. III, 1, 94. Tw. II, 4, 61. R2 V, 6, 30. H6A I, 1, 19. H6C I, 3, 28. R3 I, 2, 38. Tit. I, 35. Caes. III, 2, 111. Per. III, 2, 52. 69. V, 3, 23.

2) the crust of a paste: *and of the paste a c. will I rear and make two pasties of your shameful heads,* Tit. V, 2, 189 (cf. *Custard-coffin*).

Coffined, enclosed in a coffin: Cor. II, 1, 193. Per. III, 1, 61.

Cog, vb. intr., to cheat, to deceive, especially by smooth lies: *this scurvy, —ing companion,* Wiv. III, 1, 123. *I cannot c., I cannot prate,* III, 3, 50. *I cannot c. and say thou art this and that,* 76. *lie and c. and flout,* Ado V, 1, 95. *since you can c., I'll play no more with you,* LLL V, 2, 235. *smooth, deceive and c.* R3 I, 3, 48. *you —ing Greeks,* Troil. V, 6, 11. *you hear him c., see him dissemble,* Tim. V, 1, 98. *some —ing, cozening slave,* Oth. IV, 2, 132. Followed by an accus. indicating the result: *c. their hearts from them,* Cor. III, 2, 133.

Cogitation, thought: *c. resides not in that man that does not think,* Wint. I, 2, 271. *thoughts of great value, worthy —s,* Caes. I, 2, 50.

Cognition, perception: *I will not be myself, nor have c. of what I feel,* Troil. V, 2, 63.

Cognizance, that by which something is known, proved, or remembered: *this pale and angry rose, as c. of my blood-drinking hate,* H6A II, 4, 108. *great men shall press for tinctures, stains, relics and c.* Caes. II, 2, 89.* *the c. of her incontinency is this,* Cymb. II, 4, 127.

Co-heir, equal partaker of an inheritance: *they are —s,* Wint. II, 1, 148.

Cohere, to suit, to agree: *had time —d with place or place with wishing,* Meas. II, 1, 11. *till each circumstance of place, time, fortune, do c. and jump,* Tw. V, 259.

Coherence, agreement, accord: *the semblable c. of his men's spirits and his,* H4B V, 1, 73.

Coherent, suitable: *that time and place with this deceit so lawful may prove c.* All's III, 7, 39.

Cohort, a body of soldiers (?): *banishment of friends, dissipation of —s, nuptial breaches,* Lr. I, 2, 162. Only in Qq.

Coif, see *Quoif.*

Coign, corner: *see you yond c. o' the Capitol, yond corner-stone?* Cor. V, 4, 1 (Ff. *coin*). *no jutty, frieze, buttress, nor c. of vantage, but this bird hath made his pendent bed,* Mcb. I, 6, 7. *by the four opposing —s which the world together joins,* Per. III Prol. 17.

Coil, turmoil, bustle, confusion (sometimes = ado, q. v.): *that this c. would not infect his reason,* Tp. I, 2, 207. *here is a c. with protestation,* Gentl. I, 2, 99. *what a c. is there,* Err. III, 1, 48. *the wedding being there to-morrow, there is a great c. to-night,* Ado III, 3, 100. *yonder's old c. at home,* V, 2, 98. *all this c. is 'long of you,* Mids. III, 2, 339. *I am commanded here, and kept a c. with 'too young,'* All's II, 1, 27. *I am not worth this c.* John II, 165. *wilt thou have a reason for this c.?* Tit. III, 1, 225. *here's such a c.!* Rom. II, 5, 67. *what a c. is here!* Tim. I, 2, 236. *when we have shuffled off this mortal c.* Hml. III, 1, 67 (= this turmoil of mortality, this troublesome life).

Coin, see *Coign.*

Coin, subst. 1) stamped money: *an old Roman c.* LLL V, 2, 617. *a c. that bears the figure of an angel,* Merch. II, 7, 56. *stamped c.* Wint. IV, 4, 747. *thirty thousand marks of English c.* John II, 530. H8 III, 1, 171. III, 2, 325. Tim. III, 1, 55.

2) money in general: *the plate, c., revenues* etc. R2 II, 1, 161. *so far as my c. would stretch,* H4A I, 2, 61. *for all the c. in thy father's exchequer,* II, 2, 38. *spend his youth, his valour, c. and people,* H6B I, 1, 79. *who bates mine honour shall not know my c.* Tim. III, 3, 26. *let out their c. upon large interest,* III, 5, 108. *his c., ships, legions, may be a coward's,* Ant. III, 13, 22.

Coin, vb., 1) to stamp, to mint: *c. heaven's image in stamps that are forbid,* Meas. II, 4, 45. *let them c. his nose,* H4A III, 3, 90. *mightst have —ed me into gold,* H5 II, 2, 98. *the dog —s gold,* Tim. II, 1, 6. Caes. IV, 3, 72. Cymb. V, 4, 23. Absolutely: *they cannot touch me for —ing,* Lr. IV, 6, 83 (Ff. *crying*).

2) to fabricate, in a good as well as bad sense: *how many tales to please me hath she —ed,* Pilgr. 93. *whose gall —s slanders like a mint,* Troil. I, 3, 193. *so shall my lungs c. words till their decay*

against those measles, Cor. III, 1, 78. *this gold must c. a stratagem*, Tit. II, 3, 5. *—ing plots*, Cymb. II, 1, 64.

Coinage, 1) the stamp or impression on a coin: *I'll answer the c.* H4A IV, 2, 9. — 2) invention, forgery: *this is the very c. of your brain*, Hml. III, 4, 137.

Coiner, minter: *some c. with his tools made me a counterfeit*, Cymb. II, 5, 5.

Coistrel, see *Coystrel.*

Co-join, to join, to associate: *then 'tis very credent thou mayst c. with something*, Wint. I, 2, 143.

Colbrand, name of a Danish giant whom Guy of Warwick overcame: John I, 225. H8 V, 4, 22.

Colchos, Colchis, the country of the golden fleece: Merch. I, 1, 171.

Cold, adj. 1) not warm or hot, but the opposite: Sonn. 153, 4. Tp. II, 1, 10. Wiv. II, 3, 89. Err. I, 2, 47. Mids. III, 2, 429. Merch. II, 2, 195. Shr. Ind. I, 10. All's I, 1, 115. III, 4, 6. H6B III, 1, 223 etc. etc. Used of death: *our scarce c. conqueror*, H6A IV, 3, 50. *must our mouths be c.?* Tp. I, 1, 56. *to lie in c. obstruction and to rot*, Meas. III, 1, 119. Of the sensation of chillness: Wiv. III, 5, 23. Err. IV, 4, 33. All's I, 1, 116 (*c. wisdom waiting on superfluous folly;* i. e. wisdom exposed to and shivering in the cold). Lr. III, 2, 69. *c. terror*, Ven. 1048. *how c. it struck my heart*, H4B IV, 5, 152. *all out of work and c. for action*, H5 I, 2, 114 (i. e. not heated by taking part in the fight; cf. *dead for breath*, Mcb. I, 5, 37; *to sink for food*, Cymb. III, 6, 17). *—c. purses* = empty purses, H4A II, 4, 355 (cf. *hot*). *c. heart* = fear, cowardice: *in very sincerity of fear and c. heart*, H4A II, 3, 33; cf. IV, 3, 7.

2) insensible, wanting zeal or passion: *o'erworn, despised, rheumatic and c.* Ven. 135. *c. disdain*, Lucr. 691. *folly, age and c. decay*, Sonn. 11, 6. *unmoved, c. and to temptation slow*, 94, 4. *kept c. distance*, Compl. 237. *your c. breast*, 259. *youth is hot and bold, age is weak and c.*, Pilgr. 163. Gentl. II, 4, 203. Wiv. V, 5, 161. Meas. II, 2, 45. IV, 3, 104. Ado I, 1, 131. Merch. I, 2, 20. All's I, 1, 144. John III, 1, 105. 317. R2 II, 2, 88. H6B III, 1, 224. R3 I, 3, 312. II, 1, 40. IV, 4, 485. H8 I, 2, 61 (*c. hearts*). Tim. III, 5, 53 (*in c. blood*). Lr. I, 1, 257. I, 3, 22. Cymb. III, 1, 76. H5 III, 5, 20.

3) chaste: *c. modesty*, Compl. 293 (cf. Merch. II, 2, 195). *c. chastity*, 315. *the white c. virgin snow upon my heart*, Tp. IV, 55. *to make c. nymphs chaste crowns*, 66. *the c. fruitless moon*, Mids. I, 1, 73. II, 1, 156. *our c. maids do dead men's fingers call them*, Hml. IV, 7, 172. *as Dian had hot dreams, and she alone were c.* Cymb. V, 5, 181.

4) indifferent, unwelcome, disagreeable: *I hope my master's suit will be but c.* Gentl. IV, 4, 186. *fare you well, your suit is c.* Merch. II, 7, 73. *c. news for me*, H6B I, 1, 237. III, 1, 86. 87. *—er tidings*, R3 IV, 4, 536. *to thy c. comfort*, Shr. IV, 1, 33. *I beg c. comfort*, John V, 7, 42 (a quibble). *what cheer? as c. as can be*, Shr. IV, 3, 37 (quibble).

5) hopeless, comfortless: *and oft it hits where hope is —est*, All's II, 1, 147. *you stand in —est expectation*, H4B V, 2, 31. *a c. premeditation for my purpose*, H6C III, 2, 133.

6) cool, deliberate: *he is like to be a c.*

soldier, H4B III, 2, 134. *after this c. considerance sentence me*, V, 2, 98. *your lordship is the most —est (man) that ever turned up ace*, Cymb. II, 3, 2.

7) not affecting the scent (used of a false track): *he is now at a c. scent*, Tw. II, 5, 134. *have singled the c. fault out*, Ven. 694. *how Silver made it good in the —est fault*, Shr. Ind. 1, 20. cf. *you smell this business with a sense as c. as is a dead man's nose*, Wint. II, 1, 151.

Used adverbially: *c. and sickly*, Ant. III, 4, 7 (the suffix *ly* belonging to both words).

Cold, subst., 1) privation of heat: *rash false heat, wrapped in repentant c.* Lucr. 48. *knows not parching heat nor freezing c.* 1145. *quake with c.* 1556. *death's eternal c.* Sonn. 13, 12. *shake against the c.* 73, 3. *suspect the sun with c.* Wiv. IV, 4, 7. Err. III, 1, 71. As II, 1, 9. Shr. V, 2, 150. John V, 7, 41. R2 V, 1, 77. H5 II, 1, 10. H6A II, 1, 7. H6B I, 1, 81. II, 4, 3. III, 2, 337. R3 V, 3, 326. H8 IV, 2, 98. Caes. I, 2, 99. Ant. I, 5, 52. Per. II, 1, 77.

2) an indisposition caused by cold: *a whoreson c., a cough*, H4B III, 2, 193. *to catch c.:* Gentl. I, 2, 136. Err. III, 1, 37. Ado III, 4, 66. Troil. IV, 2, 15. Lr. I, 4, 113. Cymb. I, 4, 180. *I have caught extreme c.* Shr. IV, 1, 47. *to take c.:* Shr. IV, 1, 11. *to take a c.* H4A II, 3, 9.

Coldblooded, insensible: John III, 1, 123. cf. *cold blood:* Ado I, 1, 131. H5 II, 5, 20. H6C I, 1, 184. Tim. II, 2, 225. Cor. V, 1, 51. Ant. I, 5, 74.

Cold-hearted, wanting love, indifferent: *c. toward me*, Ant. III, 13, 158.

Coldly, 1) without heat or warmth: *who is that calls so c.?* Shr. IV, 1, 13 (= like a man benumbed). *with such warm life, as now it c. stands*, Wint. V, 3, 36. *c. embracing the discoloured earth*, John II, 306. *it* (wit) *lies as c. in him as fire in a flint*, Troil. III, 3, 257. *the funeral baked meats did c. furnish forth the marriage tables*, Hml. I, 2, 181.

2) without zeal or passion; with indifference or negligence: *yet will I woo for him, but yet so c.* Gentl. IV, 4, 111. *you charge him too c.* Wint. I, 2, 30. *the French fight c.* John V, 3, 13. *— when thou wilt inflame, how c. those impediments stand forth of wealth etc.* Compl. 269. *thou mayst not c. set our sovereign process*, Hml. IV, 3, 64 (= regard with indifference).

3) placidly, tranquilly: *if he were mad, he would not plead so c.* Err. V, 272. *bear it c. till midnight*, Ado III, 2, 132. *we c. pause for thee*, John II, 53. *modest as morning when she c. eyes the youthful Phoebus*, Troil. I, 3, 229. *reason c. of your grievances*, Rom. III, 1, 55.

Cold-moving, done with a gesture indicating indifference: *with certain half-caps and c. nods*, Tim. II, 2, 221.

Coldness, want of zeal: *whether 'twas the c. of the king, that robbed my soldiers of their heated spleen*, H6C II, 1, 122. *dull not device by c. and delay*, Oth. II, 3, 394.

Cold-pale, cold and pale: *c. weakness*, Ven. 892.

Coldspur, opposed to *Hotspur:* H4B I, 1, 50.

Co-leagued, see *Colleagued.*

Colebrook, place in England: Wiv. IV, 5, 80.

Colevile: *Sir John C. of the dale*, H4B IV, 3, 4. 42 etc.

Colic, see *Cholic.*

Collar, 1) the halter: *while you live, draw your neck out o' the c.* Rom. I, 1, 6. cf. the quibble: *a colour that I fear you will die in,* H4B V, 5, 92. 2) the part of the harness that is fastened about the horse's neck: *the —s of the moonshine's watery beams,* Rom. I, 4, 62.

Collateral, indirect: *in his bright radiance and c. light must I be comforted, not in his sphere,* All's I, 1, 99 (i. e. in the light which celestial bodies without his sphere receive from his bright radiance). *if by direct or by c. hand they find us touched,* Hml. IV, 5, 206.

Collatine, the husband of Lucrece: Lucr. Arg. 18. Lucr. 7. 10. 33. 289. 381 etc.

Collatinus, the same: Lucr. Arg. 7. 9. 11. Lucr. 218. 232. 256. 829. 1817.

Collatium, dwelling-place of Collatinus and Lucrece: Lucr. Arg. 15. Lucr. 4. 50.

Colleagued, allied, in collusion with: *thinking our state to be disjoint and out of frame, c. with the dream of his advantage,* Hml. I, 2, 21 (Capell: co-leagued).

Collect, 1) to gather, to assemble: *the sums I have —ed,* John IV, 2, 142. *c. them all together at my tent,* H5 IV, 1, 304. *have you —ed them by tribes?* Cor. III, 3, 11. Used of the raising of an army: *the navy is addressed, our power —ed,* H4B IV, 4, 5. H5 I, 2, 305. II, 4, 19. H6A IV, 4, 32. H6B III, 1, 313. Of the gathering of medicinal herbs: *thou mixture rank, of midnight weeds —ed,* Hml. III, 2, 268. *an unction —ed from all simples,* IV, 7, 145. Hence = to gather for medicinal purposes: *some prescriptions of rare and proved effects, such as his reading and manifest experience had —ed for general sovereignty,* All's I, 3, 229.

2) to gather, to infer, to conclude: *made me c. these dangers in the duke,* H6B III, 1, 35. *relate what you have —ed out of the Duke of Buckingham,* H8 I, 2, 130. *produce the grand sum of his sins, the articles —ed from his life,* III, 2, 294.

3) to recover, to compose: *be —ed; no more amazement,* Tp. I, 2, 13. *affrighted much, I did in time c. myself and thought this was so and no slumber,* Wint. III, 3, 38.

Collection, inference: *move the hearers to c.,* Hml. IV, 5, 9. *a kind of yesty c., which carries them through the most fond and winnowed opinions,* V, 2, 199. *I can make no c. of it,* Cymb. V, 5, 432.

College, a society for purposes of learning or religion: *a c. of wit-crackers,* Ado V, 4, 101. *the congregated c.* (of physicians) *have concluded,* All's II, 1, 120. *the c. of the cardinals,* H6B I, 3, 64. *together with all famous —s almost in Christendom,* H8 III, 2, 66.

Collied, blackened, darkened: *brief as the lightning in the c. night,* Mids. I, 1, 145. *passion, having my best judgment c.* Oth. II, 3, 206 (Qq. coold).

Collier, a digger or seller of coals: *since her time are —s counted bright,* LLL IV, 3, 267. *'tis not for gravity to play at cherry-pit with Satan: hang him, foul c.!* Tw. III, 4, 130 (alluding to the proverb: *like will to like, as the devil with the collier*). *we'll not carry coals; no, for then we should be —s,* Rom. I, 1, 3.

Collop, part of a man's flesh: *most dearest! my c.!* Wint. I, 2, 137.* *God knows thou art a c. of my flesh,* H6A V, 4, 18.

Collusion, blunderingly used by Dull in LLL IV, 2, 43.

Colly, see *Collied.*

Colme-kill, *Icolmkill,* the famous Iona, one of the Western Isles, where the ancient kings of Scotland were buried: Mcb. II, 4, 33.

Colmes inch, Inchcomb or Inchcolm, an island in the Firth of Forth: Mcb. I, 2, 61.

Coloquintida, colocynth: *as bitter as c.* Oth. I, 3, 355.

Colossus, the gigantic statue of Rhodes: *nothing but a c. can do thee that friendship* (to bestride thee) H4A V, 1, 123. *he doth bestride the narrow world like a c.* Caes. I, 2, 136.

Colossus-wise, like a Colossus: Troil. V, 5, 9.

Colour, subst., 1) hue, dye: Ven. 294. 1079. Lucr. 66. 1593. Sonn. 99, 14. Wiv. IV, 5, 118. Meas. IV, 3, 77. LLL I, 2, 90. Mids. I, 2, 98. III, 1, 96. As III, 4, 8. H6A IV, 1, 92. Cor. III, 1, 253 etc. etc. Denoting the fresh redness of the face: *her fear did make her c. rise,* Lucr. 257. *steals the c. from Bassanio's cheek,* Merch. III, 2, 247. *put c. in thy cheek,* Ant. IV, 14, 69. *to gain his c. I'ld let a parish of such Clotens blood,* Cymb. IV, 2, 167 (= to make him look well again). *change c.* Gentl. II, 4, 24. As III, 2, 192 etc. *What c. =* of what c. Wint. II, 1, 13. *see Falstaff in his true —s,* H4B II, 2, 187. *made all the youth in his c.* All's IV, 5, 4 (= of his c.). *you must not marvel at my course, which holds not c. with the time,* All's II, 5, 64 (= is not in keeping with the time).

Figuratively, = appearance, tinge, touch: *with —s fairer painted their foul ends,* Tp. I, 2, 143. *without all c. of base insinuating flattery,* H6A II, 4, 34. *what I have to do will want true c.; tears perchance for blood,* Hml. III, 4, 130 (cf. *truth needs no c., with his c. fixed,* Sonn. 101, 6). *though that his joy be joy, yet throw such changes of vexation on't, as it may lose some c.* Oth. I, 1, 73.

And = kind: *Sport! of what c.?* As I, 2, 107. *boys and women are for the most part cattle of this c.* III, 2, 435. *my purpose is indeed a horse of that c.* Tw. II, 3, 182. *this is a fellow of the self-same c. our sister speaks of,* Lr. II, 2, 145 (Qq *nature*).

2) specious pretence, palliation, appearance of right: *why hunt I then for c. or excuses?* Lucr. 267. *under what c. he commits this ill,* 476 (quibble). *under the c. of commending him, I have access my own love to prefer,* Gentl. IV, 2, 3. *if I find not what I seek, show no c. for my extremity,* Wiv. IV, 2, 168. *what c. for my visitation shall I hold up before him,* Wint. IV, 4, 566. *of no right, nor c. like to right,* H4A III, 2, 100. *'tis no matter if I do halt: I have the wars for my c.* H4B I, 2, 275. *this that you heard was but a c.* V, 5, 91 (quibble with collar). *we want a c. for his death,* H6B III, 1, 236. *under the c. of his usual game,* H6C IV, 5, 11. *under pretence to see the queen his aunt, for 'twas indeed his c.* H8 I, 1, 178. *the quarrel will bear no c. for the thing he is,* Caes. II, 1, 29. *seek no c. for your going,* Ant. I, 3, 32. *Caesar's ambition against all c. here did put the yoke upon us,* Cymb. III, 1, 51. — Remarkable passages: *I do fear colourable —s,* LLL IV, 2, 156 (= false pretexts; Holophernes' speech). *I love no —s,* H6A II, 4, 34 (quibble).

3) ensigns, standards, (only in the plural

form): *I must advance the —s of my love*, Wiv. III, 4, 85. *with his —s spread*, H6A III, 3, 31. H6C I, 1, 91. John II, 8. *wind up*, John V, 2, 73. *let our bloody —s wave*, H6C II, 2, 173. *their —s shall be my wind-ing-sheet*, I, 1, 127. cf. LLL III, 190. John II, 389. H6A I, 6, 1. IV, 2, 56. V, 3, 128. H6B IV, 1, 97. H6C V, 1, 58. R3 V, 3, 35 (cf. H6A III, 4, 29). *under her —s* (= upon her party) Cymb. I, 4, 20. *To fear no —s*, a proverbial phrase, originally = to fear no enemy, used in different senses: Tw. 1, 5, 6. 10. H4B V, 5, 94. cf. LLL IV, 2, 156. — With a play upon the word, used in the same sense in the singular: *under what c. he commits this ill*, Lucr. 476. *his coward lips did from their c. fly*, Caes. I, 2, 122 (but cf. Lucr. 461: *angry that the eyes fly from their lights*).

Colour, vb. 1) to dye: *my —ed hat*, Shr. I, 1, 212. *there was no link to c. Peter's hat*, IV, 1, 137. *to c. the warden pies*, Wint. IV, 3, 48. Cymb. V, 1, 2. *here's such ado to make no stain a stain as passes —ing*, Wint. II, 2, 20. *—ed sorrow* (= painted sorrow) Lucr. 1497.
2) to give a specious appearance, to palliate: *for that (his inward ill) he —ed with his high estate*, Lucr. 92. *you are partly a bawd, howsoever you c. it in being a tapster*, Meas. II, 1, 231. *never did base and rotten policy c. her working with such deadly wounds*, H4A I, 3, 109. *a kind of confession in your looks which your modesties have not craft enough to c.* Hml. II, 2, 290. *that show of such an exercise may c. your loneliness*, III, 1, 45.

Colourable, specious, plausible: *I do fear c. colours*, LLL IV, 2, 156 (Holophernes' speech).

Coloured, adj. having a colour: *a woman c. ill*, Sonn. 144, 4. *such a c. periwig*, Gentl. IV, 4, 196. *French crown c. beard*, Mids. I, 2, 98 (Qq colour). *these eyes that see thee now well c.* H6A IV, 2, 37. *not that our heads are some brown, some black, some auburn, some bald, but that our wits are so diversely c.* Cor. II, 3, 22.

Colt, subst., 1) a young horse: Ven. 419. Tp. IV, 176. LLL III, 33. Mids. V, 120. Merch. V, 72. R2 II, 1, 70. H8 I, 3, 48.
2) a young foolish fellow: *that's a c. indeed, for he doth nothing but talk of his horse*, Merch. I, 2, 44.

Colt, vb., 1) to befool: *what a plague mean ye to c. me thus? Thou liest; thou art not —ed, thou art uncolted*, H4A II, 2, 39.
2) to horse: *she hath been —ed by him*, Cymb. II, 4, 133.

Columbine, a plant, Aquilegia vulgaris: LLL V, 2, 661. Hml. IV, 5, 180 (here, perhaps, emble-matical).

Comagene, a country in ancient Syria: Ant. III, 6, 74.

Co-mart, a bargain concluded by mutual agreement: *as, by the same c. ... his fell to Hamlet*, Hml. I, 1, 93 (Ff covenant).

Co-mate, fellow, companion: *my —s and brothers in exile*, As II, 1, 1.

Comb, subst. 1) the crest of a cock: *you crow, cock, with your c. on*, Cymb. II, 1, 26 (cf. cox-comb).
2) the substance in which bees lodge their honey: *'tis seldom when the bee doth leave her c. in the dead carrion*, H4B IV, 4, 79.

Comb, vb. to adjust with a comb: Shr. IV, 1, 93. H6B III, 3, 15. *her care should be to c. your noddle with a three-legged stool*, Shr. I, 1, 64.

Combat, subst., a single fight, a duel: Ven. 365. Lucr. 1298. Pilgr. 215. Wiv. I, 1, 165. LLL V, 2, 708. Wint. II, 3, 60. V, 2, 79. John V, 2, 43. H6A I, 2, 89. IV, 1, 78. 84. H6B I, 3, 216. 224. II, 3, 48. V, 1, 67. Troil. I, 3, 335. III, 3, 236. 259. Hml. I, 1, 84. *single c.*: H6A I, 2, 95. H6B I, 3, 212. *personal c.* Ant IV, 1, 3.

Combat, vb. 1) intr. a) to fight in a duel: *wisdom and blood —ing in so tender a body*, Ado II, 3, 170. *I will not c. in my shirt*, LLL V, 2, 711. H6C II, 5, 6. Ant. III, 13, 79.
b) to fight in any manner: *his face still —ing with tears and smiles*, R2 V, 2, 32. *c. with adverse planets*, H6A I, 1, 54. *ruin c. with their palaces*, V, 2, 7.
2) trans. to oppose in single fight: *to c. a poor famished man*, H6B IV, 10, 47. *when he the am-bitious Norway —ed*, Hml. I, 1, 61.

Combatant, one who fights a duel: R2 I, 3, 117. H4A I, 3, 107. H6A IV, 1, 134. H6B II, 3, 95. Troil. IV, 5, 5. 92.

Combinate, betrothed, contracted (ac-cording to the interpretation of commentators): *her c. husband*, Meas. III, 1, 231 (perhaps = her husband joined, tied to her fortune mentioned before).

Combination, union, alliance: *a solemn c. shall be made of our dear souls*, Tw. V, 392. *this cun-ning cardinal the articles of the c. drew*, H8 I, 1, 169. *a c. and a form indeed, where every god did seem to set his seal*, Hml. III, 4, 60.

Combine, 1) trans. a) to join, to unite: *to your audit comes their distract parcels in —d sums*, Compl. 231. *where these two Christian armies might c. the blood of malice in a vein of league*, John V, 2, 37. *God c. your hearts in one*, H5 V, 2, 388. Rom. II, 3, 60. Caes. IV, 1, 43. Mcb. I, 3, 111. Hml. I, 5, 18. Ant. II, 2, 18. Absolutely: *and friendship shall c., and brotherhood*, H5 II, 1, 114 (Pistol's speech).
b) to tie, to bind: *I am —d by a sacred vow*, Meas. IV, 3, 149. Having *to* after it: *thy faith my fancy to thee doth c.* As V, 4, 156.
2) intr. to unite: *they (honour and policy) c. not there (in peace) Cor. III, 2, 45. *c. together 'gainst the enemy*, Lr. V, 1, 29.

Combless, without a crest: *a c. cock*, Shr. II, 227.

Combustion, conflagration: *kindling such a c. in the state*, H8 V, 4, 51. *prophesying of dire c. and confused events*, Mcb. II, 3, 63.

Combustious, combustible, susceptible of fire: *subject ... as dry c. matter is to fire*, Ven. 1162.

Come, to draw near, to approach, to arrive (forming its perfect with the verb *to be*): Tp. I, 2, 39. 51. 304. 332. 376. II, 2, 15. 39. V, 36. Gentl. I, 1, 54. II, 4, 78. IV, 3, 9 etc. etc. *c. cut and long-tail*, Wiv. III, 4, 47. *to c. and go*, a) = to go to and fro, to go between: Gentl. III, 1, 142. Wiv. II, 2, 130. b) = to appear and disappear: *the colour of the king doth c. and go*, John IV, 2, 76. (blood) *—ing and going with thy honey breath*, Tit. II, 4, 25. Having after it an infinitive without *to*: *we'll c. dress you straight*, Wiv. IV, 2, 84. *c. go* (let us go) Err. V, 114. H6A IV, 4, 40. Cymb. II, 1, 55. (M. Edd.

come, go). c. challenge me, LLL V, 2, 815. *to c. view fair Portia,* Merch. II, 7, 43. *c. see,* As II, 4, 86. *c. buy,* Wint. IV, 4, 230. *to c. speak with me,* H4B I, 2, 151. *c. weep with me,* Rom. IV, 1, 45. *to c. seek you out,* Lr. III, 4, 157. *to bid Cassio c. speak with you,* Oth. III, 4, 50. Caes. III, 2, 237.

Used periphrastically, when followed by an inf. with *to: if there he came to lie, why, there Love lived,* Ven. 245. *when thou comest thy tale to tell, smooth not thy tongue with filed talk,* Pilgr. 305. *howe'er you c. to know it,* Mcb. IV, 1, 51. *ere we c. to fall,* Hml. III, 3, 49. *he never can meet more mischance than c. to be but named of thee,* Cymb. II, 3, 137. *to c. to pass =* to pass, to happen: Meas. II, 1, 256. Mids. III, 2, 33. IV, 1, 83. H8 I, 2, 63. Hml. II, 2, 437. *to c. to be =* to become: *how camest thou to be the siege of this moon-calf?* Tp. II, 2, 110. *if once he c. to be a cardinal,* H6A V, 1, 32.

Having after it the partic. pres.: *she came stealing,* Ven. 344. *they both came running,* H6A II, 2, 29.

Sometimes seemingly in a general sense = to **move, to change place, to get,** but always with the latent idea of an advantageous or disadvantageous effect or purpose: *what foul play had we that we came from thence?* Tp. I, 2, 60 (sc. to our misfortune). *how camest thou in this pickle?* V, 281. *how came my man i the stocks?* Lr. II, 4, 201. *how came we ashore?* Tp. I, 2, 158 (sc. fortunately). *c. from thy ward,* 471 (sc. and yield to me). *I'll c. no more i' the basket,* Wiv. IV, 2, 50 (sc. as you wish me to do). *O, to him, to him, wench! he will relent; he's —ing, I perceive it,* Meas. II, 2, 125 (= he is about to yield). *the wind is c. about,* Merch. II, 6, 64. *to c. behind folks,* H6B IV, 7, 88 (to attack them). *shall I c. upon thee with an old saying ...,* LLL IV, 1, 121. (cf. *and c. you now with 'knocking at the gate'?* Shr. I, 2, 42.) *I was bid to c. for you,* As I, 2, 64. *and even here I brake off and came away,* R3 IV, 7, 41; cf. Cor. I, 6, 13 and Caes. I, 2, 279. *Troilus will not c. far behind him,* Troil. I, 2, 59. *c. off and on swifter than ...,* H4B III, 2, 281 (sc. to the delight of the spectator). *and over and over he —s, and up again,* Cor. I, 3, 68. *to c. in further evil,* Hml. V, 2, 69. *this villain of mine —s under the prediction,* Lr. I, 2, 119 (i. e. to my grief).

Hence, metaphorically = to **happen, to fall out,** to a person's advantage or disadvantage: *dolour —s to him,* Tp. II, 1, 19. *thou seest what's c. upon thee,* Meas. II, 1, 99. *the danger that might c.* IV, 3, 89. *to write and read —s by nature,* Ado III, 3, 16. *c. what will,* LLL V, 2, 112; cf. H4A I, 2, 162. *marriage —s by destiny,* All's I, 3, 66. *all the titles of good fellowship c. to you,* H4A II, 4, 308. *so c. to you and yours as to this prince,* H6C V, 5, 82. *the subjects' grief —s through commissions,* H8 I, 2, 57. *through our intercession this pardon —s,* I, 2, 107. *out of those many* (benefits) *which, you say, live to c. in my behalf,* Troil. III, 3, 16. *to Coriolanus c. all joy,* Cor. II, 2, 158. *this unlooked for sport —s well,* Rom. I, 5, 31. *banishment! it —s not ill,* Tim. III, 5, 112. *c. what sorrow can,* Rom. II, 6, 3. *seek and know how this foul murder —s,* V, 3, 198. cf. *what's thy interest in this sad wreck? how came it?* Cymb. IV, 2, 366. *it —s in charity to thee,* Tim. I, 2, 229. *new honours c. upon him,* Mcb. I, 3, 144. *untimely —s this hurt,* Lr. III, 7, 98. *what comfort to this great decay* (sc. Lear) *may c..* V, 3, 297. *it will c., humanity must prey on itself,* IV, 2, 48. or

came it by request, Oth. I, 3, 113. *how —s this trick upon him,* IV, 2, 129. cf. *how —s it such numbers seek for thee?* Lucr. 895. Meas. IV, 2, 136. V, 462. Err. II, 2, 121. Mids. IV, 1, 105. Wint. I, 2, 219. John II, 107. H4A V, 1, 27. H4B II, 1, 86. II, 2, 123. Cor. III, 1, 276. Tit. I, 392. Hml. II, 2, 352. Lr. II, 1, 6. *so —s it you have been mistook,* Tw. V, 266. *thus it came,* H8 II, 4, 169. *whereon it came that I was cast,* Oth. V, 2, 326.

Used of the approach of time: *all sins past and all that are to c.* Lucr. 923. Meas. II, 1, 175. Tw. II, 3, 50. H6A I, 2, 57. *To c.* = future: Sonn. 17, 1. 7. 107, 2. Tp. II, 1, 253. Wiv. III, 4, 12. Meas. IV, 2, 152. IV, 4, 33. V, 427. 436. 490. Tw. V, 364. Wint. II, 3, 151. V, 3, 31. IV, 4, 508. H4A I, 3, 171. H6B IV, 2, 138. V, 3, 31. R3 IV, 4, 387. V, 5, 33. Troil. I, 3, 346. II, 2, 202. III, 2, 180. Mcb. I, 7, 7. Cymb. V, 5, 213. Substantively: *past and to c. seems best,* H4B I, 3, 108. *that to c. shall all be done by the rule,* Ant. II, 3, 6 *(that to c.* = the future). *Come* = next, in the language of the vulgar: *c. Philip and Jacob,* Meas. III, 2, 214. *c. peascod time,* H4B II, 4, 413. *c. Lammas-eve,* Rom. I, 3, 17.* *Coming* = next: *this evening —ing,* Gentl. IV, 3, 42. *I fear we shall outsleep the —ing morn,* Mids. V, 372.

As *to c. to be,* so also *to come* alone = to **become:** *how c. you thus estranged?* LLL V, 2, 213. *how came her eyes so bright?* Mids. II, 2, 92. *how came the posterns so easily open?* Wint. II, 1, 52. *how came Falstaff's sword so hacked?* H4A IV, 4, 335. *so came I a widow,* H4B II, 3, 57. *how camest thou so* (lame)? H6B II, 1, 96. *how came it cloven?* Troil. I, 2, 133. *how came he dead?* Hml. IV, 5, 130. *how came he mad?* V, 1, 171. *if you c. slack of former services,* Lr. I, 3, 9. *how came you thus recovered?* Oth. II, 3, 296. *—s deared by being lacked,* Ant. I, 4, 44. *how came it yours?* Cymb. V, 5, 138. *how he came dead,* Per. IV, 3, 29. *how she came placed here,* V, 3, 67.

In the imperative, frequently serving as an interjection, a) to invite to acting or speaking: *mistress Ford; c., mistress Ford —,* Wiv. II, 2, 59 (i. e. speak on, tell your tale). *ay, c., quick,* IV, 5, 44. *but c., your Bergomask,* Mids. V, 368. *c., the full stop,* Merch. III, 1, 17. *c., where is this young gallant?* As I, 2, 212. *c., shall we go and kill us venison?* II, 1, 21. *a better instance, I say, c.* III, 2, 59. *c., blow thy blast,* Cor. I, 4, 12. *your hands, c. then,* Hml. II, 2, 388. *draw, and c.* Ant. IV, 14, 84. b) or to express rebuke: *c., thou canst not hide it,* Wiv. III, 3, 70. *c., you are a tedious fool,* Meas. II, 1, 119. *c., sir, I know what I know,* III, 2, 161. *c., I will fasten on this sleeve of thine,* Err. II, 2, 175. *c., talk not of her,* Ado II, 1, 262. *nay, c. again, good Kate; I am a gentleman,* Shr. II, 219. *c., sir, you peevishly threw it to her,* Tw. II, 2, 14. *c., half all Cominius' honours are to Marcius,* Cor. I, 1, 276. *c., sermon me no further,* Tim. II, 2, 181 etc. etc. — Iterated: *c., c., open the matter in brief,* Gentl. I, 1, 135. *c., fool, c., try me in thy paper,* III, 1, 299. *c., c., a hand from either,* V, 4, 116. *c., c., sans compliment, what news abroad?* John V, 6, 16. *c., Dromio, c.; these jests are out of season,* Err. I, 2, 68. *c., c., no longer will I be a fool* II, 2, 205. *c., c., you know I gave it you even now,* V, 1, 55. *c., c., do you think I do not know you?* Ado II, 1, 126. *c., lady, c., you have lost the heart of Signior Benedick,* 285. *c., c., you're mocking,* Shr. I, 1, 132. All's II, 5, 78. Wint.

IV, 4, 427. John V, 2, 60. H4A IV, 3, 16. R3 I, 3, 74. IV, 4, 284. H8 V, 3, 167. Troil. IV, 2, 29 etc. etc.

Followed by prepositions: 1) *to c. by* = to acquire, to get possession of: *as thou got'st Milan, I'll c. by Naples,* Tp. II, 1, 292. *every thing that he can c. by,* Gentl. III, 1, 125. *how camest thou by this ring?* V, 4, 96. *your heart cannot c. by her,* LLL III, 43. *how I caught it, found it, or came by it,* Merch. I, 1, 3. *superfluity —s sooner by white hairs,* I, 2, 9. Shr. I, 2, 14. IV, 1, 9. Tw. I, 5, 131. II, 5, 6. R2 III, 4, 80. H4B II, 1, 89. IV, 5, 219. R3 V, 3, 248. Tim. I, 1, 209. Caes. II, 1, 169. 259. Mcb. V, 1, 25. Oth. V, 2, 319. Cymb. II, 4, 46. 118.

2) *to c. from* = a) to be descended from: *—ing from a king,* Lucr. 1002. b) to proceed, to issue from: *if I perceive the love c. from her,* Ado II, 3, 234. *acquaint my daughter no further than —s from her demand,* Lr. I, 5, 3. Hence = to be spoken, uttered by: *this is unwonted which now came from him,* Tp. I, 2, 498. *I will set down what —s from her,* Mcb. V, 1, 37.

3) *to c. of* = a) to be descended from: *of what kind should this cock c.* As II, 7, 90. *—s of a very dull kindred,* III, 2, 32. *c. of the Bentivolii,* Shr. I, 1, 13. *you came not of one mother,* John I, 58. *thou camest not of the blood royal,* H4A I, 2, 156. *as ever you came of women,* H5 II, 1, 122. — b) to be caused by, to be the result of: *thereof —s the proverb,* Gentl. III, 1, 305. *thereof —s that the wenches say,* Err. IV, 3, 53. V, 68. *of sufferance —s ease,* H4B V, 4, 28. *hereof —s it that ...,* IV, 3, 127. *what would c. of it!* Caes. III, 2, 151. *nothing will c. of nothing,* Lr. I, 1, 92. I, 4, 312. *what's to c. of my despised time is nought but bitterness,* Oth. I, 1, 162. — Similarly preceded by *thence* and *whence:* Sonn. 111, 5. Meas. I, 2, 128. H6A I, 4, 99.

4) *to c. over:* said *I came o'er his heart; and trow you what he called me? qualm* perhaps, LLL V, 2, 278 (a quibble between overcame or conquered, and befell, worked upon); cf. *in so high a style that no man living shall c. over it,* Ado V, 2, 7 (style and stile; surpass and get over). *nor came any of his bounties over me,* Tim. III, 2, 85 (were bestowed on me). *how he —s o'er us with our wilder days,* H5 I, 2, 267 (wakes us to sad remembrance); cf. *it —s o'er my memory,* Oth. IV, 1, 20.

5) *To c. to sth.* = a) to reach, to attain: *being c. to knowledge,* Meas. V, 153. *how came you to this?* Ado I, 3, 59 (= whence do you know this?). *let me c. to her,* Mids. III, 2, 328. *I cannot c. to Cressid but by Pandar,* Troil. I, 1, 98. *young men will do't, if they c. to't,* Hml. IV, 5, 60. *he came unto himself* (= he recovered his senses) Caes. I, 2, 264. — b) to be brought to a state or condition: *to c. to growth,* Lucr. 1062. *to c. to death,* Wint. V, 2, 93. H6C III, 3, 187. *came early to his grave,* John II, 5. *to ill end,* III, 1, 94. *to ruin,* Cor. III, 2, 125. *to good,* Hml. I, 2, 158. Lr. III, 7, 100. *to bliss,* Oth. V, 2, 250. *to deadly use,* Lr. IV, 2, 36. *to the full,* Ant. II, 1, 11. *to words,* II, 6, 3. *to harvest,* II, 7, 26. *to composition,* Meas. I, 2, 1. *this we came not to,* 153. *his fact came not to an undoubtful proof,* IV, 2, 142. *his neck will c. to your waist* (i. e. have a cord about it) III, 2, 42. *c. to such penury,* As I, 1, 42. *to the arbitrement of swords,* H5 IV, 1, 168. *to this change,* Tim. IV, 3, 65. *to what issue,* Hml. I, 4, 89. *he's the second time c. to*

them (swaddling-clouts) II, 2, 402. *I came to it* (to be a grave-digger) V, 1, 155. *is it c. to this?* Ado I, 1, 199. H6A V, 4, 67. H6B II, 1, 38. Caes. IV, 3, 50. Lr. III, 4, 50. *what will this c. to?* Tim. I, 2, 197. *To c. to it* = to reach the age of puberty, to attain full growth: *grow till you c. unto it,* H4B III, 2, 270. *the other is not c. to it; you shall tell me another tale, when the other is c. to it,* Troil. I, 2, 90 (a quibble; cf. Hml. IV, 5, 60). — c) to fall to: *the other half —s to the privy coffer of the state,* Merch. IV, 1, 354. 371. — d) to begin to speak of: *c. me to what was done to her,* Meas. II, 1, 121. *now I c. to it,* V, 194. — e) to amount: *I have purchased as many diseases under her roof as ... c. to three thousand dolours,* Meas. I, 2, 47. *what —s the wool to?* Wint. IV, 3, 35. *a million of beating may c. to a great matter,* 63. *I would not be a young count in your way, for more than blushing —s to,* H8 II, 3, 42. *so much the rent of his land —s to,* Lr. I, 4, 148. Similarly: *to lack humanity so much as this fact —s to,* Cymb. III, 2, 17. *deserved so long a breeding as his white beard came to,* V, 3, 17.

Joined with adverbs: 1) *to c. about* (cf. above: *the wind is c. about,* Merch. II, 6, 64) = to be effected, to be brought to bear: *how a jest shall c. about,* Rom. I, 3, 45. *how these things came about,* Hml. V, 2, 391.

2) *to c. forth* (besides its original sense of going out, f. i. Caes. II, 1, 194) = to appear: *when —s your book forth?* Tim. I, 1, 26. *let the world see his nobleness well acted, which your death will never let c. forth,* Ant. V, 2, 46.

3) *to c. in* = a) to enter: Meas. III, 1, 45. Err. V, 40. H5 II, 1, 122 etc. *we came in with Richard Conqueror,* Shr. Ind. 1, 4. — b) to come home: *you must c. in earlier,* Tw. I, 3, 4. Troil. IV, 2, 54. — c) to appear, to arrive at a certain place in a critical moment: *had not the old man c. in,* Wint. IV, 4, 628. *whilst I was big in clamour came there in a man,* Lr. V, 3, 208. *Iago in the interim came in and satisfied him,* Oth. V, 2, 318. Especially to be combatant or bring assistance in a fight: *to c. in against me,* As I, 1, 131. *I would be loath to foil him, if he c. in,* 137. *I c. but in to try with him the strength of my youth,* I, 2, 181. *upon which better part our prayers c. in,* John III, 1, 293. *and then c. in the other,* H4A II, 4, 201. *stay till all c. in,* IV, 3, 29. *the more and less came in with cap and knee,* 68. *and —s not in, o'erruled by prophecies,* IV, 4, 18. *here came in strong rescue,* H6A IV, 6, 26. — Hence d) to intervene: *let mine own judgement pattern out my death, and nothing c. in partial,* Meas. II, 1, 31. *who can c. in and say that I mean her?* As II, 7, 77. — e) to be gained, to accrue: *if fairings c. thus plentifully in,* LLL V, 2, 2. *we may boldly spend upon the hope of what is to c. in,* H4A IV, 1, 55. *our credit —s not in like the commodity,* Per. IV, 2, 33. — f) to be mentioned: *how came that widow in?* Tp. II, 1, 77. *that 'only' came well in,* Shr. II, 365. *it came in too suddenly,* Cymb. I, 4, 130. — g) to make a pass in fencing: *I followed me close, came in foot and hand,* H4A II, 4, 241. *and c. you in and c. you in,* H4B III, 2, 302. — h) to begin: *then —s in the sweet o' the year,* Wint. IV, 3, 3. *now —s in the sweetest morsel of the night,* H4B II, 4, 396. *now —s in the sweet o' the night,* V, 3, 52 (perhaps to be registered

under e)). — i) *his spirit is c. in,* John V, 2, 70 (= he repents).

4) *to c. near* = to touch to the quick: *I have heard herself c. thus near,* Tw. II, 5, 29. *you c. near me now,* H4A I, 2, 14. *am I c. near ye now?* Rom. I, 5, 22.

5) *to c. off* = a) to get off, to get away, to escape: *my chief care is to c. fairly off from the great debts,* Merch. I, 1, 128. *thou mayst in honour c. off again,* As I, 2, 31. *came you off with so little,* All's IV, 1, 42. *to c. halting off,* H4B II, 4, 54. *he's settled, not to c. off, in his displeasure,* H8 III, 2, 23. *if the dull Ajax c. safe off,* Troil. I, 3, 381. *aidless came off,* Cor. II, 2, 116. *if I c. off and leave her in such honour,* Cymb. I, 4, 164. *c. off,* II, 2, 33. — b) to acquit one's self: *bravely came we off,* John V, 5, 4. H5 III, 6, 77. *we are c. off like Romans,* Cor. I, 6, 1. And similarly of things: *it came hardly off,* Gentl. II, 1, 116. *this —s off well; here's a wise officer,* Meas. II, 1, 57. *most incony vulgar wit! when it —s so smoothly off,* LLL IV, 1, 145. *this —s off well and excellent,* Tim. I, 1, 29. *this overdone, or c. tardy off,* Hml. III, 2, 28 (but cf. below). — c) to come down with a sum, to pay: *they must c. off; I'll sauce them,* Wiv. IV, 3, 13.

6) *to c. on* = a) to advance, to approach: Meas. III, 1, 43. V, 400. All's IV, 3, 329. Shr. V, 2, 180. Mcb. I, 5, 9 etc. — b) to accompany, to follow, to go with a person: *c. on, we'll visit Caliban,* Tp. I, 2, 307. *c. on; obey,* 483. 493. *c. on, Panthino,* Gentl. I, 3, 76. II, 5, 8. Meas. IV, 2, 57. V, 282. LLL I, 1, 312. V, 2, 136. Shr. I, 1, 150. H6C IV, 7, 87. Rom. I, 5, 127. Sometimes used as a phrase of salutation: *c. on, sir; give me your hand,* H4B III, 2, 1. *c. on, where is your boar-spear, man?* R3 III, 2, 74. — c) like the simple *come,* used as an interjection implying an exhortation or rebuke: *c. on then; down and swear,* Tp. II, 2, 157. *c. on, let us sing,* III, 2, 129. *now, sir, c. on, what was done to Elbow's wife?* Meas. II, 1, 144. *c. on, sir knave, have done your foolishness,* Err. I, 2, 72. LLL I, 1, 59. Merch. III, 4, 57. Shr. V, 2, 133. Tw. IV, 1, 34. II, 3, 32. Wint. II, 1, 27. IV, 4, 161. H4B V, 4, 8. H6A II, 4, 55. Mcb. III, 2, 26. Hml. I, 5, 151. V, 2, 265. 291. Lr. II, 2, 49. Oth. II, 1, 110. 121. — *To c. upon* = to c. on, Troil. IV, 3, 3.

7) *to c. up* = a) to arrive, H4A IV, 3, 20 etc. — b) to become a fashion: *since gentlemen came up,* H6B IV, 2, 10. — c) *to c. up to* = to approach near: *will not c. up to the truth,* Wint. II, 1, 193. — d) *marry c. up,* a vulgar phrase of reproof: *are you so hot? marry c. up, I trow,* Rom. II, 5, 64. *marry, c. up, my dish of chastity,* Per. IV, 6, 159.

To c. home, used of an anchor that will not hold: *when you cast out, it still came home,* Wint. I, 2, 214.

To c. short = to fall short, not to reach: *how far a modern quill doth come too short,* Sonn. 83, 7. *her proportions came short of composition,* Meas. V, 220. Ado III, 5, 45. Hml. IV, 7, 91. cf. *Short.* Similarly: *if you c. slack of former services,* Lr. I, 3, 9. *this overdone, or c. tardy of,* Hml. III, 2, 28 (but see above).

Comeddle, to mix, to temper: *whose blood and judgment are so well —d,* Hml. III, 2, 74 (Ff and M. Edd. *comingled*).

Comedian, a player: *are you a c.?* Tw. I, 5, 194. *the quick —s extemporally will stage us,* Ant. V, 2, 216.

Comedy, a merry play: Wiv. III, 5, 76. LLL V, 2, 462. 886. Mids. I, 2, 12. III, 1, 9. IV, 2, 45. Shr. Ind. 2, 132. Hml. II, 2, 416. III, 2, 304. Lr. I, 2, 147.

Comeliness, grace: *when youth with c. plucked all gaze his way,* Cor. I, 3, 7.

Comely, becoming, decent, graceful: *bashful sincerity and c. love,* Ado IV, 1, 55. *in most c. truth, thou deservest it,* V, 2, 7. *what is c. envenoms him that bears it,* As II, 3, 14. *he is a man of c. virtues,* Tim. III, 5, 15. *this is a happier and more c. time than when ...* Cor. IV, 6, 27.

Comely-distant, at a becoming distance: *and c. sits he by her side,* Compl. 65.

Comer, one that comes: Merch. II, 1, 21. Troil. III, 3, 168.

Comet, a blazing star: Shr. III, 2, 98. H4A III, 2, 47. H6A I, 1, 2. III, 2, 31. Caes. II, 2, 30. Per. V, 1, 87.

Comfect, comfit, dry sweetmeat: *Count C., a sweet gallant,* Ado IV, 1, 18.

Comfit-maker, one who makes comfits: *you swear like a —'s wife,* H4A III, 1, 253.

Comfort, subst., 1) assistance, rescue: *I spy c.; I cry bail,* Meas. III, 2, 44. *thy —s can do me no good at all,* Lr. IV, 1, 17. V, 3, 297.

2) consolation: *I have great c. from this fellow,* Tp. I, 1, 30. *he receives c. like cold porridge,* II, 1, 10. II, 2, 47. 57. Wiv. II, 1, 73. Meas. III, 1, 235. 280. IV, 1, 8. V, 403. Err. I, 1, 27. IV, 2, 66. As II, 3, 45. Wint. V, 3, 1. H6A I, 4, 90. II, 5, 16. R3 I, 3, 4 *(entertain).* Lr. V, 3, 297 etc. etc. *there is another c. than this world,* Meas. V, 49. *have c.!* Tp. I, 2, 25. Ado IV, 1, 119. R3 II, 2, 101. *to give c. or —s:* Meas. IV, 2, 73. Wint. IV, 4, 568. John III, 4, 100. Ant. V, 1, 62. *to put in c.* LLL IV, 3, 52. *speak c. to that grief,* Ado V, 1, 21. *take c.* Mids. I, 1, 202. Per. III, 1, 22. *take good c.* H8 IV, 2 119 (cf. Sonn. 37, 4). *what's the c.? as all —s are,* Meas. III, 1, 54. *what c. is for Claudio?* IV, 2, 80. *what c., man? how is't with aged Gaunt?* R2 II, 1, 72. *comfort!* (sometimes in the sense of 'courage'!): R2 III, 2, 75. H4B IV, 4, 112. H6B III, 2, 38. H6C IV, 8, 28. R3 II, 2, 89. *c., good c.* Wint. IV, 4, 848. *best of c.!* Ant. III, 6, 89. *courage and c.!* John III, 4, 4.

3) encouragement, cheering influence: *give him a show of c. in his suit,* Wiv. II, 1, 98. *I thank you for that c.* III, 4, 54. *tarry for the c. of the day,* Mids. II, 2, 38. *shine —s from the east,* III, 2, 432. cf. *to remain here in the cheer and c. of our eye,* Hml. I, 2, 116. *would he not be a c. to our travel,* As I, 3, 133. *a c. of retirement lives in this,* H4A IV, 1, 56. *smooth —s false, worse than true wrongs,* H4B Ind. 40. *keep c. to you,* H8 V, 1, 145. *lay —s to your bosom,* Lr. II, 1, 128. *returned me expectations and —s of sudden respect and acquaintance,* Oth. IV, 2, 192. *death will seize her, but your c. makes the rescue,* Ant. III, 11, 48. *I will reward thee once for thy spritely c., and tenfold for thy good valour,* IV, 7, 15. — *To be of c.* = to have courage, to be of good cheer: Tp. I, 2, 495. Tw. III, 4, 372. *be of good c.:* John V, 3, 9. V, 7, 25. *though he speak of c.* (= encouragingly?) Oth. II, 1, 31.

4) joy, happiness, delight: *take all my c. of thy worth,* Sonn. 37, 4. *thou ... most worthy c., now my greatest grief,* 48, 6. *so that other mine thou wilt restore, to be my c. still,* 134, 4. *two loves I have of*

c. and despair, 144, 1. *weigh our sorrow with our c.*
Tp. II, 1, 9. *a life whose very c. is still a dying horror*,
Meas. II, 3, 41. *to make her heavenly —s of despair*,
IV, 3, 114. *trouble being gone, c. should remain*, Ado
I, 1, 101. *my clerk hath some good —s too for you*,
Merch. V, 289. *whose hand thou shalt soon feel to thy
cold c.* Shr. IV, 1, 33. *we make us —s of our losses*,
All's IV, 3, 77. *the crown and c. of my life*, Wint. III,
2, 95. *as now she might have done* (viz lived), *so much
to my good c.* V, 3, 33. *Warwick, my son, the c. of my
age*, H6B I, 1, 190. *all c. that the dark night can afford
be to thy person*, R3 V, 3, 80. *this oracle of c. hath
so pleased me*, H8 V, 5, 67. *which should make our
eyes flow with joy, hearts dance with —s*, Cor. V, 3,
99. *but dawning day new c. hath inspired*, Tit. II, 2,
10. *such c. as do lusty young men feel when well-
apparel'd April on the heel of limping winter treads*,
Rom. I, 2, 26. *which feeling, periods his c.* Tim. I, 1,
99. *I'll beweep these —s*, V, 1, 161. *my soul hath her
content so absolute that not another c. like to this succeeds in unknown fate*, Oth. II, 1, 194. *I dote in mine
own —s*, 209. *c. forswear me!* IV, 2, 159. *the elements ... make thy spirits all of c.* Ant. III, 2, 41. *all
strange and terrible events are welcome, but — s we
despise*, IV, 15, 4. *I'll make't my c. he is a man*, Cymb.
III, 6, 71. *let them be joyful too, for they shall taste
our c.* V, 5, 403. cf. I, 6, 9.

5) comfortableness, ease: *I will piece out
the c. with what addition I can*, Lr. III, 6, 2. cf. *the
fire is dead with grief, being create for c.* John IV, 1,
107 (with a play upon the word).

Comfort, vb., to assist, to help: *god c. thy
capacity*, LLL IV, 2, 45 (Holophernes' speech). *dare
less appear so* (viz your loyal servant) *in —ing your
evils, than such as most seem yours*, Wint. II, 3, 56.
why dost not c. me and help me out ..., Tit. II, 3, 209.
if I find him —ing the king, Lr. III, 5, 21.

2) to console: *more widows than we bring men
to c. them*, Tp. II, 1, 134. V, 147. Meas. IV, 3, 55.
Err. III, 2, 26. Ado IV, 1, 339. LLL I, 2, 67. As II,
4, 6. H6A IV, 3, 15. H6B III, 2, 39. R3 I, 1, 139.
IV, 4, 164 etc. etc. *Be —ed!* Mcb. IV, 3, 213. Lr.
IV, 7, 78. Ant. IV, 15, 2. — Absolutely: *—ing therein,
that when old robes are worn out, there are members
to make new*, Ant. I, 2, 170.

3) to encourage: *King Henry's issue, Rich-
mond, —s thee*, R3 V, 3, 123. *live a little, c. a little,
cheer thyself a little*, As II, 6, 5 (*thyself* being object
to both verbs).

4) to cheer: *love —eth like sunshine after rain*,
Ven. 799. *in his bright radiance and collateral light
must I be —ed*, All's I, 1, 100. *he that —s my wife
is the cherisher of my flesh and blood*, I, 3, 49. *entreat
the north to c. me with cold*, John V, 7, 41. *to repair
our nature with —ing repose*, H8 V, 1, 4. *to keep
with you at meals, c. your bed*, Caes. II, 1, 284. *thy
eyes do c. and not burn*, Lr. II, 4, 176. cf. Tim. V, 1, 134.

Comfortable, 1) inclined to help, serviceable, benevolent: *be c. to my mother, your
mistress*, All's I, 1, 86. *O c. friar! where is my lord?*
Rom. V, 3, 148. *had I a steward so true, so just,
and now so c.* Tim. IV, 3, 498. *a daughter who is kind
and c.* Lr. I, 4, 328. Perhaps also in the following
passages: *no c. star did lend his light*, Lucr. 164. *by
thy c. beams I may peruse this letter*, Lr. II, 2, 171
(but it may here be = cheerful).

2) affording consolation: *a c. doctrine*,
Tw. I, 5, 239. *speak c. words*, R2 II, 2, 76.

3) cheerful: *for my sake be c.* As II, 6, 9. *what c.
hour canst thou name that ever graced me in thy company?* R3 IV, 4, 173. *sing, or express yourself in a
more c. sort*, Cor. I, 3, 2. *his c. temper has forsook him*,
Tim. III, 4, 71. *keep your mind peaceful and c.* Per.
I, 2, 36.

Comforter, 1) he who, or that which brings
solace: *it* (sleep) *seldom visits sorrow; when it doth,
it is a c.* Tp. II, 1, 196. *a solemn air and the best c.
to an unsettled fancy*, V, 58. *let no c. delight mine ear*,
Ado V, 1, 6. *to be your c. when he is gone*, R3 I, 3, 10.

2) cheerer: (the sun) *the world's c.* Ven. 529.

Comfort-killing, destroying joy and delight,
cheerless: *O c. Night*, Lucr. 764.

Comfortless, 1) disconsolate: *grim and c.
despair*, Err. V, 80. *the queen is c.* H8 II, 3, 105.

2) giving no comfort or help: *news fitting
to the night, black, fearful, c.* John V, 6, 20. *that kiss
is c. as frozen water to a starved snake*, Tit. III, 1,
251. *all dark and c.* Lr. III, 7, 85.

Comic, raising mirth: *a peaceful c. sport*,
H6A II, 2, 45. *with stately triumphs, mirthful c. shows*,
H6C V, 7, 43.

Comical, the same, used in compounds: *pastoral - c.* Hml. II, 2, 416. *tragical - c. - historical -
pastoral*, 418.

Coming-in, subst., income, revenue: *eleven
widows and nine maids is a simple c. for one man*,
Merch. II, 2, 171. *what are thy rents? what are thy
—s-in?* H5 IV, 1, 260.

Comingle, to mingle, temper: *whose blood
and judgement are so well —d*, Hml. III, 2, 74 (Qq
comeddled).

Coming-on, 1) adj., complaisant: *now I will
be your Rosalind in a more c. disposition*, As IV, 1,
113.)

2) subst. a) advancing, making an attack:
*the men do sympathise with the mastiffs in robustious
and rough c.* H5 III, 7, 159. — b) futurity: *referred
me to the c. of time*, Mcb. I, 5, 9.

Cominius, name in Cor. I, 1, 241 etc.

Comma, the shortest pause in reading:
no levelled malice infects one c. in the course I hold,
Tim. I, 1, 48.

Figuratively = that which separates or
keeps asunder: *as peace should still her wheaten
garland wear and stand a c. 'tween their amities*, Hml.
V, 2, 42, i. e. keep their amities from falling together
by the ears. (The concordance of O. Edd. is a sufficient refutation of modern emendations, particularly
as the expression of Hamlet is purposely burlesque;
cf. the following *Ases*).*

Command, subst., 1) order: Tp. I, 2, 273.
297. 500 *(do)*. Gentl. IV, 3, 5. Meas. IV, 2, 176. IV,
3, 84. Merch. III, 4, 36. As V, 2, 131. All's I, 1, 5.
Tw. III, 4, 29. H5 III, 3, 24. Hml. I, 3, 123. II, 2, 28.
493. Lr. II, 4, 266. Cymb. I, 1, 172. III, 2, 13. V, 1,
6 *(do)* etc. *move only in c.* Mcb. V, 2, 19. *At a person's c.* = a) at his service: *my heels are at your c.*
Merch. II, 2, 33 (only in Q1; the other O. Edd. *commandment*). *that man should be at woman's c.* All's
I, 3, 96. *she is content to be at your c.* H6A V, 5, 19.
at your best c. John I, 197. b) by his order: Tp. V,
48. LLL V, 1, 128. Shr. III, 2, 224. IV, 4, 89. All's

V, 3, 252. *At c.* = at pleasure: *they have had my house a week at c.* Wiv. IV, 3, 12 (= my house was at their c.). *hast thou not worldly pleasure at c.* H6B I, 2, 45. cf. *take all these similes to your c.* Compl. 227 (to your service, to do with them as you please). — *By a person's c.* = by his order: Gentl. IV, 2, 79. Wint. V, 1, 138. Ant. V, 2, 198. — *On his c.*, in the same sense: Wint. II, 1, 55. Ant. IV, 14, 66. Cymb. I, 1, 170. *On c.* = a) according to an order given: *we do upon c.* R3 I, 4, 198. b) at pleasure: *take upon c. what help we have,* As II, 7, 125. — *Under a person's c.:* *a servant under his master's c. transporting a sum of money,* H5 IV, 1, 158. — *With a person's c.:* *with thy c. let him be brought forth,* Err. V, 159.

2) sway, authority: *hast thou c.?* Lucr. 624. *deal in her* (the moon's) *c.* Tp. V, 271. *thy face bears a c. in it,* Cor. IV, 5, 67. *many people under two —s,* Lr. II, 4, 244. *I have lost c.* Ant. III, 11, 23. *thou that hast upon the winds c.* Per. III, 1, 3. Used of military affairs: *there was an excellent c.* All's III, 6, 51. *that was not to be blamed in the c. of the service,* 55. *men of estimation and c. in arms,* H4A IV, 4, 32. *a soldier-like word, and a word of exceeding good c.* H4B III, 2, 84 (Bardolph seems to mean: well beseeming a commander). *disguise the holy strength of their c.* Troil. II, 3, 136. *in the c. of Caesar,* Ant. III, 13, 25.

3) a body of troops headed by a particular officer: *and four shall quickly draw out my c., which men are best inclined,* Cor. I, 6, 84.

Command, vb., 1) to order; a) trans., followed by an accus. and an infin. with or without *to: her father hath —ed her to slip away,* Wiv. IV, 6, 23. *command thy son and daughter to join hands,* John II, 532. H6A I, 3, 30. 76. H6B II, 4, 93. R3 I, 4, 92. IV, 4, 487. Tim. I, 2, 198 etc. *I c. her come to me,* Shr. V, 2, 96. *c. our officers at arms be ready,* R2 I, 1, 204. *c. the citizens make bonfires,* H6A I, 6, 12. *compassion on the king —s me stoop,* III, 1, 119. *I c. thee go,* IV, 5, 36. *when I c. them kill,* H6B IV, 8, 5. *necessity —s me name myself,* Cor. IV, 5, 63. *c. our present numbers be mustered,* Cymb. IV, 2, 343. — *you may c. us,* H8 IV, 1, 117. *as I was —ed from you,* All's II, 5, 59 (= from your part). — Having after it a clause preceded by *that: hath —ed that thou shalt do no murder,* R3 I, 4, 201.

To c. sth. = to order sth. to be done: *dost unwillingly what I c.* Tp. I, 2, 369. *it was —ed so,* Meas. V, 463. *shall I c. thy love?* LLL IV, 1, 82. *Sir Pierce —s the contrary,* R2 V, 5, 101. *your highness shall c. a peace,* H6A IV, 1, 117. *to hear what thou —est,* H6C IV, 8, 16. — Hence = to demand imperatively: *I think I shall c. your welcome here,* Shr. V, 1, 13. *then shalt thou give me with thy kingly hand what husband in thy power I will c.* All's II, 1, 197. *my life thou shalt c., but not my shame,* R2 I, 1, 166. *c. a mirror hither,* IV, 265. *canst thou, when thou —est the beggar's knee, c. the health of it?* H5 IV, 1, 273. *this place —s my patience,* H6A III, 1, 8. *c. the conquest, Charles, it shall be thine,* V, 2, 19. *c. in Anjou what your honour pleases,* V, 3, 147. *c. silence,* H6B IV, 2, 39. *let my sovereign c. my eldest son, nay, all my sons as pledges,* V, 1, 49. *the strong necessity of time —s our services,* Ant. I, 3, 42. *through whom I might c. it* (Herod's head) III, 3, 6. *c. what cost your heart has mind to,* III, 4, 37. *wherefore you have —ed of me these most poisonous compounds,* Cymb. I, 5, 8.

With a double accus.: *will your grace c. me any service to the world's end,* Ado II, 1, 271. *please it your majesty c. me any service to her,* LLL V, 2, 312. *c. him tasks,* Oth. IV, 1, 196. *the last service that I shall c. you,* Ant. IV, 14, 132. *I am ignorant in what I am —ed,* Cymb. III, 2, 23. *that is the second thing that I have —ed thee,* III, 5, 157. — When preceding, the person is in the dative: *and to you the tribunes, for this immediate levy, he —s his absolute commission,* Cymb. III, 7, 9 (most M. Edd. commends).

To c. a person to sth.: *if you can c. these elements to silence,* Tp. I, 1, 23. *that to close prison he —ed her,* Gentl. III, 1, 235. *but these cannot I c. to any utterance of harmony,* Hml. III, 2, 377.

To c. a p. from sth. (= to order him to abstain, or to leave): *from a pure heart c. your rebel will,* Lucr. 625. *to c. the captain and all the rest from their functions,* Meas. I, 2, 13. *c. these fretting waters from your eyes,* IV, 3, 151. *thy beck might from the bidding of the gods c. me,* Ant. III, 11, 61.

Similarly: *we were all —ed out of the chamber,* Wint. V, 2, 6. *c. him away,* Err. V, 335. *I am —ed here,* All's II, 1, 27 (= to remain here). *c. a mirror hither,* R2 IV, 265.

b) intr.: *Juno does c.* Tp. IV, 131. *please you c.* Gentl. II, 1, 121. *that it* (the horse) *may know he can c.* Meas. 1, 2, 166. Merch. II, 9, 45. Tw. II, 5, 115. H6B III, 2, 2. IV, 1, 122. H6C III, 1, 93. IV, 6, 59. R3 I, 2, 39. I, 4, 199. IV, 4, 345. H8 II, 2, 105.

2) to have at one's disposal and service: *which to requite c. me while I live,* Gentl. III, 1, 23. *to know what service it is your pleasure to c. me in,* IV, 3, 10. *it is in mine authority to c. the keys of all the posterns,* Wint. I, 2, 463. *c. all the good lads in Eastcheap,* H4A II, 4, 15. *such aid as I can spare you shall c.* H6B IV, 5, 7. *c. no more content than I,* IV, 9, 2. *something I can c.* H8 IV, 1, 116. *what shall be done to him that victory —s,* Troil. IV, 5, 66. *you shall c. me,* 286. *—ing one another's fortunes,* Tim. I, 2, 109. *to supply his life, or that which can c. it,* IV, 2, 47. *such answer as I can make you shall c.* Hml. III, 2, 335. — Intransitively: *let your highness c. upon me,* Mcb. III, 1, 16 (cf. Per. III, 1, 3). *the Nevils are thy subjects to c.* H6B II, 2, 8. *what I am truly, is thine and my poor country's to c.* Mcb. IV, 3, 132.

3) to force: *my sick heart —s mine eyes to watch,* Ven. 584. *as doth a sail c. an argosy to stem the waves,* H6C II, 6, 36 (cf. III, 1, 88). *when nature —s the mind to suffer with the body,* Lr. II, 4, 109. *—ed tears* = forced, feigned tears, Shr. Ind. 1, 125.

4) to sway, to rule: a) trans.: *—ed by the motion of thine eyes,* Sonn. 149, 12. *hath not one spirit to c.* Tp. II, 2, 102. *how many should be —ed that c.* Merch. II, 9, 45. *this gallant will c. the sun,* Shr. IV, 3, 198. *Falconbridge —s the narrow seas,* H6C I, 1, 239. *—s the empire of the sea,* Ant. I, 2, 191. Tw. II, 5, 127. IV, 3, 17. H4A III, 1, 56. H4B V, 1, 83. H6A I, 1, 38. H6C III, 1, 88. 92. III, 2, 166. R3 III, 1, 108. IV, 4, 104. Cor. IV, 7, 43. Tim. III, 4, 4. — Used of a height overlooking and overruling the neighbourhood: *the eastern tower, whose height —s as subject all the vale,* Troil. I, 2, 3. Of a key opening a door: *this other doth c. a little door,* Meas. IV, 1, 32.

b) intr.: *—ing in his monarchy,* Compl. 196. *subjected tribute to —ing love,* John I, 264. *with such a* *proud* —*ing spirit*, H6A IV, 7, 88. *the great* —*ing Warwick*, H6C III, 1, 29. *every horse bears his* —*ing rein*, R3 II, 2, 128. *deserving to* c. H6A I, 1, 9. *you shall more* c. *with years than with your weapons*, Oth. I, 2, 60 (= exercise more power). Used of military affairs: *if he* (Caesar) *had been there to* c. All's III, 6, 57. *to be* —*ed under Cominius*, Cor. I, 1, 266 (= to have a command). *the man —s like a full soldier*, Oth. II, 1, 35.

Commandement (quadrisyll.) = command: *let his deservings and my love withal be valued 'gainst your wife's* c. Merch. IV, 1, 451 (M. Edd. *command-ment*). *from him I have express* c. H6A I, 3, 20 (M. Edd. *commandment*). *At* c. = at pleasure: *if to women he be bent, they have at* c. Pilgr. 418.

Commander, 1) chief, leader: Lucr. 1387. Gentl. IV, 1, 67. All's III, 5, 6. IV, 3, 153. H5 III, 6, 74. IV, 1, 97. H6A IV, 3, 48. H6C II, 2, 67. Troil. I, 3, 55. II, 3, 47. Caes. IV, 2, 48. IV, 3, 139. Oth. II, 3, 279.

2) lord, master: *invisible* c. (Death) Ven. 1004. *ay, my* c. Tp. IV, 167. *I was the world's* c. LLL V, 2, 565. c. *of this hot malicious day*, John II, 314. *Saturnine, king and* c. *of our commonweal*, Tit. I, 247. *Lord of my life,* c. *of my thoughts*, IV, 4, 28.

Commandment, 1) command, order: As II, 7, 109. Wint. II, 2, 8. Troil. I, 3, 93. Cor. II, 3, 238. Hml. I, 5, 102. III, 2, 329 *(do)*. V, 2, 381. 385. *have I* c. *on the pulse of life?* John IV, 2, 92. *At a person's* c. = at his service: Merch. II, 2, 33 (Q1 *command*). H4B V, 3, 142. *At* c. = at pleasure: H4B III, 2, 27.

2) a precept of the decalogue: *the ten* —*s*, Meas. I, 2, 8. 12. Ludicrously, *my ten —s =* my ten fingers: *I'ld set my ten —s in your face*, H6B I, 3, 145.

Commence, to begin: 1) intr. Phoen. 21. Tim. IV, 3, 268. Mcb. I, 3, 133.

2) trans. Ado II, 3, 52. H4A I, 1, 4. H4B Ind. 5. IV, 2, 118. H6A IV, 7, 7. H6B III, 2, 118. Per. II, 5, 53. *and learning a mere hold of gold kept by a devil, till sack —s it and sets it in act and use*, H4B IV, 3, 125 (Tyrwhitt: 'an allusion to the Cambridge Commencement and the Oxford Act: for by those different names our two universities have long distinguished the season at which each of them gives to her respective students a complete authority to use those hoards of learning which have entitled them to their several degrees in arts, law, physic, and divinity').

Commencement, beginning: Hml. III, 1, 185. Oth. I, 3, 350. In Troil. II, 3, 140 Q has: *the passage and whole stream of his* c. (*his* being apparently a misprint for *this;* c. having the sense of undertaking, enterprise). Ff. *this action.*

Commend, subst., 1) recommendation: *better than his outward show can any way speak in his just* c. Per. II, 2, 49.

2) compliment, greeting: *besides —s and courteous breath*, Merch. II, 9, 90. *I send to her my kind —s*, R2 III, 1, 38. *speak to his gentle hearing kind —s*, III, 3, 126.

Commend, vb., 1) to recommend: *one by nature's outwards so —ed*, Compl. 80. c. *thy grievance to my holy prayers*, Gentl. I, 1, 17. *to* c. *their service to his will*, I, 3, 42. *under the colour of —ing him*, IV, 2, 3. *when to her beauty I* c. *my vows*, 9. Wiv. II, 1, 149. II, 2, 256. Merch. IV, 1, 143. Wint. II, 2, 36. H8 II, 3, 61. Troil. III, 3, 104. V, 5, 3. Cor. IV, 5, 150. Lr. II, 1, 116. Ant. IV, 8, 12. Cymb. I, 4, 32 etc.

2) to recommend to remembrance, to remember: *if thou seest her before me,* c. *me*, Wiv. I, 4, 168. *I'll* c. *you to my master*, Gentl. I, 1, 155. Wiv. II, 2, 95. 137. Meas. I, 4, 88. III, 2, 73. Ado I, 1, 278. LLL II, 180. Mids. III, 1, 190. Merch. IV, 1, 273. Shr. IV, 3, 170. All's II, 2, 68. John V, 4, 40. R2 I, 2, 62. H6C V, 2, 42. R3 III, 1, 181 etc. — Reflectively: —*s himself most affectionately to you*, Troil. III, 1, 73. Usually the personal pronoun reflectively: *I* c. *me from our house in grief*, Lucr. 1308. *your friends are well and have them much —ed*, Gentl. II, 4, 123. *Antonio —s him to you*, Merch. III, 2, 235. As IV, 3, 92. R2 II, 1, 147. H4B II, 2, 136. III, 2, 66. H5 IV, 6, 3. R3 III, 2, 8. Hml. I, 5, 184. V, 2, 203 (In the first signification, to recommend, the full form of the reflective pronoun: Wiv. II, 2, 256. Troil. III, 3, 104. Lr. II, 1, 116). Misapplied: LLL I, 1, 188.

3) to praise: *every one —ed the virtues of his own wife*, Lucr. Arg. 6. *even so as foes* c. Sonn. 69, 4. *well learned is that tongue that well can thee* c. Pilgr. 64. Gentl. III, 1, 102. IV, 2, 40. Merch. IV, 1, 159. As II, 2, 12. IV, 3, 183. Shr. II, 176. All's IV, 3, 94. Tw. II, 5, 166. H4A II, 3, 22. H4B III, 2, 158. Caes. II, 1, 271. Mcb. IV, 1, 39. H6B V, 1, 54.

4) to commit, to deliver: *his eye —s the leading to his hand*, Lucr. 436. *I* c. *you to your own content*, Err. I, 2, 32. LLL I, 1, 234. *to her white hand see thou do* c. *this sealed-up counsel*, Hml. 169. *that thou c. it strangely to some place ...*, Wint. II, 3, 182. *to the hazard of all incertainties himself —ed*, III, 2, 170. c. *them to her service*, IV, 4, 388. c. *these waters to those baby eyes*, John V, 2, 56. *his glittering arms he will* c. *to rust*, R2 III, 3, 116. c. *a secret to your ear*, H8 V, 1, 17. —*s the ingredients of our chalice to our own lips*, Mcb. I, 7, 11. *and so I do* c. *you to their backs*, III, 1, 39. *I did* c. *your highness' letters to them*, Lr. II, 4, 28. III, 1, 19. c. *unto his lips thy hand*, Ant. IV, 8, 23.

Commendable, 1) worthy of recommendation or praise: Ado III, 1, 71. 73. Merch. I, 1, 111. III, 5, 50. Shr. IV, 3, 102. H4B III, 2, 77. H6A IV, 6, 57. Hml. I, 2, 87. (In Merch. I, 1, 111 perhaps *comméndable*).

2) bestowing praise: *and power, unto itself most* c., *hath not a tomb so evident as a chair to extol what it hath done*, Cor. IV, 7, 51 (but here also the first signification is admissible).

Commendation, 1) recommendation: *the gentleman is come to me, with* c. *from great potentates*, Gentl. II, 4, 79. *the* c. *is not in his wit, but in his villany*, Ado II, 1, 145. All's II, 2, 70. IV, 3, 92. Tw. III, 2, 40. Cymb. I, 4, 166.

2) greeting: *a word or two of —s sent from Valentine*, Gentl. I, 3, 53. Wiv. II, 2, 99. LLL II, 181 *(do)*. H6A V, 3, 176. H8 IV, 2, 118.

3) praise: *only this* c. *I can afford her*, Ado I, 1, 175. *shall turn all into my —s*, Cymb. IV, 1, 23. Merch. IV, 1, 166. As I, 2, 275. All's I, 1, 49. 53. H4A III, 1, 189. H8 V, 3, 122. Tim. I, 1, 166. Mcb. I, 4, 55. Per. II, 2, 9.

Comment, subst., 1) talk, discourse, reasoning: —*s of your praise, richly compiled*, Sonn. 85, 2. *making lascivious —s on. thy sport*, 95, 6. *a vulgar* c. *will be made of it*, Err. III, 1, 100. *forgive the* c. *that my passion made upon thy feature*, John IV, 2, 263. *the idle —s that it* (his brain) *makes*, V, 7, 4.

that every nice offence should bear his c. Caes. IV, 3, 8.

2) discourse of thought, judgment: *even with the very c. of thy soul observe mine uncle*, Hml. III, 2, 84.

Comment, vb., to discourse, to reason: *love can c. upon every woe*, Ven. 714. *this huge stage presenteth nought but shows whereon the stars in secret influence c.* Sonn. 15, 4. *say that thou didst forsake me for some fault, and I will c. upon that offence*, 89, 2. *is a physician to c. upon your malady*, Gentl. II, 1, 42. *weeping and —ing upon the sobbing deer*, As II, 1, 65. *view his breathless corpse, and c. then upon his sudden death*, H6B III, 2, 133. *fearful —ing is leaden servitor to dull delay*, R3 IV, 3, 51.

Commentaries, the memoirs (Commentarii) of Caesar: H6B IV, 7, 65.

Commerce, intercourse, transaction: *he is now in some c. with my lady*, Tw. III, 4, 191. *peaceful c. from dividable shores*, Troil. I, 3, 105. *all the c. that you have had with Troy*, III, 3, 205. *could beauty have better c. than with honesty?* Hml. III, 1, 110.

Commingle, see *Comingle*.

Commiseration, compassion: Tit. V, 3, 93. Rom. V, 3, 68 (M. Edd. *conjurations*). Followed by *on:* LLL IV, 1, 64. By *of:* Merch. IV, 1, 30.

Commission, (once of four syllables in the middle of a line: H8 II, 4, 1), 1) charge, mandate: *there is our c., from which we would not have you warp*, Meas. I, 1, 14. *give out a c. for more heads*, II, 1, 253. *this is from my c.* Tw. I, 5, 201. *have you any c. from your lord to negotiate with my face?* 249. *let not her penance exceed the king's c.* H6B II, 4, 75. 76. *a c. to a blank of danger*, Troil. III, 3, 231. Hml. V, 2, 18. 26. 32. Lr. V, 3, 252. Oth. IV, 2, 225 (Q1 *command*). Cymb. II, 4, 12. III, 7, 10. 14. Per. IV, 1, 83. *to be in c.* = to be trusted with an office: H4B III, 2, 97. Mcb. I, 4, 2.

2) a warrant by which any trust is held, or power exercised: *things out of hope are compassed oft with venturing, chiefly in love, whose leave exceeds c.* Ven. 568. cf. *thou (affection) mayst cojoin with something; and thou dost, and that beyond c.* Wint. I, 2, 144. *take thy c.* Meas. I, 1, 48. 61. *I might ask you for your c.* As IV, 1, 138. *you are more saucy with lords and honourable personages than the c. of your birth and virtue gives you heraldry*, All's II, 3, 279. cf. *arbitrating that which the c. of thy years and art could to no issue of true honour bring*, Rom. IV, 1, 64. *I'll give him my c. to let him there a month*, Wint. I, 2, 40. *from whom hast thou this great c.?* John II, 110. III, 3, 11. H4B IV, 1, 162. H6A V, 4, 95 (*letters of c.*). R3 I, 4, 90. H8 I, 2, 20. 57. 92. 101. II, 2, 6. 104. II, 4, 1. 92. III, 2, 233. 320. V, 3, 141. Cor. I, 2, 26. IV, 5, 144. IV, 7, 14. Hml. II, 2, 74. III, 3, 3. Lr. V, 3, 65. Oth. I, 3, 282. II, 1, 29. Ant. II, 3, 41. Per. I, 3, 13.

3) persons joined in a trust or office: *you are of the c.; sit you too*, Lr. III, 6, 40 (cf. *to be in c.* H4B III, 2, 97). Mcb. I, 4, 2. Cor. IV, 7, 14).

Commissioner, a person entrusted with an office or power: H5 II, 2, 61.

Commit, I) trans. 1) to do, to perpetrate: *under what colour he —s this ill*, Lucr. 476. *his —ed evil*, 972. *sin, alone —ed*, 1480. Sonn. 9, 14. 41, 1. 119, 5. Gentl. V, 4, 154. Wiv. I, 1, 31. V, 5, 238.

Meas. II, 2, 89. II, 3, 27. Err. V, 147. Ado IV, 2, 52. V, 1, 219. Mids. III, 2, 346. Merch. II, 6, 37. All's I, 3, 11. II, 1, 34. Wint. I, 2, 58. III, 2, 14. V, 2, 161. R2 IV, 224. V, 3, 33. H4A IV, 3, 101. H4B IV, 5, 126. H5 II, 1, 40. H6B I, 3, 177. R3 II, 1, 57. V, 3, 190. H8 III, 1, 49. Troil. III, 2, 110. Tit. III, 1, 275. Tim. III, 5, 72. Mcb. II, 3, 11. Lr. I, 1, 220. Oth. V, 2, 212. Ant. I, 2, 148. II, 2, 21. Cymb. II, 1, 32. V, 3, 20. Per. IV, 2, 128. IV, 4, 5. Emphatically of carnal sins: *what ignorant sin have I —ed? What —ed!* Oth. IV, 2, 70. 72. 76. 80. Used in a good sense: *c. me for —ing honour*, Wint. II, 3, 49 (for the quibble's sake). *excellent services —ed at the bridge*, H5 III, 6, 4 (Fluellen's speech).

2) to entrust, to surrender, to give up: *what thy memory cannot contain, c. to these waste blanks*, Sonn. 77, 10. *and so I c. you to the tuition of God*, Ado I, 1, 282. *and c. yourself into the hands of one that loves you not*, Mids. II, 1, 215. *her gentle spirit —s itself to yours*, Merch. III, 2, 166. III, 4, 24. As IV, 3, 145. *—s his body to painful labour*, Shr. V, 2, 148. *c. them to the fire*, Wint. II, 3, 95. Tw. I, 2, 60. John IV, 2, 67. R2 II, 1, 98. H4B V, 2, 113. H6A V, 1, 50. H8 II, 2, 87. II, 4, 214. Cor. II, 1, 232. Tit. I, 55. 59. V, 3, 170. Caes. II, 1, 235. Lr. I, 1, 275.

3) to imprison: *why they are —ed*, Ado V, 1, 227. *c. me for —ing honour*, Wint. II, 3, 49. H4B I, 2, 63. V, 2, 83. 112. H5 II, 2, 40. R3 I, 1, 48. 61. II, 4, 44. 47. H8 V, 1, 147. Having *to* after it, to denote the person charged with keeping guard, or the place of confinement: *and here c. you to my lord cardinal to keep*, H6B III, 1, 137. *he is new —ed to the bishop of York*, H6C IV, 4, 11. *c. them to their bonds*, John III, 4, 74. *to the Tower*, H8 I, 2, 193. V, 3, 54. *bear me to prison where I am —ed*, Meas. I, 2, 121. *we will c. thee hither* (to the Tower) H6B IV, 9, 39.

II) intr. to sin: *I do as truly suffer as e'er I did c.* Gentl. V, 4, 77. Applied particularly to incontinence: *c. not with man's sworn spouse*, Lr. III, 4, 83 (cf. Oth. IV, 2, 72. 76. 80).

Commix, 1) trans. to mingle, to confuse: *and, nowhere fixed* (her eyes), *the mind and sight distractedly —ed*, Compl. 28.

2) intr. to mingle: *that it* (her sigh) *would fly from so divine a temple, to c. with winds*, Cymb. IV, 2, 55.

Commixtion (Ff *commixion*), mixture, blending of ingredients: *were thy c. Greek and Trojan so that thou couldst say ...*, Troil. IV, 5, 124.

Commixture, a mass formed by mingling different things; composition, compound: *their damask sweet c.* LLL V, 2, 296. *now I fall, thy tough c. melts*, H6C II, 6, 6 (F1 —*s*).

Commodious, convenient, serviceable: *a c. drab*, Troil. V, 2, 194.

Commodity, 1) convenience: *the c. that strangers have with us in Venice*, Merch. III, 3, 27. *to me can life be no c.* Wint. III, 2, 94.

2) profit, advantage: *that smooth-faced gentleman, tickling c., c., the bias of the world* etc. John II, 573 etc. *break faith upon c.* 597. *our mere defects prove our —ies*, Lr. IV, 1, 23. *I will turn diseases to c.* H4B I, 2, 278.

3) merchandize: *some offer me —ies to buy,*

Err. lV, 3, 6. *we are like to prove a goodly c., being taken up of these men's bills,* Ado III, 3, 190. 192. cf. the same quibble: *take up —ies upon our bills,* H6B IV, 7, 135. *neither have I money nor c. to raise a sum,* Merch. I, 1, 178. *'twas a c. lay fretting by you,* Shr. II, 330. *'tis a c. will lose the gloss,* All's I, 1, 166. *our credit comes not in like the c., nor the c. wages not with the danger,* Per. IV, 2, 34.

4) quantity of wares, parcel: *he is in for a c. of brown paper and old ginger,* Meas. IV, 3, 5. *now Jove, in his next c. of hair, send thee a beard,* Tw. III, 1, 50. *where a c. of good names were to be bought,* H4A I, 2, 93.* *such a c. of warm slaves,* IV, 2, 19.

Common, adj., 1) belonging equally to more than one: *why should my heart think that a several plot which my heart knows the wide world's c. place?* Sonn. 137, 10. *homo is a c. name to all men,* H4A II, 1, 104. *your grief, the c. grief of all the land,* H6B I, 1, 77. *the c. enemy of man,* Mcb. III, 1, 69. *In c. =* to be equally participated by all: *all things in c. nature should produce,* Tp. II, 1, 159. *all the realm shall be in c.* H6B IV, 2, 74. *all things shall be in c.,* IV, 7, 21.

2) pertaining to the people or multitude (in contradistinction to what belongs to the nobility or gentry): *and that supposed by the c. rout against your estimation,* Err. III, 1, 101. *thou c. dog,* H4B I, 3, 97 (= dog-like people). *though the c. people favour him,* H6B I, 1, 158. *ill beseeming any c. man, much more a knight,* H6A IV, 1, 31. *our gentlemen, the c. file,* Cor. I, 6, 43. *hear me, my masters and my c. friends,* III, 3, 108. *to pluck the c. bosom on his side,* Lr. V, 3, 49. *the c. men are now in action,* Cymb. III, 7, 2 (opposed to the gentry).

3) of no rank, ordinary, mean: *I am a spirit of no c. rate,* Mids. III, 1, 157. *I will not jump with c. spirits,* Merch. II, 9, 32. *like a c. and an outward man,* All's III, 1, 11. *by the swords of c. soldiers slain,* H6C I, 1, 9. *berattle the c. stages —so they call them,* Hml. II, 2, 358. *grow themselves to c. players,* 365.

4) low, base, prostitute: *thou dost c. grow,* Sonn. 69, 14. *to link my dear friend to a c. stale,* Ado IV, 1, 66. *use their abuses in c. houses,* Meas. II, 1, 43. *thou pale and c. drudge 'tween man and man,* Merch. III, 2, 103. *a c. gamester,* All's V, 3, 188. *from the —est creature pluck a glove,* R2 V, 3, 17. *as c. as the way between Saint Albans and London,* H4B II, 2, 184. *base, c. and popular,* H5 IV, 1, 38. *you c. cry of curs,* Cor. III, 3, 120. *lips as c. as the stairs ...,* Cymb. I, 6, 105.

5) general: *c. speech gives him a worthy pass,* All's II, 5, 57. *surpassing the c. praise it bears,* Wint. III, 1, 3. *to be cast forth in the c. air,* R2 I, 3, 157. *Arthur's death is c. in their mouths,* John IV, 2, 187. *he loves the land and c. profit of his country,* H6B I, 1, 206. *that old c. arbitrator Time,* Troil. IV, 5, 225. *before the c. distribution,* Cor. I, 9, 35. *I have not been c. in my love,* II, 3, 101. cf. *a c. laugher,* Caes. I, 2, 72. *have by c. voice chosen Andronicus,* Tit. I, 21. *not one that rejoices in the c. wreck, as c. bruit doth put it,* Tim. V, 1, 196. *in a general honest thought and c. good to all,* Caes. V, 5, 72.

6) public: *set me in the c. stocks,* Wiv. IV, 5, 123. *the terms for c. justice,* Meas. I, 1, 12. *strewed it in the c. ear,* I, 3, 15. *a c. executioner,* IV, 2, 9; cf.

As III, 5, 3. *the c. ferry which trades to Venice,* Merch. III, 4, 53. *a thievish living on the c. road,* As II, 3, 33. *some way of c. trade,* R2 III, 3, 156. *that in c. view he may surrender,* R2 IV, 155. *the time misordered doth in c. sense crowd us and crush us to this monstrous form,* H4B IV, 2, 33 (not from private hatred). *old Free-town, our c. judgement-place,* Rom. I, 1, 109. *I hear from c. rumours,* Tim. III, 2, 5. *a c. slave,* Caes. I, 3, 15. *the c. pulpits,* III, 1, 80.

7) usual, vulgar, not extraordinary: *so did this horse excel a c. one,* Ven. 293. *the earth can yield me but a c. grave,* Sonn. 81, 7. *sweets grown c. lose their dear delight,* 102, 12. Tp. II, 1, 4. V, 207. *thou c. friend, that's without faith or love, for such is a friend now,* Gentl. V, 4, 62. Meas. II, 3, 5. IV, 2, 190. Err. III, 1, 24. 25. *things hid and barred from c. sense,* LLL I, 1, 57. 64. cf. *what impossibility would slay in c. sense, sense saves another way,* All's II, 1, 181. *his trespass, in our c. reason, is not almost a fault,* Oth. III, 3, 64. *strike more dead than c. sleep,* Mids. IV, 1, 87. Shr. I, 1, 35. All's IV, 3, 26. V, 3, 190. John III, 1, 8. H4A III, 2, 88. H6C II, 1, 126. R3 II, 2, 91. Hml. I, 2, 72. 74. Lr. II, 2, 151 etc. etc.

Used substantively: *exceed the c.* Cor. IV, 1, 32. *female, which in the c. is woman,* As V, 1, 54 (i. e. in the language of the vulgar; Touchstone's speech).

Used adverbially, at least in appearance: *I am more than c. tall,* As I, 3, 117 (perhaps = than is c.).

Common, subst., 1) an open ground equally used by many: *and make a c. of my serious hours,* Err. II, 2, 29. *my lips are no c.* LLL II, 223. *for enclosing the —s of Melford,* H6B I, 3, 24. *graze in —s,* Caes. IV, 1, 27.

2) the common people (opposed to the nobility): *touching the weal o' the c.* Cor. I, 1, 155. *hath he not passed the noble and the c.* III, 1, 29. Usually in the plural: *the —s hath he pilled,* R2 II, 1, 246. II, 2, 88. 129. H4B II, 3, 51. H6B I, 1, 192. I, 3, 131. III, 1, 28. 116. 240. 374. III, 2, 125. 243. IV, 1, 100. IV, 2, 192. H8 I, 2, 104. II, 1, 49. Cor. II, 1, 282. III, 3, 14. V, 6, 4. Caes. III, 2, 135.

3) *the —s =* the lower house of parliament: R2 IV, 154. H5 I, 1, 71.

Commonalty, the common people, the commons: H8 I, 2, 170. Cor. I, 1, 29.

Commoner, 1) one of the common people: *and then the vital —s and inland petty spirits muster me all to their captain,* H4B IV, 3, 119. *the —s, for whom we stand,* Cor. II, 1, 243.

2) a prostitute: *a c. o' the camp,* All's V, 3, 194. *thou public c.* Oth. IV, 2, 73.

Common-hackneyed, vulgarized: *so c. in the eyes of men,* H4A III, 2, 40 (not hyphened in O. Edd.).

Common-kissing, kissing anybody and anything: *the greedy touch of c. Titan,* Cymb. III, 4, 166.

Commonly, usually: Shr. II, 411. Wint. II, 1, 109. H6A V, 5, 71. Oth. III, 4, 43.

Commonweal, commonwealth, body politic: Meas. II, 1, 42. H6A III, 1, 98. H6B I, 1, 189. I, 4, 46. II, 1, 22. 191. Tit. I, 114. 227. 247. II, 1, 24.

Commonwealth, body politic: Tp. II, 1, 147. 157. Meas. I, 2, 108. Ado III, 3, 181. LLL IV, 1, 41. IV, 2, 79. Merch. III, 5, 37. 40. All's I, 1,

137. R2 II, 3, 166. III, 4, 35. H4A II, 1, 89 and 92 (used as a fem.). IV, 3, 80. H4B I, 3, 87. IV, 1, 94. V, 2, 76. H5 I, 1, 41. H6A III, 1, 73. H6B I, 3, 127. 157. IV, 2, 6. 174. H6C IV, 1, 37. Cor. IV, 6, 14. Tit. I, 313. Tim. IV, 3, 352. Caes. III, 2, 48.

Commotion, insurrection, rebellion: *when tempest of c., like the south, ... doth begin to drop upon our heads,* H4B II, 4, 392. *if damned c. so appeared,* IV, 1, 36. 93. *to make c.* H6B III, 1, 29. 358. —*s, uproars,* H8 V, 3, 28. — Figuratively: *some strange c. is in his brain,* H8 III, 2, 112. *c. in the winds,* Troil. I, 3, 98. *Achilles in c. rages and batters down himself,* II, 3, 185.

Cómmune (in Wint. perhaps commúne) to converse, to take counsel: *I would c. with you of such things,* Meas. IV, 3, 108. *I have more to c. with Bianca,* Shr. I, 1, 101. *what need we c. with you of this,* Wint. II, 1, 162. *I must c. with your grief,* Hml. IV, 5, 202. (In H5 III, 1, 7 O. Edd. *c.,* M. Edd. rightly *summon).*

Communicate, 1) trans. to impart: *she did c. to herself her own words to her own ears,* All's I, 3, 112. *till he c. his parts to others,* Troil. III, 3, 117.

2) to converse, to associate: *whose weakness, married to thy stronger state, makes me with thy strength to c.* Err. II, 2, 178. *thou* (affection) —*st with dreams; with what's unreal thou coactive art,* Wint. I, 2, 140.

Communication, intercourse, conference: *in the way of argument and friendly c.* H5 III, 2, 104. *what did this vanity but minister c. of a most poor issue?* H8 I, 1, 86.

Communicative, acting together: *let us be c. in our revenge,* Oth. I, 3, 374 (Ff *conjunctive).*

Community, 1) a society living under the same regulations: —*ies, degrees in schools and brotherhoods in cities,* Troil. I, 3, 103.

2) commonness, frequency: *sick and blunted with c.* H4A III, 2, 77.

Commutual (cf. *Mutual),* united, being as one: *Hymen did our hands unite c. in most sacred bands,* Hml. III, 2, 170.

Comonty, Sly's blunder for comedy: Shr. Ind. 2, 140.

Compáct, subst. (only in H6A *cómpact),* contract, accord: *patience once more, whiles our c. is urged,* As V, 4, 5. *all the ceremony of this c. sealed in my function,* Tw. V, 163. *take this c. of a truce,* H6A V, 4, 163. *the c. is firm and true in me,* R3 II, 2, 133. *but what c. mean you to have with us?* Caes. III, 1, 215. *who, by a sealed c., did forfeit all his lands,* Hml. I, 1, 86. In an ill sense, = plot, confederacy: *what is the course and drift of your c.?* Err. II, 2, 163.

Compáct, vb., 1) to join closely: *the poisonous simple sometimes is* —*ed in a pure compound,* Lucr. 530.

2) to consolidate: *such reasons of your own as may c. it more,* Lr. I, 4, 362.

Compáct, adj., 1) composed: *love is a spirit all c. of fire,* Ven. 149. *being c. of credit,* Err. III, 2, 22. *are of imagination all c.* Mids. V, 8. *if he, c. of jars, grow musical,* As II, 7, 5. *my heart is not c. of flint,* Tit. V, 3, 88. Absolutely: *my dimensions are as well c.* Lr. I, 2, 7.

2) solid, corporeal: *much imaginary work was there* (in a picture); *conceit deceitful, so c., so*

kind, Lucr. 1423 (so bodily, so corporeal and so natural).

3) confederated, leagued: *c. with her that's gone,* Meas. V, 242. *when he, c. and flattering his displeasure, tripped me behind,* Lr. II, 2, 125 (Qq *conjunct).*

Companion, subst. (fem. in Meas. IV, 1, 55. Wint. V, 1, 11. H6A V, 3, 149. V, 5, 58. Per. V, 1, 78). 1) one who is in the company of another: *set Caliban and his* —*s free,* Tp. V, 252. 292. *take then this your c. by the hand,* Meas. IV, 1, 55.

2) one who keeps company with, and is attached to, another: *nor laugh with his* —*s at thy state,* Lucr. 1066. *I would not wish any c. in the world but you,* Tp. III, 1, 55. *at his heels a rabble of his* —*s,* Wiv. III, 5, 77. LLL V, 1, 7. V, 2, 93. R2 V, 3, 7. H4A II, 4, 494 etc. Having *to* after it: All's II, 3, 200. H4A III, 2, 68. Hml. II, 1, 23. Cymb. V, 5, 21. Having *with* after it: *c. with a king,* H6A V, 3, 149. *was he not c. with the riotous knights,* Lr. II, 1, 96. *to be c. with them,* Cymb. III, 6, 88. — Sometimes = friend: *his c., youthful Valentine, attends the emperor,* Gentl. I, 3, 26. *who is his c. now?* Ado I, 1, 72. 81. II, 1, 231. *in* —*s, whose souls do bear an equal yoke of love, there must be needs a like proportion of lineaments,* Merch. III, 4, 11. And = spouse: Wint. V, 1, 11. H6A V, 3, 149; cf. V, 5, 58.

3) a person of the same kind or order, fellow: *now, my spruce* —*s, is all ready?* Shr. IV, 1, 116. *and am glad to have you therein my c.* H8 III, 2, 143. Adjectively: *my c. peers,* R2 I, 3, 93. *I and my c. maid,* Per. V, 1, 78. *my c. friends,* 238.

4) fellow, in a bad sense: *this cogging c.* Wiv. III, 1, 123. *this c. with the saffron face,* Err. IV, 4, 64. *the other confederate c.* Meas. V, 352. *such insociable* —*s,* LLL V, 1, 21. *the pale c. is not for our pomp,* Mids. I, 1, 15. *what an equivocal c. is this!* All's V, 3, 250. *'tis too cold a c.* I, 1, 144. *swaggering* —*s,* H4B II, 4, 102. *I scorn you, scurvy c.* 132. *why, rude c., I know thee not,* H6B IV, 10, 33. *such* —*s,* Cor. IV, 5, 14. *now, you c.* V, 2, 65. *c., hence!* Caes. IV, 3, 138. *undertake every c.* Cymb. II, 1, 29. *such* —*s,* Oth. IV, 2, 141.

Companion, vb., to make to be a fellow, to make equal: *find me to marry me with Octavius Caesar, and c. me with my mistress,* Ant. I, 2, 29.

Companionship, fellowship, converse: *that it* (policy) *shall hold c. in peace with honour,* Cor. III, 2, 49. *'tis Alcibiades, and some twenty horse, all of c.* Tim. I, 1, 251 (not met by accident, but coming in a body).

Company, subst., 1) the being or going together: *I would entreat thy c. to see the wonders of the world,* Gentl. I, 1, 5. *the other takes in hand no cause of c. of her drops' spilling,* Lucr. 1236. Gentl. II, 4, 40. IV, 1, 46. IV, 3, 25. 34. IV, 4, 18. V, 2, 36. Wiv. I, 1, 271. I, 4, 163. III, 3, 25. Meas. III, 1, 182. IV, 3, 144. 185. Err. II, 1, 87. V, 226. Ado I, 1, 84. Mids. III, 2, 434. 436. Merch. I, 2, 125. IV, 2, 8 etc. *In c.* (opposed to *alone*) Err. V, 66. Rom. III, 5, 179. *From c.* = alone, H6A V, 5, 100. *For c.* = together, Shr. IV, 1, 180. *To bear c.:* Err. I, 1, 130. H6A II, 2, 53. H6C I, 3, 6. R3 II, 3, 47. H8 II, 2, 59 (cf. *bear).* *To keep c.* Tw. V, 99. *To keep a person c.:* Err. V, 398. Merch. III, 1, 16. As I, 2, 287. Tim. V, 1, 111. *How lost you c.?* (= how were you separated?) Oth. II, 1,

91. Plur. *—ies: thrust thyself into their —ies,* John IV, 2, 167. Hml. II, 2, 14.

2) c o n v e r s e, f r i e n d l y i n t e r c o u r s e: *they that fawned on him before use his c. no more,* Pilgr. 422. *her blind boy's c. I have forsworn,* Tp. IV, 90. Gentl. III, 1, 27. III, 2, 4. As II, 1, 52. *To keep c.* Mids. III, 1, 147. *To keep a p. c.* Merch. I, 1, 108. H4B V, 5, 63. *To keep c. with:* Wiv. III, 2, 73. LLL IV, 3, 179.

3) t h e p e r s o n o r p e r s o n s with whom one is or lives together; c o m p a n i o n o r c o m p a n i o n s: *sad souls are slain in merry c.* Lucr. 1110. *to thee and thy c. I bid a hearty welcome,* Tp. V, 110. 254. *to seek new friends and stranger —ies,* Mids. I, 1, 219. *I would have him see his c.* (sc. Parolles) *ana-tomized,* All's IV, 3, 37. *his —ies unlettered,* H5 I, 1, 55. Gentl. I, 3, 43. Wiv. I, 1, 187. III, 2, 14. IV, 2, 35. LLL V, 2, 514. Mids. II, 1, 223. Merch. I, 1, 59. H4A II, 1, 51 etc. *grace and good c.!* Meas. III, 1, 44 (i. e. the company of good spirits, instead of evil ones).

4) a n a s s e m b l a g e o f p e r s o n s: *the c. parts,* Gentl. IV, 2, 81. *forbear till this c. be past,* LLL I, 2, 131. *is all our c. here?* Mids. I, 2, 1. *honest c., I thank you all,* Shr. III, 2, 195. Gentl. IV, 4, 12. Wiv. III, 3, 251. Mids. V, 361. Shr. I, 1, 247. III, 2, 96.

Hence sometimes = p e o p l e: *brings home his lord and other c.* Lucr. 1584. *forbear; here's c.* Wiv. II, 3, 17. *more c.! the fiend is strong within him,* Err. IV, 4, 110. *c.! stay,* LLL IV, 3, 77 (= there is some-body coming). *we shall be dogged with c.* Mids. I, 2, 106. *here comes more c.* (viz Oliver), As IV, 3, 75. *what c. is this?* Shr. I, 1, 46. *but soft! c. is coming here,* W, 5, 26. *to break a jest upon the c. you overtake,* IV, 5, 73. *search what —ies are near,* Cymb. IV, 2, 69. *no —ies abroad?* 101.

5) a s u b d i v i s i o n o f a r e g i m e n t, under the command of a captain: All's IV, 3, 187. H4A IV, 2, 46. Caes. IV, 3, 140. *gentlemen of —ies,* H4A IV, 2, 27 (non-commissioned officers?). *I am a gentleman of a c.* H5 IV, 1, 39.

6) t h e c r e w o f a s h i p: *the king and all our c. else being drowned,* Tp. II, 2, 179. *we have safely found our king and c.* V, 222.

Company, vb. tr., to be the c o m p a n i o n o f: *I am the soldier that did c. these three in poor beseem-ing,* Cymb. V, 5, 408.

Comparative, adj., 1) q u i c k a t c o m p a r i-s o n s: *the most c. young prince,* H4A I, 2, 90. — 2) serving as a comparison, to express the respect-ive value of things: *thou wert dignified enough, if it were made c. for your virtues, to be styled the under-hangman of his kingdom,* Cymb. II, 3, 134.

Comparative, subst. (cf. *Diminutive*), a d e a l e r i n c o m p a r i s o n s (q. v.), o n e w h o a f f e c t s w i t: *stand the push of every beardless vain c.* H4A III, 2, 67.

Compare, subst., c o m p a r i s o n: *sweet above c.* Ven. 8. *so rich a thing, braving c.* Lucr. 40. Sonn. 21, 5. 35, 6. 130, 14. Mids. III, 2, 290. Shr. V, 2, 174. Tw. II, 4, 104. Troil. III, 2, 182. Rom. II, 5, 43. III, 5, 238. Per. IV, 3, 9.

Compare, vb., 1) trans. to e s t i m a t e b y c o n-s i d e r i n g t h e r e l a t i v e q u a l i t i e s, t o m a k e c o m p a r i s o n b e t w e e n: *c. our faces,* John I, 79. *their reasons,* Caes. III, 2, 9. Followed by *to* and *with,*

indiscriminately: *his grief may be —d well to one sore sick,* Ven. 701. *—ing it to her Adonis' breath,* 1172. *green dropping sap, which she —s to tears,* 1176. Lucr. 1102. 1565. Sonn. 18, 1. LLL V, 2, 37. Mids. III, 2, 138. R2 V, 5, 1. Tim. IV, 3, 319. Per. II, 1, 32. *c. them with the bettering of the time,* Sonn. 32, 5. 90, 14. 142, 3. R3 IV, 4, 119. Rom. I, 2, 91. Mcb. IV, 3, 54. *nothing —ing to his* = in comparison with his, Tim. III, 2, 24.

2) intr. a) to make a comparison: *else he never would c. between,* R2 II, 1, 185.

b) to think one's self equal; followed by *with:* *what wicked and dissembling glass of mine made me c. with Hermia's sphery eyne?* Mids. II, 2, 99. *I will not c. with an old man,* Tw. I, 3, 126. *shall pack-horses ... c. with Caesars?* H4B II, 4, 180. *I should c. with him in excellence,* Hml. V, 2, 146. *there would be something failing in him that should c.* Cymb. I, 1, 22.

Comparison, 1) the act of comparing, or the state of being compared: Ado III, 5, 18. LLL IV, 1, 80. Merch. III, 2, 45. H4A II, 4, 277. H5 IV, 7, 26. 47. H6A V, 4, 150. Troil. I, 1, 43. I, 2, 65. I, 3, 194. III, 2, 187. Cymb. I, 4, 76. *her hand, in whose c. all whites are ink,* Troil. I, 1, 56. *to lay his gay —s apart and answer me declined,* Ant. III, 13, 26 (i. e. all that which is in his favour, when compared with me. But cf. *Gay.* Pope: *caparisons*).

2) sarcasm, scoff: *he'll but break a c. or two on me,* Ado II, 1, 152. *a man replete with mocks, full of —s and wounding flouts,* LLL V, 2, 854.

Compass, subst. 1) c i r c l e: *like to the Garter's c., in a ring,* Wiv. V, 5, 70. *my life is run his c.* Caes. V, 3, 25. *a sibyl that had numbered in the world the sun to course two hundred —es,* Oth. III, 4, 71.

2) c i r c u l a r e x t e n t: *what c. will you wear your farthingale?* Gentl. II, 7, 51. *thy crown, whose c. is no bigger than thy head,* R2 II, 1, 101. *my mind exceeds the c. of her* (Fortune's) *wheel,* H6C IV, 3, 47.

3) e x t e n t i n g e n e r a l, l i m i t: *why should we in the c. of a pale keep law,* R2 III, 4, 40. *lived well and in good c.; and now I live out of all c.* H4A III, 3, 22. 23. 25. 26. *you would sound me from my lowest note to the top of my c.* Hml. III, 2, 384 (extent of the voice).

4) r e a c h: *though rosy lips and cheeks within his* (Time's) *bending sickle's c. come,* Sonn. 116, 10. *draw within the c. of suspect the honour of your wife,* Err. III, 1, 87. *above the reach or c. of thy thought,* H6B I, 2, 46. *nor thou within the c. of my curse,* R3 I, 3, 284. *beyond thought's c.* H8 I, 1, 36. *fall into the c. of a praemunire,* III, 2, 340. *few come within the c. of my curse,* Tit. V, 1, 126. *it strains me past the c. of my wits,* Rom. IV, 1, 47. *within the c. of man's wit,* Oth. III, 4, 21. *is it within reason and c.?* IV, 2, 224. (In Oth. II, 1, 244: *for the better c. of his affection;* Qq and M. Edd. *compassing*).

5) t h e i n s t r u m e n t b y w h i c h m a r i n e r s s t e e r: *to all points o' the c.* Cor. II, 3, 26.

Compass, vb., 1) to make circular, to bend in the form of a circle: *to be —ed, like a good bilbo, in the circumference of a peck,* Wiv. III, 5, 112. *Com-passed,* adjectively, = round, arched: *his —ed crest,* Ven. 272. *with a small —ed cape,* Shr. IV, 3, 140. *the —ed window,* Troil. I, 2, 120.

2) to encircle, to surround: *all the blessings of a glad father c. thee about,* Tp. V, 180. *she is too*

big, I hope, for me to c. Err. IV, 1, 111 (quibble). *Alençon, Reignier c. him about,* H6A IV, 4, 27. *a lady fairer than ever Greek did c. in his arms,* Troil. I, 3, 276. *I see thee —ed with thy kingdom's pearl,* Mcb. V, 8, 56.

3) **to go round:** *we the globe can c. soon,* Mids. IV, 1, 102.

4) **to obtain, to get possession of:** *things out of hope are —ed oft with venturing,* Ven. 567. *that his foul thoughts might c. his fair fair,* Lucr. 346. *to c. her I'll use my skill,* Gentl. II, 4, 214. IV, 2, 92. *he —ed a motion of the Prodigal Son,* Wint. IV, 3, 102. H5 IV, 1, 311. Oth. I, 3, 367. II, 1, 244. Per. I, 1, 24.

5) **to bring about, to effect:** *how now shall this be —ed?* Tp. III, 2, 66. *the knave bragged of that he could not c.* Wiv. III, 3, 212. *that were hard to c.* Tw. I, 2, 44. *to c. wonders,* H6A V, 4, 48.

Compassed, adj., **round, circular;** see *Compass,* vb. 1.

Compassion, subst., **pity:** Tp. I, 2, 27. John IV, 1, 89. R2 V, 1, 48. H6A V, 4, 125 *(of c. =* out of c.). R3 IV, 3, 7. Cor. V, 3, 196. Tim. III, 5, 5. Followed by *of:* H6A IV, 1, 56. By *on:* H6A III, 1, 119.

Compassion, vb. **to pity:** *can you hear a good man groan, and not relent, or not c. him?* Tit. IV, 1, 124.

Compassionate, 1) **full of pity:** Lucr. 594. Tit. II, 3, 217.

2) **pitiful, moving pity:** *it boots thee not to be c.* R2 I, 3, 174.

Compeer, subst. **associate, mate:** *no, neither he, nor his —s by night giving him aid, my verse astonished,* Sonn. 86, 7.

Compeer, vb. **to mate, to equal:** *he —s the best,* Lr. V, 3, 69.

Compel, 1) **to force;** a) **absol.:** *if she cannot entreat, I can c.* Mids. III, 2, 248. H5 II, 4, 101. Ant. I, 2, 141.

b) **trans.:** *the son, —ed, been butcher to the sire,* R3 V, 5, 26. H8 I, 2, 34. Followed by an infinitive preceded by *to:* *a dog that is —ed to fight,* John IV, 1, 116. H4B III, 1, 74. IV, 1, 116. H6A III, 1, 85. Caes. III, 2, 161. V, 1, 75. Mcb. I, 2, 30. Hml. III, 3, 62. Ant. V, 1, 29. Followed by a noun preceded by *to:* *c. him to her recompense,* Meas. III, 1, 262. *I was —ed to her,* All's IV, 2, 15 (i. e. to marry her). Wint. II, 3, 88. Oth. II, 1, 238. Per. III, 2, 26.

2) **to enforce, to exact:** *he hath forced us to c. this offer,* H4B IV, 1, 147. 158. Followed by *from: there be nothing —ed from the villages,* H5 III, 6, 116. *c. from each the sixth part of his substance,* H8 I, 2, 57. By *of: an I were not a very coward, I'ld c. it of you,* All's IV, 3, 357.

Compelled = enforced, involuntary: *and why not (should I clear myself) from this —ed stain,* Lucr. 1708. *our —ed sins,* Meas. II, 4, 57. *a —ed restraint,* All's II, 4, 44. *this —ed fortune,* H8 II, 3, 87. *a —ed valour,* Hml. IV, 6, 17.

Compensation, amends: *your c. makes amends,* Tp. IV, 1, 2.

Competence, sufficient means of subsistence: *c. of life I will allow you,* H4B V, 5, 70.

Competency, the same: *that natural c. whereby they live,* Cor. I, 1, 143. Opposed to superfluity:

superfluity comes sooner by white hairs, but c. lives longer, Merch. I, 2, 9.

Competent, sufficient: *his indignation derives itself out of a very c. injury,* Tw. III, 4, 270. *against the which a moiety c. was gaged by our king,* Hml. I, 1, 90 (adequate).

Competitor, 1) one who seeks to obtain what another seeks: Gentl. II, 6, 35. Tit. I, 63. II, 1, 77.

2) associate: *his —s in oath,* LLL II, 82. *the —s enter,* Tw. IV, 2, 12. *every hour more —s flock to their aid,* R3 IV, 4, 506. *it is not Caesar's natural vice to hate our great c.* Ant. I, 4, 3. *these three world-sharers, these —s,* II, 7, 76. *thou, my brother, my c. in top of all design,* V, 1, 42.

Compile, to write, to compose: *be most proud of that which I c.* Sonn. 78, 9. *comments of your praise, richly —d,* 85, 2. *Longaville did never sonnet for her sake c.* LLL IV, 3, 134. V, 2, 52. 896.

Complain, 1) intr. a) to lament: *the poor counterfeit of her —ing,* Lucr. 1269. 1570. *to c. how far I toil,* Sonn. 28, 7. *to hear her so c.* Pilgr. 387. Gentl. I, 2, 127. V, 4, 5. Err. II, 1, 37. R3 IV, 1, 88 (Qq *complaints*). Cymb. IV, 2, 375. — Followed by *to: —ing to her deity,* R3 I, 1, 76. *to his foe supposed he must c.* Rom. II Chor. 7.

b) to present an accusation: *thou camest here to c.* Meas. V, 114. *if they did c., what could the belly answer?* Cor. I, 1, 127. — Followed by *to: to whom should I c.?* Meas. II, 4, 171. *let us c. to them what fools were here,* LLL V, 2, 302. *c. unto the king,* R3 I, 3, 43. By *of: that he hath cause to c. of,* Meas. II, 1, 121. *c. of good breeding,* As III, 2, 31, i. e. of not having received it; cf. *the shepherd that —ed of love,* III, 4, 51. *yet —est thou of obstruction,* Tw. IV, 2, 43. H4B IV, 2, 114. H6A IV, 1, 87. By *of* and *to: you'll c. of me to the king,* Wiv. I, 1, 112. *c. unto the duke of this indignity,* Err. V, 113. By *on: c. on theft,* Ven. 160. *on drouth,* 544. By *on* and *to: shall I c. on thee to our mistress?* Shr. IV, 1, 31.

2) trans.: *by chaste Lucrece' soul that late —ed her wrongs to us,* Lucr. 1839. *what I want it boots not to c.* R2 III, 4, 18.

3) refl.: *to all the host of heaven I c. me,* Lucr. 598. *of weariness he did c. him,* 845. *where then may I c. myself? to God,* R2 I, 2, 42.

Complainer, one who complains: *speechless c., I will learn thy thought,* Tit. III, 2, 39.

Complaining, subst., murmuring: *with these shreds they vented their —s,* Cor. I, 1, 213. cf. Lucr. 1269. 1570. R3 IV, 1, 88. Cymb. IV, 2, 375.

Complaint, 1) lamentation: *the pitiful —s of such as your oppression feeds upon,* H6A IV, 1, 57. *not barren to bring forth —s,* R3 II, 2, 67 (Qq *laments*). *I pity thy —s,* IV, 1, 88 (Ff *complaining*).

2) accusation: *let me not find you before me again upon any c.* Meas. II, 1, 261. IV, 4, 14. V, 24. 251. All's III, 3, 163 *(this c. we bring).* Wint. IV, 4, 730. H6B I, 3, 100. R3 I, 3, 61. H8 I, 2, 173. III, 2, 1. V, 1, 48. Cor. II, 1, 54 *(the first c. =* the first deposition of the plaintiff?). Lr. I, 4, 348. Oth. I, 2, 19. — Followed by *against:* Meas. V, 153. Mids. I, 1, 22. H4B V, 1, 44. H5 I, 2, 26. By *of: the —s I have heard of you,* All's I, 3, 9. *the —s I hear of thee,* H4A II, 4, 486. By *to: the c. they have to the king,* Wint. IV, 4, 869.

Complement, subst. (M. Edd. make a distinction between *complement* and *compliment* unknown to the orthography of O. Edd.) 1) e x t e r n a l s h o w , f o r m : *not only in the simple office of love, but in all the accoutrement, c. and ceremony of it,* Wiv. IV, 2, 5. *manhood is melted into courtesies, valour into c.* Ado IV, 1, 322. *a man of —s* (viz Armado) LLL I, 1, 169. *thine, in all —s of devoted and heart-burning heat of duty,* 279. *these* (viz this outward display of love) *are —s,* III, 23. *sans c., what news abroad?* John V, 6, 16. *garnished and decked in modest c.* H5 II, 2, 134 (i. e. in a corresponding outward appearance).*fain would I dwell on form, fain, fain deny what I have spoke: but farewell c.!* Rom. II, 2, 89. *he* (viz Tybalt) *is the courageous captain of —s,* II, 4, 20.*when my outward action doth demonstrate the native act and figure of my heart in c. extern,* Oth. I, 1, 63.

2) c o u r t e s y : *stay not thy c.* LLL IV, 2, 147 (cf. *courtesy*). *that they call c. is like the encounter of two dog-apes,* As II, 5, 26. *since lowly feigning was called c.* Tw. III, 1, 110. *even now I met him with customary c.* Wint. I, 2, 371. *in dialogue of c.* John I, 201. *there is further c. of leave-taking between France and him,* Lr. I, 1, 306. *the time will not allow the c. which very manners urges,* V, 3, 233. *to stand on more mechanic c.* Ant. IV, 4, 32.

Complemental, c o u r t e o u s : *I will make a c. assault upon him,* Troil. III, 1, 42.

Complete, *1) cómplete* (but see the article 'Changeable Accent' in the Appendix I, 1). a) f u l l , e n t i r e : *all the c. armour that thou wearest,* R3 IV, 4, 189. *in c. steel,* Hml. I, 4, 52. *a thousand c. courses of the sun,* Troil. IV, 1, 27. *a pestilent c. knave,* Oth. II, 1, 252.

b) p e r f e c t : *believe not the dribbling dart of love can pierce a c. bosom,* Meas. I, 3, 3. *a maid of grace and c. majesty,* LLL I, 1, 137. *a c. man,* I, 2, 47. H8 I, 2, 118. Troil. III, 3, 181. *my c. master,* LLL III, 11. *the most c. champion,* H6B IV, 10, 58. *that honourable, c., free-hearted gentleman,* Tim. III, 1, 10. *in c. glory,* H6A I, 2, 83.

2) *compléte,* a) f i l l e d , f u l l : *the one is filling still, never c.* Tim. IV, 3, 244. *how many* (minutes) *make the hour full c.* H6C II, 5, 26. *he is c. in feature and in mind with all good grace,* Gentl, II, 4, 73.

b) a c c o m p l i s h e d : *she is a gallant creature, and c. in mind and feature,* H8 III, 2, 49. Both significations joined: *such as she is, in beauty, virtue, birth, is the young Dauphin every way c.: if not c. of* (i. e. full of those qualities), *say he is not she,* John II, 433.

Complexion, 1) t e m p e r a m e n t , n a t u r a l d i s p o s i t i o n : *then it is the c. of them* (young birds) *all to leave the dam,* Merch. III, 1, 32. *by the o'ergrowth of some c., oft breaking down the pales and forts of reason,* Hml. I, 4, 27. *methinks it is very sultry and hot for my c.* V, 2, 102. Quibbling: *of what c.? of all the four, or the three, or the two, or one of the four. Tell me precisely of what c. Of the sea-water green,* LLL I, 2, 82.

2) e x t e r n a l a p p e a r a n c e , particularly when expressive of some natural disposition: *thou art no man, though of a man's c.* Ven. 215. *his c. is perfect gallows,* Tp. I, 1, 32. *how near the god drew to the c. of a goose!* Wiv. V, 5, 9. *we* (women) *are soft as our —s are,* Meas. II, 4, 129. *thou* (life) *art not certain, for thy c. shifts to strange effects, after the moon,*

Meas. III, 1, 24. *grace, being the soul of your c., shall keep the body of it ever fair,* 187. *know love's grief by his c.* Ado I, 1, 315. *what kind of woman is't? of your c.* Tw. II, 4, 27. *should she fancy, it should be one of my c.* II, 5, 30. *your changed —s are to me a mirror,* Wint. I, 2, 381. *men judge by the c. of the sky the state and inclination of the day,* R2 III, 2, 194. *it discolours the c. of my greatness to acknowledge it,* H4B II, 2, 6. *impious war ... with his smirched c.* H5 III, 3, 17. *ridges horsed with variable —s, all agreeing in earnestness to see him,* Cor. II, 1, 228. *the c. of the element in favour's like the work we have in hand, most bloody, fiery, and most terrible,* Caes. I, 3, 128. *hath now this dread and black c.* (of his arms) *smeared with heraldry more dismal,* Hml. II, 2, 477. *turn thy c. there, Patience, thou young and rose-lipped cherubin, —ay, there look grim as hell,* Oth. IV, 2, 62. *gentlemen of all fashions; you shall have the difference of all —s,* Per. IV, 2, 85.

3) t h e c o l o u r o f t h e s k i n , particularly of the f a c e : *often is his* (the sun's) *gold c. dimmed,* Sonn. 18, 6. *all they foul that thy c. lack,* 132, 14. *the purple pride which on thy* (the violet's) *soft cheek for c. dwells,* 99, 4. *curses all Eve's daughters, of what c. soever,* Wiv. IV, 2, 25. *what c. is she of? swart,* Err. III, 2, 103. Ado II, 1, 305. LLL IV, 3, 234. 268. Merch. I, 2, 143. II, 1, 1. II, 7, 79. As III, 4, 56. III, 5, 116. IV, 3, 171. Epil. 20. Tw. II, 3, 172. Wint. IV, 4, 585. R2 III, 3, 98. Troil. I, 2, 107. 111. 113. Oth. III, 3, 230. *that you lose so much c.* (= colour) H5 II, 2, 73; cf. As IV, 3, 171. *good my c.!* As III, 2, 204 (referring to v. 192: *change you colour?*).

Complice, c o n f e d e r a t e , ally (cf. *Accomplice*): *which is held by Bushy, Bagot and their —s,* R2 II, 3, 165. *to fight with Glendower and his —s,* III, 1, 43. *the lives of all your loving —s lean on your health,* H4B I, 1, 163. *to quell the rebels and their —s,* H6B V, 1, 212. *in despite of thee thyself and all thy —s,* H6C IV, 3, 44.

Compliment, see *Complement.*

Complimental, see *Complemental.*

Complot, subst. (*cómplot* and *complót*), p l o t , concerted plan: *their c. is to have my life,* H6B III, 1, 147. *Lord Hastings will not yield to our —s,* R3 III, 1, 192. *we may digest our —s in some form,* 200. *this fatal writ, the c. of this timeless tragedy,* Tit. II, 3, 265. *—s of mischief,* V, 1, 65. *Revenge now goes to lay a c. to betray thy foes,* V, 2, 147.

Complot, vb. (*cómplot* and *complót*), to p l o t , to p l a n : *all the treasons —ed and contrived in this land,* R2 I, 1, 96. *to plot, contrive and c. any ill,* I, 3, 189.

Comply, 1) to be courteous, formal; followed by *with*: *let me c. with you in this garb,* Hml. II, 2, 390. *he did c. with his dug, before he sucked it,* V, 2, 195.

2) to y i e l d , to be o b s e q u i o u s : *not to c. with heat,* Oth. I, 3, 264.

Compose, 1) trans. a) to c o n s t i t u t e , to f o r m : *this —d wonder of your frame,* Sonn. 59, 10. *he's —d of harshness,* Tp. III, 1, 9. Ado V, 1, 257. Mids. I, 1, 48. All's I, 2, 21. Troil. IV, 4, 79. V, 2, 170. Mcb. I, 7, 73. Hml. III, 1, 98. Per. V Prol. 5.

b) to m a k e o r w r i t e a s a p o e t : *sonnets whose —d rhymes ...* Gentl. III, 2, 69. All's III, 7, 40. H5 III, 7, 46.

2) intr. to come to a composition, to adjust differences: *if we c. well here, to Parthia,* Ant. II, 2, 15.

Composition, 1) the forming a whole of different ingredients, as well as the compound thus formed: *until life's c.* (of four elements) *be recured,* Sonn. 45, 9. *so weak a c.* (small beer) H4B II, 2, 10. *who, in the lusty stealth of nature, take more c. and fierce quality* etc. Lr. I, 2, 12. *nothing but the c. of a knave, beggar, coward* etc. II, 2, 22.

2) constitution: *the large c. of this man,* John I, 88. *O, how that name* (Gaunt) *befits my c.!* R2 II, 1, 73. *as you did mistake the outward c. of his body,* H6A II, 3, 75.

3) compact, agreement, accord: *if the duke come not to c. with the duke of Hungary,* Meas. I, 2, 2. *her proportions came short of c.* V, 220. All's I, 1, 217. IV, 3, 22. John II, 561. Cor. III, 1, 3. Mcb. I, 2, 59.*Ant. II, 6, 58. *there is no c. in these news,* Oth. I, 3, 1 (i. e. no accord or consistency).

Compost, manure: Hml. III, 4, 151.

Composture, the same: Tim. IV, 3, 444.

Composure, 1) the materials or ingredients of which something consists: *thou art of sweet c.* Troil. II, 3, 251. *his c. must be rare indeed whom these things cannot blemish,* Ant. I, 4, 22.

2) combination, bond: *it was a strong c. a fool could disunite,* Troil. II, 3, 109 (Ff *counsel*).

Compound, subst. 1) composition, mixture: *the poisonous simple sometimes is compacted in a pure c.* Lucr. 531. *with eager —s we our palates urge,* Sonn. 118, 2. cf. *to new-found methods and to —s strange,* 76, 4. Wiv. III, 5, 93. Cor. II, 1, 64. Rom. V, 1, 82. Cymb. I, 5, 8. 19.

2) mass, lump: *behold that c.* H4A II, 4, 136. *thou whoreson mad c. of majesty,* H4B II, 4, 319.

Compound, adj., 1) composed, mixed: *for c. sweet foregoing simple savour,* Sonn. 125, 7. *as c. love to physic your cold breast,* Compl. 259.

2) compact, solid: *this solidity and c. mass,* Hml. III, 4, 49.

Compound, vb. 1) to compose, to mix: *when I perhaps —ed am with clay,* Sonn. 71, 10. cf. H4B IV, 5, 116 and Hml. IV, 2, 6. *simple were so well —ed,* Phoen. 44. As IV, 1, 16. H8 I, 1, 12. Cymb. III, 5, 73. V, 5, 254.

2) to make, to constitute: *c. a boy,* H5 V, 2, 221. *—ed thee,* Tim. IV, 3, 273. *all what state —s,* IV, 2, 35.

3) to compose, to settle amicably: *c. this quarrel,* Shr. I, 2, 27. *this strife,* II, 343. H6B II, 1, 58. R3 II, 1, 74.

4) intr. to come to terms, to agree: *c. with him by the year,* Meas. IV, 2, 25. *till you c. whose right is worthiest,* John II, 281. *as manhood shall c.* H5 II, 1, 103 (Pistol's speech). *for thy ransom,* IV, 3, 80. *I must c. with mistful eyes, or they will issue too,* IV, 6, 33. *what we have —ed on,* Cor. V, 6, 84. *my father —ed with my mother under the dragon's tail,* Lr. I, 2, 139.

Comprehend, to imagine: *all this beforehand counsel —s,* Lucr. 494. *deeper sin than bottomless conceit can c. in still imagination,* 702. *where all those pleasures live that art* (= study) *can c.* Pilgr. 62 and LLL IV, 2, 114. *shaping fantasies that apprehend more than cool reason ever —s,* Mids. V, 6. *if it would*

but apprehend some joy, it —s some bringer of that joy, 20. Blunderingly in Ado III, 3, 25 and III, 5, 50.

Comprise, to contain, to include: R2 III, 3, 111. H5 V, 2, 96.

Compromise, subst. (O. Edd. *compremise* and *comprimise*), amicable agreement between parties in controversy: Wiv. I, 1, 33. John V, 1, 67. R2 II, 1, 253. H6A V, 4, 149.

Compromised, agreed: *when Laban and himself were c. that* ..., Merch. I, 3, 79.

Compt, subst.. account, reckoning: *that thou didst love her, strikes some scores away from the great c.* All's V, 3, 57. *have the dates in c.* Tim. II, 1, 35 (sc. for the better computation of the interest due upon them. O. Edd. *have the dates in. Come.*) *your servants ever have what is theirs in c., to make their audit* ..., Mcb. I, 6, 26. *when we shall meet at c.* Oth. V, 2, 273 (Q1 *count*), i. e. at the judgment-day.

Compter, see *Counter.*

Comptible (properly quick at reckoning) sensitive: *I am very c., even to the least sinister usage,* Tw. I, 5, 187.

Comptroller, see *Controller.*

Compulsative (Ff) or **Compulsatory** (Qq), operating by force: *by strong hand and terms c.* Hml. I, 1, 103.

Compulsion, force applied, constraint: Merch. IV, 1, 183. All's III, 6, 31. John II, 218. V, 2, 44. H4A II, 4, 261. 263. Troil. II, 2, 153. Lr. I, 2, 133.

Compulsive, acting by constraint: *when the c. ardour gives the charge,* Hml. III, 4, 86. *the Pontic sea, whose icy current and c. course ne'er feels retiring ebb,* Oth. III, 3, 454.

Compunctious, pricking the conscience: *c. visitings of nature,* Mcb. I, 5, 46.

Computation, calculation: Err. II, 2, 4. R3 III, 5, 89.

Comrade (*cómrade* and *comráde*), mate, companion: H4A IV, 1, 96. Hml. I, 3, 65. *to be a c. with the wolf and owl,* Lr. II, 4, 213.

Con, 1) to learn by heart: Mids. I, 2, 102. V, 80. As III, 2, 289. Tw. I, 5, 186. H5 III, 6, 79. Cor. IV, 1, 11. Troil. II, 1, 18. *to c. by heart,* LLL V, 2, 98. *without book,* Tw. II, 3, 161.*by rote,* Caes. IV, 3, 98.

2) *to c. thanks* = to be thankful: *I c. him no thanks for it,* All's IV, 3, 174. *thanks I must you c.* Tim. IV, 3, 428.

Concave, hollow: *a hill whose c. womb reworded a plaintful story,* Compl. 1. *for his verity in love, I do think him as c. as a covered goblet,* As III, 4, 26. *in her c. shores,* Caes. I, 1, 52.

Concavity, hollow space: *the —ies of it* (the mines) *is not sufficient,* H5 III, 2, 64 (Fluellen's speech).

Conceal, to hide, to keep secret: Ven. 333. Lucr. 675. Sonn. 88, 7. Compl. 317. Gentl. III, 1, 5. 19. Wiv. IV, 5, 45. 46 (used wrongly). Meas. III, 1, 53. Ado IV, 1, 242. Mids. I, 1, 212. As III, 2, 210. Shr. IV, 3, 78. All's II, 3, 283. Tw. I, 2, 53 (*c. me what I am*). IV, 3, 28. Wint. IV, 4, 697. John V, 2, 139. R2 V, 2, 96. H4B V, 3, 115. H6C IV, 7, 60. R3 III, 1, 159. H8 II, 1, 145. Tit. II, 4, 36. Lr. II, 1, 65. III, 2, 58. Cymb. V, 5, 142. Per. I, 4, 12. *my —ed lady,* Rom. III, 3, 98 (= secretly married).

Concealment, 1) forbearance of disclosure, secrecy: *let c., like a worm i' the bud, feed on her damask cheek*, Tw II, 4, 114. *imprison't not in ignorant c.* Wint. I, 2, 397. *'twere a c. worse than a theft, to hide your doings*, Cor. I, 9, 21. *some dear cause will in c. wrap me up awhile*, Lr. IV, 3, 54 (= hinder me from disclosing who I am).

2) secret: *profited in strange —s*, H4A III, 1, 167.

Conceit, subst. 1) conception, idea, image in the mind: *the c. of this inconstant stay sets you most rich in youth before my mind*, Sonn. 15, 9. 26, 7. *finding the first c. of love there bred, where time and outward form would show it dead*, 108, 13. *passing all c.* Pilgr. 110. *the good c. I hold of thee*, Gentl. III, 2, 17. *I am press'd down with c.* Err. IV, 2, 65. *if he be so* (jealous) *his c. is false*, Ado II, 1, 309. *you have a noble and a true c. of god-like amity*, Merch. III, 4, 2. *thy c. is nearer death than thy powers*, As II, 6, 8. *take up my mistress' gown for thy master's use. what's your c. in that?* Shr. IV, 3, 162. *with mere c. and fear of the queen's speed*, Wint. III, 2, 145. *'tis nothing but c.* R2 II, 2, 33. *infusing him with self and vain c.* III, 2, 166. *there's some c. or other likes him well*, R3 III, 4, 51. *the fair c. the king hath of you*, H8 II, 3, 74. *c., more rich in matter than in words*, Rom. II, 6, 30. *the horrible c. of death and night*, IV, 3, 37. *when thy first griefs were but a mere c.* Tim. V, 4, 14. *could force his soul so to his own c.* Hml. II, 2, 579. *his whole function suiting with forms to his c.* 583. *c. in weakest bodies strongest works*, III, 4, 114.*c. may rob the treasury of life*, Lr. IV, 6, 42. *hadst shut up in thy brain some horrible c.* Hml. III, 3, 115. *dangerous —s are poisons*, 326. *cannot remove the strong c. that I do groan withal*, V, 2, 55 (Q1; the rest of O. Edd. *conception*).

2) fanciful thought or device, invention: *let it be as humours and —s shall govern*, Merch. III, 5, 69. *she would applaud Andronicus' c.* Tit. IV, 2, 30. *most delicate carriages, and of very liberal c.* Hml. V, 2, 160. cf. *c. deceitful, so compact, so kind*, Lucr. 1423. *though he seem with forged quaint c. to set a gloss upon his bold intent*, H6A IV, 1, 102. Singular use: *c. upon her father*, Hml. IV, 5, 45.*rings, gawds, —s*, Mids. I, 1, 33 (i. e. presents fancifully devised. cf. *device* in Compl. 232).

3) mental faculty, comprising the understanding as well as the imagination: *deeper sin than bottomless c. can comprehend in still imagination*, Lucr. 701. *c. and grief an eager combat fight* etc. 1298. *unripe years did want c.* Pilgr. 51. *Spenser, whose deep c. is such* etc. 109. *lay open to my earthy gross c. the folded meaning*, Err. III, 2, 34. *his fair tongue, —'s expositor*, LLL II, 72. *a good lustre of c. in a tuft of earth*, IV, 2, 90. *their —s have wings*, V, 2, 260. *cut me to pieces with thy keen c.* 399. *drest in an opinion of wisdom, gravity, profound c.* Merch. I, 1, 92. *thy c. is soaking, will draw in more than the common blocks*, Wint. I, 2, 224. *make reply without a tongue, using c. alone*, John III, 3, 50. *there's no more c. in him than is in a mallet*, H4B II, 4, 263. *enticing lines, able to ravish any dull c.* H6A V, 5, 15. *a strutting player, whose c. lies in his hamstring*, Troil. I, 3, 153. *who* (the child) *if it had c., would die*, Per. III, 1, 16.

4) extraction, birth? (cf. *conceive*). Rosalind, in order to convince Orlando of her pretended knowledge of mysteries, says to him: *I know you are a gentleman of good c.* As V, 2, 59. This cannot be = a gentleman of good parts, of wit; for 'there needs no magician to tell him this.'

Conceit, vb. to form an idea, to judge: 1) intr.: *one that so imperfectly —s*, Oth. III, 3, 149 (Q1 *conjects*). — 2) tr.: *him and his worth you have right well —ed*, Caes. I, 3, 162. *one of two bad ways you must c. me, either a coward or a flatterer*, III, 1, 192.

Conceited, adj. 1) possessed with an idea: *he is as horribly c. of him*, Tw. III, 4, 322.

2) fanciful, imaginative; of persons as well as of things: *which the c. painter drew so proud*, Lucr. 1371. *an admirable c. fellow*, Wint. IV, 4, 204. *c. characters*, Compl. 16. *is not the humour c.?* Wiv. I, 3, 26. *well c.* H4B V, 1, 39.

Conceitless, stupid: *so shallow, so c.* Gentl. IV, 2, 96.

Conceive, 1) to receive into the womb; a) absol.: *to see the sails c. and grow big-bellied*, Mids. II, 1, 128. *the ewes then —ing*, Merch. I, 3, 88. Hml. II, 2, 186. With *by*: Shr. V, 2, 23. Wint. IV, 4, 94. H5 V, 2, 51. — b) trans. (= to bear, to bring forth): *a woman —d me*, Ado I, 1, 240. As IV, 1, 216. Wint. V, 1, 126. H8 II, 4, 189. cf. Caes. V, 3, 69. *I cannot c. you. Sir, this young fellow's mother could*, Lr. I, 1, 12.

2) to admit into the mind, to form, to feel: *to serve all hopes —d*, Shr. I, 1, 15. *the displeasure he hath—d against your son*, All's IV, 5, 80. *such a pleasure as incaged birds c.* H6C IV, 6, 13. *O error, soon —d*, Caes. V, 3, 69 (quibbling).

3) to form an idea, to imagine, to think; abs.: *you say well, and well you do c.* Shr. I, 2, 271. *shows much more his own —ing*, Cymb. III, 3, 98. Followed by *of*: *the grieved commons hardly c. of me*, H8 I, 2, 105. *I hope his honour will c. the fairest of me*, Tim. III, 2, 60. *and will c. the worst of me*, Cymb. II, 3, 158. *By* instead of *of*: *thus I c. by him*, Shr. V, 2, 22 (cf. *By*). — b) trans.: *—ing the dishonour of his mother*, Wint. II, 3, 13. *tongue nor heart cannot c. nor name thee*, Mcb. II, 3, 70. *what does this gentleman c.?* Oth. IV, 2, 95. *we shall, as I c. the journey, be at the Mount before you*, Ant. II, 4, 6. A clause following: *would c. for what I gave the ring*, Merch. V, 195. *what he is, more suits you to c. As I, 2, 179. as he does c. he is dishonoured*, Wint. I, 2, 454.

4) to form by thought, to devise: *this device ... we had —d against him*, Tw. V, 370. *'tis —d to scope*, Tim. I, 1, 72 (= devised to the purpose).

5) to understand; trans. and intr.: Tp. IV, 1, 50. Wiv. I, 1, 250. Meas. II, 4, 141. LLL V, 2, 340. Mids. IV, 1, 219. Wint. III, 2, 198. H4B II, 2, 124. Rom. II, 4, 51. Tim. III, 6, 72. Lr. I, 1, 12. IV, 2, 24.

Concent, a needless emendation of some M. Edd. for *Consent* in H5 I, 2, 181. 206.

Conception, 1) the first formation of the embryo: *joy had the like c. in our eyes and at that instant like a babe sprung up*, H4A V, 2, 115. *at whose c. nature this dowry gave*, Per. I, 1, 8. *c. is a blessing*, Hml. II, 2, 185 (a quibble). Figuratively: *I have a young c. in my brain*, Troil. I, 3, 312. *the passions of the mind, that have their first c. by mis-dread*, Per. I, 2, 12.

2) an evil thought: *and in my heart the strong and swelling evil of my c.* Meas. II, 4, 7. *not this dangerous c.* H8 I, 2, 139. *—s only proper to myself,*

Caes. I, 2, 41. *c. is a blessing*, Hml. II, 2, 185 (quibble). *thou but rememberest me of mine own c.* Lr. I, 4, 73. *no c. concerning you* Oth. III, 4, 156. *thou hast taken against me a most just c.* IV, 2, 211 (Ff and M. Edd. *exception*). *cannot remove the strong c.* V, 2, 55 (Q₁ *conceit*).

Conceptious, apt to conceive, fruitful: *thy fertile and c. womb.* Tim. IV, 3, 187.

Concern, vb. 1) to be of importance, to touch near, to interest; a) intr.: *deliver this paper into the royal hand of the king; it may c. much,* LLL IV, 2, 146. *which to deny —s more than avails,* Wint. III, 2, 87. cf. Gentl. I, 2, 77.

b) trans. *α*) to import: *what doth c. your co-ming?* H4B IV, 1, 30. *what —s his freedom unto me?* H6A V, 3, 116. — *β*) to be of importance to, to interest: *nothing —ing me,* Gentl. I, 2, 75. 76. *what I would speak of —s him,* Ado III, 2, 88. *as it* (Cyprus) *more —s the Turk than Rhodes,* Oth. I, 3, 22. 28. Mids. I, 1, 126. All's V, 3, 137. Tw. I, 5, 224. Wint. IV, 4, 870. H6A I, 1, 84. Cl, 2, 8. Tit. II, 1, 50. Tim. I, 2, 183. Ant. I, 2, 100. II, 2, 30. IV, 9, 25. Cymb. I, 6, 94. 182. Followed by an infinitive: *it —s me to look into the bottom of my place,* Meas. I, 1, 78. V, 255. Shr. III, 2, 130. All's I, 3, 125. H5 II, 4, 2. Tit. IV, 3, 27. *it does not c. me* = it is not for me, I do not choose: *what course I mean to hold shall nothing benefit your knowledge, nor c. me the reporting,* Wint. IV, 4, 515. *to sound your name it not —ed me,* Ant. II, 2, 35. Similarly: *nor how it may c. my modesty, in such a presence here to plead my thoughts,* Mids. I, 1, 60 (= how it may suit, beseem, my modesty).

2) to relate to: *all that may c. thy love-affairs,* Gentl. III, 1, 254. *—ing Jaquenetta,* LLL I, 1, 203. *what c. they? the general cause?* Mcb. IV, 3, 195. H8 V, 3, 3. — *Concerning* = with respect to: Wiv. I, 1, 228. Meas. IV, 1, 42. Tw. IV, 2, 54. H5 I, 2, 6. H8 I, 2, 155. V, 3, 150. Oth. III, 4, 157. *As concerning,* in the same sense: LLL V, 1, 125 (Holophernes' speech).

Concernancy, the import: *the c., sir?* Hml. V, 2, 128 (= what does all this import? what do you mean?)

Concerning, subst., affair, concern: *we shall write to you, as time and our —s shall importune,* Meas. I, 1, 57. *who … would from a paddock such dear —s hide?* Hml. III, 4, 191.

Concerning, with respect to, see *Concern* 2.

Concert (O. Edd. *consort;* see *Consort* and *Sort*), subst., a company of musicians playing: Gentl. III, 2, 84. H6B III, 2, 327.

Conclave, the college of the cardinals: H8 II, 2, 100.₁

Conclude, 1) to close, to end; a) trans.: *thousands more, that yet suspect no peril, will not c. their plotted tragedy,* H6B III, 1, 153. *his fault —s but what the law should end, the life of Tybalt,* Rom. III, 1, 190. *be it —ed, no barricado for a belly,* Wint. I, 2, 203 (= to conclude, in short).

b) intr.: *her heavy anthem still —s in woe,* Ven. 839. *—ing: 'stay, not yet,'* Tp. I, 2, 36. *thou —st like the sanctimonious pirate,* Meas. I, 2, 7. *she —d with a sigh,* Ado V, 1, 173. *quail, crush, c. and quell,* Mids. V, 292. *— s in hearty prayers,* H4B IV, 1, 14. *and so her death —s,* H6A V, 4, 16. *'tis wonder that thy life and wits at once had not —d all,* Lr. IV, 7, 42. *her*

life, which, being cruel to the world, —d most cruel to herself, Cymb. V, 5, 32. — *To c.* = in short: *and to c., they are lying knaves,* Ado V, 1, 223. Err. III, 2, 144. Shr. II, 298. H4A II, 3, 108. II, 4, 19. H6B IV, 1, 101. H6C II, 5, 47. Mcb. I, 2, 57. *to c. with truth,* H6C II, 1, 128.

2) to settle finally; a) trans. *to c. a peace,* All's IV, 3, 47. H6A V, 4, 107. 113. H6B I, 1, 42. H8 I, 1, 89. *a league,* III, 2, 321. *I hope, my absence doth neglect no great designs, which by my presence might have been —d,* R3 III, 4, 26. Followed by an infinitive or a clause, in the sense of to make up one's mind, to come to a decision: *I will c. to hate her,* Cymb. III, 5, 78. *the congregated college have —d that labouring art can never ransom nature,* All's II, 1, 120.

b) intr. to come to a final arrangement or agreement: *c. and be agreed,* R2 I, 1, 156. *where gentry, title, wisdom, cannot c. but by the yea and no of general ignorance,* Cor. III, 1, 145. Followed by *of* and *on: to have a godly peace —d of,* H6A V, 1, 5. *Suffolk —d on the articles,* H6B I, 1, 217. *'tis so —d on,* Hml. III, 4, 201.

3) to resolve: *they did c. to bear dead Lucrece thence,* Lucr. 1850. *the senate have —d to give …,* Caes. II, 2, 93. *till you c. that you shall …,* H6A II, 4, 40. *c. with me that Margaret shall be queen,* V, 5, 77. *is it —d he shall be protector?* R3 I, 3, 14. *is it so —d?* Troil. IV, 2, 68. *it is – d,* Mcb. III, 1, 141.

4) to collect by reasoning, to infer: *that she —s the picture was belied,* Lucr. 1533. *c. he is in love,* Ado III, 2, 64. *O, then c. minds swayed by eyes are full of turpitude,* Troil. V, 2, 111.

Hence by a peculiar use, a) to prove by an inference: *you c. that my master is a shepherd,* Gentl. I, 1, 76. *thou didst c. hairy men plain dealers without wit,* Err. II, 2, 87. *the text most infallibly —s it,* LLL IV, 2, 170. *the other two —s it, —o, u,* V, 1, 59. *this —s: my mother's son did get your father's heir,* John I, 127. *then you c. that he is dead,* R3 II, 2, 12. — b) to perceive by drawing an inference, to acknowledge: *reprove my allegation, if you can, or else c. my words effectual,* H6B III, 1, 41.

Conclusion, 1) end, close: *the c. shall be crowned with your enjoying her,* Wiv. III, 5, 138. *the c. is, she shall be thine,* Ado I, 1, 329. *man is a giddy thing, and this is my c.* V, 4, 110. Wiv. I, 1, 184. Meas. V, 95. LLL IV, 1, 75. As V, 4, 132. H5 II, 1, 27.●III, 6, 142. R3 I, 3, 316. Oth. II, 1, 162. 269.

In c. = a) finally: *and in c. he did beat me here,* Err. II, 1, 74. *and in c. dumbly have broke off,* Mids. V, 98. Tw. V, 70. Mcb. II, 3, 38. Lr. II, 4, 179. — b) in short: *in c., I stand affected to her,* Gentl. II, 1, 90. *and, in c., she shall watch all night,* Shr. IV, 1, 208. *it draws toward supper in c. so,* John I, 204. *and in c. drove us to seek out this head of safety,* H4A IV, 3, 102. *and in c. wins the king from her,* H6C III, 1, 50. *and in c. nonsuits my mediators,* Oth. I, 1, 15.

2) inference: Gentl. II, 5, 39. Err. II, 2, 110. LLL V, 2, 41. Tw. II, 3, 6. V, 23. Wint. I, 2, 81. *your wife Octavia, with her modest eyes and still c., shall acquire no honour, demuring upon me,* Ant. IV, 15, 28 (i. e. silently drawing inferences in surveying and examining my appearance).

3) that from which an inference is

drawn; a) an experience made and leading to consequences: *but this denoted a foregone c.* Oth. III, 3, 428. — b) an experiment: *the blood and baseness of our natures would conduct us to most preposterous —s,* Oth. I, 3, 333. *she hath pursued —s infinite of easy ways to die,* Ant. V, 2, 358. *is't not meet that I did amplify my judgement in other —s?* Cymb. I, 5, 18. *to try a c.* or *—s:* Lucr. 1160. Merch. II, 2, 39 (only in Q1; the rest of O. Edd. *confusions*). Hml. III, 4, 195. — c) a riddle: *read the c. then,* Per. I, 1, 56 (perhaps also in LLL V, 2, 41).

Concolinel, scrap of a song not yet explained in LLL III, 3.

Concord, subst., 1) agreement of minds: Mids. IV, 1, 148. V, 60. Mcb. IV, 3, 98.

2) harmony of sounds: Sonn. 8, 5. 128, 4. Gentl. I, 2, 94. Merch. V, 84. All's I, 1, 186. R2 V, 5, 47.

Concordant, agreeing: *how true a twain seemeth this c. one,* Phoen. 46.

Concubine, a kept mistress: H6C III, 2, 98.

Concupiscible, desirous, lustful: *his c. intemperate lust,* Meas. V, 98.

Concupy, subst. concupiscence, lust: *he'll tickle it for his c.* Troil. V, 2, 177.

Concur, to agree: *this —s directly with the letter,* Tw. III, 4, 73. *to establish here a peace indeed, —ing both in name and quality,* H4B IV, 1, 87. *as Hector's leisure and your bounties shall c. together,* Troil. IV, 5, 274.

Condemn, 1) to sentence, to doom: Meas. II, 1, 40. II, 2, 18. 37. 38. 80. III, 2, 190. V, 70. 449. 487. Wint. I, 2, 445. John V, 7, 48. H6A V, 4, 36. 84. H6B II, 3, 16. III, 1, 168. 237. III, 2, 24. R3 V, 3, 195. Ant. I, 3, 49 etc. *to stand —ed,* Lr. I, 4, 5. cf. Ado III, 1, 108. R2 II, 2, 132. II, 3, 119. Troil. III, 3, 219. *To c. of sth.* = to find guilty of: *till forging Nature be —ed of treason,* Ven. 729. *To sth.: we do c. thee to the very block,* Meas. V, 419. Wint. II, 3, 192. IV, 4, 388. R2 III, 1, 29. *thou wilt be —ed into everlasting redemption,* Ado IV, 2, 58 (Dogberry's speech). An infin. following: *—ed to die,* Err. I, 1, 26. Meas. II, 2, 34. H6A II, 4, 97. V, 4, 1. *c. myself to lack the courage of a woman,* Ant. IV, 14, 59 (cf. *To*). — *For sth.: — ed Lucius Pella for taking bribes,* Caes. IV, 3, 2. *the lily I —ed for thy hand,* Sonn. 99, 6 (found it guilty of having stolen its whiteness from thy hand).

Condemned = doomed to die, to be an easy prey to the enemy: *the poor —ed English,* H5 IV Chor. 22 (cf. III, 6, 143). *you have shamed me in your —ed seconds,* Cor. I, 8, 15.

2) to censure, to blame, to reprove: *travellers ne'er did lie, though fools at home c. them,* Tp. III, 3, 27. Ado III, 1, 108. *we cannot greatly c. our success,* All's III, 6, 58. *I could c. it as an improbable fiction,* Tw. III, 4, 141. R2 II, 2, 132. Troil. III, 3, 219. Caes. IV, 3, 10. Lr. I, 4, 365. Ant. II, 7, 86. Cymb. I, 6, 141. *to imagine an Antony, were nature's piece 'gainst fancy, —ing shadows quite,* Ant. V, 2, 100 (i. e. far surpassing them and showing them, by this, defective). Cor. V, 3, 134.

Condemnation, the act of condemning: Meas. II, 4, 174. H5 III, 6, 143. Cymb. III, 5, 98.

Condescend, to vouchsafe: H6A V, 3, 17. 120.

Condign, well deserved: *c. punishment,* H6B III, 1, 130. *c. praise,* LLL I, 2, 27 (Armado's speech).

Condition, subst. 1) term of a contract, stipulation: H4B IV, 1, 165. 184. 187. H5 II, 4, 144. V, 2, 326. H6A V, 1, 38. V, 4, 119. H8 I, 3, 24. Troil. IV, 5, 72. Cor. V, 1, 69. Caes. I, 2, 174. IV, 3, 32. Cymb. I, 4, 168. *upon c. I may quietly enjoy ...,* H6A V, 3, 153. *upon c. thou wilt swear ...,* V, 4, 129. *upon c. Publius shall not live,* Caes. IV, 1, 4. *to leave her on such slight —s,* Gentl. V, 4, 138 (i. e. for being obliged to fight for her). *on good c.* Cor. I, 10, 2. *on like —s,* V, 3, 205. *on such —s,* Qq in Lr. I, 1, 209. *with this c., to be whipped,* Shr. I, 1, 136. *with this c., to be thus taunted,* R3 I, 3, 108. — *Absolutely,* = on condition, even though: *himself! alas, poor Troilus! I would he were. So he is. C., I had gone barefoot to India,* Troil. I, 2, 80. cf. Lord Cromwell V, 4: *would 'twere otherwise, c. I spent half the wealth I have.*

2) contract, treaty: *mark his c. and the event,* Tp. I, 2, 117. 120. *if you repay me not such sum or sums as are expressed in the c.* Merch. I, 3, 149. *your oaths are words and poor —s, but unsealed,* All's IV, 2, 30. *shall our c. stand?* H6A V, 4, 165.

3) state, situation: *I will forget the c. of my estate, to rejoice in yours,* As I, 2, 16. *let no quarrel nor no brawl to come taint the c. of this present hour,* Tw. V, 365. *foretelling this same time's c.* H4B III, 1, 78. *suffer the c. of these times to lay a heavy hand upon our honours,* IV, 1, 101. V, 2, 11. *O hard c., twin-born of greatness,* H5 IV, 1, 250. *fitteth my degree or your c.* R3 III, 7, 143. *this throne, this Fortune, and this hill ... would be well expressed in our c.* Tim. I, 1, 77 (= would find a striking parallel in our state). *your weak c.* (= constitution) Caes. II, 1, 236. *I would not my unhoused free c. put into circumscription,* Oth. I, 2, 26. *as the time, the place, and the c. of this country stands,* II, 3, 302.

4) rank: *I am in my c. a prince,* Tp. III, 1, 59. *of what c. are you, and of what place?* H4B IV, 3, 1. *I, in my c., shall better speak of you than you deserve,* IV, 3, 90 (i. e. in my official capacity). *this day shall gentle his c.* H5 IV, 3, 63. *one so rude and of so mean c.* H6B V, 1, 64. *you see how all —s, how all minds tender down their services to Timon,* Tim. I, 1, 52.

5) quality: *here is the cate-log of her c.* Gentl. III, 1, 273. *our haste from hence is of so quick c.* Meas. I, 1, 54. *which is the hot c. of their blood,* Merch. V, 74. *in the gentle c. of blood,* As I, 1, 48 (= being of gentle blood). *the c. of that fardel,* Wint. IV, 4, 739. *a rage whose heat hath this c.* John III, 1, 341. *let me know my fault: on what c. stands it and wherein? even in c. of the worst degree,* R2 II, 3, 107. *Plural: all his senses have but human —s,* H5 IV, 1, 108. *suited in like —s as our argument,* Troil. Prol. 25. *one that knows him not; — yes, and his ill —s,* Ado III, 2, 68. *they know his —s and lay him in straw,* All's IV, 3, 288. *in such —s,* Ff. in Lr. I, 1, 209.

6) temper, character, habit: *a light c. in a beauty dark,* LLL V, 2, 20. *the c. of a saint, and the complexion of a devil,* Merch. I, 2, 143. *such is now the duke's c. that he misconstrues all that you have done,* As I, 2, 276. *demand of him my c.* All's IV, 3, 196. *our soft —s,* Shr. V, 2, 167. *I will rather be myself, mighty and to be feared, than my c.* H4A I, 3, 6. *let a Welsh correction teach you a good English c.* H5 V, 1, 83. *our tongue is rough, and my c. is not*

smooth, V, 2, 314. *I have a touch of your c.* R3 IV, 4, 157. *of true c.* H8 I, 2, 19. *all that time, acquaintance, custom and c. made tame and most familiar to my nature,* Troil. III, 3, 9. *'tis a c. they account gentle,* Cor. II, 3, 103. *that so short a time can alter the c. of a man,* V, 4, 10. *I'll trust to your —s,* Tim. IV, 3, 139. Caes. II, 1, 254. Lr. I, 1, 301. IV, 3, 35. Oth. II, 1, 255. IV, 1, 204. Ant. II, 2, 115. Cymb. V, 5, 165. Per. III, 1, 29.

Conditionally, on condition: *c., that here thou take an oath,* H6C I, 1, 196.

Conditioned, 1) of a certain quality or temper: *the best c. and unwearied spirit,* Merch. III, 2, 295. -- 2) limited by a condition: *live rich and happy; but thus c.: thou shalt build from men,* Tim. IV, 3, 533.

Condole, to mourn: *let us c. the knight,* H5 II, 1, 133 (Pistol's speech). Used blunderingly by Bottom: Mids. I, 2, 29. 43.

Condolement, sorrow, mourning: *to persever in obstinate c.* Hml. I, 2, 93. Used incorrectly: *there are certain —s, certain vails,* Per. II, 1, 156.

Conduce, to lead, to tend: *the reasons you allege do more c. to the hot passion of distempered blood,* Troil. II, 2, 168. *within my soul there doth c. a fight of this strange nature that a thing inseparate divides ...,* V, 2, 147; i. e. a fight of this nature (reason combating itself) brings me there (= to that state or extremity) to see two quite different things in one.

Conduct, subt. 1) guidance: *will to some provision give thee quick c.* Lr. III, 6, 104.

2) leading, command: *led by the impartial c. of my soul,* H4B V, 2, 36. *In the c. of:* As V, 4, 163. Troil. II, 2, 62. Rom. III, 3, 131. *Under the c. of:* John IV, 2, 129. H4B I, 1, 134. Tit. IV, 4, 65. Cymb. IV, 2, 340.

3) escort, guard: *give him courteous c. to this place,* Merch. IV, 1, 148. Tw. III, 4, 265. John I, 29. Cymb. III, 5, 8. *in my c.* H4A III, 1, 92. 197. *and under your fair c., crave leave to view these ladies,* H8 I, 4, 70. *in the c. of Iago,* Oth. II, 1, 75. *convey him with safe c.* H5 I, 2, 297. cf. *safe-conduct,* Troil. III, 3, 277. 288.

4) abstr. pro concr., = he who, or that which guides or escorts: *extinguishing his c.* (the torch) Lucr. 313. *there is in this business more than nature was ever c. of,* Tp. V, 244. *I will be his c.* R2 IV, 157. *although thou hast been c. of my shame,* H6B II, 4, 101. *appointed this c. to convey me to the Tower,* R3 I, 1, 45. *fury be my c. now,* Rom. III, 1, 129. *come, bitter c., come, unsavoury guide,* V, 3, 116.

Conduct, vb. 1) to bring along, to attend: Meas. II, 3, 18. LLL II, 96. IV, 3, 374. As III, 4, 58. Shr. Ind. 1, 107. All's III, 5, 44. Wint. II, 2, 7. John V, 6, 43. R2 IV, 103. H6A IV, 7, 51. V, 5, 100. R3 II, 4, 73. V, 3, 103. H8 I, 4, 58. Troil. III, 2, 3. V, 2, 184. Cor. I, 6, 63. I, 7, 7. Tit. II, 3, 79. Mcb. I, 6, 29. Oth. I, 3, 333. Per. II, 3, 108.

2) to lead as a commander: *will he c. you through the heart of France,* H6B IV, 8, 38. *hasten his musters and c. his powers,* Lr. IV, 2, 16.

Conductor, leader: *who is c. of his people?* Lr. IV, 7, 88.

Conduit, 1) a pipe for the conveyance of water: *all the —s of my blood froze up,* Err. V, 313. *that our best water brought by —s hither,* Cor. II, 3, 250.

2) a human figure on a well spouting water: *a pretty while these pretty creatures stand, like ivory —s coral cisterns filling,* Lucr. 1234. *the old shepherd which stands by like a weather-bitten c.* Wint. V, 2, 60. *as from a c. with three issuing spouts,* Tit. II, 4, 30. *a c., girl?* Rom. III, 5, 129.

Coney, rabbit: Ven. 687. As III, 2, 357 (fem.). H6C I, 4, 62. Cor. IV, 5, 226.

Coney-catch, to cheat, to sharp: Wiv. I, 1, 128. I, 3, 36. Shr. IV, 1, 45 (used improperly). V, 1, 102 (part. *coney-catched*).

Confect, see *Comfect.*

Confection, a composition of drugs: *our king himself doth woo me oft for my —s,* Cymb. I, 5, 15. *that c. which I gave him for cordial,* V, 5, 246.

Confectionary, subst., a place for sweetmeats: *who had the world as my c.* Tim. IV, 3, 260.

Confederacy, league, alliance, conspiracy: *she is one of this c.* Mids. III, 2, 192. *heard of our c.* H4A IV, 4, 38. *under the countenance and c. of Lady Eleanor,* H6B II, 1, 168. *a full-charged c.* H8 I, 2, 3. *what c. have you with the traitors?* Lr. III, 7, 44.

Confederate, subst., associate (mostly, but not always, in an ill sense): Tp. IV, 140. Err. IV, 1, 17. V, 236. H4B IV, 3, 79. H6A II, 2, 21. H6B I, 2, 86. R3 IV, 4, 504. Tit. I, 303. 344.

Confederate, adj., allied: *the other c. companion,* Meas. V, 352. *all the swords in Italy, and her c. arms,* Cor. V, 3, 208. *c. in the fact,* Tit. IV, 1, 39. *c. season,* Hml. III, 2, 267. Followed by *with:* Err. IV, 4, 105. R2 V, 3, 53. Tit. V, 1, 108. Cymb. III, 3, 68.

Confederate, vb. intr. to unite in a league: *—s with the king of Naples,* Tp. I, 2, 111.

Confer, 1) trans., to bestow; followed by *on:* *c. fair Milan on my brother,* Tp. I, 2, 126. Tim. I, 1, 122. Lr. I, 1, 41 (Qq *confirming*). 84 (Qq *confirmed*). Followed by *to:* *that gem, —ed by testament to the sequent issue,* All's V, 3, 197.

2) intr. to discourse, to talk: *they sit —ing by the parlour fire,* Shr. V, 2, 102. H6C V, 6, 6. Cymb. IV, 1, 9. — Followed by *with:* *to c. with thee,* Gentl. III, 2, 19. 61. H6A V, 3, 130. H6B I, 2, 74. R3 I, 3, 35. Followed by *about:* *we have some secrets to c. about,* Gentl. III, 1, 2. H6A V, 4, 101. Followed by *of:* *to c. of home affairs,* Gentl. II, 4, 119. III, 1, 253. Lr. I, 2, 98. By *with* and *of:* *c. with you of something,* Mids. I, 1, 125. Tit. V, 2, 34.

Conference, 1) discourse, conversation: Err. V, 62. Ado I, 3, 62. III, 1, 25. LLL II, 32. V, 2, 260. Mids. II, 1, 187. II, 2, 46. As I, 2, 270. Shr. II, 253. Wint. II, 2, 17. II, 3, 40. John II, 150. H6C II, 2, 171. R3 I, 1, 104. H8 II, 2, 81. II, 3, 51. Caes. IV, 2, 51. Mcb. III, 1, 80. Hml. III, 1, 1 (Ff *circumstance*). 193. Ant. I, 1, 45. Per. II, 4, 17. Cymb. I, 4, 141. *the c. was sadly borne,* Ado II, 3, 229. *to have some c. with your grace,* R2 V, 3, 27. H4A III, 2, 2. *the mutual c. that my mind hath had with you,* H6B I, 1, 25. R3 I, 1, 86. III, 7, 69. *to hold c. with:* Ado II, 1, 279. *to use:* H6C III, 3, 111. Caes. IV, 2, 17.

2) discussion: *being crossed in c. by some senators,* Caes. I, 2, 188.

Confess, 1) intr. a) to own: Wiv. I, 1, 94. Meas. V, 277. LLL IV, 3, 205. H6B III, 3, 11. IV, 2, 114. H6C III, 3, 6 etc. *marry, to c., could he get me?* John I, 236 (= sooth to say!).

b) to disclose to a priest the state of

one's conscience: *I should c. to you*, Rom.
IV, 1, 23.

2) trans. a) to own; followed by an accus.:
Ven. 1001. Wiv. I, 1, 106. Meas. II, 2, 138. II, 3,
29. V, 113. 162. Ado IV, 1, 94. 274. LLL I, 1, 287.
II, 156. Merch. III, 2, 34. As IV, 3, 166. John V, 4,
43. H6A II, 4, 67. H6B II, 3, 96. Tim. V, 1, 146
etc. *wherein I c. me much guilty*, As I, 2, 196. *c. thyself —*, Hml. V, 1, 44 (viz to be a blockhead). *—ed
it, hanged it*, Tim. I, 2, 22; cf. *to c., and be hanged
for his labour*, Oth. IV, 1, 38; and: *c. and live*, Merch.
III, 2, 35. — Followed by an accus. and dative: *thy
cheeks c. it, th' one to th' other*, All's I, 3, 183. —
Followed by a clause: *let me c. that we two must be
twain*, Sonn. 36, 1. Ven. 1117. Gentl. II, 4, 137.
Wiv. III, 4, 13. Meas. I, 3, 51. V, 184. Err. IV, 4,
102. V, 260. Mids. I, 1, 111. II, 2, 131. V, 68. Merch.
III, 2, 26. As I, 1, 53. II, 2, 11. III, 2, 408. R3 IV,
4, 210 etc. — By a dative and a clause: *—ing to
this man how ...*, Ado V, 1, 241. Shr. I, 1, 157. Wint.
IV, 3, 115. Rom. IV, 1, 25.

b) to acknowledge: *if you dare not trust that
you see, c. not that you know*, Ado III, 2, 123. *I c. the
wench*, LLL I, 1, 285 (do not disavow). *do you c.
the bond?* Merch. IV, 1, 181. *I c. the cape*, Shr. IV,
3, 141. 143. *Cleopatra does c. thy greatness*, Ant.
III, 12, 16. *now I have —ed that he is thine*, Sonn.
134, 1. *it is a judgment maimed and most imperfect
that will c. perfection so could err*, Oth. I, 3, 100.

c) to hear the confession of a penitent, to shrive:
I have —ed her, Meas. V, 533.

3) refl. to disclose the state of the conscience to a priest: *he hath —ed himself to Morgan, whom he supposes to be a friar*, All's IV, 3, 124.
c. yourself to heaven, Hml. III, 4, 149. *c. yourself freely
to her*, Oth. II, 3, 323. *c. thee freely of thy sin*, V, 2, 53.

Confession, 1) acknowledgment of something
to one's disadvantage: Meas. I, 2, 39. V, 377.
Ado V, 2, 75. LLL V, 2, 432. Merch. III, 2, 36. H4B
I, 1, 94. H8 I, 2, 6. II, 1, 16. Troil. III, 2, 161. Hml.
II, 2, 288. Oth. IV, 1, 37. With *of: to some c. of his
true state*, Hml. III, 1, 9.

2) the act of disclosing sins to a priest:
Gentl. IV, 3, 44. V, 2, 41. All's IV, 3, 130. H8 I, 2,
164. Rom. II, 3, 56. III, 5, 233. IV, 1, 22.

3) avowal, acknowledgment: *loves his mistress more
than in c.* Troil. I, 3, 269. *he made c. of you, and gave
you such a masterly report*, Hml. IV, 7, 96.

Confessor (cónfessor and conféssor). 1) a priest
who hears confessions: Meas. II, 1, 35. III, 1, 168.
IV, 3, 133. H8 I, 1, 218. I, 2, 149. I, 4, 15. II, 1, 21.
Rom. II, 6, 21. III, 3, 49.

2) surname of the Anglo-Saxon King Edward:
Edward —'s crown, H8 IV, 1, 88.

Confidence, 1) trust: Tp. I, 2, 97. R2 II, 4, 6.
H6A I, 2, 97. Troil. Prol. 23. Tim. III, 4, 31.

2) assurance, security: All's II, 1, 172.
Wint. I, 2, 414. John V, 1, 56. H8 I, 2, 167. Cor.
IV, 6, 93. Caes. II, 2, 49. Cymb. I, 4, 121. *they take
it already upon their c.* H4A II, 4, 10 (Qq *salvation).
in all c., he's not for Rhodes*, Oth. I, 3, 31.
Misapplied for *conference:* Wiv. I, 4, 172. Ado
III, 5, 3. Rom II, 4, 133.

Confident, adj. 1) trusting, without suspicion: *a man may be too c.* Wiv. II, 1, 194. *be c.
to speak; we three are but thyself*, R2 II, 1, 274. *let

me have it* (your secret); *I do not talk much. I am c.;
you shall, sir*, H8 II, 1, 146. *we are c., we shall hear
music*, Troil. I, 3, 72. *Rome, be as just and gracious
unto me as I am c. and kind to thee*, Tit. I, 61. Followed by *of: no lesser of her honour c. than I did
truly find her*, Cymb. V, 5, 187.

2) sure, assured: *c. I am last night 'twas on
mine arm*, Cymb. II, 3, 150. *yet c. I'll keep what I
have swore*, LLL I, 1, 114 (= I am sure to keep.
Or perhaps used adverbially).

3) full of assurance, without fear of
miscarriage: *art thou so c.?* All's II, 1, 162. *his
forces strong, his soldiers c.* John II, 61. *as c. as is
the falcon's flight*, R2 I, 3, 61. *c. against the world in
arms*, H4A V, 1, 117. *all too c., to give admittance to
a thought of fear*, H4B IV, 1, 152. *the c. and overlusty French*, H5 IV Chor. 18. — Peculiar expressions: *that water-walled bulwark, still secure and c.
from foreign purposes*, John II, 28 (= confidently
secure from). *these three, three thousand c., in act as
many*, Cymb. V, 3, 29 (i. e. equalling three thousand
in confidence; after the analogy of: *three thousand
strong).

Hence = bold, in a good and ill sense: *not
lions more c.* John II, 452. *a c. brow*, H4B II, 1, 121.
the c. tyrant keeps still in Dunsinane, Mcb. V, 4, 8.

Confidently, with strong assurance,
without fear of failure: *which you hear him so c. undertake to do*, All's III, 6, 21. 93.

Confine, vb., 1) to shut up: *she did c. thee into
a cloven pine*, Tp. I, 2, 274. 361. V, 7. John V, 7, 47.
H4B IV, 4, 119. H5 Prol. 20. Epil. 3. Cor. IV, 6,
86. Mcb. III, 4, 24. Hml. I, 5, 11. Ant. V, 1, 53.
Refl. *you c. yourself most unreasonably*, Cor. I, 3, 84.
c. yourself but in a patient list, Oth. IV, 1, 76.

2) to bound, to limit: *my verse to constancy —d,
one thing expressing*, Sonn. 105, 7. *a god in love, to
whom I am —d*, 110, 12. *supposed as forfeit to a
—d doom*, 107, 4 (i. e. to mortality). *whose honour
cannot be measured or —d*, Tp. V, 122. *thy —ing
shores*, John II, 338. *keep the wild flood —d*, H4B
I, 1, 154. H5 V, 2, 295. Troil. II, 3, 260. III, 2, 89.
Lr. I, 2, 25. IV, 1, 77. Refl.: *you must c. yourself
within the modest limits of order*, Tw. I, 3, 8.

3) to restrain to or from a certain place
or space, to assign the abode for: *I must be here
—d by you, or sent to Naples*, Tp. Epil. 4. *from our
free person she should be —d*, Wint. II, 1, 194. *to c.
yourself to Asher-house*, H8 III, 2, 230. *to England
send him, or c. him where your wisdom best shall think*,
Hml. III, 1, 194. cf. I, 5, 11.

4) to state with precision, to limit exactly: *acquitted by a true substantial form and present execution of our wills to us and to our purposes
—d*, H4B IV, 1, 175 (most M. Edd. *consigned). this
tablet lay upon his breast, wherein our pleasure his
full fortune doth c.* Cymb. V, 4, 110.

Confine, subst. (cónfine and confíne), 1) bound,
limit: *vow, bond, nor space, in thee* (love) *hath neither
sting, knot, nor c.* Compl. 265. *put into circumscription
and c.* Oth. I, 2, 27.

2) prison: *in which there are many —s, wards
and dungeons*, Hml. II, 2, 252. *the poor third is up,
till death enlarge his c.* Ant. III, 5, 13.

3) the space within the borders of which
some thing is restrained: *in whose c. immured

is the store which should example where your equal grew? Sonn. 84, 3. *this c. of blood and breath,* John IV, 2, 246. *nature in you stands on the very verge of her c.* Lr. II, 4, 150.

4) district, territory: *when he enters the —s of a tavern,* Rom. III, 1, 6. *spirits which I have from their —s called,* Tp. IV, 121. *the erring spirit hies to his c.* Hml. I, 1, 155. *here in these —s slily have I lurked,* R3 IV, 4, 3. *should in their own —s have their round haunches gored,* As II, 1, 24. *from our quiet —s fright fair peace,* R2 I, 3, 137. *measure our —s with such peaceful steps,* III, 2, 125. *now, neighbour —s, purge you of your scum,* H4B IV, 5, 124. *shall in these —s cry havock,* Caes. III, 1, 272.

Confineless, boundless: *my c. harms,* Mcb. IV, 3, 55.

Confiner, generally interpreted as borderer, but more probably meaning the inhabitant of a territory: *the senate hath stirred up the —s and gentlemen of Italy,* Cymb. IV, 2, 337 (cf. *Confine,* subst.).

Confirm, 1) to make firm, to strengthen: *let confusion of one part c. the other's peace,* John II, 359. *which elder days shall ripen and c. to more approved service,* R2 II, 3, 43. *his alliance will c. our peace,* H6A V, 5, 42. *to c. that amity with nuptial knot,* H6C III, 3, 54. *thou dost c. his happiness for ever,* R3 I, 2, 209. *whose strength I will c. with oath,* Cymb. II, 4, 64. — Partic. *confirmed =* firmly fixed, stably settled, not to be shaken: *in vain I spurn at my —ed despite,* Lucr. 1026. *like a constant and —ed devil,* 1513. *of approved valour and —ed honesty,* Ado II, 1, 395. *which I will do with —ed countenance,* V, 4, 17. *has such a —ed countenance,* Cor. I, 3, 65. *thy age —ed, proud, subtle,* R3 IV, 4, 171 (but perhaps *age —ed =* riper age). cf. *True-confirmed.*

2) to corroborate, to make more obligatory: *c. his welcome with some special favour,* Gentl. II, 4, 101. *to c. it* (your oath) *plain, you gave me this,* LLL V, 2, 452. *—ed by mutual joinder of your hands,* Tw. V, 160. *and to c. his goodness, tied it by letters-patents,* H8 III, 2, 249. *this, to c. my welcome, I, 4, 37. which to c., this coronet part betwixt you,* Lr. I, 1, 140.

3) to put past doubt, to ratify: *these likelihoods c. her flight,* Gentl. V, 2, 43. *his incivility —s no less,* Err. IV, 4, 49. Ado III, 3, 169. IV, 1, 152. All's IV, 3, 69. Tw. III, 4, 205. V, 260. H8 II, 1, 159. Mcb. V, 1, 21. V, 3, 31. V, 8, 41. Oth. III, 3, 7. Cymb. II, 4, 139. III, 4, 130. IV, 2, 328. Per. V, 1, 203. *I have told more of you to myself than you can with modesty speak in your own behalf; and thus far I c. you,* Tim. I, 2, 98 (i. e. to that extent I am past doubt concerning you; my belief in you goes the length of what I told myself about you).

4) to assent to, to establish by assent, to ratify: *—ed, sealed, ratified by you,* Merch. III, 2, 149. *our souls religiously c. thy words,* John IV, 3, 73. *have —ed conspiracy with fearful France,* H5 II Chor. 27. *what she says I'll c.* H6A I, 2, 128. *c. it so, mine honourable lord,* IV, 1, 122. *what we do establish, he —s,* H6B III, 1, 317. *let me c. my princely brother's greeting,* Troil. IV, 5, 174. *I would the Gods had nothing else to do but to c. my curses,* Cor. IV, 2, 46. *c. the crown to me and to mine heirs,* H6C I, 1, 172. *he's not —ed; we may deny him yet,* Cor. II, 3, 217.

Confirmation, 1) firmer establishment,

strengthening: *to thee it shall descend with better quiet, better opinion, better c.* H4B IV, 5, 189.

2) asseveration, assurance: *a second time receive the c. of my promised gift,* All's II, 3, 56. *let heaven witness, how dear I hold this c.* H8 V, 3, 174.

3) additional evidence: *the particular —s, to the full arming of the verity,* All's IV, 3, 71. *for a greater c. I have dispatched ...,* Wint. II, 1, 180. *for c. that I am much more,* Lr. III, 1, 44. *trifles are to the jealous —s,* Oth. III, 3, 323. Cymb. I, 6, 174. Per. V, 3, 54.

Confirmer, that which confirms: *the oath of a lover is no stronger than the word of a tapster; they are both the c. of false reckonings,* As III, 4, 35. *be these sad signs —s of thy words?* John III, 1, 24.

Confirmity, a blunder of Mrs Quickly for *infirmity:* H4B II, 4, 64.

Confiscate, adj. (*confiscate* and *cónfiscate*), forfeited to the public treasury: Err. I, 2, 2. Merch. IV, 1, 332. H6C IV, 6, 55 (F2F3F4 *—d;* M. Edd. *be c.*). Cymb. V, 5, 323. Followed by *to:* Err. I, 1, 21. Merch. IV, 1, 311.

Confiscation, forfeiture; adjudging to the public treasury: Meas. V, 428 (O. Edd. *confutation*).

Confixed, fastened: *or else for ever be c. here, a marble monument,* Meas. V, 232.

Conflict, subst., combat: Ven. 345. Ado I, I, 66. LLL IV, 3, 369. H6B III, 2, 164 (*hold*). H6C II, 5, 62. IV, 6, 94. Tit. II, 3, 21. Tim. III, 5, 66. Mcb. I, 2, 53. Lr. III, 5, 24. V, 3, 197.

Conflict, vb. to combat: *the —ing elements,* Tim. IV, 3, 230. *the to and fro —ing wind and rain,* Lr. III, 1, 11.

Confluence, a crowding, concourse: *you see this c., this great flood of visitors,* Tim. I, 1, 42.

Conflux, a flowing together: *knots, by the c. of meeting sap,* Troil. I, 3, 7.

Conform, vb. to make suitable: *and to my humble seat c. myself,* H6C III, 3, 11.

Conformable, compliant, obsequious: *c. as other household Kates,* Shr. II, 280. *to your will c.* H8 II, 4, 24.

Confound, 1) to mingle so as to make indistinguishable: *like a drop of water that in the ocean seeks another drop, who ... —s himself,* Err. I, 2, 38.

2) to perplex, to confuse: *even so —ed in the dark she lay,* Ven. 827. *that eye which looks on her —s his wits,* Lucr. 290. *the wiry concord that mine ear —s,* Sonn. 128, 4. Phoen. 41. John V, 7, 20. R3 IV, 4, 261. H6A V, 3, 71.

3) to amaze: *the timorous yelping of the hounds appals her senses and her spirit confounds,* Ven. 882. *which with cold terror doth men's minds c.* 1048. Lucr. 456. Caes. III, 1, 87. Hml. II, 2, 591.

4) to destroy, to ruin, to make away with: *when he himself himself —s,* Lucr. 160. *c. and kill all pure effects,* 250. *my shame be his that did my fame c.* 1202. *one man's lust these many lives —s,* 1489. *never-resting time leads summer on to hideous winter and —s him there,* Sonn. 5, 6. 60, 8. 64, 10. 69, 7. Gentl. V, 4, 73. Meas. IV, 4, 31. LLL V, 2, 397. 520. Mids. III, 2, 93. Merch. III, 2, 278. Shr. V, 2, 140. All's II, 3, 127. John IV, 2, 29. V, 7, 58. R2 III, 4, 60. IV, 141. V, 3, 86. H4B IV, 4, 41. R3 II, 1, 14. IV, 4, 399. Rom. II, 6, 13. Tim. IV, 3, 339.

V, 1, 106. Mcb. II, 2, 12. IV, 1, 54. IV, 3, 99. Ant. III, 2, 58. Cymb. I, 4, 54. Per. V, 2, 14. *all is —ed* = all is lost, H5 IV, 5, 3. — Used by way of a curse: *war and lechery c. all!* Troil. II, 3, 82. *the Roman Gods c. you both!* Tit. IV, 2, 6. Tim. I, 1, 244. IV, 1, 37. IV, 3, 75. Ant. II, 5, 92. *—ed be your strife!* H6A IV, 1, 123. *—ed be thyself,* Tim. IV, 3, 128. *O, c. the rest!* Hml. III, 2, 187 (= speak no more).

Without an object: *—ing age's cruel knife,* Sonn. 63, 10. *the shaft —s, not that it wounds, but tickles still the sore,* Troil. III, 1, 128*) *—ing contraries,* Tim. IV, 1, 20. *—ing odds,* IV, 3, 392. *come, tears, c.!* Mids. V, 300 (Pyramus' speech).   *) O. Ed. without comma.

5) to waste, to wear away: *who —s in singleness the parts that thou shouldst bear,* Sonn. 8, 7. *as doth a galled rock o'erhang and jutty his —ed base, swilled with the wild and wasteful ocean,* H5 III, 1, 13. Applied to time: *he did c. the best part of an hour,* H4A I, 3, 100. *how couldst thou in a mile c. an hour,* Cor. I, 6, 17. *let's not c. the time with conference harsh,* Ant. I, 1, 45. *to c. such time as drums him from his sport, 'tis to be chid,* I, 4, 28.

Confront, to face, to meet, to oppose: *we four indeed —ed were with four in Russian habit,* LLL V, 2, 367. *power —ed power,* John II, 330. H4B V, 3, 108. Tit. IV, 4, 3. Mcb. I, 2, 55. *whereto serves mercy but to c. the visage of offence?* Hml. III, 3, 47. In John II, 215 O. Edd. *comfort,* most M. Edd. *confront,* Coll. M. *come 'fore.*

Confused, indistinguishably mixed, disordered, indistinct: *sounds c.* H5 III Chor. 10. *howls c.* III, 3, 39. *a din c.* Cor. III, 3, 20. *c. cries,* Tit. II, 3, 102. *I never heard a passion so c.* Merch. II, 8, 12. *c. wrong,* John V, 2, 23 (no more to be distinguished from right). *c. events,* Mcb. II, 3, 63 (i. e. disorders, revolutions). *'tis here, but yet c.* Oth. II, 1, 320.

Confusedly, in disorder: *stakes plucked out of hedges they pitched in the ground c.* H6A I, 1, 118.

Confusion, 1) tumultuous medley, indistinct combination, disorder: *and fright her with c. of their cries,* Lucr. 445. *the musical c. of hounds and echo,* Mids. IV, 1, 115. *I will try —s with him,* Merch. II, 2, 39 (Q1 *conclusions*). *there is such c. in my powers,* III, 2, 179. As V, 4, 131. R2 II, 2, 19. H4A V, 1, 82. Rom. IV, 5, 66. Hml. III, 1, 2. Cymb. V, 3, 41. Per. IV, 1, 65.

2) ruin, overthrow: *they that lose half with greater patience bear it than they whose whole is swallowed in c.* Lucr. 1159. *infect thy sap and live on thy c.* Err. II, 2, 182. Mids. I, 1, 149. John II, 359. IV, 3, 152. H6A IV, 1, 77. 194. H6B II, 1, 187. Cor. III, 1, 110. 190. Rom. IV, 5, 65. Tim. IV, 1, 21. IV, 3, 127. 369. V, 4, 52. Mcb. II, 3, 71. III, 5, 29. Lr. III, 2, 92. Ant. III, 13, 115. Cymb. III, 1, 66. IV, 2, 92. — Used as a curse: *shame and c.!* H6B V, 2, 31. *crying c.* Cor. IV, 6, 29. *plague! death! c.!* Lr. II, 4, 95.

Confutation, refutation: H6A IV, 1, 98. = conviction in Meas. V, 428 (M. Edd. *confiscation*).

Confute, to refute, to put to silence: *my sisterly remorse —s mine honour,* Meas. V, 100. *nothing —s me but eyes,* H4A V, 4, 129.

Conge, see *Congy.*

Congeal, 1) trans. to coagulate, to make to freeze: *sadness hath —ed your blood,* Shr. Ind. 2,

134. — 2) intr. to coagulate, to freeze: *lest zeal, now melted ..., cool and c. again,* John II, 479. — Partic. *—ed: blood,* Ven. 1122. Lucr. 1744. *ice,* Meas. III, 2, 118. *—ed white, high Taurus' snow,* Mids. III, 2, 141. *flaws,* H4B IV, 4, 35. *blood,* H6C I, 3, 52. V, 2, 37. R3 I, 2, 56.

Congealment, coagulated blood: *wash the c. from your wounds,* Ant. IV, 8, 10.

Conger, the sea-eel, (regarded as a provocative): *eats c. and fennel,* H4B II, 4, 266. Applied to Falstaff, as a term of reproach: *you muddy c.* H4B II, 4, 58.

Congest, to gather in a mass: *must for your victory us all c.* Compl. 258.

Congratulate, to make glad, to amuse, to give pleasure to: *it is the king's pleasure to c. the princess at her pavilion in the posteriors of this day,* LLL V, 1, 93 (cf. *Gratulate*).

Congree, to agree: *—ing in a full and natural close,* H5 I, 2, 182 (Qq *congrueth*).

Congreet, to have a friendly meeting: *that face to face and royal eye to eye, you have —ed,* H5 V, 2, 31.

Congregate, to come together, to assemble: *where merchants most do c.* Merch. I, 3, 50. *the —d college,* All's II, 1, 120. *—d sands,* Oth. II, 1, 69.

Congregation, 1) assemblage, collection: *a foul and pestilent c. of vapours,* Hml. II, 2, 315. — 2) assembly of persons: Cor. III, 2, 11. Persons met for a religious purpose: Ado III, 2, 127. III, 3, 173.

Congrue, to agree: *—th with a mutual consent,* H5 I, 2, 182 (reading of the spurious Qq; Ff *congreeing*). *letters —ing to that effect,* Hml. IV, 3, 66 (Ff *conjuring*).

Congruent (used only by Armado and Holophernes) apt, suitable: *a c. epitheton,* LLL I, 2, 14. *the posterior of the day is liable, c. and measurable for the afternoon,* V, 1, 97.

Congy, to take leave: *I have —ied with the duke,* All's IV, 3, 100 (most M. Edd. *conged*).

Conject, vb. to guess: *one that so imperfectly —s,* Oth. III, 3, 149 (Ff *conceits*).

Conjectural, founded on conjecture, formed by guess: *makest c. fears to come into me,* All's V, 3, 114. *give out c. marriages,* Cor. I, 1, 198.

Conjecture, subst. 1) guess: H4B Ind. 16. I, 3, 23. H8 I, 1, 41 *('tis likely, by all —s).* Troil. IV, 5, 250.

2) suspicion: *on my eyelids shall c. hang,* Ado IV, 1, 107. *as gross as ever touched c.* Wint. II, 1, 176. *strew dangerous —s in ill-breeding minds,* Hml. IV, 5, 15.

3) idea, notion: *in my simple —s,* Wiv. I, 1, 30 (Evans' speech). *now entertain c. of a time,* H5 IV Chor. 1.

Conjoin, 1) trans. to join, to unite: Ado IV, 1, 13. V, 4, 29. H6A V, 2, 12. R3 V, 5, 31. Hml. III, 4, 126.

2) intr. to join, to league: Mids. III, 2, 193. H4B IV, 5, 64.

Conjointly, jointly, together: John II, 379. Caes. I, 3, 29.

Conjunct, joined, in a near connexion: *c. and flattering his displeasure,* Lr. II, 2, 125 (Ff *compact*). *c. and bosomed with her,* V, 1, 12.

Conjunction, union, connection: Mids. IV, 1, 116. John II, 468. III, 1, 227. H4A IV, 1, 37 (*our small c.* = our small assembled force). H4B II, 4, 286 (*Saturn and Venus in c.*). V, 1, 77. H5 V, 2, 380. R3 V, 5, 20. H8 III, 2, 45.

Conjunctive, closely united: *she's so c. to my life and soul,* Hml. IV, 7, 14. *let us be c. in our revenge,* Oth. I, 3, 374 (Qq *communicative*).

Conjuration, 1) incantation: *buz these —s in her brain,* H6B I, 2, 99. *what c. and what mighty magic,* Oth. I, 3, 92.

2) obsecration: *mock not my senseless c.* R2 III, 2, 23. *under this c. speak,* H5 I, 2, 29. *I do defy thy —s,* Rom V, 3, 68 (Q2 *commiration,* Ff *commiseration*). *an earnest c. from the king,* Hml. V, 2, 38.

Cónjure (conjúre in Err. III, 1, 34. Rom. II, 1, 26. Hml. V, 1, 279. Oth. I, 3, 105. III, 3, 294), 1) to influence by magic, to engage by incantations; a) absolutely: *dost thou c. for wenches, that thou callest for such store?* Err. III, 1, 34. *if you would c. in her,* H5 V, 2, 319. *I'll c. too,* Rom. II, 1, 6. Caes. I, 2, 146. Troil. V, 2, 125. Per. IV, 6, 156.

b) trans.: *I would to God some scholar would c. her,* Ado II, 1, 264. H5 II, 1, 57. H6A I, 5, 5. Troil. II, 3, 6. Hml. V, 1, 279. Followed by an infinitive, to denote the effect: *all these spirits thy power hath —d to attend,* Tim. I, 1, 7. Lr. II, 1, 41. Followed by an adverb: *till she had laid it and —d it down,* Rom. II, 1, 26. *to c. up:* Mids. III, 2, 158. H5 V, 2, 316. 320. H6B V, 1, 199. R3 I, 2, 34. Caes. II, 1, 323. cf. *the habitation which your prophet —d the devil into,* Merch. I, 3, 35. *magic, which has my evils —d to remembrance,* Wint. V, 3, 40. *you c. from the breast of civil peace such bold hostility,* H4A IV, 3, 43. — *Conjured* = charmed by incantations: *some dram —d to this effect,* Oth. I, 3, 105. — Comically, *to c.* = to make one pay dear for conjuring: *I'll c. you, I'll fortune-tell you,* Wiv. IV, 2, 195.

2) to call on with solemnity, to obsecrate; a) absol.: *with letters —ing to that effect,* Hml. IV, 3, 66 (Qq *congruing*). — b) trans.: *I do c. thee,* Gentl. II, 7, 2. Meas. V, 48. Err. IV, 4, 60. As Epil. 11. John IV, 2, 269. Mcb. IV, 1, 50. Hml. II, 2, 294. Followed by an infin: *I c. thee to leave me,* Err. IV, 3, 68. Cor. V, 2, 81. *she —s him ... that he make retire,* Lucr. 568. *that thou declare,* Wint. I, 2, 400. *she should ever keep it,* Oth. III, 3, 294. The effect denoted by a preposition: *he hath —d me beyond them* (my occasions) Tim. III, 6, 13.

Cónjurer, one who lays or raises spirits: Err. IV, 4, 50. V, 177. 242. H6A I, 1, 26. H6B I, 2, 76. II, 1, 172. IV, 2, 99.

Connive, to close the eyes upon a fault: *the gods do this year c. at us, and we may do any thing,* Wint IV, 4, 692.

Conquer, 1) to vanquish, to overcome; a) trans.: Lucr. 488. 1210. Sonn. 90, 6. Pilgr. 50. Err. III, 2, 28. R2 II, 1, 65. H6C II, 5, 12. IV, 6, 19. R3 V, 3, 145. Cor. V, 3, 142. Tit. I, 336. Ant. V, 2, 225 etc. — b) intr.: Ven. 100. LLL V, 2, 566. H5 V Chor. 28. H6A I, 1, 16. I, 5, 22. II, 1, 26. IV, 7, 95. V, 3, 1. R3 V, 3, 150. Troil. I, 3, 352. Cor. III, 3, 26. Tim. IV, 3, 104. Ant. II, 7, 113. III, 7, 66. III, 13, 75.

2) to subdue: All's IV, 2, 57. H5 V, 2, 195. H6A V, 4, 110. H6B I, 1, 82. 102. H6C I, 4, 63. III, 3, 86. Ant. III, 6, 34. Cymb. III, 1, 5.

Conqueror, 1) victor: Ven. 549. LLL I, 1, 8. V, 2, 570. 575. 578. 582. Mids. V, 51. As IV, 2, 4. John II, 310. H6A III, 2, 81. H6C II, 5, 12. III, 2, 3. R3 II, 4, 61. III, 1, 87. IV, 4, 184. 334. V, 3, 128. Tit. I, 104. Caes. V, 5, 55. Hml. I, 1, 89. Lr. IV, 6, 271. Ant. III, 11, 66 (fem.). IV, 14, 62 (fem.). V, 2, 27.

2) one that subdues: Shr. Ind. 1, 5 (*Richard C.*). John V, 7, 113. H6A IV, 3, 50. V, 5, 73. 74.

Conquest, 1) victory: *the foul boar's c. on her fair delight,* Ven. 1030. *to outlook c.* John V, 2, 115. *it is a c. for a prince to boast of,* H4A I, 1, 77. *princes fleshed with c.* H4B I, 1, 149. IV, 2, 89. H5 II, 2, 24. H6A I, 1, 130. V, 2, 19. H6C V, 1, 71. V, 2, 10. R3 IV, 4, 335. Tim. IV, 3, 103. Caes. II, 2, 66. III, 1, 149. V, 5, 38. Hml. V, 2, 361. Ant. V, 2, 135. *To make c.* = to gain a victory: *better c. never canst thou make,* John III, 1, 290. Followed by *of:* shall *rotten death make c. of the stronger,* Lucr. 1767. *England hath made a shameful c. of itself,* R2 II, 1, 66. *death makes no c. of this conqueror,* R3 III, 1, 87. *make a c. of unhappy me,* Per. I, 4, 69.

2) acquisition by superior force: H6A III, 4, 11. IV, 1, 148. IV, 3, 50. H6B I, 1, 96. H6C I, 1, 132. Cymb. III, 1, 22 (*make*).

3) that which is acquired by force, prey, booty: *as the grim lion fawneth o'er his prey, sharp hunger by the c. satisfied,* Lucr. 422. *mine eye and heart are at a mortal war how to divide the c. of thy sight,* Sonn. 46, 2. *to be death's c.* 6, 14. *the coward c. of a wretch's knife,* 74, 11. *what c. brings he home?* Caes. I, 1, 37. *put in the roll of c.* Ant. V, 2, 181.

Conrade, name in Ado III, 3, 102. 104. IV, 2, 16.

Consanguineous, of the same blood: Tw. II, 3, 82.

Consanguinity, relation by blood: Troil. IV, 2, 103.

Conscience, 1) the involuntary moral judgment of our own actions: Lucr. 247. Sonn. 151, 1. 2. 13. Tp. I, 2, 470. II, 1, 275. 278. Wiv. III, 3, 235. IV, 2, 221. V, 5, 32. Meas. II, 3, 21. Ado I, 1, 291. V, 2, 86. LLL IV, 2, 2. V, 2, 333 (*—s*). Mids. V, 230. Merch. II, 2, 1 etc. As III, 2, 410 (*—s*). Tw. III, 3, 17. John I, 42. V, 4, 43. H4A V, 2, 88 (*—s*). H5 I, 2, 31. III, 3, 13. IV, 1, 8 (*—s*). H6B III, 1, 141. III, 2, 235. H6C I, 1, 150. R3 I, 2, 235. I, 3, 222. I, 4, 124. III, 7, 174. IV, 3, 20. V, 2, 17. V, 3, 179. Troil. V, 10, 28 etc. etc. *I cannot with c. take it,* Wint. IV, 4, 660 (Autolycus' speech). *made it no c. to destroy a prince,* John IV, 2, 229. *that I shall clear myself, I make as little doubt as you do c. in doing daily wrongs,* H8 V, 3, 67 (cf. *make no c. of the law,* in the spurious Q1 of Rom. 20, 52). *is 't not perfect c.* Hml. V, 2, 67.

2) consciousness in general, private judgment, inmost thoughts: *I appeal to your own c., how I was in your grace,* Wint. III, 2, 47. *canst thou the c. lack to think I shall lack friends?* Tim. IV, 2, 184. *thus c. does make cowards of us all,* Hml. III, 1, 83 (= thought, consideration). *now must your c. my acquittance seal,* IV, 7, 1. *this will witness outwardly, as strongly as the c. does within,* Cymb. II, 2, 36. *I will speak my c. of the king,* H5 IV, 1, 123. *shall I speak my c.?* H6B III, 1, 68. — *In c.* = in truth, indeed: *dost thou in c. think ...,* Oth. IV, 3, 61. *In my c.:* Merch. II, 2, 29. Tw. III, 1, 33

Wint. III, 3, 4. H5 III, 6, 14. IV, 1, 81. H6B V, 1, 177. Tim. III, 3, 16. — *On my c.: and wot you what I found there, on my c., put unwillingly?* H8 III, 2, 123. *on my Christian c., this one christening will beget a thousand,* V, 4, 37. *tell me, even upon thy c., is Edward your true king?* H6C III, 3, 113. *and, o' my c., wish him ten fathom deep,* H8 II, 1, 50. *o' my conscience, twenty of the dog-days reign in's nose,* V, 4, 42. *they are too unwholesome, a c.* Per. IV, 2, 23 (M. Edd. *o' c.* cf. *A*).

Conscienced, in *Soft-conscienced.*

Conscionable, conscientious: *no further c. than in putting on the mere form of civil and humane seeming,* Oth. II, 1, 242.

Consecrate, vb. 1) to make sacred: *c. commotion's bitter edge,* H4B IV, 1, 93. *we'll c. the steps that Ajax makes,* Troil. II, 3, 193.

2) to devote: *to Saturnine ... I c. my sword,* Tit. I, 248. *to his honours ... did I my soul and fortunes c.* Oth. I, 3, 255.

Partic. *consecrated* = sacred: *her —d wall,* Lucr. 723. *at the —d fount,* Meas. IV, 3, 102. *her close and —d bower,* Mids. III, 2, 7. *that —d roof,* Tw. IV, 3, 25. *the —d snow that lies on Dian's lap,* Tim. IV, 3, 386.

Partic. *consecrate;* 1) sacred: *with this field-dew c.* Mids. V, 422. — 2) devoted: *c. to thee,* Sonn. 74, 6. *this body, c. to thee,* Err. II, 2, 134. *the imperial seat, to virtue c.* Tit. I, 14. *her sacred wit to villany and vengeance c.* II, 1, 121.

Consecration, act of devoting to the service of God: *all vows and —s giving place,* Compl. 263.

Consent, subst. 1) accord; a yielding of the mind or will to something proposed: *—s bewitched, ere he desire, have granted,* Compl. 131. *to seal our happiness with their —s,* Gentl. I, 3, 49. *not by my c.* Wiv. III, 2, 72. *the wealth I have waits on my c.* 78. III, 3, 116. Meas. II, 4, 161. IV, 1, 67. Mids. I, 1, 25. III, 2, 231. As V, 2, 15. All's V, 3, 69. John IV, 3, 135. H6B II, 4, 72. III, 1, 316. H6C II, 2, 88. II, 6, 102. Cor. III, 1, 201. Rom. I, 2, 17. Hml. I, 2, 60. Oth. I, 1, 122. *by c.* R2 I, 1, 128. *with c.* Shr. III, 2, 139. IV, 4, 47. *to give c.: I give c. to go along with you,* Gentl. IV, 3, 39. Lucr. 1854. Wiv. IV, 6, 45. All's II, 1, 156. R2 IV, 249. H6A V, 3, 136. V, 4, 124. V, 5, 23. H6C II, 6, 11. R3 III, 4, 40. *to yield c.:* H6C II, 2, 24. IV, 6, 36. 46. — Followed by *shall* or *should: my c. that she should be your wife,* Mids. IV, 1, 163. *give c. thy daughter shall be wedded to my king,* H6A V, 3, 136. V, 4, 124. H6C II, 6, 11. R3 III, 4, 40. IV, 2, 23. Followed by *may:* H6A V, 5, 23. By the subjunctive: H8 V, 3, 53. By *to:* Lucr. 1854. All's II, 1, 156. H6C II, 1, 172.

2) vote, counsel: *thou shouldst a husband take by my c., as I by thine a wife,* Wint. V, 3, 136. *by my c., we'll even let them alone,* H6A I, 2, 44. *I yield thee my free c.* H6C IV, 6, 36 (= I vote for thee). *if you shall cleave to my c., when 'tis, it shall make honour for you,* Mcb. I, 1, 25.

3) agreement, unity of opinion: *with one c. they all vowed,* Lucr. Arg. 21. 25. *do in c. shake hands to torture me,* Sonn. 28, 6. Shr. IV, 4, 35. H4B V, 1, 78. H5 I, 2, 181 (M. Edd. *concent*). 206 (M. Edd. *concent*). II, 2, 22. H6B I, 1, 42. Troil. III, 3, 176. Cor. V, 3, 71. Followed by *of* (= about): *their*

c. of one direct way should be at once to all the points o' the compass, Cor. II, 3, 24.

4) concert, intelligence: *they fell together all, as by c.* Tp. II, 1, 203. *here was a c. to dash it* (our merriment) LLL V, 2, 460. *some villains of my court are of c. and sufferance in this,* As II, 2, 3.

Consent, vb. 1) to agree, to yield to something proposed: *I will c. to act any villany,* Wiv. II, 1, 101. *she hath —ed,* IV, 6, 25. Meas. IV, 3, 59. Err. IV, 1, 72. Mids. I, 1, 40. 82. All's III, 7, 19. John IV, 2, 239. H6A V, 3, 136. H6B III, 1, 275. H6C IV, 6, 46. Cor. I, 9, 37. Caes. IV, 1, 2. Hml. I, 5, 152. Used of a promise of marriage: As IV, 1, 69. V, 2, 8. H5 V, 2, 332. Followed by *shall:* Shr. II, 271. Hml. I, 1, 172. By the subjunctive: Troil. I, 3, 362. Caes. III, 1, 232. By *to:* Wiv. II, 2, 245 *(to c. to you).* Meas. III, 1, 71. V, 424. Cor. IV, 6, 144. In the following passages it may have the second signification: *if thou didst but c. to this most cruel act,* John IV, 3, 125. *thou dost c. in some large measure to thy father's death,* R2 I, 2, 25. *the bad revolting stars that have —ed unto Henry's death,* H6A I, 1, 5. *—ed unto Salisbury's death,* I, 5, 34.

2) to agree, or to come to an agreement: *'tis well —ed,* Ado IV, 1, 253. *all your writers do c. that ipse is he,* As V, 1, 48. *'tis but the boldness of his hand, which his heart was not —ing to,* All's III, 2, 80. *c. with both that we may enjoy each other,* As V, 2, 10. *c. upon a sure foundation,* H4B I, 3, 52. *as you and Lord Aeneas c. upon the order of their fight, so be it,* Troil. IV, 5, 90. *did you and he c. in Cassio's death?* Oth. V, 2, 297 (= did you together plan Cassio's death? cf. the last passages sub 1.).

Consequence, 1) that which follows, either in effect, or in time, or in attendance; a) in effect: *the c. is then thy jealous fits have scared thy husband from the use of wits,* Err. V, 85. Merch. III, 2, 107. Rom. I, 4, 107. Caes. I, 3, 124. Mcb. I, 7, 3. — b) in time: *a dire induction am I witness to, and will to France, hoping the c. will prove as bitter,* R3 IV, 4, 6. *he closes with you in this c.: Good sir, or so,* Hml. II, 1, 45. 52. 54 (= in thus following up your remark). *if c. do but approve my dream, my boat sails freely,* Oth. II, 3, 64. — c) in attendance: *when it falls, each small annexment, petty c., attends the boisterous ruin,* Hml. III, 3, 21.

2) that which must follow or come to pass in the course of things; the result of time, a necessary and inevitable event: *ever your fresh whore and your powdered bawd: an unshunned c.; it must be so,* Meas. III, 2, 63. *but Edward lives. True, noble prince. O bitter c., that Edward still should live,* R3 IV, 2, 15.* *the spirits that know all mortal —s have pronounced me thus,* Mcb. V, 3, 5.

3) succession: *you are curbed from that enlargement by the c. o' the crown,* Cymb. II, 3, 126 (perhaps belonging to 1 c, and meaning: by the considerations attending the crown).

4) influence, importance: *in matter of heavy c.* All's II, 5, 49. R2 V, 2, 61. H5 II, 4, 146. H8 II, 4, 214 (c. of dread = dreadful importance). *win us with honest trifles, to betray us in deepest c.* Mcb. I, 3, 126.

Consequently, pursuantly, thereafter: *and c. sets down the manner how,* Tw. III, 4, 79. *didst let thy heart consent, and c. thy rude hand to act the* deed, John IV, 2, 240. *and c., like a traitor coward, sluiced out his innocent soul*, R2 I, 1, 102.

Conserve, vb. 1) to preserve, to save: *thou art too noble to c. a life in base appliances*, Meas. III, 1, 88. — 2) to preserve, to confect: *it was dyed in mummy which the skilful — d of maidens' hearts*, Oth. III, 4, 75 (Qq *with the skilful conserves*, or *conserve*).

Conserve, subst. 1) sweetmeat made of fruits: Shr. Ind. 2, 3. 7. 8. 2) a similar preparation for medicinal or magical purposes: *with the skilful —s of maidens' hearts*, Oth. III, 4, 75 (Ff and M. Edd. *which the skilful conserved*).

Consider, 1) to view attentively, to observe, to examine: *I have —ed so much, and with some care; so far that I have eyes under my service which look upon his removedness*, Wint. IV, 2, 39. *is man no more than this? c. him well*, Lr. III, 4, 107.

2) to take into consideration, to think on, to ponder; a) trans.: Tp. III, 2, 106. Gentl. I, 3, 19. V, 2, 25. Wiv. III, 5, 51. Merch. IV, 1, 198. H4A I, 3, 70. H4B I, 2, 196. H6A V, 1, 35. R3 III, 7, 176. IV, 2, 87. H8 V, 1, 100. Cor. III, 1, 320. III, 3, 49. Caes. I, 2, 168. I, 3, 62. Mcb. II, [2, 30 *(c. it not so deeply)*. Hml. III, 2, 48. Oth. I, 3, 19. Per. V, 1, 136. Followed by a clause: *when I c. every thing that grows holds in perfection but a little moment*, Sonn. 15, 1. Err. IV, 1, 68. LLL II, 2. IV, 3, 291. Mids. V, 112. As III, 4, 3. All's II, 3, 175. Tw. III, 4, 108. Wint. I, 2, 374. V, 1, 26. H4A V, 2, 77. H5 II, 2, 41. H6B I, 1, 151. R3 I, 4, 261. H8 I, 1, 106. III, 1, 159. Cor. I, 1, 30. Tim. III, 4, 12. Lr. III, 7, 30. Oth. III, 3, 216. Ant. III, 13, 54. Cymb. III, 3, 11.

b) intr.: *'twere to c. too curiously, to c. so*, Hml. V, 1, 227. *let her c.* Cymb. II, 3, 20. *you're best c.* III, 2, 79. Followed by *of: bid them o'erread these letters, and well c. of them*, H4B III, 1, 3. H5 II, 4, 113. III, 6, 133. H6C III, 2, 16. Cor. I, 2, 17. Caes. III, 2, 114. Mcb. III, 1, 75. Cymb. III, 4, 114.

To c. with one's self, trans. and intr.: *I have —ed with myself the title ...*, H6B V, 1, 175. *you ought to c. with yourselves*, Mids. III, 1, 30.

Considering = taking into account: Shr. IV, 1, 10. Rom. II, 2, 64.

3) to have regard to: *you that have worn your eyes almost out in the service, you will be —ed*, Meas. I, 2, 114.

4) to requite, to pay: *which (services) if I have not enough —ed*, Wint. IV, 2, 19. *being something gently —ed, I'll bring you where he is*, IV, 4, 825. *if this penetrate, I will c. your music the better*, Cymb. II, 3, 32.

Considerance, consideration, sober reflection: H4B V, 2, 98.

Considerate, thoughtful, circumspect: *none are for me that look into me with c. eyes*, R3 IV, 2, 30. *your c. stone*, Ant. II, 2, 112.

Consideration, 1) meditation, reflection: *startles and frights c.* John IV, 2, 25. *c., like an angel, came*, H5 I, 1, 28. *and in thy best c. check this hideous rashness*, Lr. I, 1, 152. *let's to supper, and drown c.* Ant. IV, 2, 45.

2) regard: *dubbed on carpet c.* Tw. III, 4, 258. *albeit —s infinite do make against it*, H4A V, 1, 102. H4B II, 1, 124. II, 2, 14. H8 I, 2, 66 *(give it quick c.)*. Tim. IV, 3, 196.

Considered, adj., fit for reflection: *at our more c. time we'll read*, Hml. II, 2, 81.

Considering, subst., consideration, reflection: *many mazed —s did throng and pressed in with this caution*, H8 II, 4, 185. III, 2, 135.

Consign, 1) intr. to agree, to come to the same terms: *God —ing to my good intents*, H4B V, 2, 143. *we'll c. thereto*, H5 V, 2, 90. 326. *all lovers must c. to thee and come to dust*, Cymb. IV, 2, 275 (= come to the same state, submit to the same terms).

2) to assign, to allot: *as many farewells as be stars in heaven, with distinct breath and —ed kisses to them*, Troil. IV, 4, 47 (= kisses allotted to them). — In H4B IV, 1, 175 some M. Edd. *consigned*, O. Edd. *confined*, q. v.

Consist, 1) followed by *in* = to be comprised in, to be effected by, to depend on: *if their purgation did c. in words*, As I, 3, 55. *in her —s my happiness*, R3 IV, 4, 406. *no man is the lord of any thing, though in and of him there be much —ing, till he communicate his parts to others*, Troil. III, 3, 116 (i. e. though much may depend on his cooperation and power). *all goodness that —s in bounty expect even here*, Per. V, 1, 70.

2) followed by *of*, = to be composed of: *the trade and profit of the city —eth of all nations*, Merch. III, 3, 31. *does not our life c. of the four elements?* Tw. II, 3, 10. 12. H4A IV, 2, 25. R3 V, 3, 294. Ant. III, 7, 44.

3) followed by *on*, = to insist, to stand on, to claim: *such large terms and so absolute as our conditions shall c. upon*, H4B IV, 1, 187. *welcome is peace, if he on peace c.* Per. I, 4, 83.

Cónsistory, 1) any council or solemn assembly: *my other self, my counsel's c.* R3 II, 2, 151.*— 2) the college of the cardinals: H8 II, 4, 92. 93.

Consolate, to comfort: *may report my flight, to c. thine ear*, All's III, 2, 131.

Consolation, comfort: Shr. II, 191. Ant. I, 2, 175.

Consonancy, accord, agreement: Tw. II, 5, 141. Hml. II, 2, 295.

Consonant, a letter which cannot be sounded by itself: *quis, quis, thou c.?* LLL V, 1, 55 (an attempt at jesting of Holophernes).

Consort, subst., 1) with the accent on the last syll., company, fellowship: *will thou be of our c.?* Gentl. IV, 1, 64. *he was of that c.* Lr. II, 1, 99.

2) with the accent on the first syll., a company of musicians playing together (M. Edd. *concert*): *visit by night your lady's chamber-window with some sweet c.* Gentl. III, 2, 84. *screech-owls make the c. full*, H6B III, 2, 327 (cf. *sort*).

Consórt, vb. 1) trans. to accompany, to attend: *and afterward c. you till bed-time*, Err. I, 2, 28. LLL II, 178. Rom. III, 1, 135. Caes. V, 1, 83.

2) intr. to keep company, to associate; followed by *with: who bids them still c. with ugly night*, Ven. 1041. Mids. III, 2, 387. Troil. V, 3, 9. Rom. III, 1, 48. 49 (cf. subst. *Consort* 2). Mcb. II, 3, 141.

Consorted, associated: *Collatine and his c. lords*, Lucr. 1609. *that c. crew*, R2 V, 3, 138. V, 6, 15. Followed by *with: sorted and c. ... with a wench*, LLL I, 1, 261. *c. with that harlot strumpet Shore*, R3 III, 4, 73. III, 7, 137. Rom. II, 1, 31.

Conspectuity, sight, eye: *your bisson —ies,* Cor. II, 1, 70 (a word of Menenius' making).

Conspiracy, a combination of men for an evil purpose; a plot: Tp. II, 1, 301. IV, 139. Wiv. IV, 2, 123. Wint. III, 2, 72. R2 V, 2, 96. V, 3, 59. H5 II Chor. 27. Caes. II, 1, 77. II, 3, 8. Lr. I, 2, 58.

Conspirant, engaged in a plot: *c. 'gainst this high-illustrious prince,* Lr. V, 3, 135.

Conspirator, one who engages in a plot: R2 V, 6, 19. H6A I, 3, 33. Tit. IV, 4, 26. Caes. III, 2, 237. III, 3, 30. 36. V, 1, 51. V, 5, 69. Followed by *with: whispering c. with close-tongued treason and the ravisher,* Lucr. 769.

Conspire, 1) intr. a) to plot, to hatch treason: *hath —d to kill us here,* H5 II, 2, 89. *that moved pale Cassius to c.* Ant. II, 6, 15. Followed by *with:* Mids. III, 2, 196. Wint. III, 2, 16. John I, 241. *thou, —d with that irregulous devil,* Cymb. IV, 2, 315. Followed by *against:* H5 II, 2, 167. Used of the machinations of a single person: *'gainst thyself thou stickest not to c.* Sonn. 10, 6. *to whisper and c. against my youth,* Gentl. I, 2, 43. *I would c. against destiny,* Troil. V, 1, 70. *thou dost c. against thy friend,* Oth. III, 3, 142. Rom. V, 3, 212.

b) to agree in general, to concur: *an they have —d together, I will not say you shall see a masque,* Merch. II, 5, 22. *the times c. with you,* John III, 4, 146. *what mutter you, or what c. you, lords?* H6C I, 1, 165.

2) trans. to plot: *that do c. my death,* R3 III, 4, 62. cf. H6C I, 1, 165.

Conspirer, conspirator: Mcb. IV, 1, 91.

Constable, 1) a high functionary who had the care of the common peace in deeds of arms and matters of war: *when I came hither, I was lord high c.* H8 II, 1, 102.

2) in France, the officer who held the highest military command: H5 II, 4, 41. III, 5, 40. III, 7, 8. IV, 8, 97 etc.

3) an officer of the peace, invested with the power of arresting and imprisoning: Tp. III, 2, 29 *(to justle a c.).* Wiv. IV, 5, 122. Meas. II, 1, 48. 79 etc. Ado III, 3, 10. 17. 24. 79. 178. IV, 2, 8. V, 1, 234. LLL III, 1, 178. All's II, 2, 33. H4B V, 4, 4. Rom.I, 4, 40.

Constance, female name in John I, 32. II, 540 etc.

Constancy, 1) firmness of mind: All's II, 1, 87. H8 III, 2, 2 (?). Troil. I, 3, 21. Caes. II, 1, 227. 299. II, 4, 6. Mcb. II, 2, 68.

2) faithfulness: *there is written in your brow, provost, honesty and c.* Meas. IV, 2, 163. *whose —ies expire before their fashions,* All's I, 2, 62. Especially in love: Sonn. 105, 7. 117, 14. 152, 10. Phoen. 22. Gentl. II, 2, 8. Tw. II, 4, 78. H5 V, 2, 161. Troil. III, 2, 168. Cymb. I, 4, 137.

3) consistency: *all the story ... grows to something of great c.* Mids. V, 26. Perhaps also in H8 III, 2, 2: *if you will now unite in your complaints, and force them with a c., the cardinal cannot stand under them* (but cf. Ado II, 2, 55).

Constant, 1) firm, unshaken, persevering: *still c. in a wondrous excellence,* Sonn. 105, 6. *c. stars,* 14, 10; cf. Caes. III, 1, 60. Tp. I, 2, 207. Meas. III, 2, 239. Ado II, 2, 55. Merch. III, 2, 250. Tw. II, 4, 19. John III, 1, 291. H4A II, 3, 111. H5 II, 2,

133. II, 4, 35. Cor. I, 1, 243. V, 2, 100. Caes. III, 1, 22. 72. 73. Lr. I, 1, 44. V, 1, 4. *do not turn me about; my stomach is not c.* Tp.II,2,119 (= is queasy).

2) uniform, confirmed: *variable passions throng her c. woe,* Ven. 967. *like a c. and confirmed devil,* Lucr. 1513. *'twas just the difference betwixt the c. red and mingled damask,* As III, 5, 123. *and perish c. fools,* Cor. IV, 6, 105.

3) faithful: *none like you for c. heart,* Sonn. 53, 14. *were man but c., he were perfect,* Gentl. V, 4, 111. 115. Ado II, 1, 182. Merch. II, 6, 57. As II, 3, 57. H4A II, 3, 19. H4B II, 4, 293. H5 II, 2, 5. H6C III, 3, 240. IV, 1, 77. Troil. III, 2, 119. 210. Oth. II, 1, 298. Cymb. I, 4, 65. I, 5, 75. *with rich and c. pen,* Per. IV Prol. 28. Followed by *to: though to myself forsworn, to thee I'll c. prove,* Pilgr. 59. Gentl. II, 6, 31. Ado II, 3, 67. Tw. V, 115. Wint. IV, 4, 45. 698. H8 III, 1, 134. Hml. V, 2, 208. Cymb. II, 5, 30.

4) consistent, logical: *I am no more mad than you are: make the trial of it in any c. question,* Tw. IV, 2, 53.

Constantine, the first Christian emperor: H6A I, 2, 142.

Constantinople, the town on the Bosporus: H5 V, 2, 222.

Constantly, firmly; 1) with firmness of mind: *to meet all perils very c.* Caes. V, 1, 92. 2) fixedly: *and fixed his eyes upon you? most c.* Hml. I, 2, 234. 3) certainly, for certain: *I do c. believe you,* Meas. IV, 1, 21. *I c. do think,* Troil. IV, 1, 40. 4) faithfully: *since patiently and c. thou hast stuck to the bare fortune of Posthumus,* Cymb. III, 5, 119. 5) consistently: *the devil a puritan that he is, or any thing c., but a time-pleasor,* Tw. II, 3, 160.

Constant-qualified, faithful: Cymb. I, 4, 65 (not hyphened in O. Edd.).

Constellation, a group of stars, and figuratively, an assemblage of good qualities: *I know thy c. is right apt for this affair,* Tw. I, 4, 35.

Conster, see *Construe.*

Constitution, the state of being, the frame of the mind or the body: *else nothing in the world could turn so much the c. of any constant man,* Merch. III, 2, 249. *the excellent c. of thy leg,* Tw. I, 3, 141.

Constrain, 1) to force: H4B I, 1, 196. Mcb. V, 4, 13. Followed by *to:* Cymb. III, 5, 47. By the infinitive with *to:* Ado I, 1, 208. Mids. III, 2, 428. Tw. II, 3, 69. H6A II, 1, 7. Rom. II, 4, 57. Ant. III, 6, 56. Cymb. V, 5, 141. By the inf. without *to:* *—s them weep,* Cor. V, 3, 100.

2) to do violence to, to violate: *her spotless chastity you —ed and forced,* Tit. V, 2, 178. cf. *being —ed with dreadful circumstance,* Lucr. 1703 (cf. *Enforce* and *Force*). The latter passage may fall under def. 3.

3) to produce or put on in opposition to nature: *—s the garb quite from his nature,* Lr. II, 2, 103. *—ed blemishes,* Ant. III, 13, 59. *gyves, desired more than —ed,* Cymb. V, 4, 15.

Constraint, force, compulsion: All's III, 2, 121. IV, 2, 16. IV, 3, 139. John II, 244. V, 1, 28 *(on c.).* H5 II, 4, 97. Per. III, 2, 55.

Constringe, to strain into a narrow compass, to cramp: *the dreadful spout which shipmen* *do the hurricano call, —d in mass by the almighty sun,* Troil. V, 2, 173.

Construction, interpretation: Wiv. II, 2, 232. Ado III, 4, 50. Tw. II, 3, 190. III, 1, 126. H8 Epil. 10. Cor. V, 6, 21. Mcb. I, 4, 12. Cymb. V, 5, 433. 444.

Construe (O.Edd. often *Conster*), to interpret: Lucr. 324. Pilgr. 188. Gentl. I, 2, 56. Wiv. I, 3, 50. LLL V, 2, 341. Shr. III, 1, 30. 41 (= to translate). Tw. III, 1, 63. H4B IV, 1, 104 (cf. *To*). Caes. I, 2, 45. I, 3, 34. II, 1, 307. Oth. IV, 1, 102.

Consul, 1) the chief magistrate of ancient Rome: Lucr. Arg. 26. Cor. II, 1, 238. 248 etc. Ant. I, 4, 58.

2) senator: *the bookish theoric, wherein the tongued —s can propose as masterly as he,* Oth. I, 1, 25. *many of the —s are at the duke's already,* I, 2, 43. Cymb. IV, 2, 385.

Consulship, the office of consul: Cor. II, 2, 2. II, 3, 80.

Consult, vb. intr. to take counsel together: Ven. 972. Wiv. II, 1, 111. H6B IV, 7, 140. R3 V, 3, 45. H8 I, 1, 91. Tit. IV, 2, 132.

Consume, 1) trans. to devour, to destroy, to waste: Sonn. 73, 12. Shr. II, 134. All's V, 3, 38. Wint. II, 3, 134. R2 II, 1, 39. V, 6, 2. R3 I, 1, 140. Troil. II, 2, 5. Cor. IV, 6, 78. 116. Tit. I, 129. III, 1, 62. Tim. V, 1, 137. V, 4, 71. Caes. II, 2, 49. Per. IV, 1, 24. Absolutely: *thy —ing canker,* H6A II, 4, 71. *—ing sorrow,* Tit. III, 1, 61.

2) refl. to perish, to dwindle: *fair flowers rot and c. themselves in little time,* Ven. 132. *thou —st thyself in single life,* Sonn. 9, 2. *virginity —s itself to the very paring,* All's I, 1, 154.

3) intr. to waste away, to pass away, to perish: *smoke from Aetna, that in air —s,* Lucr. 1042. *c. away in sighs,* Ado III, 1, 78. *c. away in rust,* John IV, 1, 65. *c. to ashes,* H6A IV, 4, 92. *fire and powder, which as they kiss c.* Rom. II, 6, 11.

Consummate, to perform: *to c. this business happily,* John V, 7, 95. *there shall we c. our spousal rites,* Tit. I, 337. Partic. *consummate:* Meas. V, 383. Ado III, 2, 2.

Consummation, end, death: *'tis a c. devoutly to be wished,* Hml. III, 1, 63. *burning, scalding, stench, c.* Lr. IV, 6, 131 (Ff *consumption*). *quiet c. have,* Cymb. IV, 2, 280.

Consumption, decay of the body, phthisis: Ado V, 4, 97. H4B I, 2, 264. Tim. IV, 3, 151 (—s). 201. Lr. IV, 6, 131 (Qq *consummation*).

Contagion, communication of a disease by contact: *strumpeted by the c.* Err. II, 2, 146. Hence = infection, pestilence: *it is dulcet in c.* Tw. II, 3, 59. *all the c. of the south,* Cor. I, 4, 30. *that nest of death, c. and unnatural sleep,* Rom. V, 3, 152. *to dare the vile c. of the night,* Caes. II, 1, 265. *hell itself breathes out c. to this world,* Hml. III, 2, 408. *I'll touch my point with this c.* IV, 7, 148 (sc. poison).

Contagious, poisonous, pestilential, pernicious: *c. fogs,* Mids. II, 1, 90. *breath,* Tw. II, 3, 56. *this night, whose black c. breath,* John V, 4, 33. *clouds,* H4A I, 2, 222. *prison,* H4B V, 5, 36 (Pistol's speech). *clouds,* H5 III, 3, 31. *darkness,* H6B IV, 1, 7. *sickness,* H8 V, 3, 26. *blastments,* Hml. I, 3, 42. Misapplied by Fluellen: H5 IV, 8, 22.

Contain, 1) to hold, to inclose: *the worth of that* (viz the body) *is that which it —s,* Sonn. 74,

13. *—ing fire to harm mine eye,* John IV, 1, 66. *hast made my heart too great for what —s it,* Cor. V, 6, 104 (viz the chest). *if after two days' shine Athens c. thee,* Tim. III, 5, 101. Compl. 189. LLL IV, 3, 353. Merch. II, 7, 11. 48. II, 9, 5. R2 III, 3, 24. H4A V, 4, 89. H5 I, 1, 31. H6A II, 3, 56. H6B III, 2, 410. Hml. IV, 5, 87. Lr. III, 1, 46. Cymb. I, 4, 103.

2) to comprise as a writing, to have for contents: *a sonnet —ing her affection unto Benedick,* Ado V, 4, 90. All's V, 3, 94. John II, 101. R2 IV, 234. H4B IV, 1, 169. IV, 4, 101. H6A IV, 1, 66. H8 IV, 1, 13. Rom. III, 2, 83. Cymb. III, 2, 30.

3) to keep, to retain, to restrain: *what thy memory cannot c.* Sonn. 77, 9. *cannot c. their urine,* Merch. IV, 1, 50. *to c. the ring,* V, 201. — Reflectively, = to restrain one's self: *we can c. ourselves,* Shr. Ind. 1, 100. Troil. V, 2, 180. Tim. II, 2, 26.

Containing, subst., contents: *this label, whose c. is so from sense,* Cymb. V, 5, 430.

Contaminate, to pollute, to taint: Caes. IV, 3, 24. Partic. *contaminated:* Ado II, 2, 25. H5 IV, 5, 16. H6A IV, 6, 21. Troil. IV, 1, 71. Oth. IV, 1, 221. Partic. *contaminate:* Err. II, 2, 135.

Contemn, to despise: Gentl. II, 4, 129. Tw. I, 5, 289. John V, 2, 13. Cor. I, 3, 46 (Ff *contenuing, contending*). II, 2, 161. Lr. II, 2, 150 (by conjecture). IV, 1, 1. 2. IV, 2, 32. Ant. III, 6, 1. Cymb. I, 6, 41. *what am I that thou shouldst c. me this?* Ven. 204 (cf. *This*).

Contemplate, to muse, to meditate: *so many hours must I c.* H6C II, 5, 33.

Contemplation, thought, meditation: LLL IV, 3, 321. As. II, 1, 64. Tw. II, 5, 35. H5 I, 1, 63. H8 III, 2, 131. Troil. II, 3, 29. Tit. V, 2, 9. Lr. I, 2, 151. Followed by *of: the sundry c. of my travels,* As IV, 1, 18. Oth. II, 3, 322. — Holy meditation: Merch. III, 4, 28. John V, 4, 48. R3 III, 7, 94.

Contemplative, given to thought: LLL I, 1, 14. As II, 7, 31. Tw. II, 5, 23.

Contempt, 1) the act of despising, disdain: Wiv. I, 1, 258 (O. Edd. *content*). Err. II, 2, 174. Ado III, 1, 109. LLL V, 2, 149. All's I, 2, 36. II, 2, 6. II, 3, 164. III, 2, 34. V, 3, 48. Tw. II, 3, 131. III, 1, 158. Wint. I, 2, 189. 373. John II, 88. R2 V, 2, 27. H4A I, 3, 183. H5 II, 4, 117. H6B V, 1, 209. R3 I, 2, 173. IV, 2, 124. H8 II, 4, 42. Cor. II, 3, 210. 229. Tit. IV, 4, 4. V, 1, 12. Lr. I, 4, 309. Cymb. III, 5, 42. 144. Plural —s: Tit. IV, 4, 34. Ant. I, 2, 127. Followed by *of,* to express the thing despised: Gentl. II, 4, 133. Tim. IV, 3, 8. *hold in c.* R3 I, 3, 80. *placed in c.* Tw. I, 5, 307. *put into c.* Cymb. III, 4, 92. *in c.* = contemptuously: H4A V, 2, 51. H6A I, 4, 31. H6B IV, 1, 78. Cor. II, 3, 208. *in c. of question* = without doubt, Tw. II, 5, 97. *in c. of man* = in spite of humanity, Lr. II, 3, 8.

2) the state of being despised: Tw. II, 5, 223. H5 II, 2, 172. Rom. V, 1, 71. Tim. IV, 2, 15. 32. IV, 3, 10. Cymb. IV, 2, 27.

Misapplied: LLL I, 1, 191.

Contemptible, 1) despicable, mean: *my c. estate,* H6A I, 2, 75.

2) scornful, disdainful: *the man hath a c. spirit,* Ado II, 3, 187.

Contemptuous, 1) disdainful: *this c. city,* John II, 384.

2) despicable: *c. base-born callet as she is,* H6B I, 3, 86.

Contemptuously, disdainfully: *trampling c. on thy disdain,* Gentl. I, 2, 112.

Contend, 1) to strive: *in sequent toil all* (waves) *forwards do c.,* Sonn. 60, 4. *one that, above all other strifes, —ed especially to know himself,* Meas. III, 2, 246.

2) to quarrel, to combat, to fight: *—ing kings,* Lucr. 939. Gentl. I, 2, 129. Merch. III, 2, 142. All's I, 1, 72. H5 I, 2, 24. V, 2, 377. H6C II, 5, 102. Mcb. I, 3, 92. II, 2, 7. Hml. IV, 1, 7. Ant. II, 2, 80. Per. II, 3, 24 (*c. not* = do not contradict, make no words about it). Followed by *against:* Cor. IV, 5, 119. Mcb. II, 4, 17. Per. I, 2, 17. By *with:* Ven. 820. Pilgr. 223. H6B III, 2, 384. H6C II, 5, 2. Lr. III, 1, 4. *Contending* = making war: *till he take truce with her —ing tears,* Ven. 82. *a foul —ing rebel,* Shr. V, 2, 159. cf. Mcb. II, 4, 17.

3) to vie: *they c. with thee in courtesy,* Troil. IV, 5, 206. *I'll make death love me, for I will c. even with his pestilent scythe,* Ant. III, 13, 193. *—s in skill with Marina,* Per. IV Prol. 30. Followed by *against: all our service were poor and single business to c. against those honours,* Mcb. I, 6, 16.

Content, subst. 1) contentedness, satisfaction: Wiv. I, 1, 258. IV, 5, 127. Meas. III, 1, 270. As I, 3, 139 (*in c.*). III, 2, 26. All's I, 3, 4. IV, 5, 83. V, 3, 337. R2 V, 5, 23. H6C III, 1, 64. 66. 67. H8 II, 3, 20 (*in c.*). 22. Mcb. II, 1, 17. III, 2, 5. Lr. III, 2, 76. Oth. III, 3, 348. III, 4, 120. Hence = applause, delight: *not without much c. in many singularities,* Wint. V, 3, 11. *how one another lends c.* Rom. I, 3, 84 (= how one sets off another's beauty, to satisfy the eye).

2) happiness, joy: *so I return rebuked to my c.* Sonn. 119, 13. *thy like ne'er was for a sweet c.* Pilgr. 295. As II, 3, 68. *the fulness of my heart's c.* H6B I, 1, 35. *could command no more c. than I,* IV, 9, 2. *repaired with double riches of c.* R3 IV, 4, 319. *this night he dedicates to fair c. and you,* H8 I, 4, 3. *it gives me wonder great as my c. to see you here,* Oth. II, 1, 185. *my soul hath her c. so absolute,* 193. *which drives o'er your c. these strong necessities,* Ant. III, 6, 83. *of my lord's health; of his c.* Cymb. III, 2, 31.

3) that which is the condition of happiness or satisfaction, a) that which to attain would make one happy; desire, wish, will: *within thine own bud buriest thy c.* Sonn. I, 11. *who ever ... forced examples, 'gainst her own c., to put the by-past perils in her way?* Compl. 157. *how does your c. tender your own good fortune?* Tp. II, 1, 269. *so will I in England work your grace's full c.* H6B I, 3, 70. *God hold it, to your honour's good c.* R3 III, 2, 107. *though my heart's c. firm love doth bear,* Troil. I, 2, 320 (= though my heart is desirous of love). Hence the phrases: *I leave your honour to your heart's c.* Ven. Dedic. 7 (= to see your wishes fulfilled). *I commend you to your own c.* Err. I, 2, 32. *I wish your ladyship all heart's c.* Merch. III, 4, 42.

b) meek submission, resignation, acquiescence: *forced to c., but never to obey, panting he lies,* Ven. 61. *his face, though full of cares, yet showed c.* Lucr. 1503. *to whose high will we bound our calm —s,* R2 V, 2, 38.

4) In the plural only, = that which is contained, comprised in a writing: Lucr. 948. Compl. 19. 56. Sonn. 55, 3. Tp. II, 2, 147. Gentl.

I, 2, 36. Wiv. IV, 6, 13. Meas. IV, 2, 211. IV, 3, 98. LLL IV, 2, 103. V, 2, 518. Merch. III, 2, 246. As IV, 3, 8. 21. V, 4, 136. All's III, 2, 66. Wint. III, 1, 20. H8 IV, 2, 154. Hml. V, 2, 44. Lr. I, 2, 43. 73. II, 4, 34. Cymb. II, 2, 27.

Content, vb., 1) to satisfy, to answer the expectation or hope: Meas. III, 1, 192. As V, 2, 126. John II, 547. H4A II, 3, 120. H6B IV, 10, 21. Tit V, 2, 68. Lr. I, 1, 280. Oth. II, 1, 307. Per. I, 4, 35. = to pay: *come the next Sabbath, and I will c. you,* R3 III, 2, 113. *I will c. your pains,* Oth. III, 1, 1. Absolutely: *this —s,* Shr. I, 1, 168.

Contented = satisfied, not demanding more: Sonn. 151, 11. Shr. IV, 1, 172. Merch. IV, 1, 393. All's I, 3, 54. R2 V, 5, 11. H5 IV, 1, 132. H6C II, 6, 47. Used of things: *that —ed hap,* R3 I, 3, 84. Adjectively: *the duke and all his —ed followers,* As V, 2, 17. Followed by *with:* Sonn. 29, 8. H6C IV, 3, 37.

2) to gratify, to please: *statue —ing but the eye alone,* Ven. 213. *to c. ye as much as me my dukedom,* Tp. V, 170. *a woman sometimes scorns what best —s her,* Gentl. III, 1, 93. LLL V, 2, 518. Mids. V, 113. As III, 3, 3. Shr. IV, 3, 180. Wint. II, 1, 159. H6B III, 2, 26. H8 III, 1, 132. Hml. III, 1, 24. Ant. V, 2, 68.

3) Reflectively, used in the imperative only, = compose yourself, keep your temper, be at ease: Ado V, 1, 87. Shr. I, 1, 90. 203. II, 343. H6C I, 1, 85. Troil. III, 2, 151. Tit. I, 210. Rom. I, 5, 67. *c. you in my discontent,* Shr. I, 1, 80. *O, c. thee,* Cymb. I, 5, 26 (= do not trouble thyself about it). Similarly *be contented,* imperatively: Sonn. 74, 1. Wiv. III, 3, 177. Lr. III, 4, 115.

4) Hence *to be contented* = to acquiesce, to consent, to agree: *to sell myself I can be well —ed, so thou wilt buy and pay,* Ven. 513. *are you —ed to resign the crown?* R2 IV, 200. *if the deed were ill, be you —ed to have a son set your decrees at nought,* H4B V, 2, 84. H6C III, 1, 67. H8 V, 1, 106. Caes. III, 1, 240. V, 1, 109. *well —ed!* = agreed! Mcb. II, 3, 140.

Content, adj. 1) satisfied, not demanding more: Tp. V, 144. Mids. V, 134. Merch. III, 2, 135. IV, 1, 394. As II, 4, 18. Tim. IV, 3, 247. Oth. III, 3, 172. Followed by *with:* Mids. II, 2, 111. R2 II, 1, 188. H6A V, 1, 26. H6C IV, 7, 24.

2) willing, well pleased: *the gods for murder seemed so c. to punish them, although not done, but meant,* Per. V, 3, 99. Preceded by *can: I could be well c. to be mine own attorney in this case,* H6A V, 3, 165. *and could be c. to give him good report for it,* Cor. I, 1, 32. *though soft-conscienced men can be c. to say it was for his country, he did it to please his mother,* I, 1, 38. *they could be c. to visit other places,* Caes. V, 1, 8.

3) not disinclined, satisfied so as not to oppose, agreed: *I have been c. you should lay my countenance to pawn,* Wiv. II, 2, 4. *are you c. to be our general?* Gentl. IV, 1, 61. *I will be c. to be a lawful hangman,* Meas. IV, 2, 17. Merch. IV, 1, 382. Shr. I, 1, 221. III, 2, 203. All's IV, 1, 89. H4A II, 1, 78. H6A IV, 1, 70. 71. V, 3, 126. 127. V, 5, 19. H6B III, 1, 319. IV, 2, 167. H6C IV, 6, 48. Cor. III, 3, 45. 47. Tit. V, 3, 2. Hml. IV, 5, 210. *I must be c.* = I cannot help, I cannot but: Cor. II, 1, 65. Lr. II, 4, 238. Oth. I, 3, 227. *Content!* = agreed! Merch. I, 3, 153. Shr. V, 2, 70. 74. H6A III, 1, 146. Cor. II, 3, 53. Ant. IV, 3, 26.

cry Content to that which grieves my heart, H6C III, 2, 183.

4) acquiescing, not grieved: *glad of other men's good, c. with my harm*, As III, 2, 79. *Be c.* = be quiet, be calm: Wiv. I, 4, 73. Meas. II, 2, 79. 105. Mids. II, 2, 110. Tw. V, 359. John III, 1, 42. 43. R2 V, 2, 82. Cor. III, 2, 130. Caes. IV, 2, 41. Oth. III, 3, 450. *hold you c.* Ado V, 1, 92. *Be c.* = don't be uneasy: Caes. I, 3, 142. Oth. IV, 2, 165. Cymb. V, 4, 102. *pray you, c.!* Lr. I, 4, 336.

Contention, 1) debate, dispute: *it was in a place where I could not breed no c. with him*, H5 V, 1, 11. *no quarrel, but a slight c.* H6C I, 2, 6. *'twas a c. in public*, Cymb. I, 4, 58.

2) combat, fight: *in the very heat and pride of their c.* H4A I, 1, 60. Troil. IV, 1, 16. IV, 5, 205. Oth. II, 1, 92.

3) discord: *c., like a horse full of high feeding, madly hath broke loose*, H4B I, 1, 9. *let this world no longer be a stage to feed c. in a lingering act*, 156.

Contentious, eager for combat: *c. waves*, Tp. II, 1, 118. *storm*, Lr. III, 4, 6.

Contentless, discontented: Tim. IV, 3, 245.

Contents, see *Content*, subst.

Contest, vb., to vie: *and do c. as hotly and as nobly with thy love*, Cor. IV, 5, 116.

Contestation, contention, contest: Ant. II, 2, 43.

Continence, forbearance of lewd pleasures (probably meaning moderation in the indulgence of sexual enjoyment): *to virtue consecrate, to justice, c. and nobility*, Tit. I, 15.

Continency, moderation in the indulgence of sexual enjoyment: Meas. III, 2, 185. Shr. IV, 1, 185.

Continent, subst., that which contains and encloses some thing; 1) the cover: *a plot which is not tomb enough and c. to hide the slain*, Hml. IV, 4, 64. *rive your concealing —s*, Lr. III, 2, 58. *heart, once be stronger than thy c.* Ant. IV, 14, 40. — 2) the land, as enclosing rivers and seas: *they (the rivers) have overborne their —s*, Mids. II, 1, 92. *gelding the opposed c. as much as on the other side it takes from you*, H4A III, 1, 110. *thou globe of sinful —s*, H4B II, 4, 309. *make the c., weary of solid firmness, melt itself into the sea*, III, 1, 47. — 3) a receptacle: *and all those swearings keep as true in soul as doth that orbed c. the fire that severs day from night*, Tw. V, 278 (viz the sun as the seat and source of light). Hence, figuratively = the abstract, inventory: *my c. of beauty*, LLL IV, 1, 111. *here's the scroll, the c. and summary of my fortune*, Merch. III, 2, 131. *you shall find in him the c. of what part a gentleman would see*, Hml. V, 2, 115.

Continent, adj. 1) restraining: *have a c. forbearance till the speed of his rage goes slower*, Lr. I, 2, 182. — 2) free from concupiscence: *my past life hath been as c. as chaste*, Wint. III, 2, 35.

In the following passages it may be taken in either sense: *contrary to thy established proclaimed edict and c. canon*, LLL I, 1, 262. *my desire all c. impediments would o'erbear*, Mcb. IV, 3, 64.

Continual, incessant, perpetual: Ven. 606. Lucr. 591. Sonn. 123, 12. Wiv. III, 5, 73. 118. LLL I, 1, 86. H4B Ind. 6. IV, 4, 53. V, 1, 88. H5 I, 2, 185. H6A V, 5, 63. H8 IV, 2, 28. Tit. III, 1, 229. Hml. V, 2, 221. Per. IV, 2, 8.

Continually, perpetually: H4A II, 1, 88. R3 V, 3, 84. Mcb. V, 1, 27.

Continuance, 1) duration: *c. tames the one* (viz old woes), Lucr. 1097. *long c. and increasing*, Tp. IV, 107. *a bawd of eleven years' c.* Meas. III, 2, 208. Merch. I, 1, 125. John V, 7, 14. H4A IV, 3, 105.

2) permanence: *this maid hath yet in her the c. of her first affection*, Meas. III, 1, 249. Tw. I, 4, 6. Rom. I Chor. 10.

3) abode, residence: *cloyed with long c. in a settled place*, H6A II, 5, 106.

Continuantly, a word of Mrs Quickly's making, perhaps for *incontinently*: H4B II, 1, 28.

Continuate, adj., continual, uninterrupted: *an untirable and c. goodness*, Tim. I, 1, 11. *I shall in a more c. time strike off this score of absence*, Oth. III, 4, 178; i. e. in a time unbroken by other business, or in a time more continually dedicated to you. Q1 *in a more convenient time.*

Continue, 1) trans. a) not to cease, to pursue, to persevere in: *she shall not long c. love to him*, Gentl. III, 2, 48. *the heavens c. their loves*, Wint. I, 1, 35. cf. H6A IV, 1, 161 and Oth. I, 3, 348. *c. these favours*, Tw. I, 4, 1. *shall c. our graces*, Mcb. I, 6, 30. *this united league*, R3 II, 1, 2. *c. fault*, Wint. I, 2, 85. *your resolve*, Shr. I, 1, 27. *war*, All's I, 2, 2. *I will c. that I broached in jest*, Shr. I, 2, 84. *our humble author will c. the story*, H4B V, 5, 144.

b) to leave as before: *how shall we c. Claudio*, Meas. IV, 3, 88 (= let live). *what friend of mine... did I c. in my liking*, H8 II, 4, 33.

2) intr. a) to go on, to persevere: *so you may c.* Tp. II, 1, 178. *c. in his courses*, Meas. II, 1, 196. LLL V, 2, 875. H6B IV, 9, 17. Cor. II, 3, 245. IV, 2, 30. Cymb. V, 5, 380. *mark how he —s*, Oth. IV, 1, 292.

b) to do without interruption: *I have known her c. in this* (washing her hands) *a quarter of an hour*, Mcb. V, 1, 34.

c) to be as before, to remain: *if she would c. in it*, Tp. II, 1, 184. *extremity of weather —ing*, Wint. V, 2, 129. *c. thankful*, All's V, 1, 17. *c. friends*, John III, 1, 252 and Cymb. II, 4, 49. *c. long in his favour*, H8 III, 2, 395. *c. where he is*, Cymb. I, 5, 54. *in this likeness of death*, Rom. IV, 1, 105. *your emperor —s still a Jove*, Ant. IV, 6, 29. *—s well my lord?* Cymb. I, 6, 56 (= is he well as he was?).

d) to be continually: *I thought you had —d in it* (your office) *some time*, Meas. II, 1, 276.

e) to last: *his folly will c. the standing of his body* (= as long as he lives) Wint. I, 2, 430. *more than three hours the fight —d*, H6A I, 1, 120. *but this cannot c.* H8 II, 2, 84 (= last long).

f) to be sequel, to follow: *takes no account how things go from him, nor resumes no care of what is to c.* Tim. II, 2, 5.

Elbow blundering in the use of the word in Meas. II, 1, 200.

Continuer, one who holds out without tiring: *I would my horse had the speed of your tongue, and so good a c.* Ado I, 1, 143.

Contract, subst. 1) *contráct*, treaty, agreement: *c., succession... none*, Tp. II, 1, 151. *how joyful am I made by this c.* H6A III, 1, 143. V, 4, 156. 2) *contráct* and *cóntract*, marriage-contract, espousals: Tp. IV, 19. Meas. I, 2, 149. III, 1, 223.

V, 209. All's II, 3, 185. Wint. IV, 4, 428. **V**, 1, 204. H6A V, 1, 46. V, 5, 28. R3 III, 7, 6. Rom. II, 2, 117. Cymb. II, 3, 120. *a c. of true love*, Tp. IV, 84. 133. Tw. V, 159. *the c. of her marriage*, As III, 2, 332. *his c. with Lady Lucy*, R3 III, 7, 5. Cymb. II, 3, 118.

Contráct, vb. 1) to draw together; a) to shorten: *extended or —ed all proportions*, All's V, 3, 51. cf. Hml. V, 1, 71. b) to cripple, to palsy: *aches c. and starve your supple joints*, Tim. I, 1, 257. c) to wrinkle, to knit: *our whole kingdom to be —ed in one brow of woe*, Hml. I, 2, 4. *didst c. and purse thy brow together*, Oth. III, 3, 113.

2) to stipulate: *the articles of —ed peace*, H6B I, 1, 40.

3) to betroth: *c. us 'fore these witnesses*, Wint. IV, 4, 401. Partic. —ed: Sonn. 56, 10. Wiv. V, 5, 236. Wint. V, 3, 5. H4A IV, 2, 17. Followed by *to:* Sonn. 1, 5. Meas. V, 380. Tw. V, 268. Lr. V, 3, 228. Partic. *contract: he was c. to Lady Lucy*, R3 III, 7, 179.

Contracting, subst. betrothing: *perform an old c.* Meas. III, 2, 296.

Contraction, marriage-contract: *such a deed as from the body of c. plucks the very soul*, Hml. III, 4, 46.

Contradict, to speak against, to oppose: Lucr. 1631. Wint. III, 2, 24. John II, 280. H6B III, 2, 252. H8 II, 4, 28. Rom. V, 3, 153. Mcb. II, 3, 94. Lr. V, 3, 87 *(your bans)*.

Contradiction, 1) denial, opposition: *to have his worth of c.* Cor. III, 3, 27 (i.e. to gain what he thinks worth disputing). *Without c.* = certainly: *shall be accomplished without c.* R2 III, 3, 124. *without c., I have heard that*, Ant. II, 7, 41. *'twas a contention in public, which may, without c., suffer the report*, Cymb. I, 4, 59.

2) inconsistency, incongruity of things: *of this c. you shall now be quit*, Cymb. V, 4, 169.

Contrariety, contradiction, inconsistency: *how can these —ies agree?* H6A II, 3, 59. *he and Aufidius can no more atone than violentest c.* Cor. IV, 6, 73.

Contrarious, contrary, adverse: *c. winds*, H4A V, 1, 52. It has, perhaps, the same sense in Meas. IV, 1, 62: *volumes of report run with these false and most c. quests upon thy doings.* But it may be = contradictory, inconsistent.

Contrariously, in opposed directions: *many things, having full reference to one consent, may work c.* H5 I, 2, 206.

Cóntrary, subst. 1) the opposite side: *wafting his eyes to the c.* Wint. I, 2, 372. *the king's attorney on the c. urged*, H8 II, 1, 15.

2) a proposition or fact opposite to another: Gentl. II, 4, 16. Meas. IV, 2, 103. Ado I, 1, 198. LLL I, 2, 35. All's II, 3, 237. Tw. V, 15. R2 V, 5, 102. H6A V, 5, 64. H6C I, 2, 20. I, 4, 131. R3 IV, 1, 17. Rom. IV, 5, 90. Tim. IV, 3, 304. Plur. *—ies*: Tp. II, 1, 147. Tim. IV, 1, 20. *— In the c.* = in the opposite case, on the other side: *the honour of it does pay the act of it; as in the c. the foulness is the punishment*, H8 III, 2, 182. *I do not find that thou dealest justly with me. What in the c.?* Oth. IV, 2, 175. *To the c.* = to the opposite effect: Wiv. II, 1, 38. 41. Meas. IV, 2, 123. Ado V, 2, 87. Merch. I, 3, 14. Wint. II, 2, 8. John III, 1, 10. H8 V, 1, 148. Per. II Prol. 15.

3) a thing or state of opposite qualities: *these —ies such unity do hold*, Lucr. 1558. *a falsehood in its c. as great*, Tp. I, 2, 95. *no — ies hold more antipathy*, Lr. II, 2, 93.

4) perversity, wrong conception: *is't good to soothe him in these —ies?* Err. IV, 4, 82.

Contrary, adj. (usually *cóntrary*, but *contráry* in Wint. V, 1, 45. John IV, 2, 198. Tim. IV, 3, 144 and Hml. III, 2, 221). 1) opposite, adverse: *my lord should to the heavens be c.* Wint. V, 1, 45. R3 IV, 4, 216. Seemingly used as an adverb: *mine own self-love quite c. I read*, Sonn. 62, 11. *and wouldst thou turn our offers c.?* H4A V, 5, 4. *what storm is this that blows so c.?* Rom. III, 2, 64. *our wills and fates do so c. run*, Hml. III, 2, 221. Followed by *to:* Lucr. Arg. 2. LLL I, 1, 261. Wint. III, 2, 19. H4B II, 4, 373. H6B III, 1, 58. *c. to the king*, H6B IV, 7, 40.

2) contradictory: *'tis pity love should be so c.* Gentl. IV, 4, 88. *in the divorce his c. proceedings are all unfolded*, H8 III, 2, 26.

3) different: *hath appointed them c. places*, Wiv. II, 1, 217. *they are gone a c. way*, All's III, 5, 8. *yet may your pains, six months, be quite c.* Tim. IV, 3, 144.

4) wrong: *set a deep glass of rhenish wine on the c. casket*, Merch. I, 2, 105. *slippers which his nimble haste had falsely thrust upon c. feet*, John IV, 2, 198. Adverbially: *so shall your loves woo c.* LLL V, 2, 135.

Contráry, vb., to oppose, to cross: *you must c. me*, Rom. I, 5, 87.

Contribution, tax, impost: *a trembling c.* H8 I, 2, 95. What is paid for the support of an army: *they have grudged us c.* Caes. IV, 3, 206.

Contributor, one who pays for a common purpose: Shr. I, 2, 215.

Contrite, extremely penitent: Lucr. 1727. H5 IV, 1, 313.

Contrive, 1) to devise, to plan; a) intr. to lay schemes: *the letters too of many our —ing friends in Rome petition us at home*, Ant. I, 2, 189. Perhaps also in Shr. I, 2, 276. — b) tr. to devise, to excogitate: *some loathsome dash the herald will c.* Lucr. 206. *she that her fame so to herself —s*, Compl. 243. *by whom this great assembly is —d*, H5 V, 2, 6. *the still and mental parts that do c. how many hands shall strike*, Troil. I, 3, 201. *c. the means of meeting*, Hml. II, 2, 216. *one that slept in the —ing of lust*, Lr. III, 4, 92.

2) Mostly in an ill sense, = to plot; a) intr. *the Fates with traitors do c.* Caes. II, 3, 16. *most generous and free from all —ing*, Hml. IV, 7, 136. Followed by *against:* Merch. IV, 1, 352. 360. All's IV, 3, 28. — b) trans. *all the treasons complotted and —d in this land*, R2 I, 1, 96. I, 3, 189. *premeditated and —d murder*, H5 IV, 1, 171; cf. Oth. I, 2, 3. H6A I, 1, 27. I, 4, 77. II, 1, 15. Hml. I, 5, 85. Followed by an infinitive: *have you with these —d to bait me?* Mids. III, 2, 196. As IV, 3, 135. H6A I, 3, 34. Cor. III, 3, 62.

3) to spend, to pass away: *please ye we may c. this afternoon, and quaff carouses to our mistress' health*, Shr. I, 2, 276 (more probably to be taken in the sense of 1, a).

Contriver, schemer, plotter: *we shall find of him a shrewd c.* Caes. II, 1, 158. *a secret and villanous c. against me*, As I, 1, 151. *the damned c. of* *this deed*, Tit. IV, 1, 36. *the close c. of all harms*, Mcb. III, 5, 7.

Control, subst., command, restrictive authority: *a true soul when most impeached stands least in thy c.* Sonn. 125, 14. *are their males' subjects and at their —s,* Err. II, 1, 19. *an austere regard of c.* Tw. II, 5, 74. *to be a secondary at c.* John V, 2, 80.

Hence = check, constraint, restraint: *the proud c. of fierce and bloody war,* John I, 17. *where his lustful eye, without c., listed to make his prey,* R3 III, 5, 84.

Control, vb. 1) to exercise restrictive authority, to command, to rule; a) intr.: *lightens forth —ing majesty,* R2 III, 3, 70. *to act —ing laws,* H6B V, 1, 103. — b) tr. to rule, to overrule, to dispose of: *—ing what he was —ed with,* Ven. 270. *which in her prescience she —ed still,* Lucr. 727. *I should in thought c. your times of pleasure,* Sonn. 58, 2. *could c. the moon,* Tp. V, 270. *with the same austerity and garb as he —ed the war,* Cor. IV, 7, 45. *to c. the world,* Tit. I, 199. *who can c. his fate?* Oth. V, 2, 265.

2) to overpower, to be superior to: *a man in hue, all hues in his —ing,* Sonn. 20, 7. *not mine own fears, nor the prophetic soul of the wide world ... can yet the lease of my true love c.* 107, 3. *his art ... would c. my dam's god,* Tp. I, 2, 373. *not having the power to do the good it would, for the ill which doth c. it,* Cor. III, 1, 161.

3) to check, to restrain; a) intr. *two such —ing bounds shall you be,* John II, 444. b) tr. to check, to rebuke, to confute: *and justly thus —s his thoughts unjust,* Lucr. 189. *folly doctor-like —ing skill,* Sonn. 66, 10. *the duke of Milan and his more braver daughter could c. thee,* Tp. I, 2, 439. *now no more will I c. thy griefs,* Tit. III, 1, 260. *soon I heard the crying babe —ed with this discourse,* V, 1, 26. *if then they chanced to slack you, we could c. them,* Lr. II, 4, 249.

4) to hinder: *her eyes are by his flaming torch dimmed and —ed,* Lucr. 448. *nothing can affection's course c.* 500. *till with her own white fleece her voice —ed entombs her outcry,* 678. *who* (viz his tongue) *mad that sorrow should his use c.* 1781. *highly moved to wrath to be —ed in that he freely gave,* Tit. I, 420. *which men may blame, but not c.* Lr. III, 7, 27.

Controller, 1) superintendent: *this night to be —s,* H8 I, 3, 67 (O. Edd. *comptrollers*). — 2) censurer, detractor: *an arrogant c.* H6B III, 2, 205. *saucy c. of our private steps,* Tit. II, 3, 60.

Controlment, constraint, compulsion: *c. for c.* John I, 20. *without c.* = without restraint: Ado I, 3, 21. Tit. II, 1, 68.

Controversy, 1) dispute, quarrel: Compl. 110. Meas. I, 2, 26. Err. V, 20. Merch. IV, 1, 155. Shr. V, 1, 64. John I, 44. Cor. II, 1, 80. 85. Hml. II, 2, 371.

2) combat: *shall be swallowed in this c.* H5 II, 4, 109. *stemming it with hearts of c.* Caes. I, 2, 109 (= hearts eager for combat).

Contumelious, making infamous; a) contemptuous, insolent, taunting: *with scoffs and scorns and c. taunts,* H6A I, 4, 39. *his c. spirit,* H6B III, 2, 204. — b) attended with dishonour: *giving our holy virgins to the stain of c., beastly, mad-brained war,* Tim. V, 1, 177.

Contumeliously, tauntingly, contemptuously: *that you, being supreme magistrates, thus c. should break the peace,* H6A I, 3, 58.

Contumely, contemptuous treatment, taunts: *the proud man's c.* Hml. III, 1, 71 (Ff *the poor man's c.*).

Contusion, bruise: *that winter lion, who in rage forgets aged —s,* H6B V, 3, 3 (= the hurts of old age).

Convenience, 1) favourable circumstances, advantage: *I'll beat him, if I can meet him with any c.* All's II, 3, 253. *weigh what c. both of time and means may fit us to our shape,* Hml. IV, 7, 150. *which, if c. will not allow, stand in hard cure,* Lr. III, 6, 106.

2) cause of ease, accommodation, comfort: *exposed myself, from certain and possessed —s, to doubtful fortunes,* Troil. III, 3, 7. *for want of these required —s,* Oth. II, 1, 234.

3) propriety: *and the place answer to c.* Meas. III, 1, 258. *will lay upon him all the honour that good c. claims,* All's III, 2, 75.

Conveniency, 1) favour of circumstances, advantage: *and rather keepest from me all c. than suppliest me with the least advantage of hope,* Oth. IV, 2, 178.

2) propriety: *with all brief and plain c. let me have judgment and the Jew his will,* Merch. IV, 1, 82 (= with all becoming briefness and plainness).

Convenient, 1) fit: *c. place,* Mids. III, 1, 2. H6B I, 3, 212. H8 II, 2, 138. cf. H6A II, 4, 4. *time,* H5 IV, 1, 218. *the most c. messenger,* All's III, 4, 34. *c. convoy,* IV, 4, 10. *numbers,* Cor. I, 5, 13. *more c. is he for my hand than for your lady's,* Lr. IV, 5, 31.

2) easy, commodious: *at your c. leisure,* Wiv. III, 5, 136. Adverbially: *I this morning know where we shall find him most c.* Hml. I, 1, 175 (Ff *conveniently*).

3) proper, becoming, decent: *'tis not c. you should be cozened,* Wiv. IV, 5, 83. *c. is it,* Meas. IV, 3, 107. *with all c. speed,* Merch. III, 4, 56. *it shall be c. that you be by her aloft,* H6B I, 4, 10. *I'll frame c. peace,* Cor. V, 3, 191. *it were c. you had such a devil,* Tit. V, 2, 90. *that under covert and c. seeming hast practised on man's life,* Lr. III, 2, 56. *'tis most c.* V, 1, 36.

Conveniently, 1) properly: *such fair ostents of love as shall c. become you there,* Merch. II, 8, 45.

2) commodiously, with ease: *if he may be c. delivered, I would he were,* Tw. IV, 2, 73. *till I c. could send to Romeo,* Rom. V, 3, 256. *where we shall find him most c.* Hml. I, 1, 175 (Qq *convenient*). *action may c. the rest convey,* Per. III Prol. 56.

Convent, subst. see *Covent.*

Convent, vb., to summon: *whensoever he's —ed,* Meas. V, 158. *to the council-board he be —ed,* H8 V, 1, 52. *we are —ed upon a pleasing treaty,* Cor. II, 2, 58.

2) to be convenient, to suit: *when golden time —s* Tw. V, 391 (or = invites?).

Conventicle, secret and plotting assembly: H6B III, 1, 166.

Conversant, 1) having intercourse, familiar; followed by *with: nor c. with ease and idleness,* John IV, 3, 70. *c. with pain,* Per. III, 2, 25.

2) versed; followed by *in: c. in general services,* Cymb. IV, 1, 13.

Conversation, 1) familiar discourse, talk:

Cor. II, 1, 104 (*more of your c. would infect my brain*).

2) **intercourse:** *the king had from the c. of my thoughts haply been absent,* All's I, 3, 240. *his c. with Shore's wife,* R3 III, 5, 31. Hml. III, 2, 60. Cymb. I, 4, 113.

3) **address, deportment:** *what an unweighed behaviour hath this drunkard picked out of my c.* Wiv. II, 1, 25. *till their —s appear more wise,* H4B V, 5, 106. *have not those soft parts of c. that chamberers have,* Oth. III, 3, 264. *Octavia is of a holy, cold and still c.* Ant. II, 6, 131. *the good in c.* Per. II Prol. 9.

Convérse, subst. 1) **conversation, talk:** *your party in c.* Hml. II, 1, 42 (= your interlocutor). *that your c. and business may be more free,* Oth. III, 1, 40.

2) **intercourse:** *if overboldly we have borne ourselves in the c. of breath,* LLL V, 2, 745 (i. e. in conversation).

Converse, vb., 1) **to associate, to hold intercourse:** Gentl. I, 3, 31. II, 4, 63. LLL V, 2, 861. Merch. I, 2, 78. III, 4, 12. As V, 2, 66. H4A II, 4, 494. H4B V, 1, 75. H6A II, 1, 25. H6B II, 1, 195. III, 1, 368. R3 IV, 2, 28. Cor. II, 1, 56. Lr. I, 4, 16.

2) **to talk, to discourse:** Err. II, 2, 162. Ado IV, 1, 183. LLL V, 1, 6. H6A II, 4, 81.

Conversion, change for the better: *my c. to sweetly tastes,* As IV, 3, 137. *'tis too respective and too sociable for your c.* John I, 189.

Convert, vb. 1) to turn off; a) trans. *the eyes, 'fore duteous, now —ed are from his low tract,* Sonn. 7, 11. *was —ed both from his enterprise and from the world,* As V, 4, 167. — b) intr. *when thou from youth —est,* Sonn. 11, 4. *if from thyself to store thou wouldst c.* 14, 12.

2) to change; a) trans: *may I be so —ed?* Ado II, 3, 23. III, 4, 91. Hml. III, 4, 128. Followed by *from:* Sonn. 49, 7. By *into:* Ado II, 3, 70. H4B V, 2, 60. By *to:* Hml. IV, 7, 21. V, 1, 234. Used in a religious or moral sense: *—ing Jews to Christians,* Merch. III, 5, 37. *seeks to c. you,* Tim. IV, 3, 140. H8 I, 3, 43. Denoting a change of property, = to appropriate: *myself and what is mine to you and yours is now —ed,* Merch. III, 2, 168.

b) intr.: *stones dissolved to water do c.* Lucr. 592. 691. Ado I, 1, 123. R2 V, 1, 66. V, 3, 64. Rom. I, 5, 94. Tim. IV, 1, 7. Mcb. IV, 3, 229.

Convertite, a convert: Lucr. 743. As V, 4, 190. John V, 1, 19.

Convey, 1) to carry, to transport (to or from a place): *our fraughtage I have —ed aboard,* Err. IV, 1, 88. *see him safe —ed home,* IV, 4, 125. *c. what I will set down to my lady,* Tw. IV, 2, 118. Shr. Ind. I, 37. R2 II, 1, 137. IV, 316. H6A I, 4, 110. II, 5, 120. H6B II, 4, 93. IV, 1, 68. 103. H6C III, 2, 120. IV, 3, 52. R3 I, 1, 45. V, 1, 28 (Ff lead). H8 V, 3, 89. Tit. I, 287. V, 1, 44. V, 3, 191. Rom. III, 5, 50. Lr. III, 7, 15. V, 3, 107. Ant. III, 11, 52. Absolutely: *by interims and —ing gusts we have heard the charges of our friends,* Cor. I, 6, 5.

2) to carry, to bear, or lead away: *some hole through which I may c. this troubled soul,* Lucr. 1176. *their mistress ... through the skies in her light chariot quickly is —ed,* Ven. 1192. *c. my tristful queen,* H4A II, 4, 434. *c. him with safe conduct,* H5 I, 2, 297. *to have him suddenly —ed away* (viz to hell) R3 IV,

4, 76. *the weight we must c. with us,* Ant. III, 1, 36. *which never could I so c., unless your thoughts went on my way,* Per. IV Prol. 49.

3) to carry or carry away secretly or mysteriously: *thence she cannot be —ed away,* Gentl. III, 1, 37. *how shall I best c. the ladder thither?* 128. *I'll c. thee through the city-gate,* 252. *if you have a friend here, c. him out,* Wiv. III, 3, 125. *they —ed me into a buck-basket,* III, 5, 87. *there was one —ed out of my house in this basket,* IV, 2, 152. *an onion ... which in a napkin being close —ed,* Shr. Ind. 1, 127. *he was —ed by Richard Duke of Gloster,* H6C IV, 6, 81. *into her womb c. sterility,* Lr. I, 4, 300. Reflectively: *behind the arras I'll c. myself,* Hml. III, 3, 28. cf. *c. thy deity aboard our dancing boat,* Per. III, 1, 12.

4) to do or manage with secrecy: *if she c. letters to Richmond, you shall answer it,* R3 IV, 2, 96 (= send secretly). *you may c. your pleasures in a spacious plenty,* Mcb. IV, 3, 71 (= indulge them secretly). *I will c. the business as I shall find means,* Lr. I, 2, 109. *—ed himself as heir to the lady Lingare,* H5 I, 2, 74.

5) Hence used as a cant term for to steal: *c. the wise it call,* Wiv. I, 3, 32. *O, good! c.? conveyers are you all,* R2 IV, 317. cf. *that a king's children should be so —ed,* Cymb. I, 1, 63. cf. H6C IV, 6, 81.

6) to communicate, to impart: *what obscured light the heavens did grant did but c. unto our fearful minds a doubtful warrant of immediate death,* Err. I, 1, 68. *the assault ... fortune hath —ed to my understanding,* Meas. III, 1, 189. *if seriously I may c. my thoughts in this my light deliverance,* All's II, 1, 84. *action may the rest c.* Per. III Prol. 56.

Conveyance, 1) the act of transporting or carrying away, conduct, convoy: *madest quick c. with her good aunt Anne,* R3 IV, 4, 283 (soon foundest means to send her off, to get rid of her; cf. def. 5). *to his c. I assign my wife,* Oth. I, 3, 286.

2) means of transporting: *bethink you of some c.* Wiv. III, 3, 135. *these pipes and these —s of our blood* (viz the veins) Cor. V, 1, 54.

3) the act or deed by which a right or property is transferred, a grant: *craves the c. of a promised march over his kingdom,* Hml. IV, 4, 3 (according to others = to be convoyed by Danish troops). *the very —s of his lands will hardly lie in this box,* V, 1, 119.

4) artful management, jugglery: *huddling jest upon jest with such impossible c. upon me,* Ado II, 1, 253.

5) dishonest practice, trickery: *since Henry's death, I fear, there is c.* H6A I, 3, 2. *till I make king Lewis behold thy sly c. and thy lord's false love,* H6C III, 3, 160.

Conveyer, cheater, thief: *—s are you all,* R2 IV, 317.

Convict, convicted, proved to be guilty: *before I be c. by course of law,* R3 I, 4, 192.

Convicted, defeated, overpowered (cf. *Convince*): *a whole armado of c. sail,* John III, 4, 2 (M. Edd. convented, connected etc.).

Convince, 1) to persuade, to satisfy: *that persuasion could but thus c. me, that ...,* Troil. III, 2, 171.

2) to evince, to prove: *the holy suit which fain it would c.* LLL V, 2, 756

3) to prove guilty: *else might the world c. of levity as well my undertakings as your counsels*, Troil. II, 2, 130.

4) to overcome, to defeat: *his two chamberlains will I with wine and wassail so c.* Mcb. I, 7, 64. *their malady —s the great assay of art*, IV, 3, 142. *having —ed or supplied them*, Oth. IV, 1, 28. *to c. the honour of my mistress*, Cymb. I, 4, 104. *time this truth shall ne'er c.* Per. I, 2, 123.

Convive, to feast: *there in the full c. we*, Troil. IV, 5, 272.

Convocation, assembly, synod: *our spiritual c.* H5 I, 1, 76. *a certain c. of politic worms*, Hml. IV, 3, 21.

Convoy, subst. 1) conveyance, means of transporting: *entertained my c.* All's IV, 3, 103. *to which place we have convenient c.* IV, 4, 10. *crowns for c. put into his purse*, H5 IV, 3, 37. *this sailing Pandar our doubtful hope, our c. and our bark*, Troil. I, 1, 107. *which (cords) must be my c.* Rom. II, 4, 203. *the winds give benefit and c. is assistant*, Hml. I, 3, 3.

2) attendance for defence in war: *at such a breach, at such a c.* H5 III, 6, 76.

Convulsion, spasm: *grind their joints with dry —s*, Tp. IV, 260.

Cony and **Cony-catch** see *Cony* and *Coney-catch*.

Cook, subst., one whose profession is to prepare victuals for the table; masc.: Err. I, 2, 66 (M. Edd. rightly *clock*). Ado I, 3, 75. Shr. IV, 1, 47. 165. H4B II, 4, 48. V, 1, 12. H5 V, 2, 156. Tit. V, 2, 205. Rom. IV, 2, 2. 6. Tim. III, 4, 119. Ant. II, 1, 24. Cymb. III, 6, 30. IV, 2, 164. 299. Feminine: Wiv. I, 2, 4. Wint. IV, 4, 56.

Cook, vb. to prepare for the table: Cymb. III, 6, 39. *if you be ready for that, you are well —ed*, V, 4, 156 (cf. *over-roasted*, 154).

Cookery, art of preparing victuals: Ant. II, 6, 64. Cymb. IV, 2, 49.

Cool, adj. moderately and agreeably cold: *c. shadow*, Ven. 315. *c. well*, Sonn. 154, 9. *shade*, LLL V, 2, 89. Figuratively: *a c. rut-time*, Wiv. V, 5, 15. *c. reason*, Mids. V, 6. *the c. and temperate wind of grace*, H5 III, 3, 30. *c. in zeal*, H6B III, 1, 177. *c. patience*, Hml. III, 4, 124. *when the blood was c.* Cymb. V, 5, 77.

Cool, vb. 1) tr. to abate the heat of; properly and figuratively: Ven. 190. 387. Lucr. 682. Sonn. 154, 14. Pilgr. 76. Tp. I, 2, 222. Wiv. III, 5, 24. 122. Err. IV, 4, 34. Merch. I, 1, 22. III, 1, 59. 65. Shr. Ind. 1, 58. John III, 1, 277. III, 4, 149. R2 I, 1, 51. H4B III, 1, 44. H6B IV, 10, 10. Troil. V, 1, 2. Tit. II, 1, 134. II, 3, 14. Mcb. IV, 1, 37. Lr. III, 2, 79. Oth. I, 3, 334. Ant. I, 1, 10. II, 2, 209. Per. I, 1, 161.

2) intr. to lose heat: Wiv. I, 3, 109. IV, 2, 240. Ado II, 3, 214. Merch. I, 1, 82. All's IV, 3, 373. John II, 479. IV, 2, 194. H6B III, 2, 166. H6C V, 1, 49. Troil. I, 1, 25. Cor. IV, 1, 43. Tit. III, 1, 242. Tim. III, 6, 76. Caes. IV, 2, 19. Mcb. IV, 1, 154. V, 5, 10. Lr. I, 2, 115.

Cooling card, see *Card 3.*

Coop, vb. to shut up, to confine (for protection): *and —s from other lands her islanders*, John II, 25. *I am not —ed here for defence*, H6C V, 1, 109.

Copartner, fellow: *so should I have —s in my pain*, Lucr. 789.

Copatain hat, a high-crowned hat, of the form of a sugar-loaf: Shr. V, 1, 69.

Cope, subst. firmament: *the cheapest country under the c.* Per. IV, 6, 132.

Cope, vb. 1) trans. to meet, to encounter, to have to do with; either in a friendly manner: *three thousand ducats we freely c. your courteous pains withal*, Merch. IV, 1, 412. *I love to c. him in these sullen fits*, As II, 1, 67. *is again to c. your wife*, Oth. IV, 1, 87 (= to lie by her). Or as an adversary: *who shall c. him first*, Ven. 888. *to c. malicious censurers*, H8 I, 2, 78. *he —d Hector in the battle*, Troil. I, 2, 34. II, 3, 275. Lr. V, 3, 124 (Qq *c. withal*).

2) intr. followed by *with*, in the same sense: *she that never —d with stranger eyes*, Lucr. 99. *the royal fool thou —st with*, Wint. IV, 4, 435. *as just a man as e'er my conversation —d withal*, Hml. III, 2, 60. *the men we should have —d withal*, H4B IV, 2, 95. H6B III, 2, 230. H6C I, 3, 24. R3 V, 3, 315. Rom. IV, 1, 75.

Copesmate, companion: *misshapen Time, c. of ugly Night*, Lucr. 925.

Cophetua, name of an imaginary king who married a beggar: LLL IV, 1, 66. H4B V, 3, 106 (Q *Covetua*, Ff *Covitha*). Rom. II, 1, 14.

Copious, abounding in words: *their c. stories ... are never done*, Ven. 845. *be c. in exclaims*, R3 IV, 4, 135.

Copped, rising to a prominent top: *the blind mole casts c. hills towards heaven*, Per. I, 1, 101.

Copper, the metal Cuprum: LLL IV, 3, 386. *that ring was c.* H4A III, 3, 98. 162. 163. *c. nose*, Troil. I, 2, 115. *c. crowns*, IV, 4, 107.

Copper-spur, name in Meas. IV, 3, 14.

Coppice, a low wood: LLL IV, 1, 9.

Copse, the same: Ven. 259.

Copulation, coition: As III, 2, 84. Lr. IV, 6, 116.

Copulative, subst., one who is desirous of coition: *the rest of the country —s*, As V, 4, 58.

Copy, subst., 1) the original, the archetype, that from which a transcript or print is made: *thou shouldst print more, not let that c. die*, Sonn. 11, 14. *we took him setting of boys' —ies*, H6B IV, 2, 95.

2) example: *such a man might be a c. to these younger times*, All's I, 2, 46. *the c. of your speed was learned by them*, John IV, 2, 113. *he was the mark and glass, c. and book, that fashioned others*, H4B II, 3, 31. *be c. now to men of grosser blood*, H5 III, 1, 24. — Perhaps also = a law to be followed, a rule to be observed: *it was the c. of our conference*, Err. V, 62. *takes virtuous —ies to be wicked*, Tim. III, 3, 32.

3) a transcript, or a book printed after the original; properly and tropically: *almost the c. of my child*, Ado V, 1, 298. *and leave the world no c.* Tw. I, 5, 261. All's IV, 3, 355. Wint. I, 2, 122. II, 3, 99.

4) copyhold, tenure: *but in them nature's c. is not eterne*, Mcb. III, 2, 38.

Copy, vb. to transcribe, to write after an original: Sonn. 84, 9. Hml. I, 5, 101. *to c. out*, John V, 2, 1. = to imitate in general: Oth. III, 4, 190.

Copy-book, a book in which copies are written or printed for learners to imitate: *fair as a text B in a c.* LLL V, 2, 42.

Coragio, courage: Tp. V, 258. All's II, 5, 96 Used by Stephano and Parolles.

Coral, the solid secretions of zoophytes; supposed to be petrifactions and to be always red: *c. is far more red,* Sonn. 130, 2. *of his bones are c. made,* Tp. I, 2, 397.

Adjectively: *c. mouth,* Ven. 542. *lips,* Lucr. 420. *ivory conduits c. cisterns filling,* 1234. *c. clasps and amber studs,* Pilgr. 366 (not Shakespearian). *lips,* Shr. I, 1, 179.

Coram, a Latin preposition, supposed by Slender to be a title: Wiv. I, 1, 6 (part of the formula: *jurat coram me*).

Corambus, name in All's IV, 3, 185.

Coranto (O. Edd. *Carranto*) a quick lively dance: *he's able to lead her a c.* All's II, 3, 49. *why dost thou not go to church in a galliard and come home in a c.?* Tw. I, 3, 137. *swift —s,* H5 III, 5, 33.

Cord, 1) a small rope: Gentl. II, 4, 182. III, 1, 117. Meas. III, 2, 43. Err. V, 289. Merch. IV, 1, 366. John IV, 3, 127. H4A I, 3, 166. H5 III, 6, 50. Tit. II, 4, 10. Rom. II, 4, 201. III, 2, 34. 132. Lr. II, 2, 80. Oth. III, 3, 388. Cymb. V, 4, 170. V, 5, 213.

2) string, fibre: *that would fret the string, the master c. on's heart,* H8 III, 2, 106 (or = *chord,* string of a musical instrument?).

Corded, made of cords: *a c. ladder,* Gentl. II, 6, 33. III, 1, 40.

Cordelia, female name in Lr. I, 1, 63 etc.

Cordelion, ancient orthography for *Coeur-de-lion,* q. v.

Cordial, subst., a medicine raising the spirits; anything that comforts and gladdens the heart: R3 II, 1, 41. H8 III, 1, 106. Tit. I, 166. Rom. V, 1, 85. Cymb. V, 5, 247.

Cordial, adj., reviving the spirits: *which draught to me were c.* Wint. I, 2, 318. *c. comfort,* V, 3, 77. *what is more c.* Cymb. I, 5, 64. IV, 2, 327.

Core, 1) the heart, the central part: *most putrefied c. so fair without,* Troil. V, 8, 1. *in my heart's c., ay, in my heart of heart,* Hml. III, 2, 78.

2) an ulcer or boil: *were not that a botchy c.?* Troil. II, 1, 7. *thou c. of envy,* V, 1, 4 (Q *cur*). In both passages quibbling with 'heart.'

Coridon, see *Corydon.*

Corin, a pastoral name: Mids. II, 1, 66.*As II, 4, 23. 25.

Corinth, Greek town: Err. I, 1, 88. 94. 112. V, 351. Cant term for a house of ill repute: Tim. II, 2, 73.

Corinthian, a spirited fellow: *a C., a lad of mettle,* H4A II, 4, 13 (cf. *Ephesian*).*

Coriolanus: Cor. I, 9, 65 etc. Tit. IV, 4, 68.

Corioli (O. Edd. *Corioles* and *Coriolus*) Volscian town: Cor. I, 2, 27 etc.

Co-rival, vb. tr., to vie with, to pretend to equal: *whose weak untimbered sides —ed greatness,* Troil. I, 3, 44 (cf. *Corrival*).

Cork, subst., stopple: As III, 2, 213. Wint. III, 3, 95.

Corky, resembling the rough and cleft bark of the cork-tree, shrivelled, withered: *bind fast his c. arms,* Lr. III, 7, 29.

Cormorant, a glutton: *light vanity, insatiate c., consuming means, soon preys upon itself,* R2 II, 1, 38.

Adjectively, = ravenous: *c. devouring time,* LLL I, 1, 4. *in hot digestion of this c. war,* Troil. II, 2, 6. *the c. belly,* Cor. I, 1, 125.

Corn, 1) the plants the seeds of which are made

into bread: Lucr. 281. Meas. IV, 1, 76. LLL I. 1, 96. Mids. II, 1, 94. R2 III, 3, 162. H6B I, 2, 1. III, 2, 176. H6C V, 7, 3. H8 V, 5, 32. Tit. II, 3, 123. V, 3, 71. Mcb. IV, 1, 55. Lr. III, 6, 44. IV, 4, 6. *playing on pipes of c.* Mids. II, 1, 67 (pipes made by slitting the joint of a green stalk of corn).*

2) the grains of which bread is made: Tp. II, 1, 153. LLL IV, 3, 383. H4B IV, 1, 195. H6A III, 2, 5. 41. H8 V, 1, 112. Cor. I, 1, 11. 193. II, 3, 17. III, 1, 114 etc. Per. I, 4, 95. III, 3, 18.

3) an excrescence on the feet: Rom. I, 5, 19. 22. Lr. III, 2, 33.

Cornelia; 1) the mother of the Gracchi: Tit. IV, 1, 12. 2) *C. the midwife,* IV, 2, 141.

Cornelius: Hml. I, 2, 34. Cymb. V, 5, 248.

Corner, 1) the horn: *upon the c. of the moon there hangs a vaporous drop,* Mcb. III, 5, 23.

2) the angle: *the west c. of thy garden,* LLL I, 1, 249. *at the hedge-corner,* Shr. Ind. 1, 20. All's IV, 1, 2. *at the c. of the orchard,* Tw. III, 4, 194. *at every c. have them kiss,* H6B IV, 7, 145. *down Saint Magnus' c.* IV, 8, 2. *at the park c.* H6C IV, 5, 19.

3) the angle as part of the interior of a room: *he keeps them, like an ape, in the c. of his jaw,* Hml. IV, 2, 19. Used as the appropriate place for things neglected: *I may sit in a c.* Ado II, 1, 332. *unregarded age in —s thrown,* As II, 3, 42. Or for things kept secret: *the old fantastical duke of dark —s,* Meas. IV, 3, 164. *if you thus get my wife into —s,* Merch. III, 5, 32. *skulking in —s,* Wint. I, 2, 289. *there's nothing I have done yet, deserves a c.* H8 III, 1, 31. *than keep a c. in the thing I love for others' uses,* Oth. III, 3, 272.

4) region, direction: *sits the wind in that c.?* Ado II, 3, 103. *from the four —s of the earth they come,* Merch. II, 7, 39. *I'll to yond corner. And I to this. And here will Talbot mount,* H6A II, 1, 33. *winds of all the —s,* Cymb. II, 4, 28.

5) quarter, part of the world: *all —s else o' the earth let liberty make use of,* Tp. I, 2, 491. *till that utmost c. of the west salute thee for her king,* John II, 29. *come the three —s of the world in arms,* V, 7, 116. *doth belie all —s of the world,* Cymb. III, 4, 39.

Corner-cap, the keystone: *thou makest the triumviry, the c. of society,* LLL IV, 3, 53.*

Corner-stone, the stone which forms the corner of the foundation of an edifice: Cor. V, 4, 2.

Cornet, a troop of horse: *that Somerset, who in proud heart doth stop my —s, were in Talbot's place,* H6A IV, 3, 25.

Corn-field, a field where corn is growing: As V, 3, 19.

Cornish, pertaining to Cornwall: *le Roy! a C. name,* H5 IV, 1, 50.

Cornuto, a cuckold: Wiv. III, 5, 71.

Cornwall, the south-western part of England: Lr. I, 1, 2 etc.

Corollary, a surplus: *bring a c. rather than want a spirit,* Tp. IV, 1, 57.

Coronation, the solemnity of crowning a sovereign: John IV, 2, 40. R2 IV, 320. V, 5, 77. H4B III, 2, 195. V, 2, 141. V, 5, 4. H6A III, 4, 27. V, 1, 10. H6B I, 2, 1, 74. H6C II, 6, 96. R3 III, 1, 62. 173. III, 4, 2. 16. H8 III, 2, 46. 407. IV, 1, 3. 16. Hml. I, 2, 53.

Coroner, a blundering emendation of some M. Edd. for *chroniclers* of the O. Edd. in As IV, 1,

105. The Shakespearian form of the word is *Crowner*, q. v.

Coronet, 1) an inferior crown worn by noblemen: *'twas not a crown neither, 'twas one of these —s,* Caes. I, 2, 238. Tp. I, 2, 114. H5 II Chor. 10. H6A III, 3, 89. H8 IV, 1, 54. Used for *crown: adorn his temples with a c., and yet retain but privilege of a private man,* H6A V, 4, 134. *this c. part betwixt you,* Lr. I, 1, 141.

2) garland: *with c. of fresh and fragrant flowers,* Mids. IV, 1, 57. *there her c. weeds clambering to hang,* Hml. IV, 7, 174.

Corporal, subst., the lowest officer of the infantry: Wiv. II, 1, 128. 137. H4A IV, 2, 26. H4B II, 4, 166. III, 2, 244. H5 II, 1, 1. 14. 29. 41. 107. III, 2, 3. *and I to be a c. of his* (Cupid's) *field,* LLL III, 189 (= his adjutant).

Corporal, adj. 1) bodily: Meas. III, 1, 80. All's I, 2, 24. H5 I, 1, 16. Caes. IV, 1, 33. Mcb. I, 7, 80. Cymb. II, 4, 119.

2) material, not spiritual: *she is not c.* LLL IV, 3, 86. *what seemed c. melted as breath into the wind,* Mcb. I, 3, 81.

Corporate, united in a body: *they answer in a joint and c. voice,* Tim. II, 2, 213. — Misapplied for *corporal:* H4B III, 2, 235.

Corpse (unchanged in the plural: H4A I, 1, 43 and H4B I, 1, 192), dead body: Tw. II, 4, 63. Wint. V, 1, 58. H6A II, 2, 13. H6B III, 2, 132. R3 V, 3, 266. Caes. III, 2, 62. 162. Per. III, 1, 64. *dead c.* H4A I, 1, 43. Tit. V, 1, 105. = the body without the soul: *my lord your son had only but the c., but shadows and the shows of men, to fight,* H4B I, 1, 192 (cf. *Incorpsed*).

Corpulent, fleshy, bulky: H4A II, 4, 464.

Correct, vb. 1) to set right, to counteract whatever is injurious: *whose* (the sun's) *medicinable eye —s the ill aspects of planets evil,* Troil. I, 3, 92. Absolutely: *where some, like magistrates, c. at home,* H5 I, 2, 191.

2) to chastise: Sonn. 111, 12. Meas. IV, 2, 87. Ado V, 1, 331. John II, 87. R2 I, 2, 5. H6B I, 3, 202. H8 III, 2, 335. Troil. V, 6, 3. Cor. III, 2, 78. V, 3, 57. Per. I, 3, 23.

Correction, chastisement: Sonn. 111, 12. Gentl. II, 4, 138. III, 1, 395. Meas. III, 2, 33. R2 I, 2, 4. II, 3, 105. IV, 77. V, 1, 32. H4A V, 1, 111. H4B IV, 1, 213. IV, 4, 85. H5 II, 2, 51. V, 1, 83. Troil. V, 6, 5. Lr. II, 2, 149. Misapplied: LLL I, 1, 215.

Under c. = under favour, if you do not take it ill: *under your good c., I have seen ...,* Meas. II, 2, 10. *not so, sir; under c., sir,* LLL V, 2, 489. 493. *I think, under your c., there is not many,* H5 III, 2, 130. *under the c. of bragging be it spoken,* V, 2, 144.

Correctioner, one who inflicts chastisement: *you blue-bottle rogue, you filthy famished c.* H4B V, 4, 23 (Doll Tearsheet's speech).

Correspond, to agree, to suit: *well —ing with your stiff age,* Cymb. III, 3, 31.

Correspondence, agreement, congruity: *what eyes hath love put in my head, which have no c. with true sight,* Sonn. 148, 2.

Correspondent, agreeing, obsequious: *I will be c. to command,* Tp. I, 2, 297.

Corresponsive, fitting. adapted: *massy staples and c. and fulfilling bolts,* Troil. Prol. 18.

Corrigible, 1) submissive to correction, docile: *bending down his c. neck,* Ant. IV, 14, 74.

2) corrective: *the power and c. authority of this lies in our wills,* Oth. I, 3, 329.

Corrival (cf. *Co-rival*), subst. 1) rival, competitor: *wear without c. all her dignities,* H4A I, 3, 207.

2) companion (cf. *Rival*): *and many moe —s and dear men of estimation,* H4A IV, 4, 31.

Corroborate, a word used nonsensically by Pistol: *his heart is fracted and c.* H5 II, 1, 130.

Córrosive, subst. a medicament giving pain: *though parting be a fretful c., it is applied to a deathful wound,* H6B III, 2, 403.

Córrosive, adj. fretting, giving pain: *care is no cure, but rather c.* H6A III, 3, 3.

Corrupt, vb., 1) trans. to vitiate, to deprave: *which* (heart) *once —ed takes the worser part,* Lucr. 294. *her sacred temple spotted, spoiled, —ed,* 1172. *—ed blood,* 1748. *myself —ing,* Sonn. 35, 7. *a —ed heart,* Wiv. V, 5, 91. *disdain rather c. me ever,* All's II, 3, 123. *my son —s a well-derived nature with his inducement,* III, 2, 90. *three —ed men,* H5 II Chor. 22. *attainted, —ed and exempt from ancient gentry,* H6A II, 4, 93. *whose conscience with injustice is —ed,* H6B III, 2, 235. *—ed the youth in erecting a grammar-school,* IV, 7, 36. *I'll c. her manners, stain her beauty,* R3 IV, 4, 206. *the dead carcasses that do c. my air,* Cor. III, 3, 123. Tit. III, 1, 9. Lr. II, 4, 228. Hml. III, 3, 57. Oth. I, 3, 272. Ant. IV, 5, 17.

Special sorts of depraving: a) by bribery: All's IV, 3, 309. H6C III, 2, 155. H8 III, 1, 101. Troil. IV, 4, 74. Oth. IV, 2, 190. Cymb. II, 4, 116. Followed by the preposition *to: to c. him to a revolt,* All's IV, 3, 204. Absolutely: *—ing gold,* R3 IV, 2, 34.

b) by debauching: *Angelo had never the purpose to c. her,* Meas. III, 1, 163. All's III, 5, 73. Cor. IV, 3, 33. And in a more general sense = to seduce: *would c. my saint to be a devil,* Sonn. 144, 7. Gentl. IV, 2, 6. John III, 1, 55. H4A I, 2, 102. Oth. I, 3, 60.

c) by perversion and falsification: *you c. the song,* All's I, 3, 85. *we must not so stain our judgement, or c. our hope,* II, 1, 123. *purchase —ed pardon of a man,* John III, 1, 166. *by underhand —ed foul injustice,* R3 V, 1, 6. *if this law of nature be —ed through affection,* Troil. II, 2, 177.

2) intr. to become putrid: *do as the carrion does, not as the flower, c. with virtuous season,* Meas. II, 2, 168. *—ing in its own fertility,* H5 V, 2, 40.

Corrupt, adj. vitiated, depraved, perverted: *eyes c. by over-partial looks,* Sonn. 137, 5. *c. and tainted in desire,* Wiv. V, 5, 94. *the c. deputy,* Meas. III, 1, 265. *in law, what plea so tainted and c.* Merch. III, 2, 75. H4B II, 4, 320. H5 I, 2, 73. H6A V, 4, 45. H8 I, 1, 156. I, 2, 116. V, 1, 133. Compar. *—er,* Lr. II, 2, 108.

Corrupter, perverter; seducer: *her c. of words,* Tw. III, 1, 41. *— s of my faith,* Cymb. III, 4, 85.

Corruptibly, so as to be corrupted: *it is too late: the life of all his blood is touched c.* John V, 7, 2.

Corruption, 1) depravation, depravity, wickedness: *what c. in this life that it will let this man live,* Meas. III, 1, 241. *where I have seen c. boil and bubble,* V, 320. *no man that hath a name, by falsehood and c. doth it shame,* Err. II, 1, 113. *his c. being* *ta'en from us*, H4A V, 2, 22. *c. wins not more than honesty*, H8 III, 2, 445.

2) **bribery:** *the name of Cassius honours this c.* Caes. IV, 3, 15. *c. in the place!* Lr. III, 6, 58.

3) **perversion, false representation:** *I wish no other speaker of my living actions, to keep mine honour from c.* H8 IV, 2, 71. *their virtues else shall in the general censure take c. from that particular fault*, Hml. I, 4, 35.

4) **impurity of blood,** by which a person is disabled to inherit lands: *that you resign the supreme seat to the c. of a blemished stock*, R3 III, 7, 122. *to draw forth your noble ancestry from the c. of abusing times*, 199.

5) **putrid and infectious matter,** figuratively: *any taint of vice whose strong c. inhabits our frail blood*, Tw. III, 4, 390. *when it breaks, I fear will issue thence the foul c. of a sweet child's death*, John IV, 2, 81. *sin gathering head shall break into c.* R2 V, 1, 59 and H4B III, 1, 77 (cf. also H4A V, 2, 22). *stewed in c., honeying and making love over the nasty sty*, Hml. III, 4, 93. *it will but skin and film the ulcerous place, whilst rank c., mining all within, infects unseen*, 148.

Corruptly, in a vicious and perverse manner: Merch. II, 9, 42.

Corse, dead body: Wint. IV, 4, 129. H4A I, 3, 44. IV, 1, 123. H6A I, 1, 62. R3 I, 2, 32. 33. 226. II, 1, 80. IV, 1, 67. Troil. II, 3, 35. V, 5, 10. Cor. V, 6, 145. Rom. III, 2, 54. 128. IV, 5, 80. V, 2, 30. Tim. V, 4, 70. Caes. III, 1, 199. Hml. I, 2, 105. I, 4, 52. V, 1, 181. 243. Cymb. IV, 2, 229. Per. III, 2, 63.

Used for a body in general: *not like a c.; or if, not to be buried, but quick and in mine arms*, Wint. IV, 4, 131. cf. *Corpse.*

Corslet, cuirass: Cor. V, 4, 21.

Corydon, pastoral name in Pilgr. 296.

Cosmo, name in All's IV, 3, 186.

Cost, subst. 1) **expense:** Sonn. 146, 5. Pilgr. 180. Ado I, 1, 98. Merch. III, 4, 19. H4A I, 3, 91. H4B I, 3, 44. H6A I, 1, 74. R3 I, 2, 160. H8 I, 1, 89. Rom. IV, 4, 6. Ant. III, 4, 37. Per. III, 2, 71 (*this queen, worth all our mundane c.* = worth all that the world can pay? or = worth all the pomp of our world?). Plur. —*s: for* —*s and charges*, H6B I, 1, 134. — *At a person's c.* = at his expense: Tw. V, 327. R3 V, 3, 324. Tim. I, 1, 124. — *Of a person's c.*, in the same sense: H6B I, 1, 61. IV, 6, 3. — *On* and *upon a person's c.*, in the same sense: As II, 7, 80. H5 IV, 3, 25. — *To a person's c.* = to his prejudice: *he is at Oxford still, is he not? Indeed, to my c.* H4B III, 2, 13. *we will meet, to thy c.*, H6A I, 3, 82. III, 4, 43.

2) **ornament, pomp:** *the rich proud c. of outworn buried age*, Sonn. 64, 2. *prouder than garments' c.* 91, 10. *whose bare outbragged the web it seemed to wear, yet showed his visage by that c. more dear*, Compl. 96. *where youth and c. and witless bravery keeps*, Meas. I, 3, 10. *the city-woman bears the c. of princes on unworthy shoulders*, As II, 7, 76.

Used for a costly building: *leaves his part-created c. a naked subject to the weeping clouds*, H4B I, 3, 60.

Cost, vb., to be bought at the expense of; with an accus., or a dative and accus.: Lucr. 146. Wiv. I, 1, 159. Err. III, 1, 123. Ado I, 1, 90. II, 1, 387. Mids. III, 2, 97. Merch. III, 1, 88. Shr. V, 2, 128. All's IV, 5, 11. H4B II, 1, 12. H6B I, 3, 134. H6C I,

1, 268. II, 2, 177. Troil. IV, 5, 223. V, 8, 2. Tim. I, 1, 217. Hml. III, 2, 259. Lr. V, 3, 173. Oth. II, 3, 93. Cymb. III, 6, 81. *it will c. thee dear*, Oth. V, 2, 255. *what she doth c. the holding*, Troil. II, 2, 51. *did these bones c. no more the breeding*, Hml. V, 1, 100.

Costard, 1) ludicrous expression for the **head:** Wiv. III, 1, 14. LLL III, 71. R3 I, 4, 159. Lr. IV, 6, 247.

2) name in LLL I, 1, 180. 224. I, 2, 124. 133. IV, 2, 93. IV, 3, 197 etc.

Costermonger, a petty dealer, a mercenary **soul:** *virtue is of so little regard in these* —*s' times*, H4B I, 2, 191 (Ff *in these* —*s;* Q *in these costermongers times;* M. Edd. *in these costermonger times*).

Costly, 1) **sumptuous, expensive:** Ado II, 1, 341. Shr. II, 354. H4B III, 1, 13. H6B III, 2, 106. H8 I, 1, 165. Troil. IV, 1, 60. Caes. III, 1, 258. Compar. —*ier*, Cymb. III, 2, 78. Adverbially: *painting thy outward walls so c. gay*, Sonn. 146, 4.

2) **richly adorned, gorgeous:** *how c. summer was at hand*, Merch. II, 9, 94. *a c. suit*, Shr. Ind. 1, 59. *c. thy habit as thy purse can buy*, Hml. I, 3, 70 (cf. *Cost*, subst. 2).

Co-supreme, fellow in supremacy: *the phoenix and the dove,* —*s and stars of love*, Phoen. 51.

Cote, subst. cottage: As II, 4, 83. III, 2, 448.

Cote, vb., to **pass by,** to **leave behind:** *we* —*d them on the way*, Hml. II, 2, 330. Taken by some in the same sense in LLL IV, 3, 87; but cf. *Quote*, which is often spelt *Cote.*

Cotquean, a man who busies himself with women's affairs: Rom. IV, 4, 6.

Cotsale or **Cotsall,** a corruption of *Cotswold:* Wiv. I, 1, 92. H4B III, 2, 23.

Cotswold, open downs in Glocestershire, where public games took place: R2 II, 3, 9.

Cottage, hut: Merch. I, 2, 15. As II, 4, 92. III, 5, 107. Wint. IV, 2, 50. IV, 4, 456. H6B IV, 2, 132.

Cotus, name in Cor. IV, 5, 3. 4.

Couch, subst. place for rest, bed: Lucr. 1037. Wiv. I, 3, 108. Shr. Ind. 2, 39. John III, 4, 27. H4B III, 1, 16. Oth. I, 3, 231. IV, 1, 72. Hml. I, 5, 83.

Couch, vb. 1) intr. a) to **lie:** *as fortunate a bed as ever Beatrice shall c. upon*, Ado III, 1, 46. Merch. V, 305. Oth. IV, 3, 57. Ant. IV, 14, 51.

b) to **lie down in the manner of a beast,** and hence to **stoop:** *a lioness lay* —*ing, head on ground*, As IV, 3, 116. H4A III, 1, 153. Per. III Prol. 6. *I'll wink and c.; no man their works must eye*, Wiv. V, 52. *England shall c. down in fear*, H5 IV, 2, 37.

c) to **lie close and hidden, to stand close:** *there I c. when owls do cry*, Tp. V, 90. *we'll c. in the castle-ditch*, Wiv. V, 2, 1. *but c., lo! here he comes*, All's IV, 1, 24. *where bloody murder or detested rape can c. for fear*, Tit. V, 2, 38. *c. we awhile and mark*, Hml. V, 1, 245. *this night, wherein the cub-drawn bear would c.* Lr. III, 1, 12.

2) trans. a) to **lay down:** *his body* —*ed in a curious bed*, H6C II, 5, 53. *c. his limbs*, Rom. II, 3, 38. Singular expression: *I espy virtue with valour* —*ed in thine eye*, R2 I, 3, 98 (= lying, dwelling).

b) to **make to stoop and lie close:** *a falcon towering in the skies* —*eth the fowl below with his wings' shade*, Lucr. 507. Partic. *couched* = lying or standing close and concealed: *they are all* —*ed in a pit*, Wiv. V, 3, 14. *is* —*ed in the woodbine coverture*, Ado III, 1, 30. *sorrow that is* —*ed in seeming gladness.*

Troil. I, 1, 39. *one cloud of winter showers, these flies are* —*ed,* Tim. II, 2, 181. *when he lay* —*ed in the ominous horse,* Hml. II, 2, 476.

c) to fix a spear in the rest: *a braver soldier never* —*ed lance,* H6A III, 2, 134.

d) to express, to clothe: *ignominious words, though clerkly* —*ed,* H6B III, 1, 179.

Couching, subst., stooping, bow: *these* —*s and these lowly courtesies,* Caes. III, 1, 36.

Cough, subst., violent effort of the lungs to throw off offending matter: Mids. II, 1, 54. H4B III, 2, 193.

Cough, vb., to make a noisy effort to throw offending matter from the lungs: LLL V, 2, 932. Troil. I, 3, 173. Rom. III, 1, 27. Oth. IV, 2, 29. Ant. I, 4, 63 (*which beasts would c. at*).

Coulter, see *Culter.*

Council, any deliberating assembly: *in our maiden c.* LLL V, 2, 789. *that the great figure of a c. frames by self-unable motion,* All's III, 1, 12. R3 III, 1, 179. III, 2, 12. H8 II, 4, 51. Troil. II, 3, 276. Caes. II, 1, 67. IV, 1, 45. Oth. I, 2, 92. Ant. I, 4, 75. Especially the body of privy counsellors: Wiv. I, 1, 35. 120. R2 I, 3, 124. H4A I, 1, 32. 103. I, 2, 95. III, 2, 32. H5 V, 2, 79. 304. H6A I, 1, 89. H6B I, 1, 89. III, 1, 27. IV, 2, 15. H6C I, 1, 36. R3 II, 3, 13. H8 V, 1, 43. V, 3, 2. 136. Mcb. III, 1, 23. Per. II, 4, 18. *board of c.* H8 I, 1, 79. *privy c.* H6B II, 1, 176. H8 IV, 1, 112.

Council and *counsel* often confounded, f. i. All's IV, 3, 53: *you are not of his c.*

Council-board, the body of privy counsellors: H4A IV, 3, 99. H8 V, 1, 51. cf. *board of council,* H8 I, 1, 79.

Council-house, the house where the privy council meets: H6B I, 1, 90. R3 III, 5, 38.

Councillor, a member of the privy council: H8 V, 2, 17. V, 3, 49. 143.

Counsel, subst. 1) advice: Gentl. I, 3, 34. II, 4, 185. Wiv. II, 1, 42. III, 3, 146. Meas. II, 1, 267. Ado III, 1, 102. IV, 1, 203. V, 1, 3. 23. Mids. II, 1, 218. Merch. I, 2, 22. II, 2, 32. As III, 2, 425. Shr. I, 1, 169. All's I, 1, 224. Tw. IV, 3, 8. Wint. II, 1, 164 (—*s*). IV, 4, 506 (—*s*). V, 1, 52. R2 III, 2, 214. H6A II, 5, 118. III, 1, 185. H6C II, 6, 102. IV, 8, 1. R3 I, 3, 261. II, 3, 20 etc. *to give c.:* Ado V, 1, 5. As III, 2, 383. H6B III, 1, 289. H6C II, 3, 11. *to take c. of a p.:* Ven. 640. Pilgr. 303. *I will take your c.* H4B III, 1, 106.

2) consultation: *the father should hold some c. in such a business,* Wint. IV, 4, 420 (= should be consulted). *I hold as little c. with weak fear,* H4A IV, 3, 11 (= do not consult fear). *your deeds of war and all our c. die,* H6B I, 1, 97. H6C II, 1, 208. Cor. I, 1, 154. I, 2, 2. V, 6, 97. Rom. I, 3, 9.

3) reflection, deliberation: *all this beforehand c. comprehends,* Lucr. 494. *c. may stop awhile what will not stay,* Compl. 159. *war with good c.* Gentl. I, 1, 68. *let her wear it out with good c.* Ado II, 3, 210. *thy thoughts and* —*s of thy heart,* IV, 1, 103. *my c. is my shield,* R3 IV, 3, 56. *this man hath had good c.* Lr. I, 4, 345. Perhaps also in Mids. II, 1, 218.

4) secret and inmost thought: *emptying our bosoms of our c. sweet,* Mids. I, 1, 216. *Buckingham no more shall be the neighbour to my c.* R3 IV, 2, 43 (Ff —*s*). *my* —*'s consistory,* II, 2, 151. *so stumblest on my c.* Rom. II, 2, 53.

5) privity to another's secret thoughts: *myself in c.* Gentl. II, 6, 35. *all the c. that we two have shared,* Mids. III, 2, 198. *what to your sworn c. I have spoken,* All's III, 7, 9. *he was of my c. in my whole course of wooing,* Oth. III, 3, 111. Hence = accord: *it was a strong c. a fool could disunite,* Troil. II, 3, 109 (Qq *composure*).

6) secret: *it were better for you if it were known in c.* Wiv. I, 1, 122. *this sealed-up c.* (viz a letter) LLL III, 170; cf. *these locks of c.* Cymb. III, 2, 36. *their several* —*s they unbosom shall,* LLL V, 2, 141. Troil. III, 2, 141. Tit. IV, 2, 118. *to keep c.:* Wiv. IV, 6, 7. Ado III, 3, 92. Mids. III, 2, 308. Tit. IV, 2, 144; cf. Rom. II, 4, 209. Caes. II, 1, 298. II, 4, 9. Hml. III, 2, 152. IV, 2, 11. Lr. I, 4, 34. Oth. IV, 2, 94.

7) one who gives counsel in law, a counsellor: *as I was then advised by my learned c.* H4B I, 2, 154. *we will have these things set down by lawful c.* Cymb. I, 4, 178.

Counsel, vb. to advise; absolutely: *c., Lucetta,* Gentl. II, 7, 1. Merch. II, 2, 23. III, 2, 6. H4A IV, 3, 6. Lr. II, 4, 312. trans.: Gentl. I, 1, 51. I, 2, 2. Ado III, 1, 83. V, 1, 21. Merch. II, 2, 30. As I, 2, 273. III, 3, 96. Shr. Ind. I, 136. I, 1, 162. H6B I, 3, 96. R3 I, 4, 258. III, 1, 64. H8 V, 5, 30. Cor. III, 2, 28 (*be* —*ed*). Rom. III, 5, 210. Mcb. II, 1, 29 (*I shall be* —*ed*). With *to:* *would c. you to a more equal enterprise,* As I, 2, 187. *to c. Cassio to this parallel course,* Oth. II, 3, 355. — *To c. sth.* = to recommend sth.: *he* —*s a divorce,* H8 II, 2, 31. *and c. every man the aptest way for safety and revenge,* H4B I, 1, 212.

In Per. I, 1, 113 some M. Edd.: *to c. of your days,* O. Edd. *cancel.*

Counsel-keeper, one who keeps secrets: H4B II, 4, 290.

Counsel-keeping, keeping secrets, not blabbing: Tit. II, 3, 24.

Counsellor, 1) one who gives advice: Wiv. II, 1, 6. As II, 1, 10. All's I, 1, 184 (fem.). Wint. II, 3, 55 (fem.). H4B IV, 4, 63. H5 II, 3, 55. II, 4, 33. H6B IV, 2, 182. Rom. III, 5, 239 (fem.).

2) a member of a privy council (cf. *Councillor*): Tp. I, 1, 23. Gentl. II, 4, 77. H4B IV, 5, 121. H8 I, 3, 9. Cor. I, 1, 120. Per. V, 1, 184.

3) a lawyer, advocate: *good* —*s lack no clients,* Meas. I, 2, 109.

4) a confident, one entrusted with another's secrets: *but he, his own affections' c.* Rom. I, 1, 153. *those linen cheeks of thine are* —*s to fear,* Mcb. V, 3, 17. *love's c. should fill the bores of hearing to the smothering of the sense,* Cymb. III, 2, 59.

5) a talker, prater: *is he not a most profane and liberal c.?* Oth. II, 1, 165. cf. *this c. is now most still,* Hml. III, 4, 213, and Tp. I, 1, 23.

Count, subst., a title of foreign nobility: Ado I, 1, 211. I, 2, 9. I, 3, 66. II, 1, 1. 190. 218. 296 etc. II, 2, 1. 34. III, 2, 87. III, 4, 62. IV, 1, 10. 318. 331. Merch. I, 2, 64 (*C. Palatine*). All's I, 2, 18. I, 3, 161. II, 3, 200. Tw. I, 3, 114. I, 4, 9. I, 5, 109 etc. II, 1, 44. III, 2, 7 etc. V, 263 (the same person being titled Duke in I, 2, 25). John IV, 3, 15. V, 4, 9. Equivalent to *earl:* H8 II, 3, 41.

Count, subst. (cf. *Compt*), 1) account, reckoning: *this fair child of mine shall sum my c.* Sonn. 2, 11. *I know not what* —*s harsh fortune casts upon my face,* Ant. II, 6, 54. *by my c.* Rom. I, 3, 71. *by this* *c.* III, 5, 46. *out of all c.* and *out of c.,* = incalculable, infinite, but otherwise defined by Speed: Gentl. II, 1, 62. 63.

2) account, answer at law: *why to a public c. I might not go,* Hml. IV, 7, 17 (= bring an action against him).

Count, vb., 1) to number, to reckon: *c. the clock,* Sonn. 12, 1. *to c. atomies,* As III, 2, 245. *c. thy way with sighs,* R2 V, 1, 89. H6A I, 4, 60. R3 I, 1, 162. Rom. II, 6, 32. Caes. II, 1, 192. Cymb. II, 4, 142. *to c. o'er,* Hml. III, 2, 172.

2) to account, to esteem, to think: —*ing best to be with you alone,* Sonn. 75, 7. —*ing no old thing old,* 108, 7. 121, 8. 127, 1. 141, 13. Gentl. V, 4, 70. Wiv. V, 5, 122. LLL II, 18. IV, 3, 263. 267. As V, 3, 40. All's II, 1, 155. Wint. l, 2, 245. III, 2, 28. John III, 1, 171. III, 3, 21. IV, 2, 66. R2 II, 3, 46. H6B II, 4, 39. H6C V, 6, 91. R3 IV, 1, 47. Rom. III, 5, 144. IV, 1, 9. Tim. III, 2, 62. Hml. II, 2, 261. Cymb. I, 5, 20. III, 2, 15.

3) Followed by *of,* = to attend to, to take notice of: *no man —s of her beauty,* Gentl. II, 1, 65. *c. of this, the count's a fool,* All's IV, 3, 258. Transitively in the same sense? *I'll c. his favours,* Hml. V, 2, 78 (M. Edd. *court*). cf. *nor mother, wife, nor England's — ed queen,* R3 IV, 1, 47.

Count-cardinal: H8 I, 1, 172. Is Wolsey called so in derision of his low birth? Pope: *court-cardinal.*

Countenance, subst. 1) face, air: As IV, 1, 37. Shr. IV, 2, 200. Wint. I, 2, 343. V, 2, 52. H6A I, 4, 47. Troil. IV, 5, 195. Tit. I, 263. Lr. I, 4, 30. Ant. IV, 14, 85. Cymb. III, 4, 14. cf. the quibble in LLL V, 2, 611. 623 and Ant. II, 2, 181. *such Ethiope words, blacker in their effect than in their c.* As IV, 3, 36. The following passages lead over to the subsequent significations: *which I will do with confirmed c.* Ado V, 4, 17. *such a confirmed c.* Cor. I, 3, 65. *lift up your c.* Wint. IV, 4, 49 (= be gay, take courage). *do but mark the c. that he will give me,* H4B V, 5, 8. *change my c.* H6B III, 1, 99. *subject to your c.* H8 II, 4, 26. *some news is come that turns their —s,* Cor. IV, 6, 59.

2) calmness of mien, assurance: *Biron was out of c.* LLL V, 2, 272. *put out of c.* 611. 624. *we have put thee in c.* 623. *set your c.* Shr. IV, 4, 18. *sleep day out of c.* Ant. II, 2, 181.

3) appearance, deportment: *the something that nature gave me, his c. seems to take from me,* As I, 1, 19. *therefore put I on the c. of stern commandment,* II, 7, 108. *puts my apparel and my c. on,* Shr. I, 1, 234. *in gait and c. like a father,* IV, 2, 65. *he seems to cozen somebody under my c.* V, 1, 41. *he did bear my c. in the town,* 129. *how he holds his c.* H4A II, 4, 432. *by unkind usage, dangerous c.* V, 1, 69. *his* (the horse's) *c. enforces homage,* H5 III, 7, 30. *his altered c.* H6B III, 1, 5. Troil. I, 2, 218. Lr. I, 2, 172.

4) authority, credit, patronage: *when your c. filled up his line, then lacked I matter,* Sonn. 86, 13. *you should lay my c. to pawn,* Wiv. II, 2, 5. *unfold the evil which is here wrapped up in c.* Meas. V, 118. *under whose c. we steal,* H4A I, 2, 33. *want c.* 175. *gave his c. to laugh at gibing boys,* III, 2, 65. *abuse the c. of the king,* H4B IV, 2, 13. 24. *a knave should have some c. at his friend's request,* V, 1, 49. *under the c. of Lady Eleanor,* H6B II, 1, 168. *he waged me with his c.* Cor. V, 6, 40. *that which would appear offence in us, his c. will change to virtue,* Caes. I, 3,

159. *hath given c. to his speech with almost all the holy vows of heaven,* Hml. I, 3, 113. *soaks up the king's c.* IV, 2, 16. *should have c. to drown themselves,* V, 1, 30. *we'll use his c. for the battle,* Lr. V, 1, 63.

Countenance, vb., to keep in countenance, to support, to favour: *as if the heavens should c. his sin,* Lucr. 343. Meas. V, 322. H4B IV, 1, 35. V, 1, 41. 57. Hml. IV, 1, 32. Hence = to be in keeping with: *walk like sprites, to c. this horror,* Mcb. II, 3, 85. And = to grace, to honour: *you must meet my master to c. my mistress. Why, she hath a face of her own. I call them forth to credit her,* Shr. IV, 1, 101.

Counter, subst. a round piece of metal used in calculations: As II, 7, 63. Wint. IV, 3, 38 (O. Edd. *compters*). Troil. II, 2, 28. Caes. IV, 3, 80. Cymb. V, 4, 174.

Counter, adv., the wrong way, (in the language of huntsmen): *a hound that runs c. and yet draws dry-foot well,* Err. IV, 2, 39 (a quibble intended, there being two prisons called *the Counter* in the city of London). *you hunt c.* H4B I, 2, 102. *this is c., you false Danish dogs,* Hml. IV, 5, 110.

Counter-caster, reckoner, arithmetician: Oth. I, 1, 31.

Counterchange, subst. exchange, reciprocation: *the c. is severally in all,* Cymb. V, 5, 396.

Countercheck, subst., rebuke, check: *the c. quarrelsome,* As V, 4, 84. 99. *have brought a c. before your gates,* John II, 224.

Counterfeit, that which is made in imitation of something, 1) a likeness, portrait: *the poor c. of her complaining,* Lucr. 1269. *much liker than your painted c.* Sonn. 16, 8. *describe Adonis, and the c. is poorly imitated after you,* 53, 5. *fair Portia's c.* Merch. III, 2, 115. *thou drawest a c. best in all Athens,* Tim. V, 1, 83. *this downy sleep, death's c.* Mcb. II, 3, 81.

2) simulation, feigning: *there was never c. of passion came so near the life of passion,* Ado II, 3, 110. *this was not c.* As IV, 3, 170. 173. *you gave us the c. fairly last night? what c. did I give you? the slip,* Rom. II, 4, 48. *two or three groan: these may be —s,* Oth. V, 1, 43.

3) deceitful imitation: *I fear thou art another c.* H4A V, 4, 35. *I am no c.; to die, is to be a c., for he is but the c. of a man who hath not the life of a man,* V, 4, 116. 126. *this is the king's ring; 'tis no c.* H8 V, 3, 102.

4) false coin: *seem you that you are not? Haply I do. So do —s,* Gentl. II, 4, 12. *never call a true piece of gold a c.* H4A II, 4, 540. Figuratively: *thou c. to thy true friend!* Gentl. V, 4, 53. *you c., you puppet,* Mids. III, 2, 288. *his own judgements, wherein so curiously he had set this c.* All's IV, 3, 39. *a c. resembling majesty, which, being touched and tried, proves valueless,* John III, 1, 99. *remembered a gilt c.* Troil. II, 3, 28. *some coiner made me a c.* Cymb. II, 5, 6.

Counterfeit, adj. 1) portrayed: *the c. presentment of two brothers,* Hml. III, 4, 54.

2) fictitious, false: *a c. assurance,* Shr. IV, 4, 92. *c. supposes,* V, 1, 120. *this c. lump of ore,* All's III, 6, 39. *this c. module,* IV, 3, 113. *a c. stone,* Wint. IV, 4, 608.

3) dissembling: *an arrant c. rascal,* H5 III, 6, 64. *a c. cowardly knave,* V, 1, 73. *the c. matron,* Tim. IV, 3, 112.

Counterfeit, vb. 1) to copy or imitate; a) absolutely: *—ing actors,* H6C II, 3, 28. *thou —est most lively,* Tim. V, 1, 85 (equivocally). — b) trans.: *—ing the action of an old woman,* Wiv. IV, 5, 121. *I c. him,* Ado II, 1, 121. H4A V, 4, 28. H6A II, 4, 62. 66. V, 3, 63. R3 III, 5, 5. Cor. II, 3, 108. Rom. III, 5, 132. Oth. III, 3, 356. Followed by an inf.: *—s to die with her,* Lucr. 1776.

2) to feign, to forge; a) absolutely: *she doth but c.* Ado II, 3, 107. Err. II, 2, 171. As IV, 3, 167. 168. 183. Tw. IV, 2, 22. 122. H4A V, 4, 114. H6C II, 6, 65. Lr. III, 6, 64. — b) trans.: *c. sad looks,* Mids. III, 2, 237. R2 I, 4, 14. H4A V, 4, 118. H4B IV, 2, 27. *stamp and c. advantages,* Oth. II, 1, 247. Followed by an inf.: *c. to swoon,* As III, 5, 17. V, 2, 28. *c. to be a man,* IV, 3, 174.

Counterfeitly, feignedly: *and be off to them most c.* Cor. II, 3, 107.

Counter-gate, the gate of the prison called *Counter:* Wiv. III, 3, 85.

Countermand, subst., repeal of a former order: Meas. IV, 2, 95. 100. R3 II, 1, 89.

Countermand, vb. 1) to contradict, to oppose: *my heart shall never c. mine eye,* Lucr. 276.

2) to prohibit: *one that —s the passages of alleys,* Err. IV, 2, 37.

Countermine, subst. a mine made to meet that of the enemy: H5 III, 2, 67 (Rom. I, 4, 84, in the spurious Q1).

Counterpart, copy: Sonn. 84, 11.

Counterpoint, counterpane, coverlet: *my arras —s,* Shr. II, 353.

Counterpoise, subst., the weight in the other scale: *too light for the c. of so great an opposition,* H4A II, 3, 14. = equal weight or fortune: *to whom I promise a c., if not to thy estate a balance more replete,* All's II, 3, 182.

Counterpoise, vb., to counterbalance, to equal in weight: Ado IV, 1, 29. H6B IV, 1, 22. H6C III, 3, 137. Cor. II, 2, 91. V, 6, 78. Tim. I, 1, 145.

Counterseal, vb. to seal with another: Cor. V, 3, 205.

Countervail, vb. to balance, to equal: Rom. II, 6, 4. Per. II, 3, 56.

Countess, the consort or heiress of an earl or count: Tw. II, 2, 1. V, 100. H6A II, 2, 38. R3 I, 3, 20. *—es,* H8 IV, 1, 53.

Countless, innumerable, infinite: *this c. debt,* Ven. 84. *were the sum of these c. and infinite,* Tit. V, 3, 159. *her c. glory,* Per. I, 1, 31. *c. eyes,* 73.

Country, 1) a tract of land, a region: *he's a justice of peace in his c.* Wiv. I, 1, 226. *have I sought every c. far and near,* H6A V, 4, 3. *I do dismiss you to your several —ies,* H6B IV, 9, 21. *here in this c.* H6C III, 1, 75. *skirr the c. round,* Mcb. V, 3, 35.

2) the rural parts of a territory: *the c., city, court,* As II, 1, 59. III, 2, 48. All's III, 2, 14. *in cities mutinies, in —ies discord, in palaces treason,* Lr. I, 2, 117. Adjectively: *in c. footing,* Tp. IV, 138. *a c. fire,* Wiv. V, 5, 256. *girl,* LLL I, 2, 122. *proverb,* Mids. III, 2, 458. *folks,* As V, 3, 25. *copulatives,* V, 4, 58. *manners,* John I, 156. *cocks,* H5 IV Chor. 15. *servant-maid,* R3 I, 3, 107. *lord,* H8 I, 3, 44. *base,* Cymb. V, 3, 20. *gentleman,* Per. II, 3, 33. Obscure

passage: *I mean, my head upon your lap. Ay, my lord. Do you think I meant c. matters?* Hml. III, 2, 123 (thought by some to be an allusion to a certain French word of a similar sound).

3) the whole territory of a state: *king of this c.* Tp. IV, 243. V, 106. Meas. III, 2, 230. Err. III, 2, 117. Ado III, 2, 34. Merch. II, 8, 30. As III, 2, 126. Tw. I, 2, 21. R2 IV, 98. H6A V, 1, 62. R3 I, 3, 152. Troil. II, 2, 95. Caes. V, 3, 49 etc. Followed by *of:* our *c. of Greece,* Per. II, 1, 68. Followed a name without *of: the c. Maine and Anjou,* H6A V, 3, 154. — *My picked man of —ies,* John I, 193 (= traveller). *the rest of thy low —ies have made a shift to eat up thy holland,* H4B II, 2, 25. — = the inhabitants of a territory: *all the c. cried hate upon him,* H4B IV, 1, 136. *how will the c. misthink the king,* H6C II, 5, 107.

4) the land of nativity: *bleed, bleed, poor c.* Mcb. IV, 3, 31. *in spite of nature, of years, of c., credit, every thing,* Oth. I, 3, 97. *forgive me, c. and sweet countrymen,* H6A III, 3, 81. *your own c.* As IV, 1, 35. *my c.* Wint. IV, 2, 5. H6A I, 2, 81. II, 3, 41. III, 3, 44. V, 1, 27. H6B I, 1, 206. II, 3, 12. H5 V, 2, 58. Troil. IV, 1, 68. Cor. I, 9, 17. Mcb. I, 3, 114. Ant. IV, 14, 80. Adjectively: *by all our c. rights in Rome maintained,* Lucr. 1838. *I know our c. disposition well,* Oth. III, 3, 201. *to match you with her c. forms,* 237. *our c. mistresses,* Cymb. I, 4, 62.

Perhaps used as a trisyllable in Tw. I, 2, 21 and Cor. I, 9, 17 (cf. *Henry*).

Countryman, 1) one born in the same country with another: Gentl. II, 4, 54. III, 2, 11. Err. I, 1, 7. 12. Merch. III, 2, 226. 287. Shr. I, 1, 202. I, 2, 190. IV, 2, 77. All's III, 5, 50. Tw. V, 238. R2 I, 4, 34. II, 4, 2. V, 2, 20. H5 II, 2, 189. IV, 6, 1. IV, 7, 110. H6A I, 2, 29. I, 5, 27. III, 1, 137. III, 2, 27. III, 3, 38. 74. 81. IV, 1, 45. H6B IV, 7, 121. IV, 8, 11. Cor. I, 1, 56. V, 1, 38. Tit. I, 3. IV, 2, 152. Tim. V, 1, 172. V, 4, 38. Caes. I, 1, 61. II, 1, 122. Mcb. IV, 3, 160. Hml. I, 1, 125. Oth. V, 1, 89. Ant. IV, 15, 57. Cymb. I, 4, 42. II, 4, 20 etc.

2) one who inhabits the rural parts: *a simple c. that brought her figs,* Ant. V, 2, 342.

Country-mistresses, ladies native of a person's country: Cymb. I, 4, 62 (M. Edd. without hyphen).

Countrywoman, a woman born in the same country: Troil. IV, 1, 67. Per. V, 1, 103.

County, 1) a shire: Wiv. I, 1, 5. John V, 1, 8. H4B II, 1, 199. III, 2, 64. IV, 2, 61. H6A V, 3, 158. H6B III, 1, 313. H6C V, 3, 23. H8 I, 2, 98.

2) a French *comté,* a province: *the c. of Maine,* H6B I, 1, 51. *these —ies were the keys of Normandy,* 114.

3) count: Ado II, 1, 195 (Ff *count*). 370 (Ff *count*). IV, 1, 317. Merch. I, 2, 49. All's III, 7, 22. Tw. I, 5, 320. Rom. I, 2, 68. I, 3, 105. III, 5, 115. 219. IV, 1, 71. IV, 2, 23. 29. IV, 4, 21. IV, 5, 6. 10. V, 3, 174.

Couple, subst., 1) a tie that holds dogs together: *I'll go in —s with her,* Wint. II, 1, 135.

2) two, a brace: *a c. of Ford's knaves,* Wiv. III, 5, 99. Ado III, 5, 34. Wint. V, 1, 132. H4B V, 1, 28. Tit. IV, 4, 44.

3) a male and female joined: *this young c.* Tp. IV, 1, 40. V, 202. Mids. IV, 1, 186. V, 414. As V, 4, 36. Shr. III, 2, 242. Wint. V, 1, 134. 190.

Couple, vb. 1) to tie together: *c. Clowder with the deep-mouthed brach,* Shr. Ind. 1, 18. —*d and linked together with all religious strength of sacred vows,* John III, 1, 228.

2) to join, to pair, to marry: —*d in bands of perpetuity,* H6A IV, 7, 20. *let your mind be* —*d with your words,* Troil. V, 2, 15. *but one word with one of us? c. it with something,* Rom. III, 1, 42. *still we went* —*d and inseparable,* As I, 3, 78. *to c. us,* III, 3, 45. *shall I c. hell?* Hml. I, 5, 93 (= add). Followed by *to: will c. my reproach to Tarquin's shame,* Lucr. 816. Gentl. I, 2, 127. As III, 3, 30. John II, 349. Tim. V, 1, 228.

3) intr. to pair: *begin these woodbirds but to c. now?* Mids. IV, 1, 145.

Couplement, combination: *making a c. of proud compare, with sun and moon, with earth and sea's rich gems,* Sonn. 21, 5. — Used for *couple* by Don Armado: LLL V, 2, 535.

Couplet, couple, pair: *we'll whisper o'er a c. or two of most sage saws,* Tw. III, 4, 412. *patient as the female dove, when that her golden c. are disclosed,* Hml. V, 1, 310 (Qq —*s*).

Courage, 1) bravery: Ven. 556. 1158. Meas. I, 2, 112. III, 2, 166. Ado V, 1, 132. Merch. IV, 1, 111. As II, 4, 8. III, 3, 51. John II, 82. III, 4, 4. H4A II, 3, 53. H6A I, 2, 36. 89. I, 5, 10. III, 3, 87. H6B I, 3, 57. I, 4, 7. IV, 4, 35. H6C I, 4, 10. IV, 3, 24. R3 V, 3, 349. Cymb. II, 4, 24 (—*s*) etc. etc.

2) heart, mind, disposition in general: *this soft c. makes your followers faint,* H6C II, 2, 57. *nor check my c. for what they can give,* Cor. III, 3, 92. *mother, where is your ancient c.* IV, 1, 3. *I'd such a c. to do him good,* Tim. III, 3, 24. Hence = desire: *shows his hot c. and his high desire,* Ven. 276. cf. 294.

Courageous, brave: Lucr. 1828. Merch. II, 2, 10.*As II, 4, 7. H4B III, 2, 170. H6A III, 2, 93. R3 V, 2, 14. V, 5, 3. Rom. II, 4, 20. Ant. II, 3, 20. Misapplied: Wiv. IV, 1, 4. Mids. IV, 2, 27.

Courageously, bravely: Ven. 30. Mids. I, 2, 111. R3 I, 3, 115.

Courier, a messenger sent in haste: Tim. V, 2, 6. *heaven's cherubin, horsed upon the sightless* —*s of the air,* Mcb. I, 7, 23 (i. e. the winds). cf. *Vauntcourier.*

Course, subst. 1) race, career: *what rounds, what bounds, what c., what stop he makes,* Compl. 109. *when he has run his c. and sleeps in blessings,* H8 III, 2, 398. *when he doth run his c.* Caes. I, 2, 4. *see the order of the c.* 25.

2) progress, passage, way: *his* (a river's) *strong c.* Ven. 960. *who with a lingering stay his c. doth let,* Lucr. 328. *nothing can affection's c. control,* 500. *make war against proportioned c. of time,* 774. *O time, cease thou thy c.* 1765. *by chance or nature's changing c. untrimmed,* Sonn. 18, 8. *him in thy* (time's) *c. untainted do allow,* 19, 11. *divert strong minds to the c. of altering things,* 115, 8. *perfected by the swift c. of time,* Gentl. I, 3, 23. *when his* (the river's) *fair c. is not hindered,* II, 7, 27. 33. *what is the c. and drift of your compact?* Err. II, 2, 163. *this c. of fortune,* Ado IV, 1, 159. *the c. of true love never did run smooth,* Mids. I, 1, 134. cf. *their c. of love,* Rom. V, 3, 287. *in the common c. of all treasons,* All's IV, 3, 26. *all impediments in fancy's c. are motives of more fancy,* V, 3, 214. *that from the bloody c. of war your*

son may hie, III, 4, 8. *restraining honesty from c. required,* Wint. I, 2, 245. *justice, which shall have due c.* III, 2, 6. cf. *the duke cannot deny the c. of law,* Merch. III, 3, 26. *o'erswell with c. disturbed thy shores,* John II, 338. *it makes the c. of thoughts to fetch about,* IV, 2, 24. *kept on his c.* R2 V, 2, 10. *found no c. of breath within your majesty,* H4B IV, 5, 151 (= current). *denied our c.* H6C V, 6, 22. *direct his c. as please himself,* R3 II, 2, 129. *draw forth your noble ancestry unto a lineal true-derived c.* III, 7, 200. *thus hath the c. of justice wheeled about,* IV, 4, 105. Cor. I, 1, 71. *steering with due c. towards Rhodes,* Oth. I, 3, 34. *whose icy current and compulsive c. ne'er feels retiring ebb,* III, 3, 454. *the lethargy must have his quiet c.* IV, 1, 54. — To bear one's c.: H4A III, 1, 108. To bend one's c.: Err. I, 1, 118. H6C IV, 8, 58. R3 IV, 5, 14 (Ff *power*). To hold one's c.: Ven. 1193. Wint. IV, 4, 513. H5 III Chor. 17. H6C V, 3, 19. To keep a c.: H6C V, 3, 1. V, 4, 22. To make one's c.: R3 IV, 4, 529 (Qq *made away*). Hml. I, 1, 37. To take one's c.: H4B IV, 2, 103. Caes. III, 2, 266.

A c. of the sun = a year (cf. Hml. III, 2, 165. Oth. III, 4, 71): *five hundred* —*s of the sun,* Sonn. 59, 6. *the yearly c. that brings this day about,* John III, 1, 81. *after so many* —*s of the sun enthroned,* H8 II, 3, 6. *a thousand complete* —*s of the sun,* Troil. IV, 1, 27. cf. *ourself, by monthly c., shall our abode make with you,* Lr. I, 1, 134 (i. e. every month alternately).

3) way, manner, habit: *to be aged in any kind of c.* Meas. III, 2, 238. *a prodigal c. is like the sun's,* Tim. III, 4, 12. *I could not answer in that c. of honour as she had made the overture,* All's V, 3, 98. *divert his grain from his c. of growth,* Troil. I, 3, 9. *in our circumstance and c. of thought 'tis heavy with him,* Hml. III, 3, 83. *meet the old c. of death,* Lr. III, 7, 101.

Plural —*s* = habits, way of life, conduct: *let him continue in his* —*s,* Meas. II, 1, 196. *bad* —*s,* R2 II, 1, 213. *all the* —*s of my life do show,* H4A III, 1, 42. *each heart being set on bloody* —*s,* H4B I, 1, 159. *the* —*s of his youth promised it not,* H5 I, 1, 24. *his addiction was to* —*s vain,* 54. *follow your envious* —*s,* H8 III, 2, 243. *his own* —*s will denote him,* Oth. IV, 1, 290. *that we have taken no care to your best* —*s,* Per. IV, 1, 39. *and bear his* —*s to be ordered by Lady Fortune,* IV, 4, 47.

4) process, order: *as it appears in the true c. of all the question,* Ado V, 4, 6. *whate'er the c., the end is the renown,* All's IV, 4, 36. *fourteen weeks before the c. of time,* John I, 113. *the plot and the general c. of the action,* H4A II, 3, 23. *with every c. in his particular,* H4B IV, 4, 90. *ere I had heard the c. of it so far,* IV, 5, 143. *to admit the excuse of time, of numbers and due c. of things,* H5 V Chor. 4. *c. of direct session,* Oth. I, 2, 86.

In c. of, or *in the c. of* = in the progress, in the working, in consequence of: *who threats, in c. of this revenge, to do as much as ever Coriolanus did,* Tit. IV, 4, 67. *which doth give me a more content in c. of true delight,* Per. III, 2, 39. *in the c. of justice, none of us should see salvation,* Merch. IV, 1, 199. *you do not well in obstinacy to cavil in the c. of this contract,* H6A V, 4, 156. *thou canst not, in the c. of gratitude, but be a diligent follower of mine,* Cymb. III, 5, 121.

In c., as it seems, = the modern *of course: this being granted in c.* Meas. III, 1, 259

5) proceeding: *who should not upbraid our c.* Tp. II, 1, 287. *you know the c. is common,* Meas. IV, 2, 190. IV, 3, 153. Err. IV, 3, 96. Ado IV, 1, 214. LLL II, 25. Merch. IV, 1, 8. All's II, 5, 63. John III, 1, 178. H4B II, 1, 89. H6C III, 1, 25. R3 I, 4, 224. III, 1, 31. H8 V, 3, 35. Tim. III, 3, 41. V, 1, 106. Caes. II, 1, 162. Oth. I, 3, 111 (*—s*). *by c. of justice:* Meas. V, 35. *by c. of law:* H6B III, 1, 237. R3 I, 4, 192; cf. Merch. III, 3, 26 and H4B V, 2, 87. — *To hold my very c.,* Lr. I, 3, 26 (= to do like me). *to run a c.: did entreat your highness to this c. which you are running here,* H8 II, 4, 216. *you shall run a certain c.* Lr. I, 2, 89. *to take a c.:* Wint. II, 3, 48. H6A IV, 1, 132. Troil. V, 3, 74. Cymb. V, 1, 3.

6) study, occupation: *a c. of learning and ingenious studies,* Shr. I, 1, 9. *shut myself up in some other c.* Oth. III, 4, 121. *stick to your journal c.* Cymb. IV, 2, 10.

7) the dishes placed at once upon the table; Mcb. II, 2, 39.*cf. Oth. IV, 2, 93. Cor. 1, 5, 17.

8) bear-baiting: *bear-like I must fight the c.* Mcb. V, 7, 2. *I am tied to the stake, and I must stand the c.* Lr. III, 7, 54.

9) a sail: *set her two —s off to sea again,* Tp. I, 1, 53 (i. e. the main sail and fore sail). cf. *Maincourse.*

Course, vb. 1) to run: *she did so c. o'er my exteriors,* Wiv. I, 3, 72. *had numbered the sun to c. two hundred compasses,* Oth. III, 4, 71 (Q1 make). Used of a quick circulation of the blood: *the sherris warms it* (the blood) *and makes it c. from the inwards to the parts extreme,* H4B IV, 3, 115. cf. *but love ... —s as swift as thought in every power,* LLL IV, 3, 330. *swift as quicksilver it —s through the natural gates and alleys of the body,* Hml. I, 5, 66.

2) to hunt, to chase: *I am —ing myself,* LLL IV, 3, 2. *the —ing snatchers,* H5 I, 2, 143 (= hunting after booty, or = careering, fleet?). *say thou wilt c.* Shr. Ind. 2, 49. Transitively, = to hunt, to pursue hotly: *the big round tears —d one another,* As II, 1, 39. *we —d him at the heels,* Mcb. I, 6, 21. *to c. his own shadow,* Lr. III, 4, 58. *to c. your flying flags,* Ant. III, 13, 11.

Courser, horse: Ven. 31. 261. 403. R2 I, 2, 21. H4B IV, 1, 119. H5 III, 7, 47. H6C V, 7, 9. Tim. I, 2, 217. Oth. I, 1, 113. Ant. I, 2, 200.*Per. II, 1, 164.

Court, subst., 1) court-yard: *in the base c. he doth attend to speak with you,* R2 III, 3, 176. 180. 182.

2) the place of residence of a prince; the prince with his retinue: Compl. 59. Tp. V, 166. Gentl. III, 1, 27. 165. Wiv. I, 4, 62. II, 2, 63. III, 3, 57. LLL I, 1, 13. II, 24. As I, 3, 44. II, 1, 4. 59. H5 II, 4, 133 (*the mistress c. of Europe*). H6A II, 5, 105 etc. Preceded by *at* and in indiscriminately: *at your c.* Gentl. III, 1, 57. *at the new c.* As I, 1, 102. *at the c.* III, 2, 47. 49. *at c.* Wiv. IV, 3, 3. IV, 4, 89. As III, 2, 40. All's I, 1, 203. II, 2, 9. *in his royal c.* Gentl. I, 3, 27. 67. LLL I, 1, 52. All's IV, 5, 52. Tw. II, 1, 46. H6B I, 3, 46. Mcb. III. 6, 26. *in the c. of heaven,* John III, 4, 87. *in the c.* Wiv. IV, 3, 6. As III, 2, 19. H6A IV, 1, 189. *in c.* Compl. 234. LLL IV, 1, 100. As III, 2, 34. All's I, 3, 259. H6A III, 2, 135. H6B I, 2, 25. I, 3, 82. H8 II, 3, 82. Cymb. I, 1, 46 etc.*

Court holy-water (Fr. *eau bénite de la cour*) = vain compliments, flattery: *c. holy-water in a dry*

house is better than this rain-water out o' door, Lr III, 2, 10.

3) any jurisdiction, as well as the room in which, and the persons by whom, justice is administered: *the Archbishop of Canterbury held a late c. at Dunstable,* H8 IV, 1, 27. *I may dismiss this c.* Merch. IV, 1, 104. 144. 149. 172. 204. 300. 303. 389. H8 II, 4, 62. *the c. of Rome,* II, 2, 105. *you will come into the c. and swear,* Merch. I, 2, 76. *call the Jew into the c.* IV, 1, 14. *come into the c.* H8 II, 4, 7. *that the queen appear in c.* Wint. III, 2, 10.

Inns of c. = colleges in which students of law reside and are instructed: H4B III, 2, 14. H6B IV, 7, 2.

4) the legislative body: *call we our high c. of parliament,* H4B V, 2, 134. H6B V, 3, 25.

5) a place for playing the game of tennis: *all the —s of France will be disturbed with chaces,* H5 I, 2, 265.

6) *Court of guard* = the main guard-house: *at the c. of guard,* H6A II, 1, 4. *the lieutenant to-night watches on the c. of guard,* Oth. II, 1, 220. *on the c. and guard of safety,* II, 3, 216. *we must return to the c. of guard,* Ant. IV, 9, 2. 32.

Court, vb., to endeavour to please, to seek favour by blandishments; 1) absolutely: *I have forgot to c.* Gentl. III, 1, 85. *their purpose is to parle, to c. and dance,* LLL V, 2, 122. *see how they kiss and c.* Shr. IV, 2, 27. Followed by *it: knows to c. it with words,* Tit. II, 1, 91.

2) trans.: *did c. the lad with many a lovely look,* Pilgr. 45. *a most auspicious star, whose influence if now I c. not,* Tp. I, 2, 183. Ado V, 1, 244. LLL V, 2, 131. Shr. I, 1, 54. I, 2, 137. III, 1, 49. IV, 2, 34. Wint. IV, 4, 864. R3 I, 1, 15. Rom. III, 3, 142. Hml. I, 5, 54. V, 2, 78 (*I'll c. his favours; O. Edd. count*). Oth. IV, 3, 57. Per. I, 2, 6.

Court-contempt, the disdain felt by a courtier: Wint. IV, 4, 759.

Court-cupboard (O. Edd. *cubbert* and *cubbord*) a moveable buffet or closet, in which plate and other articles of luxury were displayed: *remove the c., look to the plate,* Rom. I, 5, 8.

Courteous, 1) polite, civil: Merch. II, 9, 90. IV, 1, 148. As V, 4, 76. 97. Shr. II, 247. All's IV, 5, 111. H6C I, 2, 43. Rom. II, 4, 60. II, 5, 57. Tim. III, 6, 105. Hml. I, 4, 60. Ant. I, 3, 86. II, 2, 227. Followed by *to:* Mids. III, 1, 167. Cor. II, 2, 30.

2) kind, benevolent: *thanks, c. wall,* Mids. V, 179. *your c. pains,* Merch. IV, 1, 412. *an affable and c. gentleman,* Shr. I, 2, 98. *do me this c. office,* Tw. III, 4, 278. *my c. lord,* Troil. V, 2, 185. *O c. Tybalt!* Rom. III, 2, 62.

Courteously, politely: Troil. IV, 4, 123.

Courtesy, subst. (ordinarily trisyllabic; dissyllabic in Ven. 888. Meas. II, 4, 175. Shr. IV, 2, 111. All's V, 3, 324. Cor. V, 3, 27. Rom. I, 4, 72. Lr. II, 4, 182. III, 7, 26) 1) politeness: Ven. 888. Ado I, 1, 123. LLL V, 2, 755. 790. Mids. II, 2, 56. Merch. V, 141. As III, 2, 51. Tw. I, 5, 222. IV, 2, 38. R2 I, 4, 26. III, 3, 193. H4A I, 3, 251. II, 4, 11. H4B IV, 3, 47. H6A II, 2, 58. R3 I, 3, 49. Troil. IV, 5, 82. V, 6, 15. Rom. II, 4, 55. Hml. III, 2, 326. Oth. II, 3, 36. *In c.* = out of c.: *kissed his hand away in c.* LLL V, 2, 324. 366. Mids. V, 258. R3 IV, 2, 107.

2) any act or show of politeness: *they do discharge their shot of c.* Oth. II, 1, 56 (i. e. of salu-

tation). *our power shall do a c. to our wrath*, Lr. III, 7, 26 (i. e. obey it). *outward —ies*, Meas. V, 15. *manhood is melted into —ies*, Ado IV, 1, 322. *nod to him, elves, and do him —ies*, Mids. III, 1, 177. *for these —ies I'll lend you moneys*, Merch. I, 3, 129. Oth. II, 1, 171 (Ff *courtship*). *remember thy c., I beseech thee, apparel thy head*, LLL V, 1, 103 (i. e. put on your hat). In the same sense: *pray you, leave your c., good mounsieur*, Mids. IV, 1, 21 (cf. *I beseech you, remember —*, Hml. V, 2, 108; and: *stay not thy compliment, I forgive thy duty*, LLL IV, 2, 147).

In particular, = a bow in the knees, a kind of reverence made by men as well as women: *a new-devised c.* LLL I, 2, 66. *with soft low tongue and lowly c.* Shr. Ind. 1, 114. *let thy —ies alone*, All's V, 3, 324. *first my fear, then my c.* H4B V, 5, 116. *the match is made, she seals it with a c.* H6C III, 2, 57. Rom. I, 4, 72. II, 4, 55 — 57. Caes. III, 1, 36. Oth. II, 1, 177. *To make c.:* Ado II, 1, 56. 58. As Epil. 23. H4B II, 1, 135 (Ff without *make*). Tropically: *bidding the law make c. to their will*, Meas. II, 4, 175 (i. e. bow; cf. Lr. III, 7, 26).

3) good manners, good breeding: *if you were civil and knew c.* Mids. III, 2, 147. *I was beset with shame and c.* Merch. V, 217.*the c. of nations allows you my better*, As I, 1, 49.*

4) complaisance, kindness: *if thou scorn our c., thou diest*, Gentl. IV, 1, 68. *to do me both a present and a dangerous c.* Meas. IV, 2, 172. *for your many —ies I thank you*, Ado V, 1, 191. *these ladies' c. might well have made our sport a comedy*, LLL V, 2, 885. *he was wont to lend money for a Christian c.* Merch. III, 1, 52. *the best conditioned and unwearied spirit in doing —ies*, III, 2, 296. *never trained to offices of tender c.* IV, 1, 33. *to do you c., this will I do*, Shr. IV, 2, 91. 111. *as we change our —ies*, All's III, 2, 100. *marry, hang you! and your c., for a ring-carrier*, III, 5, 95. *some of us never shall a second time do such a c.* H4A V, 2, 101 (i. e. embrace each other). *if thou wert sensible of c.* V, 4, 94. *I thank your grace for this high c.* V, 5, 32. *and then I need not crave his c.* H6A V, 3, 105. *bounteous Buckingham, the mirror of all c.* H8 II, 1, 53. *how shall this bosom multiplied digest the senate's c.?* Cor. III, 1, 132. *thou hast never in thy life showed thy dear mother any c.* V, 3, 161. *the offices of nature, bond of childhood, effects of c., dues of gratitude*, Lr. II, 4, 182. *return and force their scanted c.* III, 2, 67. *this c. forbid thee shall the duke instantly know*, III, 3, 22. *the queen shall then have c., so she will yield us up*, Ant. III, 13, 15. *O dissembling c.!* Cymb. I, 1, 84. *hopeless to have the c. your cradle promised*, IV, 4, 28. *how c. would seem to cover sin*, Per. I, 1, 121. *a c. which if we should deny ...*, V, 1, 58.

Courtesy, vb. (of two syllables), to make a reverence, to bow (in the knees); properly and metaphorically: Tp. I, 2, 378. LLL V, 2, 221. Shr. IV, 1, 95. H4A III, 2, 127. H4B II, 1, 135 (Q *make c.*). Rom. II, 4, 58. Cymb. III, 3, 55. Followed by *to:* Lucr. 1338. Merch. I, 1, 13. Tw. II, 5, 67. H5 V, 2, 293. Tit. V, 3, 74.

Courtezan, a prostitute: H6A III, 2, 45. H6B I, 1, 223. R3 III, 7, 74. Lr. III, 2, 79. Cymb. III, 4, 126.

Court-gate, the gate of the court: H4B III, 2, 33. H8 I, 3, 18.*

Court-hand, the manner of writing used in judicial proceedings: *he can make obligations and write c.* H6B IV, 2, 101.

Courtier, 1) one who attends or frequents the courts of princes: Wiv. II, 2, 62. III, 2, 8. LLL I, 2, 65. As II, 7, 36. III, 2, 51. IV, 1, 12. V, 4, 42. 73. All's I, 1, 80. Tw. III, 1, 97. H6B IV, 4, 36. H8 I, 3, 22. Troil. I, 3, 234. Rom. I, 4, 72. Tim. IV, 3, 241. Hml. I, 2, 117. III, 1, 159. V, 1, 90 etc.

Feminine: Wiv. III, 3, 66. All's I, 1, 169. H8 II, 3, 83.

2) courter, wooer: *—s of beauteous freedom*, Ant. II, 6, 17.

Court-like, adj. becoming the court, polite, elegant: Wiv. II, 2, 237.

Courtly, adj. 1) relating or belonging to a court: *sent him forth from c. friends, with camping foes to live*, All's III, 4, 14. *in c. company*, H6B I, 1 27. *to promise is most c. and fashionable*, Tim. V, 1, 29.

2) elegant, polite: *you have too c. a wit for me*, As III, 2, 72. *I am too c.* Troil. III, 1, 30. *very c. counsel*, IV, 5, 22. *she hath all c. parts more exquisite than lady*, Cymb. III, 5, 71.

Courtney, name: *Sir Edward C.*, R3 IV, 4, 502.

Court-odour, the smell of a court: *receives not thy nose c. from me?* Wint. IV, 4, 758.

Courtship, 1) civility, elegance of manners: *trim gallants, full of c. and of state*, LLL V, 2, 363. *rated them at c., pleasant jest and courtesy* 790. *observed his c. to the common people*, R2 I, 4, 24. *I thought king Henry had resembled thee in courage, c. and proportion*, H6B I, 3, 57. *I will gyve thee in thine own c.* Oth. II, 1, 171 (Q1 *courtesies*).

2) courting, wooing: *employ your chiefest thoughts to c. and such fair ostents of love*, Merch. II, 8, 44.

The two significations blent: *who was in his youth an inland man, one that knew c. too well, for there he fell in love*, As III, 2, 364. *more validity, more honourable state, more c. lives in carrion-flies than Romeo*, Rom. III, 3, 34.

Courtsy, see *Courtesy.*

Court-word, a term used at court: *advocate is the c. for a pheasant*, Wint. IV, 4, 768.

Cousin, 1) the son or daughter of an uncle or aunt; a) masc.: Wiv. I, 1, 7. 137 etc. Ado I, 2, 2. Merch. III, 4, 50. R2 IV, 304 etc. H6A IV, 1, 114 etc. H6C I, 1, 66 etc. b) femin.: Meas. I, 4, 45. 46. Ado I, 1, 35. 192. II, 1, 55. 391. III, 1, 2. V, 1, 300. As I, 1, 113. I, 2, 152 etc. — Having *of* before the following name: *c. of Hereford*, R2 I, 1, 28. *good —s both of York and Somerset*, H6A IV, 1, 114. H6B I, 1, 65. 167. H6C I, 1, 72. IV, 8, 34. R3 III, 4, 37. *my c. king*, R2 II, 3, 123. H4A I, 3, 158.

2) any kinsman or kinswoman: Ado I, 2, 25. = nephew: Ado I, 2, 2. John III, 3, 71. H4A I, 3, 187. V, 1, 105. R3 III, 1, 2. 101. IV, 4, 221. V, 3, 151. Hml. I, 2, 64. 117. III, 2, 97. = niece: As I, 2, 164. I, 3, 44. Tw. I, 3, 5. R2 II, 2, 105. Troil. I, 2, 44. III, 2, 206. Tit. II, 4, 12. = uncle: Tw. I, 5, 131. V, 313. = brother-in-law: H4A III, 1, 51. = grandchild: John III, 3, 17. R3 II, 2, 8. II, 4, 9. Oth. I, 1, 113.

3) a title given by princes to other princes and distinguished noblemen: Meas. V,

1. 165. 246. All's I, 2, 5. III, 1, 7. H4A III, 1, 3. H5 V, 2, 4. 308. H6C I, 1, 72. IV, 8, 34. R3 III, 4, 37.

Cousin-german, first-cousin, son of the father's brother or sister: Troil. IV, 5, 121 (cf. *Cozen-German*).

Covenant, contract, stipulation: *my heart this c. makes*, R2 II, 3, 50. Hml. I, 1, 93 (Qq *comart*). Cymb. I, 4, 177. II, 4, 50. Plur. *—s* = conditions, articles of a contract: *that —s may be kept on either hand*, Shr. II, 128. *if we conclude a peace, it shall be with such strict and severe —s*, H6A V, 4, 114. *agree to any —s*, V, 5, 88. *let there be —s drawn between us*, Cymb. I, 4, 155.

Covent, convent, monastery: Meas. IV, 3, 133. H8 IV, 2, 19.

Coventry, English town: R2 I, 1, 199. I, 2, 45. 56. H4A IV, 2, 1. 42. H4B IV, 1, 135. H6C IV, 8, 32. 58. 64.

Cover, subst. any thing laid over another to hide or screen or contain it: *the c. of the salt hides the salt*, Gentl. III, 1, 369. *they* (the news) *have a good c.; they show well outward*, Ado I, 2, 8. *death is the fairest c. for her shame*, IV, 1, 117. *my form ... is yet the c. of a fairer mind*, John IV, 2, 258. *that small model of the barren earth which serves as paste and c. to our bones*, R2 III, 2, 154. *this unbound lover only lacks a c.* (like a book) Rom. I, 3, 88. *the c.* (of the carriage) *of the wings of grasshoppers*, I, 4, 60.

Cover, vb. 1) trans. a) to overspread; to hide or shelter by laying or putting something on: *when that churl Death my bones with dust shall c.* Sonn. 32, 2. *the hair that —s the wit*, Gentl. III, 1, 371. *help to c. your master*, Wiv. III, 3, 151. *—ed fire*, Ado III, 1, 77. Mids. III, 2, 356. V, 336. R2 III, 2, 110. R3 IV, 4, 239. Tit. II, 3, 199. *c. the table*, Merch. III, 5, 65 (= spread the cloth for dinner). *a —ed goblet*, As III, 4, 26. *—ed dishes*, Tim. III, 6, 55. *c. thy head*, As V, 1, 19. R2 III, 2, 171. *pray be —ed*, As III, 3, 78 (= put on your hat). V, 1, 20. *the desk that's —ed o'er with Turkish tapestry*, Err. IV, 1, 104.

b) to clothe: *all that beauty that doth c. thee*, Sonn. 22, 5. Compl. 317. Meas. III, 1, 96. H5 II, 4, 38. Cymb. V, 4, 135. *I am rapt and cannot c. the monstrous bulk of this ingratitude with any size of words*, Tim. V, 1, 67.

c) to conceal: *misty night —s the shame*, Lucr. 357. 1252. Sonn. 95, 11. Ado IV, 1, 37. 176. LLL II, 125. H6C IV, 2, 22. Rom. I, 5, 58. Caes. V, 3, 44. Lr. I, 1, 284. III, 1, 20. V, 3, 242. Per. I, 1, 121.

d) to horse: *you'll have your daughter —ed with a Barbary horse*, Oth. I, 1, 111.

2) absol.: *the —ing sky*, Wint. I, 2, 294. Cymb. V, 5, 350. = to spread the cloth: *c. is the word*, Merch. III, 5, 57. As II, 5, 32. H4B II, 4, 11. = to put on one's hat: Merch. II, 9, 44. III, 5, 58.

Covering, subst. = cover: *bring some c. for this naked soul*, Lr. IV, 1, 46. *without c., save yon field of stars*, Per. I, 1, 37. *under the c. of a careful night*, I, 2, 81.

Coverlet, the cover of a bed: Lucr. 394. Shr. IV, 1, 205.

Covert, subst., thicket: *you must retire yourself into some c.* Wint. IV, 4, 664. *in this c. will we make our stand*, H6C III, 1, 3. *stole into the c. of the wood*, Rom. I, 1, 132.

Covert, adj secret, hid, disguised: *to lock it in the wards of c. bosom*, Meas. V, 10. *c. enmity*, H4B Ind. 9. *the —est sheltered traitor*, R3 III, 5, 33. *how c. matters may be best disclosed*, Caes. IV, 1, 46. *that under c. and convenient seeming hast practised on man's life*, Lr. III, 2, 56.

Covertly, closely, not openly: *so c. that no dishonesty shall appear in me*, Ado II, 2, 9.

Coverture, cover, shelter: *couched in the woodbine c.* Ado III, 1, 30. *in night's c.* H6C IV, 2, 13. In Cor. I, 9, 46 some M. Edd. *coverture*, O. Edd. *overture*.

Covet, to desire; 1) trans.: Lucr. 134. H5 IV, 3, 28. R3 III, 7, 163. Cor. II, 2, 130. Mcb. IV, 3, 127. — 2) intr., followed by *for:* H6A V, 4, 145.

Coveting, subst. desire: Cymb. II, 5, 25.

Covetous, 1) desirous; followed by *of* or *for: c. of wisdom*, H8 V, 5, 25. *of praise*, Troil. II, 3, 248. *for gold*, H5 IV, 3, 24.

2) absol. greedy of gain, avaricious: Sonn. 134, 6. Err. IV, 3, 75. H6A III, 1, 29. Tim. IV, 3, 515. Cor. I, 1, 44. Caes. IV, 3, 79.

Covetously, avariciously: *if he c. reserve it*, Tim. IV, 3, 408.

Covetousness, 1) eagerness, desire: *when workmen strive to do better than well, they do confound their skill in c.* John IV, 2, 29.

2) eagerness for gain, avarice: As III, 5, 91. Tw. V, 51. H4B I, 2, 256.

Cow, subst. the female of the bull: Ado V, 4, 49. As II, 4, 50. John I, 124. Tit. V, 1, 31. Ant. III, 10, 14. *God sends a curst c. short horns*, Ado II, 1, 25. *and that I would not for a c., God save her!* H8 V, 4, 27 (? Coll. M. *a crown*. Perhaps a cow of one's own was thought a considerable property). — Plur. *kine:* H4A II, 4, 520 (*Pharaoh's lean k.*). cf. *Milch*.

Cow, vb., to depress with fear, to quell: *it hath —ed my better part of man*, Mcb. V, 8, 18.

Coward, subst. poltroon: Ven. 569. 1158. Lucr. 273. 1391. Tp. III, 2, 30. Wiv. II, 3, 32. Meas. III, 1, 137. V, 337. 505. Ado V, 2, 59. LLL V, 2, 86. Mids. III, 2, 405. Merch. III, 2, 83. As I, 3, 123. All's I, 1, 112. III, 6, 11. IV, 3, 321. Tw. III, 4, 421. R2 I, 1, 69. H6A I, 1, 131. I, 2, 23. II, 1, 16. II, 4, 31. IV, 1, 28. IV, 2, 52. IV, 3, 27. H6B III, 2, 220. IV, 1, 43. IV, 7, 88. IV, 10, 79. H6C I, 4, 40. II, 2, 114. V, 4, 40. R3 I, 4, 138. 286. III, 2, 90 etc.

Coward, adj., destitute of courage, basely timid: *thy c. heart*, Ven. 1024. *the c. captive*, Lucr. 75. *the c. conquest of a wretch's knife*, Sonn. 74, 11. As III, 5, 13. John II, 158. H5 II, 4, 69. H6A IV, 6, 47. H6B III, 2, 307. R3 V, 3, 179. Caes. I, 2, 122. Lr. II, 4, 43. Cymb. IV, 4, 37. Per. IV, 3, 25. *some, turned c. but by example*, Cymb. V, 3, 35.

Coward, vb., to make timorous: *what read you there, that hath so —ed and chased your blood out of appearance?* H5 II, 2, 75.

Cowardice, want of courage: Gentl. III, 2, 32. V, 2, 21. Ado V, 1, 149. Mids. II, 1, 234. III, 2, 302. R2 I, 2, 34. H4B II, 4, 353. IV, 3, 114. H6A III, 2, 55. H6C I, 1, 41. I, 4, 47. IV, 2, 7. Troil. I, 3, 197. Tit. II, 1, 132. Tim. III, 5, 16. Caes. II, 2, 41.

Coward-like, cowardly, timorous: Lucr. 231.

Cowardly, adj. wanting courage: Wiv. III, 1, 68. Mids. III, 1, 197. Wint. IV, 3, 112. H4A II, 3,

16. H5 IV, 7, 6. V, 1, 73. H6A III, 2, 109. R3 I, 4, 264. Cor. I, 1, 207. I, 6, 3. IV, 6, 122. Caes. V, 1, 104. Lr. II, 2, 59.

Cowardly, adv. in the manner of a coward: H4A I, 3, 63. H6A I, 1, 134. R3 I, 4, 104. Ant. IV, 15, 56.

Cowardship, cowardice: Tw. III, 4, 423.

Cow-dung, the excrement of cows: Lr. III, 4, 137.

Cower, to squat, to bend down: *—s i' the hams,* Per. IV, 2, 113. *the splitting rocks —ed in the sinking sands and would not dash me with their ragged sides,* H6B III, 2, 97.

Cowish, cowardly: Lr. IV, 2, 12.

Cowl-staff, a pole on which a weight is borne between two persons: Wiv. III, 3, 156.

Cowslip, a sort of primrose: Tp. V, 89. Mids. II, 1, 10. 15. V, 339. H5 V, 2, 49. Cymb. I, 5, 83. II, 2, 39.

Cox: *c. my passion!* All's V, 2, 42 (cf. *Cock*).

Coxcomb, 1) a fool's cap: *shall I have a c. of frize?* Wiv. V, 5, 146. *what is your crest? a c.?* Shr. II, 226 (viz a cock's comb). *here's my c. ... you were best take my c.* Lr. I, 4, 105. 109. 114. 116. 117. 121.

2) a fool: Err. III, 1, 32. Ado IV, 2, 71. LLL IV, 3, 84. All's III, 6, 122. Tw. V, 213. H5 IV, 1, 79. Cor. IV, 6, 134 (quibbling). Oth. V, 2, 233.

3) the head (jocularly): *I will knog your urinals about your knave's c.* Wiv. III, 1, 91. *a bloody c.* Tw. V, 179. 193. 195. H5 V, 1, 45. *your broken c.* 57. *she knapped 'em o' the —s with a stick,* Lr. II, 4, 125.

Coy, adj. 1) disdainful, contemptuous, inaccessible to love: *flint-hearted boy, 'tis but a kiss I beg; why art thou c.?* Ven. 96. *yet was he servile to my c. disdain,* 112. *scorn is bought with groans, c. looks with heart-sore sighs,* Gentl. I, 1, 30. *but she is nice and c.* III, 1, 82. *as c. and wild as haggards of the rock,* Ado III, 1, 35. *'twas told me you were rough and c. and sullen,* Shr. II, 245.

2) soft: *if not, enforced hate, instead of love's c. touch, shall rudely tear thee,* Lucr. 669.

Coy, vb. 1) to disdain: *if he —ed to hear Cominius speak, I'll keep at home,* Cor. V, 1, 6.

2) to stroke softly, to caress: *while I thy amiable cheeks do c.* Mids. IV, 1, 2.

Coystril, a mean paltry fellow: *he's a coward and a c.* Tw. I, 3, 43. *doorkeeper to every c.* Per. IV, 6, 176.

Coz, a contraction of *cousin:* Wiv. I, 1, 24. 213. 251. III, 4, 36. 54 etc. Ado III, 4, 39. 103. As I, 2, 1. 25. 244. 260. III, 2, 228. IV, 1, 209. Rom. I, 1, 189. 201 *(my c.).* 213 *(fair c.).* Mcb. IV, 2, 14 *(my dearest c.)* etc. = uncle: *seek the crowner and let him sit o' my c.* Tw. I, 5, 143. = nephew: John III, 3, 17. Rom. I, 5, 67. = brother-in-law: H4A III, 1, 78. Used as a title given by princes to other princes and noblemen: H4A I, 1, 91. III, 1, 58. H4B IV, 2, 83. H5 IV, 3, 30. 73. V, 2, 313.

Cozen, to cheat; 1) intr.: *a —ing quean,* Wiv. IV, 2, 180. *—ing hope,* R2 II, 2, 69. *some cogging, —ing slave,* Oth. IV, 2, 132.

2) trans.: Wiv. IV, 5, 95. 96. V, 5, 218. Ado II, 2, 39. Merch. II, 9, 38. Shr. III, 2, 170. V, 1, 40. All's IV, 2, 76. IV, 4, 23. Wint. IV, 4, 254. H4A I, 2, 136. Hml. III, 4, 77. Lr. V, 3, 154. With *of,* =

to defraud of sth.: *—ing the pillow of a lawful kiss,* Lucr. 387. Wiv. IV, 5, 38. 79. V, 5, 175. All's IV, 5, 28. R3 IV, 4, 222. Tit. V, 3, 101.

Cozenage, cheat, deceit: Wiv. IV, 5, 64. Err. I, 2, 97. Hml. V, 2, 67.

Cozener, sharper: Wiv. IV, 5, 67. Wint. IV, 4, 256. H4A I, 3, 255. Lr. IV, 6, 167.

Cozen-Germans, German swindlers, a word of Evans' making: Wiv. IV, 5, 79 (cf. *Cousin-german*).*

Cozier, botcher, cobbler: *ye squeak out your —s' catches,* Tw. II, 3, 97.*

Crab, 1) crawfish: Hml. II, 2, 206.

2) wild apple: Tp. II, 2, 171. LLL IV, 2, 6. V, 2, 935. Mids. II, 1, 48. *you must not look so sour. It is my fashion, when I see a c.* Shr. II, 230. *she's as like this as a c. is like an apple; ... she will taste as like this as a c. does to a c.* Lr. I, 5, 16. 18 (the crab being the emblem of a morose person; cf. *Crabbed*).

3) name of a dog: Gentl. II, 3, 5. 44. IV, 4, 26.

Crabbed, peevish, morose: Pilgr. 157. Tp. III, 1, 8. Meas. III, 2, 104. *three c. months had soured themselves to death,* Wint. I, 2, 102.

Crab-tree, the tree that bears crab-apples: H6B III, 2, 214. H8 V, 4, 8. Cor. II, 1, 205.

Crack, subst., a pert little boy, an imp: *when a' was a c. not thus high,* H4B III, 2, 34. *'tis a noble child. A c., madam,* Cor. I, 3, 74.

Crack, subst. 1) disruption, fissure, breach; in a moral sense: *my love to thee is sound, sans c. or flaw,* LLL V, 2, 415. *I cannot believe this c. to be in my dread mistress,* Wint. I, 2, 322. *this c. of your love shall grow stronger than it was before,* Oth. II, 3, 330.

2) a burst of sound: *the fire and —s of sulphurous roaring,* Tp. I, 2, 203. *thunder's c.* Tit. II, 1, 3. Mcb. I, 2, 37. IV, 1, 117 (*to the c. of doom*). Ant. V, 1, 15.

3) change of voice in puberty: *our voices have got the mannish c.* Cymb. IV, 2, 236.

Crack, vb. 1) trans. a) to break with a noise, to split: *—ing the stones of the prunes,* Meas. II, 1, 110. *a fusty nut,* Troil. II, 1, 111. *nuts,* Rom. III, 1, 21. *—ed many a ring,* Compl. 45. *my lace,* Wint. III, 2, 174. *a vial,* R2 I, 2, 19. *a mirror,* IV, 289. R3 II, 2, 52. *c. the glass of her virginity,* Per. IV, 6, 151. *—ing ten thousand curbs,* Cor. I, 1, 72.

b) to break, to rend in any manner, in a physical as well as moral sense: *c. my sinews,* Tp. III, 1, 26. *he —s his gorge,* Wint. II, 1, 44. *the tackle of my heart is —ed,* John V, 7, 52. *—ed crowns,* H4A II, 3, 96. *from my shoulders c. my arms,* H6A I, 5, 11. *c. thy lungs,* Troil. IV, 5, 7. *a —ed drachm,* Cor. I, 5, 6. *c. your cheeks,* Lr. III, 2, 1. *nature's moulds,* 8. *heart, c. thy frail case,* Ant. IV, 14, 41. *—ing the strong warrant of an oath,* R2 IV, 235. *he has —ed the league,* H8 II, 2, 25. *though all the world should c. their duty,* H8 II, 2, 193. *the unity of states,* Troil. I, 3, 99. *a —ed heart,* Cor. V, 3, 9. Lr. II, 1, 92. *the bond 'twixt son and father,* I, 2, 118. *her bond of chastity,* Cymb. V, 5, 207. *word and oath,* Per. I, 2, 121.

c) to impair, to weaken: *not to c. the wind of the poor phrase,* Hml. I, 3, 108 (cf. *Wind*). *no reason I should reserve my —ed one* (sc. life) *to more care,* Cymb. IV, 4, 50. Used of the voice, = to make hoarse and soundless: *O time's extremity, hast* thou so —ed and splitted my poor tongue, Err. V, 308. c. my clear voice with sobs, Troil. IV, 2, 114. c. the lawyer's voice, Tim. IV, 3, 153. pray God, your voice, like a piece of uncurrent gold, be not —ed within the ring, Hml. II, 2, 448 (cf. the subst. in Cymb. IV, 2, 236).

d) to open and drink: c. a quart together, H4B V, 3, 66.

e) to utter in a blustering manner: our brags were —ed of kitchen-trulls, Cymb. V, 5, 177.

2) intr. a) to break, to burst: my charms c. not, Tp. V, 2. my heart is ready to c. Wiv. II, 2, 301. cf. Hml. V, 2, 370 and Per. III, 2, 77. as thunder when the clouds in autumn c. Shr. I, 2, 96. make your shoulders c. John II, 146. the strings of life began to c. Lr. V, 3, 217. the heaven's vault should c. 259. his shipping —ed 'gainst our rocks, Cymb. III, 1, 28.

b) to bluster, to brag: Ethiopes of their sweet complexion c. LLL IV, 3, 268.

Cracker, blusterer, swaggerer: what c. is this same that deafs our ears, John II, 147.

Crack-hemp, a rogue that deserves to be hanged: come hither, c. Shr. V, 1, 46.

Cradle, subst., a bed for babes: LLL IV, 3, 245. Merch. III, 2, 69. As I, 1, 113. R2 I, 3, 132. H6B IV, 9, 3. R3 IV, 1, 101. H8 IV, 2, 50. V, 5, 19. Tim. V, 4, 40. Mcb. I, 6, 8. Lr. I, 1, 15. Cymb. IV, 4, 28. in this hollow c. take thy rest, Ven. 1185 (viz on the breast). so near the c. of the fairy queen, Mids. III, 1, 80. rock his brains in c. of the rude imperious surge, H4B III, 1, 20. if drink rock not his c. Oth. II, 3, 136. does thoughts unveil in their dumb —s, Troil. III, 3, 200 (trisyllabic?).

Cradle, vb., to lie as in a cradle: husks wherein the acorn —d, Tp. I, 2, 464.

Cradle-babe, an infant lying in the cradle: H6B III, 2, 392.

Cradle-clothes, swaddling-clothes: H4A I, 1, 88.

Craft, 1) power, skill: catching all passions in his c. of will, Compl. 126. had you that c., to reave her of what should stead her most, All's V, 3, 86. that taught me c. to counterfeit oppression of such grief, R2 I, 4, 13. wooing poor craftsmen with the c. of smiles, 28. the serpentine c. of thy caduceus, Troil. II, 3, 13.

2) manual art, trade: he is not his —'s master, H4B III, 2, 297. you have made fair hands, you and your —, Cor. IV, 6, 118.

3) cunning, artifice, guile: false-creeping c. and perjury, Lucr. 1517. Compl. 295. Pilgr. 320. Wiv. V, 5, 239. Meas. III, 2, 10. 291. All's IV, 2, 33 (plur. —s). Tw. V, 169. H4A II, 4, 503. H5 III, 6, 153. Troil. III, 2, 160. IV, 4, 105. Cor. I, 10, 16. Hml. II, 2, 290. III, 4, 188. 210 (—s). Lr. II, 2, 108. Cymb. V, 5, 55.

Craft, vb., to make good handiwork (a word of Menenius' making): you and your crafts, you have —ed fair! Cor. IV, 6, 118.

Craftily, cunningly, slily: Meas. II, 4, 75 (O. Edd. crafty). Oth. II, 3, 41.

Craftsmen, mechanics: R2 I, 4, 28.

Crafty, cunning, sly: Ado III, 1, 22. Shr. II, 406. H4A II, 4, 504. H6B I, 2, 100. III, 1, 254. 367. Troil. V, 4, 10. Tit. II, 4, 41. Hml. III, 1, 8. Cymb. II, 1, 57. you may think my love was c. love and call it cunning, John IV, 1, 53 (i. e. feigned love; cf. crafty-sick).

Crafty-sick, feigning illness: H4B Ind. 37 (cf. John IV, 1, 53, and sly frantic wretch, in Tit. IV, 4, 59).

Craggy, abounding with broken rocks, rugged: Pilgr. 356 (not Shakespearian).

Cram, 1) to thrust in, to press: you c. these words into mine ear, Tp. II, 1, 106. —ed in the basket, Wiv. III, 5, 98. c. within this wooden O the very casques, H5 Prol. 12. With up: —ed up in a sheet of paper, LLL V, 2, 7. —s his rich thievery up, Troil. IV, 4, 45.

2) to fill, to stuff: to c. a maw, Meas. III, 2, 23. manhood and honour should have hare-hearts, would they but fat their thoughts with this —ed reason, Troil. II, 2, 49 (= full of considerations?). — Mostly followed by with: —ed with observation, As II, 7, 40. whose skull Jove c. with brains, Tw. I, 5, 122. II, 3, 163. Wint. I, 2, 91. H5 IV, 1, 287. H8 II, 4, 110. Cor. I, 1, 83. Rom. V, 3, 48.

Cramp, subst. spasm, convulsion: Lucr. 856. Tp. I, 2, 325. 369 (old —s, cf. Lucr. 855). IV, 261 (aged — s). V, 286. As IV, 1, 105. All's IV, 3, 324.

Crank, subst., winding passage, zigzag: through the —s and offices of man, Cor. I, 1, 141.

Crank, vb., to run in windings: he (the hare) —s and crosses with a thousand doubles, Ven. 682. this river comes me —ing in, H4A III, 1, 98.

Cranmer, name in H8 II, 4, 238. III, 2, 63. 71. 102. 400. IV, 1, 105 etc.

Crannied, chinky: that had in it a c. hole or chink, Mids. V, 159 (in the comedy of the clowns).

Cranny, fissure, chink: Lucr. 310. 1086. Err. II, 2, 31. Mids. III, 1, 73. V, 164.

Crants, garland: but here she is allowed her virgin c. Hml. V, 1, 255 (Ff rites).

Crare, a small vessel, skiff; a word introduced into the text by conjecture only: O melancholy! who ever yet could sound thy bottom? find the ooze, to show what coast thy sluggish c. might easiliest harbour in? Cymb. IV, 2, 205 (O. Edd. care).

Crash, subst., loud sound of things falling and breaking: Hml. II, 2, 498.

Crassus, 1) the Roman triumvir: Ant. III, 1, 2. — 2) name in Meas. IV, 5, 8.

Crave, 1) to beg, to demand (the person or thing wished for being the object): so offers he to give what she did c. Ven. 88. a beggar's orts to c. Lucr. 985. at your hand the account of hours to c. Sonn. 58, 3. Pilgr. 139. Wiv. IV, 4, 90. Meas. II, 2, 14. IV, 1, 22. IV, 2, 170. IV, 4, 10. V, 431. 432. 481. Err. I, 2, 26. LLL V, 1, 123. Merch. IV, 1, 206. Shr. V, 2, 152. John II, 234. H5 I, 1, 92. II, 4, 66. H6A I, 1, 159. I, 4, 32. II, 3, 13. 77. III, 3, 37. IV, 1, 84. 100. V, 3, 105. 130. H6C II, 1, 208. III, 1, 30. 43. III, 3, 32. 53. R3 II, 2, 106. H8 I, 4, 71. Cor. II, 3, 121. III, 1, 65. 283. Tit. V, 1, 159. Rom. I, 5, 113. II, 2, 190. III, 3, 5. Tim. I, 2, 63. Mcb. I, 2, 59. IV, 3, 20. Hml. IV, 4, 3 (Ff claims). Lr. I, 1, 197. Oth. I, 3, 237. Ant. II, 5, 98. Per. I, 4, 81. II, 1, 11. II, 3, 47. — Followed by an inf.: when ladies c. to be encountered, H6A II, 2, 46. II, 3, 29. R2 I, 3, 53. Tim. II, 2, 237. Cymb. IV, 2, 362. Per. V, 1, 5. by a clause: and c. I may have liberty to venge this wrong, H6A III, 4, 41. Ant. II, 6, 58. nature —s all dues be rendered to their owners, Troil. II, 2, 173. —

Of before the person of whom something is asked: *I —d nothing of thee*, Pilgr. 140. 141. Tw. II, 1, 5. H6B IV, 5, 4. H6C IV, 6, 8. Ant. III, 12, 17. — Absolutely: *you said you could not beg. I did but c.* Per. II, 1, 91.

2) to ask for, to demand to know: *if she deny to wed, I'll c. the day when I shall ask the banns*, Shr. II, 180. *—ing your opinion of my title*, H6B II, 2, 4.

3) to require: *the cause —s haste*, Lucr. 1295. *this must c. a most strange story*, Tp. V, 116. *business —ing quick despatch*, LLL II, 31. *to do that well —s a kind of wit*, Tw. III, 1, 68. *his designs c. haste*, R2 II, 2, 44. *till time and vantage c. my company*, H4B II, 3, 68. *a breach that —s a quick expedient stop*, H6B III, 1, 288. *that —s wary walking*, Caes. II, 1, 15. *cause of state —ing us jointly*, Mcb. III, 1, 34. Cor. III, 2, 33. IV, 1, 8. Rom. IV, 1, 69. Lr. II, 1, 130. IV, 2, 82.

Craven, subst. coward: H5 IV, 7, 139. H6A IV, 1, 15. Used of a beaten cock: *no cock of mine, you crow too like a c.* Shr. II, 228.

Craven, adj. cowardly: *his c. heart*, H6A II, 4, 87. *some c. scruple*, Hml. IV, 4, 40.

Craven, vb. to make cowardly: *a prohibition so divine that —s my weak hand*, Cymb. III, 4, 80.

Craver, euphemism for beggar, devised by the fisherman in Per. II, 1, 92.

Crawl, to creep: Sonn. 60, 6. Mids. II, 2, 146. III, 2, 444. Hml. III, 1, 130. Lr. I, 1, 42. *—ed into the favour of the king*, H8 III, 2, 103 (cf. *Creep*).

Craze, to break, to impair: *so many miseries have —d my voice*, R3 IV, 4, 17. *the grief hath —d my wits*, Lr. III, 4, 175.

Crazed, adjectively, 1) invalid: *yield thy c. title to my certain right*, Mids. I, 1, 92.*2) deranged in intellect: *to half a soul and to a notion c.* Mcb. III, 1, 83 (cf. *Care-crazed*, R3 III, 7, 184).

Crazy, decrepit, weak: *fitter for sickness and for c. age*, H6A III, 2, 89.

Creak, to make a grating sound: *let not the —ing of shoes betray thy heart*, Lr. III, 4, 97. Transitively = to cause to make a grating sound: *—ing my shoes on the plain masonry*, All's II, 1, 31.

Cream, subst., the oily part of milk: As III, 5, 47. Wint. IV, 4, 161. H4A IV, 2, 65.

Cream, vb. to gather a covering on the surface, to mantle: *whose visages do c. and mantle like a standing pond*, Merch. I, 1, 89.

Cream-faced, white, pale: *thou c. loon*, Mcb. V, 3, 11.

Create, 1) to bring into being, to produce; a) absol.: *great —ing Nature*, Wint. IV, 4, 88. b) trans.: Sonn. 20, 9. 81, 10. Err. III, 2, 39. Mids. III, 2, 204. All's II, 3, 150. IV, 5, 10. R2 V, 5, 91. H5 IV, 1, 264. V, 2, 244. H6B V, 1, 105. H6C II, 5, 39. H8 V, 5, 42. Troil. V, 2, 124. Cor. III, 2, 9. Mcb. IV, 3, 187. Lr. I, 2, 14. Cymb. V, 4, 124. With *of*: *—d of every creature's best*, Tp. III, 1, 47. *c. her child of spleen*, Lr. I, 4, 304. H5 II, 2, 31. Rom. I, 1, 183.

Create = created: *the issue there c.* Mids. V, 412. *being c. for comfort*, John IV, 1, 107. *hearts c. of duty and of zeal*, H5 II, 2, 31. *O any thing, of nothing first c.* Rom. I, 1, 183 (F1 *created*).

2) to form, to make: *—ing every bad a perfect best*, Sonn. 114, 7. *king Richard might c. a perfect guess*, H4B III, 1, 88.

3) to choose, to appoint: *we c. our uncle York lord governor of England*, R2 II, 1, 219. *he were —d knight*, H6B V, 1, 77. *that you c. your emperor's eldest son*, Tit. I, 224. *we c. lord Saturninus Rome's great emperor*, 231. *will c. thee empress of Rome*, 320. *I c. thee here my lord and master*, Lr. V, 3, 77. *he —s Lucius proconsul*, Cymb. III, 7, 7. *I c. you companions to our person*, V, 5, 20. — Especially = to invest with a peerage: John II, 551. H6A II, 4, 119. III, 1, 173. III, 4, 26. IV, 7, 62. H6B I, 1, 64. H6C II, 6, 103. IV, 3, 34.

Creation, 1) the act of creating, of calling into existence: *heaven in thy c. did decree that in thy face sweet love should ever dwell*, Sonn. 93, 9. *not made after this downright way of c.* Meas. III, 2, 113. *when I consider what great c. and what dole of honour flies where you bid it*, All's I, 3, 176 (i. e. how you can make her what you please; cf. v. 150). *this bodiless c. ecstasy is very cunning in*, Hml. III, 4, 138.

2) the thing created: *men their c. (viz women) mar in profiting by them*, Meas. II, 4, 127. *a dagger of the mind, a false c., proceeding from the heat-oppressed brain*, Mcb. II, 1, 38.

3) the act of bringing the world into existence: *from the c. to the general doom*, Lucr. 924. R3 IV, 3, 19.

4) nature: *slandering c. with a false esteem*, Sonn. 127, 12. *what demi-god hath come so near c.?* Merch. III, 2, 116. *and in the essential vesture of c. does tire the ingener*, Oth. II, 1, 64.

Creator, the Being that has created the world: H6C IV, 6, 44. Troil. II, 3, 72.

Creature, 1) a living being: Ven. 677. 1081. Lucr. 1147. 1627. Sonn. 1, 1. 113, 10. 143, 2. Tp. I, 2, 7. 31. III, 1, 48. III, 3, 74. V, 182. Gentl. II, 4, 153. Wiv. III, 4, 61. Meas. IV, 3, 71. Err. II, 2, 212. V, 92. Ado I, 1, 71. IV, 1, 185. Mids. II, 1, 172. Merch. II, 1, 4. III, 2, 277. As I, 2, 45. H6B II, 1, 7. H6C II, 2, 26. R3 V, 2, 24. Lr. IV, 6, 161 etc. *if thou canst like this c. as a maid*, All's II, 3, 149. *—s of prey*, Wint. III, 3, 12. *guilty —s*, Hml. II, 2, 618. *out of —s*, Per. IV, 2, 6 (without a sufficient supply of women). Used of things personified: *that mercy which fierce fire and iron extends, —s of note for mercy-lacking uses*, John IV, 1, 121. — Used in contempt as well as in tenderness: *a very beastly c.* Err. III, 2, 88. *pretty —s*, Lucr. 1233. Pilgr. 134. Tp. III, 1, 25. Wiv. IV, 2, 137. Err. III, 2, 33. R2 I, 2, 132 etc.

2) a servant, dependant: *new created the —s that were mine*, Tp. I, 2, 82. *tangled in affection to a c. of the queen's*, Lady Anne Bullen, H8 III, 2, 36. *this fellow here, Lord Timon, this thy c. by night frequents my house*, Tim. I, 1, 116. *hundreds call themselves your —s, who by you have been restored*, Per. III, 2, 45. (but here more probably = owing their lives to you).

Credence, belief, confidence: *his love and wisdom may plead for amplest c.* All's I, 2, 11. *we lay our best love and c. upon thy promising fortune*, III, 3, 2. *there is a c. in my heart*, Troil. V, 2, 120.

Credent, 1) credulous: *lending ... c. soul to that strong-bonded oath*, Compl. 279. *if with too c. ear you list his songs*, Hml. I, 3, 30.

2) **credible:** *my authority bears of a c. bulk,* Meas. IV, 4, 29 (= weight of credit). *'tis very c. thou mayst cojoin with something,* Wint. I, 2, 142.

Credible, deserving belief: All's I, 2, 4.

Credit, subst. 1) belief, faith; a) subjectively: *make us but believe, being compact of c., that you love us,* Err. III, 2, 22. *to dissever so our great self and our c., to esteem a senseless help when help past sense we deem,* All's II, 1, 126. *and there I found this c. that he did range the town to seek me out,* Tw. IV, 3, 6 (= this belief, opinion). *though c. be asleep and not an ear open,* Wint. V, 2, 67.

b) objectively: *beyond c.* Tp. II, 1, 59. *want c.* III, 3, 25. *swear by your double self, and there's an oath of c.* Merch. V, 246. *lack I c.?* Wint. II, 1, 157. *that which I shall report will bear no c.* V, 1, 179. *former fabulous story got c.* H8 I, 1, 37. *there is no composition in these news that gives them c.* Oth. I, 3, 2. *'tis apt and of great c.* II, 1, 296. *letters of good c.* Per. V, 3, 77.

2) a good opinion entertained of a p. and influence derived from it: *whose credit with the judge could fetch your brother from the manacles of law,* Meas. II, 4, 92. *how canst thou thus glance at my c. with Hippolyta?* Mids. II, 1, 75. *I was in that c. with them that I knew of their going to bed,* All's V, 3, 262. *what c. I have with the duke,* IV, 3, 196; cf. 200. *give us better c.* Wint. II, 3, 146. *I have but a very little c. with your worship,* H4B V, 1, 54. *my c. now stands on such slippery ground,* Caes. III, 1, 191. *if on my c. you dare build so far,* Lr. III, 1, 35. *she shall undo her c. with the Moor,* Oth. II, 3, 365. *the c. that thy lady hath of thee deserves thy trust, and thy most perfect goodness her assured c.* Cymb. I, 6, 157. — In particular, = trust with regard to property: *of c. infinite,* Err. V, 6. *try what my c. can in Venice do,* Merch. I, 1, 180. *I have used my c.* H4A I, 2, 63. *my reliances on his fracted dates have smit my c.* Tim. II, 1, 23.

3) reputation: *testimonies against his worth and c.* Meas. V, 244. *the one ne'er got me c., the other mickle blame,* Err. III, 1, 45. *consider how it stands upon my c.* IV, 1, 68. *thus will I save my c. in the shoot,* LLL IV, 1, 26. *to-morrow I wrestle for my c.* As I, 1, 133. *his name and c. shall you undertake,* Shr. IV, 2, 106. *you must hold the c. of your father,* All's I, 1, 89. *upon my reputation and c.* IV, 3, 154. H4A II, 1, 80. H6A IV, 1, 36. H6B II, 3, 71. H6C III, 3, 116. H8 III, 2, 265. Oth. I, 3, 97. Per. IV, 2, 33. *'tis a goodly c. for you,* Wiv. IV, 2, 200 (= it does you much honour). *this is much c. to you,* Tw. II, 3, 117.

Credit, vb. 1) to believe: Sonn. 138, 7. Tp. I, 2, 102. All's I, 3, 245. R2 III, 3, 120. H6B IV, 2, 159. Caes. V, 1, 79. Per. V, 1, 124.

2) to do honour: *I call them forth to c. her,* Shr. IV, 1, 106 (misunderstood by Grumio who replies: *Why, she comes to borrow nothing of them*).

Creditor, one to whom a debt is owed: Meas. I, 1, 40. I, 2, 136. Err. IV, 4, 123. Merch. III, 1, 118. III, 2, 318. III, 3, 34. John III, 3, 21. H4B V, 5, 129. Tim. I, 1, 96. III, 4, 105. *Debitor and c.* = the credit and debit sides: *belee'd and calmed by debitor and c.* Oth. I, 1, 31. *you have no true debitor and c. but it,* Cymb. V, 4, 172.

Credulity, aptness to believe and be deceived: Wint. II, 1, 192.

Credulous, apt to believe, easily deceived: Ven. 986. Lucr. 1522. Tp. II, 2, 149. Shr. IV, 2, 67. Lr. I, 2, 195. Oth. IV, 1, 46. Cymb. V, 5, 210. Followed by *in: c. in this mad thought,* Tit. V, 2, 74. By *of: so c. of cure,* All's II, 1, 118. By *to: c. to false prints,* Meas. II, 4, 130.

Creed, a summary of the articles of faith: *I love him not, nor fear him; there's my c.:* as *I am made without him, so I'll stand, if the king please,* H8 II, 2, 51.

Creek, 1) a small river: *I'll throw it into the c. behind our rock, and let it to the sea,* Cymb. IV, 2, 151 (cf. 184: *I have sent Cloten's clotpoll down the stream*).

2) a narrow passage, alley, lane: *one that countermands the passages of alleys, —s and narrow lands,* Err. IV, 2, 38.

Creep, 1) to move with the belly to the ground: *the snail... fearing to c. forth,* Ven. 1036. *the little worms that c.* Lucr. 1248. *love will c. in service where it cannot go,* Gent. IV, 2, 20. *the smallest mouse that —s on floor,* Mids. V, 223. *any —ing venomed thing,* R3 I, 2, 20. *he's more than a —ing thing,* Cor. V, 4, 14. *no sooner was I crept out of my cradle,* H6B IV, 9, 3. *from forth the kennel of thy womb hath crept a hell-hound,* R3 IV, 4, 47.

2) to move slowly or feebly: *the poor, lame, blind, halt, c., cry out for thee,* Lucr. 902. *see time, how slow it —s,* 1575. *the —ing hours of time,* As II, 7, 112. *c. like shadows by him,* Wint. II, 3, 34. *c. time ne'er so slow,* John III, 3, 31. *—s in this petty pace from day to day,* Mcb. V, 5, 20. *—ing like snail unwillingly to school,* As II, 7, 146. *she —s; her motion and her station are as one,* Ant. III, 3, 21.

3) to move with servility and bending down: *to come as humbly as they used to c. to holy altars,* Troil. III, 3, 73.

4) to move stealthily or imperceptibly: *which drives the —ing thief to some regard,* Lucr. 305. 736. 1627. *time whose millioned accidents c. in 'twixt vows,* Sonn. 115, 6. *what incidency of harm is —ing toward me,* Wint. I, 2, 404. *as wild geese that the —ing fowler eye,* Mids. III, 2, 20. *till o'er their brows death-counterfeiting sleep with leaden legs and batty wings doth c.* 365. *the deep of night is crept upon our talk,* Caes. IV, 3, 226. — Used of the motion of the air and sounds: *this music crept by me upon the waters,* Tp. I, 2, 391. *those dulcet sounds that c. into the dreaming bridegroom's ear,* Merch. III, 2, 52. *let the sounds of music c. in our ears,* V, 56. *the invisible and —ing wind,* H5 III Chor. 11. *—ing murmur and the poring dark fills the wide vessel of the universe,* IV Chor. 2.

5) to get into a hiding-place: *in thy weak hive a wandering wasp hath crept,* Lucr. 839. *my best way is to c. under his gaberdine,* Tp. II, 2, 40. *he may c. in here,* Wiv. III, 3, 138. 150. III, 5, 148. IV, 2, 56. 59. *c. in crannies,* Err. II, 2, 31. *now will he c. into sedges,* Ado II, 1, 209. *his jesting spirit is crept into a lute-string,* III, 2, 61. *c. into acorn-cups,* Mids. II, 1, 31. *the moon may through the centre c.* III, 2, 54. *I could have crept into any alderman's thumb-ring,* H4A II, 4, 364. *the day is crept into the bosom of the sea,* H6B IV, 1, 2. *to make thy sepulchre and c. into it far before thy time,* H6C I, 1, 237. *in those holes ... there were crept reflecting gems,* R3 I, 4, 30. *in the basket c.* Hml. III, 4, 195.

6) to get to or into a place or thing secretly and unexpectedly: *are you crept before us?* Gentl. IV, 2, 18. *are you crept hither to see the wrestling?* As I, 2, 165. *the marriage with his brother's wife has crept too near his conscience; no, his conscience has crept too near another lady,* H8 II, 2, 18. *how comes it he is to sojourn with you? how —s acquaintance?* Cymb. I, 4, 25 (a very odd expression; = how does acquaintance come to be between you?). *the idea of her life shall sweetly c. into his study of imagination,* Ado IV, 1, 226. *I feel this youth's perfections to c. in at mine eyes,* Tw. I, 5, 317. cf. *you shall secretly into the bosom c. of that same noble prelate,* H4A I, 3, 266. *I am crept in favour with myself,* R3 I, 2, 259. *Pompey —s apace into the hearts of such,* Ant. I, 3, 50. *reproach and beggary is crept into the palace of our king,* H6B IV, 1, 102. *how some men c. in skittish Fortune's hall, whiles others play the idiots in her eyes,* Troil. III, 3, 134. *as if that whatsoever god who leads him were slily crept into his human powers and gave him graceful posture,* Cor. II, 1, 236. *whilst emulation in the army crept,* Troil. II, 2, 212. *lust and liberty c. in the minds and marrows of our youth,* Tim. IV, 1, 26. And inversely: *c. into the jaundice by being peevish,* Merch. I, 1, 85.

Creeple, see *Cripple.*

Crescent, subst. the increasing moon, half-moon: *he is no c.* Mids. V, 246.

Crescent, adj. increasing: *nature, c., doth not grow alone in thews and bulk,* Hml. I, 3, 11. *my powers are c., and my auguring hope says it will come to the full,* Ant. II, 1, 10. *he was then of a c. note,* Cymb. I, 4, 2.

Crescive, the same: *grew like the summer grass, fastest by night, unseen, yet c. in his faculty,* H5 I, 1, 66.

Cresset, a fire made in a high place or suspended in the air: *the front of heaven was full of fiery shapes, of burning —s,* H4A III, 1, 15.

Cressid = *Cressida:* Merch. V, 6. All's II, 1, 100. H5 II, 1, 80. Troil. I, 1, 30. 98 etc.

Cressida, the mistress of Troilus: Tw. III, 1, 59. 62. Troil. I, 2, 195. III, 1, 36. 95 etc.

Cressy, town in Picardy: *C. battle,* H5 II, 4, 54.

Crest, subst., 1) the helmet topping an armorial ensign: *like coats in heraldry, due but to one and crowned with one c.* Mids. III, 2, 214. *this is the very top, the height, the c., or c. unto the c., of murder's arms,* John IV, 3, 46.

2) coat-armour: *when tyrants' —s and tombs of brass are spent,* Sonn. 107, 14. *each fair instalment, coat and several c.* Wiv. V, 5, 67. *what is your c.? a coxcomb?* Shr. II, 226. *old Nevil's c., the rampant bear,* H6B V, 1, 202. *thou hast stroke upon my c.* Tit. I, 364 (cf. Lucr. 828).

3) any badge: *let's write good angel on the devil's horn; 'tis not the devil's c.* Meas. II, 4, 17. *beauty's c. becomes the heavens well,* LLL IV, 3, 256 (i. e. the brightness which is the badge of beauty). *it* (the horn) *was a c. ere thou wast born,* As IV, 2, 15.

4) helmet: *his lance, his battered shield, his uncontrolled c.* Ven. 104. *no plume in any English c.* John II, 317. H4A V, 4, 72. H6A IV, 6, 10. V, 3, 25. Troil. IV, 5, 143. Mcb. V, 8, 11.

5) the top: *this night whose black contagious breath already smokes about the burning c. of the old,*

feeble and day-wearied sun, John V, 4, 34. cf. IV, 3, 46.

6) the raised head and neck of certain animals: *his* (the horse's) *braided hanging mane upon his compassed c. now stand on end,* Ven. 272. *high c., short ears,* 297. *throwing the base thong from his bending c.* 395. *now for the bare-picked bone of majesty doth dogged war bristle his angry c.* John IV, 3, 149. *they* (the horses) *fall their —s,* Caes. IV, 2, 26. — Figuratively of men: *which makes him prune himself, and bristle up the c. of youth against your dignity,* H4A I, 1, 99. *and make him fall his c. that prouder than blue Iris bends,* Troil. I, 3, 380. *when they shall see his c. up again,* Cor. IV, 5, 225.

Crest, vb. to form the crest of, to top: *his reared arm —ed the world,* Ant. V, 2, 83 (Percy: 'an allusion to some of the old crests in heraldry, where a raised arm on a wreath was mounted on the helmet').

Crest-fallen, dispirited, humbled: *they would whip me with their fine wits till I were as c. as a dried pear,* Wiv. IV, 5, 102. *shall I seem c. in my father's sight?* R2 I, 1, 188. *let it make thee c.* H6B IV, 1, 59.

Crestless, not dignified with coat-armour, ignoble: H6A II, 4, 85.

Crest-wounding, attainting nobility, disgraceful: *c. private scar,* Lucr. 828 (cf. Tit. I, 364).

Cretan, belonging to the isle of Crete: *the C. strond,* Shr. I, 1, 175.

Crete, the island to the south of the Archipelago: Mids. IV, 1, 118. 131. H5 II, 1, 77. H6A IV, 6, 54. H6C V, 6, 18.

Crevice, a fissure: *through the c. of a wall,* Tit. V, 1, 114.

Crew, company, band: *Collatine and all his lordly c.* Lucr. 1731. *we'll bring thee to our —s,* Gentl. IV, 1, 74(?). *a c. of patches,* Mids. III, 2, 9. *so dissolute a c.* R2 V, 3, 12. *that consorted c.* 138. *art thou of Cornish c.?* H5 IV, 1, 50 (Pistol's speech). *all the c. of them,* H6B II, 2, 72. *to London all the c. are gone,* H6C II, 1, 174. *with a valiant c.* R3 IV, 5, 12. *a c. of wretched souls,* Mcb. IV, 3, 141. *a c. of pirates,* Per. V, 1, 176.

Crewel, worsted: *he wears c. garters,* Lr. II, 4, 7 (a quibble; Ff *cruel*).

Crib, subst. 1) manger: *let a beast be lord of beasts, and his c. shall stand at the king's mess,* Hml. V, 2, 88.

2) hovel: *why rather, sleep, liest thou in smoky —s,* H4B III, 1, 9.

Cribbed, caged: *but now I am cabined, c., confined,* Mcb. III, 4, 24.

Cricket, 1) an insect chirping about fireplaces: Shr. IV, 3, 110. Wint. II, 1, 31. H4A II, 4, 100 (*as merry as —s*) Rom. I, 4, 63. Mcb. II, 2, 16. Cymb. II, 2, 11. Per. III Prol. 7.

2) name of a fairy: Wiv. V, 5, 47.

Crier, the officer whose business is to make proclamation: Wiv. V, 5, 45. John II, 134 (cf. *Town-crier*).

Crime, a heavy offence: Lucr. 224. 772. 931. 993. 1252. Sonn. 120, 8. 124, 14. Tp. Epil. 19. Gentl. IV, 1, 52. Meas. II, 3, 7. III, 2, 287. Err. II, 2, 143. LLL IV, 1, 31. All's IV, 3, 86. Wint. IV, 1, 4. R2 IV, 223. H5 II, 2, 56. IV, 1, 139. H6A III, 1, 11.

H6B III, 1, 134. R3 I, 2, 76 (Qq *evils*). Tim. III, 5, 58. 83. V, 4, 37. Mcb. IV, 3, 96. Hml. I, 5, 12. II, 1, 43. III, 3, 81. Lr. I, 3, 4. III, 2, 52. IV, 2, 79. Oth. V, 2, 26. Per. IV, 4, 5.

Crimeful, criminal, wicked: Lucr. 970. Hml. IV, 7, 7 (Qq *criminal*).

Crimeless, free from crime, innocent: H6B II, 4, 63.

Criminal, adj. 1) involving a crime: Wint. III, 2, 90. Cor. III, 3, 81. Hml. IV, 7, 7 (Ff *crimeful*). 2) tainted with crime: *being c. in double violation of sacred chastity and of promise-breach*, Meas. V, 409.

Crimson, subst., red colour: *the virgin c. of modesty*, H5 V, 2, 323.

Crimson, adj. red: Ven. 76. 506. Lucr. 1738. Mids. II, 1, 108. John IV, 2, 253. R2 III, 3, 46. H5 IV, 4, 16. H6B III, 1, 259. III, 2, 200. Tit. II, 4, 22. V, 2, 22. Rom. V, 3, 95. Cymb. II, 2, 38.

Crimson, vb. to dye red: *—ed in thy lethe*, Caes. III, 1, 206.

Cringe, to distort: *whip him, till like a boy you see him c. his face*, Ant. III, 13, 100.

Cripple, subst. a lame person: Pilgr. 308. Merch. I, 2, 22. H6B II, 1, 133. R3 II, 1, 89. Adjectively: *the c. tardy-gaited night*, H5 IV Chor. 20 (O. Edd. *creeple*).

Cripple, vb. to make lame: *c. our senators*, Tim. IV, 1, 24. In John V, 2, 36 O. Edd.: *and c. thee unto a pagan shore*; M. Edd. *grapple*.

Crisp, curled: *leave your c. channels*, Tp. IV, 130. *the Severn ... hid his c. head*, H4A I, 3, 106. *c. heaven*, Tim. IV, 3, 183 (so called from the curled clouds).

Crisped, curled: *those c. snaky golden locks*, Merch. III, 2, 92.

Crispian, name of a saint: *this day is called the feast of C.* H5 IV, 3, 40 (i. e. the 25th of October). 43. 46. *Crispin Crispian*, 57.

Crispianus, the same: *on the day of Crispin Crispianus*, H5 IV, 7, 94.

Crispin, a saint, brother to Crispian: *on —'s day*, H5 IV, 3, 48 (25th Oct.). *C. Crispian*, 57. 67. *C. Crispianus*, IV, 7, 94.

Critic, subst. a censurer, carper: *my adder's sense to c. and to flatterer stopped are*, Sonn. 112, 10. *a very beadle to a humorous sigh, a c., nay, a nightwatch constable*, LLL III, 178. *do not give advantage to stubborn —s, apt for depravation*, Troil. V, 2, 131.

Critic, adj. censorious, snarling: *c. Timon laugh at idle toys*, LLL IV, 3, 170.

Critical, the same: *some satire, keen and c.* Mids. V, 54. *I am nothing, if not c.* Oth. II, 1, 120.

Croak, vb. to caw, to cry as a raven: Troil. V, 2, 191. Hml. III, 2, 264. Lr. III, 6, 33. Transitively: *the raven himself is hoarse that —s the fatal entrance of Duncan*, Mcb. I, 5, 40.

Crocodile, the animal Crocodilus: *the mournful c.* H6B III, 1, 226. *eat a c.* Hml. V, 1, 299. *each drop she falls would prove a c.* Oth. IV, 1, 257. Ant. II, 7, 31. 46. *the tears of it are wet*, 55.

Cromer, name: *Sir James C.* H6B IV, 7, 118.

Cromwell, 1) *Lord C. of Wingfield* (one of Talbot's titles) H6A IV, 7, 66. — 2) *Thomas C.*, servant to Wolsey: H8 III, 2, 76. 372 etc. IV, 1, 108.

Crone, old woman: *give't to thy c.* Wint. II, 3, 76.

Crook, to bend: *c. the pregnant hinges of the knee*, Hml. III, 2, 66 (cf. *Knee-crooking, Low-crooked*).

Crook-back, hunchback: H6C II, 2, 96. V, 5, 30. — Adjectively: *where's that valiant c. prodigy*, H6C I, 4, 75.

Crooked, 1) curved: *c. beak*, Lucr. 508. *knife*, Sonn. 100, 14. *curls*, Compl. 85. *deformed, c.* Err. IV, 2, 19. *lame, foolish, c.* John III, 1, 46. *c. age*, R2 II, 1, 133. *a c. figure*, H5 Prol. 15. *shape*, H6B V, 1, 158 *c. noses*, Cymb. III, 1, 37. *our c. smokes*, V, 5, 477. Tropically: *indirect c. ways*, H4B IV, 5, 185. *I make a c. face at it*, Cor. II, 1, 62 (= a wry face). 2) perverse, false: *their c. titles usurped from you*, H5 I, 2, 94. 3) malignant: *c. eclipses 'gainst his glory fight*, Sonn. 60, 7. *ill-nurtured, c., churlish*, Ven. 134. *if c. fortune had not thwarted me*, Gentl. IV, 1, 22. *as c. in thy manners as thy shape*, H6B V, 1, 158. *since the heavens have shaped my body so, let hell make c. my mind*, H6C V, 6, 79. *c. malice*, H8 V, 3, 44 (cf. Tp. I, 2, 259).

Crooked-pated, having a curved head: *to betray a she-lamb of a twelvemonth to a c. old cuckoldly ram*, As III, 2, 86.

Crook-kneed, bandylegged: (hounds) *c. and dew-lapped*, Mids. IV, 1, 127.

Crop, subst. harvest: Lucr. 958. As III, 5, 101. All's I, 3, 48. Tim. IV, 1, 29. Cymb. I, 6, 33.*IV, 2, 180.

Crop, vb. 1) to cut off, to mow, to pluck: *c. a weed*, Ven. 946. *the stalk*, 1175. *their waxen thighs*, Mids. III, 1, 172. *a flower*, R2 II, 1, 134. V, 2, 51. *the budding honours*, H4A V, 4, 73. *the flower-de-luces*, H6A I, 1, 80. *roses*, II, 4, 41. *a plant*, H6C V, 5, 62. *the golden prime of this young prince*, R3 I, 2, 248. *the seeded pride*, Troil. I, 3, 318. *the ears*, Cymb. II, 1, 14. *my life*, Per. I, 1, 141. 2) to reap: *he ploughed her, and she —ed*, Ant. II, 2, 233.

Crop-ear, a horse with curtailed ears: H4A II, 3, 72.

Crosby House (Ff) or **Crosby Place** (Qq), a house in Bishopsgate Street, where Richard III lived before his accession: R3 I, 2, 213. I, 3, 345. III, 1, 190.

Cross, subst. 1) the ensign of the Christian religion: Err. II, 1, 79. Merch. V, 31. R2 IV, 94. H4A I, 1, 20. 26. II, 4, 372.*Used as the emblem of human suffering: Sonn. 34, 12. 42, 12. Mids. I, 1, 153. R2 IV, 241. 2) any thing that thwarts, vexation, hinderance, mischance: *I see what —es my attempt will bring*, Lucr. 491. *a thousand —es keep them from thy aid*, 912. *one silly c. wrought all my loss*, Pilgr. 257. Ado II, 2, 4. Mids. I, 1, 136. As V, 4, 137. R2 II, 2, 79. H4B III, 1, 55. R3 III, 1, 4. Lr. V, 3, 278. Per. II, 1, 127. 3) money stamped with the figure of a cross: *—es love not him*, LLL I, 2, 36. *I should bear no c. if I did bear you*, As II, 4, 12. *you are too impatient to bear —es*, H4B I, 2, 253.

Cross, adj. 1) passing in different directions, cutting each other, zigzag: *the c. blue lightning*, Caes. I, 3, 50. *quick c. lightning*, Lr. IV, 7, 35. 2) perverse: *what c. devil made me put this main secret in the packet I sent the king?* H8 III, 2, 214. *my state, which is c. and full of sin*, Rom. IV, 3, 5. 3) malapert: *nor hast thou pleasure to be c. in* talk, Shr. II, 251. *my lord of York will still be c. in talk*, R3 III, 1, 126. *be c. with him*, Tit. II, 3, 53.

Cross, adv. athwart: *give him another staff; this last was broke c.* Ado V, 1, 139 (cf. *Across*).

Cross, prepos. across, athwart: *when you come c. his humour*, H4A III, 1, 172 (Ff *do c.*). *waft me safely c. the Channel*, H6B IV, 1, 114.

Cross, vb. 1) to lay athwart: *I have no one to blush with me, to c. their arms and hang their heads with mine*, Lucr. 793. *with your arms —ed*, LLL III, 19.

2) to sign with a cross: *I c. me for a sinner*, Err. II, 2, 190.

3) to come across a person's way, to meet, to face: *your precious self had then not —ed the eyes of my young play-fellow*, Wint. I, 2, 79. *send danger from the east unto the west, so honour c. it from the north to south*, H4A I, 3, 196. *what is thy name that in the battle thus thou —est me*, V, 3, 2. *what chance is this that suddenly hath —ed us?* H6A I, 4, 72. *I'll c. it, though it blast me*, Hml. I, 1, 127. — Absolutely: *I am that way going to temptation, where prayers c.* Meas. II, 2, 159.*

4) to zigzag (cf. *Adj.*): *he cranks and —es with a thousand doubles*, Ven. 682. Transitively: *without any slips of prolixity or —ing the plain highway of talk*, Merch. III, 1, 13 (i. e. without deviating from the straight way).

5) to pass from side to side; a) absol.: *thence we have —ed, to execute the charge*, Wint. V, 1, 161. *was embarked to c. to Burgundy*, R3 I, 4, 10. — b) trans.: *Leander —ed the Hellespont*, Gentl. I, 1, 22. *—ed the Severn*, Cymb. III, 5, 17. *the sea*, H6A III, 1, 180. IV, 1, 89. V, 5, 90. H6C II, 6, 97. III, 3, 235. R3 IV, 1, 42. Cymb. I, 6, 202. IV, 2, 334.

6) to thwart, to hinder: *to c. the curious workmanship of nature*, Ven. 734. *with some mischance c. Tarquin in his flight*, Lucr. 968. *the world is bent my deeds to c.* Sonn. 90, 2. Gentl. II, 6, 40. III, 1, 18. IV, 1, 12. V, 2, 55. Wiv. IV, 5, 130. V, 5, 40. Meas. IV, 2, 178. Ado I, 3, 70. II, 2, 3. 8. LLL V, 2, 138. Mids. I, 1, 150. II, 1, 119. Merch. II, 4, 36. II, 5, 56. III, 1, 23. John III, 1, 91. H6A IV, 3, 52. H8 III, 2, 234. Rom. IV, 5, 95. V, 3, 20. Tim. I, 2, 166. III, 3, 29. Mcb. III, 1, 81. Cymb. III, 5, 168. V, 4, 101. — Followed by *from: to c. me from the golden time I look for*, H6C III, 2, 127.

7) to cut short, to contradict: *both which so c. him with their opposite persuasion, that now he vows a league, and now invasion*, Lucr. 286. *I love not to be —ed*, LLL I, 2, 34. *we cannot c. the cause why we were born*, IV, 3, 218. *when did she c. thee with a bitter word?* Shr. II, 28. *I'll say so; who can c. it?* Per. IV, 3, 16. Shr. IV, 1, 75. IV, 3, 195. IV, 5, 10. H4A III, 1, 147. Caes. I, 2, 188. IV, 3, 150. Ant. I, 3, 9. Per. III Prol. 41.

8) to furnish with money? cf. *when all's spent, he'ld be —ed then, an he could*, Tim. I, 2, 168 (a quibble intended?).

Cross-bow, a bow having the form of a cross: H5 IV, 8, 99. H6C III, 1, 6.*

Cross-gartered, wearing the garters crossed on the leg: Tw. II, 5, 167. 181. 185. 219. III, 4, 55.

Cross-gartering, subst. wearing the garters crossed: Tw. III, 4, 22.

Crossing, subst. cutting short, contradiction: *of many men I do not bear these —s*, H4A III, 1, 36.

Crossly, adversely: *c. to thy good all fortune goes*, R2 II, 4, 24.

Crossness, spirit of contradiction: *she will die, if he woo her, rather than she will bate one breath of her accustomed c.* Ado II, 3, 184.

Cross-row, the alphabet: *and from the c. plucks the letter G*, R3 I, 1, 55.

Crossway, the place where two roads intersect each other: *damned spirits all, that in —s and floods have burial*, Mids. III, 2, 383.

Crotchet, 1) perverse conceit, odd fancy: *thou hast some —s in thy head*, Wiv. II, 1, 159. *the duke had —s in him*, Meas. III, 2, 135.

2) a character in music: *these are very —s that he speaks: note, notes, forsooth, and nothing*, Ado II, 3, 58 (quibble). *I will carry no —s; I'll re you, I'll fa you*, Rom. IV, 5, 120 (quibbling; cf. *to carry coals, s. Carry* 1).

Crouch, to lie close to the ground, to stoop, to cringe: *to c. in litter of your stable planks*, John V, 2, 140. *when —ing marrow in the bearer strong cries of itself 'No more,'* Tim. V, 4, 9. *must I stand and c. under your testy humour?* Caes. IV, 3, 45. Followed by *for* = to fawn in order to obtain sth.: *at his heels, leashed in like hounds, should famine, sword and fire c. for employment*, H5 Prol. 8.

Crow, subst. 1) the bird Corvus Cornix: Ven. 324. Lucr. 1009. Sonn. 70, 4. 113, 12. Phoen. 17 (*treble-dated c.*). Err. III, 1, 81. Ado I, 1, 133. Mids. II, 1, 97. III, 2, 142. Merch. V, 102. All's IV, 3, 319. Wint. III, 2, 192. IV, 4, 221. H5 II, 1, 91. IV, 2, 51. H6B IV, 10, 90. V, 2, 11. Troil. I, 2, 265. IV, 2, 9. Cor. III, 1, 139. IV, 5, 45. Rom. I, 2, 92. I, 5, 50. Caes. V, 1, 85. Mcb. III, 2, 50. Lr. IV, 6, 13. Cymb. I, 3, 15. III, 1, 83. III, 3, 12. V, 3, 93. Per. IV Prol. 32. The French cock called so in contempt: *at the crying of your nation's c.* John V, 2, 144. (cf. *Night-crow*). *To pluck a c. together* = to quarrel, to have a dispute about sth.: Err. III, 1, 83.

2) a bar of iron to force open doors: Err. III, 1, 80. 84. Rom. V, 2, 21.

Crow, vb. (Impf. *crew*: Hml. I, 1, 147. I, 2, 218. Partic. *crowed*: Rom. IV, 4, 3) to cry as a cock: Tp. II, 1, 29. Mids. II, 1, 267. Shr. II, 228. H5 IV Chor. 15. Rom. IV, 4, 3. Hml. I, 1, 147. 157. I, 2, 218. Cymb. II, 1, 26. = to laugh merrily: *you were wont, when you laughed, to c. like a cock*, Gentl. II, 1, 28. *my lungs began to c. like chanticleer*, As II, 7, 30. *these wise men that c. so at these set kind of fools*, Tw. I, 5, 95. = to strut like a cock crowing in triumph: *and yet he'll be —ing as if he had writ man ever since his father was a bachelor*, H4B I, 2, 30.

Crowd, subst. a throng of people: *where have you been broiling? among the c. i' the Abbey*, H8 IV, 1, 57.

Crowd, vb. 1) intr. to press: *the general ... c. to his presence*, Meas. II, 4, 29. *he burst his head for —ing among the marshal's men*, H4B II, 2, 347.

2) tr. to press: *the time misordered doth, in common sense, c. us and crush us to this monstrous form*, H4B IV, 2, 34. *the poor mechanic porters —ing in their heavy burdens at his narrow gate*, H5 I, 2, 200. *a man into whom nature hath so —ed humours that his valour is crushed into folly*, Troil. I, 2, 23. *the throng will c. a feeble man almost to death*, Caes. II, 4, 35.

Crow-flower, Lychnis flos-cuculi: Hml. IV, 7, 170 (at present = buttercup).

Crow-keeper, 1) a scarecrow: *scaring the ladies like a c.* Rom. I, 4, 6.

2) a field-guard: *that fellow handles his bow like a c.* Lr. IV, 6, 88.

Crown, subst. 1) the gold ornament worn on the head as a badge of regal or imperial dignity: Lucr. 216. Tp. I, 2, 114. II, 1, 208. Meas. II, 2, 60. Merch. IV, 1, 189. R2 III, 3, 95. H4A II, 4, 420. H4B II, 4, 188. H6A I, 1, 150. III, 1, 69. IV, 1, 1. 156. V, 3, 119. H8 I, 1, 61. IV, 1, 88 etc. etc. —*s imperial,* —*s and coronets,* H5 II Chor. 10. Used for *coronet: Err.* I, 1, 144. *the triple c.* (of the pope) H6B I, 3, 66.

Figuratively, = the top, the height, that which accomplishes any thing: *and on this couple drop a blessed c.* Tp. V, 202 (i. e. supreme bliss). *wedding is great Juno's c.* As V, 4, 147. *the fine is the c.* All's IV, 4, 35. *the c. and comfort of my life,* Wint. III, 2, 95. *make Cressid's name the very c. of falsehood,* Troil. IV, 2, 106. *O that husband! my supreme c. of grief,* Cymb. I, 6, 4. *the c. o' the earth doth melt,* Ant. IV, 15, 63.

2) a garland: *to make cold nymphs chaste —s,* Tp. IV, 1, 66. *with your sedged —s,* 129. *an olive branch and laurel c.* H6C IV, 6, 34.

3) the top: *upon the c. o' the cliff,* Lr. IV, 6, 67.

4) the top of the head: *from toe to c.* Tp. IV, 233. *from the c. of his head to the sole of his foot,* Ado III, 2, 9. *from the c. to the toe,* Mcb. I, 5, 43. Mids. II, 1, 109.

Hence = the head: *I'll have this c. of mine cut from my shoulders,* R3 III, 2, 43. R2 III, 3, 96. H4A II, 3, 96. H5 IV, 1, 245. H6B II, 1, 51. Mcb. III, 4, 81. *a French c.* = a bald head: Meas. I, 2, 52. Mids. I, 2, 99. All's II, 2, 23.

5) the half of an eggshell: *give me an egg, nuncle, and I'll give thee two —s. What two —s shall they be? Why, after I have cut the egg i' the middle and eat up the meat, the two —s of the egg,* Lr. I, 4, 174.

6) a coin (= five shillings sterling): Pilgr. 409. LLL II, 1, 130. As I, 1, 3. II, 3, 38. Shr. I, 2, 57. II, 123. 352. V, 2, 70. R2 IV, 16. H4A I, 2, 147. II, 4, 420. H4B II, 2, 99. H5 II Chor. 22. IV, 3, 37. H6B IV, 1, 16. 18. IV, 10, 29. H6C II, 2, 144. II, 5, 57. Tim. III, 4, 28. Hml. II, 2, 73. Per. IV, 2, 121. *French c.* (= a hundred and nine cents): Meas. I, 2, 52. LLL III, 142. Mids. I, 2, 97 (*French c. colour beard*). All's II, 2, 23. H4B III, 2, 237. H5 IV, 1, 245. H6B IV, 2, 166. *some with cunning gild their copper —s,* Troil. IV, 4, 107.

Plays on the different significations: Meas. I, 2, 52. Mids. I, 2, 99. All's II, 2, 23. R2 III, 3, 96. H4A II, 3, 96. II, 4, 420. H5 IV, 1, 243. 245. H6B IV, 2, 166. Lr. I, 4, 171. Per. IV, 2, 121.

Crown, vb. 1) to invest with a crown: John IV, 2, 1. H6A III, 1, 180. IV, 1, 157. R3 I, 3, 175 etc. *to c. himself,* H6B IV, 4, 31. *to c. himself king,* H6A I, 3, 68. *c. her queen,* H6B I, 1, 48. —*ed king,* H6A I, 1, 92. *queen,* V, 5, 90.

2) to adorn with a garland: —*s him with flowers,* Mids. II, 1, 27. —*ed with rank fumiter,* Lr. IV, 4, 3. *like a Fury —ed with snakes,* Ant. II, 5, 40.

3) Figurative use: a) to top, to cover as

with a crown: *with each end of thy blue bow dost c. my bosky acres,* Tp. IV, 80. *coats in heraldry —ed with one crest,* Mids. III, 2, 214. — b) to glorify: *thy outward thus with outward praise is —ed,* Sonn. 69, 5. *whether doth my mind, being —ed with you, drink up the monarch's plague, this flattery,* 114, 1. *incertainties now c. themselves assured,* 107, 7. —*ing the present, doubting of the rest,* 115, 12. *love is —ed with the prime,* As V, 3, 33. *and c. thee for a finder of madmen,* Tw. III, 4, 154. *though you were —ed the nonpareil of beauty,* I, 5, 272. *as if allegiance in their bosoms sat,* —*ed with faith and constant loyalty,* H5 II, 2, 5. *no day without a deed to c. it,* H8 V, 5, 59. *Achilles whom opinion —s the sinew and the forehead of our host,* Troil. I, 3, 142. *and in some sort these wants of mine are —ed, that I account them blessings,* Tim. II, 2, 190. *willing misery outlives incertain pomp, is —ed before,* IV, 3, 243. *this grief is —ed with consolation,* Ant. I, 2, 174. *when my turpitude thou dost so c. with gold,* IV, 6, 34. Ironically: *to be a queen, and —ed with infamy,* H6B III, 2, 71. *for queen, a very caitiff —ed with care,* R3 IV, 4, 100. *thy saints for aye be —ed with plagues,* Tim. V, 1, 56. — c) to perfect, to complete, to accomplish: *nativity ... crawls to maturity, wherewith being —ed, crooked eclipses 'gainst his glory fight,* Sonn. 60, 6. *c. what I profess with kind event,* Tp. III, 1, 69. *the conclusion shall be —ed with your enjoying her,* Wiv. III, 5, 138. *one day shall c. the alliance on't,* Tw. V, 326. *each your doing —s what you are doing in the present deed,* Wint. IV, 4, 145. *beheld one joy c. another,* V, 2, 48. *the end —s all,* Troil. IV, 5, 224. *to c. my thoughts with acts,* Mcb. IV, 1, 149. *To c. up,* in the same sense: *'as true as Troilus' shall c. up the verse,* Troil. III, 2, 189. — d) to instate as master: *whether beauty, birth, or wealth, or wit, entitled in their parts do —ed sit,* Sonn. 37, 7. *him will I tear out of that cruel eye, where he sits —ed in his master's spite,* Tw. V, 131. *and on your eyelids c. the god of sleep,* H4A III, 1, 217.

Crowner, coroner: Tw. I, 5, 142. Hml. V, 1, 4. 24.

Crownet, crown, coronet: —*s regal,* Troil. Prol. 6. *crowns and —s,* Ant. V, 2, 91. *whose bosom was my c., my chief end,* IV, 12, 27.

Crown-imperial, Fritillaria imperialis: Wint. IV, 4, 126.

Crudy, raw: *foolish and dull and c. vapours,* H4B IV, 3, 106.

Cruel, adj. 1) hardhearted, savage: Ven. 624. Lucr. 1460. Sonn. 60, 14. 63, 10. 129, 4. 131, 2. 133, 5. 140, 1. Pilgr. 269. Meas. II, 4, 109. III, 2, 281. V, 207. Mids. II, 2, 150. Merch. III, 2, 318. IV, 1, 217. As IV, 3, 31. H6A III, 3, 46. H6C I, 3, 17. R3 II, 1, 105. Lr. II, 4, 7 etc. etc. Substantively: *O c.!* Sonn. 149, 1. Compar. *crueller:* Cor. V, 2, 71. Superl. *cruellest:* Tw. I, 5, 259. — Followed by *to:* Sonn. 1, 8. Cymb. V, 5, 32. 33. By *with:* Rom. I, 1, 27.

2) hard, painful: *O c. speeding,* Pilgr. 269. *a c. fever,* Meas. IV, 3, 74. *with c. pain,* Mids. V, 80. *c. death,* I, 2, 12. Cor. V, 2, 71. *you have seen c. proof of this man's strength,* As I, 2, 184 etc.

Cruel, subst. cruel being: *all —s else subscribe,* Lr. III, 7, 65 (cf. Sonn. 149, 1).

Cruel-hearted: Gentl. II, 3, 10.

Cruelly, 1) in a barbarous, savage manner: Lucr. Arg. 2. Tp. V, 71. All's V, 2, 29. Tim. III, 5, 9.

2) extremely: *I love thee c.* H5 V, 2, 216.

Cruelty, inhumanity, savageness: Mids. III, 2, 59. Merch. III, 4, 21 (Q1 *misery*). IV, 1, 21. 64. As IV, 3, 38. Tw. III, 2, 69. Wint. II, 3, 191. H4A IV, 3, 45. H6B I, 3, 135. IV, 1, 132. V, 2, 60. H8 V, 3, 76. Cor. IV, 5, 80. Mcb. I, 5, 44. IV, 2, 71. Oth. V, 2, 333. Ant. V, 2, 129. Followed by *to: to brother born a household c.* H4B IV, 1, 95. — Abstr. pro concr.: *farewell, fair c.* Tw. I, 5, 307. *get thee to yond same sovereign c.* II, 4, 83.

Crum, subst. the soft part of bread: *rub your chain with —s,* Tw. II, 3, 129.* *he that keeps nor crust nor c.* Lr. I, 4, 217.

Crumble, to fall into pieces: *my bowels c. up to dust,* John V, 7, 31.

Crupper, the strap of leather reaching from the saddle to the tail of the horse: Err. I, 2, 56. Shr. III, 2, 61. IV, 1, 84.

Crusado, see *Cruzado.*

Crush, vb. 1) to press, to squeeze: *you c. me, let me go,* Ven. 611. *c. this herb into Lysander's eye,* Mids. III, 2, 366. *crowd us and c. us to this monstrous form,* H4B IV, 2, 34. *a man into whom nature hath so crowded humours that his valour is —ed into folly,* Troil. I, 2, 23. *c. him together rather than unfold his measure duly,* Cymb. I, 1, 26.

2) to force, to strain: *to c. our old limbs in ungentle steel,* H4A V, 1, 13 (*in* = into). *this simulation is not as the former: and yet, to c. this a little, it would bow to me,* Tw. II, 5, 152. *that is but a —ed necessity,* H5 I, 2, 175 (= forced, strained).*

3) to destroy by pressing or striking, to bruize, to break: *the iron bit he —eth 'tween his teeth,* Ven. 269. *with time's injurious hand —ed and o'erworn,* Sonn. 63, 2. *now thou —est the snake,* LLL V, 1, 146. Wint. IV, 4, 489. H5 III, 7, 155. R3 V, 3, 111 (*c. down*). Cor. I, 10, 14. Absolutely: Mids. V, 292. Cor. II, 3, 211. R2 V, 5, 34 (*—ing penury*).

4) to overwhelm, to destroy: *who cannot be —ed with a plot?* All's IV, 3, 360. *we did our main opinion c. in taint of our best man,* Troil. I, 3, 373.

5) to drink, to crack: *come and c. a cup of wine,* Rom. I, 2, 86.

Crust, subst., rind, incrustation: *with vile and loathsome c.* Hml. I, 5, 72. = the outer hard part of bread: Gentl. III, 1, 346. R3 II, 4, 28. Lr. I, 4, 217.

Crust, vb. to incrust, to cover with a rind: *of man and beast the infinite malady c. you quite o'er,* Tim. III, 6, 109.

Crusty, hard, surly: *thou c. batch of nature,* Troil. V, 1, 5.

Crutch, subst. a support used by old people and invalids: Ado II, 1, 373. Wint. I, 1, 44. 50. H4B I, 1, 145. H6B III, 1, 189. H6C III, 2, 35. R3 II, 2, 58. H8 I, 1, 172. Troil. V, 3, 60. Cor. I, 1, 246. Rom. I, 1, 83. Tim. IV, 1, 14.

Figuratively, = old age: *gives the c. the cradle's infancy,* LLL IV, 3, 245. *to have turned my leaping-time into a c.* Cymb. IV, 2, 200.

Cruzado, name of a Portuguese coin: *lost my purse full of —es,* Oth. III, 4, 26.

Cry, subst. 1) clamour: *the c. did knock against*

my heart, Tp. I, 2, 8. *the most piteous c. of the poor souls,* Wint. III, 3, 91. *what suppliant makes this eager c.* R2 V, 3, 75. *the c. of women,* Mcb. V, 5, 8. Plural *cries:* Lucr. 445. 1459. H5 II, 4, 106. H6B V, 2, 4. R3 I, 2, 52. 1, 4, 60. II, 2, 61. Cor. II, 2, 114. Tit. II, 3, 102. Lr. II, 4, 43. Per. II, 1, 22. *Hue and c.,* see *Hue.*

2) exclamation: *the c. of Talbot,* H6A II, 1, 79.

3) report: *the c. goes that you shall marry her,* Oth. IV, 1, 127. *the c. went once on thee,* Troil. III, 3, 184 (i. e. thou wast once in men's mouths).

4) barking, howling: *ceasing their clamorous c.* Ven. 693. 870. 885. *every region near seemed all one mutual c.* Mids. IV, 1, 122. Plural: *owls' and wolves death-boding cries,* Lucr. 165.

5) a pack of hounds: *a c. more tuneable was never holla'd to,* Mids. IV, 1, 128. *you common c. of curs,* Cor. III, 3, 120. *you and your c.* IV, 6, 148. *not like a hound that hunts, but one that fills up the c.* Oth. II, 3, 370.

Hence = company in general: *a fellowship in a c. of players,* Hml. III, 2, 289.

Cry, vb. 1) to utter a loud voice: *I did begin to start and c.* Lucr. 1639. *when screech-owls c.* H6B I, 4, 21. Tp. I, 2, 32. V, 90. Wiv. I, 1, 309. Err. IV, 2, 27. Ado V, 1, 32. John V, 2, 144. H6B V, 1, 154. H6C II, 1, 16. V, 6, 45. Mcb. II, 2, 16 etc. etc. *c. cock-a-diddle-dow,* Tp. I, 2, 386. *c. baa,* Gentl. I, 1, 98. *though he c. cuckoo,* Mids. III, 1, 139. *c. sleep to death,* Lr. II, 4, 120.

2) to weep, to lament: *thy —ing self,* Tp. I, 2, 132. *to c. to the sea that roared to us,* 149. Gentl. II, 3, 8. Wiv. III, 1, 22. Err. II, 1, 35. III, 1, 59. As II, 4, 5. Wint. III, 3, 32. Troil. II, 2, 97. 99. 111 etc. *c. it o'er again,* Tp. I, 2, 134. *c. myself awake,* Cymb. III, 4, 46.

3) to exclaim, to call out: *cried 'Hell is empty,'* Tp. I, 2, 214. *I shaked you and cried,* II, 1, 319. IV, 1, 45. Gentl. IV, 4, 82. Mcb. II, 2, 23. 27. 40. 44 etc. etc. *To c. aim,* see *Aim.* *I c. bail,* Meas. III, 2, 44. *to c. amen to that,* H5 V, 2, 21. *very envy cried fame and honour on him,* Tw. V, 62. *the affair cries haste,* Oth. I, 3, 277. *all the country cried hate upon him,* H4B IV, 1, 137. *c. havock,* see *Havock.* *or both yourself and me c. lost,* Wint. I, 2, 411. *I'll c. a match,* Rom. II, 4, 74. *c. shame upon her,* Rom. I, 1, 123. *c. woe,* R3 III, 3, 7. Lr. III, 2, 33. *monarchs' hands that let not bounty fall where want cries some, but where excess begs all,* Compl. 42 (i. e. where want cries, 'some bounty!'). Singular passage: *whose judgements in such matters cried in the top of mine,* Hml. II, 2, 459, i. e. whose judgements were more audible, better listened to than mine; cf. *my griefs c. louder than advertisement,* Ado V, 1, 32. — Followed by *to: would c. to a sailor 'Go hang,'* Tp. II, 2, 53. *cries 'cuckold' to my father,* Hml. IV, 5, 118. — Dative without *to: I c. you mercy,* Wiv. III, 5, 27 (= I beg your pardon). Ado I, 2, 26. Meas. IV, 1, 10. H6A V, 3, 109. *I c. your worships' mercy,* Mids. III, 1, 182. *O c. you mercy,* Gentl. V, 4, 94 (cf. *Mercy*). *I c. you gentle pardon,* Oth. V, 1, 93. *and c. these summoners grace,* Lr. III, 2, 59. 4, 176.

4) to proclaim; a) intr. to make proclamation: *when time shall serve, let but the herald c., and I'll appear,* Lr. V, 1, 48. b) trans.: *that fame may c. you loud,* All's II, 1, 17. *this masque was cried incomparable,*

H8 I, 1, 27. *c. it about the streets,* Caes. III, 1, 79. *hast thou cried her through the market? I have cried her almost to the number of her hairs,* Per. IV, 2, 99.

5) Followed by prepositions; a) by *against,* = to exclaim against, to accuse vehemently: *for then my guiltless blood must c. against them,* H8 II, 1, 68. *what is the matter that you c. against the noble senate?* Cor. I, 1, 190. cf. Cymb. V, 4, 88.

b) by *for,* = to demand eagerly: *for restful death I c.* Sonn. 66, 1. *he cries for you,* Err. V, 182. *—ing for a surgeon,* H5 IV, 1, 145. H6A V, 4, 53. H6B III, 2, 378. H8 II, 1, 90. Mcb. I, 2, 42.

The same sense expressed by an infinitive: *her neglected child cries to catch her,* Sonn. 143, 6. *when I waked, I cried to dream again,* Tp. III, 2, 152. *his means of death, his obscure funeral ... c. to be heard,* Hml. IV, 5, 216. *oft our displeasures, to ourselves unjust, destroy our friends and after weep their dust: our own love waking cries to see what's done,* All's V, 3, 65 *(what's done* = what is destroyed; cf. *Do).*

c) by *to,* = to call upon, to implore: *how he cried to me for help,* Wint. III, 3, 97. *he cried to me; I saw him prisoner,* Cor. I, 9, 84. *my uses c. to me,* Tim. II, 1, 20. *we poor ghosts will c. to the shining synod of the rest against thy deity,* Cymb. V, 4, 88.

d) by *on* or *upon,* = to name with emotion, to utter the cry of: *and cried in fainting upon Rosalind,* As IV, 3, 150. *some —ing for a surgeon, some upon their wives left poor behind them, some upon the debts they owe, some upon their children rawly left,* H5 IV, 1, 145. *no longer on Saint Denis will we c.* H6A I, 6, 28. *their souls came to my tent and cried on victory,* R3 V, 3, 231. *his mangled Myrmidons that come to him, —ing on Hector,* Troil. V, 5, 35. *and then on Romeo cries, and then down falls again,* Rom. III, 3, 101. *this quarry cries on havock,* Hml. V, 2, 375. *whose noise is this that cries on murder?* Oth. V, 1, 48. — Used of hounds, = to yelp on a scent: *how cheerfully on the false trail they c.! O, this is counter, you false Danish dogs,* Hml. IV, 5, 109. *he cried upon it at the merest loss,* Shr. Ind. 1, 23. *Sowter will c. upon it for all this, though it be as rank as a fox,* Tw. II, 5, 135. cf. Wiv. IV, 2, 208.

6) Joined with adverbs; a) with *down,* = to decry, to depreciate, to overwhelm with cries: *and from a mouth of honour quite c. down this Ipswich fellow's insolence,* H8 I, 1, 137.

b) with *up,* = to extol: *what worst, as oft is cried up for our best act,* H8 I, 2, 84.

c) with *out* = to cry; *α)* to utter a loud voice, to clamour: *your drums, being beaten, will c. out, and so shall you, being beaten,* John V, 2, 166. *men, wives and children stare, c. out and run,* Caes. III, 1, 97. *eyasses that c. out on the top of question,* Hml. II, 2, 355. *others whom the rigour of our state forced to c. out,* Lr. V, 1, 23. Used of a woman in labour: *is she —ing out?* H8 V, 1, 67.

β) to weep, to lament: *how I cried out then,* Tp. I, 2, 133. *hark, how Troy roars, how Hecuba cries out!* Troil. V, 3, 83.

γ) to exclaim, to call out: *a space whose every cubit seems to c. out 'How shall that Claribel etc.* Tp. II, 1, 258. Meas. V, 412. Err. V, 245. Tw. I, 5, 293. H5 II, 3, 19. H6A I, 1, 128. Troil. II, 2, 13. Caes. III, 1, 80. Lr. IV, 6, 76. Ant. III, 4, 17.

δ) to make proclamation: *wisdom cries out in the streets,* H4A I, 2, 99. *my fate cries out and makes each petty artery as hardy ...,* Hml. I, 4, 81. Transitively: *if you do love Rosalind so near the heart as your gesture cries it out,* As V, 2, 69. *art thou a man? thy form cries out thou art,* Rom. III, 3, 109.

ε) Followed by prepositions; by *against: whereof the execution did c. out against the nonperformance,* Wint. I, 2, 260. — By *for: the poor, lame, blind, halt, creep, c. out for thee,* Lucr. 902. H6A IV, 4, 15. H6B III, 2, 395. H6C V, 2, 41. Oth. II, 3, 226. Cymb. IV, 2, 372. — By *of,* = to cry on: *they say he cried out of sack and of women,* H5 II, 3, 29. *giddy censure will then c. out of Marcius 'O, if he had borne the business!'* Cor. I, 1, 273. — By *on: who cries out on pride, that can therein tax any private party,* As II, 7, 70. *where honourable rescue and defence cries out upon the name of Salisbury,* John V, 2, 19. *cries out upon abuses,* H4A IV, 3, 81. *that same word* (necessity) *even now cries out on us,* H4B III, 1, 94. Used of hounds being on a scent: *if I c. out thus upon no trail, never trust me when I open again,* Wiv. IV, 2, 208.

Crystal, subst. crystal glass, f i n e g l a s s: *her eyes and tears ... both —s, where they viewed each other's sorrow,* Ven. 963. Compl. 37. *all his senses were locked in his eye, as jewels in c.* LLL II, 243. *to what shall I compare thine eyne? c. is muddy,* Mids. III, 2, 139. — Used for the eyes by Pistol: *go, clear thy —s,* H5 II, 3, 56.

Crystal, adj. 1) m a d e o f c r y s t a l: *through c. walls each little mote will peep,* Lucr. 1251.

2) b r i g h t: *the more fair and c. is the sky,* R2 I, 1, 41. *comets, brandish your c. tresses in the sky,* H6A I, 1, 3. *thy c. gate ope,* Cymb. V, 4, 81. Used of eyes: Ven. 633. Sonn. 46, 6. Gentl. II, 4, 89. LLL IV, 3, 142. Rom. I, 2, 101. Of tears: Ven. 491. 957. Compl. 286. John II, 171.

Crystal-button, having buttons of crystal: H4A II, 4, 78 (in the description of an inn-keeper).

Crystalline, b r i g h t: *mount, eagle, to my palace c.* Cymb. V, 4, 113.

Cub, subst. a w h e l p: *pluck the young sucking —s from the she-bear,* Merch. II, 1, 29. *O thou dissembling c.* Tw. V, 167.

Cubbert or **Cubbord,** subst., in *Court-cupboard,* q.v.

Cubbord, vb. (M. Edd. *cupboard*), vb. t o h o a r d: *idle and unactive, still —ing the viand,* Cor. I, 1, 103.

Cub-drawn, sucked by cubs and made hungry by it: *this night, wherein the c. bear would couch,* Lr. III, 1, 12.

Cubiculo, a p a r t m e n t: Tw. III, 2, 56; see Sh.'s Latin in the Appendix.

Cubit, a measure of eighteen i n c h e s: *a space whose every c. seems to cry out,* Tp. II, 1, 257.

Cuckold, subst. a man whose wife is false to his bed: Wiv. II, 2, 293. 298. 313. 328. III, 5, 106. V, 5, 113. Meas. V, 523. Ado II, 1, 46. LLL V, 1, 73. Merch. V, 265. 281. All's I, 3, 49. II, 2, 26. Tw. I, 5, 56. Wint. I, 2, 191. 269. H4A II, 4, 371. H8 V, 4, 25. Troil. II, 3, 78. III, 3, 64. IV, 1, 61. V, 1, 61. V, 7, 9. Cor. IV, 5, 244. Hml. IV, 5, 118. Oth. III, 3, 167. IV, 3, 76. Ant. I, 2, 70. 81. Cymb. II, 4, 146.

Cuckold, vb. to make a cuckold: Wiv. III, 5, 140. Oth. I, 3, 375. IV, 1, 211.

Cuckoldly, having a false wife: *poor c. knave,* Wiv. II, 2, 281. 286. V, 5, 114. As III, 2, 87.

Cuckold-mad, interpretation of h o r n - m a d: Err. II, 1, 58.

Cuckold-maker, one who makes another a cuckold: H8 V, 4, 25. Troil. V, 7, 9.

Cuckoo, the bird C u c u l u s : *—s hatch in sparrows' nests,* Lucr. 849. LLL V, 2, 896. Merch. V, 112. H4A III, 2, 75. *as that ungentle gull, the —'s bird, useth the sparrow,* V, 1, 60. *the hedge-sparrow fed the c. so long, that it's had it head bit off by it young,* Lr. I, 4, 235. *the c. builds not for himself,* Ant. II, 6, 28. Used as a term of contempt: *o' horseback, ye c., but afoot he will not budge a foot,* H4A II, 4, 387. — Its note prognosticating the destiny of cuckoldom: LLL V, 2, 908 etc. Mids. III, 1, 134. 139. All's I, 3, 67.

Cuckoo-bird, the same: *take heed, ere summer comes or —s do sing,* Wiv. II, 1, 127.

Cuckoo-bud, the b u d o f the cowslip: *—s of yellow hue,* LLL V, 2, 906 (or = buttercup?).*

Cuckoo-flower, c o w s l i p : Lr.IV,4,4 (doubtful).

Cudgel, subst. a s t i c k t o s t r i k e w i t h : Wiv. II, 2, 292. IV, 2, 91. 216. V, 5, 117. Merch. II, 2, 71. H5 V, 1, 54. 69. 81. H8 V, 4, 19. Cor. IV, 5, 156.

Cudgel, vb. t o b e a t w i t h a s t i c k : Wiv. IV, 5, 99. Ado V, 4, 115. Tw. II, 5, 145. John II, 464. V, 2, 138. H4A III, 3, 100. 123. 159. H5 V, 1, 90. Troil. III, 3, 249. Oth. II, 3, 372. *c. thy brains no more about it,* Hml. V, 1, 63 (the clown's speech; cf. *Beat.*)

Cudgelled, c a u s e d b y a c u d g e l : *and patches will I get unto these c. scars,* H5 V, 1, 93.

Cue, the c a t c h - w o r d : Wiv. III, 3, 39. Ado II, 1, 316. Mids. III, 1, 78. 102. IV, 1, 205. V, 186. R3 III, 4, 27. Lr. I, 2, 147. Hence = sign, hint, motive: *the clock gives me my c.* Wiv. III, 2, 46. *now we speak upon our c.* H5 III, 6, 130. *what would he do, had he the motive and the c. for passion that I have?* Hml. II, 2, 587. *were it my c. to fight,* Oth. I, 2, 83.

Cuff, subst. 1) a b l o w w i t h t h e f i s t : Shr. III, 2, 165. IV, 1, 67. Hml. II, 2, 373.

2) the f o l d a t t h e e n d o f a s l e e v e : *with ruffs and —s,* Shr. IV, 3, 56.

Cuff, vb., t o s t r i k e w i t h t h e f i s t : Shr. II, 221. Tw. III, 4, 428. H6A I, 3, 48.

Cuisses (O. Edd. *cushes*) armour for the thighs: H4A IV, 1, 105.

Cull, to p i c k o u t , t o s e l e c t f r o m m a n y : LLL V, 3, 234. V, 1, 98. John II, 40. H5 III Chor. 24. H6C III, 1, 4. Troil. II, 3, 274. Rom. IV, 3, 7. V, 1, 40. Followed by *from: —ed these fiery spirits from the world,* John V, 2, 114. H4B IV, 5, 75. Tit. IV, 1, 44. By *out of: ye familiar spirits that are —ed out of the powerful regions under earth,* H6A V, 3, 10. Joined with *forth: Fortune shall c. forth out of one side her happy minion,* John II, 391. *c. the infected forth,* Tim. V, 4, 43. With *out: do you now c. out a holiday?* Caes. I, 1, 54.

Cullion, mean wretch: Shr. IV, 2, 20. H5 III, 2, 22. H6B I, 3, 43.

Cullionly, base, wretched: Lr. II, 2, 36.

Culpable, guilty: *he be approved in practice c.* H6B III, 2, 22.

Culter (M. Edd. *coulter*), plough-iron: H5 V, 2, 46.

Culverin, a sort of cannon: H4A II, 3, 56.

Cumber, to l o a d , t o v e x : *let it not c. your better remembrance,* Tim. III, 6, 52. *civil strife shall c. all the parts of Italy,* Caes. III, 1, 264.

Cumberland, English county: H6B V, 2, 1. 6. Mcb. I, 4, 39. 48.

Cunning, subst. 1) k n o w l e d g e , f o r e - t h o u g h t : *as if that luck, in very spite of c.,* bade him win all, Troil. V, 5, 41. *shame that they wanted c. in excess hath broke their hearts,* Tim. V, 4, 28. *if he be not one that truly loves you, that errs in ignorance and not in c.* Oth. III, 3, 49.

2) p o w e r : *is this thy c., thou deceitful dame?* H6A II, 1, 50. *we have been guided by thee hitherto and of thy c. had no diffidence,* III, 3, 10. *would ye not think his* (Saint Alban's) *c. to be great, that could restore this cripple to his legs again?* H6B II, 1, 132. *fortune's blows when most struck home, being gentle wounded craves a noble c.* Cor. IV, 1, 9.

3) a r t , s k i l l : *yet eyes this c. want to grace their art: they draw but what they see, know not the heart,* Sonn. 24, 13. *a sorcerer, that by his c. hath cheated me of the island,* Tp. III, 2, 49. *if I read it not truly, my ancient skill beguiles me; but in the boldness of my c. I will lay my self in hazard,* Meas. IV, 2, 165. *some sport wherein your c. can assist me much,* Shr. Ind. 1, 92. *I have no c. in protestation,* H5 V, 2, 150. *I'll prove more true than those that have more c. to be strange,* Rom. II, 2, 101. *an excellent play, set down with as much modesty as c.* Hml. II, 2, 461. *guilty creatures sitting at a play have by the very c. of the scene been struck so to the soul,* 619. *we'll make a solemn wager on your —s,* IV, 7, 156. *virtue and c. were endowments greater than nobleness and riches,* Per. III, 2, 27. *in our sports my better c. faints under his chance,* Ant. III, 3, 34. *try thy c.* III, 12, 31.

Hence = profession: *shame not these woods by putting on the c. of a carper,* Tim. IV, 3, 208.

4) c r a f t : *my c. shall not shame me,* Ado II, 2, 56. *with c. hast thou filched my daughter's heart,* Mids. I, 1, 36. *a child shall get a sire, if I fail not of my c.* Shr. II, 413. *the c. of her passion invites me in this churlish messenger,* Tw. II, 2, 23. *to force that on you in a shameful c., which you knew none of yours,* III, 1, 127. *his false c. taught him to face me out of his acquaintance,* V, 1, 85. *it was not brought me; there's the c. of it,* Lr. I, 2, 64. H8 II, 4, 107. Lr. III, 7, 49.

5) d i s s i m u l a t i o n , f a l s e n e s s : *what needest thou wound with c. when thy might is more than my o'erpressed defence can bide?* Sonn. 139, 7. *hence, bashful c.!* Tp. III, 1, 81. *you do advance your c. more and more,* Mids. III, 2, 128. *you may think my love is crafty love and call it c.,* John IV, 1, 54. *while some with c. gild their copper crowns, with truth and plainness I do wear mine bare,* Troil.IV,4,107. *deaths put on by c. and forced cause,* Hml. V, 2, 394. *time shall unfold what plaited c. hides,* Lr. I, 1, 283. *in c. I must draw my sword upon you,* II, 1, 31. *there is division, although as yet the face of it be covered with mutual c.* III, 1, 21. *this cannot be c. in her,* Ant. I, 2, 155. *O c., how I got it!* Cymb. V, 5, 205.

Cunning, adj. 1) k n o w i n g , w e l l i n s t r u c t e d : *to make the c. hounds mistake their smell,* Ven. 686. *this learned constable is too c. to be understood,* Ado V, 1, 234. *to c. men* (as schoolmasters) *I will be very kind,* Shr. I, 1, 97. *to get her c. schoolmasters,* 192. *c. in music and the mathematics,* II, 56. *c. in Greek,*

81. *whose red and white nature's own sweet and c. hand laid on,* Tw. I, 5, 258. *so c. in fence,* III, 4, 312. *wherein c. but in craft?* H4A II, 4, 503. *a c. man did calculate my birth,* H6B IV, 1, 34. *c. cooks,* Rom. IV, 2, 2. *this bodiless creation ecstasy is very c. in,* Hml. III, 4, 139.

2) powerful: *Margery Jourdain, the c. witch,* H6B I, 2, 75. *your silence, c. in dumbness, from my weakness draws my very soul of counsel,* Troil. III, 2, 140.

3) skilful: *I will so plead that you shall say my c. drift excels,* Gentl. IV, 2, 83. *be c. in the working this,* Ado II, 2, 53. *to sell a bargain well is as c. as fast and loose,* LLL III, 103. *so c. and so young is wonderful,* R3 III, 1, 135.

4) made or done or devised with skill, artful: *like a c. instrument cased up,* R2 I, 3, 163. *thou —est pattern of excelling nature,* Oth. V, 2, 11 (Qq *cunning*). *what c. match have you made with this jest of the drawer,* H4A II, 4, 101. *I'll find some c. practice,* Tit. V, 2, 77. *if there be any c. cruelty that can torment him,* Oth. V, 2, 333.

5) crafty: *which c. love did wittily prevent,* Ven. 471. *O c. love, with tears thou keepest me blind,* Sonn. 148, 13. *the c. manner of our flight,* Gentl. II, 4, 180. *O c. enemy,* Meas. II, 2, 180. III, 1, 95. *whatsoever c. fiend it was,* H5 II, 2, 111. *I am too courtly and thou art too c.* Troil. III, 1, 30. H8 I, 1, 168. Oth. I, 3, 102.

6) dexterous and trickish in dissembling: *to cloak offences with a c. brow,* Lucr. 749. *what authority and show of truth can c. sin cover itself withal,* Ado IV, 1, 37. *the seeming truth which c. times put on to entrap the wisest,* Merch. III, 2, 100. *trust not those c. waters of his eyes,* John IV, 3, 107. *most c. in my patience,* Oth. IV, 1, 91. *that c. whore of Venice,* IV, 2, 89. *she is c. past man's thought,* Ant. I, 2, 150.

Cunningly, dexterously, craftily: Gentl. III, 1, 44. H6A IV, 1, 110. Troil. IV, 4, 93. Tit. II, 3, 6.

Cup, subst. 1) a sort of drinking-vessel: Sonn. 114, 12. Wiv. II, 2, 77. Err. V, 270. As V, 1, 46. Shr. Ind. 2, 2. Wint. I, 2, 316. II, 1, 39. H4A I, 2, 8. II, 2, 49. II, 4, 129. H5 IV, 3, 55. H6B II, 3, 60. IV, 1, 56. R3 I, 4, 166. Cor. II, 1, 52. Rom. I, 2, 86. III, 1, 9. V, 3, 161. Caes. IV, 3, 161. Hml. V, 2, 283. Oth. II, 3, 38. 40. Ant. II, 7, 60. IV, 2, 21. Cymb. V, 3, 71 etc. *the sour c. of prosperity,* LLL I, 1, 315. *fill the c. of alteration with divers liquors,* H4B III, 1, 52. *all foes shall taste the c. of their deservings,* Lr. V, 3, 304. *plenty's c.* Per. I, 4, 52. *this would drink deep; 'twould drink the c. and all,* H5 I, 1, 20 (i. e. all the prerogatives of the church).

2) a sort of plate, probably a soup-plate: *there, take it to you, trenchers, —s and all,* Shr. IV, 1, 168. *his viands sparkling in a golden c.* H6C IV, 5, 52.

3) the cupula of an acorn: Mids. II, 1, 31.

Cup, vb. to supply with full cups: *c. us till the world go round,* Ant. II, 7, 124.

Cup-bearer, he who conveys wine to others: Wint. I, 2, 313. 345.

Cupboard, see *Cubbord.*

Cupid, the God of love: Ven. 581. Sonn. 153, 1. 14. Wiv. II, 2, 141. V, 5, 32. Ado I, 1, 40. 186.

256. 273. II, 1, 400. III, 1, 22. 106. III, 2, 11. LLL I, 2, 67. 181. II, 254. III, 182. 204. IV, 3, 24. 58. 366. V, 2, 9. 87. Mids. I, 1, 169. 235. II, 1, 157. 161. 165. III, 2, 103. 440. IV, 1, 78. Merch. II, 6, 38. II, 9, 100. As I, 3, 1. IV, 1, 48. All's I, 1, 189. III, 2, 16. Troil. III, 1, 120. III, 2, 15. 81. III, 3, 222. Rom. I, 1, 215. I, 4, 4. 17. II, 1, 13. II, 5, 8. Lr. IV, 6, 141. Oth. I, 3, 270. Cymb. III, 2, 39. Per. I, 1, 38. Plur. *—s:* Ant. II, 2, 207. Cymb. II, 4, 89.

Cur, term of contempt for a dog: Gentl. II, 3, 10. IV, 4, 2. 11. 52. Wiv. I, 1, 97. Merch. I, 3, 119. 123. As I, 3, 5. Shr. Ind. 1, 17. R2 II, 2, 139. H6A IV, 2, 47. H6B III, 1, 18. V, 1, 146. H6C I, 4, 56. Troil. I, 3, 391. Cor. III, 3, 120. Caes. III, 1, 46. V, 1, 43. Lr. I, 4, 89 etc. Designating a particular species of dogs: *as hounds and greyhounds, mongrels, spaniels, —s,* Mcb. III, 1, 93.

Used as a term of reproach for men: Tp. I, 1, 46. Mids. III, 2, 65. Merch. III, 3, 18. H5 II, 1, 44. R3 IV, 4, 56. Troil. II, 1, 44. Cor. V, 6, 107 etc.

Curan, name in Lr. II, 1, 1.

Curate, a parish priest: LLL V, 1, 120. V, 2, 538. Tw. IV, 2, 3. 25.

Curb, subst. bridle: Ven. 285. Meas. I, 3, 20. As III, 3, 81. H4A I, 2, 68. H4B IV, 4, 62. Cor. I, 1, 72. Tim. IV, 3, 446.

Curb, vb. 1) to bridle, to refrain: *no exclamation can c. his heat,* Lucr. 706. *we must c. it* (our blood) Compl. 163. *so is the will of a living daughter —ed by the will of a dead father,* Merch. I, 2, 26. *and thus I'll c. her mad and headstrong humour,* Shr. IV, 1, 212. *in the —ed time,* All's II, 4, 46 (i. e. in the time of restraint and abstinence). *Harry from —ed licence plucks the muzzle of restraint,* H4B IV, 5, 131. *to c. those raging appetites,* Troil. II, 2, 181. *to c. the will of the nobility,* Cor. III, 1, 39. *—ing his lavish spirit,* Mcb. I, 2, 57. *my sanctity will to my sense bend no licentious ear, but c. it,* Per. V, 3, 31. *— To c. from =* to restrain from: *the fair reverence of your highness —s me from giving reins and spurs to my free speech,* R2 I, 1, 54. *you are —ed from that enlargement,* Cymb. II, 3, 125. *To c. of,* in the same sense: *c. the cruel devil of his will,* Merch. IV, 1, 217. *and —s himself even of his natural scope when you come cross his humour,* H4A III, 1, 171.

2) intr. to bow or bend (Fr. *courber*): *virtue itself of vice must pardon beg, yea, c. and woo for leave to do him good,* Hml. III, 4, 155.

Curd, vb. to cause to coagulate: *does it c. thy blood to say I am thy mother?* All's I, 3, 155. *and c. the thin and wholesome blood,* Hml. I, 5, 69.

Curds, coagulated milk: Wint. IV, 4, 161. H6C II, 5, 47. Tit. IV, 2, 179.

Curdy, vb. to congeal: *chaste as the icicle that's —ied by the frost from purest snow,* Cor. V, 3, 66.

Cure, subst. healing, remedy: Ven. 505. Lucr. 732. 1821. Sonn. 153, 8. 13. 154, 13. Meas. III, 1, 245. Ado IV, 1, 254. All's I, 3, 254. II, 1, 163. John II, 546. III, 4, 105. R2 II, 1, 98. H5 IV, 1, 269. H8 I, 4, 33. II, 2, 76. Rom. I, 1, 161. IV, 5, 65. Tim. III, 3, 12. Mcb. IV, 3, 142. Lr. III, 6, 107 (*stand in hard c.*). Oth. II, 1, 51 (*stand in bold c.*).* Cymb. III, 5, 37. Per. III, 2, 33. *Past c. =* incurable: All's II, 1, 161. John IV, 2, 86. Rom. IV, 1, 45. *past her c.,* Tp. V, 141. *past c. of the thing you wot of,* Meas. II,

1, 115. *past c. of the fives,* Shr. III, 2, 54. *past c. I am, now reason is past care,* Sonn. 147, 9. *past c. is still past care,* LLL V, 2, 28. *care is no c.* H6A III, 3, 3.

Cure, vb. 1) trans. to **heal**: Ven. 372. Lucr. 861. 1581. Sonn. 34, 8. 111, 14. 118, 12. Pilgr. 36. Tp. I, 2, 106. V, 59. Meas. III, 2, 107. 236. Ado I, 1, 90. LLL IV, 3, 67. As III, 2, 423. 426. 442. 446. 447. All's I, 3, 235. Wint. I, 2, 170. John III, 1, 277. III, 4, 112. R2 I, 1, 172. H6B V, 1, 101. H6C II, 2, 122. R3 II, 2, 103. IV, 4, 516. H8 II, 4, 101. III, 1, 158. III, 2, 380. IV, 2, 122. Troil. III, 2, 78. Cor. III, 1, 235. 297. Tim. IV, 3, 227. Mcb. IV, 3, 152. 215. Hml. IV, 3. 69. Lr. IV, 6, 34. IV, 7, 15. 79 (Ff *killed*). Oth. II, 1, 311. Ant. IV, 14, 78. Cymb. II, 3, 109. V, 4, 6. *To c. a p. of an evil:* All's II, 1, 71. Wint. I, 2, 296. H4B IV, 2, 41. Mcb. V, 3, 39. Oth. II, 3, 149.

2) intr. to **heal**: *one desparate grief —s with another's languish,* Rom. I, 2, 49 (cf. *Unrecuring*).

Cureless, incurable: *my c. crime,* Lucr. 772. *fall to c. ruin,* Merch. IV, 1, 142 (Ff *endless*). *c. are my wounds,* H6C II, 6, 23.

Curer, healer, physician: Wiv. II, 3, 40. Troil. V, 1, 55.

Curfew, the ringing of a bell at night, as a signal to retire to rest: *ye elves ... that rejoice to hear the solemn c.* Tp. V, 40. *since the c. rung,* Meas. IV, 2, 78. *he begins at c. and walks till the first cock,* Lr. III, 4, 121. — *C. bell* = the bell ordinarily used for that purpose: *the second cock hath crowed, the c. bell hath rung, 'tis three o' clock,* Rom. IV, 4, 4.

Curio, name in Tw. I, 1, 16.

Curiosity, nicety, exactness, scrupulousness: *when thou wast in thy gilt and thy perfume, they mocked thee for too much c.* Tim. IV, 3, 303. *qualities are so weighed, that c. in neither can make choice of either's moiety,* Lr. I, 1, 6. *wherefore should I ... permit the c. of nations to deprive me,* I, 2, 4. *which I have rather blamed as mine own jealous c. than as a very pretence and purpose of unkindness,* I, 4, 75.

Curious, 1) careful, accurate, scrupulous: *if my slight Muse do please these c. days,* Sonn. 38, 13. *letters with sleided silk feat and affectedly enswathed, and sealed to c. secrecy,* Compl. 49. *for c. I cannot be with you, of whom I hear so well,* Shr. IV, 4, 36. *frank nature, rather c. than in haste, hath well composed thee,* All's I, 2, 20. *what care I what c. eye doth quote deformities?* Rom. I, 4, 31. *you shall not find, though you be therein c., the least cause for what you seem to fear,* Ant. III, 2, 35. *I am something c., to have them in safe stowage,* Cymb. I, 6, 191.

2) elegant, nice: *to cross the c. {worksmanship of nature,* Ven. 734. *his body couched in a c. bed,* H6C II, 5, 53. *mar a c. tale in telling it,* Lr. I, 4, 35. *he was lapped in a most c. mantle,* Cymb. V, 5, 361. *her face the book of praises, where is read nothing but c. pleasures,* Per. I, 1, 16. *those mothers who, to nousle up their babes, thought nought too c.* I, 4, 43.

3) requiring care, embarrassing: *I am so fraught with c. business that I leave out ceremony,* Wint. IV, 4, 525. *what too c. dreg espies my sweet lady in the fountain of our love?* Troil. III, 2, 70.

Curious-good, done with art and care, nice: *this is too c., this blunt and ill,* Lucr. 1300.

Curious-knotted, laid out in nice plots: *thy c. garden,* LLL I, 1, 249.

Curiously, carefully, nicely, minutely: *the which if I do not carve most c., say my knife's naught,* Ado V, 1, 157. *the sleeves c. cut,* Shr. IV, 3, 144. *that he might take a measure of his own judgements, wherein so c. he had set this counterfeit,* All's IV, 3, 39. *'twere to consider too c., to consider so,* Hml. V, 1, 227.

Curl, subst. a ringlet of hair; always used in the plural: Sonn. 12, 4. Compl. 85. All's I, 1, 105. Hml. III, 4, 56.

Curl, vb. 1) tr. to **form into ringlets**: *his —ed hair,* Lucr. 981. *a —ed pate,* H5 V, 2, 169. Lr. III, 4, 88. *the wealthy —ed darlings of our nation,* Oth. I, 2, 68. *the —ed Antony,* Ant. V, 2, 304. Used of clouds: *to ride on the —ed clouds,* Tp. I, 2, 192. Of waves: *—ing their monstrous heads,* H4B III, 1, 23. *swell the —ed waters,* Lr. III, 1, 6.

2) intr. to **form ringlets**: *it will not c. by nature,* Tw. I, 3, 105.

Curled-pate, having curled hair: *make c. ruffians bald,* Tim. IV, 3, 160.

Currance (F2.3.4 *current*) current, flow: *never came reformation in a flood, with such a heady c. scouring faults,* H5 I, 1, 34.

Currant, small dried grape: Wint. IV, 3, 40.

Current, subst. 1) the flowing, the progressive motion of water: *a river running from a fount with brinish c.,* Compl. 284. *this stream through muddy passages hath held his c.* R2 V, 3, 63. H5 I, 1, 34 (F1 *currance*). R3 II, 2, 68. Used of the sea: *on such a full sea are we now, and we must take the c. when it serves,* Caes. IV, 3, 223. *the Pontic sea, whose icy c. ...,* Oth. III, 3, 454. Figuratively: *enterprises of great pith and moment with this regard their —s turn awry,* Hml. III, 1, 87.

2) stream, river: *thus ebbs and flows the c. of her sorrow,* Lucr. 1569. *the c. that with gentle murmur slides,* Gentl. II, 7, 25 (masc. v. 28). Meas. III, 1, 251. John II, 335. 441. R2 III, 3, 108. H4A I, 3, 192. III, 1, 101. Cor. III, 1, 96. Tim. I, 1, 24. Oth. IV, 2, 59.

3) course: *to excuse the c. of thy cruelty,* Merch. IV, 1, 64. *and all the c. of a heady fight,* H4A II, 3, 58 (Qq *currents*). *in the corrupted —s of this world,* Hml. III, 3, 57.

Current, adj. 1) in general circulation, common: *speak 'pardon' as 'tis c. in our land,* R2 V, 3, 123.

2) generally received, of full value, sterling, having currency: *thy word is c. with him for my death,* R2 I, 3, 231. *let not his report come c. for an accusation,* H4A I, 3, 68. *it holds c. that I told you yesternight,* II, 1, 59 (i. e. it remains in force, proves to be true). *we must have bloody noses and cracked crowns, and pass them c. too,* II, 3, 97. *no soldier ... should go so general c. through the world,* IV, 1, 5. *the one you may do with sterling money, and the other with c. repentance,* H4B II, 1, 132. *thou canst make no excuse c. but to hang thyself,* R3 I, 2, 84. *your fire-new stamp of honour is scarce c.* I, 3, 256. *and yet go c. from suspicion,* II, 1, 94 (i. e. and yet are thought honest and free from suspicion). *to try if thou be c. gold indeed,* IV, 2, 9. *held c. music,* H8 I, 3, 47 (thought to be a good musician).

Currish, 1) becoming a dog: *she says your dog was a cur, and tells you c. thanks is good enough for such a present,* Gentl. IV, 4, 53. *Lucentio slipped me like his greyhound ... A good swift simile, but something c.* Shr. V, 2, 54.

2) malicious: *thy c. spirit governed a wolf,*
Merch. IV, 1, 133. *to change this c. Jew,* 292. *his c.
riddles sort not with this place,* H6C V, 5, 26.*

Curry, vb. intr. to curry favour, to seek favour
by flattery: *I would c. with Master Shallow that
no man could better command his servants,* H4B V,
1, 82.

Curse, subst. 1) malediction: *I give him —s,*
Mids. I, 1, 196; cf. Cymb. IV, 2, 313. *the c. never fell
upon our nation till now,* Merch. III, 1, 89. H6A V, 4,
86. H6B III, 2, 155. 310. H6C I, 4, 164. R3 I, 2,
69. 233. I, 3, 174 etc. etc.

2) great vexation, great drawback: *you
to your beauteous blessings add a c.* Sonn. 84, 13. *'tis
the c. in love, when women cannot love where they're
beloved,* Gentl. V, 4, 43. Wint. II, 3, 87. H6B IV, 10,
83 etc. Abstr. pro concr.: *what can happen to me above
this wretchedness? all your studies make me a c. like
this,* H8 III, 1, 124, i. e. so cursed and wretched a
being.

Curse, vb. 1) intr. to utter maledictions:
Tp. I, 2, 364. II, 2, 4. Err. IV, 2, 28. Ado II, 3, 154.
V, 1, 212. Mids. III, 2, 46. V, 184. H6A V, 3, 43.
H6B III, 2, 319. R3 I, 3, 319 etc. *—ing cries,* R3 I,
2, 52. *c. away a winter's night,* H6B III, 2, 335. *did
c. against the Volsces,* Cor. III, 1, 9.

2) tr. to load with a malediction, to wish evil
to: Ven. 945. Lucr. 209. 970. 996. Sonn. 29, 4.
Tp. I, 2, 339. V, 179. Gentl. III, 1, 146. Wiv. IV, 2,
24. Meas. III, 1, 31. Merch. I, 3, 52. John III, 1, 173
(stand —d). H6A I, 1, 23. IV, 3, 44. H6B III, 2, 88.
308. R3 I, 2, 80. Troil. IV, 2, 15 etc. etc.

The partic. *cursed* monosyll.: Tp. V, 179. Mids.
V, 182. Merch. I, 3, 52. H6B III, 2, 88. R3 I, 2, 14 (Qq.).
I, 3, 319 etc. Dissyllabic: Tp. I, 2, 339. John III, 1,
173. H6A V, 4, 26. R3 I, 2, 16 etc. Always of two
syllables in the sense of 'hateful, abominable':
to make him c. this cursed crimeful night, Lucr. 970.
O frowning Fortune, cursed, fickle dame, Pilgr. 259.
Wiv. V, 5, 242. Wint. IV, 3, 469. R2 IV, 147. H6A
I, 3, 39. II, 2, 6. II, 5, 58. V, 4, 32. R3 I, 2, 80. Tit.
V, 1, 16. V, 2, 144. V, 3, 97. Rom. III, 3, 104. V,
3, 19. Tim. IV, 3, 19. 93. Caes. III, 2, 181. Mcb. II,
1, 8. V, 8, 55. Hml. I, 5, 62. 188. III, 3, 43. V, 1, 270.
Oth. V, 2, 276. Per. IV Prol. 43. V Prol. 11. V, 3,
96. *Cursedst* = most wretched: *to make me blest or
cursedst among men,* Merch. II, 1, 46.

Always monosyllabic and spelt *curst* in the sense
of shrewish, waspish, and, in speaking of beasts,
wicked: *finding their enemy* (the boar) *to be so curst,*
Ven. 887. *she is curst; well, the best is, she hath no
teeth to bite,* Gentl. III, 1, 347. *she's too curst. Too
curst ist more than curst; I shall lessen God's sending
that way; for it is said, 'God sends a curst cow short
horns,' but to a cow too curst he sends none,* Ado II,
1, 22. *do not curst wives hold that self-sovereignty,*
LLL IV, 1, 36. *I was never curst,* Mids. III, 2, 300.
nor longer stay in your curst company, 341. *here she
comes, curst and sad,* 439. *her eldest sister is so curst
and shrewd,* Shr. I, 1, 185. *curst and shrewd,* I, 2, 70.
Katharine the curst, 128. *Kate the curst,* II, 187. *if
she be curst, it is for policy,* 294. *she shall still be
curst in company,* 307. *thou hast tamed a curst shrew,*
V, 2, 188. *be curst and brief,* Tw. III, 2, 46. *they
(bears) are never curst but when they are hungry,*
Wint. III, 3, 135. *curst melancholy,* H4A II, 3, 49

(M. Edd. blunderingly *cursed*). *terms as curst, as harsh
and horrible to hear,* H6B III, 2, 312. *sweet saint, for
charity, be not so curst,* R3 I, 2, 49. *with curst speech
I threatened to discover him,* Lr. II, 1, 67. — Compar. *curster: curster than she? why, 'tis impossible,*
Shr. III, 2, 156. Superl. *curstest: how tame a meacock
wretch can make the curstest shrew,* Shr. II, 315.

Cursed-blessed, partly happy, partly unhappy:
to hold their c. fortune long, Lucr. 866.

Cursorary (writing of most M. Edd. after Q3;
the other Qq *cursenary;* Ff *curselary*) cursory,
hasty: *I have but with a c. eye o'erglanced the articles,*
H5 V, 2, 77.

Curst, adj. see *Curse* vb.

Curstness, quarrelsomeness, ill humour:
*touch you the sourest points with sweetest terms, nor c.
grow to the matter,* Ant. II, 2, 25.

Curtail, vb. to cut short, to put a stop
to: *when a gentleman is disposed to swear, it is not
for any standers-by to c. his oaths,* Cymb. II, 1, 12.
To c. of sth. = to cut off from: *I that am —ed of
this fair proportion,* R3 I, 1, 18.

Curtail, adj. see *Curtal.*

Curtain, subst. a cloth hanging to shut out
the light or conceal something: *the —s being close
(of the bed)* Lucr. 367. *spread thy close c., love-
performing night,* Rom. III, 2, 5. *wherefore have these
gifts a c. before 'em?* Tw. I, 3, 134. *To draw the c.*
or *—s* = a) to close it: Merch. II, 7, 78. II, 9, 84.
Wint. V, 3, 59. 68. 83. H6B III, 3, 32. H8 V, 2, 34.
Lr. III, 6, 90. Oth. V, 2, 104. b) to open it: Lucr.
374. Merch. II, 7, 1 *(draw aside).* II, 9, 1. Tw. I,
5, 251. H4A IV, 1, 73. H4B I, 1, 72. Troil. III, 2,
49. Rom. I, 1, 142. — Used for the eyelids: *the fringed
—s of thine eye advance,* Tp. I, 2, 408. For ensigns:
their ragged —s poorly are let loose, H5 IV, 2, 41.

Curtained, enclosed with curtains: *c. with
a counsel-keeping cave,* Tit. II, 3, 24. *wicked dreams
abuse the c. sleep,* Mcb. II, 1, 51.

Curtal, adj. having a docked tail: *my c.
dog plays not at all,* Pilgr. 273. *hope is a c. dog in
some affairs,* Wiv. II, 1, 114 (such a dog being thought
unfit for the chase). *she had transformed me to a c.
dog and made me turn i' the wheel,* Err. III, 2, 151. —
Used of a horse: *I'ld give bay C. and his furniture,*
All's II, 3, 65.

Curtis, name in Shr. IV, 1, 12. 17. 20 etc.

Curtle-axe, cutlass, a broad, curving sword:
a gallant c. upon my thigh, As I, 3, 119. *scarce blood
enough to give each naked c. a stain,* H5 IV, 2, 21.

Curtsy, see *Courtesy.*

Curvét, subst. the bound of a horse: *the
bound and high c. of Mars's fiery steed,* All's II,
3, 299.*

Curvét, vb. to leap, to bound: *he rears
upright, —s and leaps,* Ven. 279. *cry holla to thy
tongue, it —s unseasonably,* As III, 2, 258.

Cushes, see *Cuisses.*

Cushion, subst. a pillow for a seat: Ado IV, 2,
2. Mids. III, 2, 205. Shr. II, 355. H4A II, 4, 416.*
H4B V, 4, 17. Cor. I, 5, 6. II, 1, 98. III, 1, 101. V,
3, 53. Caes. IV, 3, 243. Lr. III, 6, 36. Cymb. IV, 2,
212. *from the casque to the c.* = from war to peace,
Cor. IV, 7, 43.

Custalorum, a corruption of *Custos Rotulorum:*
Wiv. I, 1, 7.

Custard, a composition of eggs, milk and sugar: *like him that leaped into the c.* All's II, 5, 41 ('It was a piece of foolery practised at city entertainments, for a jester to jump into a large deep custard set for the purpose.' Singer).

Custard-coffin, the upper crust covering a custard: Shr. IV, 3, 82.

Custody, a keeping, guarding: *gaoler, take him to thy c.* Err. I, 1, 156. *how darest thou trust so great a charge from thine own c.?* I, 2, 61. *whilst 'tis in my c.* Oth. III, 3, 164.

Custom, 1) common use, received order: *contrary to the Roman laws and —s,* Lucr. Arg. 3. *to plant and o'erwhelm c.* Wint. IV, 1, 9. H5 II, 4, 83. V, 2, 293. H8 I, 3, 2. IV, 1, 16. 20. Troil. I, 3, 88. Cor. I, 10, 23. II, 2, 140. II, 3, 124. 150. Rom. IV, 5, 80. Tim. IV, 1, 19. Mcb. IV, 1, 100. Hml. I, 4, 12. IV, 5, 104. Lr. I, 2, 3. Oth. II, 3, 36.

2) habit, regular practice: *I am more serious than my c.* Tp. II, 1, 219. *'tis a c. with him in the afternoon to sleep,* III, 2, 95. *till c. make it their perch,* Meas. II, 1, 3. Ado I, 1, 169. Merch. I, 3, 65. IV, 1, 268. As II, 1, 2. Wint. IV, 4, 12. Troil. III, 3, 9. Hml. I, 5, 60. III, 4, 37. 161. IV, 7, 188. V, 1, 75. Oth. I, 3, 230. Ant. II, 2, 240. Cymb. I, 4, 150. IV, 2, 10. Per. Prol. 29. Followed by *of*: *c. of fell deeds,* Caes. III, 1, 269. *all c. of exercises,* Hml. II, 2, 308. — *Of c.* = customary: *our dance of c.* Wiv. V, 5, 79. *think of this but as a thing of c.* Mcb. III, 4, 97. *tricks of c.* Oth. III, 3, 122.

3) habit of buying of a p.: *you shall hop without my c.* Shr. IV, 3, 99. Hence = customers, purchasers: *Julio Romano, who would beguile Nature of her c.* Wint. V, 2, 108. *you'll lose nothing by c.* Per. IV, 2, 150.

Customary, 1) according to received usage and order: *it is a c. cross,* Mids. I, 1, 153. *take from Time his charters and his c. rights,* R2 II, 1, 196. Cor. II, 3, 93. Hml. I, 2, 78.

2) habitual: *you would be prouder of the work than c. bounty can enforce you,* Merch. III, 4, 9. *I met him with c. compliment,* Wint. I, 2, 371.

Customed, customary, common: *to wring the widow from her c. right,* H6B V, 1, 188. *no common wind, no c. event,* John III, 4, 155.

Customer, 1) frequent visitor, purchaser: Meas. IV, 3, 4. Wint. IV, 4, 192. Per. IV, 6, 21. Contemptuously = visitor, guest: *you minion you, are these your —s?* Err. IV, 4, 63.

2) a prostitute: *I think thee now some common c.* All's V, 3, 287. *I marry her? what? a c.!* Oth. IV, 1, 123.

Custom-shrunk, having fewer customers than formerly: Meas. I, 2, 85.

Cut, subst. 1) stroke, gash, wound: *this was the most unkindest c. of all,* Caes. III, 2, 187. *if there were no more women but Fulvia, then had you indeed a c.* Ant. I, 2, 173.

2) the manner in which a thing is cut, shape, fashion: *beard of formal c.* As II, 7, 155. *the c. of a certain courtier's beard,* V, 4, 73. *a beard of the general's c.* H5 III, 6, 81. *their clothes are after such a pagan c.* H8 I, 3, 14.

3) a lot made of chips of unequal lengths: *we'll draw —s for the senior,* Err. V, 422.

4) a slope in a garment: *cloth o' gold, and*

—s, and laced with silver, Ado III, 4, 19. *here's snip and nip and c. and slish and slash,* Shr. IV, 3, 90; cf. 122. 127. 147.

5) a docked (or gelded?) horse: *if thou hast her not in the end, call me c.* Tw. II, 3, 203 (cf. *call me horse,* H4A II, 4, 215). *beat C.'s saddle,* H4A II, 1, 6 (cf. *Curtal,* and *Cut and long-tail* in *Cut* vb.).

Cut, vb. 1) to penetrate with an edged instrument, to separate the parts of a body; a) absol.: *let us be keen and rather c. a little,* Meas. II, 1, 5. LLL II, 50. Merch. IV, 1, 280. — b) trans.: *c. his wezand,* Tp. III, 2, 99. cf. *to c. his throat,* Wiv. I, 4, 114. H6B IV, 1, 20. IV, 2, 29. *he hath twice or thrice c. Cupid's bow-string,* Ado III, 2, 11. *a razor —ing a smaller hair,* LLL V, 2, 258. *if I c. my finger,* Mids. III, 1, 186. *c. thread and thrum,* V, 291. *I would the —ing of my garments would serve the turn,* All's IV, 1, 50. *c. my lace,* Wint. III, 2, 174; cf. R3 IV, 1, 34 and Ant. I, 3, 71. *my buckler c. through,* H4A II, 4, 186. *the flint doth c. my feet,* H6B II, 4, 34. *our general is c. in the middle,* Cor. IV, 5, 210. *c. the winds,* Rom. I, 1, 118. *I am c. to the brains,* Lr. IV, 6, 197. *c. me to pieces,* LLL V, 2, 399; cf. Shr. IV, 3, 128 and John IV, 3, 93. *into as many gobbets will I c. it,* H6B V, 2, 58. *that hand that c. thy youth in twain,* Rom. V, 3, 99 (as the Fates do the thread of life). *c. my heart in sums,* Tim. III, 4, 93. Singular phrase: *hold or c. bow-strings,* Mids. I, 2, 114 ('When a party was made at butts, assurance of meeting was given in the words of that phrase; the sense of the person using them being, that he would keep promise, or they might cut his bowstrings, demolish him for an archer'. Capell).

2) to carve: *I can c. the mutton to't,* Tw. I, 3, 130.

3) to divide, to cleave by passing through: *—ing the clouds towards Paphos,* Tp. IV, 93. Mids. III, 2, 379. *to see the fish c. the silver stream,* Ado III, 1, 27. *c. the sea to France,* H6C II, 6, 89. Ant. III, 7, 23. Per. III Prol. 46. Intr.: *behold the strong-ribbed bark through liquid mountains c.* Troil. I, 3, 40. — Similarly: *c. their passage through the force of France,* H5 II, 2, 16 (cf. *c. out*).

4) to clip: *c. your hair,* Gentl. II, 7, 44. *to c. French crowns,* H5 IV, 1, 245 (a quibble). *easy it is of a c. loaf to steal a shive,* Tit. II, 1, 87. *that I will, come c. and long-tail,* Wiv. III, 4, 47 (properly = come any kind of dogs, curtal ones or long-tailed; and then = come who will to contend with me). *she was washed and c. and trimmed,* Tit. V, 1, 95 (= her hair was cut; with a quibble).

5) to separate from the body: *in the —ing it* (a pound of flesh) Merch. IV, 1, 309. *cut most of their festival purses,* Wint. IV, 4, 627. *who 'twas that c. thy tongue,* Tit. II, 4, 2. 27. *the one* (hand) *will help to c. the other,* III, 1, 78. *they c. thy sister's tongue,* V, 1, 92. *c. her hands,* 93. Followed by *from*: *and from my false hand c. the wedding ring,* Err. II, 2, 139. *to c. the forfeiture from that bankrupt,* Merch. IV, 1, 122. *I'll have this crown of mine c. from my shoulders,* R3 III, 2, 43.

6) to form by cutting, to shape: *c. their passage,* H5 II, 2, 16. Used of a beard: As V, 4, 75. 77. 78 etc. of a gown: Shr. IV, 3, 122 (cf. *c. out*); of statues and pictures carved in stone: *an agate very vilely c.* Ado III, 1, 65. *like his grandsire c. in ala-*

baster, Merch. I, 1, 84. *what fine chisel could ever yet c. breath?* Wint. V, 3, 79.

7) to make, in the phrase '*to c. a caper*': Tw. I, 3, 129. Per. IV, 2, 116.

8) Followed by *from*, = to preclude or shut out: *he shall never c. from memory my sweet love's beauty*, Sonn. 63, 11. *c. the entail from all remainders*, All's IV, 3, 313. *he —s me from my tale*, H4A V, 2, 91 (= interrupts me, puts a stop to my tale; cf. *c. off*).

Joined with adverbs; 1) *to c. away*, a) to separate from the body: *of England's coat one half is c. away*, H6A I, 1, 81. *he's a disease that must be c. away*, Cor. III, 1, 295. *c. away her tongue*, Tit. V, 3, 57. — b) to make away with: *if all obstacles were c. away*, R3 III, 7, 156.

2) *to c. off*, a) to separate from the body: *c. off a man's head*, Meas. IV, 2, 1. John V, 4, 16. R2 II, 2, 102. H4B II, 1, 50. H6B IV, 10, 88. H6C V, 1, 55. Caes. II, 1, 163. *a pound of your flesh*, Merch. I, 3, 151. IV, 1, 233. *my left hand*, V, 177.

b) to cancel, to destroy, to make an end of: *c. off the sequence of posterity*, John II, 96. *and there my rendezvous is quite c. off*, H5 V, 1, 88. *that winter should c. off our springtime so*, H6C II, 3, 47. *I'll c. the causes off*, III, 2, 142. *c. off all fears*, Troil. II, 2, 133. *he that —s off twenty years of life —s off so many years of fearing death*, Caes. III, 1, 101. *how to c. off some charge in legacies*, IV, 1, 9. *to grudge my pleasures, to c. off my train*, Lr. II, 4, 177.

c) to put to death: *c. off by course of justice*, Meas. V, 35. 112. As II, 3, 25. H4B IV, 5, 210. H5 III, 6, 114. H6A III, 1, 185. H6C V, 5, 66. R3 I, 3, 214. I, 4, 225. Cor. V, 6, 140. Tit. IV, 4, 26. Caes. III, 1, 162. Mcb. IV, 3, 79. Hml. I, 5, 76. Lr. IV, 5, 38. IV, 6, 268. Cymb. IV, 2, 316.

d) to put a stop to, to break off: *to c. off the argument*, As I, 2, 49. *all strife*, Shr. III, 1, 21. *more circumstance*, John II, 77. *his tale*, IV, 2, 202. *the ceremonious vows of love*, R3 V, 3, 98.

e) to preclude, to prevent: *from which lingering penance of such misery doth she c. me off*, Merch. IV, 1, 272. *beauty starved with her severity —s beauty off from all posterity*, Rom. I, 1, 226. *from which advantage shall we c. him off*, Caes. IV, 3, 210.

3) *to c. out*, a) to remove by cutting: *c. out my tongue*, John IV, 1, 101. b) to form or shape by cutting: *I bid thy master c. out the gown*, Shr. IV, 3, 127 (i. e. make slopes in it). 147. *be his own carver and c. out his way*, R2 II, 3, 144. *c. out the burly-boned clown in chines of beef*, H6B IV, 10, 60. *take him and c. him out in litt'le stars*, Rom. III, 2, 22. Hence = to form, to shape in any way: *by the pattern of mine own thoughts I c. out the purity of his*, Wint. IV, 4, 393.

4) *to c. short* = to c. off, to make away with: *—ing short that fraudful man*, H6B III, 1, 81. *rather than bloody war should c. them short*, IV, 4, 12. *c. short all intermission*, Mcb. IV, 3, 232.

Cutlass, see *Curtle-axe*.

Cutler, one whose occupation is to make knives: *like —s' poetry upon a knife*, Merch. V, 149.

Cutpurse, a thief: Wint. IV, 4, 686. H5 III, 6, 65. V, 1, 91. Lr. III, 2, 88. *a c. of the empire and the rule*, Hml. III, 4, 99. Adjectively: *you c. rascal*, H4B II, 4, 137.

Cutter, sculptor: Cymb. II, 4, 83.

Cutter-off, interrupter: *when Fortune makes Nature's natural the c. of Nature's wit*, As I, 2, 53.

Cut-throat, a butcher of men: Mcb. III, 4, 17. Adjectively: *c. dog*, Merch. I, 3, 112.

Cuttle, swaggerer, bully: *I'll thrust my knife in your mouldy chaps, an you play the saucy c. with me*, H4B II, 4, 139. (= *cutter*, which Cotgrave translates by *balaffreux, taillebras, fendeur de naseaux*. Coles: *a cutter, gladiator, latro*).*

Cyclops, name of the gigantic servants of Vulcan: *men framed of the C. size*, Tit. IV, 3, 46. *never did the —' hammers fall on Mars's armour*, Hml. II, 2, 511.

Cydnus, river in Cilicia: Ant. II, 2, 192. V, 2, 228. Cymb. II, 4, 71.

Cygnet, young swan: John V, 7, 21 (O. Edd. *symet*). H6A V, 3, 56 (O. Edd. *signets*). Troil. I, 1, 58 (O. Edd. *cignets*).

Cymbal, a brass instrument producing a sharp ringing sound, when two are struck together: Cor. V, 4, 53.

Cymbeline, name in Cymb. III, 1, 62. III, 3, 58. V, 4, 76 etc.

Cyme, name of a laxative in Mcb. V, 3, 55: *what rhubarb, c., or what purgative drug would scour these English hence?* F2 and F3 *caeny*, F4 and most M. Edd. *senna*.

Cynic, a follower of Diogenes, a rude man: *how vilely doth this c. rhyme!* Caes. IV, 3, 133.

Cynthia, Diana, the Goddess of the moon and of chastity: Ven. 728. Rom. III, 5, 20. Per. II, 5, 11.

Cypher, see *Cipher*.

Cypress, the tree Cupressus: *in c. chests my arras counterpoints*, Shr. II, 353 (O. Edd. *Cypros*). *at the c. grove*, Cor. I, 10, 30. Emblem of mourning: *come away, death, and in sad c. let me be laid*, Tw. II, 4, 53 (a cypress coffin, or cypress branches laid in the coffin; according to some it means here 'crape'). *their sweetest shade a grove of c. trees*, H6B III, 2, 323.

Cypress (O. Edd.) or **Cyprus** (some M. Edd.) crape: *a c., not a bosom, hideth my heart*, Tw. III, 1, 132. *c. black as e'er was crow*, Wint. IV, 4, 221.

Cyprus, island in the Mediterranean: Oth. I, 1, 29. 151. I, 2, 39. I, 3, 8 etc. Ant. III, 6, 10.

Cyrus, the Persian king, slain by Tomyris: H6A II, 3, 6.

Cytherea, Venus: Pilgr. 43. 73. Shr. Ind. 2, 53. Wint. IV, 4, 122. Cymb. II, 2, 14.

D.

D, the fourth letter of the alphabet: LLL V, 1, 24.

D, note in music: Shr. III, 1, 77.

D, abbreviation for penny: LLL III, 140. For pence: H4A II, 4, 585 — 589.

Dabble (cf. *Bedabble*), vb. to spatter, to sprinkle: *hair —d in blood*, R3 I, 4, 54.

Dace, the fish Cyprinus Leuciscus: H4B III, 2, 356.

Dad, father, in the language of infants: Tw. IV, 2, 140. John II, 467. H6C I, 4, 77.

Daedalus, the fabulous artist, who invented the art of flying: H6C V, 6, 21. Alluded to in H6A IV, 6, 54.

Daemon, see *Demon.*

Daff, vb. (cf. *doff*) 1) to take off: *my white stole of chastity I —ed,* Compl. 297. Ant. IV, 4, 13 (F2.3.4 *doff*).

2) to put aside, to turn away: *and —ed me to a cabin hanged with care,* Pilgr. 183. *I would have —ed all other respects,* Ado II, 3, 176. *canst thou so d. me?* V, 1, 78. *his comrades, that —ed the world aside and bid it pass,* H4A IV, 1, 96. *every day thou —est me with some device,* Oth. IV, 2, 176 (only in F1; the other O. Edd. *doffest*).

Daffodil (O. Edd. *daffadil*), Narcissus pseudo-Narcissus: *when —s begin to peer,* Wint. IV, 3, 1. *—s, that come before the swallow dares, and take the winds of March with beauty,* IV, 4, 118.

Dagger, 1) poniard: Ado IV, 1, 110. Mids. V, 150. Merch. III, 1, 115. III, 4, 65. Shr. IV, 1, 138. All's IV, 3, 164. Tw. IV, 1, 30. Wint. I, 2, 156. H4A II, 4, 336. 416. H4B IV, 5, 107. H5 IV, 1, 56. H6A I, 3, 79. H6C V, 6, 27. R3 I, 3, 212. III, 1, 110. H8 I, 2, 204. Tit. IV, 1, 118. Rom. IV, 5, 120. V, 3, 203. Caes. I, 3, 89. Mcb. II, 1, 33 etc. Hml. III, 2, 414 (*speak —s;* cf. Ado II, 1, 255). Cymb. IV, 2, 79 etc.

2) a blunt blade with a basket hilt used for defence, introduced in the poet's time in the place of the buckler used formerly: *playing at sword and dagger,* Wiv. I, 1, 295. *what's his weapon? rapier and d.* Hml. V, 2, 152. *the rapier and d. man,* Meas. IV, 3, 16.

3) *Dagger of lath,* the wooden weapon given to the Vice in the old Moralities: *like to the old Vice, who with d. of lath, in his rage and his wrath, cries 'ah ha'! to the devil,* Tw. IV, 2, 136. H4A II, 4, 151. *and now is this Vice's d. become a squire,* H4B III, 2, 343. *every one may pare his nails with a wooden d.* H5 IV, 4, 77 (i. e. may offer him any insult).

Dagonet, a foolish knight at the court of King Arthur: H4B III, 2, 300.

Daily, adj. 1) happening by day: *with nightly tears and d. heart-sore sighs,* Gentl. II, 4, 132.

2) happening every day: Lucr. 649. Err. I, 1, 60. John II, 569. H6C IV, 6, 85. R3 II, 2, 15 (Ff *earnest*). H8 V, 3, 68. 115. Cor. IV, 7, 38. Hml. I, 1, 73. Oth.V, 1, 19 *(he hath a d. beauty in his life).*

Daily, adv. every day: Sonn. 28, 13. 56, 11. 76, 13. Gentl. I, 3, 58. Ado IV, 1, 20. Wint. III, 2, 243. R2 II, 1, 249. V, 3, 6. H4A III, 2, 70. H4B IV, 5, 195. H6A IV, 3, 32. V, 4, 161. H6B I, 3, 127. H6C II, 5, 91. R3 I, 3, 81. H8 III, 2, 167. Troil. I, 1, 94. Cor. I, 1, 84. Tim. IV, 3, 91. 174. 380. Cymb. III, 5, 49.

Daintily, 1) deliciously: *baked in that pie, whereof their mother d. hath fed,* Tit. V, 3, 61.

2) delicately, fastidiously: *famine ... whom thou foughtest again, though d. brought up,* Ant. I, 4, 60.

Daintiness, fastidiousness: *here have I the d. of ear to check time broke,* R2 V, 5, 45.

Daintry, Daventry: H6C V, 1, 6.

Dainty, subst. (used only in the plural) delicacy: *torches are made to light, —ies to taste,* Ven. 164. Err. III, 1, 21. LLL IV, 2, 25. Shr. II, 190.

Dainty, adj. 1) pleasing to the palate, delicious: *a table full of welcome makes scarce one d. dish,* Err. III, 1, 23. LLL I, 1, 26. Troil. V, 8, 20. *as at English feasts, so I regreet the —iest last,* R2 I, 3, 68. *worse than gall the —iest that they taste,* H6B III, 2, 322.

2) delicate, enticing, lovely: *that's my d. Ariel,* Tp. V, 95. *O, a most d. man! to see him walk before a lady and to bear her fan,* LLL IV, 1, 146. *her feet were much too d. for such tread,* IV, 3, 279. *O d. duck, O dear!* Mids. V, 286 and Wint. IV, 4, 324. *basins and ewers to lave her d. hands,* Shr. 2, 350. *she is a d. one,* H8 I, 4, 94. *and gives memorial d. kisses to it,* Troil. V, 2, 80. *single you thither then this d. doe,* Tit. II, 1, 117. II, 2, 26. *your laboursome and d. trims,* Cymb. III, 4, 167.

3) nice, fastidious: *Love's tongue proves d. Bacchus gross in taste,* LLL IV, 3, 339. *no shape but his can please your d. eye,* H6A V, 3, 38. *the hand of little employment hath the —ier sense,* Hml. V, 1, 78. *To make d. =* to give one's self airs, to look prim: *that makes d., she, I'll swear, hath corns,* Rom. I, 5, 21 (cf. *Nice*).

4) minute: *the king is weary of d. and such picking grievances,* H4B IV, 1, 198.

5) Followed by *of,* = over-solicitous about, taking too much care of: *grows d. of his worth,* Troil. I, 3, 145.* *let us not be d. of leave-taking, but shift away,* Mcb. II, 3, 150.

Daisied, full of daisies: *the prettiest d. plot,* Cymb. IV, 2, 398.

Daisy, the plant Bellis perennis: *whose perfect white showed like an April d. on the grass,* Lucr. 395. *—ies pied,* LLL V, 2, 904. *there's a d.* Hml. IV, 5, 184 (of what significance?). IV, 7, 170.

Dale, valley: Ven. 232. Lucr. 1077. Pilgr. 355. Mids. II, 1, 2. 83. Wint. IV, 3, 2. H4B IV, 3, 4. 6. 10.

Dalliance, 1) trifling, toying, wanton play: *do not give d. too much the rein,* Tp. IV, 1, 51. *you use this d. to excuse your breach of promise,* Err. IV, 1, 48. 59. H5 II Chor. 2. H6A V, 1, 23. Hml. I, 3, 50.

2) tarrying: *keep not back your powers in d.* H6A V, 2, 5.

Dally, 1) to trifle, to wanton, to play: *to sport and dance, to toy, to wanton, d., smile and jest,* Ven. 106. Lucr. 554. Err. I, 2, 59. Tw. II, 4, 48. H4A V, 3, 57. R3 II, 1, 12. Hml. III, 2, 257. V, 2, 308. Followed by *with: grief —ied with nor law nor limit knows,* Lucr. 1120. LLL V, 1, 109. Tw. III, 1, 16. 23. R3 I, 3, 265. III, 7, 74. *d. not with the gods,* Shr. IV, 4, 68 (= take not their name in vain). cf. *that high All-seer that I —ied with hath turned my feigned prayer on my head,* R3 V, 1, 20.

2) to delay, to tarry: *come, d. not, be gone,* H6A IV, 5, 11. *if thou shouldst d. half an hour,* Lr. III, 6, 100.

Dalmatian, subst. inhabitant of Dalmatia: Cymb. III, 1, 74. III, 7, 3.

Dam, subst. female parent, used of birds: Merch. III, 1, 33. Mcb. IV, 3, 218. Of quadrupeds: Mids. V, 227. H6B III, 1, 214. H6C III, 2, 162. H8 I, 1, 176. Tit. II, 3, 142. IV, 1, 97. V, 2, 144. — *The devil and his d.:* Wiv. I, 1, 151. IV, 5, 108. Err. IV, 3, 51. Shr. I, 1, 106. III, 2, 158. John II, 128. H6A I, 5, 5. Tit. IV, 2, 65. Oth. IV, 1, 153.

Used of human mothers, in contempt: Tp. I, 2, 320. 373. III, 2, 109. Merch. IV, 1, 136. Wint. I, 2, 137. II, 3, 94. H6C II, 2, 135. Cor. III, 1, 293. Tit. V, 1, 27. V, 2, 191. Used as a term of endearment: *blemished his gracious d.* Wint. III, 2, 199.

Dam, subst. that which confines water: *no more —s I'll make for fish,* Tp. II, 2, 184.

Dam, vb., to stop up: *the strait pass was —ed with dead men,* Cymb. V, 3, 11. Joined with *up: voice —ed up with woe,* Lucr. 1661. *the more thou —est it* (the fire) *up, the more it burns,* Gentl. II, 7, 24 (cf. the following simile). *I'll have the current —ed up,* H4A III, 1, 101. *now will I d. up this thy yawning mouth,* H6B IV, 1, 73.

Damage, subst. injury, loss: *it can do me no d.* H8 I, 2, 183. *all d. else, as honour, loss of time, expense ... shall be struck off,* Troil. II, 2, 3 (Q *domage*).

Damage, vb. tr. to injure: *all hopes whose growth may d. me,* R3 IV, 2, 60.

Damascus: *this be D., be thou cursed Cain,* H6A I, 3, 39 (Damascus was supposed to be the place where Cain slew Abel).

Damask, subst. 1) a mixture of red and white: *the difference between the constant red and mingled d.* As III, 5, 123. — 2) pale red colour: *the war of white and d. in their cheeks,* Cor. II, 1, 232.

Damask, adj. 1) of a mingled red and white: *their d. sweet commixture show,* LLL V, 2, 296. *her d. cheek,* Tw. II, 4, 115. — 2) pale red: *a lily pale, with d. dye to grace her,* Pilgr. 89. — 3) of Damascus: *gloves as sweet as d. roses,* Wint. IV, 4, 222.

Damasked, of a mingled red and white: *I have seen roses d., red and white,* Sonn. 130, 5.

Dame, 1) mistress, a) a woman who governs: *since thou* (viz the hand) *couldst not defend thy loyal d.* Lucr. 1034. *both d. and servant,* Wint. IV, 4, 57. — b) a woman beloved or courted: *when as thine eye hath chose the d.* Pilgr. 299. *fare thee well, d.* Ant. IV, 4, 29.

2) mother: *the sire, the son, the d. and daughter die,* Lucr. 1477. *my old d. will be undone now,* H4B III, 2, 123. 245 (cf. *Dam* and *Stepdame*).

3) lady: *such a peerless d.* Lucr. 21. 51. 1628. 1714. Err. II, 2, 149. LLL V, 2, 160. Mids. V, 298. H6A V, 3, 124. V, 5, 12. H6C III, 3, 255. Cor. II, 1, 231. Tit. I, 317. IV, 1, 90. IV, 2, 41. Mcb. IV, 2, 65. IV, 3, 73. Lr. IV, 6, 120. Oth. IV, 1, 47. Per. Prol. 31. I, 4, 26. Before names: *thy d. Partlet,* Wint. II, 3, 75; cf. H4A III, 3, 60. *d. Mortimer,* II, 4, 123. *d. Margaret,* H6B I, 2, 39. *d. Eleanor,* I, 2, 91. I, 3, 150. II, 3, 1.

Used as a term of contemptuous address: *Fortune, cursed, fickle d.* Pilgr. 259. *how now, d.!* Shr. II, 23. H6A II, 1, 50. H6B I, 2, 42. I, 3, 79. Lr. V, 3, 154.

Damn, 1) to condemn: *with a spot I d. him,* Caes. IV, 1, 6. *perform't, or else we d. thee,* Ant. I, 1, 24. (the style of gods imitated?).

2) to doom to eternal torments in a future life: *thereof comes that the wenches say 'God d. me,'* Err. IV, 3, 54. *if I do not, d. me,* All's IV, 1, 96 (= God d. me). H4B II, 4, 181. Oth. III, 3, 398. 475. *—s himself to do,* All's III, 6, 95 (i. e. says 'God d. me, if I do not'). *the devil d. thee black,* Mcb. V, 3, 11. Partic. *—ed: a torment to lay upon the —ed,* Tp. I, 2, 290. *the devil will not have me —ed,* Wiv. V, 5,

38. *I am —ed in hell,* II, 2, 9. *—ed to hell for this,* R2 IV, 43. Mids. III, 2, 382. Merch. III, 1, 34. III, 5, 6. 17. As III, 2, 36. All's I, 3, 18. III, 6, 96. Tw. III, 4, 313; cf. H4B II, 4, 169. Hml. V, 2, 68 (*is't not to be —ed*). Oth. IV, 2, 36. Cymb. V, 3, 37 etc. Unintelligible passage: *a fellow almost —ed in a fair wife,* Oth. I, 1, 21.*

3) to cause to be doomed to the torments of hell, to bring to damnation: *if they should speak, would almost d. those ears which, hearing them, would call their brothers fools,* Merch. I, 1, 98. *do you d. others, and let this d. you,* Tim. IV, 3, 165. *the devil ... abuses me to d. me,* Hml. II, 2, 632. *if thou wilt needs d. thyself, do it a more delicate way than drowning,* Oth. I, 3, 360. *come, swear it, d. thyself,* IV, 2, 35. *hence, vile instrument! thou shalt not d. my hand,* Cymb. III, 4, 76.

4) The partic. *damned* = hateful, detestable: *surfeits, imposthumes, grief and d. despair,* Ven. 743. *ink would have seemed more black and d. here,* Compl. 54. *this d. witch Sycorax,* Tp. I, 2, 263. Wiv. II, 2, 300. Meas. III, 1, 96 (*damnedst*). IV, 3, 127. Err. IV, 4, 105. Merch. III, 2, 78. All's II, 3, 147. John V, 4, 52. H6A III, 2, 38. H6B IV, 10, 83. R3 II, 4, 64. Hml. II, 2, 482 etc.

Damnable, 1) deserving damnation: *if it were d., why would he for the momentary trick be perdurably fined?* Meas. III, 1, 113. IV, 3, 73. As V, 2, 68. R3 I, 4, 197.

2) odious, detestable: *thou d. fellow, did not I pluck thee by the nose?* Meas. V, 342. All's IV, 3, 251. H4A I, 2, 101. Troil V, 1, 29. Hml. III, 2, 263.

Adverbially: *is it not meant d. in us, to be trumpeters of our unlawful intents?* All's IV, 3, 31 (i. e. is not our drift a damnable one?). *inconstant and d. ingrateful,* Wint. III, 2, 188.

Damnably, detestably: *I have misused the king's press d.* H4A IV, 2, 14.

Damnation, condemnation to everlasting torments: Wiv. III, 2, 40. Ado IV, 1, 174. As III, 2, 45. John IV, 2, 218. H5 IV, 1, 162. 184. Tim. III, 1, 55. Hml. IV, 5, 133. Oth. III, 3, 372. *death and d!* 396.

2) a sin deserving eternal torments: *'twere d. to think so base a thought,* Merch. II, 7, 49. *bungle up d. with patches, colours,* H5 II, 2, 115. *his virtues will plead against the deep d. of his taking off,* Mcb. I, 7, 20. cf. *ancient d.! O most wicked fiend!* Rom. III, 5, 235 (or abstr. pro concr., = old sinner?).

Damon, name in a song: Hml. III, 2, 292.

Damosel, see *Damsel.*

Damosella, damsel: *d. virgin, was this directed to you?* LLL IV, 2, 132 (Holophernes' speech).

Damp, subst. moist air, fog: *with rotten —s ravish the morning air,* Lucr. 778. *in murk and occidental d.* All's II, 1, 166. *the poisonous d. of night,* Ant. IV, 9, 13.

Damsel, lass, wench: *it was a spite unto the silly d.* Pilgr. 218. *I was taken with a d.* LLL I, 1, 292. 293. 294 (Ff Q2 *damosell*). *for this d., I must keep her at the park,* I, 2, 135. *d., I'll have a bout with you,* H6A III, 2, 56. *d. of France, I think I have you fast,* V, 3, 30.

Damson, a small black plum: H6B II, 1, 102.

Dan (Ff Q2 *Don*), lord, master: *D. Cupid,* LLL III, 182.

Dance, subst. sportive motion regulated by music:

Wiv. V, 5, 79. Ado I, 2, 14. II, 1, 114. V, 4, 120. LLL IV, 3, 379. V, 1, 160. V, 2, 212. Mids. II, 1, 254. V, 32. 361. R2 I, 3, 291. *wealth is burden of my wooing d.* Shr. I, 2, 68.

Dance, vb. 1) to move sportively with measured steps regulated by music; a) intr. Ven. 105. 148. Lucr. Arg. 10. Gentl. III, 2, 81. Wiv. III, 2, 68. LLL II, 114. V, 2, 122. 213. Mids. II, 1, 140. IV, 1, 94. Shr. II, 33. All's II, 1, 33. H4B IV, 5, 125. Oth. II, 2, 5. III, 3, 185. Ant. I, 3, 4 etc. *—ing measures,* As V, 4, 199. *—ing shoes,* Rom. I, 4, 14. *the —ing horse,* LLL I, 2, 57 (a horse exhibited by one Bankes and celebrated for its curious performances). Ironically: *I'll make him d.* Wiv. III, 2, 91 (cf. Lr. V, 3, 277. Wiv. II, 1, 237). Used of any similar motion: *the —ing banners of the French,* John II, 308. *the emptier* (bucket) *ever —ing in the air,* R2 IV, 185. *a city on the inconstant billows —ing,* H5 III Chor. 15. *and* (let my head) *sooner d. upon a bloody pole,* H6B IV, 1, 127.

b) trans.: *do you sing it* (Light o' love) *and I'll d. it,* Ado III, 4, 46. *to d. our ringlets,* Mids. II, 1, 86. V, 403. LLL V, 1, 161. All's II, 1, 77. Wint. IV, 4, 58. Ant. II, 7, 110. *and so d. out the answer,* Ado II, 1, 75.

2) to triumph, to exult: *my —ing soul doth celebrate this feast of battle,* R2 I, 3, 91. *make our hearts d. with comfort,* Cor. V, 3, 99. *hell only —th at so harsh a chime,* Per. I, 1, 85. cf. R2 II, 4, 12. Applied to the quivering light of the heavenly bodies as indicating joy: *there was a star —d, and under that was I born,* Ado II, 1, 349. *shall we make the welkin d. indeed?* Tw. II, 3, 59. *make the sun d.* Cor. V, 4, 54. Used of the throbbing of the heart in a more general sense: *my heart —s, but not for joy,* Wint. I, 2, 110.

3) Ludicrously, = to stick fast: *there —ing up to the chins,* Tp. IV, 183. *I have some of them in Limbo Patrum, and there they are like to d. these three days,* H8 V, 4, 68.

Similarly as a vb. trans. in the phrase *to d. attendance* = to wait on a person without being admitted: *I —d attendance on his will,* H6B I, 3, 174. *I d. attendance here,* R3 III, 7, 56. *to d. attendance on their lordships' pleasure,* H8 V, 2, 31.

4) to cause to dance, a) to fill with joy: *but that I see thee here, more —s my rapt heart than ...* Cor. IV, 5, 122. — b) to dandle: *he —d thee on his knee,* Tit. V, 3, 162.

Dancer, one who dances: Ado II, 1, 111. Ant. III, 11, 36.

Dancing-rapier, a sword worn only for ornament at dancing: *although our mother, unadvised, gave you a d. by your side,* Tit. II, 1, 39 (cf. *no sword worn but one to dance with,* All's II, 1, 33. *kept his sword e'en like a dancer,* Ant. III, 11, 36).

Dancing-school: H5 III, 5, 32.

Dandle, to rock on the knee, to fondle: *like the froward infant stilled with —ing,* Ven. 562. H6B I, 3, 148. Tit. IV, 2, 161.

Dane, a native of Denmark: All's IV, 1, 78. Hml. V, 1, 281. V, 2, 352. Danes known as great drinkers: Hml. I, 4, 19. Oth. II, 3, 79. 85.

= king of Denmark: *liegemen to the D.* Hml. I, 1, 15. *you cannot speak of reason to the D. and lose your voice,* I, 2, 44. I, 4, 45. V, 2, 336.

Danger, subst. peril, hazard: Ven. 206. 788.

Lucr. 128. 184. 1265. Tp. II, 1, 297. III, 2, 76. Meas. I, 2, 184. IV, 3, 89. Merch. IV, 1, 38. 362. As V, 2, 75. All's I, 3, 248. H6A IV, 5, 8. H6B II, 4, 66. III, 1, 35. H6C IV, 1, 74 etc. etc. *with d. of my life,* H6B II, 1, 103. *I am hurt to d.* Oth. II, 3, 197. *do much d.* Rom. V, 2, 20. Caes. II, 1, 17.* Personified: *d. knows full well that Caesar is more dangerous than he,* Caes. II, 2, 44. — *My d.* = a) the danger I am in: *in thy d. commend thy grievance to ...,* Gentl. I, 1, 15. *regard thy d.* III, 1, 256. *thy age and —s make thee dote,* Err. V, 329. *draw not on thy d.* H6C III, 3, 75. Cymb. III, 5, 103. b) the danger threatened by me: *come not within his d.* Ven. 639. *you stand within his d., do you not?* Merch. IV, 1, 180 (according to some, = you are in his debt; but Antonio's answer: *Ay, so he says,* excludes this interpretation). cf. *full of d. is the duke of Gloster,* R3 II, 3, 27. *into the d. of this adverse town,* Tw. V, 87. *remains in d. of her former tooth,* Mcb. III, 2, 15. *nor tempt the d. of my true defence,* John IV, 3, 84. cf. Troil. V, 10, 14. *'tis d.,* Lr. IV, 7, 79.

Danger, vb. to endanger: *whose quality the sides o' the world may d.* Ant. I, 2, 199.

Dangerous, 1) full of danger, exposing to danger: Gentl. IV, 3, 24. V, 4, 41. Wiv. I, 3, 112. Meas. II, 2, 181. III, 2, 237. IV, 2, 171. IV, 4, 32. Ado III, 3, 179. V, 1, 97. V, 2, 21. LLL I, 1, 129. I, 2, 112. Merch. I, 1, 31. III, 1, 5. III, 2, 98. As IV, 1, 194. All's II, 5, 12. IV, 3, 248. Wint. I, 2, 158. John IV, 2, 54. R2 III, 2, 124. V, 3, 81. H4A IV, 1, 34. H6A III, 2, 33. IV, 2, 29. 56. H6B I, 1, 164. II, 1, 21. II, 2, 69. III, 1, 74. H6C IV, 3, 15. R3 I, 1, 32. I, 4, 138. 146. II, 2, 126. III, 1, 12. 182. III, 5, 23. IV, 4, 90. H8 I, 2, 139. Rom. IV, 1, 9 etc. etc.

2) exposed to danger: *to drive infection from the d. year,* Ven. 508. *so thrive I in my enterprise and d. success of bloody wars,* R3 IV, 4, 236 (Qq *d. attempt of hostile arms*).

Adverbially: *either slain or wounded d.* H6C I, 1, 11 (the spurious Qq and M. Edd. *dangerously*).

Dangerously, perilously: John IV, 2, 186. H6B II, 1, 171. H6C I, 1, 11 (Ff *dangerous*). Cor. V, 3, 188.

Dangle, to hang and swing: *yon —ing apricocks,* R2 III, 4, 29.

Daniel, the prophet celebrated for his sagacity as a judge: Merch. IV, 1, 223. 333. 340.

Danish, appertaining to Denmark: Hml. IV, 3, 63. IV, 4, 1. IV, 5, 110. V, 2, 50. 170.

Dank, adj. damp: *the d. earth,* Lucr. 1130. *on the d. and dirty ground,* Mids. II, 2, 75. *peas and beans are as d. here as a dog,* H4A II, 1, 9. *night's d. dew,* Rom. II, 3, 6. *the humours of the d. morning,* Caes. II, 1, 263.

Dankish, dampish: *in a dark and d. vault,* Err. V, 247.

Dansker, Dane: Hml. II, 1, 7.

Daphne, the nymph loved by Apollo and changed into a laurel: Mids. II, 1, 231. Shr. Ind. 2, 59. Troil. I, 1, 101.

Dapple, vb. to spot, to variegate: *the gentle day —s the drowsy east with spots of grey,* Ado V, 3, 27. *the poor —d fools,* As II, 1, 22.

Dardan, 1) the country of Troy: *from the strond of D.* Lucr. 1436. Adjectively: *on D. plains,* Troil. Prol. 13. — 2) one of the six gates of Troy: Troil. Prol. 16.

Dardanian, adj. Trojan: *the D. wives,* Merch. III, 2, 58.

Dardanius, name in Caes. V, 5, 8. 9.

Dare, subst. 1) b o l d n e s s: *it lends a lustre and more great opinion, a larger d. to our great enterprise, than if the earl were here,* H4A IV, 1, 78.

2) d e f i a n c e: *Pompeius hath given the d. to Caesar,* Ant. I, 2, 191.

Dare, vb. (3 d̲ person *dare* and *dares* indiscriminately, but in the sense to c h a l l e n g e or d e f y *dares* only. Preterit *durst,* but only in the first two significations. Partic. *dared,* = ventured: Meas. II, 2, 91. Wint. III, 2, 130. R2 II, 3, 91. 92. H5 Prol. 9. = d e f i e d: H6A I, 3, 45. Rom. II, 4, 12. Hml. I, 1, 84. Ant. III, 7, 31).

1) to h a v e c o u r a g e, to be bold enough, to v e n t u r e; a) usually followed by an inf. without *to:* Ven. 401. Lucr. 458. 605. 1314. Sonn. 57, 5. 131, 7. Pilgr. 196. Tp. I, 2, 470. III, 1, 77. III, 2, 62. Gentl. I, 2, 42. II, 3, 63. V, 4, 162. Wiv. II, 1, 25. II, 2, 253. Meas. III, 1, 77. IV, 3, 160. V, 316. Err. I, 2, 60. IV, 1, 75. V, 31. Ado III, 1, 74. III, 2, 12. IV, 1, 300. LLL I, 1, 229. IV, 3, 227. 270. Mids. III, 1, 136. III, 2, 336. 422. V, 253. Merch. II, 4, 36. III, 1, 47. Tw. III, 4, 347. Wint. II, 2, 37. V, 2, 184. John I, 271. III, 1, 132. H4A III, 3, 163. H5 III, 7, 156. H6A I, 2, 89. I, 3, 44. II, 4, 2. 32. III, 4, 31. H6B I, 1, 229. II, 1, 39. 42. III, 2, 201. IV, 8, 4. V, 1, 95. H6C III, 3, 178. R3 IV, 2, 70. H8 II, 1, 72. V, 3, 50. Troil. I, 3, 271. V, 2, 94. Tit. II, 1, 59. Rom. II, 4, 12. Mcb. I, 7, 46. 47. IV, 3, 33. V, 3, 28. Hml. I, 1, 161 (Ff *can*). III, 4, 39 etc. *Durst:* Lucr. 1223. Tp. I, 2, 140. Ado V, 4, 89. LLL IV, 3, 346. Mids. II, 2, 76. III, 2, 69. As V, 4, 89. Shr. IV, 1, 166. All's V, 3, 46. Wint. II, 2, 50. R2 I, 1, 66. H4A I, 3, 116. V, 1, 63. H6A I, 1, 123. I, 4, 48. II, 4, 87. H6B IV, 10, 4. H6C I, 1, 63. II, 2, 108. IV, 1, 112. V, 2, 22. H8 I, 1, 33. Tit. IV, 1, 62. Mcb. I, 7, 49. Per. I, 2, 54 etc.

b) followed by an inf. with *to:* *then may I d. to boast how I do love thee,* Sonn. 26, 13. *he —s to tread,* Wiv. IV, 4, 59. *had not —d to do that evil,* Meas. 2, 91. H5 II, 2, 81. H6B IV, 1, 80. V, 1, 22. Cymb. III, 3, 34. *I durst to wager she is honest,* Oth. IV, 2, 12 (*I durst wager,* Per. V, 1, 42). — *To* before a second inf.: *—s better be damned than to do it,* All's III, 6, 96.

c) followed by an accus.: *the roe which no encounter d.* Ven. 676. *my heart ... not —ing the reports of my tongue,* All's IV, 1, 34 (i. e. not —ing to perform what the tongue speaks). *what —s not Warwick,* H6B III, 2, 203. *he that —s most,* H8 V, 3, 131. *what man d., I d.* Mcb. III, 4, 99. Cor. IV, 5, 99.

d) absolutely: *how he —s, being —d,* Rom. II, 4, 12.

2) m a y; and negatively, m u s t n o t: *we d. trust you in this kind,* Gentl. III, 2, 56. *my robe ... is all I d. now call my own,* H8 III, 2, 455. *what I d. too well do, I d. not do,* All's II, 3, 210 (i. e. what I am bold enough to do, I must not, it is not well for me, to do). *durst inhabit on a living brow,* Sonn. 68, 4. *I durst have denied that,* Err. II, 2, 67. *how they might hurt their enemies, if they durst,* Ado V, 1, 98. *she durst not lie near this lack-love,* Mids. II, 2, 76. *my face so thin that in mine ear I durst not stick a rose lest men should say ...,* John I, 142. *I durst so far free him,*

Cor. IV, 7, 47. *durst I have done my will,* Caes. V, 3, 48. — *I d. say:* H5 IV, 1, 129. H6A II, 4, 133. *I d. not say:* Gentl. V, 4, 65. *I d. assure you:* Shr. IV, 3, 191. Caes. V, 4, 21. *I d. vouch:* Cor. III, 1, 300

Passing, as *may* also does, into the sense of w i l l and c a n; a) of w i l l: *I d. be bound again, my soul upon the forfeit, that your lord will never more break faith,* Merch. V, 251. *and —s better be damned than to do it,* All's III, 6, 96 (= would rather). *I d. lay any money 'twill be nothing yet,* Tw. III, 4, 432. *let Titan rise as early as he d.* Troil. V, 10, 25. *death do what he d.* Rom. II, 6, 7. *Surrey durst better have burnt that tongue than said so,* H8 III, 2, 253. *I love you and durst commend a secret to your ear,* V, 1, 17. *I durst wager,* Per. V, 1, 42. — b) Of c a n: *although the king have mercies more than I d. make faults,* H8 II, 1, 71. *more miseries than my weak-hearted enemies d. offer,* III, 2, 390. *exposing what is mortal and unsure to all that fortune, death and danger d.* Hml. IV, 4, 52 (= may or can do).

3) to c h a l l e n g e, to d e f y: *am I —d and bearded to my face,* H6A I, 3, 45. *if false Suffolk d. him,* H6B III, 2, 203. *—ing the event to the teeth,* H8 I, 2, 36. *but d. all imminence,* Troil. V, 10, 13. *how he —s, being —d,* Rom. II, 4, 12. *do you d. our anger?* Tim. III, 5, 96. *to d. the vile contagion of the night,* Caes. II, 1, 265. *I d. damnation,* Hml. IV, 5, 133. Followed by *to: I dare thee but to breathe upon my love,* Gentl. V, 4, 131. *and —s him to set forward,* R2 I, 3, 109. *I d. him to lay his gay comparisons apart,* Ant. III, 13, 25. *unless a brother should a brother d. to gentle exercise,* H4A V, 2, 54. *I d. your quenchless fury to more rage,* H6C I, 4, 28. *—ing an opposite to every danger,* R3 V, 4, 3. *d. me to the desert,* Mcb. III, 4, 104. *was by Fortinbras —d to the combat,* Hml. I, 1, 84. *he —s us to't,* Ant. III, 7, 30. *—d him to single fight,* 31. *—s me to personal combat,* IV, 1, 3. *I d. you to this match,* Cymb. I, 4, 157. — *To d.* on: *he goes before me and still —s me on,* Mids. III, 2, 413.

Singular passages: *their neighing coursers —ing of the spur,* H4B IV, 1, 119 (probably = their coursers, by neighing, challenging the spur to give the signal of setting off. cf. *Of,* concerning the use of this preposition after participles). *how might she tongue me! yet reason —s her no,* Meas. IV, 4, 28 (perhaps = reason defies her denial of my assertions).

4) to a m a z e, to make couch down in f e a r (used of birds caught by means of small mirrors fastened on scarlet cloth, or by keeping a hawk hovering aloft): *let his grace ... d. us with his cap like larks,* H8 III, 2, 282. *our approach shall so much d. the field that England shall couch down in fear and yield,* H5 IV, 2, 36.

Dareful, full of d e f i a n c e: *we might have met them d., beard to beard,* Mcb. V, 5, 6.

Daring, bold (in a good and ill sense): Lucr. 1173. Gentl. III, 1, 155. Merch. II, 1, 28. R2 IV, 8. H4A V, 1, 91. H6A III, 2, 113. R3 IV, 4, 170. H8 II, 4, 215. III, 2, 207.

Daring-hardy, a u d a c i o u s: R2 I, 3, 43.

Darius, king of Persia: *the rich-jewelled coffer of D.* H6A I, 6, 25 (i. e. the casket in which Alexander the Great kept the Iliad).

Dark, adj., 1) v o i d o f l i g h t: *'tis d.* Ven. 719. *it grows d.* LLL V, 2, 633. *I should wish it d.* Merch. V, 304. *d. night,* Ven. 727. Lucr. 729. 1625

Pilgr. 200. Wiv. V, 2, 13. Ado III, 3, 167. LLL I, 1, 45. Mids. III, 2, 177. H6B I, 4, 19. *earth's d. womb*, Lucr. 549. *d. harbour*, 768. *desert*, 1144. *your light grows d.* LLL I, 1, 79. *corners*, Meas. IV, 3, 164. *vault*, Err. V, 247 etc. Superl. *—est:* Shr. IV, 3, 175. Hml. V, 2, 267. — Madmen kept in a dark house or room: Err. IV, 4, 97. V, 247. As III, 2, 421. Tw. III, 4, 148. V, 350.

2) opposed to f a i r: *art as black as hell, as d. as night*, Sonn. 147, 14. *a light condition in a beauty d.* LLL V, 2, 20. *an her hair were not somewhat —er than Helen's*, Troil. I, 1, 41. cf. R2 I, 1, 169.

3) g l o o m y, dismal: *with a heavy, d., disliking eye*, Ven. 182. *what freezings have I felt, what d. days seen*, Sonn. 97, 3. *his affections d. as Erebos*, Merch. V, 87. *war is no strife to the d. house and the detested wife*, All's II, 3, 309. *d. dishonour*, R2 I, 1, 169. *death, that d. spirit*, Cor. II, 1, 177. *this d. monarchy* (hell), R3 I, 4, 51. *the fate of that d. hour*, Mcb. III, 1, 138. *fortune*, Cymb. III, 4, 147. *more d. and d. our woes*, Rom. III, 5, 36.

4) i n d i s c e r n i b l e, obscure, not known: *if thou destroy them not in d. obscurity*, Ven. 760. *in the d. backward and abysm of time*, Tp. I, 2, 50. *the duke would have d. deeds darkly answered*, Meas. III, 2, 187. *what's your d. meaning*, LLL V, 2, 19. *d. oblivion*, R3 III, 7, 129. *our —er purpose*, Lr. I, 1, 37. — Hence = m e a n: *if you could wear a mind d. as your fortune is*, Cymb. III, 4, 147; cf. R2 I, 1, 169.

Dark, adv. in the dark, without light: *than without candle may go d. to bed*, As III, 5, 39. *I'll keep him d.* All's IV, 1, 104.

Dark, subst. darkness, want of light: *in the d.* Ven. 827. Tp. II, 2, 6. Meas. IV, 1, 43. LLL V, 2, 24. Mcb. IV, 1, 25. Hml. V, 2, 13. Lr. II, 1, 40. Oth. IV, 3, 67. V, 1, 63. 112. *in d.* Sonn. 43, 4. Rom. V, 3, 105. *with the d. I'll steal away*, All's III, 2, 132 *the poring d.* H5 IV Chor. 2. *befits the d.* Rom. II, 1, 32. *through the blanket of the d.* Mcb. I, 5, 54. *the wanderers of the d.* Lr. III, 2, 44. *we are for the d.* (viz death) Ant. V, 2, 194. *d. needs no candles now, for d. is light*, LLL IV, 3, 269. *d. shall be my light and night my day*, H6B II, 4, 40.

Dark, vb. to darken, 1) trans.: *this so —s in Philoten all graceful marks*, Per. IV Prol. 35.

2) intr.: *even with the vail and —ing of the sun*, Troil. V, 8, 7 (Q *darkning*).

Darken, 1) to make d a r k: *by —ing my clear sun*, H8 I, 1, 226. Figuratively, a) to obscure: *their blaze shall d. him for ever*, Cor. II, 1, 275. *you are —ed in this action*, IV, 7, 5. *gain which —s him*, Ant. III, 1, 24. — b) to sully, to foul: *lend it not* (thy light) *to d. her whose light excelleth thine*, Lucr. 191. *—ing thy power to lend base subjects light*, Sonn. 100, 4. *evils enough to d. all his goodness*, Ant. I, 4, 11. *careless heirs may the two latter* (nobleness and riches) *d. and expend*, Per. III, 2, 29. — c) to make g l o o m y: *d. not the mirth of the feast*, Wint. IV, 4, 41. — d) to deprive of intellectual vi- sion: *if your knowledge be more, it is much —ed in your malice*, Meas. III, 2, 157.

2) to grow dark: *with the vail and —ing of the sun*, Troil. V, 8, 7 (Ff *darking*).

Dark-eyed: *d. night*, Lr. II, 1, 121.

Darkling, adv., in the dark: Mids. II, 2, 86. Lr. I, 4, 237. Ant. IV, 15, 10.

Darkly, 1) in a situation void of light: *when I sleep, in dreams they* (my eyes) *look on thee, and d. bright are bright in dark directed*, Sonn. 43, 4.

2) gloomily: *my stars shine d. over me*, Tw. II, 1, 4.

3) n o t c l e a r l y, obscurely: *I will go d. to work with her*, Meas. V, 279. *therefore I'll d. end the argument*, LLL V, 2, 23. *when I spake d. what I pur- posed*, John IV, 2, 232. R3 I, 4, 175.

4) secretly: *the duke yet would have dark deeds d. answered; he would never bring them to light*, Meas. III, 2, 188. *I will tell you a thing, but you shall let it dwell d. with you*, All's IV, 3, 13.

Darkness, 1) absence of light: Ven. 1128. Lucr. 118. 398. 462. 752. Sonn. 27, 8. Tp. I, 2, 130. V, 66. LLL I, 1, 78. Mids. I, 1, 148. V, 393. Tw. IV, 2, 34. 47. 62. V, 312. H4B I, 1, 160. H6A II, 1, 7. V, 4, 89. H6B II, 1, 67. IV, 1, 7. R3 I, 3, 269. V, 3, 86. H8 V, 5, 45. Rom. II, 3, 3. Caes. II, 1, 278. Mcb. II, 4, 9. Per. II, 3, 44.

2) d e a t h, in a physical and moral sense: *I will encounter d. as a bride*, Meas. III, 1, 84. cf. R3 I, 3, 269 and 327.

3) hell: *this thing of d.* Tp. V, 275. *thy state of d.* Err. IV, 4, 59. *the prince of d.* All's IV, 5, 45. Lr. III, 4, 148. *the sons of d.* H4A II, 4, 191. III, 3, 42. *descend to d.* H6B I, 4, 42. *the instruments of d.* Mcb. I, 3, 124. *d. and devils!* Lr. I, 4, 273. IV, 6, 130. *send to d. all that stop me*, Ant. III, 13, 182. *to d. fleet souls that fly backwards*, Cymb. V, 3, 25. *the act of d.*, Lr. III, 4, 90, and *the deed of d.* Per. IV, 6, 32, i. e. for- nication.

4) secrecy: *though lately we intended to keep in d. what occasion now reveals*, Tw. V, 156.

Dark-seated, lying in darkness: *d. hell*, H6B III, 2, 328.

Darksome, dark: Lucr. 379.

Dark-working, working in darkness (in secrecy, or by infernal means?): *d. sorcerers*, Err. I, 2, 99.

Darling, subst. one very dear, a favourite: Tp. III, 3, 93. H6B III, 1, 216. H6C I, 4, 78. Oth. I, 2, 68 (Ff *dearling.* cf. *Minion*). Per. I, 4, 44. Used of things: All's II, 1, 110. Oth. III, 4, 66.

Adjectively: *the d. buds of May*, Sonn. 18, 3.

Darnel, the plant L o l i u m t e m u l e n t u m: H5 V, 2, 45. Lr. IV, 4, 5. Thought to be injurious to the eyes: H6A III, 2, 44.

Darraign, to range: *d. your battle*, H6C II, 2, 72.

Dart, subst. missile weapon, arrow: Ven. 941. 948. Meas. I, 3, 2. H6B III, 1, 362. 366. Cor. I, 6, 61. Caes. V, 3, 76. Oth. IV, 1, 278. Ant. IV, 14, 70. Cymb. IV, 2, 211. Per. I, 2, 53.

Dart, vb. tr. to throw, to shoot: *thine eye —s forth the fire that burneth me*, Ven. 196. *which* (eye) *after him she —s*, 817. Sonn. 139, 12. LLL V, 2, 396. As III, 5, 25. Shr. V, 2, 137. R2 III, 2, 43. V, 2, 14. *all curses ... be —ed on thee*, Cymb. IV, 2, 314. *where 'twill not extend, thither he —s it* (viz his sword) H8 I, 1, 112. *d. your flames into her eyes*, Lr. II, 4, 167. — Absolutely: *—ing Parthia*, Ant. III, 1, 1.

Dash, subst. 1) mark of infamy: *some loath- some d. the herald will contrive, to cipher me how fondly I did dote*, Lucr. 206. *had I not the d. of my former life in me*, Wint. V, 2, 122.

2) at first d. = from the first: *she takes upon her bravely at first d.* H6A I, 2, 71.

Dash, vb. 1) to smite, to strike, to knock; with the idea of violence and rapidity: *when we have —ed them* (the walls) *to the ground,* John II, 405. *their heads —ed to the walls,* H5 III, 3, 37.

Joined with *out,* = to knock out: *Troilus had his brains —ed out,* As IV, 1, 98. Wint. II, 3, 140. Rom. IV, 3, 54. Mcb. I, 7, 58.

2) to shatter, to crash, to crush; absol.: *run on the —ing rocks thy weary bark,* Rom. V, 3, 118. Transitively: *the rocks ... would not d. me with their ragged sides,* H6B III, 2, 98. Usually with the words *to pieces: a brave vessel ... —ed all to pieces,* Tp. I, 2, 8. Caes. IV, 3, 82. And reflectively: *touch ground and d. themselves to pieces,* H4B IV, 1, 18. R3 I, 3, 260.

3) to destroy, to frustrate: *here was a consent, to d. it like a Christmas comedy,* LLL V, 2, 462. *with a full intent to d. our late decree,* H6C II, 1, 118.

4) to put out of countenance, to depress: *an honest man and soon —ed,* LLL V, 2, 585. *this hath a little —ed your spirits,* Oth. III, 3, 214.

5) to throw water on suddenly: *this tempest, —ing the garment of this peace, aboded the sudden breach on't,* H8 I, 1, 93 (cf. *Bedash*). Joined with *out* = to put out, to quench: *the sea ... —es the fire out,* Tp. I, 2, 5.

Dastard, subst. coward: R2 I, 1, 190. H6A I, 2, 23. IV, 1, 19. H6B IV, 8, 28. H6C II, 2, 114.

Dastard, adj. cowardly: H6A I, 1, 144. I, 4, 111. Cor. IV, 5, 81.

Dat, French pronunciation of *that,* very often in Wiv. and H5.

Datchet-lane, a lane in Windsor: Wiv. III, 5, 101.

Datchet-mead: Wiv. III, 3, 15. 141. 157.

Date, subst. the fruit of the date-tree: All's I, 1, 172. Wint. IV, 3, 49. Troil. I, 2, 280. Rom. IV, 4, 2.

Date, subst. 1) time stipulated or prescribed: *thy end is truth's and beauty's doom and d.* Sonn. 14, 14. *my reliances on his fracted —s have smit my credit,* Tim. II, 1, 22. *take the bonds along with you, and have the —s in compt,* 35.

2) time in general, duration: *an expired d., cancelled ere well begun,* Lucr. 26. *enchained me to endless d. of never ending woes,* 935. *through her wounds doth fly life's lasting d. from cancelled destiny,* 1729. *summer's lease hath all too short a d.* Sonn. 18, 4. *so long as youth and thou are of one d.* 22, 2. *eternal numbers to outlive long d.* 38, 12. *beyond all d., even to eternity,* 122, 4. *our —s are brief,* 123, 5. *here comes the almanac of my true d.* Err. I, 2, 41. *with league whose d. till death shall never end,* Mids. III, 2, 373. *your d. is better in your pie than in your cheek,* All's I, 1, 172. *will weep my d. of life out for his sweet life's loss,* John IV, 3, 106. R2 V, 2, 91. H4A II, 4, 552. H6A IV, 6, 9. R3 IV, 4, 254. Troil. I, 2, 281. Tit. I, 168. Rom. I, 4, 3. 108. V, 3, 229. Per. III, 4, 14.

Date-broke: *d. bonds,* Tim. II, 2, 37; an emendation received into the text by most M. Edd.; O. Edd. quite intelligibly: *with clamorous demands of debt, broken bonds.*

Dated, in *New-dated* and *Treble-dated,* q. v.

Dateless, termless, eternal: *death's d. night,* Sonn. 30, 6. *a d. lively heat, still to endure,* 153, 6. *the d. limit of thy dear exile,* R2 I, 3, 151. *a d. bargain,* Rom. V, 3, 115.

Daub, to colour, to paint: *d. her lips with her own children's blood,* H4A I, 1, 6. *d. the wall of a jakes with him,* Lr. II, 2, 71. Figuratively: *so smooth he —ed his vice with show of virtue,* R3 III, 5, 29. *I cannot d. it further,* Lr. IV, 1, 54 (cf. *Bedaub*).

Daubery, colouring, false pretences: *we are simple men; we do not know what's brought to pass under the profession of fortune-telling; she works by charms, by spells, by the figure, and such d. as this is, beyond our element: we know nothing,* Wiv. IV, 2, 186 (i. e. in fact she is a go-between).

Daughter, female child: Tp. I, 2, 17. 57. 439. Gentl. II, 4, 49. Wiv. I, 1, 46 etc. etc. *Eve's —s,* Wiv. IV, 2, 24. *that d. here of Spain,* John II, 423. *—s of the game,* Troil. IV, 5, 63. Used for a daughter-in-law: R3 IV, 1, 5. Cor. I, 3, 1. Used by clergymen as a paternal form of addressing young women: Meas. II, 3, 30. IV, 1, 71. IV, 3, 116. Rom. IV, 1, 39. Neuter, in speaking of a new-born child: *hath brought you forth a d.; here 'tis; commends it to your blessing,* Wint. II, 3, 66. Rhyming to *after* in Shr. I, 1, 245.

Daughter-beamed, a word formed by Boyet in derision of *sun-beamed,* LLL V, 2, 171 (cf. H6C II, 1, 41).

Daughter-in-law, a son's wife: All's I, 3, 173. III, 2, 21. IV, 5, 4.

Daunt, to intimidate, to dishearten: Lucr. 462. Shr. I, 2, 200. H4B I, 1, 110. H6A V, 3, 69. H6B III, 1, 100. IV, 1, 119. Tit. I, 268.

Dauntless, fearless: John II, 72. V, 1, 53. H6C III, 3, 17. Mcb. III, 1, 52.

Dauphin (O. Edd. *Dolphin*), the eldest son of the king of France, and heir apparent of the crown: John II, 425 etc. H5 I, 2, 221 etc. H6A I, 1, 92. 96. 149. I, 2, 46 (*the Prince D.*) etc. H6B I, 3, 128. IV, 7, 31 etc. H6C II, 2, 151. Lr. III, 4, 104 (here M. Edd. also *Dolphin*).* — Used without an article: *if D. and the rest will be but ruled,* H6A III, 3, 8. *Prince D.* the usual form of address: John II, 524. H5 II, 4, 6. 29 etc. Quibbling with the name of the fish: H6A I, 4, 107.

Daventry (cf. *Daintry*), town in England: H4A IV, 2, 51.

Davy, name; 1) *St. D.'s day* (26th of Aug.), the day of the battle of Crecy, in whose memory the Welsh wore leek in their caps: H5 IV, 1, 55. IV, 7, 108. V, 1, 2. — 2) a servant of Justice Shallow: H4B V, 1, 2. 8. 10 etc. V, 3, 10. 11. 65. — 3) *D. Gam,* slain at Agincourt: H5 IV, 8, 109.

Daw, the bird Corvus monedula, jackdaw: Ado II, 3, 264. LLL V, 2, 915. Tw. III, 4, 39. Troil. I, 2, 265. Oth. I, 1, 65. Thought a foolish bird: *I am no wiser than a d.* H6A II, 4, 18. *then thou dwellest with —s too? No, I serve not thy master,* Cor. IV, 5, 48.

Dawn, subst. break of day, morning-light: Meas. IV, 2, 226. H5 IV, 1, 291.

Dawn, vb., to grow light: *—ing day,* Tit. II, 2, 10.

Dawning, subst., morning light: Meas. IV, 2, 97. H5 III, 7, 141. Hml. I, 1, 160. Cymb. II, 2, 48. *good d. to thee,* Lr. II, 2, 1 (Qq *even*).

Day, 1) the time between the rising and setting of the sun: *she prays she never may behold the d.* Lucr. 746. *d. night's scapes doth open lay,* 747. *'tis almost d.* Gentl. IV, 2, 139. Lucr. 806. Sonn.

28, 9. LLL V, 2, 733. R3 IV, 4, 118. Hml. I, 5, 11 etc. etc. Used as a masc.: *I tell the d., to please him thou art bright,* Sonn. 28, 9. = light: *clear as d.* H6B II, 1, 108. *O thou d. of the world,* Ant. IV, 8, 13. Strange expression: *a hand open as d. for melting charity,* H4B IV, 4, 32. — *Good d.!* Gentl. IV, 4, 113 Ado V, 1, 112. Wint. I, 2, 366. Troil. III, 3, 62. *good d. and happiness!* As IV, 1, 30. *g. day to you,* Ado V, 1, 46. H4B IV, 2, 2. Cor. I, 3, 51. *d. and night,* Ven. 1186. *night and d.* Troil. III, 2, 122. *by d.:* Sonn. 27, 13. Gentl. III, 1, 109. Err. IV, 1, 18. Merch. II, 5, 47. V, 100. 104. Wint. III, 3, 56. H6B I, 1, 26. H6C V, 4, 56. H8 V, 1, 16. *by d. and night:* Tp. I, 2, 336. Tit. IV, 3, 28. Lr. I, 3, 4. *by d. or night,* Wiv. II, 1, 16. *by night and d.* Err. IV, 2, 60. *By d. and night* used as an oath: H8 I, 2, 213 and perhaps Lr. I, 3, 4 (Ff *by d. and night, he wrongs me*). *O d. and night, but this is wondrous strange,* Hml. I, 5, 164. *by this day!* Ado II, 3, 254. *by this good d.!* V, 4, 95. H4B III, 2, 81. *as sure as d.* H4A III, 1, 255. — *In the d.* = by day: *thou singest not in the d.* Lucr. 1142. *in the living d.* Sonn. 43, 10. *unless I look on Silvia in the d., there is no d. for me,* Gentl. III, 1, 180.

2) a time of twenty four hours: Tp. I, 2, 298. 421. 490 etc. IV, 1, 29. Gentl. I, 3, 85. V, 4, 172. R3 II, 1, 1. IV, 4, 188. Cor. I, 3, 9. Caes. V, 1, 72 etc. etc. *a twelvemonth and a d.* LLL V, 2, 837. 887. *for ever and a d.* As IV, 1, 145. Shr. IV, 4, 97. *this d.* = to-day, Merch. IV, 1, 409. *what is the time of the d.?* Tp. I, 2, 238. LLL II, 122. H4A I, 2, 1. *how's the d.?* (= what o' clock is it?) Tp. V, 3. *an it be not four by the d.* (= four o' clock) H4A II, 1, 2 (the carrier's speech). *'tis a chronicle of d. by d.,* Tp. V, 163. *d. by d.* = every day, always: Sonn. 75, 13. 117, 4. All's III, 1, 18. *from. d. to d.,* in the same sense: LLL V, 2, 860. *a whole week by —s* = every day of a whole week, Troil. IV, 1, 10. *fair,* or *good,* or *happy time of d.,* used as a form of salutation: LLL V, 2, 339. H4B I, 2, 107 (Ff. *time of the d.*). H5 V, 2, 3. R3 I, 1, 122. I, 3, 18. II, 1, 47. IV, 1, 6. Tim. III, 6, 1. *in the morn, when every one will give the time of d.* H6B III, 1, 14. *not worth the time of d.* (i.e. not worth greeting) Per. IV, 3, 35. *nor to us hath tendered the duty of the d.* Cymb. III, 5, 32 (i. e. has omitted the morning-salutation). Proverbial phrase: *there live we as merry as the d. is long,* Ado II, 1, 52. *I should be as merry as the d. is long,* John IV, 1, 18. — Prepositions before it: a) *at: at the d. of judgement,* Wiv. III, 3, 226 (Evans' speech). *at the latter d.* H5 IV, 1, 143 (a common soldier's speech). — b) *in; α)* = within, during: *lost, and recovered in a d. again,* H6A III, 2, 115. *you made in a d. whole towns to fly,* H6B II, 1, 164. *when that hour o'erslips me in the d. wherein I sigh not,* Gentl. II, 2, 9. β) = on: *in the hottest day shall he be set,* Wint. IV, 4, 817. *a d. wherein the fortune of ten thousand men must bide the touch,* H4A IV, 4, 9. *that our armies join not in a hot d.* H4B I, 2, 234. *in the d. of battle,* R3 IV, 4, 188. *the d. wherein I wished to fall,* V, 1, 16. *two lions littered in one d.* Caes. II, 2, 46. *they met me in the d. of success,* Mcb. I, 5, 1. c) *on: on a d.* Pilgr. 227. *one meal on every d.* LLL I, 1, 40. cf. *on his wedding-day, on Saturday* etc.: Ado V, 1, 169. LLL IV, 1, 6. Mids. I, 2, 7. Merch. I, 3, 127. II, 5, 25.

3) a day of battle, combat: *victor of the d.*

Pilgr. 223. *by losing of this d.* John III, 4, 116. *how goes the day with us?* V, 3, 1. H4B I, 2, 167. Cor. II, 2, 99. Cymb. V, 2, 17. Hence = victory: *the d. is ours,* H4A V, 4, 163. R3 V, 5, 2. Cymb. V, 5, 75. *to win the d.,* H6A I, 6, 17. H6C II, 1, 136. R3 V, 3, 145. *if my young lord your son have not the d.* H4B I, 1, 52. *doubt not of the d.* H6C IV, 7, 87. *the d. almost itself professes yours,* Mcb. V, 7, 27. *to whom in favour she* (Fortune) *shall give the d.* John II, 393. Singular passage: *we will live to see their d. and them our fortune give,* H6B V, 2, 89 (= a victory like theirs).

4) time; in the sing.: *never see d. that the happy sees,* R2 V, 3, 94. *I have not sought the d. of this dislike,* H4A V, 1, 26. *these seven years' d.* H6B II, 1, 2. *never's my d.* Troil. IV, 5, 52. *the d. serves well for them now,* Cor. IV, 3, 32. *I have seen the d.* Lr. V, 3, 276. *this d.* = at this time: *there's not one so young and so villanous this d. living,* As I, 1, 161. *at this d.:* H5 I, 2, 53. H6B IV, 2, 157. *one d.* = in future time: Wiv. III, 3, 88. H8 II, 2, 22. *another d.,* in the same sense: *'twill be thine another d.,* LLL IV, 1, 109. *this quarrel will drink blood another d.* H6A II, 4, 134 (concerning *the other d.* see *Other*). *one of these days,* in the same sense: As I, 2, 91. Wint. II, 1, 18. H5 II, 1, 92. Proverbially: *to have one's day* = to have one's time or turn: *the worst is death, and death will have his d.,* R2 III, 2, 103. *the cat will mew and dog will have his d.* Hml. V, 1, 315. *Alack the d.!* (an exclamation of pity or grief): Pilgr. 227. LLL IV, 3, 101. Merch. II, 2, 73. R2 III, 3, 8. IV, 257. Rom. III, 2, 39. IV, 5, 23. Lr. IV, 6, 185. *Alas the d.:* Wiv. III, 5, 39. IV, 2, 71. As III, 2, 231. Tw. II, 1, 25. II, 2, 39. H4B II, 1, 14. Troil. III, 2, 50. Rom. III, 2, 72. Mcb. II, 4, 23. Oth. III, 4, 158. IV, 2, 42. 124. *Woe the d.:* Tp. I, 2, 15. *Well a d.,* see *Well-a-day.*

Plural: *the wits of former —s,* Sonn. 59, 13. 67, 14. 68, 1. 106, 13. 38, 13. Gentl. II, 4, 68. LLL IV, 1, 22. IV, 3, 262. John IV, 2, 58. H6B II, 2, 69. III, 1, 142. R3 I, 3, 145. IV, 4, 28. V, 5, 34. H8 V, 3, 29 (*of late —s*). Remarkable use: *let not the hours of this ungodly day wear out the days in peace,* John III, 1, 110 (M. Edd. *wear out the day*). *'tis but early days,* Troil. IV, 5, 12 (genitive? cf. *now-a-days*). *see that you take no longer days, but send the midwife presently to me,* Tit. IV, 2, 166 (quite = time).

5) In the plural, = life: *wretched hateful —s,* Lucr. 161. *that tongue that tells the story of thy —s,* Sonn. 95, 5. *as I hope for quiet —s,* Tp. IV, 1, 24. *once in my —s I'll be a madcap,* H4A I, 2, 159. *like a hermit overpassed thy —s,* H6A II, 5, 117. *outlive thy father's —s,* Tit. I, 167.

6) age (mostly in the plural): *all the treasure of thy lusty —s,* Sonn. 2, 6. *painting my age with beauty of thy —s,* 62, 14. *my —s are past the best,* 138, 6. Gentl. I, 1, 3. Ado V, 1, 65. R2 II, 3, 43. Hml. II, 2, 11. — In the singular: *some flowers that might become your time of d.* Wint. IV, 4, 114.

Day-bed, a couch, a sofa: Tw. II, 5, 54. R3 III, 7, 72 (Ff *love-bed*).

Daylight, the light of the day: Pilgr. 199. Merch. V, 124. Tw. II, 5, 173. Troil. III, 2, 51. Rom. I, 1, 145. II, 2, 20. III, 5, 12. Lr. IV, 7, 52. *by d.:* Ado II, 1, 86. Mids. III, 2, 427. 433. *To burn d.* = to lose time: Wiv. II, 1, 54. Rom. I, 4, 43.

Day-wearied, weary of the labours of the day: *d. sun,* John V, 4, 35.

Day-woman, a woman hired by the day, a chairwoman: LLL I, 2, 136.

Dazzle, 1) tr. to overpower with light or splendour: Lucr. 377. Gentl. II, 4, 210. H5, I, 2, 279. H6A I, 1, 13.

2) to lose the power of seeing well: *upon his hurt she looks so steadfastly, that her sight —ing makes the wound seem three,* Ven. 1064. LLL I, 1, 82. *d. mine eyes, or do I see three suns?* H6C II, 1, 25. *thou shalt read when mine begin to d.* Tit. III, 2, 85.

Dazzled trisyll.: Gentl. II, 4, 210 (F2.3.4: —*d so*).

De, wrong pronunciation of *the:* H5 III, 4, 8 etc. V, 2, 178 etc. cf. *Do de.*

Dead, adj. 1) deprived of life: Tp. II, 2, 25. 34. 115. III, 1, 6. Gentl IV, 2, 106. IV, 4, 80 etc. etc. *well-nigh d. for me,* Ado V, 4, 81 (languishing for me). *almost d. for breath,* Mcb. I, 5, 37 (instead of *for want of breath;* cf. *to sink for food,* Cymb. III, 6, 17; *cold for action,* H5 I, 2, 114). *the d.:* Sonn. 31, 7. 68, 5. Mids. V, 356. *our English d.* H5 IV, 8, 107. *these d.* H6A IV, 7, 81. *the d.* = the dead man, Caes. III, 2, 131 etc. *to do him d.* H6C I, 4, 108. *felled him d.* Lr. IV, 2, 76. *kill her d.* Mids. III, 2, 269. Hml. III, 2, 194. *hit me d.* Troil. IV, 5, 251 (cf. *Strike*). *d. men's fingers,* = the plant orchis mascula: Hml. IV, 7, 173. *He's but a d. man* = he must die: Wiv. IV, 2, 44. *d. men's cries do fill the empty air,* H6B V, 2, 4. *thou art d.* Cymb. V, 5, 299.

To be d. sometimes = to have died: *the lady is d upon mine accusation,* Ado V, 1, 249. *my Nell is d. in the spital of malady of France,* H5 V, 1, 86. *who finds the partridge in the puttock's nest, but may imagine how the bird was dead, although the kite soar with unbloodied beak?* H6B III, 2, 192. *if that I had been d., thou wouldest not have mourned so much for me,* IV, 4, 23. *my wife is d. to-night,* Rom. V, 3, 210. *your eldest daughters have fordone themselves, and desperately are d.* Lr. V, 3, 292.

Figurative use: *my love to her is d.* Gentl. II, 6, 28. *he will awake my mercy which lies d.* John IV, 1, 26. *d. coals,* Wint. V, 1, 68. John V, 2, 83. *by the d. and drowsy fire,* Mids. V, 399. John IV, 1, 106. *thou d. elm,* H4B II, 4, 358. *our decrees, d. to infliction, to themselves are d.* Meas. I, 3, 28. *why should false painting imitate his cheek and steal d. seeing of his living hue?* Sonn. 67, 6 (*d. seeming?*).

2) similar to death: *we were d. of sleep,* Tp. V, 230. *strike more d. than common sleep of all these five the sense,* Mids. IV, 1, 86. *he drinks your Dane d. drunk,* Oth. II, 3, 85. *so dull, so d. in look, so woe-begone,* H4B I, 1, 71. *honest Iago, that lookest d. with grieving,* Oth. II, 3, 177 (= deadly pale). R2 III, 2, 79.

3) bringing death, deadly: *so should a murderer look, so d., so grim,* Mids. III, 2, 57. *we free thee from the d. blow of it* (our displeasure) Wint. IV, 4, 445. *you breathe these d. news in as d. an ear,* John V, 7, 65. *in that d. time when Gloster's death was plotted,* R2 IV, 10 (or = dark and dreary?).

4) still as death: *d. midnight,* Sonn. 43, 11. Meas. IV, 2, 67. H5 III Chor. 19. R3 V, 3, 180. *the night's d. silence,* Gentl. III, 2, 85. *at d. time of the night,* Tit. II, 3, 99. *at this d. hour,* Hml. I, 1, 65. *in the d. vast and middle of the night,* I, 2, 198.

Dead, subst., perfect stillness: *the d. of night, when heavy sleep hath closed up mortal eyes,* Lucr. 162. *in d. of night,* 449. *in the dreadful d. of dark*

midnight, 1625. *in the d. of night,* Tw. I, 5, 290. H4B I, 1, 72. *in the d. of darkness,* Tp. I, 2, 130.

Dead-killing, deadly: *with a cockatrice' d. eye,* Lucr. 540. *d. news,* R3 IV, 1, 36.

Deadly, adj. 1) belonging or relating to death, like death: *a d. groan,* Ven. 1044. H6C II, 6, 43. *pale and d. looks,* Err. IV, 4, 96. *d. divorce step between me and you,* All's V, 3, 319. *with such a suffering, such a d. life,* Tw. I, 5, 284. *d. night* (= death) H6A II, 4, 127. *all's cheerless, dark and d.* Lr. V, 3, 290. *a d. deed* = a deed of death: Lucr. 1730. Tit. V, 3, 66.

2) causing death, mortal: *d. bullet,* Ven. 461. *cares,* Lucr. 1593. *banishment,* Gentl. III, 1, 173. *doom,* 185. *poisons,* Err. V, 70. Cymb. I, 5, 10. *sickness,* Shr. IV, 3, 14. *thy assailant is quick, skilful and d.* Tw. III, 4, 246. *d. bloodshed,* John IV, 3, 55. *wounds,* H4A I, 3, 109. H6C II, 6, 27. *quarrel,* H6C II, 5, 91. *stroke,* R3 I, 2, 178. *eye,* I, 3, 225. *web,* 243. *venom,* IV, 1, 62. *holes,* V, 3, 125. *theme,* Troil. IV, 5, 181. *time,* V, 2, 39. *point,* Rom. III, 1, 165. III, 3, 103. *grief,* Mcb. IV, 3, 215. *use,* Lr. IV, 2, 36. *breach,* Oth. I, 3, 136. *sorrow,* Ant. I, 2, 75.

3) aiming to kill, implacable: *d. enmity,* Lucr. 503. Tit. V, 1, 131. *enemies,* Lucr. 674. *hate,* R2 II, 2, 131. III, 2, 136. H6B III, 2, 314. R3 I, 1, 35.

4) wicked, flagitious, detestable: *d. sin,* LLL II, 105. Rom. III, 3, 24. *the d. seven sins,* Meas. III, 1, 111. *this d. blot in thy digressing son,* R2 V, 3, 66. *this is the d. spite that angers me,* H4A III, 1, 192. *O d. gall,* Troil. IV, 5, 30.

Deadly, adv. 1) in a manner relating to or resembling death: *how darkly and how d. dost thou speak,* R3 I, 4, 174. *d. pale,* III, 7, 26.

2) mortally: *d. hurt,* Troil. V, 5, 12 (in Err. V, 70 it is adj.).

3) implacably: *hate him d.* Ado V, 1, 178. All's V, 3, 117. H6C I, 4, 84.

4) wickedly, detestably: *they lie d. that tell you you have good faces,* Cor. II, 1, 67.

Deadly-handed: *the d. Clifford slew my steed,* H6B V, 2, 9.

Deadly-standing (not hyphened in O. Edd.) menacing death: *what signifies my d. eye,* Tit. II, 3, 32.

Deadman (as one word in O. Edd., as two in M. Edd.): Mcb. IV, 3, 170. Cymb. V, 3, 12. Perhaps also in Err. V, 241. cf. *Man* and *Finger.*

Deaf, adj. wanting the sense of hearing: Ven. 435. Lucr. 495. Sonn. 29, 3. Gentl. IV, 2, 64. Err. V, 316. John II, 451. R2 I, 1, 19. 112. H4B I, 2, 77. H6B III, 2, 76. 144. H6C I, 4, 53. Cor. IV, 5, 239. Tit. II, 1, 128. II, 3, 160. IV, 4, 98. V, 1, 46. Caes. I, 2, 213. Mcb. V, 1, 81. Followed by *to:* H4B I, 2, 80. Troil. II, 2, 172. V, 3, 16. Rom. III, 1, 163. 197. Tim. I, 2, 257. Ant. I, 3, 98.

Deaf, vb., to deafen: *—ed with the clamours of their own dear groans,* Lucr. V, 2, 874. *—s our ears with this abundance of superfluous breath,* John II, 147.

Deafen, to make deaf, to stun: H4B III, 1, 24. Per. III, 1, 5. *make a battery through his —ed parts,* V, 1, 47.

Deafness, incapacity of hearing: Tp. I, 2, 106. H4B I, 2, 134.

Deal, subst., a quantity: *the fellow has a d. of that too much, which holds him much to have,* All's

III, 2, 92. *a great d. of* = much: Wiv. V, 3, 11. All's III, 6, 100. H6A I, 2, 101. Troil. II, 1, 108. Cor. II, 1, 32. Tim. III, 2, 53. *a great d.*, adverbially: *you are not of his council. So should I be a great d. of his act*, All's IV, 3, 55. *greater a great d. in evil*, 321. *you pay a great d. too dear*, Wint. I, 1, 18. *words him a great d. from the matter*, Cymb. I, 4, 17. *you are a great d. abused*, 124. *great d.* (without the article): *great d. misprizing the knight*, Troil. IV, 5, 74. — *an infinite d. of nothing*, Merch. I, 1, 114. *this intolerable d. of sack*, H4A II, 4, 592. *my shepherd's pipe can sound no d.* Pilgr. 271 (= nothing). *to weep with them that weep doth ease some d.* Tit. III, 1, 245. *such a d. of wonder*, Wint. V, 2, 26. *such a d. of spleen*, H4A II, 3, 81. III, 1, 154. *such a d. of stinking breath*, Caes. I, 2, 247. *such a d. of man*, Lr. II, 2, 127. *what a d. of scorn*, Tw. III, 1, 157. *what a d. of world I wander*, R2 I, 3, 269. *what a candy d. of courtesy*, H4A I, 3, 251. *what a d. of brine*, Rom. II, 3, 69.

Deal, vb. (impf. and part. *dealt*); 1) trans. to give, to bestow: *Jupiter is yonder, —ing life*, Troil. IV, 5, 191. *I could d. kingdoms to my friends*, Tim. I, 2, 226. *as rich men d. gifts*, IV, 3, 516. cf. the quibble in Tw. V, 32.

2) intr. to do, to act, to proceed: *I will incense Page to d. with poison*, Wiv. I, 3, 110. *I will d. in this as secretly and justly as your soul should with your body*, Ado IV, 1, 249. *do not you meddle, let me d. in this*, V, 1, 101. *we cannot d. but with the very hand of stern injustice*, John V, 2, 22. *from the king I come to learn how you have dealt for him*, 121. *I never dealt better since I was a man*, H4A II, 4, 188. *and doubt not so to d. as all things shall redound unto your good*, H6B IV, 9, 46. *foes to my rest are they that I would have thee d. upon*, R3 IV, 2, 76 (= proceed against). *men shall d. unadvisedly sometimes*, IV, 4, 292. *let us d. justly*, Lr. III, 6, 42. *heavens, d. so still!* IV, 1, 69. *and, to d. plainly, I fear I am not in my perfect mind*, IV, 7, 62. *he alone dealt on lieutenantry*, Ant. III, 11, 39 (= acted by substitutes; cf. *On*). *God above d. between thee and me!* Mcb. IV, 3, 121 (i. e. God may intervene and conduct business between us, not the negotiators of the devilish Macbeth). cf. *Plain-dealing*.

To d. in = to have to do, to meddle with: *could d. in her* (the moon's) *command without her power*, Tp. V, 271 (i. e. could command her). *marriage is a matter of more worth than to be dealt in by attorney-ship*, H6A V, 5, 56. *I should not d. in her* (love's) *soft laws*, H6C III, 2, 154.

To d. with = to have to do with: *—ing with witches and with conjurers*, H6B II, 1, 172. *he privily —s with our cardinal*, H8 I, 1, 184. *away she started to d. with grief alone*, Lr. IV, 3, 34. Per. IV, 6, 29. Hence = to cope with: *I am never able to d. with my master, he hath learnt so much fence*, H6B II, 3, 78. *show me a murderer, I'll d. with him*, Tit. V, 2, 93 (= I'll do his business for him).

To d. with a person in a certain manner = to treat, to use: *I will d. in poison with thee*, As V, 1, 59. *that like a father you will d. with him*, Shr. IV, 4, 44. *we must d. gently with him*, Tw. III, 4, 106. R2 II, 1, 69. H6B I, 3, 160. III, 1, 323. R3 I, 3, 275. IV, 4, 499. Rom. IV, 4, 178 (*if you should d. double with her*). Hml. II, 2, 284. IV, 6, 20. Oth. IV, 2, 173. Cymb. V, 5, 420. Per. IV, 6, 147.

Dealer, in *Double-dealer* and *Plain-dealer*. Dromio makes a comparative of the latter word: *the plainer dealer, the sooner lost*, Err. II, 2, 89.

Dealing (cf. *Double-dealing* and *Plain-dealing*) subst. 1) proceeding, manner of acting: *revealed the actor and whole manner of his d.* Lucr. Arg. 21. *in plain d., I shall have you whipt*, Meas. II, 1, 264 (= to be plain with you). *the justice of your d.* IV, 2, 201. H4B II, 1, 40. H6B II, 4, 73. R3 III, 6, 14. H8 III, 1, 39. Rom. II, 4, 181. Lr. III, 3, 2. Plural *—s*: Merch. I, 3, 163. R3 III, 1, 49. Oth. III, 3, 260.

2) treatment: *so thou wilt buy and pay and use good d.* Ven. 514. *you should find better d.* Tw. III, 3, 18.

Deanery, the house of a dean: Wiv. IV, 6, 31. V, 3, 3. V, 5, 216.

Dear, adj. 1) bearing a high price: *is it possible that any villany should be so d.?* Ado III, 3 118 (i. e. should cost a thousand ducats). *shall render me a d. account*, IV, 1, 337; cf. R2 I, 1, 130. *making graces d.* LLL II, 1, 10. *it is a d. expense*, Mids. I, 1, 249. *the —est ring in Venice will I give you*, Merch. IV, 1, 435. *I have been d. to him*, Tw. III, 2, 58. *my thanks are too d. a halfpenny*, Hml. II, 2, 282.

2) asking a high price: *at the —est chandler's in Europe*, H4A III, 3, 52. *whose tailors are as d. as yours*, Cymb. II, 3, 84.

3) precious, valuable, of worth; a) of things: *wail my d. time's waste*, Sonn. 30, 4. *a —er birth than this his love had brought*, 32, 11. *thou art too d. for my possessing*, 87, 1. *that may express my love or thy d. merit*, 108, 4. *sold cheap what is most d.* 110, 3. *showed his visage by that cost more d.* Compl. 96. *sonnets that did amplify each stone's d. nature*, 210. *the fault's your own; so is the —est of the loss*, Tp. II, 1, 135. *supportable to make the d. loss*, V, 146; cf. R3 II, 2, 77. 78. 79. *I hold your dainties cheap, and your welcome d.* Err. III, 1, 21; cf. H8 V, 3, 174 and Troil. V, 3, 27. *sighs of love that costs the fresh blood d.* Mids. III, 2, 97. cf. *thy —est blood*, H6A III, 4, 40. H6C I, 1, 223. V, 1, 69. *your worth is very d. in my regard*, Merch. I, 1, 62. *a —er merit, not so deep a maim, have I deserved*, R2 I, 3, 156. *that's the —est grace it renders you*, H4A III, 1, 182. *here the Trojans taste our —est repute with their finest palate*, Troil. I, 3, 337. *that his country's —er than himself*, Cor. I, 6, 72. *to earn a —er estimation of them*, Cor. II, 3, 103. *a heart —er than Plutus' mine*, Caes. IV, 3, 102. *three of the carriages are very d. to fancy*, Hml. V, 2, 159 (cf. Meas. II, 2, 150). Hence = important: *to lay so dangerous and d. a trust on any soul removed*, H4A IV, 1, 34. *the letter was not nice but full of charge and d. import*, Rom. V, 2, 19. *a ring that I must use in d. employment*, V, 3, 32. *and dare, upon the warrant of my note, commend a d. thing to you*, Lr. III, 1, 19. *some d. cause will in concealment wrap me up*, IV, 3, 53. 46. *they have used their —est action in the tented field*, Oth. I, 3, 85.

b) used of persons: *many moe corrivals and d. men of estimation*, H4A IV, 4, 31. *death hath not struck so fat a deer to-day, though many —er, in this bloody fray*, V, 4, 108. *the d. man holds honour far more precious-dear than life*, Troil. V, 3, 27 (i. e. the worthy, estimable man. Some M. Edd. *brave man*).

4) beloved, cherished: Lucr. 687. Tp. I, 2, 1. 17. 305. III, 1, 21. V, 172. Gentl. I, 2, 17. II, 7, 12

etc. etc. Followed by *to:* Tp. III, 1, 39. Gentl. II, 6, 23. Tw. III, 2, 57 etc. Sometimes approaching to the sense of lovely: *prodigal of all d. grace,* LLL II, 9. *d. perfection,* All's V, 3, 18. cf. Compl. 96, and *dearly* in Cymb. II, 2, 18. Singular use (cf. in German das liebe Leben, die liebe Unschuld, der liebe Himmel, etc.): *O d. discretion, how his words are suited!* Merch. III, 5, 70. *beat at this gate, that let thy folly in and thy d. judgment out,* Lr. I, 4, 294. *the gods to their d. shelter take thee,* I, 1, 185. *from him* (viz death) *d. life redeems you,* Wint. V, 3, 103.

Often substantively: *my d.* Lucr. 1293. Mids. II, 2, 43. *d., they durst not,* Tp. I, 2, 140. Mids. V, 286. Wint. V, 1, 215. Cor. V, 3, 47. Ant. III, 13, 158. IV, 15, 21. *sweet d.* Shr. IV, 2, 10. *— est!* Tp. III, 1, 86. Wint. I, 2, 137. *best of —est,* Sonn. 48, 7. *my —est,* Wint. I, 2, 88. *thy —est quit thee,* Ant. III, 13, 65. *a counsellor, a traitress and a d.* All's I, 1, 184.

Quite as a subst., = lover, sweetheart: *will court thee for his d.* LLL V, 2, 131. *Lord Biron is my d.* 457. *it is thy d.* Mids. II, 2, 33. *yonder is thy d.* III, 2, 176. *deflowered my d.* V, 297. *minion, your d. lies dead,* Oth. V, 1, 33. In the plural: *for my lads to give their dears,* Wint. IV, 4, 227 (Autolycus' song).

5) heartfelt: *d. religious love,* Sonn. 31, 6. *and our d. love lose name of single one,* 39, 6. 117, 3. 124, 1. *so d. the love my people bore me,* Tp. I, 2, 141. Wiv. IV, 6, 9. Meas. III, 2, 160. As I, 2, 288. John II, 157. *effects of terror and d. modesty,* Compl. 202 (i. e. the chaste bashfulness of the heart). *what d. good will I bear unto the banished Valentine,* Gentl. IV, 3, 14. *where we swore to you d. amity,* John V, 4, 20. *sweets grown common lose their d. delight,* Sonn. 102, 12. *praising what is lost makes the remembrance d.* All's V, 3, 20. *surprise her with discourse of my d. faith,* Tw. I, 4, 25. *if thou wert sensible of courtesy, I should not make so d. a show of zeal,* H4A V, 4, 95 (= such a hearty, sincere show. Ff and Q2 *great*). *out of d. respect,* H8 V, 3, 119. *strangles our d. vows even in the birth,* Troil. IV, 4, 39. *O, a root! d. thanks!* Tim. IV, 3, 192. Hence = earnest: *thine, in the —est design of industry,* LLL IV, 1, 88 (Armado's letter). *you towards York shall bend you with your —est speed,* H4A V, 5, 36. *consort with me in loud and d. petition,* Troil. V, 3, 9.

Used as well of disagreeable affections: *deafed with the clamours of their own d. groans,* LLL V, 2, 874. *if she had partaken of my flesh and cost me the —est groans of a mother,* All's IV, 5, 11. *made lame by fortune's —est spite,* Sonn. 37, 3. *your grace is perjured much, full of d. guiltiness,* LLL V, 2, 801. *whom thou in terms so bloody and so d. hast made thine enemies,* Tw. V, 74 (= so touching the heart). *thou art the issue of my d. offence,* John I, 257 (= the offence burdening my conscience). *the dateless limit of thy d. exile,* R2 I, 3, 151 (= sad, grieving the heart). *this d. and deep rebuke,* H4B IV, 5, 141 (= earnest). *true repentance of all your d. offences,* H5 II, 2, 181 (= grievous). *how canst thou urge God's dreadful law to us, when thou hast broke it in so d. degree?* R3 I, 4, 215. *which in his —est need will shrink from him,* V, 2, 21 (Qq *greatest*). *O thou sweet king-killer, and d. divorce twixt natural son and sire,* Tim. IV, 3, 382 (but here it may be = cherished). *strain what other means is left unto us in our d. peril,* V, 1, 231 (= felt grievously). *and I a heavy interim shall support by*

his d. absence, Oth. I, 3, 260. *thy other banished son, with this d. sight struck pale and bloodless,* Tit. III, 1, 257 (unless Hanmer be right here in writing *dire*)

Used of persons, = zealous, earnest, ardent, in a good as well as bad sense: *bountiful Fortune, now my d. lady,* Tp. I, 2, 179. *with no less nobility of love than that which —est father bears his son,* Hml. I, 2, 111. *which art my nearest and —est enemy,* H4A III, 2, 123. *would I had met my —est foe in heaven,* Hml. I, 2, 182.*

6) inmost, vital: *summon up your —est spirits,* LLL II, 1. *to my d. doting heart thou art the fairest and most precious jewel,* Sonn. 131, 3. *my d. heart's —er heart,* Err. III, 2, 62. *I'll empty all these veins and shed my d. blood drop by drop in the dust,* H4A I, 3, 134. (cf. Mids. III, 2, 97. H6A III, 4, 40. H6C I, 1, 223. V, 1, 69). *though that her jesses were my d. heart-strings,* Oth. III, 3, 261. *since my d. soul was mistress of her choice,* Hml. III, 2, 68. *love is my sin, and thy d. virtue hate,* Sonn. 142, 1.

Hence = true, very: *I love none. A d. happiness to women,* Ado I, 1, 129. *this is d. mercy, and thou seest it not,* Rom. III, 3, 28 (Q1 *mere*).

Dear, subst. see *Dear* adj. 4.

Dear, adv. 1) at a high price: *to buy sth. dear,* Err. IV, 1, 81. Mids. III, 2, 426. Merch. III, 2, 315. H4A V, 3, 7. 23. H6B I, 1, 252. II, 1, 100. V, 1, 5. H8 III, 1, 184. *aby it d.* Mids. III, 2, 175. *the touches —est prized,* As III, 2, 160. *for which I shall pay d.* Tw. III, 3, 37. Wint. I, 1, 18. *dearest valued,* John III, 1, 343. *won them —er,* H4B IV, 3, 73. *sell his life d.* H6A IV, 2, 53. *some will d. abide it,* Caes. III, 2, 119. *cost thee d.* Oth. V, 2, 255.

2) heartily: *to love one d.* Sonn. 115, 2. Merch. III, 2, 315. Shr. II, 339. R3 III, 5, 24. H8 II, 2, 111. IV, 2, 155 (the *—est*). Tit. IV, 1, 23. Rom. II, 3, 66. *shall it not grieve thee —er than thy death,* Caes. III, 1, 196. Lr. I, 1, 57. III, 4, **174.**

Dear, vb.; partic. deared = endeared, beloved: Ant. I, 4, 44, only a conjecture of M. Edd. for *feared* of O. Edd.

Dear-beloved, heartily loved: Tp. V, 309.

Dear-bought, purchased at a high price: H6B I, 1, 252 (not hyphened in O. Edd.).

Dearest-valued: John III, 1, 343 (not hyphened in O. Edd.).

Dearlings, reading of Ff in Oth. I, 2, 68; Qq *darlings.*

Dear-loved: Rom. III, 2, 66 (only in Q1; the other O. Edd. *dearest*). Tim. II, 2, 151 (F1 *loved*).

Dearly, 1) at a high price: *d. bought,* Merch. IV, 1, 100. *riders d. hired,* As I, 1, 14. *pay full d. for ...,* H4A V, 1, 84. *as the upper Germany can d. witness,* H8 V, 3, 30. *she hath bought the name of whore thus d.* Cymb. II, 4, 128. *held thee d.* H6C II, 1, 102 and Tit. V, 1, 36.

2) exquisitely: *man, how d. ever parted,* Troil. III, 3, 96 (= richly gifted). *rubies unparagoned, how d. they do't!* Cymb. II, 2, 18.

3) heartily: *as we d. grieve for that which thou hast done,* Hml. IV, 3, 43. *most d. welcome,* Wint. V, 1, 130. Troil. IV, 5, 18. *and greets your highness d.* Cymb. I, 6, 13. *how d. would it touch thee to the quick,* Err. II, 2, 132. *to adore d.* Ant. III, 2, 8. *to cherish d.* John III, 3, 24. *to hate d.* As I, 3, 35. *to love,* Sonn. 42, 2. Tp. IV, 1, 49. Meas. II, 4, 120. Ado V, 1, 179

As I, 3, 31. 33. All's I, 3, 218. IV, 2, 26. **V**, 3, 317. Tw. II, 2, 34. H6C III, 2, 37. R3 II, 2, 26. H8 IV, 2, 138. Cor. V, 4, 15. Rom. III, 4, 3. Caes. III, 2, 186. Lr. III, 4, 94. Oth. IV, 2, 158. Ant. I, 3, 6. II, 2, 153. Per. II, 1, 136. 144. *to tender,* As V, 2, 77. Tw. V, 129. Rom. III, 1, 75. Hml. I, 3, 107.

Dearn, adj. dreadful: *if wolves had at thy gate howled that d. time,* Lr. III, 7, 63 (Ff *stern). by many a d. and painful perch of Pericles the careful search ... is made,* Per. III Prol. 15.

Dearness; *in d. of heart* = heartily dear: *I think he holds you well and in d. of heart,* Ado III, 2, 101 (M. Edd.: *he holds you well, and in d. of heart hath holp* etc.).

Dear-purchased, bought at a high price: Sonn. 117, 6.

Dearth, 1) scarcity which makes food dear, famine: Sonn. 14, 4. R2 III, 3, 163. R3 II, 3, 35. Cor. I, 1, 69. 74. I, 2, 10. Lr. I, 2, 158. Ant. II, 7, 22. Figuratively = want in general: *he with her plenty pressed, she faint with d.* Ven. 545. Sonn. 146, 3. Gentl. II, 7, 16. Followed by *of: a scarcity and barren d. of daughters and of sons,* Ven. 754.

2) high price: *and his infusion of such d. and rareness,* Hml. V, 2, 123.

Death, extinction of life, state of being without life: Tp. I, 1, 72. II, 1, 260. III, 3, 77. Gentl. I, 1, 158. III, 1, 170. 185. IV, 1, 27. V, 4, 41. 126 etc. etc. Plur. *—s:* Sonn. 54, 12. 140, 7. Wiv. III, 5, 110. Meas. III, 1, 40. Tw. V, 136. Wint. IV, 4, 809. R2 III, 1, 7. H4A I, 3, 186. V, 3, 44. H6B II, 2, 76. IV, 8, 13. R3 I, 2, 117. 192. IV, 3, 8. Cor. III, 3, 70. Tit. II, 1, 78. Hml. V, 2, 394. Ant. V, 2, 340. *divers —s in d.* Wint. V, 1, 202. The singular relating to several persons: *I and ten thousand had left no mourning widows for our d.* H6C II, 6, 19. — *this thought is as a d.* Sonn. 64, 13. *when in swinish sleep their drenched natures lie as in a d.* Mcb. I, 7, 68. *how Caesar hath deserved to lie in d.* Caes. III, 1, 132. *on my face he turned an eye of d.* H4A I, 3, 143 (cf. *Dead,* adj. 2. Johnson: 'an eye menacing death'). *I am out of fear of d. or —'s hand,* IV, 1, 136. *they'll give him d. by inches,* Cor. V, 4, 42. *do on them some violent d.* Tit. V, 2, 108. *and sure as d. I swore,* Tit. I, 487 (= as surely as death awaits us). cf. *he took it on his d. that this my mother's son was none of his,* John I, 110 (i. e. he said that it was as certain as his death). *I'll take it upon my d. I gave him this wound,* H4A V, 4, 154 (cf. *take it upon their salvation,* II, 4, 9. *take it of my soul,* Tim. III, 4, 70; see *Take). 'tis d. for any one in Mantua to come to Padua,* Shr. IV, 2, 81 (i. e. he is liable to be punished with death). *be it d. proclaimed to boast of this,* H5 IV, 8, 119. *whoso draws a sword, 'tis present d.* H6A III, 4, 39. *Mantua's law is d. to any he that utters them,* Rom. V, 1, 67. *if doing nothing be d. by the law,* Tim. I, 1, 195. cf. *never joyed since the price of oats rose; it was the d. of him,* H4A II, 1, 14. *what life is in that, to be the d. of this marriage,* Ado II, 2, 19. *to take one's d.* = to die: H6B II, 3, 90. H6C I, 3, 35. *came to his d.* H6C III, 3, 187. — Meaning the manner of dying: *die a flea's d.* Wiv. IV, 2, 158. *that d. is too soft for him,* Wint. IV, 4, 807. *devise strange —s,* H6B III, 1, 59. — = spiritual death, damnation: *made her thrall to living d. and pain perpetual,* Lucr. 726.

To d. = with a deadly effect, mortally: *wounding itself to d.* Lucr. 466. *a vengeful canker eat him up to d.* Sonn. 99, 13. *sick to d.* Pilgr. 233. H8 IV, 2, 1. Tim. III, 1, 64. *bowled to d.* Wiv. III, 4, 91. cf. Tp. II, 2, 158. III, 2, 38. V, 276. Meas. II, 1, 6. V, 528. Ado III, 1, 76. IV, 1, 186. V, 1, 88. Merch. IV, 1, 258. As II, 4, 66. John V, 4, 9. H6B III, 2, 412. V, 1, 148. H6C I, 4, 127. II, 4, 13. R3 III, 3, 12. *to do to d.* = to kill: Ado V, 3, 3. H6B III, 2, 179. *strike me to d.* Cymb. V, 5, 235. *I with my trespass never will dispense, till life to d. acquit my forced offence,* Lucr. 1071. *till it* (the drum) *cry sleep to d.* Lr. II, 4, 120 (till it strike the sleepers dead by the terror of its sound).

To the d. = 1) mortally, with a deadly effect: *wounded to the d.* H4B I, 1, 14. *his venom tooth will rankle to the d.* R3 I, 3, 291. *hurt to the d.* Oth. II, 3, 163. 2) on peril of death; though death should be the consequence: *you are both sure, and will assist me? to the d.* Ado I, 3, 72. *no, to the d., we will not move a foot,* LLL V, 2, 146. *I'll follow you unto the d.* John I, 154. *and in that quarrel use it* (my sword) *to the d.* H6C II, 2, 65. *I will not do it to the d.* R3 III, 2, 55.

The d., in general, = a violent death: *and humbly beg the d. upon my knee,* R3 I, 2, 179. *she hath betrayed me and shall die the d.* Ant. IV, 14, 26. *die the d.!* Cymb. IV, 2, 96. More particularly = death by judicial sentence: *die the d.* Meas. II, 4, 165. Mids. I, 1, 65. *adjudged to the d.* Err. I, 1, 147. *condemns you to the d.* R2 III, 1, 29. *bear Worcester to the d.* H4A V, 5, 14. *where they feared the d., they have borne life away,* H5 IV, 1, 181.

D. used as an imprecation: *d.! my lord, their clothes are after such a pagan cut,* H8 I, 3, 13. Lr. III, 4, 72. *d. of thy soul!* Mcb. V, 3, 16. *life and d.!* Lr. I, 4, 318. *d. on my state!* II, 4, 113. *d. and damnation!* Oth. III, 3, 396.

Used as a masculine: *d. to me subscribes, since spite of him I'll live in this poor rhyme,* Sonn. 107, 10, *thou art —'s fool; for him thou labourest by thy flight to shun and yet runnest towards him still,* Meas. III, 1, 11 (cf. *Fool). bequeath to d. your numbness, for from him dear life redeems you,* Wint. V, 3, 102. John V, 7, 15. Rom. IV, 1, 75. — Personified: Ven. 930. LLL V, 2, 616 (*a —'s face in a ring;* cf. *Death's- head). Merch. II, 7, 63 (a carrion D.).* John II, 352. 453. R2 III, 2, 162. H4B V, 4, 32 (*goodman D.) H6A IV, 7, 18. Cymb. V, 3, 69.

Death-bed, the bed in which a person dies: Sonn. 73, 11. Merch. III, 2, 47. John I, 109. R2 II, 1, 95. V, 1, 39. H6B V, 1, 164. Rom. II Chor. 1. Hml. IV, 5, 193. Oth. V, 2, 51. Evans says: *upon his death's bed,* Wiv. I, 1, 53.

Death-boding, portending death: Lucr. 165.

Death-counterfeiting, resembling death: *d. sleep,* Mids. III, 2, 364.

Death-darting: *the d. eye of cockatrice,* Rom. III, 2, 47.

Death-divining: *the d. swan,* Phoen. 15.

Deathful, deadly: *a d. wound,* H6B III, 2, 404.

Death-like, deadly: *d. dragons here affright thee hard,* Per. I, 1, 29.

Death-marked, destined to die: *the fearful passage of their d. love,* Rom. Prol. 9.

Death-practised, threatened with death by stratagems: Lr. IV, 6, 284.

Death's-head, a naked skull as the emblem of death: Merch. I, 2, 55. H4A III, 3, 34. H4B II, 4, 255. cf. *Death's face,* LLL V, 2, 616.

Deaths-man, executioner: Lucr. 1001. H6B III, 2, 217. H6C V, 5, 67. Lr. IV, 6, 263.

Death-tokens, the spots which indicate the approaching death of persons infected with the plague: *he is so plaguy proud that the d. of it cry 'No recovery;'* Troil. II, 3, 187 (see *Token* and *Tokened*).

Death-worthy, deserving death: Lucr. 635.

Debar, to deprive of: *that am —ed the benefit of rest,* Sonn. 28, 2.

Debase, to degrade: R2 III, 3, 127. 190. R3 I, 2, 247 (Ff *abase*).*Cor. III, 1, 135.

Debate, subst. contest, quarrel: *for thee against myself I'll vow d., for I must ne'er love him whom thou dost hate,* Sonn. 89, 13. *lost in the world's d.* LLL I, 1, 174. *this same progeny of evils comes from our d., from our dissension,* Mids. II, 1, 116. *this d. that bleedeth at our doors,* H4B IV, 4, 2. *I am no further than your enemy; she is not worth our d.* Cymb. I, 4, 173.

Debate, vb. 1) to combat: *but for loss of Nestor's golden words, it seemed they would d. with angry swords,* Lucr. 1421. Transitively, = to combat about, to decide by combat: *nature and sickness d. it at their leisure,* All's I, 2, 75. *two thousand souls and twenty thousand ducats will not d. the question of this straw,* Hml. IV, 4, 26.

2) to contend in words, to dispute: *idle words, d. where leisure serves with dull debaters,* Lucr. 1019. *in —ing which was best,* Err. III, 1, 67.

3) to speak about, to discuss; a) trans.: *I will d. this matter at more leisure,* Err. IV, 1, 100. *who accused her upon the error that you heard —d,* Ado V, 4, 3. *a wise council that did d. this business,* H8 II, 4, 52. 173. Tit. V, 3, 20. Ant. II, 2, 20. Followed by a clause: *—ing to and fro how France and Frenchmen might be kept in awe,* H6B I, 1, 91. H6C IV, 7, 51. 53. *where wasteful time —th with decay, to change your day of youth to sullied night,* Sonn. 15, 11. — b) intr.: *hear him d. of commonwealth affairs,* H5 I, 1, 41. *your several suits have been considered and —d on,* H6A V, 1, 35.

4) to consider: *in his inward mind he doth d. what following sorrow may on this arise,* Lucr. 185. *—ing, die!* 274. *I have —d, even in my soul, what wrong, what shame, what sorrow I shall breed,* 498. *I am —ing of my present store,* Merch. I, 3, 54 (cf. *Of*). *I and my bosom must d. awhile,* H5 IV, 1, 31. *my state stands on me to defend, not to d.* Lr. V, 1, 69.

Debatement, consideration: *after much d. my sisterly remorse confutes mine honour,* Meas. V, 99. *that without d. further he should the bearers put to sudden death,* Hml. V, 2, 45.

Debater, disputant, controvertist: Lucr. 1019.

Debauched, see *Deboshed.*

Debile, weak: All's II, 3, 39. Cor. I, 9, 48.

Debility, weakness: As II, 3, 51.

Debitor and Creditor, an accounting-book: Oth. I, 1, 31.*Cymb. V, 4, 171.

Debonair, gentle, meek: *courtiers as free, as d., unarmed, as bending angels,* Troil. I, 3, 235.

Déborah, the heroine of Israel (Judges Chap. 4): H6A I, 2, 105.

Deboshed (some M. Edd. *debauched*), debased, base: *thou d. fish,* Tp. III, 2, 29. *the mere word's a slave d. on every tomb,* All's II, 3, 145. *with all the spots o' the world taxed and d.* V, 3, 206. *men so disordered, so d. and bold,* Lr. I, 4, 263.

Debt (pronounced *det,* to the mortification of Holofernes: LLL V, 1, 23), that which is due from one person to another: Ven. 84. 521. Lucr. 329. 649. Sonn. 83, 4. Meas. III, 2, 67. 264. Err. IV, 4, 121. 124. LLL V, 1, 24. Mids. III, 2, 85. Merch. III, 2, 309. Tw. I, 1, 34. H4A I, 3, 185. R3 II, 2, 92. IV, 4, 21. Hml. III, 2, 203 etc. Plur. —s: Tp. III, 2, 140. Merch. I, 1, 128. III, 2, 321. Shr. IV, 4, 25. H5 IV, 1, 248. Troil. III, 2, 58 etc. — *To be in d.* Err. IV, 2, 48. 57. *no squire in d.* Lr. III, 2, 86. *what he speaks is all in d.* Tim. I, 2, 204. *go hence in d.* Wint. I, 2, 6. *die in d.* LLL V, 2, 333. Rom. I, 1, 244. *to be in d. to:* Tim. III, 5, 78. *being no more in d. to years than thou,* H4A III, 2, 103. *in like manner was I in d. to my business,* Tim. III, 6, 15. *was in my d.* R2 I, 1, 129. R3 III, 2, 112.

Debted, indebted: *three odd ducats more than I stand d. to this gentleman,* Err. IV, 1, 31.

Debtor, one who owes something to another: Lucr. 964. 1155. Sonn. 134, 11. Wiv. II, 2, 138. LLL V, 2, 43. Merch. I, 1, 152. As II, 3, 76. H4B V, 5, 132. Troil. IV, 5, 51. Ant. V, 2, 205. Cymb. I, 4, 38. II, 4, 8. III, 3, 34. V, 4, 19. Per. II, 1, 149.

Decay, subst. 1) decline from a better to a worse state: *who lets so fair a house fall to d.* Sonn. 13, 9. *wasteful time debateth with d., to change your day of youth to sullied night,* 15, 11. 16, 3. 100, 11. Pilgr. 184. Wiv. V, 5, 152. Merch. V, 64. Tim. IV, 3, 466. Lr. V, 3, 288. Abstr. pro concr.: *what comfort to this great d. may come,* Lr. V, 3, 297 (= ruin).

2) fall, ruin, perdition, end: *in thy bed I purpose to destroy thee: that done, some worthless slave of thine I'll slay, to kill thine honour with thy life's d.* Lucr. 516. *the light will show, charactered on my brow, the story of sweet chastity's d.* 808. *to feed oblivion with d. of things,* 947. *herein lives wisdom, beauty and increase; without this, folly, age and cold d.* Sonn. 11, 6. *my love was my d.* 80, 14. *be thou the trumpet of our wrath and sullen presage of your own d.* John I, 28. *vast confusion waits, as doth a raven on a sick-fallen beast, the imminent d. of wrested pomp,* IV, 3, 154. *cry woe, destruction, ruin and d.* R2 III, 2, 102. *with what wings shall his affections fly towards fronting peril and opposed d.!* H4B IV, 4, 66. *good king Henry, thy d. I fear,* H6B III, 1, 194. *till then fair hope must hinder life's d.* H6C IV, 4, 16. *death, desolation, ruin and d.* R3 IV, 4, 409. *so shall my lungs coin words till their d. against those measles,* Cor. III, 1, 78.

Decay, vb. 1) intr. a) to pass from a better to a worse state; to become weak: *when that (the flesh) —s, the guilty rebel for remission prays,* Lucr. 713. *his leaves will wither and his sap d.* 1168. *and in mine own love's strength seem to d.* Sonn. 23, 7. *and state itself confounded to d.* 64, 10. *the which (your health) must perforce d.* H4B I, 1, 165. *my weak —ing age,* H6A II, 5, 1. *swifter than blood —s,* Troil. III, 2, 170. *when love begins to sicken and d.* Caes. IV, 2, 20. Partic. decayed: Sonn. 79, 3. Err. II, 1, 98. IV, 3, 26. All's V, 2, 24. Cor. V, 2, 47.

b) to perish, to end: *O happiness as soon*

—*ed and done as is the morning's dew*, Lucr. 23. *let your love even with my life d.* Sonn. 71, 12. *had not churchmen prayed, his thread of life had not so soon* —*ed*, H6A I, 1, 34. *whiles we are suitors to their throne,* —*s the thing we sue for*, Ant. II, 1, 4.

2) trans. a) to impair: *rocks impregnable are not so stout, nor gates of steel so strong, but time* —*s*, Sonn. 65, 8. *infirmity, that* —*s the wise*, Tw. I, 5, 82.

b) to destroy: *every day that comes comes to d. a day's work in him*, Cymb. I, 5, 56 (perhaps also Sonn. 65, 8).

Decayer, destroyer: *your water is a sore d. of your whoreson dead body*, Hml. V, 1, 188.

Decease, subst. death: Ven. 1002. Sonn. 13, 7. 97, 8. H6A II, 5, 58. H6B III, 1, 25. H6C I, 1, 175.

Decease, vb. to die: Sonn. 1, 3. 32, 4. 72, 7. Mids. V, 53. Merch. II, 2, 67. Shr. I, 2, 54. 102. John I, 8. II, 65. IV, 2, 85. H4B III, 1, 81 *(times* —*d).* H6B IV, 4, 56. Rom. IV, 5, 23. Cymb. I, 1, 39.

Deceit, 1) fraud, fallacy, deception: Lucr. 585. 1507. Compl. 172. Wiv. V, 5, 239. Meas. III, 1, 269. IV, 1, 75. All's III, 7, 38. John I, 215. V, 4, 27. H5 V, 2, 121. H6A II, 1, 14. H6B III, 1, 57. 79. 264. H6C III, 3, 68. V, 4, 26. R3 II, 2, 27. 30. III, 1, 8. Tit. III, 1, 189. Rom. III, 2, 84. Per. I, 4, 75.

2) delusion, misconception: *the folded meaning of your words' d.* Err. III, 2, 36.

Deceitful, 1) full of fallacy, fraudulent: Gentl. II, 7, 72. Shr. IV, 4, 83. H6A II, 1, 50. H6B IV, 7, 109. H6C III, 3, 141. Mcb. IV, 3, 58.

2) delusive: *conceit d., so compact, so kind*, Lucr. 1423.

3) disappointing expectation: *they fall their crests and like d. jades sink in the trial*, Caes. IV, 2, 26.

Deceivable, delusive, deceptious: *there's something in't that is d.* Tw. IV, 3, 21. *not thy knee, whose duty is d. and false*, R2 II, 3, 84.

Deceive, 1) to beguile, to cheat; a) absol.: *in either's aptness, as it best* —*s*, Compl. 306. *the* —*ing father of a deceitful son*, Shr. IV, 4, 83. John I, 214. V, 4, 26. H6C III, 2, 189. R3 I, 3, 48. — b) trans.: Ven. 781. Lucr. 585. Sonn. 93, 2. Gentl. IV, 2, 98. 127. Wiv. III, 1, 13. 109. IV, 6, 46. Shr. V, 1, 121. R3 V, 3, 92. Tit. III, 1, 187. 190. Ant. V, 2, 14 etc. Followed by *of*, = to cheat out of sth.: *thou of thyself thy sweet self dost d.* Sonn. 4, 10.

2) to mislead the mind, to cause to err; a) absol.: *most* —*ing when it seems most just*, Ven. 1156. — b) trans.: Ven. 601. Sonn. 39, 12. Gentl. IV, 4, 73. Wiv. III, 3, 137. 190. Err. I, 2, 98. V, 331. Ado III, 3, 168. V, 1, 238. LLL II, 230. V, 2, 135. Mids. II, 2, 140. Merch. III, 2, 74 etc. *To be* —*d* = to be mistaken: Sonn. 104, 12. Meas. III, 2, 131. Ado V, 4, 76. 79. LLL IV, 1, 98. V, 2, 544. Merch. II, 3, 13. V, 111. As V, 3, 38. Shr. III, 1, 62. H6A II, 3, 51. V, 4, 72. H6C I, 1, 155. IV, 7, 41. Troil. IV, 2, 40. Hml. II, 2, 394. Lr. IV, 6, 9. *be not* —*d*, Caes. I, 2, 37. *to be* —*d in a person:* Meas. III, 1, 197. III, 2, 178. As I, 2, 209. All's III, 6, 6. Reflectively: *if thou thyself* —*st*, Sonn. 40, 7. *thou* —*st thyself*, R3 I, 4, 249.

3) to disappoint; a) absol.: *many* —*ing promises of life*, Meas. III, 2, 260. b) trans.: *curst be thy stones for thus* —*ing me*, Mids. V, 182.

Deceiver, impostor: Ado II, 3, 65. one who

---

has robbed another of sth. by fraud: I have my dukedom got and pardoned the d. Tp. Epil. 7.

December, the last month in the year: Sonn. 97, 4. Ado I, 1, 195. As IV, 1, 148. Tw. II, 3, 90. Wint. I, 2, 169. R2 I, 3, 298. Cymb. III, 3, 37.

Decent, becoming, noble: *d. carriage*, H8 IV, 2, 145.

Deceptious, delusive: *as if those organs had d. functions*, Troil. V, 2, 123.

Decern, misapplied for *concern*: Ado III, 5, 4.

Decide, to bring to an issue, to determine: LLL V, 2, 752. H4B IV, 1, 182. H6A IV, 1, 119.

Decimation, selection of every tenth for punishment: Tim. V, 4, 31.

Decipher, 1) to unfold, to detect: *we should have seen* —*ed there more rancorous spite*, H6A IV, 1, 184. *you are both* —*ed for villains marked with rape*, Tit. IV, 2, 8.

2) to distinguish, to make distinguishable: *the white will d. her well enough*, Wiv. V, 2, 10. *which is the natural man, and which the spirit? who* —*s them?* Err. V, 334.

Decision, determination of a difference: All's III, 1, 3. Troil. II, 2, 173. Mcb. V, 4, 17.

Decius: *D. Brutus* (for Decimus): Caes. I, 3, 148. II, 1, 95 etc.

Deck, subst. 1) the covering or floor of a ship: Tp. I, 2, 197. Wiv. II, 1, 94. Tim. IV, 2, 20. Cymb. I, 3, 11. Per. III Prol. 59. IV, 1, 57. V, 1, 115.

2) a pack of cards: *whiles he thought to steal the single ten, the king was slily fingered from the d.* H6C V, 1, 44.

Deck, vb. 1) to cover, to dress: *coats to d. our soldiers for these Irish wars*, R2 I, 4, 62. *in black my lady's brows are* —*ed*, LLL IV, 3, 258. *and see another* —*ed in thy rights*, R3 I, 3, 206. Singular passage: *when I have* —*ed the sea with drops full salt*, Tp. I, 2, 155 (according to some commentators a provincialism for sprinkled; but to speak of floods as being increased by tears is an hyperbole too frequent with Sh.. Prospero means to say that he shed so many tears as to cover the surface of the sea with them).

2) to adorn: *the orator, to d. his oratory, will couple my reproach to Tarquin's shame*, Lucr. 815. *sweet ornament that* —*s a thing divine*, Gentl. II, 1, 4. *'tis your thoughts that now must d. our kings*, H5 Prol. 28. *I thought thy bride-bed to have* —*ed*, Hml. V, 1, 268. Joined with *up: help to d. up her*, Rom. IV, 2, 41. Followed by *with:* —*s with praises Collatine's high name*, Lucr. 108. Tp. III, 2, 105. Mids. I, 1, 211. Shr. I, 1, 16. IV, 3, 60. H6A I, 2, 99. H6C III, 1, 63. Caes. I, 1, 70. By *in:* H5 II, 2, 134. H6C III, 2, 149.

Declare, 1) to make known, to tell explicitly and openly: *that it shall please you to d. whether ever I did broach this business to your highness*, H8 II, 4, 145. *d. thine office*, Ant. III, 12, 10.

2) to explain, to unfold: *my scutcheon plain* —*s that I am Alisander*, LLL V, 2, 567. *I conjure thee that thou d. what incidency thou dost guess of harm is creeping toward me*, Wint. I, 2, 402. *to know his embassy, which I could with a ready guess d.* H5 I, 1, 96. *and now d., why didst thou say, of late thou wert despised*, H6A II, 5, 41. *d. the cause my father lost*

his head, 53. *read, and d. the meaning,* Cymb. V, 5, 434.

Declension, 1) a declining towards a worse state, deterioration: *from a God to a bull? a heavy d.* H4B II, 2, 193 (Q *descension*). *seduced the pitch and height of all his thoughts to base d.* R3 III, 7, 189. *fell into a sadness, then into a fast, ... and by this d. into the madness,* Hml. II, 2, 149.

2) inflexion of nouns: Wiv. IV, 1, 76.

Decline, vb. 1) trans. a) to bend down: —*ing their rich aspect to the hot breath of Spain,* Err. III, 2, 139. *d. your head,* Lr. IV, 2, 22.

b) to inflect (in grammar): Wiv. IV, 1, 42.

c) to run through from first to last, to take into exact consideration: *d. all this, and see what now thou art,* R3 IV, 4, 97. *I'll d. the whole question,* Troil. II, 3, 55.

2) intr. a) to sink down, to fall: *with head —d,* Lucr. 1661. Ant. III, 11, 47. *with —ing head into his bosom,* Shr. Ind. 1, 119. *she had one eye —d for the loss of her husband,* Wint. V, 2, 81. *not letting it d.* (viz his sword), Troil. IV, 5, 189. *which* (arm) *being advanced, —s, and then men die,* Cor. II, 1, 178. *not one accompanying his —ing foot,* Tim. I, 1, 89. *his sword which was —ing on the milky head of reverend Priam,* Hml. II, 2, 500.

b) to sink down or fall in a moral sense, to come to a less perfect state: *every fair from fair sometime —s,* Sonn. 18, 7. *he straight —d, drooped,* Wint. II, 3, 14. *in this —ing land,* R2 II, 1, 240. *can thy spirit wonder a great man should d.* H8 III, 2, 375. *who thrives and who —s,* Cor. I, 1, 197. Tim. IV, 1, 20 (*d. to ..*). *ready to d.* Caes. IV, 3, 217. *and to d. upon a wretch,* Hml. I, 5, 50. *sons at perfect age, and fathers —ing,* Lr. I, 2, 78 (Ff —*d*). *I am —d into the vale of years,* Oth. III, 3, 265. *I must perforce have shown to thee such a —ing day,* Ant. V, 1, 38. *Declined* = fallen: *what the —d is he shall as soon read in the eyes of others as feel in his own fall,* Troil. III, 3, 76. *not letting it* (his sword) *d. on the —d,* IV, 5, 189. *answer me —d, sword against sword,* Ant. III, 13, 27.

c) to incline, or to bow down? *far more to you do I d.* Err. III, 2, 44.

Decoct, to boil, to heat: *can sodden water d. their cold blood to such valiant heat?* H5 III, 5, 20.

Decorum, propriety, decency: Meas. I, 3, 31. Ant. I, 2, 77. V, 2, 17.

Decrease, vb. 1) trans. to make less: *which I have bettered rather than —d,* Shr. II, 119.

2) intr. to grow less: Sonn. 15, 7. H4B I, 2, 205. Per. I, 2, 85. Misapplied: Wiv. I, 1, 255.

Decree, subst. resolution, 1) decision: *poor hand, why quiverest thou at this d.?* Lucr. 1030. *change —s of kings,* Sonn. 115, 6. All's V, 3, 40. R2 IV, 213. H4B IV, 5, 118. V, 2, 85. H6C II, 1, 118. Cor. I, 6, 34. Tit. V, 2, 11. Rom. III, 5, 138.

2) established law: *our —s, dead to infliction, to themselves are dead,* Meas. I, 3, 27. *young blood doth not obey an old d.* LLL IV, 3, 217. *a hot temper leaps o'er a cold d.* Merch. I, 2, 20. *the —s of Venice,* IV, 1, 102. 219. LLL I, 1, 117. 148. H4A IV, 3, 79. Caes. III, 1, 38.

Decree, vb. to resolve, to determine: *heaven in thy creation did d. that in thy face sweet love should ever dwell,* Sonn. 93, 9. *it hath in solemn synods been — d,* Err. I, 1, 13. *I have —d not to sing in*

my cage, Ado I, 3, 35. As I, 2, 111. R2 I, 3, 122. H4A I, 1, 32. Tit. II, 3, 274. Rom. III, 3, 146. Per. II, 3, 35. *Decreed* = ordained, fated: *what is —d must be,* Tw. I, 5, 330. *it is —d Hector the great must die,* Troil. V, 7, 8. *it is —d he dies to-night,* Cor. III, 1, 289. *which read and not expounded, 'tis —d, as these before thee thou thyself shalt bleed,* Per. I, 1, 57.

Decrepit, worn with age: Ven. 1148. Sonn. 37, 1. LLL I, 1, 139. H6A V, 4, 7.

Dedicate, vb. 1) to devote, to inscribe: *in —ing my unpolished lines to your lordship,* Ven. Dedic. 1. *the love I d. to your lordship,* Lucr. Dedic. 1. *all —d to closeness,* Tp. I, 2, 89. Meas. II, 2, 154. Ado II, 3, 9. H6B V, 2, 37. H8 I, 4, 2. Cymb. I, 6, 136. *the —d words which writers use of their fair subject, blessing every book,* Sonn. 82, 3 (= the dedicatory words).

2) to commit, to grant: *nor doth he d. one jot of colour unto the weary and all-watched night,* H5 IV Chor. 37. *what folly I commit, I d. to you,* Troil. III, 2, 110. *the bud bit with an envius worm, ere he can spread his sweet leaves to the air, or d. his beauty to the sun,* Rom. I, 1, 159. *his poor self, a —d beggar to the air,* Tim. IV, 2, 13 (= a beggar committed to the air). *to devour so many as will to greatness d. themselves,* Mcb. IV, 3, 75. *to the face of peril myself I'll d.* Cymb. V, 1, 29.

Partic. *dedicated:* Sonn. 82, 3. Tp. I, 2, 89. Tim. IV, 2, 13. *dedicate:* Meas. II, 2, 154. H6B V, 2, 37.

Dedication, 1) devotedness: *my love ... all his in d.* Tw. V, 85.

2) something devoted or inscribed: *you are rapt in some work, some d. to the great lord,* Tim. I, 1, 19.

3) committing, giving up: *a cause more promising than a wild d. of yourselves to unpathed waters,* Wint. IV, 4, 577.

Deed, 1) act, action; a) a thing having been done: Lucr. Arg. 23. Lucr. 195. 226. 252. 502. 610. 1003. 1566. Tp. III, 3, 72. Meas. II, 2, 93. III, 1, 135. III, 2, 187. IV, 4, 23. Err. III, 2, 20. Merch. IV, 1, 206. V, 91. As I, 2, 240. Wint. I, 2, 97. H6A I, 1, 15. 156. H6B I, 1, 97. 191 etc. etc.

b) a thing being done; doing: *thou grantest no time for charitable —s,* Lucr. 908. *to talk in —s,* 1348. *do —s of youth,* Sonn. 37, 2. *into my —s to pry,* 61, 6. *they look into the beauty of thy mind, and that in guess they measure by thy —s,* 69, 10. *the world is bent my —s to cross,* 90, 2. *sweetest things turn sourest by their —s,* 94, 13. *the guilty goddess of my harmful —s,* 111, 2. *in nothing art thou black save in thy —s,* 131, 13. *and controversy hence a question takes, whether the horse by him became his d.,* or he *his manage by the well-doing steed,* Compl. 111. *each your doing crowns what you are doing in the present d.* Wint. IV, 4, 145. *to stop devoted charitable —s,* R3 I, 2, 35. *if it be known to him that I gainsay my d.* H8 II, 4, 96. *my father loved you; he said he did, and with his d. did crown his word upon you,* III, 2, 155. *we are yet but young in d.* Mcb. III, 4, 144. *what is't you do? a d. without a name,* IV, 1, 49. *in my true heart I find she names my very d. of love,* Lr. I, 1, 73. *did I but speak thy —s,* Oth. IV, 2, 76. *I will hope of better —s to-morrow,* Ant. I, 1, 62. Tp. V, 71. Gentl. II, 2, 18. Meas. I, 3, 38. V, 451. Merch. IV, 1, 202. As II, 4, 82. III, 3, 18. H6A III, 2, 49. IV, 7, 8. H8 III, 2, 153. 154 etc.

Euphemistically = copulation (cf. *Do*): *one that will do the d. though Argus were her eunuch,* LLL III, 200. *in the doing of the d. of kind,* Merch. I, 3, 86. *Io ... beguiled and surprised, as lively painted as the d. was done,* Shr. Ind. 2, 58. *all other circumstances made up to the d.* Wint. II, 1, 179. *give her —s,* Troil. III, 2, 58. *edifies another with her —s,* V, 3, 112. *not in d.* Ant. I, 5, 15.

Followed by *of,* = performance: *do you think he will make no d. at all of this that so seriously he does address himself unto?* All's III, 6, 102. *the d. of saying is quite out of use,* Tim. V, 1, 28 (= the performance of what has been said. cf. *may give his saying d.* Hml. I, 3, 27).

2) written evidence of a legal act: *draw a d. of gift,* Merch. IV, 1, 394. 396. IV, 2, 1. V, 292. *ere this hand, by thee to Romeo sealed, shall be the label to another d.* Rom. IV, 1, 57.

Deed-achieving, gained by deeds (—*ing* gerund): *by d. honour,* Cor. II, 1, 190.

Deedless, inactive: *speaking in deeds and d. in his tongue,* Troil. IV, 5, 98.

Deem, subst. idea, thought: *I true! how now! what wicked d. is this?* Troil. IV, 4, 61.

Deem, vb. 1) to judge, to estimate: *Imogen, that best could d. his dignity,* Cymb. V, 4, 57. Followed by *of*: *how the world may d. of me,* H6B III, 2, 65. *what it should be more than his father's death, that thus hath put him so much from the understanding of himself, I cannot d. of,* Hml. II, 2, 10 (Qq *dream*).

2) to think; mostly followed by a double accus.: *speed more than speed but dull and slow she —s,* Lucr. 1336. Sonn. 54, 3. 121, 3. LLL II, 1, 174. All's II, 1, 127. Tw. I, 5, 100. Wint. V, 3, 64. H6A I, 4, 49. H8 II, 4, 53. III, 2, 142. Followed by *for*: *so are those errors to truths translated and for true things —ed,* Sonn. 96, 8. By a clause: *that the souls of men may d. that you are worthily deposed,* R2 IV, 227.

Deep, adj. 1) descending far, entering far: *d. sounds,* Lucr. 1329. *as d. as hell,* Wiv. III, 5, 14. Meas. III, 1, 94. *d. glass,* Merch. I, 2, 104. *well,* R2 IV, 184. Rom. III, 1, 99. *dungeon,* H4B IV, 3, 9. *brook,* H6B III, 1, 53. *grave,* III, 2, 150. *bosom of the ocean,* R3 I, 1, 4. *pit,* Tit. II, 3, 240. *sea,* Rom. II, 2, 134. *waters,* Per. IV, 2, 159. *healths five fathom d.* Rom. I, 4, 85. (*potations pottle-d.* Oth. II, 3, 56). *the anchor is d.* Wiv. I, 3, 56. *so d. a root,* H6A II, 4, 85. *d. nook,* Tp. I, 2, 227. *it shall not wind with such a d. indent,* H4A III, 1, 104. *d. wound,* Sonn. 133, 2. Gentl. V, 4, 71. Tit. III, 1, 247. *scars,* Err. V, 193. H6B I, 1, 87. *hurt,* Rom. III, 1, 99. *so d. a maim,* R2 I, 3, 156. *incision,* I, 1, 155. Tropically: *those honours d. and broad,* Mcb. I, 6, 17 (extensive in all directions). *d. oblivion,* R3 III, 7, 129 (Qq *dark; as it were, buried*). *in this sin he is as d. as I,* I, 4, 220. Hence = far from the outer part: *some dark d. desert,* Lucr. 1144. And used of time: *d. night,* H6B I, 4, 19. *midnight,* Mids. I, 1, 223. *—est winter,* Tim. III, 4, 14.

2) loud, full-toned, sonorous: *and with d. groans the diapason bear,* Lucr. 1132. *the thunder, that d. and dreadful organ-pipe,* Tp. III, 3, 98. *the d. dread-bolted thunder,* Lr. IV, 7, 33. *between two dogs, which hath the —er mouth,* H6A II, 4, 12. *the tongues of dying men enforce attention like d. harmony,* R2 II,

1, 6. cf. *from his d. chest laughs out a loud applause,* Troil. I, 3, 163 (see *Deeply*).

3) Very variously used in a figurative sense; a) coming from, or dwelling in the inmost heart, heartfelt; and therefore intense: *d. delight,* Pilgr. 113. *desire,* Ven. 389. Mcb. I, 4, 51. *contempt,* R3 IV, 2, 124 (wanting in Ff). *curses, not loud but d.* Mcb. V, 3, 27. *despair,* H6C III, 3, 12. *disgrace,* R3 I, 1, 111. *extremes,* Tit. III, 1, 216. *exclaims,* R3 I, 2, 52. *grief,* Hml. IV, 5, 76. *groans,* Ven. 377. Lucr. 1132. 1276. Gentl. III, 1, 230. cf. *sighs,* Pilgr. 275. Rom. I, 1, 139. *kindness,* Sonn. 152, 9. *laments,* Tit. III, 2, 46. *my heart's d. languor,* Tit. III, 1, 13. *loathing,* Mids. II, 2, 138. *true zeal and d. integrity,* R2 V, 3, 108. *love,* Gentl. I, 1, 21. 23. Rom. II, 2, 134. *melancholy,* H6B V, 1, 34. *prayers,* R3 I, 4, 69. *this dear and d. rebuke,* H4B IV, 5, 141. *repentance,* Mcb. I, 4, 7. *shame,* Err. V, 253. John IV, 2, 235. *sorrow,* Tit. III, 1, 217. *torture,* Lucr. 1287. *unrest,* 1725. *vexation,* 1779. *vow,* 1847. cf. *oaths,* Sonn. 152, 9. LLL I, 1, 23 (see *Deep-sworn,* and Cymb. II, 3, 96: *I swear I love you. If you but said so, 'twere as d. with me*). *d. woes,* Lucr. 1118. *natures of such d. trust,* Lr. II, 1, 117. *intending d. suspicion,* R3 III, 5, 8. H8 III, 1, 53. *malice,* R2 I, 1, 155. Cor. IV, 6, 41. *to fill the mouth of d. defiance up,* H4A III, 2, 116. *d. enemies,* R3 IV, 2, 73. *with such a d. demeanour in great sorrow,* H4B IV, 5, 85. *of thy d. duty more impression show,* Cor. V, 3, 51. *why should you fall into so d. an O?* Rom. III, 3, 90. *O, that our night of woe might have remembered my —est sense how hard true sorrow hits,* Sonn. 120, 10.

b) sagacious, penetrating, profound: *sad pause and d. regard beseem the sage,* Lucr. 277. 1400. *by d. surmise,* 1579. *policy,* 1815. *question,* Compl. 121. *conceit,* Pilgr. 109. *a chough of as d. chat,* Tp. II, 1, 266. *a d. story of a —er love,* Gentl. I, 1, 23. *the spirit of d. prophecy she hath,* H6A I, 2, 55. *hold me pace in d. experiments,* H4A III, 1, 49. *d. intent,* R3 I, 1, 149. *plots,* Hml. V, 2, 9 (Ff *dear*). In an ill sense, = artful, insidious: *d. deceit,* H6B III, 1, 57. *d. traitors,* R3 I, 3, 224. *d., hollow, treacherous,* II, 1, 38.

c) proficient, versed, well skilled: *how d. you were within the books of God,* H4B IV, 2, 17. *counterfeit the d. tragedian,* R3 III, 5, 5. *meditating with two d. divines,* III, 7, 75. *d. clerks she dumbs,* Per. V Prol. 5.

d) touching near, important: *I'll read you matter d. and dangerous,* H4A I, 3, 190. *d. designs and matters of great moment,* R3 III, 7, 67. *my d. service,* IV, 2, 123 (or = having gone such lengths?). *to betray us in —est consequence,* Mcb. I, 3, 126. *if you said so, 'twere as d. with me,* Cymb. II, 3, 96.

e) heavy, grievous: *'tis much d.* (viz a debt), Tim. III, 4, 30. *the d. damnation of his taking off,* Mcb. I, 7, 20. *sin,* Lucr. 701. R2 I, 1, 187 (Ff *foul*). R3 III, 1, 43 (Ff *great*). *vice,* R3 II, 2, 28 (Qq *foul guile*).

f) Used of colours, = dark, intense: *the canker-blooms have full as d. a dye as the perfumed tincture of the roses,* Sonn. 54, 5. *the d. vermilion in the rose,* 98, 10.

Deep, adv., far below the surface, or far down: *d. in the thigh* (viz wounded) Pilgr. 127. *I'll seek him —er than e'er plummet sounded,* Tp. III, 3,

101. V, 56. Merch. IV, 1, 280. As IV, 1, 209. All's IV, 1, 62. V, 3, 24. John V, 2, 60. H4B III, 2, 172. H5 IV, 7, 82. H8 II, 1, 51. Troil. I, 1, 50. II, 3, 277. IV, 2, 86. Rom. I, 3, 98. Tim. III, 4, 15. Hml. II, 2, 602. Ant. I, 5, 29. Cymb. IV, 2, 388. *drink d.* H4A II, 4, 16. H5 I, 1, 20. Hml. I, 2, 175. *our fears in Banquo stick d.* Mcb. III, 1, 50.

Figurative use (cf. the adjective): *so d. sticks it in my penitent heart,* Meas. V, 480. *touches me —er,* R3 I, 1, 112. *fall d. in love,* Cor. I, 5, 22. *whose loss hath pierced him d.* Tit. IV, 4, 31. *that trick of state was a d. envious one,* H8 II, 1, 45. *d. damned,* John IV, 3, 122. *—er read and better skilled,* Tit. IV, 1, 33. *our tongues and sorrows do sound d. our woes into the air,* Per. I, 4, 13.

Deep, subst. 1) the sea, the ocean: *your soundless d.* Sonn. 80, 10. *the salt d.* Tp. I, 2, 253. Err. I, 1, 64. LLL IV, 3, 31. Mids. III, 1, 161. III, 2, 48. Shr. I, 1, 23. H4A I, 3, 203. R3 I, 4, 32. III, 4, 103. Lr. IV, 1, 77. IV, 2, 50. Plur. —s: Gentl. III,2,81. Troil.III,3,198 (Q *depth*). Per.II Prol. 30.

2) the infernal region: *I can call spirits from the vasty d.* H4A III, 1, 52. *to Pluto's damned lake, to the infernal d.* H4B II, 4, 170. *bind them* (the winds) *in brass, having called them from the d.* Per. III, 1, 4.

3) the midst, the most still part: *in d. of night,* Wiv. IV, 4, 40. *the d. of night,* Caes. IV, 3, 226.

Deep-brained, ingenious: *d. sonnets,* Compl. 209.

Deep-contemplative, given to profound meditation: As II, 7, 31.

Deep-divorcing: Err. II, 2, 140 (probably it ought to be *deep divorcing vow,* not hyphened; cf. *deep vow,* Lucr. 1847. *deep oaths,* Sonn. 152, 9. LLL I, 1, 23).

Deep-drawing, sinking deep into the water: *d. barks,* Troil. Prol. 12.

Deep-drenched, submerged: *d. in a sea of care,* Lucr. 1100.

Deep-fet, deep-fetched: *my d. groans,* H6B II, 4, 33.

Deep-green, of a dark green colour: *the d. emerald,* Compl. 213.

Deeply, 1) far below the surface: *he is d. in,* Tw. II, 5, 47. *to know if your affiance were d. rooted,* Cymb. I, 6, 164. *both dissemble d. their affections,* Shr. IV, 4, 42.

2) in the inmost recesses of the heart, most feelingly: *entertained them d. in the heart,* Gentl. V, 4, 102. *I will d. put the fashion on and wear it in my heart,* H4B V, 2, 52. *d. distressed,* Ven. 814. *took it d.* Wint. II, 3, 14. *wine loved I d.* Lr. III, 4, 93 (Ff. *deerely). how d. you touch me,* Cymb. IV, 3, 4. Used of vows: *thou art sworn as d. to effect what we intend,* R3 III, 1, 158. *'tis d. sworn,* Hml. III, 2, 235.

3) profoundly: *that most d. to consider,* Tp. III, 2, 106. *consider it not so d.* Mcb. II, 2, 30.

4) intensely, very much: *not so sound and half so d. sweet,* H4B IV, 5, 26. *d. indebted for this piece of pains,* H6B I, 4, 47. *she's with the lion d. still in league,* Tit. IV, 1, 98.

5) loudly: *passion on passion d. is redoubled,* Ven. 832. *hearing thy beauty sounded, but not so d. as to thee belongs,* Shr. II, 194.

Deep-mouthed, having a loud and sonorous voice: *the d. brach,* Shr. Ind. 1, 18. *thunder,* John V, 2, 173. *sea,* H5 V Chor. 11.

Deep-premeditated, carefully prepared: *comest thou with d. lines,* H6A III, 1, 1.

Deep-revolving, profoundly considering: *the d. witty Buckingham,* R3 IV, 2, 42.

Deep-searched, scrutinized: *the sun that will not be d. with saucy looks,* LLL I, 1, 85.

Deep-sore, very painful: *heart's d. wounding,* Ven. 432.

Deep-sweet, intensely sweet: *ear's d. music,* Ven. 432.

Deep-sworn, earnestly promised by oath: *d. faith,* John III, 1, 231.

Deep-vow, name in Meas. IV, 3, 14.

Deep-wounded: Pilgr. 126.

Deer (not inflected in the plural), 1) any animal? *mice and rats, and such small d.* Lr. III, 4, 144 (perhaps = game).

2) quadruped of the genus Cervus: Ven. 231. Lucr. 1149. Pilgr. 300. Wiv. V, 5, 18. 123. Err. II, 1, 100. LLL IV, 1, 35. 115. IV, 2, 3 etc. As II, 1, 47. 66. III, 3, 57. IV, 2, 1. 5. 11. Shr. V, 2, 56. Wint. I, 2, 118. H4A V, 4, 107. H6B V, 2, 15. H6C III, 1, 22. Tit. III, 1, 89. 91. Caes. III, 1, 209. Hml. III, 2, 282. Cymb. III, 4, 112. Plural: Ven. 689. Wiv. I, 1, 115. V, 5, 252. All's I, 3, 59. H6A IV, 2, 46. 48. 54. H6C III, 1, 2. 4. IV, 5, 17. Mcb. IV, 3, 206. Cymb. II, 3, 75. — Quibbling with *dear:* Ven. 231. Pilgr. 300. Wiv. V, 5, 18. 123. LLL IV, 1, 115. Shr. V, 2, 56. H4A V, 4, 107. H6A IV, 2, 54. Tit. III, 1, 91. Mcb. IV, 3, 206.

Deface, 1) to disfigure, to soil: Lucr. 719. Sonn. 6, 1. 64, 1. Pilgr. 90. H5 II, 4, 60. H6A III, 3, 45. V, 5, 29. H6B IV, 1, 42. R3 II, 1, 122. III, 7, 126.

2) to blot, to obliterate: *pay him six thousand, and d. the bond,* Merch. III, 2, 301. *blotting your names from books of memory, razing the characters of your renown, —ing monuments of conquered France,* H6B I, 1, 102. Perhaps also in R3 II, 1, 122; but cf. H5 II, 4, 60.

Defacer, one who disfigures or destroys: *that foul d. of God's handiwork,* R3 IV, 4, 51. *—s of a public peace,* H8 V, 3, 41.

Defame, subst. infamy: Lucr. 768. 817. 1033.

Defamed, disreputed, infamous: *England was —d by tyranny,* H6B III, 1, 123.

Default, fault: *we are penitent for your d.* Err. I, 2, 52. *this was your d.* H6A II, 1, 60. *Talbot perisheth by your d.* IV, 4, 28. *in the d.* = at a need: *that I may say in the d. he is a man I know,* All's II,3,242.

Defeat, subst. ruin, destruction: *made d. of her virginity,* Ado IV, 1, 48. *making d. on the full power of France,* H5 I, 2, 107. *a king whose property and life a damned d. was made,* Hml. II, 2, 598. *so may a thousand actions be all well borne without d.* H5 I, 2, 213 (Qq *defect). their d. does by their own insinuation grow,* Hml. V, 2, 58.

Defeat, vb. 1) to undo, to destroy: *it is my love that doth my rest d.* Sonn. 61, 11. *my honour's at the stake; which to d. I must produce my power,* All's II, 3, 156 (i. e. to defeat the danger threatening my honour). *your activity may d. and quell the source of all erection,* Tim. IV, 3, 163. *with a —ed joy,* Hml. I,

2, 10. *my stronger guilt —s my strong intent*, III, 3, 40. *his unkindness may d. my life*, Oth. IV, 2, 160.

2) **to disappoint:** *if these men have —ed the law and outrun native punishment*, H5 IV, 1, 175. *alleged many sharp reasons to d. the law*, H8 II, 1, 14. *therein, you gods, you tyrants do d.* Caes. I, 3, 92. *thou strikest not me, 'tis Caesar thou —est*, Ant. IV, 14, 68. *lest by some mortal stroke she do d. us*, V, 1, 65. Followed by *of: nature ... by addition me of thee —ed*, Sonn. 20, 11. *to have —ed you and me, you of your wife and me of my consent*, Mids. IV, 1, 162.

3) **to disfigure:** *d. thy favour with an usurped beard*, Oth. I, 3, 346.

Defeature, disfigurement: Ven. 736. Err. II, 1, 98. V, 299.

Defect, 1) **fault, imperfection:** *having no —s, why dost abhor me?* Ven. 138. Sonn. 49, 2. 70, 1. Tp. III, I, 44. Shr. I, 2, 124. R3 III, 7, 160. Troil. I. 3, 172. Hml. I, 4, 31. II, 2, 102. Lr. IV, 1, 22. Ant. II, 2, 55. 236. *d. of sth.* = want of sth.: *d. of that we have*, Lucr. 151. *d. of spirit*, 1345. *of manners*, H4A III, 1, 184. *of judgment*, Cor. IV, 7, 39. Cymb. IV, 2, 111.

2) **deficiency:** *all my best doth worship thy d.* Sonn. 149, 11. *our will became the servant to d.* Mcb. II, 1, 18.

Misapplied: Mids. III, 1, 40. Merch. II, 2, 152.

Defective, 1) **faulty, vicious:** *our vineyards, fallows, meads and hedges, d. in their natures, grow to wildness*, H5 V, 2, 55.

2) **wanting, coming short:** *we, poising us in her d. scale, shall weigh thee to the beam*, All's II, 3, 161. *our state is d. for requital*, Cor. II, 2, 54. *this effect d. comes by cause*, Hml. II, 2, 103. *all which the Moor is d. in*, Oth. II, 1, 233.

Defence, 1) **resistance made against an attack:** *nothing 'gainst time's scythe can make d.* Sonn. 12, 13. 89, 4. 139, 8. Pilgr. 110. John II, 81. IV, 3, 84. V, 1, 76. V, 2, 18. V, 7, 88. H5 I, 2, 153. III, 3, 43. H6C V, 1, 109. Tim. IV, 3, 346. Mcb. IV, 2, 78. *for the d. of a town*, Cor. IV, 5, 178. *in d.* Tim. III, 5, 55. *in d. of:* LLL V, 2, 85. H6A IV, 1, 99. H6C I, 1, 160. II, 2, 32. 79. Troil. II, 2, 198. Mcb. I, 3, 99. Hml. V, 1, 7. Lr. V, 3, 115. Used of the warding off of temptations: *I could drive her from ... a thousand other her —s*, Wiv. II, 2, 259. All's I, 1, 127. III, 5, 77. John I, 258.

2) **protection:** *God, the widows' champion and d.* R2 I, 2, 43. *let the heavens give him d. against the elements*, Oth. II, 1, 45. *we'll no d.* Cymb. III, 4, 81.

3) **armament, preparation for war:** *who but Rumour, who but only I, make fearful musters and prepared d.* H4B Ind. 12. *to answer royally in our —s*, H5 II, 4, 3. *—s, musters, preparations should be maintained*, 18. *in cases of d. 'tis best to weigh the enemy more mighty than he seems: so the proportions of d. are filled*, 43. 45. *desperation is all the policy, strength and d. that Rome can make against them*, Cor. IV, 6, 127.

Hence = arms, offensive as well as defensive: *that d. thou hast, betake thee to it*, Tw. III, 4, 240. *thy wit ... like powder in a skilless soldier's flask, is set afire by thine own ignorance, and thou dismembered with thine own d.* Rom. III, 3, 134. *go put on thy —s*, Ant. IV, 4, 10; cf. Cymb. III, 4, 81.

4) **readiness for combat, means or practice of fighting:** *by how much d. is better than no*

skill, *by so much is a horn more precious than to want*, As III, 3, 62. *now is it manhood, wisdom and d., to give the enemy way*, H6B V, 2, 75. *the city being but of small d.* H6C V, 1, 64. *whilst we, lying still, are full of rest, d. and nimbleness*, Caes. IV, 3, 202. *gave you such a masterly report for art and exercise in your d. and for your rapier most especially*, Hml. IV, 7, 98.

Defend, 1) trans. a) **to protect from violence or injury:** *what thorns the growing rose —s*, Lucr. 492. 1034. Wiv. III, 3, 126. Tw. V, 88. John I, 242. IV, 3, 88. R2 II, 2, 113. H6C IV, 7, 38. R3 I, 4, 213. Troil. I, 2, 284 etc. Cor. I, 1, 219. Tim. II, 2, 158 *(what shall d. the interim?)*. Hml. V, 2, 335. Lr. III, 6, 101. Per. I, 2, 30. II, 1, 135. *O d. me!* Tp. II, 2, 92. *O God, d. me!* Ado IV, 1, 78. Tw. III, 4, 331. R3 V, 3, 117. Caes. II, 3, 9. Lr. V, 3, 256. Per. IV, 2, 95. *God d. the right!* LLL I, 1, 216. R2 I, 3, 101. H6B II, 3, 55. *so d. thee heaven*, R2 I, 3, 15. 25. 41. Oth. III, 3, 373 (Ff *forgive*). *angels and ministers of grace d. us!* Hml. I, 4, 39.

Reflectively: *d. thyself*, H4A V, 4, 34. H5 I, 2, 179. H6C IV, 1, 45. R3 III, 5, 19. Cor. III, 2, 94. Lr. II, 1, 32. Oth. II, 3, 203.

Followed by *from: d. me from what is past*, Lucr. 1684. *heavens d. me from that Welsh fairy*, Wiv. V, 5, 85. Meas. III, 1, 268. Merch. I, 2, 57. R2 I, 1, 187. H5 I, 2, 141. 218. H6B IV, 5, 5. V, 3, 19. H6C IV, 3, 22. R3 I, 4, 114. Caes. V, 4, 23. Lr. III, 4, 31. Oth. III, 3, 175.

b) **to maintain by force or by argument, to secure:** *fair fall the wit that can so well d. her*, Ven. 472. *I lost the ring —ing it*, Merch. V, 178. 204. *let this d. my loyalty*, R2 I, 1, 67. *which in myself I boldly will d.* 145. *when Helen is —ed*, Troil. II, 2, 158. IV, 1, 58. Hml. IV, 4, 23. Lr. V, 1, 69.

c) **to forbid:** *hath he seen majesty? Isis else d.!* Ant. III, 3, 46. *heaven d. your good souls that you think ...*, Oth. I, 3, 267. *God d. the lute should be like the case*, Ado II, 1, 98. R2 I, 3, 18. R3 III, 7, 81 (Qq *forbid*). 173. *God d. but God should go before such villains*, Ado IV, 2, 21. *God d. but still I should stand so*, H4A IV, 3, 38.

2) intr. **to be prepared against attack, to make armaments:** *lay down our proportions to d. against the Scot*, H5 I, 2, 137.

Defendant, subst., the party that opposes a complaint or demand: Sonn. 46, 7. Merch. IV, 1, 361. H6B II, 3, 49.

Defendant, adj. **defensive:** *repair our towns of war with men of courage and with means d.* H5 II, 4, 8.

Defender, one who protects: Cor. III, 3, 128. V, 2, 42. Tit. I, 77.

Defensible, in a state of making defence, able to fight: *where nothing but the sound of Hotspur's name did seem d.* H4B II, 3, 38. *we no longer are d.* H5 III, 3, 50.

Defensive, serving to protect: *a moat d. to a house*, R2 II, 1, 48. *holy Joan was his d. guard*, H6A II, 1, 49.

Defer, 1) trans. **to delay, to postpone:** *d. the spoil of the city until night*, H6B IV, 7, 142. *—ed the visitation of my friends*, R3 III, 7, 107 (Qq *neglect*).

2) intr. **to delay, to tarry:** *d. no time, delays have dangerous ends*, H6A III, 2, 33.

Defiance, 1) **challenge to fight:** John I,

21. R2 III, 3, 130. H4A V, 2, 43. H4B III, 1, 65. H5 II, 4, 117. III, 5, 37. III, 6, 142. Troil. IV, 1, 12. Rom. I, 1, 117. Caes. V, 1, 64. *to fill the mouth of deep d. up,* H4A III, 2, 116 (or perhaps = feud, enmity?).

2) rejection, declaration that one will have nothing to do with another: *take my d.! die, perish!* Meas. III, 1, 143.

Deficient, 1) failing, fainting: *and the d. sight topple down headlong,* Lr. IV, 6, 23. — 2) defective: *being not d., blind, or lame of sense,* Oth. I, 3, 63.

Defile, vb. 1) to make unclean, to render dirty: *they that touch pitch will be —d,* Ado III, 3, 60. *pitch that —s,* LLL IV, 3, 3. H4A II, 4, 456. H6B II, 1, 196. Quibbling: *—s the pitchy night,* All's IV, 4, 24. *in a pitched field; ay, —d land,* Tim. I, 2, 231. *houses are —d for want of use,* Per. I, 4, 37.

2) to pollute, to sully: Lucr. 787. 1029. 1545. Wiv. I, 3, 108. Ado V, 4, 63. Mids. III, 2, 410. All's V, 3, 301. R2 V, 3, 63. H5 III, 3, 35. Lr. III, 6, 119. Per. I, 1, 131.

Absolutely: *vows were ever brokers to —ing,* Compl. 173.

Defiler, one who pollutes: *thou bright d. of Hymen's purest bed,* Tim. IV, 3, 383.

Define, to explain the meaning, to describe the distinctive properties of sth., to describe: *d., d., well-educated infant,* LLL I, 2, 99. *to d. true madness, what is't but to be nothing else but mad?* Hml. II, 2, 93. *and for myself mine own worth do d., as I all other in all worths surmount,* Sonn. 62, 7. *behold, as may unworthiness d., a little touch of Harry,* H5 IV Chor. 46.

Definement, description: *his d. suffers no perdition in you,* Hml. V, 2, 117.

Definite, resolved, free from hesitation: *idiots in this case of favour would be wisely d.* Cymb. I, 6, 43.

Definitive, the same: *never crave him; we are d.* Meas. V, 432.

Definitively, positively: *d. thus I answer you,* R3 III, 7, 153.

Deflower or **Deflour** (rhyming to *Moor,* Tit. II, 3, 191) to ravish: Meas. IV, 4, 24. Tit. II, 3, 191. II, 4, 26. V, 3, 38. Rom. IV, 5, 37. Absolutely: *I must d.* Lucr. 348. Misapplied: Mids. V, 297.*

Deform, to disfigure: Gentl. II, 1, 68. 70. Err. I, 2, 100. LLL V, 2, 767.

Deformed, adj. 1) misshaped, ill-favoured: Ven. Dedic. 5. Err. IV, 2, 19. Ado III, 3, 131. LLL IV, 2, 24. Tw. III, 4, 402. H6C V, 6, 51. R3 I, 1, 20. Superl. *—'st:* Sonn. 113, 10.

2) apt to deform or disfigure: *careful hours with time's d. hand have written strange defeatures in my face,* Err. V, 298.

Deformed, taken for a name by Dogberry: Ado III, 3, 132. 182. 184. V, 1, 317.

Deformity, bad shape, ugliness: Gentl. II, 1, 82. H6C III, 2, 158. R3 I, 1, 27. I, 2, 57. Lr. IV, 2, 60. Plur. *—ies:* Rom. I, 4, 31.

Deftly, neatly, dexterously: *thyself and office d. show,* Mcb. IV, 1, 68.

Defunct, dead, deadened: *abhor to make his bed with the d.* Cymb. IV, 2, 358. *the organs, though d. and dead before,* H5 IV, 1, 21. *in my d. and proper satisfaction,* Oth. I, 3, 265 (most M. Edd. *in me d.*).

Defunction, death: *after d. of king Pharamond,* H5 I, 2, 58.

Defunctive, funereal: *d. music,* Phoen. 14.

Defuse (most M. Edd. *diffuse,* q. v.), to make indiscernible and shapeless: *if but as well I other accents borrow, that can my speech d.* Lr. I, 4, 2. Partic. *—d* = shapeless: *to swearing and stern looks, —d attire and every thing that seems unnatural,* H5 V, 2, 61.* *—d infection of a man,* R3 I, 2, 78.

Defy, 1) to dare, to brave with contempt: *thy registers and thee* (time) *I both d.* Sonn. 123, 9. Tp. III, 2, 140. Wiv. II, 2, 74. Meas. II, 1, 86. As IV, 3, 32. John II, 155. R2 I, 1, 60. H4A III, 3, 71. H6A III, 1, 27. H6B IV, 10, 67. H6C II, 2, 118. 170. H8 V, 4, 58. Cor. III, 3, 79. Rom. V, 1, 24 (only in Q1; the rest of O. Edd. *deny*). V, 3, 68.

2) to slight, to despise, to renounce: *age, I do d. thee,* Pilgr. 167. *love's denying, faith's —ing,* 250. *complexions that liked me, and breaths that I —ed not,* As Epil. 21. *fools that for a tricksy word d. the matter,* Merch. III, 5, 75. *I d. lechery,* Tw. I, 5, 133. *d. the devil, consider he's an enemy to mankind,* III, 4, 108. *I d. all counsel, all redress,* John III, 4, 23. *all studies here I solemnly d.* H4A I, 3, 228. *I cannot flatter, I d. the tongues of soothers,* IV, 1, 6. *and so, proud-hearted Warwick, I d. thee, and to my brother turn my blushing cheeks,* H6C V, 1, 98. *d. the foul fiend,* Lr. III, 4, 101. *we d. augury,* Hml. V, 2, 230. *have you that a man may deal withal, and d. the surgeon?* Per. IV, 6, 29.

3) to challenge: *I dare and do d. thee for a villain,* Err. V, 32. *if you offend him, I for him d. you,* Tw. III, 4, 345. John II, 406. H4A V, 2, 32. H5 II, 1, 76. III, 3, 5 (*d. us to our worst*). Ant. II, 2, 160. Cymb. III, 1, 68.

Degenerate, adj. fallen from the virtue of the ancestors: R2 I, 1, 144. II, 1, 262. H4A III, 2, 128. H6C I, 1, 183. Tit. III, 1, 66. Lr. I, 4, 275. IV, 2, 43. Used of things: *the baser is he, coming from a king, to shame his hope with deeds d.* Lucr. 1003. *can it be that so d. a strain as this should once set footing in your generous bosoms?* Troil. II, 2, 154.

Hence = corrupt, base: *the more d. and base art thou,* Gentl. V, 4, 136. John V, 2, 151. H6B IV, 4, 2.

Degrade, to reduce to a lower rank: H6A IV, 1, 43. H6C IV, 3, 33.

Degree, 1) step or round of a staircase or ladder: *scorning the base —s by which he did ascend,* Caes. II, 1, 26. *his ascent is not by such easy —s,* Cor. II, 2, 29. Figuratively: *and in these —s have they made a pair of stairs to marriage,* As V, 2, 41. *I pity you; that's a d. to love,* Tw. III, 1, 134. *as were our England in reversion his, and he our subjects' next d. in hope,* R2 I, 4, 36. *the next d. is England's royal throne,* H6C II, 1, 193. *who stands so eminent in the d. of this fortune as Cassius does?* Oth. II, 1, 241.

2) a step of progression: *what future evils are now to have no successive —s,* Meas. II, 2, 98. *the —s of the lie,* As V, 4, 92. *in the third d. of drink,* Tw. I, 5, 143. *I'll answer thee in any fair d. or chivalrous design of knightly trial,* R2 I, 1, 80 (i. e. to any length that is compatible with the honour of knighthood). *so both the —s* (age and youth) *prevent my curses,* H4B I, 2, 259. *—s in schools and brotherhoods in cities,* Troil. I, 3, 104. *hadst thou, like us*

from our first swath, proceeded the sweet —s that this brief world affords, Tim. IV, 3, 253 (i. e. the different stages of enjoyment). *in the highest d.* Tw. I, 5, 61. IV, 2, 128. Cor. V, 6, 85. *in the highest d., in the direst d., in each d.* R3 V, 3, 196—198. *in the least d.* LLL I, 1, 157. *in no less d.* As V, 4, 154. *of the worst d.* R2 II, 3, 108. *in so dear d.* R3 I, 4, 215. *of such unnatural d.* Lr. I, 1, 222. *Hector is not Troilus in some —s,* Troil. I, 2, 74. *by d.* = step by step: *festered members rot but by d.* H6A III, 1, 192. *by —s:* LLL V, 2, 418. Shr. III, 2, 145. Oth. II, 3, 377. Ant. III, 13, 163.

3) **rank:** *under the d. of a squire,* Wiv. III, 4, 48. *I know not the d. of the Worthy,* LLL V, 2, 508. *O, that estates, —s and offices were not derived corruptly!* Merch. II, 9, 41. Tw. I, 3, 116. 125. III, 4, 86. Wint. II, 1, 85. H4B IV, 3, 6. H5 IV, 1, 263. IV, 7, 143. V, 1, 38. H6A II, 4, 111. III, 1, 20. IV, 1, 17. V, 1, 29. H6B V, 1, 73. R3 I, 1, 87. III, 7, 143. 188 (Qq *all his thoughts*). Troil. I, 3, 83. 86. 101. 108. Tim. IV, 1, 19. V, 1, 211. Mcb. III, 4, 1. Lr. V, 3, 111. Oth. II, 3, 97. III, 3, 230.

Deify, to **adore as a deity:** Compl. 84. As III, 2, 381.

Deign, 1) followed by an inf., := to **condescend, to think worthy:** Shr. V, 2, 145. H6A I, 2, 78. V, 3, 151. H6C IV, 7, 39.

2) followed by an accus., a) to **condescend to give, to grant:** *if thou wilt d. this favour,* Ven. 15. *nor would we d. him burial of his men,* Mcb. I, 2, 60.

b) to **condescend to take, not to disdain:** *Julia would not d. my lines,* Gentl. I, 1, 160. *thy palate then did d. the roughest berry,* Ant. I, 4, 63.

Deiphobus, son of Priam: Troil. I, 2, 247. III, 1, 148. IV, 2, 63.

Deity (of two or three syllables, indiscriminately): Godhead: Tp. II, 1, 278. IV, 92. LLL IV, 3, 74. Tw. V, 234. Wint. IV, 4, 26. R3 I, 1, 76. Troil. IV, 4, 29. Cor. IV, 6, 91. Tim. III, 6, 82. Ant. I, 2, 168. Cymb. V, 4, 90. Per. III, 1, 12.

Deject, vb. to **depress, to lower:** *nor once d. the courage of our minds,* Troil. II, 2, 121. Partic. *—ed,* a) = lowered, humbled: *you have the start of me, I am —ed,* Wiv. V, 5, 171. *the lowest and most —ed thing of fortune,* Lr. IV, 1, 3. *the —ed state wherein he is,* Per. II, 2, 46. b) = cast down, low-spirited: *this —ed Mariana,* Meas. III, 1, 277. *the —ed haviour of the visage,* Hml. I, 2, 81. *Antony is valiant, and —ed,* Ant. IV, 12, 7.

Partic. *deject: reason and respect make livers pale and lustihood d.* Troil. II, 2, 50. *and I, of ladies most d. and wretched,* Hml. III, 1, 163.

Delabreth, French name, properly *d' Albret:* H5 III, 5, 40. IV, 8, 97.

De la Pole, name: H6A V, 3, 67.

Delate, to **carry, to convey:** *more than the scope of these —d articles allow,* Hml. I, 2, 38 (Ff *dilated,* q. v.).*

Delation, denunciation, accusation: *such things ... are close —s working from the heart,* Oth. III, 3, 123 (F 1 Q 2. 3 *dilations,* Q1 *denotements*).

Delay, subst., lingering, procrastination: Wiv. II, 1, 99. Mids. V, 205. As III, 2, 207. All's II, 4, 45. Tw. II, 3, 51. R2 V, 1, 101. H5 II, 4, 142. H6A IV, 3, 46. H6B I, 1, 170. H6C III, 2, 18. R3 IV, 1, 52. IV,

3, 52. H8 I, 2, 59. II, 4, 67. Rom. I, 4, 44. II, 5, 33. Hml. III, 1, 72. Lr. I, 2, 100. Oth. II, 3, 394. Plur. *—s:* Ven. 909. Lucr. 1719. Err. I, 1, 75. H6A I, 2, 146. III, 2, 33. H6C IV, 8, 40. Tit. IV, 3, 42. Hml. IV, 7, 121. *make no d.* Mids. III, 2, 394. *hold him in d.* Tw. I, 5, 112. *use d.* H6C IV, 8, 60.

Delay, subst., name of a ship: Err. IV, 3, 40.

Delay, vb. to **put off, to defer, to retard;** absol.: *the powers, —ing, not forgetting,* Tp. III, 3, 73. *d. not,* H6C III, 3, 246. Caes. III, 1, 9. *while men d.* H4A III, 2, 180. Trans.: *the doors, the wind, the glove, that did d. him,* Lucr. 325. *his unhallowed haste her words —s,* 552. Sonn. 126, 11. Meas. IV, 2, 174. Wint. IV, 4, 474. H6A IV, 3, 10. Cor. I, 6, 60. Rom. III, 5, 201. Oth. III, 4, 114. Hml. IV, 3, 57. Ant. II, 1, 3. Cymb. V, 4, 102. Per. II, 5, 22. Hence = to **detain, to keep back:** *let me stay the growth of his beard, if thou d. me not the knowledge of his chin,* As III, 2, 222. *what safe and nicely I might well d. by rule of knighthood, I disdain and spurn,* Lr. V, 3, 144 (i. e. I disdain to refuse it). Dubious passage: *God d. our rebellion!* All's IV, 3, 23 (= make us slow in sinning?).

Délectable, delightful: *making the hard way sweet and d.* R2 II, 3, 7. *full of nimble fiery and d. shapes,* H4B IV, 3, 108.

Deliberate, vb., to **pause and consider:** *d. a day or two,* Gentl. I, 3, 73. *and not to d., not to remember,* H4B V, 5, 22.

Deliberate, adj., considerate: *these d. fools,* Merch. II, 9, 80. *your most grave belly was d.* Cor. I, 1, 131. Of things: *whose settled visage and d. word,* Meas. III, 1, 90. *d. pause,* Hml. IV, 3, 9.

Delicate, adj. 1) tender: *a spirit too d. to act her earthy commands,* Tp. I, 2, 272. *led by a d. and tender prince,* Hml. IV, 4, 48. *her d. cheek,* Lr. IV, 3, 15. Ant. II, 2, 209. *when the mind is free, the body is d.* Lr. III, 4, 12. *abused her d. youth with drugs,* Oth. I, 2, 74. *her d. tenderness will find itself abused,* II. 1, 235.

2) lovely, graceful: *d. Ariel,* Tp. I, 2, 441. IV, I, 49. *a d. wench,* II, 1, 43. *a most d. monster,* II, 2, 93. *thou ever young, fresh, loved and d. wooer,* Tim. IV, 3, 385. *a most fresh and d. creature,* Oth. II, 3, 20. *these d. creatures,* III, 3, 269.

3) delicious: *of subtle, tender and d. temperance,* Tp. II, 1, 42. *soft and d. desires,* Ado I, 1, 305. *more moving, d. and full of life,* IV, 1, 230. *the climate's d.* Wint. III, 1, 1. *such d. burthens,* IV, 4, 195. *roots that shall first spring and be most d.* H5 II, 4, 40. *the air is d.* Mcb. I, 6, 10. *do it a more d. way than drowning,* Oth. I, 3, 360. *in soft and d. Lethe,* Ant. II, 7, 114. *proud of that most d. lodging,* Cymb. II, 4, 136. *a d. odour,* Per. III, 2, 61.

4) fine, ingenious, artful; of persons and things: *so d. with her needle,* Oth. IV, 1, 199. *O most d. fiend! who is't can read a woman?* Cymb. V, 5, 47. *d. fine hats,* All's IV, 5, 110. *most d. carriages,* Hml. V, 2, 160. *it were a d. stratagem,* Lr. IV, 6, 188.

Delicate, subst. a delicacy: *far beyond a princes —s,* H6C II, 5, 51.

Delicious, highly pleasing to the taste: Lucr. 699. Shr. Ind. I, 39. Tit. IV, 4, 93. Ant. I, 5, 27.

Deliciousness, highly pleasing taste: Rom. II, 6, 12.

Delight, subst. 1) high degree of pleasure or satisfaction: *my day's d. is past,* Ven. 380.

his other agents aim at like d. 400. Lucr. 12. 357. 385.
742. 927. Sonn. 36, 8. 47, 14. Pilgr. 113. 314. LLL
I, 1, 71. Mids. II, 1, 254. V, 114. Merch.II, 6, 67. John
IV, 3, 69. R2 III, 4, 7. Rom. I, 2, 28. II, 5, 77. Hml. I,
2, 13. Oth. I, 1, 68. Ant. IV, 4, 21. Per. III, 2, 39. Plur.
—*s*: As V, 4, 204. Rom. II, 6, 9. Ant. V, 2, 88. Followed
by *in: their labour d. in them sets off*, Tp. III, 1, 2.
Of d. == delightful: *figures of d. drawn after you*,
Sonn. 98, 11. *pageants of d.* Gentl. IV, 4, 164. *affections
of d.* H4B II, 3, 29. *To give d.* Tp. III, 2, 145. *to have
d.* Sonn. 75, 11. Err. IV, 4, 118. R3 I, 1, 25. Oth. II, 1,
228. *have a d.* Meas. II, 1, 134. *to take d.* Sonn. 37,
1. 75, 11. LLL I, 2, 134. *to take d. in sth.*: As I, 2,
168. Mids. III, 2, 455. Shr. I, 1, 92. Tw. I, 5, 89. II, 4,
12. H6A III, 1, 111. Hml. II, 2, 341.

2) that which gives pleasure: *the foul boar's
conquest on her fair d.* Ven. 1030. *marks thee for my
earth's d.* Lucr. 487. Wiv. V, 5, 158. Mids. V, 41. Merch.
II, 8, 53. Troil. V, 2, 140. Per. IV, 4, 12. Plur. —*s*:
LLL I, 1, 29. H6A V, 5, 17. H8 V, 1, 3. Troil. II, 2,
143. Mcb. IV, 1, 128. Hml. III, 1, 27.

3) the faculty of giving pleasure, the
charm: *her best is bettered with a more d.* Ven. 78.
of more d. than hawks or horses be, Sonn. 91, 11. *sweets
grown common lose their sweet d.* 102, 12. 130, 7. *paint
the meadows with d.* LLL V, 2, 907. *find d. writ there
with beauty's pen*, Rom. I, 3, 82.

Delight, vb. 1) trans. to affect with great
pleasure: *to d. his ear*, Pilgr. 47. Ado V, 1, 6. H6A
I, 4, 62. H6C V, 7, 35. Hml. II, 2, 321. 327. Per. I, 4,
40. Partic. —*ed*, LLL V, 2, 671. —*ed with*, Sonn. 141,
5. Reflectively: *that mine eyes —ed them in any other
form*, Oth. IV, 2, 155.

2) intr. to take great pleasure: *how you d.,
my lords*, *I know not*, LLL I, 1, 175. *such a thing as
thou, to fear, not to d.* Oth. I, 2, 71. *not so much to feed
on as d.* Per. I, 4, 29. Followed by an inf.: *do I d. to
die?* Ven. 496. Sonn. 24, 12. All's III, 4, 27. H6B IV,
8, 29. R3 I, 2, 53. Tit. II, 4, 46. Followed by *in: others
d. in such-like circumstance*, Ven. 843. Lucr. 430.
697. Sonn. 8, 2. Gentl. II, 4, 148. IV, 2, 66. Err. I, 1,
107. Ado II, 1, 144. LLL V, 2, 346. Shr. I, 1, 113.
Tw. 1, 3, 120. Tit. IV, 1, 60. Rom. III, 2, 116. Mcb.
II, 3, 55. IV, 3, 129. Hml. II, 2, 328.

Delighted, adj. (derived from the subst.) endowed with delight, delightful: *and the d. spirit
to bathe in fiery floods*, Meas. III, 1, 121 (i. e. the spirit
having the power of giving delight, rich in delight).
if virtue no d. beauty lack, Oth. I, 3, 290. *to make my
gift, the more delayed, d.* Cymb. V, 4, 102.

Delightful, highly pleasing: Ven. 236. LLL
V, 1, 118. R2 I, 3, 291. R3 I, 1, 8. Tit. III, 1, 82. Per.
II, 1, 164. II, 5, 28.

Delinquent, subst. the criminal: *did he not
straight the two —s tear?* Mcb. III, 6, 12.

Deliver, 1) to set free, to release: Wiv.
IV, 5, 122. Err. IV, 3, 41. V, 284. Merch. IV, 1, 287.
416. Tw. IV, 2, 74. V, 323. H4B V, 5, 41. R3 I, 1, 115.
Cor. I, 9, 89. Followed by *from*: Meas. IV, 4, 14. Err.
IV, 3, 44. LLL I, 2, 63. Merch. III, 3, 22. Shr. I, 1, 66.
R3 I, 1, 69. I, 4, 254 (quibble). Troil. II, 3, 17. Caes.
I, 3, 90. Lr. IV, 6, 273. Followed by *of: how I may be
—ed of these woes*, John III, 4, 55. *we'll d. you of your
great danger*, Cor. V, 6, 14. Joined with *up*, == to set
at liberty: *d. them up without their ransom*, H4A I, 3,
260. *d. up my lord of Westmoreland*. V, 2, 29.

2) to disburden (of a child): *she is something
before her time —ed*, Wint. II, 2, 25. *a gasping new
—ed mother*, R2 II, 2, 65. Tit. IV, 2, 61. 142. Oth. II,
1, 129. Per. III, 4, 7. Followed by *of*: —*ed of such a
burden*, Err. I, 1, 55. H4B II, 2, 97. H8 V, 1, 164. Tit.
V, 3, 120. Figuratively: Hml. II, 2, 215.

3) to bear, to bring forth: *those children
nursed, —ed from thy brain*, Sonn. 77, 11. *thirty three
years have I but gone in travail of you, and till this
present hour my heavy burthen ne'er —ed*, Err. V, 402.
*these (ideas etc.) are —ed upon the mellowing of occa-
sion*, LLL IV, 2, 72. *from the inward motion to d. sweet
poison for the age's tooth*, John I, 212. *there are many
events in the womb of time which will be —ed*, Oth. I,
3, 378. *I am great with woe, and shall d. weeping*, Per.
V, 1, 107.

4) to surrender, to transfer, to give: *it
(the eye) no form —s to the heart*, Sonn. 113, 5. *money*,
Gentl. I, 1, 138 (quibble). *a dog*, IV, 4, 7. *a ring*, 77.
I will d. his wife into your hand, Wiv. V, 1, 31. *I have
—ed to Lord Angelo my absolute power*, Meas. I, 3,
11. *to d. his head in the view of Angelo*, IV, 2, 177.
Err. IV, 4, 91. LLL IV, 2, 145. Merch. II, 7, 59. Shr.
IV, 2, 90. Wint. III, 2, 128. H4A II, 1, 27. H6A V, 1,
53. V, 3, 157. H6B I, 1, 51. I, 3, 3. R3 I, 4, 92. Troil.
IV, 2, 65. Tit. IV, 2, 61 (quibble). Cymb. I, 1, 73 etc.
Often used of letters: *the post attends, and she —s it*,
Lucr. 1333. *for —ing your letter*, Gentl. I, 1, 145. I,
3, 54. II, 1, 167. III, 1, 54. 249. Meas. IV, 5, 1. Ado IV,
1, 20. Merch. II, 2, 123. Tw. V, 296. H6A IV, 1, 11 etc.
received and did d. to our age this tale, Wiv. IV, 4,
37. —*ed him to his liberty*, Meas. IV, 2, 137. *d. him to
safety*, John IV, 2, 158 (i. e. put him to prison). —*ed
me to my sour cross*, R2 IV, 241. *now he —s thee from
this world's thraldom to the joys of heaven*, R3 I, 4, 254
(quibble). *God d. to a joyful resurrections*, Wiv. I, 1,
53 (Evans' speech).

Joined with adverbs; a) back: *'twill be —ed back*,
Cor. I, 10, 2. b) out: *though all at once cannot see what
I do d. out to each*, Cor. I, 1, 147 (== distribute). c)
over: *see him —ed o'er*, LLL I, 1, 307. *see them —ed
o'er to execution*, R2 III, 1, 29. *which, —ed o'er to the
voice*, H4B IV, 3, 109. —*ed her over to me*, V, 4, 4.
released and —ed over to the king, H6B I, 1, 59 (cf.
51). d) up: *so d. I up my apes*, Ado II, 1, 49. John IV,
2, 152. H4A V, 5, 27. H4B V, 2, 111. H6B I, 1, 12.
122. Troil. II, 2, 152. cf. H4A I, 3, 260 and V, 2, 29.

5) to let go, to send: *in —ing my son from
me, I bury a second husband*, All's I, 1, 1. *in fine, —s
me to fill the time, herself most chastely absent*, III, 7,
33. And == to let fly: —*ed such a shower of pebbles*,
H8 V, 4, 59.

6) to utter, to speak, to communicate:
as he most learnedly —ed, Tp. II, 1, 45. *I'll d. all*, V,
313. *that the money and the matter may be both at once
—ed*, Gentl. I, 1, 138 (quibble). *if his enemy d. it*, III,
2, 35. *more depends on it than we must yet d.* Meas.
IV, 2, 128. *her very words didst thou d. to me*, Err. II,
2, 166. LLL II, 73. All's I, 3, 121. III, 6, 32. IV, 3,
175. Tw. 1, 5, 222. II, 3, 140. V, 299. Wint. IV, 4, 371
(quibble). 509. V, 2, 4. 29. R2 III, 1, 39. III, 2, 92.
IV, 9. H4A I, 3, 26. V, 2, 26. H4B IV, 2, 69. H5 III, 6,
176. H6B III, 2, 313. H6C V, 2, 46. R3 III, 4, 17. IV,
4, 447. H8 I, 2, 143. Cor. IV, 6, 63. Rom. III, 5, 139.
Caes. III, 1, 181. Mcb. III, 3, 2. Hml. V, 2, 186 (with
affectation: *shall I d. you e'en so?* Ff *re-deliver*).

Cymb. I, 6, 88 etc. Absolutely, = to speak: *and thus d.* R2 III, 3, 34. *an't please you, d.* Cor. I, 1, 98.

7) to discover, to show: *and might not be —ed to the world,* Tw. I, 2, 42. *the sorrow that —s us thus changed makes you think so,* Cor. V, 3, 39. *I'll d. myself your loyal servant, or endure your heaviest censure,* V, 6, 141.

Deliverance, 1) release: Meas. III, 1, 105. IV, 2, 13. Merch. III, 2, 38. H4B II, 1, 138. H8 II, 2, 46.

2) the state of being disburdened of a child: *ne'er mother rejoiced d. more,* Cymb. V, 5, 370.

3) utterance: *if seriously I may convey my thoughts in this my light d.* All's III, 1, 85. *you have it from his own d.* II, 5, 4. *and at each word's d. stab poniards in our flesh,* H6C II, 1, 97.

Delivery, 1) release: R3 I, 1, 75. I, 4, 253.

2) surrender: *the hour prefixed of her d. to this valiant Greek,* Troil. IV, 3, 2.

3) communication, account: *I make a broken d. of the business,* Wint. V, 2, 10.

Delphos, Delphi, the oracle of Apollo: Wint. II, 1, 183. II, 3, 195. III, 2, 127. Thought to be an island: III, 1, 2.

Delude, to dupe: *thou false —ing slave,* Shr. IV, 3, 31. *O give me leave, I have —d you,* H6A V, 4, 76. *let loose on me the justice of the state for thus —ing you,* Oth. I, 1, 141.

Deluge, inundation: R3 I, 2, 61. Tit. III, 1, 230.

Delve, vb. to dig: *—s the parallels in beauty's brow,* Sonn. 60, 10. *I will d. one yard below their mines,* Hml. III, 4, 208. *what's his name and birth? I cannot d. him to the root,* Cymb. I, 1, 28. cf. *Earth-delving.*

Delver, one who digs: Hml. V, 1, 15.

Demand, subst. 1) request; suit; a) Wiv. I, 1, 233. Meas. III, 1, 254. John II, 56. R2 III, 3, 123. H5 II, 4, 121. V, 2, 71. 89. 96. H6A V, 3, 144. H6B V, 1, 40. H6C III, 2, 80. R3 IV, 2, 87 and 97 (Ff request). Ant. V, 2, 10. *a visage of d.* Tim. II, 1, 29. *they gave us our —s,* Cor. III, 1, 135. *make thy d.* All's II, 1, 194. Troil. V, 5, 130. *make d.* Troil. III, 3, 17. Followed by *of: —s of debt,* broke bonds, Tim. II, 2, 37. *for the d. of our neglected tribute,* Hml. III, 1, 178. — b) All's II, 1, 89. H4B IV, 1, 144. H6C III, 3, 66. 259. IV, 8, 39.

2) question: *an answer that must fit all —s,* All's II, 2, 35. IV, 3, 52. H8 II, 3, 52. Cor. III, 2, 45. Hml. II, 1, 12. III, 1, 13. Lr. I, 5, 3. Cymb. I, 6, 89. IV, 2, 23. *make that d. of the prover,* Troil. II, 3, 72 (Ff *to the creator*). *let Patroclus make —s to me,* III, 3, 272. *he'll make d. of her,* Ant. V, 2, 305.

Demand, vb. 1) to claim, to request: *to deny, if they d.* All's II, 1, 21. *he doth d. to have repaid a hundred thousand crowns,* LLL II, 143. 144. The thing claimed in the accus.: *what is't thou canst d.?* Tp. I, 2, 245. *I will please you what you will d.* Err. IV, 4, 52. All's I, 3, 109. III, 7, 22. John IV, 2, 84. H4A I, 3, 23. 47. H6B I, 1, 133. R3 II, 1, 98. Tit. IV, 4, 106. V, 1, 160. Rom. V, 3, 298. Oth. III, 4, 189. Ant. III, 6, 37. Cymb. V, 5, 99. Per. IV, 3, 13. *Of before the person applied to: yet did I not d. of him,* Compl. 149. *the pound of flesh which I d. of him,* Merch. IV, 1, 99.

2) to question, to ask: *well —ed,* Tp. I, 2, 139. *d. what 'tis,* Meas. II, 4, 33. Wint. V, 3, 153.

John III, 1, 140. H5 V, 2, 32. Cor. III, 3, 43. Caes. III, 2, 21. Mcb. IV, 1, 61. Hml. IV, 5, 129. The person asked in the accus.: *to be —ed of a sponge,* Hml. IV, 2, 12. *d. that demi-devil why he hath...,* Oth. V, 2, 301. *d. me nothing,* 303. *being —ed that,* Per. V, 1, 190. Or preceded by *of: you will d. of me why I do this,* Meas. I, 3, 17. All's IV, 3, 148. 180. H4B I, 1, 40. H8 I, 2, 153. Caes. V, 1, 6. The thing asked for in the accus.: *—ed the cause of her sorrow,* Lucr. Arg. 19. *why d. you this?* LLL V, 2, 386. H4A I, 2, 5. 12. Lr. V, 3, 62. Cymb. IV, 2, 362. V, 5, 389. *To d. sth. of a p.: d. of him my condition,* All's IV, 3, 196. John III, 1, 146. R2 I, 3, 7. The thing asked for preceded by *of: why may not I d. of thine affairs?* John V, 6, 4. *—ing of king Henry's life and death,* H6B II, 1, 175. *we'll mannerly d. thee of thy story,* Cymb. III, 6, 92. Preceded by *after: —ing after you,* Lr. III, 2, 65.

Demean, vb. refl., to behave: *Antipholus is mad, else would he never so d. himself,* Err. IV, 3, 83. *he —ed himself rough, rude and wildly,* V, 88. H6B I, 1, 188. I, 3, 106. H6C I, 4, 7.

Demeanour, 1) motion expressive of sentiment, external deportment, gesture: *which he by dumb d. seeks to show,* Lucr. 474. *with such a deep d. in great sorrow,* H4B IV, 5, 85 (i. e. a demeanour deep in sorrow, or of deep sorrow). *I perceive but cold d. in Octavius' wing,* Caes. V, 2, 4.

2) behaviour: *fashion your d. to my looks,* Err. II, 2, 33. *ignoble in d.* H6B III, 2, 210.

Demerit, subst. desert, in a good as well as ill sense: *opinion shall of his —s rob Cominius,* Cor. I, 1, 276. *my —s may speak unbonneted,* Oth. I, 2, 22. *not for their own —s, but for mine, fell slaughter on their souls,* Mcb. IV, 3, 226.

Demesnes, 1) estate in lands: *a gentleman of noble parentage, of fair d.* Rom. III, 5, 182.

2) district, territory: *the d. that there adjacent lie,* Rom. II, 1, 20. *this rock and these d. have been my world,* Cymb. III, 3, 70.

Demetrius, name in Mids. I, 1, 24. 40. 52 etc. and in Tit. II, 1, 29 etc.

Demi-Atlas, half an Atlas, bearing half of the world: *the d. of this earth,* Ant. I, 5, 23.

Demi-cannon, a kind of ordnance: Shr. IV, 3, 88.

Demi-devil, half a devil: Tp. V, 272. Oth. V, 2, 301.

Demi-god, half a God: Meas. I, 2, 124. LLL IV, 3, 79. Merch. III, 2, 115.

Demi-natured, having half the nature of another, half grown together with another: *incorpsed and d. with the brave beast,* Hml. IV, 7, 88.

Demi-paradise, half a Paradise: R2 II, 1, 42.

Demi-puppet, half a puppet, smaller than a puppet: *you —s,* Tp. V, 36.

Demise, vb., to bequeath: *what state... canst thou d. to any child of mine?* R3 IV, 4, 247 (Ff 2. 3. 4 *devise*).*

Demi-wolf, a mongrel dog between a dog and a wolf: Mcb. III, 1, 94.

Demon (O. Edd. *Daemon*), 1) the genius: *thy d., that thy spirit which keeps thee, is noble,* Ant. II, 3, 19.

2) an evil spirit, devil: *if that same d. that hath gulled thee thus should...,* H5 II, 2, 121.

Demonstrable, proved, apparent: *some un-*

hatched practice made d. here in Cyprus to him, Oth.
III, 4, 142.

Démonstrate or **Demónstrate,** 1) to show:
*description cannot suit itself in words to d. the life of
such a battle,* H5 IV, 2, 54. *a thousand moral paintings
I can show that shall d. these quick blows of Fortune's
more pregnantly than words,* Tim. I, 1, 91. *and even
the like precurse of fierce events ... have heaven and
earth together —d unto our climatures,* Hml. I, 1, 124.
*when my outward action doth d. the native act and
figure of my heart,* Oth. I, 1, 61.

2) to prove: *every thing about you —ing a careless desolation,* As III, 2, 400. *which would d. them now
but goers backward,* All's I, 2, 47. *this may help to
thicken other proofs that do d. thinly,* Oth. III, 3, 431.

Demonstration, exhibition: *by a familiar d.
of the working,* LLL I, 2, 9. *did your letters pierce the
queen to any d. of grief?* Lr. IV, 3, 12.

Demonstrative, exhibitive, showing and proving
with clearness: *this most memorable line, in every
branch truly d.* H5 IV, 4, 89.

Demure, adj. grave, sober, modest, considerate: *her mistress she doth give d. good-morrow,
with soft-slow tongue, true mark of modesty,* Lucr. 1219.
after a d. travel of regard, Tw. II, 5, 59. *none of these
d. boys come to any proof,* H4B IV, 3, 97. *with d. confidence this pausingly ensued,* H8 I, 2, 167.

Demure, vb. to look with affected modesty:
Octavia shall acquire no honour —ing upon me, Ant.
IV, 15, 29.

Demurely, soberly, gravely: *look d.* Merch.
II, 2, 201. *the drums d. wake the sleepers,* Ant. IV,
9, 31.

Den, 1) a cave: Tp. IV, 1, 25. H4B V, 5, 39.
Especially the habitation of a lion: LLL IV, 1, 95.
John II, 291. V, 1, 57. H6C II, 2, 12. II, 5, 74. Ant.
V, 1, 17.

2) a pit: Tit. II, 3, 215.

3) a hollow, a glen: Tit. IV, 1, 59.

Den, abbreviation for *evening* or *even* in *Good
den:* Ado III, 2, 83. V, 1, 46. John I, 185. Rom. III,
1, 41. cf. *Godgigoden* and *Good-den.*

Denay, subst. denial: Tw. II, 4, 127.

Denay, vb., to deny: *then let him be —ed the
regentship,* H6B I, 3, 107.

Denial, 1) negation: *word of d. in thy labras
here!* Wiv. I, 1, 166 (Pistol's speech).

2) refusal: Lucr. 242. 324. Tw. I, 5, 154. 285.
H6C III, 3, 130. Tim. II, 1, 17. Plur. —s: Cor. V, 3,
81. Cymb. II, 3, 53. *To make d.:* Meas. III, 1, 167.
Shr. II, 281. All's I, 2, 9.

Denier, the smallest piece of money: *not
a d.* Shr. Ind. I, 9. *I'll not pay a d.* H4A III, 3, 91.
my dukedom to a beggarly d. R3 I, 2, 252.

Denis, orthogr. of some M. Edd. for *Dennis,* q. v.

Denmark, a European state and country: Hml.
I, 2, 49. 52. I, 4, 90. IV, 5, 21 etc. = *king of D.:*
I, 1, 48. I, 2, 69. 125 etc.

Dennis, 1) name of the national saint of France
(St. Denis): LLL V, 2, 87. H5 V, 2, 193. 220. H6A
I, 6, 28. III, 2, 18.

2) name of a servant in As I, 1, 93.

Denny, name in H8 V, 1, 82.

Denote, to indicate, to mark: *love doth well
d. love's eye is not so true as all men's No,* Sonn. 148,
7. *to d. her to the doctor,* Wiv. IV, 6, 39. *thy acts d.*

the fury of a beast, Rom. III, 3, 110. *shapes of grief
that can d. me truly,* Hml. I, 2, 83. *this —d a foregone
conclusion,* Oth. III, 3, 428. *his own courses will d.
him so,* IV, 1, 290.

Denotement, sign, indication: *in a man
that's just they are close —s, working from the heart,*
Oth. III, 3, 123 (only in Q1; the rest of O. Edd. *delations*). In II, 3, 323 some M. Edd. blunderingly
denotement, for *devotement* of O. Edd.

Denounce, 1) to speak or proclaim in a
threatening manner: *I will d. a curse upon his head,*
John III, 1, 319. *tongues of heaven, —ing vengeance
upon John,* III, 4, 159. *his curses —ed against thee,*
R3 I, 3, 180.

2) to declare: *if not —d against us* (viz war)
Ant. III, 7, 5.

Denunciation, proclamation, formal declaration: *she is fast my wife, save that we do the
d. lack of outward order,* Meas. I, 2, 152.

Deny, 1) absol. to say No: *love's —ing,* Pilgr.
249. *if thou d., then force must work my way,* Lucr.
513. *if law, authority and power d. not, it will go hard
with poor Antonio,* Merch. III, 2, 291. All's II, 1, 20.
H6C II, 2, 129. R3 III, 1, 35.

2) to contradict, to declare sth. not to be
true; a) followed by a simple accus.: *—es all that
you have said,* Meas. V, 283. Wiv. I, 1, 193. Meas.
IV, 2, 145. V, 418. Err. II, 2, 17. 67. IV, 1, 67. IV,
4, 99. V, 3, 16. 22. 305. 379. Ado I, 3, 33. IV, 1,
123. 175. 274. LLL I, 1, 298. Merch. V, 187. All's
II, 1, 144. H4A II, 4, 516. H6B IV, 2, 154. R3 I, 1,
96. Hml. V, 2, 247 etc. b) followed by a dative and
accus.: *both one and other he —es me now,* Err. IV,
3, 86. By a dative alone: *if you will d. the sheriff,* H4A
II, 4, 544 (i. e. say No to him). The dative preceded
by *to: do not d. to him that you love me,* Rom. IV, 1,
24. — c) followed by a clause: *d. that thou bearest
love to any,* Sonn. 10, 1. Meas. II, 1, 18. Tw. V, 339.
Rom. IV, 1, 24. Lr. II, 2, 31. Cymb. II, 4, 145. Superfluous negative: *he —ed you had in him no right,* Err.
IV, 2, 7. *you may d. that you were not the cause,* R3
I, 3, 90. The negatived verb followed by *but: it must
not be —ed but I am a plain-dealing villain,* Ado I, 3,
33. All's V, 3, 166. Cor. IV, 5, 243. Singular expression:
that's as much as you would be —ed of your fair courtesy,
Per. II, 3, 106 (= as if you would have your courtesy
denied).

3) to disown, to disavow: *that I did d. my
wife and house,* Err. III, 1, 9. *wherefore doth Lysander
d. your love,* Mids. III, 2, 229. *d. him, forswear him,*
Shr. V, 1, 114. *will you d. me now?* Tw. III, 4, 381. *as
I d. the devil,* John I, 252. *I d. my sacred state,* R2
IV, 209. 213. *wilt thou d. thy parentage?* H6A V, 4,
14. *d. me not,* 20. *d. thy father and refuse thy name,*
Rom. II, 2, 34. *I d. you, stars,* V, 1, 24 (Q1 *defy*).
Followed by *for: and d. himself for Jove,* Pilgr. 243.
LLL IV, 3, 119. *—ed my house for his, me for his wife,*
Err. II, 2, 161. Double accus.: *hast thou —ed thyself
a Faulconbridge?* John I, 251.

4) to contradict, to object to: *the defendant doth plea d.* Sonn. 46, 7. *that I can d. by
a circumstance,* Gentl. I, 1, 84. *I d. your major,* H4A
II, 4, 544.

5) to refuse; a) to refuse to do sth.: *if you d. to
dance,* LLL V, 2, 228. Shr. II, 180. V, 2, 103. Wint.
V, 2, 139. R3 V, 3, 343. Rom. I, 5, 21. Lr. II, 4, 89.

b) to refuse to accept, to decline: *I would not d. you,* Ado V, 4, 94. *thou wouldst have — ed Beatrice,* V, 4, 115. cf. *d. my love,* As IV, 3, 62, and *do they all d. her?* All's II, 3, 92. *you may not d. it* (the combat) LLL V, 2, 712. *not to d. this imposition,* Merch. III, 4, 33. *d. his offered homage,* R2 II, 1, 204.

c) to refuse to give, not to grant; α) the thing withheld in the accus.: *how to grant suits, how to d. them,* Tp. I, 2, 80. LLL V, 2, 821. Merch. III, 3, 26. III, 4, 71. IV, 1, 38. As IV, 1, 79. John IV, 1, 119. H4A I, 3, 25. 29. H5 V, 2, 324. H6A V, 3, 75. H6B V, 1, 123. H6C III, 2, 5. V, 6, 22. Cor. V, 2, 85. Hml. II, 1, 109. Ant. II, 1, 3. — β) the person from whom something is withheld in the accus.: *you must not d. me,* Merch. II, 2, 187. IV, 1, 101. 424. Cor. II, 3, 2. 214. Caes. IV, 3, 82. *by self-example mayst thou be —ed,* Sonn. 142, 14. *Florence is —ed,* All's I, 2, 12. *would be —ed,* R2 V, 3, 103. *I'll know his grievance, or be much —ed,* Rom. I, 1, 163. Tim. III, 2, 15. 69. — γ) *to d. a person sth.:* *—ies thee vantage,* Meas. V, 418. *no bedroom me d.* Mids. II, 2, 51. *they d. him justice,* Merch. III, 2, 281. IV, 1, 429. V, 165. 212. 227. As I, 2, 197. Tw. V, 93. Wint. IV, 2, 2. John IV, 2, 59. V, 7, 43. H6C III, 2, 9. Tim. III, 2, 26. 81. Mcb. IV, 1, 104. H8 V, 3, 161. *be not —ed access,* Tw. I, 4, 16. *myself the child-bed privilege —ed,* Wint. III, 2, 104. H4B IV, 1, 78. Ant. V, 2, 234. — δ) *to d. a person to do sth.* = to forbid: *to be your fellow you may d. me,* Tp. III, 1, 85. Err. IV, 4, 67. R2 II, 3, 129. H6C II, 2, 172. Tit. II, 3, 174. Lr. III, 2, 66. — ε) *to d. sth. to a p.:* *d. it to a king,* H4B III, 1, 30. *give to dogs what thou —est to men,* Tim. IV, 3, 537. *if you d. your griefs to your friend,* Hml. III, 2, 352.

Depart, subst. 1) a going away; always in the phrase *at my d.:* Gentl. V, 4, 96. H6B I, 1, 2. H6C IV, 1, 92.

2) death: *tidings were brought me of your loss and his d.* H6C II, 1, 110.

Depart, vb. 1) intr. a) to go away, to withdraw: *prays her that he may d.* Ven. 578. *he thence —s a heavy convertite,* Lucr. 743. *when you d. from him,* Meas. IV, 1, 69. *d. in patience,* Err. III, 1, 94. 107. IV, 4, 79. V, 108. Ado III, 3, 73. V, 1, 334. V, 2, 44. 54. Merch. I, 1, 64. As V, 1, 63. Tw. III, 4, 192. IV, 1, 19. Wint. I, 2, 238. II, 1, 40. V, 3, 97. John I, 23. R2 I, 2, 63. H5 IV, 3, 36. H6A I, 3, 89. H6C V, 4, 49. R3 I, 4, 196. III, 7, 141. Troil. V, 2, 36. Tit. V, 2, 145. Rom. I, 1, 110. III, 1, 56. V, 3, 277. Tim. IV, 3, 232. Caes. III, 1, 142. III, 2, 49. 60. 65. Mcb. IV, 1, 111. Hml. IV, 5, 55. Ant. IV, 14, 36. Joined with *away:* *they d. away with shame,* LLL V, 2, 156. *all the rest d. away,* Rom. I, 1, 105.

Implying the idea of a previous stay: *praise in —ing,* Tp. III, 3, 39. *that I may venture to d. alone,* Gentl. IV, 3, 36. *why thou —edst from thy native home,* Err. I, 1, 30. Ado I, 1, 101. LLL V, 2, 1. Wint. I, 2, 54. H6B III, 2, 388. IV, 1, 140. Rom. V, 3, 108. Hml. I, 2, 175. Lr. II, 4, 1. Cymb. III, 6, 68. V, 4, 164. Per. I, 3, 18. Followed by *for:* *they stay the first —ing of the king for Ireland,* R2 II, 1, 290. By *to:* *—ed with the rest back to the camp,* Lucr. Arg. 13. *and then d. to Paris,* H6A III, 2, 128. *both d. to him,* H6C IV, 1, 138. *he must hence d. to Tyre,* Per. III Prol. 39.

b) to die: *what could death do, if thou shouldst d.* Sonn. 6, 11. *hearing how hastily you are to d.* Meas. IV, 3, 54. *tolling a —ing friend,* H4B I, 1, 103. H6A III, 2, 110. *—ed souls,* H6B IV, 7, 123. H8 IV, 2, 156.

c) to part: *a deadly groan, like life and death's —ing,* H6C II, 6, 43. *ere we d., we'll share a bounteous time in different pleasures,* Tim. I, 1, 263. *the loathness to d. would grow,* Cymb. I, 1, 108. Followed by *from:* *as easy might I from myself d.* Sonn. 109, 3. Followed by *with,* = to resign, to give up: *which* (Aquitaine) *we much rather had d. withal,* LLL II, 147. *hath willingly —ed with a part,* John II, 563.

2) trans. to leave: *from that which thou —est,* Sonn. 11, 2. *d. the chamber,* H4B IV, 5, 91. *I would your highness would d. the field,* H6C II, 2, 73. *ere I d. his house,* Lr. III, 5, 1.

Departure, 1) a going away: Gentl. III, 1, 160. IV, 4, 140. Merch. I, 2, 121. As III, 2, 311. All's IV, 3, 108. Wint. I, 2, 450. III, 2, 78. IV, 2, 10. John III, 4, 115. R2 II, 2, 21. 25. H4A I, 3, 123. III, 1, 144. IV, 1, 23. H6A II, 3, 30. R3 V, 3, 229. Lr. I, 5, 54. Ant. I, 2, 139. Cymb. IV, 3, 10. Per. I, 3, 12.

2) death: *shall ring thy dire d. out,* H6A IV, 2, 41.

Depend, 1) to hang down, to lean: *two winking Cupids, each on one foot standing, nicely —ing on their brands,* Cymb. II, 4, 91.

2) to serve, to attend: *canst thou believe thy living is a life, so stinkingly —ing?* Meas. III, 2, 28. *you d. on him, I mean,* Troil. III, 1, 4. *the remainder, that shall still d.* Lr. I, 4, 271 (but here perhaps in another sense).

3) to impend: *in me moe woes than words are now —ing,* Lucr. 1615. *that is the curse —ing on those that war for a placket,* Troil. II, 3, 21 (Ff *dependant*). *this day's black fate on moe days doth d.* Rom. III, 1, 124. *we'll slip you for a season, but our jealousy does yet d.* Cymb. IV, 3, 23 (here perhaps = to be in suspense).

4) to be connected with, to be influenced by; followed by *on:* *it* (life) *—s upon that love of thine,* Sonn. 92, 4. *a better state to me belongs than that which on thy humour doth d.* 92, 8. 101, 3. Compl. 274. Tp. I, 2, 181. Gentl. I, 3, 62. Meas. IV, 2, 128. Merch. I, 2, 114. IV, 1, 434. As I, 3, 59. John IV, 2, 65. H4B IV, 5, 159. H6C I, 2, 11. Hml. I, 3, 20. III, 3, 14. Oth. I, 3, 203. II, 3, 379. Ant. I, 2, 182. Per. III, 3, 41. Perhaps also Lr. I, 4, 271.

5) to rely, to confide; followed by *on:* *bidding me d. upon thy stars,* John III, 1, 125. *I do d. upon the lord,* Troil. III, 1, 5. Cor. I, 1, 183. III, 1, 166. Caes. III, 1, 217. Oth. I, 3, 369. Cymb. V, 4, 127.

Dependance, the state of being influenced and determined by sth.: *'tis a cause that hath no mean d. upon our joint and several dignities,* Troil. II, 2, 192.

Dependancy or **Dependency,** 1) concatenation, consistency: *such a d. of thing on thing, as e'er I heard in madness,* Meas. V, 62.

2) the state of being influenced and determined: *though it be allowed in meaner parties to knit their souls, on whom there is no more d. but brats and beggary,* Cymb. II, 3, 123.

3) reliance: *let me report to him your sweet d.* Ant. V, 2, 26.

Dependant or **Dependent,** subst. retainer: Meas. IV, 3, 95. LLL III, 134. Tim. I, 1, 85. Lr. I, 4, 65. *the lords —s,* III, 7, 18.

Dependant or **Dependent,** adj. 1) relating to and occasioned by something previous: *promise-breach thereon d.* Meas. V, 411.

2) impending: *the curse d. on those*, Troil. II, 3, 21 (Q *depending*).

Depender, dependant, retainer: *to be d. on a thing that leans*, Cymb. I, 5, 58.

Deplore, to complain: *to their instruments tune a —ing dump*, Gentl. III, 2, 85. *never more will I my master's tears to you d.* Tw. III, 1, 174.

Depopulate, vb. to unpeople: *would d. the city and be every man himself*, Cor. III, 1, 264.

Depose, 1) to divest of office, to dethrone: John II, 372. R2 II, 1, 107. 108. III, 2, 56. 150. 157. III, 3, 144. III, 4, 67. 77. IV, 192. 227. 234. V, 1, 27. 50. H4A I, 3, 152. II, 4, 478. IV, 3, 90. H5 I, 2, 65. H6A II, 5, 64. H6B I, 4, 33. 62. II, 2, 24. H6C I, 1, 41. 153. III, 1, 45. 69. R3 I, 3, 162. III, 7, 209. Followed by *of*: *that Lepidus of the triumvirate should be —d*, Ant. III, 6, 29.

2) to declare upon oath, to swear: *I'll d. I had him in mine arms*, Meas. V, 198. *seeing 'twas he that made you to d.*, *your oath is vain*, H6C I, 2, 26.

3) to put under oath, to cause to swear: *d. him in the justice of his cause*, R2 I, 3, 30.

Depositary, one with whom a thing is lodged in trust: Lr. II, 4, 254.

Depravation, detraction: *critics apt, without a theme, for d.* Troil. V, 2, 132.

Deprave, to detract, to slander: *lie and cog and flout, d. and slander*, Ado V, 1, 95. *who lives that's not —d or —s?* Tim. I, 2, 145.

Depraved, corrupt, wicked: *thou'lt not believe with how d. a quality*, Lr. II, 4, 139.

Depress, to press down, to humble: *—ed he is already*, R2 III, 4, 68.

Deprive, 1) to bereave; followed by *of*: *—d him of his life*, H4A IV, 3, 91. *—d of honour*, H6A II, 5, 27. Rom. IV, 1, 102. Hml. V, 1, 272. Lr. I, 1, 232. Without *of*: *permit the curiosity of nations to d. me*, Lr.I, 2, 4 (= to disinherit). *Of* omitted: *is wretchedness —d that benefit?* Lr. IV, 6, 61.

2) to rob, to take away: *'tis honour to d. dishonoured life*, Lucr. 1186. *that life was mine that thou hast here —d*, 1752. *which might d. your sovereignty of reason*, Hml. I, 4, 73.

Depth, 1) the deepness, the measure of a thing from the surface downward; properly and figuratively: *to sound the d. of this knavery*, Shr. V, 1, 141. *a spirit raised from d. of under-ground*, H6B I, 2, 79. *to make less the d. of grief*, H6C II, 1, 85. *I was come to the whole d. of my tale*, Rom. II, 4, 104. *I were damned beneath all d. in hell*, Oth. V, 2, 137. *beyond my d.* H8 III, 2, 361 (i. e. where I could not touch the bottom). cf. *past d.* Tim. III, 5, 12 (= bottomless).

2) a deep place: *sounded all the —s and shoals of honour*, H8 III, 2, 437. *finds bottom in the uncomprehensive d.* Troil. III, 3, 198 (Ff *deeps*).

Deputation, the office of a substitute, vicegerency: Meas. I, 1, 21. H4A IV, 1, 32. IV, 3, 87. Ant. III, 13, 74 (O. Edd. *disputation*). *thy topless d. he puts on*, Troil. I, 3, 152, i. e. thy dignity as Jove's substitute; cf. *deputy* in LLL I, 1, 221. John III, 1, 136. R2 I, 2, 38.

Depute, to substitute: *—ing Cassio in his government*, Oth. IV, 1, 248. *to d. Cassio in Othello's place*, IV, 2, 226. *not the king's crown, nor the —d sword*, Meas. II, 2, 60, i. e. the sword of his deputy, or the sword which serves to represent his dignity.

Deputy, substitute, vicegerent: Meas. I, 2, 161. 186. III, 1, 89. 265. III, 2, 19. 35. IV, 1, 27. IV, 2, 81. 197. IV, 3, 79. V, 88. LLL I, 1, 221. John II, 365. III, 1, 136. R2 I, 2, 38. III, 2, 57. IV, 126. H6A V, 3, 161. H6B III, 2, 286. R3 III, 7, 6. H8 II, 1, 42. III, 2, 260. *the d. of the ward* (i. e. the police-officer of the district) H4A III, 3, 130. cf. H4B II, 4, 92.

Deracinate, to unroot, extirpate: H5 V, 2, 47. Troil. I, 3, 99.

Derby, name: R2 I, 3, 35. R3 I, 3, 17. 20. 22. 30 etc. (some M. Edd. *Stanley*).

Dercetas, name in Ant. V, 1, 5 (O. Edd. Decretas).

Dere, French corruption of *there*, often in Wiv. and H5.

Deride, to laugh to scorn: *who cover faults, at last shame them —s*, Lr. 1, 1, 284 (reading of Qq).

Derision, laughing in contempt, scorn: Mids. III, 2, 123. 159. 197. 370. Troil. III, 3, 44.

Derivation, descent, extraction: *in the d. of my birth*, H5 III, 2, 141 (Fluellen's speech). *my d. was from ancestors who stood equivalent with mighty kings*, Per. V, 1, 91.

Derivative, subst. that which is transmitted by descent: *for honour, 'tis a d. from me to mine*, Wint. III, 2, 45.

Derive, 1) to draw as from a source, to gain: *from thine eyes my knowledge I d.* Sonn. 14, 9. *to find out this abuse, whence 'tis —d*, Meas. V, 247. LLL IV, 3, 302. 350. Wint. I, 2, 112. H4B I, 1, 206. Tim. I, 2, 8. III, 4, 69. IV, 3, 162. Lr. I, 2, 87. *O, that estates, degrees and offices were not —d corruptly*, Merch. II, 9, 42 (= got, gained). *how is this —d?* H4B I, 1, 23 (= whence do you know this?). Reflectively, = to originate: *his indignation —s itself out of a very competent injury*, Tw. III, 4, 269.

2) to draw upon one, to cause: *things which would d. me ill will to speak of*, All's V, 3, 265. *what friend of mine that had to him —d your anger, did I continue in my liking?* H8 II, 4, 32.

3) to receive by descent: *treason is not inherited; or if we did d. it from our friends, what's that to me?* As I, 3, 64. *she —s her honesty and achieves her goodness*, All's I, 1, 52. *honours thrive, when rather from our acts we them d. than our foregoers*, II, 3, 143. *his true titles to some certain dukedoms —d from Edward*, H5 I, 1, 89.

Reflectively, = to be inherited, to descend: *this shame —s itself from unknown loins*, Ado IV, 1, 137. *this crown ... which —s itself to me*, H4B IV, 5, 43.

4) Partic. *derived* = descended: *thou wast not to this end from me —d*, Lucr. 1755. *you are well —d*, Gentl. V, 2, 23. V, 4, 146. Mids. I, 1, 99. All's V, 3, 159. R2 II, 2, 34. H5 II, 4, 91. H6A II, 5, 74. 84. H6C I, 4, 119 (*of*). Caes. II, 1, 322.

5) to deduce, to prove logically: *d. this*, Troil. II, 3, 66 (cf. *Decline*).

Dern, see *Dearn*.

Derogate, vb. to disparage; used with purposed ambiguity: *is there no derogation in it? You cannot d., my lord. You are a fool granted: therefore your issues, being foolish, do not d.* Cymb. II, 1, 48. 51.

Derogate, partic. or adj. depraved, corrupt: *from her d. body never spring a babe*, Lr. I, 4, 302.

Derogately, disparagingly: *that I should once name you d.* Ant. II, 2, 34.

Derogation, disparagement: *is there no d. in it?* Cymb. II, 1, 47.

Desartless, desertless, misapplied by Dogberry: Ado III, 3, 9.

Descant, subst. 1) the treble: *and mar the concord with too harsh a descant,* Gentl. I, 2, 94.

2) comment: *on that ground I'll build a holy d.* R3 III, 7, 49.

Déscant, vb. 1) to sing: *while thou on Tereus —est better skill,* Lucr. 1134.

2) to comment: *to d. on the doubts of my decay,* Pilgr. 184. *and d. on mine own deformity,* R3 I, 1, 27.

Descend, 1) intr. a) to go or come down: *the heat of this —ing sun,* Ven. 190. *night —ed to hell,* Lucr. 1081. *let her d.* Wiv. IV, 5, 22. Merch. II, 6, 40. Wint. V, 3, 88. 99. R2 I, 3, 54. H6A V, 3, 143. H6B I, 4, 42. III, 2, 163. Tit. II, 3, 248. Rom. III, 5, 42. V, 3, 28. Tim. V, 4, 55. 64. Caes. III, 2, 164. Mcb. II, 2, 17. Lr. II, 1, 21. Cymb. I, 6, 169. *if he be chaste, the flame will back d.* Wiv. V, 5, 89 (instead of rising). — Tropically: *those oaths —ed into perjury,* Gentl. V, 4, 49. *pardon me that I d. so low,* H4A I, 3, 167.

b) to be derived or extracted: *hadst thou —ed from another house,* As I, 2, 241. *—ing now from him,* R2 IV, 111. H6B IV, 2, 47. H6C III, 3, 87. *To be —ed,* in the same sense: H5 I, 2, 66. H6A V, 4, 8. Partic. *—ed:* H6B IV, 4, 29. Cor. II, 3, 253. Ant. V, 2, 330. Cymb. V, 5, 303. Followed by *from:* As I, 2, 241. R2 IV, 111. H6B IV, 4, 29. H6C III, 3, 87. By *of:* H5 I, 2, 66. H6A V, 4, 8. H6B IV, 2, 47. Ant. V, 2, 330.

c) to pass by inheritance: *to thee it shall d. with better quiet,* H4B IV, 5, 188. H5 I, 2, 100.

2) trans. to go or fall down from: *some (hair) untucked —ed her sheaved hat,* Compl. 31. *d. my throne* H6C I, 1, 74.

Descending, subst. lineage: *that thou camest from good d.* Per. V, 1, 129 (Ff descent).

Descension, decline, degradation: *from a God to a bull, a heavy d.* H4B II, 2, 193 (Ff declension).

Descent, 1) a motion downward: *not the dreadful spout … shall dizzy with more clamour Neptune's ear in his d.* Troil. V, 2, 175. Singular passage: *from the extremest upward of thy head to the d. and dust below thy foot,* Lr. V, 3, 137 (i. e. from the extremest upward to the extremest downward).

2) extraction, lineage: Gentl. III, 2, 32. Shr. Ind. 2, 15. R2 I, 1, 107. H6A III, 1, 166. H6B III, 1, 21. 48. H6C I, 4, 72. II, 1, 92. IV, 1, 70. R3 III, 2, 54. Cymb. V, 5, 308. Per. II, 5, 60. *Edward king, the third of that d.* H6A II, 5, 66 (= of that house).

3) transmission by inheritance: *a ring that downward hath succeeded in his house from son to son, some four or five —s since the first father wore it,* All's III, 7, 24 (or = generations?). *my inheritance of free d.* R2 II, 3, 136.

4) origin, source: *and know their spring, their head, their true d.* Rom. V, 3, 218.

Describe, to show or represent in words: Sonn. 53, 5. Merch. I, 2, 40. Troil. II, 3, 219. Tit. IV, 1, 57. Caes. IV, 2, 18.

Description, 1) representation in words: Sonn. 106, 2. LLL V, 2, 523. Merch. I, 2, 41. As IV, 3, 85. All's IV, 3, 294. Wint. V, 2, 63. H5 III, 6, 39. IV, 2, 53. H6A V, 5, 1. Tim. IV, 3, 412. **V,**

3, 1. Oth. II, 1, 62. Ant. II, 2, 203. II, 7, 56. Cymb. II, 4, 93. IV, 1, 26. V, 5, 178. Per. IV, 2, 109. Misapplied by Evans in Wiv. I, 1, 222.

2) kind, sort: *a friend of this d.* Merch. III, 2, 303 (= such as you described).

Descry, subst. discovery: *the main d. stands on the hourly thought,* Lr. IV, 6, 217, i. e. every hour the main body is expected to come in sight.

Descry, vb. to espy, to discover: *marks —ed in men's nativity,* Lucr. 538. *we are —ed,* LLL V, 2, 389. *I killed a man and fear I was —ed,* Shr. I, 1, 237. *what's past and what's to come she can d.* H6A I, 2, 57. *who hath —ed the number of the foe?* R3 V, 3, 9. *to d. the true ground of these woes,* Rom. V, 3, 181. *to d. the strength o' the enemy,* Lr. IV, 5, 13.*d. a sail,* Oth. II, 1, 4. *he is —ed,* Ant. III, 7, 55. *we have —ed a portly sail of ships make hitherward,* Per. I, 4, 60. *in Helicanus may you well d. a figure of truth,* V, 3, 91.

Desdemon, female name in Oth. III, 1, 56. III, 3, 55. IV, 2, 41. V, 2, 204. 281 (Qq always *Desdemona).*

Desdemona, the same: Oth. I, 2, 25 etc. etc.

Desért, subst. 1) that which is due to a person; that which entitles to a reward, or demands a punishment: *against that time do I ensconce me here within the knowledge of mine own d.* Sonn. 49, 10. *to do more for me than mine own d.* 72, 6. *wherein I should your great —s repay,* 117, 2. *my patience, more than thy d., is privilege for thy departure,* Gentl. III, 1, 159. *some sign of good d.* III, 2, 18. *dispose of them as thou knowest their —s,* V, 4, 159. *challenge me by these —s,* LLL V, 2, 815. *I will assume d.* Merch. II, 9, 51. *are my —s no better?* 60. *nor would I have him till I do deserve him, yet never know how that d. should be,* All's I, 3, 206. *shackle up my love and her d.* II, 3, 160. *would I were able to load him with his d.* H5 III, 7, 86. *not of any challenge of d.* H6A V, 4, 153. *my d. is honour,* H6C III, 3, 192. *my d. unmeritable shuns your high request,* R3 III, 7, 154. *the duke found his —s,* H8 III, 2, 267. *plead your —s,* Tit. I, 45. *I give thanks in part of thy —s,* 236. *I chiefly that set thee on to this d.* Cymb. I, 5, 73. *it is your grace's pleasure to commend, not my d.* Per. II, 5, 30. — *Without d.* = without cause: *not without d. so well reputed,* Gentl. II, 4, 57. *my wife — but I protest, without d. — hath oftentimes upbraided me,* Err. III, 1, 112. *that all without d. have frowned on me,* R3 II, 1, 67.

2) merit, claim to honour and reward: Sonn. 17, 2. 66, 2. Pilgr. 325. Meas. V, 9. R2 II, 3, 44. H4A IV, 3, 46. H4B IV, 3, 60. H5 II, 2, 34. H6A III, 4, 25. H6C III, 3, 132. R3 I, 3, 97. IV, 4, 415. Troil. III, 2, 101. III, 3, 172. Cor. II, 3, 71. 72. Tit. I, 16. 256. III, 1, 171. Tim. I, 1, 65. III, 5, 79. Hml. II, 2, 553. 555. Lr. II, 4, 141. Ant. I, 2, 194. Per. I, 1, 31. Followed by *to,* to indicate the person of whom somebody has well deserved: *that my —s to you can lack persuasion,* Tw. III, 4, 382. *these good —s; not half so bad as thine to England's king,* H6B I, 4, 49. *surnamed Pius for many good and great —s to Rome,* Tit. I, 24.

Désert, subst. uninhabited tract of land, solitude: Lucr. 1144. Gentl. V, 4, 2. Merch. II, 7, 41. As II, 6, 18. II, 7, 110. III, 2, 133. Wint. III, 3, 2. Mcb. III, 4, 104. Oth. I, 3, 140.

Desert, adj. uninhabited, unpeopled: Tp. II, 1, 35. Mids. II, 1, 218. As II, 1, 23. II, 4, 72. IV, 3, 142. Wint. II, 3, 176. *words that would be howled out in the d. air, where hearing should not latch them,* Mcb. IV, 3, 194.

Desertless, see *Desartless.*

Deserve, 1) trans. to be worthy of, to merit; applied to good and evil; a) followed by an accus.: *her pleading hath —d a greater fee,* Ven. 609. *—d more than a prison,* Tp. I, 2, 362. Sonn. 2, 9. 39, 8. 79, 6. Pilgr. 32. Gentl. I, 2, 48. II, 4, 59. II, 7, 82. V, 4, 147. Wiv. II, 2, 125. III, 3, 81. 89. Meas. III, 1, 45. V, 11. 530. Ado I, 1, 12. III, 1, 45. 47. V, 2, 8. Mids. II, 2, 124. 127. IV, 2, 23. Merch. I, 2, 131. II, 7, 7. II, 9, 59. IV, 1, 446. V, 181. 265. As I, 2, 274. III, 2, 421. V, 4, 193. All's I, 3, 205. R2 I, 3, 158. V, 1, 68. H6A III, 3, 89. H6B IV, 3, 11. H6C II, 6, 26. III, 3, 249. V, 1, 104. R3 I, 2, 223. III, 1, 49. III, 4, 61. 68. H8 Prol. 7. IV, 1, 113. Troil. IV, 1, 53 (Ff *merits*). Cor. III, 1, 60. III, 3, 140. Tim. I, 1, 102. Ant. III, 6, 34 etc.

b) *To d. sth. of a p.: what he —s of you and me,* H8 III, 2, 14. *the people d. such pity of him as the wolf does of the shepherds,* Cor. V, 6, 110. *of whom I have —d this hearing,* Tim. II, 2, 207. *something you may d. of him through me,* Mcb. IV, 3, 15.

c) Followed by an inf.: *how I may d. to be your porter,* Wiv. II, 2, 180. Sonn. 142, 12. LLL IV, 3, 208. All's II, 5, 37. Wint. III, 2, 179. R2 II, 1, 193. H4B IV, 3, 91 (*better than you d.,* viz to be spoken of). H6A I, 1, 9. H6C I, 1, 219. IV, 1, 47. Cor. V, 3, 206. Caes. III, 1, 132. Mcb. I, 3, 111. Per. II, 1, 107. *I have —d all tongues to talk their bitterest,* Wint. III, 2, 216.

2) intr. to be worthy: *others say thou dost d.* Ado III, 1, 115. *I shall study —ing,* Lr. I, 1, 32. *a —ing woman,* Oth. II, 1, 146. Modified by an adverb: *she —s well,* LLL I, 2, 124. *d. well at my hands,* Ado V, 2, 2. *you have well —d,* As I, 2, 254. I, 3, 37. All's IV, 3, 332. Tw. IV, 2, 86. H6C V, 1, 93. *I know her virtuous and well —ing,* H8 III, 2, 98. *I hope she will d. well,* IV, 2, 136. *Richard hath best —d of all my sons,* H6C I, 1, 17. *very nobly have you —d,* Wint. IV, 4, 529. *let me d. so ill as you,* Cor. III, 1, 51. *doth ill d. by doing well,* Cymb. III, 3, 54. *God grant that some d. not worse than Clarence,* R3 II, 1, 93. *would thou hadst less —d,* Mcb. I, 4, 18. *hast no less —d,* 30. *how pitiful I d.* Ado V, 2, 29.

Followed by *of: wherein have I so —d of you?* Meas. V, 507. Ado IV, 1, 263. Cor. II, 2, 27. II, 3, 94.

The partic. *deserved* = having deserved: *unpitied let me die, and well —d,* All's II, 1, 192. *whose gratitude towards her —d children is enrolled in Jove's own book,* Cor. III, 1, 292 (= well deserving, meritorious).

Deservedly, justly: Tp. I, 2, 361.

Deserver, he who is worthy of sth.: *the lily-beds proposed for the d.* Troil. III, 2, 14. Mcb. I, 4, 42. Ant. I, 2, 193.

Deserving, subst. = desert, q. v., 1) that which is due to a person, or that for which he may claim something: *for that riches where is my d.?* Sonn. 87, 6. *reputation is oft got without merit and lost without d.* Oth. II, 3, 270. *death is my d.* Meas. V, 482. *how much unlike my hopes and my —s,* Merch. II, 9, 57. IV, 1, 450. *all foes* (shall taste) *the cup of their —s,* Lr. V, 3, 304. *I shall give thee thy d.* Ant. IV, 12, 32. *I confess me knit to thy d. with cables of perdurable*

toughness, Oth. I, 3, 343, i. e. to that which is due to thee, viz Desdemona's love.

2) merit: *we make foul the clearness of our —s,* All's I, 3, 7. *all her d. is a reserved honesty,* III, 5, 64. H4A IV, 3, 35. V, 2, 58. H4B IV, 3, 48. Cor. I, 9, 20. Lr. III, 3, 24.

Design, subst., 1) scheme, plan: *his givings-out were of an infinite distance from his true-meant d.* Meas. I, 4, 55. Wint. II, 1, 50. II, 2, 49. H8 I, 2, 181. Cymb. II, 2, 23.

2) a work in hand, enterprise, cause: *'tis a meritorious fair d. to chase injustice with revengeful arms,* Lucr. 1692. *lending soft audience to my sweet d.* Compl. 278. *being then appointed master of this d.* Tp. I, 2, 163. LLL IV, 1, 88 and V, 1, 105 (both times used by Armado). *the fated sky gives us free scope, only doth backward pull our slow —s when we ourselves are dull,* All's I, 1, 234. *hinder not the honour of his d.* III, 6, 44. *a vessel rides fast by, but not prepared for this d.* Wint. IV, 4, 513. *I'll answer thee in any fair degree, or chivalrous d. of knightly trial,* R2 I, 1, 81. *officers appointed to direct these fair —s,* I, 3, 45. *his —s crave haste,* II, 2, 44. *leave these sad —s to him that hath more cause to be a mourner,* R3 I, 2, 211. *I hope my absence doth neglect no great —s, which by my presence might have been concluded,* III, 4, 25. *in deep —s and matters of great moment,* III, 7, 67. *be not peevish-fond in great —s,* IV, 4, 417. *the ample proposition that hope makes in all —s begun on earth below,* Troil. I, 3, 4. 102. 146. *there you touched the life of our d.* II, 2, 194 (= our cause). *unless I lame the foot of our d.* Cor. IV, 7, 8. *murder ... towards his d. moves like a ghost,* Mcb. II, 1, 55. *the heart of brothers sway our great —s,* Ant. II, 2, 151. *my competitor in top of all d.* V, 1, 43. *that thou wilt be a voluntary mute to my d.* Cymb. III, 5, 159. *away to Britain post I in this d.* V, 5, 192.

Design, vb. to designate, to point out: *we shall see justice d. the victor's chivalry,* R2 I, 1, 203 (*justice* being the object of *design*). *the article —ed,* Hml. I, 1, 94 (= pointed out, mentioned before. Qq and F1 *design*).

Designment (cf. *Design* 2) enterprise: *served his —s in mine own person,* Cor. V, 6, 35. *their d. halts,* Oth. II, 1, 22.

Desire, subst. 1) wish: *to grow unto himself was his d.* Ven. 1180. Lucr. 1606. Sonn. 57, 2. 123, 7. Wiv. II, 2, 189. Meas. IV, 2, 188. LLL I, 1, 10. Mids. III, 2, 445 etc. *with duty and d. we follow you,* Mids. I, 1, 127 (i. e. obediently and gladly). *makes her d. along to go,* Per. III Prol. 40 (= desires, asks). *your heart's —s be with you!* As I, 2, 211 (i. e. may your wishes be accomplished). *sweet health and fair —s consort your grace!* LLL II, 178. *fair —s ... guide them!* Troil. III, 1, 47 (cf. *thoughts* in R3 IV, 1, 94 Troil. III, 1, 49). *most fair return of greetings and —s,* Hml. II, 2, 60. *to have d.,* Tw. III, 3, 45. Troil. III, 3, 46. *to have a d.,* Merch. II, 2, 136. As V, 1, 37. All's II, 3, 240. *I have a great d. to ...,* Mids. IV, 1, 37. *the great d. I had,* Shr. I, 1, 1. Followed by *of: my desire of having,* Tw. V, 50. R3 III, 7, 236. cf. *I burn with d. to have d.* H6A I, 2, 108. By *to: I have a great d. to a bottle of hay,* Mids. IV, 1, 37. *I have no d. to it,* Per. IV, 1, 44. By *for: —s for sport,* Oth. IV, 3, 102.

2) love, affection: *then can no horse with my*

d. keep pace, Sonn. 51, 9. *a votary to fond d.* Gentl. I, 1, 52. *to tangle her —s*, III, 2, 68. Wiv. I, 1, 245. Especially sensual affection, lust, appetite: *d. doth lend her force*, Ven. 29. 276. 386. 547. 773. Lucr. 2. 171. 175. 642. Sonn. 147, 8. 154, 7. Gentl. V, 4, 59. Wiv. II, 2, 256. V, 5, 94. 100. Mids. I, 1, 4 etc. Personified, like love, in the masc. gender: Lucr. 703. LLL I, 2, 64.

3) the thing wished for: *now hast thou thy d.* John I, 176. *have thy d.* R2 V, 3, 38. H4A IV, 3, 49. Hml. V, 2, 14. *God send every one their hearts' d.* Ado III, 4, 61. *give him his d.* Tw. III, 4, 271. *be inheritor of thy d.* R3 IV, 3, 34. *being now trimmed in thine own —s*, H4B I, 3, 94. *where our d. is got without content*, Mcb. III, 2, 5. *your —s are yours*, Ant. III, 4, 28. *the queen of audience nor d. shall fail*, III, 12, 21. Used as a trisyll.: *that have inflamed d. in my breast*, Per. I, 1, 20 (Ff *within my breast*).

Desire, vb. 1) to wish for; followed by an accus.: *do I delight to die or life d.?* Ven. 496. Lucr. 1011. Sonn. I, 1. 29, 7. 89, 6. 153, 11. Wiv. I, 3, 21. II, 1, 10. Meas. I, 4, 3. IV, 1, 52. Ado IV, 1, 259. LLL I, 1, 105. Merch. I, 3, 60. Tw. III, 2, 72. H6B II, 1, 102. H6C IV, 7, 6. R3 II, 1, 61. Hml. I, 4, 59 etc. = to lust after: *being —d yielded*, Compl. 149. *d. her foully*, Meas. II, 2, 174. *finding yourself —d of such a person*, II, 4, 91. — *d* = loved: *you shall be well —d in Cyprus*, Oth. II, 1, 206. *her —d Posthumus*, Cymb. III, 5, 62. — Followed by an inf.: *d. to be invited*, Sonn. 141, 7. Tp. III, 1, 78. Wiv. I, 1, 38. IV, 3, 1. Meas. II, 2, 171. 178. IV, 2, 59. Mids. III, 1, 155. V, 166. All's V, 3, 157. R3 II, 1, 58. Tim. IV, 3, 248 etc. Followed by *should: dost thou d. my slumbers should be broken*, Sonn. 61, 3. *and most d. should meet the blow of justice*, Meas. II, 2, 30.

2) to ask, to entreat, to request: *consents bewitched, ere he d., have granted*, Compl. 131. *To d. sth.: I do d. thy worthy company*, Gentl. IV, 3, 25. cf. Wiv. I, 1, 271 and Meas. IV, 3, 144. *—s access to you*, Meas. II, 2, 19. II, 4, 18. Wint. V, 1, 87. *if you should need a pin, you could not with more tame a tongue d. it*, Meas. II, 2, 46. *I d. better acquaintance*, Tw. I, 3, 55. *d. it not*, II, 1, 39. *he —s some private speech with you*, All's II, 5, 61. *your queen — s your visitation*, H8 V, 1, 169. *that longer you d. the court*, II, 4, 62 (= demand a longer trial). *my lord —s you presently*, Ant. III, 5, 22. *of thy intents —s instruction*, V, 1, 54. *d. my man's abode where I did leave him*, Cymb. I, 6, 53 (i. e. bid him stay where etc.) etc.

To d. sth. of a p.: I d. more acquaintance of you, Wiv. II, 2, 168. *I shall d. more love and knowledge of you*, As I, 2, 297. *d. some conduct of the lady*, Tw. III, 4, 265. *I d. of you a conduct over-land*, Cymb. III, 5, 7.

To d. a p. of sth.: I shall d. you of more acquaintance, Mids. III, 1, 185. 193 (Ff *of you more*). *I humbly do d. your grace of pardon*, Merch. IV, 1, 402. *I d. you of the like*, As V, 4, 56. *Of* omitted: *I d. you more acquaintance*, Mids. III, 1, 200 (F 3. 4 and M. Edd. *your more acquaintance*).

To d. a p. to sth. = to invite: shall we dance, if they d. us to it? LLL V, 2, 145. *d. them all to my pavilion*, H5 IV, 1, 27. *I would d. my famous cousin to our Grecian tents*, Troil. IV, 5, 150. cf. *d. them home*, 157.

Followed by an inf.: *let me d. to know*, Meas. III, 2, 253. H8 V, 1, 169. Ant. III, 13, 67. Inf. without *to: —s you let the dukedoms that you claim hear no more*

of you, H5 I, 2, 256. *I d. you do me right and justice, and to bestow your pity on me*, H8 II, 4, 13. *d. her call her wisdom to her*, Lr. IV, 5, 35. — *—ing thee that Publius may have* ..., Caes. III, 1, 53.

To d. a p. to do sth.: Gentl. IV, 3, 32. Wiv. II, 2, 118. III, 5, 46. V, 5, 181. Meas. I, 1, 77. I, 3, 3. III, 2, 164. IV, 3, 43. 101. V, 75. Err. II, 1, 60. Mids. I, 2, 102. Merch. II, 2, 124. II, 6, 2. John V, 3, 6. H8 V, 1, 65. Cor. II, 2, 46. II, 3, 61. Hml. V, 2, 215. Lr. I, 4, 268. Ant. III, 13, 67 etc.

Desirer, one who wishes: *give it bountiful to the —s*, Cor. II, 3, 109.

Desirous, wishing for, longing after; followed by *of:* H6C IV, 8, 44. Tit. V, 1, 4. Tim. I, 2, 122. By an inf.: As I, 2, 213. Hml. III, 4, 171. By *should: my niece is d. you should enter*, Tw. III, 1, 83.

Desist, to abandon a purpose: Ant. II, 7, 86. Per. I, 1, 39. V, 1, 95. *d. to build*, H4B I, 3, 47.

Desk, a writing-table with a repository under it: Err. IV, 1, 103. IV, 2, 29. 46. Hml. II, 2, 136.*

Desolate, adj. 1) desert, uninhabited, solitary: *in this d. isle*, Tp. III, 3, 80. *subverts your towns and in a moment makes them d.* H6A II, 3, 66. *seek out some d. shade*, Mcb. IV, 3, 1.

2) forsaken, left alone: *alas, poor lady, d. and left*, Gentl. IV, 4, 179. *let him not come there; d. will I hence and die*, R2 I, 2, 73. *makes them leave me d.* H6B IV, 8, 60.

Desolation, 1) destitution, solitariness: *you have lived in d. here*, LLL V, 2, 357. *where thou art not*, (there is) *d.* H6B III, 2, 364. *my d. does begin to make a better life*, Ant. V, 2, 1. *there were d. of gaolers and gallowses*, Cymb. V, 4, 213.

2) depopulation, waste: John II, 386. H5 II, 2, 173. III, 3, 18. R3 IV, 4, 409. Per. I, 4, 89.

3) want of comfort, despair: *a careless d.* As III, 2, 400.

Misapplied: LLL I, 2, 165.

Despair, subst. perfect hopelessness: Ven. 743. 955. 988 etc. Lucr. 131. Sonn. 99, 9. 144, 1. Tp. Epil. 15. Meas. IV, 3, 114. Err. V, 80. Merch. III, 2, 109. All's II, 1, 147. Wint. III, 2, 211. John III, 1, 297. R2 I, 2, 29. II, 2, 47. III, 2, 66. 205. H4B I, 3, 40. H6A V, 4, 90. H6B II, 1, 67. III, 3, 23. H6C II, 3, 9. III, 3, 12. 215. IV, 4, 17. R3 I, 2, 85. II, 2, 36. Cor. III, 3, 127. Rom. I, 5, 106. Mcb. IV, 3, 152. Lr. IV, 6, 33. V, 3, 191. 254. Ant. III, 11, 19. Cymb. I, 1, 137. III, 5, 60. Plur. *—s:* H6A II, 5, 28. H8 II, 2, 29.

Despair, vb. to be without hope, to despond: Lucr. 1447. Sonn. 140, 9. Gentl. III, 1, 247. Shr. III, 1, 45. All's IV, 3, 86. Wint. I, 2, 198. John IV, 3, 126. R2 II, 2, 67. 68. H6C I, 1, 178. R3 I, 2, 86. V, 3, 120. 200. Tit. II, 1, 91. Rom. I, 1, 228. Cymb. V, 5, 61. Followed by *of:* Lucr. 983. H6A II, 1, 17.

Transitively: *d. thy charm*, Mcb. V, 8, 13 (or is it = may thy charm despair?).

Despatch, see *Dispatch*.

Desperate, 1) hopeless: *d. in his suit*, Ven. 336. *whose d. hands themselves do slay*, Ven. 765. Tp. III, 3, 104. Tw. II, 2, 8. John III, 1, 32. H4A III, 1, 198. H6A IV, 2, 50. IV, 6, 54. H6C I, 4, 42. R3 II, 2, 99. H8 I, 2, 35. Tit. V, 3, 75. Rom. IV, 3, 54. V, 1, 36. V, 3, 59. 117. 263. Hml. V, 1, 243. Cymb. V, 5, 58. Used of things, = suggested by despair: *to find some d. instrument of death*, Lucr. 1038. *she will do a d. outrage to herself*, Ado II, 3, 159. Wint. IV, 4, 496. R3 V, 3

319. Hml. II, 1, 104. Oth. V, 2, 207. Followed by *of*: *I am d. of obtaining her*, Gentl. III, 2, 5. *d. of their bones*, H5 IV, 2, 39. *I am d. of my fortunes*, Oth. II, 3, 337.

2) put beside one's self, mightily agitated: *will he not wake and in a desperate rage post hither*, Lucr. 219. *she d. with her nails her flesh doth tear*, 739. *he waxes d. with imagination*, Hml. I 4, 87. *go after her, she's d., govern her*, Lr. V, 3, 161.

3) despaired of, irremediable, not to be saved; or at least extremely dangerous: *and I d. approve desire is death*, Sonn. 147, 7. *my suit then is d.* Wiv. III, 5, 127. All's I, 3, 235. Tw. II, 2, 38. H6C IV, 1, 129. R3 IV, 4, 232. Rom. I, 2, 49. IV, 1, 70. Tim. III, 4, 103. IV, 3, 469. Hml. IV, 3, 9. IV, 7, 26. Cymb. IV, 3, 6.

4) reckless, regardless of danger or any other consideration: *careless lust stirs up a d. courage*, Ven. 556. *tutored in the rudiments of many d. studies by his uncle*, As V, 4, 32 (i. e. forbidden by law). *and venture madly on a d. mart*, Shr. II, 329. *skill infinite or monstrous d.* All's II, 1, 187. *this is a fond and d. creature*, V, 3, 178. *as dissolute as d.* R2 V, 3, 20. *an enterprise more venturous or d. than this*, H6A II, 1, 45. *unheedful, d., wild adventure*, IV, 7, 7. *thy school-days frightful, d., wild and furious*, R3 IV, 4, 169. *though he be grown so d. to be honest*, H8 III, 1, 86. *are you so d. grown, to threat your friends*, Tit. II, 1, 40. *I will make a d. tender of my child's love*, Rom. III, 4, 12 (i. e. overbold). *a d. execution*, IV, 1, 69. *d. appliance*, Hml. IV, 3, 10. *a d. train*, Lr. II, 4, 308. *quietness would purge by any d. change*, Ant. I, 3, 54.

Followed by *of*: *d. of shame and state*, Tw. V, 67 (= reckless of disgrace and danger).

5) Hence used to mark any bad quality predominating in a high degree: *virginity should be buried in highways as a d. offendress against nature*, All's I, 1, 153. *Salisbury is a d. homicide*, H6A I, 2, 25. *the d. tempest hath so banged the Turks*, Oth. II, 1, 21.

Desperately, 1) in despair: *and d. are dead*, Lr. V, 3, 292. *insensible of mortality, and d. mortal*, Meas. IV, 2, 152 (probably = destined to die without hope of salvation).

2) recklessly: *d. he hurried through the street*, Err. V, 140. *a bloody deed, and d. dispatched*, R3 I, 4, 278.

3) extremely: *not knowing how to find the open air, but toiling d. to find it out*, H6C III, 2, 178.

Desperation, 1) despair: Cor. IV, 6, 126. Hml. III, 2, 228.

2) utter recklessness, a state of mind bordering on madness: *played some tricks of d.* Tp. I, 2, 210. *the very place puts toys of d. into every brain*, Hml. I, 4, 75.

Despise, to contemn, to treat with contempt: Lucr. 187. Sonn. 29, 9. 100, 12. 129, 5. 141, 3. 149, 10. Gentl. III, 2, 3. IV, 2, 102. IV, 4, 99. 100. Wiv. I, 1, 69. 70. Meas. III, 2, 293. LLL V, 2, 441. Mids. II, 2, 73. III, 2, 235. Merch. I, 2, 68. H4B V, 5, 55. H6A II, 2, 47. II, 5, 36. 42. H6C I, 1, 188. H8 III, 2, 291. Troil. IV, 5, 187 (Ff *scorning*). Cor. III, 1, 22. III, 3, 133. Tit. IV, 2, 113. V, 3, 101. Rom. I, 4, 110. IV, 5, 59. Tim. III, 6, 82. Mcb. IV, 3, 201. Hml. III, 1, 72 (Ff *disprized*). Lr. I, 1, 254. III, 2, 20. Oth. I, 1, 8. 162. II, 3, 278. 299. Ant. IV, 15, 4. Cymb. III, 5, 149. Per. II, 3, 26. *with war and ostentation of —d arms*, R2 II, 3, 95 (= not taken notice of, not

thought worth opposing). *we'll make foul weather with —d tears*, III, 3, 161 (= unnoticed).

Despised, quite adjectively, = not worth regarding, despicable: *o'erworn, —d, rheumatic and cold*, Ven. 135. *then I am not lame, poor, nor —d*, Sonn. 37, 9. *nor mark prodigious, such as are —d in nativity*, Mids. V, 420. *—d substance of divinest show*, Rom. III, 2, 77. *is yond —d and ruinous man my lord?* Tim. IV, 3, 465. Sometimes it seems almost = creating despite, hateful, f. i. Rom. I, 4, 110. IV, 5, 59. Oth. I, 1, 162; and this may be the sense in R2 II, 3, 95.

Despiser, contemner: As II, 7, 92.

Despite, subst. malice, aversion, contemptuous hate: *in vain I spurn at my confirmed d.* Lucr. 1026. *thy intercepter, full of d.* Tw. III, 4, 243. *hag of all d.* H6A III, 2, 52. *who crowned the gracious duke in high d.* H6C II, 1, 59. *that I in all d. might rail at him*, II, 6, 81. *d. o'erwhelm thee*, Cor. III, 1, 164. *follow him with all d.* III, 3, 139. *has thrown such d. and heavy terms upon her*, Oth. IV, 2, 116. Followed by *of*: *thou wast ever an obstinate heretic in the d. of beauty*, Ado I, 1, 237.

In d. = 1) out of malice: *on whom, as in d., the sun looks pale*, H5 III, 5, 17. *scant our former having in d.* Oth. IV, 3, 92.

2) in defiance of another's power or inclination: *when beauty boasted blushes, in d. virtue would stain that o'er with silver white*, Lucr. 55. *we come but in d.* Mids. V, 112. *an onion ... shall in d. enforce a watery eye*, Shr. Ind. I, 128. *and in d. I'll cram thee with more food*, Rom. V, 3, 48. Followed by *of*: Ven. 731. Sonn. 141, 4. Wiv. V, 5, 132. Ado II, 1, 398. III, 2, 68. III, 4, 89. As I, 3, 25. II, 5, 49. Shr. Ind. 2, 129. John III, 3, 52. H6B I, 1, 94. IV, 8, 63. H6C I, 1, 154. I, 1, 158 (*in d. of me*). IV, 1, 146. IV, 3, 43. Hml. III, 4, 192. Cymb. V, 5, 58. *in my d.* Tit. I, 361. Cymb. IV, 1, 16. *in thy d.* H6A IV, 7, 22. *in your d.* Cymb. I, 6, 135. Singular passage: *I will depart in quiet, and in d. of mirth mean to be merry*, Err. III, 1, 108; i. e. I will defy mirth itself to keep pace with me; I will outjest mirth itself (cf. the German trotz).

Despite, prepos., in despite of, in defiance of: *d. thy* (time's) *wrong, my love shall in my verse ever live young*, Sonn. 19, 13. 60, 14. 123, 14. Ado V, 1, 75. H6B I, 1, 179. V, 1, 210. Lr. V, 3, 132. Oftener followed by *of*: *d. of fruitless chastity ... be prodigal*, Ven. 751. Lucr. 732. Sonn. 3, 12. 44, 3. Meas. I, 2, 25. 27. LLL V, 2, 129. Shr. III, 2, 144. R2 I, 1, 168. H6A IV, 6, 8. Lr. V, 3, 244.

Despite, vb. to annoy, to vex: *only to d. him, I will endeavour any thing*, Ado II, 2, 31.

Despiteful, 1) full of aversion and contemptuous hate, malicious: *to seem d. and ungentle to you*, As V, 2, 86. *his d. Juno*, All's III, 4, 13. *the most d. gentle greeting*, Troil IV, 1, 32 (Ff *despitefullest*). *d. and intolerable wrongs*, Tit. IV, 4, 50.

2) hateful, annoying: *d. love*, Shr. IV, 2, 14. *d. tidings*, R3 IV, 1, 37. *d. Rome*, Ant. II, 6, 22.

Despitefully, maliciously: *d. I mean to bear thee unto the base bed of some rascal groom*, Lucr. 670.

Despoil, to strip, to deprive: *—ed of your honour in your life*, H6B II, 3, 10.

Destined, doomed or ordained by fate:

the d. ill she must herself assay, Compl. 156. *being d. to a drier death,* Gentl. I, 1, 158. *putting on the d. livery,* Meas. II, 4, 138. *d. to a fairer death,* R3 IV, 4, 219. *take thou the d. tenth,* Tim. V, 4, 33.

Destiny, fate: Lucr. 1729. Tp. III, 3, 53. Wiv. V, 5, 43. Mids. I, 1, 151. Wint. IV, 4, 46. John IV, 2, 91. R3 IV, 4, 217. Troil. V, 1, 70. IV, 5, 184; cf. Cor. II, 2, 116. Oth. III, 3, 275. Ant. III, 6, 84. *by that d. to perform an act,* Tp. II, 1, 252. *his d.* I, 1, 34. As IV, 1, 57. Mcb. III, 5, 17. *my d.* Merch. II, 1, 15. H4B III, 2, 252. Proverbial: *hanging and wiving goes by d.* Merch. II, 9, 83. *your marriage comes by d.* All's I, 3, 66.

The Destinies = the Parcae: Ven. 733. 945. Merch. II, 2, 65. As I, 2, 111. R2 I, 2, 15. H6C II, 2, 137. Per. I, 2, 108.

Destitute, adj. 1) forsaken: *whose ranks of blue veins, as his hand did scale, left their round turrets d. and pale,* Lucr. 441. With *of,* = stripped, deprived of: *the king himself of his wings d.* Cymb. V, 3, 5.

2) wanting: *wherein we are not d. for want,* Per. V, 1, 57.

Destroy, to ruin, to bring to nought: Ven. 346. Lucr. 215. 1369. Sonn. 9, 12. Wint. V, 2, 17. R2 I, 3, 242. IV, 291. V, 3, 120. H6A III, 1, 114. Cor. IV, 5, 149. IV, 6, 42. V, 3, 133. 147. Mcb. II, 3, 76. III, 2, 6. Hml. III, 2, 207. Per. II, 5, 86. = to kill: Ven. 760. 1163. Lucr. 514. Tp. I, 2, 139. III, 2, 53. 123. 155. All's V, 3, 64. Wint. V, 1, 11. John IV, 2, 229. R2 II, 1, 105. III, 2, 184. H4A I, 3, 62. H5 III, 3, 43. H6A IV, 1, 147. IV, 6, 25. R3 I, 4, 250 (Qq *slaughter*). Troil. IV, 5, 243. Tit. V, 2, 59. Mcb. IV, 3, 84. Lr. IV, 6, 234. Ant. III, 4, 19. Absolutely: *death's —ing wound,* R2 III, 2, 139. *as if a God had —ed in such a shape,* Ant. IV, 8, 26.

Destroyer, killer, murderer: Cor. IV, 5, 241. Tim. III, 6, 105.

Destruction, subversion, ruin: John II, 409. V, 7, 77. R2 III, 2, 102. H6B I, 3, 154. Tit. II, 3, 50. Caes. I, 3, 13. Mcb. IV, 1, 60. Ant. V, 2, 132. Per. V, 3, 89. Especially = death, slaughter: R2 V, 3, 139. H4B I, 3, 33. H5 III, 3, 4. H6A IV, 2, 27. IV, 3, 21. R3 II, 4, 53. IV, 1, 40. V, 1, 9. V, 3, 319. H8 V, 1, 141. Troil. III, 2, 24 *(swooning d.).* V, 10, 9 (in V, 2, 41 and V, 3, 85 Q and M. Edd. *distraction*). Cor. II, 1, 259. III, 1, 214. Tit. III, 1, 170. Tim. III, 6, 92. IV, 3, 23. 62. Caes. III, 1, 265. Mcb. III, 2, 7. Oth. I, 3, 177.

Det, pronunciation of *debt,* blamed by Holophernes, LLL V, 1, 23.

Detain, 1) to restrain from proceeding: Ven. 577. Ado I, 1, 151. Merch. III, 2, 9. As I, 2, 286. Shr. III, 2, 105. H6A II, 5, 56. Lr. IV, 3, 49. Ant. II, 2, 173.

2) to withhold, not to give: Sonn. 126, 10. Err. II, 1, 107. R2 I, 1, 90. Lr. I, 2, 42. Ant. III, 6, 29. IV, 5, 13.

Detect, to discover, to find out, to betray: *I will d. my wife,* Wiv. II, 2, 325. *to be —ed with a jealous bell-wether,* III, 5, 111 *(with = by). I never heard the absent duke much —ed for women,* Meas. III, 2, 130. *groaning every hour would d. the lazy foot of time,* As III, 2, 322. *to let thy tongue d. thy base-born heart,* H6C II, 2, 143. R3 I, 4, 141. Tit. II, 4, 27. Hml. III, 2, 94. Per. II, 1, 55.

Detection, discovery: *could I come to her with any d. in my hand,* Wiv. II, 2, 255.

Detector, he who discovers: *that this treason were not, or not I the d.* Lr. III, 5, 14.

Detention, withholding: *the d. of long since due debts,* Tim. II, 2, 39.

Determine, vb. to circumscribe, to limit: *the sly slow hours shall not d. the dateless limit of thy dear exile,* R2 I, 3, 150.

Determinate, adj. 1) limited, fixed: *my bonds in thee are all d.* Sonn. 87, 4.* *my d. voyage is mere extravagancy,* Tw. II, 1, 11.

2) decisive: *ere a d. resolution, he did require a respite,* H8 II, 4, 176. *unless his abode be lingered by some accident: wherein none can be so d. as the removing of Cassio,* Oth. IV, 2, 232.

Determination, 1) circumscription, limit: *so should that beauty which you hold in lease find no d.* Sonn. 13, 6.

2) decision: *he humbles himself to the d. of justice,* Meas. III, 2, 258. *to make up a free d. 'twixt right and wrong,* Troil. II, 2, 170.

3) resolution: *did she change her d.?* Wiv. III, 5, 69. *acquainted me with their —s,* Merch. I, 2, 111. *would you were of our d.* H4A IV, 3, 33. *I have in quick d. thus set it down,* Hml. III, 1, 176.

Determine, 1) trans. a) to limit: *a restraint to a —ed scope,* Meas. III, 1, 70. Hence = to put an end to: *till his friend sickness hath —d me,* H4B IV, 5, 82. *to my —d time thou gavest new date,* H6A IV, 6, 9.

b) to resolve on, to decide, to settle: *by their verdict is —d the clear eye's moiety,* Sonn. 46, 11. *d. our proceedings,* Gentl. III, 2, 97. *I will d. this before I stir,* Err. V, 167. Merch. IV, 1, 106. John II, 584. H6B IV, 7, 93. H6C IV, 6, 56. R3 I, 3, 15. III, 1, 193 (Qq *do*). III, 2, 13. V, 1, 19. Tit. I, 407. V, 2, 139. Rom. III, 1, 136. Hml. III, 2, 197. Ant. III, 6, 84. IV, 4, 37. Followed by a dative and accus.: *she —s herself the glory of a creditor,* Meas. I, 1, 39 (= settles, fixes). By an inf.: *you have —d to bestow her on Thurio,* Gentl. III, 1, 13. *I d. to fight lustily for him,* H5 IV, 1, 201. By a clause: *wildly —ing which way to fly,* Lucr. 1150. *d. what we shall do straight,* John II, 149. R3 II, 2, 141. III, 5, 52. Caes. IV, 1, 8.

Determined = resolved: Ado V, 4, 36. R3 I, 1, 30. Caes. V, 1, 100. Oth. II, 3, 227.

2) intr. a) to end: *must all d. here?* Cor. III, 3, 43. *I purpose not to wait on fortune till these wars d.* V, 3, 120. *as it —s, so dissolve my life,* Ant. III, 13, 161. *it will d. one way,* IV, 3, 2.

b) to resolve, to decide: *as the flesh and fortune shall better d.* Meas. II, 1, 268. *till you know how he —s further,* H8 I, 1, 214. Lr. V, 3, 45. Oth. I, 3, 276. Ant. V, 1, 59. Followed by *of: our marriage hour —d of,* Gentl. II, 4, 181. *to d. of what conditions we shall stand upon,* H4B IV, 1, 164. *to d. of the coronation,* R3 III, 4, 2. *having —d of the Volsces,* Cor. II, 2, 41. *brief sounds d. of my weal or woe,* Rom. III, 2, 51 (Qq *determine my weal*). By *on: stir not till you have well —d upon these slanderers,* Meas. V, 258. *d. on some course,* Cor. IV, 1, 35. *on our proceedings,* Lr. V, 1, 31.

Detest, to abhor: Lucr. 1566. Gentl. IV, 1, 73. V, 4, 39. Meas. II, 1, 74. Mids. III, 2, 434. All's II, 3, 309. III, 5, 68. Tw. II, 5, 220. H8 V, 3, 39. Tit.

III, 1, 248. V, 2, 37. Ant. IV, 14, 57. Cymb. II, 5, 33. Misapplied: Wiv. I, 4, 160. Meas. II, 1, 69. 75.

Detested = abominable: LLL IV, 1, 31. R2 II, 3, 109. III, 2, 44. H4A I, 3, 162. R3 I, 3, 233. Tit. II, 3, 74. 93. 224. Tim. III, 6, 104. Lr. I, 2, 81. I, 4, 284. II, 4, 220. *ay me, —ed! how am I beguiled!* Tw. V, 142.

Detestable, abominable: Wint. IV, 3, 65. John III, 4, 29. Tit. V, 1, 94. Rom. IV, 5, 56. V, 3, 45. Tim. IV, 1, 33.

Detract, 1) to take away: *shall I d. so much from that prerogative,* H6A V, 4, 142.

2) to derogate: *to utter foul speeches and to d.* Tp. II, 2, 96.

Detraction, speaking ill, defamation: *happy are they that hear their —s and can put them to mending,* Ado II, 3, 238. *more d. at your heels than fortunes before you,* Tw. II, 5, 149. *d. will not suffer it,* H4A V, 1, 141. *unspeak mine own d.* Mcb. IV, 3, 123.

Detriment, misfortune, suffering: *being from the feeling of her own grief brought by deep surmise of others' d.* Lucr. 1579.

Deucalion, the Noah of the Greeks: Wint. IV, 4, 442. Cor. II, 1, 102.

Deuce-ace, one and two thrown at dice: LLL I, 2, 49; cf. *Ames-ace.*

Devest, see *Divest.*

Device, 1) contrivance, conceit, stratagem: *the shame that from them no d. can take,* Lucr. 535. *O excellent d.* Gentl. II, 1, 145. Wiv. I, 1, 43. Meas. IV, 4, 15. Err. I, 2, 95. LLL V, 1, 144. Mids. III, 1, 17. As I, 1, 157. IV, 3, 20. Shr. I, 2, 135. Tw. II, 3, 176. II, 5, 199. III, 4, 143. 144. 153. V, 368. H4A II, 4, 290. 344. H6A I, 2, 41. H6C III, 3, 141. R3 I, 4, 162. III, 6, 11. H8 I, 1, 204. III, 2, 217. Troil. I, 3, 375. Tit. I, 395. II, 1, 78. IV, 4, 52. Oth. IV, 2, 177.

2) plan, scheme: *this is our d.* Wiv. IV, 4, 41. *husband your d.* IV, 6, 52. *I'll tell thee all my whole d.* Merch. III, 4, 81. Mids. I, 2, 107. Shr. I, 1, 198. Tit. III, 1, 134. V, 2, 120. 143. Hml. III, 2, 222. IV, 7, 66. Oth. II, 3, 394.

3) any thing fancifully conceived; as an embroidery: *this d. was sent me from a nun,* Compl. 232 (cf. *conceit* in Mids. I, 1, 33). The cut and ornaments of a garment: *not alone in habit and d., exterior form, outward accoutrement,* John I, 210. The emblem on a shield: *to explain the labour of each knight in his d.* Per. II, 2, 15. 19. 25. The form into which plate is wrought: *plate of rare d.* Cymb. I, 6, 189. A dramatic performance, a mask played by private persons: *but I will forward with my d.* LLL V, 2, 669. *that is an old d. and it was played ...,* Mids. V, 50. *entertained me with mine own d.* Tim. I, 2, 155 (perhaps also in LLL V, 1, 144. Mids. I, 2, 107. III, 1, 17).

4) manner of thinking, cast of mind: *I hate not love, but your d. in love, that lends embracements unto every stranger,* Ven. 789. *he's gentle, never schooled and yet learned, full of noble d.* As I, 1, 174.

Devil, in O. Edd. **Divel** (ordinarily monosyll., but sometimes dissyll., f. i. Tp. IV, 188. Wiv. I, 3, 61. Mids. V, 9. Tw. I, 5, 270. H8 II, 1, 21) fiend; *the d.:* Tp. I, 2, 319. III, 2, 89. V, 129. Meas. II, 4, 16. V, 29. 294. Err. IV, 3, 50. IV, 4, 131. H4A I, 2, 131 etc. *a d.:* Sonn. 144, 7. Tp. III, 2, 138. IV, 188. Meas. III, 1, 92.

Err. IV, 2, 33. LLL V, 2, 106. Shr. III, 2, 158. H6B I, 2, 92 etc. *this d.* Lucr. 85. *some d.* John III, 2, 2. *what d.* Wiv. III, 3, 230 etc. *—s:* Tp. I, 2, 215. II, 2, 59. 91. III, 3, 36. Wiv. I, 3, 61. II, 2, 312. Err. IV, 3, 72. LLL IV, 3, 257. Mids. V, 9 etc. *the d. and his dam,* Wiv. I, 1, 151. Err. IV, 3, 51. Shr. III, 2, 158. H6A I, 5, 5. Oth. IV, 1, 153 etc. (cf. *Dam*). *in the —'s name,* H4A III, 1, 69. *with the —'s name,* Wiv. II, 1, 24. Used as a feminine: Wint. I, 2, 82. John III, 1, 196. Cymb. II, 1, 57. Proverbial phrases: *he must have a long spoon that must eat with the d.* Err. IV, 3, 65. *give the d. his due,* H4A I, 2, 132. H5 III, 7, 127. *he must needs go that the d. drives,* All's I, 3, 32. *the d. rides upon a fiddlestick,* H4A II, 4, 534 (cf. *the d. fiddle them,* H8 I, 3, 42). *be mad, cry: the d.* Err. IV, 4, 131. *tell truth and shame the d.* H4A III, 1, 62. *the d. can cite Scripture,* Merch. I, 3, 99. *as good a gentleman as the d.* H5 IV, 7, 145; cf. Lr. III, 4, 148. *more haughty than the d.* H6A I, 3, 85; cf. Tw. I, 5, 270. — Used for any great evil: *d. Envy,* Troil. II, 3, 23. *the d. Luxury,* V, 2, 55. *the d. drunkenness,* Oth. II, 3, 297. *the d. wrath,* 298. — Noting extraordinary skill or boldness: *set spurs and away, like three German —s,* Wiv. IV, 5, 70. *the finest mad d. of jealousy,* V, 1, 19. *thou most excellent d. of wit,* Tw. II, 5, 226. *he is a d. in a private brawl,* Tw. III, 4, 259. *he's a very d.* 301. *I have persuaded him the youth's a d.* 321. *one that will play the d. with you,* John II, 135. *he will foin like any d.* H4B II, 1, 18. *fight like —s,* H5 III, 7, 162. *he's the d.* Cor. I, 10, 16. — Serving as an expletive to express wonder or vexation: *what the d. should move me ...,* All's IV, 1, 37. *what the d. art thou?* John II, 134. *what the d. hast thou brought here?* H4B II, 4, 1. *what a d. hast thou to do with the time of the day?* H4A I, 2, 6. *what a d. dost thou in Warwickshire?* IV, 2, 56. *where the d. should he learn our language?* Tp. II, 2, 69. Rom. II, 4, 1. *why the d. should we keep knives,* H5 II, 1, 95. *why the d. took he upon him ...,* H8 I, 1, 72. Rom. III, 1, 107. — Used as a ludicrous negative: *the d. a puritan that he is, or any thing constantly, but a timepleaser,* Tw. II, 3, 159.

Devilish, diabolical: Meas. III, 1, 65. Shr. II, 26. 152. H5 III Chor. 33. H6B III, 1, 46. IV, 1, 83. IV, 7, 80. R3 I, 2, 90. I, 4, 265. III, 4, 62. Mcb. IV, 3, 117. Oth. II, 1, 249. Cymb. I, 5, 16.

Devilish-holy (not hyphened in O. Edd.) wicked and good at the same time: *when truth kills truth, O d. fray!* Mids. III, 2, 129.

Devil-monk, not hyphened in O. Edd.: H8 II, 1, 21.

Devil-porter, the porter of hell; used, by the addition of *it,* as a verb: *I'll d. it no further* Mcb. II, 3, 19 (= play no longer the porter of hell).

Devise, 1) trans. to contrive, to excogitate, to invent: *danger —th shifts,* Ven. 690. Lucr. 969. Sonn. 83, 14. Gentl. III, 1, 38. Wiv. IV, 2, 75. Ado IV, 1, 281. V, 4, 130. LLL I, 1, 124. 133. I, 2, 66. IV, 3, 372. Merch. I, 2, 19. 32. As I, 2, 25. I, 3, 137. III, 2, 158. IV, 3, 182. Wint. IV, 4, 451. John III, 1, 149. 250. R2 I, 1, 77. II, 1, 249. III, 4, 1. IV, 330. H4B V, 1, 87. V, 3, 139. H5 I, 2, 55. H6A III, 1, 2. III, 3, 17. H6B III, 1, 59. 121. IV, 8, 71. H6C II, 6, 71. IV, 1, 35. R3 II, 2, 22. V, 3, 306. 310. H8 I, 2, 51. Troil. III, 2, 86. Cor. II, 2, 128. Tit. V, 1, 128. Rom. II, 4, 191. V, 3, 240. Tim. I, 2, 15. Caes. III, 1, 246. Hml. IV, 7, 70. V, 2, 32. Lr. V, 1, 64. Oth. III, 1, 39. IV, 2, 221. *which* *is more than history can pattern, though —d and played to take spectators,* Wint. III, 2, 37, i. e. adorned by poetical fiction. = to l i e, to f o r g e: *d. some virtuous lie,* Sonn. 72, 5. *—ing impossible slanders,* Ado II, 1, 143. III, 1, 84. H4A III, 2, 23. Oth. III, 4, 12. IV, 2, 133.

Followed by an inf. or a clause: *when they have —d what strained touches rhetoric can lend,* Sonn. 82, 9. *d. how you'll use him, and let us two d. to bring him thither,* Wiv. IV, 4, 27. Ado II, 1, 274. Mids. I, 1, 213. III, 2, 35. As I, 3, 102. Cor. IV, 1, 38. Rom. III, 1, 72. 2) intr. to invent, to lay s c h e m e s: *d., wit; write, pen,* LLL I, 2, 190. *or my reporter —d well for her* (= fabled), Ant. II, 2, 194. *then she plots, then she ruminates, then she —s,* Wiv. II, 2, 321. *for his safety there I'll best d.* H6A I, 1, 172. = to t h i n k, to p o n d e r: *the other instruments did see and hear, d., instruct, walk, feel,* Cor. I, 1, 105. Followed by *on: where are you? what d. you on?* H6A I, 2, 124.

Devoid, adj. v o i d, destitute: *d. of pity,* Tit. V, 3, 199.

Devonshire, English county: R3 IV, 4, 500.

Devote, vb. (used only in the partic. *—ed*) to c o n s e c r a t e, to a d d i c t: *he hath —d and given up himself to the contemplation . . .,* Oth. II, 3, 321. *—ed yours,* Lucr. Dedic. 4. *a true —ed pilgrim,* Gentl. II, 7, 9. *the substance of your perfect self is else —ed,* IV, 2, 125. LLL I, 1, 280. *this is your —d friend,* All's IV, 3, 264. *thy poor —d suppliant,* R3 I, 2, 207. = pious, holy: *to stop —d charitable deeds,* R3 I, 2, 35.

Devote, adj. a d d i c t e d: *d. to Aristotle's checks,* Shr. I, 1, 32.

Devotement, devotion, d e v o t e d l o v e and v e n e r a t i o n: *he hath devoted and given up himself to the contemplation, mark and d. of her parts and graces,* Oth. II, 3, 322 (most M. Edd., after the later Ff and Qq, *denotement*). The use of the prepos. *of* is to be accounted for by what in grammar is called Ζεῦγμα; cf. Sonn. 48, 12. Meas. II, 4, 1. John II, 27.

Devotion, 1) strong affection, engrossing l o v e: *the faithfullest offerings that e'er d. tendered,* Tw. V, 118. *in the d. of a subject's love,* R2 I, 1, 31. *it shows my d.* H4B V, 5, 19. *upon the like d. as yourselves, to gratulate the gentle princes,* R3 IV, 1, 9. *with pure heart's love, immaculate d.* IV, 4, 404. Ant. I, 1, 5. Leading over to the second signification: *to his image did I d.* Tw. III, 4, 397.

2) d e v o u t n e s s, p i e t y: *camest thou here by chance, or of d., to this holy shrine?* H6B II, 1, 88. H6C II, 1, 164. IV, 6, 43. R3 III, 7, 103. Troil. IV, 4, 28. Rom. I, 5, 100. IV, 1, 41. Mcb. IV, 3, 94. Hml. III, 1, 47.

3) z e a l: *he seeks their hate with greater d. than they can render it him,* Cor. II, 2, 21. *I have no great d. to the deed,* Oth. V, 1, 8.

Devour, 1) to eat up ravenously, to s w a l l o w u p: Ven. 57. Sonn. 19, 1. 2. Ado III, 1, 28. LLL I, 1, 4. Mids. III, 1, 198. Tw. V, 236. John V, 6, 41. V, 7, 64. Cor. II, 1, 10. Mcb. IV, 3, 74. Per. II, 1, 35. *to d. up:* Mids. I, 1, 148. All's IV, 3, 249. *and with a greedy ear d. up my discourse,* Oth. I, 3, 150.

2) to c o n s u m e, to d e s t r o y, to a n n i h i l a t e: *his taste delicious, in digestion souring, —s his will* (i. e. his cupidity) *that lived by foul —ing,* Lucr. 700. *what virtue breeds iniquity —s,* 872. *not that —ed, but that which doth d., is worthy blame,* 1256. *they d. their*

reason, Tp. V, 155 (annul it by diffidence). *what dangers may drop upon his kingdom and d. incertain lookers on,* Wint. V, 1, 28. *—ing pestilence hangs in our air,* R2 I, 3, 284. *he seemed in running to d. the way,* H4B I, 1, 47. *the wretch that trembles under his* (the lion's) *—ing paws,* H6C I, 3, 13. *whatever praises itself but in the deed, —s the deed in the praise,* Troil. II, 3, 167. *good deeds past, which are —ed as fast as they are made, forgot as soon as done,* III, 3, 148. *the present wars d. him,* Cor. I, 1, 262. *the cruelty and envy of the people hath —ed the rest,* IV, 5, 82. *this fell —ing receptacle,* Tit. II, 3, 235. *the good-years shall d. them,* Lr. V, 3, 24.

3) to a b s o r b: *a grace it had —ing,* Tp. III, 3, 84 (M. Edd. *a grace it had, devouring*). cf. Wint. III, 1, 10 and 11. *Pericles, in sorrow all —ed,* Per. IV, 4, 25.

Devourer, one who devours: Tit. III, 1, 57.

Devout, pious, religious: Tw. III, 4, 424. John V, 4, 48. H5 I, 1, 9. R3 III, 7, 92. Troil. II, 3, 38. Rom. I, 2, 93. Oth. III, 4, 41. *but more d. than this in our respects have we not been,* LLL V, 2, 792 (i. e. we have not treated the business as a matter of holy importance).

Devoutly, with devotion, earnestly: *she d. dotes, dotes in idolatry,* Mids. I, 1, 109. *prayed d.* H8 IV, 1, 84. *d. to be wished,* Hml. III, 1, 84.

Dew, subst. moisture precipitated by the cooling of the atmosphere: Lucr. 24. 396. Tp. I, 2, 228. 321. Mids. III, 2, 443. IV, 1, 58. 126. Merch. V, 7. Shr. II, 174. John II, 285. H6B V, 2, 53. R3 V, 3, 46 (Qq *air*). Tit. II, 3, 201. Rom. I, 1, 138. II, 3, 6. III, 5, 127. Hml. I, 1, 167. I, 2, 130. I, 3, 41. Oth. I, 2, 59. Cymb. I, 5, 1. IV, 2, 284. Plur. *—s:* Cor. II, 3, 35. Caes. V, 3, 64. Hml. I, 1, 117. Used of tears: *such relenting d. of lamentations,* Lucr. 1829. LLL IV, 3, 29. Wint. II, 1, 109. John V, 2, 45. R2 V, 1, 9. Used of things refreshing and beneficent: *the golden d. of sleep,* R3 IV, 1, 84. *the honey-heavy d. of slumber,* Caes. II, 1, 230. *this coal, which God's d. quench,* H8 II, 4, 80. Cymb. V, 5, 351. Likewise *—s: his —s fall everywhere,* H8 I, 3, 57. *the —s of heaven fall thick in blessings on her,* IV, 2, 133. *he watered his new plants with —s of flattery,* Cor. V, 6, 23.

Corrupted from the French *dieu:* H5 IV, 4, 7.

Dew, vb. to wet as with dew, to m o i s t e n: Ven. 66. Mids. II, 1, 9. H6B III, 2, 340. Rom. V, 3, 14. Mcb. V, 2, 30. In H6A IV, 2, 34 O. Edd. *dew,* M. Edd. *due.*

Dew-bedabbled, sprinkled with dew: Ven. 703. cf. *Bedabble.*

Dewberry, the fruit of Rubus caesius: Mids. III, 1, 169.

Dewdrop, a drop of dew: Mids. II, 1, 14. Troil. III, 3, 224.

Dew-dropping, wetting, rainy: *the d. south,* Rom. I, 4, 103.

Dewlap (O. Edd. *dewlop*) hanging breast: *against her lips I bob and on her withered d. pour the ale,* Mids. II, 1, 50.*

Dewlapped, having flesh hanging from the throat: *d. like bulls,* Tp. III, 3, 45. *d. like Thessalian bulls,* Mids. IV, 1, 127.

Dewy, moist with dew, or consisting of dew: *weep like the d. night,* Lucr. 1232. *the d. morn,* Pilgr. 71. *I would these d. tears were from the ground,* R3 V, 3, 283.

Dexter, right, opposed to left: *my mother's blood runs on the d. cheek,* Troil. IV, 5, 128.

Dexteriously, adroitly: Tw. I, 5, 66.

Dexterity, nimbleness: *in youth quick bearing and d.* Lucr. 1389. *my admirable d. of wit,* Wiv. IV, 5, 121. *with as quick d.* H4A II, 4, 286. *d. so obeying appetite,* Troil. V, 5, 27. Rom. III, 1, 168. *to post with such d. to incestuous sheets,* Hml. I, 2, 157.

Diablo, the Spanish name for the devil: Oth. II, 3, 160.

Diadem, the crown: H6A II, 5, 89. H6B I, 1, 246. I, 2, 7. 40. IV, 1, 82. H6C I, 4, 104. II, 1, 153. II, 2, 82. IV, 7, 66. Tit. I, 6. Hml. II, 2, 530. III, 4, 100. Ant. V, 2, 345.

Dial, 1) an instrument for measuring time by the shadow of the sun: Sonn. 77, 2. 7. Err. V, 118. H4A I, 2, 9. H5 I, 2, 210. H6C II, 5, 24. Oth. III, 4, 175.

2) clock, watch: *as those bars which stop the hourly d., who with a lingering stay his course doth let, till every minute pays the hour his debt,* Lucr. 327. *he drew a d. from his poke,* As II, 7, 20. 33. *then my d. goes not true,* All's II, 5, 6. *whereto my finger, like a —'s point, is pointing still,* R2 V, 5, 53. *if life did ride upon a —'s point, still ending at the arrival of an hour,* H4A V, 2, 84. *the bawdy hand of the d. is now upon the prick of noon,* Rom. II, 4, 119 (but cf. *Dial-hand*).

Dialect, peculiar language, manner of expression: *he had the d. and different skill, catching all passions in his craft of will,* Compl. 125. *in her youth there is a prone and speechless d., such as move men,* Meas. I, 2, 188. *to go out of my d. which you discommend so much,* Lr. II, 2, 115.

Dial-hand, the hand of a clock, or a gnomon: *yet doth beauty, like a d., steal from his figure and no pace perceived,* Sonn. 104, 9.

Dialogue, subst. dramatic conversation: Ado III, 1, 31. LLL V, 2, 895. All's IV, 3, 112. Tw. I, 5, 214. John I, 201. Troil. I, 3, 155.

Dialogue, vb. to act both parts in a conversation: *and —d for him what he would say, asked their own wills, and made their wills obey,* Compl. 132. *how dost, fool? Dost d. with thy shadow?* Tim. II, 2, 52 (i. e. dost thou play the part of thy shadow, asking thee that question?).

Diameter, the longest line in a circle: *whose whisper o'er the world's d. transports his poisoned shot,* Hml. IV, 1, 41.

Diamond, the most precious gem: Compl. 211. Wiv. III, 3, 59. Err. IV, 3, 70. V, 391. LLL V, 2, 3. Merch. III, 1, 87. H6A V, 3, 169. H6B III, 2, 107. H6C III, 1, 63. Tim. III, 6, 131. Mcb. II, 1, 15. Lr. IV, 3, 24. Cymb. I, 1, 112. I, 4, 78. 81. 154. 163. II, 4, 98. V, 5, 137. Per. II, 3, 36. II, 4, 53. III, 2, 102.

Dian, 1) the goddess of the moon and of chastity: Ven. 725. Sonn. 153, 2. Ado IV, 1, 58. Shr. II, 260. 262. All's I, 3, 119 (only by conjecture). 218. II, 3, 80. H6C IV, 8, 21. Cor. V, 3, 67. Tit. II, 3, 57. 61. Rom. I, 1, 215. Tim. IV, 3, 387. Oth. III, 3, 387. Cymb. II, 4, 82. II, 5, 7. V, 5, 180. Per. IV Prol. 29. V, 1, 251. V, 2, 13. V, 3, 1. 37. 69. *Dian's bud,* Mids. IV, 1, 78 (the bud of Agnus Castus or Chaste tree).

2) name in All's IV, 3, 238. 256.

Diana, the same, 1) the goddess: Mids. I, 1, 89. Merch. I, 2, 117. V, 66. As III, 4, 17. IV, 1, 154. Tw.

I, 4, 31. H4A I, 2, 29. Troil. V, 2, 91. Cymb. I, 6, 133. II, 3, 74. Per. II, 5, 10. III, 2, 105. III, 3, 28. III, 4, 13. IV Prol. 4. IV, 2, 161, V, 3, 17. 25.

2) female name in All's III, 5, 11. 19. IV, 2, 2. IV, 3, 241. 355. IV, 4, 26.

Diapason, deep notes harmoniously accompanying high ones: *and with deep groans the d. bear,* Lucr. 1132.

Diaper, a towel: *another bear the ewer, the third a d.* Shr. Ind. 1, 57.

Dibble, subst. a pointed instrument to make holes for planting seeds: Wint. IV, 4, 100.

Dice, vb. to game with dice: H4A III, 3, 18.

Dicer, a player at dice: *as false as —s' oaths,* Hml. III, 4, 45.

Dich, a corruption of *do it: much good d. thy good heart,* Tim. I, 2, 73.

Dick, diminutive of Richard: LLL V, 2, 923. Tw. V, 202. H4A II, 4, 9. H6B IV, 2, 27. IV, 3, 1. H6C V, 5, 35. Cor. II, 3, 123. *some mumble-news, some trencher-knight, some D.* LLL V, 2, 464 (cf. *Jack*).

Dickens, the devil: *I cannot tell what the d. his name is,* Wiv. III, 2, 19.

Dickon = Dick: R3 V, 3, 305.

Dicky, the same: H6C I, 4, 76.

Dictator, a Roman magistrate invested with absolute power: Cor. II, 2, 93.

Diction, language, expression: *to make true d. of him, his semblable is his mirror,* Hml. V, 2, 123.

Dictynna (O. Edd. *Dictisima, Dictissima, Dictima* and *Dictinna*), a title of Diana: LLL IV, 2, 37. 38.

Dido, the queen of Carthage, in love with Aeneas: Tp. II, 1, 76. 78. 81. 100. 101. Merch. V, 10. H6B III, 2, 117. Tit. II, 3, 22. V, 3, 82. Rom. II, 4, 43. Hml. II, 2, 468. Ant. IV, 14, 53. Not named, but alluded to: Shr. I, 1, 159.

Die, subst. and vb. = colour, see *Dye.*

Die, subst., a small cube marked with numbers, used in gaming: Mids. V, 312 (quibbling with the verb *to die*). Wint. IV, 3, 27. R3 V, 4, 10. Tim. V, 4, 34 (quibbling). Plural *dice:* Wiv. III, 1, 38. Ado II, 1, 290. LLL V, 2, 326. Wint. I, 2, 133. Lr. III, 4, 93. Ant. II, 3, 33. *to play at dice:* Merch. II, 1, 32. H5 IV Chor. 19. IV, 5, 8. *well run, dice!* LLL V, 2, 233.

Die, vb. to lose life, to expire: Tp. I, 2, 279. II, 1, 216. II, 2, 45. III, 1, 79. III, 2, 140. Gentl. III, 1, 171. IV, 1, 68. IV, 3, 20 etc. etc. = to be killed: *if thou scorn our courtesy, thou —st,* Gentl. IV, 1, 68. *if you go out, you d.* Wiv. IV, 2, 68. IV, 5, 45 etc. etc. *I'll d. on him that says so but yourself,* Gentl. II, 4, 114 (i. e. challenge him to a mortal combat). *to d. upon the hand I love so well,* Mids. II, 1, 244. *He that —s and lives by bloody drops,* As III, 5, 7 (i. e. who earns his subsistence by killing people). *at this sport Sir Valour —s,* Troil. I, 3, 176 (expires with laughter). Followed by *of: —d of a cruel fever,* Meas. IV, 3, 74. *she of that boy did d.* Mids. II, 1, 135. *—d thy sister of her love?* Tw. II, 4, 122. H4B V, 5, 146. Ant. V, 2, 254. Cymb. I, 1, 158.

Dying, substantively, for the act of death: *and death once dead, there's no more —ing then,* Sonn. 146, 14. *to counterfeit —ing,* H4A V, 4, 119. *whom to leave is only bitter to him, only —ing,* H8 II, 1, 74. *—ing* *fear through all her body spread,* Lucr. 1266 (= fear of death). *a life whose very comfort is still a —ing horror,* Meas. II, 3, 42. *dyed in the —ing slaughter of their foes,* John II, 323. *Edward for Edward pays a —ing debt,* R3 IV, 4, 21 (= a debt of death).* *—ing cries,* Cor. II, 2, 114. *leaked is our bark, and we, poor mates, stand on the —ing deck,* Tim. IV, 2, 20 (the deck on which we are to die).

Becoming transitive, when joined with *death: d. a dry death,* Tp. I, 1, 72. *a flea's death,* Wiv. IV, 2, 158. *a fair death,* H4A II, 2, 14. *a violent death,* H6B I, 4, 34. *a guiltless death,* Oth. V, 2, 122. *a thousand deaths,* Tw. V, 136. *a hundred thousand deaths,* H4A III, 2, 158. *to d. the death* (= to perish by the sword of justice) Meas. II, 4, 165. Mids. I, 1, 65. Ant. IV, 14, 26. Cymb. IV, 2, 96 (cf. *Death*). *that we the pain of death would hourly d. rather than d. at once,* Lr. V, 3, 185 (Qq *with the pain*).

To d. for sth. = to pine for sth.: *and in despite of all, —s for him,* Ado III, 2, 69. *I d. for food,* As II, 6, 2. II, 7, 104. *take thought and d. for Caesar,* Caes. II, 1, 187. *to this I witness call the fools of time, which d. for goodness, who have lived for crime,* Sonn. 124, 14 (i. e. who feel or, at least, express a perpetual longing for what is good, but nevertheless indulge their bad propensities).

Applied to things, = to perish in any manner, to be extinguished, to fade, to vanish, to be forgotten, to cease etc.: *a —ing coal,* Ven. 338. Lucr. 1378. 1379. *here —s the dusky torch of Mortimer,* H6A II, 5, 122. *here burns my candle out, ay, here it —s,* H6C II, 6, 1. *a flower that —s when first it gins to bud,* Pilgr. 171. *her vine unpruned —s,* H5 V, 2, 42. *when —ing clouds contend with growing light,* H6C II, 5, 2. *that strain again! it had a —ing fall,* Tw. I, 1, 4.* *the appetite may sicken and so d.* 3. *debating, d.!* Lucr. 274. *else his project —s,* Tp. II, 1, 299. *so —s my revenge,* Ado V, 1, 301. *the contents —s in the zeal of that which it presents,* LLL V, 2, 519. *fancy —s in the cradle where it lies,* Merch. III, 2, 68. *health shall live free, and sickness freely d.* All's II, 1, 171. *d. thou, and d. our fear,* H6C V, 2, 1. *shall these labours and these honours d.?* H6B I, 1, 97. *this day all quarrels d.* Tit. I, 465. *but d. thy thoughts when thy first lord is dead,* Hml. III, 2, 225. *the cease of majesty —s not alone,* III, 3, 16. *the sweat of industry would dry and d. but for the end it works to,* Cymb. III, 6, 31. *one good deed —ing tongueless,* Wint. I, 2, 92. *whate'er lord Harry Percy then had said, may reasonably d. and never rise,* H4A I, 3, 74. *enough of this: let it d. as it was born,* Cymb. I, 4, 131.

Diet, subst. 1) **food, fare:** *I will bespeak our d.* Tw. III, 3, 40. *you owe money for your d. and by-drinkings,* H4A II, 3, 84. *in speech, in gait, in d., in affections of delight,* H4B II, 3, 29. *spare in d.* H5 II, 2, 131. *your d. shall be in all places alike,* Tim. III, 6, 74. *for food and d.* Hml. I, 1, 99. *your worm is your only emperor for d.* IV, 3, 23. *feed upon such nice and waterish d.* Oth. III, 3, 15. *breaths rank of gross d.* Ant. V, 2, 212.

2) **regimen prescribed** (especially for persons suffering from the French disease): *to fast like one that takes d.* Gentl. II, 1, 25. *unless they kept very good d.* Meas. II, 1, 116. *bring down rose-cheeked youth to the tub-fast and the d.* Tim. IV, 3, 87. *he hath kept an evil d. long,* R3 I, 1, 139.*

Diet, vb. 1) to feed: *they must be —ed like mules,* H6A I, 2, 10. *to d. my revenge,* Oth. II, 1, 303.

2) **to feed by the rules of medicine:** *I will attend my husband, be his nurse, d. his sickness,* Err. V, 99. *to d. rank minds sick of happiness,* H4B IV, 1, 64. Hence = to adjust, to set right by a certain manner of feeding: *disciplined, ay, —ed in grace,* Compl. 261. *as if I loved my little should be —ed in praises sauced with lies,* Cor. I, 9, 52. *I'll watch him till he be —ed to my request,* V, 1, 57. *thou art all the comfort the gods will d. me with,* Cymb. III, 4, 183.

3) **to keep fasting, to constrain to fast:** *we shall not then have his company to-night? Not till after midnight, for he is —ed to his hour,* All's IV, 3, 35. *you that have turned off a first so noble wife, may justly d. me,* V, 3, 221 (obsc. pass.).

Dieter, one who prepares food by medicinal rules: *sauced our broths, as Juno had been sick, and he her d.* Cymb. IV, 2, 51.

Differ, to be other, to be unlike: Wiv. II, 1, 72. R3 I, 4, 83. Tim. I, 1, 170. III, 1, 49 (cf. *difference* in Lr. V, 3, 288). Ant. II, 2, 116. Cymb. III, 6, 86. IV, 2, 4. Followed by *from:* Ado V, 1, 33. As I, 1, 10.

Difference, 1) **the state of being unlike,** dissimilarity: *our drops this d. bore,* Compl. 300. Gentl. IV, 4, 195. Merch. IV, 1, 368. Wint. IV, 4, 17. John III, 1, 204. H8 I, 1, 139. Tit. II, 1, 31. Hml. III, 4, 76. Oth. I, 3, 7. Per. IV, 2, 85. *making such d. twixt wake and sleep as is the d. betwixt day and night,* H4A III, 1, 219. *let him bear it for a d. between himself and his horse,* Ado I, 1, 69 (= a mark of distinction, in heraldry). cf. *wear your rue with a d.* Hml. IV, 5, 183. *that from your first of d. and decay have followed your sad steps,* Lr. V, 3, 288 (= from your first turn of fortune? cf. *differ* in Tim. III, 1, 49: *is't possible the world should so much differ, and we alive that lived?*). Followed by *between* or *betwixt:* Merch. III, 1, 41. As III, 5, 122. All's I, 3, 116. Wint. I, 1, 4. H5 II, 4, 134. Lr. I, 4, 151. Cymb. V, 5, 194. By *of:* the d. of old Shylock and Bassanio, Merch. II, 5, 2. Lr. IV, 2, 26. Plur. *—s: stand off in —s so mighty,* All's II, 3, 128. *I'll teach you —s,* Lr. I, 4, 100.

2) **variety:** *my verse to constancy confined, one thing expressing, leaves out d.* Sonn. 105, 8. *the seasons' d.* As II, 1, 6. *full of most excellent —s,* Hml. V, 2, 112 (= different excellencies).

3) **distinction:** *as long as I have an eye to make d. of men's liking,* Wiv. II, 1, 57.

4) **quarrel, dissension, contention:** Merch. IV, 1, 171. John II, 355. III, 1, 238. R2 I, 1, 201. IV, 86. H4B IV, 1, 181. H8 I, 1, 101. III, 1, 58. Cor. V, 6, 18. Lr. II, 1, 125. II, 2, 56. Ant. II, 1, 49. II, 2, 21. Cymb. I, 4, 57. *I am glad thou hast set thy mercy and thy honour at d. in thee,* Cor. V, 3, 201 (= set at variance). *vexed I am with passions of some d.* Caes. I, 2, 40 (= with conflicting affections).

Differency, dissimilarity: Cor. V, 4, 11 (F2. 3. 4 *difference*).

Different, 1) **unlike, dissimilar:** *much d. from the man he was,* Err. V, 46. *d. in blood,* Mids. I, 1, 135. John III, 4, 60. Rom. 1, 5, 92. II, 3, 14. Lr. IV, 3, 37.

2) **various, other, not the same:** *the sweet smell of d. flowers in odour and in hue,* Sonn. 98, 6. Compl. 125. Wiv. II, 1, 77. Tim. I, 1, 264. IV, 3, 257. Hml. III, 1, 179.

Difficult, hard, not easy: *it shall be full of poise and d. weight,* Oth. III, 3, 82 (i. e. a weight not easy to handle, or a heavy difficulty. Q1 *of poise and difficulty*).

Difficulty, hardness to be done, opposed to easiness: Meas. IV, 2, 221. All's IV, 3, 107. Troil. II, 2, 139. III, 2, 87. Oth. III, 3, 82 (Ff *difficult weight*). 397.

Diffidence, distrust, suspicion: *thou dost shame thy mother and wound her honour with this d.* John I, 65. *and of thy cunning had no d.* H6A III, 3, 10. *needless —s, banishment of friends,* Lr. I, 2, 161.

Diffuse, 1) to pour out, to scatter: *who with thy saffron wings upon my flowers —st honey-drops,* Tp. IV, 1, 79.

2) Partic. *diffused* = defused, q. v., wild, uncouth: *with some —d song,* Wiv. IV, 4, 54. (In H5 V, 2, 61; R3 I, 2, 78 and Lr. I, 4, 2 O. Edd. *defused*).

Dig (impf. and partic. *digged*) 1) to turn up the earth with a spade or other instrument: *you must d. with mattock and with spade,* Tit. IV, 3, 11. Hml. V, 1, 42. Cymb. IV, 2, 389. Transitively, to denote the result: *the adversary is digt himself four yard under the countermines,* H5 III, 2, 66 (Fluellen's speech).

2) to form by digging, to excavate: *his snout —s sepulchres,* Ven. 622. *deep trenches,* Sonn. 2, 2. R2 III, 3, 169. H4B IV, 5, 111. H6B IV, 10, 55. V, 1, 169. H6C V, 2, 21. Tit. II, 3, 270. Hml. V, 1, 141. With *up: if I —ed up thy forefathers' graves,* H6C I, 3, 27. Rom. V, 3, 6.

3) to gain by turning up the earth: *will d. thee pig-nuts,* Tp. II, 2, 172. H4A I, 3, 60. H6A I, 4, 45. Mcb. IV, 1, 25. With *up: oft have I —ed up dead men from their graves,* Tit. V, 1, 135.

4) to lower by digging: *who —s hills because they do aspire,* Per. I, 4, 5.

Digest, 1) to concoct in the stomach; properly and figuratively: *I do d. the poison of thy flesh,* Err. II, 2, 145. *it can never be they will d. this harsh indignity,* LLL V, 2, 289 (i. e. take up with it). *howsoe'er thou speakest, 'mong other things I shall d. it,* Merch. III, 5, 95. Tw. II, 4, 104. Wint. IV, 4, 12. H5 II, 2, 56. III, 6, 136. H8 III, 2, 53. Caes. I, 2, 305. IV, 3, 47. *with my two daughters' dowers d. this third,* Lr. I, 1, 130 (= enjoy it).

2) to reduce to nothing, as if by concoction: *my son* (sc. a son-in-law), *in whom my house's name must be —ed,* All's V, 3, 74. *linger your patience on, and we'll d. the abuse of distance,* H5 II Chor. 31.*d. your angry choler on your enemies,* H6A IV, 1, 167 (= void it on your enemies).

3) to dispose in due method, to arrange: *that we may d. our complots in some form,* R3 III, 1, 200. *starting thence away to what may be —ed in a play,* Troil. Prol. 29. *an excellent play, well —ed in the scenes,* Hml. II, 2, 460. *matters are so well —ed,* Ant. II, 2, 179 (O. Edd. *disgested*).

4) to comprehend, to understand: *examine their counsels and their cares, d. things rightly touching the weal o' the common,* Cor. I, 1, 154 (O. Edd. *disgest*). *how shall this bisson multitude d. the senate's courtesy,* III, 1, 131.

Digestion, the act of concocting food in the stomach; properly and tropically: Lucr. 699. Err. V, 74. R2 I, 3, 236. H5 V, 1, 27. H8 I, 4, 62. Troil. II, 2, 6. II, 3, 44. 120. Mcb. III, 4, 38.

Dighton, name in R3 IV, 3, 4. 9. 17.

Dignify, 1) to invest with honor, to exalt: *so shall these slaves be king, and thou their slave: thou nobly base, they basely —ed,* Lucr. 660. *she shall be —ed with this high honour, to bear my lady's train,* Gentl. II, 4, 158. *thou wert —ed enough, to be styled the under-hangman of his kingdom,* Cymb. II, 3, 132.

2) to give lustre to, to honour: *he that writes of you, if he can tell that you are you, so —es his story,* Sonn. 84, 8. *both truth and beauty on my love depends; so dost thou too, and therein —ed,* 101, 4. Gentl. I, 1, 64. All's II, 3, 133. H4B I, 1, 22. Troil. IV, 5, 103. Cor. II, 2, 89. Rom. II, 3, 22. Per. IV, 6, 42.

Dignity, 1) worthiness, worth, estimation, merit: *if that flower with base infection meet, the basest weed outbraves his d.* Sonn. 94, 12. *in her fair cheek, where several worthies make one d.* LLL IV, 3, 236. *things base and vile, holding no quantity, love can transpose to form and d.* Mids. I, 1, 233. *the great d. that his valour hath here acquired for him,* All's IV, 3, 80. *so he that doth redeem her* (honour) *thence might wear without corrival all her —ies,* H4A I, 3, 207. *this* (viz wisdom) *hath not a finger's d.* Troil. I, 3, 204. *it holds his estimate and d. as well wherein 'tis precious of itself as in the prizer,* II, 2, 54. *a cause that hath no mean dependance upon our joint and several —ies,* II, 2, 193. *from me, whose love was of that d. that it went hand in hand even with the vow,* Hml. I, 5, 48. *use them after your own honour and d.* II, 2, 557. *to throw Pompey the Great and all his —ies upon his son,* Ant. I, 2, 195. *immoment toys, things of such d. as we greet modern friends withal,* V, 2, 166. *clay and clay differs in d.* Cymb. IV, 2, 4. *Imogen, that best could deem his d.* V, 4, 57.

2) elevation, grandeur: *the d. of this act was worth the audience of kings,* Wint. V, 2, 86. *not unconsidered leave your honour, nor the d. of your office,* H8 I, 2, 16.

3) elevated rank, high office: *his hand, as proud of such a d., marched on ...,* Lucr. 437. *Prospero the prime duke, being so reputed in d.* Tp. I, 2, 73. *let none presume to wear an undeserved d.* Merch. II, 9, 40. Err. I, 1, 144. Wint. IV, 4, 486. V, 1, 183. John II, 490. H4A I, 1, 99. H4B V, 2, 93. H5 V, 2, 88. H6A V, 4, 132. H6B III, 2, 209. IV, 7, 40. R3 IV, 4, 246. 314. H8 II, 4, 227. Rom. Prol. 1. Mcb. V, 1, 62. Plural: Wint. I, 1, 27. H4B V, 3, 130. H6A I, 3, 50. H8 III, 1, 142. III, 2, 329. 379. Tim. V, 1, 145. Caes. III, 1, 178. Mcb. I, 6, 19. Cymb. V, 5, 22.

Emphatically, = sovereignty, royal power: *forget this new-fallen d.* As V, 4, 182. *my cloud of d. is held from falling with so weak a wind,* H4B IV, 5, 99. *not a thought but thinks on d.* H6B III, 1, 338. *I am resolved for death or d.* V, 1, 194. *take to your royal self this proffered benefit of d.* R3 III, 7, 196. *a dream of what thou wert, a breath, a bubble, a sign of d.* IV, 4, 89. *to the d. and height of honour,* 243.

Digress, 1) to deviate, to swerve: *I am come to keep my word, though in some part enforced to d.* Shr. III, 2, 109. *—ing from the valour of a man,* Rom. III, 3, 127.

2) to transgress, to offend: *thy —ing son,* R2 V, 3, 66. *I do d. too much, citing my worthless praise,* Tit. V, 3, 116.

Digression, 1) deviation, departure from the

main subject: *but this is mere d. from my purpose,* H4B IV, 1, 140.

2) transgression, offence: *my d. is so vile,* Lucr. 202. *that I may example my d. by some mighty precedent,* LLL I, 2, 121.

Dig-you-den, in the phrase '*God d.*' = give you good evening, LLL IV, 1, 42.

Dilate, vb. 1) to expand, to enlarge; part. —*d* = expansive: *thy wisdom which, like a bourn, a pale, a shore, confines thy spacious and —d parts,* Troil. II, 3, 261.

2) to relate at large, to enlarge upon: *d. at full what hath befallen of them,* Err. I, 1, 123. *that I would all my pilgrimage d.* Oth. I, 3, 153.

Dilated = detailed, copious, particular: *take a more —d farewell,* All's II, 1, 59. *more than the scope of these —d articles allow,* Hml. I, 2, 38 (Qq *delated*).

Dilatory, full of delays, tardy: *this d. sloth and tricks of Rome,* H8 II, 4, 237. *wit depends on d. time,* Oth. II, 3, 379.

Dildo, a burden in popular songs: *with such delicate burthens of —s and fadings,* Wint. IV, 4, 195.

Dilemma, a difficult choice, perplexing situation: *in perplexity and doubtful d.* Wiv. IV, 5, 87. *I will pen down my —s,* All's III, 6, 80.

Diligence, assiduity, due attention: *which being done with speedy d.* Lucr. 1853. *with whispering and most guilty d.* Meas. IV, 1, 39. *there wants no d. in seeking him,* Cymb. IV, 3, 20. *the search is made with all due d.* Per. III Prol. 19.

More especially, = assiduity in service, officiousness, serviceableness: *hence with d.* Tp. I, 2, 304. *he shall think by our true d. he is no less than what we say he is,* Shr. Ind. 1, 70. *your accustomed d. to me,* H6A V, 3, 9. *I will receive it with all d. of spirit,* Hml. V, 2, 94. *the best of me is d.* Lr. I, 4, 38. *if your d. be not speedy, I shall be there before you,* I, 5, 4. Abstr. pro concr.: *was't well done? Bravely, my d.* Tp. V, 241.

Diligent, assiduous, attentive (opposed to negligent): *hath into bondage brought my too d. ear,* Tp. III, 1, 42. *by d. discovery,* Lr. V, 1, 53. Especially = officious: *how d. I am to dress thy meat myself,* Shr. IV, 3, 39. *he knows you are too d.* Tim. III, 4, 40. *a d. follower of mine,* Cymb. III, 5, 121. *a page so kind, so duteous, d.* V, 5, 86.

Dim, adj. 1) not seeing clearly: *these eyes wax dim,* H6A II, 5, 9. H8 IV, 2, 164.

2) not easily penetrated by the eye, dusky: *d. darkness,* Lucr. 118. *mist,* 548. 643. 765. 1588. Wint. III, 3, 56. H4B IV, 5, 101. Tit. III, 1, 212. Rom. III, 5, 203. V, 3, 107. Caes. II, 1, 84.

3) lacklustre, wanting brightness; a) tarnished: *that fresh fair mirror, d. and old,* Lucr. 1760. — b) wanting the fresh aspect of life and health: *showing life's triumph in the map of death, and death's d. look in life's mortality,* Lucr. 403. *he will look as hollow as a ghost, as d. and meagre as an ague's fit,* John III, 4, 85. — c) wanting beauty, homely: *violets d., but sweeter than the lids of Juno's eyes,* Wint. IV, 4, 120.*

Dim, vb. 1) to impair the sight of, to hinder from seeing, either by dazzling or clouding the eyes: *her eyes are by his flaming torch —ed and controlled,* Lucr. 448. *some sudden qualm hath struck me at the heart and —ed mine eyes,* H6B I, 1, 55. I, 2, 6. III, 1, 218. H6C V, 2, 16.

2) to make invisible or less visible, to darken, to tarnish: *often is his* (the sun's) *gold complexion —ed,* Sonn. 18, 6. R2 III, 3, 66. R3 II, 2, 102. IV, 4, 16. Tit. IV, 4, 82. Figuratively: *let not sloth d. your honours new-begot,* H6A I, 1, 79. H6B I, 1, 125. And = to eclipse: *so doth the greater glory d. the less,* Merch. V, 93.

Dimension, body, bodily shape: *in d. and the shape of nature a gracious person,* Tw. I, 5, 280. *a spirit I am indeed, but am in that d. grossly clad which from the womb I did participate,* V, 244. In the plural, as it seems, = the single parts of the body: *hath not a Jew hands, organs, —s, senses, affections, passions?* Merch. III, 1, 62. *a' was so forlorn, that his —s to any thick sight were invincible,* H4B III, 2, 336. *my —s are as well compact,* Lr. I, 2, 7.

Diminish, vb. trans. 1) to lessen: Err. II, 2, 130. As V, 4, 145. Lr. IV, 6, 19.

2) to take from in a hurtful manner, to injure: *if springing things be any jot —ed, they wither in their prime,* Ven. 417. *your swords may as well wound the loud winds as d. one dowle that's in my plume,* Tp. III, 3, 64.

Diminution, the state of growing less: Ant. III, 13, 198. Cymb. I, 3, 18.

Diminutive, adj. very small: *spans and inches so d.* Troil. II, 2, 31. *the most d. of birds,* Mcb. IV, 2, 10.

Diminutive, subst. a most insignificant thing or person: *such waterflies, —s of nature,* Troil. V, 1, 38. *most monster-like, be shown for poorest —s, for dolts,* Ant. IV, 12, 37 (cf. *Comparative*).

Dimple, subst. a small cavity in the cheek or chin: Ven. 242. Wint. II, 3, 101.

Dimpled, set with dimples: *d. chin,* Lucr. 420. Troil. I, 2, 134. *boys,* Ant. II, 2, 207. *smiles,* Tim. IV, 3, 119.

Din, subst. loud noise: *beasts shall tremble at thy d.* Tp. I, 2, 371. II, 1, 314. Shr. I, 1, 178. I, 2, 200. Cor. II, 2, 119. III, 3, 20. Cymb. V, 4, 111. Per. III Prol. 2. *trumpeters, with brazen d. blast you the city's ear,* Ant. IV, 8, 36. *minstrelsy and pretty d.* Per. V, 2, 7.

Dine, to eat the chief meal of the day: Gentl. II, 1, 177. II, 4, 141. Wiv. III, 2, 56. Err. I, 2, 23. II, 1, 6. II, 2, 209. 221. III, 1, 40. IV, 1, 109 etc. LLL I, 1, 61. IV, 2, 159. Mids. IV, 2, 35. Merch. I, 3, 33. Shr. III, 2, 187. 197. IV, 3, 59. H6C II, 2, 128. R3 III, 4, 79. Cor. V, 1, 50. Rom. I, 1, 179. Caes. I, 2, 294. Oth. III, 3, 58 etc. *to d. and sup with water and bran,* Meas. IV, 3, 159. *the men are not yet cold, nor the bear half —d on the gentleman,* Wint. III, 3, 108 (the clown's speech). *when my lust hath —d,* Cymb. III, 5, 146.

Ding, a word imitating the song of birds: *when birds do sing, hey d. a. d. d.* As V, 3, 21.

Ding-dong, imitation of the sound of bells: Tp. I, 2, 403. 404. Merch. III, 2, 71.

Dining-chamber, a room to dine in: Gentl. IV, 4, 9. H4B II, 1, 154.

Dinner, the principal meal of the day: Tp. I, 2, 330. Gentl. I, 2, 131. II, 1, 30. Wiv. III, 3, 239. Meas. II, 1, 292. Err. I, 2, 75. II, 1, 5. II, 2, 189. Merch. I, 1, 104. II, 1, 44. III, 5, 52. IV, 1, 401. As II, 6, 18. III, 2, 102 (—*s*). Shr. I, 2, 218. H5 IV, 2, 57 (—*s*). H6A II, 4, 133. R3 III, 2, 122. Caes. I, 2, 296 etc. etc. *at d.*

Err. I, 2, 62. II, 2, 99. IV, 3, 69. V, 415. LLL V, 1, 3. Merch. IV, 2, 8. As IV, 1, 184. R3 III, 4, 96 etc. *we have a hot venison pasty to d.* Wiv. I, 1, 202. *shall 't be to-night at supper? to-morrow d.?* Oth. III, 3, 58. *the d. is on the table,* Wiv. I, 1, 270. *the d. attends you,* 279. *forward to the bridal d.* Shr. III, 2, 221.

Dinner-time: Gentl. I, 2, 67. II, 1, 176. Err. I, 2, 11. II, 1, 62. II, 2, 56. Merch. I, 1, 70. 105. Shr. IV, 3, 190. H4A III, 3, 222. *by to-morrow d.* II, 4, 564.

Dint, subst. impression: *as new-fallen snow takes any d.* Ven. 354. *you feel the d. of pity,* Caes. III, 2, 198. *By d. of* = by force of: *that by indictment and by d. of sword have since miscarried under Bolingbroke,* H4B IV, 1, 128. cf. *Undinted.*

Diomed, 1) one of the heroes before Troy: Troil. III, 3, 32. IV, 1, 10 etc. etc. 2) name in Ant. IV, 14, 114. 116. 128.

Diomede, the Greek hero: H6C IV, 2, 19.

Diomedes, the same: Troil. III, 3, 30. IV, 2, 67.

Dion, name in Wint. II, 1, 184. II, 3, 194. III, 2, 126.

Dionyza, female name in Per. I, 4, 1. IV Prol. 43 etc.

Dip, vb. tr. to plunge, to immerse: followed by *in: this cloth thou dippedst in blood,* H6C I, 4, 157. Tim. I, 2, 41. Caes. III, 2, 138. Hml. IV, 7, 19. 143. Absolutely: *who can call him his friend that —s in the same dish?* Tim. III, 2, 73.

Dire, dismal, dreadful, horrible: Ven. 975. 1159. Lucr. 972. Err. I, 1, 142. R2 I, 3, 127. V, 6, 16. H6A IV, 2, 41. R3 IV, 4, 5. 143. V, 3, 197 (*—st*). V, 5, 28. Troil. II, 2, 134. Tit. V, 2, 6. V, 3, 178. Rom. V, 3, 247, Mcb. I, 5, 44 (*—st*). II, 3, 63. IV, 3, 188. Hml. III, 2, 270. Oth. I, 1, 75. Cymb. IV, 2, 196.

Diréct, adj. (twice *díréct:* Tim. IV, 3, 20. Oth. I, 2, 86). 1) straight, right on: *hedge aside from the d. forthright,* Troil. III, 3, 158. *their consent of one d. way,* Cor. II, 3, 25.

2) plain, express: *yield me a d. answer,* Meas. IV, 2, 7. *the lie d.* As V, 4, 86. 91. 101. *there's nothing level in our cursed natures, but d. villany,* Tim. IV, 3, 20.

3) tending to an end as by a straight line or course, immediate: *by d. or indirect attempts,* Merch. IV, 1, 350. *in mine own d. knowledge,* All's III, 6, 9. *by d. or by collateral hand,* Hml. IV, 5, 206.

4) not brought about by irregular means, ordinary: *till fit time of law and course of d. session call thee to answer,* Oth. I, 2, 86.

5) honest, upright: *indirection thereby grows d.* John III, 1, 276. *be even and d. with me,* Hml. II, 2, 298. *to be d. and honest is not safe,* Oth. III, 3, 378.

Direct, vb. 1) to point or aim in a certain line: *and darkly bright (my eyes) are bright in dark —ed,* Sonn. 43, 4. *d. thy feet where thou and I may never meet,* Tw. V, 171. *d. mine arms I may embrace his neck,* H6A II, 5, 37. *may d. his course as please himself,* R3 II, 2, 129.

2) to mark out a way, to show, to address: *I have —ed you to wrong places,* Wiv. III, 1, 110. *d. me where Aufidius lies,* Cor. IV, 4, 7. *I was —ed hither,* Tim. IV, 3, 198. *d. me to him,* Hml. IV, 6, 33. *none want eyes to d. them the way,* Cymb. V, 4, 193. Used of letters and words: *was this —ed to you?* LLL IV,

2, 132. *to whom they are —ed,* H4A IV, 4, 4. *words sweetly placed and modestly —ed,* H6A V, 3, 179.

3) to lead, to guide, to regulate, to advise: *I am —ed by you,* Meas. IV, 3, 141. *some god d. my judgment,* Merch. II, 7, 13. *her gentle spirit commits itself to yours to be —ed,* III, 2, 166. *whom heavens —ing,* Wint. V, 3, 150. *be ready to d. these home alarms* R2 I, 1, 205. I, 3, 45. *d. not him whose way himself will choose,* II, 1, 29. *the duke is —ed by an Irishman,* H5 III, 2, 70. *they thus —ed, we will follow in the main battle,* R3 V, 3, 298 (cf. *Direction* 2). H8 I, 1, 147. Troil. V, 2, 110. Rom. I, 4, 113. Hml. I, 4, 91. Cymb. III, 4, 196. V, 4, 186.

4) to prescribe, to instruct, to assign: *I'll first d. my men what they shall do,* Wiv. IV, 2, 101. *she hath —ed how I shall take her from her father's house,* Merch. II, 4, 30. *we'll d. her how 'tis best to bear it,* All's III, 7, 20. *no further go in this than I by letters shall d. your course,* H4A I, 3, 293. *I'll d. thee how thou shalt escape,* H6A IV, 5, 10. Cor. II, 3, 51. *a letter which —ed him to seek her on the mountains,* Cymb. V, 5, 280. *your rule d. to any,* Per. I, 2, 109.

Direction, 1) aim, tendency: *makes it take head from all d., purpose, course, intent,* John II, 580. *by indirections find —s out,* Hml. II, 1, 66.

2) guidance, superintendence: *led by nice d. of a maiden's eyes,* Merch. II, 1, 14. *I do commit his youth to your d.* John IV, 2, 68. Troil. II, 3, 33. Mcb. IV, 3, 122. Used of military command: *if there be no better —s,* H5 III, 2, 68. 76. 84. 107 (Fluellen's speech). *call for some men of sound d.* R3 V, 3, 16. *'tis time to arm and give d.* 236. *a good d.* 302. *I have but an hour of love, of worldly matters and d.* Oth. I, 3, 300. *he is a soldier fit to stand by Caesar and give d.* II, 3, 128.

3) prescription, instruction, order: *men will kiss even by their own d.* Ven. 216. *they lack no d.* Wiv. III, 3, 19. Ado II, 1, 386. Merch. I, 3, 174. Shr. IV, 3, 117. Wint. IV, 4, 534. H4A II, 1, 56. R3 II, 2, 153. IV, 4, 225. Rom. II, 2, 79. Mcb. III, 3, 4 (*to the d.* = according to the d.; cf. *To*). Oth. II, 3, 4. Plur. *—s:* R2 II, 3, 35 (Ff *direction*). H4B V, 2, 121. H6B III, 2, 12.

Direction-giver, counsellor: Gentl. III, 2, 90.

Directitude, a word coined by a servant and not understood by his fellow-servant: Cor. IV, 5, 222. 223.

Directive, able to be directed: *swords and bows d. by the limbs,* Troil. I, 3, 356.

Directly, 1) in a straight line: *the path which shall d. lead thy foot to England's throne,* John III, 4, 129. *to wind, to stop, to run d. on,* Caes. IV, 1, 32. *which lead d. to the door of truth,* Oth. III, 3, 407.

2) just, exactly: *this concurs d. with the letter,* Tw. IV, 4, 73. *that you d. set me against Aufidius,* Cor. I, 6, 58. *stand you d. in Antonius' way,* Caes. I, 2, 3. *the high east stands, as the Capitol, d. here,* II, 1, 111. *'tis most sweet, when in one line two crafts d. meet,* Hml. III, 4, 210.

3) not by secondary means, straightforwardly: *indirectly and d. too thou hast contrived against the life of the defendant,* Merch. IV, 1, 359. *nor is't d. laid to thee, the death of the young prince,* Wint. III, 2, 195. *to counsel Cassio to this parallel course, d. to his good,* Oth. II, 3, 356.

4) without ambiguity, without further

ceremony: *whether that my angel be turned fiend,* *suspect I may, but not d. tell,* Sonn. 144, 10. *not take interest, not d. interest,* Merch. I, 3, 78. *answer me d. unto this question,* H4A II, 3, 89. H4B IV, 2, 52. Caes. I, 1, 12. III, 3, 10. 17. 21. 22. 25. *but d. to say I love you,* H5 V, 2, 130. *you would swear d. their very noses had been counsellors to Pepin,* H8 I, 3, 8. *he was too hard for him d.* Cor. IV, 5, 197. *who in want a hollow friend doth try, d. seasons him his enemy,* Hml. III, 2, 219. *I shall flying fight, rather d. fly,* Cymb. I, 6, 21.

5) honestly: *I have dealt most d. in thy affair,* Oth. IV, 2, 212. *that is, what villany soe'er I bid thee do, to perform it d. and truly,* Cymb. III, 5, 113.

6) manifestly: *Desdemona is d. in love with him,* Oth. II, 1, 221. *if you give me d. to understand you have prevailed,* Cymb. I, 4, 171.

7) straightways, immediately: *will she go now to bed? d.* Mcb. V, 1, 78.

Direful, dreadful, dismal: Ven. 98. Lucr. 741. Tp. I, 2, 26. R3 I, 2, 17. IV, 4, 85. Tit. V, 3, 144. Rom. V, 3, 225. Mcb. I, 2, 26. Oth. V, 1, 38.

Dire-lamenting, very mournful: *d. elegies,* Gentl. III, 2, 82.

Direness, horror: Mcb. V, 5, 14.

Dirge, funeral song: Lucr. 1612. Rom. IV, 5, 88. Hml. I, 2, 12.

Dirt, filth, mire: Shr. IV, 1, 59. 80. H6B IV, 1, 71. Hml. V, 1, 116. V, 2, 90. Lr. I, 4, 177. Cymb. III, 6, 54. *Paris is d. to him,* Troil. I, 2, 259. *to match us in comparisons with d.* I, 3, 194. *as ignorant as d.* Oth. V, 2, 164.

Dirt-rotten, changed to dirt by putrefaction: *d. livers,* Troil. V, 1, 23.

Dirty, adj. nasty, filthy: Mids. II, 2, 75. Tw. II, 4, 85. H4B V, 5, 38. H5 III, 5, 13. IV, 1, 47. Hml. V, 1, 110. Cymb. III, 6, 55.

Dis, the God Pluto: Tp. IV, 89. Wint. IV, 4, 118.

Disability, incapacity, unworthiness: Gentl. II, 4, 109 (or = disparagement?)

Disable, 1) to impair: *strength by limping sway —d,* Sonn. 66, 8. *how much I have —d mine estate,* Merch. I, 1, 123.

2) to disparage, to undervalue: *to be afeard of my deserving were but a weak —ing of myself,* Merch. II, 7, 30. *d. all the benefits of your own country,* As IV, 1, 34. *he —d my judgment,* V, 4, 80. *d. not thyself,* H6A V, 3, 67.*

Disadvantage, unfavourable state: H4B II, 3, 36. *we have at d. fought,* Cor. I, 6, 49.

Disagree, to be at variance: H6A IV, 1, 140.

Disallow, to refuse: *what follows if we d. of this?* John I, 16.

Disanimate, to discourage: H6A III, 1, 183.

Disannul, to annul, to cancel: Err. I, 1, 145. H6C III, 3, 81.

Disappointed, unfurnished, unprepared, unready, (cf. *Appoint* 3): *cut off even in the blossoms of my sin, unhousel'd, d., unanel'd,* Hml. I, 5, 77.

Disarm, to deprive or divest of arms: Sonn. 154, 8. Tp. I, 2, 472. Wiv. III, 1, 78. Troil. III, 1, 167.

Disaster, subst. 1) obnoxious planet: *stars with trains of fire and dews of blood, —s in the sun,* Hml. I, 1, 118.*

2) mischance, misfortune: All's I, 1, 187. III, 6, 55. IV, 3, 127. V, 3, 112. Troil. I, 3, 5. Mcb. III, 1, 112. Lr. I, 1, 177 (Qq *diseases*). I, 2, 131. Per. V, 1, 36.

Disaster, vb. to injure, rather blunderingly used by a servant in Ant. II, 7, 18: *holes where eyes should be, which pitifully d. the cheeks.*

Disastrous, unfortunate, calamitous: *d. chances,* Oth. I, 3, 134.

Disbench, to drive from the seat: *I hope my words —ed you not,* Cor. II, 2, 75.

Disbranch, to pull off, to slip off from a tree: *she that herself will sliver and d. from her material sap,* Lr. IV, 2, 34.

Disburse, to pay out: Lucr. 1203. Err. IV, 1, 38. LLL II, 132. R2 I, 1, 127. Mcb. I, 2, 61.

Disburthen, to unload, to disencumber: *ere't (my heart) be —ed with a liberal tongue,* R2 II, 1, 229.

Discandy, to thaw (cf. *Candy*): *by the —ing of this pelleted storm,* Ant. III, 13, 165 (O. Edd. *discandering*). *the hearts that spaniel'd me at heels ... do d., melt their sweets on blossoming Caesar,* IV, 12, 22.

Discard, to cast off, to expel: *welcome home again —ed faith,* John V, 4, 12. *I here d. my sickness,* Caes. II, 1, 321 (cf. *discharge* in Wint. II, 3, 11). *the fountain from the which my current runs, to be —ed thence!* Oth. IV, 2, 61. Especially, = to dismiss from service: Wiv. I, 3, 6. II, 1, 182. Tw. III, 4, 99. H4A IV, 2, 30. Used in contempt: H4A I, 3, 178. Lr. III, 4, 74.

Disease, to undress, to unmask: *I will d. me, and myself present as I was sometime Milan,* Tp. V, 85. *d. thee instantly,* Wint. IV, 4, 648.

Discern, 1) to distinguish: *I could d. no part of his face from the window,* H4B II, 2, 86. *an eye —ing thine honour from thy suffering,* Lr. IV, 2, 52.

2) to see, to perceive, to distinguish by the eye; a) absol.: *as far as I could well d. for smoke,* H6A II, 2, 26. *as I d., it burneth in the Capels' monument,* Rom. V, 3, 126. b) trans.: Lucr. 619. Wint. III, 3, 138. H6A III, 2, 24. Lr. II, 4, 151. Oth. II, 1, 1. III, 3, 102. Cymb. I, 6, 84. Per. V, 1, 116.

Discerner, judge, one who has the power of distinguishing: *no d. durst wag his tongue in censure,* H8 I, 1, 32.

Discerning, subst., intellectual faculty: *his —s are lethargied,* Lr. I, 4, 248.

Discharge, subst. 1) volley: *by d. of their artillery,* H4A I, 1, 57. Used of sighs: As II, 1, 37. Troil. IV, 4, 43.

2) payment: *will keep me here without d., money, or furniture,* H6B I, 3, 172. *of what's past, is, and to come, the d.* Cymb. V, 4, 173.

3) dismission from service: *thy soldiers have took their d.* Lr. V, 3, 105.

4) performance, execution: *an act whereof what's past is prologue, what to come in yours and my d.* Tp. II, 1, 254.

Discharge, vb. 1) to unburden, to deliver, to free: *I d. thee of thy prisoner,* Ado V, 1, 328. *d. yourself of our company,* H4B II, 4, 147 (quibbling; cf. v. 121. 123). *that the trunk may be —d of breath,* Rom. V, 1, 63.

2) to disembark: *the bark that hath —d her fraught,* Tit. I, 71. Figuratively: *infected minds to*

their deaf pillows will d. their secrets, Mcb. V, 1, 81 (but cf. def. 3).

3) to let off, to shoot: *—d cannon,* Lucr. 1043. *to d. their birding-pieces,* Wiv. IV, 2, 58. H8 V, 4, 47. Oth. II, 1, 56. Absolutely: *d. upon mine hostess,* H4B II, 4, 121. 123. III, 2, 280. Figuratively = to vent: *ere once she can d. one word of woe,* Lucr. 1605. *he did d. a horrible oath,* H8 I, 2, 206. cf. Mcb. V, 1, 81.

4) to dismiss: *after two days I will d. thee,* Tp. I, 2, 299. R2 III, 2, 211. H4B IV, 2, 61. 92. IV, 3, 137. H6C IV, 1, 109. V, 5, 87. Followed by *from: we here d. your grace from being regent,* H6B I, 1, 66. *he was from thence —d,* H8 II, 4, 34. By *of: I do d. you of your office,* Meas. V, 466. — Figuratively: *'tis hoped his sickness is —d,* Wint. II, 3, 11 (cf. *discard* in Caes. II, 1, 321).

4) to pay; used of sums owed as well as of creditors: *I will d. my bond,* Err. IV, 1, 13. *the money,* Merch. IV, 1, 208. *death can be paid but once, and that she has —d,* Ant. IV, 14, 28. *see him presently —d,* Err. IV, 1, 32. IV, 4, 122. Merch. III, 2, 276. Tim. II, 2, 12.

5) to perform: *the sun will set before I shall d. what I must strive to do,* Tp. III, 1, 22. *I will d. it in your straw-colour beard,* Mids. I, 2, 95. IV, 2, 8. V, 206. 368. All's I, 3, 127. H6B II, 4, 103. Troil. III, 2, 94. Cor. II, 3, 150. III, 2, 106. Cymb. III, 7, 16.

Disciple, subst. pupil, follower: *the devil and his —s,* H8 V, 3, 112.

Disciple, vb., to train, to teach: *and was —d of the bravest,* All's I, 2, 28.

Discipline, subst. 1) instruction: *this d. shows thou hast been in love,* Gentl. III, 2, 88. *we do admire this virtue and this moral d.* Shr. I, 1, 30 (cf. v. 18). *heaven bless thee from a tutor, and d. come not near thee,* Troil. II, 3, 32.

2) subjection to laws: H5 III, 6, 58 (Fluellen's speech). *thy acts in Ireland, in bringing them to civil d.* H6B I, 1, 195.

3) military skill and experience: *our chiefest men of d.* John II, 39. 261. 413. *O negligent and heedless d.* H6A IV, 2, 44. R3 III, 7, 16. V, 3, 17. Oth. II, 1, 275. Cymb. II, 4, 23. Often used by Captain Fluellen: H5 III, 2, 63. 76. 77. 86. 103. 107. III, 6, 12.

Discipline, vb. to train, to instruct: *—d, ay, dieted in grace,* Compl. 261. *he that —d thy arms to fight,* Troil. II, 3, 255. *has he —d Aufidius soundly?* Cor. II, 1, 139.

Disclaim, to disown, to disavow; absol.: *let my —ing from a purposed evil free me so far,* Hml. V, 2, 252. *nature —s in thee,* Lr. II, 2, 59 (cf. *In*).

Transitively: *I have —ed Sir Robert and my land,* John I, 247. R2 I, 1, 70. Cor. III, 1, 35. Tim. IV, 3, 490. Lr. I, 1, 115.

Disclose, vb., 1) to uncover, to unfold, to open: *when summer's breath their masked buds —s,* Sonn. 54, 8. Hml. I, 3, 40. Of eggs, = to hatch: *as patient as the female dove, when that her golden couplets are —d,* Hml. V, 1, 310.

2) to reveal: *that which thyself now hast —d to me,* Gentl. III, 1, 32. LLL II, 229. 251. V, 2, 467. All's I, 3, 195. R3 II, 4, 46. Caes. II, 1, 298. IV, 1, 46. Oth. II, 1, 157.

Disclose, subst., the hatch, production: *the hatch and the d. will be some danger,* Hml. III, 1, 174.

Discolour, to dye ill; mostly = to stain with blood: John II, 306. H5 III, 6, 171. H6B IV, 1, 11. Rom. V, 3, 143. = to make sallow: *with lank and lean —ed cheek,* Lucr. 708. = to put to the blush: *though it —s the complexion of my greatness to acknowledge it,* H4B II, 2, 5.

Discomfit, subst. discouragement (cf. *Recomfiture*): *uncurable d. reigns in the hearts of all our present parts,* H6B V, 2, 86.

Discomfit, vb. 1) to defeat: H4A I, 1, 67. III, 2, 114. H6B V, 1, 63.

2) to discourage: *go with me and be not so —ed,* Shr. II, 164 (cf. *Recomfiture*).

Discomfiture, defeat: H6A I, 1, 59.

Discomfort, subst. 1) want of hope, discouragement: *d. guides my tongue,* R2 III, 2, 65. Mcb. I, 2, 28.

2) uneasiness, sorrow: H4B I, 2, 118. Mcb. IV, 2, 29. Ant. IV, 2, 34.

Discomfort, vb. 1) to discourage: Troil. V, 10, 10. Caes. V, 3, 106. — 2) to make uneasy, to grieve: Hml. III, 2, 176.

Discomfortable, wanting hope? or discouraging? R2 III, 2, 36.

Discommend, to disapprove: Lr. II, 2, 116.

Disconsolate, desperate: Caes. V, 3, 55.

Discontent, subst. 1) dissatisfaction, vexation: *nor falls under the blow of thralled d. whereto the inviting time our fashion calls,* Sonn. 124, 7. *can you make no use of your d.?* Ado I, 3, 40. John III, 4, 179. IV, 2, 53. R2 IV, 331. Cymb. II, 3, 160. Plur. *—s:* Ven. 1161. John IV, 3, 151. H4A I, 3, 189. Applied to single persons: Tit. I, 443. Tim. V, 1, 227.

2) sorrow, grief: *losing her woes in shows of d.* Lucr. 1580. *why art thou thus attired in d.?* 1601. *not prizing her poor infant's d.* Sonn. 143, 8. Compl. 56. Pilgr. 142 (*thy d.* = mourning for thee?). Meas. IV, 1, 9. Shr. I, 1, 80. H6B III, 1, 201. III, 2, 301. H6C III, 3, 173. R3 I, 1, 1. Tit. I, 267. Tim. III, 4, 71.

3) a malcontent: *fickle changelings and poor —s,* H4A V, 1, 76. *to the ports the —s repair,* Ant. I, 4, 39.

Discontented, dissatisfied, out of humour: John IV, 2, 127. V, 1, 8. R2 III, 3, 63. H6A III, 1, 163. R3 IV, 2, 36. IV, 4, 312. V, 1, 7. H8 III, 2, 91. Cor. I, 1, 115. V, 1, 44. Tim. III, 5, 115. Ant. II, 6, 6. *here's another d. paper,* Oth. V, 2, 314 (a letter full of dissatisfaction).

Discontenting, being discontented, vexed: *your d. father strive to qualify,* Wint. IV, 4, 543.

Discontinue, to cease using, to give up, to leave: *I must d. your company,* Ado V, 1, 192. *I have —d a school above a twelvemonth,* Merch. III, 4, 75.

Discord, subst. 1) dissonance: Ven. 431. Mids. IV, 1, 123. As II, 7, 6. All's I, 1, 186. Plur. *—s:* H6C V, 6, 48. Rom. III, 1, 51. III, 5, 28.

2) dissension: Tp. IV, 1, 20. Err. I, 1, 5. John III, 1, 111. H4B II, 4, 61. H6A III, 1, 106. 194. IV, 1, 188. IV, 4, 22. V, 5, 63. Hml. IV, 1, 45. Lr. I, 2, 117. Plur. *—s:* Rom. V, 3, 294. Oth. II, 1, 200 (*make*). — = contradiction: *how shall we find the concord of this d.?* (viz lying in the words: tragical mirth) Mids. V, 60.

The two significations blent: Lucr. 1124. Troil. I, 3, 110. Tit. II, 1, 70.

Discordant, disagreeing: *the still d. wavering multitude,* H4B Ind. 19.

Discourse, subst. 1) conversation: *in their —s after supper,* Lucr. Arg. 6. *now no d., except it be of love,* Gentl. II, 4, 140. Ado III, 1, 5. R2 II, 3, 6. R3 V, 3, 99. Rom. III, 5, 53. Hml. III, 4, 118 *(hold).* Oth. III, 1, 55. Cymb. III, 6, 91. *your honesty should admit no d. to your beauty,* Hml. III, 1, 108.

2) that which one says or tells, speech, saying, tale: *a kind of excellent dumb d.* Tp. III, 3, 39. *which I'll waste with such d. . . . ,* V, 303. *I dare be bold with our d. to make your grace to smile,* Gentl. V, 4, 163. *are my —s dull?* Err. II, 1, 91. Ado I, 1, 288. *it is an epilogue or d., to make plain some obscure precedence,* LLL III, 82. Mids. IV, 1, 183. H6B I, 1, 104. H6C III, 3, 88. R3 III, 7, 19. Cor. IV, 5, 209. Tit. V, 1, 26. Oth. I, 3, 150. Followed by *of: leave off d. of disability,* Gentl. II, 4, 109 (= speak no more of etc.). *surprise her with d. of my dear faith,* Tw. I, 4, 25. *list his d. of war,* H5 I, 1, 43.

3) the art and manner of speaking and conversing: *my thoughts and my d. as madmen's are,* Sonn. 147, 11. *hear sweet d., converse with noblemen,* Gentl. I, 3, 31. *how likes she my d.?* V, 2, 15. *of excellent breeding, admirable d.* Wiv. II, 2, 235. *to affect speech and d.* Meas. I, 1, 4. *voluble and sharp d.* Err. II, 1, 92. *a wench of excellent d.* III, 1, 109. *of such enchanting presence and d.* III, 2, 166. *of good d.* Ado II, 3, 35. *so sweet and voluble is his d.* LLL II, 76. *his d. peremptory,* V, 1, 11. *d. will grow commendable in none only but parrots,* Merch. III, 5, 50. *beauty, good shape, d.* Troil. I, 2, 275. *put your d. into some frame,* Hml. III, 2, 320.

4) reasoning, thought, reflection: *when she will play with reason and d.* Meas. I, 2, 190. *yet doth this accident and flood of fortune so far exceed all instance, all d.* Tw. IV, 3, 12. *imagined worth holds in his blood such swoln and hot d.* Troil. II, 3, 183. *is your blood so madly hot that no d. of reason can qualify the same?* II, 2, 116. *O madness of d., that cause sets up with and against itself,* V, 2, 142. *a beast that wants d. of reason,* Hml. I, 2, 150. *he that made us with such large d., looking before and after,* IV, 4, 36. *either in d. of thought or actual deed,* Oth. IV, 2, 153 (Qq *d. or thought*).

Discourse, vb. 1) to speak; a) intr. *bid me d., I will enchant thine ear,* Ven. 145. *stand not to d.* Gentl. V, 2, 44. *it is the wittiest partition that ever I heard d.* Mids. V, 169. *it is no time to d.* H5 III, 2, 112. *her eye —s,* Rom. II, 2, 13. Followed by *of: when I d. of love and peace,* Gentl. V, 2, 17. Having after it an accus., to denote the result: *how shall we d. the freezing hours away,* Cymb. III, 3, 38.

b) trans.: *it will d. most eloquent music,* Hml. III, 2, 374. *d. fustian with one's shadow,* Oth. II, 3, 282.

2) to be affable and conversable: *she —s, she carves,* Wiv. I, 3, 49.

3) to relate, to tell; a) intr. *let lion etc. at large d.* Mids. V, 152. *d., I prithee, on this turret's top,* H6A I, 4, 26. Followed by *of:* Caes. III, 1, 295.

b) trans.: *hear at large —d all our fortunes,* Err. V, 395. *I am to d. wonders,* Mids. IV, 2, 29. *the manner of their taking may appear at large —d in this paper,* R2 V, 6, 10. *he did d. to Dido's ear the story,* Tit. V, 3, 81. *I'll then d. our woes,* Per. I, 4, 18.

Discourser, narrator, orator: H8 I, 1, 41.

Discoursive, in *Dumb-discoursive,* q. v.

Discourtesy, unkindness: *I shall unfold equal d. to your best kindness,* Cymb. II, 3, 101.

Discover, 1) to lay open to view: *daylight and champain —s not more,* Tw. II, 5, 173. *d. the several caskets to this noble prince,* Merch. II, 7, 1. *what good is covered with the face of heaven, to be —ed,* R3 IV, 4, 240.

2) to detect: *some offences that thou wouldst d.* Meas. II, 1, 195. Ado V, 1, 239. Tit. II, 3, 287.

3) to find out: *to d. islands far away,* Gentl. I, 3, 9. *I think I can d. him,* Oth. I, 1, 179.

4) to recognise: *Angelo hath seen them both, and will d. the favour,* Meas. IV, 2, 185. *then you should d. a brace of unmeriting magistrates,* Cor. II, 1, 46. *by no means I may d. them by any mark of favour,* Caes. II, 1, 75.

5) to reveal, to betray: *that which I would d., the law of friendship bids me to conceal,* Gentl. III, 1, 4. *I will open my lips in vain, or d. his government,* Meas. III, 1, 199. *he has —ed my design,* Wint. II, 1, 50. *I threatened to d. him,* Lr. II, 1, 68. Gentl. II, 1, 173. V, 4, 171. Wiv. II, 2, 190. Ado I, 2, 12. II, 3, 161. III, 2, 97. All's IV, 1, 80. IV, 3, 339. Wint. IV, 4, 742. H5 II, 2, 151. H6A V, 4, 60. H8 V, 3, 71. Troil. V, 2, 5. Tit. IV, 1, 74. V, 1, 85. Rom. II, 2, 106. Caes. III, 1, 17. Cymb. I, 6, 98. III, 5, 95. V, 5, 277. Absolutely: *that you have —ed thus,* Ado II, 2, 40 (*—ed this?*).

6) to show: *frame some feeling line that may d. such integrity,* Gentl. III, 2, 77. *so near the life of passion as she —s it,* Ado II, 3, 111. *when the oracle shall the contents d.* Wint. III, 1, 20. *most wisely hath Ulysses here —ed the fever,* Troil. I, 3, 138. Caes. I, 2, 69. Per. V Prol. 24. With a double accus.: *leaves nothing undone that may fully d. him their opposite,* Cor. II, 2, 23.

7) to tell: *d. how, and thou shalt find me just,* Err. V, 203. *d. more at large what cause that was,* H6A II, 5, 59. *I can d. all the unlucky manage of this fatal brawl,* Rom. III, 1, 147.

8) to espy, to reconnoitre: *we —ed two ships,* Err. I, 1, 92. *to d. what power the duke of York had levied there,* R2 II, 3, 33. H6A I, 4, 12. IV, 3, 6. Ant. IV, 10, 8. IV, 12, 2. Cymb. IV, 2, 130. Absolutely: *thou hast painfully —ed: are his files as full as thy report?* Tim. V, 2, 1.

Discoverer, scout, explorer: H4B IV, 1, 3.

Discovery, 1) the act of finding out or of bringing to light: *pretending in her —ies of dishonour,* Meas. III, 1, 246. *one inch of delay more is a South-sea of d.* As III, 2, 207 (i. e. a South-sea to be searched for discoveries). *he will for a week escape a great deal of —ies,* All's III, 6, 100. *by the d. we shall be shortened in our aim,* Cor. I, 2, 22. *so far from sounding and d.* Rom. I, 1, 157. = that which is brought to light: *to bring forth this d.* All's V, 3, 151.

2) the act of revealing, disclosure: *she dares not thereof make d.* Lucr. 1314. *do it so cunningly that my d. be not aimed at,* Gentl. III, 1, 45. *'tis an office of d.* Merch. II, 6, 43. *my fortunes which are here by this d. lost,* Wint. I, 2, 441. *at the d. of most dangerous treason,* H5 II, 2, 162. *so shall my anticipation prevent your d.* Hml. II, 2, 305 (= confession).

3) the act of espying or perceiving: *ambition cannot pierce a wink beyond, but doubt d. there,* Tp. II, 1, 243. *make d. err in report of us,* Mcb. V, 4,

6. *here is the guess of their true strength and forces by diligent d.* Lr. V, 1, 53.

4) the act of showing or bringing to view: *a satire against the softness of prosperity, with a d. of the infinite flatteries that follow youth and opulency,* Tim. V, 1, 37. The abstr. for the concr.: *confounded in the dark she lay, having lost the fair d. of her way,* Ven. 828 (i. e. him who showed, by whose light she perceived her way). — Doubtful passage: *and the rivelled fee-simple of the tetter take and take again such preposterous —ies,* Troil. V, 1, 28 (perhaps an indecent quibble between perception or sight and uncovering).*

Discredit, subst. disgrace: *it would not have relished among my other —s,* Wint. V, 2, 133.

Discredit, vb. 1) to deprive of credibility: *promises of life, which I have —ed to him,* Meas. III, 2, 261.

2) to bring into disgrace or disrepute: Meas. IV, 2, 30. John IV, 2, 33. Troil. I, 3, 195. IV, 5, 247. Ant. I, 2, 161. II, 2, 49.

Discreet, wise, judicious: Tw. I, 5, 103. IV, 3, 19. H4B II, 4, 272. Cor. III, 1, 150. Rom. I, 1, 199. Lr. I, 4, 233. Oth. II, 1, 227.

Discreetly, wisely: Shr. I, 1, 247. Misapplied by Evans for *Discretion:* Wiv. I, 1, 148.

Discretion, 1) good sense, common sense, reason, wisdom: *I will not adventure my d. so weakly,* Tp. II, 1, 188. *I have need of such a youth that can with some d. do my business,* Gentl. IV, 4, 70. *nor do I think the man of safe d. that does affect it,* Meas. I, 1, 72. Ado II, 3, 198. LLL V, 1, 78. V, 2, 734. Mids. V, 1, 235. 237. 239. 241. 257. Merch. III, 5, 70. H4A V, 4, 121. H5 II, 4, 38. H6A IV, 1, 158 (*—s*). H8 I, 1, 50. V, 3, 137. Troil. I, 2, 24. 273. Cor. I, 1, 206. Hml. I, 2, 5. II, 1, 117. II, 2, 489. III, 2, 19. Lr. II, 4, 151. Ant. II, 7, 11. Per. I, 3, 5. Misapplied by Evans: Wiv. I, 1, 44. 261. IV, 4, 1.

2) becoming regard, consideration: *old folks, you know, have d., as they say, and know the world,* Wiv. II, 2, 135. *they would have no more d. but to hang us,* Mids. I, 2, 83. *you do not use me with that affability as in d. you ought to use me,* H5 III, 2, 139. *let's teach ourselves that honourable stop, not to outsport d.* Oth. II, 3, 3.

Use thy d. = use thy pleasure, As I, 1, 152. *well, do your d.* Oth. III, 3, 34.

Discuss, to tell; a word used only by Nym, Pistol, Fluellen and such like persons: Wiv. I, 3, 104. IV, 5, 2. H5 III, 2, 65. IV, 1, 37. IV, 4, 5. 30.

Disdain, subst. 1) contempt, aversion: *barren hate, sour-eyed d. and discord,* Tp. IV, 1, 20. Ado I, 1, 119. 121. III, 1, 51. H6C IV, 1, 98. *to hold in d.:* Ven. 394. 761. H5 I, 2, 48. Especially contempt of love: *pouted in a dull d.* Ven. 33. 112. 241. 501. Lucr. 691. Sonn. 132, 2. 140, 2. Pilgr. 221. Gentl. I, 2, 112. As III, 4, 57. All's II, 3, 166. H6C III, 3, 127. Implying the idea of haughtiness and overbearing pride: *d. rather corrupt me ever,* All's II, 3, 122 (than to degrade myself thus). *pride, haughtiness, opinion and d.* H4A III, 1, 185. *ambitions, covetings, change of prides, d.* Cymb. II, 5, 25.

2) the state of being despised, ignominy: *reproach, d. and deadly enmity,* Lucr. 503. *thy kinsmen hang their heads at this d.* 521. *the d. and shame whereof hath ever since kept Hector fasting,* Troil. I,

2, 35 (unless it be here his wounded pride at being defeated by such a despised adversary).

Disdain, vb. 1) absol. = to be haughty, to show contempt: *therefore I will not d.* Wint. IV, 4, 774. *it shall be so, d. they ne'er so much,* H6A V, 3, 98. *where one part does d. with cause,* Cor. III, 1, 143.

2) tr. to think unworthy, to scorn, to treat with contempt; followed by an accus.: Ven. 358. Lucr. 844. 987. Sonn. 3, 6. 33, 13. Err. III, 1, 121. Ado I, 3, 30. Shr. II, 3. All's I, 2, 61. II, 3, 124. R2 V, 5, 83. H4B V, 2, 95. H6A I, 4, 32. H6B III, 1, 17. R3 III, 4, 85. Troil. I, 3, 129. V, 6, 15. Cor. I, 1, 264. I, 4, 26. Tit. III, 1, 71. Tim. IV, 3, 22. Mcb. I, 2, 17. Lr. V, 3, 145. 188. Cymb. I, 6, 147. III, 4, 20. III, 5, 75. V, 5, 105. Per. V, 1, 120. Followed by an inf.: *d. to him —ed scraps to give,* Lucr. 987. Gentl. II, 4, 162. H6B IV, 1, 88. R3 V, 3, 278. By a clause: *my heart —ed that my tongue should so profane the word,* R2 I, 4, 12. *which we d. should tetter us,* Cor. III, 1, 79.

Disdained, adj., disdainful: *revenge the jeering and d. contempt of this proud king,* H4A I, 3, 183.

Disdainful, contemptuous, haughty: Ado II, 1, 134. III, 1, 34. Mids. II, 1, 261. II, 2, 130. As III, 4, 53. Shr. IV, 2, 39. H5 III, 6, 118. Ant. III, 13, 142. Followed by an inf.: *d. to be tried by it,* H8 II, 4, 123.

Disdainfully, contemptuously: Lucr. 40. Troil. III, 3, 53.

Disease, subst. 1) any thing which causes uneasiness; vexation, trouble: *according to the fool's bolt, and such dulcet —s,* As V, 4, 68 (= such sweet mortifications). *in that ease, I'll tell thee my d.* H6A II, 5, 44. *thou d. of a friend, and not himself,* Tim. III, 1, 56. *to shield thee from —s of the world,* Lr. I, 1, 177 (Ff *disasters*).

2) disorder, illness: Sonn. 147, 2. Tp. II, 2, 3. Wiv. III, 3, 204. Meas. I, 2, 46. 53. Ado I, 1, 87. Mids. II, 1, 105. Merch. III, 1, 64. Shr. Ind. 1, 62. Shr. I, 2, 81. All's I, 1, 26. 243. Wint. I, 2, 207. 386. John III, 4, 112. H4B I, 2, 5. 136. 138. 266. 278. II, 4, 46. 49. H, 1, 39. III, 2, 192. IV, 1, 57. IV, 5, 64. V, 1, 85. H6B IV, 7, 94. H8 I, 1, 125. I, 3, 37. Troil. I, 21. V, 10, 57. Cor. III, 1, 222. 295. Tim. III, 1, 63. IV, 2, 14. IV, 3, 84. 539. Mcb. IV, 3, 146. V, 1, 65. V, 3, 51. Hml. IV, 1, 21. IV, 3, 9. Lr. I, 1, 167. II, 4, 225. Ant. V, 1, 37. Per. IV, 6, 105.

Disease, vb. to make uneasy, to put out of humour: *she will but d. our better mirth,* Cor. I, 3, 117. Writing of F2. 3. 4 in Mcb. V, 3, 21.

Diseased, sick: Sonn. 118, 8. 154, 12. Wint. I, 2, 297. H4A III, 1, 27. H4B III, 2, 191. IV, 1, 54. Tim. IV, 3, 207. Mcb. V, 3, 40. Hml. III, 2, 334. Cymb. I, 6, 123.

Disedge, to take off the edge of appetite, to surfeit: *when thou shalt be —d by her,* Cymb. III, 4, 96.

Disembark, to carry to land: Gentl. II, 4, 187. Oth. II, 1, 210.

Disfigure, to deform: Err. V, 183. LLL IV, 3, 59. Mids. I, 1, 51. Shr. I, 2, 114. John IV, 2, 22. R2 III, 1, 10. Misapplied: Mids. III, 1, 62.

Disfurnish, to deprive of means: *to d. myself against such a good time,* Tim. III, 2, 49. Followed by of, = to deprive: *of which if you should here* *d. me,* Gentl. IV, 1, 14. *she'll d. us of all our cavaliers,* Per. IV, 6, 12.

Disgest, writing of O Edd. for *digest* in Cor. I, 1, 154. Caes. I, 2, 305 and Ant. II, 2, 179.

Disgestion, writing of O. Edd. for *digestion* in H5 V, 1, 27.

Disgorge, to vomit: As II, 7, 69. Troil. Prol. 12. Per. III Prol. 48. Followed by *of,* = to empty by vomiting: *so didst thou d. thy glutton bosom of the royal Richard,* H4B I, 3, 97.

Disgrace, subst, the opposite of grace (q. v.); 1) a state of being out of favour: *in d. with fortune and men's eyes,* Sonn. 29, 1. *nor my own d.* R2 II, 1, 168. *Macduff lives in d.* Mcb. III, 6, 23 (also in IV, 2, 29?).

2) any thing that turns to the disparagement of a person; a) dishonour, shame: *every eye can see the same d.* Lucr. 751. *martyred with d.* 802. 827. 1320. Sonn. 127, 8. *thy grace being gained cures all d. in me,* Pilgr. 36 and LLL IV, 3, 67. Tp. IV, 209. All's II, 3, 249. R2 I, 1, 133. 194. H4B II, 2, 15. H6B I, 2, 49. H6C I, 1, 253. R3 III, 7, 217. Tit. IV, 2, 60. Rom. I, 1, 49. Ant. III, 7, 39. IV, 14, 66.

b) an offence, ill treatment, humiliation: *no man well of such a salve can speak that heals the wound and cures not the d.* Sonn. 34, 8. *like tears that did their own d. bewail,* Mids. IV, 1, 61. *his d. is to be called boy,* LLL I, 2, 186. *I will take it as a sweet d.* H4B I, 1, 89. *the d. we have digested,* H5 III, 6, 135. 140. *and in d. bespoke him thus,* H6A IV, 6, 20. *have laid —s on my head,* H6B III, 1, 162. *you shall sustain moe new —s,* H8 III, 2, 5. *pray heaven, he sound not my d.* V, 2, 13. *that in their country did them that d.* Troil. II, 2, 95. Cor. I, 1, 97.

c) a state of being abashed, of being exposed to contempt; discredit: *the red rose blush at her own d.* Lucr. 479. *look in your glass, and there appears a face that overgoes my poor invention quite, dulling my lines and doing me d.* Sonn. 103, 8. *or brook such d. well as he shall run into,* As I, 1, 140. *if thou dost him any slight d.* 155. *—s have of late knocked too often at my door,* All's IV, 1, 31. *I have forgot my part, and I am out, even to a full d.* Cor. V, 3, 42.

d) dejected state, fall, overthrow, calamity: *till we have brought Duke Humphrey in d.* H6B I, 3, 99. *how eagerly ye follow my —s,* H8 III, 2, 240.

e) any thing misbecoming in behaviour or appearance: *this deep d. in brotherhood,* R3 I, 1, 111. *it would be my d. and your discomfort,* Mcb. IV, 2, 29 (perhaps: I should shed tears, which would not become me). *parcel the sum of my —s by addition of his envy,* Ant. V, 2, 163. Hence = disfigurement: (the sun) *stealing unseen to west with this d.* (viz of being hidden by clouds) Sonn. 33, 8. *let fame ... grace us in the d. of death,* LLL I, 1, 3.

Disgrace, vb. 1) to put out of favour: *your grace is welcome to a man —d,* Gentl. V, 4, 123. *—d me in my happy victories,* H4A IV, 3, 97. R3 I, 3, 79.

2) to dishonour: Ven. 412. Lucr. 718. 1833. Gentl. III, 1, 29. Wiv. IV, 4, 16. Ado III, 2, 130. IV, 2, 56. V, 1, 245. Merch. III, 1, 56. As II, 4, 4. R2 I, 1, 170. H6A I, 5, 8. III, 1, 99. III, 4, 29. V, 5, 48. H6C IV, 3, 32. R3 IV, 4, 371. Tim. III, 3, 13. *so —d a part* (= disgraceful) Wint. I, 2, 188.

3) to discredit, to baffle, to lower in estimation: *right perfection wrongfully – d,* Sonn. 66, 7. *thou canst not d. me half so ill, as I'll myself d.* 89, 5. 7. *that her skill may time d. and wretched minutes kill,* 126, 8. *words are very rascals since bonds —d them,* Tw. III, 1, 25. *who came off bravely, who —d,* H5 III, 6, 77. *we shall much d. the name of Agincourt,* IV Chor. 49. *let it not d. me, if I demand ...,* V, 2, 31. *if the trial of the law o'ertake ye, you'll part away —d,* H8 III, 1, 97.

Disgraceful, unbecoming: *away with these d. wailing robes!* H6A I, 1, 86.

Disgracious, wanting grace, not finding grace in another's eyes: *that seems d. in the city's eyes,* R3 III, 7, 112. *if I be so d. in your sight,* IV, 4, 177.

Disguise, subst. false appearance; 1) a dress intended to conceal a person: Gentl. V, 4, 107. Wiv. II, 1, 246. IV, 6, 21. Ado I, 1, 323. III, 2, 33. Shr. IV, 2, 18. Tw. I, 2, 54. II, 2, 28. H4A II, 2, 78. Lr. V, 3, 219.

2) false show, deceitful semblance: *so d. shall by the disguised pay with falsehood false exacting,* Meas. III, 2, 294; cf. All's IV, 2, 75. *when his d. and he is parted,* III, 6, 112.

3) the state of being inflamed with wine: *the wild d. hath almost anticked us all,* Ant. II, 7, 131.

Disguise, vb. 1) to hide by any counterfeit appearance: *her cheeks with chaps and wrinkles were —d; of what she was no semblance did remain,* Lucr. 1452. *so disguise shall by the —d* etc. Meas. III, 2, 294. *known unto these and to myself —d,* Err. II, 2, 216. John IV, 1, 127. H5 III, 1, 8. Troil. II, 3, 136. Mcb. III, 2, 35. Cymb. III, 4, 147.

2) to conceal by an unusual dress: Lucr. 1815. Gentl. II, 6, 37. Wiv. IV, 2, 69. 70. Err. I, 2, 101. LLL V, 2, 83. 96. 301. 303. 433. Merch. II, 4, 2. As I, 1, 131. Shr. I, 2, 132. III, 1, 33. Wint. IV, 2, 61. John IV, 3, 4. H6B IV, 1, 48. Rom. III, 3, 168. Per. IV, 6, 18.

Disguiser, he who, or that which changes appearance and prevents recognition: *death's a great d.* Meas. IV, 2, 186.

Dish, subst. 1) a vessel in which food is served up: Tp. II, 2, 187. Meas. II, 1, 95. 96. 97. 98. 103. LLL IV, 3, 82. As III, 3, 37. Shr. IV, 3, 65. R2 III, 3, 150. Troil. II, 3, 129. Tim. III, 2, 73. III, 6, 55. *a d. of stewed prunes,* Wiv. I, 1, 296. *a d. of doves,* Merch. II, 2, 144. *of skim milk,* H4A II, 3, 35. *of butter,* II, 4, 134. *of prawns,* H4B II, 1, 104. *of apple-johns,* II, 4, 5. *of caraways,* V, 3, 3. *of leather-coats,* 44. *thou full d. of fool,* Troil. V, 1, 10. *my d. of chastity,* Per. IV, 6, 160. (= table? Cymb. IV, 2, 35.)

2) the meat served up in such a vessel; a particular kind of food: Wiv. III, 5, 121. Err. III, 1, 23. Ado II, 1, 283. II, 3, 23. Shr. IV, 3, 24. 44. Tw. II, 5, 123. Wint. IV, 3, 8. Tim. IV, 3, 299. Caes. II, 1, 173. Hml. III, 2, 99. IV, 3, 26. Oth. III, 3, 78. Ant. II, 6, 134. V, 2, 275. Cymb. II, 3, 119. V, 4, 158.

Dish, vb. to serve up at table: *for conspiracy, I know not how it tastes, though it be —ed for me to try how,* Wint. III, 2, 73.

Dishabit, vb. to dislodge: *those sleeping stones ... from their fixed bed of lime had been —ed,* John II, 220.

Dishclout, a cloth used for washing and wiping dishes: LLL V, 2, 720. *Romeo is a d. to him*, Rom. III, 5, 221.

Dishearten, to discourage, to depress: H5 IV, 1, 117. Mcb. II, 3, 37.

Dishevelled, not bound up, flowing, loose: *with long d. hair*, Ven. 147. Lucr. 1129.

Dishonest, 1) dishonourable: Meas. III, 1, 137. V, 262. As V, 3, 4. Tw. III, 4, 420. IV, 2, 35.

2) unchaste, lewd: Wiv. III, 3, 196. IV, 2, 104. Tw. I, 5, 46.°49. 51. H5 I, 2, 49.

Dishonestly, without good faith: Err. V, 3. Cymb. IV, 2, 40.

Dishonesty, 1) want of probity: Ado II, 2, 10. — 2) baseness: Tw. III, 4, 421. Wint. II, 3, 47. — 3) lewdness: Wiv. IV, 2, 140.

Dishonour, subst., disgrace, ignominy: Lucr. 198. 621. 654. 844. Tp. III, 1, 27. IV, 209. Meas. III, 1, 236. 246. V, 385. All's III, 6, 59. Wint. II, 3, 13. R2 I, 1, 169. V, 3, 70. H4A I, 1, 85. H6B II, 3, 18. III, 1, 298. IV, 1, 39. H6C III, 2, 9. III, 3, 9. 75. H8 II, 3, 4. Troil. IV, 1, 59. Cor. III, 1, 157. III, 2, 124. Tit. I, 13. II, 1, 56. Tim. I, 1, 157. Caes. IV, 3, 109. Mcb. IV, 3, 29 *(—s)*. Ant. III, 11, 54. IV, 14, 56. Cymb. III, 4, 32. III, 5, 63.

Dishonour, vb. to disgrace, to blast with infamy: Lucr. 1185. 1186. Meas. IV, 4, 34. V, 22. Err. V, 199. Ado IV, 1, 65. 304. V, 1, 44. Wint. I, 2, 455. R2 IV, 21. H5 III, 1, 22. H6A III, 1, 9. III, 2, 90. IV, 5, 14. V, 3, 102. H6B II, 1, 199. H6C III, 3, 184. IV, 1, 33. R3 IV, 4, 367. 375. Cor. III, 2, 58. III, 3, 60. IV, 6, 83. Tit. I, 295. 303. 340. 345. 385. 425. 432. 435. IV, 1, 90. Rom. IV, 3, 26. Hml. II, 1, 21. Per. I, 2, 21.

Dishonourable, destitute of honour, shameful: R2 IV, 65. H4B IV, 2, 26. H6A I, 1, 20. Rom. III, 1, 76. Caes. I, 2, 138.

Adverbially: *more d. ragged than an old faced ancient*, H4A IV, 2, 33.

Dishonoured, adj. dishonourable: *nor has Coriolanus deserved this d. rub*, Cor. III, 1, 60. *no unchaste action or d. step*, Lr. I, 1, 231.

Dishorn, to strip of horns: *d. the spirit*, Wiv. IV, 4, 63.

Disinherit, to deprive of an inheritance: H6C I, 1, 193. 225. 226. 250. II, 2, 24. R3 I, 1, 57.

Disjoin, 1) tr. to part, to sunder: *—ing hands*, John III, 1, 197. 262. *scattered and —ed from fellowship*, III, 4, 3. *it —s remorse from power*, Caes. II, 1, 18.

2) intr. to part, to rid one's self: *till breathless he —ed*, Ven. 541.

Disjoint, to fall out of joint, to fall to pieces: *let the frame of things d.* Mcb. III, 2, 16. Not inflected in the partic.: *thinking our state to be d. and out of frame*, Hml. I, 2, 20.

Disjunction, separation: Wint. IV, 4, 540.

Dislike, subst. 1) disapprobation: *d. of our proceedings kept the earl from hence*, H4A IV, 1, 64.

2) displeasure, disfavour: *in pain of your d.* H6B III, 2, 257. *your —s doth cloud my joys*, H6C IV, 1, 73 (M. Edd. *dislike*). *in fear to kindle your d.* H8 II, 4, 25. *for no d. against the person of the good queen*, 223.

3) dissension, discord: *I have not sought the day of this d.* H4A V, 1, 26. *you feed too much on*

this d. Troil. II, 3, 236. *each fancy, each complaint, d.* Lr. I, 4, 348.

Dislike, vb. 1) to disapprove, to regard with ill-will or disgust; a) tr.: Meas. I, 2, 18. Merch. I, 2, 26. As V, 4, 73. All's II, 3, 129. Tw. I, 5, 119. Cor. II, 2, 25. Hml. V, 2, 227. Lr. IV, 2, 10. Ant. II, 2, 113.

b) absol.: *with a heavy, dark, —ing eye*, Ven. 182. *not minding whether I d. or no*, Per. II, 5, 20. Followed by *of*: *thou —st of virtue*, All's II, 3, 130.

2) to displease: *if either thee d.* Rom. II, 2, 61 (Q1 *displease*). *it —s me*, Oth. II, 3, 49.

Disliken, to make unlike, to disguise: *d. the truth of your own seeming*, Wint. IV, 4, 666.

Dislimn, to efface, to blot: *that which is now a horse, even with a thought the rack —s*, Ant. IV, 14, 10.

Dislocate, to disjoint: *to d. and tear thy flesh and bones*, Lr. IV, 2, 65.

Dislodge, vb. intr. to retire, to march off: *the Volscians are —d, and Marcius gone*, Cor. V, 4, 44.

Disloyal, faithless, false, especially to a sovereign or to the marriage bed: Gentl. IV, 2, 95. Ado III, 2, 107. 111. Wint. II, 3, 203. Mcb. I, 2, 52. Oth. III, 3, 121. 409. Cymb. I, 1, 131. III, 2, 6. Followed by *to*: R2 I, 3, 114. V, 2, 105. Cymb. III, 4, 33.

Disloyalty, want of fidelity in love: Err. III, 2, 11. Ado II, 2, 49.

Dismal, striking the mind with sorrow or dismay: *be this d. sight the closing up of our most wretched eyes*, Tit. III, 1, 262. *this torture should be roared in d. hell*, Rom. III, 2, 44. *my d. scene I needs must act alone*, IV, 3, 19. *my fell of hair would at a d. treatise rouse and stir*, Mcb. V, 5, 12. *the sight is d.* Hml. V, 2, 378.

More especially = ill-boding, fatal: *this d. cry* (of the hounds) *rings sadly in her ear*, Ven. 889. *I am wrapped in d. thinkings*, All's V, 3, 128. *and Bolingbroke my sorrow's d. heir*, R2 II, 2, 63. *a raven's note, whose d. tune bereft my vital powers*, H6B IV, 2, 41. *like to a d. clangor heard afar*, H6C II, 3, 18. *his* (the screech-owl's) *d. threatening sound*, II, 6, 58. *chattering pies in d. discords sung*, V, 6, 48. *so full of d. terror was the time* (of sleep) R3 I, 4, 7. *for more slander to thy d. seat* (Pomfret), R3 III, 3, 13. *a d. yew*, Tit. II, 3, 107. *a joyless, d., black and sorrowful issue*, IV, 2, 67. *unto a d. and a fatal end*, Mcb. III, 5, 21. *smeared with heraldry more d.* Hml. II, 2, 478. *this ornament makes me look d.* Per. V, 3, 74. *a d. fight*, H6A I, 1, 105; cf. *Norway began a d. conflict*, Mcb. I, 2, 53.

Superl. *dismallest*: Tit. I, 384 and II, 3, 204.

Dismal-dreaming, full of ill-boding dreams: *and drives away dark d. night*, Pilgr. 200.

Dismantle, to strip; properly and figuratively: *muffle your face, d. you*, Wint. IV, 4, 666. *this realm —d was of Jove himself*, Hml. III, 2, 293. *to d. so many folds of favour*, Lr. I, 1, 220.

Dismask, to divest of a mask: LLL V, 2, 296.

Dismay, subst. fear, apprehension: Tp. V, 14. Merch. I, 3, 181. III, 2, 61. Hml. IV, 1, 45.

Dismay, vb. 1) tr. to fill with fear and apprehension: *she shall not d. me*, Wiv. III, 4, 27. *—ed not this our captains?* Mcb. I, 2, 33. Partic. *—ed*: Ven. 896. Lucr. 273. Tp. IV, 147. Wiv. III,

4, 26. LLL V, 2, 570. Merch. V, 9. H6A I, 2, 50. II, 3, 73. R3 V, 3, 174. Cor. IV, 6, 150. Oth. V, 2, 269.

2) intr. to take fright: *d. not, princes, at this accident*, H6A III, 3, 1.

Disme, the tenth: *every tithe soul, 'mongst many thousand —s, hath been as dear as Helen*, Troil. II, 2, 19.

Dismember, to tear limb from limb, to dilacerate: John III, 1, 330. Rom. III, 3, 134. Caes. II, 1, 170.

Dismiss, 1) to let go, to send away: LLL IV, 3, 209. Wint. V, 1, 164. H6A II, 5, 30. H6B IV, 9, 21. H6C III, 2, 78. Cor. II, 3, 162. IV, 2, 7. V, 1, 66. Mcb. IV, 1, 72. Oth. IV, 3, 8. 14. Reflectively: *life never lacks power to d. itself*, Caes. I, 3, 97.

2) to discard from an office or service: Meas. IV, 2, 27. R2 III, 3, 78. H4A IV, 3, 100. Lr. II, 4, 207. 210. Used of an army, = to disband: John V, 1, 64. H4A IV, 4, 37. H4B IV, 2, 96. H6A V, 4, 173. H6B IV, 9, 40. V, 1, 44. Cor. V, 3, 82. Tit. I, 44. 53.

3) to send away from court, to adjourn: *I may d. this court*, Merch. IV, 1, 104. *d. the controversy bleeding*, Cor. II, 1, 85.

4) to reject, to refuse: *the —ed bachelor*, Tp. IV, 1, 67. *to d. it* (the suit) Tw. I, 5, 117.

5) to discontinue: *d. your vows, your feigned tears*, Ven. 425.

6) to remit, to pardon: *a —ed offence*, Meas. II, 2, 102.

Dismission, 1) discharge from an office: Ant. I, 1, 26. — 2) rejection, refusal of a love-suit: *save when command to your d. tends*, Cymb. II, 3, 57.

Dismount, 1) to alight from a horse: Tit. II, 3, 76. V, 2, 54.

2) to throw down (from a horse): *your horse would trot as well, were some of your brags —ed*, H5 III, 7, 84.

3) to remove cannon from their carriages; hence: *d. thy tuck* (= draw thy rapier from the scabbard), Tw. III, 4, 244. Figuratively: *his eyes he did d.* Compl. 281; cf. v. 22.

Disnatured, unnatural: Lr. I, 4, 305.

Disobedience, 1) want of observance due to lawful authority: Wiv. V, 5, 240. Wint. III, 2, 69. H4A I, 3, 16. H6A IV, 1, 142. Cor. III, 1, 117. Followed by *to*: *d. to your father's will*, Mids. I, 1, 87. By *against*: *my d. 'gainst the king my father*, Cymb. III, 4, 91.

2) irreverence to parents, undutifulness: *to speak on the part of virginity, is to accuse your mothers: which is most infallible d.* All's I, 1, 150.

Disobedient, not observant of lawful authority: Gentl. III, 1, 69. Troil. II, 2, 182. Rom. III, 5, 161. IV, 2, 18.

Disobey, to refuse to do what is commanded; absol.: R3 I, 2, 37. trans.: Tp. IV, 1, 77. H5 IV, 1, 152. H6A V, 4, 170.

Disorbed, unsphered: *like a star d.* Troil. II, 2, 46.

Disorder, subst. 1) want of order, confusion: John III, 4, 102. R2 IV, 142. H5 IV, 5, 17. H6B V, 2, 32. Troil. I, 3, 95. Cymb. V, 2, 15.

2) discomposure, derangement of the

mental functions: *the marrow-eating sickness whose attaint d. breeds by heating of the blood*, Ven. 742. *you have displaced the mirth with most admired d.* Mcb. III, 4, 110.

3) offence, misconduct: *she's nothing allied to your —s*, Tw. II, 3, 105. *machination, hollowness, treachery, and all ruinous —s*, Lr. I, 2, 123. *his own —s deserved much less advancement*, II, 4, 202.

Disordered, 1) deranged, confused, irregular: Mids. V, 126. R2 III, 4, 46. 48. V, 5, 46. H5 V, 2, 44.

2) deranged in habits, of bad conduct: *men so d., so deboshed and bold*, Lr. I, 4, 263. 277.

Disorderly, deranged, confused: *to order these affairs thus thrust d. into my hands*, R2 II, 2, 110.

Disparage, to speak contemptuously of, to vilify: *I will d. her no farther till you are my witnesses*, Ado III, 2, 131. *d. not the faith thou dost not know*, Mids. III, 2, 174.

Disparagement, offence, injury: *committed —s unto you*, Wiv. I, 1, 31 (Evans' speech). *do him d.* Rom. I, 5, 72. *passed sentence may not be recalled but to our honour's great d.* Err. I, 1, 149.

Dispark, to treat (a private park) as a common (by divesting it of its enclosures etc.): *—ed my parks and felled my forest woods*, R2 III, 1, 23.

Dispatch, subst. 1) a sending away: *the words of your commission will tie you to the numbers and the time of their d.* Cymb. III, 7, 16.

2) the getting rid of sth., doing away: *what needed, then, that terrible d. of it into your pocket!* Lr. I, 2, 33 (terrible = fearful).

3) the finishing or winding up of a business: *to have a d. of complaints*, Meas. IV, 4, 14. *serious business, craving quick d.* LLL II, 31. *take and give back affairs and their d.* Tw. IV, 3, 18. *the business that seeks d. by day*, H8 V, 1, 16. *let's hence and hear how the d. is made*, Cor. I, 1, 281. *you shall put this night's great business into my d.* Mcb. I, 5, 69. Almost = business: *after some d. in hand at court, thither we bend again*, All's III, 2, 56. *and between these main parcels of d. effected many nicer needs*, IV, 3, 104.

4) decisive answer given: *to-day we shall have our d.* LLL IV, 1, 5. *yet give us our d.* Cor. V, 3, 180. *the several messengers from hence attend d.* Lr. II, 1, 127.

5) *Swift d.* = speed, haste: *makes all swift d. in pursuit of the thing*, Sonn. 143, 3. H5 II, 4, 6. *write from us to him, post-post-haste d.* Oth. I, 3, 46.

Dispatch, vb., 1) to send: *Lucrece hastily —eth messengers*, Lucr. Arg. 17. Gentl. I, 3, 38. All's III, 4, 34. Wint. II, 1, 182. John I, 99. V, 7, 90. R2 II, 2, 103. III, 1, 40. H6A IV, 4, 40. Cor. I, 7, 2. Tim. II, 2, 196. Hml. I, 2, 33.

2) to make ready for going, and then to prepare in general: *d. me hence*, Gentl. II, 7, 88. *d. you with your safest haste and get you from our court*, As I, 3, 43. *whilst a field should be —ed and fought, you are disputing of your generals*, H6A I, 1, 72.

3) to finish, to wind up (a business); a) absol.: *have you —ed?* Wiv. V, 5, 189. *we'll d. indeed*, Ant. V, 2, 230. Followed by *with*, = to come to an agreement: *d. with Angelo, that it may be quickly*, Meas. III, 1, 278. *they have —ed with Pompey*, Ant. III, 2, 2.

b) trans.: *d. it quickly*, Wiv. V, 3, 3. Meas. IV, 3, 82. *d. all business*, Merch. III, 2, 325. Shr. Ind. I, 129. All's IV, 3, 98. R3 I, 3, 341 (Qq *to d. this deed*, Ff *to d. this thing*). I, 4, 278 (Qq *performed*). IV, 2, 84 (Ff *I will d. it straight; Qq 'tis done, my gracious lord*). Tit. III, 1, 193. Hml. III, 3, 3. Oth. I, 3, 148. Ant. II, 2, 168. Cymb. I, 3, 39. *will you d. us here under this tree?* As III, 3, 66 (i. e. marry us).

4) to satisfy, to answer decisively: *d. us with all speed*, H5 II, 4, 141. *you shall be soon —ed*, 144. *they are well —ed*, Per. II, 5, 15.

5) to put to death: R2 III, 1, 35. H6B III, 2, 2. 6. H6C V, 5, 69. R3 I, 3, 341 (Ff *to d. this thing*, Qq *to d. this deed*). Cor. III, 1, 286. Tit. IV, 2, 86. Rom. V, 1, 79. Mcb. III, 4, 15. Lr. IV, 5, 12. Ant. IV, 14, 104. Absolutely: *therefore I will be sudden and d.* John IV, 1, 27. *nay, now d.* R3 I, 2, 182.* *and found — d.!* Lr. II, 1, 60. *I am sworn and will d.* Per. IV, 1, 92. — Followed by *of,* = to deprive of by death, to tear away from by death: *thus was I sleeping, by a brother's hand of life, of crown, of queen, at once —ed*, Hml. I, 5, 75 (*of* = from; cf. *Of*).

6) to make haste: *and now d. we toward the court*, H4B IV, 3, 82. Mostly in the imper. *dispatch* = be quick, make haste: Gentl. V, 2, 48. Wiv. IV, 2, 112. Meas. IV, 3, 96. Err. IV, 1, 52. Mids. IV, 1, 113. Wint. IV, 4, 654. R2 IV, 243. H4B II, 4, 14. V, 5, 4. H6B II, 3, 94. R3 I, 3, 356. III, 3, 8. III, 4, 96. 104. Cor. V, 6, 8. Mcb. V, 3, 50. Oth. IV, 2, 30. IV, 3, 33. Ant. III, 12, 26. IV, 4, 15. IV, 5, 17. V, 2, 309. 325. Cymb. I, 5, 3. III, 4, 98.

Dispensation, 1) exemption from law, granting of a license: *a d. may be had*, H6A V, 3, 86.

2) a tampering with sth., a specious pretence for evading a duty, a plausible excuse: *and with good thoughts makes d., urging the worser sense for vantage still*, Lucr. 248. *he rather means to lodge you in the field, than seek a d. for his oath*, LLL II, 87.

Dispense, to come to easy terms, to tamper with: *d. with trifles*, Wiv. II, 1, 47. *we must of force d. with this decree*, LLL I, 1, 148. *how shall we then d. with that contract*, H6A V, 5, 28. *canst thou d. with heaven for such an oath?* H6B V, 1, 181. Hence = to do without, to spare: *might you d. with your leisure, I would by and by have some speech with you*, Meas. III, 1, 154. *men must learn now with pity to d.* Tim. III, 2, 93. And = to excuse, to pardon: *and with my trespass never will d.* Lucr. 1070. *with my fault I thus far can d.* 1279. *may my poor mind with the foul act d.* 1704. *mark how with my neglect I do d.* Sonn. 112, 12. *nature —s with the deed so far that it becomes a virtue*, Meas. III, 1, 135. *unfeeling fools can with such wrongs d.* Err. II, 1, 103.

Disperse, 1) to scatter, to drive asunder: *in troops I have —d them 'bout the isle*, Tp. I, 2, 220. *the fleet which I —d*, 233. R2 II, 3, 27. III, 2, 74. III, 3, 2. H4B IV, 2, 102. H6B IV, 9, 34. R3 IV, 4, 523. Joined with *scatter: our soldiers, scattered and —ed*, H6A II, 1, 76. R3 IV, 4, 513. Tit. V, 2, 78. Reflectively: *we will d. ourselves*, R2 II, 4, 4. H6B V, 1, 45. Caes. II, 1, 222.

2) to dissipate, to make to vanish: *thy sea within a puddle's womb is hearsed, and not the puddle in thy sea —d*, Lucr. 658. *—d those vapours*, Err. I, 1, 90. *—d are the glories*, H6A I, 2, 137. H6C V, 3, 10. H8 III, 1, 2.

3) to spread: *every alien pen hath got my use and under thee their poesy d.* Sonn. 78, 4. *those tongues that durst d. it* (the rumour) H8 II, 1, 153. *poison such as will d. itself through all the veins*, Rom. V, 1, 61. *the —d air*, Lucr. 1805 (= spreading everywhere).

4) intr. a) to be scattered, to separate: *away, d.* Wiv. V, 5, 78. b) to vanish: *a circle in the water, which never ceaseth to enlarge itself, till by broad spreading it d. to nought*, H6A I, 2, 135.

Dispiteous, pitiless: John IV, 1, 34.

Displace, 1) to remove from the proper place: *to d. it* (the corner-stone) *with your little finger*, Cor. V, 4, 4. *he would d. our heads where they grow, and set them on Lud's town*, Cymb. IV, 2, 122.

2) to depose: H4B IV, 5, 209. H6B I, 1, 177.

3) to cancel, to banish: *thou plantest scandal and —st laud*, Lucr. 887. *you have —d the mirth*, Mcb. III, 4, 109.

Displant, 1) to transplant, to transpose: *unless philosophy can make a Juliet, d. a town, reverse a prince's doom*, Rom. III, 3, 59.

2) to depose: *whose qualification shall come into no true taste again but by the —ing of Cassio*, Oth. II, 1, 283.

Display, vb. 1) to unfold, to open, to spread wide: *when his gaudy banner is —ed*, Lucr. 272. cf. John II, 309. 320. Per. I, 4, 72. *till sable Night upon the world dim darkness doth d.* Lucr. 118. *whose fair flower being once —ed*, Tw. II, 4, 40. *his hands abroad —ed*, H6B III, 2, 172.

2) to show openly: *light's ... which they will at once d. to the night*, Wiv. V, 3, 17. *these black masks proclaim an enshield beauty ten times louder than beauty could —ed*, Meas. II, 4, 81. *with visages —ed*, LLL V, 2, 144. *and to sun's parching heat —ed my cheeks*, H6A I, 2, 77.

3) to show in general: *and —ed the effects of disposition gentle*, H8 II, 4, 86. *d. at last, what God will have discovered*, Tit. IV, 1, 73.

4) intr. to bristle up, to look big: *the very fellow that of late —ed so saucily against your highness*, Lr. II, 4, 41.

Displease, not to meet with approbation, to be disagreeable, to offend: absol.: *—ing service*, H4A III, 2, 5. *—ing play*, H4B V, 5, 125. Trans.: Meas. IV, 1, 13. Mids. III, 2, 54. Shr. I, 1, 76. H4A I, 3, 122. Rom. III, 5, 232. Caes. I, 2, 262. Oth. IV, 3, 17.

Displeased = discontented, offended: —ed: Gentl. II, 7, 66. Err. II, 2, 19. Merch. V, 213. H6B I, 1, 155 (*at*). R3 II, 2, 89. Tit. I, 270 (*with*).

Displeasure, 1) dislike, disfavour, hate: *this may prove food to my d.* Ado I, 3, 68. *I am sick in d. to him*, II, 2, 6. All's V, 2, 6. 22. V, 3, 235. Wint. II, 3, 45. IV, 4, 444. H4B V, 5, 117. H5 IV, 1, 211. H8 II, 4, 20. III, 2, 23. 392. Cor. II, 2, 24. IV, 5, 78. Lr. I, 1, 202. III, 3, 5. Oth. III, 3, 43. Ant. III, 4, 34. Per. II, 5, 54. Plur. *—s:* All's V, 3, 63 (and H5 IV, 7, 38 in Fluellen's speech). *to incur a person's d.:* All's IV, 3, 11. Cymb. I, 1, 103. *to run into d.:* All's II, 5, 38. H8 I, 2, 110. *to take d.* or *a d.:* Tp. IV, 202 (in the sense of anger). As I, 2, 290. Per. I, 3, 21. *d. against a p.:* Tp. IV, 202. As I, 2, 290. All's IV, 5, 80. *d. at:* Per. I, 3, 21. *to:* Ado II, 2, 6. *your d.* = the disfavour you are in: H8 III, 2, 392. Oth. III, 1, 45. *though I should win your* *d. to entreat me to it,* Lr. II, 2, 119 (scornfully opposed to the title *'your grace'*). Used as a masc.: *run to meet d. farther from the doors, and grapple with him ere he comes so nigh,* John V, 1, 60.

2) **anger, indignation:** *if I should take a d. against you,* Tp. IV, 202. *you would abate the strength of your d.* Merch. V, 198. Troil. V, 2, 37. Rom. III, 1, 160. Tim. III, 5, 87. Lr. I, 2, 172. 177. II, 2, 125. III, 7, 6. Oth. II, 1, 154. III, 4, 128.

3) **that which displeases, offence:** *hast thou delight to see a wretched man do outrage and d. to himself?* Err. IV, 4, 119. *doing d. to the citizens by rushing in their houses,* V, 142.

Disponge, see *Dispunge.*

Disport, subst. **sport, pastime:** Lucr. Arg. 11. Oth. I, 3, 272.

Disport, vb. refl. **to amuse one's self:** *to d. himself,* H6C IV, 5, 8. Tim. I, 2, 141.

Dispose, subst. 1) **disposal:** *all that is mine I leave at thy d.* Gentl. II, 7, 86. *which, with ourselves, all rest at thy d.* IV, 1, 76. *his goods confiscate to the duke's d.* Err. I, 1, 21. *needs must you lay your heart at his d.* John I, 263.

2) **disposition, temper:** *carries on the stream of his d. in will peculiar,* Troil. II, 3, 174. *he hath a person and a smooth d. to be suspected,* Oth. I, 3, 403.

Dispose, vb. 1) **to arrange, to regulate;** a) absol.: *where they* (her eyes) *resign their office and their light to the —ing of her troubled brain,* Ven. 1040. *put his cause and quarrel to the —ing of the cardinal,* John V, 7, 92. *you did suspect she had —d with Caesar,* Ant. IV, 14, 123 (= settled matters). b) trans.: *how thou pleasest, God, d. the day,* H5 IV, 3, 132. *all was royal: to the —ing of it nought rebelled,* H8 I, 1, 43.

2) **to bring to bear, to make the best of:** *so hot a speed with such advice —d,* John III, 4, 11. *four or five most vile and ragged foils, right ill —d in brawl ridiculous,* H5 IV Chor. 50. *when these so noble benefits shall prove not well —ed,* H8 I, 2, 116. *his blows are well —d,* Troil. IV, 5, 116.

3) **to apply or turn to a certain place or purpose, to bestow, to use, to do with;** a) tr. *the mariners say how thou hast —d,* Tp. I, 2, 225. *the children thus —d,* Err. I, 1, 84. *tell me how thou hast —d thy charge,* I, 2, 73. *now to the Goths, there to d. this treasure,* Tit. IV, 2, 173. *we intend so to d. you as yourself shall give us counsel,* Ant. V, 2, 186.

b) With *of: d. of them as thou knowest their deserts,* Gentl. V, 4, 159. *my daughter is —d of,* Wiv. III, 4, 74. Ado V, 1, 303. R2 II, 2, 117. H4A V, 5, 24. H5 III, 3, 49. IV, 1, 149. IV, 7, 85. Cor. IV, 7, 40. Caes. III, 1, 178. Lr. V, 3, 76. The purpose or place indicated: *d. of her to some more fitter place,* Meas. II, 2, 16. *as she is mine, I may d. of her, which shall be either to this gentleman or to her death,* Mids. I, 1, 42. *I'll d. of thee among a sisterhood,* Rom. V, 3, 156.

c) Reflectively, = to do, to go (by): *to your own bents d. you,* Wint. I, 2, 179. *by whose letters I'll d. myself,* Per. I, 2, 117.

4) **to make inclined:** *there is an idle banquet attends you: please you to d. yourselves,* Tim. I, 2, 161 (i. e. to fall to). *—ed* = inclined: *—d to set me light,* Sonn. 88, 1. *to sleep,* Tp. II, 1, 202. H4B IV, 5, 17. *to be merry,* As IV, 1, 156. *to stir your hearts,* Caes. III, 2, 127. *to swear,* Cymb. II, 1, 11. *to mirth,* Ant.

I, 2, 86. Cymb. I, 6, 58. And = affected, tempered: *to see how Fortune is —d to us,* H4A IV, 1, 38. *he's —d as the hateful raven,* H6B III, 1, 76. Cor. III, 2, 22. Caes. I, 2, 314.

Disposed, absolutely, = inclined to merriment: *Boyet is —d,* LLL II, 250. *to make my lady laugh when she's —d,* V, 2, 466. *he does well enough if he be —d,* Tw. II, 3, 88. cf. *Ill-disposed.*

Disposer, perhaps one who may dispose of another, who can bring him to do anything: *my d. Cressida,* Troil. III, 1, 95. 98. 101.

Disposition, 1) **arrangement, settlement:** *I crave fit d. for my wife,* Oth. I, 3, 237.

2) **inclination:** *I have a great —s to cry,* Wiv. III, 1, 22 (Evans' speech). *Orlando hath a d. to come in,* As I, 1, 131. *the king, of* (Ff *on*) *his own royal d., and not provoked by any suitor else,* R3 I, 3, 63. *let him wave thus, to express his d., and follow Marcius,* Cor. I, 6, 74. *how stands your d. to be married?* Rom. I, 3, 65.

3) **humour, mood, caprice:** *now I will be your Rosalind in a more coming-on d.* As IV, 1, 113. *this drum sticks sorely in your d.* All's III, 6, 47. *which will now be so unsuitable to her d.* Tw. II, 5, 221. *grace and good d. attend your ladyship!* III, 1, 146. *entertain a cheerful d.* R2 II, 2, 4. *it goes so heavily with my d.* Hml. II, 2, 309. *let his d. have that scope that dotage gives it,* Lr. I, 4, 314. *O well divided d.!* Ant. I, 5, 53. Plural: *lesser had been the thwartings of your —s,* Cor. III, 2, 21. *if our father carry authority with such —s as he bears,* Lr. I, 1, 309 (Ff *d.*) *put away these —s that of late transform you from what you rightly are,* I, 4, 242.

4) **natural constitution of the mind, temper, character, sentiments:** *the warrant I have of your honourable d.* Lucr. Dedic. 2. Lucr. 1695. *his d. would have gone to the truth of his words,* Wiv. II, 1, 61. *the villanous inconstancy of man's d.* Wiv. IV, 5, 111. *I do it not in evil d., but from Lord Angelo by special charge,* Meas. I, 2, 122. *of what d. was the duke?* III, 2, 244. *he is of a very melancholy d.* Ado II, 1, 6. *the base, though bitter d. of Beatrice,* 215. *my father's rough and envious d.* As I, 2, 253. *of churlish d.* II, 4, 80. *dost thou think I have a doublet and hose in my d.?* III, 2, 206. *the royal d. of that beast,* IV, 3, 118. *guiltless and of free d.* Tw. I, 5, 99. *against thy better d.* Wint. III, 3, 28. *this robe of mine does change my d.* IV, 4, 135. *displayed the effects of d. gentle,* H8 II, 4, 87. *the true knowledge he hath in their d.* Cor. II, 2, 15. *away, my d., and possess me some harlot's spirit!* III, 2, 111. *I thought thy d. better tempered,* Rom. III, 3, 115. *strange even to the d. that I owe,* Mcb. III, 4, 113. *a truant d.* Hml. I, 2, 169. *with much forcing of his d.* III, 1, 12. *his goatish d.* Lr. I, 2, 138. *whose d. will not be rubbed,* II, 2, 160. *your brother's evil d.* III, 5, 7. *I fear your d.* IV, 2, 31. *so blessed a d.* Oth. II, 3, 326. *as they pinch one another by the d.* Ant. II, 7, 8 (i. e. by their foible; a servant's speech). Plural: *her —s she inherits,* All's I, 1, 47. *give your —s the reins,* Cor. II, 1, 33.

5) **nature, quality in general, manner of thinking and acting:** *to practise his judgment with the d. of natures,* Meas. III, 1, 165. *the bitter d. of the time will have it so,* Troil. IV, 1, 48. *shall think meet to put an antic d. on,* Hml. I, 5, 172. *so horribly to shake our d. with thoughts,* I, 4, 55. *I know our country d. well,* Oth. III, 3, 201.

Dispossess, to deprive of possession: *d. the soul of thy grandam*, Tw. IV, 2, 64. *to d. that child*, John I, 131. Tim. I, 1, 139. With *of* = to deprive of: Meas. II, 4, 22. John IV, 3, 23.

Dispraise, subst., blame, censure: Gentl. III, 2, 47. LLL IV, 3, 264. Tim. I, 1, 165.

Dispraise, vb., to blame, to censure; absol.: Sonn. 95, 7. Transit.: Gentl. III, 2, 55. IV, 4, 107. H4A V, 2, 60. H4B II, 4, 341. 346. H5 V, 2, 213. Troil. I, 1, 46. IV, 1, 76. Rom. III, 5, 237. Ant. II, 5, 107. Cymb. V, 5, 173.

Dispraisingly, with blame: Oth. III, 3, 72.

Disprize, to undervalue, to despise: *—ing the knight opposed*, Troil. IV, 5, 74 (Q *misprizing*). *the pangs of —d love*, Hml. III, 1, 72 (Qq *despised*).

Disproperty, to take away: *—ied their freedoms*, Cor. II, 1, 264.

Disproportion, subst., inconsistency, irregularity, unnatural tendency: *a will most rank, foul d., thoughts unnatural*, Oth. III, 3, 233 (Ff *—s*). cf. *Proportion*.

Disproportion, vb. (to deprive of symmetry) to disfigure: *to d. me in every part, like to a chaos, or an unlicked bear-whelp*, H6C III, 2, 160. *he is as —ed in his manners as in his shape*, Tp. V, 290.

Disproportioned = contradictory, inconsistent: *there is no composition in these news that gives them credit. Indeed, they are —ed*, Oth. I, 3, 2.

Disprove, to gainsay, to refute: Gentl. V, 4, 66. Meas. V, 161. H6C I, 1, 89. Caes. III, 2, 105. Oth. V, 2, 172. Cymb. IV, 2, 34.

Dispunge, to pour down: *the poisonous damp of night d. upon me*, Ant. IV, 9, 13 (M. Edd. *disponge*; cf. *Spongy*).

Dispurse, to disburse, to pay: H6B III, 1, 117 (F4 *disbursed*).

Disputable, disputatious: *he is too d. for my company*, As II, 5, 36.

Disputation, 1) controversy, debate, discussion: *thus, graceless, holds he d. 'tween frozen conscience and hot-burning will*, Lucr. 246. *if that (my good name) be made a theme for d., the branches of another root are rotted*, 822. *so she holds d. with each thing she views*, 1101 (v. 1093: *thus cavils she with every thing she sees*). *say to great Caesar this in d., I kiss his conquering hand*, Ant. III, 13, 74 (perhaps = say to Caesar this as the plea which I put in. M. Edd. *this: in deputation*).

2) conversation: *I understand thy kisses and thou mine, and that's a feeling d.* H4A III, 1, 206. cf. H5 III, 2, 101 (Fluellen's speech).

Dispute, vb. 1) intr. a) to contend by argument, to altercate: *you are —ing of your generals*, H6A I, 1, 73. *d. not with her; she is lunatic*, R3 I, 3, 254. *I'll have 't —d on*, Oth. I, 2, 75.

b) to argue, to reason: *thou —st like an infant*, LLL V, 1, 69. *though my soul —s well with my sense, that this may be some error, but no madness*, Tw. IV, 3, 9. *let me d. with thee of thy estate*, Rom. III, 3, 63.

2) trans. a) to call in question: *whether your grace be worthy, yea or no, d. not that: York is the worthier*, H6B I, 3, 111.

b) to discuss, to reason upon: *can he know man from man? d. his own estate?* Wint. IV, 4, 411. *d. it like a man. I shall do so, but I must also feel it as a man*, Mcb. IV, 3, 220.

Disquantity, vb. to diminish: *to d. your train*, Lr. I, 4, 270.

Disquiet, subst. uneasiness, vexation: Ado II, 1, 268. Ant. II, 2, 70 (*did you too much d.*).

Disquiet, adj. being in a passion, impatient: *be not so d.: the meat was well*, Shr. IV, 1, 171.

Disquietly, in a manner destroying tranquillity and ease: *machinations, hollowness, treachery, and all ruinous disorders, follow us d. to our graves*, Lr. I, 2, 124.

Disrelish, vb. to loathe: Oth. II, 1, 236.

Disrobe, to divest, to strip: *d. the images*, Caes. I, 1, 69. With *of*: *d. the lion of that robe*, John II, 142. *I'll d. me of these Italian weeds*, Cymb. V, 1, 22.

Disseat, to unseat, to dethrone; only by conjecture in Mcb. V, 3, 21; F1 *dis-eate*, F2.3.4. *disease*.

Dissemble, 1) intr. a) to assume a false appearance: Ven. 641. Wiv. III, 3, 152. As III, 4, 7. Shr. II, 9. Tw. IV, 2, 7. V, 167. H6A III, 1, 140. IV, 1, 63. H6B V, 1, 13. R3 I, 2, 237. II, 2, 31. Troil. V, 4, 8. Tim. V, 1, 98. Oth. III, 4, 34. Ant. I, 3, 79. Cymb. I, 1, 84. *I would d. with my nature*, Cor. III, 2, 62 (i. e. I would be hypocritical to myself). — Sometimes, seemingly, = to be false in any way: *—ing villain, thou art false in both. —ing harlot, thou art false in all*, Err. IV, 4, 103. 104. *all —ing set aside, tell me for truth the measure of his love*, H6C III, 3, 119. *that —ing abominable varlet Diomed*, Troil. V, 4, 2. And so perhaps in R3 I, 1, 19: *cheated of feature by —ing nature* (but it may be: nature which in other cases knows so well to feign and to hide a bad mind by a fair show).

b) to give a false appearance: *what wicked and —ing glass of mine made me compare with Hermia's sphery eyne?* Mids. II, 2, 98.

2) tr. a) to hide by a false appearance: *—d her delight*, Pilgr. 314. 336. *or both d. deeply their affections*, Shr. IV, 4, 42. *d. not your hatred, swear your love*, R3 II, 1, 8 (= do not gloss it over). Tit. I, 438. 443. Per. II, 5, 23.

b) to make unrecognizable, to disguise: *I will d. myself in it*, Tw. IV, 2, 5.

Dissembler, hypocrite: Ado V, 1, 53. R3 I, 2, 185. Rom. III, 2, 87.

Dissembly, Dogberry's word for *assembly*: Ado IV, 2, 1.

Dissension, disagreement, discord: Ven. 1160. Mids. II, 1, 116. H5 IV, 8, 70. H6A III, 1, 33. 72. 189. IV, 1, 116. 139. V, 5, 84. H6C IV, 6, 40. *on a d. of a doit*, Cor. IV, 4, 17.

Dissentious, apt to breed discord, seditious: Ven. 657. H6A III, 1, 15. R3 I, 3, 46. Cor. I, 1, 167. IV, 6, 7.

Dissever, to separate: All's II, 1, 125. Wint. V, 3, 155. John II, 388.

Dissipation, dissolution: *d. of cohorts*, Lr. I, 2, 161. Only in Qq.

Dissolute, wanton, lewd, debauched: Wiv. III, 3, 204. R2 V, 3, 12. 20.

Dissolutely, lewdly: H4A I, 2, 39. Misapplied by Slender: Wiv. I, 1, 260. 262.

Dissolution, 1) melting, liquefaction: *against love's fire fear's frost hath d.* Lucr. 355. *a man of continual d. and thaw*, Wiv. III, 5, 118.

2) separation, division: —*s of ancient amities*, Lr. I, 2, 158.

3) death, destruction: *there is so great a fever on goodness, that the d. of it must cure it*, Meas. III, 2, 236. *reproach and d. hangeth over him*, R2 II, 1, 258.

Dissolve, 1) trans. a) to melt: *as if the world were all —d to tears*, R2 III, 2, 108.

b) to loose, to undo: *who quickly would d. the bands of life*, R2 II, 2, 71. *the bonds of heaven are slipped, —d and loosed*, Troil. V, 2, 156 (cf. *Indissoluble*).

c) to put an end to, to destroy: *lest his ungoverned rage d. the life*, Lr. IV, 4, 19.

d) to separate: *nothing can d. us*, Wiv. V, 5, 237. —*d from my hive*, All's I, 2, 66. *they are —d*, Cor. I, 1, 208.

2) intr. a) to be melted: *my smooth moist hand would in thy palm d.* Ven. 144. *what wax so frozen but —s with tempering*, 565. Lucr. 592. Gentl. III, 2, 8. Mids. I, 1, 245. R2 V, 1, 9. Lr. V, 3, 203 (*I am ready to d.*, i. e. to tears). Ant. III, 13, 162. V, 2, 302.

b) to fade away, so fall to nothing: *the charm —s apace*, Tp. V, 64. *all shall d.* IV, 154. Misapplied by Slender: Wiv. I, 1, 259.

Dissuade, 1) to divert by reasons: *I would fain d. him*, As I, 2, 170. With *from*: Sonn. 141, 10. Ado II, 1, 171. As I, 1, 147. All's II, 3, 215. Lr. II, 1, 66. Cymb. V, 5, 463.

2) to speak against, to counteract: *example cannot for all that d. succession*, All's III, 5, 25.

Distaff, the staff from which the flax is drawn in spinning: Tw. I, 3, 109. Wint. I, 2, 37. Lr. IV, 2, 17. *could have turned a d. to a lance*, Cymb. V, 3, 34, i. e. women to men.

Distaff-woman, a spinner: R2 III, 2, 118.

Distain, to stain, to defile: (cf. *Tear-distained*): *the silver-shining queen he would d.* Lucr. 786. *you having lands, and blest with beauteous wives, they would restrain the one, d. the other*, R3 V, 3, 322. *the worthiness of praise —s his worth, if that the praised himself bring the praise forth*, Troil. I, 3, 241. In Err. II, 2, 148: *I live —ed, thou undishonoured*, Heath's emendation '*thou dishonoured*' speaks for itself. In Per. IV, 3, 31 M. Edd. *she did d. my child*; O. Edd. *disdain*.

Distance, subst. 1) intervening space, remoteness: Sonn. 44, 2. Phoen. 30. Wiv. II, 1, 109. Meas. I, 4, 54. H5 II Chor. 32. Per. I, 2, 10. *hold a long d.* All's III, 2, 27. Mcb. III, 6, 44. *fell off a d. from her*, H8 IV, 1, 65. *to meet his grace just d. 'tween our armies*, H4B IV, 1, 226. Technical term for the space kept between two antagonists in fencing: Wiv. II, 1, 233. II, 3, 27. Rom. II, 4, 22. Quibbling in All's V, 3, 212.

2) alienation: *so is he mine* (viz enemy) *and in such bloody d., that every minute of his being thrusts against my nearest of life*, Mcb. III, 1, 115.

3) cautious restraint, reserve: *with safest d. I mine honour shielded*, Compl. 151. *kept cold d.* 237. *she knew her d. and did angle for me*, All's V, 3, 212. *hold their honours in a wary d.* Oth. II, 3, 58. *in a politic d.* III, 3, 13.

Distant, remote: Mids. II, 2, 60. Hml. II, 1, 13. Per. II, 1, 111. III, 4, 13. Misapplied: Meas. II, 1, 94.

Distaste, vb. 1) intr. to be unsavoury, to be distasteful: *a single famished kiss, —ing with the salt of broken tears*, Troil. IV, 4, 50 (Qq *distasted*). *poisons, which at the first are scarce found to d.* Oth. III, 3, 327.

2) tr. a) to make distasteful, to embitter: *her brain-sick raptures cannot d. the goodness of a quarrel*, Troil. II, 2, 123. —*ed with the salt of broken tears*, IV, 4, 50 (Ff *distasting*).

b) to disrelish, to loathe, to dislike: *although my will d. what it elected*, Troil. II, 2, 66. *if he d. it, let him to our sister*, Lr. I, 3, 14 (Qq *dislike*).

Distasteful, repulsive: *after d. looks and these hard fractions ... they froze me into silence*, Tim. II, 2, 220.

Distemper, subst. 1) indisposition: *if you are sick at sea, or stomach-qualmed at land, a dram of this will drive away d.* Cymb. III, 4, 194.

2) mental derangement, perturbation: *I would not have your d. in this kind for the wealth of Windsor Castle*, Wiv. III, 3, 231. *instigated by his d.* III, 5, 78. *any madness I ever yet beheld seemed but tameness to this his d.* IV, 2, 28. *there is a sickness which puts some of us in d., but I cannot name the disease*, Wint. I, 2, 385. *little faults proceeding on d.* H5 II, 2, 54 (i. e. committed in the state of drunkenness; cf. v. 42 and *distempering draughts*, Oth. I, 1, 99). *he hath found the head and source of all your son's d.* Hml. II, 2, 55. *what is your cause of d.?* III, 2, 351. *upon the heat and flame of thy d. sprinkle cool patience*, III, 4, 123.

Distemper, vb. to put out of temper, to make ill-humoured: *the malignancy of my fate might perhaps d. yours*, Tw. II, 1, 5. (jealousy) —*ing gentle love in his desire*, Ven. 653. *full of supper and —ing draughts*, Oth. I, 1, 99 (cf. Hml. III, 2, 312. 313). Mostly in the participle —*ed:* 1) ill-humoured: *never saw I him touched with anger, so —ed*, Tp. IV, 145. —*ed lords*, John IV, 3, 21. *the king is marvellous —ed*, Hml. III, 2, 312. 2) diseased, bodily or mentally deranged: *a sad —ed guest*, Sonn. 153, 12. *you taste with a —ed appetite*, Tw. I, 5, 98. *it is but as a body yet —ed*, H4B III, 1, 41. *the hot passion of —ed blood*, Troil. II, 2, 169. *it argues a —ed head*, Rom. II, 3, 33. *he cannot buckle his —ed cause within the belt of rule*, Mcb. V, 2, 15. Used of bad weather: *no —ed day*, John III, 4, 154. And figuratively: *this —ed messenger of wet, the many-coloured Iris*, All's I, 3, 157.

Distemperance, mental derangement: Per. V, 1, 27 (Q 1. 2. *distemperature*).

Distemperature, disorder, 1) of the body: *a huge infectious troop of pale —s*, Err. V, 82. *our grandam earth, having this d.* H4A III, 1, 34. 2) of the mind: *thou art uproused by some d.* Rom. II, 3, 40. *upon what ground is his d.* Per. V, 1, 27 (Ff *distemperance*). 3) of the weather: *thorough this d. we see the seasons alter*, Mids. II, 1, 106. *how bloodily the sun begins to peer above yon bosky hill! the day looks pale at his d.* H4A V, 1, 3.

Distill, 1) tr. a) to let fall in drops: *drops of new-shed blood as fresh as morning's dew —ed on flowers*, Tit. II, 3, 201. *tears —ed by moans*, Rom. V, 3, 15 (falling at every moan? or = the extract and quintessence of moans?).

b) to extract the finest and purest parts

from, as by means of an alembic: *flowers —ed, though they with winter meet, leese but their show,* Sonn. 5, 13. *let not winter's ragged hand deface in thee thy summer, ere thou be —ed,* 6, 2. *my verse —s your truth,* 54, 14 (as they do the odour of the rose). *Siren tears, —ed from limbecks foul as hell within,* 119, 2. *—ed Carduus Benedictus,* Ado III, 4, 73. *earthlier happy is the rose —ed,* Mids. I, 1, 76. *balm his foul head in warm —ed waters,* Shr. Ind. I, 48 (i. e. in rose-water). *sweets, which they d. now in the curbed time,* All's II, 4, 46. *choice doth boil, as 'twere from forth us all, a man —ed out of our virtues,* Troil. I, 3, 350.

c) Hence in general = to take the quintessence from: *nature presently —ed Helen's cheek, but not her heart,* As III, 2, 152. *there is some soul of goodness in things evil, would men observingly d. it out,* H5 IV, 1, 5. *upon the corner of the moon there hangs a vaporous drop profound; I'll catch it ere it come to ground: and that —ed by magic sleights shall raise such artificial sprites,* Mcb. III, 5, 26.

d) to melt: *—ed almost to jelly with the act of fear,* Hml. I, 2, 204 (Ff *bestill'd*).

2) intr. a) to fall in drops: *with rain that shall d. from these two ancient urns,* Tit. III, 1, 17.

b) to practise distillation: *to make perfumes, d., preserve,* Cymb. I, 5, 13.

c) Partic. *—ing* = distilled, exquisite, delicate: *wishing her cheeks were gardens full of flowers, so they were dewed with such —ing showers,* Ven. 66. *this —ing liquor drink thou off,* Rom. IV, 1, 94 (the spurious Q1 and M. Edd. *distilled*).

Distillation, the substance extracted by distilling: *were not summer's d. left, a liquid prisoner pent in walls of glass,* Sonn. 5, 9 (i.e. rose-water). *to be stopped in like a strong d.* Wiv. III, 5, 115.

Distilment, the same: Hml. I, 5, 64.

Distinct, subst., a thing apart: *two —s, division none,* Phoen. 27.

Distinct, adj. 1) *distinct*, marked out, specified: *and make d. the very breach,* Troil. IV, 5, 245. 2) *distinct*, different, separate: Merch. II, 9, 61. Troil. IV, 4, 47. But cf. Appendix I, 1.

Distinction, the act of separating and distinguishing, discrimination: All's II, 3, 127. III, 4, 40. IV, 5, 27. Tw. II, 3, 175. Troil. I, 3, 27. III, 2, 28. Cor. III, 1, 323. Ant. III, 1, 29. Cymb. IV, 2, 248. V, 5, 384.

Distinctively, distinctly, accurately; reading of F2.3.4 in Oth. I, 3, 155: *whereof by parcels she had something heard, but not d.* F1 *instinctively,* Qq *intentively.*

Distinctly, 1) separately, not blent in one: *on the topmast, the yards and bowsprit, would I flame d., then meet and join,* Tp. I, 2, 200. *and bury all, which yet d. ranges, in heaps and piles of ruin,* Cor. III, 1, 206. *the centurions and their charges, d. billeted,* IV, 3, 48. *I remember a mass of things, but nothing d.* Oth. II, 3, 290.

2) intelligibly: *thou dost snore d.* Tp. II, 1, 217.

3) explicitly: *I do not in position d. speak of her,* Oth. III, 3, 235.

4) visibly, in a striking manner: *the office did d. his full function,* H8 I, 1, 45.

Distinguish, 1) trans. a) to know and dis-

criminate from other things: Err. I, 1, 53. Shr. I, 1, 205. With *from*: Cymb. I, 3, 10.

b) to make discernible by exhibiting differences: *perspectives which eyed awry d. form,* R2 II, 2, 20. *the valued file —es the swift, the slow,* Mcb. III, 1, 96.

c) to discern, to understand: *no man could d. what he said,* Lucr. 1785. *that mought not be —ed,* H6C V, 2, 45. *nor more can you d. of a man than of his outward show,* R3 III, 1, 9. *every one hears that which can d. sound,* Lr. IV, 6, 215.

2) intr. to perceive difference; followed by *betwixt*: Oth. I, 3, 314. Cymb. I, 6, 34. By *of*: *sight may d. of colours,* H6B II, 1, 129. *since my dear soul was mistress of her choice and could of men d.* Hml. III, 2, 69 (Qq *could of men d. her election, s' hath* etc.)

Distinguishment, distinction: Wint. II, 1, 86.

Distract, vb. 1) to parcel, to disjoin, to divide: *supply it with one gender of herbs, or d. it with many,* Oth. I, 3, 327. *d. your army, which doth most consist of war-marked footmen,* Ant. III, 7, 44. Partic. *—ed: to the brightest beams —ed clouds give way,* All's V, 3, 35. Partic. *distract: to your audit comes their d. parcels in combined sums,* Compl. 231.

2) to confound, to put beside one's self, to madden: *this news —s me,* Wiv. II, 2, 140 (with joy). *poverty hath —ed her,* H4B II, 1, 116. *silence those whom this vile brawl —ed,* Oth. II, 3, 256. Partic. *—ed;* a) confused: *in most uneven and —ed manner,* Meas. IV, 4, 3. b) harassed, heart-broken, wretched: *accept —ed thanks,* Troil. V, 2, 189. *you only speak from your —ed soul,* Tim. III, 4, 115. *best state, contentless, hath a —ed and most wretched being,* IV, 3, 246. *while memory holds a seat in this —ed globe,* Hml. I, 5, 97. c) mad, out of one's senses: *abide all three —ed,* Tp. V, 12. *my poor —ed husband,* Err. V, 39. *in this —ed fear,* Mids. III, 2, 31. *they stared and were —ed,* Mcb. II, 3, 110. *he feels himself —ed,* Hml. III, 1, 5. *he's loved of the —ed multitude,* IV, 3, 4.

Partic. *distract;* a) beside one's self, desperate: *with this she fell d., and, her attendants absent, swallowed fire,* Caes. IV, 3, 155. b) mad: *the fellow is d.* Err. IV, 3, 42. *poor gentleman, he's much d.* Tw. V, 287. *mine hair be fixed on end, as one d.* H6B III, 2, 318. *to see thy noble uncle thus d.* Tit. IV, 3, 26. Hml. IV, 5, 2. Lr. IV, 6, 288.

Distractedly, disjointly: (her eyes) *anon their gazes lend to every place at once, and, nowhere fixed, the mind and sight d. commixed,* Compl. 28. *she did speak in starts d.* Tw. II, 2, 22 (= brokenly).

Distraction, 1) division, detachment: *his power went out in such —s as beguiled all spies,* Ant. III, 7, 77.

2) perturbation of mind, despair, perplexity: *in her invention and Ford's wife's d.* Wiv. III, 5, 87. *as if you held a brow of much d.* Wint. I, 2, 149. *countenances of such d.* V, 2, 52. *you flow to great d.* Troil. V, 2, 41 (Q *destruction*). *d., frenzy and amazement,* V, 3, 85 (Q *destruction*). *tears in his eyes, d. in's aspect,* Hml. II, 2, 581. *make boot of his d.* Ant. IV, 1, 9.

3) derangement of the mind, madness: *in the d. of his madding fever,* Sonn. 119, 8. *all knit up in their —s,* Tp. III, 3, 90. *I know not what 'twas but d.* Tw. V, 71. *this savours not much of d.* 322. *this is a mere d.* H8 III, 1, 112. *how I am punished with sore d.* Hml. V, 2, 241.

Distrain, to seize, to take possession of: *my father's goods are all —ed and sold*, R2 II, 3, 131. *hath here —ed the Tower to his use*, H6A I, 3, 61.

Distraught, distracted, mad: R3 III, 5, 4. Rom. IV, 3, 49. cf. *Bestraught.*

Distress, subst. affliction, painful situation, misery: Lucr. 1127. 1444. Wiv. III, 3, 198. As II, 7, 91. 95. All's V, 2, 26. H6A II, 5, 87. IV, 1, 37. R3 I, 4, 273. II, 2, 64. Cor. V, 1, 35. Tit. III, 1, 38. Tim. V, 1, 15. Hml. IV, 7, 179. Lr. IV, 4, 18. Cymb. III, 6, 79. Plur. *—es*: Gentl. V, 4, 6. Mcb. IV, 3, 188.

Distressed, afflicted, miserable, pressed hard: Ven. 814. Lucr. 465. Err. IV, 4, 62. H6A IV, 3, 30. H6B IV, 9, 31. H6C III, 3, 213. R3 II, 2, 86. III, 7, 185. IV, 4, 98. H8 II, 1, 110. Tit. I, 103. IV, 4, 32. Rom. IV, 5, 59. Lr. IV, 3, 40. Oth. I, 3, 157 (Ff *distressful*). Cymb. IV, 2, 47. Per. I, 4, 7. II, 5, 46.

Distressful, attended with misery: *d. bread*, H5 IV, 1, 287. *war*, H6A V, 4, 126. *times*, R3 IV, 4, 318. *stroke*, Oth. I, 3, 157 (Q *distressed*).

Distribute, 1) to deal out: *as much as one sound cudgel of four foot could d.* H8 V, 4, 20. *the spoil was ne'er —d*, Cor. III, 3, 5.
2) to administer: *the ministers that do d. it* (justice) Cor. III, 3, 99.

Distribution, dealing out, dispensation: Cor. I, 9, 35. Lr. IV, 1, 73.

Distrust, subst. 1) suspicion: H6A III, 3, 31. Ant. III, 2, 34. 2) want of self-confidence: *let not the world see fear and sad d. govern the motion of a kingly eye*, John V, 1, 46.

Distrust, vb. 1) to doubt, not to confide in: Tw. IV, 3, 13. 2) to be solicitous about: *you are so sick of late that I d. you. Yet, though I d., discomfort you it nothing must*, Hml. III, 2, 175.

Distrustful, diffident: H6A I, 2, 126.

Disturb, vb. to excite from a state of rest, to trouble; absol.: *—ing jealousy*, Ven. 649. Trans.: Ven. 340. 450. Lucr. 454 *(from sleep)*. 974. Tp. IV, 160. Err. V, 84. 215. Mids. II, 1, 87. V, 395. John II, 338. H4A II, 3, 62. H5 I, 2, 265. H6A I, 2, 121. IV, 1, 127. H6B III, 2, 256. III, 3, 25. IV, 8, 6. V, 1, 12. H8 II, 2, 61. Cor. IV, 5, 57. Tit. I, 101. Rom. I, 1, 98. IV, 1, 41. Caes. I, 3, 39. Per. I, 2, 1.

Disturb, subst. disturbance: *my sweet sleep's —s*, R3 IV, 2, 74 (Ff *disturbers*).

Disturbance, interruption of a settled state: *the —s that nature works*, Per. III, 2, 37.

Disturber, troubler: R3 IV, 2, 74 (Qq *disturbs*). Tit. IV, 4, 6.

Disunite, to divide, to part: *it was a strong composure a fool could d.* Troil. II, 3, 109.

Disvalue, to depreciate: *her reputation was —ed in levity*, Meas. V, 221.

Disvouch, to contradict: *every letter he hath writ hath —ed other*, Meas. IV, 4, 1.

Ditch, a trench cut in the ground: Wiv. III, 3, 16. Err. V, 122. Cor. III, 1, 96. Tim. IV, 3, 166. Mcb. III, 4, 26. Ant. IV, 6, 38. V, 2, 57.

Ditch-delivered, brought forth in a ditch: Mcb. IV, 1, 31.

Ditch-dog, a dead dog thrown into a ditch: Lr. III, 4, 138.

Ditched, closed in by a ditch: *d. and walled with turf*, Cymb. V, 3, 14.

Ditcher, digger: Hml. V, 1, 34.

Ditty, song: *a woeful d.* Ven. 836. (the lark) *doth welcome daylight with her d.* Pilgr. 199. *the dolefullest d.* 383. Tp. I, 2, 405. Ado II, 3, 72. Mids. V, 402. As V, 3, 36. H4A III, 1, 124. 209.

Diurnal, performed in a day: *ere twice the horses of the sun shall bring their fiery torcher his d. ring*, All's II, 1, 165.

Dive, to plunge or sink in a fluid: Tp. I, 2, 191. John V, 2, 139. H4A I, 3, 203. Tit. IV, 3, 43. Tim. IV, 1, 2. Per. III Prol. 49. Figuratively: *to d. into their hearts*, R2 I, 4, 25. *d., thoughts, down to my soul*, R3 I, 1, 41. *hath not yet —d into the world's deceit*, III, 1, 8. *he —s into the king's soul, and there scatters dangers, doubts*, H8 II, 2, 27.

Dive-dapper, didapper, dab-chick: *a d. peering through a wave*, Ven. 86.

Divel, ancient orthogr. for *Devil*, q. v.

Diver, one that goes under water: Ant. II, 5, 16.

Divers, 1) differing, deviating: *new opinions, d. and dangerous*, H8 V, 3, 18.
2) different: *time travels in d. paces with d. persons*, As III, 2, 326. *how chance's mocks and changes fill the cup of alteration with d. liquors*, H4B III, 1, 53. H5 I, 2, 184. Rom. II, 3, 11.
3) several, sundry: *d. philosophers hold*, Wiv. I, 1, 236. Tw. I, 5, 263. Wint. V, 1, 202. John III, 4, 7. H4A I, 3, 262. H6A IV, 1, 25. R3 I, 2, 218. H8 II, 1, 17. Caes. IV, 1, 20. Followed by *of*: *d. of Antonio's creditors*, Merch. III, 1, 118.

Divers-coloured, of different colours: Ant. II, 2, 208.

Diversity, variety: *d. of sounds*, Tp. V, 234.

Diversly, differently: *that our wits are so d. coloured*, Cor. II, 3, 22.

Divert, to turn off: *time's accidents ... d. strong minds to the course of altering things*, Sonn. 115, 8. *sometime —ed their poor balls are tied to the orbed earth*, Compl. 24. *the malice of a —ed blood and bloody brother*, As II, 3, 37 (= turned off from the course of nature). All's III, 4, 21. H5 II Chor. 15. Troil. I, 3, 8. 99.

Dives, the rich man of the parable (St. Luke XVI): H4A III, 3, 36.

Divest, vb. refl. 1) to undress: *like bride and groom —ing them for bed*, Oth. II, 3, 181 (O. Edd. *devesting*).
2) to resign, to abdicate: *that you d. yourself and lay apart the borrowed glories*, H5 II, 4, 78. *we will d. us, both of rule, interest of territory, cares of state*, Lr. I, 1, 50.

Dividable, divided, separated, different: *peaceful commerce from d. shores*, Troil. I, 3, 105 (cf. *Individable*).

Dividant, separated, different: *twinned brothers of one womb, whose procreation, residence and birth scarce is d., touch them with several fortunes*, Tim. IV, 3, 5.

Divide, 1) trans. a) to part into different pieces: *d. me like a bribed buck*, Wiv. V, 5, 27. Merch. III, 2, 15. As IV, 1, 45. R2 II, 2, 17. V, 1, 60. H4A II, 3, 34. III, 1, 70. 72. V, 5, 34. H4B I, 3, 74. H5 I, 2, 183. H6A IV, 5, 49. V, 2, 11. H6C II, 5, 30. Troil. II, 3, 256. Caes. IV, 1, 14. Hml. V, 2, 118. Lr. I, 1, 38. Oth. I, 3, 181. Ant. I, 5, 53. IV, 14, 32. *hindering their* (the vapours') *present fall by this —ing*, Lucr.

551 (= scattering). *and she a fair —d excellence, whose fulness of perfection lies in him,* John II, 439 (i. e. a fraction only, a half).

b) to separate, sever: *let us —d live,* Sonn. 39, 5. *we were —d from them,* Tp. V, 239. R2 V, 1, 81. H4B I, 1, 194. R3 III, 1, 179 (cf. III, 2, 20). Troil. I, 3, 72. IV, 5, 69. Rom. III, 5, 30. Hml. IV, 5, 85. Ant. II, 3, 2. *d. the sunday from the week,* Hml. I, 1, 76 (= distinguish).

c) to disunite: *he little thought of this —d friendhip,* R3 I, 4, 244. V, 5, 27. 28. *that our stars should d. our equalness to this,* Ant. V, 1, 47.

d) to distribute in shares: *how to d. the conquest of thy sight,* Sonn. 46, 2. *pledges the breath of him in a —d draught,* Tim. I, 2, 49. *take that, d. it,* Ant. III, 11, 5.

Reflectively: *o'er and o'er —s him 'twixt his unkindness and his kindness,* Wint. IV, 4, 562. *all the fiends d. themselves between you,* Cymb. II, 4, 130 (take every one a piece of you).

e) to share, to communicate: *her grievance with his hearing to d.* Compl. 67. *I will d. my crown with her,* H6A I, 6, 18.

2) intr. a) to part, to go asunder: *it* (her blood) *doth d. in two slow rivers,* Lucr. 1737. *I'ld d.* Tp. I, 2, 198. *so doth valour's show and valour's worth d. in storms of fortune,* Troil. I, 3, 46. *that a thing inseparate —s more wider than the sky and earth,* V, 2, 149.

b) to be disunited, to fall out: *brothers d.* Lr. I, 2, 116.

c) to share, to partake: *you shall in all d. with us,* Cor. I, 6, 87.

Divination, prophecy: Ven. 670. H4B I, 1, 88. Troil. II, 2, 114. Cymb. IV, 2, 351.

Divine, adj. 1) partaking of the nature of God, or proceeding from God or the Gods: *stealing moulds from heaven that were d.* Ven. 730. Lucr. 1164. Tp. I, 2, 159. 418. Meas. V, 374. Err. II, 1, 20. III, 2, 32. All's III, 6, 33. Wint. III, 2, 29. V, 1, 37. R2 I, 1, 38. V, 5, 12. H4B IV, 1, 92. H6C V, 6, 81. R3 III, 3, 42. Troil. III, 3, 203. IV, 2, 105. Cor. III, 1, 141. IV, 5, 110. Hml. IV, 4, 49. Lr. I, 2, 136. Cymb. III, 4, 79. IV, 2, 170.

2) excellent in the highest degree, heavenly: *sweet ornament that decks a thing d.* Gentl. II, 1, 4. II, 4, 147. 151. II, 7, 13. Ado II, 3, 60. LLL IV, 3, 83. 248. Mids. III, 2, 137. 226. H6A V, 5, 16. H6C I, 4, 132. R3 I, 2, 75. Oth. II, 1, 73. Cymb. II, 1, 62. IV, 2, 55.

Superl. —st: —st creature, H6A I, 6, 4. Rom. III, 2, 77. *Lucina, O —st patroness,* Per. III, 1, 11.

3) pious, holy: *before you blot with your uncleanness that which is d.; offer pure incense to so pure a shrine,* Lucr. 193. *that eye which looks on her confounds his wits; that eye which him beholds, as more d., unto a view so false will not incline,* 291. *like prayers d., I must each day say o'er the very same,* Sonn. 108, 5. *buy terms d. in selling hours of dross,* 146, 11. *I know him for a man d. and holy,* Meas. V, 144. *turning ... your tongue d. to a loud trumpet,* H4B IV, 1, 51. *bids thee with most d. integrity welcome,* Troil. IV, 5, 170.

Divine, subst. a priest: Meas. III, 2, 221. Merch. I, 2, 16. Wint. III, 1, 19. R3 III, 7, 75. Cor. II, 3, 64. Rom. III, 3, 49. Mcb. V, 1, 82.

Divine, vb. 1) to foretel, to prophesy: *darest thou d. his downfall?* R2 III, 4, 79. Intr: *if I were bound to d. of this unity, I would not prophesy so,* Ant. II, 6, 124.

2) to forebode, to guess, to conjecture: *they looked but with —ing eyes,* Sonn. 106, 11. *my —ing thoughts,* H6C IV, 6, 69. *the danger that his soul —s,* R3 III, 2, 18. *from Cyprus, as I may d.* Oth. I, 2, 39. *which mulier I d. is this most constant wife,* Cymb. V, 5, 448. cf. *True-divining.*

Divinely, holily, devoutly: *in this right hand, whose protection is most d. vowed upon the right of him it holds,* John II, 237. *d. bent to meditation,* R3 III 7, 62.

Divineness, perfection, excellence in a supreme degree: *behold d. no elder than a boy,* Cymb. III, 6, 44.

Diviner, one who can prophesy: *this drudge or d. laid claim to me,* Err. III, 2, 144.

Divinity, 1) something divine or superhuman: *there is d. in odd numbers,* Wiv. V, 1, 4. *to your ears d., to any other's profanation,* Tw. I, 5, 233. 236. *there's such d. doth hedge a king,* Hml. IV, 5, 123. *there's a d. that shapes our ends,* V, 2, 10.

2) theology: *trust not my age, my reverence, calling, nor d.* Ado IV, 1, 170. *hear him but reason in d.* H5 I, 1, 38. *Ay and No too was no good d.* Lr. IV, 6, 101. *d. of hell!* Oth. II, 3, 356. *to have d. preached there,* Per. IV, 5, 4.

In Ado IV, 1, 170, Oth. II, 3, 356 and Per. IV, 5, 4 it may as well be = devotion, holiness.

Division, 1) separation: *two distincts, d. none,* Phoen. 27. *saw d. grow together,* 42. *how have you made d. of yourself?* Tw. V, 229. *the spacious breadth of this d. admits no orifex ...,* Troil. V, 2, 150.

2) sharing out, repartition: *I'll make d. of my present with you,* Tw. III, 4, 380. *in the d. of the kingdom,* Lr. I, 1, 4.

3) fraction: *the d. of the twentieth part of one poor scruple,* Merch. IV, 1, 329.

4) body of an army: *his —s are in three heads,* H4B I, 3, 70.

5 methodical arrangement, disposition: *rightly reasoned and in his own d.* Ado V, 1, 230. *that never set a squadron in the field, nor the d. of a battle knows more than a spinster,* Oth. I, 1, 23.

6) disunion, difference: *the woefullest d.* R2 IV, 146. *the quality and hair of our attempt brooks no d.* H4A IV, 1, 62. *the d. of our amity,* H4B III, 1, 79. H6A IV, 1, 193. R3 V, 5, 28. Cor. IV, 3, 19. Caes. IV, 3, 235. Lr. I, 2, 149. 159. III, 1, 19. III, 3, 9. Oth. IV, 1, 242. Ant. II, 1, 48. III, 4, 13.

7) variation, modulation: *ditties sung by a fair queen with ravishing d.* H4A III, 1, 211. *the lark makes sweet d.* Rom. III, 5, 29. *abound in the d. of each several crime, acting it many ways,* Mcb. IV, 3, 96.*

Divorce, subst. 1) legal dissolution of the bonds of matrimony: H8 II, 2, 31. III, 2, 26. 33. 65. Cymb. II, 1, 67.

2) any separation of love: *in this unjust d. of us,* Err. I, 1, 105. *deadly d. step between me and you!* All's V, 3, 319. *mark your d.* Wint. IV, 4, 428. *made a d. betwixt his queen and him,* R2 III, 1, 12. *to make d. of their incorporate league,* H5 V, 2, 394. *those that weep this lamentable d.* Cymb. I, 4, 20.

3) that which separates (the abstr. for the concr.): *hateful d. of love — thus chides she Death,* Ven. 932. *as the long d. of steel falls on me,* H8 II, 1, 76 (viz the axe of the executioner). *O thou sweet king-killer and dear d. 'twixt natural son and sire,* Tim. IV, 3, 382.

Divorce, vb. 1) to separate legally a husband or wife from the other: *she was —d,* H8 IV, 1, 32. *he will d. you,* Oth. I, 2, 14. cf. *Deepdivorcing,* Err. II, 2, 140.

2) to separate in general, a) from the intercourse of love: *doubly —d,* R2 V, 1, 71. *I here d. myself both from thy table and thy bed,* H6C I, 1, 247. *beguiled, —d,* Rom. IV, 5, 55. b) from other things: *that contempt will quite d. his memory from his part,* LLL V, 2, 150. *souls and bodies hath he —d three,* Tw. III, 4, 260. *d. this terror from my heart,* R2 V, 4, 9. *d. not wisdom from your honour,* H4B I, 1, 162. *a sleep that from this golden rigol hath —d so many English kings,* IV, 5, 36. *if that quarrel, fortune, do d. it from the bearer,* H8 II, 3, 14. *I would d. me from thy mother's tomb,* Lr. II, 4, 133. Singular passage: *nothing but death shall e'er d. my dignities,* H8 III, 1, 142 (viz from me).

Divorcement, divorce: *though he do shake me off to beggarly d.* Oth. IV, 2, 158.

Divulge, to make public, to proclaim: *d. Page for a secure and wilful Actaeon,* Wiv. III, 2, 43. *a —d shame traduced by odious ballads,* All's II, 1, 174. *in voices well —d,* Tw. I, 5, 279 (= of good reputation). *that shall be —d,* Troil. V, 2, 163. *to keep it from —ing,* Hml. IV, 1, 22 (= from becoming known).

Dizy, name in Meas. IV, 3, 13.

Dizzy, adj. causing giddiness: *how fearful and d. 'tis to cast one's eye so low!* Lr. IV, 6, 12.

Dizzy, vb. to make giddy, to stun: *d. with more clamour Neptune's ear,* Troil. V, 2, 174. *would d. the arithmetic of memory,* Hml. V, 2, 119.

Dizzy-eyed, having a giddy sight, dazzled: *d. fury,* H6A IV, 7, 11.

Do (2. p. *doest* and *dost,* 3. p. *does* and *doth* indiscriminately; 2. p. impf. *didst;* once *diddest* in two syll., Hml. IV, 7, 58). 1) to act, to deal; a) intr.: *do as thou wilt,* Rom. III, 5, 205. *do how I can,* As II, 3, 35. *done like a Frenchman: turn, and turn again,* H6A III, 3, 85. *while some men leave to do* (= to be active) Troil. III, 3, 133 etc. etc. *being mad before, how doth she now for wits?* Ven. 249 (= how should she come by good sense?). *how shall we do for money?* R2 II, 2, 104. *how wilt thou do for a father?* Mcb. IV, 2, 38. *how will you do to content this substitute?* Meas. III, 1, 192. *so said, so done, is well,* Shr. I, 2, 186. *well done!* Tp. IV, 142. LLL V, 1, 145. Mcb. IV, 1, 39. Cymb. I, 5, 82. *you have done well, that men must lay their murders on your neck,* Oth. V, 2, 169. Followed by *with: heaven doth with us, as we with torches do,* Meas. I, 1, 33. *do with your injuries as seems you best,* V, 256. *To have to do with* = to have concern or business with, to deal with: *when truth and virtue have to do with thee, a thousand crosses keep them from thy aid,* Lucr. 911. *nor need you have to do with any scruple,* Meas. I, 1, 64. Ado V, 1, 77. H6A V, 4, 42. H6B V, 2, 56. R3 I, 3, 292. *With* omitted: *day hath nought to do what's done by night,* Lucr. 1092.

Doing, substantively, = deed, action, manner of acting: *God is much displeased that you take with unthankfulness his doing,* R3 II, 2, 90. *ignorant tongues which will be the chronicles of my doing,* H8 I, 2, 74. *those that have beheld the doing,* Cor. I, 9, 40. *please you that I may pass this doing,* II, 2, 143. Plural: *volumes of report run ... upon thy doings,* Meas. IV, 1, 63. *among the infinite doings of the world,* Wint. I, 2, 253. *to hide your doings,* Cor. I, 9, 23. *valiant doings in their country's cause,* Tit. I, 113. *and buzz lamenting doings in the air,* III, 2, 62 (= lamentations).

b) trans. to act, to transact, to practise: *what do you here?* Tp. I, 1, 41. *there's something else to do,* IV, 126. *what's to do here?* Meas. I, 2, 115. *what's to do?* Tw. III, 3, 18. *you saw the ceremony? that I did,* H8 IV, 1, 60 etc. etc. *To do* = yet undone: *the best is yet to do,* As I, 2, 121. *O that it were to do!* H6B III, 2, 3. *To do* = ado: *there has been much to do on both sides, and the nation holds it no sin to tarre them to controversy,* Hml. II, 2, 369. *What have you to do* = what is that to you? it does not concern you: *what have you to do whither they bear it?* Wiv. III, 3, 164. *what had he to do to chide at me?* As III, 5, 129. *perhaps him and her, sir: what have you to do?* Shr. I, 2, 226. *I will be angry: what hast thou to do?* III, 2, 218. — Followed by *with: what shall be done with the groaning Juliet?* Meas. II, 2, 15. cf. Wiv. IV, 4, 45. H6A IV, 7, 94. H6C V, 7, 37. Rom. III, 5, 61 etc. Followed by *to: do whate'er thou wilt to the wide world,* Sonn. 19, 6. *what dost thou to mine eyes?* 137, 1. Meas. II, 1, 120. 149. All's IV, 3, 194. H6C I, 4, 65. R3 IV, 4, 252. Troil. IV, 2, 108. Caes. II, 1, 331. Hml. I, 4, 66 etc. *To* omitted: *who does me this?* Hml. II, 2, 601 (cf. *harm,* wrong etc.). — Elliptical use of the infinitive: *I will not stir from this place, do what they can,* Mids. III, 1, 124. *yet this I will not do, do how I can,* As II, 3, 35. *do what you can, yours will not be entreated,* Shr. V, 2, 89.

2) to perform, to effect: *the wills above be done,* Tp. I, 1, 72. *I have done nothing but in care of thee,* I, 2, 16. *what shall I do?* I, 2, 300. *what will this do?* Ado IV, 1, 211 (= avail). *this business, which he knows is not to be done; damns himself to do and dares better be damned than to do't,* All's III, 6, 95. *I shall do good* (= I shall speed, succeed) Wint. II, 2, 54. *no woman can do more than I do with her,* Wiv. I, 4, 137. *O, it is much that a lie with a slight oath and a jest with a sad brow will do with a fellow,* H4B V, 1, 93. *when your words are done, my woes end likewise with the evening sun,* Err. I, 1, 27 (= are carried into execution). cf. *yet let that be, which the eye fears, when it is done, to see,* Mcb. I, 4, 53. *this is my doing,* Wiv. III, 4, 99. *it is Jove's doing,* Tw. III, 4, 83. *this is the cardinal's doing,* H8 II, 2, 20. *To do to death* = to put to death: Ado V, 3, 3. H6B III, 2, 179. 244. H6C II, 1, 103. III, 3, 103. *to do him dead,* H6C I, 4, 108. — *To do so* = to act according to what is said before (v. *So*); *to do it* = to perform, to execute: *see thou do it,* Err. II, 2, 141. *get thee gone, but do it,* Merch. IV, 1, 397. *here is man shall do it,* Wint. IV, 4, 829. *do it, England,* Hml. IV, 3, 67. *I will do't, my lord,* IV, 7, 7. Particularly used, when the sense is restricted by an adjunct: *I should do it with more ease,* Tp. III, 1, 29. *do it so cunningly that my discovery be not aimed at,* Gentl. III, 1, 44. *if I can do it by aught that I can speak in his dispraise,* III, 2, 46. *I do it not in evil disposition,* Meas. I, 2, 122. *if you like else-*

where, do it by stealth, Err. III, 2, 7. *I shall do it on a full stomach*, LLL I, 2, 153. *anoint his eyes, but do it when the next thing he espies may be the lady*, Mids. II, 1, 262. *he does it under name of perfect love*, Shr. IV, 3, 12. *let us do it with no show of fear*, H5 II, 4, 23. *he did it unconstrained*, H6C I, 1, 143. *with a true heart and brother-love I do it*, H8 V, 3, 173. *now might I do it pat*, Hml. III, 3, 73. *we then can do't at land*, Ant. III, 7, 54. *do it at once*, IV, 14, 82. *I cannot do it better than in gyves*, Cymb. V, 4, 14. *To do it* = to do so: *the duke of Milan and his daughter could control thee, if now 'twere fit to do't*, Tp. I, 2, 440. *and did it to minister occasion to these gentlemen*, II, 1, 173. — Substantives as objects: *our own doth little advantage*, Tp. I, 1, 34 (or verb?). *and did the third a blessing*, Lr. I, 4, 115. *to do me business in the veins o' the earth*, Tp, I, 2, 255. All's III, 6, 95. *charity*, Lr. III, 4, 61. *have done some wanton charm upon this man*, Tp. IV, 94. *do all points of my command*, I, 2, 499. *does not all commands*, Cymb. V, 1, 6. *I will do your mother's commandment*, Hml. III, 2, 329. *Lucius will do his commission*, Cymb. II, 4, 12. *our coronation done*, H4B V, 2, 141. *the neglecting it may do much danger*, Rom. V, 2, 20. *he may do danger*, Caes. II, 1, 17. *do on them some violent death*, Tit. V, 2, 108. *do your discretion*, Oth. III, 3, 34. *do thy duty*, Shr. IV, 1, 38. *my mother did but duty*, All's IV, 2, 12. *did him peculiar duties*, Lucr. 14. *do my duties to the senate*, Oth. III, 2, 2 (cf. *Duty*). *may it do him ease*, Shr. V, 2, 179. H6C V, 5, 72. Tit. III, 1, 121. Hml. I, 1, 131. *I will do you any embassage*, Ado II, 1, 277. *my best endeavours shall be done*, Merch. II, 2, 182. *the last enchantment you did here*, Tw. III, 1, 123. *a fault that he did*, Gentl. IV, 4, 16. Wiv. V, 5, 9. *your favours done to me*, Gentl. III, 1, 6. Err. I, 1, 123. Tw. III, 2, 7. H6B I, 1, 71. *nor that full star doth half that glory to the sober west*, Sonn. 132, 8. *to do a person grace*, Sonn. 132, 11. Err. II, 1, 87. V, 164. Shr. I, 2, 131. R2 III, 3, 181. H4A II, 1, 78. V, 4, 161. H4B V, 5, 6. Caes. III, 2, 62. Hml. I, 1, 131. II, 2, 53. *harm*, Tp. I, 2, 15 etc. cf. *Harm. doing damned hate upon thyself*, Rom. III, 3, 118. *each eye doth homage to his sight*, Sonn. 7, 3. Tp. I, 2, 113 etc. *doing the honour of thy lordliness to one so meek*, Ant. V, 2, 161. *to do justice*, q. v. *six of his labours you'ld have done*, Cor. IV, 1, 18. *to do our country loss*, H5 IV, 3, 21. *your message done*, Gentl. IV, 4, 93. 95. Troil. I, 3, 219. Tit. IV, 1, 117. IV, 4, 104. Rom. II, 5, 66. *do my good morrow to them*, H5 IV, 1, 26. *do the murder first*, Tp. IV, 232. Rom. V, 1, 81. Hml. III, 2, 248. III, 3, 54. *I will make thee do thy right nature*, Tim. IV, 3, 44. *do no outrages on silly women*, Gentl. IV, 1, 71. cf. Lucr. 605. Err. IV, 4, 119. Ado II, 3, 159. Lr. II, 4, 24. *you may do the part of an honest man*, Ado II, 1, 172 (cf. *Part*). *I have done penance*, Gentl. II, 4, 129. H6B II, 3, 11. II, 4, 105. *foul play*, Lr. III, 7, 31. *your pleasure*, R3 IV, 2, 21. *thou dost thyself a pleasure*, Oth. I, 3, 376. *does foul pranks*, Oth. II, 1, 143. *at thy request I will do reason*, Tp. III, 2, 128. *to do myself this reason and this right*, Tit. I, 279. *you shall do small respect*, Lr. II, 2, 137. *and I, to do you rest, a thousand deaths would die*, Tw. V, 136. *do them reverence*, Merch. I, 1, 13. Caes. III, 2, 125. *do right unto this princely duke of York*, H6C I, 1, 166 etc. (cf. *Right*). *do all rites*, Ado IV, 1, 209. V, 3, 23. H4A V, 4, 98. H5 IV, 8, 127. *do*

present sacrifice, Caes. II, 2, 5. Per. V, 1, 242. *hath twice done salutation to the morn*, R3 V, 3, 210. Caes. IV, 2, 5. *I have done thee worthy service*, Tp. I, 2, 247. IV, 267 etc. *to do him shame*, Lucr. 597. Sonn. 36, 10. LLL IV, 3, 204. Tw. III, 4, 400. *to do obsequious sorrow*, Hml. I, 2, 92. *and do my spiriting gently*, Tp. I, 2, 298. *such transformation done*, H4A I, 1, 45. *trespass*, Ant. II, 1, 40. *do our work*, Tp. III, 2, 158 etc. *did us but loving wrong*, Tp. I, 2, 151 etc.

3) Used for other verbs to spare the repetition of them: *when beauty lived and died as flowers do now*, Sonn. 68, 2. *both truth and beauty on my love depends: so dost thou too*, 101, 4. Tp. I, 2, 52. 61. 88. II, 1, 267. II, 2, 23. III, 1, 29. III, 2, 111. Gentl. I, 1, 78. II, 4, 11. II, 6, 17. II, 7, 38. III, 2, 24. 27. Meas. II, 1, 262. Err. II, 2, 103. IV, 4, 78. Ado V, 1, 129. 189. V, 4, 46. LLL I, 2, 79. IV, 2, 98. 130. Mids. III, 1, 120. III, 2, 167. 251. IV, 1, 71. V, 155. Tw. II, 5, 143. Wint. II, 1, 73. II, 3, 48. R2 II, 3, 17. H5 V Chor. 35. H6A II, 5, 105. H6B V, 2, 59. H6C I, 1, 221. R3 III, 2, 67. H8 V, 3, 67. Troil. I, 2, 194. Cor. II, 3, 131. III, 2, 110. Tit. I, 213. Rom. II, 2, 20. Mcb. I, 3, 10. Hml. IV, 5, 152. Ant. III, 4, 10 etc.

4) Used, with some latitude, of any kind of work or performance; = to play, to act, to perform: *you could never do him so ill-well*, Ado II, 1, 122. *do the part of an honest man*, 172. *if I do it, let the audience look to their eyes*, Mids. I, 2, 28. *you may do it extempore*, 70. *we will do it in action as we will do it before the duke*, III, 1, 5. *thou didst it excellent*, Shr. Ind. I, 89. *our interpreter does it well*, All's IV, 3, 236. = to write, to copy: *since mind at first in character was done*, Sonn. 59, 8. *are they not lamely writ? No, boy, but as well as I can do them*, Gentl. II, 1, 98. *'tis very clerkly done*, 115. *the precedent was full as long a doing*, R3 III, 6, 7. = to express: *which lames report to follow it and undoes description to do it*, Wint. V, 2, 63. = to found, to build: *unwilling to outlive the good that did it*, H8 IV, 2, 60. *at whose expense it (the monument) is done*, Per. IV, 3, 46. = to paint, or to cut: *how could he see to do them?* Merch. III, 2, 124. *is't not well done?* Tw. I, 5, 253. *a piece of work so bravely done*, Cymb. II, 4, 73. *who was he that otherwise than noble nature did, hath altered that good picture?* IV, 2, 364. *a piece many years in doing*, Wint. V, 2, 104. *he so near to Hermione hath done Hermione*, 109. *her dead likeness excels whatever yet you looked upon or hand of man hath done*, V, 3, 17. *masterly done*, 65. = to fashion: *how it (the gown) should be done*, Shr. IV, 3, 118.

5) Used, likewise, for the most different verbs implying any notion of activity: *the noble thanes do bravely in the war*, Mcb. V, 7, 26. *and to such wondrous doing brought his horse*, Hml. IV, 7, 87. *do bravely, horse!* Ant. I, 5, 22 (i. e. move with grace and majesty). *provoke not battle, till we have done at sea*, III, 8, 4. *I am not able to do* (i. e. lend money) Tim. III, 2, 55. — The imperative used as a term of encouragement (= go on!): *do, do: we steal by line and level*, Tp. IV, 239. *aye, do, persever, counterfeit sad looks*, Mids. III, 2, 237. *you woreson cur! Do, do. Thou stool for a witch. Ay, do, do*, Troil. II, 1, 45. *do, rudeness; do, camel; do, do*, 58. *thou art proclaimed a fool, I think. Do not, porpentine, do not: my fingers itch*, 27. — Used for the act of cohabitation: *my Collatine would else have come to me when Tarquin did*, Lucr. 917. *for*

doing I am past, All's II, 3, 246. *doing is activity, and he will still be doing*, H5 III, 7, 107. *you bring me to do, and then you flout me too*, Troil. IV, 2, 27. Actively: *what has he done? a woman*, Meas. I, 2, 88. *I have done thy mother*, Tit. IV, 2, 76. cf. *do't in your parents' eyes*, Tim. IV, 1, 8. Quibbling: *I would fain be doing. I doubt it not, but you will curse your wooing*, Shr. II, 74; cf. I, 2, 227. *they would do that which should undo more doing*, Wint. I, 2, 312. *things won are done: joy's soul lies in the doing*, Troil. I, 2, 313.

To do well = to be convenient, to fit, to succeed, to thrive: *will it do well?* Wiv. II, 3, 82. *though it do well, I do not relish well their loud applause*, Meas. I, 1, 70. *that thinks he hath done well in people's eyes*, Merch. III, 2, 143. *words do well when he that speaks them pleases those that hear*, As III, 5, 111. *it would do well to set the deer's horns upon his head*, IV, 2, 4. Shr. Ind. I, 126. Tw. I, 3, 143. II, 3, 87. John I, 236. R2 III, 3, 170. H4B III, 2, 307. H6B II, 3, 61. H8 I, 4, 87. Cor. IV, 1, 21. Tit. II, 3, 305. Hml. III, 1, 184. V, 1, 52. Ant. II, 1, 8. III, 13, 188. *the gashes do better upon them*, Mcb. V, 8, 3. *you can do better yet*, Ant. I, 3, 81. *my favour to him that does best*, H8 II, 2, 115.

To do it = to be what is wanted: *you can do it!* H4B III, 2, 157 (= that is a good joke! German: ihr versteht's!). *this piece of toasted cheese will do't*, Lr. IV, 6, 90 (comes pat to the purpose). *how dearly they do't*, Cymb. II, 2, 18 (what a delicate effect and appearance they have!)

Absolutely, = to serve: *'twould not do*, All's IV, 1, 56. *all would not do*, H4A II, 4, 188. *if all this will not do, I'll drown you*, R3 I, 4, 276 (Qq serve). *if they smile and say 'twill do, I know, within a while all the best men are ours*, H8 Epil. 12. cf. *when I cannot live any longer, I will do as I may*, H5 II, 1, 17 (= shift). *I could not do withal* = I could not help it, Merch. III, 4, 72.

6) **to fare**, to be in a state with regard to health: *how does thine ague?* Tp. II, 2, 139. III, 2, 26. IV, 103. Gentl. II, 4, 122. IV, 2, 55. Wiv. I, 1, 84. 91. I, 4, 142. 146. II, 1, 169. III, 4, 34. Ado IV, 1, 114. V, 2, 90. Merch. III, 2, 236. As I, 2, 231. III, 3, 75. All's II, 4, 19. Tw. III, 4, 26. 106. H4A III, 3, 107. R3 IV, 1, 14. Troil. III, 3, 63. Rom. III, 3, 97. Mcb. V, 3, 37. Lr. I, 4, 107 etc. *how have ye done since last we saw in France?* H8 I, 1, 1.

7) Used, when joined with the infinitive of other verbs, as a mere expletive: not only in interrogative and negative sentences (Tp. I, 2, 78. 106. 250. I, 2, 40. 310. 355. I, 1, 14. I, 2, 138 etc.) but, without any emphasis, in affirmative ones: *you do assist the storm*, Tp. I, 1, 15. I, 2, 8. 94. 102. 129. 153. 163. 181. 242. 249. 251. 274. 278. 280. 282. 287. 288. 311. 343. 347. 350. 359. 399. 405. 426. 433. 453 etc. etc. *do not do your cousin such a wrong*, Ado III, 1, 87. *do not be so bitter with me*, Mids. III, 2, 306. *which do not be entreated to*, Ant. II, 6, 32.

8) The partic. *done* = a) finished, at an end: *her words are done*, Ven. 254. *ere summer half be done*, 802. 846. Err. V, 224. Ado II, 1, 114. Shr. I, 1, 259. III, 1, 23. All's V, 3, 335. Tw. II, 3, 113. V, 416. R2 IV, 196. H4A I, 3, 30. V, 3, 16. H6A II, 5, 62. H6C IV, 1, 104. Cor. I, 6, 31. II, 3, 149. Rom. I, 5, 52. Caes. I, 2, 178. Lr. V, 1, 67. Oth. II, 1, 20. Ant. I, 2, 101. V, 2, 193. *When all's done* = after all: *a horn for my money, when all's done*, Ado II, 3, 63. *we must leave*

the killing out, when all is done, Mids. III, 1, 16. *this is the best fooling, when all is done*, Tw. II, 3, 31. *when all's done, you look but on a stool*, Mcb. III, 4, 67.

I have done, Tp. II, 1, 26. *have done!* Lucr. 645, Gentl. II, 4, 99. LLL V, 2, 559. John II, 183. H6B I, 4, 31. 42. R3 I, 3, 273. Rom. III, 5, 72. Ant. III, 7, 20. III, 13, 153. Cymb. IV, 2, 229. Followed by a gerund or an accus.: *I have done weeping*, Gentl. II, 3, 2. Troil. III, 2, 108. *when other petty griefs have done their spite*, Sonn. 90, 10. Err. I, 2, 72. R3 I, 3, 215. Tim. V, 1, 226. Caes. IV, 2, 51. Ant. IV, 12, 17. Cymb. IV, 2, 282. Followed by *with: ha' done with words*, Shr. III, 2, 118. H6C II, 2, 117. *have done with woes*, Tit. V, 3, 176. *I have done with thee*, Rom. III, 5, 205.

b) ruined, lost: *were I not immortal, life were done*, Ven. 197. *wasted, thawed and done*, 749. *as soon decayed and done*, Lucr. 23. *a beauty spent and done*, Compl. 11. *though there my hope be done*, All's IV, 2, 65. *our own love waking cries to see what's done*, V, 3, 65. R2 I, 1, 183. H6A IV, 3, 38. IV, 6, 7. H6C III, 3, 33. 58. Troil. I, 2, 313. Rom. I, 4, 39. Hml. III, 2, 172.

c) a match, agreed: *done!* Tp. II, 1, 32. *a match! 'tis done*, Shr. V, 2, 74. *'tis done*, Cor. I, 4, 2.

Dobbin, name of a horse: Merch. II, 2, 100. 102.

Dock, the plant Rumex: Tp. II, 1, 144. H5 V, 2, 52.

Docked, placed as in a dry dock; Pope's conjecture in Merch. I, 1, 27. O. Edd. *docks*, some M. Edd. *decks*.

Doctor, one who has passed the degrees of a faculty, a learned man: Wiv. IV, 5, 71. Err. IV, 4, 50. 125. V, 170. Merch. III, 4, 50. IV, 1, 105. 144. 168. V, 210 etc. R3 III, 5, 103. H8 II, 2, 122. II, 4, 206. —*s doubt that*, Wiv. V, 5, 184. *but then is an ape a d. to such a man*, Ado V, 1, 206.

Especially a physician: Wiv. I, 2, 1. I, 4, 3. 99. II, 1, 210. II, 3, 19. 49. IV, 4, 84 etc. H4B I, 2, 1. Mcb. IV, 3, 145. V, 1, 87. V, 3, 37. Cymb. I, 5, 4. V, 5, 30. *your —s*, Shr. Ind. 2, 133. *our most learned —s*, All's II, 1, 119. *our —s say*, R2 I, 1, 157. *his d.* Hml. III, 2, 317. *d. She*, All's II, 1, 82. *d. of physic*, Wiv. II, 1, 4 (Evans' speech).

Doctor-like, like a learned man, giving one's self airs: Sonn. 66, 10.

Doctrine, 1) instruction: *from women's eyes this d. I derive*, LLL IV, 3, 302. 350. *we knew not the d. of ill-doing, nor dream'd that any did*, Wint. I, 2, 70. *thou canst not teach me to forget. I'll pay that d.* Rom. I, 1, 244. *I hourly learn a d. of obedience*, Ant. V, 2, 31.

2) learning: *the schools, embowelled of their d., have left off the danger to itself*, All's I, 3, 247.

3) a principle of faith: *a comfortable d.*, Tw. I, 5, 239. *a worse sin than ill d.* H8 I, 3, 60.

Document, instruction: *a d. in madness*, Hml. IV, 5, 178.

Do de, inarticulate sound uttered by a person shivering with cold: Lr. III, 4, 59. III, 6, 77.

Dodge, vb. to use craft, to play mean tricks: *d. and palter in the shifts of lowness*, Ant. III, 11, 62.

Doe, a she-deer, the female of a buck: Ven. 875. Lucr. 581. Wiv. V, 5, 17. 20. As II, 7, 128. Troil. III, 1, 127. Tit. II, 1, 93. 117. II, 2, 26.

Doer, 1) one who has done any thing: Lucr. Arg. 23. All's II, 3, 133. V, 3, 154. Tw. III, 4, 91. Caes. III, 1, 95. Cymb. V, 1, 15.

2) one who is wont and ready to act: *great —s in our trade,* Meas. IV, 3, 20. *talkers are no good —s,* R3 I, 3, 352.

Doff (cf. *Daff*) 1) to take off: *d. this habit,* Shr. III, 2, 102. John III, 1, 128. H4A V, 1, 12. Troil. V, 3, 31. Ant. IV, 4, 13 (F1 *daff*). Figuratively: *d. thy name,* Rom. II, 2, 47. *d. their distresses,* Mcb. IV, 3, 188.

2) to evade: *every day thou —est me with some device,* Oth. IV, 2, 176 (F1 *dafts*).

Dog, subst. 1) the domestic animal belonging to the genus Canis: Ven. 240. Lucr. 736. Pilgr. 273 (*curtal d.*). Tp. II, 2, 144. Gentl. II, 3, 6. II, 5, 36. IV, 2, 78. Wiv. I, 1, 96. 298. II, 1, 114 (*a curtal d.*). III, 5, 8. Err. III, 2, 151 (*curtal d.*). V, 70. Mids. II, 1, 210. V, 136. Merch. IV, 1, 91. Mcb. III, 1, 95. Lr. III, 4, 96 etc. etc. *has no more pity in him than a d.* Gentl. II, 3, 12. *they called us for our fierceness English —s,* H6A I, 5, 25. *he's a very d. to the commonalty,* Cor. I, 1, 28 (i. e. unfeeling, cruel). *that bloody mind, I think, they learned of me, as true a d. as ever fought at head,* Tit. V, 1, 102. (cf. *Dogged, Dog-hearted*). *let slip the —s of war,* Caes. III, 1, 273 (i. e. famine, sword and fire; cf. H5 Prol. 7). Proverbial phrases: *you'll lie like dogs,* Tp. III, 2, 22 (quibbling). *thus I would teach a d.* Gentl. IV, 4, 7. *he shall not have a stone to throw at his d.* Wiv. I, 4, 119. cf. As I, 3, 3. Mcb. V, 3, 47. Oth. IV, 1, 147. *let no d. bark,* Merch. I, 1, 94 (= all be silent). *to be, as it were, a d. at all things,* Gentl. IV, 4, 14 (= to be well versed in all things); cf. *I am d. at a catch,* Tw. II, 3, 64. *I'ld beat him like a d.* Tw. II, 3, 154. H4A III, 3, 101. Cor. IV, 5, 57. *a staff is quickly found to beat a d.* H6B III, 1, 171. *as dank as a d.* H4A II, 1, 10. *—s must eat,* Cor. I, 1, 210. *blush like a black d.* Tit. V, 1, 122. *with an R. Ah, mocker! that's the —'s name,* Rom. II, 4, 223 (Ben Jonson: *R is the dog's letter and hurreth in the sound*). *dog will have his day,* Hml. V, 1, 315. *flattered me like a d.* Lr. IV, 6, 98.

2) a term of reproach: Tp. I, 1, 44. Mids. III, 2, 65. Merch. I, 3, 112. II, 8, 14 (*the d. Jew*). IV, 1, 128. As I, 1, 86. R2 V, 5, 70 (*sad d.*). H6A I, 2, 23. R3 I, 2, 39. IV, 3, 6 and V, 5, 2 (*bloody d.*). Tit. V, 3, 14 (*inhuman d.*). Rom. I, 1, 9. Oth. V, 1, 62 (*inhuman d.*). V, 2, 361 (*Spartan d.*), etc. etc. The Cynic Apemantus often called so in Tim. II, 2, 50. 90. IV, 3, 251 etc.

Dog, vb. to follow; 1) as the dog does his master: *to d. his heels and courtsy at his frowns,* H4A III, 2, 127.

2) to hunt, to track like a hound: *where death and danger —s the heels of worth,* All's III, 4, 15. *I have —ed him like his murderer,* Tw. III, 2, 81. R2 V, 3, 139. H6A IV, 3, 2. R3 IV, 1, 40. Troil. V, 1, 103.

3) to attend with molestation: *we shall be —ed with company,* Mids. I, 2, 106. *both our honour and our shame in this are —ed with two strange followers,* Troil. I, 3, 365. *a name whose repetition will be —ed with curses,* Cor. V, 3, 144.

Dog-ape, a dog-faced baboon? (Dyce), or a male ape? *that they call compliment is like the encounter of two —s,* As II, 5, 27.

Dogberry, name in Ado III, 3, 8.

Dog-days, the hottest days in the year: *twenty of the d. now reign in his nose,* H8 V, 4, 43.

Dogfish, a kind of shark: H6A I, 4, 107.

Dog-fox, male fox (cf. *Fox*): *that same d. Ulysses,* Troil. V, 4, 12 (or perhaps = bloody-minded, cruel fox?).

Dogged, adj. bloody-minded, unfeeling, cruel (cf. *Dog*): *I'll fill these d. spies with false reports,* John IV, 1, 129. *doth d. war bristle his angry crest,* IV, 4, 149. *d. York doth level at my life,* H6B III, 1, 158.

Dog-hearted, unfeeling, inhuman: *his d. daughters,* Lr. IV, 3, 47.

Dog-hole, a kennel: *France is a d.* All's II, 3, 291.

Dog's-leather, leather made of dogskin: H6B IV, 2, 26.

Dog-weary, extremely weary: Shr. IV, 2, 60.

Doing, subst. see *Do.*

Doit, the smallest piece of money, a trifle: Tp. II, 2, 33. Merch. I, 3, 141. H6B III, 1, 112. Cor. V, 4, 60. Tim. I, 1, 217. Per. IV, 2, 55. *irons of a d.* (= worth a d.) Cor. I, 5, 7. *a dissension of a d.* IV, 4, 17. In Ant. IV, 12, 37 O. Edd. *dolts,* M. Edd. blunderingly *doits.*

Doit, name in H4B III, 2, 21.

Dolabella, name in Ant. V, 1, 1. 69. V, 2, 68. 197 etc.

Dole, subst. 1) dealing, distribution: *that in the d. of blows your son might drop,* H4B I, 1, 169.

2) share, portion: *when I consider what great creation and what d. of honour flies where you bid it,* All's II, 3, 176. *Happy man be his d.* = a) may happiness be his portion: *I'll fight. You will! why, happy man be's d.* Wint. I, 2, 163. b) happy he who succeeds best: *if it be my luck, so; if not, happy man be his d.* Wiv. III, 4, 68. *sweet Bianca! happy man be his d.! he that runs fastest gets the ring,* Shr. I, 1, 144. *now, my masters, happy man be his d.* H4A II, 2, 81.

Dole, subst. sorrow, grief: *what dreadful d. is here!* Mids. V, 283. *making such pitiful d. over them,* As I, 2, 139. *in equal scale weighing delight and d.* Hml. I, 2, 13. *omit we all their d. and woe,* Per. III Prol. 42.

Doleful, sorrowful, sad: *the d. knell,* Lucr. 1495. Pilgr. 272. *my d. plight,* 277. *the —est ditty,* 383. *d. matter merrily set down,* Wint. IV, 4, 189. *a very d. tune,* 265. *a d. hymn,* John V, 7, 22. *my d. days,* H4B II, 4, 211. *d. dumps,* Rom. IV, 5, 129.

Doll, contraction of *Dorothy:* H4B II, 1, 176. II, 2, 167. II, 4, 39 etc. H5 II, 1, 81. V, 1, 86 (M. Edd. *Nell*).

Dollar, a silver coin: Mcb. I, 2, 62. Quibbling with *dolour:* Tp. II, 1, 17. Meas. I, 2, 50. Lr. II, 4, 54.

Dolorous, sad: *you take me in too d. a sense,* Ant. IV, 2, 39.

Dolour, sorrow, grief: Lucr. 1446. 1582. Gentl. III, 1, 240. Wint. V, 2, 95. R2 I, 3, 257. R3 II, 2, 65. Troil. V, 3, 84 (Q —s, Ff d.). Mcb. IV, 3, 8. Cymb. V, 4, 80. Quibbling with *dollar:* Tp. II, 1, 17. Meas. I, 2, 50. Lr. II, 4, 54.

Dolphin, 1) ancient spelling of *Dauphin,* q. v.* 2) name in H5 IV, 8, 100.

3) the fish Delphinus Delphis: Mids. II, 1, 150. All's II, 3, 31. Tw. I, 2, 15. H4B II, 1, 94 (*in*

my d. chamber). Quibble between 1st and 3d signif.: H6A I, 4, 107.

Dolphin-like: Ant. V, 2, 89.

Dolt, blockhead, loggerhead: Troil. I, 2, 262. Oth. V, 2, 163. Ant. IV, 12, 37 (not *doits,* as M. Edd. have it).

Domage, see *Damage.*

Dombledon, name in H4B I, 2, 33 (Q *Dommelton*).

Domestic, adj., pertaining to a person's own country or nation, intestine, not foreign: *d. broils,* R3 II, 4, 60. *d. awe, night-rest and neighbourhood,* Tim. IV, 1, 17 (i. e. all reverence for the duties of society). *d. fury,* Caes. III, 1, 263. *malice d.* Mcb. III, 2, 25. *broils,* Lr. V, 1, 30. *quarrel,* Oth. II, 3, 215. *equality of two d. powers,* Ant. I, 3, 47. *Caesar, that hath more kings his servants than thyself d. officers,* Cymb. III, 1, 65 (= officers in thy own country).

Domestic, subst. one who is in immediate and direct dependence on another, not a foreign vassal: *powers are your retainers, and your words, —s to you, serve your will as't please yourself pronounce their office,* H8 II, 4, 114.

Domination, dominion, sovereign power: *thou and thine usurp the —s, royalties and rights of this oppressed boy,* John II, 176 (F1 —s, F2.3.4 *d.'.*

Dominator, ruler: *sole d. of Navarre,* LLL I, 1, 222 (Armado's letter). *Saturn is d. over mine* (desires) Tit. II, 3, 31.

Domineer, to have one's way, to indulge one's self unrestrained, to play the master: *go to the feast, revel and d.* Shr. III, 2, 226. Followed by *over,* = to hector, to tyrannize: *a —ing pedant o'er the boy,* LLL III, 179.

Dominical, the red letter which in old almanacs denotes the Lord's day: LLL V, 2, 44.

Dominion, the territory under a prince's government: *in his d.* Cymb. III, 2, 41. Plur. *—s:* Wint. II, 3, 177. John III, 1, 154. R2 I, 3, 142. H8 II, 4, 16. Hml. II, 2, 78. Lr. I, 1, 180.

Domitius, name in Ant. III, 5, 21. IV, 2, 1 (O. Edd. *Domitian*).

Dommelton, name in H4B I, 2, 33 (Ff *Dombledon*).

Don, subst. Spanish title before the names of noblemen: *D. Alphonso,* Gentl. I, 3, 39. *D. Antonio,* II, 4, 54. Ado I, 1, 1. II, 2, 34. III, 3, 115 etc. LLL I, 1, 280. IV, 1, 89. V, 1, 9 etc. *D. Worm, his conscience,* Ado V, 2, 86. *D. Cupid,* LLL III, 182 (Q1 *Dan*).

Don, vb. to do on, to put on: *this robe,* Tit. I, 189. *his clothes,* Hml. IV, 5, 52. *his helm,* Ant. II, 1, 33.

Donalbain, name in Mcb. II, 2, 19. II, 3, 80 etc.

Donation, gift, grant: *some d. freely to estate on the blest lovers,* Tp. IV, 85. *the motive of our so frank d.* Cor. III, 1, 130. *I would have put my wealth into d.* Tim. III, 2, 90. *it was wise nature's end in the d., to be his evidence now,* Cymb. V, 5, 367.

Doncaster (Qq *Dancaster*), place in England: H4A V, 1, 42. 58.

Dong, see *Ding.*

Doom, subst. 1) decree, judgment, sentence: *for now against himself he sounds this d., that through the length of times he stands disgraced,* Lucr. 717. *when they had sworn to this advised d.* 1849. *giving gentle d.* Sonn. 145, 7. Gentl. III, 1, 185. 222.

IV, 1, 32. Meas. II, 2, 12. As I, 3, 85. John III, 1, 311. R2 I, 3, 148. V, 6, 23. H4A III, 2, 6. H6A IV, 1, 45. H6B I, 3, 208. 214. III, 1, 281. H6C III, 3, 101. R3 IV, 4, 12. 217. Tit. V, 3, 182. Rom. III, 3, 4. 59. Lr. I, 1, 151 (Ff *reserve thy state*). 167 (Ff *gift*). Per. III Prol. 32 (*obedient to their —s*). V, 2, 20. *d. of death,* Err. I, 1, 2. H5 III, 6, 46 (*give*). Tit.III,1,24. *expect your highness' d., of life or death,* H6B IV, 9, 12. *d. of mercy,* H6C II, 6, 46. *of banishment,* Tit. III, 1, 51.

2) the last judgment: *from the creation to the general d.* Lucr. 924. *to the ending d.* Sonn. 55, 12. *to the edge of d.* 116, 12. *till the perpetual d.* Wiv. V, 5, 62. *the general d.* Rom. III, 2, 67. *the great —'s image,* Mcb. II, 3, 83. *to the crack of d.* IV, 1, 117. *as against the d.* Hml. III, 4, 50.

3) the decree of destiny, fate: *forfeit to a confined d.* Sonn. 107, 4 (i. e. to the fate of mortality). *from his all-obeying breath I hear the doom of Egypt,* Ant. III, 13, 78. cf. *alter not the d. forethought by heaven,* John III, 1, 311. *unavoided is the d. of destiny,* R3 IV, 4, 217.

4) perdition, ruin, death: *to be thy partner in this shameful d.* Lucr. 672. *thy end is truth's and beauty's d. and date,* Sonn. 14, 14. *to change blows with thee for our day of d.* R2 III, 2, 189. *and triumph in thy day of d.* H6C V, 6, 93. *this is the day of d. for Bassianus,* Tit. II, 3, 42. *the death of Antony is not a single d.* Ant. V, 1, 18.

Doom, vb. 1) to judge, to decide: *nobly —ed!* Cymb. V, 5, 420.

2) to sentence, to condemn: *to d. the offenders,* R3 III, 4, 67. *the gods d. him after,* Cor. I, 8, 6. *my lord is —ed a prisoner,* R2 V, 1, 4. *—ed to die,* Err. I, 1, 155. *—ed to walk the night,* Hml. I, 5, 10. *he —ed this beauty to a grave,* John IV, 3, 39. *d. men to death,* Tit. III, 1, 47.

3) to pass sentence of: *to d. my brother's death,* R3 II, 1, 102. *will d. her death,* Tit. IV, 2, 114. *the prince will d. thee death,* Rom. III, 1, 139.

Doomsday, 1) the day of the last and universal judgment: Err. III, 2, 101. LLL IV, 3, 274. Caes. III, 1, 98. Hml. I, 1, 119. II, 2, 243. V, 1, 67. Ant. V, 2, 232.

2) the day of death; death: *d. is near: die all, die merrily,* H4A IV, 1, 134. *All-Souls' day is my body's d.* R3 V, 1, 12. *what less than d. is the prince's doom?* Rom. III, 3, 9. *their stolen marriage-day was Tybalt's d.* V, 3, 234.

Door, (of two syll. in Tit. I, 288; cf. *fire, hour* etc.) a passage into a building, or into any room of it: Wiv. IV, 2, 53. Meas. IV, 1, 32. Err. III, 1, 30. Ado I, 1, 255 etc. *—s:* Gentl. III, 1, 111. Lr. II, 4, 307. Oth. I, 1, 85 (*To beat, knock, make, shut the d.* cf. *Beat* etc.). Plur. for the sing.: *the —s are made against you,* Err. III, 1, 93. *shut —s after you,* Merch. II, 5, 53. *I will make fast the —s,* II, 6, 49. *make the —s upon a woman's wit,* As IV, 1, 162. Tw. I, 4, 16 (cf. *Gate*). *at the d.:* Wiv. III, 3, 93. IV, 2, 98. Merch. I, 2, 147 (*knocks at the d.*). IV, 1, 15. As I, 1, 97. H4A II, 4, 93. Caes. II, 1, 70. Oth. II, 3, 48. *at d.:* Wiv. IV, 2, 111. Shr. IV, 1, 123. Wint. IV, 4, 352. H4A II, 4, 318. H4B II, 4, 381 (*knocks at d.*). 402. V, 3, 75. H8 V, 2, 17. 24. V, 4, 37. Troil. IV, 2, 36. Cymb. IV, 2, 22. *at your d.* John V, 2, 137. Tw. I, 4, 16. I, 5, 157. H6B IV, 2, 190. *it would not out at* *windows nor at —s,* John V, 7, 29. *to wander forth of —s,* Caes. III, 3, 3. *beg from d. to d.* Err. IV, 4, 40. *met the knave in the d.* Wiv. III, 5, 103. *dead as nail in d.* H4B V, 3, 126 (cf. *Door-nail*). *out of d.: the goose came out of d.* LLL III, 92. *beaten out of d.* Shr. Ind. 2, 87. John IV, 1, 34. *out o' d.* (Old Edd. *out a d.*): Err. II, 1, 11. Wint. II, 3, 67. Lr. III, 2, 11. *out of —s:* Err. IV, 4, 36. As III, 1, 15. Tw. II, 3, 78. Tim. I, 2, 25. Caes. III, 2, 183. *out o' —s:* Tp. III, 2, 78. H4B II, 4, 229. *out of my d.* Wiv. I, 4, 132. IV, 2, 194. *go to the d.* (= leave the house) Cor. IV, 5, 9. *speak within d.* (Qq —s) = do not cry so loud as to be heard in the street, Oth. IV, 2, 144. — In many of the above-cited instances the word is taken in the sense of h o u s e, as in the following also: *their business lies out o' d.* Err. II, 1, 11. *come not within these —s,* As II, 3, 17. *rain within —s, and none abroad,* H4B IV, 5, 9. *this rain-water out o' d.* Lr. III, 2, 11. *to haunt about my —s,* Oth. I, 1, 96. *pictures out of d.* II, 1, 109 (Q1 *out adoors*).

Figurative use: *brought him to the d. of death,* H6C III, 3, 105. *lead directly to the d. of truth,* Oth. III, 3, 407. *is the wind in that d.?* H4A III, 3, 102. *let the foul'st contempt shut d. upon me,* H8 II, 4, 43. *to meet displeasure farther from the —s,* John V, 1, 60. *this debate that bleedeth at our —s,* H4B IV, 4, 2. *will make no wars without —s,* Ant. II, 1, 13. *all of her that is out of d. most rich,* Cymb. I, 6, 15.

Door-keeper, a bawd: Per. IV, 6, 126. 175 (cf. Oth. IV, 1, 28—30).

Door-nail: *as dead as a d.* H6B IV, 10, 43; cf. H4B V, 3, 126.

Door-particulars, h o m e a f f a i r s, p r i v a t e a f f a i r s: *these domestic d. are not the question here,* Lr. V, 1, 30 (Ff *these domestic and particular broils*).

Dorcas, name of a shepherdess in Wint. IV, 4, 73.

Dorcus, name in Troil. V, 5, 8.

Doricles, assumed name of Florizel: Wint. IV, 4, 146. 150. 168. 178.

Dormouse, the animal M y o x u s g l i s, which passes winter in sleep: *to awake your d. valour,* Tw. III, 2, 21.

Dorothy, female name in H4B II, 4, 130. 136. Cymb. II, 3, 143.

Dorset, name in R3 I, 3, 210. 333 (Qq *Vaughan*). II, 1, 19. 66 (Qq *Lord Grey*). 83. IV, 1, 39. IV, 2, 47. IV, 4, 311. 520 etc. H8 IV, 1, 38. V, 3, 170.

Dorsetshire, an English county: R3 IV, 4, 524.

Dotage, 1) i m b e c i l i t y o f m i n d, particularly in old age: Tim. III, 5, 99. Lr. I, 4, 315. 349. II, 4, 200.

2) e x c e s s i v e f o n d n e s s: Ado II, 3, 175. 224. Mids. IV, 1, 52. Oth. IV, 1, 27. Ant. I, 1, 1. I, 2, 121.

Dotant, a man whose intellect is impaired by age: *such a decayed d.* Cor. V, 2, 47 (F4 *dotard*).

Dotard, the same: Ado V, 1, 59. Shr. V, 1, 109. Wint. II, 3, 74. Cymb. I, 1, 50.

Dote, 1) to a c t or s p e a k i r r a t i o n a l l y: *dumbly she passions, franticly she —th,* Ven. 1059. *peace, —ing wizard,* Err. IV, 4, 61. V, 195. 329. LLL V, 2, 76. H4B IV, 4, 126. H5 II, 1, 65. Troil. II, 2, 58. Tit. III, 2, 23. Oth. II, 1, 208. Ant. III, 11, 15.

2) to b e f o n d, to l o v e to e x c e s s: *love makes young men thrall and old men d.* Ven. 837. Lucr. 155. 207. 643. Sonn. 131, 3. 141, 4. Compl. 235. Err. III, 2, 47. LLL IV, 3, 126. Troil. V, 4, 4. Rom. II, 3,

82. III, 3, 67. Oth. III, 3, 170. Ant. III, 10, 20. *—ing* = fond, tender: *thou art —ing father of his fruit,* Lucr. 1064. 1490. Wiv. II, 2, 203. *a grandam's name is little less in love than is the —ing title of a mother,* R3 IV, 4, 300. — Followed by *on* or *upon:* Lucr. 416. 497. Sonn. 148, 5. Tp. IV, 231. Gentl. II, 4, 173. 207. IV, 4, 87. Wiv. II, 2, 106. Ado II, 1, 320. II, 3, 99. 219. Mids. I, 1, 108. 225. 230. II, 1, 171. III, 2, 3. IV, 1, 50. 173. Merch. I, 2, 120. As I, 2, 151. All's II, 1, 48. Tw. II, 2, 36. H4A III, 1, 146. H4B IV, 1, 138. H8 II, 1, 52. Cor. II, 1, 204. Hml. V, 2, 197. Lr. I, 4, 41. Oth. I, 1, 46.

Doter, fond lover: LLL IV, 3, 260.

Double, adj. 1) t w o f o l d: Ven. 429. Lucr. 1114. Sonn. 78, 8. 111, 12. Compl. 3. Phoen. 39. Tp. V, 295. Wiv. III, 3, 187. Meas. II, 2, 184. III, 2, 205. V, 409. Err. III, 2, 17. LLL IV, 3, 331. V, 2, 762 (Coll. M. *dull*). Mids. III, 2, 180. 209. IV, 1, 195. Merch. II, 8, 19 (*d. ducats*). Shr. IV, 3, 57. Tw. III, 2, 26. John IV, 2, 9. H4A III, 3, 202. H6A III, 2, 116. R3 IV, 4, 319. 324. Mcb. I, 2, 37. I, 6, 15. Hml. V, 1, 118. Cymb. I, 6, 121 etc. *snakes with d. tongue,* Mids. II, 2, 9. III, 2, 72. R2 III, 2, 20. *your chin d.* H4B I, 2, 207. *d. beer,* H6B II, 3, 64 (O. Edd. *double-beer*). *I am not a d. man,* H4A V, 4, 141 (i. e. a fetch, an apparition). *a voice potential as d. as the duke's,* Oth. I, 2, 14 (= of twofold influence), *an he were d. and d. a lord,* All's II, 3, 254. Compar. *—r:* Mids. III, 2, 72.

2) t w o t o g e t h e r, b e i n g i n p a i r s: *why answer not the d. majesties?* John II, 480. *whose d. bosoms seem to wear one heart,* Cor. IV, 4, 13. *his d. vouchers,* Hml. V, 1, 114.

3) e q u i v o c a l, d e c e i t f u l, f a l s e: *a d. heart,* Ado II, 1, 288 (quibble). *a d. meaning,* II, 3, 267. *a d. tongue,* V, 1, 170. LLL V, 2, 245. Mids. III, 2, 72 (*—r*). *swear by your d. self,* Merch. V, 245. *d. both in his words and meaning,* H8 IV, 2, 38. *in a d. sense,* Mcb. V, 8, 20. *his purchases, and d. ones too,* Hml. V, 1, 118.

Double, adv. 1) i n t w i c e t h e q u a n t i t y, t o t w i c e t h e d e g r e e: *an he were d. and d. a lord,* All's II, 3, 254. *then you kill her d.* Wint. V, 3, 107. *England shall d. gild his treble guilt,* H4B IV, 5, 129. *all our service ... done d.* Mcb. I, 6, 15. *I'll make assurance d. sure,* IV, 1, 83.

2) f a l s e l y, d e c e i t f u l l y: *if you should deal d. with her,* Rom. II, 4, 179 (the nurse's speech).

Double, vb. 1) trans. a) to m a k e t w o o f o n e: *his face seems twain, each several limb is —d,* Ven. 1067.

b) to e n l a r g e to t w i c e t h e q u a n t i t y o r n u m b e r: Gentl. II, 4, 21. Err. III, 2, 20. Merch. III, 2, 302. R2 I, 1, 57 (Ff *doubly*). H4B III, 1, 97. H8 V, 5, 29. Cor. II, 2, 120. Tim. I, 2, 7. Mcb. IV, 1, 10. 20. 35. Ant I, 5, 40.

c) to b e t w i c e a s m u c h: *thy fifty yet doth d. five and twenty,* Lr. II, 4, 262. *he's honourable, and —ing that, most holy,* Cymb. III, 4, 180.

d) to p l a c e i n t w o r a n k s: *to instruct for the —ing of files,* All's IV, 3, 303.

2) intr. a) to i n c r e a s e to t w i c e t h e s u m: *that the debt should d.* Ven. 521.

b) to s p e a k b r o k e n l y, to s p l i t t h e w o r d s: *this knave's tongue begins to d.* H6B II, 3, 94.

Double, subst. a t u r n t o e s c a p e p u r s u i t:

he cranks and crosses with a thousand —s, Ven.
682.

Double, name in H4B III, 2, 45.

Double-beer, a strong beer, ale: H6B II,
3, 64 (M. Edd. without the hyphen).

Double-charge, to overcharge: *I will d. thee
with dignities,* H4B V, 3, 129 (quibble in the words
Pistol and *charge*).

Double-damned, damned two ways: Oth. IV,
2, 37.

Double-dealer, one guilty of duplicity;
used quibblingly: *I might have cudgelled thee out of
thy single life, to make thee a d.* Ado V, 4, 116. *I will
be so much a sinner, to be a d.: there's another,* Tw.
V, 38.

Double-dealing, duplicity: *but that it would
be d., I would you could make it another,* Tw. V, 32.

Double-fatal, dangerous or deadly two ways:
their bows of d. yew, R2 III, 2, 117 (so called on
account of the poisonous quality of the leaves, and
of the wood being used for instruments of death).

Double-henned: *now my d. sparrow!* (Q *d.
Spartan*) Troil. V, 7, 11; perhaps = sparrow with
a double-hen, i. e. with a female married to two cocks,
and hence false to both.

Double-lock, vb. to shoot the bolt twice, to
fasten with double security: *d. the door,* Ven. 448.

Double-meaning, speaking equivocally:
a d. prophesier, All's IV, 3, 114.

Doubleness, the state of being twofold: *the d.
of the benefit,* Meas. III, 1, 268.

Doublet, the inner garment of a man:
Tp. II, 1, 102. Gentl. II, 4, 20 (*my jerkin is a d.*).
Ado II, 3, 19. III, 2, 37. III, 3, 125. LLL III, 19. Merch.
I, 2, 80. Shr. Ind. 2, 9. Shr. V, 1, 68. Tw. II, 4, 76.
H4A II, 4, 84. 185. H4B V, 5, 87. H6B II, 1, 151.
H8 IV, 1, 74. Cor. I, 5, 7. Caes. I, 2, 267. Hml. II, 1,
78. Cymb. III, 4, 172. *a new d. and hose,* Wiv. III,
3, 35. *d. and hose ought to show itself courageous,*
As II, 4, 6. *I have a d. and hose in my disposition,*
III, 2, 206. 232. *we must have your d. and hose plucked
over your head,* IV, 1, 206. *in your d. and hose this
raw rheumatic day,* Wiv. III, 1, 46 (i. e. without a
coat or cloak). *he goes in his d. and hose and leaves
off his wit,* Ado V, 1, 203. *thou oughtest not to let thy
horse wear a cloak, when honester men go in their hose
and —s,* H6B IV, 7, 56.

Double-vantage, vb. to benefit twofold:
*the injuries that to myself I do, doing thee vantage, d.
me,* Sonn. 88, 12.

Doubly, in twice the quantity, number
or degree: Merch. V, 244. All's V, 3, 315. R2 I, 1,
57 (Qq *doubled*). I, 3, 167. V, 1, 71. Troil. I, 3, 122.
Cor. I, 1, 151. *thy blows, d. redoubled,* R2 I, 3, 80.
d. redoubled strokes, Mcb. I, 2, 38.

Doubt, subst. (its pronunciation: LLL V, 1, 23).
1) uncertainty of mind, irresolution, inde-
cision: *the hot scent-snuffing hounds are driven to d.*
Ven. 692. *this shall I ne'er know, but live in d.* Sonn.
144, 13. *nice affections wavering stood in d. if best
were as it was, or best without,* Compl. 97. *were you
in d., that you asked her?* Ado I, 1, 106. *still gazing
in a d. whether those peals of praise be his or no,*
Merch. III, 2, 145. *hang no more in d.* John III, 1,
219. *speaks things in d., that carry but half sense,*
Hml. IV, 5, 6 (i. e. in ambiguity; cf. *doubtful* I, 5,

175). Mids. III, 2, 279. As V, 4, 25. H6C IV, 1, 135.
IV, 7, 27. Rom. IV, 1, 87. Cymb. IV, 3, 45.

2) disposition or motive to disbelieve
sth., want of credit: *our —s are traitors,* Merch.
I, 4, 77. *I should be arguing still upon that d.* Shr. III,
1, 55. Wint. IV, 4, 633. John IV, 2, 233. R3 I, 3, 1.
H8 II, 2, 28. II, 4, 215 (*commit to d.*). III, 1, 171.
Mcb. IV, 3, 25. Oth. III, 3, 366. Per. I, 2, 97. *to make
d.* (used negatively): LLL V, 2, 151. H8 V, 3, 67.
Cor. I, 2, 18. *to make no d. of sth.:* Gentl. V, 2, 20.
Cor. V, 4, 49. *'tis d. whether our kinsman come to see
his friends,* R2 I, 4, 20. *no d. but he hath got a quiet
catch,* Shr. II, 333. Tim. I, 2, 91. *no d.* = undoubtedly:
Tp. I, 2, 7. V, 266. Mids. IV, 1, 137. Merch. I, 2, 35.
H5 I, 1, 64. II, 2, 19. IV, 3, 95. H6C V, 1, 62. R3 I,
1, 129. I, 2, 245. II, 3, 15. II, 4, 21. III, 1, 154. III,
7, 54. 170. IV, 1, 87. IV, 2, 39. IV, 4, 226. V, 3, 214.
H8 I, 3, 57. III, 2, 244. Caes. III, 2, 219. Cymb. IV,
3, 21. Per. I, 2, 86. *out of d.:* Wiv. II, 1, 79. Err. IV,
3, 82. Mids. IV, 2, 3. Merch. I, 1, 21. 155. H5 IV, 1,
20. 114. V, 1, 47. *that's past d.* Wint. I, 2, 268. II,
3, 80. *stay, past d., for greater,* Cor. II, 3, 265. *without
all d.* H8 IV, 1, 113.

3) apprehension, suspicion: *overcome by
d. and bloodless fear,* Ven. 891. *to descant on the —s
of my decay,* Pilgr. 184. *they made a d. presence
majestical would put him out,* LLL V, 2, 101. *urge
—s to them that fear,* R2 II, 1, 299. *deposed 'tis d. he
will be,* III, 4, 69 (Ff *doubted*). *to end one d. by death
revives two greater in the heirs of life,* H4B IV, 1, 199.
the d. is that he will seduce the rest, H6C IV, 8, 37. *in
whose breast d. and suspect are placed too late,* Tim.
IV, 3, 519. *bound in to saucy —s and fears,* Mcb. III,
4, 25. *shall never sag with d.* V, 3, 10. *where love is
great, the littlest —s are fear,* Hml. III, 2, 181. *to be
once in d. is once to be resolved,* Oth. III, 3, 179. *the
smallest fear or d. of her revolt,* 188. *'tis a shrewd d.,
though it be but a dream,* 429. *this is a d. nothing
becoming you,* Cymb. IV, 4, 14. *to lop that d.* Per. I,
2, 90. H6C III, 3, 238.

Doubt, vb. 1) to hesitate to believe; a)
absol.: *I d.* Meas. I, 4, 77. *wherefore should I d.?*
Shr. IV, 4, 107. R3 II, 4, 22. Cor. I, 6, 68. Tim. IV,
3, 514. Hml. II, 2, 116. *I d. whether their legs be worth
the sums,* I, 2, 238. *I not d.* Tp. II, 1, 121. V, 303.
I d. not, Meas. IV, 2, 209. Tw. II, 3, 185. H6B IV,
9, 46. *d. not,* Shr. I, 1, 63. H4A IV, 4, 33. *d. thou not,*
Troil. V, 3, 35. *I do not d.* Merch. I, 1, 149. *do not
d.* John V, 2, 180. *I do nothing d.* Cymb. I, 4, 106.

b) Followed by *of: crowning the present,* —*ing
of the rest,* Sonn. 115, 12. John I, 63. H5 II, 2, 184.
H6A I, 1, 100. H6B IV, 8, 54. H6C I, 2, 73. IV, 7, 87.
Caes. III, 1, 183. Lr. IV, 7, 24.

c) Used negatively and followed by *but: let it not
be —ed but he'll come,* Wiv. IV, 4, 43. *d. not but she
will well excuse . . .,* Err. III, 1, 92. Ado IV, 1, 236.
All's IV, 4, 18. Wint. III, 2, 31. H4B IV, 4, 11. H5 II,
2, 187. R3 III, 5, 64. V, 2, 19. Cor. II, 1, 217. 242.
Per. IV, 6, 196. 210. Followed by *but that: I do not
d. but that my noble master will appear such,* Caes.
IV, 2, 11. By an infinitive preceded by *but: I d. not
but to fashion it,* Ado II, 1, 384. Mids. IV, 2, 44. Tw.
V, 316. R2 V, 2, 115. H4A II, 2, 14. H6A II, 5, 126.

d) Followed by an accus.: *so high a hope that
even ambition cannot pierce a wink beyond, but d. discovery there,* Tp. II, 1, 243 (= d. of what it sees

there). —*ing thy birth and lawful progeny*, H6A III, 3, 61. *you do not d. my faith?* H8 II, 1, 143. *they nothing d. prevailing*, Cor. I, 3, 111. *nothing —ing your present assistance*, Tim. III, 1, 20. *I do not d. thy faith*, Per. I, 2, 111. *I d. it not*, Err. IV, 1, 84. Ado I, 1, 47. Shr. II, 75. IV, 1, 15. H6B I, 4, 48. Rom. III, 4, 14. Tim. V, 1, 95. Mcb. V, 4, 2. Hml. I, 2, 41. Ant. III, 7, 1. *doctors d. that*, Wiv. V, 5, 184. As V, 4, 44. John II, 193. H5 II, 2, 20. Cor. I, 2, 30. Tim. III, 6, 57. *which I d. not*, H5 III, 1, 28.

2) to distrust: *fearful to do a thing where I the issue —ed*, Wint. I, 2, 259. *I do not d. you*, H4B IV, 2, 77. *I speak not this as —ing any here*, H6C V, 4, 43. *his looks I fear, and his intents I d.* Rom. V, 3, 44. *unto bad causes swear such creatures as men d.* Caes. II, 1, 132. *he is not —ed*, IV, 2, 13. *and begin to d. the equivocation of the fiend*, Mcb. V, 5, 43. *who dotes, yet —s*, Oth. III, 3, 170.

3) to suspect, to fear; a) followed by an accus.: *you that love the fundamental part of state more than you d. the change on't*, Cor. III, 1, 152. *I d. some foul play*, Hml. I, 2, 256. *my general will forget my love and service. Do not d. that*, Oth. III, 3, 19.

b) followed by a clause: *I d. he be not well*, Wiv. I, 4, 42. *—ing the filching age will steal his treasure*, Sonn. 75, 6. *I d. we should have been too young for them*, Ado V, 1, 118. *I d. my uncle practises more harm to me*, John IV, 1, 19. IV, 2, 102. V, 6, 44. H4A I, 2, 203. H4B V, 5, 122. H6C IV, 3, 19. H8 I, 2, 158. Troil. I, 2, 302. Tit. II, 3, 68. Mcb. IV, 2, 67. Hml. II, 2, 56. III, 1, 174. Lr. V. 1, 6. Followed by *lest:* —*ing lest that he had erred*, Per. I, 3, 22. By an inf.: *d. truth to be a liar*, Hml. II, 2, 118.

c) *I d. me* = I fear me, I fear: Tim. I, 2, 159.

Doubtful, 1) not settled in opinion, wavering, hesitating: *in perplexity and d. dilemma*, Wiv. IV, 5, 87. *d. whether what I see be true*, Merch. III, 2, 148. *yet I am d.* Lr. IV, 7, 65. Followed by *of: I am d. of your modesties*, Shr. Ind. 1, 94.

2) not secure, suspicious, filled with apprehension: *d. thoughts and rash-embraced despair*, Merch. III, 2, 109. *that my most jealous and too d. soul may live at peace*, Tw. IV, 3, 27. *wild amazement hurries up and down the little number of your d. friends*, John V, 1, 36. *d. fear*, H6C IV, 6, 62. *dwell in d. joy*, Mcb. III, 2, 7. *I am d. that you have been conjunct and bosomed with her*, Lr. V, 1, 12.

3) uncertain, undecided, questionable: *beauty is but a vain and d. good*, Pilgr. 169. *long was the combat d.* 215; cf. H4A IV, 1, 48. H6A IV, 1, 151. R3 V, 3, 93. Mcb. I, 2, 7. *what obscured light the heavens did grant did but convey unto our fearful minds a d. warrant of immediate death*, Err. I, 1, 69. *his (supply) is certain, ours is d.* H4A IV, 3, 4. *d. hollow-hearted friends*, R3 IV, 4, 435. 493. *this sailing Pandar our d. hope*, Troil. I, 1, 107. *d. fortunes*, III, 3, 8. *it is d. yet whether Caesar will come forth*, Caes. II, 1, 193.

4) breeding suspicion: *by pronouncing of some d. phrase*, Hml. I, 5, 175 (cf. *doubt* IV, 5, 6). *her death was d.* V, 1, 250.

Doubtfully, with uncertainty of meaning, equivocally, ambiguously: *I writ at random, very d.* Gentl. II, 1, 118. *spake he so d., thou couldst not feel his meaning?* Err. II, 1, 50. 53. *whom the oracle hath d. pronounced thy throat shall cut*, Tim. IV, 3, 121.

Doubtless, adj. 1) free from fear or suspicion: *sleep d. and secure*, John IV, 1, 130. — 2) sure: *I am d. I can purge myself*, H4A III, 2, 20.

Doubtless, adv. undoubtedly, certainly: *bawd he is d.* Meas. III, 2, 72. H6A I, 2, 119. IV, 7, 44. H6C IV, 6, 90. Cor. I, 4, 48. Oth. III, 3, 242. Cymb. III, 4, 178.

Dough, unbaked paste of bread: *our cake is d. on both sides*, Shr. I, 1, 110. *my cake is d.* V, 1, 145 (i. e. I am disappointed).

Doughty-handed, stout of hands: Ant. IV, 8, 5.

Doughy, unbaked, unripe: Alls IV, 5, 3.

Douglas, name in H4A I, 1, 67. II, 4, 377. III, 2, 107 etc. H4B I, 1, 17 etc. *the D.:* H4A I, 3, 261. II, 3, 28. IV, 1, 3. V, 1, 116. V, 4, 26. V, 5, 27. H4B Ind. 31.

Dout, to put out, to extinguish: *that their hot blood may spin in English eyes, and d. them with superfluous courage*, H5 IV, 2, 11 (O. Edd. *doubt*). *I have a speech of fire, that fain would blaze, but that this folly* (viz my tears) *—s it*, Hml. IV, 7, 192 (F1 *doubts*, Qq F2. 3. 4 *drowns*).

Dout, pronunciation of *doubt*, blamed by Holofernes, LLL V, 1, 22.

Dove, the bird Columba; sacred to Venus: Ven. 1190. Lucr. 58. Pilgr. 119. Mids. I, 1, 171. Rom. II, 5, 7. Per. IV Prol. 32. Of white colour and used as the emblem of whiteness: Ven. 10. 366. 1190. Lucr. 58. Pilgr. 119. Wint. IV, 4, 374. H4B IV, 1, 46. Rom. I, 5, 50. Per. IV Prol. 32. Opposed to the crow and raven: Sonn. 113, 12. Mids. II, 2, 114. Tw. V, 134. Symbol of harmlessness and innocence: Ven. 153. Lucr. 360. Pilgr. 86. Phoen. 50. Mids. I, 2, 85. II, 1, 232. Shr. II, 295. III, 2, 159. Tw. V, 134. H4B III, 2, 171. IV, 1, 46. H6B III, 1, 71. Cor. V, 3, 27. Hml. V, 1, 309. *so —s do peck the falcon's piercing talons*, H6C I, 4, 41. II, 2, 18. Ant. III, 13, 197. Standing rhyme to *love:* Rom. II, 1, 10. Mahomet inspired with a d. H6A I, 2, 140. —*s driven away with stench*, I, 5, 23. — Used as a term of endearment: Wiv. I, 3, 107. Mids. V, 332. Hml. IV, 5, 167.

Used for *pigeon* by old Gobbo: *a dish of —s*, Merch. II, 2, 144. The words confounded on purpose: *he eats nothing but —s, and that breeds hot blood*, Troil. III, 1, 140.

Dove-cote, a small building to keep pigeons in: Cor. V, 6, 115.

Dove-drawn, on a carriage drawn by doves, Tp. IV, 94.

Dove-feathered, with white feathers like a dove: *d. raven*, Rom. III, 2, 76.

Dove-house, a building for doves: Rom. I, 3, 27. 33.

Dover, town in England: John V, 1, 31 (*D. castle*). H5 III Chor. 4 (M. Edd. *Hampton*). H6A V, 1, 49. Lr. III, 1, 36. III, 6, 98. III, 7, 19 etc.

Dowager, a widow with a jointure: Mids. I, 1, 5. 157. H8 II, 4, 180. *princess d.* III, 2, 70. IV, 1, 23.

Dowdy, a slut, a trollop: Rom. II. 4, 43.

Dower, subst. 1) the property which a woman brings to her husband in marriage: Tp. III, 1, 54 Meas. I, 2, 154. All's II, 3, 151. IV, 4, 19. V, 3, 328. H6A V, 1, 44. V, 5, 46. Lr. I, 1, 45. 110. 130. 195.

2) that which a widow possesses after the death

of her husband: Shr. II, 345. 391. IV, 2, 117. IV, 4, 45. H6C III, 2, 72.

3) any gift? *If this suit lay in Bianca's d., how quickly should you speed!* Oth. IV, 1, 108 (or indeed = marriage-portion? Qq and most M. Edd. *power*).

Dowered, furnished as with a marriage-portion: *d. with our curse,* Lr. I, 1, 207.

Dowerless, having no marriage-portion: Lr. I, 1, 259. II, 4, 215.

Dowland, name of a famous lutenist in the time of the poet: Pilgr. 107.

Dowlas, coarse linen: H4A III, 3, 79.

Dowle, fibre of down in a feather: *diminish one d. that's in my plume,* Tp. III, 3, 65.

Down, subst. 1) a tract of naked, hilly land: *pursue these fearful creatures o'er the —s,* Ven. 677. *my bosky acres and my unshrubbed d.* Tp. IV, 81.

2) *the —s,* a well-known road for shipping near Deal: *whilst our pinnace anchors in the —s,* H6B IV, 1, 9.

3) soft feathers: Lucr. 1012. Wint. IV, 4, 374. H4A I, 3, 7. H4B IV, 5, 33. Troil. I, 1, 58. Oth. I, 3, 232. Cymb. III, 6, 35. Used of tender hair: *his phoenix d.* Compl. 93.

Down, an unmeaning snatch or burden of a song: *and d., d., a d. a,* Wiv. I, 4, 44. *you must sing a d. a d., an you call him a d. a,* Hml. IV, 5, 170.

Down, adv. 1) from a higher to a lower place, in a direction to the ground or bottom: *pour d. stinking pitch,* Tp. I, 2, 3. *look d., you gods,* V, 201. *fetch her d.* Gentl. III, 1, 40. *if the bottom were as deep as hell, I should d.* Wiv. III, 5, 14. *d. sleeves,* Ado III, 4, 20 (= hanging sleeves).* *that the precipitation might d. stretch below the beam of sight,* Cor. III, 2, 4. *it will be rain to-night. Let it come d.* Mcb. III, 3, 16. *a pack of sorrows which would press you d.* Gentl. III, 1, 20. *sit d.* Tp. I, 2, 32. III, 1, 23. III, 3, 6. *set it d.* III, 1, 18. *laying them d.* Gentl. I, 2, 135 etc. etc. *up and d.* = upwards and downwards, Per. III Prol. 50. *d. with the topmast,* Tp. I, 1, 37. *d. with 'em,* Gentl. IV, 1, 2. LLL IV, 3, 368. H6B IV, 7, 2 (= throw them d., destroy them; cf. *With*). *d.* = kneel down: *d. therefore and beg mercy of the duke,* Merch. IV, 1, 363. *d. and swear,* Tp. II, 2, 157. As III, 5, 57. Cor. V, 3, 169. = to bed: *to be up early and d. late,* Wiv. I, 4, 108. *is she not d. so late?* Rom. III, 5, 66. *in your clothes, and d. again?* IV, 5, 12; cf. the quibble in V, 3, 209. = fallen or struck down, lying on the ground: *the wall is d. that parted their fathers,* Mids. V, 359. *I can tell who should d.* As I, 2, 227. *if thou see me d. in the battle,* H4A V, 1, 121. *I was d. and out of breath,* V, 4, 149. Caes. V, 4, 9. Mcb. III, 3, 20. Rom. V, 3, 209. Tropically: *if Edward repossess the crown, 'tis like that Richmond with the rest shall d.* H6C IV, 6, 100. IV, 3, 42. IV, 4, 28. *Troy had been d.* Troil. I, 3, 75. *quite, quite d.* Hml. III, 1, 162. *the great man d., you mark his favourite flies,* III, 2, 214. *to be forestalled ere we come to fall, or pardoned being d.* III, 3, 50. Hence: *the French shone d. the English* (= outshone, eclipsed) H8 I, 1, 20. — *The moon is d.* Mcb. II, 1, 2 (= set). *she goes d. at twelve,* 3. *if the wind were d.* (= had ceased) Gentl. II, 3, 59. — Implying the idea of great and threatening power, when joined to verbs indicating motion: *go d. upon him,* H5 III, 5, 53. *come d. upon us with a mighty power,* Caes. IV, 3, 169. *a woman that bears all d. with her*

brain, Cymb. II, 1, 59 (cf. *Bear*). — *To write d.* (i.e. originally: on the paper): Gentl. I, 2, 117. Ado IV, 2, 13. Wint. IV, 4, 571 etc. (cf. *Write*). *O villain, that set this d. among her vices,* Gentl. III, 1, 337 (cf. *Set*). *prick him d.* Caes. IV, 1, 3. *make us pay d. for our offence by weight,* Meas. I, 2, 125 (originally = pay on the table). *paid d. more penitence than done trespass,* Wint. V, 1, 3. *I dare pawn d. my life for him,* Lr. I, 2, 93. Hence = downright, without hesitation: *he hailed d. oaths,* Mids. I, 1, 243. *there did this goldsmith swear me d. that I this day of him received the chain,* Err. V, 227. *here's a villain that would face me d. he met me on the mart,* III, 1, 16.

2) in a horizontal direction (a use originating in a misconceived idea of high and low): *walk with me d. to his house,* Err. IV, 1, 12. *west of this place, d. in the neighbour bottom,* As IV, 3, 79. *there have been commissions sent d. among 'em,* H8 I, 2, 20. *Up and d.* = a) to march straight up and d. Ado III, 1, 16. *wander up and d. to view the city,* Err. I, 2, 31. Mids. III, 1, 126. III, 2, 396. John V, 1, 35. H6A I, 3, 51. H6B III, 1, 214. Cor. V, 4, 40. Rom. II, 5, 53. Hml. II, 2, 528. *thrice his head thus waving up and d.* II, 1, 93. *to go up and d.* = to go, to show one's self, to be seen: *a' goes up and d. like a gentleman,* Ado III, 3, 135. *all shapes that man goes up and d. in,* Tim. II, 2, 119. b) everywhere: *we have been up and d. to seek thee,* Ado V, 1, 122. Merch. III, 1, 79. *holds in chase mine honour up and d.* John I, 223. *you follow the young prince up and d. like his ill angel,* H4B I, 2, 185. *the commons scatter up and d.* H6B III, 2, 126. c) altogether (in comparisons): *here's my mother's breath up and d.* Gentl. II, 3, 32. *here's his dry hand up and d.* Ado II, 1, 124. *up and d. carved like an apple-tart,* Shr. IV, 3, 89. *for up and d. she doth resemble thee,* Tit. V, 2, 107.

3) below, at the bottom, on the ground: *the other d., unseen and full of water,* R2 IV, 187. *and break your own neck d.* Hml. III, 4, 196 (a motion from above having preceded).

Down, prepos. 1) along from a higher to a lower place: *his tears run d. his beard,* Tp. V, 16. As II, 1, 39. R2 I, 1, 57. Cor. III, 1, 266. Hml. II, 2, 518. Ant. II, 5, 35.

2) along in a level direction: *up Fish Street! d. Saint Magnus' corner!* H6B IV, 8, 1. *I'ld whistle her off and let her d. the wind,* Oth. III, 3, 262. *up and d.: thy blood, which else runs tickling up and d. the veins,* John III, 3, 44. *walk up and d. the streets,* Caes. I, 3, 25. = throughout: *she says up and d. the town that her eldest son is like you,* H4B II, 1, 114.

Down-bed, a bed of down: H8 I, 4, 18.

Downfall, 1) fall from rank or state, ruin: R2 III, 4, 79. H6B III, 1, 73. H6C V, 6, 65. R3 II, 4, 49 (Ff *ruin*). III, 7, 217.

2) a going down, setting: *from Hyperion's rising in the east until his very d. in the sea,* Tit. V, 2, 57. Figuratively: *even in the d. of his mellowed years, when nature brought him to the door of death,* H6C III, 3, 104 (cf. Rom. III, 5, 128 etc.).

Downfallen, lying on the ground, ruined: *bestride our d. birthdom,* Mcb. IV, 3, 4. *the d. Mortimer,* H4A I, 3, 135 (F1.2.3 *downfall,* Qq *down-trod*).

Down-feather, Ant. III, 2, 48.

Down-gyved: *his stockings fouled, ungartered, and d. to his ancle,* Hml. II, 1, 80. Steevens: "hanging down like the loose cincture which confines the fetters round the ancles." Q3. 4 *down-gyred*, which would be = rolled up down to his ancle (but *gyre* is no Shakespearian word).

Down-razed, levelled to the ground: *lofty towers I see d.* Sonn. 64, 3.

Downright, adj. 1) straight down, straight to the point, done without trifling: *have at thee with a d. blow,* H6B II, 3, 92. *I cleft his beaver with a d. blow,* H6C I, 1, 12. *such mercy as his ruthless arm, with d. payment, showed unto my father,* I, 4, 32.

2) unceremonious, blunt, undisguised: *not made by man and woman after this d. way of creation,* Meas. III, 2, 112. *nor I have no cunning in protestation: only d. oaths,* H5 V, 2, 150. *that I did love the Moor to live with him, my d. violence and storm of fortunes may trumpet to the world,* Oth. I, 3, 250.

Downright, adv. directly, without stopping short, without further ceremony, plainly: *grew I not faint? and fell I not d.?* Ven. 645. *they'll mock us now d.* LLL V, 2, 389; cf. Mids. II, 1, 145 and Cor. II, 3, 167. *you have heard him swear d. he was,* As III, 4, 31. *and d. languished,* Wint. II, 3, 17. *it rains d.* Rom. III, 5, 129.

Down-roping, hanging down in glutinous filaments: *the gum d. from their pale-dead eyes,* H5 IV, 2, 48.

Down-sleeves, see *Down.*

Downstairs, down by the staircase: H4A II, 4, 112. H4B II, 1, 107. II, 4, 202.

Down-trod, trampled to the ground: H4A I, 3, 135 (F1. 2. 3 *downfall,* F4 *downfaln*).

Down-trodden, the same: John II, 241.

Downward, adj. directed to the ground: *the boar, whose d. eye still looketh for a grave,* Ven. 1106.

Downward, adv. 1) from a higher place to a lower, down: Compl. 284. Ado III, 2, 35. R2 V, 5, 113. Caes. V, 1, 86.

2) in a course of lineal descent: *a ring the county wears, that d. hath succeeded in his house from son to son,* All's III, 7, 23.

Downwards = *downward* 1): Tit. III, 1, 124.

Downy, 1) covered or furnished with down or soft hair: *a d. feather,* H4B IV, 5, 32. *d. cygnets,* H6A V, 3, 56. *d. windows* (viz the eyelids) Ant. V, 2, 319.

2) soft, placid: *shake off this d. sleep,* Mcb. II, 3, 81.

Dowry, 1) the property which a woman brings to her husband: Wiv. I, 1, 247. Meas. III, 1, 226. LLL II, 8. As III, 3, 55. Shr. I, 1, 136. I, 2, 185. II, 121. 272. IV, 5, 65. V, 2, 114. Tw. II, 5, 201. John II, 469. 486. H5 III Chor. 30. H6A V, 1, 20. H6B I, 1, 62. 129 (*—ies*). H6C III, 3, 137. Hml. III, 1, 140. Lr. I, 1, 244.

2) property (of women) in general: *spend the d. of a lawful bed,* Lucr. 938. *so are those crisped snaky golden locks often known to be the d. of a second head,* Merch. III, 2, 95. *I would not have him miscarry for the half of my d.* Tw. III, 4, 70. *at whose conception nature this d. gave,* Per. I, 1, 9.

Dowsabel, female name (used in jest?): Err. IV, 1, 110.

Doxy, a woman ready to be serviceable to any man: Wint. IV, 3, 2.

Dozen, twelve in number: H4A II, 4, 93. Hml.

II, 2, 566. II, 4, 193. Oth. IV, 3, 85. Followed by a subst. without *of: a d. years,* Tp. I, 2, 279. *thirty d. moons,* Hml. III, 2, 167. Wiv. I, 1, 16. Meas. I, 2, 21. Ado V, 1, 97. LLL V, 2, 234. Shr. Ind. I, 27. John III, 4, 173. H4B II, 4, 387. 402. III, 2, 102. 310. H8 I, 4, 105. V, 4, 8. Cor. I, 3, 24. Rom. III, 4, 27. Hml. V, 2, 172. Oth. I, 2, 41. Cymb. I, 6, 185. Followed by *of: seven d. of Scots,* H4A II, 4, 116. III, 3, 77. H4B V, 1, 71. V, 4, 16. Cor. II, 3, 135. Per. IV, 6, 22. *a d. of them:* All's IV, 5, 110. R2 V, 2, 97. H4A II, 4, 183. Tim. III, 6, 88. *knock them down by the —s,* H8 V, 4, 33.

Drab, subst. a lewd wench, a strumpet: Meas. II, 1, 247. Wint. IV, 3, 27 (*die and d.*). H6A V, 4, 32. H6B II, 1, 156. Troil. V, 1, 104. V, 2, 195. V, 4, 9. Mcb. IV, 1, 31. Hml. II, 2, 615.

Drabbing, following loose women: Hml. II, 1, 26.

Drachma, an ancient Greek coin: *that do prize their hours at a crack'd d.* Cor. I, 5, 6 (O. Edd. *drachme;* M. Edd., in spite of the verse, *drachm*). Caes. III, 2, 247. IV, 3, 73.

Draff, the refuse of food given to swine: *still swine eats all the d.* Wiv. IV, 2, 109 (O. Edd. *draugh*). *eating d. and husks,* H4A IV, 2, 38.

Drag, to pull, to draw, to trail: *my affairs d. me homeward,* Wint. I, 2, 24. *what impediments d. back our expedition,* H4A IV, 3, 19. *I'll d. thee up and down,* H6A I, 3, 51. H6B III, 2, 229. IV, 1, 4. IV, 3, 14. IV, 10, 86. Troil. V, 10, 5. Tit. II, 3, 129. 283. IV, 4, 56. Rom. III, 5, 156. Hml. IV, 1, 35.

Dragon, 1) a fabulous winged serpent: John II, 68. 288. H4A III, 1, 151. H6A I, 1, 11. R3 V, 3, 350. Cor. IV, 1, 30. V, 4, 13. Rom. III, 2, 74. Tim. IV, 3, 189. Mcb. IV, 1, 22. Lr. I, 1, 124. Per. I, 1, 29. *night's swift —s cut the clouds full fast,* Mids. III, 2, 379. *the d. wing of night o'erspreads the earth,* Troil. V, 8, 17. *swift, swift, you —s of the night,* Cymb. II, 2, 48.

2) a constellation of the northern hemisphere: *my father compounded with my mother under the —'s tail, and my nativity was under Ursa major; so that it follows, I am rough and lecherous,* Lr. I, 2, 140.

Dragonish, resembling a dragon: *a cloud that's d.* Ant. IV, 14, 2.

Dragon-like, like a dragon: *fights d.* Cor. IV, 7, 23.

Drain, 1) to cause to flow, to empty, to draw off: *to d. upon his face an ocean of salt tears,* H6B III, 2, 142. *how couldst thou d. the life-blood of the child,* H6C I, 4, 138. *that any drop ... should by my mortal sword be —ed,* Troil. IV, 5, 135.

2) to make dry: *when hours have —ed his blood,* Sonn. 63, 3. *I will d. him dry as hay,* Mcb. I, 3, 18. Hence = to imbibe, suck in: *a handkerchief, which, say to her, did d. the purple sap from her sweet brothers' body,* R3 IV, 4, 276. And = to drink off: *as he —s his draughts of Rhenish down,* Hml. I, 4, 10.

Dram, 1) the eighth part of an ounce: *weigh down by the d.* Tim. V, 1, 154. *buy ladies' flesh at a million a d.* Cymb. I, 4, 147. III, 5, 89. Quibbling: *no d. of a scruple,* Tw. III, 4, 87. H4B I, 2, 148.

2) the smallest quantity: *empty from any d. of mercy,* Merch. IV, 1, 6. *every d. of it,* All's II, 3, 233. Wint. II, 1, 138. *three quarters and a d. dead,*

IV, 4, 815. *the d. of ill*, Hml.I, 4, 36. *a d. of worth*, Cymb. III, 5, 89. *a d. of this will drive away distemper*, III, 4, 193.

3) a pernicious potion: *with no rash potion, but with a lingering d.* Wint. I, 2, 320. *shall give him such an unaccustomed d.* Rom. III, 5, 91. *let me have a d. of poison*, V, 1, 60. *some d. conjured to this effect*, Oth. I, 3, 105. *the queen's d. she swallowed*, Cymb. V, 5, 381.

Draugh, see *Draff*.

Draught, 1) the act of drinking at once (without taking breath), and that which is drunk at once: *a morning's d. of sack*, Wiv. II, 2, 153. *one d. above heat*, Tw. I, 5, 140. Wint. I, 2, 318. H6B II, 3, 74. Tim. I, 2, 49. IV, 3, 194. Hml. I, 4, 10. Oth. I, 1, 99.

2) the depth a vessel sinks in water: *for shallow d. and bulk unprizable*, Tw. V, 58.

3) a sink, a jakes: *sweet d., sweet quoth a! sweet sink, sweet sewer*, Troil. V, 1, 82. *drown them in a d.* Tim. V, 1, 105.

Draught-oxen, oxen used to draw a cart or plough: Troil. II, 1, 116.

Draw (impf. *drew*, partic. *drawn*). 1) to pull along, to cause to move by force applied in advance of the thing moved; absol.: *to follow as it —s*, Meas. II, 4, 177. *this advantage, this vile —ing bias*, John II, 577. *we d. together*, Troil. V, 5, 44 (= we are yoked together, have the same work in hand). *every bearded fellow that's but yoked may d. with you*, Oth. IV, 1, 68 (= is in the same case). Trans.: *two doves will d. me through the sky*, Ven. 153. Tw. II, 5, 70. H5 III Chor. 12. Lr. I, 4, 244. II, 4, 75. *I have followed it, or it hath —n me rather*, Tp. I, 2, 394. Meas. III, 2, 289. Mids. II, 1, 195. Merch. V, 68. 80. Tw. II, 3, 61. H4B II, 4, 313. Troil. I, 3, 14. Ant. II, 5, 13. IV, 15, 13. 30. *and back the same grief d.* Lucr. 1673. *from the purple fountain Brutus drew the knife*, 1734. Compl. 36. Merch. IV, 1, 428. *to d. a tooth*, Ado III, 2, 22. *to d. a bow:* Shr. V, 2, 47. H4B III, 2, 48. Lr. I, 1, 145. *d. your arrows to the head*, R3 V, 3, 339; and absol.: *look ye d. home enough*, Tit. IV, 3, 3. *now d. 63. d. me a clothiers' yard*, Lr. IV, 6, 88. cf. *I will bid thee d., as we do the minstrels; d., to pleasure us*, Ado V, 1, 128 (i. e. the bow of thy fiddle). *to d. a sword:* Lucr. 626. Tp. II, 1, 292. Err. V, 151. Ado V, 1, 125. Mids. III, 1, 11. H6A III, 4, 39. H6B IV, 1, 92. *a dagger*, Mids. V, 150. *weapons*, Tp. II, 1, 320. 322. H6B III, 2, 237. *d. thy tool*, Rom. I, 1, 37. *to d. out =* to d.: H5 IV, 2, 22. *d. forth thy weapon*, Shr. III, 2, 238. *to d. the sword on a person:* Err. V, 262. Tw. V, 191. Rom. III, 1, 9. And absol.: *d. together*, Tp. II, 1, 294. Tw. V, 69. H4B II, 1, 50. H6A I, 3, 46. Rom. I, 1, 69. Lr. II, 1, 32. II, 2, 33 etc. *to d. on a p.:* Err. V, 43. Rom. V, 3, 284. Lr. II, 2, 131. Cymb. I, 1, 160 etc. *why are you drawn?* (= why have you drawn your sword?) Tp. II, 1, 308. *—n and ready*, Mids. III, 2, 402. H5 II, 1, 39 (O. Edd. *hewn*). Rom. I, 1, 73. — *to d. the curtain*, (= a) to pull it before sth., in order to hide it: Merch. II, 7, 78. II, 9, 84. Wint. V, 3, 59. H6B III, 3, 32. H8 V, 2, 34. Oth. V, 2, 104. b) to open it, in order to discover sth.: Lucr. 371. 374. Merch. II, 9, 1. Tw. I, 5, 251. H4A IV, 1, 73. H4B I, 1, 72. Troil. III, 2, 49. *to d. aside the curtains*, Merch. II, 7, 1. — *to d. lots:* Ant. II, 3, 35. Per. I, 4, 46. *we'll d. cuts for the senior*, Err. V, 422. *four shall quickly*

d. out my command, Cor. I, 6, 84. Hence = to win, to get: *I would not d. them* (viz the six thousand ducats): *I would have my bond*, Merch. IV, 1, 87 (or = take from the table?). *the rich stake —n*, Wint. I, 2 248. *all the world of wealth I have —n together*, H8 III, 2, 211. *that, swoopstake, you will d. both friend and foe*, Hml. IV, 5, 142. *what can you say to d. a third more opulent*, Lr. I, 1, 87. *and must d. me that which my father loses*, III, 3, 24. *to apprehend thus, —s us a profit from all things we see*, Cymb. III, 3, 18. — *to d. apart* (= to take aside) Oth. II, 3, 391. *to d. Don Pedro and the Count Claudio alone*, Ado II, 2, 33. *when I had it, drew myself apart*, Tit. V, 1, 112. *d. them to Tiber banks*, Caes. I, 1, 63. *he —s Mark Antony out of the way*, III, 1, 26. *to d. the brats of Clarence out of sight*, R3 III, 5, 107 (= to withdraw them from the eyes of the public). cf. *hath —n him and the rest from their sport*, Wiv. IV, 2, 34. Err. I, 1, 44. V, 56. Followed by *from*, in a tropical sense, = to elicit: *to utter that which else no worldly good should d. from me*, Gentl. III, 1, 9. 73. *d. a belief from you*, As V, 2, 63. *until you had —n oaths from him*, Wint. I, 2, 29. *to d. my answer from thy articles*, John II, 111 (i. e. to make me answer according to thy articles). *tears —n from her eyes by your foul wrongs*, R2 III, 1, 15. *you do d. my spirits from me with new lamenting ancient oversights*, H4B II, 3, 46. *drewest rivers from his eyes*, R3 I, 3, 176. *your silence from my weakness —s my very soul of counsel*, Troil. III, 2, 140. *his insolence —s folly from my lips*, IV, 5, 258. *to d. from her a prayer of earnest heart*, Oth. I, 3, 152. *nor from mine own weak merits will I d. the smallest fear*, Oth. III, 3, 187 (= derive, deduce). *from whose so many weights of baseness cannot a dram of worth be drawn*, Cymb. III, 5, 89. *to d. forth from =* to turn off, divert from: *to d. forth your noble ancestry from the corruption of abusing times unto a lineal course*, R3 III, 7, 198. cf. *when holy men are at their beads, 'tis hard to d. them hence*, R3 III, 7, 93. *poverty could never d. 'em from me*, H8 IV, 2, 149. *to d. to sth. =* to move, to incite, to induce: *how many actions most ridiculous hast thou been —n to by thy fantasy?* As II, 4, 31. *so much (love) as might have —n one to a longer voyage*, Tw. III, 3, 7. *such noble scenes as d. the eye to flow*, H8 Prol. 4. *if that thy artificial feat can d. him but to answer thee in aught*, Per. V, 1, 73. cf. *and d. you into madness*, Hml. I, 4, 74. *how hardly I was —n into this war*, Ant. V, 1, 74. *d. our throne into a sheep-cote*, Wint. IV, 4, 808. *profit again should hardly d. me here*, Mcb. V, 3, 62. And with *on: shall d. him on to this confusion*, Mcb. III, 5, 29. *to d. him on to pleasures*, Hml. II, 2, 15. *to d. on =* to bring on, to cause: *d. not on thy danger*, H6C III, 3, 75. *whose voice will d. on more*, Hml. V, 2, 403. *death —n on with torture*, Cymb. IV, 4, 14. *= to d. within the compass of suspect =* to make suspected: Err. III, 1, 87. cf. *to d. me in these vile suspects*, R3 I, 3, 89. *to d. out =* to spin out, to lengthen: *my laments would be —n out too long*, Lucr. 1616. *thy unkindness shall his death d. out to lingering sufferance*, Meas. II, 4, 166. *he —eth out the thread of his verbosity*, LLL V, 1, 18. *to eke it and to d. it out in length*, Merch. III, 2, 23. *rough uneven ways —s out our miles*, R2 II, 3, 5. *'tis but the time and —ing days out that we stand upon*, Caes. III, 1, 100. *a man may d. his heart out, ere 'a pluck one*, All's I, 3, 93 (perhaps quibbling: may pluck his heart out, and: *may spend his life*). *to d.*, simply, = to draw out, to lengthen: *the hand of time shall d. this brief into as huge a volume*, John II, 103. *how long her face is —n*, H8 IV, 2, 97. — *to d. breath* = to breathe: *any that —s breath in Italy*, Merch. III, 2, 298. *cheerly —ing breath*, R2 I, 3, 66. *—s the sweet infant breath of gentle sleep*, 133. *that no man might d. short breath to-day*, H4A V, 2, 49. *d. thy breath in pain, to tell my story*, Hml. V, 2, 359. *so she at these sad signs —s up her breath*, Ven. 929 (= draws a deep breath). — *to d.* = to drag to the place of execution (used in quibbles only): *they* (tapsters) *will d. you, and you will hang them*, Meas. II, 1, 215. *I have the toothache. Draw it! hang it!* Ado III, 2, 22. *—n in the flattering table of her eye, hanged in the frowning wrinkle of her brow*, John II, 504.

2) **to suck, to drink up**: *she will d. his lips' rich treasure dry*, Ven. 552. *well —n, monster!* Tp. II, 2, 151. *a lioness with udders all —n dry*, As IV, 3, 115 (cf. *Cub-drawn*). *from my dugs he drew not this deceit*, R3 II, 2, 30. Applied to the sun: *there the sun shall greet them and d. their honours reeking up to heaven*, H5 IV, 3, 101. *O blessed sun, d. from the earth rotten humidity*, Tim. IV, 3, 1. *fogs —n by the powerful sun*, Lr. II, 4, 169. *to d. in: thy conceit is soaking, will d. in more than the common blocks*, Wint. I, 2, 224. *I d. in many a tear*, H6C IV, 4, 21.

3) **to tap, to broach**: *he shall d., he shall tap*, Wiv. I, 3, 11. *they* (tapsters) *will d. you*, Meas. II, 1, 215. *the wine of life is —n, and the mere lees is left this vault to brag of*, Mcb. II, 3, 100. cf. *I never come into any room in a taphouse, but I am —n in*, Meas. II, 1, 220 (quibbling = I am bled in it, I am swindled out of my money). Followed by *of*: *the purse too light, being —n of heaviness*, Cymb. V, 4, 168 (= emptied of). *to d. blood* = to spill blood: *where it* (the knife) *—s blood*, Hml. IV, 7, 144. Followed by *from*: *for every bloody drop was —n from him*, H6A II, 2, 8. *one drop of blood —n from thy country's bosom*, III, 3, 54. *drew blood from thee*, H6C IV, 6, 16. 43. Followed by *on*: *blood will I d. on thee*, H6A I, 5, 6. *some blood —n on me*, Lr. II, 1, 35. By *out of*: Cor. IV, 5, 105.

4) Used of military affairs, a) **to assemble, to levy**: *d. our puissance together*, John III, 1, 339. *that such an army could be —n in France*, 2, 118. *before I drew this gallant head of war*, V, 2, 113. H4A III, 1, 89. IV, 1, 33. 126. IV, 4, 28. H4B I, 3, 76. 109. Cymb. III, 5, 25. And in general = to assemble: *a good quarrel to d. emulous factions*, Troil. II, 3, 79. *when you have —n your number*, Cor. I, 3, 261. *there were —n upon a heap a hundred ghastly women*, Caes. I, 3, 22. — b) **to range in battle, to array**: *Troy before the which is —n the power of Greece*, Lucr. 1368. *my foreward shall be —n in length*, R3 V, 3, 293 (Q1 *be —n out all in length*). With *up*: *d. up your powers*, Lr. V, 1, 51.

5) **to withdraw**: *d. the action*, H4B II, 1, 162. *wilt thou d. thy forces hence*, H6C V, 1, 25. *the Roman legions, all from Gallia —n*, Cymb. IV, 3, 24 (or = assembled?). *I was fain to d. mine honour in*, H8 V, 4, 60 (= to retreat into the house).

6) **to mark with lines, or to represent by a picture, to paint**: *which the conceited painter drew so proud*, Lucr. 1371. 1520. Sonn. 16, 4. 19, 10. 24, 10. 98, 12. Ado III, 1, 63. LLL V, 2, 38. Shr. Ind. 2, 62. All's I, 1, 104. John II, 503. V, 7, 32. H4B I,

3, 42. V, 2, 13. Tim. V, 1, 83. Caes. II, 1, 232. Hml. II, 1, 91. *the lines of my body are as well —n as his*, Cymb. IV, 1, 10. *drawn in little* = reduced to a smaller shape, formed in miniature: *on his visage was in little —n what largeness thinks in Paradise was sawn*, Compl. 90. *if all the devils of hell be —n in little and Legion itself possessed him*, Tw. III, 4, 94.

7) **to write down, to sketch, to chalk out**: *I will d. a bill of properties*, Mids. I, 2, 107. *d. a deed of gift*, Merch. IV, 1, 394. *let specialties be —n*, Shr. II, 127. *there it is in writing, fairly —n*, III, 1, 70. H4A III, 1, 80. 141. H6A V, 1, 38. H6C III, 3, 135. R3 V, 3, 24. H8 I, 1, 169. Cymb. I, 4, 155.

8) As a hunting term, = **to trace, to track**: *a hound that runs counter and yet —s dry-foot well*, Err. IV, 2, 39. *no more truth in thee than in a —n fox*, H4A III, 3, 129 (i. e. a fox scented and driven from cover; such a one being supposed to be full of tricks).

9) **to move, to advance, to approach**: *a reverend man ... towards this afflicted fancy drew*, Compl. 61. *how near the god drew to the complexion of a goose*, Wiv. V, 5, 8. *nature to her bias drew in that*, Tw. V, 267 (or = pulled, attracted?). *it —s towards supper*, John I, 204. *it now —s toward night*, H5 III, 6, 179. *—ing to their exigent*, H6A II, 5, 9. *when mine oratory drew toward end*, R3 III, 7, 20 (Qq *grew to an end*). *d. to her succour*, H8 V, 4, 54. *an you d. backward*, Troil. III, 2, 47. *to d. toward an end with you*, Hml. III, 4, 216. *let your best love d. to that point, which seeks best to preserve it*, Ant. III, 4, 21. *to d. near* = a) to approach: R2 I, 3, 123. H6C III, 3, 138. Cor. III, 3, 39. Tim. III, 1, 41 *(nearer)*. Lr. IV, 7, 25. *it —s something near to the speech we had*, Meas. I, 2, 78. Err. V, 12. *Pyramus —s near the wall*, Mids. V, 170. Tit. I, 117. 118. Hml. I, 4, 5. b) **to come in, to enter**: Tp. V, 318. All's III, 2, 101. Tim. II, 2, 46; cf. *d. nigh*, Tit. V, 3, 24. *d. homewards* = come home, As IV, 3, 179. *to d. on* = to approach: *the hour —s on*, Wiv. V, 3, 25. Meas. IV, 3, 82. Mids. I, 1, 2. *the minute —s on*, Wiv. V, 5, 2.

10) **to sink in water**: *greater hulks d. deep*, Troil. II, 3, 277 (cf. *Deep-drawing, Draught*).

Drawbridge, a bridge which may be raised up: R3 III, 5, 15.

Drawer, waiter: Wiv. II, 2, 165. H4A II, 4, 7. 33. 102. H4B II, 2, 191. II, 4, 109. 312. Rom. III, 1, 9.

Drawl, to speak slowly and with affectation: *such a —ing, affecting rogue*, Wiv. II, 1, 145.

Drayman, a kind of carrier, a man who attends a dray or cart on which beer is carried: R2 I, 4, 32. Troil. I, 2, 270.

Dread, subst. 1) great fear: Lucr. 117. 171. Wint. IV, 4, 17. R2 I, 1, 73. R3 II, 3, 38. *consequence of d.* = dreadful consequence, H8 II, 4, 214. *have d. to speak*, Lr. I, 1, 149. The thing feared following with *of*: *the d. and fear of kings*, Merch. IV, 1, 192. Hml. III, 1, 78.

2) a person highly revered: *but having thee at vantage, wondrous d.*, (the boar) *would root these beauties as he roots the mead*, Ven. 635.

Dread, adj. 1) awful, terrible: *this d. night*, Lucr. 965. *make his d. trident shake*, Tp. I, 2, 206. *the d. rattling thunder*, V, 44; cf. *Jove's d. clamours*, Oth. III, 3, 356. *that d. penalty*, LLL I, 1, 128; cf. *d. correction*, H4A V, 1, 111, and *sentence of d. banishment*, R2 III, 3, 134. *by your d. Verily*, Wint. I, 2, 55.

how d. an army, H5 IV Chor. 36. *d. curses*, H6B III, 2, 330. R3 I, 3, 191. *d. Fury*, Tit. V, 2, 82. *d. exploits*, Mcb. IV, 1, 144. Lr. II, 2, 130. *this d. and black complexion*, Hml. II, 2, 477. *the d. summit of this chalky bourn*, Lr. IV, 6, 57.

2) awful, venerable, inspiring with fear and reverence: *d. prince of plackets*, LLL III, 186. *I cannot believe this crack to be in my d. mistress*, Wint. I, 2, 322. *as surely as my soul intends to live with that d. king that took our state upon him*, H6B III, 2, 154. *Henry, our d. liege*, V, 1, 17. *our d. father*, Troil. II, 2, 27. *your d. pleasures*, Hml. II, 2, 28. *your d. command*, III. 4, 109. Used in addressing princes: *my d. lord*, Meas. V, 371. H5 I, 2, 103. R3 III, 1, 97 (Ff *dear*). Hml. I, 2, 50 (Ff *d. my lord*). *d. lord*, H6B III, 2, 243. H6C III, 2, 32. H8 V, 2, 114. 148. Per. I, 2, 52. *d. sovereign*, R2 I, 1, 165. H5 I, 2, 97. *d. queen*, Tit. V, 3, 26. Ant. III, 3, 9. *d. Priam*, Troil. II, 2, 10. *most d. liege*, H8 V, 1, 122.

Dread, vb. 1) to fear; a) followed by an accus.: Lucr. 270. Merch. IV, 1, 89. Wint. II, 3, 79. John III, 1, 164. H6C II, 6, 92. Cor. IV, 6, 55. Tit. II, 3, 50. Ant. V, 2, 334. Cymb. V, 1, 15. By a clause: *—ing the winter's near*, Sonn. 97, 14. Ant. IV, 14, 127. Cymb. V, 5, 253. *that he should draw his several strengths together need not be —ed*, H4B I, 3, 78.

2) to be solicitous about: *—ing my love*, Pilgr. 94.

Dreaded, adjectively, = awful: *in the presence of —ed justice*, Cor. III, 3, 98. *touching this —ed sight*, Hml. I, 1, 25.

Dread-bolted, armed with a terrible bolt: *d. thunder*, Lr. IV, 7, 33.

Dreadful, 1) terrible: Ven. 928. Lucr. 1625. 1703. Pilgr. 67. Tp. I, 2, 202. III, 3, 98. Wiv. IV, 4, 34. Meas. I, 3, 33. LLL III, 205. Mids. III, 1, 32. V, 283. Merch. III, 2, 273. All's III, 2, 64. Wint. V, 1, 154. John IV, 2, 78. 125. 173. 255. R2 I, 3, 135. H5 II Chor. 13. IV Chor. 14. H6A I, 1, 29. 30. 110. II, 3, 7. H6B III, 2, 91. 158. IV, 1, 92. V, 2, 27. H6C I, 1, 187. II, 1, 44. II, 2, 138. III, 3, 259. R3 I, 2, 46. I, 4, 22. Troil. IV, 4, 129. IV, 5, 4. V, 2, 171. Tit. I, 88. Rom. III, 2, 67. Caes. I, 3, 56. II, 1, 63. III, 1, 266. Mcb. II, 4, 3. III, 2, 44. Hml. I, 4, 70. Lr. III, 2, 50 etc. = awful: *your most d. laws*, H4B V, 2, 94. *God's d. law*, R3 I, 4, 214.

2) filled with fear, timorous: *from forth dull sleep by d. fancy waking*, Lucr. 450. *our d. marches* (changed) *to delightful measures*, R3 I, 1, 8. *this to me in d. secrecy impart they did*, Hml. I, 2, 207. *silence that d. bell*, Oth. II, 3, 175 (rung in fear and spreading fear).

Dreadfully, 1) terribly: Lucr. 444. 2) abominably: *I am most d. attended*, Hml. II, 2, 276. 3) with dread: *apprehends death no more d. but as a drunken sleep*, Meas. IV, 2, 150.

Dream, subst. thought or vision in sleep: Sonn. 129, 12. Tp. I, 2, 45. 486. IV, 157. V, 239. Gentl. V, 4, 26. Wiv. III, 3, 172. III, 5, 142. Meas. II, 2, 4. Err. II, 2, 184. Mids. II, 2, 147. H6B I, 1, 26. I, 2, 22 etc. etc. *I have dreamt a fearful d.* R3 V, 3, 212. *I dreamt a d. to-night*, Rom. I, 4, 50. Hence = idle fancy: Meas. IV, 1, 64. Tw. II, 2, 27. II, 5, 211. Wint. III, 2, 82. Lr. I, 4, 346. *a d. of what thou wert*, R3 IV, 4, 88. Tim. IV, 2, 34. Hml. I, 2, 21. II, 2, 578. *if consequence do but approve my d.* Oth. II, 3, 64.

Dream, vb. 1) to have ideas or images in sleep: Tp. III, 2, 149. 152. Wiv. III, 3, 171. Err. V, 346. Ado IV, 1, 67. Mids. IV, 1, 199. Merch. III, 2, 52. Shr. Ind. I, 64. Tw. IV, 1, 67 etc. etc. *look how thou —est*, R3 IV, 2, 57. *four nights will quickly d. away the time*, Mids. I, 1, 8. Trans.: *ne'er —ed a joy beyond his pleasure*, H8 III, 1, 135. *did I d. it so?* Rom. V, 3, 79. *I have —ed a fearful dream*, R3 V, 3, 212. Rom. I, 4, 50. Followed by *of*: Ado II, 1, 360. Merch. II, 5, 18. R3 V, 3, 165. Rom. I, 4, 71. 78. 81. 83. By *on*: Meas. III, 1, 34. Tw. II, 3, 191. H6C III, 2, 134. R3 V, 3, 151. Rom. I, 4, 72. 73. 74.

2) to think, to imagine; to have a presentiment: *that he should d. the full Caesar will answer his emptiness*, Ant. III, 13, 34. *nor Cymbeline —s that they are alive*, Cymb. III, 3, 81. Followed by *of*: *if Collatinus d. of my intent*, Lucr. 218. *strange news that you yet —ed not of*, Ado I, 2, 4. H4A II, 1, 77. H6C II, 1, 199. Hml. I, 5, 167. II, 2, 10. Ant. II, 2, 148. By *on*: *unstained thoughts do seldom d. on evil*, Lucr. 87. Sonn. 107, 2. Gentl. II, 4, 172. II, 7, 64. IV, 4, 86. Meas. II, 2, 179. Ado IV, 1, 214. H6B III, 1, 73. H6C III, 2, 168. R3 I, 2, 100. V, 3, 330.

Dreamer, 1) one who dreams: *—s often lie*, Rom. I, 4, 51 (quibbling in both words).

2) a visionary, a fantastic: *thou idle d.* John IV, 2, 153. *the d. Merlin and his prophecies*, H4A III, 1, 150. *he is a d.* Caes. I, 2, 24.

Dreary, dismal, gloomy: *to step out of these d. dumps*, Tit. I, 391 (Qq *dririe*, Ff *sudden*).

Dreg (sing. in Troil. III, 2, 70; everywhere else plur. *—s*). 1) the lees, grounds: *thou hast but lost the —s of life* (viz the body) Sonn. 74, 9. *more —s than water*, Troil. III, 2, 72. *drink up the lees and —s of a flat tamed piece*, IV, 1, 62.

2) the last residue: *I will here shroud till the —s of the storm be past*, Tp. II, 2, 42 (cf. v. 21). *some certain —s of conscience are yet within me*, R3 I, 4, 124. *the good gods assuage thy wrath, and turn the —s of it upon this varlet here*, Cor. V, 2, 84.

3) that which spoils a thing, corrupts its purity: *what too curious d. espies my sweet lady in the fountain of our love?* Troil. III, 2, 70. *friendship is full of —s*, Tim. I, 2, 239.

Drench, subst. physic for a horse: H4A II, 4, 120. H5 III, 5, 19 (cf. *Horse-drench*).

Drench, vb. (cf. *Bedrench, Indrenched, Deep-drenched*) to steep in moisture, to wet thoroughly: Ven. 494. 1054. Tp. II, 1, 62. Gentl. I, 3, 79. H5 IV, 3, 80. H6A IV, 7, 14. Mcb. I, 7, 68. Lr. III, 2, 3. Ant. II, 6, 18.

Dress, subst. equipment: *till I shall see you in your soldier's d., which will become you both, farewell*, Ant. II, 4, 4.

Dress, vb. to put in order; used of a garden: *he had not so trimmed and —ed his land as we this garden*, R2 III, 4, 56. 73. Of meat prepared for the table: *d. meat and drink*, Wiv. I, 4, 102. Shr. IV, 3, 40. Tw. II, 5, 123. Ant. V, 2, 276. Cymb. III, 6, 90. Of the rubbing and combing of horses: R2 V, 5, 80. Of wounds: Tw. V, 211. Oth. V, 1, 124. Of the adjusting and trimming of a chamber: *d. your sister's chamber up*, Shr. III, 1, 83. Of any preparation and equipment: *lent him our terror, —ed him with our love*, Meas. I, 1, 20. *—ed in a little brief authority*, II, 2, 118. *to be —ed in an opinion of wisdom*, Merch. I, 1,

91. —*ed myself in such humility,* H4A III, 2, 51. *he was the glass wherein the noble youth did d. themselves,* H4B II, 3, 22. *to d. the ugly form of insurrection with your fair honours,* IV, 1, 39. *that we should d. us fairly for our end,* H5 IV, 1, 10. *being —ed to some oration,* Troil. I, 3, 166. *we'll d. him up in voices,* 382 (= trim him up). *was the hope drunk wherein you —ed yourself,* Mcb. I, 7, 36. *the abilities that Rhodes is —ed in,* Oth. I, 3, 26. — Used of garments and what is like them: Sonn. 68, 12. 76, 11. 98, 2. Wiv. IV, 2, 84. 100. IV, 4, 48. Ado II, 1, 36. III, 4, 103. Shr. Ind. I, 106. H4A I, 3, 33. H4B II, 4, 302. H6B IV, 2, 6 (quibble). Rom. IV, 5, 12. Mcb. I, 3, 108.

Dresser, a table on which meat is prepared: Shr. IV, 1, 166.

Dressing, subst., trimming up, ornamental habiliment: *they are but —s of a former sight,* Sonn. 123, 4 (cf. Sonn. 68, 12. 76, 11). *in all his —s, characts, titles, forms,* Meas. V, 56.

Dribling (M. Edd. *dribbling*), falling weakly like a drop: *the d. dart of love,* Meas. I, 3, 2 (perhaps *dribbing; dribber* and *dribbed* being, according to Collier and Steevens, terms of archery, denoting a bad shot).

Drift, 1) things driven along at once, a shower: *their d. of bullets,* John II, 412.

2) direction, turn: *the sole d. of my purpose doth extend not a frown further,* Tp. V, 29. *finding by this encompassment and d. of question that they do know my son,* Hml. II, 1, 10. *can you by no d. of circumstance get from him ...,* III, 1, 1 (Qq *d. of conference*).

3) tendency, aim, intention, meaning, scheme: *love, lend me wings to make my purpose swift, as thou hast lent me wit to plot this d.* Gentl. II, 6, 43. *cross my friend in his intended d.* III, 1, 18. *you shall say my cunning d. excels,* IV, 2, 83. *O, understand my d.* Wiv. II, 2, 251. *hold you ever to our special d.* Meas. IV, 5, 4. *what is the course and d. of your compact?* Err. II, 2, 163. *I will tell you my d.* Ado II, 1, 403. *the king not privy to my d.* H6C I, 2, 46. *the author's d.* Troil. III, 3, 113 (= what he aims at). *we know your d.* Cor. III, 3, 116 (what you intend to say). *be plain and homely in thy d.* Rom. II, 3, 55 (in what you have to say). *in the mean time shall Romeo by my letters know our d.* IV, 1, 114. *my free d. halts not particularly,* Tim. I, 1, 45. *here's my d.* Hml. II, 1, 37. *if our d. look through our bad performance,* IV, 7, 152.

Drily, see *Dryly.*

Drink, subst. 1) liquor to be swallowed, beverage, potion· Ven. 92. Lucr. 577. LLL V, 2, 372. Mids. II, 1, 38. As V, 1, 45. Tw. I, 3, 42. I, 5, 47. 49. Wint. I, 1, 15. H4A II, 4, 83. H4B IV, 3, 98. H6B III, 2, 321. III, 3, 17. H6C II, 5, 48. Cor. II, 1, 61. Tit. III, 2, 35. Caes. I, 2, 127. Mcb. II, 1, 31. II, 3, 27. Hml. III, 2, 314. IV, 7, 160. V, 2, 320. Lr. I, 4, 137. Oth. II, 3, 136. Ant. II, 7, 9. Cymb. V, 4, 164. *meat and d.* Wiv. I, 4, 102. H4B V, 3, 31. *that's meat and d. to me* (= I like it best of all): Wiv. I, 1, 306. As V, 1, 11. Figuratively: *her garments, heavy with their d.* Hml. IV, 7, 182.

2) carousing: *his days are foul and his d. dangerous,* Tim. III, 5, 73. *shall we dance now the Egyptian Bacchanals, and celebrate our d.?* Ant. II, 7, 111.

3) drunkenness: *the poor monster's in d.* Tp. II, 2, 162. *he was gotten in d.* Wiv. I, 3, 25. *he's in the* third degree of d. Tw. I, 5, 144. V, 197. H4A II, 4, 458. *a beggar in his d.* Oth. IV, 2, 120. *the slaves of d. and thralls of sleep,* Mcb. III, 6, 13.

Drink, vb. (Impf. *drank*: Shr. Ind. 2, 6. Tit. IV, 3, 85. *drunk*: All's II, 3, 106. H4A II, 4, 168. Ant. II, 5, 21. Partic. *drunk*). 1) to swallow liquor; absol.: Meas. I, 2, 40. 134. Merch. I, 3, 38. H4A II, 4, 168. Tit. IV, 3, 85 etc. etc. *to d. deep,* H4A II, 4, 16. Hml. I, 2, 175. *d. of Circe's cup,* Err. V, 270. —*ing,* Tp. II, 2, 88. IV, 171 etc. *glasses is the only —ing,* H4B II, 1, 155. —*ings and swearings,* Wiv. V, 5, 168 (Evans' speech). *to d. to* (to d. a person's health): Tp. III, 2, 3. Tw. I, 3, 41. H4B IV, 2, 68. V, 3, 49. 61. H6B II, 3, 59. 68. Tim. I, 2, 112. Hml. V, 2, 289. Per. II, 3, 75. IV, 3, 11. *I d. to the general joy of the whole table,* Mcb. III, 4, 89. *the king shall d. to Hamlet's better breath,* Hml. V, 2, 282. *I d. to you in a cup a sack,* H6B II, 3, 59. *it hath served me instead of a quart pot to d. in,* IV, 10, 16. Remarkable use: *I shall d. in pipe-wine first with him,* Wiv. III, 2, 90.

Trans.: Sonn. 119, 1. Tp. I, 2, 462. II, 2, 78. III, 2, 2. 31. Wiv. III, 2, 89. Meas. III, 2, 3. Ado V, 1, 253. LLL IV, 2, 27. Shr. Ind. 2, 6. All's II, 3, 106 etc. *this do I d. to thee,* Rom. IV, 3, 58. *d. carouses to the next day's fate,* Ant. IV, 8, 34. Figuratively: *the iron would d. my tears,* John IV, 1, 62. —*ing my griefs* (= full of my tears) R2 IV, 189; cf. H6C V, 4, 75. Tit. III, 1, 140. *thy brother's blood the thirsty earth hath drunk,* H6C II, 3, 15. R3 I, 2, 63. *this quarrel will d. blood,* H6A II, 4, 134. — *To d. a health:* Shr. III, 2, 198. Tw. I, 3, 40. H8 I, 4, 106. Hml. I, 2, 125. Ant. I, 2, 12. The accus. denoting the result: *had drunk himself out of his five sentences,* Wiv. I, 1, 179. *d. down all unkindness,* 204. —*ing oceans dry,* R2 II, 2, 146. *he —s your Dane dead drunk,* Oth. II, 3, 84. *I drunk him to his bed,* Ant. II, 5, 21. — *To d. off* (= to d. at a draught): —*s off candles' ends,* H4B IV, 4, 267. Rom. IV, 1, 94. V, 1, 78. Hml. V, 2, 337. *to d. up* (= to drink without flinching): *would d. up the lees and dregs of a flat tamed piece,* Troil. IV, 1, 61. *woo't d. up eisel,* Hml. V, 1, 299.

Drunk = intoxicated (only in the predicate; cf. *Drunken*): Tp. II, 1, 146. V, 278. Wiv. I, 1, 175. Meas. III, 2, 136. IV, 2, 157. 158. V, 188. Ado III, 3, 45. V, 1, 17. Merch. I, 2, 94. Shr. Ind. 1, 31. Tw. I, 3, 38. H4B II, 4, 230 etc. *dead drunk,* Oth. II, 3, 85. *where hath our intelligence been drunk?* John IV, 2, 116. *drunk with choler,* H4A I, 3, 129. *England's lawful earth, unlawfully made drunk with innocents' blood,* R3 IV, 4, 30. *with his own tears made drunk,* Rom. III, 3, 83. *was the hope drunk?* Mcb. I, 7, 35.

2) Figuratively, to take in by any inlet, to inhale, to hear, to see: *his nostrils d. the air,* Ven. 273. *what he breathes out, his breath —s up again,* Lucr. 1666. *make sacred even his stirrup and through him d. the free air,* Tim. I, 1, 83. *to d. their vapour,* Ant. V, 2, 213. *d. up the monarchs' plague, this flattery,* Sonn. 114, 2. 10. *take the cork out of thy mouth that I may d. thy tidings,* As III, 2, 214. *how his silence —s up this applause,* Troil. II, 3, 211. *my ears have not yet drunk a hundred words of that tongue's utterance,* Rom. II, 2, 58. *thither write, and with mine eyes I'll d. the words you send,* Cymb. I, 1, 100.

3) to swallow up, to devour, to consume:

I d. the air before me and return or ere your pulse twice beat, Tp. V, 102 (= I annihilate distance). *is not my teeming date drunk up with time?* R2 V, 2, 91. *this would d. deep. 'twould d. the cup and all,* H5 I, 1, 20. *the air will d. the sap,* H8 I, 2, 98. *dry sorrow —s our blood,* Rom. III, 5, 59. *and spend our flatteries, to d. those men upon whose age we void it up again,* Tim. I, 2, 142.

Drive, vb. (Impf. *drave:* As III, 2, 438. Troil. III, 3, 190. Rom. I, 1, 127 (Q2 *drive*). Ant. I, 2, 98. *drove:* Wiv. V, 5, 131. H4A IV, 3, 102. H6A I, 1, 13. H6C II, 2, 107. Cor. II, 2, 95. Tim. IV, 3, 402. Per. V, 1, 38. Partic. *driven:* Ven. 692. Err. IV, 4, 36. As V, 2, 71. All's I, 3, 31. Wint. IV, 4, 220 etc. *droven:* Ant. IV, 7, 5. *drove:* H6B III, 2, 84, where it, however, may be taken as an imperf.). 1) trans. a) to compel or urge forward, to propel, to expel: *to d. infection from the dangerous year,* Ven. 508. *I could d. the boat with my sighs,* Gentl. II, 3, 60. Wiv. II, 2, 257. Err. IV, 4, 36. Mids. III, 2, 65. All's I, 3, 31. 32. III, 2, 109. H4A I, 3, 200. II, 4, 151. V, 4, 11. H6A I, 2, 54. 148. V, 5, 7. H6C II, 2, 107. Cor. I, 6, 12. II, 2, 95. Caes. II, 1, 54. IV, 1, 23. Hml. III, 1, 27. III, 2, 362. Lr. II, 2, 90. Ant. I, 2, 98. I, 4, 73. III, 6, 82 (like clouds). III, 12, 22. IV, 7, 5. Per. I, 2, 26. II, 1, 34. II, 3, 85. *to d. away:* Pilgr. 200. John IV, 1, 79. H6A I, 5, 24. Caes. I, 1, 75. Per. IV, 6, 139. *to d. away the heavy thought of care,* R2 III, 4, 2. *to d. away the time,* H4A II, 4, 31 (= not to feel its tediousness). *will d. away distemper,* Cymb. III, 4, 194. *to d. back:* John III, 3, 12. H6A I, 1, 13. I, 3, 41. I, 5, 22. H6B III, 2, 84. IV, 9, 34. Rom. II, 5, 6. *to d. out:* Gentl. II, 4, 193. Cor. IV, 7, 54. Caes. III, 1, 171.

b) to force, to induce, to cause: *which —s the creeping thief to some regard,* Lucr. 305. *shall d. some of them to a noncome,* Ado III, 5, 67. *none can d. him from the envious plea,* Merch. III, 2, 284. *this —s me to entreat you,* All's II, 5, 68. *—s me to these habits of her liking,* Tw. II, 5, 183. *d. the gentleman into a most hideous opinion of his rage,* III, 4, 211. *he will d. you out of your revenge,* H4B II, 4, 323. *I shall d. you then to confess,* 338. *drove us to seek out this head of safety,* H4A IV, 3, 102. *till mischief and despair d. you to break your necks,* H6A V, 4, 91. *drave great Mars to faction,* Troil. III, 3, 190. Rom. I, 1, 127. *judgment must be driven to find out practices of cunning hell,* Oth. I, 3, 101. *may d. us to a render where we have lived,* Cymb. IV, 4, 11.

c) to bring, to carry (to a point or state): *the hounds are driven to doubt,* Ven. 692. *what error —s our eyes and ears amiss?* Err. II, 2, 186. *I drave my suitor from his mad humour of love to a living humour of madness,* As III, 2, 438. *I know into what straits of fortune she is driven,* V, 2, 71. *and driven into despair an enemy's hope,* R2 II, 2, 47. *the sharp points of my alleged reasons d. this forward,* H8 II, 4, 225. *drove him into this melancholy,* Tim. IV, 3, 402. *a sister driven into desperate terms,* Hml. IV, 7, 26. *the disaster that drove him to this,* Per. V, 1, 38 (= brought him so low). Hence = to raise or to reduce: *drove the grossness of the foppery into a received belief,* Wiv. V, 5, 131. *to d. liking to the name of love,* Ado I, 1, 302. *the other half comes to the general state, which humbleness may d. unto a fine,* Merch. IV, 1, 372.

d) to purify by motion, to sift: *lawn as white as driven snow,* Wint. IV, 4, 220 (or = driven together by the wind?). *my thrice driven bed of down,* Oth. I, 3, 232.

2) intr. a) to be carried by wind and waves: *our —ing boat,* Tw. I, 2, 11. *up and down the poor ship —s,* Per. III Prol. 50. *d. a-land,* III, 2, 69.

b) to pass in a carriage: *sometime she —th o'er a soldier's neck,* Rom. I, 4, 82.

c) to betake one's self with haste: *lay him in it* (viz a litter) *and d. towards Dover,* Lr. III, 6, 98.

d) Followed by *at* or *upon,* = to rush upon, to attack: *Pyrrhus at Priam —s,* Hml. II, 2, 494. *the hounds should d. upon thy new transformed limbs,* Tit. II, 3, 64. *to let d.* (= to aim strokes at, to strike at): *four rogues in buckram let d. at me,* H4A II, 4, 217. *came at my back and let d. at me,* 247.

Drivelling, doting, foolish: *this d. love,* Rom. II, 4, 95.

Drizzle, vb. tr. to shed in small slow drops: *in sap-consuming winter's —d snow,* Err. V, 312. *it —s rain,* Ado III, 3, 111. *the air* (Ff and the earlier Qq *earth*) *doth d. dew,* Rom. III, 5, 126. *which —d blood upon the Capitol,* Caes. II, 2, 21.

Drollery, as it seems, = a painting of a humorous kind: *what are these? a living d.* Tp. III, 3, 21 (Nares and Dyce: a puppet-show). *a pretty slight d., or the story of the Prodigal, or the German hunting in water-work, is worth a thousand of these bed-hangings,* H4B II, 1, 156.

Dromio, name in Err. I, 2, 10. 68. II, 2, 1. 5. 156. 189 etc.

Drone, the male bee that makes no honey: Merch. II, 5, 48. H5 I, 2, 204. H6B IV, 1, 109. Per. II Prol. 18. II, 1, 51. Hence = a sluggard: *Dromio, thou d., thou snail,* Err. II, 2, 196 (O. Edd. *Dromio*).

Drone, the largest tube of the bagpipe, which emits a continued deep note: *the d. of a Lincolnshire bagpipe,* H4A I, 2, 85.

Drone-like, not making honey: *my honey lost, and I a d. bee,* Lucr. 836.

Droop, 1) intr. a) to sink, to lean downward: *keep my —ing eyelids open,* Sonn. 27, 7. *—ing fog,* Mids. III, 2, 357. *from the orient to the —ing west,* H4B Ind. 3. *thus —s this lofty pine and hangs his sprays,* H6B II, 3, 45. *good things of day begin to d. and drowse,* Mcb. III, 2, 52. *as patient as the female dove, his silence will sit —ing,* Hml. V, 1, 311.

b) to decline, to fail, to faint, to languish: *make them* (the flowers) *d. with grief and hang the head,* Ven. 666. *my fortunes will ever after d.* Tp. I, 2, 184. *that makes your servants d.* Shr. Ind. 2, 29. *declined, —ed, took it deeply,* Wint. II, 3, 14. John V, 1, 44. R2 II, 1, 292. H4A IV, 1, 28. H6A V, 2, 1. V, 3, 29. IV, 5, 5 (—*ing chair,* i. e. fit for declining age). H6B I, 2, 1. H6C I, 1, 6. III, 3, 21. Cor. IV, 1, 20. Cymb. V, 3, 90.

2) trans. to let sink, to hang down: *a withered vine that —s his sapless branches to the ground,* H6A II, 5, 12. In H5 IV, 2, 47 F1 *dropping,* F2.3.4 *drooping.*

Drop, subst. a globule of any fluid, and what is like it: Ven. 1170. Lucr. 1375. Tp. I, 1, 62. III, 2, 2. V, 16. Err. I, 2, 35. II, 2, 128. Ado III, 2, 19. IV, 1, 143. LLL IV, 3, 27. Merch. IV, 1, 113

310. As III, 5, 7. Shr. V, 2, 145. H6A II, 2, 8. III, 3, 54. H6C I, 1, 97. R3 V, 3, 181. Mcb. III, 5, 24 etc. *d. by d.* Wiv. IV, 5, 100. H4A I, 3, 134. *with the —s of this most balmy time my love looks fresh,* Sonn. 107, 9 (as with rain). *allay with some cold —s of modesty thy skipping spirit,* Merch. II, 2, 195. *the crimson —s in the bottom of a cowslip,* Cymb. II, 2, 38. *—s of tears,* R3 IV, 4, 321. H8 II, 4, 72. *d., alone,* = tear: *falls an orient d.* Ven. 981. *so shall I die by —s of hot desire,* 1074. Lucr. 1228. 1236. Compl. 300. Tp. I, 2, 155. V, 64. Merch. II, 3, 13. As II, 7, 123. John III, 4, 63. V, 2, 49. H4B IV, 3, 14. R3 I, 2, 155. Caes. III, 2, 198. Mcb. I, 4, 35. Ant. IV, 2, 38. = drop of blood: *sweat —s of gallant youth,* H5 III, 5, 25 (cf. H6A IV, 4, 18). *any d. thou borrowedst from thy mother,* Troil. IV, 5, 133. = a small quantity, a trifle: *a d. of patience,* Oth. IV, 2, 53. *a d. of pity,* Cymb. IV, 2, 304. cf. Err. IV, 3, 73.

Drop, vb. 1) intr. a) to fall in drops: *the tide* (of tears) *that in the sweet channel of her bosom —ed,* Ven. 958. *green —ing sap,* 1176. Lucr. 686. Tp. I, 2, 323. *lest resolution d. out at mine eyes in tender womanish tears,* John IV, 1, 35. Figuratively: *when tempest of commotion ... doth begin to melt and d. upon our heads,* H4B II, 4, 394. cf. the quibble in IV, 5, 101. *it* (mercy) *—eth as the gentle rain from heaven upon the place beneath,* Merch. IV, 1, 185. *so much the more must pity d. upon her,* H8 II, 3, 18. cf. Wint. V, 2, 123.

b) to fall in general: *make thy weapon d.* Tp. I, 2, 473. *a crown —ing upon thy head,* II, 1, 209. cf. III, 2, 151. *hast thou not —ed from heaven,* II, 2, 140. *the weakest kind of fruit —s earliest to the ground,* Merch. IV, 1, 116. Err. II, 2, 100. As III, 2, 248. Wint. III, 2, 203. V, 1, 28. H4A IV, 1, 108. R3 IV, 4, 2. Troil. I, 3, 160. Lr. IV, 3, 24. Oth. III, 3, 311. Ant. III, 13, 161. V, 2, 92. = to fall dead: *they —ed as by a thunder-stroke,* Tp. II, 1, 204. *till one d. down a corse,* H4A IV, 1, 123. *that your son might d.* H4B I, 1, 169. H5 III, 2, 8. Cor. IV, 4, 4. Caes. II, 1, 119. Ant. V, 2, 347. — *To d. in* = to come in: *and do not d. in for an after-loss,* Sonn. 90, 4.

2) trans. a) to let fall in drops: *d. sweet balm in Priam's wound,* Lucr. 1466. *d. the liquor in her eyes,* Mids. II, 1, 178. *my heart —ed love, my power rained honour on you,* H8 III, 2, 185. *a tempest —ing fire,* Caes. I, 3, 10 (= raining; cf. Lucr. 1552). Especially of tears: Lucr. 1552. R2 III, 3, 166. III, 4, 104 (Q1 *fall*). V, 3, 101. R3 I, 3, 354. Oth. V, 2, 350. And of blood: H5 I, 2, 19. H6A IV, 4, 18. Cor. I, 5, 19. III, 1, 301. Caes. IV, 3, 73. Cymb. V, 5, 148. — Absolutely: *with a —ing industry they skip from stem to stern,* Per. IV, 1, 63 (i. e. dripping well). And *to d.* = to weep: *in summer's drought I'll d. upon thee still,* Tit. III, 1, 19. *with an auspicious and a —ing eye,* Hml. I, 2, 11.

b) to let fall in general: *—ed a precious jewel in a flood,* Ven. 824. *on this couple d. a blessed crown,* Tp. V, 202. *I'll d. the paper,* LLL IV, 3, 43; cf. Tw. II, 3, 168. III, 2, 83. Caes. II, 1, 49. *you d. manna in the way of starved people,* Merch. V, 294. *d. gold,* All's IV, 3, 252. *she —s booties in my mouth,* Wint. IV, 4, 863. *—ing the hides and hips,* H5 IV, 2, 47 (F2.3.4. *drooping*). *—ed his knife,* Tit. II, 4, 50. *whose loves I may not d.* Mcb. III, 1, 122. *to d. down: he*

—s down the knee before him, Tim. I, 1, 60. *to d. forth,* of a tree yielding its fruit: *when it —s forth such fruit,* As III, 2, 250; and = to bring forth in general: *women's gentle brain could not d. forth such giant-rude invention,* IV, 3, 34.

c) to submerge, to plunge, to drown: *he'll d. his heart into the sink of fear,* H5 III, 5, 59. (the gods) *in our own filth d. our clear judgments,* Ant. III, 13, 113.

Drop-heir, name in Meas. IV, 3, 16.

Droplet, little drop, tear: Tim. V, 4, 76.

Dropping, subst. that which is infused by drops: *like eager —s into milk,* Hml. I, 5, 69.

Dropsied, diseased with dropsy: *where great additions swell's, and virtue none, it is a d. honour,* All's II, 3, 135.

Dropsy, unsound collection of water in the body: *the d. drown this fool!* Tp. IV, 230. *that swollen parcel of —ies,* H4A II, 4, 496.

Dross, refuse, worthless matter: *hours of d.* Sonn. 146, 11. *it is d.* Err. II, 2, 179. Merch. II, 7, 20. John III, 1, 165. Troil. IV, 4, 9 (Ff *cross*).

Drossy, futile, frivolous: *the d. age,* Hml. V, 2, 197.*

Drought, dryness, aridity: Tit. III, 1, 19.

Drouth, want of drink, thirst: *complain on d.* Ven. 544. *crickets sing at the oven's mouth, e'er the blither for their d.* Per. III Prol. 8.

Drovier, dealer in cattle: Ado II, 1, 201 (M. Edd. *drover*).

Drown, 1) trans. a) to overwhelm in or cover with water: *I'll d. my book,* Tp. V, 57. *in the —ed field,* Mids. II, 1, 96. *to d. my clothes and say I was stripped,* All's IV, 1, 57. *rivers d. their shores,* R2 III, 2, 107. R3 I, 2, 70. Hml. II, 2, 587. Tit. III, 1, 141. 230. Mcb. V, 2, 30. *pleasure d. the brim,* All's II, 4, 48. Used of flowing tears: *they d. their eyes,* Lucr. 1239. 1680. Sonn. 30, 5. All's IV, 3, 79. Tw. II, 1, 32. Wint. II, 1, 112. H6C II, 1, 104.

b) to suffocate in water: Lucr. 266. Tp. III, 2, 15. Wiv. III, 5, 11. H6B III, 2, 94. H6C III, 2, 186. R3 I, 4, 277. Tit. III, 2, 20. Tim. V, 1, 105. Hml. V, 1, 20. Oth. I, 3, 341. Figuratively: R3 IV, 4, 251. Tit. V, 3, 90. 107. Mcb. I, 7, 25. Ant. IV, 2, 45. Tp. III, 2, 14. Per. V, 1, 196. Passive: *we are less afraid to be —ed than thou,* Tp. I, 1, 48. I, 2, 405. II, 1, 244. II, 2, 91. 113. 179. III, 3, 8. 92. Gentl. I, 3, 79. Meas. III, 2, 52. Err. III, 2, 52. As III, 2, 305. IV, 1, 105. Tw. I, 2, 5. I, 5, 139. II, 1, 31. V, 248. H4A I, 3, 205. H5 IV, 7, 79. H6A I, 2, 12. H6C IV, 4, 23. V, 6, 20. Hml. IV, 7, 166. 184. Oth. I, 3, 368. Reflectively: *hang and d. their proper selves,* Tp. III, 3, 59. *to d. me,* Err. III, 2, 46. *d. thyself,* John IV, 3, 130. Hml. V, 1, 6. 11. 13. 18. 20. 31. Oth. I, 3, 306. 340. 360.

c) to overpower: *I in deep delight am —ed,* Pilgr. 113. Merch. II, 3, 14. H6B III, 1, 198. H6C III, 3, 14. Tim. IV, 3, 89. = to make perish: *the dropsy d. this fool,* Tp. IV, 230. *d. desperate sorrow in dead Edward's grave,* R3 II, 2, 99. *there my hopes lie —ed,* Troil. I, 1, 49. = to make completely drunk: *the sluttish ground, who is but drunken, when she seemeth —ed,* Ven. 984. *a third* (draught) *—s him,* Tw. I, 5, 141. *a sin that often —s him,* Tim. III, 5, 69; cf. *d. themselves in riot,* IV, 1, 28. == to sound louder, to make unheard by a louder sound: *the mean is —ea* *with your unruly base*, Gentl. I, 2, 96. *coughing —s the parson's saw*, LLL V, 2, 932. *to d. thy cries*, R3 II, 2, 61. *thus will I d. your exclamations*, IV, 4, 153.

2) intr. to perish in water: *an unpractised swimmer —s for want of skill*, Lucr. 1099. 1114. Sonn. 124, 12. Tp. I, 1, 31. 42. 49. 60. II, 2, 61. V, 218. Gentl. IV, 4, 4. Merch. II, 2, 172. R3 I, 4, 21. Oth. I, 3, 361.

Drowse, to be heavy with sleepiness: H4A III, 2, 81. Mcb. III, 2, 52.

Drowsily, sleepily: Caes. IV, 3, 240.

Drowsiness, sleepiness: Tp. II, 1, 199.

Drowsy, sleepy, heavy, dull: *sleep when I am d.* Ado I, 3, 17. John III, 4, 109. R3 V, 3, 228. Rom. IV, 1, 96. *dapples the d. east with spots of grey*, Ado V, 3, 27. H5 IV Chor. 16. *the d. race of night*, John III, 3, 39. H6B IV, 1, 5. *from their d. beds*, H6A II, 2, 23. *by the dead and d. fire*, Mids. V, 399. *d. hums*, Mcb. III, 2, 42. *make heaven d. with the harmony*, LLL IV, 3, 345. *puts the d. and neglected act freshly on me*, Meas. I, 2, 174. *the organs break up their d. grave*, H5 IV, 1, 22. *their d. spirits*, Troil. II, 2, 210. V, 5, 32. *all the d. syrups of the world*, Oth. III, 3, 331 (= disposing to sleep).

Drudge, subst. one employed in mean service, a slave: *he is contented thy poor d. to be*, Sonn. 151, 11. Merch. III, 2, 103. All's I, 3, 49. Rom. II, 5, 77 (fem.). Used as a term of reproach: Err. III, 2, 144 (fem.). Shr. IV, 1, 132. H6B IV, 1, 105. IV, 2, 159. *a very d. of nature's*, Cymb. V, 2, 5 (cf. *the slave of nature*, R3 I, 3, 230, i. e. born for baseness).

Drudgery, hard servile work: H4B III, 2, 125.

Drug, subst. 1) a medicinal substance: Sonn. 118, 4. Err. V, 104. Mcb. V, 3, 55. Cymb. I, 5, 4. 36. III, 5, 57. IV, 2, 38. 326. = poison: Tit. I, 154 (Ff *grudges*). Rom. V, 1, 66. V, 3, 120. Hml. III, 2, 266. Oth. I, 2, 74. I, 3, 91. Ant. IV, 15, 25.

2) = drudge, according to most interpreters: *the sweet degrees that this brief world affords to such as may the passive —s of it freely command*, Tim. IV, 3, 254; but it may mean: all things in passive subserviency to salutary as well as pernicious purposes.

Drug, vb. to season with ingredients: *I have —ed their possets*, Mcb. II, 2, 6.

Drug-damned, detested for its drugs or poisons: *d. Italy*, Cymb. III, 4, 15.

Drum, subst., instrument of military music: Ado II, 3, 14. LLL I, 2, 188. Merch. II, 5, 29. All's II, 5, 96. III, 3, 11. III, 5, 91. III, 6, 21 etc. John II, 76. III, 1, 303. H4A III, 3, 230. H6A III, 3, 29. IV, 2, 39. V, 4, 174. H6B V, 3, 32. H6C I, 1, 118. V, 1, 11. R3 III, 5, 16. IV, 4, 135 (Ff *trumpet*) etc. etc. *has led the d. before the English tragedians*, All's IV, 3, 298. *to beat the d.:* John V, 2, 166. Cor. V, 6, 151. Tim. IV, 3, 96. Lr. IV, 6, 292. *at their chamber-door I'll beat the d.* Lr. II, 4, 119 (= I'll knock hard at their door). *strike, d.* Rom. I, 4, 114. *let our —s strike*, Tim. V, 4, 85. Lr. V, 3, 81. *strike up our —s*, H4B IV, 2, 120. H6C II, 1, 204. V, 3, 24. R3 IV, 4, 179. Cor. IV, 5, 230. *strike up the d. towards Athens*, Tim. IV, 3, 169. *whilst any trump did sound, or d. struck up*, H6A I, 4, 80. *if you give him not John —'s entertainment, your inclining cannot be removed*, All's III, 6, 41 (= if you do not beat him).* *he's a good d., but a naughty orator*, V, 3, 253. *good Tom D., lend me a*

handkercher, 322 (equivocal allusions to Parolles' military character and his feat in fetching off his lost drum).

Drum, vb. to beat a drum: Lucr. 435. All's IV, 3, 331. Rom. I, 4, 86 (or subst.?). Ant. I, 4, 29.

Drumble, to be sluggish: Wiv. III, 3, 156.

Drummer, one whose office is to beat the drum: H6C IV, 7, 50.

Drunkard, one given to ebriety: Tp. I, 1, 59. II, 2, 170. V, 296. Wiv. II, 1, 24. Err. III, 1, 10. Ado III, 3, 112. LLL IV, 3, 50. As IV, 1, 7. Shr. Ind. 1, 107. 113. 133. H4A II, 4, 124. Tit. III, 1, 232. Rom. II, 3, 3. Hml. I, 4, 19. Lr. I, 2, 134. II, 1, 36. Oth. II, 3, 61. 307.

Drunken, 1) intoxicated: *a d. brain*, Ven. 910. *is but d.* 984. Lucr. 703. Tp. II, 2, 155. 183. Wiv. I, 1, 190. Err. IV, 1, 96. Shr. Ind. I, 36. Tw. I, 5, 138. V, 207. 412. H6C II, 3, 23. R3 III, 4, 101. Ant. V, 2, 219.

2) done in a state of intoxication: *d. sleep*, Meas. IV, 2, 150. *d. prophecies*, R3 I, 1, 33. *a d. slaughter*, II, 1, 122. *d. spilth of wine*, Tim. II, 2, 169.

3) given to drink: *my d. butler*, Tp. V, 277. *your d. cousin*, Tw. V, 312. *so d. an officer*, Oth. II, 3, 280.

Drunkenly, in a drunken manner: *d. caroused*, R2 II, 1, 127.

Drunkenness, 1) intoxication: *it hath pleased the devil d. to give place to the devil wrath*, Oth. II, 3, 297.

2) addiction to drink: *d. is his best virtue*, All's IV, 3, 285. Tw. II, 5, 81. III, 4, 389.

Dry, adj., 1) destitute of moisture, not wet: *to fan and blow them d.* (the wetted cheeks) Ven. 52. *she will draw his lips' rich treasure d.* 552. *many a d. drop seemed a weeping tear*, Lucr. 1375. *if the river were d.* Gentl. II, 3, 58. III, 2, 75. Merch. III, 2, 206. As IV, 3, 115. Wint. V, 3, 48. R2 II, 2, 146. H4A III, 1, 132. H6C III, 2, 139. IV, 8, 55. Tit. III, 1, 125. Rom. III, 2, 131. Hml. IV, 2, 22. Lr. III, 1, 14. III, 2, 10. III, 6, 79. *a d. death* (i. e. on land) Tp. I, 1, 72. *a drier death*, Gentl. I, 1, 158. *his d. nurse*, Wiv. I, 2, 4 (misapplied by Evans).

2) sapless, not succulent, not green: *d. combustious matter*, Ven. 1162. *d. oats*, Mids. IV, 1, 36. *d. toasts*, H4B IV, 4, 63. *d. cheese*, Troil. V, 4, 11. *stubble*, Cor. II, 1, 274. *drier logs*, Rom. IV, 4, 15. *d. meat* supposed to make choleric, Err. II, 2, 60.

3) sapless, barren: *graze on my lips, and if those hills be d., stray lower*, Ven. 233. (an oak) *d. with bald antiquity*, As IV, 3, 106. Hence used of the flaccidity of age: *here's his d. hand up and down*, Ado II, 1, 123. cf. H4B I, 2, 204. *these six d., round, old, withered knights*, II, 4, 8. *d. convulsions*, Tp. IV, 260 (cf. *old, and aged cramps*). *the d. serpigo*, Troil. II, 3, 81. *I will drain him d. as hay*, Mcb. I, 3, 18. *A d. hand* indicating want of generative faculty: Tw. I, 3, 77.

4) thirsty: *none so d. or thirsty will touch one drop of it*, Shr. V, 2, 144. *when I was d. with rage and extreme toil*, H4A I, 3, 31. *when I have been d., it hath served me instead of a quart pot to drink in*, H6B IV, 10, 14. Troil. II, 3, 234. Tit. III, 1, 14. Rom. III, 5, 59. Hml. IV, 7, 158. cf. the quibbles in LLL V, 2, 373 and Tw. I, 5, 49. Followed by *for: so d. he was for sway*, Tp. I, 2, 112.

5) stupid, insipid: *his brain, which is as d. as the remainder biscuit after a voyage,* As II, 7, 39. *his brain is d. enough,* Troil. I, 3, 329. *this jest is d. to me,* LLL V, 2, 373. *you 're a d. fool,* Tw. I, 5, 45. *what's your jest? a d. jest,* I, 3, 81 (i. e. a jest about stupidity).

6) hard, severe: *a d. basting,* Err. II, 2, 64. (cf. *Dry-beat*).

Dry, vb. 1) trans. a) to free from moisture: *d. your eyes,* Meas. IV, 3, 132. R2 III, 3, 202. R3 IV, 4, 278 (Ff *wipe*). H8 III, 2, 432. Tit. III, 1, 138. *to d. thy cheeks,* H6C I, 4, 83.

b) to wipe away, or to make evaporate: *d. his tears,* Ven. 1092. Sonn. 34, 6. Meas. III, 1, 234. H6C I, 4, 174. IV, 8, 43. R3 I, 3, 177. *sorrow that friendly sighs sought still to d.* Ven. 964. Wint. V, 3, 51. *shall d. your pities,* II, 1, 110 (i. e. tears). *dew,* Rom. II, 3, 6. *vapours,* H4B IV, 3, 105. — Joined with *up: the lamp —es up his oil to lend the world his light,* Ven. 756. *the sun —ed up the dewy morn,* Pilgr. 71. *d. those vapours up,* H6C V, 3, 12. *d. up your tears,* Rom. IV, 5, 79.

c) to deprive of natural juice, sap, or greenness: *to d. the old oak's sap,* Lucr. 950. *a —ed pear,* Wiv. IV, 5, 103. *—ed peas,* Mids. IV, 1, 42. *a neat's tongue —ed,* Merch. I, 1, 112. H4A II, 4, 271. *cakes,* H4B II, 4, 159. *branches,* R2 I, 2, 14. *a —ed herring,* Rom. II, 4, 39. *oats,* Lr. V, 3, 38. With *away: 'twas* (viz the meat) *burnt and —ed away,* Shr. IV, 1, 173.

d) to wither, to make strengthless and barren: *time hath not yet so —ed this blood of mine,* Ado IV, 1, 195. *which* (heart) *being —ed with grief, will break to powder,* Ant. IV, 9, 17. With *up: d. up thy marrows, vines and plough-torn leas,* Tim. IV, 3, 193. *d. up in her organs of increase,* Lr. I, 4, 301. Used of the brain, = to make senseless or stupid: *have I laid my brain in the sun and —ed it,* Wiv. V, 5, 144. *O heat, d. up my brains,* Hml. IV, 5, 154.

2) intr. to lose moisture, to become dry: *great seas have —ed,* All's II, 1, 143. *the blood upon your visage — es,* Cor. I, 9, 93. Cymb. III, 6, 31. With *up:* Oth. IV, 2, 60.

Dry-beat, to thrash, to cudgel soundly: *all —en with pure scoff,* LLL V, 2, 263. *and as you shall use me hereafter, d. the rest of the eight,* Rom. III, 1, 82. *I will d. you with an iron wit,* IV, 5, 126.

Dry-foot, the scent of the game, as far as it can be traced (perhaps so called, because, according to sportsmen, in water the scent is lost): *a hound that runs counter and yet draws d. well,* Err. IV, 2, 39.*

Dryly, not succulently: *like one of our French withered pears, it looks ill, it eats d.* All's I, 1, 176.

Dryness, enervation: *the d. of his bones,* Ant. I, 4, 27.

Dub, to knight: Tw. III, 4, 257. John I, 245. H6C II, 2, 59. *to d. a p. knight:* H5 IV, 8, 91. *—ed them gentlewomen,* R3 I, 1, 82. *to d. thee with the name of traitor,* H5 II, 2, 120. *do me right and d. me knight,* H4B V, 3, 78; referring to a custom of the time: he who drank a large potation, on his knees, to the health of his mistress, was said to be dubbed a knight, and retained the title for the evening.

Ducat, a coin, generally of gold: Gentl. I, 1, 145. Meas. III, 2, 134. Err. IV, 1, 30. 105. IV, 3, 84 etc. Ado II, 2, 54. III, 3, 116. IV, 2, 50. Merch. I, 3,

1. 9. 27. II, 3, 4. II, 6, 50. II, 8, 15. III, 1, 88 etc. Shr. II, 371. Tw. I, 3, 22. Rom. V, 1, 59. Hml. II, 2, 383. III, 4, 23. IV, 4, 20. Cymb. I, 4, 138. *double —s,* Merch. II, 8, 19.

Ducdame, burden of a song in As II, 5, 56. 60, not understood by the hearer, nor, as it seems, by the singer himself (some M. Edd. *duc ad me,* others *huc ad me*).*

Duchess, the wife of a duke: Ado III, 4, 16. Mids. I, 2, 6. 77. R2 II, 2, 97. H6B I, 2, 87. 98. 105. I, 4, 1. II, 4, 7. 98. III, 1, 45. H6C II, 1, 146. H8 II, 3, 38. 99. III, 2, 85. IV, 1, 52. V, 3, 169. Lr. I, 1, 247 III, 5, 15. *I, his forlorn d,* H6B II, 4, 45. *the duke of Cornwall and Regan his d.* Lr. II, 1, 4.

Duchy, the territory governed by a duke: H6B I, 1, 50. 58. 110.

Duck, subst. the waterfowl Anas: Tp. II, 2, 133. 134. 136. H4A II, 2, 108. Troil. III, 2, 56. Per. III Prol. 49. Used as a term of endearment: Mids. V, 286. Wint. IV, 4, 324. H5 II, 3, 54. Troil. IV, 4, 12.

Duck, vb. 1) to dive: Ven. 87 *(—s in).* Oth. II, 1, 190. *go a —ing,* Ant. III, 7, 65.

2) to bow: *d. with French nods,* R3 I, 3, 49. *the learned pate —s to the golden fool,* Tim. IV, 3, 18. *—ing observants,* Lr. II, 2, 109.

Dudgeon, the handle of a dagger: Mcb. II, 1, 46.*

Due, adj. 1) owed, to be paid as a deb *how grows it d.? d. for a chain,* Err. IV, 4, 137. *penalty which here appeareth d. upon the bond,* Merca. IV, 1, 249. Followed by *to: three thousand ducats d. unto the Jew,* Merch. IV, 1, 411. More particularly = expired, of an expired date: *since Pentecost the sum is d.* Err. IV, 1, 1. *'tis not d. yet,* H4A V, 1, 128. *claim it when 'tis d.* Troil. IV, 5, 51. *'twas d. on forfeiture six weeks,* Tim. II, 2, 30. *long since d. debts,* 39. *give 't these fellows to whom 'tis instant d.* 239. *what is now d. debt,* Cymb. IV, 2, 233.

2) to be justly claimed as a right or property, appropriate, becoming, proper: *fair payment for foul words is more than d.* LLL IV, 1, 19. *justice shall have d. course,* Wint. III, 2, 6. *a d. sincerity governed his deeds,* Meas. V, 451. R2 II, 1, 287. III, 4, 41. H5 V Chor. 4. H6B III, 1, 274. V, 1, 8. H6C IV, 6, 5. Troil. I, 3, 31. Hml. IV, 5, 212. Oth. I, 3, 238. III, 3, 461. Cymb. IV, 4, 46. V, 4, 79. V, 5, 258. Per. III Prol. 19. V, 3, 86. Followed by *to: my errand, d. unto my tongue, I bare home upon my shoulders,* Err. II, 1, 72. *her obedience, which is d. to me,* Mids. I, 1, 37. Wint. III, 2, 59. R3 I, 3, 112. Troil. IV, 5, 291. Lr. IV, 2, 27. Oth. I, 3, 189. Cymb. V, 5, 212. Per. II, 4, 5.

3) belonging: *I am d. to a woman,* Err. III, 2, 81. *a customary cross d. to love,* Mids. I, 1, 154. *two of the first, like coats in heraldry, d. but to one,* III, 2, 214. *is it a fee-grief d. to some single breast?* Mcb. IV, 3, 197.

4) such as a thing ought to be, direct, exact, precise: *I have ta'en a d. and wary note upon it,* Meas. IV, 1, 38; cf. *that all the kingdom may have d. note of him,* Lr. II, 1, 85. *the time approaches that will with d. decision make us know,* Mcb. V, 4, 17 (= make us know exactly). *shall our abode make with you by d. turns,* Lr. I, 1, 137 (= punctually alternating). *I would unstate myself, to be in a d. resolution,* I, 2,

108 (i. e. to have perfect certainty). *holding d. course to Harfleur,* H5 III Pιol. 17 (= direct, straight). *steering with d. course towards the isle of Rhodes,* Oth. I, 3, 34.

Due, subst. 1) debt: *to have the d. and forfeit of my bond,* Merch. IV, 1, 37. *here is a note of certain —s,* Tim. II, 2, 16. *stop the mouth of present —s,* 157.

2) that which may be claimed as a right: *his d. writ in my testament,* Lucr. 1183. *to eat the world's d.* Sonn. I, 14. 31, 12. 39, 8. 46, 13. 69, 3. 74, 7. Meas. III, 2, 71. LLL V, 2, 334. All's II, 4, 43. H4A I, 2, 59. H4B IV, 2, 116. IV, 5, 37(*thy d. from me;* cf. 41). H5 III, 7, 4. R3 III, 7, 120. 158. IV, 2, 91. IV, 4, 27. V, 1, 29. H8 V, 1, 132. Troil. I, 3, 106. II, 2, 174 *(—s).* Tim. III, 1, 37. Mcb. I, 4, 21. I, 5, 13 *(—s).* III, 6, 25. Lr. II, 4, 182 *(—s).* Cymb. III, 5, 11. *give the devil his d.* H4A I, 2, 133. H5 III, 7, 127.

Due, adv. exactly, directly, straight on: *there lies your way, d. west,* Tw. III, 1, 145. *whose current keeps d. on to the Propontic,* Oth. III, 3, 455. *every third word a lie, —r paid to the hearer than the Turk's tribute,* H4B III, 2, 330.

Due, vb. to endue: *this is the latest glory of thy praise that I, thy enemy, d. thee withal,* H6A IV, 2, 34. O. Edd. *dew,* which may be right, the praise being considered as a last refreshment before 'withering and pale' death; cf. v. 38.

Duellist, one expert in the rules of duelling: Rom. II, 4, 24.

Duello, the rules of duelling, as prescribed in certain books of the time: *the passado he respects not, the d. he regards not,* LLL I, 2, 185. *the gentleman will have one bout with you: he cannot by the d. avoid it,* Tw. III, 4, 337.

Duff, = Macduff: *dear D.* Mcb. II, 3, 94.

Dug, pap, teat; used in the sing. of human mothers: *with mother's d. between its lips,* H6B III, 2, 393. Rom. I, 3, 26. 31. 32. Hml. V, 2, 195. (In Ant. V, 2, 7 some blundering M. Edd. *dug* for *dung* of O. Edd.). In the plur. of beasts as well as women: Ven. 875. As II, 4, 50. R2 V, 3, 90. R3 II, 2, 30.

Duke, subst. a title of some sovereign princes; in England one of the highest order of nobility: Tp. I, 2, 54. 58. 72. 103. 437. Gentl. IV, 1, 49. IV, 4, 20. V, 2, 30. V, 4, 122 etc. etc. *Suffolk's d. for the duke of Suffolk:* H6B I, 1, 124. Meaning the doge of Venice: Merch. II, 8, 4. III, 2, 279. Shr. IV, 2, 83; and throughout in Oth. Confounded with *king* by Dull, Armado and Dogberry: LLL I, 1, 182. I, 2, 38. 132. Ado III, 5, 22. Even by the princess: LLL II, 38. And perhaps on purpose by Hamlet: Hml. III, 2, 249 (cf. *Count*). The swaggering Pistol calls Fluellen *great d.* H5 III, 2, 23 (= *dux,* leader, commander?).

Duke, vb. followed by *it,* == to play the duke: *Lord Angelo —s it well,* Meas. III, 2, 100.

Dukedom, 1) the territory of a duke: Tp. I, 2, 110. 115. 126. 168. V, 118. 133. 168. 211. Epil. 6. As I, 3, 61. V, 4, 175. H4B IV, 3, 93. H5 I, 1, 87. I, 2, 227. 247. III Chor. 31. III, 5, 12. H6B I, 1, 219. I, 3, 90. H6C IV, 7, 9. 23. *d. of Lancaster,* H4A V, 1, 45. *of Maine,* H6B IV, 2, 170.

2) the dignity of duke: *his d. and his chair with me is left,* H6C II, 1, 90. 93. *Gloster's d. is too ominous,* II, 6, 107. R3 I, 2, 252.

Dulcet, sweet to the ear: *such d. and harmonious breath,* Mids. II, 1, 151. *d. sounds in break of day,* Merch. III, 2, 51. *according to the fool's bolt, and such d. diseases,* As V, 4, 68. *a d. and a heavenly sound,* Shr. Ind. I, 51. *discord d.* All's I, 1, 186. *to hear by the nose, it is d. in contagion,* Tw. II, 3, 58.

Dull, adj. 1) unfeeling, insensible: *blushed and pouted in a d. disdain,* Ven. 33. *looks on the d. earth with disturbed mind,* Ven. 340. *lent a fire even to the —est peasant,* H4B I, 1, 113. *sleep in d. cold marble,* H8 III, 2, 434. *the woods are ruthless, dreadful, deaf and d.* Tit. II, 1, 128. *nature, as it grows again toward earth, is fashioned for the journey, d. and heavy,* Tim. II, 2, 228. Used of the operation of the senses and denoting either, actively, bad perceptivity, or, passively, bad perceptibility: *my d. deaf ears* (have) *a little use to hear,* Err. V, 316. *a savour that may strike the —est nostril,* Wint. I, 2, 421. *my sight is very d.* Tit. II, 3, 195. *this is a d. sight; are you not Kent?* Lr. V, 3, 282.* *picked out the —est scent,* Shr. Ind. I, 24. *d. of tongue and dwarfish,* Ant. III, 3, 19 (i. e. of a low soundless voice).

2) spiritless, lifeless, faint: *well-painted idol, image d. and dead,* Ven. 212. *their courage with hard labour tame and d.* H4A IV, 3, 23. *so faint, so spiritless, so d., so dead in look,* H4B I, 1, 71. *in their pale d. mouths the gimmal bit lies foul with chewed grass,* H5 IV, 2, 49. *when the blood is made d. with the act of sport,* Oth. II, 1, 230. Hence = weary, sleepy: *from forth d. sleep by dreadful fancy waking,* Lucr. 450. *while she was in her d. and sleeping hour,* Mids. III, 2, 8. *vexing the d. ear of a drowsy man,* John III, 4, 109. *O thou d. God* (viz Sleep) H4B III, 1, 15. *unless some d. and favourable hand will whisper music to my weary spirit,* IV, 5, 2 (disposing to sleep with a drowsy music). *the night's d. ear,* H5 IV Chor. 11. *my spirits grow d., and fain I would beguile the tedious day with sleep,* Hml. III, 2, 236. *at this oddeven and d. watch o' the night,* Oth. I, 1, 124. *O sleep, lie d. upon her,* Cymb. II, 2, 31. Per. V, 1, 163. cf. Tit. II, 3, 195 and 196.

3) slow, heavy, indolent, inert: *if the d. substance of my flesh were thought,* Sonn. 44, 1; cf. *he is only an animal, only sensible in the —er parts,* LLL IV, 2, 28. *the slow offence of my d. bearer when from thee I speed,* Sonn. 51, 2. *no d. flesh, in his fiery race,* 11. *is not lead a metal heavy, d. and slow?* LLL III, 60. *d. lead,* Merch. II, 7, 8. *like d. and heavy lead,* H4B I, 1, 118. *the d. elements of earth and water,* H5 III, 7, 23. *turn back, d. earth, and find thy centre out,* Rom. II, 1, 2 (cf. Tim. II, 2, 228). *speed more than speed but d. and slow she deems,* Lucr. 1336. *a d. fighter,* H4A IV, 2, 86. *give way, d. clouds, to my quick curses,* R3 I, 3, 196. *leaden servitor to d. delay,* IV, 3, 52. *I cannot bound a pitch above d. woe,* Rom. I, 4, 21. *you are d., Casca,* Caes. I, 3, 57. *—er shouldst thou be than the fat weed,* Hml. I, 5, 32. *a d. and muddy-mettled rascal,* II, 2, 594. *spur my d. revenge,* IV, 4, 33.

4) tedious, irksome: *debate where leisure serves with d. debaters,* Lucr. 1019. *she excels each mortal thing the d. earth dwelling,* Gentl. IV, 2, 52 (cf. *d. earth* in Ven. 340. Rom. II, 1, 2 and Tim. II, 2, 228, and cf. *Sullen*). *are my discourses d.?* Err. II, 1, 91. *that I was —er than a great thaw,* Ado II, 1, 251. *in this d. and long-continued truce,* Troil. I,

3, 262. *within a d., stale, tired bed,* Lr. I, 2, 13. *shall I abide in this d. world?* Ant. IV, 15, 61. *the sober eye of d.* Octavia, V, 2, 55.

5) **awkward, stupid:** *he* (Death) *insults o'er d. and speechless tribes,* Sonn. 107, 12. *d. thing, I say so,* Tp. I, 2, 285. *this d. fool,* V, 297. Gentl. II, 6, 41. Meas. IV, 4, 24. Ado II, 1, 143. Merch. III, 2, 164. As I, 2, 56. III, 2, 32. 121. All's I, 1, 234. R2 I, 3, 168. H'B IV, 2, 22. H6A V, 5, 15. R3 IV, 2, 17. IV, 4, 444. Troil. I, 3, 381. II, 2, 209. Cor. I, 9, 6. V, 3, 40. Tim. V, 1, 26. Oth. V, 2, 225. Cymb. V, 5, 197.

6) **out of tune, gloomy, melancholy:** *if they sing, 'tis with so d. a cheer,* Sonn. 97, 13. *when I am d. with care and melancholy,* Err. I, 2, 20. *d. melancholy,* V, 79. *dumps so d. and heavy,* Ado II, 3, 73. *the motions of his spirit are d. as night,* Merch. V, 86. *my d. and heavy eye,* R2 III, 2, 196. *with d. unwillingness to repay a debt,* R3 II, 2, 92. cf. Rom. I, 4, 21. cf. *Dull-eyed.*

7) **not bright, dim, clouded:** *the foolish and d. and crudy vapours,* H4B IV, 3, 106. *is not their climate foggy, raw and d.* H5 III, 5, 16. cf. *d. clouds,* R3 I, 3, 196. *sparkles this stone as it was wont? or is't not too d. for your good wearing?* Cymb. II, 4, 41. *mark her eye and tell me for what d. part in it you chose her,* Wint. V, 1, 64. cf. R2 III, 2, 196. Tit. II, 3, 195. Lr. V, 3, 282.

8) **blunt, obtuse:** *the murderous knife was d. and blunt,* R3 IV, 4, 226. Double sense: *my words are d.; O quicken them with thine! Thy woes will make them sharp,* 124.

Dull, vb. 1) **to make insensible, to deprive of fine feeling:** *—ed and cloyed with gracious favours,* H5 II, 2, 9. *do not d. thy palm with entertainment of each new-hatched comrade,* Hml. I, 3, 64.

2) **to benumb, to stupify:** *attached with weariness to the —ing of my spirits,* Tp. III, 3, 6. *will stupify and d. the sense awhile,* Cymb. I, 5, 37.

3) **to weary, to bore:** *I would not d. you with my song,* Sonn. 102, 14.

4) **to make inert and lazy:** *peace itself should not so d. a kingdom,* H5 II, 4, 16. *d. not device by coldness and delay,* Oth. II, 3, 394.

5) **to make stupid:** *that overgoes my blunt invention quite, —ing my lines and doing me disgrace,* Sonn. 103, 8.

6) **to blunt:** *borrowing —s the edge of husbandry,* Hml. I, 3, 77.

Dull, name in LLL I, 1, 271. IV, 2, 37. V, 1, 156.

Dullard, an **idiot:** Lr. II, 1, 76. *makest thou me a d. in this act? wilt thou not speak to me?* Cymb. V, 5, 265 (i. e. a person stupidly insensible and indifferent to what is going on).

Dull-brained, **stupid:** R3 IV, 4, 332.

Dull-eyed, **looking sad:** *I'll not be made a soft and d. fool, to shake the head, relent and sigh,* Merch. III, 3, 14. *d. melancholy,* Per. I, 2, 2.

Dully, **sluggishly, tediously:** *the beast that bears me plods d. on,* Sonn. 50, 6. *d. sluggardized at home,* Gentl. I, 1, 7. *the time shall not go d. by us,* Ado II, 1, 379.

Dulness, 1) **insensibility, indolence:** *kill the spirit of love with a perpetual d.* Sonn. 56, 8. *when*

light-winged toys of feathered Cupid seel with wanton d. my speculative and officed instruments, Oth. I, 3, 270. *even till a Lethe'd d.* Ant. II, 1, 27.

2) **drowsiness:** *'tis a good d.* Tp. I, 2, 185.

3) **stupidity:** As I, 2, 58. Tim. IV, 3, 335.

Duly, 1) as it ought to be, in a **suitable manner:** *as d., but not as truly, as bird doth sing on bough,* H5 III, 2, 19. H6B IV, 1, 62. H8 II, 3, 68. Cymb. I, 1, 27.

2) **exactly:** *let this be d. performed,* Meas. IV, 2, 127. *I d. am informed his grace is at Marseilles,* All's IV, 4, 8. *disbursed I d.* R2 I, 1, 127. *have their wages d. paid,* H8 IV, 2, 150.

Dumain (rhyming to *pain* and *twain,* LLL IV, 3, 171 and V, 2, 47): name: LLL I, 1, 15. 28. II, 56. IV, 3, 82. 127. V, 2, 276. 285.*All's IV, 3, 200. 210. 277. 316.

Dumb, adj. 1) **destitute of the power of speech:** Sonn. 23, 10. 38, 7. 78, 5. Gentl. III, 1, 90. Ado I, 1, 212. V, 3, 10. All's IV, 3, 213. H6A II, 4, 26. H6B III, 2, 32. R3 III, 7, 25. Troil. III, 3, 200. Cor. II, 1, 278. Tit. V, 3, 114. Caes. III, 1, 260. III, 2, 229. Cymb. II, 4, 84. *d. deaf,* H6B III, 2, 144.

2) **not speaking, silent:** Ven. 406. Lucr. 268. 1105. 1780. Sonn. 83, 10. 85, 14. 101, 9. Gentl. III, 1, 207. Mids. V, 334. Merch. I, 1, 106. V, 279. All's II, 3, 146. Tit. V, 3, 184. Hml. I, 2, 206. IV, 6, 26. Per. V, 2, 267. *d. to us,* Hml. I, 1, 171. *to strike d.* Ven. 1146. Gentl. II, 2, 21. John IV, 2, 235. *mute and d.* Lucr. 1123. R3 IV, 4, 18 (Ff *still and mute).* Hml. II, 2, 137.

3) **not accompanied by words:** *d. action,* Tit. IV, 2, 40. *demeanour,* Lucr. 474. *discourse,* Tp. III, 3, 39. *play,* Ven. 359. *show,* Ado II, 3, 226. Merch. I, 2, 78. Tit. III, 1, 131. Hml. III, 2, 14. *what's d. in show,* Per. III Prol. 14.

Dumb, vb. **to put to silence:** *deep clerks she —s,* Per. V Prol. 5. *what I would have spoke was beastly —ed by him,* Ant. I, 5, 50 (O. Edd. *dumbe* and *dumb).*

Dumb-discoursive, **speaking without words:** Troil. IV, 4, 92.

Dumbe, name of a minister: H4B II, 4, 95.

Dumbly, **silently, without speaking:** Ven. 1059. Mids. V, 98. R2 V, 1, 95.

Dumbness, 1) **incapacity to speak:** Lr. IV, 1, 63.

2) **silence:** Tw. III, 2, 25. Wint. V, 2, 15. Troil. III, 2, 140.

3) **show without words:** *to the d. of the gesture one might interpret,* Tim. I, 1, 33.

Dumb-show, **pantomime:** Ado II, 3, 226. Merch. I, 2, 78. Tit. III, 1, 131. Hml. III, 2, 14.

Dump, 1) (only in the plur.) **ill humour, low spirits, melancholy:** *sing no more ditties, sing no mo of —s so dull and heavy,* Ado II, 3, 73. *in your —s?* Shr. II, 286. *to step out of these dreary —s,* Tit. I, 391. *doleful —s the mind oppress,* Rom. IV, 5, 129.

2) **a melancholy strain in music:** *distress likes —s,* Lucr. 1127. *tune a deploring d.* Gentl. III, 2, 85. *play me some merry d.* Rom. IV, 5, 108 (Peter's speech).

Dun, adj. **dark, swarthy:** *if snow be white, why then her breasts are d.* Sonn. 130, 3. *the —est smoke of hell,* Mcb. I, 5, 52. *I am done. Tut, dun's* *the mouse*, Rom. I, 4, 40 (a proverbial saying, perhaps used, without any distinct meaning, to quibble on the word *done*).

Dun, subst. a d u n h o r s e: *if thou art d.*, *we'll draw thee from the mire*, Rom. I, 4, 41 (allusion to a rural pastime called *'dun in the mire'*, in which a log of wood represented a horse and was to be lifted by the company).

Dun, corruption from *Don:* LLL IV, 3, 199 (Costard's speech).

Duncan, name of the king in Mcb. I, 5, 40 etc. etc.

Dung, m a n u r e, f i l t h; (cf. *Cow - dung*, *Dung- hill*): *never palates more the d.*, *the beggars' nurse and Caesars'*, Ant. V, 2, 7 (cf. Ant. I, 1, 35 and Tim. IV, 3, 444. Some M. Edd. *dug!*)

Dungeon, a d e e p, d a r k p l a c e o f c o n f i n e- m e n t: LLL IV, 3, 255. All's IV, 3, 273. H4B IV, 3, 8. H6A II, 5, 57. R3 I, 2, 111. Caes. I, 3, 94. Hml. II, 2, 252. Oth. III, 3, 271. Cymb. I, 6, 87.

Dung-hill, a h e a p o f d u n g: Wiv. I, 3, 70. LLL V, 1, 81. 83. As I, 1, 16. H5 IV, 3, 99. H6B IV, 10, 87. Lr. III, 7, 97. Used to denote a base ex- traction: *d. curs*, H4B V, 3, 108. *d. grooms*, H6A I, 3, 14. H6B I, 3, 196. A term of reproach for a per- son meanly born: *out, d.!* John IV, 3, 87. Lr. IV, 6, 249.

Dungy, consisting of dung, f i l t h y: *the whole d. earth*, Wint. II, 1, 157. Ant. I, 1, 35.

Dúnsinane (Dunsínane in Mcb. IV, 1, 93), the castle of Macbeth: Mcb. IV, 1, 93. V, 2, 12. V, 3, 2. 60. V, 4, 9. V, 5, 45. 46. V, 8, 30.

Dunsmore, place in England: H6C V, 1, 3.*

Dunstable, place in England: H8 IV, 1, 27.

Dup, to do up, to open: *and —ed the chamber- door*, Hml. IV, 5, 53.

Durance, i m p r i s o n m e n t: *perpetual d.* Meas. III, 1, 67. *set thee from d.* LLL III, 130. *is now in d.* Tw. V, 283. H4B V, 5, 36. Quibbling: *gives them suits of d.* Err. IV, 3, 27 (the dress worn in prisons, and a lasting dress). *is not a buff jerkin a most sweet robe of d.?* H4A I, 2, 49.

Dure, in *Ever-during*, *Long-during*, q. v.

During, prepos. for or in t h e t i m e of: Lucr. Arg. 4. Err. V, 328. Mids. IV, 2, 20. H4A II, 4, 21. 302. V, 3, 39. H6A I, 2, 31. II, 5, 67. IV, 7, 50. R3 I, 4, 15. H8 III, 2, 249. Troil. IV, 1, 11. Cor. II, 1, 239. Lr. V, 3, 299. Cymb. IV, 4, 7.

Dusky, h a l f d a r k, g l o o m y: *d. Dis*, Tp. IV, 89. *d. vapours of the night*, H6A II, 2, 27. *d. torch*, II, 5, 122. *sky*, H6B III, 2, 104. *spectacles*, 112. *graves*, R3 IV, 4, 70.

Dust, 1) f i n e, d r y p a r t i c l e s o f e a r t h, covering the ground and raised by the wind: Lucr. 1381. Gentl. II, 3, 35. Mids. V, 397. R2 III, 2, 146. III, 3, 43. V, 2, 6. 30. H4A I, 3, 134. H4B I, 3, 103. H6C V, 1, 56. V, 2, 23. Cor. III, 1, 171. Tit. III, 1, 12. Tim. V, 2, 16. Hml. V, 1, 274. Lr. IV, 6, 201. V, 3, 137. Ant. III, 6, 48. Per. I, 1, 97. II, 2, 55. *to grind to d.* Cor. III, 2, 103. Tit. V, 2, 187. *crumble up to d.* John V, 7, 31.

2) a s i n g l e p a r t i c l e of e a r t h: *was in mine eye the d. that did offend it*, All's V, 3, 55. *blow each d., each straw, each little rub out of the path*, John III, 4, 128. *a grain, a d., a gnat*, IV, 1, 93. *to touch a d. of England's ground*, R2 II, 3, 91.

3) Used figuratively, a) for any worthless thing: *vile gold, dross, d.* John III, 1, 165. H6C V, 2, 27.

Troil. III, 3, 178. Caes. III, 1, 116. Lr. IV, 2, 30. — b) as the emblem of age and oblivion: *smear with d. their glittering golden towers*, Lucr. 945. *the d. and injury of age*, Sonn. 108, 10. *are they like to take d.?* Tw. I, 3, 135. R2 II, 1, 294. H5 II, 4, 87. Cor. II, 3, 126. — c) as the common origin of all things in existence: *a thousand grains that issue out of d.* Meas. III, 1, 21. *a piece of valiant d.* Ado II, 1, 64. Hml. II, 2, 321. Cymb. IV, 2, 5. — d) as that to which all things return in death: Sonn. 32, 2. All's II, 3, 147. Wint. IV, 4, 469. John III, 4, 32. IV, 2, 120. H4A IV, 4, 85. H4B IV, 5, 116. H6A V, 3, 29. H6B III, 3, 14. Rom. V, 3, 13. Hml. I, 2, 71. IV, 2, 6. V, 1, 232. Cymb. IV, 2, 247. 263. = the remains of the dead: *weep their d.* All's V, 3, 64. *the d. of Alexander*, Hml. V, 1, 225.

Dusty, r e d u c e d t o d u s t: *mighty states character- less are grated to d. nothing*, Troil. III, 2, 196. *all our yesterdays have lighted fools the way to d. death*, Mcb. V, 5, 23.

Dutch, pertaining to Holland: *half stewed in grease, like a D. dish*, Wiv. III, 5, 121. *German or Dane, low D.* All's IV, 1, 78.

Dutchman, H o l l a n d e r: Ado III, 2, 33. *veal, quoth the D.* LLL V, 2, 247. *lustique, as the D. says*, All's II, 3, 46. *like an icicle on a —'s beard*, Tw. III, 2, 29.

Duteous, r e s p e c t f u l, o b s e q u i o u s: *the d. vassal scarce is gone*, Lucr. 1360. *the eyes*, *'fore d.* Sonn. 7, 11. *release all d. oaths*, R2 IV, 210 (Qq *duty's rites*). *his d. land*, H4A IV, 3, 44. *my d. spirit*, H4B IV, 5, 148. *d. love*, R3 II, 1, 33. *service*, 63. *our d. citizens*, III, 5, 65. *a d. and knee-crooking knave*, Oth. I, 1, 45. *be but d.* Cymb. III, 5, 159. V, 5, 86. Followed by *to: d. to the vices of thy mistress*, Lr. IV, 6, 258.

Dutiful, the same: H5 II, 2, 127. Troil. V, 3, 72

Duty, 1) that which a person is bound to do *to get it is thy d.* Ven. 168. *'gainst law or d.* Lucr. 497. Err. V, 107. Ado II, 1, 55. IV, 1, 3. LLL I, 1, 269. Merch. III, 5, 60. R3 I, 3, 250 (quibble). I, 4, 230. Tit. I, 414. Mcb. III, 1, 18. Lr. I, 1, 279 etc. *my mother did but d.* All's IV, 2, 12. *do thy d. and have thy d.* Shr. IV, 1, 38. Speaking of military ser- vice, = guard: *keep your —ies*, Cor. I, 7, 1. cf. Oth. II, 3, 151.

2) o b e d i e n c e, s u b m i s s i o n:* *fleet-winged d. with thought's feathers flies*, Lucr. 1216. *which I was much unwilling to proceed in but for my d. to your lady- ship*, Gentl. II, 1, 113. *disobedient, stubborn, lacking d.* III, 1, 69. *what a foolish d. call you this? I would your d. were as foolish*, Shr. V, 2, 125. *my lady char- ged my d. in this business*, Lr. IV, 5, 18. *At d.* = at command: *who had the mouths, the tongues, the eyes and hearts of men at d.* Tim. IV, 3, 262.

3) r e v e r e n c e, r e s p e c t, p i e t y: *your honour's in all d.* Ven. Dedic. 9. Lucr. Ded. 7. *were my worth greater, my d. would show greater*, Lucr. Ded. 4. *his kindled d. kindled her mistrust*, Lucr. 1352. *my d. will I boast of*, Gentl. II, 4, 111. *her child-like d.* III, 1, 75. *in the modesty of fearful d.* Mids. V, 1, 101. *all adoration, d. and observance*, As V, 2. 102. *tongues spit their —ies out*, H8 I, 2, 61. Sonn. 26, 2. 4. Compl. 130. Gentl. III, 1, 8. 17. Ado I, 1, 157. LLL I, 1, 280. V, 2, 199. Mids. I, 1, 127. V, 83. 86. As I, 2, 177. II, 3, 58. Shr. Ind. 1, 82. H5 II, 2, 31. H6A

II, 1, 37. IV, 4, 34. H6B I, 3, 161. V, 1, 173. H6C V, 7, 28. R3 II, 2, 108. Troil. III, 1, 169. Cor. V, 3, 51. 55. Tim. IV, 3, 523. Hml. IV, 4, 6 etc.

4) **act of reverence, homage, compliment**: *where mortal stars did him peculiar —ies,* Lucr. 14. *my d. to you,* All's III, 2, 27; cf. H5 V, 2, 23. *such d. to the drunkard let him do,* Shr. Ind. I, 113. *pay that d. to him,* John II, 247. *he gave you all the —ies of a man,* H4A V, 2, 56. *set your knee against my foot, and in reguerdon of that d. done ....,* H6A III, 1, 170. III, 4, 4. H6B III, 1, 17. R3 I, 3, 251. Mcb. I, 4, 24.*III, 4, 92. IV, 1, 132. Hml. I, 2, 88. Ir. I, 1, 99. II, 2, 110. Oth. I, 3, 41. III, 2, 2. Ant. III, 13, 82. Cymb. II, 3, 55. III, 5, 32 etc. *stay not thy compliment; I forgive you d.* LLL IV, 2, 147 (= depart without further ceremony; cf. Merch. III, 5, 60).

5) **that which is due**; only in the phrase: *do thy d. and have thy d.* Shr. IV, 1, 39.

Dwarf, a person far below the common size of men: Wiv. III, 2, 6. Mids. III, 2, 328. H6A II, 3, 22. Troil. II, 3, 146.

Dwarfish, very small: Mids. III, 2, 295. John V, 2, 135. H8 I, 1, 22. Mcb. V, 2, 22. Ant. III, 3, 19.

Dwell, 1) to have one's habitation, a) in a house or what is like it: Ven. 1173. Sonn. 71, 4. Tp. I, 2, 457. 459. Gentl. I, 1, 43. Wiv. I, 2, 2. II, 2, 48. Meas. II, 1, 261. Ado V, 1, 186. Merch. II, 2, 49. II, 6, 25. As III, 2, 352. 357. V, 4, 62. Tw. III, 1, 9. Wint. II, 1, 30. R2 I, 2, 72. H6B IV, 10, 68. H8 IV, 2, 126. Rom. III, 2, 84. V, 1, 38. Caes. II, 1, 285. III, 3, 7. 15. 27. Per. IV, 6, 83. V, 1, 123. b) in a country: Tp. II, 1, 246. Epil. 7. Gentl. IV, 2, 52. All's II, 3, 301. Tw. II, 3, 84. R2 I, 3, 177. H6C III, 1, 74. Cor. IV, 5, 40. 47. Hml. I, 5, 123. Oth. I, 1, 70. Per. V Prol. 15.

2) **to abide, to remain, to continue**: *I'll rather d. in my necessity,* Merch. I, 3, 157. *you shall let it d. darkly with you,* All's IV, 3, 13 (i. e. keep it secret). *he should still d. in his musings,* H8 III, 2, 133.

3) **to have one's seat, to live, to exist**: *out none (viz face) where all distress and dolour —ed,* Lucr. 1446. *Sinon in this cold hot-burning fire doth dwell,* 1557. *the lovely gaze where every eye doth d.* Sonn. 5, 2. *you live in this and d. in lovers' eyes,* 55,

14. *lean penury within that pen doth d.* 84, 5. *in my tongue thy name no more shall d.* 89, 10. 93, 10. 99, 4. Compl. 129. Wiv. III, 5, 72. Err. III, 1, 104. Mids. I, 1, 206. H5 IV, 3, 27. R3 I, 2, 59. IV, 2, 67. Rom. II, 2, 187. Mcb. III, 2, 7. Oth. IV, 1, 84. Per. III, 2, 36.

4) **to lie, to depend on, to be in the power of**; followed by *in*: *my hopes in heaven do d.* H8 III, 2, 460. *though't be a sportful combat, yet in the trial much opinion —s,* Troil. I, 3, 336. *—s not in particular will,* II, 2, 53. *whose easy-borrowed pride —s in the fickle grace of her he follows,* Lr. II, 4, 189. Followed by *upon*: *what great danger —s upon my suit?* Ven. 206. By *with*: *to be wise and love exceeds man's might; that —s with gods above* Troil. III, 2, 165.

5) Followed by *on,* = a) to stand on, to stick to, to make much of: *she —s so securely on the excellency of her honour,* Wiv. II, 2, 251. *fain would I d. on form,* Rom. II, 2, 88. b) to continue long in: *sweet discourse, which so long sundered friends should d. upon,* R3 V, 3, 100. *more than I have said, the leisure and enforcement of the time forbids to d. upon,* 239.

Dweller (followed by *on*) one who makes much of sth.: *have I not seen —s on form and favour lose all,* Sonn. 125, 5.

Dwelling, 1) habitation, lodging: Compl. 82. Wint. IV, 4, 740. Caes. III, 3, 26. — 2) the country in which a man lives; home: *your accent is something finer than you could purchase in so removed a d.* As III, 2, 360. *my name is called Vincentio, my d. Pisa,* Shr. IV, 5, 55. *you have here a goodly d. and a rich,* H4B V, 3, 7.

Dwelling-house: John V, 7, 3.

Dwelling-place: As II, 1, 63. H6A I, 3, 77.

Dwindle, to shrink, to fall away: H4A III, 3, 3. Mcb. I, 3, 23.

Dye, subst. color: Sonn. 54, 5. Pilgr. 89. 284. Mids. III, 2, 102. H8 I, 1, 208. Hml. I, 3, 128 (Ff *eye*).

Dye, vb. to color: Sonn. 99, 5. 101, 2. Tp. II, 1, 63. As IV, 3, 156. John II, 323. H4A II, 4, 16. H6A II, 4, 61. H6C I, 2, 33. Oth. III, 4, 74.

Dyer, one whose occupation is to dye cloth and the like: Sonn. 111, 7.

E.

E, 1) the fifth letter of the alphabet: LLL V, 1, 24. 58. — 2) a note in music: *e la mi,* Shr. III, 1, 78.

Each, 1) used of an indefinite number, a) = every, any: *would move e. part in me that were but sensible,* Ven. 436. *e. envious brier his weary legs doth scratch, e. shadow makes him stop, e. murmur stay,* 705. *from whom e. lamp and shining star doth borrow,* 861. Lucr. 309. 334. 818. 1101. Sonn. 7, 2. 48, 2. 127, 5. Pilgr. 92. Tp. I, 2, 329. 354. III, 3, 48. V, 251. Gentl. I, 2, 119. II, 7, 35. IV, 2, 51. Wiv. V, 5, 67. LLL I, 1, 107. Mids. V, 405. 409. Tw. V, 258. Wint. II, 3, 154. IV, 4, 1. 143. John III, 4, 128. H4A I, 1, 64. V, 2, 93. H4B I, 1, 158. H6B III, 1,

221. H6C V, 6, 12. R3 V, 3, 25. 198. Tim. IV, 3, 423 etc. etc. *e. day* = every day, daily: Sonn. 108, 6. R2 I, 1, 22. H6B III, 1, 63. Alternating with *every*: *e. passion labours so, that every present sorrow seemeth chief,* Ven. 969. *e. one* = every one: *the locks between her chamber and his will, e. one by him enforced,* Lucr. 303. *e. one, tripping on his toe, will be here,* Tp. IV, 46. *she would to e. one sip,* Wint. IV, 4, 62. *through this grate I count e. one and view the Frenchmen,* H6A I, 4, 60. *thanks to all at once and to e. one,* Mcb. V, 8, 74. *e. particular saint,* Meas. V, 243. *e. several paper,* Gentl. I, 2, 108. Mids. V, 424. H4B IV, 1, 170. Mcb. IV, 3, 96. Per. IV, 4, 6. *bide the penance*

of e. three years' day, LLL I, 1, 115 (= of every day in the space of three years). *at e. his needless heavings*, Wint. II, 3, 35.

b) every one, every body: *like a school broke up, e. hurries toward his home*, H4B IV, 2, 105. *compel from e. the sixth part of his substance*, H8 I, 2, 57. 94. *gazed e. on other*, R3 III, 7, 26. *men of heart looked wondering e. on other*, Cor. V, 6, 100. *this shouldering of e. other in the court*, H6A IV, 1, 189. *whiles they e. other cross*, IV, 3, 52.

2) used of a definite and limited number; a) joined to a subst.: *in e. cheek appears a pretty dimple*, Ven. 242. *with e. end of thy blue bow*, Tp. IV, 80. *in e. eye one*, Merch. V, 245. *the true succeeders of e. royal house*, R3 V, 5, 30. *e. man apart*, Tim. V, 1, 110. *e. one: e. one with ireful passion*, Err. V, 151. *the whole world again cannot pick out five such, take e. one in his vein*, LLL V, 2, 548. *e. one to this office*, Shr. Ind. I, 73. V, 2, 66. Wint. V, 3, 153. R2 III, 2, 132. H6C II, 1, 26. 36. Tit. III, 1, 278. Cymb. V, 3, 49.

b) absolutely, = every one out of a certain number: *e. leaning on their elbows*, Ven. 44. *e. do in consent shake hands*, Sonn. 28, 5. *e. doth good turns unto the other*, 47, 2. Wiv. V, 5, 27. Ado V, 3, 29. LLL IV, 3, 162. 297. V, 2, 148. All's II, 3, 63. IV, 3, 187. H5 III, 7, 169. H6B II, 4, 61. Troil. IV, 1, 65. Tim. IV, 2, 27. Mcb. I, 3, 44 etc. *e. other*, α) separated by a prepos.: *which e. to other hath so strongly sworn*, LLL I, 1, 309. *wink e. at other*, Mids. III, 2, 239. Tim. V, 5, 83. Mcb. I, 3, 155. Ant. II, 2, 138. β) placed together: *white and red e. other did destroy*, Ven. 346. Wiv. II, 2, 114. Mids. III, 2, 363. As V, 2, 11. Tw. V, 222. John II, 406. R2 I, 1, 27. I, 3, 184. H5 III, 2, 146. R3 I, 3, 189. I, 4, 243. Troil. I, 3, 391. Ant. III, 6, 78. *both crystals, where they viewed e. other's sorrow*, Ven. 963. *they interchange e. other's seat*, Lucr. 70. *both stood wondering e. other's chance*, 1596. *we still did meet e. other's man*, Err. V, 386. H5 IV Chor. 7. V, 2, 379. R3 II, 2, 114.

Each, alone, = each other: *but being both from me, both to e. friend, I guess one angel in another's hell*, Sonn. 144, 11. *ten masts at e. make not the altitude which thou hast perpendicularly fell*, Lr. IV, 6, 53 (= each joined to another). cf. *matched in mouth like bells, e. under e.* Mids. IV, 1, 129. *mark how one string, sweet husband to another, strikes e. in e. by mutual ordering*, Sonn. 8, 10 (= the strings strike each other mutually, one making the other sound).

Eager, 1) sharp, sour, acid: *with e. compounds we our palate urge*, Sonn. 118, 2. *like e. droppings into milk*, Hml. I, 5, 69.

2) keen, biting: *a nipping and an e. air*, Hml. I, 4, 2.

3) full of asperity, bitter: *the bitter clamour of two e. tongues*, R2 I, 1, 49. *vex him with e. words*, H6C II, 6, 68.

4) impetuous, vehement: *conceit and grief an e. combat fight*, Lucr. 1298. *what shrill-voiced suppliant makes this e. cry?* R2 V, 3, 75. *hunger will enforce them to be more e.* H6A I, 2, 38. *my followers to the e. foe turn back*, H6C I, 4, 3.

5) ardently desirous: *gazed for tidings in my e. eyes*, Lucr. 254. *with e. feeding food doth choke the feeder*, R2 II, 1, 37.

Eagerly, ardently, impetuously: *how e. ye follow my disgraces*, H8 III, 2, 240. *where e. his sickness pursued him still*, IV, 2, 24. *who, having some advantage on Octavius, took it too e.* Caes. V, 3, 7.

Eagerness, ardent desire: *madding my e. with her restraint*, All's V, 3, 213.

Eagle, the bird Aquila: Lucr. 1015. LLL IV, 3, 334. R2 III, 3, 69. H4A II, 4, 363. IV, 1, 99. H6A I, 2, 141. H6B III, 1, 248. IV, 1, 109. H6C I, 1, 268. II, 1, 91. V, 2, 12. R3 I, 1, 132. I, 3, 71. Troil. I, 2, 265. Cor. III, 1, 139. V, 6, 115. Tit. IV, 4, 83. Rom. III, 5, 221. Tim. I, 1, 49. IV, 3, 224 (*outlived the e.*). Caes. V, 1, 81. Mcb. I, 2, 35. Ant. II, 2, 186. Cymb. I, 1, 139. III, 3, 21. V, 3, 42. Per. IV, 3, 48. *Jove's bird, the Roman e.* Cymb. IV, 2, 348; cf. V, 4, 113. 115. V, 5, 427. 473. Used as a fem.: Ven. 55. H5 I, 2, 169. Cymb. V, 5, 470. As a masc.: Phoen. 11. John V, 2, 149.

Eagles, name of a mistress of Theseus', in the writing of O. Edd., Mids. II, 1, 79. M. Edd. *Aegle*.

Eagle-sighted, able, like the eagle, to look at the sun: LLL IV, 3, 226 (cf. H6C II, 1, 91).

Eagle-winged, soaring high like an eagle: *e. pride*, R2 I, 3, 129.

Ean, to yean, to bring forth young: H6C II, 5, 36. *in —ing time*, Merch. I, 3, 88. *on my —ing time*, Per. III, 4, 6.

Eanling, young lamb just dropped: Merch. I, 3, 80.

Ear, subst. 1) the organ of hearing: Tp. I, 2, 37. 85. II, 1, 106. 313. 314. III, 1, 42. III, 2, 147. IV, 176. 178. Gentl. III, 1, 205. Wiv. II, 3, 66. III, 1, 82. Meas. IV, 1, 56. IV, 3, 109. V, 139. 310. 542 etc. etc. *you have a quick e.* Gentl. IV, 2, 63. Mids. III, 2, 178. R2 II, 1, 234. Per. IV, 1, 70. *if that his head have e. in music*, Cymb. III, 4, 178; cf. Mids. IV, 1, 31. *every one give e.* LLL IV, 1, 59. V, 2, 286. Tw. V, 308. *give e. to his motions*, Wiv. I, 1, 221. H8 IV, 2, 8. V, 1, 48. Hml. I, 3, 68. Lr. II, 4, 236. Ant. II, 1, 32. *lend thine e.* All's IV, 1, 62. R3 IV, 2, 80. *lend me your —s*, Caes. III, 2, 78. *lend e. to*, Cor. V, 3, 19. *lend favourable e. to our request*, R3 III, 7, 101 (Qq *ears*). *lend no e. unto my purposes*, H4A I, 3, 217. *give some evening music to her e.* Gentl. IV, 2, 17. Hml. II, 2, 128. *give't me in mine e.* Wint. II, 1, 32. *breathe it in mine e.* Gentl. III, 1, 239. *buzzed into his —s*, R2 II, 1, 26. *hark in thine e.* Tp. I, 2, 318. *in his e. I'll holla 'Mortimer'*, H4A I, 3, 222. *rounded in the e.* John II, 566. *to tell you in your e.* Wiv. I, 4, 109. II, 2, 100. Ant. III, 2, 46. *whisper in your lady's e.* LLL V, 2, 436. 443. John I, 1, 42. IV, 2, 189. *a word in your e.* Ado IV, 2, 29. V, 1, 144. As III, 5, 59. All's IV, 3, 260. Troil. V, 2, 34. *his plausive words he scattered not in —s, but grafted them*, All's I, 2, 54. *when the blast of war blows in our —s*, H5 III, 1, 5. *our person to arraign in e. and e.* Hml. IV, 5, 94 i. e. by mutual whisperings). *if it should come to the e. of the court*, Wiv. IV, 5, 97. *so I have strewed it in the common e.* Meas. I, 3, 15. *in theirs and in the commons' —s*, Cor. V, 6, 4. *I'll be placed in the e. of all their conference*, Hml. III, 1, 192 (= within hearing). *hath to the public e. professed the contrary*, Meas. IV, 2, 102. *read it to public e.* Ant. III, 4, 5. *know you such a one? but by the e.* All's III, 5, 53 (= by hearsay). *I have no —s to his request*, Ant. III, 12, 20. *fasten your e. on my advisings*, Meas

III, 1, 203. *all their other senses stuck in —s*, Wint. IV, 4, 621. *take the —s strangely*, Tp. V, 313. *he hears with —s*, Wiv. I, 1, 150 (Pistol's speech). *what fire is in mine —s*, Ado III, 1, 107 (no allusion to the proverbial saying, that when our ears glow, some people are talking of us, but simply meaning: what fire pervades me by what I have heard!). *pitchers have —s*, (= we may be overheard): Shr. IV, 4, 52. R3 II, 4, 37.

Taken only as a part of the head: *a box of the e.* Merch. I, 2, 86. H4B I, 2, 218. *a box o' the e.* Meas. II, 1, 189. H5 IV, 7, 133. 181. H6B IV, 7, 91. *a box on the e.* H5 IV, 1, 232. (cf. *Box*). *I will bite thee by the e. for that jest*, Rom. II, 4, 81. *I come to draw you out by the —s*, H4B II, 4, 314. *sowl the porter of Rome gates by the —s*, Cor. IV, 5, 214. *will you pluck your sword out of his pilcher by the —s*, Rom. III, 1, 84 (In Tw. II, 5, 71 F1 *with ears;* M. Edd. *with cars;* Hanmer rightly *by the ears*). *to be by the —s* = to scuffle: All's I, 2, 1. Cor. I, 1, 237. *I would fain be about the —s of the English*, H5 III, 7, 91. *make haste, lest mine* (sword) *be about your —s*, Rom. III, 1, 85. *shall we beat the stones about thine —s*, H6C V, 1, 108. *let them pull all about mine —s*, Cor. III, 2, 1. *he will shake your Rome about your —s*, IV, 6, 99. *I will fetch off my bottle, though I be o'er —s for my labour*, Tp. IV, 214 (i. e. though I should be drowned in the morass). *o'er head and —s a forked one*, Wint. I, 2, 186. *up to the —s in blood*, H4A IV, 1, 117. *love, wherein thou stickest up to the —s*, Rom. I, 4, 43. *go shake your —s*, Tw. II, 3, 134 (i. e. grumble at your pleasure). *turn him off, like to the empty ass, to shake his —s and graze in commons*, Caes. IV, 1, 26.

Figuratively used of inanimate things: *hangeth like a jewel in the e. of caelo*, LLL IV, 2, 5 (Holofernes' speech). *hang a pearl in every cowslip's e.* Mids. II, 1, 15. *my house's —s, I mean my casements*, Merch. II, 5, 34. *send the breath of parley into his* (the castle's) *ruined —s*, R2 III, 3, 34.

2) the handle; in the phrase: *pitchers have —s*, which see above.

3) the spike óf corn: As III, 5, 102. Hml. III, 4, 64.

Ear, vb. to cultivate, to till, to plough: *e. so barren a land*, Ven. Dedic. 5. All's I, 3, 47. R2 III, 2, 212. Ant. I, 2, 115. I, 4, 49.

Ear-bussing, told in the ear: *e. arguments*, Lr. II, 1, 9 (Ff *ear-kissing*).

Ear-deafening, stunning the ear with noise: Wint. III, 1, 9.

Ear-kissing, told in the ear: Lr. II, 1, 9 (Qq *ear-bussing*).

Earl, English title of nobility: Ven. Dedic Lucr. Dedic. Wiv. II, 2, 78. II, 3, 96. John II, 552. R2 II, 1, 215. 256. H4A I, 1, 67. IV, 1, 65. V, 4, 146. H4B I, 1, 1. 6. 11. 162. H5 I, 1, 13. H6A I, 1, 159. II, 5, 54. 90. III, 4, 26. IV, 7, 61. V, 3, 53. H6B I, 1, 8. II, 2, 36. 87. 45. 48. H6C I, 1, 54. V, 1, 32. R3 II, 1, 68. IV, 4, 534. V, 3, 69. H8 I, 1, 199. II, 1, 43. IV, 1, 19. IV, 2, 12. Lr. IV, 2, 59. III, 7, 103. Introduced into Scotland by Malcolm: Mcb. V, 8, 63.

Used of foreign noblemen, = count: All's III, 5, 12. 19. H5 IV, 8, 103. H6A V, 5, 34. 37. Rom. III, 4, 21.

Earldom, 1) the seigniory and dignity of an earl: H6C I, 1, 78. R3 III, 1, 195. IV, 2, 93. 105.

2) county: H6A III, 3, 26.

Earliness, rising before the usual time: *thy e. doth me assure*, Rom. II, 3, 39.

Early, adj. coming before the usual time: *the —iest fruit*, As III, 2, 125. *an e. spring*, H4B I, 3, 38. Particularly used of the time before the day is much advanced: *one e. morn*, Sonn. 33, 9. *an e. stirrer*, H4B III, 2, 3. H5 IV, 1, 6. *the e. village cock*, R3 V, 3, 209. *'tis but e. days*, Troil. IV, 5, 12. *what e. tongue*, Rom. II, 3, 32. *at these e. hours*, Per. III, 2, 22. *to-morrow with your —iest let me have speech with you*, Oth. II, 3, 7 (as soon as you are up).

Early, adv., in good season, betimes: Ven. 528. Lucr. Arg. 16. Lucr. 1801. Compl. 78. Gentl. IV, 3, 9. Wiv. I, 4, 108. Mids. IV, 1, 137. Merch. IV, 1, 456. As II, 2, 6. All's II, 1, 28. Tw. I, 5, 132. II, 3, 8. John II, 5. H4A I, 2, 139. IV, 3, 110. H6B I, 1, 91. R3 III, 2, 36. V, 3, 88. H8 II, 3, 84. Troil. I, 2, 52. IV, 1, 34. IV, 2, 48. V, 10, 25. Tit. II, 2, 15. Rom. I, 1, 130. I, 2, 13. I, 4, 106. I, 5, 141. III, 4, 10. 35. III, 5, 36. 113. IV, 1, 42. IV, 3, 46. V, 3, 23. 188. 208. 209. 275. Caes. II, 2, 110. IV, 3, 230. V, 3, 5. Ant. IV, 4, 22. Cymb. II, 3, 38. Per. III, 2, 12. 19. V, 3, 22. Compar. —*ier:* Tw. I, 3, 5. Per. IV, 6, 82. Superl. —*iest:* Merch. IV, 1, 116.

Earn, 1) ancient spelling of *yearn*, q. v.

2) a) to acquire as a reward or wages: Ado III, 3, 115 (sth. of a p.). As III, 2, 77. Tw. III, 4, 199. Wint. I, 2, 107. H4B I, 2, 29. II, 4, 155. Troil. IV, 5, 141. Cor. I, 1, 278. II, 3, 103. Oth. IV, 2, 163. Ant. III, 13, 46. Per. IV Prol. 13.

b) to deserve: *his excellence did e. it, ere he had it*, Ado III, 1, 99. *I and my sword will e. our chronicle*, Ant. III, 13, 175. *feast the army; we have store to do't, and they have —ed the waste*, IV, 1, 16.

Earnest, subst., handsel, a part paid beforehand as a pledge: Wint. IV, 4, 659. Tim. IV, 3, 47. 168. Per. IV, 2, 49. Quibbling in Gentl. II, 1, 163 and Err. II, 2, 24. Followed by *of:* H5 II, 2, 169. Mcb. I, 3, 104. 132. Lr. I, 4, 104. Cymb. I, 5, 65. *in e.:* Ado II, 1, 42. H5 V, 1, 67. H6A V, 3, 16.

Earnest, subst. seriousness, true meaning; opposed to jest: *did you perceive her e.?* Gentl. II, 1, 163 (quibble). *it was a passion of e.* As IV, 3, 172. *now your jest is e.* Err. II, 2, 24 (quibble . *in e.:* Gentl. II, 5, 13. Err. IV, 2, 3. Ado V, 1, 197. Mids. III, 2, 277. Wint. IV, 4, 656. R2 V, 3, 100. H4A II, 4, 334. R3 V, 1, 22. Cor. I, 3, 106. Tit. I, 277. *in good e.:* As I, 2, 29. I, 3, 26. IV, 1, 192. Wint. I, 2, 150. H4B II, 1, 168 (Q *so God save me*). *in most profound e.* Ado V, 1, 198.

Earnest, adj. 1) zealous with sincerity, eager in heart: *her e. eye did make him more amazed*, Lucr. 1356 (= searching, intent). *an e. advocate to plead for him*, R3 I, 3, 87. *e. in the service of my God*, III, 7, 106. *a prayer of e. heart*, Oth. I, 3, 152. *so e. to have me filch it*, III, 3, 314.

2) not feigned, heartfelt, urgent: *my tongue should stumble in my e. words*, H6B III, 2, 316. *with e. prayers*, R3 II, 2, 15 (Qq *daily*). *an e. motion made to the queen*, H8 II, 4, 233. *an e. inviting*, Tim. III, 6, 11. *an e. conjuration*, Hml. V, 2, 38.

Earnest-gaping, looking intently: *my e. sight*, H6B III, 2, 105.

Earnestly, eagerly, devoutly, urgently, intently: *why dost thou whet thy knife so e.?* Merch. IV, 1, 121. *he wishes e.* Wint. IV, 1, 32. *have e. implored* *a general peace*, H6A V, 4, 98. *how e. he cast his eyes upon me*, H8 V, 2, 12. *how e. they knock*, Troil. IV, 2, 41. *how e. are you set a-work, and how ill requited!* V, 10, 37. *as I e. did fix mine eye upon the wasted building*, Tit. V, 1, 22. *why so e. seek you to put up that letter?* Lr. I, 2, 27. *I e. beseech*, Ant. II, 2, 23.

Earnestness, zeal, heartfelt eagerness: *it shows my e. of affection*, H4B V, 5, 17 (Ff *in affection*). *all agreeing in e. to see him*, Cor. II, 1, 229. *the nobles in great e. are going all to the senate-house*, IV, 6, 57. *with a solemn e. he begged of me to steal it*, Oth. V, 2, 227.

Ear-piercing, shrill, of a sharp sound: *the e. fife*, Oth. III, 3, 352.

Earth, subst. 1) the globe which we inhabit: Tp. I, 2, 255. IV, 82. Err. I, 1, 89. Mids. II, 1, 156. 175. III, 2, 53. Troil. III, 2, 186 (*as true as e. to the centre*) etc.
2) the visible surface of the globe, the ground: *looks on the dull e.* Ven. 340. *where should this music be? i' the air or the e.?* Tp. I, 2, 387. Wiv. III, 4, 90. Merch. II, 8, 35. As I, 2, 213. R2 II, 4, 20. IV, 52. H6B I, 2, 5. I, 4, 14. H6C II, 3, 35. Tit. IV, 1, 84. Rom. III, 5, 127 etc. *it is as positive as the e. is firm*, Wiv. III, 2, 49. *cf. the huge firm e.* John III, 1, 72. *sure and firm-set e.* Mcb. II, 1, 56. cf. Caes. I, 3, 3. Without the article: *when the wind —'s foundation shakes*, Ven. 1047. *from —'s dark womb some gentle gust doth get*, Lucr. 549. *—'s increase*, Tp. IV, 110. *I'll not put the dibble in e.* Wint. IV, 4, 100. *the powerful regions under e.* H6A V, 3, 11. *it grows again toward e.* Tim. II, 2, 227. *darkness doth the face of e. entomb*, Mcb. II, 4, 9. *within the hollow mine of e.* Oth. IV, 2, 79. *as far from fraud as heaven from e.* Gentl. II, 7, 78. *unfolds both heaven and e.* Mids. I, 1, 146. *glance from heaven to e., from e. to heaven*, V, 13. Wint. I, 2, 315. *crawling between e. and heaven*, Hml. III, 1, 130 (Ff *heaven and e.*). *now heaven walks on e.* Tw. V, 100. — Imagined now as the source, now as the grave of life: Sonn. 19, 2. Wint. IV, 4, 501. Rom. II, 3, 9. Sonn. 74, 7. 81, 2. Gentl. IV, 2, 116. R2 III, 3, 168. IV, 69. H4B IV, 5, 191. R3 IV, 4, 75. Rom. I, 2, 14. III, 2, 59 etc.
3) the world in which we live, as opposed to other scenes of existence: *no sound that the e. owes*, Tp. I, 2, 407. 491. Err. III, 2, 32. R3 IV, 4, 52. 166. Ant. IV, 6, 30 etc. *in the e.: where shall it find a harbour in the e.?* H6B V, 1, 168. *I am not vexed more at any thing in the e.* Cymb. II, 1, 20. *on the e.:* Ven. 753. Gentl. II, 4, 153. IV, 2, 52. Merch. II, 1, 28. R3 I, 2, 140. Without the article: *—s sovereign salve*, Ven. 28. 933. Lucr. 487. Wiv. V, 5, 84. Rom. III, 5, 208. Tp. III, 1, 68. Gentl. V, 4, 80. Err. III, 2, 64. Lr. I, 2, 105. *in e. or heaven*, Ven. 493. *'tis set down so in heaven, but not in e.* Meas. II, 4, 50. Err. II, 2, 214. All's II, 4, 13. H6C II, 3, 43. *on e.:* Ven. 794. Gentl. II, 4, 139. Merch. III, 5, 81. John I, 261. R2 I, 2, 7. III, 2, 68. H4A I, 3, 57. H6A V, 4, 41. H6B II, 1, 19. 35. III, 2, 372. R3 II, 1, 6. IV, 4, 166. Rom. III, 5, 207 etc.
4) the country, the land: *although my foot did stand upon the farthest e. removed from thee*, Sonn. 44, 6. *upon the e. of its right father*, Wint. III, 3, 45. *this e. of majesty*, R2 II, 1, 41. 50. *the e. this climate overlooks*, John II, 344. *so greet I thee, my e.* R2 III, 2, 10. *if this rebellious e. have any resting for her true king's queen*, V, 1, 5. *never so needful on the e. of*

France, H6A IV, 3, 18. *would I had never trod this English e.* H8 III, 1, 143. — Even in the sense of land, landed property: *she is the hopeful lady of my e.* Rom. I, 2, 15.
5) dry land, opposed to water: Tp. I, 2, 11. Err. II, 1, 17. Mcb. I, 3, 79 etc.
6) the substance, thought to be an element, of which the globe and its productions consist: *the e. can have but e.* Sonn. 74, 7. *poor soul, the centre of my sinful e.* 146, 1. *the elements of air and e.* Tw. I, 5, 294. *the most peerless piece of e.* Wint. V, 1, 94. *as false as air, as water, wind, or sandy e.* Troil. III, 2, 199. *I am not of stronger e. than others*, Cor. V, 3, 29. *turn back, dull e.* Rom. II, 1, 2. *vile e., to e. resign*, III, 2, 59. *Earth and water thought to be gross and heavy elements:* Sonn. 44, 11. H5 III, 7, 23; hence *earth* serving to denote grossness or dulness: *thou e. thou*, Tp. I, 2, 314. *here lies your brother, no better than the e. he lies upon*, II, 1, 281. *make men of some other metal than e.* Ado II, 1, 63. *a good lustre of conceit in a tuft of e.* LLL IV, 2, 90. *thou little better thing than e.* R2 III, 4, 78. cf. *more than e. divine*, Err. III, 2, 32. *examples gross as e. exhort me*, Hml. IV, 4, 46. *she's dead as e.* Lr. V, 3, 261 (cf. *Earthly* and *Earthy*).
Used as a fem.: Sonn. 19, 2 and R2 V, 1, 5; cf. *his mother e.* As I, 2, 213.

Earth, vb. to inter, to bury: *who shall be of as little memory, when he is —ed*, Tp. II, 1, 234.

Earth-bound, fixed in the ground: *his* (the forest's) *e. root*, Mcb. IV, 1, 96.

Earth-delving, digging in the ground: *e. conies*, Ven. 687.

Earthen, made of clay: Rom. V, 1, 46.

Earthly, 1) pertaining to the earth: *this heavenly and e. sun*, Ven. 198. *sucked an e. mother*, 863. *this e. saint*, Lucr. 85. *e. faces*, Sonn. 17, 8. *my vow was e., thou a heavenly love*, Pilgr. 35 and LLL IV, 3, 66. cf. Pilgr. 70 and LLL IV, 2, 122. *the liquor is not e.* Tp. II, 2, 131. *an e. paragon*, Gentl. II, 4, 146 and Cymb. III, 6, 43. *no e. mean to save him*, Meas. II, 4, 95. *e. faults*, V, 488. *every e. thing*, Ado IV, 1, 122. *e. godfathers of heavens' lights*, LLL I, 1, 88. *two e. women*, Merch. III, 5, 85. *e. power*, IV, 1, 196. *e. things atone*, As V, 4, 115. *a heavenly effect in an e. actor*, All's II, 3, 28. *the e. author of my blood*, R2 I, 3, 69 (Ff *earthy*). *their e. parts*, H5 IV, 3, 102. *e. blessings*, H6B I, 1, 22. *in this e. vale*, II, 1, 70. *joyed an e. throne*, IV, 9, 1. *glory*, H8 I, 1, 14. *queens*, II, 4, 141. *audit*, III, 2, 141. *dignities*, 379. *the moon, were she e., no nobler*, Cor. II, 1, 108. *e. honour*, Tit. II, 1, 10. *this e. world*, Mcb. IV, 2, 75. *respeaking e. thunder*, Hml. I, 2, 128. *the e. Jove*, Ant. II, 7, 73. *joys*, Per. I, 1, 49. *man*, II, 1, 2. The comp. adverbially: *—er happy*, Mids. I, 1, 76.*
2) consisting of earth, or made in the earth: *a sceptre, or an e. sepulchre*, H6C I, 4, 17. *this e. prison of their bones* (viz the grave) Tit. I, 99 (Qq *earthy*. But here the first signification is applicable).
3) resembling earth or clay, lifeless: *doth shine upon the dead man's e. cheeks*, Tit. II, 3, 229 (Q1 *earthy*). cf. Lr. V, 3, 261.

Earthquake, a shaking of the earth: Ven. 648. Tp. II, 1, 315. Ado I, 1, 275. As III, 2, 196. All's I, 3, 92. John V, 2, 42. H5 II, 4, 100. Rom. I, 3, 23.

Earth-treading, moving on the earth, earthly: Rom. I, 2, 25.

Earth-vexing, plaguing the life of man: *this e. smart,* Cymb. V, 4, 42.

Earthy, 1) consisting of earth: *lie in an e. pit,* R2 IV, 219. *this e. prison of their bones,* Tit. I, 99 (Ff *earthly*).

2) resembling earth, cold and lifeless as earth: *the e. and cold hand of death lies on my tongue,* H4A V, 4, 84. *his dead and e. image,* H6B III, 2, 147. *how pale she looks, and of an e. cold,* H8 IV, 2, 98. *the dead man's e. cheeks,* Tit. II, 3, 229 (Q2 Ff *earthly*).

3) gross, low: *to act her e. and abhorred commands,* Tp. I, 2, 273. *my e. gross conceit,* Err. III, 2, 34.

4) pertaining to the earth or to this world: *what e. name to interrogatories can task the free breath of a sacred king?* John III, 1, 147. *the e. author of my blood,* R2 I, 3, 69 (Qq *earthly*).

Ear-wax, cerumen: Troil. V, 1, 58.

Ease, subst. 1) easiness, facility, freedom from difficulty: *an attempt of e. and gain,* Oth. I, 3, 29. *at what e.* = how easily: H8 V, 1, 132. *with e.* = easily, without difficulty: Sonn. 136, 7. Meas. IV, 2, 205. John II, 513. Hml. IV, 7, 137. Cymb. V, 5, 363. *with much e.* H4A II, 2, 111. *with much more e.* Tp. III, 1, 30. *with such e.* H4A IV, 1, 107.

2) quiet, tranquillity: *the younger of our sort, that surfeit on their e.* All's III, 1, 18. *nor conversant with e. and idleness,* John IV, 3, 70. *a sword rusted with e.* H6B III, 2, 198. *roots itself in e. on Lethe wharf,* Hml. I, 5, 33. *to take one's e.* = to take a nap: *shall I not take mine e. in mine inn but I shall have my pocket picked?* H4A III, 3, 93. *some come to take their e. and sleep an act or two,* H8 Epil. 2.

3) comfortableness, freedom from pain and solicitude: *the aim of all is but to nurse the life with honour, wealth and e. in waning age,* Lucr. 142. *give physic to the sick, e. to the pained,* 901. Sonn. 50, 3. As II, 5, 54. R2 II, 1, 10. V, 5, 28. H4B V, 4, 28. H6A I, 1, 142. II, 5, 44. H6B II, 3, 21. H6C IV, 6, 52. H8 IV, 2, 4. Troil. I, 3, 266. Rom. IV, 5, 102 (*'heart's e'.* the title of a song, probably sung by Pandar in Troil. IV, 4, 17). Hml. V, 2, 109. Lr. III, 4, 23. *chairs of e.* = easy-chairs, Tim. V, 4, 11. *to do a person e.* Shr. V, 2, 179. H6C V, 5, 72. Tit. III, 1, 121. Hml. I, 1, 131. *at e.* = comfortably: As III, 2, 25. Rom. II, 4, 36. Oth. III, 3, 32. *at his e.* H6C III, 3, 151. *at heart's e.* Caes. I, 2, 208. Plur. *—s* = means of comfort, of alleviating pain: *till then I'll sweat and seek about for —s,* Troil. V, 10, 56.

Ease, vb. 1) to remove a burden from, to relieve, to deliver; followed by *of: for —ing me of the carriage,* Wiv. II, 2, 179. *to e. your country of distressful war,* H6A V, 4, 126. Tim. V, 1, 201. Caes. IV, 1, 20.

2) to relieve, to repair after strong exertion: *we'll walk afoot awhile and e. our legs,* H4A II, 2, 84. *he never stood to e. his breast with panting,* Cor. II, 2, 126.

3) to appease, to free from anxiety or passion: *it —th some, though none it ever cured,* Lucr. 1581. *till he be —d with being nothing,* R2 V, 5, 40. *I will e. my heart,* H4A I, 3, 127. H5 IV, 1, 19. H6C I, 3, 29. R3 IV, 4, 131. Tit. II, 4, 35. V, 2, 31. 119.

4) to assuage, to allay: *day's oppression is not —d by night,* Sonn. 28, 3. *to e. the anguish of a torturing hour,* Mids. V, 37. H6C III, 3, 20. Troil. IV, 4, 20. Tit. II, 4, 57. III, 1, 234. — Absolutely: *to weep with them that weep doth e. some deal,* Tit. III, 1, 245. *like a spendthrift sigh, that hurts by —ing,* Hml. IV, 7, 124.

Easeful, quiet, or comfortable: *ere he (the sun) attain his e. western bed,* H6C V, 3, 6.

Easily, 1) without difficulty: Ven. 627. Wiv. II, 1, 243. Meas. III, 1, 244. Ado I, 1, 75. LLL V, 2, 190. 749. Wint. II, 1, 53. John I, 269. II, 515. R2 III, 2, 130. H4A I, 3, 264. H4B III, 1, 101. H6B III, 1, 100. 135. R3 III, 7, 50. Troil. II, 3, 111. Tit. II, 3, 287. Hml. III, 2, 404. Oth. V, 2, 345. Ant. V, 2, 35. Cymb. II, 1, 49. III, 1, 29. *Easiliest:* Cymb. IV, 2, 206.

2) without reluctance, willingly, readily: *oaths which he will break as e. as I do tear this paper,* Gentl. IV, 4, 136. *his surly nature, which e. endures not article tying him to aught,* Cor. II, 3, 204. *if he care not for it, he will supply us e.* Tim. IV, 3, 407. *would have brooked the eternal devil to keep his state in Rome as e. as a king,* Caes. I, 2, 161.

3) quietly: *the one sleeps e. because he cannot study,* As III, 2, 339.

4) commodiously, without shaking or jolting: *your wit ambles well, it goes e.* Ado V, 1, 159. *he will bear you e. and reins well,* Tw. III, 4, 358. *O for a chair, to bear him e. hence,* Oth. V, 1, 83.

Easiness, freedom from emotion, evenness of temper, unconcernedness: *if we suffer, out of our e. and childish pity to one man's honour, this contagious sickness,* H8 V, 3, 25. *that shall lend a kind of e. to the next abstinence,* Hml. III, 4, 166. *custom hath made it in him a property of e.* V, 1, 76.

East, 1) the quarter where the sun rises: Sonn. 132, 6. Pilgr. 193. Ado V, 3, 27. LLL IV, 3, 223. Mids. III, 2, 432. R2 III, 2, 50. III, 3, 64. H4A I, 3, 195. III, 1, 222. R3 V, 3, 279. Rom. I, 1, 126. 141. II, 2, 3. Caes. II, 1, 101. 110. Oth. IV, 2, 144. *in the E.:* John V, 4, 32. Tit. V, 2, 56. Rom. III, 5, 8. *within the e.* (in the same sense): Rom. V, 3, 86. *to the e.* = eastward: Cymb. IV, 2, 255. — Used without the article, when joined with other names of the same kind: *from e., west, north and south,* Wint. I, 2, 203. *from e. to west,* Troil. II, 3, 274. *for e. or west,* Cor. I, 2, 10. *from e. to occident,* Cymb. IV, 2, 372. *by e.* = in or to the east: *by e., north, west and south I spread my conquering might,* LLL V, 2, 566. *by e. and west let France and England mount their cannon,* John II, 381. *England, from Trent and Severn hitherto, by south and e. is to my part assigned,* H4A III, 1, 75. cf. Armado's letter in LLL I, 1, 248. Without a preposition, = a) eastward: *they take their courses e., west, north, south,* H4B IV, 2, 104. Cor. II, 3, 24. b) in the east: *this heavy-headed revel e. and west makes us traduced,* Hml. I, 4, 17. — Used adjectively: *my E. and West Indies,* Wiv. I, 3, 79. As III, 2, 93. *on the e. side of the grove,* H6B II, 1, 43.

2) the countries lying to the east of Europe: Mcb. IV, 3, 37. Ant. I, 5, 46. II, 3, 40. II, 6, 51.

Eastcheap, name of a street and tavern in London: H4A I, 2, 145. 176. II, 4, 16. 485. H4B II, 1, 76. II, 2, 161.*

Easter, the festival in memory of the Savior's resurrection: Rom. III, 1, 30.

Eastern, 1) lying to or coming from the east: Lucr. 773. Mids. III, 2, 142. 391. R2 III, 2, 42. Troil. I, 2, 2. Rom. II, 3, 2. Hml. I, 1, 167 (Qq *eastward*).

2) Oriental: *O e. star! Ant.* V, 2, 311.

Eastward, adj. lying to the east: *yon high e. hill,* Hml. I, 1, 167 (Ff *eastern*).

Easy, adj. 1) **not difficult:** Tp. II, 1, 89. Wiv. II, 2, 196. Meas. IV, 2, 221. Ado II, 3, 271. LLL I, 2, 55. Merch. I, 1, 48. I, 2, 13. As III, 2, 245. Tw. II, 2, 30. Wint. V, 3, 93. John V, 2, 106. R2 III, 2, 191. H4A I, 3, 201. H5 V, 2, 195. H6C III, 2, 53. IV, 2, 18. R3 III, 1, 161. Cor. II, 1, 272. Tit. II, 1, 87. Hml. III, 2, 372. Oth. II, 3, 345. IV, 2, 112. Ant. III, 13, 144. *'tis e. to it,* Ant. III, 10, 32 (= not difficult to get there).

2) **causing no great pain:** *in whose* (our justice's) *—est passage look for no less than death,* Wint. III, 2, 91. *all deaths are too few, the sharpest too e.* IV, 4, 809. *they should find e. penance,* H8 I, 4, 17. *e. fines,* Cor. V, 6, 65. *e. ways to die,* Ant. V, 2, 359.

3) **requiring no great labour or exertion, soon done:** *words are e. like the wind,* Pilgr. 405. *with very e. arguments of love,* John I, 36. *the e. groans of old women,* Cor. V, 2, 45. *which an e. battery might lay flat,* Cymb. I, 4, 22.

4) **commodious; well fitting** (in speaking of clothes), **smooth, not uneven** (of ways): *this woman is an e. glove; she goes off and on at pleasure,* All's V, 3, 278. *our e. robes of peace,* H4A V, 1, 12. *is my beaver —er than it was?* R3 V, 3, 50. *at last, with e. roads, he came to Leicester,* H8 IV, 2, 17. *his ascent is not by such e. degrees,* Cor. II, 2, 28.

5) **tractable,** soon persuaded, managed without difficulty: *I would your spirit were —er for advice,* Wint. IV, 4, 516. *of so e. and so plain a stop,* H4B Ind. 17. *the e. yielding spirit of this woman,* II, 1, 125 (hyphened in O. and M. Edd.). *I can never win a soul so e. as that Englishman's,* H5 II, 2, 125 (or adv.?). *when he thinks, good e. man, full surely his greatness is a ripening,* H8 III, 2, 356. *your lady being so e.* Cymb. II, 4, 47.

6) **not to be minded, slight, inconsiderable:** *'tis all as e. falsely to take away a life true made as … to make a false one,* Meas. II, 4, 46. *which is for me less e. to commit than you to punish,* Wint. I, 2, 58. *the difference is purchase of a heavy curse from Rome, or the light loss of England for a friend: forego the —er,* John III, 1, 207. *was this e.?* H4B V, 2, 71. *these faults are e.* H6B III, 1, 133. *at an e. price,* Tit. III, 1, 199. *a little water clears us of this deed: how e. is it then!* Mcb. II, 2, 68.

Easy, adv. 1) **without difficulty:** *as e. might I from myself depart,* Sonn. 109, 3. Wiv. III, 2, 33. Meas. II, 4, 126. Err. II, 2, 127. Mids. V, 22. All's V, 3, 125. John IV, 3, 142. Mcb. II, 3, 143. V, 8, 9. Compar. *—er:* Wiv. II, 2, 195. Ado IV, 1, 300. LLL V, 1, 45. Merch. I, 2, 17. Hml. III, 2, 386.

2) **commodiously, fitly:** *this new garment sits not so e. on me as you think,* H4B V, 2, 45. *lest our old robes sit —er than our new,* Mcb. II, 4, 38.

3) **without jolting or pitching:** *which with a snaffle you may pace e.* Ant. II, 2, 64. *on whose foolish honesty my practices ride e.* Lr. I, 2, 198.

Easy-borrowed (not hyphened in O. Edd.) assumed with ease, gained without pains (cf. *Pride 2,* = prime, glory): *this is a slave, whose e. pride dwells in the fickle grace of her he follows,* Lr. II, 4, 188.

Easy-held (not hyphened in O. Edd.) **free from constraint:** *this her e. imprisonment hath gained thy daughter princely liberty,* H6A V, 3, 139.

Easy-melting, soft, easily touched and wrought into another shape: *wrought the e. king like wax,* H6C II, 1, 171.

Easy-yielding, flexible, pliant: *practised upon the e. spirit of this woman,* H4B II, 1, 125.

Eat (O. Edd. mostly *eate*); Impf. *eat:* Sonn. 99, 12. Mids. II, 2, 149. As I, 3, 76. Shr. IV, 1, 200. Tim. III, 4, 50. Mcb. II, 4, 18. Ant. II, 2, 231. Partic. *eat:* Ado IV, 1, 196. LLL IV, 2, 26. As II, 7, 88. John I, 234. R2 V, 5, 85. H4B IV, 5, 165. H6B IV, 10, 41. Hml. IV, 3, 29. Lr. I, 4, 174. *Eaten:* Gentl. I, 1, 46. Wiv. IV, 2, 1. Meas. II, 1, 104. III, 2, 59. Ado I, 1, 43. LLL I, 1, 43. As IV, 1, 108. Shr. III, 2, 208. Wint. III, 3, 134. IV, 4, 185. H4B I, 2, 245. II, 1, 80. II, 4, 372. H6A V, 4, 31. Cor. IV, 5, 201. Mcb. I, 3, 84. IV, 1, 64. Hml. IV, 3, 21. Oth. III, 3, 391.

1) **to take food, to chew and swallow with the mouth:** a) trans.: Tp. I, 2, 330. Wiv. I, 1, 290. IV, 2, 109. V, 5, 179. Meas. II, 1, 104. III, 2, 192. Err. II, 2, 61. Ado I, 1, 43. II, 1, 156 *(no supper).* III, 4, 90. LLL IV, 2, 26. V, 1, 43. Mids. II, 2, 149 *(away).* IV, 2, 43. As II, 5, 42 *(food).* II, 7, 88. IV, 1, 108. Shr. IV, 2, 208. IV, 1, 200. Wint. III, 3, 134. John I, 234. R2 V, 5, 85. H4B II, 4, 372. H5 III, 7, 156 *(his breakfast).* H6A V, 4, 31. H6B IV, 10, 41. Cor. IV, 5, 201. Mcb. II, 4, 18. III, 2, 17 *(our meal).* IV, 1, 64. Hml. IV, 3, 21. Ant. II, 2, 231. V, 2, 272. 274 etc. *to e. up:* Sonn. 146, 8. Meas. III, 2, 59. Shr. IV, 3, 50. H4B I, 3, 99. Troil. I, 3, 124. Cor. III, 1, 294. Lr. I, 4, 174. — Figurative use: *as he had —en ballads,* Wint. IV, 4, 185. *to e. the air* = to be deluded with hopes: H4B I, 3, 28. Hml. III, 2, 99. *to e. one's word* = to retract: Ado IV, 1, 280. As V, 4, 155. H4B II, 2, 149. *to e. a sword* = to receive it into the body, to be hurt by it, to fight: *by my sword, thou lovest me. Do not swear, and e. it. I will make him e. it that says I love not you,* Ado IV, 1, 279. *a' should not bear it so, a' should e. swords first,* Troil. II, 3, 227. cf. *when valour preys on reason, it —s the sword it fights with,* Ant. III, 13, 200 (= it is hurt by its own sword, or it destroys its own sword?). *I'll make thee e. iron like an ostrich, and swallow my sword,* H6B IV, 10, 30. Similarly, in an obscene sense: *ladies e. lords,* Tim. I, 1, 209 (cf. *eater* in Per. I, 1, 130).

b) absolutely: Tp. I, 2, 412. Meas. III, 2, 26. Err. IV, 3, 65. Shr. IV, 3, 13. 52. All's V, 2, 58. Wint. V, 3, 111. R2 IV, 73. H4B V, 3, 18. H5 III, 7, 162. 166. Cor. I, 1, 210. Caes. I, 2, 296 etc. = to dine or to sup: *I will not e. with you,* Merch. I, 3, 38. *e. together,* As I, 3, 76. *to e. with us,* All's III, 5, 101. Troil. IV, 5, 158. Followed by *of:* Merch. I, 3, 34. Tit. V, 3, 29. Tim. III, 4, 50. Hml. IV, 3, 29. By *on: have we —en on the insane root,* Mcb. I, 3, 84. Followed by an accusative denoting the effect: *he hath —en me out of house and home,* H4B II, 1, 80.

c) intr. = to taste, or relish: *it —s drily,* All's I, 1, 175.

2) **to devour, to consume, to waste, to destroy;** a) trans. *earth, gape open wide and e. him*

quick, R3 I, 2, 65. *the ocean —s not the flats with more impetuous haste*, Hml. IV, 5, 100. *the most forward bud is —en by the canker*, Gentl. I, 1, 46. John III, 4, 82. H6A II, 4, 71. *to be —en to death with a rust*, H4B I, 2, 245. *to e. the world's due*, Sonn. 1, 14. *seemed in —ing him to hold him up*, R2 III, 4, 51. *I e. not lords*, Tim. I, 1, 207. *what a number of men e. Timon!* I, 2, 40. *that monster custom, who all sense doth e.* Hml. III, 4, 161. *To e. up*, in the same sense: *this canker that —s up love's tender spring*, Ven. 656. *a vengeful canker e. him up to death*, Sonn. 99, 12. Rom. II, 3, 30. *time's office is to e. up errors by opinion bred*, Lucr. 937. *your sorrow hath —en up my sufferance*, Wiv. IV, 2, 1. *nor* (hath) *age so e. up my invention*, Ado IV, 1, 196. *made a shift to e. up thy holland*, H4B II, 2, 25. *hast e. thy bearer up*, H4B IV, 5, 165. *if the wars e. us not up*, Cor. I, 1, 87. *he that is proud —s up himself*, Troil. II, 3, 164. *till famine and the ague e. them up*, Mcb. V, 5, 4. *—en up with passion*, Oth. III, 3, 391.

b) absol. *the —ing canker*, *—ing love*, Gentl. I, 1, 43. Followed by *in* or *into*, = to gnaw, to make way by corrosion: *like water that doth e. in steel*, Lucr. 755. *how one man —s into another's pride, while pride is feasting in his wantonness*, Troil. III, 3, 136.

Eater, 1) one who eats: *a great e. of beef*, Tw. I, 3, 90. *of broken meats*, Lr. II, 2, 15. Per. I, 1, 130; cf. *to eat* in Tim. I, 1, 209.

2) devourer, destroyer: *e. of youth*, Lucr. 927.

Eath, in *Uneath*, q. v.

Eaves, the edge of the roof which overhangs the house: Tp. V, 17. *to chide him from our e.* All's III, 7, 42. cf. *House-eaves.*

Eaves-dropper, a listener: R3 V, 3, 221.

Ebb, subst. the reflux of the tide: Tp. V, 270. H4B IV, 4, 125. Oth. III, 3, 455. *mine eyes, never since at e.* Tp. I, 2, 435. Figuratively, = decline, decay: H4A I, 2, 42. H4B II, 2, 22. H6C IV, 8, 56. Tim. II, 2, 150. *Ebb and flow* an image of capriciousness: *his pettish lines, his —s, his flows*, Troil. II, 3, 139.

Ebb, vb. to flow back towards the sea: Lucr. 1569. Tp. V, 35. LLL IV, 3, 215. H4B V, 2, 131. Rom. III, 5, 134. Ant. II, 7, 24. Figuratively, = to decline, decay: *sorrow —s, being blown with wind of words*, Lucr. 1330. *to e. hereditary sloth instructs me*, Tp. II, 1, 222. *—ing men*, 226. *the means do e.* As II, 7, 73. (your verse) *is shrewdly —ed*, Wint. V, 1, 102. *the fortune of us that are the moon's men doth e. and flow*, H4A I, 2, 36. *packs and sects of great ones, that e. and flow by the moon*, Lr. V, 3, 19. *ne'er e. to humble love*, Oth. III, 3, 458. *the —ed man*, Ant. I, 4, 43.

Ebon, black, dark: *death's e. dart*, Ven. 948. *rouse up revenge from e. den*, H4B V, 5, 39.

Ebon-coloured, black: LLL I, 1, 246.

Ebony, the black wood of the tree Diospyrus Ebenum: LLL IV, 3, 247. Tw. IV, 2, 42.

Ebrew = Hebrew: *a Jew, an e. Jew*, H4A II, 4, 198.

Eche (rhyming to *speech* in Per.) to eke (q. v.), to piece out: *to e. it and to draw it out in length*, Merch. III, 2, 23 (Q1 *eck*, Q2.3.4 *ech* and *eech*, Ff *ich*). *e. out our performance with your mind*, H5 III Chor. 35 (M. Edd. *eke*). *and time … with your fine fancies quaintly e.* Per. III Prol. 13. cf. *Eke.*

Echo, subst. repercussion of sound: Ven. 695. 834 (*—es*). 840. Mids. IV, 1, 116. Shr. Ind. 2, 48 (*—es*). Tw. II, 4, 21. John V, 2, 168. H4B III, 1, 97. Tit. II, 3, 17. Rom. II, 2, 162 (*the cave where E. lies*). Mcb. V, 3, 53.

Echo, name of a dog: Shr. Ind. I, 26.

Echo, vb. 1) intr. to resound: *all the church did e.* Shr. III, 2, 181. Tit. II, 2, 6. = 2) trans. to reverberate, to repeat in sound: *he —es me*, Oth. III, 3, 106.

Eclipse, subst. obscuration of a luminous body: Sonn. 35, 3. 60, 7. 107, 5. Mcb. IV, 1, 28. Hml. I, 1, 120. Lr. I, 2, 112. 148. 154. Oth. V, 2, 99.

Eclipse, vb. to darken, to extinguish: *born to e. thy life this afternoon*, H6A IV, 5, 53. *by doubtful fear my joy of liberty is half —ed*, H6C IV, 6, 63. *our terrene moon is now —ed*, Ant. III, 13, 154.

Ecstasy, any state of being beside one's self; a) extreme delight, rapture: *allay thy e.; in measure rein thy joy*, Merch. III, 2, 112. b) excitement, violent passion, extreme disquietude: *thus stands she in a trembling e.* Ven. 895. *which may her suffering e. assuage*, Compl. 69. *hinder them from what this e. may now provoke them to*, Tp. III, 3, 108. *the e. hath so much overborne her that my daughter is sometime afeard she will do a desperate outrage to herself*, Ado II, 3, 157. *attend him in his e.* Tit. IV, 1, 125. *than on the torture of the mind to lie in restless e.* Mcb III, 2, 22. *violent sorrow seems a modern e.* IV, 3, 170. *this bodiless creation e. is very cunning in. E.! my pulse, as yours, doth temperately keep time*, Hml. III, 4, 138. 139. c) madness: *how he trembles in his e.!* Err. IV, 4, 54. *his feigned —ies shall be no shelter to these outrages*, Tit. IV, 4, 21. *this is the very e. of love*, Hml. II, 1, 102. *that unmatched form and feature of blown youth blasted with e.* III, 1, 168. *sense to e. was ne'er so thralled but it reserved some quantity of choice*, III, 4, 74; cf. 138. d) a fainting fit, a swoon: *laid good 'scuse upon your e.* Oth. IV, 1, 80.

Eddy, a whirlpool: Lucr. 1669.

Eden, Paradise: R2 II, 1, 42.

Edgar, name in Lr. I, 2, 16 etc.

Edge, subst. 1) extreme border, brink, margin: *to the e. of doom*, Sonn. 116, 12. *upon the e. of yonder coppice*, LLL IV, 1, 9. Merch. II, 2, 173. All's III, 3, 6. Troil. IV, 5, 68. Ant. II, 2, 117. Per. III, 3, 35.

2) the cutting side of a blade: Sonn. 95, 14. LLL I, 1, 6. V, 2, 257. H4B III, 2, 286. H5 II, 1, 25. H6C II, 2, 166. V, 2, 11. H8 I, 1, 110. Troil. III, 1, 165. V, 5, 24. Cor. I, 4, 29. Mcb. IV, 1, 151. V, 7, 19. Ant. IV, 15, 26. Plur. *—s*: Cor. V, 6, 113. Ant. II, 6, 39. *give e. unto the swords* = make them sharp, cutting: H5 I, 2, 27. *to turn the e.* = make it fall flat: H6B II, 1, 180. IV, 10, 60. *let not Bardolph's vital thread be cut with e. of penny cord*, H5 III, 6, 50 (Pistol's speech). Figuratively: *wit whose e. hath power to cut*, LLL II, 50. Tit. II, 1, 26. Cymb. III, 4, 36. *the e. of war*, H4A I, 1, 17. *commotion's bitter e.* H4B IV, 1, 93. *borrowing dulls the e. of husbandry*, Hml. I, 3, 77. *abate the e. of traitors*, R3 V, 5, 35.

Used for any thing very narrow: *he walked o'er perils on an e.* H4B I, 1, 170.

3) keenness, desire, appetite: *thy* (viz love's) *e. should blunter be than appetite*, Sonn. 56, 2. *rebate and blunt his natural e. with profits of the mind,*

Meas. I, 4, 60. *affection's e.* Shr. I, 2, 73. *cloy the hungry e. of appetite,* R2 I, 3, 296. *give him farther e., and drive his purpose on to these delights,* Hml. III, 1, 26 (cf. H5 I, 2, 27). *to take away* or *to take off the e. =* to blunt it: Tp. IV, 1, 29. Hml. III, 2, 260. *to set on e. =* to sharpen, to make eager: *set my pugging tooth on e.* Wint. IV, 3, 7. And with an inverse form of expression: *set this bateless e. on his keen appetite,* Lucr. 9. = to take off the appetite, to disgust: *that would set my teeth nothing on e., nothing so much as mincing poetry,* H4A III, 1, 133 (properly = to grate on the teeth).

Edge, vb., to sharpen, to whet: *with spirit of honour —d more sharper than your swords,* H5 III, 5, 38. *thy —d sword,* H6A III, 3, 52.

Edgeless, blunt, unfit to cut: *fall thy e. sword,* R3 V, 3, 135. 163.

Édict or **Edíct,** decree, law: Meas. II, 2, 92. LLL I, 1, 11. 262. Mids. I, 1, 151. H4A IV, 3, 79. H6B III, 2, 258. R3 I, 4, 203. Cor. I, 1, 84. Per. I, 1, 111. *make thine own e. for thy pains, which we will answer as a law,* Ant. III, 12, 32 (i. e. decree the reward for thy pains).

Edifice, building: Wiv. II, 2, 225. Merch. I, 1, 30. Cor. IV, 4, 3.

Edify, 1) to raise in thought or improve by moral instruction (used ironically): *look then to be well —ed when the fool delivers the madman,* Tw. V, 298. *but —es another with her deeds,* Troil. V, 3, 112 (perhaps = to gratify, satisfy in general).

2) to instruct: *you must be —ed by the margent,* Hml. V, 2, 162. *can you inquire him out, and be —ed by report?* Oth. III, 4, 14.

Edition, publication and republication of a writing: *these* (letters) *are of the second e.* Wiv. II, 1, 78.

Edmund: 1) *E. Langley Duke of York:* R2 I, 2, 62. H6A II, 5, 85. H6B II, 2, 15. — 2) *E. Mortimer Earl of March:* H6B II, 2, 36. IV, 2, 144. — 3) *son of Roger of March:* H4A I, 3, 156. II, 3, 26. H6A II, 5, 7. H6B II, 2, 38 (confounded by Sh. with Nr. 2). — 4) *E. duke of Somerset:* H6B I, 2, 29. IV, 9, 38. — 5) the natural son of the Earl of Gloster in Lr. I, 1, 25 etc.

Edmundsbury, place in England: John IV, 3, 11. V, 4, 18.

Educate, to instruct: *do you not e. youth at the charge-house?* LLL V, 1, 86 (Armado's speech).

Education, instruction, formation of mind and manners: As I, 1, 22. 72. Shr. Ind. 2, 20. II, 99. All's I, 1, 46. John II, 493. Oth. I, 3, 182. Per. II, 3, 82. IV Prol. 9.

Edward, 1) *E. Confessor:* H8 IV, 1, 88. Mcb. III, 6, 27. 2) *E. the Third:* R2 I, 2, 11. II, 1, 121. H4B IV, 4, 128. H5 I, 1, 89. I, 2, 248. H6A I, 2, 31. II, 4, 84. II, 5, 66. H6B II, 2, 10. — 3) *E. the Black Prince:* H5 I, 2, 105. II, 4, 56. IV, 7, 97. H6A II, 5, 64. H6B II, 2, 11. — 4) *E. Prince of Wales, son of Henry VI:* H6C I, 1, 259. II, 2, 60. III, 3, 31 etc. R3 I, 2, 10 etc. — 5) *E. the Fourth:* H6C I, 2, 40. I, 4, 11. 74 etc. R3 I, 1, 36 etc. — 6) *E. the Fifth:* R3 I, 3, 199 etc. — 7) *E. the Sixth: two E. shovel-boards,* Wiv. I, 1, 159; cf. *Shovel-board.* — 8) *E. duke of York:* H5 IV, 8, 108. — 9) *E. duke of Bar:* H5 IV, 8, 103. — 10) *Sir E. Courtney:* R3 IV, 4, 502 (Qq *William*). — 11) *E. Bohun* (duke of Buckingham): H8 II, 1, 103.

Eel, the fish Anguilla: LLL I, 2, 28. Shr. IV, 3, 179. Lr. II, 4, 124. Per. IV, 2, 155 (*thunder shall not so awake the beds of —s*).

Eel-skin, the skin of an eel: *my arms such —s stuffed,* John I, 141. *thrust him and all his apparel into an e.* H4B III, 2, 351.

E'en, see *Even.*

E'er, see *Ever.*

Effect, subst. 1) execution, performance, realization: *thoughts are but dreams till their —s be tried,* Lucr. 353. *attained the e. of your own purpose,* Meas. II, 1, 13. *thou art the cause and most accursed e.* R3 I, 2, 120. 121 (abstr. pro concr.). *no compunctious visitings of nature shake my fell purpose, nor keep peace between the e. and it,* Mcb. I, 5, 48. *our wishes may prove —s,* Lr. IV, 2, 15. *thy thoughts touch their —s in this,* Ant. V, 2, 333.

2) action, working, manifestation: *the warm —s which she in him finds missing she seeks to kindle,* Ven. 605. *which* (viz the worser sense) *in a moment doth confound and kill all pure —s,* Lucr. 251. *though it alter not love's sole e., yet doth it steal sweet hours from love's delight,* Sonn. 36, 7. *I had him in mine arms with all the e. of love,* Ven. 199. *I found the e. of love in idleness,* Shr. I, 1, 156. *to receive at once the benefit of sleep, and do the —s of watching,* Mcb. V, 1, 12. *lest with this piteous action you convert my stern —s,* Hml. III, 4, 129. *that good —s may spring from words of love,* Lr. I, 1, 188. *thou better knowest the offices of nature, ... —s of courtesy,* II, 4, 182.

3) outward manifestation, expression, show, sign, token: *such devils steal —s from lightless hell,* Lucr. 1555. *bloodless white and the encrimsoned mood, —s of terror and dear modesty, encamped in hearts, but fighting outwardly,* Compl. 202. *losing his verdure even in the prime and all the fair —s of future hopes,* Gentl. I, 1, 50. *thy complexion shifts to strange —s, after the moon,* Meas. III, 1, 24. *what —s of passion shows she?* Ado II, 3, 112. *that we, whose baser stars do shut us up in wishes, might with —s of them follow our friends,* All's I, 1, 198. *there is not a white hair on your face but should have his e. of gravity,* H4B I, 2, 183. *notwithstanding the poor and untempering e. of my visage,* H5 V, 2, 241. *displayed the —s of disposition gentle,* H8 II, 4, 86. *I do invest you jointly with my power, pre-eminence and all the large —s that troop with majesty,* Lr. I, 1, 133.

4) that which is produced by an agent or cause, operation, result, consequence, fruit: *lust's e. is tempest after sun,* Ven. 800. *every beauty robbed of his e.* 1132. *being so applied, the poison in e. is purified,* Lucr. 532. Compl. 293. *to make you understand this in a manifested e.* Meas. IV, 2, 169 (i. e. so that its being manifest may be the effect or result of my exposition). Err. IV, 3, 57. V, 215. As IV, 3, 52. Shr I, 2, 93. All's I, 3, 228. II, 3, 27. Wint. IV, 1, 18. H4B I, 2, 133. Tit. IV, 4, 30. Rom. I, 5, 108. Caes. II, 1, 250. Hml. I, 5, 64. II, 2, 101. 103. III, 3, 54. Lr. I, 2, 115. 156. Oth. I, 2, 13 (*in his effect,* i. e. the voice's e.). I, 3, 225. Cymb. I, 5, 23. 25. 43. *to take e.* = to operate: Rom. V, 3, 244. *of none e.* = invalid: H8 IV, 1, 33. *to no e.* = in vain, resultless: Tit. V, 2, 12. *to so base e.* Gentl. II, 7, 73. *to this e.* = to this end: H6A V, 4, 102. Oth. I, 3, 105. *to e.* = to the purpose·

I have written to e.; there's not a god left unsolicited, Tit. IV, 3, 59. *few words, but to e. more than all yet,* Lr. III, 1, 52.

5) tenour, import, meaning, sense: *then others for the breath of words respect, me for my dumb thoughts, speaking in e.* Sonn. 85, 14. *the e. of my intent is to cross theirs,* LLL V, 2, 138. *words blacker in their e. than in their countenance,* As IV, 3, 35. *too fairly* (writ) *for so foul e.* John IV, 1, 38. *answer in the e. of your reputation, and satisfy the poor woman,* H4B II, 1, 142 (i. e. act up to what your reputation promises). *our just demands, whose tenours and particular —s you have … in your hands,* H5 V, 2, 72. *mere words, no matter from the heart; the e. doth operate another way,* Troil. V, 3, 109. *'tis in few words, but spacious in e.* Tim. III, 5, 97. *I shall the e. of this good lesson keep,* Hml. I, 3, 45. *wilt thou know the e. of what I wrote?* V, 2, 37. *let thy* (the book's) *—s so follow, to be … as good as promise,* Cymb. V, 4, 135. *to this e.* = with this tendency or aim (in diesem Sinne): *to this e. we breathed our counsel,* John IV, 2, 35. *to this e. have I moved you,* Troil. III, 3, 216. *shall I redeliver you e'en so? To this e., after what flourish your nature will,* Hml. V, 2, 187 (i. e. such be the general import of what you are to say). *daily prayers all to that e.* R3 II, 2, 15. *all the bitterest terms that ever ear did hear to such e.* Tit. II, 3, 111. *he spoke Greek. To what e.?* Caes. I, 2, 283 (in welchem Sinne?).

Effect, vb. 1) to execute, to perform, to fulfil: *in hand with all things, nought at all —ing,* Ven. 912. *fell exploits —ing,* Lucr. 429. *the purpose that you resolved to e.* Tp. III, 3, 13. *to e. your suits,* Wint. IV, 4, 828; cf. Oth. III, 4, 167. *the ancient proverb will be well —ed,* H6B III, 1, 170. *e. your rage,* Troil. V, 10, 6. Wiv. II, 2, 322. Mids. II, 1, 265. III, 2, 395. All's IV, 3, 104. V, 3, 42. R2 IV, 329. H4B IV, 4, 24. H5 II, 2, 157. H6B I, 2, 84. R2 III, 1, 158. 186. H8 I, 1, 107. Troil. IV, 2, 70. Cor. I, 9, 18. Tit. II, 3, 6. Ant. III, 1, 31. Cymb. V, 5, 60.

2) to bring about, to cause to be, to produce: *how willingly I would e. the match,* Gentl. III, 2, 22. *as much as I can do, I will e.* 66. *to e. your marriage,* Ado III, 2, 102. *our good will —s Bianca's grief,* Shr. I, 1, 86. *to e. one thing,* 120. *his death was so —ed,* All's III, 2, 119. *I wish it —ed,* IV, 5, 84. *to e. this knot of amity,* H6A V, 1, 15. *this marriage,* H6C II, 6, 98.

Effectless, bootless, vain: Tit. III, 1, 76. Per. V, 1, 53.

Effectual, 1) operative, efficacious: *the doom, which, unreversed, stands in e. force,* Gentl. III, 1, 223. *to teach you gamut in a briefer sort, more pleasant, pithy and e.* Shr. III, 1, 66.

2) full of import, grave, decisive: *or else conclude my words e.* H6B III, 1, 41. *a reason mighty, strong and e.* Tit. V, 3, 43 (cf. *Effect* subst. 5).

Effectually, 1) efficaciously, in a manner productive of the expected consequence: *your bidding shall I do e.* Tit. IV, 4, 107. -- 2) in its function and operation: (mine eye) *seems seeing, but e. is out, for it no form delivers to the heart,* Sonn. 113, 4.

Effeminate, adj. like a woman; 1) soft, tender-hearted: *well we know your tenderness of heart and gentle, kind, e. remorse,* R3 III, 7, 211.

2) weak, unmanly, cowardly: *none do you*

like but an e. prince, H6A I, 1, 35. *shall we at last conclude e. peace?* V, 4, 107. *an e. man in time of action,* Troil. III, 3, 218. Rom. III, 1, 119.

3) capricious, humorous: *at which time would I, being but a moonish youth, grieve, be e., changeable,* As III, 2, 430. *which he, young wanton and e. boy, takes on the point of honour to support,* R2 V, 3, 10.

Effigies, effigy, image, likeness: *as mine eye doth his e. witness most truly limned and living in your face,* As II, 7, 193.

Effuse, subst. effusion, loss: *much e. of blood doth make me faint,* H6C II, 6, 28.

Effuse, vb. to shed: *whose maiden blood, thus rigorously —d,* H6A V, 4, 52.

Effusion, 1) shedding, spilling: *of blood,* H5 III, 6, 138. H6A V, 1, 9. *of tears,* John V, 2, 49.

2) that which is poured out: (thy children) *the mere e. of thy proper loins,* Meas. III, 1, 30.

Eftest, most convenient: *that's the e. way,* Ado IV, 2, 38 (Dogberry's speech).

Eftsoons, by and by: *e. I'll tell thee why,* Per. V, 1, 256.

Egal = equal; 1) being on the same terms: *whose souls do bear an e. yoke of love,* Merch. III, 4, 13 (Q1 *equal*). 2) impartial: *e. justice,* Tit. IV, 4, 4 (F2.3.4 *equal*).

Egally, in the same degree: R3 III, 7, 213 (F2.3.4 *equally*).

Egeus, name in Mids. I, 1, 21. 115. IV, 1, 140. 184.

Egg, that from which the young of birds and some other animals are produced: Wiv. III, 5, 31. As II, 5, 14. III, 2, 39. H5 I, 2, 171. Troil. I, 2, 145. 146. Rom. III, 1, 26. Caes. II, 1, 32. Lr. I, 4, 170. 173. 175. III, 7, 106. IV, 6, 51. *an e. and butter,* H4A I, 2, 23. II, 1, 65. *as full of quarrels as an e. is full of meat,* Rom. III, 1, 24. *as like as —s,* Wint. I, 2, 130. Used to denote any thing worthless: *he will steal an e. out of a cloister,* All's IV, 3, 280. *will you take —s for money?* Wint. I, 2, 161*(cf. the passage in Lr. I, 4, 170 etc.). *not worth an e.* Cor. IV, 4, 21. Term of reproach for a malapert boy: Mcb. IV, 2, 83; cf. *pigeon-egg,* LLL V, 1, 78; *finch-egg,* Troil. V, 1, 41.

Egg-shell, the shell of an egg: Cymb. III, 1, 28. Denoting a thing without value: Hml. IV, 4, 53.

Eglamour, name in Gentl. I, 2, 9. IV, 3, 6. V, 1, 8. V, 2, 32. 51 etc.

Eglantine, the sweet briar: Mids. II, 1, 252. Cymb. IV, 2, 223.

Egma, corruption of *enigma:* LLL III, 73.

Egregious, extraordinary, enormous: *e. indignity,* All's II, 3, 228. *e. dog,* H5 II, 1, 49. *e. ransom,* IV, 4, 11. *e. murderer,* Cymb. V, 5, 211.

Egregiously, in an enormous, shameful manner: *making him e. an ass,* Oth. II, 1, 318.

Egress, subst. licence of going out of a place: Wiv. II, 1, 225 (used by the host).

Egypt, 1) country in Northern Africa: *a brow of E.* Mids. V, 11. *all the first-born of E.* As II, 5, 63 (see *First-born*). *for all the mud in E.* H8 II, 3, 92 Ant. I, 1, 29. I, 5, 12 etc.

2) the king of Egypt: *—'s widow,* Ant. II, 1, 37 the queen of Egypt (Cleopatra): I, 3, 41. 78. I, 5, 43 III, 9, 51. 56. IV, 14, 15. IV, 15, 18. 70. V, 2, 114.

Egyptian, subst. a native of Egypt: Tw. IV, 2,

48. Ant. II, 2, 223. III, 7, 64. III, 13, 164. IV, 12, 10. Per. III, 2, 84. = gipsy: Oth. III, 4, 56.

Egyptian, adj., pertaining to Egypt: *the E. thief*, Tw. V, 121 (the robber Thyamis in the Aethiopics of Heliodorus). Ant. I, 2, 120. II, 6, 64. 134. II, 7, 110. III, 10, 2. V, 2, 208.

Eight, twice four: Wiv. III, 3, 210. III, 5, 47. 55. 132. 134. Meas. IV, 2, 67. Ado III, 2, 74 (*e. or nine wise words*). As III, 2, 101. V, 4, 134. Tw. V, 205. R2 I, 1, 88. II, 1, 286. H4A II, 2, 26. 67. II, 4, 27. 184. III, 3, 83. H4B III, 1, 60. V, 1, 52. H5 I, 2, 64. II, 1, 98. IV, 8, 90. H8 IV, 2, 26. Cor. V, 4, 17. Rom. III, 1, 83. Caes. II, 2, 114. Hml. V, 1, 183. Lr. I, 5, 40. Oth. III, 4, 174. Ant. II, 2, 183. *it shall be written in e. and six*, Mids. III, 1, 25 (i. e. in lines alternately of eight and six syllables, like the popular English ballads).

Eighteen, eight and ten: Err. I, 1, 126. R2 I, 1, 95. H4A II, 4, 346. H6B I, 1, 42. 67. Cymb. II, 1, 61.

Eighth (O. Edd. *Eight*), the ordinal of eight: H8 II, 1, 116. Caes. II, 1, 213. Mcb. IV, 1, 119.

Eight-penny, of the worth of eight pence: *some e. matter*, H4A III, 3, 119.

Eighty, ten times eight: R3 IV, 1, 96.

Eight-year-old, of the age of eight years: *an e. horse*, Cor. V, 4, 17 (not hyphened in O. Edd.).

Eisel, see *Esile* and *Eysell*.

Either, 1) one of two, the one or the other: *to leave the master loveless, or kill the gallant knight: to put in practice e., alas, it was a spite*, Pilgr. 217. *here is neither cheer nor welcome: we would fain have e.* Err. III, 1, 66. *if e. of you know any impediment*, Ado IV, 1, 12. Merch. I, 2, 56. As IV, 1, 5. Shr. I, 1, 52. All's I, 2, 15. Tw. III, 1, 2, 43. Troil. II, 1, 110. Lr. I, 1, 7. Ant. II, 1, 16 etc.

2) each of two, both: *of —'s colour was the other queen*, Lucr. 66. *the sovereignty of e. being so great*, 69. *the face of e. ciphered —'s heart*, 1396. 1165. Sonn. 44, 14. Phoen. 36. 43. Gentl. V, 4, 116. LLL V, 2, 459. Shr. I, 2, 181. Wint. II, 3, 38. R2 III, 4, 11. R3 II, 1, 15. Before a subst.: *at e. end*, Err. I, 1, 86. *on e. hand*, H6A IV, 2, 23. *on e. side*, H4A V, 1, 99. R3 V, 3, 299. V, 5, 12. Cor. V, 3, 138. Cymb. V, 3, 81. *with e. part's agreement*, Shr. IV, 4, 50. *the hum of e. army*, H5 IV Chor. 5. *till the prince came, who parted e. part*, Rom. I, 1, 122. = each, used of more than two: *in a plenitude of subtle matter, applied to cautels, all strange forms receives, of burning blushes, or of weeping water, or swooning paleness; and he takes and leaves, in —'s aptness, as it best deceives*, Compl. 306.

3) each other: *each* (viz day and night) *though enemies to —'s reign, do in consent shake hands to torture me*, Sonn. 28, 5. *they are both in —'s powers*, Tp. I, 2, 450. *treason and murder ever kept together, as two yoke-devils sworn to —'s purpose*, H5 II, 2, 106. *unfold the imagined happiness that both receive in e. by this dear encounter*, Rom. II, 6, 29.

4) *e. which* = whichsoever: *my virtue or my plague, be it e. which*, Hml. IV, 7, 13.

5) *e. — or*, a) = whether — or, both — and: *but what needs e. your mum or her budget?* Wiv. V, 2, 9. *future evils, e. now or by remissness new conceived*, Meas. II, 2, 96. *O perilous mouths, that bear in them one and the self-same tongue, e. of condemnation or*

approof, II, 4, 174. *e. death or life shall thereby be the sweeter*, III, 1, 5. *e. at flesh or fish, a table full of welcome makes scarce one dainty dish*, Err. III, 1, 22. *it is certain that e. wise bearing or ignorant carriage is caught*, H4B V, 1, 84. *I shall offend, e. to detain or give it*, Lr. I, 2, 42. Of more than two things: *there is divinity in odd numbers, e. in nativity, chance or death*, Wiv. V, 1, 4.

b) disjunctively, granting only one of two alternatives (in senses a & b sometimes a monosyllable: Sonn. 70, 10. Mids. II, 1, 32. II, 2, 156. H4B IV, 1, 108. H6C II, 1, 94. R3 I, 2, 64. Caes. IV, 1, 23. Oth. IV, 2, 153): *till it. gorge be stuffed, or prey be gone*, Ven. 58. Sonn. 47, 9. 70, 10. Wiv. II, 1, 197. Meas. II, 2, 150. II, 4, 74. 95. IV, 2, 137. V, 31. Err. III, 1, 33. IV, 1, 56. 72. Ado II, 1, 225. V, 2, 58. Mids I, 1, 43. 65. 86. Merch. II, 1, 39. As I, 1, 139. II, 6, 7. III, 2, 212. H6A I, 1, 163. I, 5, 27. III, 3, 58. H6C I, 1, 11. II, 3, 31. IV, 4, 8. R3 IV, 4, 151 etc. In a negative sentence: *it not appears to me e. from the king or in the present time that you should have an inch of any ground to build a grief on*, H4B IV, 1, 108. *yet is't not probable to come alone, e. he so undertaking, or they so suffering*, Cymb. IV, 2, 142. Of more than two things: *e. this is envy in you, folly, or mistaking*, Meas. III, 2, 149.

Why either = whether: *why e. were you ignorant to see't, or, seeing it, of such childish friendliness, to yield your voices?* Cor. II, 3, 182.

Superfluous after *or*: *wilt thou set thy foot o' my neck? Or o' mine e.?* Tw. II, 5, 206.

Eject, to expel, banish: *to e. him hence*, Cor. III, 1, 287.

Eke, adv. also (used only by Pistol, the Host, and Flute): Wiv. I, 3, 105. II, 3, 77. Mids. III, 1, 97.

Eke, vb. (cf. *Eche*), to add to, to lengthen, to piece out: *to e. it and to draw it out in length*, Merch. III, 2, 23 (Q1 *eck*, Ff Q2.3.4 *ich* and *eech*). *and mine, to e. out hers*, As I, 2, 208. *to e. out that wherein toward me my homely stars have failed*, All's II, 5, 79.

Elbe, see *Elve*.

Elbow, subst. the next joint of the arm below the shoulder: Ven. 44. John I, 194. H4B I, 2, 81. Troil. II, 1, 49. Caes. III, 1, 107. *my e. itched; I thought there would a scab follow*, Ado III, 3, 106. *at his e.* = near him: Ado III, 3, 105. Merch. II, 2, 3. H4B II, 1, 22. R3 I, 4, 150. Oth. V, 1, 3. *out at e.* = having a torn coat, in bad circumstances: Meas. II, 1, 61. *to rub the e.*, an attitude of exultation: LLL V, 2, 109. H4A V, 1, 77.

Elbow, name in Meas. II, 1, 48. 59. 101 etc.

Elbow, vb., to haunt, to harass: *a sovereign shame so —s him*, Lr. IV, 3, 44.

Elbow-room, room for motion, free scope: *now my soul hath e.* John V, 7, 28.

Eld, subst. old age: *the superstitious idle-headed e. received and did deliver to our age this tale ... for a truth*, Wiv. IV, 4, 36. *all thy blessed youth becomes as aged, and doth beg the alms of palsied e.* Meas. III, 1, 36. In Troil. II, 2, 104 Ff *old*, Q *elders*, M. Edd. *eld*.

Elder, subst., the plant Sambucus: *my heart of e.* Wiv. II, 3, 30 (i. e. weak, faint; spoken to Caius who does not understand it). *Judas was hanged on an e.* LLL V, 2, 610 (according to a tradition generally received). *that's a perilous shot out of an e. gun*, H5 IV, 1, 210 (i. e. doing little hurt).* *let the stinking e., grief, untwine his perishing root with the increasing vine*, Cymb. IV, 2, 59. cf. *Elder-tree.*

Elder, adj. 1) = older, more advanced in age: *how can I then be e. than thou art?* Sonn. 22, 8. *how much more e. art thou than thy looks!* Merch. IV, 1, 251. H5 V, 2, 246. R3 III, 2, 62 (Ff *older*). Troil. I, 2, 88. Rom. I, 5, 40. Caes. II, 2, 47. IV, 3, 56. Lr. I, 1, 20. Ant. III, 10, 13. Cymb. III, 6, 45. Per. I, 2, 15. *e. days* = a more advanced age: R2 II, 3, 43. V, 3, 21. *some e. masters of known honour*, Hml. V, 2, 259. *to second ills with ills, each e. worse*, Cymb. V, 1, 14 (i. e. committed at a more advanced age).*

2) as it is now used, = born before another: Shr. I, 1, 51. I, 2, 268. John I, 57. H6B IV, 2, 150. H6C IV, 1, 118. *e. brother*, As I, 1, 56. IV, 3, 121. John II, 104. 239. H6C III, 3, 102. R3 IV, 4, 503 (Qq *his brother there*). Tit. II, 1, 74. Tim. II, 2, 130. *e. sister*, Shr. I, 2, 263. Wint. I, 2, 98. *e. son*, H6B II, 2, 51.

Used substantively, a) a person older than another: *you are my e.* Err. V, 420. LLL V, 2, 609. *I know my duty to my —s*, Shr. II, 7. *let the woman take an e. than herself*, Tw. II, 4, 31.

b) aged person: *whether the withered e. hath not his poll clawed*, H4B II, 4, 281. *wrinkled —s*, Troil. II, 2, 104 (Ff *old*, M. Edd. *eld*). *our —s say*, Caes. I, 2, 7.

c) a senator: *our best —s*, Cor. I, 1, 230. *most reverend and grave —s*, II, 2, 46.

Elder-tree, the tree Sambucus: Tit. II, 3, 272. 277.

Eldest, 1) = oldest: *your e. acquaintance cannot be three hours*, Tp. V, 186. *my youngest boy, and yet my e. care*, Err. I, 1, 125. *it hath the primal e. curse upon 't, a brother's murder*, Hml. III, 3, 37.

2) born before others, having the right of primogeniture: As I, 1, 47. I, 2, 133. Shr. Ind. 1, 84. I, 1, 185. Ii, 94. All's III, 5, 79. Tw. I, 5, 121. Wint. II, 1, 144. John I, 51. II, 177. H4A I, 1, 71. H4B II, 1, 114. H6B II, 2, 22. 43. V, 1, 49. H6C III, 3, 242. Tit. I, 103. 224. Mcb. I, 4, 38. Lr. V, 3, 291. Cymb. I, 1, 58. The eldest son a spoiled favourite: *like my lady's e. son, evermore tattling*, Ado II, 1, 10. *that blind priest, like the e. son of fortune, turns what he list*, H8 II, 2, 21; cf. Tw. I, 5, 121.

Eldest-born, first-born: Lr. I, 1, 55.

Ele, in *Unaneled*, q. v.

Eleanor, 1) daughter of Roger Earl of March: H6B II, 2, 38. 2) E. Cobham, Duchess of Gloster: H6B I, 2, 41. 42. I, 3, 150. II, 1, 169. II, 3, 1 etc. Misprint for *Margaret:* III, 2, 79. 100.

Elect, adj. chosen: *his captain, steward, deputy e.* R2 IV, 126. *the e. o' the land*, H8 II, 4, 60.

Elect, vb. to pick out, to choose: Meas. I, 1, 19. R2 III, 2, 57. H6A IV, 1, 4. Troil. II, 2, 66. Cor. III, 1, 211. Tit. I, 228. Cymb. III, 4, 112.

Election, act of choosing, choice: Merch. II, 9, 3. III, 2, 24. Troil. I, 3, 349. II, 2, 61. Cor. II, 3, 227. 237. 263. Tit. I, 16. 22. 183. 235. Hml. III, 2, 69. V, 2, 65. 366. Lr. I, 1, 209. Oth. I, 1, 27. Cymb. I, 1, 53. I, 6, 175. Per. II, 4, 33. *to make e.:* All's II, 3, 61. H6B I, 3, 165. Cymb. I, 2, 30.

Elegancy, fine polish, gracefulness: LLL IV, 2, 126 (Holofernes' speech).

Elegy, a plaintive poem: Gentl. III, 2, 82. As III, 2, 380.

Element, 1) the first or constituent part of any thing; all existing things being supposed to consist of fire, air, water and earth: *receiving nought by —s so slow* (viz earth and water) *but heavy tears*, Sonn. 44, 13. *these quicker —s* (air and fire) 45, 5. *the —s of whom your swords are tempered*, Tp. III, 3, 61. *there's little of the melancholy e. in her*, Ado II, 1, 357 (choler being ascribed to fire, blood to air, phlegm to water, and melancholy to earth). *does not our life consist of the four —s?* Tw. II, 3, 10. *the dull —s of earth and water never appear in him*, H5 III, 7, 23. *the —s so mixed in him*, Caes. V, 5, 73. *the very —s of this warlike isle*, Oth. II, 3, 59 (a pure extract, as it were, the very quintessence of the isle). *the —s once out of it, it transmigrates*, Ant. II, 7, 50 (= after its dissolution). *I am fire and air, my other —s I give to baser life*, Ant. V, 2, 292.

2) fire, air, water and earth, such as they, separately, appear in nature: *you should not rest between the —s of air and earth*, Tw. I, 5, 294. *meet with no less terror than the elements of fire and water*, R2 III, 3, 55. *bounding between the two moist —s*, Troil. I, 3, 41 (i. e. air and water). *native and indued unto that e.* Hml. IV, 7, 181.

3) More especially the air and sky that surrounds us: *these water-galls in her dim e.* (like rainbows in the sky) *foretell new storms*, Lucr. 1588. *the e. itself shall not behold her face at ample view*, Tw. I, 1, 26. *o'ershine you as much as the full moon doth the cinders of the e.* (i. e. the stars) H4B IV, 3, 58. *the e. shows to him as it doth to me*, H5 IV, 1, 107. *the complexion of the e.* Caes. I, 3, 128. *contending with the fretful e.* Lr. III, 1, 4. And in the plural: *then to the —s!* Tp. V, 317 (i. e. into the air). *love, with the motion of all —s, courses as swift as thought in every power*, LLL IV, 3, 329. *by the —s!* Cor. I, 10, 10 (= by the heavens!); cf. *you —s that clip us round about*, Oth. III, 3, 464. *she's framed as fruitful as the free —s*, II, 3, 348 (as the air that blows on any body). Used of the air in commotion by tempests: *if you can command these —s to silence*, Tp. I, 1, 24. *to the conflicting —s exposed*, Tim. IV, 3, 230. *I tax not you, the —s, with unkindness*, Lr. III, 2, 16. *let the heavens give him defence against the —s*, Oth. II, 1, 45. *the —s be kind to thee*, Ant. III, 2, 40. *the unfriendly —s forgot thee utterly*, Per. III, 1, 58.

4) proper and natural habitation or sphere: *such daubery as this is, beyond our e.* Wiv. IV, 2, 186. *out of my welkin, I might say e., but the word is overworn*, Tw. III, 1, 65. *I am not of your e.* III, 4, 137 (= above you). *thou climbing sorrow, thy e. is below*, Lr. II, 4, 58. *above the e. they lived in*, Ant. V, 2, 90. Singular expression: *one that promises no e. in such a business*, H8 I, 1, 48 (= of whom it would not be expected, that he should find his proper sphere in such a business).

Elephant, 1) the animal Elephas, the largest quadruped: Troil. I, 2, 22. II, 3, 2. 113. Caes. II, 1, 205. — 2) name of an inn: Tw. III, 3, 39. 48. IV, 3, 5.

Elevate, to raise: *another* (eye) *—d that the oracle was fulfilled*, Wint. V, 2, 82.

Eleven, one more than ten: Wiv. II, 2, 87. 88. 95. 275. Meas. II, 1, 291. III, 2, 208. Merch. II, 2, 171 (Ff Q2.3.4 *a 'leven*). As II, 7, 25. Tw. III, 2, 37.

Wint. II, 1, 144. H4A II, 4, 242. H4B V, 4, 17. R3 III, 6, 5. Troil. III, 3, 296. Cor. I, 3, 26. Rom. I, 3, 23. Hml. I, 2, 252. Oth. II, 2, 11. Per. IV, 2, 16. 17. *that teacheth tricks e. and twenty long, to tame a shrew and charm her chattering tongue*, Shr. IV, 2, 57 (a phrase of an origin as yet unknown).

Eleven-pence: *e. farthing better*, LLL III, 172 (O. Edd. *a 'leven-pence*).

Eleventh, the next in order to the tenth: H4A III, 2, 166. H5 I, 1, 2.

Elf, subst. a diminutive spirit, a fairy: Mids. V, 400. Plur. *elves:* Tp. V, 33. Wiv. V, 5, 46. 60. Err. II, 2, 192 (F1 *sprites*, F2.3.4 *elves sprites*, some M. Edd. *elvish sprites*). Mids. II, 1, 17. 30. II, 2, 5. III, 1, 177. Mcb. IV, 1, 42.

Elf, vb. to entangle, to mat together: *e. all my hair in knots*, Lr. II, 3, 10.

Elf-lock, hair clotted together by the agency of the elves or fairies: Rom. I, 4, 90.

Elf-skin, the skin of a fairy: *you starveling, you e.* H4A II, 4, 270 (equalling in bigness not even an elf, but only his cast skin. Hanmer: *eel-skin*).

Eliads, see *Oeillades*.

Elisabeth, 1) the daughter of Edward IV: R3 IV, 3, 41. IV, 4, 203. IV, 5, 18. V, 5, 29. — 2) the daughter of Henry VIII, the famous queen: H8 V, 5, 4. 10.

Ell, a measure of forty five inches: Err. III, 2, 112. H4A III, 3, 83. Rom. II, 4, 88.

Ellen, female name in H4B III, 2, 8.

Elm, the tree Ulmus: *thou art an e., my husband, I a vine*, Err. II, 2, 176. *the female ivy so enrings the barky fingers of the e.* Mids. IV, 1, 49. Poins calls Falstaff a *dead e.*, H4B II, 4, 358, perhaps on account of the weak support which he had given to Doll Tearsheet.

Eloquence, oratory, forcible language: Lucr. 563. Sonn. 23, 9. Gentl. III, 1, 83. Mids. V, 103. Merch. III, 2, 106. Shr. II, 177. H4A II, 4, 113. H5 V, 2, 149. 302. Cor. III, 2, 76. Tit. III, 1, 83. Rom. III, 2, 33. Ant. III, 12, 26.

Eloquent, speaking forcibly: Tw. III, 2, 47. H5 III, 7, 37. R3 IV, 4, 357. Hml. III, 2, 375 (Ff *excellent*).

Else, 1) other; a) other than this; in the phrase *'what e.'?* = of course: *will her ladyship behold and hear our exorcisms? Ay, what e.?* H6B I, 4, 6. H6C IV, 6, 56. Cor. IV, 6, 149. Ant. III, 7, 29. III, 11, 27. Singular expressions: *bastards, and e.* John II, 276 (= and such like). *God forbid e.* = God forbid that it should be otherwise: All's III, 5, 77. H8 II, 2, 115.

b) besides: *what seest thou e. in the dark backward and abysm of time?* Tp. I, 2, 49. 99. III, 1, 72. III, 3, 25. IV, 126. Gentl. I, 1, 58. Meas. II, 1, 226. Err. III, 2, 29. As I, 2, 149 etc. etc.

c) except this: *invisible to every eyeball e.* Tp. I, 2, 303. 491. II, 2, 179. Gentl. II, 1, 38 etc. etc.

2) otherwise, under other circumstances; a) in another place: *since the substance of your perfect self is e. devoted, I am but a shadow*, Gentl. IV, 2, 125 (i. e. since you love another). *hath not e. his eye strayed his affection in unlawful love?* Err. V, 50. cf. *Elsewhere*.

b) in the other case; if the fact were different: *thou didst prevent me; I had peopled e. this isle with Calibans*, Tp. I, 2, 350. II, 1, 299. III, 3, 80. Gentl.

III, 1, 9. Wiv. V, 5, 40. Meas. I, 2, 193. Err. II, 2, 203. IV, 3, 83 etc. *the fire is dead with grief ...; see e. yourself*, John IV, 1, 108 (i. e. if you will not believe me).

Or *else* = α) or if it be not so, in the contrary case: *speak fair words, or e. be mute*, Ven. 208. *pity the world, or e. this glutton be*, Sonn. 1, 13. 14, 13. *be more abstemious, or e. good night your vow*, Tp. IV, 1, 54. *be mute, or e. our spell is marred*, 127. Epil. 12. Gentl. I, 2, 47. II, 1, 10. IV, 1, 35. IV, 2, 22. IV, 4, 208. V, 4, 126. Wiv. I, 1, 158. 266. II, 2, 7. III, 3, 91. Meas. II, 4, 97. 165. III, 1, 103. V, 106. 232. Err. II, 1, 105. II, 2, 38. IV, 1, 44. IV, 3, 78. Ado II, 1, 58. LLL V, 2, 447. Mids. I, 1, 88. 119. III, 2, 346. Merch. IV, 1, 391. As IV, 1, 161. V, 2, 42. Shr. V, 3, 28. 78. All's IV, 3, 62. V, 3, 294. V, 4, 22. Wint. I, 2, 274. H5 I, 2, 231. H6A III, 2, 76. H6B I, 3, 222. III, 1, 41. IV, 1, 16. H6C I, 4, 16. II, 2, 174. II, 5, 136. III, 2, 88. V, 1, 49. R3 IV, 4, 498 etc.

β) simply = ôr, without a contradistinction: *whether it is that she reflects so bright, that dazzleth them, or e. some shame supposed*, Lucr. 377. *or kills his life, or e. his quality*, 875. *thyself thou gavest, thy own worth then not knowing, or me, to whom thou gavest it, e. mistaking*, Sonn. 87, 10; cf. 8, 4. *this or e. nothing will inherit her*, Gentl. III, 2, 87. *will you give thanks, or e. shall I?* Shr. IV, 1, 162. *is it true, or is it e. your pleasure to break a jest?* IV, 5, 71. *is it upon record, or e. reported from age to age?* R3 III, 1, 72. *pour our treasures into foreign laps, or e. break out in peevish jealousies*, Oth. IV, 3, 90. Tp. I, 2, 83. Gentl. I, 1, 35. II, 1, 172. Err. III, 2, 65. V, 337. LLL IV, 2, 61. Mids. I, 1, 137. 139. II, 1, 33. As II, 7, 92. Shr. II, 65. Tw. V, 169. H6A II, 4, 6. V, 4, 30. Hml. III, 2, 213. Cymb. V, 4, 146 etc. *nor e.* = nor: *a lion fell, nor e. a lion's dam*, Mids. V, 227.

Elsewhere, in another place or in other places: Sonn. 61, 13. 139, 12. Err. III, 1, 121. Shr. IV, 3, 6. R2 I, 1, 93. H4A I, 2, 61. H6C IV, 1, 58. Cor. III, 3, 135. *if you like e.* Err. III, 2, 7 (= if you love another). *thou lovest e.* Sonn. 139, 5.

Elsinore, residence of the Danish kings in Hml. I, 2, 174. II, 2, 278. 387. 573.

Eltham, place in England: H6A I, 1, 170. 176. *at E. Place*, III, 1, 156.

Elve (M. Edd. *Elbe*), river in Germany: H5 I, 2, 45. 52.

Elvish, writing of M. Edd. in Err. II, 2, 192; O. Edd. *elves sprites*.

Elvish-marked, marked and disfigured by the fairies: R3 I, 3, 228.

Ely, 1) seat of a bishop in England: *my lord of E.* R3 III, 4, 32. *at E. House* R2 I, 4, 58. II, 1, 216.* 2) the bishop of Ely: R3 IV, 3, 46. 49. IV, 4, 468 (Ff in all the three passages: *Morton*).

Elysium, Paradise: Ven. 600. Gentl. II, 7, 38. Tw. I, 2, 4. H5 IV, 1, 291. H6B III, 2, 399. H6C I, 2, 30. Cymb. V, 4, 97.

'Em, see *They*.

Emballing: *for little England you'ld venture ar e.* H8 II, 3, 47, i. e., according to the best commentators, to be distinguished by the *ball*, the ensign of royalty, used with the sceptre at coronations.

Embalm, to fill with aromatics against putrification: H8 IV, 2, 170. Tim. IV, 3, 40.

Embark, 1) trans. a) to put on shipboard: Err. V, 409. H5 III Chor. 5. Hml. I, 3, 1. — b) to engage: *he's —ed to the Cyprus wars,* Oth. I, 1, 150.

2) intr. to go on shipboard: *to e. for Milan,* Gentl. I, 1, 71. *the — ed traders,* Mids. II, 1, 127. *was —ed,* R3 I, 4, 10. *he —ed at Milford,* Cymb. III, 6, 62. Per. IV, 4, 27.

Embarquement: *nor fane nor Capitol, the prayers of priests nor times of sacrifice, —s all of fury, shall lift up their rotten privilege and custom 'gainst my hate,* Cor. I, 10, 22; probably = embargo, restraint, stop, hinderance.*

Embassade = embassy, H6C IV, 3, 32.

Embassador, see *Ambassador.*

Embassage, message, errand: *to thee I send this written e.* Sonn. 26, 3. *I have almost matter enough in me for such an e.* Ado I, 1, 282. *do you any e. to the Pigmies,* II, 1, 277. *conned his e.* LLL V, 2, 98. *nimble mischance, doth not thy e. belong to me?* R2 III, 4, 93. *I expect an e. from my Redeemer to redeem me hence,* R3 II, 1, 3.

Embassy, 1) a public message concerning state affairs; a) the sending and employment of a public minister: *comes in e.* LLL I, 1, 135. *dispatched him in an e.* John I, 99. *on your Greekish e.* Troil. IV, 5, 216.

b) the commission delivered by him: *what's his e.* LLL II, 3. *hear the e.* John I, 6. *my e.* 22. II, 44. H5 I, 1, 95. I, 2, 240. II, 4, 32. Cor. V, 3, 17.

2) any message: *in tender e. of love,* Sonn. 45, 6. *another e. of meeting,* Wiv. III, 5, 132. *hear Orsino's e.* Tw. I, 5, 176. *loving —ies,* Wint. I, 1, 31. *in e. to his mother,* Cymb. IV, 2, 185.

Embattle (O. Edd. *embattail*), 1) trans. to array for battle: *her defences, which now are too strongly —d against me,* Wiv. II, 2, 260. *—d and ranked,* John IV, 2, 200 (of four syll.). *the English are —d,* H5 IV, 2, 14.

2) to be arrayed: *we shall e. by the second hour,* Ant. IV, 9, 3.

Embayed, land-locked: *ensheltered and e.* Oth. II, 1, 18.

Embellish, to adorn: *—ed with rubies,* Err. III, 2, 137.

Ember-eves, the evenings before the ember-days, Per. Prol. 6.

Embers, cinders: Lucr. 5. Ant. II, 2, 13.

Emblaze, to glorify before the world (cf. *Blaze*): *thou shalt wear it* (the blood) *as a herald's coat, to e. the honour that thy master got,* H6B IV, 10, 76.

Emblem, sign, symbol: *his cicatrice, an e. of war,* All's II, 1, 44. *the rod, and bird of peace, and all such —s,* H8 IV, 1, 89.

Embody, to incorporate, to unite in one body: *I by vow am so —ed yours,* All's V, 3, 173.

Embolden, to make bold, to encourage: Wiv. II, 2, 173. Tim. III, 5, 3. Per. I, 1, 4.

Emboss, vb. (French *embusquer*, Ital. *imboscare*) to ambuscade, to close round (a game): *we have almost —ed him,* All's III, 6, 107; cf. 110 (O. Edd. *Imbost*).

Embossed (O. Edd. *imbossed* and *imbost*), 1) protuberant, tumid, swollen (cf. the French *bosse*): *all the e. sores and headed evils,* As II, 7, 67. *an e.*

carbuncle, Lr. II, 4, 227. *e. rascal,* H4A III, 3, 177. *who once a day with his e. froth the turbulent surge shall cover,* Tim. V, 1, 220.

2) foaming at the mouth in consequence of hard hunting, or covered with foam: *the poor cur is e.* Shr. Ind. I, 17.* *the boar of Thessaly was never so e.* Ant. IV, 13, 3.

Embounded, inclosed: *that sweet breath which was e. in this beauteous clay,* John IV, 3, 137.

Embowel, to eviscerate: H4A V, 4, 109. 111. R3 V, 2, 10. Tropically, = to exhaust, to empty: *the schools, —ed of their doctrine, have left off the danger to itself,* All's I, 3, 247.

Embrace, subst., clasp, fond pressure in the arms: Ven. 539. 811. 874. Wint. IV, 4, 450. H6A III, 3, 82. Rom. V, 3, 113.

Embrace, vb. 1) to clasp in the arms: Pilgr. 147. Tp. V, 109. 121. Err. V, 413. Shr. IV, 5, 34. Tw. V, 258. Wint. V, 2, 57. V, 3, 111. John II, 306. H4A V, 2, 74. H6A II, 5, 37. V, 3, 171. H6B IV, 6. H6C I, 1, 202. II, 3, 45. R3 II, 1, 25. H8 V, 3, 158. 172. Troil. IV, 5, 135. 199. 201. Tit. V, 2, 69. V, 3, 108. Lr. V, 3, 176. Cymb. V, 4, 139. Per. V, 1, 223. V, 3, 55. Absolutely: *her hard —ing,* Ven. 559. *—ing bushes,* 629. *locks her in —ing,* Wint. V, 2, 84. *let me e. too,* Troil. IV, 4, 15. *let me e. with old Vincentio,* Shr. IV, 5, 68. *their breaths —d together,* Oth. II, 1, 266. Used of sexual intercourse: Lucr. 518. Ado IV, 1, 50.

2) to join in an embrace, to clasp each other: *now kiss, e.* Gentl. I, 2, 129. *after we had —d,* Wiv. III, 5, 74. *let us e.* LLL IV, 3, 213. H4A V, 2, 99. H4B IV, 2, 63. R3 III, 3, 24. *—d from the ends of opposed winds,* Wint. I, 1, 33. *e. and kiss,* H6B III, 2, 354. *they join,* as H6C II, 1, 29. Of sexual intercourse: *your brother and his lover have —d,* Meas. I, 4, 40.

3) to surround, to encompass: *you'll see your Rome —d with fire,* Cor. V, 2, 7. Quibbling: *and girdle with —ing flames the waist of Collatine's fair love,* Lucr. 6. *hugged and —d by the strumpet wind,* Merch. II, 6, 16. *—d by a piece of tender air,* Cymb. V, 4, 139. Figuratively: *let grief and sorrow still e. his heart,* Tp. V, 214. *even such a passion do h e. my bosom,* Troil. III, 2, 37 (cf. *Engirt*).

4) to welcome, to receive with joy; a) of persons: *when first I did e. him,* Cor. IV, 7, 10. *whom this beneath world doth e. and hug with amplest entertainment,* Tim. I, 1, 44. *with joy he will e. you,* Cymb. III, 4, 179. b) of things: *yet strive I to e. mine infamy,* Lucr. 504. *you e. your charge too wilingly,* Ado I, 1, 103. V, 1, 303. *you e. the occasion to depart,* Merch. I, 1, 64. *let thy blood and spirit e. them* (thy Fates), Tw. II, 5, 150. *his enfranchisement,* R2 I, 3, 89. *the one and other* (salutation and lefiance) *Diomed —s,* Troil. IV, 1, 14. *I e. it freely,* Hml. V, 2, 263.

5) to tend, to cherish: *quicken his —d heaviness,* Merch. II, 8, 52. *to e. your own safety and give over this attempt,* As I, 2, 189. *you never shall e. each other's love in banishment,* R2 I, 3, 184. *he knows that you e. not Antony as you did love, but as you feared him,* Ant. III, 13, 56.

6) to take, to accept: *to e. your offer,* Tw. V, 328. *e. but my direction,* Wint. IV, 4, 534. *we must e. this gentle offer of the perilous time,* John IV, 3, 12.

the means that heaven yields must be —*d,* R2 III, 2, 29. *let it be a quarrel between us. I e. it,* H5 IV, 1, 221. *e. we then this opportunity,* H6A II, 1, 13. *e. his pardon,* H6B IV, 8, 14. *he would e. no counsel,* Tim. III, 1, 27. *he would e. the means to come by it,* Caes. II, 1, 259. *with sorrow I e. my fortune,* Hml. V, 2, 399. *which do not be entreated to, but weigh what it is worth* —*d,* Ant. II, 6, 33. *I e. these conditions,* Cymb. I, 4, 168. *I will e. your offer,* Per. III, 3, 38.

7) *to undergo, to suffer, to submit to: e. thy death,* Gentl. V, 4, 126. *what cannot be eschewed must be* —*d,* Wiv. V, 5, 251. *which* (death) *though myself would gladly have* —*d,* Err. I, 1, 70. *whom* (death) *I myself e. to set him free,* All's III, 4, 17. *I e. this fortune patiently,* H4A V, 5, 12. *let me e. thee, sour adversity,* H6C III, 1, 24. *Fleance must e. the fate of that dark hour,* Mcb. III, 1, 137. *thou unsubstantial air that I e.* Lr. IV, 1, 7 (cf. *Air*).

Embracement, a clasp in the arms, e m b r a c e: Ven. 312. 790. Err. I, 1, 44. Shr. Ind. 1, 118. Wint. V, 1, 114. R3 II, 1, 30. H8 I, 1, 10. Troil. IV, 5, 148. Cor. I, 3, 4. Tit. V, 2, 68. Cymb. I, 1, 116. Per. I, 1, 7.

Embrasure, e m b r a c e: Troil. IV, 4, 39.

Embroidered, adorned with figures of needlework: Pilgr. 364 (not Shakespearian). cf. *Rich-embroidered.*

Embroidery, ornamental needle-work: Wiv. V, 5, 75.

Embrue, see *Imbrue.*

Emerald, a precious stone: *the deep-green e., in whose fresh regard weak sights their sickly radiance do amend,* Compl. 213. *e. tufts,* Wiv. V, 5, 74 (Ff Q₃ *emrold* .

Emilia , name in Wint. II, 2, 12 etc. and Oth. II, 1, 163 etc.

Emilius, see *Aemilius.*

Eminence, 1) high place, distinction: H8 II, 3, 29. Troil. I, 3, 90. Mcb. III, 2, 31. Lr. V, 3, 131.

2) excellence, sublimity: *whether the tyranny be in his place, or in his e. that fills it up,* Meas. I, 2, 168. *to have the e. of* = to be better than: Troil. II, 3, 266.

Eminent, 1) high, conspicuous: *bowed his e. top to their low ranks,* All's I, 2, 43. *who stands so e. in the degree of this fortune as Cassio does?* Oth. II, 1, 240 (Qq *eminently*).

2) of high rank: *by an e. body that enforced the law against it,* Meas. IV, 4, 25. *allied to e. assistants,* H8 I, 1, 62. *an e. monsieur,* Cymb. I, 6, 65. *a pantler, not so e.* II, 3, 129.

Eminently, high: *who stands so e. in the degree of this fortune,* Oth. II, 1, 240 (= on so high a stepping-stone. Ff *eminent*).

Emmanuel, the name given to Jesus in the Old Testament, formerly prefixed to public deeds: H6B IV, 2, 106.

Emmew, to mew, to coop up, to keep d o w n: *and follies doth e. as falcon doth the fowl,* Meas. III, 1, 91. Edinb. Rev. Oct. 72 proposes *enew.*

Empale, see *Impale.* **Emperator,** see *Imperator.*

Emperial, used by the clown for *emperor* and *imperial:* Tit. IV, 3, 94. IV, 4, 40.

Emperor, title of the sovereigns of Rome: Tit. I, 184 etc. Ant. II, 7, 109. III, 7, 21. IV, 6, 28. IV,

14, 90. V, 2, 76 etc. Cymb. I, 6, 187. III, 5, 2 etc. Hence, of the lords paramount of Germany: John I, 100. H5 I, 2, 76. IV, 1, 42. V Chor. 38. H6A V, 1, 2. H8 I, 1, 176. 185. 188. II, 1, 162 etc. of the sovereign of Russia: Meas. III, 2, 93. Wint. III, 2, 120. Uncertain what prince may be meant by it: Gentl. I, 3, 27. 38. 41. 58. II, 4, 77 (the duke of Milan?). Used of the queen-bee: H5 I, 2, 196. Of any supreme degree of human power and splendour: *a present for any e.* Tp. II, 2, 72. Wiv. I, 3, 9. John IV, 3, 89. Rom. V, 1, 9. Hml. IV, 3, 22. Oth. IV, 1, 195.

Empery = empire, 1) supreme dominion: *ruling in large and ample e. o'er France,* H5 I, 2, 226. *strive for rule and e.* Tit. I, 19. 22. 201.

2) country subject to a prince's dominion: *your right of birth, your e., your own,* R3 III, 7, 136. *a lady so fair, and fastened to an e.* Cymb. I, 6, 120.

Emphasis, stress of utterance: *whose grief bears such an e.* Hml. V, 1, 278. *be choked with such another e.* Ant. I, 5, 68.

Empierced, see *Enpierced.*

Empire, 1) supreme power, sovereignty: All's I, 1, 72. Ant. I, 2, 192. III, 6, 66. V, 1, 43. *that beasts may have the world in e.* Tim. IV, 3, 393.

2) the territory and dominion of an emperor: H6B I, 1, 153. Tit. I, 183. 307. Ant. I, 1, 34. IV, 2, 22. Cymb. V, 5, 461. *a maid too virtuous for the contempt of e.* All's III, 2, 34 (i. e. of an emperor).

3) any dominion: R3 IV, 4, 471. Hml. l, 1, 119. Hml. III, 4, 99. Per. II, 1, 54.

Empiric, subst. a q u a c k: *to prostitute our past-cure malady to* —*s,* All's II, 1, 125.

Empiricutic (a word coined, probably, by old Menenius), adj. q u a c k i s h: *the most sovereign prescription in Galen is but e.* Cor. II, 1, 128.

Employ, to occupy, to set to work, to trust with an office, to use: Meas. V, 391. LLL III, 152. V, 1, 159. As I, 1, 38. III, 5, 96. 98. Wint. II, 1, 49. IV, 4, 387. John I, 96. 98. R2 II, 3, 132. III, 4, 37. H4A I, 3, 265. II, 4, 562. H6A IV, 1, 72. H6B III, 1, 291. III, 2, 273. H6C I, 2, 44. R3 II, 1, 36. H8 II, 2, 15. III, 2, 158. Troil. I, 3, 386. II, 2, 40. Tit. III, 1, 282. IV, 3, 39. V, 2, 149. Hml. II, 2, 74. Oth. I, 3, 48. Ant. V, 1, 72. Cymb. I, 1, 173. Followed by *to:* *e. your chiefest thoughts to courtship,* Merch. II, 8, 43. *if you'll e. me to him,* Ant. V, 2, 70 (use my service with him). cf. *to e. you towards this Roman,* Cymb. III, 3, 68. *I will e. thee back again,* Ant. III, 3, 39. Followed by *in: there's some great matter she'ld e. me in,* Gentl. IV, 3, 3. IV, 4, 45. Meas. V, 537. Mids. I, 1, 124. III, 2, 374. John IV, 2, 226. H4B IV, 2, 24. H6A II, 1, 69. R3 I, 1, 108. III, 1, 180. Armado says: *I must e. him in a letter to my love,* LLL III, 6. Followed by the inf.: *you shall be* —*ed to hasten on this expedition,* Gentl. I, 3, 76. Merch. IV, 1, 117. Tim. III, 3, 39.

Reflectively: *e. thee for our good,* H6A III, 3, 16.

Employer, one that sets to work: *Troilus the first e. of pandars,* Ado V, 2, 31.

Employment, 1) use: *wit may be made a Jack-a-Lent, when 'tis upon ill e.* Wiv. V, 5, 135. *the which* (money) *he hath detained for lewd* —*s,* R2 I, 1, 90. Rom. V, 3, 32. Hml. V, 1, 77.

2) office, service, commission: *fit for*

great e. Gentl. V, 4, 157. *you have no e. for me,* Ado II, 1, 280. LLL II, 35. IV, 2, 140 *(your ladyship's in all desired e.).* All's II, 2, 71. Tw. III, 4, 204. H5 Prol. 8. H8 II, 1, 48. Tim. IV, 3, 262. Hml. V, 2, 57. Lr. V, 3, 32. Cymb. III, 4, 113. III, 5, 110. *at your e.* = at your service, John I, 198. *upon hasty e.* H4B II, 1, 139. Lr. II, 2, 136.

3) work, business: *what e. have we here?* Tw. II, 5, 91. *is there not wars? is there not e.?* H4B I, 2, 85.

Empoison, to destroy: *how much an ill word may e. liking,* Ado III, 1, 86. *a man by his own alms —ed, and with his charity slain,* Cor. V, 6, 11 (cf. *Poison*).

Empress (sometimes trisyll. in Tit.; f. i. I, 240. 320. II, 1, 20. II, 3, 66. IV, 2, 143), 1) the consort of an emperor: Gentl. II, 4, 76. V, 4, 141. H5 V, 2, 255. H6B I, 3, 81. Tit. I, 240. 320. 459. II, 1, 20. II, 3, 66. IV, 2, 143. IV, 3, 73. V, 3, 32 etc.

2) a female sovereign: *the general of our gracious e.* H5 V Chor. 30. *madam, O good e.* Ant. III, 11, 33. IV, 15, 71. V, 2, 71.

3) sovereign mistress: *e. of my love,* LLL IV, 3, 56. *of my soul,* Tit. II, 3, 40.

Emptiness, state of containing nothing, inanity: H4B I, 3, 75. Ant. III, 13, 36. Cymb. I, 6, 45.

Empty, adj. 1) containing nothing: Tp. I, 2, 214. IV, 111. Mids. II, 1, 96. Merch. II, 7, 63. Tw. III, 4, 404. John V, 1, 40. R2 I, 2, 59. 68. IV, 186. H4B II, 4, 67. H5 IV, 4, 73 (Proverb: *the e. vessel makes the greatest sound.* cf. H4B II, 4, 66 and Lr. I, 1, 155). R3 I, 2, 59. Rom. I, 4, 67. V, 1, 45. V, 3, 204. Tim. I, 2, 199. III, 1, 16. IV, 2, 12. Hml. V, 2, 136. Oth. II, 1, 53. Ant. III, 13, 146. Cymb. IV, 2, 113. V, 4, 166. *the e. air,* H6B V, 2, 4. R3 I, 4, 39. *through the e. skies,* Ven. 1191. *weep our bosoms e.* Mcb. IV, 3, 2.

2) vacant, unfilled: *e. place,* As I, 2, 205. *chair,* H4B IV, 5, 95. R3 IV, 4, 470. H8 V, 3, 10.

3) uncharged, not supplied, having nothing to carry: *an e. messenger,* Tim. III, 6, 40. *the e. ass,* Caes. IV, 1, 26.

4) void, destitute; followed by *of: e. of that fault,* LLL V, 2, 878. *of defence,* H5 I, 2, 153. *of reasons,* Troil. II, 2, 34. *of all thought,* IV, 2, 6. *of all things,* Cymb. III, 4, 71. Followed by *from: void and e. from any dram of mercy,* Merch. IV, 1, 5. By *in: that in civility thou seemest so e.* As II, 7, 93.

5) vain, hollow: *e. words,* Meas. II, 4, 2. *so e. a heart,* H5 IV, 4, 72. *e. vanities,* H8 II, 3, 69.

6) hungry: *an e. eagle,* Ven. 55. H6B III, 1, 248. H6C I, 1, 268. *falcon,* Shr. IV, 1, 193. *tigers,* Rom. V, 3, 39.

Empty, vb. 1) to deprive of the contents: Wiv. III, 3, 15. IV, 2, 149. As V, 1, 47. R2 II, 2, 130. H4A I, 3, 86. 133. H4B IV, 4, 37. With *of: —ing our bosoms of their counsel,* Mids. I, 1, 216. *old receptacles of filth,* Per. IV, 6, 185.

2) to make vacant: *the untimely —ing of the happy throne,* Mcb. IV, 3, 68.

3) to pour out, to discharge: *—ed all their fountains in my well,* Compl. 255. *—es itself into the main of waters,* Merch. V, 96. *the —ing of our fathers' luxury,* H5 III, 5, 6 (= the efflux, issue).

Empty-hearted, destitute of feeling: Lr. I, 1, 155.

Emulate, vb. to vie with: *thine eye would e. the diamond,* Wiv. III, 3, 58.

Emulate, adj., envious, jealous: *pricked on by a most e. pride,* Hml. I, 1, 83.

Emulation, 1) rivalry: Lucr. 1808. As IV, 1, 11. Cor. I, 10, 12.

2) jealousy, envy, envious contention: *such factious —s,* H6A IV, 1, 113. *keep off aloof with worthless e.* IV, 4, 21. *e. now, who shall be nearest,* R3 II, 3, 25. *an envious fever of pale and bloodless e.* Troil. I, 3, 134. *e. in the army crept,* II, 2, 212. III, 3, 156. IV, 5, 123. *shouting their e.* Cor. I, 1, 218. *virtue cannot live out of the teeth of e.* Caes. II, 3, 14.

Emulator, an envier: *an envious e. of every man's good parts,* As I, 1, 150.

Emulous, 1) desirous of superiority, ambitious: *but in mine e. honour let him die,* Troil. IV, 1, 28.

2) envious: *e. factions,* Troil. II, 3, 79. *he is not e. as Achilles is,* 242. *whose glorious deeds made e. missions 'mongst the gods,* III, 3, 189.

Enact, subst., doing, working, action: *betray with blushing the close —s and counsels of the heart,* Tit. IV, 2, 118.

Enact, vb. 1) to act, to perform: *—ed wonders with his sword,* H6A I, 1, 122. *what murder hath been —ed through your enmity,* III, 1, 116. *the king —s more wonders than a man,* R3 V, 4, 2. Used of a part in a play: *to e. my present fancies,* Tp. IV, 121. *what did you e.? I did e. Julius Caesar,* Hml. III, 2, 107. 108.

2) to set down, to record: *a little harm done to a great good end for lawful policy remains —ed,* Lucr. 529. *it is —ed in the laws of Venice,* Merch. IV, 1, 348. *it is —ed thus,* H6A V, 4, 123.

Enactor, actor, performer: *the violence of either grief or joy their own —s with themselves destroy,* Hml. III, 2, 207 (Qq *enactures*).*

Enacture, action, representation: Hml. III, 2, 207 (Ff *enactors*).*

Enamelled, glossy and variegated: Gentl. II, 7, 28. Err. II, 1, 109. Mids. II, 1, 255.

Enamoured, in love; followed by *of:* Mids. III, 1, 141. IV, 1, 82. Rom. III, 3, 2. By *on:* Ado II, 1, 170. H4A V, 2, 70. H4B I, 3, 102.

Encamp, vb. trans. to form into a camp, to place in tents: *e. his soldiers where they are,* Tit. V, 2, 126. Reflectively: H5 III, 6, 180. Rom. II, 3, 27 (= to be at war). Partic. *—ed,* Compl. 203 (= at war). H4A IV, 2, 82 (= in the field). H6C IV, 2, 14.

Encave, to hide: *do but e. yourself,* Oth. IV, 1, 82.

Enceladus, a giant of ancient fable: Tit. IV, 2, 93.*

Enchafe, to chafe, to enrage: *the —d flood,* Oth. II, 1, 17. *their royal blood —d,* Cymb. IV, 2, 174.

Enchain, to bind, to tie: *—ed me to endless date of never ending woes,* Lucr. 934.

Enchant, 1) to charm, to make efficient by witchcraft: *Medea gathered the —ed herbs,* Merch. V, 13. *—ing all that you put in,* Mcb. IV, 1, 43. cf. *some —ed trifle to abuse me,* Tp. V, 112 (= produced by witchcraft).

2) to bewitch, to subdue by charms: *whose —ing story,* Lucr. 1521. *e. him with thy words,*

H6A III, 3, 40. *I will e. the old Andronicus with words,*
Tit. IV, 4, 89. *thou hast —ed her,* Oth. I, 2, 63. *such
a holy witch that he —s societies into him,* Cymb. I,
6, 167. Absolutely: *I want art to e.* Tp. Epil. 14.
this —ing queen, Ant. I, 2, 132.

3) to c h a r m, to d e l i g h t, to r a v i s h: Ven.
145. 247. Lucr. 83. Compl. 89. 128. Err. III, 2, 166.
LLL I, 1, 168. II, 247. Troil. III, 1, 164. III, 2, 21.
Tit. III, 1, 86.

Enchantingly, as if by means of charms: *of all
sorts e. beloved,* As I, 1, 174.

Enchantment, c h a r m: Tw. III, 1, 123. Abstr.
pro concr.: *and you, e.* Wint. IV, 4, 445 (= enchantress).

Enchantress, s o r c e r e s s: *fell banning hag, e.*
H6A V, 3, 42.

Enchase, to s t u d, to s e t, to a d o r n: *king
Henry's diadem, —d with all the honours of the world,*
H6B I, 2, 8.

Encircle, to surround: Wiv. IV, 4, 56. H4B
IV, 2, 6.

Enclog, to e n c u m b e r, to c h e c k, to s t o p:
traitors ensteeped to e. the guiltless keel, Oth. II, 1,
70 (Qq *clog*).

Enclose, 1) to s h u t i n, to e n v e l o p: *blind
they are (viz his eyes) and keep themselves —d,* Lucr.
378; cf. Cymb. II, 2, 21. *in what sweets dost thou thy
sins e.* Sonn. 95, 4. *the glowing roses that flame through
water which their hue —s,* Compl. 287. *beauty, truth,
and rarity here —d in cinders lie,* Phoen. 55; cf. *the
dead – d in clay,* H5 IV, 8, 129. *my honesty, that lies
—d in this trunk,* Wint. I, 2, 435. *thy breast —s my
poor heart,* R3 I, 2, 205.

2) to s e p a r a t e f r o m c o m m o n g r o u n d s b y
a f e n c e: *for —ing the commons of Melford,* H6B
I, 3, 24.

3) to s u r r o u n d, to e n c o m p a s s: *their silent
war of lilies and of roses in their pure ranks his traitor
eye —s,* Lucr. 73. *—ed were they with their enemies,*
H6A I, 1, 136. Caes. V, 3, 8. 28.

Enclouded, enveloped as by a cloud: *in their
thick breaths shall we be e.* Ant. V, 2, 212.

Encompass, 1) to e n c l o s e, surround: *—ed
with a winding maze,* Lucr. 1151. *round —ed and set
upon,* H6A I, 1, 114. *—ed with thy lustful paramours,*
III, 2, 53. H6C II, 1, 15. *—ed with your crown,* II, 2,
3. R3 I, 2, 204. *her wide walks —ed but one man,*
Caes. I, 2, 155.

2) to o b t a i n, g e t p o s s e s s i o n o f, c o m e
b y: *have I —ed you?* Wiv. II, 2, 159 (cf. *Compass*).

Encompassment, a coming round one, c i r c u m -
v e n t i o n: *by this e. and drift of question,* Hml. II,
1, 10.

Encounter, subst. 1) m e e t i n g, a s e e i n g o r
f i n d i n g e a c h o t h e r: *fair e. of two most rare affections,*
Tp. III, 1, 74. *these lords at this e. do so much admire,*
V, 154. Gentl. II, 7, 41. Shr. I, 2, 105. Wint. I, 1, 29.
V, 2, 62. H8 IV, 1, 4. Rom. II, 6, 29. Caes. I, 3, 156.
Hml. III, 1, 34. Ant. I, 4, 79. More particularly, a)
an amorous meeting, a r e n d e z v o u s: *comes me in
the instant of our e.* Wiv. III, 5, 74. Meas. III, 1, 261.
Ado III, 3, 161. IV, 1, 94. All's III, 7, 32. Troil. III,
2, 217. b) a hostile meeting, c o m b a t: *uncouple at
the roe which no e. dare,* Ven. 676. *—s mounted are
against your peace,* LLL V, 2, 82 (abstr. pro concr.:
= encounterers, combatants). H4A II, 2, 64. V, 1,

84. R3 I, 2, 115. Cor. IV, 5, 129. Lr. II, 1, 56. Ant.
I, 2, 98. The two significations blent: *now is she in
the very lists of love, her champion mounted for the
hot e.* Ven. 596. Ado I, 1, 327. Rom. I, 1, 219. Cymb.
II, 5, 19.

2) m a n n e r o f a d d r e s s o r a c c o s t i n g, b e h a v i o u r:
that with your strange e. much amazed me, Shr. IV, 5,
54. *that they call compliment is like the e. of two dog-
apes,* As II, 5, 27. *since he came, with what e. so
uncurrent I have strained to appear thus,* Wint. III, 2,
50. *mark the e.* Hml. II, 2, 164. *only got the tune of
the time and outward habit of e.* V, 2, 199.

Encounter, vb. 1) trans., a) to m e e t: Tp. IV,
137. Gentl. I, 2, 5. Meas. III, 1, 84. Ado II, 3, 132.
LLL I, 1, 244. H5 IV, 7, 165. H6A IV, 7, 37. Troil.
III, 2, 40. Cor. II, 1, 94. IV, 3, 40. Mcb. III, 4, 9.
Cymb. I, 3, 32. Opposed to *avoid: the fashion of the
world is to avoid cost, and you e. it,* Ado I, 1, 98 (= go
to meet it, seek it). cf. *will you e. the house?* Tw. III,
1, 82 (affectedly, = go towards). Passively: *we were
—ed by a mighty rock,* Err. I, 1, 102. *two nights together
had these gentlemen been thus —ed,* Hml. I, 2, 199.
well —ed = well met, LLL V, 1, 37. H4B IV, 2, 1.
Cymb. III, 6, 66. Used of a hostile meeting, = to
fight, to assail: R2 V, 3, 48. H4B I, 1, 133. H6A
III, 2, 9. IV, 6, 18. H6B V, 2, 10. H6C I, 1, 15. I,
4, 13. IV, 8, 36. Rom. II, 4, 17. Passively: *he shall
be —ed with a man as good as himself,* H6B IV, 2,
124. *Titan's face blushing to be —ed with a cloud,*
Tit. II, 4, 32. *that I am thus —ed with clamorous
demands of date-broke bonds,* Tim. II, 2, 36.

b) to b e f a l l: *good time e. her!* Wint II, 1, 20.
all the plagues of hell should at one time e. such revolt,
Cymb. I, 6, 112.

2) intr. to m e e t: *mountains may be removed with
earthquakes and so e.* As III, 2, 196. *when we —ed,*
Tim. III, 6, 5. Followed by *with: when ladies crave
to be —ed with,* H6A III, 2, 46. *I will e. with Andronicus,*
Tit. V, 2, 2. *let not your hate e. with my love,* All's I,
3, 214; i. e. do not hate, while I love; cf. *the great
dignity that his valour hath here acquired for him shall
at home be —ed with a shame as ample,* IV, 3, 81.
Used of a hostile conflict, = to fight, to combat: *let
belief and life e. so,* John III, 1, 31. *our powers, with
smiling fronts —ing,* Cor. I, 6, 8. Followed by *with:
if thou e. with the boar,* Ven. 672. Wint. II, 3, 138.
H4A I, 3, 114. H6C V, 3, 5.

Encounterer, one who m e e t s a n o t h e r h a l f -
w a y: *these —s that give a coasting welcome ere it come,*
Troil. IV, 5, 58.

Encourage, to e m b o l d e n, to i n c i t e, to i n s p i r i t:
Lucr. 1402. As I, 2, 252. All's III, 6, 80. Wint. III,
2, 165. R3 III, 1, 175. Caes. IV, 3, 209.

Encouragement, i n s p i r i t i n g, i n c r e a s e o f
c o n f i d e n c e: Meas. I, 2, 192. R3 V, 2, 6.

Encrimsoned, red coloured: Compl. 201.

Encroach, to u s u r p t h e r i g h t s o f o t h e r s:
—ing tyranny, H6B IV, 1, 96.

Encumber, *with arms —ed thus, or this head-
shake,* Hml. I, 5, 174; = folded arms?

End, subst. 1) the e x t r e m e p a r t o f a n y t h i n g:
at which e. of the beam should bow, Tp. II, 1, 131. *each
e. of thy blue bow,* IV, 80. *to the west e. of the wood,*
Gentl. V, 3, 9. *to the world's e.* Ado II, 1, 272. *the e.
of his club,* LLL V, 1, 139. V, 2, 897. Merch. I, 3,
82. As III, 3, 55. Wint. I, 1, 34. H4B V, 5, 124.

R3 III, 7, 35 etc. *to the opposed e. of our intents,* LLL V, 2, 768. *the latter e. of his commonwealth,* Tp. II, 1, 157. Wiv. I, 4, 9. LLL V, 2, 630. Mids. IV, 1, 223. All's II, 5, 31. H4A IV, 2, 85. H5 V, 2, 341 (quibbling). *I'll woo you like a soldier, at arms 'e.* Gentl. V, 4, 57 (quibbling in the word *arms*). *hold death awhile at the arm's e.* As II, 6, 10. cf. *he holds Belzebub at the staves' e.* Tw. V, 292. *candles' —s,* H4B II, 4, 267. *blessed fig's e.* Oth. II, 1, 256. *thou hast it at the fingers' e.* LLL V, 1, 81. Tw. I, 3, 83. *pick strong matter of revolt and wrath out of the bloody fingers' —s of John,* John III, 4, 168. *smile upon his fingers' —s,* H5 II, 3, 16. *every lane's e.* Wint. IV, 4, 701. *a rope's e.* Err. IV, 1, 16. 98. IV, 4, 16. 45. *at upper e. o' the table,* Wint. IV, 4, 59. *at the tongue's e.* LLL III, 1, 12. *at town's e.* H4A IV, 2, 10. *they are for the town's e.* V, 3, 39. Without the sign of the genitive: *at street e.* Wiv. IV, 2, 40. *unto Long-lane e.* Shr. IV, 3, 187. *at the orchard e.* Tw. III, 4, 244. *at either e. the mast,* Err. I, 1, 86 (cf. *Of*). *to stand on e.* = to bristle up: Ven. 272. R3 I, 3, 304 (Ff *an end*). *my hair be fixed on e.* H6B III, 2, 318 (Ff *an end*). *to stand an e.* Hml. I, 5, 19. III, 4, 122.

2) extremity in general, conclusion, close: *sweet beginning, but unsavoury e.* Ven. 1138. *without e.* Lucr. Dedic. 1. Lucr. 238. *my weary travel's e.* Sonn. 50, 2. *my life hath e.* 92, 6. *'I hate' she altered with an e.* 145, 9. Tp. IV, 115. Meas. V, 46. Merch. III, 1, 20. Troil. IV, 5, 224 etc. *to make an e. of sth.:* Wiv. I, 2, 12. Wint. III, 3, 99. Cor. IV, 2, 26. Tim. III, 4, 55. Hml. IV, 5, 57. Ant. IV, 14, 105. *to have an e.* Lr. V, 1, 45. *to have e.* Sonn. 92, 6. Ant. I, 2, 95. *grew to an e.* R3 III, 7, 20 (Ff *drew toward e.*). *an e., sir,* All's II, 2, 66. Cor. V, 3, 171. *at an e.* LLL V, 2, 430. H6C III, 2, 81. *at e.* Cor. IV, 7, 4. *there's an e.* (= there is no more to say about it): Ado II, 1, 129. H4A V, 3, 65. H5 II, 1, 11. III, 2, 153. Cymb. III, 1, 84. *there an e.,* in the same sense: Gentl. I, 3, 65. II, 1, 168. Shr. V, 2, 98. R2 V, 1, 69. H4B III, 2, 358. Troil. I, 1, 91. Rom. III, 4, 28. Mcb. III, 4, 80. *has hurt me, and there's the e. on't,* Tw. V, 202. *in the e.* = finally: All's IV, 2, 68. Tw. II, 3, 203. R3 I, 3, 272. H4B I, 1, 79. H6B III, 1, 364. H6C I, 2, 14. Cor. I, 9, 5. Tim. III, 3, 30. Hml. IV, 2, 18. Lr. III, 7, 101. *I'll catch the fly in the latter e.* H5 V, 2, 341 (quibbling). *for an e.* in the same sense: *so it must fall out to him or our authorities, for an e.* Cor. II, 1, 260.

3) perdition, destruction, death: *beauty's waste hath in the world an e.* Sonn. 9, 11. *thy e. is truth's and beauty's doom and date,* 14, 14. *my e. was wrought by nature,* Err. I, 1, 34. 159. *to the world's e.* II, 2, 108. cf. Troil. III, 2, 209 and Cor. III, 1, 304. Err. IV, 4, 44. Merch. IV, 1, 274. R2 II, 1, 11. H6A II, 5, 7. H8 II, 1, 97. *I shall see an e. of him,* As I, 1, 171. *he makes a swanlike e.* Merch. III, 2, 44. *a made a finer e.* H5 II, 3, 11. *made a good e.* Hml. IV, 5, 186. *this apoplexy will certain be his e.* H4B IV, 4, 130. *either of you to be the other's e.* R3 II, 1, 15. *take his e.* H6B I, 4, 36. *is this the promised e.?* Lr. V, 3, 263.

4) issue, result, that which is found or met with at the close: *most poor matters point to richest —s,* Tp. III, 1, 4. *in this forest let us do those —s that here were well begun,* As V, 4, 176. *delays have dangerous —s,* H6A III, 2, 33. *these violent delights*

have violent —s, Rom. II, 6, 9. *bring noblest minds to basest —s,* Tim. IV, 3, 471. *what can be avoided whose e. is purposed by the mighty gods?* Caes. II, 2, 27. cf. *the cardinal is the e. of this,* H8 II, 1, 40 (= he is at the bottom of it).

5) fragment, scrap: *ere you flout old —s any further,* Ado I, 1, 290. *with odd old —s stolen out of holy writ,* R3 I, 3, 337 (Qq *old odd —s*).

6) purpose, intention, aim: *neglecting worldly —s,* Tp. I, 2, 89. *their foul —s,* 143. *to work mine e. upon their senses,* V, 53. Meas. I, 3, 5. LLL I, 1, 55. Mids. V, 111. As III, 3, 53. H8 I, 1, 58. II, 1, 124. Cor. V, 3, 4. Ant. III, 2, 37. III, 12, 8. Cymb. III, 5, 63. V, 5, 57. *to this e.* Lucr. 1755. Ado I, 1, 312. H4B IV, 1, 54. *to that e.* Err. IV, 4, 16. As I, 1, 13. III, 3, 42. H6C IV, 1, 64. R3 III, 5, 67. Cor. I, 1, 37. *to what e.* Err. IV, 1, 97. IV, 4, 15. Ado II, 3, 162. LLL V, 2, 304. H4A II, 4, 33. R3 III, 7, 84. *to the e. to crave your assistance,* LLL V, 1, 122. *to the e. they were created,* H6C II, 5, 39. *to no other e.* H6B V, 1, 39. *to a great good e.* Lucr. 528. *bitter to sweet e.* Meas. IV, 6, 8. *to as much e. as give a crutch to the dead,* H8 I, 1, 171.

7) *Still an e.* = ever and anon: *a slave that still an e. turns me to shame,* Gent. IV, 4, 67 (corrupted from *still and anon?*).

End, vb. 1) trans. a) to finish, to cease: *the world's comforter his day's hot task had —ed,* Ven. 530. Lucr. 579. 1079. Pilgr. 226. Tp. IV, 148. Err. I, 1, 2. Mids. II, 2, 63. V, 321. Merch. I, 1, 104. Wint. III, 1, 18. R3 II, 4, 64. Cymb. V, 4, 144 etc. Absolutely: *where she —s, she doth anew begin,* Ven. 60. *to the —ing doom,* Sonn. 55, 12. *as —ing anthem of my endless dolour,* Gentl. III, 1, 240. *and O shall e.* Tw. II, 5, 144.

b) to bring to a close or decision, to consummate, to achieve, to decide: *when wilt thou sort an hour great strifes to e.?* Lucr. 899. *the sword should e. it,* Wiv. I, 1, 41. *to hear it and e. it between them,* 144. *I shall e. this strife,* Merch. II, 3, 20. *here let them e. it,* H6B II, 3, 55. *and kissed the fatal knife, to e. his vow,* Lucr. 1843. *this —ed action,* Ado I, 1, 299. *you have —ed my business,* Cor. IV, 3, 41. *this same day must e. that work the ides of March begun,* Caes. V, 1, 114. *rewards his deeds with doing them, and is content to spend the time to e. it,* Cor. II, 2, 133 (i. e. and is, in achieving what he does, content to have a pastime). *help to reap the fame which he did e. all his,* V, 6, 37 (i. e. I helped to gather the harvest which he consummated as his alone. Perhaps a technical phrase of harvest-work).

c) to destroy, to kill: *for —ing thee no sooner,* Meas. III, 1, 32. Wint. II, 3, 183. H4A V, 3, 9. V, 4, 69. Ant. III, 11, 38. Reflectively: *to e. itself by death,* Lr. IV, 6, 62. *to e. ourselves,* Ant. IV, 14, 22. Absolutely: *time must friend or e.* Troil. I, 2, 84. cf. Gentl. III, 1, 240.

2) intr. a) to be finished, to come to a close, to cease: *then the story aptly —s,* Ven. 716. 846. Sonn. 30, 14. Tp. IV, 265. Gentl. II, 4, 31. Err. I, 1, 28. 138. LLL III, 100. V, 2, 221. 884. Mids. II, 2, 61. 63. III, 2, 373. As V, 4, 204. All's III, 2, 131. IV, 4, 35. V, 1, 25. Tw. II, 3, 44. H6A I, 2, 136. H6B IV, 2, 188. H6C I, 4, 26 etc.

b) to die: *ere they live, to e.* Meas. II, 2, 99. *thus Thisby —s,* Mids. V, 353. Tw. II, 1, 22. H4B

IV, 5, 80. H8 V, 1, 20. Caes. V, 3, 24. Cymb. V, 5, 30. Per. V, 1, 213.

End-all, that which concludes the whole: *that but this blow might be the be-all and the e. here,* Mcb. I, 7, 5.

Endamage, to do mischief to, to injure: Gentl. III, 2, 43. H6A II, 1, 77.

Endamagement, injury, harm: *have hither marched to your e.* John II, 209.

Endanger, to put in hazard: Gentl. V, 4, 133. Wiv. II, 2, 16.

Endart, to let fly and pierce like an arrow: *but no more deep will I e. mine eye,* Rom. I, 3, 98.

Endeared, 1) made dear, raised in price: *thy bosom is e. with all hearts, which I by lacking have supposed dead,* Sonn. 31, 1. *to be e. to a king,* John IV, 2, 228.

2) bound, obliged: *you broke your word, when you were more e. to it than now,* H4B II, 3, 11. *we are so virtuously bound, so infinitely e.* Tim. I, 2, 233. *I am so much e. to that lord; he's ever sending,* III, 2, 36.

Endeavour, subst. effort, labour, exertion: *without sweat or e.* Tp. II, 1, 160. LLL I, 1, 5. V, 2, 863. Merch. III, 4, 48. John II, 81. H4B IV, 3, 130. H5 I, 2, 185. Troil. V, 10, 39. Hml. II, 2, 353. Lr. II, 1, 36. Ant. IV, 10, 9. *your best e.* H6B III, 1, 163. Plur. —*s:* LLL V, 2, 740. All's I, 3, 5. II, 1, 156. H5 V, 2, 25. H8 III, 2, 169. *my best* —*s,* Merch. II, 2, 182. Wint. IV, 4, 542.

Endeavour, vb. 1) trans. to attempt, to strive to effect: *I will e. any thing,* Ado II, 2, 31. —*ed my advancement to the throne,* H6A II, 5, 69. *I'll e. deeds,* Troil. IV, 5, 259. With an infinitive: —*s to trust to himself,* R3 I, 4, 147. Reflectively: *e. thyself to sleep,* Tw. IV, 2, 104 (= strive to sleep).

2) intr. to exert one's self, to do one's best: *you will e. for your French part of such a boy,* H5 V, 2, 228. *we with our travels will e.* Per. II, 4, 56 (M. Edd. *e. it or e. us*).

Ender, he who, or that which makes an end: *to you, my origin and e.* Compl. 222, i. e. the source of my life and of my death, my alpha and omega, beginning and ending.

Ending, subst. 1) close, conclusion: *the world hath e. with thy life,* Ven. 12. *my e. is despair,* Tp. Epil. 15. *here our play has e.* Per. V, 3, 102.

2) destruction, death: *the sad dirge of her certain e.* Lucr. 1612. *the e. of mortality,* John V, 7, 5. *the king is not bound to answer the particular* —*s of his soldiers,* H5 IV, 1, 164. *to the e. of the world,* IV, 3, 58.

3) termination: *a babbling rhyme; very ominous* —*s,* Ado V, 2, 40.

Endless, 1) perpetual, eternal: *e. date of never ending woes,* Lucr. 935. *olives of e. age,* Sonn. 107, 8. *e. night,* R2 I, 3, 177. 222. *right and wrong, between whose e. jar justice resides,* Troil. I, 3, 117.

2) infinite, excessive, unlimited: *my e. dolour,* Gentl. III, 1, 240. *it will fall to e. ruin,* Merch. IV, 1, 142 (Qq *cureless*). *an infinite and e. liar,* All's III, 6, 11. *thou and e. night have done me shame,* John V, 6, 12 (i.e. extremely dark. M. Edd. *eyeless*). *sing her e. praise,* H6A I, 6, 20. *heaven, from thy e. goodness,* H8 V, 5, 1.

Endow, 1) to settle a dower on, to portion: *though she were* —*ed with all that Adam had*

left him, Ado II, 1, 259. *myself and all, will I withal e. a child of thine,* R3 IV, 4, 249. *how shall she be* —*ed,* Tim. I, 1, 139. *thy half o' the kingdom wherein I thee* —*ed,* Lr. II, 4, 184.

2) to furnish, enrich: *whom she best* —*ed,* Sonn. 11, 11. *I do not think so fair an outward . . .* —*s a man but he,* Cymb. I, 1, 24. Followed by *with:* —*ed thy purposes with words,* Tp. I, 2, 357.

Endowment, 1) property, revenue: *base men by his* —*s are made great,* R2 II, 3, 139.

2) gift, accomplishment: Cymb. I, 4, 6. Per. III, 2, 27. V, 1, 117.

Endue, see *Indue.*

Endurance (O. Edd. *indurance*), suffering, sufferance: *past the e. of a block,* Ado II, 1, 246. *the thousandth part of my e.* Per. V, 1, 137. *and to have heard you without e. further,* H8 V, 1, 122 (i.e. without further suffering; according to some Intpp. = durance, confinement).

Endure, 1) intr. a) to last: *their verdure still e.* Ven. 507. *a dateless lively heat, still to e.* Sonn. 153, 6. *youth's a stuff will not e.* Tw. II, 3, 53.

b) to remain, to continue: *my mind . . . still pure doth in her poisoned closet yet e.* Lucr. 1659. *to e. friends,* Cor. I, 6, 58.

c) to suffer with patience, to bear up under adversity: *have patience and e.* Ado IV, 1, 256. *'tis past* —*ing,* Wint. II, 1, 2. *I will e.* Lr. III, 4, 18. V, 3, 211. 316.

2) trans. a) to bear, to sustain without breaking or yielding, to bear up against: *e. the tooth-ache patiently,* Ado V, 1, 36. *to e. her loud alarums,* Shr. I, 1, 131. *mortal ears might hardly e. the din,* 178. *'twill e. wind and weather,* Tw. I, 5, 255. *whose honour and whose honesty till now* —*d all weathers,* Wint. V, 1, 195. *not able to e. the sight of day,* R2 III, 2, 52. H4A I, 2, 212. H4B II, 1, 87. H5 II, 1, 10. II, 2, 180. H6B I, 4, 41. II, 4, 8. IV, 2, 60. R3 I, 2, 45. 127. H8 III, 2, 389. V, 4, 67. Tim. III, 5, 43. Caes. I, 2, 99. IV, 2, 25. V, 3, 192. 193. Lr. III, 4, 3. Ant. III, 10, 18. Per. IV, 1, 56. With an inf.: *he that can e. to follow with allegiance a fallen lord,* Ant. III, 13, 43.

b) to bear or suffer without opposition, to allow, to take up with: *e. this wooden slavery,* Tp. III, 1, 61. *I could not e. a husband with a beard,* Ado II, 1, 32. *not to be* —*ed,* III, 3, 37. *whether you can e. the livery of a nun,* Mids. I, 1, 70. *I will no longer e. it,* As I, 1, 25. 75. III, 5, 96. IV, 3, 69. Shr. V, 2, 94. Wint. IV, 4, 481. H4A I, 3, 18. H5 V, 2, 337. H6A II, 4, 115. H6B V, 1, 90. R3 I, 3, 42. III, 7, 230. Cor. II, 3, 204. Tit. II, 3, 88. IV, 4, 51. Rom. I, 5, 78. Caes. IV, 3, 29. 41. Mcb. V, 4, 9. Hml. III, 3, 5. Lr. I, 3, 6. I, 4, 223. V, 1, 15. V, 2, 9. Oth. III, 3, 390. IV, 2, 180. Ant. I, 2, 179. Cymb. III, 5, 5. *I cannot e.* = I cannot bear, cannot abide: Ado II, 1, 284. II, 3, 248. H4B II, 4, 3. 203. cf. *I could e. any thing before but a cat,* All's IV, 3, 266. And without *can, not to e.* = to detest: *howbeit that I e. him not,* Oth. II, 1, 297. Followed by an inf.: *she cannot e. to hear tell of a husband,* Ado II, 1, 362. H6B IV, 7, 44. H8 III, 2, 278. *the lion did e. to have his princely paws pared all away,* Tit. II, 3, 151. Inf. without *to: your betters have* —*ed me say my mind,* Shr. IV, 3, 75.

c) to suffer, to have to bear, to undergo,

to be exposed to: *their dolour others have —d,* Lucr. 1582. *the mortal moon hath her eclipse —d,* Sonn. 107, 5. *this I e. for thee,* Gentl. V, 3, 15. *when he shall e. the like,* Ado V, 1, 30. LLL I, 1, 132. V, 2, 353. As V, 4, 179. R2 V, 5, 30. H6A I, 4, 57. II, 3, 38. R3 I, 3, 106. IV, 4, 304. Cor. V, 6, 142. Tim. II, 2, 148. Caes. I, 2, 326. Mcb. V, 5, 36. Lr. III, 7, 60. Cymb. II, 1, 62. V, 5, 299. Per. III, 2, 6. V, 1, 88.

Endymion, a youth loved by the goddess of the moon: Merch. V, 109.

Enemy, 1) foe, adversary: Ven. 887. Lucr. 674. 1171. 1470. Sonn. 139, 10. Tp. 1, 2, 179. 466. III, 3, 89. IV, 264. Gentl. II, 6, 29. III, 2, 35. IV, 1, 8. Wiv. III, 4, 93. Ado IV, 1, 301. V, 1, 98. Mids. IV, 1, 147. Merch. I, 3, 136. III, 1, 60. III, 2, 265. As I, 2, 238. 267. II, 3, 11. 18. II, 5, 7. V, 4, 47 etc. etc. *be —ies with me,* H5 II, 1, 108 (after the analogy of the preceding *'be friends with me'*). *that thrust had been mine e. indeed,* Oth. V, 1, 24. Followed by *to:* Sonn. 28, 5. Tp. I, 2, 121. All's I, 1, 65. Tw. III, 4, 108. John II, 243. H6A III, 1, 18. H6B III, 1, 258. III, 2, 57. H6C V, 4, 28. R3 II, 2, 37. Tit. II, 3, 183 etc.

Used adjectively: *this e. town,* Cor. IV, 4, 24. *followed his e. king,* Lr. V, 3, 220. *she would not hold out e. for ever,* Merch. IV, 1, 447. *that which all the Parthian darts, though e., lost aim,* Ant. IV, 14, 71.

2) fiend, devil: *O cunning e., that, to catch a saint, with saints dost bait thy hook,* Meas. II, 2, 180. *wherein the pregnant e. does much,* Tw. II, 2, 29; cf. III, 4, 108 and Mcb. III, 1, 69.

Enew, a term of falconry, = to drive back to the water, as the hawk does water-fowl; and hence = to pursue eagerly; conjectured for *emmew* in Meas. III, 1, 91.

Enfeeble, to weaken: Sonn. 86, 14. H5 III, 6, 154. H6A I, 4, 69 (*—d* quadrisyll.). Cymb. V, 2, 4.

Enfeoff, to give in vassalage, to make subservient: *—ed himself to popularity,* H4A III, 2, 69.

Enfetter, to enchain, to tie: *his soul is so —ed to her love,* Oth. II, 3, 351.

Enfold, see *Infold.*

Enforce, 1) to force, constrain, oblige; to urge: *art —d to seek some fresher stamp,* Sonn. 82, 7. *inward joy —d my heart to smile,* Gentl. I, 2, 63. Ado V, 4, 8. LLL V, 2, 864. Merch. III, 2, 33. III, 4, 9. V, 216. Shr. III, 2, 109. R2 I, 4, 45. H4A V, 1, 65. H5 III, 6, 99. H6A I, 2, 38. H6B IV, 4, 17. H6C I, 1, 229. 230. Rom. V, 3, 47. *e. them to this place,* Tp. V, 100. *what Tranio did, myself —d him to,* Shr. V, 1, 132. *to e. a poor widow to so rough a course,* H4B II, 1, 89. IV, 3, 55. *that lack of means e. you not to evil,* V, 5, 71. R3 III, 5, 46. III, 7, 223. With an inf. without *to: my father would e. me marry Thurio,* Gentl. IV, 3, 16. *if wrongs be evils and e. us kill,* Tim. III, 5, 36. Absolutely: *now I want spirits to e., art to enchant,* Tp. Epil. 14.

2) to obtain by force, to cause or provoke irresistibly: *drops, —d by sympathy,* Lucr. 1229. *thou —st laughter,* LLL III, 76. *shall I e. thy love,* IV, 1, 82. *e. a thievish living on the common road,* As II, 3, 32. Shr. Ind. 1, 128. John I, 18. II, 448. R2 I, 1, 6. H5 III, 7, 31. Tim. V, 4, 45. Partic. *—d* = a) involuntary: *forgive me this —d wrong,* Merch. V, 240. *this —d cause,* John V, 2, 30. *an —d pilgrimage,* R2 I, 3, 264. *by an —d obedience of planetary*

influence, Lr. I, 2, 135. b) constrained, counterfeited, not coming from the heart: *—d smiles,* R3 III, 5, 9. *an —d ceremony,* Caes. IV, 2, 21.

Followed by prepositions, a) *from,* = α) to obtain by force from: *as from this cold flint I —d this fire,* Lucr. 181. Ant. I, 3, 7. Cymb. IV, 3, 11. V, 5, 283. — β) to drive with violence from: *and are —d from our most quiet there by the rough torrent of occasion,* H4B IV, 1, 71. *as swift as stones —d from the old Assyrian slings,* H5 IV, 7, 65 (cf. *enforcement* in H4B I, 1, 120). — b) by *on,* = to press sth. upon: *I will no more e. my office on you,* All's II, 1, 129. — c) by *to,* in the same sense: *I will e. it easily to my love,* John II, 515.

3) to open with violence: *the locks, each one by him —d, retires his ward,* Lucr. 303. Hence = to violate, to ravish: *lamenting some —d chastity,* Mids. III, 1, 205. *she was —d, stained and deflowered,* Tit. V, 3, 38. *thy mistress —d,* Cymb. IV, 1, 18. cf. *love is blind and —s,* H5 V, 2, 328. *—d* adjectively: *—d hate, instead of love's coy touch, shall rudely tear thee,* Lucr. 668 (i. e. the hateful proceeding of rape, of ravishment).

4) to urge, to ply hard: *if he evade us here, e. him with his envy to the people,* Cor. III, 3, 3. *the flint who, much —d, shows a hasty spark,* Caes. IV, 3, 112.

5) to urge, to demand with importunity: *when he's returned, against Aumerle we will e. his trial,* R2 IV, 90. *e. the present execution of what we chance to sentence,* Cor. III, 3, 21. *e. their charity,* Lr. II, 3, 20.

6) to urge, to set off, to lay much stress upon: *abide here and e. them* (his speeches) *against him,* Meas. V, 267. *e. his pride, and his old hate unto you,* Cor. II, 3, 227. *his glory not extenuated, nor his offences —d,* Caes. III, 2, 43. *e. no further the griefs between you,* Ant. II, 2, 99. Absolutely: *we will extenuate rather than e.* Ant. V, 2, 125.

7) to put in act with severity, to cause to take effect with strictness: *to e. or qualify the laws,* Meas. I, 1, 66. *—d the law against it,* IV, 4, 25. *the torture, O, e. it,* Oth. V, 2, 369. Joined with *on: the law, with all his might to e. it on,* Oth. I, 2, 16.

Enforcedly, involuntarily: Tim. IV, 3, 241.

Enforcement, 1) force applied, constraint: As II, 7, 118. All's V, 3, 107. H4B I, 1, 120 (*upon e.*). R3 III, 7, 233.* V, 3, 238.

2) violation, rape: *what wrong else by foul e. might be done to me,* Lucr. 1623. *his e. of the city wives,* R3 III, 7, 8.

Enfranch, to set free from slavery: *my —ed bondman,* Ant. III, 13, 149 (some M. Edd. *enfranchised*).

Enfranchise, to set at liberty, to deliver: Ven. 396. Gentl. II, 4, 90. III, 1, 151. Ado I, 3, 34. LLL III, 121. Wint. II, 2, 61. R3 I, 1, 110. Tit. IV, 2, 125. Tim. I, 1, 106. Ant. I, 1, 23.

Enfranchisement, 1) release from prison or slavery, deliverance: John IV, 2, 52. R2 I, 3, 90. H6B V, 1, 113. Caes. III, 1, 81.

2) restoration to public rights, repeal from exile: *to beg e. immediate on his knees,* R2 III, 3, 114. *to beg e. for Publius Cimber,* Caes. III, 1, 57.

Enfree, to set at liberty: *to render him, for the —d Antenor, the fair Cressid,* Troil. IV, 1, 38.

Enfreedom, to set at liberty: LLL III, 125 (Armado's speech).

Engage, 1) to pawn, to pledge: *I to thee —d a prince's word*, Err. V, 162. *I have —d myself to a dear friend, —d my friend to his mere enemy*, Merch. III, 2, 264. 265. *this to be true, I do e. my life*, As V, 4, 172. *there is my honour's pawn; e. it to the trial*, R2 IV, 56. 71 (= take it up as a pawn). *I will e. my word to thee*, H4A II, 4, 563. *suffered his kinsman March to be —d in Wales, there without ransom to lie forfeited*, IV, 3, 95.* *Westmoreland, that was —d, did bear it*, V, 2, 44. *let all my land be sold. 'tis all —d*, Tim. II, 2, 155. *what other oath than honesty to honesty —d*, Caes. II, 1, 127. *I here e. my word*, Oth. III, 3, 462.

2) to bind by contract or promise: *enough, I am —d; I will challenge him*, Ado IV, 1, 335. *hold it sin to break the vow I am —d in*, LLL IV, 3, 178. *too old, to be —d to young*, Mids. I, 1, 138. *come —d by my oath*, R2 I, 3, 17. *I do stand —d to many Greeks, in the faith of valour, to appear to them*, Troil. V, 3, 68.

3) to enlist, to embark in an affair, to venture: *under whose blessed cross we are impressed and —d to fight*, H4A I, 1, 21. *a quarrel which hath our several honours all —d to make it gracious*, Troil. II, 2, 124. *—ing and redeeming of himself with such a careless force*, V, 5, 39. *we have —d ourselves too far*, Ant. IV, 7, 1.

4) to bind, to tie: *we all that are —d to this loss*, H4B I, 1, 180. *O limed soul, that, struggling to be free, art more —d*, Hml. III, 3, 69.

Engagement, obligation? or affair, enterprise embarked in?: *all my —s I will construe to thee*, Caes. II, 1, 307.

Engaol, to imprison: *within my mouth you have —ed my tongue*, R2 I, 3, 166.

Engender, to beget, to produce: LLL IV, 3, 295. Merch. III, 2, 67. As II, 7, 123. Shr. IV, 1, 175. H6A III, 1, 39. 181. H6C V, 3, 13. Troil. II, 3, 170; cf. Tim. IV, 3, 181. Caes. V, 3, 71. Oth. I, 3, 409. Ant. III, 13, 159.

Engild, to gild, to make splendent: Mids. III, 2, 187.

Engine, 1) any device or contrivance: *their promises, enticements, oaths, tokens, and all these —s of lust*, All's III, 5, 21. *she shall file our —s with advice*, Tit. II, 1, 123. *devise —s for my life*, Oth. IV, 2, 221.

2) any instrument or implement: *the e. of her thoughts* (viz the tongue) Ven. 367. Tit. III, 1, 82. *an e. fit for my proceeding*, Gentl. III, 1, 138 (i. e. a rope-ladder). Especially any machine for purposes of war: *sword, pike, knife, gun, or need of any e., would I not have*, Tp. II, 1, 161. *the ram that batters down the wall, they place before his hand that made the e.* Troil. I, 3, 208. *let him, like an e. not portable, lie under this report*, II, 3, 143. *when he walks, he moves like an e.* Cor. V, 4, 19. *the fatal e.* Tit. V, 3, 86 (the Trojan horse). *you mortal —s* (cannon) Oth. III, 3, 355. An instrument of torture: *that, like an e. wrenched my frame of nature from the fixed place*, Lr. I, 4, 290.

Enginer (the later Ff and some M. Edd. *engineer*), contriver, inventor: *does tire the e.* Oth. II, 1, 65 (O. Edd. *ingeniver*). Especially = contriver of means for military purposes; a pioneer: *there's Achilles, a rare e.! if Troy be not taken till these two*

undermine it, the walls will stand, Troil. II, 3, 8. *'tis the sport to have the e. hoist with his own petar: and 't shall go hard but I will delve one yard below their mines*, Hml. III, 4, 206.

Engirt, to surround, encompass, enclose: *so white a friend —s so white a foe*, Ven. 364. *that gold must round e. these brows*, H6B V, 1, 99. Partic. engirt: *this siege that hath e. his marriage*, Lucr. 221. *grossly e. with daring infamy*, 1173 (enclosed as by a besieging enemy). *my body round e. with misery*, H6B III, 1, 200 (cf. *Embrace* 3.).

England (perhaps trisyll. in R2 IV, 17), 1) the country: Tp. II, 2, 29. Wiv. I, 1, 303. Err. III, 2, 128. Merch. I, 2, 72. I, 3, 21. II, 7, 55. III, 2, 271. As I, 1, 123. Tw. III, 2, 51. Mcb. II, 3, 143. III, 1, 31. III, 6, 46. IV, 1, 142. IV, 3, 148. Hml. III, 1, 177. IV, 3, 48. V, 1, 162 etc. Oth. II, 3, 78. 91. Very often in the Histories. Fem.: H5 II, 4, 24. R3 V, 5, 23. Neut.: John II, 95. 202. V, 7, 112. 118. R2 II, 1, 65. H5 II, 4, 9.

2) the king of England: John II, 56. 341. 424. III, 4, 8 (*bloody E. into E. gone*). H5 III, 5, 48 (*Harry E.*). III, 6, 131. V, 2, 12 etc. Mcb. IV, 3, 43. 189.

English, adj. pertaining to England: Wiv. II, 3, 62. Meas. I, 2, 34. All's IV, 3, 299. IV, 5, 41. Mcb. II, 3, 15. III, 6, 26. V, 2, 1. V, 3, 8. 18. Very often in the Histories (*E. John*, John II, 10. *E. Henry*, H6A II, 1, 36. III, 2, 80. III, 3, 66. *E. John Talbot*, IV, 2, 3. 30).

Substantively, 1) the English language: Wiv. I, 3, 55. I, 4, 6 (*the king's E.*). II, 1, 143. III, 1, 80. IV, 3, 8. V, 5, 142. 152. Merch. I, 2, 77. R2 I, 3, 160. H4A II, 4, 27. III, 1, 121. H8 III, 1, 46. V, 5, 15.

2) the English people or army: Merch. II, 8, 29. All's II, 3, 100. Mcb. V, 3, 56. Oth. II, 3, 81. Very often in the Histories, f. i.: *fly, noble E.* John V, 4, 10. Sometimes = Englishmen: *when E. measure backward their own ground*, V, 5, 3. *the blood of E. shall manure the ground*, R2 IV, 137. *a power of E.* H4A I, 1, 22. H4B IV, 4, 98. cf. H5 I, 2, 111. IV, 3, 104.

Englished, translated into English: Wiv. I, 3, 52.

Englishman, a native of England: Pilgr. 212. Wiv. II, 3, 65. Merch. I, 2, 87. John V, 2, 145. V, 4, 42. R2 I, 1, 66. I, 3, 309. H5 II, 2, 125. IV, 7, 129. R3 II, 1, 69. H8 III, 1, 84. Oth. II, 3, 82. Plur. *Englishmen*: R2 III, 3, 44. H5 III, 7, 169. V, 2, 395. H6B III, 1, 311. = English: *and put the Englishmen unto the sword*, H6B III, 1, 284.

Englishwoman: *the princess is the better E.* H5 V, 2, 124 (= speaks better English).

Englut, to swallow: H5 IV, 3, 83. Tim. II, 2, 175. Oth. I, 3, 57.

Engraffed (cf. *Graff*), rooted, fixed deep and firm: *the imperfections of long e. condition*. Lr. I, 1, 301 (Qq *engrafted*). *one of an e. infirmity*, Oth. II, 3, 145 (Edd. *ingraft*). Followed by *to*, = firmly attached, grown into one: *so much e. to Falstaff*, H4B II, 2, 67 (cf. *Enrooted*).

Engraft, to inoculate: *as he* (viz time) *takes from you, I e. you new*, Sonn. 15, 14. *Engrafted* = rooted: *in the —ed love he bears to Caesar*, Caes. II, 1, 184. Lr. I, 1, 301 (Ff *engraffed*). With *to*, = firmly attached: *I make my love —ed to this store*, Sonn. 37, 8.

Engrave, to cut as with a chisel, to imprint: R3 IV, 4, 272. Part. *—d*: Gentl. II, 7, 4. H6A II, 2, 15. *Engraven*: Lucr. 203.

Engross, 1) to make gross, to fatten: *not sleeping, to e. his idle body,* R3 III, 7, 76.

2) to amass: *Percy is but my factor, to e. up glorious deeds on my behalf,* H4A III, 2, 148. *for this they have —ed and piled up the cankered heaps of strange-achieved gold,* H4B IV, 5, 71. *your mariners are muleters, reapers, people —ed by swift impress,* Ant. III, 7, 37.

3) to purchase or seize in the gross, to take the whole of: *my next self thou harder hast —ed,* Sonn. 133, 6. *—ed opportunities to meet her,* Wiv. II, 2, 203. *if thou —est all the griefs,* All's III, 2, 68. *seal with a righteous kiss a dateless bargain to —ing death,* Rom. V, 3, 115.

4) to make a fair copy of: *which in a set hand fairly is —ed,* R3 III, 6, 2.

Engrossment, amassment, accumulation: H4B IV, 5, 80.

Enguard, to surround as with a guard, to arm: *he may e. his dotage with their powers, and hold our lives in mercy,* Lr. I, 4, 349.

Enigma, riddle: LLL III, 72. Cor. II, 3, 96.

Enigmatical, like a riddle, darkly expressed: Ado V, 4, 27.

Enjoin, 1) to bind, to oblige; followed by *to: I would bend under any heavy weight that he'll e. me to,* Ado V, 1, 287. *I am —ed by oath to observe three things,* Merch. II, 9, 9. *to be by oath —ed to this,* Wint. III, 3, 53. *— ed,* absolutely, = bound in duty or by oath: *of — ed penitents there's four or five, to great Saint Jaques bound, already at my house,* All's III, 5, 97.

2) to order, to charge: *those logs that you are —ed to pile,* Tp. III, 1, 17. *she —ed me to write some lines,* Gentl. II, 1, 93. 110. Rom. IV, 2, 19. Per. II, 4, 55. *we e. thee, that thou carry this bastard hence,* Wint. II, 3, 173. *it was —ed him,* LLL V, 2, 718.

Enjoint, see *Injoint.*

Enjoy, 1) to feel, obtain or possess with pleasure: *they that love best their loves shall not e.* Ven. 1164. *O happiness —ed but of a few,* Lucr. 22. 512. Sonn. 9, 10. 129, 5. Wiv. II, 2, 249. 265. III, 5, 138. V, 5, 116. Meas. I, 2, 194. LLL III, 46. Merch. II, 6, 13. III, 2, 29. As V, 2, 4. 11. Shr. III, 2, 138. Tw. III, 4, 99. Wint. IV, 4, 539. V, 1, 215. John I, 135. R2 II, 1, 111. II, 3, 16. H4B IV, 4, 12. 108. H5 IV, 1, 254. 299. H6A V, 3, 154. 159. V, 4, 73. 132. H6B II, 4, 39. IV, 10, 19. H6C I, 1, 175. I, 2, 12. II, 5, 50. III, 1, 65. III, 2, 95. IV, 6, 52. R3 I, 3, 84. 152. 154. 155. IV, 1, 84. V, 3, 336. V, 5, 7. H8 III, 2, 248. Troil. III, 3, 88. Cor. V, 3, 106. Tit. I, 311. II, 3, 22. Rom. III, 2, 28. Caes. II. 1, 230. Lr. I, 2, 56. V, 1, 58. V, 3, 78. Oth. I, 3, 365. IV, 2, 220. Cymb. I, 4, 161. I, 6, 91. II, 1, 70. II, 4, 43. 126.

2) to possess or obtain: *with what I most e. contented least,* Sonn. 29, 8. *what we have we prize not to the worth whiles we e. it,* Ado IV, 1, 221. *all that he —s,* John II, 240. *to lose what they e.* R2 II, 4, 13. *wherein it shall appear that your demands are just, you shall e. them,* H4B IV, 1, 145. *it is not worth the —ing,* H6B III, 1, 334. *e. thy plainness,* Ant. II, 6, 80 (i. e. lose it not). *what do you esteem it at? more than the world —s,* Cymb. I, 4, 86. Absolutely: *to e. by rage and war,* R2 II, 4, 14.

Enjoyer, possessor, proprietor: *now proud as an e. and anon doubting the filching age will steal his treasure,* Sonn. 75, 5.

Enkindle, to kindle, to put in a flame, to inflame: John IV, 2, 163. V, 2, 87. Troil. II, 2, 63. Caes. II, 1, 249. Lr. III, 7, 86. *that trusted home might yet e. you unto the crown,* Mcb. I, 3, 121 (= incite, stimulate).

Enlard, to fatten: *to e. his fat already pride,* Troil. II, 3, 205 (cf. *lard* in Tim IV, 3, 12).

Enlarge, 1) to set at large, to give free scope to, to spread abroad, to vent: *to tie up envy evermore —d,* Sonn. 70, 12. *in other places she —th her mirth so far that there is shrewd construction made of her,* Wiv. II, 2, 231. *one body should be filled with all graces wide —d,* As III, 2, 151 (= spread through the world). *lest your displeasure should e. itself to wrathful terms,* Troil. V, 2, 37. *in my tent e. your griefs,* Caes. IV, 2, 46. *her obsequies have been as far —d as we have warrantise,* Hml. V, 1, 249 (= extended, exempt from restrictions).

2) to set at liberty: *he shall e. him,* Tw. V, 285. H4A III, 2, 115. H5 II, 2, 40. 57. *the poor third is up, till death e. his confine,* Ant. III, 5, 13.

3) to extend, to spread, to make of greater extent: *and doth e. his rising with the blood of fair king Richard,* H4B I, 1, 204. *a circle in the water which never ceases to e. itself,* H6A I, 2, 134.

Enlargement, 1) release from confinement: *give e. to the swain,* LLL III, 5. *for e. striving,* H4A III, 1, 31. H6A II, 5, 30. H6C IV, 6, 5.

2) liberty: *you are curbed from that e. by the consequence of the crown,* Cymb. II, 3, 125.

Enlighten, to shed light on, to make bright: *and to e. thee, gave eyes to blindness,* Sonn. 152, 11 (i. e. to make thee bright, I made myself blind).

Enlink, to connect, to join: *all fell feats —ed to waste and desolation,* H5 III, 3, 18.

Enmesh, to ensnare: *the net that shall e. them all,* Oth. II, 3, 368.

Enmew, see *Emmew.*

Enmity, the state of being an enemy, hateful opposition: Lucr. 503. Sonn. 55, 9. Tp. II, 1, 116. Err. I, 1, 5. Mids. IV, 1, 150. H4B Ind. 9. H6A III, 1, 116. H6C II, 5, 75. IV, 6, 98. R3 II, 1, 50. V, 5, 21. Troil. II, 2, 137. Cor. IV, 4, 18. V, 3, 104. Tit. V, 1, 131. V, 3, 107. Rom. II, 2, 73. V, 3, 304. Lr. II, 4, 212. *to be at e.:* R2 II, 2, 68. R3 II, 1, 60. *holds such an e. with . .,* Hml. I, 5, 65. *—ies,* Ant. II, 1, 43.

Ennoble, to raise to the rank of nobility: All's II, 3, 179. R3 I, 3, 81.

Enobarbe, name in Ant. II, 7, 129.

Enobarbus, the same: Ant. I, 2, 88. II, 2, 1. III, 2, 53 etc.

Enormity, perversity: *in what e. is Marcius poor in, that you two have not in abundance? He's poor in no one fault,* Cor. II, 1, 18.

Enormous, perverse, disordered: *from this e. state,* Lr. II, 2, 176.

Enough (rhyming to *off,* Gentl. V, 1, 12), 1) sufficient quantity, sufficient, sufficiently; used as a subst. as well as an adj. (relating to a sing. or plur. indiscriminately) and adv.: *he hath e.* Merch. II, 2, 160. *room e.* Tp. I, 1, 9. *targe e.* I, 2, 110. *bolts e.* Meas. V, 350. *we cannot misuse him e.* Wiv. IV, 2, 105. Sonn. 34, 5. 111, 14. Tp. I, 2, 314. 492. II, 2, 165. Gentl. II, 4, 143. III, 2, 67. Wiv. III, 3, 47. III, 5, 56. IV, 1, 69. IV, 2, 72. V, 2, 11. Meas. I, 4, 2. II, 2, 170. III, 2, 240. IV, 3, 178. V, 215. 308. Err.

IV, 1, 41. V, 58. Mids. I, 2, 78. II, 2, 125. Merch. IV, 1, 127. 159. Tw. I, 1, 7. V, 78 (*on base and ground e.* = from a sufficient motive) etc. etc. Followed by *of: e. of this,* Rom. I, 3, 49. Cymb. I, 4, 130. *you may have e. of Hector,* Troil. IV, 5, 263. Preceding the word to which it relates: *there is not e. leek to swear by,* H5 V, 1, 52 (Fluellen's speech). *not e. barbarous,* Per. IV, 2, 70. *the greatness whereof I cannot e. commend,* Merch. IV, 1, 159. Relating to an adj. preceding its subst.: *with simular proof e.* Cymb. V, 5, 200 (cf. Ado IV, 2, 87 and Troil. V, 1, 57).

2) very much, very, quite, pretty well, rather: *beat him e.: after a little time I'll beat him too,* Tp. III, 2, 93. *if thou be'st rated by thy estimation, thou dost deserve e., and yet e. may not extend so far as to the lady,* Merch. II, 7, 27. *more free than he is jealous. That's e.* Wint. II, 3, 30. *a wild dedication of yourselves to miseries e.* IV, 4, 579. *a rich fellow e.* Ado IV, 2, 87. *an honest fellow e.* Troil. V, 1, 57. *I have reason good e.* Tw. II, 3, 158. *if we recover that, we are sure e.* Gentl. V, 1, 12. *your thief thinks it little e.* Meas. IV, 2, 49. Merch. II, 5, 46. H4A II, 4, 164. *like e.* = very probably: Sonn. 87, 2. Ado II, 3, 108. As IV, 1, 69. H4A IV, 4, 7. Oth. III, 4, 190. Ant. III, 13, 29. *well e.* = pretty well, quite well: Gentl. II, 1, 55. Ado II, 1, 116. Tw. I, 3, 106. II, 3, 87. H4A II, 2, 29. III, 3, 73. Ant. III, 3, 50 etc.

Enow, adj. sufficient, used as the plural of *enough: we were Christians e.* Merch. III, 5, 24. *his losses, e. to press a royal merchant down,* IV, 1, 29. *we have French quarrels e.* H5 IV, 1, 240. IV, 2, 28. IV, 3, 20. IV, 5, 19. H6A V, 4, 56. Mcb. II, 3, 7. IV, 2, 57. Ant. I, 4, 11.

Enpatron, to be the patron saint of, to have under one's patronage or guardianship: *for these must your oblations be, since I their altar, you e. me,* Compl. 224.

Enpierced, pierced, wounded: *I am too sore e. with his shaft,* Rom. I, 4, 19.

Enquire, see *Inquire.*

Enrage, to put in rage, to make furious: H4B IV, 1, 211. Troil. I, 3, 38. Cor. I, 3, 69. Mcb. III, 4, 118. IV, 3, 229. Partic. —*d,* 1) furious: Lucr. 1562. Gentl. II, 6, 38. Ado III, 3, 170. Tw. V, 81. John II, 451. V, 2, 57. H4B I, 1, 152. H5 III, 3, 25. H6A I, 1, 124. Lr. IV, 2, 75 (*thereat*). IV, 6, 71 (Qq *enridged*). Ant. IV, 12, 31 (*against*). — 2) raging as in a fever: *being now* —*d with grief,* H4B I, 1, 144. 3) mad with love and desire: *being so* —*d, desire doth lend her force,* Ven. 29. *his love, perceiving how he is* —*d,* 317. *she loves him with an* —*d affection,* Ado II, 3, 105.

Enrank, to place in order: *no leisure had he to e. his men,* H6A I, 1, 115.

Enrapt, transported, inspired: *am like a prophet suddenly e.* Troil. V, 3, 65.

Enrich, to make rich or precious: *and much e. thy book,* Sonn. 77, 14. *as art and practice hath* —*ed any,* Meas. I, 1, 13. *the captive is* —*ed,* LLL IV, 1, 76; cf. H6A V, 5, 51. Mids. I, 1, 250. As I, 1, 108. R2 I, 3, 141. II, 3, 61. R3 III, 7, 77. Oth. III, 3, 160. Cymb. II, 2, 30. Followed by *with: e. the poor with treasures,* Ven. 1150. *such fiery numbers as the prompting eyes of beauty's tutors have* —*ed you with,* LLL IV, 3, 323. H4A III, 3, 181. H5 III Chor. 22. R3 II, 3, 19. III, 1, 85. V, 5, 33. Tim. V, 1, 6.

Hence = to make dear, to adorn, to give higher worth to: *with the annexions of fair gems* —*ed,* Compl. 208. *what lady is that which doth e. the hand of yonder knight?* Rom. I, 5, 43. *her pretty action did outsell her gift, and yet* —*ed it too,* Cymb. II, 4, 103.

Enridged, formed into ridges (cf. Ven. 820. Lucr. 1439): *horns whelked and waved like the e. sea,* Lr. IV, 6, 71 (Ff *enraged*).

Enring, to encircle: Mids. IV, 1, 49.

Enrobe, to attire: Wiv. IV, 6, 41. Merch. I, 1, 34.

Enrolled, registered, recorded: Meas. I, 2, 170. LLL I, 1, 38. 41. 46. H6C II, 1, 173. H8 I, 2, 119. Cor. III, 1, 292. Caes. III, 2, 41.

Enrooted, grown into one, coalesced: *his foes are so e. with his friends that, plucking to unfix an enemy, he doth unfasten so and shake a friend,* H4B IV, 1, 207 (cf. *Engraffed*).

Enround, to surround, enclose: H5 IV Chor. 36.

Enscheduled, written down: H5 V, 2, 73.

Ensconce, see *Insconce.*

Enseamed, defiled, filthy: *in the rank sweat of an e. bed,* Hml. III, 4, 92 (*Enseam* was the technical name for the whole process of cleansing the hawk from internal defilement).

Ensear, to dry up: *e. thy fertile and conceptious womb,* Tim. IV, 3, 187.

Ensheltered, sheltered, covered from injury: Oth. II, 1, 18.

Enshield, enshielded, as within a shield, covered, protected: *these black masks proclaim an e. beauty,* Meas. II, 4, 80.

Enshrine, to enclose as in a shrine, to sanctify: H6A III, 2, 119.

Ensign, 1) banner, standard: Ven. 107. R2 IV, 94. H6A V, 4, 174. Rom. V, 3, 94. Caes. V, 1, 80. V, 3, 3. Cymb. V, 5, 480.

2) sign, badge: *mine honour's* —*s humbled at thy feet,* Tit. I, 252.

Ensinewed, joining one's sinews to those of another, allied: *all members of our cause that are e. to this action,* H4B IV, 1, 172 (cf. John V, 2, 63. Ff *insinewed*).

Enskyed, placed in heaven, celestial: Meas. I, 4, 34.

Ensnare, to lay snares or nets for: Lucr. 584. R3 I, 3, 243. Oth. II, 1, 170. V, 2, 302. *thy beauty hath* —*d thee to this night,* Lucr. 485, i. e. has entrapped thee to the advantage of this night.

Ensteeped, steeped, lying under water: Oth. II, 1, 70.

Ensue, 1) to follow, to come after: a) trans.: *repentant tears e. the deed,* Lucr. 502. *let not to-morrow then e. to-day,* R2 II, 1, 197.

b) intr.: *what canst thou boast of things long since, or any thing* —*ing,* Ven. 1078. *as one shifts, another straight* —*s,* Lucr. 1104. *heart-sorrow and a clear life* —*ing,* Tp. III, 3, 82. Gentl. II, 2, 11. As I, 3, 32 (to follow as a consequence). H4B III, 1, 55. H6B I, 1, 50. H8 I, 1, 27. I, 2, 168. Cor. V, 3, 148. Oth. II, 3, 9. Ant. IV, 14, 77. Per. Prol. 41.

2) to happen in a train of events: *shame that might e. by that her death,* Lucr. 1263. *to bear up against what would e.* Tp. I, 2, 158. Wiv. I, 3, 35.

Err. II, 2, 193. V, 78. John IV, 3, 61. V, 1, 16. H6A III, 1, 188. Troil. IV, 5, 217. Fer. III Prol. 53. With *of: of thy misprision must perforce e. some true love turned,* Mids. III, 2, 90. *what will e. hereof,* R2 II, 1, 212. *what of her —s I list not prophesy,* Wint. IV, 1, 25 (= what becomes of her).

3) to be about to happen: *to effect your —ing marriage,* Ado III, 2, 102. *would the scandal vanish with my life, how happy then were my —ing death,* R2 II, 1, 68. *men's minds mistrust —ing dangers,* R3 II, 3, 43 (Ff *pursuing danger*). *at hand —s his piteous end,* R3 IV, 4, 74. *inkling of an —ing evil,* H8 II, 1, 141. *nor here, nor what — s,* Cymb. III, 2, 81. *left me breath nothing to think on but —ing death,* Per. II, 1, 7.

Enswathed, enwrapped, enveloped: *with sleided silk e.* Compl. 49.*

Entail, subst., hereditary property: *and cut the e. from all remainders,* All's IV, 3, 313.

Entail, vb. 1) to bestow as an hereditary possession: *I here e. the crown to thee and to thine heirs,* H6C I, 1, 194.

2) to appoint hereditary possessor: *to e. him and his heirs unto the crown,* H6C I, 1, 235.

Entame, to tame, subdue: *that can e. my spirits to your worship,* As III, 5, 48.

Entangle, 1) to make confused and intricate: *dismiss the controversy bleeding, the more —d by your hearing,* Cor. II, 1, 86.

2) to ensnare, to involve in difficulties: *to be —d with those mouth-made vows,* Ant. I, 3, 30. *very force —s itself with strength,* IV, 14, 48.

Enter, 1) intr. a) to go in, come in: Ven. 780. 890. Tp. IV, 216. Meas. II, 2, 152. Err. II, 2, 212. 220. Ado II, 1, 87. III, 1, 9. H6A III, 2, 25. V, 2, 18 (cf. *On*). H6C I, 3, 22. Cor. III, 1, 111 etc. With *at: pity —s at an iron gate,* Lucr. 595. *e. at her window,* Gentl. III, 1, 113. *at the abbey,* Err. V, 278. *term such as will e. at a lady's ear,* H5 V, 2, 100. *fame late —ing at his heedful ears,* H6C III, 3, 63. Joined with the adv. *in: longs to e. in,* R2 I, 3, 2 (= to e. the lists). *by fair or foul means, must we e. in,* H6C IV, 7, 14. Followed by the prepos. *in, into* and *within: may with foul intrusion e. in and dwell upon your grave,* Err. III, 1, 103. *to e. in my house,* IV, 4, 67. V, 92. *—ed in a brake,* Mids. III, 2, 15. *let it not e. in your mind of love,* Merch. II, 8, 42. *to e. in the castle,* R2 II, 3, 160. *the sweetest sleep that ever —ed in a drowsy head,* R3 V, 3, 228. *are —ed in the Roman territories,* Cor. IV, 6, 40. *swift to e. in the desperate thoughts of men,* Rom. V, 1, 36. *these words e. in our ears like ....,* Tim. V, 1, 199. *these words like daggers e. in mine ears,* Hml. III, 4, 95. *—ing into some monastery,* Meas. IV, 2, 217. *e. into that brake,* Mids. III, 1, 77. *Pucelle is —ed into Orleans,* H6A I, 5, 36. *that we e., as into our dukedom,* H6C IV, 7, 9. *within this bosom never —ed yet the dreadful motion of a murderous thought,* John IV, 2, 254.

b) to make a solemn entry: *I am bound to e. publicly,* Meas. IV, 3, 101. IV, 4, 10. IV, 6, 15. H6C IV, 7, 9.

c) as a technical term of the stage, = to appear on the scene: *Pyramus e.* Mids. III, 1, 103. *she is to e. now,* V, 186. *the competitors e.* Tw. IV, 2, 12. Substantively: *his e. and exit shall be strangling a snake,* LLL V, 1, 141.

d) to have a passage, to find room between: *so wide as a bristle may e.* Tw. I, 5, 3. *admits no orifex for a point as subtle as Ariachne's broken woof to e.* Troil. V, 2, 152.

e) to engage: *I am here —ed in bond for you,* Err. IV, 4, 128; cf. R2 V, 2, 65. *e. into a quarrel,* Ado II, 3, 203. *since I have —ed into these wars,* H6A I, 2, 132. *sith I am —ed in this cause so far,* Oth. III, 3, 411.

2) trans. a) to come or go into: *e. this sweet city,* Lucr. 469. *you shall see her chamber-window —ed,* Ado III, 2, 116. *e. his forbidden gates,* LLL II, 26. Merch. II, 5, 35. V, 273. As II, 3, 28. H6B III, 2, 132. IV, 10, 27. R3 I, 3, 195. Cor. II, 2, 114. V, 6, 6. Rom. III, 1, 6 etc. *terrible to e. human hearing,* Tp. I, 2, 265 (cf. Merch. II, 5, 35 and R3 I, 3, 195). *to e. the cloister,* Meas. I, 2, 182 (= to become a nun). *to e. the lists,* (viz as a combatant), H6B II, 3, 50; cf. R2 I, 3, 2.

b) to pierce: *his sides are better proof than thy spear's point can e.* Ven. 626. *thorns which —ed their frail shins,* Tp. IV, 181. *that it may e. Mowbray's breast,* R2 I, 2, 48. I, 3, 75. *this respite shook the bosom of my conscience, —ed me, yea, with a splitting power,* H8 II, 4, 182.

c) to engage in, to begin: *e. talk with lords,* H6A III, 1, 63. *have you —ed the action?* H4B II, 1, 1 (= have you brought an action? commenced a lawsuit?). cf. *I have —ed him and all,* 10 (blunderingly = the action against him).

d) to initiate: *'tis our hope, after well —ed soldiers, to return,* All's II, 1, 6. *they of Rome are —ed in our counsels,* Cor. I, 2, 2. cf. *Man-entered.* Hence = to introduce favourably, to recommend: *this sword shall e. me with him,* Ant. IV, 14, 113.

Enterprise, subst. attempt, undertaking: Lucr. 184. Mids. III, 2, 157. Meas. IV, 1, 66. As I, 2, 188. V, 4, 168. All's III, 6, 70. John V, 2, 90. H4A II, 3, 86. III, 2, 113. IV, 1, 29. 78. V, 1, 71. 88. H5 I, 2, 121. II, 2, 164. H6A II, 1, 44. V, 3, 7. H4B I, 1, 178. H6C I, 2, 37. R3 IV, 4, 235. Troil. I, 3, 103. Caes. I, 2, 302. I, 3, 123. II, 1, 133. II, 4, 41. III, 1, 13. 16. Mcb. I, 7, 48. Hml. I, 1, 99. II, 2, 78. III, 1, 86. Per. I, 1, 5. Followed by *of: now, lords, to France: the e. whereof shall be to you, as us, like glorious,* H5 II, 2, 182. Sometimes very nearly = doing, affair, business: *so far blameless proves my e. that I have 'nointed an Athenian's eyes,* Mids. III, 2, 350. *words, vows, gifts, tears, and love's full sacrifice, he offers in another's.* Troil. I, 2, 309. *it greets me as an e. of kindness,* Per. IV, 3, 38.

Entertain, subst. reception, entertainment: *your e. shall be as doth befit our honour,* Per. I, 1, 119. In II, 3, 64 some M. Edd. *e. for entrance* of O. Edd.

Entertain, vb. 1) to receive hospitably, to treat: *was royally —ed and lodged by Lucrece,* Lucr. Arg. 15. *in Tarquin's likeness I did e. thee,* 596. 842. Ado I, 3, 45. Shr. I, 1, 44. Tit. V, 3, 32. Tim. II, 2, 45.

2) to amuse: *approach, rich Ceres, her to e.* Tp. IV, 75. *to e. him with hope,* Wiv. II, 1, 68. *to e. them sprightly,* Wint. IV, 4, 53. *—ed me with mine own device,* Tim. I, 2, 155.

3) to receive in general: *since mine own doors refuse to e. me,* Err. III, 1, 120. *then e. him, then for-*

swear him, As III, 2, 436. *heaven, set ope thy everlasting gates, to e. my vows*, H6B IV, 9, 14. *burn, bonfires, to e. great England's lawful king*, V, 1, 4. *there's few or none will e. it* (viz conscience) R3 I, 4, 135. *Cancer when he burns with —ing great Hyperion*, Troil. II, 3, 207. *e. them, give them guide to us*, Tim. I, 1, 252. *let the presents be worthily —ed*, I, 2, 191. Even = to meet as an enemy: *O noble English, that could e. with half their forces the full pride of France*, H5 I, 2, 111.

4) to treat in general: *I'll e. myself like one that I am not acquainted withal*, Wiv. II, 1, 89. *thou with mildness —est thy wooers*, Shr. II, 252. *yet tellest thou not how thou wert —ed*, H6A I, 4, 38. *I am sorry that with reverence I did not e. thee as thou art*, II, 3, 72. *your highness is not —ed with that ceremonious affection*, Lr. I, 4, 63.

5) to enter into, to admit, not to refuse (Germ. eingehen auf etwas): *awake, thou Roman dame, and e. my love*, Lucr. 1629. cf. *if thou —est my love, let it appear in thy smiling*, Tw. II, 5, 159 (and perhaps As III, 2, 436). *I'll e. the offered fallacy*, Err. II, 2, 188. *how should that be? but e. it, and I will give thee all the world*, Ant. II, 7, 69.

6) to take or keep in service: *e. him to be my fellow-servant*, Gentl. II, 4, 104. 110. IV, 4, 68. 75. 96. *I will e. Bardolph*, Wiv. I, 3, 10. *as many devils e.* 61. *—ed for a perfumer*, Ado I, 3, 60. *—ed my convoy*, All's IV, 3, 103. *e. some score or two of tailors*, R3 I, 2, 257. Tim. IV, 3, 496. Caes. V, 5, 60. Lr. III, 6, 83. Cymb. IV, 2, 394.

7) to maintain, to keep: *he —ed a show so seeming just*, Lucr. 1514. *and do a wilful stillness e.* Merch. I, 1, 90. *I quake, lest thou a feverous life shouldst e.* Meas. III, 1, 75. *here we e. a solemn peace*, H6A V, 4, 175 (?).

8) to pass, to spend (time) agreeably: *the weary time she cannot e.* Lucr. 1361. *to e. the time with thoughts of love*, Sonn. 39, 11. *I play the noble housewife with the time, to e. it so merrily with a fool*, All's II, 2, 63. *it cannot be that the misplaced John should e. an hour, one minute, nay, one quiet breath of rest*, John III, 4, 133. *I could be well content to e. the lag-end of my life with quiet hours*, H4A V, 1, 24. *to e. these fair well-spoken days*, R3 I, 1, 29.

9) to conceive, to harbour, to feel, to keep: *all —ed, each passion labours so*, Ven. 969. *when every grief is —ed that's offered*, Tp. II, 1, 16. *—ed ambition*, V, 75. *—ed them* (thy oaths) *deeply in her heart*, Gentl. V, 4, 102. *e. a cheerful disposition*, R2 II, 2, 4. *e. no more of it* (sorrow) H4B V, 2, 54. *now e. conjecture of a time*, H5 IV Chor. 1. *e. good comfort*, R3 I, 3, 4. *which* (opinion) *—ed*, Troil. I, 3, 354. *had but newly —ed revenge*, Rom. III, 1, 176. *they have —ed cause enough to draw their swords*, Ant. II, 1, 46. — In Per. II, 2, 14 M. Edd. *explain*, but this is no Shakespearian word. Read '*interpret*'.

Entertainer, one who harbours, or who treats (quibbling): Tp. II, 1, 17.

Entertainment, 1) hospitable reception, kind treatment, kindness: *I spy e. in her*, Wiv. I, 3, 48. *the stealth of our most mutual e.* Meas. I, 2, 158. *this e. may a free face put on*, Wint. I, 2, 111. 118. *this great favour done, in e. to my princely queen*, H6B I, 1, 72. *whom this beneath world doth embrace and hug with amplest e.* Tim. I, 1, 45. *do not dull thy*

palm with e. of each new-hatched comrade, Hml. I, 3, 64. *lest my extent to the players should more appear like e. than yours*, II, 2, 392. *desires you to use some gentle e. to Laertes*, V, 2, 216. *instruct her what she has to do, that she may not be raw in her e.* Per. IV, 2, 60.

2) reception, treatment in general: *witness the e. that he gave*, Ven. 1108. *I will resist such e.* Tp. I, 2, 465. *for an entrance to my e.* Shr. II, 54. *have you so soon forgot the e. her sister welcomed you withal?* III, 1, 2. *the rudeness that hath appeared in me have I learned from my e.* Tw. I, 5, 231. H4B IV, 5, 174 (*give*). Cor. IV, 5, 10. V, 2, 69. Hml. II, 2, 329. Ant. III, 13, 140. Cymb. I, 4, 167.

3) provisions of the table, any accommodation of guests, feast: *if love or gold can in this desert place buy e.* As II, 4, 72. *gave me fresh array and e.* IV, 3, 144. *John Drum's e.* All's III, 6, 41 (i. e. blows). Tw. II, 1, 34. Wint. I, 1, 9. Lr. II, 4, 209. *set a fair fashion on our e.* Tim. I, 2, 152 (= feast). Evans, blunderingly, calls guests *—s*, Wiv. IV, 5, 77.

4) amusement: *let us devise some e. for them*, LLL IV, 3, 373. Tim. I, 2, 185. Oth. II, 3, 37. Per. II, 3, 55. *some e. of time* = pastime: LLL V, 1, 125 (Holofernes' speech; cf. *Entertain*, def. 8).

5) service: *worthy your lordship's e.* All's III, 6, 13. *some band of strangers in the adversary's e.* IV, 1, 17. *already in the e.* Cor. IV, 3, 49. *if your lady strain his e.* Oth. III, 3, 250 (his readmission into service). *have e., but no honourable trust*, Ant. IV, 6, 16.

6) conception, expectation: *advised him for the e. of death*, Meas. III, 2, 225 (cf. *Entertain*, def. 9).

Entertissued, see *Intertissued*.

Enthralled, 1) deprived of liberty, captive: *what though I be e.?* H6A V, 3, 101.

2) reduced to the servitude of love, in love: *my e. eyes*, Gentl. II, 4, 134. *being e. as I am*, Wint. IV, 4, 234. With *to: too high to be e. to low*, Mids. I, 1, 136. *so is mine eye e. to thy shape*, III, 1, 142.

Enthroned, sitting on a throne: Merch. IV, 1, 194. H8 II, 3, 6. Troil. I, 3, 90. Ant. II, 2, 220. III, 6, 5.

Entice, to allure; absol.: *—ing lines*, H6A V, 5, 14. *—ing birds*, H6B I, 3, 92. Trans.: Lucr. 1411. Pilgr. 416. Mids. II, 1, 199. With *to:* H6A III, 3, 19. Per. Prol. 27. I, 1, 30.

Enticement, allurement: All's III, 5, 20.

Entire (as for the accent, see Appendix I, 1). 1) whole, undivided, unbroken: *divides one thing e. to many objects*, R2 II, 2, 17. *a carbuncle e.* Cor. I, 4, 55. *one e. and perfect chrysolite*, Oth. V, 2, 145.

2) complete, total: *the one half of an e. sum*, LLL II, 131. *the man e.* Caes. I, 3, 155.

3) unalloyed, unqualified, pure: *your e. affection to Bianca*, Shr. IV, 2, 23. *pure fear and e. cowardice*, H4B II, 4, 352.

4) essential, chief: *love's not love when it is mingled with regards that stand aloof from the e. point*, Lr. I, 1, 243.

Entirely, 1) completely, not only in part, without restriction: *drunk many times a day, if not many days e. drunk*, Meas. IV, 2, 158 (i. e. continually, without an intervening time of sobriety). *subdue my father e. to her love*, Oth. III, 4, 60. *my mistress loved thee and her fortunes mingled with thine e.* Ant. IV, 14, 25.

2) with the whole power or activity, merely: *other slow arts e. keep the brain*, LLL IV, 3, 324.

3) with all one's heart, as much as can be: *they are e. welcome*, Merch. III, 2, 228. *that Benedick loves Beatrice so e.* Ado III, 1, 37. All's I, 3, 104. Lr. I, 2, 105. *whom I with all the office of my heart e. honour*, Oth. III, 4, 114.

Entitle, to call: *that which we lovers e. affected*, LLL II, 232. *I may e. thee my loving father*, Shr. IV, 5, 61. *I am as ignorant in that as you in so —ing me*, Wint. II, 3, 70. *that which in mean men we e. patience*, R2 I, 2, 33.

Entitled, having a title or claim: *let our hands part, neither e. in the other's heart*, LLL V, 2, 822 (i. e. neither having a claim to the other's heart). *for whether beauty, birth, or wealth, or wit, or any of these all, or all, or more, e. in their parts, do crowned sit*, Sonn. 37, 7 (i. e. or more excellencies having a just claim to the first place as their due. Blundering M. Edd. *e. in thy parts*).*

Entomb, to bury; properly and figuratively: Lucr. 390. 679. 1121. Sonn. 81, 8. Troil. III, 3, 186. Cor. II, 1, 99. Tim. V, 4, 66. Mcb. II, 4, 9.

Entrails, internal parts, bowels: Tp. I, 2, 295. Wiv. V, 5, 162. H5 III, 7, 14. H6C I, 4, 87. R3 IV, 4, 23. 228. Tit. I, 144. II, 3, 230. Caes. II, 2, 39. V, 3, 96. Mcb. IV, 1, 5.

Entrance, subst. (trisyll. in Rom. I, 4, 8. Per. II, 3, 64 and perhaps Mcb. I, 5, 40). 1) the passage by which something may be entered: *his heart granteth no penetrable e. to her plaining*, Lucr. 559. *no more the thirsty e. of this soil shall daub her lips with her own children's blood*, H4A I, 1, 5 (i. e. the surface of the earth). *Achilles stands in the e. of his tent*, Troil. III, 3, 38. *the stony e. of this sepulchre*, Rom. V, 3, 141.

2) the act of entering: *shut against his e.* Err. IV, 3, 90. *I will answer you with gait and e.* Tw. III, 1, 93. Wint. IV, 4, 449. John II, 85. R2 III, 3, 22. H6A II, 1, 30. H8 IV, 2, 107. Tit I, 383. Rom. I, 4, 8. Mcb. I, 5, 40. II, 3, 120. Per. II, 3, 64 (= arrival). *to give e.* = to give permission to enter: John II, 450. Cor. IV, 5, 13. *to have e.* H6A III, 2, 6. = enter, appearance on the scene: *they have their exits and their —s*, As II, 7, 141.

3) the entering upon, beginning; followed by *to: for an e. to my entertainment, I do present you with a man of mine*, Shr. II, 54. *beware of e. to a quarrel*, Hml. I, 3, 66.

Entranced, seemingly dead: Per. III, 2, 94.

Entrap, to catch insidiously, to ensnare: Merch. III, 2, 101. 122. As I, 1, 157. H4A IV, 3, 98. H6A IV, 4, 37. Per. II, 5, 45.

Entreasured, richly furnished, enriched: *balmed and e. with full bags of spices*, Per. III, 2, 65.

Entreat, subst., entreaty, earnest petition: R3 III, 7, 225 (Ff entreaties). Tit. I, 449. 483.

Entreat, vb. 1) to ask earnestly, to beseech; absol.: *still she —s, and prettily —s*, Ven. 73. Shr. IV, 2, 33. IV, 3, 7. 8. H6B III, 2, 282. R3 III, 7, 219. IV, 4, 345. *e. for life*, R3 I, 4, 269. *e. for her*, As IV, 3, 73. R3 I, 4, 272. Lr. II, 2, 161. III, 3,

6. With an accus. indicating a) the person applied to: Ven. 97. Meas. II, 2, 43. Shr. III, 2, 200. 203. All's II, 5, 70. H4A III, 1, 176. H6B IV, 1, 120. R3 III, 7, 201. Tit. II, 3, 304. IV, 4, 94. 95. Caes. I, 2, 166. III, 2, 65. Ant. V, 2, 158. Cymb. I, 6, 181. III, 4, 99. b) the thing asked for: *I rather would e. thy company*, Gentl. I, 1, 5. *e. an hour of revels with 'em*, H8 I, 4, 71 (i. e. beg permission to pass an hour). *we must e. the time alone*, Rom. IV, 1, 40 (beg to be left alone for the present). Gentl. IV, 4, 116. Meas. V, 482. Ado V, 4, 18. LLL III, 154. IV, 1, 83. Merch. IV, 2, 7. All's II, 1, 130. Wint. I, 2, 97. H8 IV, 2, 104. Tim. I, 2, 193. Caes. II, 1, 100. Oth. II, 3, 229. Ant. II, 2, 227. Cymb. V, 5, 84. With a double accus.: *—s her a little favour of speech*, Oth. III, 1, 28.

The person following in the accus., the thing wished for with *to: being —ed to it by your friend*, Gentl. III, 2, 45. *e. him to a peace*, Tw. V, 389. *e. you to your wonted furtherance*, H6A V, 3, 21. *did e. your highness to this course*, H8 II, 4, 216. *to e. me to't*, Lr. II, 2, 120. *to e. your captain to soft and gentle speech*, Ant. II, 2, 2. *which do not be —ed to*, II, 6, 32. Similarly: *the senators e. thee back to Athens*, Tim. V, 1, 144.

The thing asked for expressed by an inf.: *I did not then e. to have her stay*, As I, 3, 71. Ant. III, 13, 53. Per. V, 1, 62. The person asked in the accus., the thing required in the inf: *—ed me to call*, Gentl. IV, 3, 2. Meas. V, 266. Ado III, 1, 40. Mids. I, 1, 58. I, 2, 102. III, 1, 42. Merch. II, 2, 210. III, 2, 232. Shr. V, 2, 86. All's III, 2, 95. 97. John V, 7, 39. R2 I, 4, 56. R3 III, 7, 59. H8 III, 2, 32. Cor. II, 2, 141. Rom. II, 2, 16. Tim. III, 1, 17. Caes. II, 1, 55. Hml. I, 1, 26. III, 1, 22. 190. Lr. II, 4, 250. 302. IV, 1, 47. Oth. II, 3, 329. III, 3, 244. Per. II, 4, 45. The inf. without *to: let me e. you speak the former language*, Meas. II, 4, 140. *you would e. me rather go than stay*, Shr. III, 2, 194. *e. her hear me*, Tit. II, 3, 138. *e. her show a woman pity*, 147. Shr. III, 2, 199. H4A II, 4, 567. H6B III, 2, 339. H8 IV, 2, 119. Rom. V, 3, 260. Tim. I, 2, 175. Oth. III, 3, 77. Per. II, 1, 65.

The thing asked for expressed by a dependant clause: *and do e. thou pardon me my wrongs*, Tp. V, 118. *and e. that you vouchsafe*, LLL V, 2, 740. All's II, 5, 68. H5 V, 2, 64. H6A II, 2, 40. H6C V, 6, 59. Tit. I, 39. Hml. II, 2, 10. Oth. IV, 1, 273.

The person with *of: let me e. of you to pardon me*, Shr. Ind. 2, 120. *I must e. of you some of that money*, Tw. III, 4, 374. *I e. true peace of you*, R3 II, 1, 62. III, 1, 138. Tit. I, 362. III, 1, 31. — The thing with *of: the Dauphin whom of succours we —ed*, H5 III, 3, 45.

2) to prevail on by solicitation: *if she cannot e., I can compel*, Mids. III, 2, 248. *I would she were in heaven, so she could e. some power to change this currish Jew*, Merch. IV, 1, 292. As I, 2, 159. 171. 218. Shr. V, 2, 89. H4B V, 5, 133. Troil. IV, 5, 265. *I could hardly e. him back*, Tw. III, 4, 64.

3) to obtain by solicitation: *when we can e. an hour to serve, we would spend it in some words upon that business*, Mcb. II, 1, 22.

4) to invite: *if he e. you to his bed*, Meas. III, 1, 274. *I e. you home with me to dinner*, Merch. IV, 1, 401. H4B II, 1, 194. *dost thou e. me, Hector?* Troil. IV, 5, 268. *severally e. him*, 274.

5) to treat, to use: *fairly let her be —ed,* R2 III, 1, 37. *I'll write unto them and e. them fair,* H6C I, 1, 271. *be patient and e. me fair,* R3 IV, 4, 151. *e. her fair,* Troil. IV, 4, 115. *e. her not the worse in that I pray you use her well,* H6B II, 4, 81.

6) to treat, to negociate: *I'll send some holy bishop to e.* H6B IV, 4, 9.

Entreatment, invitation: *from this time be somewhat scanter of your maiden presence; set your —s at a higher rate than a command to parley,* Hml. I, 3, 122 (the invitations which you receive).*

Entreaty, petition, solicitation: Meas. IV, 1, 68. As I, 2, 250. IV, 1, 80. Wint. I, 2, 232. John V, 2, 125. H6A V, 4, 85. H6C III, 1, 91. R3 III, 1, 40. III, 7, 225 (Qq *entreats*). H8 V, 1, 150. Troil. IV, 5, 149. Cor. I, 3, 9. IV, 5, 212. V, 1, 74. Tim. V, 2, 11. Hml. II, 2, 29. 76. Ant. II, 7, 9. *at a person's e.:* Wint. I, 2, 220. R3 III, 7, 115 (Ff *on*). Lr. I, 2, 175. *upon e.* Shr. IV, 3, 5. R3 III, 7, 115 (Qq *at*).

Entrench (cf. *Intrench*), to cut: *this very sword —ed it,* All's II, 1, 45.

Entry, passage to enter a house, gate: *I hear a knocking at the south e.* Mcb. II, 2, 66.

Entwist, to wreathe around: Mids. IV, 1, 48.

Envelop, to wrap, surround, enclose: *the best and wholesomest spirits of the night e. you,* Meas. IV, 2, 77. *leaving his body as a paradise, to e. and contain celestial spirits,* H5 I, 1, 31.

Envenom, 1) to taint with poison: *—ed sting,* H6B III, 2, 267. *darts,* Caes. V, 3, 76. Hml. V, 2, 328. 332. Tropically: *this report of his did Hamlet so e. with his envy,* Hml. IV, 7, 104.

2) to poison, to kill by poison, and to destroy in general: *what is comely —s him that bears it,* As II, 3, 15. *e. him with words,* John III, 1, 63.

Envious, 1) malignant, mischievous, spiteful: *each e. briar his weary legs doth scratch,* Ven. 705. *an e. sneaping frost,* LLL I, 1, 100. Merch. III, 2, 284. As I, 2, 253. II, 1, 4. Shr. Ind. 2, 67. R2 II, 1, 62. H6A III, 1, 26. III, 4, 33. IV, 1, 90. H6B II, 4, 12. 35. III, 1, 157 (*the e. load* = the load of malice) H6C III, 2, 157. V, 6, 25. R3 I, 3, 26. I, 4, 37. H8 II, 1, 45. III, 2, 447. Tit. III, 1, 96. Rom. I, 1, 156. III, 1, 173. III, 2, 40. III, 5, 7. Caes. II, 1, 178. III, 2, 179. Hml. IV, 7, 174.

2) jealously pained by the excellence or good fortune of another: Meas. III, 2, 154. As I, 1, 149. R2 III, 3, 65. H6A III, 1, 194. H8 III, 2, 243. Troil. I, 3, 133. III, 3, 174. Rom. II, 2, 4. 7 (most of these passages may as well be taken in the first signification).

Enviously, spitefully: *spurns e. at straws,* Hml. IV, 5, 6.

Environ, vb. to surround, to envelop: Gentl. I, 1, 16. H4B IV, 3, 106. H6A V, 4, 90. H6C I, 1, 242. II, 1, 50. II, 4, 4. R3 I, 4, 59 (*about*). Tit. III, 1, 94. Rom. IV, 3, 50. Per. II, 2, 36. The passive always followed by *with.*

Envy, subst. 1) jealous mortification at the sight of another's excellence: *very e. and the tongue of loss cried fame and honour on him,* Tw. V, 61. *rival-hating.* R2 I, 3, 131. *defensive against the e. of less happier lands,* II, 1, 49. H4A I, 1, 79. H6A IV, 1, 193. H6B III, 2, 315. H8 III, 2, 239. V, 3, 44. Troil. IV, 4, 30. Hml. IV, 7, 75. 104. Cymb. II, 3, 133. Per. IV Prol. 12. 37. Perhaps also Lucr.

909. With *at: full of e. at his greatness,* Troil. II, 1, 36. With *of: e. of so rich a thing,* Lucr. 39. H5 V, 2, 379. *in e. of Caesar,* Caes. V, 5, 70. Hendiadis: *not Afric owns a serpent I abhor more than thy fame and e.* Cor. I, 8, 4 (= thy envied fame; cf. *And*).

2) malice, spite, hate: *who with age and e. was grown into a hoop,* Tp. I, 2, 259. *carry me out of his —'s reach,* Merch. IV, 1, 10. 126. R2 I, 2, 21. H4A V, 2, 67. R3 IV, 1, 100. H8 III, 1, 113. Cor. IV, 5, 80. 109. Tit. II, 1, 4. Tim. I, 2, 144. Caes. II, 1, 164. Ant. V, 2, 164. Followed by *to: his e. to the people,* Cor. III, 3, 3. Especially malice shown by calumny and depreciation: *to tie up e. evermore enlarged,* Sonn. 70, 12. *stands at a guard with e.* Meas. I, 3, 51. *either this is e. in you, folly, or mistaking,* III, 2, 149. *she bore a mind that e. could not but call fair,* Tw. II, 1, 30. *either e. or misprision,* H4A I, 3, 27. *gather wealth, I care not with what e.* H6B IV, 10, 23. *exempt from e., but not from disdain,* H6C III, 3, 127 (= above calumny). H8 II, 1, 85. II, 2, 89. III, 1, 36. Troil. II, 3, 23. III, 2, 104. V, 1, 4. 29. Tit. I, 153.

Envy, vb. (⏌ or ⏌⏌) 1) to feel jealousy and mortification at sth.; a) trans.; *to e. a person:* Sonn. 128, 5. As III, 2, 78. Shr. II, 18. Per. II, 3, 26. *to e. sth.:* R2 I, 1, 23. H4A IV, 3, 35. H6B III, 1, 206. R3 I, 3, 75. IV, 1, 64. Cor. I, 1, 116. 234. Per. II, 3, 14. A dependant clause following: *e. much thou hast robbed me of this deed,* Cymb. IV, 2, 158.

b) intr., with *at: I e. at their liberty,* John III, 4, 73. *whose honesty the devil and his disciples only e. at,* H8 V, 3, 112.

2) to show malice and ill-will, particularly by derogatory and calumnious speeches (cf. *Envy,* subst. def. 2) to rail, to depreciate; a) trans.: *such (sounds) as become a soldier rather than e. you,* Cor. III, 3, 57 (= are intended to depreciate you). b) intr. *for that he has, as much as in him lies, from time to time —ed against the people, seeking means to pluck away their power,* Cor. III, 3, 95.

Enwheel, to surround, encompass: *the grace of heaven e. thee round,* Oth. II, 1, 87.

Enwombed, conceived in the womb, born of one's own body: *and put you in the catalogue of those that were e. mine,* All's I, 3, 150.

Enwrap, to envelop: *though 'tis wonder that —s me thus,* Tw. IV, 3, 3.

Ephesian, a jolly companion: Wiv. IV, 5, 19. H4B II, 2, 164. cf. *Corinthian.*

Ephesus, Greek town in Asia Minor: Err. I, 1, 17. 20. 31. 135. 153. II, 1, 2, 150. IV, 1, 83. IV, 4, 6. Per. III, 2, 43. IV Prol. 3. V, 1, 241. 255. V, 2, 17.

Epicure, a man given to luxury, a sybarite: Mcb. V, 3, 8. Ant. II, 7, 58.

Epicurean, adj. luxurious: Wiv. II, 2, 300. Ant. II, 1, 24.

Epicurism, luxury: Lr. I, 4, 265.

Epicurus, the celebrated Greek philosopher: Caes. V, 1, 76.

Epidamium (M. Edd. *Epidamnum*) the ancient Illyrian town of Epidamnus or Dyrrhachium: Err. I, 1, 42. 63. I, 2, 1. IV, 1, 85. 94. V, 349. 353.

Epidarus, writing of O. Edd. in Err. I, 1, 94. M. Edd. *Epidaurus;* but perhaps a misprint for *Epidamnus.*

Epigram, a short sarcastic poem: *dost thou think I care for a satire or an e.?* Ado V, 4, 103.

Epilepsy, a fit of the falling sickness: *my lord is fallen into an e.* Oth. IV, 1, 51.

Epileptic, affected with the falling sickness: *a plague upon your e. visage,* Lr. II, 2, 87 (called so for constrained grinning).

Epilogue, a speech addressed to the spectators after the conclusion of a play: Mids. V, 360. 362. 369. As Epil. 2. 5. 7. 8. Used confusedly by Armado, LLL III, 82.

Epistle, letter: *—s of love,* Tw. II, 3, 169. *a madman's —s are no gospels,* V, 294.

Epistrophus, name in Troil. V, 5, 11.

Epitaph, inscription upon a tomb: Sonn. 81, 1. Ado IV, 1, 209. V, 1, 293. LLL IV, 2, 51. Merch. IV, 1, 118. All's I, 2, 50. R2 III, 2, 145. H4A V, 4, 101. H5 I, 2, 233. Tim. IV, 3, 380. V, 1, 188. Hml. II, 2, 550. III, 2, 143. Cymb. III, 3, 52. Per. IV, 3, 43.

Epithet, term, expression, phrase: *suffer love! a good e.!* Ado V, 2, 67. *the —s are sweetly varied,* LLL IV, 2, 8. *a most singular and choice e.* V, 1, 17. *they will not answer to that e.* V, 2, 170. *horribly stuffed with —s of war,* Oth. I, 1, 14.

Epitheton, the same, used by Armado: LLL I, 2, 15. (O. Edd. *apethaton, apathaton*).

Epitome, abridgment: Cor. V, 3, 68.

Equal, adj. 1) being of the same quantity or quality: Merch. III, 4, 13 (Ff Q2. 3 *egal,* q. v.). All's I, 2, 2. Tw. III, 4, 16. John II, 358. H5 V, 2, 23. H8 I, 1, 29. II, 2, 108. Cor. I, 10, 14. Hml. III, 2, 73. Ant. III, 4, 35. With *to: unfold e. discourtesy to your best kindness,* Cymb. II, 3, 101. Per. II, 1, 117. With *with: now grown in grace e. with wondering,* Wint. IV, 1, 25 (her beauty equalled, deserved the admiration it caused). *my vows are e. partners with thy vows,* H6A III, 2, 85. *let thy tongue be e. with thy heart,* H6B V, 1, 89 (= speak what you think). *wishing his foot were e. with his eye,* H6C III, 2, 137 (wishing to be at the distance which he sees from far).

Substantively: *he has no e.* (in pride) Cor. I, 1, 257. *as some my —s did,* Compl. 148 (some in the same situation).

Adverbially: *he is e. ravenous as he is subtle,* H8 I, 1, 159.

2) of the same rank: *bestow thy fawning smiles on e. mates,* Gentl. III, 1, 158. *mated with an e. husband,* Tim. I, 1, 140. cf. *on e. terms,* R2 IV, 22. *in e. rank,* H4B V, 2, 137.

Substantively: *where your e. grew,* Sonn. 84, 4. *she is no e. for his birth,* Ado II, 1, 171. *his e. had awaked them,* All's I, 2, 38. *this and my food are —s,* Tim. I, 2, 61.

3) of the same weight, counter-poising each other: *e. poise of sin and charity,* Meas. II, 4, 68. *let the forfeit be nominated for an e. pound of your fair flesh,* Merch. I, 3, 150 (= an exact pound, just of the weight of a pound). *in justice' e. scales,* H6B II, 1, 204. H4B IV, 1, 67. H6C II, 5, 13. Hml. I, 2, 13. Cymb. III, 6, 78. Figuratively: *son and father weep with e. strife,* Lucr. 1791. *a more e. enterprise,* As I, 2, 188 (not beyond one's power). Adverbially: *her dowry shall weigh e. with a queen,* John II, 486. *his taints and honours waged e. with him,* Ant. V, 1, 31.

4) just, impartial: *justice always whirls in e. measure,* LLL IV, 3, 384. *having here no judge indifferent, nor no more assurance of e. friendship and proceeding,* H8 II, 4, 18.

Equal, vb. 1) to be as large, as great, or as good as: *my homely stars have failed to e. my great fortune:* All's II, 5, 81. Wint. IV, 4, 397. V, 1, 101. H4A III, 1, 97. H6A II, 5, 22. H6B IV, 2, 127. H6C III, 2, 145. R3 I, 2, 250. Ant. IV, 15, 77. Per. IV, 3, 8. V, 1, 89. 99. 132. Absolutely: *his* (sum) *had —ed,* Tim. III, 4, 32.

2) to match; a) trans.: *they that stabbed Caesar shed no blood at all, nor were not worthy blame, if this foul deed were by to e. it,* H6C V, 5, 55. b) intr.: *we are a body strong enough to e. with the king,* H4B I, 3, 67.

Equality, the same quantity or strength: John II, 327. Lr. I, 1, 5 (Ff *qualities*). Ant. I, 3, 47.

Equally, 1) in the same manner, at the same time: Ado I, 1, 12. Lr. V, 3, 45. Ant. III, 4, 36. Cymb. III, 4, 32. In R3 III, 7, 213 Qq F1 *egally.*

2) in the same proportion: As I, 2, 35. H4A III, 1, 73. R3 V, 3, 294.

3) alike in weight or dignity: *you weigh e.* Meas. IV, 2, 31. *ne'er settled e., but high or low,* Ven. 1139.

Equalness, partnership: *that our stars should divide our e. to this,* Ant. V, 1, 48.

Equinoctial, subst. the equator: Tw. II, 3, 24 (the fool's speech).

Equinox, the equal length of the day and the night: *see his vice; 'tis to his virtue a just e., the one as long as the other,* Oth. II, 3, 129.

Equipage, accoutrements: *to march in ranks of better e.* Sonn. 32, 12 (Some M. Edd., following the spurious Qq in Wiv. II, 2, 3: *I will retort the sum in e.*; quite unintelligibly).

Equity, justice: John II, 241. H4A II, 2, 106. H6B III, 1, 146. Lr. III, 6, 39.

Equivalent, of equal rank and dignity: *e. with mighty kings,* Per. V, 1, 92.

Equivocal, of doubtful meaning, ambiguous: *what an e. companion is this!* All's V, 3, 250. *these sentences, to sugar or to gall, being strong on both sides, are e.* Oth. I, 3, 217.

Equivocate, vb. 1) intr. to use ambiguous expressions by way of deceit: *could not e. to heaven,* Mcb. II, 3, 12. 2) trans. to effect by duplicity: *—s him in a sleep,* II, 3, 39 (the porter's speech).

Equivocation, ambiguity: Mcb. V, 5, 43. Hml. V, 1, 149.

Equivocator, one who uses ambiguous language: Mcb. II, 3, 9. 13. 35.*

Ercles, corruption from Hercules: Mids. I, 2, 31. 42.

Ere, conj. (dissyll. in H6A I, 3, 88); 1) sooner than, before: *e. he says adieu,* Ven. 537. *the merchant fears e. rich at home he lands,* Lucr. 336. Ven. 462. Lucr. 567. 704. 1277. 1688. Sonn. 68, 8. Tp. I, 2, 51. II, 1, 280. III, 2, 18. Gentl. II, 4, 31. III, 1, 253. V, 4, 29. 113. Wiv. II, 1, 127. Meas. II, 2, 99. III, 2, 34. IV, 3, 92. V, 340. Err. I, 1, 95. 101. II, 1, 29. V, 2, 54. IV, 4, 2. 122 etc. etc. Followed by the subjunctive: *treason works e. traitors be espied,* Lucr. 361. *e. he go to bed, knit clouds about his head,* 776. *e. he arrive his weary noon-tide prick,* 781. Sonn. 6, 2. *sexes both consents, e. he desire, have granted,* Compl. 131. Pilgr. 315. Gentl. I, 1, 46. Wiv. IV, 2, 51. V, 5, 54. Meas. II, 2, 38. Err. I, 2, 7. LLL I, 2, 152. R2 I, 3, 198. II, 1, 229. H4A IV, 4, 36. H6A II, 5, 62. IV,

2, 35. IV, 7, 24. H6B II, 3, 22. H6C II, 3, 35. R3 III, 2, 62. IV, 4, 184. Tit. III, 1, 192 etc. *e. it be long =* shortly: Meas. IV, 2, 79. H6A III, 2, 75. H6C III, 3, 232. IV, 1, 111. Elliptical phrases: *cancelled e. well begun,* Lucr. 26. *Priam found the fire e. he his tongue,* H4B I, 1, 74. *to fright them e. destroy,* Cor. IV, 5, 149. *there be many Caesars e. such another Julius,* Cymb. III, 1, 12. *to die e. sick,* IV, 2, 9.

2) rather than: *she will die, e. she make her love known,* Ado II, 3, 182. Usually followed by *will, would, shall, should,* according to the verbal form of the principal sentence: *I will be thrown into Etna, e. I will leave her,* Wiv. III, 5, 129. *so I will grow, so live, so die, e. I will yield my virgin patent up,* Mids. I, 1, 80. Merch. I, 2, 107. H6B V, 1, 112. R3 III, 1, 44 (Ff. *before*). cf. *let the frame of things disjoint, e. we will eat our meal in fear,* Mcb. III, 2, 17. *the impression of keen whips I'ld wear as rubies, ere I'ld yield my body up to shame,* Meas. II, 4, 103. *e. he would have hanged a man ... he would have paid,* III, 2, 124. Oth. I, 3, 316. *the Jew shall have my flesh e. thou shalt lose ...,* Merch. IV, 1, 113. John III, 1, 345. R2 I, 1, 190. *I should have given him tears, e. he should thus have ventured,* As I, 2, 251. H6A III, 1, 120. Elliptically: *I will find you twenty lascivious turtles e. one chaste man,* Wiv. II, 1, 83. *saw the lion's shadow e. himself,* Merch. V, 8. *a devil would have shed water out of fire e. done it,* Wint. III, 2, 194. *I will die a thousand deaths ere break ...,* H4A III, 2, 159. H6B V, 2, 85. R3 III, 4, 40. Cor. I, 1, 247. 223.

Ere that, in both significations: *to be diseased e. that there was true needing,* Sonn. 118, 8. *e. that we will suffer such a prince to be disgraced, we will fight,* H6A III, 1, 97.

Or ere, likewise in both significations: 1) *return or e. your pulse twice beat,* Tp. V, 103. Shr. IV, 5, 8. *'twill be two days or e. we meet,* John IV, 3, 20. V, 6, 44. Mcb. IV, 3, 173. Hml. I, 2, 147. Cymb. III, 2, 67. 2) *I would have sunk the sea within the earth or e. it should the good ship so have swallowed,* Tp. I, 2, 11. *this heart shall break or e. I weep,* Lr. II, 4, 289. *those that would die or e. resist,* Cymb. V, 3, 50.

Ere, prepos. before, in a temporal sense: *e. the break of day,* Lucr. 1280. *e. day,* Mids. III, 2, 395. *e. the next Ascension day,* John IV, 2, 151. *e. this day,* H6C III, 3, 131. *e. morning,* Meas. IV, 2, 98. Merch. V, 48. *e. night,* Pilgr. 312. H6C II, 5, 59. V, 4, 69. Caes. V, 3, 109. *e. sunrise,* Meas. II, 2, 153. *e. sunset,* John III, 1, 110. H6C II, 2, 116. Mcb. I, 1, 5. *e. noon,* Mcb. III, 5, 22. *e. dinner time,* H4A III, 3, 222. *e. supper time,* Tp. III, 1, 95. *e. the thirtieth of May,* H6B I, 1, 49. *e. the ninth hour,* Ant. II, 5, 21. *e. that hapless time,* H6A III, 1, 201. *e. the time of her awaking,* Rom. V, 3, 257. *e. the first sacrifice,* Troil. IV, 2, 66. *e. a determinate resolution,* H8 II, 4, 176. *e. long =* before long, shortly: *which thou must leave e. long,* Sonn. 73, 14. *e. long espied a fickle maid,* Compl. 5. Tp. V, 87. Meas. III, 1, 46. Mids. V, 441. John IV, 2, 102. H6A I, 3, 88. II, 1, 22. III, 2, 46. IV, 1, 171. H6C I, 1, 146. III, 1, 91. Cor. V, 1, 61. *e. now =* a) formerly, times ago: *I have loved e. now,* As II, 4, 24. *I have e. now been better known to you,* All's V, 2, 2. *spent time worse e. now,* Wint. IV, 1, 30. *twice and once e. now,* H4B V, 3, 43. *what you have been e. now, and what you are,* R3 I, 3, 132 (Ff *e. this*). b) not now for the first time, formerly as well as now: *your kin-*

dred hath made my eyes water e. now, Mids. III, 1, 200. *there have been cuckolds e. now,* Wint. I, 2, 191. H6A V, 3, 107. Cor. II, 3, 214. Rom. IV, 4, 9. Mcb. III, 4, 75. *Ere this =* a) long ago, before this time: *thou hadst been gone e. this,* Ven. 613. *I have inly wept, or should have spoke e. this,* Tp. V, 201. *shortly mean to touch our shore, perhaps they had done e. this,* R2 II, 1, 289. *which long e. this we offered to the king,* H4B IV, 1, 75. R3 III, 1, 21. *e. this I should have fatted ...,* Hml. II, 2, 606. b) formerly, heretofore: *as I e. this was pure to Collatine,* Lucr. 826. *slanders him with cowardice whose frown hath made thee faint and fly e. this,* H6C I, 4, 48. *what you have been e. this, and what you are,* R3 I, 3, 132 (Qq *e. now*).

Erebus, Tartarus, hell: Merch. V, 87. H4B II, 4, 171. Caes. II, 1, 84.

Erect, vb. to raise, to set up, to build: Wiv. II, 2, 226. Ado V, 2, 80. H6A II, 2, 12. III, 2, 119. H6B III, 2, 80. IV, 7, 36. Troil. IV, 5, 108. Tim. V, 4, 23.

Erection, 1) the act of building: H4B I, 3, 44. — 2) the tension of the yard: *your activity may defeat and quell the source of all e.* Tim. IV, 3, 164. A blunder of Mrs. Quickly for *direction:* Wiv. III, 5, 41.

Erewhile, a little while ago, even now: LLL IV, 1, 99. Mids. III, 2, 274. As II, 4, 89. III, 5, 105. Oth. IV, 1, 77 (Q1 *e. mad;* the other O. Edd. *o'er-whelmed*).

Ergo (cf. *Argo, Argal,* and Latin in the appendix), Lat. adv., consequently: Err. IV, 3, 57. Merch. II, 2, 59. 63. Shr. IV, 3, 129. All's I, 3, 53.

Eringo, sea-holly: *let it snow —es,* Wiv. V, 5, 23 (supposed to possess aphrodisiac qualities).

Ermengare, daughter of Charles of Lorraine: H5 I, 2, 82.

Ern, see *Yearn.*

Eros, name in Ant. III, 5, 1. IV, 4, 1 etc.

Erpingham: *Sir Thomas E.* R2 II, 1, 283. H5 IV, 1, 13. 96.

Err, 1) to deviate from the true course, to stray: *if I can check my —ing love, I will,* Gentl. II, 4, 213. *my jealous aim might e.* III, 1, 28. Mids. I, 1, 230. Hml. III, 4, 73. Oth. I, 3, 62. 100 (*against all rules; cf. error* in Ado IV, 1, 165). III, 3, 227 (*nature —ing from itself*).

2) to be mistaken: Sonn. 131, 7. 137, 13. Err. V, 317. Tw. IV, 2, 46. H8 I, 1, 174. Mcb. V, 4, 7. Cymb. V, 5, 35. Per. I, 2, 43.

3) to offend: *whether you had not sometime in your life —ed in this point,* Meas. II, 1, 15. II, 2, 134. All's II, 3, 190. III, 7, 12. H6C IV, 8, 46. Troil. V, 2, 111. Oth. III, 3, 49. IV, 3, 100. Cymb. I, 6, 176. Per. I, 3, 22.

4) to wander, to roam: *how brief the life of man runs his —ing pilgrimage,* As III, 2, 138. *the extravagant and —ing spirit,* Hml. I, 1, 154. *a frail vow betwixt an —ing barbarian and a supersubtle Venetian,* Oth. I, 3, 362 (cf. I, 1, 137).

Errand, 1) a verbal message: Err. II, 1, 72. As IV, 3, 6. John III, 1, 137. Rom. III, 3, 79. Caes. II, 4, 3. Ant. III, 13, 104. *to do an e.* Shr. IV, 4, 14. *he came of an e.* Wiv. I, 4, 80. III, 4, 114. IV, 2, 182. *of a sleeveless e.* Troil. V, 4, 9. *go a mile on his e.* Meas. III, 2, 39. Ado II, 1, 273. Caes. IV, 1, 13.

2) any oral communication to be made:

there is no lady living so meet for this great e. Wint. II, 2, 46. *first I'll do my e.* II, 3, 64. *upon which e. I now go toward him,* V, 1, 231. H4B I, 1, 69. H5 IV, 1, 324. Cor. V, 2, 65 (O. Edd. *arrant*).

Errant, deviating: *tortive and e. from his course of growth,* Troil. I, 3, 9.

Erroneous, 1) deviating from the right course, irregular, unnatural: *what stratagems, how fell, how butcherly, e., mutinous and unnatural,* H6C II, 5, 90.

2) mistaking, misled: *e. vassal!* R3 I, 4, 200.

Error, 1) mistake, deception, false opinion: Ven. 898. Lucr. 937. Sonn. 116, 13. Meas. I, 2, 54. Err. II, 2, 186. III, 2, 35. V, 388. 397. Ado IV, 1, 165 (*the —s that these princes hold against her maiden truth;* cf. Oth. I, 3, 100 . IV, 1, 172. V, 4, 3. LLL V, 1, 137. V, 2, 471. Mids. III, 2, 368. Merch. III, 2, 78. Shr. IV, 3, 146. All's I, 3, 211. Tw. IV, 3, 10. Wint. IV, 1, 2. John II, 230 (*to make a faithless e. in your ears;* cf. Troil. V, 3, 111; = deception). H6A II, 4, 6 (*to be in the e.*). 67. Troil. V, 2, 110. 111. V, 3, 111 (cf. John II, 230). Cor. II, 3, 127. Caes. V, 3, 67. 69. Hml. V, 2, 406. Oth. I, 3, 10. 357. Ant. III, 13, 114. Cymb. V, 5, 260. Per. I, 1, 46.

2) deviation from the right course, aberration, irregularity: *this is the greatest e. of all the rest: the man should be put into the lanthorn,* Mids. V, 250. *many an e. by the same example will rush into the state,* Merch. IV, 1, 221. *it is the very e. of the moon,* Oth. V, 2, 109. cf. All's I, 3, 211.

3) moral offence: Sonn. 96, 7 (the different significations blent). 117, 9. 119, 5. 141, 2. Compl. 184. Gentl. V, 4, 111. LLL V, 2, 781.

Erst, formerly, once: Sonn. 12, 6. As III, 5, 95. H5 V, 2, 48. H6B II, 4, 13. Tit. IV, 1, 64. V, 3, 80. Per. I, 1, 49.

Erudition, culture of the mind, learning: Troil. II, 3, 254.

Eruption, a breaking forth, a violent commotion: LLL V, 1, 121. H4A III, 1, 28. Caes. I, 3, 78. Hml. I, 1, 69.

Escalus, name: Meas. I, 1, 1. 46. IV, 3, 135. V, 16. 245 etc. All's III, 5, 80.

Escanes, name: Per. II, 4, 1. IV, 4, 13.

Escape (cf. *Scape*) subst. 1) a getting out of danger: Tp. II, 1, 2. Shr. I, 1, 235. Tw. I, 2, 19. H6C II, 1, 7. IV, 6, 80. *by strong e.* Err. V, 148.

2) flight: *privy to this their late e.* Wint. II, 1, 95. *tell the king of this e.* IV, 4, 677.

3) sally: *thousand —s of wit,* Meas. IV, 1, 63.

4) transgression: *Rome will despise her for this foul e.* Tit. IV, 2, 113. *thy e. would teach me tyranny, to hang clogs on them,* Oth. I, 3, 197 (double sense).

Escape, vb. 1) intr. to get out of danger: Tp. II, 2, 126. 132. Wiv. IV, 2, 74. Meas. IV, 2, 157 (*hence*). John V, 6, 42. H6A IV, 5, 10. H6C II, 6, 38. IV, 6, 78 (*from*). Ant. IV, 8, 4. = to come off alive: H5 IV, 1, 192.

2) trans. to be saved from, to avoid, to shun: Merch. III, 1, 110. As I, 1, 133. All's III, 6, 99. H6A III, 2, 40. H6C I, 1, 1. H8 I, 2, 26. Hml. III, 1, 141. IV, 7, 162. Lr. II, 3, 3. Ant. IV, 14, 94.

Escapen, archaism for *escape*: *ne aught —ed but himself,* Per. II Prol. 36 (M. Edd. *escapen*).

Eschew, to avoid: *what cannot be —ed must be embraced,* Wiv. V, 5, 251.

Escot, vb. to pay for, to maintain: *how are they —ed?* Hml. II, 2, 362.

Esile, see *Eysell*.

Especial, particular, concerning a single person or purpose: *upon e. cause,* H6A IV, 1, 55. *for thine e. safety,* Hml. IV, 3, 42. *there is e. commission come from Venice,* Oth. IV, 2, 225.

Adverbially: *for your rapier most e.* Hml. IV, 7, 99 (Ff *especially*).

Especially, 1) particularly, principally: Gentl. III, 2, 41. Meas. III, 2, 247. Ado II, 1, 93. II, 3, 122. As I, 1, 176. All's IV, 3, 10. H6A III, 1, 155. V, 4, 71. Troil. III, 1, 48. Cor. II, 1, 22. V, 4, 6. Tim. III, 1, 45. Hml. II, 2, 468. IV, 7, 99 (Qq *especial*). Ant. I, 2, 181. Per. IV, 2, 104.

2) in particular, apart: *you were born under a charitable star. Under Mars, I. I e. think, under Mars,* All's I, 1, 207. *would you proceed e. against Caius Marcius?* Cor. I, 1, 26. *drink is a great provoker of three things. What three things does drink e. provoke?* Mcb. II, 3, 29.

Esperance, hope: Troil. V, 2, 121. Lr. IV, 1, 4. Motto of the Percies: H4A II, 3, 74. V, 2, 97 (quadrisyll.).

Espial, spy: H6A I, 4, 8. IV, 3, 6. Hml. III, 1, 32.

Espouse, vb. 1) to marry, to unite by the marriage-ceremony: *I have performed my task and was —d,* H6B I, 1, 9.

2) to take to wife: H5 II, 1, 81. H6B I, 1, 46. R3 IV, 5, 18. Tit. I, 242. 328.

Espoused to = joined, associated with: *kings might be —d to more fame,* Lucr. 20. *and so —d to death,* H5 IV, 6, 26.

Espy, 1) to perceive, to see, to discover: Ven. 261. Lucr. 361. Compl. 5. Mids. II, 1, 262. III, 2, 105. R2 I, 3, 97. Troil. III, 2, 71. Tit. II, 3, 194. Per. V Prol. 18. Double accus.: *he doth e. himself love's traitor,* John II, 506.

2) to watch, to observe: *we are —ed,* Tit. II, 3, 48.

Esquire, a title of dignity, next in degree below a knight: Wiv. I, 1, 4. 110. H4B III, 2, 63. IV, 3, 140. H5 I, 1, 14. IV, 8, 89. 109. H6B IV, 10, 46. V, 1, 75.

Essay, subst. = *assay,* q. v.: Sonn. 110, 8. Lr. I, 2, 47.

Essence, 1) existence, life: *love in twain had the e. but in one,* Phoen. 26 (= had but one life). *she is my e.* Gentl. III, 1, 182 (the cause of my life). *his glassy e.* Meas. II, 2, 120. 2) a being: *her honour is an e. that's not seen,* Oth. IV, 1, 16.

Essential, existent, real: *and in the e. vesture of creation does tire the ingener,* Oth. II, 1, 64.

Essentially, really: *thou art e. mad, without seeming so,* H4A II, 4, 540. *he that loves himself hath not e. but by circumstance the name of valour,* H6B V, 2, 39. *that I e. am not in madness, but mad in craft,* Hml. III, 4, 187.

Essex, English county: H6C I, 1, 156.

Establish, 1) to settle, to fix: *e. him in his true sense again,* Err. IV, 4, 51. *one raised in blood, and one in blood —ed,* R3 V, 3, 247.

2) to enact, ordain, appoint: *thy —ed edict,* LLL I, 1, 262. Merch. IV, 1, 219. H5 I, 2, 50. H6B III, 1, 317. Cor. I, 1, 85.

3) to make or appoint by decree: *we were —ed the people's magistrates*, Cor. III, 1, 201. *to e. Caesar as a king*, Caes. I, 3, 86.

4) to confirm, to ratify: *to e. here a peace*, H4B IV, 1, 86. H6A V, 3, 92.

5) to bestow by a settlement of inheritance: *we will e. our estate upon our eldest*, Mcb. I, 4, 37.

Estate, subst. 1) condition, situation: *his letter there will show you his e.* Merch. III, 2, 239. *my e. is very low*, 318. *I will forget the condition of my e., to rejoice in yours*, As I, 2, 17. *labouring art can never ransom nature from her inaidible e.* All's II, 1, 122. Wint. V, 2, 159. H5 IV, 1, 99. H6B III, 1, 206. H6C III, 3, 150. IV, 3, 18. H8 V, 1, 74. Rom. III, 3, 63. Lr. V, 3, 209. Ant. IV, 2, 152. Cymb. V, 5, 74.

2) state, peculiar form of existence: *when I came to man's e.* Tw. V, 402. *showing, as in a model, our firm e.* R2 III, 4, 42. *it gives me an e. of seven years' health*, Cor. II, 1, 125. *supported his e.* Tim. III, 2, 76. *and wish the e. o' the world were now undone*, Mcb. V, 5, 50. Hence *all —s = all kinds of people*: LLL V, 2, 855. R3 III, 7, 213.

3) interest, affairs: *know man from man, dispute his own e.* Wint. IV, 4, 411. *we sin against our own e., when we may profit meet, and come too late*, Tim. V, 1, 44. Especially = public interest, state-affairs, interest of government: *how wildly then walks my e. in France*, John IV, 2, 128. *the e. is green and yet ungoverned*, R3 II, 2, 127. *business of e.* H8 II, 2, 70. *the terms of our e. may not endure hazard so dangerous*, Hml. III, 3, 5.

4) rank, dignity: *and was, according to his e., royally entertained*, Lucr. Arg. 14. *for that he coloured with his high e.* Lucr. 92. Merch. II, 9, 41. Shr. III, 2, 102. All's I, 3, 117. Tw. I, 2, 44. H6A I, 2, 75. Hml. V, 1, 244. Cymb. V, 5, 22. Per. IV, 4, 14. = royal dignity: *we will establish our e. upon our eldest*, Mcb. I, 4, 37. *he poisons him in the garden for his e.* Hml. III, 2, 273.

5) fortune, property, possessions: Merch. I, 1, 43. 123. All's II, 3, 182. III, 7, 4. Tw. I, 3, 116. I, 5, 278. Wint. IV, 2, 46. H4B I, 3, 53. H8 I, 1, 82. Tim. I, 1, 119. II, 2, 150. 233. III, 2, 7. III, 3, 5. IV, 3, 521. V, 1, 44. Cymb. I, 4, 119. 133. Per. IV, 2, 36.

Estate, vb. (used only in the infinitive), to settle as a possession, to bestow; with *on: some donation freely to e. on the blest lovers*, Tp. IV, 85. *all the revenue will I e. upon you*, As V, 2, 13. With *unto: all my right of her I do e. unto Demetrius*, Mids. I, 1, 98.

Esteem, subst. 1) estimation, opinion of merit: *slandering creation with a false e.* Sonn. 127, 12. *most dear in the e. and poor in worth*, Troil. III, 3, 129. *precious in the world's e.* LLL II, 4. *high in his e.* Mids. III, 2, 294. *labour for a greater e.* As V, 2, 62. *a coward in thine own e.* Mcb. I, 7, 43.

2) high estimation, great regard, worth: *we lost a jewel of her, and our e. was made much poorer by it*, All's V, 3, 1 (we are worth less by her loss). *prisoners of e.* H6A III, 4, 8. V, 5, 27. Rom. I, 3, 70. *of no e.* Cymb. V, 5, 253. *nor should thy prowess want praise and e.* H6B V, 2, 22. *of good e.* Gentl. I, 3, 40. Shr. IV, 5, 64. H6B III, 2, 21. *of so high e.* Shr. Ind. 2, 16. *in much e. with the king*, H8 IV, 1, 109.

Esteem, vb. 1) to estimate, to value: *that love is merchandized whose rich —ing the owner's tongue doth publish every where*, Sonn. 102, 3 (= estimation, price). *—ed above thy life*, Merch. IV, 1, 285. *what do you e. it at?* Cymb. I, 4, 85. Double accus.: *he nought —s that face of thine*, Ven. 631. Gentl. III, 1, 83. *be —ed nothing*, Ant. I, 2, 144.

2) to prize, to rate high, to respect: *the basest jewel will be well —ed*, Sonn. 96, 6. 100, 7. *me and my possessions she —s not*, Gentl. III, 1, 79. LLL V, 2, 894. All's II, 1, 126. Troil. I, 2, 144. I, 3, 199. III, 1, 69. Tim. II, 2, 112. Cymb. I, 1, 52.

3) to think, consider, repute; a) trans. α) with a double accus.: *'tis better to be vile than vile —ed*, Sonn. 121, 1. LLL II, 44. Mids. III, 2, 353. As I, 2, 237. Shr. Ind. 1, 27. 122. H5 IV, 4, 64. H6A IV, 1, 5. Mcb. I, 7, 42. Hml. I, 1, 85. Oth. IV, 2, 65. β) with *as, how* and *so: whom she —eth as his friend*, Gentl. III, 2, 37. *the sullen passage of thy weary steps e. as foil*, R2 I, 3, 266. *e. him as a lamb*, Mcb. IV, 3, 54. *how —est thou me?* Gentl. II, 1, 66. *how is the man —ed here?* Err. V, 4. *he with the Romans was —ed so as silly jeering idiots are with kings*, Lucr. 1811.

b) intr.: *beseech you so to e. of us*, Wint. II, 3, 148.

Estimable, 1) valuable: Merch. I, 3, 167. 2) estimating, or attending the estimation of sth.: *though I could not with such e. wonder over-far believe that*, Tw. II, 1, 28, i. e. with such admiration caused by the estimation; with such admiring judgment; cf. Walkers' Crit. Exam. I, pag. 183.

Estimate, subst., estimation, value, price: Sonn. 87, 2. R2 II, 3, 56. Troil. II, 2, 54. Cor. III, 3, 114. Tim. I, 1, 14. *to have e.* = to be brought into account: *all that life can rate worth name of life, in thee hath e.* All's II, 1, 183.

Estimation, 1) the act of estimating, of adjusting proportional value: *if the scale do turn but in the e. of a hair*, Merch. IV, 1, 331. *who, in a cheap e., is worth all your predecessors*, Cor. II, 1, 101. II, 3, 103.

2) value, worth: *whose e. do you mightily hold up*, Ado II, 2, 24. *if thou be'st rated by thy e., thou dost deserve enough*, Merch. II, 7, 26. *your son lacked the sense to know her e. home*, All's V, 3, 4. Abstr. pro concr., = thing of worth: *beggar the e. which you prized richer than sea and land*, Troil. II, 2, 91. *your ring may be stolen too: so your brace of unprizable —s*, Cymb. I, 4, 99.

3) reputation, honour: *he cannot plead his e. with you*, Meas. IV, 2, 28. *to be of worth and worthy e.* Gentl. II, 4, 56. *your yet ungalled e.* Err. III, 1, 102. LLL I, 1, 272. H4A IV, 4, 32. V, 1, 98. H5 III, 6, 16. Hml. II, 2, 348. Oth. I, 3, 275.

4) esteem, respect: *to let him lack a reverend e.* Merch. IV, 1, 163. *bonneted into their e. and report*, Cor. II, 2, 31. *he would use me with e.* V, 2, 56. 66.

5) conjecture, supposition: *I speak not this in e., as what I think might be*, H4A I, 3, 272.

Estranged, alienated: *e. from thyself*, Err. II, 2, 122. *how come you thus e.* LLL V, 2, 213.

Estridge, ostrich: H4A IV, 1, 98. *the dove will peck the e.* Ant. III, 13, 197 (Douce: = goshawk).*

Etcetera, and the rest, and so forth: *come we to full points here, and are —s nothing?* H4B II, 4, 198 (Pistol's speech). *captain-general of the Grecian* *army, Agamemnon, e.* Troil. III, 3, 280. *O that she were an open e.* Rom. II, 1, 38 (i. e. an open-arse; only in Q1).

Eternal, subst. God: *by penitence the —'s wrath is appeased,* Gentl. V, 4, 81.

Eternal, adj. everlasting, endless: Ven. 951. Lucr. 345. Sonn. 13, 12. 18, 9. 12. 38, 12. 64, 4. 108, 9. Compl. 238. Wiv. II, 1, 50. 104. LLL I, 1, 158. All's II, 3, 246. III, 2, 24. Tw. V, 159. John III, 4, 18. H5 IV, 5, 10. H6A V, 3, 48. H6B I, 4, 28. III, 2, 263. III, 3, 19. H6C III, 3, 124.*R3 I, 3, 269. V, 3, 62. H8 IV, 2, 90. Troil. V, 2, 166. Tit. I, 155. 168. II, 4, 15. III, 1, 21. Rom. IV, 5, 70. Mcb. III, 1, 68. IV, 1, 105. Hml. I, 5, 21 *(this e. blazon =* this account of things e., of eternity). Oth. III, 3, 361. Ant. V, 1, 66 *(her life in Rome would be e. in our triumph =* would be for ever recorded as the most glorious trophy of our triumph).

Used to express extreme abhorrence: *would have brooked the e. devil to keep his state in Rome,* Caes. I, 2, 160.*O proud death, what feast is toward in thine e. cell,* Hml. V, 2, 376. *some e. villain,* Oth. IV, 2, 130.

Adverbially: *to be boy e.* Wint. I, 2, 65.

Eternally, for ever: *these couples shall e. be knit,* Mids. IV, 1, 186.

Eterne, eternal, everlasting: Mcb. III, 2, 38. Hml. II, 2, 512.

Eternity, endless time, immortality: Lucr. 214. 967. Sonn. 77, 8. 122, 4. 125, 3. Phoen. 58. LLL I, 1, 7. Wint. V, 2, 106. H6B II, 4, 90. Troil. II, 3, 256. Cor. V, 4, 25. Hml. I, 2, 73. Ant. I, 3, 35.

Eternize, to immortalize: H6B V, 3, 31.

Ethiop, a native of Ethiopia: Pilgr. 242 and LLL IV, 3, 118. Gentl. II, 6, 26. Ado V, 4, 38. LLL IV, 3, 268. Mids. III, 2, 257. Rom. I, 5, 48. Per. II, 2, 20. Adjectively: *such E. words, blacker in their effect than in their countenance,* As IV, 3, 35.

Ethiopian, the same: Wiv. II, 3, 28. Wint. IV, 4, 375.

Etna, see *Aetna.*

Eton, town in England: Wiv. IV, 4, 75. IV, 5, 68. IV, 6, 24. V, 5, 194.

Eunuch (the indef. art. *an* before it), one castrated: LLL III, 201 *(though Argus were her e. and her guard).* Mids. V, 45. All's II, 3, 94. Tw. I, 2, 56. 62. H6B IV, 2, 175. Cor. III, 2, 114. Tit. II, 3, 128. Ant. I, 5, 8. 10. II, 5, 5. III, 7, 15. IV, 14, 25. Cymb. II, 3, 34.

Euphrates, river in Asia: Ant. I, 2, 106.

Euriphile, name in Cymb. III, 3, 103. IV, 2, 234. 238. V, 5, 340.

Europa, 1) the quarter of the earth: Ado V, 4, 45. — 2) the daughter of Agenor carried away by Jove in the shape of a bull: Wiv. V, 5, 4. Ado V, 4, 46. Not named, but indicated: Shr. I, 1, 173.

Europe, the quarter of the earth: Tp. II, 1, 124. Wint. II, 2, 3. H4A III, 3, 52. H4B II, 2, 146. IV, 3, 24. H5 II, 4, 133. III, 7, 5. H6A I, 1, 156. H6C II, 1, 71. Cymb. II, 3, 149.

Evade, to elude by shuffling excuses: Cor. III, 3, 2. Oth. I. 1, 13.

Evans, name in Wiv. I, 4, 34.

Evasion, 1) shuffling excuse, subterfuge: Meas. I, 1, 51. Troil. II, 3, 123. Lr. I, 2, 137.

2) any trick or artifice in disputing: *there can be no e. to blench from this and to stand firm*

by *honour,* Troil. II, 2, 67. *his —s have ears thus long,* II, 1, 75.

Eve, the wife of Adam: Sonn. 93, 13. Gentl. III, 1, 342. Wiv. IV, 2, 24. LLL I, 1, 267. V, 2, 322. Tw. I, 5, 30. R2 III, 4, 75.

Eve, the evening before a holiday: *All-hallond e.* Meas. II, 1, 130.

Even, subst. the latter part of the day: Ven. 495. Sonn. 28, 12. 132, 7. H5 III, 1, 20. *this e.* Gentl. V, 2, 42. *good e.* Gentl. II, 1, 104. IV, 2, 85. Wiv. II, 1, 203. Meas. III, 2, 227. IV, 3, 154. As II, 4, 69. III, 3, 74. V, 1, 15. Rom. II, 6, 21. Tim. II, 2, 9. Hml. I, 2, 167.

Even, adj. 1) level, plain, smooth: *a very e. way,* Ado IV, 1, 266. *in the e. road of a blank verse,* V, 2, 33. *upon e. ground,* John II, 576. *give e. way unto my rough affairs,* H4B II, 3, 2. *the e. mead,* H5 V, 2, 48. *that my path were e. to the crown,* R3 III, 7, 157. *the e. field,* Caes. V, 1, 17. *the ground is e.* Lr. IV, 6, 3.

2) level, parallel, of the same height: *lay this Angiers e. with the ground,* John II, 399. *who in a moment e. with the earth shall lay your towers,* H6A IV, 2, 12. Figuratively, = conformable: *nought hath passed, but e. with law,* Tit. IV, 4, 8.

3) balanced, of an equal weight: *your vows to her and me will e. weigh,* Mids. III, 2, 133. *while they weigh so e., we hold our town for neither,* John II, 332. Tropically = impartial: *weigh thy value with an even hand,* Merch. II, 7, 25. *to bear one's self e.* = to behave with equanimity, to guard one's composure: *bear ourselves as e. as we can, the king will always think him in our debt,* H4A I, 3, 285. *how smooth and e. they do bear themselves,* H5 II, 2, 3. cf. *to bear all smooth and e., this sudden sending him away must seem deliberate pause,* Hml. IV, 3, 7. *he could not carry his honours e.* Cor. IV, 7, 37 (= with equanimity, without losing his equilibrium).

4) uniform, equal: *all must be e. in our government,* R2 III, 4, 36. *both sides are e.: here I'll sit in the midst,* Mcb. III, 4, 10.

5) quite up to a certain measure, full (cf. *equal* in Merch. I, 3, 150): *let us from point to point this story know, to make the e. truth in pleasure flow,* All's V, 3, 326. *to make even =* to fulfil: *make thy demand. But will you make it e.?* All's II, 1, 194; cf. As V, 4, 18. Substantively: *the king hath run bad humours on the knight; that's the e. of it,* H5 II, 1, 128 (= the full truth, the whole).

6) straight, direct: *the world, who of itself is peised well, made to run e. upon e. ground,* John II, 576. *then he runs straight and e.* H4A III, 1, 114. Figuratively, = fair, honest: *in plain shock and e. play of battle,* H5 IV, 8, 114. *be e. and direct with me,* Hml. II, 2, 298.

7) extricated from difficulties, plain, smooth: *death we fear that makes these odds all e.* Meas. III, 1, 41. *to make these doubts all e.* As V, 4, 25 (cf. 18). *when earthly things made e. atone together,* 115. Applied to a person: *to make e. o'er* = to give a full insight into, a clear perception of: Lr. IV, 7, 80 *(to make him e. o'er the time he hath lost).*

8) without a flaw or blemish, pure: *I know my life so e.* H8 III, 1, 37. *a soul as e. as a calm,* 166. *do not stain the e. virtue of our enterprise,* Caes. II, 1, 133.

9) having accounts balanced, quit: *he would be e. with you,* H6B I, 3, 204 (be quit with you). IV, 7, 100. Troil. IV, 5, 44. Oth. II, 1, 308 (Ff *evened).* Ant. III, 7, 1. *and make us e. with you,* Mcb. V, 8, 62 (= reward you according to your deserts).

10) capable of being divided into two equal parts; opposed to *odd: now the number is e.* LLL IV, 3, 211. *you're an odd man; give e.,* or *give none,* Troil. IV, 5, 41. *e. or odd,* Rom. I, 3, 16. cf. Meas. III, 1, 41.

Even, vb. 1) to act up to, to keep pace with: *to e. your content,* All's I, 3, 3. *but we'll e. all that good time will give us,* Cymb. III, 4, 184 (= we'll profit by any advantage offered).

2) to place in a state in which nothing is due on either side; to make quits: *till I am —ed with him,* Oth. II, 1, 308 (Q1 *even).*

Even, adv. 1) equally, likewise, as well: *a man may rot e. here,* Lr. V, 2, 8. 10. *not your knowledge, your personal pain, but e. your purse, still open, hath built Lord Cerimon such strong renown,* Per. III, 2, 46. *her mother, e. strong against that match and firm for Doctor Caius,* Wiv. IV, 6, 27 (= equally strong). *e. daughter, welcome,* As V, 4, 154. *to go e.* = to accord: *were you a woman, as the rest goes e., I should my tears let fall upon your cheek,* Tw. V, 246. *rather shunned to go e. with what I heard than in my every action to be guided by others' experiences,* Cymb. I, 4, 47 (cf. *Evenly*). *e ... and* = both ... and, Cor. V, 6, 4.

2) up to a certain measure, fully, quite: *O, that record could with a backward look, e. of five hundred courses of the sun, show me your image,* Sonn. 59, 6 (= of full five hundred). *mine eyes, e. sociable to the show of thine,* Tp. V, 63. *whom to call brother would e. infect my mouth,* V, 131. *these sweet thoughts do e. refresh my labours,* III, 1, 14; cf. *your father's wrath could not be so cruel to me, as you would e. renew me with your eyes,* Cymb. III, 2, 43. *answered my affection e. to my wish,* Wiv. IV, 6, 12. *e. like an o'er-grown lion,* Meas. I, 3, 22. *my affairs do e. drag me homeward,* Wint. I, 2, 24 (= quite). *we are blest in this man, e. blest,* IV, 4, 859. *and e. these three days have I watched,* H6A I, 4, 16 (= all these etc.). *e. as thou wilt,* H6C II, 6, 99. *a soldier e. to Cato's wish,* Cor. I, 4, 57. *of all these bounds, e. from this line to this,* Lr. I, 1, 64. *the ingratitude of this Seleucus does e. make me wild,* Ant. V, 2, 154. *which to read would be e. mortal to me,* Cymb. III, 4, 18. *a wench full grown, e. ripe for marriage-rite,* Per. IV Prol. 17. Contracted to *e'en: they have e'en put my breath from me,* Tim. III, 4, 104. *I am e'en sick of shame,* III, 6, 46. *we'll e'en to it like French falconers,* Hml. II, 2, 449. Lr. IV, 7, 53. *e'en like a dancer,* Ant. III, 11, 36.

3) at the same moment, the very time: *let your love e. with my life decay,* Sonn. 71, 12. *and having that, do choke their service up e. with the having,* As II, 3, 62. *how long have you professed apprehension? e. since you left it,* Ado III, 4, 69. *and e. since then hath Richard been obscured,* H6A II, 5, 26. Hence = this very moment, just now: *e. a toy in hand here,* As III, 3, 77. *the king who had e. tuned his bounty to sing happiness to him,* All's IV, 3, 11. *e. already they clap the lubber Ajax on the shoulder,* Troil. III, 3, 138. *E'en: how near is your master? e'en at hand,* Shr. IV, 1, 120. *O joy, e'en made away ere't can be born!* Tim. I, 2, 110. *she's e'en setting on water,* II, 2, 71.

politic worms are e'en at him, Hml. IV, 3, 22 (cf. the German *eben).*

4) just, precisely, exactly: *e. at this word she hears a merry horn,* Ven. 1025. *so* (obscured) *are you e. in the lovely garnish of a boy,* Merch. II, 6, 45. *e. at that time,* III, 2, 196. *the wise man's folly is anatomized e. by the squandering glances of the fool,* As II, 7, 57. *e. thou, that hast a heart so tender o'er it, e. thou and none but thou,* Wint. II, 3, 132. *e. for his sake am I pitiless,* Tit. II, 3, 162. *e. at noon-day,* Caes. I, 3, 27. *E'en: e'en as many as could well live,* Merch. III, 5, 24. cf. Hml. III, 2, 59. *what have we here? e'en that you have there,* All's III, 2, 20. *e'en a crow of the same nest,* IV, 3, 319. *e'en with losing his wits,* Hml. V, 1, 174. *Even as:* Ven. I. 55. 338. 458. 601. Gentl. I, 1, 10. II, 4, 192. IV, 4, 5. Wiv. II, 2, 272. Merch. III, 2, 49. H6A I, 2, 1. H6B I, 1, 238. V, 2, 53 etc. *e'en as,* Merch. III, 5, 24. Tim. III, 4, 23. *e. here,* Err. II, 2, 14. Wint. IV, 4, 452. *e. there,* Lucr. 348. Sonn. 41, 11. Merch. I, 3, 50. II, 8, 46. *e. before,* John III, 1, 233. *e. like,* H6A II, 5, 3. *e. such,* Sonn. 106, 8. Merch. III, 5, 88. *e. thus,* Pilgr. 147. 149. 151. H6B III, 2, 353. Oth. IV, 1, 47. *e. now,* 1) of things past, = just now: *e. now we heard a hollow burst of bellowing,* Tp. II, 1, 311. Wiv. II, 3, 66. IV, 5, 26. Meas. V, 521. Err. II, 2, 14. IV, 1, 55. IV, 3, 7. John V, 7, 12. H6C V, 2, 32 etc. 2) of things present, = now, at this moment: *the time is come e. now,* Meas. IV, 1, 22. *and e. now, but now, this house ... is yours,* Merch. III, 2, 171. Ado III, 1, 29. Wint. V, 1, 52. H6B III, 2, 378. H6C V, 2, 25. R3 I, 4, 149. Oth. I, 1, 152. 3) of future things, = immediately, presently: *the steed is stalled up, and e. now to tie the reader she begins to prove,* Ven. 39. *when I have required some heavenly music, which e. now I do,* Tp. V, 52. *e. now about it!* Gentl. III, 2, 98. *so swift a pace hath thought that e. now you may imagine him upon Blackheath,* H5 V Chor. 15. *away e. now,* H6B III, 2, 229. *and e. now my burthened heart would break, should I not curse them,* 320. *e. now be gone,* 352. *e. but now:* Sonn. 45, 11. Mids. III, 2, 225. Merch. V, 272 (Ff. *but e. now).* Hml. I, 1, 81. Lr. I, 1, 217. III, 2, 65. Oth. III, 2, 327. *but e. now:* Tp. V, 232. Merch. I, 1, 35. V, 272 (Qq *e. but now).* As II, 7, 3. Wint. III, 3, 79. John V, 3, 12 (cf. *but e. too well,* Wint. IV, 4, 188, in the clown's speech). — *Even so,* 1) = just so, exactly so: *e. so she kissed his brow,* Ven. 59. 603. 827. 881. Sonn. 33, 9. 69, 4. Gentl. I, 1, 47. Meas. I, 4, 43. II, 4, 26. V, 55. Merch. III, 2, 147. V, 189. R2 II, 1, 176. H6B III, 1, 213. III, 2, 194. R3 IV, 1, 79. Cor. I, 1, 116 etc. 2) used to answer in the affirmative, = indeed, yes: *with child, perhaps? unhappily, e. so,* Meas. I, 2, 160. *'tis e. so,* Ado III, 2, 78. *dead, for my life! e. so,* LLL V, 2, 730. As III, 3, 56. H6C V, 1, 47. Troil. I, 2, 52. Caes. IV, 3, 157. Lr. V, 3, 242. *e'en so:* Hml. V, 1, 77. 96. 220. 3) expressing surprise or discontent: *is it e. so? begin you to grow upon me?* As I, 1, 91. *his eyes do show his days are almost done. Is't e. so?* Tw. II, 3, 114. *is it e. so? nay, then, I see ...* H6A II, 2, 44. R3 IV, 2, 123 (Ff *thus).* Rom. V, 1, 24. *is it e'en so? why, then, I thank you all,* Rom. I, 5, 125. *your brother cannot live. E. so!* Meas. II, 4, 34. *no man shall have private conference with his brother. E. so,* R3 I, 1, 88. *he cannot come out on's grave. E. so?* Mcb. V, 1, 72. *Ajax was here the voluntary, and you as under an impress. E'en so,*

Troil. II, 1, 108. — *E. when*, 1) = just when: *to die, e. when they to perfection grow*, Tw. II, 4, 42. 2) = whenever: *e. when you please*, R3 III, 7, 243. *e. where* = wherever: *draw me through the sky e. where I list to sport me*, Ven. 154. *stretched to their servants, daughters, wives, e. where his lustful eye listed to make his prey*, R3 III, 5, 83. *e. what* = whatever: *e. what fashion thou best likest*, Gentl. II, 7, 52. Pleonasm: *e. just*, Err. IV, 1, 7. H5 II, 3, 12.

5) *very*, in the sense this word has when placed before a subst.: *that e. for anger makes the lily pale*, Lucr. 478 (for *very a.*). *a swallowing gulf that e. in plenty wanteth*, 557. *e. in the moment that we call them ours*, 868. *your praise shall still find room e. in the eyes of all posterity*, Sonn. 55, 11. 116, 12. Tp. V, 239. Gentl. I, 1, 49. I, 3, 37. III, 1, 250. Wiv. V, 5, 87. Meas. II, 2, 162. IV, 2, 83. V, 413. Err. III, 2, 3. V, 200. LLL V, 2, 768. Merch. II, 9, 30. IV, 1, 135. As II, 7, 153. Tw. I, 1, 14. I, 5, 187. 290. Wint. V, 1, 65. 228. John II, 338. R2 I, 3, 138. 208. H6B IV, 2, 189. V, 2, 12. H6C I, 1, 51. I, 2, 34. III, 3, 104. V, 1, 69. R3 II, 1, 116. III, 7, 186. IV, 4, 302. Lr. IV, 6, 194 etc. *I have debated e. in my soul*, Lucr. 498 (i e. my very, my inmost soul). *give me welcome e. to thy pure and most most loving breast*, Sonn. 110, 14. *I do desire thee, e. from a heart as full of sorrows*, Gentl. IV, 3, 32 (= from the depth of a heart). *and e. in kind love I do conjure thee*, II, 7, 2 (= in what is kindness and love itself, in true sincerity of love). cf. Err. III, 2, 163. Tw. I, 4, 14. Wint. III, 2, 2. Tit. V, 3, 172. H6C III, 3, 113. Like the adj. *very*, sometimes = *mere, alone: e. for the service that long since I did thee, e. for the blood that then I lost for thee, now grant me justice*, Err. V, 191 (i. e. if for nothing else, at least for the service). *I assure ye e. that your pity is enough to cure me*, Sonn. 111, 14. *to chide myself e. for this time I spend in talking to thee*, Gentl. IV, 2, 104. *e. for your son's sake*, Wint. I, 2, 336. John IV, 1, 74. H6B V, 1, 207. V, 2, 49. H6C III, 1, 13. *e. for revenge mock my destruction*, R3 V, 1, 9. *give me a kiss: e. this repays me*, Ant. III, 11, 71 (this alone is sufficient to ...). *I honour him e. out of your report*, Cymb. I, 1, 55.

Pleonasm: *e.very: e. her very words*, Err. II, 2, 165. Ado V, 1, 238. Caes. I, 3, 52. Hml. III, 2, 84. Oth. I, 3, 252.

6) Serving to denote identity of persons or things: *e. I* = I myself, Sonn. 35, 5. Ado V, 1, 273. *e. he* = the same: Ado I, 3, 53. Merch. V, 214. As I, 2, 161. *e. she*, Gentl. II, 1, 48. II, 4, 145. Ado III, 2, 109. *e. of yourself*, H8 II, 2, 126. *those lines that I before have writ do lie, e. those that said I could not love you dearer*, Sonn. 115, 2 (= those same). *e. by the self-same sky*, 15, 6. *e. for this*, 39, 5. *e. in this thought*, Lucr. 729. *e. with such-like valour*, Tp. III, 3, 59. *e. that power*, Gentl. II, 6, 4. *my will is e. this*, IV, 2, 93. *e. for that*, Mids. II, 1, 202. *e. for that I thank you*, Merch. II, 1, 22. *e. with those wings which have used with fearful flight, make war*, H6C II, 2, 29. *e. with the word*, R3 I, 2, 189. *this? e'en that*, Hml. V, 1, 201. *e. here*, Err. II, 2, 14. R3 V, 3, 1. *e. then* = at the same moment: H6C II, 2, 156. Hml. I, 2, 218. Oth. III, 3, 276. *thus*, Cor. I, 1, 112.

7) Serving to introduce what is less expected (which is now its principal use): *I have been wooed ... e. by the stern and direful god of war*, Ven. 98. *and e. thence thou wilt be stolen*, Sonn. 48, 13. Tp. II, 1,

241. Meas. II, 2, 84. Wint. IV, 2, 27. H4A III, 2, 151. V, 1, 104. V, 5, 31. H6C I, 4, 162. Tim. I, 1, 63.

8) Serving to lay an emphasis on a word or phrase *there appears much joy in him, e. so much that joy could not show itself modest*, Ado I, 1, 21 (= nay, so much). cf. Troil. I, 3, 283. *e. so quickly may one catch the plague?* Tw. I, 5, 314. *O once tell true, e. for my sake*, Mids. III, 2, 68. *I swear to thee, e. by thine own fair eyes*, Merch. V, 242; cf. Tit. V, 1, 86. *e. with the swiftness of putting on*, Tw. II, 5, 186. *furbish new the name of John of Gaunt, e. in the lusty haviour of his son*, R2 I, 3, 77. *be it known unto thee by these presence, e. the presence of Lord Mortimer*, H6B IV, 7, 32. *e. here*, Tp. III, 3, 7 and R3 IV, 4, 112. Before *till* and *to* it indicates the end and term of an action: *fill thy hungry eyes e. till they wink with fulness*, Sonn. 56, 6. Mids. III, 2, 391. As II, 1, 9. John II, 26. 386. *bears it out even to the edge of doom*, Sonn. 116, 12. 122, 4. Tp. IV, 193. Ado V, 1, 93. Merch. I, 1, 181. All's II, 4, 37. Tw. III, 4, 286. Wint. II, 1, 36. III, 2, 7. John V, 4, 57. H4A IV, 1, 30. Tim. II, 2, 206. Caes. III, 1, 108. Per. II, 4, 10. Cor. I, 1, 140. V, 6, 76.

9) Lastly used to reduce the mind to a lower and more common level, and expressing acquiescence in what cannot be helped: *therefore I will e. take sixpence in earnest of the bearward*, Ado II, 1, 42. *by my consent, we'll e. let them alone*, H6A I, 2, 44. *Mark Antony will e'en but kiss Octavia*, Ant. II, 4, 3. *no more, but e'en a woman, and commanded by such poor passion*, IV, 15, 72. Applied to a matter of course in general: *men will kiss e. by their own direction*, Ven. 216 (= for it is the characteristic of men to kiss etc.). *whither? e. to the next willow*, Ado II, 1, 194 (= whither else than, or of course to the next willow). *whither away so fast? e. to the hall*, H8 II, 1, 2. cf. *you still shall live where breath most breathes, e. in the mouths of men*, Sonn. 81, 14. *what state ... canst thou demise to any child of mine? e. all I have*, R3 IV, 4, 248 (Germ. *eben*).

Even-christian, fellow Christian: Hml. V, 1, 32 (the clown's speech).

Even-handed, impartial: Mcb. I, 7, 10 (cf. Merch. II, 7, 25).

Evening, the latter part of the day: Lucr. Arg. 5. Pilgr. 291. Gentl. IV, 2, 17. IV, 3, 42. V, 1, 7. Wiv. II, 2, 102. Err. I, 1, 28. III, 1, 96. Ado II, 1, 31. II, 3, 40. Mids. V, 39. All's III, 6, 79. John II, 285. H4A II, 3, 109. H6B II, 1, 43. H6C I, 4, 34. H8 III, 2, 226. Rom. IV, 1, 38. Caes. III, 2, 176. Lr. I, 2, 101. II, 1, 103.

Evenly, 1) in a straight line, directly: *Trent shall run in a new channel, fair and e.* H4A III, 1, 103. *e. derived from his most famed of famous ancestors*, H5 II, 4, 91.

2) conformably: *whatsoever comes athwart his affection ranges e. with mine*, Ado II, 2, 7 (cf. *to go even* = to accord; *Even* adv. def. 1).

Even-pleached, interwoven so as to have a smooth and even surface: *hedges e.* H5 V, 2, 42.

Event, 1) that which happens, incident, occurrence: Ven. 1159. Lucr. 1598. Tp. V, 227. LLL I, 1, 245. Merch. V, 297. As V, 4, 133. John III, 4, 155. R2 V, 2, 37. H4B IV, 2, 82. H6C II, 1, 32. II, 5, 63. Tit. V, 3, 178. 204. Tim. III, 4, 17. Mcb. II, 3, 63. V, 4, 15 (*the true e.* = that which happens indeed, and is not only suspected\. Hml. I, 1, 121. Oth. I, 3, 377. Ant. IV, 15, 3. V, 2, 363. Per. IV Prol. 45.

2) consequence, issue, result: Tp. I, 2, 117. III, 1, 69. Ado I, 2, 7. Shr. III, 2, 129. Tw. III, 4, 431. Wint. III, 1, 11. R2 II, 1, 214. H4B I, 1, 166. H6A IV, 1, 191. V, 5, 105 (almost = chance, cf. All's III, 2, 107). H8 I, 2, 36. Troil. II, 2, 120. Hml. IV, 4, 50. Lr. I, 4, 371. Cymb. III, 5, 14.

3) an affair in hand, business, enterprise: *but leave we him to his —s, with a prayer they may prove prosperous*, Meas. III, 2, 252. *success will fashion the e. in better shape*, Ado IV, 1, 237. *dream on the e.* Tw. II, 3, 191. *you and I must talk of that e.* H6B III, 1, 326. *ears and eyes for the time, but hearts for the e.* Cor. II, 1, 286 (= for our purpose). *some craven scruple of thinking too precisely on the e.* Hml. IV, 4, 41.

Eventful, rich in incidents and changes of fortune: As II, 7, 164.

Ever, 1) at any time: *would I might but e. see that man*, Tp. I, 2, 169. 419. II, 2, 63. 73. V, 244. Gentl. I, 1, 16. II, 1, 145. III, 1, 167. IV, 3, 19. Meas. III, 1, 197. V, 187. Err. II, 2, 48 etc. etc. The indef. art. omitted after it: *was there e. man a coward that hath drunk so much?* Tp. III, 2, 30. *deeper than did e. plummet sound*, V, 56. H6B III, 2, 211. Cor. V, 6, 145. Rom. III, 2, 74. 83. Cymb. I, 6, 160. II, 1, 1. Even when being the object: *the rankest smell that e. offended nostril*, Wiv. III, 5, 94. *roared as e. I heard bull-calf*, H4A II, 4, 287.

Contracted to *e'er:* Tp. I, 2, 321. 445. II, 1, 99. III, 1, 89. V, 242. 289. Gentl. IV, 2, 141. V, 4, 77. Meas. V, 63. 361. Merch. II, 4, 34. V, 223. H6A I, 2, 35. V, 4, 66. H6B II, 3, 34 etc. The indef. art. omitted: Tp. III, 3, 101. Wint. IV, 4, 221. V, 1, 11. All's I, 3, 122.

Following *how* and *what*, but severed from them: *how dearly ever parted*, Troil. III, 3, 96. *what bloody business ever*, Oth. III, 3, 469. *what goddess e'er she be*, Troil. I, 1, 27.

Used as a word of enforcement: *that ever this fellow should have fewer words than a parrot*, H4A II, 4, 110. *shall rue the hour that ever thou wast born*, H6C V, 6, 43. *performance is e. the duller for his act*, Tim. V, 1, 26. *truth can never be confirmed enough, though doubts did e. sleep*, Per. V, 1, 204. *has the old man e'er a son?* Wint. IV, 4, 810. *I love thee better than I love e'er a scurvy young boy*, H4B II, 4, 295. *as loud as e'er thou canst*, H6A I, 3, 72.

Or ever = rather than: *would I had met my dearest foe in heaven or e. I had seen that day*, Hml. I, 2; 183 (Ff *ere I had ever*). *Or e'er*, see *Ere.*

2) at all times, through all time: Pilgr. 228. Tp. I, 2, 184. III, 1, 87. Gentl. I, 1, 2. II, 1, 71. III, 1, 36. Meas. I, 2, 76. I, 3, 8. II, 2, 186. III, 1, 188. III, 2, 62. IV, 2, 138. Err. V, 172. Shr. V, 1, 85 etc. etc. = eternally: Ven. 447. Sonn. 19, 4. Tp. IV, 122 etc. *e. right. Menenius e.*, e. Cor. II, 1, 208 (= ever the same). *for e.:* Tp. II, 1, 132. 284. IV, 218. Gentl. V, 4, 119. Wiv. III, 3, 103. Meas. V, 232. Err. III, 1, 106. Merch. IV, 2, 14. H6A II, 4, 109 etc. *for e. and a day:* As IV, 1, 145. Shr. IV, 4, 97. *e. yet:* Ven. 453. Gentl. III, 1, 30. *e. and anon:* LLL V, 2, 101. H4A I, 3, 38. *e. among:* H4B V, 3, 23 (see *Among*). *not e.* = not always: *not e. the justice*

and the truth o' the question carries the due o' the verdict with it, H8 V, 1, 130.

= for ever: *your lordship e. binds him*, Tim. I, 1, 104. *I gave it freely e.* I, 2, 10. *this push will cheer me e., or disseat me now*, Mcb. V, 3, 21. *your poor servant e.* Hml. I, 2, 162.

Contracted to *e'er* only when followed by *since: my desires e'er since pursue me*, Tw. I, 1, 23. *and e'er since sits on his horse*, John II, 288. *my true lip hath virgined it e'er since*, Cor. V, 3, 48.

Ever-angry: *e. bears*, Tp. I, 2, 289.

Ever-burning: *hell*, Tit. III, 1, 243. *lights above*, Oth. III, 3, 463.

Ever-during, everlasting: *an e. blame*, Lucr. 224.

Ever-esteemed, always respectfully observed: *my e. duty*, LLL I, 1, 268 (Armado's letter).

Ever-fired, continually burning: *quench the guards of the e. pole*, Oth. II, 1, 15 (Ff *ever-fixed*).

Ever-fixed, never changing place: *an e. mark*, Sonn. 116, 5. *the e. pole*, Oth. II, 1, 15 (Qq *ever-fired*).

Ever-gentle: Lr. IV, 6, 221 (O. Edd. without the hyphen).

Ever-harmless: Tp. IV, 129.

Everlasting, enduring for ever, eternal: Lucr. 1855. Wiv. III, 3, 31. Meas. III, 1, 59. Err. IV, 2, 33 (*an e. garment*, i. e. a robe of durance, q. c.). Ado IV, 2, 59. Mids. I, 1, 85. All's IV, 3, 11. John II, 284. V, 4, 20. H4A III, 2, 47. H5 IV, 5, 4. H6B II, 1, 18. IV, 9, 13. Troil. V, 3, 5. Tit. III, 1, 51. V, 1, 148. Rom. II, 6, 17. V, 3, 110. Tim. V, 1, 218. Caes. V, 1, 116. Mcb. II, 3, 22. Substantively, *the E* = God: Hml. I, 2, 131.

Everlastingly, for perpetuity: Gentl. II, 4, 163. John V, 7, 105. R2 III, 2, 207. R3 IV, 4, 349.

Ever-living, immortal: *that e. man of memory*, H6A IV, 3, 51.

Evermore = ever; 1) at any time; but only negatively, *not e.* = nevermore: *I may not e. acknowledge thee*, Sonn. 36, 9. *I will not tarry, no, nor e. upon this business my appearance make in any of their courts,* H8 II, 4, 131.

2) at or through all times: Sonn. 70, 12. Meas. IV, 2, 155. Ado II, 1, 11. LLL I, 1, 143. Mids. III, 2, 307. Merch. I, 1, 52. Shr. IV, 5, 10. R2 II, 3, 65. H6B II, 4, 2. H8 III, 2, 172. Troil. IV, 5, 34. Rom. III, 5, 70. 131. Oth. II, 3, 134. III, 3, 295. Per. V, 3, 101. *for e.:* Mids. IV, 1, 181. John V, 7, 107.

3) for ever: *so shall I e. be bound to thee*, Wiv. IV, 6, 54. *e. be blest*, V, 5, 68. Merch. IV, 1, 414. All's I, 1, 6. Tit. IV, 2, 56. Hml. II, 2, 123.

Adjectively? *frantic-mad with e. unrest*, Sonn. 147, 10 (Q *ever-more; ever more?*).

Ever-preserved, never abandoned: *our e. love*, Hml. II, 2, 296.

Ever-running, never stopping: *follows so the e. year*, H5 IV, 1, 293.

Ever-valiant, never daunted: H4A I, 1, 54.

Every, one by one out of an indefinite number; opposed to *no:* Tp. I, 1, 62. I, 2, 195. 197. 303. II, 1, 257. II, 2, 8. 152. Gentl. I, 3, 32. II, 7, 29 etc. etc. *e. third thought*, Tp. V, 311. *e. 'leven wether*, Wint. IV, 3, 33. *in e. ten*, Ant. V, 2, 278. *e. these happened accidents*, Tp. V, 249. *all and e. part*, John

IV, 2, 38. *all my soul and all my e. part*, Sonn. 62, 2. *on thy e. part*, LLL IV, 1, 87. *in my e. action*, Cymb. I, 4, 48. *whose e. passion*, Ant. I, 1, 50. *whose e. touch*, Cymb. I, 6, 101. *e. day*, Tp. II, 1, 4. Gentl. I, 2, 5 etc. *when are you married? why, e. day, to-morrow*, Ado III, 1, 101. *e. man*, Tp. V, 256. Cor. III, 1, 265. Caes. II, 1, 90 etc. *e. one*, Sonn. 53, 3. Tp. IV, 137. Wiv. V, 5, 255. Err. III, 2, 157. IV, 3, 3. LLL V, 2, 123. 331. Merch. II, 9, 17. H4B II, 4, 389. H5 I, 2, 26. H6A II, 2, 14. H6B III, 1, 14 etc. *when e. one to rest themselves betake*, Lucr. 125 (Q1 *himself betakes*). *God send e. one their heart's desire*, Ado III, 4, 60. *e. thing*, Lucr. 602. Tp. II, 1, 49. Gentl. III, 1, 125 etc. etc.

Every, alone, = every one: *e. of this happy number*, As V, 4, 178. *e. of your wishes*, Ant. I, 2, 38.

Used for *each*: *they had gathered a wise council to them of e. realm* (viz Spain and England) H8 II, 4, 52. cf. Lucr. 1739. Caes. II, 1, 90.

Everywhere, 1) in every place: Sonn. 84, 12. 97, 4. 100, 12. 102, 4. Merch. I, 2, 82. As III, 2, 8. Tw. III, 1, 44. V, 235. R2 I, 2, 72. H4B IV, 4, 87. H8 II, 2, 39. Troil. V, 5, 26. Tit. IV, 4, 18. Oth. I, 1, 138 (*of here and e.; cf. Tw. V, 235*).

2) to every place: Mids. I, 1, 6. Tw. II, 4, 80. H6A I, 1, 124. H8 I, 3, 57. Tit. IV, 1, 2.

3) in every part, thoroughly, altogether: *beauty o'ersnowed, and bareness e.* Sonn. 5, 8. *ill faced, worse bodied, shapeless e.*, Err. IV, 2, 20. *the boy Love is perjured e.* Mids. I, 1, 241. cf. Troil. IV, 5, 256.

Evidence, 1) witness, testimony, proof: *thou art too fine in thy e.* All's V, 3, 270. *upon this e.* H8 II, 1, 26. *to be his e. now*, Cymb. V, 5, 368. Plur. —*s*, Wint. V, 2, 41. *bear e. against my soul*, R3 I, 4, 67 (Ff. *give e.*). *to give in e.* Hml. III, 3, 64. *give true e. to his love*, Ant. I, 3, 74.

2) one that bears witness: *his scarlet lust came e. to swear*, Lucr. 1650 (= came as e.). Ado IV, 1, 38. Lr. III, 6, 37. Not inflected in the plur.: *true e. of good esteem*, H6B III, 2, 21. *where are the e.* R3 I, 4, 188 (Ff *is the e.*).

Evident, 1) apparent, manifest: Sonn. 10, 4. Tw. II, 5, 128. Wint. II, 2, 43. H6A II, 4, 23.

2) fit to serve as evidence, conclusive: *render to me some corporal sign about her, more e. than this*, Cymb. II, 4, 120.

3) certain, indubitable: *power … hath not a tomb so e. as a chair to extol what it hath done*, Cor. IV, 7, 52. *we must find an e. calamity, though we had our wish, which side should win*, V, 3, 112.

Evil, subst. 1) any thing which impairs the happiness or perfection of a being: *better is by e. still made better*, Sonn. 119, 10. *my female e. tempteth my better angel from my side*, 144, 5. *our natures do pursue a thirsty e.* Meas. I, 2, 134. *no e. lost is wailed*, Err. IV, 2, 24. Mids. II, 1, 115. As II, 7, 132. H4B IV, 4, 78. Troil. I, 3, 319. Tim. III, 5, 36. Hml. V, 2, 70.

2) wickedness, depravity: *unstained thoughts do seldom dream on e.* Lucr. 87. *O unlooked-for e., when virtue is profaned in such a devil*, 846. *ensconced his secret e.* 1515. *unless this general e. they maintain, all men are bad*, Sonn. 121, 13. Wiv. III, 5, 97. V, 2, 15. All's IV, 3, 321. Wint. I, 2, 303. H5 II, 2, 101. H6B III, 1, 73. Per. Prol. 28.

3) injury, mischief: *we must do good against e.* All's II, 5, 53. *do good for e.* R3 I, 3, 335. *are

you of good or e.? Oth. V, 1, 65. cf. Caes. III, 2, 80. Lr. I, 1, 169. Hml. V, 2, 252.

4) moral offence, crime: *the dire thought of his committed e.* Lucr. 972. *cave-keeping* —*s*, 1250. *to do that e.* Meas. II, 2, 91. 95. *I do repent me, as it is an e.* II, 3, 35. II, 4, 6. III, 2, 21. V, 117. 501. LLL IV, 3, 286. Merch. III, 2, 77. Wint. V, 1, 5. V, 3, 40. H4B V, 5, 71. R3 I, 2, 76. 78 (Ff *crimes*). III, 4, 69 (Qq *this ill*). Tit. V, 3, 186. Caes. II, 1, 79. Mcb. IV, 3, 57. Lr. V, 3, 156. Cymb. V, 5, 60. Per. I, 4, 104.

5) bad quality, imperfection, defect: *maintained so politic a state of e. that they will not admit any good part to intermingle with them*, Ado V, 2, 63. *the principal* —*s that he laid to the charge of women*, As III, 2, 370. All's I, 1, 113. Mcb. IV, 3, 112. Oth. II, 3, 140. 149. Ant. I, 4, 11.

6) disease: *all the embossed sores and headed* —*s*, As II, 7, 67.* *comforting your* —*s*, Wint. II, 3, 56. —*s that take leave*, John III, 4, 114. *would increase his e.* Cor. I, 1, 183. *'tis called the e.* Mcb. IV, 3, 146 (viz the King's Evil).

7) misfortune: *that I may bear my* —*s alone*, Tw. II, 1, 6. *to acquaint you with this e.* John V, 6, 25. *an ensuing e.* H8 II, 1, 141. —*s imminent*, Caes. II, 2, 81. *accidental* —*s*, IV, 3, 146. *too true an e.* Oth. I, 1, 161.

8) a privy, a draught house? At least it has been interpreted so in the following passages: *to raze the sanctuary and pitch our* —*s there*, Meas. II, 2, 172. *build their* —*s on the graves of men*, H8 II, 1, 67 (cf. 2 Kings 10, 27).

Evil, adj. 1) bad, having qualities tending to injury and mischief: *I do it not in e. disposition*, Meas. I, 2, 122. *ill deeds are doubled with an e. word*, Err. III, 2, 20. *like an e. angel*, IV, 3, 20. LLL I, 2, 178. H4B I, 2, 186 (Q *ill*). *planets e.* Troil. I, 3, 92. *thy e. spirit*, Caes. IV, 3, 282. *evils that take leave, on their departure most of all show e.* John III, 4, 115. *things e.* H5 IV, 1, 4. *an e. diet*, R3 I, 1, 139. *an e. sign*, H6C V, 6, 44. *in e. mixture*, Troil. I, 3, 95.

2) wicked, morally corrupt: *an e. nature*, Tp. I, 2, 93. *e. deeds*, Meas. I, 3, 38. *an angel is not e.* LLL V, 2, 105. Lucr. 1245. Merch. I, 3, 100. H6B III, 3, 5. H6C I, 4, 117. H8 IV, 2, 45. Lr. I, 2, 136. III, 5, 7.

Adverbially: *how e. it beseems thee*, H6C IV, 7, 84. *were he e. used*, H8 I, 2, 207. Lr. I, 1, 169.

Evil-eyed, malicious: *e. unto you*, Cymb. I, 1, 72.

Evilly, badly, ill: *this act so e. born*, John III, 4, 149. *good deeds e. bestowed*, Tim. IV, 3, 467.

Evitate, to avoid: Wiv. V, 5, 241.

Ewe, female sheep: Pilgr. 246. Tp. V, 38. Ado III, 3, 74. Merch. I, 3, 81. 87. 96. IV, 1, 74. As III, 2, 54. 81. 83. Wint. IV, 4, 461. H4B III, 2, 55. H6C II, 5, 35. Oth. I, 1, 89.

Ewer, a kind of pitcher, used to bring water for washing the hands: Shr. Ind. 1, 57. II, 350. Tim. III, 1, 7.

Exact, adj. (ŏ—; but see Appendix I, 1: Chang. Acc.) accurate, precise, strict: *the true and e. performer*, All's III, 6, 65 (who is precisely, really the performer). *to set the e. wealth of all our states all at one cast*, H4A IV, 1, 46. *severals and generals of grace e.* Troil. I, 3, 180 (the minutest peculiar and general excellencies). *I have with e. view perused thee*, IV, 5, 232. *the —est auditors*, Tim. II, 2, 165. *an e. command*, Hml. V, 2, 19. *and in the most e. regard support the worships of their name*, Lr. I, 4, 287.

Exact, vb. to demand authoritatively, to extort: Tp. I, 2, 99. Meas. III, 2, 295. Merch. I, 3, 138. IV, 1, 22. H6B IV, 7, 42.

Exaction, compulsion to pay, extortion: Merch. I, 3, 166. R2 II, 1, 249. H8 I, 2, 25. 47. 52. 54.

Exactly, 1) accurately: Tp. I, 2, 238. 499. Hml. I, 2, 200. Ant. V, 2, 139. Cymb. II, 4, 75.

2) earnestly? or expressly? *and e. begged your grace's pardon*, R2 I, 1, 140.

Exalt, to raise on high, to elevate: *in his own grace he doth e. himself more than in your addition*, Lr. V, 3, 67. Partic. —*ed* = high: *with a more —ed respect*, Tw. II, 5, 31. *the most —ed shores*, Caes. I, 1, 65. *to be —ed with the threatening clouds*, I, 3, 8 (cf. *With*).

Examination, inquiry by interrogatories, trial: Ado III, 5, 53 *(take their e.).* IV, 2, 68. All's III, 6, 29. H8 I, 1, 116. II, 1, 16. Used by Dogberry for examine: Ado III, 5, 64 (Ff *examine*).

Examine, 1) to inspect carefully, to inquire into, to explore: Wiv. I, 3, 67. Ado I, 1, 291. II, 3, 216. Mids. I, 1, 68. John I, 89. H5 IV, 1, 69. Cor. I, 1, 153. Rom. I, 1, 234. I, 3, 83.

2) to interrogate as in a judicial proceeding: Ado III, 5, 51. 64 (Qq *examination*). IV, 2, 6. 8. 36. V, 1, 322. As IV, 1, 203. H4A II, 4, 413. H6B IV, 2, 105.

3) to question, to doubt: *all her deserving is a reserved honesty, and that I have not heard —d*, All's III, 5, 66.

Example, subst. 1) pattern, precedent for imitation; in a good as well as a bad sense: Lucr. 1194. Compl. 157. 268. Meas. III, 1, 191. Ado V, 1, 332. Merch. III, 1, 74. IV, 1, 221. All's III, 5, 23. John V, 1, 52. H4B IV, 1, 82. H5 II, 2, 45. IV, 1, 19. H6B IV, 2, 190. H8 I, 2, 90. I, 3, 62. IV, 2, 11. 44. Cor. II, 2, 108. Hml. IV, 4, 46. Ant. III, 10, 28. Cymb. V, 3, 36. *to make a person an e.*: Meas. I, 4, 68. Wint. IV, 4, 847. Oth. II, 3, 251. *the wars must make —s out of their best*, III, 3, 65 (Ff *example*).

2) instance: Meas. IV, 2, 100. Tw. II, 5, 44. Wint. I, 2, 357. John III, 4, 13. H5 II, 4, 12. Cor. IV, 6, 50. *there's much e. for 't*, Tim. I, 2, 47. *for e.*: Meas. I, 2, 26. H6B IV, 7, 58.

Example, vb. 1) to give a precedent for: *that I may e. my digression by some mighty precedent*, LLL I, 2, 121. *ill, to e. ill*, IV, 3, 124. *bloodshed ... —d by this heinous spectacle*, John IV, 3, 56. *hear her but —d by herself*, H5 I, 2, 156. *every step, —d by the first pace*, Troil. I, 3, 132. *I'll e. you with thievery*, Tim. IV, 3, 438.

2) to give an instance of: *the store which should e. where your equal grew*, Sonn. 84, 4. *I will e. it*, LLL III, 84.

Exasperate, vb. to provoke, to make angry: Tw. III, 2, 20. Lr. V, 1, 60. Unchanged in the partic.: *why art thou then e.*, Troil. V, 1, 34. *this report hath so e. the king*, Mcb. III, 6, 38.

Exceed, 1) trans. a) to go beyond: *in love whose leave —s commission*, Ven. 568. *which far —s*

his barren skill to show, Lucr. 81. *your own science —s the lists of all advice*, Meas. I, 1, 6. *e. all instance*, Tw. IV, 3, 12. *thy cruelty hath —ed law*, H6B I, 3, 136. *let not her penance e. the king's commission*, II, 4, 75. *my mind —s the compass of her wheel*, H6C IV, 3, 47. *to be wise and love —s man's might*, Troil. III, 2, 164. *e. the common*, Cor. IV, 1, 32. *a return —ing all use of quittance*, Tim. I, 1, 290. *let it not e. three days*, Oth. III, 3, 63. *do not e. the prescript of this scroll*, Ant. III, 8, 4.

b) to surpass: Ven. 292. Sonn. 32, 8. 83, 3. 150, 8. Gentl. III, 1, 166. Ado I, 1, 193. Merch. III, 2, 159. As I, 2, 256. All's V, 3, 338. H4A IV, 3, 28. H6A I, 1, 15. I, 2, 56. 90. R3 I, 3, 218. Cor. IV, 2, 39. 42. IV, 5, 236. Tim. I, 2, 210. Hml. V, 2, 173. Ant. IV, 7, 3. Cymb. I, 4, 156. V, 2, 9.

2) intr. a) to be greater: *the guilt being great, the fear doth still e.* Lucr. 229.

b) to be paramount: *O, that —s*, Ado III, 4, 17. *to make some good, but others to e.* Per. II, 3, 16. Partic. —*ing* = extraordinary, surpassing: Gentl. II, 1, 100. All's V, 1, 1. H6A V, 4, 41. H6B V, 1, 70. Oth. III, 3, 258. The gerund substantively: *to —ing good*, Tw. III, 4, 174 (= to excess, eminently).

Exceeding, adv. uncommonly, extremely (never joined to verbs): Err. I, 1, 57. Ado II, 3, 167. III, 4, 25. 53. V, 4, 118. LLL V, 2, 532. Merch. I, 1, 67. II, 2, 54. H4A IV, 2, 75. H4B II, 2, 1. III, 2, 84. 293. IV, 5, 11. V, 2, 3. H8 I, 4, 28. IV, 2, 52. Cymb. I, 6, 59.

Exceedingly, the same; mostly followed by *well*: LLL III, 144. H4A I, 3, 282. III, 1, 166. Oth. II, 3, 372. *methinks it is very sultry and hot ... e., my lord*, Hml. V, 2, 103.

Excel, 1) trans. to surpass: Ven. 293. Lucr. 191. Tp. II, 1, 168. Gentl. IV, 2, 51. LLL I, 2, 78. All's IV, 3, 321. Wint. V, 3, 16. Rom. II, 5, 41. III, 5, 225. Oth. II, 1, 63. Cymb. I, 4, 80. *valour and pride e. themselves in Hector*, Troil. IV, 5, 79.

2) intr. to be excellent or exquisite: Ven. 443. 1131. Sonn. 5, 4. Gentl. IV, 2, 50. 83. LLL IV, 3, 41. H6A V, 5, 38. Oth. V, 2, 11.

Excellence, 1) the state of possessing good qualities in an eminent degree: Sonn. 94, 8. Meas. I, 1, 38. Ado III, 1, 99. LLL IV, 3, 300. John II, 439. IV, 3, 66. H5 II, 2, 113. Hml. V, 2, 146. Cymb. I, 6, 44.

2) high degree, uncommon manner: *kind is my love to-day, to-morrow kind, still constant in a wondrous e.* Sonn. 105, 6. *loves him with that e. that angels love good men with*, H8 II, 2, 34.

3) any laudable quality, eminent skill: *what is thy e. in a galliard?* Tw. I, 3, 127. Wint. V, 3, 30. Hml. IV, 7, 132. V, 2, 143.

4) a title of honour given a) to kings: H6A V, 1, 4. H6B I, 1, 3. I, 3, 122. b) to princes of the royal house: H6A V, 4, 94. H6B I, 1, 161.

Excellency, high quality, eminence: Wiv. II, 2, 252. Ado II, 3, 48. Tw. II, 3, 163. Oth. II, 1, 65 *(does bear an e.; Ff does tire the ingeniver). is there not a double e. in this?* Wiv. III, 3, 187.

Excellent, adj. highly praiseworthy, eminent: Sonn. 38, 3. Pilgr. 102. Tp. III, 2, 118. III, 3, 39. IV, 244. Gentl. II, 1, 100. 145. Wiv. II, 2, 234. III, 3, 246. H7. IV, 4, 69. Meas. II, 2, 107. Err. III, 1, 109. Ado I, 1, 52. II, 1, 7. 127. 337. II, 3, 36. 87. III, 1, 89. III, 4, 23. 63. LLL I, 2, 179. IV, 3, 354. V, 1, 144.

Mids. III, 2, 247. V, 219. Merch. IV, 1, 246. As I, 2, 129. 197. III, 4, 12. Shr. Ind. I, 67. All's I, 1, 32. III, 6, 51. Tw. I, 3, 100. II, 1, 13. II, 5, 140. H4A II, 3, 20. H4B II, 4, 22. H6A I, 2, 110. H6B III, 1, 230. R3 I, 4, 162. Cor. I, 3, 101. Rom. I, 2, 52. Tim. III, 3, 27 etc. etc. In a bad sense: *that e. grand tyrant of the earth,* R3 IV, 4, 52. *e. falsehood!* Ant. I, 1, 40. *this is the e. foppery of the world,* Lr. I, 2, 128. Tit. II, 3, 7.

Excellent, adv. well in a high degree, eminently: *he hath an e. good name,* Ado III, 1, 98. As V, 1, 29. *thou didst it e.* Shr. Ind. I, 89. *it becomes me well enough, does't not? e.* Tw. I, 3, 108. *e. good,* II, 3, 46. H4B II, 2, 36. II, 4, 25. *this comes off well and e.* Tim. I, 1, 29. *e. well,* Hml. II, 2, 174. *how fares our cousin Hamlet? e.* III, 2, 98. *e. well,* Oth. II, 3, 121. *e. good,* IV, 1, 226. *operate most vilely; for my vantage e.* Cymb. V, 5, 198.

Excellently, 1) eminently, extremely well: Ado III, 4, 13. All's IV, 3, 237. Tw. I, 5, 185. 254. III, 4, 206.

2) in a high degree: *no man alive can love in such a sort the thing he means to kill more e.* Troil. IV, 1, 24 (cf. *Excellence,* def. 2).

Except, vb. 1) trans. a) to take out of a number, to exclude: *e. not any,* Gentl. II, 4, 154. *—ing one,* R2 IV, 31. R3 I, 1, 99. *—ing none,* H6B I, 1, 193 (used blunderingly by Verges: Ado III, 5, 33). *only you —ed,* Ado I, 1, 126. As III, 2, 103. *always —ed my dear Claudio,* Ado III, 1, 93.

b) to object to, to protest against, to refuse: *desire is death, which physic did e.* Sonn. 147, 8. *let her e. before —ed,* Tw. I, 3, 7 (allusion to a law-phrase). *my high blood's royalty, which fear, not reverence, makes thee to e.* R2 I, 1, 72. *within the bond of marriage ... is it —ed I should know no secrets?* Caes. II, 1, 281 (made a reservation).

2) intr. to object: *let her e.* Tw. I, 3, 7. Followed by *against:* Gentl. I, 3, 83. II, 4, 155.

Except, prepos. taken out, not included: Gentl. I, 2, 120. II, 1, 164. II, 4, 154. John II, 489. R2 I, 3, 44. H6A I, 1, 91. Caes. I, 2, 60. Hml. II, 2, 221. Preceded by the noun: *Richard e.* R3 V, 3, 243.

Except, conj. 1) unless; followed by the subjunctive: Gentl. II, 4, 140. III, 1, 178. Err. V, 55. H5 IV, 4, 10. H6A I, 1, 43. II, 5, 111. III, 1, 34. 113. 117. H6B III, 1, 267. V, 1, 9. H6C III, 2, 47. Mcb. I, 2, 39. Cymb. I, 5, 81. By an inf.: Merch. II, 1, 12. John I, 73. R2 II, 2, 139. *e. thou wilt ...,* Gentl. II, 4, 155.

2) with the exception that: *more I know not, e. he had the honour ...,* All's IV, 3, 300. *e. the north-east wind awaked the sleeping rheum,* R2 I, 4, 6.

Exception, contradiction, objection, disapprobation: *knew the true minute when e. bid him speak,* All's I, 2, 40. *he doth deny his prisoners, but with proviso and e.* H4A I, 3, 78. *how modest in e.* H5 II, 4, 34. *'tis positive 'gainst all —s,* IV, 2, 25. *what I have done, that might your nature, honour and e. roughly awake, I here proclaim was madness,* Hml. V, 2, 242. *to take —s =* to disapprove, to find fault; followed by *at:* Gentl. V, 2, 3. H6A IV, 1, 105. By *to:* Gentl. I, 3, 81. Tw. I, 3, 6. H6C III, 2, 46. By *against:* *thou hast taken against me a most just e.* Oth. IV, 2, 211 (Qq conception).

Exceptless, making no exception, extending to all: *forgive my general and e. rashness,* Tim. IV, 3, 502.

Excess, 1) superfluity, too much of a thing: Merch. III, 2, 113. All's I, 1, 67. Rom. II, 6, 33. Lr. IV, 1, 73. Interest on money called so contemptuously: Merch. I, 3, 63. With *of:* Gentl. III, 1, 220. Tw. I, 1, 2. H5 II, 2, 42. Oth. IV, 1, 100.

2) immoderate indulgence; a) intemperance: *the profit of e. is but to surfeit,* Lucr. 138. *not where want cries some, but where e. begs all,* Compl. 42. *the blood of youth burns not with such e.* LLL V, 2, 73. *shame that they wanted cunning in e., hath broke their hearts,* Tim. V, 4, 28. b) profusion: *worms, inheritors of this e.* Sonn. 146, 7. *wasteful and ridiculous e.* John IV, 2, 16.

Excessive, immoderate: *e. pride,* Lucr. Arg. 1. *grief,* All's I, 1, 65.

Exchange, subst. 1) the act of giving and receiving reciprocally: Ado II, 1, 320. Wint. IV, 4, 689. 691. *the allusion holds in the e.* LLL V, 2, 42 (in applying one word for the other). *to make e.* Gentl. II, 2, 6. *make an e.* Wint. IV, 4, 647. *made e. of vow,* Rom. II, 3, 62. *the e. of thy vow for mine,* II, 2, 127. *in e. of it =* for it: Wiv. II, 2, 243. *I have got, in e. of a hundred and fifty soldiers, three hundred and odd pounds,* H4A IV, 2, 14. *desired my Cressid in right great e.* Troil. III, 3, 21 (i. e. in a fair e. for a person of importance).

2) the thing given or received in return: *it cannot countervail the e. of joy that one short minute gives me in her sight,* Rom. II, 6, 4. *and the e. my brother,* Lr. IV, 6, 280. *there's my e.* V, 3, 97. *if Hamlet give the first or second hit, or quit in answer of the third e.* Hml. V, 2, 280 (i. e. the third hit received).

3) the act of transferring money by bills: *I have bills for money by e. from Florence,* Shr. IV, 2, 89.

4) the place where merchants meet? It may be meant in the blunder of Dull: *the collusion holds in the e.* LLL IV, 2, 43. Meant, but not called so in Merch. I, 3, 50.

5) change, transmutation: *I am much ashamed of my e.* Merch. II, 6, 35.

Exchange, vb. 1) to give and take reciprocally: *—d our children,* H4A I, 1, 87. *let's e. charity,* Lr. V, 3, 166. Having *for* before the thing received: *e. the bad for better,* Gentl. II, 6, 13. H4A III, 2, 146. H6A I, 4, 29. Tim. IV, 3, 527. Oth. III, 3, 180. Cymb. I, 1, 119. *For* before the thing given: *what shalt thou e. for rags? robes,* LLL IV, 1, 84 (Armado's speech). *With* before the person receiving the thing given: Shr. V, 1, 128. Wint. IV, 4, 284. Hml. V, 2, 340. *With* before the thing received: *to shift his being is to e. one misery with another,* Cymb. I, 5, 55.

2) to change, to alter: *not with the time —d,* Sonn. 109, 7.

Exchequer, treasury: Sonn. 67, 11. Gentl. II, 4, 43. Wiv. I, 3, 78. R2 II, 3, 65. H4A II, 2, 39. 57. III, 3, 205. H5 III, 6, 137.

Excite, to rouse, stir up: *the push and enmity of those this quarrel would e.* Troil. II, 2, 138. With *to =* to impel: *every reason —s to this, that my lady loves me,* Tw. II, 5, 178. *what —s your most worshipful thought to think so?* H4B II, 2, 64 (O. Edd. *accites*). *to the grim alarm,* Mcb. V, 2, 5. *—d me to treason,* Cymb. V, 5, 345.

Excitement, impulsion, exhortation, encouragement: —*s to the field, or speech for truce,* Troil. l, 3, 182. —*s of my reason and my blood,* Hml. IV, 4, 58.

Exclaim, subst. outcry, cry of distress: Troil. V, 3, 91. Plur. —*s:* R2 I, 2, 2. R3 I, 2, 52. IV, 4, 135. Tit. IV, 1, 86.

Exclaim, vb. 1) to cry, to declare aloud: *the French —ed the devil was in arms,* H6A I, 1, 125. *that thus you do e. you'll go with him,* H6B IV, 8, 37.

2) to cry out querulously or outrageously: Ven. 886. All's I, 3, 123. H6A IV, 1, 83. R3 III, 4, 104. With *against* = to rail at: *she —s against repose and rest,* Lucr. 757. *against the thing he sought he would e.* Compl. 313. *e. against their own succession,* Hml. II, 2, 367. *e. no more a. it* (viz wine) Oth. II, 3, 314. With *on* = to accuse loudly: —*s on Death,* Ven. 930. *on the direful night,* Lucr. 741. Merch. III, 2, 176. H6A III, 3, 60. IV, 4, 30. V, 3, 134. R3 III, 3, 15 (not in Qq).

Exclamation, vociferous reproach: Lucr. 705. John II, 558. H4B II, 1, 88. R3 IV, 4, 153. H8 I, 2, 52. Misapplied in Ado III, 5, 28.

Exclude, to shut out, to keep off: —*s all pity from our threatening looks,* Err. I, 1, 10.

Excommunicate, excommunicated, interdicted from the rites of the church: *stand cursed and e.* John III, 1, 173. *stand e. and cursed,* 223.

Excommunication, Dogberry's blunder for *examination:* Ado III, 5, 69.

Excrement, 1) alvine discharges: *the earth's a thief, that feeds and breeds by a composture stolen from general e.* Tim. IV, 3, 445.

2) that which grows out of the body, hair, beard: *why is Time such a niggard of hair, being, as it is, so plentiful an e.?* Err. II, 2, 79. *dally with my e., with my mustachio,* LLL V, 1, 109. *assume but valour's e.* (the beard of Hercules) Merch. III, 2, 87. *let me packet up my pedlar's e.* Wint. IV, 4, 734. *your bedded hair, like life in —s, starts up,* Hml. III, 4, 121.

Excusable, admitting of justification, pardonable: Ant. III, 4, 2.

Excuse, subst. 1) plea offered in extenuation, apology: *you do it for increase: O strange e.!* Ven. 791. Lucr. 267. 1073. 1316. 1614. Gentl. I, 3, 82. III, 1, 168. Ado IV, 1, 176. LLL V, 2, 432. Mids. III, 2, 245. V, 363. Merch. II, 4, 37. As III, 3, 94. Wint. V, 1, 47. John II, 119. IV, 2, 31. H4A III, 2, 19. V, 2, 17. H4B V, 1, 6. 7. H5 V Chor. 3. H6C II, 6, 71. Troil. II, 3, 173. III, 1, 156. Ant. II, 2, 56. Cymb. III, 2, 67. *I will not have e.* Per. II, 3, 96. *to make e.* or —*s:* Ven. 188. Lucr. 114. 225. 1653. R3 I, 2, 84.

2) the act of apologizing: *in way of thy e.* Tw. I, 5, 3. *pleading so wisely in e. of it,* H4B IV, 5, 181. Rom. I, 4, 1. III, 1, 197. *make my old e.* Sonn. 2, 11 (= e. of my old age). *make your e.* Tw. I, 5, 33. Troil. III, 1, 85. 99 (Q *makes e.; i. e. make his e.*). Rom. II, 5, 33.

3) justification, pardon: *this desire might have e.* Lucr. 235. 238. Sonn. 51, 5. Shr. Ind. 2, 126. Cor. V, 6, 69. *to give e.* = to pardon: Lucr. 1715. Cor. I, 3, 114.

Excuse, vb. 1) to plead for, to justify, vindicate; a) absol.: *never e.* Mids. III, 363. b) trans.: Ven. 403. Sonn. 35, 8. 42, 5. 51, 1. 101,

10. 139, 9. Gentl. II, 6, 8. Wiv. III, 3, 206. Meas. II, 4, 119. IV, 1, 12. Err. III, 1, 1. 92. IV, 1, 48. Merch. IV, 1, 64. As IV, 1, 172. Shr. III, 2, 110. All's V, 3, 55. John IV, 2, 30. H8 V, 3, 149. Cor. IV, 7, 11. Rom. III, 1, 69. V, 3, 227. Tim. II, 2, 141. Oth. V, 1, 94. Ant. I, 4, 24. V, 2, 290. Cymb. III, 2, 66.

2) to apologize for not doing: *e. it not, for I am peremptory,* Gentl. I, 3, 71 (= do not decline it). *I must e. myself,* Wiv. III, 2, 54 (= I cannot come). *you must e. me,* H4B V, 1, 3. 5. 6. 7. *e. me to the king,* H6C V, 5, 46 (account for my absence). *the reason that I have to love thee doth much e. the appertaining rage to such a greeting,* Rom. III, 1, 66 (= account for the want of rage). *the excuse that thou dost make in this delay is longer than the tale thou dost e.* II, 5, 34.

3) to pardon, to acquit: *we cite our faults that they may hold —d our lawless lives,* Gentl. IV, 1, 54. *pitied and —d of every hearer,* Ado IV, 1, 218. R2 V, 3, 65. H5 V, 2, 329. H6A V, 5, 98. H8 II, 4, 156. 161. Troil. I, 2, 87. Tit. IV, 2, 105. Cymb. III, 5, 46. *stand —d:* John IV, 3, 51. R3 I, 2, 86. *to e. one's self* = to clear one's self from guilt: *pray God the Duke of York e. himself,* H6B I, 3, 181. R3 I, 2, 82.

Execrable, abominable: Tit. V, 3, 177.

Execrations, detestations, curses: H6B III, 2, 305. Troil. II, 3, 7.

Execute, 1) to carry into execution, to effect, to perform: Lucr. 877. Tp. II, 1, 148. Meas. V, 527. Merch. III, 1, 75. Shr. I, 1, 251. Tw. III, 4, 30. Wint. IV, 2, 17. V, 1, 162. H4A I, 2, 180. III, 1, 82. H6B III, 1, 256. IV, 1, 130. H8 I, 1, 198. Troil. III, 3, 50. IV, 1, 13. Cor. IV, 5, 232. Tit. V, 2, 15. With *on: to e. the like upon thyself,* H6C II, 4, 10. *this vengeance on me had they —d,* Tit. II, 3, 113. *were there worse end than death, that end upon them should be —d,* 303. Absol.: *work thou the way, and thou shalt e.* H6C V, 7, 25.

2) to practise, to let work, to indulge: —*ing the outward face of royalty,* Tp. I, 2, 104. *wounding flouts, which you on all estates will e.* LLL V, 2, 855. *e. thy wrath in me alone,* R3 I, 4, 71 (cf. Tit. II, 3, 113). *in fellest manner e. your arms,* Troil. V, 7, 6. *when my lust hath dined, which I will e. in the clothes ...,* Cymb. III, 5, 147. Intrans.: *Cassio following him with determined sword, to e. upon him,* Oth. II, 3, 228 (= to wreak his anger upon him; sich an ihm auszulassen).

3) to put to death in a legal form: Gentl. IV, 4, 35. Meas. II, 1, 34. IV, 2, 124. 132. 137. 167. 182. IV, 3, 35. H5 III, 6, 107. 111. H6A II, 4, 91. R3 V, 3, 96. Tim III, 5, 103. Per. IV, 6, 137.

4) to kill, to destroy: *didst send two of thy men to the noble duke, R2 IV, 82. whom with my bare fists I would e.* H6A I, 4, 36. Absol.: *if murdering innocents be —ing,* H6C V, 6, 32.

Execution, 1) a carrying into effect, performance: Gentl. I, 3, 36. Meas. I, 1, 60. II, 2, 11. Wint. I, 2, 260. H4B IV, 1, 174. H6A V, 5, 99. R3 I, 3, 346. Troil. III, 2, 89. Cor. II, 1, 257. III, 3, 21. Rom. IV, 1, 69. Caes. I, 2, 301. Mcb. III, 1, 105.

2) action, working: *scarce I can refrain the e. of my big-swoln heart upon that Clifford,* H6C II, 2, 111. *by reason guide his* (the ram's) *e.* Troil. I, 3, 210. *the sway, revenue, e. of the rest,* Lr. I, 1, 139. *the e. of his wit, hands, heart,* Oth. III, 3, 466.

3) any deed of hostility and violence, blows, slaughter, destruction: *be swift like lightning in the e.* R2 I, 3, 79. *holds his infant up and hangs resolved correction in the arm that was upreared to e.* H4B IV, 1, 214. *retreat is made and e. stayed,* IV, 3, 78. *doing the e. and the act for which we have assembled them,* H5 II, 2, 17. *hath done to-day mad and fantastic e.* Troil. V, 5, 38. *to do some fatal e.* Tit. II, 3, 36. *his brandished steel, which smoked with bloody e.* Mcb. 1, 2, 18. With *on*: *do e. on the watch,* H6A III, 2, 35. Tit. IV, 2, 84. V, 3, 76. *thy cruelty in e. upon offenders hath exceeded law,* H6B I, 3, 135.

4) death lawfully inflicted: Gentl. IV, 2, 134. Meas. I, 4, 74. IV, 2, 24. 159. Err. V, 121. Wint. 1, 2, 446. R2 III, 1, 30. H4B IV, 3, 80. H5 III, 6, 58. H6A II, 5, 99. V, 4, 54. H6B II, 3, 6. R3 III, 5, 46. H8 IV, 2, 121. Cor. V, 2, 52. V, 4, 8. Cymb. III, 2, 72. *is e. done on Cawdor?* Mcb. I, 4, 1.

Executioner, 1) he who puts to death in pursuance of a legal warrant: Meas. IV, 2, 9. 222. As III, 5, 3. 8. R2 III, 4, 33. H6C II, 2, 123. V, 6, 30. 33. Cymb. IV, 2, 128.

2) Euphemism for murderer: H6B III, 1, 276. R3 I, 2, 119. 186. I, 3, 339.

Exécutor, 1) one who executes, carries into effect: *such baseness had never like e.* Tp. III, 1, 13.

2) one who disposes of another's heritage: *thy unused beauty must be tombed with thee, which, used, lives the e. to be,* Sonn. 4, 14. *let's choose —s and talk of wills,* R2 III, 2, 148. *and their —s, the knavish crows, fly o'er them, all impatient for their hour,* H5 IV, 2, 51.

3) executioner: *delivering o'er to —s pale the lazy drone,* H5 I, 2, 203 (in this sense accented on the first syll.)

Exempt, adj. 1) free from, not liable to; followed by *from*: *the king is not e. from envious malice of thy swelling heart,* H6A III, 1, 25. *e. from fear,* H6B IV, 1, 129. *from envy,* H6C III, 3, 127. *yourself are not e. from this,* R3 II, 1, 18 (Qq *in this*).

2) cut off, kept far: *be it my wrong you are from me e.* Err. II, 2, 173. *this our life e. from public haunt finds tongues in trees,* As II, 1, 15. *corrupted and e. from ancient gentry,* H6C IV, 1, 4, 93. *who would not wish to be from wealth e., since riches point to misery and contempt,* Tim. IV, 2, 31.

Exempt, vb. to rid, to keep far: *things done well e. themselves from fear,* H8 I, 2, 89. *—ed be from me the arrogance to choose from forth the royal blood of France,* Alls II, 1, 198.

Exequies, funeral rites: H6A III, 2, 133.

Exercise, subst. 1) any kind of habitual practice or exertion to acquire skill, knowledge, or grace: *for any or for all these —s* (viz war, travels, studies) Gentl. I, 3, 11. *be in eye of every e. worthy his youth,* 32. *allow me such —s as may become a gentleman,* As I, 1, 76. *less frequent to his princely —s,* Wint. IV, 2, 37. *deny his youth the rich advantage of good e.* John IV, 2, 60. *gentle e. and proof of arms,* H4A V, 2, 55. *friends, whose house, whose bed, whose meal and e. are still together,* Cor. IV, 4, 14. *forgone all custom of e.* Hml. II, 2, 308 (Qq *—s*). *show of such an e.* (viz reading) *may colour your loneliness,* III, 1, 45.

2) skill acquired: *to invest their sons with arts and martial —s,* H4B IV, 5, 74. *swelling o'er with arts and e.* Troil. IV, 4, 80. *gave you such a masterly report for art and e. in your defence,* Hml. IV, 7, 98.

3) bodily exertion, action, motion: *thy e. hath been too violent for a second course of fight,* Cor. I, 5, 16. *hard at hand comes the master and main e., the incorporate conclusion,* Oth. II, 1, 269.

4) act of devotion, performance of religious duties: *once a day I'll visit the chapel where they lie, and tears shed there shall be my recreation: so long as nature will bear up with this e., so long I daily vow to use it,* Wint. III, 2, 242. *I am in your debt for your last e.* R3 III, 2, 112. *to draw him from his holy e.* III, 7, 64. *much castigation, e. devout,* Oth. III, 4, 41.

5) occupation in general, ordinary task, habitual activity: *urchins shall forth at vast of night, that they may work all e. on thee,* Tp. I, 2, 328 (all their wonted mischievous doing). *he's all my e., my mirth, my matter,* Wint. I, 2, 166. *hunting was his daily e.* H6C IV, 6, 85. *those mouths ... are now starved for want of e.* Per. I, 4, 38.

Exercise, vb. 1) trans. to perform, to practise: *no longer e. upon a valiant race thy injuries,* Cymb. V, 4, 82.

2) intr. to practise gymnastics: *in the common show-place, where they e.* Ant. III, 6, 12. As for Tp. I, 2, 328, see Subst. def. 5.

Exeter, English town: R3 IV, 2, 106. *bishop of E.* IV, 4, 503. *the Duke of E.* R2 II, 1, 281. *Duke of E.,* uncle to King Henry V: H5 II, 2, 39. III, 3, 51. III, 6, 6 etc. IV, 3, 9. 53 etc. V, 2, 83. H6A III, 1, 200. H6C I, 1, 72. 80 etc. II, 5, 137. IV, 8, 34. 48.

Exhalation, a bright phenomenon, a meteor: *no natural e. in the sky,* John II, 4, 153. *do you see these meteors? do you behold these —s?* H4A III, 4, 352. *I shall fall like a bright e. in the evening,* H8 III, 2, 226. *the —s whizzing in the air give so much light,* Caes. II, 1, 44.

Exhale, to draw out: *the grave doth gape, and doting death is near; therefore e.* H5 II, 1, 66 (= draw your sword; Pistol's speech). *'tis thy presence that —s this blood from cold and empty veins,* R3 I, 2, 58. *what these sorrows could not thence* (from my eyes) *e., thy beauty hath,* 166. Used of the sun drawing up vapours and thus causing meteors: *with rotten damps ravish the morning air: let their —d unwholesome breaths make sick the life of purity,* Lucr. 779. *breath a vapour is; then, thou fair sun, e. this vapour now; in thee it is,* Pilgr. 39 and LLL IV, 3, 70. *be no more an —d meteor, a prodigy of fear and a portent,* H4A V, 1, 19. *it is some meteor that the sun —s,* Rom. III, 5, 13. cf. *Hale.*

Exhaust, to draw out wholly, to drain: *spare not the babe, whose dimpled smiles from fools e. their mercy,* Tim. IV, 3, 119.

Exhibit, to present, to offer officially: Wiv. II, 1, 29. Meas. IV, 4, 11. H6A III, 1, 151. Misapplied: Merch. II, 3, 10.

Exhibiter, he who presents (a bill): H5 I, 1, 74.

Exhibition, allowance, pension: Gentl. I, 3, 69. Lr. I, 2, 25. Oth. I, 3, 238. IV, 3, 75. Cymb. I, 6, 122. Used blunderingly by Verges: Ado IV, 2, 5.

Exhort, to incite by words, to impel: H6B IV, 10, 79. Hml. IV, 4, 46.

Exhortation, admonition: Merch. I, 1, 104 (supposed to be an allusion to the long sermons of the Puritans, the last part of which was termed so).

Exigent, subst. 1) exigence, pressing necessity, decisive moment: *why do you cross me in this e.?* Caes. V, 1, 19. *thou art sworn, that when the e. should come, ... thou then wouldst kill me,* Ant. IV, 14, 63.

2) end: *these eyes wax dim, as drawing to their e.* H6A II, 5, 9.

Exile, subst. 1) banishment (*éxile* and *exíle*): Pilgr. 189. Gentl. III, 2, 3. V, 4, 155. As I, 1, 107. 115. II, 1, 1. R2 I, 3, 151. 217. H6B III, 2, 382. Cor. I, 6, 35. III, 3, 89. IV, 6, 132. V, 3, 45. 96. Rom. III, 3, 13. 20 (*world's e. is death*). 43. 140. V, 3, 211. Cymb. II, 3, 46. III, 5, 36. IV, 4, 26.

2) one banished (*éxile*): Tit. III, 1, 285. Cymb. I, 1, 166.

Exile, vb. (*exíle;* as for *exiled,* see Appendix I, 1) to banish: Lucr. Arg. 25. Lucr. 640. Mids. III, 2, 386. As V, 4, 171. R2 I, 3, 283. Rom. III, 1, 192. III, 2, 133. Mcb. V, 8, 66. Cymb. V, 4, 59. *From omitted: and equity —d your highness' land,* H6B III, 1, 146.

Exion, blunder of Mrs. Quickly for action: H4B II, 1, 32.

Exist, to live: Meas. III, 1, 20 (*exists* for *existest*). Lr. I, 1, 114. Oth. III, 4, 112.

Exit, departure of a player from the stage: LLL V, 1, 141. V, 2, 598. As II, 7, 141.

Exorciser, conjurer, one who can raise spirits: Cymb. IV, 2, 276.

Exorcism, conjuration for raising spirits: H6B I, 4, 5.

Exorcist, conjurer, one who can raise spirits: Alls V, 3, 305. Caes. II, 1, 323.

Expect, subst. expectation: *and be't of less e.* Troil. I, 3, 70.

Expect, vb. 1) to look for, to have a previous apprehension of: Ven. 718. Lucr. 149. 432. Tp. IV, 1, 42. Meas. IV, 3, 115. Err. IV, 3, 61. Ado, I, 1, 17. V, 1, 305. LLL IV, 1, 85. Merch. I, 3, 160. II, 5, 20. IV, 1, 34. V, 275. Shr. IV, 4, 91 (F 2.3.4 and some M. Edd. *except*). Alls II, 3, 189. Wint. I, 2, 450. John V, 3, 10. H5 I, 2, 123. H6A I, 2, 131. IV, 3, 12. H6B I, 4, 2. III, 1, 328. IV, 9, 12. H6C V, 1, 10. R3 II, 1, 3. 35. II, 3, 35. 37. III, 1, 39. IV, 4, 438. H8 V, 3, 94. Epil. 8. Troil. 1, 3, 83. IV, 4, 119. V, 6, 21. Cor. V, 1, 19. Tit. III, 1, 96. Rom. III, 5, 111 (*—s* for *—est*). Tim. IV, 3, 517. V, 2, 14. Caes. I, 2, 297. Ant. II, 1, 30. IV, 2, 43. IV, 7, 3. Cymb. I, 4, 2. I, 5, 57. II, 4, 38. III, 4, 25. IV, 2, 341. Per. I, 4, 59. II, 3, 5. IV, 1, 35. V, 1, 71.

2) to wait for: *my father at the road —s my coming,* Gentl. I, 1, 54. *let's in, and there e. their coming,* Merch. V, 49. *here I will e. thy coming,* H6A V, 3, 145. *and at the port e. you,* Ant. IV, 4, 23. *—ing overthrow,* Per. I, 4, 94.

Expectance, expectation, state of wondering what is to ensue: *there is e. here from both the sides what further you will do,* Troil. IV, 5, 146.

Expectancy, hope: *the e. and rose of the fair state,* Hml. III, 1, 160 (Qq *expectation*). *every minute is e. of more arrivance,* Oth. II, 1, 41.

Expectation, the act of looking forward to sth.: Ven. Ded. 8. Ado I, 1, 16. II, 3, 220. Alls II, 1, 145. John IV, 2, 7. H4A II, 3, 20 (*full of e.* = hopeful, promising). III, 2, 36. H4B I, 3, 23. 65. IV, 5, 104. V, 2, 126. H5 II Chor. 8. II, 4, 20. III, 3, 44. Troil. Prol. 20. III, 2, 19. Tim. V, 1, 25. Caes.

I, 1, 46. Mcb. II, 3, 5. III, 3, 10. Oth. II, 1, 287. IV, 2, 191 (Qq *e.*, Ff *—s*). Ant. III, 6, 47. Cymb. III, 5, 28. *you stand in coldest e.* H4B V, 2, 31. *our preparation stands in e. of them,* Lr. IV, 4, 23.

Expecter, one looking for the issue of an affair: *signify this loving interview to the —s of our Trojan part,* Troil. IV, 5, 156.

Expedience, 1) haste: *are making hither with all due e.* R2 II, 1, 287. *will with all e. charge on us,* H5 IV, 3, 70.

2) expedition, enterprise, campaign: *what our council did decree in forwarding this dear e.* H4A I, 1, 33. *I shall break the cause of our e. to the queen,* Ant. I, 2, 185.

Expedient, 1) convenient, suitable, proper: *it is most e. for the wise to be the trumpet of his own virtues,* Ado V, 2, 85. *whose ceremony shall seem e. on the now-borne brief,* Alls II, 3, 186.

2) expeditious, quick: *his marches are e. to this town,* John II, 60. *with much e. march,* 223. *with all e. haste,* IV, 2, 268 (or = convenient, due?). *e. manage must be made,* R2 I, 4, 39. *a breach that craves a quick e. stop,* H6B III, 1, 288. *I will with all e. duty see you,* R3 I, 2, 217 (or = convenient, proper?).

Expediently, quickly: As III, 1, 18.

Expedition, 1) haste, dispatch: Gentl. I, 3, 37. III, 1, 164. Wint. I, 2, 458. H4B IV, 3, 37. R3 IV, 3, 54. Tim. V, 2, 3. Mcb. II, 3, 116. Used as the name of a ship: Err. IV, 3, 38.

2) march of an army: *before your e. to Shrewsbury,* H4B I, 2, 116. *let us deliver our puissance into the hand of God, putting it straight in e.* H5 II, 2, 191. *who intercepts my e.?* R3 IV, 4, 136 (Ff *me in my e.*). *bending their e. toward Philippi,* Caes. IV, 3, 170.

3) warlike enterprise: John I, 49. II, 79. H4A I, 3, 150. IV, 3, 19. H4B I, 2, 249. H5 I, 2, 301. H6A IV, 4, 2. 32. Cor. II, 1, 169. Oth. I, 3, 229.

4) any enterprise implying a change of place: Gentl. I, 3, 77. V, 1, 6. Misapplied by Fluellen: H5 III, 2, 82.

Expeditious, speedy: Tp. V, 315.

Expel, to drive out, to banish: *the dire imagination,* Ven. 976. *remorse,* Tp. V, 76. *another heat,* Gentl. II, 4, 192. *inconveniences,* H5 V, 2, 66. *him thence,* Cor. IV, 7, 33. *sickness,* Tim. III, 1, 66. *this matter in his heart,* Hml. III, 1, 180. *the winter's flaw,* V, 1, 239 (cf. *sun-expelling*).

Expend, to spend, to waste, to give away: *I would e. it* (my life) *with all willingness,* H6B III, 1, 150. *to e. your time with us,* Hml. II, 2, 23. Oth. I, 3, 391. *riches .. careless heirs may e.* Per. III, 2, 29.

Expense, 1) the spending, consuming: *husband nature's riches from e.* Sonn. 94, 6. *after the e. of so much money,* Wiv. II, 2, 147. *my state being galled with my e.* III, 4, 5. *so much e. of thy sweet breath,* LLL V, 2, 523. *to have the e. and waste of his revenues,* Lr. II, 1, 102 (Q2 *the waste and spoil*).

2) cost, charge, money spent: Err. III, 1, 123. Mids. I, 1, 249. H6A I, 1, 76. V, 5, 92. H8 III, 2, 108. Troil. II, 2, 4. Tim. II, 2, 1. 135. Mcb. V, 8, 60. Per. III Prol. 20. V Prol. 19. *at a person's e.:* IV, 3, 46. *at what e.* Hml. II, 1, 9. *—s* = drinking-money: Tw. III, 1, 49.

3) loss: *moan the e. of many a vanished sight*

Sonn. 30, 8.*cf. *the e. of spirit in a waste of shame is lust in action*, 129, 1.

Experience, subst. 1) knowledge gained by observation or trials: Compl. 152. Gentl. I, 3, 22. II, 4, 69. Wiv. II, 2, 212. LLL III, 27. As IV, 1, 26. 27. Shr. I, 2, 52. All's I, 3, 229. II, 1, 110. II, 5, 10. H6B V, 1, 171. R3 IV, 4, 326. Tit. V, 3, 78. Oth. II, 3, 373. Ant. I, 4, 32. III, 10, 23. Per. I, 2, 37.

2) observation, trial: *guided by others' —s,* Cymb. I, 4, 49. *e., O thou disprovest report,* IV, 2, 34. With *of: your long e. of her wisdom,* Err. III, 1, 89.

Experienced, full of experience, skilful or wise by practice or observation: Wint. I, 2, 392. Troil. I, 3, 68. Cor. IV, 5, 145. Per. I, 1, 164 (Ff *experient*).

Experient, skilful: *a well e. archer,* Per. I, 1, 164 (Qq *experienced*).

Experiment, trial, something done to discover the effect: Wiv. IV, 2, 36. All's II, 1, 157. Tit. II, 3, 69. *hold me pace in deep —s,* H4A III, 1, 49.

Experimental, pertaining to experience: *with e. seal,* Ado IV, 1, 168 (= with the seal of experience).

Expert, experienced, skilful: H5 III, 7, 139. H6A III, 2, 127. Oth. II, 1, 49. II, 3, 82 (Ff *exquisite*).

Expertness, skill derived from practice: All's IV, 3, 202. 296.

Expiate, to bring to a close, to finish: *then look I death my days should e.* Sonn. 22, 4. Not inflected in the partic.: *make haste: the hour of death is e.* R3 III, 3, 23 (F2.3.4 *now expired*; Qq *the limit of your lives is out.* cf. the old play of King Leir p. 424: *and seek a means to e. his wrath*).

Expiration, termination, close: LLL V, 2, 814. R2 II, 3, 111. Lr. II, 4, 205.

Expire, 1) intr. a) to die: *whereon it* fire) *must e.* Sonn. 73, 11. *thus —ing do foretell of him,* R2 II, 1, 32.

b) to perish, to end: *when body's work's —d,* Sonn. 27, 4. *whose constancies e. before their fashions,* All's I, 2, 63. *your breathing shall e.* John V, 4, 36. cf. *men's lives e.* Mcb. IV, 3, 172. *I would his troubles likewise were —d,* H6A II, 5, 31.

c) to elapse, to go by, to cease: Lucr. 26. Merch. I, 3, 160. H4B V, 5, 111. H6B I, 1, 68. Per. I, 1, 89. II, 4, 47. III, 3, 2. III, 4, 14.

2) trans. to finish: *some consequence shall … e. the term of a despised life,* Rom. I, 4, 109.

Explain, only by conjecture in Per. II, 2, 14.

Explicable, in *Inexplicable,* q. v.

Explication, explanation, interpretation: LLL IV, 2, 14 (Holophernes' speech).

Exploit, subst. 1) a deed of renown: Merch. III, 2, 60. All's III, 6, 72. H4A I, 2, 192. I, 3, 199. H5 I, 2, 121. H6A II, 1, 43. II, 3, 5. R3 V, 3, 330. Troil. III, 1, 89. Tit. V, 1, 11. Caes. II, 1, 317. *to do —s,* H6A IV, 5, 27. H6B I, 1, 196. Used ironically: Err. IV, 3, 27. Mids. III, 2, 157. H4B I, 2, 169. Hml. IV, 7, 65. Lr. II, 2, 130. Of deeds of great wickedness: Lucr. 429. R3 IV, 2, 35. Mcb. IV, 1, 144.

2) combat, war: *sick for breathing and e.* All's I, 2, 17. *I must give myself some hurts, and say I got them in e.* IV, 1, 41.

Expose, 1) to cast out to chance: *to e. the child,* Wint. V, 2, 78.

2) to give up, to leave to the mercy of; followed by *to:* Tp. III, 3, 71. All's III, 2, 106. Wint. III, 3, 50. V, 1, 153. Troil. III, 3, 6. IV, 4, 70. Tim.

III, 5, 42. IV, 3, 230. Hml. IV, 4, 51. Lr. III, 4, 34. Cymb. III, 4, 164. By *into* instead of *unto: —d myself into the danger of this town,* Tw. V, 86. By *against: to be —d against the warring winds,* Lr. IV, 7, 32 (Ff and M. Edd. *opposed*).

Exposition, a laying open the sense, interpretation: Merch. IV, 1, 237. Rom. II, 4, 60. Per. I, 1, 112. With *on: your e. on the holy text,* H4B IV, 2, 7. Used by Bottom for *disposition:* Mids. IV, 1, 43.

Expositor, interpreter: LLL II, 72.

Expostulate, to discuss, to speak, to converse: *the time now serves not to e.* Gentl. III, 1, 251. *stay not to e., make speed,* H6C II, 5, 135. *more bitterly could I e.* R3 III, 7, 192. *to e. what majesty should be,* Hml. II, 2, 86. *I'll not e. with her, lest her body and beauty unprovide my mind again,* Oth. IV, 1, 217.

Expostulation, speech, conversation: *we must use e. kindly,* Troil. IV, 4, 62.

Exposture, exposure, state of being exposed: *a wild e. to each chance,* Cor. IV, 1, 36.

Exposure, state of being unprovided, want of sufficient defence: *to weaken and discredit our e., how rank soever rounded in with danger,* Troil. I, 3, 195.*when we have our naked frailties hid, that suffer in e.* Mcb. II, 3, 133.

Expound, to explain, to interpret: Mids. IV, 1, 212. Shr. IV, 4, 79. H5 IV, 4, 62. Caes. II, 2, 91. Cymb. I, 6, 152. Per. I, 1, 57. 90.

Express, adj., 1) given in direct terms, not left to inference: *an e. command,* Meas. IV, 2, 176. Wint. II, 2, 8. H6A I, 3, 20. *charge,* H5 III, 6, 114. *and bid me tell my tale in e. words,* John IV, 2, 234 (cf. App.1, 1). *let me have your e. opinions,* H6A I, 4, 64.

2) expressive, significative: *in form and moving how e. and admirable,* Hml. II, 2, 317.

Express, vb. 1) trans. a) to indicate by signs, to exhibit: *whose inward ill no outward harm —ed,* Lucr. 91. *her joy with heaved-up hand she doth e.* 111. *her womb —eth his full tilth,* Meas. I, 4, 44. *if you be one, as you are well —ed by all external warrants,* II, 4, 136. LLL II, 237. Alls V, 3, 337. John IV, 2, 142. Cor. I, 6, 74. III, 1, 132. Tim. I, 1, 76. I, 2, 88. Cymb. I, 3, 13. V, 4, 112.

b) to show in general, to make appear: *to e. the like kindness, I freely give unto you this young scholar,* Shr. II, 77. *yet I e. to you a mother's care,* Alls I, 3, 154. *I can e. no kinder sign of love than this kind kiss,* H6B I, 1, 18. *as I in justice and true right e. it* (viz my prowess) V, 2, 25. *costly thy habit, but not —ed in fancy,* Hml. I, 3, 71 (i. e. let not the costliness appear by fantasticalness). *what so poor a man may do, to e. his love,* I, 5, 185. *patience and sorrow strove who should e. her goodliest,* Lr. IV, 3, 19.

c) to convey in words, to tell: *my tongue cannot e. my grief,* Ven. 1069. *more it is than I can well e.* Lucr. 1286. Sonn. 23, 12. 105, 8. 106, 7. 108, 4. 140, 3. Meas. II, 4, 148. LLL IV, 3, 122. V, 2, 412. As III, 2, 418. Alls V, 3, 332 (construe: *the progress of that and all*). Wint. V, 2, 27. Tim. V, 4, 74. Oth. IV, 3, 29. Per. II, 2, 9 (*to e. my commendations great*). Absolutely: *past all —ing,* Merch. III, 5, 78.

d) to declare in words: *such sums as are —ed in the condition,* Merch. I, 3, 149. *as I do —ed, but what of that?* IV, 1, 260. *—ed and not —ed,* III, 2, 185. *scorned a fair colour, or —ed it stolen,* Alls V, 3, 50. *mine integrity being counted falsehood, shall, as*

I e. it, be so received, Wint. III, 2, 28. Troil. V, 2, 162. Hml. IV, 4, 6. Lr. I, 1, 37. Per. IV, 3, 44.

e) **to speak:** *my thoughts and my discourse as madmen's are, at random from the truth vainly —ed,* Sonn. 147, 12. *—ing, although they want the use of tongue, a kind of excellent dumb discourse,* Tp. III, 3, 37.

2) refl. a) **to make one's self known:** *it charges me in manners to e. myself,* Tw. II, 1, 16. — b) **to show one's self, to appear:** *hath —ed himself in all his deeds a father and a friend to thee,* Tit. I, 422. *e. yourself in a more comfortable sort,* Cor. I, 3, 1. — c) **to speak one's mind,** to expose one's views: *ere he e. himself, or move the people with what he would say,* Cor. V, 6, 55.

Expressive, communicative, open-hearted: *be more e. to them,* Alls II, 1, 54.

Expressly, 1) in direct terms: LLL I, 1, 62. Merch. IV, 1, 307. Shr. Ind. 2, 123. IV, 1, 174. H5 II, 4, 112. IV, 7, 1. H8 III, 2, 235. Rom. III, 1, 91. Tim. II, 2, 32.

2) expressively, distinctly: *their face their manners most e. told,* Lucr. 1397. *who in his circumstance e. proves that no man is the lord of any thing,* Troil. III, 3, 114.

Expressure, 1) expression, form of language suited to the subject: *an operation more divine than breath or pen can give e. to,* Troil. III, 3, 204.

2) accurate description: *wherein by the colour of his beard, the shape of his leg, the e. of his eye, forehead, and complexion, he shall find himself most feelingly personated,* Tw. II, 3, 171.

3) impression, trace: *the e. that it bears, green let it be,* Wiv. V, 5, 71.

Expulse, to expel: *for ever should they be —d from France,* H6A III, 3, 25.

Expulsion, a driving away, banishment: Cor. V, 4, 46. Cymb. II, 1, 65.

Exquisite, excellent: *her beauty is e.* Gentl. II, 1, 59. *the most e.* Claudio, Ado I, 3, 52. *e. beauty,* Tw. I, 5, 181. *thy e. reason,* II, 3, 155. 157. *most e. Sir Topas,* IV, 2, 67. *beauty,* Rom. I, 1, 235. *my very e. friend,* Tim. III, 2, 32. *a most e. lady,* Oth. II, 3, 18. *e. in his drinking,* 82 (Q1 *expert*). *song,* 101. *form,* Cymb. I, 6, 190. *parts,* III, 5, 71.

Exsufflicate, (O. Edd. *exufflicate*): *when I shall turn the business of my soul to such e. and blown surmises,* Oth. III, 3, 182. Dyce: "swollen, puffed out." Nares: "contemptible, abominable. From exsufflare, low Lat. which Du Cange explains 'contemnere, despuere, rejicere.'" Probably synonymous to *blown,* = empty, unsubstantial, frivolous.

Extant, 1) in being, still existing: Sonn. 83, 6. Wiv. V, 5, 127. H4A II, 4, 132. Hml. III, 2, 273.

2) present: *in this e. moment,* Troil. IV, 5, 168.

Extemporal, unpremeditated: *some e. god of rhyme,* LLL I, 2, 189 (Armado's speech). *e. epitaph,* IV, 2, 50. *e. speech,* H6A III, 1, 6.

Extemporally, without premeditation: Ven. 836. Ant. V, 2, 217.

Extempore, without previous meditation: Mids. I, 2, 70. Shr. II, 265. Wint. IV, 4, 692. H4A II, 4, 309. 347.

Extend, 1) trans. a) to stretch, to reach forth: *I e. my hand to him thus,* Tw. II, 5, 72.

b) to spread: *the report of her is —ed more than can be thought to begin from such a cottage,* Wint. IV, 2, 49.

c) to amplify, to increase: *ne worse of worst —ed, with vilest torture let my life be ended,* Alls II, 1, 176 (i. e. nor would that be an increase of ill; it would not be the worst mended by what is still worse).*

—ed or contracted all proportions to a most hideous object, V, 3, 51. *if much you note him, you shall offend him and e. his passion,* Mcb. III, 4, 57. *you do e. these thoughts of horror further than you shall find cause,* Ant. V, 2, 62. *you speak him far. I do e. him, sir, within himself,* Cymb. I, 1, 25 (=I magnify, extol him not more than he deserves). *the approbation of those ... are wonderfully to e. him,* I, 4, 21 (= to praise him above his merit). *towards himself, his goodness forespent on us, we must e. our notice,* II, 3, 65.

d) to apply, to use, to show: *sometimes they do e. their view right on,* Compl. 25. *and supplicant their sighs to you e.* 276. *when vice makes mercy, mercy's so —ed, that for the fault's love is the offender friended,* Meas. IV, 2, 115. *to buy his favour, I e. this friendship,* Merch. I, 3, 169. *Love (was) no god, that would not e. his might, only where qualities were level,* Alls I, 3, 118. *the duke shall e. to you what further becomes his greatness,* III, 6, 73. *you do lack that mercy which fierce fire and iron —s,* John IV, 1, 120. *till he behold them (viz his parts) formed in the applause where they're —ed,* Troil. III, 3, 120. *that we our largest bounty may e.* Lr. I, 1, 53. *that I e. my manners,* Oth. II, 1, 99.

e) to seize upon (a law term): *Labienus hath —ed Asia,* Ant. I, 2, 105.

2) intr. to stretch, to reach: Tp. V, 29. Merch. II, 7, 28. H8 I, 1, 111. Tim. II, 2, 160.

Extent, 1) space, length: *the very head and front of my offending hath this e., no more,* Oth. I, 3, 81.

2) application, use, maintenance: *for the e. of egal justice,* Tit. IV, 4, 3.

3) behaviour, deportment, conduct: *in this uncivil and unjust e. against thy peace,* Tw. IV, 1, 57.* *lest my e. to the players should more appear like entertainment than yours,* Hml. II, 2, 390.

4) seizure: *make an e. upon his house and lands,* As III, 1, 17.

Extenuate, 1) to palliate (opposed to aggravate): Ven. 1010. Meas. II, 1, 27. Ado IV, 1, 51. Troil. II, 2, 187. Oth. V, 2, 342. Ant. V, 2, 125.

2) to mitigate: *which (law) by no means we may e.* Mids. I, 1, 120.

3) to undervalue, to detract from: *his glory not —d,* Caes. III, 2, 42.

Extenuation, alleviation, mitigation: H4A III, 2, 22.

Exterior, adj. external, outward: Ado IV, 1, 41. John I, 211. H4B IV, 5, 149. Hml. II, 2, 6.

Exteriorly, outwardly: John IV, 2, 257.

Exteriors, outward parts, outside: *she did so course o'er my e.* Wiv. I, 3, 72.

Extermine, to exterminate, destroy: As III, 5, 89.

Extern, external, outward: Oth. I, 1, 63. Substantively, = outward show: *with my e. the outward honouring,* Sonn. 125, 2.

External, outward: Sonn. 53, 13. Meas. II, 4, 137. Shr. V, 2, 168. John II, 571. R2 IV, 296. H6A

V, 5, 3. Ant. V, 2, 349. In H6C III, 3, 124 M. Edd. rightly *eternal.*

Extinct, adj. extinguished, quenched: *my oil-dried lamp shall be e. with age,* R2 I, 3, 222. *these blazes ... e. in both,* Hml. I, 3, 118.

Extincted, extinguished, quenched: *give renewed fire to our e. spirits,* Oth. II, 1, 81.

Extincture, extinction, quenching: Compl. 294.

Extinguish, 1) to quench: Lucr. 313. — 2) to obscure: *natural graces that e. art,* H6A V, 3, 192.

Extirp, to extirpate, root out: Meas. III, 2, 110. H6A III, 3, 24.

Extirpate, to root out, to remove completely: *e. me and mine out of the dukedom,* Tp. I, 2, 125.

Extol, to praise, to magnify: Lucr. Arg. 7. Gentl. III, 1, 102. Meas. V, 508. Cor. I, 9, 14. IV, 7, 53. Tim. I, 1, 167.

Extolment, praise: Hml. V, 2, 121.

Exton, name in R2 V, 5, 100. 110. V, 6, 34.

Extort, to draw by force, to wring, wrest: *—ed gold,* H6B IV, 7, 105. Hml. I, 1, 137. *e. a poor soul's patience,* Mids. III, 2, 160 (cf. *to move,* or *wake a person's patience* = to make impatient, Ado V, 1, 102. R3 I, 3, 248). With *from:* Tw. II, 1, 14. III, 1, 165. Cymb. III, 1, 48. IV, 4, 12.

Extortion, rapacious and illegal exaction: H6B I, 3, 132. H8 III, 2, 285.

Extract, to draw out: *putting the hand in the pocket and —ing it clutched,* Meas. III, 2, 50. *compounded of many simples, —ed from many objects,* As IV, 1, 17. *a most —ing frenzy of mine own from my remembrance clearly banished his,* Tw. V, 288 (i. e. drawing other thoughts from my mind. F2.3.4 *exacting;* some M. Edd. *distracting;* cf. v. 287). *that foreign hire could out of thee e. one spark of evil,* H5 II, 2, 101. Partic. *extraught* = derived: *knowing whence thou art extraught,* H6C II, 2, 142.

Extraordinarily, in an uncommon degree: H4B I, 2, 235. Misapplied by Mrs Quickly: II, 4, 26.

Extraordinary, (of six syllables), uncommon, rare: Wiv. III, 3, 75. As I, 2, 7. Wint. I, 2, 227. H4A III, 1, 41. III, 2, 78.

Extraught, see *Extract.*

Extravagancy, vagrancy: *my determinate voyage is mere e.* Tw. II, 1, 12.

Extravagant, vagrant: *a foolish e. spirit, full of forms, figures etc.* LLL IV, 2, 68. *the e. and erring spirit hies to his confine,* Hml. I, 1, 154. *an e. and wheeling stranger of here and everywhere,* Oth. I, 1, 137.

Extreme, adj. (as for the accent, see Appendix I, 1: Chang. Accent) 1) outermost, utmost: *to the e. verge of hazard,* All's III, 3, 6. Lr. IV, 6, 26. *makes it course from the inwards to the parts e.* H4B IV, 3, 116 (Q F1.2 *—s;* perhaps *extremest*). Superl. *—st: to the —st shore of my modesty,* Meas. III, 2, 266. As II, 1, 42. H4B IV, 3, 38. Troil. I, 3, 167. Lr. V, 3, 136.

2) last: *the e. parts of time extremely forms all causes to the purpose of his speed,* LLL V, 2, 750. Superl.: *my —st means,* Merch. I, 1, 138. *to the —st point of mortal breathing,* R2 IV, 47.

3) utmost, greatest, most violent: Lucr. 230. Gentl. II, 7, 22. Shr. II, 136. IV, 1, 47. H4A I, 3, 31. R3 III, 5, 44. IV, 4, 185. Cor. IV, 5, 75. Tit. V, 1,

113. Rom. II Chor. 14. *—st:* R3 I, 2, 232. Cor. III, 3, 82. Tim. III, 5, 54.

4) immoderate, excessive: *savage, e., rude, cruel,* Sonn. 129, 4. *had, having, and in quest to have, e.* 10. *be not as e. in submission as in offence,* Wiv. IV, 4, 11. Tit. V, 1, 113.

Extreme, subst. 1) the utmost point, the point at the greatest distance from another: *his heart, twixt two —s of passion, joy and grief, burst smilingly,* Lr. V, 3, 198. *between the —s of hot and cold,* Ant. I, 5, 51. *no midway 'twixt these —s,* III, 4, 20.

2) highest degree: *thy (love's) weal and woe are both of them —s,* Ven. 987. Lucr. 1337. *by so much is the wonder in —s,* H6C III, 2, 115. *perplexed in the e.* Oth. V, 2, 346.

3) anything in its highest degree; a) calamity, danger, suffering: *devise —s beyond extremity, to make him curse this night,* Lucr. 969. *fierce —s in their continuance will not feel themselves,* John V, 7, 13. *resolute in most —s,* H6A IV, 1, 38. *who can be patient in such —s,* H6C I, 1, 215. *do to this body what —s you can,* Troil. IV, 2, 108. *'twixt my —s and me this bloody knife shall play the umpire,* Rom. IV, 1, 62. b) cruelty: *the fire is dead with grief, being create for comfort, to be used in undeserved —s,* John IV, 1, 108. c) passion: *do not break into these deep —s,* Tit. III, 1, 216. d) mirth: *the over-merry spleen which otherwise would grow into —s,* Shr. Ind. 1, 138. *to chide at your —s it not becomes me,* Wint. IV, 4, 6.

Extremely, very much: LLL V, 2, 750. Mids. V, 80. H8 II, 1, 33. Epil. 6. Tim. III, 2, 14.

Extremity, 1) the utmost point: *to the edge of all e. pursue each other,* Troil. IV, 5, 68. *the middle of humanity thou never knewest, but the e. of both ends,* Tim. IV, 3, 301.

2) highest degree: *devise extremes beyond e.* Lucr. 969. *swift e.* Sonn. 51, 6 (= highest degree of swiftness, extreme swiftness). *the e. of dire mishap,* Err. I, 1, 142. V, 48. As IV, 3, 23. Wint. V, 2, 20. Troil. IV, 5, 78. Tit. IV, 1, 19. Lr. V, 3, 207. *in e.:* Mids. III, 2, 3. As IV, 1, 5. Rom. I, 3, 103. Hml. III, 2, 178.

3) anything in the highest degree: a) distress, danger, difficulty: Lucr. 1337. Shr. IV, 2, 102. R2 II, 2, 72. H4A I, 2, 212. H8 V, 1, 19. Cor. III, 2, 41. IV, 1, 4. IV, 5, 84. Rom. II Chor. 14. Hml. II, 2, 192. Per. V, 1, 140. b) rigor, violence, cruelty: *O time's e., hast thou so cracked and splitted my poor tongue,* Err. V, 307. *e. of weather continuing,* Wint. V, 2, 129; cf. *this e. of the skies,* Lr. III, 4, 106. *'tis she that tempers him to this e.* R3 I, 1, 65. *what he is, augmented, would run to these and these —ies,* Caes. II, 1, 31. *I did proceed upon just grounds to this e.* Oth. V, 2, 139. *thy tongue may take off some e.* Cymb. III, 4, 17. c) folly, extravagancy: *any e. rather than a mischief,* Wiv. IV, 2, 75. *show no colour for my e.* 169.

Exufflicate, see *Exsufflicate.*

Exult, to rejoice, to triumph: Tw. II, 5, 8. With *over:* As III, 5, 36.

Exultation, delight, triumph: Wint. V, 3, 131.

Eyas (originally *a nias,* French *niais*) a nestling: Hml. II, 2, 355.

Eyas-musket, a young sparrow-hawk: Wiv. III, 3, 22.

Eye (plur. —*s;* the obsolete plur. *eyne,* for the sake of the rhyme: Ven. 633. Lucr. 643. Compl. 15. LLL V, 2, 206. Mids. I, 1, 242. II, 2, 99. III, 2, 138. V, 178. As IV, 3, 50. Shr. V, 1, 120. Ant. II, 7, 121. Without the constraint of the rhyme: Lucr. 1229, and in Gower's Prol. Per. III, 5). 1) the organ of sight: Tp. I, 2, 25. 135. 398. 435. II, 1, 191. 214. 319. V, 156. Gentl. II. 1, 41. 77. IV, 2, 46. IV, 4, 197. V, 2, 13 etc. etc. *to have one's —s* = to be able to see: Merch. II, 2, 79. H5 V, 2, 337 (cf. *if I had my mouth, I would bite,* Ado I, 3, 36). Caes. I, 2, 62. cf. Cor. IV, 5, 13. *to put the finger in the eye* = to weep in a childish manner: Err. II, 2, 206. Shr. I, 1, 79. *all —s* = consisting of nothing but eyes: Troil. I, 2, 31; cf. Tp. IV, 1, 59. *what a haste looks through his —s,* Mcb. I, 2, 46. *peep through their —s,* Merch. I, 1, 52 (= are chuckling inwardly). *tended her in the —s,* Ant. II, 2, 212 (= showed her submissive reverence by their looks). *look how thy e. turns pale,* Troil. V, 3, 81 (= grows dim as if by death). *the setting of thine e. and cheek,* Tp. II, 1, 229 (i. e. thy look). *thy —s are almost set in thy head,* Tp. III, 2, 10 (i. e. closed; a phrase used of drunken persons); cf. *his —s were set at eight in the morning,* Tw. V, 205. *thou art come to set mine e.* John V, 7, 51 (= to close it up); cf. H6B III, 3, 32. *at the first sight they have changed —s,* Tp. I, 2, 441 (= fallen in love with each other); cf. *mingle —s with one that ties his points,* Ant. III, 13, 156 (= change amorous looks). *and thence from Athens turn away our —s,* Mids. I, 1, 218 (= leave Athens). *whither do you follow your —s?* Cor. II, 1, 109. *—s of youth,* Wiv. III, 2, 68. *an e. of favour,* Ado V, 4, 22. *of love,* 24. *—s of pity,* Wint. III, 2, 123. Merch. IV, 1, 27. *an e. of death,* H4A I, 3, 143. *shuts up sorrow's e.* Mids. III, 2, 435. *it opens the —s of expectation,* Tim. V, 1, 25. *close the e. of anguish,* Lr. IV, 4, 15. Regarded as a most precious thing: *would give an e. to boot,* Troil. I, 2, 260 (but Ff *money*). *worth a Jew's e.* Merch. II, 5, 43 (see *Jew*). *to hit him in the e.* Tw. II, 5, 52. *have at the very e. of that proverb,* H5 III, 7, 129. *if the streets were paved with thine —s,* LLL IV, 3, 278. *I'll spurn thine —s like balls before me,* Ant. I, 5, 63.

Figurative use: *the flowerets' —s,* Mids. IV, 1, 60. Cymb. II, 3, 26. *your city's —s, your winking gates,* John II, 215. *the e. of mind,* Lucr. 1426. Hml. I, 1, 112. I, 2, 185. *the e. and prospect of his soul,* Ado IV, 1, 231. *religious love put out religion's e.* Compl. 250. Very often applied to the sun: *spread their fair leaves at the sun's e.* Sonn. 25, 6. 33, 2. Pilgr. 81. Wint. IV, 4, 819. John III, 1, 79. Troil. I, 3, 91. *the e. of heaven* = the sun: Lucr. 356. Sonn. 18, 5. Err. II, 1, 16. LLL V, 2, 375. John IV, 2, 15. R2 I, 3, 275. III, 2, 37. Tit. II, 1, 130. *yon grey is not the morning's e.* Rom. III, 5, 19. *O e. of —s* (i. e. the sun) Lucr. 1088. *all yon fiery oes and —s of light,* Mids. III, 2, 188 (== stars).

2) sight, look: *all askance he holds her in his e.* Ven. 342. *from Venus' e., which after him she darts,* 817. *in disgrace with fortune and men's —s,* Sonn. 29, 1. *brought me to her e.* Compl. 247. *banished from your e.* Tp. II, 1, 126. *gave me good —s,* Wiv. I, 3, 67. *have open e.* Wiv. II, 1, 126. *as you have one e. upon my follies,* II, 2, 192. *I have —s upon him,* Ant. III, 6, 62. *keep —s upon her,* Mcb. V, 1, 85. *have an e. to Cinna,* Caes. II, 3, 2. *I have an e. of you,* Hml. II, 2, 301

(= I see your drift). *set e. upon Zenelophon,* LLL IV, 1, 66. *no single soul can we set e. on,* Cymb. IV, 2, 131. *in thy e. that shall appear,* Mids. II, 2, 32. *gambol in his — s,* III, 1, 168. *that next came in her e.* III, 2, 2. *in —s of men,* Sonn. 16, 12. *hath done well in people's —s,* Merch. III, 2, 143. *sweats in the e. of Phoebus,* H5 IV, 1, 290. *do 't in your parents' —s,* Tim. IV, 1, 8. *in the public e.* Ant. III, 6, 11. *kill him, and in her —s,* Cymb. III, 5, 142. *there it lies in your e.* Tw. II, 2, 16. *we shall express our duty in his e.* Hml. IV, 4, 6. *be thou as lightning in the —s of France,* John I, 24 (i. e. return to France with the swiftness of lightning). *him in e., still him in praise,* H8 I, 1, 30. *and be in e. of every exercise,* Gentl. I, 3, 32 (= see, witness)'. *set we our squadrons on yond side o' the hill, in e. of Caesar's battle,* Ant. III, 9, 2. *if it stand, as you yourself still do, within the e. of honour,* Merch. I, 1, 137 (= if honour is not lost sight of, not disregarded). *place my merit in the e. of scorn,* Sonn. 88, 2. *and feast upon her —s,* Meas. II, 2, 179. *we are glad to behold your —s,* H5 V, 2, 14. *I beg leave to see your kingly —s,* Hml. IV, 7, 45. *I could live and die i' the —s of Troilus,* Troil. I, 2, 264. *to the —s of* = to the face of: *her shall you hear disproved to her —s,* Meas. V, 161 (cf. I, 1, 69). *even to the —s of Richard gave him defiance,* H4B III, 1, 64.

3) view of the mind, opinion: *black men are pearls in beauteous ladies' —s,* Gentl. V, 2, 12. *pleasing in thine e.* Err. II, 2, 117. Ado I, 1, 189. IV, 1, 132. LLL IV, 3, 85. Wint. II, 1, 132. H6B IV, 4, 46. H6C III, 3, 117. R3 III, 7, 112. IV, 4, 177 (Qq *sight*). Cymb. V, 4, 56 etc. *to choose love by another's —s,* Mids. I, 1, 140. *I looked upon her with a soldier's e.* Ado I, 1, 300 etc.

4) a small hole or perforation: *to thread the postern of a needle's e.* R2 V, 5, 17. *the e. of Helen's needle,* Troil. II, 1, 87. As to John V, 4, 11: *unthread the rude e. of rebellion,* see the articles *Thread* and particularly *Unthread.* John II, 583*.

5) a tinge, shade of colour: *tawny, with an e. of green in it,* Tp. II, 1, 55. In Hml. I, 3, 128: *not of the e. which their investments show,* Qq and most M. Edd. *dye.*

Eye, vb. 1) to see: *when first your eye I —d,* Sonn. 104, 2. *capering to e. her,* Tp. V, 238. *no man their works must e.* Wiv. V, 5, 52. *wild geese that the creeping fowler e.* Mids. III, 2, 20. 40. *perspectives... —d awry distinguish form,* R2 II, 2, 19. *clambering the walls to e. him,* Cor. II, 1, 226. *saving those that e. thee,* V, 3, 75. *he —s us not,* Cymb. V, 5, 124.

2) to look on, to observe, to hold in view: *many a lady I have —d with best regard,* Tp. III, 1, 40. *e. your master's heels,* Wiv. III, 2, 4. *I —d them even to their ships,* Wint. II, 1, 35. *when she coldly —s the youthful Phoebus,* Troil. I, 3, 229. *my proceedings e.* V, 7, 7. *wherefore —st him so?* Cymb. V, 5, 114.

3) intr. to look, appear: *my becomings kill me, when they do not e. well to you,* Ant. I, 3, 97.

Eye-ball, the globe or apple of the eye: John III, 4, 30. H6A IV, 7, 79. H6B III, 2, 169. = eye: *look in mine —s, there thy beauty lies,* Ven. 119. *rolling his greedy —s in his head,* Lucr. 368. *invisible to every e. else,* Tp. I, 2, 303. Mids. III, 2, 369. As III, 5, 47. H6B III, 2, 49. Mcb. IV, 1, 113. Cymb. III, 4, 104.

Eye-beam, a glance, a look: LLL IV, 3, 28. **Eyebrow**, the hairy arch over the eye: As II, 7, 149. Wint. II, 1, 13. 15.

Eye-drop, a tear: H4B IV, 5, 88.

Eye-glass, the window-pane of the eye, the retina: *or your e. is thicker than a cuckold's horn*, Wint. I, 2, 268.

Eyeless, destitute of sight, blind: Rom. V, 3, 126. Tim. IV, 3, 182. Lr. III, 1, 8. III, 7, 96. IV, 6, 231. In John V, 6, 12 some M. Edd. *e.*, O. Edd. *endless.*

Eyelid, the membrane that covers the eye: Ven. 956. Sonn. 27, 7. 61, 2. Tp. II, 1, 201. IV, 177. Ado IV, 1, 107. LLL III, 13. Mids. II, 1, 170. II, 2, 81. As II, 7, 116. H4A III, 1, 217. III, 2, 81. H4B III, 1, 7. Hml. V, 1, 290. Per. III, 2, 99.

Eye-offending, injuring the eye: *e. brine*, Tw. I, 1, 30. = shocking: *foul moles and e. marks*, John III, 1, 47.

Eyesight, the sense of seeing, the eye: LLL I, 1, 76. II, 239. V, 2, 445. H4A V, 4, 138. Rom. I, 1, 239. III, 5, 57. Lr. I, 1, 57.

Eye-sore, a blemish: *an e. in my golden coat*, Lucr. 205. *doff this habit, an e. to our solemn festival*, Shr. III, 2, 103.

Eye-string, the tendon by which the eye is moved: Cymb. I, 3, 17.

Eye-wink, a look, a glance (of intelligence). *they could never get an e. of her*, Wiv. II, 2, 72.

Eyliad, see *Oeillade.* **Eyrie**, see *Aery.*

Eysell, vinegar: *I will drink potions of e. 'gainst my strong infection*, Sonn. 111, 10 (vinegar being esteemed efficacious in preventing the communication of the plague and other contagious distempers). *woo't weep? woo't fight? woo't fast? woo't tear thyself? woo't drink up e.? eat a crocodile?* Hml. V, 1, 299 (Qq *esill*, Ff *esile* in italics; Keightley *Yssel*, Hanmer *Nile*, Capell *Nilus*. About *to drink up* see *Drink* and *Up.* Hamlet's questions are evidently ludicrous, and drinking vinegar, in order to produce '*a vinegar aspect*', seems much more to the purpose than drinking up rivers. As for the crocodile, it must be remembered, that it is a *mournful* animal; cf. H6B III, 1, 226 and Oth. IV, 1, 257; and therefore the most convenient meat for such a mourner as Laertes).

F.

Fa, the fourth note in the gamut: *ut, re, sol, la, mi, fa*, LLL IV, 2, 102. *C fa ut*, Shr. III, 1, 76. *fa, sol, la, mi*, Lr. I, 2, 149. Used as a verb: *I'll try how you can sol, fa*, Shr. I, 2, 17. *I'll re you, I'll fa you*, Rom. IV, 5, 121.

Fabian, name in Tw. II, 5, 1. III, 4, 281 etc.

Fable, subst. 1) a fiction: *these antique —s*, Mids. V, 3. *but that's a f.* Oth. V, 2, 286.

2) a lie (euphemistically): *sans f.* Err. IV, 4, 76. *I recount no f.* LLL V, 1, 111.

Fable, vb. 1) to tell fictitious tales: H6C V, 5, 25. 2) to tell falsehoods: H6A IV, 2, 42.

Fabric, 1) structure, frame: Tp. IV, 151. Wint. I, 2, 429. Cor. I, 1, 123.

2) a large building: *manhood is called foolery, when it stands against a falling f.* Cor. III, 1, 247.

Fabulous, 1) fictitious: H8 I, 1, 36. 2) full of lies: *report is f. and false*, H6A II, 3, 18.

Face, subst. 1) the visage: Ven. 157. Sonn. 17, 8. Tp. II, 1, 206. III, 1, 49. IV, 173. Gentl. II, 1, 142. III, 1, 103. IV, 4, 72. 160. 190. V, 2, 8. V, 4, 114 etc. etc. *to make —s* = to distort one's f.: LLL V, 2, 649. Cor. II, 1, 83. Mcb. III, 4, 67. *leave thy damnable —s*, Hml. III, 2, 263. *can any f. of brass hold longer out?* LLL V, 2, 395. *I have not the f. to say . . .*, Cor. IV, 6, 116. *to put a strange f. on his own perfection*, Ado II, 3, 49. *if he break, thou mayst with better f. exact the penalty*, Merch. I, 3, 137. *turn thy f. in peace*, John V, 2, 159 (= depart). *so buxom, blithe, and full of f.* Per. Prol. 23 (= beautiful? or of a full face, of a florid appearance?). *hadst thou Narcissus in thy f. I'll tell thee wonders. With that f.?* LLL I, 2, 145 (Jaquenetta's reply, evidently implying doubt). *from f. to foot*, Cor. II, 2, 112. *f. to f.*: Ado V, 1, 307. John II, 390. R2 I, 1, 15. H5 V, 2, 30. H8 V, 3, 47. *breatheth in her f.* Ven. 62; cf. Err. II, 2, 137. H4A II, 4, 214 etc. *break it in your f.* Err. III, 1, 76 (= before your eyes). *stand in his f. to contradict his claim*, John II, 280. *slept in his f.* H4A III, 2, 82. *laughed in his f.* H6C II, 1, 60. *look in this gentleman's f.* Meas. II, 1, 154. John II, 495 etc. *look me in the f.* Mids. III, 2, 424. H6A I, 1, 140. Ant. III, 3, 12 etc. *he smiled me in the f.* H5 IV, 6, 21. *pale destruction meets thee in the f.* H6A IV, 2, 27. *ravish your daughters before your —s*, H6B IV, 8, 32. H6C II, 2, 14. II, 6, 39. Caes. V, 3, 35 etc. *the prayers of holy saints and wronged souls, like high-reared bulwarks, stand before our —s*, R3 V, 3, 242. *wilt thou flout me thus unto my f.?* Err. I, 2, 91. *it shall be read to his f.* All's IV, 3, 131. *speak treason to thy f.* R2 V, 3, 44. H6A I, 3, 44. 45. H6B IV, 7, 42. V, 1, 86. H8 II, 1, 18. Rom. IV, 1, 28. Oth. V, 2, 77. *to show one's f.* = to have the courage to appear: Wiv. II, 3, 33. LLL V, 2, 271. Troil. V, 5, 45. Mcb. V, 7, 14. — The controverted passage in Caes. II, 1, 114: *if not the f. of men* etc. may be understood literally: having manly faces, looking like men, you ought to act like men.

Figurative use: *to ride with ugly rack on his* (heaven's) *celestial f.* Sonn. 33, 6. *spits in the f. of heaven*, Merch. II, 7, 45. R3 IV, 4, 239. Mcb. IV, 3, 6. *to see this morning's f.* Rom. IV, 5, 41. *to the f. of peril myself I'll dedicate*, Cymb. V, 1, 28 (i. e. to look peril in the face . cf. *stays but to behold the f. of that occasion*, H4A I, 3, 275. *against the f. of death I sought the purchase*, Per. I, 2, 71. *fled from that great f. of war*, Ant. III, 13, 5.

2) look, appearance, form: *so love's f. may still seem love to me*, Sonn. 93, 2. *executing the outward f. of royalty*, Tp. I, 2, 104. *I have felt so many quirks of joy and grief, that the first f. of neither, on the start, can woman me to it*, All's III, 2, 52. *in this*

the antique and well noted f. of plain old form is much disfigured, John IV, 2, 21. you taught me how to know the f. of right, V, 2, 88. thinking by this f. to fasten in our thoughts that they have courage, Caes. V, 1, 10. there is division, although as yet the f. of it be covered, Lr. III, 1, 20.

3) surface: about the mourning and congealed f. of that black blood a watery rigol goes, Lucr. 1744. the f. to sweeten of the whole dungy earth, Wint. II, 1, 156. shall ill become the flower of England's f. R2 III, 3, 97. the earth's cold f. H6C II, 3, 35. R3 V, 3, 266. Tim. IV, 3, 190. Mcb. II, 4, 9. cf. LLL IV, 2, 7.

Face, vb. 1) trans. a) to meet in front, to oppose: give me them that will f. me, H4A II, 4, 167. f. them in the field, H4B IV, 1, 24. if at Philippi we do f. him, Caes. IV, 3, 211. till he —d the slave, Mcb. I, 2, 20.

b) to brave, to bully: f. not me, Shr. IV, 3, 125. 126. —d and braved me, V, 1, 124.

c) to trim, to edge: to f. the garment of rebellion with some fine colour, H4A IV, 1, 74. cf. thou hast —d many things, Shr. IV, 3, 123. Figuratively, = to embellish, to give a lustre to: the face that —d so many follies, R2 IV, 285 (or = countenanced?).

d) to patch: an old —d ancient, H4A IV, 2, 34.

2) intr. a) to uphold a false appearance, to lie with effrontery: Suffolk doth not flatter, f. or feign, H6A V, 3, 142. a villain that would f. me down he met me on the mart, Err. III, 1, 6 (me is the dative).

b) to get through one's business by effrontery; followed by a superfluous it: a vengeance on your crafty withered hide! yet I have —d it with a card of ten, Shr. II, 407 (Nares: "a common phrase, originally expressing the confidence or impudence of one who with a ten, as at brag, faced, or outfaced one who had really a faced card against him"). a' —s it out, but fights not, H5 III, 2, 35. Followed by an accus. denoting the result: that thinks with oaths to f. the matter out, Shr. II, 291. to f. me out of my wits, Tw. IV, 2, 101. to f. me out of his acquaintance, V, 91. for fear I should be —d out of my way, H5 III, 7, 90.

Face-royal, a kingly visage, and the visage stamped on the coin called a royal: he will not stick to say his face is a f.: God may finish it when he will, 'tis not a hair amiss yet: he may keep it still at a f., for a barber shall never earn sixpence out of it, H4B I, 2, 26—28 (i. e. he may keep it at the full value of a royal. F 2.3.4 and M.Edd. he may keep it still as a f.).

Facile, easy: so may he with more f. question bear it, Oth. I, 3, 23.

Facility, ease, easiness: it argues f. LLL IV, 2, 57. the elegancy, f. and golden cadence of poesy, 126. he drinks you with f. your Dane dead drunk, Oth. II, 3, 84.

Facinerious, a word coined by Parolles with as little regard to grammar as to sense: he 's of a most f. spirit that will not acknowledge it to be —, All's II, 3, 35 (most M. Edd., being better Latinists than Parolles: facinorous). cf. Dexterious, Robustious.

Facing, that which is put on the outside by way of decoration, a trimming: stands for the f. Meas. III, 2, 11.

Facinorous, see Facinerious.

Fact, evil deed, crime: Lucr. 239. 349. Meas. IV, 2, 141. V, 439. All's III, 7, 47. Wint. III, 2, 86. H6A IV, 1, 30. H6B I, 3, 176. II, 1, 173. Tit. IV, 1, 39. Tim. III, 5, 16. Mcb. III, 6, 10. Cymb. III, 2, 17. Per. IV, 3, 12.

Faction, 1) a going into parties, dissension, conspiracy: I will bandy with thee in f., I will o'errun thee with policy, As V, 1, 61. how such an apprehension may turn the tide of fearful f. H4A IV, 1, 67. this brawl to-day, grown to this f. in the Temple-garden, H6A II, 4, 125. drave great Mars to f. Troil. III, 3, 190. to commit outrages, and cherish —s, Tim. III, 5, 73. equality of two domestic powers breed scrupulous f. Ant. I, 3, 48.

2) the forming a party, joining, alliance: their fraction is more our wish than their f. Troil. II, 3, 108.

3) party; a) the side, the cause followed: I have forsaken your pernicious f. (viz the English) and joined with Charles, H6A IV, 1, 59. Hamlet is of the f. that is wronged, Hml. V, 2, 249. in arms upon his f. R2 III, 2, 203 (Qq party). a tower of strength, which they upon the adverse f. want, R3 V, 3, 13 (Qq party). — b) the persons acting in union, the adherents of a cause: R2 II, 2, 57. H6A I, 1, 71. II, 4, 109. H6C V, 3, 17. R3 I, 3, 57. Troil. I, 3, 80. II, 3, 80. Cor. I, 1, 197. Tit. I, 18. 214. 404. 451. Tim. III, 5, 30. Caes. II, 1, 77.

4) company: this fellow were a king for our wild f. Gentl. IV, 1, 37. I will keep where there is wit stirring and leave the f. of fools. Troil. II, 1, 130.

Factionary, adj. taking part in a quarrel or dissension: always f. upon the party of your general, Cor. V, 2, 30.

Factious, 1) joining a cause, taking part in a quarrel: make up no f. numbers for the matter; in thine own person answer thy abuse, H6B II, 1, 40. you and your husband were f. for the house of Lancaster, R3 I, 3, 128. you have been f. one against the other, II, 1, 20. be f. for redress, Caes. I, 3, 118.

2) dissentious, rebellious: H6A IV, 1, 113. 190. H6B V, 1, 135. H6C I, 1, 74. Troil. I, 3, 191. II, 2, 209.

Factor, 1) agent, substitute in mercantile affairs: Err. I, 1, 42. H4A III, 2, 147. R3 III, 7, 134. IV, 4, 72. Cymb. I, 6, 188.

2) any substitute: chief —s for the gods, Ant. II, 6, 10.

Faculty, 1) power, ability: so long as brain and heart have f. by nature to subsist, Sonn. 122, 6. notes whose —ies inclusive were more than they were in note, All's I, 3, 232. and such other gambol —ies he has, H4B II, 4, 273. Duncan hath borne his —ies so meek, Mcb. I, 7, 17. how infinite in f. Hml. II, 2, 317.

2) quality, peculiar nature, essential virtue: unseen, yet crescive in his f. H5 I, 1, 66. which neither know my —ies nor my person, H8 I, 2, 73. change their natures and preformed —ies to monstrous quality, Caes. I, 3, 67. amaze the —ies of eyes and ears, Hml. II, 2, 592.

Fade, 1) to lose the colour of life, to wither: they (the canker-blooms) live unwooed and unrespected f. Sonn. 54, 10. Mids. I, 1, 129. Rom. IV, 1, 99. this is a man, old, wrinkled, —d, Shr. IV, 5, 43.

2) to disappear or lose strength gradually, to fail, to vanish, to grow dim, to die: such day as after sun-

set —*th in the west,* Sonn. 73, 6. *like this unsubstantial pageant* —*d,* Tp. IV, 155. *some* —*ing glimmer,* Err. V, 315. —*ing in music,* Merch. III, 2, 45. *my* —*ing breath,* H6A II, 5, 61. *it* —*d on the crowing of the cock,* Hml. I, 1, 157. *rise and f.* Cymb. V, 4, 106.

3) to be perishable: *thy eternal summer shall not f.* Sonn. 18, 9. *all her* —*ing sweets,* 19, 7. *why so large cost dost thou upon thy* —*ing mansion spend?* 146, 6. *nothing of him that doth f. but doth suffer a sea-change,* Tp. I, 2, 399. *one* —*ing moment's mirth,* Gentl. I, 1, 30.

Fadge, to succeed, to turn out well: *we will have, if this f. not, an antique,* LLL V, 1, 154. *how will this f.?* Tw. II, 2, 34.

Fading, a common burden of songs: *such delicate burthens of dildos and* —*s,* Wint. IV, 4, 195.

Fadom, see *Fathom.*

Faggot, a bundle of sticks or twigs used for fuel: H6A V, 4, 56. Tit. III, 1, 69.

Fail, subst. 1) failure, omission: *mark and perform it, for the f. of any point in it shall be death to thyself,* Wint. II, 3, 170.

2) want, deficiency: *his highness' f. of issue,* Wint. V, 1, 27. *by this my issue's f.* H8 II, 4, 198. *how grounded he his title to the crown, upon our f.?* I, 2, 145 (= in case of our want of issue).

3) offence: *the public body ... hath sense of its own f.* Tim. V, 1, 151 (O. Edd. *fall*). *goodly and gallant shall be false and perjured from thy great f.* Cymb. III, 4, 66.

Fail, vb. 1) intr. a) to become deficient, to cease to be sufficient, to cease: *it* (thy dignity) *cannot f. but by the violation of my faith,* Wint. IV, 4, 487 (= cease). *my sight* —*s,* H4B IV, 4, 110. *sweet honey and sweet notes together f.* Troil. V, 10, 45.

b) to be wanting: *though thy speech doth f.,* one *eye thou hast,* H6A I, 4, 82. *till Lionel's issue* —*s, his should not reign,* H6B II, 2, 56. *fall Greeks, f. fame,* Troil. V, 1, 48. *on whom depending, their obedience* —*s to the greater bench,* Cor. III, 1, 166. *which* (letter) —*ing, periods his comfort,* Tim. I, 1, 98. *obedience f. in children,* IV, 1, 4. *there would be something* —*ing,* Cymb. I, 1, 21.

c) to lose strength, to decline: *full of decay and* —*ing,* Tim. IV, 3, 466. Euphemistically, = to die: *had the king in his last sickness* —*ed,* H8 I, 2, 184.

d) to stay away, not to appear: *she will not f., for lovers break not hours,* Gentl. V, 1, 4. *wherein it is at our pleasure to f.* H4A I, 2, 191. Ado V, 1, 339. As V, 2, 132. All's IV, 2, 64. Caes. II, 1, 214.

e) not to act up to expectation: *if you fail in our request, the blame may hang upon your hardness,* Cor. V, 3, 90. *if my sight f. not,* H8 IV, 2, 108. *either my eyesight* —*s, or thou lookest pale,* Rom. III, 5, 57. Hence = to be mistaken, to err, to offend: *if he chance to f., he hath sentenced himself,* Meas. III, 2, 271. *one man holding troth, a million f.* Mids. III, 2, 93. *I have found myself to f. as often as I guessed,* All's III, 1, 15. *deceived by him that in such intelligence hath seldom* —*ed,* IV, 5, 88. *to f. in the disposing of those chances,* Cor. IV, 7, 40.

f) to miss, not to obtain, to miscarry; followed by *of: if I fail of the right casket,* Merch. II, 9, 11; cf. II, 2, 80 (Launcelot's speech). *if he f. of that, he will have other means,* As II, 3, 24. —*ing of her end,* Cymb. V, 5, 57. Hence = to want, to be

destitute: *if I f. not of my cunning,* Shr. II, 413. *the queen of audience nor desire shall f.* Ant. III, 12, 21.

g) not to succeed, to be frustrated, to fall short; used of persons: *if you f.* Merch. II, 9, 7. 15. H6A II, 1, 31. H6C II, 1, 190. R3 I, 1, 149. Troil. I, 3, 382. Mcb. I, 7, 59. 61. Oth. II, 1, 309. Ant. III, 7, 53. Of things: Tp. Epil. 12. Merch. III, 2, 270. All's II, 1, 145. Wint. II, 2, 42. H5 II, 4, 101. III, 2, 17. H6B II, 1, 52. H8 V, 1, 124. Troil. I, 3, 5. Cor. IV, 7, 55. Rom. III, 5, 242. Cymb. II, 4, 7.

2) trans. a) not to assist, to disappoint: *he might in a main danger f. you,* All's III, 6, 17. *if truth and upright innocency f. me,* H4B V, 2, 39. *if thou f. us, all our hope is done,* H6C III, 3, 33.

b) to be wanting to: *my life will be too short, and every measure f. me,* Lr. IV, 7, 3.

c) to neglect, to omit, not to afford: *he* —*ed his presence at the tyrant's feast,* Mcb. III, 6, 21. *would f. her obligation,* Lr. II, 4, 144. *I will never f. beginning nor supplyment,* Cymb. III, 4, 181. Followed by an infinitive: *f. not to do your office,* Meas. IV, 2, 129. All's II, 5, 80. H8 II, 3, 74. V, 1, 149. Rom. II, 2, 170. Hml. I, 2, 22.

d) to stay away from, to leave alone: *I will not f. your ladyship,* Gentl. IV, 3, 45. Wiv. II, 2, 96. Ado I, 1, 279. Mids. I, 2, 109. Merch. I, 1, 72. II, 4, 21. *f. not our feast,* Mcb. III, 1, 28.

Fain, adj. 1) glad, pleased: *are glad and f. by flight to save themselves,* H6A III, 2, 114. With *of: man and birds are f. of climbing high,* H6B II, 1, 8.

2) contented, yielding to necessity, putting a good face on it: *I must be f. to bear with you,* Gentl. I, 1, 127. *I must be f. to pawn my plate,* H4B II, 1, 153. *horns, which such as you are f. to be beholding to your wives for,* As IV, 1, 59.

3) constrained, obliged: Wiv. II, 2, 25. Meas. IV, 3, 159. 182. LLL V, 2, 9. All's IV, 3, 269. H6B IV, 2, 172. H8 V, 4, 60. Lr. IV, 7, 38.

Fain, adv. gladly, willingly; never used but joined to *would;* followed by a clause: *the good old man would f. that all were well,* H6C IV, 7, 31. Oftener by an inf.: *I would f. die a dry death,* Tp. I, 1, 72. Gentl. II, 1, 180. Wiv. II, 2, 151. Meas. V, 15. 21. 120. Err. III, 1, 66. Ado II, 1, 383. III, 5, 32. V, 1, 124. LLL V, 2, 372. As I, 2, 170. III, 3, 46. Shr. II, 74. All's V, 3, 115. Wint. V, 2, 96. H4B II, 4, 13. H5 I, 1, 85. III, 7, 91. IV, 7, 171. R3 III, 1, 29. Troil. III, 1, 149. V, 4, 5. Rom. II, 4, 214. Caes. I, 2, 240. Mcb. V, 3, 28. Hml. II, 2, 131. 153. Lr. I, 2, 70. I, 4, 30. 196. Oth. II, 3, 32. *full f.* H5 III, 2, 127 (Jamy's speech). *you would not have him die. No man alive so f. as I,* H6B III, 1, 244. *I would very f. speak with you,* Oth. IV, 1, 175. Severed from *would: I would forget it f.* Rom. III, 2, 109. Preceding *would: and now she f. would speak,* Ven. 221. LLL V, 2, 756. H4B II, 3, 65. H6A II, 3, 9. V, 3, 65. H6B III, 2, 141. R3 I, 4, 74. H8 II, 1, 25. Rom. II, 2, 88. Hml. III, 2, 236. IV, 7, 191. *most f. would steal,* All's II, 5, 86. *how f. would I wash my hands,* R3 I, 4, 279. *how f. would I have hated all mankind,* Tim. IV, 3, 506.

Faint, adj. 1) weak, feeble: *what strength I have's mine own, which is most f.* Tp. Epil. 3. *my f. means,* Merch. I, 1, 125. *such a man, so f., so spiritless,* H4B I, 1, 70. *f. souls past corporal toil,* H5 I, 1, 16. *too f. a number,* III, 6, 139. *f. Henry,* H6C II, 1,

153. *the f. defects of age,* Troil. I, 3, 172. *fear hath made thee f.* Tit. II, 3, 234. *a f. cold fear,* Rom. IV, 3, 15. Peculiar expressions: *upon f. primrose-beds,* Mids. I, 1, 215 (so called because flowers are the emblems of weakness? or for having a faint smell?): *in thy f. slumbers,* H4A II, 3, 50 (= disturbed, broken slumbers).

2) languid, exhausted: *f. with dearth,* Ven. 545. *grew I not f.?* 645. *agues pale and f.* 739. *this pale f. swan,* John V, 7, 21. V, 3, 17. V, 5, 4. H4A I, 3, 32. H4B I, 1, 108. H6A I, 1, 158. H6C I, 4, 23. Caes. II, 4, 43. Cymb. IV, 2, 63. V, 4, 163.

3) spiritless, weak-hearted: *who is so f. that dare not be so bold to touch the fire, the weather being cold?* Ven. 401. *faint not, f. heart,* Lucr. 1209. *women and children of so high a courage, and warriors f.* H6C V, 4, 51.

4) cold, without zeal, not forward to do one's duty: *chanting f. hymns to the cold fruitless moon,* Mids. I, 1, 73. *to set a gloss on f. deeds,* Tim. I, 2, 16. *has friendship such a f. and milky heart?* III, 1, 57. *their f. reply,* III, 3, 25. *a most f. neglect,* Lr. I, 4, 73. *longest, but in a —er kind,* Cymb. III, 2, 57.

Faint, vb. 1) intr. a) to become feeble: *as if with grief or travail he had —ed,* Lucr. 1543. Mids. II, 2, 35. As II, 4, 66. 75 *(—s for succour; cf. For).* Tit. II, 3, 233. Rom. II, 4, 72. Ant. II, 3, 34. *one —ing kiss,* H6A II, 5, 40 (as of a dying man). *my —ing words,* 95.

b) to swoon: Lucr. 1486. Err. I, 1, 46. As IV, 3, 149. H6C II, 6, 28. Rom. III, 1, 111. Lr. V, 3, 311. Oth. V, 1, 84. Ant. II, 5, 110. III, 6, 47. Cymb. V, 5, 149.

c) to lose courage, to be dispirited: *affection —s not like a pale-faced coward,* Ven. 569. *how I f., when I of you do write,* Sonn. 80, 1. Lucr. 1209. John V, 7, 78. R2 II, 1, 297. II, 2, 32. H6C I, 1, 129. I, 4, 48. II, 2, 57. R3 V, 3, 172. Troil. II, 2, 142.

2) trans. to deject, to sadden: *it —s me, to think what follows,* H8 II, 3, 103.

Faint-hearted, 1) weak, spiritless: H6C I, 1, 183. Tit. III, 1, 65.

2) void of zeal, not forward to do one's duty, hollow-hearted: *f. Woodvile, prizest him 'fore me?* H6A I, 3, 22.

Faintly, 1) in a feeble, languid manner: Ven. 482. Lucr. 740. R2 I, 3, 281. H5 IV, 2, 44. H6A I, 2, 8. Rom. I, 4, 7. Oth. III, 3, 282.

2) without zeal, not earnestly, not forcibly, slightly: *I f. broke with thee of Arthur's death,* John IV, 2, 227. *he prays but f. and would be denied,* R2 V, 3, 103. *'twas very f. he said Rise,* Cor. V, 1, 66. *I have told you what I have seen, but f.* Lr. I, 2, 191. *now he denies it f.* Oth. IV, 1, 113.

Faintness, 1) exhaustion, weariness: Mids. III, 2, 428. 2) want of spirit: H6A IV, 1, 107.

Fair, subst. a stated meeting of buyers and sellers: Err. I, 1, 18. LLL IV, 3, 235. V, 2, 318. All's V, 3, 148. Wint. IV, 3, 109. H4B III, 2, 43. V, 1, 26. H8 V, 4, 73. Lr. III, 6, 78.

Fair, adj., 1) beautiful, handsome; used of things as well as persons: Ven. 7. 115. Lucr. 1600. Sonn. 13, 9. 54, 3. 95, 12. 106, 2. 127, 1. 144, 3. Compl. 208 (*gems*). Pilgr. 38 (*sun*). Tp. I, 2, 126 (*Milan*). 458. II, 1, 70. 129. Gentl. II, 1, 54. II, 4, 199. II, 6, 2. 25. IV, 2, 41. IV, 4, 153. 154. V, 2,

11 (*pearls*) etc. etc. *wine and sugar of the best and the —est,* Wiv. II, 2, 70 (Mrs. Quickly's speech). *where you may make the —est shoot,* LLL IV, 1, 10. *thy f. virtue's force,* Mids. III, 1, 143 (= thy beauty's force).

Substantively, a) beauty: *having no f. to lose,* Ven. 1083. *to rob him of his f.* 1086. *neither in inward worth, nor outward f.* Sonn. 16, 11. *every fair from f. sometime declines,* 18, 7. *that f. thou owest,* 10. *these bastard signs of f.* 68, 3. *to your f. no painting set,* 83, 2. *my decayed f. a sunny look of his would soon repair,* Err. II, 1, 98. *where f. is not, praise cannot mend the brow,* LLL IV, 1, 17. *O heresy in f.* 22. *Demetrius loves your f.* Mids. I, 1, 182. *let no f. be kept in mind but the f. of Rosalind,* As III, 2, 99.

b) a beautiful person; applied to a man: *speak, f.* Ven. 208. To women: *that his foul thoughts might compass his f. f.* Lucr. 346. *his f.* Sonn. 21, 4. *from many a several f.* Compl. 206. *gentle and f.* Meas. I, 4, 24. *looking on —est of f.* LLL II, 241. *twenty thousand —s,* V, 2, 37. *O happy f.* Mids. I, 1, 182. *I'll be thine, my f.* Wint. IV, 4, 42. *speak, my f.* H5 V, 2, 177. *farewell, revolted f.* Troil. V, 2, 186. *that f. for which love groaned,* Rom. II Chor. 3.

c) anything beautiful: *the life of purity, the supreme f.* (viz the sun) Lucr. 780. *every f.* Sonn. 18, 7. 21, 4. *slander's mark was ever yet the f.* 70, 2. *they hide the f.* Rom. I, 1, 237. *'tis much pride for f. without the f. within to hide,* I, 3, 90.

2) clear, fine, not dim and cloudy: *f. welkin,* Lucr. 116. *the f. and fiery-pointed sun,* 372. *f. was the morn,* Pilgr. 117. *f. weather,* Ado I, 3, 25. LLL I, 2, 149. *f. blessed beams,* Mids. III, 2. 392. *since the more f. and crystal is the sky,* R2 I, 1, 41. *f. time of day,* H5 V, 2, 3. *so foul and f. a day,* Mcb. I, 3, 38. *f. daylight,* Lr. IV, 7, 52.

3) clear, unspotted, pure: *lest f. humanity abhor the deed,* Lucr. 195. *his f. f.* 346 (= his pure, innocent mistress). *thou their f. life, and they thy fouler grave,* 661. *f. founts,* 850. *f. nature is both kind and tame,* Compl. 311. *f. issue,* Tp. IV, 1, 24; cf. Wint. II, 1, 150. *when his f. course is not hindered,* Gentl. II, 7, 27. *Silvia is too f., too true, too holy, to be corrupted with my worthless gifts,* IV, 2, 5. *each f. instalment,* Wiv. V, 5, 67. *bear a f. presence, though your heart be tainted,* Err. III, 2, 13. *my f. name,* R2 I, 1, 167. *the arms are f.* H4A V, 2, 88. *let fools do good, and f. men call for grace,* Tit. III, 1, 205. *divided from herself and her f. judgement,* Hml. IV, 5, 85 etc.

4) of a white complexion: Ado I, 1, 174 (quibbling). LLL V, 2, 32. As IV, 3, 86. Tit. IV, 2, 69. 154. Opposed to black: Sonn. 127, 1. 11. 144, 3. 147, 13. Gentl. V, 2, 9. LLL IV, 3, 253. 261. As III, 2, 97. Tit. III, 1, 205. IV, 2, 69. Oth. I, 3, 291. II, 1, 130 etc.

5) becoming, honorable, equitable: *with colours —er painted their foul ends,* Tp. I, 2, 143. *f. encounter of two most rare affections,* III, 1, 74. *f. play,* V, 175; cf. John V, 2, 118 and H8 IV, 2, 36. *keep f. quarter with his bed,* Err. II, 1, 108. II, 2, 147. *too brown for a f. praise,* Ado I, 1, 174. *death is the —est cover for her shame,* IV, 1, 117. *teach us some f. excuse,* LLL V, 2, 432. *I like not f. terms and a villain's mind,* Merch. I, 3, 181. III, 4, 36. *there is a f. behaviour in thee,* Tw. I, 2, 47. R2 I, 1, 54. III, 3,

53. 123. 188. H4A II, 2, 14. H6B IV, 6, 11. H6C IV, 7, 14. Troil. II, 2, 148. Ant. V, 2, 10 etc. etc.

6) being as a thing ought to be, in order, in a good state: *the ways are f. enough*, Merch. V, 264. *have you laid f. the bed?* H6B III, 2, 11. *I will go wash, and when my face is f.,...* Cor. I, 9, 69. *they* (the horses) *are f. with their feeding*, As I, 1, 12. *how art thou a king but by f. sequence and succession?* R2 II, 1, 199. *that's even as f. as 'at hand, quoth the chamberlain'*, H4A II, 1, 54. *f. health*, Sonn. 45, 12 and LLL V, 2, 834. *your f. safety*, John III, 3, 16. *'tis a f. hand*, Merch. II, 4, 12 (= plain, legible). *having our f. order written down*, John V, 2, 4. *f. five hundred pound a year*, John I, 69 (= full); cf. *he would have lived many a f. year*, As IV, 1, 101.

7) favourable, auspicious: *points on me graciously with f. aspect*, Sonn. 26, 10. *found such f. assistance*, 78, 2. *all the f. effects of future hopes*, Gentl. I, 1, 50. *made use and f. advantage of his days*, II, 4, 68. *her f. influence*, III, 1, 183. *God grant them a f. departure*, Merch. I, 2, 121. *this most f. occasion*, John V, 4, 51. *f. be all thy hopes*, H6A II, 5, 113. *f. hope must hinder life's decay*, H6C IV, 4, 16. *lines of f. comfort*, R3 V, 2, 6. *my consent and f. according voice*, Rom. I, 2, 19.

Substantively: *f. be to you*, Troil. III, 1, 46. *f. befall your mask*, LLL II, 124. Shr. V, 2, 111. R2 II, 1, 129. R3 I, 3, 282. III, 5, 47. *f. fall the wit that can so well defend her*, Ven. 472. *f. fall the bones*, John I, 78.

8) kind: *speak f. words*, Ven. 208. *at the price of one f. word*, Cor. III, 3, 91. *guileful f. words*, H6A I, 1, 77. *only f. speech*, Cor. III, 2, 96. *Venus salutes him with this f. good morrow*, Ven. 859. *f. praise*, LLL IV, 1, 23. *f. prayer*, Meas. I, 4, 69. Mids. II, 2, 62. *one f. look*, Gentl. V, 4, 23. Shr. V, 2, 153. R3 III, 4, 100 (Ff *good*). *f. humility*, III, 7, 17. *hold f. friendship with his majesty*, LLL II, 141. *f. harbour in my house*, II, 175. *f. payment for foul words*, V, 1, 19. *f. speechless messages*, Merch. I, 1, 164. *f. ostents of love*, II, 8, 44. *render f. return*, H5 II, 4, 127. *made f. love of hate*, R3 II, 1, 50. *time, with his —er hand*, Tim. V, 1, 126 etc. *so f. an offered chain*, Err. III, 2, 186 (i. e. a chain which is so kind an offer, so kindly offered). *your company is —er than honest*, Meas. IV, 3, 185 (= more kind than decent).

9) good, accomplished, such as would be desired or loved: *our best-moving f. solicitor*, LLL II, 29. *his f. tongue, conceit's expositor*, 72. *bless it to all f. posterity*, Mids. IV, 1, 95. *f. thoughts and happy hours attend on you*, Merch. III, 4, 41. *many f. promotions*, R3 I, 3, 80. 95. *if there be one among the —est of Greece that holds his honours higher than his ease*, Troil. I, 3, 265; cf. Tit. IV, 2, 69. Hence serving as an expletive of courtesy: *f. sir*, LLL V, 2, 310. Merch. I, 3, 127. IV, 2, 5. Shr. IV, 5, 53. *the f. Sir Eglamour*, Gentl. I, 2, 9. *fare you well, f. gentlemen*, As I, 2, 260. *f. cousin*, R2 III, 3, 190. IV, 304. H5 IV, 3, 19. *f. nephew*, H6A II, 5, 55. *f. Lords*, Lucr. 1688. H6C II, 1, 95. IV, 8, 23. *my —est friend*, Wint. IV, 4, 112. *f. lovers*, Mids. IV, 1, 182. *my f. guests*, H8 I, 4, 35. *f. Saint George*, R3 V, 3, 349. *f. Diomed*, Troil. IV, 1, 75. *f. Greek*, IV, 4, 115. *this f. assembly*, Ado V, 4, 34. As V, 4, 159. *f. knighthood's bending knee*, Wiv. V, 5, 76 etc. etc. Even in such phrases: *f. torch, burn out thy light*, Lucr. 190. *had notice of your f. approach*,

LLL II, 81. *a pound of your f. flesh*, Merch. I, 3, 151. Ridiculed in Troil. III, 1, 46: *f. be to you, my lord, and to all this f. company! f. desires, in all f. measure, fairly guide them! especially to you, f. queen! f. thoughts be your f. pillow!*

Opposed, in all its significations, to *foul:* Ven. 1030. Lucr. 661. Tp. I, 2, 143. Ado IV, 1, 104. LLL IV, 1, 19. 23. H6C IV, 7, 14. Tim. IV, 3, 28. Mcb. I, 1, 11. I, 3, 38 etc.

Adv. 1) beautifully, finely: *shall hate be —er lodged than gentle love?* Sonn. 10, 10. *all the pictures —est lined*, As III, 2, 97. *you will have Gremio to keep you f.* Shr. II, 17. *things that do sound so f.* Mcb. I, 3, 52. Used with irony: *she bears me f. in hand*, Shr. IV, 2, 3. *you fought f.* H4A II, 4, 329. *you have crafted f.* Cor. IV, 6, 118.

2) bright, clearly: *the moon shines f.* H4A III, 1, 142.

3) in a good and legible hand: *is it not f. writ?* John IV, 1, 37. *wrote it f.* Hml. V, 2, 32. *to write f.* 34.

4) auspiciously, fortunately: *the wind blows f. from land*, Err. IV, 1, 91. *the wind sits f.* R2 II, 2, 123. H5 II, 2, 12. *rest you f., good signior*, Merch. I, 3, 60. *yourself stood as f. as any comer for my affection*, II, 1, 20. *chance as f. and choose as true*, III, 2, 132. *since this business so f. is done*, H4A V, 5, 43. *should he 'scape Hector f.* Troil. I, 3, 372.

5) honestly, equitably: *my mother played my father f.* Meas. III, 1, 141. *we offer f.* H4A V, 1, 114.

6) kindly, gently: *speak f.* Err. III, 2, 11. R2 III, 3, 128. R3 I, 3, 47 (Ff *look*). Cor. III, 2, 70. Tit. I, 46. Hml. IV, 1, 36. *didst speak him f.* Err. IV, 2, 16. IV, 4, 157. Mids. II, 1, 199. Shr. I, 2, 180. H4B V, 2, 33. H6B IV, 1, 120. H6C V, 4, 24. Cor. III, 1, 263. Tit. V, 2, 140. Rom. III, 1, 158. *speak me f. in death* (= speak well of me after my death) Merch. IV, 1, 275. *I bespake you f.* Tw. V, 192. *entreat them f.* H6C I, 1, 271. R3 IV, 4, 151. Troil. IV, 4, 115. *look f.* R3 I, 3, 47 (Qq *speak*). *tap for tap, and so part f.* H4B II, 1, 207. *I hope his honour will conceive the —est of me*, Tim. III, 2, 60. *so f. an offered chain*, Err. III, 2, 186; cf. Adj. def. 8.

7) soft, gently, still: *soft and f., friar*, Ado V, 4, 72. *the silver Trent shall run f. and evenly*, H4A III, 1, 103 (instead of: fairly and evenly). *stand f., I pray thee, let me look on thee*, Troil. IV, 5, 235.

Fair, vb. to make beautiful: *—ing the foul with art's false borrowed face*, Sonn. 127, 6 (cf. *Unfair*).

Fair-betrothed, fairly, honourably affianced: Per. V, 3, 71; O. Edd. not hyphened.

Fairest-boding, of a very good omen: R3 V, 3, 227.

Fair-faced, 1) of a white complexion: Ado III, 1, 61. 2) looking kindly: *f. league*, John II, 417.

Fairing, a present (originally one given at a fair): LLL V, 2, 2.

Fairly, 1) beautifully, gracefully, finely: *and that unfair which f. doth excel*, Sonn. 5, 4 (= with respect to beauty, by beauty). *after some oration f. spoke*, Merch. III, 2, 180. *thou offerest f. to thy brother's wedding*, As V, 4, 173. *I'll have them very f. bound*, Shr. I, 2, 146. Rom. III, 2, 84. *the true blood which peepeth f. through it*, Wint. IV, 4, 148. *the unworthiest shows as f. in the mask*, Troil. I, 3, 84. *this purpose, that so f. shows*, Ant. II, 2, 147.

2) in a good and legible hand: Shr. III, 1, 70. III, 2, 62. John IV, 1, 38. R3 III, 6, 2.

3) in a becoming manner, decently, honourably: *f. spoke,* Tp. IV, 1, 31. *f. offered,* Wint. IV, 4, 389. *f. answered,* H8 III, 2, 179. *my chief care is to come f. off from the great debts,* Merch. I, 1, 128. *to be said an honest man and a good housekeeper goes as f. as to say a careful man and a great scholar,* Tw. IV, 2, 11. *thou doest thy office f.* H5 III, 6, 148. *we should dress us f. for our end,* IV, 1, 10. *now you're f. seated,* H8 I, 4, 31. *would I were f. out on't,* V, 3, 109. *what Troy means f. shall be spoke aloud,* Troil. I, 3, 259. *furnish you f. for this interchange,* III, 3, 33. *he bears all things f.* Cor. IV, 7, 21. *how f. this lord strives to appear foul,* Tim. III, 3, 31.

4) kindly, gently: *they parted very f. in jest,* Gentl. II, 5, 14. *then f. I bespoke the officer,* Err. V, 233. *f. let her be entreated,* R2 III, 1, 37. *speak, my fair, and f., I pray thee,* H5 V, 2, 177. *how long f. shall her sweet life last?* R3 IV, 4, 352 (= without danger from foul practices). *they are f. welcome,* Tim. I, 2, 182. *I shall accept them f.* 190. *my extent to the players, which must show f. outward,* Hml. II, 2, 391. *greet them f.* Per. V, 1, 10.

5) auspiciously, fortunately: *f. met,* Meas. V, 1. H5 V, 2, 10. *heavens so shine, that they may f. note this act of mine,* Tw. IV, 3, 35. *my fortunes every way as f. ranked as Demetrius',* Mids. I, 1, 101. *our soldiers stand full f. for the day,* H4A V, 3, 29. *such a day, so f. won,* H4B I, 1, 21. *we f. hope,* H5 V, 2, 18. *fair desires f. guide them,* Troil. III, 1, 48. *a second hope, as f. built as Hector,* IV, 5, 109. Probably in this passage also: *let them say 'tis grossly done; so it be f. done, no matter,* Wiv. II, 2, 149 (= so as to bid fair to make its fortune?)

6) well, finely: *we may blow our nails together, and fast it f. out,* Shr. I, 1, 109. *you gave us the counterfeit f. last night,* Rom. II, 4, 48.

Fairness, 1) beauty: Merch. III, 2, 94. Oth. II, 1, 130. Cymb. V, 5, 168.

2) spotlessness, unstained honour: *to the f. of my power,* Cor. I, 9, 73 (alluding to v. 69).

Fair-play, courteous intercourse between enemies: *shall we send f. orders ... to arms invasive?* John V, 1, 67. *according to the f. of the world, let me have audience,* V, 2, 118 (not hyphened by some M. Edd).

Fair-shining, bright: *three f. suns,* H6C II, 1, 40.

Fair-spoken, eloquent: H8 IV, 2, 52 (cf. *Well-spoken* and *Better-spoken*).

Fairy, a diminutive spirit, of the same nature as the elves: Ven. 146. Wiv. IV, 4, 61. 71. 79. V, 2, 2. V, 3, 13. V, 4, 1. V, 5, 77. 95 etc. Mids. II, 1, 61. 144. 256. III, 1, 160. IV, 1, 46. 65. V, 390. 400. 409. Rom. I, 4, 69. Mcb. IV, 1, 42. *the f. kingdom,* Mids. II, 1, 144. *f. king,* IV, 1, 98. *f. lord,* III, 2, 378. *f. queen,* Wiv. IV, 6, 20. Mids. II, 1, 8. II, 2, 12. III, 1, 80. IV, 1, 75. *f. land,* Err. II, 2, 191. Mids. II, 1, 65. 122. IV, 1, 66. *the f. oyes,* Wiv. V, 5, 45. *that hour of f. revel,* IV, 4, 58. *'tis almost f. time,* Mids. V, 371. *a f. song,* Mids. II, 2, 1. *these f. toys,* V, 1, 3. Of different sex: Wiv. V, 5, 85. Cymb. III, 6, 41. IV, 2, 217. Of different colour: Wiv. IV, 4, 49. V, 5, 41. Their benign influence: Mids. II, 1, 12. V, 408 etc. Wint. III, 3, 121. 127. Lr. IV, 6, 29. Cymb.

IV, 2, 217. V, 4, 133. Their malignity: Tp. IV, 196. 212. Err. II, 2, 191. IV, 2, 35. Hml. I, 1, 163. Cymb. II, 2, 9. Not consisting of flesh and blood: Per. V, 1, 155. Taking no food: Cymb. III, 6, 41. Exchanging children: H4A I, 1, 87; cf. *the —ies' midwife,* Rom. I, 4, 54. Danger of seeing or speaking to them: Wiv V, 5, 51.

Used to denote a person of more than human power: *to this great f. I'll commend thy acts,* Ant. IV, 8, 12.

Fairy-like, in the manner of fairies: Wiv. IV, 4, 57.

Faith, 1) belief: *it is his grounds of f. that all that look on him love him,* Tw. II, 3, 164. Wint. I, 2, 430. V, 3, 95. H5 V, 2, 217. Lr. I, 1, 225. With *in:* H8 I, 3, 30. Especially religious belief: Wiv. IV, 4, 10. Err. III, 2, 150. Ado I, 1, 258. Merch. IV, 1, 130. All's IV, 1, 83. Tw. I, 5, 137. R2 V, 5, 13 (Qq word). H4A III, 1, 155. H6A V, 1, 14. Cymb. III, 4, 85.

2) truth, truthfulness, veracity: *all my honest f. in thee is lost,* Sonn. 152, 8. *upon my f. and honour,* Meas. V, 224. All's II, 1, 83. *how can these things in me seem scorn to you, bearing the badge of f.* (viz tears) *to prove them true?* Mids. III, 2, 127. 174. *do you mean good f.?* Merch. III, 2, 212. *by the f. of my love, I will,* As III, 2, 449. *Lady Constance speaks not from her f., but from her need,* John III, 1, 210. H4A III, 3, 174. *so deep suspicion, where all f. is meant,* H8 III, 1, 53. *by my f.!* Ado II, 1, 242. As III, 5, 38. IV, 1, 21. V, 4, 65. John II, 545. H4A I, 2, 154. V, 4, 125. H6B IV, 2, 54 etc. *by my two —s and troths,* Ado I, 1, 228. *by the f. of men!* Cor. II, 1, 204. *by the f. of man,* Oth. I, 1, 10. *on my f.* Meas. V, 224. Wint. II, 1, 70. Rom. IV, 5, 115. *in f.* = in sooth, indeed: Sonn. 141, 1. Pilgr. 322. Wiv. I, 4, 9. Ado I, 1, 199. 227. II, 1, 22. 324. III, 5, 13. IV, 1, 298. V, 1, 57. Merch. II, 4, 12. V, 143. 174. Shr. Ind. 1, 1. Tw. II, 4, 109. Wint. IV, 4, 505. H4A II, 3, 82 (Ff *in sooth*). 90 (Ff *indeed*) etc. *i' f.:* Wiv. I, 1, 290. I, 4, 4. 170. Ado I, 1, 173. I, 1, 307. III, 4, 15. III, 5, 39. V, 1, 155. LLL IV, 1, 135. IV, 3, 9. Mids. III, 2, 284. Merch. I, 1, 111. I, 3, 153. As III, 2, 228. III, 4, 11. IV, 3, 176. V, 3, 15. Shr. I, 1, 61 etc. *in good f.:* Sonn. 131, 5. LLL V, 2, 280. All's II, 2, 36. Tw. I, 5, 28. Lr. II, 1, 111 (Qq *sooth*) etc. *good f.!* Wiv. I, 4, 160. As III, 2, 269. All's II, 1, 70. II, 3, 233. H6A II, 4, 18. H6C III, 2, 23. R3 II, 4, 16. III, 2, 117. Rom. IV, 4, 20. Per. V, 1, 179. *faith!* (in the same sense; sometimes written *'faith*): Tp. I, 2, 437. III, 3, 43. Wiv. II, 1, 39. 159. Meas. II, 1, 282. III, 2, 65. V, 509. Err. III, 1, 49. III, 2, 134. Ado I, 1, 46. II, 1, 55. II, 3, 79. 108. LLL V, 2, 586. Merch. III, 2, 213. As IV, 1, 116. V, 1, 3. V, 4, 51. Shr. I, 1, 138. All's I, 3, 34. 105. H6A II, 4, 7. H6B II, 1, 38. R3 I, 4, 124. IV, 4, 175 etc. Joined to imperatives, to make the demand more urgent: *f., stay here this night,* Err. IV, 4, 155. Mids. I, 2, 49. As I, 3, 36. III, 5, 45. IV, 1, 94. Troil. IV, 1, 51. Similarly *i' f.: go to, i' f.* Ado I, 1, 202. Joined to questions: *what years, i' f.?* Tw. II, 4, 28. *but what, in f., make you from Wittenberg?* Hml. I, 2, 168.

3) faithfulness, fidelity: *purest f. unhappily forsworn,* Sonn. 66, 4. *upon whose f. and honour I repose,* Gentl. IV, 3, 26. Ado I, 1, 75. II, 1, 187. Wint. III, 2, 20. John II, 568. 597. III, 1, 95. 212.

V, 2, 10. V, 4, 12. R2 III, 2, 101. III, 3, 37. H4A II, 1, 35. III, 3, 125. 127. H6B III, 1, 205. R3 IV, 4, 497. V, 1, 17. Caes. III, 1, 137. IV, 2, 22. Ant. III, 13, 43. —*s:* John IV, 2, 6. V, 7, 75. H4B IV, 1, 193. = trustworthy discretion: *you do not doubt my f.?* H8 II, 1, 143. *'twill require a strong f. to conceal it,* 145.

Especially faithfulness in love: Sonn. 152, 3 *(torn)*. Pilgr. 58. 96. 250. 255. Gentl. IV, 2, 11. IV, 4, 107. V, 4, 47. 50. 52. 62. Mids. II, 1, 79. Merch. II, 6, 7. As V, 2, 95. V, 4, 156. 194. Tw. I, 4, 25. Wint. IV, 4, 35. 488.

4) word or honour pledged, vow: *plight your honourable* —*s to me,* Lucr. 1690. *being by f. enforced to call Claudio to a reckoning,* Ado V, 4, 8. *if I break f.* LLL I, 1, 154. *break f. and troth,* IV, 3, 143. *f. so infringed,* 146. *our f. not torn,* 285. Merch. V, 253. *hold little f.* Tw. V, 174. John V, 2, 7. R2 IV, 76. H6C III, 3, 247. Troil. V, 3, 69. Mcb. IV, 3, 128.

Especially a vow of love: *quick Biron hath plighted f. to me,* LLL V, 2, 283. *my f. and this the princess I did give,* 454. *to solemnize the bargain of your f.* Merch. III, 2, 195. V, 169. Wint. IV, 4, 471. H6A V, 3, 162.

5) true love: *all the f., the virtue of my heart, is only Helena,* Mids. IV, 1, 174. *stealing her soul with many vows of f.* Merch. V, 19. *his f., his sweet disaster,* All's I, 1, 187. *plight me the full assurance of your f.* Tw. IV, 3, 26. *since you to non-regardance cast my f.* V, 124. *lest f. turn to despair,* Rom. I, 5, 106.

Faith-breach, breach of fidelity, disloyalty: Mcb. V, 2, 18.

Faithed, credited: *would the reposal of any trust, virtue, or worth in thee make thy words f.,* Lr. II, 1, 72.

Faithful, 1) of true fidelity, loyal: Pilgr. 406. 430. Meas. V, 2. LLL V, 2, 50. 844. Mids. IV, 1, 96. As II, 4, 99. V, 2, 87. V, 4, 14. John I, 50. III, 4, 66. V, 7, 104. R2 III, 3, 100. 118. H5 I, 2, 13. II, 2, 161. H6A III, 4, 21. V, 5, 91. R3 III, 7, 149. H8 II, 1, 61. V, 4, 76. Tit. V, 1, 1. Rom. II, 2, 127. V, 3, 232. 302. Mcb. III, 6, 36. Hml. II, 2, 130. V, 2, 39. Cymb. I, 1, 174. With *to:* LLL IV, 2, 111. Caes. III, 2, 90. Adverbially: *day serves not light more f. than I'll be,* Per. I, 2, 110.

2) believing in the truth of religion: R3 I, 4, 4.

3) true; veracious: *a f. verity,* Meas. IV, 3, 131. *I will be f.* Hml. II, 2, 115.

4) full of true love, coming from the heart: *whether that thy youth and kind will the f. offer take of me and all,* As IV, 3, 60. *to whose ingrate and unauspicious altars my soul the* —*est offerings hath breathed out,* Tw. V, 117.

Faithfully, 1) with good faith, loyally: LLL II, 157. V, 2, 841. H8 IV, 2, 141.

2) honestly, conformably to truth: *we will answer all things f.* Merch. V, 299. *I'll speak that which you will wonder at. But wilt thou f.?* All's IV, 1, 95. *her death was f. confirmed by the rector of the place,* IV, 3, 68. *their own authors f. affirm.* H5 I, 2, 43.

3) from the heart, earnestly: *if that you were the good Sir Rowland's son, as you have whispered*

f. you were, As II, 7, 192. *hast thou denied thyself a Faulconbridge? As f. as I deny the devil,* John I, 252. *if thou dost love, pronounce it f.* Rom. II, 2, 94. *I should not urge it half so f.* Tim. III, 2, 46.

Faithfulness, 1) fidelity, loyalty: Per. I, 1, 154.

2) true love: *nor ask advice of any other thought but f. and courage,* Per. I, 1, 63.

Faithless, 1) disloyal, perfidious: John II, 230. H8 II, 1, 123.

2) not to be trusted: *O f. coward!* Meas. III, 1, 137.

3) unbelieving, infidel: *a f. Jew,* Merch. II, 4, 38.

Faitor, evildoer: *down, dogs! down,* —*s!* H4B II, 4, 173 (Pistol's speech. Q *faters,* Ff *fates*).

Falchion, a scimitar: Lucr. 176. 509. 1046. 1626. LLL V, 2, 618. H6C I, 4, 12. R3 I, 2, 94. Lr. V, 3, 276.

Falcon, a female hawk trained for sport (the smaller and weaker male being called *tercel* or *tassel,* q. v.): Ven. 1027. Lucr. 506. 511. Meas. III, 1, 92. As III, 3, 81. Shr. IV, 1, 193. Wint. IV, 4, 15. R2 I, 3, 61. H6B II, 1, 5. 12. H6C I, 4, 41. Troil. III, 2, 55. Mcb. II, 4, 12.

Falconbridge, name: LLL II, 42. 205. Merch. I, 2, 71. John I, 56. 134. 176. 251. III, 4, 171. IV, 3, 94. V, 3, 5 etc. H5 III, 5, 44 (M. Edd. after Holinshed: *Fauconberg*). H6A IV, 7, 67. H6C I, 1, 239.*

Falconer, one who trains or uses hawks for sport: Rom. II, 2, 159. Hml. II, 2, 450 *(like French* —*s)*.

Fall, subst. 1) the act of dropping from a higher to a lower place: *a f. off a tree,* H6B II, 1, 96. Tit. II, 3, 203. *the f. of every Phrygian stone,* Troil. IV, 5, 223. cf. *the f. of a sparrow,* Hml. V, 2, 231. Used of fruits: Pilgr. 136. Of leaf: R2 III, 4, 49.

2) the act of tumbling from an erect posture: Troil. III, 3, 87. Cor. I, 3, 69. Cymb. I, 2, 39.

3) the act of being thrown down at wrestling: *in despite of a f.* As I, 3, 25. Hence = a round in wrestling: *try a f.* As I, 1, 132. I, 2, 216.

4) the descent of fluids; of a river: Lucr. 650. Wiv. III, 1, 17. Of rain: Lucr. 551. R3 IV, 4, 512. Of blood: *without much f. of blood,* H5 I, 2, 25.

5) the ebb, decrease: *that now they are at f., want treasure,* Tim. II, 2, 214.

6) the stroke of a sword: *that they may crush down with a heavy f. the helmets ...,* R3 V, 3, 111. *I heard the clink and f. of swords,* Oth. II, 3, 234.

7) a cadence, a sinking of tone: *that strain again: it had a dying f.* Tw. I, 1, 4.

8) destruction, death, overthrow: *to procure my f.* Err. I, 1, 1. *what shall I gain by young Arthur's f.* John III, 4, 141. H6C V, 2, 10. R3 I, 2, 4. Cor. V, 6, 18. 49. Caes. III, 2, 194. Mcb. III, 1, 122. Hml. V, 2, 231. Per. I, 1, 149.

9) downfall, degradation, loss of greatness: All's II, 1, 13. III, 6, 108. R2 II, 4, 15. IV, 318. V, 1, 44 (Qq *tale*). V, 5, 88. H4A III, 2, 38. H5 III, 5, 68. H6A III, 2, 32. H6B I, 2, 106. III, 1, 52. Troil. III, 3, 78. V, 10, 49. Tim. V, 2, 17. V, 3, 10. Mcb. IV, 3, 69. Ant. III, 13, 155. V, 2, 172. Cymb. IV, 2, 403.

10) defection from virtue, sin: *to make a*

second f. of cursed man, R2 III, 4, 76. *thy f. hath left a kind of blot*, H5 II, 2, 138. *like another f. of man*, 142. *to stay him from the f. of vanity*, R3 III, 7, 97. *hath sense of its own f.* Tim. V, 1, 151 (M. Edd. *fail*). *ere we come to f.* Hml. III, 3, 49. Used for *fault* by Evans: Wiv. I, 1, 262.

Fall, vb. (impf. *fell;* partic. usually *fallen,* f. i. Ven. 354. Tp. II, 1, 181. Meas. II, 4, 178. Ado IV, 1, 141. Mids. III, 2, 417. Merch. IV, 1, 266. As III, 5, 66. V, 4, 182. Shr. IV, 1, 57. All's V, 1, 12 etc. Three times *fell:* Tit. II, 4, 50. Tim. IV, 3, 265. Lr. IV, 6, 54). A) intr. 1) **to drop from a higher place:** Ven. 314. 354. 527. Lucr. 1139. Pilgr. 136. Tp. II, 2, 24. IV, 1, 18. Gentl. I, 2, 73. Err. I, 2, 37. Ado IV, 1, 141. Mids. II, 1, 90. 108. 165. Shr. IV, 1, 57. Tw. V, 247. R2 II, 1, 153. H6B III, 2, 412 (*this way f. I to death;* i. e. so as to die). H8 IV, 1, 55; cf. Ant. IV, 14, 106. H8 I, 1, 203. Rom. V, 1, 62 (*f. dead*). Tim. IV, 3, 265. Lr. IV, 6, 54 etc. etc. Used of the foot, = to tread: *that the blind mole may not hear a foot f.* Tp. IV, 195. *though he go as softly as foot can f.* As III, 2, 346. Of the coming down of a sword: *an it had not —en flatlong,* Tp. II, 1, 181. Mcb. V, 8, 11.

2) **to drop from an erect posture:** Ven. 719. Tp. II, 1, 203. II, 2, 16. Gentl. V, 4, 9; cf. Ant. I, 1, 34. Err. V, 114. Ado II, 3, 152. Mids. III, 2, 25. 417 etc. etc.

3) **to disembogue:** *there —s into thy boundless flood black lust, dishonour,* Lucr. 653.

4) **to sink, to decrease, to decay:** *her price is —en,* Lr. I, 1, 200. *a good leg will f.* H5 V, 2, 167. With *away: am I not —en away vilely since this last action?* H4A III, 3, 1. *till bones and flesh and sinews f. away,* H6A III, 1, 193. And with *off: what a —ing off was there!* Hml. I, 5, 47 (= what a change for the worse).

5) **to be degraded or destroyed, to perish:** Sonn. 151, 12. Meas. II, 1, 38. John III, 4, 139. H6A II, 5, 90. III, 1, 174. H6B III, 1, 22. H8 IV, 1, 55. Hml. I, 1, 114. Ant. III, 13, 44 etc. = to be slain: All's III, 1, 22. H4B Ind. 29. Rom. III, 1, 179. Cymb. III, 3, 91. V, 4, 72 etc.

6) **to depart from the path of virtue, to sin:** Compl. 321. Meas. II, 1, 18. II, 3, 11. II, 4, 178. III, 1, 191. H4A III, 3, 186. Rom. II, 3, 80.

7) **to be brought forth:** *the eanlings should f. as Jacob's hire,* Merch. I, 3, 81. *that their burthens may not f. this day,* John III, 1, 90.

8) **to rush with violence:** *they fell on,* H8 V, 4, 56. *all the dukes f. upon the king,* Meas. I, 2, 3. *they fell upon me, bound me,* Err. V, 246. *tear me, take me, and the gods f. upon you,* Tim. III, 4, 100. Caes. V, 1, 81. Ant. II, 2, 75.

9) **to come, to get:** *f. to decay,* Sonn. 13, 9. *it will f. to cureless ruin,* Merch. IV, 1, 141. *in twenty pieces,* Rom. II, 5, 50. *grieve not that I am —en to this for you,* Merch. IV, 1, 266. *to f. before the lion,* Tw. III, 1, 140 (= to meet the lion). *how fell you besides your five wits?* IV, 2, 92. *you f. 'mongst friends,* Cymb. III, 6, 75. *he fell to himself again,* H8 II, 1, 35 (= he came to himself). *which —s into mine ears as profitless as water in a sieve,* Ado V, 1, 4; cf. *the repetition, in a woman's ear, would murder as it fell,* Mcb. II, 3, 91; and: *what a strange infection is —en into thy ear?* Cymb. III, 2, 4. *—s into forfeit,* Meas.

I, 4, 66. *into the cinque pace,* Ado II, 1, 82. *into a cough,* Mids. II, 1, 54. *into revelry,* As V, 4, 183. *into dreams,* Shr. Ind. 2, 128. *into abatement,* Tw. I, 1, 13. *into thy hand,* II, 5, 155. *into apoplexy,* H4B I, 2, 123. 135. *into revolt,* IV, 5, 66. *into a slower method,* R3 I, 2, 116. *in broil,* Cor. III, 1, 33. *into the sear,* Mcb. V, 3, 23. *in fright,* Oth. II, 3, 232. *into such vile success,* III, 3, 222. *fell in praise of our country mistresses,* Cymb. I, 4, 61. *to f. asleep,* Sonn. 153, 1. H4A III, 3, 112. Tit. II, 4, 50 (cf. *Asleep*). *to f. in love:* Gentl. I, 2, 2. Ado II, 3, 12. As I, 2, 26. *to f. in love with:* Ado II, 1, 396. V, 2, 61. As III, 5, 66. 72. Cor. I, 5, 22 etc. (cf. *Love*). *f. into so strong a liking with Rowland's son,* As I, 3, 27. *if he f. in rage with their refusal,* Corr. II, 3, 266.

10) **to become:** *she fell distract,* Caes. IV, 3, 155. *shall we f. foul for toys?* H4B II, 4, 183 (= quarrel; Pistol's speech). *f. mad,* Tit. II, 3, 104. *f. sick,* Sonn. 118, 14. Merch. III, 4, 71. H8 IV, 2, 15. *at jars,* H6B I, 1, 253.

11) **to begin, to get into;** followed by the gerund: *nature, as she wrought thee, fell a doting,* Sonn. 20, 10. *she fell a turning,* Pilgr. 100. *the people f. a hooting,* LLL IV, 2, 61. *he —s a capering,* Merch. I, 2, 65. *my nose fell a bleeding,* II, 5, 24. *the people fell a shouting,* Caes. I, 2, 222. *f. a cursing,* Hml. II, 2, 615.

12) **to happen, to come to pass:** *as it fell upon a day,* Pilgr. 373. *if anything f. to you upon this, more than thanks and good fortune,* Meas. IV, 2, 190. *it will f. pat as I told you,* Mids. V, 188. *an the worst f. that ever fell,* Merch. I, 2, 96. *as the matter —s,* III, 2, 204. *whate'er —s more,* All's V, 1, 37. *howe'er the matter f.* V, 3, 121. *this sudden mischief never could have —en,* H6A II, 1, 59. *an ensuing evil, if it f., greater than this,* H8 II, 1, 141. *my misgiving still —s shrewdly to the purpose,* Caes. III, 1, 146. *I know not what may f.* 243. *for fear of what might f.* V, 1, 105. *it —s right,* Hml. IV, 7, 71. *there's —en between him and my lord an unkind breach,* Oth. IV, 1, 237.

13) Followed by *to,* = a) **to begin, to get into:** *with measure heaped in joy, to the measures f.* As V, 4, 185. *but you f. to some discord,* H4B II, 4, 61. *f. to thy prayers,* V, 5, 51. *makes me from wondering f. to weeping joys,* H6B I, 1, 34. *f. to blows,* II, 3, 80. *fell so roundly to a large confession,* Troil. III, 2, 161. *his soldiers fell to spoil,* Caes. V, 3, 7. *he —s to such perusal of my face,* Hml. II, 1, 90. *before you f. to play,* V, 2, 216. *f. to quarrel,* Lr. IV, 6, 37. *may f. to match you with her country forms,* Oth. III, 3, 237. — b) **to lay hands on, to assail:** *as he* (Mars) *fell to her* (Venus), *so fell she to him* (Adonis), Pilgr. 146. *f. to their throats,* Ant. II, 7, 78. Hence c) **to apply one's self:** *f. to them* (mathematics) *as you find your stomach serves you,* Shr. I, 1, 38. *f. to it* = be busy, be not idle: Tp. I, 1, 3. *if we be forbidden stones, we'll f. to it with our teeth,* H6A III, 1, 90. *so f. to it* = help yourself, eat: Tim. I, 2, 71. *f. to,* in the same sense: As II, 7, 171. R2 V, 5, 98. H5 V, 1, 38. Tit. III, 2, 34. — d) **to become the share of:** *since this fortune —s to you,* Merch. III, 2, 134. *to each of you one fair and virtuous mistress f.* All's II, 3, 64. *from her will f. some blessing to this land,* H8 III, 2, 51. *his fell to Hamlet,* Hml. I, 1, 95. cf. *new-fallen* = recently fallen to the share of a person: As V, 4, 182. H4A V, 1, 44. — e) **to become**

subject to: *when majesty —s to folly,* Lr. I, 1, 151 (Qq *stoops*). *f. to reprobation,* Oth. V, 2, 209.

14) Followed by *from,* a) to forsake, to quit the party of: *f. from this faith,* Ado I, 1, 257. *I will f. from thee,* John III, 1, 320. H6C III, 3, 209. — b) to become a stranger to, to lose: *that you are not —en from the report that goes upon your goodness,* All's V, 1, 12. *—en from favour,* H8 III, 1, 20. *and be not from his reason —en thereon,* Hml. II, 2, 165.

15) Followed by *on,* a) used of evils, = to come down, to light: *all the infections ... on Prosper f.* Tp. II, 2, 2. III, 3, 80. *a blasting breath to f. on him,* Meas. V, 122. *her death shall f. heavy on you,* Ado V, 1, 150. Merch. III, 1, 89. All's I, 1, 79. R2 IV, 147. H4A V, 5, 13. R3 III, 3, 15. V, 1, 14. Mcb. IV, 1, 105. IV, 3, 227. Oth. I, 3, 120. — b) of benign influences, = to bless: *all comfort may hourly f. upon you,* H8 V, 5, 8. *for which the people's prayers still f. upon you,* Per. III, 3, 19. — c) to become the share of, to be enjoyed by: *seeing thou —est on me so luckily,* H4A V, 4, 33 (= becomest my prey). *such a flood of greatness fell on you,* V, 1, 48. *what in me was purchased, —s upon thee in a fairer sort,* H4B IV, 5, 201. *the victory fell on us,* Mcb. I, 2, 58. *the sovereignty will f. upon Macbeth,* II, 4, 30. *preferment —s on him that cuts him off,* Lr. IV, 5, 38. — d) Peculiar use: *and f. on my side so,* H6A II, 4, 51 (= leave your party for mine).

16) Joined with adverbs: *mortals that f. back to gaze on him,* Rom. II, 2, 30 (= to bend back). *though we here f. down, we have supplies to second our attempt,* H4B IV, 2, 44 (= to get the worse). to f. *away* (cf. def. 4) = to forsake, to leave a party: *f. away like water from ye,* H8 II, 1, 129. *Canidius and the rest that fell away,* Ant. IV, 6, 17. to f. *from,* in the same sense: *the —ing from of his friends,* Tim. IV, 3, 401. to f. *off* = a) to keep far, to stay behind: *fell off a distance from her,* H8 IV, 1, 64. b) to prove faithless: *inconstancy —s off ere it begins,* Gentl. V, 4, 113. *he never did f. off,* H4A I, 3, 94. *friendship —s off,* Lr. I, 2, 116. John V, 5, 11. Tim. V, 1, 62. Cymb. III, 7, 6. (cf. def. 4). — to f. *in* = to join, to be on friendly terms: *let's f. in with them,* H6B IV, 2, 32. *after he once fell in with Mistress Shore,* R3 III, 5, 51. *—ing in, after —ing out,* Troil. III, 1, 112. — to f. *over* = to go over, to desert to: *dost thou now f. over to my foes?* John III, 1, 127. — to f. *out* = a) to fall at odds, to quarrel: Mids. IV, 1, 55. Shr. IV, 1, 57. All's IV, 5, 61. R3 I, 3, 158. Troil. III, 1, 93. 112. III, 3, 75. Cor. IV, 3, 34. Rom. I, 3, 32. III, 1, 29. Hml. II, 1, 59. Lr. II, 2, 92. II, 4, 111. Cymb. V, 4, 32. b) to come to pass: Meas. II, 4, 117. Ado IV, 1, 219. Mids. III, 2, 35. IV, 2, 32. Merch. II, 5, 26. John IV, 2, 154. R3 III, 2, 66. Cor. II, 1, 259. Rom. III, 4, 1. Hml. II, 2, 127. III, 1, 16. Oth. II, 3, 231. IV, 2, 242. Cymb. I, 4, 61. d) to turn out, to prove: *their events can never f. out good,* R2 II, 1, 214. *if all things f. out right,* H6A II, 3, 4. *wishes f. out as they're willed,* Per. V, 2, 16.

B) trans. 1) to let fall, to drop: *every tear he —s,* Lucr. 1551. Tp. V, 64. R2 III, 4, 104 (Ff Q 2.3 *drop*). R3 I, 3, 354 (Qq *drop*). Oth. IV, 1, 257. Ant. III, 11, 69. *to f. it* (your hand) *on Gonzalo,* Tp. II, 1, 296. As III, 5, 5. R3 V, 3, 135. 163. *rather cut a little, than f. and bruise to death,* Meas. II, 1, 6. f.

a drop of water in the breaking gulf, Err. II, 2, 127. *her mantle she did f.* Mids. V, 143. *—ing a lip of much contempt,* Wint. I, 2, 372. *f. his crest,* Troil. I, 3, 379. Caes. IV, 2, 26.

2) to bring forth: *f. parti-coloured lambs,* Merch. I, 3, 89.

3) to befall, to happen to: *fair f. the wit that can so well defend her,* Ven. 472. LLL II, 125. John I, 78. *no disgrace shall f. you for refusing him at sea,* Ant. III, 7, 40.

Fallacy, illusion, mistake: *I'll entertain the offered f.* Err. II, 2, 188.

Fallen-off, revolted: Cymb. III, 7, 6.

Fallible, liable to error: *hopes,* Meas. III, 1, 170. Misapplied by the clown in Ant. V, 2, 258 (O. Edd. *falliable*).

Falling-from, defection: *the f. of his friends,* Tim. IV, 3, 401 (O. Edd. not hyphened).

Falling-off, a change for the worse (cf. *Fall,* vb. def. A 4): *what a f. was there!* Hml. I, 5, 47.

Falling-sickness, epilepsy: Caes. I, 2, 256. 258 (O. Edd. not hyphened).

Fallow, subst. arable land untilled: Meas. I, 4, 42. H5 V, 2, 54.

Fallow, adj. 1) of a pale red or yellow colour: *your f. greyhound,* Wiv. I, 1, 91.

2) untilled: *her f. leas,* H5 V, 2, 44.

False, adj. 1) not true: *that sometime true news, sometime f. doth bring,* Ven. 658. Gentl. V, 2, 107. Meas. V, 156. 292. Err. V, 179. 209. 268. Ado V, 1, 219. All's V, 3, 229 *(the story goes f.).* H4B Ind. 8. H6B I, 3, 158. Caes. II, 2, 63. Ant. II, 1, 18 etc.

2) not right, wrong, erroneous: *f. alarms,* Ven. 651. *with f. bethinking,* 1024. *a f. esteem,* Sonn. 127, 12. *f. compare,* 130, 14. *a f. interpreter,* Gentl. I, 2, 78. *f. and most contrarious quests,* Meas. IV, 1, 62. *his conceit is f.* Ado II, 1, 309. *a f. gallop,* III, 4, 94; cf. As III, 2, 119. *f.; we have given thee faces,* LLL V, 2, 625. *I smell f. Latin,* V, 1, 83; cf. *my f. French,* H5 V, 2, 236. *f. reckonings,* As III, 4, 35. *play f. strains upon thee,* IV, 3, 68; cf. *the strings are f.* Caes. IV, 3, 292. *with f. aim,* All's III, 2, 113. *a f. conclusion,* Tw. II, 3, 6. *on the f. trail,* Hml. IV, 5, 109. *f., f.; this, this,* Ant. IV, 4, 7 etc.

3) not real: *to worship shadows and adore f. shapes,* Gentl. IV, 2, 131. *a dagger of the mind, a f. creation,* Mcb. II, 1, 38. *frighted with f. fire,* Hml. III, 2, 277.

4) not genuine: *why should f. painting imitate his cheek,* Sonn. 67, 5. *f. art,* 68, 14. 127, 6. *to put metal in restrained means and make a f. one* (viz life) Meas. II, 4, 49. *f. prints,* 130. *ravish doters with a f. aspect,* LLL IV, 3, 260. *to bring f. generations,* Wint. II, 1, 148. *f. coin,* H8 III, 1, 171. *f. dice,* Ado II, 1, 290. Wint. I, 2, 132.

5) misrepresenting the truth, deceitful: *why should others' f. adulterate eyes give salutation to my sportive blood?* Sonn. 121, 5; cf. 148, 5; *millions of f. eyes are stuck upon thee,* Meas. IV, 1, 60. *with f. sorrow's eye,* R2 II, 2, 26. *I do despise one that is f.* Wiv. I, 1, 70 (Evans' speech); cf. *affection makes him f.* Rom. III, 1, 182 (or vb.?). *thy f. seeming,* Meas. II, 4, 15. *the f. sweet bait that we lay,* Ado III, 1, 33. *words are grown so f.* Tw. III, 1, 28. *f. witness,* H6B III, 1, 168. *she is fooled with a most f. effect,* Cymb. I, 5, 43

6) **inconstant** (especially in love), **faithless**: *fickle, f. and full of fraud*, Ven. 1141. Sonn. 20, 4. 5. 109, 1. Pilgr. 90. Tp. I, 2, 77. 92. Gentl. II, 4, 197. IV, 2, 95. IV, 4, 110. 141. V, 4, 35. Wiv. II, 2, 305. Err. II, 2, 139. III, 2, 8. IV, 4, 104. LLL V, 2, 783. Mids. I, 1, 174. As III, 5, 73. Wint. IV, 4, 151. *as f. as air, as water, wind, or sandy earth*, Troil. III, 2, 198. *f. as water*, Oth. V, 2, 134 etc. With *to:* Sonn. 41, 14. Gentl. IV, 2, 1. LLL V, 2, 782. R3 IV, 4, 207. V, 1, 15. Cor. III, 2, 15. Lr. V, 3, 134. Oth. V, 2, 142. Ant. I, 3, 29. Cymb. III, 4, 42 etc. *to be f. with* = a) to deceive one: *and I the truer, so to be f. with her*, Cymb. I, 5, 44. b) to commit adultery with: *she f. with Cassio!* Oth. V, 2, 182. *let her beauty look through a casement to allure f. hearts and be f. with them*, Cymb. II, 4, 35.

7) **not to be depended on, not to be trusted**; a) **cowardly**: *cowards, whose hearts are all as f. as stairs of sand*, Merch. III, 2, 83. *I am no fighter: I am f. of heart that way*, Wint. IV, 3, 116. b) **dishonest**: *f. desire*, Lucr. 2. *rash f. heat*, 48. *without f. vantage or base treachery*, Gentl. IV, 1, 29. *pay with falsehood f. exacting*, Meas. III, 2, 295. *in a f. quarrel there is no true valour*, Ado V, 1, 120. *to fashion this f. sport*, Mids. III, 2, 194.

Substantively: *my f. o'erweighs your true*, Meas. II, 4, 170. *from f. to f.* Troil. III, 2, 197.

False, adv. 1) **not truly, without truth**: *her f. speaking tongue*, Sonn. 138, 7. *thou speakest f.* Err. IV, 4, 103. John IV, 3, 91. H8 II, 4, 136. Mcb. V, 5, 38. *dream often so, and never f.* Cymb. IV, 2, 353.

2) **not rightly, wrongly, amiss**: *you play me f.* Tp. V, 172 (quibbling). *he plays f. How? out of tune on the strings?* Gentl. IV, 2, 59 (quibbling). *if all aim but this be levelled f.* Ado IV, 1, 239. *thou judgest f.*, H4A I, 2, 74. *I should be f. persuaded I had daughters*, Lr. I, 4, 254. *that I interpret f.* Per. I, 1, 124.

3) **faithlessly, perfidiously**: *to play f.* Err. II, 2, 144. John I, 118. Mcb. I, 5, 22. cf. Gentl. IV, 2, 59. *they played me f.* H6B III, 1, 184. cf. Tp. V, 172. *his mother played f. with a smith*, Merch. I, 2, 48. *has packed cards with Caesar and f. played my glory unto an enemy's triumph*, Ant. IV, 14, 19. *mine ear, therein f. struck, can take no greater wound*, Cymb. III, 4, 117.

False, vb.: *not sure, in a thing —ing*, Err. II, 2, 95, = apt to be falsified? In Rom. III, 1, 182 and Cymb. III, 3, 74 it may be adj.

False-boding, prophesying amiss: *f. woman*, R3 I, 3, 247. O. Edd. not hyphened, perhaps meaning: false prophetess.

False-creeping, moving insidiously and imperceptibly: *f. craft*, Lucr. 1517. O. Edd. not hyphened, meaning: perfidious and slowly approaching craft.

False-derived, not based on truth: *every slight and f. cause*, H4B IV, 1, 190.

False-faced, hypocritical: Cor. I, 9, 44.

False-heart, adj. perfidious: *a f. traitor*, H6B V, 1, 143.

False-hearted, deceitful, perfidious: Troil. V, 1, 95.

Falsehood, 1) **untruth, lie**: *to unmask f. and bring truth to light*, Lucr. 940. R2 IV, 39. H6A III, 4, 71. H6C III, 3, 99. H8 II, 4, 97. Rom. I, 2, 94. Hml. II, 1, 63. Cymb. III, 6, 13. V, 5, 134.

2) **deceit, imposture**: *why of eyes' f. hast thou forged hooks*, Sonn. 137, 7. *pay with f. false exacting*, Meas. III, 2, 295. *excellent f.* Ant. I, 1, 40.

3) **perfidy**: Tp. I, 2, 95. H6A V, 4, 109. H6C IV, 4, 8. R3 II, 1, 14.

4) **inconstancy**: Gentl. III, 2, 32. IV, 2, 130. Err. II, 1, 113. John III, 1, 95. Troil. III, 2, 198. 202. IV, 2, 106. Cymb. I, 6, 107. With *to: my f. to my friend*, Gentl. IV, 2, 8.

5) **dishonesty**: *that to my use it might unused stay from hands of f.*, Sonn. 48, 4, i. e. thieves; cf. *a man of f.* H4A II, 1, 71. *I shall be forsworn, which is a great argument of f.* LLL I, 2, 175; cf. V, 2, 785. *what a goodly outside f. has*, Merch. I, 3, 103. Wint. III, 2, 28. *this is mere f.*, 142 (= foul play). *f. f. cures*, John III, 1, 277. *if you suspect my husbandry of f.* Tim. II, 2, 164.

Falsely, 1) **not truly, lyingly**: *thou speakest it f.* All's V, 3, 113. *most f. doth he lie*, R2 I, 1, 68.

2) **not rightly, wrongly, erroneously**: *where is my judgement fled, that censures f. what they (my eyes) see aright?* Sonn. 148, 4. *f. accused*, Ado V, 2, 99. H6B I, 3, 192. *he's indicted f.* Oth. III, 4, 154. *f. to draw me in these vile suspects*, R3 I, 3, 89. *f. murdered*, Oth. V, 2, 117. *f. thrust upon contrary feet*, John IV, 2, 198. *thy speaking of my tongue, most truly f.* H5 V, 2, 204.

3) **dishonestly, perfidiously**: *f. pocket up his report*, Tp. II, 1, 67. *f. to take away a life true made*, Meas. II, 4, 47. *truth the while doth f. blind the eyesight*, LLL I, 1, 76. *how can that be true love which is f. attempted?* I, 2, 177. *England's chair, where he is f. set*, R3 V, 3, 251. *laid f. in the plain way of his merit*, Cor. III, 1, 60. *f. borne in hand*, Hml. II, 2, 67.

Falseness, 1) **untruth, lie**: Per. V, 1, 121. 2) **perfidy**: Compl. 105. H4B III, 1, 90.

False-play, vb., writing of M. Edd. in Ant. IV, 14, 19; O. Edd. not hyphened; cf. *False* adv. def. 3.

False-speaking, writing of M. Edd. in Sonn. 138, 7; O. Edd. not hyphened; cf. *False* adv. def. 1.

Falsify, to show to be false, to disprove: *by how much better than my word I am, by so much shall I f. men's hopes*, H4A I, 2, 235.

Falstaff: *Sir John F.*, name in Wiv., H4A, H4B and H5. cf. *Fastolfe.*

Falter, to totter, to be like to fall: *shall rotten death make conquest of the stronger and leave the —ing feeble souls alive*, Lucr. 1768. *ere her native king shall f. under foul rebellion's arms*, R2 III, 2, 26.

Fame, subst. 1) **rumour, report**: *I have played the part of Lady F.* Ado II, 1, 221; cf. Troil. III, 3, 210 and Tit. II, 1, 126. *all-telling f. doth noise abroad*, LLL II, 1, 21. *thou art no less than f. hath bruited*, H6A II, 3, 68. H6C III, 3, 63. *having heard by f. of this assembly*, H8 I, 4, 66. *so is the f.* Ant. II, 2, 166. *vulgar f.* III, 13, 119. *f. answering the most strange inquire*, Per. III Prol. 22. *when f. had spread their cursed deed*, V, 3, 95.

2) **renown**: Lucr. 20. 106. 1054. 1188. 1491. 1638. Sonn. 80, 4. 100, 13. Ado V, 3, 6. 8. LLL IV, 1, 32. All's II, 1, 17. Tw. III, 3, 23. H4B IV, 3, 56. V, 5, 46. H5 I, 2, 162 (fem.). III, 2, 11. 13. IV, 1, 45. H6A III, 2, 76. IV, 4, 46. IV, 6, 39. 45. H6B I, 1, 99. V, 2, 60. R3 III, 1, 81. 88. IV, 5, 13. H8 V, 5, 47. Troil. I, 3, 144. 244. II, 2, 202. III, 3, 228. IV, 5, 143 (fem). V, 1, 48. Cor. I, 1, 267. I, 3, 14. I, 8, 4. II, 1,

181. V, 6, 36. 126. Tit. I, 390. Hml. IV, 4, 61. Oth. III, 1, 48. Ant. III, 1, 15. Cymb. III, 3, 51. Per. III, 2, 98.

3) reputation: *beauty and virtue strived which of them both should underprop her f.* Lucr. 53. *my shame be his that did my f. confound,* 1202. *she that her f. so to herself contrives,* Compl. 243. *shame hath a bastard f., well managed,* Err. III, 2, 19. *f. that all hunt after,* LLL I, 1, 1. *too much to know is to know nought but f.* I, 1, 92, i. e. outward estimation without intrinsic worth; cf. R3 I, 4, 83. *it confounds thy f.* Shr. V, 2, 140. *I am in good name and f. with the very best,* H4B II, 4, 82. *he wrongs his f.* H6A II, 1, 16. *my meed hath got me f.* H6C IV, 8, 38. *that's their f. in peace,* Troil. I, 3, 236.

4) high praise, panegyric: *the noblemen yielded Collatinus the victory, and his wife the f.* Lucr. Arg. 12. *I have letters sent me that set him high in f.* All's V, 3, 31. *very envy and the tongue of loss cried f. and honour on him,* Tw. V, 62. *I have been the book of his good acts, whence men have read his f. unparalleled, haply amplified,* Cor. V, 2, 16. *set a double varnish on the f. the Frenchman gave you,* Hml. IV, 7, 133. *a maid that paragons description and wild f.* Oth. II, 1, 62. *your fine Egyptian cookery shall have the f.* Ant. II, 6, 65.

Fame, vb. 1) to make famous: *such a counterpart shall f. his wit,* Sonn. 84, 11. —*d* = famous: All's I, 2, 71. H5 II, 4, 92. IV, 3, 100. Caes. I, 2, 153. Cymb. III, 1, 30.

2) to report, repute: —*d for mildness, peace, and prayer,* H6C II, 1, 156. *your grace hath still be —d for virtuous,* IV, 6, 26.

3) to extol, to panegyrize: —*d be thy tutor, and thy parts of nature thrice —d, beyond all erudition,* Troil. II, 3, 253.

Familiar, adj. 1) pertaining to the house and family, attached and serviceable to men: *it is a f. beast to man,* Wiv. I, 1, 21. *good wine is a good f. creature,* Oth. II, 3, 313. *that affable f. ghost which nightly gulls him with intelligence,* Sonn. 86, 9. *now, ye f. spirits,* H6A V, 3, 10 (cf. *Familiar,* subst.).

2) pertaining to home, domestic, such as to make one feel at home: *that haunted us in our f. paths,* H5 II, 4, 52. *tame and most f. to my nature,* Troil. III, 3, 10. *our names, f. in his mouth as household words,* H5 IV, 3, 52.

3) kind without any constraint: *quenching my f. smile,* Tw. II, 5, 73. *with humble and f. courtesy,* R2 I, 4, 26. *be thou f., but by no means vulgar,* Hml. I, 3, 61.

4) intimate, on friendly terms: *so f.!* Troil. V, 2, 8. Cor. V, 2, 91. Caes. IV, 2, 16. Cymb. I, 4, 112. Followed by *with:* H4B II, 1, 108. II, 2, 115. 138. Oth. I, 3, 402. Ant. III, 13, 124. Lr. V, 1, **16.**

5) well acquainted: *f. with men's pockets,* H5 III, 2, 51. Rom. III, 3, 6.

6) well known; with *to:* H4B V, 2, 139. H5 III, 7, 40. Cymb. V, 5, 93. Per. III, 2, 34. Without *to:* *the Gordian knot of it he will unloose, f. as his garter,* H5 I, 1, 47.

7) accustomed, habitual: *I can construe the action of her f. style,* Wiv. I, 3, 51. *'tis my f. sin with maid's to seem the lapwing,* Meas. I, 4, 31.

8) of daily occurrence, ordinary, trivial: *let wonder seem f.* Ado V, 4, 70. *to make modern and f.,*

things supernatural and causeless, All's II, 3, 2. *dreadful objects shall be so f.* Caes. III, 1, 266. *direness, f. to my slaughterous thoughts,* Mcb. V, 5, 14.

9) easy to understand: *by a f. demonstration of the working,* LLL I, 2, 9. *I do not strain at the position, —it is f. — but at the author's drift,* Troil. III, 3, 113.

Familiar, subst. 1) a particular friend: LLL V, 1, 101. H4B II, 2, 144. Tim. IV, 2, 10.

2) a demon or attendant spirit: *love is a f* LLL I, 2, 177. *her old f. is asleep,* H6A III, 2, 122. *he has a f. under his tongue,* H6B IV, 7, 114 (cf. *Familiar* adj. def. 1).

Familiarity, intimate converse, unconstrained intercourse: Wiv. I, 1, 257. All's V, 2, 3. Wint. II, 1, 175. In the language of Mrs. Quickly, = *familiar:* H4B II, 1, 108 (Ff. *familiar*).

Familiarly, unceremoniously, with the unconcern arising from intimate acquaintance: Err. II, 2, 26. John II, 459. H4B III, 2, 344. R3 IV, 4, 316.

Family, 1) the body of persons belonging to the same household: Oth. I, 1, 84.

2) race, kindred, lineage: Lucr. Arg. 22. Ado IV, 1, 208. H5 II, 2, 129. H6C I, 1, 65. Tit. I, 239. 345. 451.

Famine, 1) hunger: *f. and no other hath slain me,* H6B IV, 10, 64. 81. *f. is in thy cheeks,* Rom. V, 1, 69. *upon the next tree shalt thou hang alive, till f. cling thee,* Mcb. V, 5, 40. *yet f., ere clean it o'erthrow nature, makes it valiant,* Cymb. III, 6, 19.

2) general distress for want of provisions: Sonn. 1, 7. H4B III, 2, 337. H5 Prol. 7. H6A IV, 2, 11. Mcb. V, 5, 4. Ant. I, 2, 50. I, 4, 59.

Famish, 1) tr. to starve, to distress with hunger: Ven. 20. Merch. II, 2, 113. Shr. IV, 3, 3. H4B V, 4, 22. H5 II, 5, 57. H6A I, 2, 7. I, 4, 68. H6B I, 3, 175. IV, 10, 47. R3 V, 3, 329. Tit. V, 3, 179. Tim. IV, 3, 535. *a single —ed kiss,* Troil. IV, 4, 49 (i. e. hungry, longing for more). *mine eye is —ed for a look,* Sonn. 47, 3.

2) intr. to die of hunger: H6B IV, 10, 2. H6C V, 4, 32. Cor. I, 1, 5. 82. Tit. II, 3, 154. Per. I, 4, 12. With an accus. denoting the result: *thou shalt f. a dog's death,* Tim. II, 2, 91 (some M. Edd. *f., a dog's death*).

Famous, 1) renowned: Tp. V, 192. Err. V, 367. All's I, 1, 29. R2 II, 1, 52. V, 6, 36. H5 II, 4, 92. IV, 7, 95. H6A I, 1, 6. II, 3, 5. II, 5, 85. III, 3, 13. H6B I, 1, 5. V, 2, 69. V, 3, 30. H6C II, 1, 155. V, 4, 52. R3 III, 1, 84. 164. III, 7, 100. H8 III, 2, 66. V, 2, 61. Troil. IV, 5, 151. Hml. III, 4, 194. Ant. V, 2, 363. Cymb. III, 1, 6. Per. I, 1, 34.

2) notorious, in a bad sense: Shr. I, 2, 254. Wint. III, 3, 12. H4B IV, 3, 69. Ant. I, 4, 48.

Famoused, renowned: Sonn. 25, 9. (A verb *to famous* in Lodge's Rosalind, ed. Collier, p. 17).

Famously, gloriously: R3 II, 3, 19. Cor. I, 1, 37.

Fan, subst. 1) instrument used by ladies to cool themselves by moving the air: Wiv. II, 2, 12. LLL IV, 1, 147. Shr. IV, 3, 57. H4A II, 3, 25. H6B I, 3, 141. Rom. II, 4, 112. 232. Oth. IV, 2, 9. Ant. I, 1, 9. II, 2, 208.

2) instrument to winnow grain: Troil. I, 3, 27.

3) the fanning, agitating the air: *falls even in*

the f. and wind of your fair sword, Troil. V, 3, 41, (or rather a hendiadis = the fanning wind).

Fan, vb. 1) to blow as with a fan: Ven. 52. 306. Mids. III, 1, 176. III, 2, 142. All's III, 2, 128. Wint. IV, 4, 375. H5 III Chor. 6 (O. Edd. *fayning*). IV, 1, 212. Cor. III, 3, 127. Mcb. I, 2, 50.

2) to winnow, to try: *the love I bear him made me to f. you thus*, Cymb. I, 6, 177.

Fanatical, extravagant? *I abhor such f. phantasimes, such insociable and point-devise companions,* LLL V, 1, 20 (Holofernes' speech).

Fancy, subst. 1) the power of forming mental images, imagination: Tp. V, 59. LLL IV, 2, 129. Mids. V, 25. Wint. V, 3, 60. H5 III Chor. 7. H8 IV, 2, 94. V, 1, 60 (*when my f. is on the play* = when I play with attention). Cor. II, 1, 216. Hml. V, 1, 204. Lr. IV, 2, 86. Ant. V, 2, 98. 99. Per. III Prol. 13. V, 2, 20. With the article: *where we see the f. outwork nature,* Ant. II, 2, 206.

2) image, conception, a thought not founded on reason, but on imagination: Lucr. 450. Tp. IV, 122. Meas. IV, 1, 65. Ado III, 1, 95 (*speaking my f.* = speaking as I think). As IV, 3, 102. Shr. Ind. 1, 44. Tw. IV, 1, 66. Wint. II, 3, 119. III, 2, 182. H6A IV, 1, 178 (*that was but his f.*). H8 II, 3, 101. Mcb. III, 2, 9. V, 3, 38. Lr. I, 4, 348. Oth. IV, 2, 26.

3) fantasticalness: *this child of f. that Armado hight,* LLL I, 1, 171. *costly thy habit, but not expressed in f.* Hml. I, 3, 71.

4) liking, taste: *stones whose rates are either rich or poor, as f. values them,* Meas. II, 2, 151. *a f. that he hath to strange disguises,* Ado III, 2, 32. *unless he have a f. to this foolery,* 37. *to fit your —ies to your father's will,* Mids. I, 1, 118. *we must every one be a man of his own f.* All's IV, 1, 20. *very dear to f.* Hml. V, 2, 159 (i. e. to amateurs). *be as your —ies teach you,* Oth. III, 3, 88.

5) love: *a martial man to be soft —'s slave,* Lucr. 200. Pilgr. 214. 302. Ado III, 2, 31. 38. Mids. I, 1, 155. IV, 1, 168. Merch. III, 2, 63. 68. 70. As III, 5, 29. V, 4, 156. All's I, 1, 108. II, 3, 175. V, 3, 214. 215. Tw. I, 1, 14. II, 4, 34. V, 397. Wint. IV, 4, 493. H6A V, 3, 91. Troil. IV, 4, 27. Oth. III, 4, 63. The abstr. for the concr.: *a reverend man towards this afflicted f. fastly drew,* Compl. 61. *what tributes wounded —ies sent me,* 197.

6) a love-song, or a song in general? *sware they were his —ies or his good-nights,* H4B III, 2, 342. *an old hat and 'the humour of forty —ies' pricked in it for a feather,* Shr. III, 2, 70 (Nares: one part of the collection called Wit's Recreations, is entitled "Fancies and Fantastics." Another publication gives us, "Wits, Fits, and Fancies.")

Fancy, vb. to like, to love: *win her to f. him,* Gentl. III, 1, 67. *that special face which I could f. more than any other,* Shr. II, 12. *you f. riches more,* 16. *Bianca doth f. any other,* IV, 2, 2. *we f. not the cardinal,* H6B I, 3, 97. Absolutely: *should she f., it should be one of my complexion,* Tw. II, 5, 29. *never did young man f. with so eternal and so fixed a soul,* Troil. V, 2, 165.

Fancy-free, free from the power of love: Mids. II, 1, 164.

Fancy-monger, love-monger, one who makes love his business: As III, 2, 382.

Fancy-sick, love-sick: Mids. III, 2, 96.

Fane, temple: Cor. I, 10, 20. Cymb. IV, 2, 242.

Fang, subst., the pointed tooth, tusk: *—s,* Ven. 663. Merch. III, 3, 7. John II, 353. Lr. III, 7, 58. Figuratively: *the icy f. and churlish chiding of the winter's wind,* As II, 1, 6. *by the very —s of malice I swear,* Tw. I, 5, 196 (O. Edd. *phangs*).

Fang, name of a sheriff's officer: H4B II, 1, 1. 27. 44.

Fang, vb. to seize with the teeth, to tear: *destruction f. mankind,* Tim. IV, 3, 23.

Fanged, armed with sharp teeth: *adders f.* Hml. III, 4, 203.

Fangled (cf. *New-fangled*) given to tinsel-finery: *be not, as is our f. world, a garment nobler than that it covers,* Cymb. V, 4, 134.

Fangless, toothless: *a f. lion,* H4B IV, 1, 218.

Fantasied, filled with fancies or imaginations: *I find the people strangely f.* John IV, 2, 144.

Fantastic, 1) imaginary, existing only in imagination: *by thinking on f. summer's heat,* R2 I, 3, 299.

2) indulging the vagaries of imagination, capricious: *soothing the humour of f. wits,* Ven. 850. *to be f. may become a youth,* Gentl. II, 7, 47. *f. tricks,* Meas. II, 2, 121. *f. garlands,* Hml. IV, 7, 169.

3) incredible, prodigious: *who hath done to-day mad and f. execution,* Troil. V, 5, 38.

Fantastical, 1) imaginary: *are ye f., or that indeed which outwardly ye show?* Mcb. I, 3, 53. *whose murder yet is but f.* 139.

2) indulging the vagaries of imagination, capricious, whimsical: *this is fery f. humours,* Wiv. III, 3, 181. *a mad f. trick,* Meas. III, 2, 98. *the old f. duke,* IV, 3, 164. *like a Scotch jig, and full as f.* Ado II, 1, 79. *a very f. banquet,* II, 3, 22. *the schoolmaster is exceeding f.* LLL V, 2, 532. *proud, f., apish,* As III, 2, 431. *a f. knave,* III, 3, 107. *the musician's melancholy, which is f.* IV, 1, 12. Wint. IV, 4, 779.

3) imaginative: *so full of shapes is fancy, that it alone is high f.* Tw. I, 1, 15.

4) incredible, prodigious: *telling her f. lies,* Oth. II, 1, 226.

Fantastically, oddly, capriciously: *with a head f. carved upon it,* H4B III, 2, 334. *her sceptre so f. borne by a vain, giddy youth,* H5 II, 4, 27.

Fantastico, a fantastical, coxcomical person: Rom. II, 4, 30; only in the spurious Q1; the rest of O. Edd. *fantacies* and *fantasies.*

Fantasy, 1) imagination, the power of imagining: Wiv. V, 5, 55. Mids. V, 5. H4B V, 2, 13. Rom. I, 4, 98. Caes. III, 3, 2. *the main opinion he held once of f., of dreams and ceremonies,* II, 1, 197 (i. e. of the faculty of imagination to foreshow the future). *art thou alive? or is it f. that plays upon our eyesight?* H4A V, 4, 138; cf. Hml. I, 1, 23. 54.

2) mental image, conceit: *a causeless f.* Ven. 897. *full of hateful —ies,* Mids. II, 1, 258. *legions of strange —ies,* John V, 7, 18. *no figures nor no —ies, which busy care draws in the brains of men,* Caes. II, 1, 231.

3) love (or rather love-thoughts): *fie on sinful f.* Wiv. V, 5, 97. *and stolen the impression of her f.* Mids. I, 1, 32. *how many actions most ridiculous hast thou been drawn to by thy f.?* As II, 4, 31. *it* (love) *is to be all made of f., all made of passion and all made of wishes,* V, 2, 100.

4) a whim, caprice: *such antic, lisping, affecting —s,* Rom. II, 4, 30 (the spurious Q1 and M. Edd. *fantasticoes*). *for a f. and trick of fame,* Hml. IV, 4, 61. *to please his f.* Oth. III, 3, 299.

Fap, drunk: Wiv. I, 1, 183 (in Bardolph's speech, not understood by Slender).

Far, name: *Monsieur La F.* Lr. IV, 3, 10.

Far, adv. (never adj.) 1) at or to a great distance: *how f. I toil,* Sonn. 28, 8. *so f. from Italy removed,* Tp. II, 1, 110. *f. from the ground,* Gentl. III, 1, 114. II, 7, 78. Meas. I, 4, 33. Err. IV, 2, 27. Mids. II, 2, 60. As I, 3, 111. Shr. IV, 2, 73. R2 I, 3, 199. H6B I, 3, 154. Mcb. III, 1, 24. Hml. IV, 5, 139 etc. *f. away,* Gentl. I, 3, 9; cf. Err. IV, 2, 27. *f. off:* Ven. 301. 697. Tp. V, 316. John I, 174. Caes. III, 2, 171 etc. *f. remote,* Sonn. 44, 4. *f. and near,* H6A V, 4, 3. Lr. II, 1, 84. *f. and wide,* Rom. II, 4, 90. *from f.:* Err. I, 1, 93. Mids. I, 2, 38. All's III, 4, 10. H6C II, 3, 18 etc. *as f. as God has any ground,* Merch. II, 2, 117. *as f. as who goes farthest,* Caes. I, 3, 119. *as f. as to the sepulchre of Christ,* H4A I, 1, 19. *from Venice as f. as Belmont,* Merch. V, 17. Shr. IV, 2, 75. R2 IV, 13. H4A II, 1, 27. H4B V, 5, 113. Rom. II, 2, 82. *thus f.:* R3 V, 2, 3. H8 II, 1, 55 (cf. *Thus*).

2) at or to a distance of time, long: *'tis f. off,* Tp. I, 2, 44 (= long ago). *f. before thy time,* H6C I, 1, 237. *it shall be so f. forth friendly maintained till we set his youngest free,* Shr. I, 1, 140.

3) distantly in a figurative sense: *f. from the purpose,* Lucr. 113. *f. from accident,* Sonn. 124, 5. *f. be it we should honour such,* H6B IV, 1, 123. *so f. as my coin would stretch,* H4A I, 2, 61. *not extend so f. as to the lady,* Merch. II, 7, 28. cf. Gentl. II, 4, 71. IV, 2, 101. Wiv. II, 1, 107. Merch. III, 2, 127 etc. *f. off* = only by hints, indirectly: *or shall we sparingly show you f. off the Dauphin's meaning?* H5 I, 2, 239. *as it were f. off,* sound thou Lord Hastings, R3 III, 1, 170. *touch this sparingly, as 'twere f. off,* III, 5, 93. *f. in* or *into* = deep in or into: *he did look f. into the service of the time,* All's I, 2, 26. *do not plunge thyself too f. in anger,* II, 3, 222. *I am now so f. in offence with my niece,* Tw. IV, 2, 75. In a temporal sense: *too f. in years to be a pupil,* R2 I, 3, 171. *how f. into the morning is it?* R3 V, 3, 234.

4) at or to a high point or degree, much: *which f. exceeds his skill,* Lucr. 81. Tp. III, 2, 110. Gentl. III, 1, 166. LLL IV, 3, 41. V, 2, 677. All's IV, 3, 306. R3 III, 1, 104. Cymb. I, 4, 70. *f. poorer,* Lucr. 693. 1647. Sonn. 94, 14. 119, 12. Gentl. V, 4, 51. Err. III, 2, 44. H6B IV, 10, 50. Ant. I, 2, 16. *inferior f.* Sonn. 80, 7. *better f.* H6A II, 1, 29. H6C I, 1, 130. Rom. V, 3, 38. *f. too huge,* John V, 2, 86. *a baser man of arms by f.* H6A I, 4, 30. *thou thinkest me as f. in the devil's book as thou,* H4B II, 2, 49. *she enlargeth her mirth so f. that there is shrewd construction made of her,* Wiv. II, 2, 232. *nature dispenses with the deed so f. that it becomes a virtue,* Meas. III, 1, 135. *so f. deceived in him,* All's III, 6, 6. *my lord's almost so f. transported that he'll think anon it lives,* Wint. V, 3, 69. H5 III, 6, 144. H8 V, 1, 47. Tim. I, 2, 178. cf. *thus f.* Wint. V, 3, 74. *how f. my praise doth wrong this shadow,* Merch. III, 2, 126. *reposing too f. in his virtue,* All's III, 6, 15. *York is too f. gone with grief,* R2 II, 1, 184 (cf. *Go*). Hml. II, 2, 190. *you strain too f.* H4A IV, 1, 75. *you may fear too f. Safer than trust too f.* Lr. I, 4, 351. *press not a falling*

man too f. H8 III, 2, 333; cf. *you press me f.* Merch. IV, 1, 425. *to mingle friendship f. is mingling bloods,* Wint. I, 2, 109. *you never read so f. to know the cause,* Shr. III, 1, 9 (= studied so much). *your late censure, which was too f.* H8 III, 1, 65 (i. e. too severe). *thus f. give me leave to speak him,* IV, 2, 32 (i. e. to say so much of him). *ere you had spoke so f.* Lr. V, 3, 63 (= gone such lengths in your pretensions). *you speak him f.* Cymb. I, 1, 24 (= say much of him, praise him much). *in that he spake too f.* V, 5, 309. cf. *thus f.* Tw. II, 1, 29. *whose f. unworthy deputy I am,* H6B III, 2, 286. *f. unfit to be a sovereign,* H6C III, 2, 92. *still f. wide,* Lr. IV, 7, 50. *as f. as* = in as much as: *as f. as I could well discern,* H6A II, 2, 26. H8 I, 3, 5. Troil. II, 2, 9. Lr. V, 1, 13. *so f. as* = in so much as: *so f. be mine as my true service shall deserve your love,* R2 III, 3, 198. *so f. as to mine enemy,* I, 3, 193 (= in so much as I may speak to my adversary). *so f. blameless,* Mids. III, 2, 350. *so f. am I glad,* 352. *thus f.* Lucr. 1279. Sonn. 136, 4. 141, 13. Err. V, 254. All's III, 7, 15. Tw. II, 1, 29. Wint. V, 3, 74. H6C IV, 7, 2. H8 II, 1, 121. III, 2, 432. IV, 2, 32. V, 3, 147 (cf. *Thus*). *so f. forth as* = in so much as: *so f. forth as herself might be her chooser,* Wiv. IV, 6, 11. cf. *how f. forth you do like their articles,* H4B IV, 2, 53. *know thus f. forth,* Tp. I, 2, 177.

The compar. *farther* and superl. *farthest* are adj. as well as adv.; 1) adj. a) more, most distant: *'tis a space for —ther travel,* Ant. II, 1, 31. *the —thest earth,* Sonn. 44, 6. *the —thest steppe,* Mids. II, 1, 69. *brother-in-law was the —thest off you could have been to him,* Wint. IV, 4, 722. *the —thest limit,* John I, 22. *in the —thest east,* Rom. I, 1, 141. *the —thest sea,* II, 2, 83. *are you at the —thest?* Shr. IV, 2, 73.

b) *farther* = other, more: *stays no —ther reason,* Sonn. 151, 8. *have you nuns no —ther privileges?* Meas. I, 4, 1. *use no —ther means,* Merch. IV, 1, 81. H4B IV, 4, 72 (Q *further*). H5, I, 1, 5. Rom. I, 1, 108. Cymb. I, 5, 65. III, 5, 92. Per. IV, 2, 52.

c) *farthest* = latest: *spring come to you at the —thest in the very end of harvest,* Tp. IV, 114. Merch. II, 2, 122. = utmost: *such a wife as my thoughts make thee, and as my —thest band shall pass on thy approof,* Ant. III, 2, 26.

2) adv. a) at or to a greater, at or to the greatest distance; —*ther:* Sonn. 47, 11. Ado V, 1, 236. Shr. I, 2, 51. IV, 2, 75. John V, 1, 60. R3 IV, 1, 8. Rom. II, 2, 178 (Ff *further*). Ant. IV, 14, 47. —*ther off:* Sonn. 28, 8. Tp. III, 2, 81. 92. H6C III, 2, 195. Lr. IV, 6, 30 (Ff *further*). *please you,* —*ther,* Tp. I, 2, 65 (= proceed); cf. Meas. III, 1, 212. —*thest:* Sonn. 117, 8. Caes. I, 3, 120.

b) *farther* = more: *'tis time I should inform thee —ther,* Tp. I, 2, 23. *thou must now know —ther,* 33. *I will disparage her no —ther,* Ado III, 2, 131. *no —ther wise than Percy's wife,* H4A II, 3, 110 (Ff *further*). Shr. I, 1, 48. Wint. II, 1, 136. IV, 4, 460. V, 3, 75. Caes. IV, 3, 36. Oth. III, 1, 242 (Q *farder,* Ff *further*). Cymb. II, 4, 52. Cor. II, 3, 117. = deeper: *seeing —ther than the eye hath shown,* Sonn. 69, 8.

Far, as a contracted compar., = *farther* (cf. *Near*): *f. than Deucalion off,* Wint. IV, 4, 442 (O. Edd. *farre*). cf. Shr. IV, 2, 73.

Farced, stuffed, tumid: *the f. title running 'fore the king,* H5 IV, 1, 280. see *Force,* def. 7.

Fardel or **Farthel,** a pack, a bundle: Wint.

IV, 4, 728. 739. 781. 783. V, 2, 4. 125. Hml. III, 1, 76.

Fardingale, see *Farthingale*.

Fare, subst. fortune, hap, cheer: *how fares your majesty? Poisoned, —ill f. — dead*, John V, 7, 35. *how now, fair lords? what f.? what news abroad?* H6C II, 1, 95.

Fare, vb. 1) to happen, to fall out: *so —s it with this faulty lord of Rome*, Lucr. 715. *so will it f. with Claudio*, Ado IV, 1, 224. *how would it f. with your departed souls?* H6B IV, 7, 123.

2) to be in any state or under any circumstances: *so surfeit-taking Tarquin —s this night*, Lucr. 698. *which I will keep so chary as tender nurse her babe from —ing ill*, Sonn. 22, 12. *f. well I could not*, Pilgr. 186 (quibble). *so f. my limbs with long imprisonment*, H6A II, 5, 4. *farewell, and better than I f.* H6B II, 4, 100. *so —d our father with his enemies*, H6C II, 1, 18. *this battle —s like to the morning's war*, II, 5, 1. *well f. you, gentlemen*, Tim. I, 1, 163. Very often in questions: *how —s the king?* Tp. V, 7. *how —s my gracious sir?* 253. LLL V, 2, 736. Shr. Ind. 2, 102. Wint. II, 2, 21. H6B III, 2, 33. III, 3, 1. H6C II, 1, 8. R3 II, 4, 40 (Ff *doth*). III, 1, 96. IV, 1, 38. V, 3, 82. Hml. III, 2, 97. Cymb. V, 5, 236 etc. *how —st thou?* Merch. III, 5, 75 (Ff Q2.3.4 *cheerest*). H6A I, 4, 74. Ant. II, 6, 72. *how f. you?* Tim. III, 6, 28. *how dost thou f.?* H6A IV, 6, 27. *to ask her how she —s*, Lucr. 721. 1594. *and see our gentle queen how well she —s*, H6C V, 5, 89. And in the imper. with *well*, to express a kind wish to those who leave or are left: *f. thee well*, Wiv. II, 2, 137. Mids. II, 1, 245. Merch. II, 3, 4. Tw. III, 4, 183. Ant. III, 2, 39. 41 etc. *f. thou well*, Tp. V, 318. *f. ye well*, Meas. IV, 3, 172. Mids. III, 2, 243. Merch. I, 1, 58. Tw. II, 1, 40 etc. *f. you well*, Wiv. III, 2, 85. V, 3, 7. Meas. I, 1, 59. 73. II, 1, 265. III, 1, 280. Err. III, 2, 183. LLL I, 2, 137. Mids. II, 2, 131. Tw. I, 3, 64 etc. etc.

3) to feed, to be entertained: *feast your ear with the music awhile, if they will f. so harshly o' the trumpet's sound*, Tim. III, 6, 37. Quibbling: *f. well I could not, for I supped with sorrow*, Pilgr. 186. *how —s my noble lord? Marry, I f. well, for here is cheer enough*, Shr. Ind. 2, 103. *how —s our cousin Hamlet? Excellent, of the chameleon's dish*, Hml. III, 2, 97. *if you fall in the adventure, our crows shall f. the better for you*, Cymb. III, 1, 83. *you shall taste gentlemen of all fashions, you shall f. well*, Per. IV, 2, 84.

Farewéll or **Fàrewell**, a kind wish at parting: Sonn. 87, 1. Pilgr. 185. 293. Tp. I, 1, 65. II, 2, 182. III, 1, 90. Gentl. I, 1, 62. II, 2, 16. IV, 2, 84. IV, 4, 183. Wiv. III, 2, 88. Meas. II, 1, 222. III, 1, 176. Err. I, 2, 30. Mids. I, 1, 220. II, 1, 16. V, 1, 352. Merch. II, 3, 8. II, 5, 45. Caes. V, 1, 117 etc. etc. With *to: f. to your worship*, Wiv. I, 4, 176. Shr. III, 2, 198. Caes. V, 5, 31 etc. *and so we bid f.* R3 III, 5, 71. *bid me f.* As Epil. 24. H6C V, 2, 49. R3 IV, 1, 104. *bidding f. to so sweet a guest*, R2 II, 2, 8. *nor bade f. to him*, Mcb. I, 2, 21 (cf. *Bid*). Substantively: *welcome ever smiles, and f. goes out sighing*, Troil. III, 3, 169. *take a more dilated f.* All's II, 1, 59. H6C II, 1, 22. Caes. V, 1, 116. Cymb. III, 4, 188. *let Andronicus make this his latest f. to their souls*, Tit. I, 149. *a happy f.* H6C IV, 8, 31. *a brief f.* Cor. IV, 1, 1. *long f.* Ant. V, 2, 295. *a long f. to all my greatness*, H8 III, 2, 351. *we bid a loud f. to these great fellows*,

Ant. II, 7, 139. *a volume of —s*, R2 I, 4, 18. *as many —s as be stars in heaven*, Troil. IV, 4, 46.

Used at parting from persons or things renounced or irrecoverably lost; with *to: so f. to the little good you bear me*, H8 III, 2, 350. *bid f. to your good life*, Wiv. III, 3, 127. Oftener without *to: then f. his great renown*, Pilgr. 420. Ado II, 1, 189. III, 1, 109. R2 III, 2, 170. H6A IV, 3, 16. 23. H6B III, 2, 356. H8 III, 2, 281. 459. V, 3, 27. Rom. II, 2, 89. *but f. it, for I will use no art*, Hml. II, 2, 99. *bid Bianca f.* Shr. IV, 4, 97.

Far-fet, (far-fetched) rich in deep stratagems: *if York, with all his f. policy, had been the regent there instead of me, he never would have stayed in France so long*, H6B III, 1, 293.

Farm, subst. 1) ground let to a tenant: *at my f. I have a hundred milch-kine*, Shr. II, 358. *leased out ... like to a tenement or pelting f.* R2 II, 1, 60. *let me be no assistant for a state, but keep a f. and carters*, Hml. II, 2, 167.

2) a small, poor estate: *to buy a slobbery and dirty f.* H5 III, 5, 13. *I had sold my f. to buy my crown*, V, 2, 129. *low —s, poor pelting villages*, Lr. II, 3, 17.

3) lease: *the Earl of Wiltshire hath the realm in f.* R2 II, 1, 256.

Farm, vb. 1) to let on lease: *we are enforced to f. our royal realm*, R2 I, 4, 45.

2) to take the lease of: *to pay five ducats, I would not f. it*, Hml. IV, 4, 20.

Farmer, a cultivator of ground, a husbandman: Shr. Ind. 1, 84. I, 2, 210. Mcb. II, 3, 5. Lr. IV 6, 158.

Farm-house, residence of a farmer: Wiv. II, 3, 91.

Far-off, adj. distant: *one might see those f. eyes look sad*, Lucr. 1386. *like f. mountains turned into clouds*, Mids. IV, 1, 193. *if we did but glance a f. look*, H6B III, 1, 10. *spies a f. shore*, H6C III, 2, 136.

Farrow, a litter of pigs: *that hath eaten her nine f.* Mcb. IV, 1, 65.

Farthel, see *Fardel*.

Farther and **Farthest**, see *Far*.

Farthing (cf. *Three-farthings*) the fourth of a penny: LLL III, 138. 149. 172.

Farthingale, a hoop petticoat: Gentl. II, 7, 51. IV, 4, 42. Wiv. III, 3, 69. Shr. IV, 3, 56 (O. Edd. *fardingales*).

Fartuous, Mrs Quickly's form of *virtuous*: Wiv. II, 2, 100.

Fashion, subst. 1) the make or form, shape: *the fineness of the gold and chargeful f.* Err. IV, 1, 29. Especially of articles of dress: *the f. of his hat*, Ado I, 1, 76. cf. II, 3, 18. III, 3, 125. 128. 129. III, 4, 23. Shr. IV, 3, 130. Lr. III, 6, 84. *what f. shall I make your breeches?* Gentl. II, 7, 49. 52. *your gown 's a most rare f.* Ado III, 4, 15. Tw. II, 5, 219. III, 4, 417.

2) external appearance in general: *when sighs and groans and tears may grace the f. of her disgrace*, Lucr. 1319. *that thou but leadest this f. of thy malice to the last hour of act*, Merch. IV, 1, 18. *'tis some odd humour pricks him to this f.* Shr. III, 2, 75. *I will deeply put the f. on*, H4B V, 2, 52. *I scorn thee and thy f.* H6A II, 4, 76 (viz thy adorning thyself with a red rose). *I will, or let me lose the f. of a man,*

H8 IV, 2, 159. *set a fair f. on our entertainment,* Tim. I, 2, 152. *puts him thus from f. of himself,* Hml. III, 1, 183.

3) **way, manner:** *as is false women's f.* Sonn. 20, 4. *I heard your guilty rhymes, observed your f.* LLL IV, 3, 139. *it is my f.* Shr. II, 230. H4B II, 4, 60. Caes. IV, 3, 135. *after his unpolished f.* LLL IV, 2, 19. Caes. I, 2, 180. I, 3, 34. Ant. IV, 15, 87. *in the same f.* Tp. V, 8. Wiv. III, 4, 83. LLL V, 2, 794. Troil. I, 3, 178. Cor. I, 1, 281. Hml. I, 3, 111. *what f. will you wear the garland of?* Ado II, 1, 195. *why doest thou garter up thy arms a this f.?* All's II, 3, 265 (M. Edd. *o' this f.*). *Alexander looked o' this f.* Hml. V, 1, 219 (Qq *a this f.*). *upon this f.* As I, 1, 2. *this shepherd's passion is much upon my f.* II, 4, 62. *two and two, Newgate f.* H4A III, 3, 104.

4) **kind, sort:** *thou friend of an ill f.* Gentl. V, 4, 61. *which 'longs to women of all f.* Wint. III, 2, 105. *gentlemen of all —s,* Per. IV, 2, 84. *this reasoning is not in the f. to choose me a husband,* Merch. I, 2, 23 (i. e. not of a kind, not well suited to etc. Ff *in f.*).

5) **custom, prevailing practice:** *the pretty babes, that mourned for f., ignorant what to fear,* Err. I, 1, 74. *the f. of the world is to avoid cost,* Ado I, 1, 97. Wiv. III, 3, 183. As II, 1, 56. II, 3, 59. Epil. 1. Shr. III, 1, 80. H5 V, 2, 284. 296. 299. H6B I, 3, 46. Troil. V, 2, 196. Caes. V, 5, 5. Lr. III, 4, 74. Particularly the prevailing mode of dress or ornament: Ado III, 3, 140 etc. LLL IV, 3, 262. Shr. IV, 3, 95. All's I, 2, 63. R2 II, 1, 21. H4B III, 2, 340. V, 1, 89. R3 I, 2, 258. Caes. IV, 1, 39. *out of f.* All's I, 1, 170. Troil. III, 3, 152. Cymb. III, 4, 53.

6) **that which good breeding requires,** the tastes and usages of good society (der gute Ton): *thralled discontent, whereto the inviting time our f. calls,* Sonn. 124, 8. *long agone I have forgot the court; besides, the f. of the time is changed,* Gentl. III, 1, 86. *to be so odd and from all —s,* Ado III, 1, 72. *a man in all the world's new f. planted,* LLL I, 1, 165. *—'s own knight,* 179. *for f. sake, I thank you,* As III, 2, 271 (pro forma). *though it appear a little out of f., there is much care and valour in this Welshman,* H5 IV, 1, 85. *w:t would be out of f.* Troil. II, 3, 226. *wars and lechery: nothing else holds f.* V, 2, 196. *for Hamlet and the trifling of his favour, hold it a f. and a toy in blood,* Hml. I, 3, 6. 112. *these are now the f.* II, 2, 357. *the appurtenance of welcome is f. and ceremony,* 389. *the glass of f. and the mould of form,* III, 1, 161. *I prattle out of f.* Oth. II, 1, 208.

Fashion, vb. *) to shape, to form:* *sometimes —ing them like Pharaoh's soldiers,* Ado III, 3, 142. *—ing our humours to the opposed end of our intents,* LLL V, 2, 767. *that self mould that —ed thee,* R2 I, 2, 23. *he was the copy and book that —ed others,* H4B II, 3, 32. *to be —ed into what pitch he please,* H8 II, 2, 49. *—ed to much honour from his cradle,* IV, 2, 50. Used of the cut of garments: *a better —ed gown,* Shr. IV, 3, 101. *so new a —ed robe,* John IV, 2, 27. With a double accus.: *—ed thee that instrument of ill,* H6A III, 3, 65 (= formed, made thee to be that i.). *all with me's meet that I can f. fit,* Lr. I, 2, 200.

2) to shape, to adapt to a purpose, to **accommodate:** *how shall I f. me to wear a cloak,* Gentl. III, 1, 135. *f. your demeanour to my looks,* Err. II, 2, 33. *his present portance, which he did f. after the inveterate*

hate he bears you, Cor. II, 3, 233. *nature, as it grows again toward earth, is —ed for the journey, dull and heavy,* Tim. II, 2, 228.

3) to work from one shape into another, to **frame:** *since the quarrel will not bear colour for the thing he is, f. it thus,* Caes. II, 1, 30. *I'll f. him,* 220. Hence = to counterfeit, to pervert: *to f. a carriage to rob love from any,* Ado I, 3, 30. *God forbid that you should f., wrest, or bow your reading.* H5 I, 2, 14.

4) to frame, to contrive, to bring about: *I doubt not but to f. it,* Ado II, 1, 384. *I will so f. the matter that Hero shall be absent,* II, 2, 47. *success will f. the event in better shape than I can lay it down in likelihood,* IV, 1, 237. *a sonnet —ed to Beatrice,* V, 4, 88. *they have conjoined to f. this false sport,* Mids. III, 2, 194. *a thing not in his power to bring to pass, but swayed and —ed by the hand of heaven,* Merch. I, 3, 94. *where you and Douglas, as I will f. it, shall happily meet,* H4A I, 3, 297. *his going hence, which I will f. to fall out between twelve and one,* Oth. IV, 2, 242. *to f. in* = to contrive to put in or insert: *'be thou true' say I, to f. in my sequent protestation; be thou true, and I will see thee,* Troil. IV, 4, 67.

Fashionable, such as the prevailing practice is, customary: *time is like a f. host that slightly shakes his parting guest by the hand,* Troil. III, 3, 165. *to promise is most courtly and f.* Tim. V, 1, 29.

Fashion-monger, one who affects gentility: Rom. II, 4, 34.

Fashion-monging (F2.3.4 *mongring*), affecting gentility, foppish: Ado V, 1, 94.

Fashions (corrupted from *farcins*), a disease of the skin in horses: Shr. III, 2, 53.

Fast, subst. **abstinence from food:** Ven. 55. Meas. I, 2, 130. R2 II, 1, 80. Hml. II, 2, 147. Especially voluntary abstinence from food as a religious mortification: Lucr. 891. Meas. I, 4, 61. LLL I, 1, 24. Plur. *—s:* Gentl. II, 4, 131. LLL V, 2, 811. Cor. V, 1, 56. *to break one's f.:* John I, 235. *kept a tedious f.* R2 II, 1, 75.

To break one's f. = to breakfast: Gentl. II, 4, 141. Err. I, 2, 50. H6C II, 2, 127 (*broke their —s*).

Fast, vb. (impf. *—ed,* Gentl. II, 1, 29. In Cymb. IV, 2, 347: *I fast and prayed,* the termination *ed* belongs to both verbs), to **abstain from food:** Gentl. II, 1, 25. 29. Err. I, 2, 89. LLL I, 1, 303. I, 2, 134. 151. 160. IV, 3, 122. Shr. IV, 1, 176. 180. Wint. IV, 4, 612. R2 II, 1, 81. H6A III, 2, 42. R3 IV, 4, 118. Troil. I, 2, 37. III, 3, 137 (Ff *feasting*). Hml. V, 1, 298. *—ing* = hungry: John III, 1, 260. H5 IV, 2, 58. Cymb. III, 6, 91. = before breakfast: *she is not to be kissed —ing,* Gentl. III, 1, 326. — With *from: f. from all,* Ant. II, 7, 108 (= abstain from all food). With an accus. denoting the result: *f. it fairly out,* Shr. I, 1, 109.

Used of abstinence from food for the mortification of the flesh: Meas. II, 2, 154. Err. I, 2, 51. LLL I, 1, 48. IV, 3, 292. 294. As III, 5, 58. Wint. III, 2, 212. Hml. I, 5, 11.*Oth. III, 4, 40. Cymb. IV, 2, 347.

Fast, adj. 1) **close, firmly fixed:** *make f. the doors,* Merch. II, 6, 49. *the gates made f.* H6C IV, 7, 10. *all f.?* H8 V, 2, 3 (= closed). *whom we raise we will make f. within a hallowed verge,* H6B I, 4, 25. *f. and loose* (a cheating game of gipsies and other vagrants): LLL I, 2, 162. III, 104. John III, 1, 242. Ant. IV, 12, 28.

2) close, deep, sound: *in a most f. sleep*, Mcb. V, 1, 9.

3) firm, confirmed: *remain f. foe to the plebeii*, Cor. II, 3, 192. *'tis our f. intent*, Lr. I, 1, 39. With *to*, = firm in adherence, faithfully devoted: *wilt thou be f. to my hopes, if I depend on the issue?* Oth. I, 3, 369. *and will continue f. to your affection*, Cymb. I, 6, 138.

4) quick: *idle weeds are f. in growth*, R3 III, 1, 103. *springs out into f. gait*, H8 III, 2, 116.

Fast, adv. 1) closely, tightly: *to bind f.* Sonn. 134, 8. Err. V, 40. Merch. II, 5, 54 (*f. bind, f. find*). Tit. II, 1, 16. V, 2, 166. Lr. III, 7, 29. *hold f.* Troil. V, 3, 59. Tim. IV, 1, 8. Mcb. IV, 3, 3. *kept f.* Ven. 575. *the green* (plum) *sticks f.* 527. *the hand which was f. belocked in thine*, Meas. V, 210. *this hand, f. wound about thy hair*, H6C V, 1, 54. *I have you f.* H6A V, 3, 30. *to entrap the hearts of men —er than gnats in cobwebs*, Merch. III, 2, 123.

2) close: *f. by*, Wint.IV,4,512. H6B III,2,189.

3) deeply, soundly: *the dove sleeps f.* Lucr. 360. *as f. locked up in sleep*, Meas. IV, 2, 69. *f. asleep*, Tp. II, 1, 215. Gentl. III, 1, 25. IV, 2, 136. H4A II, 4, 577. Tit. II, 3, 194. Caes. II, 1, 229. *f.*, alone, = f. asleep: *Juliet! f., I warrant her, she*, Rom. IV, 5, 1 (the nurse's speech).

4) firmly, immovably, unchangeably: *she is f. my wife, save that we do the denunciation lack of outward order*, Meas. I, 2, 151. *that thou art so f. mine enemy*, H6B V, 2, 21. *friends now f. sworn*, Cor. IV, 4, 12. *are you f. married?* Oth. I, 2, 10. *sit you f.* H6C IV, 1, 119. *to stand f.* = a) to stand still, stop: Gentl. IV, 1, 1. Caes. V, 1, 22. b) to show constancy or courage, not to yield: John III, 1, 208. H4A II, 2, 75. Troil. II, 3, 273. V, 2, 187. Cor. I, 4, 41. III, 1, 231. Caes. III, 1, 87. With *to: stand f., good Fate, to his hanging*, Tp. I, 1, 32 (= persist in thy purpose of hanging him).

5) swiftly, quickly: Lucr. 262. 1334. 1670. Sonn. 11, 1. Tp. II, 2, 75. Gentl. III, 1, 51. Err. III, 2, 72. IV, 2, 30. Ado II, 1, 82. LLL II, 120. IV, 3, 186. Mids. I, 1, 129. III, 2, 379. 416. Merch. I, 3, 97. V, 25. As III, 5, 116. Shr. I, 1, 145. Wint. IV, 4, 184. John IV, 2, 269. H4A II, 4, 163. 442. H5 I, 1, 65. H6B I, 4, 78. III, 2, 367. H6C V, 4, 63. R3 II, 3, 1. Rom. II, 5, 5. Ant. II, 2, 201. = soon, readily: *which they 'll do f. enough of themselves*, Wiv. IV, 1, 69. *thou wouldst sin the —er*, Tim. I, 2, 246. *as f. as* = as soon as: Sonn. 114, 8. As IV, 1, 134. Used of sounds, words, strokes, tears etc. = thickly, in rapid succession: *didst vent thy groans as f. as mill-wheels strike*, Tp. I, 2, 281. *as f. as she answers thee with frowning looks, I'll sauce her with bitter words*, As III, 5, 68. *kiss on kiss she vied so f.* Shr. II, 311. *pelt so f. at one another's pate*, H6A III, 1, 82. *York as f. upon your Grace exclaims*, IV, 4, 30. *—er than spring-time showers comes thought on thought*, H6B III, 1, 337. *weeping as f. as they stream forth thy blood*, Caes. III, 1, 201. *drop tears as f. as the Arabian trees their gum*, Oth. V, 2, 350.

The different significations confounded: *give my love fame —er than time wastes life*, Sonn. 100, 13 (i. e. a fame whose stability is greater than the haste of time). *ten times —er Venus' pigeons fly to seal*

love's bonds new made, than they are wont to keep obliged faith unforfeited, Merch. II, 6, 5. *bids the other grow —er than thought or time*, Wint. IV, 4, 565.

Fast-closed, closely shut: John II, 447.

Fasten, 1) trans. a) to fix firmly, to bind tightly: Ven. 68. Err. I, 1, 86. Tit. V, 3, 183. With *to:* Err. I, 1, 80. With *on:* Ven. 38.

b) to link, to join: *a lady so fair, and —ed to an empery*, Cymb. I, 6, 120.

c) to fix, to attach: *mine eye oft was —ed to it*, All's V, 3, 82. *f. your ear on my advisings*, Meas. III, 1, 203. *—ed and fixed the shame on't in himself*, Wint. II, 3, 15.

d) to put or palm upon by persuasion: *thinking by this face to f. in our thoughts that they have courage*, Caes. V, 1, 11. *if I can f. but one cup upon him*, Oth. II, 3, 50.

e) Partic. *—ed* = confirmed, hardened: *strong and —ed villain*, Lr. II, 1, 79.

2) intr. to lay a clinching hold on, to cling to; with *on: I will f. on this sleeve of thine*, Err. II, 2, 175. *with his strong arms he —ed on my neck*, Lr. V, 3, 212.

Fast-falling: *f. tears*, H6C I, 4, 162.

Fast-growing, quickly developed: *our f. scene*, Per. IV Prol. 6.

Fasting-day, a day of abstinence from fleshmeat: Per. II, 1, 86.

Fast-lost (O. Edd. not hyphened), lost by fasting: *feast-won, f.* Tim. II, 2, 180.

Fastly, hastily: Compl. 61.

Fastolfe, (O. Edd. *Falstaff*), name: *Sir John F.* H6A I, 1, 131. I, 4, 35. III, 2, 104.

Fat, subst. 1) the oily parts of the body: Wiv. IV, 5, 100. R3 V, 3, 258.

2) vat, large tub: Ant. II, 7, 122 (most M. Edd. *vats*).

Fat, adj. 1) fleshy, corpulent: Gentl. IV, 1, 36. Wiv. II, 1, 56. IV, 2, 29. 77. 233. IV, 5, 16. V, V, 14 etc. Err. III, 2, 94. V, 414. LLL I, 1, 26. As II, 1, 55. Shr. Ind. 2, 23. H4A I, 2, 210 etc. H4B II, 1, 82 etc. Caes. I, 2, 192. 198. Hml. IV, 3, 24. V, 2, 298. Ant. II, 6, 66.

2) well-fed: *a f. goose*, LLL III, 103. *horse*, Mids. II, 1, 45. *sheep*, As III, 2, 28. *oxen*, Shr. II, 360. *tripe*, IV, 3, 20. *tame things*, Wint. I, 2, 92. *deer*, H4A V, 4, 107. *bull-beeves*, H6A I, 2, 9. *to feed f.* = to give ample food to: *I will feed f. the ancient grudge I bear him*, Merch. I, 3, 48. *advantage feeds him f., while men delay*, H4A III, 2, 180. *feed and be f., my fair Calipolis*, H4B II, 4, 193.

3) rich, fertile: *the f. earth's store*, Lucr. 1837. *a f. marriage*, Err. III, 2, 94. *the f. ribs of peace*, John III, 3, 9. *f. purses*, H4A I, 2, 141. *the —est soil*, H4B IV, 4, 54.

4) oily, greasy, nauseous: *come out of that f. room*, H4A II, 4, 1. *too much cloyed with f. meat*, H4B V, 5, 143.

5) heavy, dull: *a f. l'envoy; ay, that's a f. goose*, LLL III, 105. *well-liking wits they have; gross, gross; f., f.* V, 2, 268. *it is as f. and fulsome to mine ear as howling after music*, Tw. V, 112. *duller than the f. weed that roots itself in ease on Lethe wharf*, Hml. I, 5, 32.

Fat, vb. 1) trans. a) to fatten: Mids. II, 1, 97. Hml. II, 2, 607. IV, 3, 23. 24.

b) to **nourish**: *manhood and honour should have hare-hearts, would they but f. their thoughts with this crammed reason*, Troil. II, 2, 48. Figuratively, to refresh, to delight: *how this villany doth f. me with the very thoughts of it*, Tit. III, 1, 204.

2) intr. to **grow fat**: *he is franked up to —ing for his pains*, R3 I, 3, 314 (perhaps here also trans.).

Fatal, 1) instrumental to destiny: *Parca's f. web*, H5 V, 1, 21. *the Thracian f. steeds*, H6C IV, 2, 21.

2) foreboding mischief and death: *that f. screech-owl to our house, that nothing sung but death to us and ours*, H6C II, 6, 56. *the nightly owl or f. raven*, Tit. II, 3, 97. Err. V, 348. Wint. IV, 2, 22. H6A III, 1, 195. H6B I, 1, 99. H6C II, 5, 98. Tit. II, 3, 264. Rom. Prol. 5. Caes. V, 1, 88. Mcb. I, 5, 40. II, 1, 36. II, 2, 3.

3) pernicious, deadly; used of persons as well as things: *wreathed up in f. folds*, Ven. 879. *the most skilful, bloody and f. opposite*, Tw. III, 4, 293. Lucr. 1843. Merch. III, 1, 5. R2 V, 6, 35. H4A V, 4, 26 *(to)*. H5 III Chor. 27. H6A I, 4, 76. III, 2, 28. V, 4, 57. H6B I, 1, 234. III, 2, 267. H6C I, 4, 22. V, 1, 87. V, 4, 27. V, 6, 16. R3 I, 2, 14. III, 3, 10. III, 4, 103. Tit. II, 3, 36. 202. V, 3, 86. Rom. III, 1, 148. 171. V, 1, 65. Mcb. III, 5, 21. Oth. V, 2, 20. 37. *the f. and neglected English*, H5 II, 4, 13, i. e. the fatally neglected E., neglected to our destruction.

Fatally, perniciously: H5 II, 4, 54.

Fatal-plotted (O. Edd. not hyphened), plotted to a pernicious end: Tit. II, 3, 47.

Fat-already (O. Edd. not hyphened), already too well fed: *to enlard his f. pride*, Troil. II, 3, 205.

Fat-brained, dull, stupid: H5 III, 7, 143.

Fate, subst. 1) destiny: Lucr. 1069. Sonn. 29, 4. Wiv. V, 5, 246. Mids. III, 2, 92. Tw. I, 5, 329. II, 1, 4. Wint. III, 3, 28. H4B III, 1, 45. H6A IV, 6, 8. Troil. V, 3, 26. Mcb. I, 5, 30. III, 1, 71. 137. III, 5, 30. Oth. II, 1, 195. Ant. IV, 8, 34 etc. Plur. *—s: whom the —s have marked to bear...*, Err. I, 1, 141. *the foolish —s*, Mids. I, 2, 40. *thy —s open their hands*, Tw. II, 5, 159. *O, the —s! how would he look*, Wint. IV, 4, 20. *where —s await the duke of Suffolk?* H6B I, 4, 35. H6C IV, 3, 58. Caes. I, 2, 139. II, 3, 16. Hml. I, 1, 122. III, 2, 221. Per. III, 3, 8.

2) the Goddess of destiny: *stand fast, good F., to his hanging*, Tp. I, 1, 33. III, 3, 61. Wiv. III, 5, 106. LLL V, 2, 68. Plur. *—s:* Mids. V, 199. 290. Merch. II, 2, 65. Caes. III, 1, 98. Per. IV, 3, 14.

3) evil destiny, death, perdition: *O f., take not away thy heavy hand*, Ado IV, 1, 116 (i. e. death). *if to my sword his f. be not the glory*, Troil. IV, 1, 26. *where our f. may rush and seize us*, Mcb. II, 3, 127. cf. Meas. III, 1, 145. Tim. III, 5, 14.

4) great good fortune ordained by destiny: *let us fear the native mightiness and f. of him*, H5 II, 4, 64. *Caesar sits down in Alexandria, where I will oppose his f.* Ant. III, 13, 169. cf. Per. V, 1, 72 (M. Edd., without cause, *feat*).

Fate, vb., to ordain, to destine: *as it hath —d her to be my motive*, All's IV, 4, 20. Part. *—ed* = doomed, decreed by destiny: *one midnight —ed to the purpose*, Tp. 1, 2, 129. Lr. III, 4, 70. Oth. III, 3, 276.

Fated, adj. invested with the power of destiny: *the f. sky gives us free scope*, All's I, 1, 232.

Fat-guts, paunch-belly: H4A II, 2, 33.

Father, subst. 1) he by whom one is begotten: Tp. I, 2, 1. 21. 54. 55. 57. 390 etc. Gentl. I, 1, 53. I, 2, 131 etc. etc. *f. of Warwick* = f. Warwick, H6C V, 1, 81 (cf. *Of*). Figurative use: *surfeit is the f. of much fast*, Meas. I, 2, 130. *make thee the f. of their idle dreams*, IV, 1, 64. *whose judgements are mere —s of their garments*, All's I, 2, 62. *every minute now should be the f. of some stratagem*, H4B I, 1, 8. *thy wish was f. to that thought*, IV, 5, 93.

2) God: *O, the f., how he holds his countenance!* H4A II, 4, 432. *good f., 'tis day*, Rom. IV, 4, 20 (F2.3.4 and most M. Edd. *faith*).

3) ancestor: *O f. Abram*, Merch. I, 3, 162. *our —s*, H5 III, 5, 6. R3 V, 3, 333. Caes. I, 3, 82. *f. of many kings*, Mcb. III, 1, 5. 60.

4) father-in-law: Ado IV, 1, 24. Merch. II, 6, 25. Shr. II, 292. V, 1, 10. H4A III, 1, 87. 147. R3 I, 3, 135. Rom. IV, 1, 2 etc.

4) one who exercises paternal care over another: *so kind a f. of the commonweal*, H6A III, 1, 98. *Timon has been this lord's f.* Tim. III, 2, 74. cf. Troil. II, 3, 267.

5) appellation given to any old man: Compl. 71. 288. Gentl. IV, 2, 59. Meas. III, 2, 14 (*good brother f.*). Wint. IV, 4, 353. 461. Troil. II, 3, 264. Tim. I, 1, 110. Mcb. II, 4, 4 etc. *now I perceive thou art a reverend f.* Shr. IV, 5, 48. *that f. ruffian*, H4A II, 4, 500. *the plain bald pate of f. Time*, Err. II, 2, 71. *the rusty curb of old f. antic the law*, H4A I, 2, 69. Title given to senators: Tit. III, 1, 1.

6) a priest or dignitary of the church: Tw. V, 145. R3 III, 5, 100. III, 7, 61. H8 II, 4, 58. 205. IV, 1, 26. *our holy f.* = the pope: John III, 1, 145. *ghostly f.* = confessor: Meas. IV, 3, 32. V, 126. H6C III, 2, 107. Rom. II, 2, 189. Used in addressing priests: Meas. I, 3, 1. 39. II, 3, 29. III, 1, 178. 281. III, 2, 13. 227. IV, 1, 66. IV, 2, 194. Tw. IV, 3, 34. John III, 1, 181. III, 4, 76. H4B IV, 1, 38. H8 IV, 2, 20. Rom. II, 3, 31 etc.

7) an ecclesiastical writer of the first centuries: *being of an old —'s mind*, LLL IV, 2, 33. *as a certain f. saith*, 153.

Father, vb. 1) to supply with a father: *the lady —s herself*, Ado I, 1, 112. *being so —ed and so husbanded*, Caes. II, 1, 297. *—ed he is, and yet he's fatherless*, Mcb. IV, 2, 27. *he childed as I —ed*, Lr. III, 6, 117.

2) to be father to: *Charles must f. it*, H6A V, 4, 71. *cowards f. cowards and base things sire base*, Cymb. IV, 2, 26. *rather f. thee than master thee*, 395.

Father-house, paternal house: Ant. II, 7, 135 (F2.3.4 and M. Edd. *father's house*).

Father-in-law, 1) the father of a man's wife: Lucr. Arg. 2. R3 I, 4, 49. H8 III, 2, 8. 256.

2) stepfather: R3 V, 3, 81.

Fatherless, destitute of a father: Mcb. IV, 2, 27. *our f. distress*, R3 II, 2, 64 (our grief at being bereft of our father).

Fatherly, adj. paternal: Ado IV, 1, 75. Shr. II, 288.

Fatherly, adv. in a paternal manner: *he cannot choose but take this service I have done f.* Cymb. II, 3, 39.

Fathom or **Fadom** (the latter the more usual orthography) subst. 1) a measure of length containing six feet, used to measure deeps: *f. and half*, Lr. III, 4, 37. Unchanged in the plur.: Tp. I, 2, 396. As IV, 1, 210. All's IV, 1, 63. Wint. IV, 4, 281. H8 II, 1, 51. Rom. I, 4, 85. Lr. IV, 6, 50. Plur. —s: Tp. V, 55. Troil. I, 1, 50. Hml. I, 4, 77.

2) depth: *for all ... the profound sea hides in unknown —s*, Wint. IV, 4, 502.

3) reach, penetration (in the language of the seaman Iago): *another of his f. they have none*, Oth. I, 1, 153.

Fathomless, immeasurable: *buckle in a waist most f. with spans and inches*, Troil. II, 2, 30.

Fathom-line, lead-line: H4A I, 3, 204.

Fatigate, fatigued, exhausted: *his doubled spirit requickened what in flesh was f.* Cor. II, 2, 121.

Fat-kidneyed, gross, paunched: H4A II, 2, 5.

Fatness, fullness of flesh, grossness, gross and dull sensuality: *in the f. of these pursy times virtue itself of vice must pardon beg*, Hml. III, 4, 153.

Fat-witted, heavy-witted, stupid: H4A I, 2, 2.

Faucet-seller, see *Fosset-seller*.

Fauconberg, name restituted by M. Edd., after Holinshed, in H5 III, 5, 44 and IV, 8, 104; O. Edd. *Faulconbridge*.

Faulchion, see *Falchion*.

Faulconbridge, see *Falconbridge*.

Fault, 1) defect, imperfection: Sonn. 148, 14. Gentl. II, 3, 3. III, 1, 328. 362. 373. 376. 377. V, 4, 112. Wiv. I, 4, 13. 15. III, 4, 32. Meas. II, 1, 28. V, 1, 444. Err. III, 2, 55. 107. Merch. II, 2, 192. As III, 2, 298. 299. 301. Shr. I, 1, 134. I, 2, 88. All's III, 6, 120 (*that's all the f.*). Tw. I, 5, 47. H4A III, 1, 180. 245 etc. *to find f.* = to be displeased, to blame: Troil. Prol. 30. *to find f. with*, All's I, 3, 89. *with* and *about*, Shr. IV, 1, 202. *the cold f.* = cold scent, loss of scent: *till they have singled the cold f. cleanly out*, Ven. 694. *Silver made it good in the coldest f.* Shr. Ind. 1, 20. *the cur is excellent at —s*, Tw. II, 5, 140.

2) offence, transgression, crime: *the shame and f. finds no excuse nor end*, Lucr. 238. *the f. unknown is as a thought unacted*, 527. 629. Sonn. 89, 1. 118, 10. Tp. V, 132. Epil. 18. Gentl. I, 2, 40. 52. IV, 1, 31. 53. IV, 4, 15. Meas. I, 3, 35. II, 1, 40. 10. 2, 35. II, 4, 72. 133. III, 2, 282. V, 110. 417. 461. Err. I, 2, 65. V, 206. Ado II, 1, 228. LLL I, 2, 105. 106. Merch. V, 186. As I, 3, 48. All's III, 4, 7. IV, 3, 85. V, 3, 60 (*our rash —s* = our inconsiderateness, our offence in being rash). Wint. I, 2, 85 (*continue f.*). III, 2, 61. John I, 262. IV, 2, 71. R2 I, 3, 240. II, 3, 105. H6B I, 3, 202. III, 1, 47. 64. H6C II, 1, 197. II, 6, 71. III, 2, 164. V, 1, 101. R3 I, 4, 230. Tit. V, 2, 173. Tim. III, 5, 1 etc. *to do a f.* Wiv. V, 5, 9. *to make a f.* Lucr. 804. Sonn. 35, 5. Wint. III, 2, 218. 220. R2 I, 2, 5. *the f. thou gavest him* (= inputedst) H8 III, 2, 262. *'tis your f.* (= you are to blame for it) Ven. 381. Lucr. 482. Tp. II, 1, 135. Wiv. III, 5, 40. Meas. I, 2, 162. II, 2, 162. Err. II, 1, 95. Mids. I, 1, 200. III, 2, 243. Merch. III, 2, 304. All's II, 1, 25. H6C II, 2, 7. *lay the f. on me*, H6A II, 1, 57. *Margaret was in some f. for this*, Ado V, 4, 4. *the children are not in the f.* H4B II, 2, 29. *is Antony or we in f. for this?* Ant. III, 13, 2. *mine eyes were not in f.* Cymb. V, 5, 63. — With *against* and *to*: *'tis a f. to heaven, a f. against the dead, a f. to nature*, Hml. I, 2, 101.

3) want, default: *for f. of a better*, Wiv. I,

4, 17. H4B II, 2, 45. *for f. of a worse*, Rom. II, 4, 129.

4) ill hap, misfortune: *'tis your f.; 'tis a good dog*, Wiv. I, 1, 95. *the more my f. to scape his hands where I was like to die*, Per. IV, 2, 79. Perhaps also in Wiv. III, 3, 233.

Faultful, guilty, criminal: Lucr. 715.

Faultiness, the state of being faulty, defectiveness: *round even to f.* Ant. III, 3, 33.

Faultless, innocent: *look thyself be f.* H6B II, 1, 189. *any malice should prevail, that f. may condemn a nobleman*, III, 2, 24. *a clout steeped in the f. blood of pretty Rutland*, R3 I, 3, 178.

Faulty, criminal, guilty: *wherein my youth hath f. wandered and irregular*, H4A III, 2, 27. *that I am f. in Duke Humphrey's death*, H6B III, 2, 202. *men so noble, however f., yet should find respect*, H8 V, 3, 75.

Faustus, the celebrated German magician: Wiv. IV, 5, 71.

Favour, subst. 1) kind regard, benevolence, friendly disposition: Tp. IV, 204. Ado V, 4, 22. Merch. I, 3, 169. Tw. II, 3, 131. III, 2, 19. V, 126. 344. Wint. II, 3, 179 etc. *I am in the f. of Margaret*, Ado II, 2, 13. *best in f.* H8 I, 4, 108. *in f. with a person*, Sonn. 25, 1. R3 I, 1, 79. *out of f.* Tw. II, 5, 9. Lr. I, 4, 111. *receive him to f.* Tit. I, 421. *in f.* = favourably disposed: *to whom in f. she* (Fortune) *shall give the day*, John II, 393. *fortune in f. makes him lag behind*, H6A III, 3, 34. Plur. —s: *outward courtesies would fain proclaim —s that keep within*, Meas. V, 16. *is he inconstant in his —s?* Tw. I, 4, 7. *hangs on princes' —s*, H8 III, 2, 367. *he that depends upon your —s*, Cor. I, 1, 184. *I'll court his —s*, Hml. V, 2, 78.

2) a kind act, benevolence shown, countenance: *if thou wilt deign this f.* Ven. 15. Gentl. II, 4, 101. 161. R3 I, 2, 208 etc. Plur. —s: Gentl. III, 1, 161. Shr. IV, 2, 30. H4B II, 2, 138 etc. *to do a f.* or —s *to a person*: Gentl. III, 1, 6. Err. I, 1, 123. Tw. III, 2, 7. R2 III, 2, 11 (Q1 —s, the other O. Edd. *f.*). H6B I, 1, 71. Tit. I, 234.

3) a present, a token of love: *a thousand —s from a maund she drew*, Compl. 36. *you have a f. too: who sent it?* LLL V, 2, 30. 125. 130. 292. 468. 722. Mids. II, 1, 12. IV, 1, 54. All's V, 3, 74. R2 V, 3, 18. H4A V, 4, 96. H5 IV, 7, 160.

4) lenity, charitableness: *pity, she cries, some f., some remorse*, Ven. 257. *that for this f. he presently become a Christian*, Merch. IV, 1, 386. *untaught to plead for f.* H6B IV, 1, 122. *justice with f. have I always done*, H6B IV, 7, 72. *begged a' pardon? he did ask f.* Ant. III, 13, 133.

5) leave, good will, pardon: *speak on with f.; we are bent to hear*, John II, 422. *pray, give me f.* H8 I, 1, 168. *give me your f.: my dull brain was wrought with things forgotten*, Mcb. I, 3, 149. *your leave and f. to return to France*, Hml. I, 2, 51. *entreats her a little f. of speech*, Oth. III, 1, 28. *by thy f., I must sigh in thy face*, LLL III, 68. *by your f.* Tw. II, 4, 25. Lr. IV, 6, 215. *by your good f.* Meas. IV, 2, 33. H8 V, 3, 74. *under f.* Tim. III, 5, 40.

6) that which conciliates affection; attraction, charm: *she told him stories to delight his ear; she showed him —s to allure his eye*, Pilgr. 48. *her beauty is exquisite, but her f. infinite*, Gentl. II, 1, 60 (quibble).

as frowning at the —s of the world, H6B I, 2, 4. *thought and affliction, passion, hell itself, she turns to f. and to prettiness*, Hml. IV, 5, 189. *even his stubbornness, his checks, his frowns, have grace and f. in them*, Oth. IV, 3, 21.

7) **aspect, look, appearance:** *have I not seen dwellers on form and f. lose all*, Sonn. 125, 5 (i. e. outward appearance, seeming). *I do love the f. and the form of this most fair occasion*, John V, 4, 50. *which to reduce into our former f. you are assembled*, H5 V, 2, 63. *the complexion of the element in f. is like the work we have in hand*, Caes. I, 3, 129 (O. Edd. *is —s; some M. Edd. is favoured*). *much o' the f. of other your new pranks*, Lr. I, 4, 258. Particularly used of the exterior of persons, = figure, features, countenance: *both f., savour, hue and qualities, are on the sudden wasted*, Ven. 747. *if it see the most sweet f. or deformed'st creature*, Sonn. 113, 10. *Angelo will discover the f.* Meas. IV, 2, 185. *a good f. you have, but that you have a hanging look*, 34. Ado II, 1, 97. III, 3, 19. LLL IV, 3, 262. V, 2, 33 (quibble). Mids. I, 1, 186. As IV, 3, 87. V, 4, 27. All's I, 1, 94. 107. V, 3, 49. Tw. II, 4, 24. III, 4, 363. 416. Wint. V, 2, 53. R2 IV, 168. Troil. I, 2, 101 (*a brown f.*). IV, 5, 213. Caes. I, 2, 91. II, 1, 76. Mcb. I, 5, 73. Hml. V, 1, 214. Oth. I, 3, 346. Ant. II, 5, 38. Cymb. IV, 2, 104. —*s* = features, applied to a single person: *and stain my —s in a bloody mask*, H4A III, 2, 136.* *my hospitable —s*, Lr. III, 7, 40. — Cymb. I, 6, 42*.

Favour, vb. 1) **to regard with kindness and predilection:** Gentl. II, 1, 158. H6B I, 1, 158. H6C I, 1, 67. H8 II, 1, 47. Tit. IV, 4, 79. *you may call it melancholy, if you will f. the man*, Troil. II, 3, 94. *commend unto his lips thy —ing hand*, Ant. IV, 8, 23 (O. Edd. *savouring*).

2) **to countenance, befriend, support:** Err. I, 1, 150. H6A II, 1, 47. IV, 1, 81. H6C IV, 1, 144. Cor. II, 1, 54. III, 3, 8. Tit. I, 139.

Favourable, 1) **friendly, kind:** *unless some dull and f. hand will whisper music to my weary spirit*, H4B IV, 5, 2 (cf. *favouring hand*, Ant. IV, 8, 23). *lend f. ears to our request*, R3 III, 7, 101.

2) **propitious:** *f. stars*, Shr. IV, 5, 40. *till the heavens look with an aspect more f.* Wint. II, 1, 107. *most f. and happy speed*, Oth. II, 1, 67.

Favourably, propitiously, advantageously: *which the time shall more f. minister*, Oth. II, 1, 277.

Favoured, featured; only by conjecture in Caes. I, 3, 129 (O. Edd. *is favours*; some M. Edd. *in favour 's*); cf. *Hard-favoured, Well-favoured, Ill-favoured.*

Favourer, one who favours and assists, a friend: *as —s, not as foes*, Per. I, 4, 73. With *of:* H8 V, 3, 80. Tit. I, 9. With *to:* Cymb. V, 3, 74.

Favourite, subst. a person treated with predilection: Sonn. 25, 5. Ado III, 1, 9. R2 III, 2, 88. H4A IV, 3, 86. H4B IV, 2, 25. H6A IV, 1, 190. H6C I, 1, 56. Hml. III, 2, 214.

Fawn, subst. a **young deer:** Ven. 876. As II, 7, 128.

Fawn, subst. wheedling courtesy, flattery: *spend a f. upon 'em*, Cor. III, 2, 67.

Fawn, vb. 1) **to wag the tail:** *as the grim lion —eth o'er his prey*, Lucr. 421. *when he —s, he bites*, R3 I, 3, 290. Cor. I, 6, 38. Caes. V, 1, 41.

2) **to wheedle, to cringe, to be overcourteous:** *thy —ing smiles*, Gentl. III, 1, 158. LLL V, 2, 62. Merch. I, 3, 42. H4A I, 3, 252. Caes. III, 1, 45. Hml. III, 2, 67 (Ff *feigning*). With *upon* (= to court servilely and in the manner of a dog): Sonn. 149, 6. Pilgr. 421. Gentl. IV, 2, 15. Mids. II, 1, 204. R2 I, 3, 170. III, 2, 130. V, 1, 33. H6A IV, 4, 35. H6C IV, 1, 75. IV, 8, 49. Tim. III, 4, 51. Caes. I, 2, 75.

Fay, faith: *by my f.* Shr. Ind. 2, 83. Rom. I, 5, 128. Hml. II, 2, 271.

Fealty, fidelity, loyalty: Gentl. II, 4, 91. H6B V, 1, 50. Cymb. V, 4, 73. With *to:* R2 V, 2, 45. Tit. I, 257.

Fear (dissyll. in H4A IV, 3, 7) subst. 1) **apprehension, dread:** Ven. 1153. Sonn. 86, 12. Gentl. II, 7, 68. Ado II, 3, 200. 203 etc. Plur. —*s:* Lucr. 456. Sonn. 107, 1. Compl. 298. Meas. IV, 2, 207. Mids. V, 97. LLL I, 2, 107 etc. With *of:* Gentl. III, 1, 33. Wiv. I, 1, 37. 189. II, 2, 24. Err. V, 195. Merch. IV, 1, 192 etc. *to give fear to use and liberty*, Meas. I, 4, 62. *put f. to valour*, Ven. 1158 (= make valour timorous). *stand in f.* Meas. II, 3, 34. H6B IV, 2, 67. *all his men upon the foot of f.* H4A V, 5, 20 (= flying). *for f.* Lucr. 610. Err. IV, 2, 56. H6A III, 1, 85. R3 V, 2, 20 etc. *for f. of sth.:* Tp. II, 2, 116. Gentl. I, 4, 48. Caes. V, 1, 105. *for f. lest ...:* Wiv. III, 5, 104. Mids. III, 2, 385. *for f. = lest, that not: and never after ear so barren a land, for f. it yield me still so bad a harvest*, Ven. Ded. 6. *receive the money now, for f. you ne'er see chain nor money more*, Err. III, 2, 182. *make it less, for f. I surfeit*, Merch. III, 2, 114. *out of f. =* a) for or from fear: *you speak it out of f.* H4A IV, 3, 7. b) without f.: *I am out of f. of death*, IV, 1, 135. cf. *this will put them out of f.* Mids. III, 1, 23. Personified: *honest f. doth too soft betake him to retire*, Lucr. 173. *thy angel becomes a f.* Ant. II, 3, 22 (or = *a-fear*, i. e. in fear, afeard?).

2) **doubt, mistrust:** *so I, for f. of trust, forget to say*, Sonn. 23, 5 (see *Fear*, vb. def. 3. b).

3) **timidity:** *do so near the bottom run by their own f. or sloth*, Tp. II, 1, 228. *it is the baseness of thy f. that makes thee strangle thy propriety*, Tw. V, 149.

4) **dreadfulness, formidableness:** *the f. of your adventure would counsel you to a more equal enterprise*, As I, 2, 187. *my love and f. glued many friends to thee*, H6C II, 6, 5. *there is no f. in him: let him not die*, Caes. II, 1, 190. *what should be the f.?* Hml. I, 4, 64. *put thyself into a haviour of less f., ere wildness vanquish my staider senses*, Cymb. III, 4, 9.

5) **a thing to be dreaded, an object of fear:** *imagining some f.* Mids. V, 21. *when we should submit ourselves to an unknown f.* All's II, 3, 6 (or = the fear of something unknown?). *shall we buy treason? and indent with —s, when they have lost and forfeited themselves?* H4A I, 3, 87. *and hold'st it f. or sin to speak a truth*, H4B I, 1, 95. *all these bold —s thou seest with peril I have answered*, IV, 5, 196. *environed with all these hideous —s*, Rom. IV, 3, 50. *we will fetters put upon this f. which now goes too free-footed*, Hml. III, 3, 25.

Fear, vb. 1) **to be afraid, to dread; a) absol.:** Ven. 1154. Tp. III, 3, 43. Gentl. V, 3, 13. Meas. V, 403. LLL I, 2, 108 etc. **b) followed by an accus.:**

Lucr. 172. Pilgr. 94. Sonn. 115, 9 *(—ing of time's tyranny;* cf. *Of).* Tp. V, 284. Gentl. II, 1, 26. III, 1, 71. IV, 1, 6. Meas. I, 3, 27. III, 1, 74. 132. V, 402. Err. I, 1, 74. Ado II, 3, 201. 205. Tw. V, 153 etc. *—ed gods!* Cymb. IV, 2, 305. *he shall never more be —ed of doing harm,* Lr. II, 1, 113. c) by a double accus.: *the thief doth f. each bush an officer,* H6C V, 6, 12. *cardinal sins and hollow hearts I f. ye,* H8 III, 1, 104. d) by an inf.: Gentl. I, 3, 80. Wiv. IV, 4, 39. Meas. 1, 4, 79. Tw. I, 5, 327. IV, 2, 63 etc. e) by a clause: Pilgr. 347. Tp. I, 2, 443. II, 1, 132. V, 116. Gentl. I, 1, 37. 147. Meas. I, 3, 34. Err. I, 2, 105 etc. *f. not but that she will love you,* Gentl. III, 2, 1. *I —ed lest I might anger thee,* Tp. IV, 168. Gentl. III, 1, 28.

I f. me = I f.: Tp. V, 283. Gentl. II, 1, 7, 61. 67. Meas. V, 33. Tw. III, 1, 125. R2 II, 2, 149. III, 2, 67. H6A III, 1, 24. 136. V, 5, 102. H6B I, 1, 150. 163. III, 1, 343. IV, 4, 23. H6C III, 2, 60. R3 I, 2, 195. Cor. IV, 6, 88. Tim. I, 2, 247. Ant. II, 7, 37.

2) to affright, to terrify: *he would not f. him,* Ven. 1094. *to f. the birds of prey,* Meas. II, 1, 2. *this aspect hath —ed the valiant,* Merch. II, 1, 9. *f. boys with bugs,* Shr. I, 2, 211. *uncleanly scruples f. not you,* John IV, 1, 7 (M. Edd. *scruples!*). *the people f. me,* H4B IV, 4, 121. *more —ed than harmed,* H5 I, 2, 155. *go f. thy king withal,* H6C III, 3, 226. *a bug that —ed us all,* V, 2, 2. *how I may be censured, something —s me to think,* Lr. III, 5, 4. *such a thing as thou, to f., not to delight,* Oth. I, 2, 71. *thou canst not f. us,* Ant. II, 6, 24.

3) to be concerned, to be in solicitude, to be anxious; a) absol. *f. not,* Ado V, 4, 44. Mids. II, 1, 268. Merch. I, 3, 158. Shr. Ind. I, 100. H6C IV, 7, 37. *f. not you,* Gentl. IV, 2, 82. Meas. I, 2, 109. *f. you not,* IV, 1, 71. Merch. V, 123 etc. b) trans. 1) to be concerned, solicitous, alarmed about, to fear for: *I —ed thy fortune,* Ven. 642. *you need not to f. the bawds,* Meas. II, 1, 248. *f. me not,* Meas. IV, 1, 70. *f. me not, man, I will not break away,* Err. IV, 4, 1. *f. you not my part of the dialogue,* Ado III, 1, 31. *a toy: your grace needs not f. it,* LLL IV, 3, 201. *which makes me f. the enjoying of my love,* Merch. III, 2, 29. *I f. you,* III, 5, 3. *I'll f. no other thing so sore as keeping safe Nerissa's ring,* V, 306. *f. you not him,* Shr. IV, 4, 10. 13. *you shall not need to f. me,* All's III, 5, 31. *he was much —ed by his physicians,* H4A IV, 1, 24. *never f. me,* IV, 2, 64. *f. not your advancements,* H4B V, 5, 84. *I f. her not,* H6C III, 2, 24. *his physicians f. him,* R3 I, 1, 137. *f. me not,* Troil. V, 2, 62. *f. thy dangerous stoutness,* Cor. III, 2, 126. *f. me not,* Rom. I, 1, 42. *do' not f. our person,* Hml. IV, 5, 122. The significations confounded: *if any f. lesser his person than an ill report,* Cor. I, 6, 69. 2) to suspect, to doubt: *you need not f. us,* Merch. III, 5, 33. *—ed thy faith,* H6B III, 1, 205. *I speak not 'be thou true' as —ing thee,* Troil. IV, 4, 64. *I f. Cassio with my night-cap too,* Oth. II, 1, 316. *f. not you that* (= do not doubt of it) Wiv. IV, 4, 78. H6B IV, 3, 19. H6C IV, 2, 5. *f. you not her courage,* H6B I, 4, 6. *Sebastian are you? —est thou that, Antonio?* Tw. V, 228. *if you shall see Cordelia, as f. not but you shall,* Lr. III, 1, 47. — Meas. II, 4. 9*.

Feared, adj. tainted, mixed with fear: *quake in the present winter's state and wish that warmer days would come: in these f. hopes,* Cymb. II, 4, 6.

Fearful, 1) filled with fear, afraid: *whereon with f. eyes they long have gazed,* Ven. 927. Meas. IV, 2, 204. Err. I, 1, 68. Mids. V, 101. 165. John IV, 2, 191 *(action).* R2 III, 2, 110. III, 3, 73. H4A IV, 1, 67 *(faction).* H4B Ind. 12 *(musters).* H6B III, 1, 331. H6C II, 2, 30. II, 5, 130. V, 4, 44. R3 IV, 2, 126. IV, 3, 51. IV, 4, 311. V, 1, 18. V, 3, 181. H8 V, 1, 87. Rom. III, 3, 1. Oth. I, 3, 12 *(in f. sense)* etc. *f. to do a thing,* Wint. I, 2, 258. *grow f. that you protect this course,* Lr. I, 4, 225. With *of* = a) fearing: *f. of him,* Ven. 630. *of infection,* Rom. V, 2, 16. b) fearing for: *f. of his life,* H6C V, 6, 87.

2) timorous, cowardly: *pursue these f. creatures,* Ven. 677. *virtue is bold, and goodness never f.* Meas. III, 1, 216. *of a f. heart,* As III, 3, 49. Wint. I, 2, 250. H6B III, 2, 224. IV, 4, 2. IV, 8, 44. H6C I, 1, 25. 178. V, 4, 7. Caes. V, 1, 10 *(with f. bravery).*

3) causing apprehension (Germ. bedenklich): *my house, left in the f. guard of an unthrifty knave,* Merch. I, 3, 176. *holy seems the quarrel upon your grace's part, black and f. on the opposer,* All's III, 1, 5. *you have some hideous matter to deliver, when the courtesy of it is so f.* Tw. I, 5, 222. *a f. eye thou hast,* John IV, 2, 106. *full of difficult weight and f. to be granted,* Oth. III, 3, 83.

4) dreadful, terrible: *bare and unpeopled in this f. flood,* Lucr. 1741. *O f. meditation!* Sonn. 65, 9. *he's gentle and not f.* Tp. I, 2, 468. *this f. country,* V, 106. Gentl. I, 2, 121. Meas. III, 1, 116. Mids. III, 1, 33. Wint. V, 1, 153. John I, 38. III, 1, 238. V, 6, 20. R2 II, 4, 11. H4A III, 2, 167. H4B IV, 1, 16. H5 IV, 3, 5. H6A IV, 2, 15. R3 I, 1, 11. I, 4, 14 (Ff *heavy*). 24. V, 3, 97. 212. Tit. III, 1, 253. Rom. Chor. 9. Caes. I, 3, 78 etc. Superl. *—est,* R3 III, 4, 106. With *to: f. to their eyes,* H6C II, 2, 27.

Fearfully, 1) in fear, timorously: Ven. 886. Sonn. 99, 8. Pilgr. 288. Merch. V, 7. John IV, 2, 74. H4A I, 3, 105. Per. IV, 2, 127.

2) terribly: H5 III, 1, 12; cf. Lr. IV, 1, 77. Rom. V, 3, 133.

Fearfulness, awe, dread: *in servile f.* Caes. I, 1, 80.

Fearless, free from fear, bold: R2 I, 1, 123. H6C IV, 7, 62. With *of:* Meas. IV, 2, 151.

Fear-surprised, overcome by fear: *f. eyes,* Hml. I, 2, 203.

Feast, subst. 1) a festival: *therefore are —s so solemn and so rare, since, seldom coming, in the long year set, like stones of worth they thinly placed are,* Sonn. 52, 5. Wint. IV, 3, 40. IV, 4, 10. 42. 68. 237. John V, 2, 58. R2 I, 3, 92. H4A III, 2, 58. H5 IV, 3, 40. H6A I, 1, 154. Caes. I, 1, 72. Per. V Prol. 17.

2) the celebration of a solemn event, especially of a marriage: *one f., one house, one mutual happiness,* Gentl. V, 4, 173. *at a marriage f.* LLL II, 40. *three and three, we'll hold a f. in great solemnity,* Mids. IV, 1, 190. Merch. III, 2, 214. Shr. II, 318. III, 2, 226. 250. V, 1, 146. All's II, 3, 187. John III, 1, 302. H8 IV, 1, 94.

3) a repast, entertainment, banquet Ven. 447. 450. Sonn. 141, 8. Compl. 181. Meas. I, 2, 57 *(impiety has made a f. of thee).* Err. III, 1, 26. V, 405. 407. Ado V, 1, 154. LLL V, 1, 40. Merch. II, 6, 8. 48. As II, 7, 115. 122. Wint. I, 2, 344. IV,

3, 43. R2 I, 3, 67. 297. H4A IV, 2, 85. H4B IV, 4, 106. H6A IV, 5, 7. Troil. I, 3, 191. Rom. I, 2, 20. IV, 5, 87 (*a burial f.*). Tim. I, 1, 270. I, 2, 62. III, 6, 76. Mcb. II, 2, 40. III, 1, 12. 28. III, 4, 33. III, 6, 22. 35. Hml. II, 2, 52. Ant. II, 2, 187 (*monstrous matter of f.*). II, 6, 75. Cymb. III, 3, 75 etc.

Feast, vb. 1) trans. to entertain, to treat; a) absol.: *his new —ing,* Tim. III, 6, 9. *you should have feared false times when you did f.* IV, 3, 520 (i. e. when you invited your friends to banquets). — b) with an object: *I do f. to-night my best-esteemed acquaintance,* Merch. II, 2, 180. *you are retired, as if you were a —ed one,* Wint. IV, 4, 63 (= a guest). *f. his neighbours,* H5 IV, 3, 45. H6A II, 3, 82. Troil. V, 1, 3. Cor. IV, 4, 9. Tit. I, 489. Tim. III, 4, 114. Ant. II, 2, 76. II, 6, 61. IV, 1, 15. Figuratively: *to f. thine eyes,* Tim. I, 2, 133. *your ears,* III, 6, 36. = to treat in general: *how shall I f. him? what bestow on him?* Tw. III, 4, 2. *'tis like you would not f. him like a friend,* H6B III, 2, 184. Singular passage: *the place which I have —ed,* Tim. III, 4, 83 (= which I have made festive?).

2) intr. a) to banquet, to eat and drink sumptuously: Lucr. 891. 906. Wiv. II, 3, 92. Err. V, 205. LLL I, 1, 62. Merch. II, 5, 37. Shr. IV, 3, 185. John II, 354. H6A I, 6, 13. H6B IV, 1, 58. Troil. I, 3, 308. IV, 5, 229. 280. Tit. V, 2, 128. 185. Rom. II, 3, 49. Caes. III, 3, 1. Hml. II, 2, 84. Ant. II, 6, 66. Per. I, 3, 40. *a —ing presence,* Rom. V, 3, 86. With *on: —ing on your sight,* Sonn. 75, 9. *f. upon her eyes,* Meas. II, 2, 179. *to f. upon whole thousands of the French,* John V, 2, 178. *With,* in the same sense: *with my love's picture then my eye doth feast,* Sonn. 47, 5. *f. with the best,* Shr. V, 2, 8. Followed by a superfluous *it: revel and f. it at my house,* Err. IV, 4, 65.

b) to enjoy one's self, to indulge in pleasures: *that does take your mind from —ing,* Wint. IV, 4, 357. *since Richard and Northumberland, great friends, did f. together,* H4B III, 1, 59. *there is full liberty of —ing from this present hour of five till the bell have told eleven,* Oth. II, 2, 10. *f. here awhile, until our stars lend us a smile,* Per. I, 4, 107.

Feast-finding, attending banquets: *f. minstrels,* Lucr. 817.

Feast-won, got by feasts: *f., fast-lost,* Tim. II, 2, 180 (the same quibble in Lucr. 891).

Feat, subst. exploit: Ado I, 1, 15. V, 4, 50. Shr. I, 2, 267. Wint. II, 3, 111. H4B III, 2, 328. H5 I, 2, 116. IV, 3, 51. H6A I, 2, 64. H8 I, 1, 61. Cor. II, 2, 99. Oth. I, 3, 87. Ant. IV, 8, 9. Cymb. III, 1, 7. III, 3, 90. Per. V, 1, 72 (only by conjecture; O. Edd. rightly *fate*). V, 2, 6 (Walker rightly *feasts*). Used of deeds of great wickedness: H5 III, 3, 17. Mcb. I, 7, 80. Hml. IV, 7, 6.

Feat, adj. dexterous, neat, trim: *never master had a page so kind.... so f., so nurse-like,* Cymb. V, 5, 88. *how well my garments sit upon me, much —er than before,* Tp. II, 1, 273. In Compl. 48: *f. and affectedly,* the termination *ly* belongs to both words; see *Featly.*

Feat, vb. to make neat, to fashion: *to the more mature a glass that —ed them,* Cymb. I, 1, 49.*

Feather, 1) the plume of birds: Ven. 56. Sonn. 78, 7; cf. H5 I, 2, 307 and Caes. I, 1, 77. Tp. I, 2, 322. Meas. IV, 2, 31. Err. III, 1, 79. 81. 82.

Shr. IV, 3, 178. Wint. II, 3, 154; cf. H6B IV, 8, 57 and H6C III, 1, 84. H4B II, 4, 108. IV, 5, 32. H5 IV, 1, 213. H6B III, 1, 75. Rom. I, 1, 186. Tim. II, 1, 30. Hml. II, 2, 306 (*moult no f.*). Lr. IV, 6, 49. V, 3, 265. Ant. III, 2, 48. Per. IV Prol. 33. *he starts at stirring of a f.* Ven. 302. *every f. starts you,* All's V, 3, 232. *the best f. of our wing,* Cymb. I, 6, 186. Worn as an ornament in caps and hats: Shr. III, 2, 71. All's IV, 5, 111. H5 IV, 3, 112. H8 I, 3, 25. Hml. III, 2, 286. Plur. *—s* = wings: *with thought's —s,* Lucr. 1216. *set —s to thy heels,* John IV, 2, 174. *to soar with his light —s,* Rom. I, 4, 20.

2) kind of birds, kind in general: *check at every f.* Tw. III, 1, 71. *of their f. many moe proud birds,* H6C II, 1, 170. *birds of selfsame f.* III, 3, 161. *what plume of —s is he that indited this letter?* LLL IV, 1, 96. *I am not of that f. to shake off my friend,* Tim. I, 1, 100.

Feather-bed: Merch. II, 2, 174.

Feathered, 1) furnished with feathers: *f. wings,* Ven. 306. *breasts,* Lucr. 1122. *creatures,* Sonn. 143, 2. Phoen. 11.

2) winged: *f. Mercury,* H4A IV, 1, 106. *Cupid,* Oth. I, 3, 270. *in f. briefness,* Per. V, 2, 15.

Featly, neatly, adroitly: *with sleided silk feat and affectedly enswathed,* Compl. 48 (the termination *ly* belonging to both adverbs). *foot it f.* Tp. I, 2, 380. *she dances f.* Wint. IV, 4, 176.

Feature, the shape, make, exterior, the whole turn or cast of the body: *it shapes them to your f.* Sonn. 113, 12. *how —s are abroad, I am skilless of,* Tp. III, 1, 52. *complete in f. and in mind,* Gentl. II, 4, 73. *doth my simple f. content you?* As III, 3, 3 (not understood by Audrey). *nor know I you by voice or any f.* Tw. III, 4, 387. *thou hast done good f. shame,* 400. *liker in f. to his father Geffrey than thou and John in manners,* John II, 126. *the comment that my passion made upon thy f.* IV, 2, 264. *her peerless f.* H6A V, 5, 68. *cheated of f.* R3 I, 1, 19. *complete in mind and f.* H8 III, 2, 50. *that unmatched form and f. of blown youth,* Hml. III, 1, 167. *to show virtue her own f.* III, 2, 25. *bemonster not thy f.* Lr. IV, 2, 63. *report the f. of Octavia,* Ant. II, 5, 112. *for f., laming the shrine of Venus,* Cymb. V, 5, 163.

Featured, shaped: Sonn. 29, 6. Ado III, 1, 60.

Featureless, ugly: Sonn. 11, 10 (cf. *Shapeless*).

February, the second month in the year: *a F. face, so full of frost,* Ado V, 4, 41.

Fecks, faith: *art thou my boy? Ay, my good lord. I' f.?* Wint. I, 2, 120.

Fedary, accomplice: *let my brother die, if not a f., but only he owe and succeed thy weakness,* Meas. II, 4, 122 (F 2.3.4 and M. Edd. *feodary,* as if it came from *feod,* and not from *foedus*). *art thou a f. for this act, and lookest so virgin-like without?* Cymb. III, 2, 21 (O. Edd. *foedary*).

Federary, the same: *Camillo is a f. with her,* Wint. II, 1, 90.

Fee, subst. 1) a landed property: *to pay five ducats, five, I would not farm it; nor will it yield to Norway or the Pole a ranker rate, should it be sold in f.* Hml. IV, 4, 22. Hence, as it seems, property in general: *the rest of your —s, O Gods, the senators of Athens, make suitable for destruction,* Tim. III, 6, 89 (most M. Edd. *foes*).

2) reward, recompense, payment: Ven-

393. 538. Sonn. 120, 13. Ado II, 2, 54. Mids. III, 2, 113.*John II, 170. R3 I, 2, 170. I, 4, 284. III, 5, 96. Troil. III, 3, 49. Tit. II, 3, 179. Hml. II, 2, 73 (*three thousand crowns in annual f.*). Per. III, 2, 74. *I do not set my life at a pin's f.* Hml. I, 4, 65 (i. e. a pin would be too high a payment for it). Especially gratuities to professional men, properly and figuratively: Ven. 609. Lucr. 913. Gentl. I, 2, 48. Err. IV, 1, 76. Merch. IV, 1, 423. V, 164. 290. All's II, 1, 192. Wint. I, 2, 53. H6B III, 2, 217. H6C IV, 6, 5. Rom. I, 4, 73. Lr. I, 1, 166.

Fee, vb., to reward, to pay, to hire: Wiv. II, 2, 204. Merch. III, 1, 131. All's II, 1, 64 (O. Edd. see). Tw. I, 5, 303. H6C I, 4, 92. H8 III, 2, 213. Mcb. III, 4, 132.

Feeble, weak: *f. age*, Ven. 941. Lucr. 1768. Sonn. 7, 10. John V, 4, 35. H6B V, 3, 13. R3 II, 2, 58. Tit. II, 3, 288. III, 1, 208. Caes. II, 1, 130. *f. Desire*, Lucr. 710 (= exhausted). Pilgr. 319. Gentl. II, 7, 10. H5 IV, 6, 22. *a lady's f. voice*, John III, 4, 41. Err. V, 310. Caes. II, 1, 313. *every f. rumour*, Cor. III, 3, 125. *to help the f. up*, Tim. I, 1, 107. Caes. I, 2, 129. II, 4, 36. Denoting want of military strength: H4B I, 3, 19. H5 II, 4, 22. Mental weakness: Err. III, 2, 35. H6B V, 1, 2. *ere my tongue shall wound my honour with such f. wrong*, R2 I, 1, 191 (with the wrong of such weakness, such cowardice).

Feeble, name in H4B III, 2, 158 etc.

Feeble, vb. to weaken: John V, 2, 146. Cor. I, 1, 199.

Feebleness, weakness, imbecility: Tit. I, 188.

Feebly, weakly: *the deeds of Coriolanus should not be uttered f.* Cor. II, 2, 87.

Feed', subst. pasture: *his flocks and bounds of f. are now on sale*, As II, 4, 83. *the other* (sheep) *rotted with delicious f.* Tit. IV, 4, 93 (Ff *food*).

Feed, vb. (impf. and partic. *fed*) 1) trans. a) to supply with food, to nourish: Ven. 170. 876. 1104. Sonn. 146, 12. Tp. I, 1, 164. Mids. III, 1, 169. Merch. III, 1, 63. As I, 2, 99. II, 3, 43. All's II, 2, 3 (*highly fed and lowly taught*). II, 4, 39 (*well fed*). R2 III, 2, 12. Tit. IV, 2, 122. Hml. III, 2, 100 etc. *to f. fat* = to nourish well and copiously: Merch. I, 3, 48. H4A III, 2, 180. cf. H4B III, 4, 193. Figurative use: *a mountain-spring that —s a dale*, Lucr. 1077. *the spring that those shrunk pipes had fed*, 1455. *to f. a fire*, John V, 2, 85. H6B III, 1, 303. Tit. I, 144. *desire, fed in heart*, Wiv. V, 5, 101. *fancy ... with gazing fed*, Merch. 146, 12. *to f. my means*, 266. *her sad behaviour —s his vulture folly*, Lucr. 556. *sparing justice —s iniquity*, 1687. *such meet food to f. it* (disdain) Ado I, 1, 122. *it will f. my revenge*, Merch. III, 1, 56. *to f. contention*, H4B I, 1, 156. *to f. oblivion with decay of things*, Lucr. 947. *they nourished disobedience, fed the ruin of the state*, Cor. III, 1, 117.

b) to entertain, to indulge: *to f. my humour, wish thyself no harm*, R3 IV, 1, 65. *f. his humour kindly*, Tit. IV, 3, 29. *to f. his brain-sick fits*, V, 2, 71. *he doth me wrong to f. me with delays*, IV, 3, 42 (= to keep me in vain hopes, to put me off).

c) to delight: *the object that did f. her sight*, Ven. 822. *he fed them with his sight*, 1104. *the sight of lovers —eth those in love*, As III, 4, 60. *makes me see and cannot f. mine eye*, All's I, 1, 236. *her eye must be fed*, Oth. II, 1, 228. *follow my disgraces, as if it fed ye*, H8 III, 2, 241. *f. yourselves with questioning*, As V, 4, 144. *in his commendations I am fed*, Mcb. I, 4, 55. *I f. myself with most delicious poison*, Ant. I, 5, 26. *please your thoughts in —ing them with those my former fortunes*, IV, 15, 53.

d) to eat, to consume: *virginity consumes itself to the very paring, and so dies with —ing his own stomach*, All's I, 1, 155 (corrupt?)

2) intr. a) to eat: Lucr 905. Sonn. 56, 3. 118, 6. Tp. III, 3, 49. Meas. I, 4, 41. Err. V, 64. As I, 1, 20. II, 4, 73. II, 7, 105. 168. R2 II, 1, 37. H4B II, 4, 193. H6B IV, 1, 57. Tit. V, 3, 54. Tim. IV, 3, 444. Mcb. III, 4, 35. 58. Ant. V, 2, 187 etc. Used of animals, = to graze, to take fodder: Ven. 232. Pilgr. 245. Err. II, 1, 101. As I, 1, 12. H4A V, 2, 14. H4B II, 2, 160. Tim. V, 1, 52 etc. *we both have fed as well*, Caes. I, 2, 98 (have been nourished with as good food). *my wife is fair, —s well, loves company*, Oth. III, 3, 184 (i. e. eating and drinking takes well with her). *fed well*, 340 (only in Ff.; = ate with appetite). Followed by *of*: *never fed of the dainties*, LLL IV, 2, 25. Tit. V, 3, 61. Hml. IV, 3, 30. Oftener by *on*: Ven. 63. 169. Sonn. 147, 3. Gentl. I, 2, 106. II, 1, 179. II, 4, 27. LLL II, 220. As II, 4, 86. Shr. IV, 3, 24. John III, 3, 10. Tim. IV, 3, 306. Caes. I, 2, 149 etc. Figurative use: *when his glutton eye so full hath fed*, Ven. 399. 548. *the vulture of sedition —s in the bosom of such great commanders*, H6A IV, 3, 48. *my half-supped sword, that frankly would have fed*, Troil. V, 8, 19. *the pleasure that some fathers f. upon*, R2 II, 1, 79. *you have fed upon my signories*, III, 1, 22.

b) to eat away, to consume, to destroy: *under whose* (love's) *simple semblance he* (lust) *hath fed upon fresh beauty*, Ven. 795. *time —s on the rarities of nature's truth*, Sonn. 60, 11. *so shalt thou f. on death, that —s on men, and death once dead, there's no more dying then*, 146, 13. *to f. upon the prodigal Christian*, Merch. II, 5, 14. *the care on thee depending hath fed upon the body of my father*, H4B IV, 5, 160. *such as your oppression —s upon*, H6A IV, 1, 58. *a mortal mineral, which should by the minute f. on life*, Cymb. V, 5, 51.

c) to indulge in a thought, to be taken up with it: *and f. upon the shadow of perfection*, Gentl. III, 1, 177. *I have fed upon this woe already*, 219. *you f. too much on this dislike*, Troil. II, 3, 235. *— s on his wonder*, Hml. IV, 5, 89 (Ff *keeps on his wonder*; Qq *feeds on this wonder*).

Feeder, 1) one who gives food: *nurse and f. of the other four* (senses), Ven. 446. *the tutor and the f. of my riots*, H4B V, 5, 66. *I will your very faithful f. be*, As II, 4, 99; i. e. your shepherd, he who feeds your flocks.

2) eater: *a huge f.* Merch. II, 5, 46. *the —s digest it with a custom*, Wint. IV, 4, 11. *food doth choke the f.* R2 II, 1, 37. *thou, beastly f., art so full of him*, H4B I, 3, 95.

3) one who receives food at the table of a great one, a parasite: *when all our offices have been oppressed with riotous —s*, Tim. II, 2, 168. *abused by one that looks on —s*, Ant. III, 13, 109. According to some, it means a servant in As II, 4, 99. Tim. II, 2, 168 and Ant. III, 13, 109.

Feeding, subst. 1) pasturage: *boasts himself to have a worthy f.* Wint. IV, 4, 169.

2) taking food: *to bitter sauces did I frame my f.* Sonn. 118, 6. *a horse full of high f.* H4B I, 1, 10. *with wine and f.* Cor. V, 1, 55.

Fee-farm: *a kiss in f.* Troil. III, 2, 53. Malone: "a kiss of a duration that has no bounds; a fee-farm being a grant of lands in fee, that is for ever, reserving a certain rent."

Fee-grief, a peculiar sorrow, a grief that has a particular owner: *the general cause, or is it a f. due to some single breast?* Mcb. IV, 3, 196.

Feel (impf. and part. *felt*; 2. p. *feltst*, Err. II, 2, 19). 1) to perceive by the touch; trans.: Meas. I, 2, 166. Err. II, 1, 53. III, 2, 134. IV, 4, 26. Mids. I, 1, 244. Wint. II, 1, 152. Ant. V, 2, 325 etc. *let me f. thy cloak upon me,* Gentl. III, 1, 136. *f. you your legs?* Lr. IV, 6, 65. Absolutely: *each —ing part,* Ven. 892. *the instruments that f.* Wint. II, 1, 154. *instruct, walk, f.* Cor. I, 1, 105. *finds not till it —s,* III, 3, 129. Tim. II, 2, 7. *I understand thy kisses and thou mine, and that's a —ing disputation,* H4A III, 1, 206 (quibbling).

2) to touch, to handle: *my smooth moist hand, were it with thy hand felt,* Ven. 143. *her other tender hand his fair cheek —s,* 352. 373. *let me f. your pulse,* Err. IV, 4, 55. V, 243. H5 II, 3, 25. H6B III, 2, 145. Absolutely: *then I felt to his knees,* H5 II, 3, 26.

3) to try, to sound: *howsoever you speak this to f. other men's minds,* H5 IV, 1, 131. *he hath wrote this to f. my affection to your honour,* Lr. I, 2, 94.

4) to perceive by the mind, to have the sense of: *I f. not this deity in my bosom,* Tp. II, 1, 277. *I f. the best is past,* III, 3, 50. *never —s the wanton stings and motions,* Meas. I, 4, 58. *couldst not f. his meaning,* Err. II, 1, 51. *I hope, thou feltst I was displeased,* II, 2, 19. *that I love her, I f.* Ado I, 1, 230. Troil. III, 3, 78. *fierce extremes will not f. themselves,* John V, 7, 14. *now I f. of what coarse metal ye are moulded,* H8 III, 2, 238. *I f. now the future in the instant,* Mcb. I, 5, 58. *to the felt absence now I f. a cause,* Oth. III, 4, 182. With a double acc.: *when thou —est it cold,* Sonn. 2, 14. *my conscience which I then did f. full sick,* H8 II, 4, 204. *I f. me much to blame,* H4B II, 4, 390. *how dost thou f. thyself now?* R3 I, 4, 123. *for then, and not till then, he felt himself, and found the blessedness of being little,* H8 IV, 2, 65. *he —s himself distracted,* Hml. III, 1, 5. With an inf.: *—ing it (my heart) break,* Compl. 275. *now does he f. his title hang loose about him,* Mcb. V, 2, 20. *I f. this youth's perfections ... to creep in at mine eyes,* Tw. I, 5, 315.

5) to be touched and affected by, to suffer, to enjoy, to experience: Tp. I, 2, 209. 487. Gentl. IV, 4, 177. All's III, 2, 51. H6C IV, 1, 82. H8 III, 1, 144. Rom. III, 5, 76. 77. Tim. V, 1, 74. Mcb. V, 2, 17. Lr. V, 3, 324. Oth. III, 3, 455 (Ff *keeps*) etc. *the felt absence,* Oth. III, 4, 182. *not imagined, felt,* Cymb. IV, 2, 307. Absolutely: *as if it felt with Scotland,* Mcb. IV, 3, 7.

Feeling = making itself felt, heartfelt, coming from and going to the heart: *have of my suffering youth some —ing pity,* Compl. 178. *frame some —ing line,* Gentl. III, 2, 76. *to whose —ing sorrows I might be some allay,* Wint. IV, 2, 8. *a —ing disputation,* H4A III, 1, 206 (quibbling). *let me weep for such a —ing loss,* Rom. III, 5, 75. *who, by the art of known and —ing sorrows, am pregnant to good pity,* Lr. IV, 6, 226.

Feeler, one who touches: *this hand, whose touch would force the —'s soul to the oath of loyalty,* Cymb. I, 6, 101.

Feeling, subst. 1) the sense of touch: Sonn. 141, 6. LLL IV, 3, 337. Wint. IV, 4, 625. Tit. IV, 2, 28. Mcb. II, 1, 37. Hml. III, 4, 78. *the sense of f.* Ven. 439.

2) sensation, perception: R2 I, 3, 301. Lr. III, 4, 13. Cymb. V, 5, 68. With *of:* Lucr. 1578. Tp. V, 21. Meas. I, 2, 38. R2 II, 3, 141. Hml. V, 1, 73. Lr. IV, 6, 287.

3) experience, knowledge: *he had some f. of the sport,* Meas. III, 2, 127. *thou hast no f. of it,* LLL III, 115.

4) sensibility: Lucr. 1317. LLL IV, 2, 30. R2 III, 2, 24. R3 I, 4, 257.

Feelingly, 1) by feeling, by making itself felt: *these are counsellors that f. persuade me what I am,* As II, 1, 11. *you see how this world goes. I see it f.* Lr. IV, 6, 152.

2) in a heartfelt manner: *true sorrow then is f. sufficed when with like semblance it is sympathized,* Lucr. 1112. *here f. she weeps Troy's painted woes,* 1492.

3) so as to hit a thing exactly, so as to hit home: *do I speak f. now?* Meas. I, 2, 36. *he shall find himself most f. personated,* Tw. II, 3, 172. *to speak f. of him,* Hml. V, 2, 113 (= to speak him home).

Feeling-painful, causing a deep-felt pain, wringing the heart: *my woe too sensible thy passion maketh more f.* Lucr. 1679.

Feere, see *Fere.*

Fee-simple, absolute fee, hereditary and unconditional property: *my woeful self, that did in freedom stand, and was my own f., not in part,* Compl. 144. *if the devil have not in f.* Wiv. IV, 2, 225. *for a quart d'écu he will sell the f. of his salvation, the inheritance of it,* All's IV, 3, 312. *for entering his f. without leave,* H6B IV, 10, 27. *the rivelled f. of the tetter,* Troil. V, 1, 26. *an I were so apt to quarrel as thou art, any man should buy the f. of my life for an hour and a quarter,* Rom. III, 1, 35.

Feign, 1) to invent, to image; a) trans.: *the poet did f. that Orpheus drew trees,* Merch. V, 80. *all that poets f. of bliss and joy,* H6C I, 2, 31. *I have upon a high and pleasant hill —ed Fortune to be throned,* Tim. I, 1, 64. *thou hast —ed him a worthy fellow,* 229. 230. b) absol.: *as poets f.* Pilgr. 115. *the truest poetry is the most —ing,* As III, 3, 20.

2) to pretend, to counterfeit, to dissemble; a) trans.: *your —ed tears,* Ven. 425. *it is the more like to be —ed,* Tw. I, 5, 208. H6A III, 1, 190. H6C IV, 2, 11. R3 V, 1, 21. Tit. IV, 4, 21. Cymb. III, 2, 76. V, 5, 279. b) intr. *with —ing voice verses of —ing love,* Mids. I, 1, 31. *most friendship is —ing,* As II, 7, 181. III, 3, 22. 27. Tw. III, 1, 110. V, 140. H4B IV, 5, 152. H6A V, 3, 142. Rom. II, 5, 16. Hml. III, 2, 67 (Qq *fawning*).

Felicitate, made happy: *I am alone f. in your dear highness' love,* Lr. I, 1, 76.

Felicity, bliss: *a wife of such wood were f.* LLL IV, 3, 249. *absent thee from f. awhile,* Hml. V, 2, 358.

Fell, subst. skin: *their —s are greasy,* As III, 2, 55. *my f. of hair would at a dismal treatise rouse,* Mcb. V, 5, 11. *the good-years shall devour them, flesh and f.* Lr. V, 3, 24.

Fell, adj. fierce, savage, cruel, pernicious: *Oberon is passing f. and wrath,* Mids. II, 1, 20. *to-morrow do I meet thee, f. as death,* Troil. IV, 5, 269. *more f. than anguish, hunger, or the sea,* Oth. V, 2, 362. *you say he is so f.* Cymb. IV, 2, 109. Mostly joined to a subst.: Lucr. 145. 429. 766. Sonn. 64, 1. 74, 1. Compl. 13. Mids. V, 227. 289. Merch. IV, 1, 135. Tw. I, 1, 22. John III, 4, 40. V, 7, 9. R2 I, 2, 46. I, 3, 302. H4B IV, 5, 207. V, 5, 39. H5 III, 3, 17. V, 2, 391. H6A V, 3, 42. H6B III, 1, 351. III, 2, 266. V, 1, 153. H6C I, 4, 149. II, 5, 13. IV, 4, 12. H8 V, 1, 49. Cor. I, 3, 48. Tit. II, 3, 235. 281. V, 3, 100. Tim. IV, 3, 61. Caes. III, 1, 269. Mcb. I, 5, 47. IV, 2, 71. IV, 3, 219. Hml. II, 2, 495. V, 2, 347 (see *Fell-incensed*). Lr. II, 1, 52. Superl. *—est:* Troil. V, 7, 6. Cor. IV, 4, 18.

Fell, vb. to hew down: *—ed my woods,* R2 III, 1, 23. H6C II, 1, 55. Tim. V, 1, 210. *I'll f. thee down,* H6B IV, 2, 123. *—ed him dead,* Lr. IV, 2, 76. *all save thee I f. with curses,* Tim. IV, 3, 508.

Fell-incensed, writing of some M. Edd. in Hml. V, 2, 61; O. Edd. without the hyphen.

Fell-lurking, lurking to do mischief: H6B V, 1, 146.

Fellow, subst. 1) companion, comrade: *he hath lost his —s,* Tp. I, 2, 416. *I and my —s are ministers of fate,* III, 3, 60. IV, 35. Gentl. IV, 1, 1. Err. I, 2, 37. Ado III, 3, 92. Mids. III, 2, 24. Merch. II, 2, 164. III, 5, 64. Tw. II, 5, 170. III, 4, 84. Wint. II, 3, 142. III, 2, 39. V, 1, 34. H4A V, 2, 76. H6C IV, 3, 54. R3 V, 2, 1. H8 II, 4, 160. Cor. I, 4, 27. IV, 5, 194. Rom. I, 5, 51. Tim. IV, 2, 3. Mcb. I, 5, 36. IV, 3, 129. Lr. I, 3, 13. III, 1, 48. Ant. IV, 2, 13. Adject. (in M. Edd. mostly hyphened): *thy f. birds,* Pilgr. 397. *every one fault seeming monstrous till his f. fault came to match it,* As III, 2, 373. *a f. counsellor,* H8 V, 2, 17. *f. kings,* H6B IV, 2, 173. *her f. maids,* Per. V, 1, 50. *my f. ministers,* Tp. III, 3, 65. *my f. partner,* Meas. IV, 2, 19. *my f. peers,* Per. I, 3, 11. *my f. scholars,* LLL I, 1, 17. *my f. schoolmaster,* Shr. III, 2, 140. *my f. servant,* Gentl. II, 4, 105. *f. soldier,* H6C IV, 7, 70. *f. student,* Hml. I, 2, 177. *your f. tribune,* Cor. III, 1, 52. V, 4, 39.

2) an equal: *my brother's servants were then my —s,* Tp. II, 1, 274. *to be your f. you may deny me,* III, 1, 84. *good hay hath no f.* Mids. IV, 1, 38; cf. Merch. III, 5, 88 and H8 I, 3, 41. *and be his f. so,* R2 III, 2, 99. *if he be not f. with the best king,* H5 V, 2, 261. *of whose quality there is no f. in the firmament,* Caes. III, 1, 62. *it is impossible that ever Rome should breed thy f.* V, 3, 101. *my young remembrance cannot parallel a f. to it,* Mcb. II, 3, 68. *the suits of princely —s,* Cymb. III, 4, 93. Hence = one of a pair: *his* (the shaft's) *f. of the self-same flight,* Merch. I, 1, 141. *here is the f. of it* (a glove) H5 IV, 8, 30. 42.

3) Used as an appellation of familiarity, and sometimes of contempt: Tp. I, 1, 29. V, 218. 274. Gentl. IV, 1, 37. IV, 4, 26. Wiv. II, 1, 143. 237. Meas. III, 2, 139. Err. IV, 2, 36. Merch. I, 1, 51. III, 4, 64. All's II, 3, 308. Tw. III, 4, 67. H5 V, 1, 8. V, 2, 262. Cor. I, 4, 52. Mcb. IV, 3, 183. Ant. IV, 7, 140. Cymb. II, 3, 60 etc. Used in addressing a person: Meas. I, 2, 120. LLL I, 1, 183. IV, 1, 102. Cor. V, 2, 63. Lr. III, 2, 69. IV, 1, 31. *—s:* Meas. IV, 3, 69. Shr. I, 2, 280. R3 V, 1, 10. Lr. III, 7, 67. Ant. IV, 14, 135. Before a name: *f. Trinculo,* Tp. II, 2, 180, *f. Hector,*

LLL V, 2, 678. *f. Grumio,* Shr. IV, 1, 112. *—s =* servants, people: *I am more bound to you than your —s, for they are but lightly rewarded,* LLL I, 2, 156. *whose —s are these?* H4A IV, 2, 68. cf. *my shoulders for the f. of this walk,* Wiv. V, 5, 29, i. e. for the forester.

Fellow, vb. to pair with: *affection.... with what's unreal thou coactive art, and —est nothing,* Wint. I, 2, 142.

Fellowly, sociable, companionable: *mine eyes, even sociable to the show of thine, fall f. drops,* Tp. V, 64.

Fellowship, 1) company, a state of being together: *scattered and disjoined from f.* John III, 4, 3. *parted our f.* Oth. II, 1, 93. *kneels and holds up hands for f.* Cor. V, 3, 175.

2) equality of fortune, companionship in adversity: *f. in woe doth woe assuage,* Lucr. 790. Rom. III, 2, 116. Lr. III, 6, 114. *sweet f. in shame,* LLL IV, 3, 49. *fears his f. to die with us,* H5 IV, 3, 39. *a royal f. of death,* IV, 8, 106.

3) association, alliance, partnership: *security enough to make —s accurst,* Meas. III, 2, 241. *everlasting bond of f.* Mids. I, 1, 85 (i. e. marriage). *out upon this half-faced f.* H4A I, 3, 208. *his f. in the cause against your city,* Tim. V, 2, 12. *a f. in a cry of players,* Hml. III, 2, 289. *this it is to have a name in great men's f.* Ant. II, 7, 13.

4) communion, familiar intercourse: *all the f. I hold now with him is only my obedience,* H8 III, 1, 121. *by the rights of our f.* Hml. II, 2, 294.

5) companionableness, a spirit and disposition as they ought to be among comrades: *nor good f. in thee,* H4A I, 2, 156. *all the titles of good f. come to you,* II, 4, 307. *in the soul of sound good f.* Troil. IV, 1, 52 (some M. Edd. *good-fellowship*).

Felly, subst. the exterior part of a wheel: *break all the spokes and —s from her wheel,* Hml. II, 2, 517.

Felon, probably a robber, or burglarian: *murder indeed I tortured above the f. or what trespass else,* H6B III, 1, 132. *apprehend thee for a f. here,* Rom. V, 3, 69. In Tim. III, 5, 49 O. Edd. *fellow,* M. Edd. *felon.*

Felonious, pillaging with violence: *or foul f. thief that fleeced poor passengers,* H6B III, 1, 129.

Felony, robbery, burglary: Tp. II, 1, 160. Misapplied by Cade: H6B IV, 2, 73.

Felt, a stuff made of wool, wrought by pressure into a compact substance: Lr. IV, 6, 189.

Female, subst. a she, one of the sex which brings forth young: Ven. 309. Err. II, 1, 24. LLL I, 1, 267. Mids. III, 2, 441. As V, 1, 54. R2 V, 5, 6. H4B III, 2, 140. V, 3, 20. H5 I, 2, 50. 89. 92.

Female, adj., pertaining to the sex which produces young: *my f. evil,* Sonn. 144, 5. *the f. ivy,* Mids. IV, 1, 48. *f. bastard,* Wint. II, 3, 175. *this law and f. bar,* H5 I, 2, 42 (i. e. exclusion of women). *fresh f. buds,* Rom. I, 2, 29. *the f. dove,* Hml. V, 1, 309. *a f. heir,* Per. Prol. 22. Hence = womanly, tender: *of f. favour,* As IV, 3, 87. *their f. joints,* R2 III, 2, 114. *with f. fairies will his tomb be haunted,* Cymb. IV, 2, 217 (Douce: 'harmless and protecting spirits, not fairies of a mischievous nature').

Femetary, see *Fumitory.*

Feminine, female: *a soul f. saluteth us,* LLL IV, 2, 83 (Holofernes' speech).

Fen, a bog: Tp. I, 2, 322. II, 1, 48. II, 2, 2. Cor. III, 3, 121. IV, 1, 30.

Fence, subst. 1) defence, guard: *the seas which He hath given for f. impregnable,* H6C IV, 1, 44.

2) the art of using the sword, skill in fencing: Wiv. I, 1, 295. Ado V, 1, 75. 84. Tw. III, 4, 312. John II, 290. H6B II, 1, 52. II, 3, 79.

Fence, vb. 1) to defend, to guard: *the red should f. the white,* Lucr. 63. *where's captain Margaret, to f. you now?* H6C II, 6, 75. *Oxford, that did ever f. the right,* III, 3, 98. *O thou wall, dive in the earth, and f. not Athens,* Tim. IV, 1, 3. *the tops of trees, which f. the roots they grow by,* Per. I, 2, 30.

2) to inclose: *a sheep-cote —d about with olive trees,* As IV, 3, 78. cf. Tim. IV, 1, 3.

3) to practise fencing, to fight according to art: Wiv. II, 3, 15. Merch. I, 2, 66. Tw. I, 3, 98. H4B II, 1, 206. Hml. II, 1, 25. Figuratively: *without any more virginal —ing,* Per. IV, 6, 63 (= evasions).

Fencer, a master of fence, one who teaches the art of using the sword: Ado V, 2, 13. Tw. III, 4, 307.

Fennel, the plant Foeniculum vulgare, considered as an inflammatory herb, and used also as an emblem of flattery: H4B II, 4, 267. Hml. IV, 5, 180.

Fenny, bred in bogs: *a f. snake,* Mcb. IV, 1, 12.

Fen-sucked, drawn out of bogs: *f. fogs,* Lr. II, 4, 169.

Fenton, name in Wiv. I, 4, 155. III, 4, 34. 101 etc.

Feodary, see *Fedary.*

Fer, French name in H5 IV, 4, 27. 28. 29. *Master Fer! I'll fer him,* 29.

Ferdinand, 1) F. the Catholic, king of Spain: H8 II, 4, 47. 2) the son of King Alonso of Naples: Tp. I, 2, 212. II, 1, 244. III, 3, 92. IV, 1, 8. V, 139. 3) a cousin of Petruchio's: Shr. IV, 1, 154.

Fere, spouse: *the woeful f. of that dame,* Tit. IV, 1, 89. In Per. Prol. 21 O. Edd. *peer,* M. Edd. *fere* or *pheere.*

Fern-seed, the seed of the plant Filix, supposed to have the power of rendering persons invisible: H4A II, 1, 96. 98.

Ferrara, Italian principality: H8 III, 2, 323.

Ferrers (O. Edd. *Ferris*), name in R3 V, 5, 13.

Ferret: *Cicero looks with such f. and such fiery eyes,* Caes. I, 2, 186 (Intpp.: with eyes red like those of the ferret or Mustela furo).

Ferret, vb. to worry as a ferret does the rabbit: *I'll fer him, and firk him, and f. him,* H5 IV, 4, 30. 33 (cf. the old King Leir, ed. Nichols, p. 461: *I'll f. you ere night for that word*).

Ferry, a place where persons are conveyed over a river: Merch. III, 4, 53.

Ferryman, one who transports passengers over a river: R3 I, 4, 46.

Fertile, 1) fruitful: *barren place and f.* Tp. I, 2, 338. II, 2, 152. Wint. III, 1, 2. H4A III, 1, 77. H5 V, 2, 37. H6A III, 3, 44. H6B I, 1, 238. III, 1, 88. Tim. IV, 3, 187. Hml. V, 2, 88. *a f. climate,* Oth. I, 1, 70. *and f. every wish,* Ant. I, 2, 39 (O. Edd. *foretel*).

2) abundant, ample: *f. tears,* Tw. I, 5, 274. *good store of f. sherris,* H4B IV, 3, 131.

3) bountiful, liberal: *from heartiness, from bounty, f. bosom,* Wint. I, 2, 113.

Fertile-fresh, of a luxuriant verdure: Wiv. V, 5, 72.

Fertility, fruitfulness: R2 III, 4, 39. H5 V, 2, 40.

Fervency, eagerness: *your diver did hang a salt-fish on his hook, which he with f. drew up,* Ant. II, 5, 18.

Fervour, ardor, zeal: All's III, 4, 11. Tw. I, 5, 306. Cymb. III, 5, 61. Per. V Prol. 20.

Feste, name of the clown in Tw. II, 4, 11.

Fester, 1) to rankle, to grow virulent: *this —ed joint,* R2 V, 3, 85. *—ed members rot but by degree,* H6A III, 1, 192. *well might they* (the wounds) *f. 'gainst ingratitude,* Cor. I, 9, 30.

2) to rot: *lilies that f.* Sonn. 94, 14. *their poor bodies must lie and f.* H5 IV, 3, 88. *—ing in his shroud,* Rom. IV, 3, 43.

Festinate, hasty: Lr. III, 7, 10.

Festinately, hastily: LLL III, 6.

Festival, subst. a time of public joy, a day kept sacred and celebrated: H6A I, 6, 26. Rom. III, 2, 29. Per. Prol. 5. *our solemn f.* Shr. III, 2, 103 (i. e. our marriage-feast). *I cannot woo in f. terms,* Ado V, 2, 41. *their f. purses,* Wint. IV, 4, 627.

Festival, adj. celebrated with joy, joyous: *this day shall be kept f.* John III, 1, 76. *all things that we ordained f.* Rom. IV, 5, 84.

Fet (cf. *Deep-fet, Far-fet*), fetched: *whose blood is f. from fathers of war-proof,* H5 III, 1, 18. R3 II, 2, 121.

Fetch, subst. a shift, a stratagem: *it is a f. of wit,* Hml. II, 1, 38 (Ff *f. of warrant*). *mere —es,* Lr. II, 4, 90.

Fetch, vb. 1) to go and bring: Tp. I, 2, 228. V, 32. 84. Meas. V, 253. 474. Err. I, 2, 74. II, 1, 75. III, 1, 84. LLL III, 50. As II, 2, 17. Shr. Ind. 1, 11. Tw. IV, 2, 126. R3 II, 2, 121 (Ff *fet*) etc. *to f. a p. sth.:* Ado II, 1, 274. 276. Mids. II, 1, 133. 169. III, 1, 161. IV, 1, 40. Shr. Ind. 2, 51 etc. Absolutely: *she can f. and carry,* Gentl. III, 1, 274. *to f. down:* Gentl. III, 1, 40. H6C II, 6, 52. *to f. in:* Tp. I, 2, 312. 366. II, 2, 185. Shr. IV, 1, 142. *to f. off:* Tp. IV, 213. All's III, 6, 20. 45. Tw. I, 5, 114. Cor. I, 4, 62. *to f. out:* Meas. IV, 3, 36. Err. V, 157. *to f. up:* As III, 3, 2. Ant. IV, 15, 35.

2) to call for, to come to attend: *to f. you to church,* Ado III, 4, 102. *to f. him,* Caes. II, 1, 212. *I come to f. you to the senate-house,* II, 2, 59. 108. *to f. in* = to go to meet, to attend with solemnity: *go forth and f. their conquering Caesar in,* H5 V Chor. 28.

3) to derive, to draw as from a source: *think you I can a resolution f. from flowery tenderness?* Meas. III, 1, 82. *all the treasons f. from false Mowbray their first head and spring,* R2 I, 1, 97. *they will be kin to us, or they will f. it from Japhet,* H4B II, 2, 128. *forms being —ed from glistering semblances of piety,* H5 II, 2, 116. *I f. my life and being from men of royal siege,* Oth. I, 2, 21.

4) to draw forth, to heave: *thy hounds shall f. shrill echoes from the hollow earth,* Shr. Ind. 2, 48. *as she —ed breath,* Pilgr. 153. Per. I, 4, 15. *how hard he —es breath,* H4A II, 4, 579. *—es her wind so short,* Troil. III, 2, 33. *—es her breath as short,* 35.

5) to recover, to deliver: *whose credit could f. your brother from the manacles of the all-building law,* Meas. II, 4, 93. cf. *f. off,* Tp. IV, 213. All's III, 6, 20. 45. Cor. I, 4, 62.

6) to make, to take (speaking of motions): —*ing mad bounds*, Merch. V, 73. *I'll f. a turn about the garden*, Cymb. I, 1, 81. Intr. *to f. about* = to turn, to veer round: *like a shifted wind unto a sail, it makes the course of thoughts to f. about*, John IV, 2, 24.

7) With *in*, = a) to apprehend, to seize, to take prisoner: *within our files there are enough to f. him in*, Ant. IV, 1, 14. *and swear he 'ld f. us in*, Cymb. IV, 2, 141. b) to take in, to dupe: *you speak this to f. me in*, Ado I, 1, 225.

8) With *off*, = a) to make away with: *will f. off Bohemia*, Wint. I, 2, 334. b) to fleece, to make a prey of: *as I return, I will f. off these justices*, H4B III, 2, 324.

Fetlock, the tuft of hair that grows behind the pastern joint of horses: Ven. 295. H5 IV, 7, 82. H6C II, 3, 21.

Fetter, to shackle, to enchain, to tie: Meas. III, 1, 67. Ado V, 1, 25. All's II, 3, 251. Tw. III, 1, 167. H5 I, 2, 243. H6C V, 7, 11. Tit. II, 1, 15. V, 3, 6. Cymb. V, 4, 8.

Fetters, chains: Hml. III, 3, 25. Ant. I, 2, 120.

Fettle, to dress, to prepare: *f. your fine joints 'gainst Thursday next*, Rom. III, 5, 154.

Feud, quarrel, contention: *wherein my sword had not impressure made of our rank f.* Troil. IV, 5, 132.

Fever, subst. a disease characterised by increase of heat and preternatural thirst: *burning —s, agues pale*, Ven. 739. *the raging fire of f.* Err. V, 75. *this tyrant f. burns me up*, John V, 3, 14. *a burning f.* H4B IV, 1, 56. *fiery f.* H5 IV, 1, 270. *till the high f. seethe your blood*, Tim. IV, 3, 433. Sonn. 147, 1. Phoen. 7. Meas. III, 2, 235. IV, 3, 74. V, 152. LLL IV, 3, 95. 97. John V, 3, 3. Tim. IV, 1, 22. Caes. I, 2, 119. Cymb. IV, 3, 2. Figuratively, = extreme agitation, wild excitement: *in the distraction of this madding f.* Sonn. 119, 8. *felt a f. of the mad*, Tp. I, 2, 209. *an envious f. of emulation*, Troil. I, 3, 133. 134. 139. *life's fitful f.* Mcb. III, 2, 23. Denoting a violent shaking: *to make a shaking f. in your walls*, John II, 228.

Fever, vb. to put in a fever: *the white hand of a lady f. thee*, Ant. III, 13, 138.

Feverous, feverish, affected with a fever: *a f. pulse*, Troil. III, 2, 38. *as if the world were f.* Cor. I, 4, 61. Mcb. II, 3, 66. Figuratively: *a f. life*, Meas. III, 1, 75.

Fever-weakened, debilitated by a fever: H4B I, 1, 140.

Few, not many, a small number: Lucr. 1613. Sonn. 73, 2. Tp. II, 1, 7. V, 166. Meas. II, 1, 282. Ado I, 1, 7. IV, 1, 143. LLL V, 1, 147. Wint. IV, 4, 809. H6A I, 1, 161. H6B II, 4, 69. H6C IV, 1, 86. IV, 6, 29. R3 I, 4, 134. Hml. I, 3, 58. 68 etc. Comp. —*er*: H4A II, 4, 111. H4B I, 3, 47. H5 IV, 3, 22. Superl. —*est*: H6A II, 4, 41. 44. *some f.*: Tp. V, 255. R2 III, 3, 4. III, 4, 86. H4B IV, 5, 102. H6C III, 3, 204. *a f.* = 1) some few: Merch. III, 2, 254. H4A II, 1, 7. H5 II, 2, 89. III, 5, 5. H6C II, 1, 16. Cor. V, 6, 46. Mcb. III, 2, 4. Cymb. IV, 2, 283. 2) few: *O happiness enjoyed but of a f.* Lucr. 22. *where small experience grows but in a f.* Shr. I, 2, 52 (i. e. except in few; M. Edd.: *grows. But in a few,*). *love all, trust*

a f. All's I, 1, 73. *I am solicited, not by a f.* H8 I, 2, 18. — *In f.* = 1) in few words: *thus, then, in f.* H5 I, 2, 245. 2) in short: Tp. I, 2, 144. Meas. III, 1, 237. H4B I, 1, 112. Hml. I, 3, 126. *in a f.*, in the same sense, only by a blunder of M. Edd. in Shr. I, 2, 52; see above.

Fewness, paucity of words, brevity: *f. and truth, 'tis thus*, Meas. I, 4, 39.

Fickle, inconstant, unstable, changeable: Ven. 1141. Sonn. 126, 2. Pilgr. 85. 259. 401. Compl. 5. John II, 583. H4A V, 1, 76. H5 III, 6, 28. H6A IV, 1, 138. Rom. III, 5, 60. 61. 62. Lr. II, 4, 189 (Ff. *fickly*).

Fickleness, inconstancy: H6A V, 3, 134.

Fico (cf. *Figo*), a fig (Spanish): *a f. for the phrase*, Wiv. I, 3, 33.

Fiction, poetical invention, unreal imagination: *an improbable f.* Tw. III, 4, 141. *for thy f., why, thy verse swells with stuff*, Tim. V, 1, 86. *but in a f., in a dream of passion*, Hml. II, 2, 578.

Fiddle, subst. a violin: H8 I, 3, 41.

Fiddle, vb.: *a French song and a fiddle has no fellow. The devil f. 'em*, H8 I, 3, 42; i. e. the devil may treat them with his fiddlestick.

Fiddler, one who plays upon a fiddle: Shr. II, 158 (trisyll.). III, 1, 1. *the f. Apollo*, Troil. III, 3, 305.

Fiddlestick, the bow with which a fiddler plays upon a violin: *the devil rides upon a f.* H4A II, 4, 535 (perhaps = here we have a pretty sight! this is wondrous sport!). *here's my f.* Rom. III, 1, 51.

Fidele, name assumed by Imogen: Cymb. III, 6, 60. IV, 2, 148 etc.

Fidelity, apparently = faith: *by my f., this is not well*, Wiv. IV, 2, 160.

Fidiused, a partic. jocularly formed from the name of Aufidius: *I would not have been so f.* Cor. II, 1, 144; i. e. dealt with, beaten.

Fie, an exclamation of contempt or dislike: Ven. 185. Tp. II, 1, 24. Wiv. I, 1, 181. IV, 5, 24. Meas. II, 4, 42. III, 2, 20. Err. II, 1, 86. II, 2, 154. Mids. II, 1, 239. Merch. III, 4, 79. H6A I, 3, 57. III, 1, 127. V, 4, 17. R3 III, 1, 22 etc. *fie, fie*: Gentl. II, 6, 14. Wiv. III, 3, 229. Ado IV, 1, 96. Merch. I, 1, 46 etc. *fie, fie, fie*: Wiv. II, 2, 328. Meas. II, 2, 172. III, 1, 148 etc. Followed by *on*: Gentl. III, 1, 290. Wiv. IV, 1, 64. 70. V, 5, 97. Meas. IV, 2, 29. Err. V, 27. Ado III, 4, 28. Merch. IV, 1, 101. As II, 7, 62. Shr. IV, 1, 1. H6B IV, 10, 1 etc.

Expressing impatience rather than contempt or disdain: *f. f., you crush me*, Ven. 611. *f. f., fond love, thou art so full of fear*, 1021. *f. f. f. now would she cry; tereu, tereu by and by*, Pilgr. 385. *f. f., how wayward is this foolish love*, Gentl. I, 2, 57. *f. f., he'll never come*, Wiv. IV, 4, 19. *self-harming jealousy! f., beat it hence*, Err. II, 1, 102. *f., now you run this humour out of breath*, IV, 1, 57. *f., painted rhetoric! O, she needs it not*, LLL IV, 3, 239. *f. f., you counterfeit*, Mids. III, 2, 288. *f. f., Gratiano, where are all the rest?* Merch. II, 6, 62. *f. f., no thought of him!* Wint. II, 3, 18. *f. on this storm!* Lr. III, 1, 49. Cor. IV, 2, 53.

Field, 1) plain ground not built on, nor covered with wood; open country: Ven. 8. Pilgr. 355. Wiv. II, 3, 81. 90. V, 5, 72. LLL II, 85. 94. V, 2, 345. Mids. II, 1, 96. As III, 2, 18. Shr. III, 2, 233. H6A II, 2, 25. H6B I, 1, 80. IV, 2, 54. Lr. III, 4, 117 etc. Opposed to the town: Mids. II, 1, 238. III, 2, 398.

Cor. II, 2, 125. Opposed to the sea: *betokened wreck to the seaman, tempest to the f.* Ven. 454. *moving accidents by flood and f.* Oth. I, 3, 135. Figurative use: *why labour you to make it wander in an unknown f.* Err. III, 2, 38. *without covering, save yon f. of stars,* Per. I, 1, 37. *our blest —s,* Cymb. V, 4, 117. Sonn. 2, 2.

2) the ground where war is waged: *Percy is already in the f.* H4A IV, 2, 81. R3 IV, 3, 48. *the power that Edward hath in f.* H6C IV, 8, 35. *to become the f.* John V, 1, 55. *traitors brave the f.* R3 IV, 3, 57. *brave our —s,* John V, 1, 70.

3) the ground where a battle is fought: *making my arms his f.* Ven. 108. *in her fair face's f.* Lucr. 72 (quibbling). 107. R3 I, 4, 56 etc.

4) battle, combat, war: *dare not stay the f.* Ven. 894. *I to be a corporal of his f.* LLL III, 189. *to the f.!* IV, 3, 366. All's III, 1, 23. *won three —s of Sultan Solyman,* Merch. II, 1, 26. *those Italian —s, where noble fellows strike,* All's II, 3, 307. *knighted in the f.* John I, 54. *the noise and rumour of the f.* V, 4, 45. *till —s and blows and groans applaud our sport,* H4A I, 3, 302. *how goes the f.* V, 5, 16. *to get the f.* H6A V, 3, 12 and H6C I, 4, 1. H5 IV, 7, 93. H6A I, 1, 72. I, 4, 81. III, 2, 96. IV, 7, 60. H6B I, 3, 113. IV, 7, 85. H6C I, 1, 90. III, 2, 1 *(slain at Saint Alban's f.).* R3 V, 3, 64. Troil. III, 3, 188. IV, 4, 144. Caes. V, 3, 107. V, 5, 80. Mcb. V, 1, 4 etc. Without the article: *to f.* Lucr. 1430. Troil. I, 1, 5. IV, 4, 145. *from f.* Troil. III, 1, 161 (Q *the f.*). *in f.* LLL V, 2, 556. Figuratively: *in a f. of feasts,* Ant. II, 1, 23.

5) any combat or contention: *the f. is won,* Shr. IV, 5, 23. *to challenge him the f.* Tw. II, 3, 137 (i. e. a single combat); cf. *divided by any voice or order of the f.* Troil. IV, 5, 70. *go before to f.* Rom. III, 1, 61. *the very parings of our nails shall pitch a f.* H6A III, 1, 103. *to the f.* Cymb. IV, 2, 42 (i. e. to the chase).

6) the surface of a shield: *beauty, in that white intituled, from Venus' doves doth challenge that fair f.* Lucr. 58. cf. the quibble in v. 72. A similar quibble perhaps intended in H6B IV, 2, 54.

Field-bed (properly a bed contrived for carrying into the field) a bed in the open air: *this f. is too cold for me,* Rom. II, 1, 40.

Field-dew, dew taken from the field: Mids. V, 422.

Fielded, engaged in fight: *our f. friends,* Cor. I, 4, 12.

Fiend, devil: Ven. 638. Sonn. 144, 9 (cf. Pilgr. 23). 145, 11. Compl. 317. Phoen. 6. Tp. III, 3, 102. Wiv. II, 2, 313. Err. II, 2, 35. IV, 4, 110. Merch. II, 2, 2. 10. 11 etc. Shr. III, 2, 157. Tw. III, 4, 101. 124. 237. IV, 2, 29. John IV, 3, 123. V, 7, 47. R2 IV, 270. H4A II, 4, 404. H4B II, 4, 196. 359. H5 II, 1, 97. II, 2, 111. III, 3, 16. H6A II, 1, 46. H6B I, 4, 43. III, 3, 21. R3 I, 2, 34. I, 4, 58. IV, 4, 75. Cor. IV, 5, 98. Tit. II, 3, 100. IV, 2, 79. Rom. III, 2, 75. 81. Mcb. IV, 3, 233. V, 5, 43. V, 8, 19. Hml. II, 2, 519. Lr. I, 4, 281. III, 4, 46. 52 etc. III, 6, 18. 31. IV, 1, 61. IV, 2, 60. IV, 6, 72. 79. 129. Oth. IV, 1, 71. V, 2, 275. Cymb. III, 4, 129. III, 5, 83. V, 5, 210. Applied to women: Err. IV, 3, 66. Shr. I, 1, 88. H6A III, 2, 45. 52. Rom. III, 5, 235. Lr. IV, 2, 66. Cymb. V, 5, 47.

Fiend-like, devilish: Tit. V, 1, 45. Mcb. V, 8, 69.

Fierce, 1) savage, furious: Sonn. 19, 3. 23,

3. Mids. III, 2, 325. John I, 17. II, 68. IV, 1, 74. 120. V, 2, 158. R2 II, 1, 173. V, 5, 110. H5 III, 3, 23. R3 I, 2, 71. Troil. V, 5, 6. Cor. I, 10, 27. Tit. II, 3, 165. Rom. V, 3, 38. Caes. II, 2, 19. III, 1, 263. Lr. II, 4, 175. III, 7, 57. Per. V, 3, 88.

2) passionate, wild, impetuous: *there is no following her in this f. vein,* Mids. III, 2, 82. *such temperate order in so f. a cause,* John III, 4, 12. *f. extremes in their continuance will not feel themselves,* V, 7, 13. *his rash f. blaze of riot,* R2 II, 1, 33. *in f. tempest is he coming,* H5 II, 4, 99 (dissyll.?). *such f. alarums both of hope and fear,* H6A V, 5, 85. *yet have I f. affections,* Ant. I, 5, 17.

3) wild, disordered, irregular: *think no more of this night's accidents but as the f. vexation of a dream,* Mids. IV, 1, 74. *this f. abridgment hath to it circumstantial branches,* Cymb. V, 5, 382. *the like precurse of f. events,* Hml. I, 1, 121.

4) immoderate, excessive: *what had he to do in these f. vanities,* H8 I, 1, 54. *the f. wretchedness that glory brings us,* Tim. IV, 2, 30.

5) fiery, ardent, strenuous: *with all the f. endeavour of your wit,* LLL V, 2, 863; cf. *would beget opinion of my more f. endeavour,* Lr. II, 1, 36. *f. to their skill, and to their fierceness valiant,* Troil. I, 1, 8. *not f. and terrible only in strokes,* Cor. I, 4, 57. *take more composition and f. quality,* Lr. I, 2, 12. Perhaps in this sense, but more probably in that of the French *fier,* proud, from which it is derived, in H6B IV, 9, 45: *he is f. and cannot brook hard language.* Adverbially: *England his approaches makes as f. as waters,* H5 II, 4, 9. *midday sun f. bent against their faces,* H6A I, 1, 14 (as if it came from *fire;* cf. def. 5).

Fiercely, strenuously: *both sides f. fought,* H6C I, 1, 121.

Fierceness, savageness, rough valour: *my name is Pistol called. It sorts well with your f.* H5 IV, 1, 63. *they called us for our f. English dogs,* H6A I, 5, 25. *fierce to their skill, and to their f. valiant,* Troil. I, 1, 8 (cf. *Fierce,* def. 5).

Fiery, 1) consisting of fire: Meas. III, 1, 122. LLL V, 2, 375. Mids. II, 1, 161. All's II, 1, 165. John IV, 1, 63. R2 III, 3, 64. H4A III, 1, 14. H4B II, 4, 288. H6C II, 6, 12. R3 V, 3, 20. 350. Troil. V, 3, 53. Cor. III, 2, 91. V, 3, 60. Rom. II, 3, 4. Caes. I, 3, 130. II, 2, 19.

2) splendent, bright: *the f. glow-worm,* Mids. III, 1, 173. *yon f. oes,* III, 2, 188. *your skill shall, like a star i' the darkest night, stick f. off,* Hml. V, 2, 268. *more f. by night's blackness,* Ant. I, 4, 13. *the f. orbs above,* Cymb. I, 6, 35.

3) hot: *the f. fever,* H5 IV, 1, 270.

4) ardent, spirited: Sonn. 51, 11. LLL IV, 3, 322. Shr. III, 1, 48. All's II, 3, 300. John II, 67. 358. V, 2, 114. R2 V, 2, 8. H4A IV, 1, 109. H4B IV, 3, 108. H6C I, 4, 87. R3 IV, 3, 54. Hml. II, 1, 33. IV, 3, 45.

5) irritable, passionate: *the f. Tybalt,* Rom. I, 1, 116. *the f. quality of the duke,* Lr. II, 4, 93. 97. 105. *f. eyes* = angry eyes: Ven. 219. H6C II, 5, 131. Caes. I, 2, 186. *how f. and how sharp he looks,* Err. IV, 4, 53.

Fiery-footed, having feet of fire: Rom. III, 2, 1.

Fiery-kindled (O. Edd. not hyphened), inflamed: *f. spirits,* John II, 358.

Fiery-pointed (O. Edd. not hyphened) throwing darts with points of fire: *the fair and f. sun,* Lucr. 372.

Fiery-red, red with fire, red as fire: *the eastern gate, all f.* Mids. III, 2, 391. *f. with haste,* R2 II, 3, 58.

Fife, a small pipe used as a wind-instrument: *the drum and the f.* Ado II, 3, 14. Oth. III, 3, 352. *the drum and the vile squealing of the wry-necked f.* Merch. II, 5, 30 (meaning here, according to some, the musician himself). *trumpets, sackbuts, psalteries and —s,* Cor. V, 4, 52.

Fife, Scotch county: H4A I, 1, 71. 95. Mcb. I, 2, 48. II, 4, 36. IV, 1, 72. 151. V, 1, 47.

Fift, see *Fifth.*

Fifteen, five and ten: Wiv. II, 2, 14. III, 5, 11. Merch. II, 2, 170. Shr. Ind. 2, 81. 83. 115. All's IV, 3, 190. Wint. IV, 2, 4. IV, 3, 34. John II, 275. H4B II, 1, 186. H5 I, 1, 13. III, 7, 136. IV, 8, 84. Caes. II, 1, 59 (some M. Edd. *fourteen*).

Fifteenth, used as a subst., the fifteenth part of all the personal property of a subject: *demand a whole f.* H6B I, 1, 133. Plur. *fifteens:* IV, 7, 25.

Fifth (O. Edd. *fift;* in Per. II, 2, 36 Ff *fifth*), the next to the fourth: LLL V, 1, 57. Merch. I, 2, 137. As V, 4, 99. Shr. Ind. I, 13. John IV, 2, 183. H4B IV, 5, 120. V, 3, 119. H6A I, 1, 6. 52. I, 4, 79. II, 5, 82. III, 1, 196. IV, 3, 52. V, 1, 31. H6B II, 2, 15. 46. IV, 8, 17. Troil. II, 1, 134. Per. II, 2, 36 etc.

Fifty, five times ten: Wiv. III, 4, 49. Meas. III, 2, 134. LLL IV, 2, 62. IV, 3, 243. As V, 1, 63. Shr. I, 2, 81. All's IV, 3, 184. 187. 188. Wint. IV, 4, 802. H4A II, 4, 205. 467. IV, 2, 15. H4B III, 1, 96. H6A III, 4, 6. IV, 7, 73. Troil. I, 2, 171. 175. Tim. II, 2, 201. Hml. II, 2, 383. Lr. I, 4, 316. II, 4, 210. 240. 262. Ant. I, 2, 27 etc.

Fifty-fold, fifty times told: *f. a cuckold,* Ant. I, 2, 69.

Fig, subst. the fruit of the tree Ficus: Mids. III, 1, 170. John II, 162. Ant. V, 2, 235. 342. *I love long life better than —s,* Ant. I, 2, 32 (a proverbial phrase). Used to denote a contemptible trifle: *a f. for Peter!* H6B II, 3, 67. *virtue! a f.!* Oth. I, 3, 322. *she's full of most blessed condition. Blessed —'s end!* II, 1, 256. *the f. of Spain,* H5 III, 6, 62 (an expression of contempt, pretended to be of Spanish origin, which consisted in thrusting out the thumb between the first and second fingers).

Fig, vb. to insult by thrusting out the thumb between the two first fingers: *and f. me like the bragging Spaniard,* H4B V, 3, 123 (Pistol's speech).

Fight, subst. 1) combat, battle: Ven. 114 (*the god of f.*). 746. Lucr. 62. Sonn. 25, 9 (*famoused for f.*). Pilgr. 280. Meas. I, 3, 42. Merch. III, 2, 62. John I, 266. H6A I, 5, 27. II, 2, 22. III, 1, 93. IV, 2, 56 etc. etc. *single f.* = a combat between two persons, H4A V, 1, 100. V, 2, 47. H6C IV, 7, 75. Ant. III, 7, 31. IV, 4, 37. *fight,* alone, = single combat: Gentl. IV, 1, 28. As V, 2, 33. H6A IV, 1, 116. Troil. IV, 5, 90.

2) cloth and canvass to screen the combatants in ships: *up with your —s,* Wiv. II, 2, 142.

Fight, vb. (impf. and part. *fought; well-foughten* in H5 IV, 6, 18); 1) intr. to contend in arms, to combat; absol. or with *against* or *with* before the persons or party opposed: Lucr. 68. 230. 273. 428.

1402. 1436. Compl. 203. Wiv. II, 1, 19. LLL I, 1, 230. V, 2, 659. Mids. II, 1, 241. H6A I, 2, 127. III, 1, 100. III, 3, 74. Ant. III, 7, 28 etc. etc. *—ing men* = armed soldiers, combatants: R2 III, 2, 70. H5 IV, 3, 3. *this is fought indeed!* Ant. IV, 7, 4 (cf. *Be*). Used of single combats: Wiv. I, 4, 28. II, 1, 240. II, 3, 24. Ado IV, 1, 301. V, 1, 118. Mids. III, 2, 354. Wint. V, 2, 140. H6B II, 3, 57. 71. Ant. IV, 2, 1. Cymb. II, 1, 21. 23 etc. *I cannot f.* = I am ignorant of the use of arms, H6B I, 3, 217. Used of beasts: John IV, 1, 116. Tit. V, 1, 102. Of mental combats: *the —ing conflict of her hue,* Ven. 345. *leaden slumber with life's strength doth f.* Lucr. 124. *desire doth f. with grace,* 712. *crooked eclipses 'gainst his glory f.* Sonn. 60, 7. *upon thy side against myself I'll f.* 88, 3. *to f. against his passion,* Ado III, 1, 83. *her —ing soul,* Hml. III, 4, 113. *in my heart there was a kind of —ing,* V, 2, 4. Followed by an accus. indicating the result: *you shall f. your hearts out,* Troil. III, 2, 54 (i. e. till you have enough of it. Similarly of an amorous encounter: H6C III, 2, 23). With an accus. denoting a measure: *I shall never be able to fight a blow,* H6B I, 3, 220 (not differing, in a grammatical view, from: *we fought a long hour,* H4A V, 4, 151).

2) trans.: *to f. a battle,* H5 IV, 7, 98. H6A I, 1, 31. Tit. I, 66. Lr. IV, 7, 97. V, 1, 40. *a combat,* Lucr. 1298. Pilgr. 215. Wint. V, 2, 80. John V, 2, 43. *a course,* Mcb. V, 7, 2. *a field,* H6A I, 1, 72. *a fray,* Wiv. II, 1, 208. H6C II, 1, 107. *a quarrel,* As V, 4, 49. *wars,* John II, 4. *to fight out* = not to cease fighting for a cause, till it be decided: *that true hand that fought Rome's quarrel out,* Tit. V, 3, 102. *f. it out,* H6A I, 1, 99. I, 2, 128. III, 2, 66. H6C I, 1, 117. I, 4, 10. *To fight a p.* = to fight against? *I'll fight their legions o'er,* Tp. III, 3, 103 (= against all their legions, one after another? or: I'll fight, till their legions, one by one, are made away with? in which latter case it would be the accus. of the result. Perhaps *to fight over* = to outfight; cf. *Over*).

Fighter, 1) a combatant, a warrior: *to the latter end of a fray ... fits a dull f.* H4A IV, 2, 86.

2) a swordsman: Wiv. II, 3, 44. Tw. III, 4, 265. Wint. III, 3, 116.

Fig-leaves, leaves of a fig-tree: Ant. V, 2, 354.

Figo (cf. *Fico*), fig, a contemptible trifle: *f. for thy friendship,* H5 III, 6, 60. *the f. for thee,* IV, 1, 60 (= I do not care for thee).

Figure, subst. 1) form, shape: *—s of delight, drawn after you,* Sonn. 98, 11. *a f. trenched in ice,* Gentl. III, 2, 6. *before so noble and so great a f. be stamped upon it,* Meas. I, 1, 50; cf. Merch. II, 7, 56 and Cymb. V, 4, 25. *in the f. of a lamb,* Ado I, 1, 15. *as a form of wax resolveth from his f. 'gainst the fire,* John V, 4, 25. *when we see the f. of the house,* H4B I, 3, 43. *key-cold f. of a holy king,* R3 I, 2, 5. *whose f. even this instant cloud puts on,* H8 I, 1, 225. *that unbodied f. of the thought,* Troil. I, 3, 16. *in such indexes is seen the baby f. of the giant mass of things to come,* 345. *a gate of steel fronting the sun receives and renders back his f.* III, 3, 123. *in the same f. like the king,* Hml. I, 1, 41. *this portentous f.* 109. *a f. like your father,* I, 2, 199. *what would your gracious f.?* III, 4, 104. *the native act and f. of my heart,* Oth. I, 1, 62. *a fixed f. for the time of scorn,* IV, 2, 54. *in as like a f.* Cymb. III, 3, 96.

2) an image formed by any kind of art: *the silken —s,* Compl. 17 (i. e. embroidery). *to leave the f. or disfigure it,* Mids. I, 1, 51. *there shall no f. at such rate be set,* Rom. V, 3, 301. *these pencilled —s,* Tim. I, 1, 159. *—s such and such,* Cymb. II, 2, 26. *never saw I —s so likely to report themselves,* II, 4, 82.

3) image in general, representation: *bravely the f. of this harpy hast thou performed,* Tp. III, 3, 83. *what f. of us think you he will bear?* Meas. I, 1, 17. *the f. of God's majesty,* R2 IV, 125. *in Helicanus may you well descry a f. of truth, of faith, of loyalty,* Per. V, 3, 92.

4) idea, imagination: *a spirit full of forms, —s, shapes,* LLL IV, 2, 68. *that the great f. of a council frames by self-unable motion,* All's III, 1, 12. *he apprehends a world of —s here, but not the form of what he should attend,* H4A I, 3, 209. Denoting idle fancies tending to disquiet the mind: *to scrape the —s out of your husband's brains,* Wiv. IV, 2, 231. *thou hast no —s nor no fantasies which busy care draws in the brains of men,* Caes. II, 1, 231.

5) a character denoting a number: *we fortify in paper and in — s,* H4B I, 3, 56. *a crooked f. may attest in little place a million,* H5 Prol. 15. *thou art an O without a f.* Lr. I, 4, 212. *hearts, tongues, —s . . . . cannot think, speak, cast . . .* Ant. III, 2, 16. Quibbling: *yet doth beauty, like a dial-hand, steal from his f. and no pace perceived,* Sonn. 104, 10. *a most fine f. To prove you a cipher,* LLL I, 2, 58. *there I shall see mine own f. Which I take to be either a fool or a cipher,* As III, 2, 307.

6) a character in writing, a letter: *and write in thee the —s of their love, ever to read them thine,* Tim. V, 1, 157. *our captain hath in every f. skill, an aged interpreter,* V, 3, 7. Perhaps, at least quibbling, also in Oth. I, 1, 62.

7) a turn of rhetoric: *she wooes you by a f.* Gentl. II, 1, 154. *a most fine f.* LLL I, 2, 58. *what is the f.?* V, 1, 67. *—s pedantical,* V, 2, 408. *it is a f. in rhetoric,* As V, 1, 45. *there is —s in all things,* H5 IV, 7, 35. *a foolish f.* Hml. II, 2, 98. Quibbling: *he will throw a f. in her face,* Shr. I, 2, 114 (alluding perhaps to what is called the ten commandments).

8) a peculiar mode of fortune-telling: *she works by charms, by spells, by the f.* Wiv. IV, 2, 185 (certainly not by the horoscope, as Johnson interprets it, but perhaps, after an old German custom, by throwing molten lead into cold water and interpreting the fantastical figures thus formed).

Figure, vb. 1) to mark or adorn with figures: *the vaulty top of heaven —d quite o'er with burning meteors,* John V, 2, 53. *my —d goblets,* R2 III, 3, 150.

2) to represent or indicate by a typical resemblance: *wings and no eyes f. unheedy haste,* Mids. I, 1, 237. *white investments f. innocence,* H4B IV, 1, 45.

3) to show, to reveal: *there is a history in all men's lives, —ing the nature of the times deceased,* H4B III, 1, 81. *in this the heaven —s some event,* H6C II, 1, 32. *I would I knew thy heart. 'tis —d in my tongue,* R3 I, 2, 194.

4) to indicate not directly, but by signs: *he refused to take her —d proffer,* Pilgr. 52.

5) to imagine: *what's in the brain that ink may character which hath not —d to thee my true spirit?* Sonn. 108, 2. *—ing that they their passions likewise lent me,* Compl. 199. *thou art always —ing diseases in me,* Meas. I, 2, 53 (cf. *Self-figured*).

Filbert, the hazel nut: Tp. II, 2, 175.

Filch, to steal, to pilfer; 1) intr.: Sonn. 75,6. Wiv. I, 3, 28. H5 III, 2, 48.

2) tr.: Mids. I, 1, 36. Oth. III, 3, 315. With *from:* Oth. III, 3, 159.

File, subst. 1) a line or wire on which papers are strung in due order for preservation: *either it is there, or it is upon a f. with the duke's other letters in my tent,* Alls IV, 3, 231.

2) list, catalogue: *the muster f. amounts not to fifteen thousand,* Alls IV, 3, 189. *our present musters grow upon the f. to five and twenty thousand,* H4B I, 3, 10. *he makes up the f. of all the gentry,* H8 I, 1, 75. *the valued f. distinguishes the swift, the slow,* Mcb. III, 1, 95 (i. e. the list which states the value of each). *if you have a station in the f.* 102. *I have a f. of all the gentry,* V, 2, 8.

3) the number, multitude: *the greater f. of the subject held the duke to be wise,* Meas. III, 2, 144. *and front but in that f. where others tell steps with me,* H8 I, 2, 42. *a f. of boys behind them,* V, 4, 59. *but for our gentlemen, the common f.* Cor. I, 6, 43. *I mean us of the right-hand f.* II, 1, 26. *three performers are the f. when all the rest do nothing,* Cymb. V, 3, 30.

4) line, rank of soldiers: *great Mars, I put myself into thy f.* Alls III, 3, 9. *to instruct for the doubling of —s,* IV, 3, 303. *let him choose out of my —s my best and freshest men,* Cor. V, 6, 34. *are his —s as full as thy report?* Tim. V, 2, 1. *his eyes that o'er the —s und musters of the war have glowed,* Ant. I, 1, 3. *within our —s there are enough to fetch him in,* IV, 1, 12.

File, vb. 1) to rub with a file: *—d steel,* Tw. III, 3, 5. *—d keys off,* Wint. IV, 4, 624. Hence = to polish, to refine: *precious phrase by all the Muses —d,* Sonn. 85, 4. *when your countenance —d up his line,* 86, 13 (O. Edd. *fild,* some M. Edd. *filled*). *—d talk,* Pilgr. 306. *his tongue is —d,* LLL V, 1, 12. *she shall f. our engines with advice,* Tit. II, 1, 123.

2) to defile, to stain: *for Banquo's issue have I —d my mind,* Mcb. III, 1, 65.

3) to march in a line, to keep pace: *my endeavours have ever come too short of my desires, yet —d with my abilities,* H8 III, 2, 171 (O. Edd. *fill'd*).

Filial, pertaining to or becoming a child in relation to the parents: Compl. 270. H4B IV, 5, 39. Hml. I, 2, 91. Lr. III, 4, 14.

Fill, subst. the shaft or thill of a carriage: *an you draw backward, we'll put you in the —s,* Troil. III, 2, 48 (cf. *Fill-horse*).

Fill, subst. as much as is enough to satisfy desire: *gaze your f.* Shr. I, 1, 73. *flowed their f.* H6C II, 5, 72. 113. Troil. IV, 5, 236. Tim. V, 4, 73. Hml. IV, 5, 129. *thou hast thy f. of blood,* Troil. V, 8, 4.

Fill, vb. 1) trans. a) to make full, to replenish: Lucr. 1234. Sonn. 112, 1. Tp. V, 81. II, 2, 181; cf. H4A IV, 2, 2; H4B V, 3, 56. R3 V, 3, 63 and Ant. III, 13, 184. Meas. IV, 3, 160. As V, 1, 46. Alls I, 2, 69 (*I f. a place*). Wint. III, 3, 22. IV, 4, 465 (*to f. his grave*). R3 IV, 4, 91 (*to f. the scene*). Cor. II, 1, 227. Caes. III, 2, 94. Cymb. III, 2, 59 etc. *to f. a sail* = to swell it: Tp. Epil. 11. H6C II, 6, 35. Per. V, 2, 15. *to f. your song* (= to give it a full concord by accompanying it) Gentl. I, 2, 95. *delivers me to f. the time*, Alls III, 7, 33 (= to do what must be done in that time). — Followed by *with:* Lucr. 946. 1804. Sonn. 17, 2. 63, 3. Tp. I, 2, 370. IV, 233. Gentl. II, 3, 58. V, 4, 112. Meas. III, 2, 182. As III, 2, 150. Tw. III, 1, 115. Wint. III, 2, 167 (*—ed with honour*). John IV, 1, 129 (*I'll f. these dogged spies with false reports*); cf. H6A II, 2, 43 and Mcb. III, 1, 32. R2 II, 2, 131. H4A III, 2, 101. H6A V, 4, 35. H6B III, 2, 69. H6C III, 3, 13. H8 V, 3, 15. Troil. II, 2, 102. Ant. I, 3, 63. III, 13, 18 etc. *my endeavours have ever come too short of my desires, yet —ed with my abilities*, H8 III, 2, 171 (i. e. they had the full support of my abilities. Most M. Edd. *filed*). *to f. full: f. it full with wills*, Sonn. 136, 6. *have —ed their pockets full of pebble stones*, H6A III, 1, 80. R3 I, 4, 143. Cor. I, 3, 94. *to f. up* = 1) to fill: *in his eminence doth —s it up* (viz the place) Meas. I, 2, 168; cf. As I, 2, 204; John III, 4, 93; H4A IV, 2, 35 and Oth. III, 3, 247 (= the simple *fill* in Alls I, 2, 69). *time as long would be —ed up with our thanks*, Wint. I, 2, 4. *f. up her enemies' ranks*, John V, 2, 28. *f. up chronicles*, H4A I, 3, 171. *his hours —ed up with riots*, H5 I, 1, 56. *are my chests —ed up with extorted gold?* H6B IV, 7, 105. *goodness and he f. up one monument*, H8 II, 1, 94 (cf. *fill:* Wint. IV, 4, 465). *have your mouth —ed up*, H, 3, 87. *f. up the time*, Mcb. III, 1, 24. *f. up the cistern of my lust*, IV, 3, 62. *to f. up your will*, 88. 2) to fill entirely and to the brim: *—ed up with mud*, Mids. II, 1, 98. *f. up the measure of her will*, John II, 556. *—ed up with guts*, H4A III, 3, 175. Hence 3) to close: *I'll f. your grave up*, Wint. V, 3, 101. *to f. the mouth of deep defiance up*, H4A III, 2, 116 (= to stop, to put to silence; cf. Mouth). 4) to make complete: *as minutes f. up hours*, Lucr. 297. *your countenance —ed up his line*, Sonn. 86, 13 (O. Edd. *fild*, some M. Edd. *filed*). *how many inches doth f. up one mile*, LLL V, 2, 193. *one that —s up the cry*, Oth. II, 3, 370. 5) to fulfil: *to f. up your grace's request in my stead*, Merch. IV, 1, 160.

b) to satisfy, to satiate: *although to-day thou f. thy hungry eyes*, Sonn. 56, 5. *with a body —ed*, H5 IV, 1, 286. *to see meat f. knaves*, Tim. I, 1, 271. Absolutely: *the one is —ing still, never complete.* Tim. IV, 3, 244.

c) to occupy: *thy place is —ed*, H6C III, 1, 16.

d) to pour in: *f. me some wine*, Tim. III, 1, 9. Absolutely: *f., Lucius, till the wine o'erswell the cup*, Caes. IV, 3, 161. *f. full*, Mcb. III, 4, 88. *f. till the cup be hid*, Ant. II, 7, 93. *f. to your mistress' lips*, Per. II, 3, 51.

2) intr. to grow full, to be satiated: *she feeds, yet never —eth*, Ven. 548.

Fillet, 1) a band tied round the head: Compl. 33. 2) meat rolled together and tied round: *f. of a fenny snake*, Mcb. IV, 1, 12.

Fill-horse (Q1 *pil-horse*, Ff Q 2. 3. 4 *phil-horse*, some M. Edd. *thill-horse*) shaft-horse: Merch. II, 2, 100.

Fillip, to strike with a jerk of the finger: H4B I, 2, 255.* Troil. IV, 5, 45. Cor. V, 3, 59 (Ff *fillop*).

Filly foal, a female colt: Mids. II, 1, 46.

Film, subst. the thin skin which separates the seeds in pods: Rom. I, 4, 63.

Film, vb. to cover with a thin skin: *it will but skin and f. the ulcerous place*, Hml. III, 4, 147.

Filorio, see *Philario.*

Filth, 1) dirt: Lucr. 1010. Meas. III, 1, 93. H6B IV, 1, 71. Lr. II, 3, 9. Per. IV, 6, 186.

2) pollution: *when we in our viciousness grow hard, the gods in our own f. drop our clear judgements*, Ant. III, 13, 113.

3) Used as a term of extreme contempt, when applied to persons: *f. as thou art*, Tp. I, 2, 346. *the f. and scum of Kent*, H6B IV, 2, 130. *sweep the court clean of such f. as thou art*, IV, 7, 35. *to general —s convert, green virginity*, Tim. IV, 1, 6 (i. e. drabs, prostitutes; cf. *Filthy* def. 3). *—s savour but themselves*, Lr. IV, 2, 39. *f., thou liest*, Oth. V, 2, 231.

Filthy, 1) dirty: *in the f. mantled pool*, Tp. IV, 182 (some M. Edd. *filthy-mantled*). *this f. witness* (viz blood) Mcb. II, 2, 47.

2) foggy, thick: *o'erblows the f. and contagious clouds*, H5 III, 3, 31. *hover through the fog and f. air*, Mcb. I, 1, 12.

3) foul, scurvy, low, extremely contemptible, applied to things as well as persons: *'tis lewd and f.* (viz a cap) Shr. IV, 3, 65. *dowlas, f. dowlas*, H4A III, 3, 79. *a f. piece of work*, Tim. I, 1, 202. *her most f. bargain*, Oth. V, 2, 157. *f. scurvy lord*, Alls II, 3, 250. *you f. bung*, H4B II, 4, 137. *you f. famished correctioner*, V, 4, 22. *a very f. rogue*, Troil. V, 4, 31. *f. hags!* Mcb. IV, 1, 115. *f. knave*, Lr. II, 2, 17. *O f. traitor*, III, 7, 32. Synonymous to lewd, bawdy, debauched, obscene: *these f. vices*, Meas. II, 4, 42. III, 2, 24. *a f. officer he is in those suggestions for the young earl*, Alls III, 5, 18. *sung to f. tunes*, H4A II, 2, 49. *the worst is f. and would not hold taking*, Tim. I, 2, 158. *hates the slime that sticks on f. deeds*, Oth. V, 2, 149.

Fin, the limb by which the fish balances its body: Tp. II, 2, 35. Err. III, 1, 79. 82. Cor. I, 1, 184.

Finally, lastly: *lastly and f.* Wiv. I, 1, 142 (Evans' speech).

Finch, the bird Fringilla: Mids. III, 1, 133. *f. egg*, used as a term of contempt: Troil. V, 1, 41 (cf. *Egg*).

Find, (impf. and part. *found*) 1) to discover by seeking; a) absol.: *hopeless to f.* Err. I, 1, 136. *without seeking f.* Cymb. V, 4, 139. b) tr.: Tp. I, 2, 417. III, 3, 9. Gentl. I, 2, 119. IV, 4, 64. Wiv. III, 3, 211. III, 5, 83. Meas. I, 2, 180 etc. etc. With *forth: to f. his fellow forth*, Err. I, 2, 37. *to f. the other forth*, Merch. I, 1, 143. With *out:* Gentl. III, 1, 259. Wiv. III, 3, 173. Err. III, 2, 117. Merch. II, 8, 51. H6A V, 4, 4. H6B V, 1, 169 etc.

2) to discover, to make out, to trace out: *I gave him gentle looks thereby to f. that which thyself hast now disclosed to me*, Gentl. III, 1, 31. *to f. his title with some shows of truth*, H5 I, 2, 72 (= to trace out; most M. Edd., following the spurious Q.: *to fine*). *inspire me, that I may this treason f.* Tit. IV, 1, 67. *the old man hath found their guilt*, IV, 2, 26. *f. me to marry me with Octavius Caesar*, Ant. I, 2, 28. With *out:* Lucr. 1146. Wiv. II, 1, 130. Meas. II, 2, 75. IV, 6, 10. V, 239. Err. III, 2, 120. Mids. II, 2, 39. IV, 1, 108 etc.

3) to meet with, to light upon, to get: *the shame and fault —s no excuse nor end*, Lucr. 238. *what torment I did f. thee in*, Tp. I, 2, 287. *there shalt thou f. the mariners asleep*, V, 98. *in one voyage did Claribel her husband f. at Tunis, and Ferdinand, her brother, found a wife*, 209. 210. 280. Gentl. II, 1, 175. IV, 4, 94. Wiv. I, 4, 68. III, 2, 47 etc. etc. *we*

must have you f. your legs, H6B II, 1, 147. Absol.: *fast bind, fast f.* Merch. II, 5, 54. (*to f. in one's heart,* see *Heart*).

4) to see, to perceive, to experience: *by my prescience I f. my zenith doth depend upon a most auspicious star,* Tp. I, 2, 181. III, 3, 33. 47. IV, 1, 10. Wiv. III, 3, 88. III, 4, 95. Meas. IV, 1, 54. Shr. I, 1, 156. H6A III, 2, 98. H8 IV, 2, 66. Oth. I, 3, 357. Ant. IV, 14, 122 etc. With a double accus.: —*ing yourself desired of such a person,* Meas. II, 4, 91. *you shall f. her the infernal Ate,* Ado II, 1, 263. *what a sprat you shall f. him,* Alls III, 6, 113. *they shall f. dear deer of us,* H6A IV, 2, 54. *found false,* R3 V, 1, 14. *you shall f. me a grave man,* Rom. III, 1, 101. With an inf.: *thou shalt f. those children nursed ... to take a new acquaintance,* Sonn. 77, 10. *till I found it to be true,* Shr. I, 1, 153. *I have found myself to fail,* Alls III, 1, 14. *you shall f. yourself to be well thanked,* V, 1, 36. Absolutely: *your ignorance which —s not till it feels,* Cor. III, 3, 129. Singular expression: *in what he did profess, well found,* Alls II, 1, 105; cf. Cor. II, 2, 48.

5) to feel: *I f. they (my eyes) are inclined to do so,* Tp. II, 1, 192. *I f. not myself disposed to sleep,* II, 1, 201. *the poor beetle —s a pang as great as when a giant dies,* Meas. III, 1, 80. *we must f. an evident calamity, though we had our wish,* Cor. V, 3, 111.

6) to think, to judge; absol. *I speak but as I f.* Shr. II, 66. trans.: —*ing his usurpation most unjust,* H6A II, 5, 68. *is he found guilty?* H8 II, 1, 7. *the crowner hath sat on her, and —s it Christian burial,* Hml. V, 1, 5. *'tis found so,* 8. *bring us what she says, and what you f. of her,* Ant. V, 1, 68.

7) to detect, to unmask, to see through: *I have now found thee,* Alls II, 3, 216. II, 4, 32. *you were the first that found me,* V, 2, 46. *you have found me,* H4A I, 3,3. *I am a king that f. thee,* H5 IV, 1, 276. *if she f. him not, to England send him,* Hml. III, 1, 193. *there I found 'em, there I smelt 'em out,* Lr. IV, 6, 104. *the woman hath found him already,* Oth. II, 1, 253. With *out*: *but when you f. him out, you have him ever after,* Alls III, 6, 100.

Finder, discoverer: *we will bring the device to the bar and crown thee for a f. of madmen,* Tw. III,4, 154. In Oth. II, 1, 246 Ff *a f. of occasions,* Qq *a finder-out.*

Finder-out, discoverer: Wint. V, 2, 131. Oth. II, 1, 246 (Ff *finder*).

Find-fault, fault-finder, detractor: H5 V, 2, 298.

Finding, subst. a thing found: *go you the next way with your —s,* Wint. III, 3, 132.

Fine, subst. 1) end, conclusion: *the f. is, I will live a bachelor,* Ado I, 1, 247. *the f. is the crown,* Alls IV, 4, 35. *is this the f. of his —s,* Hml. V, 1, 115. *in f.* = finally, in the end: Alls III, 7, 19. 33. IV, 3, 62. V, 3, 215. H6A I, 4, 34. Hml. II, 2, 69. IV, 7, 134. V, 2, 15. Lr. II, 1, 50.

2) pecuniary punishment, mulct: Merch. IV, 1, 372. 381. H6A I, 3, 64. H8 V, 4, 84. Cor. III, 3, 15. Rom. III, 1, 195. (= a sum of money, by way of quibbling, in Err. II, 2, 76). Sometimes = punishment in general: *the faults whose f. stands in record,* Meas. II, 2, 40. *paying the f. of rated treachery even with a treacherous f. of all your lives,* John V, 4, 37. 38. *what faults he made before the last, I think*

might have found easy —s, Cor. V, 6, 65. In Rom. I, 5, 96 O. Edd. *sin,* M. Edd., quite unnecessarily, *fine.*

3) a sum of money paid to the lord by his tenant, for permission to alienate or transfer his lands to another: *a great buyer of land, with his statutes, his recognizances, his —s, his double vouchers, his recoveries,* Hml. V, 1, 114. 115. *with f. and recovery,* a term of law denoting absolute ownership: *if the devil have him not in fee-simple, with f. and recovery,* Wiv. IV, 2, 225. Somewhat loosely used in Err. II, 2, 75: *there's no time for a man to recover his hair that grows bald by nature. May he not do it by f. and recovery? Yes, to pay a f. for a periwig and recover the lost hair of another man* (Perhaps *by f. and recovery* = by finery and re-covery, i. e. by making himself fine and re-covering his head with another man's hair).

Fine, vb. 1) to punish: *to f. the faults,* Meas. II, 2, 40. *why would he for the momentary trick be perdurably —d?* III, 1, 115. *the nobles hath he —d for ancient quarrels,* R2 II, 1, 247 (here undoubtedly meaning a pecuniary punishment).

2) to fix as the sum to be paid: *I have —d these bones of mine for ransom,* H5 IV, 7, 72.

3) to refine, to purify: *time's office is to f. the hate of foes,* Lucr. 936 (or is it = to end?). *to f. his title with some shows of truth,* H5 I, 2, 72 (so the spurious Q and some M. Edd.; Ff *find*; see *Find,* def. 2).

Fine, adj. 1) thin, slender, minute: *to twist so f. a story,* Ado I, 1, 313. *a f. wit ... True, a f. little one,* V, 1, 162. Adverbially: *he draweth out the thread of his verbosity —r than the staple of his argument,* LLL V, 1, 19.

2) thin, keen, smoothly sharp: *blunting the f. point of seldom pleasure,* Sonn. 52, 4. *what f. chisel could ever yet cut breath?* Wint. V, 3, 78.

3) made of fine threads, not coarse: *f. linen,* Shr. II, 355. *stuff so f. and smooth,* Tim. V, 1, 87.

4) pure, free from foreign matter: *a cup of wine that's brisk and f.* H4B V, 3, 48. *other (gold) less f. in carat, is more precious,* IV, 5, 162. 164.

5) refined, accomplished: *to hear with eyes belongs to love's f. wit,* Sonn. 23, 14; cf. Gentl. I, 1, 44; Wiv. IV, 5, 102 and Ado V, 1, 161. *a f., quaint graceful fashion,* Ado III, 4, 22. *a most f. figure,* LLL I, 2, 58. *your accent is something —r,* As III, 2, 359. *a f. musician,* Shr. I, 2, 174. *not noted but of the —r natures,* Wint. I, 2, 226. *if speaking truth in this f. age were not thought flattery,* H4A IV, 1, 2. *in respect of a f. workman, I am but a cobbler,* Caes. I, 1, 10. *the —st part of pure love,* Ant. I, 2, 152. *your f. cookery,* II, 6, 64.

6) nice, delicate, tender: *a heart of that f. frame,* Tw. I, 1, 33. *here the Troyans taste our dearest repute with their —st palate,* Troil. I, 3, 338. *some joy too f., too subtle-potent,* III, 2, 24. *the grief is f., full, perfect, that I taste,* IV, 4, 3. *the f. strains of honour,* Cor. V, 3, 149. *nature is f. in love,* Hml. IV, 5, 161. *f. fancies,* Per. III Prol. 13. Adverbially: *how f. this tyrant can tickle where she wounds,* Cymb. I, 1, 84.

7) neat, elegant, beautiful: *f. apparition,* Tp. I, 2, 317. *spirit,* 420. *Ariel,* 494. *things,* II, 2, 120. *how f. my master is,* V, 262. *a knight well-spoken, neat and f.* Gentl. I, 2, 10. *f. change in the music,*

IV, 2, 68. *I have a f. hawk,* Wiv. III, 3, 247. *spirits are not finely touched but to f. issues,* Meas. I, 1, 37. *some mistress f.* LLL I, 1, 63. *in a f. frenzy,* Mids. V, 12. *a f. tragedy,* 367. *a f. youth,* Merch. III, 4, 69. *your f. frame,* Alls IV,2, 4. *f. hats,* IV, 5, 111. *a f. new prince,* Wint. II, 1, 17. *some f. colour that may please the eye,* H4A V, 1, 75. *a' shot a f. shoot,* H4B III, 2, 49. *made a —r end,* H5 II, 3, 11. *a f. forehead,* Troil. III, 1, 117. *a f. spot,* Cor. I, 3, 56. *her f. foot,* Rom. II, 1, 19. *he will make the face of heaven so f.* III, 2, 23. *more handsome than f.* Hml. II, 2, 467 (i. e. neat, elegant, nice). *f. word, legitimate,* Lr. I, 2, 18. *a f. woman! a fair woman!* Oth. IV, 1, 189. Often used ironically: *a f. volley of words,* Gentl. II, 4, 33. *f., in faith,* Mids. III, 2, 284. *our f. musician,* Shr. III, 1, 63. *you have made a f. hand,* H8 V, 4, 74. *fettle your f. joints,* Rom. III, 5, 154. *here's f. revolution,* Hml. V, 1, 98. *to have his f. pate full of f. dirt,* 116. *I was a f. fool,* Oth. IV, 1, 155. *'tis a noble Lepidus, a very f. one,* Ant. III, 2, 7.

8) **subtle:** *the —st mad devil of jealousy,* Wiv. V, 1, 19. *thou art too f. in thy evidence,* Alls V, 3, 270. *O for a f. thief,* H4A III, 3, 211. *his f. pate,* Hml. V, 1, 116. Wint. I, 2, 226.

9) **trim, showy:** *my Katharine shall be f.* Shr. II, 319. *f. array,* 325. *there were none f. but Adam,* IV, 1, 139. *O f. villain,* V, 1, 68. *of the newest and —st wear,* Wint. IV, 4, 327. *such gain the cap of him that makes 'em f.* Cymb. III, 3, 25. Adverbially: *I may go the — r,* Ado I, 1, 248. *I'll confine myself no —r,* Tw. I, 3, 10.

Fine-baited, subtly seducing: *lead him on with a f. delay,* Wiv. II, 1, 99 (O. Edd. not hyphened).

Fineless, infinite: *riches f.* Oth. III, 3, 173.

Finely, 1) in minute parts: *such and so f. bolted didst thou seem,* H5 II, 2, 137.

2) so as to taste well: *brew me a pottle of sack f.* Wiv. III, 5, 30. *a tripe f. broiled,* Shr. IV, 3, 20.

3) nicely, delicately: *spirits f. touched,* Meas. I, 1, 36.

4) adroitly, cleverly, well: *we'll betray him f.* Wiv. V, 3, 22. *f. put off,* LLL IV, 1, 112. 114. 118. *we will turn it f. off,* V, 2, 511.

5) neatly, beautifully: *f. attired in a robe of white,* Wiv. IV, 4, 72.

Fineness, 1) purity, freedom from base mixtures: Err. IV, 1, 29. Troil. I, 3, 22.

2) capacity for refined conceptions, ingenuity: *those that with the f. of their souls by reason guide his execution,* Troil. I, 3, 209.

Finger, subst. 1) one of the extreme flexible parts of the hand: Ven. 228. Sonn. 96, 5. 128, 3. Tp. IV, 246. Gentl. IV, 4, 141. Err. IV, 4, 142. V, 276. LLL V, 1, 109. Mids. III, 1, 72. 186. Merch. III, 2, 186. V, 168. H4A II, 3, 90. H6A II, 4, 49. H6B IV, 10, 51. H8 III, 2, 115. IV, 1, 57. Troil. I, 3, 204. Rom. I, 4, 66. IV, 2, 4. 7. 8 etc. *to put* (the) *f. in the eye* = to weep in a childish manner: Err. II, 2, 206. Shr. I, 1, 79. *I'll never put my f. in the fire,* Wiv. I, 4, 91 (= I will not burn my fingers by imprudent meddling). *my —s iich* = I have a great mind to beat you: Troil. II, 1, 27. Rom. III, 5, 165. *my f. itches to make one* (viz at fighting) Wiv. II, 3, 48. *thou hast it at the —s' ends* (= thou knowest how to do it) LLL V, 1, 81. Tw. I, 3, 83. *smile upon his —s' ends,* H5 II, 3, 1f. *pick strong matter of revolt and wrath out of the bloody —s' ends of John,* John

III, 4, 168. *lay thy f. on thy lips* = be silent, Troil. I, 3, 240. Hml. I, 5, 187. *with his f. and his thumb* (= snapping his fingers) LLL V, 2, 111. *'twixt his f. and his thumb,* H4A I, 3, 37. H4B IV, 3, 141. *you had not kissed your three —s so oft,* Oth. II, 1, 174. Figurative use: *he shall not knit a knot in his fortunes with the f. of my substance,* Wiv. III, 2, 76. *the female ivy so enrings the barky —s of the elm,* Mids. IV, 1, 49 (what are the fingers of the elm?). *long purples that ... our cold maids do dead men's —s call,* Hml. IV, 7, 172 (the plant orchis mascula). A hurt in the finger proverbial for a little injury: Meas. V, 316. As I, 1, 153. H5 II, 2, 102. H8 V, 3, 106. Tim. II, 1, 24. Oth. III, 4, 146.

2) the measure of the breadth of a finger: *three —s on the ribs,* H4A IV, 2, 80.

3) the hand: *the devil take your —s,* Tp. III, 2, 89. *lay-to your —s,* IV, 251. *I will kiss thy royal f.* LLL V, 2, 891 (Armado's speech). *not worthy to touch Fortune's — s,* Tw. II, 5, 171. *to thrust his icy — s in my maw,* John V, 7, 37. H6A V, 3, 48. H6B III, 2, 145. H8 I, 1, 53. Caes. I, 2, 243. III, 1, 198. IV, 3, 24. Hml. V, 1, 283. Cymb. V, 5, 466. cf. *—s' ends,* John III, 4, 168.

Finger, vb. 1) to handle with the fingers: *you would be —ing them* (the papers) Gentl. I, 2, 101.

2) to take thievishly, to pilfer: *whiles he thought to steal the single ten, the king was slily — ed from the deck,* H6C V, 1, 44. *—ed their packet,* Hml. V, 2, 15.

3) to touch, to play on an instrument: *to teach her —ing,* Shr. II, 151. *to learn the order of my —ing,* III, 1, 65. *if you can penetrate her with your —ing,* Cymb. II, 3, 16. *the strings, who, —ed to make man his lawful music,* Per. I, 1, 82.

Finger-end, the end of the finger: *with trial-fire touch me his f.* Wiv. V, 5, 88.

Finical, spruce, foppish: Lr. II, 2, 19.

Finish, vb. 1) to end; a) trans.: LLL II, 221. Tw. V, 254. H5 IV, 7, 46. H6A IV, 2, 36. Ant. IV, 9, 18. Cymb. IV, 2, 273. — b) intr.: *that reason wonder may diminish, how thus we met, and these things f.* As V, 4, 146. *his days may f. ere that hapless time,* H6A III, 1, 201. = to die: *f., good lady,* Ant. V, 2, 193. *were present when she —ed,* Cymb. V, 5, 36. *I had you down and might have made you f.* 412.

2) to perform: *the nuptial —ed, let him be whipped,* Meas. V, 518. *that is —ed too,* Mids. III, 2, 38. *what he bids be done is —ed with his bidding,* Cor. V, 4, 24.

3) to complete: *he is the half part of a blessed man, left to be —ed by such as she,* John II, 438. *God may f. it* (his face) H4B I, 2, 27. *her monument is —-ed,* Per. IV, 3, 43. With *up: how many days will f. up the year,* H6C II, 5, 28.

Finisher, performer: *he that of greatest works is f.* Alls II, 1, 139.

Finless, destitute of fins: H4A III, 1, 151.

Finny, having fins: Per. II, 1, 52.

Finsbury, a large field near London (now covered with buildings) in which the trainbands used to exercise, and the usual resort of the plainer citizens: H4A III, 1, 257.

Firago, Lat. *virago,* a termagant woman; an expression used at random by Sir Toby to frighten Sir Andrew who *"has not bestowed his time in the tongues:"* Tw. III, 4, 302.

Fire, subst. (mostly monosyll.; sometimes dissyll., f. i. Pilgr. 97. Tp. I, 2, 5. Gentl. I, 2, 30. Shr. II, 133. R2 I, 3, 294. II, 1, 34. V, 1, 48. Tit. I, 127. Caes. III, 1, 171. Rhyming to *liar:* Rom. I, 2, 94); 1) heat and light joined, c a l o r i c, supposed to be an element: Pilgr. 97. Tp. V, 45. Gentl. I, 2, 30. II, 7, 19. Err. IV, 3, 57. Ado I, 1, 234. III, 1, 77. Mids. II, 1, 5 etc. etc. *f.* and *air* the lighter and more sprightly elements: Sonn. 45, 1. Ant. V, 2, 292 (cf. *Air*). *f. drives out f.* Caes. III, 1, 171. John III, 1, 277. Cor. IV, 7, 54. Rom. I, 2, 46. *men all in f.* Caes. I, 3, 25 (= *fiery*). *to be on f.* = to burn: *the heavens were all on f.* H4A III, 1, 24. Figuratively = to burn with desire or impatience: *Percy is on f. to go,* H4A III, 1, 269. IV, 1, 117. H5 II Chor. 1. *to stand on f.,* in the same sense: *I stand on f.: come to the matter,* Cymb. V, 5, 168. *to set on f.* = to kindle, to cause to burn: Ven. 388. Wiv. V, 5, 40. John II, 351. H6B IV, 6, 16. Tim. III, 3, 34. *set f. on barns* = set barns on f. Tit. V, 1, 133. *run through f. and water* (= do any-thing) Wiv. III, 4, 107. Mids. II, 2, 103. *to give f.* = to discharge fire-arms: Wiv. II, 2, 143. Figura-tively: *three times with sighs she gives her sorrow f., ere once she can discharge one word of woe,* Lucr. 1604. *you gave the f.* Gentl. II, 4, 38. *to take f.* = to begin to burn, Wiv. V, 5, 92. *hasty as f.* R2 I, 1, 19. *as red as f.* H6C III, 2, 51. *the coal of f.* Cor. I, 1, 177. *f. and brimstone* (a curse): Tw. II, 5, 56. Oth. IV, 1, 245. With the article: *or in the ocean drenched or in the f.* Ven. 494. *to swim, to dive into the f.* Tp. I, 2, 191. *the f. seven times tried this,* Merch. II, 9, 63.

2) any thing burning, a flame, a conflagration: *dashes the f. out,* Tp. I, 2, 5. 203. *he does make our f.* 311. *thus have I shunned the f.* Gentl. I, 3, 78. *like a waxen image 'gainst a f.* II, 4, 201. II, 7, 22. *I'll ne'er put my finger in the f.* Wiv. I, 4, 91 (i. e. com-promit myself by meddling). *by a country 'f.* V, 5, 256. Ado II, 1, 262. Mids. I, 1, 173. Wint. II, 3, 114. 140. R2 I, 3, 294. V, 1, 48. Tit. I, 127 etc. Plur. —s: Lucr. 647. 1353. Wiv. V, 5, 48. Shr. II, 133. Wint. III, 2, 177. R2 II, 1, 34. Cor. I, 4, 39 (*the* —s *of heaven*). III, 3, 68. Rom. I, 2, 94. Hml. I, 5, 11. Cymb. IV, 4, 18.

3) h e a t in general: *the raging f. of fever,* Err. V, 75. In a moral sense, a) ardor of temper: *O that false f. which in his cheek so glowed,* Compl. 324. *your love's hot f.* Tp. I, 7, 21. *what f. is in mine ears,* Ado III, 1, 107 (= how is my heart inflamed by what I have just heard). *unbated f.* Merch. II, 6, 11. *sighs of f.* Tw. I, 5, 275. *his sparkling eyes, replete with wrathful f.* H6A I, 1, 12. *f. and fury,* Rom. III, 1, 129 (the spurious Q1 and M. Edd. *fire-eyed fury*). *time qualifies the spark and f. of it* (love) Hml. IV, 7, 114. b) sensual desire, lust: *and to Collatium bears the lightless f.* Lucr. 4. *straw to the f. i' the blood,* Tp. IV, 1, 53. Wiv. II, 1, 68. V, 5, 99. Alls III, 7, 26. The syphilis called so: Tim. IV, 3, 142.

Fire, vb. (dissyll. in H6C II, 1, 83 and Caes. III, 2, 260). 1) to set on fire, to k i n d l e: *another wind that —s the torch,* Lucr. 315. *he* (the sun) *—s the proud tops of the eastern pines,* R2 III, 2, 42. *hasty powder —d,* Rom. V, 1, 64. *f. the traitors' houses,* Caes. III, 2, 260. *a beacon —d,* Per. I, 4, 87. Tropi-cally, = to inflame: *that —s all my breast,* H6C II, 1, 83. *a heart new —d,* Caes. II, 1, 332. *might f. the blood of ordinary men,* III, 1, 37.

2) to d r i v e b y f i r e: *till my bad angel f. my good one out,* Sonn. 144, 14 (cf. Cor. IV, 7, 54 and Caes. III, 1, 171). *f. us hence like foxes,* Lr. V, 3, 23.

3) to d i s c h a r g e: *that lead which is —d from a gun,* LLL III, 63. *let all the battlements their ord-nance f.* Hml. V, 2, 281.

Firebrand, a burning piece of wood: Tp. II, 2, 6. H4B II, 2, 97. Troil. II, 2, 110. Caes. III, 3, 41.

Fire-drake, fiery dragon; a man with a red nose called so: H8 V, 4, 45.*

Fire-eyed, grim-lo o k i n g: *the f. maid of smoky war,* H4A IV, 1, 114. *f. fury,* Rom. III, 1, 129 (only in the spurious Q1; the rest of O. Edd. *fire and fury*).

Fire-new, fresh from the mint, bran-new: LLL I, 1, 179. Tw. III, 2, 23. R3 I, 3, 256. Lr. V, 3, 132.

Fire-robed, c l a d in fire: *the f. god, golden Apollo,* Wint. IV, 4, 29.

Fire-shovel, an instrument for taking up coals of fire: H5 III, 2, 48.

Firework, pyrotechnical exhibition: LLL V, 1, 119. —s, H8 I, 3, 27.

Firing, subst. fuel: Tp. II, 2, 185.

Firk, vb., to b e a t, to d r u b: *I'll fer him, and f. him, and ferret him,* H5 IV, 4, 29. 33.

Firm, 1) s t r o n g l y f i x e d, not giving way, not easily shaken: *the f. soil,* Sonn. 64, 7. Wiv. III, 2, 49. John III, 1, 72. *stand as f. as faith,* Wiv. IV, 4, 10. *stand as f. as rocky mountains,* H4B IV, 1, 188. *hold f. the walls of thy honour,* Cymb. II, 1, 67. *thou art not f. enough,* H4B IV, 5, 204. *the f. fixture of thy foot,* Wiv. III, 3, 67. *before his legs be f. to bear his body,* H6B III, 1, 190.

2) s t e a d y, c o n s t a n t, unshaken, to be re-lied on: *who was so f., so constant, that this coil would not infect his reason?* Tp. I, 2, 207. *love's f. votary,* Gentl. III, 2, 58. *f. for Doctor Caius,* Wiv. IV, 6, 28. *a soldier f. and sound of heart,* H5 III, 6, 26. *to stand f. by honour,* Troil. II, 2, 68. *f. of word,* IV, 5, 97. *who so f. that cannot be seduced?* Caes. I, 2, 316. *I have sworn: I am f.* Lr. I, 1, 248. *the f. Roman to great Egypt sends this treasure,* Ant. I, 5, 43 (= constant, faithful). *a man of stricture and f. abstinence,* Meas. I, 3, 12. *her wits are not f.* V, 33. *f. and irrevocable is my doom,* As I, 3, 85. *your f. re-solve,* Shr. II, 93. H6C III, 3, 129. *fix most f. thy resolution,* Oth. V, 1, 5. *your f. promise,* Shr. II, 387. *were my worth as is my conscience f.* Tw. III, 3, 17. *keep our faiths f.* John V, 2, 7. R3 IV, 4, 497 (Ff *look your heart be f.*). Troil. III, 2, 116. *our f. estate,* R2 III, 4, 42. *thou art framed of the f. truth of valour,* H5 IV, 3, 14. *thy f. loyalty,* H6C III, 3, 239. *the compact is f. and true in me,* R3 II, 2, 133. *f. love,* Troil. I, 2, 320. *my f. nerves,* Mcb. III, 4, 102. *the charm is f. and good,* IV, 1, 38. *this f. bosom,* Hml. III, 2, 412. *f. security,* Ant. III, 7, 49. *could behold the sun with as f. eyes as he,* Cymb. I, 4, 13.

3) d e t e r m i n e d, positive, distinctly sta-ted: *here is no f. reason to be rendered why he cannot abide a gaping pig,* Merch. IV, 1, 53. *the king hath granted every article ... according to their f. proposed natures,* H5 V, 2, 362.

Firmament, the sky: Wint. III, 3, 86. R2 II, 4, 20. Tit. V, 3, 17. Caes. III, 1, 62. Hml. II, 2, 312 (not in Ff.). Lr. I, 2, 144.

Firmly, steadily, steadfastly, securely, constantly: Lucr. 416. Pilgr. 255. Wiv. II, 1,

242. Shr. I, 1, 49. I, 2, 157. IV, 2, 28 (*here I f. vow*). H6B III, 1, 88. H6C III, 3, 219. Tit. V, 2, 73. Lr. V, 3, 101.

Firmness, 1) fixedness, stability: *the continent weary of solid f.* H4B III, 1, 48. 2) steadiness, constancy: *the unstooping f. of my upright soul,* R2 I, 1, 121.

Firm-set, strongly fixed: *thou sure and f. earth,* Mcb. II, 1, 56.

First, adj. num., the ordinal of *one;* 1) that which is in time or order before any other: Ven. Ded. 4. Sonn. 114, 9. Tp. I, 2, 214. 440. 445. II, 1, 103. V, 165. Gentl. V, 4, 46. Wiv. II, **2**, 40. III, 4, 14. Meas. I, 1, 47. II, 2, 92. 106. V, 361. Err. V, 422. LLL I, 2, 183. Mids. III, 1, 144. As I, 2, 219 etc. etc. *rob me the exchequer the f. thing thou doest,* H4A III, 3, 205. *from f. to last* = from the beginning to the end: John II, 326. Oth. III, 3, 96. *from the f. to last,* As IV, 3, 140. Substantively, = beginning, commencement: *I am a man that from my f. have been inclined to thrift,* Tim. I, 1, 118. *many unrough youths that even now protest their f. of manhood,* Mcb. V, 2, 11. *upon our f. he sent out to suppress his nephew's levies,* Hml. II, 2, 61 (i. e. as soon as we approached him, applied to him). *from your f. of difference and decay,* Lr. V, 3, 288. *The f.,* a term of heraldry, denoting a particular form of dividing the shield from the highest part to the lowest: *two of the f., like coats in heraldry, due but to one and crowned with one crest,* Mids. III, 2, 213 (O. Edd. *first life coats*). — At the f. = a) from the beginning, at the outset: *I knew you at the f. you were a moveable,* Shr. II, 197. *that take it on you at the f. so roundly,* III, 2, 216. *at the f. I saw the treasons planted,* Ant. I, 3, 25. *even at the f. thy loss is more than can thy portage quit,* Per. III, 1, 34. b) in the beginning: *playing, whose end, both at the f. and now, was and is ....,* Hml. III, 2, 23. *poisons which at the f. are scarce found to distaste,* Oth. III, 3, 327. — At f. = a) what it signifies at present, in the beginning: *ruined love, when it is built anew, grows fairer than at f.* Sonn. 119, 12. *scorn at f. makes after-love the more,* Gentl. III, 1, 95. H6A II, 1, 51. Tim. I, 2, 15. Hml. I, 2, 190. Oth. II, 3, 358. *at f. and last* = from the beginning to the end: *grief, I fear me, both at f. and last,* H6A V, 5, 102. *at f. and last the hearty welcome,* Mcb. III, 4, 1. b) from the beginning, at the very outset, directly: *struck dead at f. what needs a second striking,* Ven. 250. *so shall I taste at f. the very worst of fortune's might,* Sonn. 90, 12. *every offence is not a hate at f.* Merch. IV, 1, 68. *you touched my vein at f.* As II, 7, 94. *whom would to God I had well knocked at f.* Shr. I, 2, 34. *he whose wife is most obedient to come at f. when he doth send for her,* V, 2, 68. *at f. I stuck my choice upon her,* Alls V, 3, 44. *but what mean I to speak so true at f.?* H4B Ind. 28. *had we done so at f., we had droven them home with clouts about their heads,* Ant. IV, 7, 5. *we are familiar at f.* Cymb. I, 4, 112. *in an hour — was 't not? — or less, — at f.?* II, 5, 15. c) first, in its different significations; 1) before others: *true is it that I receive the general food at f.* Cor. I, 1, 135. 2) firstly: *at f. the infant, ... and then ...* As II, 7, 143. 3) the first time, originally: *at f. I did adore a twinkling star, but now I worship a celestial sun,* Gentl. II, 6, 9. *your highness will take again your queen, as yours at f.* Wint. I, 2, 336. *let it rest where it began*

at f. H6A IV, 1, 121. *a word devised at f. to keep the strong in awe,* R3 V, 3, 310. *from whence at f. she weighed her anchorage,* Tit. I, 73. *since at f.* = ever since: *since mind at f. in character was done,* Sonn. 59, 8. *I could not speak with Dromio since at f. I sent him from the mart,* Err. II, 2, 5.

2) the best, noblest: *through all the signories it was the f.* Tp. I, 2, 71. *a buck of the f. head,* LLL IV, 2, 10. H4A IV, 4, 15. V, 1, 33. Rom. II, 4, 25. Remarkable passage: *my f. son, whither wilt thou go?* Cor. IV, 1, 33 (i. e. my eldest and therefore most beloved son; cf. Ado II, 1, 10).

First, adv. 1) before any other: *mine eye loves it and doth f. begin,* Sonn. 114, 14. *which f. begins to crow,* Tp. II, 1, 29. Wiv. I, 1, 320. II, 1, 75. Err. IV, 1, 51. Tw. IV, 1, 38 etc. etc.

2) before any thing else in order of proceeding: *having f. seized his books,* Tp. III, 2, 97. 100. *do the murder f.* IV, 232. V, 120. Wiv. II, 2, 262. III, 2, 91. Meas. IV, 5, 10. V, 362. 513. Mids. I, 2, 8. H6A IV, 1, 116. Lr. V, 3, 2 etc. Hence = sooner, rather: *I'll be hanged f.* Meas. III, 2, 178. *the stars will kiss the valleys f.* Wint. V, 1, 206. *I'll see her damned f.* H4B II, 4, 169.

3) the first time, at the beginning: *as you were when f. your eye I eyed,* Sonn. 104, 2; cf. Tw. I, 1, 19. *a flower that dies when f. it gins to bud,* Pilgr. 171. *when thou camest f. thou strokedst me,* Tp. I, 2, 332. II, 1, 69. V, 6. 225. Gentl. II, 6, 4. Err. IV, 2, 7. 15. V, 261. Ado II, 3, 75. Merch. II, 6, 12. III, 2, 256 etc.

4) originally: *for a woman wert thou f. created, till Nature, as she wrought thee, fell a doting,* Sonn. 20, 9. *I am all the subjects that you have, which f. was mine own king,* Tp. I, 2, 342. *thou camest from Corinth f.?* Err. V, 362. *f. he was a noble servant to them, but he could not carry his honours even,* Cor. IV, 7, 35.

5) in the first place, firstly: Gentl. II, 1, 18. Wiv. III, 5, 110. Meas. II, 1, 169. III, 1, 255. IV, 3, 4. V, 107. Err. II, 2, 46. Mids. III, 1, 11. Merch. II, 9, 10 etc.

First-begotten, eldest: H6A II, 5, 65.

First-born, first produced, eldest: Sonn. 21, 7. LLL I, 1, 101. As I, 1, 50. H4B I, 1, 157. Tit. I, 5. 120. IV, 2, 92. *I'll rail against all the f. of Egypt,* As II, 5, 63 (Johnson and after him other commentators say that this expression means high-born persons; but perhaps it means such persons as may be railed at with impunity; cf. Exodus XI, 5 and 6).

First-conceived, first heard: *the f. sound,* H6B III, 2, 94.

First-fruits, first produce: *my second joy and f. of my body,* Wint. III, 2, 98 (O. Edd. not hyphened).

First-good, of the best quality; only by conjecture in H8 I, 4, 6; O. Edd. *as first, good company.*

Firstling, the first produce or offspring: *our play leaps o'er the vaunt and —s of those broils, beginning in the middle,* Troil. Prol. 27 (i. e. the first acts). *the very —s of my heart shall be the —s of my hand,* Mcb. IV, 1, 147.

Fish, subst. 1) an animal that lives in water and breathes by means of gills: Tp. II, 1, 112. II, 2, 25. 29 etc. III, 2, 30. 32. V, 266. Wiv. I, 1, 22. Err. III, 1, 82. Ado II, 3, 114. III, 1, 26 (fem.). Alls III, 6,

92. Wint. IV, 4, 279. 284. V, 2, 91. H4A III, 1, 151. Rom. I, 3, 89. Hml. IV, 3, 29. Per. II, 1, 122. Unchanged in the plur.: Tp. II, 2, 184. Err. II, 1, 23. III, 1, 79. Merch. III, 1, 55. H4B I, 1, 200. Tit. IV, 4, 91. Cor. IV, 7, 34. Cymb. IV, 2, 36. Plur. —*es*: Ven. 1100. Err. II, 1, 18. R3 I, 4, 25. H8 I, 2, 79. Rom. V, 1, 44. Tim. IV, 3, 426. Ant. II, 5, 12. Cymb. IV, 2, 153. Per. II, 1, 70. *as whole as a f.* Gentl. II, 5, 20.

2) the flesh of fish, used as food: Alls V, 2, 9. Lr. I, 4, 18. Per. II, 1, 86. *'tis well thou art not f.* Rom. I, 1, 36. *at flesh or f.* Err. III, 1, 22. *neither f. nor flesh*, H4A III, 3, 144. *half f., half flesh*, Per. II, 1, 27.

Fish, vb. 1) to be employed in catching fish: Tp. II, 2, 165. Hml. IV, 3, 28. Ant. I, 4, 4. With *for:* Merch. I, 1, 101. Figuratively, = to catch at sth., to seek to obtain by artifice: *that sort was well —ed for*, Tp. II, 1, 104. *others f. with craft for great opinion*, Troil. IV, 4, 105. *here's nothing to be got, unless thou canst f. for it*, Per. II, 1, 74.

2) to search in quest of fish: *his pond —ed by his next neighbour*, Wint. I, 2, 195.

Fisher, one whose occupation is to catch fish: Ven. 526. Err. I, 1, 116. Rom. I, 2, 41. Per. II, 1, 53.

Fishermen, people whose occupation is to catch fish: Wiv. IV, 5, 100. Err. I, 1, 112. V, 351. Lr. IV, 6, 17. Per. II, 1, 56.

Fishify, to change to fish: *O flesh, how art thou —ed*, Rom. II, 4, 40.

Fish-like, resembling fish: *f. smell*, Tp. II, 2, 27.

Fish-meal, a dinner on fish instead of flesh: H4B IV, 3, 99.

Fishmonger, a seller of fish: Hml. II, 2, 174. 190. (Malone: "Perhaps a joke was here intended. *F.* was a cant term for a wencher.")

Fishpond, a pond in which fish are kept: Alls V, 2, 22.

Fish-street, street in London: H6B IV, 8, 1.

Fisnomy, physiognomy: Alls IV, 5, 42.

Fist, subst. the hand closed: John II, 465. H5 II, 1, 71 (*give me thy f.; Pistol's speech*). IV, 1, 46. H6A I, 4, 36. H6B I, 1, 245. IV, 10, 51. H6C II, 1, 154. Troil. II, 1, 43. II, 3, 212.

Fist, vb. to grasp: *an I but f. him once*, H4B II, 1, 23. —*ing each other's throat*, Cor. IV, 5, 131. *to the choleric —ing of every rogue thy ear is liable*, Per. IV, 6, 177.

Fistula, a sinuous ulcer: Alls I, 1, 39.

Fit, subst. 1) a violent attack of disease, a paroxysm: Lucr. 856. Tp. II, 2, 76. 79. John III, 4, 85. 114. H4B I, 1, 142. IV, 4, 114. Caes. I, 2, 120. Mcb. III, 4, 21. Oth. IV, 1, 52.

2) an attack of mental disorder: *a f. of madness*, Err. V, 76. 139. Hence = madness: *unless some f. or frenzy do possess her*, Tit. IV, 1, 17. *in his lawless f.* Hml. IV, 1, 8. *thus awhile the f. will work on him*, V, 1, 308. Plur. —*s:* Tp. III, 3, 91. Err. IV, 3, 91. Tit. IV, 4, 12. V, 2, 71.

3) any irregular and violent affection of the mind: *thy jealous —s*, Err. V, 85. *I love to cope him in these sullen —s*, As II, 1, 67. *what f. is this?* Wint. III, 2, 175. *I feel the last f. of my greatness*, H8 III, 1, 78. *a charm to calm these —s*, Tit. II, 1, 134 (meaning hot desire). *to take the indisposed and sickly f. for the sound man*, Lr. II, 4, 112. *still waving, as the*

—*s and stirs of's mind could best express*, Cymb. I, 3, 12 (= emotion). *a woman's fitness comes by —s*, IV, 1, 6. Used of other things, = caprice, distemperature: *a f. or two o' the face*, H8 I, 3, 7 (i. e. a grimace). *the violent f. o' the time craves it as physic*, Cor. III, 2, 33. *and best knows the —s o' the season*, Mcb. IV, 2, 17.

4) a division of a song or tune: *you say so in —s*, Troil. III, 1, 62 (quibbling, as the intpp. suppose, but not very intelligibly).

Fit, adj. 1) convenient, proper: *if now 'twere f. to do it*, Tp. I, 2, 440. *it were f. you knew him*, Alls III, 6, 14. —*er is my study and my books than wanton dalliance*, H6A V, 1, 22. Tit. IV, 3, 95. Tim. V, 1, 57. Caes. IV, 1, 13. Lr. IV, 7, 43. Cymb. I, 6, 110 etc. etc. *at f. time*, Meas. IV, 5, 1. V, 498. As I, 3, 137. Cor. IV, 3, 33. —*er place*, Meas. II, 2, 17. IV, 6, 10. —*est course*, Err. IV, 3, 96. —*er matter*, Alls IV, 5, 81 etc. *I thought your marriage f.* Meas. V, 425. *the soft way which were f. for thee to use*, Cor. III, 2, 83. With *for* or an inf.: *in some better place*, —*er for sickness*, H6A III, 2, 89. *strewings —est for graves*, Cymb. IV, 2, 285. *how f. a word is that vile name to perish on my sword*, Mids. II, 2, 106. *thou art —er to be worn in my cap*, H4B I, 2, 17. H6C III, 2, 91 etc.

2) of the right measure, suiting, tallying: *one o' these maids' girdles for your waist should be f.* LLL IV, 1, 50. *these fixed evils sit so f. on him*, Alls I, 1, 113. *Julia's gown which served me as f. as if the garment had been made for me*, Gentl. IV, 4, 167. *how f. his garments serve me!* Cymb. IV, 1, 2. Figuratively: *will your answer serve f. to all questions?* Alls II, 2, 20. *botch the words up f. to their own thoughts*, Hml. IV, 5, 10. *all with me's meet that I can fashion f.* Lr. I, 2, 200.

3) well qualified, adapted, becoming: *an officer f. for the place*, Gentl. I, 2, 45. *an engine f. for my proceeding*, III, 1, 138. V, 4, 157. Ado III, 3, 23. LLL IV, 1, 22. Tw. IV, 1, 52. H6A V, 3, 33. H6B I, 3, 67. R3 I, 2, 105. Hml. I, 1, 66. Tim. III, 1, 52. Caes. II, 1, 173. *none so f. as to present the Nine Worthies*, LLL V, 1, 130. *f. to play in our interlude*, Mids. I, 2, 5. Shr. I, 1, 112 etc.

4) well disposed, prepared, ready: *if I do find him f., I'll move your suit*, Oth. III, 4, 166. *the maid will I frame and make f. for his attempt*, Meas. III, 1, 266. *f. for treasons*, Merch. V, 85. *tell Valeria we are f. to bid her welcome*, Cor. I, 3, 47. *I have already f.* — *'tis in my cloak-bag* — *doublet, hat, hose*, Cymb. III, 4, 171. cf. *more f. to do another such offence than die for this*, Meas. II, 3, 14. *why should his mistress not be f. too*, Cymb. IV, 1, 5. Hml. V, 2, 229.

5) such as a person or thing ought to be, answering the purpose: *I find him a f. fellow*, H8 II, 2, 117. *leave him out; indeed, he is not f.* Caes. II, 1, 153. *in state as wholesome as in state 'tis f.* Wiv. V, 5, 63. *when it comes so smoothly off, so f.* LLL IV, 1, 145. *what will serve is f.* Ado I, 1, 320. *folly that he wisely shows is f.* Tw. III, 1, 74. *find their f. rewards*, H8 III, 2, 245. *drugs f.* Hml. III, 2, 266.

Fit, vb. 1) trans. a) to be adapted to, to be of the right measure for, to suit: *every true man's apparel —s your thief*, Meas. IV, 2, 46. Alls II, 2, 17. Figuratively: *an answer that —s all questions*, Alls II, 2, 16. *weigh what convenience both of time and means* *may f. us to our shape,* Hml. IV, 7, 151. *it doth not f. me,* Tw. III, 3, 38 (= it does not suit me, would not be well done). *where, it —s not you to know,* Wint. IV, 4, 304. *she'll f. it,* Wiv. II, 1, 166 (= she will be the very person required for it, she will do her business well). *how both did f. it,* LLL IV, 1, 131. *he cannot but with measure f. the honours which we devise him,* Cor. II, 2, 127 (so that the honours, as it were, sit fit on him).

b) to agree, to accord, to be in harmony with: *it better —s my blood to be disdained,* Ado I, 3, 29. *it —s my humour well,* As III, 2, 20. *this* (cap) *doth f. the time,* Shr. IV, 3, 69 (= is according to the prevailing fashion). *that time best —s the work,* H6B I, 4, 23. *she better would have —ed me,* H6C IV, 1, 54. *this valley —s the purpose passing well,* Tit. II, 3, 84.

c) to become, to behove: *few words shall f. the trespass best,* Lucr. 1613. *the humble salve which wounded bosom —s,* Sonn. 120, 12. *a silly answer and —ing well a sheep,* Gentl. I, 1, 81. IV, 4, 125. Ado III, 2, 119. LLL I, 2, 42. John I, 206. H4A IV, 2, 86. H5 II, 4, 11. H6A III, 1, 57. R3 III, 7, 143. Troil. V, 3, 38. Tit. I, 187. Hml. I, 1, 173. Oth. III, 4, 150. Cymb. III, 5, 22. V, 5, 98. Per. I, 1, 129. I, 2, 43.

d) to prepare, to qualify for some purpose: *he may be so —ed that his soul sicken not,* Meas. II, 4, 40. *I am not —ed for it* (viz death) IV, 3, 47. *no time shall be omitted that will betime, and may by us be —ed,* LLL IV, 3, 382. *f. thy thoughts to mount aloft,* Tit. II, 1, 12. *when she had —ed you with her craft,* Cymb. V, 5, 55.

e) to make accordant; followed by *to: f. thy consent to my sharp appetite,* Meas. II, 4, 161. *f. his mind to death,* 187. *think you of a worse title, and I will f. her to it,* Ado III, 2, 114. *to f. your fancies to your father's will,* Mids. I, 1, 118. *we'll f. him to our turn,* Shr. III, 2, 134. *f. you to the custom,* Cor. II, 2, 146. *f. you to your manhood,* Cymb. III, 4, 195. Followed by *with: I had a thing to say, but I will f. it with some better tune,* John III, 3, 26. The partic. *—ed* = fit, doing well, conformable to the object in view: *I hope here is a play —ed,* Mids. I, 2, 67. *not one word apt, one player —ed,* V, 65. *that part was aptly —ed and naturally performed,* Shr. Ind. 1, 87. *plots —ed for rape,* Tit. II, 1, 116. *a document in madness, thoughts and remembrance —ed,* Hml. IV, 5, 179.

f) to furnish, to accommodate: *f. me with such weeds,* Gentl. II, 7, 42. *I will f. thee with the remedy,* Ado I, 1, 321. II, 1, 61. II, 3, 44. Wint. IV, 4, 78. 192. H8 II, 1, 99. Cymb. V, 5, 21. Without *with: I'll f. you,* Alls II, 1, 93. Tit. IV, 1, 114. Part. *—ed* = equipped, appointed: *well —ed in arts,* LLL II, 45. *well are you —ed, had you but a Moor,* Tit. V, 2, 85.

2) intr. a) to be adapted, to serve fit: *and now the happy season once more —s,* Ven. 327. *that —s as well as 'Tell me' ...,* Gentl. II, 7, 50. *this opportunity as —ing best to quittance their deceit,* H6A II, 1, 14. *are all things —ing for that royal time?* R3 III, 4, 4 (Ff ready). *left nothing —ing for the purpose untouched,* III, 7, 18.

b) to agree, to accord; with *to: news —ing to the night,* John V, 6, 19. With *with: it —s not with this hour,* Tit. III, 1, 266. *must make content with his fortunes f.* Lr. III, 2, 76.

c) to be convenient, to become: *oft it hits*

where hope is coldest and despair most —s, Alls II, 1, 147 (O. Edd. *shifts*). *any thing that is —ing to be known,* Wint. IV, 4, 741. H6B I, 1, 247. II, 3, 44. H8 V, 1, 108. Rom. I, 5, 77.

Fitchew, the pole-cat: Troil. V, 1, 67. Thought to be very amorous: Lr. IV, 6, 124. Hence a term for a wanton woman: Oth. IV, 1, 150.

Fitful, full of paroxysms: *life's f. fever,* Mcb. III, 2, 23.

Fitly, 1) with propriety, reasonably, well: *even so most f. as you malign our senators,* Cor. I, 1, 116. *cats, that can judge as f. of his worth as I can of those mysteries,* IV, 2, 34. *if aught within that little seeming substance, ... and nothing more, may f. like your grace,* Lr. I, 1, 203. *I can compare our rich misers to nothing so f. as to a whale,* Per. II, 1, 33.

2) pat to the purpose, opportunely: *here, my lord. So f.?* Tim. III, 4, 111. *I will f. bring you to hear my lord speak,* Lr. I, 2, 184.

Fitment, 1) equipment: *in poor beseeming; 'twas a f. for the purpose I then followed,* Cymb. V, 5, 409.

2) that which is proper and becoming, duty: *when she should do for clients her f., she has me her quirks,* Per. IV, 6, 6 (the bawd's speech).

Fitness, adaptedness, the quality of answering the purpose: *an answer of such f. for all questions,* Alls II, 2, 31. *they* (time and place) *have made themselves, and that their f. now does unmake you,* Mcb. I, 7, 53.

2) serviceableness, ability: *dispossessing all my other parts of necessary f.* Meas. II, 4, 23. *of no more soul nor f. for the world than camels in the war,* Cor. II, 1, 266.

3) opportunity, convenience: *how many hands shall strike, when f. calls them on,* Troil. I, 3, 202. *if his f. speaks, mine is ready,* Hml. V, 2, 209. *a woman's f. comes by fits,* Cymb. IV, 1, 6.

4) propriety, decency: *the queen being absent, 'tis a needful f. that we adjourn this court,* H8 II, 4, 231. *were 't my f. to let these hands obey my blood,* Lr. IV, 2, 63.

Fitted, worked and vexed by paroxysms: *how have mine eyes out of their spheres been f. in the distraction of this madding fever,* Sonn. 119, 7.

Fitzwater, name in R2 IV, 43. 60. V, 6, 17.

Five, four and one: Sonn. 59, 6. Tp. I, 2, 47. 396. II, 1, 184. III, 2, 6. 16. Gentl. II, 5, 10. Wiv. III, 3, 237. Meas. IV, 2, 127. V, 217. 222. Err. I, 1, 101. 133. I, 2, 26. IV, 1, 10. IV, 4, 13. V, 118. Ado III, 3, 84. 141. LLL IV, 2, 36. V, 1, 56 etc. etc. cf. *Putterout, Sense, Wit.*

Five-finger-tied, tied with all the fingers of the hand, eagerly made: *and with another knot, f., the fractions of her faith .... are bound to Diomed,* Troil. V, 2, 157.

Five-fold, quintuple: Tw. I, 5, 312.

Fives, (properly *vives*) a disease of horses, consisting in an inflammation of the parotid glands: Shr. III, 2, 54.

Fivescore, a hundred: LLL IV, 2, 41. IV, 3, 242.

Fix, 1) to set or place steadily and immovably: *f. thy foot,* Cor. I, 8, 4. *there thy —ed foot shall grow,* Tw. I, 4, 17. *stars shot from their —ed places,* Lucr. 1525. Sonn. 21, 12. *every —ed star.*

LLL I, 1, 89. John IV, 2, 183. R2 II, 4, 9. H8 V, 5, 48. *—es no bourn 'twixt his and mine*, Wint. I, 2, 133. *continual motion, to which is —ed, as an aim or butt, obedience*, H5 I, 2, 186. *wrenched my frame of nature from the —ed place*, Lr. I, 4, 291. *their —ed beds of lime*, John II, 219. *the horsemen sit like —ed candlesticks*, H5 IV, 2, 45. *if yet your gentle souls fly in the air and be not —ed in doom perpetual*, R3 IV, 4, 12. *delivered strongly through my —ed teeth*, H6B III, 2, 313 (i. e. set). In a moral sense: *where her faith was firmly —ed in love*, Pilgr. 255; cf. H6C III, 3, 125. *never did young man fancy with so eternal and so —ed a soul*, Troil. V, 2, 166. *f. most firm thy resolution*, Oth. V, 1, 5. *the hour is —ed*, Wiv. II, 2, 303. *heirs of —ed destiny*, V, 5, 43. *my intents are —ed*, All's I, 1, 244. *had not —ed his canon 'gainst self-slaughter*, Hml. I, 2, 131. *how unremovable and —ed he is in his own course*, Lr. II, 4, 94. *truth needs no colour, with his colour —ed*, Sonn. 101, 6 (i. e. native and unchangeable). *these —ed evils sit so fit in him*, All's I, 1, 113. *whose patience is as a virtue —ed*, Troil. I, 2, 5. *he's your —ed enemy*, Cor. II, 3, 258. *that's most —ed*, Tim. I, 1, 9 (= certain).

2) to direct steadily: *against my heart will f. a sharp knife*, Lucr. 1138. Particularly of the eye: *whose* (her eye's) *beams upon his hairless face are —ed*, Ven. 487. *her eyes are sadly —ed in the remorseless wrinkles of his face*, Lucr. 561. Compl. 27. Err. I, 1, 85. LLL I, 1, 81. H6B I, 2, 5 (*to*). Tit. V, 1, 22. Tim. I, 1, 68. Hml. I, 2, 234. Cymb. I, 6, 104. Similarly: *his contemplation were —ed on spiritual object*, H8 III, 2, 132. *on whom our care was —ed*, Err. I, 1, 85.

3) to set, to place in general: *an ass's nole I —ed on his head*, Mids. III, 2, 17. *fastened and —ed the shame on't in himself*, Wint. II, 3, 15; cf. *where the greater malady is —ed*, Lr. III, 4, 8. *the statue is newly —ed*, Wint. V, 3, 47. *her foot is —ed upon a spherical stone*, H5 III, 6, 37. *the —ed sentinels almost receive the secret whispers*, IV Chor. 6. *mine hair be —ed on end*, H6B III, 2, 318. *—ed his head upon our battlements*, Mcb. I, 2, 23. *a massy wheel, —ed on the summit of the highest mount*, Hml. III, 3, 18. *a —ed figure for the time of scorn to point his finger at*, Oth. IV, 2, 54. cf. *Transfix.*

Fixture, (F 2.3.4 *fixure*) setting: *the firm f. of thy foot would give an excellent motion to thy gait in a farthingale*, Wiv. III, 3, 67.

Fixure, 1) stability: *deracinate the unity and married calm of states quite from their f.* Troil. I, 3, 101 (F 3.4 *fixture*).

2) direction: *the f. of her eye has motion in 't*, Wint. V, 3, 67.

Flag, subst. 1) banner, standard: John II, 207. R3 IV, 4, 89. Rom. V, 3, 96. Ant. III, 13, 11.

2) an ensign by which signs are made: *the bloody f.* H5 I, 2, 101. *set up the bloody f. against all patience*, Cor. II, 1, 84. *by the semblance of their white —s they bring us peace*, Per. I, 4, 72. *f. of truce*, H6A III, 1, 138. *a f. and sign of love*, Oth. I, 1, 157.

3) the water-plant Iris: Ant. I, 4, 45.

Flag, vb. to hang loose, to droop: *drowsy, slow and —ing wings*, H6B IV, 1, 5.

Flagon, a bottle: *poured a f. of Rhenish on my head*, Hml. V, 1, 197.

Flail, the tool of the thrasher: H6C II, 1, 131.

Flake, flock, thin tuft: *these white —s*, Lr. IV, 7, 30 (thin white hair).

Flaky, loosely hanging together, scattering like flakes: *f. darkness breaks within the east*, R3 V, 3, 86.

Flame, subst. fire rising from burning bodies: Lucr. 180. Sonn. 1, 6. Wiv. V, 5, 89. All's I, 2, 59. H6A III, 1, 191. Mcb. IV, 1, 67. Cymb. II, 2, 19. Per. I, 1, 138. *through fire and through f.* Lr. III, 4, 53. *by the f. of yonder glorious heaven*, Troil. V, 6, 23. Plur. *—s:* H5 III, 3, 16. III, 6, 109. IV Chor. 8. H6B V, 2, 41. H6C II, 1, 84. Caes. I, 2, 113. Hml. I, 5, 3. II, 2, 528. Lr. II, 4, 167. Figuratively used of love: Sonn. 109, 2. 115, 4. Compl. 191. Troil. III, 2, 167. Hml. IV, 7, 115. *in so true a f. of liking*, All's I, 3, 217. *if I did love you in my master's f.* Tw. I, 5, 283. Of passionate desire: Lucr. 6. Wiv. V, 5, 101. Of poetry: Tim. I, 1, 23. Of ambition: R3 IV, 4, 328. Of passion: Hml. III, 4, 123. Of war: H4B Ind. 26.

Flame, vb. to blaze, to burn with rising fire: Lucr. 448. 1627. Pilgr. 97. Phoen. 35. Tp. I, 2, 200. Cor. IV, 3, 21. V, 2, 49. Caes. I, 3, 16. Hml. II, 2, 497. Oth. V, 2, 8. With an accus. denoting the result: *I —d amazement*, Tp. I, 2, 198.* Figuratively: Compl. 287. All's II, 3, 86. H6B V, 2, 55. Troil. I, 2, 113. Hml. III, 4, 84.

Flame-coloured, bright yellow: H4A I, 2, 11. Rowe's conjecture in Tw. I, 3, 144; O. Edd. *dam'd coloured.*

Flamen, a (Roman) priest: Cor. II, 1, 229. Tim. IV, 3, 155.

Flaminius, name of a servant in Tim. II, 2, 194. III, 1, 7. 8. 15. 33.

Flanders, county in the Low Countries: H6C IV, 5, 21. H8 III, 2, 319.

Flank, the side of the human body between the ribs and the hip: Ven. 1053. 1115.

Flannel, a soft nappy stuff of wool; ludicrously used to designate a Welshman: *I am not able to answer the Welsh f.* Wiv. V, 5, 172 (Wales being famous for the manufacture of it).

Flap, a piece of cloth hanging loose: *thou green sarcenet f. for a sore eye*, Troil. V, 1, 36.

Flap-dragon, subst. a small combustible body, set on fire and put afloat in a glass of liquor, to be swallowed flaming: LLL V, 1, 45. H4B II, 4, 267.

Flap-dragon, vb. to swallow: *how the sea —ed it*, Wint. III, 3, 100.

Flap-eared, having broad pendulous ears: *beetle-headed f. knave*, Shr. IV, 1, 160.

Flap-jack, a pancake: Per. II, 1, 87.

Flap-mouthed, having broad hanging lips: *another f. mourner* (viz a dog) Ven. 920.

Flare, vb. to glitter, to flutter with a splendid show: *ribands pendent, —ing 'bout her head*, Wiv. IV, 6, 42.

Flash, subst. 1) a burst of light, a sudden blaze: *lightning f.* Tit. II, 1, 3. Caes. I, 3, 52. Per. III, 1, 6. Cymb. IV, 2, 270.

2) a sudden burst or outbreak of high spirits: *the f. and outbreak of a fiery mind*, Hml. II, 1, 33. *your —es of merriment*, V, 1, 210.

Flash, vb. 1) to burst on the sight with a sudden blaze: *—ing fire will follow*, H5 II, 1, 56. Trans.: *it —ed forth fire, as lightning from the sky*, Ven. 348.

2) to shine, to dazzle the eye: *which —es now a Phoenix,* Tim. II, 1, 32.

3) to break out: *he —es into one gross crime or other,* Lr. I, 3, 4.

Flask, a powder-horn: LLL V, 2, 619. Rom. III, 3, 132.

Flat, subst. 1) low level ground: Tp. II, 2, 2. John V, 6, 40. Hml. IV, 5, 100. V, 1, 275. Cymb. III, 3, 11.

2) a shallow, a sand bank: Merch. I, 1, 26. III, 1, 5.

Flat, adj. 1) without eminences, plain, level: *f. meads,* Tp. IV, 63. *smite f. the thick rotundity of the earth,* Lr. III, 2, 7.

2) prostrate, level with the ground: *I'll fall f.* Tp. II, 2, 16. *to lay f.* == to destroy: *to lay all f.* Cor. III, 1, 198. 204. Cymb. I, 4, 23. *down with the nose, down with it f.* Tim. IV, 3, 158.

3) stale, insipid, dull: *the f. unraised spirits,* H5 Prol. 9. *drink up the lees and dregs of a f. tamed piece,* Troil. IV, 1, 62. *weary, stale, f. and unprofitable,* Hml. I, 2, 133. *that we are made of stuff so f. and dull,* IV, 7, 31.

4) depressed, low: *now you are too f. and mar the concord,* Gentl. I, 2, 93 (quibbling; cf. v. 91).

5) absolute, downright: *f. blasphemy,* Meas. II, 2, 131. *f. transgression of a schoolboy,* Ado II, 1, 229. *f. perjury,* IV, 2, 44. 52. LLL IV, 3, 293. Shr. V, 1, 37. John III, 1, 298. *that's f.* = that's certain: LLL III, 102. H4A I, 3, 218. IV, 2, 43.

Flatlong, not edgewise, but with the flat side downward: *what a blow was there given! an it had not fallen f.* Tp. II, 1, 181.

Flatly, downright: *at his look she f. falleth down,* Ven. 463. *he tells me f. there is no mercy for me in heaven,* Merch. III, 5, 34. Shr. I, 2, 77. John V, 2, 126. H4A II, 4, 3.

Flatness, downrightness, absoluteness, completeness: *the f. of my misery,* Wint. III, 2, 123.

Flatter, to flutter, to drive in disorder: *like an eagle in a dove-cote, I —ed your Volscians in Corioli,* Cor. V, 6, 116 (cf. the German *flattern.* M. Edd. *fluttered*).

Flatter, 1) to treat with praise or blandishments; a) trans.: Pilgr. 403. Sonn. 138, 14. Gentl. II, 4, 147. 148. IV, 4, 192. Merch. II, 5, 13. As III, 5, 54. V, 4, 46. Shr. IV, 2, 31. R2 I, 1, 25. II, 1, 87. H6A V, 5, 25. H6B I, 3, 169. R3 I, 2, 224. Caes. II, 1, 208 etc. b) absol.: Ven. 284. Pilgr. 413. Gentl. III, 1, 102. IV, 3, 12. Wiv. III, 2, 7. As IV, 1, 188. John II, 503. 504. H6A V, 3, 142. H6C V, 6, 3. Mcb. III, 2, 33 etc. Followed by *with: should dying men f. with those that live?* R2 II, 1, 88.

2) to gratify or encourage with hopes or favourable representations; a) trans.: *reviving joy bids her rejoice and —s her it is Adonis' voice,* Ven. 978. *despair and hope makes thee ridiculous: the one doth f. thee in thoughts unlikely,* 989. *—ing himself in project of a power,* H4B I, 3, 29. Lucr. 296. 1061. 1559. 1560. Sonn. 28, 11. 33, 2. R2 V, 5, 23. H5 V, 2, 239. H6A II, 1, 51. H6C III, 2, 143. Hml. III, 4, 145 etc. b) absol.: *the one sweetly —s, th' other feareth harm,* Lucr. 172. 641. Sonn. 87, 13. H6B I, 1, 163. R3 IV, 4, 85. Rom. V, 1, 1. Followed by *with: unless I f. with myself too much,* Gentl. IV, 4, 193. *desire him not to f. with his lord nor hold him up with hopes,* Tw. I, 5, 322.

3) to blandish, to soothe, to please: *thou dost give me —ing busses,* H4B II, 4, 291. *to f. up these powers of mine with rest,* LLL V, 2, 824, i. e. to indulge in, to give myself completely up to rest.

Flatterer, 1) one who flatters, a fawner, wheedler: Sonn. 112, 11. R2 II, 1, 100. 242. IV, 306. H6A II, 4, 31. Cor. I, 9, 43. III, 1, 45. Tim. I, 1, 58. 233. I, 2, 83. III, 2, 72. IV, 3, 206 etc. Caes. II, 1, 206. III, 1, 193. IV, 3, 91. V, 1, 44. 45. Lr. II, 2, 117. Per. I, 2, 60.

2) that which gratifies and deludes with hopes: *and fear to find mine eye too great a f. for my mind,* Tw. I, 5, 328. *if thine eye be not a f., come thou on my side,* R3 I, 4, 271. Quibbling: *I will put off hope and keep it no longer for my f.* Tp. III, 3, 8. cf. R2 II, 2, 69.

Flattering-sweet, (O. Edd. not hyphened), very gratifying: Rom. II, 2, 141.

Flattery, 1) adulation: Ven. 425. Sonn. 114, 2. Gentl. IV, 2, 97. Err. III, 2, 28. As II, 1, 10. H4A IV, 1, 2. H5 III, 7, 125 (*there is f. in friendship,* a proverb). IV, 1, 268. V, 2, 315. H6A II, 4, 35. H6B III, 1, 28. H8 V, 3, 124. V, 5, 17. Cor. III, 2, 137. V, 6, 23. Tim. I, 2, 257. Caes. III, 1, 52. Cymb. V, 5, 64. Per. I, 2, 39. IV, 4, 45. Plur.: Tim. I, 2, 142. III, 6, 101. Lr. I, 3, 20.

2) gratifying deception, delusion: *my friend and I are one; sweet f.! then she loves but me alone,* Sonn. 42, 14. *some f. for this evil,* LLL IV, 3, 286. *he does me double wrong that wounds me with the —ies of his tongue,* R2 III, 2, 216. *would I had never trod this English earth, nor felt the —ies that grow upon it,* H8 III, 1, 144. *now farewell, f., die, Andronicus; thou dost not slumber,* Tit. III, 1, 254. *the infinite —ies that follow youth and opulency,* Tim. V, 1, 37. *she is persuaded I will marry her, out of her own love and f., not out of my promise,* Oth. IV, 1, 133.

Flaunts, subst. finery, showy apparel: *in these my borrowed f.,* Wint. IV, 4, 23.

Flavius, name: Meas. IV, 5, 6. 10. Tim. I, 2, 163. Caes. I, 2, 289. V, 3, 108 (O. Edd. *Flavio*).

Flaw, subst. 1) breach, crack, fissure: *my love to thee is sound, sans crack or f.* LLL V, 2, 415. *this heart shall break into a hundred thousand —s,* Lr. II, 4, 288. Figuratively: *observe how Antony becomes his f.* Ant. III, 12, 34.*

2) a sudden burst of wind, a gust: *gusts and foul —s to herdmen and to herds,* Ven. 456. *as humorous as winter and as sudden as —s congealed in the spring of day,* H4B IV, 4, 35 (i. e. probably gusts carrying ice with them. According to Edwards and Dyce: small blades of ice). *calm the fury of this madbred f.* H6B III, 1, 354. *a great sea-mark, standing every f.* Cor. V, 3, 74. *to expel the winter's f.* Hml. V, 1, 239. *I do not fear the f.* Per. III, 1, 39. Tropically, = impetuosity, storm of passion: *falling in the —s of her own youth,* Meas. II, 3, 11. *these —s and starts would well become a woman's story,* Mcb. III, 4, 63.

Flaw, vb. to damage by a fissure, to make a rent in: *France hath —ed the league,* H8 I, 1, 95. *which hath —ed the heart of all their loyalties,* I, 2, 21. *his —ed heart...burst,* Lr. V, 3, 196 (cf. *Honour-flawed*).

Flax, the fibres of the plant Linum, cleansed and combed for the spinner: Wiv. V, 5, 159. Tw. I, 3, 108. H6B V, 2, 55. Lr. III, 7, 106.

Flaxen, of the colour of flax: *all f. was his poll,* Hml. IV, 5, 196.

Flax-wench, a woman whose occupation is to dress flax: Wint. I, 2, 277.

Flay, to strip of the skin, to skin: Wint. III, 2, 177. IV, 4, 812. 835. 845. Cor. I, 6, 22. III, 3, 89. Lr. I, 4, 330. Jocularly = to undress: *the gentleman is half —ed already,* Wint. IV, 4, 655 (O. Edd *fled*).

Flea, the insect Pulex: Wiv. IV, 2, 158. LLL V, 2, 698. Shr. IV, 3, 110. Tw. III, 2, 67. H4A II, 1, 16. 23. H5 II, 3, 42. III, 7, 156.

Fleance, (dissyll., except Mcb. III, 1, 36) name of the son of Banquo: Mcb. III, 1, 36. 135. III, 2, 37. III, 3, 17. III, 4, 18. 20. III, 6, 6. 7. 20.

Fleckled (the spurious Q1 and M. Edd. *flecked,* Pope *fleckered*) spotted, dappled: *f. darkness like a drunkard reels,* Rom. II, 3, 3.

Fledged, already covered with feathers: *Shylock knew the bird was f.* Merch. III, 1, 32. Used, in jest, of a beard: *whose chin is not yet f.* H4B I, 2, 23.

Flee (only once, LLL III, 66, in the present; in all other passages the impf. or partic. *fled*) 1) to run from danger, and to hasten away in general; a) intr.: Ven. 793. 1037. Sonn. 71, 3. 148, 3. Pilgr. 130. 291. Phoen. 23. Gentl. V, 2, 35. 47. V, 3, 10. Wiv. IV, 5, 73. Err. V, 154. 263. Ado V, 1, 193. 209. Mids. III, 2, 405. V, 143. Merch. II, 8, 16. All's II, 3, 305. H6A I, 2, 23. II, 2, 1. H6B III, 2, 151. IV, 8, 68. IV, 10, 70. R3 V, 5, 16 (*the soldiers fled* = the soldiers who are fled) etc. etc. With *from: the rogue fled from me,* H4B II, 4, 248. Rom. I, 1, 136. *fled from words,* Cor. II, 2, 76. Oth. II, 1, 152.

b) trans.: *Stafford fled the field,* H4B I, 1, 18. *that which we have fled during the life,* H6A IV, 7, 49. *so fled his enemies my warlike father,* H6C II, 1, 19. Mcb. V, 7, 67.

2) to fly, to be borne through the air with rapidity: *love's golden arrow at him should have fled,* Ven. 947. *I shoot thee at the swain. Thump then and I flee,* LLL III, 66. *arrows fled not swifter toward their aim,* H4B I, 1, 123.

Fleece, subst. 1) the wool shorn from a sheep at once: As II, 4, 79. H6C II, 5, 37. V, 6, 8. Figuratively: *I would you had won the f. that he hath lost,* Merch. III, 2, 245.

2) the skin of a sheep covered with wool: *with her own white f. her voice controlled,* Lucr. 678. *the golden f.* Merch. I, 1, 170. III, 2, 244. *the Golden F.* the highest order of knighthood in Burgundy: H6A IV, 7, 69.

3) curled hair: *ere beauty's dead f. made another gay,* Sonn. 68, 8. *my f of woolly hair,* Tit. II, 3, 34.

Fleece, vb. to strip, to rob, to plunder: H4A II, 2, 90. H6B III, 1, 129.

Fleer, subst. sneer, look of contempt: Oth. IV, 1, 83 (Qq *jeeres*).

Fleer, vb. to make a wry face, to grin ("to make an evil countenance with the mouth by uncovering of the teeth", cf. Halliwell, dictionary of archaisms, I, 361): *one rubbed his elbow thus, and —ed and swore a better speech was never spoke before,* LLL V, 2, 109. *a man that is no —ing tell-tale,* Caes. I, 3, 117. With *at: never f. and jest at me,* Ado V, 1, 58. *to f. and scorn at our solemnity,* Rom. I, 5, 59.

Fleet, subst. a squadron of ships: Tp. I, 2, 226. 232. V, 316. Ado II, 1, 148. Tw. V, 60. H5 III Chor. 5. 16. H6C III, 3, 253. Oth. I, 3, 8. 35. II, 1, 10. 17. 24. II, 2, 4. Ant. III, 7, 37. IV, 12, 11.

Fleet, the prison for insolvent debtors in London: H4B V, 5, 97.

Fleet, adj. swift: LLL V, 2, 261. Shr. Ind. 1, 26. 2, 50.

Fleet, vb. 1) to flit, to fly, to pass away with rapidity: *make glad and sorry seasons as thou* (time) *—s,* Sonn. 19, 5. *from thee, the pleasure of the —ing year,* 97, 2; cf. *so cares and joys abound, as seasons f.* H6B II, 4, 4. *how all the other passions f. to air,* Merch. III, 2, 108. *from the gallows did his fell soul f.* IV, 1, 135. *those souls that to their everlasting residence shall f.* John II, 285. *and I, hence —ing, here remain with thee,* Ant. I, 3, 104. *to darkness f. souls that fly backwards,* Cymb. V, 3, 25. Hence *—ing* = inconstant: *a dream, a breath, a froth of —ing joy,* Lucr. 212. *false, —ing, perjured Clarence,* R3 I, 4, 55. *the —ing moon no planet is of mine,* Ant. V, 2, 240.

2) to float: *our severed navy have knit again and f., threatening most sea-like,* Ant. III, 13, 171.

3) tr. to make pass lightly and swiftly: *f. the time carelessly,* As I, 1, 124.

Fleet-foot, swift: *the f. roe,* Ven. 561.

Fleet-winged, flying swiftly: *f. duty,* Lucr. 1216.

Flegmatic, see *Phlegmatic.*

Fleming, a native of Flanders: *I will rather trust a F. with my butter,* Wiv. II, 2, 316.

Flemish, resembling a Fleming, unwieldy and given to drink like a Fleming: *this F. drunkard,* Wiv. II, 1, 23.

Flesh, subst. the animal substance investing the bones and covered with the skin: Ven. 56. 142. Lucr. 739. Sonn. 44, 1. Tp. III, 3, 46. Wiv. V, 5, 91. Err. II, 2, 145. Ado IV, 1, 145. Merch. I, 3, 151. 166. 168. III, 2, 288. As IV, 3, 148. H6B III, 1, 301. Hml. I, 2, 129 etc. *get thyself in f.* Rom. V, 1, 84 (= recruit your flesh). *you shall be yet far fairer than you are. He means in f.* Ant. I, 2, 17 (= you shall gather flesh). *my trembling f.* R3 V, 3, 181. *makes my f. tremble,* Rom. I, 5, 92. *devour them, f. and fell,* Lr. V, 3, 24. *she would not exchange f. with one that loved her,* Wint. IV, 4, 285 (refused his love). — Serving to denote the whole body, the animal part of man in general: *the mountain of mad f. that claims marriage of me,* Err. IV, 4, 159. *a pretty piece of f.* Ado IV, 2, 85. LLL III, 156. Tw. I, 5, 30. As III, 2, 68. *the liver-vein, which makes f. a deity,* LLL IV, 3, 74. *a thing stuck on with oaths upon your finger, and so riveted with faith unto your f.* Merch. V, 169. Similarly *f. and blood:* Tp. V, 114. LLL I, 1, 186. All's I, 3, 38. Tw. V, 36. H6B I, 1, 233. Denoting relationship: *thou art a collop of my f.* H6A V, 4, 18. *man and wife is one f.* Hml. IV, 3, 54; cf. *best of my f.* Cor. V, 3, 42; *I feed on mother's f.* Per. I, 1, 65. 130. *f. and blood, you, brother mine,* Tp. V, 74 (i. e. my f. and blood, yea, my brother). *thou art mine own f. and blood,* Merch. II, 2, 98. III, 1, 37. 40. All's I, 3, 50. Tit. IV, 2, 84. Serving as the emblem of human frailty in general, and of sensuality in particular: *no dull f.* Sonn. 51, 11. *capable of our f.* H8 V, 3, 12. *his doubled spirit requickened what in f. was fatigate,*

Cor. II, 2, 121. *I will be f. and blood*, Ado V, 1, 34. *as true we are as f. and blood can be*, LLL IV, 3, 214. *mock not f. and blood with solemn reverence*, R2 III, 2, 171. *men are f. and blood and apprehensive*, Caes. III, 1, 67. *the f. being proud, desire doth fight with grace*, Lucr. 712. *f. stays no farther reason*, Sonn. 151, 8. *to hearken after the f.* LLL I, 1, 220. Wiv. IV, 4, 24. Meas. II, 1, 267. All's I, 3, 31. H4B II, 4, 379. H6A I, 1, 41. Troil. V, 10, 46. Tim. IV, 3, 156. *I will tarry in despite of the f. and the blood*, Shr. Ind. 2, 130 (Sly's speech).

Denoting animal food: *over-roasted f.* Shr. IV, 1, 178. *didst eat strange f.* Ant. I, 4, 67. Quibbling: *suffering f. to be eaten*, H4B II, 4, 372. *when f. is cheap*, V, 3, 20. Opposed to *fish*: *at f. or fish*, Err. III, 1, 22. *neither fish nor f.* H4A III, 3, 144. Rom. II, 4, 40. Per. II, 1, 27. 85.

Flesh, vb. 1) to feed with flesh, to satiate: *this night he —es his will in the spoil of her honour*, All's IV, 3, 19. *the wild dog shall f. his tooth on every innocent*, H4B IV, 5, 133. *the kindred of him hath been —ed upon us*, H5 II, 4, 50.

2) to make fierce and eager for combat (as a dog fed with flesh only): *put up your iron: you are well —ed; come on*, Tw. IV, 1, 43. *shall a beardless boy f. his spirit in a warlike soil*, John V, 1, 71. *the head which princes —ed with conquest aim to hit*, H4B I, 1, 149. Part. *—ed* = fierce, hardened: *the —ed soldier, rough and hard of heart*, H5 III, 3, 11. *—ed villains, bloody dogs*, R3 IV, 3, 6.*

3) to feed with flesh for the first time, to initiate: *full bravely hast thou —ed thy maiden sword*, H4A V, 4, 133. *did f. his puny sword in Frenchmen's blood*, H6A IV, 7, 36. *come, I'll f. ye; come on, young master*, Lr. II, 2, 49.

Flesh-fly, a fly that feeds on flesh and deposits her eggs in it: Tp. III, 1, 63.

Fleshly, corporeal: John IV, 2, 245.

Fleshment, insolence, fierceness: *and in the f. of this dread exploit, drew on me here again*, Lr. II, 2, 130.

Fleshmonger, a fornicator: Meas. V, 337.

Flewed, having large hanging chaps: *my hounds are bred out of the Spartan kind, so f., so sanded*, Mids. IV, 1, 125.

Flexible, bending, pliant: *when the splitting wind makes f. the knees of knotted oaks*, Troil. I, 3, 50. Hence = tractable, soft: H6C I, 4, 141.

Flexure, the act of bending: H5 IV, 1, 272. Troil. II, 3, 115.

Flibbertigibbet, name of a fiend: Lr. III, 4, 120.* IV, 1, 64.

Flickering (Qq *flitkering* and *fletkering*, Ff *flicking*) twinkling: *the wreath of radiant fire on f. Phoebus' front*, Lr. II, 2, 114.

Flier, one that flees, a fugitive: Cor. I, 4, 45. 49. II, 2, 107. Cymb. V, 3, 2.

Flight, 1) hasty or secret departure: Lucr. 968. Gentl. II, 4, 180. II, 6, 37. V, 2, 43. Ado V, 4, 127. Mids. I, 1, 212. 246. V, 310 (*take thy f.*). Merch. III, 1, 28. As I, 3, 139. All's II, 5, 97. III, 2, 130. Wint. II, 1, 174. IV, 4, 519. 554. H6C IV, 6, 89. Mcb. IV, 2, 3. 13. Cymb. III, 5, 100. V, 5, 46. Per. I, 1, 142. = faithless desertion: *Theseus' perjury and unjust f.* Gentl. IV, 4, 173. *we will untread the steps of damned f.* John V, 4, 52. 60.

2) the act of fleeing from an enemy: Compl. 244. Meas. III, 1, 12. H4B I, 1, 130. H6A III, 2, 105. 114. IV, 2, 24. IV, 5, 11. 26. 41. IV, 6, 52. H6C II, 2, 30. II, 3, 12. II, 6, 24. III, 3, 36 (*put to f.*). Troil. V, 10, 12. Cor. I, 4, 38. Tim. V, 4, 13. Lr. III, 4, 10. Ant. III, 10, 28.

3) the act of passing through the air: Lucr. 695. Mids. IV, 1, 104. R2 I, 3, 61. H4A III, 2, 31. H6C II, 1, 130. Mcb. III, 1, 141. III, 2, 41. *to make a f.* Gentl. II, 7, 12. Wint. IV, 4, 15. *flies an eagle f.* Tim. I, 1, 49. *his fellow of the self-same f.* Merch I, 1, 141 (i. e. flying to the same distance).

4) a flock of birds, or other beings passing through the air together: *a f. of fowl scattered by winds*, Tit. V, 3, 68. *—s of angels sing thee to thy rest*, Hml. V, 2, 371.

5) a kind of light and well-feathered arrow: *challenged Cupid at the f.* Ado I, 1, 40.

Flighty, swift: *the f. purpose never is o'ertook unless the deed go with it*, Mcb. IV, 1, 145.

Flinch, not to stand the test, to come short, to fail: *if I break time, or f. in property of what I spoke, unpitied let me die*, All's II, 1, 190. *if he f., chide me for it*, Troil. III, 2, 114.

Fling, subst. a contemptuous remark, sarcasm: *else would I have a f. at Winchester*, H6A III, 1, 64.

Fling, vb. (impf. and part. *flung*) 1) trans. to throw: *the water, whose enmity he flung aside*, Tp. II, 1, 116. *here I'll f. the pillow*, Shr. IV, 1, 204. *the mouth of passage shall we f. wide ope*, John II, 449. *f. up his cap*, H6B IV, 8, 15. *f. it at thy face*, H6C V, 1, 51. *which (accusations) he fain would have flung from him*, H8 II, 1, 25. *f. away ambition*, III, 2, 441. *matrons flung gloves upon him*, Cor. II, 1, 279.

2) intr. to rush: *he's flung in rage from this ingrateful seat of monstrous friends*, Tim. IV, 2, 45. *Duncan's horses broke their stalls, flung out*, Mcb. II, 4, 16 (or is it, by a hysteron-proteron, = kicked out?).

Flint, 1) a stone commonly used to strike fire. Lucr. 176. 181. LLL IV, 2, 90. H6B III, 2, 317. Troil. III, 3, 257. Tim. I, 1, 22. Caes. II, 1, 36. IV, 3, 111.

2) any hard stone: *harder than f., for stone at rain relenteth*, Ven. 200. *the ruthless f. doth cut my tender feet*, H6B II, 4, 34. *I could have up rocks and fight with f.* V, 1, 24. Cor. V, 3, 53. Tit. II, 3, 141. Rom. II, 6, 17. Cymb. III, 6, 34. Per. IV, 4, 43. Plur. *—s: shards, —s and pebbles should be thrown on her*, Hml. V, 1, 254. Symbol of hardness: *love make his heart of f.* Tw. I, 5, 305. Merch. IV, 1, 31 (Q2 F1 *—s*). Tit. V, 3, 88. *being incensed, he's f.* H4B IV, 4, 33. R3 I, 3, 140. *f. bosom*, R2 V, 1, 3. *throw my heart against the f. and hardness of my fault*, Ant. IV, 9, 16.

Flint castle, a castle in Wales: R2 III, 2, 209.

Flint-hearted, hard-hearted: Ven. 95.

Flinty, 1) consisting of hard stones: John II, 384. R2 V, 5, 20. H6A II, 1, 27. H6B II, 4, 8. Oth. I, 3, 231.

2) hard, hard-hearted: Ven. 199. All's IV, 4, 7. H6B III, 2, 99. H6C I, 4, 142. II, 1, 202. Tim. IV, 3, 491.

Flirt-gills (O. Edd. *flurt-gills*) women of light behaviour: *I am none of his f.* Rom. II, 4, 162.

Float, vb. to be borne along on water: Err. I,

1, 87. V, 348. John II, 74. Cor. IV, 1, 7. Mcb. IV, 2, 21.

Flock, subst. 1) a lock of wool: *put a few —s in the point*, H4A II, 1, 7.

2) a crowd, a company: *when the rich golden shaft hath killed the f. of all affections else*, Tw. I, 1, 36. *like a f. of wild geese*, H4A II, 4, 152. *gathered —s of friends*, H6C II, 1, 112. *this f. of drunkards*, Oth. II, 3, 61.

3) Especially a number of sheep grazing together: Ven. 685. Pilgr. 245. 286. Mids. II, 1, 97. Merch. IV, 1, 114. As II, 4, 83. 88. 92. III, 5, 81. Wint. IV, 4, 70. 109. H6B II, 2, 73. III, 1, 258. H6C II, 5, 31. H8 I, 4, 70. Applied to a congregation: *when that your f., assembled by the bell* (as sheep by the bell-wether) *encircled you*, H4B IV, 2, 5.

Flock, vb., to gather and repair in crowds: *they f. together in consent*, H4B V, 1, 78. *many young gentlemen f. to him*, As I, 1, 123. H6C IV, 8, 5. *f. to follow him*, H4B I, 1, 209. *f. to their aid*, R3 IV, 4, 507.

Flood, 1) any great body and flow of water: Ven. 824. Lucr. 266. 1118. 1677. Pilgr. 84. Mids. II, 1, 5. III, 2, 383. Merch. V, 80. All's II, 1, 142. John IV, 2, 139. V, 4, 53. H5 II, 1, 97. R3 IV, 4, 512. Cor. IV, 5, 137. Tit. III, 1, 126. = the sea: Lucr. 653. Mids. II, 1, 127. Merch. I, 1, 10. IV, 1, 72 (*the main f.*). John III, 4, 1. H4B I, 1, 62. 154. V, 2, 132. H5 V Chor. 10. H6C II, 5, 9. V, 4, 5. R3 I, 4, 37. H8 III, 2, 197. Troil. I, 1, 105. Tit. IV, 2, 103. Tim. V, 1, 219. Hml. I, 4, 69. Oth. II, 1, 2. 17. Per. III Chor. 45. *moving accidents by f. and field*, Oth. I, 3, 135 (= by sea and land). Used of rivers: Compl. 44. Ado I, 1, 318. H4A I, 3, 103. H5 I, 2, 45. R3 I, 4, 45. Caes. I, 2, 103. Of flowing tears: Err. III, 2, 46. Shr. Ind. 2, 67. H6A III, 3, 56. H6B III, 1, 199. Tit. V, 3, 90. Of a stream of blood: Lucr. 1741. *fiery —s*, Meas. III, 1, 122.

2) the great deluge: *Noah's f.* Err. III, 2, 108. As V, 4, 35. Caes. I, 2, 152.

3) opposed to ebb, the flowing of the tide: *lose the f.* Gentl. II, 3, 46. John V, 7, 64. *taken at the f.* Caes. IV, 3, 219. cf. *the moon, the governess of —s*, Mids. II, 1, 103.

4) overflowing, abundance, plenty: *this accident and f. of fortune*, Tw. IV, 3, 11. *such a f. of greatness fell on you*, H4A V, 1, 48. *never came reformation in a f. with such a heady currance*, H5 1, 1, 33. *this great f. of visitors*, Tim. I, 1, 42. *such a sudden f. of mutiny*, Caes. III, 2, 215 (similar to a raging sea). *in f* = overflowing: *his youth in f., I'll prove this truth with my three drops of blood*, Troil. I, 3, 300. *his eyes in f. with laughter*, Cymb. I, 6, 74.

Floodgate, a sluice: Ven. 959. H4A II, 4, 435. Adjectively: *my grief is of so f. and o'erbearing nature*, Oth. I, 3, 56 (i. e. has the impetuosity of a mighty flood rushing through an opened sluice).

Floor, subst. 1) a level ground, a plain: *look how the f. of heaven is thick inlaid with patines of bright gold*, Merch. V, 58.

2) the bottom of a room: *mouse that creeps on f.* Mids. V, 223. *o' the f.* Cymb. IV, 2, 212. *i' the f.* III, 6, 50.

Flora, the goddess of flowers: Wint. IV, 4, 2.

Florence, 1) town and dukedom in Italy: Shr. I, 1, 14. IV, 2, 90. All's III, 2, 54. 71. IV, 3, 18 etc. Oth. I, 3, 45.

2) the duke of F.: *and F. is denied*, All's I, 2, 12.

Florentine, a native of Florence: Ado I, 1, 11. Shr. I, 1, 209. All's I, 2, 1. III, 6, 23. V, 3, 130. 158. Oth. I, 1, 20. III, 1, 43. *the F.* = —s: All's I, 2, 6. IV, 1, 80. IV, 3, 326.

Florentius, name of a knight in Gower's Confessio Amantis: *be she as foul as was —' love*, Shr I, 2, 69 (Nares: "Florentius bound himself to marry a deformed hag, provided she taught him the solution of a riddle, on which his life depended").

Florizel, name in Wint. IV, 1, 22. IV, 2, 29. IV, 3, 13. V, 1, 85.

Flote, flood, sea: *and are upon the Mediterranean f.* Tp. I, 2, 234.

Flour, the finer part of meal: *all from me do back receive the f. of all, and leave me but the bran*, Cor. I, 1, 149 (Ff *flowre*; some M. Edd. *flower*).

Flourish, subst. 1) varnish, gloss, ostentatious embellishment: *time doth transfix the f. set on youth*, Sonn. 60, 9. *my beauty ... needs not the painted f. of your praise*, LLL II, 14. *lend me the f. of all gentle tongues*, IV, 3, 238. *poor painted queen, vain f. of my fortune*, R3 I, 3, 241. IV, 4, 82 (a mere varnish representing what I was indeed). *since brevity is the soul of wit, and tediousness the limbs and outward —es*, Hml. II, 2, 91. *shall I redeliver you even so? To this effect, sir; after what f. your nature will*, V, 2, 187.

2) a sounding of trumpets in triumph: *then music is even as the f. when true subjects bow to a new-crowned monarch*, Merch. III, 2, 49. *a f., trumpets!* R3 IV, 4, 148.

Flourish, vb. 1) intr. a) to blow, to blossom: *one —ing branch of his most royal root*, R2 I, 2, 18. *until it* (the rose) *wither with me to my grave or f. to the height of my degree*, H6A II, 4, 111. *wither one rose, and let the other f.* H6C II, 5, 101. *like the lily, that once was mistress of the field and —ed*, H8 III, 1, 152.

b) to thrive, to be prosperous: *—ing peopled towns*, Gentl. V, 4, 3. *'tis youth in ladies' eyes that —eth*, Shr. II, 342. *a seducer —es, and a poor maid is undone*, All's V, 3, 146. Wint. I, 2, 359. H6B II, 2, 57. R3 V, 3, 130. 138. 158. H8 IV, 2, 125. V, 5, 53. Tit. I, 38. Tim. V, 1, 13. Hml. V, 2, 40. Cymb. V, 4, 145. Per. II, 2, 47.

c) to brandish a sword: *give that changing piece to him that —ed for her with his sword*, Tit. I, 310. *all of us fell down, whilst bloody treason —ed over us*, Caes. III, 2, 196.

d) to sound in triumph: *why do the emperor's trumpets f. thus?* Tit. IV, 2, 49.

2) trans. a) to colour, to varnish: *the justice of your title to him doth f. the deceit*, Meas. IV, 1, 75. cf. *O'erflourish*.

b) to brandish: *—es his blade*, Rom. I, 1, 85.

Flout, subst. a mock, a gibe: LLL V, 2, 269. 397. 854. *I could have given my uncle's grace a f.* R3 II, 4, 24.

Flout, vb. to mock, to make a fool of; 1) trans.: Tp. III, 2, 130. 131. Err. I, 2, 91. II, 2, 22. 46. Ado II, 3, 148. Mids. II, 2, 128. III, 2, 327. Shr. II, 29. John II, 373. H6A I, 3, 14. IV, 1, 75. R3 II, 1, 78. Troil. IV, 2, 27. Cor. II, 3, 168. Mcb. I, 2, 49.

2) intr. with *at*: *never f. at me*, Ado V, 4, 108.

As I, 2, 47. Tit. III, 1, 246. Absolutely: Ado I, 1, 186. V, 1, 95. As V, 1, 13. With an accus. denoting the result: *a college of wit-crackers cannot f. me out of my humour*, Ado V, 4, 102. *f. me out of my calling*, As III, 3, 108. *ere you f. old ends any further*, Ado I, 1, 290 (i. e. recite old ends to mock me).

Flouting-stock, a laughing-stock: Wiv. III, 1, 120 and IV, 5, 83 (Evans' speeches).

Flow, subst. 1) the streaming, running of a fluid: *whom from the f. of gall I name not*, H8 I, 1, 152. *set mine eyes at f.* Tim. II, 2, 172. *scornedst our brain's f.* V, 4, 76 (i. e. tears).

2) the high tide, opposed to the ebb: *make —s and ebbs*, Tp. V, 270. Figuratively: H4A I, 2, 43. Troil. II, 3, 139. Tim. II, 2, 151.

3) height of water in general: *add to his* (the sea's) *f.*, *but alter not his taste*, Lucr. 651. *they take the f. of the Nile by certain scales i' the pyramid*, Ant. II, 7, 20. Figuratively: *nor cease his f. of riot*, Tim. II, 2, 3.

Flow, vb. (impf. —*ed*: Wint. V, 1, 102. Rom. II, 4, 41. partic. —*ed*: H4B IV, 4, 125. V, 2, 130. H6C II, 5, 72. *flown*: All's II, 1, 142) 1) to stream, to run: Tp. II, 1, 222. Meas. I, 3, 52. All's II, 1, 142. H6C IV, 8, 54. Used of tears: Compl. 284. LLL IV, 3, 29. H6A I, 1, 83. H6B III, 1, 199. H6C II, 5, 72. Of the eye shedding tears: *an eye unused to f.* Sonn. 30, 5. *draw the eye to f.* H8 Prol. 4. *our eyes f. with joy*, Cor. V, 3, 99. Figuratively, = to descend: *he did not f. from honourable sources*, Per. IV, 3, 27.

2) to rise, opposed to ebb: *ebbs and —s*, Lucr. 1569. LLL IV, 3, 215. H4A I, 2, 36. Rom. III, 5, 134. Lr. V, 3, 19. *doth it* (pride) *not f. as hugely as the sea*, As II, 7, 72. H4B IV, 4, 125. V, 2, 130. *the princely blood —s in his cheek*, Cymb. III, 3, 93.

3) Hence serving to express any kind of fulness, abundance and plenty: *if wit f. from it*, Wint. II, 2, 52. *what expense by the hour seems to f. from him*, H8 III, 2, 109. *he is so full of grace that it —s over on all that need*, Ant. V, 2, 24. *f., f., you heavenly blessings, on her!* Cymb. III, 5, 166. —*ing cups*, H5 IV, 3, 55. Oth. II, 3, 60. *let the health go round. Let it f. this way*, Tim. I, 2, 55 (i. e. let it be drunk with full cups; an expression ridiculed by Apemantus). *your verse —ed with her beauty once*, Wint. V, 1, 102 (was full of the praise of her beauty). *the numbers that Petrarch —ed in*, Rom. II, 4, 41. *I f. in grief*, Ado IV, 1, 251. *to make the even truth in pleasure f.* All's V, 3, 326. *you f. to great distraction*, Troil. V, 2, 41 (i. e. your heart is so full that it will overflow and vent itself in madness). *does purpose honour to you no less —ing than marchioness of Pembroke*, H8 II, 3, 62. *with gifts of nature —ing, and swelling o'er with arts and exercise*, Troil. IV, 4, 80.

Flower, subst. (usually monosyll., but dissyll. in Lucr. 1227. Sonn. 124, 4. Mids. III, 2, 102. Caes. I, 1, 55). 1) the displayed bud of a plant: *women are as roses, whose fair f. being once displayed, doth fall that very hour*, Tw. II, 4, 39.

2) the expanded blossom with its stalk: Ven. 8. 65. Lucr. 870. Sonn. 65, 4. 94, 9. 124, 4. Compl. 75. 147. Tp. IV, 1, 78. Gentl. II, 4, 162. Wiv. V, 5, 66. 74. Meas. II, 2, 167. Mids. II, 1, 27. 247. III, 2, 204 etc. etc. *maiden —s*, H8 IV, 2, 169 (see *Maiden*).

3) beauty: *shall ill become the f. of England's*

face, change the complexion of her maid-pale peace to scarlet indignation, R2 III, 3, 97. *how she gins to blow into life's f. again*, Per. III, 2, 96.

4) one who is the ornament of his class: *this is the f. that smiles on every one*, LLL V, 2, 331. *I am that f.* (viz Hector) 661. *thou hast slain the f. of Europe for his chivalry*, H6C II, 1, 71. *he's one of the —s of Troy*, Troil. I, 2, 203. *come knights from east to west and cull their f.*, *Ajax shall cope the best*, II, 3, 275. *f. of warriors*, Cor. I, 6, 32. *he's a f., in faith, a very f.* Rom. I, 3, 78. *he is not the f. of courtesy*, II, 5, 44. *f. as she was*, Rom. IV, 5, 37. V, 3, 12. cf. also II, 4, 62.

Flower-de-luce, the white lily: Wint. IV, 4, 127. Armorial emblem of France: H6A I, 1, 80. I, 2, 99. H6B V, 1, 11. Hence King Henry calls Princess Katharine so: H5 V, 2, 224.

Flowered, decked with flowers: Tit. V, 1, 15. Rom. II, 4, 64.

Floweret, small flower: Mids. IV, 1, 60. H4A I, 1, 8.

Flowering, 1) blooming: *f. infants*, H5 III, 3, 14. *all my f. youth*, H6A II, 5, 56.

2) covered with flowers: *the snake rolled in a f. bank*, H6B III, 1, 228. *O serpent heart, hid with a f. face*, Rom. III, 2, 73.

Flower-soft, soft, delicate as flowers: *the silken tackle swell with the touches of those f. hands*, Ant. II, 2, 215.

Flowery, 1) pertaining to a flower: *think you I can a resolution fetch from f. tenderness?* Meas. III, 1, 83 (i. e. from the exhortations of a delicate woman).

2) full of flowers: Mids. III, 1, 132. IV, 1, 1. All's IV, 5, 56.

Fluellen, name of a Welsh captain in H5 III, 2, 58 etc. etc.

Fluent, affluent, copious (cf. *flowing*): *it is a theme as f. as the sea*, H5 III, 7, 36.

Flush, adj. being in its prime, having its full vigour, lusty: *now the time is f., when crouching marrow in the bearer strong cries of itself 'No more'*, Tim. V, 4, 8. *with all his crime broad blown, as f. as May*, Hml. III, 3, 81 (Ff *fresh*). *f. youth revolt*, Ant. I, 4, 52.

Flushing, transient redness? *ere yet the salt of most unrighteous tears had left the f. in her galled eyes*, Hml. I, 2, 155 (ere her tears had had time to redden her eyes?)

Fluster, to make hot with drinking: *three lads of Cyprus .... have I to night —ed with flowing cups*, Oth. II, 3, 60.

Flute, a wind-instrument: Ant. II, 2, 200. 7, 138. Name in Mids. I, 2, 44. 58. IV, 1, 207.

Flutter, see *Flatter*.

Flux, the flow: *thus misery doth part the f. of company*, As II, 1, 52. *civet is the very uncleanly f. of a cat*, III, 2, 70.

Fluxive, flowing with tears: *these often bathed she in her f. eyes*, Compl. 50.

Fly, subst. the insect Musca: Ven. 316. As IV, 1, 111. Wint. IV, 4, 551. 820. H5 V, 2, 336 (*like flies at Bartholomew tide, blind, though they have their eyes*). Troil. II, 3, 17. Cor. IV, 6, 95. Tit. III, 2, 53 etc. Rom. II, 4, 34. III, 3, 41. Tim. III, 6, 106; cf. II, 2, 181. Mcb. IV, 2, 32. Lr. IV, 1, 38. IV, 6, 114. Oth. I, 1, 71. II, 1, 170. Ant. II, 2, 186. III, 13, 166. Cymb. IV, 2, 210. 388. V, 4, 31. Per. IV, 3, 50 etc.

Fly, vb. (impf. *flew* — never = fled —: Compl. 60. Merch. III, 1, 30. H6A I, 1, 124. H6B II, 1, 6. H8 IV, 1, 74. Troil. IV, 5, 246. Lr. IV, 2, 76. Part. *flown:* Sonn. 145, 12. Wint. IV, 3, 105. H4B IV, 5, 229. Mcb. III, 2, 40. Lr. IV, 6, 92. Cymb. III, 5, 61). 1) to pass through the air by the aid of wings or other means: Ven. 304. Lucr. 1010. 1014. 1216. Sonn. 78, 6. Tp. I, 2, 190. IV, 74. V, 91. Gentl. II, 7, 11. III, 1, 141. Mids. II, 1, 156. Merch. I, 1, 14. II, 6, 5. III, 1, 30. As II, 7, 86. IV, 1, 165. All's III, 2, 113 *(bullets).* John IV, 2, 175. H6A I, 1, 75. II, 4, 11. IV, 5, 55. R3 I, 4, 133 *(out).* V, 2, 23. H8 IV, 1, 74 *(up).* Tit. IV, 4, 82. Lr. IV, 6, 92 etc. Followed by an accus. denoting a measure: *what a pitch she flew,* H6B II, 1, 6. *f. an ordinary pitch,* Caes. I, 1, 78. —*s an eagle flight,* Tim. I, 1, 49. *ere the bat hath flown his cloistered flight,* Mcb. III, 2, 40.

2) to move rapidly and eagerly: *as falcon to the lure, away she* —*es,* Ven. 1027. *the very instant that I saw you did my heart f. to your service,* Tp. III, 1, 65. *f., run, hue and cry,* Wiv. IV, 5, 93. *in the morning early will we both f. toward Belmont,* Merch. IV, 1, 457. *here, there, and every where, enraged he flew,* H6A I, 1, 124. *the duke of Alençon* —*eth to his side,* H6A I, 1, 95. *all f. to him,* 96. *we will not f., but to our enemies' throats,* 98. *made the lame to leap and f. away,* H6B II, 1, 162. *many f. to him,* H6C II, 2, 71. *f. to the duke,* R3 IV, 4, 443. *do they still f. to the Roman,* Cor. IV, 7, 1. *flew on him,* Lr. IV, 2, 76. *she's flown to her desired Posthumus,* Cymb. III, 5, 61. *to f. out* = to rush out, to break out: *their blood thinks scorn, till it f. out and show them princes born,* Cymb. IV, 4, 54. *my valour ....for him shall f. out of itself,* Cor. I, 10, 19 (= shall break out of, leave, deny, its own nature). *his spirits f. out into my story,* Cymb. III, 3, 90 (i. e. he loses consciousness and identifies himself with the hero of my story). *having flown over many knavish professions, he settled only in rogue,* Wint. IV, 3, 105 (= having tried in a flippant manner).

3) to pass away, to depart: *observed (the hours) as they flew,* Compl. 60. *what is infirm from your sound parts shall f.* All's II, 1, 170. *health with youthful wings is flown from ....,* H4B IV, 5, 229. *the breach whereout Hector's great spirit flew,* Troil. IV, 5, 246.

4) to proceed: *O, that forced thunder from his heart did f.* Compl. 325. *all the honours that can f. from us shall on them settle,* All's III, 1, 20. *his words do from such passion f. that he believes himself,* Tw. III, 4, 407. *yet have I gold* —*es from another coast,* H6B I, 2, 93. cf. Lucr. 177. 1406.

5) to flee; a) intr.: Ven. 674. 894. Lucr. 230. 740. 1150. Sonn. 143, 7. 145, 12. Gentl. IV, 3, 29. Wiv. II, 2, 215. IV, 4, 55. V, 5, 107. Err. V, 184. LLL V, 2, 86. Mids. II, 1, 231. 234. As I, 3, 102. H6A III, 2, 107. H6C I, 4, 40. Ant. III, 13, 11 etc. *to f. from* = 1) to leave, to forsake: *from thy altar do I f.* All's II, 3, 80. *before young Talbot from old Talbot f.* H6A IV, 6, 46. H6C V, 4, 34. *wilt thou, O God, f. from such gentle lambs?* R3 IV, 4, 22. V, 2, 21 (Qq *shrink*). Mcb. V, 3, 49. 2) to part with: *the eyes f. from their lights,* Lucr. 461. *through her wounds doth f. life's lasting date from cancelled destiny,* 1728. *f. I hence, I f. away from life,* Gentl. III, 1, 187. 3) to flee from: *so runnest thou after that which* —*es from thee,* Sonn. 143, 9. Err. III, 2, 160. H5 IV, 1, 177. H6A I, 1, 97. I, 2, 103. I, 5, 32.

H6C V, 6, 7. R3 V, 3, 185. Cymb. V, 4, 92. — b) trans. = 1) to leave, to desert, to avoid: *she would the caged cloister f.* Compl. 249. *f. this place,* Mids. I, 1, 203. Lr. II, 1, 22. *ere thou f. the realm,* R2 I, 3, 198. Mcb. IV, 2, 1. *like the current* —*es each bound,* Tim. I, 1, 24. *f. pride,* Err. IV, 3, 81. *thou shalt f. him,* Mids. II, 1, 246. As III, 5, 9. All's V, 3, 156. *he'll quickly f. my friendship too,* Cymb. V, 3, 62. 2) to flee from: *f. him when he comes back,* Tp. V, 35. *I f. not death,* Gentl. III, 1, 185. V, 2, 50. Wiv. II, 2, 216. H6A IV, 5, 37. H6C I, 4, 23. R3 III, 2, 28. Cymb. IV, 2, 71.

6) to fall off, to revolt (cf. 5. a. 1): *you made in a day whole towns to f.* H6B II, 1, 164. With *off:* *the images of revolt and* — *ing off,* Lr. II, 4, 91. *and never f. off our loves again,* Ant. II, 2, 155.

7) to let a falcon rise to pursue its game: —*ing at the brook,* H6B II, 1, 1 (cf. *Brook*). *we'll e'en to it like French falconers, f. at any thing we see,* Hml. II, 2, 450.

Fly-bitten, stained by flies: *these f. tapestries,* H4B II, 1, 159.

Fly-blowing, stains made by flies: *I shall not fear f.* Tp. V, 284.

Fly-blown, stained by flies: H6A IV, 7, 76.

Fly-slow, tardy: R2 I, 3, 150 (only in F2 and some M. Edd.; the rest of O. Edd. *sly slow*).

Foal, subst. a colt: *a filly f.* Mids. II, 1, 46.

Foal, vb. to bring forth colts: *it* —*s me straight, and able horses,* Tim. II, 1, 9.

Foam, subst. the white substance which agitation forms on the surface of waters: Lucr. 1442. Tim. IV, 3, 379. V, 1, 53.

Foam, vb. to gather foam, to froth: Tp. I, 2, 211. Caes. I, 3, 7. Oth. II, 1, 11 (Q1 *banning*). Ant. II, 6, 21. —*ing bottles,* H5 III, 6, 82. *his* —*ing courser,* R2 I, 2, 51. H6C II, 1, 183. —*s at mouth,* Troil. V, 5, 36. Caes. I, 2, 255. Oth. IV, 1, 55. —*ed at the mouth,* Cymb. V, 5, 276.

Foamy, foaming, frothy: *the sea's enraged and f. mouth,* Tw. V, 81.

Fob, vb. (cf. *Fub*) to cheat, to delude, to trick: *resolution thus* —*ed with the rusty curb of old father antic the law,* H4A I, 2, 68. *and have been* —*ed off from this day to that day,* H4B II, 1, 37 (O. Edd. *fubbed*). *to f. off our disgrace with a tale,* Cor. I, 1, 97. *and begin to find myself* —*ed in it,* Oth. IV, 2, 197 (O. Edd. *fopt*).

As a subst. by conjecture in Err. IV, 3, 25 (O. Edd. *sob*).

Fodder, food for sheep: Gentl. I, 1, 92.

Foe, enemy: Ven. 364. 684. 699. Lucr. 77. 471. 936. 988. 1035. 1196. 1608. Sonn. 40, 14. 69, 4. 139, 11. Pilgr. 430. Gentl. V, 4, 72. 118. Wiv. III, 3, 70. Err. V, 82 *(to).* LLL V, 2, 556. Mids. III, 2, 44. John III, 1, 127. H6A I, 1, 43. I, 2, 115. I, 3, 62 *(to).* II, 4, 105. III, 1, 101. 174. III, 2, 32. III, 3, 46. H6B I, 1, 94. II, 4, 57. III, 1, 271. III, 2, 59 *(to).* H6C I, 1, 205. I, 4, 3. R3 IV, 2, 74 *(to).* H8 I, 1, 140 etc. etc. The sing. used to denote an opposing army: *the number of the f.* R3 V, 3, 9 (Ff *traitors*). *yielded to the f.* Ant. IV, 12, 11. Mcb. I, 2, 38 etc.

Foeman, enemy in war: H4B III, 2, 285. H6A I, 1, 144. H6C II, 5, 82. V, 7, 3. Tit. IV, 1, 127.

Fog, dense vapor, thick mist: Mids. II, 1, 90. III, 2, 357. Tw. IV, 2, 48. Cor. II, 3, 34. Tit. III, 1, 213. Mcb. I, 1, 12. Lr. I, 4, 321. II, 4, 169. Cymb. III, 2, 81.

Foggy, full of vapours, misty: Lucr. 771. As III, 5, 50. H5 III, 5, 16. Mcb. III, 5, 35.

Foh, exclamation of contempt or abhorrence: Wiv. I, 3, 33. Meas. V, 356. All's V, 2, 17. Troil. V, 2, 22. 48. Hml. II, 2, 617. Lr. III, 4, 188. Oth. III, 3, 232 (Qq *fie*. V, 1, 123 (om. Ff.).

Foil, subst. 1) defeat, miscarriage: *one sudden f. shall never breed mistrust*, H6A III, 3, 11. *take my soul, before that England give the French the f.* V, 3, 23.

2) blemish, shortcoming: *some defect in her did quarrel with the noblest grace she owed and put it to the f.* Tp. III, 1, 46. *yet must Antony no way excuse his —s, when we do bear so great weight in his lightness,* Ant. I, 4, 24 (M. Edd. *soils*).

Foil, subst. that on which a jewel is placed to set it off; and hence anything serving to give lustre to another thing: Compl. 153. R2 I, 3, 266. H4A I, 2, 239. R3 V, 3, 250. Hml. V, 2, 266.

Foil, subst. a rapier used in fencing: Ado V, 2, 13. H5 IV Chor. 50. Hml. II, 2, 334. IV, 7, 137. V, 2, 182. 265. 270. 276.

Foil, vb. 1) to defeat: Ven. 114. Sonn. 25, 10. As I, 1, 136. I, 2, 199. II, 2, 14. H6C V, 4, 42. Troil. I, 3, 372. Cor. I, 9, 48.

2) to make inefficacious, to undo, to mar: *she framed the love, and yet she —ed the framing,* Pilgr. 99. *when light-winged toys of feathered Cupid f. with wanton dulness my speculative and officed instruments,* Oth. I, 3, 270 (Qq *foyles,* Ff *seel*). *and must not f. the precious note of it* (the crown) *with a base slave,* Cymb. II, 3, 126 (M. Edd. *soil*).

Foin, subst. a thrust in fencing: Lr. IV, 6, 251.

Foin, vb. to make a thrust in fencing: Wiv. II, 3, 24. Ado V, 1, 84. H4B II, 1, 17. II, 4, 252.

Foison, rich harvest: *speak of the spring and f. of the year; the one doth shadow of your beauty show, the other as your bounty doth appear,* Sonn. 53, 9. Tp. II, 1, 163. IV, 110. Meas. I, 4, 43. Mcb. IV, 3, 88. Ant. II, 7, 23.

Foist, vb. to humbug, to hoax: *our dates are brief, and therefore we admire what thou dost f. upon us that is old,* Sonn. 123, 6.

Foix, French name: H5 III, 5, 45. IV, 8, 104.

Fold, subst. an enclosure for sheep, a pen: Ven. 532. Mids. II, 1, 96. H6B III, 1, 253. Tim. V, 4, 43. Figuratively: Lucr. 679.

Fold, subst. 1) the doubling of cloth, the complication, plait: *to dismantle so many —s of favour,* Lr. I, 1, 221 (a favour which covered Cordelia like a wide garment?).

2) the roll of a snake: *an adder wreathed up in fatal —s,* Ven. 879.

3) the embrace: *the weak wanton Cupid shall from your neck unloose his amorous f.* Troil. III, 3, 223.

Fold, vb. 1) to double, to lay in plaits: *—ed schedules* (i. e. letters) Compl. 43. *take forth paper, f. it,* Mcb. V, 1, 7. *thus will I f. them one upon another,* Gentl. I, 2, 128. *—ed arms* = crossed arms, LLL III, 183. Tit. III, 2, 7. With *up: here —s she up the tenour of her woe* (viz the letter) Lucr. 1310. Hml. V, 2, 51. *to have me f. up Parca's fatal web,* H5 V, 1, 21 (i. e. to make an end of it, put thee to death. Pistol's speech). *to f. down* = to turn down: *f. down the leaf where I have left,* Cymb. II, 2, 4.

2) to double, to multiply: *from a pound to a pin? f. it over and over, 'tis threefold too little for carrying a letter,* Gentl. I, 1, 115.

3) to enclose, to wrap: *f. it* (the knife) *in the oration,* Tit. IV, 3, 116. With *in: the fires i' the lowest hell f. in the people,* Cor. III, 3, 68. *his fame —s in this orb o' the earth,* V, 6, 126. With *up: they shoot but calm words —ed up in smoke,* John II, 229.

4) to embrace: *we will descend and f. him in our arms,* R2 I, 3, 54.

5) to wrap up, to cover, to conceal: *nor f. my fault in cleanly coined excuses,* Lucr. 1073. *lay open to my earthy-gross conceit the —ed meaning,* Err. III, 2, 36. *that man's face can f. in pleasing smiles such murderous tyranny,* Tit. II, 3, 266. With *in: so did the merciless and pitchy night f. in the object,* Ven. 822. With *up: shame —ed up in blind concealing night,* Lucr. 675. *whose beams thy cloudy wrath hath in eternal darkness —ed up,* R3 I, 3, 269.

Folio, the largest size of books: *whole volumes in f.* LLL I, 2, 192.

Folk, people; sing.: LLL IV, 3, 212. H4B IV, 4, 126. Hml. V, 1, 30. Lr. IV, 6, 243. Plur. *—s:* Wiv. I, 4, 128. II, 2, 134. As V, 3, 25. Shr. I, 2, 139. V, 2, 38. R2 V, 1, 41. H6B IV, 7, 89. Rom. II, 5, 16. Cymb. II, 3, 106. III, 6, 9.

Follow, 1) to go, come or be after; locally and temporally; a) intr.: Ven. 54. Lucr. 186. Tp. I, 2, 464. 501. III, 2, 159. III, 3, 109. Gentl. III, 1, 324. V, 2, 53. Wiv. I, 3, 14. II, 1, 202. IV, 2, 206. Meas. II, 4, 177. III, 1, 259. IV, 2, 58. Ado I, 1, 207. III, 3, 107. LLL I, 1, 207. III, 1, 94. Tw. II, 5, 154. H4A V, 4, 166. H6A III, 2, 59. Hml. II, 2, 432. Oth. IV, 2, 220. Cymb. IV, 2, 387 etc. etc. *I will talk with you, walk with you, and so —ing,* Merch. I, 3, 37 (= and so forth). With *after: which —s after,* Wint. IV, 1, 28. With *upon: it —ed hard upon,* Hml. I, 2, 179. — b) trans.: Lucr. 357. Tp. I, 2, 393. 459. 494. III, 2, 157. III, 3, 107. IV, 179. Gentl. I, 1, 92. 93. 95. V, 2, 48. 50 etc. etc. *whither do you f. your eyes?* Cor. II, 1, 109 (= where are you going?).

2) to pursue, to chase, to prosecute: *to f. that which flies,* Sonn. 143, 7. *Moyses and Valerius f. him,* Gentl. V, 3, 8. *f. no further now,* H4B IV, 3, 27. *they f. us with wings,* H6C II, 3, 12. *f. him, as he hath —ed you, with all despite,* Cor. III, 3, 139. *I have ever —ed thee with hate,* IV, 5, 104. *O Antony, I have —ed thee to this!* Ant. V, 1, 36.

3) to ensue: *to do this deed, promotion —s,* Wint. I, 2, 357. *what —s if we disallow of this?* John I, 16. H5 II, 4, 96. R3 IV, 4, 407. Troil. I, 3, 110. Cymb. III, 3, 69. V, 4, 174.

4) to be the consequence, to result: *it —s not that she will love Sir Thurio,* Gentl. III, 2, 50. All's II, 3, 119. H5 I, 2, 174. R3 I, 1, 59. Cor. II, 1, 69. III, 1, 148. Hml. I, 3, 79. Lr. I, 2, 141. Trans.: *what —s this?* Wint. IV, 4, 376.

5) to observe, to obey, to act up to: *and —s close the rigour of the statute,* Meas. I, 4, 67. *I shall f. it* (your counsel) II, 1, 267. Merch. I, 2, 12. 16. 18. Wint. II, 1, 162. H4B I, 2, 147. H5 III, 1, 33. H8 III, 2, 243.

6) to be the next thing to be said or done: *then it —s thus: thou shalt be master in my stead,* Shr. I, 1, 206. *this —s: make for Sicilia,* Wint. IV, 4, 553. *well, sir, what —s?* H8 V, 1, 79 (= what is the matter?).

now this —s: Charles the emperor came to whisper Wolsey, I, 1, 174. *now —s that you know,* Hml. I, 2, 17.

7) to be in consonance, to agree: *the spring is near when green geese are a breeding. How —s that?* LLL I, 1, 98. *to make Judas hang himself. Begin, sir, you are my elder. Well —ed: Judas was hanged on an elder,* V, 2, 610. *how ill it —s, after you have laboured so hard, you should talk so idly,* H4B II, 2, 31. *be not a garment nobler than that it covers: let thy effects so f., to be most unlike our courtiers, as good as promise,* Cymb. V, 4, 136.

8) to attend, to wait on: *she would have —ed her exile,* As I, 1, 114. *does your business f. us?* All's II, 1, 102. *the liberty that —s our places,* H5 V, 2, 297. *heavenly blessings f. such creatures,* H8 II, 3, 58. *how eagerly ye f. my disgraces,* III, 2, 240. *the flatteries that f. youth,* Tim. V, 1, 37. *the love that —s us sometime is our trouble,* Mcb. I, 6, 11.*Intr.: *temptation —s where thou art,* Sonn. 41, 4.

9) to seek after, to court: *you are there —ed by a faithful shepherd,* As V, 2, 87. *I f. him not by any token of presumptuous suit,* All's I, 3, 203. *are they so —ed?* Hml. II, 2, 349.

10) to adhere to, to side with: *we'll f. Cade,* H6B IV, 8, 35. *we'll f. the king,* 55. *we —ed then our lord, our lawful king,* R3 I, 3, 147. *had rather have us win than him they f.* V, 3, 244.

11) to serve; a) intr.: *for a little f. and do me service,* Tp. IV, 267. *I'll f., as they say, for reward,* H4A V, 4, 166 (cf. Gentl. I, 1, 94 and H6B II, 3, 109). *and —s but for form,* Lr. II, 4, 80. b) trans.: *I'll bear him no more sticks, but f. thee,* Tp. II, 2, 167. *a loyal sir to him thou —est,* V, 70. *thou for wages —est thy master,* Gentl. I, 1, 94. *she uses me with a more exalted respect than any one else that —s her,* Tw. II, 5, 32. Troil. III, 1, 2. Lr. I, 1, 143. Ant. V, 2, 151 etc.

12) to pursue, to apply one's self to: *the dire imagination she did f.* Ven. 975. *that I f. thus a losing suit against him,* Merch. IV, 1, 61. 177. *the justice of thy plea, which if thou f.* 204. *had I but —ed the arts!* Tw. I, 3, 99. *f. arms,* John II, 31 and H6A II, 1, 43. *f. your function,* Cor. IV, 5, 35. *he will never f. any thing that other men begin,* Caes. II, 1, 151. *assaulted for —ing her affairs,* Lr. II, 2, 157. Ant. I, 4, 10. Cymb. V, 5, 410.

13) to pursue, to continue, to carry through (what is now to follow up): *how with a sportful malice it* (the device) *was —ed,* Tw. V, 373. *such a day, so fought, so —ed and so fairly won,* H4B I, 1, 21. *'the time shall come', thus did he f. it,* III, 1, 75. *this chase is hotly —ed,* H5 II, 4, 68. *f. me this jest now till thou hast worn out thy pump,* Rom. II, 4, 65.

14) to imitate, to copy: *we have laughed to see the sails conceive and grow big-bellied with the wanton wind; which she, with pretty and with swimming gait, —ing would imitate,* Mids. II, 1, 131. *such another encounter, which lames report to f. it,* Wint. V, 2, 62. *to f. still the changes of the moon,* Oth. III, 3, 178.

Follower, 1) one who goes behind another: *a pointing-stock to every idle rascal f.* H6B II, 4, 47. *go before to field, he'll be your f.* Rom. III, 1, 61 (quibbling; cf. Wiv. III, 2, 2). *beware my f.* Lr. III, 4, 146.

2) pursuer: *the fatal —s do pursue,* H6C I, 4, 22. *'tis for the —s, not for the fliers,* Cor. I, 4, 44.

3) attendant, associate: Tp. V, 7. Err. II, 2, 109. Mids. I, 1, 155. As V, 2, 17. Wint. V, 2, 74. R2 IV, 280. H4B IV, 4, 53. 75. V, 5, 104. Troil. I, 3, 365.

4) one under the command of another, especially in war: R2 III, 2, 217. IV, 224. H4B I, 1, 191. H5 II Chor. 11. III, 6, 143. III, 7, 144. IV, 3, 85. H6A III, 1, 139. IV, 5, 45. H6B IV, 8, 66. H6C I, 1, 208. I, 4, 3. II, 2, 57. IV, 3, 13. V, 4, 67. Tit. I, 3. 9. 44. Ant. IV, 14, 111.

5) servant, retainer: Gentl. II, 4, 45. Wiv. I, 3, 5. III, 2, 2 (quibbling). Merch. II, 2, 157. Tw. IV, 3, 17. V, 284. Wint. I, 2, 437. R3 III, 7, 34. IV, 4, 481. Cor. V, 6, 39. Rom. III, 1, 61 (quibbling). Lr. I, 4, 316. II, 4, 145. 240. 296. Ant. IV, 2, 24. IV, 14, 134. Cymb. III, 5, 121.

Folly, 1) perversity of judgment, absurdity: Lucr. 992. 1810. Sonn. 11, 6. Gentl. I, 1, 34. 48. I, 2, 15. 65. II, 1, 81. Meas. III, 2, 149. Ado II, 3, 243. LLL V, 2, 70. 118. Mids. III, 2, 315. As V, 4, 111 etc.

2) absurd act: As II, 4, 34. H4B II, 2, 196. Plur. —*ies:* Gentl. II, 1, 40. Ado II, 3, 11. Merch. II. 6, 37. Wint. II, 3, 128. Lr. III, 7, 91 etc.

3) weakness of intellect, stupidity: *and f. doctor-like controlling skill,* Sonn. 66, 10. *the f. of this island!* Tp. III, 2, 5. *this is your own f.* Wiv. V, 5, 206. *cold wisdom waiting on superfluous f.* All's I, 1, 116.

4) inordinate desire, wantonness: *her sad behaviour feeds his vulture f.* Lucr. 556. *why should tyrant f. lurk in gentle breasts?* 851. *the f. of my soul dares not present itself,* Wiv. II, 2, 253. *he gives her f. motion and advantage,* III, 2, 35. *whose settled vision and deliberate word nips youth i' the bud and —ies doth emmew,* Meas. III, 1, 91. *your fault was not your f.* John I, 262. *tempt me no more to f.* Troil. V, 2, 18. *even her f. helped her to an heir,* Oth. II, 1, 138. *she turned to f., and she was a whore,* V, 2, 132. *cf.* also Ven. 838. Wiv. II, 2, 193. LLL IV, 3, 44. Mids. I, 1, 200.

Folly-fallen, grown foolish: Tw. III, 1, 75.

Fond, adj. 1) foolish, silly: Ven. 1021. Lucr. 216. 1094. Sonn. 3, 7. Meas. V, 105. Mids. III, 2, 317. Merch. II, 9, 27. III, 3, 9. All's V, 3, 178. Wint. IV, 1, 18. IV, 4, 437. R2 V, 2, 95. 101. H4B I, 3, 91. H6A II, 3, 45. V, 3, 81. H6B III, 1, 36. 74. R3 III, 2, 26 (Ff simple). III, 4, 83. V, 3, 330. Cor. IV, 1, 26. Tit. II, 3, 172. Rom. III, 3, 52. Tim. I, 2, 65. III, 5, 42. Caes. III, 1, 39. Lr. I, 2, 52. I, 4, 323. IV, 7, 60. Oth. I, 3, 320. III, 3, 445. Compar. —*er:* Troil. I, 1, 10. Adverbially: *f. done, done f.* All's I, 3, 76.

2) slight, trifling, trivial, not worth considering, nugatory: *not with f. shekels of the tested gold,* Meas. II, 2, 149. *full of foul hope and full of f. mistrust,* Lucr. 284. *trivial f. records,* Hml. I, 5, 99. *a kind of yesty collection, which carries them through and through the most f. and winnowed opinions,* V, 2, 200 (*f. and winnowed* = trite, trivial). *these are old f. paradoxes to make fools laugh i' the alehouse,* Oth. II, 1, 139.

3) doting, tender: *f. desire,* Lucr. 314. Gentl. I, 1, 52. *when men were f., I smiled,* Meas. II, 2, 187. *pretty, f. adoptious christendoms,* All's I, 1, 188. *this f. delay,* R2 V, 1, 101. *I am too f.* Rom. II, 2, 98. *f. nature bids us all lament,* IV, 5, 82. *if you are so f. over her iniquity, give her patent to offend,* Oth. IV, 1, 208 (i. e. if you grow so tender in thinking of her iniquity). With *of* = a) doting on, loving: Wint. I, 2, 164. John III, 4, 92. 98. Oth. V, 2, 157. b) desirous:

f. of no second brood, Cor. V, 3, 162. *then old and f. of issue,* Cymb. I, 1, 37. With *on* = loving: *being f. on praise,* Sonn. 84, 14. *more f. on her than she upon her love,* Mids. II, 1, 266. With *with: are with gain so f.* Lucr. 134. With the inf. = desirous: *why would you be so f. to overcome the bonny priser,* As II, 3, 7.

The first and third significations blent: Lucr. 1473. Gentl. IV, 4, 201. Meas. I, 3, 23. Err. II, 1, 116. Mids. II, 2, 88. III, 2, 114.

Fond, adv. see *Fond,* adj. def. 1.

Fond, vb. to d o t e: *my master loves her dearly: and I, poor monster, f. as much on him,* Tw. II, 2, 35 (but it may very well be the adj.).

Fondling, darling: Ven. 229.*

Fondly, 1) f o o l i s h l y: Lucr. 207. Err. IV, 2, 57. Shr. IV, 2, 31. John II, 258. R2 III, 3, 185. H4B IV, 2, 119. H6C II, 2, 38. R3 III, 7, 147.

2) in a t r i f l i n g, nugatory m a n n e r: *how f. dost thou spur a forward horse,* R2 IV, 72. Perhaps also in R3 III, 7, 147.

3) t e n d e r l y: R2 III, 2, 9.

Fondness, l o v e: Meas. II, 4, 28. All's I, 3, 176. H8 III, 1, 131.

Font, b a p t i s t e r y: Merch. IV, 1, 400. R2 IV, 256.

Fontibell, female name: All's IV, 2, 1.

Food, victuals, n o u r i s h m e n t: Lucr. 1115. Sonn. 75, 1. Tp. I, 2, 160. 462. Gentl. I, 1, 93. Wiv. I, 3, 38. Err. V, 83 (*in f.*). LLL I, 1, 39. Mids. IV, 1, 178. Merch. III, 1, 63. III, 2, 102. As II, 3, 31. II, 4, 65. II, 5, 42. II, 6, 2. Shr. IV, 3, 16. R2 II, 1, 37 etc. Figuratively: *his looks are my soul's f.* Gentl. II, 7, 15; cf. Mids. I, 1, 223. *it would give eternal f. to his jealousy,* Wiv. II, 1, 104; cf. Ado I, 1, 122; I, 3, 68; LLL IV, 1, 95; Lr. IV, 1, 24. *my f., my fortune, and my sweet hope's aim,* Err. III, 2, 63; cf. John III, 4, 104. *chewing the f. of sweet and bitter fancy,* As IV, 3, 102. *if music be the f. of love,* Tw. I, 1, 1; cf. Ant. II, 5, 1. *f. for powder,* H4A IV, 2, 71 etc.

Fool, subst. 1) one who acts or thinks absurdly: Lucr. 1568. Tp. III, 1, 73. III, 3, 27. 60. IV, 223. V, 297. Gentl. I, 1, 36. I, 2, 53. III, 1, 99. Err. II, 2, 205. Ado III, 4, 59. Mids. III, 2, 115. IV, 1, 89 etc. etc. *to make a f. of one,* Tw. II, 3, 138. *a f. go with thy soul,* H4A V, 3, 22 (i. e. go thy ways, fool that thou art; cf. Wiv. I, 4, 11. H4B V, 3, 70. Tim. V, 1, 111). *call me not f. till heaven hath sent me fortune,* As II, 7, 19 (cf. the German proverb: God is the guardian of the silly). *a —'s bolt is soon shot,* H5 III, 7, 132; cf. As V, 4, 67. *if you should lead her into a —'s paradise,* Rom. II, 4, 175 (i. e. if you make a fool of her, deceive her). *not a holiday f. there but would give a piece of silver,* Tp. II, 2, 30. (cf. As I, 3, 14). *we play the —s with the time,* H4B II, 2, 154 (we make jests, when, under so heavy circumstances, we ought to be grave). *bad is the trade that must play f. to sorrow,* Lr. IV, 1, 40 (Qq *the f.*). *he should be my f. and I his fate,* LLL V, 2, 68 (= I should make a fool of him, he should be my dupe). *now I am your f.* Tw. III, 1, 156 (you make sport of me). *I'll be your f. no more,* Troil. V, 2, 32; cf. III, 2, 157. *none of these rogues and cowards but Ajax is their f.* Lr. II, 2, 132 (they make sport of Ajax, the fiercest of the Greek warriors). *my f. usurps my body,* IV, 2, 28. *thus do I ever make my f. my purse,* Oth. I, 3, 389. *love is not time's f.* Sonn. 116, 9 (is not made a sport of by time, is not subject to time). *to*

this I witness call the —s of time, 124, 13 (i. e. those who are 'subject to time's love or to time's hate', v. 3). *merely thou* (life) *art death's f.* Meas. III, 1, 11. *thought's the slave of life, and life time's f.* H4A V, 4, 81. *I am fortune's f.* Rom. III, 1, 141; cf. Lr. IV, 6, 195. *mine eyes are made the —s o' the other senses,* Mcb. II, 1, 44. *and we —s of nature so horridly to shake our disposition with thoughts beyond the reaches of our souls,* Hml. I, 4, 54. In quite another sense Tim. III, 6, 106: *you —s of fortune, trencher-friends;* i. e. foolish followers of fortune.

Adjectively: *this f. gudgeon, this opinion,* Merch. I, 1, 102. *the f. multitude,* II, 9, 26. Abstr. pro concr.: *much f. may you find in you,* All's II, 4, 36. *thou full dish of f.* Troil. V, 1, 10. *this is not altogether f.* Lr. I, 4, 165. *they will not let me have all f. to myself,* 169 (Q2 *all the f.*).

2) an i d i o t, a b l o c k h e a d: *unfeeling —s can with such wrongs dispense,* Err. II, 1, 103. *he's a very f. and a prodigal,* Tw. I, 3, 25. *f. Lepidus,* Ant. III, 5, 18.

3) a licensed jester (*"a fellow in a long motley coat guarded with yellow"*, H8 Prol. 15; see *Motley;* *with his hair cut,* Err. V, 175): Ado I, 1, 41. II, 1, 211. Mids. IV, 1, 215. Tw. I, 5, 39. 42. 45. 48 etc. II, 3, 15. 19 etc. III, 1, 36 etc. etc. *use you for my f. and chat with you,* Err. II, 2, 27. *he was whipped for getting the shrieve's f. with child,* All's IV, 3, 213 (Douce: "female idiots were retained in families for diversion as well as male"). *there is no slander in an allowed f., though he do nothing but rail,* Tw. I, 5, 101. *or tie my treasure up in silken bags, to please the f. and death,* Per. III, 2, 42 (an allusion, according to Steevens, to an old print, in which Death is exhibited in the act of plundering a miser of his bags, and the Fool is standing behind and grinning at the process. But the expression would be pretty clear even without such an allusion).

4) a term of endearment and pity: *do not weep, good —s,* Wint. II, 1, 118. *the poor f. prays her that he may depart,* Ven. 578. *alas poor f., why do I pity him,* Gentl. IV, 4, 98. *you have a merry heart..... I thank it, poor f.* Ado II, 1, 326. *the poor dappled —s,* As II, 1, 22. *alas, poor f., how have they baffled thee,* Tw. V, 377. *so many weeks ere the poor —s will ean,* H6C II, 5, 36. *and my poor f. is hanged,* Lr. V, 3, 305. *poor venomous f., be angry,* Ant. V, 2, 308. *felt it bitter, pretty f.* Rom. I, 3, 31. 48. And without an adj.: *she's a lamb, a dove, a f. to him,* Shr. III, 2, 159.

Fool, vb. 1) trans. a) to make a fool of, to m o c k: *being —ed, by foolery thrive,* All's IV, 3, 374. *we will f. him black and blue,* Tw. II, 5, 12. *you are —ed, discarded and shook off by him,* H4A I, 3, 178. *f. me not so much to bear it tamely,* Lr. II, 4, 278.

b) to impose on, to d e c e i v e: *I do not now f. myself,* Tw. II, 5, 177. *to f. their preparation,* Ant. V, 2, 225. *she is —ed with a most false effect,* Cymb. I, 5, 42.

2) intr. to act or talk like a fool: *while I stand —ing here,* R2 V, 5, 60. *why old men f. and children calculate,* Caes. I, 3, 65 (O. Edd. *why old men, fooles,* and etc.). With an accus. noting the result: *you can f. no more money out of me,* Tw. V, 44. *they f. me to the top of my bent,* Hml. III, 2, 401. With a superfluous *it: rather than f. it so, let the high office and the honour go,* Cor. II, 3, 128.

The gerund —*ing*, substantively, = jesting in the style of a fool: Tp. II, 1, 177. Meas. I, 2, 71. Merch. II, 2, 88. Tw. I, 5, 36. 119. II, 3, 23. 31. 86. Troil. V, 2, 101.

Fool-begged, idiotical, stupid: *this f. patience in thee will be left*, Err. II, 1, 41 (properly "so foolish that the guardianship of it might well be begged." Nares. cf. *Beg*. Might it not be simply: such patience begged, demanded foolishly?).

Fool-born or **Fool-borne?** foolish from the birth, or tolerated by none but fools? (O. Edd. always *borne*, never *born*): *reply not to me with a f. jest: presume not that I am the thing I was*, H4B V, 5, 59.

Foolery, 1) absurdity: Wiv. IV, 2, 38. Ado III, 2, 37. LLL IV, 3, 163. V, 2, 76. As I, 2, 96. Wint. III, 2, 185 (—*ies*). Cor. III, 1, 246. Hml. V, 2, 225.

2) habitual folly: All's IV, 3, 374. Tw. III, 1, 43. Tim. II, 2, 124.

3) jesting, buffoonery: Err. IV, 3, 34. As I, 3, 14. Tw. I, 5, 13. Wint. IV, 4, 341. Caes. I, 2, 236. 291. Cymb. III, 2, 75.

Fool-hardiness, temerity: Cor. I, 4, 46.

Fool-hardy, temerarious: All's IV, 1, 32. R2 V, 3, 43.

Fooling, see *Fool*, vb.

Foolish, 1) unwise, absurd, perverse: Sonn. 141, 10. Tp. I, 2, 479. Gentl. I, 2, 57. Meas. II, 4, 24. V, 241. LLL V, 2, 374. Mids. III, 2, 319. Merch. II, 3, 13. As II, 2, 21. IV, 1, 105. V, 3, 41. Tw. V, 73. H6A III, 2, 112. H6B III, 1, 225. H6C II, 6, 108. R3 IV, 1, 104. Troil. V, 3, 79. Caes. II, 2, 105. Lr. I, 2, 197 etc.

2) behaving ridiculously, in the manner of a jester: Lucr. 1813. Err. II, 2, 30. LLL IV, 2, 68. V, 2, 584. Mids. III, 1, 137.

3) stupid: Gentl. II, 4, 174. IV, 4, 71. Wiv. III, 3, 205. Shr. IV, 1, 130. John III, 1, 46. H4A II, 4, 446. R3 IV, 2, 56. Ant. III, 3, 34.

4) Used as a term of modesty in recommending a thing: *he, of all the men that ever my f. eyes looked upon, was the best deserving a fair lady*, Merch. I, 2, 130. *we have a trifling f. banquet towards*, Rom. I, 5, 124.

Foolish-compounded, composed of absurdity: *this f. clay, man*, H4B I, 2, 8.

Foolishly, unwisely, absurdly: Meas. I, 2, 196. As I, 2, 93. II, 7, 54. H4B IV, 2, 119. Oth. IV, 2, 181.

Foolishness, absurdity: Err. I, 2, 72.

Foolish-witty, wise in folly and foolish in wisdom: Ven. 838.

Fool's-head, the emblems of a fool on the head: *you shall have An f. of your own*, Wiv. I, 4, 134.

Foot, subst. 1) the part of the leg which treads the earth: Lucr. 555. 1427. Tp. II, 2, 153. V, 34. Wiv. I, 3, 69. III, 3, 67. Ado II, 1, 15. 276. II, 3, 66. III, 2, 10 etc. Plur. *feet*: Tp. I, 2, 461. IV, 174. 184. LLL III, 13. IV, 3, 279. Tw. III, 4, 306. John IV, 2, 198. H6A II, 5, 13 etc. *my stay, my guide and lantern to my feet*, H6B II, 3, 25. (cf. Psalm 119, 105). *that the blind mole hear not a foot fall*, Tp. IV, 195. *as softly as f. can fall*, As III, 2, 346. *let him walk from whence he came, lest he catch cold on's feet*, Err. III, 1, 37. *do not you know my lady's foot by the squier?* LLL V, 2, 474 (do not you know her thoroughly?). *never dare misfortune cross her foot*, Merch. II, 4, 36. *to lame the foot of our design*, Cor. IV, 7, 7. *have secret feet in*

some of our best ports, Lr. III, 1, 32 (= have secretly landed; Q1 *fee*). *I'ld with thee every f.* Cor. IV, 1, 57 (very eagerly). *his death, which I did think with slower foot came on*, Meas. V, 400. *it requires swift f.* Tim. V, 1, 231. *near and on speedy f.* Lr. IV, 6, 217. *horses swift and sure of f.* Mcb. III, 1, 38. *the better foot before* = at a quick pace: John IV, 2, 170. Tit. II, 3, 192. *upon the foot of fear* (= flying), H4A V, 5, 20. *nor our strong sorrow upon the f. of motion*, Mcb. II, 3, 131 (having free scope). *with license of free f.* As II, 7, 68 (unbounded license). *to give thee all, and in his waning age set f. under thy table*, Shr. II, 404. *when I from France set f. at Ravenspurgh*, H4A III, 2, 95. *I will set this f. of mine as far as who goes farthest*, Caes. I, 3, 119. *set on your f.* II, 1, 331. *my f. my tutor?* Tp. I, 2, 469 (proverbial; cf. Tim. I, 1, 94). *I followed me close, came in f. and hand*, H4A II, 4, 241. *fighting f. to f.* Ant. III, 7, 67. *from face to f.* Cor. II, 2, 112. *from head to f.* Err. III, 2, 115. Troil. II, 1, 29. Hml. I, 2, 228. Ant. V, 2, 239. Cymb. I, 6, 19. *head to f. now is he total gules*, Hml. II, 2, 478. *at f.* = at one's heels: *follow him at f.* Hml. IV, 3, 56. cf. *at whose f., to mend the petty present, I will piece her throne with kingdoms*, Ant. I, 5, 44 (cf. *at heel of that*, II, 2, 160). *at one's foot* = lying, or kneeling, or prostrate before one: Merch. III, 1, 92. John V, 2, 76. V, 7, 113. R2 I, 1, 165. H6A IV, 6, 53. Rom. II, 2, 147. *at one's feet*: Gentl. III, 1, 225. Err. V, 114. R2 III, 3, 39. H6A IV, 7, 76. V, 3, 194. H6B II, 3, 35. H6C I, 1, 75. R3 II, 1, 107. Tit. I, 252. II, 4, 51. Hml. II, 2, 31. Ant. III, 13, 76. *at the feet sat Caesarion*, III, 6, 5. *set your knee against my f.* H6A III, 1, 169. *fall before his feet*, John V, 4, 13. *lets fall his sword before your highness' feet*, H6A III, 4, 9. *success be strewed before your feet*, Ant. I, 3, 101. *fall his princely feet before*, LLL IV, 1, 92 (Armado's poetry). *place your hands below your husband's foot*, Shr. V, 2, 177. *on foot* = a) walking, not on horseback: Shr. IV, 3, 188. R3 V, 4, 4. b) standing, not fallen: *'tis this fever that keeps Troy on f.* Troil. I, 3, 135. c) raised, levied, under arms: *a power on f.* As V, 4, 162. Cor. IV, 5, 125. d) in motion, action, or process of execution: *when thou hast on f. the purblind hare*, Ven. 679. *while other jests are on f.* Wiv. IV, 6, 22. *since love's argument was first on f.* LLL V, 2, 757. Wint. I, 1, 3. John III, 4, 169. H4B I, 3, 37. H5 I, 2, 310. Cor. IV, 3, 49. *hurl down my gage upon this overweening traitor's foot*, R2 I, 1, 147. *I'll strike thee to my f.* R3 I, 2, 41. *as low as to thy f. doth Cassius fall*, Caes. III, 1, 56. *throw it under f.* Shr. V, 2, 122. *tread it under f.* H6B V, 1, 209. *laid his love and life under my f.* H4B III, 1, 63. *under my feet I stamp thy cardinal's hat*, H6A I, 3, 49.

2) the lower part, the base: *the cedar stoops not to the base shrub's f.* Lucr. 664. *that shore whose f. spurns back the ocean's roaring tides*, John II, 24. *the f. of the ladder*, H4A I, 2, 42. *from top of honour to disgrace's feet*, H6B I, 2, 49. *yond towers ... must kiss their own feet*, Troil. IV, 5, 221. cf. Gent. V, 2, 46.

3) a measure of twelve inches: *we will not move a f.* LLL V, 2, 146. *he will not budge a f.* H4A II, 4, 388. H6A I, 3, 38. *thy horn is a f.* Shr. IV, 1, 30. *a f. of honour better*, John I, 182. 183. *within a f. of ...*, Lr. IV, 6, 25. *when he sees me go back one f.* H6A I, 2, 21. H6B V, 3, 6. Rom. I, 1, 87 (Ff *a f.*). *loves her by the f.* LLL V, 2, 674 (probably an obscene

quibble intended). *give no f. of ground*, H6C I, 4, 15. *every f.* John I, 146. Cor. IV, 1, 57. plural: *three foot*, John IV, 2, 100. *four f.* H4A II, 2, 13. H8 V, 4, 19. *twelve f.* Wint. IV, 4, 347.

4) infantry: H4A II, 4, 597. III, 3, 209. H4B II, 1, 186. H6A IV, 1, 165. R3 V, 3, 294. 297. Ant. IV, 10, 4.

5) a certain number of syllables constituting part of a verse: *more feet than the verses would bear*, As III, 2, 174. *I carry winged time post on the lame feet of my rhyme*, Per. IV Prol. 48.

Foot, vb. 1) to tread, to walk: *thieves do f. by night*, Wiv. II, 1, 126 (Pistol's speech). *S. Withold —ed thrice the old*, Lr. III, 4, 125 (old song). Followed by *it*, = to dance nimbly, to skip: *f. it featly here and there*, Tp. I, 2, 380. *f. it, girls*, Rom. I, 5, 28.

2) to kick: *you that did f. me as you spurn a stranger cur*, Merch. I, 3, 119. *I'll f. her home again*, Cymb. III, 5, 148. In speaking of an eagle, = to grasp or strike with the talon: *stooped as to f. us*, Cymb. V, 4, 116 (cf. the subst. *foot* in Lucr. 555).

3) to add the lowest part: *I'll sew nether stocks and mend them and f. them too*, H4A II, 4, 130.

Football, a ball consisting of an inflated bladder, cased in leather, to be driven by the foot: Err. II, 1, 83. Lr. I, 4, 95.

Footboy, a lackey: Shr. III, 2, 72. H6A III, 2, 69. H8 V, 2, 25. V, 3, 139.

Footcloth, housings of a horse, used by the nobility: *thou dost ride in a f.* H6B IV, 7, 51. *my f. mule*, IV, 1, 54. *my f. horse*, R3 III, 4, 86.

Footed, 1) furnished with a foot, in *fiery-footed*, *nimble-footed* etc.

2) landed: *he is f. in this land already*, H5 II, 4, 143. *there's part of a power already f.* Lr. III, 3, 14 (Qq *landed*). *the traitors late f. in the kingdom*, III, 7, 45.

Footfall, tread: *mount their pricks at my f.* Tp. II, 2, 12.

Footing, 1) step, tread: *the earth, in love with thee, thy f. trips*, Ven. 722. *I hear the f. of a man*, Merch. V, 24. *the wooden dialogue and sound 'twixt his stretched f. and the scaffoldage*, Troil. I, 3, 156. *to set f.* = a) to arrive, to step on, to touch: *set no f. on this unkind shore*, H6B III, 2, 87. *when she set f. here*, H8 III, 1, 103. b) to get a firm position, to gain ground: *who strongly hath set f. in this land*, R2 II, 2, 48. *when Talbot hath set f. once in France*, H6A III, 3, 64. *that so degenerate a strain should once set f. in your generous bosoms*, Troil. II, 2, 155.

2) landing: *whose f. here anticipates our thoughts*, Oth. II, 1, 76.

3) dance: *and these fresh nymphs encounter in country f.* Tp. IV, 138.

4) the ground to tread on: *there your charity would have lacked f.* Wint. III, 3, 114. *shall we, upon the f. of our land, send fair-play orders to arms invasive?* John V, 1, 66. *on the unsteadfast f. of a spear*, H4A I, 3, 193. *upon the giddy f. of the hatches*, R3 I, 4, 17. *blind fear finds safer f. than blind reason*, Troil. III, 2, 77.

5) footprint: *dance on the sands, and yet no f. seen*, Ven. 148.

Foot-land-raker (M. Edd. not hyphened), pedestrian vagabond: H4A II, 1, 81.

Foot-licker, meanest servant: *and I for aye thy f.* Tp. IV, 218.

Footman, 1) a pedestrian: *a horseman or a f.* Wint. IV, 3, 67. 68 (quibbling v. 69).

2) a soldier serving on foot: *war-marked footmen*, Ant. III, 7, 45.

3) a hired runner, a running footman: *and by the waggon-wheel trot, like a servile f., all day long*, Tit. V, 2, 55.

Footpath, a narrow way for pedestrians: Wint. IV, 3, 132 (*the f. way*). Lr. IV, 1, 58.

Footstep, the step: *it shall strew the —s of my rising*, John I, 216.

Footstool, that which supports the feet in sitting: *and made our f. of security*, H6C V, 7, 14.

Fop, subst. a fool, a dunce: *a whole tribe of —s, got 'tween asleep and wake*, Lr. I, 2, 14.

Fop, vb. to make a fool of, to dupe: *and begin to find myself —ed in it*, Oth. IV, 2, 197 (M. Edd. *fobbed*).

Foppery, 1) folly: *I had as lief have the f. of freedom as the morality of imprisonment*, Meas. I, 2, 138. *let not the sound of shallow f. enter my sober house*, Merch. II, 5, 35. *this is the excellent f. of the world*, Lr. I, 2, 128.

2) dupery, tricking, deceit: *drove the grossness of the f. into a received belief*, Wiv. V, 5, 131.

Foppish, foolish: *wise men are grown f.* Lr. I, 4, 182.

For, prepos. 1) in the place of: *f. Achilles' image stood his spear*, Lucr. 1424 (cf. *Stand*). *to have no screen between this part he played and him he played it f.* Tp. I, 2, 108. *the best that ever I heard. Ay, the best f. the worst*, LLL I, 1, 283 (you say the best, but mean the worst; for in such a case the greatest absurdity is the most amusing). *f. charitable prayers, shards, flints and pebbles should be thrown on her*, Hml. V, 1, 253 etc.

2) in exchange of, as the price of, or at the price of: *now would I give a thousand furlongs of sea f. an acre of barren ground*, Tp. I, 1, 70. *I will not take too much f. him; he shall pay f. him*, II, 2, 80. 81. *I shall have my music f. nothing*, III, 2, 154. *though I be o'er ears f. my labour*, IV, 214. *here's a garment f. it*, 242. *I would not f. the world*, V, 173. *f. a score of kingdoms you should wrangle*, 174. *gave me nothing f. my labour*, Gentl. I, 1, 103. *war f. war, and blood f. blood*, John I, 19. *dead f. a ducat*, Hml. III, 4, 24. *here's money f. my meat*, Cymb. III, 6, 50 etc. Hence the following phrases: *I dare not f. my head fill my belly*, Meas. IV, 3, 160 (originally = though it cost my life, though I should die of hunger; and then used as a mere form of asseveration). *an thou darest f. thy heart*, H4B II, 4, 242. *f. the heavens, rouse up a brave mind*, Merch. II, 2, 12. *master, f. my hand, both our inventions meet and jump in one*, Shr. I, 1, 194. *f. my life, to break with him about Beatrice*, Ado III, 2, 76. *dead, f. my life!* LLL V, 2, 728. *now, f. my life, the knave doth court my love*, Shr. III, 1, 49. IV, 3, 1. H6B II, 4, 18. H6C I, 4, 170. R3 IV, 1, 3 (but cf. *Before* and *Fore*).

3) in the character or quality of, as: *and give it* (the island) *his son f. an apple*, Tp. II, 1, 91. *keep it* (hope) *no longer f. my flatterer*, III, 3, 8. *bring it hither f. stale to catch the thieves*, IV, 187. *place it f. her chief virtue*, Gentl. III, 1, 339. *which he must carry f. a present to his lady*, IV, 2, 79. *piled f. a French velvet*, Meas. I, 2, 35. *she that even my soul doth f. a wife*

abhor, Err. III, 2, 164. *hang me up f. the sign of blind Cupid*, Ado I, 1, 256. *your daughter here the princes left f. dead*, IV, 1, 204. *two pitch-balls stuck in her face f. eyes*, LLL III, 199. *I marvel thy master hath not eaten thee f. a word*, V, 1, 43. *the king will court thee f. his dear*, V, 2, 131. *that 'a wears next his heart f. a favour*, 721. *even such a husband hast thou of me as she is f. a wife*, Merch. III, 5, 89. *'twill be recorded f. a precedent*, IV, 1, 220. *I'll have that doctor f. my bed-fellow*, V, 233. *I take thee f. wife*, As IV, 1, 136. *set the deer's horns upon his head f. a branch of victory*, IV, 2, 5. *he excels his brother f. a coward*, All's IV, 3, 321. *crown thee f. a finder of madmen*, Tw. III, 4, 154. *the light loss of England f. a friend*, John III, 1, 206. *doth any one accuse York f. a traitor?* H6B I, 3, 182. *I refuse you f. my judge*, H8 II, 4, 82. *it is turned out of all towns f. a dangerous thing*, R3 I, 4, 146. *be burnt f. liars*, Rom. I, 2, 96. Cor. III, 1, 57. IV, 6, 161. V, 4, 23. Caes. II, 2, 80. Mcb. IV, 3, 125. *we here dispatch you f. bearers of this greeting*, Hml. I, 2, 35 (Ff *bearing*). *f. a robe a blanket*, II, 2, 530. *you must put me in your heart f. friend*, IV, 7, 2. *as poor f. a subject as he is f. a king*, Lr. I, 4, 22. *to course his own shadow f. a traitor*, III, 4, 58. *attach thee f. an abuser of the world*, Oth. I, 2, 78. *stands up f. the main soldier*, Ant. I, 2, 198. *will appear there f. a man*, III, 7, 19. Hence a peculiar use: *I cross me f. a sinner*, Err. II, 2, 190 (= sinner that I am). *I defy thee f. a villain*, V, 32 (= villain that thou art). *what is he f. a fool that betroths himself to unquietness?* Ado I, 3, 49 (= who is he, fool that he is; who is that fool?). *Mars dote on you f. his novices*, All's II, 1, 48. *Lord have mercy on thee f. a hen*, II, 3, 224. *marry, hang you! and your courtesy, f. a ring-carrier*, III, 5, 95. *I will grace the attempt f. a worthy exploit*, III, 6, 71. *I'll tickle ye f. a young prince*, H4A II, 4, 489. *was I with you there f. the goose?* Rom. II, 4, 78. *a pestilence on him f. a mad rogue!* Hml. V, 1, 196. *I forgive thee f. a witch*, Ant. I, 2, 40. — Sometimes after verbs else followed by an inf. or a double accus.: *chronicled f. wise*, Gentl. I, 1, 41. *denied my house f. his, me f. his wife*, Err. II, 2, 161. *an idiot holds his bauble f. a god*, Tit. V, 1, 79. *I know him f. a man divine and holy*, Meas. V, 144. *he might have more diseases than he knew f.* H4B I, 2, 6. *what dost thou know me f.?* Lr. II, 2, 14. *I knew it f. my bond*, Ant. I, 4, 84. *since fate hath made thy person f. the thrower-out of my poor babe*, Wint. III, 3, 29. *whom late you have named f. consul*, Cor. III, 1, 196. *renowned f. hardy and undoubted champions*, H6C V, 7, 6. *the king, your father, was reputed f. a prince most prudent*, H8 II, 4, 45. *the conceit is deeper than you think f.* Shr. IV, 3, 163 (cf. *Think*).

4) in behalf or advantage of (cf. *Sake*): *your reason f. raising this storm*, Tp. I, 2, 177. *the first that e'er I sighed f.* Tp. I, 2, 446. *speak not f. him*, 460. 501. *I'll fish f. thee*, II, 2, 165. *that f. which I live*, IV, 4. *every man shift f. all the rest*, V, 256. *let no man take care f. himself*, 257. (cf. the vb. *Care*). *I leave myself and friends and all f. love*, Gentl. I, 1, 65. *the more is f. your honesty*, Ado III, 3, 56. *f. love and courtesy lie further off*, Mids. II, 2, 56. *I'll die f. it, but some woman had the ring*, Merch. V, 208. *f. your father's remembrance, be at accord*, As I, 1, 66. *we'll fast f. company*, Shr. IV, 1, 180. *wear this jewel f. me*, Tw. III, 4, 228. *make work upon ourselves, f. heaven*

or hell, John II, 407. *let no eye profane a tear f. me*, R2 I, 3, 60. *the wind sits fair f. news to go to Ireland*, R2 II, 2, 123. *let it not be believed f. womanhood*, Troil. V, 2, 129. *his throat is cut; that I did f. him*, Mcb. III, 4, 16. *if thy speech be sooth, I care not if thou dost f. me as much*, V, 5, 41. *the pox upon her green-sickness f. me*, Per. IV, 6, 15. *I hope all's f. the best*, H6C III, 3, 170 (cf. *Better*, *Best*, *Worse*, *Worst*, *Once*, *Nonce* etc).

5) in favour of, siding with: *till time had made them f. us*, Meas. I, 2, 157. *he's f. a jig or a tale of bawdry*, Hml. II, 2, 522. *to the health of our general! I am f. it*, Oth. II, 3, 89 (= I make one). *he's f. his master*, Cymb. I, 5, 28.

6) assigned or due to, at the service of: *there's other business f. thee*, Tp. I, 2, 315. *they are f. you*, Gentl. II, 1, 131. *money f. these wars*, R2 II, 2, 104. *two tender playfellows f. dust*, R3 IV, 4, 385. *'tis f. me to be patient*, Err. IV, 4, 20. *it were f. me to throw my sceptre at the injurious gods*, Ant. IV, 15, 75. *times to repair our nature ... and not f. us to waste these times*, H8 V, 1, 4. *gave sign f. me to leave you*, Caes. II, 1, 247. *To be f.* = to be at a person's service; either amicably: *I am f. you, though it cost me ten nights' watchings*, Ado II, 1, 387. *sit, and a song. We are f. you*, As V, 3, 10. *I am f. you again*, Wint. II, 1, 22. Or for combat: *I am f. thee straight*, Shr. IV, 3, 152. *nay, if you be an undertaker, I am f. you*, Tw. III, 4, 350. Rom. I, 1, 61. III, 1, 86. Oth. I, 2, 58. cf. the adjectives *Fit*, *Ready* etc., and the use after *too*: *too massy f. your strengths*, Tp. III, 3, 67. *she is too big f. me to compass*, Err. IV, 1, 111. *a punishment too good f. them*, Ado III, 3, 5. Similarly: *a heavy reckoning f. you*, Cymb. V, 4, 159 etc. etc.

7) toward, to, on the way to: *to embark f. Milan*, Gentl. I, 1, 71. *I am arrived f. fruitful Lombardy*, Shr. I, 1, 3. *take your way f. home*, All's II, 5, 69. *away f. England!* John III, 3, 6. *f. England go*, 71. III, 4, 181. *are there no posts dispatched f. Ireland?* R2 II, 2, 103. *news to go f. Ireland*, 123 (Ff and M. Edd. *to*). *made their march f. Bordeaux*, H6A IV, 3, 8. *at my depart f. France*, H6B I, 1, 2. *I'll ship them all f. Ireland*, III, 1, 329. *you sent me deputy f. Ireland*, H8 III, 2, 260. *but come: f. England!* Hml. IV, 3, 51. *every thing is bent f. England*, 47. *the Turkish preparation makes f. Rhodes*, Oth. I, 3, 14. *straight away f. Britain*, Cymb. I, 4, 179. *from whence he moves his war f. Britain*, III, 5, 26. After *will* and *to be*: *his lordship will next morning f. France*, All's IV, 3, 91. *we will f. Ireland*, R2 II, 1, 218. *I am f. France*, All's IV, 3, 353. *I am f. the air*, Mcb. III, 5, 20. *he's not f. Rhodes*, Oth. I, 3, 31. *Publicola and Caelius are f. sea*, Ant. III, 7, 74. *we are f. the dark*, Ant. V, 2, 194. *I am again f. Cydnus*, 228. Armado even says: *I am f. whole volumes in folio*, LLL I, 2, 191 (= I am about to write whole volumes).

8) with a view to, tending to, in order to obtain, to serve as: *a piece of skilful painting, made f. Priam's Troy*, Lucr. 1367 (= to represent Troy). *the herd gone to the hedge f. shade*, Pilgr. 72. *the ministers f. the purpose*, Tp. I, 2, 131. *which of he or Adrian, f. a good wager, first begins to crow?* II, 1, 28. *what a sleep were this f. your advancement!* II, 1, 268. *f. more assurance I embrace thy body*, V, 108. *the sheep f. fodder follow the shepherd*, Gentl. I, 1, 92. *a corded ladder f. which the youthful lover now is gone,*

III, 1, 41. *to stick it in their children's sight, f. terror,* not to use, Meas. I, 3, 26. *be it f. nothing but to spite my wife,* Err. III, 1, 118. *we'll draw cuts f. the senior,* V, 422. *f. night-tapers crop their waxen thighs,* Mids. III, 1, 172. *work f. bread,* III, 2, 10. *the business is f. Helen to come hither,* All's I, 3, 100. *f. sealing the injury of tongues,* Wint. I, 2, 337. *want ye corn f. bread?* H6A III, 2, 41. *follow us f. thy reward,* H6B II, 3, 109. *watching f. your good,* IV, 7, 90. *when Tarquin made a head f. Rome,* Cor. II, 2, 92. *thou wouldst have told this tale f. virtue, not f. such an end,* Cymb. I, 6, 143.

9) in quest of, with a desire of, in order to come by: *that sort was well fished f.* Tp. II, 1, 104. *your father calls f. you,* Gentl. I, 3, 88. *he cries f. you,* Err. V, 182. *if you look f. a good speech now, you undo me,* H4B V, 5, 119. *Caesar did write f. him to come to Rome,* Caes. III, 1, 278. *how shall we do f. money?* R2 II, 2, 104. *how wilt thou do f. a father?* Mcb. IV, 2, 38. *haste we f. it,* Ant. II, 2, 167 (cf. *Ask, Come, Hope, Long, Stay, Wait, Wish* etc.). Particularly after words implying desire: *I am ambitious f. a motley coat,* As II, 7, 43. *I am not covetous f. gold,* H5 IV, 3, 24. *so dry he was f. sway,* Tp. I, 2, 112. *he was mad f. her,* All's V, 3, 260. *the king was weeping-ripe f. a good word,* LLL V, 2, 274. *to die f. sth.* = to languish for: *the fools of time, which die f. goodness, who have lived for crime,* Sonn. 124, 14. *dies f. him,* Ado III, 2, 69. *take thought and die f. Caesar,* Caes. II, 1, 187. *I die f. food,* As II, 6, 2. II, 7, 104. *almost dead f. breath,* Mcb. I, 5, 37. *starve f. a merry look,* Err. II, 1, 88. *starved f. meat,* Shr. IV, 3, 9. *faints f. succour,* As II, 4, 75. — Elliptically, without a governing word: *alack, f. pity!* Tp. I, 2, 132. *alack f. mercy!* 436. *O f. my beads!* Err. II, 2, 190. *God, f. thy mercy!* IV, 4, 147. *good lord, f. alliance!* Ado II, 1, 330. *O f. your reason!* LLL V, 2, 244. *away, and f. our flight!* All's II, 5, 97. *alack, f. lesser knowledge!* Wint. II, 1, 38. *O Proserpina, f. the flowers now,* IV, 4, 117. *now f. a true face,* H4A II, 4, 550. *O f. a fine thief!* III, 3, 212. *O f. a Muse of fire,* H5 Prol. 1. *Oh f. my husband!* R3 II, 2, 71. *Lord, f. thy justice!* H8 III, 2, 93. *O f. a falconer's voice!* Rom. II, 2, 159. *O f. a chair!* Oth. V, 1, 82. *O f. a horse with wings!* Cymb. III, 2, 50. *now f. our mountain sport!* III, 3, 10. *now f. the counsel of my son and queen!* IV, 3, 27.

10) on account of, because of, with: *red f. shame,* Ven. 36. *that even f. anger makes the lily pale,* Lucr. 478. *pale f. sorrow,* Pilgr. 119. *now should not the shoe speak a word f. weeping,* Gentl. II, 3, 28. *giddy f. lack of sleep,* Shr. IV, 3, 9. *as far as I could well discern f. smoke and dusky vapours,* H6A II, 2, 27. *these cheeks are pale f. watching,* H6B IV, 7, 90 (F 2.3.4 *with*). *my heart f. anger burns,* H6C I, 1, 60. *if thou canst f. blushing, view this face,* I, 4, 46. *if that I could f. weeping,* Cor. IV, 2, 13. *shakes f. age and feebleness,* Tit. I, 188. *Cydnus swelled above the banks, or f. the press of boats or pride,* Cymb. II, 4, 71. *thus by day my limbs, by night my mind, f. thee and f. myself no quiet find,* Sonn. 27, 14 (= on account of thee). *the lily I condemned f. thy hand,* 99, 6. *and I* (banished) *from Mantua f. a gentleman, who in my mood I stabbed unto the heart,* Gentl. IV, 1, 50. *he dares not come there f. the candle,* Mids. V, 253. *happy f. so sweet a child,* H6A V, 3, 148. *he hates me f. my*

father Warwick, R3 IV, 1, 86. *my valour ... f. him shall fly out of itself* Cor. I, 10, 18. *leave nothing out f. length,* II, 2, 53. *not having the power to do the good it would, f. the ill which doth control it,* III, 1, 161. III, 3, 134. Caes. III, 2, 13. Mcb. III, 1, 121. *to trash f. o'ertopping,* Tp. I, 2, 81. *the red plague rid you f. learning me your language,* 365. *torment me f. bringing wood in slowly,* II, 2, 16. *'twill weep f. having wearied you,* III, 1, 19. *smote the air f. breathing in their faces,* IV, 173. *I was taken up f. laying them down,* Gentl. I, 2, 135. *I was chidden f. being too slow,* II, 1, 12. *banished f. practising to steal away a lady,* IV, 1, 48. *our peace will grow stronger f. the breaking,* H4B IV, 1, 223. *banished f. mischiefs manifold,* Tp. I, 2, 264. *f. one thing she did they would not take her life,* 266. *f. this thou shalt have cramps,* 325. *I'll free thee f. this,* 421. *f. every trifle are they set upon me,* II, 2, 8. *I will give him some relief, if it be but f. that,* 70. *f. several virtues have I liked several women,* III, 1, 42. *do not, f. one repulse, forego the purpose,* III, 3, 12. *apprehended f. arrival here,* Err. I, 2, 4. *f. which, I hope, thou feltst I was displeased,* II, 2, 19. *scape being drunk f. want of wine,* Tp. II, 1, 146. Gentl. II, 1, 31. *I hid me f. fear of the storm,* Tp. II, 2, 116. Gentl. I, 3, 78. II, 3, 52. *it is f. love,* Gentl. II, 4, 4. Mids. III, 2, 311. *f. what cause thou comest to Ephesus,* Err. I, 1, 31. *f. the great desire I had to see fair Padua, I am arrived,* Shr. I, 1, 1. *leave pricking it f. pity,* Cor. I, 3, 96. *alack, f. woe!* R2 III, 3, 70. *I thank thee f. that jest,* Tp. IV, 241. I, 2, 175. II, 1, 123. *which speed, I hope, the better f. our words,* Merch. V, 115. *he were the worse f. that, were he a horse,* Ant. III, 2, 52. *if it were not f. one trifling respect, I could come to such honour,* Wiv. II, 1, 44. *were 't not f. laughing, I should pity him,* H4A II, 2, 117. *he would have lived many a fair year, if it had not been f. a hot midsummer night,* As IV, 1, 102. *But for,* in the same sense, = if there had not been: *these mine eyes, but f. thy piteous lips, no more had seen,* Ven. 504 (cf. *But*). *Save for* = except: *then was this island, save f. the son that she did litter here, not honoured with a human shape,* Tp. I, 2, 282. *of all one pain, save f. a night of groans,* R3 IV, 4, 303.

Peculiar use: *the which* (treasure) *he will not every hour survey, f. blunting the fine point of seldom pleasure,* Sonn. 52, 4 (i. e. because it would blunt, = lest it should blunt). *here they shall not lie, f. catching cold,* Gentl. I, 2, 136. *now will I dam up this thy yawning mouth f. swallowing the treasure of the realm,* H6B IV, 1, 74. *and advise thee to desist f. going on death's net,* Per. I, 1, 40. Troil. I, 2, 293.

11) in spite of (when followed by *all*): *yet f. all that let him be a handsome fellow,* Ado II, 1, 57. V, 1, 177. Merch. III, 4, 73. All's IV, 3, 242. V, 3, 193. Caes. I, 2, 240. *f. all this,* Merch. II, 5, 41. Tw. II, 5, 135. Mcb. IV, 3, 44. Lr. II, 4, 54. *f. all this same,* Rom. V, 3, 43. *the priest was good enough, f. all the old gentleman's saying,* As V, 1, 3. Mcb. IV, 2, 37. *draw, men, f. all this privileged place,* H6A I, 3, 46. *f. all this flattering gloss, he will be found a dangerous protector,* H6B I, 1, 163. *f. all his wings, the fool was drowned,* H6C V, 6, 20. *f. all her cherubin look,* Tim. IV, 3, 63. Hence *for all* = though: *taking no notice that she is so nigh, f. all askance he holds her in his eye,* Ven. 342. *f. all he was in woman's apparel, I would not have had him,* Wiv. V, 5, 204. *there are*

verier knaves desire to live, f. all he be a Roman, Cymb. V, 4, 209 (cf. *All*).

12) with respect to, concerning (cf. *As*): *like none f. constant heart,* Sonn. 53, 14. *I'll warrant him f. drowning,* Tp. I, 1, 49. *f. the liberal arts without a parallel,* I, 2, 73. *I claim the promise f. her heavenly picture,* Gentl. IV, 4, 92. *it would neither serve f. the writing nor the tune,* LLL I, 2, 119. *marvellous well f. the pen,* IV, 2, 158. *I am a right maid f. my cowardice,* Mids. III, 2, 302. *a very paramour f. a sweet voice,* IV, 2, 12. *a very fox f. his valour,* V, 234. *thus much f. greeting,* Shr. IV, 1, 115. *observe his reports f. me,* All's II, 1, 46. *the charge my father gave me f. visiting your highness,* Wint. V, 1, 163. *what store of parting tears were shed? Faith, none f. me,* R2 I, 4, 6. *a second Hector f. his grim aspect,* H6A II, 3, 20. *no way to that f. weakness,* III, 2, 25. *the flower of Europe f. his chivalry,* H6C II, 1, 71. *so much f. him,* Hml. I, 2, 25. *this f. him,* Ant. III, 12, 15. *f. the rest o' the fleet, they all have met again,* Tp. I, 2, 232. *but f. the miracle, few can speak like us,* II, 1, 6. *f. you.... I do forgive ...,* V, 130. *cf. f. me, I force not argument a straw,* Lucr. 1021. *f. me, I am the mistress of my fate,* 1069. Gentl. IV, 2, 100. Wiv. V, 5, 13. Mids. I, 1, 117. Meas. IV, 3, 148. H6B II, 1, 190. III, 2, 59. IV, 8, 32. Ant. III, 13, 51. *f. this new-married man ... you must pardon,* Meas. V, 405. *f. Angelo, his act did not o'ertake his bad intent,* 455. 158. 488. Ado III, 2, 100. LLL I, 1, 211. I, 2, 135. Shr. II, 3. H6A II, 4, 100. III, 1, 21. H6B I, 1, 106. H6C II, 1, 145. V, 5, 3. Ant. III, 12, 19. *But for* and *now for,* used to introduce a new theme: *but f. your conscience?* Tp. II, 1, 275..*but f. the bloody napkin?* As IV, 3, 139. *but f. the seventh cause?* V, 4, 69. *now f. your answer,* Merch. IV, 1, 52. *now f. the rebels which stand out in Ireland,* R2 I, 4, 38. *now f. our Irish wars,* II, 1, 155. *now, lords, f. France,* H5 II, 2, 182. *now f. ourself and f. this time of meeting,* Hml. I, 2, 26. *cf. f. your dwelling, briefly,* Caes. III, 3, 26. *f. aught I know,* and *f. anything I know* = *as far as I know,* H4B V, 5, 146. Per. II, 5, 78 (cf. *Anything* and *Aught*). *f. aught I could ever read,* Mids. I, 1, 132. *f. aught that I can tell,* III, 2, 76.

Followed by an inf. and having the sense of a conditional clause: *f. Coriolanus neither to care whether they love or hate him manifests the true knowledge he has,* Cor. II, 2, 13. *f. their tongues to be silent were a kind of injury,* 34. *f. the multitude to be ingrateful were to make a monster of the multitude,* II, 3, 10. *f. me to put him to his purgation would perhaps plunge him into far more choler,* Hml. III, 2, 317. *'twould braid yourself too near f. me to tell it,* Per. I, 1, 93. Caes. II, 2, 97.

13) through the space of, during: *f. many miles about there's scarce a bush,* Lr. II, 4, 304. *he's safe f. these three hours,* Tp. III, 1, 21. *f. a little follow,* IV, 266. *f. this one night,* V, 302. *f. this nineteen years,* Meas. I, 3, 21. *f. long,* I, 4, 63. *f. three months,* Tw. V, 97. *f. these eighteen years,* R2 I, 1, 95. *f. this my lifetime,* H6C I, 1, 171. *f. this many a day,* Hml. III, 1, 91 etc. *f. ever,* see *Ever.*

14) following, answering, one after another, by: *I'll aid thee tear f. tear,* H6C II, 5, 76. *get goal f. goal of youth,* Ant. IV, 8, 22.

For, conj. 1) Used, as at present, to introduce a reason by a coordinate sentence (Fr. car, Germ. denn): *let's assist them, f. our case is as theirs,* Tp. I, 1, 58.

sit down, f. thou must now know farther, I, 2, 33. 40 467. II, 1, 2. 108. 148. 189 etc. etc.

2) Introducing a reason by a subordinate clause, = because, as: *and f., poor bird, thou singest not in the day, some dark deep desert will we find out,* Lucr. 1142. *but f. their virtue only is their show, they live unwooed,* Sonn. 54, 9. *and f. they looked but with divining eyes, they had not skill enough your worth to sing,* 106, 11. *and f. thou wast a spirit too delicate, ... she did confine thee,* Tp. I, 2, 272. *my foolish rival that her father likes only f. his possessions are so huge,* Gentl. II, 4, 175. *I curse myself, f. they are sent by me, that they should harbour where their lord would be,* III, 1, 148. *you may not so extenuate his offence, f. I have had such faults,* Meas. II, 1, 28. *those, f. their parents were exceeding poor, I bought,* Err. I, 1, 57. *and f. the morning now is something worn, our purposed hunting shall be set aside,* Mids. IV, 1, 187. *why should this a desert be? f. it is unpeopled?* As III, 2, 134. *you are come in happy time, the rather f. I have some sport in hand,* Shr. Ind. 1, 91. Shr. I, 1, 92. All's III, 5, 45. 56. Wint. III, 3, 33. IV, 4, 86. John II, 591. R2 I, 3, 127. 129. I, 4, 12. 43. II, 1, 159. H6B I, 3, 169. R3 I, 1, 58. II, 2, 95. Cor. III, 1, 10. Tit. V, 1, 74. Lr. I, 1, 227. Oth. I, 3, 269 (Ff *when*). III, ?, 263. 265. III, 4, 161. Cymb. III, 4, 54. IV, 2, 129.

For that, in the same sense: *f. that I love your daughter, I must advance the colours of my love,* Wiv. III, 4, 82. *which was broke off, partly f. that her promised proportions came short of composition,* Meas. V, 219. *else imputation, f. that he knew you, might reproach your life,* 426. *f. that it is not night when I do see your face, therefore I think I am not in the night,* Mids. II, 1, 220. Merch. I, 3, 44. Tw. III, 1, 166. Wint. IV, 4, 759. John V, 4, 42. R2 I, 1, 129. I, 3, 125. II, 1, 125. H6A II, 3, 31. II, 5, 71. V, 5, 80. H6C IV, 6, 11. Cor. I, 1, 117. I, 9, 47. III, 3, 93. Tit. III, 1, 40. Tim. II, 2, 209. Mcb. IV, 3, 185. Lr. I, 2, 5. Oth. I, 3, 24. II, 3, 234. Ant. III, 7, 30. Per. II, 1, 81.

For because, in the same sense: *why so? not f. because your brows are blacker,* Wint. II, 1, 7. *why rail I on this Commodity? but f. because he hath not wooed me yet,* John II, 588. *and f. because the world is populous, ... I cannot do it,* R2 V, 5, 3.

3) = in order that (followed by *shall* or *should*): *and f. the time shall not seem tedious, I'll tell thee what befel me,* H6C III, 1, 9. *love forswore me in my mother's womb, and f. I should not deal in her soft laws, she did corrupt frail nature,* III, 2, 154.

4) *For to,* followed by an inf., a) = in order to: *think women still to strive with men, to sin and never f. to saint,* Pilgr. 342. *send down Justice f. to wreak our wrongs,* Tit. IV, 3, 51. *which f. to prevent, I have thus set it down,* Hml. III, 1, 175 (Ff *to,* and *how to* prevent). *had not overboard thrown me f. to seek my mother,* Per. IV, 2, 71. b) to: *let your highness lay a more noble thought upon mine honour than f. to think ....,* All's V, 3, 181. *forbid the sea f. to obey the moon,* Wint. I, 2, 427. *here lacks but your mother f. to say amen,* Tit. IV, 2, 44. *we'll teach you f. to drink,* Hml. I, 2, 175 (Ff *to drink deep*). Shr. III, 2, 249.

5) Used as an expletive without meaning: *a pickaxe and a spade, a spade, f. and a shrouding sheet,* Hml. V, 1, 103 (song of the clown).

Concerning *for why,* see *Why.*

Forage, subst. the act of preying, ravage,

destructive rage: *and he* (the lion) *from f. will incline to play,* LLL IV, 1, 93 (cf. Edward 3 II, 1: *the lion doth become his bloody jaws, and grace his foragement, by being mild when vassal fear lies trembling at his feet*).

Forage, vb. to prey: *with blindfold fury she begins to f.* Ven. 554. *f. and run to meet displeasure farther from the doors,* John V, 1, 59 (= pounce upon your prey). *to behold his lion's whelp f. in blood of French nobility,* H5 I, 2, 110.

Forager, one who goes in search of food, one who is on the prowl: *when that the general is not like the hive to whom the —s shall all repair, what honey is expected?* Troil. I, 3, 82.

Forbear (impf. not used; partic. *forborne:* Ant. III, 13, 107) 1) tr. a) to **abstain from:** *f. it therefore* (i. e. lamenting) Meas. IV, 3, 129. *f. laughing,* LLL I, 1, 198. 200. *f. your food awhile,* As II, 7, 127. Tw. III, 2, 87. H6B IV, 10, 57. H6C IV, 1, 6. R3 I, 1, 104. Rom. III, 1, 90. Ant. II, 7, 104. III, 13, 107. Cymb. III, 5, 39. Per. II, 4, 41. 46 (corr. pass.). Followed by an infin.: *f. to glance thine eye aside,* Sonn. 139, 6. H6B III, 3, 31. IV, 7, 81. H6C IV, 1, 75. R3 IV, 4, 118.

b) to **avoid,** to **leave alone:** *f. his presence,* Lr. I, 2, 175. *f. me,* Ant. I, 2, 125. *f. me till anon,* II, 7, 44.

c) to **spare,** to **let alone:** *no fisher but the ungrown fry —s,* Ven. 526. *thou mightst my seat f.* Sonn. 41, 9. *canst thou not f. me half an hour,* H4B IV, 5, 110. *f. him,* Hml. V, 1, 296. *I did full hard f. him,* Oth. I, 2, 10. *ghost unlaid f. thee,* Cymb. IV, 2, 278.

2) intr. a) to **abstain** from doing what was purposed: *f.* Gentl. III, 1, 202. 204 (i. e. do not strike). *f., I say; it is my lord the duke,* V, 4, 122 (i. e. cease your crying). Wiv. II, 3, 17. IV, 1, 57. LLL V, 2, 439. Merch. III, 2, 3. As II, 7, 88. 97. Shr. III, 1, 1. Wint. V, 3, 80. R2 IV, 30. H6A III, 1, 105. IV, 7, 49. H6B II, 4, 58. III, 2, 46. H8 V, 3, 86. Tit. V, 2, 163. Lr. I, 1, 164. Oth. IV, 1, 53. Ant. I, 3, 11.

b) to be **patient:** *better f. till Proteus make return,* Gentl. II, 7, 14. *love, lend me patience to f. awhile,* V, 4, 27. *till he come home again, I would f.* Err. II, 1, 31. *I say, sing. F. till this company be past,* LLL I, 2, 131. *my lord, it were your duty to f.* H6A III, 1, 52. H6C III, 1, 27. Rom. V, 3, 220. Lr. II, 4, 110. Ant. I, 3, 73. Cymb. V, 5, 124.

c) to **leave a place,** to **withdraw:** *either f., quit presently the chapel, or resolve you for more amazement,* Wint. V, 3, 85. *f., Seleucus,* Ant. V, 2, 175. *we must f.* Cymb. I, 1, 68.

Forbearance, 1) act of abstaining, refraining: *true noblesse would learn him f. from so foul a wrong,* R2 IV, 120. *me of my lawful pleasure she restrained and prayed me oft f.* Cymb. II, 5, 10.

2) reserve: *here is a mannerly f.* H6A II, 4, 19. *one of your great knowing should learn f.* Cymb. II, 3, 103.

3) act of withdrawing, keeping aloof: *I crave your f. a little,* Meas. IV, 1, 22. *have a continent f. till the speed of his rage goes slower,* Lr. I, 2, 182; cf. v. 175.

Forbid (impf. *forbade;* partic. usually *forbid; forbidden:* Sonn. 6, 5. LLL II, 6. H6A III, 1, 79. 89. Rom. III, 1, 92 Qq *forbid,* Ff *forbidden. forbod:* Compl.

164). 1) to **prohibit,** to **interdict,** to command to forbear; absol.: *the cardinal of Winchester —s,* H6A I, 3, 19. H6B III, 2, 264. With an inf.: *more the leisure and enforcement of the time —s to dwell upon,* R3 V, 3, 239. *To f. a person to do sth.: forbade my tongue to speak,* Lucr. 1648. Ado III, 2, 7. LLL I, 1, 60. 62. Merch. IV, 1, 75. Shr. IV, 1, 174. John III, 1, 190. H4A I, 3, 220. H6A III, 1, 79. Mcb. I, 3, 46. Hml. I, 5, 13. Elliptically: *finding myself in honour so f.* Compl. 150. *wilt thou flout me thus, being f.?* Err. I, 2, 92. *why have those banished and —en legs dared once to touch . . . ,* R2 II, 3, 90. The inf. without *to: the treason that my haste —s me show,* R2 V, 3, 50. With *for to: f. the sea for to obey the moon,* Wint. I, 2, 427. A subordinate clause following with *should: forbade the boy he should not pass those grounds,* Pilgr. 124. The accus. indicating the thing prohibited: *—en usury,* Sonn. 6, 5. *in stamps that are f.* Meas. II, 4, 46. *he —s it,* H5 V Chor. 19. *that which the kings' king —s,* R3 IV, 4, 346. Troil. IV, 5, 122. Cor. V, 1, 12. Rom. III, 1, 92. Double accus.: *to be forbod the sweets that seem so good,* Compl. 164. *I f. thee one most heinous crime,* Sonn. 19, 8. *f. the smiling courtesy of love the holy suit,* LLL V, 2, 755. *if we be —en stones,* H6A III, 1, 89. Troil. V, 3, 75. Tim. I, 1, 127. Lr. III, 3, 22. V, 1, 47. The thing prohibited with *from: from whose obedience I f. my soul,* John IV, 3, 64.

2) to **command not to enter:** *to f. Sir Valentine her company and my court,* Gentl. III, 1, 26. *forbade her my house,* Wiv. IV, 2, 88. 181. *his —en gates,* LLL II, 26. *let love f. sleep his seat on thy eyelid,* Mids. II, 2, 80.

3) to **prevent,** to **avert:** *who his spoil of beauty can f.?* Sonn. 65, 12. *f. the sun to enter,* Ado III, 1, 9. *this shall f. it,* Rom. IV, 3, 23. *and therefore I f. my tears,* Hml. IV, 7, 187. *do that which heaven hath f. the Ottomites,* Oth. II, 3, 171. Mostly used to express a wish; absol.: *God f.* Merch. II, 2, 69. Shr. IV, 2, 78. V, 151. R2 II, 2, 51. IV, 114. H4A V, 2, 36. H6C V, 4, 48. Rom. I, 3, 4. *God f. else,* H8 II, 2, 115; cf. All's III, 5, 77. *the gods f.* Mids. III, 2, 276. Troil. V, 1, 3. Cor. III, 1, 233. Ant. IV, 2, 19. V, 2, 213. *now gods f.* Per. II, 1, 82. *heaven f.* Oth. II, 3, 261. V, 1, 72. *Jupiter f.* Troil. II, 3, 208. *the Lord f.* H8 III, 2, 54. *the higher powers f.* Wint. III, 2, 203. *wrinkles f.* Ant. I, 2, 19. With an accus.: *O f. it, God,* R2 IV, 129 (Qq *forefend*). *as God f. the hour,* H6C II, 1, 190. *God f. that,* III, 2, 25. *heavens f. such scarcity of youth,* Troil. I, 3, 302. Passively: *let it be f.* All's IV, 3, 54. *be it f., my lord,* Wint. I, 2, 241. Followed by a clause: *fortune f. my outside have not charmed her,* Tw. II, 2, 19. *God f. I say true,* R2 II, 1, 200. Mostly with *should: God f. I should in thought control your times of pleasure,* Sonn. 58, 1. *God f. it should be so,* Ado I, 1, 219. R2 III, 3, 101. H4A V, 4, 11. H5 I, 2, 13. H6B III, 2, 23. IV, 4, 10. H6C I, 2, 18. IV, 1, 21. R3 III, 1, 40. III, 7, 81 (Ff *defend*). Troil. II, 2, 127. Cor. III, 1, 290. Tit. IV, 3, 90. Per. I, 2, 61. *God f. but a knave should have some countenance,* H4B V, 1, 48 (= that not). *the heavens f. but that our loves and comforts should increase,* Oth. II, 1, 196.

4) to **curse,** to **blast:** *he shall live a man f.* Mcb. I, 3, 21.

Forbiddenly, in an unlawful manner: *that you have touched his queen f.* Wint. I, 2, 417.

Forbidding, subst. hinderance, obstacle: *all these poor —s could not stay him,* Lucr. 323.

Force, subst. 1) strength, vigour: *desire doth lend her f.* Ven. 29. *some glory in their bodies' f.* Sonn. 91, 2. *her feeble f. will yield,* Pilgr. 319. Compl. 248. Wint. IV, 4, 385. John I, 265. H6A I, 5, 1. 21. IV, 4, 36. Troil. III, 1, 166. IV, 1, 18. V, 5, 40. Cor. I, 10, 14 *(in an equal f. = by an e. f.; cf. In).* V, 2, 95. Tim. II, 2, 176. Ant. IV, 14, 48. Cymb. V, 5, 414. *never could maintain his part but in the f. of his will,* Ado I, 1, 239 (see *Will,* subst.).

2) power, faculty: *sweet love, renew thy f.* Sonn. 56, 1. *much is the f. of heaven-bred poesy,* Gentl. III, 2, 72. *take her hearing prisoner with the f. and strong encounter of my amorous tale,* Ado I, 1, 326. *Dian's bud hath such f.* Mids. IV, 1, 79; cf. III, 1, 143. *let us on your imaginary —s work,* H5 Prol. 18. Merch. II, 9, 30. IV, 1, 190. As III, 5, 26. All's V, 3, 7. Tw. I, 5, 329. H6A V, 5, 79. H6B III, 2, 332. Hml. I, 3, 26 (Ff *sect* and *f.*; Qq *act* and *place*). III, 3, 48. *of f.* = weighty: *those occasions were of f.* H6A III, 1, 157. *some reason of no little f.* H6B I, 3, 166. *arguments of mighty f.* H6C II, 2, 44.

3) virtue, efficacy, operation: *this flower's f. in stirring love,* Mids. II, 2, 69. *use our commission in his utmost f.* John III, 3, 11. *the potion's f. should cease,* Rom. V, 3, 249. R3 IV, 4, 351. H8 I, 1, 64. Hml. III, 1, 113. Cymb. I, 5, 18.

4) validity: *which (doom) stands in effectual f.* Gentl. III, 1, 223. *our late edict shall strongly stand in f.* LLL I, 1, 11. *there is no f. in the decrees of Venice,* Merch. IV, 1, 102. John I, 130. 132. H8 I, 2, 101.

5) violence: *f. must work my way,* Lucr. 513. *sweetens the aloes of all —s, shocks and fears,* Compl. 273; cf. Troil. IV, 2, 107. As II, 7, 103. R2 III, 3, 207. H6C IV, 4, 33. Troil. I, 3, 116. *by f.* Lucr. 1243. Err. V, 352. H6B II, 2, 30. H6C I, 1, 29. Tit. II, 1, 118. *by main f.* H6B I, 1, 210. *f. perforce =* a) by violence, against one's will: John III, 1, 142. H4B IV, 1, 116. H6B I, 1, 258. b) of necessity, absolutely, by all means: *as f. perforce the age will pour it in,* H4B IV, 4, 46.

6) necessity; only in the phrase *of f.,* joined to the verb *must: these of f. must your oblations be,* Compl. 223. LLL I, 1, 148. Mids. III, 2, 40. Merch. IV, 1, 56. 421. Wint. IV, 4, 434. H4A II, 3, 120. Caes. IV, 3, 203. cf. def. 5: *f. perforce.*

7) warlike preparation, army, troops: All's IV, 1, 94. H5 I, 2, 150. II, 2, 16. H6A II, 1, 32. IV, 4, 3. H6B V, 1, 22. Mcb. V, 3, 18. Ant. I, 2, 96. 104. III, 13, 169. IV, 11, 2. *of f. enough to bid his brother battle,* H6C V, 1, 77. *not fearing outward f.* Cor. III, 1, 77. *our old love made a particular f.,* Tim. V, 2, 8 (i. e. made an army, a party of its own). Plur. *—s:* John II, 54. 61. H4A III, 2, 178. H4B I, 3, 81. II, 1, 185. H5 I, 2, 112. 147. H6A III, 2, 102. III, 3, 83. IV, 4, 11. H6B IV, 2, 122. V, 1, 60. H6C IV, 8, 62. V, 1, 9. 25. R3 V, 3, 109. Lr. V, 1, 52. Cymb. III, 7, 11. Per. I, 2, 24.

Force, vb. 1) to reinforce, to strengthen: *were they not —d with those that should be ours,* Mcb. V, 5, 5.

2) to constrain: *art thou king and wilt be —d?* H6C I, 1, 230. *with much —ing of his disposition,* Hml. III, 1, 12. Followed by an inf. with *to:* Lucr. 261. Sonn. 41, 12. Meas. III, -2, 268. Err.

I, 1, 75. Ado V, 1, 64. Shr. III, 2, 8. Wint. I, 2, 52. H4B I, 1, 105. IV, 1, 147. H6C II, 5, 6. 8. III, 3, 26. R3 V, 1, 23. H8 III, 2, 430. Cor. I, 6, 19. V, 6, 106. Lr. V, 1, 23. Ant. V, 2, 213. Without *to: rain added to a river will f. it overflow the bank,* Ven. 72. *I'll f. thee yield to my desire,* Gentl. V, 4, 59. *I'll f. the wine peep through their scars,* Ant. III, 13, 190. *this secret will f. him think,* Cymb. II, 2, 41. Followed by a subst. with *to: —d to content,* Ven. 61. *so Lucrece must I f. to my desire,* Lucr. 182. As II, 7, 102. R3 IV, 4, 279 (Ff *move*). Tit. IV, 1, 72. Ant. V, 1, 56. Cymb. I, 6, 101. Per. III, 2, 22. Partic. *—d =* constrained, unnatural, false: *that —d thunder from his heart did fly,* Compl. 325. *if thou takest up the princess by that —d baseness which he has put upon it,* Wint. II, 3, 78. *with these —d thoughts darken not the mirth o' the feast,* IV, 4, 41. *'tis like the —d gait of a shuffling nag,* H4A III, 1, 135.

3) to bring about or effect by constraint or violence: *this —d league doth f. a further strife,* Lucr. 689. *which —d such way,* H8 II, 4, 184. *f. their scanted courtesy,* Lr. III, 2, 66. *my —d offence,* Lucr. 1071. *—d stain,* 1701. *—d marriage,* Wiv. V, 5, 243 and H6A V, 5, 62. *a visitation —d by need,* Wint. V, 1, 91. *his little kingdom of a —d grave,* John IV, 2, 98. *—d drops of blood,* H5 IV, 1, 314. *a —d affection,* Caes. IV, 3, 205. *—d breath,* Hml. I, 2, 79 (i. e. heavy, panting). *a —d content,* Oth. III, 4, 120. *—d even =* violent: *deaths put on by cunning and —d cause,* Hml. V, 2, 394. *indirect and —d courses,* Oth. I, 3, 111.

Followed by prepositions or adverbs, = to put or drive or draw by constraint or by an effort: *to f. him after,* Wint. IV, 4, 679. *f. her hence,* II, 3, 61. *it shall not force this lineal honour from me,* H4B IV, 5, 45. H5 IV, 6, 28. H6A IV, 6, 24. H6C III, 3, 206. *—d him on so fast,* Lucr. 1670. *to f. that on you,* Tw. III, 1, 127. *—ing faults upon Hermione,* Wint. III, 1, 16. *—d out,* Tim. I, 2, 208. *f. the letter to my view,* Gentl. I, 2, 54. *could f. his soul so to his own conceit,* Hml. II, 2, 579.

4) to ravish, to violate; absol.: *hot and —ing violation,* H5 III, 3, 21. Trans.: *that* (viz my mind) *was not —d,* Lucr. 1657. *would have —d your honour and your love,* Gentl. V, 4, 22. *I'll woo you like a soldier ... and f. ye,* 58. *to f. a spotless virgin's chastity,* H6B V, 1, 186. *—d in the gloomy woods,* Tit. IV, 1, 53. *her spotless chastity you —d,* V, 2, 178.

5) to urge: *—d examples 'gainst her own content,* Compl. 157. *when he would f. it* (the law) Meas. III, 1, 110. *if you will now unite in your complaints and f. them with a constancy,* H8 III, 2, 2. *why f. you this?* Cor. III, 2, 51.

6) to value, to care for: *I f. not argument a straw,* Lucr. 1021. *your oath once broke, you f. not to forswear,* LLL V, 2, 440 (cf. *Forceless).*

7) to farce, to stuff: *f. him with praises,* Troil. II, 3, 232. *wit larded with malice, and malice —d with wit,* V, 1, 64. Perhaps also in H5 II Chor. 32: *f. a play;* but the passage is evidently corrupt.

Forceful, powerful, strong: *follow our f. instigation,* Wint. II, 1, 163.

Forceless, strengthless: *f. flowers,* Ven. 152. *engaging and redeeming of himself with such a careless force and f. care,* Troil. V, 5, 40. But it may mean here: heedless, regardless (cf. *Force,* vb. def. 6); in any case the sense is: with so little care.

Forcible, powerful, strong: *so f. is thy wit,* Ado V, 2, 56. *most f.* Feeble, H4B III, 2, 179. *reasons strong and f.* H6C I, 2, 3.

Forcibly, by force, by violence: *to enforce these rights so f. withheld,* John I, 18. *f. prevents our locked embrasures,* Troil. IV, 4, 38.

Ford, subst. a shallow current: *deep sounds make lesser noise than shallow —s,* Lucr. 1329. *through f. and whirlipool,* Lr. III, 4, 53 (Ff *sword*). Quibbling: *Mistress Ford! I have had f. enough; I was thrown into the f.; I have my belly full of f.* Wiv. III, 5, 36.

Ford, name in Wiv. I, 1, 198. I, 3, 39. II, 1, 118 etc. etc.

Fordo (orthogr. of M. Edd.) or **Foredo** (orth. of O. Edd.) 1) to undo, destroy: *—es itself,* Hml. II, 1, 103. *f. its own life,* V, 1, 244. *she fordid herself,* Lr. V, 3, 255. *have —ne themselves,* 291. *this is the night that either makes me or —es me,* Oth. V, 1, 129. 2) to overcome, to exhaust: *all with weary task —ne,* Mids. V, 381.

Fore (M. Edd. *'fore*). prepos. = before (q. v.) in its various significations: *at any time f. noon,* Meas. II, 2, 160. *the grace f. meat,* Cor. IV, 7, 3. *the farced title running f. the king,* H5 IV, 1, 280. *a mighty whiffler f. the king,* V Chor. 12. *what would you f. our tent?* Troil. I, 3, 215. *couches f. the mouse's hole,* Per. III Prol. 6. *f. whose throne 'tis needful to kneel,* All's IV, 4, 3 (O. Edd. *for*). *f. who please to come,* Wint. III, 2, 42. *contract us f. these witnesses,* IV, 4, 401. *present yourself f.* Leontes, 556. *to bring my whole cause f. his holiness,* H8 II, 4, 120. *f. all the Greekish heads,* Troil. I, 3, 221. *many an heir of these fair edifices f.* *my wars have I heard groan and drop,* Cor. IV, 4, 3. *whip him f. the people's eyes,* IV, 6, 60. V, 6, 120. *f. noble Lucius present yourself,* Cymb. III, 4, 175. *you must not so far prefer her f. ours,* Cymb. I, 4, 70. *prizest him f. me,* H6A I, 3, 22. *f. God!* Ado II, 3, 192 (Q *before*). IV, 2, 32. All's II, 3, 51. H4B III, 2, 186 (Ff *trust me*). 317 (Ff om.). V, 3, 6 (Ff om.). H5 II, 2, 1. Hml. II, 2, 488. Oth. II, 3, 66. *f. me, I speak in respect,* All's II, 3, 31. *f. me, this fellow speaks!* Cor. I, 1, 124.

Fore, adv.: *the eyes, f. duteous, now converted are,* Sonn. 7, 11.

Fore, conj.: *not a month f. your queen died, she was more worth such gazes,* Wint. V, 1, 226. *to stop their marches f. we are inflamed,* John V, 1, 7.

Fore-advised, pre-admonished: Cor. II, 3, 199.

Fore-bemoaned, bewailed in former times: Sonn. 30, 11.

Fore-betrayed, beguiled, seduced before: Compl. 328.

Forecast, foresight, policy: H6C V, 1, 42.

Foredo, see *Fordo.*

Fore-doom, vb. to sentence beforehand: *your eldest daughters have —ed themselves,* Lr. V, 3, 291 (Ff and M. Edd. *foredone*).

Fore-end, earlier part: *paid more pious debts to heaven than in all the f. of my time,* Cymb. III, 3, 73.

Forefather, ancestor: R2 II, 2, 35. H6B IV, 7, 37. H6C I, 3, 27. Rom. IV, 3, 51.

Forefend, to avert, forbid: *heavens f.!* Wint. IV, 4, 541. R2 IV, 129 (Ff *forbid*). H6A V, 4, 65. H6B III, 2, 30. Tit. I, 434. Oth. V, 2, 32. 186. Cymb. V, 5, 287. *which peril heaven f.!* H6C II, 1, 191. *have*

you never found my brother's way to the —ed place? Lr. V, 1, 11 (= forbidden).

Forefinger, the finger next to the thumb, the index: All's II, 2, 24. Rom. I, 4, 56 (but cf. H4A II, 4, 364).

Forefoot, one of the anterior feet of a quadruped: *give me thy fist, thy f. to me give,* H5 II, 1, 71.

Forego, 1) to give up, renounce: Sonn. 125, 7. Tp. III, 3, 12. John III, 1, 207. R2 I, 3, 160. IV, 212. H8 III, 2, 423. Troil. V, 8, 9. Hml. II, 2, 308. Ant. III, 7, 46.

2) to forfeit: *mine eyes f. their light,* Lucr. 228. *let us not f. that for a trifle that was bought with blood,* H6A IV, 1, 149.

Foregoers, ancestors: *honours thrive, when rather from our acts we them derive than our f.* All's II, 3, 144.

Foregone, 1) former, past: *grieve at grievances f.* Sonn. 30, 9. *remembrances of days f.* All's I, 3, 140. 2) gone before, previous: *but this denoted a f. conclusion,* Oth. III, 3, 428.

Forehand, 1) preference, advantage: *had the f. and vantage of a king,* H5 IV, 1, 297. 2) the thing preferred to others: *the sinew and the f. of our host,* Troil. I, 3, 143.

Adjectively: *and so extenuate the f. sin,* Ado IV, 1, 51 (= anticipated, done too early). *carried you a f. shaft a fourteen and fourteen and a half,* H4B III, 2, 52 (an expression not yet sufficiently explained).

Forehead, the part of the face above the eyes: Lucr. 1091. Tp. IV, 250. Gentl. IV, 4, 198. Wiv. IV, 2, 26. Err. III, 2, 126. Ado I, 1, 243. 266. LLL IV, 3, 125. As II, 3, 50. III, 3, 60. All's IV, 3, 263. Tw. II, 5, 37. Wint. II, 3, 100. John V, 2, 176. H4B I, 3, 8. R3 IV, 4, 140. Troil. III, 1, 117. Cor. I, 3, 45. Rom. II, 1, 18. Hml. III, 4, 43. Oth. III, 3, 284. Ant. III, 3, 35. Figuratively: *a promised glory as smiles upon the f. of this action,* Troil. II, 2, 205. *converses more with the buttock of the night than with the f. of the morning,* Cor. II, 1, 57. *compelled, even to the teeth and f. of our faults, to give in evidence,* Hml. III, 3, 63.

Forehorse, the horse in a team which goes foremost: *I shall stay here the f. to a smock,* All's II, 1, 30 (i. e. ushering in and squiring ladies).

Foreign, 1) of another country, alien, extraneous: Merch. II, 7, 46. All's I, 3, 152. John II, 28. IV, 2, 111. 244. V, 1, 11. R2 I, 3, 272. III, 1, 20. H4B IV, 5, 215. H5 II, 2, 10. 100. H6A III, 3, 55. IV, 1, 144. H6B IV, 7, 82. H6C IV, 1, 38. 149. R3 IV, 4, 312. 531. H8 I, 3, 29. I, 4, 56. II, 2, 129 (= living abroad). III, 2, 314. Cor. V, 3, 114. Rom. I, 4, 83. Mcb. III, 2, 25. Hml. I, 1, 74. Lr, IV, 3, 46.

2) pertaining to strangers, not related: *pour our treasures into f. laps,* Oth. IV, 3, 89. *I love the king, your father, and yourself with more than f. heart,* Per. IV, 1, 34.

Foreigner, one of another country: John IV, 2, 172. cf. *Mountain-foreigner.*

Foreknowing, 1) partic. foreseeing: Ven. 245. John IV, 2, 154. 2) subst. prescience: Hml. I, 1, 134.

Foreknowledge, prescience: Tw. I, 5, 151.

Foremost, 1) going before others, most advanced: *thou goest f.* Cor. I, 1, 162. *my wife comes f.* V, 3, 22.

2) first in place and dignity: *goes f. in report*, Ado III, 1, 97. *you shall have f. hand*, H4B V, 2, 140. *the f. man of all this world*, Caes. IV, 3, 22.

Forenamed, mentioned before: Meas. III, 1, 248.

Forenoon, the time of the day to the meridian: Cor. II, 1, 78. Ant. I, 2, 26.

Forepast, antecedent: *my f. proofs shall tax my fears of little vanity*, All's V, 3, 121.

Fore-rank, first rank, front: *she is our capital demand, comprised within the f. of our articles*, H5 V, 2, 97.

Fore-recited, exposed before: H8 I, 2, 127.

Forerun, to come before as a sign or earnest of something following: *—ing more requital*, Meas. V, 8. LLL IV, 3, 380. R2 II, 4, 15. III, 4, 28. H4B IV, 2, 82. Rom. V, 1, 53.

Forerunner, 1) messenger sent before, harbinger: Merch. I, 2, 136. Tim. I, 2, 124.

2) predecessor, ancestor: *that great f. of thy blood*, John II, 2.

Fores (O. Edd. *Sores*), place in Scotland: Mcb. I, 3, 39.

Foresaid, mentioned before: Meas. II, 1, 110. LLL IV, 2, 163. John III, 1, 145. H5 I, 2, 83. H8 I, 1, 190. Hml. I, 1, 103.

Foresay, to decree: *let ordinance come as the gods f. it*, Cymb. IV, 2, 146 (cf. *Forethink*).

Foresee, 1) to see beforehand, to divine, prophesy; absol.: *Cassandra doth f.* Troil. V, 3, 64. trans.: Tp. II, 1, 297. H6A V, 4, 111. Troil. I, 2, 10. Ant. I, 2, 14.

2) to provide for: *who ... —ing those fell mischiefs our reasons laid before him, hath commanded...*, H8 V, 1, 49. *of him that, his particular to f., smells from the general weal*, Tim. IV, 3, 159.

3) to perceive, to be aware of: *that you f. not what impediments draw back our expedition*, H4A IV, 3, 18.

Foreshow, to prognosticate: Cymb. V, 5, 473. Per. IV, 1, 86.

Foresight, prescience: Lucr. 728.

Foreskirt, the loose and pendulous part of a coat before: *honour's train is longer than his f.* H8 II, 3, 98.

Foreslow (M. Edd. *forslow*), to delay: *f. no longer*, H6C II, 3, 56.

Forespeak (M. Edd. *forspeak*), to gainsay: *thou hast forespoke my being in these wars*, Ant. III, 7, 3.

Forespent, 1) previously bestowed: *his goodness f. on us*, Cymb. II, 3, 64.

2) past, foregone: *his vanities f.* H5 II, 4, 36.

3) exhausted: *almost f. with speed*, H4B I, 1, 37. *f. with toil*, H6C II, 3, 1 (M. Edd. *forspent*).

Forespurrer, one that rides before, a harbinger: Merch. II, 9, 95.

Forest, a tract of land covered with trees: Sonn. 104, 4. Gentl V, 1, 11. V, 2, 38. Wiv. IV, 4, 29. V, 5, 15. 112. Mids. II, 1, 25. 83. II, 2, 66. As I, 1, 120. I, 3, 109. II, 4, 15. II, 6, 6. II, 7, 12. III, 2, 130. 242. III, 3, 45 etc. R2 III, 1, 23 (*my f. woods*). H4B IV, 1, 1. 19. H6C IV, 6, 83. V, 7, 12. Tit. II, 1, 114. II, 3, 59. Tim. IV, 3, 352. Caes. III, 1, 207. Mcb. IV, 1, 95. V, 3, 60. Hml. III, 2, 286. Lr. I, 1, 65.

Forestall, 1) to anticipate, to be beforehand with, to prevent: *thus I f. thee, if thou mean to*

chide, Lucr. 484. *her foresight could not f. their will*, 728. *might not you f. our sport*, LLL V, 2, 473. *but for my tears, I had —ed this rebuke*, H4B IV, 5, 141. *I shall f. thee*, Troil. IV, 5, 230. *to be —ed ere we come to fall*, Hml. III, 3, 49. *I will f. their repair hither*, V, 2, 228.

2) to deprive: *may this night f. him of the coming day*, Cymb. III, 5, 69.

3) to judge beforehand, to regard with prejudice: *they f. prescience and esteem no act but that of hand*, Troil. I, 3, 199. *never shall you see that I will beg a ragged and —ed remission*, H4B V, 2, 38.*

Forest-bear, a bear living in a forest: H6C II, 2, 13.

Forest-born, born in the forest: As V, 4, 30.

Forester, an officer of the forest: LLL IV, 1, 7. Mids. III, 2, 390. IV, 1, 108. 113. As III, 2, 315. IV, 2, 6. H4A I, 2, 29.

Foretell, 1) to predict, to prophesy: Lucr. 1589. R2 II, 1, 32. H4A V, 1, 6. H4B III, 1, 78. H8 IV, 2, 27. Troil. IV, 5, 217. V, 1, 100.

2) to foretoken, to show: *'tis good speed, —s the great Apollo suddenly will have the truth of this appear*, Wint. II, 3, 199. *many men that stumble at the threshold are well foretold that danger lurks within*, H6C IV, 7, 12. John V, 7, 5. H4B I, 1, 61. H6C II, 1, 43.

3) to tell or communicate before: *these our actors, as I foretold you, were all spirits*, Tp. IV, 149.

Forethink, 1) to foresee, to anticipate: *doth f. thy fall*, H4A III, 2, 38. *—ing this, I have already fit ... doublet* etc. Cymb. III, 4, 171.

2) to ordain, decree: *alter not the doom forethought by heaven*, John III, 1, 312 (cf. *Foresay*).

Forevouched, affirmed before: Lr. I, 1, 223.

Foreward, the vanguard: *my f. shall be drawn out all in length*, R3 V, 3, 293.

Forewarn, 1) to admonish beforehand: *f. him that he use no scurrilous words*, Wint. IV, 4, 215.

2) to caution beforehand: H6B III, 2, 85. H6C IV, 1, 113.

3) to inform previously: *we were —ed of your coming*, H6C IV, 7, 17.

Forewearied (M. Edd. *forwearied*) quite worn out, exhausted: John II, 233.

Forfeit, subst. 1) transgression, infringement, breach, neglect of an obligation entered: *I dare be bound again, my soul upon the f.* Merch. V, 252. *your lives shall pay the f. of the peace*, Rom. I, 1, 104 (or is it the penalty or fine for the breach of the peace?).

2) the losing of something in consequence of the breach of some obligation; forfeiture: *your brother's life falls into f.* Meas. I, 4, 66. *I will be bound to pay it ten times o'er, on f. of my hands, my head, my heart*, Merch. IV, 1, 212. *with the divine f. of his soul upon oath*, All's III, 6, 34. *make f. of his head*, H6C II, 1, 197.

3) the loss or penalty incurred by a trespass or breach of condition: *the strong statutes stand like the —s in a barber's shop*, Meas. V, 323 (cf. *Barber*). *thy slanders I forgive, and therewithal remit thy other —s*, 526. *let the f. be nominated for an equal pound of your flesh*, Merch. I, 3, 149. *to have the due and f. of my bond*, IV, 1, 37. 207. *what is it thou de-*

mandest? the f. of my servant's life, R3 II, 1, 99 (= the forfeited life of my servant). *he could not but think her bond of chastity quite cracked, I having ta'en the f.* Cymb. V, 5, 208 (i. e. what she lost, viz her chastity). Hence = loss of life, death: *despising many —s and subduements*, Troil. IV, 5, 187 (i. e. many lives having, as it were, become due and payable like debts).* *expire the term of a despised life by some vile f. of untimely death*, Rom. I, 4, 111.

4) one obnoxious to capital punishment: *your brother is a f. of the law*, Meas. II, 2, 71. *Claudio is no greater f. to the law than Angelo*, IV, 2, 167.

Forfeit, vb. 1) absol. not to keep an obligation: *if he f., thou wilt not take his flesh*, Merch. III, 1, 53. *I will have the heart of him, if he f.* 132.

2) trans. a) to lose in consequence of an engagement: *I will not f. it*, Merch. I, 3, 157. *'tis all engaged, some —ed and gone*, Tim. II, 2, 155. With *to*, = to give up, to resign sth. to another: *his vows are —ed to me*, All's V, 3, 142. *f. all those lands to the conqueror*, Hml. I, 1, 88.

b) to lose in general, to put to extreme hazard: *myself I'll f., so that other mine thou wilt restore*, Sonn. 134, 3. *—ing our own brains*, H8 Prol. 19. *to f. all your goods*, III, 2, 342. *he —s his own blood that spills another*, Tim. III, 5, 88.

c) to give up for lost, to abandon, to forsake: *undone and —ed to cares*, All's II, 3, 284. *indent with fears, when they have lost and —ed themselves*, H4A I, 3, 88. *to be engaged in Wales, there without ransom to be —ed*, IV, 3, 96. *so should we save a valiant gentleman, by —ing a traitor*, H6A IV, 3, 27.

Forfeit, partic. adj. 1) liable to penal seizure; lost by breach of laws or conditions: *all the souls that were were f. once*, Meas. II, 2, 73. *still f. in the same kind*, III, 2, 206. *our states are f.* LLL V, 2, 425. *stand f.* 427. *my bond to the Jew is f.* Merch. III, 2, 319. *this bond is f.* IV, 1, 230. With *to*: *thy wealth being f. to the state*, Merch. IV, 1, 365.

2) subject, due: *f. to a confined doom*, Sonn. 107, 4. *his brains are f. to the next tile that falls*, All's IV, 3, 216.

Forfeiter, one who incurs a penalty by failing his obligations: Cymb. III, 2, 38.

Forfeiture, 1) that which is lost on engagement: *by the exaction of the f.* Merch. I, 3, 165. *loose the f.* IV, 1, 24. *to cut the f. from that bankrupt there*, 122. *take thy f.* 335. *thou shalt have nothing but the f.* 343.

2) the falling due of a debt: *the envious plea of f., of justice and his bond*, Merch. III, 2, 285. *I oft delivered from his —s many*, III, 3, 22. *will never grant this f. to hold*, 25. *'twas due on f.* Tim. II, 2, 30.

Forfend, see *Forefend.*

Forge, subst. a furnace in which iron is heated and beaten into form: Troil. IV, 5, 255. Oth. IV, 2, 74. Tropically: Wiv. IV, 2, 239. H5 V Chor. 23.

Forge, vb. 1) to shape by heating and hammering: Hml. II, 2, 512.

2) to frame in general: *the best wishes that can be —d in your thoughts*, All's I, 1, 85. *to me the difference —s dread*, Wint. IV, 4, 17. H4A V, 1, 68. Cor. III, 1, 258. V, 1, 14.

3) to frame falsely or to a bad intent, to counterfeit, to coin; a) absol.: *—ing nature*, Ven. 729. *think not that I have —d*, H6A III, 1, 12.

b) trans.: Ven. 804. Sonn. 137, 7. All's IV, 1, 26. R2 IV, 40. H4B IV, 1, 92. H6A III, 1, 90. IV, 1, 102. H8 I, 2, 181. Tit. V, 2, 71. Mcb. IV, 3, 82. Hml. I, 5, 37. Cymb. IV, 2, 318.

Forgery, 1) invention, excogitation: *in f. of shapes and tricks*, Hml. IV, 7, 90.

2) deception, lie: Lucr. 460. 920. Pilgr. 4. Mids. II, 1, 81. H6C III, 3, 175. Hml. II, 1, 20.

Forget (impf. *forgot*: H4A V, 1, 58. H8 III, 1, 132. Hml. V, 2, 76. Cymb. III, 5, 133. Per. III, 1, 59. Partic. usually *forgot*; fifteen times *forgotten*, and only in this form joined, adjectively, to a subst.: *a forgotten matter*, Tw. II, 3, 174. *forgotten dust*, H4B IV, 5, 116. *things forgotten*, Mcb. I, 3, 150.) 1) to lose the memory of, to let go from the remembrance; absol.: *the powers, delaying, not —ing*, Tp. III, 3, 73. Wiv. I, 1, 78. R2 I, 1, 156. H5 IV, 3, 49. Lr. IV, 7, 84. trans.: Lucr. 536. 1644. Sonn. 25, 12. 71, 7. 72, 3. 81, 4. 149, 3. Pilgr. 253. Tp I, 2, 250. 257. 259. 263. II, 1, 157. IV, 139. Gentl. II, 4, 195. III, 2, 10. 29. IV, 4, 86. 124. V, 4, 142. Wiv. I, 4, 180. IV, 1, 79. V, 5, 80. Meas. III, 1, 23. LLL I, 1, 142. III, 30. IV, 3, 95. Mids. II, 2, 36. III, 2, 201. V, 174. Merch. I, 3, 140. As I, 2, 5. II, 4, 32. II, 7, 186. Shr. III, 1, 2. V, 1, 50. All's V, 3, 9. Tw. II, 3, 174. John III, 4, 50. H4A V, 1, 58. H4B IV, 5, 116. V, 2, 72. H5 IV, 3, 49. H6B II, 4, 26. IV, 1, 133. R3 I, 2, 240. I, 3, 117. H8 III, 1, 132. III, 2, 433. Troil. III, 3, 40. Mcb. I, 3, 150. III, 1, 11. Hml. III, 2, 138. 144. Cymb. I, 6, 113. Per. III, 1, 59 etc. Followed by a depending clause: Gentl. II, 6, 27. Ado IV, 2, 80. H4A III, 3, 8. H6A IV, 1, 52. H6B I, 2, 26. By an inf.: Sonn. 23, 5. 100, 1. 117, 3. Ado V, 1, 263. H4A I, 2, 5. Cymb. III, 4, 157. III, 5, 133 etc.

2) to unlearn, to lose the habit or faculty of: *her voice is stopped, her joints f. to bow*, Ven. 1061. *—ing shame's pure blush*, 558. *long agone I have forgot to court*, Gentl. III, 1, 85. *I will f. to drink after thee*, Meas. I, 2, 40. *you have quite forgot a husband's office*, Err. III, 2, 1. *we meet like men that had forgot to speak*, H4B V, 2, 22. *hath thy knee forgot to bow?* H6B V, 1, 161. *laboured much how to f. that learning*, Hml. V, 2, 35.

3) not to respect, to neglect: *my father's precepts I therein do f.* Tp. III, 1, 59. *when once our grace we have forgot, nothing goes right*, Meas. IV, 4, 36. *f. to pity him*, R2 V, 3, 57. *to f. my place*, H4B V, 2, 77. *forgot honour and virtue*, H6B II, 1, 194. *all was either pitied in him or forgotten*, H8 II, 1, 29. *—s the shows of love to other men*, Caes. I, 2, 47. Hml. V, 2, 17. Lr. I, 5, 35. Oth. II, 3, 167. Cymb. II, 3, 110.

4) Used reflectively, = a) to lose consciousness of one's self, to lose remembrance of what one has been: *would not the beggar then f. himself?* Shr. Ind. 1, 41. Tw. V, 144. John III, 4, 49. R2 III, 2, 83. H6B II, 4, 27. R3 IV, 4, 420. Troil. III, 2, 192. Hml. I, 2, 161. Cymb. I, 6, 113. b) to act rashly and without reflection: *thou dost f. thyself*, John III, 1, 134. *I would not have you f. yourself*, IV, 3, 83. *so far f. yourselves*, H8 V, 3, 142. *you f. yourself, to hedge me in*, Caes. IV, 3, 29. 35. *that to Laertes I forgot myself*, Hml. V, 2, 76.

5) Absol., in the same two significations: a) *I f., but these sweet thoughts do even refresh my labours*, Tp. III, 1, 13. *I do f. Do not muse at me*, Mcb. III, 4,

84. b) *the best sometimes f.* Oth. II, 3, 241. *how comes it, Michael, you are thus forgot?* 188.

Forgotten = forgetful: *my oblivion is a very Antony, and I am all forgotten,* Ant. I, 3, 91 (quibbling?).

Forgetful, 1) easily losing the memory of things: H4A I, 3, 161. Caes. IV, 3, 255.

2) heedless, neglectful: *return, f. Muse,* Sonn. 100, 5. *f. in our long absence,* H8 II, 3, 105.

3) rash, inconsiderate: *when that rash humour which my mother gave me makes me f.* Caes. IV, 3, 121.

Forgetfulness, 1) loss of memory, cessation to remember: Sonn. 122, 14. H4B III, 1, 8. Cor. V, 2, 92.

2) oblivion, the state of being forgotten: *blind f. and dark oblivion,* R3 III, 7, 129.

3) neglect, lack of duty: *my love's f.* Gentl. II, 2, 12. *they confess toward thee f.* Tim. V, 1, 147.

Forgetive, inventive: *apprehensive, quick, f.* H4B IV, 3, 107.

Forgive, 1) to pardon; absol.: R2 I, 1, 156. R3 I, 2, 174. Lr. IV, 7, 84 etc. *to f. sth.:* Sonn. 40, 9. Tp. V, 131. Wiv. III, 3, 226. V, 5, 35. Meas. V, 525. All's V, 3, 9 etc. *to f. a person:* Tp. V, 78. Gentl. V, 4, 74. Wiv. II, 2, 58. Meas. II, 1, 37. V, 538. Merch. I, 2, 68. I, 3, 53. H6A III, 3, 81. Cymb. V, 5, 419. *to f. a p. sth.:* Tp. III, 2, 139. Merch. V, 22. 240. All's III, 4, 12. Wint. III, 3, 125. H6A I, 2, 20 etc. *God f. thee for it,* H4A I, 2, 103. A clause following: Gentl. II, 4, 172. V, 4, 154 etc.

2) to remit, not to exact: *f. that sum,* Wiv. V, 5, 178 (not in Ff.). *I f. thy duty,* LLL IV, 2, 147. *f. a moiety of the principal,* Merch. IV, 1, 26. *I f. you the praise,* Tw. I, 5, 204.

Forgiveness, pardon: Tp. V, 198. Meas. IV, 2, 54. Wint. IV, 4, 560. V, 2, 57. R2 V, 3, 84. V, 5, 90. Hml. V, 2, 340. Lr. II, 4, 154. V, 3, 11.

Forgo, see *Forego.*

Fork, any thing dividing into two: *thou dost fear the soft and tender f. of a poor worm,* Meas. III, 1, 16 (i. e. the forked tongue of a snake). *adder's f.* Mcb. IV, 1, 16. *though the f. invade the region of my heart,* Lr. I, 1, 146 (i. e. the barbed arrow-head). *whose face between her —s presages snow,* IV, 6, 121 (i. e. between her legs; cf. III, 4, 113).

Forked, dividing into two: *f. heads,* As II, 1, 24 (= barbed arrow-heads). *o'er head and ears a f. one,* Wint. I, 2, 186 (= a horned cuckold); cf. Troil. I, 2, 178 and Oth. III, 3, 276. *a serpent with f. tongue,* H6B III, 2, 259. *he was like a f. radish,* H4B III, 2, 334. *a f. animal,* Lr. III, 4, 113 (two-legged). *a f. mountain,* Ant. IV, 14, 5.

Forlórn (cf. Append. I, 1), 1) partic. ruined, made unhappy: *love hath f. me,* Pilgr. 265.

2) participial adj. a) lost, not to be found: *the f. soldier that so nobly fought,* Cymb. V, 5, 405.

b) desolate: *to some f. and naked hermitage,* LLL V, 2, 805.

c) abandoned, forsaken, outcast: *ravens foster f. children,* Tit. II, 3, 153. *with swine and rogues f.* Lr. IV, 7, 39. Substantively: *forced to live in Scotland a f.* H6C III, 3, 26.

d) unhappy, wretched: *and whom she finds f. she doth lament,* Lucr. 1500. *and from the f. world his visage hide,* Sonn. 33, 7. *so great and so f.* Wint. II, 2, 22. H6A I, 2, 19. H6B II, 4, 45. III, 2, 77. IV, 1, 65. H6C III, 1, 54. Tit. V, 2, 81. V, 3, 75. Ap-

plied to unhappy lovers: *poor queen of love, in thine own law f.* Ven. 251. *so do thy lips make modest Dian cloudy and f.* 725. *she leaps that was but late f.* 1026. Pilgr. 73. 381. Gentl. I, 2, 124. V, 4, 12.

e) of a wretched appearance, meager, bare: *a' was so f. that his dimensions to any thick sight were invincible,* H4B III, 2, 335 (the only passage in prose, in which the word occurs). *the trees, though summer, yet f. and lean,* Tit. II, 3, 94.

Form, subst. 1) shape, figure, external appearance: *saint-like —s,* Lucr. 1519. *so fair a f. lodged not a mind so ill,* 1530. *when your sweet issue your sweet f. should bear,* Sonn. 13, 8. *how would thy shadow's f. form happy show,* 43, 6 (i. e. thy person, whose shadow only I now see). 108, 14. 113, 5. Compl. 99. 241. Tp. I, 2, 411. Gentl. III, 2, 8. Wiv. V, 5, 10. Err. II, 2, 200. LLL IV, 2, 68. Mids. I, 1, 49. V, 15. Tw. III, 4, 291. Wint. II, 1, 69. John I, 160. III, 4, 97. IV, 2, 256. V, 4, 50. V, 7, 26. H4A I, 3, 210. R3 III, 7, 14. Troil. V, 3, 12. Hml. I, 5, 100. Oth. III, 3, 237. IV, 2, 155. Ant. V, 2, 98 etc.

2) image, picture, more especially likeness, portrait: *that thou no f. of thee hast left behind,* Sonn. 9, 6. 24, 2. *O thou senseless f., thou shalt be worshipped,* Gentl. IV, 4, 203. Meas. II, 4, 126. LLL II, 237. Merch. II, 7, 61. Tw. II, 2, 31. John V, 7, 32.

3) manner of arranging particulars: *in polished f. of well-refined pen,* Sonn. 85, 8. *observation, the which he vents in mangled forms,* As II, 7, 42. *what f. of prayer can serve my turn?* Hml. III, 3, 51.

4) manner of behaving, deportment: *in him a plenitude of subtle matter all strange —s receives,* Compl. 303. *if the gentle spirit of moving words can no way change you to a milder f.* Gentl. V, 4, 56. *in such —s as here were presupposed on thee,* Tw. V, 358. John I, 211. Cor. II, 2, 148. Caes. I, 2, 303. Hml. I, 2, 210. II, 2, 583. III, 1, 161.

5) external appearance, empty show: *dwellers on f. and favour,* Sonn. 125, 5. *O place, O f., how often dost thou wrench awe from fools,* Meas. II, 4, 12. V, 56. LLL V, 2, 325. Rom. V, 3, 246. Lr. II, 4, 80. Oth. IV, 2, 138.

6) good semblance: *to set a f. upon desired change,* Sonn. 89, 6. *makes most f. in mirth,* LLL V, 2, 520. *things base and vile love can transpose to f. and dignity,* Mids. I, 1, 233. *in goodly f. comes on the enemy,* H4B IV, 1, 20. H5 II, 2, 116. *to bring manslaughter into f.* Tim. III, 5, 27.

7) outline, plan: *the f. of my intent,* Tw. I, 2, 55. *the f. and model of our battle,* R3 V, 3, 24.

8) method, order: *in manner and f. following,* LLL I, 1, 207. *their f. confounded,* LLL V, 2, 520. *I will not keep this f. upon my head, when there is such disorder in my wit,* John III, 4, 101. III, 1, 253. R2 III, 4, 41. H6B III, 1, 58. R3 III, 1, 200. Hml. III, 1, 171.

9) established practice, ceremony, ritual: *by cold gradation and weal-balanced f.* Meas. IV, 3, 104. *the plain f. of marriage,* Ado IV, 1, 2. John IV, 2, 22. R2 III, 2, 173. H4B IV, 5, 119. Rom. II, 2, 88. II, 4, 36. Cor. III, 1, 325.

10) a long seat: LLL I, 1, 209. Wint. I, 2, 313. Caes. III, 2, 264. Quibbling in Rom. II, 4, 36.

Form, vb. to shape, to make: Lucr. 1241. 1243. Sonn. 3, 2. 43, 6. Tp. I, 2, 83. III, 1, 56. LLL V, 2, 750. 772. Tw. I, 3, 142. John II, 498. IV, 3, 45. Troil. II, 2, 120. III, 3, 119.

Formal, 1) regular, orderly, accurate, according to rule and custom: *her hair, nor loose, nor tied in f. plat,* Compl. 29. *beard of f. cut,* As II, 7, 155. *the f. vice Iniquity,* R3 III, 1, 82 (= customary).* *no noble right nor f. ostentation,* Hml. IV, 5, 215. *to make of him a f. man again,* Err. V, 105 (i.e. an ordinary man, a man in his senses; cf. *Informal*). *this is evident to any f. capacity,* Tw. II, 5, 128. *thou shouldst come like a Fury crowned with snakes, not like a f. man,* Ant. II, 5, 41 (= common, ordinary).

2) precise, pedantic: *are you so f.?* Shr. III, 1, 61. *f. in apparel,* IV, 2, 64.

3) grave, dignified: *and flow henceforth in f. majesty,* H4B V, 2, 133. *with untired spirits and f. constancy,* Caes. II, 1, 227.

Formally, regularly, according to custom or established rites: *how I may f. in person bear me like a true friar,* Meas. I, 3, 47. *and f., according to our law, depose him,* R2 I, 3, 29.

Former, 1) most forward, anterior: *our f. ensign,* Caes. V, 1, 80.

2) preceding: *this simulation is not as the f.* Tw. II, 5, 152. *a third is like the f.* Mcb. IV, 1, 115. *o'erborne in the f. wave,* Cymb. V, 3, 48.

3) previous, antecedent, aforesaid: *speak your f. language,* Meas. II, 4, 140. *we do lock our f. scruple in our strong-barred gates,* John II, 370. *speak again, not all thy f. tale, but this one word,* III, 1, 25. *bear my f. answer back,* H5 IV, 3, 90. *maintain the f. words thou spakest,* H6A IV, 4, 31. *the f. agents, if they did complain, what could the belly answer?* Cor. I, 1, 127. *your f. promise,* 242. *my f. sum,* Tim. II, 1, 2. *my f. speeches have but hit your thoughts,* Mcb. III, 6, 1 (= what I said hitherto). *my f. lecture,* Hml. II, 1, 67 (= given hitherto). *my f. suit,* Oth. III, 4, 110. *our f. having,* IV, 3, 92. *thou must not take my f. sharpness ill,* Ant. III, 3, 38.

4) first mentioned of two (opposed to *latter*): Ant. III, 13, 80. Per. III, 2, 30.

5) having happened or existed in time past; old, gone: Sonn. 56, 4. 59, 4. 13. 123, 4. Gentl. II, 4, 194. V, 4, 142. Ado V, 4, 65. Mids. III, 2, 457. As V, 4, 192. Shr. Ind. 2, 124. IV, 2, 30. Wint. V, 1, 30. 79. V, 2, 122. R2 V, 1, 18. H4B III, 1, 42. IV, 5, 216. V, 5, 62. H5 I, 2, 124. V, 2, 63. 67. H6A IV, 4, 6. H6C I, 4, 45. III, 3, 7. 195. 198. R3 II, 1, 24. H8 I, 1, 18. 36. Cor. II, 1, 150. V, 3, 202 (*a f. fortune* = a fortune like that of old). Tim. V, 1, 127. 128. Mcb. I, 2, 65. II, 4, 4. III, 2, 15. Hml. III, 2, 174. Lr. I, 3, 9. Oth. V, 2, 9. Ant. I, 2, 33 (*a fairer f. fortune*). III, 13, 145. IV, 15, 53.

Formerly, 1) previously, before: *the danger f. by me rehearsed,* Merch. IV, 1, 362.

2) in time past: All's I, 1, 176. Wint. IV, 2, 37. H8 I, 1, 83. Cor. IV, 1, 53. Ant. III, 5, 11.

Formless, shapeless, chaotic: *all form is f.* John III, 1, 253. *f. ruin of oblivion,* Troil. IV, 5, 167.

Fornication, lewd commerce of the sexes: Wiv. V, 5, 166. Meas. II, 1, 82. V, 70. 195. H8 V, 4, 36.

Fornicatress, a woman who without marriage cohabits with a man: Meas. II, 2, 23.

Forrest, name: R3 IV, 3, 4. 10. 15.

Forsake (impf. *forsook,* partic. *forsook* and *forsaken*): 1) to refuse: *thou hast power to choose, and they none to f.* All's II, 3, 62. *if you f. the offer of their love,* H6A IV, 2, 14. *were your godheads to borrow of men, men would f. the gods,* Tim. III, 6, 84. *hath she forsook so many noble matches,* Oth. IV, 2, 125. Abs.: *till my soul f., shall cry for blessings on him,* H8 II, 1, 89 (Germ. versagen.).

2) to leave, to quit: *the shadow had forsook them,* Ven. 176. *the breeder... doth f. him,* 321. *leviathans f. unsounded deeps to dance on sands,* Gentl. III, 2, 81. *forsook his scene and entered in a brake,* Mids. III, 2, 15. *I must f. the court,* Wint. I, 2, 362. John I, 148. R2 II, 3, 26. H6A I, 2, 40. V, 5, 32. H6B IV, 4, 50. R3 II, 1, 85. H8 I, 4, 104. II, 1, 132. Tim. III, 4, 72. Oth. V, 2, 330. Ant. II, 7, 43.

3) to desert, to fall off from, to be faithless to: Sonn. 89, 1. 133, 7. Gentl. IV, 4, 151. Ado II, 1, 226. John V, 7, 35. H6A IV, 1, 59. V, 3, 24. H6B IV, 2, 132. IV, 8, 10. H6C III, 1, 54. IV, 7, 85. V, 2, 25. R3 I, 3, 135. II, 1, 109. Cor. IV, 5, 82. Rom. II, 3, 67. Lr. I, 1, 254. Reflectively: Ven. 161. Lucr. 157. Sonn. 12, 11. All's IV, 2, 39.

4) to reject, to renounce: *"it cannot be" she in that sense forsook, and turned it thus,* Lucr. 1538. *and bid you f. your liberty,* Err. IV, 3, 20.

Forslow, see *Foreslow.*

Forsooth, in truth, certainly; used by low persons as a phrase of honest asseveration: *ay, f.* Wiv. I, 4, 19. 26. 49. 87. II, 1, 169. II, 2, 89. V, 2, 4. Rom. IV, 2, 12. *yes, f.* Tit. IV, 4, 40. Lr. I, 4, 214. Ant. V, 2, 281. *no, f.* Wiv. I, 4, 22. Shr. IV, 3, 1. H6B I, 3, 33. *I thank you f.* Wiv. I, 1, 277. 280. *I had rather f. go,* III, 2, 5. III, 3, 163. IV, 1, 78. IV, 5, 107. All's I, 3, 100. H4A II, 4, 46. H6B II, 1, 63. 93. II, 3, 82.

Implying some contempt, when used by well-bred persons: *and f. to search his house,* Wiv. III, 5, 78. *this pernicious slave, f., took on him as a conjurer,* Err. V, 242. Ado II, 3, 59. LLL III, 175. Mids. II, 1, 70. III, 2, 230. 293. As III, 2, 380. Shr. III, 2, 8. H4A I, 3, 140. IV, 3, 78. H6A IV, 1, 157. V, 4, 83. H6B I, 3, 118. III, 2, 183. R3 I, 3, 44. H8 III, 1, 87. III, 2, 124. Troil. I, 3, 172. Cor. III, 2, 85. Oth. I, 1, 19.

Forspeak, see *Forespeak.*

Forspend, see *Forespend.*

Forswear, (impf. *forswore,* partic. *forsworn*), 1) trans. a) to refuse or renounce upon oath, to swear that one will have nothing to do with a person or thing: *a woman I forswore,* Pilgr. 33. 34 and LLL IV, 3, 64. 65. *her and her blind boy's company I have forsworn,* Tp. IV, 91. Gentl. III, 1, 212. 214. III, 2, 4. LLL IV, 3, 297. 310. 319. 355. V, 2, 410. Mids. II, 1, 62. As III, 2, 437. 440. Shr. IV, 2, 26. 29. 47. Tw. I, 3, 93. Wint. I, 2, 361. R2 IV, 211. H4A I, 2, 208. II, 2, 16. H4B II, 4, 219. IV, 3, 134. V, 4, 23. H6C I, 1, 251. III, 2, 153. Tim. IV, 3, 133. Oth. IV, 2, 159. Followed by an inf.: *f. to wear iron about you,* Tw. III, 4, 276. Cor. V, 3, 80. Rom. I, 1, 229. Reflectively: *f. themselves as often as they speak,* Wint. V, 1, 200 (= curse themselves). Absol.: *would all the world but he had quite forsworn,* Shr. IV, 2, 35.

b) to deny upon oath: *you'll f. this again,* Meas. III, 2, 177. IV, 3, 183. Err. V, 24. 25. 261. Ado V, 1, 169. Shr. V, 1, 114. All's I, 3, 189. Rom. I, 5, 54. With an inf.: *that chain which he forswore to have,* Err. V, 11. With a subordinate clause: —*ing that he is forsworn,* H4A V, 2, 39.

2) refl., to swear falsely, to perjure one's

self: *f. not thyself*, Gentl. II, 5, 3. Wiv. IV, 5, 103. Mids. I, 1, 240. H6C V, 5, 75. R3 I, 3, 136. Tit. V, 1, 130.

3) intr. **to swear falsely, to commit perjury:** *love bids me f.* Gentl. II, 6, 6. LLL V, 2, 440. As V, 4, 58. R3 I, 4, 207. Partic. *forsworn* = perjured: Ven. 726. Sonn. 66, 4. 88, 4. 152, 1. Pilgr. 57. Gentl. II, 6, 1. 2. 3. IV, 2, 10. Meas. IV, 1, 2. V, 38. Err. IV, 2, 10. V, 212. Ado I, 1, 155. LLL I, 1, 150. 155. I, 2, 175. II, 98. IV, 2, 109. IV, 3, 47. 116. 219. 283. 363. 385 *(men forsworn).* V, 2, 471. 842. Merch. III, 2, 11. 14. As I, 2, 71. 82. John III, 1, 62. 101. 284. 286. 287. V, 4, 31. R2 IV, 52 *(forsworn Aumerle).* H4A V, 2, 39. H5 IV, 8, 13. H6C I, 2, 18. Troil. V, 2, 22. Cor. V, 3, 28. Rom. III. 2, 87. III, 5, 197. 236. Mcb. IV, 3, 126. With *to: to myself forsworn*, Pilgr. 59 and LLL IV, 2, 111.

Fort, a fortified place, castle, fortress: H6B IV, 1, 89. Figuratively: Lucr. 482. 1175. Hml. I, 4, 28.

Forted, fortified, strong: *it deserves, with characters of brass, a f. residence 'gainst the tooth of time*, Meas. V, 12.

Forth, adv. 1) **off, away, abroad:** *and f. with bashful innocence doth hie*, Lucr. 1341. *travel f. without my cloak*, Sonn. 34, 2. *if a virgin, and your affection not gone f.* Tp. I, 2, 448. *graves let 'em (their sleepers) f.* V, 49. *put f. their sons to seek preferment out*, Gentl. I, 3, 7. *what honest clothes you send f. to bleaching*, Wiv. IV, 2, 126. *the heavens lead f. and bring you back in happiness*, Meas. I, 1, 75. *the heedful slave is wandered f. to seek me out*, Err. II, 2, 3. *if any bark put f.* III, 2, 155. *is there any ship puts f. to-night?* IV, 3, 35. *turn melancholy f. to funerals*, Mids. I, 1, 14. *every one (grave) lets f. his sprite*, V, 388. *had I such venture f.* Merch. I, 1, 15. *it is meet I presently set f.* IV, 1, 404. *to travel f. so far*, As I, 3, 111. *is gone f. to sleep*, IV, 3, 5. *when I am f., bid me farewell and smile*, Cor. IV, 1, 49. *I am the turned f.* Tit. V, 3, 109. *they are all f.; well, I will walk myself*, Rom. IV, 2, 44. *it waves me f. again*, Hml. I, 4, 68. *his best force is f. to man his galleys*, Ant. V, 11, 3 etc. *her husband will be f.* Wiv. II, 2, 276 (= not at home). *he dines f.* Err. II, 2, 212. *I am bid f. to supper*, Merch II, 5, 11. *feasting f.* 37. *I am promised f.* Caes. I, 2, 293. V, 3, 80.

2) **from another place to that of the speaker; here, hither** (cf. *Away*, def. 3): *come f.* Tp. I, 2, 315. 320. *and sends me f. to keep them living*, II, 1, 298. *when I suddenly call you, come f.* Wiv. III, 3, 11. *his hinds were called f. by their mistress*, III, 5, 100. IV, 2, 125. Meas. IV, 1, 50. *you must call f. the watch*, Ado IV, 2, 36. 39. *call her f., brother*, V, 4, 39. LLL V, 2, 899. *bring your music f. into the air*, Merch. V, 53. *call f. an officer*, Shr. V, 1, 94. *swinge me them soundly f. unto their husbands*, V, 2, 104. *bring f. this counterfeit module*, All's IV, 3, 113. *call f. the holy father*, Tw. V, 145. *I shall bring Emilia f.* Wint. II, 2, 15. *bring f. his oracle*, III, 2, 118. John IV, 1, 8. H6A II, 2, 4. IV, 2, 3. V, 3, 128. H6B IV, 1, 8. Ant. IV, 2, 9 etc.

3) **out; from confinement or indistinction into open view:** *f., my sword*, Oth. V, 1, 10. *beat f. our brains*, Tit. V, 3, 133. *blaze f. her wrongs*, Ven. 219. *his malice will suddenly break f.* As I, 2, 295 (cf. *Break*, as well as the other verbs to which it is joined). *thus breathes she f. her spite*, Lucr. 762. *let your ser-*

vants bring my husband f. Err. V, 93. *bring Deformed f.* Ado III, 3, 185 (= before the judge). *to bring f.* = to beget, procreate: Pilgr. 284. Tp. II, 1, 93. 162. III, 2, 113. V, 170. H6C V, 6, 50 etc. cf. *to body f.* and *to drop f.*, in the same sense: Mids. V, 14. As III, 2, 250. IV, 3, 34; and *to throe f.* Ant. III, 7, 81. *called f. the mutinous winds*, Tp. V, 42. *call f. your actors*, Mids. I, 2, 16. H6A I, 1, 83. *it is you that have chalked f. the way which brought us hither*, Tp. V, 203. *if thou beest Trinculo, come f.* II, 2, 107. Mids. III, 2, 19. Merch. III, 2, 59. *when comes your book f.?* Tim. I, 1, 26. *which out of a great deal of old iron I chose f.* H6A I, 2, 101. *thine eye darts f. the fire that burneth me*, Ven. 196. *draw f. thy weapon*, Shr. III, 2, 238. *to find his fellow f.* Err. I, 2, 37. Merch. I, 1, 143. *it flashed f. fire*, Ven. 348. *to give f. the corn o' the storehouse*, Cor. III, 1, 113. Lr. II, 4, 116. *dying eyes gleamed f. their ashy lights*, Lucr. 1378. *Caesar shall go f.* Caes. II, 2, 8. 28. 48; cf. II, 1, 194. and Cymb. II, 3, 43. *ere the writs go f.* H6B V, 3, 26 (= are issued). *if he had gone f. consul*, Cor. IV, 6, 35 (= if he had been chosen c.). *heaved f. such groans*, As II, 1, 36. *I shall inquire you f.* Gentl. II, 4, 186. *lay f. the gown*, Shr. IV, 3, 62. *embalm me, then lay me f.* H8 IV, 2, 171. *whose great decision hath much blood let f.* All's III, 1, 3. *lock me f.* Err. IV, 4, 98. 100. *make f.* Caes. V, 1, 25. *peeping f.* Lucr. 447. Hml. III, 4, 119. *which shall point you f. what you must say*, Wint. IV, 4, 572. *this is put f. too truly*, Wint. I, 2, 14. *his negligence sometime puts f.* 254. *put f. thy hand, reach at the glorious gold*, H6B I, 2, 11. *roar these accusations f.* H6A III, 1, 40. *and f. she rushes*, Ven. 262. *and f. again... vapours doth she send*, Ven. 273. *send him f.* Err. V, 158. *to set f.* = to recommend, to cry up: Lucr. 32. Pilgr. 310. Merch. III, 5, 95. *to shoot f. thunder*, H6B IV, 1, 104. *shrills her dolours f.* Troil. V, 3, 84. *sighed f. proverbs*, Cor. I, 1, 209. *he singled Clifford f.* H6C II, 1, 12. *stand f.*, Demetrius, Mids. I, 1, 24 (= step forward from among your companions). III, 1, 83. As I, 2, 75. R2 IV, 7. H6B II, 3, 1. H8 V, 3, 47. *now step I f. to whip hypocrisy*, LLL IV, 3, 151. *she throws f. Tarquin's name*, Lucr. 1717. *to trumpet f. my infamy*, Per. I, 1, 145. *there my father's grave did utter f. a voice*, Meas. III, 1, 87. *weeping his welcomes f.* Wint. IV, 4, 560. *yield you f. to public thanks*, Meas. V, 7 (evidently = yield f. public thanks to you).

Forth of = out of: Tp. V, 160. Meas. I, 1, 35. R2 III, 2, 204. H6C II, 2, 157. R3 IV, 4, 176. Caes. III, 3, 3. Oth. V, 1, 35 *(Ff for).* Ant. I, 5, 12.

From f. = from out: Ven. 259. Lucr. 373. 450. 1068. 1834. Wiv. IV, 4, 53. All's II, 1, 199. John IV, 2, 148. IV, 3, 143. V, 4, 45. R2 II, 1, 106. II, 3, 102. R3 IV, 4, 47. Troil. I, 3, 350. Tit. I, 327. Rom. Chor. 5. Tim. I, 1, 138. IV, 3, 186. *Forth from: arise f. from the couch of lasting night*, John III, 4, 27.

4) **on, forward:** *to hear this matter f.* Meas. V, 255 (= to hear the further process of the matter). *go f.; try what my credit can do*, Merch. I, 1, 179. *as he f. walked on his way*, Shr. IV, 1, 149. *go thou f., and fortune play upon thy prosperous helm*, All's III, 3, 6. *flies an eagle flight, bold and f. on*, Tim. I, 1, 49. Caes. IV, 1, 35. *Fidele's sickness did make my way long f.* Cymb. IV, 2, 149. Especially, = in or to the field, ready to meet the enemy: *then f., dear country-*

men! H5 II, 2, 189. *now f., lord constable and princes all*, III, 5, 67. *when we first marched f.* John II, 320. *the dukes of Berri and of Bretagne shall make f.* H5 II, 4, 5. *Samsons it sendeth f. to skirmish*, H6A I, 2, 34 *when thou art f. in the incursions*, Troil. II, 1, 32. *some parcels of their power are f. already*, Cor. I, 2, 32. *the Volsces have an army f.* I, 3, 108. *are my brother's powers set f.?* Lr. IV, 5, 1. *our troops set f. to-morrow*, 16. cf. *when thou wilt inflame, how coldly those impediments stand f. of wealth* etc. Compl. 269. *'gainst death and all-oblivious enmity shall you pace f.* Sonn. 55, 10. *to furnish f.* = to provide with what is necessary: H4B I, 2, 251. Hml. I, 2, 181.

And so f. = et caetera: LLL IV, 2, 96. Tw. I, 5, 267. III, 4, 82. H4B V, 3, 4. Troil. I, 2, 277 (Q *and such like*). *or so f.:* Hml. II, 1, 61 (cf. *So-forth*).

Redundantly after *far: know thus far f.* Tp. I, 2, 177. *so far f. as herself might be her chooser*, Wiv. IV, 6, 11. *it shall be so far f. friendly maintained till...*, Shr. I, 1, 140. *how far f. you do like their articles*, H4B IV, 2, 53. Similarly after *from this day* or *time: from this day f. I'll use you for my mirth*, Caes. IV, 3, 48. *I would not, from this time f., have you so slander any moment leisure*, Hml. I, 3, 132. *from this time f. my thoughts be bloody*, IV, 4, 65.

Forth, prepos. o u t o f: *steal f. thy father's house*, Mids. I, 1, 164. *drive the English f. the bounds of France*, H6A I, 2, 54. *he that loosed them f. their brazen caves*, H6B III, 2, 89. *issue f. their city*, Cor. I, 4, 23. *peered f. the golden window of the east*, Rom. I, 1, 126. *they have put f. the haven*, Ant. IV, 10, 7.

Forthcoming, appearing before the judge, t r i e d at l a w: *see that he be f.* Shr. V, 1, 96. *we'll see your trinkets here all f.* H6B I, 4, 56. *your lady is f. yet at London*, II, 1, 179.

Forthlight, name in Meas. IV, 3, 17.

Forthright, a s t r a i g h t p a t h: Tp. III, 3, 3. Troil. III, 3, 158.

Forthwith, i m m e d i a t e l y, without delay: Lucr. 178. Err. IV, 4, 123. Merch. I, 3, 173. Shr. IV, 3, 184. V, 2, 87. R2 V, 1, 70. H4A I, 1, 22. H6A I, 1, 153. I, 5, 14. H6C III, 3, 135. 243. IV, 3, 52. IV, 4, 31. IV, 6, 54. 97. R3 II, 2, 121. H8 II, 2, 109. V, 3, 88. Troil. I, 3, 389. IV, 2, 65. Tit. V, 3, 193. Hml. III, 3, 3. Oth. IV, 3, 8. Cymb. V, 3, 41.

Fortification, the works erected to defend a place: Oth. III, 2, 5.

Fortify, 1) trans. to strengthen and secure by works of defence: John III, 4, 10. H5 III, 3, 53. H6A IV, 2, 19. H6C I, 2, 52. Mcb. V, 2, 12. Figuratively: *f. yourself in your decay*, Sonn. 16, 3. *he's —ied against any denial*, Tw. I, 5, 153. *let us assail your ears that are so —ed against our story*, Hml. I, 1, 32. Cymb. I, 4, 21. With *from*, = to secure, protect from: *which —ed her visage from the sun*, Compl. 9.

2) intr. to raise works of strength: *for such a time do I now f. against confounding age's cruel knife*, Sonn. 63, 9. *we f. in paper and in figures*, H4B I, 3, 56. *view the Frenchmen how they f.* H6A I, 4, 61.

Fortinbras, name in Hml. I, 1, 82. II, 2, 68. IV, 4, 2 etc.

Fortitude, 1) c o n s t a n c y, firmness of mind: Tp. I, 2, 154. H8 III, 2, 388. Mcb. IV, 3, 94.

2) v i g o u r, f o r c e, s t r e n g t h: *despairing of his own arm's f.* H6A II, 1, 17. *the f. of the place is best known to you*, Oth. I, 3, 222.

Fortnight, the space of two weeks: Wiv. I, 1, 212. Mids. V, 376. Merch. III, 1, 131. H4A II, 3, 41. H4B III, 1, 104. R3 III, 2, 62. Cor. I, 1, 59. Rom. I, 3, 15. Lr. I, 4, 317. IV, 6, 245.

Fortress, subst. fortified place, stronghold: R2 II, 1, 43. H6A II, 1, 26 (*God is our f.*). III, 4, 6. Ant. III, 2, 31.

Fortressed, fortified, guarded: *weakly f. from a world of harms*, Lucr. 28.

Fortunate, successful, prosperous, favoured by fortune; used of persons: Mids. III, 2, 233. V, 413. Merch. I, 1, 176. All's II, 4, 14. Wint. IV, 4, 662. H4A V, 1, 38. H6A I, 2, 91. V, 2, 21. H6C IV, 6, 25. IV, 8, 27. Cor. IV, 3, 39. Tit. II, 1, 32. Caes. III, 2, 27. Ant. IV, 14, 76. Cymb. V, 4, 144. Of things: Ado III, 1, 45. Caes. II, 2, 84.

Fortunately, by good fortune, luckily: Mids. IV, 1, 182. Lr. II, 2, 174. Oth. II, 1, 61.

Fortunate-unhappy, favoured by fortune, rich in the outward means of happiness, but miserable in soul: Tw. II, 5, 172.

Fortune, subst. 1) the power supposed to distribute the lots of life according to her humour: *lame by —'s dearest spite*, Sonn. 37, 3. *which heaven and f. still rewards with plagues*, Gentl. IV, 3, 31. IV, 1, 22. Meas. II, 1, 268. Err. I, 1, 106. Merch. II, 1, 36. As II, 1, 19. John V, 2, 58. R2 II, 4, 24. Troil. II, 2, 90. Cor. V, 3, 119 etc. etc. Figured as a Goddess: Lucr. 351. Sonn. 29, 1. 124, 2. Pilgr. 259. Wiv. III, 3, 69. Merch. II, 2, 175. IV, 1, 267. As I, 2, 37. All's I, 3, 115. Tw. II, 2, 19. II, 5, 171. John III, 1, 54. 60. 61. H5 V, 1, 85. H6B I, 2, 67. Troil. IV, 5, 293. Cor. I, 5, 21. Tim. I, 1, 64. *bountiful F., now my dear lady*, Tp. I, 2, 178. *lady F.* As II, 7, 16. Wint. IV, 4, 51. Per. IV, 4, 48. Represented with a wheel as the emblem of mutability: Lucr. 952. As I, 2, 34. H5 III, 6, 28. 32. H6C IV, 3, 46. Lr. II, 2, 180. Ant. IV, 15, 44. *on —'s cap we are not the very button*, Hml. II, 2, 233.

2) the good or ill that befalls man: *I feared thy f.* Ven. 642. *to try their f.* Gentl. I, 3, 8. IV, 1, 43. *if it were my master's f. to have her or no*, Wiv. IV, 5, 49. Err. V, 355. H4A V, 5, 12. Hml. III, 4, 32 etc. *good f.* Tp. II, 1, 270. Wiv. III, 4, 105. Meas. IV, 2, 191. Merch. II, 1, 45. II, 2, 168. Shr. I, 2, 168. All's II, 4, 16 (M. Edd. *—s*). John I, 180. Oth. IV, 1, 62 (Qq *—s*) etc. *to try her gracious f. with lord Angelo*, Meas. V, 76. *ill f.* H6A III, 2, 109. *no worse f.* Wiv. I, 4, 34. H4B II, 2, 152. *the fouler f. mine*, Shr. V, 2, 98. *followed both my —s faithfully*, H8 IV, 2, 141.

Often used in the plural: *my —s will ever after droop*, Tp. I, 2, 183. *knit a knot in his —s*, Wiv. III, 2, 76. *hear all our —s*, Err. V, 395. *belonging to whom? to my —s and me*, LLL II, 224. *my —s every way as fairly ranked*, Mids. I, 1, 101. *I will go buy my —s*, As I, 1, 79. *to question you about your —s*, II, 7, 172. 200. Shr. IV, 2, 104. Tw. II, 5, 77. III, 4, 6. H6B III, 1, 221. H6C II, 2, 157. Oth. I, 3, 228 etc. etc. *your good —s*, Merch. I, 2, 5. *in their best —s*, Ant. III, 12, 30.

3) c h a n c e, f a t e, a c c i d e n t: *nor can I f. to brief minutes tell*, Sonn. 14, 5. *all is but f.* Tp. V, 257 and Tw. II, 5, 27. *the assault ... f. hath conveyed to my understanding*, Meas. III, 1, 189. *nor is my whole estate upon the f. of this present year*, Merch. I, 1, 44. *whatever f. stays him from his word*, Shr. III, 2, 23.

each circumstance of place, time, f. Tw. V, 259. *to prove more —s thou art tired,* Cor. IV, 5, 99. *the battles, sieges, —s, that I have passed,* Oth. I, 3, 130. *by f.* = by accident: Sonn. 32, 3. Merch. II, 1, 34. As I, 2, 47. Oth. V, 2, 226. *at f.* = at hazard, at random: *and let her down the wind, to prey at f.* Oth. III, 3, 263.

4) good luck, happy success, prosperity: *reckoning his f. at such high-proud rate,* Lucr. 19. *cancelled my —s,* 934. *thou letst thy f. sleep,* Tp. II, 1, 216. *partner of his f.* Gentl. I, 3, 59. *I read your f. in your eye,* II, 4, 143. *myself do want my servants' f.* III, 1, 147. *good bringing up, f. and truth,* IV, 4, 74. *flies her f. when it follows her,* V, 2, 50. *my food, my f. and my sweet hope's aim,* Err. III, 2, 63. *I thank my f. for it,* Merch. I, 1, 41. *if I do fail in f. of my choice,* II, 9, 15. *f. now to my heart's hope!* 19. *share the good of our returned f.* As V, 4, 180. *this accident and flood of f.* Tw. IV, 3, 11. *I may not wish the f. thine,* John III, 1, 333. *it rained down f. showering on your head,* H4A V, 1, 47. *f. and victory sit on thy helm,* R3 V, 3, 79. *pride which out of daily f. ever taints the man,* Cor. IV, 7, 38. *will you be put in mind of his blind f.* V, 6, 118. *held you so under f.* Mcb. III, 1, 78. *what art thou that hast this f. on me?* Lr. V, 3, 165.

5) estate, possessions, wealth: *to hold their cursed-blessed f. long,* Lucr. 866. Meas. III, 1, 230. As II, 7, 19. Tim. I, 1, 55. Lr. I, 1, 251 etc. Plural: *take my daughter, and with her my —s,* Ado II, 1, 314. Merch. I, 1, 177. As II, 4, 77. Wint. IV, 4, 601. John II, 69. Tim. I, 1, 293. Oth. V, 2, 366 etc.

Fortune, vb.) 1) to happen, to come to pass: *you will wonder what hath —d,* Gentl. V, 4, 169.

2) to regulate the fortune of: *f. him accordingly,* Ant. I, 2, 77.

Fortune-tell, a verb used in jest, = to teach to tell fortune: *I'll conjure you, I'll f. you,* Wiv. IV, 2, 196.

Fortune-teller, one who predicts future events: Err. V, 239.

Fortune-telling, the art or practice of predicting future events: Wiv. IV, 2, 184.

Forty, four times ten: R2 I, 3, 159. H4A IV, 1, 130. Tit. I, 193. Rom. IV, 1, 105. V, 1, 59. Lr. I, 4, 42. Oth. I, 3, 4. Used for an indefinite number, where no exact reckoning was needed: *when f. winters shall besiege thy brow,* Sonn. 2, 1. *I had rather than f. shillings,* Wiv. I, 1, 205; Tw. II, 3, 20 and V, 180. *f. more,* Meas. IV, 3, 20. *worth f. ducats,* Err. IV, 3, 84. 97; cf. H4A III, 3, 95. 117 and H5 IV, 4, 14. *in f. minutes,* Mids. II, 1, 176. *f. fancies,* Shr. III, 2, 70. *I myself fight not once in f. year,* H6A I, 3, 91. *f. pence,* H8 II, 3, 89 (proverbial expression of a small wager). *within these f. hours,* III, 2, 253. *f. truncheoners,* V, 4, 54. *I could beat f. of them,* Cor. III, 1, 243. *hop f. paces,* Ant. II, 2, 234. *f. days longer,* Per. I, 1, 116. *is not the king's name f. thousand names?* R2 III, 2, 85 (Ff *twenty*). *f. thousand fathom above water,* Wint. IV, 4, 281. *f. thousand brothers,* Hml. V, 1, 292. *f. thousand lives,* Oth. III, 3, 442.

Forward, adj. 1) anterior, fore: *his f. voice,* Tp. II, 2, 94. *whoever charges on his f. breast,* All's III, 2, 116. *let's take the instant by the f. top,* V, 3, 39.

2) advanced, going far: *she is as f. of her breeding as she is in the rear our birth,* Wint. IV, 4, 591 (cf. *Of*). *when a jest is so f., and afoot too, I hate it,* H4A II, 2, 50.

3) not behindhand, ready, willing, making the first steps to meet another: *am bold to show myself a f. guest within your house,* Shr. II, 51. *you are marvellous f.* 73. *speak England first, that hath been f. first to speak unto this city,* John II, 482. *what need I be so f. with him that calls not on me?* H4A V, 1, 130. *nor do we find him f. to be sounded,* Hml. III, 1, 7. *our expectation that it would be thus hath made us f.* Cymb. III, 5, 29.

4) eager, zealous: *how fondly dost thou spur a f. horse,* R2 IV, 72. *his f. spirit would lift him where most trade of danger ranged,* H4B I, 1, 173. *let 'em have their rights, they are ever f.* H8 IV, 1, 9. *thus f. in his banishment,* H6B III, 2, 253. *thus f. in my right,* Tit. I, 56. *f. upon his party,* R3 III, 2, 46. *on thy side,* V, 3, 94. *most f. to doom the offenders,* III, 4, 66. *f. of revenge,* H6C IV, 8, 46.

5) bold, immodest, malapert: *you'll still be too f.* Gentl. II, 1, 11. *you grow too f.* Shr. III, 1, 1. *how fiery and f. our pedant is,* 48.

6) early ripe, premature: *the f. violet thus did I chide,* Sonn. 99, 1. *the most f. bud,* Gentl. I, 1, 45. *a very f. March-chick,* Ado I, 3, 58. *short summers lightly have a f. spring,* R3 III, 1, 94. *a violet f., not permanent,* Hml. I, 3, 8.

7) promising, hopeful, highly gifted: *good wit seconded with the f. child Understanding,* As III, 3, 14. *long live thou and these thy f. sons,* H6C I, 1, 203. *you promised knighthood to our f. son,* II, 2, 58. *bold, quick, ingenious, f.* R3 III, 1, 155.

Forward, adv. 1) before, toward the fore-part, opposed to *back: and bending f. struck his armed heels . . .,* H4B I, 1, 44 (Ff *forwards*). *I came into the world with my legs f.* H6C V, 6, 71. *he fled f. still, toward your face,* Cymb. I, 2, 16. *look f. on the journey you shall go,* Meas. IV, 3, 61.

2) onward, on: *f., old man, do not break off so,* Err. I, 1, 97 (= continue). LLL V, 2, 623. *f., I pray, since we have come so far,* Shr. IV, 5, 12 (= do not stop). H6C II, 5, 139. *f. with your tale,* Tp. III, 2, 91. Ado III, 3, 109. *f. to the temple,* Merch. II, 1, 44. *f. to the bridal dinner,* Shr. III, 2, 221. *I will f. with my device,* LLL V, 2, 669. *we'll f. towards Warwick,* H6C IV, 7, 82. *brought him f. to his answer,* H8 IV, 2, 13 (= before the judge; cf. *Forth*). *the sharp thorny points of my alleged reasons drive this f.* H8 II, 4, 225. *to go f.* = a) to continue: H8 I, 2, 177. b) to continue in one's courses: *gramercies, lad, go f.* Shr. I, 1, 168. *go f. and be choked with thy ambition,* H6A II, 4, 112. (the king is) *angry, if you go f.* H6B IV, 2, 135. *let his grace go f.* H8 III, 2, 281. c) to move, to go off: *can I go f. when my heart is here?* Rom. II, 1, 1. d) to proceed, take place, to come to pass: *let our plot go f.* Wiv. IV, 4, 13. *then the play is marred, it goes not f.* Mids. IV, 2, 6. 17. As I, 2, 193. H6C III, 3, 58. Cor. IV, 5, 228. *march f.* H6C IV, 7, 82. *roll f.* Lucr. 1118. *to set f.* John IV, 3, 19. R2 I, 3, 109. 117. H4A II, 3, 30. 38 (Ff *forwards*). III, 2, 173. H4B IV, 1, 227. Cymb. V, 5, 479.

Forward, vb. to advance, promote: *in —ing this dear expedience,* H4A I, 1, 33.

Forwardness, 1) readiness, ardor, zeal: H6A I, 1, 100. H6C IV, 5, 23. V, 4, 65. Cymb. IV, 2, 342.

2) immodest assurance, confidence, pertness: *since the youth will not be entreated, his own peril on his f.* As I, 2, 159.

Forwards = *forward:* Sonn. 60, 4. In R2 I, 3, 109, H4A II, 3, 38 and H4B I, 1, 44 Qq *forward,* Ff *forwards.*

Forwearied, see *Forewearied.*

Fosset-seller (F1.2.3 *forset-seller,* F4 *fauset-seller*), one who sells fossets or faucets, pipes to be inserted in a cask for drawing liquor: Cor. II, 1, 79.*

Foster, to nurse, feed, nourish: Gentl. III, 1, 184. LLL I, 1, 223. R2 I, 3, 126. Tit. II, 3, 153. Cymb. III, 3, 119. Per. II, 5, 89. IV, 3, 15. *a lion —ed up at hand,* John V, 2, 75.

Foster-nurse, nourisher, supporter: As II, 3, 40. Lr. IV, 4, 12.

Foul, adj. the opposite of *fair* (q.v.) and often joined to it in contradistinction (f. i. Ven. 1030. Lucr. 412. Ado IV, 1, 104. LLL IV, 1, 23. H4B IV, 4, 104. H6C IV, 7, 14. Tim. III, 3, 32. IV, 3, 28. Mcb. I, 1, 11. I, 3, 38). 1) ugly: *hard-favoured, f.* Ven. 133. *beauty hath nought to do with such f. fiends,* 638. *the f. boar's conquest on her fair delight,* 1030. *all they f. that thy complexion lack,* Sonn. 132, 14. *be she as f. as was Florentius' love,* Shr. I, 2, 69. Ado III, 1, 64. IV, 1, 104. LLL IV, 3, 87. As III, 3, 36. 39. III, 5, 62. Tw. III, 4, 130. John III, 1, 47. H4B IV, 4, 104. H5 IV Chor. 4. 21. R3 V, 1, 157. Tim. IV, 3, 28. Oth. II, 1, 141. Ant. I, 2, 76 etc.

2) filthy, dirty, muddy: *the f. lake o'erstunk their feet,* Tp. IV, 183. *the reasonable shore that now lies f. and muddy,* V, 82. *f. linen,* Wiv. III, 3, 139. H4B V, 1, 38. *shirts,* Wiv. III, 5, 91. *clothes,* 101. 108. *balm his f. head,* Shr. Ind. 1, 48. *a f. hill,* IV, 1, 69. *f. ways,* IV, 1, 2. H4A II, 1, 93. *your lips grow f.* LLL IV, 1, 139. *f. bogs,* H5 III, 7, 61. *it grows —er,* Ant. II, 7, 106. *the —est ditch,* IV, 6, 38 etc.

3) impure, polluted: *her f. tainted flesh,* Ado IV, 1, 145 (some M. Edd. *foul-tainted*). *and make f. the clearness of our deservings,* All's I, 3, 6. *the purest of their wives is f. as slander,* Oth. IV, 2, 19.

4) unsound, diseased, corrupted: *cleanse the f. body of the infected world,* As II, 7, 60. *the f. corruption of a sweet child's death,* John IV, 2, 81. *f. sin gathering head shall break into corruption,* R2 V, 1, 58. *you perceive the body of our kingdom, how f. it is,* H4B III, 1, 39. *f. disease,* Hml. IV, 1, 21. Lr. I, 1, 167.

5) not clear, cloudy, troubled, stormy: *gusts and f. flaws,* Ven. 456. *f. weather,* 972. Tp. II, 1, 141. As V, 4, 142. R2 III, 3, 161. H4A III, 1, 68. *yond same black cloud looks like a f. bombard,* Tp. II, 2, 21. *so f. a sky clears not without a storm,* John IV, 2, 108. *the f. and ugly mists,* H4A I, 2, 226. *so f. and fair a day,* Mcb. I, 3, 38. *f. and violent tempest,* Oth. II, 1, 34.

6) wicked: *like a f. usurper,* Lucr. 412. *f. night-waking cat,* 554. *wooing his purity with her f. pride,* Sonn. 144, 8. *the f. witch Sycorax,* Tp. I, 2, 258. *f. deed,* III, 3, 72. *that f. conspiracy,* IV, 139. *a f. fault,* Wiv. V, 5, 12 (quibbling). *answering one f. wrong,* Meas. II, 2, 103. 128. II, 4, 113. 146. III, 1, 213. H6A V, 4, 93. Tim. III, 3, 32. Lr. III, 4, 46. 52 etc. Oth. IV, 1, 213. 215. V, 2, 200. Ant. IV, 12, 10 etc. *f. play* = wicked proceeding, ill dealing: *what f. play had we that we came from thence?* Tp. I, 2, 60. 62. *played f. play with our oaths,* LLL V, 2, 766. *I doubt some f. play,* Hml. I, 2, 256. *do me no f. play,* Lr. III, 7, 31. *by fair or f. means,* H6C IV, 7, 14.

7) disgraceful, derogatory, detractive· *f. words and frowns must not repel a lover,* Ven. 573 Ado V, 2, 50. *his backward voice is to utter f. speeches,* Tp. II, 2, 96. *in f. mouth to call him villain,* Meas. V, 309. *that may with f. intrusion enter in and dwell upon your grave,* Err. III, 1, 103. *fair payment for f. words,* LLL IV, 1, 19; cf. 139. *this f. derision,* Mids. III, 2, 197. *f. whisperings are abroad,* Mcb. V, 1, 79. *if you grow f. with me,* H5 II, 1, 59 (= if you use scornful language to me). *shall we fall f. for toys?* H4B II, 4, 183 (= quarrel; Pistol's speech). *and take f. scorn to fawn on him by sending,* H6A IV, 4, 35.

8) bad, in its widest sense: *some f. mischance,* Gentl. II, 2, 11. *'tis a f. thing when a cur cannot keep himself in all companies,* IV, 4, 11. *f. breath,* Ado V, 2, 53. *f. ways,* LLL V, 2, 926. *I am a f. way out,* Tw. II, 3, 201. *the —er fortune mine,* Shr. V, 2, 98. *f. shrewd news,* John V, 5, 14. *our —est wares,* Troil. I, 3, 359.

Adverbially: *ere I will see the crown so f. mis-placed,* R3 III, 2, 44.

Foul, vb. to dirty, to soil: *his stockings —ed,* Hml. II, 1, 79.

Foul-faced, showing a wicked and ugly countenance: *black scandal or f. reproach,* R3 III, 7, 231.

Foully, 1) wickedly: Meas. II, 2, 174. All's V, 3, 154. Mcb. III, 1, 3.

2) disgracefully, derogatorily: *f. spoken of,* H4A I, 3, 154.

Foul-mouthed, speaking ill of others, given to calumny and detraction: All's I, 3, 60. H4A III, 3, 122. H4B II, 4, 77 *(—st).*

Foulness, 1) ugliness: *praised be the gods for thy f.* As III, 3, 40. *he's fallen in love with your f.* III, 5, 66.

2) wickedness, badness: *speaking of her f., washed it with tears,* Ado IV, 1, 155. *as i' the contrary the f. is the punishment,* H8 III, 2, 183. *no vicious blot, murder, or f.* Lr. I, 1, 230.

Foul-reeking (not hyphened in O. Edd.) exhaling bad vapours: *O night, thou furnace of f. smoke,* Lucr. 799.

Foul-spoken, using improper language: *f. coward, that thunderest with thy tongue,* Tit. II, 1, 58.

Found, vb. to lay the basis of, to establish as on something solid, to base: *—ed as the rock,* Mcb. III, 4, 22. *hath —ed his good fortunes on your love,* Oth. III, 4, 94.

Foundation, 1) the basis or groundwork on which any thing stands: Ven. 1047. Wint. I, 2, 429. II, 1, 101. John IV, 2, 104. H4A III, 1, 16. H4B I, 3, 52. Cor. III, 1, 205. Mcb. IV, 1, 58.

2) an establishment for a charitable purpose: *God save the f.* Ado V, 1, 327 (the customary phrase of such as received alms at religious houses). *—s fly the wretched, such, I mean, where they should be relieved,* Cymb. III, 6, 7 (quibbling between fixed places and charitable establishments).

Founder, subst. the author, he from whom something originates: *the f. of this law,* H5 I, 2, 42. 59.

Founder, vb. 1) tr. to knock up or disable (a horse) by overriding: *Phoebus' steeds are —ed,* Tp. IV, 30. *I have —ed nine score and odd posts,* H4B IV, 3, 39.

2) intr. to fail, miscarry: *all his tricks f.* H8 III, 2, 40.

Fount, a spring or source of water: Lucr. 850. Compl. 283. Meas. IV, 3, 102. H6C IV, 8, 54. H8 I, 1, 154.

Fountain, 1) a spring or source of water: Ven. 234. Lucr. 577. 1707. 1734. Sonn. 35, 2. Compl. 255. Mids. II, 1, 29. 84. IV, 1, 121 (*mountains?*). Shr. V, 2, 142. R2 V, 3, 61. Troil. III, 2, 71. III, 3, 311. 313. Tit. II, 4, 23. III, 1, 123. 127. Rom. I, 1, 92. Mcb. II, 3, 103. Oth. IV, 2, 59.

2) artificial spring, spout of water: As IV, 1, 155. Caes. II, 2, 77.

Four, twice two: Ven. 446. Sonn. 45, 7. Tp. I, 2, 47. II, 2, 62. 93. Gentl. IV, 4, 4. 19. Wiv. II, 1, 237. IV, 4, 48. V, 5, 129. Meas. IV, 2, 56. 124. IV, 3, 11. LLL V, 2, 367. Mids. I, 1, 2. III, 2, 438. Merch. I, 1, 168 etc. etc. Remarkable use: *it's f. to one*, Tw. I, 3, 112. *any time these f. hours*, Wint. V, 2, 148. *if I travel but f. foot*, H4A II, 2, 12. *I will beat his pate f. days*, H5 V, 1, 43. *'tis not f. days gone*, Cor. I, 2, 6. *he walks f. hours together here in the lobby*, Hml. II, 2, 160. *I had rather fast from all f. days*, Ant. II, 7, 108.

Four-inched, four inches broad: Lr. III, 4, 57.

Fourscore, 1) eighty: Wiv. III, 1, 56. Meas. II, 1, 127. 204. Merch. III, 1, 114. 116. 117. As II, 3, 71. 74. Wint. IV, 4, 464. Tim. II, 2, 120. Lr. IV, 1, 14. IV, 7, 61.

2) the eightieth: *on Wednesday the f. of April*, Wint. IV, 4, 280 (Autolycus' speech).

Fourteen, twice seven: Meas. I, 3, 21 (some M. Edd. *nineteen*). Ado III, 3, 141. Shr. Ind. 2, 24. All's II, 3, 107. Tw. IV, 1, 24. Wint. II, 1, 147. John I, 113. H4A I, 1, 26. II, 4, 121. III, 1, 88. IV, 1, 126. H4B III, 2, 53. H5 II, 1, 35. H6B III, 1, 327. Rom. I, 2, 9. I, 3, 12. 14. 17. Caes. II, 1, 59 (O. Edd. *fifteen*). Lr. I, 2, 5. Per. V, 3, 8. 74.

Fourth, the ordinal of four: LLL V, 2, 114. Merch. I, 3, 21. As V, 4, 98. Shr. Ind. I, 13. R2 IV, 112. H4B V, 3, 119. H6A II, 5, 63. 78. H6B II, 2, 23. 55. H6C I, 1, 132. 139. III, 3, 83. IV, 7, 71. Cor. II, 3, 36. Mcb. IV, 1, 116. Cymb. V, 3, 86. Per. II, 2, 31.

Foutra or **Foutre** (Q *footre*, Ff *footra*), an expression of contempt: *a f. for the world*, H4B V, 3, 103. *a f. for thine office*, 120 (Pistol's speech).

Fowl, subst. **bird:** Phoen. 10. Lucr. 507 (masc.). Wiv. V, 5, 11. Meas. II, 2, 85. III, 1, 92. Ado II, 1, 209. II, 3, 95. H4A IV, 2, 21 (*a struck f. or a hurt wild-duck.* Perhaps here and in some other passages the woodcock is meant). H6B II, 1, 45. H6C V, 6, 19. Plur. —s: Lucr. 1335. Err. II, 1, 18. III, 1, 79. Plur. *f.*: Lucr. 511. Tw. IV, 2, 55. Tit. V, 3, 68. Cymb. I, 4, 97.

Fowler, a sportsman who pursues birds: Mids. III, 2, 20.

Fox, 1) the animal Vulpes: Wiv. III, 3, 174. LLL III, 85. 90. 96. Mids. V, 237. 240. All's III, 6, 111. H4A V, 2, 9. H6B III, 1, 256. H6C IV, 7, 25. Lr. I, 4, 340 (fem.). III, 4, 96. Opposed to the lamb as its natural enemy: Gentl. IV, 4, 97. Meas. V, 300. H6B III, 1, 55. 253. Troil. III, 2, 200. Tim. IV, 3, 332. *will you eat no grapes, my royal f.?* All's II, 1, 73. *fire us hence like* —*es*, Lr. V, 3, 23. *hide f., and all after*, Hml. IV, 2, 33 (a sport of children). *Sowter will cry upon't for all this, though it be as rank as a f.* Tw. II, 5, 136. *to wake a wolf is as bad as to smell*

a f. H4B I, 2, 176. Emblem of ingratitude: *now, you she* —*es*, Lr. III, 6, 24. I, 4, 340. III, 7, 28. Of cunning: Ven. 675. Meas. III, 2, 9. Mids. V, 234. H4A III, 3, 129. Cor. I, 1, 176. Tim. IV, 3, 331. Cymb. III, 3, 40. Hence = a cunning fellow: Shr. II, 405. Tw. I, 5, 86. H8 I, 1, 158.

2) a sword: *thou diest on point of f.* H5 IV, 4, 9 (Pistol's speech. The figure of a fox was frequently engraved on blades).

Foxship, ingratitude: *hadst thou f. to banish him that struck more blows for Rome than thou hast spoken words?* Cor. IV, 2, 18.

Fracted, broken: *his heart is f.* H5 II, 1, 130 (Pistol's speech). *his f. dates*, Tim. II, 1, 22.

Fraction, 1) breach, discord: *their f. is more our wish than their faction*, Troil. II, 3, 107.

2) fragment, scrap: *the* —*s of her faith, orts of her love*, Troil. V, 2, 158. *after distasteful looks and these hard* —*s*, Tim. II, 2, 220.

Fragile, easily broken: Tim. V, 1, 204.

Fragment, a scrap, a poor remnant: *the body of your discourse is sometime guarded with* —*s*, Ado I, 1, 288. *the* —*s, scraps, the bits and greasy relics of her o'er-eaten faith*, Troil. V, 2, 159. *it is some poor f., some slender ort of his remainder*, Tim. IV, 3, 400. *you were a f. of Cneius Pompey's*, Ant. III, 13, 117. *our cowards, like* —*s in hard voyages, became the life o' the need*, Cymb. V, 3, 44. Applied to persons as a term of extreme contempt: *from whence, f.?* Troil. V, 1, 9. *get you home, you* —*s*, Cor. I, 1, 226.

Fragrant, sweet-scented, odorous: Sonn. 95, 2. Wiv. III, 1, 20. Mids. IV, 1, 57. Tit. II, 2, 2. II, 4, 54.

Frail, weak, in a physical as well as moral sense: Lucr. 227. Sonn. 121, 7. Tp. IV, 181. Meas. II, 4, 121. 124. 128. As III, 5, 12. Tw. III, 4, 391. John V, 7, 3. R2 I, 3, 196. H5 III, 6, 163. H6C III, 2, 155. R3 IV, 4, 498. H8 III, 2, 148. V, 3, 11. Oth. I, 3, 362. II, 1, 155. Ant. IV, 14, 41. Cymb. I, 4, 100. Per. I, 1, 42.

Frailty, weakness, in a physical as well as moral sense: Sonn. 109, 10 (—*ies*). 121, 7 (—*ies*). Wiv. II, 1, 242. III, 5, 52. Meas. III, 1, 190. III, 2, 260. Tw. II, 2, 32. John V, 7, 23. H4A III, 3, 189. H8 V, 3, 12. Troil. IV, 4, 98. Mcb. II, 3, 132 (—*ies*). Hml. I, 2, 146. Oth. IV, 3, 100. 102. Ant. V, 2, 123 (—*ies*).

Frame, subst. 1) fabric, structure: *the f. and huge foundation of the earth shaked*, H4A III, 1, 16. *let the f. of things disjoint*, Mcb. III, 2, 16. *this goodly f., the earth*, Hml. II, 2, 310. *that f.* (viz the gallows-maker's) *outlives a thousand tenants*, V, 1, 49. *wrenched my f. of nature from the fixed place*, Lr. I, 4, 290.

2) a case or structure to enclose and support a picture: *my body is the f. wherein 'tis held* (viz the picture) Sonn. 24, 3.

3) a mould for castings: *the very mould and f. of hand, nail, finger*, Wint. II, 3, 103. Figuratively: *chid I for that a frugal nature's f.* (viz for having but one child) Ado IV, 1, 130 (= did I grumble against the niggardness of nature's casting-mould?).

4) shape, form: *this composed wonder of your f.* Sonn. 59, 10. *faults may shake our* —*s*, Meas. II, 4, 133; cf. Oth. V, 2, 44. Meas. V, 61. All's IV, 2, 4. Tw. I, 1, 33. H4B III, 2, 155. H6A II, 3, 54. Tim. I,

1, 69. *out of f.* = out of shape, disordered: LLL III, 193. Hml. I, 2, 20. *put your discourse into some f.* III, 2, 321.

5) contrivance, devising, scheming: *whose spirits toil in f. of villanies,* Ado IV, 1, 191.

Frame, vb. 1) to compose, to shape, to form: *moulds wherein she —d thee,* Ven. 731. *—ing thee so fair,* 744. Sonn. 5, 1. Mids. V, 296. Merch. I, 1, 51. R3 I, 2, 244. IV, 3, 19. Cor. V, 3, 23. 63. Tit. IV, 2, 119. IV, 3, 46. Lr. IV, 6, 231. Oth. II, 3, 347. Per. II, 3, 15. IV, 2, 150. With *of: nature never —d a woman's heart of prouder stuff,* Ado III, 1, 49. *composed and —d of treachery,* V, 1, 257. H5 IV, 3, 14.

2) to beget, to produce, to breed: *she —d the love, and yet she foiled the —ing,* Pilgr. 99. *fear —s disorder,* H6B V, 2, 32.

3) to devise, to contrive, to plan: *f. some feeling line,* Gentl. III, 2, 76. *yet had he —d to himself many deceiving promises of life,* Meas. III, 2, 259. *this* (scandal) *of hers, —d by thy villany,* Ado V, 1, 71. *here he hath —d a letter,* LLL IV, 2, 142. *that the great figure of a council —s by self-unable motion,* All's III, 1, 12. *'tis not a visitation —d, but forced by need,* Wint. V, 1, 91 (= planned, premeditated). *I —d to the harp many an English ditty,* H4A III, 1, 123. *to f. our sovereign's fall,* H6B III, 1, 52. *but you f. things that are known alike,* H8 I, 2, 44. *I'll f. convenient peace,* Cor. V, 3, 191. *more than I could f. employment,* Tim. IV, 3, 262.

4) to manage: *and either end in peace, which God so f.!* H4B IV, 1, 180. *f. the business after your own wisdom,* Lr. I, 2, 107. *that yarely f. the office,* Ant. II, 2, 216.

5) to mould, to fashion, to work into a certain shape: *the maid will I f. and make fit for his attempt,* Meas. III, 1, 266. *it is needful that you f. the season for your own harvest,* Ado I, 3, 26. *like to Lysander sometime f. thy tongue,* Mids. III, 2, 360. *thou wilt f. thyself hereafter theirs,* Cor. III, 2, 84. *'twas time and griefs that —d him thus,* Tim. V, 1, 126. Followed by *to,* = to conform: *to bitter sauces did I f. my feeding,* Sonn. 118, 6. *to her will f. all thy ways,* Pilgr. 323. *f. your mind to mirth,* Shr. Ind. 2, 137. *f. your manners to the time,* I, 1, 232. H6A II, 4, 8. 9. H6C III, 2, 185. Cor. III, 2, 97. Ant. V, 1, 55. Cymb. II, 3, 51. IV, 2, 177. Per. II, 5, 81. Followed by an inf.: *if his going I could f. to serve my turn,* Wint. IV, 4, 520. H6C IV, 6, 72. Oth. I, 3, 404.

6) intr.: *the beauty of this sinful dame made many princes thither f.* Per. Prol. 32 (= to go, to resort?).

Frampold, quarrelsome: *she leads a very f. life with him,* Wiv. II, 2, 94 (Mrs Quickly's speech).

France, 1) the country of the French: Wiv III, 3, 57. 183. Err. III, 2, 125. LLL II, 30. 153. IV, 1, 6. 122. V, 2, 558. Merch. I, 2, 81. As I, 1, 149 etc. etc. *malady of F.* H5 V, 1, 87.

2) the French king: All's III, 1, 7. John I, 1. 20. II, 110. H5 II Chor. 20. III, 6, 166. V, 2, 2. Lr. I, 1, 46 etc.

Frances (O. Edd. *Francis*) female name: LLL III, 122.

Franchise, subst. liberty: *your —s confined into an auger's bore,* Cor. IV, 6, 86. *whose* (our laws') *repair and f. shall be our good deed,* Cymb. III, 1, 57 (= free exercise).

Franchised, free (q. v.), unstained, innocent: *so I keep my bosom f.* Mcb. II, 1, 28.

Francis, name: Ado III, 5, 62. IV, 1, 1. Mids. I, 2, 44. R2 II, 1, 284. H4A II, 4, 9. 35 etc. H4B II, 4, 305. III, 2, 23. 158. *Saint F.:* All's III, 5, 39. Rom. II, 3, 65. V, 3, 121.

Franciscan, belonging to the order of St. Francis: *F. friar,* Rom. V, 2, 1.

Francisco, 1) name: Hml. I, 1, 7. — 2) Frenchman: *is he dead, my F.?* Wiv. II, 3, 28 (the host's speech).

Frank, subst. an enclosure for swine, a sty: *doth the old boar feed in the old f.?* H4B II, 2, 160.*

Frank, name (= Francis): Wiv. II, 1, 155.

Frank, adj. 1) free, unrestrained: *thy f. election make,* All's II, 3, 61.

2) open, using no disguise: *with f. and with uncurbed plainness tell us the Dauphin's mind,* H5 I, 2, 244. *bearing with f. appearance their purposes toward Cyprus,* Oth. I, 3, 38. *to show the love and duty that I bear you with —er spirit,* III, 3, 195.

3) liberal, bountiful: *being f. she* (Nature) *lends to those are free,* Sonn. 4, 4. *f. nature hath well composed thee,* All's I, 2, 20. *our so f. donation,* Cor. III, 1, 130. *to be f., and give it thee again,* Rom. II, 2, 131. *whose f. heart gave all,* Lr. III, 4, 20. *'tis a good hand, a f. one,* Oth. III, 4, 44.

Franked up, shut up in a frank or sty: R3 I, 3, 314. IV, 5, 3.

Frankfort, German town: Merch. III, 1, 89.

Franklin, a yeoman: *let boors and —s say it,* Wint. V, 2, 173. *a f. in the wild of Kent,* H4A II, 1, 60. *no costlier than would fit a —'s housewife,* Cymb. III, 2, 79.

Frankly, 1) freely, without restraint: *my half-supped sword, that f. would have fed,* Troil. V, 8, 19. *to be controlled in that he f. gave,* Tit. I, 420 (or = bountifully?) *men and men's fortunes could I f. use,* Tim. II, 2, 188.

2) openly, without disguise: *to forgive me f.* H8 II, 1, 81. *speak f. as the wind,* Troil. I, 3, 253. *very f. he confessed his treasons,* Mcb. I, 4, 5.

3) without reserve, without ceremony, readily: *I'ld throw it* (life) *down for your deliverance as f. as a pin,* Meas. III, 1, 106 (or = liberally, bountifully?). *to make me f. despise myself,* Oth. II, 3, 299.

4) with a free and not preoccupied mind: *we may of their encounter f. judge,* Hml. III, 1, 34. *and will this brothers' wager f. play,* V, 2, 264.

Frankness, openness, candor: H5 V, 2, 318.

Frantic, mad: *f. with grief,* Lucr. 762. *he is f. too,* Err. IV, 4, 116. LLL V, 1, 29. *the lover, all as f., sees Helen's beauty in a brow of Egypt,* Mids. V, 10. As I, 3, 51. Shr. III, 2, 12. R2 III, 3, 185. V, 3, 89. H6A III, 3, 5. R3 I, 3, 247. II, 4, 64. IV, 4, 68 (Qq *tragic*). Tit. IV, 4, 59. V, 3, 64.

Franticly, madly: *f. she doteth,* Ven. 1059. *how f. I square my talk,* Tit. III, 2, 31.

Frantic-mad, quite mad: Sonn. 147, 10.

Frateretto, name of a fiend: Lr. III, 6, 7.

Fraud, 1) deceit, treachery, stratagem: Lucr. 1243. H6C IV, 4, 33. R3 I, 4, 154 (Ff *strong-framed,* Qq *strong in fraud*).

2) falseness, faithlessness: *it* (love) *shall be fickle, false and full of f.* Ven. 1141. *his heart as far from f. as heaven from earth,* Gentl. II, 7, 78. *the*

f. of men was ever so, Ado II, 3, 74. *the f. of England, not the force of France, hath now entrapped the noble-minded Talbot*, H6A IV, 4, 36.

Fraudful, deceitful, treacherous: H6B III, 1, 81.

Fraught, subst., 1) freight, cargo: Tw. V, 64. Tit. I, 71.

2) load, contents: *swell, bosom, with thy f.* Oth. III, 3, 449.

Fraught, vb. to load, to burden: *if after this command thou f. the court with thy unworthiness,* Cymb. I, 1, 126. Partic. *—ed: O cruel speeding, —ed with gall*, Pilgr. 270. Partic. *fraught,* = a) laden, loaded: Merch. II, 8, 30. Troil. Prol. 4. b) filled, charged, stored: *whose composed rhymes should be full f. with vows*, Gentl. III, 2, 70. *I am so f. with curious business*, Wint. IV, 4, 525. *to mark the full f. man and best indued with some suspicion*, H5 II, 2, 139. Followed by *of: that good wisdom whereof I know you are f.* Lr. I, 4, 241. — Gerund *—ing: the —ing souls within her*, Tp. I, 2, 13, = constituting the cargo.

Fraughtage, cargo: Err. IV, 1, 87. Troil. Prol. 13.

Fraughting, see *Fraught*, vb.

Fray, subst. 1) a fight, a battle: *to the latter end of a f.* H4A IV, 2, 85. *in this bloody f.* V, 4, 108. *after that bloody f. at Wakefield fought*, H6C II, 1, 107.

2) a violent riot attended with bloodshed: *he was not at this f.* Rom. I, 1, 124. 179. III, 1, 146. 156. Caes. II, 4, 18.

3) a single combat, whether with swords or words or at fisticuffs: *there is a f. to be fought between Sir Hugh and Caius*, Wiv. II, 1, 208. *to part a f.* Ado V, 1, 114; LLL V, 2, 484; Shr. I, 2, 23. Mids. III, 2, 129. 342. 447. *thou that makest the f.* Merch. III, 2, 62. III, 4, 68.

Fray, vb. to fright: *as if she were —ed with a sprite*, Troil. III, 2, 34.

Freckled, spotted: *a f. whelp*, Tp. I, 2, 283. *the f. cowslip*, H5 V, 2, 49.

Freckles, spots: *in those f. live their savours,* Mids. II, 1, 13.

Frederick, name: Meas. III, 1, 217. 224. As I, 2, 87. 246. V, 4, 160.

Free, adj. (compar. *freer*: Wiv. III, 2, 86. R2 I, 3, 88. Lr. IV, 2, 95. Ant. I, 5, 11. Cymb. V, 4, 204). 1) at liberty, not confined, not restrained: Sonn. 134, 5. Tp. V, 87, 241. Ado IV, 1, 25. As II, 7, 68. H4A V, 5, 28. H5 III, 6, 44. H6A V, 3, 59. R3 III, 6, 9. Rom. III, 3, 42. Tim. I, 1, 45. Hml. III, 3, 68. Lr. II, 4, 134. Ant. I, 5, 11. Cymb. V, 4, 202. 204. *as f. as mountain winds*, Tp. I, 2, 498. Cor. I, 9, 89. *drink the f. air*, Tim. I, 1, 83. *thought is f.* Tp. III, 2, 132. Tw. I, 3, 73. *to set f.* Tp. I, 2, 442. V, 252. Epil. 20. Shr. I, 1, 142. 2, 268. All's III, 4, 17. H6A III, 3, 72. H6C IV, 6, 16. Tit. I, 274. *to set him f. from his captivity*, H6C IV, 5, 13. Per. IV, 6, 107. *then to the elements be f.* Tp. V, 318. *I am not bound to that all slaves are f. to*, Oth. III, 3, 135 (Ff without *to*).

2) independent, not enslaved, not subject to another: Merch. IV, 1, 94. John III, 1, 148. H6A I, 3, 64. V, 3, 114. 115. H6B III, 1, 223 (*f. lords*, i.e. being, by the departure of the king, restored to independence and liberty of discussion). IV, 7, 132. Troil. II, 2, 170 (*to make up a f. determination*, i. e. not influenced by passion). Cor. V, 6, 26. Tim. III, 4, 81.

Caes. I, 2, 97. III, 2, 25. V, 3, 47. Mcb. III, 6, 36 (*f. honours*, i.e. honours of free men, not, as under Macbeth, of slaves). V, 8, 55. Oth. I, 2, 26. Ant. II, 5, 27. 57. IV, 14, 81. Cymb. I, 6, 72. III, 1, 49.

3) not encumbered, affected or stained with; generally followed by *from: from that thy Lucrece is not f.* Lucr. 1624. *from our faults, as faults from seeming f.* Meas. III, 2, 41. V, 141. Err. IV, 4, 70. As II, 1, 4. Tw. III, 4, 249. IV, 1, 44. John II, 453. R2 I, 1, 33. V, 6, 27. H5 II, 2, 132. V Chor. 20. H6A V, 3, 155. H6B III, 1, 101. III, 2, 251. IV, 7, 108. Caes. V, 5, 54. Hml. IV, 7, 136. Per. II, 4, 2. Followed by *of: infirmities that honesty is never f. of*, Wint. I, 2, 264. *if he know that I am f. of your report, he knows I am not of your wrong*, H8 II, 4, 99. *heaven make thee f. of it* (my death) Hml. V, 2, 343. *f. of grace*, LLL III, 67 (Armado's speech, expressing the contrary of what he means to say).

4) not obstructed, unhindered, affording or having the liberty of acting or moving: *f. vent of words*, Ven. 334. *we shall have the —r wooing*, Wiv. III, 2, 86. *I breathe f. breath.* LLL V, 2, 732. *are not the streets as f. for me as for you*, Shr. I, 2, 233. *f. access*, II, 1, 98. *f. scope*, All's I, 1, 233. *is f. for me to ask*, II, 1, 203. *health shall live f.* 171. R2 II, 3, 136. H5 V, 2, 86. H8 II, 2, 94. Troil. V, 10, 30. Cor. III, 3, 73. Caes. II, 1, 79. Lr. II, 3, 3. IV, 2, 95. Oth. I, 2, 98. III, 1, 41. Per. II, 4, 33. *from our f. person she should be confined*, Wint. II, 1, 194 (i. e. accessible to all). *when the day serves, before black-cornered night, find what thou wantest by f. and offered light,* Tim. V, 1, 48 (i. e. common to all, withheld from none). *I am your f. dependant*, Meas. IV, 3, 95 (= at your free disposal).

5) unconstrained, voluntary, gratuitous: *is it a f. visitation?* Hml. II, 2, 283. *making God so f. an offer*, H5 IV, 1, 193. *by my f. consent*, Wint. V, 1, 70. H6C IV, 6, 36. *f. pardon*, Meas. II, 4, 111. H6B IV, 8, 9. H8 I, 2, 100 (but *f. pardon* may be as well = a pardon restoring to full liberty, an absolute pardon).

6) willing, ready, eager: *that my love may appear plain and f., all that was mine in Silvia I give thee*, Gentl. V, 4, 82. *Leontes opening his f. arms and weeping his welcomes forth*, Wint. IV, 4, 559. *never did captive with a —r heart cast off his chains of bondage*, R2 I, 3, 88. *courageously and with a f. desire attending but the signal to begin*, 115. *Lord Lucius, out of his f. love, hath presented to you four horses*, Tim. I, 2, 188. *and thy f. awe pays homage to us*, Hml. IV, 3, 63. *Montano with his f. duty recommends you thus*, Oth. I, 3, 41. *provided I have your commendation for my more f. entertainment*, Cymb. I, 4, 167.

7) open, candid, unreserved: *to have f. speech with you*, Meas. I, 1, 78. R2 I, 1, 55. 123. Oth. III, 4, 129. *I will be f. in words*, Shr. IV, 3, 79. *to be a speaker f.* Troil. IV, 4, 133. *he did solicit you in f. contempt*, Cor. II, 3, 208. *f. and friendly conference*, Caes. IV, 2, 17. *let us speak our f. hearts*, Mcb. I, 3, 155. *the Moor is of a f. and open nature*, Oth. I, 3, 405.

8) liberal, bountiful, communicative: *being frank she lends to those are f.* Sonn. 4, 4. *and now be you as f. to us*, Meas. V, 393. *she hath been liberal and f.* H6A V, 4, 82. *his heart and hand both open and both f.* Troil. IV, 5, 100. *they have pardons,*

being asked, as f. as words to little purpose, Cor. III, 2, 88. *in grateful virtue I am bound to your f. heart*, Tim. I, 2, 6. *being f. itself, it thinks all others so*, II, 2, 242. *to be f. and bounteous to her mind*, Oth. I, 3, 266. *she's framed as fruitful as the f. elements*, II, 3, 348. *most f. in his reply*, Hml. III, 1, 14 (= communicative). With *of: maiden-tongued he was, and thereof f.* Compl. 100 (= very conversable). *f. of speech*, Oth. III, 3, 185. *you have of your audience been most f. and bounteous*, Hml. I, 3, 93.

9) not affected with any disease or distress of the body or mind; sound, happy, careless, unconcerned: *whether thou art tainted or f.* Meas. I, 2, 44; cf. LLL V, 2, 422 (= sound). *the f. maids that weave their thread with bones*, Tw. II, 4, 46 (careless). *if thou hatest curses, stay not; fly, whilst thou art blest and f.* Tim. IV, 3, 542. *when the mind's f., the body's delicate*, Lr. III, 4, 11. *leaving f. things and happy shows behind*, III, 6, 112. *bear f. and patient thoughts*, IV, 6, 80. *he bears the sentence well that nothing bears but the f. comfort which from thence he hears*, Oth. I, 3, 213. *was f. and merry*, III, 3, 340. *laughs from his f. lungs*, Compl. I, 6, 68.

10) guiltless, innocent, harmless: *if he be f., why then my taxing like a wild-goose flies*, As II, 7, 85. *to be generous, guiltless and of f. disposition*, Tw. I, 5, 99. *this entertainment may a f. face put on*, Wint. I, 2, 112. *in every one of those no man is f.* 251. *your f. undertaking cannot miss a thriving issue*, II, 2, 44. *a gracious innocent soul, more f. than he is jealous*, II, 3, 30. *would all other women could speak this with as f. a soul*, H8 III, 1, 32. *make mad the guilty and appal the f.* Hml. II, 2, 590. *we that have f. souls, it touches us not*, III, 2, 252. *this advice is f. I give and honest*, Oth. II, 3, 343. *hold her f.* III, 3, 255.

11) of a pure and generous mind, and hence of a noble and blameless conduct; gentle, gracious: *in voices well divulged, f., learned and valiant*, Tw. I, 5, 279. *like f. and honest men*, H8 III, 1, 60. *courtiers as f., as debonair, unarmed, as bending angels*, Troil. I, 3, 235. *thou art too gentle and too f. a man*, IV, 5, 139. *she is of so f., so kind a disposition*, Oth. II, 3, 325. *I would not have your f. and noble nature be abused*, III, 3, 199.

Used adverbially: *I as f. forgive you as I would be forgiven*, H8 II, 1, 82. *which else should f. have wrought*, Mcb. II, 1, 19.

Free, vb. 1) to set at liberty, to release: *f. that soul which wretchedness hath chained*, Lucr. 900. *I'll f. thee within two days*, Tp. I, 2, 420. Meas. III, 1, 66. 99. Wint. II, 2, 61. H4B III, 2, 261. H6A V, 3, 61. Tim. I, 1, 103.

2) to disengage, to deliver; with *from: let guiltless souls be —d from guilty woe*, Lucr. 1482. *from what a torment I did f. thee*, Tp. I, 2, 251. II, 1, 293. H6A I, 2, 81. H6B III, 2, 155. H6C III, 2, 180. IV, 3, 63. R3 V, 3, 261. H8 I, 1, 52. II, 2, 44. Rom. IV, 1, 118.

3) to acquit, to absolve, to show or declare to be guiltless: *my life's foul deed, my life's fair end shall f. it*, Lucr. 1208. *—s all faults*, Tp. Epil. 18. *mine honour, which I would f.* Wint. III, 2, 112. *we f. thee from the dead blow of it*, IV, 4, 444. *I f. you from it*, H8 II, 4, 157. *I dare so far f. him*, Cor. IV, 7, 47. *f. me so far in your most generous thoughts*, Hml. V, 2, 253.

4) to remove, to do away: *f. from our feasts and banquets bloody knives*, Mcb. III, 6, 35. *he wrings at some distress: would I could f. it!* Cymb. III, 6, 80.

Freedom, 1) liberty, opposed to confinement: Meas. I, 2, 138. Err. V, 250. R3 IV, 4, 223. H8 I, 2, 200. Cor. I, 9, 87. Tim. I, 2, 69. Cymb. V, 4, 16. Opposed to banishment: R2 I, 3, 273. Caes. III, 1, 54. Lr. I, 1, 184.

2) liberty, opposed to a state of subjection, independence: Ven. 160. Compl. 143 (*stand in f.*). Tp. II, 2, 190. III, 1, 89. V, 96. Tw. II, 5, 207. H6A V, 3, 116. H6B IV, 8, 28. Tit. I, 17. Caes. III, 1, 78. 81. 110. Ant. II, 6, 17. *thou shalt have the air at f.* Tp. IV, 266. *where I have lived at honest f.* Cymb. III, 3, 71.

3) exemption, the state of not being affected with a thing: *age from folly could not give me f.* Ant. I, 3, 57.

4) franchise, warranted right: *mine eye my heart thy picture's sight would bar, my heart mine eye the f. of that right*, Sonn. 46, 4. *doth impeach the f. of the state, if they deny him justice*, Merch. III, 2, 280. *let the danger light upon your charter and your city's f.* IV, 1, 39. *I speak it in the f. of my knowledge*, Wint. I, 1, 12. *dispropertied their —s*, Cor. II, 1, 264.

5) unreservedness, openness: *you cannot with such f. purge yourself.* H8 V, 1, 103 (or is it = so as to prove your perfect innocence?).

Free-footed, not restrained in marching: Hml. III, 3, 26 (cf. As II, 7, 68).

Free-hearted, liberal, bountiful: Tim. III, 1, 10.

Freely, (compar. *freelier*, Cor. I, 3, 3) 1) at liberty, without hinderance: *thou shalt live as f. as thy lord, to call his fortune thine*, Tw. I, 4, 39. *to such as may the passive drugs of it f. command*, Tim. IV, 3, 255. *my boat sails f.* Oth. II, 3, 65. *shall bear the olive f.* Ant. IV, 6, 7. *and sing our bondage f.* Cymb. III, 3, 44. *opposing f. the beauty of her person to the people*, H8 V, 1, 67 (= so as to be seen without impediment).

2) voluntarily, of one's own accord: *that I am f. dissolved*, Wiv. I, 1, 259 (Slender's speech). *as f. as God did give her me*, Ado IV, 1, 27. *I do it f.* 260. *health shall live free and sickness f. die*, All's II, 1, 171. *committing f. your scruple to the voice of Christendom*, H8 II, 2, 87. *your better wisdoms, which have f. gone with this affair along*, Hml. I, 2, 15. *you do f. bar the door upon your own liberty*, III, 2, 351 (Qq *surely*).

3) openly, candidly, frankly: *confess f.* All's IV, 3, 276. Tw. V, 367. Oth. II, 3, 324. V, 2, 53. *speak f.* Err. V, 285. R2 I, 1, 17. IV, 327. H6C IV, 1, 28. H8 I, 2, 131. Cor. IV, 6, 64. Oth. III, 1, 58. Cymb. V, 5, 119. Per. I, 2, 102. *I f. told you*, Merch. III, 2, 257. cf. H5 I, 2, 238. H8 II, 2, 112. H8 V, 3, 48. Hml. II, 2, 338. Ant. V, 2, 23.

4) honestly, sincerely: *whose love had spoke from an infant, f. that it was yours*, Wint. III, 2, 71. *that f. rendered me these news for true*, H4B I, 1, 27. *that noble lady or gentleman, that is not f. merry, is not my friend*, H8 I, 4, 36. *I think it f.* Oth. II, 3, 335.

5) plentifully, copiously: *all their petitions are as f. theirs as they themselves would owe them*, Meas. I, 4, 82. *I am half your self, and I must f. have the half of any thing*, Merch. III, 2, 252. *you would*

drink f. H4B IV, 2, 75. *our history shall with full mouth speak f. of our acts,* H5 I, 2, 231. *pledge him f.* Per. II, 3, 78.

6) willingly, readily, heartily, gladly: *hear me speak. F., good father,* Tim. I, 1, 110. *come f. to gratulate thy plenteous bosom,* I, 2, 130. *to look so green and pale at what it did so f.* Mcb. I, 7, 38. *I embrace it f.* Hml. V, 2, 263. *I should —ier rejoice in that absence,* Cor. I, 3, 3. Frequently joined to verbs implying the notion of a gift or offer: Tp. IV, 85. Merch. IV, 1, 412. Shr. II, 79. All's I, 2, 14. Wint. I, 1, 19. R2 III, 3, 41. H6B IV, 1, 12. H6C III, 2, 55. Tim. I, 2, 10. Hml. II, 2, 31.

Free-man, one who is not a slave: Caes. III, 2, 25 (most M. Edd. not hyphened). V, 3, 41.

Freeness, bounty, generosity: *we'll learn our f. of a son-in-law; pardon's the word to all,* Cymb. V, 5, 421.

Freestone-coloured, of the colour of freestone or sandstone: As IV, 3, 25. [= "of a dirty brown". J. C. Smith, Warwick Sh.]

Free-town, Villafranca in Italy: Rom. I, 1, 109.

Freeze, subst. see *Frize.*

Freeze, vb. (impf. *froze,* Tim. II, 2, 222; partic., when serving to form the preterit or passive, *froze:* Err. V, 313. H4B I, 1, 199; when joined to a subst., *frozen:* Ven. 565. Lucr. 247. Gentl. III, 2, 9. LLL V, 2, 265. 925. Shr. IV, 1, 40. R2 I, 1, 64. I, 3, 211. II, 1, 117. H6B V, 2, 35. R3 II, 1, 115. Tit. III, 1, 252. Rom. I, 4, 101) 1) intr. a) to be congealed by cold: *my very lips might f. to my teeth,* Shr. IV, 1, 7. *the mountain tops that f.* H8 III, 1, 4. *frozen,* Ven. 565. Gent. III, 2, 9 *(her frozen thoughts;* cf. *Melt).* LLL V, 2, 925. R2 I, 1, 64. Tit. III, 1, 252. Rom. I, 4, 101. With *up:* Err. V, 313.

b) to be extremely cold: *f., thou bitter sky,* As II, 7, 184. *—ing cold,* Lucr. 1145. *—ing hours,* Cymb. III, 3, 39. *frozen* = cold: *six frozen winters,* R2 I, 3, 211.

c) to have the sensation of cold: *you must not f.* H8 I, 4, 21. *frozen to death,* Shr. IV, 1, 40. R3 II, 1, 115.

d) Figuratively, to be or grow cold, to cool: *thy love doth f.* Shr. II, 340. *thy kindness —th,* R3 IV, 2, 22. *frozen* = cold: Lucr. 247. LLL V, 2, 265. R2 II, 1, 117. H6B V, 2, 35.

2) trans. to congeal, to chill: *would f. thy young blood,* Hml. I, 5, 16. With *up:* Rom. IV, 3, 16. Figuratively, to cool, to abate the ardor of: *cold hearts f. allegiance in them,* H8 I, 2, 61. *they froze me into silence,* Tim. II, 2, 222. *to f. the god Priapus,* Per. IV, 6, 3. With *up: f. up their zeal,* John III, 4, 150. H4B I, 1, 199.

Freezing, subst. chilling cold: *what —s have I felt,* Sonn. 97, 3.

French, adj. pertaining to France: Wiv. I, 4, 99. II, 1, 209. III, 1, 61. LLL I, 1, 136. I, 2, 65. Merch. I, 2, 58 etc. etc. *a F. brawl,* LLL III, 9 (quibbling); cf. *F. quarrels,* H5 IV, 1, 240. *F. crown,* meaning 1) the emblem of French royalty; 2) a coin; 3) the crown of a Frenchman's head; 4) baldness produced by a certain disease; and hence used with equivocation: Meas. I, 2, 52. LLL III, 142. Mids. I, 2, 97. 99. All's II, 2, 23. H4B III, 2, 237. H5 IV, 1, 242. H6B IV, 2, 166. *F. hose,* H5 III, 7, 56. Mcb. II, 3, 16. cf. Merch. I, 2, 80. *F. falconers,* Hml. II, 2, 450. *duck with F. nods,* R3 I, 3, 49. *F. withered*

pears, All's I, 1, 175. *rapiers, poniards and swords,* Hml. V, 2, 156. 168. *slop,* Rom. II, 4, 47; cf. H8 I, 3, 31. *a F. song and a fiddle,* H8 I, 3, 41. *F. thrift,* Wiv. I, 3, 93. *velvet,* Meas. I, 2, 35.

Substantively, = 1) the French language: Merch. I, 2, 75. R2 V, 3, 124. H5 V, 2, 236. H6B IV, 2, 176. in F. LLL III, 10. R2 V, 3, 119. H5 IV, 4, 24. 30. V, 2, 188. 367.

2) the French nation or army: Merch. II, 8, 29. All's II, 3, 101. John IV, 2, 161. V, 1, 5. R2 II, 1, 178. H4B I, 3, 71. H6A I, 1, 25. 87. 106. I, 4, 100. II, 1, 23. H6B I, 1, 214. I, 3, 209 etc. etc. *our F.,* All's II, 1, 20. *these F.* John II, 214. *all F.* H6A III, 3, 60.

3) Frenchmen: *a dozen F.* John III, 4, 173. *certain F.* H5 I, 2, 47.

4) a single Frenchman: *F. and Welsh,* Wiv. III, 1, 99 (the host's speech). *if there be here German, or Dane, low Dutch, Italian, or F., let him speak to me,* All's IV, 1, 79. *the F. might have a good prey of us, if he knew of it,* H5 IV, 4, 80. *had death been F.* H6A IV, 7, 28.

Frenchman, a native of France: Wiv. II, 1, 230. Ado III, 2, 33. Merch. I, 2, 88. II, 8, 27. H5 I, 1, 97. H6A III, 3, 85. Hml. IV, 7, 134. Cymb. I, 6, 64. 76 etc. Plur. *Frenchmen* = 1) men native of France: All's II, 1, 12. IV, 2, 73. John II, 42. 316. H5 III, 6, 159. H6A II, 2, 9. IV, 6, 34. IV, 7, 36. 2) French, i. e. the French nation or army: *view the Frenchmen, how they fortify,* H6A I, 4, 61. 106. 111. II, 1, 11. IV, 7, 77. V, 3, 1. V, 4, 115. V, 5, 43. H6B I, 1, 92. IV, 2, 179.

Frenchwoman, a woman native of France: H6B I, 3, 143. H6C I, 4, 149.

Frenzy, 1) madness: Wiv. V, 1, 21. Err. IV, 4, 84. Shr. Ind. 2, 135. Tw. V, 288. John IV, 2, 122. Troil. V, 10, 29. Tit. IV, 1, 17. IV, 4, 12. Cymb. IV, 2, 134.

2) any violent agitation of the mind approaching to distraction: Lucr. 1675. Mids. V, 12. Troil. V, 3, 85. Cymb. V, 5, 282. Plur. *—ies,* Ven. 740.

Frequent, adj. 1) having intercourse, conversant, intimate: *I have f. been with unknown minds,* Sonn. 117, **5.**

2) addicted: *less f. to his princely exercises,* Wint. IV, 2, 36.

Frequent, vb. 1) tr. to visit often: Tim. I, 1, 117. Per. IV, 6, 202.

2) intr. to pay regular visits: *there he daily doth f.* R2 V, 3, 6.

Fresh, subst. a sweet-water spring: *where the quick —es are,* Tp. III, 2, 75.

Fresh, adj. 1) not faded, not vapid or stale, unimpaired and healthy: *with f. variety,* Ven. 21. *love's gentle spring doth always f. remain,* 801. *a spreading flower, f. to myself,* Compl. 76. *the f. lap of the crimson rose,* Mids. II, 1, 108. IV, 1, 57. All's V, 3, 327. Tw. I, 1, 31. Wint. I, 2, 420. R2 III, 3, 47. V, 1, 10. Rom. I, 2, 29. Cymb. II, 2, 15. *f. morning drops,* LLL IV, 3, 27. Rom. I, 1, 138. *a —er clime,* R2 I, 3, 285. *—er air,* H8 I, 4, 101. *the f. streams ran by her,* Oth. IV, 3, 45. *how f. she looks,* Per. III, 2, 79. *f. days of love,* Mids. V, 29.

2) not yet used, untouched, not worn off: *our garments are now as f. as when we put them*

on first, Tp. II, 1, 68. 97. 102; cf. I, 2, 219. *a withered serving-man a f. tapster*, Wiv. I, 3, 19. *ever your f. whore and your powdered bawd*, Meas. III, 2, 62. *cannot use such vigilance as when they are f.* Tp. III, 3, 17. *they all are f.* H5 IV, 3, 4. Troil. Prol. 14. V, 6, 20. Cor. V, 6, 35. *thus did I keep my person f.* H4A III, 2, 55. *f. and stainless youth*, Tw. I, 5, 278.

3) full of new life and vigour: *'tis f. morning with me*, Tp. III, 1, 33. *cast thy humble slough and appear f.* Tw. II, 5, 162; cf. H5 IV, 1, 23. *thy friendship makes us f.* H6A III, 3, 86. Cymb. I, 5, 42.

4) brisk, lively, full of alacrity: *the fair sun, when in his f. array*, Ven. 483. *O spirit of love, how quick and f. art thou*, Tw. I, 1, 9. *f. as a bridegroom*, H4A I, 3, 34. Troil. IV, 4, 147. *in appointment f. and fair*, IV, 5, 1. *look f. and merrily*, Caes. II, 1, 224. *I am f. of spirit*, V, 1, 91.

5) youthful, florid, in the prime of life: *f. beauty*, Ven. 164. *that f. fair mirror, dim and old*, Lucr. 1760. *the world's f. ornament*, Sonn. I, 9. *my love looks f.* 107, 10. *since first I saw you f.* 104, 8. *Adonis, lovely, f. and green*, Pilgr. 44. *these f. nymphs*, Tp. IV, 137. Gentl. V, 4, 115. LLL IV, 3, 28. Mids. III, 2, 97; cf. H4A II, 3, 47. As III, 5, 29. Shr. IV, 5, 29. 37. Wint. I, 1, 44. IV, 4, 433. 562. H5 III, 3, 14. Tim. IV, 3, 385. Oth. II, 3, 20. III, 3, 386.

6) new: *to seek some —er stamp of the time-bettering days*, Sonn. 82, 8. *f. and new*, Wiv. IV, 5, 9. *f. array*, As IV, 3, 144; cf. All's V, 2, 4; H5 IV, 2, 57; IV, 3, 117. Lr. IV, 7, 22; Per. V, 1, 216. *f. in murmur*, Tw. I, 2, 32. *f. horses*, Wint. III, 1, 21. John IV, 2, 7. H4A II, 4, 200. H6C III, 3, 237. Troil. II, 3, 272. Cor. V, 3, 17. Tit. III, 1, 111. Mcb. I, 2, 33. Oth. II, 1, 231. III, 3, 179. Cymb. V, 2, 16. Per. IV, 2, 10.

7) refreshing: *the emerald, in whose f. regard weak sights their sickly radiance do amend*, Compl. 213. *under a f. tree's shade*, H6C II, 5, 49. *f. cups, soft beds*, Cymb. V, 3, 71.

8) unripe, inexperienced: *how green you are and f. in this old world*, John III, 4, 145. cf. Fresh-new.

9) holding good, unchanging, constant: *the —est things now reigning*, Wint. IV, 1, 13. *ever since a f. admirer of what I saw*, H8 I, 1, 3. *that slander is found a truth now, for it grows again —er than e'er it was*, II, 1, 155. *'tis so lately altered, that the old name is f. about me*, IV, 1, 99. *whose remembrance is yet f. in their grief*, Cymb. II, 4, 15.

10) not salt: *the petty streams that pay a daily debt to their salt sovereign, with their f. falls' haste*, Lucr. 650. Tp. I, 2, 160. 338. Wiv. I, 1, 22. Tw. III, 4, 419 (quibbling). H5 I, 2, 209. Tit. III, 1, 128. Adverbially: *bleeding f.* H6B III, 2, 188.

Fresh-brook, a rivulet of sweet water: Tp. I, 2, 463.

Fresh-fish (O. Edd. not hyphened) a novice: *and you, a very f. here*, H8 II, 3, 86.

Freshly, 1) in an unimpaired state: *where we, in all her trim, f. beheld .. our ship*, Tp. V, 236.

2) healthily, well: *looks he as f.* As III, 2, 243. H5 IV Chor. 39.

3) anew: *puts the drowsy act f. on me*, Meas. I, 2, 175. *shall f. grow*, Cymb. V, 4, 143.

4) with unabated sympathy, constantly: *in their flowing cups f. remembered*, H5 IV, 3, 55. *f. pitied in our memories*, H8 V, 3, 31.

Freshness, 1) unimpaired state: *our garments hold their f.* Tp. II, 1, 63. — 2) bloom of youth: *whose youth and f. wrinkles Apollo's*, Troil. II, 2, 78.

Fresh-new (O. Edd. not hyphened) unpractised: *this f. sea-farer*, Per. III, 1, 41.

Fret, subst. the stop of a musical instrument which regulates the vibration of a string: *as —s upon an instrument*, Lucr. 1140. *she mistook her —s*, Shr. II, 150. *—s call you these?* 153.

Fret, vb. (partic. *fretted*; in Merch. IV, 1, 77 Qq *fretten*, Ff *fretted*), 1) to corrode, to eat or wear away: *rust the hidden treasure —s*, Ven. 767. *I would 'twere something that would f. the string, the master-cord on 's heart*, H8 III, 2, 105 (quibbling; see subst. Fret). Absolutely: *command these —ing waters from your eyes*, Meas. IV, 3, 151. Hence = to form by wearing away, to dig: *till they have —ed us a pair of graves*, R2 III, 3, 167. *f. channels in her cheeks*, Lr. I, 4, 307. Intransitively, = to be worn away, to corrupt, to rot: *stinking clothes that —ed in their own grease*, Wiv. III, 5, 115. *'twas a commodity lay —ing by you*, Shr. II, 330. *he —s like a gummed velvet*, H4A II, 2, 2 (velvet, being stiffened with gum, as it was customary, quickly rubbed and fretted itself out).

2) to agitate violently: *do not f. yourself too much in the action*, Mids. IV, 1, 14. *when they (pines) are —ed with the gusts of heaven*, Merch. IV, 1, 77 (Qq *fretten*). Absolutely: *a sail, filled with a —ing gust*, H6C II, 6, 35.

3) to be vexed, to be angry, to chafe: Ven. 69. 75. 621. Lucr. 648. Err. II, 1, 6. Shr. III, 2, 230. H4A II, 2, 2 (quibbling). H5 IV, 7, 82. H6A I, 2, 16. V, 2, 20. H6B I, 1, 230. H6C I, 4, 91. Caes. IV, 3, 42. Mcb. V, 5, 25. Ant. III, 6, 27. Transitively, by way of quibbling, = to make angry: *though you can f. me, yet you cannot play upon me*, Hml. III, 2, 388; cf. H8 III, 2, 105.

4) to variegate: *yon gray lines that f. the clouds*, Caes. II, 1, 104. *Fretted =* a) various: *his —ed fortunes give him hope and fear*, Ant. IV, 12, 8. b) embossed, adorned: *this majestical roof —ed with golden fire*, Hml. II, 2, 313. *the roof o' the chamber with golden cherubins is —ed*, Cymb. II, 4, 88.

Fretful, 1) eating away, gnawing: *though parting be a f. corrosive*, H6B III, 2, 403.

2) angry, peevish: H4A III, 3, 13. Hml. I, 5, 20. Lr. III, 1, 4.

Friar (of one or two syll. indiscriminately) brother or member of a mendicant order: Gentl. IV, 1, 36. IV, 3, 43. V, 1, 3. V, 2, 37. Meas. I, 3, 48. II, 3, 2. III, 2, 13 (*bless you, good father f. And you, good brother father*). 81. IV, 3, 56. 142. V, 125. 241. 248. 363. 484 etc. Ado IV, 1, 1. 7. 24. 115. V, 4, 18 etc. Shr. IV, 1, 148. All's II, 2, 28. IV, 3, 125. H6A I, 6, 19. R3 III, 5, 104. H8 I, 2, 148. Rom. II, 4, 193. III, 5, 241. IV, 2, 31. V, 2, 1 etc.

Friday, the sixth day of the week: Meas. III, 2, 192. As IV, 1, 116. Troil. I, 1, 78.

Friend, subst. one joined to another in benevolence and intimacy; masc.: Tp. I, 2, 488. II, 1, 290. 298. II, 2, 95. 106. V, 120. Gentl. I, 1, 59. I, 3, 54. V, 4, 54 etc. etc. fem.: Wiv. III, 3, 146. III, 4, 93. Err. V, 414. Mids. III, 2, 216. H6A II, 1, 54 etc. *it* *is a hard matter for —s to meet,* As III, 2, 195 (allusion to the proverb: *friends may meet, but mountains never greet*). *a f. i' the court is better than a penny in purse,* H4B V, 1, 34. *you cannot tell who's your f.* Tp. II, 2, 89. *nature thy f.* Wiv. III, 3, 70. *good expedition be my f.* Wint. I, 2, 458. Lr. IV, 6, 262. Cymb. I, 6, 18. *stand these poor people's f.* H8 IV, 2, 157. With *to:* Sonn. 144, 11. H6A I, 3, 25 etc. *at f. =* on terms of friendship: *all greetings that a king at f. can send his brother,* Wint. V, 1, 140 (F2.3.4 *as f.*). *to f. =* for f.: *you have them ill to f.* All's V, 3, 182. *we shall have him well to f.* Caes. III, 1, 143. *as I shall find the time to f.* Mcb. IV, 3, 10. *had I admittance and opportunity to f.* Cymb. I, 4, 116. *to be f. with: France f. with England,* John III, 1, 35. Oftener *to be —s: you'll never be —s with him,* LLL V, 2, 13. 552. *I would be —s with you,* Merch. I, 3, 139. H4B II, 4, 71. H5 II, 1, 107. IV, 8, 65. H6C IV, 1, 115. Caes. III, 1, 220. Lr. IV, 1, 37. Ant. II, 5, 44. 47. Cymb. I, 1, 105. *I am good —s with my father,* H4A III, 3, 203. *to-night all —s,* Troil. IV, 5, 270. *I will hold —s with you,* Ado I, 1, 91. *that she make —s to the strict deputy,* Meas. I, 2, 185 (= gain his friendship). *make —s, invite,* Shr. III, 2, 16 (some M. Edd. *make feasts, invite friends*). H8 II, 1, 127. Adjectively: Caes. V, 3, 18.

Used for near relations, particularly parents: *he leaves his —s to dignify them more,* Gentl. I, 1, 64. II, 4, 123. *she is promised by her —s unto a gentleman,* III, 1, 106. *a dower remaining in the coffer of her —s,* Meas. I, 2, 155. *if we did derive it from our —s,* As I, 3, 64. *'tis doubt whether our kinsman come to see his —s,* R2 I, 4, 22. *young, strong, and of good —s,* H4B III, 2, 114. *thou art no father nor no f. of mine,* H6A V, 4, 9. *you envy my advancement and my —s',* R3 I, 3, 75. *at their —s' doors,* Tit. V, 1, 136.

Synonymous to lover, paramour, sweetheart; masc.: *if you have a f. here, convey him out,* Wiv. III, 3, 124. *I will never love that which my f. hates,* Ado V, 2, 72. *to be naked with her f. in bed,* Oth. IV, 1, 3. *from Egypt drive her all-disgraced f.* Ant. 3, 22. *I profess myself her adorer, not her f.* Cymb. I, 4, 74. fem.: *he hath got his f. with child,* Meas. I, 4, 29. *never come in vizard to my f.* LLL V, 2, 404.

Used as a familiar compellation: Wiv. III, 1, 2. Shr. I, 2, 190. Ant. III, 5, 1 etc.

Friend, vb. to favour; absol.: *time must f. or end,* Troil. I, 2, 84. trans.: *for the fault's love is the offender —ed,* Meas. IV, 2, 116. *disorder, that hath spoiled us, f. us now,* H5 IV, 5, 17. *not —ed by his wish,* H8 I, 2, 140. *be —ed with aptness of the season,* Cymb. II, 3, 52.

Friending, subst. favour, friendship: *to express his love and f. to you,* Hml. I, 5, 185.

Friendless, destitute of friends: H8 III, 1, 80.

Friendliness, kindness, good nature: *of such childish f. to yield your voices,* Cor. II, 3, 183.

Friendly, adj. 1) being on terms of friendship: *I will have my lord and you again as f. as you were,* Oth. III, 3, 7. *take our f. senators by the hands,* Cor. IV, 5, 138. *nothing but himself is f. with him,* Tim. V, 1, 122.

2) amicable, benevolent, kind: Ven. 964. Gentl. I, 3, 62. Ado V, 4, 83. Mids. III, 2, 217. Merch. II, 2, 32. Shr. Ind. 1, 103. Wint. I, 2, 350. John II, 481. H5 III, 2, 104. H6A III, 1, 185. V, 1, 38.

H6C IV, 1, 141. R3 II, 1, 59. Caes. IV, 2, 17. IV, 3, 89.

3) favourable, propitious, serviceable: *let me buy your f. help thus far,* All's III, 7, 15. *a prosperous south-wind f.* Wint. V, 1, 161. *standing your f. lord,* Cor. II, 3, 198. *left no f. drop to help me after,* Rom. V, 3, 163. *the gods to-day stand f.* Caes. V, 1, 94. *my f. knave, I thank thee,* Lr. I, 4, 103. *now let thy f. hand put strength enough to it,* IV, 6, 234. With *to: I must think of that which company would not be f. to,* H8 V, 1, 76.

Friendly, adv. in the manner of friends, amicably: As III, 5, 59. Shr. I, 1, 141. IV, 2, 107. H4B IV, 2, 63. Cor. IV, 6, 9. Tit. I, 219. IV, 2, 40. Tim. V, 4, 49. Ant. II, 6, 47. Cymb. III, 5, 13. V, 5, 481.

Friendship, 1) mutual attachment, intimacy: Lucr. 569. Gentl. III, 1, 5. Ado II, 1, 182. Mids. III, 2, 202. Merch. I, 3, 134. As II, 7, 181. Wint. I, 2, 344. H5 II, 1, 114. III, 7, 125. H6A III, 1, 145. III, 3, 86. H6C IV, 1, 116. R3 I, 4, 244. Troil. III, 3, 173. IV, 4, 22. Rom. V, 3, 41. Tim. I, 2, 18. 239. III, 1, 45. 57. IV, 1, 31. IV, 2, 34. Caes. III, 1, 203. Hml. II, 2, 277. Lr. I, 2, 116. Ant. II, 6, 129. Cymb. V, 3, 62. *hold fair f. with,* LLL II, 141. *to mingle f.* Wint. I, 2, 109. *in f. =* a) benevolently, kindly: Pilgr. 188. Wiv. III, 1, 89. As I, 2, 273. b) on friendly terms: All's I, 2, 25. Ant. II, 2, 115.

2) kind disposition, good-will: *you have no cause to hold my f. doubtful,* R3 IV, 4, 493. *no more assurance of equal f. and proceeding,* H8 II, 4, 18.

3) kind service: *to buy his favour, I extend this f.* Merch. I, 3, 169. Ado IV, 1, 265. Wint. IV, 2, 22. H4A V, 1, 124. Tim. IV, 3, 70. 72. Oth. III, 3, 21. *some f. will it* (the hovel) *lend you 'gainst the tempest,* Lr. III, 2, 62.

Frieze, the part of the entablature of a column which separates the architrave from the cornice: Mcb. I, 6, 6.

Fright, subst. violent fear, terror: Wiv. III, 5, 110. *fall in f.* Oth. II, 3, 232. Plur. —*s:* Wint. II, 2, 23. H4B IV, 4, 221. Troil. I, 3, 98.

Fright, vb. to terrify: Ven. 1098. Lucr. 308. 445. 814. 1149. Tp. II, 1, 314. II, 2, 5. Err. IV, 3, 77. LLL IV, 3, 275. Mids. I, 2, 77. II, 1, 35. III, 1, 124. As II, 1, 62. Shr. V, 2, 43. Tw. III, 4, 214. V, 243. Wint. II, 1, 28. III, 2, 93. IV, 4, 117. John III, 1, 11. IV, 2, 25. V, 1, 58. R2 II, 3, 80. 94. II, 4, 9. H4A I, 1, 2. III, 1, 40. H4B I, 1, 67. III, 1, 6. H5 V, 2, 246. H6A IV, 7, 82. H6B III, 2, 50. V, 1, 126. R3 I, 1, 11. I, 2, 24. H8 Epil. 4. Troil. V, 4, 34. Cor. I, 9, 5. IV, 5, 149. Tit. IV, 1, 24. Rom. I, 4, 87. Caes. II, 2, 14. IV, 3, 40. Mcb. IV, 2, 70. Hml. III, 2, 277. Ant. III, 13, 6. Cymb. II, 3, 145. With an adverb or prepositional phrase denoting the result: *to f. them hence,* LLL I, 1, 128. *he'll f. you up,* Rom. IV, 5, 11. *from our confines f. fair peace,* R2 I, 3, 137. Oth. II, 3, 175. Per. V, 3, 3. —*s English out of his wits,* Wiv. II, 1, 143. Ado IV, 2, 55. Mids. I, 2, 82. Ant. III, 13, 196.

Frightful, impressing terror, dreadful: H6B III, 2, 326. R3 IV, 4, 169.

Fringe, an ornamental appendage of garments, consisting of loose threads: As III, 2, 354. Used of eyelashes: Per. III, 2, 101.

Fringed, bordered with fringe: *the f. curtains of thine eye,* Tp. I, 2, 408.

Frippery, a place where old clothes are sold: Tp. IV, 225.

Frisk, to skip, to gambol: Wint. I, 2, 67.

Fritter, a fragment, shred: *one that makes —s of English,* Wiv. V, 5, 151.

Frivolous, slight, of no moment: *to leave f. circumstances,* Shr. V, 1, 28. *for so slight and f. a cause,* H6A IV, 1, 112. *your oath is vain and f.* H6C I, 2, 27.

Frize, a kind of coarse woollen stuff: *shall I have a coxcomb of f.?* Wiv. V, 5, 146 (Wales being celebrated for this kind of cloth). *my invention comes from my pate as birdlime does from f.* Oth. II, 1, 127 (O. Edd. *freeze*).

Fro, 1) prepos. = from: *copest with death himself to scape f. it,* Rom. IV, 1, 75 (Qq *from*). *why did you throw your wedded lady f. you?* Cymb. V, 5, 261 (M. Edd. *from*).

2) adv. *to and fro* = hither and thither, up and down: H6A II, 1, 69. H6B IV, 8, 58. *the to and fro conflicting wind and rain,* Lr. III, 1, 11. *debating to and fro,* H6B I, 1, 91.

Frock, an outer garment: *a f. or livery, that aptly is put on,* Hml. III, 4, 164.

Frog, the animal **Rana**: Mcb. IV, 1, 14. Lr. III, 4, 134.

Frogmore, a place near Windsor: Wiv. II, 3, 78. 90. III, 1, 33.

Froissart (O. Edd. *Froysard*), name of a French historian: H6A I, 2, 29.

Frolic, gay, merry: *we fairies now are f.* Mids. V, 394. *and therefore f.* Shr. IV, 3, 184.

From, prepos. 1) Denoting emission, by indicating the origin, source or starting-point of a thing or action: *I commend me f. our house in grief,* Lucr. 1308 ("The usual formula at the conclusion of letters was *from the house of the writer.*" Dyce); cf. Ado I, 1, 283. *f. fairest creatures we desire increase,* Sonn. I, 1. *a fortitude f. heaven,* Tp. I, 2, 154; cf. *music f. the spheres,* Tw. III, 1, 121. *he furnished me f. mine own library with volumes,* Tp. I, 2, 167. *to fetch dew f. the Bermoothes,* 229. *brushed dew f. unwholesome fen,* 322. *this is unwonted which now came f. him,* 498. *she that f. Naples can have no note,* II, 1, 247. *infections that the sun sucks up f. bogs,* II, 2, 2. *dropped f. heaven,* 140. *no woman's face remember, save f. my glass mine own,* III, 1, 50. *they expect it f. me,* IV, 42. *receiving them f. such a worthless post,* Gentl. I, 1, 161. *f. our infancy we have conversed,* II, 4, 62; cf. R3 IV, 3, 19. *to cram a maw f. such a filthy vice,* Meas. III, 2, 24 (= by means of). *many a knight f. tawny Spain,* LLL I, 1, 174. *a sweet look f. Demetrius' eye,* Mids. II, 2, 127. *the greater throw may turn by fortune f. the weaker hand,* Merch. II, 1, 34. *f. hour to hour we ripe,* As II, 7, 26; cf. *heir f. heir shall hold this quarrel up,* H4B IV, 2, 48 (quite = heir by heir). *I am f. humble, he f. honoured name,* All's I, 3, 162. *this calf bred f. his cow,* John I, 124. *to draw my answer f. thy articles,* II, 111. *holds f. all soldiers chief majority,* H4A III, 2, 109 (= by the consent of). *nor ever had one penny bribe f. France,* H6B III, 1, 109. *proceed no straiter 'gainst our uncle Gloster than f. true evidence he be approved culpable,* III, 2, 21. *I speak f. certainties,* Cor. I, 2, 31. *add more, f. thine invention, offers,* Ant. III, 12, 29. *f. every one the best she hath,* Cymb. III, 5, 73. cf. Compl. 68. Tp. I, 1, 30. Meas. III, 1, 1. Mids. I, 1, 244 etc. etc. *the setting of thine eye proclaims a matter f. thee,* Tp. II, 1, 230. *couldst thou perceive so much f. her?* Gentl. I, 1, 142 (quibbling). *upon agreement f. us to his liking,* Shr. I, 2, 183 (= proceeding from us; on our side). *make thee a fortune f. me,* Ant. II, 5, 49. *civility not seen f. other,* Cymb. IV, 2, 179 (German: abgesehen). *how f. the finny subject of the sea these fishers tell the infirmities of men,* Per. II, 1, 52 (applying to men truths perceived by, and taken from, the observation of fishes). *your highness claiming f. the female,* H5 I, 2, 92; cf. *Henry doth claim the crown f. John of Gaunt,* H6B II, 2, 54 (as the heir of Gaunt). *this was sent me f. a nun,* Compl. 232; cf. Gentl. I, 2, 38. I, 3, 53. LLL IV, 2, 94. V, 2, 47. H5 I, 2, 221. H6A IV, 1, 49. H6B III, 2, 277. H6C II, 1, 146. III, 3, 164. *let me hear f. thee,* Gentl. I, 1, 57. II, 4, 103. Merch. V, 35. H6B III, 2, 405. Hml. I, 3, 4. *tell him f. me,* Gentl. IV, 4, 123. H6B IV, 10, 78. *as I was commanded f. you,* All's II, 5, 59. *I do it f. Lord Angelo by special charge,* Meas. I, 2, 123. *a certainty vouched f. our cousin Austria,* All's I, 2, 5. *I have this present evening f. my sister been well informed of them,* Lr. II, 1, 103 (= by a letter of my sister). *of that I shall have also cause to speak, and f. his mouth whose voice will draw on more,* Hml. V, 2, 403. *I had other things to have spoken with her too f. him,* Wiv. IV, 5, 42 (= by his order, in his name). *I come to speak with Paris f. the prince Troilus,* Troil. III, 1, 41. *thus once again says Nestor f. the Greeks,* II, 2, 2. *he bade me f. him call thee thane f. of Cawdor,* Mcb. I, 3, 105. *her gentle spirit commits itself to yours to be directed, as f. her lord,* Merch. III, 2, 167. *a pension of thousands to be paid f. the Sophy,* Tw. II, 5, 196. *an arrow shot f. a well-experienced archer,* Per. I, 1, 164 (quite = by). *I do desire thee, even f. a heart full of sorrows,* Gentl. IV, 3, 32. Rom. III, 5, 228. *speak it f. your souls,* H6B III, 1, 247. R3 I, 4, 243. IV, 1, 89. IV, 4, 255. H8 II, 4, 81. Rom. III, 5, 228. *f. bitterness of soul,* R3 I, 3, 179. *you only speak f. your distracted soul,* Tim. III, 4, 115. *speaks not f. her faith, but f. her need,* John III, 1, 210. *but nothing spake in warrant f. himself,* R3 III, 7, 33.

2) Denoting departure, separation and privation: *his rider loved not speed, being made f. thee,* Sonn. 50, 8. *we came f. thence,* Tp. I, 2, 60. *Sycorax f. Argier was banished,* 265. *come f. thy ward,* 471. *banished f. your eye,* II, 1, 126. *why thou departedst f. thy native home,* Err. I, 1, 30. *ran f. you,* IV, 4, 152 (cf. *Run*). *fled f. me,* H4B II, 4, 248 (cf. *Flee*). *away f. me,* H6B I, 2, 50. *until his army be dismissed f. him,* IV, 9, 40. *we will not f. the helm,* H6C V, 4, 21; cf. *Signior Iachimo will not f. it,* Cymb. I, 4, 184 (= will stand by it, will persevere) etc. *pluck my garment f. me,* Tp. I, 2, 24. *justled f. your senses,* V, 158. *divided f. them,* 239. *weed her love f. Valentine,* Gentl. III, 2, 49. *unwind her love f. him,* 51. *set thee f. durance,* LLL III, 129. *grow f. the king's acquaintance,* H8 III, 1, 161 etc. *that rich jewel he should keep unknown f. thievish ears,* Lucr. 35; cf. John I, 124 (see *Keep*). *that to my use it might unused stay f. hands of falsehood,* Sonn. 48, 4. *to give them f. me,* 122, 11; cf. Lr. I, 1, 128. *to win it f. me,* Tp. I, 2, 456. *f. me he got it,* III, 2, 61 (cf. *Take*). *suck the soil's fertility f. wholesome flowers,* R2 III, 4, 39 (so as to make wholesome flowers perish). *if aught possess thee f. me, it is dross,* Err. II, 2, 179 (= and dispossess me). *to smother up*

his beauty f. the world, H4A I, 2, 223. *their titles usurped f. you*, H5 I, 2, 95. *so great an honour as one man more would share f. me*, IV, 3, 32 (i. e. depriving me of it). *shakes all our buds f. growing*, Cymb. I, 3, 37 (cf. *Command, Hide, Hinder* and *Prevent*). *void and empty f. any dram of mercy*, Merch. IV, 1, 6. *which robs my tongue f. breathing native breath*, R2 I, 3, 173. Similarly: *we must starve our sight f. lovers' food*, Mids. I, 1, 223. *the maid is mine f. all the world*, Shr. II, 386. *who in that sale sells pardon f. himself*, John III, 1, 167 (forfeits his own salvation). *giving full trophy ... quite f. himself to God*, H5 V Chor. 22. It is the same use after the words of deliverance and protection: *weakly fortressed f. a world of harms*, Lucr. 28. *canopy the herd f. heat*, Sonn. 12, 6. *fortified her visage f. the sun*, Compl. 9. *f. what a torment I did free thee*, Tp. I, 2, 251. II, 1, 293. *release me f. my bands*, Epil. 9. *as you f. crimes would pardoned be*, 19. cf. *Guard* and *Save.*

3) Denoting election, = among: *humbly entreating from your royal thoughts a modest one*, All's II, 1, 130. *why have you that charitable title from thousands?* Tim. I, 2, 94.

4) Denoting the cause of an effect, = in consequence of, on account of: *how are they wrapped in with infamies that f. their own misdeeds askance their eyes*, Lucr. 637. *f. whom we all were sea-swallowed*, Tp. II, 1, 250. *he would give't thee, f. this rank offence, so to offend him still*, Meas. III, 1, 100. *called so f. his grandfather*, Shr. III, 1, 53. *whom f. the flow of gall I name not but f. sincere motions*, H8 I, 1, 152. *heaven, f. thy endless goodness, send prosperous life*, V, 5, 1. *f. broad words Macduff lives in disgrace*, Mcb. III, 6, 21. *f. her* (his soul's) *working all his visage wanned*, Hml. II, 2, 580. *f. what cause*, III, 1, 6. *f. whom we do exist and cease to be*, Lr. I, 1, 114. *he wears the rose of youth upon him, f. which the world should note something particular*, Ant. III, 13, 21. *your highness shall f. this practice but make hard your heart*, Cymb. I, 5, 24. *goodly and gallant shall be false and perjured f. thy great fail*, III, 4, 66.

5) Denoting distance, = away from, far from: *both f. me, both to each friend*, Sonn. 144, 11. *which is f. my remembrance*, Tp. I, 2, 65. *so far f. Italy*, II, 1, 110. *f. whom my absence was not six months old*, Err. I, 1, 45. *feeds f. home*, II, 1, 101. *f. our free person she should be confined*, Wint. II, 1, 194. *he is seldom f. the house of a most homely shepherd*, IV, 2, 43. *I am best pleased to be f. such a deed*, John IV, 1, 86. *powers f. home*, IV, 3, 151 (= foreign powers). *stand f. him*, H4B II, 1, 74 and IV, 4, 116; cf. Caes. III, 2, 169. *where, f. company, I may revolve my grief*, H6A V, 5, 100. *f. thy sight, I should be raging mad*, H6B III, 2, 394. *f. thee to die*, 401. *he lived f. all attainder of suspect*, R3 III, 5, 32; cf. II, 1, 94. *live with Richmond, f. the reach of hell*, IV, 1, 43. *thou shalt build f. men*, Tim. IV, 3, 533. *it must be done to-night, and something f. the palace*, Mcb. III, 1, 132. *f. thence* (viz home) *the sauce to meat is ceremony*, III, 4, 36. *what make you f. Wittenberg?* Hml. I, 2, 164. *to answer f. our home*, Lr. II, 1, 126.

6) Denoting change, by indicating a form left for another: *as a form of wax resolveth f. his figure 'gainst the fire*, John V, 4, 25. *our scene is altered f. a serious thing*, R2 V, 3, 79. *exposed myself, from certain and possessed conveniences, to doubtful fortunes,*

Troil. III, 3, 7. *the icicle that's curdied by the frost f. purest snow*, Cor. V, 3, 66.

7) Expressing difference and discrepancy, = otherwise than, differently from: *so f. himself impiety hath wrought*, Lucr. 341. *at random f. the truth vainly expressed*, Sonn. 147, 12. *to be so odd and f. all fashions*, Ado III, 1, 72. *you can wish none* (joy) *f. me*, Merch. III, 2, 193. *this is f. my commission*, Tw. I, 5, 201. *write f. it, if you can*, V, 340 (= otherwise, differently). *hold a wing quite f. the flight of all thy ancestors*, H4A III, 2, 31. *quite f. the answer of his degree*, H5 IV, 7, 142. *so f. thy soul's love didst thou love her brothers*, R3 IV, 4, 259 (quibbling). *and will be led at your request a little from himself*, Troil. II, 3, 191. *'twas f. the canon*, Cor. III, 1, 90. *of him that, his particular to foresee, smells f. the common weal*, Tim. IV, 3, 160. *clean f. the purpose*, Caes. I, 3, 35. *beasts f. quality and kind*, 64. 66. I, 2, 314. *quite f. the main opinion he held once*, II, 1, 196. *whereby he does receive particular addition, f. the bill that writes them all alike*, Mcb. III, 1, 100. *any thing so overdone is f. the purpose of playing*, Hml. III, 2, 22. *that f. the sense of all civility I thus would trifle*, Oth. I, 1, 132. *this is f. the present*, Ant. II, 6, 30 (= not now the question). *words him a great deal f. the matter*, Cymb. I, 4, 17. *so f. sense in hardness*, V, 5, 431.

8) Used for *of* by Fluellen: *I must speak with him f. the pridge*, H5 III, 6, 91.

Preceding adverbs and other prepositions: *sacred f. above*, H6A I, 2, 114. *she culled it f. among the rest*, Tit. IV, 1, 44. *come f. behind*, H6A I, 2, 66. *threw me off f. behind one of them*, Wiv. IV, 5, 69. *f. below your duke to beneath your constable*, All's II, 2, 32. *f. below their heads*, Tim. IV, 3, 32. *f. forth a sawpit*, Wiv. IV, 4, 53. All's II, 1, 199 etc. (cf. *Forth*). *f. off a hill*, Compl. 1. *f. off the head of this Athenian*, Mids. IV, 1, 70. Merch. IV, 1, 139. 302. All's IV, 3, 191. John I, 145. II, 325. R2 III, 1, 6. III, 2, 45. IV, 204. H5 IV, 3, 87. H6A II, 4, 30. H6C II, 6, 52. Cor. III, 3, 103. Rom. IV, 1, 78. Cymb. III, 1, 26. *f. out* = *out of:* Merch. III, 4, 21. John V, 2, 136. R2 III, 3, 64. IV, 206. R3 I, 4, 186. *f. under ground*, H6B II, 1, 174. *f. under this terrestrial ball*, R2 III, 2, 41.

From, adv. *off: the falling f. of his friends*, Tim. IV, 3, 402 (M. Edd. *off*, or *from him*).

Front, subst. 1) the forehead, brow: *why stand these royal —s amazed thus?* John II, 356. *the f. of heaven was full of fiery shapes*, H4A III, 1, 14. *two monarchies, whose high upreared and abutting —s the ocean parts*, H5 Prol. 21. *grim-visaged war hath smoothed his wrinkled f.* R3 I, 1, 9. *our powers, with smiling —s encountering*, Cor. I, 6, 8 (quibbling). *f. to f. bring thou this fiend of Scotland and myself*, Mcb. IV, 3, 232. *had he his hurts before? ay, on the f.* V, 8, 47. Lr. II, 2, 114. Hml. III, 4, 56. *to take the safest occasion by the f.* Oth. III, 1, 52. *a tawny f.* Ant. I, 1, 6. Metaphorically: *the very head and f. of my offending*, Oth. I, 3, 80.

2) the van of an army: *our main battle's f.* H6C I, 1, 8. *companion in the f. of war*, Ant. V, 1, 44. Quibbling in Cor. I, 6, 8.

3) the foremost part, the beginning: *Philomel in summer's f. doth sing*, Sonn. 102, 7. *Flora peering in April's f.* Wint. IV, 4, 3.

Front, vb. 1) trans. a) to face, to oppose, to defy, to meet: *what well-appointed leader --s* *us here?* H4B IV, 1, 25. *death doth f. thee with apparent spoil,* H6A IV, 2, 26. *f. him to his face,* H6B V, 1, 86. Cor. V, 2, 44. Ant. I, 4, 79. Absol.: *towards —ing peril,* H4B IV, 4, 66.

b) to attack: *f. her, board her,* Tw. I, 3, 59. *you four shall f. them in the narrow lane,* H4A II, 2, 62. *those wars which —ed mine own peace,* Ant. II, 2, 61.

c) to stand over against: *a gate of steel —ing the sun,* Troil. III, 3, 122.

d) to form an outwork for, to fortify: *yonder walls that f. your town,* Troil. IV, 5, 219.

2) intr. to march in the front or first rank: *and f. but in that file where others tell steps with me,* H8 I, 2, 42.

Frontier, an outwork in fortification: *of palisadoes, —s, parapets,* H4A II, 3, 55. *goes it against the main of Poland, or for some f.?* Hml. IV, 4, 16 (i. e. some border territory). Metaphorically: *the moody f. of a servant brow,* H4A I, 3, 19 (in which "*the eye pries through the portage of the head like the brass cannon,*" H5 III, 1, 10).

Frontlet, a band for the forehead: *what makes that f. on?* Lr. I, 4, 208.*

Frost, freezing cold: Sonn. 5, 7. Tp. I, 2, 256. Ado V, 4, 42. LLL I, 1, 100. Shr. IV, 1, 23. H8 III, 2, 355. Cor. V, 3, 66. Tit. IV, 4, 71. Rom. IV, 5, 28. Plur. —*s:* Lucr. 331. LLL V, 2, 811. Mids. II, 1, 107. Shr. V, 2, 139. H4B I, 3, 41. Merch. II, 4, 75. Hml. III, 4, 87. Metaphorically: Lucr. 355. Merch. II, 4, 75. Hml. III, 4, 87.

Frosty, causing congelation, very cold: As II, 3, 53. R2 I, 3, 295. Tit. III, 1, 5. Used of hair, = grey, hoary: *the f. head,* H6B V, 1, 167. *my f. signs and chaps of age,* Tit. V, 3, 77. Metaphorically, = cold: Ven. 36. H4A IV, 1, 128. H5 III, 5, 22. 24.

Frosty-spirited, cold, dull: H4A II, 3, 21.

Froth, subst. spume, foam: Wint. III, 3, 95. Tim. IV, 3, 433. V, 1, 220. Metaphorically, = any thing vain and empty: *a dream, a breath, a f. of fleeting joy,* Lucr. 212. *f. and scum, thou liest,* Wiv. I, 1, 167.

Froth, name: Meas. II, 1, 104. 154 etc.

Froth, vb. to make a tankard foam: *let me see thee f. and lime,* Wiv. I, 3, 15 (Ff. *f. and live*).

Frothy, foamy: *whose* (the boars') *f. mouth,* Ven. 901.

Froward (rhyming to *coward:* Ven. 570. to *toward:* Pilgr. 56. Shr. IV, 5, 78. V, 2, 183) not willing to obey or comply, refractory: Ven. 562. 570. Pilgr. 56. Gentl. III, 1, 68. Shr. I, 1, 69. I, 2, 90. II, 295. IV, 5, 78. V, 2, 119. 157. 169. 183. H6A III, 1, 18. H6C IV, 7, 84.

Frown, subst. a stern and surly look: Ven. 465. Sonn. 25, 8. 117, 11. Tp. V, 30. 127. As IV, 1, 110. Shr. V, 2, 172. Wint. II, 3, 100. John III, 1, 104. H6B V, 1, 100. H6C I, 4, 48. IV, 5, 28. Troil. I, 3, 26. Tit. I, 458. II, 1, 11. Lr. V, 3, 6. Cymb. IV, 2, 264. *you are too much i' the f.* Lr. I, 4, 209. *to look back in f.* Cymb. V, 3, 28. Plur. —*s:* Ven. 573. Sonn. 93, 8. Mids. I, 1, 195. H4A III, 2, 127. H5 III, 5, 18. H6C I, 1, 72. II, 6, 32. IV, 1, 75. Rom. I, 5, 75. Oth. IV, 3, 20. Per. I, 2, 53.

Frown, vb. to look stern and surly: Ven. 45. 571. Pilgr. 259. 311. 419. Gentl. I, 2, 62. III, 1, 96. Err. II, 2, 112. Merch. I, 2, 50. 64. III, 2, 85. As III, 5, 68 (—*ing looks*). Shr. II, 173. 249. III, 2,

95. V, 1, 144. Tw. II, 5, 65. Wint. III, 3, 54. John II, 505. IV, 2, 213. R2 I, 1, 16. H6C II, 3, 7. R3 I, 4, 190. IV, 4, 37. H8 I, 4, 33. III, 2, 205. V, 1, 88. Cor. III, 1, 107. III, 2, 67. IV, 5, 69. Rom. I, 1, 46. II, 2, 96. II, 3, 1. Hml. I, 1, 62. Lr. I, 4, 211. Cymb. I, 1, 1. III, 5, 18. Per. I, 4, 108. *f. on, you heavens,* Troil. V, 10, 6. Followed by *against: when he —ed, it was against the French,* R2 II, 1, 178. By *at* (= on account or on occasion of): H6B I, 2, 4. H6C III, 3, 168. Ant. II, 7, 128. By *on* or *upon* (= to regard angrily): Sonn. 49, 2. 149, 6. Gentl. II, 4, 3. Mids. I, 1, 194. As III, 5, 15. Tw. V, 346. Wint. III, 3, 6. John IV, 1, 58. IV, 3, 96. 159. H4B I, 1, 152. H5 III, 6, 41. H6A IV, 2, 9. H6C V, 1, 101. R3 II, 1, 67. V, 3, 283. 287. V, 5, 21.

Frowningly, sternly, with a look of displeasure: *looked he f.?* Hml. I, 2, 231.

Fructify, to bear fruit: *those parts that do f. in us,* LLL IV, 2, 30. Fructful, see *Fruitful.*

Frugal, not prodigal, sparing: *f. nature,* Ado IV, 1, 130. With *of: I was then f. of my mirth,* Wiv. II, 1, 28.

Fruit, 1) the produce of a tree or other plant in which the seeds are contained: Merch. IV, 1, 115. As III, 2, 126. John II, 473. R2 II, 1, 153. H6C V, 6, 52. V, 7, 32. R3 III, 7, 167. Rom. II, 1, 35. Oth. II, 3, 383. Per. I, 1, 21. 28. Collectively: *he dies that touches any of this f.* As II, 7, 98. III, 2, 123. 250. H4A II, 4, 471. H4B I, 3, 39. H5 I, 1, 62. III, 5, 18. H6C III, 3, 126. Troil. II, 3, 129. Cor. IV, 6, 100. Hml. II, 2, 200. Cymb. III, 3, 61. V, 5, 263. Constituting the dessert at table: *the f. to that great feast,* Hml. II, 2, 52.

2) offspring, child: Lucr. 1064. Sonn. 97, 10. H4B V, 4, 15. H6A V, 4, 13. 63. H6B III, 2, 214. H6C IV, 4, 24. H8 V, 1, 20. Tit. V, 1, 43. 48.

3) production, effect, consequence: *the —s of the sport,* Tw. II, 5, 216. *to taste their —s of duty,* R2 III, 4, 63. H6C III, 2, 58. 59. R3 II, 1, 134. Oth. II, 3, 9. *she took the —s of my advice,* Hml. II, 2, 145 (= profited by my advice).

Plur. for the sing.: *my second joy and first —s of my body,* Wint. III, 2, 98 (M. Edd. *first-fruits*). *this is the —s of whoring,* Oth. V, 1, 116 (Qq *fruit*).

Fruit-dish, a vessel used for serving up fruit: Meas. II, 1, 95.

Fruiterer, a seller of fruit: H4B III, 2, 36.

Fruitful, 1) bearing fruit, covered with fruit: *Adonis' gardens that one day bloomed and f. were the next,* H6A I, 6, 7. Of a woman: *to make this creature f.* Lr. I, 4, 299.

2) very productive, fertile: Lucr. 107. LLL V, 2, 857. Shr. I, 1, 3. II, 372. H6A V, 4, 127. R3 V, 2, 8. In LLL Q1 *fructful.*

3) plenteous, copious: *one f. meal would set me to it,* Meas. IV, 3, 161. *with a recompense more f. than their offence can weigh down,* Tim. V, 1, 153. *the f. river in the eye,* Hml. I, 2, 80. *ram thou thy f. tidings in mine ears, that long time have been barren,* Ant. II, 5, 24. *in Britain where was he that could stand up his parallel, or f. object be in eye of Imogen?* Cymb. V, 4, 55 (i. e. copious, rich enough to engross her attention).

4) liberal, bountiful: *a hand as f. as the land that feeds us,* H8 I, 3, 56. *she's framed as f. as the free elements,* Oth. II, 3, 347. *if an oily palm be*

not a f. prognostication, Ant. I, 2, 53 (i. e. betrays a woman of an amorous temper).

Fruitfully, copiously, fully: *you understand me? most f.* All's II, 2, 73. *time and place will be f. offered*, Lr. IV, 6, 270.

Fruitfulness, liberality, bountifulness: *this argues f. and liberal heart*, Oth. III, 4, 38 (cf. *fruitful* in Ant. I, 2, 53).

Fruition, enjoyment: *where I may have f. of her love*, H6A V, 5, 9.

Fruitless, 1) barren, having no offspring: *upon my head they placed a f. crown*, Mcb. III, 1, 61. 2) empty, vain, idle: *a dream and f. vision*, Mids. III, 2, 371. *f. pranks*, Tw. IV, 1, 59. 3) averse to love, cold: *despite of f. chastity*, Ven. 751. *chanting faint hymns to the cold f. moon*, Mids. I, 1, 73.

Fruit-tree, a tree bearing fruit: R2 III, 4, 45. 58. Rom. II, 2, 108.

Frush, to bruise, to batter: *I like thy armour well; I'll f. it and unlock the rivets all*, Troil. V, 6, 29 (Fr. *froisser*).

Frustrate, vb. 1) to disappoint: *to f. prophecies*, H4B V, 2, 127. *f. his proud will*, Lr. IV, 6, 64. 2) to make null, to render of no effect: *to f. both his oath and what beside may make against the house of Lancaster*, H6C II, 1, 175.

Frustrate, partic. adj. vain, ineffectual: *our f. search*, Tp. III, 3, 10. *being so f., tell him he mocks the pauses that he makes*, Ant. V, 1, 2 (refer *f.* to *pauses*).

Frutify, used by Launcelot for *notify:* Merch. II, 2, 142.

Fry, subst. a swarm of little fishes just produced from the spawn: Ven. 526. All's IV, 3, 250. Per. II, 1, 34. Used of a dense crowd of people: *what a f. of fornication is at door!* H8 V, 4, 36. Of young people, in contempt: *young f. of treachery*, Mcb. IV, 2, 84.

Fry, vb. to suffer the action of fire, to be roasted, to broil: Shr. II, 340. Troil. V, 2, 57.

Fub (cf. *Fob*), to delude, to shift off: *—ed off from this day to that day*, H4B II, 1, 37.

Fuel, that which feeds fire: Sonn. 1, 6. Tp. I, 2, 366. H5 II, 3, 45. H6B III, 1, 303. H6C V, 4, 70.

Fugitive, 1) adj. flying: Ant. III, 1, 7. 2) subst. a deserter: *thrust out like a f.* H6A III, 3, 67. *a master-leaver and a f.* Ant. IV, 9, 22.

Fulfil, 1) to make full, to fill completely: *they* (women) *are so —ed with men's abuses*, Lucr. 1258. *Will will f. the treasure of thy love*, Sonn. 136, 5. *charity itself —s the law*, LLL IV, 3, 364 (= is the contents of the law). *corresponsive and —ing bolts*, Troil. Prol. 18 [= "close-fitting" Herford]. 2) to execute, to perform: *I found you where you did f. the act of lust*, Lucr. 1635. *see his exequies —ed*, H6A III, 2, 133. 3) to accomplish, to answer by compliance or execution: *thy princely office how canst thou f.* Lucr. 628. *thus far my love-suit f.* Sonn. 136, 4. *servants must their masters' minds f.* Err. IV, 1, 113. *it does f. my vow*, Wint. IV, 4, 497. *their purposes*, V, 1, 36. *the oracle is —ed*, V, 2, 25. 82. *spurn at his edict and f. a man's*, R3 I, 4, 203. *your pleasure be —ed*, H8 II, 4, 57. V, 2, 19. Caes. III, 1, 159. *his commandment is —ed*, Hml. V, 2, 381. *his prince' desire*, Per. II Prol. 21.

Full, adj. 1) replete, filled, containing all that can be contained: *fill it f. with wills*, Sonn. 136, 6; cf. R3 I, 4, 143 and Mcb. III, 4, 88. *on a f. stomach*, LLL I, 2, 154. *the f. stream of the world*, As III, 2, 440. *f. measure*, Shr. III, 2, 227. *f. hogshead*, H4B II, 4, 68. *the f. moon*, IV, 3, 57; cf. Lr. IV, 6, 70. *with both hands f.* H4B IV, 4, 103. *entertain with half their forces the f. pride of France*, H5 I, 2, 112. *speak with f. mouth*, 230. *Volumnia is worth of consuls a city f.* Cor. V, 4, 57. *the table's f.* Mcb. III, 4, 46. *my heart is f.* Oth. V, 2, 175 etc. *the proud f. sail of his verse*, Sonn. 86, 1 (= swelled). *what a f. fortune does the thicklips owe*, Oth. I, 1, 66 (= stored with all that can make happy). *his f. fortune*, Cymb. V, 4, 110 (cf. *Full-fortuned*). *the f. Caesar will answer his emptiness*, Ant. III, 13, 35 (= favoured by every advantage). *never (have I liked) any with so f. soul*, Tp. III, 1, 44. *the grief is fine, f., perfect*, Troil. IV, 4, 3 (= filling the whole soul). *the f. stop*, Merch. III, 1, 17; cf. *come we to f. points here?* H4B II, 4, 198 (Pistol's speech). *thou lovest me not with the f. weight that I love thee*, As I, 2, 9. *in his f. and ripened years*, R3 II, 3, 14 (= when he is a full-grown man). *that f. meridian of my glory*, H8 III, 2, 224. *I did never know so f. a voice issue from so empty a heart*, H5 IV, 4, 72 (= sonorous); cf. *congreeing in a f. and natural close, like music*, I, 2, 182. *a —er blast ne'er shook our battlements*, Oth. II, 1, 6 (= stronger). *a f. eye* = not sunk, hollow, and dim, but lively and bright: Ven. 296. Wint. V, 1, 53. H5 V, 2, 170. cf. *that f. star that ushers in the even*, Sonn. 132, 7. *my most f. flame* (= bright) Sonn. 115, 4.

2) having in abundance; followed by *of:* *gardens f. of flowers*, Ven. 65. *f. of fraud*, 1141. *of riot*, 1147. *of care*, Sonn. 56, 13 and Pilgr. 158. *of blame*, Sonn. 129, 3. *of pleasure*, Tp. III. 2, 125. *of our displeasure*, Wint. IV, 4, 444. *f. of rest* = refreshed, H4A IV, 3, 27 and Caes. IV, 3, 202. Tp. III, 2, 144. IV, 172. Gentl. II, 4, 177. III, 1, 65. IV, 3, 33. IV, 4, 134. V, 4, 156. Wiv. III, 5, 38. Meas. I, 2, 54 (*f. of error*). Err. I, 2, 97. III, 1, 23. Ado V, 1, 105 (*true and f. of proof*). LLL V, 2, 45. Mids. I, 1, 22. II, 1, 258. Merch. I, 2, 54. As II, 1, 53. All's I, 1, 220. H4B I, 1, 10. Tim. IV, 3, 466 (*f. of decay*). V, 1, 4 (*he's so f. of gold*). Mcb. I, 4, 29 (*to make thee f. of growing*). Oth. II, 1, 254. Ant. V, 2, 24 etc. etc.

3) complete, entire, not defective or partial: *f. perfection*, Ven. 634. *to give f. growth to that which still doth grow*, Sonn. 115, 14. *a f. year*, Tp. I, 2, 250; cf. Meas. IV, 2, 12 and Cor. V, 6, 78. *with f. and holy rite*, Tp. IV, 1, 17. *with f. line of his authority*, Meas. I, 4, 56. *her womb expresseth his f. tilth*, 44. *to veil f. purpose*, IV, 6, 4. *make f. satisfaction*, Err. V, 399. *brings home f. numbers*, Ado I, 1, 9; cf. *make a —er number up*, Caes. IV, 3, 208. *you must not make the f. show of this*, Ado I, 3, 20. *her affections have their f. bent*, II, 3, 232. *the intent and purpose of the law hath f. relation to the penalty*, Merch. IV, 1, 248; cf. H5 I, 2, 205 and Ant. V, 2, 23. *thy huntress' name that my f. life doth sway*, As III, 2, 4; cf. *my f. heart remains in use with you*, Ant. I, 3, 43. *the f. power of France*, H5 I, 2, 107. *giving f. trophy, signal and ostent to God*, V Chor. 21. *your grace's f. content*, H6B I, 3, 70. *screech-owls make the concert f.* III, 2, 327. *with a f. intent*, H6C II, 1, 117. *your breath of*

f. consent, Troil. II, 2, 74. 132; cf. *passed for consul with f. voice*, Cor. III, 3, 59. *whom our f. senate call all in all sufficient*, Oth. IV, 1, 275. *o'er my spirit thy f. supremacy thou knewest*, Ant. III, 11, 59 etc. *you have it f.* = you are the man, you will do: Ado I, 1, 110. cf. *content thee, for I have it f.* Shr. I, 1, 203.

4) filled with food, satiated, crammed: *all f. with feasting on your sight*, Sonn. 75, 9. *as those that feed grow f.* Meas. I, 4, 41. *glutted, gorged, and f.* H4A III, 2, 84. *because we now are f.* Troil. II, 2, 72. *when they are f., they belch us*, Oth. III, 4, 105. *f. surfeits*, Ant. I, 4, 27. *to feed again, though f.* Cymb. II, 4, 138. *With of: f. of your ne'ercloying sweetness*, Sonn. 118, 5. *thou beastly feeder art so f. of him*, H4B I, 3, 95.

5) accomplished, perfect: *the man commands like a f. soldier*, Oth. II, 1, 36 (ein ganzer Soldat). *one that but performs the bidding of the —est man*, Ant. III, 13, 87 (properly one that has more of man in him than anybody else). As to Ado III, 1, 45 and Per. Prol. 23 see *Full* adv. and *Face.*

Used substantively, when preceded by prepositions; *at f.* = a) fully, completely: *be thou at f. ourself*, Meas. I, 1, 44. *dilate at f.* Err. I, 1, 123. Merch. V, 297. All's II, 1, 135. H4B I, 1, 135. H5 II, 4, 140. H6B II, 2, 6. 77. H8 I, 4, 60. IV, 1, 8. Hml. IV, 3, 65. b) in the state of fulness: *you took the moon at f.* LLL V, 2, 214. *at f. of tide*, Ant. III, 2, 49. *In the f.* = not separately, but in full company, all together: *there in the f. convive we*, Troil. IV, 5, 272. *To the f.* = a) fully: *your passions have to the f. appeached*, All's I, 3, 197. *we'll see these things effected to the f.* H6B I, 2, 84. b) to the state of fulness: *it will come to the f.* Ant. II, 1, 11 (my hope, like the moon). *to behold his visage, even to my f. of view*, Troil. III, 3, 241 (to the satisfaction of my eyes).

Full, adv. 1) fully, completely, quite: *f. as deep a dye*, Sonn. 54, 5. *deserve as f. as fortunate a bed*, Ado III, 1, 45 (some M. Edd. *deserve as f., as fortunate a bed*). *f. as lovely*, Gentl. IV, 4, 191. V, 4, 38. Ado II, 1, 79. LLL IV, 3, 253. R2 IV, 53. H6B III, 2, 314. H6C I, 4, 11. III, 2, 37. V, 3, 17. R3 III, 6, 7. Mcb. I, 4, 54. *f. fathom five*, Tp. I, 2, 396. *f. three thousand ducats*, Merch. I, 3, 57. *not f. a month*, Wint. V, 1, 117. John I, 113. R2 V, 3, 2. H5 I, 1, 13. R3 II, 4, 29. Hml. III, 2, 165. *f. charactered with lasting memory*, Sonn. 122, 2. *I am now f. resolved*, Gentl. III, 1, 76. *make up f. clear*, Meas. V, 157. *to be f. like me*, Wint. I, 2, 129. *f. expired*, H6B I, 1, 68. *f. complete*, H6C II, 5, 26. *inform her f. of my particular fear*, Lr. I, 4, 360. *the legions are f. weak to undertake these wars*, Cymb. III, 7, 5. *f. bent with sin*, Per. II Prol. 23.

2) to satiety: *when his glutton eye so f. hath fed*, Ven. 399. *I have supped f. with horrors*, Mcb. V, 5, 13.

3) Placed emphatically before adjectives and adverbs: *f. dearly*, H4A V, 1, 84. *f. fast*, Mids. III, 2, 379. *f. gently*, Ven. 361. H6C II, 1, 123. *f. ghastly*, H6B III, 2, 170. *f. hard*, Oth. I, 2, 10. *f. joyous*, Shr. IV, 5, 70. *little*, H8 III, 1, 75. *low*, R2 III, 2, 140. *f. many a*, Sonn. 33, 1. Tp. III, 1, 39. Mids. III, 1, 135. *merrily*, LLL V, 2, 481. Troil. V, 10, 42. *oft*, Pilgr. 339. All's I, 1, 115. *often*, Mids. II, 1, 125. V, 190. H6B III, 1, 367. *pale*, Compl. 5. *poor*, Tp. I, 2, 20. *salt*, 155. *scarce*, H6A I, 1, 112. *sick*, H8 II, 4, 204. *soon*, Lucr. 370. Rom. II, 3, 30. *sorry*,

Ant. I, 1, 59. *suddenly*, Lr. II, 1, 58. *true*, All's I, 3, 65. *warm*, John V, 2, 59 (O. Edd. *f. warm of blood*, M. Edd. *f. of warm blood*). *well*, Wint. IV, 4, 306. H6B III, 1, 358. H6C II, 2, 43.

Full-acorned, having fed to the full on acorns. Cymb. II, 5, 16.

Fullam, a kind of false dice: Wiv. I, 3, 94.

Full-charged, charged or loaded to the full: *I stood in the level of a f. confederacy*, H8 I, 2, 3.

Fuller, one whose trade is to cleanse cloth: H8 I, 2, 33.

Full-fed, fed to fulness: Lucr. 694.

Full-flowing, freely venting its passion: *from a f. stomach*, Lr. V, 3, 74.

Full-fortuned, at the height of prosperity: Ant. IV, 15, 24; cf. Oth. I, 1, 66. Cymb. V, 4, 110.

Full-fraught, see *Fraught.*

Full-gorged, fed to fulness, sated: *till she (the falcon) stoop she must not be f.* Shr. IV, 1, 194.

Full-hearted, full of courage and confidence: Cymb. V, 3, 7.

Full-hot, very fiery: H8 I, 1, 133 (Ff not hyphened).

Full-manned, completely furnished with soldiers: Ant. III, 7, 52.

Full-replete (Ff not hyphened) completely filled: H6A V, 5, 17.

Full-winged, having perfect wings: *the f. eagle*, Cymb. III, 3, 21.

Fully, 1) completely, entirely, thoroughly: *thy history f. unfold*, Meas. I, 1, 30. *to instruct her f. in those sciences*, Shr. II, 57. All's V, 3, 97. Cor. II, 2, 23. Tim. II, 2, 134. *f. sealed up*, H6A I, 1, 130. *f. satisfied*, H8 II, 4, 148. *our hour is f. out*, Ant. IV, 9, 33.

2) so as to be complete or to satisfy: *Nathaniel's coat was not f. made*, Shr. IV, 1, 135. *having f. dined before*, Cor. I, 9, 11. *it will stuff his suspicion more f.* Lr. III, 5, 22.

3) from a full soul, with all one's might: *to oppose his hatred f.* Cor. III, 1, 20. *whose every passion f. strives to make itself admired*, Ant. I, 1, 50.

Fulness, 1) completeness: John II, 440. H6B I, 1, 35.

2) plenty, affluence: *with ample and brim f. of his force*, H5 I, 2, 150. *my plenteous joys, wanton in f.* Mcb. I, 4, 34. *to lapse in f. is sorer than to lie for need*, Cymb. III, 6, 12.

3) satiety: *although to-day thou fill thy hungry eyes even till they wink with f.* Sonn. 56, 6.

Fulsome, 1) disgusting, nauseous: Tw. V, 112. John III, 4, 32. R3 V, 3, 132.*Oth. IV, 1, 37.

2) lustful, wanton: *the f. ewes*, Merch. I, 3, 87.

Fulvia, the wife of Antony: Ant. I, 1, 20 etc. etc.

Fum, interj. expressing disgust: *fie, foh, and f.* Lr. III, 4, 188.

Fumble, 1) intr. to make awkward endeavours to do any thing: *I saw him f. with the sheets*, H5 II, 3, 14. *with a palsy —ing on his gorget*, Troil. I, 3, 174. *thou —st*, Ant. IV, 4, 14.

2) tr. to handle or manage awkwardly: *what dost thou wrap and f. in thine arms?* Tit. IV, 2, 58. *as many farewells ... he —s up into a loose adieu*, Troil. IV, 4, 48.

Fume, subst. 1) vapor: *love is a smoke raised with the f. of sighs*, Rom. I, 1, 196.

2) a delusion, a fantasm, any thing hindering, like a mist, the function of the brain: *the ignorant —s that mantle their clearer reason,* Tp. V, 67. *memory shall be a f., and the receipt of reason a limbeck only,* Mcb. I, 7, 66. *shot at nothing, which the brain makes of —s,* Cymb. IV, 2, 301.

3) a passion which deprives the mind of self-control: *bites the poor flies in his f.* Ven. 316. *her f. needs no spurs,* H6B I, 3, 153.

Fume, vb. 1) to smoke: *that* (smoke) *which from discharged cannon —s,* Lucr. 1043.

2) to be as in a mist, to be dulled and stupefied: *keep his brain —ing,* Ant. II, 1, 24.

3) to be in a rage: *frets call you these? I'll f. with them,* Shr. II, 253.

Fumiter (Qq *femiter,* Ff *fenitar*) the plant Fumaria: Lr. IV, 4, 3.

Fumitory (O. Edd. *femetary*) the same: H5 V, 2, 45.

Function, 1) office, employment, occupation: Meas. I, 2, 14. II, 2, 39. III, 2, 264. As II, 7, 79. Tw. IV, 2, 8. V, 164. Wint. IV, 4, 143. H5 I, 2, 184. III, 7, 41. H6A I, 1, 173. III, 1, 50. H8 I, 1, 45. Cor. IV, 5, 35. IV, 6, 9. Hml. II, 2, 582. Oth. IV, 2, 27. Used of the appropriate action of the organs of the body: Sonn. 113, 3. LLL IV, 3, 332. Mids. III, 2, 177. H8 III, 2, 187. Troil. V, 2, 123. Hml. III, 2, 184. Cymb. V, 5, 258.

2) the operation of the mental faculties: *f. is smothered in surmise,* Mcb. I, 3, 140. *as her appetite shall play the god with his weak f.* Oth. II, 3, 354.

Fundamental, serving for the foundation, essential: *the f. reasons of this war,* All's III, 1, 2. *the f. part of state,* Cor. III, 1, 151.

Funeral, subst. solemn burial, obsequies: Tp. II, 2, 47. Mids. I, 1, 14. John V, 7, 98. H6A I, 1, 82. II, 5, 112. Tit. IV, 2, 163. Caes. III, 1, 230. 233. 249. III, 2, 89. III, 3, 22. Hml. I, 2, 12. 176. IV, 5, 213 (Ff, more properly, *burial*). Ant. V, 2, 367. Per. II, 4, 32. *—s in the* (sense of *f.*: *plead for his —s,* Tit. I, 381. *his —s shall not be in our camp,* Caes. V, 3, 105.

Funeral, adj. pertaining to a solemn burial: H6C II, 5, 117. Tit. I, 176. V, 3, 196. Rom. IV, 5, 85. Caes. III, 1, 245. Hml. I, 2, 180.

Fur, subst. the haired skin of animals: Lr. III, 1, 14.

Fur, vb. to line with haired skins: Troil. II, 2, 38. Partic. *—ed:* Meas. III, 2, 8. 9. H6B IV, 2, 51 (*her —ed pack,* i. e. consisting of fur).* Lr. IV, 6, 169. *—ed moss,* Cymb. IV, 2, 228 (= similar to fur).

Furbish, to rub to brightness, to burnish: R2 I, 3, 76 (Ff *furnish*). Mcb. I, 2, 32.

Furious, enraged, wildly passionate, impetuously valiant (cf. subst. *Fury*): Tw. III, 4, 334. H4A I, 1, 13. H4B I, 1, 126. IV, 3, 42. H5 II, 1, 64. III, 6, 29. H6A IV, 1, 185. H6B II, 1, 34. R3 IV, 4, 169. Tit. II, 1, 75. Rom. III, 1, 126. Mcb. II, 3, 114. Ant. III, 13, 195. Cymb. II, 3, 7. IV, 2, 259.

Furlong, the eighth part of a mile: Tp. I, 1, 69. Wint. I, 2, 95 (in both passages *a thousand —s* opposed to *an acre*).

Furnace, subst. an enclosed fireplace: Ven. 274. Lucr. 799. As II, 7, 148. H8 I, 1, 140.

Furnace, vb. to exhale like a furnace: *he —s the thick sighs from him,* Cymb. I, 6, 66.

Furnace-burning, hot like a furnace: *my f. heart,* H6C II, 1, 80.

Furnish, 1) to supply with what is necessary, to equip, to fit out: *to f. me upon my longing journey,* Gentl. II, 7, 85. *we have two hours to f. us,* Merch. II, 4, 9. *we are not —ed like Bohemia's son,* Wint. IV, 4, 599. R2 I, 4, 46. H4A IV, 1, 97. H8 II, 2, 3. 141. Troil. III, 3, 33. Ant. I, 4, 77. Per. II, 2, 53. Followed by *to: to f. thee to Belmont,* Merch. I, 1, 182. All's II, 3, 307. In a more restricted sense, = to supply with money: Merch. I, 3, 59. H8 III, 2, 328. Tim. III, 1, 20. = to dress: *which* (attire) *is the best to f. me,* Ado III, 1, 103. *he was —ed like a hunter,* As III, 2, 258. *I am not —ed like a beggar,* Epil. 10. *semblably —ed like the king,* H4A V, 3, 21. *ornaments to f. me to-morrow,* Rom. IV, 2, 35 (cf. Merch. II, 4, 9. Troil. III, 3, 33. Per. II, 2, 53). Followed by *with,* = to supply with: *he —ed me with volumes,* Tp. I, 2, 166. II, 2, 146. Meas. III, 2, 221. Err. IV, 1, 34. Merch. II, 4, 32. IV, 1, 157. Shr. II, 349. R2 II, 1, 285. H4B I, 1, 31. H5 II, 2, 87. H6C III, 3, 203. Caes. III, 1, 66. Oth. III, 3, 477. Joined to the adverbs *forth* and *out: lend me a thousand pound to f. me forth,* H4B I, 2, 251. *f. forth the marriage tables,* Hml. I, 2, 181. *to f. out a moderate table,* Tim. III, 4, 116.

2) to endow, to enrich, to improve: *what heaven more will, that thee may f., fall on thy head,* All's I, 1, 78. *he then that is not —ed in this sort doth but usurp the sacred name of knight,* H6A IV, 1, 39. *he may f. and instruct great teachers,* H8 I, 2, 113. Followed by *with:* Tw. III, 4, 255. Cymb. I, 4, 8. I, 6, 16.

Furnishings, dressings, appendages, outward signs: *or something deeper, whereof perchance these are but f.* Lr. III, 1, 29.

Furniture, equipment: *neither art thou the worse for this poor f. and mean array,* Shr. IV, 3, 182 (= dress). *I'ld give bay Curtal and his f.* All's II, 3, 65 (= trappings). *there shalt thou know thy charge, and there receive money and order for their f.* H4A III, 3, 226. *without discharge, money or f.* H6B I, 3, 172. *see the barge be ready, and fit it with such f. as suits the greatness of his person,* H8 II, 1, 99.

Furnival, name in H6A IV, 7, 66 (*Lord F. of Sheffield,* one of the many titles of Talbot).

Furrow, subst. a trench in the earth made by the plough: Tp. IV, 135. Hence a hollow made by wrinkles in the face: Sonn. 22, 3.

Furrow, vb. to make hollows in: *to f. me with age,* R2 I, 3, 229. *the —ed sea,* H5 III Chor. 12.

Furrow-weeds, weeds growing on ploughed land: Lr. IV, 4, 3.

Further, adj. (cf. *Farther,* for which it is often substituted by M. Edd.) 1) more distant, later: *that we adjourn this court till f. day,* H8 II, 4, 232. *they are ready to-morrow, or at f. space, to appear,* Lr. V, 3, 53.

2) beyond this: *my thoughts aim at a f. matter,* H6C IV, 1, 125. *to suppress his f. gait,* Hml. I, 2, 31. *could not endure a f. view,* Ant. III, 10, 18.

3) additional, more, other, new: *this forced league doth force a f. strife,* Lucr. 689. *let's make f. search,* Tp. II, 1, 323. III, 2, 76. Wiv. IV, 2, 221. Meas. IV, 2, 106. Ado III, 2, 115. As III, 5, 97. All's II, 3, 41. II, 4, 54. III, 5, 29. R2 I, 4, 40. III, 3, 112.

H4B IV, 4, 72 (Ff *farther*). H6A V, 3, 16. H6B III, 1, 138. V, 3, 10. H6C III, 1, 111. H8 II, 1, 69. III, 2, 337. V, 1, 104. Cor. II, 2, 31. III, 1, 268. 284. Tit. III, 1, 134. Rom. V, 3, 212. Hml. I, 2, 36. III, 1, 26. III, 2, 346. IV, 1, 33. V, 2, 45 (*without debatement f.*). 70. Lr. I, 1, 306. I, 2, 100. IV, 7, 82. Oth. III, 3, 98. IV, 2, 251. Cymb. I, 5, 44. II, 4, 134. IV, 2, 91. Per. II, 5, 87. *no f.* = nothing else (cf. *No*): *apprehends no f. than this world*, Meas. V, 486. *I have no f. with you*, Cor. II, 3, 181 (= I'll have no more to do with you). *I'll now no f.* III, 3, 87.

Further, adv. 1) at a greater distance: *lie f. off*, Mids. II, 2, 44. 57. *your best friends shall wish I had been f.* Caes. II, 2, 125.

2) to a greater distance: *I can go no f.* Tp. III, 3, 1. Mids. III, 2, 316. 444. As II, 4, 10. II, 6, 1. Tw. II, 3, 43. *go thou f. off*, Lr. IV, 6, 30 (Qq *farther*). *get thee f.* All's V, 2, 15. *as if thou never walk'st f. than Finsbury*, H4A III, 1, 257. *I would have thee gone, and yet no f. than a wanton's bird*, Rom. II, 2, 178 (Qq *farther*). *can fly no f.* H6C I, 4, 40. Caes. V, 3, 9. Metaphorically: *I will go f. than I meant, to pluck all fears out of you*, Meas. IV, 2, 206. H8 I, 2, 69. *if I strayed no f., but chose here*, Merch. II, 7, 25. *lest this affection spread f.* Cor. III, 1, 311 etc.

3) in pursuance of some thing begun: *this way she runs, and now she will no f.* Ven. 905. *hear a little f.* Tp. I, 2, 135. *ere you flout old ends any f.* Ado I, 1, 290. *if I travel but four foot f.* H4A II, 2, 13. *I can read no f.* H6B I, 1, 55. *I urged you f.* Caes. II, 1, 243. *hark f.* Ant. IV, 9, 11. *I will look f. into it* (= I will continue to be on the look-out) Wiv. II, 1, 245. Lr. I, 4, 76. *see f.* = continue to watch her, Cymb. V, 5, 124. 127. *but I'll see f.* Per. IV, 1, 100.

4) a greater space: *his eyeballs f. out than when he lived*, H6B III, 2, 169.

5) greater lengths, to a greater extent: *the sole drift of my purpose doth extend not a frown f.* Tp. V, 30. *let's obey his humour a little f.* Wiv. IV, 2, 210. *I must attempt you f.* Merch. IV, 1, 421. *I will no f. offend you than becomes me for my good*, As I, 1, 84. *I hope I need not to advise you f.* All's III, 5, 27. *I know not how I shall assure you f.* III, 7, 2. *do they charge me f.?* V, 3, 167. *it may awake my bounty f.* Tw. V, 47. *being no f. enemy to you than ....* John II, 243. *f. I will not flatter you... than this*, 516. *and be no f. harmful than in show*, V, 2, 77. *mistake not f. than you should*, R2 III, 3, 15. *so far will I trust you... not an inch f.* H4A II, 3, 117. *question no f. of the case*, H6A II, 1, 72. *can vengeance be pursued f. than death?* Rom. V, 3, 55. *nor construe any f. my neglect*, Caes. I, 2, 45. *which is no f. than the main voice of Denmark goes withal*, Hml. I, 3, 27. *you extend these thoughts of horror f. than you shall find cause*, Ant. V, 2, 63. Lr. I, 5, 2.

6) more: *interrupt the monster one word f.* Tp. III, 2, 77. *we will hear f. of it by your daughter*, Ado II, 3, 213. Wiv. IV, 2, 233. All's I, 3, 133. III, 6, 82. H8 III, 2, 232. Mcb. I, 5, 72. *no f.* = no more: *I will no f. chide you*, Tw. III, 3, 3. *no f. wise than Percy's wife*, H4A II, 3, 110 (Qq *farther*). Wiv. V, 5, 253. Mids. III, 2, 316. H4A V, 1, 44. Cor. III, 2, 8 etc.

7) besides, in addition, again: *for f. I could say 'this man's untrue,'* Compl. 169. *the duke shall both speak of it, and extend to you what f. be-* *comes his greatness*, All's III, 6, 74. *f. I say and f. will maintain*, R2 I, 1, 98. *and shall it in more shame be f. spoken, that ...*, H4A I, 3, 177. *and f. I have learned*, IV, 1, 90. *it is f. agreed between them*, H6B I, 1, 57. *then f. tell me for truth*, H6C III, 3, 119. *as I f. have to understand*, IV, 4, 10.

Further, vb. to promote, to forward: *f. this act of grace*, Ant. II, 2, 149.

Furtherance, a helping forward, assistance: *that may give f. to our expedition*, H5 I, 2, 301. *entreat you to your wonted f.* H6A V, 3, 21. *by your f.* Per. II, 1, 160.

Furtherer, abettor: Tp. V, 73.

Furthermore, moreover, besides: Merch IV, 2, 10. H6B IV, 2, 169. Per. II, 3, 73.

Furthest (cf. *farthest*, for which it has sometimes been substituted by M. Edd.) most distant: Err. I, 1, 133. Ado II, 1, 275. R2 I, 1, 93.

Fury, 1) a goddess of vengeance: Tit. V, 2, 82. Ant. II, 5, 40. *possessed with a F.* Ado I, 1, 193. *is as a F. to torment my soul*, H6C I, 3, 31. Plur. *—ies:* Mids. V, 289. All's V, 3, 261. H4B V, 3, 110. R3 I, 4, 57.

2) a storm of anger, rage: Ven. 318. Tp. V, 26. Mids. IV, 1, 167. Merch. IV, 1, 11. Tw. III, 4, 213. Wint. IV, 4, 482. John V, 2, 127. H6A III, 1, 123. IV, 2, 10. IV, 3, 28. IV, 7, 11. H6B V, 1, 27. H6C I, 4, 23. V, 5, 57. Tim. III, 5, 18. 71 etc. *I understand a f. in your words, but not the words*, Oth. IV, 2, 32. Used of the elements: Lucr. 648. Tp. I, 2, 392. H6B III, 1, 354. H6C II, 5, 8. Plur. *—ies:* H5 IV, 7, 37 (Fluellen's speech).

3) impetuosity: Ven. 554. Lucr. 501. Gentl. IV, 1, 45. Wiv. II, 1, 92. John I, 265. Ant. IV, 6, 9. Cymb, III, 1, 68. V, 5, 8 *the f. spent, anon did this break from her*, Wint. III, 3, 26 (i. e. her violent fit of weeping).

4) madness, frenzy: Err. V, 147. Tim. III, 6, 118.

5) enthusiasm, exaltation of fancy: *spendest thou thy f. on some worthless song?* Sonn. 100, 3. *what zeal, what f. hath inspired thee now?* LLL IV, 3, 229. *a sibyl ... in her prophetic f. sewed the work*, Oth. III, 4, 72.

6) name of a dog: Tp. IV, 258.

Furze (O. Edd. *firrs* and *firzes*), gorse: Tp. I, 1, 71. IV, 180.

Fust, to grow mouldy: Hml. IV, 4, 39.

Fustian, subst. 1) a coarse cotton stuff: Shr. IV, 1, 49.

2) high-sounding nonsense: *discourse f. with one's own shadow*, Oth. II, 3, 282 (or merely nonsense?)

Fustian, adj. high-sounding and at the same time nonsensical: *a f. riddle*, Tw. II, 5, 119. *I cannot endure such a f. rascal*, H4B II, 4, 203 (or merely = nonsensical?).

Fustilarian, a term of reproach: H4B II, 1, 66 (one who goes in fustian?).

Fusty, mouldy: Troil. I, 3, 161. II, 1, 111. Cor. I, 9, 7.

Future, subst. the time to come: All's IV, 2, 63. Tim. II, 2, 157. Mcb. I, 5, 59. Cymb. III, 2, 29. *in f.* Tim. I, 1, 141.

Future, adj. to come: Gentl. I, 1, 50. Meas. II, 2, 95. Wint. V, 1, 32. R2 IV, 138. H6A V, 3, 4. H6B V, 2, 84. H8 III, 2, 422. Lr. I, 1, 45.

Futurity, the time to come: *in f.* Oth. III, 4, 117.

G.

G, the seventh letter of the alphabet: R3 I, 1, 39. 55. 56. 58.

Gabble, subst. inarticulate sounds resembling language: All's IV, 1, 22.

Gabble, vb. to utter inarticulate sounds instead of language: Tp. I, 2, 356. Tw. II, 3, 95.

Gaberdine, a long and loose outer garment: Tp. II, 2, 40. 115. Merch. I, 3, 113.

Gabriel, name of a servant: Shr. IV, 1, 136.

Gad, subst. a sharp point of metal: *and with a g. of steel will write these words,* Tit. IV, 1, 103. *upon the g.* = suddenly: Lr. I, 2, 26 (upon the spur? but cf. this Caes. V, 3, 29).

Gad, vb. to ramble idly: *where have you been —ing?* Rom. IV, 2, 16.

Gadshill, 1) name of a person: H4A I, 2, 118. 143. 182. II, 1, 58. 2) of a place: H4A I, 2, 139.* III, 3, 43. H4B I, 2, 170. II, 4, 333.

Gag, to prevent from speaking by thrusting something into the mouth: Tw. I, 5, 94. V, 384.

Gage, subst. pledge, pawn: R2 I, 1, 69. 146. 161. 174. 176. 186. IV, 25. 46. 83. H5 IV, 1, 223. IV, 7, 127. *there is my g. in g. to thine,* R2 IV, 34. 1, 9. *rest under g.* 86. 105. *lay to g.* = to leave in pawn, Lucr. 1351.

Gage, vb. (cf. *Gauge*) 1) to pledge, to pawn: *one for all, or all for one we g.* Lucr. 144. *a moiety competent was —d by our king,* Hml. I, 1, 91.
2) to engage, to bind: *the great debts wherein my time hath left me —d,* Merch. I, 1, 130. *that men of your nobility and power did g. them both in an unjust behalf,* H4A I, 3, 173. *—ing me to keep an oath,* Troil. V, 1, 46. cf. *Ingaged.*

Gain, subst. profit, any thing advantageous obtained by industry or good fortune: Lucr. 730. Sonn. 42, 9. 141, 13. Pilgr. 220. Gentl. I, 1, 32. LLL I, 1, 67. Shr. II, 331. 332. All's IV, 3, 79. Wint. II, 1, 169. John I, 242. II, 598. H4B I, 1, 183. H6A II, 1, 52. H6C V, 1, 71. V, 7, 20. R3 II, 4, 59. III, 7, 134. IV, 2, 64. V, 3, 267. Cor. I, 1, 22. Tim. V, 1, 225. Lr. II, 4, 79. Oth. I, 3, 29. V, 1, 14 (Qq game). Ant. III, 1, 24. Per. IV, 2, 129. Plur. —s: Merch. III, 1, 59. R2 V, 6, 12. R3 I, 1, 162. Mcb. IV, 1, 40. Synonymous to riches: *with g. so fond,* Lucr. 134. *having no other pleasure of his g.* 860. *Nature lives upon his —s,* Sonn. 67, 12. With an objective genitive: *g. of care,* R2 IV, 197. *to upbraid my g. of it* (the crown) H4B IV, 5, 194. *hopes to find you forward upon his party for the g. thereof* (the crown) R3 III, 2, 47. *double g. of happiness,* IV, 4, 327.

Gain, vb. to obtain or acquire by industry or good fortune; absol. = to profit, to have advantage: *despair to g. doth traffic oft for —ing,* Lucr. 131. All's II, 1, 3. Err. III, 2, 51. Cor. II, 3, 78. Ant. II, 6, 53. Per. IV, 6, 193 (some M. Edd. *g. aught*). Trans.: Lucr. 138. 211. Sonn. 64, 5. 119, 14. Compl. 79. Pilgr. 36. Err. III, 2, 250. 340. Merch. I, 3, 164. II, 7, 5. As I, 1, 14. IV, 1, 26. John III, 4, 137. 141. H5 IV, 1, 192. H6A IV, 6, 36. V, 3, 32. V, 4, 115. H8 I, 2, 170. III, 2, 212. V, 3, 182. Tit. II, 4, 20. Mcb. III, 2, 20. Hml. IV, 4, 18. V, 2, 184. Oth. I, 3,

390. Cymb. I, 1, 33. Per. I, 1, 31. II Prol. 8. II, 1, 110. IV Prol. 8. *to g. my thoughts* (= dispose them favourably) All's V, 3, 183. *our audience,* H4B IV, 1, 76. *a language,* IV, 4, 69 (= learn it). *to g. the inn,* Mcb. III, 3, 7. *the cap of him,* Cymb. III, 3, 25. *his colour,* IV, 2, 167 (= to restore it). With a dat. and accus.: *—ed thy daughter princely liberty,* H6A V, 3, 140.

= to make a gainer, to make victorious: *the foul opinion you had of her pure honour —s or loses your sword or mine,* Cymb. II, 4, 59 (= will be the triumph or perdition of etc.).

Gainer, one who receives advantage: Sonn. 88, 9. Wiv. II, 2, 147.

Gain-giving, misgiving: Hml. V, 2, 226.

Gainsay, 1) to contradict: *you are too great to be by me —d,* H4B I, 1, 91. *what I should say my tears g.* H6C V, 4, 74.
2) to deny: *to g. what they did,* Wint. III, 2, 57. *whosoe'er —s king Edward's right,* H6C IV, 7, 74. *that I g. my deed,* H8 II, 4, 96.
3) to say no, to refuse: *I'll no —ing,* Wint. I, 2, 19.
4) to forbid: *the just gods g. that any drop ... should by my mortal sword be drained,* Troil. IV, 5, 132.

'Gainst, see Additions.

Gait, 1) the manner of walking: *an humble g., calm looks,* Lucr. 1508. *I know her by her g.* Tp. IV, 102. Wiv. III, 3, 68. LLL IV, 3, 185. V, 1, 12. Mids. II, 1, 130. Shr. Ind. 1, 132. II, 261. IV, 2, 65. All's II, 1, 56. Wint. IV, 4, 756. H4A III, 1, 135. H4B II, 3, 23. 28. H6B III, 1, 373. Troil. I, 1, 54. Caes. I, 3, 132. Hml. III, 2, 35. Lr. V, 3, 175. Oth. V, 1, 23. Ant. III, 3, 20. *the manner of his g.* Tw. II, 3, 171. Troil. IV, 5, 14.
2) marching, walking: *the world's comforter, with heavy g., his day's hot talk hath ended,* Ven. 529. *solemn night with slow sad g.* Lucr. 1081. *o'er whom thy fingers walk with gentle g.* Sonn. 128, 11. *strut in his g.* Wiv. I, 4, 31. *the heavy g. of night,* Mids. V, 375. *every fairy take his g.* 423. *address thy g. unto her,* Tw. I, 4, 15. *I will answer you with g. and entrance,* III, 1, 93. *with his lion g.* H5 II, 2, 122. *springs out into fast g.* H8 III, 2, 116. *stay not here thy g.* Tim. V, 4, 73. *go your g.* Lr. IV, 6, 242 (Edgar's speech in the character of a peasant).
3) proceeding: *to suppress his further g. herein,* Hml. I, 2, 31.

Galathe, name of Hector's horse: Troil. V, 5, 20.

Gale, a moderate wind: *auspicious —s,* Tp. V, 314. *happy g.* Shr. I, 2, 48. *a little g.* H6C V, 3, 10. *every g. and vary of their masters,* Lr. II, 2, 85.

Galen, a celebrated physician of antiquity: Wiv. II, 3, 29. III, 1, 67. All's II, 3, 12. H4B I, 2, 133. Cor. II, 1, 128.

Gall, subst. 1) the bile: H4B I, 2, 199. Mcb. I, 5, 49. IV, 1, 27. Oth. IV, 3, 93.
2) an ingredient of ink: Tw. III, 2, 52. Cymb. I, 1, 101.
3) any thing bitter and disagreeable: *thy*

honey turns to g., thy joy to grief, Lucr. 889. Pilgr 270. H6B III, 2, 322. Troil. II, 2, 144. IV, 5, 30. Rom. I, 1, 200. I, 5, 94. Lr. I, 4, 127. cf. Cymb. I, 1, 101.

4) bitterness of mind, rancor: *to tie the g. up in the slanderous tongue,* Meas. III, 2, 199. *thou grievest my g.* LLL V, 2, 237. H5 II, 2, 30. H6A I, 2, 16. H8 I, 1, 152. Troil. I, 3, 193. 237. Hml. II, 2, 605. Lr. I, 4, 292. cf. Tw. III, 2, 52. H4B I, 2, 199. Mcb. I, 5, 49. Oth. IV, 3, 93. The abstr. for the concr.: *out, g.!* Troil. V, 1, 40.

Gall, vb. 1) to hurt by friction, to excoriate: *let the —ed jade wince, our withers are unwrung,* Hml. III, 2, 253. *—ing his kingly hands, haling ropes,* Per. IV, 1, 54.

2) to hurt by touching roughly: *I am loath to g. a new healed wound,* H4B I, 2, 166. *he —s his kibe,* Hml. V, 1, 153.

3) to wear away: *their* (the waves') *ranks began to break upon the —ed shore,* Lucr. 1440. *as doth a —ed rock o'erhang his confounded base,* H5 III, 1, 12.* Used of eyes injured by tears: *reigns in —ed eyes of weeping souls,* R3 IV, 4, 53. *the flushing in her —ed eyes,* Hml. I, 2, 155. cf. *O'ergalled.*

4) to wound or hurt anyhow: *hath he not hit you here? 'a has a little —ed me,* Shr. V, 2, 60. *stand by, or I shall g. you,* John IV, 3, 94. 95. *the huntsman that has —ed him* (the lion) H8 III, 2, 207. *the Bull, being —ed, gave Aries such a knock,* Tit. IV, 3, 71. *the canker —s the infants of the spring,* Hml. I, 3, 39. *if I g. him slightly, it may be death,* IV, 7, 148.

5) to injure, to harass, to annoy: *my state being —ed with my expense,* Wiv. III, 4, 5. *to strike and g. them for what I bid them do,* Meas. I, 3, 36. II, 2, 102. As II, 7, 50. Wint. I, 2, 316. H4A I, 3, 229; cf. H4B I, 2, 258. IV, 1, 89. H5 I, 2, 151. Cor. II, 3, 203. Oth. I, 1, 149. I, 3, 216. II, 1, 98.

6) Intr. with *at,* = to quiz, to scoff: *gleeking and —ing at this gentleman,* H5 V, 1, 78 (Gower's speech).

Gallant, subst. a person of rank and mettle: *all the —s of the town,* Ado III, 4, 101. *our French —s,* H5 IV, 2, 22. *like a g. in the brow of youth,* H6B V, 3, 4. Hence = a spruce fellow, a young blood, mostly used ironically: Tp. I, 2, 413. Wiv. II, 1, 22. III, 2, 1. Ado IV, 1, 319. LLL V, 2, 126. 308. 321. 363. As I, 2, 212. II, 2, 17. Shr. III, 2, 89. IV, 3, 198. R2 V, 3, 15. H6C V, 5, 12. H8 I, 3, 19. Hml. IV, 7, 85. Oth. II, 3, 31. 46. Per. IV, 2, 4. Used as a familiar compellation: *—s, I am not as I have been,* Ado III, 2, 15. H4A II, 4, 306. H6A III, 2, 41.

Gallant, adj. (superl. *—est,* Tit. I, 317) 1) highspirited, chivalrous: Pilgr. 216. LLL V, 1, 128. 133. As I, 2, 242. All's III, 5, 81. IV, 3, 117. 161. John V, 2, 148. H4A I, 1, 52. III, 2, 140. IV, 4, 26. V, 3, 20. H4B III, 2, 68. H5 III, 5, 29. III, 6, 17. 97. III, 7, 102. IV, 2, 15. IV, 7, 11. IV, 8, 89. H6C V, 1, 40. Troil. I, 2, 40. 231. I, 3, 321. III, 3, 161. IV, 5, 183. Tit. IV, 2, 164. Rom. III, 1, 122. III, 5, 114.

2) splendid, fine, noble, beautiful: *our royal, good and g. ship,* Tp. V, 237. *a g. lady,* LLL II, 196; cf. H8 III, 2, 49; Tit. I, 317; 400; Cymb. III, 4, 65; Per. V, 1, 66. *such g. chiding,* Mids. IV, 1, 120. *a g. curtle-axe upon my thigh,* As I, 3, 119. *it is a g. child,* Wint. I, 1, 42. *this g. head of war,* John V, 2,

113. *a g. prize,* H4A I, 1, 75. *make g. show,* Caes. IV, 2, 24. V, 1, 13.

Adverbially: *a lover that kills himself most g. for love,* Mids. I, 2, 25 (Quince's speech).

Gallantly, 1) bravely, nobly: H5 III, 6, 95. Ant. IV, 4, 36. — 2) splendidly, finely: *g. armed,* H4A IV, 1, 105.

Gallantry, a body of gallants: *Hector, Deiphobus, Helenus, Antenor, and all the g. of Troy,* Troil. III, 1, 149.

Gallant-springing (O. Edd. not hyphened) growing up in beauty: R3 I, 4, 227.

Galled, adj. full of gall, rancorous: *some g. goose of Winchester would hiss,* Troil. V, 10, 55.

Gallery, a kind of walk along the floor of a house: Wint. V, 3, 10. H6A II, 3, 37. H8 V, 1, 86. Per. II, 2, 59.

Galley, a flat-built vessel driven with oars, formerly used in the Mediterranean: Shr. II, 381. Tw. III, 3, 26. Oth. I, 2, 40. I, 3, 3. 13. Ant. II, 6, 82. IV, 11, 3.

Gallia, 1) the Latin name of Wales: Wiv. III, 1, 99. 2) of Gaul: H5 I, 2, 216. H6A IV, 7, 48. H6C V, 3, 8. Cymb. I, 6, 201. II, 4, 18. III, 5, 24. III, 7, 4. IV, 2, 333. IV, 3, 24. *in the G. wars,* H5 V, 1, 94 (Pistol's speech).

Gallian, pertaining to Gaul: H6A V, 4, 139. Cymb. I, 6, 66.

Galliard, a nimble and lively dance: Tw. I, 3, 127. 137. 142. H5 I, 2, 252.

Gallias, a large galley: Shr. II, 380.

Gallimaufry, a medley, hotchpotch: Wiv. II, 1, 119. Wint. IV, 4, 335 (used by Pistol and the shepherd's servant).

Gallon, a measure containing four quarts: H4A II, 4, 587.

Gallop, subst., twice used in the phrase *a false g.: what pace is this thy tongue keeps? Not a false g.* Ado III, 4, 99. *this is the very false g. of verses,* As III, 2, 119 (cf. Jaehns' interesting work: Ross und Reiter I, p. 67).*

Gallop, vb. 1) to move by leaps: Mcb. IV, 1, 140. Rom. III, 2, 1.

2) to ride at the pace which is performed by leaps: H5 IV, 7, 89.

3) to move with speed: LLL IV, 3, 187. As III, 2, 329. 344. H6B I, 3, 154. Rom. I. 4, 70. 77.

4) trans. to run through: *the sun ... —s the zodiac in his glistering coach,* Tit. II, 1, 7 (or is it the accus. of measure?).

Gallow, vb. to frighten: *the wrathful skies g. the very wanderers of the dark,* Lr. III, 2, 44.

Galloway nags, common hackneys: H4B II, 4, 205 (Pistol's speech).*

Gallowglasses, heavy-armed foot soldiers of Ireland and the western isles: H6B IV, 9, 26. Mcb. I, 2, 13.

Gallows, 1) a beam on two posts, on which criminals are hanged: Tp. V, 217. Meas. I, 2, 84. Merch. IV, 1, 135. 400. As III, 2, 345. Wint. IV, 3, 28. H4A I, 2, 43. H4B II, 2, 105. IV, 3, 32. H5 III, 6, 44. H6B II, 3, 8. IV, 2, 131. H8 V, 4, 6. Hml. V, 1, 52. 54. 55. Cymb. V, 4, 207. *a fat pair of g.* H4A II, 1, 74. Plur. *g.: shall there be g. standing,* H4A I, 2, 66. *—es:* Cymb. V, 4, 214 (the gaoler's speech).

2) one that deserves to be hanged: *his complexion*

is perfect g. Tp. I, 1, 32. *a shrewd unhappy g.* LLL
V, 2, 12.

Gallows-maker, one whose trade is to build
gallows: Hml. V, 1, 49.

Gallus, name in Ant. V, 1, 69.

Gam, name in H5 IV, 8, 109.

Gambol, subst. a high leap, a caper: Merch.
III, 2, 93. Shr. Ind. 2, 140. Wint. IV, 4, 335. Hml.
V, 1, 209. *g. faculties,* H4B II, 4, 273.

Gambol, vb. to skip, to frisk: Mids. III, 1,
168. *I the matter will reword, which madness would g.
from,* Hml. III, 4, 144.

Game, subst. 1) sport of any kind: *mocking
intended g.* LLL V, 2, 155. *pleasant g.* 360. *as wag-
gish boys in g. themselves forswear,* Mids. I, 1, 240.

2) a match at play: *lost at a g. of tick-tack,*
Meas. I, 2, 196. *seest a g. played home, the rich stake
drawn,* Wint. I, 2, 248. *so thrive it* (foul play) *in your
g.* John IV, 2, 95. *the best cards for the g.* V, 2, 105.
play at subtle —s, Troil. IV, 4, 89. *the bull has the
g.* V, 7, 12. *the g. was ne'er so fair,* Rom. I, 4, 39.
play at that g. Tim. I, 2, 12. *at g.* Hml. III, 3, 91
(Ff *gaming*). *every way makes my g.* Oth. V, 1, 14
(Ff *gain*). *play with him at any g.* Ant. II, 3, 25.

3) amorous sport, gallantry: *daughters of
the g.* Troil. IV, 5, 63. *full of g.* Oth. II, 3, 19. Quibbling: *he knows the g.: how true he keeps the wind,*
H6C III, 2, 14. cf. Troil. V, 7, 12.

4) field sport, the chase: *the gentles are at
their g.* LLL IV, 2, 172. *under the colour of his usual
g.* H6C IV, 5, 11.

5) a solemn contest exhibited to the people
in antiquity: *at the Olympian —s,* H6C II, 3, 53. *the
—s are done,* Caes. I, 2, 178.

6) the animal pursued in the chase: *the
g. is afoot,* H4A I, 3, 278. H5 III, 1, 32. *the g. is
roused,* Cymb. III, 3, 98. *the g. is up,* 107. *that way
goes the g.* Mids. III, 2, 289 (= this it is you aim at).
this way lies the g. H6C V, 5, 14. *follow where the g.
makes way,* Tit. II, 2, 23. *followed the sugared g.
before thee,* Tim. IV, 3, 259. In Wiv. II, 3, 93 O. Edd.
cried game, M. Edd. *cried I aim,* perhaps wrongly,
for the bantering host may well have modified the
common phrase by way of telling Doctor Caius,
"which way his game lay."

Game, vb. (used only in the partic. pres. and
gerund) to play for a stake: Hml. II, 1, 24. 58. III,
3, 91 (Qq *game*).

Gamesome, fond of games, sportive, gay: Shr.
II, 247. Caes. I, 2, 28. Cymb. I, 6, 60.

Gamester, 1) one addicted to play, or one engaged at play: Wiv. III, 1, 37. LLL I, 2, 44. H5 III,
6, 119.

2) a frolicksome fellow, a merry rogue: *now will
I stir this g.* As I, 1, 170. *sirrah young g.* Shr. II, 402.
you are a merry g. H8 I, 4, 45.

3) a prostitute: *was a common g. to the camp,* All's
V, 3, 188. *were you a g. at five?* Per. IV, 6, 81.

Gammon, a smoked ham: *a g. of bacon,* H4A
II, 1, 26.

Gamut (O. Edd. *gamoth* and *gamouth*) the scale
of musical notes: Shr. III, 1, 67. 71. 72. 73.

Gangrened, mortified: Cor. III, 1, 307.

Ganymede, 1) Jove's page: As I, 3, 127. 2) the
name taken by Rosalind: As III, 2, 91. IV, 3, 158.
160. V, 2, 92 etc.

Gaol (O. Edd. now *gaol,* now *jail;* rhyming to
bail: Sonn. 133, 12) a prison: Ven. 362. Sonn. 133,
12. Ado III, 5, 64. 69. Shr. V, 1, 95. 97. 135. H6B
IV, 3, 18. Tim. III, 4, 82. Lr. IV, 6, 272.

Gaoler, the keeper of a prison: Meas. IV, 2, 90.
Err. I, 1, 156. IV, 4, 112. 145. Merch. III, 3, 1. 3.
9. 35. Wint. I, 2, 59. R2 I, 3, 169. Cor. V, 1, 65.
Ant. II, 5, 52. Cymb. I, 1, 73. V, 4, 204. 213.

Gap, 1) an opening, a breach: *when two
authorities are up, how soon confusion may enter 'twixt
the g. of both,* Cor. III, 1, 111.

2) a void: *made a g. in nature,* Ant. II, 2,
223.

3) a passage: *stop this g. of breath with dust,*
John III, 4, 32. *stands in the g. and trade of mo preferments,* H8 V, 1, 36.

4) an interstice, vacuity: *in this wide g. of
time,* Wint. V, 3, 154. Ant. I, 5, 5. Cymb. III, 2, 64.
that wide g. Wint. IV, 1, 7. *stand in the —s to teach
you,* Per. IV, 4, 8.

5) a defect, a flaw: *break a foul g. into the
matter,* Wint. IV, 4, 198. *a g. in our feast,* Mcb. III,
1, 12. *a great g. in your honour,* Lr. I, 2, 91.

Gape, 1) to open the mouth wide: Tp. I,
1, 63. Per. II, 1, 37. *made g. the pine,* Tp. I, 2, 292.
the graves all —ing wide, Mids. V, 387. H4B V, 5,
57. H5 II, 1, 65. *may that ground g. and swallow me,*
H6C I, 1, 161. R3 I, 2, 65. IV, 4, 75. Tit. II, 3, 249.
Hml. I, 2, 245. *a —ing wound,* Merch. III, 2, 268.
H4B II, 4, 212. *mouths* (of cannon) *—ing on Harfleur,*
H5 III Chor. 27.

2) to stare with open mouth, to gaze intently:
a press of —ing faces, Lucr. 1408. John II, 375.
H4A V, 1, 77. *would you grossly g. on,* Oth. III, 3,
395. cf. *Earnest-gaping.*

3) to open the mouth with hope and expectation,
to long for: *young affection —s to be his heir,* Rom.
II Chor. 2. *let gallows g. for dog,* H5 III, 6, 44 (Pistol's speech).

4) to cry with open mouth: *a —ing pig,*
Merch. IV, 1, 47. 54 (according to some, a pig prepared for the table). *leave your —ing,* H8 V, 4, 3.

Gar, Dr. Caius' pronunciation of the word *God:
by g.* Wiv. I, 4, 114. 117. 118. 123. 125 etc. etc.

Garb, form, manner, way, mode of doing
some thing: *he could not speak English in the native g.*
H5 V, 1, 80. *commanding peace even with the same
austerity and g. as he controlled the war,* Cor. IV, 7,
44. *let me comply with you in this g.* Hml. II, 2, 390.
constrains the g. quite from his nature, Lr. II, 2, 103.
abuse him to the Moor in the rank g. Oth. II, 1, 315.

Garbage, offal: Hml. I, 5, 57. Cymb. I, 6, 50.

Garboils, disturbances, commotions: Ant.
I, 3, 61. II, 2, 67.

Garden, a piece of ground planted with herbs,
flowers or fruit-trees, or laid out for pleasure: Ven.
65. Sonn. 16, 6. Meas. IV, 1, 28. 33. Ado V, 1, 182.
LLL I, 1, 250. Shr. IV, 4, 100. Wint. I, 2, 178. IV,
4, 84. 98. R2 III, 4, 1. 43. 57. 73. H5 IV, 7, 103.
H6A I, 6, 6. II, 4, 4. H6B III, 1, 32. IV, 10, 8. 35.
67. R3 III, 4, 34. Hml. I, 2, 135. III, 2, 272. Lr. IV,
6, 200. Oth. I, 3, 323. Ant. III, 5, 17. Cymb. I, 1,
81. *Lombardy, the g. of Italy,* Shr. I, 1, 4. H5 V, 2,
36. Epil. 7.

Garden-door: Tw. III, 1, 103.

Gardener, one whose occupation is to tend a

garden: R2 III, 4, 24. 100. H5 II, 4, 39. H6B IV, 2,
142. Hml. V, 1, 34. Oth. I, 3, 324.

Garden-house, a house standing in a garden, a
summer-house: Meas. V, 212. 229.

Gardiner, name of a well-known prelate: H8 II,
2, 109. 116. 121. IV, 1, 101.*

Gardon, Costard's blunder for *guerdon:* LLL III,
171. 173.

Gargantua, Rabelais' giant: As III, 2, 238.

Gargrave, name in H6A I, 4, 63. 88.

Garish, gaudy, showy: *a g. flag*, R3 IV, 4,
89. *pay no worship to the g. sun*, Rom. III, 2, 25.

Garland, 1) a wreath, chaplet: Gentl. IV,
2, 53. Ado II, 1, 196. 226. 235. Wint. IV, 4, 128.
H4A V, 4, 73. H6C III, 3, 228, R3 IV, 4, 333. H8
IV, 2, 91. Cor. II, 1, 138. Caes. V, 3, 85. Hml. IV,
7, 169. V, 2, 41. Oth. IV, 3, 51. Ant. I, 2, 5. III, 1,
11. Emblem of glory: *call him noble that was now
your hate, him vile that was your g.* Cor. I, 1, 188.
Marcius wears this war's g. I, 9, 60. *he lurched all
swords of the g.* II, 2, 105. *withered is the g. of the
war*, Ant. IV, 15, 64.

2) the crown: *so thou the g. wearest success-
ively*, H4B IV, 5, 202. V, 2, 84. R3 III, 2, 40. 41.

Garlic, the plant Allium sativum: Meas. III,
2, 195. Mids. IV, 2, 43. Wint. IV, 4, 162. H4A III,
1, 162.

Garlic-eater: Cor. IV, 6, 98.

Garment, an article of dress (plur. —*s =*
clothes, dress): Ven. 415. Sonn. 91, 3. Compl. 316.
Tp. I, 2, 24. 164. 218. 474. II, 1, 61. 68. 96. 272. IV,
241. 244. Gentl. IV, 4, 168. Wiv. V, 5, 208. Err.
III, 1, 70. IV, 2, 33. Ado V, 1, 245. Mids. II, 1, 264.
III, 2, 349. Merch. III, 4, 51. As III, 2, 111. IV, 3,
86. Shr. IV, 3, 173. All's I, 2, 62. IV, 1, 50. Tw. V,
282. Wint. IV, 3, 70. IV, 4, 649. 776. V, 2, 53.
John III, 4, 97. H4A I, 2, 202. II, 4, 342. III, 2, 135.
V, 1, 74. H4B V, 2, 44. H5 IV, 3, 26. IV, 8, 55. R3
I, 3, 283. II, 1, 116. H8 I, 1, 93. Cor. II, 3, 154.
III, 1, 180. Mcb. I, 3, 145. Hml. IV, 7, 182. Lr. III,
6, 84. IV, 7, 22 etc. Cymb. II, 3, 138. III, 4, 53 etc.
Per. II, 1, 155. V, 1, 216.

Garner, a granary: Tp. IV, 111. Cor. I, 1,
254.

Garner, vb., to lay up, to treasure: *where
I have —ed up my heart*, Oth. IV, 2, 57.

Garnish, subst. equipment: *in the lovely g. of
a boy*, Merch. II, 6, 45.

Garnish, vb. 1) to deck, to adorn: —*ed
with such bedecking ornaments of praise*, LLL II, 78.
*with taper-light to seek the beauteous eye of heaven to
g.* John IV, 2, 15. —*ed and decked in modest complement*, H5 II, 2, 134.

2) to equip, to supply, to fit out: *a many
fools, that stand in better place, —ed like him*, Merch.
III, 5, 74.

Garret, a room immediately under the roof of a
house: H6B I, 3, 194.

Garrison, subst. a body of troops stationed in a
town or fortified place: H6B III, 1, 117. *our towns
of g.* H6A V, 4, 168.

Garrisoned, 1) manned with troops: *it is already
g.* Hml. IV, 4, 24. 2) stationed: *the legions g. in Gallia*,
Cymb. IV, 2, 333.

Garter, subst. 1) a string or riband by which a
stocking or hose is tied to the leg: Mids. V, 366.

Shr. IV, 1, 94. H5 I, 1, 47. Lr. II, 4, 7. Oth V, 1, 82.

2) the badge of the highest order of English
knighthood: Wiv. V, 5, 70. H4A II, 2, 47 *(—s)*.
H6A IV, 1, 15. 34. R3 IV, 4, 366. 370.

3) name of an inn: Wiv. I, 1, 143. I, 3, 1. II, 1,
100. 187 etc.

Garter, vb. to bind with or as with a garter:
Gentl. II, 1, 83. Shr. III, 2, 69. *why dost thou g. up
thy arms a this fashion? dost make hose of thy sleeves?*
All's II, 3, 265.

Gash, subst. a deep and wide wound: Ven. 1066.
H4A IV, 1, 43. H5 IV, 6, 13. Troil. I, 1, 62. Cor.
II, 1, 171. Mcb. I, 2, 42. III, 4, 27. IV, 3, 40. V, 8,
2. Ant. IV, 8, 11. Per. V, 1, 193.

Gashed, cut deep and wide, yawning: *his g.
stabs*, Mcb. II, 3, 119.

Gaskins, loose breeches: Tw. I, 5, 27.

Gasp, subst. catch of breath; always applied to
the agonies of death: *to the last g.* As II, 3, 70. H6A
I, 2, 127. *at last g.* Cymb. I, 5, 53. *my latter g.* H6A
II, 5, 38. *his latest g.* H6C II, 1, 108. *to the latest g.*
V, 2, 41.

Gasp, vb. to catch breath with labour: Wint.
III, 3, 25. R2 II, 2, 65. H4B I, 1, 208. H6B III, 2,
371. With *out*, trans.: *nor g. out my eloquence*, H5 V,
2, 149.

Gasted, see *Ghasted.*

Gastness, see *Ghastness.*

Gate, a large door which gives entrance into a
city, or a large building, or an enclosed ground: Tp.
I, 2, 130. Meas. IV, 5, 9. Mids. I, 1, 213. John II,
17. H6A III, 2, 1. H6B IV, 8, 24. Tim. V, 1, 200
etc. Err. II, 2, 208. III, 1, 48. 73. LLL I, 1, 109.
II, 172. Mids. I, 2, 36. Merch. I, 2, 147. II, 9, 86.
Tw. I, 5, 107. 125. H6A I, 3, 4 etc. Meas. IV, 1, 30.
H4B I, 1, 5. Lr. IV, 1, 58. *bring me out at g.* Cor.
IV, 1, 47. *met him at g.* Lr. III, 7, 17. —*s of steel*,
Sonn. 65, 8. Troil. III, 3, 121. Plur. for the sing.:
to meet him at the —s, Meas. IV, 3, 136. IV, 4, 6. *the
abbess shuts the —s on us*, Err. V, 156. *at my --s*,
Ado IV, 1, 134. *before we enter his forbidden – s*,
LLL II, 26. *thou (viz Samson) didst excel me in carry-
ing —s*, I, 2, 79. *while we shut the —s upon one wooer*,
Merch. I, 2, 147. *at my —s*, Tw. I, 5, 210. *open the
—s*, H6A I, 3, 4. *these are the city —s*, III, 2, 1. *off
with his head, and set in on York —s*, H6C I, 4, 179.
see him out at —s, Cor. III, 3, 138. 1, 124. *thrust him
out at —s*, Lr. III, 7, 93 (cf. *Door*).

Figurative use: *sings hymns at heaven's g.* Sonn.
29, 12. H6A V, 4, 53. H6C II, 3, 40. Cymb. II, 3,
21. *the g. of hell*, Ado II, 1, 45. *the eastern g.* Mids.
III, 2, 391. H6C II, 1, 21. *to love's alarms it* (my
heart) *will not ope the g.* Ven. 424. *soft pity enters at
an iron g.* Lucr. 595. *stolen from forth thy g.* 1068.
with crystal g. Compl. 286 *(gait?)*. *I'll lock up all the
—s of love*, Ado IV, 1, 106. *eyes shut their coward
—s on atomies*, As III, 5, 13. *his —s of breath*, H4B
IV, 5, 31. *the —s of mercy shall be all shut up*, H5
III, 3, 10. *through the natural —s and alleys of the
body*, Hml. I, 5, 67.

Gather, 1) trans. a) to bring together, to
assemble: *to g. our soldiers scattered*, H6A II, 1,
76. III, 2, 102. IV, 1, 73. H6B IV, 6, 13. H6C II, 1, 112.
they had —ed a wise council to them, H8 II, 4, 51. *to
g. head* = 1) to assemble an army: *the French have
—ed head*, H6A I, 4, 100. H6B IV, 5, 10. Tit. IV, 4, 63.

2) to generate pus or matter, to become ripe: *foul sin —ing head shall break into corruption,* R2 V, 1, 58. H4B III, 1, 76.

b) to collect: *to g. in some debts,* Shr. IV, 4, 25. *among the people g. up a tenth,* H6A V, 5, 93.

c) to pluck: *flowers that are not —ed in their prime,* Ven. 131. Sonn. 124, 4. Merch. V, 13. Tit. III, 1, 113. Lr. IV, 6, 15. Cymb. I, 5, 1.

d) to acquire, to gain: *and I of him will g. patience,* Ado V, 1, 19. *thus may we g. honey from the weed,* H5 IV, 1, 11. *come to g. money for their corn,* H6A III, 2, 5. *g. wealth, I care not with what envy,* H6B IV, 10, 23. *of him I —ed honour,* Cymb. III, 1, 71.

e) to deduce by reasoning, to infer: *g. the sequel by that went before,* Err. I, 1, 96. *the reason that I g. he is mad,* IV, 3, 87. *by this we g. you have tripped since,* Wint. I, 2, 75. H6A II, 3, 69. II, 5, 96. R3 I, 3, 68. Hml. II, 2, 15. III, 1, 35. Lr. IV, 5, 32. Cymb. I, 5, 22.

2) intr. a) to become ripe: *now does my project g. to a head,* Tp. V, 1.

b) to draw inferences, to gain information: *will lead thee on to g. from thee,* All's IV, 1, 91. *now g. and surmise,* Hml. II, 2, 108.

Gaud, see *Gawd.*

Gaudy, disposed and dressed as for a festival; gay and showy: *under whose brim the g. sun would peep,* Ven. 1088. *when his* (love's) *g. banner is displayed,* Lucr. 272. *only herald to the g. spring,* Sonn. 1, 10. *the g. blossoms of your love,* LLL V, 2, 812. *thou g. gold,* Merch. III, 2, 101. *the g., blabbing and remorseful day,* H6B IV, 1, 1. *rich, not g.* Hml. I, 3, 71. *let us have one other g. night,* Ant. III, 13, 183.

Gauge (O. Edd, *gage`,* vb. to measure, to judge of: *you shall not g. me by what we do to-night,* Merch. II, 2, 208.

Gaul, ancient name of France: Wiv. III, 1, 99.

Gaultree (Ff *Gualtree*), name of a forest in Yorkshire: H4B IV, 1, 2.

Gaunt, name of the father of Henry IV: R2 I, 1, 1. I, 2, 22. II, 1, 72 etc. H4A II, 2, 70. V, 1, 45. H4B III, 2, 49. 345. 349. H6A II, 5, 77. H6B II, 2, 14. 22. H6C I, 1, 19. III, 3, 81. 83.

Gaunt, adj. lean, meager: R2 II, 1, 74 (cf. *Arm-gaunt*).

Gauntlet, an iron glove: John V, 2, 156. H4B I, 1, 146. Troil. IV, 5, 177. Lr. IV, 6, 91.

Gawd, any worthless thing giving joy, a bawble, a toy: *rings, —s, conceits,* Mids. I, 1, 33. *as the remembrance of an idle g. which in my childhood I did dote upon,* IV, 1, 172. *for these other —s, I'll pull them off,* Shr. II, 3 (O. Edd. *goods*). *the proud day is all too wanton and too full of —s to give me audience,* John III, 3, 36. *all with one consent praise new-born —s,* Troil. III, 3, 176.

Gawded, in *Nicely-gawded,* q. v.

Gawdy, see *Gaudy.*

Gawsey, name in H4A V, 4, 45. 58.*

Gay, fine, showy: *rich caparisons or trapping g.* Ven. 286. *ere beauty's dead fleece made another g.* Sonn. 68, 8. *so costly g.* 146, 4. *the learned man hath got the lady g.* Pilgr. 225. *g. vestments,* Err. II, 1, 94. *my g. apparel,* R2 III, 3, 149. V, 2, 66. *g. new coats,* H5 IV, 3, 118. *g. ornaments,* H6C III, 2, 149. *never lacked gold and yet went never g.* Oth. II, 1, 151. *to lay his g. comparisons apart,* Ant. III, 13, 26.

Gayness, finery: *our g. and our gilt are all besmirched,* H5 IV, 3, 110.

Gaze, subst. 1) intent regard, look of eagerness or wonder: Ven. 632. Compl. 26. Pilgr. 193. LLL II, 247. Merch. V, 78. Wint. V, 1, 226. H4A III, 2, 78. Troil. IV, 5, 282. Cor. I, 3, 8. Oth. I, 3, 19. Per. IV, 3, 33. *to stand at g.* = to stare: Lucr. 1149.

2) an object eagerly looked on: *the lovely g. where every eye doth dwell,* Sonn. 5, 2. *live to be the show and g. of the time,* Mcb. V, 8, 24.

Gaze, vb. to look intently and eagerly: Lucr. 424. Sonn. 125, 8. Err. III, 2, 57. V, 53. Merch. III, 2, 68. 145. Shr. III, 2, 96. Wint. IV, 4, 110. H5 IV Chor. 27. H6B I, 2, 9 (*g. on*). II, 4, 20. Caes. I, 3, 59. Ant. III, 13, 12. IV, 14, 52. With *against: —ing 'gainst the sun,* H6C II, 1, 92. With *in: —d for tidings in my eyes,* Lucr. 254. *—ing in mine eyes,* Err. V, 243. *in the fountain shall we g. so long,* Tit. III, 1, 127. With *on* or *upon:* Ven. 224. 818. 927. Lucr. 366. 496. 1015. 1355. 1384. 1531. Sonn. 2, 3. 20, 6. 24, 12. Gentl. II, 1, 46. Err. I, 1, 89. I, 2, 13. III, 2, 56. Merch. II, 5, 33. Wint. V, 3, 60. R2 II, 2, 18. H6B I, 2, 6. II, 4, 11. R3 I, 4, 35. III, 7, 26 (Ff *stared*). Tit. V, 1, 21. Rom. II, 2, 30. III, 1, 56. Ant. II, 2, 222. Per. V, 1, 87. 139. Followed by an accus. denoting the result: *g. an eagle blind,* LLL IV, 3, 334. *g. your fill,* Shr. I, 1, 73.

Gazer, one who looks intently: Ven. 748. Sonn. 96, 11. H6B III, 2, 53. H6C III, 2, 187. Per. II, 1, 165.

Gear, 1) stuff: *I'll grow a talker for this g.* Merch. I, 1, 110 (i. e. for what you have said against silent people). *if Fortune be a woman, she's a good wench for this g.* II, 2, 176 (= respecting this article). *Cupid grant all tongue-tied maidens here bed, chamber, Pandar, to provide this g.* Troil. III, 2, 220. *a dram of poison, such soon-speeding g.* Rom. V, 1, 60. And in contempt, = dress: *disguised like Muscovites, in shapeless g.* LLL V, 2, 303.

2) affair, matter, business: *to this g. the sooner the better,* H6B I, 4, 17. *I will remedy this g. ere long,* III, 1, 91. *come, shall we do this g.?* R3 I, 4, 158. *will this g. ne'er be mended?* Troil. I, 1, 6. *come, to this g.* Tit. IV, 3, 52. *here's goodly g.* Rom. II, 4, 107.

Geck, a dupe: *made the most notorious g. and gull,* Tw. V, 351. *to become the g. and scorn o' the other's villany,* Cymb. V, 4, 67.

Geffrey, name of the elder brother of King John, and father of Prince Arthur: John I, 8. II, 99. III, 4, 46 etc.

Geld, (partic. *gelded,* but once *gelt:* Merch. V, 144) 1) to castrate: Meas. II, 1, 242. Merch. V, 144. Wint. II, 1, 147. H6B IV, 2, 174. Per. IV, 6, 133.

2) to deprive of an essential part: *Aquitaine so —ed as it is,* LLL II, 149. *—ing the opposed continent,* H4A III, 1, 110. With *of: to g. a codpiece of a purse,* Wint. IV, 4, 623. *—ed of his patrimony,* R2 II, 1, 237.

Gelding, a castrated horse: Wiv. II, 2, 319. H4A II, 1, 39. 105.

Gem, a precious stone, a jewel: Sonn. 21, 6. Compl. 208. Merch. II, 7, 54. All's V, 3, 196. Tw. II, 4, 88. R3 I, 4, 31. H8 II, 3, 78. Metaphorically: *he is the brooch and g. of all the nation,* Hml. IV, 7, 95. *a g. of women,* Ant. III, 13, 108.

Geminy, a twinned pair: *a g. of baboons,* Wiv. II, 2, 8.

Gender, subst. 1) r a c e, k i n d, s o r t: *and thou treble-dated crow, that thy sable g. makest with the breath thou givest and takest,* Phoen. 18. *the love the general g. bear him,* Hml. IV, 7, 18. *supply it with one g. of herbs,* Oth. I, 3, 326.

2) grammatical distinction of sex: Wiv. IV, 1, 73.

Gender, vb. to b e g e t, to b r e e d: *a cistern for foul toads to knot and g. in,* Oth. IV, 2, 63.

General, adj. 1) not particular or especial, but pertaining to or concerning all: *with one consent and a g. acclamation the Tarquins were exiled,* Lucr. Arg. 25. *the g. doom,* 924. Rom. III, 2, 67. cf. *the g. trumpet,* H6C V, 2, 43; *the g. all-ending day,* R3 III, 1, 78. *all these I better in one g. best,* Sonn. 91, 8 (= best in every respect). *unless this g. evil they maintain,* 121, 13 (badness of all mankind). *g. honour,* Meas. IV, 3, 141 (honour paid by everybody). *he is the g. challenger,* As I, 2, 180. *thou art a g. offence,* All's II, 3, 270. *in a g. voice,* H4B IV, 1, 136. *g. wreck,* H6A I, 1, 135. *a g. peace,* V, 4, 98. *their woes are parcelled, mine are g.* R3 II, 2, 81. *g. applause,* III, 7, 39. *a g. welcome from his grace salutes ye all,* H8 I, 4, 1. *this challenge, however it is spread in g. name, relates in purpose only to Achilles,* Troil. I, 3, 322. *I receive the g. food at first,* Cor. I, 1, 135. *the g. hunting in this forest,* Tit. II, 3, 59. *forgive my g. and exceptless rashness,* Tim. IV, 3, 502 (i. e. the opinion which I rashly formed of all mankind). *a g. shout,* Caes. I, 2, 132. *I drink to the g. joy of the whole table,* Mcb. III, 4, 89. *all you gods, in g. synod,* Hml. II, 2, 516. *never loved Cassio but with such g. warranty of heaven as I might love,* Oth. V, 2, 60 etc. *his attorneys g.* R2 II, 1, 203 (not partially commissioned, but trusted with all his interests). *heir g.* H5 I, 2, 66. *captain g.* Troil. III, 3, 279. *Rome hath sent one g. tongue unto us, this good man,* H8 II, 2, 96 (i. e. speaking in the name of the whole college). *collected for g. sovereignty,* All's I, 3, 230 (excellency in every respect). *whose private with me of the Dauphin's love is much more g. than these lines import,* John IV, 3, 17 (= goes greater lengths, is not so restricted as the contents of the letter). *thou wouldst have plunged thyself in g. riot,* Tim. IV, 3, 256 (wouldst have indulged every vice). *they confess toward thee forgetfulness too g. gross,* V, 1, 147 (thorough forgetfulness; Dyce: *general-gross*). *as broad and g. as the casing air,* Mcb. III, 4, 23 (i. e. as free to go everywhere).

2) o r d i n a r y, c o m m o n: *too g. a vice,* Meas. III, 2, 106. *I knew it the most g. way,* Tim. II, 2, 209.

3) c o l l e c t i v e, w h o l e, a l l: *our g. forces at Bridgenorth shall meet,* H4A III, 2, 178. *all our g. force might with a sally of the very town be buckled with,* H6A IV, 4, 3. *to square the g. sex by Cressid's rule,* Troil. V, 2, 132 (the whole female sex). *the blot and enemy to our g. name,* Tit. II, 3, 183. *a great abatement of kindness appears as well in the g. dependants as in the duke himself,* Lr. I, 4, 65. *if the g. camp had tasted her body,* Oth. III, 3, 345. cf. *the g. world,* LLL II, 11. As II, 7, 69.

4) i n a l l, taken as a w h o l e: *his g. behaviour vain, ridiculous,* LLL V, 1, 13. *commends the plot and the g. course of the action,* H4A II, 3, 23. *whose virtue and whose g. graces speak that which none else can utter,* Ant. II, 2, 132.

5) r e l a t i n g to the p e o p l e or the politic community; c o m m o n, p u b l i c: *he did in the g. bosom reign of young, of old,* Compl. 127. *even so the g. subject to a well-wished king quit their own part,* Meas. II, 4, 27 (M. Edd. *general, subject* etc. cf. *Subject*). *g. ceremony,* H5 IV, 1, 256. *followed with the g. throng,* H8 Prol. 28. *to g. filths convert o' the instant, green virginity,* Tim. IV, 1, 6 (= common prostitutes). *cleave the g. ear with horrid speech,* Hml. II, 2, 589. *never alone did the king sigh, but with a g. groan,* III, 3, 23. *the other half comes to the g. state,* Merch. IV, 1, 371; cf. *concluded by Priam and the g. state of Troy,* Troil. IV, 2, 69; *the g. state can scarce entreat you to be odd with him,* IV, 5, 264. *to gripe the g. sway into your hand,* H4A V, 1, 57. *my brother g., the commonwealth,* H4B IV, 1, 94. *our g. grievances,* 169. *every man ... broke into a g. prophecy,* H8 I, 1, 92 (but this may as well be a prophecy pronounced by everybody). *you will rather show our g. louts how you can frown,* Cor. III, 2, 66. cf. III, 1, 146. V, 3, 6. Tim. IV, 3, 160. *though in g. part we were opposed,* V, 2, 7 (i. e. in politics). *did the g. coffers fill,* Caes. III, 2, 94. *in a g. honest thought and common good to all,* V, 5, 71 (= with true public spirit). *disbursed ten thousand dollars to our g. use,* Mcb. I, 2, 62. *the g. cause, or is it a fee-grief?* IV, 3, 196. *we must emply you against the g. enemy,* Oth. I, 3, 49. *the g. care,* 54. *alike conversant in g. services, and more remarkable in single oppositions,* Cymb. IV, 1, 13.

Adverbially: *should go so g. current,* H4A IV, 1, 5.

General, subst. 1) the w h o l e, the t o t a l, that which comprehends the several parts: *the success, although particular, shall give a scantling of good or bad unto the g.* Troil. I, 3, 342. *in g.* = total, entire, whole: *so are the horses of our enemy in g.* H4A IV, 3, 26 (= all the horses, not only part of them). *these predictions are to the world in g. as to Caesar,* Caes. II, 2, 29. *the greater part, the horse in g., are come with Cassius,* IV, 2, 29 (= the whole horse). cf. *for one's offence why should so many fall, to plague private sin in g.?* Lucr. 1484 (= in all mankind). *'twere better she were kissed in g.* Troil. IV, 5, 21 (= by all). *thou art a grave and noble counsellor, most wise in g.* Per. V, 1, 185 (= in all things).

2) that which is c o m m o n to all: *all our abilities ... severals and — s of grace,* Troil. I, 3, 180.

3) the p e o p l e, the p u b l i c b o d y: *I know no personal cause to spurn at him, but for the g.* Caes. II, 1, 12. *'twas caviare to the g.* Hml. II, 2, 457. Perhaps subst. in Meas. II, 4, 27 (O. Edd. *general subject,* M. Edd. *general, subject*) and H4B IV, 1, 94.

4) the l e a d e r, c h i e f: *the g. of hot desire,* Sonn. 154, 7, *our g.* (viz of a band of outlaws) Gentl. IV, 1, 61. *sole imperator and great g. of trotting paritors,* LLL III, 187. *g. of your woes,* Rom. V, 3, 219. Especially = commander of an army, or of a division of an army: All's III, 3, 1. IV, 1, 89. IV, 3, 144. 145. H4B IV, 1, 27. 141. H5 V Chor. 30. H6A I, 1, 73. IV, 2, 2. V, 2, 8. H6B IV, 2, 118. IV, 4, 13. H6C I, 2, 68. Troil. I, 3, 81. IV, 5, 19. Cor. IV, 1, 23. Caes. IV, 3, 124. Lr. IV, 3, 8 etc. etc.

Generally, not partially or severally, but universally, throughout, with no exception: *g. allowed,* Wiv. II, 2, 236; cf. *g. condemned,* R2 II, 2, 132. *so many giddy offences as he hath g. taxed their whole sex withal,* As III, 2, 367. *you were best to call them* *g.* Mids. I, 2, 2. *to whom we all rest g. beholding,* Shr. I, 2, 274. *to be g. thankful,* All's II, 3, 43. *he that so g. is at all times good must of necessity hold his virtue to you,* I, 1, 8. *they are g. fools and cowards,* H4B IV, 3, 102 (not = in general, usually, but without exception). *his true titles to some certain dukedoms and g. to the crown and seat of France,* H5 I, 1, 88. *this is noted, and g., whoever the king favours, the cardinal instantly will find employment,* H8 II, 1, 47. *how, if he had boils? full, all over, g.* Troil. II, 1, 3. *and g. in all shapes this spirit walks in,* Tim. II, 2, 119.

Generation, 1) the act of begetting, procreation: *the work of g.* Merch. I, 3, 83. *is this the g. of love?* Troil. III, 1, 144.

2) propagation: *heir from heir shall hold this quarrel up whiles England shall have g.* H4B IV, 2, 49. *the gods revenge it upon me and mine to the end of g.* Per. III, 3, 25.

3) one gradation in the scale of genealogical descent: *on him, being but the second g. removed from thy womb,* John II, 181.

4) the people of the same period; an age: *undo a whole g.* Per. IV, 6, 4.

5) progeny, offspring: *to bring false —s,* Wint. II, 1, 148. *these two beget a g. of still-breeding thoughts,* R2 V, 5, 8. *is love a g. of vipers?* Troil. III, 1, 146. *he that makes his g. messes,* Lr. I, 1, 119.

6) race, kind: *our human g.* Tp. III, 3, 33. *ere twice the sun hath made his journal greeting to the under g.* Meas. IV, 3, 93. *thy mother is of my g.* Tim. I, 1, 204.

Generative, probably = produced in the way of procreation, begot: *he is a motion g.* Meas. III, 2, 119 (a puppet born of a female being). cf. Walker's Crit. Exam. I, p. 179, as to the passive use of adjectives in *ive*.

Generosity, nobility, the order of nobles: *to break the heart of g.* Cor. I, 1, 215.

Generous, 1) noble, of noble birth: *the g. and gravest citizens,* Meas. IV, 6, 13. *most g. sir,* LLL V, 1, 96. *of a most select and g. chief in that,* Hml. I, 3, 74. *the g. islanders by you invited,* Oth. III, 3, 280.

2) noble-minded, magnanimous, honorable: LLL V, 2, 632. Tw. I, 5, 98. Troil. II, 2, 155. Hml. IV, 7, 136. V, 2, 253. Lr. I, 2, 8.

Genitive case, the second case in declension: Wiv. IV, 1, 59. 61. 63.

Genius, 1) a good or evil spirit supposed to direct the actions of man: *the strongest suggestion our worser genius can,* Tp. IV, 1, 27. *one of these men is g. to the other,* Err. V, 332. *his very g. hath taken the infection of the device,* Tw. III, 4, 142. *the g. so cries 'come' to him that instantly must die,* Troil. IV, 4, 52. *the g. and the mortal instruments are then in council,* Caes. II, 1, 66.*under him my g. is rebuked,* Mcb. III, 1, 56 (cf. Ant. II, 3, 19).

2) a spirit embodied, a bodily representation of something incorporeal: *a' was the very g. of famine,* H4B III, 2, 337.

Gennet, see *Jennet.*

Genoa (O. Edd. *Genowa* in Merch., *Genoa* in Shr.), town in Italy: Merch. III, 1, 84. 103. 112. 113. Shr. IV, 4, 4.

Gentile, a pagan: *a g. and no Jew,* Merch. II, 6, 51 (quibbling with *gentile.* Q2 F1 *gentle*).

Gentility, 1) good extraction: *mines my g. with my education,* As I, 1, 22.

2) good manners, politeness: *a dangerous law against g.* LLL I, 1, 129 (Q1 *gentlety*).

Gentle, adj. (compar. *—r:* Shr. I, 1, 60. Wint. IV, 4, 93. H5 III, 6, 119. IV, 5, 15. H6A III, 2, 135. V, 4, 8. Cor. III, 1, 55. Rom. III, 3, 10. Oth. IV, 3, 11. Superl. *—st:* Per. III, 3, 37). 1) well born, well descended, noble: *should tyrant folly lurk in g. breasts,* Lucr. 851. *our parents' noble names, in whose success we are g.* Wint. I, 2, 394. *we marry a —r scion to the wildest stock,* IV, 4, 93. *mean and g. all,* H5 IV Chor. 45. *a slave, no —r than my dog,* IV, 5, 15. *to boast of g. blood,* H6A IV, 1, 44. *I am descended of a —r blood,* V, 4, 8. *there's many a g. person made a Jack,* R3 I, 3, 73. *he was g., but unfortunate,* Cymb. IV, 2, 39. *came of a g. kind,* Per. V, 1, 68.

2) amiable, lovely, full of endearing qualities: *the g. lark mounts up on high,* Ven. 853. *what thinkest thou of the g.* Proteus? Gentl. I, 2, 14. *whom your g. daughter hates,* III, 1, 14. *she is pretty, and honest, and g.* Wiv. I, 4, 149. *I hope it some pardon for the most g. Claudio,* Meas. IV, 2, 75. *let me bail these g. three,* V, 362. *the g. day,* Ado V, 3, 25. *he's g.* As I, 1, 172. *I love the g. Desdemona,* Oth. I, 2, 25 etc. Very often in compellations, = good, dear, sweet: *I thank you, g. servant,* Gentl. II, 1, 114. *have patience, g. Julia,* II, 2, 1. II, 4, 136. II, 7, 1. 42. IV, 2, 19. IV, 4, 178. V, 4, 12. Wiv. I, 3, 313. Meas. I, 4, 7. II, 2, 143. II, 4, 139. V, 433. Err. III, 2, 25 etc. etc.

Substantively: *g. and fair,* Meas. I, 4, 24. *be merry, g.* Wint. IV, 4, 46. *g., hear me,* Ant. IV, 15, 47.

3) kind: *the rough beast that knows no g. right,* Lucr. 545. *let beasts bear g. minds,* 1148. *giving g. doom,* Sonn. 145, 7. 41, 5. Tp. I, 2, 468. III, 1, 8. Epil. 11. Gent. III, 1, 31. V, 4, 55. Meas. II, 2, 89. Err. III, 1, 110. III, 2, 165. IV, 4, 158. LLL V, 2, 632. As I, 1, 48. Shr. I, 1, 60. II, 244. IV, 3, 71. Tw. IV, 2, 37. John IV, 3, 13. H5 III, 6, 119. H6A III, 2, 135. Cor. III, 1, 55. Rom. III, 3, 10. Mcb. IV, 3, 231. Oth. IV, 1, 204. IV, 3, 11. Ant. V, 2, 58 etc. With *to:* *be g. to her,* Ant. V, 2, 68.

4) soft, tender, meek, bland, opposed to wild, rough and harsh: *whose g. wind shall cool the heat,* Ven. 189; cf. Lucr. 549. H6C II, 6, 21. Per. III, 3, 37. *a g. flood,* Lucr. 1118; cf. Gent. II, 7, 25. 34. H4A I, 3, 98. *it droppeth as the g. rain from heaven,* Merch. IV, 1, 185. *he trots with g. majesty,* Ven. 278; cf. *with g. gait,* Sonn. 128, 11. *a g. kiss,* Gentl. II, 7, 29. *touching but my g. vessel's side,* Merch. I, 1, 32. *conducted to a g. bath,* Cor. I, 6, 63. *you would not use a g. lady so,* Mids. III, 2, 152. *will you tear impatient answers from my g. tongue,* 287. *as g. and as jocund as to jest go I to fight,* R2 I, 3, 95 (= meek, tranquil). *the g. Archbishop of York is up,* H4B I, 1, 189 (= meek, peaceable).

5) not violent, harmless: *it is no g. chase,* Ven. 883. *a g. riddance,* Merch. II, 7, 78. *to g. exercise and proof of arms,* H4A V, 2, 55. *with g. travail,* H8 V, 1, 71. Hence = tame: *she was old and g.* H5 III, 7, 55. *to make them g.* H8 V, 3, 22. *the air nimbly and sweetly recommends itself unto our g. senses,* Mcb. I, 6, 3 (our senses which become gentle and kind by its influence. See Prolepsis in Appendix).

Adverbial use: *as g. tell me,* Troil. IV, 5, 287

G   471

(Q *but g.*). *every time --r than other*, Caes. I, 2, 230.
how calm and g. I proceeded, Ant. V, 1, 75.

Gentle, subst. (cf. adj. def. 2) in the plur. —*s*,
= gentlefolks, gentlemen, persons of good birth: *the
—s are at their game*, LLL IV, 2, 172. Mostly used
as a familiar compellation: Wiv. III, 2, 92. LLL II,
225. Shr. III, 2, 95. Especially in addressing an
audience: Mids. V, 128. 436. H5 Prol. 8. II Chor. 35.

Gentle, vb. to **ennoble**: *be he ne'er so vile,
this day shall g. his condition*, H5 IV, 3, 63.

Gentle-aged, writing of some M. Edd. in Tit.
III, 1, 23; O. Edd. not hyphened.

Gentlefolks, persons of good family: R3 I, 1, 95.

Gentle-hearted, kind-hearted: H6C I, 4, 176.

Gentle-kind, kind, courteous (cf. *Mankind*):
their manners are more g. Tp. III, 3, 32 (O. Edd. not
hyphened).

Gentleman, 1) a man of birth, though not
a nobleman: *a g. and well derived*, Gent. V, 4, 146.
some of us are gentlemen, IV, 1, 44. *a g. born*, Wiv.
I, 1, 8. 286. Merch. III, 2, 258. Wint. I, 2, 391. H5
IV, 7, 141. 144. H6A II, 4, 27. H6B III, 2, 10. R3
I, 3, 72. Lr. III, 4, 148. Cymb. IV, 2, 338 (cf. III, 7,
7) etc.

2) a man of honour and good breeding:
'tis an ill office for a g. Gent. III, 2, 40. *thou art a g.,
valiant, wise, remorseful, well accomplished*, IV, 3, 11.
Wiv. II, 1, 200. II, 2, 264. IV, 6, 4; cf. LLL I, 1,
236 and R2 III, 3, 120. Ado III, 3, 135. LLL III,
1, 100. Merch. III, 4, 6. H6A III, 2, 70. Cor. I, 6,
42. Hml. III, 1, 11. IV, 5, 148 etc.

3) any man, by way of complaisance: Tp. II,
1, 173. 182. Gent. I, 2, 4. I, 3, 40. II, 4, 55. 74. III,
1, 107. 121. III, 2, 95. Mids. I, 1, 43, III, 1, 167.
John II, 573. R2 III, 1, 9. H6B IV, 1, 19. Tim. III,
1, 11. Lr. I, 1, 25. Oth. IV, 2, 95 etc. Serving as a
compellation, a) in the sing.: *your name, honest g.?*
Mids. III, 1, 187. *g., wear this for me*, As I, 2, 257.
260. Tw. V, 199. Cor. I, 5, 23. Rom. II, 2, 100.
Tim. I, 1, 163. Oth. I, 3, 308. b) oftener in the plur.:
Gent. II, 4, 33. 47. IV, 2, 86. Wiv. I, 1, 193. IV, 2,
206. Mids. III, 2, 299. R3 I, 2, 55 etc.

4) attendant of a person of rank: *the
count's g.* Tw. V, 183. 186. 284. H8 I, 2, 5. 125. Tim.
I, 1, 142. Lr. I, 3, 1. II, 2, 156. *gentlemen of the shade*,
H4A I, 2, 29.

5) a subordinate officer in the army: *gentlemen of companies*, H4A IV, 2, 26. *I am a g. of a
company*, H5 IV, 1, 39.

Gentleman-like, like or becoming a man of
birth and breeding: Gent. IV, 4, 19. Mids. I, 2, 90. As
I, 1, 73. Wint. V, 2, 156. Rom. II, 4, 190.

Gentleness, mild temper, kindness: Tp. I, 2,
165. II, 1, 137. LLL V, 2, 745. Mids. II, 2, 132.
Merch. IV, 1, 25. As II, 7, 102. 103. 118. 124. Tw.
II, 1, 45. III, 4, 123. H8 II, 4, 137. Troil. I, 2, 276.
IV, 1, 20. Tit. I, 237. Caes. I, 2, 33. Lr. I, 4, 364.

Gentle-sleeping (O. Edd. not hyphened): R3
I, 3, 288.

Gentlety, reading of Q1 in LLL I, 1, 129; Ff
gentility, q. v.

Gentlewoman, 1) a woman of good family: Wiv. III, 4, 45. R3 I, 1, 82. Hml. V, 1, 27.
Cymb. II, 3, 83.

2) any female person, lady: Gent. IV, 2, 74. IV,
4, 41. 146. 185. Wiv. I, 1, 63. I, 4, 87. II, 2, 198.

Meas. II, 3, 10. III, 1, 227. V, 282. Err. II, 2, 162.
V, 373. Shr. Ind. 1, 85. 132. I, 2, 87. IV, 3, 70. IV,
5, 29. 62. All's I, 1, 19. 42. I, 3, 2. IV, 3, 17. IV,
5, 9. H4B II, 2, 169. II, 4, 328. 354. V, 5, 137. H5
II, 1, 35. V, 2, 211. Rom. II, 4, 177. 180. Used in
compellations; a) sing.: Gentl. IV, 4, 113. Wint. II,
2, 20. H4B II, 4, 377. Rom. II, 4, 116. 121. Lr. I,
4, 257. b) plur.: Ado V, 4, 10.

3) a female attendant of a lady of high rank:
Ado II, 3, 223. III, 3, 154. As II, 2, 10. All's I, 3,
72. 103. Tw. I, 5, 172. H8 III, 2, 94. Oth. III, 1, 26.
Ant. II, 2, 211.

Gently, 1) mildly, kindly, tenderly: *the
tiger would be tame and g. hear him*, Ven. 1096.
speak you so g.? As II, 7, 106. Tw. III, 4, 106. 123.
Wint. IV, 4, 825. John V, 2, 76. R2 II, 2, 71. H4A
V, 2, 37. H4B II, 4, 106. H5 Prol. 34. H6C II, 1,
123. II, 6, 45. R3 II, 2, 119. Tit. V, 3, 138. Tim.
I, 2, 207. Ant. II, 2, 20. Per. III, 1, 5.

2) without reluctance, willingly: *and do my
spiriting g.* Tp. I, 2, 298. *the castle is g. rendered*,
Mcb. V, 7, 24.

3) softly: *full g. now she takes him by the hand*,
Ven. 361. *when thou g. swayest the wiry concord*, Sonn.
128, 3. Mids. I, 2, 85. IV, 1, 48. Merch. V, 2. Shr.
Ind. 1, 46. R2 I, 1, 79. H6A V, 3, 49. H6C II, 1, 132.
H8 IV, 2, 31. Caes. IV, 2, 31. Hml. III, 2, 6. Ant. V,
2, 297.

Gentry, 1) rank by birth: *she conjures him
by knighthood, g.* Lucr. 569. *thou shouldst not alter
the article of thy g.* Wiv. II, 1, 53. *which no less adorns
our g. than our parents' noble names*, Wint. I, 2, 393.
exempt from ancient g. H6A III, 4, 93. *g., title, wisdom*,
Cor. III, 1, 144.

2) the class of gentlemen, the people of
good birth and breeding: All's I, 2, 16. John V, 2, 31.
H8 I, 1, 76. Cor. II, 1, 254. Mcb. V, 2, 9. Cymb. III,
7, 7. V, 1, 18. V, 2, 8.

3) courtesy: *to show us so much g. and good
will*, Hml. II, 2, 22. *he is the card and calendar of g.*
V, 2, 114.

George, 1) *Saint G.*, the patron saint of England:
LLL V, 2, 620. Shr. II, 237. H5 V, 2, 220. *swinged
the dragon*, John II, 288. His name a war-cry: *mine
innocency and Saint G. to thrive*, R2 I, 3, 84. *cry
'Saint G.'* H6C II, 2, 80. R3 V, 3, 301. 349. *England
and Saint G.* H5 III, 1, 34. *God and Saint G.* H6A
IV, 2, 55. H6C II, 1, 204. IV, 2, 29. R3 V, 3, 270.
Saint G. and victory, H6A IV, 6, 1. H6C V, 1, 113.
our great Saint —'s feast, H6A I, 1, 154. *Saint —'s
field* (a field near London): H4B III, 2, 207. H6B V,
1, 46. *the noble order of Saint G.* H6A IV, 7, 68.

2) the figure of the Saint on horseback worn by
knights of the garter: *look on my G.* H6B IV, 1, 29.
by my G. R3 IV, 4, 366. 369.

3) Christian name of several persons; a) of the
duke of Clarence: H6C I, 4, 74. II, 1, 138. 143. II,
6, 104. R3 I, 1, 46 etc. b) of the son of Lord Stanley
R3 IV, 4, 497. IV, 5, 3 etc. c) of Mr. Page: Wiv. II,
1, 153. V, 5, 213. d) of one Seacole: Ado III, 3, 11.
e) of one Barnes: H4B III, 2, 22. d) of an imagined
person: John I, 186.

Gerard, name in All's I, 1, 30. 42. II, 1, 104.

German, subst. a native of Germany: Wiv. IV
3, 1. IV, 5, 73. Ado III, 2, 35. Merch. I, 2, 90. All's
IV, 1, 78. H6C IV, 8, 2. Oth. II, 3, 80.

German, adj. pertaining to Germany: Wiv. IV, 5, 70. H5 I, 2, 48. *like a G. clock, still a repairing,* LLL III, 192. *the G. hunting in water-work,* H4B II, 1, 157. *a full acorned boar, a G. one,* Cymb. II, 5, 16 (O. Edd. *Jarmen*).

German, adj. akin: *those that are g. to him,* Wint. IV, 4, 802. *g. to the lion,* Tim. IV, 3, 344. *the phrase would be more g. to the matter,* Hml. V, 2, 165 (cf. *Cousin-german*).

Germane, subst. a near relation: *you'll have coursers for cousins and gennets for —s,* Oth. I, 1, 114.

Germany, the country of the Germans: Wiv. IV, 5, 89 (*Jamany* is Dr. Caius' pronunciation). Merch. I, 2, 81. John I, 100. H5 I, 2, 44. 53. H8 V, 3, 30. Lr. IV, 7, 91.

Germens (O. Edd. *germains*), germs, seeds: Mcb. IV, 1, 59. Lr. III, 2, 8.

Gertrude, name of the queen in Hml. II, 2, 54. III, 1, 28. IV, 1, 6. 28. 38. IV, 5, 77 etc.

Gest, a stage for rest in a progress, a limited place and time of staying (Fr. *giste, gîte*): *I'll give him my commission to let him there a month behind the g. prefixed for his parting,* Wint. I, 2, 41.

Gests, deeds, exploits; only by conjecture in Ant. IV, 8, 2; O. Edd. *guests.*

Gesture, action or motion of the body expressive of sentiment: Tp. III, 3, 37. As V, 2, 69. Wint. V, 2, 15. H5 IV Chor. 25. Tim. I, 1, 33. Hml. IV, 5, 11. Oth. IV, 1, 88. 103. 142.

Get (impf. *got; gat* in Per. II, 2, 6 on account of the rhyme. Partic. *got; gotten* in Wiv. I, 3, 25. R2 V, 5, 74. H6B IV, 4, 49. H6C III, 3, 90. IV, 7, 88). A) trans. 1) to obtain; to receive, to come by: *where Cupid got new fire,* Sonn. 153, 14. *what he —s more of her than sharp words,* Wiv. II, 1, 190. Err. IV, 3, 13. LLL IV, 1, 138. Mids. III, 2, 78. Merch. II, 2, 99. V, 224. R2 V, 5, 74. Cor. II, 2, 74. Cymb. IV, 2, 236. Per. I, 1, 168 etc. *To have got =* to have: *who hath got an ague,* Tp. II, 2, 68 (Stephano's speech). *ye 've got a humour there does not become a man,* Tim. I, 2, 26. (Troil. II, 3, 252 Q *gat,* Ff *got*).

2) to gain, to win, to acquire: *sells eternity to g. a toy,* Lucr. 214. *every alien pen hath got my use,* Sonn. 78, 3. *what a mansion have those vices got,* 95, 9. *the learned man hath got the lady,* Pilgr. 225. *as thou got'st Milan,* Tp. II, 1, 291. III, 2, 60. IV, 89. Epil. 6. Gentl. IV, 1, 75. Wiv. III, 4, 1. V, 5, 224. Meas. I, 2, 150; cf. Err. III, 1, 106. Err. I, 2, 34. III, 2, 70. Ado I, 1, 65. II, 1, 18. LLL IV, 3, 369 (*g. the sun of them*). Merch. II, 3, 12 (Qq and F1 *and do not g. thee;* F2.3.4 *and M.* Edd. *and get thee*). H6A V, 3, 12; cf. H6C I, 4, 1. H6A III, 2, 79. 84. H6B I, 1, 84. 121. III, 2, 70. IV, 4, 49. H6C I, 1, 132. III, 3, 90. IV, 7, 88. Troil. I, 2, 317 (*love got*). Cor. III, 3, 4; cf. Ant. IV, 14, 98 (followed by *on*). Caes. I, 2, 130 (*get the start of*). II, 1, 326 (*g. the better of*). Mcb. III, 2, 5. Hml. V, 2, 198. Ant. IV, 8, 22 (*get goal for goal of youth*). Absol.: R2 III, 3, 201. H6A IV, 3, 32. H8 IV, 2, 55.

3) to earn by labour: *you should g. your living by reckoning,* LLL V, 2, 497. *pleased with what he —s,* As II, 5, 43. *g. that I wear,* III, 2, 78. Absol.: *none of his own —ing,* As III, 3, 56. *is it a shame to g. when we are old?* Per. IV, 2, 32.

4) to procure: *did his picture g.* Compl. 134; cf. Ado II, 3, 273. *g. a new man,* Tp. II, 2, 189. *I*

must g. a sconce for my head, Err. II, 2, 37. Merch. III, 2, 197. H4B I, 1, 214. Troil. III, 2, 62. Mcb. II, 2, 46. Oth. I, 1, 167. 180. With a dative: *g. thee wood enough,* Tp. II, 2, 165. 175. *I'll g. you such a ladder,* Gent. III, 1, 126. Err. III, 1, 45. Merch. III, 2, 198. Ant. I, 5, 76. *I'll g. me one,* Gent. III, 1, 133. IV, 4, 196. Ado II, 1, 20. III, 4, 73. V, 4, 124. Tw. IV, 1, 23. H6B IV, 2, 1.

5) to lay hold on, to seize: *where he the lamb may g.* Lucr. 878. *I'll potch at him some way or wrath or craft may g. him,* Cor. I, 10, 16. *the plebeians have got your fellow tribune and hale him,* V, 4, 39. *every puny whipster — s my sword,* Oth. V, 2, 244.

6) to learn, to hear, to be informed of what was kept secret: *thou shalt never g. such a secret from me,* Gent. II, 5, 40. *from whose simplicity I think it not uneasy to g. the cause of my son's resort thither,* Wint. IV, 2, 56. *g. from him why he puts on this confusion,* Hml. III, 1, 2. *where the dead body is bestowed, we cannot g. from him,* IV, 3, 13. *which yet from her by no means can I g.* Per. II, 5, 6.

7) to beget, to procreate: Sonn. 7, 14. Tp. I, 2, 319 (with *upon*). Wiv. I, 3, 25. Meas. II, 3, 13. III, 2, 125. Ado II, 1, 337. V, 4, 50. Merch. III, 5, 12. Shr. II, 412. All's I, 1, 140. II, 3, 101. III, 2, 44. IV, 2, 10. Wint. II, 3, 105. III, 3, 76. John I, 108. 237. 259 (*were I to g. again =* to be got). H4B II, 2, 12. IV, 3, 101. H6C II, 2, 133. R3 III, 7, 10. 190. H8 II, 3, 44 (used of a woman). Troil. II, 3, 252. Tit. IV, 2, 90. Mcb. I, 3, 67. Lr. I, 2, 15. II, 1, 80. III, 4, 151. IV, 6, 118. Ant. III, 13, 107. Per. II, 2, 6 etc. Absol.: *to g. it is thy duty,* Ven. 168. *one of your father's —ing,* Ado II, 1, 336.

8) to cause, to make: *our youth got me to play the woman's part,* Gent. IV, 4, 165. *g. the learned writer to set down our excommunication,* Ado III, 5, 68. Mids. IV, 1, 220. Shr. I, 2, 38. Tw. III, 4, 131. H6A I, 4, 25. Lr. III, 7, 103. The inf. without *to: they could never g. her so much as sip on a cup,* Wiv. II, 2, 76 (Mrs Quickly's speech).

9) to work or procure to be or go or come: *once did I g. him bound,* Err. V, 145. *we must g. her ravished,* Per. IV, 6, 5. *g. this done,* IV, 2, 66. *to g. our stuff aboard,* Err. IV, 4, 162. *g. your weapons in your hand,* Mids. IV, 1, 10. *g. your apparel together,* IV, 2, 35; cf. As I, 3, 136. *g. it ready,* Lr. I, 4, 8. *to g. on =* to put on: *g. on thy boots,* H4B V, 3, 136. *g. on your cloak,* Tim. II, 1, 15. Mcb. II, 2, 70. *to g. with child,* see *Child. I'll g. them all three all ready,* Tw. III, 1, 102 (= learn by heart; Sir Andrew's speech). *to g. my palfrey from the mare,* Ven. 384. *your commendations g. from her tears,* All's I, 3, 53. *I could ne'er g. him from it,* Tim. III, 1, 30. *g. me hither paper,* Lucr. 1289. *if you thus g. my wife into corners,* Merch. III, 5, 32. *g. me a taper in my study,* Caes. II, 1, 7. *g. thyself in flesh,* Rom. V, 1, 84. *to g. myself into more work,* Caes. I, 1, 34. *when the fox hath once got in his nose,* H6C IV, 7, 25. *g. him to bed,* Tw. V, 214. *the —ing up of the negro's belly,* Merch. III, 5, 41.

Most frequent is the reflective use (never with the full reflective pronouns *myself* etc.) in the sense of to betake one's self, to go: *go g. thee hence,* Gent. IV, 4, 64. R3 IV, 1, 39. *g. you home,* Wiv. II, 1, 158. Err. III, 1, 114. *g. thee away,* I, 2, 16. *g. thee from the door,* III, 1, 33. As I, 3, 44. H6A III, 2, 71. *g. you in,* Err. III, 2, 25. As I, 1, 81. Shr. I, 1, 75. *g.*

thee further, All's V, 2, 15. *g. you on,* Tw. III, 4, 270.
—s him to rest, H5 IV, 1, 287. *I'll g. me to a place
more void,* Caes. II, 4, 37. Ado II, 1, 47. III, 3, 45.
III, 5, 62. H6B III, 2, 8. *g. you with him,* As I, 1, 86
etc. As frequent is the phrase *g. thee gone, g. you
gone:* Gent. III, 1, 101. Meas. II, 1, 216. Err. IV, 1,
19. Mids. II, 1, 194. III, 2, 318. Merch. III, 4, 55. IV,
1, 397 etc. *And go g. thee gone* (cf. *Go*): Gent. I, 2,
100. Err. III, 1, 84 etc. etc.

B) Intr. 1) to make one's way, to go, to come:
from earth's dark womb some gentle gust doth g. Lucr.
549. *g. to Naples,* Tp. II, 2, 71. *g. aboard,* Wint. III,
3, 7. IV, 4, 669. *g. before him to the king,* R2 V, 2,
112. *we shall to London g.* H6B V, 2, 81. *the air
hath got into my wounds,* H6C II, 6, 27. *g. higher on
that hill,* Caes. V, 3, 20. *if I g. down,* John IV, 3, 6.
we cannot g. in, Err. III, 1, 69. H8 V, 4, 17. 18. *more
likely to fall in than to g. o'er,* H4B I, 1, 171. *g. off,*
Cor. II, 1, 141. *how got she out?* Oth. I, 1, 170. *to g.
out of this wood,* Mids. III, 1, 153. *to g. up* = to
mount, H4B II, 1, 85. = to sit no longer, but get on
one's legs: H8 V, 4, 93. *some g. within him,* Err. V, 34
(= close with him, seize him so as to prevent him
from using his sword).

2) to become, to come to be; only in the
phrase *to g. clear* = to get rid, to be delivered: *to g.
clear of all the debts,* Merch. I, 1, 134. *they got clear
of our ship,* Hml. IV, 6, 19.

Getter, begetter: Cor. IV, 5, 240.

Ghasted (O. Edd. *gasted*) frightened: *g. by the
noise I made,* Lr. II, 1, 57.

Ghastly, ghostlike, dismal, horrible: *some g.
sprite,* Lucr. 451. *g. shadows,* 971. *in g. night,* Sonn.
27, 11. *this g. looking,* Tp. II, 1, 309. R3 III, 5, 8. *g ,
gaping wounds,* H4B II, 4, 212 (Pistol's speech). *g.
dreams,* R3 I, 4, 3 (Ff *fearful*). *g. women,* Caes. I, 3, 23.
Adverbially: *staring full g. like a strangled man,*
H6B III, 2, 170.

Ghastness, ghastliness, haggard look: *do you
perceive the g. of her eye?* Oth. V, 1, 106 (Qq *gestures*).

Ghost, subst. 1) the spirit of a deceased
person: Meas. V, 440; cf. H6B I, 4, 22. Err. V,
337. Mids. III, 2, 381. Wint. V, 1, 63. 80. John III,
4, 84. R2 III, 2, 158. H4B II, 3, 39. H5 IV Chor.
28. H6A I, 1, 52. I, 2, 7. IV, 7, 87. V, 2, 16. H6B
III, 2, 231. 373. R3 I, 2, 8. III, 1, 144. IV, 4, 26.
Rom. IV, 3, 55. Caes. I, 3, 63. II, 2, 24. V, 5, 17.
Mcb. II, 1, 56. V, 7, 16. Hml. I, 5, 4. 96. 125. 138.
III, 2, 87. 297. Lr. V, 3, 313. Ant. IV, 14, 52. Cymb.
IV, 2, 278. V, 4, 88. 94.

2) a spirit in general, a supernatural being:
*that affable familiar g. which nightly gulls him with
intelligence,* Sonn. 86, 9.

3) a spectre: *grim-grinning g.* Ven. 933 (Death
called so).

4) life, soul: *to give up the g.* (= to die) H6C
II, 3, 22. Caes. V, 1, 89. *to yield the g.* H6A I, 1, 67.
R3 I, 4, 37.

5) a dead body: *a timely-parted g., of ashy
semblance, meagre, pale and bloodless,* H6B III, 2, 161.
I'll make a g. of him that lets me, Hml. I, 4, 85.

Ghost, vb. to haunt after death: *who at Philippi
the good Brutus —ed,* Ant. II, 6, 13.

Ghostly, spiritual: *your g. father,* Meas. IV,
3, 51. V, 126. H6C III, 2, 107. Rom. II, 2, 189. II,
3, 45. II, 6, 21. III, 3, 49.

Giant, a person of extraordinary size and power:
Meas. II, 2, 108. 109. III, 1, 81. Ado V, 1, 205.
Tw. I, 5, 218. John I, 225. V, 2, 57. H4B I, 2, 1. IV,
5, 45. Troil. I, 3, 345. II, 3, 147. Mcb. V, 2, 21. **Lr.**
IV, 6, 91. Cymb. III, 3, 5. Adjectively, = enormous,
monstrous: *a g. traitor,* H8 I, 2, 199.

Giant-dwarf, a dwarf with the power of a giant:
this senior-junior, g. Dan Cupid, LLL III, 182.

Giantess, a female giant: *I had rather be a g.
and lie under Mount Pelion,* Wiv. I*.* 1, 81 (alluding
to the ancient fable of the Gigantomachy).

Giant-like, like a giant, ruthless, rude: *that
same cowardly g. ox-beef hath devoured many a gentleman of your house,* Mids. III, 1, 197. *what is the
cause that thy rebellion looks so g.?* Hml. IV, 5, 121
(with allusion to the ancient Gigantomachy).

Giant-rude, rude after the manner of a giant:
such g. invention, As IV, 3, 34.

Gib, an old Tom-cat: *who would from a paddock,
from a bat, a g., such dear concernings hide?* Hml. III,
4, 190 (cf. *Gib-cat*).

Gibber, to speak inarticulately, to gabble:
Hml. I, 1, 116.

Gibbet, subst. a gallows: Wiv. II, 2, 17. H4A
IV, 2, 40. Mcb. IV, 1, 66. Ant. V, 2, 61. Cymb. V,
4, 207.

Gibbet, vb. to hang: *swifter than he that —s
on the brewer's bucket,* H4B III, 2, 282 ("This alludes
to the manner of carrying a barrel, by putting it on
a sling." Nares' Glossary, q. v.)

Gibbet-maker, the clown's corruption from
Jupiter: Tit. IV, 3, 80.

Gib-cat, an old Tom-cat: *as melancholy as a g.*
H4A I, 2, 83.

Gibe, subst. sneer, scoff: Wiv. III, 3, 259.
IV, 5, 82. H5 IV, 7, 52. Hml. V, 1, 209. Oth. IV, 1,
83. Cymb. III, 4, 161.

Gibe, vb. to scoff, to flout: LLL V, 2, 868.
H4A III, 2, 66. Ant. II, 2, 74.

Giber, a scoffer, a jester: *a perfecter g. for
the table than a necessary bencher for the Capitol,* Cor.
II, 1, 91.

Gibingly, scoffingly: Cor. II, 3, 232.

Giddily, 1) with various turnings, incon-
stantly: *how g. a' turns about all the hot bloods,*
Ado III, 3, 140.

2) carelessly, heedlessly, negligently:
*the parts that fortune hath bestowed upon her, I hold
as g. as fortune,* Tw. II, 4, 87.

Giddiness, inconsiderateness: *neither call
the g. of it in question,* As V, 2, 6.

Giddy, 1) having in the head a sensation of circular motion, and therefore wavering and inclined to
fall: Merch. III, 2, 145. Shr. IV, 3, 9. V, 2, 20. John
IV, 2, 131. H4B IV, 4, 110. Troil. III, 2, 19. Rom.
I, 2, 48. Used of things causing that sensation: *upon
the high and g. mast,* H4B III, 1, 18. *the g. footing of
the hatches,* R3 I, 4, 17.

2) turning, ever varying, inconstant: *the g.
round of Fortune's wheel,* Lucr. 952; cf. *g. Fortune's
fickle wheel,* H5 III, 6, 28. *art not thou thyself g. with
the fashion too?* Ado III, 3, 150. *man is a g. thing,*
V, 4, 109. *our fancies are more g. and unfirm,* Tw. II,
4, 34. *an habitation g. and unsure hath he that buildeth
on the vulgar heart,* H4B I, 3, 89.

3) thoughtless, flighty, harebrained:

so many g. offences, As III, 2, 367. *more g. in my de-sires than a monkey*, IV, 1, 153. *the g. loose suggestions*, John III, 1, 292. *go, ye g. goose*, H4A III, 1, 232. *a vain, g., shallow, humorous youth*, H5 II, 4, 28. *many have their g. brains knocked out*, H6A III, 1, 83.**how the g. multitude do point*, H6B II, 4, 21. *many g. people flock to him*, H6C IV, 8, 5. *g. censure will then cry out*, Cor. I, 1, 272.

4) rash, hot-brained, excitable: *to busy g. minds with foreign quarrels*, H4B IV, 5, 214. *a g. neighbour to us*, H5 I, 2, 145. *'twill prove a g. world*, R3 II, 3, 5 (Qq *troublous*). *the g. men of Rome*, Tit. IV, 4, 87. *disperse the g. Goths*, V, 2, 78.

Giddy-paced, skipping, flighty: *these most brisk and g. times*, Tw. II, 4, 6.

Gift, 1) a thing given or bestowed, a present: Sonn. 11, 12. 60, 8. 122, 1. Tp. IV, 1, 8. 13. Gent. III, 1, 89. IV, 4, 62. V, 4, 148. Wiv. II, 2, 67. III, 5, 9. Meas. II, 2, 147. Err. III, 2, 188. Ado III, 3, 15. IV, 1, 29. Merch. II, 9, 91. IV, 1, 444. V, 167. As I, 2, 34. 43. All's II, 1, 4. 115. Shr. II, 76. Wint. I, 1, 31. H4A IV, 3, 71. H6B IV, 7, 73. H6C V, 1, 31. R3 IV, 2, 91. Tim. I, 2, 178. IV, 3, 516. Hml. III, 1, 101 etc. *to give a g.* H6B I, 1, 15. R3 III, 1, 115. With *to:* —*s to women*, As I, 2, 38. Tim. I, 1, 289. Oth. V, 1, 17.

2) the act of giving, donation: *the cause of this fair g. in me is wanting*, Sonn. 87, 7. *draw a deed of g.* Merch. IV, 1, 394. *I will not take her on g. of any man*, As III, 3, 69. *by g. of heaven*, H5 II, 4, 79. *by Warwick's g.* H6C V, 1, 35. *of their friend's g.* Tim. I, 2, 147. *jewels of Timon's g.* III, 4, 19. *the one may be given, if there were ... merit for the g.* Cymb. I, 4, 91. With an obj. gen.: *by g. of my chaste body to his lust*, Meas. V, 97. *a g. of all*, Merch. IV, 1, 388. V, 292.

3) quality, faculty, endowment: *your graces and your* —*s*, Sonn. 103, 12. Gent. IV, 2, 6. Wiv. I, 1, 64. Ado III, 5, 47. LLL IV, 2, 67. V, 2, 651. As III, 2, 161. Shr. I, 1, 107. All's I, 1, 47. Tw. I, 3, 29. H4B I, 2, 194. H6A V, 1, 43. V, 5, 3 etc. With an obj. gen.: *which by a g. of learning did bear the maid away*, Pilgr. 224. *the g. of tongue* (= eloquence) H4A V, 2, 78. With *in: his g. is in devising impos-sible slanders*, Ado II, 1, 143. *I have no g. in shrew-ishness*, Mids. III, 2, 301. *have not more g. in taci-turnity*, Troil. IV, 2, 75. *you have a goodly g. in horn-ing*, Tit. II, 3, 67. With an inf.: *they have the g. to know it*, As II, 7, 38. Shr. Ind. 1, 124. H5 V, 2, 162.

Gig, a top (cf. *Whirligig*): LLL IV, 3, 167. V, 1, 70. 73.

Giglet or **Giglot,** 1) subst. a lewd woman, a wanton: Meas. V, 352.

2) adj.: *a g. wench*, H6A IV, 7, 41. *g. fortune*, Cymb. III, 1, 31 [= "fickle, inconstant", Wyatt, Warwick Sh.]

Gilbert, name: R3 IV, 5, 10. H8 I, 1. 219. II, 1, 20.

Gild (impf. —*ed:* Wiv. I, 3, 69. partic. ordi-narily — 20 times — —*ed;* 6 times gilt: LLL V, 2, 652. John II, 316. H4B IV, 3, 55. Troil. II, 3, 27. III, 3, 178. Tit. II, 1, 6), to overlay with gold: Sonn. 55, 1. 101, 11. LLL V, 2, 652. Merch. II, 7, 69. John IV, 2, 11. R2 I, 1, 179. H4B IV, 3, 55. Troil. II, 3, 27. III, 3, 178. IV, 4, 107. Cymb. V, 5, 4. Metaphorically: 1) to make bright and shining like gold; used of the sun: Sonn. 28, 12. 33, 4. Gent.

V, 1, 1. R2 I, 3, 147. H5 IV, 2, 1. H8 III, 2, 412. Tit. II, 1, 6. Similarly of the eye: *an eye —ing the object whereupon it gazeth*, Sonn. 20, 6. *the beam of her view —ed my foot*, Wiv. I, 3, 69. *could have —ed pale looks*, Cymb. V, 3, 34.* —*ed* = bright, shining, gay-coloured: *a —ed snake*, As IV, 3, 109. Lr. V, 3, 84. *the —ed newt*, Tim. IV, 3, 182. *a —ed butterfly*, Cor. I, 3, 66. Lr. V, 3, 13. —*ed wings*, Tit. III, 2, 61. *a —ed fly*, Lr. IV, 6, 114. *the —ed puddle which beasts would cough at*, Ant. I, 4, 62 (covered with a film of a golden hue). — 2) to make red: *gilt with French-men's blood*, John II, 316. *I'll g. the faces of the grooms* (with blood) Mcb. II, 2, 56. *this grand liquor that hath —ed them*, Tp. V, 280 (= flustered them, made them red with drinking; with an allusion to the grand elixir). cf. *beauty's red, which virtue gave the golden age to g. their silver cheeks*, Lucr. 60. — 3) to make fair, to adorn, to embellish: —*ed honour shamefully misplaced*, Sonn. 66, 5. *deceits were —ed in his smiling*, Compl. 172. *I'll g. it* (the lie) *with the happiest terms I have*, H4A V, 4, 162. *hath a little —ed over your night's exploit*, H4B I, 2, 169. *England shall double g. his treble guilt*, IV, 5, 129. *we lose our heads to g. his horns*, Troil. IV, 5, 31. *that great me-dicine hath —ed thee*, Ant. I, 5, 37. — 4) to supply with gold, to make rich: *and g. myself with some more ducats*, Merch. II, 6, 49. *Anjou and fair Touraine ... shall g. her bridal bed*, John II, 491. *offence's —ed hand may shove by justice*, Hml. III, 3, 58.

Gilder, see *Guilder*.

Gill, the organ of respiration in fishes: Ven. 1100.

Gill, a familiar term for a woman, in *Flirt-gill*, q. v. cf. *Jill*.

Gilliams, name of a servant in H4A II, 3, 68.

Gillian, name of a female servant in Err. III, 1, 31.

Gillyvor (most M. Edd. *gilliflower*) the flower Dianthus caryophyllus: Wint. IV, 4, 82. 98.

Gilt, subst. 1) gold laid on the surface, gilding; metaphorically = fair show: *the double g. of this opportunity*, Tw. III, 2, 26. *the dust that hides our sceptre's g.* R2 II, 1, 294; cf. Troil. III, 3, 179. *our gayness and our g. are all besmirched*, H5 IV, 3, 110. *iron of Naples hid with English g.* H6C II, 2, 139. *as cherubins, all g.* H8 I, 1, 23. *it more becomes a man than g. his trophy*, Cor. I, 3, 43. *when thou wast in thy g. and thy perfume*, Tim. IV, 3, 302.

2) gold, money: *have for the g. of France — O guilt indeed! — confirmed conspiracy*, H5 II Chor. 26.

Gimmal (O. Edd. *Jymold*), consisting of links or rings: *in their pale dull mouths the g. bit lies foul with chewed grass*, H5 IV, 2, 49 (cf. Edward III I, 2, 29: *lay aside their jacks of gymold mail*).*

Gimmors (F2.3.4 *gimmals*), a gimcrack, a curious contrivance: *by some odd g. or device their arms are set like clocks*, H6A I, 2, 41.

Gin, subst. a snare, a springe: Tw. II, 5, 92. H6B III, 1, 262. H6C I, 4, 61. Mcb. IV, 2, 35.

Gin, vb. (impf. *gan; can* in LLL IV, 3, 106), to begin; followed by an accus.: Mcb. I, 2, 25. By an inf. with *to:* Ven. 6. 46. Pilgr. 171. Tp. III, 3, 106. Mcb. V, 5, 49. Hml. I, 5, 90. Cymb. V, 3, 37. Per. III, 2, 95. By an inf. without *to:* Ven. 95. Lucr. 1228. Compl. 177. Pilgr. 232. LLL IV, 3, 106. H4B I, 1, 129. Cor. II, 2, 119. Cymb. II, 3, 22. V, 5, 197.

Ging, a gang, a pack: *there's a knot, a g.,*

a pack, a conspiracy against me, Wiv. IV, 2, 123 (F1 *gin*).

Ginger, a s p i c e taken from the plant Zingiber officinale: Meas. IV, 3, 6. 8. Merch. III, 1, 10. Tw. II, 3, 126. Wint. IV, 3, 50. H4A II, 1, 27. H5 III, 7, 21.

Gingerbread, a kind of cake with an admixture of ginger: LLL V, 1, 75. cf. *Pepper-gingerbread.*

Gingerly, n i c e l y , c a r e f u l l y : *what is't that you took up so g.?* Gent. I, 2, 70.

Ginn, a female name, from *Jenny:* Err. III, 1, 31.

Ginyes, Mrs. Quickly's corruption from *genitive:* Wiv. IV, 1, 64 (M. Edd. *Jenny's*).

Gipe, Fluellen's pronunciation of *gibe:* H5 IV, 7, 52.

Gipsy, one of a race of vagabonds of a dark complexion, supposed to have come from Egypt: *both in a tune like two —es on a horse,* As V, 3, 16. Cleopatra, the famous queen of Egypt, called so in contempt: Rom. II, 4, 44. Ant. I, 1, 10. IV, 12, 28.

Gird, subst. a s a r c a s m : Shr. V, 2, 58. H6A III, 1, 131.

Gird, vb. tr. and intr. to q u i z , to r e f l e c t o n : *men of all sorts take a pride to g. at me,* H4B I, 2, 7. *he will not spare to g. the gods,* Cor. I, 1, 260.

Gird, vb. (partic. —ed and *girt.* cf. *Girt*) 1) t o b i n d round: *summer's green all —ed up in sheaves,* Sonn. 12, 7.

2) to e n c l o s e , to i n v e s t : *—ing with grievous siege castles and towns,* H5 I, 2, 152. *on —ed Harfleur,* III Chor. 27. *girt in with the ocean,* H6C IV, 8, 20.

Girdle, subst. a b e l t drawn round the waist: LLL IV, 1, 50. H4B I, 2, 45. Tim. III, 4, 91. Hml. V, 2, 157. Lr. IV, 6, 128. *if he be* (angry) *he knows how to turn his g.* Ado V, 1, 143 (perhaps = he knows how to vent his anger in a harmless way. Holt White: "Large belts were worn with the buckle before; but for wrestling the buckle was turned behind, to give the adversary a fairer grasp at the girdle. To turn the buckle behind, therefore, was a challenge." Halliwell interprets: "you may change your temper or humour, alter it to the opposite side."). *an I do, I pray God my g. break,* H4A III, 3, 171 (alluding to the proverb: *ungirt unblest?*). Figuratively: *I'll put a g. round about the earth in forty minutes,* Mids. II, 1, 175. *the beachy g. of the ocean,* H4B III, 1, 50. *within the g. of these walls,* H5 Prol. 19. *in our salt-water g.* Cymb. III, 1, 81.

Girdle, vb. to e n c l o s e : Lucr. 6. John II, 217. H5 V, 2, 349. H6A IV, 3, 20. R3 IV, 3, 10. With *in:* Tim. IV, 1, 2.

Girl, a young unmarried woman: Lucr. 1270. Tp. I, 2, 61. Gent. II, 7, 1. III, 2, 29. V, 2, 49. V, 4, 134. Wiv. I, 4, 35. LLL I, 1, 315. I, 2, 123. IV, 2, 151. IV, 3, 371. V, 2, 58. Merch. II, 5, 15. II, 8, 21. III, 2, 161. As I, 3, 100. Shr. III, 2, 27. All's II, 1, 19. Wint. I, 2, 78. III, 2, 183. R2 III, 4, 9. H6A II, 4, 15. V, 4, 80. Troil. V, 3, 99. Rom. I, 5, 28. Caes. I, 2, 128. Cymb. V, 5, 107 etc. etc. Used, in fondness, of married women: Oth. V, 2, 275. Ant. IV, 8, 19.

Girt, vb. (some M. Edd. *gird*) to g i r d : *I g. thee with the valiant sword of York,* H6A III, 1, 171. H6B I, 1, 65 (cf. *Engirt*).

Girth, a band by which the saddle of a horse is made fast: Ven. 266. Shr. III, 2, 61.

Gis, a corruption of *Jesus: by G. and by Saint Charity,* Hml. IV, 5, 58.

Give (partic. *given* mostly monosyll., sometimes

dissyll., f. i. R2 IV, 249. H8 III, 2, 46. Hml. 1, 5, 35. II, 2, 128. Per. IV Prol. 35. Partic. *gave,* Ven. 571. *Gi' = give,* according to M. Edd. in Rom. I, 2, 58; O. Edd. *Godgigoden,* q. v.). I) trans. 1) to i m p a r t , to d e l i v e r , to c o m m u n i c a t e , to h a n d ; absol.: *when maidens sue, men g. like gods,* Meas. I, 4, 81. *reserve still to g.* Tim. III, 6, 81. With an accus., or an accus. and dative: Tp. I, 1, 69. I, 2, 113. 424. II, 1, 91. II, 2, 86. III, 3, 105. Gent. I, 1, 99. I, 2, 37. II, 1, 164. 165. V, 4, 93 etc. etc. *to g. life* = a) to beget: R2 II, 3, 155. H4B IV, 5, 117. H6C II, 5, 92. Tit. IV, 2, 123. b) to save: *you have given me life,* Merch. V, 286. *his life I gave him,* Tw. V, 83. *I gave thee life, and rescued thee from death,* H6A IV, 6, 5. c) to spare: *that gave thee life, when well he might have slain thee,* Tit. II, 3, 159 (cf. *Life*). *g. me your hands* = clap: Mids. V, 444. *to g. the woman* (= to give her away in the ceremony of marriage; to express consent to her marriage): As III, 3, 68. 70; cf. V, 4, 19; and *g. away* in Shr. III, 2, 196. *I g. her father's heart from her,* Lr. I, 1, 127 (cf. *From*). *to g. in charge,* Tp. V, 8. H6C IV, 1, 32. R3 IV, 3, 25; passively: *so am I —n in charge,* H6B II, 4, 80 (cf. *Charge*); cf. *was —n to understand,* Merch. Ii, 8, 7 (cf. *Understand*). *g. me to know,* Oth. II, 3, 209. *they gave us our demands,* Cor. III, 1, 135. *to g. it* = to beat, to strike: *hob, nob, is his word; g. 't or take 't,* Tw. III, 4, 263. *g. it Pallas,* Tit. IV, 3, 64. cf. Cor. II, 3, 109. Rom. IV, 5, 113. *g. me* = I am for, commend me to, that's the word: *let him be the devil, an he will, I care not: g. me faith, say I; well, it's all one,* Tw. I, 5, 137. *g. me them that will face me,* H4A II, 4, 167. *g. me life,* V, 3, 63. *g. me the spirit,* H4B III, 2, 278. *g. me the spare men,* 288. *g. me always a little, lean shot,* 294. *g. me worship and quietness,* H6C IV, 3, 16.

Variously combined with substantives; see *Advice; Affront* (Cymb. V, 3, 87); *Aim* (Gent. V, 4, 101); *Assay* (Hml. II, 2, 71); *Audience; Bastinado* (H4A II, 4, 370); *Being* (Shr. I, 1, 11); *Blow* (Tp. II, 1, 180. Err. III, 1, 13); *Boots* (Gent. I, 1, 27); *Charge* (Lucr. 434. Hml. III, 4, 86. Wint. V, 1, 162. H6C III, 3, 258); *Chase* (Hml. IV, 6, 16); *Chastisement* (John V, 2, 147); *Command* and *Commandment* (Hml. V, 2, 385); *Consent; Counsel; Counterfeit* (Rom. II, 4, 47); *Death* (Cor. V, 3, 42. Caes. V, 1, 103. Hml. III, 4, 177. IV, 5, 96); *Defiance* (H4B III, 1, 65); *Delight* (Tp. III, 2, 145); *Direction* (H6B III, 2, 12. R3 IV, 4, 225); *Duty* (H4A V, 2, 56); *Ear; good Even* (= to wish a good evening: Gent. II, 1, 104. cf. *g. you good morning,* Wiv. II, 2, 35. II, 3, 21. Meas. IV, 3, 117. R3 II, 3, 6. Lr. II, 2, 165. Cymb. II, 3, 66. *g. you good night,* Hml. I, 1, 16. *g. the time of day,* H6B III, 1, 14); *Excuse* (Cor. I, 3, 114); *Eyes* (*gave me good eyes,* Wiv. I, 3, 67); *Favour* (*give me thy favour still,* Tp. IV, 204); *Fear* (Meas. I, 4, 62); *Gift* (H6B I, 1, 15); *Glad* (*to give him glad,* Per. II Prol. 38, = gladness?); *Glory* (Cor. V, 4, 54); *Groan; Ground* (Tp. II, 2, 64. Cymb. I, 2, 19); *Head* (H4B I, 1, 43); *Hope* (Wint. V, 3, 127); *Horns* (LLL V, 2, 252); *Hunger* (Cymb. II, 4, 137); *Instance* (Err. I, 1, 65. H5 II, 2, 119); *Intelligence* (Wiv. III, 5, 85); *Joy; Judgment* (Merch. IV, 1, 244); *Kindness* (Caes. V, 4, 28); *Knock* (Tit. IV, 3, 71); *Leave; Leer* (Wiv. I, 3, 49); *Lie* (Sonn. 150, 3. Tp. III, 2, 85. As III, 2, 410. Mcb. II, 3, 39. 41); *Line* (Wint. I, 2, 181); *Look* (Gent. III, 1, 31. Troil. III, 3, 143. Lr. II, 4, 37. IV, 5, 25); *Love* (Meas. II, 4, 104.

As III, 5, 88.); *good Morning* and *Morrow* (see above *Even*); *Music* (Gent. IV, 2, 17. As II, 7, 173. Tw. II, 4, 1); *Night* (see above *Even*); *Notice; Oath* (= to administer an oath: Gent. II, 6, 4. LLL IV, 3, 250); *Offence* (Lr. II, 2, 121); *Onset* (Gent. III, 2, 94); *Order; Overthrow* (Caes. V, 2, 5); *Pains* (Tp. I, 2, 242); *Pause* (Hml. III, 1, 68); *Praise; Punishment* (H6B III, 1, 130); *Reason* (Tw. I, 5, 325. III, 2, 2'; *Redress* (Lucr. 1603); *Reins* (R2 I, 1, 55); *Relief* (Tp. II, 2, 70); *Report* (Hml. IV, 7, 97); *Reproof* (Wiv. II, 1, 59); *Revolt* (Mcb. V, 4, 12); *Sentence; Shame; Sign; Sound* (John II, 230); *Spurs* (R2 I, 1, 55); *Stroke* (H6B IV, 1, 22'; *Thanks; Throe* (H8 II, 4, 198); *Time of day* (H6B III, 1, 14); *Truce* (H6A III, 4, 3); *Verdict* (R2 I, 3, 234); *View* (order gave each thing v. H8 I, 1, 44); *Watch* (Hml. IV, 5, 74); *Way* (= a) to yield: Tp. I, 2, 186. Cor. IV, 6, 122. V, 6, 32. b) to give free scope: H4B V, 2, 82); *Welcome* (Err. I, 1, 115. R2 V, 2, 29. H4A IV, 3, 59); *Wonder* (Oth. II, 1, 185); *Word* (*give the word*, Caes. IV, 2, 2. V, 3, 5. *g. no words but mum*, H6B I, 2, 89. *to whom he gave the words*, H8 IV, 2, 20. *gave to me good word*, Troil. III, 3, 143. *to g. words or talk with the lord Hamlet*, Hml. I, 3, 134); *Wound* (H4A V, 4, 155) etc.

Joined with adverbs; *to g. away:* Merch. V, 179. Shr. III, 2, 196. H4A V, 5, 33. H4B IV, 3, 75. H6C II, 2, 38. Oth. III, 4, 45 etc. = to neglect: *thy solicitor shall rather die than g. thy cause away*, Oth. III, 3, 28. *to g. back*, Tw. IV, 3, 18. *to g. in evidence* = to depose: Hml. III, 3, 64. *to g. off* = to resign: *my crown I should g. off*, John V, 1, 27. *to g. over* = a) to resign, to renounce: *never g. her o'er*, Gent. III, 1, 94. *g. it not o'er so*, Meas. II, 2, 43. *g. over this attempt*, As I, 2, 189. John V, 2, 107. H4A I, 2, 107. H6A I, 2, 125. With *to: thy tender-hefted nature shall not g. thee o'er to harshness*, Lr. II, 4, 174. b) to leave off, to discontinue: *I will g. over all*, Wiv. IV, 6, 2. *g. over my trade*, Tim. IV, 3, 460. *g. o'er the play*, Hml. III, 2, 279. *I will g. over my suit*, Oth. IV, 2, 201. c) to forsake, to leave: *the visitor will not g. him o'er so*, Tp. II, 1, 11. *will you g. her o'er*, Mids. III, 2, 130. 135. *to g. you over at this first encounter*, Shr. I, 2, 105. d) to despair of: *thou art altogether —n over*, H4A III, 3, 40. *the gods have —n us over*, Tit. IV, 2, 48. *his friends, like physicians, g. him over*, Tim. III, 3, 12. — *To g. out* = a) to surrender: *I thought ye would never have —n out these arms till you had recovered your ancient freedom*, H6B IV, 8, 26 (Cade's speech). b) to show: *do plainly g. you out an unstained shepherd*, Wint. IV, 4, 149. *the behaviour of the young gentleman —s him out to be of good capacity*, Tw. III, 4, 203. *these pencilled figures are even such as they g. out*, Tim. I, 1, 160. *a better soldier none that Christendom —s out*, Mcb. IV, 3, 192. *she that, so young, could g. out such a seeming*, Oth. III, 3, 209. c) to publish, to proclaim: *you'll be glad to g. out a commission for more heads*, Meas. II, 1, 253. *it is the bitter disposition of Beatrice that so —s me out*, Ado II, 1, 216. *I will g. out divers schedules of my beauty*, Tw. I, 5, 263. *hath any friend —n out reward to him*, R3 IV, 4, 517 (Ff *proclaimed*). *g. out that Anne my wife is sick*, IV, 2, 58. *side factions and g. out conjectural marriages*, Cor. I, 1, 197. *'tis —n out that a serpent stung me*, Hml. I, 5, 35. d) to declare, to pretend, to tell, to express: *our ship which we gave out split*, Tp. V, 223. *g. out you are of Epidamnum*, Err. I, 2, 1. *gave him*

out incurable, All's II, 3, 16. *one that —s out himself Prince Florizel*, Wint. V, 1, 85. *those powers of France that thou for truth —st out are landed here*, John IV, 2, 130. *the just proportion that we gave them out*, H4B IV, 1, 23. *g. it out that he is marched to Bordeaux*, H6A IV, 3, 3. *bloodier villain than terms can g. thee out*, Mcb. V, 8, 8. *she —s it out that you shall marry her*, Oth. IV, 1, 116. *as good as I have —n out him*, Cymb. V, 5, 312. *Giving out*, substantively: *his —ing out were of an infinite distance from his true-meant design*, Meas. I, 4, 54 (M. Edd. *givings-out*). *such ambiguous —ing out, to note that you know aught of me*, Hml. I, 5, 178. *this is the monkey's own —ing out*, Oth. IV, 1, 131. — *To g. through* = to hand down, to publish through the ranks: *g. the word through*, H5 IV, 6, 38. — *To g. up* = a) to surrender, to resign: Meas. II, 2, 13. IV, 3, 137. V, 467. LLL II, 140. H6B II, 3, 23. IV, 7, 141. R3 III, 3, 14 (Ff *give to thee*). *to g. up the ghost*, H6C II, 3, 22 (cf. *Ghost*). With *to: g. up your body to such sweet uncleanness*, Meas. II, 4, 54. *all my mother came into mine eyes and gave me up to tears*, H5 IV, 6, 32. *for —ing up of Normandy to Mounsieur Basimecu*, H6B IV, 7, 30. H8 II, 1, 96. II, 4, 43. Troil. IV, 2, 67. Cor. V, 6, 92. Ant. III, 6, 66. III, 7, 48. Per. III, 3, 36. b) to devote: *and here g. up ourselves .... to be commanded*, Hml. II, 2, 30. *he hath devoted and —n up himself to the contemplation of her parts*, Oth. II, 3, 322. *Iago doth g. up the execution of his wit to wronged Othello's service*, III, 3, 465. c) to deliver: *g. me up the truth*, Hml. I, 3, 98. *what lawful quest have —n their verdict up unto the frowning judge?* R3 I, 4, 189.

2) to make a present of, to bestow without any price or reward: *that I should neither sell nor g. nor lose it*, Merch. IV, 1, 443. *I'll nor sell nor g. him*, Cor. I, 4, 6. Oth. IV, 1, 15. Cymb. I, 4, 90. Per. IV Prol. 35. Cor. III, 1, 74.

3) to grant, to allow: *he would g. 't thee, so to offend him still*, Meas. III, 1, 100. *g. me one poor request*, Hml. I, 5, 142 (cf. Cor. III, 1, 135). *to g. quiet pass through your dominions*, II, 2, 77. *'tis my breeding that —s me this bold show of courtesy*, Oth. II, 1, 100.

4) to yield: *I g. thee the bucklers*, Ado V, 2, 17 (= I yield thee the victory). *to our best mercy g. yourselves*, H5 III, 3, 3; cf. All's IV, 2, 35.

5) to commit, to surrender: *and to enlighten thee, gave eyes to blindness*, Sonn. 152, 11 (= made myself blind). *—n to the fire*, Wint. II, 3, 8. *and g. you to the gods*, Ant. III, 2, 64. Reflectively: *have —n ourselves to hell*, Wiv. V, 5, 156. *did g. ourself to barbarous licence*, H5 I, 2, 270. *gave himself to the numb cold night*, R3 II, 1, 116.

Partic. *—n* = addicted, devoted: *he is —n to prayer*, Wiv. I, 4, 13. *to musing*, 164. V, 5, 166. Meas. III, 2, 248. As III, 3, 20. H4A III, 3, 38. V, 4, 149. Caes. II, 1, 188. Ant. V, 2, 252. With an adverb, = affected, disposed, inclined: *a woman cardinally —n*, Meas. II, 1, 81. *lewdly —n*, H4A II, 4, 469. *virtuously —n*, III, 3, 16. *well —n*, H6C III, 1, 72. Caes. I, 2, 197. *cannibally —n*, Cor. IV, 5, 200.

6) to attribute, to ascribe, to impute: *the fault thou gavest him*, H8 III, 2, 262. *I will g. you the minstrel; then will I g. you the serving-creature*, Rom. IV, 5, 116. 117 (= I will call you). *those that*

gave the thane of Cawdor to me, Mcb. I, 3, 119. See above *to give the lie.*

7) **to communicate, to tell:** *g. 't me in mine ear*, Wint. II, 1, 32. *hath his solicitings all —n to mine ear*, Hml. II, 2, 128. *my mind gave me .... ye blew the fire that burns ye*, H8 V, 3, 109 (= I suspected). *my mind gave me his clothes made a false report of him*, Cor. IV, 5, 157.

8) **to represent:** *more cruel to your good report than grateful to us that g. you truly*, Cor. I, 9, 55. *men's reports g. him much wronged*, Ant. I, 4, 40.

9) **to have or show as an emblem in armorial bearings:** *they may g. the dozen white luces in their coat*, Wiv. I, 1, 16. *g. sheep in lions' stead*, H6A I, 5, 29.

10) **to consider:** *the crown and comfort of my life, your favour, I do g. lost*, Wint. III, 2, 96.

II) **intr. to yield, to submit:** *g. no foot of ground*, H6C I, 4, 15 (may be active). *whose eyes do never g. but through lust and laughter*, Tim. IV, 3, 491 (= are never subdued, never shed tears). Dubious passage: *these often bathed she in her fluxive eyes, and often kissed, and often gave to tear*, Compl. 51 (= yielded to the impulse? or devoted, betook herself? or is *tear* a subst.? Most M. Edd. *gan*). With adverbs; *to g. back* = to retire: *g. back, or else embrace thy death*, Gent. V, 4, 126. *to g. off* = to cease: *let's see how 'twill g. off*, Ant. IV, 3, 23. *to g. up* = to yield, to cease to resist: *where Philomel gave up*, Cymb. II, 2, 46. *to g. over* = to cease, to discontinue, to quit a business: *had she then gave over*, Ven. 571. *at last she smilingly with this —s o'er*, Lucr. 1567. *busy winds g. o'er*, 1790. *shall we g. o'er and drown?* Tp. I, 1, 41. *who, half through, —s o'er*, H4B I, 3, 60. *I have given over, I will speak no more*, II, 3, 5. *have the pioners —n o'er?* H5 III, 2, 92. *I'll never g. o'er*, Cymb. II, 3, 17. *and so g. over*, Per. IV, 2, 29. 39. *'twere best I did g. o'er*, V, 1, 168. *to g. o'er to* = to yield, to succumb to: *if you g. o'er to stormy passion*, H4B I, 1, 164.

Giver, one who gives or imparts: Gent. II, 4, 35. Troil. III, 3, 102. Tim. I, 1, 290. Hml. III, 1, 101.

Giving-out, anything uttered, assertion: Meas. I, 4, 54. Hml. I, 5, 178. Oth. IY, 1, 131 (see *Give* I, 1.).

Glad, adj. 1) **pleased, joyous:** Tp. V, 180. Wiv. IV, 5, 57. H8 II, 4, 26. Per. II, 5, 72. With *at: g. at the thing they scowl at*, Cymb. I, 1, 15. With *of:* Tp. III, 1, 74. 92. Gent. III, 2, 63 *(will be g. of you)*. IV, 1, 32 *(held me g. of such a doom)*. Wiv. III, 3, 124. Ado I, 1, 19. Merch. I, 2, 142. III, 1, 121. III, 2, 243. As III, 2, 79. 311. All's IV, 3, 75. H4A III, 1, 128. H4B IV, 2, 77. Cor. IV, 3, 54 *(g. of your company)*. Per. I, 4, 41 *(g. of bread)* etc. *I am g. on't:* Merch. II, 6, 67. Cor. I, 1, 229. Rom. IV, 2, 28. Caes. I, 3, 137. Oth. II, 1, 30. IV, 1, 249. Cymb. I, 1, 164. Per. II, 5, 74. Followed by a sentence: *I shall be g. if he have deceived me*, Wiv. III, 1, 12 (Evans' speech). *I am right g. that he's so out of hope*, Tp. III, 3, 11. Wiv. V, 5, 247. Ado V, 4, 7. Ant. II, 2, 178. *I am not g. that such a sore of time should seek a plaster*, John V, 2, 12. *I am g. the fat knight is not here*, Wiv. IV, 2, 29. I, 4, 94. 50. Mids. III, 2, 352. Merch. II, 2, 115. II, 6, 34. As I, 1, 165 etc. Followed by an inf.: Wiv. I, 1, 32. II, 2, 185. Meas. II, 1, 253. III, 1, 167. V, 2. Err. II, 2, 20. Ado III, 5, 30. H6B III, 2, 273 etc.

2) **causing joy:** *g. tidings*, H6B IV, 9, 7.

Glad, subst. = gladness? *till fortune, tired with doing bad, threw him ashore, to give him g.* Per. II Prol. 38 (or is it = to represent, to introduce him glad?).

Glad, vb. to affect with pleasure, **to gladden:** H6C IV, 6, 93. H8 II, 4, 196. V, 1, 71. Tit. I, 166. Per. Prol. 4. I, 1, 9. I, 4, 28. II, 3, 21.

Gladly, with pleasure, with all one's heart *(I would g.* = I should like to*)*: Sonn. 8, 3. Meas. I, 3, 18. II, 3, 23. Err. I, 1, 70. All's IV, 3, 37. Wint. V, 2, 9. R2 V, 3, 105. H4B I, 3, 6. H5 III, 6, 87. Cor. I, 9, 6. Rom. I, 1, 136. Mcb. I, 3, 155. Lr. II, 4, 295. Oth. IV, 1, 19. Ant. V, 2, 31.

Gladness, pleasure of mind, joy: As III, 5, 98. Troil. I, 1, 39. Ant. II, 2, 169.

Glamis, name of a Scottish thanedom or county: Mcb. I, 3, 48. 71. = thane of G.: I, 3, 116. I, 5, 16. 23. 55. II, 2, 42. III, 1, 1.

Glance, subst. 1) **look:** Lucr. 1399. Gent. I, 1, 4. LLL V, 2, 775. Shr. V, 2, 137. H6B I, 2, 16. Troil. III, 2, 126.

2) **censure by an oblique hint, reflection:** *the wise man's folly is anatomized even by the squandering —s of the fool*, As II, 7, 57.*

Glance, vb. 1) **intr. a) to look:** *doth g. from heaven to earth, from earth to heaven*, Mids. V, 13. *why with the time do I not g. aside to new-found methods?* Sonn. 76, 3.

b) **to hint:** *how canst thou g. at my credit with Hippolyta?* Mids. II, 1, 75. *Caesar's ambition shall be —d at*, Caes. I, 2, 324.

c) **to dart aside from the object first aimed at:** *to g. from him to the duke himself, to tax him with injustice*, Meas. V, 311. *your shafts of fortune, though they hurt you mortally, yet g. full wanderingly on us*, Per. III, 3, 7.

d) **to dart aside and miss the aim:** *your arrow hath —d*, Wiv. V, 5, 249. *the jest did g. away from me*, Shr. V, 2, 61. *they yet g. by and scarcely bruise*, Lr. V, 3, 148.

2) **trans. a) to cast:** *forbear to g. thine eye aside*, Sonn. 139, 6. *—ing an eye of pity on his losses*, Merch. IV, 1, 27. *if we did but g. a far-off look*, H6B III, 1, 10.

b) **to hint at:** *in company I often —d it*, Err. V, 66.

Glanders, a disease of horses, characterized by the discharge of sticky matter from the nose: Shr. III, 2, 51.

Glansdale, name in H6A I, 4, 63.

Glare, vb. to look with a fierce or with a ghastly and staring eye: *I met a lion, who —d upon me*, Caes. I, 3, 21 (O. Edd. *glaz'd*). *thou hast no speculation in those eyes which thou dost g. with*, Mcb. III, 4, 96. *look you, how pale he —s*, Hml. III, 4, 125. *look, where he stands and —s*, Lr. III, 6, 25.

Glass, 1) **a brittle and transparent substance** formed of fixed alkalies and sand: Ven. 980. Sonn. 5, 10. Pilgr. 87. Per. II, 3, 36. *her eyes are grey as g.* Gent. IV, 4, 197. *my kingdom stands on brittle g.* R3 IV, 2, 62. Adjectively: *g. eyes*, Lr. IV, 6, 174.

2) **things composed of that substance; a) a mirror,** a looking-glass: Ven. 1129. Lucr. 615. 619. 1526. 1758. Sonn. 3, 1. 9. 62, 9. 77, 1. 103, 6. Tp. III, 1, 50. Meas. II, 2, 95. II, 4, 125. Err. V, 417. LLL

IV, 1, 18. IV, 3, 40. Mids. I, 1, 210. II, 2, 98. As III, 5, 54. Shr. II, 234. Tw. III, 4, 415. Wint. IV, 4, 14. 609. R2 IV, 269. 276. 279. H4B II, 3, 21. 31. H5 V, 2, 154. H6B III, 2, 330. V, 1, 142. R3 I, 2, 263. II, 2, 53. Troil. I, 2, 311. II, 3, 165. III, 3, 47. Caes. I, 2, 68. II, 1, 205. Mcb. IV, 1, 119. Hml. III, 1, 161. III, 4, 19. Lr. III, 2, 36. Cymb. I, 1, 49. IV, 1, 9. Per. I, 4, 27. *if this be so, as yet the g. seems true,* Tw. V, 272 (Non liquet). *fair g. of light, I loved you,* Per. I, 1, 76 (= reflection, image of light?).

b) a vessel to drink in: Merch. I, 2, 104. As V. 1, 46. Shr. Ind. 1, 7. H4B II, 1, 155. H8 I, 1, 166. Metaphorically: *crack the g. of her virginity,* Per. IV, 6, 151.

c) an hour-glass: *Time's fickle g.* Sonn. 126, 2. *past the mid season; at least two —es,* Tp. I, 2, 240. *three —es since,* V, 223. All's II, 1, 168. Wint. I, 2, 306. IV, 1, 16. H6A IV, 2, 35.

d) Used of the eye-balls: *in the —es of thine eyes I see thy grieved heart,* R2 I, 3, 208. *schoolboys' tears take up the —es of my sight,* Cor. III, 2, 117. cf. *Glassy,* Lucr. 102.

Glassed, enclosed in glass: LLL II, 244.

Glass-faced, reflecting, like a mirror, the looks of another: *the g. flatterer,* Tim. I, 1, 58.

Glass-gazing, often contemplating one's self in a mirror: Lr. II, 2, 19.

Glassy, resembling glass: *the g. margents of such looks,* Lucr. 102 (i. e. the eyes). *his g. essence,* Meas. II, 2, 120. *g. streams,* H6A V, 3, 62. Hml. IV, 7, 168.

Glaze, to cover as with glass; to furnish (windows) with glass: *hath his windows —d with thine eyes,* Sonn. 24, 8. *—d with crystal gate the glowing roses,* Compl. 286. *sorrow's eye, —d with blinding tears,* R2 II, 2, 16. (In Caes. I, 3, 21 O. Edd. *—d,* M. Edd. rightly *glared*).

Gleam, subst. a ray; only by conjecture in Mids. V, 279; Qq F1 *beames;* F2.3.4 *streams.*

Gleam, vb. to dart, to cast as rays of light: *dying eyes — ed forth their ashy lights,* Lucr. 1378.

Glean, 1) to gather: *to g. the broken ears,* As III, 5, 102. *—ing all the land's wealth into one,* H8 III, 2, 284. *when he needs what you have —ed, it is but squeezing,* Hml. IV, 2, 21.

2) to pick out, to separate, to sift: *how much low peasantry would then be —ed from the true seed of honour,* Merch. II, 9, 46.

3) to obtain, to acquire: *not for Bohemia, nor the pomp that may be thereat —ed,* Wint. IV, 4, 500. *a wonder how his grace should g. it,* H5 I, 1, 53.

4) to disfurnish, to lay bare, to exhaust: *galling the —ed land with hot assays,* H5 I, 2, 151.

5) to conclude, to infer: *what harm can your bisson conspectuities g. out of this character,* Cor. II, 1, 71. *and to gather, so much as from occasion you may g.* Hml. II, 2, 16.

Gleeful, merry: Tit. II, 3, 11.

Gleek, subst. a scoff: *where's the Bastard's braves, and Charles his —s?* H6A III, 2, 123. *what will you give us? No money, but the g.* Rom. IV, 5, 115.

Gleek, vb. to scoff: *I can g. upon occasion,* Mids. III, 1, 150. *—ing and galling at this gentleman,* H5 V, 1, 78.

Glendower (*Glendówer* and *Gléndower*) name of a Welsh prince: R2 III, 1, 43. H4A I, 1, 40. I, 3, 83. 117. II, 3, 27. II, 4, 374. III, 1, 87. IV, 1, 124.

131. V, 5, 40 etc. H4B I, 3, 72. III, 1, 103. H6B II, 2, 41.

Glib, adj. smooth, slippery: *so g. of tongue,* Troil. IV, 5, 58. *g. and slippery creatures,* Tim. I, 1, 53. *that g. and oily art to speak and purpose not,* Lr. I, 1, 227.

Glib, vb. to geld, to castrate: *I had rather g. myself than they should not produce fair issue,* Wint. II, 1, 149.

Glide, subst. smooth and easy motion produced without change of step: *and with indented —s did slip away into a bush,* As IV, 3, 113.

Glide, vb. to move smoothly and easily: Ven. 816. Gent. II, 7, 25; cf. Tit. II, 1, 85. Mids. V, 389; cf. Caes. I, 3, 63. H6B III, 2, 260. Rom. II, 5, 5. Cymb. III, 2, 54.

Glimmer, subst. a faint light: Err. V, 315.

Glimmer, vb. to shine faintly: Mids. II, 1, 77. III, 2, 61. V, 398. H6A II, 4, 24. Mcb. III, 3, 5.

Glimpse, 1) a transient lustre: *whether it be the fault and g. of newness,* Meas. I, 2, 162.* *that thou revisit'st thus the —s of the moon,* Hml. I, 4, 53.

2) a tincture: *there is no man hath a virtue that he hath not a g. of,* Troil. I, 2, 25.

Glister, to shine, to sparkle: Ven. 275. Merch. II, 7, 65. Wint. III, 2, 171. IV, 1, 14. John V, 1, 54. R2 III, 3, 178. H5 II, 2, 117. H8 II, 3, 21. Tit. II, 1, 7.

Glittering, shining, sparkling: Lucr. 945. Mids. V, 279. John III, 1, 80. R2 III, 3, 116. IV, 51. H4A I, 2, 237. IV, 1, 100. Tim. IV, 3, 26. Per. IV, 3, 44.

Globe, 1) the terraqueous ball, the earth: Tp. IV, 153. Mids. IV, 1, 102. R2 III, 2, 38. H6B III, 2, 406 (*in this world's g.*). Troil. I, 3, 113. Tit. V, 2, 49 (O. Edd. *—s,* M. Edd. *g.*). Lr. II, 2, 170. Oth. V, 2, 100. *while memory holds a seat in this distracted g.* Hml. I, 5, 97 (according to intpp., = this head confused with thought; but perhaps = world).

2) an artificial sphere representing the earth: *her breasts, live ivory —s circled with blue, a pair of maiden worlds unconquered,* Lucr. 407. *she is spherical like a globe; I could find out countries in her,* Err. III, 2, 116. *thou g. of sinful continents,* H4B II, 4, 309.

Glooming, gloomy, cloudy, dismal: *a g. peace this morning with it brings,* Rom. V, 3, 305.

Gloomy, dismally dark: Lucr. 803. H6A V, 4, 89. Tit. IV, 1, 53.

Glorify, 1) to make glorious, to give splendor to: *the bright sun —es the sky,* Ven. 485. *such silver currents do g. the banks that bound them in,* John II, 442. *I will not return till my attempt so much be —ed as to my ample hope was promised,* V, 2, 111. *death's dishonourable victory we with our stately presence g.* H6A I, 1, 21.

2) to pay praise, to magnify in worship: *that we for thee may g. the Lord,* H6B II, 1, 75.

Glorious, 1) highly creditable, praiseworthy, famous: Lucr. 109. Ado V, 3, 8. LLL II, 45. John II, 394. R2 I, 1, 107. IV, 93. H4A III, 2, 133. 146. 148. H5 II, 2, 183. IV, 6, 18. H6A I, 1, 55. I, 6, 8. H6B III, 1, 92. V, 3, 29. H6C I, 4, 16. Troil. III, 3, 188. Oth. II, 3, 186. III, 3, 354. Per. II Prol. 14.

2) of supreme excellence and splendor, illustrious: Err. III, 2, 50. R2 III, 2, 61. H6A V, 5, 38. H6B I, 2, 11. H6C III, 2, 171. R3 I, 1, 2. Troil. V

2, 80. V, 6, 23. Cor. V, 2, 74. Tit. I, 187. Rom. II, 2, 27. Per. I, 1, 77. I, 2, 72. *the g. sun:* LLL I, 1, 84. Tw. IV, 3, 1. John III, 1, 77. H6A V, 4, 87. H6B III, 1, 353. H6C II, 1, 22. 26. V, 3, 5. Troil. I, 3, 89. cf. Lucr. 1013. Sonn. 33, 1. Pilgr. 81. Per. I, 2, 4.

3) striving for excellence and renown, d e s i r o u s o f g l o r y: *most miserable is the desire that's g.* Cymb. I, 6, 7. *the purchase is to make men g.* Per. Prol. 9.

Gloriously, s p l e n d i d l y: Ven. 857. Mids. III, 2, 106.

Glory, 1) f a m e, r e n o w n: Ado I, 3, 69. II, 1, 401. III, 1, 110. H4A V, 4, 64. H5 IV Chor. 31. H6A II, 2, 43. III, 4, 11. IV, 6, 50. IV, 7, 48. Caes. V, 5, 36. Cymb. I, 1, 32. *g. grows guilty of detested crimes,* LLL IV, 1, 31 (viz by being desired too much).

2) high praise, g l o r i f i c a t i o n: *thou in losing me shalt win much g.* Sonn. 88, 8. *in g. of my kinsman Hercules,* Mids. V, 47. *heavens have g. for this victory,* H6A III, 2, 117. *if to my sword his fate be not the g.* Troil. IV, 1, 26. *giving him g.* Cor. V, 6, 54.

3) j u s t p r i d e: *time's g. is to calm contending kings,* Lucr. 939. *which shall be most my g., being dumb,* Sonn. 83, 10. *she determines herself the g. of a creditor,* Meas. I, 1, 40. *his g. is to subdue men,* LLL I, 2, 186. *let it be your g. to see her tears,* Tit. II, 3, 139.

4) a state of greatness and supreme excellence: *g. is like a circle in the water,* H6A I, 2, 133. *Henry Monmouth, before whose g. I was great in arms,* II, 5, 24. *the fierce wretchedness that g. brings us,* Tim. IV, 2, 30. *who would be so mocked with g.* 33.

5) s p l e n d o r, m a g n i f i c e n c e: Lucr. 1523. Sonn. 25, 8. 37, 12. 60, 7. 84, 6. 132, 8 *(do g. to).* Gent. I, 3, 85. LLL IV, 3, 37. Merch. V, 93. John II, 350. H6A I, 2, 83. V, 1, 27. H6C I, 4, 103. V, 2, 23. R3 I, 3, 203 etc. *this is the latest g. of thy praise,* H6A IV, 2, 33; cf. *emboldened with the g. of her praise,* Per. I, 1, 4. Plur. *—ies:* Ven. 1014. R2 IV, 192. H5 II, 4, 79. H6A I, 2, 137. H6C II, 1, 158. V, 4, 54. R3 IV, 2, 5 (Qq *honours*). I, 4, 78. Caes. III, 1, 149. III, 2, 63. V, 5, 81.

6) a h a l o: *till I have set a g. to this hand,* John IV, 3, 71.

Glory, vb. to take pride; with *in:* Sonn. 91, 1. H8 II, 1, 66. V, 3, 164.

Glose, see *Gloze.*

Gloss, lustre of the surface, s p e c i o u s a p p e a r a n c e: Pilgr. 170. Ado III, 2, 6. LLL II, 47. 48. All's I, 1, 167. H6A IV, 4, 6. H6B I, 1, 163. H8 V, 3, 71.* Troil. II, 3, 128. Mcb. I, 7, 34. Oth. I, 3, 227. *to set g. on sth.* = to give a fair appearance: Ven. 936. *to set a g. on:* H6A IV, 1, 103. Tim. I, 2, 16. Plur. *—es:* Tp. II, 1, 63.

Gloster or **Gloucester** or **Glouster,** 1) English county: Wiv. I, 1, 5. H6C II, 6, 107.

2) English town: Lr. I, 5, 1.

3) the ducal title of the sixth son of Edward III: R2 I, 1, 100.* II, 1, 128 etc. H6B II, 2, 16.

4) the younger brother of Henry V, and protector of the realm under Henry VI: H4B IV, 4, 12. IV, 5, 48. H5 III, 2, 59. V, 2, 84. H6A I, 1, 37. 100. I, 3, 4. 52. 62. II, 4, 118. III, 1, 3. 27 etc. H6B I, 1, 69 etc. etc.

5) the son of Richard of York, who was afterwards king under the name of Richard III: H6C II, 6, 103. IV, 5, 16 etc. Very often in R3.

6) the father of Edgar and Edmund in Lr. I, 1, 35 etc.

Glostershire or **Gloucestershire,** English county: Wiv. III, 4, 44. V, 5, 191. R2 II, 3, 3. V, 6, 3. H4A I, 3, 243. III, 2, 176. H4B IV, 3, 88. 138.

Glove, subst. a cover for the hand: Lucr. 317. Gent. II, 1, 1. LLL V, 2, 48. Merch. IV, 1, 426. As IV, 3, 26. All's V, 3, 278. Tw. III, 1, 13. Wint. IV, 4, 193. 236. 610. H5 III, 2, 51. Troil. II, 2, 38. Rom. II, 2, 24. Oth. III, 3, 77. IV, 2, 9. *by these —s,* Wiv. I, 1, 156. 161. 168 (Slender's oath). *by this white g.* LLL V, 2, 411 (Biron). *by Venus' g.* Troil. IV, 5, 179. *these —s ... are an excellent perfume,* Ado III, 4, 62. *—s as sweet as damask roses,* Wint. IV, 4, 222. 253. *wear it* (a *g.) as a favour,* R2 V, 3, 17; cf. Troil. IV, 4, 73. V, 2, 79. Lr. III, 4, 88. *here's my g.; give me another of thine,* H5 IV, 1, 226 (viz as a mark to be challenged by an enemy); cf. IV, 7, 125 etc. *I will throw my g. to Death himself, that there's no maculation in thy heart,* Troil. IV, 4, 65. *throw thy g., or any token of thy honour else, that thou wilt use the wars as thy redress,* Tim. V, 4, 49. 54. *with g., or hat, or handkerchief, still waving,* Cymb. I, 3, 11. *matrons flung —s upon him,* Cor. II, 1, 279.

Glove, vb. to cover with a glove: *a scaly gauntlet now must g. this hand,* H4B I, 1, 147.

Glover, one whose trade is to make gloves: Wiv. I, 4, 21.

Glow, subst. heat, transitory redness in the face: *the red g. of scorn,* As III, 4, 57.

Glow, vb. 1) intr. to shine with heat without a flame: *coals of —ing fire,* Ven. 35. Wiv. III, 5, 122. Mids. V, 382. Per. I, 2, 41. Metaphorically, = to be hot, to burn: Lucr. 47. Sonn. 73, 9. Cor. IV, 3, 26. = to be red: *—ing roses,* Compl. 286. = to become red with animation: Ven. 337. Compl. 324. John IV, 1, 114. Caes. I, 2, 183. Hml. III, 4, 48. Per. V, 1, 96. = to be bright, to shine: *his eyes that have —ed like plated Mars,* Ant. I, 1, 4.

2) trans. to make hot, to flush: *to g. the delicate cheeks,* Ant. II, 2, 209.

Glow-worm, the beetle Lampyris: Ven. 621. Wiv. V, 5, 82. Mids. III, 1, 173. Hml. I, 5, 89. Per. II, 3, 43.

Gloze, subst. t i r a d e, words not to the purpose: *now to plain - dealing; lay these —s by,* LLL IV, 3, 370.

Gloze, vb. to make tirades, t o m a k e m e r e w o r d s: *they whom youth and ease have taught to g.* R2 II, 1, 10. *which Salique land the French unjustly g. to be the realm of France,* H5 I, 2, 40. *on the cause and question now in hand you have —d, but superficially,* Troil. II, 2, 165. *it shall become high-witted Tamora to g. with all,* Tit. IV, 4, 35. *he has found the meaning, but I will g. with him,* Per. I, 1, 110. In Meas. V, 346 some M. Edd. *gloze,* O. Edd. *close,* q. v.

Glue, vb. to join with a viscous substance: Tit. II, 1, 41. John III, 4, 65. H6C V, 2, 38. In a figurative sense: Ven. 546. H6C II, 6, 5.

Glut, to s w a l l o w: Tp. I, 1, 63.

Glutted, c l o y e d: H4A III, 2, 84.

Glutton, subst. a g o r m a n d: Ven. 803. Sonn. 1, 13. H4A IV, 2, 28 and H4B I, 2, 39; cf. S. Luke ch. XVI.

Adjectively: *his g. eye,* Ven. 399. *thy g. bosom,* H4B I, 3, 98.

Glutton, vb. to gormandize: *or —ing on all, or all away,* Sonn. 75, 14.

Glutton-like, like a glutton, greedy: Ven. 548.

Gluttonous, greedy: Tim. III, 4, 52.

Gluttony, excess of eating: H4B II, 4, 46. 48.

Gnarl, to growl, to snarl: *—ing sorrow hath less power to bite,* R2 I, 3, 292. *wolves are —ing,* H6B III, 1, 192.

Gnarled, knotty: *the unwedgeable and g. ook,* Meas. II, 2, 116.

Gnat, the insect Culex: Lucr. 1014. Err. II, 2, 30. Merch. III, 2, 123. John IV, 1, 93. H6C II, 6, 9. Tit. IV, 4, 82. Rom. I, 4, 64. Ant. III, 13, 166. Cymb. I, 3, 21. Per. II, 3, 62. *to see a king transformed to a g.* LLL IV, 3, 166 (cf. Per. II, 3, 62).

Gnaw (impf. *—ed,* R3 I, 4, 25; partic. *gnawn,* Wiv. II, 2, 307) 1) to wear off by slow corrosion with the fore teeth: H6A III, 1, 73. H6B III, 1, 192. R3 II, 4, 28. IV, 2, 27 (Qq *bites*). Cor. I, 1, 254. Tit. III, 1, 262. Tim. IV, 3, 49. Oth. V, 2, 43. With an accus. denoting the result: *—ing my bonds in sunder,* Err. V, 249. Figuratively: *the thought doth like a poisonous mineral g. my inwards,* Oth. II, 1, 306. *hell g. his bones,* IV, 2, 136. Absol. *the —ing vulture of thy mind,* Tit. V, 2, 31.

2) intr.: *my reputation gnawn at,* Wiv. II, 2, 307. *men that fishes —ed upon,* R3 I, 4, 25.

Go (impf. *went;* partic. *gone*) 1) to move step by step, to walk: *I never saw a goddess go,* Sonn. 30, 11. *as proper a man as ever went on four legs,* Tp. II, 2, 63. *I can go no further,* III, 3, 1. *love will creep in service where it cannot go,* Gent. IV, 2, 20. *your wit ambles well, it —es easily,* Ado V, 1, 159. *I can no further crawl, no further go,* Mids. III, 2, 444. *if you go — So far afoot, I shall be weary,* H4A II, 3, 86. *cannot go but thirty mile a day,* H4B II, 4, 179. *ride more than thou —est,* Lr. I, 4, 134. *—ing shall be used with feet,* III, 2, 94.

2) to walk leisurely, not to run: *we'll not run, nor go neither,* Tp. III, 2, 22. *thou must run to him, for thou hast stayed so long that —ing will scarce serve the turn,* Gent. III, 1, 388.

3) to make haste: *towards thee I'll run, and give him leave to go,* Sonn. 51, 14. *trip and go,* LLL IV, 2, 145. *I go, I go, look how I go,* Mids. III, 2, 100. *run, go!* H6B III, 2, 35.

4) to depart (the opposite of to come): *all this service have I done since I went,* Tp. V, 226. *to-morrow be in readiness to go,* Gent. I, 3, 70. *is your countryman gone?* III, 2, 12. *my daughter takes his —ing grievously,* 14. *is the duke gone?* Meas. V, 301. *pluck but his name out of his heart, and turn him —ing,* Caes. III, 3, 39. *there's no — ing but by their consent,* Per. IV, 6, 208 etc. *come go* = let us go: Err. V, 114. H6A IV, 4, 40. Cymb. II, 1, 55. *to come and go:* Tp. IV, 44. Gent. III, 1, 142. Wiv. II, 2, 130. John IV, 2, 76. H6C II, 1, 129 eic. *knocks go and come,* H5 III, 2, 8 (Pistol's speech). *To be gone* often = to go away: *be gone!* Gent. I, 1, 156. III, 1, 168. H8 V, 1, 86. Rom. I, 5, 121. Ant. III, 11, 8 etc. *will ye be gone?* Gent. I, 2, 49; cf. I, 1, 11. *that now you are come, you will be gone,* Meas. III, 1, 180. *if it prove so, I will be gone the sooner,* Err. I, 2, 103. *I'll be gone and not trouble you,* IV, 3, 71. Mids. II, 1, 16. *our intent was to be gone from Athens,* IV, 1, 157. *I'll be gone about it straight,* Merch. II, 4, 25. *you must*

be gone from hence immediately, II, 9, 8. *let us now persuade you. Not to be gone from hence,* H6A III, 2, 94. *thou must be gone from Troilus,* Troil. IV, 2, 97. *will you be gone?* Cor. IV, 2, 14. Rom. III, 5, 1. *pre-pare not to be gone,* I, 5, 123 etc. *get thee gone,* Err. IV, 1, 19 etc. (cf. *Get*).

Hence = to pass away, to vanish, to come to an end: *how things go from him,* Tim. II, 2, 4. *bruised pieces, go; you have been nobly borne,* Ant. IV, 14, 42. *she is —ing,* H8 IV, 2, 99 (= dying); cf. *now my spirit is —ing,* Ant. IV, 15, 58. *To let go* = a) to quit hold: *let go, and let me go,* Ven. 379. *let him go,* Err. IV, 4, 114. *now I let go your hand,* Tw. I, 3, 84. John III, 1, 192. Hml. II, 1, 96. IV, 5, 122. 126. V, 2, 354. Lr. IV, 6, 27. 238. Oth. II, 3, 154. Ant. III, 2, 63. b) to unloose, to unclasp: *let go that rude uncivil touch,* Gent. V, 4, 60. *let go thy hand,* Tw. IV, 1, 40. John III, 1, 195. *let go thy hold,* Lr. II, 4, 73. c) to give up for lost, to try to forget, (never mind): *let him go,* Tp. III, 3, 10. *sigh no mo, and let them go,* Ado II, 3, 68. *let the rest go,* All's II, 3, 155. *let that go,* II, 5, 81 (speak no more of it). *let it go; 'tis but a drum,* III, 6, 48. John III, 3, 33. R2 III, 3, 146. H6B II, 3, 47. Cor. III, 2, 18. Mcb. III, 1, 88. Hml. II, 2, 95. Oth. V, 2, 246. Ant. II, 5, 115.

Gone = a) past: *are they* (kisses) *not quickly told and quickly gone?* Ven. 520. *let us not burthen our remembrance with a heaviness that's gone,* Tp. V, 200. *every present time doth boast itself above a better gone,* Wint. V, 1, 97. *Tuesday night last gone,* Meas. V, 229. *'tis not ten years gone since ...,* H4B III, 1, 57. *'tis not four days gone since I heard thence,* Cor. I, 2, 6. b) finished, consumed: *till either gorge be stuffed or prey be gone,* Ven. 58. *when that* (bottle) *is gone he shall drink nought but brine,* Tp. III, 2, 73. *the fuel is gone that maintained that fire,* H5 II, 3, 45. c) va-nished, away: *the wind would blow it* (his bonnet) *off, and, being gone, play with his locks,* Ven. 1089. *'tis gone; no, it begins again,* Tp. I, 2, 394. *who is fled and gone,* Ado V, 2, 101. d) lost, ruined, dead: *all hope is gone,* Meas. I, 4, 68. *then is your cause gone too,* V, 302. *a diamond gone,* Merch. III, 1, 88. *you are gone both ways,* III, 5, 20. *the party is gone, she is gone,* LLL V, 2, 678. *I am gone for ever,* Wint. III, 3, 58. *we are gone else,* IV, 4, 851. *the suit which you demand is gone and dead,* John IV, 2, 84. *his wits are gone,* Lr. III, 6, 94. cf. *he is far gone,* Hml. II, 2, 190. *Othello's occupation's gone,* Oth. III, 3, 357. *the odds is gone,* Ant. IV, 15, 66. *he's gone,* Tp. II, 1, 122. 244. *my lord that's gone* (= dead) All's IV, 5, 67. *that she were gone, given to the fire,* Wint. II, 3, 7. *the prince is gone. How gone? is dead,* III, 2, 146. *her that's gone,* V, 1, 35. *if that young Arthur be not gone already, even at that news he dies,* John III, 4, 163. *think upon these gone,* Rom. V, 3, 60. *Portia, art thou gone?* Caes. IV, 3, 166. *'tis but a man gone,* Oth. V, 1, 10. *O quick, or I am gone,* Ant. IV, 15, 31. Lr. V, 3, 315. Cymb. IV, 2, 216. e) overpowered by a sensa-tion: *York is too far gone with grief,* R2 II, 1, 184. *thus both are gone with conscience and remorse,* R3 IV, 3, 20. cf. *Overgone.*

The imperative used as a rebuke: *you are a tame man, go,* Mids. III, 2, 259. *go, go; you are a knave,* H5 V, 1, 73. *you are a princox, go,* Rom. I, 5, 88 etc.

5) to move, to pass in any manner and to any end; properly and metaphorically: *the sound is —ing*

away, Tp. III, 2, 157. *here! go, the desk, the purse,* Err. IV, 2, 29. *went'st not to her for a purse of ducats?* IV, 4, 90. *never —ing aright, being a watch, but being watched that it may still go right,* LLL III, 194. 195. cf. *my dial —es not true,* All's II, 5, 6. *that way —es the game,* Mids. III, 2, 289. *I did go between them,* All's V, 3, 258; cf. Oth. III, 3, 100. *who —es there?* H6C IV, 3, 26. *thy slander hath gone through and through her heart,* Ado V, 1, 68 etc. etc. *to go together* = to agree, to be in keeping: *they* (viz honour and safety) *do not go together,* Ant. IV, 15, 47. *her beauty and her brain go not together,* Cymb. I, 2, 32. *to go with* = a) to attend, to be with, to be applied to: *let the proverb go with me: I'll be horn-mad,* Wiv. III, 5, 154. *good words went with her name,* Meas. III, 1, 220. *let death and honesty go with your impositions,* All's IV, 4, 29. *had rather go with sir priest than sir knight,* Tw. III, 4, 298. *that great property which still should go with Antony,* Ant. I, 1, 59. *had it* (victory) *gone with us,* Cymb. V, 5, 76. *grace go with you,* Meas. II, 3, 39. John III, 3, 71. H5 IV, 3, 11. H6B II, 4, 87. Mcb. II, 4, 40 etc. b) to agree, to accord: *your better wisdoms, which have freely gone with this affair,* Hml. I, 2, 15. *which is no further than the main voice of Denmark —es withal,* I, 3, 28. *went hand in hand even with the vow,* I, 5, 49. *—es thy heart with this?* Lr. I, 1, 107 (Qq *—es this with thy heart?*). *all my reports go with the modest truth,* IV, 7, 5. *— which went beyond all man's endeavours,* H8 III, 2, 168. *the king has gone beyond me,* III, 2, 409 (cf. *Beyond*). *you go far,* I, 1, 38. *I will go further than I meant,* Meas. IV, 2, 206 (cf. *Far* and *Further*). *on this side the verdict went,* Compl. 113. Often denoting aim and purpose: *to go about sth.,* cf. *About. —es it against the main of Poland?* Hml. IV, 4, 15. *when you went onward on this ended action,* Ado I, 1, 299. *this action I now go on is for my better grace,* Wint. II, 1, 121. *in what fashion he —es upon this present action,* Cor. I, 1, 282. *I am —ing to* = I am about to: Gent. III, 1, 54. Meas. III, 2, 272. R3 I, 3, 341 etc. *go a bat-fowling,* Tp. II, 1, 185 (cf. *A*). *go to buffets,* H4A II, 3, 35. *went to cuffs,* Hml. II, 2, 373. *go not to arms against mine uncle,* John III, 1, 308. *boys went to span-counter,* H6B IV, 2, 166. *go to horse,* Shr. IV, 3, 193. *to hazard,* H5 III, 7, 93. *to work,* Hml. II, 2, 139. *go to your bosom,* Meas. II, 2, 136 (= examine yourself). *go to your knees,* III, 1, 171 (cf. the resp. substantives). *ignorant to whom it —es,* Gent. II, 1, 116 (= to whom it is addressed). *let the high office and the honour go to one that would do thus,* Cor. II, 3, 129 (= fall to the share of). *more fierce quality than doth go to the creating a whole tribe of fops,* Lr. I, 2, 14. *go to it orderly,* Shr. II, 45. *to go to it* = a) to suffer death: *three or four of his blind brothers and sisters went to it,* Gent. IV. 4, 5. *so Guildenstern and Rosencrantz go to it,* Hml. V, 2, 56. b) to fornicate: *the wren goes to it,* Lr. IV, 6, 114. 124. *did you go to it so young?* Per. IV, 6, 80. — Followed by an inf.: a) with *to*: *to take order for the wrongs I went,* Err. V, 146. *I went to seek him,* 225. LLL IV, 1, 24. As II, 7, 128. John V, 1, 24. R2 III, 2, 211. H6A II, 3, 32 etc. b) without *to,* almost redundantly: *go make thyself like a nymph,* Tp. I, 2, 301. *go take this shape,* 303. *go sleep, and hear us,* II, 1, 190. *I must go send some better messenger,* Gent. I, 1, 159. *thou wouldst as soon go kindle fire with snow,* II, 7, 19. *go mend,* Meas. III, 2, 28.

you may as well go stand upon the beach and bid the main flood bate his usual height, Merch. IV, 1, 71. Tp. II, 2, 53. 56. IV, 1, 37. 186. 259. V, 30. Gent. I, 2, 100. IV, 4, 123. Wiv. I. 3, 80. I, 4, 7. III, 3, 35. Meas. I, 2, 82. V, 253. Err. I, 2, 9. 30. 104. II, 2, 189. III, 1, 30. 35. 64. 84. III, 2, 152. IV, 4, 116. V, 221. Ado II, 3, 273. V, 2, 103. Mids. I, 1, 246. As I, 1, 79. Shr. II, 108. 112. Tw. III, 3, 19. Wint. IV, 3, 15. R2 I, 4, 63. II, 2, 108. IV, 139. H5 IV, 5, 18. H6A I, 5, 14. II, 3, 28. H6B V, 1, 169. H6C I, 4, 159. II, 1, 160. II, 2, 84. IV, 1, 58. Troil. II, 1, 99. Tit. IV, 3, 7. Caes. I, 2, 25. Oth. IV, 3, 32 etc. etc. Joined to the following verb by *and: wouldst thou have me go and beg my food,* As II, 3, 31. Lr. I, 4, 82. Wint. III, 2, 205. *go some and pull down the Savoy,* H6B IV, 7, 1 etc.

Joined to adverbs: *who went about from this fair throne to heave the owner out,* Lucr. 412. *how he —es about to abuse me,* Meas. III, 2, 215. Ado I, 3, 12. IV, 1, 65. IV, 2, 28. Mids. IV, 1, 212. H5 IV, 1, 212 etc. (cf. *About*). *quite athwart —es all decorum,* Meas. I, 3, 31. *shall make it go quick away* (= pass) Tp. V, 304 (cf. *Away*). *gather the sequel by what went before,* Err. I, 1, 96. *let go by the actor,* Meas. II, 2, 41 (= leave him unpunished). *the first's for me; let her go by,* Shr. I, 2, 256 (leave her untouched, do not look to her). *go by, Jeronimy,* Shr. Ind. 1, 9. *had let go by the swiftest hours,* Compl. 59 (= pass). *the accidents gone by,* Tp. V, 305. *the time —es by,* Tw. III, 4, 398. *lets go by some sixteen years,* Wint. V, 3, 31. *Crispin Crispian shall ne'er go by,* H5 IV, 3, 57. *let sour words go by and language end,* Tim. V, 1, 223. *when went there by an age,* Caes. I, 2, 152. *the night gone by,* Lr. I, 2, 168. *not many moons gone by,* Ant. III, 12, 6 (cf. *By,* prepos. and adv.; see also Ado II, 1, 379). *they had gone down,* Meas. I, 2, 102 (= would have been pulled down). *down —es all before them,* H5 III Chor. 34. *the moon —es down at twelve,* Mcb. II, 1, 3 (= sets). *to go even* = to agree: *the rest —es even,* Tw. V, 246. *shunned to go even with what I heard,* Cymb. I, 4, 47. *to go far,* Wint. I, 2, 218 etc. (cf. *Far*). *if a virgin, and your affection not gone forth,* Tp. I, 2, 448. *ere the writs go forth,* H6B V, 3, 26. *if he had gone forth Consul,* Cor. IV, 6, 35. *when —es this forward?* Cor. IV, 5, 228 (cf. *Forward*). *it shall go hard but I'll prove it,* Gent. I, 1, 86. *it shall go hard but I will better the instruction,* Merch. III, 1, 75. *it shall go hard if Cambio go without her,* Shr. IV, 4, 109. *when a man's servant shall play the cur with him, it —es hard,* Gent. IV, 4, 2. *it will go hard with poor Antonio,* Merch. III, 2, 292. *'twill go hard with you,* H6B IV, 2, 108. *to go in* = a) to enter: Wiv. I, 1, 288. II, 1, 171. III, 3, 244 etc. b) to have room enough: *he is too big to go in there,* Wiv. III, 3, 142. *to go near* = to be like to: *it will go near to remove his fit,* Tp. II, 2, 78. *it will go near to be thought so,* Ado IV, 2, 24. *this passion would go near to make a man look sad,* Mids. V, 294. *would have gone near to fall in love with him,* As III, 5, 125. *you shall go near to call them knaves,* H6B I, 2, 102. *to go off* (cf. *Off*) = a) to be discharged: H4B II, 4, 147. b) to depart: *the soul and body rive not more in parting than greatness —ing off,* Ant. IV, 13, 6. c) to be deducted: *I would the friends we miss were safe arrived. Some must go off,* Mcb. V, 8, 36. d) to fall, to be cut off: *off —es your head,* H6B IV, 1, 17. R3 IV, 5, 4. H8 I, 2, 186. e) to be taken off: *this woman's* an easy glove; she —es off and on at pleasure, All's V, 3, 279. *to go on* = a) to get on one's way, to set off: *go safely on to seek thy son,* Tp. II, 1, 327. *go on before,* Gent. II, 4, 186 etc. b) to continue: Ado V, 1, 1. Wint. I, 2, 82 etc. c) to proceed: *it —es on, I see, as my soul prompts it,* Tp. I, 2, 419. *with the same haviour that your passion bears —es on my master's grief,* Tw. III, 4, 227. *whose quality, —ing on, the sides o' the world may danger,* Ant. I, 2, 198. d) to be put on: All's V, 3, 279. *to go out* = a) to leave a place: *may I not go out ere he come?* Wiv. IV, 2, 51. 66 etc. b) to set out, to march out: *there are other men fitter to go out than I,* H4B III, 2, 126 (= to march as soldiers). *his power went out in such distractions,* Ant. III, 7, 77. *upon this French —ing out,* H8 I, 1, 73. *old Joan had not gone out,* H6B II, 1, 4 (= had not taken her flight). c) to cease, to be extinguished: *thinkest thou the fiery fever will go out with titles blown from adulation?* H5 IV, 1, 270. *then out it —es* (viz the candle) H8 III, 2, 97. Lr. I, 4, 237. *to go round* = to turn round, to revolve: *nineteen zodiacs have gone round,* Meas. I, 2, 172. *cup us, till the world go round,* Ant. II, 7, 125. *to go through* = to do one's utmost: *I do it for some piece of money, and go through with all,* Meas. II, 1, 285. *I have gone through for this piece,* Per. IV, 2, 47. *to go up* = to be put up: *the sword —es up again,* Caes. V, 1, 52. *go to* = come! (a phrase of exhortation or reproof): Tp. V, 297. Gent. II, 1, 13. Wiv. I, 4, 165. II, 2, 159. II, 1, 7. III, 3, 42. Meas. II, 1, 59. II, 2, 156. III, 2, 218. LLL V, 1, 80. Merch. II, 2, 169. As IV, 1, 130. Shr. V, 1, 139. All's V, 2, 58. Tw. II, 5, 168. III, 4, 105. Wint. IV, 4, 709. I, 2, 182. H4B III, 2, 127. H8 IV, 2, 103. H6C IV, 1, 89. Troil. III, 2, 56. Lr. I, 4, 101. III, 3, 8. Oth. IV, 1, 177. IV, 2, 194. Meas. II, 2, 12. IV, 2, 31. Ado I, 1, 202. II, 1, 128. IV, 2, 86. LLL III, 203. All's II, 3, 275. I, 1, 59. John IV, 1, 97. H4A II, 1, 104. III, 3, 70. H6A V, 4, 70. H6B IV, 2, 164. 180. R3 II, 4, 35. Troil. III, 1, 73. Rom. I, 5, 79. 80. 84. II, 4, 196 etc.

6) to proceed, to have its course regulated: *loving —es by haps,* Ado III, 1, 105. *hanging and wiving —es by destiny,* Merch. II, 9, 83. *preferment —es by letter and affection,* Oth. I, 1, 36. *we go by the moon and seven stars,* H4A I, 2, 15. *his disposition would have gone to the truth of his words,* Wiv. II, 1, 61. Used of tunes and melodies: *that —es without a burden,* Ado III, 4, 44. *this tune —es manly,* Mcb. IV, 3, 235. *—es to the tune of Two Maids,* Wint. IV, 4, 295. cf. 11th definition.

7) to fare, to be in a good or ill state: *you shall hear how things go,* Wiv. IV, 5, 126. Tim. III, 6, 20. *things go ill,* Cymb. I, 6, 95. *how —es the world?* Shr. IV, 1, 36. Wint. II, 3, 72. Tim. I, 1, 2. II, 2, 36. Caes. V, 5, 22. Mcb. II, 4, 21. Hml. II, 2, 179. Lr. IV, 6, 151 (cf. *World*). *howe'er the business —es,* Wint. III, 2, 218. H8 IV, 1, 23. *how —es the day with us?* John V, 3, 1. *how —es the field?* H4A V, 5, 16. *crossly to thy good all fortune —es,* R2 II, 4, 24. *how —es our reckoning?* Tim. II, 2, 159. *how —es the night?* Mcb. II, 1, 1 (what time of night is it?). *nothing es right,* Meas. IV, 4, 37. *with princes if it shall go well,* Sonn. 14, 7. *all —es well,* LLL V, 2, 113. John III, 4, 4. H4A IV, 1, 83. H6C IV, 2, 1. Oth. II, 3, 380. Ant. III, 10, 27. *nought shall go ill,* Mids. III, 2, 462. *all —es worse,* R2 III, 2, 120. *it must go*

wrong with you, John I, 41. *it —es so heavily with my disposition,* Hml. II, 2, 309. *how it —es with us,* Meas. I, 1, 58. Wint. V, 2, 29. Mcb. IV, 3, 180. Oth. IV, 3, 11. Ant. I, 5, 38. IV, 12, 3. V, 2, 332. Cymb. III, 5, 22.

8) to exist, to live, to be: *thou among the wastes of time must go,* Sonn. 12, 10. *wit shall not go unrewarded,* Tp. IV, 242. *if you went in pain, this knave would go sore,* Err. III, 1, 65. *Benedick —es foremost in report,* Ado III, 1, 97. *thou shalt like an airy spirit go,* Mids. III, 1, 164. *I shall make shift to go without him,* Merch. I, 2, 97; cf. Shr. IV, 4, 109 and Oth. I, 3, 368. *it —es much against my stomach,* As III, 2, 21 and H5 III, 2, 56; cf. *you go against the hair of your professions,* Wiv. II, 3, 41. *commendations go with pity,* All's I, 1, 49. *the story then —es false,* V, 3, 229. *let men go free,* H5 III, 6, 44; cf. Hml. III, 1, 196. III, 3, 26. IV, 3, 2. *which of the peers have uncontemned gone by him?* H8 III, 2, 10. *yet go we under our opinion still that we have better men,* Troil. I, 3, 383. *he has done nobly, and cannot go without any honest man's voice,* Cor. II, 3, 139. *answer have I none but what should go by water,* Oth. IV, 2, 104. *she went before others,* Cymb. I, 4, 78 (= was superior to others); cf. V, 2, 8.

9) to be current: *should go so general current through the world,* H4A IV, 1, 5. *your ill angel is light; but I hope he that looks upon me will take me without weighing; and yet in some respects I cannot go, I cannot tell,* H4B I, 2, 190. *go current from suspicion,* R3 II, 1, 94. *the report —es,* Wiv. I, 3, 58. *an old tale —es,* IV, 4, 28. cf. All's V, 1, 13. Tim. V, 1, 18. *the hare of whom the proverb —es,* John II, 137; cf. Wiv. III, 5, 154. *the voice —es,* H8 IV, 2, 11. *the noise —es,* Troil. I, 2, 12. *the cry went once on thee,* III, 3, 184; cf. Oth. IV, 1, 127. *the whisper —es so,* Hml. I, 1, 80.

10) to be accepted as current, to pass: *this same shall go,* LLL IV, 3, 59. *the property by what it is should go, not by the title,* All's II, 3, 137. *the things they go under,* III, 5, 22 (= what they pretend to be); cf. Ado II, 1, 212. *to be said an honest man —es as fairly as ...,* Tw. IV, 2, 10. *in the catalogue ye go for men,* Mcb. III, 1, 92. cf. *how go maidenheads?* Troil. IV, 2, 23.

11) to be expressed in words, to run: *thus it —es,* As II, 5, 51. *and thane of Cawdor too: went it not so?* Mcb. I, 3, 87. cf. 6th definition.

12) to be dressed: *he that —es in the calf's skin,* Err. IV, 3, 18. 23. Ado I, 1, 247. V, 1, 96. 203. LLL V, 2, 717. As III, 2, 234. Shr. III, 2, 76. Tw. III, 4, 416. H6B IV, 1, 48. IV, 2, 13. 195. Troil. III, 2, 99. Tim. V, 1, 70. Lr. II, 4, 271. Oth. II, 1, 151.

13) to be pregnant: *thirty three years have I but gone in travail of you,* Err. V, 400. *the child I now go with,* H4B V, 4, 10. *went with child of Edward,* R3 III, 5, 86. *great-bellied women that had not half a week to go,* H8 IV, 1, 77. *the fruit she —es with,* V, 1, 20. *go great with tigers,* Tim. IV, 3, 188.

14) to become: *the prince will go mad,* Troil. IV, 2, 78. Lr. II, 4, 289.

15) Seemingly trans., = to enter on, to make: *look forward on the journey you shall go,* Meas. IV, 3, 61. *you go not the way to examine,* Ado IV, 2, 35. Wint. III, 3, 132. John V, 3, 7. Mcb. II, 3, 21. (cf. *Way*). *a king may go a progress through the guts of a beggar,* Hml. IV, 3, 33.

16) Peculiar phrases: *you shall go*, H4B III, 2, 127 (= march, become a soldier). *in what key shall a man take you, to go in the song?* Ado I, 1, 188 (= to join you in your song). *there it —es* = well done! Tp. IV, 257. Tit. IV, 3, 76.

Goad, subst. a pointed instrument (used to drive on beasts): *—s, thorns, nettles, tails of wasps*, Wint. I, 2, 329.

Goad, vb. to stimulate: Meas. II, 2, 182. All's V, 1, 14. Cor. II, 3, 271.

Goal, mark, aim: *but to the g.* Wint. I, 2, 96 (= to the purpose). *can get g. for g. of youth*, Ant. IV, 8, 22 (= get the better of youth in any contest). *honour be but a g. to my will*, Per. II, 1, 171.

Goat, the animal Capra Hircus: Wiv. V, 5, 146. Merch. I, 3, 168. As III, 3, 2. 7. H4A III, 1, 39. IV, 1, 103. H5 IV, 4, 20 *(mountain g.)*. V, 1, 29. 30. Cor. III, 1, 177. Tit. IV, 2, 178. Mcb. IV, 1, 27. Oth. III, 3, 180. 403. IV, 1, 274. Cymb. IV, 4, 37.

Goatish, lustful, lecherous: Lr. I, 2, 138 (cf. *Goat* in H5 IV, 4, 20. Oth. III, 3, 403. IV, 1, 274. Cymb. IV, 4, 37).

Gobbet, a mouthful, a small piece (of flesh): H6B IV, 1, 85. V, 2, 58.

Gobbo, name in Merch. II, 2, 4. 5. 8.

Go-between, subst. one who transacts business (in love-affairs) between two parties: Wiv. II, 2, 273 (cf. All's V, 3, 258. Oth. III, 3, 100).

Goblet, a drinking vessel, a cup: As III, 4, 26. R2 III, 3, 150. H4B II, 1, 94.

Goblin, a mischievous spirit: Tp. IV, 259. Err. II, 2, 192. Mids. III, 2, 399. Wint. II, 1, 26. Troil. V, 10, 29. Hml. I, 4, 40. V, 2, 22.

God, subst. the Supreme Being, a deity: Tp. I, 2, 10. 373. II, 2, 122. V, 296. Gent. IV, 4, 201. Wiv. I, 1, 37. I, 4, 5 etc. etc. Plur. *—s*, Err. I, 1, 99 etc. *O the —s!* Cor. II, 3, 60. IV, 1, 37. Ant. V, 2, 171. *O the good —s!* 221. *when maidens sue, men give like —s*, Meas. I, 4, 81. *G. is a good man*, Ado III, 5, 39 (proverbial phrase). *G. be with my old master*, As I, 1, 88. *G. buy you* (= G. be with you; cf. *Buy*), As III, 2, 273. IV, 1, 31. V, 3, 41. *G. ye good even*, As V, 1, 16. *G. ye good morrow*, Rom. II, 4, 115. *G. ye good den*, 116. *—'s book*, H6B II, 3, 4. *—'s mother*, H6A I, 2, 78. *—'s bread!* Rom. III, 5, 177. *by —'s lid*, Troil. I, 2, 228. *—'s my life!* Ado IV, 2, 72. Mids. IV, 1, 209. *—'s light!* H4A III, 3, 71. *—'s me, my horse!* H4A II, 3, 97. *by —'s will!* H6A II, 4, 82. *—'s will!* H5 IV, 3, 23. 74. H8 II, 3, 12. *—'s will and his pleasure!* H5 IV, 8, 2 (Fluellen's speech; cf. *Will*). The name of God often omitted; cf. *Bless* and *Save*. As often altered in O. Edd. by the substitution of *Heaven, Jove* etc., cf. Qq and Ff in R2 II, 1, 238. II, 2, 98. III, 1, 37. V, 3, 4. H4A I, 3, 214. II, 1, 29. II, 4, 209 etc. Used for *Goddess: are you a g.?* Err. III, 2, 9. *we, Hermia, like two artificial —s*, Mids. III, 2, 203.

God, vb. to idolize: *this old man loved me above the measure of a father; nay, —ed me indeed*, Cor. V, 3, 11.

God-a-mercy, 1) God have mercy: *G. on his soul!* Hml. IV, 5, 199 (Ff *Gramercy*). *G., Grumio, then he shall have no odds*, Shr. IV, 3, 154. *G., so should I be sure to be heart-burned*, H4A III, 3, 58.

2) gramercy, thank you: *good den, Sir Richard! G., fellow*, John I, 185. *the Lord in heaven bless thee,*

noble Harry! G., old heart, H5 IV, 1, 34. *G., that thou wilt believe me*, Troil. V, 4, 33. *how does my good Lord Hamlet?* Well, *G.* Hml. II, 2, 172.

God-daughter, a girl for whom one became sponsor at baptism: H4B III, 2, 8.

God-den, see *Godgigoden* and *Good-den*.

Goddess, a female deity: Ven. 28. Sonn. 111, 2. 130, 11. Pilgr. 34. Tp. I, 2, 421. V, 187. Meas. I, 1, 39. Ado V, 3, 12. LLL IV, 3, 65. 75. V, 2, 36. Mids. III, 2, 137. 226. As I, 2, 56. All's I, 1, 183. I, 3, 116. IV, 2, 2. Wint. II, 3, 104. IV, 4, 210. V, 1, 131. H5 III, 6, 29. Troil. I, 1, 27. I, 2, 257. Cor. I, 5, 21. Tit. II, 1, 22. Lr. I, 2, 1. I, 4, 297. Ant. I, 2, 73. III, 6, 17. III, 10, 4. Cymb. IV, 2, 169. 295. Per. V, 1, 251. V, 3, 6.

Goddess-like, like a goddess, adv. Wint. IV, 4, 10. Cymb. III, 2, 8. Per. V Prol. 4.

Godfather, sponsor at baptism: Ven. Dedic. 5. LLL I, 1, 88. 93. Merch. IV, 1, 398. R3 I, 1, 48. H8 V, 3, 163. V, 4, 39.

Godgigoden or **Godigoden**, 1) a phrase of salutation, = god give you a good evening, Rom. I, 2, 58. 2) an exclamation of reproof: *I speak no treason. O G.* Rom. III, 5, 173 (cf. *Digyouden*)

Godhead, divinity, godship: LLL V, 2, 10. As IV, 3, 44. Tim. III, 6, 84. Cymb. V, 4, 103.

Godild or **God 'ild**, a phrase used in returning thanks (corrupted from *God yield*, cf. Ant. IV, 2, 33): *G. you for your last company*, As III, 3, 76 (= thank you). *I like him very well. G. you, sir*, V, 4, 56. *how you shall bid G. us for your pains*, Mcb. I, 6, 13. *how do you, pretty lady? Well, G. you*, Hml. IV, 5, 41.

Godlike, 1) adj. divine: LLL I, 1, 58. Merch. III, 4, 3. Troil. I, 3, 31 (Ff *godly*). Hml. IV, 4, 38.

2) adv. like a God: *g. perfect*, Per. V, 1, 208.

Godliness, piety, careful observance of the laws of God: Tw. III, 4, 135. Oth. I, 2, 9.

Godly, pious, righteous, conformed to God's law: Wiv. I, 1, 187. H6A V, 1, 5. Troil. I, 3, 31 (Q *godlike*). II, 2, 32. IV, 4, 82.

Godson, one for whom another has been sponsor at baptism: Lr. II, 1, 93.

Goer back, one who gives way: Cymb. I, 1, 169.

Goer backward, one who suffers deterioration instead of improving: All's I, 2, 48.

Goer between, one who transacts business between two parties: Troil. III, 2, 208.

Goffe, name in H6B IV, 5, 11 (most M. Edd. *Gough*).

Gogs-wouns, corruption from *God's wounds*: *by G.* Shr. III, 2, 162.

Gold, subst. 1) the most precious metal: Ven. 768. Compl. 45. Tp. V, 208. Gent. II, 4, 171. Wiv. I, 1, 52. I, 3, 76. II, 2, 69. III, 4, 16 etc. *a hundred pound in g.* Wiv. IV, 6, 5. Err. II, 1, 61. III, 1, 8. H4A II, 4, 307. H5 IV, 1, 44. *g. preserving life in medicine potable*, H4B IV, 5, 163 (a solution of gold being thought to have medicinal virtues).

2) money: Lucr. 855. Err. I, 2, 70. II, 2, 1. 9. Merch. II, 4, 32. III, 2, 308. As II, 3, 45 etc. *might'st have coined me into g.* H5 II, 2, 98.

Gold, adj. made of gold: Troil. I, 3, 296. Rom. I, 3, 92. Figuratively: *his (the sun's) g. complexion*, Sonn. 18, 6. *those g. candles*, 21, 12. *her hairs were*

g. LLL IV, 3, 142. *in their* (the cowslips') *g. coats*, Mids. II, 1, 11.

Gold-bound, encompassed with gold: *g. brow*, Mcb. IV, 1, 114.

Golden, 1) consisting of gold: *Love's g. arrow*, Ven. 947; cf. Mids. I, 1, 170 and Tw. I, 1, 35. *the g. bullet*, Pilgr. 328 (i. e. bribes). *a g. fleece*, Merch. I, 1, 170; cf. *the G. Fleece*, H6A IV, 7, 69. *in a g. bed*, Merch. II, 7, 59. *the g. chest*, II, 9, 23. *rings*, Shr. IV, 3, 55. R2 III, 2, 59. IV, 1, 184. H4A II, 4, 419. IV, 5, 36. H5 II, 2, 169. H6A V, 3, 118, H6B I, 1, 243. III, 1, 352. H6C II, 5, 52. III, 2, 152. R3 III, 5, 96. IV, 1, 60. IV, 4, 140. Rom. III, 3, 22. Mcb. I, 5, 29. IV, 3, 153. Lr. I, 4, 179. Cymb. II, 4, 88. III, 1, 61. Per. I, 1, 27. *g. gifts*, Err. III, 2, 188. *g. care* (i. e. the crown) H4B IV, 5, 23; cf. *g. sorrow*, H8 II, 3, 22.

2) ornamented with gold: *my g. coat*, Lucr. 205; cf. H4A IV, 1, 100. *g. towers*, Lucr. 945; cf. *g. palaces*, H6A V, 3, 170. *g. letter*, LLL V, 2, 44. John III, 1, 85. Per. IV, 3, 44. *g. quoifs*, Wint. IV, 4, 226.

3) rich in gold: *these g. shores*, Wiv. I, 3, 89. *the learned pate ducks to the g. fool*, Tim. IV, 3, 18.

4) resembling gold in colour and brightness: *the g. splendour of the sun*, Lucr. 25; cf. 777. Sonn. 7, 8. 33, 3. LLL IV, 3, 26. Mids. V, 279. Wint. IV, 4, 30. R2 I, 3, 146. H4A III, 1, 222. H5 II, 4, 58. H6C II, 1, 21. R3 V, 3, 19. Tit. II, 1, 5. Rom. I, 1, 126. Hml. II, 2, 313. Ant. V, 2, 320. *her g. hairs*, Ven. 51; cf. Lucr. 400. Sonn. 68, 5. Err. III, 2, 48. Merch. III, 2, 92. 122. *their* (the fishes') *g. gills*, Ven. 1100; cf. Ado III, 1, 27. *his silver skin laced with his g. blood*, Mcb. II, 3, 118 (cf. *Gild*). *her g. couplets*, Hml. V, 1, 310. *to ope their g. eyes*, Cymb. II, 3, 26.

5) precious, excellent, happy, auspicious: *the g. age*, Lucr. 60. Tp. II, 1, 168. As I, 1, 125. *this thy g. time*, Sonn. 3, 12. *when g. time convents*, Tw. V, 391. *g. times*, H4B V, 3, 100. H6C III, 2, 127. *this g. day of victory*, H6A I, 6, 31. *in former g. days*, H6C III, 3, 7. *the g. prime of this prince*, R3 I, 2, 248. *g. hap*, Lucr. 42: cf. Cymb. V, 4, 132. *Fortune's g. hand*, John III, 1, 57. *the g. yoke of sovereignty*, R3 III, 7, 146; cf. IV, 4, 329. *thy g. sleep*, H4A II, 3, 44; cf. R3 IV, 1, 84. Tit. II, 3, 26. Rom. II, 3, 38. Per. III, 2, 23. *his g. enfranchisement*, R2 I, 3, 90. *in g. multitudes*, H4A IV, 3, 73. *g. service*, Tw. IV, 3, 8. *g. joys*, H4B IV, 3, 104. *opinions*, Mcb. I, 7, 33. *promises*, Tit. IV, 4, 97. *Nestor's g. words*, Lucr. 1420; cf. Hml. V, 2, 136. *with g. quill*, Sonn. 85, 3. *poets' sinews, whose g. touch ...*, Gent. III, 2, 79. *the g. cadence of poesy*, LLL IV, 2, 126. *Helen's g. tongue*, Troil. I, 2, 114. *the g. story*, Rom. I, 3, 92. *a g. mind stoops not to shows of dross*, Merch. II, 7, 20. *g. lads and girls*, Cymb. IV, 2, 262.

Goldenly, splendidly, excellently: *report speaks g. of his profit*, As I, 1, 6.

Goldsmith, one who manufactures vessels and ornaments of gold: Err. IV, 1, 15. 19. 24. IV, 3, 46. IV, 4, 85. 135. 145. V, 219. 227. As III, 2, 288.

Golgotha, the place of execution in ancient Palestine: R2 IV, 144. Mcb. I, 2, 40.

Goliath, the celebrated Philistine giant: Wiv. V, 1, 23. Plur. *Goliasses:* H6A I, 2, 33.

Gondola (O. Edd. *gondilo* and *gundello*) a pleasure-boat used at Venice: Merch. II, 8, 8. As IV, 1, 38.

Gondolier (O. Edd. *gundelier*) one who rows a gondola: Oth. I, 1, 126.

Goneril, name of the eldest daughter of King Lear: Lr. I, 1, 54 etc.

Gongarian, reading of the spurious Qq in Wiv. I, 3, 23; Ff *Hungarian*, q. v.

Gonzago, name in the interlude in Hml. II, 2, 563. III, 2, 249. 273. 275.

Gonzalo, name in Tp. I, 2, 161. II, 1, 169. 296. 316. V, 15. 62 etc.

Good, adj. having such qualities as are desired, not bad, not evil: *it should the g. ship so have swallowed*, Tp. I, 2, 16. *with his g. arms*, Tp. I, 1, 119. *by this g. light*, II, 2, 147. *of many g. I think him best*, Gent. I, 2, 21. *g. company*, I, 3, 43. *that's not g.* Meas. II, 4, 75. *a g. sharp fellow*, Ado I, 2, 19. *an army of g. hearts*, Merch. III, 5, 72. *quick, g. hands*, Ant. V, 2, 39. *she's a g. sign, but I have seen small reflection of her wit*, Cymb. I, 2, 32 etc. etc. = virtuous, well disposed: *g. wombs have borne bad sons*, Tp. I, 2, 120. *g. natures*, 359. *g. things will strive to dwell with it*, 458. *g. angels preserve the king*, II, 1, 306. *the hand that hath made you fair hath made you g.* Meas. III, 1, 185. *a song of g. life*, Tw. II, 3, 37. 39 etc. (see below *to make g.*) = kind: *like a g. parent*, Tp. I, 2, 94. *with the help of your g. hands*, Tp. Epil. 10. *your g. heart*, Wiv. I, 1, 83. *gave me g. eyes*, I, 3, 67. *you must be so g. to rise*, Meas. IV, 3, 29 (Pompey's speech). *be so g. as read me this letter*, LLL IV, 2, 92 (Jaquenetta's speech). *who builds his hopes in air of your g. looks*, R3 III, 4, 100 (Qq *fair*). *g. leave*, As I, 1, 109 Merch. III, 2, 326. John I, 231. H4A I, 3, 20. H6C III, 2, 34. *your g. pleasure*, Caes. II, 1, 286. *your g. advice*, Mcb. III, 1, 21. *be g. to me*, Meas. III, 2, 202. H4B II, 1, 69. *be g. to Rome*, Cor. IV, 6, 112. *the gods be g. unto us*, V, 4, 33. *I would be g. to thee*, Tim. I, 2, 243. *to be so g. to Caesar as to hear me*, Caes. II, 4, 29. *I will be g. to thee*, IV, 3, 266. *my g. lady, lord, master* = my patroness, patron (cf. *Lady* etc.). In compellations almost = dear: *g. boatswain*, Tp. I, 1, 10. *g. Fate*, 33. *g. sir*, I, 2, 88. 442. *be calm, g. wind*, Gent. I, 2, 118. *g. Eglamour*, V, 1, 8. *do me no harm, g. man*, Wint. IV, 4, 199. Err. III, 1, 1. IV, 4, 50 etc. *my g. lord here*, H6B II, 1, 196. *g. mine host*, Wiv. I, 3, 13. IV, 6, 18. *g. your graces*, H8 III, 1, 78. Oth. I, 3, 52. *g. my complexion*, As III, 2, 204 (cf. *My, Mine, Your, Lord* etc.). = favourable, propitious: *your own g. fortune*, Tp. II, 1, 270. *g. hap*, Gent. I, 1, 15. *your g. word*, III, 2, 42. *in g. time*, Tp. II, 1, 95. Err. II, 2, 58. 65 (cf. *Time*). *g. night, g. day, g. morrow*; cf.. *Night* etc. = fit, proper, convenient, useful: *'tis a g. dulness*, Tp. I, 2, 185. *lest it should ravel and be g. to none*, Gent. III, 2, 52. *what's that g. for?* Merch. III, 1, 54. *'tis not g. that children should know any wickedness*, Wiv. II, 2, 133. *'tis g. we do so*, Merch. II, 4, 28 (= let us do so). *'twere g. you sent him thither*, Gent. I, 3, 29. II, 4, 7. Meas. II, 4, 42. Hml. IV, 5, 14. *'twere g. you do so much*, Merch. IV, 1, 261. *he were as g. go a mile on his errand*, Meas. III, 2, 38 (Elbow's speech). *a' were as g. crack a fusty nut*, Troil. II, 1, 111 (Thersites' speech). *as g. as rotten*, Per. IV, 2, 9. *as g. to chide the waves as speak them fair*, H6C V, 4, 24 (= to as little purpose); cf. *you were as g. to shoot against the wind*, Tit. IV, 3, 57. *g. at sth.* = skilful in: *g. at such eruptions*, LLL V, 1, 120. *he's as g. at any thing*, As

V, 4, 110. *art thou g. at these kickshawses?* Tw. I, 3, 122. *ever g. at sudden commendations,* H8 V, 3, 122. *'tis g.,* in answers, = well, Meas. III, 2, 61. IV, 1, 14. Caes. II, 1, 60. Oth. III, 4, 201. And *g.* alone: *g., then, if his face be the worst thing about him, how could ...,* Meas. II, 1, 163. *would we could see you at Corinth! G., gramercy,* Tim. II, 2, 74. Troil. I, 2, 14. IV, 2, 74. Mcb. IV, 1, 96. Hml. IV, 3, 48. V, 1, 17. Oth. IV, 1, 222. Ant. V, 2, 270. *g. as the best,* Tim. V, 1, 24. = rich, wealthy: *Antonio is a g. man,* Merch. I, 3, 12. *my meaning in saying he is a g. man is to have you understand me that he is sufficient,* 16. *we are accounted poor citizens, the patricians g.* Cor. I, 1, 16. Used simply to raise and strengthen the meaning of a word: *in g. sooth,* Tp. II, 2, 150; cf. *g. deed* = indeed, Wint. I, 2, 42. *thy g. friend Trinculo,* Tp. II, 2, 106. *no great g. lover of the archbishop's,* H8 IV, 1, 104. *for a g. wager,* Tp. II, 1, 28. *may be a precedent and witness g. that thou ...,* R2 II, 1, 130. *g. cheap* = cheap, H4A III, 3, 51 (cf. *Cheap*). *bid him suppose some g. necessity touches his friend,* Tim. II, 2, 236. *that your g. beauties be the happy cause of Hamlet's wildness,* Hml. III, 1, 39. *I have g. hope thou didst not know on't,* Lr. II, 4, 191. *pregnant to g. pity,* IV, 6, 227. *is't too dull for your g. wearing?* Cymb. II, 4, 41.

I'll be as g. as my word = I'll keep my word: Wiv. III, 4, 112. Tw. III, 4, 357. H4A III, 3, 164. H4B V, 5, 90. H5 IV, 8, 33. *as g. as promise,* Cymb. V, 4, 137.

To make g. = a) to prove to be blameless: *was this inserted to make interest g.?* Merch. I, 3, 95. *I say good queen, and would by combat make her g.* Wint. II, 3, 60. b) to prove to be true: *if he make this g.* Gent. II, 4, 75. Err. V, 375. Ado V, 1, 147. Tw. I, 5, 7. R2 I, 1, 4. 37. 99. Troil. I, 3, 274. Rom. V, 3, 286. Mcb. III, 1, 8. 79. Hml. I, 2, 210. c) to maintain: *I made g. my place,* H8 V, 4, 57. *convenient numbers to make g. the city,* Cor. I, 5, 13. *our potency made g.* Lr. I, 1, 175. *made g. the passage,* Cymb. V, 3, 23 (In this sense the two words are never separated by the object). d) to perform, to carry into effect: *Silver made it g. in the coldest fault,* Shr. Ind. 1, 19. *that I may soon make g. what I have said,* Shr. I, 1, 74. *go with me to make the matter g.* IV, 2, 114. *I'll warrant they'll make it g.* H6B V, 1, 122. *make g. this ostentation,* Cor. I, 6, 86. *of no power to make his wishes g.* Tim. I, 2, 202. *what power is in Agrippa, to make this g.?* Ant. II, 2, 145.

Good, subst. 1) a good man; sing.: *unwilling to outlive the g. that did it,* H8 IV, 2, 60. Vocatively (cf. *Fair, Gentle, Sweet* etc.): *g., speak to the mariners,* Tp. I, 1, 3. *nay, g., be patient,* 16. *g., yet remember whom thou hast aboard,* 20. *g. thou, save me a piece of marchpane,* Rom. I, 5, 8. Followed by *now* (q. v.): *g. now, hold thy tongue,* Err. IV, 4, 22. *now, g. now, say so but seldom,* Wint. V, 1, 19. *ay, g. now, love,* Troil. III, 1, 122. *g. now, sit down and tell me,* Hml. I, 1, 70. *g. now, some excellent fortune,* Ant. I, 2, 25. *g. now, play one scene of excellent dissembling,* I, 3, 78. Plur.: *to make bad g., and g. provoke to harm,* Meas. IV, 1, 15. *both joy and terror of g. and bad,* Wint. IV, 1, 2. *all the virtues that attend the g.* H8 V, 5, 28 etc.

2) advantage, benefit, good fortune, welfare: *all g. befortune you,* Gent. IV, 3, 41. *lose*

the g. we oft might win, Meas. I, 4, 78. *I will keep her ignorant of her g.* IV, 3, 113. *choke your g. to come,* V, 427. *I have a motion much imports your g.* 541. *change slander to remorse: that is some g.* Ado IV, 1, 213. *the devil give him g. of it,* Merch. IV, 1, 345. *glad of other men's g.* As III, 2, 79. *what hap? what hope of g.?* H6C II, 3, 8. *love their country's g.* R3 III, 7, 21. *no less importing than our general g.* 68. *prays for Richmond's g.* V, 3, 84. *pointed to the g. of your most sacred person,* H8 III, 2, 173. *as our g. wills,* Cor. II, 1, 258. *it is not nor it cannot come to g.* Hml. I, 2, 158. *if this man come to g.* Lr. III, 7, 100. *portend no g. to us,* I, 2, 113. *let the time run on to g. or bad,* Cymb. V, 5, 129. *your danger's ours. And our g. his,* 315. With *for:* *to bring this woman to evil for your g.* Wiv. III, 5, 98. As I, 1, 85. Wint. V, 1, 32. H6A III, 3, 16. H6B I, 1, 199. IV, 7, 90. Caes. III, 2, 50. Ant. II, 1, 7. With *to:* *it shall be to your g.* As V, 2, 11. Plur. —s: *which for our —s we do no further ask,* John IV, 2, 64. *to do g. to* = to be of use to, to be profitable: Ven. 28. Lucr. 1028. 1117. Wiv. I, 4, 98. Meas. I, 2, 147. I, 4, 76. IV, 1, 52. Err. V, 164. Ado I, 1, 292. Merch III, 5, 8. As V, 2, 64. Wint. V, 2, 134. H6B I, 2, 77. *much g. do it your heart,* Wiv. I, 1, 83. Mids. I, 2, 73. Troil. I, 2, 221. 229. 234. *it did me g., before the palace gate, to brave the tribune,* Tit. IV, 2, 35. *to do g. on* = to work, to produce effect, to prevail on: *what can do g. on him?* Meas. IV, 2, 71. *one that no persuasion can do g. upon,* H4A III, 1, 200, *he may chance to do some g. on her,* Rom. IV, 2, 13. Absol., *to do g.* = to succeed: *shall I do any g.? shall I not lose my suit?* Wiv. I, 4, 152. *I shall do g.* Wint. II, 2, 54. *if we mean to thrive and do g.* H6B IV, 3, 17.

3) goodness, righteousness, virtuous and charitable deeds: *if all these petty ills shall change thy g.* Lucr. 656. *O time, thou tutor both to g. and bad,* 995. *captive g. attending captain ill,* Sonn. 66, 12. *all thy sum of g.* 109, 12. *so you o'ergreen my bad, my g. allow,* 112, 4. Gent. III, 1, 243. V, 4, 156. Meas. I, 4, 38. III, 1, 204. LLL II, 62. Merch. III, 4, 10. As II, 1, 17. II, 7, 63. All's I, 1, 46. II, 3, 135. H6C I, 4, 134. R3 I, 2, 69. H8 IV, 2, 47. V, 1, 123. Caes. III, 1, 246. III, 2, 81. Mcb. II, 4, 41. Hml. IV, 4, 34. Lr. V, 3, 200 etc.

4) property, possession: *we have no g. that we can say is ours,* Lucr. 873. *beauty is but a vain and doubtful g.* Pilgr. 169. Oftener in the plur.: Gent. II, 7, 87. Err. I, 1, 21. 43. I, 2, 2. V, 410. Merch. IV, 1, 310. 353. Shr. I, 2, 57. III, 2, 232. H6B I, 1, 225. H6C IV, 6, 55. R3 II, 4, 69. H8 III, 2, 342 etc. *many a man knows no end of his —s,* As III, 3, 53 (= knows not what to do with his riches?).

Good-bye, see *Buy.*

Good-conceited, well devised, fanciful: Cymb. II, 3, 18.

Good-deed, in very deed: Wint. I, 2, 42 (cf. *Good* adj).

Good-den (O. Edd. *godden* and *gooden*), good evening: John I, 185. H5 III, 2, 89. Cor. II, 1, 103. IV, 6, 20. 21. Tit. IV, 4, 43. Rom. I, 2, 57. II, 4, 116. 117 (*is it g.?* '*Tis no less, for the hand of the dial is now upon the prick of noon*).

Good-faced, pretty: *no, g. sir,* Wint. IV, 3, 123.

Goodfellow, another name of Puck: *or else you are that shrewd and knavish sprite called Robin G.* Mids. II, 1, 34.

Good-friday, the Friday of passion week: John I, 235. H4A I, 2, 128.

Good-jer, see *Good-year.*

Good-limbed, well shaped: H4B III, 2, 113.

Goodly (compar. *—ier:* Tp. I, 2, 483. All's III, 5, 83. superl. *—iest:* H8 IV, 1, 69. Tit. IV, 2, 11. Lr. IV, 3, 19) fair, fine: Lucr. 1247. Sonn. 80, 12. Compl. 137. Tp. I, 2, 416. IV, 113. V, 182. 260. Gent. IV, 1, 56. Err. I, 1, 51. Merch. I, 3, 102. 103. Shr. Ind. 2, 83. 86. II, 264. III, 2, 96. IV, 5, 2. All's I, 1, 160. III, 2, 9. IV, 5, 102. Wint. II, 1, 20. 66. 74. II, 2, 26. V, 1, 178. H4A I, 2, 238. II, 4, 464. H4B I, 3, 103. IV, 1, 20. V, 3, 6. H6C II, 2, 23. 34. V, 1, 31. V, 4, 17. V, 6, 52. R3 I, 3, 9. IV, 4, 320. V, 3, 21. Troil. II, 2, 109. IV, 4, 15. V, 6, 27. V, 8, 2. Cor. IV, 4, 1. IV, 5, 5. Tit. I, 261. II, 3, 67. 76. IV, 2, 11. V, 2, 172. Tim. V, 1, 175. Hml. I, 2, 186. II, 2, 251. 310. Oth. IV, 2, 71. Ant. I, 1, 2. II, 7, 40. Cymb. III, 3, 1. III, 4, 65. Per. II, 4, 36. III, 1, 23. IV, 1, 9. V, 1, 18. 36. 66. Ironically: *a g. broker!* Gent. I, 2, 41. *'tis a g. credit for you,* Wiv. IV, 2, 199. Ado III, 3, 190. III, 4, 65. IV, 1, 318. Shr. V, 2, 91. All's I, 3, 188. H4B II, 4, 214 (Ff *good*). 219. H6A V, 3, 33. Troil. V, 1, 59. V, 10, 35. Cor. III, 1, 261. IV, 6, 147. Tit. IV, 4, 19. Rom. II, 4, 107. Tim. III, 3, 27. Oth. II, 3, 159. Peculiar use: *g. lord, what a wit-snapper are you!* Merch. III, 5, 55. *from gracious England have I offer of g. thousands,* Mcb. IV, 3, 44 (= full, many thousands?).

Good-man or **Goodman** (*Goódman*) a familiar appellation, = a) gaffer: *I'll lay my head to any —'s hat,* LLL I, 1, 310. *g. baldpate,* Meas. V, 328. *g. Verges,* Ado III, 5, 10. LLL IV, 2, 37. V, 1, 156. Tw. IV, 2, 141. H4A II, 4, 106. H4B V, 3, 93. V, 4, 32. Hml. V, 1, 14. *g. boy,* Rom. I, 5, 79. Lr. II, 2, 48. b) husband: *my men should call me lord: I am your g.* Shr. Ind. 2, 107.

Goodman, name in H6B I, 3, 19.

Good-morrow, a term of salutation, good morning: Ven. 859. Lucr. 1219. Gent. II, 1, 102 etc. cf. *Morrow.*

Goodness, 1) the state of being good, good quality: *a healthful state which, rank of g., would by ill be cured,* Sonn. 118, 12. *makes beauty brief in g.* Meas. III, 1, 186. *the g. of a quarrel,* Troil. II, 2, 123. *nothing is at a like g. still,* Hml. IV, 7, 117. 118.
2) moral righteousness, virtue: *die for g.* Sonn. 124, 14. *which any print of g. wilt not take,* Tp. I, 2, 352. *the g. that is cheap in virtue,* Meas. III, 1, 185. 215. III, 2, 236. All's I, 1, 52. 72. IV, 3, 320. V, 1, 13. Wint. II, 2, 43. IV, 2, 13. V, 1, 176. R2 V, 3, 65. H8 II, 1, 94. II, 2, 91. III, 2, 282. 283. 286. 287. V, 5, 22. Mcb. IV, 3, 33. Lr. IV, 2, 38. Oth. II, 3, 367. Ant. I, 4, 11. Cymb. I, 4, 156. I, 6, 158. II, 4, 9. Per. III, 3, 26. IV, 6, 122.
3) kindness: *thanks for thy much g.* Meas. V, 534. *our natural g. imparts this,* Wint. II, 1, 164. *God's g. had been great to thee,* H6B II, 1, 84. H8 III, 2, 249. 263. IV, 2, 131. V, 5, 1. Tim. I, 1, 11. I, 2, 17. IV, 2, 38. Lr. IV, 7, 2. Oth. II, 3, 327. Cymb. II, 3, 64. *for g. sake,* H8 Prol. 23. III, 1, 159.
4) any thing good: *bliss and g. on you,* Meas. III, 2, 228. *we hear such g. of your justice,* V, 6. *there is some soul of g. in things evil,* H5 IV, 1, 4. *Talbot means no g. by his looks,* H6A III, 2, 72. *the g. of the night upon you!* Oth. I, 2, 35 (cf. Meas. IV, 2, 76.

R3 V, 3, 80). *the g. I intend upon you,* Lr. V, 1, 7. *there's no g. in thy face,* Ant. II, 5, 37. *there is no g. in the worm,* V, 2, 268. *all g. that consists in bounty expect even here,* Per. V, 1, 70. = good fortune, success: *as you hope for any g.* R3 I, 4, 194 (Qq *to have redemption). the chance of g. be like our warranted quarrel,* Mcb. IV, 3, 136.

Good-night, 1) a form of salutation in parting for the night: R3 V, 3, 30. Mcb. II, 2, 4 etc. cf. *Night.*
2) a little poem, probably to be sung in a serenade: *his fancies or his —s,* H4B III, 2, 343 (According to Chappell, = last dying speeches, made into ballads).

Goodrig, one of Talbot's baronial titles: H6A IV, 7, 64.

Goodwife, an appellation applied to women as *goodman* to men, gossip: *good morrow, g.* Wiv. II, 2, 36 (M. Edd. not hyphened). *did not g. Keech, the butcher's wife, come in then …?* H4B II, 1, 101.

Good-will, see *Will.*

Goodwins or **Goodwin sands,** name of shallows near the mouth of the Thames: Merch. III, 1, 4. John V, 3, 11. V, 5, 13.

Good-year (O. Edd. *good-ier, good-yeere, good-yere,* and *good-year*) supposed to be corrupted from *goujère,* i. e. the French disease: *the —s shall devour them,* Lr. V, 3, 24. Used as a slight curse: *we must give folks leave to prate: what, the g.!* Wiv. I, 4, 129. *what the g.! why are you sad?* Ado I, 3, 1.* *what the g.! one must bear,* H4B II, 4, 64. *what the g.! do you think I would deny her?* 191.

Goose, 1) the waterfowl Anser (the emblem of foolishness and timidity): Tp. II, 2, 136. Wiv. V, 5, 9. LLL III, 92. 98 etc. Mids. V, 235. 238. Merch. V, 105. As II, 7, 86. H4A III, 1, 232. Rom. II, 4, 75. 78 etc. Lr. II, 2, 89. *breaks his staff like a noble g.* As III, 4, 48 (?). *a green g.* LLL I, 1, 97. IV, 3, 75. *a sweet g.* Rom. II, 4, 86. *Winchester g.* H6A I, 3, 53. Troil. V, 10, 55 (cf. *Winchester*). *a g. look,* Mcb. V, 3, 12. Plur. *geese:* Gent. IV, 4, 35. Wiv. III, 4, 41. V, 1, 27. Mids. III, 2, 20. H4A II, 4, 153. Cor. I, 1, 176. I, 4, 34. Mcb. V, 3, 13. Lr. II, 4, 46.
2) a tailor's smoothing iron: *come in, tailor; here you may roast your g.* Mcb. II, 3, 17.

Gooseberry, the fruit of Ribes Grossularia: *not worth a g.* H4B I, 2, 196.

Goose-pen, a quill: Tw. III, 2, 53.

Goose-quill, the same: Hml. II, 2, 359.

Gorbellied, having a large paunch: H4A II, 2, 93.

Gorboduc (O. Edd. *Gorbodack*) name of an old British king: Tw. IV, 2, 16.

Gordian knot, the celebrated knot of the Phrygian king Gordius, untied by Alexander: H5 I, 1, 46. Cymb. II, 2, 34.

Gore, subst. blood effused from the body: Ven. 664. Mids. V, 346. H5 IV, 6, 12. IV, 7, 82. H6A III, 3, 55. Tim. III, 5, 84. Mcb. II, 3, 122. Hml. II, 2, 484. *bedaubed in blood, all in g. blood,* Rom. III, 2, 56 (the nurse's speech).

Gore, vb. to stab, to pierce: Ven. 616. As II, 1, 25. Tw. II, 5, 117. R2 I, 3, 60. Troil. I, 1, 115. Metaphorically, to wound, to hurt deeply: Sonn. 110, 3. H5 IV, 1, 174. Troil. III, 3, 228. Lr. V, 3, 320.

Gorge, subst. the throat, the swallow, the stomach: *till g. be stuffed,* Ven. 58. *he cracks his* *g*. Wint. II, 1, 44 (i. e. by endeavouring to vomit). *cast the g*. Tim. IV, 3, 40 (= vomit). *my g. rises at it*, Hml. V, 1, 207. *to heave the g*. Oth. II, 1, 236 (== to retch).

Gorge, vb. to glut, to fill: *the —d hawk,* Lucr. 694. *with his presence glutted, —d and full,* H4A III, 2, 84. Rom. V, 3, 46. Lr. I, 1, 120. Absol.: *—ing and feeding from our soldiers' hands,* Caes. V, 1, 82. cf. *Full-gorged.*

Gorgeous, magnificent, splendid: Tp. IV, 152. LLL IV, 3, 223. R2 III, 3, 148. H4A IV, 1, 102. H4B V, 2, 44. H6A V, 3, 64. Rom. III, 2, 85. Lr. II, 4, 271. 272. cf. *Thrice-gorgeous.*

Gorget, a piece of armour to defend the throat: Troil. I, 3, 174.

Gorgon, the common name of three fabulous women with snaky hairs, the sight of whom turned beholders to stone: Mcb. II, 3, 77. Ant. II, 5, 116.

Gormandize, to feed ravenously: Merch. II, 5, 3. H4B V, 5, 57.

Gory, 1) covered with blood: Rom. V, 3, 142. Mcb. III, 4, 51.

2) bloody, deadly: *the obligation of our blood forbids a g. emulation 'twixt us twain,* Troil. IV, 5, 123.

Gosling, a young goose: Cor. V, 3, 35. Per. IV, 2, 91.

Gospel, God's word as revealed by the Evangelists: *a madman's epistles are no —s,* Tw. V, 295.

Gospelled, firm in Christian faith, acting up to the precepts of the gospel: Mcb. III, 1, 88.

Goss, Genista Anglica: Tp. IV, 180.

Gossamour, the filaments floating in the air in autumn: Rom. II, 6, 18. Lr. IV, 6, 49.

Gossip, subst. 1) a sponsor at baptism (masc. and fem.): *'tis not a maid, for she hath had —s,* Gent. III, 1, 269 (sponsors for a child of hers). *go to a —s' feast,* Err. V, 405. *needful conference about some —s for your highness,* Wint. II, 3, 41. *my noble —s, you have been too prodigal,* H8 V, 5, 13.

2) Used as a familiar compellation to a female friend or neighbour: *what ho! g.* Ford, Wiv. IV, 2, 9. *did not goodwife Keech come in then and call me g.* Quickly, H4B II, 1, 102.

3) a sipping and tattling woman: *sometime lurk I in a —'s bowl,* Mids. II, 1, 47; cf. Rom. III, 5, 175. *if my g. Report be an honest woman of her word,* Merch. III, 1, 7. *as lying a g. as ever knapped ginger,* 9. *the babbling g. of the air,* Tw. I, 5, 292. *mighty —s in this monarchy,* R3 I, 1, 83. *a long-tongued babbling g.* Tit. IV, 2, 150. *speak to my g. Venus one fair word,* Rom. II, 1, 11. *smatter with your —s,* III, 5, 172.

Gossip, vb. 1) tr. to christen: *adoptious christendoms, that blinking Cupid —s,* All's I, 1, 189.

2) intr. to make merry, to drink and chat at a christening or any other feast: *with all my heart I'll g. at this feast,* Err. V, 407. *will you walk in to see their —ing,* 419. *full often hath she —ed by my side,* Mids. II, 1, 125. *at feasts, full of warm blood, of mirth, of —ing,* John V, 2, 59.

Gossip-like, resembling a tattling woman: *I will leave you now to your g. humour,* Ado V, 1, 188.

Goth, one of an ancient German tribe in the East of Europe: *Ovid was among the —s,* As III, 3, 9. Often in Tit. (I, 28. 85 etc.).

Gough, see *Goffe.*

Goujere, spelling of some M. Edd. for *Goodyear,* q. v.

Gourd, a species of false dice (perhaps with a secret cavity): Wiv. I, 3, 94.

Gourney, see *Gurney.*

Gout, 1) the arthritis: Meas. III, 1, 31. As III, 2, 338. H4B I, 2, 258. 273. Cymb. V, 4, 5. Plur. *—s,* Lucr. 856.

2) a drop: *—s of blood,* Mcb. II, 1, 46 (*Gouts* is also the term applied to the little knob-like swellings or indurated drops which appear at times on the legs and feet of the hawk. Edinb. Rev. Oct. 72).

Gouty, diseased with the arthritis: Compl. 140. Troil. I, 2, 30. Tim. IV, 3, 46.

Govern, 1) to bear sway, to rule, to reign: *I would with such perfection g.* Tp. II, 1, 167. *upon his place —s lord Angelo,* Meas. I, 4, 57. *who —s here?* Tw. I, 2, 24. H6B I, 1, 166. IV, 9, 48. R3 II, 3, 15. Tit. V, 3, 147. Mcb. IV, 3, 101. Per. IV, 4, 15.

b) to prevail, to sway: *let it be as humours and conceits shall g.* Merch. III, 5, 69. *the heart of brothers g. in our loves,* Ant. II, 2, 150.

2) tr. a) to rule as a chief magistrate, to reign over: *the best —ed nation,* H4B V, 2, 137. *God and King Henry g. England's realm,* H6B II, 3, 30. *to g. and rule multitudes,* V, 1, 94. H6C III, 3, 69. IV, 3, 35. R3 II, 3, 11. H8 I, 2, 171. Tit. IV, 4, 60. Per. II, 4, 31. IV, 6, 59.

b) to sway, to direct, to control, to regulate: *—ed him in strength, though not in lust,* Ven. 42. *kings like gods should g. every thing,* Lucr. 602. *that eye that —s me to go about,* Sonn. 113, 2. *truer stars did g. Proteus' birth,* Gent. II, 7, 74; cf. H4A I, 2, 31; R3 II, 2, 69; Caes. V, 1, 108; Lr. IV, 3, 35. *the finest mad devil of jealousy that ever —ed frenzy,* Wiv. V, 1, 20; cf. Meas. V, 451; Ado I, 1, 67; III, 2, 61; Merch. IV, 1, 134; John V, 1, 47; H4A III, 1, 237; V, 2, 19; Tit. III, 1, 219; Tim. I, 1, 292; Caes. I, 3, 83; IV, 1, 33; Ant. II, 3, 29. *I will g. it* (my tongue) H4B II, 2, 180. *though Venus g. your desires,* Tit. II, 3, 30. *how I have —ed our determined jest,* V, 2, 139. *g. these ventages with your finger,* Hml. III, 2, 372. *be —ed by your knowledge,* Lr. IV, 7, 19. *she's desperate: g. her,* V, 3, 161. *a father by thy stepdame —ed,* Cymb. II, 1, 63.

Governance, direction, control: *a pupil under Gloster's g.* H6B I, 3, 50.

Governess, a female ruler, mistress: *their dear g. and lady,* Lucr. 443. *the moon, the g. of floods,* Mids. II, 1, 103.

Government, 1) direction, control: *a sound, but not in g.* Mids. V, 124 (not a regular tune). *each part deprived of supple g.* Rom. IV, 1, 102. *quite besides the g. of patience,* Cymb. II, 4, 150.

2) self-control, evenness of temper, decency of manners: *the mild glance that sly Ulysses lent showed deep regard and smiling g.* Lucr. 1400. *men of good g.* H4A I, 2, 31. *defect of manners, want of g.* III, 1, 184. *'tis g. that makes them* (women) *seem divine,* H6C I, 4, 132. *wife-like g.* H8 II, 4, 138. *fear not my g.* Oth. III, 3, 256 (cf. *Misgoverned* and *Misgovernment*).

3) rule, authority, supreme power: *the g. I cast upon my brother,* Tp. I, 2, 75. *in the g. of Lord Angelo,* Meas. IV, 2, 141. *come underneath the yoke*

of g. H4B IV, 4, 10. *under the sweet shade of your g.* H5 II, 2, 28. *I here resign my g. to thee,* H6C IV, 6, 24. *Tarsus, o'er which I have the g.* Per. I, 4, 21.

4) conduct, chief command: *under whose g. come they along?* H4A IV, 1, 19. *that quarter whereof I had the g.* H6A II, 1, 64. *deputing Cassio in his g.* Oth. IV, 1, 248.

5) administration of public affairs: *the state g. changed from kings to consuls,* Lucr. Arg. 25. *of g. the properties to unfold,* Meas. I, 1, 3. *or discover his g.* III, 1, 199. *all must be even in our g.* R2 III, 4, 36. *g. doth keep in one consent,* H5 I, 2, 180. *is this the g. of Britain's isle?* H6B I, 3, 47. *that no dissension hinder g.* H6C IV, 6, 40. *in bearing weight of g.* 51. *in him there is a hope of g.* R3 II, 3, 12. *the kingly g. of this your land,* III, 7, 132. *his peaceable reign and good g.* Per. II, 1, 108.

Governor, 1) one invested with supreme authority: *her lord, her g., her king,* Merch. III, 2, 167. Shr. V, 2, 138. *Rome's gracious g.* Tit. V, 3, 146 (= emperor).

2) one who rules a country or place with delegated authority: Meas. I, 2, 164. 169. R2 II, 1, 220. H5 III, 3, 1. H6A I, 4, 20. IV, 1, 3. H6B IV, 1, 89. Oth. II, 1, 30. 55. V, 2, 367. Per. I, 4, 56. 85. IV, 6, 57. 87. V, 1, 4. 21. 221.

3) one who has the care of a young man, a tutor: *being ordained his* (the young king's) *special g.* H6A I, 1, 171.

Gower, name of 1) the famous old English poet: Per. I Prol. 2. II Prol. 40.

2) an attendant of the Lord Chief Justice in H4B II, 1, 145. 191. 194 etc.

3) a captain in Henry V's army: H5 III, 6, 86. IV, 7, 13 etc.

Gown, any long loose upper garment; 1) worn by women: Gent. IV, 4, 166. Wiv. IV, 2, 72. 78. 85. Ado III, 4, 15. 16. LLL V, 2, 844. Shr. IV, 3, 62. 86. 93. H4A III, 3, 4. H4B II, 1, 172. H6B I, 3, 88. Oth. IV, 3, 74.

2) worn by men: Tp. IV, 226. 227. Tim. III, 6, 120. 127. Oth. I, 1, 86. Per. II, 1, 83. 169. *a furred g.* Meas. III, 2, 8. Lr. IV, 6, 169. *an almsman's g.* R2 III, 3, 149. *black mourning --s,* H6C II, 1, 161. *wear the surplice of humility over the black g. of a big heart,* All's I, 3, 99. *one that hath two —s,* Ado IV, 2, 88.

3) the dress of a civil magistrate or a divine: Meas. II, 2, 44. H6B II, 1, 111. 115. Wiv. III, 1, 34. Tw. IV, 2, 1. 7. 70. Cor. II, 2, 141. II, 3, 44. 93 (the Roman toga).

4) a dressing gown to make one's self easy: Tw. II, 5, 54. H4B III, 2, 197. Caes. IV, 3, 231. 239. 253.

Grace, subst. 1) a goddess of beauty bestowing pleasingness: *with the garment of a G. the naked and concealed fiend he covers,* Compl. 316. *more G. than boy,* Gent. V, 4, 166. *had I a sister were a G.* Troil. I, 2, 257. *—s her subjects,* Per. I, 1, 13.

2) any excellence which conciliates love or makes well-pleasing: *in great commanders g. and majesty you might behold,* Lucr. 1387. *all jointly listening, but with several —s,* 1410. *in fresh numbers number all your —s,* Sonn. 17, 6. *in all external g. you have some part,* 53, 13. *arts with thy sweet —s graced be,* 78, 12. *they rightly do inherit heaven's —s,* 94, 5. *thou makest faults —s,* 96, 4. *of your —s and your gifts to tell,* 103, 12. *some defect in her did quarrel with the noblest g. she owed,* Tp. III, 1, 45. *he is complete in feature and in mind with all good g. to grace a gentleman,* Gent. II, 4, 74. III, 1, 102. IV, 2, 42. Ado II, 1, 128. II, 3, 30. LLL II, 9. 10. Mids. I, 1, 206. Merch. II, 7, 33. As II, 2, 13. II, 3, 11. 18. III, 2, 151. H5 III, 5, 34. H6B I, 1, 32. R3 II, 4, 13. Rom. II, 3, 15. Hml. IV, 7, 21. Lr. V, 3, 67. Oth. II, 3, 323. Ant. II, 2, 132 etc. *heaven give thee moving —s,* Meas. II, 2, 36 (i. e. the gift of persuasion). *God give him g. to groan,* LLL IV, 3, 21 (i. e. the pleasant faculty of groaning). *that's the dearest g. it renders you,* H4A III, 1, 182. Often almost equivalent to beauty, attraction, charm: *which to her oratory adds more g.* Lucr. 564. *lascivious g. in whom all ill well shows,* Sonn. 40, 13. *how the channel to the stream gave g.* Compl. 285. *a g. it had devouring,* Tp. III, 3, 84. *no ceremony ... becomes them with one half so good a g. as mercy does,* Meas. II, 2, 62. *less in your knowledge and your g. you show not than our earth's wonder,* Err. III, 2, 31. *if half thy outward —s had been placed about thy thoughts,* Ado IV, 1, 102. *wit's own g. to grace a learned fool,* LLL V, 2, 72. *the moon shines with a good g.* Mids. V, 273. *chid his truant youth with such a g.* H4A V, 2, 63. *natural —s that extinguish art,* H6A V, 3, 192. *can you deliver an oration with a g.?* Tit. IV, 3, 99. 107 (i. e. in a becoming manner). *she would catch another Antony in her strong toil of g.* Ant. V, 2, 351. *To do g.* = to embellish, to become well: *dost him g. when clouds do blot the heaven,* Sonn. 28, 10. *mourning doth thee g.* 132, 11; and in a moral sense, = to reflect credit on: *to do the profession some g.* H4A II, 1, 79. *if a lie may do thee g.* V, 4, 161 (= may make thee appear in a better light). *any good thing that may to thee do ease and g. to me,* Hml. I, 1, 131. Similarly: *by their hands this g. of kings must die,* H5 II Chor. 28 (= this ornament). *To have the g. to do sth.* = to do it in a becoming manner: *what g. hast thou thus to reprove these worms?* LLL IV, 3, 153 (= how does it become you?). *few have the g. to do it,* V, 1, 148. *we have not the g. to grace it with such show,* 320. *have the g. to consider that tears do not become a man,* As III, 4, 2 (= do, as becomes you, consider).

3) favour, kindness, kind regard: *to gain my g.* Compl. 79. Pilgr. 36. *I will pay thy —s home both in word and deed,* Tp. V, 70. *you shall have g. of the duke,* Meas. IV, 3, 140. *his company must do his minions g.* Err. II, 1, 87; cf. *to do him all the g. and good I could,* V, 164; *now shall my friend Petruchio do me g. and offer me ...,* Shr. I, 2, 131; *to come at traitors' calls and do them g.* R2 III, 3, 181; *I will make the king do you g.* H4B V, 5, 6; *do g. to Caesar's corpse,* Caes. III, 2, 62. *one woman shall not come in my g.* Ado II, 3, 31. *to win g.* LLL II, 60. *not a man of them shall have the g. to see a lady's face,* LLL V, 2, 128. *these graces challenge g.* H6C IV, 8, 48. *I confess your royal —s,* H8 III, 2, 166. *doth g. for g. and love for love allow,* Rom. II, 3, 86. *shall continue our —s towards him,* Mcb. I, 6, 30. *which by their — s I will keep,* Cymb. I, 4, 95. *the —s for his merits due,* V, 4, 79 etc.

4) honourable distinction, honour (cf. above to do g. H4A II, 1, 79. Caes. III, 2, 62): *to undergo such ample g. and honour,* Meas. I, 1, 24. *that loose g. which shallow laughing hearers give to fools,* LLL V, 2, 869.

to their penned speech render we no g. 147. *ancestry whose g. chalks successors their way,* H8 I, 1, 59. *do g. to them and bring them in,* Hml. II, 2, 53. *give me g. to lay my duty on your hand,* Ant. III, 13, 81. *in g. of* = in honour of: *came here in g. of our solemnity,* Mids. IV, 1, 139. *in g. whereof the great cannon to the clouds shall tell,* Hml. I, 2, 124.

5) mercy: *death is all the g. I beg,* Meas. V, 379. *wilt thou kneel for g.* H6C II, 2, 81; cf. Ant. V, 2, 28. *to take our brother Clarence to your g.* R3 II, 1, 76. *cry these dreadful summoners g.* Lr. III, 2, 59 etc.

6) beneficent influence of heaven, divine favour, salvation: *heavenly moisture, air of g.* Ven. 64. *heavens rain g. on that,* Tp. III, 1, 75. *of whose soft g. I have her sovereign aid,* V, 142. *swearest g. o'erboard,* 219. *curse the g. that with such grace hath blessed them,* Gent. III, 1, 146. *they have not so little g., I hope,* Wiv. II, 2, 117. *thou art a wicked villain, despite of all g.* Meas. I, 2, 27. *g. go with you,* II, 3, 39; *g. and good company!* III, 1, 44; *g. and good disposition attend your ladyship,* Tw. III, 1, 146. *his affects ... not by might mastered, but by special g.* LLL I, 1, 153. *the more my prayer, the lesser is my g.* Mids. II, 2, 89 (quibbling). *you have the g. of God, and he hath enough,* Merch. II, 2, 160 (allusion to the proverb: *the grace of God is enough*). *this action I now go on is for my better g.* Wint. II, 1, 122. *pour your —s upon my daughter's head,* V, 3, 122. *g. thou wilt have none,* H4A I, 2, 19. *by inspiration of celestial g.* H6A V, 4, 40. Ironically: *a goodly prize, fit for the devil's g.* H6A V, 3, 33. *Herb of g.* = the plant Ruta graveolens: All's IV, 5, 18. R2 III, 4, 105. Hml. IV, 5, 182. *g. grow where those drops fall,* Ant. IV, 2, 38.

7) the headspring of mercy, God: *his g. hath made the match, and all G. say Amen,* Ado II, 1, 315. *I will tell truth: by G. itself I swear,* All's I, 3, 226. *the greatest G. lending g.* II, 1, 163. *G. to boot!* Wint. I, 2, 80. *by the g. of G.* Mcb. V, 8, 72.

8) good fortune, happiness, blessedness: *curse the g. that with such g. hath blessed them,* Gent. III, 1, 146. *unless you have the g. by your fair prayer to soften Angelo,* Meas. I, 4, 69. *the more my prayer, the lesser is my g.* Mids. II, 2, 89 (quibbling). *though I be not so in g. as you,* III, 2, 232. *and I in such a poverty of g.* As III, 5, 100 (Tw. III, 1, 146? see above). *every wink of an eye some new g. will be born,* Wint. V, 2, 120. *a double blessing is a double g.* Hml. I, 3, 53. *further this act of g.* Ant. II, 2, 149. *past hope and in despair; that way, past g.* Cymb. I, 1, 137.

9) blessed disposition of mind, virtue: *desire doth fight with g.* Lucr. 712. *some say thy g. is youth,* Sonn. 96, 2. *disciplined, ay, dieted in g.* Compl. 261. *seek for g.* Tp. V, 295. *the boy hath g. in him; he blushes,* Gent. V, 4, 165. *g., being the soul of your complexion, shall keep the body of it ever fair,* Meas. III, 1, 187. *g. to stand,* III, 2, 278. *when once our g. we have forgot, nothing goes right,* IV, 4, 36. *all the g. that she hath left is that she will not add to her damnation a sin of perjury,* Ado IV, 1, 173. *falsehood turns to g.* LLL V, 2, 786. *if you have any pity, g. or manners,* Mids. II, 2, 241. *they are as innocent as g. itself,* As I, 3, 56; cf. *be they as pure as g.* Hml. I, 4, 33. *I hope your own g. will keep you where you are,* All's III, 5, 28. *put your g. in your pocket,* Tw. V, 35. *out of your g. devise some gentle order,* John III, 1,

250. *make less thy body hence, and more thy g.* H4B V, 5, 56. *a Christian king, unto whose g. our passion is subject,* H5 I, 2, 242. *these —s challenge g.* H6C IV, 8, 48 (= these virtues claim affection). *not a man of you had so much g. to put it in my mind,* R3 II, 1, 120. *bear the inventory of your best —s in your mind,* H8 III, 2, 138. *you are in the state of g.* Troil. III, 1, 15. *two such opposed kings encamp them still in man, g. and rude will,* Rom. II, 3, 28. *the king-becoming —s, as justice, verity, temperance,* Mcb. IV, 3, 91. *time be thine, and thy best —s spend it at thy will,* Hml. I, 2, 63. *conscience and g., to the profoundest pit!* IV, 5, 132. *though we have some g., yet have we some revenge,* Oth. IV, 3, 93. *past g.? obedience?* Cymb. I, 1, 136.

10) thanksgiving before meals: Wiv. I, 1, 274. LLL IV, 2, 161. H4A I, 2, 22. Cor. IV, 7, 3. *to say g.:* Meas. I, 2, 20. Merch. II, 2, 202. Tit. IV, 3, 100.

11) Used as an appellation of persons of the highest rank; of kings and queens: Tp. III, 2, 115. IV, 72. 228. 240. LLL I, 1, 51. II, 32. H6A III, 1, 153. III, 4, 12. IV, 1, 12. H6B I, 1, 4. II, 1, 177 etc. etc. *God save thy g., majesty I should say,* H4A I, 2, 19. Of royal princes and princesses: Ado II, 1, 314. LLL V, 2, 80. 673 etc. Of dukes and duchesses: Gent. III, 1, 52. 67. III, 2, 20. 96. V, 4, 123. Meas. I, 1, 26. I, 3, 31. V, 3. Err. V, 136. Mids. I, 1, 39. 62. V, 106. Merch. IV, 1, 2. H6A III, 1, 60. IV, 1, 162. H6B I, 1, 39. I, 2, 71 *(what sayst thou majesty? I am but g.).* R3 I, 1, 84. II, 4, 24. V, 1, 31 etc. Of high dignitaries of the church: H4A III, 2, 119. H8 I, 4, 21 etc. *G.! not so, friend; honour and lordship are my titles,* Troil. III, 1, 16. *I am thy lover's g.* Mids. V, 197 (Pyramus' speech).

Grace, vb. 1) to give, in any manner, a good appearance to, to set off, to adorn, to dignify, to exalt: *when sighs and groans and tears may g. the fashion of her disgrace,* Lucr. 1319. *eyes this cunning want to g. their art,* Sonn. 24, 13. *and with his presence g. impiety,* 67, 2. *arts with thy sweet graces —d be,* 78, 12. *swear that brightness doth not g. the day,* 150, 4. *their purposed trim pieces not his grace, but were all —d by him,* Compl. 119. *a lily pale, with damask dye to g. her,* Pilgr. 89. *Tunis was never —d with such a paragon,* Tp. II, 1, 74. Gent. II, 2, 18. II, 4, 74. Ado II, 3, 41. LLL I, 1, 3. V, 2, 72. 320. All's I, 1, 91. Wint. V, 1, 22. John II, 348. IV, 2, 62. R2 I, 4, 9. III, 4, 99. V, 6, 51. H4A V, 1, 92. H4B I, 1, 129. H6A V, 5, 3. H6B V, 1, 98. H6C V, 3, 2. R3 III, 5, 11. IV, 4, 383. V, 5, 6. Cor. I, 1, 268. Tit. V, 2, 17. Caes. I, 1, 39. III, 1, 120. Oth. I, 3, 88. Ant. IV, 14, 136. Cymb. V, 5, 406.

2) to do honour: *whom they doted on and blessed and —d more than the king,* H4B IV, 1, 139. *we g. the yeoman by conversing with him,* H6A II, 4, 81. *and —d thy poor sire with his bridal-day,* H6C II, 2, 155. *g. his speech tending to Caesar's glories,* Caes. III, 2, 62. *to g. us with your royal company,* Mcb. III, 4, 45. *to g. him only,* Cor. V, 3, 15. *To g. one's self* = to gain credit and honour: *if he do not mightily g. himself on thee,* As I, 1, 155. *to do yourself good and not to g. me,* V, 2, 64. *to g. himself under the form of a soldier,* H5 III, 6, 71.

3) to exalt, to praise: *I will g. the attempt for a worthy exploit,* All's III, 6, 71.

4) to favour: *—d by the emperor,* Gent. I, 3,

58. to g. *the gentry of a land remote,* John V, 2, 31. *to intrude where I am —d,* Tit. II, 1, 27. *as we list to g. him,* Lr. V, 3, 61 (or = to raise his dignity).

5) to gratify, to make happy: *what comfortable hour ... that ever —d me in thy company,* R3 IV, 4, 174.

6) Arbitrarily derived from the subst., = to speak of grace: *g. me no grace, nor uncle me no uncle,* R2 II, 3, 87 (= do not talk to me of grace).

Graced, adj. full of graces, dignified, honorable: *were the g. person of our Banquo present,* Mcb. III, 4, 41. *a g. palace,* Lr. I, 4, 267.

Graceful, 1) elegantly beautiful, attractive: Ado III, 4, 22. Cor. II, 1, 237. Per. II, 2, 41. IV Prol. 36.

2) favourable: *could not with g. eyes attend those wars,* Ant. II, 2, 60.

3) of a blessed disposition, virtuous: *you have a holy father, a g. gentleman,* Wint. V, 1, 171.

Graceless, impious, profligate: Lucr. 246. Shr. I, 2, 270. V, 2, 160. John IV, 3, 58. H6A V, 4, 14. H6B IV, 4, 38.

Gracious, 1) kind, benevolent, beneficent, salutary: *be, as thy presence is, g. and kind,* Sonn. 10, 11 (quibbling). *your g. favours,* Gent. III, 1, 6. *he is g., if he be observed,* H4A IV, 4, 30. *heaven and our Lady g. hath it pleased,* H6A I, 2, 74. *look g. on thy prostrate thrall,* 117. *heaven, be thou g. to none alive,* I, 4, 85. *those g. words revive my drooping thoughts,* H6C III, 3, 21. *look on my forces with a g. eye,* R3 V, 3, 109. *he's loving and most g.* H8 III, 1, 94. *from him plucked either his g. promise,* Cor. II, 3, 201. *so hallowed and so g. is the time,* Hml. I, 1, 164.

2) finding favour, agreeable: *is he g. in the people's eyes?* H6C III, 3, 117. *if ever Bassianus were g. in the eyes of Rome,* Tit. I, 1, 11. *g. triumpher in the eyes of Rome,* 170. *if ever Tamora were g. in those princely eyes of thine,* 429.

3) in a state of heavenly grace, pious, virtuous, holy: *she hath made him that g. denial which he is most glad to receive,* Meas. III, 1, 166. *do no stain to your own g. person,* 208. *I am a brother of g. order,* III, 2, 232. *fair and g. daughter,* IV, 3, 116. *a g. innocent soul,* Wint. II, 3, 29. *their issue not being g.* IV, 2, 30. *if this rule were true, he should be g.* R3 II, 4, 20. *God keep your lordship in that g. mind,* III, 2, 56. *to make it* (the quarrel) *g.* Troil. II, 2, 125. *his g. nature would think upon you,* Cor. II, 3, 195. *his large fortune upon his good and g. nature hanging,* Tim. I, 1, 56. *these are g. drops,* Caes. III, 2, 198. *the g. Duncan,* Mcb. III, 1, 66. III, 6, 3. 10. *what would your g. figure?* Hml. III, 4, 104. *thy state is the more g.* V, 2, 86. *a g. aged man,* Lr. IV, 2, 41.

4) happy, fortunate, prosperous: *to try her g. fortune with Lord Angelo,* Meas. V, 76. *there is but one shamed that was never g.* As I, 2, 200. *g. be the issue,* Wint. III, 1, 22. *give to a g. message an host of tongues,* Ant. II, 5, 86.

5) lovely, attractive, beautiful: *when the g. light lifts up his burning head,* Sonn. 7, 1. *be, as thy presence is, g. and kind,* 10, 11 (quibbling). *no face so g. is as mine,* 62, 5. *my g. numbers are decayed,* 79, 3. *shall will in others seem right g.* 135, 7. *that word makes the faults g.* Gent. III, 1, 378. *never shall it* (beauty) *more be g.* Ado IV, 1, 109. *apt and g. words,* LLL II, 73. *my love, her mistress, is a g. moon,* IV, 3, 230. *to make an offence g.* V, 1, 147. *to make*

it *the more g. I shall sing it at her death,* Mids. IV, 1, 224. *thy g. golden glittering gleams,* V, 279. *seasoned with a g. voice,* Merch. III, 2, 76. *a g. person,* Tw. I, 5, 281. *very g. fooling,* II, 3, 22. *the g. mark o' the land,* Wint. IV, 4, 8. *a g. creature,* John III, 4, 81. *his g. parts,* 96. *with all the g. utterance thou hast,* R2 III, 3, 125. *virtuous and fair, royal and g.* R3 IV, 4, 204. *my g. silence,* Cor. II, 1, 192.

6) Used as a courteous epithet in speaking of or to royal or noble persons: *how fares my g. sir?* Tp. V, 253. *my g. lord,* All's II, 3, 174. *commend the paper to his g. hand,* V, 1, 31. *my g. sovereign,* V, 3, 87. *our most g. mistress,* Wint. I, 2, 233. 249. 459. *come, my g. lord,* II, 1, 2. *how fares our g. lady?* II, 2, 21. *his g. dam,* III, 2, 199. *g. my lord,* IV, 4, 477. *g. couple,* V, 1, 134. *spring from one most g. head,* R2 III, 3, 108. *this g. meeting,* H5 V, 2, 13. *most g. sovereign,* H6A III, 1, 149. V, 3, 161. *to your most g. hands,* H6B I, 1, 13. *what is your g. pleasure?* Mcb. V, 3, 30. *g. England,* IV, 3, 43. *g., so please you,* Hml. III, 1, 43 etc. Used of dukes and duchesses: Gent. III, 1, 4. Meas. V, 63. 421. Err. V, 159. 190. Mids. I, 1, 26. Merch. IV, 1, 165. R3 I, 1, 122 etc. Of other nobility: *g. lords,* LLL V, 2, 739. H5 I, 2, 1. H6A I, 1, 103. *g. Olivia,* Tw. V, 108.

Graciously, 1) kindly, favourably, mercifully: *points on me g. with fair aspect,* Sonn. 26, 10. *God so g. hath brought to light this treason,* H5 II, 2, 185. *Laertes' son did g. plead for his funeral,* Tit. I, 381. *look g. on him,* 439.

2) virtuously, holily: *but g. to know I am no better,* Meas. II, 4, 77. *what he will do g., I will thankfully receive,* Per. IV, 6, 65.

Gradation, regular advance from step to step: *by cold g. and weal-balanced form,* Meas. IV, 3, 104. *preferment goes by letter and affection, and not by old g.* Oth. I, 1, 37.

Graff, subst. a scion: Lucr. 1062. Per. V, 1, 60.

Graff, vb. to impregnate with a scion: As III, 2, 124. H4B V, 3, 3. Partic. *graft:* H6B III, 2, 214. R3 III, 7, 127. cf. *Misgraffed.*

Graft, vb. 1) to insert as a scion, to make take root in and grow to: *his plausive words he scattered not in ears, but —ed them,* All's I, 2, 54. *a servant —ed in my serious trust,* Wint. I, 2, 246. *the plants thou —est,* R2 III, 4, 101. *such rude society as thou art —ed to,* H4A III, 2, 15. *all the particulars of vice so —ed,* Mcb. IV, 3, 51.

2) to impregnate with a scion: *we have some old crabtrees that will not be —ed to your relish,* Cor. II, 1, 206.

Grafter, the tree from which a scion is taken to insert it in another: *our scions, put in wild and savage stock, spirt up so suddenly into the clouds, and overlook their —s,* H5 III, 5, 9.

Grain, 1) a single seed of corn: Meas. III, 1, 20. Merch. I, 1, 116. Cor. III, 3, 90. V, 1, 27. 28. 30. H6C I, 3, 59.

2) corn: Cor. I, 1, 83. 200. Ant. II, 7, 25.

3) any minute particle, any small hard mass: *not a g. of it,* Wint. II, 1, 156. *a g., a dust, a gnat,* John IV, 1, 93. *each g. of gravel,* H8 I, 1, 155.

4) the smallest weight (the twentieth part of a scruple): *he weighs time even to the utmost g.* H5 II, 4, 138. *every g. of Plutus' gold,* Troil. III, 3, 197. *rot half a g. a day,* Oth. V, 2, 156.

5) the direction of the veins or fibres of wood: *divert his g. tortive and errant from his course of growth*, Troil. I, 3, 8. Metaphorically, = natural bias, natural temper: *against the g. to voice him consul*, Cor. II, 3, 241. *in g.* = innate, natural, not factitious (used of colours): *that is a fault that water will mend. No, sir, 'tis in g.* Err. III, 2, 108. *your purple in g. beard*, Mids. I, 2, 97. *'tis in g., 'twill endure wind and weather*, Tw. I, 5, 255.

Grained, 1) showing the grain of the wood, rough, furrowed, not smooth: *his g. bat*, Compl. 64. *my g. ash*, Cor. IV, 5, 114. Hence: *this g. face of mine*, Err. V, 311.

2) being in grain, dyed in grain: *such black and g. spots as will not leave their tinct*, Hml. III, 4, 90 (Qq *grieved*).

Gramercy, great thanks: Merch. II, 2, 128. R3 III, 2, 108. Tit. I, 495. IV, 2, 7. Tim. II, 2, 74. —*ies:* Shr. I, 1, 41. 168. Tim. II, 2, 69. In Ophelia's song, Hml. IV, 5, 199, Ff *gramercy*, Qq *God a mercy*.

Grammar, a book containing the rules of a language: Tit. IV, 2, 23.

Grammar-school, a school in which the learned languages are taught: H6B IV, 7, 37.

Grand, 1) principal, chief: *refusing her g. hests*, Tp. I, 2, 274. *this g. liquor*, V, 280 (alluding to the grand elixir of the alchemists). *the g. conspirator*, R2 V, 6, 19. *that excellent g. tyrant of the earth*, R3 IV, 4, 52. *produce the g. sum of his sins*, H8 III, 2, 293. *to unseal their g. commission*, Hml. V, 2, 18. *thy g. captain Antony*, Ant. III, 1, 9. *as petty as is the morn-dew to his g. sea*, III, 12, 10 (i. e. the ocean).

2) great, mighty: *g. preparation*, Wiv. IV, 5, 89 (Dr. Caius' speech). *under the allowance of your g. aspect*, Lr. II, 2, 112 (Ff *great*. But *grand* may here also have the sense of principal, predominant, sovereign).

Grandam, grandmother: Gent. II, 1, 24. II, 3, 13. LLL V, 2, 17. Merch. II, 2, 206. Tw. IV, 2, 56. 65. John I, 168. II, 133. 159. 160. 161. 163. 168. 194. III, 1, 334. III, 3, 3. 14. H4A III, 1, 34. R3 I, 3, 102. II, 2, 1. 12. 20. 31. II, 4, 10. 30. 32. III, 1, 145. IV, 4, 299. Troil. I, 3, 299. Mcb. III, 4, 66.

Grandchild, one in the second degree of descent: *the g. to her blood*, Cor. V, 3, 24.

Grandfather, the father's or mother's father: Gent. III, 1, 295. LLL II, 255. Shr. III, 1, 53. H4A II, 2, 71. III, 3, 94. 118. H5 IV, 7, 95. H6A II, 4, 83. II, 5, 63. III, 1, 42. H6C I, 1, 106. III, 1, 77. V, 4, 52. Tit. IV, 2, 3. Cymb. IV, 2, 82.

Grand-juror, a member of the grand jury: H4A II, 2, 96.

Grand-juryman, the same: Tw. III, 2, 17.

Grandmother, the father's or mother's mother: Tp. I, 2, 119. Gent. III, 1, 297. LLL I, 1, 266. H5 I, 2, 81.

Grandpré, French name: H5 III, 5, 44. III, 7, 138. IV, 8, 104.

Grandsire, grandfather: Wiv. I, 1, 53. 59. Merch. I, 1, 84. Shr. IV, 5, 50. John V, 4, 42. R2 II, 1, 104. III, 3, 106. H5 III Chor. 20. H6C I, 1, 125. II, 2, 37. Troil. I, 3, 292. II, 1, 115. IV, 5, 196. Tit. III, 2, 46. 49. II, 1, 18. 42. 118. IV, 2, 10. V, 3, 161. 172. Rom. I, 4, 37. II, 4, 33. Hml. II, 2, 486. Oth. I, 1, 91. Cymb. V, 4, 123.

Grange, a solitary farm-house: Meas. III, 1, 277. Wint. IV, 4, 309. Oth. I, 1, 106.

Grant, subst. the act of granting or bestowing, concession, permission: *the fairest g. is the necessity*, Ado I, 1, 319 (i. e. the necessity of granting is the best manner of granting). *having any occasion to write for matter of g.* H5 V, 2, 366 (i. e. a request). *your g., or your denial, shall be mine*, H6C III, 3, 130. *it was my will and g.* IV, 1, 49. *by the entreaty and g. of the whole table*, Cor. IV, 5, 212. With *of: with g. of our most just desires*, H4B IV, 2, 40. *in g. of all demands*, H5 II, 4, 121.

Grant, vb. 1) to give, to afford, to allow, to comply with: Lucr. 908. 915. Compl. 131. Tp. I, 2, 79. Gent. IV, 2, 101. V, 4, 150. 151. Meas. II, 4, 70 (cf. *Of*). III, 1, 259. Err. I, 1, 67. LLL I, 1, 162. II, 222. Merch. I, 1, 125. As IV, 1, 114. All's II, 3, 83. 91. III, 4, 28. Wint. IV, 2, 3. V, 1, 222. R2 III, 3, 41. IV, 1, 154. V, 3, 99. H6A V, 3, 19. H6C III, 2, 8. 63. Mcb. II, 1, 24. Cymb. II, 4, 13 etc. *a fool — ed* = an allowed, licensed fool, Cymb. II, 1, 50. *that without the which a soldier and his sword —s scarce distinction*, Ant. III, 1, 29 (= allows, admits, affords). With *to: his heart —eth no penetrable entrance to her plaining*, Lucr. 558. *the benefit is always —ed to those....*, R3 III, 1, 48. Dative without *to: g. me justice*, Err. V, 190. *heaven g. us its peace*, Meas. I, 2, 4. LLL I, 1 197. V, 2, 798. Mids. I, 1, 221. Merch. I, 2, 121. III, 3, 8. IV, 1, 423. All's V, 3, 145. Tw. V, 4. John IV, 2, 46. H6A IV, 1, 78. R3 I, 2, 219. II, 1, 125. Ant. III, 6, 35. V, 2, 11. Cymb. III, 1, 8 etc. With an inf.: *the duke will never g. this forfeiture to hold*, Merch. III, 3, 25. A double accus.: *the gods g. them true*, Cor. II, 1, 156. The dative made subj. of the pass.: *thou art —ed space*, All's IV 1, 98. *and the offender —ed scope of speech*, H6B IV, 1, 176. A dependent clause following: H4B IV, 5, 220. H6C III, 3, 112. R3 I, 2, 102. *g. I may ever love*, Tim. IV, 3, 474 (= God g.). Absol.: *how do I hold thee but by thy —ing?* Sonn. 87, 5. *and, wooing, she should g.* As V, 2, 4. Followed by *to: before I would have —ed to that act*, H6C I, 1, 245 (= said yes).

2) to admit as true: Sonn. 79, 5. 82, 1. 130, 11. Gent. IV, 2, 105. Meas. I, 2, 30. Tw. V, 342. Wint. I, 2, 114. John III, 1, 211. V, 2, 160. R2 II, 3, 124. H4B I, 2, 190. Tit. V, 1, 72. Caes. II, 1, 16. Ant. I, 4, 16. Cymb. II, 4, 92 etc. *g., if thou wilt, thou art beloved of many*, Sonn. 10, 3 (= granting, supposing). *g. that our hopes should be still-born*, H4B I, 3, 63. With a double accus.: *I g. him bloody*, Mcb. IV, 3, 57. *mad let us g. him then*, Hml. II, 2, 100. cf. *g. him there*, H5 V Chor. 7. With a dat.: *I g. you*, Mids. I, 2, 81. H4A II, 4, 390. V, 4, 149. R3 I, 2, 101 (Qq *I grant, yea*). 102. *will you g. with me that Ferdinand is dead?* Tp. II, 1, 243.

Grape, the fruit of the vine: Ven. 601. Lucr. 215. Meas. II, 1, 133 (*in the Bunch of Grapes*). Mids. III, 1, 170. As V, 1, 37. 39. All's II, 1, 73. II, 3, 105. Cor. V, 4, 18. Tim. IV, 3, 432. Oth. II, 1, 257. Ant. II, 7, 123. V, 2, 285.

Grapple, subst. close fight: Tw. V, 59. Hml. IV, 6, 18.

Grapple, vb. 1) intr. to wrestle, to contend in close fight: LLL II, 218. John III, 1, 104. V, 1, 61. H4A I, 3, 197. H6B I, 1, 257.

2) tr. to clasp: *and g. thee unto a pagan shore*, John V, 2, 36 (O. Edd. *cripple*). *g. your minds to sternage of this navy*, H5 III Chor. 18. —*s you to the*

heart and love of us, Mcb. III, 1, 106. *g. them to thy soul with hoops of steel*, Hml. I, 3, 63.

Grasp, subst. the gripe, the seizure: *the —s of love*, Troil. IV, 2, 13 (= embraces). Hence = possession, hold: *the whole space that's in the tyrant's g.* Mcb. IV, 3, 36.

Grasp, vb. to gripe, to seize: H6B V, 1, 97. H6C II, 5, 132. Caes. IV, 3, 26. Ant. IV, 12, 46. *with his arms outstretched —s in the corner*, Troil. III, 3, 168. Absol. = to grapple, to strive, to struggle: *one that —ed and tugged for life*, H6B III, 2, 172.

Grass, the common herbage of the field: Ven. 473. 1028. 1055. Lucr. 395. Tp. II, 1, 52. Err. II, 2, 202. LLL V, 2, 185. 187. Mids. I, 1, 211. Merch. I, 1, 18. All's IV, 5, 22 (quibbling with *grace*). R2 I, 3, 289. III, 3, 100. H5 I, 1, 65. III, 3, 13. IV, 2, 50. H6B III, 2, 337. IV, 2, 75 (*go to g.* = graze). IV, 10, 9. 44. Tit. IV, 4, 71. Tim. IV, 3, 425. Hml. III, 2, 358.

Grass-green, green with grass: *a g. turf*, Hml. IV, 5, 31.

Grass-hopper, the insect Gryllus: Rom. I, 4, 60.

Grass-plot, a level spot covered with grass: Tp. IV, 73.

Grassy, covered with grass: R2 III, 3, 50.

Grate, subst., iron lattice-work: Wiv. II, 2, 8. H6A I, 4, 10. 60.

Grate, vb. 1) intr. a) to produce an offensively creaking sound: *—ing shock of wrathful iron arms*, R2 I, 3, 136. *hear a dry wheel g. on the axle-tree*, H4A III, 1, 132.

b) to be offensive, to put out of humour, to vex; with *on*: *I have —ed upon my good friends for three reprieves*, Wiv. II, 2, 6. *suborned to g. on you*, H4B IV, 1, 90.

2) trans. a) to make to creak: *the threshold —s the door*, Lucr. 306. — b) to grind: *mighty states are —d to dusty nothing*, Troil. III, 2, 195. — c) to offend, to vex: *—ing all his days of quiet*, Hml. III, 1, 3. *news from Rome. — s me; the sum*, Ant. I, 1, 18.

Grateful, 1) thankful: All's II, 1, 132. Cor. I, 9, 54. Tim. I, 2, 5.

2) gratifying, agreeable: *a gift very g.* Shr. II, 76.

Gratiano, (of three or four syll.), Italian name: Merch. I, 1, 58. 77. II, 2, 124. 189. II, 4, 26. II, 8, 2 etc. Oth. V, 1, 93. V, 2, 365.

Gratify, 1) to show love to, to give pleasure to: *to g. the table with a grace*, LLL IV, 2, 161. *g. this gentleman*, Merch. IV, 1, 406.* Shr. I, 2, 273. *to g. the good Andronicus*, Tit. I, 220. *to g. your honourable youth*, IV, 2, 12. *the which when any shall not g.* Per. I, 4, 101.

2) to requite: *to g. his noble service*, Cor. II, 2, 44. *she did g. his amorous works with that recognizance*, Oth. V, 2, 213. *in these feared hopes I barely g. your love*, Cymb. II, 4, 7.

Gratii, Italian name in All's IV, 3, 186.

Gratillity, a word framed by the fool in Tw. II, 3, 27; corrupted from *gratuity?*

Gratis, without a recompense, for nothing: Lucr. 914. Wiv. II, 2, 16. Merch. I, 3, 45. III, 3, 2. IV, 1, 379. H4B IV, 3, 76. Cor. III, 1, 43. 114. 125. Hml. II, 2, 335.

Gratitude, thankfulness: All's IV, 4, 6. Cor. III, 1, 291. Lr. II, 4, 182. Cymb. III, 5, 121.

Gratulate, vb. (cf. *Congratulate*) to gratify, to give pleasure to, to make glad: *to g. the gentle princes there*, R3 IV, 1, 10. *and g. his safe return to Rome*, Tit. I, 221.* *come freely to g. thy plenteous bosom*, Tim. I, 2, 131.

Gratulate, adj. gratifying, satisfactory: *there's more behind that is more g.* Meas. V, 535.

Grave, subst. the place in which a dead body is deposited, a sepulchre: Ven. 757. 995. Lucr. 198. 661. Sonn. 1, 14. 31, 9. 77, 6. Tp. V, 48. 311. Gent. III, 1, 21. IV, 2, 114. IV, 3, 21. Meas. III, 1, 86. Err. III, 1, 104. Ado V, 3, 19. Mids. V, 387. Merch. II, 7, 51. V, 154. As II, 6, 3. John III, 4, 17. H6A II, 1, 34. II, 4, 110. IV, 3, 40. H6B I, 4, 22. IV, 1, 6. V, 1, 169. H6C I, 3, 27. R3 I, 2, 216. H8 II, 1, 86. IV, 2, 170. Cor. I, 9, 20 etc. etc.

Grave, adj. worthy, reverend, venerable: *g. Nestor*, Lucr. 1401. *g. sir, hail!* Tp. I, 2, 189. *the generous and —est citizens*, Meas. IV, 6, 13. *as shy, as g., as just, as absolute as Angelo*, V, 54. *Pisa renowned for g. citizens*, Shr. I, 1, 10. IV, 2, 95. *the reverence of the g. wearers*, Wint. III, 1, 6. *my g. sir*, IV, 4, 422. *O g. and good Paulina*, V, 3, 1. *seem they g. and learned?* H5 II, 2, 128. *you sage g. men*, R3 III, 7, 227. *let some —r eye pierce into that*, H8 I, 1, 67. *your most g. belly was deliberate*, Cor. I, 1, 132. *you are reverend g. men*, II, 1, 66. *most reverend and g. elders*, II, 2, 46. *you g. but reckless senators*, III, 1, 92. *a —r bench than ever frowned in Greece*, 106. *my g. lords*, V, 6, 106. Tit. III, 1, 1. 31. Rom. III, 1, 102. Tim. IV, 1, 5. 11. Hml. III, 4, 214. Oth. I, 1, 107. I, 3, 76. 124. 230. Cymb. I, 1, 49. Per. V, 1, 184. Used of things, = worthy, sober, dignified: *till I have honoured you with some —r labour*, Ven. Dedic. 4. *a purpose more g. and. wrinkled than the aims and ends of burning youth*, Meas. I, 3, 5. *a nuncio of more g. aspect*, Tw. I, 4, 28. *and leave you to your —r steps*, Wint. I, 2, 173. *thy g. admonishments*, H6A II, 5, 98. *these g. ornaments*, V, 1, 54; cf. Tit. III, 1, 43 and Rom. I, 1, 100. *enriched with politic g. counsel*, R3 II, 3, 20; cf. Mcb. III, 1, 22. *my frosty signs and chaps of age, g. witnesses of true experience*, Tit. V, 3, 78. *of g. and austere quality*, Tim. I, 1, 54. *our —r business frowns at this levity*, Ant. II, 7, 127. *you bear a —r purpose, I hope*, Cymb. I, 4, 151. — Peculiar passage: *this false soul of Egypt, this g. charm*, Ant. IV, 12, 25 (according to some intpp. = deadly. Perhaps corrupt).

Grave, vb. (Partic. *—d* and *—n*) 1) to entomb, to bury: *—d in the hollow ground*, R2 III, 2, 140. *ditches g. you all*, Tim. IV, 3, 166.

2) to cut a little, to wound slightly, to graze: *being steeled, soft sighs can never g. it*, Ven. 376.

3) to engrave, to insculp, to carve: *and g. upon my cheeks what helpless shame I feel*, Lucr. 755. *if time have any wrinkle —n there*, Sonn. 100, 10. *this saying —d in gold*, Merch. II, 7, 36. *where should be —n the slaughter of the prince*, R3 IV, 4, 141 (Ff branded).

Gravel, subst. 1) small pebbles, hard sand: *when we see each grain of g.* H8 I, 1, 155. *O g. heart*, Meas. IV, 3, 68 (= flint heart).

2) a disease: *loads o' g. in the back*, Troil. V, 1, 22.

Gravel'd, sticking in the sand, put to a stop: *you were better speak first, and when you were g. for lack of matter, you might take occasion to kiss*, As IV, 1, 74.

Graveless, unburied: Ant. III, 13, 166.

Gravely, with dignity: *if thou dost it half so g., so majestically*, H4A II, 4, 478.

Grave-maker, a grave-digger: Hml. V, 1, 34. 66. 154 (cf. H6A II, 1, 34. H8 II, 1, 86).

Grave-making, grave-digging: Hml. V, 1, 74.

Graveness, dignity, reverendness: *youth no less becomes the light and careless livery that it wears than settled age his sables and his weeds importing health and g.* Hml. IV, 7, 82.

Graves, ancient spelling for *greaves*, an armour for the legs: *turning your books to g.* H4B IV, 1, 50. (Such is the vulgar interpretation. But *graves* may as well be sepulchres here).

Grave-stone, tombstone: Tim. IV, 3, 380. V, 1, 222. V, 4, 67.

Gravity, dignity, solemnity of deportment or character, venerableness: *when love shall reasons find of settled g.* Sonn. 49, 8 (i. e. of a dignified reserve). *at most odds with his own g. and patience*, Wiv. III, 1, 54. *a man of his place, g. and learning*, 57. *my g., wherein I take pride*, Meas. II, 4, 9. *how ill agrees it with your g.* Err. II, 2, 170. LLL V, 2, 74. 778. Merch. I, 1, 92. Tw. III, 4, 129. H4A II, 4, 325. H4B I, 2, 183. H8 III, 1, 73. Rom. III, 5, 175. Caes. II, 1, 149. Oth. II, 3, 191.

Gravy, the juice that drips from flesh in roasting: H4B I, 2, 184.

Gray, adj. see *Grey*.

Graymalkin, a familiar spirit in the shape of a cat: Mcb. I, 1, 8.

Gray's Inn, one of the inns of court of London: H4B III, 2, 36.

Graze, 1) intr. to feed on grass: Ven. 233. LLL I, 1, 238. As III, 2, 81. Wint. IV, 4, 109. Rom. III, 5, 190. Caes. IV, 1, 27. Cymb. V, 4, 2.

2) tr. to set to feed on grass, to tend: Compl. 57. Merch. I, 3, 72. As II, 4, 79.

Graze, to touch or brush lightly in passing: H5 IV, 3, 105. Oth IV, 1, 279.

Grease, subst. fat: Wiv. II, 1, 69. III, 5, 116. 121. Err. III, 2, 97. As III, 2, 57.

Grease, vb. to smear, to soil with an unctuous matter: Tim. IV, 3, 195.

Greasily, nastily: *you talk g.* LLL IV, 1, 139.

Greasy, 1) smeared, defiled with grease: Wiv. III, 5, 92. As III, 2, 55. H4A II, 4, 252. Troil. V, 2, 159. Cor. IV, 6, 131. Ant. V, 2, 210.

2) fat, bulky, corpulent: *this g. knight*, Wiv. II, 1, 112. *g. Joan doth keel the pot*, LLL V, 2, 930. 939. *you fat and g. citizens*, As II, 1, 55.

Great, 1) large in size or dimensions: *the g. globe*, Tp. IV, 153. *the —er hides the less*, Gent. III, 1, 372. *g. chamber*, Wiv. I, 1, 157 and Rom. I, 5, 14. *a g. round beard*, Wiv. I, 4, 20. *g. ragged horns*, Wiv. IV, 4, 31. *your bum is the —est thing about you, so that in the beastliest sense you are Pompey the G.* Meas. II, 1, 228. *the g. wart on my left arm*, Err. III, 2, 148. *g. pails*, V, 173. *in such g. letters*, Ado I, 1, 267. *a word too g. for any mouth*, As III, 2, 239. *her g. P's*, Tw. II, 5, 97. *the fellow with the g. belly*, H4B I, 2, 165. *give me the spare men, and spare me the g. ones*, III, 2, 289; cf. V, 3, 92 and V, 5, 85. *a g. pin*, H6B IV, 10, 32. *g. anchors*, R3 I, 4, 26. *g. weeds do grow apace*, II, 4, 13. *you g. fellow*, H8 V, 4, 91. *—er hulks draw deep*, Troil. II, 3, 277. *the g. toe*, Cor. I, 1, 159;

cf. H4B I, 2, 274. *g. bellies*, Tim. I, 1, 210 etc. etc. *g. Italy*, Shr. I, 1, 4. *g. Dunsinane*, Mcb. V, 2, 12. *g. Media*, Ant. III, 6, 14 (Media magna). *g. with child*, Meas. II, 1, 91 (= pregnant). *go g. with tigers*, Tim. IV, 3, 188. *I am g. with woe, and shall deliver weeping*, Per. V, 1, 107. Used of the heart swelling with emotion: *my mind hath been as big, my heart as g.* Shr. V, 2, 171. *if my heart were g., 'twould burst at this*, All's IV, 3, 366 (quibbling). *my heart is g., but it must break with silence*, R2 II, 1, 228. *the heart, g. and puffed up with this retinue, doth any deed of courage*, H4B IV, 3, 121. *a thousand hearts are g. within my bosom*, R3 V, 3, 347. *thou hast made my heart too g. for what contains it*, Cor. V, 6, 104.

2) long continued: *a g. time after*, Tp. III, 3, 105. *a youth of —er time*, Gent. II, 7, 48 (i. e. older). *a g. while*, Tw. V, 414. H4B II, 2, 24 etc.

3) of a high degree, of a considerable number or quantity, high, mighty, considerable, copious: *g. comfort*, Tp. I, 1, 30. *a falsehood as g. as my trust*, I, 2, 95. *g. loss*, II, 1, 123. hope 240. *she as far surpasseth Sycorax as —est does least*, III, 2, 111. *their g. guilt*, III, 3, 104. *indignation*, IV, 200. *worth*, Gent. I, 2, 44. *impeachment*, I, 3, 15. *a g. fighter*, Wiv. II, 3, 44; cf. *a g. quarreller*, Tw. I, 3, 31; *a g. eater of beef*, 90; *our —est friends*, Cor. I, 1, 249; *— er friends*, Ant. III, 5, 48; *no g. good lover of the archbishop's*, H8 IV, 1, 104 etc. *a g. deal of heart-break*, Wiv. V, 3, 11. *so g. a fever*, Meas. III, 2, 235. *by g. injunctions*, IV, 3, 100. *small cheer and g. welcome*, Err. III, 1, 26. *a g. thaw*, Ado II, 1, 251. *as g. a soil*, III, 2, 5. *I yield upon g. persuasion*, V, 4, 95. *too g. testimony*, As IV, 3, 171. *a g. way fool*, All's I, 1, 112. *three g. oaths*, IV, 1, 64. *g. pains*, Tw. I, 5, 185. *of g. estate*, 278. *number*, III, 3, 29. *for a —er confirmation*, Wint. II, 1, 180. *gives but the —er feeling to the worse*, R2 I, 3, 301. *with as g. aim*, H4B III, 2, 285. *to raise so g. a siege*, H5 III, 3, 47. *g. truth*, Troil. IV, 4, 106. *the —est taste most palates theirs*, Cor. III, 1, 103. *bring forth the parties of suspicion. I am the —est*, Rom. V, 3, 223 (in the highest degree suspicious). *this g. clatter*, Mcb. V, 7, 21. *your g. judgment*, Cymb. I, 6, 174 etc. etc. *these g. tears*, All's I, 1, 91 (= copious?); cf. *when g. leaves fall, the winter is at hand*, R3 II, 3, 33. *it is g. morning* (= broad day) Troil. IV, 3, 1. Cymb. IV, 2, 61. *g. in our hope*, All's III, 3, 2 (= in great hope); cf. *g. in fortune*, III, 7, 14. *g. in knowledge*, II, 5, 9. *the —est of my pride is to see my ewes graze*, As III, 2, 80 (= my —est pride). *my father's skill, which was the —est of his profession*, All's I, 3, 249 (beyond which his profession could not extend). *the —est of your having lacks a half to pay your debts*, Tim. II, 2, 153.

4) of high rank or power: *my g. mind most kingly drinks it* (flattery) *up*, Sonn. 114, 10. *thy no —er father*, Tp. I, 2, 21. *his g. person*, 237. *all hail, g. master*, 189. *g. Juno*, IV, 102. *fit for g. employment*, Gent. V, 4, 157. *of g. admittance*, Wiv. II, 2, 235 (admittance to persons of rank). *too g. of birth*, III, 4, 4. *g. ones* Meas. II, 2, 59. Tw. I, 2, 33. Oth. III, 3, 273. *of a g. kindred, well allied*, Meas. III, 2, 108. *one of the —est men in this realm*, H4B V, 3, 92. *shall make you g.* V, 5, 85. *this becomes the g.* H5 III, 5, 55. *by g. preservation we live to tell it you*, R3 III, 5, 36 (= by high, divine p.). *g. tyranny, lay thou thy basis sure*, Mcb. IV, 3, 32. *g. command o'ersways the order*, Hml.

V, 1, 251 (viz the king's command). *their g. stars*, Lr. III, 1, 22. *their — er pleasures*, V, 3, 2 etc. etc. *the g. Cham*, Ado II, 1, 277. *G. Master of France*, H5 IV, 8, 100.

5) of extraordinary qualities, eminent, magnanimous: *Frederick the g. soldier*, Meas. III, 1, 217. *no — er heart in thee?* As II, 6, 4; cf. Alls IV, 3, 366. *with a g. heart heave away the storm*, John V, 2, 55. *he bears too g. a mind*, Caes. V, 1, 113. *others fish with craft for g. opinion*, Troil. IV, 4, 105. *rightly to be g. is not to stir without g. argument*, Hml. IV, 4, 53. *too short of that g. property*, Ant. I, 1, 58. *there's a g. spirit gone*, I, 2, 126. *our g. designs*, II, 2, 151. *that g. face of war*, III, 13, 4. *it is g. to do that thing*, V, 2, 4 etc. etc. *Alexander the G.* H5 IV, 7, 15. *Antiochus the G.* Per. Prol. 17. *Charles the G.* H5 I, 2, 46. *Pompey the G.* Meas. II, 1, 230. LLL V, 1, 136. H5 IV, 1, 70. Ant. I, 2, 195.

6) principal, chief, called so by way of eminence: *the g. care of goods*, Err. I, 1, 43. *the g. flood*, Caes. I, 2, 152 (the deluge). *the g. seal*, H8 III, 2, 229. 319. 347. *let the g. axe fall*, Hml. IV, 5, 218. *Imogen, the g. part of my comfort*, Cymb. IV, 3, 5.

7) Adverbially used: *'tis g. like he will*, H6B III, 1, 379.

Great-bellied, far advanced in pregnancy: Meas. II, 1, 102. H8 IV, 1, 76 (cf. Tim. I, 1, 210).

Great-grandfather, the father of the grandfather: H5 I, 1, 89. I, 2, 146. H6C II, 2, 37.

Great-grandsire, the same: H4B IV, 4, 128. H5 I, 2, 103.

Great-grown, having become powerful: H6C IV, 8, 63.

Great-kinsman, a relation removed by some degrees in the ascending line? an ancestor? Rom. IV, 3, 53.

Greatly, 1) in a high degree, much, very: Err. I, 2, 105. LLL IV, 2, 78. All's III, 6, 58. R2 IV, 263. V, 2, 48. H6B III, 1, 281. H6C II, 6, 94. Tit. II, 3, 266. Hml. IV, 4, 55. Oth. III, 1, 18. Ant. V, 2, 14.

2) illustriously: *small time, but in that small most g. lived this star of England*, H5 Epil. 5. Hml. IV, 4, 55.

Greatness, 1) high degree, large extent: *his own learning, the g. whereof...*, Merch. IV, 1, 158.

2) superior excellence, sublimity, paramount eminence: *he let him outlive that day to see his* (God's) *g.* H5 IV, 1, 195. *the g. of his name*, H8 V, 5, 52. *full of envy at his g.* Troil. II, 1, 37. *possessed he is with g.* II, 3, 180.

3) magnanimity: *though it show g., courage, blood*, H4A III, 1, 181. *model to thy inward g.* H5 II Chor. 16. *lest in her g. she do defeat us*, Ant. V, 1, 64.

4) high rank, power, elevated place: *no might nor g. can censure scape*, Meas. III, 2, 196. *O place and g.* IV, 1, 60. *in the g. of my word, you die*, As I, 3, 91 (i.e. as it is the word of a prince). *be not afraid of g.* Tw. II, 5, 157. 158. III, 4, 42. 47. 49. Wint. IV, 4, 17. V, 1, 89. John III, 1, 121. IV, 2, 94. IV, 3, 86. V, 1, 4. H4A I, 3, 11. III, 2, 16. 24. IV, 3, 74. V, 1, 48. H4B III, 1, 74. IV, 2, 15. IV, 4, 26. IV, 5, 98. H5 I, 2, 274. IV, 1, 251. 268 (*great g.*). H6B I, 1, 173. R3 III, 7, 161. 163. H8 II, 1, 100. III, 1, 78. III, 2, 223. 351. 357. IV, 2, 102. V, 5, 39. Troil. I, 3, 44. III, 3, 75. Cor. I, 1, 180. Caes. II, 1, 18. Mcb. I, 5, 12. 14. IV, 3, 75. Hml. I, 3, 17. IV, 7, 78 (Ff *wisdom*). Ant. II, 2, 93. III, 12, 16. IV, 13, 6. V, 2, 30. Cymb.

IV, 2, 25. IV, 5, 38. V, 4, 128. Per. II, 1, 8. II, 4, 12 In compellations, = highness, grace, majesty: *if thy g. will revenge it on him*, Tp. III, 2, 61. 72. *it pleaseth his g.* LLL V, 1, 113. *most esteemed g., will you hear?* V, 2, 894. All's III, 6, 74. H4B II, 2, 6. 15. V, 2, 111. Troil. I, 3, 158. II, 3, 118. Cor. V, 2, 105. Ant. V, 2, 220. Cymb. V, 5, 132.

5) bigness: *words, whose g. answers words*, H6B IV, 10, 56.

Great-oneyers, perhaps persons that converse with great ones: H4A II, 1, 84 (a word formed like *lawyer, sawyer, bowyer* etc.).

Great-sized, large, tall: Troil. III, 3, 147. V, 10, 26.

Great-uncle, the brother of the grandfather: H5 I, 2, 105. IV, 7, 96 (O. Edd. not hyphened).

Greaves, see *Graves*.

Grecian, subst. a native of Greece: All's I, 3, 75. Troil. I, 3, 279. II, 2, 43. 80. IV, 1, 70. IV, 2, 64. IV, 3, 6. IV, 4, 57. 90. 102. 123. IV, 5, 257. 268. V, 3, 40. V, 4, 17. 25.

Grecian, adj. pertaining to Greece: Sonn. 53, 8. Merch. V, 5. As IV, 1, 98. Troil. I, 3, 79. 282. 293. II, 2, 78. III, 3, 138. 279. IV, 4, 74. 78. IV, 5, 125. 151. 224. Cor. I, 3, 46.

Gree, vb. to agree; 1) tr. to stipulate: *are there no other tokens between you — d?* Meas. IV, 1, 42.

2) intr. a) to be in concord: *how g. you now?* Merch. II, 2, 108 (Q1 *agree*). *we have —d so well together*, Shr. II, 299.

b) to suit, to be accommodated: *what with his gust is —ing*, Sonn. 114, 11.

c) to come to one opinion, to come to a compromise: *all the means plotted and —d on*, Gent. II, 4, 183. Shr. II, 272. Ant. II, 6, 37.

Greece, the country of the Greeks: Lucr. 1368. Wiv. II, 3, 35. Err. I, 1, 133. Shr. Ind. 2, 95 (*old John Naps of G.* Non liquet).*H6A V, 5, 104. H6C II, 2, 146. Troil. Prol. 1. I, 2, 267. I, 3, 55. 63. 265. II, 1, 13 (*the plague of G.*; according to Johnson the plague sent by Apollo). 31. IV, 1, 46. IV, 4, 125. IV, 5, 65. 271. Cor. III, 1, 107. 115. Per. I, 4, 97. II, 1, 68.

Greedily, eagerly, ravenously: Ado III, 1, 28.

Greediness, 1) eagerness: *thither with all g. of affection are they gone*, Wint. V, 2, 111.

2) ravenousness, voracity: *the insatiate g. of his desires*, R3 III, 7, 7. *if thou wert the wolf, thy g. would afflict thee*, Tim. IV, 3, 337. Lr. III, 4, 96.

Greedy, eager, vehemently desirous: Lucr. 368. Wiv. I, 3, 73. Merch. III, 2, 278. R2 V, 2, 13. H4B I, 1, 78. Oth. I, 3, 149. Cymb. III, 4, 165.

Greek, subst. 1) a native of Greece: Lucr. 1384. 1402. 1470. H4B II, 4, 181. H6C II, 1, 52. Troil. Prol. 14. 21. I, 1, 7. 84. I, 2, 12. 268. I, 3, 246 etc. Tit. I, 2, 379. V, 3, 84. Hml. II, 2, 491. Cymb. IV, 2, 313. *foolish G.* Tw. IV, 1, 19. *she's a merry G. indeed*, Troil. I, 2, 118. *the merry —s*, IV, 4, 58 ("The Greeks were proverbially spoken of by the Romans as fond of good living and free potations." Nares).

2) the language of Greece: Shr. II, 81. Caes. I, 2, 282. 287.

Greek, adj. pertaining to Greece: As II, 5, 61. Shr. II, 101. Troil. IV, 5, 127.

Greekish, pertaining to Greece: Troil. I, 3, 67 (O. Edd. *greeks*). 221. III, 1, 166. III, 3, 211. IV, 5, 130. 185. 216. V, 1, 1. V, 4, 7.

Green, name in R2 I, 4, 23. II, 2, 62. III, 1, 2 etc.*

Green, adj. 1) of the colour of herbage and plants when growing, verdant: Ven. 1176. Lucr. 394. Sonn. 33, 3. Pilgr. 80. 283. Tp. II, 1, 53. IV, 130. V, 37. Wiv. I, 4, 47. IV, 4, 49. V, 5, 41. 71. Ado II, 1, 247. Mids. I, 1, 185. II, 1, 94. III, 1, 3. 170. As II, 7, 180. IV, 3, 109. V, 3, 19. Wint. I, 2, 156. R2 III, 3, 47. V, 2, 47. H5 II, 3, 18. V, 2, 49. Troil. I, 2, 166. V, 1, 36. Tit. II, 2, 2. II, 3, 14. Rom. V, 1, 46. Lr. III, 4, 138. Oth. IV, 3, 42. Per. II, 2, 43. *the g. sea*, Tp. V, 43. Mids. III, 2, 393. *g. Neptune*, Wint. IV, 4, 28. Ant. IV, 14, 58. *the tune of the G. Sleeves*, Wiv. II, 1, 64. V, 5, 22 (apparently a lascivious song). *his eyes were g. as leeks*, Mids. V, 342 (Thisbe's speech). *an eagle hath not so g., so quick, so fair an eye*, Rom. III, 5, 222 (the nurse's speech).

2) of a sickly and lurid complexion (cf. *Green-sickness*): *with a g. and yellow melancholy*, Tw. II, 4, 116. *her vestal livery is but sick and g.* Rom. II, 2, 8. *to look so g. and pale at what it did so freely*, Mcb. I, 7, 37.

3) unripe: *the g. plum*, Ven. 527. Pilgr. 135. Hence = inexperienced, raw: *the text is old, the orator too g.* Ven. 806. *she had a g. wit*, LLL I, 2, 94. *fancies too g. and idle for girls of nine*, Wint. III, 2, 182. *yon g. boy*, John II, 472. *how g. you are*, III, 4, 145. *the promise of his — er days*, H5 II, 4, 136. *the estate is g. and yet ungoverned*, R3 II, 2, 127. *you speak like a g. girl*, Hml. I, 3, 101. *g. minds*, Oth. II, 1, 251. *g. in judgment*, Ant. I, 5, 74.

4) fresh, new, young: *these lines shall live, and he in them still g.* Sonn. 63, 14. *since I first saw you fresh, which yet are g.* 104, 8. *Adonis, lovely, fresh and g.* Pilgr. 44. *when g. geese are a breeding*, LLL I, 1, 97. *a g. goose a goddess*, IV, 3, 75. *g. timber*, As III, 3, 90. *whiles your boots are g.* Shr. III, 2, 213. *every thing I look on seemeth g.* IV, 5, 47 (quibble). *a g. wound*, H4B II, 1, 106. H5 V, 1, 44. H6B III, 1, 287. *since griefs are g.* H4B IV, 5, 204. *it* (the compact) *is but g.* R3 II, 2, 135. *were your days as g. as Ajax'*, Troil. II, 3, 265. *Tybalt, yet but g. in earth*, Rom. IV, 3, 42. *g. virginity*, Tim. IV, 1, 7. *though of Hamlet's death the memory be g.* Hml. I, 2, 2.

Green, subst. 1) the green colour: *with an eye of g.* Tp. II, 1, 55. *of the sea-water g.* LLL I, 2, 86; (cf. Mcb. II, 2, 63). *g. is the colour of lovers*, I, 2, 90 (probably as the emblem of youth and hope. Armado speaking).

2) any thing green; a) green garments: *in g.* Wiv. IV, 6, 41. V, 3, 2. V, 5, 215. 221. *in Kendal g.* H4A II, 4, 246. 257.

b) fresh leaves and herbage: *summer's g.* Sonn. 12, 7. *making no summer of another's g.* 68, 11.

c) a grassy plain, a meadow: *trip upon the g.* Ven. 146. Tp. IV, 83. Midᵈ. II, 1, 9. 28. 99. *these — s before your town*, John II, 242. *Peter Bullcalf of the g.* H4B III, 2, 183. *Mile-end g.* 298.

d) a grave covered with grass-turf: *to strow thy g. with flowers*, Per. IV, 1, 15 (Ff grave).

Green-eyed, of a morbid sight, seeing all things discoloured and disfigured: *g. jealousy*, Merch. III, 2, 110. Oth. III, 3, 166 (cf. *Green* adj. 2).

Greenly, novice-like, sheepishly, foolishly: *I cannot look g. nor gasp out my eloquence*, H5 V, 2, 149 (or = like one that has the green-sickness?).

we have done but g., in hugger-mugger to inter him, Hml. IV, 5, 83.

Green-sickness, a disease of females, characterized by a pale, lurid complexion: H4B IV, 3, 100. Rom. III, 5, 157. Ant. III, 2, 6. Per. IV, 6, 14.

Greensward, grassy turf: Wint. IV, 4, 157.

Greenwich, English town: H8 I, 2, 188.

Greenwood, a wood in summer: *under the g. tree*, As II, 5, 1.

Greet, 1) to salute, to take courteous notice of in meeting and passing: *and scarcely g. me*, Sonn. 49, 6. *never stays to g. him*, As II, 1, 54. *not a friend g. my poor corpse*, Tw. II, 4, 62. *g. him not*, Troil. III, 3, 52.

2) to meet and address with kind wishes: *other of our friends will g. us here anon*, Meas. IV, 5, 13. *to g. me with premeditated lines*, Mids. V, 94. Shr. IV, 1, 115. Wint. V, 1, 155. R2 I, 3, 52. III, 2, 10. H4B IV, 1, 228. H6A V, 4, 94. H6B V, 1, 14. R3 III, 1, 17. IV, 1, 4. Troil. II, 3, 189. III, 1, 162. Tim. V, 1, 139. Mcb. I, 2, 65. I, 3, 55. Per. V, 1, 10.

3) to send compliments to; either in writing: *that unworthy wife that —eth thee*, Lucr. 1304. *to g. it with my lays*, Sonn. 102, 6. *to g. your lord with writing*, Cymb. I, 6, 206. Or through a messenger: *your brother kindly —s you*, Meas. I, 4, 24. *—s you from himself by me*, Wint. V, 1, 181. *my mother —s me kindly*, All's II, 4, 1. cf. Merch. IV, 1, 120. John I, 1, 2. Tim. V, 1, 132. Hml. IV, 4, 1. Oth. I, 2, 36. IV, 1, 231. Cymb. I, 6, 13. *he —s me well*, H4B III, 2, 69 and Caes. IV, 2, 6 (a phrase of thanks in return of a salutation; cf. H6B V, 1, 14).

4) to deliver compliments to: *to g. him and to give him comforts*, Wint. IV, 4, 568. *I g. your honours from Andronicus*, Tit. IV, 2, 5. *g. him from me*, Tim. II, 2, 235.

5) to address in any manner: *thus he —s your majesty*, H5 II, 4, 76. *let him g. England with our sharp defiance*, III, 5, 37. *the first that there did g. my stranger soul*, R3 I, 4, 48. Absol.: *and taught it thus anew to g.* Sonn. 145, 8 (= to speak to me).

6) to show respect or kindness to: *this diamond he —s your wife withal*, Mcb. II, 1, 15. *things of such dignity as we g. modern friends withal*, Ant. V, 2, 167. *what pageantry the regent made to g. the king*, Per. V, 2, 9. Used of things, = to gratify: *it —s me as an enterprise of kindness performed to your sole daughter*, Per. IV, 3, 38.

7) to regard, to look on: *and wordless so —s heaven for his success*, Lucr. 112. *when we g., with eyes best seeing, heaven's fiery eye*, LLL V, 2, 374. *there the sun shall g. them*, H5 IV, 3, 100. *to g. mine own land with my wishful sight*, H6C III, 1, 14. *a merrier day did never yet g. Rome*, Cor. V, 4, 45. *why so sadly g. you our victory?* Cymb. V, 5, 24.

8) to meet: *to g. the empress' friends*, Tit. IV, 2, 174. *we will g. the time*, Lr. V, 1, 54. *I g. thy love, not with vain thanks, but with acceptance bounteous*, Oth. III, 3, 469. Intr. = to meet and be amicably together: *upon the next occasion that we meet ... to talk and g.* LLL V, 2, 144. *sundered friends g. in the hour of death*, H6A IV, 3, 42. *there g. in silence and sleep in peace*, Tit. I, 90. *I cannot hope Caesar and Antony shall well g. together*, Ant. II, 2, 39.

Greeting, subst. 1) salutation, kind and courteous respect expressed at meeting: Meas. IV, 3, 92.

As V, 4, 39. H6B V, 1, 15. Troil. IV, 1, 32. IV, 5, 174. Oth. II, 1, 94. Ant. III, 6, 55.

2) a compliment sent by writing or message: All's I, 3, 258. IV, 3, 352. Wint. V, 1, 140. R2 III, 1, 39. H4B II, 2, 131. IV, 1, 27. H6C III, 3, 52. Cor. II, 1, 213. Rom. III, 5, 50. Tim. V, 1, 215. Caes. II, 2, 61. Hml. II, 2, 60. Ant. 1, 5, 77. IV, 5, 14. V, 2, 9. (*to do g.* H6C III, 3, 52. Tim. V, 1, 215. *to give g.* Wint. V, 1, 140. Oth. II, 1, 94. *to make g.* Meas. IV, 3, 92).

3) any kind of address or message: *mark my g. well,* R2 I, 1, 36. *that thou returnest no g. to thy friends,* I, 3, 254. *we hear your g. is from him, not from the king,* H5 I, 2, 236. *to whom expressly I bring g. too,* II, 4, 112. *patience perforce with wilful choler meeting makes my flesh tremble in their different g.* Rom. I, 5, 92. *the appertaining rage to such a g.* III, 1, 67. *with such prophetic g.* Mcb. I, 3, 78. *bearers of this g. to old Norway,* Hml. I, 2, 35.

Gregory, name 1) of a saint: Gent. IV, 2, 84. 2) of G. de Cassado, king Henry VIII's ambassador in Rome, H8 III, 2, 321. 3) of the famous Pope G. VII, called by Falstaff *Turk G.,* H4A V, 3, 46. 4) of servants: Shr. IV, 1, 125. 139. Rom. I, 1, 1. 69.

Gremio, name in Shr. I, 1, 95 etc. etc.

Grey, name 1) of Sir Thomas G., a conspirator under Henry V: H5 II Chor. 25. II, 2, 58. 68. 150. 2) the first husband of Edward the Fourth's queen: H6C III, 2, 2. III, 3, 174. IV, 1, 2. 25. R3 I, 1, 64. I, 3, 127. 3) his and Queen Elizabeth's son, Lord G.: R3 I, 3, 333. II, 1, 66 etc.

Grey or **Gray,** adj. 1) of the colour of ashes, between white and black: *the plain-song cuckoo g.* Mids. III, 1, 134. *the friar of orders g.* Shr. IV, 1, 148. *g. Capilet,* Tw. III, 4, 315. *the cat is g.* Lr. III, 6, 47. *g. hair* or *beard:* Ado V, 1, 68. Wint. II, 3, 162. H6A II, 5, 5. Hml. II, 2, 199. Lr. II, 2, 68. 72. *that g. iniquity,* H4A II, 4, 499. *spirits black, g., green and white,* Wiv. V, 5, 41. Used of the beginning light of daybreak: *if but once thou show me thy g. light,* Mids. III, 2, 419. *yon g. lines that fret the clouds are messengers of day,* Caes. II, 1, 103. cf. Sonn. 132, 6.

Substantively: *the gentle day dapples the drowsy east with spots of g.* Ado V, 3, 27. *yon g. is not the morning's eye,* Rom. III, 5, 19. *though g. do something mingle with our younger brown,* Ant. IV, 8, 19.

2) According to some commentators, = blue: *mine eyes are g. and bright,* Ven. 140. *her eyes are g. as glass,* Gent. IV, 4, 197. *two g. eyes,* Tw. I, 5, 266. *Thisbe a g. eye or so,* Rom. II, 4, 45. *not the morning sun of heaven better becomes the g. cheeks of the east,* Sonn. 132, 6. *it stuck upon him as the sun in the g. vault of heaven,* H4B II, 3, 19. *the morn is bright and g.* Tit. II, 2, 1 (But in all these passages it may well have the modern signification).

Grey-beard, an old man: Shr. II, 340. III, 2, 147. H6A III, 2, 50. H6C V, 6, 81. Caes. II, 2, 67.

Grey-coated, wearing a grey coat: Rom. I, 4, 64.

Grey-eyed, beginning to grow bright: *the g. morn,* Rom. II, 3, 1.

Greyhound, a tall fleet dog that chases in sight: Wiv. I, 1, 91. Ado V, 2, 11. LLL V, 2, 665. Shr. Ind. 2, 49. V, 2, 52. H4A I, 3, 252. H4B II, 4, 107. H5 III, 1, 31. H6C II, 5, 129. Cor. I, 6, 38. Tim. I, 2, 195. Mcb. III, 1, 93. Lr. III, 6, 71.

Greymalkin, see *Graymalkin.*

Grief, 1) sorrow: Ven. 666. 701. 968. 1069.

Lucr. 762. 797. 889. 1117. 1308. Sonn. 42, 1. Pilgr. 389. Tp. I, 2, 415. II, 1, 16. 127. V, 214. Gent. III, 2, 15. IV, 3, 19. 28. Meas. V, 96. Err. I, 1, 33. V, 297. 406. Ado IV, 1, 251. V, 1, 2. LLL V, 2, 762. Merch. III, 3, 32. All's III, 2, 68. Wint. II, 2, 23. John V, 7, 111. H6A II, 5, 10. Rom. I, 1, 192. Tim. V, 1, 125. Mcb. I, 7, 78. Hml. IV, 5, 150. Oth. V, 2, 192 etc. etc. *though Humphrey's pride and greatness be g. to us,* H6B I, 1, 173. *which is no g. to give,* R3 III, 1, 114. *to our g.* Wint. III, 2, 1. H6C I, 1, 93. R3 III, 1, 98. Followed by *of: and upon the g. of this died,* Ado IV, 2, 65. *g. of my son's exile hath stopped her breath,* Rom. V, 3, 211.

2) pain, suffering: *the profit of excess is but to surfeit and such —s sustain, that they prove bankrupt in this poor-rich gain,* Lucr. 139. *where lies thy g.?* LLL IV, 3, 171. John IV, 1, 48. *out of my g. and my impatience,* H4A I, 3, 51. *take away the g. of a wound,* V, 1, 134. *my limbs weakened with g.* H4B I, 1, 144. Used of the pangs of love: *know love's g. by his complexion,* Ado I, 1, 315. *they thy glory through my g. will show,* LLL IV, 3, 37. 43. *that in love's g. desirest society,* 128. *my g. in love,* As III, 5, 88. *smiling at g.* Tw. II, 4, 118. *my master's g.* III, 4, 227. *where I may revolve and ruminate my g.* H6A V, 5, 101. *add more g. to too much of mine own,* Rom. I, 1, 195.

3) cause of complaint, grievance: *I here forget all former —s,* Gent. V, 4, 142. *you give your wife too unkind a cause of g.* Merch. V, 175. *to know the nature of our —s,* H4A IV, 3, 42. *he bids you name your —s,* 48. *find our —s heavier than our offences,* H4B IV, 1, 69. *the summary of all our —s,* 73. *any ground to build a g. on,* 110. *the parcels and particulars of our g.* IV, 2, 36. *these —s shall be with speed redressed,* 59. *since —s are green,* IV, 5, 204. *the subjects' g. comes through commissions,* H8 I, 2, 56. *thy first —s were but a mere conceit,* Tim. V, 4, 14. *redress of all these —s,* Caes. I, 3, 118. III, 2, 217. IV, 2, 42. 46. *to enforce no further —s between ye,* Ant. II, 2, 100. *our —s are risen to the top,* Per. II, 4, 23. 35.

Grief-shot, sorrow-stricken: *g. with his unkindness,* Cor. V, 1, 44.

Grievance, 1) grief, sorrow, suffering: *grieve at —s foregone,* Sonn. 30, 9. *her g. with his hearing to divide,* Compl. 67. *in thy danger commend thy g. to my holy prayers,* Gent. I, 1, 17. *I pity much your —s, which since I know they virtuously are placed,* IV, 3, 37 (i. e. your pangs of love; cf. *Grief 2*); cf. *the night's dead silence will well become such sweet-complaining g.* III, 2, 86. *I'll know his g.* Rom. I, 1, 163.

2) cause of complaint: H4A V, 2, 37. H4B IV, 1, 169. IV, 2, 113. H8 I, 2, 20. Rom. III, 1, 55.

3) vexation, annoyance: *the king is weary of dainty and such picking —s,* H4B IV, 1, 198. *put upon you what restraint and g. the law will give him cable,* Oth. I, 2, 15.

Grieve, 1) trans. a) to afflict, to offend, to make sorry: *he —s my very heart-strings,* Gent. IV, 2, 61. *hast no unkind mate to g. thee,* Err. II, 1, 38. Ado II, 1, 63. LLL V, 2, 237. Merch. II, 8, 34. As I, 1, 23. V, 2, 22. Wint. II, 1, 96. John V, 2, 15. R2 II, 2, 95. H6A III, 3, 55. IV, 1, 133. H6B V, 2, 18. H6C II, 2, 55. III, 2, 100. 183. R3 II, 2, 54. II, 4, 39. H8 I, 2, 110. II, 2, 129. 142. Troil. III, 3, 209. V, 2, 46. 94. Cor. I, 9, 15. Tit. V, 1, 143. Rom. III, 5, 84. Tim. I, 2, 41. Caes. III, 1, 196. Mcb. III, 6, 11. IV

1, 110. Oth. III, 3, 3. Cymb. III, 2, 32. V, 5, 144. Per. II, 1, 21. Absol.: *it shall no longer g. without reproof*, Per. II, 4, 19 (= be offensive). *it —s me for* = I am sorry for: *it —s me for the death of Claudio*, Meas. II, 1, 294. *it —s me much more for what I cannot do for you than what befalls myself*, Tw. III, 4, 369. Partic. *—d* = sorry, displeased: Ado IV, 1, 90. Merch. II, 7, 76. As I, 3, 94. Shr. II, 37. IV, 5, 64. John III, 4, 123. V, 2, 24. R2 I, 1, 138. I, 3, 209. IV, 216. H8 I, 2, 104. Tit. II, 3, 260. Caes. I, 2, 43. Ant. III, 6, 59. With *at:* Sonn. 35, 1. Hml. II, 2, 65. With *for:* H6C II, 5, 111.

b) to be sorry for, to bemoan, to regret: *trifles thy coward heart with false bethinking —s*, Ven. 1024. *Leontes, the effects of his fond jealousies so —ing*, Wint. IV, 1, 18. *the nothing that I g.* R2 II, 2, 37. *—s at heart so many of his shadows*, H4A V, 4, 29. *you shall not g. lending me this acquaintance*, Lr. IV, 3, 55. *I thought it princely charity to g. them*, Per. I, 2, 100 (reading of Q5).

2) intr. to be afflicted, to be sorry: *—ing themselves to guess at others' smarts*, Lucr. 1238. *—d I, I had but one?* Ado IV, 1, 129. *I will die with —ing*, 326. Merch. II, 1, 38. IV, 1, 266. V, 239. As III, 2, 430. Wint. II, 1, 77. H6A I, 4, 57. III, 3, 2. H6C I, 4, 86. Cor. V, 6, 63. Tim. IV, 3, 92. Hml. III, 2, 30. 209. Oth. II, 3, 177. Ant. II, 2, 69. Cymb. III, 4, 95. V, 5, 170. With *at:* Lucr. 1117. Sonn. 30, 9. Meas. II, 2, 50. As II, 1, 26. Wint. IV, 4, 426. R2 II, 2, 12. H4B V, 5, 82. H6B III, 2, 381. H8 II, 1, 39. V, 1, 96. Cymb. IV, 3, 35. With *for:* H8 IV, 2, 117. Hml. IV, 3, 43. H6C II, 5, 111.

Grievingly, with regret: H8 I, 1, 87.

Grievous, 1) hard to be borne, heavy, painful: *a g. labour*, Gent. I, 1, 33. *imposition*, Meas. I, 2, 194. *penalties*, Merch. IV, 1, 410. *taxes*, R2 II, 1, 246. *wounds*, H4B II, 4, 212. *siege*, H5 I, 2, 152. *death*, H6B III, 2, 247. *sickness*, 370. *'tis very g. to be thought upon*, R3 I, 1, 141. *plague*, I, 3, 217. *burthen*, IV, 4, 167. *curse*, 187 (Qq *heavy*). *wreck*, Oth. II, 1, 23.

Adverbially: *g. sick*, R2 I, 4, 54 (Ff *very*). H4A IV, 1, 16.

2) deserving censure and punishment, criminal: *g. deeds*, Lucr. 1822. *fault*, Err. V, 206. Caes. III, 2, 84. *crimes*, R2 IV, 223. *complaints*, H4A II, 4, 487. H8 V, 1, 99. 100. *sin*, H6A III, 1, 128. R3 I, 4, 195. *charge*, I, 3, 326. *murder*, I, 4, 280.

Grievously, 1) painfully, heavily: Wiv. IV, 4, 22. V, 1, 21. Caes. III, 2, 85.

2) distressfully: *my daughter takes his going g.* Gent. III, 2, 14. *cry so g.* Oth. V, 1, 53.

3) criminally: *I do suspect thee very g.* John IV, 3, 134.

Griffin, a fabled animal, half a lion, and half an eagle: Mids. II, 1, 232. H4A III, 1, 152.

Griffith, name in H8 IV, 2, 1 etc.

Grim, 1) impressing terror, of a threatening aspect: Ven. 920. 1105. Lucr. 421. 452. 769. Mids. III, 2, 57. H6A II, 3, 20. IV, 3, 21. H6B III, 2, 50. Cor. I, 4, 58. IV, 5, 66. Mcb. V, 2, 4. Lr. III, 6, 71. Oth. IV, 2, 64. V, 2, 203. Per. Prol. 40.

2) gloomy, sullen: *g. care*, Lucr. 1451. *g. and comfortless despair*, Err. V, 80. *sworn brother to g. Necessity*, R2 V, 1, 21. *that g. ferryman*, R3 I, 4, 46 (Ff. *sour*).

3) of a shocking ugliness: *then was Venus like*

her mother, for her father is but g. LLL II, 256. *g. death, how foul and loathsome is thine image*, Shr. Ind. 1, 35. *if thou, that bid'st me be content, wert g., ugly...*, John III, 1, 43.

Grime, subst. foul matter, dirt: *she sweats; a man may go over shoes in the g. of it*, Err. III, 2, 106. In II, 2, 143 O. Edd. *crime*, some M. Edd. *grime.*

Grime, vb. (cf. *Begrime*), to sully, to dirt: *my face I'll g. with filth*, Lr. II, 3, 9.

Grim-grinning, grinning in a threatening manner: Ven. 933.

Grim-looked, of a threatening aspect: Mids. V, 171.

Grimly, 1) threateningly: *the skies look g.* Wint. III, 3, 3. 2) gloomily: *the augurers look g. and dare not speak their knowledge*, Ant. IV, 12, 5.

Grim-visaged, of a threatening look: R3 I, 1, 9.

Grin, to withdraw the lips from the teeth, to twist up and distort the features so as to betray malice, or scorn, or anguish: Ven. 459; cf. H6B III, 1, 18 and H6C I, 4, 56. John III, 4, 34. R2 III, 2, 163. H4A V, 3, 62. H6B III, 3, 24. IV, 1, 77. Hml. V, 1, 212 (Ff. *jeering*). Cymb. V, 3, 38.

Grind, (Partic. *ground*, Per. I, 2, 58), 1) to reduce to powder by friction: Troil. I, 1, 16. Cor. III, 2, 103. Tit. V, 2, 187. 199. Ant. III, 5, 16.

2) to whet: *mine appetite I never more will g. on newer proof*, Sonn. 110, 10. *the —ing of the axe*, Hml. V, 2, 24. Per. I, 2, 58.

3) to afflict cruelly: *g. their joints with dry convulsions*, Tp. IV, 259.

Grindstone, name in Rom. I, 5, 10.

Gripe, subst. 1) a griffin: *a white hind under the —'s sharp claws*, Lucr. 543.

2) grasp, seizure: H5 IV, 6, 22. H8 V, 3, 100. Mcb. III, 1, 62. Cymb. I, 6, 106 (cf. the verb in H8 II, 2, 136).

Gripe, vb. 1) to seize, to grasp: Lucr. 319. 1425. John IV, 2, 190. R2 II, 1, 189. III, 3, 80. H4A V, 1, 57. Oth. III, 3, 421. *we live not to be —d by meaner persons*, H8 II, 2, 136 (i. e. to join hands with. cf. the subst. in Cymb. I, 6, 106). Absol.: *many among us can g. as hard as Cassibelan*, Cymb. III, 1, 40 (= have as strong hands). Intr.: *g. not at earthly joys*, Per. I, 1, 49 (= catch at).

2) to pinch, to give pain to: *let vultures g. thy guts*, Wiv. I, 3, 94 (cf. *Gutsgriping*). *inly sorrow —s his soul*, H6C I, 4, 171. Absol.: *when —ing grief the heart doth wound*, Rom. IV, 5, 128.

Grise, see *Grize.*

Grisly, 1) somewhat grey: *his beard was g.* Hml. I, 2, 240 ((Qq and M. Edd. *grizzled*).

2) grim, full of terror: Lucr. 926. Mids. V, 140. H6A I, 4, 47. Per. III Prol. 47 (Q1 *grizzled*).

Grissel, name of the heroine of a tale of Chaucer's (the Clerk of Oxenford's tale), proverbially known as a pattern of patience: Shr. II, 297.

Grize, step, degree: *that's a degree to love. No, not a g.* Tw. III, 1, 135. *every g. of fortune is smoothed by that below*, Tim. IV, 3, 16. *which, as a g. or step, may help these lovers into your favour*, Oth. I, 3, 200.

Grizzle, subst. a tinge of grey: *when time hath sowed a g. on thy case*, Tw. V, 168.

Grizzled, somewhat grey: Hml. I, 2, 240 (Ff. *grisly*). Ant. III, 13, 17. In Per. III Prol. 47 most O. Edd. *grisly.*

Grizzly, somewhat grey, see *Grisly* 1.

Groan, subst. a mournful sound uttered in pain or sorrow, a loud sigh: Ven. 950. Lucr. 431. 588. 797. 975. 1132. 1276. 1319. Sonn. 50, 11. 13. Tp. I, 2, 280. 287. Gent. III, 1, 230. LLL V, 2, 874. Merch. I, 1, 82. As II, 1, 36. All's IV, 3, 62. R2 I, 2, 70. V, 1, 89. 100. V, 5, 56. 57. H4A I, 3, 302. H5 II, 4, 107. H6B II, 4, 33. III, 1, 221. III, 2, 60. 62. 310. H6C II, 6, 43. V, 2, 46. Cor. V, 2, 45. Tit. III, 2, 15. Rom. III, 3, 72. Mcb. IV, 3, 168. Hml. III, 3, 23. Ant. IV, 14, 31. *to give a g.* Ven. 1044. Troil. V, 10, 50. Used of a woman in labour: *you ne'er oppressed me with a mother's g.* All's I, 3, 153. *cost me the dearest —s of a mother,* IV, 5, 12. *a night of —s endured of her,* R3 IV, 4, 303. Of persons in love: *love's deep —s I never shall regard,* Ven. 377. *a thousand —s, but thinking on thy face,* Sonn. 131, 10. Compl. 275. Gent. I, 1, 29. II, 4, 131. LLL III, 184. IV, 3, 164. Tw. I, 5, 275. Rom. II, 3, 74. Hml. II, 2, 121. Of the rumbling sound of winds: *such —s of roaring wind and rain,* Lr. III, 2, 47.

Groan, vb. to utter a mournful voice in pain or sorrow: Lucr. 1362. Tp. I, 2, 156. Ado V, 1, 16. V, 3, 17. LLL V, 2, 862. R2 IV, 138. V, 1, 91. H6A I, 4, 104. H8 II, 4, 199. Cor. IV, 4, 4. Tit. I, 126. IV, 1, 123. Rom. I, 1, 206. Caes. I, 2, 61. 124. II, 2, 23. IV, 1, 22. Hml. III, 2, 259. Oth. V, 1, 42. V, 2, 56. Cymb. V, 3, 69. V, 4, 6. *to g. at* sth.: Ven. 829. Tim. III, 2, 83. *for* sth. (= to long for it): *will make them g. for it,* H8 II, 1, 106. *—ing for burial,* Caes. III, 1, 275. *to g. out:* Troil III, 1, 136. Used of a woman in labour: *what shall be done with the —ing Juliet?* Meas. II, 2, 15. *hadst thou —ed for him, thou wouldst be more pitiful,* R2 V, 2, 102. Of persons in love: *my heart longs not to g.* Ven. 785. *thy face hath not the power to make love g.* Sonn. 131, 6. *that heart that makes my heart to g.* 133, 1. LLL II, 183. III, 206. IV, 3, 21. 182. As III, 2, 321. Rom. II Chor. 3. II, 4, 92.

Groat, a piece of money valued at four pence: Wiv. I, 1, 158. All's II, 2, 22. John I, 94. R2 V, 5, 68. H4B I, 2, 263. H5 V, 1, 62. 63. 67. H6B III, 1, 113. Cor. III, 2, 10.

Groin, the part of the body next the thigh: Ven. 1116. H4B II, 4, 227.

Groom, 1) a menial, a servant, a low person: Lucr. 671. 1013. 1334. 1345. 1632. 1645. Shr. III, 2, 154. R2 V, 5, 72. H6A I, 3, 14. H6B II, 1, 185. IV, 1, 52. 128. IV, 2, 132. H8 V, 1, 174. V, 2, 18. V, 3, 144. Mcb. II, 2, 5. 50. 56. Lr. II, 4, 220. Cymb. II, 3, 132. III, 6, 70. Per. IV, 6, 201.

2) fellow: *you'll prove a jolly surly g.* Shr. III, 2, 215. *you logger-headed and unpolished —s,* IV, 1, 128. *you are gallant —s,* Tit. IV, 2, 164.

3) bridegroom (the word *bride* preceding): *like bride and g.* Oth. II, 3, 180. Cymb. III, 6, 70?

Grope, to feel along where one cannot see: *—ing for trouts in a peculiar river,* Meas. I, 2, 91. *in the dark —d I to find out them,* Hml. V, 2, 14.

Gross, adj. (comp. *—er,* superl. not found). 1) big, large, bulky: *this g. watery pumpion,* Wiv. III, 3, 43. *a g. fat man,* H4A II, 4, 560. *the crows show scarce so g. as beetles,* Lr. IV, 6, 14. Quibbling in Ado V, 1, 164. LLL I, 1, 30. V, 2, 268. H4A II, 4, 250.

2) coarse, blunt, rude, base: *love is a spirit all compact of fire, not g. to sink, but light,* Ven. 150. *though*

my g. blood is stained with this abuse, Lucr. 1655. *their g. painting,* Sonn. 82, 13. *my g. body's treason,* 151, 6. *I never saw him so g. in his jealousy,* Wiv. III, 3, 201. Meas. II, 2, 87. LLL I, 1, 29. 30. IV, 3, 339. Merch. II, 7, 50. Tw. II, 5, 176. Wint. II, 3, 108. III, 2, 198. R2 V, 5, 113. H4B IV, 4, 73. H5 III, 1, 24. H8 I, 2, 84. Tim. V, 1, 99. Hml. I, 2, 136. IV, 7, 171. Oth. I, 1, 127. Ant. V, 2, 212.

3) enormous, unseemly, shocking: *lest he should hold it her own g. abuse,* Lucr. 1315. *in g. rebellion and detested treason,* R2 II, 3, 109. *free from g. passion or of mirth or anger,* H5 II, 2, 132. R3 I, 3, 106. Rom. II, 4, 176. Tim. III, 5, 38. V, 1, 147. Lr. I, 3, 4. Oth. I, 1, 135. IV, 3, 63. V, 2, 312.

4) dull, stupid: *lay open to my earthly g. conceit,* Err. III, 2, 34. *a great g. wit,* Ado V, 1, 164; cf. LLL V, 2, 268. *this palpable g. play,* Mids. V, 374. *here shall he see g. fools,* As II, 5, 58. *a g. lout, a mindless slave,* Wint. I, 2, 301. H5 IV, 1, 299. H6B IV, 2, 178. R3 III, 6, 10. Oth. III, 3, 404.

5) easily discernible, palpable: *to prevent so g. overreaching,* Wiv. V, 5, 144. *with character too g. is writ on Juliet,* Meas. I, 2, 159. *now to all sense 'tis g. you love my son,* All's I, 3, 178. *their familiarity, which was as g. as ever touched conjecture,* Wint. II, 1, 176. *these lies are like their father: g. as a mountain, open, palpable,* H4A II, 4, 250. *the truth of it stands off as g. as black and white,* H5 II, 2, 103. *examples g. as earth,* Hml. IV, 4, 46. *if 'tis not g. in sense that thou hast practised on her,* Oth. I, 2, 72. *not to strain my speech to —er issues nor to larger reach than to suspicion,* III, 3, 219. Adverbially: *to be received plain, I'll speak more g.* Meas. II, 4, 82. *with what poor judgment he hath now cast her off appears too g.* Lr. I, 1, 295 (Ff. *grossly*).

6) whole, entire, not in parts: *how much the g. sum of deuce-ace amounts to,* LLL I, 2, 49. *the most hollow lover that may be chosen out of the g. band of the unfaithful,* As IV, 1, 199. *what is the g. sum that I owe thee,* H4B II, 1, 91.

Substantively: *we that sell by g.* LLL V, 2, 319 (= wholesale). *I cannot instantly raise up the g. of full three thousand ducats,* Merch. I, 3, 56. *the full sum of me is sum of something, which, to term in g., is an unlessoned girl,* III, 2, 160. *though they come to him by the g.* Wint. IV, 4, 208 (= in a body). *in what particular thought to work I know not, but in the g. and scope of my opinion this bodes ....* Hml. I, 1, 68.

Gross, subst. see *Gross,* adj. 6.

Gross, adv. see *Gross,* adj. 5.

Grossly, 1) coarsely, rudely: *let them say 'tis g. done,* Wiv. II, 2, 149. *speak not so g.* Merch. V, 266. *whilst this muddy vesture of decay doth g. close it in,* V, 65; cf. *a spirit I am indeed, but am in that dimension g. clad,* Tw. V, 244. Similarly: *he took my father g.* Hml. III, 3, 80, i. e. in a state of coarse sensuality.

2) stupidly: *yet g. fearest thy death,* Meas. III, 1, 18. *led so g. by this meddling priest,* John III, 1, 163. 168. *my woman's heart g. grew captive to his honey words,* R3 IV, 1, 80. *would you g. gape on?* Oth. III, 3, 395.

3) enormously, in a shocking manner: *g. engirt with daring infamy,* Lucr. 1173. *slip so g.* Meas. V, 477. *that greatness should so g. offer it* (foul play) John IV, 2, 94. *he slanders thee most g.* H4A III, 3, 150. *he has given example for our flight, most g., by his own,* Ant. III, 10, 29.

4) palpably, evidently: *the purple pride in my love's veins thou hast too g. dyed,* Sonn. 99, 5. *to counterfeit thus g. with your slave,* Err. II, 2, 171. *thine eyes see it so g. shown in thy behaviours,* All's I, 3, 184. *working so g. in a natural cause,* H5 II, 2, 107. *appears too g.* Lr. I, 1, 295 (Qq *gross*).

Grossness, 1) bulkiness, bulky appearance: *perspicuous even as substance, whose g. little characters sum up,* Troil. I, 3, 325.*

2) coarseness, want of refinement and delicacy: *drove the g. of the foppery into a received belief,* Wiv. V, 5, 131. *I will purge thy mortal g.* Mids. III, 1, 163. *weigh it but with the g. of this age,* R3 III, 1, 46.

3) enormity, shocking offence: *hiding the g. with fair ornament,* Merch. III, 2, 80.

4) stupidity: *such impossible passages of g.* Tw. III, 2, 77.

Ground, subst. 1) the surface of the earth as bearing, and being beneath, all that exists: *what seest thou in the g.?* Ven. 118. *she gazeth on the g.* 224. *clapping their proud tails to the g.* 923. *to wash the foul face of the sluttish g.* 983. *the wind, imprisoned in the g.* 1046. 1167. Lucr. 1199. 1846. Sonn. 130, 12. Pilgr. 177. Tp. II, 1, 54. IV, 173. Gent. III, 1, 114. Ado III, 1, 25. LLL I, 2, 172. Mids. II, 2, 75. IV, 1, 91. 107. As III 2, 256. R2 III, 2, 150. H4B II, 1, 152. H6A I, 1, 118. H6B I, 2, 16. R3 V, 3, 284. Rom. V, 3, 179 etc. *even g.* John II, 576. Lr. IV, 6, 3. *uneven g.* H4A II, 2, 27. *on fair g.* Cor. III, 1, 242. *plainer g.* Mids. III, 2, 404. *slippery g.* Caes. III, 1, 191. *subtle g.* Cor. V, 2, 20. *lay Angiers even with the g.* John II, 399. *the hopes touch g. and dash themselves to pieces,* H4B IV, 1, 17. *the g. is the lowest, and we are half way there,* Per. I, 4, 78. *tumble on the g.* LLL V, 2, 115. *fall upon the g.* Rom. III, 3, 69. *couching head on g.* As IV, 3, 116. *whiles yet the dew's on g.* Cymb. I, 5, 1. *pulled down to the g.* Meas. I, 2, 106. *the weakest kind of fruit drops earliest to the g.* Merch. IV, 1, 116. *dashed them to the g.* John II, 405. H6A III, 2, 17. H6B II, 3, 19. *to pluck a dainty doe to g.* Tit. II, 2, 26. *I'll catch it ere it come to g.* Mcb. III, 5, 25. *from depth of under g.* H6B I, 2, 79. *raising spirits from under g.* II, 1, 174.

2) the land, the earth as distinguished from water: *an acre of barren g.* Tp. I, 1, 70. *like a whale on g.* H4B IV, 4, 40. *Neptune's salt wash and Tellus' orbed g.* Hml. III, 2, 166.

3) the earth as the world in which we live: *the wicked'st caitiff on the g.* Meas. V, 53. *I were the fairest goddess on the g.* LLL V, 2, 36. *no man so potent breathes upon the g.* H4A IV, 1, 11. *while I remain above the g.* Cor. IV, 1, 51 (= in life). *when thou wast here above the g.* Ant. I, 5, 30. *a nobler sir ne'er lived 'twixt sky and g.* Cymb. V, 5, 146.

4) region, territory, country: *when English measure backward their own g.* John V, 5, 3. *any other g. inhabitable,* R2 I, 1, 65. *who on the French g. played a tragedy,* H5 I, 2, 106. *on any plot of g. in Christendom,* H6A II, 4, 89. *by the g. that I am banished from,* H6B III, 2, 334. 296. Caes. IV, 3, 204. Hml. I, 1, 15. V, 1, 175 (quibbling). Oth. I, 1, 29. Cymb. I, 2, 20 (quibbling).

5) land or place occupied or possessed: *in a cold valley-fountain of that g.* Sonn. 153, 4. *he should not pass those —s,* Pilgr. 124. *sighs resound through heartless g.* 279. *lead off this g.* Tp. II, 1, 323. *if the g. be*

overcharged, Gent. I, 1, 107. *a fair house built on another man's g.* Wiv. II, 2, 225. *having waste g. enough,* Meas. II, 2, 170. *now for the g. which I walked upon,* LLL I, 1, 241. *between her father's g. and mine,* Mids. V, 176. Wint. IV, 4, 16. H6B IV, 10, 36. Caes. IV, 2, 49. Hml. I, 4, 61. I, 5, 156. Cymb. V, 4, 133.

6) space occupied or to be occupied: *I will not rest till I have run some g.* Merch. II, 2, 111. *run as far as God has any g.* 118. *by the g. they hide,* H4B IV, 1, 21. *who hath measured the g.* H5 III, 7, 137. *if they get g. and vantage of the king,* H4B II, 3, 53. *I should get g. of your mistress,* Cymb. I, 4, 114. *give g.* (= yield, recede) Tp. II, 2, 64. Tw. III, 4, 334. *give no foot of g.* H6C I, 4, 15. *to give me g.* H4A II, 4, 240. Cymb. I, 2, 20. *giving no g. unto the house of York,* H6C II, 6, 16.

7) soil: *as showers are to the g.* Sonn. 75, 2. *should not find a g. to root upon,* H4B III, 1, 91. *the root was fixed in virtue's g.* H6C III, 3, 125.

8) bottom: *when would you have found the g. of beauty's excellence?* LLL IV, 3, 300. *when we know the —s and authors of it,* Tw. V, 361. *where fathom-line could never touch the g.* H4A I, 3, 204.

9) foundation: *Gamut I am, the g. of all accord,* Shr. III, 1, 73. *I have found myself in my uncertain —s to fail as often as I guessed,* All's III, 1, 15. *I shall lose the —s I work upon,* III, 7, 3. *it is his —s of faith that all that look on him love him,* Tw. II, 3, 164. Quibbling in Err. II, 1, 97 and R3 III, 7, 49.

10) cause, motive, reason, source: *the —s and motives of her woe,* Compl. 63. *then is he the g. of my defeatures,* Err. II, 1, 97. *they are the g., the books, the academes from whence doth spring the true Promethean fire,* LLL IV, 3, 303. *my g. to do it,* Wint. I, 2, 353. R3 I, 3, 69. Tit. II, 1, 48. 70. Rom. V, 3, 180. Hml. II, 2, 632. Preceded by *on: on base and g. enough,* Tw. V, 78. *on some known g. of treachery,* R2 I, 1, 11. Cor. II, 2, 13. Hml. V, 1, 175. Lr. II, 4, 146. Oth. V, 2, 138. Cymb. IV, 2, 143. Per. V, 1, 27.

11) question, matter: *I had rather you did lack* (credit) *than I upon this g.* Wint. II, 1, 159.

12) the tune on which descants are raised: *on that g. I'll build a holy descant,* R3 III, 7, 49. Quibbling: *should the empress know this discord's g., the music would not please,* Tit. II, 1, 70.

13) the first stratum in painting, the foil: *my sable g. of sin I will not paint,* Lucr. 1074. *like bright metal on a sullen g.* H4A I, 2, 236.

Ground, vb. 1) to fix firmly, to settle: *it (self-love) is so —ed inward in my heart,* Sonn. 62, 4. *no —ed malice,* R3 I, 3, 29.

2) to found, to base, to set as on a foundation or cause: *hate of my sin, —ed on sinful loving,* Sonn. 142, 2. *displeasure —ed upon no other argument,* As I, 2, 291. *how —ed he his title to the crown?* H8 I, 2, 144.

Groundling, a spectator in the pit of the theatre: Hml. III, 2, 12.

Grove, poetical term for a wood: Ven. 865. Lucr. 1129. 1249. Pilgr. 376. Tp. IV, 1, 66. V, 33. Mids. II, 1, 28. 146. 245. 259. III, 2, 5. 390. IV, 1, 120. Shr. II, 260. H4A I, 1, 82. H6B I, 2, 33. II, 1, 43. III, 2, 323. Cor. I, 10, 30. Tit. II, 3, 58. Rom. I, 1, 128. Mcb. V, 5, 38. Per. I, 4, 9.

Grovel, to lie on the face, to lie prostrate: John II, 305. H6B I, 2, 9. I, 4, 14.

Grow, (impf. *grew*, part. *grown*) 1) to become greater or larger, to increase in bulk, stature, quantity, or degree: *their pride doth g.* Lucr. 298. *so fast thou —est in one of thine,* Sonn. 11, 1. *had my friend's Muse —n with this —ing age,* 32, 10. *to give full growth to that which still doth g.* 115, 14. *—s with heat,* 124, 12. 126, 3. Tp. I, 2, 105. Gent. IV. 2, 15. Mids. II, 2, 117. H5 I, 1, 65. H6C II, 2, 169. II, 5, 2. R3 II, 4, 5. 9. 11. 13. H8 V, 4, 72. Rom. I, 3, 98 *(women g. by men).* Mcb. I, 4, 29. Oth. II, 1, 197. Cymb. I, 1, 108. Per. I, 2, 80 etc. Partic. *—n* = having attained full growth: *the —-n serpent,* Mcb. III, 4, 29. *a wench full —n,* Per. IV Prol. 16. *to g. on a person* = to gain on, to get the better, the upperhand of: *begin you to g. upon me?* As I, 1, 91.* *sickness —ing upon our soldiers,* H5 III, 3, 55. *my sickness —s upon me,* Lr. V, 3, 105. cf. *here, as I point my sword, the sun arises, which is a great way — ing on the south,* Caes. II, 1, 107 (= gaining on, encroaching on the south?) *

2) to be produced by vegetation, to shoot, to issue as plants from a soil: *the —ing rose,* Lucr. 492. *every thing that —s,* Sonn. 15, 1. *an osier —ing by a brook,* Pilgr. 75. Tp. II, 2, 171. IV, 1, 19. 112. Meas. III, 2, 284. Mids. II, 1, 250. All's V, 1, 5. R3 II, 2, 41. Ant. V, 2, 88. Cymb. IV, 2, 180 etc.

3) to take root, to be fixed: *there thy fixed foot shall g.* Tw. I, 4, 17. *would stand and make his eyes g. in my face,* Ant. I, 5, 32. With *to,* = to be united by growth, to coalesce with: *incorporate then they seem, face —s to face,* Ven. 540. *for ever may my knees g. to the earth,* R2 V, 3, 30. *till to the ground they g.* 106. *like a vine g. to him,* H8 V, 5, 50. *I would thou grewest unto the shores of the haven,* Cymb. I, 3, 1.

4) to vegetate, to be shot forth as from a soil or stem, to stand in a place as on a stalk: *how ripe in show thy lips, those kissing cherries, tempting g.* Mids. III, 2, 140. *having no other reason but that his beard grew thin and hungerly,* Shr. III, 2, 177. *that wear upon your virgin branches yet your maidenheads —ing,* Wint. IV, 4, 116. *men whose heads do g. beneath their shoulders,* Oth. I, 3, 145. *thy head, which now is —ing upon thy shoulders,* Cymb. IV, 1, 17. *displace our heads where — thank the gods! —they g.* IV, 2, 122. *to g. together* = to form one body: *we grew together like to a double cherry,* Mids. III, 2, 208. *they clung in their embracement, as* (= as if) *they grew together,* H8 I, 1, 10. Cor. III, 2, 43. With *to,* = to be incorporate, to stick to, to adhere: *in eternal lines to time thou —est,* Sonn. 18, 12. *I g. to you, and our parting is a tortured body,* All's II, 1, 36. *all men's ears grew to his tunes,* Wint. IV, 4, 186 (the servant's speech). *I lay aside that which —s to me* (my soldiership), H4B I, 2, 100. *they that my trust must g. to live not here,* H8 III, 1, 89. *he grew unto his seat,* Hml. IV, 7, 86. *here comes that which —s to the stalk,* Per. IV, 6, 45. Merch. II, 2, 18 see sub **6**.

5) to take rise, to begin to exist, to spring, to come to pass: *my beauty as the spring doth yearly g.* Ven. 141. *the womb wherein they* (thoughts) *grew,* Sonn. 86, 4. *upon familiarity will g. more contempt,* Wiv. I, 1, 258. *how her acquaintance grew with this lewd fellow,* Ado V, 1, 341. *each thing that in season —s,* LLL I, 1, 107. *whence —s this insolence?* Shr. II, 23. *how should this g.?* Wint. I, 2, 431. *I turn my glass and give my scene such —ing as you had slept*

between, IV, 1, 16. *hence grew the general wreck and massacre,* H6A I, 1, 135. *were —ing time once ripened to my will,* II, 4, 99. *some words there grew 'twixt Somerset and me,* II, 5, 46. *this late dissension —n betwixt the peers,* III, 1, 189. *this —ing image of thy fiend-like face,* Tit. V, 1, 45. *hazard so dangerous as doth hourly g. out of his lunacies,* Hml. III, 3, 6. *their defeat does by their own insinuation g.* V, 2, 59. *what —s of it, no matter,* Lr. I, 3, 23. *how grew your quarrel?* II, 2, 66. *touch you the sourest points with sweetest terms, nor curstness g. to the matter,* Ant. II, 2, 25. *his whole action —s not in the power on't,* III, 7, 69.

6) to proceed, to advance to a state, to come, to go: *so with his steerage shall your thoughts g. on,* Per. IV, 4, 19. With *to: if matters g. to your likings,* Wiv. I, 1, 79. *I trust it will g. to a most prosperous perfection,* Meas. III, 1, 271. *g. this to what adverse issue it can,* Ado II, 2, 52. *then read the names of the actors, and so g. to a point,* Mids. I, 2, 10 (come to the purpose. Ff *g. on to a point). my father did something smack, something g. to, he had a kind of taste,* Merch. II, 2, 18 (perhaps = he was like burnt milk growing to the pot and tasting disagreeably). *when they to perfection g.* Tw. II, 4, 42. *grew by our feeding to so great a bulk,* H4A V, 1, 62. *this will g. to a brawl,* H4B II, 4, 186. *g. to a greater falseness,* III, 1, 90. *which daily grew to quarrel and to bloodshed,* IV, 5, 195. *our present musters g. to five and twenty thousand men,* I, 3, 10. *as our vineyards g. to wildness,* H5 V, 2, 55. *—n to credit by the wars,* H6A IV, 1, 36. *the matter —s to compromise,* V, 4, 149. *mine oratory grew to an end,* R3 III, 7, 20 (Ff. *drew). —s to an envious fever,* Troil. I, 3, 133. *an unweeded garden that —s to seed,* Hml. I, 2, 136. *goodness —ing to a plurisy,* IV, 7, 118. *the night —s to waste,* Oth. IV, 2, 249. *the hated, —n to strength, are newly —n to love,* Ant. I, 3, 48. 49. Hence = to become: *thus policy in love ... grew to faults assured,* Sonn. 118, 10. *—s to something of great constancy,* Mids. V, 26. *this brawl to-day, —n to this faction in the Temple-garden,* H6A II, 4, 125. *if they should g. themselves to common players,* Hml. II, 2, 364. cf. *if we g. all to be pork-eaters,* Merch. III, 5, 26. *what a blunt fellow is this —n to be,* Caes. I, 2, 299. With other prepositions: *g. from the king's acquaintance,* H8 III, 1, 161 (= to become a stranger to the king). *grew in love with the song,* Wint. IV, 4, 618. *was —n into a hoop,* Tp. I, 2, 259. *g. into extremes,* Shr. Ind. 1, 138. *—n into an unspeakable estate,* Wint. IV, 2, 46. *policy —s into an ill opinion,* Troil. V, 4, 18. *a good man's fortune may g. out at heels,* Lr. II, 2, 164. *nature, as it —s again toward earth,* Tim. II, 2, 227.

7) to become: *grew kinder,* Ven. 318. *grew faint,* 645. *—s old,* Lucr. 49. Sonn. 45, 14. 102, 12. 140, 9. 11. Tp. I, 2, 76. IV, 191. Gent. II, 4, 161. V, 4, 9. Meas. I, 4, 41. II, 4, 9. Err. II, 2, 74. III, 2, 4. Mids. II, 1, 129. 152. III, 2, 262. As I, 1, 75. R3 IV, 1, 80. H8 IV, 2, 15 etc. *grew a seething bath,* Sonn. 153, 7. *grew a twenty years removed thing,* Tw. V, 92. *grew a companion to the common streets,* H4A III, 2, 68. *g. dear friends,* Cor. IV, 4, 21 etc.

8) to be, to exist, to live: *things —ing to themselves are growth's abuse,* Ven. 166. *to g. unto himself was his desire,* 1180. *what worth in you doth g.* Sonn. 83, 8. *the store which should example where your equal grew,* 84, 4. *how like Eve's apple doth thy beauty g.,*

if thy sweet virtue answer not thy show, 93, 13. *long-grown wounds*, H4A III, 2, 156 (= old). *what rank diseases g. near the heart*, H4B III, 1, 39. *we carry not a heart with us that —s not in a fair consent with ours*, H5 II, 2, 22. *our houses and ourselves and children g. like savages*, V, 2, 59. *still —ing in a majesty and pomp*, H8 II, 3, 7. *honour and policy, like unsevered friends, in the war do g. together*, Cor. III, 2, 43. *here g. no damned grudges*, Tit. I, 154 (Q1 *drugs*). *grant, as Timon —s, his hate may g. to the whole race*, Tim. IV, 1, 39.

9) to accrue, to fall to, to be due: *so thy great gift, upon misprision —ing, comes home again*, Sonn. 87, 11. *the sum is —ing to me by Antipholus*, Err. IV, 1, 18. *knowing how the debt —s, I will pay it*, IV, 4, 124. cf. *how —s it due?* 137.

10) trans. to cause to grow, to produce, to raise? *let them go to ear the land that hath some hope to g.* R2 III, 2, 212 (it may well be taken as intr.).

Growth, 1) vegetation, vegetable life: *things growing to themselves are —'s abuse*, Ven. 166. *this bastard graff shall never come to g.* Lucr. 1062. *in pride of all his g.* Sonn. 99, 12. *I cannot give it vital g. again*, Oth. V, 2, 14.

2) gradual increase of animal and vegetable bodies: Sonn. 115, 14. As I, 1, 15. III, 2, 221. H5 V, 2, 69. R3 II, 4, 7. 25. III, 1, 103. IV, 2, 60. Troil. I, 3, 9.

3) beginning, rise, springing into existence: *stops her pipe in g. of riper days*, Sonn. 102, 8. *leave the g. untried of that wide gap*, Wint. IV, 1, 6.

4) size, stature: *three or four of their g.* Wiv. IV, 4, 48. *of excellent g. and presence*, As I, 2, 130. *my g. would approve the truth*, H4B I, 2, 180.

Grub, subst. a worm: Cor. V, 4, 12. Rom. I, 4, 68. V, 3, 126.

Grub, vb. with *up*, to root out: *but for the stock, I wish it —ed up*, H8 V, 1, 23.

Grudge, subst. inveterate hatred, ill-will: Gent. V, 4, 143. Merch. I, 3, 48. H6A IV, 1, 109. H6C III, 3, 195. R3 II, 1, 65. Tit. I, 154 (Q1 *drugs*). II, 1, 48. Rom. Prol. 3. Caes. IV, 3, 125. In Tp. I, 2, 249 *without or g. or grumblings*, for *without or grudgings or grumblings.*

Grudge, vb. 1) intr. to murmur, to repine: *without g. or grumblings*, Tp. I, 2, 249 (= without grudgings) *he eats his meat without —ing*, Ado III, 4, 90. *their --ing stomachs*, H6A IV, 1, 141. *—ing hate*, R3 II, 1, 9.

2) trans. a) to give or allow reluctantly and with murmuring, to envy: *they have —d us contribution*, Caes. IV, 3, 206. *to g. my pleasures*, Lr. II, 4, 177.

b) to cherish or harbour with malice: *perish they that g. one thought against your majesty*, H6A III, 1, 176 (= that have one thought of grudge).

Gruel, a mixture made by boiling ingredients in water: *make the g. thick and slab*, Mcb. IV, 1, 32.

Grumble, to murmur with discontent, to growl: Tp. I, 2, 249. Shr. III, 2, 155. IV, 1, 170. H6B I, 3, 73. H6C I, 4, 76. Troil. II, 1, 35. Lr. III, 4, 44.

Grumio, name of Petruchio's servant in Shr. I, 2, 5 etc.

Grunt, 1) to utter a sound like a hog: Mids. III, 1, 113.

2) to groan: *to g. and sweat under a weary life*, Hml. III, 1, 77.

Gualtier, the French form of *Walter*. H6B IV, 1, 37. 38.

Gualtree forest, a forest in Yorkshire: H4B IV, 1, 2 (Q *Gaultree*).

Guard, subst. 1) a state of caution and vigilance, watch, heed: *shook off my sober —s and civil fears*, Compl. 298. *'tis best we stand upon our g.* Tp. II, 1, 321. *stands at a g. with envy*, Meas. I, 3, 51. *keeps her g. in honestest defence*, All's III, 5, 76. *betake you to your g.* Tw. III, 4, 253. *no place, that g. and most unusual vigilance does not attend my taking*, Lr. II, 3, 4. *never anger made good g. for itself*, Ant. IV, 1, 10. *the messenger came on my g.* IV, 6, 23 (when I was on duty). *court of g.*: H6A II, 1, 4. Oth. II, 1, 220. Ant. IV, 9, 2. cf. *on the court and g. of safety*, Oth. II, 3, 216. *have you had quiet g.?* Hml. I, 1, 10.

3) defence, protection: *his greatness was no g. to bar heaven's shaft*, Per. II, 4, 14. In fencing, = posture of defence: *the scrimers of their nation had neither motion, g. nor eye*, Hml. IV, 7, 102. cf. *he's out of his g. already*, Tw. I, 5, 93.

3) the act or state of keeping sure: *he broke from those that had the g. of him*, Err. V, 149. *in the fearful g. of an unthrifty knave*, Merch. I, 3, 176. *were it at home, upon my brother's g.* Cor. I, 10, 25 (when my brother had the office of protecting him; cf. Ant. IV, 6, 23). *good g.* Lr. V, 3, 1. *to send the king to some retention and appointed g.* 47. *I'll take her to my g.* Ant. V, 2, 67.

4) he who, or that which protects or keeps sure; used of things: *whoe'er keeps me, let my heart be his g.* Sonn. 133, 11. *there is between my will and all offences a g. of patience*, Troil. V, 2, 54. *the —s of the ever-fixed pole*, Oth. II, 1, 15 (the star Arctophylax). cf. H4B I, 1, 148 (quibbling). Of persons: *though Argus were her eunuch and her g.* LLL III, 201. *I will be your g.* H6A I, 2, 127. II, 1, 49. Troil. IV, 4, 130. V, 2, 184. Hml. III, 4, 104. Oth. I, 1, 125. Especially, a body of men occupied in keeping, watching, or preserving a person: Tw. III, 4, 12. H5 III, 6, 164. IV, 2, 60 (some M. Edd. *guidon*). H6A I, 4, 53. H6C IV, 2, 16. 23. IV, 3, 23. IV, 4, 8. IV, 5, 7. R3 I, 1, 42. V, 3, 76. H8 V, 3, 95. Troil. V, 1, 79. Cor. III, 3, 140. Tit. I, 283. Lr. II, 1, 18 (*set g.*). Oth. I, 1, 180. II, 3, 1. Ant. IV, 14, 104. 128. IV, 15, 9.

5) Plur. —s, trimmings, facings, ornaments: *the damned'st body to invest and cover in prenzie —s*, Meas. III, 1, 97. *the —s are but slightly basted on neither*, Ado I, 1, 289. *rhymes are —s on wanton Cupid's hose*, LLL IV, 3, 58. *velvet —s and Sunday citizens*, H4A III, 1, 261. Quibbling: *thou art a g. too wanton for the head*, H4B I, 1, 148.

Guard, vb. 1) to protect, to keep in safety, to watch; absol.: *g. with halberds*, Err. V, 185. *disorder wounds where it should g.* H6B V, 2, 33. *you g. like men*, Cor. V, 2, 2. Trans.: *I think the honey —ed with a sting*, Lucr. 493; cf. R2 III, 2, 20; H5 III Chor. 20. *draw not thy sword to g. iniquity*, Lucr. 626. Sonn. 49, 12. Tp. II, 1, 197. John I, 70. III, 3, 2. R2 III, 2, 62. H4B IV, 3, 81. IV, 5, 44. V, 2, 88. V, 5, 45. H5 I, 2, 7. IV, 4, 82. H6A I, 3, 87. II, 1, 74. V, 1, 48. H6B III, 1, 188. III, 2, 265. H6C V, 3, 21. R3 III, 5, 20. IV, 1, 93 (Ff *tend*). V, 3, 138. Troil. II, 2, 22. Cor. I, 2, 27. I, 7, 1. Tim. III, 3, 40. Caes. IV, 2, 52. Hml. IV, 3, 14. IV, 5, 97. Oth. II, 1, 77. V, 2, 241. Ant. V, 2, 36. Cymb. I, 1, 64. V, 2, 12. *g. these traitors to the block of death*, H4B IV, 2, 122. *He that wears the crown immortally, long g. it yours*, IV, 5, 145.

g. thee well, Troil. IV, 5, 253. With *from: whose wraths to g. you from*, Tp. III, 3, 79. H6B III, 1, 249. R3 V, 3, 156. Ant. V, 2, 132. Cymb. II, 2, 9. II, 5, 19.

2) to face, to trim, to ornament: *the body of your discourse is sometime —ed with fragments*, Ado I, 1, 288. *a livery more —ed than his fellows*, Merch. II, 2, 164. *to g. a title that was rich before*, John IV, 2, 10. *—ed with rags*, H4B IV, 1, 34 (O. Edd. *with rage*). *a long motley coat —ed with yellow*, H8 Prol. 16.

Guardage, guard, that which keeps and protects one: *run from her g. to the sooty bosom of such a thing as thou*, Oth. I, 2, 70.

Guardant, guard, sentinel: *when my angry g. stood alone*, H6A IV, 7, 9. *a Jack g. cannot office me from my son Coriolanus*, Cor. V, 2, 67.

Guardian, 1) one who has the care of an orphan: Ado II, 3, 174. John II, 115. Troil. V, 2, 7. 47. Lr. II, 4, 254.

2) that which keeps and guards: *Colmekill, the sacred storehouse of his predecessors, and g. of their bones*, Mcb. II, 4, 35.

Gudgeon, a small fish easily caught, of the genus Cyprinus, and hence a person easily duped: *fish not with this melancholy bait for this fool g., this opinion.* Merch. I, 1, 102.

Guerdon, subst. reward, recompense: Ado V, 3, 5. LLL III, 170 (not understood by Costard).*

Guerdoned, rewarded: H6B I, 4, 49. H6C III, 3, 191.

Guess, subst. 1) approximative estimation: *that, in g., they measure by thy deeds*, Sonn. 69, 10. *by the near g. of my memory*, Merch. I, 3, 55. *square our g. by shows*, All's II, 1, 153. *by thy g., how nigh is Clarence now?* H6C V, 1, 8. *here is the g. of their true strength and forces by diligent discovery*, Lr. V, 1, 52.

2) conjecture: H5 I, 1, 96. R3 IV, 4, 466. Oth. III, 3, 145. III, 4, 184. Cymb. I, 1, 60. *create a perfect g.* H4B III, 1, 88. *give g.* Caes. II, 1, 3. *have a likely g.* Tit. II, 3, 207.

Guess, vb. 1) trans. a) to conjecture, to suspect, to have an idea of, to divine, to conclude with probability: *I g. one angel in another's hell*, Sonn. 144, 12. *I g. the sequel*, Gent. II, 1, 122. Shr. II, 338. H4A IV, 4, 7. H6C IV, 4, 28. IV, 5, 22. H8 V, 1, 164. Followed by a clause: *—ed that it was she*, Gent. V, 2, 39. *I g. it stood in her chin*, Err. III, 2, 130. *we may g. by this what you are*, Ado I, 1, 111. All's V, 3, 329. Wint. I, 2, 403. IV, 4, 479. R3 II, 2, 19. III, 2, 45. IV, 4, 477. H8 II, 1, 7. Cor. V, 2, 68. Tit. IV, 1, 15. Ant. III, 13, 121. Absol.: *I g. not*, Meas. IV, 4, 8. *I cannot g.* H6A II, 5, 60. R3 IV, 4, 475. Tit. IV, 1, 16. *as I g.* LLL V, 2, 121. As IV, 3, 8. R2 II, 3, 68. H6C V, 5, 84. R3 IV, 1, 8. Cor. I, 6, 52. *I partly g.* As II, 4, 24. *as you g.* R3 IV, 4, 467. Oth. I, 3, 36. *to fail as often as I —ed*, All's III, 1, 16.

b) to hit upon, to reproduce by memory: *tell me their words as near as thou canst g. them*, H6C IV, 1, 90.

c) to think, to suppose, to imagine: *better far, I g., that we do make our entrance several ways*, H6A II, 1, 29. *who set the body and the limbs of this great sport together, as you g.?* H8 I, 1, 47. *we might g. they relieved us humanely*, Cor. I, 1, 18.

2) intr., with *at*, to conjecture, to divine, to find out: *grieving themselves to g. at others' smarts*, Lucr. 1238. *I g. at it*, Mcb. IV, 3, 203. *g. at her years*, Ant. III, 3, 29.

Guessingly, conjecturally, hypothetically: Lr. III, 7, 47.

Guest, a visitor, a stranger or friend entertained by another: Ven. 449. Lucr. 90. 1125. 1565. Sonn. 47, 7. 153, 12. Gent. IV, 2, 26. Wiv. II, 3, 77. IV, 3, 13. Err. I, 1, 115. III, 1, 27. LLL V, 2, 354. Merch. II, 3, 6. Shr. II, 51. 318. Wint. I, 2, 53. III, 2, 167. IV, 4, 48. R2 II, 2, 7. V, 1, 15. H4A III, 3, 194. IV, 2, 86. H4B II, 4, 101. H5 III, 3, 57. H6A II, 2, 55. H8 I, 3, 51. I, 4, 35. Troil. III, 3, 166. Cor. IV, 5, 38. Tit. I, 490. Rom. I, 2, 21. Ant. II, 2, 249 etc.

Guest-cavaleire, knightly lodger: Wiv. II, 1, 221.

Guest-justice, a justice on a visit at a place: Wiv. II, 3, 59.

Guest-wise, like a stranger: *my heart to her but as g. sojourned, and now to Helen is it home returned*, Mids. III, 2, 171.

Guiana, a rich country in South America: Wiv. I, 3, 76.

Guichard, a French name: H5 IV, 8, 100.

Guide, subst. one who directs another in his way or course: All's I, 1, 183. H4B II, 3, 6. H6B II, 3, 25. Rom. V, 3, 116. Lr. V, 3, 190. Oth. II, 3, 205. Ant. III, 13, 145. *give them g. to us* = show them in, Tim. I, 1, 252. Sing. for the plur.: *Love and Fortune be my gods, my g.* Lucr. 351. *if my instructions may be your g.* Meas. IV, 2, 181.

Guide, vb. 1) to direct in a way or course, to show the way: *some heavenly power g. us out of this country*, Tp. V, 105. *heaven g. him to thy husband's cudgel*, Wiv. IV, 2, 90. *to g. our measure*, V, 5, 83. LLL I, 2, 173. R3 IV, 1, 92. Troil. V, 1, 77. Cymb. I, 4, 49. Per. II, 1, 146. III, 2, 111.

2) to lead, to influence, to rule: *whatsoever star that —s my moving*, Sonn. 26, 9. *the devil that —s him*, Wiv. III, 5, 150. *in love the heavens themselves do g. the state*, V, 5, 245. *the affection that now —s me most*, Meas. II, 4, 168. *I give me and my service into your —ing power*, All's II, 3, 111. *Jove send her a better —ing spirit*, Wint. II, 3, 127. *we have been —ed by thee*, H6A III, 3, 9. *that god in office, —ing men*, Troil. I, 3, 231. III, 1, 48. IV, 5, 102. V, 2, 139. Cor. II, 3, 238. Mcb. III, 1, 53. Cymb. I, 1, 50.

3) to govern, to manage, to handle, to steer: *wishing Adonis had his team to g.* Ven. 179; cf. Gent. III, 1, 154 and As III, 4, 49. *'tis he that —s this hand*, Lucr. 1722. *the devil g. his cudgel*, Wiv. IV, 2, 91. *discomfort —s my tongue*, R2 III, 2, 65. *g. thou the sword*, Caes. V, 3, 45. H8 I, 1, 45. Troil. I, 3, 210. Tit. IV, 1, 69. 75.

Guider, guide: Cor. I, 7, 7.

Guiderius, the elder son of Cymbeline: Cymb. III, 3, 88. V, 5, 358. 363.

Guidon, a standard-bearer; inserted by some M. Edd. in H5 IV, 2, 60; O. Edd. *guard.*

Guienne, French province: H6A I, 1, 60.

Guildenstern, name in Hml. II, 2, 1. 33. 34 etc.

Guilder, a Dutch coin, used for money in general: Err. I, 1, 8. IV, 1, 4.

Guildford, see *Guilford.*

Guildhall, the town-house of London: R3 III, 5, 73. 102.

Guile, deceitful cunning, duplicity, treachery: Lucr. 1534. Pilgr. 335. H6A IV, 1, 63. R3 II, 1, 38. II, 2, 28. V, 3, 133.

Guiled, furnished or armed with deceit, treacherous: *ornament is but the g. shore to a most dangerous sea,* Merch. III, 2, 97. cf. *Beguiled* in Lucr. 1544.

Guileful, deceitful, treacherous: H6A I, 1, 77. Tit. V, 1, 104.

Guilford (M. Edd. *Guildford*) name in R3 IV, 4, 505. H8 I, 3, 66. I, 4, 9.

Guilt, state of having committed a crime, criminality: Lucr. 229. 635. 754. 876. 1342. Sonn. 36, 10. Tp. I, 2, 471. III, 3, 104. Gent. V, 4, 73. Tw. III, 1, 159. Wint. III, 2, 7. R2 IV, 124. V, 1, 69. V, 6, 41. H5 IV, 1, 170. H6B II, 3, 2. 104. III, 1, 169. 255. III, 2, 216. R3 I, 2, 98. III, 5, 30. Tit. II, 3, 301. IV, 2, 26. 149. Mcb. I, 7, 71. Hml. III, 2, 85. III, 3, 40. IV, 5, 19. Lr. III, 2, 57. Cymb. V, 2, 1. Quibbling with *gild* and *gilt:* H4B IV, 5, 129. H5 II Chor. 26. Mcb. II, 2, 57.

Guiltian, name in All's IV, 3, 185.

Guiltily, with a bad conscience: *g. awake,* R3 V, 3, 146.

Guiltiness, consciousness of crime: Wiv. V, 5, 130. Meas. II, 2, 139. V, 372. Ado IV, 1, 43. LLL V, 2, 801. R3 V, 3, 170. Caes. I, 1, 67. Oth. V, 1, 109. V, 2, 39.

Guiltless, innocent: Lucr. 89. 1057. 1482. Meas. IV, 2, 69. Ado IV, 1, 171. As IV, 3, 12. Tw. I, 5, 99. H5 I, 2, 25. H6A V, 4, 44. H6B III, 1, 167. IV, 1, 95. IV, 7, 108 (*g. blood-shedding* = shedding of g. blood). R3 I, 2, 98. I, 4, 72. III, 3, 14. H8 II, 1, 68. 139. Lr. I, 4, 295. Oth. II, 1, 70. IV, 1, 48. V, 2, 122. With *of:* R3 I, 4, 95 (Ff *from*). Hml. IV, 5, 149.

Guilty, 1) chargeable with a crime, not innocent: Lucr. 358. 714. 735. 1482. 1511 (*g. instance* = instance of guilt). Meas. IV, 1, 39. Err. IV, 4, 66. R2 I, 1, 73. H6A II, 4, 94. H6B III, 2, 17. H6C V, 5, 3. V, 6, 11. R3 II, 1, 135. III, 3, 11. V, 3, 142. Tit. V, 2, 184 etc. Used as a term of law: LLL IV, 3, 205. R3 V, 3, 199. *cry g.* H8 III, 2, 308. *to find one g.* H6B IV, 2, 103. H8 II, 1, 7. 27. *not g.* Wint. I, 2, 74. III, 2, 27. *he pleaded not g.* H8 II, 1, 13. Comp. *—ier:* Meas. II, 1, 21. V, 372. Followed by *in: g. in defence,* H5 III, 3, 43. *wherein am I g.?* H6B III, 1, 103. *wherein they are not g.* Hml. I, 4, 25. By *of:* Lucr. 772. 841. 918. 931. Sonn. 111, 2. 151, 4. LLL I, 2, 116. IV, 1, 31. V, 2, 746 (= in fault). Mids. III, 2, 75. Merch. III, 2, 328. All's IV, 1, 36. Wint. II, 2, 62. John IV, 3, 136. R2 II, 1, 182. IV, 79. H5 IV, 1, 183. H6A IV, 5, 47. H6B III, 2, 187. H6C III, 1, 91. R3 III, 1, 43. IV, 3, 3. Rom. V, 3, 146 etc. By *to: lest myself be g. to self-wrong,* Err. III, 2, 168. *the unthought-of accident is g. to what we wildly do,* Wint. IV, 4, 549.

2) criminal: *I heard your g. rhymes,* LLL IV, 3, 139. *this most grievous g. murder,* R3 I, 4, 280 (Ff *grievous murder*). *damned g. deeds,* Rom. III, 2, 111.

Guilty-like, like one guilty: Oth. III, 3, 39.

Guinea-hen (O. Edd. *ginny* and *gynney hen*) a term of contempt for a woman: Oth. I, 3, 317.

Guinover (some M. Edd. *Guinever*) king Arthur's queen, "not over-famous for fidelity to her husband": LLL IV, 1, 125.

Guise, fashion, custom, practice: Ven. 1177. H6B I, 3, 45. Tim. IV, 3, 472. Mcb. V, 1, 22. Cymb. V, 1, 32.

Gules, heraldic term for red: Tim. IV, 3, 59. Hml. II, 2, 479.

Gulf, 1) a whirlpool, a sucking eddy: *a swallow-ing g. that even in plenty wanteth,* Lucr. 557. *fall a drop of water in the breaking g.* Err. II, 2, 128. *England his approaches makes as fierce as waters to the sucking of a g.* H5 II, 4, 10. *thou art so near the g., thou needs must be englutted,* IV, 3, 82. *the sea whose envious g. did swallow up his life,* H6C V, 6, 25. *the swallowing g. of blind forgetfulness,* R3 III, 7, 128. *like a g. it did remain i' the midst o' the body, still cupboarding the viand,* Cor. I, 1, 101. *follow thine enemy in a fiery g.* III, 2, 91. *like a g. doth draw what's near it with it,* Hml. III, 3, 16. *wash me in steep-down —s of liquid fire,* Oth. V, 2, 280.

2) any thing englutting and absorbing, a gullet, swallow: *maw and g. of the ravined salt-sea shark,* Mcb. IV, 1, 23. cf. Lucr. 557. Cor. I, 1, 101.

Gull, subst. 1) an unfledged nestling: *that ungentle g., the cuckoo's bird,* H4A V, 1, 60. *Timon will be left a naked g.* Tim. II, 1, 31.

2) a person easily deceived, a dupe, a fool: *yond g. Malvolio is turned heathen,* Tw. III, 2, 73. *a thin-faced knave, a g.* V, 213. *made the most notorious geck and g.* 351. *'tis a g., a fool, a rogue,* H5 III, 6, 70. *Clarence I do beweep to many simple —s,* R3 I, 3, 328. *O g.!* Oth. V, 2, 163.

3) an imposition, a trick: *I should think this a g.* Ado II, 3, 123.

Gull, vb. to impose on, to trick: *that affable familiar ghost which nightly —s him with intelligence,* Sonn. 86, 10. *g. him into a nay-word,* Tw. II, 3, 145. *that same demon that —ed thee thus,* H5 II, 2, 121.

Gull-catcher, one who entraps silly persons, a trickster: Tw. II, 5, 204.

Gum, 1) the fleshy substance that invests and contains the teeth: Mcb. I, 7, 57.

2) a concrete juice exsuding through the bark of trees: Tim. I, 1, 21. Hml. II, 2, 201. Oth. V, 2, 351. Used of the rheum issuing from the eyes: H5 IV, 2, 48; cf. the passage in Hml.

Gummed, stiffened with gum: *he frets like a g. velvet,* H4A II, 2, 2.

Gun, an instrument from which shot is discharged by fire, a cannon, a musket: Ven. 461. Tp. II, 1, 161. LLL III, 63. Mids. III, 2, 22. H4A I, 3, 56. 63. H5 IV, 1, 210. H6B III, 2, 331. Rom. III, 3, 103.

Gundelier, see *Gondolier.*

Gunner, a cannonier: Tp. II, 2, 49. H5 III Chor. 32. cf. *Master-gunner.*

Gunpowder, the powder put into guns to be fired: H4A V, 4, 123. H4B IV, 4, 48. H5 IV, 7, 188.

Gun-stones, cannon-balls of stone, used for shot in old times: H5 I, 2, 282.

Gurnet, the fish Trigla; used as a term of reproach: *if I be not ashamed of my soldiers, I am a soused g.* H4A IV, 2, 13.

Gurney (O. Edd. *Gourney*), name in John I, 230.

Gush, vb. to emit in copious effusion, to shed: *mine eyes shall g. pure streams,* Lucr. 1078.

Gust, subst. a violent blast of wind: Ven. 456. Lucr. 549. Sonn. 13, 11. Merch. IV, 1, 77. Shr. II, 136. H6A V, 5, 5. H6B III, 2, 88. H6C II, 6, 35, III, 1, 88. Cor. I, 6, 5. Tit. V, 3, 69.

Gust, subst. 1) taste, relish: *mine eye well knows what with his g. is 'greeing,* Sonn. 114, 11. *the g. he hath in quarrelling,* Tw. I, 3, 33.

2) conception, notion, idea: *to kill, I grant, is sin's extremest g.* Tim. III, 5, 54.

Gust, vb. to form an idea of, to perceive: *'tis far gone, when I shall g. it last,* Wint. I, 2, 219.

Gusty, full of gusts, stormy: *a raw and g. day,* Caes. I, 2, 100.

Guts, bowels, intestines of the belly: Wiv. I, 3, 94. II, 1, 32. Ado II, 3, 61. H4A II, 4, 285. 498. III, 3, 172. 175. H5 II, 1, 61. Troil. II, 1, 80. Hml. IV, 3, 33. Used to denote gluttonous or corpulent persons: *thou clay-brained g.* H4A II, 4, 251. *I'll lug the g. into the neighbour room,* Hml. III, 4, 212.

Gutsgriping, causing pain in the bowels: *the g. ruptures,* Troil. V, 1, 21 (M. Edd. *the g., ruptures*).

Guttered, indented: *the g. rocks,* Oth. II, 1, 69.

Guy, name of a hero of romance: *I am not Samson, nor Sir G.* H8 V, 4, 22.

Guynes, name of a French town: H8 I, 1, 7.

Guysors, name of a French town: H6A I, 1, 61.

Gyve, vb. to fetter, to ensnare: *I will g. thee in thine own courtship,* Oth. II, 1, 171 (F1.3.4 *give,* Qq *catch*).

Gyves, chains, fetters: Compl. 242. Meas. IV, 2, 12. H4A IV, 2, 44. Rom. II, 2, 180. Cymb. V, 4, 14. *would convert his g. to graces,* Hml. IV, 7, 21 (an obscure passage not yet satisfactorily explained or amended. Perhaps it means: that which should be designed to fetter him, to trammel him up, would lend him a grace in the eyes of the people. As for gyves hindering grace of motion, see Compl. 242 and H4A IV, 2, 44).*

H.

H, the letter; pronounced like the subst. *ache:* Ado III, 4, 56. Ant. IV, 7, 8.

Ha, 1) an exclamation of wonder and surprise: *ha, ha! what things are these?* Tp. V, 263. *ha! the prince!* Ado II, 3, 37. 266. Merch. III, 1, 18. Tw. I, 3, 150. John II, 350. H6C IV, 1, 112. R3 I, 2, 239. IV, 2, 14. H8 III, 2, 61. Troil. III, 3, 194. Rom. III, 4, 19. IV, 4, 19. Tim. IV, 3, 30. Hml. II, 2, 603. III, 1, 103. Oth. III, 3, 35 etc. Expressive of eagerness and impatience: *ha! let me see,* Gent. II, 1, 3. *ha! thou mountain-foreigner,* Wiv. I, 1, 164. III, 5, 141. Merch II, 9, 23. III, 1, 112. John IV, 3, 120. R2 IV, 294. V, 5, 42. H4B I, 1, 48 etc. Or of indignation: *ha! not she!* Meas. II, 2, 164. *ha, fie!* II, 4, 42. *ha! little honour to be much believed,* 149. Ado IV, 1, 292. H8 I, 2, 186 etc. Sometimes joined with *hum:* Wiv. III, 5, 141. Wint. II, 1, 71. 74. Per. V, 1, 84. Denoting triumph: *ha! if I were young again,* Wiv. I, 1, 40. *ha ha! then there's more sympathy,* II, 1, 8. *the power of Scotland and of York, to join with Mortimer, ha!* H4A I, 3, 281. *this will do Helen's heart good now, ha!* Troil. I, 2, 234. *ha! art thou there?* V, 6, 8 etc. Especially when preceded by *ah* (q. c.): Wiv. II, 2, 158. Tw. III, 4, 104. IV, 2, 138. R3 III, 7, 71. Rom. I, 5, 20. Hml. I, 5, 150. Ant. II, 5, 15 etc. *ha, ah, ha!* Ado III, 3, 90. Used in laughing, when reduplicated; *ha ha!* Wint. IV, 4, 606. Troil. IV, 2, 32. *ha ha ha!* Tp. II, 1, 36. III, 2, 90. H6A II, 3, 43. Troil. III, 1, 135. 136. Tit. III, 1, 265. Lr. I, 5, 13. Oth. IV, 1, 144 etc. *ha ha he!* Troil. III, 1, 133; cf. *interjections? why then, some be of laughing, as, ah, ha, he,* Ado IV, 1, 23. Serving simply to attract attention: *sola, sola! wo ha, ho!* Merch. V, 39. *ha, ha! give me to drink mandragora,* Ant. I, 5, 3.

2) Used like the modern *eh* (yet unknown to Sh.) = what do you say? do you mean so? do you hear me? *do you put tricks upon us, ha?* Tp. II, 2, 61. *is he dead, my Francisco? ha, bully?* Wiv. II, 3, 28. *am I a woodman, ha?* V, 5, 31. *what reply? ha?* Meas. III, 2, 51. *the prince's fool, ha?* Ado II, 1, 212. II, 3, 79. LLL III, 54. Merch. II, 5, 44. As III, 5, 83. Shr. I, 1, 105. I, 2, 141. Tw. IV, 2, 85. Wint. I, 2, 230. H4A I, 1, 75. R3 I, 3, 234. V, 3, 5. H8 I, 1, 115. II, 2, 64. 67. 73. V, 1, 66. Troil. III, 3, 67. 284. Hml. V, 1, 121. Cymb. II, 1, 13 etc.

Ha', abbreviated from *have,* see *Have.*

Haberdasher, a seller of small wares, a pedlar: H8 V, 4, 49.

Haber-de-pois, see *Avoirdupois.*

Habiliment, dress, clothes: Tit. V, 2, 1. Plur. —*s:* Gent. IV, 1, 13. Shr. IV, 3, 172. R2 I, 3, 28. Ant. III, 6, 17.

Habit, 1) exterior, appearance, carriage, deportment: *now he throws that shallow h. by wherein deep policy did him disguise,* Lucr. 1814. *love's best h. is in seeming trust,* Sonn. 138, 11. *here she comes in the h. of a light wench,* Err. IV, 3, 52. *every lovely organ of her life shall come apparelled in more precious h.* Ado IV, 1, 229. *put on a sober h.* Merch. II, 2, 199. *I will speak to him like a saucy lackey and under that h. play the knave with him,* As III, 2, 314. *you seem a sober ancient gentleman by your h.* Shr. V, 1, 76. *in the h. of some sir of note,* Tw. III, 4, 81. *it is her h. only that is honest,* Tim. IV, 3, 113. *put this sour-cold h. on,* 239. *my father, in his h. as he lived,* Hml. III, 4, 135. *these thin —s and poor likelihoods of modern seeming,* Oth. I, 3, 108 (appearance, outward show). *scan the outward h. by the inward man,* Per. II, 2, 57. H8 I, 2, 122. Hml. III, 4, 162. V, 2, 198.

2) peculiar manner, custom: *how use doth breed a h. in a man,* Gent. V, 4, 1. *a better bad h. of frowning,* Merch. I, 2, 63. *some h. that too much o'erleavens the form of plausive manners,* Hml. I, 4, 29.

3) dress, garb: Lucr. Arg. 19. Gent. II, 7, 39. V, 4, 104. Wiv. IV, 6, 36. Meas. I, 3, 46. II, 4, 13. III, 1, 181. V, 389. LLL V, 2, 368. 401. Merch. III, 4, 60. Shr. III, 2, 102. IV, 3, 176. Tw. V, 223. John I, 210. H5 III, 6, 121. Tim. IV, 3, 205. Hml. I, 3, 70. Lr. V, 3, 188. Cymb. V, 3, 86. Plur. —*s:* LLL V, 2, 542. 773. Wint. III, 1, 4. H4A I, 2, 196. H8 III, 1, 117. Plur. for sing.: *drives me to these —s of her liking,* Tw. II, 5, 183. *when in other —s you are seen,* V, 396. *more valour in me than my —s show,* Cymb. V, 1, 30 (but in all the three passages it may be exterior, outward show in general).

Habitation, place of abode, dwelling: Sonn. 95, 10. Meas. III, 1, 10. Mids. V, 17. Merch. I, 3, 34. H4B I, 3, 89.

Habited, (cf. *Dishabited*) dressed, arrayed: Wint. IV, 4, 557. Tit. II, 3, 57.

Habitude, quality, form (habitudo corporis): *his real h. gave life and grace to appertainings and to ornament*, Compl. 114.

Hack, subst. a notch, a cut: *what —s are on his helmet*, Troil. I, 2, 222. 225.

Hack, vb. 1) to cut with frequent blows, to notch, to chop: Wiv. III, 1, 79. R2 I, 2, 20. H4A II, 4, 187. 288. 335. 336. H6A IV, 7, 47. R3 III, 3, 12. H8 I, 2, 97. Troil. I, 2, 253. V, 5, 34. Caes. II, 1, 163. V, 1, 40. Mcb. V, 3, 32. Ant. IV, 8, 31.

2) to do mischief? (Steevens); or to become vile and vulgar? (Johnson and Nares): *these knights will h.* Wiv. II, 1, 52. *he teaches him to hick and to h., which they'll do fast enough of themselves*, IV, 1, 68.

Hacket, name in Shr. Ind. 2, 23. 91.

Hackney, a horse much used, and hence a prostitute: *the hobby-horse is but a colt, and your love perhaps a h.* LLL III, 33.*

Hackneyed, made trite and vulgar by too much use: *so common h. in the eyes of men*, H4A III, 2, 40 (M. Edd. *common-hackneyed*).

Hag, an ugly and wicked woman: Tp. I, 2, 269. Wiv. IV, 2, 187. Wint. II, 3, 108. H6A III, 2, 52. V, 3, 42. H6B IV, 1, 79. R3 I, 3, 215. Rom. I, 4, 92. Mcb. IV, 1, 48. 115. Lr. II, 4, 281.

Hagar, the concubine of Abraham and mother of Ishmael: Merch. II, 5, 44.

Hag-born, born of a hag: Tp. I, 2, 283.

Haggard, a wild, untrained hawk: Ado III, 1, 36. Shr. IV, I, 196. IV, 2, 39. Tw. III, 1, 71. Adjectively: *if I do prove her h.* Oth. III, 3, 260 (wild, untractable, unprincipled).

Haggish, like a hag, ugly and wrinkled: *on us both did h. age steal on*, All's I, 2, 29.

Haggle, to cut, to notch, to mangle: *York, all —d over*, H5 IV, 6, 11.

Hag-seed, offspring of a hag: Tp. I, 2, 365.

Hai, see *Hay.*

Hail, subst. raindrops congealed in falling: Mids. I, 1, 244. All's V, 3, 33. Ant. III, 13, 159. Metaphorically used of any thing poured out fast and copiously, especially of language: *not a heart could scape the h. of his all-hurting aim*, Compl. 310. *as thick as h. came post with post*, Mcb. I, 3, 97 (O. Edd. *tale*). cf. Mids. I, 1, 244.

Hail, subst. a term of salutation, implying the wish of good fortune and happiness: Tp. I, 2, 189. IV, 1, 76. Meas. I, 4, 16. Mids. III, 1, 178—181. Wint. I, 2, 366. John III, 1, 136. V, 2, 68. R2 V, 5, 67. Troil. IV, 5, 65. Cor. I, 1, 167. II, 1, 192. IV, 6, 12. V, 6, 71. Tit. I, 70. Tim. V, 1, 58. Caes. III, 1, 3. V, 1, 32. Mcb. I, 2, 5. I, 5, 10. V, 8, 54. 59. Lr. IV, 6, 212. Ant. I, 5, 34. III, 6, 39. Cymb. III, 3, 7. 9. V, 5, 25. Per. V, 1, 14. 40. 83. V, 3, 1. 49. With *to*: Meas. II, 3, 1. Cor. IV, 6, 12. Tim. I, 2, 128. Mcb. I, 3, 48. 49. Hml. I, 2, 160. Lr. II, 4, 4. 129. Oth. II, 1, 85. *all h.*: Tp. I, 2, 189. LLL V, 2, 158. 339. R2 IV, 169. H6A II, 2, 34. H6C V, 7, 34. Tit. V, 3, 141. 146. Caes. II, 2, 58, Mcb. I, 3, 48—50. Per. V, 1, 39.

Hail, vb. to pour down like hail: Wiv. V, 5, 22. Mids. I, 1, 243. Ant. II, 5, 45.

Hail, vb. to salute with the cry 'hail': *they —ed him father to a line of kings*, Mcb. III, 1, 60.

Hailstone, a single ball of hail: Wiv. I, 3, 90. Cor. I, 1, 178.

Hair (rhyming to *despair:* Lucr. 981. Sonn. 99,

7. *to fair:* Compl. 204. *to bear:* Per. IV, 4, 28. *to ear:* Ven. 147 *to tear* (lacrima): Ven. 51. 191. Err. III, 2, 48. Dissyll. in Merch. III, 2, 304) 1) a single filament issuing from the skin: *there's not a h. on's head but 'tis a Valentine*, Gent. III, 1, 192. Ado II, 1, 277. LLL V, 2, 258. Shr. IV, 1, 96. All's V, 3, 77. H4A III, 3, 69. H4B I, 2, 182. Hml. I, 5, 19. Ant. I, 2, 200 etc. Used to denote a trifle: *not a h. perished*, Tp. I, 2, 217. *a rush, a h., a drop of blood, a pin*, Err. IV, 3, 73. Merch. III, 2, 304. IV, 1, 331. John IV, 1, 93. V, 7, 54. H4A III, 1, 140. III, 3, 66. H4B II, 4, 276. H8 III, 2, 259. Denoting exactness of estimation: *requital to a —'s breadth*, Wiv. IV, 2, 3. *'tis not a h. amiss yet*, H4B I, 2, 27 (quibbling). *you'll remember your brother's excuse? To a h.* Troil. III, 1, 157. *if I swerve a h. from truth*, III, 2, 191. Plur. *—s =* a) single filaments growing on the skin: *if —s be wires*, Sonn. 130, 4. *more faults than —s*, Gent. III, 1, 362. H5 III, 7, 14. Troil. I, 2, 122. Mcb. V, 8, 48. Lr. III, 7, 38. IV, 6, 99. Oth. V, 2, 75 etc. b) the whole covering of the skin: *her golden —s*, Ven. 51. 191. 306. Err. III, 2, 48. Ado V, 1, 65. LLL IV, 3, 142. Merch. I, 2, 9. III, 2, 120. John III, 4, 62. 68. 72. H4A II, 4, 514. H4B V, 5, 52. H6C II, 5, 40. Caes. II, 1, 144. Ant. II, 7, 123. Per. IV, 4, 28 *(cut his —s)* etc.

2) Collectively, the mass of filaments growing from the skin, the covering of the body: *with long dishevelled h.* Ven. 147. Lucr. 400. 981. Sonn. 99, 7. Compl. 29. 204. Tp. IV, 237. Gent. II, 7, 44 *(cut your h.).* IV, 4, 194. Wiv. I, 1, 49. Err. II, 2, 74. 77. 78. V, 173. Ado II, 3, 36. 153. LLL IV, 3, 259. Mids. I, 1, 33. I, 2, 100. IV, 1, 28. Merch. II, 2, 100. V, 158. As III, 4, 7. Wint. IV, 4, 333. John III, 4, 45 etc. *would you desire lime and h. to speak better?* Mids. V, 166. *thy stones with lime and h. knit up in thee*, 193. *boar with bristled h.* II, 2, 31; the same expression used of men struck with horror: *with h. up-staring*, Tp. I, 2, 213. *his h. upreared*, H6B III, 2, 171. *mine h. be fixed on end*, 318. R3 I, 3, 304. Caes. IV, 3, 280. Mcb. I, 3, 135. Hml. I, 5, 19. III, 4, 121. *she hath more h. than wit*, Gent. III, 1, 361; cf. Err. II, 2, 82. 84. Tw. I, 3, 101. *against the h.* = against the grain, contrary to the nature of a thing: *you go against the h. of your professions*, Wiv. II, 3, 41. *merry against the h.* Troil. I, 2, 28. *thou desirest me to stop in my tale against the h.* Rom. II, 4, 100 (very obscene quibbling). *the quality and h. of our attempt brooks no division*, H4A IV, 1, 61 (= peculiar nature).

Hair-brained, see *Hare-brained.*

Hair-breadth, narrow: *h. scapes*, Oth. I, 3, 136.

Hairless, destitute of hair: *his h. face*, Ven. 487. *h. scalps*, R2 III, 2, 112.

Hairy, 1) resembling hair: *with h. bristles armed*, Ven. 625.

2) overgrown with hair, having much hair: Err. II, 2, 87. Mids. IV, 1, 27. 56. As II, 1, 40. Wint. IV, 4, 744.

Hal, diminutive of *Harry* or *Henry*: H4A I, 2, 1. II, 2, 7 etc. H4B II, 4, 340. V, 5, 44 etc.

Halberd, a battle-axe fixed to a long pole: Err. V, 185. H6C IV, 3, 20. R3 I, 2, 40.

Halcyon, the bird Alcedo or king-fisher, said to breed during the calm weather about the winter solstice: *h. days* = calm days, H6A I, 2, 131. Its body, hung up so as to move freely, would always turn to the wind: *turn their h. beaks with every gale and vary of their masters*, Lr. II, 2, 84.

Hale, (cf. *Haul* and *Exhale*) to draw, to pull, to drag: *that sheeps' guts should h. souls out of men's bodies*, Ado II, 3, 62. *thus strangers may be —d and abused*, Shr. V, 1, 111 (pulled along, justled about against their will). *oxen and wainropes cannot h. them together*, Tw. III, 2, 64. Wint. III, 2, 102. H6A I, 1, 149. II, 5, 3. V, 4, 64. H6B IV, 1, 131. IV, 8, 59. Troil. IV, 5, 6. Cor. V, 4, 40. Tit. V, 2, 51. V, 3, 143. Oth. IV, 1, 144 (Ff *shakes*). Per. IV, 1, 55. In H4B V, 5, 37 (Pistol's speech) O. Edd. *halde* and *hall'd*, M. Edd. rightly *hauled*.

Half, (vulgarly pronounced *hauf*, according to Holophernes, LLL V, 1, 25. Plur. *halves*, Shr. V, 2, 79), subst. one of two equal parts; with the ind. art.: *lacks a h. to pay your debts*, Tim. II, 2, 153. With the def. art.: *I must have the h. of any thing*, Merch. III, 2, 252. *for the h. of my dowry*, Tw. III, 4, 70. *not a horse is h. the h. of himself*, H4A IV, 3, 24. Without art.: *they that lose h.* Lucr. 1158. Wiv. II, 2, 179. LLL V, 2, 246. R2 V, 1, 60 etc. *were h. to h. the world by the ears*, Cor. I, 1, 237. *when h. to h. the world opposed*, Ant. III, 13, 9. *h. of the which*, All's IV, 3, 190. *h. of the number*, Tit. I, 80. With a pers. pron.: *thy h. of the kingdom hast thou not forgot*, Lr. II, 4, 183. *I'll be your h.* (i. e. share your risk and profit in betting) Shr. V, 2, 78 (cf. *Half-part*). *unfold to me, your self, your h.* Caes. II, 1, 274, i. e. your wife; cf. *I'll not be your h.* LLL V, 2, 249; and the adj. in Ado II, 3, 177. Preceded by *better* and *best*: *the better h. of our possession*, H5 I, 1, 8. *the best h. should have returned to him*, Tim. III, 2, 91. *we have lost best h. of our affair*, Mcb. III, 3, 21. By one, with and without the article; not differing in sense from the simple word: *being but the one h. of an entire sum*, LLL II, 131. *the one h. of my lands*, Shr. II, 122. *thou hast the one h. of my heart*, Wint. I, 2, 348. *take the one h. of my commission*, Cor. IV, 5, 144. *my brother wears thee not the one h. so well as when thou grewest thyself*, Cymb. IV, 2, 202. *one h. of me*, Merch. III, 2, 16. IV, 1, 381. H6A I, 1, 81. Cor. IV, 5, 211. *with one h. so good a grace*, Meas. II, 2, 62. *one h. so bright*, LLL IV, 3, 30. *seize one h. his goods*, Merch. IV, 1, 353 (Q1.3.4 on). *this youth I snatched one h. out of the jaws of death*, Tw. III, 4, 394. *the other h.*: Merch. III, 2, 16. IV, 1, 353. Hml. III, 4, 158. *another h.*: H5 I, 2, 113.

Half, adj., making one of two equal parts, equal to a moiety; preceded by the def. art.: *he is the h. part of a blessed man*, John II, 437. *the h. shirt*, H4A IV, 2, 47. By a demonstr. pronoun: *this h. hour*, Tp. III, 2, 122. Tw. II, 5, 21. H6B II, 1, 64. Preceded by the ind. art. only when placed after the subst.: *seven year and a h.* Meas. II, 1, 274. All's IV, 5, 103. Wint. IV, 4, 348. H4A IV, 2, 46. H4B III, 2, 53 etc. The ind. art. placed between half and the subst.: *h. an hour*, Tp. III, 1, 91. Err. II, 2, 14. IV, 1, 65. LLL V, 2, 90. John V, 7, 83. H8 IV, 1, 66. *h. a dozen*, Ado V, 1, 97. H4A II, 4, 93. *h. a mile*, LLL V, 2, 54. R3 V, 3, 37. *h. a million*, Merch. III, 1, 57. *h. a kiss*, Wint. IV, 4, 175. *to h. a soul and to a notion crazed*, Mcb. III, 1, 83 etc. Plur. *h. tales*, Ant II, 2, 137. The def. article placed between *h.* and the subst.: *make a dark night too of h. the day*, LLL I, 1, 45. *no metal can bear h. the keenness*, Merch. IV, 1, 125. *h. the h.* H4A

IV, 3, 24. *h. the Gallian territories*, H6A V, 4, 129. *with h. the zeal*, H8 III, 2, 456. *h. the heart of Caesar, worthy Maecenas*, Ant. II, 2, 175. With a pers. pron.: *not h. your parts*, Sonn. 17, 4. *h. thy outward graces*, Ado IV, 1, 102. *h. my self*, II, 3, 177. Mids. III, 1, 37. Merch. III, 2, 251. V, 200. Tw. III, 4, 381. John V, 6, 39. H4B I, 1, 73. H5 I, 2, 112. H6C V, 4, 5. R3 IV, 4, 111. Tit. II, 4, 21 etc. With a genitive: *h. Signior Benedick's tongue*, Ado II, 1, 12. *h. all Cominius' honours*, Cor. I, 1, 277. *h. all men's hearts*, Cymb. I, 6, 168. With a demonstr. pron.: *h. that glory*, Sonn. 132, 8. *h. that wish*, Mids. II, 2, 65. *h. that face*, John I, 93. Preceded by *one*: *for this one h. year*, H4A IV, 1, 136 (M. Edd. *half-year*). *the one h. world*, Mcb. II, 1, 49. Before names: *h. Windsor*, Wiv. III, 3, 121. *h. Hector*, Troil. IV, 5, 85. Without art. before appellatives: *it is not h. way to her heart*, Shr. I, 1, 62. *h. way down hangs one*, Lr. IV, 6, 14. *we are h. way there*, Per. I, 4, 77. *h. heart, h. hand, h. Hector comes*, Troil. IV, 5, 85. *carry but h. sense*, Hml. IV, 5, 7. *within this mile and h.* Cor. I, 4, 8. *fathom and h.* Lr. III, 4, 37.

Half, adv., in an equal part, in part, not entirely: *ere summer h. be done*, Ven. 802. *thou canst not disgrace me h. so ill*, Sonn. 89, 5. *h. a fish and h. a monster*, Tp. III, 2, 32. *I am h. afraid he will have need of washing*, Wiv. III, 3, 193. III, 5, 121. LLL V, 2, 227. Mids. IV, 1, 152. Merch. II, 9, 96. As III, 2, 127. Shr. I, 2, 209. John II, 451. V, 2, 95. H6A I, 5, 30. III, 2, 55. H6B I, 3, 78. I, 4, 50. H6C I, 1, 220. IV, 1, 10. IV, 6, 63. Troil. IV, 5, 84. 93. Oth. I, 3, 176 etc.

Half-achieved, conquered only in part: H5 III, 3, 8.

Half-blooded, partly of noble, and partly of mean birth: Lr. V, 3, 80.

Half-blown, having its blossom expanded in part: *the h. rose*, John III, 1, 54.

Half-can, name in Meas. IV, 3, 19.

Half-caps, caps half taken off, slight salutations: Tim. II, 2, 221.

Half-checked: *a h. bit*, Shr. III, 2, 57 (O. Edd. *halfe-chekt*), perhaps a bit, which had only one of two necessary parts (cf. *Gimmal-bit* and the modern *Check-strap*).*

Half-cheek, a face in profile (cf. *Half-faced*): *Saint George's h. in a brooch*, LLL V, 2, 620.

Half-conquered, (O.Edd. not hyphened), gained, subdued in part: John V, 2, 95.

Half-face, a miserable look, an unpromising countenance: *he hath a f. like my father*, John I, 92.

Half-faced, 1) showing but half of the face: *a h. groat*, John I, 94 (having the king's face in profile; with a play upon the word). *our h. sun*, H6B IV, 1, 98 (half hidden by the clouds).

2) wretched-looking: *out upon this h. fellowship*, H4A I, 3, 208. *this same h. fellow Shadow*, H4B III, 2, 283. Quibbling in John I, 94.

Half-hour, (O. Edd. not hyphened) half of an hour: *within this h.* Tp. III, 2, 122. Tw. II, 5, 21. H6B II, 1, 64. *some h. past*, Lr. V, 3, 193. Cymb. I, 1, 176.

Half-kirtle, a jacket, or a petticoat attached to it (a full kirtle consisting of both together): *I'll forswear —s*, H4B V, 4, 24.

Half-moon, the moon at the quarters, and any

thing of the same shape: Wint. II, 1, 11. H4A III, 1, 100. Name of a chamber: H4A II, 4, 30.

Half-part, 1) a moiety: John II, 437 (O. Edd. not hyphened).

2) going halves with one: Per. IV, 1, 95.

Halfpenny, a coin of the value of half a penny: LLL III, 149. V, 2, 563. Hml. II, 2, 282. Plur. *halfpence:* As III, 2, 372. H5 III, 2, 47. Denoting any thing very small: *a h. purse,* Wiv. III, 5, 149. *thou h. purse of wit,* LLL V, 1, 77. *she tore the letter into a thousand halfpence,* Ado II, 3, 147. Adjectively, = of the value of half a penny: *h. loaves,* H6B IV, 2, 71.

Halfpenny-worth, a quantity of the value of half a penny: *one h. of bread,* H4A II, 4, 591.

Half-pint, the fourth part of a quart: Cor. V, 2, 60.

Half-supped, half satiated, half satisfied: *my h. sword,* Troil. V, 8, 19.

Half-sword, preceded by *at,* within half the length of a sword, in close fight: *if I were not at h. with a dozen,* H4A II, 4, 182.

Half-tale, (O. Edd. not hyphened), almost a fable: *—s be truths,* Ant. II, 2, 137.

Half-way, at or to half the distance, in the middle, on the way: *it is not h. to her heart,* Shr. I, 1, 62. *h. down hangs one that gathers samphire,* Lr. IV, 6, 14. *we are h. there,* Per. I, 4, 77.

Half-worker, one that performs half of a work: Cymb. II, 5, 2.

Half-world, (O. Edd. not hyphened) a moiety of the world: Mcb. II, 1, 49.

Half-yard, half part of a yard: Shr. IV, 3, 109.

Half-year, (O. Edd. not hyphened), a time of six months: H4A IV, 1, 136.

Halidom (cf. *Holidame*) sanctity, salvation; used in swearing: *by my h., I was fast asleep,* Gent. IV, 2, 136 (or corrupted from holy dame?).

Hall, 1) the largest room of a house: LLL V, 2, 924. Merch. V, 89. H4B V, 3, 37. Mcb. II, 3, 140. Hml. V, 2, 180. 205. *a h., a h.!* a cry to make room in a crowd: *a h., a h.! give room! and foot it, girls,* Rom. I, 5, 28.

2) the public room of a corporation: R3 III, 7, 35. H8 II, 1, 2.

3) a manor-house; the seat of a person of authority: *Kate of Kate H.* Shr. II, 189. *Priam's h.* Troil. III, 1, 161. *in skittish Fortune's h.* III, 3, 134. *of pander's h.* V, 10, 48.

Hallo, or **Halloo** (M. Edd.) or **Hallow** (O. Edd.) to cry out, to call or shout to with a loud voice: Gent. V, 4, 13. Wint. III, 3, 78. H4B I, 2, 213. Trans.: *—ing your name to the reverberate hills,* Tw. I, 5, 291.

Halloo (Ff. *alow,* Qq. *a lo*), interj. a cry used to invite attention: Lr. III, 4, 79.

Hallow, to make holy, to consecrate: Sonn. 108, 8. Compl. 228. Wiv. IV, 2, 216. Mids. V, 395. Wint. IV, 4, 613. H5 I, 2, 293. H6B I, 4, 25. IV, 10, 72. H8 II, 3, 68. Hml. I, 1, 164. Oth. III, 4, 73. Per. III, 1, 60.

Hallowmas, the feast-day of All Saints (1st of Nov.): Meas. II, 1, 128. R2 V, 1, 80. *to speak puling, like a beggar at H.* Gent. II, 1, 27 ("On All Saints' day poor people went from parish to parish, begging, in a certain lamentable tone, for a kind of cakes." Nares).

Halt, adj. lame and limping: *a cripple soon can find a h.* Pilgr. 308. In Lucr. 902 probably verb.

Halt, vb. to limp, to be lame: Lucr. 902. Sonn. 89, 3. Ado I, 1, 66. Shr. II, 258. III, 2, 91. Tw. V, 196. H4B I, 2, 275. II, 4, 54. R3 I, 1, 23. I, 2, 251. Tim IV, 1, 24. Ant. IV, 7, 16. Metaphorically, 1) to fail, to come short, to blunder: *she will outstrip all praise and make it h. behind her,* Tp. IV, 11. *a —ing sonnet,* Ado V, 4, 87. *my free drift —s not particularly, but moves itself in a wide sea of wax,* Tim. I, 1, 46 (my poetry makes no paltry and blundering comments on particularities). *the blank verse shall h. for it,* Hml. II, 2, 339. *their designment —s,* Oth. II, 1, 22. 2) to waver and shuffle, to backslide: *not trusting to this —ing legate,* John V, 2, 174. *no further —ing: satisfy me home,* Cymb. III, 5, 92.

Halter, a rope to hang malefactors: Merch. II, 2, 113. IV, 1, 379. H4A II, 4, 357. 548. H6B IV, 9, 11. Tit. V, 1, 47. Lr. I, 4, 343. III, 4, 55. Oth. IV, 2, 136.

Haltered, being in a halter: *a h. neck,* Ant. III, 13, 130.

Ham, see *Hams.*

Hames or **Ham's Castle,** a place in Picardy: H6C V, 5, 2. [="Ham" Gollancz].

Hamlet, name in Hml. I, 1, 84. 170 etc.

Hammer, subst. the instrument with which metals are beaten: John IV, 2, 193. H4B III, 2, 281. H5 IV Chor. 13. H6B II, 3, 76. Hml. II, 2, 511. Ant. V, 2, 210.

Hammer, vb. 1) to beat with a hammer, to forge; *—ed steel and iron the symbol of hardness and durability:* Lucr. 951. Sonn. 120, 4. John IV, 1, 67.

2) to work in the mind, to ponder, to forge; a) tr.: *—ing treachery,* H6B I, 2, 47. With *out: I'll h. it out,* R2 V, 5, 5. b) intr.: *whereon I have been —ing,* Gent. I, 3, 18. *—ed of this design,* Wint. II, 2, 49. *blood and revenge are —ing in my head,* Tit. II, 3, 39.

Hamper, to entangle, to ensnare, to fetter: H6B I, 3, 148.

Hampton, place in England: H5 II, 2, 91. III Chor. 4 (O. Edd. *Dover*). [="Southampton". Herford].

Hams, the knee-joints: *to bow in the h.* Rom. II, 4, 57. *weak h.* Hml II, 2, 203. *cowers i' the h.* Per. IV, 2, 114.

Hamstring, the tendon of the knee-joint: Troil. I, 3, 154.

Hand, subst. 1) the extremity of the arm, with which we seize and hold things: Ven. 143. 158. 223. 351. 352. 353. 373. 421 etc. etc. *h. in h.* = a) joining hands: *lock h. in h.* Wiv. V, 5, 81. Mids. V, 406. Mcb. I, 3, 32. Ant. IV, 14, 51. b) conjointly, together, or in union and concord: *let's go h. in h.* Err. V, 425. *the prince and Claudio, h. in h., in sad conference,* Ado I, 3, 62. *h. in h. to hell,* R3 V, 3, 313. *that hast so long walked h. in h. with time,* Troil. IV, 5, 203. *will, h. in h., all headlong cast us down,* Tit. V, 3, 132. *it* (his love) *went h. in h. even with the vow,* Hml. I, 5, 49. *foot and h.* = alertly: *came in foot and h.,* H4A II, 4, 241. *h. to h.* = in single fight: *in single opposition, h. to h.* H4A I, 3, 99. *h. to h. he would have vanquished thee,* H6C III, 1, 73. *whom h. to h. I slew in fight,* II, 5, 56. *at h.* = a) very near (in time as well as place): Wiv. III, 3, 135. Err. II, 1, 44. LLL V, 2, 308. Mids. III, 2, 111. V, 116. Merch. II, 9, 94. V, 52. 122. Shr. IV, 1, 120. John II, 77. V, 2, 169

R2 III, 2, 1. H4A II, 1, 53. H6A I, 2, 50. V, 4, 100. H6B III, 2, 10. H6C II, 2, 72. V, 1, 11. V, 4, 60. R3 III, 7, 45. IV, 4, 73. Tit. V, 3, 16. Rom. V, 1, 2. Oth. II, 1, 268. Cymb. III, 4, 2 etc. b) treated with the naked hand, without the use of violence: *like a lion fostered up at h.* John V, 2, 75 (not in a cage). *like horses hot at h.* Caes. IV, 2, 23 (i. e. fiery as long as they are led by the hand, not mounted and managed with the rein and spur; cf. H8 V, 3, 22). *out of h.* = a) off one's hands, done, ended: *were these inward wars once out of h.* H4B III, 1, 107. b) directly, at once: *gather we our forces out of h. and set upon our boasting enemy,* H6A III, 2, 102. *we will proclaim you out of h.* H6C IV, 7, 63. *I'll find some cunning practice out of h.* Tit. V, 2, 77. *a tall man of his —s* = an active, able-bodied man, who will stand the test: Wiv. I, 4, 27. *thou art a tall fellow of thy hands,* Wint. V, 2, 178. 179. 181. *I am a proper fellow of my —s,* H4B II, 2, 72 (cf. in the Nibelunge Not: *Hagne, der Sifriden sluoc, den helt ze sinen handen;* and: *er was ein helt zen handen;* str. 1846 and 2038). *in the h. of* = led or held by: *in this right h. ... stands young Plantagenet,* John II, 236. *led in the h. of her aunt,* R3 IV, 1, 2. *those that tame wild horses pace 'em not in their —s to make 'em gentle, but stop their mouths with stubborn bits,* H8 V, 3, 22 (cf. Caes. IV, 2, 23). *and in her h. the grandchild to her blood,* Cor. V, 3, 23. Tit. V, 3, 138. *in h.* = about to do or to be done, in the state of execution: *in h. with all things, naught at all effecting,* Ven. 912. *the other takes in h. no cause but company of her drops' spilling,* Lucr. 1235 (i. e. assumes as her office or incumbent duty). *we have sport in h.* Wiv. II, 1, 205. *strange things in h.* V, 1, 32. Ado I, 1, 301. Mids. V, 36. Merch. III, 4, 57. As III, 3, 77. Shr. Ind. 1, 91. V, 2, 91. All's III, 2, 56. Tw. I, 3, 69 (*do you think you have fools in h.?* = you have to do with fools). Wint. III, 3, 5. John IV, 3, 158 (*a thousand businesses are brief in h.* = quickly to be dispatched). R2 I, 4, 47. V, 3, 130. H5 I, 1, 77. H6B I, 3, 162. I, 4, 23. III, 1, 318. R3 III, 2, 116. Troil. II, 2, 164. III, 1, 89. Cor. I, 1, 56. Tit. II, 1, 112. Mcb. III, 4, 139. Lr. III, 5, 17 etc. *to bear in h.* (properly = to be always going to do and never performing) = to illude with false hopes and pretences: Meas. I, 4, 52. Ado IV, 1, 306. Shr. IV, 2, 3. H4B I, 2, 42. Mcb. III, 1, 81. Hml. II, 2, 67. Cymb. V, 5, 43. *at a person's h.* or *—s* = from: *at your h. the account of hours to crave,* Sonn. 58, 3. *receive such welcome at my h.* LLL II, 169. All's III, 5, 52. Tw. III, 2, 26. IV, 2, 87. H6C I, 4, 166. III, 3, 149. R3 I, 2, 208. Rom. III, 5, 5. Caes. II, 1, 58. *have you received no promise of satisfaction at her —s?* Wiv. II, 2, 218. Err. IV, 4, 32. Ado V, 2, 2. Mids. II, 2, 124. Shr. V, 2, 152. R2 I, 3, 158. IV, 161. H6A I, 4, 86. H6B IV, 7, 74. H6C II, 5, 67. II, 6, 26. IV, 1, 80. IV, 5, 5. V, 1, 23. 93. R3 I, 1, 120. III, 1, 197 (Ff *h.*). III, 5, 50. IV, 4, 346. Tit. I, 307. Rom. III, 5, 126 etc. *your h. is out* = you miss your aim, LLL IV, 1, 135. *give me your —s* = clap hands, applaud: Mids. V, 444; cf. *release me from my bands with the help of your good —s,* Tp. Epil. 10; *your gentle —s lend us,* All's V, 3, 340. *to have by the h.* = to hold: Tw. I, 3, 70; metaphorically: *we should not step too far till we had his assistance by the h.* H4B I, 3, 21. *to hold h. with* = to equal: *she holds h. with any princess of the world,* John II, 494. *to hold one's —s* = to abstain

from beating or striking: *hold your —s,* Err. I, 2, 93. IV, 4, 24. All's IV, 3, 215. Oth. II, 3, 154. cf. *fate held his h.* Wiv. III, 5, 107 (= kept him back). *to have a h. in* = to be concerned, to take part in: Ado V, 1, 276. R2 V, 2, 37. Caes. III, 1, 248. III, 2, 46. *to kiss one's* (own) *h.* (to show homage): LLL IV, 1, 148. V, 2, 324. As III, 2, 50. Shr. IV, 1, 97. All's II, 2, 11. Tw. III, 4, 36 etc. *to lay —s on* = to seize: Ado III, 3, 58. As I, 1, 58. Shr. V, 1, 39. H6B I, 4, 44. H6C III, 1, 26. R3 I, 4, 196. Tit. V, 2, 159. *some violent —s were laid on Humphrey's life,* H6B III, 2, 138. 156. *lay h. upon him,* Lr. IV, 6, 192 (Qq *—s*). *lay h. on heart, advise,* Rom. III, 5, 192 (= consider). *lend me thy h.* = assist me: Tp. I, 2, 23. H4A II, 4, 2. Tit. III, 1, 188. Caes. III, 1, 297. *to lie upon a person's h.* = not to find a purchaser: Ant. II, 5, 105. *to rear one's h.* = to fall to work, to strike: Tp. II, 1, 295. Caes. III, 1, 30. *to rid one's —s of* = to get rid of: Shr. I, 1, 186. *to shake —s* = to join *—s* (q.v.) in meeting or parting: Wint. I, 1, 33. Mcb. I, 2, 21. Ant. IV, 12, 20; hence = to become friends: *each, though enemies to either's reign, do in consent shake —s to torture me,* Sonn. 28, 6. As V, 4, 107. H6C I, 4, 102. *to take by the h.:* Ven. 361. Wiv. IV, 6, 37. V, 3, 3. Meas. IV, 1, 55 etc. *to take —s* = to join *—s,* to take each other by the palm: Tp. I, 2, 377. LLL V, 2, 219. 220. Mids. IV, 1, 90. Ant. II, 7, 112 etc.; forming part of the marriage-ceremony: *until they come to take —s,* Ado IV, 1, 306. *here's eight that must take —s,* As V, 4, 134. Wint. IV, 4, 394. *till you take her h. before this friar,* Ado V, 4, 56. Wint. IV, 4, 373; cf. *join —s* and *close —s,* John II, 532. 533. Hence *h.* = marriage: *more convenient is he for my h.* Lr. IV, 5, 31. *to wring one's —s,* see *Wring. a dry h.:* Ado II, 1, 124. Tw. I, 3, 77. H4B I, 2, 204 (cf. *Dry*). As the hand was given as a pledge of faith and friendship (f. i. Tp. III, 2, 119. Gent. II, 2, 8. V, 4, 116. Wiv. II, 1, 225. Troil. IV, 5, 270. Hml. II, 2, 388) it was usual to swear by it; *by this h.:* Tp. III, 2, 56. 78. IV, 1, 226. Meas. II, 1, 172. Ado IV, 1, 327. 337. Merch. V, 161. As IV, 1, 111. Tw. I, 3, 36. II, 3, 133. IV, 2, 117. John II, 343. H4A I, 3, 216. H4B II, 2, 48. H5 II, 1, 32. Hml. V, 2, 269. Oth. II, 1, 263. IV, 1, 139. 185 etc. *by my h.:* H6B V, 3, 29 (the spurious Qq and some M. Edd. *by my faith*). Cor. IV, 5, 155. *by her fair immortal h. she swears,* Ven. 80. *by Venus' h. I swear,* Troil. IV, 1, 22. *by the white h. of Rosalind,* As III, 2, 414; cf. H5 III, 7, 101. *by the h. of a soldier,* All's III, 6, 76. *by the buried h. of warlike Gaunt,* R2 III, 3, 109. Similarly *for my h.: master, for my h., both our inventions meet and jump in one,* Shr. I, 1, 194 (perhaps *'fore,* q.v.). — The h. the emblem of power, agency, action: *who once again I tender to thy h.* Tp. IV, 1, 5; cf. Wiv. I, 4, 154. II, 2, 255. Meas. V, 491. Ado III, 1, 112. Mids. II, 1, 216. Shr. V, 2, 177. H6B I, 1, 13. *'tis a great charge to come under one body's h.* Wiv. I, 4, 105. *the h. that hath made you fair hath made you good,* Meas. III, 1, 184. *nature's own cunning h.* Tw. I, 5, 258. *it is your brother's right h.* Ado I, 3, 51; cf. Gent. V, 4, 67. *time's deformed h.* Err. V, 298. *charity chased hence by rancour's h.* H6B III, 1, 144. *to die upon the h. I love so well,* Mids. II, 1, 244. *weigh thy value with an even h.* Merch. II, 7, 25. *in which you shall have foremost h.* H4B V, 2, 140. *by strong h.* (= by violence). Err. III, 1, 98. Hml. I, 1, 102. *you* *bear too stubborn and too strange a h. over your friend,* Caes. I, 2, 35. *strange things I have in head that will to h.* Mcb. III, 4, 139 (= that will be performed). *what thou wouldst do is done unto thy h.* Ant. IV, 14, 29 (ready to be received by thee). *a city on whom plenty held full h.* Per. I, 4, 22 etc. Hence = work, business: *you have made a fine h.* H8 V, 4, 74. *you have made fair —s,* Cor. IV, 6, 117.

2) form of writing, handwriting: Gent. I, 3, 46. Wiv. II, 1, 85. Err. III, 1, 12. Merch. II, 4, 12. As IV, 3, 29. Tw. II, 3, 175. II, 5, 95. III, 2, 45. III, 4, 31. V, 340. R3 III, 6, 2. Caes. I. 2, 320. Hml. IV, 7, 52.

3) signature, sign manual: *here is the h. and seal of the duke,* Meas. IV, 2, 207. *five justices' —s at it,* Wint. IV, 4, 288. *set down their —s, to kill the king,* R2 V, 2, 98. *proceeded under your —s and seals,* H8 II, 4, 222. Quibbling: LLL I, 1, 20.

4) the index of a clock or dial: All's I, 2, 41. Rom. II, 4, 119.

5) side, part: *leaving the fear of God on the left h.* Wiv. II, 2, 24. *walk by us on our other h.* Meas. V, 17. *turn up on your right h.* Merch. II, 2, 42. *turn of no h.* 45. *that covenants may be kept on either h.* Shr. II, 128. *go on the right h.* Wint. IV, 4, 856. *if promises be kept on every h.* H4A III, 2, 168. *let my woes frown on the upper h.* R3 IV, 4, 37. *come on my right h.* Caes. I, 2, 213. *upon the left h. of the even field,* V, 1, 17. *before, behind thee, and on every h.* Oth. II, 1, 86. *Of* omitted: *on either h. thee there are squadrons pitched,* H6A IV, 2, 23. *at any h., in any h.,* and *of all —s,* = at any rate, in any case: *see that at any h.* Shr. I, 2, 147. *not her that chides, at any h.* 227. *let him fetch off his drum in any h.* All's III, 6, 45. *therefore of all—s must we be forsworn,* LLL IV, 3, 219.

Obscure passage: *I would these —s might never part,* LLL V, 2, 57 (= never be disjoined by giving one to a husband?).

Hand, vb. 1) to lay hands on, to touch: *we will not h. a rope more,* Tp. I, 1, 25. *let him that makes but trifles of his eyes first h. me,* Wint. II, 3, 63.

2) to be hand in hand with, to devote one's self to: *when I was young and —ed love as you do,* Wint. IV, 4, 359.

Handed, having hands: *as poisonous-tongued as h.* Cymb. III, 2, 5.

Handfast, 1) any constraint, confinement, custody: *if that shepherd be not in h., let him fly,* Wint. IV, 4, 795.

2) contract, marriage-engagement: *to hold the h. to her lord,* Cymb. I, 5, 78.

Handful, as much as the hand can contain: Mids. IV, 1, 41. *h. of wit,* LLL IV, 1, 149.

Handicraft-man or **Handicrafts-man,** mechanic, artisan: Mids. IV, 2, 10. H6B IV, 2, 12.

Hand-in-hand, playing from one hand into the other, confounding two different things, handy-dandy, juggling: *as fair and as good, a kind of h. comparison,* Cymb. I, 4, 75.

Handiwork, work of the hand, manufacture: John I, 238. R3 IV, 4, 51. Caes. I, 1, 30.

Handkercher = handkerchief, q.v.: As IV, 3, 98. V, 2, 30. All's IV, 3, 322. John IV, 1, 42. H5 III, 2, 52. R3 IV, 4, 276 (Ff Q2.3.4. *handkerchief*). Cor. II, 1, 280. In Oth. Q. *handkercher,* Ff *handkerchief*).

Handkerchief, a piece of cloth used to clean the face or hands: Wint. V, 2, 71. R3 IV, 4, 276 (Q1 *handkercher*). Cymb. I, 3, 6. 11. In Oth. III, 3, 306. 434. IV, 4, 23 etc. Q *handkercher,* Ff *handkerchief.*

Handle, subst. that part of a thing by which it is held: Wiv. II, 2, 12. R2 III, 3, 80. Mcb. II, 1, 34.

Handle, vb. 1) to feel with the hand, to touch: *a wild bird being tamed with too much —ing,* Ven. 560. *if you —d her,* Meas. V, 276 (quibbling). As III, 2, 54. H4B IV, 1, 161 (*—ing* trisyll.). H5 V, 2, 337. Troil. I, 1, 55 (quibbling). Cor. III, 2, 80.

2) to manage, to wield: H5 V, 1, 81. H6A I, 3, 78. III, 4, 19. H6B V, 1, 7. Tit. II, 1, 42. Lr. IV, 6, 87.

3) to treat, to use: *you shall see how I'll h. her,* Meas. V, 273. *I know how to h. you,* H4B II, 4, 339. *how wert thou —d?* H6A I, 4, 24.

4) to treat or speak of, to discourse on: *points more than ail the lawyers in Bohemia can learnedly h.* Wint. IV, 4, 207. *a did in some sort h. women,* H5 II, 3, 39 (quibbling). *left nothing untouched or slightly —d,* R3 III, 7, 19. *h. not the theme,* Tit. III, 2, 29.

Handless, without hands: Troil. V, 5, 34. Tit. III, 1, 67.

Handmaid, female servant or attendant: Lucr. 787. Tw. I, 1, 25. H6A III, 3, 42. H8 II, 3, 72. Tit. I, 331. Cymb. III, 4, 159.

Handsaw, a small saw to be managed with one hand: H4A II, 4, 187. *when the wind is southerly I know a hawk from a h.* Hml. II, 2, 397 (according to Intpp. a corruption from *hernshaw,* i. e. heron; but Sh. undoubtedly thought of a real *saw*).

Handsome, well made, of a winning exterior and manners; used of male persons: Wiv. III, 4, 33. Ado II, 1, 58. All's III, 5, 83. R3 I, 3, 101. Rom. II, 5, 57. Oth. II, 1, 250. IV, 3, 36. Ant. I, 2, 75. Per. II, 1, 84. Of male attire: Ado IV, 2, 89. V, 4, 105 (= becoming, elegant, tasteful?). Of female dress: *prove that ever I dress myself h.* H4B II, 4, 303 (Doll's speech). Of horses: H8 II, 2, 4. Of the style in writing: *an honest method, as wholesome as sweet, and by very much more h. than fine,* Hml. II, 2, 466 (perhaps = becoming, fit, to the purpose).

Handsomely, 1) neatly, gracefully: Tp. V, 293. Wint. IV, 4, 777.

2) fitly, conveniently: *if we miss to meet him h.* Tit. II, 3, 268.

Handsomeness, beauty, grace, and at the same time becomingness, decency; quibbling: *I will beat thee into h. I shall sooner rail thee into wit,* Troil. II, 1, 16.

Handwriting, the form of writing peculiar to a person: Err. III, 1, 14.

Handy-dandy, a sleight of hand by which something imperceptibly is changed from one hand into the other: *change places, and h., which is the justice, which is the thief?* Lr. IV, 6, 157 (cf. *Hand-in-Hand*).

Hang, (impf. and partic. *—ed* in the sense to execute by the halter, else *hung.* In Mids. V, 366 Ff *hung,* Qq regularly *—ed. Hanged* for *hung:* Pilgr. 183. As III, 2, 182. Cymb. II, 4, 68). 1) tr. a) to suspend, to fasten to an object above: *over my altars hath he hung his lance,* Ven. 103. *like a jewel hung in ghastly night,* Sonn. 27, 11. *h. them on this line,* Tp. IV, 193. Wiv. IV, 2, 217. Meas. I, 2, 171. Ado I, 1, 243. Mids. II, 1, 15. As III, 2, 182. 379 etc. Metaphorically: *and h. more praise upon deceased I,* Sonn. 72, 7 (as on a tomb). With *out: h. out our* *banners*, Mcb. V, 5, 1. With *up*: *h. me up at the door of a brothel-house for the sign of blind Cupid*, Ado I, 1, 255. H4A II, 4, 479. H6A V, 4, 174. H6C I, 3, 28. R3 I, 1, 6. Tim. I, 2, 103.

b) to let fall, to bend down, to decline; *to h. the head*, in sign of grief: Ven. 666. 1058. Lucr. 521. 793. H6A III, 2, 124. H6B I, 2, 2. H8 III, 1, 11. 153. V, 5, 33. Tit. IV, 4, 70. Oth. IV, 3, 32. *to h. the lip* (in sheepishness and stupidity): H4A II, 4, 446. Troil. III, 1, 152. *hung their eyelids down*, H4A III, 2, 81. *the pine —s his sprays*, H6B II, 3, 45. *how would he h. his wings*, Tit. III, 2, 61.

c) to attach, to tie, to make adhere: *what passion —s these weights upon my tongue?* As I, 2, 269. *restoration h. thy medicine on my lips*, Lr. IV, 7, 26. *no hinge nor loop to h. a doubt on*, Oth. III, 3, 366.

d) to make hover and impend, and hence to make linger: *when Jove will o'er some high-viced city h. his poison in the sick air*, Tim. IV, 3, 109. *and —s resolved correction in the arm that was upreared to execution*, H4B IV, 1, 213. *thou hast hung thy advanced sword in the air*, Troil. IV, 5, 188.

e) to furnish or cover by any thing suspended: *hung with trophies*, Sonn. 31, 10. *a cabin —ed with care*, Pilgr. 183. *their heads are hung with ears that sweep away the morning dew*, Mids. IV, 1, 125. Shr. Ind. 1, 47. H6A I, 1, 1. Caes. I, 1, 74. Cymb. II, 4, 68.

f) to kill or execute by the halter: Tp. I, 1, 35. 61. III, 3, 59. Gent. II, 5, 5. IV, 4, 16. Wiv. V, 5, 191. Meas. III, 2, 124. 178. IV, 2, 42. IV, 3, 24. V, 510. Ado II, 3, 82. LLL V, 2, 610. 687. Mids. IV, 2, 23. V, 366. Merch. IV, 1, 134. 364. 367. Shr. III, 2, 228. Tw. I, 3, 13. III, 4, 136. John II, 505. H5 IV, 4, 77. H6B I, 3, 222. H6C IV, 5, 26. R3 I, 2, 84. V, 3, 331 etc. *confessed it, —ed it*, Tim. I, 2, 22. *to confess and be —ed*, Oth. IV, 1, 38. *you must h. it first, and draw it afterwards*, Ado III, 2, 24, with an obscene quibble; cf. *he that —s himself is a virgin*, All's I, 1, 150, and: *seek thou rather to be —ed in compassing thy joy than to be drowned*, Oth. I, 3, 367; perhaps also in Tw. I, 5, 20. With *up*: *h. him up*, Gent. IV, 4, 24. Err. II, 1, 67. LLL IV, 3, 54. H6B IV, 2, 190. Rom. III, 3, 57. Mcb. IV, 2, 58. Ant. V, 2, 62. Per. IV, 6, 146. *—ing*, substantively: Tp. I, 1, 33. Meas. II, 1, 250. IV, 2, 35. 42. V, 365. Merch. II, 9, 83. Tw. I, 5, 19. 20. Wint. IV, 4, 702. Cymb. I, 5, 20 etc. *be —ed*, used as a curse: *be —ed an hour*, Meas. V, 360. *Poins, Poins, and be —ed*, H4A II, 2, 4. *how got they in, and be —ed?* H8 V, 4, 17. *speak, and be —ed!* Tim. V, 1, 134. *h. me* = I'll be damned: LLL IV, 3, 9. H6B I, 3, 200. *h. thee!* Tw. II, 5, 114. Tim. IV, 3, 87. *h. him!* Wiv. II, 2, 281. 290. III, 3, 196. IV, 2, 104. Ado III, 2, 18. All's III, 5, 17. Tw. III, 4, 130. *h. her!* Wiv. IV, 2, 201. *h. it!* Ado III, 2, 23. *h. you!* All's III, 5, 94. H4A II, 2, 93. Cor. I, 1, 185. Per. IV, 6, 158. *h. 'em!* Wiv. II, 1, 179. Cor. I, 1, 194. *h. the trifle*, Wiv. II, 1, 46 etc. *h. up thy mistress*, Err. II, 1, 67. Rom. III, 3, 57. *I can as well be —ed*, Caes. I, 2, 235. H5 IV, 1, 235.

g) to cause to be executed by the halter: *you will h. them*, Meas. II, 1, 216. *that were enough to h. us all*, Mids. I, 2, 79. 80. *the usurer —s the cozener*, Lr. IV, 6, 167.

2) intr. a) to be suspended, to be supported by an object above: *his braided —ing mane*, Ven. 271. *where*

—s a piece of skilful painting, Lucr. 1366. Sonn. 24, 7. 73, 2. Pilgr. 135. Tp. III, 3, 45. V, 94. Gent. IV, 2, 122. Ado V, 1, 318. V, 3, 9. LLL V, 2, 922. Tw. I, 3, 108. Cor. I, 3, 12. Rom. V, 1, 42. Mcb. III, 5, 24. Hml. V, 1, 207 etc. *to h. quite out of fashion*, Troil. III, 3, 151; cf. Meas. I, 2, 171 and Cor. I, 3, 12. *thereby —s a tale:* Wiv. I, 4, 159. As II, 7, 28. Shr. IV, 1, 60. Oth. III, 1, 8. *a fearful — ing rock*, Gent. I, 2, 121. *to h. out*, Mids. IV, 2, 42; cf. R2 V, 2, 56. *my skin —s about me like a loose gown*, H4A III, 3, 3; cf. Mcb. V, 2, 21.

b) With *about* and *on*, = to cling to: *h. no more about me*, Wiv. II, 2, 17. *my conscience, —ing about the neck of my heart*, Merch. II, 2, 14. *she hung about my neck*, Shr. II, 310. Wint. V, 3, 112. *h. not on my garments*, Tp. I, 2, 474. Meas. II, 2, 44. *he will h. upon him like a disease*, Ado I, 1, 86. Mids. III, 2, 233. H4B II, 1, 74. II, 3, 44. Tim. II, 2, 56. Hml. I, 2, 143. With *by*: *—ing by his neck*, Ven. 593. With *off*: *h. off, thou cat, thou burr*, Mids. III, 2, 260 (= cease to hang on me, let go).

c) to hover, and hence to impend: *by the sky that —s above our heads*, John II, 397. *those musicians h. in the air*, H4A III, 1, 227. *night —s upon mine eyes*, Caes. V, 5, 41. *sleep shall neither night nor day h. upon his lid*, Mcb. I, 3, 20; cf. Per. V, 1, 236. *the clouds still h. on you*, Hml. I, 2, 66. *my cudgel shall h. like a meteor o'er the cuckold's horns*, Wiv. II, 2, 292. *devouring pestilence — s in our air*, R2 I, 3, 284. *reproach and dissolution —eth over him*, II, 1, 258. V, 3, 3. H6B II, 4, 50. Rom. I, 4, 107. Lr. III, 4, 70.

d) to dwell, to lie, to be attached: *on my eyelids shall conjecture h.* Ado IV, 1, 107. *it* (shame) *will h. upon my richest robes*, H6B II, 4, 108; cf. *contempt and beggary —s upon thy back*, Rom. V, 1, 71. *some dreadful story —ing on thy tongue*, H6C II, 1, 44. *never hung poison on a fouler toad*, R3 I, 2, 148; cf. *haply some poison yet doth h. on them* (his lips) Rom. V, 3, 165. *the blame may h. upon your hardness*, Cor. V, 3, 91. *his large fortune upon his good and gracious nature —ing*, Tim. I, 1, 56. *sundry blessings h. about his throne*, Mcb. IV, 3, 158. *that life may h. no longer on me*, Ant. IV, 9, 15.

e) to totter, to rock, to waver: *many likelihoods .... which hung so tottering in the balance*, All's I, 3, 129. *when you and those ... hung on our driving boat*, Tw. I, 2, 11. *h. no more in doubts*, John III, 1, 219. Quibbling: *which will h. upon my tongue like a new-married wife about her husband's neck*, H5 V, 2, 189; cf. H6C II, 1, 44.

f) With *together*, = 1) to hold together: *as idle as she may h. together*, Wiv. III, 2, 13 (cf. Wint. II, 2, 22). 2) to be in keeping: *mark how well the sequel —s together*, R3 III, 6, 4.

g) to rest on, to depend: *his own life hung upon the staff he threw*, H4B IV, 1, 126. *the welfare of us all —s on the cutting short that fraudful man*, H6B III, 1, 81. H8 III, 2, 367. Troil. II, 3, 217.

h) to be executed by the halter: *a good —ing prevents a bad marriage*, Tw. I, 5, 20. *if I h., I'll make a fat pair of gallows*, H4A II, 1, 74. *upon the next tree shalt thou h.* Mcb. V, 5, 39. Used as a curse: *let her go h.* Tp. II, 2, 56. *let them h.* Cor. III, 2, 23. *h., cur*, Tp. I, 1, 46. H6A III, 2, 68. Rom. III, 5, 194. *go h.* Tp. II, 2, 53. Ant. II, 7, 59.

Hanger (Qq) or **Hangers** (Ff), the part of a

sword-belt in which the weapon was suspended: Hml. V, 2, 157. 164. 167.

Hang-hog, i. e. bacon, Mrs. Quickly's interpretation of *hanc hoc:* Wiv. IV, 1, 50.

Hangings (cf. *Bed - hangings* and *Chamberhanging*) 1) tapestry: Shr. II, 351. H6B V, 3, 12.

2) fruit hanging on a tree: *a storm shook down my mellow h.* Cymb. III, 3, 63.

Hangman, a public executioner, one whose office it is to put to death in any manner: Meas. IV, 2, 18. 53. IV, 3, 28. Merch. IV, 1, 125. Wint. IV, 4, 468. 803. H4A I, 2, 76. 82. 1, 3, 166. II, 1, 70. 73. Cor. I, 5, 7. II, 1, 103. Tim. II, 2, 100. Mcb. II, 2, 28. Oth. I, 1, 34. Ant. III, 13, 130. Cymb. V, 4, 179. Per. IV, 6, 137. Cupid called so in jest as the executioner of human hearts: *the little h. dare not shoot at him,* Ado III, 2, 11. *the h. boys,* Gent. IV, 4, 60, probably the servants of the public executioner, not = the rascally boys, as Intpp. would have it.

Hannibal, the famous Carthaginian: LLL V, 2, 677. H6A I, 5, 21. Confounded with *Cannibal* by Elbow and Pistol: Meas. II, 1, 183. H4B II, 4, 180.

Hap, subst. fortune: *had not our h. been bad,* Err. I, 1, 39. *whom it was their h. to save,* 114. Shr. I, 2, 269. H6B III, 1, 314. H6C II, 3, 8. 9. Tit. V, 2, 101. Ant. II, 3, 32. *blessed h.* H6A I, 6, 10. *contented h.* R3 I, 3, 84. *my dear h.* Rom. II, 2, 190. *golden h.* Lucr. 42. *good h.* Gent. I, 1, 15. R2 I, 1, 23. Rom. III, 3, 171. *by good h.* LLL II, 210. Tim. III, 2, 27. *direful h.* R3 I, 2, 17. *ill h.* H8 Epil. 13. Plur. *—s:* *loving goes by —s,* Ado III, 1, 105. *our heavy —s,* Tit. V, 3, 202. *howe'er my —s,* Hml. IV, 3, 70.

Hap, vb. to happen, to chance, to come to pass: *if thou issueless shalt h. to die,* Sonn. 9, 3. *if it so h.* Tp. I, 1, 28. Shr. IV, 4, 108. Tw. I, 2, 60. H6A III, 1, 31. H6C III, 3, 88. Cor. III, 3, 24. Hml. I, 2, 249. Lr. III, 6, 121. Oth. V, 1, 127. Per. II Prol. 22.

Hapless, unhappy, unfortunate: Lucr. 1045. Gent. I, 1, 32. III, 1, 260. Err. I, 1, 141. H6A III, 1, 201. H6B I, 1, 226. H6C I, 4, 156. V, 6, 15.

Haply (often found in M. Edd., where O. Edd. have *happily,* q. v.) 1) fortunately: *in these thoughts myself almost despising, h. I think on thee,* Sonn. 29, 10. *if h. won, perhaps a hapless gain,* Gent. I, 1, 32. *h. I see a friend to save my life,* Err. V, 283. Shr. I, 1, 8. H6B V, 2, 79. H6C II, 5, 58.

2) perhaps: *lest I should do it wrong and h. of our old acquaintance tell,* Sonn. 89, 12. 101, 5. Gent. I, 1, 12. II, 4, 11. V, 60. Shr. Ind. 1, 136. V, 2, 171. All's III, 2, 80. III, 4, 35. IV, 1, 91. Tw. I, 2, 54. III, 3, 44. H4B I, 1, 32. H5 IV, 7, 181. H6B III, 1, 240. R3 II, 2, 137. III, 5, 60. III, 7, 144. IV, 4, 273 (Qq *happily*). Cor. V, 2, 16. Rom. V, 3, 165. Hml. III, 1, 179. III, 2, 186. Lr. I, 1, 102 (Ff *happily*). Oth. II, 1, 280 (Ff *happily*). III, 3, 263 (Qq *happily*). IV, 2, 44 (Ff *happely*). Ant. III, 13, 48. IV, 2, 26. Cymb. III, 3, 29. III, 5, 60.

3) just: *h. that name of chaste unhaply set this bateless edge on his keen appetite,* Lucr. 8 (= that very name etc.). *this love of theirs myself have often seen, h. when they have judged me fast asleep,* Gent. III, 1, 25 (just, the very moment). Perhaps also in Cymb. V, 5, 314: *I must, for mine own part, unfold a dangerous truth, though h. well for you.*

Happen, to come to pass: Ado I, 1, 271. Shr. IV,

4, 64. All's I, 3, 125. III, 2, 1. H6A II, 2, 11. H6C IV, 1, 128. H8 II, 1, 6. III, 1, 25. Hml. V, 2, 406. *these —ed accidents,* Tp. V, 250. With *to: what can h. to me?* H8 III, 1, 122. With an inf.: *to effect whatever I shall h. to devise,* R2 IV, 330. With a clause following: *how unluckily it —ed that I should purchase,* Tim. III, 2, 52.

Happily, 1) fortunately: *this gentleman is h. arrived,* Shr. I, 2, 113; cf. V, 1, 130; H8 V, 1, 85; V, 2, 9. *you are h. met,* Shr. IV, 4, 19; cf. IV, 5, 59; Rom. IV, 1, 18. *I wish it h. effected,* All's IV, 5, 84. John V, 7, 95. 101. *a Roman now adopted h.* Tit. I, 463. Dissyll.: *h. to wive and thrive,* Shr. I, 2, 56. H4A I, 3, 297. Rom. III, 5, 115.

2) in a state of felicity, with a contented mind: *how h. he lives,* Gent. I, 3, 57. *if wealthily, then h.* Shr. I, 2, 76. *he stepped before me h. for my example,* H8 IV, 2, 10. *the king hath h. received the news of thy success,* Mcb. I, 3, 89. *h., amen!* Ant. II, 2, 155.

3) favourably, in a goodly manner: *parts that become these h. enough,* Merch. II, 2, 191. *which elder years may h. bring forth,* R2 V, 3, 22.

4) perhaps: *h. you something know,* Meas. IV, 2, 98. *h. we might be interrupted,* Shr. IV, 4, 54. *the soul of your grandam might h. inhabit a bird,* Tw. IV, 2, 57. Wint. V, 2, 22. H6B III, 1, 306. Tit. IV, 3, 8 (Ff *haply*). Hml. I, 1, 134. II, 2, 402. Oth. II, 1, 280 (Qq *haply*). III, 3, 238. Cymb. IV, 1, 21. Changed to *haply* by most M. Edd, when dissyll.: All's I, 3, 241. H5 V, 2, 93. Cymb. III, 4, 150. O. Edd. differing in this case: R3 IV, 4, 273 (Ff *haply*). Lr. I, 1, 102 (Qq *haply*).

Happiness, 1) good luck, good fortune: *all h. bechance to thee in Milan,* Gent. I, 1, 61. *bring you back in h.* Meas. I, 1, 75. *a dear h. to women,* Ado I, 1, 129. *envy no man's h.* As III, 2, 79. *the victory fell on us. Great h.!* Rom. I, 2, 58. *and lo, the h.! go and importune her,* Oth. III, 4, 108. *Caesar will unstate his h.* Ant. III, 13, 30. All's IV, 3, 12. R2 I, 1, 22. H4B IV, 1, 64. H5 V, 2, 379. R3 I, 3, 41. Rom. III, 3, 142. Tim. I, 1, 76 (cf. 64). Per. II, 3, 11. Used as a form of good wishes, especially in meeting and parting: *good day and h.!* As IV, 1, 30. *health and h. betide my liege,* R2 III, 2, 91. H4B IV, 4, 81. IV, 5, 227. H6B V, 1, 124. *h. to his accomplices,* H6A V, 2, 9. *all h. unto my lord,* H6B III, 1, 93. R2 V, 6, 6. Tim. I, 1, 109. Cymb. III, 2, 46. *h. to their sheets!* Oth. II, 3, 29. Cymb. III, 5, 17. Per. I, 1, 60. *the best of h. keep with you,* Tim. I, 2, 234.

2) content, felicity: Lucr. Dedic. 6. Lucr. 22. Gent. I, 1, 14. I, 3, 49. II, 4, 183. V, 4, 173. Ado I, 1, 102. Merch. I, 2, 7. As V, 2, 48. Shr. I, 1, 19. John III, 4, 117. H4B V, 2, 61. R3 I, 2, 209. IV, 3, 26. IV, 4, 119. 324. 406. H8 IV, 2, 64. 90. Tit. I, 177. II, 4, 20. Rom. II, 6, 28. Tim. I, 2, 86. Oth. V, 2, 290. Cymb. V, 5, 26. Per. I, 1, 24. *she shall be to the h. of England an aged princess,* H8 V, 5, 57. = that which causes content, makes happy: *society is the h. of life,* LLL IV, 2, 168. *queen Margaret, England's h.* H6B I, 1, 37.

3) propriety, goodliness: *he hath indeed a good outward h.* Ado II, 3, 191 (= a happy exterior, a prepossessing appearance). *how pregnant his replies are! a h. that often madness hits on,* Hml. II, 2, 213. cf. All's II, 1, 185.

Happy, adj. 1) fortunate, lucky: *h. return be to your royal grace,* Meas. V, 3. *disgraced me in my h.*

victories, H4A IV, 3, 97. *h. always was it for that son whose father for his hoarding went to hell*, H6C II, 2, 47. *pride, which out of daily fortune ever taints the h. man*, Cor. IV, 7, 39. *not so h., yet much —er*, Mcb. I, 3, 66 (i. e. not so fortunate, but much more blessed). *a proclaimed prize! most h.!* Lr. IV, 6, 230.

2) in a state of felicity, contented and satisfied: Lucr. 16. Sonn. 6, 8. 32, 8. 92, 11. 12. Gent. III, 1, 57. V, 4, 30. 117. 148. Wiv. II, 1, 110. Meas. III, 1, 21. V, 404. Err. I, 1, 38. 139. Ado I, 1, 112. II, 3, 237. Mids. I, 1, 20. Merch. III, 2, 162. 163. 165. As V, 2, 51. All's II, 1, 185. Wint. IV, 2, 34. IV, 4, 635. R2 V, 3, 94. H6A V, 3, 148. R3 II, 1, 31. Cymb. I, 6, 6 etc. *be h.* = God bless you: Ado I, 1, 112. Wint. IV, 4, 635. *h. man be his dole:* Wiv. III, 4, 68. Shr. I, 1, 144. Wint. I, 2, 163. H4A II, 2, 80 (cf. *Dole*). *h. in* = a) fully contented, blessed by: *am I h. in thy news?* R3 IV, 3, 24. *may you be h. in your wish*, H8 III, 2, 43. *you are h. in this second match*, Rom. III, 5, 224. b) possessed of, endowed with: *have you the tongues? My youthful travel therein made me h.* Gent. IV, 1, 34. *tell him wherein you're h., which you'll make him know, if that his head have ear in music*, Cymb. III, 4, 177.

3) making happy, propitious, favourable: *I will be thankful to any h. messenger from thence*, Gent. II, 4, 53 (who brings good news). *O h. torment*, Merch. III, 2, 37. *what his —er affairs may be, are to me unknown*, Wint. IV, 2, 34. *ports and h. havens*, R2 I, 3, 276. *this is the h. wedding-torch*, H6A III, 2, 26. *the first and —est hearers of the town* (the best disposed I could find) H8 Prol. 24. *a h. star*, Tit. IV, 2, 32. *O h. dagger*, Rom. V, 3, 168. *I escaped by the h. hollow of a tree*, Lr. II, 3, 2. *a h. evening!* Gent. V, 1, 7. *h. day, my lord!* Per. II, 4, 22. *you have stayed me in a h. hour*, Ado IV, 1, 285 (= in time). H6C I, 2, 63. *omit no h. hour*, H5 I, 2, 300. *in very h. season*, H4B IV, 2, 79 (just in time). *in h. time*, in the same sense: Shr. Ind. 1, 90. All's V, 1, 6. Caes. II, 2, 60. Hml. V, 2, 214. Oth. III, 1, 32. *madam, in h. time, what day is that?* Rom. III, 5, 112 (= à propos, pray tell me).

4) well devised, fit, pleasant: *some h. mean to end a hapless life*, Lucr. 1045. *they did not bless us with one h. word*, LLL V, 2, 370. *I'll gild it with the —est terms I have*, H4A V, 4, 162. *Saint Denis bless this h. stratagem*, H6A III, 2, 18. *the —est gift that ever marquess gave*, H6B I, 1, 15. *it stains the glory in that h. verse which aptly sings the good*, Tim. I, 1, 16. Compar. *—er* adverbially: *happily met, the —er for thy son*, Shr. IV, 5, 59.

Happy, vb. to make happy, to felicitate: *that use is not forbidden usury which —es those that pay the willing loan*, Sonn. 6, 6.

Harbinger, a forerunner: Phoen. 5. Err. III. 2, 12. Mids. III, 2, 380 [Aurora's harbinger = "the morning star". W.A.Wright]. Mcb. I, 4, 45. V, 6, 10. Hml. I, 1, 122.

Harbour, subst. 1) port, haven: Tp. I, 2, 226. Merch. V, 277. Troil. I, 3, 44. Oth. II, 1, 121. 215. Ant. III, 11, 11.

2) lodging: Lucr. 768. Meas. I, 3, 4. LLL II, 175. H6B III, 1, 336. V, 1, 168. Tim. V, 4, 53 (*make their h.*).

Harbour, vb. 1) tr. a) to afford lodgings, to quarter: *any place that —s men*, Err. I, 1, 137. *she —s you as her kinsman*, Tw. II, 3, 103. *—ed in their circumference*, John II, 262.

b) to entertain, to foster (in a bad sense): Gent. I, 2, 42. H6B III, 1, 54. IV, 7, 109. H6C III, 2, 164. Lr. II, 2, 108.

2) intr. to take up one's lodging, to abide: Gent. III, 1, 140. 149. Err. III, 2, 154. R2 I, 1, 195. H6C IV, 7, 79. Used of a ship, = to be in port: Cymb. IV, 2, 206.

Harbourage, lodging, shelter: John II, 234. Per. I, 4, 100.

Hard, adj. 1) not easily pierced, not yielding to pressure, opposed to soft: Ven. 267. Sonn. 95, 14. Compl. 211. Tp. I, 2, 343. Err. II, 1, 93. LLL I, 2, 182. Merch. III, 2, 102. IV, 1, 79. As III' 2, 60. Tw. II, 2, 42. Troil. I, 1, 59. Caes. IV, 3, 74. Cymb. II, 2, 34 etc.

2) unfeeling, insensible, cruel: *thy n. heart*, Ven. 375. 500. Lucr. 978. Err. IV, 2, 34. As III, 5, 4. Cymb. III, 4, 164. *h. as steel*, Ven. 199. Gent. I, 1, 149. *—er than a stone*, Lucr. 593. 1713. Gent. I, 1, 146. 147. Merch. I, 3, 162. II, 2, 30. V, 81. Wint. I, 2, 153. R2 V, 5, 21 etc.

3) laborious, fatiguing: *making the h. way sweet and delectable*, R2 II, 3, 7. *h. labour*, H4A IV, 3, 23. Mcb. I, 7, 62. Cymb. V, 3, 44.

4) harsh, rough, difficult to be borne, evil, disagreeable: *fearing some h. news*, Lucr. 255. *to bear a h. opinion of his truth*, Gent. II, 7, 81; *punish me not with your h. thoughts*, As I, 2, 196; *under your h. construction must I sit*, Tw. III, 1, 126; *killed with your h. opinions*, H4B V, 5, 147; *you suffer too h. an exclamation*, H8 I, 2, 52; *take to you no h. thoughts*, Ant. V, 2, 117. *scorn, horn, a h. rhyme*, Ado V, 2, 38. *h. lodging and thin weeds*, LLL V, 2, 811. *by h. adventure*, As II, 4, 45. *'tis h.* All's II, 3, 314. Merch. I, 2, 27. *h. and undeserved measure*, All's II, 3, 273. *a h. bondage*, III, 5, 67. *'twere h. luck*, Wint. V, 2, 158. *h. condition*, H5 IV, 1, 250. V, 2, 326. Caes. I, 2, 174. *h. distress*, H6A II, 5, 87. *h. language*, H6B IV, 9, 45. *these h. fractions*, Tim. II, 2, 220. *h. words*, Hml. II, 1, 107. *he's at some h. point*, Cymb. III, 4, 16.

5) not easy, difficult: *faithful friends are h. to find*, Pilgr. 406. *the —est voice of her behaviour*, Wiv. I, 3, 51. *any h. lesson*, Ado I, 1, 295. Mids. III, 1, 49. Merch. II, 2, 47. IV, 1, 78. As III, 2, 194. Tw. I, 2, 44. II, 2, 42. R2 V, 5, 16. R3 III, 7, 93. Troil. III, 2, 85. Rom. I, 2, 2. II, 2, 63. Lr. II, 4, 245. III, 6, 107. Cymb. II, 2, 34. II, 4, 46 etc. *upon his will I sealed my h. consent*, Hml. I, 2, 60 (not easily obtained, reluctant). *h. of hearing* (= deafish), Shr. II, 184. *too h. for* = too powerful, getting the better of: LLL II, 258. IV, 1, 140. As I, 2, 51. H4A I, 2, 204. H8 V, 1, 57. Cor. IV, 5, 195.

6) hardened, obdurate: *thy nature did commence in sufferance, time hath made thee h. in't*, Tim. IV, 3, 269. *the initiate fear that wants h. use*, Mcb. III, 4, 143. *when we in our viciousness grow h.* Ant. III, 13, 111.

7) violent, vehement: *weary with her h. embracing*, Ven. 559.

8) heavy, wanting ease: *time's pace is so h. that it seems the length of seven year*, As III, 2, 334.

Hard, adv. 1) ill; *to bear h.* = a) to resent: *who bears h. his brother's death*, H4A I, 3, 270. b) to bear ill will: *Caesar doth bear me h.* Caes. I, 2, 317. II, 1, 215. III, 1, 157. *it goes h.* = it is a bad thing: *when a man's servant shall play the cur with him, it goes h.* Gent. IV, 4, 2. *my life, sir? how, I pray? for* *that goes h.* Shr. IV, 2, 80. *the world goes h. when Clifford cannot spare his friends an oath*, H6C II, 6, 77. *it will go h. with poor Antonio* (= he will fare ill), Merch. III, 2, 292. H6B IV, 2, 108. *it shall go hard but I will* = I shall certainly: *it shall go h. but I'll prove it*, Gent. I, 1, 86. *it shall go h. but I will better the instruction*, Merch. III, 1, 75. H4B III, 2, 354. Hml. III, 4, 207. *it shall go h. if Cambio go without her*, Shr. IV, 4, 109.

2) laboriously, earnestly, with effort: *work not so h.* Tp. III, 1, 16. *my father is h. at study*, 20. *drinking h.* Meas. IV, 3, 56. *spurred his horse so h.* LLL IV, 1, 1. *ply her h.* As III, 5, 76 and H6C III, 2, 50. *spurring h.* H4B I, 1, 36. *laboured so h.* II, 2, 32. *at your book so h.* H6C V, 6, 1. *spur your horses h.* R3 V, 3, 340. *travelled h.* Lr. II, 2, 162. II, 4, 90 (Ff *travelled all the night*). *woo h.* Cymb. III, 6, 70.

3) strongly, violently: *how h. true sorrow hits*, Sonn. 120, 10. *my next self thou —er hast engrossed*, 133, 6. *him h. beset*, Gent. II, 4, 49. *knock the door h.* Err. III, 1, 58 and Rom. III, 3, 78. *how h. he fetches breath*, H4A II, 4, 579. *strikes his breast h.* H8 III, 2, 117. *pull off my boots:* — *er,* —*er,* Lr. IV, 6, 177. *death-like dragons here affright thee h.* Per. I, 1, 29.

4) closely, tightly, fast: *holds her pulses h.* Ven. 476. *you'll kiss me h.* Wint. II, 1, 5. Oth. III, 3, 422. *he took me by the wrist and held me h.* Hml. II, 1, 87. *hug them h.* Caes. I, 2, 75. *bind him h.* Lr. III, 7, 32. Oth. III, 3, 286. *can gripe as h. as Cassibelan*, Cymb. III, 1, 41. *hold h. the breath*, H5 III, 1, 16 (= keep in).

5) close, very near: *h. at door*, Wiv. IV, 2, 111. *h. by Herne's oak*, V, 3, 14. *h. in the palm of the hand*, Err. III, 2, 123. *h. at hand*, Oth. II, 1, 268. *h. by*, Wiv. IV, 2, 40. H5 IV, 7, 91. H6B IV, 2, 121. H6C I, 2, 51. *here h. by*, Wiv. III, 3, 10. Merch. IV, 1, 145. As III, 5, 75. Tw. I, 3, 114. H4A II, 2, 79. *h. by here*, Lr. III, 2, 61. *it followed h. upon*, Hml. I, 2, 179.

6) with difficulty: *the —er matched, the greater victory*, H6C V, 1, 70. *I did full h. forbear him*, Oth. I, 2, 10.

7) heavily, slowly: *he trots h. with a young maid between the contract of her marriage and the day it is solemnized*, As III, 2, 331.

Hard-a-keeping, difficult to be observed: *too h. oath*, LLL I, 1, 65; in O. Edd. not hyphened.

Hard-believing, incredulous: Ven. 985; not hyphened in the earliest Qq.

Harden, to make hard or insensible: Lucr. 560. 978. Wint. I, 2, 146. III, 2, 53 (cf. *Heart-hardening*).

Hardest-timbered, of the hardest wood: H6C II, 1, 55.

Hard-favoured, of repulsive features, ill-looking, ugly: Ven. 133. 931. Lucr. 1632. Gent. II, 1, 53. As III, 3, 29. R2 V, 1, 14. H5 III, 1, 8. H6A IV, 7, 23. H6C V, 5, 78.

Hard-handed, having hands hard with labour: Mids. V, 72. cf. Troil. I, 1, 59. Caes. IV, 3, 74.

Hard-hearted, unfeeling, merciless: Ado V, 1, 321. Mids. II, 1, 195. Tw. I, 5, 262. R2 V, 3, 87. 121. H6C I, 4, 167. Rom. II, 4, 4.

Hardiment, boldness, bold exploit: *changing h. with great Glendower*, H4A I, 3, 101. *thus popped Paris in his h.* Troil. IV, 5, 28. *like h. Posthumus hath to Cymbeline performed*, Cymb. V, 4, 75.

Hardiness, bravery: H5 I, 2, 220. Cymb. III, 6, 22.

Hardly, 1) with difficulty: *it came h. off*, Gent. II, 1, 115. *as h. will he endure your sight*, Wint. IV, 4, 480. *these oracles are h. attained, and h. understood*, H6B I, 4, 74. *knowing how h. I can brook abuse*, V, 1, 92. *I was h. moved to come to thee*, Cor. V, 2, 78. *how h. I was drawn into this war*, Ant. V, 1, 74.

2) harshly, unfavourably, ill: *have aught committed that is h. borne by any*, R3 II, 1, 57. *the commons h. conceive of me*, H8 I, 2, 105. *we house in the rock, yet use thee not so h. as prouder livers do*, Cymb. III, 3, 8.

3) scarcely: Gent. II, 1, 33. Meas. III, 2, 162. Merch. III, 3, 33. As III, 2, 188. Shr. Ind. 2, 127. I, 1, 178. Tw. II, 3, 174. III, 2, 87. III, 4, 63. Wint. II, 3, 112. John V, 6, 42. R2 II, 4, 2. IV, 164. H5 V, 2, 191. H6A I, 1, 160. III, 2, 40. H6B I, 4, 41. H6C I, 4, 151. R3 II, 3, 2 (Qq *scarcely*). Tim. II, 2, 156. Hml. V, 1, 120 (Qq *scarcely*). Ant. I, 4, 7. Per. II, 1, 124.

4) not likely (German *schwerlich*): *I think you'll h. win her*, Gent. I, 1, 141. *h. serve*, All's IV, 1, 59. *I could be sad. Very h. upon such a subject*, H4B II, 2, 47. *you shall h. offend her*, II, 4, 125. *that can h. be*, V, 5, 81. *we shall h. see their banners*, Cor. III, 1, 7. *profit again should h. draw me there*, Mcb. V, 3, 62. *and h. shall I carry out my side*, Lr. V, 1, 61.

Hardness, 1) durity: *the flint and h. of my fault*, Ant. IV, 9, 16.

2) unfeelingness, mercilessness: *the blame may hang upon your h.* Cor. V, 3, 91. *that makes this h.* Lr. III, 6, 82 (Ff *these hard hearts*).

3) difficulty: *O h. to dissemble*, Oth. III, 4, 34. *whose containing is so from sense in h.* Cymb. V, 5, 431.

4) hardship: *a natural and prompt alacrity I find in h.* Oth. I, 3, 234. *h. ever of hardiness is mother*, Cymb. III, 6, 21.

Hardock, (Qq *hor-docks;* M. Edd. *hoar-docks, harlocks, burdocks*), burdock: Lr. IV, 4, 4.*

Hard-ruled, difficult to be guided, not easily managed: H8 III, 2, 101.

Hardy, stout, daring, bold: Tw. II, 2, 10. H6C I, 4, 14. V, 7, 6. R3 I, 3, 340. IV, 3, 47. Mcb. I, 2, 4. Hml. I, 4, 83.

Hare, the animal Lepus: Ven. 674. 679. Merch. I, 2, 21. As IV, 3, 18. Tw. III, 4, 421. John II, 137. H4A I, 3, 198. II, 4, 481. H6C II, 5, 130. Troil. II, 2, 48. III, 2, 96. Cor. I, 1, 175. I, 8, 7. Rom. II, 4, 138. 141. 144. Mcb. I, 2, 35. Ant. IV, 7, 13. Cymb. IV, 4, 37. Thought to be melancholy: H4A I, 2, 87.

Harebell, the Wild Hyacinth: Cymb. IV, 2, 222.

Hare-brained, (cf. Merch. I, 2, 21) inconsiderate, hot-headed: H4A V, 2, 19. H6A I, 2, 37.

Hare-finder, according to Intpp., one employed or skilled to find the hare in her form: Ado I, 1, 186. Perhaps originally a *hair-finder*, one who easily finds fault (cf. the German *ein Haar finden*), with an obscene double-meaning; cf. Rom. II, 4, 100 and 138.

Hare-lip, a natural fissure in the upper-lip: Mids. V, 418. Lr. III, 4, 123.

Harfleur (O. Edd. *Harflew*), town in Normandy: H5 III Chor. 17. 27. III, 3, 8. 27. 52. 57. III, 5, 49. III, 6, 128.

Ha'rford-west (reading of Q1; the other O. Edd. *Herford*, or *Hertford west*), place in Wales: R3 IV, 5, 7.

Hark, hear, listen, an imperative used to engage attention either to a noise or to what a person is saying: Tp. I, 2, 404. III, 3, 18. IV, 262. Meas. IV, 2, 72. Mids. III, 1, 88. Merch. IV, 24. 97. H6C I, 4, 22. R3 I, 4, 164 etc. *h. you, the king is coming*, H5 III, 6, 90. *h., h.!* Tp. I, 2, 382. 384. Gent. IV, 2, 36. Err. V, 184. H6A IV, 2, 39. H6C IV, 8, 51 etc. *h. what thou else shalt do me*, Tp. I, 2, 495. *h., I will tell you*, Wiv. II, 1, 218. *h. how I'll bribe you*, Meas. II, 2, 145. V, 346. LLL III, 163. Mids. III, 2, 305. Shr. I, 2, 212. *h., h., you Gods!* Per. IV, 6, 155. *h. further*, Ant. IV, 9, 11. *there, Tyrant, there, h., h.!* Tp. IV, 258 (a cry to set on dogs). *h. in thine ear*, Tp. I, 2, 318. Per. I, 2, 76. *h. you hither*, in the same sense: Wiv. III, 4, 21. H4B II, 4, 165. *h., contrymen!* H6A I, 5, 27. *h. thee*, Gent. III, 1, 127. Caes. V, 5, 5. Ant. V, 2, 192. *h. ye*, Wiv. III, 4, 29. Wint. II, 1, 15. H6A III, 4, 37. V, 4, 55. Tit. II, 1, 99. *h. you*, Wiv. II, 1, 153. Meas. II, 1, 259. Shr. I, 2, 146. H6A V, 3, 175 etc.

Harlock, see *Hardock.*

Harlot, 1) applied to men as well as women, a lewd person, a rascallion: *she with —s feasted in my house*, Err. V, 205. *away, my disposition, and possess me some —'s spirit*, Cor. III, 2, 112. *Helen and Hero hildings and —s*, Rom. II, 4, 45.

2) Applied only to women, a prostitute, only a strumpet: Err. IV, 4, 104. Tim. I, 2, 67. IV, 3, 79. Caes. II, 1, 287. Hml. III, 1, 51. IV, 5, 118. Oth. IV, 2, 239 (Ff. *harlotry*).

Adjectively: *my h. brow*, Err. II, 2, 138. *the h. king*, Wint. II, 3, 4. *that h. strumpet Shore*, R3 III, 4, 73.

Harlotry, = harlot: *he sups to-night with a h.* Oth. IV, 2, 239 (Q *harlot*). Glendower and Capulet use it like *baggage* as a term of contempt for a silly wench: *a peevish self-willed h.* H4A III, 1, 199. Rom. IV, 2, 14. Adjectively: *he doth it like one of these h. players*, H4A II, 4, 437 (= vagabond players? But perhaps Mrs Quickly means quite another thing, as f. i. *Herod* or *hero players*).

Harm, subst. 1) injury, hurt, mischief: *weakly fortressed from a world of —s*, Lucr. 28. *the other feareth h.* 172. Compl. 165. Ado V, 1, 39. Mids. II, 2, 16. Shr. Ind. 2, 138. H6A IV, 7, 30. H6C III, 2, 39. V, 7, 34. H8 I, 1, 183. Lr. I, 4, 352. IV, 7, 28 *(make)*. Ant. I, 2, 133 etc. *no h.: what more?* H4A IV, 1, 90 (= no matter, never mind). *to do h.:* Ven. 195. Tp. I, 2, 15. Mids. III, 1, 19. Merch. I, 1, 24. John III, 1, 38 etc. *to do a p. h.* or *to do h. to:* Compl. 194. Meas. II, 1, 165. III, 2, 176. Err. IV, 4, 156. Mids. III, 2, 271. Tw. I, 3, 91. H6C I, 3, 38 etc. *to do h. upon:* H4A I, 2, 103 (reading of Q1; the other O. Edd. *unto*). *would do no h. in him*, Meas. III, 2, 104. *to take no h.* Lr. III, 6, 46. *my h.* = a) the injury done by me: *inhearsed in the arms of the most bloody nurser of his —s*, H6A IV, 7, 46. cf. *the h. of unscanned swiftness*, Cor. III, 1, 313. b) the injury suffered by me: *any tragic instance of our h.* Err. I, 1, 65. *laughing at their h.* Mids. II, 1, 39. As III, 2, 80. H6C V, 4, 2. R3 II, 2, 103. Cor. I, 9, 57. Ant. II, 1, 6. *what may befall him to his h.* H6C IV, 6, 95. R3 I, 3, 248. cf. *knights should right poor ladies' —s*, Lucr. 1694. *to heal Rome's —s*, Tit. V, 3, 148.

2) evil, wickedness: *whose inward ill no outward h. expressed*, Lucr. 91. *impious act, including all foul*

—s, 199. *a little h. done to a great good end*, 528. *see any h. in his face*, Meas. II, 1, 159. *good provoke to h.* IV, 1, 15. Ado III, 4, 35. IV, 1, 108. John III, 1, 39. H4A II, 4, 512. H6A IV, 1, 179. H6B V, 1, 56. Mcb. I, 3, 123. III, 5, 7. IV, 3, 55. Caes. III, 2, 73. Lr. I, 2, 196. Oth. IV, 1, 4. 5. *when I was wont to think no h. all night*, LLL I, 1, 44, i. e. to sleep; cf. All's IV, 3, 287. Tim. IV, 3, 291.

Harm, vb. to hurt, to injure, either in body or mind: *his short thick neck cannot be easily —ed*, Ven. 627. Compl. 194. Mids. III, 2, 270. 321. John IV, 1, 66. 105. H5 I, 2, 155. Mcb. IV, 1, 81. Cymb. I, 1, 134. III, 6, 46. IV, 2, 276. *though yet he never —ed me*, All's V, 3, 300. R3 IV, 4, 238 (Qq *wronged*). Oth. III, 3, 339.

Harm-doing, wrong, evil: *she never knew h.* H8 II, 3, 5.

Harmful, hurtful, injurious, mischievous: Lucr. 1724. Sonn. 111, 2. John III, 1, 41. III, 3, 51. V, 2, 77. H6B III, 2, 262. H6C II, 2, 10. R3 IV, 4, 172. Lr. I, 4, 367. IV, 2, 77.

Harmless, not doing or meaning ill, innocent: Lucr. 510. 1347. 1507. 1723. Tp. IV, 129. 197. 212. Merch. IV, 1, 55. H4A I, 3, 61. H6B II, 2, 27. III, 1, 71. 208. 215. H6C II, 1, 62. II, 5, 75. V, 6, 8. R3 III, 5, 25. Tit. III, 2, 63. Cymb. V, 5, 394.

Harmonious, full of euphony: Tp. IV, 119. Mids. II, 1, 151.

Harmony, delightful music, euphony: Ven. 781 Tp. III, 1, 41. III, 3, 18. Ado II, 3, 41. LLL I, 1, 168. IV, 3, 345. Merch. V, 57. 63. Shr. III, 1, 5. 14. R2 I, 3, 165. II, 1, 6. H6B II, 1, 57. H6C IV, 6, 14. H8 IV, 2, 80. Troil. III, 1, 56. Tit. II, 4, 48. Hml. III, 2, 378. Cymb. V, 5, 467. Per. II, 5, 28. V, 1, 45.

Harness, 1) the furniture of a draught horse: Shr. Ind. 2, 44.

2) armour: *he doth fill fields with h.* H4A III, 2, 101. *doff thy h.* Troil. V, 3, 31. Tim. I, 2, 53. Mcb. V, 5, 52. Ant. IV, 8, 15.

Harnessed, 1) furnished with the dress for draught: H4A III, 1, 221.

2) dressed in armour: John V, 2, 132. Troil. I, 2, 8.

Harp, subst. a musical instrument strung with wire and touched with the fingers: Tp. II, 1, 87 (the allusion is to Amphion, who raised the walls of Thebes with his lyre). Mids. V, 45. R2 I, 3, 162. H4A III, 1, 123.

Harp, vb. 1) tr. to touch, to hit: *thou hast —ed my fear aright*, Mcb. IV, 1, 74.

2) intr. *with on,* to dwell on, to recur incessantly to the same theme: Meas. V, 64. R3 IV, 4, 364. Cor. II, 3, 260. Hml. II, 2, 189. Ant. III, 13, 142.

Harper, a player on the harp: LLL V, 2, 405.

Harpier, name of an unknown demon: Mcb. IV, 1, 3 (some M. Edd. *harper* or *harpy*).*

Harpy, a monster of ancient fable, with the face of a woman and the body of a bird of prey: Tp. III, 3, 83. Ado II, 1, 279. Per. IV, 3, 46.

Harrow (cf. *Harry* vb.), to vex, to fill with distress and anguish (Anglosaxon *herevjan*): *let the Volsces plough Rome and h. Italy*, Cor. V, 3, 34 (quibbling). *it —s me with fear and wonder*, Hml. I, 1, 44 (Qq *horrors* and *horrows*): *a tale whose lightest word would h. up thy soul*, I, 5, 16.

Harry, another form of *Henry*: R2 I, 3, 1. 100.

II, 1, 144. 279. II, 3, 21. IV, 220 (Ff. *Henry*). H4A I, 1, 53. I, 3, 24 etc. etc. *four H. ten shillings,* H4B III, 2, 236, i. e. pieces of the value of ten shillings, coined by Henry VII, not by Henry IV.

Harry, vb. (cf. *Harrow*) to vex, to tease, to put in fear: *I repent me much that so I —ed him,* Ant. III, 3, 43.

Harsh, 1) rugged to the touch, rough: *to whose soft seizure the cygnet's down is h.* Troil. I, 1, 58.

2) grating on the ear: *h. in voice,* Ven. 134. *too h. a descant,* Gent. I, 2, 94. III, 1, 208. LLL V, 2, 940. H4B IV, 1, 49. H6B III, 2, 312. H8 IV, 2, 95. Cor. IV, 5, 65. Rom. III, 5, 28. Hml. III, 1, 166. Per. I, 1, 85. II, 3, 97.

3) bitter and disagreeable to the taste: *sweet revenge grows h.* Oth. V, 2, 116.

4) rough, rude, repulsive: *h., featureless and rude,* Sonn. 11, 10. *this h. indignity,* LLL V, 2, 289. *h. Jew,* Merch. IV, 1, 123. *tedious it were to tell and h. to hear,* Shr. III, 2, 107. V, 2, 183. *a most h. language,* All's II, 3, 198. *thy h. rude tongue,* R2 III, 4, 74. *h. rage,* H4A III, 1, 183. *so h., so blunt, unnatural,* H6C V, 1, 86. *too h. a style,* R3 IV, 4, 360. *this h. world,* Hml. V, 2, 359. *h. conference,* Ant. I, 1, 45. *h. fortune,* II, 6, 54. *that h., noble, simple nothing, that Cloten,* Cymb. III, 4, 135. *thy h. and potent injuries,* V, 4, 83.

Harshly, with a grating sound, roughly: *'twill sound h. in her ears,* Err. IV, 4, 7. *fare so h. o'the trumpet's sound,* Tim. III, 1, 6, 37. *grating so h. all his days of quiet,* Hml. III, 1, 3.

Harshness, roughness, want of tenderness: *he's composed of h.* Tp. III, 1, 9. *turned her obedience to stubborn h.* Mids. I, 1, 38. *thy tender-hefted nature shall not give thee o'er to h.* Lr. II, 4, 175.

Harsh-resounding, grating on the ear: R2 I, 3, 135.

Harsh-sounding, grating on the ear: Ven. 431. John IV, 2, 150.

Hart, a male deer, a stag: As III, 2, 107. Tw. I, 1, 17. Troil. II, 3, 269. Tit. I, 493. Caes. III, 1, 204. Hml. III, 2, 283. Cymb. II, 4, 27. V, 3, 24. Quibbling with *heart:* As III, 2, 260. Tw. I, 1, 21. Caes. III, 1, 207.

Harvest, 1) the season and act of reaping corn or fruits: Tp. IV, 115. R3 I, 4, 249. Ant. II, 7, 26 *(come to h.).* Metaphorically: *frame the season for your own h.* Ado I, 3, 27. *when wit and youth is come to h.* Tw. III, 1, 143 (is ripened). *in's spring became a h.* Cymb. I, 1, 46.

2) the corn or fruit reaped: As III, 5, 103. H6A III, 2, 47. Metaphorically, = fruit, produce: Ven. Ded. 6. Lucr. 859. Sonn. 128, 7. LLL IV, 3, 326. H6B III, 1, 381. H6C V, 7, 21. R3 II, 2, 115. 116. V, 2, 15. Mcb. I, 4, 33. Per. IV, 2, 152.

Harvest-home, the time and act of reaping: H4A I, 3, 35. Tropically, the opportunity of gain: Wiv. II, 2, 287.

Harvest-man, a reaper, mower: Cor. I, 3, 39.

Harvey, name in H4A I, 2, 181 (M. Edd. *Bardolph*), perhaps the name of the actor who performed the part of Bardolph.

Haste, subst. speed, swift dispatch, hurry: Ven. 909. 1029. Lucr. 552. 650. 1295. 1668. Sonn. 123, 12. Meas. I, 1, 54. IV, 2, 91. V, 415. 420. LLL II, 239. Mids. I, 1, 237. Merch. IV, 1, 321. Tw. IV, 3,

22. H6C IV, 1, 129. R3 III, 5, 54. H5 IV, 2, 62. Per. I, 1, 161 (*telling your h.,* i.e. why you are in such a hurry) etc. *in h.* = speedily: Ven. 57. Lucr. 321. Err. IV, 4, 87. Merch. II, 2, 180. Cymb. I, 6, 131 etc. *all in h.* Ven. 870. *in all h.* Wiv. III, 3, 14. R3 IV, 1, 57. *in all swift h.* Troil. I, 1, 119. *in such h.* Err. II, 1, 2. H6A III, 2, 104. *in the h.* Lr. II, 1, 26. *in h. whereof* (= to do so speedily) R2 I, 1, 150. *to be in h.* = to have no time to lose: Gent. I, 3, 89. Wiv. V, 1, 25. R3 IV, 4, 161 etc. *I am in great h.* Wiv. I, 4, 174. Ado III, 5, 54. cf. *here comes one in h.* Ado V, 2, 96 (one who has no time to lose). *nature, rather curious than in h.* All's I, 2, 20. *with h.:* Mids. III, 2, 378. As I, 3, 43. H6A I, 1, 167. Caes. I, 3, 107. II, 1, 309. Hml. I, 2, 238. Ant. I, 2, 236. *to have h.* Ado V, 1, 47. *to make h.:* Gent. II, 4, 190. III, 1, 258. Meas. IV, 1, 57. Err. III, 1, 119. IV, 2, 29. Merch. III, 2, 327. IV, 1, 454. 2, 18. R3 II, 4, 15. Hml. I, 1, 13 etc. *make good h.* Meas. IV, 5, 11. *make your best h.* Wint. III, 3, 10. *make your soonest h.* Ant. III, 4, 27. *make all the speedy h. you may,* R3 III, 1, 60. *put it to the h.* Ant. V, 2, 196. *let him take his h.* Tim. V, 1, 213 (cf. *Post-haste*).

Haste, vb. 1) intr. to make haste, to use swiftness, to go speedily: Ven. 258. 865. 876. LLL II, 33. Mids. III, 2, 394. Merch. III, 4, 83. Wint. II, 3, 197. John III, 3, 6. H6A II, 5, 127. IV, 1, 10. H6C V, 4, 63. H8 III, 2, 225. Troil. IV, 1, 40. V, 5, 15. Cor. I, 5, 14. Caes. I, 3, 133. Hml. IV, 1, 37. V, 2, 397. Ant. II, 2, 167. Per. III Prol. 29.

2) trans. to push on, to urge on, to put to speed: *let it be so —d,* Merch. II, 2, 121. *I'll h. the writer,* H4A III, 1, 143. *h. on Montjoy,* H5 III, 5, 61. *h. her to the purpose,* Troil. IV, 3, 5. *h. them on,* Cor. V, 1, 74. *—s our marriage,* Rom. IV, 1, 11. *h. me to know it,* Hml. I, 5, 29 (let me quickly know it).

3) refl. to make haste, to go quickly: *I h. me to my bed,* Sonn. 27, 1. *why should I h. me thence,* 51, 3. *we will h. us,* Hml. III, 3, 26. Imperatively: *h. thee,* Meas. IV, 1, 7. John IV, 2, 260. Lr. V, 3, 251. *h. you,* Meas. III, 1, 273. All's II, 2, 74. Tim. II, 1, 15.

Hasten, 1) intr. to make haste, to move with swiftness: Sonn. 60, 2. Wint. V, 1, 189.

2) tr. to push on, to urge on, to put to speed: All's II, 3, 223. Rom. III, 3, 156. Hml. III, 2, 55. Lr. I, 4, 363. IV, 2, 16. Ant. II, 4, 1. With *on:* Gent. I, 3, 77.

Hastily, in haste, with speed: Lucr. Arg. 17. Meas. IV, 3, 54. Ado V, 1, 45. Wint. V, 3, 155. John I, 221.

Hastings, name of 1) Lord H. who rebelled against Henry IV: H4B I, 3, 15 etc. 2) Lord H. the partisan and friend of Edward IV: H6C IV, 1, 47. 134. IV, 5, 1 etc. R3 I, 1, 68 etc.

Hasty, 1) quick, speedy: *upon h. employment,* H4B II, 1, 139. *h. powder,* Rom. V, 1, 64. *a h. spark,* Caes. IV, 3, 112. *our h. sending,* Hml. II, 2, 4.

2) in haste, having no time to lose: *are you so h.?* Ado V, 1, 49. H4B IV, 5, 61. R3 IV, 4, 162.

3) rash, inconsiderate, passionate: Lucr. 49. Ado II, 1, 78. Shr. IV, 3, 169. John IV, 3, 97. R2 I, 1, 19. H6C IV, 1, 18. IV, 8, 2. R3 IV, 4, 261. Cor. II, 1, 55. IV, 7, 32. Lr. II, 4, 178. Cymb. IV, 2, 168. Adverbially: *spoke in choler, ill and h.* H8 II, 1, 34.

Hasty-footed, swift: Mids. III, 2, 200.

Hasty-witted, rash, inconsiderate: Shr. V, 2, 40.

Hat, a covering for the head; worn by men: Ven. 351. Tp. IV, 136. V, 84. Gent. II, 3, 23. Ado I, 1, 76. III, 2, 41. III, 3, 125. LLL III, 17. Mids. III, 2, 30. Merch. II, 2, 203. Shr. III, 2, 43. 69. All's IV, 5, 111. Wint. IV, 4, 664. 672. H4B II, 4, 7. H8 IV, 1, 73. Cor. II, 3, 175. Tim. III, 6, 123. Caes. II, 1, 73. Mcb. IV, 3, 208. Hml. II, 1, 79. IV, 5, 25. Cymb. I, 3, 11. III, 4, 172. Worn by women: Compl. 31. Wiv. IV, 2, 73. 81. *a cardinal's h.* H6A I, 3, 36. 49. H8 III, 2, 325. *a copatain h.* Shr. V, 1, 70. *my colour-ed h.* I, 1, 212. *to colour Peter's h.* IV, 1, 137. *by this h.!* Wiv. I, 1, 173 (Mr. Slender's oath). *to have my h.* Cor. II, 3, 105 (i. e. to be humbly saluted by me). Used as a stake in betting: *I'll lay my head to any goodman's h.* LLL I, 1, 310. *my h. to a halfpenny,* V, 2, 563. cf. *is his head worth a h.?* As III, 2, 217. The same quibble in R3 III, 2, 95.

Hatch, subst. the act of incubation and exclusion from the egg; metaphorically: H4B III, 1, 86. Hml. III, 1, 174.

Hatch, subst. 1) a half-door: *sit down at the h.* Err. III, 1, 33. *in at the window, or else o'er the h.* John I, 171 (i. e. by any way, if not the right one). *take the h.* V, 2, 138; in the same sense as *leap the h.* Lr. III, 6, 76.

2) Plur. — *es* = the deck of a ship: *the mariners all under — es stowed,* Tp. I, 2, 230. *asleep under the — es,* V, 99. *clapped under — es,* 231. *if he come under my — es, I'll never to sea again,* Wiv. II, 1, 96. *I stood upon the — es,* H6B III, 2, 103. *to walk upon the — es,* R3 I, 4, 13. 17. *we have a chest beneath the — es,* Per. III, 1, 72.

Hatch, vb. 1) tr. to brood, to disclose by sitting on: R3 IV, 1, 55. Tit. II, 3, 149. Caes. II, 1, 33. Metaphorically: Meas. II, 2, 97. LLL V, 2, 70. Shr. I, 1, 211. Cor. I, 2, 21. Mcb. II, 3, 64. Hml. I, 3, 65. Ant. I, 2, 134. Cymb. V, 5, 60.

2) intr. to be sat on, to be disclosed by incuba-tion: *why should cuckoos h. in sparrows' nests,* Lucr. 849.

Hatched, adj. closed with a half-door: *'twere not amiss to keep our door h.* Per. IV, 2, 37.

Hatched (Fr. *haché*) engraved: *h. in silver,* Troil. I, 3, 65 (relating not to Nestor, but to his speech) *

Hatchet, an axe: H6B IV, 7, 96.

Hatchment, an armorial escutcheon used at a funeral: Hml. IV, 5, 214.

Hate, subst. great dislike, aversion, the contrary to love: Lucr. 240. 668. 936. 1005. Sonn. 10, 5. 142, 1. 145, 13. Tp. IV, 1, 19. Gent. I, 2, 48. V, 2, 56. Mids. IV, 1, 150. Merch. III, 2, 6. As III, 2, 78. H6C V, 1, 104. R3 I, 1, 35. I, 2, 232. II, 1, 9. Cor. II, 2, 21 etc. Plur. — *s:* R3 II, 2, 117 (Qq *hearts*). Troil. V, 10, 27. *in h.* = prompted by h., out of h.: *if she do frown, 'tis not in h. of you,* Gent. III, 1, 96. III, 2, 34. Merch. II, 5, 14. R2 II, 1, 243. Oth. V, 2, 295. Ant. IV, 8, 25. *to bear h.:* Mids. III, 2, 190. Cor. II, 3, 234. Tit. V, 1, 3. Rom. III, 1, 63. *to do h. upon:* Rom. III, 3, 118. *to hold in h.:* Gent. III, 2, 33. *thou didst hold him in thy h.* Oth. I, 1, 7. *to render h.* Cor. II, 2, 22. With *of:* Sonn. 142, 2. Gent. V, 2, 54. Ant. IV, 8, 25. With *to:* Gent. III, 1, 46. All's II, 3, 304. Cor. I, 10, 24. Abstr. pro concr.: *thou h. and terror to prosperity,* John III, 4, 28. *call him noble that was now your h.* Cor. I, 1, 187.

Hate, vb. to dislike greatly, to regard with the passion contrary to love: Lucr. Arg. 22. 738. Sonn. 129, 7. 145, 2. 13. Tp. I, 2, 476. III, 2, 102. IV, 1, 22. Gent. III, 1, 14. III, 2, 65. Wiv. V, 5, 50. Meas. II, 4, 119. Ado V, 1, 178. Mids. II, 2, 140. III, 2, 149. R3 I, 2, 17. Cor. I, 8, 2. Ant. I, 3, 48 etc. etc. Followed by an inf.: *I h. a breaking cause to be,* LLL V, 2, 355.

Hateful, 1) exciting and deserving hate, odious: Ven. 932. 994. Lucr. 161. 240. 771. 849. 1698. Gent. I, 2, 105. Meas. III, 1, 117. V, 107. LLL IV, 3, 157. John III, 1, 179. IV, 3, 77. H4A V, 2, 41. H4B I, 1, 66. H5 II, 1, 52. H6B III, 1, 76. III, 2, 93. H6C I, 1, 266. R3 I, 3, 215. III, 5, 80. V, 3, 190. Troil. IV, 4, 33. Tit. II, 3, 236. III, 1, 132. 296. V, 2, 200. Rom. III, 3, 108. IV, 5, 43. 52. Caes. V, 3, 67. Lr. IV, 2, 87. Ant. IV, 9, 9. Cymb. II, 1, 65. With *to: h. to me,* Wiv. III, 3, 85. John III, 3, 47. Rom. II, 2, 55. Tim. IV, 3, 51. Mcb. V, 7, 9.

2) exciting great dislike, disgusting, ugly (German *hässlich*): *full of h. fantasies,* Mids. II, 1, 258. *this h. fool,* IV, 1, 54. *this h. imperfection of her eyes,* 68. *h. docks,* H5 V, 2, 52 (cf. also H4B I, 1, 66).

3) full of hate, malignant: *little office the h. com-mons will perform for us,* R2 II, 2, 138. *hide thee from their h. looks,* H6B II, 4, 23. *the noblest h. love,* Troil. IV, 1, 33.

Hatefully, odiously, or malignantly: *h. at random dost thou hit,* Ven. 940.

Hater, one who hates, an enemy: *h. of love,* All's III, 3, 11. *I wore my life to spend upon his — s,* Ant. V, 1, 9.

Hatfield; *William of H.,* second son of Edward III: H6B II, 2, 12. 33.

Hatred, hate, extreme dislike, ill-will: Sonn. 93, 5. Mids. II, 1, 211. IV, 1, 149. Wint. III, 2, 103. H5 V, 2, 380. H6C IV, 1, 80. R3 I, 2, 234. I, 3, 65. 190. II, 1, 8. 23. IV, 4, 172. H8 I, 1, 107. Cor. III, 1, 20. *to bear h.,* Rom. II, 3, 53. *to hold in h.* Cor. II, 1, 261. Never with an objective genitive, but with *to: to urge his h. more to Clarence,* R3 I, 1, 147.

Hauf, the common pronunciation of *half,* blamed by Holofernes: LLL V, 1, 25.

Haught, haughty, arrogantly proud: R2 IV, 254 (Ff *haught-insulting*). H6B I, 3, 71 (F1 *haughtie*). H6C I, 1, 169. R3 II, 3, 28.

Haughtiness, arrogant pride: H4A III, 1, 185.

Haughty, 1) arrogantly proud, insolent: H4A V, 3, 11 (Qq *proud*). H6A I, 3, 23. 85. H6B I, 1, 174. I, 3, 71 (F2.3.4 *haught*). H6C I, 1, 267. R3 IV, 4, 502. Tit. I, 302. Rom. V, 3, 49.

2) high-spirited, lofty, adventurous: *will scourge with h. arms this hateful name,* H4A V, 2, 41. *in this h. great attempt they laboured to plant the rightful heir,* H6A II, 5, 79. *these h. words of hers have battered me,* III, 3, 78. *valiant and virtuous, full of h. courage,* IV, 1, 35. *whose humble means match not his h. mind,* R3 IV, 2, 37.

Haul (cf. *Hale*) to pull, to drag: — *ed thither by most mechanical and dirty hand,* H4B V, 5, 37 (Pistol's speech. Q *halde,* Ff *hall'd*; some M. Edd. *haled*).

Haunch, the hip: Wiv. V, 5, 28. As II, 1, 25. Figuratively, = the hind part, the rear: *thou art a summer bird, which ever in the h. of winter sings the lifting up of day,* H4B IV, 4, 92.

Haunt, subst. 1) a place much frequented: *I*

will spare your —s, Mids. II, 1, 142. *sequestration from open —s and popularity,* H5 I, 1, 59. *we talk here in the public h. of men,* Rom. III, 1, 53.

2) public resort, the coming in contact with many people: *our life exempt from public h.* As II, 1, 15. *should have kept short, restrained and out of h. this mad young man,* Hml. IV, 1, 18. *Dido and her Aeneas shall want troops, and all the h. be ours,* Ant. IV, 14, 54.

Haunt, vb. 1) tr. a) to frequent, to resort to much and often: *our court is —ed with a refined traveller of Spain,* LLL I, 1, 163. *the temple —ing martlet,* Mcb. I, 6, 4. Mostly in a bad sense: *thus still to h. my house,* Wiv. III, 4, 73. Meas. I, 3, 9. As III, 2, 377. Wint. IV, 3, 109. Used of spirits and spectres appearing in places or to persons: *this —ed grove,* Mids. III, 2, 5. Cymb. IV, 2, 217. V, 4, 133. *we are —ed,* Mids. III, 1, 108. *—ed by the ghosts they have deposed,* R2 III, 2, 158. Mcb. V, 7, 16. Lr. III, 6, 31. Oth. IV, 1, 153.

b) to follow importunately, to stick to; either as an obtrusive friend: *one that claims me, one that —s me,* Err. III, 2, 82. *do not h. me thus,* Mids. II, 2, 85. *a devil —s thee in the likeness of an old fat man,* H4A II, 4, 492. *she —s me in every place,* Oth. IV, 1, 136. 152. Or as an enemy: *I do h. thee in the battle thus,* H4A V, 3, 4. *that bloody strain that —ed us in our familiar paths,* H5 II, 4, 52. *how Diomed did h. you in the field,* Troil. V, 1, 10. V, 10, 28. Or as a vexatious thought or quality: *the least of which —ing a noble man loseth men's hearts,* H4A III, 1, 186. *suspicion always —s the guilty mind,* H6C V, 6, 11. *your beauty which did h. me in my sleep,* R3 I, 2, 122. *let sorrow h. thy bed,* IV, 1, 74.

2) intr. to be much about, to resort: *following where he —ed,* Compl. 130. *where they most breed and h.* Mcb. I, 6, 9. *to h. about my doors,* Oth. I, 1, 96.

Hautboy, a wind instrument: H4B III, 2, 351 (O. Edd. *hoeboy*).

Have (abbreviated to *ha* or *ha':* Wiv. III, 3, 18. 231. Shr. III, 2, 118. IV, 1, 61. V, 2, 37. All's V, 2, 40. Wint. I, 2, 267. II, 3, 114. IV, 3, 80. H5 IV, 7, 7. H6C IV, 5, 27. H8 V, 1, 173. Cor. I, 1, 229. II, 3, 82. Tim. II, 2, 48. III, 1, 25. 30. III, 2, 51. Caes. I, 3, 19. Hml. II, 2, 565. IV, 5, 64. IV, 7, 157. V, 1, 26. Ant. II, 6, 78. II, 7, 75. 111. IV, 8, 20. Cymb. IV, 2, 390 etc. Qq *ha,* Ff *have:* Ado III, 5, 34. H4B II, 4, 258. Oth. II, 3, 40. III, 1, 3. 35. IV, 2, 113. *ha't* rhyming to *Kate:* Shr. V, 2, 181. Corrupted to *a: she might a been a grandam,* LLL V, 2, 17. Qq *a,* Ff *ha:* Hml. IV, 5, 64. *Having* monosyll. in the beginning of the verse: Ven. 828. Tp. I, 2, 479. All's V, 3, 123. Hml. II, 1, 43 etc. cf. *Being*).

1) Auxiliary vb. used to form tenses: Ven. 2. 83. 97. 101. 103. 105. 203. 204. 357. 378. 399. 413. 429. 501. 502. 530. 547. 553. 572 etc. etc. Tp. I, 2, 1. 5. 28. 33. 44. 64. 131. 179. 193. 225. 232. 247. 296. 305. 345. 350. 394. 416. 433. 479. 482 etc. etc. *had* for *should have* or *would have: she had not brought forth thee,* Ven. 204. *I had peopled,* Tp. I, 2, 350. Gent. II, 4, 88. IV, 1, 35. IV, 4, 16. 17. Wiv. II, 2, 256. Meas. II, 1, 14. Err. III, 2, 151. IV, 1, 3. Hml. I, 1, 91 etc. The inf. of the perf. seemingly for that of the pres., if that which was expected or intended has not taken place: *my curtail dog that wont to have played, plays not at all,* Pilgr. 273. *I had other things to have spoken with her,* Wiv. IV, 5, 41. *we had like*

to have had our two noses snapped off, Ado V, 1, 115. *I did think to have beaten thee,* V, 4, 111. *with Demetrius thought to have spoke thereof,* Mids. I, 1, 112. *my purpose was not to have seen you here,* Merch. III, 2, 230. *if you had pleased to have defended it,* V, 204. *he was skilful enough to have lived still, if knowledge could be set up against mortality,* All's I, 1, 34. *you might have saved me my pains, to have taken it away yourself,* Tw. II, 2, 6 (= if you had taken). Wint. IV, 4, 750. H6A II, 5, 89. H8 IV, 2, 152. Hml. V, 1, 268. Ant. II, 2, 79. II, 6, 50. V, 1, 38. Cymb. III, 6, 48. V, 5, 66. Preceded by *I had thought* (cf. subst. *Thought*): *I had thought to have learned his health of you,* R2 II, 3, 24. *I had thought to have held my peace until you had drawn oaths from him,* Wint. I, 2, 28. *which he had thought to have murdered,* H6B II, 3, 107. *I had thought to have yerked him here under the ribs,* Oth. I, 2, 5. *I had thought to have held it poor,* Ant. III, 13, 186. cf. *I had thought I had had men of some understanding of my council,* H8 V, 3, 135. Similarly after *should* and *would: he told me Paris should have married Juliet,* Rom. V, 3, 78. *I hoped thou shouldst have been my Hamlet's wife,* Hml. V, 1, 267. *you would have married her most shamefully,* Wiv. V, 5, 234. *she would have made Hercules have turned spit,* Ado II, 1, 261. *I would have told you of good wrestling,* As I, 2, 116 (= was going to tell you, but was prevented). All's II, 3, 29. 44. Tw. V, 268. H8 V, 1, 119. Tim. III, 6, 22. Caes. II, 4, 4. Ant. III, 11, 56. *had been* = was or were, if the actual state is contrary to expectation: *I thought that all things had been savage here,* As II, 7, 107. *I thought your honour had already been at Shrewsbury,* H4A IV, 2, 58. *I did not think Master Silence had been a man of this mettle,* H4B V, 3, 40. cf. *I thought King Henry had resembled thee,* H6B I, 3, 56.

2) principal verb; a) to possess, to own: *what a horse should h.* Ven. 299. *hast thou a tongue?* 427. 433. *that thou hast her,* Sonn. 42, 1, 3. Tp. I, 2, 83. 341. 412. 466. Wiv. III, 3, 231. All's III, 2, 102. Troil. III, 3, 98. Cor. I, 1, 229. Ant. II, 7, 75 etc. Pass.: *whose worthiness gives scope, being had, to triumph,* Sonn. 52, 14. *had, having, and in quest to have,* 129, 10. *grief, being altogether had,* R2 III, 4, 15. *nought's had, all's spent,* Mcb. III, 2, 4. Prov. *have is have:* John I, 173. *To h. one's eyes, one's mouth,* see *Eye, Mouth.*

b) not to be without, not to want, as something that is connected with, or inherent in one: *—ing no defects,* Ven. 138. *the sea hath bounds,* 389. *I had my load,* 430. *whom thou hast aboard,* Tp. I, 1, 20. *he hath no drowning mark upon him,* 31. *who had some noble creature in her,* I, 2, 7. *had I not four women that tended me?* 46. 48. *he's a spirit of persuasion,* II, 1, 235. *Caliban has a new master,* II, 2, 189. *we have stomachs,* III, 3, 41. *now would I have thee to my tutor,* Gent. III, 1, 84. *nobody but has his fault,* Wiv. I, 4, 15. *she has a huswife's hand,* As IV, 3, 27. *he has no pace, but runs where he will,* All's IV, 5, 70. *the present sickness that I have,* R2 II, 1, 132. *he has a familiar under his tongue,* H6B IV, 7, 114. *let her have your knees,* Oth. II, 1, 84 etc. etc. *the world hath ending,* Ven. 12. *have care,* Tp. I, 1, 10. *I have great comfort from this fellow,* I, 1, 30. *have comfort,* I, 2, 25. *you have cause of joy,* II, 1, 1. *I have hope,* V, 308. *have you a mind to sink,* I, 1, 42. *have a false* *interpreter*, Gent. I, 2, 78. *my desires had instance*, Wiv. II, 2, 256. *let's ha' no more ado*, H6C IV, 5, 27. *let's ha' some sport*, Tim. II, 2, 48. *let me have war*, Cor. IV, 5, 236 (in the sense of *give*, q. v.). etc. cf. the respective substantives. With an inf.: *I have to show to the contrary*, Wiv. II, 1, 38 (= I can prove the contrary).

c) *to receive, to get: which thou unasked shalt have*, Ven. 102. 374. *you shall have a kiss*, 536. *he shall pay for him that hath him*, Tp. II, 2, 81. *I would my master had mistress Anne*, Wiv. III, 4, 108. *howsoever he hath had intelligence*, IV, 2, 94. *sixpence that I had o' Wednesday last*, Err. I, 2, 55. *the saddler had it, sir, I kept it not*, 57. *to pay thee that I never had*, IV, 1, 74. *Jack hath not Jill*, LLL V, 2, 885. *I no question make to have it* (money), Merch. I, 1, 185. *the —ing any of these lords*, I, 2, 109. *would he were gelt that had it*, V, 144. 158. 208. *you shall ha't* (a penny) All's V, 2, 40. *I sent thee sixpence for thy leman: hadst it?* Tw. II, 3, 26. 202. R2 I, 1, 126. H5 IV, 3, 48. H8 V, 1, 173. Cor. II, 3, 82. Tit. II, 3, 145. With *from: the heat I have from thence*, Ven. 195. *the sight whereof I think you had from me*, Adv V, 4, 25. *a had him from me Christian*, H4B II, 2, 76. cf. Sonn. 75, 12. With *of: he had of me a chain*, Err. IV, 1, 10. IV, 4, 138. V, 2. *the remuneration I had of thy master*, LLL V, 1, 76. *I had it of him*, Merch. V, 258. Tim. V, 1, 6. Cymb. V, 5, 136. With *where: where had he wine?* Tp. V, 278. *where had you this pretty weathercock?* Wiv. III, 2, 18. LLL IV, 3, 196. All's V, 3, 284. H4A IV, 2, 77. *wheresoever you had it*, Oth. IV, 1, 161. Passive: *no sooner had, past reason hated*, Sonn. 129, 6. 10. *the main consents are had*, All's V, 3, 69. *whose spiritual counsel had*, Wint. II, 1, 186. *a new link to the bucket must needs be had*, H4B V, 1, 24. *that had, give't these fellows*, Tim. II, 2, 238. cf. Sonn. 75, 12.

d) *to have received or obtained, to have got or gained: this wish I h.* Sonn. 37, 14. *now hast thou thy desire*, John I, 176. Hml. V, 2, 14. *you have your wish*, H8 III, 2, 44. Cymb. III, 5, 20. *if my young lord your son have not the day*, H4B I, 1, 52. Hence = to have got, as a blow or wound: *you have it full, Benedick*, Ado I, 1, 110. *is he gone and hath nothing?* Rom. III, 1, 95. *I have it, and soundly too*, 112. *then had you a cut*, Ant. I, 2, 173.

e) *to hear, to see, to find, to enjoy in any manner: let's ha't*, Shr. IV, 1, 61. *let's have a catch*, Tw. II, 3, 18. *let me h. it* (= tell it me) Wint. I, 2, 101. II, 1, 26. H8 II, 1, 145. *we'll ha't to-morrow night*, Hml. II, 2, 565. *will you ha' the truth on't?* V, 1, 26. *we will have more of this to-morrow*, Oth. I, 3, 379 (speak of it). *let's ha't*, Ant. II, 7, 111. *there shall you have me*, Tw. III, 3, 42 (meet me, find me). *she's neither fish nor flesh; a man knows not where to h. her*, H4A III, 3, 145 (nobody knows on what terms he is with her, how he ought to treat her; Germ.: *woran er mit ihr ist*). *thou shalt ha't*, Shr. V, 2, 181 (viz the kissing of Kate; or perhaps = thou shalt carry the prize).

f) *to understand, to know, to be expert in: have you the tongues?* Gent. IV, 1, 33. *he hath neither Latin, French nor Italian*, Merch. I, 2, 74. *I have the back-trick simply as strong as any man in Illyria*, Tw. I, 3, 131. *till he had both tune and words*, Wint. IV, 4, 619. *when she has so much English*, H8 V, 5, 15. *where have you this?* Ant. II, 1, 18.

Again = to have guessed, to have hit, to have found out: *when you find him out, you have him ever after*, All's III, 6, 101. *there thou hast it*, R3 IV, 2, 73. *you have it*, Tit. IV, 2, 24. *you have me; have you not?* Hml. II, 1, 68. *I ha't*, IV, 7, 157.

g) *to experience, to suffer: the heart hath treble wrong*, Ven. 329. *she had the wrong*, H6C IV, 1, 102. (cf. *Wrong*). *what foul play had we*, Tp. I, 2, 60. *let him have all the rigour of the law*, H6B I, 3, 199. *it smites me beneath the fall I have*, Ant. V, 2, 172.

h) *to hold, to keep: such sweet observance in this work was had*, Lucr. 1385. *hast the memory of Hermione in honour*, Wint V, 1, 50. *by that God that thou hast in reverence*, Tit. V, 1, 83. cf. *Better, Best, Rather*.

i) *to be under an obligation;* followed by an infinitive: *had his team to guide*, Ven. 179 and passim. *then had you indeed a cut, and the case to be lamented*, Ant. I, 2, 173 (the case had, or would have, to be lamented). Without an inf.: *now you have left your voices, I have no further with you*, Cor. II, 3, 181 (I have nothing more to do with you). Similarly: *I have nothing with this answer; these words are not mine*, Hml. III, 2, 101.

k) *to cause, to let, to get, to see;* followed by an inf. without *to: to have their sin remain untold*, Lucr. 753. *wouldst thou have me cast my love on him?* Gent. I, 2, 25. *which they would have the profferer con°true Ay*, 56. IV, 2, 70, 72. IV, 4, 112. V, 4, 35. Meas. I, 1, 15. III, 2, 3. Ado I, 1, 169. LLL IV, 3, 150. V, 1, 116. Mids. V, 158. Merch. II, 3, 8. II, 5, 50. As II, 3, 29. Tw. III, 4, 70. Wint. IV, 4, 806. H4B II, 1, 176. V, 2, 85. H6A V, 4, 70. H6B II, 1, 147. III, 1, 243. IV, 7, 145. H6C II, 6, 95. Cor. II, 2, 79. III, 2, 17. Tim. III, 1, 27. Caes. IV, 3, 243. Ant. V, 2, 11 etc. By an inf. with *to: what would your Grace have me to do in this?* Gent. III, 1, 80. *I would not have you to think*, Tw. V, 49. Cor. II, 2, 73. IV, 2, 36. Caes. II, 2, 38. Oth. IV, 2, 237. *to* omitted and inserted: *I wish no better than have him hold that purpose and to put it in execution*, Cor. II, 1, 256. Followed by a partic. pass.: *this dumb play had his acts made plain with tears*, Ven. 359. *the waves will have him seen no more*, 819. *the threshold grates the door to have him heard*, Lucr. 306. *shalt have thy trespass cited up in rhymes*, 524. *age in love loves not to have years told*, Sonn. 138, 12. Gent. II, 1, 134. II, 4, 123. III, 1, 98. IV, 4, 106. Wiv. II, 2, 73. III, 5, 7. IV, 2, 216. V, 5, 38. Meas. II, 1, 214. 264. III, 2, 187. IV, 2, 175. Err. IV, 4, 149. Ado III, 5, 51. LLL I, 2, 120. Merch. IV, 1, 46. As II, 1, 25. IV, 1, 97. 206. Tw. II, 5, 158. Wint. II, 3, 114. H6A I, 4, 37. III, 1, 83. 101. III, 3, 15. R3 IV, 2, 19. Troil. II, 2, 148. Ant. III, 13, 88 etc. Irregular position of the partic.: *the gods will have fulfilled their purposes*, Wint. V, 1, 36 (instead of: will have their purposes fulfilled). *desire him to have borne his helmet before him*, H5 V Chor. 17. cf. *to know what she would have given*, Wiv. II, 2, 208. *with sainted vow my faults to have amended*, All's III, 4, 7. Inversely: *which has my evils conjured to remembrance*, Wint. V, 3, 39 (= has conjured my evils). Followed by a noun or an adverb.: *I had rather have it a head*, Err. II, 2, 36. *I will have it no lay*, Cymb. I, 4, 159. *we'll have you merry*, Gent. IV, 2, 30. *thrice is he armed that hath his quarrel just*, H6B III, 2, 233. *I would not have it so*, Meas. I, 2, 71. *to have me home to dinner*,

Err. II, 2, 10. *to have my love to bed and to arise,* Mids. III, 1, 174. *have by some surgeon,* Merch. IV, 1, 257 (cause to be present). *we'll have thee to a couch,* Shr. Ind. 2, 39. *if I were covetous, as he will have me,* H6A III, 1, 30. *when Oxford had me down,* R3 II, 1, 112. *I would be sure to have all well,* Tit. V, 3, 31. *I would have had thee there,* Caes. II, 4, 4. *what wouldst thou have to Athens?* Tim. IV, 3, 287 (what commission have you to Athens?).

1) Joined to adverbs and prepositions; 1) *have after* = I'll follow, or let us follow: Hml. I, 4, 89. 2) *have at it* = I'll begin it, attempt it: *have at it with you,* Wint. IV, 4, 302 (I'll sing it with you). *have at it then, by leave,* Cymb. V, 5, 315 (I'll tell my story). *have at you,* properly = my aim is at you; hence = I speak to you, listen: *have at you, then, affection's men at arms,* LLL IV, 3, 290. Oftener = I shall hit you, take care, be warned: *have at thee with a downright blow,* H6B II, 3, 92. *now have at him,* IV, 2, 129. *and so have at thee,* H6C II, 4, 11. *have at you,* H8 III, 2, 309. V, 3, 113. *have at thee,* Troil. V, 4, 24. *have at you both,* V, 6, 11. *have at thee,* 13. Rom. I, 1, 79. V, 3, 70. Hml. V, 2, 313. Used in a fight of words: *have at you with a proverb,* Err. III, 1, 51. 52. *have at you for a bitter jest,* Shr. V, 2, 45. *have at the very eye of that proverb,* H5 III, 7, 129. *have at you with my wit,* Rom. IV, 5, 125. cf. *he that will caper with me for a thousand marks, let him lend me the money, and have at him,* H4B I, 2, 217. Substantively: *I'll venture one have at him,* H8 II, 2, 85. 3) *have to it* = I will, or let us, set to it: *and then have to it afresh,* Shr. I, 1, 143. *have to my widow,* IV, 5, 78. *ha' to thee, lad,* V, 2, 37 (= I drink to you, I pledge you). 4) *have through* = I'll take my way through: *have through the very middest of you,* H6B IV, 8, 63 (cf. Euphues' Golden Legacy, ed. Collier, p. 52: *I will have amongst you with my sword*). 5) *have with thee* or *with you* = take me with you, I'll go with you: Wiv. II, 1, 161. 229. 239. III, 2, 93. LLL IV, 2, 151. As I, 2, 268. H6A II, 4, 114. R3 III, 2, 92. Troil. V, 2, 185. Cor. II, 1, 286. Oth. I, 2, 53. Cymb. IV, 4, 50.

Have-at-him, attack, thrust, stroke: *I'll venture one h.,* H8 II, 2, 85 (cf. *Have* 2, 1, 2. F1 *I'll venture one; have at him.* F2.3.4 *I'll venture one heave at him*).

Haven, harbour, port, place of safety: Shr. V, 1, 131. R2 I, 3, 276. H6C IV, 7, 8. Oth. II, 1, 3 (only in Q1; the other O. Edd. *heaven*). Ant. IV, 10, 7. Cymb. I, 1, 171. I, 3, 1. III, 2, 63. Per. I, 2, 49. cf. *Milford Haven.*

Haver, possessor: *valour is the chiefest virtue and most dignifies the h.* Cor. II, 2, 89.

Having, subst. 1) the getting possession of: *choke their service up even with the h.* (promotion) As II, 3, 62. *I wish the h. of it,* Per. II, 1, 145.

2) possession, property, estate: *the gentleman is of no h.* Wiv. III, 2, 73. *your h. in beard,* As III, 2, 396. *my h. is not much,* Tw. III, 4, 379. *of what h., breeding,* Wint. IV, 4, 740. *our content is our best h.* H8 II, 3, 23. *pared my present —s,* III, 2, 159. Cor. V, 2, 62. Tim. II, 2, 153. V, 1, 18. Mcb. I, 3, 56. Oth. IV, 3, 92 (= allowance, pin-money). Cymb. I, 2, 19.

3) endowment: *whose rarest —s made the blossoms dote,* Compl. 235. *how dearly ever parted, how much in h., or without or in,* Troil. III, 3, 97.

Haviour, (cf. *Behaviour*) external carriage and deportment, as expressive of sentiments and disposition: *I will keep the h. of reputation,* Wiv. I, 3, 86 (Nym's speech). *with the same h. that your passion bears goes on my master's grief,* Tw. III, 4, 226. *the lusty h. of his son,* R2 I, 3, 77. *thou mayst think my h. light,* Rom. II, 2, 99 (only in the spurious Q1; the rest of O. Edd. *behaviour*). *the dejected h. of the visage,* Hml. I, 2, 81. *so neighboured to his youth and h.* II, 2, 12 (Ff *humour*). *put thyself into a h. of less fear,* Cymb. III, 4, 9.

Havoc, subst. indiscriminate slaughter, merciless destruction: *wide h. made for bloody power to rush upon your peace,* John II, 220. *cry h.* 357. *pellmell h. and confusion,* H4A V, 1, 82. *cry h.* Cor. III, 1, 275. Caes. III, 1, 273. *this quarry cries on h.* Hml. V, 2, 375. With *of: nor fortune made such h. of my means,* Ado IV, 1, 197. — *who hath made this h. with them?* Tw. V, 209 (= who has brought them so low?)

Havoc, vb. to destroy, to waste: *to tear and h. more than she can eat,* H5 I, 2, 173.

Hawk, subst. a bird of prey, Falco candicans, used in sport to catch other birds: Lucr. 694. Sonn. 91, 4. Wiv. III, 3, 247. Ado III, 4, 55. Shr. Ind. 2, 45. V, 2, 72. H5 III, 7, 16. H6A II, 4, 11. H6B II, 1, 10. Hml. II, 2, 397.*

Hawk, vb. to fly hawks at birds, to practise falconry: Shr. Ind. 2, 45. H6B I, 2, 58. II, 1, 50. *to h. at* = to fly at, to attack on the wing: *a falcon was by a mousing owl —ed at and killed,* Mcb. II, 4, 13.

Hawking, hawklike, keen: *his h. eye,* All's I, 1, 105.

Hawking, forcing up phlegm, clearing the voice by hemming: *without h. or spitting or saying we are hoarse,* As V, 3, 12.

Hawthorn, the plant Crataegus Oxyacantha, white-thorn: As III, 2, 380. Lr. III, 4, 47. 102. *h. brake,* Mids. III, 1, 4. *h. bud,* Wiv. III, 3, 77. Mids. I, 1, 185. *h. bush,* H6C II, 5, 42.

Hay, grass dried for fodder: Mids. IV, 1, 37. Wint. IV, 3, 12. H6C IV, 8, 61. Mcb. I, 3, 18. Lr. II, 4, 128.

Hay, a hedge, a fence: *dance the h.* = dance in a ring, LLL V, 1, 161 (Dull's speech).

Hay, (from the Italian *hai,* habes, thou hast it) a home-thrust in fencing: *the punto reverso! the h.* Rom. II, 4, 27.

Hay-stack, a large pile of hay: Tit. V, 1, 133.

Hazard, subst. 1) chance, risk: Wint. III, 2, 169. John I, 119. H4B IV, 1, 15. R3 V, 4, 10. Cor. IV, 1, 28. Tim. V, 4, 34. Ant. III, 7, 48. *to make a h.:* Lucr. 155. Merch. II, 1, 45. John II, 71. H4A I, 3, 128 (Qq *I make a h.,* Ff *it be with h.*). *to put in h.* = to risk: *this mutiny were better put in h. than stay for greater,* Cor. II, 3, 264. *upon all —s* = at any risk, John V, 6, 7. *all is on the h.* Caes. V, 1, 68. *set so rich a main on the nice h. of one doubtful hour,* H4A IV, 1, 48. *sets all on h.* Troil. Prol. 22. With *of: without apparent h. of his life,* Gent. III, 1, 116. H4A I, 3, 128. Cor. III, 2, 61.

2) danger: *I'll lay myself in h.* Meas. IV, 2, 166. *to the extreme edge of h.* All's III, 3, 6. *we stand much h., if they bring not Timon,* Tim. V, 2, 5. *thorough the —s of this untrod state,* Caes. III, 1, 136. *endure h. so dangerous,* Hml. III, 3, 6.

3) the thing risked, the stake in gaming: *bring*

your latter h. back again, Merch. I, 1, 151. *a set shall strike his father's crown into the h.* H5 I, 2, 263 (German: *in die Schanze*, i. e. Chance, *schlagen*).*

4) evil chance, loss: *the h. therefore due fall on me by the hands of Romans*, Cymb. IV, 4, 46. *think death no h. in this enterprise*, Per. I, 1, 5.

5) a game at dice: *who will go to h. with me for twenty prisoners? You must first go yourself to h.*, *ere you have them*, H5 III, 7, 93. 95.

Hazard, vb. to venture, to risk: Gent. V, 4, 21. Err. I, 1, 132. Merch. II, 7, 9. All's II, 1, 186. H6A IV, 6, 33. 40. Cor. IV, 7, 25. Tim. III, 5, 37. IV, 3, 338. *should h. such a place with one of an ingraft infirmity*, Oth. II, 3, 144. *the circle of the Ptolemies now —ed to thy grace*, Ant. III, 12, 19 (staked and lost to thee, as at gaming). *would h. the winning both of first and last*, Cymb. I, 4, 101. Absolutely: *comes to h. for my worthless self*, Merch. II, 9, 18. *pause a day before you h.* III, 2, 2.

Hazel, adj. light-brown like the hazel-nut: *h. eyes*, Rom. III, 1, 22.

Hazel-nut, the fruit of Corylus Avellana: Shr. II, 257. Rom. I, 4, 67.

Hazel-twig, a branch of Corylus Avellana: Shr. II, 255.

He, interj. of laughter, when added to *ha:* Ado IV, 1, 23. Troil. III, 1, 133.

He, obj. case *him*, pron. of the 3 d person masc. sing. Corrupted to *a* (see *A*); *him* to *'em:* Tp. III, 2, 3; cf. II, 2, 181. *He* for *him:* thus *he that overruled I overswayed*, Ven. 109. *which, of he or Adrian, first begins to crow*, Tp. II, 1, 28 (cf. the French *qui de lui ou d'Adrien;* and: *to try whose right, of thine or mine, is most in Helena*, Mids. III, 2, 336). *there is such a league between my good man and he*, Wiv. III, 2, 26. *and he my husband best of all affects*, IV, 4, 87. *my soul hates nothing more than he*, As I, 1, 172. *not by Phoebus, he, that wandering knight*, H4A I, 2, 16. *cursed the gentle gusts and he that loosed them*, H6B III, 2, 89. *Achilles hath inveigled his fool from him. Who? Thersites? He.* Troil. II, 3, 101. *worshipped of that we hold an idol more than he*, 199. *I would wish me only he*, Cor. I, 1, 236. *no man like he doth grieve my heart*, Rom. III, 5, 83. *'tis better thee without than he within*, Mcb. III, 4, 14. *from the first corse till he that died to-day*, Hml. I, 2, 105. *I do not think so fair an outward... endows a man but he*, Cymb. I, 1, 24. *that I kiss aught but he*, II, 3, 153. *Him* for *he: him in eye, still him in praise*, H8 I, 1, 30. *damned be him that first cries Hold*, Mcb. V, 8, 34. Mostly by attraction: *abide all three distracted.... but chiefly him that you termed the good old lord Gonzalo*, Tp. V, 1, 15. *better than him I am before knows me*, As I, 1, 46. *him that thou magnifiest lies here at our feet*, H6A IV, 7, 75. *him I accuse the city ports by this hath entered*, Cor. V, 6, 5. *him you would sound.... he closes with you*, Hml. II, 1, 42. *when him we serve's away*, Ant. III, 1, 15.

1) referring to a male person named before: Ven. 4. 5. 6. 30. 36. 42. 43 etc. etc. Superfluous: *king Pandion he is dead*, Pilgr. 395. *like sir Actaeon he*, Wiv. II, 1, 122 (Pistol's speech). *which, God he kows, I saw not*, Err. V, 229; cf. John V, 7, 60; H6C I, 4, 129; R3 III, 1, 10. 26; III, 7, 235. *the king he is hunting*, LLL IV, 3, 1. *the third he capered*, V, 2, 113. *Leander he would have lived*, As IV, 1, 100. All's III,

6, 116. III, 7, 8. 17. Tw. I, 2, 4. R2 III, 4, 83. H4A III, 2, 60. H5 II, 3, 5. H6B III, 1, 222. R3 IV, 4, 65. Rom. III, 1, 169. IV, 4, 26. Lr. II, 1, 124. 2, 104. Cymb. I, 1, 40. Omitted: *was affianced to her by oath*, Meas. III, 1, 222. *left her in her tears*, 234. *poor fellow, never joyed*, H4A II, 1, 13. *which if granted, as he made semblance of his duty, would have put his knife into him*, H8 I, 2, 198. *I'ld rather than the worth of thrice the sum, had sent to me first*, Tim. III, 3, 23. Particularly before *has* (generally written *ha's* or *h'as*): *has censured him already*, Meas. I, 4, 72. Shr. IV, 4, 78. All's IV, 3, 116. 298. Tw. I, 5, 156. V, 178. 201. 293. H6B IV, 2, 97. H8 I, 3, 59. III, 1, 119. V, 5, 76. Cor. I, 3, 65. III, 1, 161. Tim. III, 2, 39. III, 3, 13. III, 5, 63. IV, 3, 454. 476. Lr. II, 4, 293.

2) denoting God, by eminence: *He that might the vantage best have took*, Meas. II, 2, 74. 76. *He that doth the ravens feed*, As II, 3, 43. *by Him that made us all*, H6C II, 2, 124. *with Him above to ratify the work*, Mcb. III, 6, 32.

3) man, male person: *I am that he, that unfortunate he*, As III, 2, 414. *I'll bring mine action on the proudest he that stops my way*, Shr. III, 2, 236. *the proudest he that holds up Lancaster*, H6C I, 1, 46. *here I stand to answer thee, or any he the proudest of thy sort*, II, 2, 97. *now let me see the proudest he but wag his finger at thee*, H8 V, 3, 131. *if I spared any, either young or old, he or she*, V, 4, 25. *Mantua's law is death to any he that utters them*, Rom. V, 1, 67.

4) this man, that man; before a relative: *he that writes of you*, Sonn. 84, 7. *he whom of all the world I loved*, Tp. I, 2, 68. II, 2, 80. Gent. I, 1, 40. Err. I, 2, 33. Ado II, 1, 7. As I, 1, 61. II, 3, 15. II, 7, 98. H6B I, 3, 75 (*he of these that can do most*) etc. etc. *who is he so fond will be the tomb of his self-love?* Sonn. 3, 7. *what's he?* Ado II, 1, 137 (= what man is that of whom you are speaking?). *what is he at the gate?* Tw. I, 5, 124. *are not you he that frights the maidens?* Mids. II, 1, 34 (= is it not you that etc.). *are you he that hangs the verses on the trees?* As III, 2, 411. *I'll have no father, if you be not he: I'll have no husband, if you be not he*, V, 4, 128. *by these gloves, then, 'twas he*, Wiv. I, 1, 168. *was he angry? So he says here*, Troil. I, 2, 56. *the fool will not, he there, that he*, II, 1, 91. *he and myself have travailed in the great shower of your gifts*, Tim. V, 1, 72. *he in the red face had it*, Wiv. I, 1, 173. *he of Wales that gave Amamon the bastinado*, H4A IV, 4, 370. *he of Winchester is held no great good lover of the archbishop's*, H8 IV, 1, 103. *the general's disdained by him one step below, he by the next*, Troil. I, 3, 130. *O, Nicholas Hopkins? He.* H8 I, 1, 221. Cor. III, 1, 57. Lr. II, 4, 114.

5) one: *like him that travels I return again*, Sonn. 109, 6. *this is he that kissed his hand away in courtesy*, LLL V, 2, 323. *he murder cries*, Mids. III, 2, 26. *or I am deceived by him that in such intelligence hath seldom failed*, All's IV, 5, 87. *he... he* = one... another: *featured like him, like him with friends possessed*, Sonn. 29, 6. *why he cannot abide a gaping pig, why he a harmless necessary cat, why he a woollen bag-pipe*, Merch. IV, 1, 54. *but he as he, the heavier for a whore*, Troil. IV, 1, 66 (the one as well as the other). *condemning some to death, and some to exile; ransoming him or pitying, threatening the other*, Cor. I, 6, 36 (cf. *his: desire his jewels and this other's house*, Mcb. IV, 3, 80).

6) *him* = himself, not only after prepositions: Tp. I, 1, 31. Gent. I, 3, 59. IV, 4, 13 etc. but after verbs: *betake him to retire*, Lucr. 174. *he did complain him*, 845. Gent. IV, 2, 47. Merch. III, 2, 235. As I, 1, 134. II, 7, 15. IV, 1, 104. IV, 3, 92. Shr. Ind. I, 76. 122. Shr. I, 1, 23. 174. Wint. IV, 4, 562. H4A III, 2, 180. H4B I, 2, 158. H6A II, 4, 14. H6B I, 1, 184. III, 2, 25. IV, 9, 9. V, 3, 5. R3 III, 2, 8. H8 I, 2, 204. II, 1, 162. Troil. I, 2, 300. V, 2, 183. Rom. I, 4, 34. I, 5, 68. II, 1, 4. Caes. I, 2, 325. I, 3, 156 etc. Dative: *let every soldier hew him down a bough*, Mcb. V, 4, 4.

Head, subst. 1) the part of the animal that contains the brain and the organs of the senses: Ven. 223. 296. Tp. II, 1, 117. 209. III, 2, 69. III, 3, 47. Gent. II, 4, 70. III, 1, 192. Wiv. IV, 4, 50 etc. etc. *to break a person's h.* (cf. *Break*): Wiv. I, 1, 125. Tw. V, 178. 188. H4A III, 1, 242. H4B II, 1, 97. III, 2, 33. *to lose the h.* (= to be beheaded): Meas. V, 71. 493. R2 III, 2, 142. H6A II, 5, 54. H6B I, 2, 34. R3 III, 4, 40. IV, 4, 242. *to hang the h.*, a gesture expressing sorrow (cf. *Hang*): Ven. 666. H6A III, 2, 124. H6B I, 2, 2. H8 III, 1, 11. 153. V, 5, 33. Tit. IV, 4, 70. Oth. IV, 3, 32. *to hold up h.*, expressing confidence and courage: *whether our present five and twenty thousand may hold up h. without Northumberland*, H4B I, 3, 17; or simply = to look up: *hold up thy head, vile Scot, or thou art like never to hold it up again*, H4A V, 4, 39. *to shake the h.*, expressing either disapprobation and denial: Ado II, 1, 377. John IV, 2, 231. Tim. II, 2, 211. Caes. I, 2, 286. Lr. IV, 6, 122. or grief and pity: *she shakes her h.* Ven. 223. *to shake the h., relent and sigh*, Merch. III, 3, 15. *what dost thou mean by shaking of thy h.?* John III, 1, 19. *thou shakest thy h. and holdest it fear or sin to speak a truth*, H4B I, 1, 95. *shakes his h. and trembling stands aloof*, H6B I, 1, 227. *shake your h. and call us wretches*, R3 II, 2, 5. *I have shook my h. and wept*, Tim. II, 2, 146. *let's shake our —s and say, We have seen better days*, IV, 2, 25. or = to nod: *and thought thee happy when I shook my h.* H6B IV, 1, 55. *to wave the h.* = to nod slowly and significantly: *waving thy h., which often, thus, correcting thy stout heart, now humble*, Cor. III, 2, 77. *thrice his h. thus waving up and down*, Hml. II, 1, 93. *from h. to foot:* Err. III, 2, 115. Troil. II, 1, 29. Hml. I, 2, 228. Ant. V, 2, 239. Cymb. I, 6, 19. *from* omitted: *h. to foot now is he total gules*, Hml. II, 2, 478. *from h. to heel*, Wint. IV, 4, 229. *from the crown of his h. to the sole of his foot*, Ado III, 2, 9. *o'er h. and ears* = entirely: *o'er h. and ears a forked one*, Wint. I, 2, 186. *by the h. and shoulders* = headlong: *thrust virtue out of our hearts by the h. and shoulders*, Wiv. V, 5, 156. *draw your arrows to the h.* R3 V, 3, 339 (bend your bows with all your might). *as true a dog as ever fought at h.* Tit. V, 1, 102 (as attacked his adversary at the front). *thou art not so long by the h. as honorificabilitudinitatibus*, LLL V, 1, 44 (Costard's speech; = that word is longer than you by the measure of a head). *thy eyes are almost set in thy h.* Tp. III, 2, 10. *hast thou never an eye in thy h.?* H4A II, 1, 32. *your death hath eyes in's h. then*, Cymb. V, 4, 184. *keep a good tongue in your h.* Tp. III, 2, 40. 121. *I have ne'er a tongue in my h.* Merch. II, 2, 166. *this tongue that runs so roundly in thy h.* R2 II, 1, 122. *with ne'er a tooth in her h.* Shr. I. 2, 80. All's II, 3, 49. *teeth hadst thou in thy h.*

H6C V, 6, 53. *lay their —s together* = consult secretly, conspire: Shr. I, 2, 139. H6B III, 1, 165. IV, 8, 61. *to turn h.* = to face the enemy: *turns h. against the lion's armed jaws*, H4A III, 2, 102. *turn h. and stop pursuit*, H5 II, 4, 69. *by my h.*, used as an oath: Troil. II, 3, 95. Rom. III, 1, 38. Considered as the seat of thought: *his h. is light*, Err. V, 72. *drunken —s*, Tw. V, 412. *I have a h. that will find out logs*, Rom. IV, 4, 17. *I have matter in my h. against you*, Wiv. I, 1, 127 (quibbling). *the matter's in my h. and in my heart*, As III, 5, 137. *'tis in my h. to do my master good*, Shr. II, 408 (= I have a design, a plan). *he's sudden, if a thing comes in his h.* H6C V, 5, 86. Mcb. III, 4, 139. Oth. IV, 2, 15.

Pars pro toto; *head* = the whole person: *take counsel of some wiser h.* Pilgr. 303. *as tall... as any is between this and his h.* Wiv. I, 4, 27. *'fore all the Greekish —s, which with one voice call Agamemnon h. and general*, Troil. I, 3, 221. *let our best —s know, that to-morrow the last of many battles we mean to fight*, Ant. IV, 1, 10. *take your houses over your —s*, H6B IV, 8, 31 (i. e. which shelter you). *I'll blast your harvest, if your h. were laid*, H6C V, 7, 21 (if you were dead); cf. H6A V, 3, 26. *guard thy h.* H6A I, 3, 87. *I know not where to hide my h.* Tp. II, 2, 23. LLL V, 2, 86. 635. Mids. III, 2, 406. R2 III, 3, 6. H4A I, 3, 106. H6A I, 5, 39. H6B V, 1, 85. Troil. IV, 4, 139. Caes. IV, 3, 16. *till then not show my h.* Sonn. 26, 14. Merch III, 1, 48. R2 V, 6, 44. Troil. V, 6, 1. Rom. V, 3, 306. *betted much money on his h.* H4B III, 2, 50. *wager on your —s*, Hml. IV, 7, 135. V, 2, 106. *to the h. of Angelo accuse him home and home*, Meas. IV, 3, 147 (= without reserve, without any fear of his person and power). *know, Claudio, to thy h.* Ado V, 1, 62. *I'll avouch it to his h.* Mids. I, 1, 106. *whose wraths else falls upon your —s*, Tp. III, 3, 81. *pour your graces upon my daughter's h.* Wint. V, 3, 123. Gent. III, 1, 19. Wiv. II, 1, 191. Mids. IV, 1, 160. Merch. IV, 1, 206. All's I, 1, 79. III, 2, 32. Wint. V, 2, 123. John I, 76. III, 1, 193. R2 V, 1, 69. V, 6, 36. H5 II, 4, 105. IV Chor. 31. H6C I, 4, 168. II, 2, 129. R3 V, 3, 206. H8 V, 4, 83. Hml. I, 5, 79 etc. Inversely: *this present enterprise set off his h.* H4A V, 1, 103.

Totum pro parte; *head* for *ear:* *a lover's ear will hear the lowest sound, when the suspicious h. of theft is stopped*, LLL IV, 3, 336. *that the appalled air may pierce the h. of the great combatant*, Troil. IV, 5, 5. *loud music is too harsh for ladies' —s*, Per. II, 3, 97 (cf. Cymb. III, 4, 178). For *mouth:* *those viands which I heaved to h.* Cymb. V, 5, 157.

2) **the horns of a deer:** *a buck of the first h.* LLL IV, 2, 10 (so a buck was called in his fifth year). *turn on the bloody hounds with —s of steel*, H6A IV, 2, 51. cf. the quibbles in Troil: *we lose our —s to gild his horns*, IV, 5, 31. *you fillip me o' the h. It were no match, your nail against his horn*, 45. 46.

3) **chief, leader, commander:** *he is his wife's h.* Meas. IV, 2, 4. Shr. V, 2, 147. *as we, under heaven, are supreme h.* John III, 1, 155. H5 II, 4, 73. H6B II, 1, 170. Troil. I, 3, 222. Cor. V, 6, 91. Hml. I, 3, 24. Adjectively: *which is the h. lady?* LLL IV, 1, 43.

4) **any thing resembling the head of an animal;** a **bud:** *whose settled visage nips youth i' the h.* Meas. III, 1, 91. the **point of an arrow:** *his best arrow*

with the golden h. Mids. I, 1, 170. *forked —s*, As II, 1, 24. the knob of a pin: LLL V, 2, 615. H4A IV, 2, 24. H4B IV, 3, 59. the purulent top of an ulcer: *foul sin gathering h. shall break into corruption,* R2 V, 1, 58. H4B III, 1, 76. Hence *to gather to a h.* = to become ripe: *now doth my project gather to a h.* Tp. V, 1.

5) the top, the summit: *set on the h. of a wasps' nest,* Wint. IV, 4, 813. *though palaces and pyramids do slope their —s to their foundations,* Mcb. IV, 1, 58. Hml. V, 1, 276. Lr. IV, 1, 76. Oth. I, 3, 141. Per. I, 4, 24. Used of waters: *Severn hid his crisp h.* H4A I, 3, 106. *the watery kingdom, whose ambitious h. spits in the face of heaven,* Merch. II, 7, 44. Metaphorically: *set quarrelling upon the h. of valour,* Tim. III, 5, 28 (think it the crown and top of valour). *the very h. and front of my offending has this extent,* Oth. I, 3, 80 (this is its height, as it were, and breadth). *on horror's h. horrors accumulate,* III, 3, 370.

6) a headland, promontory: *from the h. of Actium beat the approaching Caesar,* Ant. III, 7, 52.

7) source: *and find your salt tears' h.* All's I, 3, 178. *fetch from false Mowbray their first h. and spring,* R2 I, 1, 97. III, 3, 108. Rom. V, 3, 218. Mcb. II, 3, 103. Hml. I, 1, 106. II, 2, 55.

8) liberty of motion (a term of horsemanship), free scope, licence: *give him h.: I know he'll prove a jade,* Shr. I, 2, 249. *with that he gave his able horse the h.* H4B I, 1, 43. *hast given unto the house of York such h. as thou shalt reign but with their sufferance,* H6C I, 1, 233. *makes it take h. from all indifferency, from all direction, purpose, course, intent,* John II, 579. *to shorten you, for taking so the h., your whole —'s length,* R2 III, 3, 14.

9) armed force: *before I drew this gallant h. of war,* John V, 2, 113. H4A IV, 4, 28. *by raising of a h.* H4A I, 3, 284. V, 1, 66. H8 II, 1, 108. *made h. against my power,* H4A III, 1, 64. H4B I, 1, 168. Caes. IV, 1, 42. Oth. I, 3, 275 (metaphorically). *if we can make a h.* H4A IV, 1, 80. Cor. II, 2, 92. *making another h. to fight again,* H6C II, 1, 141. *Aufidius had made new h.* Cor. III, 1, 1. *make some stronger h.* Cymb. IV, 2, 139. *to seek out this h. of safety,* H4A IV, 3, 103. *a h. of gallant warriors,* IV, 4, 25. *a mighty and a fearful h.* III, 2, 167. *his divisions are in three —s,* H4B I, 3, 71. *for which we have in h. assembled them,* H5 II, 2, 18. *the French have gathered h.* H6A I, 4, 100. H6B IV, 5, 10. Tit. IV, 4, 63. *Laertes, in a riotous h., o'erbears your officers,* Hml. IV, 5, 101. *the powers will soon be drawn to h.* Cymb. III, 5, 25.

Head, vb. to behead, to decapitate: Meas. II, 1, 250. 251.

Headborough, a kind of village-mayor: Shr. Ind. 1, 12 (M. Edd. *third-borough*).

Headed, furnished with a head or top: *h. evils,* As II, 7, 67 (ulcers).

Headland; so by agriculturists a strip of unploughed land is called at the end of furrows, but it must in Sh. have another meaning: *shall we sow the h. with wheat?* H4B V, 1, 16 (perhaps a tract of land projecting into an expanse of waters).*

Headless, 1) having no head: Mids. III, 1, 112. H6B I, 2, 65. Cymb. IV, 2, 308. V, 5, 299.

2) having no chief: Tit. I, 186.

Headlong, adv. with the head foremost: R2 I, 2, 52. V, 1, 65. H6A I, 1, 149. Tit. V, 3, 132. Lr.

IV, 6, 24. Hence = without ceremony: *hence will I drag thee h. by the heels,* H6B IV, 10, 86.

Headlong, adj. precipitate, rash: *the h. fury of his speed,* Lucr. 501.

Headlugged, dragged, led by the head: *the h. bear,* Lr. IV, 2, 42.

Headly, reading of F1 in H5 III, 3, 32; F2.3.4 and M. Edd. *heady,* q.v.

Head-piece, armour for the head, helmet: H5 III, 7, 149. Lr. III, 2, 26; cf. 28. Used of the skull as containing the brain and seat of thought: *some severals of h. extraordinary,* Wint. I, 2, 227.

Head-shake, a significant shake of the head: Hml. I, 5, 174.

Headsman, executioner: All's IV, 3, 342.

Head-stall, that part of a bridle which covers the head: Shr. III, 2, 58.

Headstrong, obstinate, stubborn, ungovernable: Meas. I, 3, 20. Err. II, 1, 15. Shr. IV, 1, 212. V, 2, 130. Tw. III, 4, 224. H4B IV, 4, 62. H6B I, 3, 178. III, 1, 356. Troil. III, 2, 131. *how now, my h.!* Rom. IV, 2, 16.

Heady, impetuous, precipitate, hasty: H4A II, 3, 58. H5 I, 1, 34. III, 3, 32 (F1 *headly*). Compar. *—ier,* Lr. II, 4, 111.

Heady-rash, hasty, inconsiderate: Err. V, 216.

Heal, 1) tr. to cure, to restore to soundness: Lucr. 731. Sonn. 34, 8. Gent. I, 2, 115. Wiv. III, 4, 6. Meas. III, 1, 245. Merch. III, 1, 65. John V, 2, 14. H4B I, 2, 167. H5 V, 1, 62. H6C IV, 8, 41. R3 II, 2, 125. Tit. V, 3, 148. Tim. II, 1, 24. Mcb. IV, 3, 156. Ant. II, 2, 22. *to h. up:* As III, 5, 117. John II, 550.

2) to grow sound: Troil. III, 3, 229. Cor. II, 2, 73. Oth. II, 3, 377.

Health, 1) freedom from sickness: Sonn. 45, 12. 140, 8. Gent. III, 1, 57. Ado V, 1, 334. LLL V, 2, 834. Shr. Ind. 1, 121. All's II, 1, 171–II, 3, 70. John III, 4, 113. V, 2, 21. H4A IV, 1, 27. H4B I, 1, 164. I, 2, 114. IV, 2, 79. IV, 5, 227. 229. H5 IV, 1, 274. R3 I, 3, 2. 35. III, 1, 67. Troil. II, 3, 120. Cor. II, 1, 126. Rom. I, 1, 186. Caes. II, 1, 235. Mcb. III, 1, 107. III, 4, 39. 120. V, 3, 52. Lr. I, 1, 59. II, 4, 108. III, 6, 20. Ant. II, 5, 56. Cymb. III, 2, 31. IV, 2, 31. *she has her h.* All's II, 4, 2. Wint. IV, 4, 414. *he's much out of h.* Tim. III, 4, 72. *if it be so far beyond his h.* 75. *in h.* Gent. II, 4, 124. Mids. IV, 1, 179. All's II, 1, 7. R2 II, 1, 92. H4B IV, 4, 106. H5 I, 2, 18. III, 6, 157. R3 II, 4, 40. Caes. II, 1, 257. *in good h.* Gent. II, 4, 50. H8 IV, 2, 124. Per. IV, 6, 25. *in bodily h.* H4B II, 2, 111.

Sometimes = any state of the functions of the body: *to have learned his h. of you,* R2 II, 3, 24. *his h. is well,* Tim. III, 1, 12. *my long sickness of h. and living now begins to mend,* V, 1, 190. *his h., beseech you,* Cymb. I, 6, 56.

2) welfare, prosperity: *we have been praying for our husbands' h.* Merch. V, 114. *whose h. and royalty I pray for,* H8 II, 3, 73. *justice lives in Saturninus' h.* Tit. IV, 4, 24. *to the state's best h.* Tim. II, 2, 206. *have mind upon your h., tempt me no further,* Caes. IV, 3, 36. *the safety and h. of his whole state,* Hml. I, 3, 21. *be thou a spirit of h. or goblin damned,* I, 4, 40. *his (age's) sables and his weeds importing h. and graveness,* IV, 7, 82. *reasons importing Denmark's h.* V, 2, 21. Used in salutations, = hail: *h. to thy person!* Lucr. 1305. *h. to my sovereign!* H4B IV, 4, 81. H6A I, 1, 57. H8 II, 2, 62. Troil. IV, 1, 10. *so long, h.!* IV,

1, 15. *all h. unto my gracious sovereign*, H6B III, 1, 82. R3 IV, 3, 23 (Qq *hail*). *h., at your bidding, serve your majesty*, All's II, 1, 18. *sweet h. and fair desires consort your grace*, LLL II, 178. *more h. and happiness betide my liege than* ..., R2 III, 2, 91. *h. and fair greeting from our general*, H4B IV, 1, 27. V, 3, 54. H5 V, 2, 3. H6B IV, 9, 7. V, 1, 124. R3 III, 1, 18. Tim. III, 5, 5. Mcb. III, 4, 87. In drinking, = toast: Meas. I, 2, 39. Shr. III, 2, 172. H8 I, 4, 96. Rom. I, 4, 85. Tim. I, 2, 54. 57. *to drink a person's h.* Ant. I, 2, 12. *no jocund h. that Denmark drinks*, Hml. I, 2, 125. *to drink a h.* or *—s to*: Shr. III, 2, 198. Tw. I, 3, 40. H8 I, 4, 105. Per. II, 3, 52. *to give a h.*, in the same sense: H4B V, 3, 25. Ant. II, 7, 57. *I have a h. for you. I shall take it*, Ant. II, 6, 142. *carouses to our mistress' h.* Shr. I, 2, 277. *a h. to all*, Shr. V, 2, 51. H4B IV, 2, 78. Hml. V, 2, 294. Oth. II, 3, 32. 88. Ant. II, 7, 33. 90. *and to you all good h.* H8 I, 4, 38.

Healthful, 1) free from disease, sound: Sonn. 118, 11. All's II, 3, 54. H8 I, 1, 3. Caes. II, 1, 319. Hml. III, 4, 141. Oth. III, 4, 147. Ant. II, 5, 38.

2) wholesome, salutary: *a bath and h. remedy for men diseased*, Sonn. 154, 11. *makes us early stirrers, which is both h. and good husbandry*, H5 IV, 1, 7. *gave h. welcome to their shipwrecked guests*, Err. I, 1, 115 (F2. 3. 4 *helpful*).

Health-giving, wholesome: *thy h. air*, LLL I, 1, 236.

Healthsome, wholesome: Rom. IV, 3, 34.

Healthy, sound: Meas. I, 2, 55. H4B I, 2, 4.

Heap, subst. 1) things thrown together, a pile or mass: H4B IV, 5, 72. R3 I, 4, 26. Cor. III, 1, 207. *all her husbandry doth lie on —s*, H5 V, 2, 39. *lies all on a h.* Tit. II, 3, 223. *when I have laid proud Athens on a h.* Tim. IV, 3, 101.

2) great quantity, mass: *how prove you that, in the great h. of your knowledge*, As I, 2, 72. *such —s and sums of love and wealth*, Tim. V, 1, 155.

3) crowd, throng, cluster: *amongst this princely h.* R3 II, 1, 53. *let us on —s go offer up our lives*, H5 IV, 5, 18. *when they charge on —s the enemy flying*, Troil. III, 2, 29. *a hundred women drawn upon a h.* Caes. I, 3, 23.

4) the compound of the body: *hence, h. of wrath*, H6B V, 1, 157. *all thy whole h. must die*, Per. I, 1, 33.

Heap, vb. to pile, to accumulate, to lay up a great quantity of: *with measure —ed*, As V, 4, 185 (overfull, more than brimful). *if the measure of thy joy be —ed like mine*, Rom. II, 6, 25. *the —ing friendships*, Wint. IV, 2, 22 (receiving plenty of good services). *mountainous error would be too highly —ed*, Cor. II, 3, 127. *the late dignities —ed up to them*, Mcb. I, 6, 19 (cf. *To*). Followed by *on*, = to load, to bestow plenteously: Gent. III, 1, 19. H6B II, 1, 187. H6C II, 2, 158. R3 III, 7, 204. H8 III, 2, 175. IV, 2, 64. Tim. IV, 1, 22. Caes. I, 2, 134. Cymb. I, 1, 132.

Hear (impf. and partic. *heard*), 1) to perceive by the ear; trans. with a simple accus.: *do you not h. him?* Tp. I, 1, 14. *when I arrived and —d thee*, I, 2, 292. 385. 431. II, 1, 311. 313. 316. Merch. I, 2, 52. IV, 1, 149 etc. etc. *he has —d that word of some great man*, Tw. IV, 1, 12. Followed by an inf. without *to*: *which thou —dst cry*, Tp. I, 2, 32. *to h. thee speak of Naples*, 433. III, 1, 63. IV, 50. Meas. I, 2, 18. Tim. IV, 2, 21. Hml. IV, 1, 9. Cymb. V, 5, 161 etc. etc.

I have —d say, Meas. IV, 2, 38. H4B I, 2, 108. Cor. II, 2, 74. Per. IV, 6, 86. *have you not —d speak of Mariana*, Meas. III, 1, 216. Inf. with *to: who —d me to deny it*, Err. V, 25. *I had rather h. you to solicit that*, Tw. III, 1, 120. *—d a voice to call him so*, H6B II, 1, 94. Followed by a partic.: *I have —d it said*, Wint. IV, 4, 86. H6A II, 2, 55. Cor. IV, 3, 33. *her shall you h. disproved*, Meas. V, 161. *who hath not —d it spoken*, H4B IV, 2, 16. *h. her exampled by herself*, H5 I, 2, 156. H8 II, 1, 32. Epil. 5. Cor. I, 9, 29. II, 2, 81 etc. Absol.: Tw. II, 3, 58. H4A II, 1, 32. Caes. I, 2, 58 etc. *in one's —ing* = in one's presence, so as to be heard by: *in my —ing be you mute and dumb*, Lucr. 1123. *in the —ing of these many friends*, Merch. V, 241. *in —ing of all these ears*, H8 II, 4, 145. *to brave the tribune in his brothers' —ing*, Tit. IV, 2, 36. Hml. IV, 7, 73. Cymb. I, 4, 35. *within —ing* = near enough to be able to hear: Gent. II, 1, 8. H4B II, 4, 337. *out of h.* = too far to be able to hear: Mids. II, 2, 152. *no —ing, no feeling*, Wint. IV, 4, 625. *my sense of —ing*, LLL III, 1, 2 and V, 2, 670 (Armado's speeches).

Hearing, substantively, = the sense by which sounds are perceived, the ear: *would I had no —ing*, Ven. 428. *her grievance with his —ing to divide*, Compl. 67. *terrible to enter human —ing*, Tp. I, 2, 265. *out of your wits and —ing too*, III, 2, 87. *take her —ing prisoner*, Ado I, 1, 326. *it pays the —ing double recompense*, Mids. III, 2, 180. *hard of —ing*, Shr. II, 184. *speak to his gentle —ing kind commends*, R2 III, 3, 126. *these exactions are most pestilent to the —ing*, H8 I, 2, 49. *make joyful the —ing of my wife*, Mcb. I, 4, 46. *where —ing should not latch them*, IV, 3, 195. *lend thy serious —ing to what I shall unfold*, Hml. I, 5, 5. *you lie, up to the —ing of the gods*, Ant. V, 2, 95. *prevailed on thy too ready —ing*, Cymb. III, 2, 6. *fill the bores of —ing*, 59. *no more offend our —ing*, V, 4, 94. Plur. *younger —ings are quite ravished*, LLL II, 75.

2) to give allowance to speak, to attend, to listen, to lend ear to; absol.: *dost thou h.?* Tp. I, 2, 106. Gent. I, 1, 99. Shr. V, 1, 136 etc. *whose remembrance will to ears and tongues be theme and —ing ever*, Cymb. III, 1, 4. *h. you, my lords*, Ado V, 1, 47. Shr. II, 242. Troil. II, 3, 121. Hml. V, 1, 14. *h. thee, Gratiano*, Merch. II, 2, 189. *—ing*, substantively, = audience, attention: *if you will give me the —ing*, Wiv. II, 2, 183. H5 I, 1, 93. H6A III, 1, 28. V, 3, 106. Cymb. V, 5, 116. *I'll vouchsafe thee the —ing*, Wiv. II, 2, 45. *vouchsafe me —ing*, H4A IV, 3, 31. *leave me to my —ing*, Tw. III, 1, 104. *of whom I have deserved this —ing*, Tim. II, 2, 207. *we beg your —ing*, Hml. III, 2, 161.

Trans.: *the tiger would gently h. him*, Ven. 1096. Lucr. 495. Tp. II, 1, 190. Meas. III, 1, 148. Ado I, 3, 6. Tw. I, 5, 176. 235. H4B V, 5, 100 etc. *h. me with patience but to speak a word*, Rom. III, 5, 160. *h. me what I say*, H5 II, 1, 67. H6C II, 6, 63. Ant. V, 1, 51. *h. me a little*, Ado IV, 1, 157. *h. me this*, Tw. V, 123. *h. me one single word*, All's V, 2, 37. H6C I, 1, 170. Tit. II, 3, 138. Lr. V, 1, 39. *h. me this prayer*, Ant. I, 2, 70. *to-morrow we'll h. ourselves again*, Mcb. III, 4, 32 (we'll speak the matter over again; cf. *Ourselves*).

3) to be hearer, auditor of: *I will h. that play*, Mids. V, 81. *his honour never —d a play*, Shr. Ind.

1, 96. 2, 136. H5 Prol. 34. Hml. II, 2, 560. III, 2, 51. 161. *I have —d it over*, Mids. V, 77. *a lord will h. you play*, Shr. Ind. 1, 93. *'tis a good —ing when children are toward: but a harsh —ing when women are froward*, Shr. V, 2, 182 (= *'tis a pleasant spectacle*). Used of arts and science: *unfit to h. moral philosophy*, Troil. II, 2, 167. *he —s no music*, Caes. I, 2, 204 (pays no attention to m.).

4) to learn, to be told, to receive information about; trans.: *until her husband's welfare she did h.* Lucr. 263. *the blackest news that ever thou —dest*, Gent. III, 1, 286. II, 1, 145. LLL I, 1, 287. IV, 1, 97. Mids. IV, 1, 138. Merch. II, 8, 33. Shr. Ind. 2, 131. I, 2, 189. Wint. I, 2, 424. Caes. II, 2, 34. Hml. III, 2, 242 etc. *I —d no letter from my master since I wrote him*, Cymb. IV, 3, 36 (= not a jot? not a syllable?) *let those cities ... h. these tears*, Per. I, 4, 54 (be informed of them). *who since I —d to be discomfited*, H6B V, 1, 63. *I never —d the absent duke much detected for women*, Meas. III, 2, 129. *h. your own dignity so much profaned*, H4B V, 2, 93. *you shall h. the legions sooner landed*, Cymb. II, 4, 17. *I have —d* = I have been told: Wiv. II, 1, 230. Mids. I, 1, 111. Merch. IV, 1, 6. R2 II, 3, 54. Lr. II, 1, 89. Ant. II, 6, 47 etc.

Absol.: *I am sorry you must h.* Ado IV, 1, 89. *as I —d in Genoa*, Merch. III, 1, 103. *none* (news) *good to please you with the —ing*, R3 IV, 4, 458. With *from: to Milan let me h. from thee*, Gent. I, 1, 57. II, 4, 103. Meas. V, 223. Ado V, 1, 151. V, 2, 58. Merch. V, 35 etc. *'tis not four days gone since I —d thence*, Cor. I, 2, 7. With *of: you have not —d of the proclamation?* Meas. I, 2, 95. *we will h. further of it by your daughter*, Ado II, 3, 213 (cf. Cymb. II, 4, 77). IV, 1, 194. Mids. IV, 2, 3. R2 II, 1, 234. H6A III, 4, 2. H6B III, 1, 122. R3 I, 3, 184. H8 III, 2, 435 etc. *as you h. of me, so think of me*, Ado IV, 1, 338. *of whom I h. so well*, Shr. IV, 4, 37. Tim. III, 6, 29. *from* and *of:* Cor. IV, 1, 52.

I hear = I have heard, I have been told: *I h. not of him in the court*, Wiv. IV, 3, 6. *I h. you are a scholar*, II, 2, 186. *I h. your grace hath sworn*, LLL II, 104. *do you h. whether Antonio have had any loss?* Merch. III, 1, 44. *as I h., he was much bound to you*, V, 137. *and fled, as he —s since, to Burgundy*, H6C IV, 6, 79. *h. you the news abroad?* R3 II, 3, 3. *last night, I h., they lay at Northampton*, II, 4, 1. *I h. the Marquis Dorset's fled*, IV, 2, 46. *I h. that news*, 89. *h. you of it?* Tim. III, 6, 60. *I h. it by the way*, Mcb. III, 4, 130. Lr. II, 1, 107 (Qq *heard*). Ant. III, 7, 78. Cymb. IV, 3, 38 etc.

5) to attend judicially, to try in a court of law: *the council shall h. it*, Wiv. I, 1, 35. *leave you to the —ing of the cause*, Meas. II, 1, 141. *he's —ing of a cause*, II, 2, 1 (cf. *Of*). *to have —ing of this business*, III, 1, 210. *to h. this matter forth*, V, 255. *to h. the cause betwixt her and this great offender*, H8 V, 3, 120. Cor. II, 1, 78. 87. V, 6, 128.

Hearer, 1) one who attends to sounds or words: Lucr. 818. Ado I, 1, 309. LLL V, 2, 870. As II, 4, 38. John IV, 2, 190. R2 V, 1, 45. H4B III, 2, 330. H6C I, 4, 161. Troil. III, 1, 24. Mcb. III, 1, 32. Hml. II, 2, 400. IV, 5, 9. V, 1, 280.

2) one who is informed of something: *she dying .... shall be lamented, pitied and excused of every h.* Ado IV, 1, 219.

3) one of an audience: Ado II, 1, 109. H8 Prol. 17. 24.

Hearing, subst. see *Hear*.

Hearken, 1) intr. a) to listen, to prick up the ears: *to h. if his foes pursue him still*, Ven. 699. *h., sir*, Gent. II, 1, 178. *would draw heaven down and all the gods to h.* Per. I, 1, 83. With *for: she —s for his hounds and for his horn*, Ven. 868 (pricks her ears to hear). With *to*, = to listen: *to h. once again to the suit*, Tp. III, 2, 44. Mids. V, 241 (Q1 *listen*). Per. IV, 2, 107. With *after*, in Costard's language, = to listen to, to follow the dictates of: *to h. after the flesh*, LLL I, 1, 219. cf. R3 I, 1, 54.

b) to inquire, to ask about; with *after: h. after their offence*, Ado V, 1, 216. *he —s after prophecies and dreams*, R3 I, 1, 54. cf. LLL I, 1, 219.

c) to be on the alert, to lie in wait; with *for: the youngest daughter whom you h. for*, Shr. I, 2, 260 (whom you desire to gain). *said I —ed for your death*, H4A V, 4, 52. Absol.: *old Gremio is —ing still*, Shr. IV, 4, 53 (is still watching his opportunity).

2) trans. to listen to: *this king of Naples —s my brother's suit*, Tp. I, 2, 122. *h. the end*, H4B II, 4, 303 (Doll Tearsheet's speech; = listen to the end of the piece of music? or wait, and judge when all is done? Q *h. a' th end*).

Hearsay, a hearing, being told or informed by others, not by one's own eyes and perception: *let them say more that like of h. well*, Sonn. 21, 13 (that fall in love with what has been praised by others). *of this matter is little Cupid's crafty arrow made, that only wounds by h.* Ado III, 1, 23 (by hearing what others say).

Hearse, subst. a coffin on a bier: H4B IV, 5, 114. H6A I, 1, 104. R3 I, 2, 2. Caes. III, 2, 169. Per. IV, 3, 41.

Hearsed, coffined, enclosed in a coffin: *thy sea within a puddle's womb is h.* Lucr. 657. *would she were h. at my foot*, Merch. III, 1, 93. *h. in death*, Hml. I, 4, 47.

Heart, 1) the muscular viscus in the thorax which propels the blood through the arteries: Ven. 167. Gent. IV, 1, 51. Meas. II, 4, 20. Ado II, 3, 153. III, 4, 74. IV, 1, 309. Mids. II, 2, 149. Merch. III, 1, 132. IV, 1, 233 etc. Considered as the seat of any affection or emotion: *when the —'s attorney once is mute*, Ven. 335. *mine eye and h. are at a mortal war*, Sonn. 46, 1. *the cry did knock against my very h.* Tp. I, 2, 9. *my h. bleeds*, 63. Gent. I, 1, 69. I, 2, 63. I, 3, 46. IV, 2, 65. IV, 3, 19. 32. Wiv. II, 2, 301. Mids. I, 2, 73; cf. H4B III, 2, 54. H6C III, 3, 14. Rom. IV, 5, 102 etc. etc. *prays from his h.* Ado I, 1, 153 (as he is affected, sincerely); cf. Rom. III, 5, 228. *that with his very h. despiseth me*, Gent. IV, 4, 99. *I am pale at mine h. to see thine eyes so red*, Meas. IV, 3, 158. *your brother's death sits at your h.* V, 394. *since you do take it so at h.* Merch. V, 145; Tw. III, 4, 112. *I am glad at h.* Wint. III, 3, 14. *my father's disposition sticks me at h.* As I, 2, 254. *grieves at h.* H4A V, 4, 29. *some sudden qualm hath struck me at the h.* H6B I, 1, 54. *'tis warm at's h.* Cor. II, 3, 160. *touched at very h.* Cymb. I, 1, 10. *the nobles receive so to h. the banishment of Coriolanus*, Cor. IV, 3, 22. *I take all and your several visitations so kind to h.* Tim. I, 2, 225. *why should we in our peevish opposition take it to h.* Hml. I, 2, 101 etc. Hence = temper, disposition, sentiments: *thy hard h.* Ven. 375. 426. 500. Ado I,

1, 128 etc. *a kind h.* Wiv. III, 4, 106 etc. *a light h.*
LLL V, 2, 18. *a merry h.* Ado II, 1, 325. H4B V, 3,
50. *my wild h.* Ado III, 1, 112. *a corrupted h.* Wiv.
V, 5, 91. *your piteous h.* Tp. I, 2, 14. *waxen —s,* Tw.
II, 2, 31. *proud h.* H6A IV, 3, 24. *unyielding h.* Ven.
423. *the white cold virgin snow upon my h.* Tp. IV, 55.
not changing h. with habit, Meas. V, 389. *not with
better h.* Err. III, 1, 29. *thrust virtue out of our —s,*
Wiv. V, 5, 156. *liver, brain and h.* Tw. I, 1, 37 (i.e.
the organs of desire, of thought, and of sentiment).
the liver, h. and brain of Britain, Cymb. V, 5, 14. cf.
Merch. I, 1, 82. *you must bear; the h. is all,* H4B V,
3, 32. *had I the h. to do it,* Tw. V, 120. *have you the
h.?* John IV, 1, 41. *cursed be the h. that had the h. to
do it,* R3 I, 2, 15. *you scarcely have the —s to tell me
so,* I, 4, 180. 181. *how hast thou the h. to mangle me,*
Rom. III, 3, 48.

Supposed to be the prompter of will and inclination: *set all —s i' the state to what tune pleased
his ear,* Tp. I, 2, 84. *you shall have revenges to your
h.* Meas. IV, 3, 140. *h. and good will you might have
sent,* Err. IV, 4, 88. *set your h. at rest,* Mids. II, 1, 121.
if I could bid the fifth welcome with so good a h.
Merch. I, 2, 141. *as good as h. can wish,* H4A I, 1,
13. *as h. would desire,* II, 4, 26. *they had no h. to
fight,* H6C II, 1, 135. *you shall fight your —s out ere
I part you,* Troil. III, 2, 55. *say against their —s,* Cor.
I, 9, 8. *it is against my h.* Tim. III, 4, 21. *set not thy
sweet h. on proud array,* Lr. III, 4, 85 (Ff *sweet-heart*)
etc. *in h.* = heartily, sincerely, earnestly: *dost thou
not wish in h.* LLL V, 2, 55. *in h. desiring still you
may behold confusion of your foes,* H6A IV, 1, 76. *loved
her so dear in h.* H8 II, 2, 111. Tim. I, 2, 54. *I could
find in my h. to beat him,* Tp. II, 2, 160. Err. IV, 4,
160. Ado I, 1, 127. III, 5, 24. As II, 4, 4. H4A II,
4, 56. *if they can find in their —s the poor knight
shall be further afflicted,* Wiv. IV, 2, 232. *I cannot
yet find in my h. to repent,* All's II, 5, 13. *with one's
h.* = from a true impulse of the mind, sincerely: *I
thank you always with my h.* Wiv. I, 1, 86. *ay, with
my h.* Meas. V, 239. *a blister on his tongue, with my
h.* LLL V, 2, 335. *I am sure you hate me with your
—s,* Mids. III, 2, 154. *those parts that you love with
your h.* H5 V, 2, 214. *as I love Hastings with my h.*
R3 II, 1, 17. *hate a lord with my h.* Tim. I, 1, 237.
with all my h.: Err. V, 407. Mids. III, 2, 164. Merch.
III, 2, 197. III, 4, 35. IV, 1, 147. As III, 2, 454. III,
5, 136. V, 3, 3. Shr. Ind. 1, 83. IV, 4, 67. All's II,
3, 230. John I, 270. IV, 2, 180. H4A III, 1, 223.
H6A II, 3, 81. R3 I, 2, 220. II, 4, 4. III, 1, 111. III,
2, 111. Tim. III, 6, 27. Hml. III, 1, 24. Oth. I, 3,
193 etc. *do it with all thy h.* Ado IV, 1, 287. *with all
our —s,* R3 II, 2, 145. *forgave him with all their —s,*
Caes. I, 2, 276.

Principally the seat of love and amorous desire:
Ven. 374. 432. 517. Lucr. 435. Tp. III, 1, 65. 90.
Wiv. IV, 6, 51. V, 5, 101. LLL III, 37. 43. V, 2, 278
etc. etc. *so much in the h. of the world,* As I, 1, 175.
if you do love Rosalind so near the h. V, 2, 69. Opposed to the head: Merch. III, 2, 64.

Considered as the motive of activity, = courage,
spirit: *'tis the h., Master Page,* Wiv. II, 1, 235. *no
greater h. in thee?* As II, 6, 4. *our —s should be as
good,* H4B IV, 1, 157. *nothing so full of h.* Troil. I, 3,
239. *what h. receives from hence the conquering part,*
352. *boldness comes to me now and brings me h.* III,

2, 121. *men of h. looked wondering,* Cor. V, 6, 99.
despite thy valour and thy h. Lr. V, 3, 133. *where hast
thou been, my h.?* Ant. III, 13, 172. *a diminution in
our captain's brain restores his h.* 199. *out of h.* LLL
III, 46. H4A III, 3, 6. *cold h.* = cowardice, H4A IV,
3, 7 (cf. *Cold*). *to give h.* H6B IV, 4, 35. *to have good
h.* Ant. V, 1, 56. *to put in h.* Shr. IV, 5, 77. *to take h.*
Caes. IV, 3, 288. Ant. IV, 15, 85. *take a good h.* As
IV, 3, 174. Used as a compellation: *my h. of elder,*
Wiv. II, 3, 30. *great h.* H4A V, 4, 87.

Used for the soul, the mind in general: *my h. mis-
gives me,* Wiv. V, 5, 226. *ask your h. what it doth
know,* Meas. II, 2, 137. *my h. will not confess it,* All's
II, 1, 8. *half the h. of Caesar, worthy Mecaenas,* Ant.
II, 2, 175. *it angered him to the h.* H4B II, 4, 9. *anger
her to the h.* III, 2, 217. *stoop to the h.* Cor. III, 2, 32
(M. Edd. *herd*). *he lies to the h.* Oth. V, 2, 156 (= consciously). *beshrew your h.* H4B II, 3, 45. Troil. IV, 2,
29 (cf. *Beshrew*). *blessing of your h.* Gent. III, 1, 306.
blessing on his h. R2 V, 5, 64. *my h.* used as an exclamation: Wint. IV, 4, 435. H6B I, 3, 221. Caes. V, 3,
58. Sometimes almost = life: *they have murdered
this poor h. of mine,* Ven. 502. *a man may draw his
h. out, ere a pluck one,* All's I, 3, 93. *the king has
killed his h.* H5 II, 1, 93. *almost broke my h. with
laughter,* Tit. V, 1, 113 (cf. *Break*). *to prove upon thy
h., thou liest,* Lr. V, 3, 140. *for one's h.* = for one's
life: *I could not for my h. deny it him,* Merch. V, 165.
could not get him for my h. to do it, Shr. I, 2, 38. *cannot take two from twenty for his h.* Cymb. II, 1, 60.
my h. is sick, John V, 3, 4 (= I feel ill). *being strong
at h.* As IV, 3, 152 (having recovered from a swoon).
'tis bitter cold, and I am sick at h. Hml. I, 1, 9. *I am
sick at h. when I behold...,* Mcb. V, 3, 19; cf. the
quibble in LLL V, 2, 278.

Sometimes even = the mind as the power of thinking: *it* (the eye) *no form delivers to the h. of bird,
of flower,* Sonn. 113, 5. *tongue far from h.* Meas. I, 4,
33. *what his h. thinks his tongue speaks,* Ado III, 2,
14. *if I would think my h. out of thinking,* III, 4, 85.
as h. can think, H4A IV, 1, 84. *lay it to thy h.* Mcb.
I, 5, 15. Cor. II, 3, 212. *lay hand on h., advise,* Rom.
III, 5, 192. *would h. of man once think it?* Hml. I, 5,
121. *if I had played the desk or table-book, or given
my h. a winking,* II, 2, 137. *by h.* = by rote: LLL III,
36. V, 2, 98.

2) Serving as a kind and familiar compellation
to persons: *h., you swear like a comfit-maker's wife,*
H4A III, 1, 252. *take it, h.* Cymb. I, 1, 112. *I speak
to thee, my h.* H4B V, 5, 50. *my —s,* Tp. I, 1, 6. Wiv.
III, 2, 88. Tw. II, 3, 16. Rom. I, 5, 88. Ant. IV, 2,
41. *where are these —s?* Mids. IV, 2, 26. *dear h.*
Sonn. 95, 13. 139, 6. Tp. I, 2, 305. Tw. II, 3, 109.
Tit. III, 1, 211. *good h.* Wiv. II, 2, 94. III, 5, 39.
IV, 5, 115. LLL IV, 3, 153. Rom. I, 1, 190. *good —s,*
Tp. I, 1, 29. Wiv. IV, 2, 75. *there's a merry h.* H4B
V, 3, 24. *noble h.* Oth. I, 3, 303. *old h.* H5 IV, 1, 34.
poor h. H5 II, 1, 123. R3 IV, 1, 88. Tit. III, 1, 251.
my profound h. Tw. I, 5, 195. *sweet h.* LLL V, 1, 110.
sweet —s, V, 2, 1. 221. *—s of gold,* H4A II, 4, 307 etc.

3) the inmost and most vital part, the core, the
very essence: *her bare breast, the h. of all her land,*
Lucr. 439. *here is the h. of my purpose,* Wiv. II, 2,
233. *a goodly apple rotten at the h.* Merch. I, 3, 102.
the h. of my message, Tw. I, 5, 203. *in the h. of
France,* H6B I, 1, 196. IV, 8, 38. H6C II, 2, 150

my life itself and the best h. of it thanks you for this great care, H8 I, 2, 1. *flawed the h. of all their loyalties*, 21. *to stick the h. of falsehood*, Troil. III, 2, 202. *from h. of very h., great Hector, welcome*, IV, 5, 171. cf. *in my —'s core, in my h. of h.* Hml. III, 2, 78. *Aufidius, their very h. of hope*, Cor. I, 6, 55. *he outgoes the very h. of kindness*, Tim. I, 1, 286. *this was, O world, the h. of thee*, Caes. III, 1, 208. *you would pluck out the h. of my mystery*, Hml. III, 2, 382. *shake in pieces the h. of his obedience*, Lr. I, 2, 92. *beguiled me to the very h. of loss*, Ant. IV, 12, 29.

Peculiarities: used as a masc. in Sonn. 46, 5. 47, 4. All's II, 1, 8. Without the article: Meas. I, 4, 33. Mids. V, 304. H4A IV, 1, 84. H4B I, 1, 13. II, 4, 26. H6C III, 3, 14. Hml. I, 5, 121. Quibbling with *hart* (q.v.): As III, 2, 260. Tw. I, 1, 17. IV, 1, 63. Caes. III, 1, 208.

Heart-ache, any mental pain, sorrow, anguish: Hml. III, 1, 62.

Heart-blood, 1) blood shed in death, lifeblood: R2 I, 1, 172. III, 2, 131. IV, 28. H6A I, 3, 83. H6B II, 2, 66. H6C I, 1, 223.

2) the soul, the essence: *the mortal Venus, the h. of beauty*, Troil. III, 1, 34.

Heart-break, subst. overpowering sorrow: *better a little chiding than a great deal of h.* Wiv. V, 3, 11.

Heart-breaking, the same: Ant. I, 2, 74.

Heart-burned, suffering from cardialgy, affected with a bitter taste arising from the stomach: Ado II, 1, 4. H4A III, 3, 59.

Heart-burning, inflaming and consuming the heart: *h. heat of duty*, LLL I, 1, 280 (Armado's letter).

Heart-dear, tenderly loved: *my h. Harry*, H4B II, 3, 12 (Q *heart's dear*).

Heart-easing, easing, appeasing the heart: *h. words*, Lucr. 1782.

Hearted, seated in the heart: *I hate the Moor; my cause is h.* Oth. I, 3, 373. *thy crown and h. throne*, III, 3, 448. — In Ant. III, 13, 178 it makes part of the compound *treble-hearted*.

Hearten, to encourage: *h. those that fight*, H6C II, 2, 79. With *up:—s up his servile powers*, Lucr. 295.

Heart-grief, sorrow, affliction: H5 II, 2, 27.

Hearth, the fireplace in a house: Wiv. V, 5, 48. Cor. IV, 5, 27. Emblem of home and hospitality: Cor. IV, 5, 85. V, 6, 30.

Heart-hardening, rendering insensible and cruel: Cor. IV, 1, 25.

Heart-heaviness, sadness: As V, 2, 50.

Heartily, with all the heart, fully, sincerely: Ven. 404. Wiv. I, 1, 277. III, 2, 80. III, 3, 243. Ado I, 1, 151. V, 1, 175. Mids. III, 1, 182. Merch. II, 6, 52. IV, 1, 243. As I, 1, 165. II, 4, 33. II, 5, 28. Shr. IV, 1, 157. All's IV, 3, 74. Wint. IV, 4, 731. John III, 4, 124. IV, 2, 51. R2 I, 1, 150. H5 II, 2, 159. V, 1, 23. 55. R3 III, 7, 130. IV, 5, 17. H8 I, 2, 176. II, 1, 65. II, 2, 46. IV, 2, 119. V, 1, 21. 66. V, 5, 14. Cor. II, 3, 112. 118. IV, 3, 53. Tit. V, 1, 116. 143. Hml. I, 2, 41. I, 5, 134. Oth. II, 3, 303. Cymb. I, 6, 83.

Heartiness, sincere kindness, cordiality: Wint. I, 2, 113.

Heart-inflaming, kindling the passion of love: Sonn. 154, 2.

Heartless, 1) senseless, wanting sympathy: *how sighs resound through h. ground*, Pilgr. 279.

2) wanting courage, spiritless: Lucr. 471. 1392. Rom. I, 1, 73.

Heartlings, in *'od's heartlings*, an exclamation similar to *Od's bodikins*, used by Mr. Slender: Wiv. III, 4, 59.

Heart-offending, wasting the heart: *h. groans*, H6B III, 2, 60.

Heart's-ease, tranquillity of mind: H5 IV, 1, 253. Name of a song: Rom. IV, 5, 104.

Heartsick, 1) pained in the heart, sorrowful: *h. groans*, Rom. III, 3, 72. 2) sick at heart, qualmish: Cymb. IV, 2, 37.

Heart-sore, adj. paining and wasting the heart: *h. sighs*, Gent. I, 1, 30. II, 4, 132.

Heart-sorrow, sincere grief: Tp. III, 3, 81.

Heart-sorrowing, sincerely grieved: R3 II, 2, 112.

Heart-strings, the tendons supposed to brace and sustain the heart: Lucr. 1141. Gent. IV, 2, 62. R3 IV, 4, 365. Oth. III, 3, 261. Used in the sing. by Pistol: *from heart-string I love the lovely bully*, H5 IV, 1, 47.

Heart-struck (O. Edd. *heart-strook*; cf. *Strike*), aimed at and hurting the heart: *his h. injuries*, Lr. III, 1, 17.

Heart-whole, not wounded in the heart: As IV, 1, 49.

Heart-wished, desired with all the heart: *h. luxury*, Compl. 314.

Hearty, 1) coming from the heart, sincere: Tp. V, 111. Gent. V, 4, 74. Wiv. II, 2, 99. Meas V, 4. H4B IV, 1, 14. H6A III, 3, 82. Mcb. III, 4, 2. Lr. IV, 6, 228.

2) kind-hearted, good-natured: *my h. friends, you take me in too dolorous a sense*, Ant. IV, 2, 38.

Heat, subst. 1) the state of things under the action of fire, burning warmth: Ven. 91. 177. Lucr. 1145. Sonn. 12, 6. 153, 6. 154, 10. Gent. II, 4, 192. III, 2, 7. Wiv. III, 5, 117. Mids. I, 1, 244. R2 I, 3, 299. H4B IV, 5, 30. H6A I, 2, 77. H6B I, 1, 81. H6C V, 7, 18. Hml. I, 3, 118. Cymb. IV, 2, 258. Per. I, 2, 41. *he will drive you out of your revenge, if you take not the h.* H4B II, 4, 325 (alluding to the proverb: *strike the iron while it is hot*). *we must do something, and in the h.* Lr. I, 1, 312.

2) vital warmth: *it nor grows with h. nor drowns with showers*, Sonn. 124, 12. *farewell, h., and welcome, frost*, Merch. II, 7, 75. *our bloods, of colour, weight and h.* All's II, 3, 126. *h. outwardly or breath within*, Wint. III, 2, 207. *they retort that h. to them*, Troil. III, 3, 101. *freezes up the h. of life*, Rom. IV, 3, 16. *that Promethean h. that can thy life relume*, Oth. V, 2, 12. *to give my tongue that h. to ask your help*, Per. II, 1, 79.

3) fire of passion, ardour, excitement: Ven. 311. Lucr. 48. 706. 1473. Meas. V, 477. Ado IV, 1, 42. LLL V, 2, 810. H4A I, 1, 59. I, 3, 139. V, 2, 17. H4B I, 2, 198. H6B V, 1, 160. Cor. III, 1, 63. IV, 3, 19. Tit. II, 1, 134. Hml. III, 4, 4. 123. IV, 5, 154. Lr. I, 2, 177. V, 3, 56. Oth. I, 3, 264.

4) fiery temper, mettle: *neither h., affection, limb, nor beauty*, Meas. III, 1, 37. *heart-burning h. of duty*, LLL I, 1, 280 (Armado's letter). *took fire and h. away from the best-tempered courage*, H4B I, 1, 114. *decoct their cold blood to such valiant h.* H5 III, 5, 20.

5) haste, pressure, urgency: *the h. is past; follow*

no further now, H4B IV, 3, 27. *in h. of action*, Troil. IV, 5, 106. *words to the h. of deeds too cold breath gives*, Mcb. II, 1, 61. *a business of some h.* Oth. I, 2, 40.

6) the quality of being hot in the mouth: *of the h. of the ginger*, H5 III, 7, 21 (quibbling).

7) thirst: *one draught above h. makes him a fool*, Tw. I, 5, 140. *a rage whose h. hath this condition, that nothing can allay, nothing but blood*, John III, 1, 341 (quibbling).

Heat, subst. a course (at a race): *till seven years' h.* Tw. I, 1, 26 (till seven years have run their course? Some M. Edd. *seven years hence*).

Heat, vb. 1) trans. a) to make hot: Ven. 742. Sonn. 154, 14. John IV, 1, 1. 61. 105. H8 I, 1, 140. I, 4, 100. Troil. I, 1, 24. Ant. I, 2, 23. Per. IV, 1, 49. *we shall h. you thoroughly*, H6B V, 1, 159 (we shall make you sweat).

b) to warm: *when I am cold, he —s me with beating*, Err. IV, 4, 33. *his virtues shining upon others h. them*, Troil. III, 3, 101.

c) to excite, to stir up: *robbed my soldiers of their —ed spleen*, H6C II, 1, 124. *bathed thy growing with our —ed bloods*, II, 2, 169. *I'll h. his blood with Greekish wine*, Troil. V, 1, 1. *to see wine h. fools*, Tim. I, 1, 271. *with —ed visage*, Hml. III, 4, 50 (Ff. *tristful*).

d) to irritate, to rouse to anger: *thou —est my blood*, LLL I, 2, 32. *cooled my friends, —ed mine enemies*, Merch. III, 1, 60. *you'll h. my blood*, Ant. I, 3, 80.

2) intr. to become hot: *let my liver rather h. with wine*, Merch. I, 1, 81.

Partic. heat for heated: John IV, 1, 61.

Heat, vb. to run over (as at a race), to traverse: *you may ride us with one soft kiss a thousand furlongs ere with spur we h. an acre*, Wint. I, 2, 96 (*hent?*).

Heath, 1) the plant Calluna vulgaris: Tp. I, 1, 70.* 2) a tract of uncultivated land: Mcb. I, 1, 6. I, 3, 77.

Heathen, subst. a pagan: Tw. III, 2, 74. Hml. V, 1, 40.

Heathen, adj. pagan: As V, 1, 36. H8 I, 1, 19. Oth. I, 1, 30.

Heathenish, becoming a pagan, savage, barbarous: *most h. and most gross*, Oth. V, 2, 313.

Heat-oppressed, feverishly excited: *the h. brain*, Mcb. II, 1, 39.

Heave, subst. a deep sigh: *there's matter in these sighs, these profound —s*, Hml. IV, 1, 1.

Heave, vb. 1) trans. a) to raise, to lift: Compl. 15. H6B IV, 10, 54. H6C V, 7, 24. R3 IV, 4, 86. Tit. IV, 1, 40. Lr. I, 1, 93. Ant. II, 7, 15. Cymb. V, 5, 157. With *up*: Ven. 351. Lucr. 111. 638. Gent. IV, 4, 40. H6B I, 2, 13.

b) to raise or force from the breast: *—d forth such groans*, As II, 1, 36. *she —d the name of father pantingly forth*, Lr. IV, 3, 27. *to h. the gorge =* to be near vomiting, Oth. II, 1, 236.

c) to throw, to cast (in seamen's language): *a butt of sack which the sailors —d overboard*, Tp. II, 2, 127.

d) With *away* and the like adverbs, = to get away, to carry off, to remove: *from this fair throne to h. the owner out*, Lucr. 413. *my sighs, like whirlwinds, labour hence to h. thee*, 586. *by foul play were we —d thence*, Tp. I, 2, 62. *with a great heart h. away the*

storm, John V, 2, 55. *h. him away upon your winged thoughts*, H5 V Chor. 8. *to h. the traitor Somerset from hence*, H6B V, 1, 61.

2) intr. to rise, to swell: *the —ing of my lungs provokes me to smiling*, LLL III, 77 (Armado's speech). *this shoulder was ordained so thick to heave*, H6C V, 7, 23. *the performance of our —ing spleens*, Troil. II, 2, 196.

Heaven, (monosyll. and dissyll. indiscriminately) 1) the sky, the firmament; with the art.: *when clouds do blot the h.* Sonn. 28, 10. *the —'s glorious sun*, LLL I, 1, 84. *the sky, the welkin, the h.* IV, 2, 6. *the sun is in the h.* John III, 3, 34. H4A I, 1, 10. R3 V, 3, 286. Rom. II, 2, 15. Hml. I, 2, 127 (Ff *—s*. Ant. V, 2, 79. *would use his h. for thunder*, Meas. II, 2, 113. Plur.: *what obscured light the —s did grant*, Err. I, 1, 67. *I never saw the —s so dim*, Wint. III, 3, 56. H4A III, 1, 24. H6A I, 1, 1. 54. I, 2, 1. I, 4, 98. H6B III, 3, 19. Caes. I, 3, 44. Hml. I, 2, 127 (Qq *h.*). II, 2, 506. Ant. III, 12, 14. Without the art. only in the sing.: *the sun that shines from h.* Ven. 193. *like —'s thunder*, 268. *clouds that shadow —'s light*, 533. *as bright as —'s beauties*, Lucr. 13. *as h. to kiss the turrets bowed*, 1372. *h. clears*, Sonn. 148, 12. *dropped from h.* Tp. II, 2, 140. *as far as h. from earth*, Gent. II, 7, 78. *nothing situate under —'s eye*, Err. II, 1, 16. *like to a silver bow new bent in h.* Mids. I, 1, 10. *the floor of h.* Merch. V, 58. *what stars do spangle h.* Shr. IV, 5, 31. Wint. I, 2, 315. H4A III, 1, 14. H4B II, 3, 19. Rom. I, 2, 25. II, 3, 73. Mcb. IV, 3, 6 etc. *—'s air*, Sonn. 21, 8. *the gusts of h.* Merch. IV, 1, 77.

2) the habitation of God and of blessed spirits; with the art.: *why railest thou on thy birth, the h. and earth?* Rom. III, 3, 119. *away to Saint Peter for the —s*, Ado II, 1, 50. *beauty's crest becomes the —s well*, LLL IV, 3, 256. Without the art.: *hymns at —'s gate*, Sonn. 29, 12. *O h., O earth, bear witness.* III, 1, 68. *nor of h. nor earth*, Gent. V, 4, 80. *prayers that shall be up at h.* Meas. II, 2, 152. *in h. or in hell*, Err. II, 2, 214. IV, 4, 60. Ado II, 1, 47. LLL IV, 3, 345. Merch. II, 2, 68. II, 4, 34. III, 5, 81. H4B II, 3, 17. H6A I, 2, 52. H6C II, 3, 40. Lr. I, 2, 105 etc.

3) a place or state of supreme felicity: *shuts him from the h. of his thought*, Lucr. 338. *the h. that leads men to this hell*, Sonn. 129, 14. *my sole earth's h.* Err. III, 2, 64. Mids. I, 1, 207. II, 1, 243. H8 I, 4, 59. Troil. IV, 4, 120. Tit. II, 3, 41. Rom. IV, 5, 72.

4) the supreme power, God; with the art.: *the h. such grace did lend her*, Gent. IV, 2, 42. *the h. sets spies upon us*, Wint. V, 1, 203. *in this the h. figures some event*, H6C II, 1, 32. Plur.: *what priceless wealth the —s had him lent*, Lucr. 17. *as if the —s should countenance his sin*, 343. *O the —s!* Tp. I, 2, 59. 116. *no sweet aspersion shall the —s let fall*, IV, 18. *the —s themselves do guide the state*, Wiv. V, 5, 245. Meas. I, 1, 74. III, 2, 263. LLL V, 1, 78. All's V, 3, 150. Tw. II, 1, 21. III, 1, 95. IV, 2, 103. Wint. I, 1, 34. II, 1, 107. III, 2, 147. V, 1, 5. R2 I, 1, 23. III, 3, 17. H6A II, 1, 47. H6B V, 2, 73. H6C IV, 6, 33. V, 4, 68. V, 6, 78. R3 I, 3, 9. Troil. V, 3, 14. Rom. III, 6, 1. IV, 3, 4. Cymb. III, 3, 3. Without the art.: *to sing —'s praise*, Pilgr. 70. *trouble deaf h.* Sonn. 29, 3. *infused with a fortitude from h.* Tp. I, 2, 154. *here, afore h., I ratify my gift*, IV, 1, 7. *witness h.* Gent. II, 6, 25. *pray h.* II, 7, 79. IV, 3, 31. IV, 4, 112. V, 4, 36. 59. Meas. I, 1, 33. I, 2, 4. II, 2,

50. 121. II, 3, 33. II, 4, 127. Err. V, 267. All's V, 3, 171 (—'s vows; cf. *heavenly oaths*, LLL V, 2, 356). Tw. III, 4, 51. R2 I, 1, 30. H6A I, 4, 83. Caes. I, 3, 69 etc. etc. *by h.!* Sonn. 130, 13. Gent. III, 1, 166. H6B V, 1, 104 etc. *I would to h.* Meas. II, 2, 67. John III, 4, 48. IV, 1, 23. *for h. sake*, John IV, 1, 78 (cf. *Sake*). Used as a neuter: Gent. IV, 4, 112. Meas. II, 3, 33. As a masc.: *h. he knows how we shall answer him*, John V, 7, 60. *as we, under h., are supreme head, so under him that great supremacy....*, III, 1, 155. Oth. IV, 2, 47 (Ff. *they*). As a plural: *put we the quarrel to the will of h., who, when they see the hours ripe on earth*, R2 I, 2, 6. *h. that long have frowned*, R3 V, 5, 20. *there's husbandry in h.; their candles are all out*, Mcb. II, 1, 4. *heaven hath pleased it so.... that I must be their scourge and minister*, Hml. III, 4, 173. *had it pleased h. to try me with affliction; had they rained all kinds of sores on my bare head*, Oth. IV, 2, 47 (Qq *had he rained*). *if h. slumber while their creatures want*, Per. I, 4, 16 (cf. *eternal power* in Lucr. 345). Often substituted for *God* in O. Edd.; see *God*. Plur. —s: —*s thank you for it*, Tp. I, 2, 175. —*s keep him from these beasts*, II, 1, 324. III, 1, 75. III, 3, 20. Wiv. V, 5, 85. Mids. III, 2, 447. Tw. IV, 3, 34. Wint. IV, 4. 541. H6A I, 5, 9. H6C I, 1, 57. III, 3, 77. 112 etc. —*s!* Tp. I, 2, 428. V, 149. Meas. II, 4, 19. III, 1, 99. LLL IV, 1, 150. Tw. III, 4, 391 etc. Used as a sing.: *be husband to me*, —*s*, John III, 1, 108. *gentle* —*s, front to front bring thou this fiend of Scotland and myself*, Mcb. IV, 3, 231.

Heaven-bred, of divine origin: *h. poesy*, Gent. III, 2, 72.

Heaven-hued, blue: *the h. sapphire*, Compl. 215.

Heaven-kissing, touching the sky, very high: *on a h. hill*, Hml. III, 4, 59.

Heavenly, adj. 1) celestial: *calls it h. moisture, air of grace*, Ven. 64. *between this h. and earthly sun*, 198. *climbed the steep-up h. hill*, Sonn. 7, 5. 17, 8. 33, 4. Pilgr. 35; cf. LLL IV, 3, 66. Tp. IV, 86. V, 105. Gent. III, 1, 154. LLL V, 2, 166. Merch. III, 5, 84. As III, 2, 158. All's II, 3, 27. R2 III, 2, 60. H4B II, 3, 17 (Ff *h. glory*, Q *the god of heaven*). H6B III, 2, 37. H6C III, 3, 182. H8 II, 3, 57. Tim. IV, 3, 137. Mcb. IV, 3, 157. Hml. III, 1, 147. III, 4, 104. Lr. IV, 2, 132. Oth. IV, 3, 65. V, 2, 21 (*this sorrow's h.*, i. e. like that of God). V, 2, 218. Cymb. II, 2, 50. III, 5, 167. Absurdly used by Mrs Quickly: H4B II, 1, 152.

2) sanctified, holy: *a breaking cause of h. oaths*, LLL V, 2, 356. *you are full of h. stuff*, H8 III, 2, 137. *holy and h. thoughts still counsel her*, V, 5, 30. *nothing but h. business*, Troil. IV, 1, 4. *suggest with h. shows*, Oth. II, 3, 358.

3) supremely excellent: Ven. 431. 542. Lucr. 288. Pilgr. 29; cf. LLL IV, 3, 60. Pilgr. 107. Tp. V, 52. Gent. I, 3, 50. II, 4, 145. IV, 4, 92. Wiv. III, 3, 45. Meas. IV, 3, 114. LLL IV, 3, 221. V, 2, 777. 779. Merch. II, 7, 48. As I, 2, 301. Shr. Ind. 1, 51. III, 1, 5. IV, 5, 32. H6B III, 2, 361. R3 I, 2, 183. Tit. II, 4, 48. Rom. III, 2, 33. Lr. IV, 3, 32. Oth. V, 2, 278. Ant. I, 5, 59. Per. III, 2, 99. V, 1, 234.

Heavenly, adv. like a celestial being: *she was h. true*, Oth. V, 2, 135.

Heavenly-harnessed (O. Edd. not hyphened) equipped in heaven: *the h. team*, H4A III, 1, 221.

Heaven-moving, exciting the compassion of heaven: John II, 169.

Heavily, 1) so as to press down, grievously: *how h. this befell to the poor gentlewoman*, Meas. III, 1, 226. *h. punished*, LLL I, 2, 155. *the tidings which I have h. borne*, Mcb. IV, 3, 182.

2) sorrowfully, mournfully: *and h. tell o'er the sad account*, Sonn. 30, 10. *which h. he answers with a groan*, 50, 11. Ado V, 3, 18. 21. R3 I, 4, 1. II, 3, 40. Hml. II, 2, 309.

Heaviness, 1) weight, oppression: *in the h. of his sleep*, Lr. IV, 7, 21 (when he was oppressed with sleep). *the h. and guilt within my bosom*, Cymb. V, 2, 1 (= the heavy guilt). *drawn of h.* V, 4, 168 (quibbling)

2) drowsiness: *your story put h. in me*, Tp. I, 2, 307. *charming your blood with pleasing h.* H4A III, 1, 218.

3) sorrow, sadness, melancholy: Lucr. 1283. 1602. Tp. V, 200. Mids. III, 2, 84. Merch. II, 8, 52. R2 II, 2, 3. H4B IV, 2, 82. IV, 5, 8. Tit. III, 2, 49. Rom. III, 4, 11. III, 5, 109. Ant. IV, 15, 33. cf. *Heart-heaviness*.

Heaving, subst. deep sigh: Wint. II, 3, 35.

Heavy (the different significations often scarce distinguishable, as they afford much scope to quibbling), 1) weighty, ponderous: Meas. III, 1, 27. Err. V, 402. Ado V, 1, 286. Merch. IV, 1, 328. R3 I, 3, 231. II, 2, 113. III, 1, 120. 121. V, 3, 65. Troil. IV, 1, 66. Lr. IV, 6, 52. Ant. IV, 12, 46. IV, 15, 32 etc. cf. Ven. 1073. Gent. I, 2, 85. Ado III, 4, 26. LLL III, 60. Wint. III, 2, 209. R2 II, 2, 32. H4A V, 3, 34. Lr. IV, 6, 150 etc. Metaphorically: *her death shall fall h. on you*, Ado V, 1, 151. *the news I bring is h. in my tongue*, LLL V, 2, 727. *it is a charge too h. for my strength*, All's III, 3, 4. *this fever lies h. on me*, John V, 3, 4. *be Mowbray's sins so h. in his bosom*, R2 I, 2, 50. I, 3, 280. H6B V, 2, 65. R3 V, 3, 111. Cor. IV, 2, 48. Tim. III, 5, 10. Mcb. I, 4, 16 etc.

2) not easily borne; a) grievous, hard, severe: *this my mean task would be as h. to me as odious*, Tp. III, 1, 5. *an act, under whose h. sense your brother's life falls into forfeit*, Meas. I, 4, 65. *a* —*er task could not have been imposed*, Err. I, 1, 32. *h. tedious penury*, As III, 2, 342. *for thee remains a* —*er doom*, R2 I, 3, 148. *a h. sentence*, 154. *our griefs our offences*, H4B IV, 1, 69. *your* —*est censure*, Cor. V, 6, 143. *this h. task*, Tit. V, 2, 58. *at* —*est answer*, Tim. V, 4, 63. *under h. judgment*, Mcb. I, 3, 110. *'tis h. with him*, Hml. III, 3, 84 (his fate is hard). *a h. reckoning*, Cymb. V, 4, 159 and H5 IV, 1, 141.

b) oppressive, crushing: *Fate, take not away thy h. hand*, Ado IV, 1, 116. *a h. curse from Rome*, John III, 1, 205. 296. R3 III, 4, 94. IV, 4, 187 (Ff *grievous*). *to lay a h. and unequal hand upon our honours*, H4B IV, 1, 102. *whose h. hand hath bowed you to the grave*, Mcb. III, 1, 90. *such despite and h. terms*, Oth. IV, 2, 116.

c) bad, wicked: *then was your sin of* —*er kind than his*, Meas. II, 3, 28. *do not repent these things, for they are* —*er than all thy woes can stir*, Wint. III, 2, 209. *the graceless action of a h. hand*, John IV, 3, 58. *a h. deed*, Hml. IV, 1, 12.

d) annoying, wearisome: *is love so light, and may it be that thou shouldst think it h. unto thee?* Ven. 156. *the most* —*est* (night) Gent. IV, 2, 141. *this is a h. chance twixt him and you*, Shr. I, 2, 46. *from a God to a bull? a h. descension*, H4B II, 2, 192. *tedious, wearisome and h.* R3 III, 1, 5. *they are harsh and h. to me*, H8 IV, 2, 95. *discourse is h., fasting*, Cymb. III, 6, 91.

3) full of weight, important: *trust him not in matter of h. consequence*, All's II, 5, 49. *let every word weigh h. of her worth*, III, 4, 31. *some h. business hath my lord in hand*, H4A III, 3, 66. *your too much love and care of me are h. orisons 'gainst this poor wretch*, H5 II, 2, 53. *most just and h. causes*, Lr. V, 1, 27.

4) sad, sorrowful; used of persons: *a h. convertite*, Lucr. 743. *how h. do I journey on the way*, Sonn. 50, 1. *h. Saturn laughed*, 98, 4. Gent. III, 2, 62. Err. V, 45. LLL V, 2, 14. Merch. V, 130. H4B V, 2, 14. 25. 26. Rom. I, 1, 143. Caes. II, 1, 275. Per. V Prol. 22. Of things: *her h. anthem still concludes in woe*, Ven. 839. 950. 1073. 1125. Lucr. 1326. 1435. Sonn. 44, 14. Gent. I, 2, 84. Wiv. IV, 6, 2. Ado II, 3, 73. III, 2, 63. III, 4, 25. LLL I, 2, 127. V, 2, 747. Mids. III, 2, 84. All's III, 2, 35. V, 3, 100. Wint III, 3, 115. R2 II, 2, 32. II, 4, 18. III, 2, 196. 197. III, 3, 8. IV, 257. H6A IV, 2, 40. H6B III, 2, 306. 379. H6C I, 4, 160. II, 1, 43. II, 5, 63. II, 6, 42. III, 3, 37. R3 I, 4, 149. H8 III, 2, 391. Rom. IV, 5, 18. Hml. II, 2, 420. Lr. IV, 6, 150. Oth. IV, 2, 42. V, 2, 98. 371. Ant. IV, 14, 134. IV, 15, 40.

5) slow, sluggish, dull: *h. ignorance aloft to fly*, Sonn. 78, 6. *is not lead a metal h., dull and slow?* LLL III, 60. *their h. toil*, IV, 3, 326. *the h. gait of night*, Mids. V, 375. *melancholy had baked thy blood and made it h. thick*, John III, 3, 43. *cheered up the h. time*, IV, 1, 47. *O h. ignorance*, Oth. II, 1, 144. *their ships are yare, yours h.* Ant. III, 7, 39.

6) weary, drowsy, sleepy: *intending weariness with h. spright*, Lucr. 121. *though woe be h., yet it seldom sleeps*, 1574 (quibbling). *when h. sleep had closed up mortal eyes*, 163; cf. Sonn. 43, 12. *my h. eyelids*, 61, 2. *I am very h.* Tp. II, 1, 189. 198. *do not omit the h. offer of it*, 194. *upon the h. middle of the night*, Meas. IV, 1, 35. *whilst the h. ploughman snores*, Mids. V, 380. H4A V, 3, 34. R3 I, 4, 74. Caes. IV, 3, 256. Mcb. II, 1, 6. Lr. II, 2, 178.

7) gloomy: *with a h., dark, disliking eye*, Ven. 182. *with h. eye, knit brow*, Lucr. 709. *it is a h. night*, Oth. V, 1, 42.

Heavy-gaited, slow, sluggish: R2 III, 2, 15.

Heavy-hanging, (not hyphened in O. Edd.), hanging down ponderously: *a h. bell*, Lucr. 1493.

Heavy-headed, dull, brutish: *this h. revel*, Hml. I, 4, 17.

Heavy-sad, (not hyphened in O. Edd.) very sad: *sad, so h.* R2 II, 2, 30.

Heavy-thick, (O. Edd. *heavy, thick*) thick and heavy: John III, 3, 43.

Hebenon (Qq *hebona*) probably e b o n y, the juice of which was thought to be poisonous: Hml. I, 5, 62. cf. *Ebon.* (or = henbane?).*

Hebrew, (cf. *Ebrew*), a Jew: Gent. II, 5, 57. Merch. I, 3, 58. 179.

Hecate (dissyll.; trisyll. in H6A III, 2, 64), the goddess of hell and of sorcery: *the triple —'s team*, Mids. V, 391 (three-headed). H6A III, 2, 64. Mcb. II, 1, 52. III, 2, 41. III, 5, 1. Hml. III, 2, 269. Lr. I, 1, 112.

Hectic, a constitutional fever: *like the h. in my blood he rages*, Hml. IV, 3, 68.

Hector, 1) the Trojan hero: Lucr. 1430. 1486.

Ado II, 3, 196. LLL V, 2, 537. 636 etc. H4B II, 4, 237. H6A II, 3, 20. H6C IV, 8, 25. Troil. I, 1, 36 and passim. Cor. I, 3, 44. I, 8, 11. Tit. IV, 1, 88. Ant. IV, 8, 7. His name used appellatively to denote highest valour: Wiv. I, 3, 12. II, 3, 35 (the host's speech).

2) a usual name of dogs: LLL V, 2, 665.

Hecuba, the wife of Priam: Lucr. 1447. 1485. Troil. I, 2, 1. 157. V, 1, 44. V, 3, 54. 83. V, 10, 15. Cor. I, 3, 43. Tit. IV, 1, 20. Hml. II, 2, 523. 584. 585. Cymb. IV, 2, 313. Mentioned, though not named in Tit. I, 136.

Hedge, subst. a thicket planted round a field to fence it: Ven. 1094. Pilgr. 72. Ado I, 3, 28. Shr. Ind. 1, 20. All's IV, 1, 2. Wint. IV, 3, 5. R2 III, 4, 45. H4A II, 2, 74. IV, 2, 52. H5 V, 2, 42. 54. H6A I, 1, 117. Ant. I, 4, 64. *I will but look upon the h.* Wint. IV, 4, 857 (i. e. ease myself, make water). *born under a h.* H6B IV, 2, 55 (of meanest birth).

Hedge, vb. 1) to enclose, to fence: *such divinity doth h. a king*, Hml. IV, 5, 123. *England, —d in with the main*, John II, 26.

2) to confine, to restrain, to limit: *if my father had not scanted me and —d me by his wit*, Merch. II, 1, 18. *you forget yourself, to h. me in*, Caes. IV, 3, 30 (to limit my authority).

3) to creep along by the hedge, not to take the direct path: *if you give way, or h. aside from the direct forthright*, Troil. III, 3, 158 (Q turn). Hence = to shift, to shuffle: *am fain to shuffle, to h. and to lurch*, Wiv. II, 2, 26. *how he coasts and —s his own way*, H8 III, 2, 39. *this shall not h. us out: we'll hear you sing*, Troil. III, 1, 65 (by this you shall not elude us).

Hedge-born, of meanest birth: H6A IV, 1, 43. cf. H6B IV, 2, 55.

Hedgehog, the animal Erinaceus: Tp. II, 2, 10. Mids. II, 2, 10. R3 I, 2, 102.

Hedge-pig, a young hedgehog: Mcb. IV, 1, 2.

Hedge-priest, a clergyman of the lowest order: LLL V, 2, 545.

Hedge-sparrow, the bird Sylvia curruca: Lr. I, 4, 235.

Heed, subst. 1) guard, protection, means of safety: *study me how to please the eye indeed by fixing it upon a fairer eye, who dazzling so, that eye shall be his h. and give him light that it was blinded by*, LLL I, 1, 82.

2) heedfulness, attention, care: *to list me with more h.* Err. IV, 1, 101. *with better h. to resurvey them*, H5 V, 2, 80. *with all the h. I may*, R3 III, 1, 187. *give h. to't*, H8 II, 4, 169. *a h. was in his countenance*, III, 2, 80. *have you with h. perused*, Cor. V, 6, 62. *with better h. and judgment*, Hml. II, 1, 111. *to take h.* = to take care, to be careful: *let men take h. of their company*, H4B V, 1, 86. *take h. on't*, Oth. III, 4, 65. *I take no h. of thee*, Tim. I, 2, 34 (I care not for thee). *there's no h. to be taken of them*, Caes. I, 2, 276.

3) suspicious watch, caution: *those that without h. do plunge into it*, Tim. III, 5, 13. *take h.* = beware: Tp. IV, 1, 22. Wiv. II, 1, 126. 127. Merch. II, 2, 7. H6B III, 1, 80. R3 I, 4, 204. H8 I, 2, 175. Troil. V, 7, 21. Rom. III, 3, 145. Lr. I, 4, 123. *if you take not h.* H6B I, 2, 102. With *of*: *take h. of this large privilege*, Sonn. 95, 13. *take h. of them*, All's II, 1, 19. III, 5, 12. IV, 3, 241. H4B II, 1, 14.

R3 I, 3, 289. Troil. I, 2, 60. Caes. II, 3, 1. Hml. II, 1, 21. Lr. III, 4, 82. Oth. V, 2, 51. With *to: take h. to't,* Meas. V, 83. Followed by a clause; a) with the simple subjunctive: *take h. the queen come not within his sight,* Mids. II, 1, 19. Shr. III, 1, 44. R3 II, 1, 12. H8 I, 2, 173 (*good h.*). Ant. II, 7, 136. b) with *lest: take h. lest you be cony-catched,* Shr. V, 1, 101. H6B V, 1, 160. H8 III, 1, 110. c) of an interrog. form: *take h. what guests you receive,* H4B II, 4, 101. *take h. how you impawn our person,* H5 I, 2, 21. H6A III, 2, 3.

Heed, vb. 1) to attend to: *you must be so too, if h. me,* Tp. II, 1, 220. 2) to keep with care, to look after: *it* (the snake) *shall be —ed,* Ant. V, 2, 269.

Heedful, careful, attentive: Lucr. 281. 495. Err. II, 2, 2. John IV, 1, 5. H6C III, 3, 63. Hml. III, 2, 89. Superl. *—est:* All's I, 3, 231. With *of:* Err. I, 1, 83.

Heedfully, 1) attentively: Tp. I, 2, 78. LLL IV, 3, 80.

2) deliberately, consciously: *she, in worser taking, from sleep disturbed, h. doth view the sight,* Lucr. 454 (so as to observe it with consciousness). *unheedful vows may h. be broken,* Gent. II, 6, 11.

Heedless, careless, negligent: Shr. IV, 1, 169. H6A IV, 2, 44.

Heel, subst. (used only of men, horses and asses) 1) the hind part of the foot: Wiv. III, 5, 113. Shr. IV, 1, 15. Wint. IV, 4, 229. H4B I, 1, 44. Troil. II, 1, 53. Rom. III, 1, 39. Cymb. IV, 4, 40. Applied to persons attended or pursued by others: *follow my —s,* Wiv. I, 4, 132. Ant. IV, 5, 6. *eye your master's —s,* Wiv. III, 2, 4. *danger dogs the —s of worth,* All's III, 4, 15. *to dog his —s and curtsy at his frowns,* H4A III, 2, 127. *after the admired —s of Boling-broke,* H4B I, 3, 105; cf. Wiv. I, 4, 62. *to tend on Hector's —s,* Troil. IV, 4, 148. *page thy —s,* Tim. IV, 3, 224. *we will grace his —s,* Caes. III, 1, 120. *at one's —s =* behind one: *with Ringwood at thy —s,* Wiv. II, 1, 122. II, 3, 102. III, 3, 122. III, 5, 76. Err. V, 81. Tw. II, 5, 149. III, 4, 324. John V, 7, 80. H4B I, 2, 18. H5 V Chor. 27. H6B IV, 3, 14. Troil. III, 2, 2. V, 8, 6. Oth. I, 2, 42. Ant. I, 4, 58. *at the —s: dog them at the —s,* R2 V, 3, 139. *pages followed him even at the —s,* H4A IV, 3, 73. H4B I, 3, 80. H5 IV, 7, 179. R3 IV, 1, 40 (Ff *thy —s*). Cor. I, 4, 49. Caes. II, 4, 34. Mcb. I, 6, 21. Metaphorically: *here follow her vices, close at the —s of her virtues,* Gent. III, 1, 325. *is there no sequel at the —s of this mother's admiration?* Hml. III, 2, 341. *at h. of that defy him,* Ant. II, 2, 160 (cf. *at foot*). *on the h. or —s =* immediately after: *on the catastrophe and h. of pastime,* All's I, 2, 57. *when comes your book forth? upon the —s of my presentment,* Tim. I, 1, 27. *to tread on the —s =* to follow close: *with many hundreds treading on his —s,* John IV, 2, 149. *when April on the h. of limping winter treads,* Rom. I, 2, 27. *one woe doth tread upon another's h.* Hml. IV, 7, 164.

2) the whole foot (pars pro toto): *keep from my —s and beware of an ass,* Err. III, 1, 18; cf. Tim. I, 1, 282. *ye light o' love, with your —s* (i. e. by dancing) Ado III, 4, 47; cf. V, 4, 121; H5 III, 5, 34; Rom. I, 4, 36. *your wit was made of Atalanta's —s* (being so nimble) As III, 2, 294. Wint. IV, 4, 695. John IV, 2, 174. H4A II, 4, 480. H5 II Chor. 7. IV,

7, 83. H6A I, 4, 108. H6B IV, 10, 86. Troil. II, 2, 44. Tit. IV, 3, 44. Hml. IV, 5, 32. V, 1, 152. cf. Lr. I, 5, 8 and Wiv. I, 3, 34. *at his —s, leashed in like hounds,* H5 Prol. 6. *spaniel'd me at —s,* Ant. IV, 12, 21. *his —s have deserved it* (to sit in the stocks) All's IV, 3, 118. *to punish you by the —s* (i. e. to set you in the stocks) H4B I, 2, 141. *I'll lay ye all by the —s,* H8 V, 4, 83. *to trip up a person's —s =* to throw him to the ground: As III, 2, 225. Lr. II, 2, 32. cf. *trip him, that his —s may kick at heaven,* Hml. III, 3, 93. *beating his kind embracements with her —s,* Ven. 312 (= kicking at them). cf. *I scorn that with my —s,* Ado III, 4, 51. *scorn running with thy —s,* Merch. II, 2, 10. *I am almost out at —s,* Wiv. I, 3, 34 (in desolate circumstances). *a good man's fortune may grow out at —s,* Lr. II, 2, 164. *my —s are at your command =* I will run as you advise me to do: Merch. II, 2, 33. *show it a fair pair of —s* (= to flee): H4A II, 4, 53. *to trust their —s* (to flee) Mcb. I, 2, 30. *to take h. =* to take to flight: Cymb. V, 3, 67. *I'll take my —s,* Err. I, 2, 94. *betake me to my —s,* H6B IV, 8, 67. *— from head to h.* Wint. IV, 4, 229.

3) the hind part of a shoe: Shr. IV, 1, 136.

Heel, vb. to d a n c e (cf. to foot): *I cannot sing, nor h. the high lavolt,* Troil. IV, 4, 88. cf. the subst. in H5 III, 5, 34.

Hefted, see *Tender-hefted.*

Hefts, heavings, retchings: *he cracks his gorge, his sides, with violent h.* Wint. II, 1, 45.

Heifer, a c o w: Wint. I, 2, 124. H4B II, 2, 171. H6B III, 2, 188. Troil. III, 2, 200.

Heigh, a cry of encouragement and exultation· Tp. I, 1, 6. Wint. IV, 3, 2. 6. 10. H4A II, 4, 534.

Heigh-ho, an exclamation used 1) to call to a person at a distance: Mids. IV, 1, 207. H4A II, 1, 1. 2) to express joy and exultation: As II, 7, 180. 182. 190. Troil. III, 1, 137. Lr. III, 2, 75. 3) to express dejection and despondency: As IV, 3, 169. Followed by *for,* to indicate the cause of depressed spirits: *cry h. for a husband,* Ado II, 1, 332. *h.! for a hawk, a horse, or a husband?* III, 4, 54.

Height, 1) relative elevation or degree: *permit the sun to climb his wonted h.* Lucr. 776. *although his h. be taken,* Sonn. 116, 8. *punish them to your h. of pleasure,* Meas. V, 240. *bid the main flood bate his usual h.* Merch. IV, 1, 72. *I shall now put you to the h. of your breeding,* All's II, 2, 2. H5 III, 1, 17. H6A II, 4, 111. Troil. I, 2, 3.

2) size: *she is about my h.* Gent. IV, 4, 169. *complexion, h., age,* Per. IV, 2, 62.

3) altitude, elevated place, high degree, eminence: *exceeded by the h. of happier men,* Sonn. 32, 8. *impeach my h.* R2 I, 1, 189. *raised me to this careful h.* R3 I, 3, 83. IV, 4, 243. Tit. IV, 2, 34. Ant. II, 7, 22.

4) highest degree, pitch: *in the h. of this bath,* Wiv. III, 5, 120. *the very top, the h., the crest of murder's arms,* John IV, 3, 46. *the tide swelled up unto his h.* H4B II, 3, 63. *seduced the pitch and h. of all his thoughts to base declension,* R3 III, 7, 188. *at h. =* at the top, in the prime of power and strength: *at h. decrease,* Sonn. 15, 7. *our achievements, though performed at h.* Hml. I, 4, 21. *be at the h. of heart-heaviness,* As V, 2, 50. *I fear our happiness is at the h.* R3 I, 3, 41 (Qq *highest*). Tit. III, 1, 70. Caes. IV, 3, 217. *Richard falls in h. of all his pride,* R3 V, 3, 176. *leaving the fight in h.* Ant. III, 10, 21. *dishonoured me*

in the strength and h. of injury, Err. V, 200. *is he not approved in the h. a villain*, Ado IV, 1, 303. Per. II, 4, 6. *urge it no more, on h. of our displeasure*, Tim. III, 5, 87. *he's traitor to the h.* H8 I, 2, 214. *let us feast him to the h.* Troil. V, 1, 3.

5) large size, tall stature: *she hath urged her h.* Mids. III, 2, 291. *with her h. she hath prevailed with him*, 293.

6) the space overhead: *look up a h.* Lr. IV, 6, 58.

Heightened, raised high, exalted: *being so h.* Cor. V, 6, 22.

Heinous, hateful, odious, wicked; used of deeds: Lucr. 910. Sonn. 19, 8. Merch. II, 3, 16. John III, 1, 40. III, 4, 90. IV, 2, 71. IV, 3, 56. R2 IV, 131. 233. V, 3, 34. 59. R3 I, 2, 53. Tit. I, 448. 484. IV, 1, 80. V, 1, 123. V, 2, 4. Lr. V, 3, 92. Per. II, 4, 5. Used of a person: *that h. tiger Tamora*, Tit. V, 3, 195.

Heinously, odiously, villanously: *I am h. unprovided*, H4A III, 3, 213.

Heir, 1) one who is to succeed to a possession; used of females as well as of males (the word *heiress* being unknown to Sh.); a) masc.: Sonn. 1, 4. Tp. II, 1, 111. Err. III, 2, 127. LLL I, 1, 7. V, 2, 658. As I, 3, 101. Wint. III, 2, 136. H6C I, 1, 135. R3 III, 2, 54 etc. etc. b) fem.: Tp. I, 2, 58. II, 1, 253. Gent. IV, 1, 49. Ado I, 1, 297. I, 3, 57. V, 1, 299. LLL II, 41. 195. Merch. IV, 1, 94. As I, 2, 20. All's II, 3, 139. H6B II, 2, 44. 47. H6C IV, 1, 48. 52. 56. H8 V, 5, 42. Cymb. I, 1, 4. Per. Prol. 22. With *of*: Tp. II, 1, 111. 245. 256. Ado I, 3, 57. LLL I, 1, 7. II, 41. 195. V, 2, 658. H6A II, 5, 65. H6C IV, 1, 48. 52. 56. R3 V, 3, 335. Cymb. I, 1, 4. V, 5, 13 etc. With *to*: Ado V, 1, 299. As I, 2, 246. Shr. II, 118. All's II, 3, 139. Wint. IV, 4, 492. H4A I, 3, 157. H6B I, 3, 30. 187. II, 2, 44. 47. IV, 2, 139. R3I,2,25. Hml. III, 1, 63 etc.

2) child, procreation: *the first h. of my invention*, Ven. Dedic. 4. *you orphan —s of fixed destiny*, Wiv. V, 5, 43. *Bolingbroke's my sorrow's dismal h.* R2 II, 2, 63. *unfathered —s and loathly births of nature*, H4B IV, 4, 122. *helped her to an h.* Oth. II, 1, 138.

Heir-apparent, 1) certain heir: H4A I, 2, 65. II, 2, 46. II, 4, 297. 403. 2) heir presumptive: H6B I, 1, 152. Per. III Prol. 37.

Heirless, having no heir: Wint. V, 1, 10.

Helen, 1) name of the wife of Menelaus: Sonn. 53, 7. Mids. V, 11. As III, 2, 153. H4B V, 5, 35. H6C II, 2, 146. Troil. Prol. 9 and passim. Rom. II, 4, 44. Mentioned, though not by name, in Shr. I, 2, 244. 2) the mother of the emperor Constantine: H6A I, 2, 142. 3) female name in Mids. I, 1, 208. II, 2, 144. III, 2, 137. 251 etc. 4) female name in All's I, 1, 202. I, 3, 71 etc. 5) in Cymb. II, 2, 1. 6) confounded with *Hero* by Flute: Mids. V, 199.

Helena, 1) female name in Mids. I, 1, 107. 166. 179 etc. (oftener found than *Helen*). 2) in All's I, 1, 59. 3) in Rom. I, 2, 74.

Helenus, a son of Priam's: Troil. I, 2, 238 — 244. II, 2, 42. III, 1, 148.

Helias, one of the six gates of Troy: Troil. Prol. 16.

Helicane, name in Per. II Prol. 17. II, 4, 21. 26. 40. 55.

Helicanus, the same: Per. I, 2, 50. III Prol. 27. IV, 4, 13. V, 1, 1 and passim.

Helicon, mountain in Greece: H4B V, 3, 108.

Hell, 1) the habitation of the devil and of wicked

souls after death: Lucr. 764. 1082. 1287. Sonn. 144, 5. Tp. I, 2, 214. Wiv. III, 5, 14. V, 5, 39. Meas. III, 1, 94. 95. Err. II, 2, 214. IV, 2, 32. Mids. V, 9. Merch. II, 3, 2. H5 II, 2, 113. R3 I, 3, 227. Cor. III, 3, 68. Oth. III, 3, 447 (Q *cell*) etc. etc. *I am damned in h.* Wiv. II, 2, 9. *have given ourselves to h.* V, 5, 157. *ere I come to h.* R2 IV, 270. *to go to h.* Wiv. II, 1, 49. Merch. III, 2, 21. H6C II, 2, 48. Caes. I, 2, 270. Hml. III, 3, 95. Oth. V, 2, 129. *to lead apes in h.* = to die as an old maid: Ado II, 1, 43. Shr. II, 34. Used as a plural: *—'s black intelligencer, only reserved their factor*, R3 IV, 4, 71 (cf. *Heaven*).

2) a state of extreme torture and misery: *though waiting so be h.* Sonn. 58, 13. *passed a h. of time*, 120, 6. *leads men to this h.* 129, 14. Wiv. II, 2, 305. Mids. I, 1, 140. 207. II, 1, 243. III, 2, 145. Troil. IV, 1, 57 etc. Similarly used of devilish cunning: *what a h. of witchcraft lies in a tear*, Compl. 288.

3) name of the worst dungeon in prisons: *one that before the judgement carries poor souls to h.* Err. IV, 2, 40.

Hell-black, black as h., pitch-black: *h. night*, Lr. III, 7, 60.

Hell-born, born of hell: *h. sin*, Lucr. 1519.

Hell-broth, infernal porridge: Mcb. IV, 1, 19.

Hellespont, the straits now called the Dardanelles: Gent. I, 1, 22. 26. As IV, 1, 104. Oth. III, 3, 456.

Hell-fire, the fire of hell: H4A III, 3, 36. H5 II, 3, 44.

Hell-gate, the gate of hell: Mcb. II, 3, 2.

Hell-governed, directed by hell: *his h. arm*, R3 I, 2, 67.

Hell-hated, abhorred like hell: *the h. lie*, Lr. V, 3, 147.

Hell-hound, an agent of hell: R3 IV, 4, 48. Tit. V, 2, 144. Mcb. V, 8, 3.

Hellish, 1) pertaining to hell, devilish, infernal: Merch. III, 4, 21. H6A III, 2, 39. R3 III, 4, 64. Tit. II, 3, 105. IV, 2, 77. Hml. II, 2, 485. Oth. V, 2, 368.

2) wicked: *only sin and h. obstinacy tie thy tongue*, All's I, 3, 186.

Hell-kite, kite of infernal breed: Mcb. IV, 3, 217.

Hell-pains, the torments of hell: All's II, 3, 245. Oth. I, 1, 155.

Helm, subst. 1) rudder, steerage: H6B I, 3, 103. H6C V, 4, 7. 21. Cor. I, 1, 79. Ant. II, 2, 213.

2) defensive armour for the head, helmet: All's III, 3, 7. H4A III, 2, 142. H5 IV, 7, 163. R3 III, 2, 11. III, 4, 84. V, 3, 79. 351. Troil. I, 2, 253. IV, 5, 255. V, 2, 93. 169. V, 4, 5. Cor. IV, 5, 131. Lr. IV, 2, 57. IV, 7, 36. Oth. I, 3, 273. Ant. II, 1, 33.

Helm, vb. to steer: *the business he hath —ed*, Meas. III, 2, 151.

Helmet, defensive armour for the head: John II, 254. R2 I, 3, 119. IV, 51. H5 IV, 6, 6. IV, 8, 28. V Chor. 18. H6C II, 1, 163. R3 V, 3, 112. Troil. I, 2, 222. Ant. IV, 15, 56.

Help, subst. 1) assistance, aid: Lucr. 913. 1685. Sonn. 36, 4. 80, 9. LLL V, 2, 71. Mids. III, 2, 26. Merch. I, 3, 115. Wint. III, 3, 98. H6A II, 1, 18. IV, 6, 31. H6C IV, 6, 90. Tim. I, 1, 102 etc. etc. Plur. *—s: without their* (his eyes') *—s*, Hml. II, 1, 99 (Ff *h.*). *the bark is ready, and the wind at h.* Hml. IV, 3, 46 (= favourable). *to make us no better thought of,* *a little h. will serve,* Cor. II, 3, 16 (it wants but little). *my master rather played than fought, and had no h. of anger,* Cymb. I, 1, 163 (wanted the impetuosity which anger gives). *I could have looked on him without the h. of admiration,* I, 4, 5 (= without admiration; ironically). *to give h.:* All's II, 1, 212. John V, 4, 58. R3 II, 2, 66. Lr. III, 7, 70. *by h. of:* Tp. I, 2, 275. H6A V, 4, 48. *by the h. of:* As Epil. 7. *by beneficial h.* Err. I, 1, 152. *by whose h.* John II, 117. *by God's h.* H5 I, 2, 222. *with the h. of:* Tp. Epil. 10. Mids. V, 316. *with your two —s,* Ado II, 1, 397. *with their —s,* H6C IV, 1, 45. *by thy h. to this distressed queen,* H6C III, 3, 213.

2) he who, or that which gives assistance: *let's call more h.* Err. IV, 4, 149. *unless you send some present h.* V, 176. *Camillo was his h. in this,* Wint. II, 1, 46. *wish more h. from England,* H5 IV, 3, 73. 75. *the h. of Norfolk,* H6C II, 1, 178 (auxiliary troops). IV, 7, 6. Plur. *—s: with other muniments and petty —s,* Cor. I, 1, 122. *your —s are many,* II, 1, 39. *you Gods, be my —s,* Per. I, 1, 22.

3) remedy: *her h. she sees, but h. she cannot get,* Ven. 93. *for one sweet look thy h. I would assure thee,* 371 (that which would mitigate thy pain). *let him have time of time's h. to despair,* Lucr. 983. *my case is past the h. of law,* 1022. *poor helpless h., the treasure stolen away, to burn the casket,* 1056. Pilgr. 268. Gent. III, 1, 242. Wint. III, 2, 223. H6B II, 4, 67. Troil. IV, 1, 47. Cor. IV, 6, 120. *—s,* Cor. III, 1, 221.

4) cure: *I, sick withal, the h. of bath desired,* Sonn. 153, 11. *the bath for my h. lies where Cupid got new fire,* 13. *patience says it is past her cure. I rather think you have not sought her h.* Tp. V, 142. *let him be borne hence for h.* Err. V, 160. *a senseless h. when h. past sense we deem,* All's II, 1, 127. *you shall have a hempen caudle and the h. of hatchet,* H6B IV, 7, 96. *our remedies within thy h. and holy physic lies,* Rom. II, 3, 52. *my gashes cry for h.* Mcb. I, 2, 42.

Help, vb. (impf. *—ed:* R3 V, 3, 167. Oth. II, 1, 138. *holp:* John I, 240. H6B V, 3, 8. R3 I, 2, 107. IV, 4, 45. Cor. V, 3, 63. V, 6, 36. Tit. IV, 4, 59. Lr. III, 7, 62. Cymb. V, 5, 422. Partic. *—ed:* Gent. IV, 2, 48. All's II, 3, 18. Wint. III, 3, 110. 113. *holp:* Tp. I, 2, 63. Err. IV, 1, 22. Ado I, 1, 51. III, 2, 102. R2 V, 5, 62. H4A I, 3, 13. Cor. III, 1, 277. IV, 6, 81. Rom. I, 2, 48. Mcb. I, 6, 23) 1) to aid, to assist; absol.: *come, h.* Err. III, 1, 56. *hurt not those that h.* H6A III, 3, 53. Shr. I, 2, 18. V, 1, 60. R2 IV, 161 etc. *h. heaven!* Meas. II, 4, 127. *God h.* Ado III, 5, 12. *the Lord h.* H8 II, 4, 129. *God h. the while,* H4A II, 4, 145. R3 II, 3, 8 (= God have mercy on us). An inf. following; without *to: to h. unarm our Hector,* Troil. III, 1, 163. With *to: h. to celebrate a contract,* Tp. IV, 132. *h. to bear this away,* 251. Wiv. II, 2, 178. III, 3, 151. IV, 2, 167. Ado I, 1, 51. III, 2, 102. Merch. II, 5, 50. John I, 240. H4A I, 3, 13. R3 I, 2, 107. IV, 4, 45. V, 3, 78. Cor. III, 1, 277. IV, 6, 81. V, 3, 63. V, 6, 36. Tit. IV, 4, 59 etc. Followed by an accus.: *come to h. him,* Meas. II, 4, 25. IV, 2, 23. V, 355. Mids. II, 2, 145. Wint. III, 3, 110. 113. R3 I, 4, 281. Cymb. V, 5, 422 etc. *we will meet them and h. the joy,* Cor. V, 4, 65 (second the demonstrations of joy). *God h. thee,* As III, 2, 74. H4A III, 1, 246. Mcb. IV, 2, 59. *God h. me,* Ado III, 4, 67. *God h. us,* III, 5, 38. *God h. poor souls,* Err. IV, 4, 132. Ado I, 1, 88. *our Lady h. my lord,* LLL

II, 98. *so h. me heaven,* Err. V, 267. *so God h. me,* LLL V, 2, 414. H6A III, 1, 140. IV, 1, 8. H6B I, 1, 205. III, 1, 110. 120. Accus. and inf.; without *to: to h. thee curse that poisonous toad,* R3 I, 3, 246. IV, 4, 80. *to h. thee knit the cord,* Tit. II, 4, 10. *to h. me sort such ornaments,* Rom. IV, 2, 34. With *to: I will h. thee to prefer her,* Gent. II, 4, 157. Ado V, 3, 17. Mids. IV, 1, 24. R2 I, 3, 229. H6A I, 5, 17. Lr. III, 7, 62 etc. Accus. and adv. or prepositional expression: *no friendly drop to h. me after,* Rom. V, 3, 164 (to assist and enable me to follow). *h. me away,* Wiv. III, 3, 149. *h. me hence,* Mcb. II, 3, 124. *blessedly holp hither,* Tp. I, 2, 63. *if a crow h. us in,* Err. III, 1, 83. *h. me out,* Tit. II, 3, 209. *a man is well holp up that trusts to you,* Err. IV, 1, 22. *to h. the feeble up,* Tim. I, 1, 107. *h. me into some house,* Rom. III, 1, 110. *may h. these lovers into your favour,* Oth. I, 3, 200. *to h. to* = a) to assist in going to and reaching: *h. me to my closet,* R3 II, 1, 133. *hath holp him to his home before us,* Mcb. I, 6, 23. *to h. him to bed,* Cymb. V, 4, 179. b) to assist in obtaining: *to h. my cousin to a good husband,* Ado II, 1, 391. Shr. I, 1, 141. R3 I, 2, 139. *—ing me to the speech of Beatrice,* Ado V, 2, 2. *h. me to a candle,* Tw. IV, 2, 87. *—ing him to all,* R2 V, 1, 61. *holp madmen to their wits,* V, 5, 62. H4A II, 2, 43. III, 1, 246. 247. H6B V, 3, 8. R3 I, 3, 95. V, 3, 167. V, 4, 8. Oth. II, 1, 138 etc.

2) to remedy, to change for the better, to prevent: *she could not h. it,* Pilgr. 222. *cease to lament for that thou canst not h.* Gent. III, 1, 241. 359. All's V, 1, 2. H4B II, 2, 73. Cor. I, 1, 42. IV, 7, 6. Ant. II, 2, 71. In an affirmative sentence: *do thou but call my resolution wise, and with this knife I'll h. it presently,* Rom. IV, 1, 54.

3) to cure: *do wounds h. wounds, or grief h. grievous deeds?* Lucr. 1822. *I will h. his ague,* Tp. II, 2, 97. *being —ed,* Gent. IV, 2, 48. *they cannot h. him,* All's I, 3, 244. *thou thought'st to h. me,* II, 1, 133. *not —ing, death's my fee, but if I h., what do you promise me?* II, 1, 192. *not to be —ed,* II, 3, 18. *offer at my shrine, and I will h. thee,* H6B II, 1, 92. *turn giddy, and be holp by backward turning,* Rom. I, 2, 48. *the harlot's cheek, beautied with plastering art, is not more ugly to the thing that —s it,* Hml. III, 1, 52. *he that —s him take all my outward worth,* Lr. IV, 4, 10. With *of: to h. him of his blindness,* Gent. IV, 2, 47.

4) to be of use, to avail: *though what they do impart h. not at all,* R3 IV, 4, 131 (Ff *h. nothing else*). *it will h. me nothing to plead mine innocence,* H8 I, 1, 207.

5) refl. to look after one's business, to provide for one's self: *she is old and cannot h. herself,* H4B III, 2, 247 (Mouldy's speech).

Helper, 1) assistant: Meas. IV, 2, 10. H6A V, 3, 5. Per. I, 4, 37 (M. Edd. *helps*).

2) with *to,* one who assists in obtaining: *my motive and h. to a husband,* All's IV, 4, 21.

Helpful, 1) lending aid: *our h. ship,* Err. I, 1, 104. *h. swords,* R2 III, 3, 132.

2) salutary, medicinable: *gave the tongue a h. ornament,* H4A III, 1, 125 (tending to improve the language). *heavens make our presence and our practices pleasant and h. to him,* Hml. II, 2, 39.

Helpless, 1) receiving no aid, wanting support: *hopeless and h. doth Aegeon wend,* Err. I, 1, 158.

2) irremediable, incurable: *what h. shame I feel,* Lucr. 756.

3) affording no help, unprofitable, unavailing: *as those poor birds that h..berries saw,* Ven. 604 (viz painted grapes). *this h. smoke of words,* Lucr. 1027. *poor h. help,* 1056. *urging h. patience,* Err. II, 1, 39. *the h. balm of my poor eyes,* R3 I, 2, 13.

Helter-skelter, an expression denoting the utmost haste: *and h. have I rode to thee,* H4B V, 3, 98 (Pistol's words).

Hem, subst. edge, border: *upon the very h. o' the sea,* Tim. V, 4, 66.

Hem, vb. to enclose, to surround: *I have —ed thee here within the circuit of this pale,* Ven. 229. *—ed with thieves,* 1022. *all things that heaven's air —s,* Sonn. 21, 8. *—ed about with grim destruction,* H6A IV, 3, 21. *a ring of Greeks have —ed thee in,* Troil. IV, 5, 193.

Hem, a sort of voluntary half cough, used 1) by way of encouragement: *cry h., when he should groan,* Ado V, 1, 16. *if I could cry h. and have him,* As I, 3, 19.*when you breathe in your watering, they cry h. and bid you play it off,* H4A II, 4, 18. *how do you now? Better than I was, h.! Why, that's well said,* H4B II, 4, 33. *our watchword was h. boys,* III, 2, 232. *there's a man niece, h.* Troil. I, 2, 248.

2) to give a warning: *cough or cry h., if any body come,* Oth. IV, 2, 29.

Hem, vb. to cry hem: *these burrs are in my heart. H. them away,* As I, 3, 18. *now play me Nestor; h. and stroke thy beard,* Troil. I, 3, 165 (Ff *hum*). *and —s and beats her heart,* Hml. IV, 5, 5.

Hemlock, the plant Conium maculatum: H5 V, 2, 45. Mcb. IV, 1, 25. Lr. IV, 4, 4.

Hemp, that of which ropes and halters are made: H5 III, 6, 45.

Hempen, made of hemp: *h. tackle,* H5 III Chor. 8. *a h. caudle,* H6B IV, 7, 95 (a halter). Metaphorically: *h. home-spuns,* Mids. III, 1, 79 (= of coarse manners).

Hemp-seed, Mrs Quickly's word for *homicide:* H4B II, 1, 64.

Hen, the female of the cock: Shr. II, 227. H4A III, 3, 60. H4B V, 1, 28. Cor. V, 3, 162. a female pigeon: As IV, 1, 151. H4B II, 4, 108. a female pheasant: Wint. IV, 4, 771. term of contempt, to denote cowardice: All's II, 3, 224.

Hence, 1) from this place, from here to another place: *he parted h.* Gent. I, 1, 71. *dispatch me h.* II, 7, 88. III, 1, 160. 187. 246. IV, 3, 29. Meas. IV, 2, 157. V, 119. Err. II, 1, 84. II, 2, 15. IV, 4, 133 etc. etc. Adjectively: *my h. departure,* Wint. I, 2, 450. *our h. going,* Cymb. III, 2, 65. *From* superfluously before it: *when went Tarquin from hence?* Lucr. 1276. *from h. your memory death cannot take,* Sonn. 81, 3. Phoen. 24. Gent. III, 1, 169. 218. V, 2, 43. Meas. I, 1, 54. I, 4, 50. Err. IV, 3, 44. Merch. II, 9, 8. III, 2, 186. IV, 1, 395. As V, 4, 24. Tw. I, 2, 31. V, 394. H6A I, 2, 115. III, 2, 94. H6B I, 4, 30. II, 3, 5. V, 1, 61 etc. *h.* = from this world, Lr. V, 2, 10.

2) away: *my sighs, like whirlwinds, labour h. to heave thee,* Lucr. 586. *I chid Lucetta h.* Gent. I, 2, 60. *get thee h.* IV, 4, 64. *take her h. in horror,* Meas. V, 441. *jealousy, fie, beat it h.* Err. II, 1, 102. *that I were h.* III, 2, 162. *I will not h.* V, 109. *h. from her,* Ado IV, 1, 156. *let us h.* V, 3, 30. *fly h.* LLL V, 2, 86. *skip h.* Mids. II, 1, 61. *you shall h.* Merch. III, 2, 313. *h. with her,* Wint. II, 3, 67. 94. *beat them h.*

H6A I, 3, 54. *thee I'll chase h.* 55. *make we h. amain,* H6C II, 3, 56 etc. Absol., = away, be gone: Ven. 382. Sonn. 125, 13. Tp. I, 1, 17. I, 2, 304. 365. 375. 474. III, 1, 81. V, 298. Wiv. I, 3, 90. Meas. IV, 6, 15. Err. II, 1, 81. LLL IV, 3, 211. Mids. II, 1, 194. II, 2, 2. 21. 85. Shr. IV, 3, 100 etc.

3) not here, at a distance: *praising him here who doth h. remain,* Sonn. 39, 14. *thy letters may be here, though thou art h.* Gent. III, 1, 248. *else I would be h.* IV, 2, 22. *I would have thee h. and here again,* Ado II, 3, 7. *our being absent h.* Merch. V, 120. *my being here it is that holds thee h.* All's III, 2, 126. *comest thou because the anointed king is h.?* R2 II, 3, 96. *all members of our cause, both here and h.* H4B IV, 1, 171. *living h.* H5 I, 2, 270. *freedom lives h., and banishment is here,* Lr. I, 1, 184 etc. *here and h.* = in this and in another world: *this must be answered either here or h.* John IV, 2, 89. *I must die here and live h. by truth,* V, 4, 29. *both here and h. pursue me lasting strife,* Hml. III, 2, 232. Joined to terms of measure, = distant: *I have a kinsman a mile h.* Wint. IV, 3, 86. *how far h. is thy lord?* H6C V, 1, 2. *far h.* H8 III, 1, 90. *h. a mile or twain,* Lr. IV, 1, 44. With *from: Richard not far from h. hath hid his head,* R2 III, 3, 6. *hang in the air a thousand leagues from h.* H4A III, 1, 227. *'tis far from h. to France,* H6C IV, 1, 4.

From h. quite assuming the sense of from here: *kept the earl from h.* H4A IV, 1, 65. And even: *the messengers from h. attend dispatch,* Lr. II, 1, 127 (i.e. they shall receive it here, at this place).

4) out of this, from this source or cause: *controversy h. a question takes,* Compl. 110. *h. his ambition growing,* Tp. I, 2, 105. *h. shall we see,* Meas. I, 3, 53. *h. hath offence his quick celerity,* IV, 2, 113. *h. grew the general wreck,* H6A I, 1, 135. With *from: your name from h. immortal life shall have,* Sonn. 81, 5.

5) from this time forward, later, after the present time: *I teach thee how to make him seem long h. as he shows now,* Sonn. 101, 14. *farewell till half an hour h.* Tp. III, 1, 91. *I'll meet you some hour h.* Err. III, 1, 122. Ado II, 1, 375. Merch. II, 4, 27. H4A III, 2, 177. H6B V, 1, 10. R3 IV, 1, 29. Caes. II, 1, 109. III, 1, 111. Cymb. I, 1, 176.

6) henceforth, in future: *h. ever then my heart is in thy bosom,* LLL V, 2, 826. *make less thy body h., and more thy grace,* H4B V, 5, 56. With *from: from h. I'll love no friend,* Oth. III, 3, 379.

Henceforth, from this time forward, in future: Ven. 1081. Gent. I, 1, 153. I, 2, 98. II, 1, 125. Wiv. IV, 4, 6. LLL V, 2, 412. Mids. III, 2, 67. As I, 2, 35. Shr. IV, 5, 15. All's V, 2, 9. Tw. V, 172. Wint. IV, 4, 448. H4A I, 3, 118. II, 3, 106. II, 4, 490. H4B V, 2, 133. H5 V, 1, 82. H6A IV, 1, 47. 135. H6B III, 1, 324. IV, 10, 67. V, 1, 80. V, 2, 56. H6C II, 1, 77. III, 3, 196. V, 1, 102. Troil. IV, 5, 253. Tit. II, 3, 115. Rom. II, 2, 51. III, 5, 240. Tim. III, 6, 112. 114. Mcb. V, 8, 63. Lr. IV, 6, 75. Ant. I, 4, 1. III, 13, 137. Cymb. IV, 2, 317. *for h.,* in the same sense: Ado V, 1, 304. *from h.:* As I, 2, 25. John I, 160. H4A I, 3, 5. Caes. IV, 3, 121.

Henceforward, in future: H6A I, 3, 79. H6B IV, 6 5. IV, 7, 20. H6C II, 1, 39. Rom. II, 5, 66. IV, 2, 22.

Hence-going, departure: Cymb. III, 2, 65.

Henchman, a page: Mids. II, 1, 121.

Henloft, reading of the spurious Qq in Wiv. III, 4, 41; Ff and Q3 *pen.*

Henned, in *Double henned*, q. v.

Henry (sometimes trisyll.: H6A II, 5, 82. H6B IV, 8, 36. H6C I, 1, 81. 107. 139. 178. I, 2, 10. III, 1, 95. R3 II, 3, 16. In R2 IV, 112 Qq *H., fourth of that name*, Ff *H., of that name the fourth*. In R3 IV, 2, 98 Qq *I remember*, Ff *I remember me*), Christian name, 1) of the son of King John, afterwards King Henry III: John V, 6, 34. 2) of K. Henry IV: R2 I, 1, 3 etc. H4A III, 1, 64 etc. H6A II, 5, 23. 63. H6B II, 2, 21. H6C I, 1, 132 etc. 3) Henry V: H5 V, 2, 259. H6A I, 1, 6. 18. 52. I, 4, 79. II, 5, 82. III, 1, 195. IV, 3, 52. etc. H6B IV, 8, 36. H6C I, 1, 107. 4) Henry VI: H5 Epil. 9. H6A II, 1, 36. IV, 7, 70. H6C I, 1, 81. I, 2, 10. III, 2, 118. R3 II, 3, 16 etc. etc. 5) Henry VII: H6C IV, 6, 67. H8 II, 1, 112. 6) Henry VIII: H8 II, 1, 116. II, 4, 7. 7) Henry Percy: R2 II, 2, 53. H4A V, 1, 87. 8) Henry of Buckingham: H8 II, 1, 107. 9) Sir Henry Guildford: H8 I, 3, 66. 10) H. Lord Scroop: H5 II, 2, 148. 12) Henry Wriothesly Earl of Southampton: Ven. Dedic. and Lucr. Ded. 13) Henry Pimpernell: Shr. Ind. 2, 96.

Hent, subst. hold, seizure, apprehension: *up, sword, and know thou a more horrid h.* Hml. III, 3, 88.*

Hent, vb. to take, to clear, to pass beyond: *jog on the footpath way, and merrily h. the stile-a*, Wint. IV, 3, 133. Unchanged in the partic.: *the generous and gravest citizens have h. the gates, and very near upon the duke is entering*, Meas. IV, 6, 14 (have gone beyond, out of the gates to meet the duke).

Henton, name in H8 I, 2, 147. 148 (confounded with *Hopkins*).

Her, poss.pron. 1) of the third person sing.fem.: Ven. 27. 32. 49. 51 etc. etc. *a thousand other her defences*, Wiv. II, 2, 259. *one her hairs were gold*, LLL IV, 3, 142. *from Rome her enemies*, Cor.III,3,111 (M.Edd. *for Rome*). 2) of the third pers. plur., the old English use of *here* for *their* being, as it should seem, not yet quite extinct: *these water-galls in her dim element foretell new storms to those already spent*, Lucr. 1588. *were our tears wanting to this funeral, these tidings would call forth her flowing tides*, H6A I, 1, 83 (M. Edd. *their*). *the wars must make examples out of her best*, Oth III, 3, 66 (M. Edd. *their*). F1 in Troil. I, 3, 118.

Heraclitus, the ancient philosopher, not named, but alluded to in Merch. I, 2, 53.

Herald, subst. 1) an officer whose business was to record and blazon the arms of the nobility: Lucr. 206. Shr. II, 225. to order and conduct funeral processions: H6A I, 1, 45. Cor. V, 6, 145. to make proclamations: H6B IV, 2, 186. to bear challenges: H8 I, 1, 34. Lr. V, 1, 48. V, 3, 101. 109. to carry messages between hostile parties or armies: John II, 325. IV, 2, 78. H5 III, 5, 36. III, 6, 157. IV, 3, 121. 122. 127. IV, 7, 59. 69. 71. 86. IV, 8, 78. Troil. I, 3, 218. to attend messengers of the enemy: H5 IV, 7, 121. H6A IV, 7, 51. his coat without sleeves: H4A IV, 2, 48. H6B IV, 10, 75.

2) a publisher, proclaimer, harbinger: *the owl, night's h.* Ven. 531. *only h. to the gaudy spring*, Sonn. 1, 10. *let the bird of loudest lay h. sad and trumpet be*, Phoen. 3. *silence is the perfectest h. of joy*, Ado II, 1, 317. *I wish no other h.* H8 IV, 2, 69. *the lark, the h. of the morn*, Rom. III, 5, 6. *when the gods by tokens send such dreadful —s*, Caes. I, 3, 56.

3) any messenger: LLL III, 70. V, 2, 97. All's

V, 3, 46. R3 I, 1, 72. IV, 3, 55. Rom. II, 5, 4. Hml. III, 4, 58. Adjectively: Gent. III, 1, 144.

Herald, vb. to conduct solemnly: Mcb. I, 3, 102. Per. III, 1, 34.

Heraldry, 1) the art of a herald, consisting in the science treating of ensigns armorial: Mids. III, 2, 213. Oth. III, 4, 47. in the forms and ceremonies observed in a challenge and combat: Hml. I, 1, 87 *(by law and h. = by the law of h., cf. And)*.

2) blazonry, significance of armorial ensigns: *this h. in Lucrece' face was seen*, argued *by beauty's red and virtue's white*, Lucr. 64. *hath now this dread and black complexion smeared with h. more dismal*, Hml. II, 2, 478. *you are more saucy with lords than the commission of your birth and virtue gives you h.* All's II, 3, 280 (more than you are entitled to by birth and virtue, both of which may confer on a man the claim of nobility, may ennoble him).

Herb, any plant which dies to the root every year and has no wooden stem: Ven. 165. 1055. Mids. II, 1, 169. 173. 184. II, 2, 366. Merch. V, 13. All's IV, 5, 16. R2 III, 4, 46. H6B III, 1, 33. R3 II, 4, 13. Tit. III, 1, 178. Rom. II, 3, 16. 28. Oth. I, 3, 327. Cymb. IV, 2, 284. *h. of grace*: All's IV, 5, 18. R2 III, 4, 105. Hml. IV, 5, 182 (Ff *herb-grace*).

Herbert, name in R3 IV, 5, 9. V, 3, 28.

Herb-grace, reading of Ff in Hml. IV, 5, 182; Qq *herb of grace*; see *Grace*.

Herblet, small herb: Cymb. IV, 2, 287.

Herb-woman, a woman that deals in herbs: Per. IV, 6, 92.

Herculean, similar to Hercules: *this H. Roman*, Ant. I, 3, 84 (with allusion to the pretended descent of Antony from Hercules).

Hercules, the hero of antiquity, proverbial for his strength: Wiv. I, 3, 6. Ado II, 1, 261. 380. III, 3, 145. IV, 1, 324. LLL I, 2, 69. 182. IV, 3, 167. 340. V, 1, 136. 141. 145. V, 2, 539. 592. Mids. IV, 1, 117. V, 47. Merch. II, 1, 32. III, 2, 60. 85. As I, 2, 222. Shr. I, 2, 257. All's IV, 3, 283. H4A II, 4, 299. H6A II, 3, 19. H6C II, 1, 53. Cor. IV, 1, 17. IV, 6, 99. Hml. I, 2, 153. V, 1, 314. Ant. III, 7, 68. IV, 3, 16. Cymb. IV, 2, 114. 311. *do the boys carry it away? Ay, that they do; H. and his load too*, Hml. II, 2, 378 (alluding to the Globe theatre, the sign of which was Hercules bearing the globe). Corrupted to *Ercles* by Bottom: Mids. I, 2, 31. 42.

Herd, a number of beasts together: Ven. 456 689. Sonn. 12, 6. Pilgr. 72. 285. Tp. II, 1, 316. Merch. V, 71. As II, 1, 52. All's I, 3, 59. H4A III, 1, 39. H6A IV, 2, 46. H6C II, 1, 14. III, 1, 7. Troil. I, 3, 48. Ant. III, 13, 128. Applied to men in contempt: Wint. IV, 4, 620. Cor. I, 4, 31. III, 1, 33. III, 2, 32 (O. Edd. *heart*). Caes. I, 2, 266.

Herdman (Ven.) or **Herdsman**, one who tends a herd: Ven. 456. Wint. IV, 4, 344. 446. Cor. II, 1, 105.

Here, 1) in this place: Tp. I, 1, 41. I, 2, 171. 215. 270. 282 etc. etc. *h. and there*: Tp. I, 2, 380. Err. V, 147. Mids. III, 2, 381. Hml. I, 1, 97 etc. *that's neither h. nor there* = to no purpose, nonsense: Wiv. I, 4, 112 and Oth. IV, 3, 59 (Mrs Quickly's and Emilia's speeches). *nor h. nor h.* (neither to the right nor to the left) Cymb. III, 2, 80. *a wheeling stranger of h. and everywhere*, Oth. I, 1, 138. *h. and hence* = in this and in another world, see *Hence*. *'twere as good he were* (dead) *as living h. and you no* *use of him*, Rom. III, 5, 227 (i.e. in this world); cf. Mcb. I, 7, 6. Substantively: *thou losest h., a better where to find*, Lr. I, 1, 264. Used to answer to a call: *boatswain! h., master*, Tp. I, 1, 2. Wiv. III, 5, 2. Mids. I, 2, 45. 61. 64. V, 38 etc. In drinking a health: *h.'s to my love*, Rom. V, 3, 119. *h.'s to thee*, Tim. III, 1, 34. To point to a person or thing or action: *only attended by Nerissa h.* Merch. III, 4, 29. *she is desperate h.* H4A III, 1, 198. *you shall live in your country h. in banishment*, H6B II, 3, 12. *protect my lady h.* II, 4, 79. *this devil h.* III, 1, 371 (i.e. of whom I am speaking). *so he says h.* Troil. I, 2, 56. *acquaint her h. of my son Paris' love*, Rom. III, 4, 16. *Calpurnia h. stays me at home*, Caes. II, 2, 75. cf. *this lord of weak remembrance... hath h. almost persuaded*, Tp. II, 1, 234. *my riches are these poor habiliments, of which if you should h. disfurnish me*, Gent. IV, 1, 14. *hear me, O hear me h.* Meas. V, 32 (i.e. hear me yourself; do not refer me to another). *h. go; the desk, the purse; sweet now, make haste*, Err. IV, 2, 29 (i.e. go you, you whom I am addressing). *I can h. disarm thee with this stick*, Tp. I, 2, 472 (= with this stick here). *and h. by this is your brother saved*, Meas. III, 1, 263. *is h. all?* H4B III, 2, 199 (= is that the whole list? are there no more than these?). *h. I lay, and thus I bore my point*, H4A II, 4, 215 (as you see me now). Pointing to what follows (Fr. voici): *h.'s the pang that pinches*, H8 II, 3, 1. *if not so, then h. I hit it right, our Romeo hath not been in bed to-night*, Rom. II, 3, 41. *good night, and h. stands all your state*, III, 3, 166. *some comfort, nurse. Faith, h. it is*, III, 5, 214. *h.'s my drift*, Hml. II, 1, 37. *h. is* = that is, there we have, see, what a: *h. is a coil with protestation*, Gent. I, 2, 99. *h.'s a million of manners*, II, 1, 104. *h. will be an old abusing of God's patience*, Wiv. I, 4, 4. *h.'s a fellow frights English out of his wits*, II, 1, 142. Meas. I, 2, 107. II, 1, 57. Mids. I, 2, 67. II, 2, 147. Wint. II, 2, 9. John IV, 3, 116. H4B II, 4, 214. 219. H6A V, 4, 80. H6B IV, 2, 96. R3 III, 6, 10. Rom. II, 4, 87. II, 5, 67. Tim. I, 1, 18. Caes. III, 2, 257. Negatively with irony: *h.'s no knavery*, Shr. I, 2, 138. *h.'s no vanity*, H4A V, 3, 33. *h.'s no sound jest*, Tit. IV, 2, 26. Inversely: *h. much Orlando*, As IV, 3, 2 (i.e. no Orlando); cf. *Much. h.'s Agamemnon, an honest fellow enough*, Troil. V, 1, 56 (= for instance). cf. *With*.

2) at this point, on this occasion, now: *even h. she sheathed in her breast a knife*, Lucr. 1723 (= at these words). *h. cease thy questions*, Tp. I, 2, 184. *I h. forget all former griefs*, Gent. V, 4, 142. *and even h. brake off and came away*, R3 III, 7, 41 etc.

3) to this place, hither: Tp. I, 2, 51. Meas. V, 384. LLL V, 2, 218. Mids. II, 2, 20. III. 2, 98. Mcb. V, 3, 62 etc.

Hereabout, about this place: Tp. II, 2, 41. Rom. V, 3, 43. Oth. III, 4, 165 (O. Edd. *walk here about*). V, 1, 57.

Hereabouts, the same: Rom. V, 1, 38.

Hereafter, 1) in time to come, in future: Ven. 1136. Lucr. 758. 1714. Tp. V, 294. Meas. IV, 4, 15. Ado III, 2, 99. As I, 2, 296. III, 3, 41. 95. All's IV, 3, 111. Tw. II, 3, 48. R2 II, 1, 136. H4A III, 2, 92. H4B IV, 2, 76. H5 V, 1, 58. V, 2, 226. R3 II, 1, 73. III, 3, 7. H8 V, 1, 168. Cor. I, 3, 115. III, 2, 85. V, 3, 18. Rom. III, 1, 82. V, 3, 66. Caes. II, 1, 191. Mcb. I, 3, 50. I, 4, 38. Hml. I, 5, 171. Lr. I, 1, 27. Cymb. I, 4, 34. III, 4, 93. V, 5, 375. Per. III, 3, 41.

Adjectively: *that h. ages may behold*, H6A II, 2, 10. *tears to wash h. time*, R3 IV, 4, 390.

2) after this, subsequent to this: *and long h. say unto his child*, H6C II, 2, 36. *here's yet in the word h. the kneading*, Troil. I, 1, 23. *greater than both by the all-hail h.* Mcb. I, 5, 56.

3) at a later time, afterwards: *I will h. make known to you why I have done this*, Wiv. III, 3, 241. Meas. III, 1, 262. Merch. II, 6, 20. All's IV, 4, 26. Tw. III, 4, 138. Wint. IV, 4, 353. R3 I, 2, 199. Tim. V, 4, 81. Caes. I, 2, 165. Mcb. V, 5, 17. Oth. III, 3, 387. Ant. III, 5, 23. Cymb. III, 2, 68. IV, 2, 41.

Here-approach (not hyphened in O. Edd.) arrival: Mcb. IV, 3, 133.

Hereby, 1) by this: *what is meant h.* R3 I, 4, 94. 2) close by, very near: *h., upon the edge of yonder coppice*, LLL IV, 1, 9. Quibbling in I, 2, 141: *I will visit thee at the lodge. That's h.* (= as it falls out, in Jaquenetta's language).

Hereditary, possessed by inheritance, transmitted from parent to child: Tp. II, 1, 223. Wint. I, 2, 75. Cor. II, 1, 103. Tim. IV, 3, 10. 274. Lr. I, 1, 81. Ant. I, 4, 13. Somewhat improperly: *these old fellows have their ingratitude in them h.* Tim. II, 2, 224 (= inherent, natural).

Hereford or **Herford**, name of an English town and county: R2 I, 1, 3. 28. I, 2, 46. 47. I, 4, 2 etc. H4B IV, 1, 131. 138. R3 III, 1, 195. IV, 2, 93. H8 I, 1, 200. see *Ha'rford-west*.

Herefordshire, English county: H4A I, 1, 39.

Herein (cf. *In*), in this: Sonn. 11, 5. Meas. V, 527. Err. III, 1, 86. IV, 2, 26. LLL I, 1, 21. Mids. I, 1, 250. Merch. I, 1, 153. II, 2, 182. IV, 1, 267. As I, 1, 146. I, 2, 8. R2 IV, 327. V, 6, 31. H4A I, 2, 221. III, 2, 161. IV, 3, 51. H4B IV, 1, 170. H6B II, 4, 72. III, 1, 232. H6C III, 2, 75. R3 III, 4, 7. IV, 2, 25 (Ff *in this*). 26 (Ff *you h. presently*, Qq *your grace immediately*). Mcb. I, 6, 12. Hml. I, 1, 155. I, 2, 14. 31. II, 2, 76.

Hereof (cf. *Of*) of this: Err. IV, 4, 146. Shr. IV, 5, 75. R2 II, 1, 212. H4B IV, 3, 126. H6A I, 5, 39.

Here-remain, subst. (not hyphened in O. Edd.) stay, residence: *since my h. in England*, Mcb. IV, 3, 148.

Heresy, heterodoxy, opinion differing from the established faith: LLL IV, 1, 22. V, 1, 6. Mids. II, 2, 139. 141. Merch. II, 9, 82. Tw. I, 5, 246. H8 V, 3, 18. Cymb. III, 4, 84.

Heretic, one who holds opinions differing from the established faith: Sonn. 124, 9. Wiv. IV, 4, 9. Ado I, 1, 236. Wint. II, 3, 115. John III, 1, 175. H8 III, 2, 102. V, 1, 45. Rom. I, 2, 96. Lr. III, 2, 84 (the indef. art. before it never *a*, but *an*).

Hereto, till now: *a kinder value of the people than he hath h. prized them at*, Cor. II, 2, 64.

Heretofore, before: *hath he never h. sounded you?* Lr. I, 2, 74 (Ff *before*).

Hereupon, upon this: *I will h. confess I am in love*, LLL I, 2, 60.

Herford, see *Hereford*.

Heritage, estate devolved by succession: All's I, 3, 26.* Per. II, 1, 129.

Hermes, Mercury: *more musical than the pipe of H.* H5 III, 7, 19.

Hermia, female name in Mids. I, 1, 23. 46 etc

Hermione, female name in Wint. I, 2, 33. 88 etc.

Hermit, 1) an anchoret: LLL IV, 3, 242. Merch. V, 33. Tw. IV, 2, 15. H4B V, 1, 71. H6A II, 5, 117. Troil. V, 3, 45. Tit. III, 2, 41.

2) a beadsman, one bound to pray for another: *we rest your —s,* Mcb. I, 6, 20; cf. Tit. III, 2, 41.

Hermitage, the habitation of an anchoret: LLL V, 2, 805. R2 III, 3, 148.

Herne, name of a legendary hunter: Wiv. IV, 4, 28. 38. V, 5, 31. 108. his oak in Windsor park: IV, 4, 40. IV, 6, 19. V, 1, 12. V, 3, 15. V, 5, 80.

Hero, a man eminent for bravery: All's II, 1, 40. Hml. II, 2, 270.

Hero, 1) the mistress of Leander: Gent. III, 1, 119. As IV, 1, 101. 106. Rom. II, 4, 44. Confounded with Helen: Mids. V, 199. 2) female name in Ado I, 1, 198. 297 etc.

Herod, the king of Jewry, represented as a swaggering tyrant in the old dramatic performances: Wiv. II, 1, 20. H5 III, 3, 41. Hml. III, 2, 16. Ant. I, 2, 28. III, 3, 3. 4. III, 6, 73. IV, 6, 14.

Heroic, like a hero, eminently brave: H6A II, 5, 78. Writing of the spurious Qq. in Wiv. I, 3, 26.

Heroical, 1) eminently brave: LLL IV, 1, 64. H5 II, 4, 59. 2) becoming a hero: *the reasons are more potent and h.* Troil. III, 3, 192. *an h. cudgelling,* 248.

Herring, the fish Clupea harengus: Wiv. II, 3, 12. Tw. III, 1, 40. H4A II, 4, 143. H6B IV, 2, 36. Troil. V, 1, 68. Rom. II, 4, 39. *two white h.* Lr. III, 6, 33 (pickled h.).

Hers, poss. pron. of the third pers. fem. sing., used absol. with reference to a subst. going before: *h.* (viz eyes) *shone like the moon,* Ven. 491. Gent. IV, 2, 117. Mids II, 2, 93 etc. Demonstratively: Lr. II, 2, 97. Without reference to a subst.: *I am h.* Tp. V, 196. Lr. V, 1, 13. *herself and h.* Tit. IV, 2, 171. *heavens both on her and h. have laid most heavy hand,* Cymb. V, 5, 464. *of h.* = of her: *this pride of h.* Gent. III, 1, 72. *this face of mine were full as lovely as is this of h.* IV, 4, 191. *where never scandal slept, save this of h.* Ado V, 1, 71. *these haughty words of h.* H6A III, 3, 78. *what a peevish course is this of h.* R3 III, 1, 32. *nor shall ever see that face of h. again,* Lr. I, 1, 267. *that honour of h.* Cymb. I, 4, 142. Before the subst., but separated from it: *and win this ring by h. and mine adultery,* Cymb. V, 5, 186.

Herself (in two words in O. Edd.) 1) she, or her, in her own person: *h. hath taught her love,* Gent. II, 1, 174. *trust my wife with h.* Wiv. II, 2, 320. Err. I, 1, 46. Rom. I, 2, 100 etc.

2) in her own person: *the fair soul h.* Tp. II, 1, 129. Gent. V, 4, 98. Wiv. IV, 5, 41. Meas. III, 2, 60. Err. IV, 4, 75 etc.

3) refl. pron. of the third person fem. sing.: Gent. II, 3, 14. Meas. I, 1, 40 etc.

Hesione, daughter of Laomedon, not named, but alluded to: Merch. III, 2, 56. Troil. II, 2, 77.

Hesperia, see *Hisperia.*

Hesperides, the garden of antique fable with trees bearing golden apples: *is not Love a Hercules, still climbing trees in the H.?* LLL IV, 3, 341. *before thee stands this fair H. with golden fruit,* Per. I, 1, 27.

Hesperus, the evening star: *ere twice in murk and occidental damp moist H. hath quenched her sleepy lamp,* All's II, 1, 167 (M. Edd. *his sleepy lamp*).

Hest (cf. *Behest*) injunction, command, order:

Tp. I, 2, 274. III, 1, 37. IV, 1, 65 *(at thy h.).* LLL V, 2, 65. H4A II, 3, 65 (reading of Q1; the other O. Edd. less appropriately *haste;* cf. Hml. I, 1, 148).

Hew (impf. not used, partic. *—ed:* Tit. II, 4, 17. *—n:* H6C II, 2, 168. V, 4, 69), to cut, to chop, to hack: H6A IV, 7, 47. H6C II, 6, 48. Cor. IV, 5, 126. Tit. I, 97. 129. II, 4, 17. Caes. II, 1, 174. *to h. down* (a tree): H6C II, 1, 55. II, 2, 168. Cor. I, 1, 185. Mcb. V, 4, 4. *h. up,* in the same sense: *I could h. up rocks,* H6B V, 1, 24. *must by the roots be —n up,* H6C V, 4, 69. *to h. out* = to make by cutting: *or h. my way out with a bloody axe,* H6C III, 2, 181. *to h. to* = to shape by cutting (cf. *To*): *thou rather shalt enforce it with thy smile than h. to't with thy sword,* Tim. V, 4, 46 (O. Edd. *too't*). In H5 II, 1, 39 O. Edd. unintelligibly *hewn,* M. Edd. *drawn.*

Hewgh (Qq *hagh*) a sound imitative of the whizzing of an arrow: Lr. IV, 6, 93.

Hey, 1) a cry to set dogs on: Tp. IV, 256. 2) a frolicking exclamation: As V, 3, 18. 21. Tw. IV, 2, 78. V, 399. Lr. III, 2, 75 (Ff *heigh-ho*). *h. nonny,* Ado II, 3, 71. *a h. nonino,* As V, 3, 18. *h. non nonny, nonny, h. nonny,* Hml. IV, 5, 165.

Heyday (cf. *Hoyday*), a cry of exultation: Tp. II, 2, 190 (O. Edd. *highday*). Used as an appellative, = froliksome wildness: *at your age the h. in the blood is tame,* Hml. III, 4, 69.

Hick, an obviously lascivious interpretation made by Mrs Quickly of the Latin *hic:* Wiv. IV, 1, 68.*

Hide, subst. the skin of an animal: *broad buttock, tender h.* Ven. 298. *the spur that anger thrusts into his h.* Sonn. 50, 10. *an a may catch your h. and you alone,* John II, 136. 292. III, 1, 128. H5 IV, 2, 9. 47. Lr. III, 4, 109. Applied to men in contempt: Shr. II, 406. H6C I, 4, 137. Troil. V, 6, 31 (used of an armour). Hml. V, 1, 186.

Hide, vb. (impf. *hid:* Tp. II, 2, 115. LLL V, 2, 388. H4A I, 3, 106. Tit. V, 1, 107. Partic. ordinarily *hid,* nine times *hidden:* Ven. 767. Sonn. 31, 8. Meas. V, 397. As I, 3, 121. H5 III, 7, 118. R3 II, 1, 14. Caes. I, 2, 57. Mcb. I, 3, 113. Oth. II, 1, 245. The latter form used only adjectively, but never serving to form tenses), 1) to envelop, to cover: *the ivy which had hid my princely trunk,* Tp. I, 2, 86. *the cover of the salt —s the salt, and therefore it is more than the salt,* Gent. III, 1, 369. *the greater —s the less,* 372; cf. Lucr. 663. *—ing mine honour in my necessity,* Wiv. II, 2, 24; cf. *—ing his bitter jests in blunt behaviour,* Shr. III, 2, 13. *though now this grained face of mine be hid in winter's drizzled snow,* Err. V, 311. *do not h. mine eyes,* All's IV, 1, 74 (= do not blindfold me). *by the ground they h. I judge their number near the rate of thirty thousand,* H4B IV, 1, 21. *—s a sword with crowns,* H5 II Prol. 9. *gardeners do with ordure h. those roots,* II, 4, 39. *iron of Naples hid with English gilt,* H6C II, 2, 139. *a rude stream, that must for ever h. me,* H8 III, 2, 364. *when we have our naked frailties hid,* Mcb. II, 3, 132. *fill till the cup be hid,* Ant. II, 7, 93. *to h. a sword* = to sheathe it: As II, 7, 119. R3 I, 2, 176.

2) to make invisible in any manner, not to let appear, to suppress, to keep secret: *if thou dost seek to have what thou dost h., by self-example mayst thou be denied,* Sonn. 142, 13. *to h. what I have said to thee,* Gent. IV, 3, 35; cf. *would from a paddock such concernings h.* Hml. III, 4, 191; *to excuse or h. the*

liberal opposition of our spirits, LLL V, 2, 742 (= not to remember); *ere they can h. their levity in honour,* All's I, 2, 35. *shame would have it hid,* Lr. II, 1, 95. *to make the truth appear where it seems hid, and h. the false seems true,* Meas. V, 66 (make it disappear, make away with it). *obscuring and —ing from me all gentleman-like qualities,* As I, 1, 73.

3) to conceal: Ven. 339. 767. 876. Lucr. 5. 93. 371. 548. 609. 794. 1008. 1413. Sonn. 30, 6. 31, 8. 52, 10. Tp. I, 2, 229. II, 2, 115. 138. III, 1, 80. Wiv. III, 3, 71. 136. IV, 2, 65. Meas. III, 1, 40. III, 2, 285. V, 397. Err. II, 2, 31. Ado II, 3, 38. 42. III, 1, 11. V, 1, 182. LLL V, 2, 388. Mids. I, 2, 53. II, 1, 31. 227. Merch. I, 1, 116. II, 2, 84. III, 2, 80. V, 126. As I, 3, 121. Shr. Ind. 2, 53. Tw. I, 3, 133. III, 1, 133. 160. R2 III, 2, 37. H4A II, 4, 549. 553. H5 III, 7, 118. H6B II, 1, 25. IV, 10, 3. R3 II, 1, 14. III, 7, 163. Rom. III, 3, 71. Caes. I, 2, 57. Mcb. I, 3, 113. Oth. II, 1, 245 etc. *to h. one's head:* Tp. II, 2, 23. LLL V, 2, 86. 635. Mids. III, 2, 406. R2 III, 3, 6. 9. H4A I, 3, 106. H6A I, 5, 39. H6B V, 1, 85. Troil. IV, 4, 139. Caes. IV, 3, 16. *all hid, all hid; an old infant play,* LLL IV, 3, 78. *h. fox, and all after,* Hml. IV, 2, 32 (allusions to the children's play *Hide and seek*). With *from:* Sonn. 33, 7. 65, 10. Meas. I, 2, 156. LLL I, 1, 57. 64. Wint. IV, 4, 456. H6A I, 2, 68. H6B II, 4, 23. V, 1, 84. V, 2, 2. R3 III, 7, 161. Caes. II, 1, 277. Cymb. I, 6, 86. III, 1, 43. Hence = to protect, to keep in safety: *to h. us from pursuit,* As I, 3, 138. *can h. you from our messengers of war,* John II, 260. *to h. thee from this shame,* H4A II, 4, 291. *to h. thee from prevention,* Caes. II, 1, 85. *I'll h. my master from the flies,* Cymb. IV, 2, 388.

Hideous, (dissyll.; trisyll. in Wiv. IV, 4, 34) frightful, shocking, horrible: Lucr. 973. Sonn. 5, 6. 12, 2. Wiv. IV, 4, 34. Meas. I, 4, 63. All's V, 3, 52. Tw. I, 5, 221. IV, 2, 34. John IV, 2, 266. V, 4, 22. H4B II, 3, 35. H6C V, 6, 46. R3 I, 4, 60. H8 I, 1, 90. Rom. IV, 3, 50. Caes. II, 1, 65. Mcb. II, 3, 87. Hml. I, 4, 54. II, 2, 498. Lr. I, 4, 282. Oth. III, 3, 108. *drive the gentleman into a most h. opinion of his rage,* Tw. III, 4, 212 (i. e. into an opinion of the extreme hideousness of his rage). *check this h. rashness,* Lr. I, 1, 153 (shocking, in a moral sense).

Hideously, in a manner to frighten, horribly: H4B V, 2, 12. Troil. IV, 2, 13 (Qq and most M. Edd. *tediously*).

Hideousness, dreadfulness: Ado V, 1, 96.

Hie, (used only in the pres. and impf.) 1) intr. to make haste: *away she —s,* Ven. 1189. *who to her mistress —s,* Lucr. 1215. *charging the groom to h.* 1334. *doth h.* 1341. *and thither —d,* Sonn. 153, 12. Gent. IV, 4, 93. Err. IV, 3, 93. Mids. III, 2, 355. All's II, 5, 82. III, 4, 9. John III, 1, 347. H4A IV, 4, 1. H5 III, 2, 18. III, 5, 39. Tit. III, 1, 286. Rom. III, 2, 138. III, 5, 26. IV, 4, 25. Caes. I, 3, 150. III, 1, 290. Hml. I, 1, 154. Oth. V, 1, 34. Per. V Prol. 20.

2) refl. (the simple personal pronoun always serving as reflexive): *Adonis —d him to the chase,* Ven. 3. *unto the wood they h. them,* 323. Gent. IV, 2, 94. Err. I, 2, 90. IV, 4, 15. All's IV, 4, 12. R3 III, 5, 73. Oftenest in the imperative: Pilgr. 167. Err. III, 2, 152. IV, 1, 102. IV, 4, 59. Merch. I, 3, 178. II, 2, 181. Shr. IV, 4, 62. Tw. I. 5, 325. R2 V, 1, 22. H4B IV, 2, 71. R3 I, 3, 143. IV, 1, 44. V, 3, 53. Cor. I, 2, 26. Rom. II, 5, 70. 74. 79. III, 3, 164. Caes. V, 3, 78.

Mcb. I, 5, 26. III, 1, 35. Oth. IV, 3, 50. Ant. II, 3, 15. V, 2, 194. Cymb. II, 3, 143. Per. III, 1, 69. V, 1, 241.

Hiems, winter personified: LLL V, 2, 901. Mids. II, 1, 109.

High, adj. 1) having a great extent upwards, rising much above the ground or any other object: *her h. top,* Merch. I, 1, 28. *h. Taurus,* Mids. III, 2, 141. *h. Olympus,* Caes. IV, 3, 92. *h. Dunsinane hill,* Mcb. IV, 1, 93. *the wall is h.* John IV, 3, 1. R2 II, 3, 4. H4B I, 2, 44. III, 1, 18. Cor. I, 1, 203. Ant. V, 2, 61. *h. tops,* Merch. IV, 1, 76. As IV, 3, 106. Tim. V, 1, 13. *the roof of this court is too h.* LLL II, 93. *the sun is h.* H5 IV, 2, 63. *the h. east,* Caes. II, 1, 110.*h. forehead,* Gent. IV, 4, 198. Rom. II, 1, 18. *h. crest,* Ven. 297. *flies the —er pitch,* H6A II, 4, 11. *h. curvet,* All's II, 3, 299. *lavoltas h.* Troil. IV, 4, 88. *as h. a flow,* H4A I, 2, 43. *h. seas,* Oth. II, 1, 68 etc. = tall: LLL IV, 1, 46. Merch. V, 163. H4B III, 2, 34. Ant. II, 7, 48.

2) exceeding in any way the common measure: *his h. desire,* Ven. 276. *so h. a hope,* Tp. II, 1, 241. *my h. charms work,* III, 3, 88. *their h. wrongs,* V, 25. *a most h. miracle,* 177. *this h. honour,* Gent. II, 4, 158. *a h. praise,* Ado I, 1, 174. *h. deeds,* V, 1, 278; H4A III, 2, 107; V, 5, 30; H8 I, 1, 61; Tit. V, 1, 11. *a h. hope,* LLL I, 1, 196. *in the —est compulsion of base fear,* All's III, 6, 31. *h. commendation,* As I, 2, 275. *in his h. disgrace,* R2 I, 1, 194. *h. sparks of honour,* V, 6, 29. *at h. speed,* H4A II, 4, 379. *a horse full of h. feeding,* H4B I, 1, 10 (i. e. good, plentiful feeding; cf. *highly fed,* All's II, 2, 3). *in h. despite,* H6C II, 1, 59. *h. pay,* 134. *of so h. a courage,* V, 4, 50. *a h. reward,* V, 5, 10. *your h. deserts,* R3 I, 3, 97. *the h. perfection of my loss,* IV, 4, 66. *what his h. hatred would effect,* H8 I, 1, 107. *h. profits,* III, 2, 158. *h. designs,* Troil. I, 3, 102. *h. strains of divination,* II, 2, 113. *h. fortune,* Rom. II, 5, 80. *your h. displeasure,* III, 1, 160. *the other at h. wish,* Tim. IV, 3, 245 (having fully what he wishes). *the king is in h. rage,* Lr. II, 4, 299. *h. renown,* Oth. II, 3, 96. *h. and plenteous wit,* IV, 1, 201. *too h. a fame,* Ant. III, 1, 15. *see h. order in this great solemnity,* V, 2, 369. *h. expense,* Per. III Prol. 20. Often joined to words denoting estimation: *valued at the —est rate,* Err. I, 1, 24; Hml. I, 3, 122. *a place of h. respect with me,* Mids. II, 1, 209; All's V, 3, 192; H4A III, 1, 170; Mcb. III, 6, 29. *grown so h. in his esteem,* Mids. III, 2, 294; Shr. Ind. 2, 16. *misprision in the —est degree,* Tw. I, 5, 61; IV, 2, 128; R3 V, 3, 196. *make h. account of you,* R3 III, 2, 71. *h. note's ta'en of your virtues,* H8 II, 3, 59. Joined to *treason* (q. c.): Lucr. 369. Wint. III, 2, 14. R2 I, 1, 27. H4B IV, 2, 107. H5 II, 2, 145. 147. 149. H6B I, 3, 185. III, 1, 97. H8 I, 1, 201. II, 1, 27.

3) of elevated rank or birth: *that he coloured with his h. estate,* Lucr. 92. *h. birth,* Sonn. 91, 9; Troil. III, 3, 172. *too low a mistress for so h. a servant,* Gent. II, 4, 106. Wiv. III, 2, 75. Meas. IV, 2, 114; Ant. III, 6, 33. Mids. I, 1, 136. R2 I, 1, 58. H4B II, 2, 3. H6A IV, 1, 17. H6B III, 1, 48. H6C I, 4, 72. R3 IV, 4, 314. Troil. Prol. 2. Ant. I, 2, 196. 197 etc. *mark the h. noises,* Lr. III, 6, 118 (i. e. those coming from the upper region of the great ones). *h. admiral,* H6C III, 3, 252. *h. constable,* H5 II, 4, 41. IV, 8, 97. H8 II, 1, 102. *h. steward,* H8 IV, 1, 18. 41. *the h. tides in the calendar,* John III, 1, 86. *h. festivals,* H6A I, 6, 26.

4) deserving or enjoying general respect and reverence, dignified, exalted, sublime: *in that h. task*, Lucr. 80. *Collatine's h. name*, 108. *by h. almighty Jove*, 568. Tp. IV, 101. Meas. II, 2, 121. LLL II, 34. As V, 4, 150. All's I, 3, 198. II, 1, 113. II, 3, 81. IV, 2, 24. Wint. III, 2, 203. IV, 4, 7. V, 1, 88. John I, 101. IV, 2, 5. R2 I, 4, 2. III, 2, 88. IV, 109. V, 2, 38. H4A I, 3, 69. H4B IV, 4, 3. V, 2, 134. H6A III, 1, 177. H6B I, 1, 1. R3 III, 7, 155. V, 1, 20. H8 Prol. 3. Caes. I, 2, 170. III, 1, 33. V, 1, 107. Hml. IV, 7, 43. Ant. IV, 15, 87. V, 2, 363 etc. In All's II, 1, 12 read *h. Italy* (O. and M. Edd. *—er Italy*).

5) proud, lofty: *Love, whose h. imperious thoughts have punished me*, Gent. II, 4, 130. *thoughts h. for one so tender*, Wint. III, 2, 197. *with a proud majestical h. scorn*, H6A IV, 7, 39. *a lady of so h. resolve*, V, 5, 75. *in the most h. and palmy state of Rome*, Hml. I, 1, 113. *noble, courageous, h.* Ant. II, 3, 20. *plighter of h. hearts*, III, 13, 126. Used of words: *in so h. a style*, Ado V, 2, 6. *I hope in God for h. words*, LLL I, 1, 195 (= high-flown, pompous). *deserves h. speech*, Wint. II, 1, 70. *thou hast astonished me with thy h. terms*, H6A I, 2, 93. *such h. vaunts of his nobility*, H6B III, 1, 50.

6) violent, boisterous, loud: *till the h. fever seethe your blood to froth*, Tim. IV, 3, 433. *Cassio h. in oath*, Oth. II, 3, 235. *h. and boastful neighs*, H5 IV Prol. 10. *the noise was h.* Oth. V, 2, 93 (Q *here*). *the h. wind*, Ven. 305. Lucr. 335. H6B II, 1, 3. 55. Tit. V, 3, 69. Lr. II, 4, 303 (Qq *bleak*).

7) Used of time, = full, urgent: *'tis h. time that I were hence*, Err. III, 2, 162. *it is now h. supper-time*, Oth. IV, 2, 249. Of sounds, opposed to low, = sharp, acute: *in clamours of all size, both h. and low*, Compl. 21. Of colours, = vivid, deep: *if she praised him above, his complexion is —er than his; he having colour enough, and the other —er*, Troil. I, 2, 111.

High, used substantively, 1) an elevated place or region; properly and metaphorically: *the lark mounts up on h.* Ven. 854. *thine eyes that taught the dumb on h. to sing*, Sonn. 78, 5. *while you mount up on h.* R2 IV, 189. *thy seat is up on h.* V, 5, 112. *Percy stands on h.* H4A III, 3, 227. *heaved a h.* R3 IV, 4, 86.

2) persons of an elevated rank or birth: *h. and low*, Wiv. II, 1, 117. Wint. V, 1, 207. Tim. V, 1, 212. Mcb. IV, 1, 67. Cymb. IV, 2, 249. cf. Mids. I, 1, 136. Used, in a quibbling manner, of false dice turning up high or low numbers: *and h. and low beguiles the rich and poor*, Wiv. I, 3, 95.

3) The superl. *—est* = a) God: *All's IV, 2, 24.* b) the highest point or degree: *our happiness is at the —est*, R3 I, 3, 41 (Ff *height*). *wrench up thy power to the —est*, Cor. I, 8, 11. c) the farthest visible part (as the horizon seems to be raised): *let us to the —est of the field, to see what friends are living, who are dead*, H4A V, 4, 164.*

High, adv. 1) at or to a great altitude, far above the ground or any other object: *my tide swells the —er*, Lucr. 646. *to jump up —er*, 1414. *whose flames aspire —er*, Wiv. V, 5, 102. *ha, —er! Tw.* I, 3, 150. *so h. above his limits*, R2 III, 2, 109. *I will lift Mortimer as h. in the air*, H4A I, 3, 136. *sprout as h. as heaven*, H4B II, 3, 60. *h. upreared and abutting fronts*, H5 Prol. 21. *climbing h.* H6B II, 1, 8. 14. *advance thy halberd —er*, R3 I, 2, 40. *hold up h. in brass*, Troil. I, 3, 64. *lift their bosoms —er than the shores*,

112. *so h. above our heads*, Rom. III, 5, 22. *up —er toward the north*, Caes. II, 1, 109. *get —er on that hill*, V, 3, 20. *that these bodies h. on a stage be placed*, Hml. V, 2, 389. *cannot be heard so h.* Lr. IV, 6, 22. *arched so h.* Cymb. III, 3, 5. *we'll —er to the mountains*, IV, 4, 8. *the sea works h.* Per. III, 1, 48.

Figuratively: *dost advance as h. as learning my rude ignorance*, Sonn. 78, 14. *set him h. in fame*, All's V, 3, 31. *how h. thy glory towers*, John II, 350. *steps me a little —er than his vow*, H4A IV, 3, 75. *his affections are —er mounted*, H5 IV, 1, 111. *they that stand h.* R3 I, 3, 259. *actions —est reared*, Troil. I, 3, 6. *set h. in place*, Cor. II, 3, 255. *he sits h. in all the people's hearts*, Caes. I, 3, 157. *then up —er*, Cymb. I, 5, 39. Joined to expressions of price and estimation: *pitch the price so h.* Ven. 551. *grown so h. in his esteem*, Mids. III, 2, 294 (or adj.?). *to stand h. in your account*, Merch. III, 2, 157. *holds his honour —er than his ease*, Troil. I, 3, 266.

2) at or to an elevated place, in or to a high rank: *love... ne'er settled equally, but h. or low*, Ven. 1139. *mounts my love so h.* All's I, 1, 235. *I was born so h.* R3 I, 3, 263. *thus h. is Richard seated*, IV, 2, 3.

3) far: *will he travel —er, or return?* All's IV, 3, 50. *up —er to the plain*, John II, 295. Figuratively: *hold up the jest no —er*, Wiv. V, 5, 109. *if thou proceed as h. as word*, As II, 1, 213.

4) highly: *h. delightful plain*, Ven. 236. *it alone is h. fantastical*, Tw. I, 1, 15.

5) violently, passionately: *my revenges were h. bent upon him*, All's V, 3, 10. *had our weak spirits ne'er been —er reared with stronger blood*, Wint. I, 2, 72. *let me rail so h.* Ant. IV, 15, 43.

6) loudly: *neighed so h.* Ant. I, 5, 49.

7) in or to a high note: *I cannot reach so h.* Gent. I, 2, 87. *can sing both h. and low*, Tw. II, 3, 42.

High-battled, commanding proud armies: Ant. III, 13, 29.

High-blown, inflated: H8 III, 2, 361.

High-born, of high birth: John V, 2, 79. *in h. words*, LLL I, 1, 173 (perhaps *high-borne*, the spelling of *born* and *borne* not differing in O. Edd.). —

High-coloured, flushed: Ant. II, 7, 4.

High-cross, a cross anciently erected in market-places: Shr. I, 1, 137 (O. Edd. not hyph.).

High-day, holiday: *thou spendest such h. wit in praising him*, Merch. II, 9, 98.

High-engendered, created in the sky: *your h. battles*, Lr. III, 2, 23.

Highest-peering, highest, of the greatest altitude: *the h. hills*, Tit. II, 1, 8.

High-gravel-blind (not hyphened in O. Edd.) a jocular climax of the word *sand-blind*: Merch. II, 2, 38.

High-grown, overgrown with high corn: *the h. field*, Lr. IV, 4, 7.

High-judging, judging in heaven: Lr. II, 4, 231.

High-lone, erect without the assistance of others, on one's own feet: *she could stand h.* Rom. I, 3, 36 (only in Q1.2; the rest of O. Edd. *alone*).

Highly, 1) high, far above the ground: *mountainous error be too h. heaped*, Cor. III, 2, 127.

2) in an elevated place, style, or manner: *h. fed and lowly taught*, All's II, 2, 3. *ditties h. penned*, H4A III, 1, 209. *wherein thyself shalt h. be employed*, R3 III, 1, 180.

3) in a great degree, very much: *h. praised*, Ven.

Ded. 3. *things that women h. hold in hate*, Gent. III, 2, 33. *h. beloved*, Err. V, 6. *her wit values itself so h.* Ado III, 1, 53. Tit. I, 245. 419. IV, 2, 171. IV, 3, 27. V, 1, 56. Mcb. I, 5, 21. I, 6, 29. Hml. III, 2, 33.

High-minded, arrogant, overweening: *this h. strumpet*, H6A I, 5, 12.

Highmost, highest (used of the position of the sun): Sonn. 7, 9. Rom. II, 5, 9.

Highness, a title of honour given to kings and queens: Tp. II, 1, 172. V, 127. 300. LLL V, 2, 391. All's IV, 5, 79. H4B I, 2, 122. H6A I, 3, 76. III, 4, 9. IV, 1, 117. V, 1, 42. V, 5, 26. H6B I, 1, 93. I, 2, 56. I, 3, 69. R3 I, 1, 61. H8 I, 4, 93. Tit. V, 3, 32. Hml. II, 2, 65. Cymb. I, 1, 79. 175 etc. Given to other sovereign princes: Meas. V, 520. 521. Err. V, 211. Ado I, 1, 292. Mids. V, 43. As I, 3, 54. 61. 62. III, 1, 13. Used, as it seems, in flattery, to address other persons of royal blood: H6B I, 2, 78. Cymb. I, 3, 38. I, 6, 13.

High-pitched, aspiring, haughty: *his h. thoughts*, Lucr. 41.

High-placed, elevated to a high position: Mcb. IV, 1, 98.

High-proof, so as to stand any test, very much: *we are h. melancholy*, Ado V, 1, 123.

High-proud, (not hyphened in O. Edd.) very proud: *reckoning his fortune at such h. rate*, Lucr. 19.

High-reaching, aspiring, ambitious: R3 IV, 2, 31.

High-reared, high, raised to a great altitude: *h. bulwarks*, R3 V, 3, 242.

High-repented, deeply repented: All's V, 3, 36 (not hyphened in O. Edd.).

High-resolved, very resolute: Tit. IV, 4, 64.

High-sighted, supercilious: *let h. tyranny range on*, Caes. II, 1, 118.

High-soaring (not hyphened in O. Edd.) raised aloft; with *over*, = far above: *she is as far h. o'er thy praises*, Troil. IV, 4, 126.

High-steward, see *Steward*.

High-stomached, haughty: R2 I, 1, 18.

High-swoln, grown big, exasperated: *your h. hearts*, R3 II, 2, 118.

Hight (used as a characteristic archaism), is c a l l e d: *this child of fancy that Armado h.* LLL I, 1, 171. *which, as I remember, h. Costard*, 258. *this grisly beast, which lion h. by name*, Mids. V, 140. *this maid h. Philoten*, Per. IV Prol. 18.

High-viced, extremely wicked: Tim. IV, 3, 109.

Highway, a public road: Merch. III, 1, 13. V, 263. Wint. IV, 3, 29. R2 I, 4, 4. Rom. III, 2, 134. Suicides and criminals buried in —s: All's I, 1, 152. R2 III, 3, 155.

High-witted, sly, cunning: Tit. IV, 4, 35.

High-wrought, roused, going high: *a h. flood*, Oth. II, 1, 2.

Hild, for *held* (for the sake of the rhyme): Lucr. 1257.

Hilding (from the Saxon *healdan*; one who is held or kept) a base, menial wretch; used of both sexes: Shr. II, 26. Alls III, 6, 4. Rom. II, 4, 44. III, 5, 169. Cymb. II, 3, 128. Adjectively: *some h. fellow*, H4B I, 1, 57. *a h. foe*, H5 IV, 2, 29.

Hill, an eminence, a mountain: Ven. 233. 697. 858. Lucr. 390. Sonn. 7, 5. Compl. 1. Pilgr. 121. 355. Tp. V, 33. LLL IV, 1, 2. Mids. II, 1, 2. 83. Shr. IV, 1, 69. IV, 2, 61. Tw. I, 5, 291. John II, 298. R2 II, 3, 4. H4A II, 2, 9. 57. 83. II, 4, 269. 378. V, 1, 2. V, 5, 21. H4B V, 1, 43. H5 I, 2, 108. III, 3, 23. IV, 7, 60. H6C II, 5, 23. III, 1, 5. H8 I, 1, 131. Cor. III, 2, 3. Tit. II, 1, 8. Rom. II, 5, 6. 9. Tim. I, 1, 63. 73. Caes. V, 1, 3. V, 3, 12. 20. 56. Mcb. IV, 1, 93. V, 5, 33. Hml. I, 1, 167. II, 2, 518. III, 4, 59. Lr. II, 4, 73. 75. III, 4, 78. IV, 6, 1. Oth. I, 3, 141. II, 1, 189. Ant. III, 9, 1. III, 13, 127. IV, 10, 5. Cymb. III, 3, 10. Per. I, 1, 101. I, 4, 5. Holofernes nicely distinguishing between *hill* and *mountain*: LLL V, 1, 89.

Hillo or **Hilloa**, a loud exclamation to give notice of being near: Wint. III, 3, 80. Hml. I, 5, 115.

Hillock, small hill: Ven. 237.

Hilt, the handle of a sword: Wiv. III, 5, 113 Shr. III, 2, 48. H6C I, 4, 12. Hml. V, 2, 159. Plur. —s, applied to a single weapon: H4A II, 4, 229. H5 II Chor. 9* II, 1, 68. R3 I, 4, 160. Caes. V, 3, 43.

Him, see *He*.

Himself, 1) his own person; f. i. *that on h. such shame commits*, Sonn. 9, 14. *the king's son have I landed by h.* Tp. I, 2, 221 (alone, unattended); cf. Tim. I, 2, 30. *take care for h.* Tp. V, 257. *of h.* Gent. I, 2, 13. *the dog is h.* III, 3, 24. *h. would lodge*, III, 1, 143. II, 1, 146. *to die by h.* Cor. V, 2, 111 (by his own hands). Mcb. IV, 3, 150. Lr. I, 3, 6.

2) in his own person; f. i. *got by the devil h.* Tp. I, 2, 319. *he h.* III, 2, 107. V, 211. Gent. II, 1, 174. Meas. IV, 2, 112. Err. II, 2, 71. V, 119.

3) refl.; f. i. *oared h. to the shore*, Tp. II, 1, 119. Gent. III, 1, 394. Meas. III, 2, 247. All's IV, 5, 68.

Hinckley (Q *Hunckly*), a market-town in Leicestershire: H4B V, 1, 26.

Hind, the female of red deer: Lucr. 543. Mids. II, 1, 232. As III, 2, 107. All's I, 1, 102. R3 II, 4, 50. Troil. III, 2, 201. Caes. I, 3, 106.

Hind, 1) a menial, servant: Wiv. III, 5, 99. As I, 1, 20. Rom. I, 1, 73.

2) a boor, a peasant, any mean person: Err. III, 1, 77. LLL I, 2, 123. H4A II, 3, 16. H6B III, 2, 271. IV, 2, 130. IV, 4, 33. Cymb. V, 3, 77.

Hinder, adj. in a position contrary to that of the face; opposed to fore: *his h. legs*, Ven. 698.

Hinder, vb. 1) to stop, to obstruct, to keep back; absol.: *of —ing knotgrass made*, Mids. III, 2, 329 (stunting). With an accus.: *when his fair course is not —ed*, Gent. II, 7, 27. 33. *I am sorry that I have —ed you*, Err. V, 1. *these be the stops that h. study*, LLL I, 1, 70. *—ed me half a million*, Merch. III, 1, 57. *fair hope must h. life's decay*, H6C IV, 4, 16. *that no dissension h. government*, IV, 6, 40. *have —ed the passages made yonder it*, H8 II, 4, 164. *from your affairs I h. you too long*, V, 1, 54.

2) to keep back, to prevent: Lucr. 551. Err. V, 71. 77. Mids. III, 2, 318. All's III, 6, 44. Wint. I, 2, 24. R2 II, 2, 67. H5 II, 2, 187. III, 6, 169. Troil. V, 3, 57. Caes. I, 2, 30. Ant. V, 2, 335. With *from*: Tp. III, 3, 108. With an inf.: Err. IV, 3, 39. R3 II, 2, 34.

Hindmost, coming after the others, the last: Sonn. 85, 12. H6B III, 1, 2. Troil. III, 3, 160.

Hinge, subst. that on which a thing turns or depends: *whose joints, like strengthless —s*, H4B I, 1, 141. *the —s of the knee*, Hml. III, 2, 66. *that the probation bear no h. nor loop to hang a doubt on*, Oth. III, 3, 365.

Hinge, to bend like a hinge: *h. thy knee*, Tim. IV, 3, 211.

Hint, subst. that which gives matter and motive; occasion (Germ. Anlass): *it is a h. that wrings mine eyes to' t,* Tp. I, 2, 134. *our h. of woe is common,* II, 1, 3. *make them be strong and ready for this h.* Cor. III, 3, 23. *wherein of antres vast ... it was my h. to speak,* Oth. I, 3, 142. *upon this h. I spake,* 166. *when the best h. was given him, he not took it,* Ant. III, 4, 9. *take the h. which my despair proclaims,* III, 11, 18. *Posthumus took his hint,* Cymb. V, 5, 172.

Hip, the joint of the thigh with the flesh covering it, the haunch: Ven. 44. Meas. I, 2, 58. Err. III, 2, 113. 116. Ado III, 2, 36. Mids. II, 1, 55. H4B III, 1, 51. H5 IV, 2, 47. *to catch* or *have on the h.* = to lay or have hold of, to have at advantage: Merch. I, 3, 47. IV, 1, 334. Oth. II, 1, 314.

Hip, the fruit of the dogrose: Tim. IV, 3, 422.

Hipparchus, name in Ant. III, 13, 149.

Hipped (O. Edd. *hip'd*), perhaps covered on or down to the hips: *his horse h. with an old mothy saddle,* Shr. III, 2, 49 (most Intpp., inserting a comma after *h.,* explain it: sprained in the hip).

Hippocrates, the celebrated physician: Wiv. III, 1, 66 (pronounced *Hibocrates* by Evans).

Hippolyta, queen of the Amazons: Mids. I, 1, 1. 16. 122. II, 1, 75 etc.

Hire, subst. wages, remuneration: Merch. I, 3, 81. As II, 3, 39. H5 II, 2, 100. H6B III, 2, 225. R3 V, 3, 258. Cor. I, 3, 40. II, 2, 153. II, 3, 121. Hml. III, 3, 79 (Ff *h. and salary,* Qq *base and silly*). Oth. I, 1, 126. Cymb. II, 4, 129.

Hire, vb. (dissyll. in Err. IV, 1, 95. H6B I, 2, 98. H8 II, 3, 36. Tim. IV, 3, 291. Ant. V, 1, 21). 1) to engage in temporary service for wages: *—d to it by your brother,* Ado V, 1, 309. *riders dearly —d,* As I, 1, 14. H6B I, 2, 98. R3 I, 4, 234. H8 II, 3, 36. Rom. IV, 2, 2. Mcb. V, 7, 18. Lr. I, 4, 105. Ant. V, 1, 21. V, 2, 155. Cymb. I, 6, 122.

2) to procure for temporary use at a certain price: *to h. waftage,* Err. IV, 1, 95. *horse to h.* Ado I, 1, 268. Rom. V, 1, 26. *does no —d harm,* Tim. IV, 3, 291.

Hiren, i. e. Irene, name of the heroine of a tragedy by Peele, alluded to by Pistol: *have we not H. here?* H4B II, 4, 173. 189 (apparently confounded with *iron,* sword).

Hirtius, name in Ant. I, 4, 58.

His, 1) pron. poss. of *He;* a) before a subst.: Ven. 25. 30. 45. 46 etc. etc. Abbreviated to *'s: when's god's asleep,* Tp. II, 2, 155. *in's tale,* III, 2, 56. *the king and's followers,* V, 7. Gent. III, 1, 192. Wiv. III, 2, 24. Meas. V, 229. Err. III, 1, 37. Merch. V, 158. As V, 2, 17. All's IV, 2, 70. Tw. III, 4, 14. Wint. II, 3, 100. Tim. II, 2, 117. Ant. III, 7, 12. III, 13, 76. Cymb. I, 1, 46. I, 3, 12. I, 6, 68. II, 4, 12. III, 2, 72 etc. Used instead of the sign of the Anglosaxon genitive: *Mars his sword,* Sonn. 55, 7. *the king his son,* Tp. II, 1, 236. *this mis-shapen knave his mother was a witch,* V, 269. *a man of God his making,* LLL V, 2, 529 (Q2 Ff *God's*). *the count his galleys,* Tw. III, 3, 26. *Lewis his satisfaction,* H5 I, 2, 88. *Mars his true moving,* H6A I, 2, 1. *Charles his gleeks,* III, 2, 123. *France his sword,* IV, 6, 3. *Mars his idiot,* Troil. II, 1, 58. *by Mars his gauntlet,* IV, 5, 177. *Mars his helm,* 255. *Mars his heart,* V, 2, 164. *Mars his armour,* Hml. II, 2, 512 (Qq *Marses armour*). cf. *'tis not his fault the spark,* All's II, 1, 25 (M. Edd. *his fault, the spark*). the *'s* of the gen. and *his* combined: *if my brother had my*

shape, and I had his, sir Robert's his, John I, 139 Used demonstratively: *would ye not think his cunning to be great, that could restore this cripple to his legs?* H6B II, 1, 132. *desire his jewels and this other's house,* Mcb. IV, 3, 80 (= the jewels of the one; cf. *He*). *no more does mine, nor his, nor hers,* Lr. II, 2, 97 (= of him there). Referring to *one: one cannot climb it without apparent hazard of his life,* Gent. III, 1, 116.

Absol., without a subst.: *a natural guiltiness such as is his,* Meas. II, 2, 139. *to weed my vice and let his grow,* III, 2, 284. *denied my house for his,* Err. II, 2, 161 etc. = his property: *one that fixes no bourn 'twixt his and mine,* Wint. I, 2, 134. *he does deny him, in respect of his, what charitable men afford to beggars,* Tim. III, 2, 81. = the persons belonging to him, his associates or relations: *the duke and his,* H6A III, 3, 33. *points at them for his,* Mcb. IV, 1, 124. *of his* = belonging, pertaining to him: *a spirit of his,* Tp. II, 2, 15. *a sunny look of his,* Err. II, 1, 99 etc. And even: *which speechless woe of his,* Lucr. 1674. *the very tyranny and rage of his,* Merch. IV, 1, 13. *that close aspect of his,* John IV, 2, 72 (cf. the other poss. pronouns).

2) poss. of the neut. pron. *it,* = its: Ven. 359. 570. 756. 784. 854. 944. 960. 1034. 1132. 1140. Lucr. 164. 303. 328. 329. 389. 532. 548. 565. 875. 1009. 1168. 1669. Sonn. 9, 10. 14, 6. 74, 7. 84, 6. Tp. I, 2, 295. II, 1, 67. 113. 120. 302 etc. etc. Hence used also with reference to the names of countries, as in H6A IV, 6, 3, and in John II, 95, where it has been corrected and changed to *her* or *its* by some M. Edd.

Hisperia (most M. Edd. *Hesperia*) female name in As II, 2, 10.

Hiss, subst. the voice of a serpent: H6B III, 2, 326.

Hiss, vb. 1) intr. to utter a noise like a serpent: Ven. 17. Lucr. 871. Wiv. III, 5, 124. LLL V, 2, 935. Troil. V, 1, 98. Tit. II, 3, 100. Lr. III, 6, 17 (Ff *hizzing*). With an accus. denoting the effect: *h. me into madness,* Tp. II, 2, 14. Expressing contempt and disapprobation: LLL V, 1, 145. Troil. V, 10, 55. With *at:* H6B IV, 1, 78.

2) tr. to condemn by hissing, to explode: Ven. 1084. Wiv. III, 3, 41. Wint. I, 2, 189. Rom. I, 1, 119. Caes. I, 2, 261. Mcb. IV, 3, 175.

Hist, a sound uttered to attract the attention of another with the greatest possible secrecy: Rom. II, 2, 159.

Historical, giving an account of actual events: *h.-pastoral, tragical-h., tragical-comical-h.-pastoral,* Hml. II, 2, 417.

History, subst. 1) an account of the events respecting the fortune of mankind and nations: *could ever hear by tale or h.* Mids. I, 1, 133. *which is more than h. can pattern,* Wint. III, 2, 37. *there is a h. in all men's lives, figuring the nature of the times deceased,* H4B III, 1, 80. *our h. shall speak of our acts,* H5 I, 2, 230. *knows by h.* Cymb. I, 6, 70.

2) any relation of events, story: *what's her h.?* Tw. II, 4, 12. *vouchsafe me a word with you. Sir, a whole h.* Hml. III, 2, 309. *in my travels' h.* Oth. I, 3, 139. *if I should tell my h.* Per. V, 1, 119.

3) any communication: *my breast can better brook thy dagger's point than can my ears that tragic history,* H6C V, 6, 28. *this paper is the h. of my knowledge touching her flight,* Cymb. III, 5, 99. Especially communication of what is in the hearts of men: *in many's looks the false hearts' h. is writ,* Sonn. 93, 7. *there is a kind of character in thy life, that to the observer doth*

thy h. fully unfold, Meas. I, 1, 29. *made him my book, wherein my soul recorded the h. of all her secret thoughts,* R3 III, 5, 28. *Brutus' tongue hath almost ended his life's h.* Caes. V, 5, 40 (by which expression it is intimated that his tongue never swerved from truth). *often leaves the h. unspoke that it intends to do,* Lr. I, 1, 239. cf. H4B III, 1, 80.

4) a stage-play founded on historical events (*h. devised and played to take spectators,* Wint. III, 2, 37): *last scene of all, that ends this strange eventful h.* As II, 7, 164. *it is a kind of h.* Shr. Ind. 2, 144. *Chorus to this h.* H5 V Chor. 32. *tragedy, comedy, h.* Hml. II, 2, 416. *prologue to the h. of lust,* Oth. II, 1, 264 (quibbling with def. 3).

History, vb. to record: *and keep no tell-tale to his memory that may repeat and h. his loss to new remembrance,* H4B IV, 1, 203.

Hit, for *it,* see *It.*

Hit, subst. an effective stroke or thrust that does not miss the antagonist: Rom. I, 1, 214 (but here it may as well be the partic.). Hml. V, 2, 174. 185. 279. 292. 296.

Hit, vb. 1) to touch, to strike; absol.: *hatefully at random dost thou h.* Ven. 940. *how hard true sorrow —s,* Sonn. 120, 10. *the fencer's foils, which h., but hurt not,* Ado V, 2, 14. Trans.: *whose tender horns being h.* Ven. 1033. *h. with Cupid's archery,* Mids. III, 2, 103. *to h. him in the eye,* Tw. II, 5, 51. *as surely as your feet h. the ground,* III, 4, 306. H4B I, 1, 149. H6C II, 2, 166. R3 IV, 4, 202; cf. Rom. III, 1, 173. H8 V, 4, 24. 46. 52. Hml. IV, 1, 44. Cymb. III, 3, 83 (*their thoughts do h. the roofs of palaces*). III, 4, 69. V, 5, 395. Used of odours touching the sense of smelling: *a strange perfume —s the sense of the adjacent wharfs,* Ant. II, 2, 217. Per. III, 2, 62. *to h. dead =* to kill: Troil. IV, 5, 251.

2) to strike or touch after taking aim, not to miss: Ado I, 1, 260. As II, 7, 53. Shr. V, 2, 50. 57. 59. 186. H6B I, 1, 243. H8 II, 1, 165. Rom. I, 1, 213. 214. Hml. V, 2, 306. Per. I, 1, 164. II, 1, 8. In an obscene sense: LLL IV, 1, 120. 123--136. Troil. I, 2, 293. Tit. II, 1, 97. Rom. II, 1, 33. *to be h. away,* Cymb. II, 1, 3 (= to be touched, and thrust away).

3) to guess, to find out: *'twill be a hard way to h.* Merch. II, 2, 48. *thou hast h. it,* Shr. II, 199. H4A II, 4, 381. H6B IV, 2, 21. Tit. II, 1, 97. Rom. II, 3, 41. II, 4, 59. Intr., with *on: I can never h. on's name,* Wiv. III, 2, 24. *thou mightst have h. upon it here,* Tim. IV, 3, 351. *a happiness that often madness —s on,* Hml. II, 2, 213. Of instead of *on: by what wonder you do h. of mine,* Err. III, 2, 30.

4) to render like, to make resembling (in painting): *your father's image is so h. in you,* Wint. V, 1, 127.

5) to succeed, not to be disappointed; *have all his ventures failed? what, not one h.?* Merch. III, 2, 270 (or subst.?). *oft expectation fails, and oft it —s where hope is coldest,* All's II, 1, 146. *h. or miss,* Troil. I, 3, 384.

6) to meet, to agree with; trans.: *what worst, —ing a grosser quality, is cried up for our best act,* H8 I, 2, 84. *my former speeches have but h. your thoughts, which can interpret further,* Mcb. III, 6, 1. Intr.: *this —s right,* Tim. III, 1, 6 (= coincides, falls out as was prognosticated). *let's h. together,* Lr. I, 1, 308 (= let us be of one mind. Ff. *sit*).

Hither, (monosyll. in Tp. I, 2, 304, and perhaps in I, 2, 63. V, 204. As II, 5, 5. 44. II, 7, 195) to this place: Lucr. 220. 1289. Tp. I, 2, 63. 269. 304. II, 2, 125. IV, 83. 135. 186. V, 204. 228. 240. 251. Gent. II, 4, 86. V, 4, 99. Wiv. II, 1, 112. III, 3, 113. IV, 1, 17. IV, 2, 135. Meas. II, 1, 213. 222. IV, 2, 1. 63. IV, 3, 22. 112. V, 124. 154. 379. 474. Err. II, 1, 84. V, 38. 116. 251. 280. Ado II, 3, 4. 92. III, 2, 105. III, 3, 13. IV, 1, 4. V, 4, 12 etc. etc. After *welcome:* Gent. II, 4, 102. Err. III, 1, 68. Merch. III, 2, 223. As II, 7, 195. R2 III, 3, 122. Ant. III, 6, 78 etc. (cf. *Welcome*). After *arrive:* Tw. II, 2, 4 (cf. *Arrive*). *assemble the people h.* Cor. III, 3, 12. *'tis catching h., even to our camp,* H4A IV, 1, 30. *hark you h. =* hark in your ear, Wiv. III, 4, 21. H4B II, 4, 165. *I hear h. your husband's drum,* Cor. I, 3, 32 (sending its sound as far as here). *their purpose h. to this wood,* Mids. IV, 1, 166.

Hitherto, 1) to this place: *England, from Trent and Severn h.* H4A III, 1, 74.

2) to this limit, so far: *and h. doth love on fortune tend,* Hml. III, 2, 216. *I am h. your daughter,* Oth. I, 3, 185.

3) to this time: H5 V, 2, 15. H6A III, 3, 9. H6C IV, 2, 1. R3 IV, 1, 82 (Qq *ever since*). H8 V, 3, 32. Hml. I, 2, 247.

Hitherward, towards this place, this way: John V, 7, 59. H6B IV, 9, 27. H6C V, 1, 3. Cor. I, 2, 33. Lr. IV, 4, 21. Per. I, 4, 61.

Hitherwards, the same: H4A IV, 1, 89. 92.

Hive, subst. 1) a receptacle for bees: Lucr. 839. 1769. All's I, 2, 66. H4B IV, 5, 78. H6A I, 5, 24. Troil. I, 3, 81.

2) a swarm of bees: *an angry h. of bees,* H6B III, 2, 125.

3) a kind of bonnet resembling a hive: *upon her head a platted h. of straw,* Compl. 8.

Hive, vb. to reside in the manner of bees: *drones h. not with me,* Merch. II, 5, 48.

Ho, an exclamation used for several purposes; chiefly to call up to attention or service: *ho, awake!* Tp. II, 1, 308. *who's within there? ho!* Wiv. I, 4, 139. *peace, ho! be here,* Meas. IV, 3, 110; cf. I, 4, 6. *ho, open the door,* Err. III, 1, 38. LLL IV, 3, 174. Mids. IV, 1, 88. Merch. II, 6, 25. V, 66. 109 (O. Edd. *how*). As V, 4, 131. Shr. IV, 1, 43. 100. All's II, 1, 212. IV, 1, 24. Tw. I, 4, 10. Wint. II, 3, 39. John V, 6, 1. R2 V, 2, 74. H4B I, 1, 1. II, 1, 68. V, 3, 75. H6B I, 4, 82. R3 I, 4, 84. H8 V, 2, 3. Troil. IV, 1, 1. V, 2, 1. V, 3, 13. Rom. I, 1, 82. III, 5, 64. Tim. II, 1, 13. Caes. I, 2, 1. IV, 2, 1. 2. V, 4, 4. 6. Hml. III, 4, 22. IV, 1, 32. Lr. V, 3, 102. Ant. III, 13, 90 etc. *holla ho:* Shr. IV, 1, 12. *whoa ho:* Wiv. V, 5, 187 (Slender's speech). *wo ha ho:* Merch. V, 39 (Launcelot's speech). Oftenest *what ho: what ho, slave!* Tp. I, 2, 313. *what ho, Lucetta!* Gent. I, 2, 66. Wiv. IV, 2, 9. 10. 174. Meas. III, 1, 44. IV, 1, 50. IV, 2, 20. IV, 3, 25. Shr. IV, 1, 152. Tw. I, 5, 318. IV, 2, 21. R2 V, 3, 74. H4A II, 1, 52. II, 3, 68. R3 III, 2, 1 (Ff *my lord*). Troil. II, 3, 23. Rom. I, 1, 90. IV, 2, 43. Hml. III, 2, 57. III, 4, 22. Oth. I, 3, 12. Ant. IV, 14, 129. Cymb. I, 6, 139 etc. The two words separated: *what, Lucius, ho!* Caes. II, 1, 1. *what, Oswald, ho!* Lr. I, 4, 336.

Used as an expression of mockery or rebuke: *O ho, o ho! would't had been done,* Tp. I, 2, 349. *O ho, monster, we know what belongs to a frippery,* IV, 224. *ho now, you strike like the blind man,* Ado II, 1, 205. *'ware pencils, ho!* LLL V, 2, 43. *ho ho ho! coward, why comest thou not?* Mids. III, 2, 421. *have you heard any imputation to the contrary? Ho no no,* Merch. I, 3, 15. *a quarrel, ho! already,* V, 146. *O ho, Petruchio! Tranio hits you,* Shr. V, 2, 57. *o ho! entreat her,* 87. *come, we burn daylight, ho!* Rom. I, 4, 43. *peace, ho! for shame,* IV, 5, 65. *ho ho! confessed it,* Tim. I, 2, 22. *ho ho! I laugh to think,* 117. *with, ho! such bugs,* Hml. V, 2, 22. *ho! hearts, tongues .... cannot think, speak .... ho! his love,* Ant. III, 2, 16. *ho ho ho! now the witch take me, if I meant it thus,* IV, 2, 36. *O ho* sometimes = *ah ha: O ho! do you come near me now?* Tw. III, 4, 71. *O ho! do you mark that?* Hml. III, 2, 118. *O ho, I know the riddle,* Lr. V, 1, 37.

Serving as a cry of exultation: *with a hey and a ho,* As V, 3, 18. 24. 28. 32. *sweet lady, ho ho!* Tw. III, 4, 18. *with hey ho, the wind and the rain,* V, 399. 403. 407. 411. 415. *a bawd, so ho!* Rom. II, 4, 136. Used on setting out on a travel: *then westward-ho!* Tw. III, 1, 146. *on toward Calais, ho!* John III, 3, 73.

In Troil. III, 1, 131. 133. 135. 136 *oh ho,* as a cry of pain, has been changed by M. Edd. to *oh oh.*

Hoa, the usual spelling of O. Edd. for *ho,* always changed to *ho* by M. Edd., except when it seemed characteristic of the speaker's breeding.

Hoar, adj. 1) whitish: *h. leprosy,* Tim. IV, 3, 35 (the disease called elephantiasis). *a willow that shows his h. leaves,* Hml. IV, 7, 168 (Qq *hoary*).

2) mouldy: Rom. II, 4, 139. 141. 142. 144 (quibbling with *whore*).

Hoar, vb. 1) to make mouldy, to make rotten: *h. the flamen, that scolds against the quality of flesh,* Tim. IV, 3, 155.

2) to become mouldy: *when it —s ere it be spent,* Rom. II, 4, 146.

Hoard, subst. a store laid up in private, a treasure: Mids. IV, 1, 40. H4B IV, 3, 125.

Hoard, vb. to lay in hoards, to store: Lucr. 1318. Compl. 220. John III, 3, 8. R2 I, 3, 253. H6B III, 1, 113. H6C II, 2, 48. Cor. IV, 2, 11.

Hoardock, see *Hardock* and *Hordock.*

Hoarse, having the voice rough and soundless: As V, 3, 13. H6B V, 2, 7. Rom. II, 2, 161. 163. Mcb. I, 5, 39.

Hoarsely, in a soundless voice: Lucr. 1214.

Hoary, whitish: Hml. IV, 7, 168 (Ff. *hoar*).

Hoary-headed, having a white head like age: *h. frosts fall in the fresh lap of the crimson rose,* Mids. II, 1, 107.

Hob, a frequent name among the common people: Cor. II, 3, 123.

Hob (or *Hab*) a corruption of *have; hob nob* = have or have not, hit or miss, at random: *h. nob is his word; give't or take't,* Tw. III, 4, 262.

Hobbididance (cf. *Hopdance*) name of an evil spirit, taken from Harsnet's Declaration: Lr. IV, 1, 62.

Hobby-horse, 1) one of the principal parts played in the ancient morris-dance, but of late growing out of use: *the h. is forgot,* LLL III, 30. Hml. III, 2, 142. 143.

2) a term of contempt for a loose and frivolous person, either male or female: *which these —s must not hear,* Ado III, 2, 75. *callest thou my love h.?* LLL

III, 31. *my wife's a h.* Wint.I, 2, 276 (O. Edd. *holyhorse*). *give it your h.* Oth. IV, 1, 160.

Hobgoblin, name of the crier of the fairies: Wiv. V, 5, 45. a name by which Puck likes to be called: Mids. II, 1, 40.

Hobnail, a nail used for shoeing horses: H4A II, 4, 398. H6B IV, 10, 63.

Hodge-pudding, probably something similar to a hodge-podge, a pudding made of a medley of ingredients: Wiv. V, 5, 159.

Hoeboy, see *Hautboy.*

Hog, a swine: Mids. III, 1, 112. 114. Merch. III, 5, 26. As I, 1, 40. R3 I, 3, 228. Lr. III, 4, 95.

Hogshead, a large cask: Tp. IV, 252. LLL IV, 2, 88. 89. Wint. III, 3, 95. H4A III, 4, 5. H4B II, 4, 68.

Hoise, 1) to lift, to draw up: *—d sail,* R3 IV, 4, 529.

2) to carry off, to make away with, to heave away (cf. *Heave*): *there they —d us,* Tp. I, 2, 148 (O. Edd. *hoist*). *we'll h. Duke Humphrey from his seat,* H6B I, 1, 169. *'tis the sport to have the enginer —d with his own petar,* Hml. III, 4, 207 (O. Edd. *hoist*).

Hoist, to draw up (sails): *I have —ed sail to all the winds,* Sonn. 117, 7. Err. V, 21. Tw. I, 5, 215. Ant. III, 10, 15. With *up,* = to lift up: *and h. thee up to the shouting plebeians,* Ant. IV, 12, 34. V, 2, 55.

Holborn, mentioned as the residence of the bishop of Ely: R3 III, 4, 33.

Hold, subst. 1) grasp, seizure: *he that stands upon a slippery place makes nice of no vile h. to stay him up,* John III, 4, 138. *he is in the mighty h. of Bolingbroke,* R2 III, 4, 83. *let go thy h. when a great wheel runs down a hill,* Lr. II, 4, 73. *having h. of both* = holding both, having their hands in mine: John III, 1, 329. *the law hath yet another h. on you,* Merch. IV, 1, 347 (hath another way to seize you). *lay h. of him* = seize him, Cor. III, 1, 212. *he that can lay h. of her* (win her), Rom. I, 5, 118. *lay h. on him:* Meas. V, 364. Err. V, 91. Shr. V, 1, 91. Troil. V, 3, 59. Oth. I, 2, 80. *to take h.* = to gain possession: *that love should of a sudden take such h.* Shr. I, 1, 152. with *of: will not let belief take h. of him,* Hml. I, 1, 24. with *on,* = to seize, to overtake, to gain power over, possession of: *I fear thy justice will take h. on me for this,* R3 II, 1, 131. *let this tyrannous night take h. upon you,* Lr. III, 4, 156. *lest that the infection of his fortune take like h. on thee,* IV, 6, 238. *nor doth the general care take h. on me,* Oth. I, 3, 55.

2) confinement, custody: *put them in secret —s,* Meas. V, 3, 91. *he hath the jewel of my life in h.* Shr. I, 2, 119. *franked up in h.* R3 IV, 5, 3.

3) a fastness: John V, 7, 19. H4B Ind. 35. H6C I, 2, 52. Cymb. III, 3, 20. III, 6, 18.

4) the interior cavity of a ship: *a hulk better stuffed in the h.* H4B II, 4, 70.

Hold, vb. (impf. and partic. *held.* Part. *holden:* H6B II, 4, 71. *hild:* Lucr. 1257), 1) trans. a) to have or grasp in the hand: *—s her pulses hard,* Ven. 476. *—ing a trencher,* LLL V, 2, 477. *your lion that —s his pollaxe,* 580. *to h. the plough,* 893. *must I h. a candle?* Merch. II, 6, 41. *I h. the olive in my hand,* Tw. I, 5, 225. *—s his wife by the arm,* Wint. I, 2, 193. *of him it* (my hand) *—s,* John II, 238. *h. a serpent by the tongue,* III, 1, 258. *he held a pouncetbox,* H4A I, 3, 37. *h. him sure,* H4B II, 1, 27. *h. hook and line,* II, 4, 171 (i. e. become an angler in Tartarus?

Pistol's speech. cf. Lr. III, 5, 7). *h. the sceptre in his fist,* H6B I, 1, 245. *he —s vengeance in his hands,* R3 I, 4, 204. *held with a brace of harlots,* Tim. IV, 3, 79. *he held me hard,* Hml. II, 1, 87 etc.

b) to support with the hand: *help, h. his brows,* LLL V, 2, 392. *h. their hips and laugh,* Mids. II, 1, 55. *as if you held a brow of much distraction,* Wint. I, 2, 149. *I held your head,* John IV, 1, 45. *held my stirrup,* H6B IV, 1, 53. *I held the sword,* Caes. V, 5, 65 etc. *to h. up =* 1) to uphold, to support, to preserve: *your shallowest help will h. me up afloat,* Sonn. 80, 9. *he that had held up the very life of my friend,* Merch. V, 214 (Q1 *did uphold*). *us that here h. up his right,* John II, 364. *that seemed in eating him to h. him up,* R2 III, 4, 51. *to h. our safety up,* H4B IV, 2, 35. *my puissance —s it up,* H6B IV, 2, 173. *the proudest he that —s up Lancaster,* H6C I, 1, 46. 2) to bear, to carry: *no supporter but the huge firm earth can h. it up,* John III, 1, 73. *here is a hand to h. a sceptre up,* H6B V, 1, 102. 3) to carry through, to follow up, to continue: *h. up the jest no higher,* Wiv. V, 5, 109. *h. it up,* Ado II, 3, 126 (play your parts to the end). *h. the sweet jest up,* Mids. III, 2, 239 (cf. Meas. III, 1, 273). *heir from heir shall h. this quarrel up,* H4B IV, 2, 48. *they h. up Adam's profession,* Hml. V, 1, 34. 4) to encourage: *nor h. him up with hopes,* Tw. I, 5, 323. 5) to show: *what colour for my visitation shall I h. up before him?* Wint. IV, 4, 567. *to h. the mirror up to nature,* Hml. III, 2, 24. 6) to show off, to make much of: *whose estimation do you mightily h. up,* Ado II, 2, 25. *they would h. up this Salique law,* H5 I, 2, 91. *h. up high in brass,* Troil. I, 3, 64. *to h. out in the 3d sign. of h. up: well said, brazen face; h. it out,* Wiv. IV, 2, 141 (play your part to the end).

c) to bear or manage in a certain manner: *let him h. his fingers thus,* Mids. III, 1, 72. *how he —s his countenance,* H4A II, 4, 432. *h. hard the breath,* H5 III, 1, 16. *h. close thy lips,* H6C II, 2, 118. *—ing thine ear close to the ground,* Rom. V, 3, 4. *h. thee to my heart,* Mcb. I, 4, 32. *a city on whom plenty held full hand,* Per. I, 4, 22. With *off: h. off your hands,* Hml. I, 4, 80. V, 1, 286. *h. off the earth awhile, till I have caught her once more in mine arms,* V, 1, 272. *I have ever held my cap off to thy fortunes,* Ant. II, 7, 63. With *out: I will wink and h. out mine iron,* H5 II, 1, 8. *—ing out gold,* Per. II, 2, 37. With *up: h. up thy head,* Ven. 118. Wiv. I, 4, 30. IV, 1, 17. V, 1, 8. H4A V, 4, 39. H4B I, 3, 17. Caes. V, 4, 1 (cf. *Head*). *pure hands held up,* Gent. III, 1, 229. Meas. V, 443. Mids. III, 2, 143. Wint. V, 2, 51. H5 IV, 1, 316. H6B III, 3, 28. Cor. V, 3, 175. Tit. III, 1, 75. Caes. I, 3, 16. *how she —s up the neb, the bill to him,* Wint. I, 2, 183. *canst thou h. up thy heavy eyes awhile,* Caes. IV, 3, 256.

d) not to let loose, to bind, to attach: *a weak bond —s you,* Mids. III, 2, 268. *what hoop should h. us stanch,* Ant. II, 2, 117. With *to: h. you ever to our special drift,* Meas. IV, 5, 4. *whoever charges on his forward breast, I am the caitiff that do h. him to't,* All's III, 2, 117. *do not h. me to mine oath,* Troil. V, 2, 26. *his promise, which you might have held him to,* Cor. II, 3, 202.

e) to keep fast, to restrain from motion, to stop, to detain: *sad talk, wherewith my brother held you in the cloister,* Gent. I, 3, 2. *I have held him here too long,*

Err. IV, 1, 47. *what secret hath held you here?* Ado I, 1, 206. *now she —s me not,* Mids. III, 2, 335. *here's none will h. you,* Shr. I, 1, 107. *Fabian can scarce h. him yonder,* Tw. III, 4, 310. *—ing the eternal spirit in the vile prison,* John III, 4, 18. *we cannot h. mortality's strong hand,* IV, 2, 82. *the winds that held the king so long in his unlucky Irish wars,* H4A V, 1, 52. *what rein can h. licentious wickedness?* H5 III, 3, 22. *wherefore do you h. me here so long?* Caes. I, 2, 83. *I will not h. thee long,* IV, 3, 265. *fate held his hand,* Wiv. III, 5, 106. *persuade him to h. his hands,* Err. IV, 4, 23. *h. your hand or hands =* do not strike: Err. I, 2, 93. All's IV, 3, 215. H6A III, 1, 87. Lr. III, 7, 72. IV, 6, 164. Oth. I, 2, 81. II, 3, 154 etc. *h. my tongue* (= am silent): Sonn. 102, 13. Err. IV, 4, 22. As II, 5, 30. John IV, 1, 97. H6A III, 1, 61. V, 3, 42. Mcb. II, 3, 125 etc. With *from, =* to keep back from: *we for the worthiest h. the right from both,* John II, 282. *my cloud of dignity is held from falling,* H4B IV, 5, 100. *your crown and kingdom indirectly held from him,* H5 II, 4, 94. *hath held my eyes from rest,* R3 IV, 1, 82 (Qq *kept*). *may h. him from the Capitol,* Caes. II, 1, 201. *from whom this tyrant —s the due of right,* Mcb. III, 6, 25. cf. *that —s thee hence,* All's III, 2, 126. With *back:* Lucr. 1789. Sonn. 65, 11. H4B II, 3, 66. With *off:* R3 IV, 5, 5 (Qq *witholds*). Oth. III, 3, 248. With *out: h. out water in foul way,* H4A II, 1, 93. *stony limits cannot h. love out,* Rom. II, 2, 67. *mine eyes cannot h. out water,* Tim. I, 2, 111. With *in, =* not to speak of: Lr. V, 3, 202.

Hence *=* to retard, to make lose time, to cause to linger: *he held me last night nine hours in reckoning up,* H4A III, 1, 156. *h. me not with silence overlong,* H6A V, 3, 13. *he'll wrest the sense and h. us here all day,* H6B III, 1, 186. *any cruelty that can torment him much and h. him long,* Oth. V, 2, 334.

f) to contain: *my body is the frame wherein 'tis held,* Sonn. 24, 3. *that poor retention could not so much h.* 122, 9. *more devils than vast hell can h.* Mids. V, 9. *no woman's heart so big, to h. so much,* Tw. II, 4, 99. *more than my pack will h.* Wint. IV, 4, 289. *can this cockpit h. the fields of France,* H5 Prol. 11. *let me have such a bowl may h. my thanks,* H8 I, 4, 39. *as big as hell can h.* Cymb. II, 4, 140.

g) to retain, to preserve, to continue: *nor his own vision —s what it doth catch,* Sonn. 113, 8. *our garments h. their freshness,* Tp. II, 1, 62. *I'll h. my mind,* Gent. V, 4, 38. *must of necessity h. his virtue to you,* All's I, 1, 9. *you must h. the credit of your father,* 88. *thy affection cannot h. the bent,* Tw. II, 4, 38. *should h. their places,* H4B V, 2, 17. *sword, h. thy temper,* H6B V, 2, 70. *if you mind to h. your true obedience,* H6C IV, 1, 140. *God h. it,* R3 III, 2, 107 (God grant that it may be so for ever). *nothing else —s fashion,* Troil. V, 2, 196. *fame cannot better be held nor more attained than by a place below the first,* Cor. I, 1, 269. *h. that purpose,* II, 1, 256. *if you do h. the same intent,* V, 6, 13. *there's but one in all doth h. his place,* Caes. III, 1, 65. *do they h. the same estimation,* Hml. II, 2, 348. *nature her custom —s,* IV, 7, 188. *h. his purpose,* V, 2, 183. *what ribs of oak can h. the mortise,* Oth. II, 1, 9. *to h. you in perpetual amity,* Ant. II, 2, 127. *cannot h. this visible shape,* IV, 14, 14. *she —s her virtue still, and I my mind,* Cymb. I, 4, 69. 105.

h) to maintain: *—s his rank before,* Sonn. 85, 12. *I held my city,* Compl. 176. *do not curst wives h. that* *self sovereignty only for praise sake*, LLL IV, 1, 36. *he* —*s his place*, H4B II, 2, 116. *he held the right*, H6A II, 4, 38. *h. thy whore*, Troil. V, 4, 25. *h. our best advantage*, Ant. IV, 11, 4. *to h. thine own*, H6C II, 2, 42 (to maintain what is thine). *h. your own*, Shr. IV, 4, 6 (play your part well; German: *haltet euch gut*). *does she h. her own well?* H4B III, 2, 218. *Ajax, h. thine own*, Troil. IV, 5, 114.

i) to occupy: *that blood ... three foot of it doth h.* John IV, 2, 100. *Bristol castle which is held by Bushy*, R2 II, 3, 164. *go thou to the city; learn how 'tis held*, Cor. I, 10, 28.

k) to keep, to guard, to restrain: *his mistress did h. his eyes locked in her crystal looks*, Gent. II, 4, 89. *she* —*s them prisoners still*, 92; cf. Troil. II, 2, 77; Tit. II, 1, 15. *she* —*eth thee in awe*, H6A I, 1, 39. *whilst I at a banquet h. him sure*, Tit. V, 2, 76. *h. him in safety till the prince come hither*, Rom. V, 3, 183. *he held you so under fortune*, Mcb. III, 1, 77. *he may h. our lives in mercy*, Lr. I, 4, 350. *our nineteen legions thou shalt h. by land*, Ant. III, 7, 59. *h. death awhile at the arm's end*, As II, 6, 10. *your deer does h. you at a bay*, Shr. V, 2, 56. *he* —*s Belzebub at the staves' end*, Tw. V, 291. *I saw him h. lord Percy at the point*, H4A V, 4, 21.

l) to keep, to observe, to follow, to pursue: *all askance he* —*s her in his eye*, Ven. 342. —*ing their course to Paphos*, 1193; cf. Wint. IV, 4, 513; R2 V, 3, 63. H5 III Chor. 17; III, 3, 23; H6C V, 3, 19; Hml. IV, 6, 29; Ant. III, 6, 85. *these contraries such unity do h.* Lucr. 1558. *when you h. your peace* (= are silent) Gent. V, 2, 18; Wiv. IV, 1, 75; Meas. V, 79; Tw. II, 3, 68. 73. 74; Wint. I, 2, 28; H6A III, 2, 58; H6B I, 3, 179. *where there was no proportion held in love*, Wiv. V, 5, 235. *you yet shall h. your word*, 258. *h. your vow*, LLL V, 2, 345. *one man* —*ing troth*, Mids. III, 2, 92. *h. little faith*, Tw. V, 174. *h. their promises*, H5 II Chor. 29. *to h. the handfast to her lord*, Cymb. I, 5, 77. *I will h. a long distance*, All's III, 2, 27. *and h. me pace in deep experiments*, H4A III, 1, 49. *to h. your honour more precise and nice with others than with him*, H4B II, 3, 40. *to h. what distance his wisdom can provide*, Mcb. III, 6, 44. *I h. my duty, as I h. my soul, both to my God and to my king*, Hml. II, 2, 44. *you do not h. the method to enforce the like from him*, Ant. I, 3, 7. *the loyalty well held to fools*, Hml. III, 13, 42.

m) to keep, to entertain, to harbour; properly and figuratively: *the dispersed air, who,* —*ing Lucrece' life, answered their cries*, Lucr. 1805. *Verona shall not h. thee*, Gent. V, 4, 129. *this field shall h. me*, LLL V, 2, 345. *if thou didst ever h. me in thy heart*, Hml. V, 2, 357. *I do now let loose my opinion, h. it no longer*, Tp. II, 2, 36; cf. Ado II, 3, 224; Merch. IV, 1, 131; Tw. IV, 2, 62; Caes. I, 2, 323; II, 1, 196. *the good conceit I h. of thee*, Gent. III, 2, 17. *the errors that these princes h.* Ado IV, 1, 165. *you h. too heinous a respect of grief*, John III, 4, 90. —*s belief*, V, 7, 6. —*ing a weak supposal of our worth*, Hml. I, 2, 18.

n) to keep, to entertain, to maintain, to carry on, to practise: *thus* —*s he disputation 'tween conscience and will*, Lucr. 246. *how with this rage shall beauty h. a plea*, Sonn. 65, 3. *for the peace of you I h. such strife*, 75, 3. *'gainst whom the world could not h. argument*, Pilgr. 30; cf. Ado II, 3, 55; H6A II, 4, 57. *h. three words' conference with this harpy*, Ado II, 1, 278.

let's h. more chat, LLL V, 2, 228. *the difference that* —*s this present question in the court*, Merch. IV, 1, 172. *I hold as little counsel with weak fear*, H4A IV, 3, 11. *in the conflict that it* —*s with death*, H6B III, 2, 164. —*s such swoln and hot discourse*, Troil. II, 3, 183. *I would h. more talk with thee*, Caes. IV, 3, 289. *no longer session h. upon my shame*, Meas. V, 376. *our council we will h. at Windsor*, H4A I, 1, 104. *his majesty's parliament, holden at Bury*, H6B II, 4, 71. —*s her parliament*, H6C I, 1, 35. *h. divided councils*, R3 III, 1, 179. III, 2, 12 (Ff *kept*). *who* —*s his state at door*, H8 V, 2, 24. *we'll h. a feast*, Mids. IV, 1, 190. *a fortnight h. we this solemnity*, V, 376; H8 IV, 1, 94; Rom. I, 2, 20. *triumphs held at Oxford*, R2 V, 3, 14. *you h. a fair assembly*, H8 I, 4, 87. *we h. a solemn supper*, Mcb. III, 1. 14. *I had thought to have held it* (my birthday) *poor*, Ant. III, 13, 186. *h. fair friendship with his majesty*, LLL II, 141. *if with myself I h. intelligence*, As I, 3, 49. *to h. my acquaintance with thee*, All's II, 3, 240; Tw. I, 2, 16. *I have held familiarity with fresher clothes*, All's V, 2, 3. *all the fellowship I h. now with him*, H8 III, 1, 121. *h. enmity*, Hml. I, 5, 65. *amity*, Lr. II, 4, 245. *Daphne* —*s the chase*, Mids. II, 1, 231.

o) to possess; 1) to have power over, to rule: *the affliction of my mind amends, with which, I fear, a madness held me*, Tp. V, 116. *how long hath this possession held the man?* Err. V, 44. *my holy humour was wont to h. me but while one would tell twenty*, R3 I, 4, 121. 2) to own, to keep as a property; abs.: *she is not worth what she doth cost the* —*ing*, Troil. II, 2, 52 (Q *keeping*). trans.: *to h. their fortune long*, Lucr. 866. *how do I h. thee but by thy granting?* Sonn. 87, 5. *who in thy power dost h. time's fickle glass*, 126, 2. *Falstaff his gold will h.* Wiv. I, 3, 107. *h. a goodly manor for a song*, All's III, 2, 9 (M. Edd. *sold*). *with her whom here I cannot h. on shore*, Wint. IV, 4, 510. *he that* —*s his kingdom* —*s the law*, John III, 1, 188. *for him and in his right we h. this town*, II, 268. *if what in rest you have, in right you h.* IV, 2, 55. *I have and I will h. the quondam Quickly*, H5 II, 1, 82. *which* (crown) *they h. by force and not by right*, H6B II, 2, 30. —*ing Corioli in the name of Rome*, Cor. I, 6, 37. *by the power we h.* Cymb. III, 1, 58. With *of*; trans.: *he loves you well that* —*s his life of you*, Per. II, 2, 22. absol.: *men shall h. of me in capite*, H6B IV, 7, 131 (shall be my crown-vassals, by a tenure in capite).

p) to receive, to take: *we h. rumour from what we fear, yet know not what we fear*, Mcb. IV, 2, 19 (we are frightened by uncertain rumours engendered by uncertain fears). Chiefly used in the imper.: *there, h.* Gent. IV, 4, 132. *h., bear you these letters*, Wiv. I, 3, 88. *h., there's money for thee*, I, 4, 166. *h. therefore, Angelo*, Meas. I, 1, 43. Err. II, 2, 23. LLL V, 1, 75. V, 2, 130. Merch. II, 4, 20. Tw. III, 1, 49. III, 3, 38. III, 4, 381. R2 II, 2, 92. H4B III, 2, 291. 296. R3 III, 2, 108 (Ff *there, drink that for me*). Tit. IV, 3, 105. Rom. IV, 1, 122. IV, 4, 1. V, 1, 59. Caes. I, 3, 117. Mcb. II, 1, 4. The pers. pronoun following (always *thee* for *thou*): *h. thee that to drink*, Shr. IV, 4, 17. *h. thee, there's my purse*, All's IV, 5, 46. *h. thee, there's some boot*, Wint. IV, 4, 651. *h. thee, take this garland on thy brow*, Caes. V, 3, 85. *h. you, there is a groat*, H5 V, 1, 61. = hear, listen: *h., daughter*, Rom. IV, 1, 68. 89.

q) to have; in various turns of expression: *things*

base and vile, —ing no quantity, Mids. I, 1, 232. to h. a rival place with one of them, Merch. I, 1, 174. we should h. day with the Antipodes, V, 127. if truth —s true contents, As V, 4, 136. my course, which —s no colour with the time, All's II, 5, 64. the father should h. some counsel in such a business, Wint. IV, 4, 420. why —s thine eye that lamentable rheum, John III, 1, 22. and h. their level with thy princely heart, H4A III, 2, 17. h. a wing quite from the flight of all thy ancestors, 30. —s from all soldiers chief majority and military title capital, 109. such powers as might h. sortance with his quality, H4B IV, 1, 11. when they h. them (fits of the face) H8 I, 3, 8. h. you the watch tonight? Hml. I, 2, 225. wherein the spirit held his wont to walk, I, 4, 6. while memory —s a seat in this distracted globe, I, 5, 96. no contraries h. more antipathy, Lr. II, 2, 93. the trust, the office I do h. of you, Oth. I, 3, 118. your royalty —s idleness your subject, Ant. I, 3, 92.

Periphrastical use: to h. in chase = to chase: Lucr. 1736. Sonn. 143, 5. John I, 223. Cor. I, 6, 19. this ring he —s in most rich choice, All's III, 7, 25. held in contempt, R3 I, 3, 80. who of my people h. him in delay? Tw. I, 5, 112. he held such petty bondage in disdain, Ven. 394. 761. H5 I, 2, 48. h. in hate, Gent. III, 2, 33. thou didst h. him in thy hate, Oth. I, 1, 7. in what hatred he hath held them, Cor. II, 1, 262. that beauty which you h. in lease, Sonn. 13, 5. held in idle price to haunt assemblies, Meas. I, 3, 9. death doth h. us in pursuit, H6C II, 5, 127. h. me no more in your respect, All's III, 6, 4. he —s your temper in a high respect, H4A III, 1, 170. — With participles or adjectives: we cite our faults, that they may h. excused our lawless lives, Gent. IV, 1, 54 (that they may excuse). if you make a care of happy —ing her, Wint. IV, 4, 367 (= of seeing her happy). my father's eyes should h. her loathed, Oth. III, 4, 62 (= loathe her). cf. this her easy-held imprisonment, H6A V, 3, 139. Oftenest reflectively (the pers. pron. serving as refl.): my tongue-tied Muse in manners —s her still, Sonn. 85, 1 (is silent). h. you still, Err. III, 2, 69. I will not h. me still, IV, 2, 17. Troil. V, 3, 25. Mcb. III, 2, 54. I held me glad of such a doom, Gent. IV, 1, 32 (= I was glad). h. you content, Ado V, 1, 92. I can no longer h. me patient, R3 I, 3, 157.

r) to think, to judge, to consider; with an inf.: held the duke to be wise, Meas. III, 2, 145. has a deal of that too much which —s him much to have, All's III, 2, 93 (i.e. of vanity, which persuades him to have many good qualities). With a depending clause: it is held that valour is the chiefest virtue, Cor. II, 2, 87. I h. it ever, virtue and cunning were endowments greater, Per. III, 2, 26; cf. Wiv. I, 1, 236 (Evans' speech). With a double accus.: lest he should h. it her own gross abuse, Lucr. 1315. Sonn. 136, 11. 151, 13. Gent. II, 6, 29. V, 4, 133. Ado II, 1, 67. LLL IV, 3, 177. Mids. I, 1, 55. All's I, 3, 123. Wint. IV, 4, 697. John III, 4, 161. H4A I, 3, 90. H4B I, 1, 95. H6C IV, 2, 7. R3 I, 3, 50. II, 1, 55. IV, 4, 493. H8 I, 3, 47. II, 2, 124. II, 4, 83. Troil. II, 3, 199. Cor. V, 3, 81. Tit. I, 245. Caes. I, 2, 78. V, 1, 77. Cymb. IV, 3, 16. of small worth held, Sonn. 2, 4. With as: I h. you as a thing enskyed and sainted, Meas. I, 4, 34. we will h. it as a dream, Ado I, 2, 21. I h. the world but as the world, Merch. I, 1, 77. to urge the thing held as a ceremony, V, 206. as a stranger to my heart h. thee,

Lr. I, 1, 118. my life I never held but as a pawn, 157. we are held as outlaws, Cymb. IV, 2, 67. With for: h. it for no sin, Lucr. 209. for nothing h. me, Sonn. 136, 11. h. your fortune for your bliss, Merch. III, 2, 137. held for certain, H8 II, 1, 155. an idiot —s his bauble for a God, Tit. V, 1, 79.

s) to estimate: if you h. your life at any price, Tw. III, 4, 252. held at such a rate, H6C II, 2, 51. if my love thou —est at aught, Hml. IV, 3, 60. With adverbs: h. their manhoods cheap, H5 IV, 3, 66; cf. I h. your dainties cheap and your welcome dear, Err. III, 1, 21. h. dear: LLL IV, 3, 276. V, 2, 444. H6B IV, 1, 147. R3 I, 4, 239. III, 2, 80. H8 V, 3, 174. Troil. III, 3, 19. held thee dearly, H6C II, 1, 102. Tit. V, 1, 36. we held him carelessly, Rom. III, 4, 25 (treated him with indifference and neglect). the parts ... I h. as giddily as fortune, Tw. II, 4, 87 (I regard as carelessly). —s his honour higher than his ease, Troil. I, 3, 266. men very nobly held, All's IV, 3, 341 (highly respected). I h. thee reverently, H6C II, 2, 109. he —s you well, Ado III, 2, 101 (has a good opinion of you); cf. Troil. II, 3, 190. IV, 1, 77. Oth. I, 3, 396.

t) to lay, to wager: I'll h. thee any wager, Merch. II, 4, 62. I h. you a penny, Shr. III, 2, 85. Hence perhaps the phrases: she —s hand with any princess, John II, 494 (is a match for). I'll find a Marshalsea shall h. ye play these two months, H8 V, 4, 90 (shall keep you under).

u) to bear, to continue to suffer: as the ripest mulberry that will not h. the handling, Cor. III, 2, 80. would not h. taking, Tim. I, 2, 159. many corses that will scarce h. the laying in, Hml. V, 1, 182. With out: h. out this tempest, John IV, 3, 156. he cannot long h. out these pangs, H4B IV, 4, 117. nor strength to h. out flight, H6C II, 6, 24.

2) intr. a) to keep or take a thing in one's grasp: to make his anchor h., Wint. I, 2, 213 (= bite, get a good hold of the bottom). his power, like to a fangless lion, may offer, but not h. H4B IV, 1, 219. bankrupts, h. fast; rather than render back, out with your knives, Tim. IV, 1, 8.

b) to refrain: we shall be flouting; we cannot h. As V, 1, 14. if they h., when their ladies bid 'em clap, H8 Epil. 14. Mostly in the imper., = do not strike, forbear: Err. II, 2, 24. V, 33. Tw. III, 4, 351. IV, 1, 30. 34. H6B II, 3, 96. V, 2, 14. H6C I, 4, 51. V, 5, 43. Cor. V, 6, 132. Rom. III, 1, 93. Mcb. I, 5, 55. V, 8, 34. Ant. V, 2, 39. to bid you h. Lr. III, 7, 75. With in: such as can h. in, such as will strike sooner than speak, and speak sooner than drink, H4A II, 1, 85 (a rather obscure passage, the common interpretation of which is: such as can keep counsel, will not blab; cf. Lr. V, 3, 202; but it may mean in general: such as know to keep within the bounds of decency).

c) to be firm, not to break: iron may h. with her, but never lutes, Shr. II, 147. if one (point) break, the other will h. Tw. I, 5, 26. if the springe h., the cock is mine, Wint. IV, 3, 36. my heart hath one poor string to stay it by, which —s but till thy news be uttered, John V, 7, 56. if this sword h. H6C V, 1, 75. h., patience, Troil. V, 2, 29. h., h., my heart, Hml. I, 5, 93. this project should have a back or second, that might h., if this should blast in proof, IV, 7, 154. O sides, will you yet h.? Lr. II, 4, 201. can my sides h.? Cymb. I, 6, 69. to h. together = not to fall in pieces:

as well as one so great and so forlorn may h. together, Wint. II, 2, 23; cf. *hang together*, Wiv. III, 2, 13. *h. or cut bow-strings,* Mids. I, 2, 114 (probably = come what come may; a phrase not yet sufficiently explained. Usually interpreted as a cant expression of archers, = keep promise, or else cut your strings).

d) *to hold good,* to be valid, to prove true: *never faith could h., if not to beauty vowed,* Pilgr. 58 and LLL IV, 2, 110. *gourd and fullam —s,* Wiv. I, 3, 94. *if this law h. in Vienna ten year,* Meas. II, 1, 254. *the allusion —s in the exchange,* LLL IV, 2, 42. *that ever —s,* Merch. II, 6, 8. *the duke will never grant this forfeiture to h.* III, 3, 25. *it* (my privilege) *— s yet,* All's IV, 5, 98. *it —s current that I told you yesternight,* H4A II, 1, 59. *to h. in right and title of the female,* H5 I, 2, 89. *doth this news h. of good King Edward's death?* R3 II, 3, 7. *the saying did not h. in him,* II, 4, 16. *it held not,* H8 II, 1, 149. *vows to every purpose must not h.* Troil. V, 3, 24. *does the rumour h. for true?* Tim. V, 1, 4. *—s it true, that the Duke of Cornwall was so slain?* Lr. IV, 7, 85.

e) *to be fit,* to be consistent: *thou sayest well, and it —s well too,* H4A I, 2, 34; see above LLL IV, 2, 42. *this has no —ing, to swear by him whom I protest to love, that I will work against him,* All's IV, 2, 27.

f) *to continue,* to abide, not to change or fall off: *every thing —s in perfection but a little moment,* Sonn. 15, 2. *go, I'll h.* Wiv. V, 1, 1 (you may rely on me). *h. you there,* Meas. III, 1, 176 (i.e. continue in this mind; cf. *there rest,* II, 3, 36). *will this capriccio h. in thee?* All's II, 3, 310. *your resolution cannot h.* Wint. IV, 4, 36. *if this civil buffeting h.* H4A II, 4, 397. *it cannot h.* Tim. II, 1, 4 (it cannot go on thus). *will 't h.?* III, 6, 70. *if your mind h.* Caes. I, 2, 295. *that unassailable —s on his rank, unshaked of motion,* III, 1, 69 (remains, stands firm). *if your pleasure h. to play with Laertes,* Hml. V, 2, 206. *if his last purpose h.* Lr. V, 1, 1. *dost thou h. there still?* Ant. II, 5, 92 (dost thou persist in saying so?). With *out: if thou hast* (impudence) *rely upon it till my tale be heard, and h. no longer out,* Meas. V, 371 (and play your part no longer). *can any face of brass h. longer out?* LLL V, 2, 395. *she would not h. out enemy for ever,* Merch. IV, 1, 447. *well held out,* Tw. IV, 1, 5 (a part well borne). With *up: it lies much in your —ing up,* Meas. III, 1, 273 (in your not getting out of your part).

g) *to last: will this h., think you?* Cymb. I, 4, 183. *h. those justs and triumphs?* R2 V, 2, 52.

h) *to stand one's ground,* not to yield, not to surrender: *the rest will serve for a short —ing,* Cor. I, 7, 4. *our force by land hath nobly held,* Ant. III, 13, 170. With *out: nothing there —s out but Dover castle,* John V, 1, 30. Hence = to bear, to have strength enough: *how shall summer's honey breath h. out against the wreckful siege of battering days?* Sonn. 65, 6. *h. out my horse, and I will first be there,* R2 II, 1, 300. *else ne'er could they h. out so,* H6A I, 2, 43. *hath he so long held out with me untired,* R3 IV, 2, 44. *the babe cannot h. out to Tyrus,* Per. I, 1, 80.

i) *to h. friends* = to keep friendship: Ado I, 1, 91. k) With *off,* = to keep distant, to be reserved: *yet h. I off,* Troil. I, 2, 312. *I might have still held off,* IV, 2, 17. *if you love me, h. not off,* Hml. II, 2, 302.

Hold-door trade, the trade of a bawd or pimp: Troil. V, 10, 52.

Holdfast, grasping firmly: *in his h. foot the weak*

mouse panteth, Lucr. 555. Substantively: *h. is the only dog,* H5 II, 3, 54 (cf. the proverb: bray is a good dog, but holdfast is better).

Holding (cf. *Hold*), the burden of a song: *the h. every man shall bear,* Ant. II, 7, 117.

Holding-anchor, the sheet-anchor: H6C V, 4, 4.

Hole, 1) a hollow place, a cavity: Lucr. 1175. Gent. II, 3, 20. Wiv. III, 5, 143; cf. H5 III, 6, 88. LLL V, 2, 734. Mids. V, 159. 202. All's II, 2, 26. H4B II, 2, 88. III, 2, 165. R3 I, 4, 29. Hml. V, 1, 237. Ant. II, 7, 17. Used of wounds: H4B III, 2, 165. R3 I, 2, 14. V, 3, 125. Tit. III, 2, 17. Caes. V, 1, 31.

2) a pit: H4A I, 2, 120. R3 I, 4, 287. Tit. II, 3, 129. 186. 198. 210. 227. 246. V, 1, 104. Caes. II, 1, 205.

3) any hiding and lurking place: *the earth had not a h. to hide this deed,* John IV, 3, 36. *darts his light through every guilty h.* R2 III, 2, 43. Obscenely: Rom. II, 4, 97.

4) the small entrance where mice pass: *the mouse's h.* Per. III Prol. 6.

5) the hollow of the palm: *spit in the h. and tune again,* Shr. III, 1, 40 (= spit in your hand, take courage and make a new effort).

Holidam or **Holydame,** the same as *halidom,* q. v.: *by my h.* Shr. V, 2, 99. H8 V, 1, 117. Rom. I, 3, 43.

Holiday, a day of exemption from labour, a festival: Tp. IV, 136. John III, 1, 82; cf. 83. R2 III, 1, 44. H4A I, 2, 228. R3 II, 1, 73 (O. Edd. *holy day*). H8 V, 5, 77. Rom. V, 1, 56. Caes. I, 1, 2. 35. Per. II, 1, 86. *he speaks h.* Wiv. III, 2, 69 (in elegant and choice expressions); cf. *with many h. and lady terms,* H4A I, 3, 46. *a h. fool,* Tp. II, 2, 30. *h. foolery,* As I, 3, 14. *I am in a h. humour,* IV, 1, 69.

Holiday-time, gay and festive time: *in the h. of my beauty,* Wiv. II, 1, 2.

Holily, piously, virtuously, agreeably to the law of God: *how h. he works in all his business,* H8 II, 2, 24. Mcb. I, 5, 22. V, 1, 67.

Holiness, 1) sanctity: Err. V, 110. John IV, 3, 53. H6B I, 3, 58. 67. II, 1, 26. Troil. II, 1, 18.

2) a title given to the pope: Meas. III, 2, 233. John V, 1, 6. H6A V, 1, 53. H8 II, 4, 120. 235. III, 2, 32. 222.

Holla, interj. used 1) to call to a person to come near: LLL V, 2, 900. As I, 1, 93. II, 4, 66. Shr. II, 109. Hml. I, 1, 18. Joined to *ho:* Shr. IV, 1, 12.

2) to make to stop: *his flattering h.* Ven. 284. *cry h. to thy tongue,* As III, 2, 257. *h., stand there!* Oth. I, 2, 56.

3) to express surprise: *h., what storm is this?* Tit. II, 1, 25 (Qq *hollo*). *h. h., that eye that told you so looked but a-squint,* Lr. V, 3, 72.

Holla, vb. (cf. *Halloo* and *Hollo*) 1) to cry *holla:* Merch. V, 43. trans.: *he that first lights on him h. the other,* Lr. III, 1, 55 (Qq *hollow*).

2) to cry loudly: *a cry more tuneable was never —ed to,* Mids. IV, 1, 130. *h. your name to the reverberate hills,* Tw. I, 5, 291 (O. Edd. *hallow* and *hollow*). *as many lies as may be —ed in thy treacherous ear,* R2 IV, 54 (O. Edd. *hollowed*). *in his ear I'll h. Mortimer,* H4A I, 3, 222 (Qq *hollow*).

Holland, Dutch linen: H4A III, 3, 82. H4B II, 2, 26 (quibbling with the name of the country).

Hollander, Dutchman: *blunt —s,* H6C IV, 8, 2. *swag-bellied H.* Oth. II, 3, 80. 86.

Hollo, interj. expressing surprise: Tit. II, 1, 25 (Ff *holla*).

Hollo, vb., to cry holla or hollo: *she hears some huntsman h.* Ven. 973. trans. = 1) to utter loudly: *h. your name to the reverberate hills*, Tw. I, 5, 291 (O. Edd. *hallow* and *hollow*). *as many lies as may be —ed in thy ear*, R2 IV, 54. *in his ear I'll h. Mortimer*, H4A I, 3, 222 (Ff *holla*). 2) to cry to: *if I fly, h. me like a hare*, Cor. I, 8, 7. *h. the other*, Lr. III, 1, 55 (Ff *holla*).

Hollow, subst. a cavity: *love made those —s* (dimples). Ven. 243. *into this gaping h. of the earth*, Tit. II, 3, 249. *the h. of thine ear*, Rom. III, 5, 3. *by the happy h. of a tree*, Lr. II, 3, 2.

Hollow, adj. 1) excavated, having a void space within: Ven. 1185. Lucr. 1122. Wiv. IV, 2, 171. Meas. I, 2, 57. R2 II, 1, 83. III, 2, 140. 160. H4A I, 3, 106. H4B I, 3, 75. H6A V, 4, 121. Troil. I, 3, 80. Tit. III, 1, 84. III, 2, 10. V, 2, 35. Oth. III, 3, 447. Per. I, 4, 67. *h. bones*, Meas. I, 2, 57. Tim. IV, 3, 152. *h. pampered jades of Asia*, H4B II, 4, 178 (Pistol's speech). *the earth whose h. womb resounds*, Ven. 268. *the h. earth*, Shr. Ind. 2, 48. Rom. V, 3, 4. Oth. IV, 2, 79.

2) sunk deep in the orbit: *with h. eye*, Merch. IV, 1, 270. R2 II, 1, 270. H4B IV, 5, 6. H5 V, 2, 170. Per. I, 4, 51. Adverbially: *look as h. as a ghost*, John III, 4, 84.

3) deep, low, as if reverberated from a cavity: *a h. burst of bellowing*, Tp. II, 1, 311. *h. whistling in the leaves*, H4A V, 1, 5. Adverbially: *how h. the fiend speaks within him*, Tw. III, 4, 101.

4) not what one appears, not sincere, false: *the most h. lover*, As IV, 1, 197. *h. falsehood*, John III, 1, 95. *our h. parting*, R2 I, 4, 9. *h. bosoms*, H5 II Chor. 21. H6A III, 1, 136. H6B III, 2, 43. 66. H6C IV, 1, 139. R3 II, 1, 38. H8 III, 1, 104. Troil. I, 3, 80. IV, 5, 169. Rom. III, 3, 128. Tim. I, 2, 16. Caes. IV, 2, 23. Hml. III, 2, 218.

Hollow-eyed, having sunken eyes: Err. V, 240.

Hollow-hearted, not to be trusted: R3 IV, 4, 435.

Hollowly, insincerely, falsely: *if I speak h.* Tp. III, 1, 70. *try your penitence, if it be sound, or h. put on*, Meas. II, 3, 23.

Hollowness, the state of being hollow; emptiness and insincerity: *grief boundeth where it falls, not with the empty h., but weight*, R2 I, 2, 59. *whose low sound reverbs no h.* Lr. I, 1, 156. *machinations, h., treachery*, I, 2, 122.

Hollow-pampered, reading of Ff in H4B II, 4, 178; not hyph. in Q.

Hollow-swelling, reading of M. Edd. in Lucr. 1122; not hyph. in O. Edd.

Holly, Ilex aquifolium, an evergreen shrub: As II, 7, 180. 182.

Holmedon, the battle-field of Percy and Douglas: H4A I, 1, 55. 65. 70. I, 3, 24. V, 3, 14.*

Holofernes, name of the school-master in LLL IV, 2, 8. 54.

Holy (comp. *—er:* Wint V, 1, 31. Tim. IV, 3, 430. superl. *—est*, Compl. 233), 1) perfectly pure, immaculate, godlike: *by God's h. mother*, R3 I, 3, 306. III, 7, 2. *by h. Mary*, H8 V, 2, 33. *some h. angel*, Mcb. III, 6, 45. *like h. Phoebus' car*, Ant. IV, 8, 29. *by the h. Gods*, Per. III, 4, 7. V, 1, 200 etc. *plain and h. innocence*, Tp. III, 1, 82. *in the name of something h.* III, 3, 94 etc.

2) sainted: *our h. Abram*, Merch. I, 3, 73. *a h. maid*, H6A I, 2, 51. *a h. prophetess*, I, 4, 102. *h. Joan*, II, 1, 49. *by h. Paul*, R3 I, 3, 45. *the H. Land*, R2 V, 6, 49. H4B III, 1, 108. IV, 5, 211. *the h. wars in Palestine*, John II, 4.

3) consecrated by religion, sacred, reverend; used of persons of a religious order or character: *h. father*, Meas. I, 3, 1. 7. *most h. sir*, III, 1, 47. *as I was then advertising and h. to your business*, V, 388 (i. e. in the character of a priest. *I was to* = I belonged to; cf. *Be*). *this h. friar*, Ado V, 4, 58. Merch. V, 33. All's III, 5, 42. Tw. IV, 3, 23. V, 145. John III, 1, 135. III, 4, 44. V, 2, 65. H6A III, 1, 111. H6B IV, 4, 9. R3 III, 2, 117. Ant. II, 2, 244 etc. Jocularly: *a h. parcel of the fairest dames*, LLL V, 2, 160. Of religious actions, things, and institutions: *my h. order*, Meas. IV, 3, 152. *my h. errand*, John III, 1, 137. *his h. state*, H6A III, 1, 58. *the h. church*, John V, 2, 71. H5 I, 1, 23. *by the h. rood*, R3 III, 2, 77. IV, 4, 165. *by h. human law*, Lucr. 571. *h. wedlock vow*, 809. H6C III, 3, 243. *a h. and obsequious tear*, Sonn. 31, 5. *sweet beauty hath no name, no h. bower*, 127, 7. *from this h. fire of Love*, 153, 5. *h. vows*, Compl. 179. *with full and h. rite*, Tp. IV, 1, 17; Ado V, 4, 68. *h. prayers*, Gent. I, 1, 17; Err. IV, 4, 58; V, 104; Mcb. IV, 3, 154. *seal the bargain with a h. kiss*, Gent. II, 2, 7; Tw. V, 161; Rom. IV, 1, 43. *I intend h. confession*, Gent. IV, 3, 44. *between you I shall have a h. head*, Err. II, 1, 80 (by having it broken across). *in a h. band*, Ado III, 1, 114; cf. LLL V, 2, 756; Lr. II, 2, 80. *the h. edifice*, Merch. I, 1, 30. *an evil soul producing h. witness*, I, 3, 100. *our h. Sabbath*, IV, 1, 36. *h. crosses*, V, 31. *with h. bell*, As II, 7, 121. *h. bread*, H4B IV, 4, 15. *I desire your h. wishes*, All's I, 1, 68. *h. writ*, II, 1, 141; R3 I, 3, 337; Oth. III, 3, 324. *the h. text*, H4B IV, 2, 7. *in some h. place*, H6A III, 3, 14. *h. saws of sacred writ*, H6B I, 3, 61. *my h. oath*, H6C V, 1, 89. *the h. privilege of sanctuary*, R3 III, 1, 41 etc.

4) pious, godly, virtuous, righteous, of a pure heart: *in him those h. antique hours are seen*, Sonn. 68, 9. *a nun of —est note*, Compl. 233. *h. Gonzalo*, Tp. V, 62. *Silvia is too fair, too true, too h.* Gent. IV, 2, 5. 41. *the offence is h. that she hath committed*, Wiv. V, 5, 238. *as h. as severe*, Meas. III, 2, 276. *with h. abstinence*, IV, 2, 84. *so h. a man*, IV, 3, 117. V, 144. *the carriage of a h. saint*, Err. III, 2, 14. *'tis h. sport*, 27. *h. men at their death have good inspirations*, Merch. I, 2, 30. As II, 3, 15. III, 1, 5, 99. Wint. V, 1, 29. 31. John III, 3, 15 (= devout). H4B I, 1, 202. R3 I, 2, 5. III, 7, 99. Cor. III, 3, 113. Tim. IV, 3, 430. Cymb. I, 6, 166. III, 4, 62. 180 etc.

Holy-ale, a rural festival; a word substituted for the sake of the rhyme, by M. Edd. for *holydays* of O. Edd. in Per. Prol. 6.

Holy-cruel, cruel by being too virtuous: All's IV, 2, 32.

Holydame, see *Holidam*.

Holy-rood day, the fourteenth of September: H4A I, 1, 52.

Holy-thistle, the plant Centaurea benedicta: Ado III, 4, 80.

Holy-thoughted, virtuous: Lucr. 384.

Holy-water, water consecrated by the priest to sprinkle the faithful: Cymb. V, 5, 269. *court h.* Lr. III, 2, 10, the Fr. *eau bénite de la cour*, i. e. flattery.

Homage, 1) fealty and service professed to a superior lord: Tp. I, 2, 124. Tw. I, 5, 225. R2 II, 1, 204. H5 III, 7, 31. *pays h. to us,* Hml. IV, 3, 64. *to do h.* Tp. I, 2, 113. Gent. IV, 1, 66. H6A IV, 2, 7. Mcb. III, 6, 36. Ant. I, 2, 28. *do themselves h.* Oth. I, 1, 54 (know no masters but themselves).

2) respect, obeisance, reverence: H5 IV, 1, 267. *to do h.* Err. II, 1, 104. H6B III, 2, 224. *to do h. to:* Sonn. 7, 3. Shr. Ind. 1, 135. *to owe h. to:* Err. III, 2, 43.

Homager, vassal: Ant. I, 1, 31.

Home, subst. 1) one's own country: *why thou departed'st from thy native h.* Err. I, 1, 30. *to return to their h.* Merch. I, 2, 112. John II, 21. *not think of h.* 31. *at their native —s,* 69. *far from h.* R2 II, 1, 53. *how can tyrants safely govern h.* H6C III, 3, 69 etc. *at h.* = in one's own country: *though fools at h. condemn them,* Tp. III, 3, 27. Gent. I, 1, 7. 62. I, 3, 5. 14. II, 7, 62. John IV, 3, 151. H6C II, 2, 158. R3 I, 1, 135. Cor. V, 1, 7 etc. *whose contents shall witness to him I am near at h.* Meas. IV, 3, 99 (= near being at home, near home). *the letters of our friends petition us at home,* Ant. I, 2, 190 (request us to be at home, to come home). Preceded by *for: that presently you take your way for h.* All's II, 5, 69. By *toward: go thou toward h.* All's II, 5, 95. *from h.* = foreign: *now powers from h. and discontents at h. meet in one line,* John IV, 3, 151. Adjectively, = domestic: *to confer of h. affairs,* Gent. II, 4, 119. *these h. alarms,* R2 I, 1, 205.

2) one's own house: *he hath eaten me out of house and h.* H4B II, 1, 81 (Mrs Quickly's speech). *hence to your —s,* Cor. I, 1, 252. *hath holp him to his h. before us,* Mcb. I, 6, 24. *to answer from our h.* Lr. II, 1, 126 (i. e. not at home) etc. *at h.* = in one's own house: Wiv. III, 2, 12. Err. II, 1, 88. As I, 1, 8. 9. Shr. V, 2, 151. All's III, 4, 10 etc. *from h.* = a) leaving one's own house: *when I go from h.* Err. IV, 4, 37. V, 56. Lr. II, 4, 1. b) otherwhere than at home: *her husband will be from h.* Wiv. II, 2, 91. 105. *feeds from h.* Err. II, 1, 101. Merch. V, 230. H5 I, 2, 272. Lr. II, 4, 208. Oth. III, 4, 169. Cymb. III, 3, 29.

3) any place of residence, rest and comfort: *so far from h. into my deeds to pry,* Sonn. 61, 6 (i. e. from thee). *that is my h. of love,* Sonn. 109, 5. *a rendezvous, a h. to fly unto,* H4A IV, 1, 57. *he hath no h.* H6B IV, 8, 40. *many lives stand between me and h.* H6C III, 2, 173 (i. e. royalty, which alone can make me happy). *forgetting any other h. but this,* Rom. II, 2, 176. Hence = the grave: *these that I bring unto their latest h.* Tit. I, 83; cf. Hml. V, 1, 256.

4) *at h.* = in the house: *who's at h. besides yourself?* Wiv. IV, 2, 13. *yonder's old coil at h.* Ado V, 2, 98. *where be these gallants? who's at h.?* Shr. III, 2, 89. *have you dined at h.?* Rom. II, 5, 46.

Home, adv. 1) to one's own country: Tp. I, 2, 235. Gent. V, 4, 143. H6B III, 1, 298. R3 IV, 4, 313 etc. *to redeem a traitor h.* H4A I, 3, 86. 92. *welcome h.* Cor. III, 1, 20. V, 6, 51 etc. (cf. *Welcome*).

2) to one's own house: Tp. II, 1, 90. II, 2, 75. Gent. IV, 2, 94. IV, 4, 93. Wiv. II, 1, 158. Err. I, 2, 48. 75. II, 1, 31. 60. LLL V, 2, 925. Shr. IV, 3, 98. All's I, 2, 65. H6C V, 4, 56. Caes. I, 1, 1 etc. *welcomed h.* Err. IV, 4, 37. Merch. V, 113. R3 V, 3, 260 (cf. *Welcome*). *we'll be a day before our husbands h.* Merch. IV, 2, 3. *to have me h.* Err. II, 2, 10. V, 101.

H4B V, 5, 80. *wait on me h.* All's V, 3, 323. *h. to your house,* Err. I, 2, 75. Mids. III, 2, 382. Cor. III, 1, 234. Caes. III, 2, 54 etc.

3) to the house of a person spoken of: *go h. with me to dinner,* Wiv. III, 2, 81. *I pray you h. to dinner with me,* Meas. II, 1, 292. *brought you h. the head of Ragozine,* V, 538. *my way is now to hie h. to his house,* Err. IV, 3, 93. *I entreat you h. with me to dinner,* Merch. IV, 1, 401. R2 IV, 333. *I will come h. to you,* Caes. I, 2, 309. *thou shalt go h.* Per. II, 1, 85 (to our house). Caes. I, 3, 1.

4) to the place or person, to whom a thing belongs: *so thy great gift, upon misprision growing, comes h. again,* Sonn. 87, 12 (returns to thee). *now to Helen is it* (my heart) *h. returned,* Mids. III, 2, 172. *send for your ring, I will return it h.* All's V, 3, 223 (give it back to its owner). *the anchor still came h.* Wint. I, 2, 214 (did not bite, did not get hold). *where high profits might come h.* H8 III, 2, 158 (accrue to you). *the bringing h. of bell and burial,* Hml. V, 1, 256. (i. e. to the grave; cf. Tit. I, 83).

5) to the quick, sensibly, so as to make the intended effect: *who may strike h.* Meas. I, 3, 41. *push h.* H5 II, 1, 103. *charge h.* Cor. I, 4, 38. *fortune's blows, when most struck h.* IV, 1, 8. *strike her h.* Tit. II, 1, 118. II, 3, 117. *look ye draw h. enough* (your bow) IV, 3, 3. *he charges h. my unprovided body,* Lr. II, 1, 53. *wear thy good rapier bare, and put it h.* Oth. V, 1, 2. *snip, snap, quick and h.* LLL V, 1, 63 (so as to hit the adversary). *though my mocks come h. by me,* V, 2, 637. *seest a game played h., the rich stake drawn,* Wint. I, 2, 248 (in good earnest). *let my prophecy come h. to ye,* IV, 4, 663 (be effective, be fulfilled). *I will pay thy graces h.* Tp. V, 71 (fully, so as to satisfy thee). *all my services you have paid h.* Wint. V, 3, 4. *till he hath found a time to pay us h.* H4A I, 3, 288. *these injuries will be revenged h.* Lr. III, 3, 13. *I will punish h.* III, 4, 16. *accuse him h. and h.* Meas. IV, 3, 148 (so as to touch the sore). *lacked the sense to know her estimation h.* All's V, 3, 4 (to appreciate her true worth). *I cannot speak him h.* Cor. II, 2, 107 (I find no words sufficiently to set off his merit). *charge him h.* III, 3, 1. *you have told them h.* IV, 2, 48. *that trusted h. might yet enkindle you unto the crown,* Mcb. I, 3, 120 (literally). *she'll tax him h.* Hml. III, 3, 29. *look you lay h. to him,* III, 4, 1. *he speaks h.* Oth. II, 1, 166 (without reserve, without ceremony). Ant. I, 2, 109. *satisfy me h.* Cymb. III, 5, 92. *that confirms it h.* IV, 2, 328 (so as to leave no doubt). *take her h.* Per. IV, 2, 134 (treat her as she should be treated).

Home-bred, taking place in one's own country; native, domestic: *h. strife,* Ven. 764. *h. hate,* R2 I, 3, 187. *h. marriage,* H6C IV, 1, 38.

Home-keeping, remaining at home, not travelling: Gent. I, 1, 2.

Homely, 1) plain, simple, humble, not refined; used both of persons and things: *the h. villain courtsies to her low,* Lucr. 1338. *home-keeping youth have ever h. wits,* Gent. I, 1, 2. *h. meat,* All's II, 2, 49. *my h. stars,* II, 5, 80. *a most h. shepherd,* Wint. IV, 2, 43. *h. foolery,* IV, 4, 341. *with h. biggen bound,* H4B IV, 5, 27. *rich hangings in a h. house,* H6B V, 3, 12. *a h. swain,* H6C II, 5, 22. *curds,* 47. *be plain and h. in thy drift,* Rom. II, 3, 55. *a h. man's advice,* Mcb. IV, 2, 68. *make what's h. savoury,* Cymb. III, 6, 33.

2) of plain features, ugly: *upon a h. object Love can wink*, Gent. II, 4, 98. *hath h. age the alluring beauty took from my poor cheek?* Err. II, 1, 89. *I'll have thy beauty made more h. than thy state*, Wint. IV, 4, 437.

Home-return, return to one's country: Err. I, 1, 60. R2 I, 3, 267.

Homespun, subst. a coarse person: Mids. III, 1, 79.

Homeward, toward one's habitation or country: Ven. 813. Err. I, 1, 118. 135. LLL IV, 3, 375. Wint. I, 2, 24. Mcb. I, 3, 29.

Homewards, toward one's habitation: As IV, 3, 179.

Homicidal, murderous; corrupted to *honey-suckle* by Mrs. Quickly: *thou honey-suckle villain*, H4B II, 1, 56.

Homicide, a manslayer, murderer: H6A I, 2, 25. V, 4, 62. R3 I, 2, 125. V, 2, 18. V, 3, 246. Corrupted to *honey-seed* and *hemp-seed* by Mrs. Quickly: H4B II, 1, 57. 64.

Homily, a sermon: As III, 2, 164.

Honest, (comp. —*er:* Ado III, 5, 16. All's III, 5, 82. H4B II, 4, 414. H6B IV, 7, 55. Cor. IV, 5, 52. Sup. —*est:* All's III, 5, 77) 1) upright, true in words and deeds: *pawned h. looks, but laid no deeds to gage*, Lucr. 1351. *all my h. faith in thee is lost*, Sonn. 152, 8. *Germans are h. men*, Wiv. IV, 5, 74. *h. as the skin between his brows*, Ado III, 5, 13 (a proverbial phrase; cf. Germ. *eine ehrliche Haut*). *I that am h., I that hold it sin to break the vow*, LLL IV, 3, 177. V, 2, 413. Mids. V, 438. Merch. II, 2, 7. As III, 3, 26. Tw. IV, 2, 10. Wint. IV, 4, 862. H4B V, 1, 50. 54. H6B IV, 7, 55. Mcb. I, 3, 125. IV, 2, 55. Oth. III, 3, 381 etc. Often applied in a very latitudinarian sense, = fair, good, brave: *my h. lads, I will tell you*, Wiv. I, 3, 42. *to desire this h. gentlewoman to speak a good word*, I, 4, 87. *an h., willing, kind fellow*, 10. *minime, h. master*, LLL III, 61. *h. Dull*, V, 1, 162. *some h. neighbours will not make them friends*, Mids. III, 1, 148. *your name, h. gentleman?* 187. *in these h. mean habiliments*, Shr. IV, 3, 172. H4B V, 3, 58. 111. Cor. I, 1, 63 etc.

2) honorable, respectable: *h. lord*, Tp. III, 3, 34. *once again I do receive thee h.* Gent. V, 4, 78. *h. Master Page*, Wiv. I, 1, 67. *an h. gentleman*, I, 4, 177. *Master Page is an h. man*, II, 2, 121. *having an h. man to your husband*, III, 3, 107. III, 2, 88. Meas. V, 263. Err. V, 19. Ado III, 3, 20. Merch. III, 1, 14. As III, 3, 8. Shr. III, 2, 195. IV, 5, 69. H4B II, 4, 414. III, 2, 61. H8 IV, 2, 160. Caes. I, 2, 258. V, 5, 71. Oth. III, 3, 103 etc.

3) decent, fair, proper, becoming: *I thank thee for thine h. care*, Gent. III, 1, 22. *I'll ne'er be drunk but in h., civil, goodly company*, Wiv. I, 1, 187. *behold what h. clothes you send forth*, IV, 2, 126. *if it be h. you have spoke, you have courage to maintain it*, Meas. III, 2, 166. *your company is fairer than h.* IV, 3, 185. *I'll devise some h. slanders*, Ado III, 1, 84. *tractable to any h. reason*, H4A III, 3, 194.

4) chaste, not loose and wanton: *she is pretty, and h. and gentle*, Wiv. I, 4, 148. *if I find her h., I lose not my labour*, II, 1, 247. *though she appear h. to me*, II, 2, 230. *your wife is as h.* III, 3, 236. *wives may be merry, and yet h. too*, IV, 2, 107. *the h. woman, the modest wife*, 136. *an h. woman*, Meas. II, 1, 73. *with words that in an h. suit might move*, Err. IV, 2, 14. *those that she makes fair she scarce makes h.* As

I, 2, 40. III, 3, 28. All's III, 5, 77. 82. 85. III, 6, 119. Wint. II, 1, 68. 76. II, 3, 70. Cor. IV, 5, 52. Rom. II, 1, 28. Tim. IV, 3, 113. Hml. III, 1, 103. Oth. III, 3, 384. IV, 2, 12. 38. Ant. I, 5, 16 etc.

Honest-hearted, upright: Lr. I, 4, 20.

Honestly, uprightly, according to truth and law: Meas. II, 1, 106. Ado II, 1, 242. II, 2, 9. All's I, 3, 127. H5 II, 1, 36. Rom. I, 2, 65. Tim. V, 1, 16.

Honest-natured, upright, sincere, free from deceit: Tim. V, 1, 89.

Honest-true (not hyph. in O. Edd.) upright and faithful: Merch. III, 4, 46.

Honesty, 1) love of truth, upright conduct: Meas. IV, 2, 163. Ado III, 3, 56. 67. LLL V, 2, 834. As II, 4, 91. All's I, 3, 97. Wint. I, 1, 21. I, 2, 244. IV, 4, 498. 606. 696. H4A III, 3, 174. H4B II, 1, 39. H6C III, 3, 180. R3 I, 3, 55. H8 III, 2, 306. 445. Rom. III, 2, 86. Tim. II, 2, 144. Lr. I, 2, 127. 197. Oth. III, 3, 258. 376. 382. 412. Ant. II, 2, 92. III, 13, 41. *in h.* = in truth: Cymb. III, 6, 70.

2) honourableness, just claim to be respected: *of approved valour and confirmed h.* Ado II, 1, 395. *whose skill was almost as great as his h.* All's I, 1, 21. *she derives her h. and achieves her goodness*, 52. *what is his h.?* IV, 3, 279. 202. 290. 294. *infirmities that h. is never free of*, Wint. I, 2, 263. 434. II, 2, 10. V, 3, 144. H4A I, 2, 155. H8 IV, 2, 145. V, 1, 123. V, 2, 111. Tim. I, 1, 130. Caes. IV, 3, 67. Lr. II, 2, 79. Oth. I, 3, 285. II, 3, 247. III, 3, 118. 153. Coupled to honour: *I'll prove mine honour and mine h.* Err. V, 30. *whose honour and whose h. till now endured all weathers*, Wint. V, 1, 194. *affect in honour h.* H8 I, 1, 40. *you have as little h. as honour*, III, 2, 271. *why should honour outlive h.?* Oth. V, 2, 245. *by mine h.!* used as an oath: Gent. II, 5, 1. Meas. V, 59.

3) decency, love of what is noble and becoming: *have you no wit, manners, nor h., but to gabble like tinkers?* Tw. II, 3, 94. *I had thought they had parted so much h. among 'em, at least, good manners, as not thus to suffer...* H8 V, 2, 28. *every man has his fault, and h. is his*, Tim. III, 1, 29 (liberality, generosity, bounty). *I hold it not h. to have it thus set down*, Hml. II, 2, 204. *it is not h. in me to speak what I have seen*, Oth. IV, 1, 288.

4) chastity: *thou smotherest h.* Lucr. 885. *beguiled with outward h.* 1545. *translated her well, out of h. into English*, Wiv. I, 3, 55. *to wrangle with mine own h.* II, 1, 88. *the chariness of our h.* 103. *in the way of h.* II, 2, 75. *to lay an amiable siege to the h. of this Ford's wife*, 244. *h. coupled to beauty*, As III, 3, 30. 35. *I should think my h. ranker than my wit*, IV, 1, 85. *rich h. dwells like a miser in a poor house*, V, 4, 62. *no legacy is so rich as h.* All's III, 5, 14. 65. IV, 4, 28. Wint. I, 2, 288. II, 1, 155. John I, 181. H6C III, 2, 72. Troil. I, 2, 286. Tit. II, 3, 135. Hml. III, 1, 108. 110. 112. *a very honest woman, but something given to lie, as a woman should not do but in the way of h.* Ant. V, 2, 254 (a double quibbling in the words *lie* and *honesty*).

Honey, subst. 1) the sweet substance gathered by bees: Lucr. 493. 836. 889. Gent. I, 2, 106. LLL V, 2, 231. As III, 3, 31. All's I, 2, 65. Wint. IV, 4, 813. H4A I, 2, 47. III, 2, 71. H4B IV, 5, 77. H5 I, 2, 199. II, 2, 30. IV, 1, 11. Troil. I, 3, 83. II, 2, 144. V, 10, 43. 45. Tit. II, 3, 131. Rom. II, 6, 11. Per. II Prol. 18. II, 1, 51. *the h. of his language*, H8 III, 2,

22; cf. Hml. III, 1, 164. *the h. of thy breath*, Rom. V, 3, 92. Adjectively, = sweet: *h. secrets*, Ven. 16. *which to his speech did h. passage yield*, 452. *the h. fee of parting*, 538. *summer's h. breath*, Sonn. 65, 5; Tit. II, 4, 25. *h. drops*, Tp. IV, 1, 79. *his h. words*, R3 IV, 1, 80. *h. dew*, Tit. III, 1, 112. Applied to persons, in compellations: *my fair, sweet, h. monarch*, LLL V, 2, 530. *my h. love*, Shr. IV, 3, 52. *my good sweet h. lord*, H4A I, 2, 179. *sweet h. Greek*, Troil. V, 2, 18. *O h. nurse*, Rom. II, 5, 18.

2) sweet one; a fond compellation: *h., sweet husband*, H5 II, 3, 1 (F1. 2 *honey sweet*). *h., you shall be well desired in Cyprus*, Oth. II, 1, 206.

Honey, vb. to call one honey, to speak to one with fondness: *—ing and making love over the nasty sty*, Hml. III, 4, 93.

Honey-bag, the receptacle for honey in a bee: Mids. III, 1, 171. IV, 1, 13. 16. 17.

Honey-bee, a bee making honey, not a drone: H5 I, 2, 187.

Honeycomb, the cells of wax in which bees store their honey: *as thick as h.* Tp. I, 2, 329.

Honey-dew (not hyph. in O. Edd.) a substance that makes plants wither: Tit. III, 1, 112.

Honey-drop (not hyph. in O. Edd.) sweet drop: Tp. IV, 1, 79.

Honeyed, sweet: *his sweet and h. sentences*, H5 I, 1, 50.

Honey-heavy, heavy with honey, very sweet: *the h. dew of slumber*, Caes. II, 1, 230.

Honeyless, destitute of honey: Caes. V, 1, 35.

Honey-mouthed, sweet and smooth in speech: Wint. II, 2, 33.

Honey-seed, Mrs Quickly's blunder for *homicide*: H4B II, 1, 57.

Honey-stalks, probably the flower of the clover: Tit. IV, 4, 91.

Honeysuckle, the plant Lonicera Caprifolium: Ado III, 1, 8. Mids. IV, 1, 47. Mrs. Quickly's blunder for *homicidal*: H4B II, 1, 56.

Honey-sweet, very dear: H5 III, 3, 1 (F 3. 4 *honey, sweet*). *h. lord*, Troil. III, 1, 71. *h. queen*, 154.

Honey-tongued, smooth in speech: LLL V, 2, 334.

Honorificabilitudinitatibus, a word proverbial for its length: LLL V, 1, 44.*

Honour, subst. (personified as masc. All's II, 3, 141; as fem. H4A I, 3, 205) 1) high estimation, respect, veneration: *a son that well deserves the h. and regard of such a father*, Gent. II, 4, 60 (perhaps rather = who is worthy of such an honoured father). *general h.* Meas. IV, 3, 141. *h., high h. and renown to Hymen*, As V, 4, 151. *hast the memory of Hermione in h.* Wint. V, 1, 51. *cried fame and h. on him*, Tw. V, 1, 62. *when he could not but pay me terms of h.* Ant. III, 4, 7 etc.

2) good name, high reputation, renown: *unless thou take that h. from thy name*, Sonn. 36, 12. *h., riches, marriage-blessing*, Tp. IV, 106. *he after h. hunts*, Gent. I, 1, 63. Err. I, 1, 149. LLL I, 1, 6. All's II, 1, 15. Wint. III, 2, 111. H4A I, 1, 81. I, 3, 202. 205. III, 2, 106. H4B II, 3, 7. H6A I, 2, 147. III, 2, 116 etc.

3) high rank, dignity, distinction: *public h. and proud titles*, Sonn. 25, 2. *confer fair Milan with all the —s on my brother*, Tp. I, 2, 127. *dignified with this high h.* Gent. II, 4, 158. *I could come to such h.!* Wiv. II, 1, 45. *to undergo such ample grace and h.* Meas.

I, 1, 24. *take your —s*, 53. *you to your former h. I bequeath*, As V, 4, 192. *I, by the h. of my marriage-bed, claim this land for mine*, John V, 2, 93. *whose state and h. I for aye allow*, R2 V, 2, 40. *it shall make h. for you*, Mcb. II, 1, 26. *we must receive him according to the h. of his sender*, Cymb. II, 3, 63. All's III, 2, 74. John I, 182. 187. H6A V, 3, 136. H6B II, 2, 62. II, 3, 10. 43. H6C III, 3, 192. R3 I, 3, 256. Mcb. I, 3, 144. I, 6, 17. III, 6, 36. IV, 2, 66. V, 8, 64 etc.

4) a mark of respect: *to whom you show this h.* Merch. III, 4, 5. *I would do the man what h. I can*, All's IV, 3, 304. H4A V, 4, 144. H8 V, 2, 26. Ant. V, 2, 161. Cymb. III, 3, 105. *these colours that I wear in h. of my noble Lord of York*, H6A III, 4, 30. H6B I, 3, 54. Per. II, 2, 5 etc.

5) that which reflects credit on one: *Falstaff will learn the h. of the age*, Wiv. I, 3, 92 (the spurious Qq and M. Edd. *humour*). *little h. to be much believed*, Meas. II, 4, 149. *there's h. in the theft*, All's II, 1, 34. *he had the h. to be the officer at Mile-end*, IV, 3, 301. *it is an h. 'longing to our house*, IV, 2, 42. *to maintain, to the king's h., full fifteen earls*, H5 I, 1, 12. *wear it for an h. in thy cap*, IV, 8, 63. *these names in h. follows Coriolanus*, Cor. II, 1, 182. *to both your —s*, Hml. III, 1, 42. *the gods, who make them —s of men's impossibilities*, Lr. IV, 6, 73. *when I know that boasting is an h.* Oth. I, 2, 20. *his taints and —s waged equal with him*, Ant. V, 1, 30 etc.

6) personal integrity, elevated sentiments, a just claim to the respect of others felt and asserted: *finding myself in h. so forbid*, Compl. 150. *shall never melt mine h. into lust*, Tp. IV, 1, 28, *whose h. cannot be measured or confined*, V, 121. *here is her oath for love, her —'s pawn*, Gent. I, 3, 47. *how, with my h., I may undertake a journey*, II, 7, 6. *upon whose faith and h. I repose*, IV, 3, 26. *I took't upon mine h.* Wiv. II, 2, 12. *you stand upon your h.* 20. *to keep the terms of my h. precise*, 23. Meas. II, 4, 179. Err. V, 30. Ado IV, 1, 188. LLL II, 1, 170. Merch. I, 1, 137. As I, 2, 31. All's I, 2, 35. 38. II, 3, 140. V, 3, 113. Tw III, 1, 129. III, 4, 222. 232. 336. Wint. I, 2, 407. John V, 7, 85. R2 I, 1, 74. V, 3, 11. V, 6, 29. H4A IV, 1, 10. V, 1, 131. H4B V, 2, 35. H5 II Chor. 18. IV, 2, 32. V, 1, 90. H6A II, 5, 52. Cor. III, 2, 144. Mcb. I, 2, 44. IV, 3, 117. Oth. II, 3, 58 etc. *by mine h.!* Ado IV, 1, 249. Merch. V, 219. 232. As I, 2, 63. Tw. I, 5, 124. R2 V, 2, 78. H5 V, 2, 237 etc. *by the h. of my ancestry!* Gent. V, 4, 139. *vow by h. of thy house*, H6A III, 2, 77. *on or upon mine h.!* Tp. II, 1, 317. III, 2, 123. Gent. III, 1, 48. Meas. I, 1, 64. II, 4, 147. V, 524. Ado IV, 1, 89. V, 1, 104. Wint. II, 2, 65 etc. *of mine h.!* H6B IV, 2, 103 (Cade's speech).

In women it means above all purity, chastity: *with safest distance I mine h. shielded*, Compl. 151. *to violate the h. of my child*, Tp. I, 2, 348. Gent. V, 4, 22. Wiv. II, 2, 252. Meas. III, 1, 166. Ado IV, 1, 193. All's III, 5, 12. IV, 2, 45 etc.

7) a title given to the nobility, = lordship or ladyship: Ven. Ded. 3. Tp. III, 2, 26. Meas. I, 1, 84. II, 1, 8. 33. 47. 50. 92. 96. V, 82. Merch. III, 2, 194. 229. Shr. Ind. I, 54. Wint. III, 2, 115. H4A IV, 2, 58. H4B I, 1, 5. H6A II, 2, 53. II, 5, 93. V, 3, 147. H6B IV, 5, 5. R3 III, 2, 21. 107. H8 V, 3, 2. 78 (ironically). Troil. III, 1, 16. Cor. I, 2, 33. II, 2, 72. V, 6, 140. Tit. IV, 2, 5. Tim. I, 1, 109. III, 2, 28. III, 1, 91 etc.

Honour, vb. 1) to respect, to reverence: *and him by oath they truly —ed,* Lucr. 410. *that makes him —ed, or begets him hate,* 1005. *joy in that I h. most,* Sonn. 25, 4. Tp. III, 1, 73. Gent. I, 1, 4. Meas. V, 95. Mids. II, 2, 144. Merch. IV, 1, 224. As V, 4, 150. Wint. II, 2, 6. John IV, 3, 105. H4B IV, 5, 164. H6A III, 4, 35. H6B I, 1, 198. IV, 8, 16. Cor. III, 1, 306. III, 2, 121. Tit. I, 42. 49. Tim. II, 1, 23. Caes. II, 1, 91. III, 1, 128. 129. V, 4, 11. Lr. I, 1, 100. Oth. III, 4, 114. Per. I, 2, 20. II, 5, 48. III, 3, 28. Partic. *—ed,* adjectively: All's V, 3, 8. Wint. IV, 4, 504. V, 1, 113. 158. Cor. III, 3, 34. V, 3, 22. Tim. I, 2, 1. IV, 2, 28. IV, 3, 111. Mcb. I, 6, 10. Hml. I, 2, 221. Per. III, 3, 1 etc. (cf. *Honoured,* adj.).

2) to show respect, to do homage to: *till I have —ed you with some graver labour,* Ven. Ded. 4. *with my extern the outward —ing,* Sonn. 125, 2. *how shall I h. thee for this success?* H6A I, 6, 5. *who art thou? say, that I may h. thee,* V, 3, 50. *to h. me as thy king,* H6C I, 1, 198. *he hath —ed me of late,* Mcb. I, 7, 32. *every one that comes to h. them,* Per. II, 3, 61. *—ing of Neptune's triumph,* V, 1, 17 (cf. *Of*).

3) to treat with regard, to oblige: *if any come, Hector shall h. him,* Troil. I, 3, 280. *sweet sir, you h. me,* V, 1, 93. *we are —ed much by good Simonides,* Per. II, 3, 20. Followed by an inf.: *think me —ed to feast so great a warrior,* H6A II, 3, 81. *do not h. him so much to prick thy finger,* H6C I, 4, 54. *h. me so much as to advance this jewel,* Tim. I, 2, 175. By *in: our feast shall be much —ed in your marriage,* Merch. III, 2, 214. By *with: nor thou with public kindness h. me,* Sonn. 36, 11. *not —ed with a human shape,* Tp. I, 2, 283. *we h. you with trouble,* Wint. V, 3, 9. *h. such as these with humble suit,* H6B IV, 1, 123.

4) to raise to dignity, to ennoble, to reflect credit on: *h. thyself to rid me of this shame,* Lucr. 1031. *that they may prosperous be and —ed in their issue,* Tp. IV, 105. *my father's love is enough to h. him,* As I, 2, 89. *as thou lovest and —est arms,* H6C I, 1, 116. *as this title —s me and mine,* IV, 1, 72. *the name of Cassius —s this corruption,* Caes. IV, 3, 15. *kill Brutus and be —ed in his death,* V, 4, 14. *a babe to h. her,* Lr. I, 4, 303. *which hath —ed with confirmation your great judgment,* Cymb. I, 6, 174. *it —s us that we have given him cause,* III, 5, 18.

Honourable, 1) high, of distinguished rank, noble: *the match were rich and h.* Gent. III, 1, 64. *h. without the stamp of merit,* Merch. II, 9, 38. *thy place shall be h.* H4A II, 4, 596. *more h. state, more courtship lives in carrion-flies,* Rom. III, 3, 34. *he knows not yet of his h. fortune,* Oth. IV, 2, 241. *have entertainment, but no h. trust,* Ant. IV, 6, 18. Hence a term used in speaking of or to persons of quality: *to the right h. Henry Wriothesly,* Ven. and Lucr. Ded. *I leave it to your h. survey,* Ven. Ded. 6. *you lords shall plight your h. faiths to me,* Lucr. 1690. *h. ladies sought my love,* Merch. II, 4, 70. *commend me to your h. wife,* IV, 1, 273. *mine h. mistress,* All's I, 3, 145. *lords and h. personages,* II, 3, 278. *the h. lady of the house,* Tw. I, 5, 177. *I will imitate the h. Romans,* H4I II, 2, 134. *my h. lords,* H6A I, 1, 57. III, 4, 1. IV, 1, 122. H6B IV, 1, 51. IV, 2, 53. 55. H8 I, 1, 79. Tit. IV, 2, 12. Tim. I, 1, 97. I, 2, 192 etc. *you need but plead your h. privilege,* All's IV, 5, 95 (= the privilege of your rank). *all their h. points of ignorance,* H8 I, 3, 26 (becoming, in their opinion, their place in society).

2) illustrious, glorious: *has done most h. service,* All's III, 5, 4. *a resolved and h. war,* John II, 585. *h. rescue and defence,* V, 2, 18. *by the h. tomb upon your grandsire's bones,* R2 III, 3, 105. *that h. day shall ne'er be seen,* IV, 91. *is not this an h. spoil?* H4A I, 1, 74. *so h. an action,* II, 3, 36. V, 5, 26. H5 IV, 7, 105. H6A IV, 1, 41. IV, 4, 17. Tit. V, 1, 11.

3) showing respect: *an h. conduct let him have,* John I, 29. cf. H6C III, 2, 123. Ant. V, 1, 58.

4) becoming, decent: *chides the dice in h. terms,* LLL V, 2, 327. *bear himself with h. action,* Shr. Ind. 1, 110.

5) deserving respect, full of, or dictated by noble sentiments: *the warrant I have of your h. disposition,* Lucr. Ded. 2. *holy Gonzalo, h. man,* Tp. V, 62. *it's an h. kind of thievery,* Gent. IV, 1, 40. *he bears an h. mind,* V, 3, 13. Wiv. IV, 5, 23. Ado I, 1, 57. 113. III, 4, 30. 31. V, 1, 275. V, 4, 30. As I, 2, 237. III, 2, 169. III, 3, 61. Wint. I, 2, 323. II, 1, 68. 111. III, 2, 196. John V, 2, 45. R2 I, 1, 136. H4B II, 1, 134. IV, 2, 110. H5 IV, 1, 134. V, 1, 75. H6B V, 1, 170. R3 I, 2, 1. Rom. II, 2, 143. Tim. II, 2, 215 etc. *his love, which stands an h. trial,* Ant. I, 3, 75, i. e. a trial concerning its honour.

Used adverbially: *use her h.* H6C III, 2, 123 (F2. 3. 4 *—bly*). *in h. keeping her,* Troil. II, 2, 149. *thou couldst not die more h.* Caes. V, 1, 60. *how h. and how kindly we determine for her,* Ant. V, 1, 58 (the suffix *ly* belonging to both adverbs).

Not understood and wrongly applied by Elbow: Meas. II, 1, 89.

Honourable-dangerous (not hyph. in O. Edd.), honourable and dangerous: Caes. I, 3, 124.

Honourably, 1) as it becomes a man of honour: *the noble lord most h. doth uphold his word,* LLL V, 2, 449.

2) with tokens of respect: *use her h.* H6C III, 2, 123 (F1 honourable). 124. *h. received him,* H8 IV, 2, 19. *ordered h.* Caes. V, 5, 79.

3) decently, becomingly: *art not ashamed? Of what, lady? of speaking h.?* Ado III, 4, 29. *do this message h.* Tit. IV, 4, 104.

Honoured, adj. = honourable; 1) of high rank, noble: *I am from humble, he from h. name,* All's I, 3, 162. *mingling them with us, the h. number,* Cor. III, 1, 72. Applied to things relating to persons of quality: *which then he wore upon his h. finger,* Cymb. V, 5, 184 (cf. *honourable*: Ven. Ded. 6. Tim. I, 1, 97).

2) doing honour, reflecting credit on one: *a custom more h. in the breach than the observance,* Hml. I, 4, 16. *kiss the h. gashes whole,* Ant. IV, 8, 11.

3) illustrious: *he comes to an h. triumph strangely furnished,* Per. II, 2, 53.

4) consistent with honour, virtuous: *in h. love,* Lr. V, 1, 9.

Honour-flawed, of a damaged, tainted honour: Wint. II, 1, 143.

Honour-giving, conferring rank and dignity: *by the h. hand of Cordelion,* John I, 53.

Honour-owing, honourable: *his h. wounds,* H5 IV, 6, 9.

Hoo, an exclamation of triumphant joy: Cor. II, 1, 116. III, 3, 137. Ant. II, 7, 141.

Hood, Robin H., the famous outlaw, so much celebrated in popular songs: Gent. IV, 1, 36. As I, 1, 122. H4B V, 3, 107.

Hood, subst. a cowl: *all —s make not monks*, H8 III, 1, 23 (cucullus non facit monachum; cf. Meas. V, 263) A mask called so in jest: *now, by my h., a Gentile and no Jew*, Merch. II, 6, 51.

Hood, vb. 1) to dress in a cowl: Meas. V, 358.

2) to cover so as to bar sight; originally a term of falconry, as the hawk was hooded till let fly at the game: *h. mine eyes thus with my hat*, Merch. II, 2, 202. *'tis a —ed valour, and when it appears, it will bate*, H5 III, 7, 121. *h. my unmanned blood*, Rom. III, 2, 14.

Hoodman, the one blindfolded in the children's game now called blind-man's-buff: All's IV, 3, 136.

Hoodman-blind, the children's game now called blind-man's-buff: Hml. III, 4, 77.

Hoodwink, to blindfold: All's III, 6, 26. IV, 1, 90. Rom. I, 4, 4. Mcb. IV, 3, 72. Cymb. V, 2, 16. Used strangely by Caliban: *the prize I'll bring thee to shall h. this mischance*, Tp. IV, 206, = shall make harmless, ineffectual.

Hoof, the horny substance on the feet of horses: Ven. 267. R2 III, 2, 7. H4A I, 1, 8. V, 3, 43. H5 Prol. 27. III, 7, 18. Used in contempt of the human foot: *plod away i' the h.* Wiv. I, 3, 91 (F2. 3. 4 and M. Edd. *o' the h.*).

Hook, subst. any thing bent into a curve: *a pair of anchoring —s*, Gent. III, 1, 118. *a Welsh h.* H4A II, 4, 373 (a sort of bill curved at the end). Chiefly the curvated iron on which the bait is hung for fishes: Lucr. 103. Sonn. 137, 7. Meas. II, 2, 181. Ado II, 3, 114. H4B II, 4, 171 (cf. *Hold*). Rom. II Chor. 8. Ant. II, 5, 12. 17. Cymb. V, 5, 167.

Hook, vb. 1) to attach with a hook: *—ing both right and wrong to the appetite, to follow as it draws*, Meas. II, 4, 176. *but she I can h. to me*, Wint. II, 3, 7.

2) with *on*, = to apply a hook, to hold fast: *h. on, h. on*, H4B II, 1, 175.

Hook-nosed, having a curvated nose: H4B IV, 3, 45.

Hoop, subst. a circular band of wood or metal: *who with age and envy was grown into a h.* Tp. I, 2, 259 (cf. *Crooked*). *like a tumbler's h.* LLL III, 190 (such a one being bound round with ribands of various colours). *a h. of gold, a paltry ring*, Merch. V, 147. *a h. of gold to bind thy brothers in*, H4B IV, 4, 43. *the three-hooped pot shall have ten —s*, H6B IV, 2, 72. *grapple them to thy soul with —s of steel*, Hml. I, 3, 63. *what h. should hold us stanch*, Ant. II, 2, 117. As for *set cock a h.*, Rom. I, 5, 83, see *Cock-a-hoop* and *Inhooped*.

Hoop, vb. to encircle, to clasp: *or h. his body more with thy embraces*, Wint. IV, 4, 450 (O. Edd **hope**).

Hoop (M. Edd. **whoop**), 1) to shout with wonder and surprise: *wonderful out of all —ing*, As III, 2, 203. *that admiration did not h. at them*, H5 II, 2, 108.

2) to shout in an insulting manner: *to be —ed out of Rome*, Cor. IV, 5, 84.

Hoot, 1) to cry as an owl: Mids. II, 2, 6. Caes. I, 3, 28.

2) to shout with wonder: *the people fall a —ing*, LLL IV, 2, 61. *the rabblement —ed and clapped their chopped hands*, Caes. I, 2, 245 (O. Edd. *howted*).

3) to shout with contempt: *should be —ed at like an old tale*, Wint. V, 3, 116. *in —ing at Coriolanus' exile*, Cor. IV, 6, 131. With an accus. denoting the effect: *did h. him out o' the city*, Cor. IV, 6, 123.

Hop, to jump, to skip: Mids. III, 1, 168. V, 304.

401. Shr. IV, 3, 98. Rom. II, 2, 179. Ant. II, 2, 234. *to h. without* = to lose: *you shall h. without my custom*, Shr. IV, 3, 99. *would make thee quickly h. without thy head*, H6B I, 3, 140.

Hopdance, name of an evil spirit: Lr. III, 6, 32 (cf. *Hobbididance*).

Hope, subst. (personified as masc. R2 II, 2, 69), 1) an expectation indulged with pleasure: Ven. 988. Tp. II, 1, 239 — 241. III, 3, 7. Gent. III, 1, 246. IV, 2, 13. V, 4, 64. Wiv. II, 1, 68. Meas. III, 1, 3. 170. Err. I, 1, 66. Merch. II, 9, 20 *(fortune now to my heart's h.)*. As II, 7, 119. R2 II, 2, 69. H4A III, 2, 36. Tit. II, 3, 126. Ant. III, 13, 176 etc. *by all my —s!* R2 I, 1, 68. *by my —s!* H4A V, 1, 87. *to conceive —s*, Shr. I, 1, 15. *to give h.* Wiv. III, 3, 207. Wint. V, 3, 127. Ant. IV, 12, 8. *to have h.* Tp. II, 1, 238. 240. V, 308. Meas. I, 2, 187. III, 1, 4. H6B I, 1, 237. III, 1, 87. H6C II, 1, 136. Lr. II, 4, 139. *such h. have all the line of Somerset*, H6C I, 1, 19. *I have good h. thou didst not know on't*, Lr. II, 4, 191. *I have great h.* Meas. I, 2, 187. *in h.* = hoping: Meas. I, 4, 52. Merch. II, 7, 19. Tw. V, 366. Wint. V, 2, 110. H6B I, 4, 81. Tit. IV, 4, 60. Per. I, 4, 4 etc. *in the which h.* As II, 7, 119. *in that h.* H6C I, 4, 37. *to live in h.* H4B I, 3, 38. R3 I, 2, 200. *to stand in h.* Sonn. 60, 13.* Wint. V, 2, 110. Tit. II, 1, 119. *out of h.* = hopeless: *things out of h.* Ven. 567. *he's out of h.* Tp. III, 3, 11. Mids. III, 2, 279. Shr. V, 1, 146. *out of h.* = actuated by hope, in hope: *such as give their money out of h. they may believe*, H8 Prol. 8. *not out of h. to save my life*, Cor. IV, 5, 85. *past h.* = having lost all h.: Tw. V, 82. Rom. IV, 1, 45. Cymb. I, 1, 137. *past the h. of comfort*, IV, 3, 9. Followed by *in*: *I have great h. in that*, Meas. I, 2, 187. *will answer our h. in issue of a king*, H6A V, 5, 72. *we had in them no h. to win the day*, H6C II, 1, 136. *our h. in him is dead*, Tim. V, 1, 229. Followed by *of*: *in h. of action*, Meas. I, 4, 52. Merch. II, 7, 19. *I agree with you in the —s of him*, Wint. I, 1, 42. V, 2, 110. Shr. V, 1, 146. H4B I, 3, 12. H6B I, 1, 237. I, 4, 81. II, 1, 57. III, 1, 87. H6C I, 1, 58. II, 3, 8. 55. IV, 6, 93. Cymb. IV, 3, 9 etc. Followed by an inf.: *I have h. to see the nuptial*, Tp. V, 308. Meas. III, 1, 4. Shr. I, 2, 247. Wint. IV, 4, 579. R2 I, 3, 13. 15. H6A V, 5, 105. Per. I, 4, 4 etc. By a clause: Tp. II, 1, 238. Tw. V, 366. Wint. IV, 4, 678. V, 3, 127. Tit. IV, 4, 60 etc.

2) the object of an agreeable expectation: *if thou catch thy h., turn back to me*, Sonn. 143, 11. *heart hath his h., and eyes their wished sight*, Pilgr. 202. *all the fair effects of future —s*, Gent. I, 1, 50. *my affections would be with my —s abroad*, Merch. I, 1, 17. *the sweetest companion that e'er man bred his —s out*, Wint. V, 1, 12. *Lavinia is thine elder brother's h.* Tit. II, 1, 74.

3) that in which one confides: *their bravest h., bold Hector*, Lucr. 1430; cf. H6C II, 1, 51; IV, 8, 25; Tit. IV, 1, 88. *you, his false —s, keep off*, H6A IV, 4, 20. *God shall be my h.* H6B II, 3, 24; IV, 4, 55. *come hither, England's h.* H6C IV, 6, 68. *the h. o' the Strand*, H8 V, 4, 55.

4) expectancy, reversion: *if in thy h. thou darest do such outrage, what darest thou not when once thou art a king?* Lucr. 605. *to shame his h. with deeds degenerate*, 1003.

5) expectation of any kind, even fear: *by how much better than my word I am, by so much shall I*

falsify men's —*s*, H4A I, 2, 235. *friends am I with you all, upon this h. that you shall give me reasons, why and wherein Caesar was dangerous,* Caes. III, 1, 221. *the griefs are ended by seeing the worst, which late on* —*s depended,* Oth. I, 3, 203. cf. Alls I, 3, 207.

Hope, vb. 1) to expect with desire; followed by an accus.: *by* —*ing more, they have but less,* Lucr. 137. *within what space* —*est thou my cure?* All's II, 1, 163. *we h. no other from your majesty,* H4B V, 2, 62 (but cf. *Other*). *which never* —*s more heaven than rests in thee,* Tit. II, 3, 41. Perhaps also in Hml. III, 2, 62. Followed by *after: h. not after it,* As III, 5, 45. By *for: as I h. for quiet days,* Tp. IV, 1, 23. LLL I, 1, 194. Merch. IV, 1, 88. H6B III, 1, 88. R3 I, 4, 194) Ff *for any goodness,* Qq *to have redemption*). H8 II, 1, 69. III, 2, 385. By *of: you h. of pardon from Lord Angelo?* Meas. III, 1, 1. *I will h. of better deeds to-morrow,* Ant. I, 1, 61 (cf. *Of*). By an inf.: *of whom I h. to make much benefit,* Err. I, 2, 25. Ado II, 1, 60. Shr. I, 2, 193. All's I, 3, 42. Tw. I, 3, 109. H4B V, 3, 64. H5 I, 2, 299 etc. By a clause: Tp. II, 2, 114. Gent. IV, 2, 21. IV, 4, 186. Wiv. I, 1, 203. 241. 257. II, 1, 113 etc. *I h.* often = I trust: *and that, I h., is an unmeasurable distance,* Wiv. II, 1, 108. *you'll let us in, I h.* Err. III, 1, 54. cf. II, 2, 19. IV. 1, 43. 111. Mids. I, 2, 67. Shr. IV, 5, 42. Tw. III, 1, 61. H6B III, 2, 181. R3 I, 2, 201. Hml. III, 2, 40 etc. *I h. not* = I trust that it is not so: Wiv. IV, 2, 117. *I h. so:* Wint. IV, 4, 260. R3 I, 2, 114. Ant. II, 6, 58. Cymb. II, 3, 154. *so I h.* Caes. V, 1, 57. *if I h. well, I'll never see thee more,* Tim. IV, 3, 171. *I h. well of to-morrow,* Ant. IV, 2, 42.

2) to expect, to suppose, to imagine: *some of them will fall to-morrow, I h.* H5 III, 7, 77. *I cannot h. Caesar and Antony shall well greet together,* Ant. II, 1, 38.

Hoped-for, expected with desire: H6C IV, 8, 61. V, 4, 35.

Hopeful, 1) full of hope, of expectation of good fortune: *the world's h. expectation,* Ven. Ded. 8. *the h. mother,* R3 I, 2, 24.

2) exciting good hopes, likely to obtain or ensure success: Meas. I, 1, 60. Wint. II, 3, 85. III, 2, 41. H6B IV, 1, 97. H6C III, 2, 126. H8 III, 2, 420. Tit. II, 3, 49. Rom. I, 2, 15.

Hopeless, 1) destitute of hope: Lucr. 744. 1660. Err. I, 1, 158. H8 III, 1, 80. With *of: h. of their lives,* H6C I, 4, 42. With an inf.: *h. to find,* Err. I, 1, 136. Cymb. IV, 4, 27.

2) affording no hope: *the h. word of never to return,* R2 I, 3, 152. *he would pawn his fortunes to h. restitution,* Cor. III, 1, 16 (= not to be hoped for).

Hopkins, name in H8 I, 1, 221. I, 2, 147. 148 (O. Edd. *Henton*). II, 1, 22.

Horace, the celebrated Roman poet: LLL IV, 2, 104. Tit. IV, 2, 22. 24.

Horatio (seemingly of four syll. in Hml. I, 1, 53. I, 2, 180. III, 2, 57. But then these verses would have six feet), name in Hml. I, 1, 12 etc.

Horizon, the circular line in which the earth and sky seem to meet: H6C IV, 7, 81.

Horn, 1) that which grows as a weapon on the heads of some cloven-footed quadrupeds, as of sheep: Gent. I, 1, 79. LLL V, 1, 51. 68. of black cattle: Wiv. V, 5, 4. Ado I, 1, 266. II, 1, 25. V, 1, 184. LLL V, 2, 253. Troil. V, 7, 12. of deer: LLL IV, 1,

116. As IV, 2, 5. All's I, 3, 58. Tit. II, 3, 63. *the Ram's* —*s,* Tit. IV, 3, 72. cf. Ado II, 1, 28. V, 2, 38. Worn by the devil: Meas. II, 4, 16. Ado II, 1, 47. Troil. V, 2, 95. Lr. IV, 6, 71. By the hunter Herne: Wiv. IV, 4, 31. V, 1, 7. V, 2, 16. V, 5, 30. 115. In men used as the emblem of stupidity: Gent. I, 1, 79. LLL IV, 1, 116. V, 1, 71. Mids. V, 244. And particularly of cuckoldom: Wiv. II, 1, 125. II, 2, 293. III, 5, 154. V, 5, 30. Ado I, 1, 266. II, 1, 47. V, 1, 184. V, 4, 44. LLL IV, 1, 114. V, 1, 73. 2, 252 (*give* —*s,* quibbling). As III, 3, 52. 54. 56. 63. IV, 1, 59. IV, 2, 14—18. Shr. IV, 1, 29. V, 2, 41. All's I, 3, 58. II, 2, 27. Wint. I, 2, 269. John I, 219. Troil. I, 1, 115. IV, 5, 31. 46. Tit. IV, 3, 72. Ant. I, 2, 5.

2) the bony substance of which the mentioned structure consists: *there is no staff more reverend than one tipped with h.* Ado V, 4, 126. *the basest h. of his hoof,* H5 III, 7, 17.

3) a wind instrument made of it: Ado II, 3, 62. Cor. III, 1, 95 (quibbling in H5 III, 7, 17); used by messengers and forerunners: Merch. V, 47. John I, 219. by Bedlam beggars: Lr. III, 6, 78 (both to give signal of approach and to put drink in). Chiefly by huntsmen: Ven. 1025. Mids. IV, 1, 131. 143. Tit. II, 3, 18. *with h. and hounds,* Pilgr. 122. *with h. and hound,* Tit. I, 494. *hounds and* —*s,* II, 3, 27. *she hearkens for his hounds and for his h.* Ven. 868.

4) Used as the symbol of plenty (according to the ancient fable of Amalthea): *with his h. full of good news,* Merch. V, 47. *the h. of abundance,* H4B I, 2, 52.

5) —*s* = deer; *my lady goes to kill* —*s,* LLL IV, 1, 113.

6) the feeler of a snail: Ven. 1033. LLL IV, 3, 338. As IV, 1, 59. Cor. IV, 6, 44. Lr. I, 5, 33.

7) the extremity of the waxing or waning moon: Mids. V, 244. 246. Cor. I, 1, 217. Ant. IV, 12, 45.

Horn, vb. to cuckold: *you have a goodly gift in* —*ing,* Tit. II, 3, 67.

Horn-beast, deer: As III, 3, 51.

Horn-book, a primer: LLL V, 1, 49.

Horned, having horns: *the h. moon,* Mids. V, 243. *a h. man,* Oth. IV, 1, 63. *the h. herd,* Ant. III, 13, 28.

Horner, name in H6B I, 3, 29. II, 3, 59.

Horn-mad, mad like a wicked bull; mostly used with an allusion to cuckoldom: Wiv. I, 4, 51. III, 5, 155. Err. II, 1, 57; cf. 58. Ado I, 1, 272.

Horn-maker, a maker of cuckolds: As IV, 1, 63.

Hornpipe, a lively air blown to country dances: *he sings psalms to* —*s,* Wint. IV, 3, 47.

Horn-ring, a ring made of horn: Wint. IV, 4, 611.

Horologe, a clock: Oth. II, 3, 135.

Horrible, extremely dreadful, shocking, hideous: Tp. V, 234. Meas. III, 1, 128. Wint. II, 3, 152. John IV, 1, 96. V, 6, 20. H6B III, 2, 312. H8 I, 2, 206. Rom. IV, 3, 37. Tim. IV, 3, 118. Mcb. I, 3, 138. III, 4, 106. IV, 1, 122. Hml. I, 4, 72. I, 5, 80. Lr. II, 3, 17. III, 2, 19. Oth. III, 3, 115. IV, 2, 26. V, 2, 203. Ant. II, 5, 63. Adverbially: *swear h.* Tw. III, 4, 196. *h. afeard,* H4A II, 4, 402. *h. afraid,* 406 (Qq *horribly*). *h. chid,* 410 (Qq *horribly*). *h. in love,* Troil. III, 1, 106 (Q *horribly*). *h. steep,* Lr. IV, 6, 3.

Horribly, most dreadfully: Ado II, 3, 243. Tw. III, 4, 322. H4A II, 4, 406 (Ff *horrible*) 410 (Ff *horrible*). H5 V, 1, 49. Troil. III, 1, 106 (Ff *horrible*). Oth. I, 1, 14.

Horrid (comp. —*er*, Cymb. IV, 2, 331) dreadful, shocking, hideous: Tw. III, 4, 220. H5 III, 6, 81. IV Chor. 28. IV, 1, 288. H8 III, 2, 196. Tim. V, 4, 13. Caes. II, 2, 16. Mcb. I, 3, 135. I, 7, 24. IV, 3, 56. Hml. II, 2, 589. III, 3, 88. Lr. III, 2, 46. IW, 7, 87. IV, 2, 61. Cymb. II, 1, 66. IV, 2, 331.

Horridly, most dreadfully: Hml. I, 4, 55. II, 2, 479.

Horror, 1) a shuddering terror mixed with detestation: *a dying h.* Meas. II, 3, 42 (= horror of death). *take her hence in h.* V, 441. Ado II, 1, 268. R2 IV, 142. Troil. I, 3, 98. Ant. IV, 14, 66. Cymb. V, 5, 31.

2) that which causes shuddering: *outface the brow of bragging h.* John V, 1, 50. *take the present h. from the time,* Mcb. II, 1, 59. II, 3, 69. 85. V, 5, 13. Hml. II, 1, 84. Lr. I, 2, 192. V, 3, 264. Oth. III, 3, 370. Ant. V, 2, 63.

Horse, subst. 1) the animal Equus: Ven. 258. 293. 299. Sonn. 51, 9. Compl. 107. Gent. III, 1, 275. Meas. I, 2, 164. Err. III, 2, 86. Ado III, 5, 40. LLL IV, 1, 1. Mids. III, 1, 111. As III, 3, 80. V, 3, 16 etc. *the dancing h.* LLL I, 2, 57; cf. Merch. II, 6, 10 (see *Dance*). *though she have as many diseases as two and fifty —s,* Shr. I, 2, 81; cf. Lr. III, 6, 20. *as true as truest h.* Mids. III, 1, 98 (play of Pyramus). *my purpose is indeed a h. of that colour,* Tw. II, 3, 181. *I run before my h. to market,* R3 I, 1, 160 (= I count my chickens before they are hatched). Used as a term of contempt: H4A II, 4, 215. 578. III, 3, 10. Troil. II, 1, 18. III, 3, 126. Used, in a general sense, without the article: *here is good h. to hire,* Ado I, 1, 268. *as fast as h. can carry them,* H6B I, 4, 78. *I have h. will follow . . . and runs like swallows,* Tit. II, 2, 23 (M. Edd. *run like swallows*). *with h. nor hound,* 25. *h. to ride and weapon to wear,* Lr. III, 4, 142. *to take h.:* H4A I, 1, 60. H6B IV, 4, 54. R3 III, 2, 16. Lr. II, 4, 35. *when we came from h.* Cymb. III, 4, 1 (= dismounted). *ere I go to h.* Shr. IV, 3, 193. *we must to h.* All's V, 1, 37. *hie you to h.* Mcb. III, 1, 35. *to h.!* All's II, 5, 92. R2 II, 1, 299. H4A II, 2, 105. III, 1, 271. H5 IV, 2, 15. Mcb. II, 3, 149. Lr. I, 4, 359 etc. *he calls to h.* Lr. II, 4, 300. *this is to h.* Ant. III, 2, 21 (the signal of mounting). Denoting a male horse, and opposed to a mare: Ven. 322. Mids. II, 1, 45. Ant. III, 7, 7. Used as a masc.: Merch. I, 2, 45. H5 III, 7, 12. H6A II, 4, 14. R3 III, 4, 86. Tim. II, 1, 7. Cor. I, 4, 5. Caes. III, 2, 15. Plur. —*s:* Sonn. 91, 11. Wiv. II, 1, 100. IV, 3, 2. V, 5, 119. As I, 1, 11. Shr. Ind. 2, 43. I, 2, 81. IV, 1, 82. IV, 3, 187. All's II, 1, 164. H6A II, 4, 14 etc. Plur. *h.: some glory in their hawks and hounds, some in their h.* Sonn. 91, 4. *a team of h.* Gent. III, 1, 265. *tell him of his hounds and h.* Shr. Ind. 1, 61. *h. or oxen run from the leopard,* H6A I, 5, 31. V, 5, 54. H6B V, 1, 52. H6C IV, 5, 12. Tit. II, 2, 18. Mcb. IV, 1, 140. Ant. III, 6, 45. III, 7, 7. 8. Similarly unchanged in the Anglosaxon gen.: *at my h. heels,* H6B IV, 3, 14 (Cade's speech; but cf. John II, 289. H6A I, 4, 108; Troil. V, 8, 21; V, 10, 4; Lr. III, 6, 20. R2 III, 2, 7; H5 IV, 2, 12; Cor. III, 2, 2; Cymb. III, 4, 107).

2) horsemen: *Alcibiades and some twenty h.* Tim. I, 1, 250. Particularly cavalry: *the general of our h.* All's III, 3, 1. III, 6, 52. *how many h. the duke is strong,* IV, 3, 149. *six thousand h.* 170. 327. H4A III, 3, 210. IV, 3, 19. H4B II, 1, 186. R3 V, 3, 294.

297. 300. Caes. IV, 2, 29. Lr. IV, 6, 189. Ant. III, 1, 33. III, 7, 60.

Horse, vb., 1) to set as on a horse: —*ing foot on foot,* Wint. I, 2, 288. —*d* = mounted: *better* —*d,* H4B I, 1, 35. *I were manned,* —*d and wived,* I, 2, 60 (furnished with a horse). Mcb. I, 7, 22.

2) to sit on as on a horse: *ridges*—*d with variable complexions,* Cor. II, 1, 227.

Horseback, the part of the horse on which its rider sits: *sits on his h.* John II, 289. *on h.* H8 I, 1, 8. Hml. IV, 7, 85. *a h.,* in the same sense: H4A II, 3, 104. II, 4, 378. 387 (M. Edd. *o' h.*).

Horseback-breaker, one too heavy for a horse: H4A II, 4, 268.

Horse-drench, physic for a horse: Cor. II, 1, 129.

Horse-hair, the hair of horses (used in fiddle-sticks): Cymb. II, 3, 33.

Horse-leech, a large kind of leech: H5 II, 3, 57.

Horseman, a man on horseback: Wint. IV, 3, 67. 70. Plur. *horsemen* = soldiers serving on horseback: H5 IV, 2, 45. IV, 7, 60. 88. H6A I, 1, 119. IV, 1, 165. IV, 2, 43. IV, 3, 11. IV, 4, 40. H6C I, 1, 2. Caes. V, 3, 29. Cymb. III, 5, 23.

Horsemanship, the art of riding: H4A IV, 1, 110. H5 III, 7, 58.

Horse-piss, the urine of horses: Tp. IV, 199.

Horse-shoe, the iron nailed to the feet of horses: Wiv. III, 5, 123.

Horse-stealer, a thief stealing horses: As III, 4, 25.

Horse-tail, tail of a horse: Shr. IV, 1, 96.

Horse-way, a highway, opposed to a footpath: Lr. IV, 1, 58.

Hortensio, name in Shr. I, 1, 56. 95 etc.

Hortensius, name in Tim. III, 4, 1.

Hose (unchanged in the plur.) breeches, trowsers: *to garter his h.* Gent. II, 1, 83. *to put on your h.* 84.* *a round h. now's not worth a pin, unless you have a codpiece to stick pins on,* II, 7, 55. *rhymes are guards on wanton Cupid's h.* LLL IV, 3, 58. *his round h.* Merch. I, 2, 80. *his youthful h. a world too wide for his shrunk shank,* As II, 7, 160. *your h. should be un-gartered,* II, 2, 397 (after the manner of lovers; cf. Gent. II, 1, 83). *dost make h. of thy sleeves?* All's II, 3, 266. *thrust through the h.* H4A II, 4, 185. *down fell their h.* 239. *French h.* H5 III, 7, 57. Mcb. II, 3, 16. *Doublet and h.* constituting the principal parts of a male dress: *in your doublet and h.* Wiv. III, 1, 47 (i.e. without a cloak); cf. Ado V, 1, 203 and H6B IV, 7, 56. Wiv. III, 3, 35. As II, 4, 7. III, 2, 206. 232. IV, 1, 206. Shr. V, 1, 69. Cymb. III, 4, 172.

Hospitable, kind to strangers and guests: John II, 244. Cor. I, 10, 26.* Lr. III, 7, 40.

Hospital, a house built for the reception of sick paupers: *in an h.* LLL V, 2, 881.

Hospitality, kindness to strangers: Lucr. 575. As II, 4, 82.

Host, subst. (used only in verse; with *an,* not *a,* as indef. art. before it: H6B III, 1, 342. Ant. II, 5, 87) army: Lucr. 3. John III, 1, 246. H5 III, 5, 50. IV Chor. 32. IV, 2, 43. IV, 3, 34. 112. IV, 8, 119. H6A IV, 4, 31. H6B III, 1, 342. H6C II, 1, 207. Troil. I, 3, 143. 293 (Ff *mould*). II, 1, 133. V, 10, 10. Cor. I, 9, 64. V, 3, 2. Mcb. V, 4, 6. Ant. II, 5, 87. IV, 6, 27. IV, 8, 33. Cymb. IV, 2, 352. *all the h. of heaven,* Lucr. 598. Hml. I, 5, 92. *the Lord of* —*s,* H6A I, 1, 31 (= God).

Host, subst. (never immediately preceded by the indef. art.; only once the poss. pron. *my* immediately before it, H4A IV, 2, 50; else *mine* and *thine*) 1) one who hospitably lodges and entertains another at his house: Err. III, 1, 27. John V, 1, 32. Cor. I, 9, 87. Mcb. I, 6, 29. I, 7, 14. III, 4, 4. Lr. III, 7, 39. V, 2, 2. 2) an innkeeper, a landlord: *a mad h.* Wiv. III, 1, 115. *the h. of the Garter,* 124. IV, 5, 80. H4A II, 4, 518. H5 II, 1, 31. Troil. III, 3, 165. Used as a vocative: Gent. IV, 2, 73. 135. *to lie at h.* = to be put up at an inn: *our goods that lay at h. in the Centaur,* Err. V, 410. Mostly preceded by *my* and *mine: mine h. of the Garter,* Wiv. I, 1, 143. I, 4, 124. II, 1, 100. III, 1, 95. 102. III, 3, 256. IV, 5, 75. 85. Err. II, 2, 4. *my h. at Saint Albans,* H4A IV, 2, 50. *my ranting h.* Wiv. II, 1, 196. 215. In the vocative: Gent. IV, 2, 28. Wiv. I, 3, 1. 4. II, 1, 199. 202. 229. III, 1, 93. IV, 5, 26. 60. H5 II, 1, 30. 85. *my good h.* Wiv. IV, 6, 47. I, 3, 13. II, 1, 211. IV, 6, 18. *thine h.* IV, 5, 19.

Host, vb. to take up abode, to lodge: *to the Centaur, where we h.* Err. I, 2, 9. *I will bring you where you shall h.* All's III, 5, 97.

Hostage, a pledge, a surety given, whether in persons or things: *you know now your —s: your uncle's word and my firm faith,* Troil. III, 2, 115. *what they are that must be —s for Rome,* Cor. I, 10, 29. *if he stand on h. for his safety, bid him demand what pledge will please him best,* Tit. IV, 4, 105. *demand your —s,* V, 1, 160. *your —s I have,* Ant. II, 6, 1. *his body's h. for his return,* Cymb. IV, 2, 185.

Hostess (having *an* before it as ind. art.: Troil. III, 3, 253; *mine* and *thine* as poss. pron.; only twice, or rather once, *my:* H4A I, 2, 45. 54) 1) a woman who entertains guests or strangers: Lucr. 1125. Gent. II, 5, 7. All's III, 5, 45. Wint. I, 2, 60. IV, 4, 64. Mcb. I, 6, 10. 24. 31. II, 1, 16. III, 4, 5. 2) a woman who keeps an inn: *the h. of the house,* Shr. Ind. 2, 88. *ruminates like an h.* Troil. III, 3, 253. Vocative: H4A II, 4, 305. III, 3, 68. 149. 192. 229. H4B II, 1, 144. II, 4, 86. 105. 115. 404. H5 II, 1, 86 (O. Edd. *your h.,* M. Edd. *you, h.*). II, 3, 62. *my h. of the tavern,* H4A I, 2, 45. 54. *mine h.* Err. III, 1, 119. John II, 289. H4B II, 4, 122. *thine h.* 355. Jocularly: *my lady the h.* H4A II, 4, 315.

Hostessship, the office of a hostess: Wint. IV, 4, 72.

Hostile, inimical: H4A I, 1, 9. R3 IV, 4, 236 (Qq *attempt of h. arms,* Ff *success of bloody wars*). 398. Cor. III, 3, 97. Tim. V, 1, 202. Per. I, 2, 24.

Hostility, the actions of an open enemy, war, enmity: John IV, 2, 247. H4A IV, 3, 44. H6A V, 4, 162. H6C I, 1, 199.

Hostilius, 1) name of the third king of Rome: Cor. II, 3, 248. 2) of one of the three strangers in Tim. III, 2, 70.

Hostler, see *Ostler.*

Hot, 1) contrary to cold, extremely warm, burning: Ven. 35. Lucr. 682. Sonn. 104, 7. Pilgr. 77. Wiv. II, 1, 121. III, 5, 122. 124. Err. III, 2, 134. Ado I, 1, 94. Mids. V, 59. As IV, 1, 102. Shr. IV, 1, 6. 34. Wint. IV, 4, 817. John IV, 1, 1. H8 I, 1, 140. Tit. V, 1, 14 etc. *a h. pasty,* Wiv. I, 1, 202. *h. meat,* 297. *h. blood* (= warm blood) R2 I, 1, 51. H6B I, 1, 118 etc. *I am h. with haste,* John IV, 3, 74. H4A V, 3, 34. *these h. tears,* Lr. I, 4, 320. *pray God his tongue be —er* (than the glutton's) H4B I, 2, 40. *a*

—er name than any is in hell, Mcb. V, 7, 6 (worse than that of a devil in hottest hell). *while it is h., I'll put it to the issue,* H8 V, 1, 178 (alluding to the proverb: *strike the iron while it is hot*). Substantively: *the extremes of h. and cold,* Ant. I, 5, 52. Adverbially: *sometime too h. the eye of heaven shines,* Sonn. 18, 5. *the sun shines h.* H6C IV, 8, 60. *burn —er,* Wint. IV, 4, 35.

2) ardent, fiery: *youth is h. and bold,* Pilgr. 163. *a h. lover,* Gent. II, 5, 53; cf. II, 7, 21. *the first suit is h. and hasty,* Ado II, 1, 78. III, 3, 141. LLL II, 219. Merch. I, 2, 20. V, 74. R2 II, 1, 70. V, 2, 8. Caes. IV, 2, 23. Hml. I, 1, 96 etc. *I was too h. to do somebody good,* R3 I, 3, 311 (too eager). *a h. friend cooling,* Caes. IV, 2, 19. *here is more matter for a h. brain,* Wint. IV, 4, 700. cf. *your wit's too h., it speeds too fast,* LLL II, 120.

3) violent, passionate: *h. wrath,* Compl. 293. *be not so h.* Meas. V, 315. *she is so h. because the meat is cold,* Err. I, 2, 47. Shr. II, 296. IV, 1, 6. 22. Wint. II, 3, 32. H6A III, 2, 58. III, 4, 28. H6B I, 1, 137. II, 1, 25. V, 1, 151. R3 III, 4, 39. Troil. II, 3, 183. V, 3, 16 (= rash). Cymb. II, 3, 7 etc.

4) vehement, impetuous, furious: *it hath seen very h. service,* Wint. IV, 3, 71. *this h. malicious day,* John II, 314. *in this h. trial,* 342. *so h. a speed,* III, 4, 11. *h. vengeance,* R2 I, 2, 8; cf. H4A III, 2, 10. *this haste was h. in question,* H4A I, 1, 34. *h. incursions,* III, 2, 108. *he'll call you to so h. an answer,* H5 II, 4, 123 *the knocks are too h.* III, 2, 4. *our h. pursuit,* H6A II, 2, 3. *in h. digestion of this cormorant war,* Troil. II, 2, 6. *h. inroads,* Ant. I, 4, 50 etc.

5) keen in desire, amorous, lustful, lecherous: *she red and h.* Ven. 35. *his h. courage,* 276. *the h. encounter,* 596. *which the h. tyrant stains,* 797. 1074. Lucr. 434. 682. Sonn. 154, 7. Compl. 218. Pilgr. 77. Tp. IV, 98. Wiv. V, 5, 13. All's IV, 5, 42. Wint. I, 2, 108. IV, 4, 35. H4A I, 2, 10. H5 III, 3, 21. Oth. III, 3, 403. Ant. III, 13, 118. Cymb. IV, 4, 37. V, 5, 180 etc. *with liver burning h.* Wiv. II, 1, 121. *h. livers and cold purses,* H4A II, 4, 355 (cf. *Liver*).

6) heating, spirituous: *h. and rebellious liquors,* As II, 3, 49. *aqua vitae or some other h. infusion,* Wint. IV, 4, 816. *h. wine,* Cor. II, 1, 52.

7) of a strong smell or acrid taste: *the h. scent snuffing hounds,* Ven. 692 (cf. *Cold*). *h. lavender,* Wint. IV, 4, 104. *the mustard is too h. a little,* Shr. IV, 3, 25. *ginger shall be h. in the mouth,* Tw. II, 3, 127. Jocularly: *your purse is not h. enough to purchase your spice,* Wint. IV, 3, 127.

Hot-blooded, 1) amorous, lecherous: *the h. gods assist me,* Wiv. V, 5, 2. 2) passionate, rash: *the h. France,* Lr. II, 4, 215 (Ff *hot-bloodied*).

Hot-burning, 1) fiery: *and in that cold h. fire doth dwell,* Lucr. 1557 (O. Edd. *cold hot burning,* M. Edd. *cold hot-burning;* perhaps, if a change of the old writing seems necessary: *cold-hot burning*). 2) desirous, lustful; *h. will,* Lucr. 247.

Hot-house, a bagnio: Meas. II, 1, 66.

Hotly, 1) contrary to coldly, with heat: *Titan did h. overlook them,* Ven. 178. *an oven stopped burneth more h.* 332.

2) ardently, eagerly: Lucr. 716. H5 II, 4, 68. Cor. IV, 5, 117. Lr. IV, 6, 166. Oth. I, 2, 44.

Hotspur, the surname of Henry Percy: H4A I, 1, 52. 70. II, 4, 114. III, 1, 7. III, 2, 112 (O. Edd.

this H. Mars, M. Edd. *this H., Mars*). 140. V, 1, 116 (*the H.*). V, 2, 19. H4B Ind. 25. 30. 36. I, 1, 50. 121. I, 3, 26. II, 3, 37. 44.

Hound, a dog used in the chase: Ven. 678. 686. 877. 913. Lucr. 694. Sonn. 91, 4. Err. IV, 2, 39. LLL IV, 2, 130. Mids. III, 1, 111. 114. III, 2, 64. IV, 1, 111. 116. 119 (*—s of Sparta*); cf. 124. Shr. Ind. 1, 16. 61. 2, 47. Tw. I, 1, 22. H5 Prol. 7. II, 1, 77 (*h. of Crete*). H6A IV, 2, 51. Troil. V, 1, 99. Cor. V, 6, 113 (term of reproach). Tit. II, 2, 25. II, 3, 17. 63. 70. Caes. II, 1, 174. V, 1, 41. Mcb. III, 1, 93. Lr. III, 6, 72. Oth. II, 3, 370. *she hearkens for his —s and for his horn,* Ven. 868. *with horn and —s,* Pilgr. 122. *with horn and h.* Tit. I, 494. *—s and horns,* II, 3, 27. *hawk or h.* Shr. V, 2, 72.

Hour (usually monosyll.; often dissyll., f. i. Sonn. 5, 1. Tp. III, 1, 91. V, 4. Gent. III, 2, 7. Err. II, 2, 14. III, 1, 122. LLL II, 68. As II, 7, 33. V, 4, 12. Tw. V, 226. Wint. II, 3, 136. John IV, 3, 104. H6C II, 5, 26. 27. 31. 32. 33. 34. II, 6, 80. R3 IV, 1, 83. V, 3, 31. Hml. I, 4, 3. Cymb. II, 2, 2) 1) the twenty fourth part of a day, a time of sixty minutes: *three —s since,* Tp. V, 136. 186. *'twill be this h. ere I have done weeping,* Gent. II, 3, 1. *an —'s heat,* III, 2, 7. Wiv. II, 2, 327. Meas. V, 360 (*be hanged an h.; certainly long enough to be killed*). Err. I, 2, 11. III, 1, 122. V, 288. LLL I, 1, 42. II, 68. V, 2, 797. As II, 7, 24. IV, 1, 42. V, 4, 12. Wint. II, 3, 136. John IV, 3, 104. H6C II, 5, 26. 27. 31. 32. 33. 34. II, 6, 80. R3 IV, 1, 83 etc. etc. *half an h.* Tp. III, 1, 91. Err. II, 2, 14. Rom. II, 5, 2. V, 3, 130. Hml. V, 2, 326 etc. *within this half h.* Tp. III, 2, 122. *this half h.* Tw. II, 5, 21. *some half h. past,* Lr. V, 3, 193. *some half h. hence,* Cymb. I, 1, 177. *by the h. =* hourly, every hour: *what expense by the h. seems to flow from him,* H8 III, 2, 108.

2) the point of time marked by the clock: *time's fickle glass, his sickle h.* Sonn. 126, 2. *like the watchful minutes to the h.* John IV, 1, 46 (till the moment when the hour is full and the clock strikes). *if life did ride upon a dial's point, still ending at the arrival of an h.* H4A V, 2, 85 (as soon as the moment is arrived at, when the hand of the dial points to a full hour); cf. *'twixt h. and h.* Cymb. III, 2, 70. *what do you think the hour? labouring for nine,* Tim. III, 4, 8. *what h. now?* Hml. I, 4, 3. *from this present h. of five,* Oth. II, 2, 11 (cf. H8 IV, 2, 26. Rom. II, 2, 169). *ere the ninth h.* Ant. II, 5, 21. *what h. is it?* Cymb. II, 2, 2. *about the very h. that...,* Gent. V, 1, 2. *about the sixth h.* LLL I, 1, 238. H8 IV, 2, 26. Caes. II, 4, 23. *at what h.,* Meas. II, 2, 159. *at that h.* Ado IV, 1, 87. *at the h. of nine,* Rom. II, 2, 169. *at the sixth h. of morn,* Cymb. I, 3, 31. *by the second h. in the morning,* R3 V, 3, 31. Caes. II, 1, 213. Ant. IV, 9, 4. *on the sixth h.* Tp. V, 4.

3) time in general, considered either as a space, or as a point; a) as a space: *make yourself ready for the mischance of the h.* Tp. I, 1, 28. *taught thee each h. one thing or other,* I, 2, 354. *any business that we say befits the h.* II, 1, 290. *one phoenix at this h. reigning there,* III, 3, 24. *when that h. o'erslips me in the day wherein I sigh not,* Gent. II, 2, 9. *why that h. of fairy revel he dares...,* Wiv. IV, 4, 58. *reserve them till a merrier h.* Err. I, 2, 69. *the h. steals on,* IV, 1, 52. *in her dull and sleeping h.* Mids. III, 2, 8. *neglect the creeping —s of time,* As II, 7, 112. *time and the*

h. runs through the roughest day, Mcb. I, 3, 147 etc. *you were born in a merry h.* Ado II, 1, 347. *in a happy h. =* in good time: Ado IV, 1, 285. H6C I, 2, 63. *God forbid the h.!* H6C II, 1, 190 (= God forbid that such a time should come). *good h. of night!* H8 V, 1, 5. Plur. *—s =* times, time: *those —s that with gentle work did frame the lovely gaze,* Sonn. 5, 1. *when —s have drained his blood,* 63, 3. *in him those holy antique —s are seen,* 68, 9. *vainer —s,* Tp. I, 2, 174. *we have spent our —s together,* Gent. II, 4, 63. *a thousand irreligious cursed —s,* Wiv. V, 5, 242. *my serious —s,* Err. II, 2, 29. *you will temporize with the —s,* Ado I, 1, 277. *fair thoughts and happy —s attend on you,* Merch. III, 4, 41. V, 32. Tw. V, 226. R2 II, 1, 177. III, 1, 11. Tim. III, 2, 6. Lr. IV, 7, 7. Ant. II, 2, 90. III, 13, 179 etc.

b) considered as a point: *the h.'s now come,* Tp. I, 2, 36. *wherefore did they not that h. destroy us?* 139. *at this h. lie at my mercy all my enemies,* IV, 263. Gent. II, 4, 179. IV, 3, 1. Wiv. III, 5, 66. Meas. IV, 2, 176. IV, 3, 82. Err. I, 1, 54. As V, 3, 27. Shr. III, 1, 19 etc. *Humphrey h.* R3 IV, 4, 175 (see *Humphrey*). *lovers break not — s,* Gent. V, 1, 4. *when I keep not —s,* Err. III, 1, 2. *she's very near her h.* Meas. II, 2, 16 (her time of delivery). *one minute behind your h.* As IV, 1, 195. *he is dieted to his h.* All's IV, 3, 35. *prolong his h.* Tim. III, 1, 66 (his h. of death). *my h. is almost come,* Hml. I, 5, 2. *your ill —s,* Tw. I, 3, 6 (your being abroad so late).

Hour-glass, a glass which marks the time by the running of sand: Merch. I, 1, 25. H5 Prol. 31.

Hourly, adj. 1) happening every hour: Tp. IV, 108. Ado II, 1, 188. All's III, 6, 11. Cor. V, 2, 74. Lr. IV, 6, 218. Cymb. I, 1, 89. I, 6, 107. Per. II, 4, 44.

2) marking the hours: *those bars which stop the h. dial,* Lucr. 327.

Hourly, adv. every hour: Tp. I, 2, 402. Meas. III, 1, 11. All's III, 2, 85. John III, 1, 56. R2 III, 3, 157. H4A II, 2, 16. H6B III, 2, 283. H8 V, 5, 9. Tit. IV, 2, 103. Hml. III, 3, 6. Lr. I, 4, 222. V, 3, 185. Ant. V, 2, 30. Cymb. II, 1, 64. III, 4, 153.

House, subst. 1) a building for the habitation of man: Tp. I, 2, 42. II, 1, 87. III, 2, 105. IV, 186. Gent. V, 4, 173. Meas. I, 2, 98. II, 1, 255. Err. I, 2, 75. II, 1, 71. V, 1, 12. Merch. I, 3, 176. Tw. II, 3, 106 etc. *a dark h.* (to keep madmen) As III, 2, 421. Tw. IV, 2, 38. 45. 49. V, 350. *war is no strife to the dark h. and the detested wife,* All's II, 3, 309 (so comfortless as to drive mad). *bottle-ale —s,* Tw. II, 3, 29. *common —s,* Meas. II, 1, 43. *—s of resort,* I, 2, 104. *the parliament h.* H6C I, 1, 71. *the woman's maid of the h.* Shr. Ind. 2, 92. *he forbade her my h.* Wiv. IV, 2, 89. *have I not forbid her my h?* 181. *to keep the h. =* to remain at home, Meas. III, 2, 75; cf. *must keep his h.* Tim. III, 3, 42; *a goodly day not to keep h.* Cymb. III, 3, 1. *the house doth keep itself* (nobody being within) As IV, 3, 82. Cymb. III, 6, 36. *Gratiano, keep the h.* Oth. V, 2, 365 (remain in the house and look to it). *to take a h. =* to seek shelter in a house, Err. V, 36. *I commend me from our h. in grief,* Lucr. 1308; cf. *and so I commit you — To the tuition of God: from my h., if I had it,* Ado I, 1, 284 (a phrase used at the close of letters). *an honest fellow as ever servant shall come in h. withal,* Wiv. I, 4, 11 (Mrs Quickly's speech). *he hath eaten me out of h. and home,*

H4B II, 1, 80 (Mrs Quickly's speech). *at one's h.* Gent. IV, 2, 38. Wiv. II, 1, 244. III, 5, 147. V, 5, 180. Meas. IV, 4, 18. IV, 5, 6. Merch. III, 1, 78. Shr. IV, 3, 185. H8 V, 5, 76 etc.

2) any habitation: *if the ill spirit have so fair a h.* Tp. I, 2, 458; cf. *to break within the bloody h. of life,* John IV, 2, 210; *this mortal h. I'll ruin,* Ant. V, 2, 51. *my h. was at the Phoenix,* Err. II, 2, 11. *the snail carries his h. on his head,* As IV, 1, 55. Lr. I, 5, 30. *bees with smoke and doves with noisome stench are from their hives and —s driven away,* H6A I, 5, 24.

3) the management of domestic affairs; household: *I keep his h.* Wiv. I, 4, 101. *the husbandry and manage of my h.* Merch. III, 4, 25. *the mistress of the h.* V, 38. *the lady of the h.* Tw. I, 5, 177. Rom. I, 5, 115. *she could not sway her h.* Tw. IV, 3, 17. *to keep h.* = to live in plenty, in a fashionable way: *who shall bear your part and be in Padua here Vicentio's son, keep h. and ply his book,* Shr. I, 1, 201. *keep h. and port and servants,* 208. *all things that belong to h. and housekeeping,* II, 358. *if he would not keep so good a h.* Tim. III, 1, 24. *I'll forswear keeping h.* H4B II, 4, 220 (= keeping an inn; the hostess' speech).

4) the persons dwelling under the same roof: *all our h. in great perplexity,* Gent. II, 3, 9. Rom. III, 3, 156. IV, 1, 8. Mcb. II, 2, 41. Lr. II, 4, 43. *how this becomes the h.* 155 (how this would agree with the place I have in the household).*

5) family, race: Meas. II, 4, 112. Mids. III, 1, 199. As I, 2, 241. Alls IV, 2, 42. 46. Tw. II, 4, 123. R2 IV, 145. H4A II, 3, 5. H6A II, 4, 116. II, 5, 102. III, 1, 165. III, 2, 77. H6B I, 1, 257 etc. *a gentleman of the very first h.* Rom. II, 4, 25 (ridiculed as a fashionable term, certainly not meaning an upstart, as some Intpp. explain it).

House, vb. 1) tr. to lodge, to quarter: *for ever —d where it gets possession,* Err. III, 1, 106. *Satan, —d within this man,* IV, 4, 57. *we —d him in the abbey here,* V, 188. 271. *the ship should h. him safe,* Per. II Prol. 32.

2) intr. to have a lodging, to dwell: *you shall not h. with me,* Rom. III, 5, 190. *the cod-piece that will h.* Lr. III, 2, 27. *we h. i' the rock,* Cymb. III, 3, 8.

House-affairs, domestic business: Oth. I, 3, 147.
House-eaves, the edges of a roof which overhang the wall: Meas. III, 2, 186.
Household, 1) persons standing under the same domestic government: *dispersed the h. of the king,* R2 II, 3, 28. *what need I thus my well-known body to anatomize among my h.?* H4B Ind. 22. *you of my h., leave this peevish broil,* H6A III, 1, 92. *if your peevish chastity shall undo a whole h.* Per. IV, 6, 133. Adjectively: *thy (death's) h. worms,* John III, 4, 31. *all the h. servants fled with him to Bolingbroke,* R2 II, 2, 60. *call forth my h. servants,* Ant. IV, 2, 9.

2) domestic establishment, house: *she is my house, my h. stuff, my field, my barn,* Shr. III, 2, 233. *that every day under his h. roof did keep ten thousand men,* R2 IV, 282. *ornaments of h.* H8 III, 2, 126. Adjectively, = domestic, familiar, homely: *it is more pleasing stuff. What, h. stuff?* Shr. Ind. 2, 143. *and bring you from a wild Kate to a Kate conformable as other h. Kates,* II, 280. *familiar in his mouth as h. words,* H5 IV, 3, 52 (= words of everyday life). *notes of h. harmony,* H6C IV, 6, 14.

3) family, race, house: *dishonour to my —'s grave,*

Lucr. 198. *my h. coat,* R2 III, 1, 24.* *to brother born an h. cruelty,* H4B IV, 1, 95. *our —'s name,* H6A IV, 6, 38. *thy h. badge,* H6B V, 1, 201. *in our —'s monument,* Tit. V, 3, 194. *two —s, both alike in dignity,* Rom. Prol. 1. *to turn your —s' rancour to pure love,* II, 3, 92 (Ff *h.*).

Householder, 1) master of a family: Ado IV, 2, 84.

2) one that belongs to a household: *I press me none but good —s, yeoman's sons,* H4A IV, 2, 16.
Housekeeper, 1) one who keeps much at home: *you are manifest —s,* Cor. I, 3, 55.

2) one that guards the house: *the h., the hunter,* Mcb. III, 1, 97.

3) of uncertain signification: *to be said an honest man and a good h. goes as fairly as to say a careful man and a great scholar,* Tw. IV, 2, 10 (the clown's speech).
Housekeeping, a plentiful and hospitable household: *your grace hath sworn out h.* LLL II, 104. *all things that belong to house or h.* Shr. II, 358. *thy deeds, thy plainness and thy h. hath won the greatest favour of the commons,* H6B I, 1, 191.

Housel, the eucharist, in *Unhouseled,* q. v.
Houseless, wanting the shelter of a house: Lr. III, 4, 26. 30.
Housewife or **Huswife** (the latter the more usual spelling; Ff only three times *housewife:* As I, 2, 34. H8 III, 1, 24. Oth. I, 3, 273. Qq only in Oth. II, 1, 113) 1) a woman skilled in female business and superintending the concerns of a family: Sonn. 143, 1. Mids. II, 1, 37. As I, 2, 34. IV, 3, 27. Alls II, 2, 62. Tw. I, 3, 109. H8 III, 1, 24. Cor. I, 3, 76. Rom. IV, 2, 43. Tim. IV, 3, 423. Oth. I, 3, 273. Cymb. III, 2, 79. IV, 2, 45.

2) a hussy: *doth Fortune play the h. with me now?* H5 V, 1, 85. *sung those tunes to the overscutched —ves,* H4B III, 2, 341 (not in Ff). *—ves in your beds,* Oth. II, 1, 113. *a h. that by selling her desires buys herself bread and clothes,* IV, 1, 95. *that the false h. Fortune break her wheel,* Ant. IV, 15, 44 (but cf. As I, 2, 34).
Housewifery or **Huswifery** (the former spelling only in the Q of Oth. II, 1, 113), management becoming the mistress of a family: H5 II, 3, 65. Oth. II, 1, 113.
Hovel, subst. a shed: Lr. III, 2, 61. 71. 78. III, 4, 179.
Hovel, vb. to put in a shed: *wast thou fain to h. thee with swine,* Lr. IV, 7, 39.
Hovel-post, post of a shed: Merch. II, 2, 71.
Hover, 1) to hang in the air overhead or about: Compl. 319. John III, 2, 2. R3 IV, 4, 13. 15. Tit. I, 88. Mcb. I, 1, 12. Hml. III, 4, 103.

2) to be irresolute, to waver: *—ing o'er the paper with her quill,* Lucr. 1297. *a —ing temporizer,* Wint. I, 2, 302.
How, 1) in what way and manner, by what means: *being mad before, h. doth she now for wits?* Ven. 249. *h. is it that this lives in thy mind?* Tp. I, 2, 48. 52. 158. 225. 334. II, 2, 124 etc. etc. *h. and which way,* and = *h. or which way,* pleonastically: *I'll take the sacrament on't, h. and which way you will,* Alls IV, 3, 156. *if I know h. and which way to order these affairs,* R2 II, 2, 109. *h. or which way should they first break in?* H6A II, 1, 71. 73. Before an inf.: *some authority h. to proceed,* LLL IV, 3, 287. *we have*

French quarrels enow, if you could tell h. to reckon, H5 IV, 1, 241. Often superfluous: *my true eyes have never practised h. to cloak offences,* Lucr. 748; cf. Shr. III, 2, 253. *my busy care is h. to get my palfrey from the mare,* Ven. 384. *being once perfected h. to grant suits,* Tp. I, 2, 79. *instruct thee h. to snare the marmoset,* II, 2, 173. *I seek occasion h. to rise,* H6C I, 2, 45. *seek h. to redress their harms,* V, 4, 2. *laboured much h. to forget that learning,* Hml. V, 2, 35. *what is your study? h. to prevent the fiend,* Lr. III, 4, 164. *instructs you h. to adore the heavens,* Cymb. III, 3, 3. Particularly after the verbs *to know, learn* and *teach:* Lucr. 810. 1653. Sonn. 39, 13. 101, 13. 150, 9. Tp. I, 2, 364. II, 1, 222. Gent. V, 3, 4. Err. III, 2, 33. Ado II, 1, 396. V, 1, 142. Merch. III, 2, 11. As I, 1, 26. I, 2, 6. III, 2, 388. Shr. IV, 3, 7. John III, 1, 30. V, 2, 88. H5 III, 1, 25. H6B V, 1, 6. R3 I, 2, 224. Tit. V, 3, 70. Rom. III, 2, 12. Cymb. I, 5, 12 etc.

2) as: *h. thou pleasest, God, dispose the day,* H5 IV, 3, 142. *make your own purpose, h. in my strength you please,* Lr. II, 1, 114. Especially after *look: look, h. a bird lies tangled in a net, so fastened in her arms Adonis lies,* Ven. 67. *look, h. a bright star shooteth from the sky, so glides he in the night from Venus' eye,* 815. *look, how the world's poor people are amazed at apparitions, so she at these sad signs draws up her breath,* 925. *look, h. far the substance of my praise doth wrong this shadow, so far this shadow doth limp behind the substance,* Merch. III, 2, 126. *look, h. this ring encompasseth thy finger, even so thy breast encloseth my poor heart,* R3 I, 2, 204. *and look, h. many Grecian tents do stand hollow upon this plain, so many hollow factions,* Troil. I, 3, 79 (cf. *look, as:* Lucr. 372. 694 etc.).

3) of what quality: *h. features are abroad, I am skilless of,* Tp. III, 1, 52. *h. would you be, if He should judge you as you are?* Meas. II, 2, 75. *h. is the man esteemed here in the city?* Err. V, 4. cf. Ven. 79. H4A V, 2, 12 etc.

4) to what degree: *h. quick is love!* Ven. 38. *canst not feel h. want of love tormenteth,* 202. *perceiving h. he is enraged,* 317. *h. he outruns the wind,* 681. *h. strange it seems,* 985. *h. much a fool was I,* 1015. *I know not h. much tribute,* Tp. I, 2, 124. *look h. well my garments sit upon me,* II, 1, 272. *h. many fond fools serve mad jealousy,* Err. II, 1, 116. *he hath indeed better bettered expectation than you must expect of me to tell me h.* Ado I, 1, 17 etc. The ind. art. between the adj. and subst.: *h. high a pitch,* R2 I, 1, 109. *h. dread an army,* H5 IV Ch. 36 etc. *By h. much... by so much* = the more... the more: *by h. much unexpected, by so much we must awake endeavour,* John II, 80. *by h. much* correlative to a comparative: *you are the better at proverbs, by h. much a fool's bolt is soon shot,* H5 III, 7, 131. Followed by *ever: h. heinous e'er it be,* R2 V, 3, 34. *h. dearly ever parted,* Troil. III, 3, 96. by *soever:* LLL I, 1, 194 etc. (cf. *Soever*).

5) = however: *look h. he can, she cannot choose but love,* Ven. 79. *how far I toil, still farther off from thee,* Sonn. 28, 8. *I never yet saw man, h. wise, h. noble, but she would spell him backward,* Ado III, 1, 60. *be blamed for it h. you might,* Wint. II, 1, 161. *look h. we can, or sad or merrily, interpretation will misquote our looks,* H4A V, 2, 12. *whether his fall enraged him, or h. 'twas, he did so set his teeth,* Cor. I, 3, 69. *h. much the quantity, the weight as much, as I do love my father,* Cymb. IV, 2, 17. Cor. V, 1, 61.

6) = what: *h. 's the day?* Tp. V, 3 (= what time of day is it?). *h. then? shall he marry her?* Gent. II, 5, 17. *h. dost thou mean a fat marriage?* Err. III, 2, 95. *h. do you mean?* Alls III, 5, 71. *h. shall we do?* Wint. IV, 4, 598. *h. art thou called?* H6B V, 1, 73. *h. if* = what should I or what should you do if: *h. if your husband start some other where?* Err. II, 1, 30. *h. if my brother had of your father claimed this son for his?* John I, 120. *h. if it come to thee again?* R3 I, 4, 136 (Ff *what*). *h. if, when I am laid into the tomb, I wake before the time,* Rom. IV, 3, 30. *h. say you* = what do you say, what do you think or mean: Tp. II, 1, 254. Wiv. I, 4, 29. Meas. II, 4, 58. Err. IV, 4, 48. Wint. I, 2, 54. H5 V, 2, 134. H6A II, 3, 61. V, 3, 126. Tit. II, 2, 16. Mcb. III, 4, 69. Hml. I, 5, 121. Oth. II, 1, 164. With *by: h. say you by the French lord?* Merch. I, 2, 58 (cf. *By*). *h. say you by that?* Hml. II, 2, 188 (= what do you mean by this?). *h. say you by this change?* Oth. I, 3, 17. With *to: h. say you to a fat tripe?* Shr. IV, 3, 20. *h. say you to that?* Tw. I, 5, 88. With a clause: *h. sayest thou that my master is become a notable lover?* Gent. II, 5, 43. *h. sayest thou that Macduff denies his person at our great bidding?* Mcb. III, 4, 128.

7) at what price, how dear: *h. a good yoke of bullocks at Stamford fair?* H4B III, 2, 42. *h. a score of ewes now?* 54. *h. go maidenheads?* Troil. IV, 2, 23. *h. a dozen of virginities?* Per. IV, 6, 22.

8) Joined to *so,* = why: *and sped you, sir? Very ill-favoured. H. so, sir? did she change her determination?* Wiv. III, 5, 69. *Ajax goes up and down the field, asking for himself. H. so?* Troil. III, 3, 246.

9) Used as an exclamation, particularly to express surprise: *I am the best of them that speak this speech, were I but where 'tis spoken. H.? the best?* Tp. I, 2, 430. *my wife, whom I detest... H.? thy wife?* Meas. II, 1, 71. *h. h., h. h., chop-logic:* Rom. III, 5, 150 (only in Q2; the rest of O. Edd. *h. now*). *Caius Ligarius, h! Caes.* II, 1, 312. *it is not lost; but what an if it were? H.!* Oth. III, 4, 84. *h.! of adultery?* Cymb. III, 2, 1. Very often joined to *now,* q.v.

10) Placed before sentences, to lay a stress on them and draw attention to a fact: *h. like a jade he stood,* Ven. 391. *h. he outruns the wind,* 681. *h. her eyes and tears did lend and borrow!* 961. *h. her fear did make her colour rise!* Lucr. 257. *h. her hand, in my hand being locked, forced it to tremble,* 260. 1548. Tp. I, 2, 410. II, 1, 52. III, 2, 34. Gent. V, 4, 1. Err. II, 1, 86 etc. Before dependent clauses almost = that: *to note the fighting conflict of her hue, h. white and red each other did destroy,* Ven. 346. *sings extemporally a woful ditty, h. love makes young men thrall and old men dote,* 837. *I, not remembering h. I cried out then, will cry it o'er again,* Tp. I, 2, 133. *is not ignorant how his companion attends the emperor,* Gent. I, 3, 26. III, 2, 26. *none better knows than you h. I have ever loved the life removed,* Meas. I, 3, 8. *when men were fond, I smiled and wondered h.* II, 2, 187. *have informed me how the English wont to overpeer the city,* H6A I, 4, 9. *that he may have a likely guess h. these were they that made away his brother,* Tit. II, 3, 208 etc.

Howbeit (dissyll.), 1) be it as it may, nevertheless: *so do the kings of France unto this day; h. they would hold up this Salique law,* H5 I, 2, 91. *h. I thank you,* Cor. I, 9, 70.

2) Followed by *that,* = although: *the Moor, h.*

that I endure him not, is of a constant, lowing, noble *nature,* Oth. II, 1, 297.

Howe'er, 1) in whatsoever manner: *h. the business goes, you have made fault in the boldness of your speech,* Wint. III, 2, 218. *I am I, h. I was begot,* John I, 175. *h. it be, I cannot but be sad,* R2 II, 2, 29. *h. you come to know it, answer me,* Mcb. IV, 1, 51. *till I know 'tis done, h. my haps, my joys were ne'er begun,* Hml. IV, 3, 70.

2) notwithstanding, though: *it would not seem too dear, h. repented after,* All's III, 7, 28. *h. it pleases you to take it so, the ring was never hers,* V, 3, 88. *you would believe my saying, h. you lean to the nayward,* Wint. II, 1, 64. *and oft have shot at them, h. unfortunate I missed my aim,* H6A I, 4, 4. *h. thou art a fiend, a woman's shape doth shield thee,* Lr. IV, 2, 66. *this youth, h. distressed, appears he hath had good ancestors,* Cymb. IV, 2, 47.

3) in any case, at all events: *if it be so, you have wound a goodly clew; if it be not, forswear 't: h., I charge thee to tell me truly,* Alls I, 3, 189.

However, 1) in whatsoever manner: *have is have, h. men do catch,* John I, 173. *h. God or fortune cast my lot,* R2 I, 3, 85. *truly, h. else,* Lr. II, 1, 119.

2) notwithstanding, though: *there was never yet philosopher that could endure the toothache patiently, h. they have writ the style of gods,* Ado V, 1, 37. *this challenge, h. it is spread in general name, relates in purpose only to Achilles,* Troil. I, 3, 322. *h. these disturbers of our peace buzz in the people's ears, there nought hath passed but even with law,* Tit. IV, 4, 6. *so is he now, h. he puts on this tardy form,* Caes. I, 2, 303.

3) in any case, at all events: *if haply won, perhaps a hapless gain; if lost, why then a grievous labour won; h., but a folly bought with wit,* Gent. I, 1, 34. *all the land knows that; h., yet there is no great breach,* H8 IV, 1, 106.

Howl, subst. 1) the cry of a wolf: Mcb. II, 1, 54. 2) cry of anguish: H5 III, 3, 39.

Howl, vb) 1) to cry as a wolf: Tp. I, 2, 288. As V, 2, 119. H6B IV, 1, 3. Lr. III, 7, 63. as a dog: Ven. 918. Pilgr. 277. Ado II, 3, 82. Tw. V, 113. H4A III, 1, 240. H4B I, 3, 100. H6B I, 4, 21. H6C V, 6, 46. Used of bad singers: *a —ing monster,* Tp. II, 2, 183. Ado II, 3, 82.

2) to cry in anguish: Tp. I, 1, 39. I, 2, 296. V, 233. Gent. II, 3, 8. Meas. III, 1, 128. Merch. III, 2, 56. Mcb. IV, 3, 5. Lr. V, 3, 257. With *out,* tr.: *words that would be —ed out in the desert air,* Mcb. IV, 3, 194. Used of those suffering the pains of hell: *for the which I think thou wilt h.* H4B II, 4, 374. *when thou liest —ing,* Hml. V, 1, 265. Of fiends: H5 II, 1, 97. R3 I, 4, 59. *—ing,* quite substantively: *the damned use that word in hell; —ings attend it,* Rom. III, 3, 48.

Howlet (most M. Edd. *owlet*) a kind of owl: Mcb. IV, 1, 17.

Howsoe'er, 1) in whatever manner or degree: *h. you have been justled from your senses, know for certain,* Tp. V, 157. *h. thou speakest, 'mong other things I shall digest it,* Merch. III, 5, 94 (Q2 Ff *howsome'er*). *I am glad he's come, h. he comes,* Shr. III, 2, 77. *h. 'tis strange, yet it is true,* Cymb. I, 1, 65.

2) be that as it may, in any case: *but h., no simple man that sees this jarring discord, but that it doth presage some ill event,* H6A IV, 1, 187. *gold confound you h.* Tim. IV, 3, 452. *let ordinance come as the gods*

foresay it: h., my brother hath done well, Cymb. IV, 2, 146.

Howsoever, 1) in whatever manner or degree: *he talks of the basket too, h. he hath had intelligence,* Wiv. IV, 2, 94. *my form, which, h. rude exteriorly, is yet the cover of a fairer mind,* John IV, 2, 257. *h. thou pursuest this act, taint not thy mind,* Hml. I, 5, 84 (Qq *howsomever*).

2) although: *you are a bawd, h. you colour it,* Meas. II, 1, 231. *the man doth fear God, h. it seems not in him,* Ado II, 3, 205. *you love him not so ill, h. you speak this,* H5 IV, 1, 130. *h. you have been his liar, you cannot pass,* Cor. V, 2, 32.

3) be that as it may, in any case: *but h., strange and admirable,* Mids. V, 27. *h., he shall pay for me,* Troil. III, 3, 297.

Howsome'er, though: *h. their hearts are severed in religion, their heads are both one,* All's I, 3, 56. In Merch. III, 5, 94 Q2 Ff. *h.,* Q1 *howsoe'er,* q. v.

Howsomever, in whatever manner: Hml. I, 5, 84 (Ff *howsoever*).

Hox, to hough, to hamstring: Wint. I, 2, 244.

Hoy, a small vessel: Err. IV, 3, 40.

Hoyday, an exclamation of contemptuous surprise: *h., a riddle!* R3 IV, 4, 460 (most M. Edd. *heyday*). *h., spirits and fires!* Troil. V, 1, 73 (Q *heyday*). *h., what a sweep of vanity,* Tim. I, 2, 137.

Hubert, name in John III, 2, 5. III, 3, 19 etc.

Huddle, 1) tr. to put or throw in haste: *—ing jest upon jest with such impossible conveyance upon me,* Ado II, 1, 252.

2) intr. to crowd, to throng in haste: *his losses, that have of late so —ed on his back,* Merch. IV, 1, 28.

Hue, colour: Ven. 345. 398. 747. Sonn. 20, 7.* 67, 6. 82, 5. 98, 6. 104, 11. Compl. 287. LLL IV, 3, 255. V, 2, 906. Mids. III, 1, 95. 128. V, 171. Merch. II, 1, 11. II, 7, 22. Shr. II, 256. John IV, 2, 13. Tit. I, 182. 261. II, 3, 73. IV, 2, 72. 99. 100. 117. Hml. III, 1, 84. Used only in verse.

Hue and cry, a clamour in pursuit of an offender: *h., villain, go! fly, run, h.* Wiv. IV, 5, 92. 93. *a h. hath followed certain men unto this house,* H4A II, 4, 556.

Hug, 1) to press close in an embrace: Meas. III, 1, 85. Merch. II, 6, 16. All's II, 3, 297. R3 I, 4, 252. II, 2, 24. Tit. III, 1, 214. Tim. I, 1, 44. IV, 3, 207. Caes. I, 2, 75.

2) intr. to embrace each other: *to h. with swine,* John V, 2, 142.

Huge, 1) very large: Lucr. 335. 647. 959. Sonn. 15, 3. 21, 8. Tp. II, 2, 21. Gent. II, 4, 175. III, 2, 80. As III, 3, 58. John II, 103. III, 1, 72. V, 2, 86. H4A II, 4, 269. 497. III, 1, 16. 100. H4B II, 4, 68. H5 III Chor. 12. V Chor. 5. Caes. I, 2, 137. II, 4, 7. IV, 3, 92. Hml. III, 3, 19. Ant. II, 7, 16. Per. III, 2, 58.

2) great, mighty: *a h. troop,* Err. V, 81. *army,* LLL I, 1, 10. *a h. translation of hypocrisy,* V, 2, 51. *your h. store,* 377. *Pompey the H.* 692. *a h. feeder,* Merch. II, 5, 46. *Alexander the H.* H5 IV, 7, 17 (Fluellen's speech). *in that sparing makes h. waste,* Rom. I, 1, 224. *if I were a h. man,* Tim. I, 2, 51. *my h. sorrows,* Lr. IV, 6, 288. *the world's a h. thing,* Oth. IV, 3, 69. *a h. eclipse of sun and moon,* V, 2, 99. *that h. spirit,* Ant. IV, 15, 89. *will look so h.* Per. I, 2, 25.

Hugely, mightily, immensely: *h. politic*, Sonn. 124, 11. *doth it not flow as h. as the sea?* As II, 7, 72.

Hugeness, greatness, vastness: *my mistress exceeds in goodness the h. of your unworthy thinking*, Cymb. I, 4, 157.

Hugger-mugger; in h. = clandestinely: *we have done but greenly, in h. to inter him*, Hml. IV, 5, 84.

Hugh, name of 1) King H. Capet, H5 I, 2, 69. 87. 2) Sir H. Mortimer, H6C I, 2, 62. 3) Sir H. Evans, Wiv. I, 1, 1. 216 etc. 4) H. Otecake, Ado III, 3, 11. 5) H. Rebeck, Rom. IV, 5, 135.

Hulk, a large and heavy ship: *Harry Monmouth's brawn, the h. Sir John*, H4B I, 1, 19. *you have not seen a h. better stuffed in the hold*, II, 4, 70. *provokes the mightiest h. against the tide*, H6A V, 5, 6. *light boats sail swift, though greater — s draw deep*, Troil. II, 3, 277.

Hull, to float, to drive to and fro on the sea: *I am to h. here a little longer*, Tw. I, 5, 217. *there they h.* R3 IV, 4, 438.* *thus —ing in the wild sea of my conscience*, H8 II, 4, 199.

Hum, subst. 1) the noise of bees or other insects: H5 I, 2, 202 (quibbling). Mcb. III, 2, 42.

2) a low confused noise: H5 IV Chor. 5.

Hum, vb. 1) to utter a low confused sound: *burden-wise I'll h. on Tarquin still*, Lucr. 1133. *I heard a —ing*, Tp. II, 1, 317. *a thousand twangling instruments will h. about mine ears*, III, 2, 147. *—ing water must o'erwhelm thy corpse*, Per. III, 1, 64.

2) to cry *hum* or *hem*, to betray deliberation or indignation: *h. and stroke thy beard*, Troil. I, 3, 165 (Qq *hem*). *to bite his lip and h. at good Cominius*, Cor. V, 1, 49. *turns me his back and —s*, Mcb. III, 6, 42.

Hum, interj., an exclamation expressive of deliberation: Wiv. III, 5, 141. H4A III, 1, 158. Troil. III, 3, 282. 287. Tim. II, 2, 204. III, 3, 1. 9. Mcb. IV, 3, 203. Hml. II, 2, 617 (Ff om.). V, 1, 112. Lr. I, 2, 58. III, 4, 48. Oth. V, 2, 36. Cymb. III, 5, 103. Per. V, 1, 84. Substantively: *the shrug, the h. or ha*, Wint. II, 1, 71. *these —s and ha's*, 74. *his h. is a battery*, Cor. V, 4, 22.

Humane (such invariably is the spelling of O. Edd., never *human;* as for the changeable accent, see the 1st article of the Appendix, 'Grammatical Observations') 1) pertaining to man, having the qualities of man: *h. law*, Lucr. 571. *h. sense*, Pilgr. 108. *hearing*, Tp. I, 2, 265. *shape*, 284. *our h. generation*, III, 3, 33. *were I h.* V, 20. *h. reason*, Err. V, 189. *the h. mortals*, Mids. II, 1, 101 (as distinguished from the fairies who are mortal too). *h. skill*, II, 2, 119. *hanged for h. slaughter*, Merch. IV, 1, 134. *to set her before your eyes h. as she is*, As V, 2, 74 (as a human being of flesh and blood). *our h. actions*, Wint. III, 2, 30. *reason*, V, 1, 41. *the first h. principle*, H4B IV, 3, 133. *h. conditions*, H5 IV, 1, 108. *thought*, H6A I, 1, 121. *misery*, III, 2, 137. *powers*, Cor. II, 1, 236. *action*, 265. *divine and h.* III, 1, 141. *sons*, Tim. IV, 3, 185. *griefs*, V, 4, 75. *dealings*, Oth. III, 3, 260. *creatures*, Cymb. I, 5, 20.

2) worthy of man, kind, benevolent: *I have used thee with h. care*, Tp. I, 2, 346. *in h. modesty*, Mids. II, 2, 57. *touched with h. gentleness*, Merch. IV, 1, 25. *most h. and filled with honour*, Wint. III, 2, 166. *in h. gentleness*, Troil. IV, 1, 20. *it is the h. way; the other course will prove too bloody*, Cor. III, 1, 327. *the milk of h. kindness*, Mcb. I, 5, 18. *ere h. statute*

purged the gentle weal, III, 4, 76. *civil and h. seeming*, Oth. II, 1, 243.

Humanely, kindly, benevolently: Tp. IV, 190. Cor. I, 1, 19.

Humanity, the peculiar nature of man, human nature: *let (lest?) fair h. abhor the deed*, Lucr. 195. *what you see is but the smallest part and least proportion of h.* H6A II, 3, 53. *what nearer debt in all h. than wife is to the husband?* Troil. II, 2, 175. *he's opposite to h.* Tim. I, 1, 284 (a man-hater). *henceforth hated be of Timon man and all h.* III, 6, 115. *the middle of h. thou never knewest*, IV, 3, 300. *they imitated h. so abominably*, Hml. III, 2, 39. *I would change my h. with a baboon*, Oth. I, 3, 317. *a rarer spirit never did steer h.* Ant. V, 1, 32. *how look I, that I should seem to lack h. so much as this fact comes to?* Cymb. III, 2, 16 (= that I should not look like a human being).

2) mankind: *h. must perforce prey on itself*, Lr. IV, 2, 49 (cf. above H6A II, 3, 53).

Humble, adj. (compar. *—er* dissyll. in H5 IV, 7, 70 and Cor. IV, 2, 4; trisyll. in H6A III, 1, 56. Superl. *—est:* Wiv. III, 4, 20. H8 II, 4, 144. Once, but in a suspected passage, *a* before it: *a h. tongue*, LLL V, 2, 747; F2.3.4 *an*). 1) low, mean: *the h. as the proudest sail*, Sonn. 80, 6. *if thy thoughts be so h. to cast thy wandering eyes on every stale*, Shr. III, 1, 89. *I am from h., he from honoured name*, All's I, 3, 162. *my low and h. name*, II, 1, 200. *above her and her h. love*, II, 3, 89. *cast thy h. slough*, Tw. II, 5, 161. III, 4, 76. *a poor h. swain*, Wint. IV, 4, 30. H4B II, 2, 14. H6C III, 3, 11. R3 IV, 2, 37. H8 II, 3, 20. IV, 2, 49. V, 3, 166.

2) lowly, modest, submissive: *an h. gait*, Lucr. 1508. Pilgr. 330. Tp. I, 2, 482. III, 1, 87. Gent. III, 1, 226. Shr. Ind. 1, 116. All's I, 1, 185. R2 II, 3, 83. H4B V, 5, 143. H5 IV, 7, 70. H6A III, 1, 167. 168. III, 3, 42. V, 5, 18. H6B I, 2, 62. H8 II, 4, 23. 74. 144. Troil. III, 2, 102. Cor. II, 3, 161. 229. Tim. V, 4, 20. Caes. III, 1, 35. Hml. III, 4, 69 (submissive to the judgment). Ant. III, 11, 62. Often joined to certain words as a term of courtesy: *an h. prayer*, H6C IV, 6, 7. *h. service*, Tw. III, 1, 105. H6A III, 1, 168. *duty*, H4B II, 1, 137. *suit*, Wiv. III, 4, 20. LLL V, 2, 849. H6B IV, 1, 124. H6C III, 2, 13. Caes. III, 1, 5. *suitor*, H6C III, 1, 19. Tim. III, 5, 7. *suppliant*, Lucr. 897. R3 I, 1, 74. Tit. IV, 3, 117. *thanks*, Ado I, 1, 242. H6C III, 2, 62. III, 3, 221. Cymb. I, 6, 180. With to: *be h. to us*, H6A IV, 2, 6.

3) courteous, benevolent, kind (cf. *Humility*): *the h. salve which wounded bosoms fits*, Sonn. 120, 12 (i. e. the salve of kindness). *this is not generous, not gentle, not h.* LLL V, 2, 632. *a heavy heart bears not a h. tongue*, 747 (F2.3.4 *an h.;* M. Edd. *a nimble*). *with h. and familiar courtesy*, R2 I, 4, 26. *who prologuelike your h. patience pray*, H5 Prol. 33. *his lordship should be —r*, H6A III, 1, 56. *my manly eyes did scorn an h. tear*, R3 I, 2, 165. *thy voice is thunder, but thy looks are h.* I, 4, 172. *now we have shown our power, let us seem —r*, Cor. IV, 2, 4. *play the h. host*, Mcb. III, 4, 4. *ne'er ebb to h. love*, Oth. III, 3, 458.

Humble, vb. 1) to bow down: *falls not the axe upon the —d neck*, As III, 5, 5. *which (thy head) now h. as the ripest mulberry*, Cor. III, 2, 79. *all —d on your knees*, Tit. I, 472.

2) to subdue, to make submissive, to abase the

pride of: Gent. I, 2, 59. II, 4, 137. All's I, 2, 45 (*he —d* = he being —d). IV, 5, 55. Tit. I, 252. Oth. III, 3, 52. With *to: —s himself to the determination of justice*, Meas. III, 2, 258. *made great Jove to h. him to her hand*, Shr. I, 1, 174. *— ing their deities to love*, Wint. IV, 4, 26. H4B V, 2, 120. Tit. I, 51. Lr. IV, 1, 68.

Humblebee, the insect Bombus terrestris: LLL III, 85. 90. 96. Mids. III, 1, 171. IV, 1, 12. All's IV, 5, 7. Troil. V, 10, 42 (masc.).

Humble-mouthed, mild in speech: *meek and h.* H8 II, 4, 107.

Humbleness, 1) absence of pride, submissiveness: Merch. I, 3, 125. As V, 2, 103. All's II, 1, 117. H8 V, 1, 65. Tit. I, 45. IV, 2, 4.

2) benevolence, kindness; *which h. may drive unto a fine*, Merch. IV, 1, 372 (i. e. kindness on the part of the signiory).

Humble-visaged, looking submissive: LLL II, 34.

Humbly, 1) submissively: Ven. 1012. Shr. I, 1, 81. All's II, 1, 130. V, 3, 19. R2 III, 3, 104. H5 IV, 3, 129. H6B I, 1, 10. IV, 9, 11. H6C III, 1, 101. III, 3, 61. V, 1, 22. R3 I, 1, 76. I, 2, 179. II, 2, 105. IV, 4, 101. Troil. III, 3, 73. Rom. III, 1, 161. Oth. I, 3, 236. Ant. III, 1, 30. Cymb. IV, 3, 13. Joined, often as a term of mere courtesy, to certain verbs: *I h. beseech you*, Wint. V, 2, 160. H4B I, 2, 112. H8 II, 4, 53. Oth. I, 3, 220. III, 3, 212. *I h. do desire your grace*, Merch. IV, 1, 402. Troil. III, 3, 274. 285. *I h. do entreat your pardon*, H8 IV, 2, 104. *I h. pray*, H5 V Chor. 3. H8 IV, 2, 129. Tim. II, 2, 22. 28. *they h. sue unto your excellence*, H6A V, 1, 4. *most h. I do take my leave*, H6C I, 2, 61. Mcb. I, 4, 47. Hml. I, 3, 82. II, 2, 218. Cymb. I, 5, 45 (cf Dogberry's blunder in Ado V, 1, 334). *I h. thank you*, Meas. I, 4, 87. II, 1, 293. III, 1, 41. All's III, 5, 99. IV, 3, 178. H6B I, 3, 215. H8 III, 2, 381. V, 1, 109. Tit. V, 1, 18. Hml. III, 1, 92. IV, 4, 29. V, 2, 83. Oth. III, 1, 42. III, 4, 168. IV, 3, 3. Cymb. I, 1, 175. V, 5, 100. *h. I thank your lordship*, Tim. I, 1, 149. Oth. I, 3, 70. Ant. II, 2, 250.

2) benevolently, kindly: *when I do weep, they* (the stones) *h. at my feet receive my tears and seem to weep with me*, Tit. III, 1, 41.

Hume, name in H6B I, 2, 72. 85 etc.

Humidity, moisture: Wiv. III, 3, 43. Tim. IV, 3, 2.

Humility, 1) freedom from pride and arrogance, submissiveness: All's I, 1, 185. I, 3, 99. R2 V, 1, 33. H6B V, 1, 58. H8 II, 4, 109. IV, 2, 161. Cor. II, 1, 250. II, 3, 44.

2) affability, courtesy: *bowed his eminent top to their low ranks, making them proud of his h.* All's I, 2, 44. *I have sounded the very base-string of h.* H4A II, 4, 6. *dressed myself in such h. that I did pluck allegiance from men's hearts*, III, 2, 51. *your bounty, virtue, fair h.* R3 III, 7, 17.

3) kindness, benevolence, humanity: *plant in tyrants mild h.* LLL IV, 3, 349. *if a Jew wrong a Christian, what is his h.?* Revenge, Merch. III, 1, 72. *in peace there's nothing so becomes a man as modest stillness and h.* H5 III, 1, 4. *I thank my God for my h.* R3 II, 1, 72.

Humorous, 1) moist, damp: *to be consorted with the h. night*, Rom. II, 1, 31 (quibbling).

2) capricious: *the duke is h.* As I, 2, 278. II, 3, 8. *her h. ladyship* (Fortune) John III, 1, 119. *as h.*

as winter, H4B IV, 4, 34. *a vain, giddy, shallow, h. youth*, H5 II, 4, 28. *his h. predominance*, Troil. II, 3, 138.

3) obeying one's own fancies and impulses: a) merry: *'tis no marvel he* (the devil) *is so h.* H4A III, 1, 234. *I am known to be a h. patrician*, Cor. II, 1, 51. *the h. man shall end his part in peace*, Hml. II, 2, 335.*

b) sad: *a very beadle to a h. sigh*, LLL III, 177. *my often rumination wraps me in a most h. sadness*, As IV, 1, 19.

Humour, subst. 1) moisture: *suck up the —s of the dank morning*, Caes. II, 1, 262. Particularly morbid fluids of animal bodies: *the toothache, where is but a h. or a worm*, Ado III, 2, 27. *this inundation of mistempered h.* John V, 1, 12. *that trunk of —s*, H4A II, 4, 495. *through all thy veins shall run a cold and drowsy h.* Rom. IV, 1, 96. *the sun where he was born drew all such —s from him*, Oth. III, 4, 31.

2) cast of mind, temper, sentiments, spirit: *every h. hath his adjunct pleasure*, Sonn. 91, 5. *I am of your h. for that*, Ado I, 1, 132. *shall these paper bullets awe a man from the career of his h.?* II, 3, 250. *his h. is lofty*, LLL V, 1, 10. *it fits my h. well*, As III, 2, 20. *a shrew of thy impatient h.* Shr. III, 2, 29. *he kills her in her own h.* IV, 1, 183. *I'll curb her mad and headstrong h.* 212. *you either fear his h. or my negligence*, Tw. I, 4, 5. *all the unsettled —s of the land*, John II, 66. *it jumps with my h.* H4A I, 2, 78. *what h. is the prince of?* H4B II, 4, 256. *knowing dame Eleanor's aspiring h.* H6B I, 2, 97. *a bedlam and ambitious h. makes him oppose himself against his king*, V, 1, 132. *best acquainted with her h.* R3 IV, 4, 269. *you've got a h. there does not become a man*, Tim. I, 2, 26. *I'll know his h. when he knows his time*, Caes. IV, 3, 136. *except she bend her h.* Cymb. I, 5, 81. *though his h. was nothing but mutation*, IV, 2, 132. Plur. *—s: they say so most that most his —s know*, LLL II, 53. *in —s like the people of this world*, R2 V, 5, 10. *whose churchlike —s fits not for a crown*, H6B I, 1, 247.

3) temporary disposition: *in that pleasant h. they all posted to Rome*, Lucr. Arg. 8. *see what h. he is in*, Wiv. II, 3, 80. *when I am dull with care and melancholy, lightens my h. with his merry jests*, Err. I, 2, 21. 58. II, 2, 7. IV, 1, 27. Ado IV, 1, 189. LLL I, 1, 235. I, 2, 63. V, 2, 767. As III, 2, 439. IV, 1, 69. Shr. Ind. 2, 14. I, 2, 108. John V, 1, 12 (quibbling). R3 I, 2, 228. 229. I, 4, 121. Rom. I, 1, 135. 147. Oth. III, 4, 125. V, 2, 165. *to feed a person's h.* = to gratify by yielding, to humour: R3 IV, 1, 65. Tit. IV, 3, 29. The contrary is to *come 'cross, to cross a p. in his h.:* H4A III, 1, 172. Tim. I, 2, 166.

4) fancy, conceit, caprice: *tapsters answering every call, soothing the h. of fantastic wits*, Ven. 850. *such childish h. from weak minds proceeds*, Lucr. 1825. *I see a better state to me belongs than that which on thy h. doth depend*, Sonn. 92, 8. *laughing-stocks to other men's —s*, Wiv. III, 1, 88. III, 3, 181. IV, 2, 210. Err. IV, 1, 57. Ado I, 3, 19. Merch. III, 5, 68. IV, 1, 43. As V, 4, 61. Shr. III, 2, 75. Tw. II, 5, 58. Wint. II, 3, 38. John IV, 2, 209. 214. H4A III, 1, 237. H4B II, 1, 161. 163. II, 3, 30. Troil. I, 2, 23. II, 3, 222. Tit. IV, 4, 19. V, 2, 140. Rom. II, 1, 7 Tim. III, 6, 122. Caes. II, 1, 210. 250. II, 2, 56. IV, 3, 46. 109.*120.

5) mirth, merriment: *cannot flout me out of my h.*

Ado V, 4, 102. *the spirit of —s intimate reading aloud to him*, Tw. II, 5, 93. *uphold the unyoked h. of your idleness*, H4A I, 2, 220. *I am now of all —s that have showed themselves —s*, II, 4, 104.

Unexplained as yet: *the h. of forty fancies pricked in't* (his hat) Shr. III, 2, 70.＊

6) Ridiculed as a much misused phrase of fashion: *these are complements, these are —s*, LLL III, 23 (Moth's speech). *my chief h. is for a tyrant*, Mids. I, 2, 30 (Bottom). *these be good —s indeed*, H4B II, 4, 177 (Pistol.) Particularly in the slang of Nym: *slice! that's my h.* Wiv. I, 1, 135. *pass good —s*, 169. *run the nuthook's h. on me*, 171. *he was gotten in drink: is not the h. conceited?* I, 3, 26. *the good h. is to steal at a minute's rest*, 30. *the anchor is deep: will that h. pass?* 56. *the h. rises*, 63. *I thank thee for that h.* 71. *I will run no base h.* 85. *take the h. letter*, 86. *—s of revenge*, 98. cf. 103. 104. 109. 112. II, 1, 133. 134. 140—143. H5 II, 1, 58. 63. 74. 101. 121. 127. 132. II, 3, 63. III, 2, 5. 7. 27. 28.

Humour, vb. 1) to gratify and soothe by entering into another's ideas: *yielding to him — s well his frenzy*, Err. IV, 4, 84. *to h. the ignorant call I the deer a pricket*, LLL IV, 2, 52. *and —ed thus comes at the last*, R2 III, 2, 168 (perhaps rather = in this humour).

2) to tamper with, to gain: *I will teach you how to h. your cousin, that she shall fall in love with Benedick*, Ado II, 1, 396. *I would h. his men with the imputation of being near their master*, H4B V, 1, 80. *he should not h. me*, Caes. I, 2, 319.＊

3) Misapplied by Nym and Moth: *h. me the angels*, Wiv. I, 3, 63. *the —ed letter*, II, 1, 134 (cf. *the humour letter*, I, 3, 86). *h. it with turning up your eyelids*, LLL III, 13.

Humph, see *Hum.*

Humphrey or **Humphry**, name of 1) H. Duke of Gloster: H4B IV, 4, 12. H6A I, 3, 29. III, 1, 3. V, 1, 58. H6B I, 1, 76. 159 etc. 2) Sir H. Stafford: H6B IV, 2, 120. IV, 4, 34. 3) H. of Buckingham: H6B V, 1, 15.

Passage not yet satisfactorily explained: *H. hour, that called your grace to breakfast once*, R3 IV, 4, 175 (Nares: "the phrase of dining with duke Humphrey, which is still current, originated in the following manner. Humphrey, duke of Gloucester, though really buried at St. Alban's, was supposed to have a monument in old St. Paul's, from which one part of the church was termed Duke Humphrey's walk. In this, as the church was then a place of the most public resort, they who had no means of procuring a dinner, frequently loitered about, probably in hopes of meeting with an invitation, but under pretence of looking at the monuments.")

Hunch-backed, reading of the later Qq in R3 IV, 4, 81; Q1 and Ff *bunch-backed*, q. v.

Hundred, ten times ten: *a h. several times*, Gent. IV, 4, 150. *a h. and fifty pounds*, Wiv. III, 4, 49. IV, 6, 8. Meas. I, 2, 147. III, 2, 125. *a h. thousand hearts*, Mids. II, 1, 160. *tell a h.* Hml. I, 2, 238 etc. As for *an h.*, see *A*, article. *ten h.* Ven. 519. *three h.* Wiv. I, 1, 13. *five h.* Err. IV, 4, 13. *twelve h.* H6A IV, 1, 24. *fifteen h.* H4B II, 1, 186. H5 III, 7, 136. *twenty h. thousand times*, Rom. III, 3, 153 etc. Plur. *—s: many —s*, John IV, 2, 149. *by the —s*, H4A II, 4, 399. *—s he sent to hell*, H6A I, 1, 123. Per. III, 2, 44. *The H. Merry Tales*, Ado II, 1, 135 (a jest-book

then very popular, and lately reprinted). *the h. psalms*, Wiv. II, 1, 63 (M. Edd. *the hundredth psalm*). *I entertain you for one of my h.* Lr. III, 6, 83 (meaning probably his hundred knights).

Hundred-pound, a term of reproach for a snob (see *Three-suited*): *a h., filthy, worsted-stocking knave*, Lr. II, 2, 17.

Hundredth, the ordinal of hundred; only by conjecture in Wiv. II, 1, 63; O. Edd. *the hundred psalms*. *Hundred* and *thousand* were formerly also ordinals.

Hungarian, a cant term, the meaning of which originated in its consonance with the word *hunger*, = needy, beggarly: *O base H. wight, wilt thou the spigot wield?* Wiv. I, 3, 23.

Hungary, name of the country to the east of Austria: Meas. I, 2, 2. *heaven grant us its peace, but not the king of —'s*, 5 (alluding to *hunger?*).

Hunger, subst. pain and uneasiness from want of food: Lucr. 422. Ado I, 1, 252. As II, 7, 132. All's III, 2, 121. H6A I, 2, 38. H8 I, 2, 34. Oth. V, 2, 362. Cymb. II, 4, 137. III, 6, 16. 63. Per. I, 4, 12. 45. 96. With *for: in h. for bread*, Cor. I, 1, 25. Prov.: *h. broke stone walls*, 210.

Hunger, vb. to have an eager appetite: Mcb. IV, 3, 82. With *for: h. for mine empty chair*, H4B IV, 5, 95. Tim. V, 4, 32.

Hungerford, name in H6A I, 1, 146. H6C IV, 1, 48.

Hungerly, adj. wanting food, starved: *his beard grew thin and h.* Shr. III, 2, 177.

Hungerly, adv. with keen appetite: *I feed most h. on your sight*, Tim. I, 1, 262. *they eat us h.* Oth. III, 4, 105.

Hunger-starved, pinched by want of food: H6C I, 4, 5.

Hungry, 1) feeling pain from want of food, having keen appetite; properly and metaphorically: Sonn. 56, 6. 64, 5. Gent. V, 4, 33. Mids. V, 378. As IV, 3, 127. Tw. II, 4, 103. Wint. III, 3, 135. John III, 3, 10. R2 I, 3, 296. H5 II, 4, 104. H6A IV, 7, 7. H6B III, 1, 249. IV, 10, 5. H6C I, 4, 152. Cor. II, 1, 10. Rom. V, 3, 36. Tim. IV, 3, 177. Ant. II, 2, 242. Per. V, 1, 113. *their h. prey* = the prey of their hunger, H6A I, 2, 28. With *for: h. for revenge*, R3 IV, 4, 61.

2) emaciated, as if reduced by hunger: *a h. lean-faced villain*, Err. V, 237. *a lean and h. look*, Caes. I, 2, 194.

3) barren: *let the pebbles on the h. beach fillip the stars*, Cor. V, 3, 58.

Hungry-starved,= hunger-starved: H6A I, 5, 16.

Hunt, subst. 1) chase: *the h. is up*, Tit. II, 2, 1. *as if a double h. were heard at once*, II, 3, 19. *escaped the h.* Lr. II, 3, 3.

2) the game killed in the chase: *we'll go dress our h.* Cymb. III, 6, 90.

Hunt, vb. 1) to chase; absol.: Ven. 673. LLL III, 165. Shr. Ind. 1, 29. 2, 46. V, 2, 55. Tw. I, 1, 16. Wint. III, 3, 65. H4B IV, 4, 14. H6C IV, 5, 8. Cor. III, 1, 275. Tit. II, 2, 25. IV, 1, 55. 56. Tim. I, 2, 194. 196. II, 2, 197. Oth. II, 3, 370. Cymb. IV, 2, 138. 148. 162. *you h. counter* = you are at fault, H4B I, 2, 102 (Ff hyphened). Gerund *—ing:* Ven. 4. Mids. IV, 1, 188. H4B II, 1, 157 (*the German —ing*). H6C IV, 6, 85. Tit. II, 1, 112. II, 2, 20. II, 3, 59. Tim. II, 2, 8. Lr. I, 3, 7. Oth. II, 1, 313. Cymb.

IV, 2, 2. 6 (*go to* —*ing*). With an accus.: Ven. 588. 900. Tp. IV, 263. LLL IV, 3, 1. As IV, 3, 18. H5 IV, 3, 94. H6B V, 2, 15. H6C II, 4, 13. R3 IV, 4, 48. Troil. IV, 1, 19. V, 6, 31. Cor. I, 1, 240. Tit. I, 493. IV, 1, 96. Rom. III, 5, 34. Ant. IV, 1, 7.

2) to pursue; a) trans.: *lust past reason —ed*, Sonn. 129, 6. *when it hath the thing it —eth most*, LLL I, 1, 146. *this brain of mine —s not the trail of policy*, Hml. II, 2, 47.

b) with *after* or *for*: *he after glory —s*, Gent. I, 1, 63. LLL I, 1, 1. Oth. III, 4, 62. *why h. I then for colour or excuses?* Lucr. 267. R3 III, 4, 99.

Hunt-counter, reading of Ff in H4B I, 2, 102; Q and M. Edd. *hunt counter*.

Hunter, 1) one pursuing and chasing wild animals, a huntsman: Wiv. IV, 4, 28. 38. V, 5, 31. 80. 108. As II, 1, 34. III, 2, 259. Tw. III, 4, 243. Tit. II, 2, 5. 13. Caes. III, 1, 205. Cymb. III, 3, 74. V, 3, 39. With *for*: *I'll play the h. for thy life*, Troil. IV, 1, 17.

2) a dog employed in the chase: Mcb. III, 1, 97.

Huntington (most M. Edd. *Huntingdon*) name in H5 V, 2, 85.

Huntress, a woman that hunts (Diana): As III, 2, 4.

Huntsman, one who practises hunting: Ven. 973. Shr. Ind. I, 16. H6C IV, 5, 25. H8 III, 2, 207. Tit. II, 3, 269. 278. IV, 1, 101. Plur. *huntsmen*: Mids. IV, 1, 143. John II, 321. H6C IV, 5, 15. IV, 6, 84.

Hunts-up, a tune played to wake sportsmen: *hunting thee hence with h. to the day*, Rom. III, 5, 34 (the full form *the hunt is up* in Tit. II, 2, 1).

Hurdle, a sledge on which criminals are drawn to the place of execution: Rom. III, 5, 156.

Hurl, 1) tr. to throw violently and impetuously: Compl. 87. Err. II, 2, 137. Tw. III, 2, 87. R2 I, 1, 146. H6A I, 4, 46. R3 I, 3, 220. I, 4, 205. 206 (Qq *throw*). III, 7, 35 (—*ed up their caps*). IV, 4, 86. Caes. V, 1, 64. Oth. V, 2, 274. Ant. I, 2, 127.

2) intr. to move in a wild and confused manner: *these are but wild and —ing words*, Hml. I, 5, 133 (Qq *whirling*).

Hurly, much ado, commotion, tumult: *amid this h. I intend that all is done in reverend care of her*, Shr. IV, 1, 206. *I see this h. all on foot*, John III, 4, 169. *with the h. death itself awakes*, H4B III, 1, 25.

Hurly-burly, uproar, tumult: *when the h.'s done*, Mcb. I, 1, 3. Adjectively: *h. innovation*, H4A V, 1, 78.

Hurricano, a water-spout: *the dreadful spout which shipmen do the h. call*, Troil. V, 2, 172. *you cataracts and —es, spout till you have drenched our steeples*, Lr. III, 2, 2.

Hurry, subst. commotion, disorder, confusion: *in the present peace and quietness of the people, which before were in wild h.* Cor. IV, 6, 4.

Hurry, vb. 1) tr. to hasten with precipitation, to drive confusedly: *which madly —es her she knows not whither*, Ven. 904. —*ed thence me and thy crying self*, Tp. I, 2, 131. *they —ed us aboard a bark*, 144. —*ed to this place*, Wint. III, 2, 105. *amazement —es up and down the little number of your doubtful friends*, John V, 1, 35 (intr.?). —*ing me from my friends*, Per. IV, 1, 21 (Qq *whirring*).

2) to move with precipitation and disorder: *he —ed through the street*, Err. V, 140. H4B IV, 2, 105. *h. to loss*, H6A IV, 3, 53 (= are rapidly lost). *ne'er through an arch so —ed the blown tide*, Cor. V, 4, 50.

as hasty powder fired doth h. 'from the fatal cannon's womb, Rom. V, 1, 65.

Hurt, subst. 1) harm, injury, mischief: *to mend the h. that his unkindness marred*, Ven. 478. *the fall of an ass, which is no great h.* Cymb. I, 2, 39. *to do h.*: Sonn. 94, 1. As III, 5, 27. Alls I, 3, 97. 98. II, 1, 137. H4B I, 3, 34. Cymb. I, 2, 37. *thou dost me yet but little h.* Tp. II, 2, 82. Per. IV, 1, 75. *hath done to thee great h.* Cor. IV, 5, 73.

2) any bodily harm done, a wound or bruise: *upon his h. she looks so steadfastly*, Ven. 1063; cf. Tw. V, 214; Rom. III, 1, 115; Mcb. V, 8, 46; Oth. II, 3, 253. *had ta'en a h.* As II, 1, 34. *to receive a h.* Cor. II, 1, 166. Lr. II, 1, 110. III, 7, 95. *you caught h.* Per. IV, 1, 88. *I must give myself some —s*, Alls IV, 1, 40. Tw. V, 193. H5 III, 6, 11. H6A II, 4, 53. Rom. III, 1, 98. Tim. III, 5, 109. Lr. III, 7, 98.

Hurt, vb. (impf. and part. *hurt*) 1) to harm, to injure, to pain, to do mischief, to vex; absol.: *have power to h.* Sonn. 94, 1. *give delight and h. not*, Tp. III, 2, 145. III, 3, 66. Ado V, 1, 190. V, 2, 14. H6A III, 3, 53. H6C II, 6, 94. Troil. V, 3, 20. Cor. II, 2, 77. Hml. IV, 7, 124. Ant. V, 2, 299. Cymb. I, 6, 95. With an accus.: *this nor —s him nor profits you*, Meas. IV, 3, 128. *it* (wit) —*s nobody*, Ado V, 1, 165. V, 2, 16. *it —s not him that he is loved of me*, Alls I, 3, 202. John IV, 3, 33. H6C IV, 6, 20. 76. H8 III, 1, 160. Cor. IV, 6, 25. Tit. II, 3, 204. III, 1, 92. Lr. III, 4, 25. IV, 1, 18. Ant. II, 5, 81. Cymb. I, 2, 35. Per. I, 1, 100. IV, 1, 78.

2) to do bodily harm, to pain, to strike, to wound; tr.: *you h. my hand with wringing*, Ven. 421. *h. him not*, Err. V, 33. *poor h. fowl*, Ado II, 1, 209. *how they might h. their enemies*, V, 1, 98. Mids. III, 2, 269. 300. Merch. III, 1, 63. As III, 5, 25. Alls III, 5, 90. Tw. III, 2, 37. III, 4, 330. 339. V, 190. 192. 194. 201. 216. John IV, 3, 2. H4A IV, 2, 21. H4B II, 4, 227. 231. H6A III, 3, 53. Troil. I, 1, 112. I, 2, 233. 302. V, 4, 12. 14. Cor. I, 4, 37. Tit. II, 3, 203. Rom. I, 1, 119. III, 1, 93. Mcb. II, 2, 39. Hml. V, 2, 255. 335. Oth. II, 3, 163. 197. 259. III, 1, 28. IV, 1, 60. 193. Cymb. I, 2, 7. 10. 11. 12. V, 3, 12. Per. III, 3, 6. IV Prol. 25. V, 2, 163. 328.

Hurtle, to justle, to meet with noise in shock and conflict: *in which —ing from slumber I awaked*, As IV, 3, 132. *the noise of battle —d in the air*, Caes. II, 2, 22.

Hurtless, doing no harm: *the strong lance of justice h. breaks*, Lr. IV, 6, 170.

Husband, subst. 1) one who keeps house: *you will turn good h. now, you will keep the house*, Meas. III, 2, 74.

2) one careful and economical: *while I play the good h. at home, my son and my servant spend all*, Shr. V, 1, 71. *in that I deem you an ill h.* H8 III, 2, 142.

3) a husbandman, a tiller of the ground: *this Davy serves you for good uses; he is your serving-man and your h.* H4B V, 3, 12.

4) the correlative to wife, a man contracted or married to a woman: Sonn. 93, 2. Tp. III, 1, 87. V, 209. Wiv. I, 3, 59. II, 1, 103. II, 2, 85. 91. Meas. II, 1, 210. III, 1, 231. Err. II, 1, 1. 30. 43. II, 2, 137. III, 2, 2. Ado II, 1, 333 etc. With *to*: *one string, sweet h. to another*, Sonn. 8, 9. *to turn h.* = to marry, Ado I, 1, 196. *Benedick is not the unhopefulest h. that I*

know, II, 1, 393 (= most unhopeful in point of marriage). Often used vocatively: Wiv. IV, 2, 189. V, 5, 111. 255. Err. II, 2, 121. 176. 209 etc. but not, it should seem, among persons of rank: *are you my wife and will not call me h.?* Shr. Ind. 2, 106; except to give the speech a tone of peculiar tenderness and affection: John III, 1, 305. 331. R2 V, 2, 107. Cor. V, 3, 37. Rom. III, 1, 152. Ant. V, 2, 290. Cymb. I, 1, 85.

Husband, vb. 1) to till, to cultivate: *bare land, manured, —ed and tilled with good endeavour*, H4B IV, 3, 130.

2) to use with economy, to guard: *h. nature's riches from expense*, Sonn. 94, 6.

3) to manage: *h. your device*, Wiv. IV, 6, 52. *it will be pastime passing excellent, if it be —ed with modesty*, Shr. Ind. 1, 68. *and for my means, I'll h. them so well, they shall go far*, Hml. IV, 5, 138.

4) to supply with a husband, to marry: *that I —ed her bed in Florence*, Alls V, 3, 126. *so fathered and so —ed*, Caes. II, 1, 297. *if he should h. you*, Lr. V, 3, 70.

Husbandless, without a husband: John III, 1, 14.

Husbandman, reading of the later Ff in H4B V, 3, 12; Qq and earlier Ff *husband*.

Husbandry, 1) tillage, cultivation of the ground, the whole business of a farmer: *where is she so fair whose uneared womb disdains the tillage of thy h.?* Sonn. 3, 6. *her plenteous womb expresseth his full tilth and h.* Meas. I, 4, 44. *cannot so much as a blossom yield in lieu of all thy pains and h.* As II, 3, 65. *my old dame will be undone now for one to do her h. and her drudgery*, H4B III, 2, 124. *all her h. doth lie on heaps*, H5 V, 2, 39. *choke the herbs for want of h.* H6B III, 1, 33.

2) economy, thrift: *lets so fair a house fall to decay, which h. in honour might uphold*, Sonn. 13, 10. *if you suspect my h.* Tim. II, 2, 164. *there's h. in heaven; their candles are all out*, Mcb. II, 1, 4. *borrowing dulls the edge of h.* Hml. I, 3, 77.

3) care of one's business: *I commit into your hands the h. and manage of my house*, Merch. III, 4, 25. *shows good h. for the Volscian state*, Cor. IV, 7, 22. especially shown by early rising: *makes us early stirrers, which is both healthful and good h.* H5 IV, 1, 7. *like as there were h. in war, before the sun rose he was harnessed*, Troil. I, 2, 7. *that is the cause we trouble you so early; 'tis not our h.* Per. III, 2, 20.

Hush, interj. used to enjoin silence: Tp. I, 2, 477. IV, 126. Alls II, 3, 317. IV, 3, 135. Mcb. III, 1, 10. Lr. III, 4, 186. Ant. I, 2, 21. 83. Cymb. V, 4, 94.

Hush, adj. silent, still: *the orb below as h. as death*, Hml. II, 2, 508.

Hush, vb. to make silent, to still: Ven. 458. Sonn. 102, 10. Tp. IV, 207. Ado II, 3, 41. Tw. V, 110. John V, 1, 20. R2 I, 1, 53. H4B III, 1, 11. Cor. V, 3, 181. Oth. IV, 2, 79.

Husht (M. Edd. *hush*) = hush, interj.: Shr. I, 1, 68. Per. I, 3, 10.

Husks, the rind or hull of seeds, chaff: *h. wherein the acorn cradled*, Tp. I, 2, 463. *eat h. with your hogs*, As I, 1, 40. *eating draff and h.* H4A IV, 2, 38. *the shales and h. of men*, H5 IV, 2, 18. *what's past and what's to come is strewed with h. and formless ruin of oblivion*, Troil. IV, 5, 166.

Huswife, see *Housewife*.

Huswifery, see *Housewifery*.

Hutch, in *Bolting-hutch*, q. v.

Hybla, a mountain in Sicily celebrated for its honey: H4A I, 2, 47. Caes. V, 1, 34.

Hydra, the many-headed serpent killed by Hercules: H4A V, 4, 25. Cor. III, 1, 93. Oth. II, 3, 308. Adjectively: *this H. son of war*, H4B IV, 2, 38 (not to be killed by a single stroke, but putting forth new heads, when one is cut off).

Hydra-headed, not to be killed, like the heads of the Lernaean Hydra: *h. wilfulness*, H5 I, 1, 35.

Hyems, see *Hiems*.

Hyen, the hyena: *I will laugh like a h.* As IV, 1, 156.

Hymen, the god of marriage: Tp. IV, 1, 23. 97. Ado V, 3, 32. As V, 4, 118. 135. 149. 152. Tim. IV, 3, 384. Hml. III, 2, 169. Per. III Prol. 9.

Hymenaeus, nuptials: *every thing in readiness for H. stand*, Tit. I, 325.

Hymn, a solemn song: Sonn. 29, 12. 85, 7. 102, 10. Ado V, 3, 11. Mids. I, 1, 73. II, 1, 102. Merch. V, 66. John V, 7, 22. Rom. IV, 5, 88.

Hyperbole, a rhetorical exaggeration: LLL V, 2, 407. Troil. I, 3, 161.

Hyperbolical, exaggerated: *you shout me forth in acclamations h.* Cor. I, 9, 51. = using high-flown language: *out, h. fiend!* Tw. IV, 2, 29 (the clown's speech).

Hypérion, the god of the sun, Phoebus: H5 IV, 1, 292. Troil. II, 3, 207. Tit. V, 2, 56. Tim. IV, 3, 184. Hml. I, 2, 140. III, 4, 56.

Hypocrisy, false seeming, deceitful appearance, dissimulation: LLL IV, 3, 151. V, 2, 51. R2 V, 3, 107. H8 II, 3, 26. Oth. IV, 1, 6.

Hypocrite (having *an*, not *a*, before it: Meas. V, 41. H4B II, 2, 64. Per. I, 1, 122), a dissembler: Meas. V, 41. Ado I, 1, 152. H4B II, 2, 59. 64. H6A I, 3, 56. Hml. III, 2, 415. III, 4, 42. Per. I, 1, 122. Used wrongly by Dogberry: Ado V, 1, 212.

Hyrcan, Hyrcanian: *the H. tiger*, Mcb. III, 4, 101.

Hyrcania, a country on the Caspian sea: *tigers of H.* H6C I, 4, 155.

Hyrcanian, pertaining to Hyrcania: *H. deserts*, Merch. II, 7, 41. *like the H. beast*, Hml. II, 2, 472.

Hyssop (Qq *Isop*, Ff *hysope* and *hisope*) the plant Hyssopus officinalis: Oth. I, 3, 325.

Hysterica passio, see Appendix, Latin.

I.

I, the third vowel: LLL V, 1, 58. Tw. II, 5, 118. 121. 132. 147. 151. Quibbling with *ay* and *eye:* Tw. II, 5, 148. Rom. III, 2, 46.

I, the spelling of O. Edd. for *ay*, q. v. Qq *yea* and Ff *I:* R3 I, 3, 121. 126. 136. 263. II, 2, 29. See the punning in Rom. III, 2, 45—50.

I, pronoun of the first person: Ven. 18. 97. 109 etc. etc. Obj. form *me:* Ven. 138. 145. 152 etc. Preceded by adjectives: *wretched I, to imitate thee well, against my heart will fix a knife*, Lucr. 1136. *poor I am but his stale*, Err. II, 1, 101. *poor I was slain*, Tit. II, 3, 171. *poor I am stale*, Cymb. III, 4, 53. *to leave poor me*, Sonn. 49, 13. *make a conquest of unhappy me*, Per. I, 4, 69. *save poor me*, IV, 1, 91. *I for me: hang no more praise upon deceased I*, Sonn. 72, 7. *do that good mischief which may make this island thine own for ever, and I thy Caliban for aye thy foot-licker*, Tp. IV, 218. *let fortune go to hell for it, not I*, Merch. III, 2, 21. *all debts are cleared between you and I*, 321. *my father had no child but I*, As I, 2, 18. *what he is indeed, more suits you to conceive than I to speak of*, As I, 2, 279 (but cf. *a heavier task could not have been imposed than I to speak my griefs unspeakable*, Err. I, 1, 33. *I to bear this, is some burden*, Tim. IV, 3, 266. *heaven would that she these gifts should have, and I to live and die her slave*, As III, 2, 161. Similarly Gent. V, 4, 109. Cor. III, 2, 124. Cymb. III, 1, 72. On the other hand: *me, poor man, my library was dukedom large enough*, Tp. I, 2, 109). *when she exclaimed on Hastings, you and I*, R3 III, 3, after v. 15 (not in Ff and Gl. Ed). *Me for I: then ten times happy me*, Sonn. 37, 14. *the dog is me*, Gent. II, 3, 25. *get you from our court. Me, uncle?* As I, 3, 44. *that's me*, Tw. II. 5, 87. *or both yourself and me cry lost*, Wint. I, 2, 410. *me rather and my heart might feel your love*, R2 III, 3, 192. *tawny slave, half me and half thy dam*, Tit. V, 1, 27. *no mightier than thyself*, *or me*, Caes. I, 3, 76. *is she as tall as me?* Ant. III, 3, 14. cf. *O me!* John I, 220. *O me unhappy!* Gent. V, 4, 84. *woe is me!* Hml. III, 1, 168 (see *O* and *Woe*). *I* repeated at the close of the sentence: *I care not for her I*, Gent. V, 4, 132. *I'll drink no more than will do me good, for no man's pleasure I*, H4B II, 4, 129. *I do not like these several councils I*, R3 III, 2, 78. *I am no vaunter I*, Tit. V, 3, 113. *I am no baby I*, 185. *I will budge for no man's pleasure I*, Rom. III, 1, 58. *I know it I*, III, 5, 12. — *I* omitted: *beseech you*, Tp. I, 2, 473. II, 1, 1 etc. (cf. *Beseech*). *give your worship good morrow*, Wiv. II, 2, 35. R3 II, 3, 6. Hml. I, 1, 16. Lr. II, 2, 165. *and thank you too*, LLL IV, 2, 167. H8 I, 2, 13. *pray heaven*, As I, 2, 209. IV, 3, 76 etc. (cf. *Pray*). *as to a bed, that longing have been sick for*, Meas. II, 4, 103. *I show more mirth than I am mistress of, and would you yet were merrier?* As I, 2, 4 (M. Edd. *I were merrier*). *with toss-pots still had drunken heads*, Tw. V, 412. *and think me honoured*, H6A II, 3, 81. *if son to Talbot, die at Talbot's foot*, IV, 6, 53. *give thee thy due*, Tim. III, 1, 37. *for their knives care not*, V, 1, 181. *assure thee, Regan*, Lr. II, 1, 106. 4, 42. Not pronounced, or at least slurred, in its proclitical position, though inserted: *if you tarry longer, I shall give worse payment*, Tw. IV, 1, 21. *if that be true, I shall see my boy again*, John III, 4, 78. *I beseech your majesty, give me leave to go*, H6B II, 3, 20. *I beseech your graces*, Tit. I, 1, 84. 103. Similarly *let me* as one syllable: *let me see, let me see, is not the leaf turned down?* Caes. IV, 3, 273 (cf. on the other hand: Gent. I. 3, 55. II, 1, 3. LLL III, 104. Merch. II, 7, 13. II, 9, 23. H6C II, 5, 82 etc. *let me see* = now I have it, this it is: Hml. II, 2, 471. IV, 7, 155). *Me* omitted: *the justice of it pleases*, Oth. IV, 1, 222. *of me* for *my: tell thou the lamentable tale* (Ff *fall*) *of me*, R2 V, 1, 44. *not I*, used in answering: Tp. III, 3, 42. Err. V, 420 etc.

Me used as a refl. pron. = myself; accus. (cf. the resp. verbs): *I should absent me*, Shr. Ind. 2, 125. *I will address me to my appointment*, Wiv. III, 5, 135. Merch. II, 9, 19. *I will arm me*, H6C IV, 1, 113. *attire me how I can*, H6B II, 4, 109. *how I may bear me here*, Tp. I, 2, 425. *betake me to my heels*, H6B IV, 8, 67. *I cloy me*, R3 IV, 4, 62. *I commend me*, Lucr. 1308. *I complain me*, 598. *I confess me much guilty*, As I, 2, 196. *I cross me for a sinner*, Err. II, 2, 190. *I will discase me*, Tp. V, 85. *I'll disrobe me*, Cymb. V, 1, 22. *I would divorce me*, Lr. II, 4, 133. *drenched me in the sea*, Gent. I, 3, 79. *to drown me*, Err. III, 2, 46. *I ensconce me here*, Sonn. 49, 9. Wiv. III, 3, 97. *let me excuse me*, Meas. IV, 1, 12. *how shall I fashion me*, Gent. III, 1, 135. *flattering me with impossibilities*, H6C III, 2, 143. *I'll get me to a place more void*, Caes. II, 4, 37. *I hid me*, Tp. II, 2, 115. Wiv. III, 3, 36. Ado II, 3, 38. Mids II, 1, 227. H6B IV, 10, 3. R3 III, 7, 161. Cymb. I, 6, 86. *I held me glad*, Gent. IV, 1, 32. Err. IV, 2, 17. R3 I, 3, 157. Tit. I, 245. *to keep me from a most unholy match*, Gent. IV, 3, 30. *I lay me down*, H6C II, 3, 2. *I have loaden me with spoils*, H6A I, 1, 80. *I alone do me oppose*, John III, 1, 170. *to prepare me*, Meas. IV, 3, 58. *in pruning me*, LLL IV, 3, 183. *raise me from my knees*, Meas. V, 231. *rank me*, Merch. II, 9, 33. *I'll reconcile me*, Wint. III, 2, 156. R3 II, 1, 59. *I do refer me to the oracle*, Wint. III, 2, 116. *as I remember me*, R3 IV, 2, 98 (Qq only *remember*). *I'll renew me in his fall*, Cor. V, 6, 49. *I do repent me*, Meas. II, 3, 35. Mcb. II, 3, 112. *I needs must rest me*, Tp. III, 3, 4. *retire me to my Milan*, Tp. V, 310. Tim. II, 2, 171. *when I do rouse me*, H5 I, 2, 275. *I will shelter me here*, Wiv. V, 5, 24. *sit me down*, H6C II, 5, 14. *where I list to sport me*, Ven. 154. *I had squared me to thy counsel*, Wint. V, 1, 52. *subject me*, As II, 3, 36. *I did suit me like a man*, I, 3, 118. *to stage me to their eyes*, Meas. I, 1, 69. *think me honoured*, H6A II, 3, 81. *I wean me from despair*, H6C IV, 4, 17. *will wing me to some bough*, Wint. V, 3, 133. *wishing me like to one more rich*, Sonn. 29, 5. *I'll withdraw me*, H6A IV, 2, 8. *I yoke me in my brother's fault*, Cymb. IV, 2, 19 etc. — Dative: *I will buy me a son in law*, Alls V, 3, 148. *I can buy me twenty*, Mcb. IV, 2, 40. *I'll get me one of such another length*, Gent. III, 1, 133. IV, 4, 196. *make me a willow cabin*, Tw. I, 5, 287. *to procure me grace*, H6A I, 4, 7.

The dat. *me* used like the Latin dativus commodi et incommodi: *which is not yet performed me*, Tp. I, 2, 244. *to do me business in the veins o' the earth*, 255. *hark what thou else shalt do me*, 495. *will either of you bear me a challenge to him?* Tw. III, 2, 43. *heat me these irons hot*, John IV, 1, 1. *how this river comes me cranking in*, H4A III, 1, 98. *runs me up with like advantage on the other side*, 108. *I press me none but good householders*, IV, 2, 16. *the sack that thou hast drunk me would have bought me lights as cheap*, III, 3, 51. And hence, like the Latin dativus ethicus, superfluous as to the general sense, but imparting a lively colour to the expression: *he steps me to her trencher*, Gent. IV, 4, 9. *he thrusts me himself into the company*, 18. *goes me to the fellow*, 26. *he makes me no more ado*, 30. *humour me the angels*, Wiv. I, 3, 64. *I have writ me here a letter*, 65. *comes me in the instant of our encounter*, III, 5, 73. *pluck me out all the linen*, IV, 2, 155. *touch me his finger-end*, V, 5, 88. *awakes me all the enrolled penalties*, Meas. I, 2, 170. *come me to what was done to her*, II, 1, 121. *leave me your snatches*, IV, 2, 6. *comes me the prince*, Ado I, 3, 61. *I whipt me behind the arras*, 63 (Ff. *whipt behind*). *she leans me out at her mistress' window*, III, 3, 155. *study me how to please the eye*, LLL I, 1, 80. *the skilful shepherd peeled me certain wands*, Merch. I, 3, 85. *give me your present to one Master Bassanio*, II, 2, 115. *knock me here soundly*, Shr. I, 2, 8. *sayest me so?* 190. *hop me over every kennel home*, IV, 3, 98. *swinge me them soundly forth*, V, 2, 104. *deliver me this paper*, Alls V, 2, 16. *build me thy fortunes upon the basis of valour*, Tw. III, 2, 35. *challenge me the count's youth*, 36. *scout me for him at the corner of the orchard*, III, 4, 193. *hear me this*, V, 123. *imagine me, gentle spectators, that I now may be in fair Bohemia*, Wint. IV, 1, 19. *he that kills me some six or seven dozen of Scots*, H4A II, 4, 115. *I made me no more ado*, 223. *I followed me close*, 241. *rob me the exchequer*, III, 3, 205. *he steps me a little higher*, IV, 3, 75. *cut me off the heads of all the favourites*, 85. *cut me off the villain's head*, H4B II, 1, 51. *it ascends me into the brain, dries me there all the crudy vapours*, IV, 3, 105. *convey me Salisbury into his tent*, H6A I, 4, 110. *say'st thou me so?* H6B II, 1, 109. *leap me over this stool*, 144. *a strange fellow here writes me*, Troil. III, 3, 96. *they set me up, in policy, that mongrel cur Ajax*, V, 4, 13. *I pried me through the crevice of a wall*, Tit. V, 1, 114. *rests me his minim rest*, Rom. II, 4, 22. *claps me his sword upon the table*, III, 1, 6. *where I have learned me to repent the sin*, IV, 2, 17. *strike me the counterfeit matron*, Tim. IV, 3, 112. *he plucked me ope his doublet*, Caes. I, 2, 267. *you'll bear me a bang for that*, III, 3, 20. *the cloudy messenger turns me his back*, Mcb. III, 6, 41. *inquire me first what Danskers are in Paris*, Hml. II, 1, 7. *wind me into him*, Lr. I, 2, 106. *draw me a clothier's yard*, IV, 6, 88. *whip me such honest knaves*, Oth. I, 1, 49. *I fear me*, see under *Fear*.

Iachimo (trisyll.), name in Cymb. I, 4, 184. II, 4, 26. II, 5, 14. III, 4, 48. IV, 2, 340. V, 4, 63. V, 5, 411.

Iago (trisyll.; dissyll. in Oth. V, 2, 154) name in Oth. I, 1, 2 etc. etc.

Icarus, the son of Daedalus, drowned in the sea, when he attempted, after his father's example, to fly on wings: H6A IV, 6, 55. IV, 7, 16. H6C V, 6, 21.

Ice, congealed water: Gent. III, 2, 7. Meas. II, 1, 39. III, 1, 123. III, 2, 118. Mids. V, 59. Shr. IV, 1, 14. H5 IV, 1, 212. Cor. I, 1, 177. Tim. IV, 3, 226. Symbol of coldness: *boys of i.* Alls II, 3, 99. *thou art all i.* R3 IV, 2, 22. of chastity: *the very i. of chastity is in them*, As III, 4, 18. *as chaste as i.* Hml. III, 1, 140 (cf. *icicle* in Cor. V, 3, 65). *to break the ice* = to open the way: Shr. I, 2, 267. Troil. III, 3, 215. *to smooth the i.* = to do a thing superfluous: John IV, 2, 13.

Ice-brook, frozen brook: *a sword of Spain, the —'s temper*, Oth. V, 2, 253 (the allusion is to the ancient Spanish custom of hardening steel by plunging it red-hot in the rivulet Salo near Bilbilis).

Iceland dog, a sort of shaggy, sharp-eared, white dogs, much imported at that time from Iceland as lap-dogs for ladies: H5 II, 1, 44.

Icicle, a hanging conical mass of ice: LLL V, 2, 922. Merch. II, 1, 5. Tw. III, 2, 29. H5 III, 5, 23. Cor. V, 3, 65.

Icy, cold, frosty, frigid: Mids. II, 1, 109. As II, 1, 6. John V, 7, 37. R3 III, 1, 176 (O. Edd. *icy, cold;* some M. Edd. *icy-cold*). Tim. IV, 3, 258. Oth. III, 3, 454.

Idea, image: *the i. of her life shall sweetly creep into his study of imagination*, Ado IV, 1, 226. *a foolish extravagant spirit, full of forms, figures, shapes, objects, —s, apprehensions, motions, revolutions*, LLL IV, 2, 69. *I did infer your lineaments, being the right i. of your father, both in your form and nobleness of mind*, R3 III, 7, 13.

Iden, name in H6B IV, 10, 46. 77. V, 1, 74. 78. 81.

Ides of March, the fifteenth day of March in the Roman calendar: Caes. I, 2, 18. 19. 23. II, 1, 40 (O. Edd. *first of March*). III, 1, 1. IV, 3, 18. V, 1, 113.

Idiot, a stupid person, a natural, a fool: *he with the Romans was esteemed so as silly jeering —s are with kings, for sportive words and uttering foolish things*, Lucr. 1812. *Slender, though well landed, is an i.* Wiv. IV, 4, 86. *coxcomb, i., patch*, Err. III, 1, 32. *the portrait of a blinking i.* Merch. II, 9, 54. Tw. II, 5, 23. John III, 3, 45. Troil. II, 1, 58 (*Mars his i.* = Mars' licensed fool). III, 3, 135. Tit. V, 1, 79. Mcb. V, 5, 27. Cymb. I, 6, 42.

Idiot-worshipper, one who worships fools: Troil. V, 1, 7.

Idle, adj. 1) not occupied, inactive, lazy, doing nothing: *to take advantage of all i. hours*, Ven. Ded. 4. *cite each moving sense from i. rest*, Pilgr. 195. *no occupation, all men i.* Tp. II, 1, 154. 166. Gent. II, 1, 172. II, 4, 64. Wiv. III, 2, 13. R2 III, 4, 66. H4A V, 3, 41. H5 IV, 2, 31. H6B II, 4, 47. H6C II, 1, 131. R3 III, 7, 76. Cor. I, 1, 102. I, 3, 76. Tit. III, 1, 172. Rom. I, 4, 97. Caes. I, 1, 1. II, 1, 117.

2) useless, unprofitable, vain, futile: *leave this i. theme, this bootless chat*, Ven. 422. 770. *who hath she to spend the night withal but i. sounds*, 848. *out, i. words, servants to shallow fools*, Lucr. 1016. *shall above that i. rank remain*, Sonn. 122, 3. *held in i. price to haunt assemblies*, Meas. I, 3, 9. *an i. plume which the air beats for vain*, II, 4, 11. *to draw with i. spiders' strings most ponderous and substantial things*, III, 2, 289. *it is dross, usurping ivy, brier, or i. moss*, Err. II, 2, 180. *these oaths and laws will prove an i. scorn*, LLL I, 1, 311. *critic Timon laugh at i. toys*, IV, 3, 170. *will hear your i. scorns*, V, 2, 875. *never did mockers waste more i. breath*, Mids. III, 2, 168. *as the remembrance of an i. gaud*, IV, 1, 172. *this weak and i. theme*, V, 434. *I will weary you then no longer with i. talking*, As V, 2, 57. *your store, I think, is not for i. markets*, Tw. III, 3, 46. *strain their cheeks to i. merriment*, John III, 3, 46. *repent at i. times*, H4B II, 2, 140. *every i., nice and wanton reason*, IV, 1, 191. *the i. pleasures of these days*, R3 I, 1, 31. *i. weeds are fast in growth*, III, 1, 103. *thou i. immaterial skein of sleave-silk*, Troil. V, 1, 38. *there is an i. banquet*, Tim. I, 2, 160 (= trifling, insignificant). *they pass by me as the i. wind*, Caes. IV, 3, 68. *all the i. weeds that grow in our sustaining corn*, Lr. IV, 4, 5. *the unnumbered i. pebbles*, IV, 6, 21. *mine's not an i. cause*, Oth. I, 2, 95. *antres vast and deserts i.* I, 3, 140 (F2.3.4 *wild*). *if i. talk will once be necessary*, Ant. V, 2, 50.

3) wanting becoming seriousness and gravity, thoughtless, silly, absurd, foolish: *to find out shames*

and i. hours in me, Sonn. 61, 7. *make thee the father of their i. dreams*, Meas. IV, 1, 64. *shrive you of a thousand i. pranks*, Err. II, 2, 210. *heaven cease this i. humour in your honour*, Shr. Ind. 2, 14. *very i. words*, 85. *virginity is peevish, proud, i., made of self-love*, Alls I, 1, 157. *an i. lord*, II, 5, 54. *in his i. fire, to buy his will, it would not seem too dear*, III, 7, 26. *a foolish i. boy*, IV, 3, 242. *you are i. shallow things*, Tw. III, 4, 136. *fancies too green and i. for girls of nine*, Wint. III, 2, 182. *full of i. dreams*, John IV, 2, 145. *i. dreamer*, 153. *the i. comments that it* (his brain) *makes*, V, 7, 4. *and therefore is he i.?* R3 III, 1, 105. *if you love an addle egg as well as you love an i. head*, Troil. I, 2, 147. *I am no i. votarist*, Tim. IV, 3, 27. *looked upon this love with i. sight*, Hml. II, 2, 138 (wanting seriousness, taking it for a jest). *they are coming to the play; I must be i.* III, 2, 95. *you answer with an i. tongue*, III, 4, 11. *an i. and fond bondage*, Lr. I, 2, 51. *i. old man*, I, 3, 16. *reputation is an i. and most false imposition*, Oth. II, 3, 269.

Idle, vb. to be to no purpose, to play, to dally: *the gossamer that —s in the air*, Rom. II, 6, 19.

Idle-headed, foolish: *the superstitious i. eld*, Wiv. IV, 4, 36.

Idleness, 1) absence of employment, state of being unoccupied: Gent. I, 1, 8. As I, 1, 37. Shr. I, 1, 157. John IV, 3, 70. Ant. I, 2, 134. I, 4, 76.

2) want of cultivation: *conceives by i.* H5 V, 2, 51. *sterile with i., or manured with industry*, Oth. I, 3, 328.

3) frivolousness, want of gravity, vanity: *for want of other i., I'll bide your proof*, Tw. I, 5, 70. *uphold the unyoked humour of your i.* H4A I, 2, 220. *apes of i.* H4B IV, 5, 123. *but that your royalty holds i. your subject, I should take you for i. itself*, Ant. I, 2, 92. 93.

Love in i. = the flower viola tricolor: Mids. II, 1, 168; cf. Shr. I, 1, 156.

Idly, 1) without employment, lazily: Shr. I, 1, 155. H6A I, 1, 142. I, 2, 13. Troil. III, 3, 233. Cor. II, 2, 80.

2) unprofitably, vainly, frivolously: *redeem in gentle numbers time so i. spent*, Sonn. 100, 6. *mocking the air with colours i. spread*, John V, 1, 72. *so i. to profane the precious time*, H4B II, 4, 391.

3) unreasonably, foolishly, thoughtlessly: *how i. do they talk!* Err. IV, 4, 132. *I talk but i., and you laugh at me*, R2 III, 3, 171. H4B II, 2, 32. *she is so i. kinged, her sceptre so fantastically borne*, H5 II, 4, 26.

4) carelessly, regardlessly, slightly, at random, by the way: *but this from rumour's tongue I i. heard: if true or false I know not*, John IV, 2, 124 (Germ. obenhin). *the eyes of men are i. bent on him that enters next*, R2 V, 2, 25. *King Pharamond, i. supposed the founder of this law*, H5 I, 2, 59. *his guilt should be but i. posted over*, H6B III, 1, 255. *a thing slipped i. from me*, Tim. I, 1, 20.

Idol, 1) an image worshipped as God, a false God: *well-painted i., image dull and dead*, Ven. 212. Sonn. 105, 2. Gent. IV, 2, 129. Tw. III, 4, 399. H5 IV, 1, 257. Troil. V, 1, 7.

2) a person worshipped to adoration: Gent. II, 4, 144. Troil. II, 3, 199. Hml. II, 2, 109.

Idolatrous, addicted to the worship of an idol: *my i. fancy*, Alls I, 1, 108.

Idolatry, worship of an idol, excessive veneration: Sonn. 105, 1. Gent. IV, 4, 205. LLL IV, 3, 75. Mids. I, 1, 109. Troil. II, 2, 56. Rom. II, 2, 114.

If, 1) hypothetical conjunction, = in case that· followed by an indic. to express absolute assurance and certainty: *if I have ranged, like him that travels I return again*, Sonn. 109, 5 (= it being so that I have ranged; having, as I confess, ranged). *O sweet-suggesting love, if thou hast sinned, teach me to excuse it*, Gent. II, 6, 7. *if every one knows us and we know none, 'tis time to trudge*, Err. III, 2, 157. *if I stand here, I saw him*, Mcb. III, 4, 74 (= as sure as I stand here). cf. *if he had spoke, the wolf would leave his prey*, Ven. 1097 (almost = when, and alternating with when). Followed indiscriminately, or at least with a difference merely theoretical, by the indic. or subj., when the supposition admits of doubt; f.i. by the indic.: *if no harder than a stone thou art, melt at my tears*, Lucr. 593. *if thou more murmurest, I will rend an oak*, Tp. I, 2, 294. *if thou art changed to aught, 'tis to an ass*, Err. II, 2, 201. *if she lives till doomsday she'll burn a week longer than the whole world*, Err. III, 2, 100. *arrest me if thou darest*, IV, 1, 75; cf. Mids. III, 2, 422; R2 IV, 48; 56; 71; H6B III, 2, 201; 228. *if thou lovest me, steal forth thy father's house*, Mids. I, 1, 163. *if truth holds true contents*, As V, 4, 136. *if she dares trust me with her little babe*, Wint. II, 2, 37. *if thou dost love thy lord, banish the canker of ambitious thoughts*, H6B I, 2, 17. *if thou dost nod, thou breakest thy instrument*, Caes. IV, 3, 271. Subjunctive: *if the first heir of my invention prove deformed, I shall be sorry it had so noble a god-father*, Ven. Ded. 4. *that posterity which thou must have, if thou destroy them not*, Ven. 760. *if love have lent you twenty thousand tongues, yet from my ear the tempting tune is blown*, 775. *if Collatinus dream of my intent, will he not wake?* Lucr. 218. *thus I forestall thee, if thou mean to chide*, 484. *if he mount he dies*, 508. *if thou deny, then force must work my way*, 513. *if thou yield, I rest thy secret friend*, 526. *lasting shame on thee I will inflict, if thou my love's desire do contradict*, 1631. *if it so hap*, Tp. I, 1, 28. *if the ill spirit have so fair a house, good things will strive to dwell with it*, I, 2, 458. *if he have never drunk wine before, it will go near to remove his fit*, II, 2, 77. *if he awake, from toe to crown he'll fill our skins with pinches*, IV, 232. *if he make this good, he is as worthy for an empress*, Gent. II, 4, 75. *if he say Ay, it will*, II, 5, 36. *win her with gifts, if she respect not words*. III, 1, 89. *if she do frown, 'tis not in hate of you*, 96. 98. *no Valentine, if Silvia have forsworn me*, 214. *here if thou stay, thou canst not see thy love*, 244. *she'll think that it is spoke in hate. Ay, if his enemy deliver it*, III, 2, 35. *if thou scorn our courtesy, thou diest*, IV, 1, 68. *which, if my augury deceive me not, witness good bringing up*, IV, 4, 73. *if shame live in a disguise of love*, V, 4, 106. *if money go before, all ways do lie open*, Wiv. II, 2, 174. *if he start, it is the flesh of a corrupted heart*, V, 5, 90. *if power change purpose*, Meas. I, 3, 54. *if it confess a natural guiltiness*, II, 2, 138. *if ever he return*, III, 1, 197. *if the encounter acknowledge itself hereafter*, 261. *if he entreat you to his bed*, 274. *if the devil have given thee proofs for sin, thou wilt prove his*, III, 2, 31. *if he chance to fail, he hath sentenced himself*, 271. *if any thing fall to you upon this, I will plead against it*, IV, 2, 190. *if any Syracusian born come to the bay of Ephesus, he dies*, Err. I, 1, 19. *if it prove so, I will be gone the sooner*, I, 2, 103. *if thou live to see like right bereft, this fool-begged* patience in thee will be left, II, 1, 40. if aught possess thee from me, it is dross, II, 2, 179. if a crow help us in, we'll pluck a crow together, III, 1, 83. let love be drowned, if she sink, III, 2, 52. an if the wind blow any way from shore, I will not harbour in this town to-night, 153. if any hour meet a sergeant, a' turns back, IV, 2, 56. if thou follow me, I shall do thee mischief, Mids. II, 1, 236. if but once thou show me thy grey light, I'll find Demetrius, III, 2, 419. if he come not, the play is marred, IV, 2, 5. if this young gentleman have done offence, I take the fault on me, Tw. III, 4, 343. if the rascal have not given me medicines, I'll be hanged, H4A II, 2, 18. if thou love me, practise an answer, II, 4, 411. if thou have power to raise him, bring him hither, III, 1, 60. that you shall read in your own losses, if he stay in France, H5 II, 4, 139. what dares not Warwick, if false Suffolk dare him? H6B III, 2, 203. if she have restrained the riots of your followers, 'tis on such grounds as clears her, Lr. II, 4, 144. Be and were, as ambiguous forms (see Be), may be only mentioned by the way: Ven. 417. Lucr. 158. Tp. I, 1, 35. III, 2, 7. IV, 161. Gent. I, 1, 107. II, 4, 103. III, 1, 174. 352. IV, 2, 120. IV, 4, 195. V, 4, 74. Meas. I, 1, 23. Err. II, 2, 144. H4B V, 2, 65. Lucr. 587. Sonn. 127, 2. Gent. IV, 1, 30 etc. Indic. and subjunctive alternating: if there be nothing new, but that which is hath been before, how are our brains beguiled, Sonn. 59, 1. if thou dost him any slight disgrace or if he do not mightily grace himself on thee, he will practise against thee, As I, 1, 154; cf. Meas. III, 2, 37. The same uncertainty, as of a thought conceived, not a fact ascertained, expressed by shall, should and may following: if all these petty ills shall change thy good, thy sea within a puddle's womb is hearsed, Lucr. 656. and much please the absent duke, if peradventure he shall ever return, Meas. III, 1, 210. if we shall stand still, we should take root here, H8 I, 2, 85. if it should thunder as it did before, I know not where to hide my head, Tp. II, 2, 22. if in Naples I should report this, would they believe me? III, 3, 27. if I should take a displeasure against you, look you, IV, 202. 'twere false, if I should speak it, Gent. IV, 2, 107. I would not spare my brother in this case, if he should scorn me so apparently, Err. IV. 1, 78. beshrew my hand, if it should give your age such cause of fear, Ado V, 1, 56. Shr. Ind. 1, 99. H4B I, 3, 78. Cor. IV, 6, 111. he shall know you better, if I may live to report you, Meas. III, 2, 171. — A supposition contrary to reality and fact expressed by the subjunctive of the imperf. or pluperf.: if thou wert the lion, the fox would beguile thee, Tim. IV, 3, 330; cf. Merch. II, 1, 17. Cor. II, 2, 18 etc. — if not = or even: one word more shall make me chide thee, if not hate thee, Tp. I, 2, 476. If that, see That.

Omitted, with inversion of the subject: did I tell this, who would believe me? Meas. II, 4, 171. prove you that any man with me conversed, refuse me, Ado IV, 1, 183. prove it so, let fortune go to hell for it, not I, Merch. III, 2, 20. live thou, I live, 61. we will persuade him, be it possible, to put on better (attire) Shr. III, 2, 127. you'll be found, be you beneath the sky, Wint. I, 2, 180. be she honour-flawed, they'll pay for it, II, 1, 143. hold out my horse, and I will first be there, R2 II, 1, 300. were growing time once ripened to my will, H6A II, 4, 99. within thine eye sat twenty thousand deaths, I would say thou liest, Cor. III, 3, 70.

wert thou a bear, thou wouldst be killed by the horse, Tim. IV, 3, 341. go not my horse the better, I must become a borrower of the night, Mcb. III, 1, 26. do we but find the tyrant's power to-night, let us be beaten, if we cannot fight, V, 6, 7. live Roderigo, he calls me to a restitution, Oth. V, 1, 14. prove this a prosperous day, the world shall bear the olive freely, Ant. IV, 6, 6. come more, for more you're ready, Cymb. IV, 3, 30. take I your wish, I leap into the seas, Per. II, 4, 43. Indicative: pleaseth you walk with me down to his house, I will discharge my bond, Err. IV, 1, 12 (cf. Please).

2) concessive particle, = allowing that, though: I will give him some relief, if it be but for that, Tp. II, 2, 70. cf. sub 1, indic. after if.

3) whether: my love's sweet face survey, if time have any wrinkle graven there, Sonn. 100, 10. in doubt if best were as it was, Compl. 98. my prayer may know if you remain upon this island, Tp. I, 2, 423. 427. Meas. II, 3, 22. III, 2, 180. IV, 3, 112. Mids. III, 2, 1. Merch. II, 7, 10. As I, 1, 110. H4A II, 2, 34 (Q1 canst, the other O. Edd. can) etc. If... or = whether ... or: if friend or foe, let him be gently used, H6C II, 6, 45. they know if dearth or foison follow, Ant. II, 7, 22. Omitted: he left this ring behind him, would I or not, Tw. I, 5, 321. dost thou or dost thou not, heaven's curse upon thee, Tim. IV, 3, 131.

If, used as a subst.: you may avoid that too with an If, As V, 4, 103. tellest thou me of Ifs, R3 III, 4, 77.

Ignoble, 1) of low or dishonourable descent: H6A III, 1, 178. V, 4, 7. H6C IV, 1, 70. R3 III, 7, 127.

2) base, despicable: Tp. I, 2, 116. Wint. II, 3, 120. H6B II, 1, 13. III, 2, 210. R3 III, 5, 22.

Ignobly, basely, disgracefully: H6A II, 5, 35. H6B V, 2, 23. Tim. II, 2, 183. Lr. III, 7, 35.

Ignominious, scandalous, dishonourable: with other vile and i. terms, H6A IV, 1, 97. with i. words, H6B III, 1, 179. base and i. treasons, IV, 8, 66.

Ignominy, disgrace, dishonour: thy i. sleep with thee in the grave, H4A V, 4, 100 (Ff ignomy, which suits the metre better). i. and shame pursue thy life, Troil. V, 10, 33 (Ff ignomy). I blush to think upon this i. Tit. IV, 2, 115 (Qq ignomy).

Ignomy, disgrace, dishonour: Meas. II, 4, 111 (F2.3.4 ignominy, which suits the verse better). H4A V, 4, 100 (Qq ignominy). Troil. V, 10, 33 (Q ignominy). Tit. IV, 2, 115 (Ff ignominy).

Ignorance, 1) want of knowledge concerning some particular thing: his i. were wise, LLL II, 102. let me not burst in i. Hml. I, 4, 46.

2) want of knowledge and culture of the mind generally: Sonn. 78, 14. Wiv. I, 1, 182. LLL IV, 2, 24. John IV, 2, 59. R2 I, 3, 168. H4A III, 1, 213. H6B IV, 2, 178. IV, 7, 78. Tim. V, 4, 69. Cymb. III, 3, 33.

3) want of experience and skill, the state of not knowing what to do or how to behave: and heavy i. aloft to fly, Sonn. 78, 6. thine i. makes thee away, Alls I, 1, 226. I will throw thee from my care for ever into the staggers and the careless lapse of youth and i. II, 3, 171. if he have power, then vail your i.; if none, awake your dangerous lenity, Cor. III, 1, 98. set a-fire by thine own i. Rom. III, 3, 133. in mine i. your skill (in fencing) shall stick fiery off, Hml. V, 2, 266.

4) want of discernment, incapacity of distinguish-

ing between right and wrong, unconsciousness, simplicity: *I do suspect I have done some offence, and that you come to reprehend my i.* R3 III, 7, 113. *make your wantonness your i.* Hml. III, 1, 152. *errs in i. and not in cunning,* Oth. III, 3, 49.

5) stupidity, silliness: *i. itself is a plummet o'er me,* Wiv. V, 5, 172. *now his knowledge must prove i.* LLL II, 103. *thrust thy sharp wit quite through my i.* V, 2, 398. *there is no darkness but i.* Tw. IV, 2, 47. 49. 50. *leave those remnants of fool and feather with all their honorable points of i.* H8 I, 3, 26. *fonder than i.* Troil. I, 1, 10. *which short-armed i. itself knows,* II, 3, 16. *the common curse of mankind, folly and i.* 31. *such a valiant i.* III, 3, 316. *cannot conclude but by the yea and no of general i.* Cor. III, 1, 146. *till your i. deliver you to some nation,* III, 3, 129. *who resist are mocked for valiant i.* IV, 6, 104. *in a violent popular i.* V, 2, 43. *it was great i. to let him live,* Lr. IV, 5, 9. *O heavy i.! thou praisest the worst best,* Oth. II, 1, 144. *fools as gross as ignorance made drunk,* III, 3, 405. *the greater cantle of the world is lost with very i.* Ant. III, 10, 7.

Ignorant, 1) not knowing, unacquainted, not informed; absol.: *I am i. and cannot guess,* H6A II, 5, 60. *this i. present,* Mcb. I, 5, 58. Ant. II, 2, 96. Cymb. IV, 3, 11. *the i.* H4A IV, 1, 74. Hml. II, 2, 591. Followed by *in,* = not expert in: *i. in that,* Wint. II, 3, 69. *I am i. in what I am commanded,* Cymb. III, 2, 23. By *of,* = not knowing: Tp. I, 2, 18. Meas. IV, 3, 113. Merch. I, 1, 167. Shr. II, 58. All's IV, 1, 38. H6B IV, 2, 152. Mcb. I, 5, 13. Lr. I, 4, 295. Ant. II, 1, 5. By a dependent clause: Gent. I, 3, 25. II, 1, 116. III, 2, 25. IV, 3, 14. Err. I, 1, 74. LLL II, 21. 101. Wint. III, 2, 77. Hml. V, 2, 139. 143. Lr. IV, 7, 65.

2) wanting knowledge generally, untaught, unlearned: Pilgr. 65 and LLL IV, 2, 117. Tp. III, 2, 28. Meas. III, 2, 147. LLL IV, 2, 52. H8 I, 2, 72.

3) unconscious: *the i. fumes that mantle their clearer reason,* Tp. V, 67 (i. e. fumes of unconsciousness). With *of: most i. of what he's most assured, his glassy essence,* Meas. II, 2, 119.

4) dull, silly, simple: *either you are i. or seem so craftily,* Meas. II, 4, 74. 76. *this letter, being so excellently i.* Tw. III, 4, 207. *either thou art most i. by age, or thou wert born a fool,* Wint. II, 1, 173. *either wise bearing or i. carriage is caught,* H4B V, 1, 84. *were you i. to see it,* Cor. II, 3, 182. *revoke your i. election,* 227. *the eyes of the i. more learned than the ears,* III, 2, 76. *as i. as dirt,* Oth. V, 2. 164. *his shipping, poor i. baubles,* Cymb. III, 1, 27 (silly, foolish).

5) not known, undiscovered: *imprison 't not in i. concealment,* Wint. I, 2, 397. *what i. sin have I committed?* Oth. IV, 2, 70.

'Ild, see *Godild.*

Iliad, see *Oeillade.*

Ilion (O. Edd. *Illion*) the royal palace in Troy: Lucr. 1370. 1524. LLL V, 2, 658. Troil. II, 2, 109. IV, 4, 118. IV, 5, 112. 216. V, 8, 11.

Ilium, or **Illium** (both spellings in O. Edd.), the royal palace in Troy: Troil. I, 1, 104. I, 2, 46. 50. 194. Hml. II, 2, 496.

Ill, subst. 1) any evil, misfortune, pain, disease etc.: *O benefit of ill! now I find true that better is by evil still made better,* Sonn. 119, 9. 14. *that which doth preserve the ill,* 147, 3. *who ever shunned by pre-*

cedent the destined ill she must herself assay?* Compl. 156. *there is some ill a brewing,* Merch. II, 5, 17. *would not this ill do well?* R2 III, 3, 170. H5 IV, 1, 198. H6A II, 5, 129. III, 3, 65. Cor. III, 1, 161. Per. II, 1, 139. 172. Plur. —*s: rather bear those —s we have than fly to others,* Hml. III, 1, 81. *ten thousand harms, more than the —s I know,* Ant. I, 2, 133.

2) a moral evil, wickedness: *whose inward ill no outward harm expressed,* Lucr. 91. *they all rate his ill,* 304. *then had they seen the period of their ill,* 380. *under what colour he commits this ill,* 476. *him that thou taughtest this ill,* 996. *my blood shall wash the slander of mine ill,* 1207. *call them not the authors of their ill,* 1244. *in whom all ill well shows,* Sonn. 40, 13. *he thinks no ill,* 57, 14. *captive good attending captain ill,* 66, 12. *if some suspect of ill masked not thy show,* 70, 13. 118, 12. Tp. I, 2, 353. Ado II, 1, 159. LLL II, 58. IV, 1, 35. IV, 3, 124. John III, 1, 272. R2 I, 1, 86. I, 3, 189. H6B I, 2, 19. II, 3, 91. R3 III, 4, 69 (Qq *this ill,* Ff *their evil*). Tit. V, 1, 127. Rom. IV, 5, 94. Tim. III, 5, 37. Mcb. III, 2, 55. Per. I, 1, 77. Plur. —*s: if all these petty —s shall change thy good,* Lucr. 656. *to anticipate the —s that were not,* Sonn. 118, 10. *the —s we do, their —s instruct us so,* Oth. IV, 3, 104. *our —s told us is as our earing,* Ant. I, 2, 114. *second —s with —s,* Cymb. V, 1, 14.

Ill, adj. 1) bad, evil in a general sense, contrary to good: *this is too curious-good, this blunt and ill,* Lucr. 1300. *your pleasure, be it ill or well,* Sonn. 58, 14. *what care I who calls me well or ill?* 112, 13. *I am ill at reckoning,* LLL I, 2, 42; cf. *I am ill at these numbers,* Hml. II, 2, 120. *shooting well is then accounted ill,* LLL IV, 1, 25. *a mingled yarn, good and ill together,* All's IV, 3, 84. *they were ill for a green wound,* H4B II, 1, 106. *nothing can be ill,* Rom. V, 1, 17. *nothing ill come near thee,* Cymb. IV, 2, 279. Joined to substantives: *an ill advantage,* Wiv. III, 3, 116. *aspects,* Troil. I, 3, 92. *beginning,* Caes. IV, 3, 234. *chances,* H4B IV, 2, 81. *conditions,* Ado III, 2, 68. *cook,* Rom. IV, 2, 3. 6. *counsel,* Mids. II, 1, 218. Tw. V, 34. *day,* Err. V, 138. *dealing,* R3 III, 6, 14 (Qq *bad*). *deed,* Sonn. 34, 14. Err. III, 2, 20. John IV, 2, 219. H4B V, 2, 83. R3 I, 4, 216. *digestions,* Err. V, 74. *doctrine,* H8 I, 3, 60. *end,* John III, 1, 94. *event,* Lucr. 1598. H6A IV, 1, 191. *fashion,* Gent. V, 4, 61. *fortune,* H6A III, 2, 109. *friends,* R3 IV, 4, 216 (Qq *bad*). *hap,* H8 Epil. 13. *hours,* Tw. I, 3, 6. *husband,* H8 III, 2, 142. *intent,* Per. IV, 6, 116. *layer up,* H5 V, 2, 248. *life,* Wiv. II, 2, 92. *luck,* Wiv. V, 5, 120. Merch. III, 1, 98. 102. 104. H4B I, 1, 51. *manner,* Tw. I, 5, 62. *men,* Cymb. V, 5, 159. *name,* H4B II, 4, 98. *neighbourhood,* H5 I, 2, 154. *news,* Ado II, 1, 180. John IV, 2, 134. V, 6, 21. Rom. V, 1, 22. *night,* John V, 4, 36. *office,* Gent. III, 2, 40. H5 V, 2, 391. *officers,* Caes. IV, 2, 7. *opinion,* Wiv. II, 1, 73. H8 II, 2, 125. Troil. V, 4, 19. *phrase,* Hml. II, 2, 111. *planet,* Wint. II, 1, 106. *presage,* Ven. 457. *qualities,* Ado II, 1, 106. *report,* Sonn. 95, 8. Cor. I, 6, 70. Hml. II, 2, 550. Ant. II, 2, 159. *request,* Caes. V, 5, 11. *rest,* R3 I, 2, 112. *shape,* LLL II, 59. *singer,* Ado II, 3, 78. *suspicion,* Wint. V, 3, 149. *tale,* R2 III, 2, 121. *things,* Sonn. 150, 5. Rom. II, 4, 179. V, 3, 136. *thinking,* Oth. III, 4, 29. *thoughts,* Lr. V, 2, 9. *tidings,* John IV, 2, 132. Ant. II, 5, 87. *time,* Wint. III, 3, 3. *turn,* Per. IV, 1, 76. *venture,* H4B

V, 5, 127. *will*, As III, 5, 71. All's V, 3, 265. H5 III, 7, 123. *wind*, H4B V, 3, 90. *word*, Ado III, 1, 86.

2) evil in a moral sense, wicked: *end thy ill aim*, Lucr. 579. *a mind so ill*, 1530. *there's nothing ill can dwell in such a temple*, Tp. I, 2, 457. *the ill spirit*, 458. *upon ill employment*, Wiv. V, 5, 135. *a very ill house*, Meas II, 1, 67. *his ill angel*, H4B I, 2, 186. 187. *of his own body he was ill*, H8 IV, 2, 43. *ill spirit*, Caes. IV, 3, 289. *cannot be ill, cannot be good*, Mcb. I, 3, 131.

3) unwell, sick, diseased (adv.? never before the subst.): *I am ill*, Ado III, 4, 54. H4B III, 1, 104. IV, 2, 80. IV, 4, 111. H5 II, 1, 89. Lr. III, 3, 18. Ant. I, 3, 72. Cymb. IV, 2, 11. *grew so ill*, H8 IV, 2, 15. *you look very ill*, Wiv. II, 1, 36. *I see thee ill*, R2 II, 1, 92. 93. 94.

Ill, adv. not well, not rightly, badly: *speak ill of thee*, Sonn. 140, 10. Tw. III, 4, 111. *how likes she my discourse? ill*, Gent. V, 2, 16. *ill killed*, Wiv. I, 1, 84. *you do ill*, IV, 1, 67. All's I, 1, 165. Wint. IV, 4, 310. John IV, 2, 220. Per. I, 1, 104. *he takes it ill*, Err. II, 1, 12. Tim. V, 1, 93. Lr. II, 2, 152. 166. Ant. II, 2, 29. III, 3, 38. *how ill agrees it with your gravity*, Err. II, 2, 170. *suit ill spent and labour ill bestowed*, Ado III, 2, 103. *how doth your cousin? very ill*, V, 2, 92. *nothing becomes him ill*, LLL II, 46. IV, 2, 31. *to teach a teacher ill beseemeth me*, II, 108. H6A IV, 1, 31. *ill met*, Mids. II, 1, 60. *nought shall go ill*, III, 2, 462. *O knowledge ill inhabited*, As III, 3, 10. *it looks ill*, All's I, 1, 175. Tim. I, 2, 58. *when I did love you ill*, All's IV, 2, 27. *you have them ill to friend*, V, 3, 182. *we have run so ill*, John III, 4, 5. *use me ill*, IV, 1, 55. *ill left*, R2 II, 3, 154. *how ill it follows*, H4B II, 2, 31. *dies ill*, H5 IV, 1, 197. *ill blows the wind*, H6C II, 5, 55. *how ill this taper burns*, Caes. IV, 3, 275 etc.

Ill-annexed, mischievously added or joined: Lucr. 874.

Ill-beseeming, unbecoming: H4B IV, 1, 84. H6C I, 4, 113. Rom. I, 5, 76. III, 3, 113. In H6A IV, 1, 31 not hyphened.

Ill-boding, inauspicious: H6A IV, 5, 6. H6C II, 6, 59.

Ill-breeding, hatching mischief: *i. minds*, Hml. IV, 5, 15.

Ill-composed, consisting of evil ingredients: *my most i. affection*, Mcb. IV, 3, 77.

Ill-dispersing, miserably severing and scattering friends: *i. wind of misery*, R3 IV, 1, 53.

Ill-disposed, unwell, somewhat sick: Troil. II, 3, 84.

Ill-divining, misgiving: *I have an i. soul*, Rom. III, 5, 54.

Ill-doing, wrong: *we knew not the doctrine of i.* Wint. I, 2, 70.

Illegitimate, 1) spurious: Troil. V, 7, 18. 2) not rightly deduced, illogical: *i. construction*, Ado III, 4, 50.

Ill-erected, built to an evil end: *i. tower*, R2 V, 1, 2.

Ill-faced, having an ugly visage: Err. IV, 2, 20.

Ill-favoured, ill-looking, ugly: *that* (to wear a codpiece) *will be i.* Gent. II, 7, 54. *they* (bears) *are very i. rough things*, Wiv. I, 1, 311. *i. faults*, III, 4, 32. *i. children*, As III, 5, 53. *an i. thing*, V, 4, 60. *a shrewd i. wife*, Shr. I, 2, 60. *a black i. fly*, Tit. III, 2, 66.

Ill-favouredly, in a bad and ugly manner: *and*

sped you, sir? very i. Wiv. III, 5, 68. *those that she makes honest she makes very i.* As I, 2, 41. *mar no more of my verses with reading them i.* III, 2, 279. *yon island carrions i. become the morning field*, H5 IV, 2, 40.

Ill-got, gained in a bad way: H6C II, 2, 46.

Ill-headed, having a bad top: *a lance i.* Ado III, 1, 64.

Illiad, see *Oeillade*.

Ill-inhabited, badly lodged: As III, 3, 10.

Ilion and **Ilium,** see *Ilion* and *Ilium*.

Illiterate, ignorant of letters, unlearned: Lucr. 810. Gent. III, 1, 296.

Illness, iniquity, wickedness: *art not without ambition, but without the i. should attend it*, Mcb. I, 5, 21.*

Ill-nurtured, ill-bred, rude, unkind: *i., crooked, churlish*, Ven. 134. *presumptuous dame, i. Eleanor*, H6B I, 2, 42 (cf. *Nurture*).

Illo, halloo: Hml. I, 5, 114 (115: *hillo*).

Ill-resounding, of a disagreeable sound: Ven. 919.

Ill-roasted, not well cooked: *an i. egg*, As III, 2, 38.

Ill-rooted, not firmly rooted: Ant. II, 7, 2.

Ill-seeming, ill-looking: *muddy, i., thick, bereft of beauty*, Shr. V, 2, 143.

Ill-shaped, deformed: Rom. V, 1, 44.

Ill-sheathed, put in a damaged sheath: H4A I, 1, 17.

Ill-spirited, wicked: H4A V, 5, 2.

Ill-starred, unfortunate, unhappy: Oth. V, 2, 272.

Ill-ta'en, misconceived: *his i. suspicion*, Wint. I, 2, 460.

Ill-tempered, in bad temper, out of humour: Caes. IV, 3, 115. 116.

Ill-thought-on (not hyph. in O. Edd.) judged disadvantageously, seen in a bad light: Troil. I, 1, 70.

Ill-tuned, unmelodious: John II, 197.

Illume, to brighten: *to i. that part of heaven where now it burns*, Hml. I, 1, 37.

Illuminate, to give light to, to brighten: *it —th the face*, H4B III, 3, 116 (Q *illumineth*). *to i. so vile a thing as Caesar*, Caes. I, 3, 110.

Illumine, the same: *so is her face —d with her eye*, Ven. 486. *fostered, —d, cherished*, Gent. III, 1, 184. *it —th the face*, H4B IV, 3, 116 (Ff *illuminateth*).

Ill-used, misapplied: Sonn. 95, 14. R3 IV, 4, 396 (Ff *i. repast*, Qq *misused o'erpast*).

Illusion, deceptive appearance, false show: Err. IV, 3, 43. Mids. III, 2, 98. H8 I, 2, 178. Mcb. III, 5, 28. Hml. I, 1, 127.

Illustrate, adj. or partic.; illustrious: LLL IV, 1, 65 (Armado's speech). V, 1, 128 (Holophernes' speech).

Illustrate, vb. to give a clear idea of, to elucidate: *a loyal and obedient subject is therein —d*, H8 III, 2, 181.

Illustrious, 1) excellent, glorious: LLL I, 1, 178. Troil. III, 3, 278. Tim. III, 2, 87. Lr. V, 3, 135.

2) without lustre, wanting brightness: *an eye base and i. as the smoky light that's fed with stinking tallow*, Cymb. I, 6, 109 (M. Edd. *illustrous, inlustrous, unlustrous*).

Ill-uttering, speaking evil things: Ant. II, 5, 35.

Ill-weaved, of a bad texture: *i. ambition*, H4A V, 4, 88 (cf. *my weaved-up folly*, R2 IV, 229).

Ill-well: *you could never do him so i., unless you were the very man*, Ado II, 1, 122, i. e. mimicking so perfectly his peculiarities, in doing which, however, you make a sorry figure.

Ill-will, enmity, rancour: R3 I, 3, 69; not hyphened in As III, 5, 71. All's V, 3, 265. H5 III, 7, 123.

Ill-wresting, misinterpreting to disadvantage: *this i. world is grown so bad, mad slanderers by mad ears believed be,* Sonn. 140, 11.

Illyria, the country in which the comedy of Twelfth Night is laid: I, 2, 2. I, 3, 20. III, 4, 294 etc.

Illyrian, native of Illyria, a country on the Adriatic sea: *Bargulus the strong I. pirate,* H6B IV, 1, 108.

Image, subst. 1) a human figure made by a painter or sculptor: *i. dull and dead,* Ven. 212. *she sees a wretched i. bound,* Lucr. 1501. *the well-skilled workman this mild i. drew for perjured Simon,* 1520. *all this time that she with painted —s hath spent,* 1577. *like a waxen i. 'gainst the fire,* Gent. II, 4, 201. *Pygmalion's —s,* Meas. III, 2, 48. *like an i.* (i. e. dumb) Ado II, 1, 9. *the sight of my poor i. would thus have wrought you,* Wint. V, 3, 57. *glittering like —s,* H4A IV, 1, 100. *like a stony i.* Tit. III, 1, 259. *disrobe the —s,* Caes. I, 1, 69. 73.

2) a picture or statue, or any figure, representing a particular person: *for Achilles' i. stood his spear,* Lucr. 1424. *brazen —s of canonized saints,* H6B I, 3, 63. *make my i. but an alehouse sign,* III, 2, 81. *look in a glass, and call thy i. so,* V, 1, 142. *pulling scarfs off Caesar's —s,* Caes. I, 2, 289.

3) the appearance and semblance of a person: *under whose sharp fangs on his back doth lie an i. like thyself,* Ven. 664. *within his thought her heavenly i. sits,* Lucr. 288. *if in the child the father's i. lies,* 1753. *thine i. dies with thee,* Sonn. 3, 14. *where your true i. pictured lies,* 24, 6. *their —s I loved I view in thee,* 31, 13. *show me your i. in some antique book,* 59, 7. *thy i. should keep open my heavy eyelids,* 61, 1. *now thy i. doth appear in the rare semblance,* Ado V, 1, 259. *to his i. did I devotion,* Tw. III, 4, 396. *your father's i. is so hit in you,* Wint. V, 1, 127. *his dead and earthy i.* H6B III, 2, 147. *from my heart thine i. ne'er shall go,* H6C II, 5, 116. *where fame hath placed thy beauty's i.* III, 3, 64. *long mayst thou live to bear his i.* V, 4, 54. *our last king, whose i. appeared to us,* Hml. I, 1, 81.

4) appearance and semblance of any thing: *the i. of a wicked heinous fault lives in his eye,* John IV, 2, 71. *strange —s of death,* Mcb. I, 3, 97. *by the i. of my cause I see the portraiture of his,* Hml. V, 2, 77. *nothing like the i. and horror of it,* Lr. I, 2, 192. *the —s of revolt,* II, 4, 91.

5) likeness, copy, imitation: *i. of hell* (viz night) Lucr. 764. *coin heaven's i.* (viz men) Meas. II, 4, 45. *grim death, how foul and loathsome is thine i.* (drunken sleep) Shr. Ind. 1, 35. *any branch or i. of thy state,* All's II, 1, 201. *the true and perfect i. of life,* H4A V, 4, 120. *he, the noble i. of my youth,* H4B IV, 4, 55. *the precious i. of our Redeemer* (man) R3 II, 1, 123. *looking on his —s* (his children), II, 2, 50. *man, the i. of his Maker,* H8 III, 2, 443. *this growing i. of thy fiend-like face,* Tit. V, 1, 45. *see the great doom's i.* Mcb. II, 3, 83.* *to show scorn her own i.* Hml. III, 2, 26. *this play is the i. of a murder done in Vienna,* 248. *i. of that horror,* Lr. V, 3, 264.

6) that which serves to represent a person, or in which an idea is embodied: *the i. of his power lay then in me,* H4B V, 2, 74. 79. 89. *i. of pride, why should I hold my peace?* H6B I, 3, 179. *the great i. of authority,* Lr. IV, 6, 162.

7) idea, conception, imagination: *of any thing the i. tell me that hath kept with thy remembrance,* Tp. I, 2, 43. *the i. of the jest I'll show you here at large,* Wiv. IV, 6, 17. *the i. of it gives me content already,* Meas. III, 1, 270. *fancy's —s,* Mids. V, 25. *the constant i. of the creature that is beloved,* Tw. II, 4, 19. *when the i. of it leaves him he must run mad,* II, 5, 211. *my remembrance is very free and clear from any i. of offence,* III, 4, 249. *without some i. of the affected merit,* Troil. II, 2, 60. *whose horrid i. doth unfix my hair,* Mcb. I, 3, 135.

Imagery, human figures made by an artist: *that all the walls with painted i. had said at once 'Jesu preserve thee',* R2 V, 2, 16.

Imaginary, 1) pertaining to the imagination, fanciful: *much i. work was there,* Lucr. 1422. *my soul's i. sight presents thy shadow to my sightless view,* Sonn. 27, 9. *foul i. eyes of blood presented thee more hideous than thou art,* John IV, 2, 265 (=the sanguinary eyes of my imagination). *when I do shape in forms i. the unguided days that you shall look upon,* H4B IV, 4, 59 (forms created by the imagination). *let us on your i. forces work,* H5 Prol. 18. *make i. puissance,* 25. *the i. relish is so sweet,* Troil. III, 2, 20 (the mere idea of it).

2) not real, visionary, delusive: *all is i. she doth prove,* Ven. 597. *these are but i. wiles, and Lapland sorcerers inhabit here,* Err. IV, 3, 10. *which for things true weeps things i.* R2 II, 2, 27.

Imagination, 1) the faculty of the mind by which it conceives and forms ideas of things not present to the eye: Compl. 136. Tp. II, 1, 208. III, 1, 56. Ado IV, 1, 227. Mids. V, 8. 14. 18. 214. 216. All's I, 1, 93. Tim. I, 1, 32. Hml. III, 1, 128. V, 1, 206. 224 (used as a masc.). Lr. IV, 6, 133. Per. III Prol. 58. IV, 4, 3.

2) the thinking, forming an idea, imagining: *deeper sin than bottomless conceit can comprehend in still i.* Lucr. 702. *whose salt i. hath wronged your honour,* Meas. V, 406. *beyond i. is the wrong,* Err. V, 201. *beyond the i. of his neighbours,* Wint. IV, 2, 45.

3) conception, idea, thought: *tremble at the i.* Ven. 668. *the dire i. she did follow,* 975. *prove true, i.* Tw. III, 4, 409. *by bare i. of a feast,* R2 I, 3, 297. *i. of some great exploit,* H4A I, 3, 199. *my —s are as foul as Vulcan's stithy,* Hml. III, 2, 88. Especially a wrong idea, conceit: *what devil suggests this i.?* Wiv. III, 3, 231. IV, 2, 163. *how i. blows him,* Tw. II, 5, 48. 177. *with great i. proper to madmen,* H4B I, 3, 31. *for unfelt i. they often feel a world of restless cares,* R3 I, 4, 80. *he waxes desperate with i.* Hml. I, 4, 87. *woes by wrong —s lose the knowledge of themselves,* Lr. IV, 6, 290.

Imagine, 1) to form an idea of, to fancy, to create by thought; absol: *touches me deeper than you can i.* R3 I, 1, 112. With an accus.: *O then i. this,* Ven. 721. *a hand, a foot, a face, a leg, a head, stood for the whole to be —d,* Lucr. 1428. *did supply thee in her —d person,* Meas. V, 213. *i. some fear,* Mids. V, 21. *the —d voice of God,* H4B IV, 2, 19 (O. Edd. i.) H6A IV, 1, 186. Troil. II, 3, 182. Cor. IV, 5, 217. Ant. V, 2, 98. Cymb. IV, 2, 307. With a double accus.: *those that lawless and incertain thought i. howling,*

Meas. III, 1, 128. *he was to i. me his love*, As III, 2, 428. H4B V, 2, 96. H6A IV, 7, 26. Cymb. I, 4, 143. Per. IV Prol. 1. cf. *i. him upon Blackheath*, H5 V Chor. 16. The two acc. joined by *as: i. her as one by dreadful fancy waking*, Lucr.449. With a dependent clause: *i. every eye beholds their shame*, Lucr. 1343. 1622. Meas. IV, 2, 43. Shr. IV, 4, 12. R3 I, 2, 225. Acc. and dep. clause: *i. me, that I now may be in fair Bohemia*, Wint. IV, 1, 19. Acc. and inf.: *i. it to lie that way*, R2 I, 3, 286.

2) to think, to judge, to conceive in thought: *what I do i. let that rest*, H6A II, 5, 119. *when I i. ill against my king*, H6B I, 2, 19. Double acc.: *you i. me too unhurtful an opposite*, Meas. III, 2, 175. Dependent clause: *I did i. what would be her refuge*, H6A V, 4, 69. H6B III, 2, 192. R3 III, 5, 35. Hml. IV, 7, 35.

Intr., with *of: if we i. no worse of them than they of themselves, they may pass for excellent men*, Mids. V, 218.

Imagined, adj. 1) pertaining to the imagination (cf. *imaginary*): *bring them with i. speed unto the tranect*, Merch. III, 4, 52 (with the speed of imagination). *thus with i. wing our swift scene flies*, H5 III Chor. 1.

2) pertaining to thought, having its seat in the soul: *let rich music's tongue unfold the i. happiness that both receive in either*, Rom. II, 6, 28.

Imagining, subst. imagination: *present fears are less than horrible —s*, Mcb. I, 3, 138.

Imbar, to bar, to exclude: *howbeit they would hold up this Salique law to bar your highness claiming from the female, and rather choose to hide them in a net than amply to i. their crooked titles usurped from you*, H5 I, 2, 94 (O. Edd. *barre* in v. 92 and *imbarre*). The two verbs are evidently used in the same sense: they strive to exclude you, instead of excluding amply, i. e. without restriction or subterfuge, their own false titles).*

Imbecility, weakness: *strength should be lord of i.* Troil. I, 3, 114.

Imbost, see *Embossed.*

Imbrue or **Embrue**, 1) absol. to shed blood: *shall we have incision? shall we i.?* H4B II, 4, 210 (Pistol's speech). 2) tr. to shed the blood of: *come, blade, my breast i.* Mids. V, 351 (Thisbe's speech). *Lord Bassianus lies —d here*, Tit. II, 3, 222.

Imitate, 1) to endeavour to resemble, to copy: Lucr. 1137. 1438. Sonn. 67, 5. LLL IV, 3, 265. Mids. II, 1, 132. Tw. III, 4, 418. H4A I, 2, 221. H4B II, 2, 134. H5 III, 1, 6. III, 7, 46. Cor. V, 3, 150. Tim. I, 2, 13. IV, 3, 201. Hml. III, 2, 39.

2) to make in imitation, to copy: *the counterfeit is poorly —d after you*, Sonn. 53, 6.

Imitation, an attempt to resemble, act of copying: R2 II, 1, 23. Troil. I, 3, 150. Caes. IV, 1, 37. Cymb. III, 4, 174. With *of:* Troil. I, 3, 185.

Immaculate, spotless, pure: Lucr. 1656. Gent. II, 7, 76. R2 V, 3, 61. H4B IV, 3, 41. H6A V, 4, 51. R3 IV, 4, 404. Used adverbially by Armado: *my love is most i. white and red*, LLL I, 2, 95.

Immanity, ferocity: H6A V, 1, 13.

Immask, to hide in a mask: *to i. our noted outward garments*, H4A I, 2, 201.

Immaterial (cf. *Material*) of no moment, worthless, slight: *thou idle i. skein of sleave silk*, Troil. V, 1, 35.

Immediacy, state of being proximately by the side and at the place of another: *he led our powers; bore the commission of my place and person; the which i. may well stand up and call itself your brother*, Lr. V, 3, 65.

Immediate, 1) direct, without the intervention of another: *she is young, wise, fair; in these to nature she's i. heir*, All's II, 3, 139. *that which is the strength of their amity shall prove the i. author of their variance*, Ant. II, 6, 137. cf. *good name in man and woman is the i. jewel of their souls*, Oth. III, 3, 156 (needs no other considerations to enforce its importance).

2) proximate in place: *my due from thee is this imperial crown, which, as i. from thy place and blood, derives itself to me*, H4B IV, 5, 42. *send to prison the i. heir of England*, H6A V, 2, 71. *you are the most i. to our throne*, Hml. I, 2, 109.

3) instant, without intervention of time: Meas. V, 378. Err. I, 1, 69. R2 III, 3, 114. Tim. II, 1, 25. 27. Caes. III, 1, 54. Hml. V, 2, 175. Ant. I, 4, 75. Cymb. III, 7, 9.

Immediately, 1) directly, expressly: *according to our law i. provided in that case*, Mids. I, 1, 45. *and apprehended here i. the unknown Ajax*, Troil. III, 3, 124. *for that offence i. we do exile him hence*, Rom. III, 1, 192.

2) instantly, without delay: Wiv. IV, 6, 25. Err. IV, 2, 64. V, 250. LLL V, 2, 287. Mids. II, 2, 156. Merch. II, 5, 52. II, 9, 8. 16. R2 I, 4, 60. H4A III, 1, 271. V, 5, 33. H6B III, 1, 11. R3 IV, 2, 26 (Ff *presently*). Tit. V, 1, 161. Rom. III, 2, 4. Caes. IV, 3, 142. V, 1, 15. Hml. III, 2, 271.

Imminence, threatening appearance: *dare all i. that gods and men address their dangers in*, Troil. V, 10, 13.

Imminent, impending, threatening: John IV, 3, 154. H6B V, 3, 19. Troil. IV, 4, 71. Caes. II, 2, 81. Hml. I, 3, 42. IV, 4, 60. Oth. I, 3, 136 (some M. Edd. *imminent-deadly*, O. Edd. not hyphened).

Immoderate, excessive: Meas. I, 2, 131.

Immoderately, excessively: Rom. IV, 1, 6.

Immodest, 1) immoderate: *i. hatred*, Wint. III, 2, 103.

2) wanting decent reserve, indecent, indelicate: *he saith she is i.* Ven. 53. *I have took upon me such an i. raiment*, Gent. V, 4, 106. *that she should be so i. to write to one that she knew would flout her*, Ado II, 3, 148. *'tis needful that the most i. word be looked upon and learned*, H4B IV, 4, 70. *this i. clamorous outrage*, H6A IV, 1, 126.

Immodestly, indecently, unchastely (or immoderately?): *i. lies martyred with disgrace*, Lucr. 802.

Immoment, of no moment, insignificant: Ant. V, 2, 166.

Immortal, exempt from death, living for ever: Ven. 80. 197. Sonn. 81, 5. Tp. V, 189. Meas. I, 4, 35. IV, 2, 68. Merch. V, 63. Shr. V, 1, 68. All's I, 1, 23. R2 I, 1, 24. H4B II, 2, 112. H5 III, 2, 11. Troil. IV, 2, 100. Rom. II, 4, 26. III, 3, 37. V, 1, 19. Tim. I, 2, 63. IV, 3, 138. Caes. I, 2, 60. II, 3, 7. IV, 3, 157. Hml. I, 4, 67. Oth. II, 3, 263. III, 3, 356. Ant. V, 2, 284 (*i. longings* = longings for immortality). Cymb. V, 4, 118. Per. V Prol. 3. V, 3, 37. Not understood by the clown in Ant. V, 2, 247.

Immortality, eternal life · Lucr.725. Per.III,2,30.

Immortalize, to render immortal: H6A I, 2, 148.

Immortally, eternally: H4B IV, 5, 144.

Immure, subst. wall: *within whose strong —s the ravished Helen sleeps,* Troil. Prol. 8.

Immure, vb. 1) to enclose within walls: *means to i. herself,* Ven. 1194. *not to be tempted, would she be —d,* Compl. 251. LLL III, 126. R3 IV, 1, 100.

2) to enclose, to confine in any manner: *in whose confine —d is the store,* Sonn. 84, 3. *lives not alone —d in the brain,* LLL IV, 3, 328. *shall I think in silver she's —d,* Merch. II, 7, 52.

Imogen, name in Cymb. I, 1, 114 etc.

Imp, subst. youngling (used only by Armado, Holofernes and Pistol): *dear i.* LLL I, 2, 5. *Hercules is presented by this i.* V, 2, 592. *royal i. of fame,* H4B V, 5, 46. H5 IV, 1, 45.

Imp, vb. to supply with new feathers (a term of falconry): *i. out our drooping country's broken wing,* R2 II, 1, 292.

Impaint, to paint, to colour: *such water-colours to i. his cause,* H4A V, 1, 80.

Impair (Ff) or **Impare** (Q), adj. unsuitable, impertinent: *nor dignifies an i. thought with breath,* Troil. IV, 5, 103 (most M. Edd. *impure*).*

Impair, vb. to make worse, to injure, to weaken: *I i. not beauty, being mute,* Sonn. 83, 11. *i. the seeing sense,* Mids. III, 2, 179. *like a tangled chain, nothing —ed, but all disordered,* V, 126. *—ing Henry, strengthening misproud York,* H6C II, 6, 7.

Impale, to encircle, to surround: *round —d with a glorious crown,* H6C III, 2, 171. *did I i. him with the regal crown,* III, 3, 189. *i. him with your weapons round about,* Troil. V, 7, 5.

Impanneled, constituted as a jury: *to 'cide this title is i. a quest of thoughts,* Sonn. 46, 9.

Impare, see *Impair,* adj.

Impart, 1) to afford, to offer: *this no slaughter-house no tool —eth,* Lucr. 1039. *more praise than niggard truth would willingly i.* Sonn. 72, 8. With *to: some special honours it pleaseth his greatness to i. to Armado,* LLL V, 1, 113. With *toward: with no less nobility of love than that which dearest father bears his son do I i. toward you,* Hml. I, 2, 112 (i. e. with no less nobility of love than this: I bestow upon you the love of the fondest father. *Toward* is partly governed by *love*).

2) to communicate, to make known, to tell; absol: *i.* Hml. III, 2, 342 (only in Qq). With an acc.: *our natural goodness —s this,* Wint. II, 1, 165. R3 III, 1, 159. IV, 4, 130. With an acc. and *to: when I did first i. my love to you,* Merch. III, 2, 256. Shr. III, 2, 132. H6B III, 2, 299. Caes. I, 2, 84. Hml. I, 1, 169. I, 2, 207. V, 2, 92.

Impartial, 1) not favouring one party more than another, equitable, just: R2 I, 1, 115. H4B V, 2, 36. 116.

2) indifferent, not taking part: *favour, savour, hue and qualities, whereat the i. gazer late did wonder,* Ven. 748. *in this I'll be i.; be you judge of your own cause,* Meas. V, 166.

Impartment, communication: *as if it some i. did desire to you alone,* Hml. I, 4, 59.

Impasted, made into paste, concreted: *blood... baked and i.* Hml. II, 2, 481.

Impatience, 1) want of composure in pain and suffering: H4A I, 3, 51. H6C III, 3, 42. Ant. IV, 15, 79. Cymb. V, 4, 112.

2) eagerness of desire: *i. chokes her pleading tongue,* Ven. 217. *all patience and i.* As V, 2, 103.

3) anger, passion, rage: *my heart is ready to crack with i.* Wiv. II, 2, 301. *sheathe thy i.* II, 3, 88. *how i. loureth in your face,* Err. II, 1, 86. John IV, 3, 32. H6A IV, 7, 8. R3 II, 2, 38. IV, 4, 156. Cor. V, 6, 146. Caes. I, 3, 61. II, 1, 248. Lr. III, 6, 5. Ant. II, 2, 68. II, 6, 43.

Impatient (quadrisyll. in Tit. II, 1, 76) 1) wanting composure under pain and suffering: H4B I, 2, 253. Hml. I, 2, 96. With *of,* = not able to bear: *I am i. of my tarriance,* Gent. II, 7, 90. *i. of your just demands,* John II, 56. *i. of his fit,* H4B I, 1, 142. *i. of your wrongs,* Tit. V, 1, 6. *i. of my absence,* Caes. IV, 3, 152.

2) eagerly expecting, not enduring delay: *an i. child that hath new robes and may not wear them.* Rom. III, 2, 30. With *for: i. for their hour,* H5 IV, 2, 52.

3) passionate, angry: *be not i.* Wiv. III, 4, 75. *will you hear i. answers from my gentle tongue?* Mids. III, 2, 287. LLL II, 238. Shr. Ind. 1, 99. II, 152. III, 2, 29. H4A I, 3, 236. Tit. II, 1, 76. Oth. I, 3, 243. *i. with* = angry with: *wherefore is Charles i. with his friend?* H6A II, 1, 54.

Impatiently, passionately: *the current, being stopped, i. doth rage,* Gent. II, 7, 26. *i. I burn with thy desire,* H6A I, 2, 108 (eagerly). *and too i. stamped with your foot,* Caes. II, 1, 244.

Impawn, to pawn, to pledge: Wint. I, 2, 436. H4A IV, 3, 108. H5 I, 2, 21. Hml. V, 2, 155 and 171 (Ff *imponed*).

Impeach, subst. accusation, reproach: *what an intricate i. is this,* Err. V, 269. *ten to one is no i. of valour,* H6C I, 4, 60.

Impeach, vb. 1) to accuse, to reproach: Sonn. 125, 14. Err. V, 29. John II, 116. R2 I, 1, 170. H4A I, 3, 75. Rom. V, 3, 226.

2) to expose to reproach, to detract from: *you do i. your modesty too much, to leave the city,* Mids. II, 1, 214. *and doth i. the freedom of the state, if they deny him justice,* Merch. III, 2, 280. *if it be denied, will much i. the justice of his state,* III, 3, 29. *with pale beggar-fear i. my height,* R2 I, 1, 189.

Impeachment, 1) reproach, accusation: Gent. I, 3, 15. R3 II, 2, 22.

2) hinderance, impediment (Fr. *empêchement*): *to march on to Calais without i.* H5 III, 6, 151.

Impede, to hinder, to keep back: *all that —s thee from the golden round,* Mcb. I, 5, 29.

Impediment, hinderance, obstruction, objection, obstacle: Sonn. 116, 2. Compl. 269. Meas. III, 1, 251. Ado II, 2, 4. III, 2, 96. IV, 1, 13. V, 2, 87. Merch. IV, 1, 162. All's V, 3, 214. Wint. IV, 4, 729. John II, 336. H4A IV, 3, 18. H4B IV, 5, 140. H5 I, 1, 90. V, 2, 33. R3 V, 2, 4. Cor. II, 3, 236. Mcb. IV, 3, 64. Oth. II, 1, 286. V, 2, 263. Ant. II, 2, 148. *your i.* = the obstacles opposed by you, Cor. I, 1, 74.

Impenetrable, not to be moved, relentless: *the most i. cur that ever kept with men,* Merch. III, 3, 18.

Imperator, emperor: LLL III, 187 (O. Edd. *emperator*).

Imperceiverant, see *Imperseverant.*

Imperfect, 1) not finished, not settled: *something he left i. in the state,* Lr. IV, 3, 3.

2) defective: Sonn. 43, 11. Cor. II, 1, 54. Lr. IV, 6, 5. Oth. I, 3, 99. *you i. speakers,* Mcb. I, 3, 70

(not having told enough, having left too much in doubt).

Imperfection, deficiency, fault: Wiv. II, 2, 191. Mids. IV, 1, 68. H5 Prol. 23. V, 2, 69. Hml. I, 5, 79. Lr. I, 1, 300.

Imperfectly, in a deficient manner: Oth. III, 3, 149.

Imperial, 1) pertaining to an empire or emperor: *the i. diadem of Rome,* Tit. I, 6. *the i. seat,* 14. *i. lord,* 250 (Q1 *imperious*). *thy i. mistress,* II, 1, 13. *i. Caesar,* Hml. V, 1, 236 (Qq *imperious*). Cymb. V, 5, 474.

2) pertaining to royalty, royal: *the i. votaress,* Mids. II, 1, 163. *this i. crown,* H4B IV, 5, 41. *i. throne,* H5 I, 2, 35. *crowns i.* II Chor. 10. IV, 1, 278. *our voice is i.* III, 6, 131. *your most i. majesties,* V, 2, 26. *i. lord,* Epil. 8. *your high i. majesty,* H6B I, 1, 1. *the high i. type of this earth's glory,* R3 IV, 4, 244. *the i. metal,* 382. *the i. theme,* Mcb. I, 3, 129. *an i. charge,* IV, 3, 20. *the i. jointress,* Hml. I, 2, 9.

3) lordly, majestical: *i. Love,* All's II, 3, 81. *the most i. monarch,* Wint. IV, 4, 383. *Suffolk's i. tongue,* H6B IV, 1, 121. *with an i. voice,* Troil. I, 3, 187. *most i. looks,* 224. — *Crown i.,* the plant Fritillaria imperialis: Wint. IV, 4, 126.

Launce's blunder for emperor: Gent. II, 3, 5.

Imperious, 1) dictatorial, tyrannical, playing the master: Gent. II, 4, 130. H4B I, 1, 62. III, 1, 20. H6A III, 1, 44. H6B I, 3, 72. H8 II, 2, 47. Oth. II, 3, 276. Cymb. IV, 2, 35.

2) imperial, lordly, majestical: *i. supreme of all mortal things,* Ven. 996. *most i. Agamemnon,* Troil. IV, 5, 172. *Rome's i. lord,* Tit. I, 250 (Ff. *imperial*). *be thy thoughts i. like thy name,* IV, 4, 81. *be, as your titles witness, i.* V, 1, 6. *i. Caesar,* Hml. V, 1, 236 (Ff *imperial*). *the i. show of Caesar,* Ant. IV, 15, 23.

Imperiously, 1) with arrogance of command, like one who will show himself to be the master: *who's there that knocks so i.?* H6A I, 3, 5.

2) proudly, majestically: *i. he leaps,* Ven. 265.

Imperseverant, giddy-headed, flighty, thoughtless: *this i. thing loves him in my despite,* Cymb. IV, 1, 15 (needlessly corrected by M. Edd. into *imperceiverant* or *ill-perseverant*).

Impertinency, what is not to the purpose, rambling thought, folly: *O matter and i. mixed,* Lr. IV, 6, 178.

Impertinent, not to the purpose: *without the which this story were most i.* Tp. I, 2, 138. Misapplied by Launcelot: Merch. II, 2, 146.

Impeticos, a word coined by the fool, meaning *impocket* or something like it: Tw. II, 3, 27.

Impetuosity, vehemence of bearing: Tw. III, 4, 213.

Impetuous, vehement, rushing on fiercely: Hml. IV, 5, 100. Lr. III, 1, 8.

Impierced, see *Enpierced.*

Impiety, sin, wickedness: Lucr. 341. 1174. Sonn. 67, 2. Meas. I, 2, 57. Ado IV, 1, 105. H6C V, 1, 90. Tit. I, 355. Tim. III, 5, 56. Plur. —*ies:* H5 IV, 1, 185.

Impious, sinful, wicked: Lucr. 199. 809. Ado IV, 1, 105. H5 III, 3, 15. H6A V, 1, 12. H6B II, 4, 53. Hml. I, 2, 94. Per. IV, 3, 17 (M. Edd. *pious*). Irreverence to God, the primary meaning, distinctly traceable in Cymb. III, 3, 6.

Implacable, not to be appeased: Tw. III, 4, 261.

Impleached, interwoven, intertwined: Compl. 205.

Implements, utensils, instruments: *all broken i. of a ruined house,* Tim. IV, 2, 16. *i. of war,* Hml. I, 1, 74.

Implorator (Qq *imploratotors;* Pope *implorers,* which suits the verse best) one who implores or begs: —*s of unholy suits,* Hml. I, 3, 129.

Implore, to beg, to entreat, to ask earnestly: 1) a person: *i. her in my voice that she make friends to the strict deputy,* Meas. I, 2, 185. 2) a thing: *if you'll i. it* (mercy) Meas. III, 1, 66. *I do i. secrecy,* LLL V, 1, 116. *I i. so much expense,* V, 2, 523. *i. her blessing,* Wint. V, 3, 44. —*ing pardon,* H5 IV, 1, 322. *a general peace,* H6A V, 4, 98. *whose counsel I will i.* H8 II, 4, 56. —*d your highness' pardon,* Mcb. I, 4, 6.

Imply, to carry with it, to tend to, to import, to cause: *seeks not to find that her search* —*es,* All's I, 3, 222 (that which causes her search). *wherein my death might yield her any profit, or my life i. her any danger?* Per. IV, 1, 82.

Impone, to lay as a stake: Hml. V, 2, 155. 171 (a euphuism used by Osrick. Qq *impawned*).

Import, subst. 1) importance, weight, consequence: *be they* (letters) *of much i.?* Gent. III, 1, 55. *of great i. indeed,* LLL V, 1, 106. *what occasion of i. hath detained you?* Shr. III, 2, 104. *some petty towns of no i.* H6A I, 1, 91. *full of charge of dear i.* Rom. V, 2, 19. *some purpose of i.* Oth. III, 3, 316.

2) tendency, contents (of a letter): *there's letters from my mother: what the i. is, I know not yet,* All's II, 3, 294. *thousands more of semblable i.* Ant. III, 4, 3.

Import, vb. 1) to carry with it, to have in it, to tend to, to imply: *it* —*s no reason that with such vehemency he should pursue faults proper to himself,* Meas. V, 108. *I have a motion much* —*s your good,* 541. *matters of great moment, no less* —*ing than our general good,* R3 III, 7, 68. *which* —*s at full, by letters congruing to that effect, the present death of Hamlet,* Hml. IV, 3, 65. *several sorts of reasons* —*ing Denmark's health,* V, 2, 21. *which* —*s to the kingdom so much fear and danger,* Lr. IV, 3, 5. *all great fears, which now i. their dangers,* Ant. II, 2, 135.

2) to convey, to express, to mean, to signify, to show: *to keep an adjunct to remember thee were to i. forgetfulness in me,* Sonn. 122, 14. *to be your prisoner should i. offending,* Wint. I, 2, 57. *comets* —*ing change of times and states,* H6A I, 1, 2. *belike this show* —*s the argument of the play,* Hml. III, 2, 149. *what* —*s this song?* IV, 5, 27. *his sables and his weeds,* —*ing health and graveness,* IV, 7, 82. *what* —*s the nomination of this gentleman?* V, 2, 133. *your looks are pale and wild and do i. some misadventure,* Rom. V, 1, 28. *his gesture* —*s it,* Oth. IV, 1, 142. *what doth your speech i.?* IV, 2, 31. *the fit and apt construction of thy name doth i. so much,* Cymb. V, 5, 445. Absol.: *her business looks in her with an* —*ing visage,* All's V, 3, 136 (full of meaning, significant).

3) to purport; absol.: *much more general than these lines i.* John IV, 3, 17. *unwelcome news came from the north, and thus it did i.* H4A I, 1, 51 (Ff *report*). *an inventory thus* —*ing,* H8 III, 2, 124. Trans.: *with letters of entreaty, which* —*ed his fellowship i' the cause,* Tim. V, 2, 11. *to pester us with message,* —*ing the surrender of those lands,* Hml. I, 2, 23. *what might i. my sister's letter to him?* Lr. IV, 5, 6. *certain tidings now arrived,* —*ing the mere per-*

dition of the Turkish fleet, Oth. II, 2, 3. *the one of them —s the death of Cassio to be undertook*, V, 2, 310.
4) to concern: *this letter is mistook, it —eth none here*, LLL IV, 1, 57. *with such things else of quality and respect as doth i. you*, Oth. I, 3, 284 (Q *concern*). And hence = to be of consequence, to be of importance: *if you knew how much they* (letters) *do i., you would make haste*, H4A IV, 4, 5. *it doth i. him much to speak with me*, Troil. IV, 2, 52. *what else more serious —eth thee to know*, Ant. I, 2, 125.

Importance, 1) import, meaning: *the wisest beholder could not say if the i. were joy or sorrow*, Wint. V, 2, 20. *in an act of this i. 'twere most piteous to be wild*, II, 1, 181 (or =consequence, weight?).
2) subject, matter: *it had been pity you should have been put together with so mortal a purpose upon i. of so slight and trivial a nature*, Cymb. I, 4, 45.
3) pressing solicitation, urgent request, importunity: *Maria writ the letter at Sir Toby's great i.* Tw. V, 371. *at our i. hither is he come*, John II, 1, 7.

Importancy, significance, consequence (Germ. Bedeutung): *when we consider the i. of Cyprus to the Turk*, Oth. I, 3, 20.

Important, 1) full of meaning, weighty, momentous: *among other i. and most serious designs*, LLL V, 1, 104. *come to what is i. in it*, Tw. I, 5, 204. *things small as nothing he makes i.* Troil. II, 3, 180. *I have i. business*, V, 1, 89. *lets go by the i. acting of your dread command*, Hml. III, 4, 108 (or = urgent, zealous?).
2) urgent, pressing, importunate: *at your i. letters*, Err. V, 138. *if the prince be too i., tell him there is measure in every thing*, Ado II, 1, 74. *his i. blood will nought deny*, All's III, 7, 21. *France my mourning and i. tears hath pitied*, Lr. IV, 4, 26 (Ff *importuned*).

Importantly, weightily, momentously: *it is not likely when they have both their eyes and ears so cloyed i. as now, that they will waste their time upon our note*, Cymb. IV, 4, 19.*

Importless, void of meaning, insignificant: *that matter needless, of i. burden, divide thy lips*, Troil. I, 3, 71.

Importunacy, urgent solicitation: Gent. IV, 2, 112. Tim. II, 2, 42.

Importunate, pressing, urgent: Wint IV, 2, 2. Tim. II, 1, 28. III, 6, 16. Hml. IV, 5, 2. Oth. IV, 1, 26.

Importune, 1) to molest, to trouble: *I here i. death a while*, Ant. IV, 15, 19. 2) to press, to urge with eager solicitation; absol.: *as time and our concernings shall i.* Meas. I, 1, 57. Accus. indicating the person applied to: Sonn. 142, 10. Tp. II, 1, 128. Wiv. II, 2, 220. Meas. V, 438. Err. IV, 1, 2. 53. Shr. I, 1, 48. R3 II, 2, 14. Rom. I, 1, 151. Hml. I, 3, 110. Oth. III, 4, 108. With *to: nor needest thou much i. me to that*, Gent. I, 3, 17. cf. *I, their king, that hither them i.* III, 1, 145. With *for: i. him for my moneys*, Tim. II, 1, 16. With an inf.: *to i. you to let him spend his time*, Gent. I, 3, 13. Lr. III, 4, 166. Oth. IV, 1, 116. Cymb. V, 5, 249. With a clause: *—d me that his attendant might bear him company*, Err. I, 1, 127. The thing requested in the accusative: *—s personal conference with his grace*, LLL II, 32. *—s access to you*, As I, 1, 98. *i. her help*, Oth. II, 3, 324.

Importuned, adj. importunate, urgently soliciting: *my mourning and i. tears*, Lr. IV, 4, 26 (Qq and M. Edd. *important*).

Importunity, pressing solicitation, urgency: *at my i.* Merch. IV, 1, 160. *or your chaste treasure open to his unmastered i.* Hml. I, 3, 32. Oth. III, 3, 251.

Impose, subst. injunction, command: *according to your ladyship's i.* Gent. IV, 3, 8.

Impose, vb. 1) to lay on, as a burden, office, order, or penalty: Err. I, 1, 32. LLL III, 204. Wint. II, 3, 165. John III, 1, 250. H6C IV, 3, 58. Troil. III, 2, 87. Lr. II, 4, 26. With *on:* Meas. I, 3, 40. LLL III, 130. V, 2, 850. H5 IV, 1, 157. R3 III, 7, 147.
2) to enjoin, to oblige by command: *i. me to what penance your invention can lay upon my sin*, Ado V, 1, 282.

Imposition, 1) charge, accusation, imputation (cf. *impose*, H5 IV, 1, 157): *which else would stand under grievous i.* Meas. I, 2, 194. *the imposition cleared hereditary ours*, Wint. I, 2, 74 (original sin set off our account).
2) charge, injunction, order: *bound in knighthood to her i.* Lucr. 1697. Merch. I, 2, 114. III, 4, 33. All's IV, 4, 29. R3 III, 7, 232. Troil. III, 2, 86.
3) cheat, imposture: *reputation is an idle and most false i.* Oth. II, 3, 269.

Impossibility, 1) the state of being not feasible, impracticability: All's II, 1, 180. IV, 1, 39. Cor. V, 3, 61.
2) that which cannot be done: Troil. V, 5, 29. Plur. *—ies:* H6C III, 2, 143. Tim. IV, 3, 388. Lr. IV, 6, 74.

Impossible, not to be done, not feasible, impracticable: Tp. II, 1, 88. Gent. III, 1, 379. Wiv. III, 5, 151 (cf. 148). Meas. V, 51. Ado II, 1, 143. 252 (M. Edd. *impassable, importable* etc.!). II, 3, 211. V, 1, 289. LLL I, 2, 40. V, 2, 866. Shr. I, 2, 123. III, 2, 156. Tw. III, 2, 76. H6A V, 4, 47. H6C I, 2, 21. Caes. II, 1, 325. Lr. II, 4, 245. Oth. IV, 2, 134. Ant. III, 3, 18. III, 7, 57. Per. II, 5, 9. V, 1, 125. With *to: it is not i. to me*, As V, 2, 72. All's I, 1, 239. An inf. following: *it is i. to extirp it*, Meas. III, 2, 109. As V, 2, 72. R2 II, 2, 126 (Qq *unpossible*). H6B II, 1, 130. H8 V, 4, 12. An indic.: *'tis as i. that he's undrowned as he that sleeps here swims*, Tp. II, 1, 237. *it is i. they bear it out*, Oth. II, 1, 19. *should*, preceded by *that:* H6B IV, 1, 110. Caes. V, 3, 100. *without that:* Wiv. III, 4, 9. III, 5, 148. Ado I, 3, 24. Merch. III, 2, 320. Shr. II, 285. H6B I, 1, 108. H6C II, 6, 38. Oth. III, 3, 402. *may after not i.: 'tis not i. but one may seem as shy*, Meas. V, 52.

Imposthume, collection of purulent matter, abscess: Ven. 743. Troil. V, 1, 24. Hml. IV, 4, 27.

Impostor, one who cheats by a fictitious character: Tp. I, 2, 477. Mcb. III, 4, 64. fem.: All's II, 1, 158. Per. V, 1, 179.

Impotence, infirmity: Hml. II, 2, 66.

Impotent, 1) weak, feeble: *i. and snail-paced beggary*, R3 IV, 3, 53. *lame and i. conclusion*, Oth. II, 1, 162.
2) infirm, languishing under disease: *enforce the pained i. to smile*, LLL V, 2, 864. *i. and bed-rid*, Hml. I, 2, 29.

Impound, to confine in a pinfold (like stray cattle): H5 I, 2, 160.

Impregnable, not to be taken by assault, resisting any attack: Sonn. 65, 7. R2 III, 2, 168. H6C IV, 1, 44. Tit. IV, 4, 98.

Imprese, subst. a device engraved or painted anywhere: R2 III, 1, 25*(Ff *impress*).

Impress, subst. a device on an escutcheon: R2 III, 1, 25 (Qq *imprese*).

Impréss, subst. 1) a mark made, an image fixed, impression: *this weak i. of love,* Gent. III, 2, 6.

2) enforced public service, press: Troil. II, 1, 107. Hml. I, 1, 75. Ant. III, 7, 37.

Impréss, vb. (*impressed* in Lr. V, 3, 51), 1) to make an impression, to work on the mind, to touch the heart; absol.: *when thou* (love) *—est, what are precepts worth of stale example?* Compl. 267 (or = when thou compellest into thy service?).

2) to imprint; the object being a) that which makes the impression: *where love's strong passion is —ed in youth,* Alls I, 3, 139. *wears my stripes —ed upon him,* Cor. V, 6, 108. b) that which bears the impression: *his heart, like an agate, with your print —ed,* LLL II, 236. *as easy mayst thou the intrenchant air with thy keen sword i.* Mcb. V, 8, 10.

3) to compel into service, to press: H4A I, 1, 21. Mcb. IV, 1, 95. Lr. V, 3, 51.

Impression, 1) the act of making a mark by pressure: *wax yields at last to every light i.* Ven.566. *sink, my knee, in the earth: of thy deep duty more i. show than that of common sons,* Cor. V, 3, 51.

2) the mark or figure made: *the i. of strange kinds is formed in them,* Lucr. 1242. *the face, that map which deep i. bears of hard misfortune,* 1712. *your love and pity doth the i. fill which vulgar scandal stamped upon my brow,* Sonn. 112, 1. *the i. of keen whips I'ld wear as rubies,* Meas. II, 4, 101. *whose soft i. interprets for my poor ignorance,* Tim. V, 4, 68. *subscribed it, gave it the i.* Hml. V, 2, 52 (= sealed it).

3) form, figure: *which like a waxen image 'gainst the fire bears no i. of the thing it was,* Gent. II, 4, 202. *and stolen the i. of her fantasy with bracelets of thy hair,* Mids. I, 1, 32 (the form, the image dwelling in her imagination). *where the impression of mine eye infixing,* Alls V, 3, 47 (i. e. looking in her eye and seeing in it the form of mine reflected; cf. John II, 501: *I do protest I never loved myself till now infixed I beheld myself drawn in the flattering table of her eye). an unlicked bear-whelp that carries no i. like the dam,* H6C III, 2, 162.

4) effect on the mind: *such terrible i. made the dream,* R3 I, 4, 63.

Impressure, mark made by pressure, impression: As III, 5, 23. Tw. II, 5, 103 (= seal; cf. *impression* in Hml. V, 2, 52). Troil. IV, 5, 131.

Imprint, subst. impression, mark made: *the vacant leaves thy mind's i. will bear,* Sonn. 77, 3.

Imprint, vb. to form by printing, to stamp: *sweet seals in my soft lips —ed,* Ven. 511. *as a form in wax by him —ed,* Mids. I, 1, 50.

Imprison, to put to prison, to shut up, to confine: Ven. 1046. Lucr. 1456. Sonn. 52, 12. 58, 6 (*the imprisoned absence of your liberty,* i. e. separation from you, which is to me like a prison. *Of* = from; cf. *Of*). Tp. I, 2, 278. Meas. III, 1, 124. III, 2, 70. Tw. V, 349. Wint. I, 2, 396. John III, 3, 8. IV, 2, 155. H4A III, 1, 30. H6A II, 5, 55. R3 I, 3, 78. II, 2, 22. Tit. IV, 2, 124. Tim. I, 1, 94. II, 2, 234. Lr. III, 4, 140. Cymb. I, 1, 8.

Imprisonment, confinement: Meas. I, 2, 138. III, 1, 130. III, 2, 70. IV, 2, 13. Err. IV, 18. LLL I, 1,

289. H4B I, 2, 146. H6A II, 5, 4. V, 3, 139 (= captivity). H6C IV, 3, 63. IV, 6, 11. R3 I, 1, 114. 125. I, 3, 91. H8 V, 3, 150.

Improbable, not likely to be true: Tw. III, 4, 141.

Improper, not becoming: *service i. for a slave,* Lr. V, 3, 221.

Improve, to use for advantage, to turn to account: *his means, if he i. them, may well stretch so far,* Caes. II, 1, 159.

Improvident, 1) wanting forecast and care H6A II, 1, 58. 2) not circumspect, heedless, rash: *who says this is i. jealousy?* Wiv. II, 2, 302.

Impudence, shamelessness, effrontery: Meas. V, 368. Alls II, 1, 173. Wint. III, 2, 57. Per. II, 3, 69.

Impudency, the same: LLL V, 1, 5.

Impudent, shameless, saucy: Alls IV, 3, 363. V, 3, 187. H4A III, 3, 177. H4B II, 1, 123. H6C I, 4, 117. III, 3, 156. Troil. III, 3, 217. Oth. IV, 2, 81.

Impudently, shamelessly: Wint. I, 2, 274.

Impugn, to oppose, to counteract (Germ. *anfechten*): *the Venetian law cannot i. you,* Merch. IV, 1, 179. *it skills not greatly who —s our doom,* H6B III, 1, 281.

Impure (as for the accent, cf. Append.) foul, defiled: Ven. 736. Lucr. 1078. R3 III, 7, 234. In Troil. IV, 5, 103 O. Edd. *impair.*

Impurity, foulness, defilement: Lucr. 854.

Imputation, that which is thought or said of one; 1) opinion, reputation in general: *Antonio is a good man. Have you heard any i. to the contrary?* Merch. I, 3, 13. *I would humour his men with the i. of being near their master,* H4B V, 1, 81. *our i. shall be oddly poised in this wild action,* Troil. I, 3, 339. *in the i. laid on him by them, in his meed he's unfellowed,* Hml. V, 2, 149. *if i. and strong circumstances, which lead directly to the door of truth, will give you satisfaction,* Oth. III, 3, 406 (i. e. an opinion founded on strong circumstantial evidence. cf. *And*).

2) reproach, censure: *else i., for that he knew you, might reproach your life,* Meas. V, 425. *the i. of his wickedness should be imposed upon his father,* H5 IV, 1, 156.

Impute, 1) to attribute, to ascribe (in a bad sense): R2 II, 1, 141. Rom. II, 2, 105.

2) to account, to charge to account, to rate: *i. it not a crime to me,* Wint. IV, 1, 4. With *for: this silence for my sin you did i.* Sonn. 83, 9.

In, prepos. (often mutilated to *i'*, f.i. *i' faith, i' fecks,* q. v.; particularly before *the,* with which it then forms one syllable, f. i. Tp. I, 2, 84. 130. 387. II, 1, 147. II, 2, 5. Wiv. I, 3, 91. IV, 2, 50. Merch. IV, 1, 49. Wint. II, 2, 30. III, 3, 11. H8 III, 2, 100. Troil. IV, 2, 35. Ant. V, 2, 32. Cymb. III, 6, 50 etc.), denoting a local or temporal space, within which a person or thing is enclosed or contained or taking place; used of place: *tangled in a net,* Ven. 67. *in her arms,* 68. *bred more beauty in his eyes,* 70. *she bathes in water,* 94. *our sport is not in sight,* 124 (is not within seeing, cannot be seen). *in your cabin,* Tp. I, 1, 27. I, 2, 7. 197. 199. V, 2, 112 etc. etc. Before names of towns, when considered as places of extent, containing a variety of objects: *here in Troy,* Lucr. 1476. *our country rights in Rome,* 1838. LLL V, 2, 718. Caes. I, 2, 160. *keep in Tunis,* Tp. II, 1, 259. *if in Naples I should report this,* III, 3, 27. V, 149. *all happiness bechance to thee in Milan,* Gent. I, 1, 61. *there is a lady in Verona here,* III, 1, 81. Rom. Prol. 2. *never* a woman in *Windsor* knows more, Wiv. I, 4, 136. II, 2, 122. III, 3, 114. *any in Vienna,* Meas. l, 1, 23. 45. I, 3, 13. II, 1, 203. V, 269. *in Ephesus I am but two hours old,* Err. II, 2, 150. IV, 1, 83. *in Syracusa,* V, 320. *here in Messina,* Ado I, 1, 39. *in Venice,* 274. Merch. I, 1, 180. III, 3, 28. *work in Athens here,* Mids. V, 72. *any one in Mantua,* Shr. IV, 2, 81. *in Southampton,* H5 II Chor. 30. *now it is supper-time in Orleans,* H6A I, 4, 59. *the witch in Smithfield shall be burned,* H6B II, 3, 7. *to crown himself in Westminster,* IV, 4, 31 etc. Of time: *in summer's heat,* Ven. 91. *gathered in their prime,* 131. *consume themselves in little time,* 137. Tp. II, 1, 138. Err. V, 309. 319. Merch. IV, 1, 1. R3 I, 3, 127 etc.

Often used to denote a point of place or time, when modern use would demand *at: attends the emperor in his royal court,* Gent.I, 3, 27. 67 (cf. *Court*). *some say he is in Rome,* Meas. III, 2, 94. *in Syracusa was I born,* Err. I, 1, 37. *in Belmont is a lady richly left,* Merch. I, 1, 161. *cost me two thousand ducats in Frankfort,* III, 1, 88. *as ⌐I heard in Genoa,* 103. *to wive it wealthily in Padua,* Shr.I, 2, 75. *born in Verona,* 191. *born in Mantua,* II, 60. *have you ever been at Pisa? Ay, sir, in Pisa have I often been,* IV, 2, 94. *in Genoa,* IV, 4, 4. *he is a sail-maker in Bergamo,* V, 1, 81. *Gadshill lies to-night in Rochester,* H4A I, 2, 143. *crowned in Paris,* H6B I. 1, 94. *the castle in Saint Alban's,* V, 2, 68. *I, then in London,* H6C II, 1, 111. *crowned in Paris,* R3 II, 3, 17 (Qq *at*). *when I was last in Holborn,* III, 4, 33. *sojourn in Mantua,* Rom. III, 3, 169. *going back to school in Wittenberg,* Hml. I, 2, 113. *what Danskers are in Paris,* II, 1, 7. *he's now in Florence,* Oth. I, 3, 45. *in Aleppo once,* V, 2, 352. *where is he now? in Athens,* Ant. III, 6, 64 etc. Likewise of time: *in night desire sees best,* Ven. 720. *except I be by Silvia in the night,* Gent. III, 1, 178. *unless I look on Silvia in the day,* 180. *in the instant that I met with you he had of me a chain,* Err. IV, 1, 9. *you have stayed me in a happy hour,* Ado IV, 1, 285 (cf. *Hour*). *when in that moment Titania waked,* Mids. III, 2, 33. *you are come to me in happy time,* Merch. II, 4, 1, 90. *we will slink away in supper time,* Merch. II, 4, 1. *walking with thee in the night,* H4A III, 3, 49. *a day wherein the fortune of ten thousand men must bide the touch,* IV, 4, 9. *that our armies join not in a hot day,* H4B I, 2, 233. *which in the day of battle tire thee more,* R3 IV, 4, 188. *the day wherein I wished to fall,* V, 1, 16. *to infringe my vow in the same time 'tis made,* Cor. V, 3, 21. *two lions littered in one day,* Caes. II, 2, 46. *in the mature time with this paper strike the sight of the duke,* Lr. IV, 6, 282. *the duke in council! in this time of the night!* Oth. I, 2, 94. *in night,* II, 3, 216. *this is a doubt in such a time nothing becoming you,* Cymb. IV, 4, 15 etc. Sometimes superfluous: *why should we proclaim it in an hour before his entering?* Meas. IV, 4, 9. *once in a month,* Tp. I, 2, 262. *one day in a week,* LLL I, 1, 39.

Not seldom, in a local sense, = on: *what seest thou in the ground?* Ven. 118. *whose heads stood in their breasts,* Tp. III, 3, 47. *plod away i' the hoof,* Wiv. I, 3, 91 (F2.3.4 and M. Edd. *o' the*). *there is written in your brow honesty and constancy,* Meas. IV, 2, 163. *set them in my forehead,* Ado I, 1, 266. *like Pharaoh's soldiers in the reeky painting,* III, 3, 143. *in the beached margent of the sea,* Mids. II, 1, 85. *fogs falling in the land,* 90. *the blushes in my cheeks,* All's II, 3, 75. *with*

this rhyme in's forehead, IV, 3, 263. *and in the neck of that tasked the whole state,* H4A IV, 3, 92. *to be worn in my cap,* H4B I, 2, 17; cf. H5 IV, 1, 56; IV, 8, 63; Lr. III, 4, 88. *the snake rolled in a flowering bank,* H6B III, 1, 228. *in thy shoulder do I build my seat,* H6C II, 6, 100 (F2.3.4 *on*). *scattered in the bottom of the sea,* R3 I, 4, 28. *that she should lie i' the bosom of our hard-ruled king,* H8 III, 2, 100. *would he were knocked i' the head,* Troil. IV, 2, 35. *that sleeve that he'll bear in his helm,* V, 2, 169 (Q *on*). *gold strewed i' the floor,* Cymb. III, 6, 50 etc.

Expressing motion, = into: *breatheth in her face,* Ven. 62; cf. Tp. IV, 173. *look in mine eyeballs,* Ven. 119; cf. Meas. II, 1, 153; II, 2, 95; Mids. III, 2, 424; John II, 495; Ant. V, 2, 32. *brought in subjection her immortality,* Lucr. 724. *in thy weak hive a wandering wasp hath crept,* 839. *Tarquin's shape came in her mind,* 1536. *in my chamber came a creature,* 1626. *divide in two slow rivers,* 1738. *in Lucrece' bleeding stream he falls,* 1774. *in so profound abysm I throw all care,* Sonn. 112, 9. *mine eyes are bright in dark directed,* 43, 4. *which she in a river threw,* Compl. 38. *a heart which in his level came,* 309. *peg thee in his knotty entrails,* Tp. I, 2, 295. *pitch me i' the mire,* II, 2, 5. *how camest thou in this pickle?* V, 281. *delivered in the milk-white bosom of thy love,* Gent. III, 1, 250. *come in mine own great chamber,* Wiv. I, 1, 157. *thrown in the Thames,* III, 5, 6. *I'll come no more in the basket,* IV, 2, 50. *she spit in his face,* Meas. II, 1, 86. *to deliver his head in the view of Angelo,* IV, 2, 177. *creep in crannies,* Err. II, 2, 31. *I will beat this method in your sconce,* 34. *they should not drop in his porridge,* 100. *fall a drop of water in the breaking gulf,* 128 *(fall in love,* see under *Love*). *a tailor called me in his shop,* IV, 3, 7. *to enter in my house,* IV, 4, 67. V, 92. *rushing in their houses,* 143. *if you come in her presence,* Ado I, 1, 124. *one woman shall not come in my grace,* II, 3, 31. *falls into mine ears as water in a sieve,* V, 1, 5. *you may not come in my gates,* LLL II, 172. *fall in the lap of the rose,* Mids. II, 1, 108. *drop the liquor in her eyes,* 178 (cf. *pour,* Tp. II, 2, 98 and R3 I, 2, 12). *that next came in her eye,* III, 2, 2. *entered in a brake,* 15. *sink in apple of his eye,* 104. *how comes this gentle concord in the world?* IV, 1, 148. *thou stickest a dagger in me,* Merch. III, 1, 115. *his soul infused itself in thee,* IV, 1, 137. *let the sounds of music creep in our ears,* V, 56. *I will ne'er come in your bed,* 190. *never come in my sight,* As IV, 1, 41. 52. *to bring me in some grace,* Alls V, 2, 49. 53. *go not too far in the land,* Wint. III, 3, 11. *shoot in each other's mouth,* John II, 414. *snarleth in the gentle eyes of peace,* IV, 3, 150. *to enter in the castle,* R2 II, 3, 160. *never more come in my sight,* V, 2, 86. *throw the quean in the channel,* H4B II, 1, 51. *bring him in obedience,* H6A I, 1, 164. *rushing in the bowels of the French,* IV, 7, 42. *buz these conjurations in her brain,* H6B I, 2, 99. *brought Duke Humphrey in disgrace,* I, 3, 99. *breathe darkness in the air,* IV, 1, 7. *throw in the frozen bosoms hot coals of vengeance,* V, 2, 35. *stab poniards in our flesh,* H6C I, 1, 98. *if a thing comes in his head,* V, 5, 86. *I'll throw thy body in another room,* V, 6, 92. *I'll turn yon fellow in his grave,* R3 I, 2, 261. *to draw me in these vile suspects,* I, 3, 89. *breathe them in the air,* 286. *to belch it in the sea,* I, 4, 41. *chop him in the malmsey-butt,* 161. *brought me in my master's hate,* III, 2, 58. *throw them in the entrails of a wolf,* IV, 4,

23. *entered in a drowsy head*, V, 3, 228. *he'll turn your current in a ditch*, Cor. III, 1, 96. *follow thine enemy in a fiery gulf*, III, 2, 91. *cast yourself in wonder*, Caes. I, 3, 60. *in her white bosom*, Hml. II, 2, 113 (cf. Gent. III, 1, 250) etc. As for the use of such verbs as *plunge* (Tp. I, 2, 211) and *put* (Tp. I, 2, 2. 307. Wiv. III, 5, 4) and such phrases as *crack in pieces* (H6A I, 4, 52. R3 II, 2, 52. Lr. I, 2, 91), *gnawed in two* (Err. V, 289) see the resp. words.

The idea of locality gave origin to the following expressions: *leading him prisoner in a red-rose chain*, Ven. 110. *I drink to you in a cup of sack*, H6B II, 3, 60. *a quart pot to drink in*, IV, 10, 16. And when it is = among, out of: *few in millions*, Tp. II, 1, 7. *the jury may in the sworn twelve have a thief*, Meas. II, 1, 10. *every ducat in six thousand ducats*, Merch. IV, 1, 85. *there's yet one good in ten*, Alls I, 3, 83. *he, in twelve, found truth in all but one, I in twelve thousand none*, R2 IV, 170. To the same source the idea of inherence is traceable: *touched the very virtue of compassion in thee*, Tp. I, 2, 27. *some defect in her*, III, 1, 44. *are all these things perceived in me?* Gent. II, 1, 34. *there is no music in the nightingale*, III, 1, 179. *the boy hath grace in him*, V, 4, 165. *would seem in me to affect speech and discourse*, Meas. I, 1, 4. *this is envy in you*, III, 2, 149. *would behold in me this shameful sport*, Err. IV, 4, 108. *what is in you? why dost thou tear it?* LLL IV, 3, 200. *do not call it sin in me*, 115. *of strong prevailment in unhardened youth*, Mids. I, 1, 35. *he is every man in no man*, Merch. I, 2, 65. *the offender's life lies in the mercy of the duke*, IV, 1, 355. *hast any philosophy in thee?* As III, 2, 22. *that is another sin in you*, 82. *there's something in't*, All's I, 3, 248. *it is in us to plant thine honour*, II, 3, 163. *it lies in you*, V, 2, 49. *her business looks in her with an importing visage*, V, 3, 135. *there is a fair behaviour in thee*, Tw. I, 2, 47. *these lunes i' the king*, Wint. II, 2, 30. *much work for tears in many an English mother*, John II, 303. *on some known ground of treachery in him*, R2 I, 1, 11. *found truth in all but one*, IV, 171. *whose wrongs in us God pardon*, H4A I, 3, 149. *a good sack hath a two-fold operation in it*, H4B IV, 3, 104. *collect these dangers in the duke*, H6B III, 1, 35. *which time will bring to light in smooth Duke Humphrey*, 65. *in him they fear your highness' death*, III, 2, 249. *as little joy may you suppose in me*, R3 I, 3, 153. *God punish me with hate in those where I expect most love*, II, 1, 35. *in him it lies to cure me*, H8 II, 4, 100. *those twins of learning that he raised in you, Ipswich and Oxford*, IV, 2, 58. *as if he did contemn what he requested should be in them to give*, Cor. II, 2, 162. *I am in this, your wife, your son*, III, 2, 64 (we all are contained, concerned, in this question). *this is impiety in you*, Tit. I, 355. *there was no purpose in them of this remove*, Lr. II, 4, 3. *'tis not in thee to grudge my pleasures*, 194. *I cannot believe that in her*, Oth. II, 1, 254. *'tis foul in her*, IV, 1, 213. *there's nothing in her yet*, Ant. III, 3, 27 (Germ. *es ist nichts an ihr*) etc.

The idea of place and time applied to actions: *wasted in such sport*, Ven. 24. *in battle* 99. *in every jar*, 100. *rapt in secret studies*, Tp. I, 2, 77. *what to come is in yours and my discharge*, II, 1, 254. *in one voyage*, V, 208 etc. cf. *he did buffet thee and in his blows denied my house for his*, Err. II, 2, 160. *he'll have but a year in all these ducats*, Tw. I, 3, 24 (= while he has). *wept like two children in their deaths'*

sad stories, R3 IV, 3, 8. *wear our health but sickly in his life*, Mcb. III, 1, 107 (as long as he lives). *extinct even in their promise*, Hml. I, 3, 119 etc. Similarly to dispositions of mind: *trembling in her passion*, Ven. 27. *pouted in a dull disdain*, 33. *in haste*, 57. *in care of thee*, Tp. I, 2, 16. *my son is lost, and in my rate she too*, II, 1, 109. *in revenge of thy ingratitude*, Gent. I, 2, 110. *in thy opinion*, 6. *maids, in modesty, say no*, 55. *'tis not in hate of you*, III, 1, 96. *in her invention und Ford's wife's distraction*, Wiv. III, 5, 86. *in love unto Demetrius, I told him of your stealth*, Mids. III, 2, 309. *that you in pity may dissolve to dew*, R2 V, 1, 9. *my father, in kind heart and pity moved*, H4A IV, 3, 64. *as, in love and zeal, loath to depose the child*, R3 III, 7, 208. *whilst in the mildness of your sleepy thoughts, this noble isle doth want her proper limbs*, 123. *I should do so in honour*, Cor. III, 2, 64. *all's in anger*, 95. *a countenance more in sorrow than in anger*, Hml. I, 2, 232 *i 'the frown*, Lr. I, 4, 209 etc.

Used before gerunds: *quick in turning*, Ven. 140. *a piece many years in doing*, Wint. V, 2, 104 etc. Having the same meaning as a clause introduced by *when* or *while: how, in stripping it, you more invest it*, Tp. II, 1, 226. *which would be great impeachment to his age, in having known no travel in his youth*, Gent. I, 3, 16. *in paying it, it is impossible I should live*, Merch. III, 2, 320. *I am as ignorant in that as you in so entitling me*, Wint. II, 3, 70. *patches discredit more in hiding of the fault*, John IV, 2, 33. *thou hast most traitorously corrupted the youth in erecting a grammar school*, H6B IV, 7, 36 (cf. *we are forgetful in our long absence*, H8 II, 3, 106). Often quite superfluous: *is pointing still, in cleansing them from tears*, R2 V, 5, 54. *surprised by bloody hands in sleeping on your beds*, H6A V, 3, 41. *in seeming to augment it wastes it*, H8 I, 1, 145. *he raves in saying nothing*, Troil. III, 3, 249. *in roaring for a chamber-pot, dismiss the controversy bleeding*, Cor. II, 1, 86. *cast your caps in hooting at Coriolanus' exile*, IV, 6, 131.

The idea of causality originating in that of coincidence of place and time: *duty so great, which wit so pure as mine may make seem bare, in wanting words to show it*, Sonn. 26, 6. *thou movest no less with thy complaining than thy master in bleeding*, Cymb. IV, 2, 376. Hence = on account of, by means of, by: *the devil speaks in him*, Tp. V, 129. *too noble to conserve a life in base appliances*, Meas. III, 1, 89. *if your knowledge be more it is much darkened in your malice*, III, 2, 157. *I learn in this letter*, Ado I, 1, 1. *never could maintain his part but in the force of his will*, 239. *our feast shall be much honoured in your marriage*, Merch. III, 2, 214. *wearing thy hearer in thy mistress' praise*, As II, 4, 38. *the cunning of her passion invites me in this churlish messenger*, Tw. II, 2, 24. *safe in his prisonment*, John III, 4, 161. *all murders past do stand excused in this*, IV, 3, 51. *thus his royalty doth speak in me*, V, 2, 129. *what a weary way will be found in Ross and Willoughby*, R2 II, 3, 10. *thou makest me sin in envy*, H4A I, 1, 79. *as, in reproof of many tales devised, I may find pardon*, H4A III, 2, 23. *in the which better part I have saved my life*, V, 4, 122. *the king is wounded, and in the fortune of your son Prince Harry slain*, H4B I, 1, 15. *heavy in Hotspur's loss*, 121. *wherein you would have sold your king to slaughter*, H5 II, 2, 170. *and bids you, in the bowels of the Lord, deliver up the crown*, II, 4, 102 (conjuring you by). *if your father's highness do not, in grant of all demands at large, sweeten the bitter mock*, II, 4, 121. *will you yield, or guilty in defence, be thus destroyed*, III, 3, 43. *Somerset hath made the vizard famous in his death*, H6B V, 2, 69. *her life is safest in her birth. And only in that safety died her brothers*, R3 IV, 4, 213. *that my kingdom should not be gladded in't by me*, H8 II, 4, 196. *in which you brought the king to be your servant*, III, 2, 315. *all my glories in that one woman I have lost for ever*, 410. *Troy in our weakness stands, not in her strength*, Troil. I, 3, 137. *we did our main opinion crush in taint of our best man*, 374. *in second voice we'll not be satisfied*, II, 3, 149. *if in his death the gods have us befriended*, V, 9, 9. *you have shamed me in your condemned seconds*, Cor. I, 8, 15. *to crush him in an equal force*, I, 10, 14. *the people, in whose power we were elected theirs*, III, 1, 210. *in this match I hold me highly honoured*, Tit. I, 244. *lest in this marriage he should be dishonoured*, Rom. IV, 3, 26. *the Gods confound them all in thy conquest*, Tim. IV, 3, 103. *you witch me in't*, V, 1, 158. *which in his death were perfect*, Mcb. III, 1, 108. *unmanned in folly*, III, 4, 73. *in second husband let me be accurst*, Hml. III, 2, 189. *who like not in their judgment, but their eyes*, IV, 3, 5. *young Laertes, in a riotus head, o'erbears your officers*, IV, 5, 101. *strengthen your patience in our last night's speech*, V, 1, 317. *make your own purpose, how in my strength you please*, Lr. II, 1, 114. *errs in ignorance and not in cunning*, Oth. III, 3, 49. *I am most unhappy in the loss of it*, III, 4, 102. *fallen in the practice of a damned slave*, V, 2, 292. *Caesar and Antony have ever won more in their officer than person*, Ant. III, 1, 17. *make me not offended in your distrust*, III, 2, 34. *who are in this relieved, but not betrayed*, V, 2, 40. *famous in Caesar's praises, no whit less than in his feats deserving it*, Cymb. III, 1, 6. *make me blest in your care in bringing up my child*, Per. III, 3, 31. Thus also *to commence and end in sth.*: Tw. II, 3, 44. Mcb. I, 3, 133 (see the resp. articles). *In that* = as, see *That.*

Denoting the relation, the point of view, under which a thing is to be considered: *frosty in desire*, Ven. 36. *harsh in voice*, 134. *be strong in whore*, Tim. IV, 3, 141. *ignorant in that*, Wint. II, 3, 70. *harsh in sound*, Cor. IV, 5, 65. *gross in nature*, Hml. I, 2, 136. *governed him in strength, but not in lust*, Ven. 42. *being so reputed in dignity*, Tp. I, 2, 73. *their labour delight in them sets off*, III, 1, 2. *thou wast ever an obstinate heretic in the despite of beauty*, Ado I, 1, 237. *I do in birth descrve her, and in fortunes, in graces and in qualities of breeding*, Merch. II, 7, 32. *in himself too mighty, and in his parties, his alliance*, Wint. II, 3, 20. *in bestowing he was most princely*, H8 IV, 2, 56. *successful in the battles that he fights*, Tit. I, 66. *I am wealthy in my friends*, Tim. II, 2, 193. *I have no judgment in an honest face*, Oth. III, 3, 50. *your care in bringing up my child*, Per. III, 3, 32. Hence = with respect to, concerning, toward, against: *triumph in so false a foe*, Lucr. 77. *ask him some questions in his accidence*, Wiv. IV, 1, 16. *if you suspect me in any dishonesty*, IV, 2, 140. *one that can my part in him advertise*, Meas. I, 1, 42. *that power that you have in her*, Ado IV, 1, 76. *two thousand ducats in that, and other precious jewels*, Merch. III, 1, 91. *you are too young in this*, As I, 1, 57. *'tis shame such wrongs are borne in him*, R2 II, 1, 239 (that such wrongs committed

against him are borne patiently`. *thou hast saved me a thousand marks in links and torches*, H4A III, 3, 48. *execute thy wrath in me alone*, R3 I, 4, 71. *all was either pitied in him or forgotten*, H8 II, 1, 29. *ween you of better luck, I mean in perjured witness, than your master?* V, 1, 137. *all repent in their election*, Cor. II, 3, 263. *forget what we are sorry for ourselves in thee*, Tim. V, 1, 142 (to have committed against thee). *wherein my letters were slighted off*, Caes. IV, 3, 4. *our fears in Banquo stick deep*, Mcb. III, 1, 49. *the first that ever Scotland in such an honour named*, IV, 8, 64. *your intent in going back to school*, Hml. I, 2, 113. *believe so much in him, that he is young* I, 3, 124. *nature disclaims in thee*, Lr. II, 2, 60. *you may relish him more in the soldier than in the scholar*, Oth. II, 1, 167. *I will show you such a necessity in his death*, IV, 2, 247. *if in the holding or loss of that you term her frail*, Cymb. I, 4, 105. In the same way may be explained: *what in the least will you require*, Lr. I, 1, 194 (= at least; see *Least*). *what in your own part can you say to this?* Oth. I, 3, 74. *poor we may call them in their native lords*, H5 III, 5, 26 (= as regards; cf. *rich*: Gent. II, 4, 169. Tim. I, 1, 62). *in my knowing, Timon hath been this lord's father*, Tim. III, 2, 73 (cf. *know* and *knowledge*). *in himself he is* (a worthy gentleman) *but in this kind the other must be held the worthier*, Mids. I, 1, 53 (cf. on the other hand, R2 I, 1, 145). *there's little can be said in it*, Alls I, 1, 147 (concerning it, in favour of it); cf. *the which before his highness shall speak in*, H8 II, 4, 103.

Used to express habit, form and quality: *she shall be all in white*, Wiv. IV, 6, 35. *would have made all the youth in his colour*, Alls IV, 5, 4. *he in the red face*, Wiv. I, 1, 173. *if every ducat were in six parts*, Merch. IV, 1, 86. *brawling in French*, LLL III, 1, 10. *sing in Welsh*, H4A III, 1, 239. *howl in Irish*, 241. *speak in English*, H8 III, 1, 46. *when the bagpipe sings in the nose*, Merch. IV, 1, 49. *the foul fiend haunts poor Tom in the voice of a nightingale*, Lr. III, 6, 31. *in the name of the people*, Cor. III, 3, 99 (cf. *Name*). *the bloody book of law you shall yourself read in the bitter letter*, Oth. I, 3, 68. Denoting the material, of which a thing consists, = of: *I will raise her statue in pure gold*, Rom. V, 3, 299. *you are all in all in spleen*, Oth. IV, 1, 89. H8 I, 1, 19. Caes. I, 3, 25.

Indicating design and tendency, = for or to: *ought that I can speak in his dispraise*, Gent. III, 2, 47. *obey our will which travails in thy good*, Alls II, 3, 165. *shall it in more shame be further spoken*, H4A I, 3, 177. *but in mine emulous honour let him die*, Troil. IV, 1, 28. *he laboured in his country's wreck*, Mcb. I, 3, 114. *gives him three thousand crowns in annual fee*, Hml. II, 2, 73. *we will give all to you in satisfaction*, IV, 5, 209. *in sign of what you are*, Cor. I, 9, 26. Caes. II, 2, 41. Lr. I, 1, 195. This will go far to explain the following expressions: *how strange it shows, Timon in this should pay more than he owes*, Tim. III, 4, 22. and hence: *there's no purchase in money*, H4A III, 2, 46. *six pence a day in Pyramus*, Mids. IV, 2, 24.

Before pain and peril (q. v.) = on: *in pain of your dislike*, H6B III, 2, 257. *in peril of precipitation from off the rock Tarpeian never more to enter our Rome gates*, Cor. III, 3, 102.

In, adv. 1) within or into a place; joined to verbs (q. c.): *when the age is in, the wit is out*, Ado III, 5,

37. *not true in love? Yes, when he is in, but I think he is not in,* As III, 4, 29. *I am in so far in blood,* R3 IV, 2, 65. *bringing wood in,* Tp. II, 2, 16. *bring them in,* Mids. V, 84. *we will come in to dinner,* Merch III, 5, 66. *come in,* Oth. V, 2, 103. *let me creep in,* Wiv. III, 3, 150. *ducks quickly in,* Ven. 87. *fetch in our wood,* Tp. I, 2, 312. 366. *get you in,* As I, 1, 81. *he's too big to go in there,* Wiv. III, 3, 142. *go in,* Merch. III, 5, 51. *look in,* Tp. V, 167. *he ran in,* Err. V, 257. *serve in the meat,* Merch. III, 5, 65. *the moon may shine in at the casement,* Mids. III, 1, 59. *take in the topsail,* Tp. I, 1, 7. *take this fellow in,* H6B I, 3, 37. *in at his windows throw,* Caes. I, 2, 320. *in the poisoned entrails throw,* Mcb. IV, 1, 5. *walk in,* Err. V, 419. *I'll in,* Wiv. III, 3, 145. 146. R3 I, 1, 147 etc. etc. Absol.: *in, or we are spoiled,* Err. V, 37. *father, in,* Merch. II, 2, 165. *in at the window,* John I, 171. *the safest passage in,* H6A III, 2, 22. *in to our tent,* R3 V, 3, 46. *without or in,* Troil. III, 3, 97. *in, in!* Cor. IV, 5, 251. *no sooner in,* Rom. I, 4, 33. *in, and prepare,* Tim. V, 2, 16. *in, and ask thy daughter's blessing,* Lr. III, 2, 12. *in, boy,* III, 4, 26.

2) to a place and with a certain end and purpose: *how came that widow in?* Tp. I͡P, 1, 78 (why was she brought on the carpet?) *the rest will ne'er come in, if he be out,* LLL V, 2, 152. *call in my sons,* H6B V, 1, 111. *to take in a town with gentle words,* Cor. III, 2, 59 (cf. *Take*). *do receive you in with all kind love,* Caes. III, 1, 175. *this gentleman steps in to Cassio and entreats his pause,* Oth. II, 3, 229. *to come in to the cry,* V, 1, 44. *come in, and give some help,* 59. *came in and satisfied him,* V, 2, 318. *fortune brings in some boats that are not steered,* Cymb. IV, 3, 46 (cf. *Bring* and the other resp. verbs).

3) in place, in office: *who's in, who's out,* Lr. V, 3, 15.

4) engaged and bound in any manner: *this is his pardon, purchased by such sin, for which the pardoner himself is in,* Meas. IV, 2, 112 (guilty and liable to punishment). *he's in for a commodity of brown paper,* IV, 3, 5; cf. *Doll's in,* H4B V, 5, 40 (= in prison). *I would not care a pin, if the other three were in,* LLL IV, 3, 20 (guilty of the same offence). *O that I knew he were but in by the week,* V, 2, 61 (hired as my servant). *now he's deeply in,* Tw. III, 5, 47 (engaged, absorbed in his hallucinations). *I am not so well as I should be, but I'll ne'er out. Not till you have slept; I fear me you'll be in till then,* Ant. II, 7, 38 (in a fine pickle, i. e. drunk).

In, vb. (O. Edd. *inne*) to get in, to harvest, to house: *to in the crop,* All's I, 3, 48.

Inaccessible, forbidding access, not to be approached: Tp. II, 1, 37. As II, 7, 110.

In-a-door (O. Edd. without hyphen), indoor, at home: Lr. I, 4, 138.

Inaidible (M. Edd. *inaidable*), helpless, cureless: All's II, 1, 122.

Inaudible, not to be heard, making no sound: All's V, 3, 41.

Inauspicious, ill-omened, unfavourable: *i. stars,* Rom. V, 3, 111.

Incaged, confined in a cage: H6C IV, 6, 12. confined in any manner: Ven. 582. R2 II, 1, 102.

Incantations, charms performed by words: H6A V, 3, 27.

Incapable, 1) not having room sufficient to

contain; with *of: i. of more, replete with you,* Sonn. 113, 13.

2) not receptive, not susceptible: *so i. of help,* Cor. IV, 6, 120 (= not to be helped). *as one i. of her own distress,* Hml. IV, 7, 179.

3) not equal, unable; absol.: *i. and shallow innocents,* R3 II, 2, 18 (unable to comprehend). With *of: of temporal royalties he thinks me now i.* Tp. I, 2, 111. *is not your father grown i. of reasonable affairs?* Wint. IV, 4, 408.

Incardinate, Sir Andrew's blunder for *incarnate:* Tw. V, 185.

Incarnal, Launcelot's blunder for *incarnate:* Merch. II, 2, 29 (Ff Q2.3.4 *incarnation*).

Incarnardine (most M. Edd. *incarnadine*) to dye red: Mcb. II, 2, 62.

Incarnate, appearing in a human shape, true, real: Merch. II, 2, 29 (corrupted to *incarnal*). Tw. V, 185 (corr. to *incardinate*). H5 II, 3, 34 (not understood by Mrs Quickly). Tit. V, 1, 40.

Incarnation, see *Incarnal.*

Incense, subst. an offering of burned perfumes: Lucr. 194. John IV, 3, 67. Tit. I, 145. Lr. V, 3, 21.

Incénse, vb. 1) to kindle, to set on fire: *whose bosom burns with an —d fire of injuries,* H4B I, 3, 14.

2) to enkindle, to irritate: LLL V, 2, 703. All's V, 3, 25. John III, 1, 238. IV, 2, 261. H4B IV, 4, 33. H6A III, 1, 36. H8 I, 2, 65. III, 2, 61. Cor. IV, 2, 33. Mcb. III, 1, 110. Hml. IV, 5, 126. V, 2, 61. 313. Oth. I, 1, 69. Per. V, 1, 144. With *against:* Tp. III, 3, 74. Tw. III, 4, 285. H6C IV, 1, 108. R3 I, 3, 85. Cor. I, 9, 56. III, 1, 32.

3) to instigate, to provoke; with *to: what they may i. him to,* Lr. II, 4, 309. With an inf.: *I will i. Page to deal with poison,* Wiv. I, 3, 109. *Don John —d me to slander Hero,* Ado V, 1, 242. Wint. V, 1, 61. R3 III, 1, 152. III, 2, 29. Caes. I, 3, 13.

4) (according to Nares, a Staffordshire provincialism; quasi *insense*) to instruct, to inform: *I have —d the lords that he is a most arch heretic,* H8 V, 1, 43. Is this the meaning also in Ado V, 1, 242 and R3 III, 1, 152, as Nares supposes?

Incensement, irritation, exasperation: Tw. III, 4, 260.

Incertain, 1) doubtful, not to be relied on: *I have found myself in my i. grounds to fail as often as I guessed,* All's III, 1, 15. *surmise of aids i. should not be admitted,* H4B I, 3, 24. *willing misery outlives i. pomp,* Tim. IV, 3, 243. *the affairs of men rest still i.* Caes. V, 1, 96.

2) wanting certain knowledge or purpose; not knowing what to think or to do: *those that lawless and i. thought imagine howling,* Meas. III, 1, 127. *what dangers may drop upon the kingdom and devour i. lookers on,* Wint. V, 1, 29 (indifferent, not taking measures to prevent the calamity).

Incertainty, doubtfulness, precariousness: Sonn. 115, 11. Plur. *—ies* = things subject to chance, accidents of fortune: Sonn. 107, 7. Wint. III, 2, 170.

Incessant, not ceasing, continual: Err. I, 1, 71. H4B IV, 4, 118. H5 II, 2, 38. H6A V, 4, 154. H6C I, 4, 145.

Incessantly, continually: John II, 385.

Incest, sexual commerce between persons within degrees prohibited by law: Lucr. 921. Meas. III, 1,

139. Hml. I, 5, 83. Per. Prol. 26. I, 1, 126. I, 2, 76. II Prol. 2. II, 4, 2.

Incestuous, guilty of incest: Hml. I, 2, 157. I, 5, 42. III, 3, 90. V, 2, 336. Lr. III, 2, 55.

Inch, 1) the twelfth part of a foot: Rom. II, 4, 88. Hml. V, 1, 214. Plur. —*es:* Tp. II, 1, 283. LLL V, 2, 188. 193. Shr. V, 1, 29. Troil. II, 2, 31. Cymb. I, 2, 21. *I would I had thy* —*es,* Ant. I, 3, 40 (I were of thy size). Denoting any minute measure: *one i. of delay more,* As III, 2, 206. *I'll not budge an i.* Shr. Ind. 1, 14. *I'll queen it no i. farther,* Wint. IV, 4, 460; H4A II, 3, 117. *my i. of taper will be burnt,* R2 I, 3, 223. *that you should have an i. of any ground to build a grief on,* H4B IV, 1, 109. *am I not an i. of fortune better than she?* Ant. I, 2, 59. *by* —*es* = by small degrees, in a lingering manner: *they'll give him death by* —*es,* Cor. V, 4, 42. Cymb. V, 5, 52. Denoting preciseness: *from the furthest i. of Asia,* Ado II, 1, 275 (from the very farthest point). *I'll show thee every fertile i. o'the island,* Tp. II, 2, 152. *every i. of woman,* Wint. II, 1, 137. *every i. a king,* Lr. IV, 6, 109 (from top to toe). *I have speeded hither with the very extremest i. of possibility,* H4B IV, 3, 39. *we watched you at an i.* H6B I, 4, 45 (at the nicest point of time). *her stature to an i.* Per. V, 1, 110 (exactly). *tell what thou art by* —*es,* Troil. II, 1, 54. *knows the youth even to his* —*es,* IV, 5, 111.

2) an island (an Erse word): *at Saint Colmes i.* Mcb. I, 2, 61 (now called *Inchcomb*).

Incharitable, unfeeling, unkind: Tp. I, 1, 44.

Inch-meal; *by i.* = by inches, every inch, entirely: *make him by i. a disease,* Tp. II, 2, 3.

Inch-thick, adv. to the measure of an inch in thickness: Wint. I, 2, 186.

Incidency, a falling on, aptness to happen, impendence: *declare what i. thou dost guess of harm is creeping toward me,* Wint. I, 2, 403.

Incident, adj. befalling, apt to happen: *other i. throes that nature's fragile vessel doth sustain,* Tim. V, 1, 203. With *to: a malady most i. to maids,* Wint. IV, 4, 125. *plagues i. to men,* Tim. IV, 1, 21.

Incision, blood-letting: *a fever in your blood! why, then i. would let her out in saucers,* LLL IV, 3, 97. *let us make i. for your love, to prove whose blood is reddest,* Merch. II, 1, 6. *God make i. in thee! thou art raw,* As III, 2, 75 (God cure thee!). *deep malice makes too deep i.* R2 I, 1, 155; cf. 153. *shall we have i.? shall we imbrue?* H4B II, 4, 210. *make i. in their hides,* H5 IV, 2, 9.

Incite, to stir up, to stimulate, to impel: *no blown ambition doth our arms i.* Lr. IV, 4, 27. With *to:* Tp. IV, 1, 39. Ado III, 1, 113. Tw. III, 4, 75. H5 I, 2, 20. Cymb. III, 7, 6.

Incivil, impolite, rude: Cymb. V, 5, 292.

Incivility, rudeness: Err. IV, 4, 49.

Inclinable, inclined, favourably disposed: Troil. II, 2, 58 (Q *attributive*). Cor. II, 2, 60.

Inclination, 1) propensity: Lucr. 922. Wiv. III, 2, 35. H4A III, 2, 125. Hml. III, 3, 39.

2) disposition, temper: *to show, as it were, his i.* LLL IV, 2, 16. *change their gentle hearts to fierce and bloody i.* John V, 2, 158. *men judge by the complexion of the sky the state and i. of the day,* R2 III, 2, 195. *this merry i. accords not with the sadness of my suit,* H6C III, 2, 76. *give us notice of his i.* R3 III, 1, 178. *touched his spirit and tried his i.* Cor. II, 3, 200. *ob-*

serve his i. in yourself, Hml. II, 1, 71. *report the feature of Octavia, her years, her i.* Ant. II, 5, 113. *how dost thou find the i. of the people?* Per. IV, 2, 104.

Incline, 1) intr. a) to bend down, to stoop: *that eye unto a view so false will not i.* Lucr. 292. *and he from forage will i. to play,* LLL IV, 1, 93.

b) to tend, to move in a direction: *stands upon the swell at full of tide, and neither way* —*s,* Ant. III, 2, 50. *his age* —*ing to threescore,* H4A II, 4, 467.

c) to have a propension, to be favourably disposed; absol.: *'tis most easy the* —*ing Desdemona to subdue in any honest suit,* Oth. II, 3, 346. With *to: canst with thine eyes at once see good and evil,* —*ing to them both,* Wint. I, 2, 304. *doth his majesty i. to it?* H5 I, 1, 72. *I more i. to Somerset than York,* H6A IV, 1, 154. *if he would i. to the people,* Cor. II, 3, 42. *we must i. to the king,* Lr. III, 3, 14 (= side with). *this to hear would Desdemona seriously i.* Oth. I, 3, 146.

d) to be disposed in any manner: *if thou* —*est that way, thou art a coward,* Wint. I, 2, 243. *in act or will that way* —*ing,* III, 2, 53. With *to: he did i. to sadness,* Cymb. I, 6, 62.

2) trans. a) to bend, to turn: *whereto if you'll a willing ear i.* Meas. V, 542.

b) to give a tendency, to dispose favourably; 1) refl. *to i. himself to Caesar,* Ant. IV, 6, 14 (= to side with). 2) passively, *to be inclined* = to have a propensity: —*d to accessary yieldings,* Lucr. 1657. *art* —*d to sleep,* Tp. I, 2, 185. II, 1, 193. As IV, 1, 157. H4B IV, 4, 38. H6B IV, 2, 134. H6C IV, 8, 16. Tim. 1, 1, 118. Cymb. I, 6, 114.

c) to dispose in any manner; only passively, —*d* = disposed: *pity move my father to be* —*d my way,* Tp. I, 2, 447. *he was not* —*d that way,* Meas. III, 2, 130. *well* —*d,* IV, 3, 78. —*d as the wolf,* H6B III, 1, 78. *glad or sorry as I saw it* —*d,* H8 II, 4, 27. *best* —*d,* Cor. I, 6, 85. *so* —*d,* Mcb. IV, 3, 76. Hml. III, 1, 25. *lewdly* —*d,* Per. IV, 2, 156.

Inclining, 1) inclination, favourable disposition: All's III, 6, 41. Hml. II, 2, 283.

2) leaning, side, party chosen (cf. *incline:* Cor. II, 3, 42. Lr. III, 3, 14. Ant. IV, 6, 14): *both you of my i., and the rest,* Oth. I, 2, 82.

Inclip, to enclose: *whate'er the ocean pales, or sky* —*s,* Ant. II, 7, 74.

Include, 1) to comprise, to have within: *impious act,* —*ing all foul harms,* Lucr. 199. *the glories it* —*d,* H6A I, 2, 137. *the loss of such a lord* —*s all harm,* R3 I, 3, 8.

2) to conclude, to end: *we will i. all jars with triumphs,* Gent. V, 4, 160. Refl., = to terminate, to come to in the end: *then every thing* —*s itself in power, power into will, will into appetite,* Troil. I, 3, 119.

Inclusive, 1) enclosing, encircling: *the i. verge of golden metal that must round my brow,* R3 IV, 1, 59.

2) full of force and import: *notes whose faculties i. were more than they were in note,* All's I, 3, 232.

Income, the coming in, accomplishment, fulfilment: *pain pays the i. of each precious thing,* Lucr. 334.

Incomparable, without a parallel: Lucr. Arg. 7. Shr. IV, 2, 98. H6C III, 2, 85. H8 I, 1, 27. Tim. I, 1, 10.

Incomprehensible, inconceivable: *i. lies,* H4A I, 2, 209.

Inconsiderate, hasty, rash, heedless: John II, 67. Used for rude, unlearned, by Armado: LLL III, 79.

Inconstancy, unsteadiness, fickleness, faithlessness: Pilgr. 261. Gent. V, 4, 113. Wiv. IV, 5, 111. LLL IV, 3, 180. John III, 1, 322. H6B III, 2, 115.

Inconstant, unsteady, fickle, not to be relied on: Sonn. 15, 9. 92, 9. Mids. I, 1, 110. As III, 2, 432. Tw. I, 4, 7. Wint. III, 2, 187. H5 III Chor. 15. III, 6, 36. Rom. I, 4, 100. II, 2, 109. IV, 1, 119.

Incontinency, lewdness, unchastity: Hml. II, 1, 30. Cymb. II, 4, 127. III, 4, 49.

Incontinent, adj. indulging lust without restraint, unchaste: As V, 2, 43. Troil. V, 1, 106. Tim. IV, 1, 3.

Incontinent, adv. immediately: *a pair of stairs to marriage which they will climb i.* As V, 2, 42 (quibbling). *put on sullen black i.* R2 V, 6, 48. *he will return i.* Oth. IV, 3, 12.

Incontinently, immediately: *I will i. drown myself,* Oth. I, 3, 306.

Inconvenience, cause of uneasiness, evil: H5 V, 2, 66. H6A I, 4, 14.

Inconvenient, unsuitable, disagreeable: As V, 2, 73.

Incony, a word used only by Costard, apparently in the sense of fine, delicate: *my sweet ounce of man's flesh, my i. Jew,* LLL III, 136. *most i. vulgar wit,* IV, 1, 144.

Incorporal, immaterial: *the i. air,* Hml. III, 4, 118.

Incorporate, vb. to make one body: *till holy church i. two in one,* Rom. II, 6, 37. *that great vow which did i. and make us one,* Caes. II, 1, 273.

Incorporate, partic. or adj. 1) made one body: *i. then they seem; face grows to face,* Ven. 540. *undividable, i.* Err. II, 2, 124. *as if our hands, our sides, voices and minds had been i.* Mids. III, 2, 208. *to make divorce of their i. league,* H5 V, 2, 394. *my i. friends,* Cor. I, 1, 134. *the i. conclusion,* Oth. II, 1, 269 (i. e. cohabitation).

2) embodied, closely united: *I am i. in Rome,* Tit. I, 462. *i. to our attempts,* Caes. I, 3, 135.

Incorpsed, made one body: *as he had been i. and demi-natured with the brave beast,* Hml. IV, 7, 88.

Incorrect, not chastised, not subdued: *it shows a will most i. to heaven,* Hml. I, 2, 95.

Increase, subst. 1) augmentation: Sonn. 11, 5. All's I, 1, 139. 160. II, 4, 37. H6B III, 2, 292. Hml. I, 2, 144.

2) produce, progeny, offspring: *upon the earth's i. why shouldst thou feed, unless the earth with thy i. be fed?* Ven. 169. 170. *you do it for i.* 791. *from fairest creatures we desire i.* Sonn. 1, 1. *the teeming autumn, big with rich i.* 97, 6. Tp. IV, 110. Mids. II, 1, 114. H6B III, 2, 385. H6C II, 2, 164. R3 IV, 4, 297. V, 5, 38. Cor. III, 3, 114. Tit. V, 2, 192. Lr. I, 4, 301 (*the organs of i.*).

Increase, vb. 1) trans. to augment, to make grow, to make more or greater: Sonn. 64, 8. Meas. III, 2, 78. Tw, I, 5, 85. R3 IV, 1, 45. H8 III, 2, 161. Cor. I, 1, 183. IV, 5, 235 (or = to make thrive?). Ant. II, 7, 100. Cymb. II, 3, 54. Per. III, 2, 97.

2) intr. to become more and greater: Ven. 254. Sonn. 15, 5. Tp. IV, 107 (= thriving). Err. I, 1, 40. H4B I, 2, 205. II, 2, 29. V, 2, 104. R3 IV, 3, 48. IV, 4, 507 (Ff *grows strong*). Cor. V, 2, 113. Caes.

IV, 3, 216. Oth. II, 1, 196. Ant. II, 2, 165. Cymb. III, 2, 48. IV, 2, 60.

Increaseful, rich in produce: *i. crops,* Lucr. 958.

Incredible, not to be believed: *'tis i. to believe,* Shr. II, 308.

Incredulous, 1) not easily believing: H4B IV, 5, 154.

2) not easily to be believed: *no obstacle, no i. or unsafe circumstance,* Tw. III, 4, 88.

Incur, to fall into, to bring on one's self, to become liable to: Lucr. 1473. Merch. IV, 1, 361. Shr. Ind. 2, 124. All's IV, 3, 10. Wint. II, 2, 57. R3 III, 7, 152. Troil. III, 3, 6. Lr. V, 3, 4. Oth. I, 2, 69. III, 3, 67. Cymb. I, 1, 102.

Incurable, remediless: All's II, 3, 16. John V, 1, 16. H4B I, 2, 266. H6B III, 1, 286 (F1.2 *uncurable*). Troil. V, 1, 25.

Incursion, hostile encounter, a going to meet the enemy: *whose high deeds, whose hot —s and great name in arms,* H4A III, 2, 108. *when thou art forth in the —s, thou strikest as slow as another,* Troil. II, 1, 32.

Ind or **Inde**, India: Tp. II, 2, 61. LLL IV, 3, 222. As III, 2, 93.

Indebted, in debt, obliged: Merch. IV, 1, 413. H6B I, 4, 47.

Indeed, 1) really, in fact: *what should I do, seeing thee so i., that tremble at the imagination?* Ven. 667. *but when my glass shows me myself i., beated and chopped with tanned antiquity,* Sonn. 62, 9. *he did believe he was i. the duke,* Tp. I, 2, 103. *thou art very Trinculo i.* II, 2, 109. *one that takes upon him to be a dog i.* Gent. IV, 4, 13. *it is marring i.* Wiv. I, 1, 26. *none but mine own people. I.? No, certainly,* IV, 2, 15. *many a man would take you at your word, and go i.* Err. I, 2, 17. *Pyramus is not killed i.* Mids. III, 1, 20. *and there i. let him name his name,* 46 (= his real name). *what praise couldst thou bestow on a deserving woman i.* Oth. II, 1, 146 (a really deserving woman) etc.

2) in truth, to be sure: Tp. I, 2, 96. II, 1, 19. 54. 58. 226. 230. III, 1, 38. III, 2, 12. III, 3, 2. V, 261. Gent. I, 1, 74. I, 2, 97. II, 1, 162. II, 4, 9. 35. Meas. I, 2, 37 etc. etc.*

Indent, subst. indentation, zigzag direction: *it shall not wind with such a deep i.* H4A III, 1, 104.

Indent, vb. to zigzag: *then shalt thou see the dew-bedabbled wretch turn and return, —ing with the way,* Ven. 704. Partic. or adj. —ed = forming a zigzag: *with —ed glides,* As IV, 3, 113.

Indent, vb. to covenant, to bargain, to compound: *i. with fears,* H4A I, 3, 87.

Indenture, a contract: John II, 20. H4A II, 4, 53. III, 1, 80. 141. 265. Hml. V, 1, 119.* Per. I, 3, 9. IV, 6, 187.

Index, an explaining preface or prologue to a book or play: *I'll sort occasion, as i. to the story we late talked of, to part the queen's proud kindred from the king,* R3 II, 2, 149. *the flattering i. of a direful pageant,* IV, 4, 85 (pageants, or dumb shows, were perhaps introduced and explained by painted emblems). *in such —es, although small pricks to their subsequent volumes, there is seen the baby figure of the giant mass of things to come at large,* Troil. I, 3, 343. *what act, that roars so loud and thunders in the i.?* Hml. III, 4, 52. *an i. and obscure prologue to the history of lust,* Oth. II, 1, 263.

India, the country proverbially rich in southern Asia: Mids. II, 1, 69. Merch. III, 2, 272. Tw. II, 5, 17 (*my metal of India,* i. e. my girl of gold. F1 *mettle,* F2.3.4 *nettle*). H4A III, 1, 169. H8 I, 1, 21. Troil. I, 1, 103. I, 2, 80.

Indian, subst. a native of India or of America: Tp. II, 2, 34. H8 V, 4, 34. Oth. V, 2, 347 (F1 *Judean*).

Indian, adj. pertaining to India: Mids. II, 1, 22. 124. III, 2, 375. Merch. III, 2, 99. H6C III, 1, 63.

Indian-like, like an Indian: Alls I, 3, 210.

Indict (O. Ed1. *indite*) to accuse: *no matter in the phrase that might i. the author of affectation,* Hml. II, 2, 464. *he's —ed falsely,* Oth. III, 4, 154.

Indictment, accusation: Wint. III, 2, 11. H4B II, 4, 371. IV, 1, 128. R3 III, 6, 1.

Indies, the rich countries in the East and in the West: *they shall be my East and West I.* Wiv. I, 3, 79. *where America, the I.?* Err. III, 2, 136. Merch. I, 3, 19. *more lines than is in the new map with the augmentation of the I.* Tw. III, 2, 86. *our king has all the I. in his arms,* H8 IV, 1, 45.

Indifferency, moderate measure: *this commodity makes it take head from all i., from all direction, purpose, course, intent,* John II, 579 (according to some, = impartiality). *an I had but a belly of any i., I were simply the most active fellow in Europe,* H4B IV, 3, 23.

Indifferent, adj. 1) neither good nor bad, neither deserving praise nor blame, neither high nor low: *where your good word cannot advantage him, your slander never can endamage him; therefore the office is i.* Gent. III, 2, 44. *their garters of an i. knit,* Shr. IV, 1, 94 (ordinary, common, neither striking nor shocking). *this comes off well and excellent. I.* Tim. I, 1, 30. *how do ye both? As the i. children of the earth,* Hml. II, 2, 231.

2) of no moment: *dangers are to me i.* Caes. I, 3, 115.

3) taking no interest, unconcerned: *doth his majesty incline to it or no? He seems i.* H5 I, 1, 72.

4) impartial: *look on my wrongs with an i. eye,* R2 II, 3, 116. *having here no judge i.* H8 II, 4, 17.

Indifferent, adv. pretty, rather, somewhat: *I'll tell you news i. good for either,* Shr. I, 2, 181. *it does i. well,* Tw. I, 3, 143. *two lips i. red,* I, 5, 265. *Harry of Monmouth's life is come after it i. well,* H5 IV, 7, 34. *he'll fight i. well,* Troil. I, 2, 242. *I am i. honest,* Hml. III, 1, 123. *it is i. cold,* V, 2, 100.

Indifferently, 1) tolerably, pretty: *I have an humour to knock you i. well,* H5 II, 1, 58. *we have reformed that i. with us,* Hml. III, 2, 41.

2) without interest, unconcernedly: *he waved i. twixt doing them neither good nor harm,* Cor. II, 2, 19. *set honour in one eye and death i'the other, and I will look on both i.* Caes. I, 2, 87.

3) impartially: *hear me speak i. for all,* Tit. I, 430.

Indigent, needy, poor: H5 I, 1, 16.

Indigest, subst. a chaos: *you are born to set a form upon that i. which he hath left so shapeless and so rude,* John V, 7, 26.

Indigest, adj. chaotic, formless: *to make of monsters and things i. such cherubins,* Sonn. 114, 5.

Indigested, formless, shapeless: H6B V, 1, 157. H6C V, 6, 51.

Indign, unworthy, disgraceful: Oth. I, 3, 274.

Indignation, high displeasure, contemptuous anger: Tp. IV, 200. All's III, 2, 32. Tw. II, 3, 140.

III, 4, 269. John II, 212. IV, 1, 63. IV, 2, 103. V, 6, 37. R2 III, 3, 99. H5 IV, 7, 39. R3 I, 3, 220. Lr. I, 2, 86.

Indignity, 1) unworthiness, disgrace: *I shall make this northern youth exchange his glorious deeds for my —ies,* H4A III, 2, 146.

2) contemptuous injury, insult: Tp. III, 2, 42. Err. V, 113. 253. LLL V, 2, 289. All's II, 3, 229 (*give*). H4A I, 3, 2. H4B V, 2, 69. Tit. I, 8. Oth. II, 3, 245.

Indirect, 1) not tending to a purpose by the plainest course and the most obvious means, but in a circuitous and second-hand way: *that by direct or i. attempts he seek the life of any citizen,* Merch. IV, 1, 350. (R3 I, 4, 224?).

2) wrong, unfair, lawless: *till he hath ta'en thy life by some i. means or other,* As I, 1, 159. *though i., yet indirection thereby grows direct,* John III, 1, 275. *his title, the which we find too i. for long continuance,* H4A IV, 3, 105. *by what by-paths and i. crooked ways I met this crown,* H4B IV, 5, 185. *he needs no i. nor lawless course to cut off those,* R3 I, 4, 224. *what an i. and peevish course is this of hers,* III, 1, 31. *did you by i. and forced courses subdue and poison this young maid's affections?* Oth. I, 3, 111.

Indirection, 1) oblique course or means: *by —s find directions out,* Hml. II, 1, 66.

2) wrong, dishonest practice: *i. thereby grows direct,* John III, 1, 276. *to wring from the hard hands of peasants their vile trash by any i.* Caes. IV, 3, 75.

Indirectly, 1) not in a straight course, by second hand, not in express terms: *why should poor beauty i. seek roses of shadow, since his rose is true?* Sonn. 67, 7. *to speak so i. I am loath,* Meas. IV, 6, 1. *turn down i. to the Jew's house,* Merch. II, 2, 45 (misapplied by Launcelot). *i. and directly too thou hast contrived against the very life of the defendant,* IV, 1, 359. *I answered i.* H4A I, 3, 66. *thy head, all i., gave direction,* R3 IV, 4, 225.

2) wrongfully: *we shall repent each drop of blood that hot rash haste so i. shed,* John II, 49. *your crown and kingdom, i. held from him,* H5 II, 4, 94.

Indiscreet, unwise, injudicious: *it would ill become me to be vain, i. or a fool,* LLL IV, 2, 31. *so i. an officer,* Oth. II, 3, 280.

Indiscretion, want of wisdom, want of judgment: *our i. sometimes serves us well, when our deep plots do pall,* Hml. V, 2, 8. *all's not offence that i. finds and dotage terms so,* Lr. II, 4, 199.

Indisposed, unwell, slightly disordered, (cf. *Dispose*): *to take the i. and sickly fit for the sound man,* Lr. II, 4, 112.

Indisposition, disinclination (or bad humour?): *when my i. put you back,* Tim. II, 2, 139.

Indissoluble, not to be loosed, not to be untied: *a most i. tie,* Mcb. III, 1, 17.

Indistinct, not to be exactly discerned and separated from other things: *make the main and the aerial blue an i. regard,* Oth. II, 1, 40. *makes it i., as water is in water,* Ant. IV, 14, 10.

Indistinguishable, not discernible in its peculiar form and nature; of any kind: *you whoreson i. cur,* Troil. V, 1, 33. Indistinguished, see *Undistinguished.*

Indite (cf. *Indict*) to write, to pen: LLL IV, 1, 96. Blunderingly for *invite:* H4B II, 1, 30. Rom. II,

4, 135 (used by Benvolio in derision of the nurse. F2.3.4 *invite*).

Individable (cf. *Dividable*) not to be distinguished and determined by a peculiar appellation: *scene i. or poem unlimited*, Hml. II, 2, 418 (i.e. not to be called tragedy, comedy etc.).

Indrenched, overwhelmed with water: Troil. I, 1, 51.

Indubitate, doubtless, evident: LLL IV, 1, 67; used by Armado, and perhaps blunderingly.

Induce, to move, to prevail on, to determine: Meas. IV, 3, 53. H8 II, 4, 76. Cor. I, 9, 16. With o: Tw. V, 315. H8 II, 4, 151. With an inf.: Tit. V, 3, 79. Cymb. II, 4, 63. 125. Used of things, = to obtain: *to i. their mediation*, Ant. V, 2, 169.

Inducement, that which moves and determines, motive, impulse: R3 IV, 4, 279. H8 II, 4, 169. *with his i.* = impelled, instigated, seduced by him, All's III, 2, 91.

Induction, beginning, introduction: *our i. full of prosperous hope*, H4A III, 1, 2. *plots have I laid, —s dangerous*, R3 I, 1, 32. *a dire i. am I witness to*, IV, 4, 5.

Indue or **Endue**, to endow, to supply, to furnish: *Mercury i. thee with leasing*, Tw. I, 5, 105. *more strong reasons I shall i. you with*, John IV, 2, 43. *the tribunes i. you with the people's voice*, Cor. II, 3, 147. Partic. *—d* = endowed, gifted: *men —d with worthy qualities*, Gent. V, 4, 153. *—d with intellectual sense*. Err. II, 1, 22. *he is best —d in the small*, LLL V, 2, 646. *the full-fraught man and best —d*, H5 II, 2, 139. Having to after it, to denote aim and destination: *like a creature native and —d unto that element*, Hml. IV, 7, 180 (supplied with qualities for that element, suited to live in water). *let our finger ache, and it —s our other healthful members even to that sense of pain*, Oth. III, 4, 146 (it imparts to the other limbs the faculty of feeling the same pain).

Indulgence, leniency, connivance: *of partial i. to their benumbed wills*, Troil. II, 2, 178. In the Roman Catholic church, = absolution from censure and punishment: *as you from crimes would pardoned be, let your i. set me free*, Tp. Epil. 20. *givest whores —s to sin*, H6A I, 3, 35.

Indulgent, apt to connive, mild: Ant. I, 4, 16.

Indurance, see *Endurance*.

Industrious, zealous, studious: *my i. servant Ariel*, Tp. IV, 33. *they gape and point at your i. scenes and acts of death*, John II, 376. *a true i. friend*, H4A I, 1, 62. *put we on i. soldiership*, Mcb. V, 4, 16.

Industriously, studiously, deliberately, earnestly, on purpose: *if i. I played the fool, it was my negligence, not weighing well the end*, Wint. I, 2, 256 (Lat. de industria).

Industry, assiduity, zealous activity: Gent. I, 3, 22. H4A II, 4, 112. H4B IV, 5, 70. H6C V, 4, 11. Oth. I, 3, 328. Cymb. III, 5, 112. III, 6, 31. Per. IV, 1, 63. Not quite intelligibly used by Armado: *thine in the dearest design of i.* LLL IV, 1, 88 (= earnestness ?).

Inequality, incongruity, contradiction to known facts, improbability: *do not banish reason for i.* Meas. V, 65 (because it is not in accordance with your opinion. Or should it perhaps be = partiality?).

Inestimable, transcending all price: R3 I, 4, 27. Troil. II, 2, 88. Per. II, 4, 8.

Inevitable, unavoidable, not to be escaped: Merch. IV, 1, 57. Tw. III, 4, 304. Cor. IV, 1, 26. Ant. IV, 14, 65.

Inexecrable, reading of the earlier O. Edd. in Merch. IV, 1, 128: *i. dog*. F3.4 and M. Edd. *inexorable*.

Inexorable, not to be moved by entreaty, relentless: Merch. IV, 1, 128 (O. Edd. *inexecrable*). H6C I, 4, 154. Rom. V, 3, 38.

Inexplicable, unintelligible: *i. dumb shows*, Hml. III, 2, 13.

Infallible, admitting of no doubt, quite certain: Meas. III, 2, 119. LLL IV, 1, 61. All's I, 1, 150. Wint. I, 2, 287. H6B II, 2, 5.

Infallibly, without a possibility of mistaking, with a truth beyond doubt: *the text most i. concludes it*, LLL IV, 2, 169. *your lordship speaks most i. of him*, Hml. V, 2, 126.

Infamonize, Armado's word for disgrace: *dost thou i. me*, LLL V, 2, 684.

Infamous, disgraceful: H6A IV, 1, 30. Ant. IV, 9, 19.

Infamy, disgrace: Lucr. 504. 539. 794. 1025. 1055. 1173. 1638. Gent. II, 7, 64. Ado IV, 1, 135. 241. LLL V, 1, 72. H4B I, 2, 157. H5 II, 1, 79. H6A IV, 1, 143. IV, 5, 33. H6B III, 2, 71. H6C V, 1, 82. R3 III, 7, 126. IV, 4, 208. Per. I, 1, 145. Plur. *—ies*, Lucr. 636.

Infancy, the first part of life, early childhood: Tp. I, 2, 484. Gent. II, 4, 62. Wiv. V, 5, 56. LLL IV, 3, 245. Wint. V, 3, 27. H6A V, 4, 50. H6B I, 1, 93. R3 IV, 4, 168. Troil. I, 1, 12. II, 2, 105. III, 2, 177. Tit. V, 3, 165.

Infant, a young child: Ven. 562. 942. Sonn. 143, 8. LLL I, 1, 101. I, 2, 99. V, 1, 69. As II, 7, 143. Wint. III, 2, 71. V, 1, 44. John III, 4, 132. H4B IV, 1, 212. H5 III, 3, 14. 38. H6A III, 1, 16. H6B V, 2, 57. R3 II, 1, 71. IV, 4, 363. H8 V, 5, 18. 49. Troil. IV, 2, 6. Tit. IV, 1, 86. Caes. I, 1, 45. III, 1, 268. Hml. I, 3, 39. Per. III, 1, 41. III, 3, 15 (*the i. of your care*).

Adjectively: *i. sorrows*, Lucr. 1096. *an old i. play* LLL IV, 3, 78. *i. state*, John II, 97.*breath*, R2 I, 3, 133. *fortune*, II, 3, 66 and H4A I, 3, 253. *warrior*, III, 2, 113. *bands*, H5 Epil. 9. *your i. morn*, R3 IV, 4, 16. *the i. rind of this small flower*, Rom. II, 3, 23.

Infant-like, as of a little child: *your abilities are too i.* Cor. II, 1, 41.

Infect, 1) to affect in any manner, but always contrary to wishes: *Navarre is —ed. With what? With that which we lovers entitle affected*, LLL II, 230. *a fear which oft —s the wisest*, Wint. I, 2, 262. *never to be —ed with delight*, John IV, 3, 69. *if it did i. my blood with joy*, H4B IV, 5, 170. *no more —ed with my country's love than when I parted hence*, Cor. V, 6, 72.

2) to taint with disease, to pollute, to poison; absol.: *she would i. to the north star*, Ado II, 1, 257. *corruption —s unseen*, Hml. III, 4, 149. Trans.: Lucr. 850. Tp. I, 2, 208. III, 1, 31. V, 131. Err. II, 2, 182. LLL V, 2, 420. As II, 7, 60. Wint. I, 2, 305. 306. 418. II, 1, 42. H4A IV, 1, 28. H4B IV, 1, 58. H6C V, 4, 46. R3 I, 2, 149. 150. H8 I, 1, 162. I, 2, 133. V, 1, 46. Troil. I, 3, 8. Cor. I, 4, 33. II, 1, 105. Tim. I, 1, 48. IV, 1, 30. IV, 3, 3. V, 4, 43. Mcb. IV, 1, 138. V, 1, 80. Hml. III, 2, 269. Lr. II, 4, 168. Ant. I, 2,

99. Followed by *with:* As III, 2, 120. Shr. III 2, 52. H5 II, 2, 126. Hml. IV, 5, 90. Lr. I, 4, 264.

Partic. *infect,* for *—ed,* Troil. I, 3, 187.

Infected, adj. pertaining to infection; not implanted by nature, but as it were caught; factitious: *O that i. moisture of his eye,* Compl. 323. *this is in thee a nature but i.; a poor unmanly melancholy sprung from change of fortune,* Tim. IV, 3, 202.

Infection, 1) the state of being tainted with disease: *if that flower with base i. meet,* Sonn. 94, 11. *I will drink potions of eisel 'gainst my strong i.* 111, 10. *he hath ta'en the i.* Ado II, 3, 126 and Tw. III, 4, 142. *to the i. of my brains,* Wint. I, 2, 145. Cor. III, 1, 310. Rom. I, 2, 50. Lr. IV, 6, 237. Cymb. III, 2, 3.

2) a contagious disease, a plague: *their verdure still endure, to drive i. from the dangerous year,* Ven. 508 (certain herbs being supposed to keep off the plague). *advice is sporting, while i. breeds,* Lucr. 907. *wherefore with i. should he live,* Sonn. 67, 1. *all the —s that the sun sucks up,* Tp. II, 2, 1. Wint. I, 2, 423. V, 1, 169. John V, 2, 20. R2 II, 1, 44. H6B III, 2, 287. R3 I, 2, 78 (parodying v. 75). Rom. V, 2, 16. Tim. V, 1, 224.

Confounded with *affection* by Mrs Quickly and old Gobbo: Wiv. II, 2, 120. Merch. II, 2, 133.

Infectious, 1) having the plague: *like one i.* Wint. III, 2, 99. *the i. house,* Oth. IV, 1, 21 (Qq *infected*).

2) communicating a disease, contagious: *a huge i. troop of pale distemperatures,* Err. V, 81. *the i. pestilence,* Rom. V, 2, 10. Tim. IV, 1, 22. Ant. II, 5, 61. Cymb. I, 5, 26.

Infectiously, morbidly: *the will dotes that is attributive to what i. itself affects, without some image of the affected merit,* Troil. II, 2, 59.

Infer, 1) to bring in as an argument, to allege: *—ing arguments of mighty force,* H6C II, 2, 44. III, 1, 49. *i. the bastardy of Edward's children,* R3 III, 5, 75. *I did i. your lineaments,* III, 7, 12. *thus saith the duke, thus hath the duke —ed,* 32. *i. fair England's peace by this alliance,* IV, 4, 343. *what shall I say more than I have —ed?* V, 3, 314. *'tis —ed to us, his days are foul,* Tim. III, 5, 73.

2) to show, to prove, to demonstrate: *that need must needs i. this principle, that faith would live again by death of need,* John III, 1, 213. *this doth i. the zeal I had to see him,* H4B V, 5, 14. *I this i., that many things, having full reference to one consent, may work contrariously,* H5 I, 2, 204 (or = I draw this conclusion?).

Inference, that which has been alleged, reasoning: *when I shall turn the business of my soul to such exsufflicate and blown surmises, matching thy i.* Oth. III, 3, 183.

Inferior, adj. lower in station or value, subordinate; absol.: John V, 1, 50. R2 IV, 128. Cor. I, 1, 142. Oth. III, 4, 144. With *to:* Sonn. 80, 7. Shr. Ind. 2, 69. H6A III, 1, 96. V, 1, 57. H6C IV, 1, 122.

Inferior, subst. a person of a lower station: *that which any i. might have bought,* All's V, 3, 218. *my —s.* Cymb. II, 1, 32.

Infernal, pertaining to Tartarus or hell, hellish: Ado II, 1, 263. H4B II, 4, 170. Tit. V, 2, 30.

Infest, to harass, to vex: *do not i. your mind with beating on the strangeness of this business,* Tp. V, 246.

Infidel, subst. an unbeliever, one who is not a Christian: Merch. III, 2, 221. IV, 1, 334. R2 IV, 139. H4A II, 3, 32. R3 III, 5, 41.

Infinite, adj. boundless, endless, numberless, immense: Tp. IV, 210. Gent. II, 1, 60. Wiv. II, 2, 213. Meas. I, 4, 54. Err. V, 6. LLL V, 2, 199. Merch. I, 1, 114. All's II, 1, 187. III, 6, 11. Wint. I, 2, 253. John IV, 3, 117. H4A V, 1, 102. H5 IV, 1, 253. V, 2, 163. H8 III, 1, 82. Troil. III, 2, 88. IV, 4, 71. Tit. V, 3, 159. Rom. II, 2, 135. Tim. III, 6, 108. IV, 3, 178. V, 1, 37. Hml. I, 4, 34. II, 2, 261. 316. V, 1, 204. Ant. I, 2, 9. II, 2, 241. IV, 8, 17. V, 2, 358. Cymb. I, 1, 120. V, 4, 195.

Infinite, subst. infinity, boundlessness: *instances of i. of love,* Gent. II, 7, 70. *it is past the i. of thought,* Ado II, 3, 106. *will you with counters sum the past proportion of his i.?* Troil. II, 2, 29.

Infinitely, boundlessly, endlessly: *to whom I am so i. bound,* Merch. V, 135. *I love thee i.* H4A II, 3, 105. *promise you i.* H4B V, 5, 132. *so i. endeared,* Tim. I, 2, 233. *to whose kindnesses I am most i. tied,* Cymb. I, 6, 23.

Infinitive, Mrs Quickly's blunder for *infinite:* H4B II, 1, 26.

Infirm, 1) not firm, not steadfast: *i. of purpose,* Mcb. II, 2, 52.

2) weak, disabled by disease or age: All's II, 1, 170. Lr. I, 1, 302. III, 2, 20.

Infirmity, 1) moral weakness: *this ambitious foul i.* Lucr. 150. *be not disturbed with my i.* Tp. IV, 160. *allowed —ies,* Wint. I, 2, 263. *discover thine i.* H6A V, 4, 60. *a man of their i.* Cor. III, 1, 82. *bear his friends' —ies,* Caes. IV, 3, 86. *these fishers tell the —ies of men,* Per. II, 1, 53.

2) defect, imperfection: *to mingle beauty with —ies,* Ven. 735. *she speaks this in the i. of sense,* Meas. V, 47. *those —ies she owes,* Lr. I, 1, 205. *I am unfortunate in this i.* Oth. II, 3, 43. 132. 145. *assuming man's —ies,* Per. Prol. 3.

3) weakness caused by age: *i. that decays the wise doth ever make the better fool,* Tw. I, 5, 82. 84. *i. which waits upon worn times,* Wint. V, 1, 141. *'tis the i. of his age,* Lr. I, 1, 296.

4) disease: *will you be cured of your i.?* All's II, 1, 71. *it was his i.* Caes. I, 2, 274. *I have a strange i.* Mcb. III, 4, 86. *i. doth still neglect all office,* Lr. II, 4, 107. *play with all —ies for gold,* Cymb. I, 6, 124. *constrained by her i.* III, 5, 47.

5) incapability of begetting children: *leaving no posterity: 'twas not their i., it was married chastity,* Phoen. 60.

Infix, to imprint: *where the impression of mine eye —ing,* All's V, 3, 47. *I never loved myself till now —ed I beheld myself drawn in the flattering table of her eye,* John II, 502.

Inflame, 1) to set on fire: *to stop their marches 'fore we are —d,* John V, 1, 7. cf. Per. II, 2, 35.

2) to enkindle, to fire with passion, to excite; absol.: *when thou wilt i.* Compl. 268. *—ing wrath,* John III, 1, 340. *—ing love,* H6A V, 5, 82. *can as well i. as it can kill,* Per. II, 2, 35. IV, 1, 6 (corr. pass.). Trans.: H4B V, 5, 33. Caes. III, 2, 149. Lr. I, 1, 258. Oth. II, 1, 231. Per. I, 1, 20. IV, 1, 5. *—d with Lucrece' beauty,* Lucr. Arg. 12. *Mars his heart, —d with Venus,* Troil. V, 2, 165.

Inflammation, the state of being inflamed or

heated: *which some of us should be too, but for i.* H4B IV, 3, 103.

Inflict, 1) to lay on, to impose, to bring on: *lasting shame on thee and thine I will i.* Lucr. 1630. *no pain they can i. upon him,* H6B III, 1, 377.

2) to afflict, to punish, to visit: *i. our province,* Per. V, 1, 61 (M. Edd. *afflict*).

Infliction, the act of laying on, execution of a punishment: *our decrees, dead to i., to themselves are dead,* Meas. I, 3, 28.

Influence, subst. 1) a flowing in, infusion, inspiration: *be most proud of that which I compile, whose i. is thine and born of thee,* Sonn. 78, 10. *that's the way to choke a gibing spirit, whose i. is begot of that loose grace which shallow laughing hearers give to fools,* LLL V, 2, 869.

2) the power exerted by celestial bodies on terrestrial or other celestial bodies: Ven. 862. Sonn. 15, 4. Tp. I, 2, 182. Meas. III, 1, 9. All's II, 1, 56. Wint. I, 2, 426. Tim. V, 1, 66. Hml. I, 1, 119. Lr. I, 2, 136. II, 2, 113. Q in Troil. I, 3, 92. *I leave to be, if I be not by her fair i. fostered, illumined, cherished, kept alive,* Gent. III, 1, 183 (as by the sun).

Infold, to wrap, to enclose: *her arms i. him like a band,* Ven. 225; cf. *let me i. thee,* Mcb. I, 4, 31. *gilded tombs do worms i.* Merch. II, 7, 69. *unless the breath of groans mist-like i. me from the search of eyes,* Rom. III, 3, 73.

Infoldings, Autolycus' euphuism for clothes: Wint. IV, 4, 756.

Inform, 1) to form, to shape; absol.: *it is the bloody business which —s thus to mine eyes,* Mcb. II, 1, 48. trans: *the God of soldiers i. thy thoughts with nobleness,* Cor. V, 3, 71 (almost = inspire).

2) to instruct, to teach how to behave: *I shall i. them,* Cor. III, 3, 18. *nor can her heart i. her tongue,* Ant. III, 2, 48. *'twere good you leaned unto his sentence with what patience your wisdom may i. you,* Cymb. I, 1, 79. In Cor. III, 1, 47 the tribune takes the word in this sense.

3) to make acquainted, to communicate to, to tell: Tp. I, 2, 23. H4A I, 1, 104. H6A V, 1, 42. H8 V, 3, 17. Cor. III, 1, 47. Hml. I, 1, 79. Lr. II, 4, 99. 100. Ant. III, 6, 20. Cymb. II, 3, 157. With *of:* Merch. IV, 1, 173. All's I, 3, 128. Wint. I, 2, 396. H6A I, 1, 105. Cor. II, 2, 162. Lr. I, 4, 360. II, 1, 104. II, 2, 174. II, 4, 104. IV, 2, 8. Oth. II, 3, 198. Cymb. IV, 2, 361. With a dependant clause: All's IV, 4, 8. V, 3, 26. 97. H6A I, 4, 8. V, 4, 118. H6C IV, 4, 26. Ant. I, 4, 77.

Refl., = to know: *i. yourselves we need no more of your advice,* Wint. II, 1, 167.

4) to communicate, to report, to give intelligence of, to tell; trans.: *that let me i. you,* Meas. III, 2, 136. *haply thou mayst i. something to save thy life,* All's IV, 1, 91. *he did i. the truth,* Cor. I, 6, 42. Absol.: *a' will betray us all unto ourselves: i. on that,* All's IV, 1, 103. *who, were't so, would have —d for preparation,* Mcb. I, 5, 34 (would have given intelligence).

5) With *against,* = to communicate by way of accusation, to denounce: *what they will i. 'gainst any of us all, that will the king severely prosecute,* R2 II, 1, 242. *how all occasions do i. against me,* Hml. IV, 4, 32. *he —ed against him,* Lr. IV, 2, 93.

Informal, out of one's senses: Meas. V, 236 (cf. *Formal.*)

Information, 1) intelligence, notice; abstr. pro concr.: *to whip your i.* Cor. IV, 6, 53.

2) With *against,* = denouncement, accusation: *Lucio's i. against me,* Meas. III, 2, 210. *seeking tales and —s against this man,* H8 V, 3, 110.

Informer, denunciator, accuser: Ven. 655. Sonn. 125, 13.

Infortunate, not favoured by fortune, not prosperous, unlucky: John II, 178. H6B IV, 9, 18. Oth. II, 3, 42 (Qq *unfortunate*). V, 2, 283 (Ff *unfortunate*).

Infringe, to break, to transgress, to violate: Lucr. 1061. Meas. II, 2, 92. Err. I, 1, 4. LLL IV, 3, 144. 146. H6C II, 2, 8. R3 III, 1, 41. Cor. V, 3, 20.

Infuse, 1) to shed, to pour: *those clear rays which she —d on me,* H6A I, 2, 85.

2) to pour in, to instill: *these words i. new life in me,* Tit. I, 461. Reflexively: *souls of animals i. themselves into the trunks of men,* Merch. IV, 1, 132. *a wolf... —d itself in thee,* 137.

3) to inspire, to fill; in a good as well as a bad sense: *—ing them with dreadful prophecies,* Ven. 928. *—d with a fortitude from heaven,* Tp. I, 2, 154. *—d with so foul a spirit,* Shr. Ind. 2, 17. *—ing him with self and vain conceit,* R2 III, 2, 166. *i. his breast with magnanimity,* H6C V, 4, 41. *heaven hath —d them with these spirits,* Caes. I, 3, 69.

Infusion, 1) a medicinal liquor: *recovered with aqua vitae or some other hot i.* Wint. IV, 4, 816. *the blest —s that dwell in vegetives,* Per. III, 2, 35.

2) endowments, qualities: *his i. of such dearth and rareness,* Hml. V, 2, 122 (purposely affected).

Ingaged, not engaged, not bound (cf. *Gage*)*:* *thought I stood i.* All's V, 3, 96 (some M. Edd. preposterously *engaged*).

Ingener, see *Enginer.*

Ingenious, 1) dwelling in the mind, heartfelt, conscious: *a poor, decayed, i., foolish, rascally knave,* All's V, 2, 25 (= conscious of his own contemptibleness). *whose wicked deed thy most i. sense deprived thee of,* Hml. V, 1, 271. *I stand up and have i. feeling of my huge sorrows,* Lr. IV, 6, 287.

2) intellectual, mental: *a course of learning and i. studies,* Shr. I, 1, 9.

Ingenious or **Ingenuous** (used indiscriminately), of things, = artful, of curious structure: *my ingenuous instrument,* Cymb. IV, 2, 186 (M. Edd. *ingenious*). Of persons, = witty, inventive: *that an eel is ingenious,* LLL I, 2, 29 (Q2 Ff *ingenuous*). *the meaning, pretty ingenious?* III, 59 (Q2 *ingenuous*). *if their sons be ingenuous, they shall want no instruction,* IV, 2, 80 (Q1 *ingenous;* F1.2 *ingennous;* Q2 F3.4 *ingenuous*). *bold, quick, ingenious, forward, capable,* R3 III, 1, 155. *send out for torturers ingenious,* Cymb. V, 5, 215.

Ingeniously, from the heart: *i. I speak,* Tim. II, 2, 230.

Ingenuous, see *Ingenious.*

Inglorious, not bringing honour: John V, 1, 65.

Ingot, a bar or wedge of precious metal: Meas. III, 1, 26.

Ingraft, see *Engraft.*

Ingrate, ungrateful, unthankful: Shr. I, 2, 270. Tw. V, 116. John V, 2, 151. H4A I, 3, 137. Cor. V, 2, 92.

Ingrateful, unthankful: Tw. V, 80. Wint. III, 2, 188. John V, 7, 43. H5 II, 2, 95. Cor. II, 2, 35.

Tit. V, 1, 12. Tim. IV, 2, 45. IV, 3, 188. 194. Lr. II, 4, 165. III, 2, 9. III, 7, 28.

Ingratitude, unthankfulness: Gent. I, 2, 110. Merch. V, 218. As II, 7, 176. Tw. III, 4, 388. Wint. III, 2, 69. Troil. III, 3, 147 (plur.). Cor. I, 9, 30. II, 3, 10. Tit. I, 447. IV, 3, 33. Tim. II, 2, 224. III, 4, 27. V, 1, 68. V, 4, 17. Caes. I, 1, 60. III, 2, 189. Mcb. I, 4, 15. Lr. I, 4, 281. I, 5, 44. III, 4, 14. Ant. II, 6, 22. V, 2, 153.

Ingredience, that which composes a compound: *commends the i. of our poisoned chalice to our own lips,* Mcb. I, 7, 11 (M. Edd. *ingredients*). *add thereto a tiger's chaudron for the i. of our cauldron,* IV, 1, 34 (M. Edd. *ingredients*). *every inordinate cup is unblessed, and the i. is a devil,* Oth. II, 3, 311 (Ff and M. Edd. *ingredient*).

Ingredient, something entering into a compound: *the abhorred i.* Wint. II, 1, 43. *the i. is a devil,* Oth. II, 3, 311 (Qq *ingredience*). In Mcb. I, 7, 11 and IV, 1, 34 O. Edd. *ingredience.*

Ingross, see *Engross.*

Inhabit 1) to hold or occupy as a place of residence: Tw. III, 4, 391. IV, 2, 57.

2) intr. to dwell, to live, to abide: *durst i. on a living brow,* Sonn. 68, 4. *where man doth not i.* Tp. III, 3, 57. V, 105. Gent. I, 1, 44. IV, 2, 48. V, 4, 7. Err. III, 2, 161. IV, 3, 11. John IV, 2, 107. R2 IV, 143. R3 I, 4, 30.

3) to take as a habit (whether a costume or a custom), to do on: *if trembling I i. then, protest me the baby of a girl,* Mcb. III, 4, 105 (a passage much controverted and corrected).

Inhabitable, not habitable, not affording an habitation, uninhabitable: R2 I, 1, 65.

Inhabitant, dweller: H4B IV, 5, 138. Mcb. I, 3, 41.

Inhabited, lodged, in *Ill-inhabited.*

Inhearse, to enclose as in a coffin: *that did my ripe thoughts in my brain i.* Sonn. 86, 3. *—d in the arms of the most bloody nurser of his harms,* H6A IV, 7, 45.

Inherent, adhesive, sticking fast, not to be removed: *and by my body's action teach my mind a most i. baseness,* Cor. III, 2, 123.

Inherit, 1) to receive as a possession or a natural quality from a progenitor; absol.: *here's the twin-brother of thy letter, but let thine first i.* Wiv. II, 1, 74. trans.: *treason is not —ed,* As I, 3, 63. *her disposition she —s,* Alls I, 1, 47. I, 2, 22. II, 1, 13. H4B II, 2, 27. Tim. V, 4, 38. With *of: the cold blood he did naturally i. of his father,* H4B IV, 3, 128.

2) to have or take possession; absol.: *the king and all our company else being drowned, we will i. here,* Tp. II, 2, 179. *but to the girdle do the gods i.* Lr. IV, 6, 128. trans., = to have, to possess, to enjoy, to obtain, to gain: *they rightly do i. heaven's graces,* Sonn. 94, 5. *the great globe itself, yea, all which it i.* Tp. IV, 154. *this, or else nothing, will i. her,* Gent. III, 2, 87. *which with pain purchased doth i. pain,* LLL I, 1, 73. *nothing but fair is that which you i.* IV, 1, 20. *a grave, whose hollow womb —s nought but bones,* R2 II, 1, 83. *I have lived to see —ed my very wishes,* Cor. II, 1, 215. *to bury so much gold under a tree, and never after to i. it,* Tit. II, 3, 3. *such delight shall you i. at my house,* Rom. I, 2, 30. *how Wales was made so happy as to i. such a haven,* Cymb. III, 2, 63.

3) to put in possession, to possess: *it must be great that can i. us so much as of a thought of ill in him,* R2 I, 1, 85.

Inheritance, 1) a possession or estate received by right of succession: John I, 72. IV, 2, 97. R2 II, 3, 136. H5 I, 2, 99. H6A II, 5, 27. III, 1, 164. H6B I, 1, 82. IV, 10, 20. H6C I, 1, 78.

2) possession in general: *for a cardecue he will sell the fee-simple of his salvation, the i. of it,* Alls IV, 3, 312. *spend a fawn upon 'em for the i. of their loves,* Cor. III, 2, 68. *which had returned to the i. of Fortinbras, had he been vanquisher,* Hml. I, 1, 92.

Inheritor, 1) heir: Sonn. 146, 7. H4B IV, 5, 169. Troil. IV, 1, 64. Per. I, 4, 64.

2) possessor, owner: *the sole i. of all perfections that a man may owe,* LLL II, 5. *be i. of thy desire,* R3 IV, 3, 34. *the very conveyances of his lands will hardly lie in this box, and must the i. himself have no more?* Hml. V, 1, 121.

Inheritrix, heiress: H5 I, 2, 51.

Inherse, see *Inhearse.*

Inhibited, prohibited, forbidden: *the most i. sin in the canon,* Alls I, 1, 157. *a practiser of arts i.* Oth. I, 2, 79.

Inhibition, prohibition, hinderance: *how chances it they travel? their residence, both in reputation and profit, was better both ways. I think their i. comes by the means of the late innovation,* Hml. II, 2, 346 (their hinderance to reside, to take a fixed abode, comes from the new law which limited theatrical performances to two theatres, viz the Globe and the Fortune).

Inhooped, enclosed in a hoop: *his quails ever beat mine i.* Ant. II, 3, 38 (Cocks or quails were sometimes made to fight within a broad hoop, to keep them from quitting each other. cf. *Cock-a-hoop*).

Inhospitable, unkind to strangers: Per. V, 1, 254.

Inhuman (O. Edd. *inhumane;* cf. *Humane*) cruel, savage: Merch. IV, 1, 4. Alls V, 3, 116. H5 II, 2, 95. H6C I, 4, 154. R3 I, 2, 60. Tit. V, 2, 178. V, 3, 14. Oth. V, 1, 62.

Iniquity, wickedness: Lucr. 626. 872. 1687. Sonn. 62, 12. Wint. IV, 4, 694. H5 IV, 1, 160. H6B IV, 2, 29. Oth. I, 2, 3. IV, 1, 208. Per. IV, 6, 93. Abstr. pro concr.: Per. IV, 6, 28. It was one of the names of the Vice, the established buffoon of the old Moralities: *which is the wiser here? Justice or I.?* Meas. II, 1, 181. *like the formal vice I.* R3 III, 1, 82. The same allusion perhaps in H4A II, 4, 500: *that reverend vice, that grey i.*

Initiate, subst. or adj.? novice, or pertaining to a novice: *the i. fear that wants hard use,* Mcb. III, 4, 143.

Injoint, to join: *have there —ed them with an after fleet,* Oth. I, 3, 35 (cf. *Insinewed*).

Injunction, 1) imposition, obligation, engagement: *by great —s I am bound to enter publicly,* Meas. IV, 3, 100 (urgent motives). *to these —s every one doth swear,* Merch. II, 9, 17.

2) command, order: Tp. III, 1, 11. Tw. II, 5, 182. Lr. III, 4, 155.

Injure, 1) to hurt: *I fly thee, for I would not i. thee,* As III, 5, 9.

2) to wrong: H6B IV, 7, 107. H6C I, 1, 179. R3 I, 3, 56. Rom. III, 1, 71.

Injurer, one who wrongs: *monstrous i. of heaven and earth,* John II, 174

Injurious, 1) wrongful, unjust: *by whose i. doom my brother was done to death,* H6C III, 3, 101.

2) detractory, hurting reputation, insulting: *i. duke, that threatest where's no cause,* H6B I, 4, 51. *i. Margaret,* H6C III, 3, 78. *call me a traitor! thou i. tribune,* Cor. III, 3, 69. *i. thief, hear but my name,* Cymb. IV, 2, 86.

3) hurtful, offensive, mischievous, pernicious, contrary to beneficial: *robbed and ransacked by i. theft,* Lucr. 838. *i. shifting time,* 930. *i. distance should not stop my way,* Sonn. 44, 2. *with time's i. hand crushed,* 63, 2. *i. wasps, to feed on such sweet honey and kill the bees,* Gent. I, 2, 106. *O i. love, that respites me a life,* Meas. II, 3, 40. *i. world!* IV, 3, 127. *i. Hermia!* Mids. III, 2, 195. *like a false traitor and i. villain,* R2 I, 1, 91. *i. time now with a robber's haste crams his rich thievery up,* Troil. IV, 4, 44. *the i. Gods,* Ant. IV, 15, 76. *the i. Romans did extort this tribute,* Cymb. III, 1, 48.

Injury (the different significations scarcely to be kept asunder) 1) injustice, wrong: *without accusing you of i.* Sonn. 58, 8. *the —ies of a wanton time,* H4A V, 1, 50. *they did me too much i.* V, 4, 51. *whose bosom burns with an incensed fire of —ies,* H4B I, 3, 14. *it is the time, and not the king, that doth you —ies,* IV, 1, 106. *those wrongs, those bitter —ies,* H6A II, 5, 124. *you do me shameful i.* R3 I, 3, 88. *you do him i. to scorn his corse,* II, 1, 80. *not confess so much, were a kind of ingrateful i.* Cor. II, 2, 35. *one's i. =* a) the wrong done by one: *her i. the beadle to her sin,* John II, 188. *stooped my neck under your —ies,* R2 III, 1, 19. *saints in your —ies,* Oth. II, 1, 112. *he does buy my —ies, to be friends,* Cymb. I, 1, 105. *thy harsh and potent —ies,* V, 4, 84. b) the wrong suffered by one: *do with your —ies as seems you best,* Meas. V, 256. *his i. the gaoler to his pity,* Cor. V, 1, 64.

2) offence, insult: *dishonoured me even in the strength and height of i.* Err. V, 200. *till I torment thee for this i.* Mids. II, 1, 147. *you would not do me thus much i.* III, 2, 148. *I alone do feel the i.* 219. *his indignation derives itself out of a very competent i.* Tw. III, 4, 270. *return an i.* H5 IV, 7, 189. *what said Warwick to these —ies?* H6C IV, 1, 107. *this shall not excuse the —ies that thou hast done me,* Rom. III, 1, 69. *my i. =* the offence offered to me: Tw. V, 319. Tim. III, 5, 34.

3) any thing contrary to a benefit, mischief, damage, annoyance, hurt, ill: *it is a greater grief to bear love's wrong than hate's known i.* Sonn. 40, 12. *the —ies that to myself I do,* 88, 11. *weighs not the dust and i. of age,* 108, 10. *they elsewhere might dart their —ies,* 139, 12. *the i. of many a blasting hour,* Compl. 72. *conceit, my comfort and my i.* Err. IV, 2, 66. *out of all eyes, tongues, minds and —ies,* Ado IV, 1, 245. Mids. I, 1, 17. As I, 2, 203. Shr. III, 2, 28. Tw. V, 375. Wint. I, 2, 338. John II, 187. H4B V, 2, 8. Troil. IV, 4, 35. Cor. V, 6, 154. Lr. II, 4, 306. III, 1, 17. III, 3, 12. Oth. I, 3, 207. 314. Ant. V, 2, 117. Cymb. II, 4, 80. III, 4, 125. Per. V, 1, 131.

4) a crime (euphemistically): *a party in this i.* Oth. V, 1, 86.

5) a hurt or disease of the body: *thought not good to bruise an i. till it were full ripe,* H5 III, 6, 129.

6) any thing futile and contemptible, a naughtiness: *if thy pocket were enriched with any other —ies but these,* H4A III, 3, 182.

Injustice, 1) want of equity, the quality of being unjust: Meas. V, 312. Wint. III, 2, 148. R2 III, 1, 34. R3 V, 1, 6. H8 II, 4, 89. Tit. IV, 4, 18 (Qq *unjustice*).

1) an unjust action, a wrong: Lucr. 1693. Meas. IV, 4, 11. John V, 2, 23. H6B III, 2, 235.

Ink, the black liquor used for writing: Lucr. 1289. Sonn. 65, 14. 108, 1. Compl. 54. Gent. III, 1, 288. III, 2, 75. Err. III, 1, 13. LLL I, 1, 246. IV, 2, 27. IV, 3, 347. V, 2, 41. Tw. III, 2, 48. 53. IV, 2, 15. 88. 118. H4B IV, 1, 50. H6A V, 3, 66. R3 V, 3, 23. 49. 75. Troil. I, 1, 56. Tit. IV, 3, 106. Rom. V, 1, 25. Ant. I, 5, 65. Cymb. I, 1, 101. III, 2, 20. Per. III, 1, 66. *she is fallen into a pit of i., that the wide sea hath drops too few to wash her clean again,* Ado IV, 1, 142.

Inkhorn, an inkstand made of horn: Ado III, 5, 63. H6B IV, 2, 117. *an i. mate =* a bookish man: H6A III, 1, 99.

Inkle, a kind of tape: LLL III, 140. Wint. IV, 4, 208. Per. V Prol. 8.

Inkling, a hint, a vague intimation: *I can give you i. of an ensuing evil,* H8 II, 1, 140. *they have had i. this fortnight what we intend to do,* Cor. I, 1, 59.

Inky, 1) made with ink: *bound in with shame, with i. blots and rotten parchment bonds,* R2 II, 1, 64.

2) black: *i. brows,* As III, 5, 46. *my i. cloak,* Hml. I, 2, 77.

Inland, a word of a very vague signification, not so much denoting remoteness from the sea or the frontier, as a seat of peace and peaceful civilization; (perhaps opposed to mountainous districts as the seats of savage barbarousness; cf. Tw. IV, 1, 52; H5 V, 1, 37; Cymb. IV, 2, 100 & 370; and meaning the flat country): *a wall sufficient to defend our i. from the pilfering borderers,* H5 I, 2, 142. Adjectively: *yet am I i. bred and know some nurture,* As II, 7, 96. *who was in his youth an i. man, one that knew courtship too well,* III, 2, 363. *then the vital commoners and i. petty spirits muster me all to their captain, the heart,* H4B IV, 3, 119 (given till then to the arts of peace). Similarly perhaps in the following passage: *his state empties itself, as doth an i. brook into the main of waters,* Merch. V, 96 (a brook running through a well cultivated plain).

Inlay, to diversify and decorate by inserting something in the substratum: *the floor of heaven is thick inlaid with patines of bright gold,* Merch. V, 59. *they are worthy to i. heaven with stars,* Cymb. V, 5, 352.

Inlustrous, see *Illustrious.*

Inly, adj. inward: *the i. touch of love,* Gent. II, 7, 18. *how i. sorrow gripes his soul,* H6C I, 4, 171.

Inly, adv. inwardly: *I have i. wept,* Tp. V, 200. *sit patiently and i. ruminate the morning's danger,* H5 IV Chor. 24.

Inmost, deepest within, remotest from the surface: Tit. IV, 3, 12. Hml. III, 4, 20.

Inn, 1) the town-house of a nobleman: *thou most beauteous i.* R2 V, 1, 13.

2) a college of common law professors and students: *a must to the —s o' court,* H4B III, 2, 14. *Clement's i.* 15. *Gray's i.* 36. *in all the —s o' court,* 25. H6B IV, 7, 2.

3) a house of entertainment for travellers, a tavern: Err. I, 1, 54. I, 2, 14. 23. H4A III, 3, 93 (*shall I not take mine ease in mine i.*). Mcb. III, 3, 7. Lr. I, 4, 265.

Inn or Inne, vb. see *In,* vb.

Innkeeper, one who keeps a house for the entertainment of travellers: H4A IV, 2, 51.

Innocence, 1) freedom from a particular guilt, guiltlessness: Wint. III, 2, 31. R2 I, 3, 84 (M. Edd. *innocency*). H4B IV, 1, 45. H6B II, 3, 106. IV, 4, 59. R3 III, 5, 20 (Ff Q2.3.4.5 *innocency*). H8 I, 1, 208. III, 2, 301. V, 1, 142. Tit. I, 437.

2) freedom from any thought of evil, harmlessness, purity and simplicity of heart: Lucr. 1341. Tp. III, 1, 82. Mids. II, 2, 45. III, 2, 202. Merch. I, 1, 145. Tw. II, 4, 48. III, 1, 169. Wint. I, 2, 69. II, 2, 41. John IV, 1, 64. Tim. I, 1, 199. Per. I, 2, 93.

3) plainness and artlessness bordering on silliness: *who has not only his i., which is much, to excuse him,* Wint. V, 2, 70. Perhaps also in Merch. I, 1, 145.

Innocency, 1) freedom from a particular guilt: John IV, 3, 110. R2 I, 3, 84 (O. Edd. *innocence*). H4B V, 2, 39. R3 III, 5, 20 (Q1 *innocence*).

2) freedom from any thought of evil: Meas. III, 2, 10. H4A III, 3, 186. IV, 3, 63.

Innocent, name: *Pope I.* John III, 1, 139. 146.

Innocent, adj. 1) not guilty, free from a particular crime: Ado V, 1, 291. V, 4, 1. As I, 3, 56. Wint. II, 2, 29. John IV, 2, 252. IV, 3, 89. R2 I, 1, 103. H6B III, 1, 141. R3 I, 4, 187. Tit. III, 1, 115. Mcb. III, 1, 79. Ant. II, 5, 76. With *from: i. from meaning treason,* H6B III, 1, 69. *how i. I was from any private malice,* H8 III, 2, 267. With *of: be i. of the knowledge,* Mcb. III, 2, 45.

2) free from any thought of sin, quite harmless: Tp. II, 1, 155. 164. III, 3, 72. Ado IV, 1, 162. V, 1, 63. 194. 273. As II, 1, 39. Wint. II, 3, 29. III, 2, 101. 135. John IV, 1, 25. IV, 2, 259. H6B III, 2, 53. IV, 2, 86. H6C I, 3, 8. R3 I, 3, 182. II, 4, 52 (*the i. and aweless throne,* i. e. occupied by an innocent and unrespected child). IV, 3, 11. Tit. III, 2, 56. Mcb. I, 5, 66. II, 2, 36. IV, 3, 16. Hml. III, 4, 43. Cymb. III, 4, 70.

3) childish, silly: *an i. rhyme,* Ado V, 2, 38.

Innocent, subst. 1) a person free from guilt or any thought of evil: *it: the wild dog flesh his tooth on every i.* H4B IV, 5, 133. *accuse some i.* Tit. V, 1, 130. *thou hast killed the sweetest i.* Oth. V, 2, 199. *some —s scape not the thunderbolt,* Ant. II, 5, 77. Especially a little child: *to save the i.* Wint. II, 3, 166. *the guiltless blood of —s,* H6A V, 4, 44. *murdering —s,* H6C V, 6, 32. *incapable and shallow —s,* R3 II, 2, 18. *drunk with —s' blood,* IV, 4, 30 (Ff *innocent*).

2) an idiot: *a dumb i. that could not say him nay,* Alls IV, 3, 213. *pray, i., and beware the foul fiend,* Lr. III, 6, 8. *unless you play the pious i.* Per. IV, 3, 17.

Innovation, a change (for the worse): *rub the elbow at the news of hurlyburly i.* H4A V, 1, 78. *their inhibition comes by the means of the late i.* Hml. II, 2, 347 (cf. *Inhibition*). *I have drunk but one cup, and behold what i. it makes here,* Oth. II, 3, 42.

Innovator, an introducer of changes (for the worse): *a traitorous i.* Cor. III, 1, 175.

Innumerable, not to be counted, immense: H8 III, 2, 326.

Inobled, reading of F1 in Hml. II, 2, 525. 526. 527: *the i. queen.* The other O. Edd. *mobled. I.* perhaps = stripped of her majesty.

Inoculate, to graft, to bud: *virtue cannot so i. our old stock,* Hml. III, 1, 119.

Inordinate, improper, immoderate: *nothing in him seemed i.* Lucr. 94. *such i. and low desires,* H4A

III, 2, 12. *every i. cup is unblessed,* Oth. II, 3, 311 (Q1 *unordinate*).

Inquire, subst. a seeking for information, search: *make i. of his behaviour,* Hml. II, 1, 4 (Ff *inquiry*). *fame answering the most strange i.* Per. III Prol. 22.

Inquire, vb. (trisyll. in Shr. I, 2, 166), to ask questions, to seek for information; 1) absol.: *i. at London,* R2 V, 3, 5. *did prompt me to i.* Rom. II, 2, 80. Followed by *about: I promised to i. about a schoolmaster,* Shr. I, 2, 166. By *after: you have not been —d after,* Meas. IV, 1, 19. *would you buy her, that you i. after her?* Ado I, 1, 181. As III, 4, 50. Alls V, 2, 55. By *for: go i. for my master,* Wiv. I, 4, 42. Meas. IV, 1, 17. As IV, 3, 90. Per. IV, 6, 176. By *of,* in the same sense: *my father hath a power; i. of him,* R2 III, 2, 186. By an interr. clause: *i. where money is,* Merch. I, 1, 183. H4A III, 3, 61. Hml. II, 1, 7.

2) trans. to ask for, to seek out by asking: *you must i. your way,* Cor. III, 1, 54. *my brother never did urge me in this act: I did i. it,* Ant. II, 2, 46. With *forth: I shall i. you forth,* Gent. II, 4, 186. With *out. i. my lodging out,* Merch. II, 2, 162. IV, 2, 1. John IV, 3, 115. H4A IV, 2, 17. R3 IV, 2, 54. Tit. V, 2, 123. Rom. II, 4, 173. Tim. IV, 2, 48. Oth. III, 4, 14.

Inquiry (cf. *After-inquiry,* Cymb. V, 4, 189); *to make i. of* = to seek for information about: *we have made i. of you, and we hear such goodness of your justice,* Meas. V, 5. *to make i. of his behaviour,* Hml. II, 1, 4 (Qq *inquire*).

Inquisition, an asking or seeking for, search, inquiry: *left me to a bootless i.* Tp. I, 2, 35. *let not search and i. quail,* As II, 2, 20.

Inquisitive, asking for, seeking: *my youngest boy became i. after his brother,* Err. I, 1, 126. *falling there to find his fellow forth, unseen, i., confounds himself,* I, 2, 38.

Inroad, incursion: Ant. I, 4, 50.

Insane root, a root causing madness (probably hemlock or henbane): *have we eaten of the i. root,* Mcb. I, 3, 84.

Insanie, madness: *it insinuateth me of i.* LLL V, 1, 28 (O. Edd. *infamie*). cf. *Sanity.*

Insatiate, greedy so as not to be satisfied: R2 II, 1, 38. R3 III, 5, 87 (Qq *unsatiate*). III, 7, 7. Tit. V, 1, 88.

Insconce, to shelter, to hide: *he entertained a show so seeming just, and therein so —d his secret evil,* Lucr. 1515. *against that time do I i. me here within the knowledge of mine own desert,* Sonn. 49, 9. *you will i. your rags under the shelter of your honour,* Wiv. II, 2, 27. *I will i. me behind the arras,* III, 3, 96. *I must get a sconce for my head and i. it too,* Err. II, 2, 38. *we make trifles of terrors, —ing ourselves into seeming knowledge,* Alls II, 3, 4.

Inscribe, to write on: *in all you writ to Rome, Ego et Rex meus was still —d,* H8 III, 2, 315.

Inscription, words written on something: Merch. II, 7, 4. 14.

Inscroll, to write on a scroll: Merch. II, 7, 72.

Inscrutable, not to be traced out and understood, impenetrable: Gent. II, 1, 141.

Insculp, to carve, to cut: Merch. II, 7, 57.

Insculpture, an inscription cut in stone: Tim. V, 4, 67.

Insensible, 1) having no sense, void of feeling: *peace is ... deaf, sleepy, i.* Cor. IV, 5, 239. With *of:*

i. of mortality, Meas. IV, 2, 152 (indifferent to, not caring for, death).

2) not to be felt, imperceptible: *'tis i. then*, H4A V, 1, 140.

Inseparable, not to be parted: As I, 3, 78. John III, 4, 66.

Inseparate, indivisible: *that a thing i. divides more wider than the sky and earth*, Troil. V, 2, 148.

Insert, to put in, to take notice of in speaking or writing: LLL IV, 2, 19. Merch. I, 3, 95. Hml. II, 2, 568.

Inset, to set, to infix: *I will i. you neither in gold nor silver*, H4B I, 2, 19 (Ff *set*).

Inshelled, hid in the shell: Cor. IV, 6, 45.

Inshipped, embarked: H6A V, 1, 49.

Inside, the internal part: Wint. IV, 4, 833. John V, 2, 110. H4A III, 3, 8. H8 III, 2, 78. *kissing with i. lip*, Wint. I, 2, 286; i.e. very fervently, in the manner described by Iago in Oth. III, 3, 423.

Insinewed (Q *ensinewed*), joined in sinews, adding one's power, allied: *i. to this action*, H4B IV, 1, 172 (cf. John V, 2, 63 and *Injoint*).

Insinuate, 1) to ingratiate one's self (in a bad sense): *to i., flatter, bow*, R2 IV, 165. *base —ing flattery*, H6A II, 4, 35. *sly —ing Jacks*, R3 I, 3, 53. *the —ing nod*, Cor. II, 3, 106. *to see so great a lord basely i.* Tit. IV, 2, 38. *some busy and —ing rogue*, Oth. IV, 2, 131. Followed by *with*, = to make favour with: *with Death she humbly doth i.* Ven. 1012. *i. with you*, As Epil. 9.

2) to intermeddle: *thinkest thou, for that I i., or toaze from thee thy business, I am therefore no courtier?* Wint. IV, 4, 760. *take the devil in thy mind, and believe him not: he would i. with thee but to make thee sigh*, R3 I, 4, 152.

3) to give an intimation to, to put in mind: *it —th me of insanie*, LLL V, 1, 27 (Holofernes' speech; a doubtful passage).

Insinuation, 1) the act of making favour with a person: *make compromise, i., parley and base truce to arms invasive*, John V, 1, 68.

2) meddling: *their defeat does by their own i. grow*, Hml. V, 2, 59.

3) intimation, suggestion: *most barbarous intimation! yet a kind of i., as it were, in via, in way, of explication*, LLL IV, 2, 14 (Holofernes' speech).

Insist, to persist in demanding: *yet I —ed*, Caes. II, 1, 245. With *on: —ing on the old prerogative*, Cor. III, 3, 17.

Insisture, persistency, constancy: Troil. I, 3, 87 ("a word not found but in this place." Nares).

Insnare, see *Ensnare.*

Insociable (of five syll. in LLL V, 2, 809) 1) not companionable: LLL V, 1, 20. 2) retired from society: V, 2, 809.

Insolence, impudent overbearing, sauciness, petulancy: Shr. II, 23. H6A I, 3, 37. H6B I, 1, 175. I, 3, 125. II, 1, 31. II, 2, 70. H8 I, 1, 138. Troil. IV, 5, 258. Cor. I, 1, 266. II, 1, 270. III, 1, 70. Tim. V, 4, 12. Hml. III, 1, 73. Ant. III, 6, 20.

Insolent, overbearing, impudent, saucy: Tp. I, 1, 46. John II, 122. H6B III, 1, 7. Troil. I, 3, 369. II, 3, 218. Cor. IV, 6, 30. V, 6, 131. Lr. I, 4, 221. Oth. I, 3, 137.

Insomuch, seeing that, since, as: *I speak not this that you should bear a good opinion of my knowledge, i. I say I know you are*, As V, 2, 60.

Inspiration, 1) the operation of a higher being on the mind: Err. II, 2, 169. H6A V, 4, 40.

2) a sudden thought, conceit: *holy men at their death have good —s*, Merch. I, 2, 31.

Inspire, 1) to animate by supernatural infusion, to fill with ideas from a higher source: Alls II, 1, 151. R2 II, 1, 31. H8 I, 1, 91. Tit. IV, 1, 67. Cymb. II, 3, 55. Followed by *with*, to denote the agent or the medium: *was Mahomet —d with a dove? thou with an eagle art —d then?* H6A I, 2, 140. *—d with the spirit of putting down kings*, H6B IV, 2, 38. *i. us with the spleen of fiery dragons*, R3 V, 3, 350.

2) to rouse the mind of, to animate in general: *what zeal, what fury hath —d thee now?* LLL IV, 3, 229.

3) to breathe into, to infuse: *dawning day new comfort hath —d*, Tit. II, 2, 10.

Install, to place in a rank or office, to instate: *—ed me in the diadem*, H6A II, 5, 89. *—ed in that high degree*, IV, 1, 17. *is my lord of Winchester —ed*, V, 1, 28. H6C III, 1, 46. *Cranmer is —ed lord archbishop*, H8 III, 2, 402.

Instalment, the act of instating in a rank or office: *each fair i., coat and several crest, with loyal blazon, evermore be blest*, Wiv. V, 5, 67. *the i. of this noble duke in the seat royal*, R3 III, 1, 163.

Instance, that which drives to a thought or action; that by which something is perceived or occasioned; 1) cause, motive: *wherefore? what's the i.?* Alls IV, 1, 44. *gave thee no i. why thou shouldst do treason*, H5 II, 2, 119. *his fears are shallow, wanting i.* R3 III, 2, 25. *Troy had been down, but for these —s*, Troil. I, 3, 77. *the —s that second marriage move are base respects of thrift*, Hml. III, 2, 192.

2) argument, proof: *what i. of the contrary?* Gent. II, 4, 16. *one of our covent gives me this i.* Meas. IV, 3, 134. *they will scarcely believe this without trial: offer them —s*, Ado II, 2, 42. *i., briefly*, As III, 2, 53. *a better i.* 59. 62. 71. *for i., sir, that you may know you shall not want, one word*, Wint. IV, 4, 604. *the examples of every minute's i., present now, hath put us in these ill-beseeming arms*, H4B IV, 1, 83. *I have received a certain i. that Glendower is dead*, III, 1, 103. *what i. gives Lord Warwick for his vow?* H6B III, 2, 159. *i., O i., strong as Pluto's gates ... i., O i., strong as heaven itself*, Troil. V, 2, 153. 155. *not with such familiar —s as he hath used of old*, Caes. IV, 2, 16 (= proofs of familiarity).

3) sign, symptom, token: *blushing red no guilty i. gave*, Lucr. 1511 (= no sign of guilt). *—s of infinite of love*, Gent. II, 7, 70. *before the always wind-obeying deep gave any tragic i. of our harm*, Err. I, 1, 65.

4) a single case by which something is proved, example, precedent: *my desires had i. and argument to commend themselves*, Wiv. II, 2, 256. *the reason that I gather he is mad, besides this present i. of his rage*, Err. IV, 3, 88. *yet doth this accident and flood of fortune so far exceed all i.* Tw. IV, 3, 12.

5) a pattern, a sample, a specimen from which the whole may be known: *why should that gentleman that rode by Travers give then such —s of loss?* H4B I, 1, 56 (= details). *nature is fine in love, and where 'tis fine, it sends some precious i. of itself after the thing it loves*, Hml. IV, 5, 162.

6) a sentence, a saw, a proverb, any thing alleged to support one's own opinion: *an old i. that lived in*

he time of good neighbours, Ado V, 2, 78. *full of wise saws and modern —s,* As II, 7, 156. *what verse for it? what i. for it?* Troil. V, 10, 41.

Instant, subst. 1) the present moment: *let's take the i. by the forward top,* Alls V, 3, 39. *I feel now the future in the i.* Mcb. I, 5, 59. *whose virtue and obedience doth this i. so much commend itself,* Lr. II, 1, 115. *at this i.:* Meas. V, 151. H8 I, 1, 127. Lr. I, 2, 177. II, 2, 101. Cymb. V, 5, 469. *for the i.* Ant. II, 2, 104. *from this i.* Cor. III, 3, 101. Mcb. II, 3, 97. Oth. IV, 2, 208. *on* or *upon the i.* = immediately: LLL III, 42. Oth. I, 2, 38. III, 3, 471. IV, 3, 7. Cymb. III, 5, 97. *o' the i.,* in the same sense: Tim. II, 2, 207. IV, 1, 7. *to this i.* Err. IV, 4, 31. *until this i.* H5 IV, 7, 59.

2) any moment: *to make some special i. special blest,* Sonn. 52, 11. *the very i. that I saw you, did my heart fly to your service,* Tp. III, 1, 64. *till that i. shut my woeful self up,* LLL V, 2, 817. Tw. I, 1, 21. Wint. V, 2, 75. *at the very i. of Falstaff's and our meeting,* Wiv. V, 3, 16. Ado II, 2, 16. Tim. I, 2, 116. *at an i.* = at the same moment, at once: *did he send you both these letters at an i.?* Wiv. IV, 4, 4. As I, 3, 76. H4A V, 4, 151. *in the i.* Wiv. III, 5, 73. Err. IV, 1, 9. Merch. IV, 1, 152. John III, 4, 113. Rom. I, 1, 115. *in an i.* = at once, at the same time: *wilt thou show the whole wealth of thy wit in an i.?* Merch. III, 5, 62. As III, 2, 225. Lr. V, 3, 229. *on the i.* = at that moment: *dying upon the i. that she was accused,* Ado IV, 1, 217. *the French ambassador upon that i. craved audience,* H5 I, 1, 91. *on the i. they got clear of our ship,* Hml. IV, 6, 18. Cymb. I, 5, 50.

Instant, adj. 1) present, happening or offering itself at this moment: *from the time of his remembrance to this very i. disaster of his setting i' the stocks,* Alls IV, 3, 127. *the i. action,* H4B I, 3, 37. *whose figure even this i. cloud puts on,* H8 I, 1, 225. *take the i. way,* Troil. III, 3, 153 (= serve the present time). *your good tongue, more than the i. army we can make, might stop our countryman,* Cor. V, 1, 37.

2) immediate, without delay: *that you will take your i. leave,* Alls II, 4, 49. *to wage an i. trial with the king,* H4A IV, 4, 20. Tim. III, 1, 18. III, 2, 41. Hml. I, 5, 71. II, 2, 538. Lr. I, 4, 268. II, 1, 130. V, 3, 149. Cymb. V, 5, 278.

Adverbially, = immediately, without delay: *to whom 'tis i. due,* Tim. II, 2, 239. *grow not i. old,* Hml. I, 5, 94.

Instantly, 1) immediately, without delay: Meas. V, 253. 382. Ado I, 2, 16. Merch. I, 3, 56. II, 9, 52. IV, 1, 281 (Q1 *presently*). As IV, 3, 146 (in this one passage used of the past). Wint. II, 3, 134. III, 3, 14. IV, 4, 648. John V, 7, 76. H6B V, 2, 27. H8 II, 1, 48. Troil. I, 2, 297. IV, 4, 53. Cor. II, 3, 221. Tim. II, 2, 35. Caes. III, 1, 9. Hml. II, 2, 35. Lr. III, 3, 23. III, 7, 4. V, 3, 36. Ant. I, 2, 145. Per. I, 1, 148.

2) at the same time, at once: *as if he mastered there a double spirit of teaching and of learning i.* H4A V, 2, 65.

Instate, to put in possession, to invest: *for his possessions ... we do i. and widow you withal,* Meas. V, 249.

Instead of, in place of, to make up for: Lucr. 669. As II, 4, 52. John II, 227. H4A V, 3, 8. H4B I, 3, 57. H6A I, 1, 46. 87. 117. H6B III, 1, 294. IV, 7, 143. IV, 10, 15. H6C I, 1, 98. II, 6, 54. R3 I, 1, 10. V, 4, 12. Troil. I, 1, 61.

Insteeped, steeped, drenched: H5 IV, 6, 12.

Instigate, to prick on, to incite: Lucr. 43. Wiv. III, 5, 77. H6B III, 1, 51.

Instigation, pricking on, incitement (used as a vox media): Wint. II, 1, 163. R3 III, 7, 139. Caes. II, 1, 49. Somewhat blunderingly used by Horner: *I am come hither, as it were, upon my man's i.* H6B II, 3, 88 (i. e. my man has been the occasion of my coming).

Instinct, natural impulse, knowledge not acquired by experience, but inborn: H4A II, 4, 299. 300. 349. 409. 543. H6B III, 2, 250. Cor. V, 3, 35. Cymb. IV, 2, 177. V, 5, 381. *by i.:* Sonn. 50, 7. H4B I, 1, 86. R3 II, 3, 42. *on i.:* H4A II, 4, 301. 331. 389. 390.

Instinctively, by natural impulse: Tp. I, 2, 148. In Oth I, 3, 154 F1 erroneously *i.,* Quarto *intentively,* F2.3.4 *distinctively.*

Institute, 1) to establish, to appoint: *we i. your grace to be our regent,* H6A IV, 1, 162.

2) to set on foot, to begin: *i. a course of learning,* Shr. I, 1, 8.

Institutions, rules and forms of government: Meas. I, 1, 11.

Instruct. 1) to teach as or like a tutor; absol.: Alls IV, 3, 302. H6A IV, 1, 159. Cor. I, 1, 105. Oth. IV, 3, 104. Trans.: Meas. IV, 2, 57. Shr. I, 1, 95. 192. I, 2, 134. 174. II, 57. H4B II, 2, 95. H8 I, 2, 113. Troil. II, 3, 262. V, 7, 17. Tit. V, 1, 98. Oth. II, 1, 224. Followed by an inf.: Tp. II, 2, 173. H6A III, 1, 133. Ant. III, 11, 7. Cymb. III, 3, 3. By a subord. clause: Meas. I, 3, 46. Tim. I, 1, 133. Per. IV, 2, 59.

2) to inform, to furnish with knowledge: *in all these circumstances I'll i. you,* Shr. V, 2, 119. *of what strength and nature, I am not yet —ed,* Meas. I, 1, 81. Of following: *he'll then i. us of this body,* Cymb. IV, 2, 360.

3) to direct, to furnish with orders or precepts: *she well —s me,* Hml. V, 2, 218. *if thou dost as this —s thee,* Lr. V, 3, 29. With an inf.: *I will i. my sorrows to be proud,* John III, 1, 68. With a clause: *i. my daughter how she shall persever,* Alls III, 7, 37. With *to: that —ed him to mercy,* Meas. III, 2, 128.

4) to inspire, to prompt: *to ebb hereditary sloth —s me,* Tp. II, 1, 223. *I speak as my understanding —s me,* Wint. I, 1, 21. *as your charities shall best i. you,* II, 1, 114. *some powerful spirit i. the kites and ravens to be thy nurses,* II, 3, 186. *with what vehe mency the occasion shall i. you,* H8 V, 1, 150. *very nature will i. her in it,* Oth. II, 1, 237.

Instruction, 1) teaching, tutoring: *I would be glad to receive some i.* Meas. IV, 2, 19. *they shall want no i.* LLL IV, 2, 81. *my i. shall serve to naturalize thee,* Alls I, 1, 222. cf. Cor. I, 4, 22. *i.,* manners, Tim. IV, 1, 18. *have by their brave i. got upon me a nobleness in record,* Ant. IV, 14, 98. Denoting spiritual advice: *I am going with i. to him,* Meas. II, 3, 38. III, 2, 33. cf. Merch. I, 2, 16.

2) a precept conveying knowledge: *it is a good divine that follows his own —s,* Merch. I, 2, 16. *I will better the i.* III, 1, 76. *I cannot say 'tis pity she lacks —s,* Wint. IV, 4, 593. *we but teach bloody —s,* Mcb. I, 7, 9. *and let —s enter,* Cymb. I, 5, 47.

3) information: *the queen my mistress of thy intents desires i.* Ant. V, 1, 54.

4) authoritative information, direction: *that you*

will some good i. give how I may bear me here, Tp. I, 2, 424. *of my i. hast thou nothing bated,* III, 3, 85. *if my —s may be your guide,* Meas. IV, 2, 181. *keep your i.* IV, 5, 3. *I'll give thee more —s,* Shr. Ind. 1, 130. *under my poor —s,* Alls IV, 4, 27.

5) prompting, suggestion: *yet had he framed to himself, by the i. of his frailty, many deceiving promises of life,* Meas. III, 2, 259. *now it lies you on to speak to the people, not by your own i., but with such words that are but roted in your tongue,* Cor. III, 2, 53. *nature would not invest herself in such shadowy passion without some i.* Oth. IV, 1, 41.

Instrument, 1) tool, organ; applied to things: Lucr. 1038. Tp. III, 3, 54 (cf. *To*). Wint. II, 1, 154. John IV, 1, 104. R2 V, 5, 107. H4B IV, 1, 217. H6C V, 1, 87. Troil. Prol. 4. I, 3, 354. Cor. I, 1, 104. Rom. V, 3, 200. Caes. I, 3, 70. III, 1, 154. Mcb. II, 1, 43. Hml. V, 2, 327. Lr. V, 3, 171. Oth. I, 3, 271. Cymb. III, 4, 75. V, 4, 10. To persons: Meas. V, 237. Alls V, 3, 202. Wint. I, 2, 415. IV, 4, 637. V, 2, 77. John V, 2, 81. H6A III, 3, 65. H6C IV, 6, 18. Mcb. I, 3, 124. III, 1, 81. IV, 3, 239. Ant. V, 2, 236. Per. IV Prol. 44.

2) agent, author: *I partly know the i. that screws me from my true place in your favour,* Tw. V, 125. *that cause ... was cursed i. of his decease,* H6A II, 5, 58. *if haply you my father do suspect an i. of this your calling back,* Oth. IV, 2, 45.

3) a document: *I kiss the i. of their pleasures,* Oth. IV, 1, 232.

4) any tool or machine to make music: Lucr. 1140. 1464. Tp. III, 2, 146. Gent. III, 2, 84. As IV, 3, 68. Shr. I, 1, 82. 93. II, 100. 155. III, 1, 22. 25. 38. 64. Alls III, 6, 69. R2 I, 3, 163. II, 1, 149. H4A V, 2, 98. Troil. III, 1, 104. Cor. I, 9, 41. Rom. IV, 5, 86. Tim. I, 2, 102. Caes. IV, 3, 239. 257. 271. 293. Hml. III, 2, 387. Oth. III, 1, 3. 6. 10. IV, 2, 169. Cymb. IV, 2, 186.

Instrumental, serving as a tool, helpful, serviceable: *the hand more i. to the mouth,* Hml. I, 2, 48.

Insubstantial, incorporeal, created out of nothing, shadowy: *this i. pageant,* Tp. IV, 155.

Insufficience, want of the requisite power, incompetency: Wint. I, 1, 16.

Insufficiency, the same: Sonn. 150, 2. Mids. II, 2, 128.

Insuit, the unintelligible reading of O. Edd. in Alls V, 3, 216; most M. Edd. *infinite.*

Insult, vb. to exult, to triumph as a victorious enemy: *under his —ing falchion lies harmless Lucretia,* Lucr. 509. *no lord of thine, thou haught —ing man,* R2 IV, 254 (Ff *haught-insulting*). *now am I like that proud —ing ship which Caesar and his fortunes bare at once,* H6A I, 2, 138. *thy* (death's) *—ing tyranny,* IV, 7, 19. *—ing Charles,* V, 4, 147. *hath that poor monarch taught thee to i.?* H6C I, 4, 124. *the proud —ing queen,* II, 1, 168. *proud —ing boy,* II, 2, 84. *-- ing tyranny begins to jet upon the innocent and aweless throne,* R3 II, 4, 51. *i. without all reason,* Cor. III, 1, 144. *being down, —ed,* Lr. II, 2, 126. With *on: I will i. on him,* Tit. III, 2, 71. With *over: death —s o'er dull and speechless tribes,* Sonn. 107, 12. *that you i., exult, and all at once, over the wretched,* As III, 5, 36. *I might have let alone the —ing hand of Douglas over you,* H4A V, 4, 54. *so he walks, —ing o'er his prey,* H6C I, 3, 14.

Insulter, a triumphing enemy: *her lips are conquerors, his lips obey, paying what ransom the i. willeth,* Ven. 550.

Insultment, exultation, triumph over a conquered enemy: *he on the ground, my speech of i. ended on his dead body,* Cymb. III, 5, 145.

Insupportable, intolerable, insufferable: Alls II, 3, 243. Caes. IV, 3, 151. Oth. V, 2, 98.

Insuppressive, insuppressible, not to be kept down: *the i. mettle of our spirits,* Caes. II, 1, 134.

Insurrection, seditious rising, rebellion: Lucr. 722. H4A V, 1, 79. H4B I, 1, 201. IV, 1, 40. Cor. I, 1, 225. IV, 3, 13. Caes. II, 1, 69.

Integrity, freedom from any falseness and dishonesty, perfect uprightness: Gent. III, 2, 77. Meas. IV, 2, 205. V, 107. LLL V, 2, 356. Alls IV, 2, 33. Wint. I, 2, 240. III, 2, 27. R2 V, 3, 108. H8 II, 4, 59. III, 1, 51. V, 1, 115. V, 3, 145. Troil. IV, 5, 170. Cor. III, 1, 159 (or is it here a sound and untainted state in general?). Tit. I, 48. Mcb. IV, 3, 115. Cymb. V, 5, 44. With *to: my i. to heaven,* H8 III, 2, 454. *my i. and truth to you,* Troil. III, 2, 172.

Intellect, 1) understanding: LLL I, 1, 71. IV, 2, 27. V, 1, 64. R2 V, 1, 28.

2) meaning, or (according to Baynes) = sign, signature? LLL IV, 2, 137 (*intellection* being a schoolterm for synecdoche).

Intellectual, pertaining to the understanding: Err. II, 1, 22. H5 III, 7, 148.

Intelligence, 1) mental intercourse, terms of mutual understanding: *that affable familiar ghost which nightly gulls him with i.* Sonn. 86, 10. *if with myself I hold i. or have acquaintance with mine own desires,* As I, 3, 49. *last night the very gods showed me a vision, — I fast and prayed for their i.* Cymb. IV, 2, 347.

2) notice, information, news: Wiv. IV, 2, 154. Mids. I, 1, 248. Alls III, 6, 32. IV, 5, 88. Wint. IV, 2, 51. R2 II, 1, 278. III, 3, 1. H4A V, 5, 10. H5 II Chor. 12. R3 II, 1, 54. H8 I, 1, 153. Troil. V, 2, 193. Cor. IV, 3, 30. Mcb. I, 3, 76. Cymb. I, 6, 114. *to give i.:* Wiv. III, 5, 85. Ado I, 3, 46. Lr. II, 1, 23. *to have i.:* Wiv. IV, 2, 95. Alls IV, 3, 70. Wint. IV, 2, 42. R3 III, 2, 24. Abstr. pro concr., = spy, informer: *where hath our i. been drunk?* John IV, 2, 116. *sought to entrap me by i.* H4A IV, 3, 98.

Intelligencer, one who entertains the communication and intercourse between two parties, an agent, mediator: *the very opener and i. between the grace, the sanctities of heaven and our dull workings,* H4B IV, 2, 20. *Richard yet lives, hell's black i., only reserved their factor, to buy souls and send them thither,* R3 IV, 4, 71.

Intelligencing, going between parties: *a most i. bawd,* Wint. II, 3, 68.

Intelligent, bearing intelligence, giving information, communicative: *be i. to me,* Wint. I, 2, 378. *which are to France the spies and speculations i. of our state,* Lr. III, 1, 25. *which approves him an i. party to the advantages of France,* III, 5, 12. *our posts shall be swift and i. betwixt us,* III, 7, 12.

Intemperance, want of moderation, licentiousness: H4A III, 2, 156 (Ff *intemperature*). Mcb. IV, 3, 66.

Intemperate, unrestrained, immoderate: Meas. V, 98. Ado IV, 1, 60.

Intemperature, reading of Ff in H4A III, 2, 156; Qq *intemperance.*

Intend, 1) to tend, to be apt: *and i. to chide myself even for this time I spend in talking to thee,* Gent. IV, 2, 103. *any thing that —s to laughter,* H4B I, 2, 9 (Ff *tends*).

2) to bend, to direct: *my thoughts i. a zealous pilgrimage to thee,* Sonn. 27, 6. *as they did battery to the spheres i.* Compl. 23. *if he should i. this voyage towards my wife,* Wiv. II, 1, 188. *if thou dost i. never so little show of love to her,* Mids. III, 2, 333. *the king is set forth, or hitherwards —ed speedily,* H4A IV, 1, 92. *Caesar through Syria —s his journey,* Ant. V, 2, 201. *and to Tarsus i. my travel,* Per. I, 2, 116.

3) to mean, to design, to purpose; absol.: *as I i.* LLL V, 2, 429. *after the measure as you —ed well,* Cor. V, 1, 47. *as I —ed,* Rom. V, 3, 245. *I i. so,* Oth. IV, 1, 173. With an obj.: Gent. III, 1, 18. IV, 3, 44. V, 2, 41. Meas. V, 154. Ado I, 3, 47. II, 2, 46. LLL V, 2, 155. Mids. III, 2, 12. John V, 4, 61. R2 V, 3, 33. H5 II, 2, 6. 157. H6B III, 1, 265. IV, 4, 37. V, 1, 56. 60. R3 III, 1, 158. III, 5, 70. H8 Prol. 21. II, 4, 235. Cor. V, 2, 49. Tit. I, 78. II, 1, 122. Caes. III, 1, 151. Hml. II, 1, 5. Lr. I, 1, 228. Oth. IV, 1, 119. Followed by *for: —s you for his swift ambassador,* Meas. III, 1, 58 (= to be). *what I i. for thee,* John III, 3, 68 (in thy favour). By *to* or a simple dative: *here's no harm —ed to thee,* Wint. IV, 4, 642. R3 IV, 4, 237. Troil. II, 2, 39. Caes. III, 1, 90. Lr. V, 1, 66. By *towards: any harm's —ed towards him,* Caes. II, 4, 31. By *upon: the goodness I i. upon you,* Lr. V, 1, 7. Governing an inf.: *he —s to hunt the boar,* Ven. 587. Lucr. Arg. 8. Gent. III, 1, 11. Shr. Ind. I, 29. 81. Tw. V, 155. Wint. V, 2, 112. John V, 1, 55. H4A V, 2, 94. H6A I, 1, 176. I, 3, 88. III, 1, 4. H6B III, 2, 16. 255. H6C I, 2, 50. II, 5, 139. IV, 2, 25. R3 IV, 4, 263 (Qq *mean*). Troil. IV, 1, 78. Cor. I, 1, 60. II, 2, 159. V, 6, 7. Tit. IV, 1, 116. Rom. V, 3, 34. Lr. I, 1, 240. Oth. V, 2, 64. Ant. V, 2, 186. Inf. without *to: how long within this wood i. you stay?* Mids. II, 1, 138 (perhaps subst.).

4) to mean, to purport, to understand: *that is —ed in the general's name,* H4B IV, 1, 166. *so help me God, as I dissemble not! So help me God, as I i. it not,* H6A III, 1, 141 (do not mean what my words express). *I speak no more than what my soul —s,* H6C III, 2, 94. *how i. you, practised?* Ant. II, 2, 40. Used by Dr. Caius even in the sense of to understand = the French *entendre: i. vat I speak,* Wiv. I, 4, 47.

5) to wish: *as I i. to thrive in this new world,* R2 IV, 78. *as my soul —s to live with that dread king,* H6B III, 2, 153. *as I i. to thrive to-day,* H6B V, 2, 17. *as I i. to prosper and repent,* R3 IV, 4, 397. Followed by a subordinate clause with *shall: he doth i. she shall be England's queen:* H6A V, 1, 45. Gent. II, 6, 39. Wiv. IV, 6, 38 (cf. *Intent*).

6) to pretend: *—ing weariness with heavy spright,* Lucr. 121. *i. a kind of zeal both to the prince and Claudio,* Ado II, 2, 35. *I i. that all is done in care of her,* Shr. IV, 1, 206. *—ing deep suspicion,* R3 III, 5, 8. *i. some fear,* III, 7, 45. *—ing other serious matters,* Tim. II, 2, 219.

Intendment, 1) intention, purpose: Ven. 222. As I, 1, 140. Oth. IV, 2, 206.

2) direction, bent, aim: *we do not mean the coursing snatchers only, but fear the main i. of the Scot,* H5 I, 2, 144.*

Intenible, incapable of retaining: *in this captious and i. sieve,* All's I, 3, 208.

Intent, 1) bent, direction, aim: *with swift i. he goes to quench the coal,* Lucr. 46. *that their business might be every thing, and their i. every where,* Tw. II, 4, 80.

2) intention, purpose, design: Ven. 469. Lucr. 218. Sonn. 115, 7. Meas. V, 124. 456. 457. 459. LLL V, 2, 137. 138. 140. 467. 768. Mids. IV, 1, 138. 156. V, 79. 114. All's I, 1, 244. III, 4, 21. IV, 3, 32. IV, 4, 4. Tw. I, 2, 55. John II, 580. IV, 1, 96. R2 IV, 329. H4A V, 2, 89. H4B V, 2, 143. H6A V, 5, 20. H6B III, 1, 355. III, 2, 251. H6C I, 2, 39. II, 1, 117. R3 I, 1, 149. 158. III, 5, 69. Troil. I, 3, 306. V, 3, 8. Cor. II, 2, 160. V, 6, 13. Tit. IV, 2, 151. Rom. V, 3, 44. 134. 154. Mcb. I, 7, 26. Hml. I, 4, 42. Lr. I, 1, 39. 2, 88. 4, 2. II, 1, 66. IV, 7, 9. V, 3, 296. Ant. V, 1, 54. V, 2, 126. 226. Per. IV, 6, 116. V, 1, 259. *to that i.* = for that purpose: Shr. I, 2, 199. Oth. I, 2, 56. *to have an i.* All's I, 3, 224. *to have no i.* Ado I, 1, 195. H4B III, 1, 72. *had i.* Per. II Prol. 24 (Q1 *hid i.*). Followed by *towards: in his i. towards our wives,* Wiv. II, 1, 181; cf. Tim. V, 1, 23.

3) wish: *humble my —s to your directions,* H4B V, 2, 120. *for your i. in going back to school,* Hml. I, 2, 112. *my stronger guilt defeats my strong i.* III, 3, 40. *to have i.,* followed by *shall,* = to wish, to desire: *he hath i. his wonted followers shall all be very well provided for,* H4B V, 5, 104. *belike his majesty hath some i. that you shall be new-christened,* R3 I, 1, 49.

4) that which is meant or understood by word or letter; meaning, purport, thought: *the i. and purpose of the law hath full relation to the penalty,* Merch. IV, 1, 247. *their* (the letters') *cold i., tenour and substance,* H4B IV, 1, 9; cf. H6A V, 1, 3. *to-morrow shall you bear our full i. back to our brother England,* H5 II, 4, 114. *to set a gloss upon his bold i.* H6A IV, 1, 103. *you may be pleased to catch at mine i. by what did here befall me,* Ant. II, 2, 41.

Intention, bent, drift, aim: *she did so course o'er my exteriors with such a greedy i., that the appetite of her eye did seem to scorch me up,* Wiv. I, 3, 73. *affection, thy i. stabs the centre,* Wint. I, 2, 138.

Intentively, with a mind bent on something, with close application: *whereof by parcels she had something heard, but not i.* Oth. I, 3, 155 (F1 *instinctively,* F2.3.4 *distinctively*).

Inter, to bury: John V, 7, 99. H5 IV, 1, 312. H6A II, 2, 13. R3 I, 2, 30. 214. V, 5, 15. H8 IV, 2, 172. Tit. I, 146. 375. Rom. V, 3, 87. Caes. III, 2, 81. Hml. I, 4, 49 (Ff *inurned*). IV, 5, 84. Cymb. IV, 2, 401.

Intercept, 1) to take in the way, to stop in progress: Gent. III, 1, 43. H4A I, 3, 151. H6C II, 1, 114. R3 IV, 4, 136 (Ff. *who —s me in my expedition?* Qq *who —s my expedition?*). H8 III, 2, 286.

2) to put a stop to, to restrain: *to i. this inconvenience,* H6A I, 4, 14. *being —ed in your sport,* Tit. II, 3, 80. *they will not i. my tale,* III, 1, 40. With *from: she that might have —ed thee from all the slaughters,* R3 IV, 4, 137.

Intercepter, one who stops another in his way: Tw. III, 4, 242.

Interception, the stopping and seizing of something in its passage: H5 II, 2, 7.

Intercession, a petition in favour of another: Gent. III, 1, 233. H6A V, 4, 148. H8 I, 2, 106. Cor. V, 2, 47. V, 3, 32. Rom. II, 3, 54.

Intercessor, one who pleads in favour of another: Merch. III, 3, 16.

Interchained, linked together: *two bosoms i. with an oath,* Mids. II, 2, 49 (Ff *interchanged*).

Interchange, subst. 1) mutual giving and receiving: Wint. I, 1, 30. R3 II, 1, 26. V, 3, 99. Troil. III, 3, 33.

2) alternation, vicissitude: *when I have seen such i. of state, or state itself confounded to decay,* Sonn. 64, 9.

Interchange, vb. to exchange, to give and receive mutually: *they i. each other's seat,* Lucr. 70. —*d love-tokens with my child,* Mids. I, 1, 29. *two bosoms* —*d,* II, 2, 49 (Qq *interchained*). —*ing blows,* H6A IV, 6, 19. Rom. I, 1, 120. *I shall i. my waned state for Henry's regal crown,* H6C IV, 7, 3.

Interchangeably, 1) in return: *and i. hurl down my gage,* R2 I, 1, 146.

2) mutually: *and i. set down their hands,* R2 V, 2, 98. *being seeled i.* H4A III, 1, 81. *in witness whereof the parties i.* Troil. III, 2, 62.

Interchangement, exchange, mutual giving and receiving: Tw. V, 162.

Interdict, to exclude, to prohibit: *from this cession i. every fowl of tyrant wing,* Phoen. 9.

Interdiction, exclusion from a right: *since that the truest issue of thy throne by his own i. stands accursed,* Mcb. IV, 3, 106.

Interest, subst. (dissyll.; but at the end of the verse sometimes trisyll.: Sonn. 74, 3. Merch. I, 3, 76. H4A IV, 3, 49. H6A V, 4, 167. R3 IV, 4, 323), 1) concern, advantage: *no more that thane of Cawdor shall deceive our bosom i.* Mcb. I, 2, 64. *I bar it in the i. of my wife,* Lr. V, 3, 85.

2) share, participation: *my life hath in this line some i. which for memorial still with thee shall stay,* Sonn. 74, 3. *if ever love had i. in his liver,* Ado IV, 1, 233. *you claim no i. in any of our towns of garrison,* H6A V, 4, 167. *so much i. have I in thy sorrow,* R3 II, 2, 47. *I have an i. in your hate's proceeding,* Rom. III, 1, 193. *since my lord hath i. in them, I will keep them in my bedchamber,* Cymb. I, 6, 195. *what's thy i. in this sad wreck?* IV, 2, 365.

3) right, claim: *how many a tear hath love stolen from mine eye as i. of the dead,* Sonn. 31, 7. *let the tongue of war plead for our i. and our being here,* John V, 2, 165. *the shes of Italy should not betray mine i. and his honour,* Cymb. I, 3, 30. With *in: he hath no i. in me,* As V, 1, 8 (Audrey's speech, rather ambiguous). With *to: acquainted me with i. to this land,* John V, 2, 89. *he hath more worthy i. to the state than thou,* H4A III, 2, 98. *to whose young love the vines of France and milk of Burgundy strive to be i.* Lr. I, 1, 87 (the respective riches of the two countries vie with each other to found a claim to the love of Cordelia. M. Edd. *interested*).*

4) possession, property: *thy i. was not bought basely with gold, but stolen from forth thy gate,* Lucr. 1067. *in the i. of thy bed a stranger came,* 1619. *do not take away my sorrow's i.* 1797. *if that the youth of my new i. here have power to bid you welcome,* Merch. III, 2, 224. *the unowed i. of proud-swelling state,* John IV, 3, 147. *all your i. in those territories*

is utterly bereft you, H6B III, 1, 84. *where life hath no more i. but to breathe,* Tit. III, 1, 250. *we will divest us, both of rule, i. of territory, cares of state,* Lr. I, 1, 51.

5) profit derived from money lent, usury: *my well-known thrift, which he calls i.* Merch. I, 3, 52. 76. 95. Tim. I, 2, 206. III, 4, 52. III, 5, 108 (*upon i.*). Metaphorically: Ven. 210. Gent. II, 1, 108. H4A IV, 3, 49. R3 IV, 4, 323.

Intergatory (M. Edd. *inter'gatory*), interrogatory, a question asked upon oath: *charge us upon* —*ies,* Merch. V, 298. *the first i. that my Nerissa shall be sworn on,* 300. *let me answer to the particular of the* —*ies,* All's IV, 3, 207. In Cymb. V, 5, 392 O. Edd. *interrogatories,* some M. Edd. *intergatories.*

Interim, intervening time, interval: Sonn. 56, 9. Ado II, 1, 380. LLL I, 1, 172. As III, 2, 333. Tw. V, 98. H5 V Chor. 43. Cor. I, 6, 5. Tim. II, 2, 158. Caes. II, 1, 64. Mcb. I, 3, 154. Hml. V, 2, 73. Oth. I, 3, 259. V, 2, 317 (Qq *nick*). Per. V, 2, 14.

Interior, subst. inside: Merch. II, 9, 28.

Interior, adj., internal, being or done within: *your i. hatred,* R3 I, 3, 65. *make an i. survey of your good selves,* Cor. II, 1, 43.

Interjection, a word not expressing a certain thought, but indicative of emotion: Ado IV, 1, 22.

Interjoin, to join mutually, to marry: *i. their issues,* Cor. IV, 4, 22.

Interlace, to intermix, to put in by way of variety: *and here and there the painter* —*s pale cowards,* Lucr. 1390.

Interlude, a play performed in the intervals of a festivity: Mids. I, 2, 6. V, 156. Tw. V, 380. Lr. V, 3, 89.

Intermingle, 1) tr. to mix: *I'll i. every thing he does with Cassio's suit,* Oth. III, 3, 25.

2) intr. to be mixed: *they will not admit any good part to i. with them,* Ado V, 2, 64.

Intermission (of five syll. at the end of the verse in Merch. and As) cessation, delay: *for i. no more pertains to me than you,* Merch. III, 2, 201 (O. Edd. *for i., no more*). *I did laugh sans i. an hour,* As II, 7, 32. *cut short all i.* Mcb. IV, 3, 232. *delivered letters spite of i.* Lr. II, 4, 33 (though my business was thus interrupted and the answer delayed which I was to receive).

Intermissive, having a temporary cessation: *their i. miseries,* H6A I, 1, 88.

Intermit, to suspend, to delay: *to i. the plague that needs must light on this ingratitude,* Caes. I, 1, 59.*

Intermixed, having an admixture, alloyed: *best is best, if never i.* Sonn. 101, 8. *thoughts of things divine are i. with scruples,* R2 V, 5, 12.

Interpose, 1) to place between, to thrust in; refl.: *what watchful cares do i. themselves betwixt your eyes and night?* Caes. II, 1, 98.

2) intr. to step in between: *please you to i.* Wint. V, 3, 119.

Interposer, that which comes between: *no rest be i. 'twixt us twain,* Merch. III, 2, 329.

Interpret, to explain, to expound, to decipher; absol.: *whose soft impression* —*s for my poor ignorance,* Tim. V, 4, 69. *your thoughts which can i. further,* Mcb. III, 6, 2. Oth. V, 2, 73. Per. I, 1, 124. Trans.: Tit. III, 2, 36. Caes. II, 2, 83. A subord. clause following: *your beards forbid me to i. that you* *are so*, Mcb. I, 3, 46. Used of the explanation given of a puppet-show (motion) or what is like it; trans.: *then the eye —s to the ear the heavy motion that it doth behold*, Lucr. 1325. *one, but painted thus, would be —ed a thing perplexed*, Cymb. III, 4, 7. Intr. (= to play the interpreter): *O excellent motion! O exceeding puppet! now will he i. to her*, Gent. II, 1, 101. *to the dumbness of the gesture one might i.* Tim. I, 1, 34. *I could i. between you and your love, if I could see the puppets dallying*, Hml. III, 2, 256.

Interpretation, explanation, construction: Wint. IV, 4, 364. H4A V, 2, 13. H4B II, 2, 99. Cor. IV, 7, 50. V, 3, 69.

Interpreter, 1) explainer, expounder: Gent. I, 2, 78. Merch. III, 4, 80. Wint. V, 1, 150. H8 I, 2, 82. Tim. V, 3, 8.

2) a mediator between persons who do not understand each other's language: All's IV, 1, 6. 8. 23. IV, 3, 236. H5 V, 2, 282.

Interrogatory (cf. *Intergatory*) examination, question: John III, 1, 147. Cymb. V, 5, 392 (M. Edd. *intergatories*).

Interrupt, to make to cease, to hinder from proceeding by coming between: Lucr. 1170. Tp. III, 2, 77. LLL V, 2, 91. 725. Shr. IV, 4, 54. John II, 542. H6C I, 1, 123. Troil. III, 3, 93. Cor. III, 1, 249. Rom. V, 3, 27. Per. V, 1, 167.

Interrupter, one who hinders in proceeding by coming between: Tit. I, 208.

Interruption, stop, hinderance in proceeding caused by breaking in: John II, 76. III, 4, 9. R3 III, 7, 102.

Inter-tissued (O. Edd. *enter-tissued*) interwoven, variegated: *the i. robe of gold and pearl*, H5 IV, 1, 279.

Intervallum, intervening time, interval: *without —s*, H4B V, 1, 91.

Interview, a meeting: LLL II, 167. H5 V, 2, 27. H8 I, 1, 165. 180. Troil. IV, 5, 155.

Intestate, having died without a testament, gone without leaving anything behind: *airy succeeders of i. joys*, R3 IV, 4, 128 (Ff *intestine*).

Intestine, domestic, coming to pass between people of the same nation: Err. I, 1, 11. H4A I, 1, 12. In R3 IV, 4, 128 Ff *intestine*, Qq rightly *intestate*.

Intil = into (the clown's song): *and hath shipped me i. the land*, Hml. V, 1, 81.

Intimate, vb. to suggest, to cause to think of: *your father here doth i. the payment of a hundred thousand crowns*, LLL II, 129. *thou this to hazard needs must i. skill infinite*, All's II, 1, 186 (thy hazarding this must suggest the idea of infinite skill). *the spirit of humours i. reading aloud to him*, Tw. II, 5, 94.

Intimation, suggestion: LLL IV, 2, 13 (Holofernes' speech).

Intitle, see *Entitle.*

Intituled, 1) having a name or title: *i., nominated, or called, Don Adriano de Armado*, LLL V, 1, 8 (Sir Nathaniel's speech).

2) having a claim: *beauty, in that white i.* Lucr. 57.*

Into (accented sometimes on the first, sometimes on the second syllable, perhaps oftener on the latter) 1) noting entrance (the origin discernible in R3 V, 3, 46: *in to our tent*; Ff *into my tent*): *the spur that anger thrusts i. his hide*, Sonn. 50, 10. *to dive i. the*

fire, Tp. I, 2, 191. *you cram these words i. mine ears*, II, 1, 106. *hath i. bondage brought my ear*, III, 1, 41. *knock a nail i. his head*, III, 2, 69. *return no more i. my sight*, Gent. I, 2, 47. *let us i. the city*, III, 2, 91. *thrust himself i. secrets*, III, 1, 394. *I will look further i. it*, Wiv. II, 1, 245; cf. *to look i. happiness through another man's eyes*, As V, 2, 48 (see *Look*). *slighted me i. the river*, Wiv. III, 5, 9. 37. 88. 122. *they fled i. this abbey*, Err. V, 155. *we came i. the world*, 424. *thrust a cork i. a hogshead*, Wint. III, 3, 95. *if the midnight bell did sound on into the drowsy race of night*, John III, 3, 39 (sounded, in striking twelve, as if it should never cease. Most M. Edd. *sound one unto*; as if the midnight bell ever struck one!). *it ascends me i. the brain*, H4B IV, 3, 105. *you would have me seek i. myself*, Caes. I, 2, 64 (cf. *Seek*). *I will myself i. the pulpit first*, III, 1, 236; cf. III, 2, 68. *thou fellest i. my fury*, Ant. IV, 12, 41. *he enchants societies i. him*, Cymb. I, 6, 167 (i. e. makes their hearts his; cf. *puts the world i. her person*, Ado II, 1, 216, = gives out her opinion for that of the world) etc. Temporally: *how far i. the morning is it?* R3 V, 3, 234.

The idea of motion not yet extinct in some expressions, with which modern English connects that of rest: *she did confine thee i. a cloven pine*, Tp. I, 2, 277. 361. Cor. IV, 6, 87. *ensconcing ourselves i. seeming knowledge*, All's II, 3, 5. *a jewel locked i. the wofullest cask*, H6B III, 2, 409. *a man i. whom nature hath so crowded humours*, Troil. I, 2, 22. *every thing includes itself in power, power i. will, will i. appetite*, I, 3, 120. After *to lay: is all my armour laid i. my tent?* R3 V, 3, 51. *when I am laid i. the tomb*, Rom. IV, 3, 30. After *to put: what he puts i. the press*, Wiv. II, 1, 80. *to put me i. everlasting liberty*, III, 3, 31. *shall I put him i. the basket*, IV, 2, 48. *put not yourself i. amazement*, Meas. IV, 2, 220. *who put unluckily i. this bay*, Err. V, 125. Ado I, 1, 184. Mids. V, 251. As III, 3, 36. V, 1, 38. All's III, 6, 81. IV, 1, 45. R2 I, 3, 164. H4B II, 1, 81. III, 2, 289. IV, 5, 45. H8 III, 1, 93. 118. 170 etc.

2) Noting an effect or result: *was grown i. a hoop*, Tp. I, 2, 259. *a sea-change i. something rich*, 401. *hiss me i. madness*, II, 2, 14. *thou didst then rend thy faith i. a thousand oaths*, Gent. V, 4, 48. *I was beaten i. all the colours*, Wiv. IV, 5, 118. *he hath turned a heaven i. a hell*, Mids. I, 1, 207 (Q1 *unto*). *turns i. yellow gold his salt green streams*, III, 2, 393. *did he not moralize this spectacle? O yes, i. a thousand similes*, As II, 1, 45. *gull him i. a nay-word*, Tw. II, 3, 146. *banged the youth i. dumbness*, III, 2, 25. *laugh yourselves i. stitches*, 73. *he does smile his face i. more lines*, 84. *is grown i. an unspeakable estate*, Wint IV, 2, 46. *the hand of time shall draw this brief i. as huge a volume*, John II, 103. *I should quickly leap i. a wife*, H5 V, 2, 145 (win a wife by leaping). *his valour is crushed i. folly*, Troil. I, 2, 23. *I will beat thee i. handsomeness*, II, 1, 16. *your nurse i. a rapture lets her baby cry*, Cor. II, 1, 223. *knee the way i. his mercy*, V, 1, 6. *you know the very road i. his kindness*, 59. *swear the gods i. shudders*, Tim. IV, 3, 137. *whom I will beat i. clamorous whining*, Lr. IV, 2, 24. *the water-flies blow me i. abhorring*, Ant. V, 2, 60. *to work her son i. the adoption of the crown*, Cymb. V, 5, 56 etc. Perhaps also in the following passage: *who having i. truth by telling of it, made such a sinner of his memory, to credit his own lie*, Tp. I, 2, 100 (i. e. by tell-

ing it into truth, by telling it with such assurance and so often as to make it appear like truth, even in his own eyes).

3) = unto, to: *return i. France*, All's IV, 3, 50. *bloody England i. England gone*, John III, 4, 8. *went with his forces i. France*, H5 I, 2, 147. *sending i. France*, 246. *at his return i. London*, III, 6, 72. *crossing the sea from England i. France*, H6A IV, 1, 89. *to carry i. Flanders the great seal*, H8 III, 2, 319. *I have borne this corse i. the market-place*, Caes. III, 1, 292. *sent i. England*, Hml. V, 1, 161. *he went i. France*, V, 2, 220. Lr. I, 4, 79. *he goes i. Mauritania*, Oth. IV, 2, 229. Similarly: *pray God's blessing i. thy attempt*, All's I, 3, 260. *did I expose myself i. the danger of this adverse town*, Tw. V, 87. *look back i. your mightly ancestors*, H5 I, 2, 102 (cf. *look i. Master Froth here*, Meas. II, 1, 126; Pompey's speech). *am become as new i. the world*, Troil. III, 3, 12. *you would have sold your king to slaughter, his princes and his peers to servitude, and his whole kingdom i. desolation*, H5 II, 2, 173 (perhaps denoting the effect). *put your dread pleasures more into command than to entreaty*, Hml. II, 2, 28. As *in* is used for *on*, so *into* also, with the idea of motion: *with declining head i. his bosom*, Shr. Ind. 1, 119. *my heart leaps to be gone into my mother's bosom*, Per. V, 3, 45. *dive i. the bottom of the deep*, H4A I, 3, 203.

Intolerable, 1) not to be endured, insufferable: Wiv. III, 5, 110. Shr. V, 2, 94. H6A V, 4, 79. H6B I, 1, 175. III, 1, 172. Tit. IV, 4, 50.

2) enormous, monstrous: *withered and of i. entrails*, Wiv. V, 5, 161. *one halfpenny-worth of bread to this i. deal of sack*, H4A II, 4, 592. Perhaps also in H6B I, 1, 175.

Adverbially: *she is i. curst*, Shr. I, 2, 89.

Intomb, see *Entomb.*

Intoxicates, Fluellen's word for inebriated: *a little i. in his prains*, H5 IV, 7, 39.

Intreasured, laid up, stored: *which in their seeds and weak beginnings lie i.* H4B III, 1, 85 (cf. *Entreasured*).

Intrenchant, not to be cut, indivisible, invulnerable: *as easy mayst thou the i. air with thy keen sword impress*, Mcb. V, 8, 9. cf. *Entrench.*

Intrenched, fortified with a ditch and parapet: H6A I, 4, 9.

Intricate, entangled, not easy to unravel: *an i. impeach*, Err. V, 269.

Intrinse, internal, intimate, deep-rooted: *bite the holy cords a-twain which are too i. to unloose*, Lr. II, 2, 81.

Intrinsicate, the same: *with thy sharp teeth this knot i. of life at once untie*, Ant. V, 2, 307 (or confounded with *intricate?*).

Intrude, 1) intr. to thrust one's self in without having a right to do so: *to i. where I am graced*, Tit. II, 1, 27. *thou wretched, rash, —ing fool*, Hml. III, 4, 31. *where's that palace whereinto foul things sometimes i.* Oth. III, 3, 138.

2) tr. to enter without a right to do so, to invade: *why should the worm i. the maiden bud?* Lucr. 848.

Intruder, one who thrusts himself in without a just claim: Gent. III, 1, 157. Tit. II, 3, 65.

Intrusion, entrance without permission or right: Wiv. II, 2, 174. Err. II, 2, 181. III, 1, 103. Rom. I, 5, 93.

Inundation, overflow of waters, flood: Compl. 290. John V, 1, 12. V, 2, 48. Rom. IV, 1, 12.

Inure, to habituate, to accustom: *this glove to wanton tricks is not —d*, Lucr. 321. *to i. thyself to what thou art like to be, cast thy humble slough*, Tw. II, 5, 160.

Inurned, entombed: *the sepulchre wherein we saw thee quietly i.* Hml. I, 4, 49 (Qq interred).

Invade, 1) to enter, to penetrate into: *though the fork i. the region of my heart*, Lr. I, 1, 146. *this contentious storm —s us to the skin*, III, 4, 7.

2) to attack, to make an inroad into: *to i. the French*, H5 I, 2, 136. *France —s our land*, Lr. V, 1, 25.

Invasion, attack, inroad: Lucr. 287. John IV, 2, 173.

Invasive, hostilely overrunning the country: *arms i.* John V, 1, 69.

Invective, subst. a railing and reproachful speech or expression; with *against: with a bitter i. against the tyranny of the king*, Lucr. Arg. 24. *breathe out —s 'gainst the officers*, H6C I, 4, 43.

Invectively, railingly: *thus most i. he pierceth through the body of the country*, As II, 1, 58.

Inveigh, to exclaim, to rail; with *against: no man i. against the withered flower*, Lucr. 1254.

Inveigle, to seduce: *Achilles hath —d his fool from him*, Troil. II, 3, 99.

Invent, to find out, to excogitate, to devise, to frame by the imagination; absol.: *how can my Muse want subject to i.?* Sonn. 38, 1. Trans.: *what of thee thy poet doth i.* 79, 7. *she never did i. this letter*, As IV, 3, 28. *the brain of man is not able to i. any thing that tends to laughter more than I i. or is —ed on me*, H4B I, 2, 9. 10. *I would i. as bitter-searching terms*, H6B III, 2, 311. *he lies, for I —ed it myself*, IV, 2, 163. *i. some other custom*, Oth. II, 3, 36.

Invention, 1) something new found out or devised: *our brains labouring for i. bear amiss the second burden of a former child*, Sonn. 59, 3. *to change true rules for old —s*, Shr. III, 1, 81. *those palates must have —s to delight the taste*, Per. I, 4, 40.

2) imagination, imaginative faculty as well as poetic fiction: *if the first heir of my i. prove deformed*, Ven. Ded. 5. *thou thyself dost give i. light*, Sonn. 38, 8. *keep i. in a noted weed*, 76, 6. *a face that overgoes my blunt i. quite*, 103, 7. *in this change is my i. spent*, 105, 11. *if your love can labour aught in sad i.* Ado V, 1, 292. *smelling out the odoriferous flowers of fancy, the jerks of i.* LLL IV, 2, 129. *neither savouring of poetry, wit, nor i.* 166. *a verse that I made yesterday in despite of my i.* As II, 5, 49. *ascend the brightest heaven of i.* H5 Prol. 2. *my i. comes from my pate as birdlime does from frize*, Oth. II, 1, 126. Perhaps also in Tw. V, 352: *made the most notorious geck and gull that e'er i. played on*, i. e. that e'er was a theme of comedy.

3) activity of the mind generally, faculty of thinking and excogitating any thing: *heaven hath my empty words, whilst my i., hearing not my tongue, anchors on Isabel*, Meas. II, 4, 3. *nor hath age so eat up my i.* Ado IV, 1, 196. *impose me to what penance your i. can lay upon my sin*, V, 1, 282. *of so high and plenteous wit and i.* Oth IV, 1, 201. *add more, from thine i., offers*, Ant. III, 12, 29.

4) thought, idea, device: *both our —s meet and jump in one*, Shr. I, 1, 195. *if this letter speed and*

my i. thrive, Lr. I, 2, 20. Used of thoughts couched in writing: *much like a press of people at a door throng her —s, which shall go before*, Lucr. 1302. *this is a man's i. and his hand*, As IV, 3, 29. *women's gentle brain could not drop forth such giant-rude i.* 34. *eloquent and full of i.* Tw. III, 2, 47. *say 'tis not your seal, not your i.* V, 341. *do it without i., suddenly*, H6A III, 1, 5 (not "with premeditated lines", v. 1).

5) skill employed in contriving any thing to meet a difficulty: *what excuse can my i. make?* Lucr. 225. *in her i. and Ford's wife's distraction*, Wiv. III, 5, 84. *i. is ashamed, against the proclamation of thy passion, to say thou dost not*, All's I, 3, 179.

6) a device, a forgery, a falsehood: *he will return with an i. and clap upon you two or three probable lies*, All's III, 6, 106. *it must be a very plausive i. that carries it*, IV, 1, 29. *what if both Lewis and Warwick be appeased by such i. as I can devise?* H6C IV, 1, 35. *let them accuse me by i.* Cor. III, 2, 143. *filling their hearers with strange i.* Mcb. III, 1, 33.

Inventor, contriver, author: Mcb. I, 7, 10. Hml. V, 2, 396.

Inventorially, in the manner of a catalogue: Hml. V, 2, 118.

Inventory, subst. a detailed account, a catalogue: H4B II, 2, 20. H8 III, 2, 124. 137. 452 (*to take*). Cor. I, 1, 21. Cymb. II, 2, 30.

Inventory, vb. to make a catalogue of: *it shall be —ed*, Tw. I, 5, 264.

Inverness (O. Edd. *Envernes*) Scottish town: Mcb. I, 4, 42.

Invert, to change to the contrary: *i. the attest of eyes and ears*, Troil. V, 2, 122. With *to: i. what best is boded me to mischief*, Tp. III, 1, 70.

Invest, 1) to array, to dress: *how, in stripping it, you more i. it*, Tp. II, 1, 226. *the damned'st body to i. and cover in prenzie guards*, Meas. III, 1, 96. *i. me in my motley*, As II, 7, 58. *in the official marks —ed*, Cor. II, 3, 148. *nature would not i. herself in such shadowing passion*, Oth. IV, 1, 40.

2) to place in possession of a dignity or rank, to install: *our substitutes well —ed*, H4B IV, 4, 6. *i. thee with my honours*, IV, 5, 96. *which honour must not i. him only*, Mcb. I, 4, 40. *gone to Scone to be —ed*, II, 4, 32. *i. you with my power*, Lr. I, 1, 132. *in my rights by me —ed*, V, 3, 69.

3) to adorn, to endow: *to i. their sons with arts*, H4B IV, 5, 73.

4) to be about, to attend: *their gesture sad —ing lank-lean cheeks and war-worn coats*, H5 IV Chor. 26 (a passage thought corrupt by many M. Edd.). — In Hml. I, 3, 83 Qq —s, Ff rightly *invites*.

Investments, dress: H4B IV, 1, 45. Hml. I, 3, 128.

Inveterate, of long standing, deep-rooted, obstinate: *an enemy to me i.* Tp. I, 2, 122. *i. canker*, John V, 2, 14. *malice*, R2 I, 1, 14. *hate*, Cor. II, 3, 234.

Invincible, 1) unconquerable: H6A IV, 2, 32. H6B I, 4, 9. Cor. IV, 1, 10. With *against: i. against all assaults of affection*, Ado II, 3, 120.

2) not to be evinced, not to be made out, indeterminable: *his dimensions to any thick sight were i.* H4B III, 2, 337 (some M. Edd. *unvisible*).

Inviolable, not to be broken: John V, 2, 7. H6C II, 1, 30. R3 II, 1, 27 (Qq *unviolable*).

Invised, perhaps inspected, investigated, tried: *the diamond was beautiful and hard, whereto his i. pro-*

perties did tend, Compl. 212 (according to commentators, = invisible).

Invisible, 1) not perceptible by the eye: Ven. 434. 1004. Lucr. 827. Tp. IV, 185. V, 97. Gent. II, 1, 141. Err. V, 187. Ado I, 1, 244. LLL V, 2, 257. Mids. II, 1, 186. V, 246. As I, 2, 223. III, 5, 30. Tw. I, 5, 316. III, 1, 35. John V, 7, 16. H4A II, 1, 96. H5 III Chor. 11. Troil. III, 1, 35. Mcb. III, 2, 48. Hml. IV, 4, 50. Oth. II, 3, 283. With *to:* Tp. I, 2, 302.

2) not to be accounted for by what is seen, inexplicable: *a strange i. perfume hits the sense*, Ant. II, 2, 217. *an i. instinct*, Cymb. IV, 2, 177.

Invitation, allurement: *she gives the leer of i.* Wiv. I, 3, 50.

Invite, to ask, to call on, to summon, to solicit; absol.: *the —ing time*, Sonn. 124, 8. *till now did ne'er i., nor never woo*, Compl. 182. *an —ing eye*, Oth. II, 3, 24. With an obj.: *—s me in this churlish messenger*, Tw. II, 2, 24. *Rome, —d by your noble self, hath sent*, H8 II, 2, 95. *the bell —s me*, Mcb. II, 1, 62. Hml. I, 3, 83. Cymb. III, 4, 108. Per. V, 1, 86. The thing required in the accus.: *the lamentation of the French —s the king of England's stay at home*, H5 V Chor. 37. *to i.* = to ask to come as a guest: Err. II, 1, 4. IV, 3, 4. Ado I, 1, 149. LLL IV, 2, 170. Rom. IV, 2, 1. Tim. I, 2, 45. II, 1, 11. III, 4, 118. Oth. I, 3, 128. III, 3, 281. Followed by *to: —d to any sensual feast*, Sonn. 141, 7. *I i. your highness to my poor cell*, Tp. V, 300. Wiv. III, 3, 245. Err. I, 2, 24. H8 IV, 2, 88. Troil. III, 3, 285. Rom. I, 2, 21. Mcb. I, 7, 63. Ant. II, 2, 170. 225. cf. *thither will I i. the duke*, As V, 2, 16. *aboard my galley I i. you*, Ant. II, 6, 82. Followed by an inf.: *i. my lords to sup with me*, H6B I, 4, 83. *to i. the Trojan lords to see us*, Troil. III, 3, 236. 275. Tim. V, 1, 209. Mcb. V, 8, 75. Hml. V, 2, 401.

Confounded with *indite:* H4B II, 1, 30. Rom. II, 4, 135.

Inviting, invitation, request to come as a guest: *he hath sent me an earnest i.* Tim. III, 6, 11.

Invocate, to invoke, to pray to: Sonn. 38, 10. H6A I, 1, 52. R3 I, 2, 8.

Invocation, the calling on a superior power for its assistance: Lucr. 1831. LLL I, 2, 102. As II, 5, 61. John III, 4, 42. Rom. II, 1, 27.

Invoke, to call on, to pray to: Sonn. 78, 1. H5 I, 2, 104.

Invulnerable, not to be wounded: Tp. III, 3, 66. John II, 252. Cor. V, 3, 73 (F *unv.*) Hml. I, 1, 145.

Inward, adj. 1) internal, interior: *an i. bruise*, H4A I, 3, 58. *i. sickness*, IV, 1, 31. *these i. wars*, H4B III, 1, 107. *the i. man*, Hml. II, 2, 6. Per. II, 2, 57. *his i. soul* = his inmost soul, the depth of his soul: Lucr. 1779; cf. 185. John III, 1, 227. R2 II, 2, 11. 28. H4B IV, 5, 148.

2) seated in the mind: *that i. beauty*, Ven. 434. *i. ill*, Lucr. 91. *i. vice*, 1546. *in i. worth*, Sonn. 16, 11. 46, 14. Tp. V, 77. Gent. I, 2, 63. John I, 212. H5 I, 1, 39. II Chor. 16. R3 I, 4, 79. Troil. V, 10, 31. Hml. I, 3, 13. Ant. III, 13, 33.

3) not known to many, confidential, private: *if either of you know any i. impediment why you should not be conjoined*, Ado IV, 1, 12. *what is i. between us, let it pass*, LLL V, 1, 102.

4) privy to one's thoughts, familiar: *who is most i. with the royal duke?* R3 III, 4, 8.

Inward, adv. internally: *it is so grounded i. in my heart,* Sonn. 62, 4. *i. searched,* Merch. III, 2, 86. *the imposthume that i. breaks,* Hml. IV, 4, 28.

Inward, subst. 1) the inside, the interior: *the tender i. of thy hand,* Sonn. 128, 6. *wherefore breaks that sigh from the i. of thee?* Cymb. III, 4, 6.

2) Plur. —*s,* = the inner parts of the body, the bowels: *makes it course from the —s to the parts extreme,* H4B IV, 3, 115. *doth gnaw my —s,* Oth. II, 1, 306.

3) one privy to another's thoughts, an intimate: *I was an i. of his,* Meas. III, 2, 138.

Inwardly, internally, in the soul: *let Benedick waste i.* Ado III, 1, 78. *my heart bleeds i.* H4B II, 2, 51. Tim. I, 2, 211.

Inwardness, intimacy: *my i. and love is very much unto the prince,* Ado IV, 1, 247.

Io, a mistress of Jove's: Shr. Ind. 2, 56.

Ionia, Greek country in Asia Minor: Ant. I, 2, 107.

Ionian sea, the sea between Italy and Greece: Ant. III, 7, 23.

Ipswich, English town, birthplace of Wolsey: H8 I, 1, 138. IV, 2, 59.

Iras, female name in Ant. I, 2, 43 etc.

Ire (used only in verse) anger, wrath: Err. V, 216. R2 I, 1, 18. H6A IV, 3, 28. H6C I, 3, 29. Per. II, 1, 1.

Ireful, (used only in verse) angry, wroth: Ven. 628. Err. V, 151. H6A IV, 6, 16. H6C II, 1, 57. II, 5, 132.

Ireland (trisyll. at the end of the verse in H6B I, 1, 194. III, 1, 329. H8 III, 2, 260) the large island to the west of Great Britain: Err. III, 2, 119 *(bogs).* John I, 11. II, 152. R2 I, 4, 38. 52. II, 1, 218. 290. II, 2, 42. 103. 123. 141. H5 III, 7, 56 *(a kern of I.).* V Chor. 31. V, 2, 258. H6B I, 1, 194. 232. III, 1, 282. 310. 312. 329. 348. 380. IV, 9, 24. V, 1, 1. H6C IV, 7, 73. R3 IV, 2, 109 *(a bard of I.).* H8 II, 1, 42. III, 2, 260. Mcb. II, 3, 144. III, 1, 31.

Iris, the Goddess of the rainbow and messenger of Juno: Tp. IV, 60 (performing a part in the pageant, but not named). *that this distempered messenger of wet, the many-coloured I., rounds thine eye,* All's I, 3, 158 (see for an explanation Lucr. 1586). *I'll have an I. that shall find thee out,* H6B III, 2, 407. *his crest that prouder than blue I. bends,* Troil. I, 3, 380.

Irish, pertaining to Ireland: *I was an I. rat,* As III, 2, 188 (rats were supposed to be killed by certain mystic rhymes). *I. wolves,* V, 2, 119. *I. wars,* R2 I, 4, 62. II, 1, 155. 259. H4A I, 3, 150. IV, 3, 88. V, 1, 53. Substantively, = Irish language: *howl in I.* H4A III, 1, 241.

Irishman, a native of Ireland: *trust an I. with my aqua-vitae bottle,* Wiv. II, 2, 318. H5 III, 2, 71. Pl. *Irishmen* = Irish: *try your hap against the Irishmen,* H6B III, 1, 314.

Irk, impers. vb.; *it* —*s* = it gives pain, it annoys, it mortifies: *it* —*s me,* As II, 1, 22. *it* —*s his heart,* H6A I, 4, 105. *it* —*s my very soul,* H6C II, 2, 6.

Irksome, disagreeable, offensive: As III, 5, 95. Shr. I, 2, 188. H6B II, 1, 56.

Iron (monosyll. in John IV, 1, 120. IV, 2, 194. R3 V, 3, 110) 1) the hard metal Ferrum: Pilgr. 88. Ado IV, 1, 153. Shr. II, 147. John IV, 1, 67. IV, 2,

194. Troil. III, 2, 186. Cor. IV, 5, 235. Caes. I, 3, 94. *strike now, or else the i. cools,* H6C V, 1, 49. Used as a symbol of hardheartedness: *you draw not i., for my heart is true as steel,* Mids. II, 1, 196. *with an aspect of i.* H5 V, 2, 245. *i. of Naples hid with English gilt,* H6C II, 2, 139. *hearts of i.* H8 III, 2, 425.

2) any thing made of iron: *heat me these —s,* John IV, 1, 1. 39. 61. 75. 82. 120. 125. *a great deal of old i.* H6A I, 2, 101. —*s of a doit,* Cor. I, 5, 7. *the wrenching i.* Rom. V, 3, 22. *ne'er wore i. on his heel,* Cymb. IV, 4, 40. —*s* = chains: Tim. III, 5, 50. Denoting particularly weapons, offensive and defensive: *runs not this speech like i. through your blood?* Ado V, 1, 252. *put up your i.* Tw. IV, 1, 42. *bind my brows with i.* H4B I, 1, 150. H5 II, 1, 8. III, 7, 161. H6A IV, 3, 20. H6B IV, 10, 30. R3 V, 3, 110.* Troil. II, 3, 18. Ant. IV, 4, 3.

Iron, adj. made of iron: Ven. 269. Err. III, 1, 84. Mids. V, 370. John II, 212. III, 3, 38. R2 I, 3, 136. H4B IV, 2, 8. H6A I, 4, 10. 49. Rom. IV, 5, 126. V, 2, 21. Metaphorically, = heardhearted, unfeeling, rude: *soft pity enters at an i. gate,* Lucr. 595. *in this i. age,* John IV, 1, 60. *tales of i. wars,* H4A II, 3, 51. *with an i. wit,* Rom. IV, 5, 126. *an i. heart,* Tim. III, 4, 84.

Iron-witted, unfeeling, insensible: *I will converse with i. fools and unrespective boys,* R3 IV, 2, 28 (cf. Rom. IV, 5, 126).

Irreconciled, not atoned for, unremitted: *die in many i. iniquities,* H5 IV, 1, 160.

Irrecoverable, beyond redemption, lost for ever: *the fiend hath pricked down Bardolph i.* H4B II, 4, 360.

Irregular, lawless, unprincipled: *leaving our rankness and i. course,* John V, 4, 54. *against the i. and wild Glendower,* H4A I, 1, 40. *wherein my youth hath faulty wandered and i.* III, 2, 27.

Irregulous, the same: *conspired with that i. devil Cloten,* Cymb. IV, 2, 315.

Irreligious, impious, ungodly: *a thousand i. cursed hours,* Wiv. V, 5, 242. *O cruel i. piety,* Tit. I, 130. *an i. Moor,* V, 3, 121.

Irremovable, immovable, inflexible: Wint. IV, 4, 518.

Irreparable, not to be made up for, irretrievable: *i. is the loss,* Tp. V, 140.

Irresolute, not firm in purpose, wavering: *an i. purpose,* H8 I, 2, 209.

Irrevocable, not to be reversed or retracted: As I, 3, 85. H6B III, 2, 294. H6C III, 3, 247.

Isabel, the ordinary form of *Isabella;* name of 1) the grandmother of Lewis the Tenth of France: H5 I, 2, 81. 2) the sister of Claudio in Meas. II, 4, 18. IV, 3, 163. Dissyll.: II, 2, 68. II, 4, 144. 154. III, 1, 106. IV, 2, 79. IV, 3, 119. V, 386. 435. Trisyll.: II, 4, 4. 184. III, 1, 115. 148. IV, 3, 111. 126. V, 204. 211. 270. 441. 442.

Isabella, female name in Meas. I, 4, 7. 18. 23. III, 1, 151. IV, 3, 157.

Isbel, the clown's spelling of *Isabel* in All's I, 3, 20. 25. III, 2, 13. 14.*

Iscariot, the betrayer of Christ: LLL V, 2, 601.

Isidore, name in Tim. II, 1, 1. II, 2, 11. 27.

Isis, the principal Goddess of ancient Egypt: Ant. I, 2, 66. 70. 72. 77. I, 5, 70. III, 3, 18. 46. III, 6, 17.

Island, a tract of land surrounded by water:

Lucr. 1740. Tp. I, 2, 171. 281. 331. 344. 389. 423. 455. II, 1, 35. 90. 93. 325. II, 2, 152. III, 2, 5. 50. III, 3, 30. 56. IV, 217. V, 176. Epil. 8. Gent. I, 3, 9. John I, 10. H5 III, 7, 150. H6B III, 1, 148. III, 3, 3. H6C IV, 8, 20. Oth. II, 3, 133. 147. Ant. V, 2, 91. Per. V, 1, 52. Adjectively: *yon i. carrions*, H5 IV, 2, 39. *the i. kings*, Troil. III, 1, 167.

Islander, inhabitant of an island: Tp. II, 2, 37. III, 3, 29. John II, 25. V, 2, 103. H6B IV, 1, 137. Oth. III, 3, 280.

Isle, = island (fem. in John V, 2, 25. Oth. II, 3, 175. In R3 III, 7, 125 Qq *her*, Ff *his*): Tp. I, 2, 220. 223. 337. 351. II, 1, 143. II, 2, 67. III, 2, 6. 60. 144. III, 3, 80. V, 124. 212. 287. 306. Wint. III, 1, 2. John IV, 2, 99. V, 2, 25. R2 II, 1, 40. H5 III, 5, 14. H6A I, 1, 50. H6B I, 1, 125. I, 3, 47 (*Britain's i.*). II, 3, 13. II, 4, 78. IV, 7, 66. R3 III, 1, 164. III, 7, 110. 125. V, 2, 11. H8 II, 3, 79. Troil. Prol. 1. Mcb. I, 2, 12. Oth. I, 3, 34. II, 1, 43. 206. II, 3, 59. 63. 175. Ant. III, 6, 26. Cymb. III, 1, 18.

Isop, see *Hyssop*.

Israel, the nation of the Jews: *O Jephthah, judge of I.* Hml. II, 2, 422.

Issue, subst. 1) that which comes from sth., a turning out, final event, end: *let burnt sack be the i.* Wiv. III, 1, 112. *see the i. of his search*, III, 3, 186. IV, 2, 207. Ado II, 2, 52. III, 2, 133. V, 3, 32. Merch. III, 2, 60. Wint. I, 2, 188. 259. II, 2, 45. II, 3, 153. III, 1, 22. V, 2, 9. V, 3, 128. R2 II, 3, 152. H4A I, 1, 61. II, 4, 103. H5 V, 2, 12. R3 III, 7, 54. H8 I, 2, 90. Troil. IV, 5, 148. Hml. I, 4, 89. V, 2, 72. Oth. I, 3, 370. II, 3, 372. *better i.* = better fortune: *whose better i. in the war*, Ant. I, 2, 97.

2) decision of a law-suit or what is compared with it: *while it is hot, I'll put it to the i.* H8 V, 1, 178 (I'll make a trial of it). *with fearful bloody i. arbitrate*, John I, 38. *arbitrating that which the commission of thy years and art could to no i. of true honour bring*, Rom. IV, 1, 65. *certain i. strokes must arbitrate*, Mcb. V, 4, 20.

3) that which proceeds from a man; action, deed: *spirits are not finely touched but to fine —s*, Meas. I, 1, 37. *how the people take the cruel i. of these bloody men*, Caes. III, 1, 294. *you are a fool granted: therefore your —s, being foolish, do not derogate*, Cymb. II, 1, 51.

4) produce, fruit, result, consequence: *this abundant i. seemed to me but hope of orphans*, Sonn. 97, 9. *look you for any other i.?* Ado II, 2, 30. *the dearest i. of his practice*, All's II, 1, 109. *thou art the i. of my dear offence*, John I, 257. *now see the i. of your peace*, III, 4, 21. *communication of a most poor i.* H8 I, 1, 87. *why do you now the i. of your proper wisdoms rate?* Troil. II, 2, 89. *I'll see some i. of my spiteful execrations*, II, 3, 7. *the i. of it being so proper*, Lr. I, 1, 18. *to that full i. for which I razed my likeness*, I, 4, 3. *not to strain my speech to grosser —s nor to larger reach than to suspicion*, Oth. III, 3, 219.

5) progeny, offspring, child or children, or descendants farther removed: Ven. 1178. Lucr. 37. 522. Sonn. 13, 8. Tp. IV, 1, 24. 105. V, 205. Ado IV, 1, 134. Mids. V, 412. 417. Merch. II, 4, 38. All's I, 3, 27. V, 3, 197. Wint. II, 1, 150. II, 3, 93. 193. III, 3, 43. IV, 2, 30. V, 1, 27. 46. John II, 186. R2 I, 3, 20. H4B V, 2, 14. H5 V, 2, 377. H6A II, 5, 94. V, 5, 72. H6B II, 2, 32. 35. 37. 38. 51. 56. H6C II, 2, 22.

III, 2, 131. R3 I, 1, 57. I, 3, 232. III, 5, 90. IV, 4, 57. 296. V, 3, 123. H8 I, 2, 134. II, 4, 191. 198. III, 2, 291. Cor. I. 3, 23. IV, 4, 22.* Tit. IV, 2, 66. 67. V, 3, 121. Tim. IV, 3, 371. Caes. III, 2, 142. Mcb. III, 1, 65. 89. IV, 1, 87. 102. IV, 3, 106. Lr. I, 2, 9. IV, 3, 37. Ant. III, 6, 7. Cymb. I, 1, 37. V, 5, 330. 331. 457. Per. I, 2, 73. Lr. I, 1, 67 Ff —*s*, Qq *i.*

Issue, vb. 1) intr. a) to pass out, to go out, to flow or run out: *when it breaks, I fear will i. thence the foul corruption*, John IV, 2, 80. *from it —d drops of blood*, H5 IV, 1, 314. *I did never know so full a voice i. from so empty a heart*, IV, 4, 72. *the blood that Clifford made i. from the bosom of the boy*, H6C I, 4, 81. II, 6, 82. R3 IV, 1, 69. Rom. I, 1, 92. *sweet music —s thence*, Troil. III, 2, 142. *if all our wits were to i. out of one skull*, Cor. II, 3, 23.

b) to get out, to sally forth: *watch the door with pistols, that none shall i. out*, Wiv. IV, 2, 54. Used especially of troops in a fortified place: *the citizens of Corioli have —d*, Cor. I, 6, 10. And with *forth* and *out:* H6A IV, 2, 20. H6C I, 2, 71. V, 1, 63. Cor. I, 4, 23.

c) to proceed, to come as from a source: *grains that i. out of dust*, Meas. III, 1, 21. *it —s from the rancour of a villain*, R2 I, 1, 143. *he that meets Hector —s from our choice*, Troil. I, 3, 347.

d) to descend: *such a slip of wilderness ne'er —d from his blood*, Meas. III, 1, 143. Part. —*d: and princess no worse —d*, Tp. I, 2, 59. —*d from the progeny of kings*, H6A V, 4, 38.

2) tr. to send out, to pour forth: *a gaping wound —ing life-blood*, Merch. III, 2, 269. Absol.: *I must compound with mistful eyes, or they will i. too*, H5 IV, 6, 34. *a conduit with three —ing spouts*, Tit. II, 4, 30.

Issueless, childless: Sonn. 9, 3. Wint. V, 1, 174.

It (the primary form *hit* perhaps preserved in Alls V, 3, 195 and Mcb. I, 5, 48, where M. Edd. write *it;* but the passages may be explained otherwise. Often contracted to '*t* before and behind other words: '*t had, 't has, 'tis, 't was, 't were, 't will, 't would, did 't, do 't, does 't, be 't, is 't, was 't, were 't, take 't, by 't, for 't, in' t, on 't, to 't, with 't* etc. etc.; see f. i. Tp. I, 2, 22. 44. 61. 87. 135. 175. 176. 185. 190. 245. 304. 309. 310. 334. 349. 359. 394. 409. 440. 459. II, 1, 48. 55. 176. 276. 277. 312. 314. III, 1, 19. IV, 242 etc. etc) 1) pers. pron. of the neuter gender, relating to single nouns as well as to sentences, and used, without a certain reference, before impersonal verbs and expressions, as: *how is it with our general?* Cor. V, 6, 10. *since that time it is eleven years*, Rom. I, 3, 35. *it will be rain*, Mcb. III, 3, 16. *if it were now to die*, Oth. II, 1, 191. *till it cry: sleep to death*, Lr. II, 4, 120(?) etc. Sometimes a reference borne in mind, but not expressed: *grow till you come unto it*, H4B III, 2, 270. *th' other's not come to it*, Troil. I, 2, 90. (cf. *Come*). *make it their walk*, Mcb. III, 3, 14. *I cannot daub it further*, Lr. IV, 1, 54. *you stayed well by't in Egypt*, Ant. II, 2, 179. *there's hope in't yet*, III, 13, 176. *there's sap in't*, 192.

Emphatically: *beauty's effect with beauty were bereft, nor it nor no remembrance what it was*, Sonn. 5, 12. *were some child of yours alive that time, you should live twice, in it and in my rhyme*, 17, 14. *why does my blood thus muster to my heart, making both it unable for itself, and dispossessing all my other parts of necessary fitness?* Meas. II, 4, 21. *that's it that al-*

ways makes a good voyage of nothing, Tw. II, 4, 80. does not the stone rebuke me for being more stone than it? Wint. V, 3, 38. it holds current that I told you, H4A II, 1, 58. you are welcome into our kingdom; use us and it, H8 II, 2, 78. there was it for which my sinews shall be stretched upon him, Cor. V, 6, 44. if it please me which thou speakest, Tit. V, 1, 59. this dagger hath mista'en, for lo, his house is empty on the back of Montague, and it missheathed in my daughter's bosom, Rom. V, 3, 205 (Ff and later Qq is). you and I must part, but that's not it, Ant. I, 3, 87. 'tis not my profit that does lead mine honour, mine honour it, II, 7, 83. another stain as big as hell can hold, were there no more but it, Cymb. II, 4, 141. you have no true debitor and creditor but it, V, 4, 172.

Superfluous: my life's foul deed, my life's fair end shall free it, Lucr. 1208. perspective it is best painter's art, Sonn. 24, 4. the rain it raineth every day, Tw. V, 401. and now be it known to you my full intent, Tit. IV, 2, 151. unless to defend ourselves it be a sin, Oth. II, 3, 203. Before subord. clauses: what lets it but he would be here, Err. II, 1, 105. publish it that she is dead, Ado IV, 1, 206. I take it your own business calls on you, Merch. I, 1, 63 (cf. Take). my boon I make it that you know me not, Lr. IV, 7, 10 etc.

Omitted: long she thinks till he return again, Lucr. 1359. the less you meddle or make with them, the more is for your honesty, Ado III, 3, 56. 's not so good, III, 4, 9. 's but a night-gown, 18. being that I flow in grief, IV, 1, 251; cf. being two hours to day, Merch. V, 303; being holiday, the beggar's shop is shut, Rom. V, 1, 56; being done, there is no pause, Oth. V, 2, 82; and being that we detain all his revenue, Ant. III, 6, 29; being so frustrate, tell him he mocks the pauses, V, 1, 2. if they should speak, would almost damn those ears, Merch. I, 1, 98. if it be denied, will much impeach the justice of his state, III, 3, 29. happiest of all is that her gentle spirit commits itself to yours to be directed, III, 2, 165. at the Elephant is best to lodge, Tw. III, 3, 40. thus let be, H8 I, 1, 171 (cf. Be). remains that you do meet the senate, Cor. II, 3, 147. if so be thou darest not this, IV, 5, 98. sufficeth not that we are brought to Rome, Tit. I, 109. let us give him burial, as becomes, 347. have I thought long to see this morning's face, Rom. IV, 5, 41. so please him come unto this place, Caes. III, 1, 140 (cf. Please). as becomes a friend, 229. shall not be long but I'll be here again, Mcb. IV, 2, 23. and now remains that we find out the cause, Hml. II, 2, 100. grates me, Ant. I, 1, 18. by her election may be truly read what kind of man he is, Cymb. I, 1, 53. be what it is, V, 4, 149. and that in Tarsus was not best longer for him to make his rest, Per. II Prol. 25. more, if might, shall be discovered, V Prol. 23.

Used for he or she, before is: is this Mistress Satan? It is the devil, Err. IV, 3, 50. it is a good divine that follows his own instructions, Merch. I, 2, 15. it is the most impenetrable cur that ever kept with men, III, 3, 18. here's Wart; you see what a ragged appearance it is, H4B III, 2, 279. 'tis a gull, a fool, H5 III, 6, 70. it is some carpenter, H6A V, 3, 90. a peevish harlotry it is, Rom. IV, 2, 14. Tp. I, 2, 309. As I, 1, 148. Tim. III, 1, 23. Troil. III, 2, 34. Oth. V, 2, 239. Mcb. I, 4, 58. laying these slight sullies on my son, as 'twere a thing a little soiled in the working, Hml. II, 1, 40. 'tis a noble Lepidus, Ant. III, 2, 6.

Relating to persons; a) to designations of chil-

dren: if thou takest up the princess by that forced baseness which he has put upon't, Wint. II, 3, 79. grandam will give it a plum, John II, 161. when it (little Juliet) did taste the wormwood, Rom. I, 3, 30. 32. 48. 51. 52. 54. 57. a little daughter; for the sake of it be manly, Per. III, 1, 21. Jocularly applied to Cressida by Pandarus: would he not, a naughty man, let it sleep? Troil. IV, 2, 34. b) to persons of either sex: a wretched soul we bid be quiet when we hear it cry, Err. II, 1, 35. will make or man or woman madly dote upon the next like creature that it sees, Mids. II, 1, 172. see where it comes, LLL V, 2, 337. c) to self: me to whom thou gavest it (viz thy self) Sonn. 87, 10. since I am crept in favour with my self, I will maintain it with some little cost, R3 I, 2, 260.

Used after intr. verbs, formed sometimes for the purpose, to give the expression a peculiar emphasis: if I do not act it, hiss me, Wiv. III, 3, 40 (if I do not play my part with a vengeance). love bears it out even to the edge of doom, Sonn. 116, 12. nor should that nation boast it so with us, H6A III, 3, 23. I'll go brave it at the court, Tit. IV, 1, 121. how to bride it, Shr. III, 2, 253. she hears them chant it lustily, Ven. 869. knows to court it with words, Tit. II, 1, 91. nature and sickness debate it at their leisure, Alls I, 2, 75. I'll devil-porter it no further, Mcb. II, 3, 19. how dearly they do't, Cymb. II, 2, 18. Lord Angelo dukes it well, Meas. III, 2, 100. I have faced it with a card of ten, Shr. II, 407. a faces it out, but fights not, H5 III, 2, 35. revel and feast it at my house, Err. IV, 4, 65. fight it out, H6A I, 1, 99 (cf. Fight). rather than fool it so, Cor. II, 3, 128. foot it featly, Tp. I, 2, 380. foot it, girls, Rom. I, 5, 28. let the music knock it, H8 I, 4, 108. I see them lording it in London streets, H6B IV, 8, 47. to mince it in love, H5 V, 2, 130. a trull that noises it against us, Ant. III, 6, 96. many cowards that do outface it with their semblances, As I, 3, 124. to prince it much beyond the trick of others, Cymb. III, 3, 85. I'll queen it no inch farther, Wint. IV, 4, 460. would hire me to queen it, H8 II, 3, 37. to revel it with him, H6C III, 3, 225. roaming it thus, Hml. I, 3, 109 (Qq wrong, M. Edd. running). smoothest it so with king and commonweal, H6B II, 1, 22. she sweeps it through the court with troops of ladies, I, 3, 80. he'll tickle it for his concupy, Troil. V, 2, 177. my true lip hath virgined it e'er since, Cor. V, 3, 48. I come to wive it wealthily, Shr. I, 2, 75.

2) = there: 'tis no trusting to yond foolish lout, Gent. IV, 4, 71. Perhaps also in: 'tis your brother Cassius at the door, who doth desire to see you, Caes. II, 1, 70.

3) = its: she knows it cowardice, Gent. V, 2, 21 (perhaps = she knows it to be cowardice). the innocent milk in it most innocent mouth, Wint. III, 2, 101. the public body hath sense of it own fall, Tim. V, 1, 151. it had it head bit off, Lr. I, 4, 236. woman it pretty self, Cymb. III, 4, 160. The earlier O. Edd. it, the later its: of it own kind, Tp. II, 1, 163. leave it to it own protection, Wint. II, 3, 178. it hath it original from much grief, H4B I, 2, 131. corrupting in it own fertility, H5 V, 2, 40. it had upon it brow a bump, Rom. I, 3, 52. it lifted up it head, Hml. I, 2, 216. fordo it own life, V, 1, 244. nature which contemns it origin, Lr. IV, 2, 32. moves with it own organs, Ant. II, 7, 49. of it own colour, 53.

4) Used for the def. article in the language of

little children: *go to it grandam, child; it grandam will give it a plum,* John II, 160. 161.

Italian, subst. 1) a native of Italy: Alls IV, 1, 79. Cymb. II, 1, 40. 53. III, 2, 4.

2) the language of Italy: ·Merch. I, 2, 75. Hml. III, 2, 274.

Italian, adj. pertaining to Italy: Shr. II, 405. Alls II, 3, 307. Wint. V, 2, 105. John III, 1, 153. Cymb. V, 1, 18. 23. V, 5, 196. 210.

Italy, the country to the south of the Alps: Lucr. 106 (*fruitful I.*). Tp. II, 1, 110. Ado III, 1, 92. 97. V, 1, 174. Merch. I, 2, 80 (*bought his doublet in I.*). II, 2, 167. III, 2, 298. Shr. I, 1, 4. II, 69. Alls II, 1, 12 (read: *high I.*). 19. II, 3, 275. R2 II, 1, 21 (*fashions in proud I.*). IV, 97. Cor. V, 3, 34. 208. Rom. III, 1, 13. Caes. I, 3, 88. III, 1, 264. Ant. I, 2, 97. I, 3, 44. I, 4, 51. II, 5, 23. III, 5, 21. Cymb. I, 3, 29. I, 4, 71. 103. III, 4, 15 (*drug-damned I.*). 51. III, 6, 62. IV, 2, 338. IV, 3, 34. V, 4, 64. V, 5, 161.

Itch, subst. 1) a cutaneous disease accompanied by an uneasy sensation in the skin eased by rubbing: *rubbing the poor i. of your opinion,* Cor. I, 1, 169. —*es, blains,* Tim. IV, 1, 28.

2) a teasing desire: *the i. of his affection,* Ant. III, 13, 7.

Itch, vb. to feel that uneasiness in the skin which is removed by scratching: *my elbow* —*ed; I thought there would a scab follow,* Ado III, 3, 106. Troil. II, 1, 29. *mine eyes do i.; doth that bode weeping?* Oth. IV, 3, 58. Hence = to have a teasing desire: *a tailor might scratch her where'er she did i.* Tp. II, 2, 55. *an* —*ing palm,* Caes. IV, 3, 10. *my finger* —*es to make one,* Wiv. II, 3, 48. *my fingers i.* = I have a great mind to strike: Troil. II, 1, 28. Rom. III, 5, 165.

Item, see Latin in the Appendix.

Iterance, repetition: Oth. V, 2, 150 (Qq *iteration.* cf. *Reprobance*).

Iteration, 1) repetition: Oth. V, 2, 150 (Ff *iterance*).

2) allegation, quotation: *thou hast damnable i. and art indeed able to corrupt a saint,* H4A I, 2, 101. *truth tired with i.,* *as true as steel, as plantage to the moon* etc. Troil. III, 2, 183.

Ithaca, the island of Ulysses: Troil. I, 3, 70. Cor. I, 3, 94.

Its, poss. pronoun of the 3$\underline{d}$ person, relating to neuters; a word just coming into use in Shakespeare's time, but not nearly so frequent as *his* (q. v.): Tp. I, 2, 95. 393. Meas. I, 2, 4. Wint. I, 2, 151. 152. 157. 266. III, 3, 46. H6B III, 2, 393. The earlier O. Edd. *it,* the later *its:* Tp. II, 1, 163. Wint. II, 3, 178. H4B I, 2, 131. H5 V, 2, 40. Rom. I, 3, 52. Hml. I, 2, 216. V, 1, 244. Lr. IV, 2, 32. Ant. II, 7, 49. 53.

Even absolutely, contrary to the present use: *each following day became the next day's master, till the last made former wonders its,* H8 I, 1, 18.

Itself (O. Edd. ordinarily in two words), 1) its own nature or substantiality: *beauty within i. should not be wasted,* Ven. 130. *beauty i. doth of i. persuade,* Lucr. 29. *state i. confounded to decay,* Sonn. 64, 10. *without all ornament, i. and true,* 68, 10. *though to i. it only live and die,* 94, 10. *the great globe i.* Tp. IV, 153. *it assaults mercy i.* Epil. 18. *most precious in i.* Gent. II, 6, 24. IV, 4, 188. Wiv. III, 5, 32. V, 5, 172. Meas. II, 2, 135. II, 4, 21. III, 1, 150. Ado I, 1, 8 etc. etc. *of i.,* see *Of. Hero i.* Ado IV, 1, 83 (i. e. the name of Hero itself). Separated by an adj.: *woman it pretty self,* Cymb. III, 4, 160.

2) refl. pronoun of the 3$\underline{d}$ person applied to things: Sonn. 67, 4. Tp. III, 1, 80. Wiv. II, 2, 253. Meas. I, 1, 55. II, 4, 79. III, 1, 262. V, 540. LLL IV, 3, 265 etc.

Ivory, subst. the substance of which the tusks of elephants consist: Ven. 363. Merch. III, 1, 42.

Ivory, adj. 1) consisting of ivory: Lucr. 407. 1234. Shr. II, 352.

2) white and smooth like ivory: Ven. 230. Lucr. 464. Tim. I, 1, 70.

Ivy, the plant Hedera: Pilgr. 365. Tp. I, 2, 86. Err. II, 2, 180. Mids. IV, 1, 48. Wint. III, 3, 69.

I-wis (most M. Edd. *I wis,* i. e. I know), adv. surely, certainly: Merch. II, 9, 68. Shr. I, 1, 62. R3 I, 3, 102. Per. II Prol. 2. In H6A IV, 1, 180 some M. Edd. *I wist,* O. Edd. *I wish.*

J.

Jack, 1) diminutive of John, Christian name of Rugby, Falstaff and Cade: Wiv. I, 4, 61. II, 3, 1. 3. 8. 13 etc. Wiv. II, 2, 144. H4A I, 2, 111. 126. II, 2, 73. II, 4, 522. III, 3, 187 etc. H6B IV, 2, 5. 162. IV, 4, 13 etc. Evidently a favourite name among the peasantry; hence the proverbial phrases: *J. hath not Jill,* LLL V, 2, 885. *J. shall have Jill,* Mids. III, 2, 461. *be the* —*s fair within, the jills fair without,* Shr. IV, 1, 51 ("a play upon the words, which signify two drinking measures as well as men and maid-servants." Steevens). And the beginning of a song: *J., boy, ho, boy,* Shr. IV, 1, 43.

2) a term of contempt for saucy and paltry, or silly fellows: *I vill kill de J. priest,* Wiv. I, 4, 123. II, 3, 32 (Dr. Caius' speech). *boys, apes, braggarts,* —*s, milksops,* Ado V, 1, 91. *the prince is a J., a sneak-cup,* H4A III, 3, 99. 158. *if I be not J. Falstaff, then am I a J.* V, 4, 143. *since every J. became a gentleman, there's many a gentle person made a J.* R3 I, 3, 72. *twenty such* —*s,* Rom. II, 4, 160. *thou art as hot a J. in thy mood as any in Italy,* Rom. III, 1, 12. *hang him, J.* IV, 5, 149. *take hence this J. and whip him,* Ant. III, 13, 93. *this J. of Caesar's,* 103. *bragging* —*s,* Merch. III, 4, 77. *rascal fiddler and twangling J.* Shr. II, 159. *a swearing J.* 290. *no proud J. like Falstaff,* H4A II, 4, 12. *long I will not be J. out of office,* H6A I, 1, 175. *insinuating* —*s,* R3 I, 3, 53. *a J. guardant cannot office me from my son,* Cor. V, 2, 67. *your fairy has done little better than played the J. with us,* Tp. IV, 198, alluding perhaps to the Jack o'lantern or ignis fatuus; but cf. *do you play the flouting J.?* Ado I, 1, 186.

3) a figure striking the bell in old clocks: *I stand fooling here, his J. o'the clock,* R2 V, 5, 60. *like a J thou keepest the stroke betwixt thy begging and my meditation,* R3 IV, 2, 117. *cap and knee slaves, vapours, and minute* —*s,* Tim. III, 6, 107 (marking every minute, changing with every minute?).

4) a key of a virginal: *I envy those —s that nimble leap to kiss the tender inward of thy hand*, Sonn. 128, 5. 13.

5) a bowl aimed at in the game of bowling: *when I kissed the j., upon an up-cast to be hit away*, Cymb. II, 1, 2.

6) a drinking measure (half a pint): Shr. IV, 1, 51 (quibbling; see sub 1).

Jack-a-lent, a small stuffed puppet thrown at during Lent: *you little J., have you been true to us?* Wiv. III, 3, 27. *see now how wit may be made a J., when 'tis upon ill employment*, V, 5, 134.

Jack-a-nape or **Jack-'nape**, Dr. Caius' form for *Jack-an-apes:* Wiv. I, 4, 113. 116. II, 3, 87.

Jack-an-apes, an ape, a monkey: *sit like a j., never off*, H5 V, 2, 148. Used as a term of contempt: *I will be like a j. also*, Wiv. IV, 4, 67. *that j. with scarfs*, Alls III, 5, 88. *a whoreson j. must take me up for swearing*, Cymb. II, 1, 4.

Jack-dog, a word coined by Dr. Caius, to express his utmost contempt: Wiv. II, 3, 65.

Jack-sauce, Fluellen's blunder for *saucy Jack:* H5 IV, 7, 148.*

Jack-slave, a mean fellow: *every J. hath his bellyful of fighting*, Cymb. II, 1, 22.

Jacob, 1) the patriarch: Merch. I, 3, 72. 73. 78. 81. 89. 92. II, 5, 36.

2) the apostle, whose feast is on the first of May: *come Philip and J.* Meas. III, 2, 214.

Jade, subst. 1) a term of contempt or pity for a worthless, or wicked, or maltreated horse: Ven. 391. Lucr. 707. Sonn. 51, 12. Gent. III, 1, 277. Meas. II, 1, 269. Shr. I, 2, 249. IV, 1, 1. Alls II, 3, 301. R2 III, 3, 179. V, 5, 85. H4A II, 1, 7. 11. H4B I, 1, 45. II, 4, 178. H5 III, 5, 19. III, 7, 26. IV, 2, 46. H6B IV, 1, 3.* Caes. IV, 2, 26. Hml. III, 2, 253. —*'s tricks:* Ado I, 1, 145. Alls IV, 5, 64. Troil. II, 1, 21.

2) a term of extreme contempt, when applied to persons, male as well as female: *no such j. as you*, Shr. II, 202. *I'ld play incessantly upon these —s*, John II, 385. *I had as lief have my mistress a j.* H5 III, 7, 63.

Jade, vb. 1) to treat like a jade, to spurn, to kick: *the honourable blood of Lancaster must not be shed by such a —d groom*, H6B IV, 1, 52 (the spurious Qq *jady*). *to be thus —d by a piece of scarlet*, H8 III, 2, 280. *the ne'er yet beaten horse of Parthia we have —d out o' the field*, Ant. III, 1, 34.

2) to make appear like a jade, to make ridiculous and contemptible: *I do not now fool myself, to let imagination j. me*, Tw. II, 5, 178.

Jail, see *Gaol.*

Jailer, see *Gaoler.*

Jakes, a privy: Lr. II, 2, 72. Concealed in the name of *Ajax:* LLL V, 2, 581.

Jamany, Dr. Caius' blunder for *Germany:* Wiv. IV, 5, 89.

James, Christian name of 1) J. Gurney: John I, 230. 231. 2) Sir J. Cromer: H6B IV, 7, 117. 3) J. Tyrrel: R3 IV, 2, 68. 4) Sir J. Blunt: R3 IV, 5, 11. 5) J. Soundpost: Rom. IV, 5, 138. — Used by Fluellen for Jamy: H5 III, 2, 90.

Jamy, 1) = Jacob: *Saint J.* Shr. III, 2, 84 (Biondello's song). 2) name of a Scottish captain: H5 III, 2, 80. 81.

Jane, female name: As II, 4, 48. H4B III, 2, 210.

Jangle, 1) intr. to sound discordantly: *kept such a —ing of the bells*, Per. II, 1, 45. Hence = to quarrel, to altercate, to wrangle: *good wits will be —ing*, LLL II, 225. *their —ing I esteem a sport*, Mids. III, 2, 353.

2) to make to sound discordantly, to put out of tune: *like sweet bells —d, out of tune and harsh,* Hml. III, 1, 166.

January, the coldest month in the year: Ado I, 1, 94. Wint. IV, 4, 111.

Janus. a Roman God with two faces: *by two-headed J.* Merch. I, 1, 50. *by J.* Oth. I, 2, 33.

Japhet, the eldest son of Noah: H4B II, 2, 128.

Jaquenetta, female name in LLL I, 1, 204. 275. 314. I, 2, 150. III, 132. IV, 1, 58. V, 2, 686. 892.

Jaques, (dissyll.), name of 1) Saint J. le Grand, whose sanctuary at Florence is resorted to by Helena in Alls III, 4, 4. III, 5, 37. 98. IV, 3, 58. 2) J. Falcon-bridge: LLL II, 42. 3) J. Chatillon, admiral of France: H5 III 5, 43. IV, 8, 98. 4) the melancholy J. in As II, 1, 26. 41. 43. 54. I, 5, 11. 20. V, 4, 200. 5) a brother of Oliver and Orlando: As I, 1, 5. 6) an officer in Alls IV, 3, 185.

Jar, subst. 1) the tick of a clock: *I love thee not a j. o' the clock behind what lady-she her lord*, Wint. I, 2, 43.

2) harsh sound, discord: *if he, compact of —s, grow musical*, As II, 7, 5 (quibbling).

3) discord, quarrel, contention, combat: *conquers in every j.* Ven. 100. *include all —s with triumphs*, Gent. V, 4, 160. Err. I, 1, 11. H6A I, 1, 44. Troil. I, 3, 117. *fallen at —s*, H6B I, 1, 253. *live at j.* IV, 8, 43.

Jar, vb. 1) to tick: *my thoughts are minutes, and with sighs they j. their watches on unto mine eyes*, R2 V, 5, 51 (cf. *Watch*).

2) to be discordant, to be out of tune: *you delight not in music. Not a whit, when it —s so*, Gent. IV, 2, 67. *the treble —s*, Shr. III, 1, 39. Metaphorically: *our —ing notes agree*, Shr. V, 2, 1. Alls I, 1, 186. H6B II, 1, 57. Lr. IV, 7, 16.

3) to clash, to quarrel: *'tis the base knave that —s*, Shr. III, 1, 47. *that two such noble peers should j.* H6A III, 1, 70. IV, 1, 188. Tit. II, 1, 103. Lr. IV, 7, 32 (Ff —*ing*, Qq *warring*).

Jason, the chief of the Argonauts: Merch. I, 1, 172. III, 2, 244.

Jaunce, subst. a wild ramble, a roving about, a coursing: *what a j. have I had!* Rom. II, 5, 26 (Ff *jaunt*).

Jaunce, vb. to ride hard, to work the horse wildly, to rove about in a harassing manner (Germ. *tummeln*): *spurred, galled and tired by —ing Boling-broke*, R2 V, 5, 94.* *to catch my death with —ing up and down*, Rom. II, 5, 53 (Ff *jaunting*).

Jaundice, a disease characterized by yellowness of the eyes and skin: Merch. I, 1, 85. Troil. I, 3, 2.

Jaunt, a wild and fatiguing ramble: Rom. II, 5, 26 (Qq *jaunce*).

Jaunt, to rove about in a harassing manner: Rom. II, 5, 53 (Qq *jauncing*).

Javelin, a boar-spear: Ven. 616.

Jaw, the mouth of a beast (Germ. *Rachen*): *he keeps them, like an ape, in the corner of his j.* Hml. IV, 2, 20. Plur. —*s*, in the same sense: Sonn. 19, 3. Mids. I, 1, 148. Tw. III, 4, 394. John V, 2, 116. H4A III, 2, 102. H5 II, 4, 105. H6B IV, 1, 6. Troil. I, 3, 73. Rom. V, 3, 47. Hml. I, 4, 50. Ant. II, 5, 13.

Jaw-bone, the bone in which the teeth are fixed: Hml. V, 1, 85.*

Jay, the bird Corvus glandarius: Tp. II, 2, 173. Shr. IV, 3, 177. Wint. IV, 3, 10. Denoting a loose woman: *we'll teach him to know turtles from —s*, Wiv. III, 3, 44. *some j. of Italy hath betrayed him*, Cymb. III, 4, 51.

Jealous, 1) suspicious in love: Wiv. II, 2, 276. 283. 316. III, 3, 184. III, 5, 102. 111. IV, 2, 137. 170. Err. V, 69. 85. Ado II, 1, 305. Mids. II, 1, 24. 61. Wint. II, 3, 30. III, 2, 135. R3 I, 1, 81. 92. Troil. IV, 5, 107. Cor. V, 3, 46. Oth. III, 3, 183. 198. III, 4, 28. 29. 99. 156. 159. 160. 161. V, 2, 345. Followed by *of*, to denote a) the person feared: Merch. III, 5, 31. Lr. V, 1, 56. b) the person feared about: Err. IV, 2, 23. As IV, 1, 150.

2) suspicious in any way: *let not the j. day behold that face*, Lucr. 800. *nor dare I question with my j. thought where you may be*, Sonn. 57, 9. *fearing lest my j. aim might err*, Gent. III, 1, 28. *a soldier j. in honour*, As II, 7, 151. *our first merriment hath made thee j.* Shr. IV, 5, 76. R3 III, 1, 36. Rom. V, 3, 33. Lr. I, 4, 75. With *of: j. as the stung are of the adder*, Lr. V, 1, 56. With *on: be not j. on me*, Caes. I, 2, 71. With a clause: *you are j. now that this is from some mistress*, Oth. III, 4, 185.

3) suspiciously fearful, doubtful: *that my most j. and too doubtful soul may live at peace*, Tw. IV, 3, 27. With *of: j. of catching*, Ven. 321 (fearing to be caught). *your nobles, j. of your absence*, H5 IV, 1, 302 (concerned about). *so loving j. of his liberty*, Rom. II, 2, 182. With a clause: *that you do love me, I am nothing j.* Caes. I, 2, 162 (I do not doubt).

Jealous-hood, jealousy (abstr. pro concr.): Rom. IV, 4, 13.

Jealousy, 1) suspicion in love: Ven. 1137. Gent. II, 4, 177. Wiv. II, 1, 104. 107. II, 2, 302. 324. III, 3, 201. III, 5, 73. IV, 2, 155. 208. V, 1, 20. Err. II, 1, 102. 116. Mids. II, 1, 81. IV, 1, 149. Tw. V, 122. Wint. I, 2, 451. H5 V, 2, 391. Troil. IV, 4, 82. Oth. II, 1, 310. III, 3, 165 (*the green-eyed monster*). 176. 177. 192. IV, 1, 102. Cymb. V, 4, 66. Plur. —*ies*: Wiv. III, 3, 182. IV, 2, 164. V, 5, 139 (Evans' speeches). Wint. III, 2, 114. 181. IV, 1, 18. Oth. IV, 3, 90.

2) suspicion in any way, apprehension: *j., that sour unwelcome guest*, Ven. 449. *where love reigns, disturbing j. doth call himself affection's sentinel*, 649. *j. itself could not mistrust*, Lucr. 1516. *to find out shames and idle hours in me, the scope and tenour of thy j.* Sonn. 61, 8. *j. shall be called assurance*, Ado II, 2, 49. *shuddering fear and green-eyed j.* Merch. III, 2, 110. *j. what might befall your travel*, Tw. III, 3, 8. H5 II, 2, 126. Hml. II, 1, 113. IV, 5, 19. Oth. III, 3, 147. Cymb. IV, 3, 22. Plur.: *transported by my —ies*, Wint. III, 2, 159. *surmises, —ies, conjectures*, H4B Ind. 16. Mcb. IV, 3, 29. Ant. II, 2, 134. — = *jealous*, Wiv. II, 2, 93 (Mrs Quickly).

Jeer, subst. scoff, taunt, gibe: *mark the —s, the gibes*, Oth. IV, 1, 83 (Ff *fleers*).

Jeer, vb. to scoff, to flout: *esteemed so as silly —ing idiots are with kings*, Lucr. 1812. *dost thou j. and flout me in the teeth?* Err. II, 2, 22. —*ing and disdained contempt*, H4A I, 3, 183. *to mock your own —ing*, Hml. V, 1, 212 (Qq *grinning*).

Jelly, viscous and gluy substance: Wint. I, 2, 418. Hml. I, 2, 205. Lr. III, 7, 83.

Jennet, a kind of horse: *a breeding j.* Ven. 260. —*s for germans*, Oth. I, 1, 113.

Jenny's case, Mrs Quickly's blunder for *Genitive case:* Wiv. IV, 1, 64 (O. Edd. *Ginyes case*).

Jeopardy, danger: *look to thyself, thou art in j.* John III, 1, 346.

Jephthah (O. Edd. *Jepha, Jeptha, Jepthah* and *Jephta*), the judge of Israel who sacrificed his daughter: H6C V, 1, 91. Hml. II, 2, 422. 429. 430.

Jerk, subst. a sudden spring, a sally, a flash: *the —s of invention*, LLL IV, 2, 129 (Holofernes' speech).

Jerkin, a short coat: Tp. IV, 236. 237. 238. Gent. II, 4, 19. 20. Wiv. I, 3, 18. Shr. III, 2, 44. H4A I, 2, 48. 52. II, 4, 77. H4B II, 2, 189. II, 4, 18. Troil. III, 3, 266.

Jeronimy, Sly's form of *Hieronimo*, the principal character in the Spanish Tragedy of Thomas Kyd: *go by, J.* Shr. Ind. 1, 9.

Jerusalem, 1) the Holy City: John II, 378. H4A I, 1, 102. H6A V, 5, 40. H6B I, 1, 48. H6C I, 4, 122. V, 7, 39.

2) Paradise: *so part we sadly in this troublous world, to meet with joy in sweet J.* H6C V, 5, 8.

3) name of a chamber: H4B IV, 5, 235. 238. 241.

Jesses, straps of leather or silk, with which hawks were tied by the legs: *though her j. were my heart-strings*, Oth. III, 3, 261.

Jessica, name of the daughter of Shylock: Merch. II, 4, 20. 29 etc.

Jest, subst. 1) any thing ludicrous and amusing uttered or done: Tp. IV, 241. Gent. II, 1, 141. 160. Wiv. II, 1, 224. II, 2, 116. III, 4, 39. 60. IV, 2, 237. IV, 6, 17. V, 5, 109. Err. I, 2, 21. 68. II, 2, 21. III, 1, 123. Ado I, 3, 15. II, 1, 252. II, 3, 141. 206. LLL II, 71. IV, 1, 144. IV, 3, 174. V, 2, 46. Mids. III, 2, 239. Merch. I, 1, 56. As I, 3, 26. Shr. V, 2, 91. H4A I, 2, 208. H6B I, 1, 132. R3 II, 4, 30. Hml. V, 1, 204 (*a fellow of infinite j.*). Ant. III, 13, 181 etc. *to break —s:* Ado V, 1, 189. Shr. IV, 5, 72. Troil. I, 3, 148. *to make a j.:* H6C V, 1, 30.

2) the object of laughter, a laughing-stock: *let me be your j., I deserve it*, Wiv. III, 3, 161.

3) the contrary to earnest; what is not meant as it was pretended: *let us confess and turn it to a j.* LLL V, 2, 390. *rated them at courtship, pleasant j. and courtesy*, 790. *our letters showed much more than j.* 795. *'tis no j. that I do hate thee*, Mids. III, 2, 280. *if that be j., then all the rest was so*, Shr. II, 22. *takest it all for j.* Wint. I, 2, 249. *in j.* = not in earnest: Gent. II, 5, 14. LLL I, 1, 54. Shr I, 2, 84. R2 V, 3, 101. H4A II, 3, 102. H6B III, 2, 400. H6C II, 3, 28. R3 V, 1, 22. Hml. III, 2, 244.

Jest, vb. 1) to make merry by words or actions, to joke: Ven. 106. Tp. III, 2, 52. Wiv. IV, 2, 108. Err. I, 2, 62. II, 2, 65. Ado III, 2, 60. LLL V, 2, 477. 881. Shr. I, 1, 231. Alls I, 2, 33. Tw. II, 5, 24. H4A V, 3, 57. *j. on* = continue to jest: H6C III, 2, 116. R3 III, 2, 77. With *at: j. at every offer*, Pilgr. 54. *at my exile*, 189. Ado V, 1, 58. Rom. II, 2, 1. With *on: your sauciness will j. upon my love*, Err. II, 2, 28 (= to play, to trifle with my love). *he must observe their mood on whom he —s*, Tw. III, 1, 69. cf. *to break a jest upon the company*, Shr. IV, 5, 72. With *to: I j. to Oberon and make him smile*, Mids. II, 1, 44. With *with: great men may j. with saints*, Meas. II, 2, 127. Err. II, 2, 8. 32.

2) to act or speak in sport, not to be in earnest: *no, sweet Death, I did but j.* Ven. 997. Meas. IV, 3, 52. Err. II, 2, 23. Ado V, 1, 147. LLL V, 2, 66. Mids. III, 2, 265. Shr. II, 19. IV, 2, 48. John III, 1, 16. R2 I, 3, 95 (*as jocund as to j.,* = as if I were going to a mock-fight). Troil. I, 2, 224. Tit. II, 3, 253. Rom. III, 5, 191. Hml. III, 2, 244. Followed by *with: with maids to j., tongue far from heart,* Meas. I, 4, 32. Shr. II, 20. John III, 1, 242. H6C III, 2, 91. Cor. I, 3, 103.

Jester, 1) one who cracks jokes, a scoffer: *—s do oft prove prophets,* Lr. V, 3, 71.

2) one who knows to take a joke, one not over-earnest: *the parson is no j.* Wiv. II, 1, 218.

3) a buffoon, a licensed fool: Ado II, 1, 142. 251. Tw. II, 4, 11. H4A III, 2, 61. H4B V, 5, 52. Hml. V, 1, 199.

Jesting, subst. that which is not meant honestly: *her faith, her oaths, her tears, and all were —s,* Pilgr. 96.

Jesu, the name of the Saviour: R2 IV, 93. V, 2, 17. H4A II, 2, 86 (Qq *Jesus*). II, 4, 314 (om. in Ff). 430 (Ff *O rare!*). 533 and III, 3, 96 (om. in Ff). H4B II, 4, 317 (Ff *what*). III, 2, 36 (Ff *Oh*). H6B I, 1, 161. I, 3, 6. V, 1, 214. R3 I, 3, 136. V, 3, 178. Rom. II, 3, 69 (*J. Maria*). II, 4, 31. II, 5, 29.

Jesus, the same: H4A II, 2, 86 (Ff *Jesu*). H6B I, 2, 70. H6C V, 6, 75.

Jet, subst. a fossil of a velvet-black colour: Compl. 37. Merch. III, 1, 42. H6B II, 1, 112. Tit. V, 2, 50.

Jet, vb. to stalk, to strut: *how he —s under his advanced plumes,* Tw. II, 5, 36. *arched so high that giants may j. through,* Cymb. III, 3, 5. *whose men and dames so —ed and adorned,* Per. I, 4, 26. With *on,* = to insult over, to treat with insolence: *tyranny begins to j. upon the aweless throne,* R3 II, 4, 51* (Ff *jut*). *to j. upon a prince's right,* Tit. II, 1, 64 (Qq *iet,* Ff *set*). In Err. II, 2, 28 O. Edd. *jest.*

Jew, a Hebrew; 1) masc.: Gent. II, 5, 58. Merch. I, 3, 154. 178. II, 2, 2. II, 4, 18. 34 (and passim in this play). *here dwells my father J.* Merch. II, 6, 25. *the villain J.* II, 8, 4. *the dog J.* 14. *a J. would have wept to have seen our parting,* Gent. II, 3, 12. *if I do not love her, I am a J.* Ado II, 3, 272. *I am a J., if I serve the J. any longer,* Merch. II, 2, 119. *my master's a very J.* 112. *I am a J. else, an Ebrew J.* H4A II, 4, 198. *liver of blaspheming J.* Mcb. IV, 1, 26 (as an ingredient in the cauldron of the witches). Confounded with *jewel: my incony J.* LLL III, 136. *most lovely J.* Mids. III, 1, 97.

2) fem.: *most sweet J.* Merch. II, 3, 11. *a Gentile and no J.* II, 6, 51. *there will come a Christian by, will be worth a —'s eye,* II, 5, 43 (O. Edd. *Jewes,* M. Edd. *Jewess',* a word unknown to Sh.; cf. *heir, tiger* etc. as fem. As for the metre, cf. *whale's* dissyll. in LLL V, 2, 332; *moon's,* Mids. II, 1, 7; *rope's,* Err. IV, 1, 98 etc. It was common in the middle ages to extort sums of money from the Jews by threatening them with mutilations, if they refused to pay. The threat of losing an eye must have had a powerful effect. In our passage, of course, a quibble is intended).

Jewel, any personal ornament of gold or precious stones: Ven. 163. 824. Sonn. 27, 11. 48, 5. 52, 8. 96, 6. Gent. III, 1, 90. Meas. II, 1, 24. Err. II, 1, 109. V, 144. LLL II, 243. IV, 2, 5. V, 2, 455. Mids. III, 1, 161. IV, 1, 196. Merch. II, 4, 32. II, 8, 20.

III, 1, 91. 93. V, 224 (a ring). As I, 3, 136. II, 1, 14. III, 2, 94. Tw. II, 4, 126. II, 5, 67. III, 4, 228 (a picture). Wint. V, 2, 37. John V, 1, 40. R2 I, 1, 180 I, 3, 267. H4B I, 2, 22. II, 4, 52. H6A V, 1, 47. H6B III, 2, 106. 409. R3 I, 4, 27. H8 II, 2, 32. Cor. I, 4, 56. Tit. III, 1, 199. Rom. I, 5, 48. Tim. I, 1, 12 (and passim). Lr. IV, 6, 28. Ant. V, 2, 138. Cymb. I, 4, 165 (a ring). I, 6, 189. II, 3, 146 (a bracelet). II, 4, 96. V, 5, 143. Per. II, 1, 162. II, 2, 12. III, 1, 67. III, 4, 1. V, 3, 24. Metaphorically: Lucr. 34. 1191. Sonn. 65, 10. 131, 4. Compl. 154. Tp. III, 1, 54. Gent. II, 4, 169. IV, 4, 51. Wiv. II, 2, 213. III, 3, 45. Ado I, 1, 183. Shr. I, 2, 119. Alls IV, 2, 46. V, 3, 1. Wint. V, 1, 116. R2 I, 3, 270. Mcb. III, 1, 68.*Lr. I, 1, 271. Oth. I, 3, 195 (*for your sake, j., I am glad*). III, 3, 156. Ant. IV, 15, 78. Cymb. I, 1, 91. I, 4, 165. Per. III, 2, 99. IV, 6, 164.

Jewel-house, the place where the regal ornaments are reposited: H8 IV, 1, 111. V, 1, 34.

Jeweller, one who deals in jewels: Alls V, 3, 297. Tim. I, 1, 8.

Jewel-like, brilliant like a precious stone: Per. V, 1, 111.

Jewess, writing of M. Edd. in Merch. II, 5, 43; see *Jew.*

Jewish, pertaining to a Jew: *my J. gaberdine,* Merch. I, 3, 113. *his J. heart,* IV, 1, 80.

Jewry, the country of the Jews: Wiv. II, 1, 20. R2 II, 1, 55. H5 III, 3, 40. Ant. I, 2, 28. III, 3, 3. III, 6, 73. IV, 6, 12.

Jezebel, the name of the proud queen in the 2. Book of Kings ch. 9, not very accurately applied to Malvolio by Sir Andrew: Tw. II, 5, 46.

Jig, subst. a facetious metrical composition, a ludicrous ballad; or a merry dance accompanying it: *all my merry —s are quite forgot,* Pilgr. 253. *a Scotch j.* Ado II, 1, 77. *profound Salomon to tune a j.* LLL IV, 3, 168. *my very walk should be a j.* Tw. I, 3, 138. *he's for a j. or a tale of bawdry,* Hml. II, 2, 522.*

Jig, vb. to sing in the tune of a jig; to compose jigs; to walk like one who dances a jig: *to j. off a tune at the tongue's end,* LLL III, 11. *what should the wars do with these —ing fools?* Caes. IV, 3, 137. *you j., you amble, and you lisp,* Hml. III, 1, 150.

Jig-maker, a writer or composer of jigs: Hml. III, 2, 131.

Jill (cf. *Gill*), a familiar name for a woman: *Jack hath not J.* LLL V, 2, 885. *Jack shall have J.* Mids. III, 2, 461. *be the jacks fair within, the —s fair without,* Shr. IV, 1, 52. cf. *Jack.*

Jingle, to clink, to sound with a fine, sharp rattle: *—ing chains,* Tp. V, 233.

Joan, 1) female noun prop.: a) of J. la Pucelle or J. of Arc: H6A I, 4, 101. I, 6, 3. 17. 29. II, 1, 49. II, 2, 20. III, 3, 17. V, 4, 2. 6. 17. 20. 49. 60. b) of a hawk: H6B II, 1, 4.

2) designation of a peasant girl: *some men must love my lady and some J.* LLL III, 207. *groan for J.* IV, 3, 182 (Q1 *love*). *while greasy J. doth keel the pot,* V, 2, 930. 939. *Alice madam, or J. madam?* Shr. Ind. 2, 112. *now can I make any J. a lady,* John I, 184.

Job, the hero of the Book of Job: *as poor as J.* Wiv. V, 5, 164. H4B I, 2, 144.

Jockey, a diminutive of John: *J. of Norfolk, be not too bold,* R3 V, 3, 304.

Jocund, gay, lively, brisk: Lucr. 296. Tp. III,

2, 126. Tw. V, 135. R2 I, 3, 95. R3 III, 2, 86. V, 3, 232. Rom. III, 5, 9. Mcb. III, 2, 40. Hml. I, 2, 125.

Jog, to trot: *you may be —ing whiles your boots are green*, Shr. III, 2, 213. *j. on, j. on, the foot-path way*, Wint. IV, 3, 132.

John, Christian name of 1) King J.: John II, 10. III, 1, 137. III, 4, 133 etc. 2) J. of Gaunt: R2 I, 1, 1 etc. H4A II, 2, 70 etc. H6A II, 5, 77. H6B II, 2, 14. H6C I, 1, 19. III, 3, 81. 3) Prince J. of Lancaster: H4A III, 2, 171. IV, 1, 89 etc. 4) Prester J., a fabulous monarch in the East: Ado II, 1, 276. 5) a companion of Robin Hood: *Robin Hood, Scarlet and J.* H4B V, 3, 107. Bardolph called *Scarlet and John* by Falstaff on account of his red face: Wiv. I, 1, 177. 6) Don J., brother of Don Pedro in Ado II, 1, 1. III, 3, 116. 160. IV, 1, 190. IV, 2, 42. V, 1, 242 etc. 7) a friar in Rom. V, 2, 2. V, 3, 250. 8) a priest in R3 III, 2, 111. 9) J. Bates: H5 IV, 1, 87. 10) Sir J. Bracy: H4A II, 4, 367. 11) J. Cade: H6B III, 1, 357 etc. 12) Sir J. Colevile: H4B IV, 3, 42. 13) J. de la Car: H8 I, 1, 218. 14) J. Doit: H4B III, 2, 21. 15) Sir J. Falstaff: Wiv. I, 1, 3. 31. 71 etc. H4A I, 2, 125. II, 1, 75. II, 2, 69 etc. 16) Sir J. Fastolfe: H6A I, 1, 131. 17) J. Goodman: H6B I, 3, 19. 18) J. Hume: H6B I, 2, 68 etc. 19) Sir J. Montgomery: H6C IV, 7, 40. 20) Sir J. Mortimer: H6C I, 2, 62. 21) Sir J. Norbery: R2 II, 1, 284. 22) J. Duke of Norfolk: R3 V, 3, 296. 23) J. Naps of Greece: Shr. Ind. 2, 95. 24) Sir J. Ramston: R2 II, 1, 283. 25) J. Rugby: Wiv. I, 4, 1 etc. 26) a servant of Ford's: Wiv. III, 3, 1. 27) J. Southwell: H6B I, 4, 14. 28) Sir J. Stanley: H6B II, 3, 13. II, 4, 77 etc. 29) John Talbot: H6A IV, 2, 3 etc. 30) his son, young Talbot: H6A IV, 3, 35. IV, 5, 1 etc. 31) Sir J. Umfrevile: H4B I, 1, 34. *St. J.* Ff in R3 I, 1, 138.

J. Drum's entertainment, i. e. blows as the drum receives: Alls III, 6, 41. cf. *Poor-John, Apple-John.*

John-a-dreams, a dreamy, idle fellow: Hml. II, 2, 595.

Join, 1) tr. to couple, to combine, to unite: *to j. hands*, John II, 532. *—ed in love*, III, 1, 240. *to j. your hearts in love*, H6A III, 1, 68. *j. our powers*, III, 3, 90. *j. your hands*, H6C IV, 6, 39. *God —ed my heart and Romeo's*, Rom. IV, 1, 55. Tim. III, 5, 79. Caes. I, 3, 17. Hml. III, 2, 91. Ant. II, 2, 154. Per. II, 5, 86. *to j. together:* As III, 3, 88. H6C II, 1, 37. IV, 1, 22. R3 II, 2, 118. Per. III Prol. 18. *to following: her lips to mine how often hath she —ed*, Pilgr. 91. *a charm, —ed to their suffered labour*, Tp. I, 2, 231. *false blood to false blood —ed*, John III, 1, 2. R2 II, 2, 66. H6A III, 2, 27. H6C III, 3, 242. Cymb. V, 5, 457. *with following: j. her hand with his*, As V, 4, 120. *York is —ed with Bolingbroke*, R2 III, 2, 200. *I am —ed with no foot-land-rakers*, H4A II, 1, 81. H6A I, 1, 93. I, 4, 101. V, 5, 68. H8 II, 2, 106. Cor. IV, 6, 66. 89. Tim. III, 3, 25. Caes. V, 1, 62. Lr. III, 2, 22. Cymb. I, 1, 29. I, 6, 106.

3) intr. a) to unite, to combine, to become as one: *they* (currents of blood) *j.* Lucr. 1442. *meet and j.* Tp. I, 2, 201. Mids. III, 2, 150. As V, 4, 135. Alls I, 1, 238. John II, 441. III, 1, 52. H6A III, 1, 145. H6C II, 1, 29. IV, 8, 62. Tit. II, 1, 103. IV, 2, 136. *to j. together:* Ven. 971. H5 IV, 1, 143. H6B I, 1, 199. Followed by *with: j. with the spite of fortune*, Sonn. 90, 3. *I will j. with you to disgrace her*, Ado III, 2, 130. Mids. III, 2, 216. R2 II, 1, 132. V, 1, 16. H4A

I, 3, 132. 281. V, 1, 86. H4B II, 3, 54. H5 II, 2, 168. H6A II, 1, 18. III, 3, 62. 75. IV, 1, 60. IV, 3, 8. H6B I, 1, 167. I, 3, 98. IV, 4, 52. H6C II, 1, 139. III, 3, 217. IV, 1, 36. R3 II, 2, 36. IV, 4, 491. Cor. IV, 7, 14. Tit. IV, 3, 32. V, 2, 4. Tim. I, 1, 127. Mcb. III, 3, 1. Hml. IV, 1, 33. Ant. II, 1, 22. Cymb. V, 5, 88. A noun, preceded by *with*, understood, though not expressed: *and his own notion shall j. to thrust the lie unto him*, Cor. V, 6, 109 (i. e. shall j. with what I have alleged, shall contribute to thrust etc.).

b) to meet, to engage in close fight: *if once they j. in trial*, H4A V, 1, 85. *that our armies j. not in a hot day*, H4B I, 2, 233. *as the battles —ed*, H6C I, 1, 15. *our battles —ed*, II, 1, 121. *j. bravely*, R3 V, 3, 312. *yet they are not —ed*, Ant. IV, 12, 1.

Joinder, a joining, conjunction: *confirmed by mutual j. of your hands*, Tw. V, 160.

Joindure, in *rejoindure*, q. v.

Joiner, a maker of wooden furniture: Mids. I, 2, 66. III, 1, 47. V, 226. Rom. I, 4, 68.

Joint, subst. 1) a juncture of parts admitting of motion, articulation, hinge: *a scaly gauntlet with —s of steel*, H4B I, 1, 146. *this broken j. between you and her husband entreat her to splinter*, Oth. II, 3, 328. Especially the articulation of limbs: *her —s forget to bow*, Ven. 1061. *suppler —s*, Tp. III, 3, 107. *grind their —s*, IV, 259. *we'll touse you j. by j.* Meas. V, 314. R2 III, 3, 75. V, 3, 98. H4B I, 1, 140. Rom. IV, 5, 25. Tim. I, 1, 257. *out of j.* = dislocated: H4B V, 4, 3. Troil. I, 2, 28. Hml. I, 5, 188.

2) limb: *my —s did tremble*, Ven. 642. *will not my frail —s shake*, Lucr. 227. 452. *because of his great limb or j.* LLL V, 1, 135. *clap their female —s in stiff unwieldy arms*, R2 III, 2, 114. *this festered j. cut off*, V, 3, 85. 105. H4A IV, 1, 83. H5 IV, 3, 123. H6B III, 2, 319. Troil. I, 3, 238. IV, 1, 29. IV, 5, 57. 233. Tit. II, 3, 212. Rom. III, 5, 154. IV, 3, 51. V, 3, 35. Quibbling: *he hath the —s of every thing, but every thing so out of j.* Troil. I, 2, 28. *the elephant hath —s, but none for courtesy: his legs are legs for necessity, not for flexure*, II, 3, 113.

3) the limb of an animal cut up by the butcher: *a j. of mutton*, H4B III, 4, 375. V, 1, 28. *if I have bargained for the j.* Per. IV, 2, 141.

Joint, adj. shared by different persons, common: *a j. burden laid upon us all*, H4B V, 2, 55. *hath no mean dependance upon our j. and several dignities*, Troil. II, 2, 193. *in a j. and corporate voice*, Tim. II, 2, 213.

Joint, vb., to unite, to join (cf. *Injoint*): *—ing their force 'gainst Caesar*, Ant. I, 2, 96. *—ed to the old stock*, Cymb. V, 4, 142. V, 5, 440.

Joint-labourer, fellow-labourer: *make the night j. with the day*, Hml. I, 1, 78.

Jointly, 1) together, in concert: *we shall j. labour with your soul to give it due content*, Hml. IV, 5, 211.

2) in common, all in company: *all j. listening*, Lucr. 1410. *then j. to the ground their knees they bow*, 1846. *they j. swear to spoil the city*, H6B IV, 4, 52. *cause of state craving us j.* Mcb. III, 1, 35. *I do invest you j. with my power*, Lr. I, 1, 132.

Jointress, a dowager: *the imperial j. to this warlike state*, Hml. I, 2, 9.

Joint-ring, a ring with joints in it, so as to consist of two halves: Oth. IV, 3, 73.

Joint-servant, colleague: *made him j. with me*, Cor. V, 6, 32.

Joint-stool (O. Edd. *join'd-stool* and *join-stool*) a stool made with joints, a folding-chair: H4A II, 4, 418. H4B II, 4, 269. Rom. I, 5, 7. In allusion to the proverb '*Cry you mercy, I took you for a j.*': Shr. II, 199. Lr. III, 6, 54.

Jointure, estate settled on a woman in case of her husband's decease: Wiv. III, 4, 50. As IV, 1, 56. Shr. II, 372. H6C III, 3, 136. Rom. V, 3, 297.

Jole or **Jowl**, cheek: *I'll go with thee, cheek by j.* Mids. III, 2, 338 (cheek to cheek, closely).

Joll, see *Joul.*

Jollity, 1) high merriment, gayety: Err. II, 2, 90. Mids. IV, 1, 97. V, 377. Wint. IV, 4, 25. Cymb. IV, 2, 194.

2) gayness of dress, finery: *needy nothing trimmed in j.* Sonn. 66, 3.

Jolly, merry, gay: As II, 7, 183. Shr. III, 2, 215. Tw. IV, 2, 78. John II, 321. R3 IV, 3, 43. Lr. III, 6, 43. Ant. II, 7, 65. IV, 8, 30. Cymb. I, 6, 67.

Jolt-head, blockhead, dunce: Gent. III, 1, 290. Shr. IV, 1, 169.

Jordan, a chamber-pot: H4A II, 1, 22. H4B II, 4, 37.

Joseph, a servant's name: Shr. IV, 1, 91.

Joshua, Moses' successor, one of the Nine Worthies: LLL V, 1, 133.

Jot, a point, a tittle, the least quantity imaginable: *if springing things be any j. diminished*, Ven. 417. *if you break one j. of your promise*, As IV, 1, 194. *if one j. beyond the bound of honour*, Wint. III, 2, 51. *brings a thousand-fold more care to keep than in possession any j. of pleasure*, H6C II, 2, 53. *if this salute my blood a j.* H8 II, 3, 103. Mostly with a negative: Meas. IV, 2, 64. IV, 3, 128. Merch. IV, 1, 306. Shr. I, 1, 241. Tw. III, 2, 1. III, 4, 363. Wint. V, 1, 217. H5 IV Chor. 37. R3 II, 1, 70. Cor. II, 2, 145. Tim. IV, 3, 126. Hml. V, 1, 122. 229. Lr. I, 4, 8. Oth. III, 3, 215. Ant. IV, 5, 13.

Joul or **Jowl** or **Joll**, to thrust, to throw, to dash: *they may j. horns together*, As I, 3, 59. *how the knave —s it to the ground*, Hml. V, 1, 84.

Jourdain, (O. Edd. *Jordane*) name of a sorceress in H6B I, 2, 75. I, 4, 13.

Journal, diurnal, daily: *ere twice the sun hath made his j. greeting*, Meas. IV, 3, 92. *stick to your j. course*, Cymb. IV, 2, 10.

Journey, subst. a travel: Sonn. 27, 3. Gent. II, 7, 7. 60. 65. 85. Meas. III, 1, 27. IV, 3, 61. Shr. Ind. 1, 76. Tw. II, 3, 44. Wint. III, 1, 11. John IV, 3, 20. H6B II, 4, 106. H8 I, 1, 85. I, 2, 155. Troil. IV, 5, 218. Cor. I, 10, 33. IV, 3, 12. Rom. II, 5, 10. Tim. II, 2, 228. Mcb. I, 7, 62. Hml. III, 2, 171. Lr. V, 3, 321. Oth. II, 1, 284. V, 2, 267. Ant. II, 4, 6. V, 2, 201. Cymb. II, 4, 43. V, 4, 190. Per. II, 1, 112.

Journey, vb. to travel: Sonn. 50, 1. Gent. I, 3, 41. Shr. IV, 5, 8. R3 II, 2, 146.

Journey-bated, exhausted by travelling: H4A IV, 3, 26.

Journeyman, a hired workman: R2 I, 3, 274. Hml. III, 2, 37.

Jove, Jupiter, the supreme god of the Romans: Ven. 1015. Lucr. 568. Pilgr. 67. 84. 241. Tp. I, 2, 201. V, 45. Gent. IV, 4, 208. Wiv. V, 5, 3. 10. Meas. II, 2, 111. Ado II, 1, 100. V, 4, 46. 48. LLL IV 2

119. IV, 3, 117. 141. 144. V, 2, 495. Mids. V, 179. As I, 3, 126. II, 4, 61. III, 2, 249 (—'s tree; cf. Tp. V, 45). III, 3, 11. Shr. I, 1, 174. All's IV, 2, 25 (M. Edd. *God*). V, 3, 288. Tw. I, 5, 121. II, 5, 107. 186. 193. III, 1, 50. III, 4, 83. 91. IV, 2, 13. Wint. II, 3, 126. III, 1, 10. IV, 4, 16. H4B II, 2, 193. V, 5, 50. H5 II, 4, 100. IV, 3, 24. H6B IV, 1, 49. IV, 10, 62 (the spurious Qq and M. Edd. *God*). H6C V, 2, 14 (—'s tree; cf. As III, 2, 249). R3 IV, 3, 55. Troil. I, 3, 20. II, 2, 45 (and passim). Cor. II, 1, 282. III, 1, 86 (and passim). Tit. II, 3, 70. IV, 1, 66. IV, 3, 40. IV, 4, 14. Rom. II, 2, 93. Tim. IV, 3, 108. Hml. III, 2, 294. III, 4, 56. Lr. II, 4, 231. Oth. II, 1, 77. II, 3, 17. III, 3, 356. Ant. I, 2, 157. II, 7, 73. III, 4, 29. III, 13, 85. IV, 6, 29. IV, 15, 36. Cymb. II, 4, 98. III, 3, 88. III, 6, 6. IV, 2, 348. Per. I, 1, 7. 104. II, 3, 28.

Jovial, 1) Jove-like, belonging to Jove: *his J. face*, Cymb. IV, 2, 311. *our J. star*, V, 4, 105.

2) merry: Mcb. III, 2, 28. Lr. IV, 6, 203.

Jowl, subst. see *Jole.*

Jowl, vb., see *Joul.*

Joy, subst. 1) the state of feeling happy, delight, gladness, happiness: Ven. 405. 600. Lucr. 111. 690. 889. 1107. 1431. Sonn. 8, 2. 42, 13. 91, 6. 129, 12. Pilgr. 345. Tp. II, 1, 207. Gent. I, 2, 63. II, 4, 139. III, 1, 175. Meas. II, 3, 36. Ado I, 1, 21. 28. II, 1, 317. Mids. V, 19. 20. Merch. III, 2, 107 etc. etc. Plur. — *s*: Tp. IV, 108. H4B V, 3, 99. H4A I, 1, 34. H6B I, 1, 251. R3 I, 4, 255. II, 2, 100. Mcb. I, 4, 33 etc. *to give j.* = to make happy: Mids. II, 1, 73. R2 V, 3, 95. H6A I, 6, 14. *to take j.* = to rejoice, to delight: *I take some j. to say you are*, As IV, 1, 90. *it should take j. to see her in your arms*, Wint. V, 1, 80. *for j.* = out of gladness: LLL V, 2, 291. Wint. I, 2, 111. V, 2, 54. R2 III, 2, 4. H6C II, 1, 196. R3 III, 1, 184. Caes. V, 3, 32. Cymb. III, 1, 29. *in j.* = glad, happy: Err. I, 1, 40. As V, 4, 185. R2 I, 3, 261. Cor. I, 3, 17. Followed by *in*: H6B IV, 2, 366. R3 I, 3, 110. By *of*: *I wish him j. of her*, Ado II, 1, 200. V, 1, 9. *God give thee j. of him*, LLL V, 2, 448. *to leap out of himself for j. of his found daughter*, Wint. V, 2, 54. *my j. of liberty*, H6C IV, 6, 63. R3 III, 1, 184. Tit. I, 400. Rom. II, 2, 117. Ant. V, 2, 261. Cymb. III, 1, 29.

Used to express kind wishes: *j. to you!* Meas. V, 532. *j., gentle friends!* Mids. V, 29. *good j., my lord and lady*, Merch. III, 2, 190. *all j. befall your grace*, Cymb. III, 5, 9. *I drink to the general j. o'the whole table*, Mcb. III, 4, 89. *heaven give thee j.* Wiv. V, 5, 250. Ado II, 1, 312. 350. III, 4, 24. LLL V, 2, 448. As III, 3, 47. Shr. IV, 2, 52. Cor. II, 3, 118. 142. Tit. I, 400. IV, 3, 76. *God send you j.* Shr. II, 321. *that doth not wish you j.* Tp. V, 215. Ado II, 1, 200. Ant. V, 2, 261.

2) that which causes delight or happiness: *makes him all her j.* Mids. II, 1, 27. IV, 1, 4. *was this king Priam's j.?* All's I, 3, 77. *my second j.* Wint. III, 2, 97. John III, 4, 104. H4B II, 4, 52 (Ff *marry*). H6A I, 4, 23. H6B III, 2, 79. H6C III, 3, 242. Tit. I, 382. Lr. I, 1, 84. Ant. I, 5, 58.

Joy, vb. 1) tr. a) to gladden, to make happy: *much it —s me too to see you are become so penitent*, R3 I, 2, 220. *—ed are we that you are*, Cymb. V, 5, 424. *neither pleasure's art can j. my spirits*, Per. I, 2 9.

b) to enjoy, to delight in possessing: *and with it*

j. thy life, R2 V, 6, 26. *live thou to j. thy life*, H6B III, 2, 365. *was ever king that —ed an earthly throne*, IV, 9, 1. *to j. and weep their gain and loss*, R3 II, 4, 59. *let her j. her raven-coloured love*, Tit. II, 3, 83.

2) intr. a) to be glad: *this told, I j.* Sonn. 45, 13. *nothing can make me j.* John III, 4, 107. *hope to j.* R2 II, 3, 15. *until you bid me j.* V, 3, 95. *never —ed*, H4A II, 1, 13. H6C II, 1, 9. 77. Cor. V, 4, 60. Hml. III, 2, 209. Ant. IV, 6, 20. Per. II, 1, 165. With *at: to j. at weeping*, Ado I, 1, 28. With *in*, = to take delight: *you j. not in a love-discourse*, Gent. II, 4, 127. *why should I j. in any abortive birth?* LLL I, 1, 104. *we'll j. in such a son*, Per. I, 1, 118. With *over: I do j. o'er myself, prevented from a damned enterprise*, H5 II, 2, 163 (= I am pleased with myself). Followed by an inf.: *she —ed to jest at my exile*, Pilgr. 189. *how we j. to see your wit restored*, Shr. Ind. 2, 79. By a clause: *and j. that thou becomest king Henry's friend*, H6C III, 3, 201. Caes. V, 5, 34.

b) to enjoy, to delight in possessing; with *in: j. in that I honour most*, Sonn. 25, 4. *where are thy children? wherein dost thou j.?* R3 IV, 4, 93. *although I j. in thee, I have no j. of this contract to-night*, Rom. II, 2, 116.

Joyful, 1) glad, feeling happy: Wiv. I, 1, 54. Err. I, 1, 51. LLL V, 1, 80. R2 V, 2, 29. H6A III, 1, 143. R3 I, 3, 19. III, 7, 203. IV, 4, 99. H8 III, 2, 6. IV, 2, 93. Cor. IV, 3, 51. Tit. III, 1, 116. Rom. II, 4, 185. III, 5, 116. 118. Mcb. I, 4, 45. Cymb. V, 5, 402. *j. tears* = tears of joy: H8 V, 3, 175. Ant. IV, 8, 9. With *of: j. of your reformation*, LLL V, 2, 879. *j. of thy company*, Shr. IV, 5, 52. *of your sights*, Tim. I, 1, 255.

2) glad, making happy: *the j. day*, As V, 3, 1. H4B V, 3, 131. R3 IV, 1, 6. *j. tidings*, H4B I, 1, 35. Rom. III, 5, 105. V, 1, 2. *j. births*, H5 V, 2, 35. *a j. issue*, Tit. IV, 2, 66. *a j. trouble*, Mcb. II, 3, 53.

Joyfully, gladly: H5 IV, 3, 8. R3 III, 7, 245. Hml. II, 2, 41.

Joyless, sad, unhappy: Lucr. 1711. R3 I, 3, 156. Tit IV, 2, 67.

Joyous, glad: H5 V, 2, 9. With *of:* Shr. IV, 5, 70.

Judas, name of 1) J. Maccabaeus: LLL V, 1, 134. V, 2, 540. 599. 602. 603. 604. 633. 2) J. Iscariot: LLL V, 2, 601. 608. As III, 4, 9. R2 III, 2, 132. IV, 170. H6C V, 7, 33.

Jude, a Jew: LLL V, 2, 629. 631.

Judean, a Jew; reading of F1 in Oth. V, 2, 347; the rest of O. Edd. *Indian*.

Judge, subst. 1) an officer appointed to determine questions of law and to administer justice: Lucr. 1648. Meas. I, 4, 27. II, 2, 61. 69. 177. II, 4, 92. III, 1, 65. III, 2, 257. V, 166. Merch. III, 1, 36. IV, 1, 224. 236. 246. 250. 253. 301. 304. 313. 317. 323. 399. V, 143. 157. 180. All's II, 1, 142. Tw. V, 362. Wint. III, 2, 117. John II, 112. 115. R2 I, 3, 237. IV, 118. H4A I, 2, 73. H6A IV, 1, 42. R3 I, 4, 190. H8 I, 2, 71. II, 4, 17. 78. 82. III, 1, 100. V, 3, 60. 101. Tit. III, 1, 50. Tim. III, 5, 50. Cymb. IV, 2, 128. Fem.: *being j. in love, she cannot right her cause*, Ven. 220.

2) one who decides upon the merit of any question: Gent. V, 4, 36. Merch. II, 5, 1. IV, 1, 276. V, 157. As IV, 1, 220. John I, 79. II, 519. H6B IV, 10, 82. Tit. I, 426. Hml. V, 2, 290. Oth. I, 1, 38. 59.

3) the chief magistrate of ancient Israel before the time of the kings: Hml. II, 2, 422.

Judge, vb. 1) to hear and determine in causes on trial, to pass sentence; absol.: *to offend and j. are distinct offices*, Merch. II, 9, 61. *j. you between us*, H6A II, 4, 10. H6B III, 3, 31. Hml. IV, 5, 205. trans. = to pass sentence on, to decide, to determine: *it could not be —d*, Wiv. I, 1, 93. *so God j. me*, 191. *if He should but j. you as you are*, Meas. II, 2, 77. *the strangest controversy to be —d by you*, John I, 45. R2 IV, 123. 128. H6B II, 3, 15. III, 2, 136. H8 II, 2, 107. II, 4, 121. Caes. IV, 2, 38.

2) to form or give an opinion of any kind; absol.: *you shall j.* Gent. IV, 4, 18. *j. when you hear*, Mids. IV, 1, 132. As I, 2, 283. III, 2, 130. H4A I, 2, 74. II, 4, 483. H6B I, 3, 208. H6C II, 1, 128. Caes. III, 2, 18. With *of: and then j. of my merit*, Wiv. III, 5, 52. *if I can j. of her*, Merch. II, 6, 53. Cor. IV, 2, 34. Hml. III, 1, 34. With a dependant clause: *I j. by his blunt bearing he will keep his word*, H5 IV, 7, 184. *j. if I have done amiss*, H6A IV, 1, 27. R3 I, 3, 257. Tit. V, 3, 125. Caes. III, 2, 186. Oth. I, 2, 72. With an accus.: *men j. by the complexion of the sky the state and inclination of the day*, R2 III, 2, 194. *kindly to j. our play*, H5 Prol. 34.

3) to guess: *to what, I pray? J.* Meas. I, 2, 49.

4) to think, to hold, to be of opinion; absol.: *we j. no less*, H5 II, 2, 39. *you are a churchman, or, I'll tell you, cardinal, I should j. now unhappily*, H8 I, 4, 89. *at least he —d so*, Per. I, 3, 21. With a dependant clause: *although you j. I wink*, Gent. I, 2, 139. H6B III, 2, 67. Cor. II, 3, 28. With a double accus.: *when they have —d me fast asleep*, Gent. III, 1, 25. H4B IV, 1, 21. H6A V, 4, 47. H6B III, 1, 232. R3 III, 4, 6. Lr. I, 2, 97.

Judgment, 1) the act and power of administering justice and passing sentence: *I have seen when, after execution, j. hath repented o'er his doom*, Meas. II, 2, 11. *He which is the top of j.* II, 2, 76. *a Daniel come to j.* Merch. IV, 1, 223. *if j. lie in them*, R2 II, 2, 133. *struck me in my very seat of j.* H4B V, 2, 80. *j. only doth belong to thee*, H6B III, 2, 140. *Rome, the nurse of j.* H8 II, 2, 94. *his royal self in j. comes to hear*, V, 3, 120.

2) a sentence passed, a doom: *let mine own j. pattern out my death*, Meas. II, 1, 30. *let me have j.* Merch. IV, 1, 83. 89. 103. 240. 244. H8 II, 1, 32. 58. III, 2, 33. Rom. III, 3, 10. Tim. III, 5, 102. Mcb. I, 3, 110. I, 7, 8. Hml. V, 2, 291.

3) a dispensation of Providence in punishing crimes: *God's secret j.* H6B III, 2, 31. *this was a j. on me*, H8 II, 4, 194. *accidental —s*, Hml. V, 2, 393. *this j. of the heavens that makes us tremble*, Lr. V, 3, 231.

4) the last doom: *till the j. that yourself arise*, Sonn. 55, 13. *heaven forgive my sins at the day of j.* Wiv. III, 3, 227. Err. IV, 2, 40. R3 I, 4, 109. Troil. V, 7, 22. Lr. I, 4, 17.

5) the faculty of discerning the truth, discernment, good sense, understanding: *my j. knew no reason why my most full flame should afterwards burn clearer*, Sonn. 115, 3. *where is my j. fled*, 148, 3. *let it not tell your j. I am old*, Compl. 73. *O appetite, from j. stand aloof*, 166. *his j. ripe*, Gent. II, 4, 70. Meas. III, 1, 164. V, 478. Ado III, 1, 88. Mids. I, 1, 57. 236. III, 2, 134. Merch. II, 7, 13. 71. II, 9, 64. As I, 2, 186. V, 4, 80. All's I, 2, 61. II, 1, 123. 141. III, 6, 34. Tw. III, 2, 16. Wint. II, 1, 171. H4B I, 2, 16. 215. H5 II,

2, 136. III, 7, 58. IV, 7, 50. H6A II, 4, 16. H6C III, 3, 133. IV, 1, 12. 61. H8 II, 4, 47. Troil. I, 2, 99. II, 2, 65. II, 3, 134. IV, 5, 102. Cor. II, 3, 213. III, 1, 158. IV, 7, 39. V, 6, 106. Tim. III, 3, 10. V, 1, 31. Caes. II, 1, 147. III, 2, 109. Hml. II, 1, 111. II, 2, 458 (Qq —*s*, Ff *j.*) III, 2, 74. III, 4, 70. IV, 3, 5. IV, 5, 85. 151. Lr. I, 1, 294. I, 4, 294. Oth. I, 3, 9. 99. II, 1, 311. II, 3, 206. III, 3, 50. 236. IV, 2, 215. Ant. I, 4, 33. I, 5, 74. II, 2, 55. III, 3, 28. III, 13, 31. 37. 113. Cymb. I, 4, 49. I, 5, 17. I, 6, 41. 174. III, 5, 76. IV, 2, 111. 302. Abstr. pro concr.: *one of the soundest* —*s in Troy*, Troil. I, 2, 208 (Ff *j.*).

6) manner of thinking about sth., opinion, notion: *not from the stars do I my j. pluck*, Sonn. 14, 1. *on better j. making*, 87, 12. *whereto the j. of my heart is tied*, 137, 8. *do you question me for my simple true j.?* Ado I, 1, 168. 171. LLL II, 15. Mids. I, 1, 57. As II, 7, 45. All's IV, 3, 38. H4B I, 3, 20. Troil. I, 3, 329. Cor. II, 3, 226. Rom. I, 4, 46. Hml. I, 3, 69. III, 2, 91. Lr. I, 1, 153. Cymb. I, 4, 22. Per. I Prol. 41. IV, 6, 100. *by all men's* —*s*, Gent. IV, 4, 167. *in my j.* = in my opinion: Gent. IV, 4, 156. R3 III, 4, 45 (Qq *in mine opinion*). *in my* —*'s place*, in the same sense: Sonn. 131, 12. *to my j.*, in the same sense: Lr. I, 4, 62. Blunderingly used by Evans: Wiv. III, 1, 97.

Judgment-day, doomsday: H6A I, 1, 29. R3 I, 4, 106.

Judgment-place, seat of a court of justice: Rom. I, 1, 109.

Judicious, 1) pertaining to a judge or connoisseur: *examined my parts with most j. oeillades*, Wiv. I, 3, 68.

2) discerning, wise: Mcb. IV, 2, 16. Hml. III, 2, 29. Lr. III, 4, 76.

3) judicial, as practised in the distribution of public justice: *his last offences shall have j. hearing*, Cor. V, 6, 128.

Jug, a drinking vessel with a swelling belly: Shr. Ind. 2, 90.

Jug, diminutive of a name, probably of *Joan: whoop, J., I love thee*, Lr. I, 4, 245.

Juggle, vb. to play tricks, to practise imposture: John III, 1, 169. H6A V, 4, 68. Troil. II, 3, 77. V, 2, 24. Mcb. V, 8, 19. Hml. IV, 5, 130. With an accus. denoting the effect: *the spells of France should j. men into such strange mysteries*, H8 I, 3, 1.

Juggler, one who practises tricks by sleight of hand, a cheat, a charlatan: *nimble* —*s that deceive the eye*, Err. I, 2, 98. *a threadbare j.* V, 239. *O me, you j.* Mids. III, 2, 282. *you basket-hilt stale j.* H4B II, 4, 141.

Juice, 1) the sap of vegetables: Wiv. V, 5, 66. Mids. II, 1, 170. 176. 257. Hml. I, 5, 62. Ant. V, 2, 285.

2) the sap of animal bodies: *barren, lean and lacking j.* Ven. 136.

Juiced, in *Precious-juiced*, q. v.

Jule, abbreviation of *Juliet:* Rom. I, 3, 43 (F2.3.4 *Juliet*).

Julia, female name in Gent. I, 1, 66. 100. 160. I, 2, 109 etc.

Juliet, female name, 1) in Meas. I, 2, 118. 159. I, 4, 45. II, 2, 15. II, 4, 142. 2) in Rom. I, 3, 4 etc.

Julietta, the same as Juliet: Meas. I, 2, 74. 150.

Julio Romano, a famous Italian painter: Wint. V, 2, 106.

Julius, the gentile name of Caesar: R2 V, 1, 2. H6A I, 1, 56. H6B IV, 1, 137. R3 III, 1, 69. 84. Caes.

III, 1, 204. IV, 3, 19. Hml. I, 1, 114. III, 2, 108. Ant. II, 6, 12. III, 2, 54. Cymb. II, 4, 21. III, 1, 2. 12.

July, the seventh month of the year: Ado I, 1, 285. Wint. I, 2, 169. H8 I, 1, 154.

Jump, subst. stake, hazard: *our fortune lies upon this j.* Ant. III, 8, 6.

Jump, vb. 1) intr. a) to leap, to skip, to spring: *to j. up higher*, Lucr. 1414. *sorel* —*s from thicket*, LLL IV, 2, 60. *a careless herd* —*s along by him*, As II, 1, 53. —*s twelve foot*, Wint. IV, 4, 347. —*s upon joint-stools*, H4B II, 4, 269. —*ing o'er times*, H5 Prol. 29.

b) to agree, to tally: *both our inventions meet and j. in one*, Shr. I, 1, 195. *till each circumstance cohere and j.* Tw. V, 259. *they j. not on a just account*, Oth. I, 3, 5. Followed by *with: I will not j. with common spirits*, Merch. II, 9, 32. *it* —*s with my humour*, H4A I, 2, 78. *which (outward show) seldom or never* —*eth with the heart*, R3 III, 1, 11.

2) tr. a) to overleap: *nimble thought can j. both sea and land*, Sonn. 44, 7. Perhaps = to throw to the ground: *j. her and thump her*, Wint. IV, 4, 195.

b) to put to stake, to hazard: *to j. a body with a dangerous physic*, Cor. III, 1, 154.*we'ld j. the life to come*, Mcb. I, 7, 7. *or j. the after-inquiry on your own peril*, Cymb. V, 4, 188.

Jump, adv. exactly, just, pat: *j. at this dead hour*, Hml. I, 1, 65 (Ff *just*). *since, so j. upon this bloody question, you from the Polack wars, and you from England, are here arrived*, V, 2, 386. *bring him j. when he may Cassio find*, Oth. II, 3, 392.

June, the sixth month of the year: Sonn. 104, 7. H4A II, 4, 397. III, 2, 75. Ant. III, 10, 14.

Junius, the gentile name of the elder Brutus: Lucr. Arg. 18. Cor. I, 1, 220. Tit. IV, 1, 91.

Junkets, sweetmeats: Shr. III, 2, 250.

Juno, the highest goddess of the Romans, wife of Jupiter: Pilgr. 242 and LLL IV, 3, 118. Tp. IV, 102. 109. 125. 131. As I, 3, 77 (—*'s swans*).*V, 4, 147 (wedding is great —'s crown). All's III, 4, 13. Wint. IV, 4, 121. Troil. I, 2, 133. Cor. II, 1, 111. Lr. II, 4, 22. Ant. III, 11, 28. IV, 15, 34. Cymb. III, 4, 168. IV, 2, 50. V, 4, 32. Per. II, 3, 30 (queen of marriage). V, 1, 112. Alluded to, but not named: Cor. V, 3, 46.

Juno-like, resembling Juno: *in anger J.* Cor. IV, 2, 53.

Jupiter, the supreme god of the Romans: Tp. IV, 77. Wiv. V, 5, 7. As II, 4, 1. III, 2, 163 (some M. Edd. *pulpiter*). Wint. IV, 4, 27. Troil. I, 2, 65. 177. II, 3, 208. IV, 5, 191. V, 1, 59. Cor. I, 3, 41. I, 9, 90. II, 1, 115. IV, 5, 109. Tit. IV, 3, 66. 79. 83. 84. Lr. I, 1, 181. II, 4, 21. Ant. II, 2, 6. III, 2, 9. Cymb. II, 3, 130. II, 4, 121. 122. III, 5, 84. III, 6, 43. V, 3, 84. V, 4, 77. 85. 91. 119. V, 5, 427. 482.

Jure, a word ludicrously formed by Falstaff: *you are grandjurors, are ye? we'll j. ye, faith*, H4A II, 2, 97.

Jurisdiction, extent of judicial power: H6B IV, 7, 29. H8 III, 2, 312.

Juror, one that serves on a jury: H8 V, 3, 60. Tim. IV, 3, 345.

Jury, twelve persons impanneled and sworn to give a verdict according to their conscience: Meas. II, 1, 19. H8 III, 2, 269.

Juryman, in *Grand-Juryman*, q. v.

Just, subst. a tilt, a tournament: R2 V, 2, 52.

Just, vb. to tilt: Per. II, 1, 116.

Just, adj. (superl. —*est:* Ant. II, 1, 2) 1) conforming to the laws and principles of justice, equitable: Meas. I, 2, 127. II, 2, 41. II, 4, 52. IV, 2, 88. V, 54. Err. V, 203. All's III, 1, 8. Wint. II, 3, 204. R2 III, 3, 119. H6A II, 5, 29. H6B III, 2, 233. V, 1, 68. H6C III, 3, 32. 77. Ant. II, 1, 1. 2. Cymb. V, 1, 7 etc.

2) well founded, legitimate: *j. cause of hate,* Sonn. 150, 10. Ado II, 3, 173. Wint. V, 1, 61. *who can blot that name with any j. reproach?* Ado IV, 1, 82. *nature, stronger than his j. occasion,* As IV, 3, 130. *your request is j.* Wint. III, 2, 118. *whether I in any j. term am affined to love the Moor,* Oth. I, 1, 39 etc.

3) honest, upright, to be relied on: (love) *most deceiving when it seems most j.* Ven. 1156. *when shall he think to find a stranger j., when he himself himself confounds,* Lucr. 159. *he entertained a show so seeming j.* 1514. *she always hath been j. and virtuous,* Ado V, 1, 311. *which* (displeasure of your master) *on your j. proceeding I'll keep off,* All's V, 3, 236. H6A V, 3, 144. H6A III, 1, 95. H8 III, 1, 60. Tim. IV, 3, 498. Caes. III, 2, 90. Mcb. IV, 3, 30. Hml. III, 2, 59. Lr. III, 6, 120 (*in thy j. proof* = in thy proving honest). Oth. III, 3, 122. 385. V, 1, 31.

4) right, true, founded in fact (Germ. *richtig*): on *j. proof surmise accumulate,* Sonn. 117, 10 (= on what is proved to be true). *and the j. pleasure lost which is so deemed not by our feeling, but by others' seeing,* 121, 3 (= real. Or = the pleasure of being honest?). *my j. censure,* Wint. II, 1, 37 (= correct opinion). *the things I speak are j.* H4B V, 3, 126. *it is very j.* III, 2, 89. *is not this j.?* H5 II, 1, 116. '*tis j. to each of them.* Troil. I, 2, 75. *my report is j. and full of truth,* Tit. V, 3, 115. Lr. III, 1, 37. Tim. V, 1, 17. '*tis j.* Caes. I, 2, 54. *my j. belief,* Per. V, 1, 239 (= what I think to be true). Used in answers: *Perpetual durance? Ay, j.* Meas. III, 1, 68. V, 202. Ado II, 1, 29. V, 1, 164. As III, 2, 281. All's II, 3, 21. H5 III, 7, 158. Tit. IV, 2, 24.

5) exact, precise: *a j. sevennight,* Ado II, 1, 375. *a j. pound,* Merch. IV, 1, 327. *the j. proportion that we gave them out,* H4B IV, 1, 23. *to meet his grace j. distance 'tween our armies,* 226. *bring me j. notice of the numbers dead,* H5 IV, 7, 122. *by j. computation of the time,* R3 III, 5, 89 (Ff *true*). *usurp the j. proportion of of my sorrow,* IV, 4, 110. *part in j. proportion our small strength,* V, 3, 26. *j. opposite to what thou justly seemest,* Rom. III, 2, 78. *jump not on a j. account,* Oth. I, 3, 5. '*tis to his virtue a j. equinox,* II, 3, 129.

Just, adv. exactly, precisely: *now was she j. before him as he sat,* Ven. 349. *j. in his way,* 879. *j. to the time,* Sonn. 109, 7. *have j. our theme of woe,* Tp. II, 1, 6. *j. as you left them,* V, 9. *j. twixt twelve and one,* Wiv. IV, 6, 19; cf. I, 1, 51 (Evans' speech). Meas. IV, 3, 77. Ado II, 1, 8. II, 3, 22. 263. V, 4, 51. Merch. IV, 1, 326. As II, 1, 56. III, 2, 286. III, 5, 122. Shr. IV, 3, 117. All's I, 1, 171. IV, 2, 69. Tw. V, 15. H6B I, 4, 64. H8 I, 4, 28. Troil. I, 3, 164. Tit. III, 2, 2. 17. Rom. III, 3, 85. Tim. III, 2, 71. Mcb. III, 3, 4. Hml. I, 1, 65 (Qq *jump*). Ant. II, 7, 48. *even j.:* Err. IV, 1, 7. H5 II, 3, 13.

Just-borne, borne in the cause of right: *our j. arms,* John II, 345.

Justeius (O. Edd. *Justeus* and *Justius*), name in Ant. III, 7, 73.

Justice, (personified as a fem. in R2 II, 1, 227.

Oth. V, 2, 17. Per. V, 1, 122) 1) equal distribution of right, conformity to the laws and the principles of equity, either as a quality or as a rule of acting: Lucr. 1649. Meas. II, 2, 100. III, 2, 268. V, 20. Err. V, 133. 190. 197. Merch. II, 8, 17. III, 2, 281. IV, 1, 315. Wint. II, 1, 67. H8 III, 1, 116 (*if you have any j.*). Tit. IV, 3, 15. 49. Tim. IV, 1, 16. Mcb. IV, 3, 92. Oth. IV, 1, 223 etc. *reprieve him from the wrath of greatest j.* All's III, 4, 29 (i. e. God). *in j.* = justly, assisting the cause of right and truth: *I will in j. charge thee,* Wint. II, 3, 180. *God in j. hath revealed,* H6B II, 3, 105. V, 2, 25. H6C II, 2, 130. III, 2, 5. V, 4, 81. R3 V, 3, 254. Tit. I, 180. Cymb. V, 5, 464. *to do j.:* H8 III, 2, 396. Cor. IV, 4, 25. *to do a p. j.:* John II, 172. H8 II, 4, 13. Lr. V, 3, 128. Ant. III, 6, 88. *to give j.:* Meas. V, 25. 27. *to have j.* = to be dealt with justly: Meas. V, 453. Merch. IV, 1, 316. Tit. IV, 3, 79. 104.

2) judicial proceeding, operation of the laws: *j. is feasting while the widow weeps,* Lucr. 906. *sparing j. feeds iniquity,* 1687. *the terms for common j.* Meas. I, 1, 12. *liberty plucks j. by the nose,* I, 3, 29. 32. II, 1, 21. 180. II, 2, 30. III, 2, 258. IV, 2, 83. 101. V, 6. 35. LLL IV, 3, 384. Merch. III, 3, 29. All's V, 3, 154; cf. H4B V, 2, 109. Wint. III, 2, 6. 91. 125. R2 I, 3, 235. H6B II, 1, 204. H8 V, 3, 46. Mcb. I, 7, 10 etc. *to do j.* = to execute the law: H4B V, 2, 109. H6B IV, 7, 72.

3) justness, well-founded right: *the j. of my flying hence,* Gent. IV, 3, 29. *the j. of your title,* Meas. IV, 1, 74. *if the duke avouch the j. of your dealing,* IV, 2, 200. *to mitigate the j. of thy plea,* Merch. IV, 1, 203. *depose him in the j. of his cause,* R2 I, 3, 30; cf. H6C II, 1, 133 and Tit. I, 2. *i' the j. of compare,* Per. IV, 3, 9. Dubious passage: *keep thy word's j.* Lr. III, 4, 83 (Qq *word justly*).

4) one commissioned to hold courts, a judge: *my brother j.* Meas. III, 2, 267. *and then the j.* As II, 7, 153. IV, 1, 203. V, 4, 103. All's V, 2, 35. Wint. IV, 4, 288. H4B V, 4, 30. R3 II, 3, 46. Lr. IV, 6, 155. 157. *my lord chief j.* H4B V, 2, 1. V, 3, 144. V, 5, 48. *you are right, j.* (= chief-j.): H4B V, 2, 102. *j. of peace:* Wiv. I, 1, 5. 225. 283. H6B IV, 7, 45. —*s of the peace:* H4B III, 2, 64. *of peace omitted:* Wiv. II, 3, 49. 59. H4B III, 2, 324. 327. V, 1, 75. *J. Shallow:* Wiv. I, 1, 77. H4B III, 2, 62 (Evans' and Bardolph's speeches).

5) In drinking, = a pledge: *I'll do you j.* Oth. II, 3, 90.

Justice-like, resembling a justice of peace: H4B V, 1, 76.

Justicer, administrator of justice, judge: Lr. III, 6, 59. Cymb. V, 5, 214. In Lr. III, 6, 23 O. Edd. *justice,* M. Edd. *justicer;* in IV, 2, 79 Q2 *justicers,* the rest of O. Edd. *justices.*

Justification, vindication, defence: Lr. I, 2, 46.

Justify, to make appear as just; 1) to clear from guilt, to vindicate: Sonn. 139, 1. Meas. V, 159. Wint. I, 1, 10. H6B II, 3, 16. H8 II, 4, 162. Pcr. Prol. 42.

2) to ratify, to confirm, to prove: *I could j. you traitors,* Tp. V, 128. *how is this —ed?* All's IV, 3, 64. *say 't and j. it,* Wint. I, 2, 278. *who has not only his innocence to j. him,* V, 2, 71 (to confirm what he declares). *here —ed by us,* V, 3, 145. *I'll hear him his confessions j.* H8 I, 2, 6. *more particulars must j. my knowledge,* Cymb. II, 4, 79. *when thou shalt kneel*

and j. in knowledge she is thy very princess, Per. V, 1, 219.

Justle, 1) to push, to press, to force: *howsoe'er you have been —d from your senses,* Tp. V, 158. *let not the cloud of sorrow j. it from what it purposed,* LLL V, 2, 758. *where injury of chance puts back leave-taking, —s roughly by all time of pause,* Troil. IV, 4, 36.

2) to shoulder, to cope with, to wrestle, to fight; absol.: *how has he the leisure to be sick in such a —ing time?* H4A IV, 1, 18. Trans.: *I am in case to j. a constable,* Tp. III, 2, 29.

Justly, 1) conformably to justice, by right, equitably: *if that the injuries be j. weighed,* Tw. V, 375. H4B IV, 1, 67. *our purposes God j. hath discovered,* H5 II, 2, 151. *I am j. killed with mine own treachery,* Hml. V, 2, 318. 338. *let us deal j.* Lr. III, 6, 42.

2) with good reason, rightly: *one j. weeps,* Lucr. 1235. *in this the madman j. chargeth them,* Err. V, 213. *you may j. diet me,* Alls V, 3, 221. *the visitation which he j. owes him,* Wint. I, 1, 8. *that I may j. say,* H4B IV, 3, 44. *one that did j. put on the vouch of very malice itself,* Oth. II, 1, 147. *more than some can j. boast of,* Cymb. II, 3, 85. *and j. too, I think, you fear the tyrant,* Per. I, 2, 103.

3) conformably to truth and fact: *look you speak j.* Meas. V, 298. *j. and religiously unfold,* H5 I, 2, 10. *his grace has spoken well and j.* H8 II, 4, 65. *so j. to your grave ears I'll present,* Oth. I, 3, 124.

4) honestly, honourably: *and j. thus controls his thoughts unjust,* Lucr. 189. *I will deal in this as secretly and j.* Ado IV, 1, 250. *by him that j. may bear his betrothed from all the world away,* Tit. I, 285. *no man can j. praise but what he does affect,* Tim. I, 2, 221. *deal j. with me,* Hml. II, 2, 284. *that j. thinkest and hast most rightly said,* Lr. I, 1, 186. *keep thy word j.* III, 4, 83 (Ff *thy word's justice*). *I do not find that thou dealest j. with me,* Oth. IV, 2, 173.

5) exactly, accurately: *if you do keep your promises in love but j., as you have exceeded all promise, your mistress shall be happy,* As I, 2, 256. *in cash most j. paid,* H5 II, 1, 120. *just opposite to what thou j. seemest,* Rom. III, 2, 78. *a grief might equal yours, if both were j. weighed,* Per. V, 1, 89.

Justness, justice, propriety: *we may not think the j. of each act such and no other than event doth form it,* Troil. II, 2, 119.

Jut, to project, to thrust forth: *serving of becks and —ing out of bums,* Tim. I, 2, 237. In R3 II, 4, 51 Ff *jut,* Qq *jet,* q. v.

Jutty, subst. or adj.? projection or projecting? *no j. frieze, buttress, nor coign of vantage,* Mcb. I, 6, 6 (M. Edd. *jutty, frieze*).

Jutty, vb. to project beyond: *as doth a galled rock o'erhang and j. his confounded base,* H5 III, 1, 13.

Juvenal (used only by Armado, Flute, and by Falstaff in jesting) a youth: LLL I, 2, 8. III, 67. Mids. III, 1, 97. H4B I, 2, 22.

K.

Kam, crooked, awry: *this is clean k.* Cor. III, 1, 304.

Kate, diminutive of *Catherine:* Tp. II, 2, 51. Meas. III, 2, 211. LLL IV, 3, 83. Shr. II, 21. 168. 183. 186. 274—280 (and passim). H4A II, 3, 39 etc. H5 V, 2, 148 etc. H8 II, 4, 133.

Kated, provided with a Kate (or a cat?): Shr. III, 2, 247.

Kate-hall, name of a manor coined by Petruchio: Shr. II, 189.

Katharina, female name in Shr. I, 1, 52. 100. I, 2, 99. 125. II, 1, 43. V, 2, 6. 99.

Katharine, female name: LLL II, 195. V, 2, 47. Shr. I, 2, 128. 129. 184. II, 62. 185. 269 etc. H4B V, 5, 145. H5 III Chor. 30. V, 2, 4 etc. H6A I, 2, 100 *(Saint K.).* H8 II, 1, 149. II, 4, 10. 229. III, 2, 69. IV, 1, 22.

Kecksy, the dried stem of hemlock: H5 V, 2, 52.

Keech, the fat of an ox or cow, rolled up by the butcher in a round lump; hence a name given to a butcher's wife in H4B II, 1, 101, and to the butcher's son Wolsey in H8 I, 1, 55.

Keel, subst. the principal timber in a ship, which supports the whole frame; used for the whole ship: Oth. II, 1, 70. Ant. I, 4, 50. Per. III Prol. 46.

Keel, vb. to scum (Germ. kielen): *while greasy Joan doth k. the pot,* LLL V, 2, 930. 939 (according to most commentators, = to cool).

Keen, 1) sharp: *k. teeth,* Sonn. 19, 3. As II, 7, 177. *whips,* Meas. II, 4, 101. *edge,* LLL I, 1, 6. V, 2, 256. *knife,* Merch. IV, 1, 124. Mcb. I, 5, 53. *arrows,* As III, 5, 31. *sword,* Mcb. V, 8, 10. Metaphorically, of persons: *let us be k., and rather cut a little,* Meas. II, 1, 5.

2) bitter, acrimonious: *thy k. conceit,* LLL V, 2, 399; cf. 256. *this k. mockery,* Mids. II, 2, 123. *when she's angry, she's k. and shrewd,* III, 2, 323. *some satire, k. and critical,* V, 54. *my k. curses,* John III, 1, 182. *this k. encounter of our wits,* R3 I, 2, 115. *you are k., my lord,* Hml. III, 2, 258 (quibbling).

3) eager: *k. appetite,* Lucr. 9. Sonn. 118, 1. Merch. II, 6, 9. *advice is often seen by blunting us to make our wits more k.* Compl. 161. *so k. and greedy to confound a man,* Merch. III, 2, 278. *a dull fighter and a k. guest,* H4A IV, 2, 86. *assailed with fortune fierce and k.* Per. V, 3, 88.

Keen-edged, sharp: H6A I, 2, 98.

Keenness, sharpness, bitterness: *no metal can bear half the k. of thy sharp envy,* Merch. IV, 1, 125.

Keep, subst. custody, guard: *in Baptista's k. my treasure is,* Shr. I, 2, 118.

Keep, vb. (impf. and partic. *kept.* 2d person *keptest:* Alls V, 3, 330), I. trans. 1) to hold, to retain, not to part with: *k. still possession of thy gloomy place,* Lucr. 803. *she may detain, but not still k., her treasure,* Sonn. 126, 10. *if I k. them, I needs must lose myself,* Gent. II, 6, 20. *I will k. my sides to myself,* Wiv. V, 5, 28. *the saddler had it* (the money), *I kept it not,* Err. I, 2, 57. *k. thy Hermia,* Mids. III, 2, 169. *the impressure thy palm some moment —s,* As III, 5, 24. *you might k. that check,* As IV, 1, 169 (i.e. suppress it, not utter it). *k. your hundred pounds to yourself,* Shr. V, 1, 24. *k. it to yourself,* Alls I, 3, 128 (do not speak of it); cf. H6B I, 2, 53 and R3 III, 2, 104. *to* *k. them on*, Alls II, 4, 18 (to have them in future). *k. your purse*, Tw. I, 5, 303. *might have kept this calf from all the world*, John I, 123 (might have retained it, though all the world claimed it). *so I may k. mine eyes*, IV, 1, 102. *I will not k. her long*, R3 I, 2, 230. *in honourable —ing her*, Troil. II, 2, 149. *k: seat*, Mcb. III, 4, 54. *he that —s nor crust nor crum*, Lr. I, 4, 217. *but kept a reservation*, II, 4, 255 (whereas everything else was given away). *to k. her still, and men in awe*, Per. Prol. 36 (used in two significations: to retain her possession, and to deter men from wooing her) etc.

2) *to guard: under twenty locks kept fast*, Ven. 575. *the honey which thy chaste bee kept*, Lucr. 840. *whoe'er —s me, let my heart be his guard*, Sonn. 133, 11. *them* (the sheep) *to k.* Tp. IV, 1, 63. *the key whereof myself have ever kept*, Gent. III, 1, 36. *keys kept safe*, 111. *heaven k. your honour*, Meas. II, 2, 42; II, 4, 34; Ado V, 1, 332; As I, 1, 168; H4B III, 2, 308; Cor. IV, 6, 25; Ant. III, 2, 36. *your money that I had to k.* Err. I, 2, 8. *k. the gate*, II, 2, 208. *—s the prison*, IV, 3, 17. *that you k. Costard safe*, LLL I, 2, 133; cf. Meas. II, 2, 157. *the house doth k. itself*, As IV, 3, 82; Cymb. III, 6, 36. *I hope your own grace will k. you where you are*, Alls III, 5, 28. *I'll keep my stables where I lodge my wife*, Wint. II, 1, 134 (cf. Ado III, 4, 48. Antigonus may be in dread of the coachman). *k. this boy*, John III, 2, 5. *I'll k. him so, that he shall not offend your majesty*, III, 3, 64. *to k. him safely till his day of trial*, R2 IV, 153. *who —s the gate here?* H4B I, 1, 1. *had all our quarters been as safely kept*, H6A II, 1, 63. *commit you to my lord cardinal to k.* H6B III, 1, 138. *you had the good lord to k.* III, 2, 183. *I'll k. London with my soldiers*, H6C I, 1, 207. *must gently be preserved, cherished and kept*, R3 II, 2, 119. *who —s the tent now?* Troil. V, 1, 11. *k. then this passage to the Capitol*, Tit. I, 12. *k. the door*, Hml. IV, 5, 115. *Gratiano, k. the house*, Oth. V, 2, 365 etc. *With from*, = to protect from: *heavens k. him from these beasts*, Tp. II, 1, 324. *to k. me from a most unholy match*, Gent. IV, 3, 30. *—s you from dishonour*, Meas. III, 1, 246. *to k. him from stumbling*, Shr. III, 2, 59. *that —s you from the blow of the law*, Tw. III, 4, 168. *k. his princely heart from Richard's hand*, John I, 267. *that this good blossom could be kept from cankers*, H4B II, 2, 102. *to k. your royal person from treason's knife*, H6B III, 1, 173. *kept low shrubs from winter's powerful wind*, H6C V, 2, 15. *God k. you from them*, R3 III, 1, 15. 16. *to k. itself from noyance*, Hml. III, 3, 13 etc.

3) *to occupy, to inhabit, to be or remain in: let him k. his loathsome cabin*, Ven. 637. *which three till now never kept seat in one*, Sonn. 105, 14. *k. your cabins*, Tp. I, 1, 15. *they do no more adhere and k. place together*, Wiv. II, 1, 62. *that Adam that kept the Paradise*, Err. IV, 3, 16. *you will k. the house*, Meas. III, 2, 75 (remain within doors), *who cannot k. his wealth, must k. his house*, Tim. III, 3, 42; *a goodly day not to k. house*, Cymb. III, 3, 1 (see *House*). *other slow arts entirely k. the brain*, LLL IV, 3, 324. *making that idiot laughter k. men's eyes*, John III, 3, 45. *doth he k. his bed?* H4A IV, 1, 21 (cf. *Bed*). *like peasant foot-boys do they k. the walls*, H6A III, 2, 69. *the Earl of Pembroke —s his regiment*, R3 V, 3, 29 (remains with). *—s his tent*, Troil. I, 3, 190. *the hart Achilles —s thicket*, II, 3, 270. *k. then the path*, III, 3, 155 (occupy,

enter on). *did ever dragon k. so fair a cave*, Rom. III, 2, 74. *—s his chamber*, Tim. III, 4, 73; Cymb. II, 3, 78. *k. the hills*, Caes. V, 1, 3. *our hostess —s her state*, Mcb. III, 4, 5. *thy spirit which —s thee*, Ant. II, 3, 19. *he did k. the deck*, Cymb. I, 3, 10 etc.

4) *to hold, to hold up, to maintain: if I k. not my rank*, As I, 2, 113. *to k. this city*, John II, 455. *hath power to k. you king*, R2 III, 2, 28. *— s the bridge most valiantly*, H5 III, 6, 11. *yet k. the French the field*, IV, 6, 2. *k. the town*, Cor. I, 7, 5. *kept his credit with his purse*, Tim. III, 2, 75. With *up:* John III, 1, 216.

5) *to preserve, to retain: both were kept for heaven and Collatine*, Lucr. 1166. *k. her husband's shape in mind*, Sonn. 9, 8; cf. As III, 2, 99. *k. this remembrance*, Gent. II, 2, 5. *I will k. your counsel*, Wiv. IV, 6, 7; Mids. III, 2, 308 (cf. *Counsel*). *let it k. one shape*, Meas. II, 1, 3. *lose a thing that none but fools would k.* III, 1, 8 (wish to preserve). *which I did make him swear to k. for ever*, Merch. IV, 2, 14; V, 156. *k. thy friend under thy own life's key*, Alls I, 1, 75. *thou keptst a wife herself, thyself a maid*, Alls V, 3, 330. *I will not k. this form upon my head*, John III, 4, 101. *to k. by policy what Henry got*, H6B I, 1, 84. *k. comfort to you*, H8 V, 1, 145. *k. this sleeve*, Troil. V, 2, 66. *k. this holy kiss*, Rom. IV, 1, 43. *k. his wealth*, Tim. III, 3, 42. *I shall the effect of this good lesson k.* Hml. I, 3, 45. *k. it, my Pericles*, Per. II, 1, 132. 134.

6) *to hold and preserve in any state, to cause to continue or to be: the staring ruffian shall it k. in quiet*, Ven. 1149. *kept in awe*, Lucr. 245. *let my good name be kept unspotted*, 821. *to k. thy sharp woes waking*, 1136. *k. open my heavy eyelids*, Sonn. 61, 1. *k. invention in a noted weed*, 76, 6. *with tears thou —est me blind*, 148, 13. *he kept his head above the waves*, Tp. II, 1, 118. *to k. them living*, 299. *night kept chained below*, IV, 1, 31. *fire that's closest kept*, Gent. I, 2, 30. *kept alive*, III, 1, 184. *that I'll k. shut*, 358. *to k. him above deck*, Wiv. II, 1, 94. *to k. the terms of my honour precise*, II, 2, 22. *k. their limbs whole*, III, 1, 79. *k. the body ever fair*, Meas. III, 1, 188. *to k. him warm*, III, 2, 8. *I will k. her ignorant of her good*, IV, 3, 113. *k. me in patience*, V, 116. *so clean kept*, Err. III, 2, 105. *to k. obliged faith unforfeited*, Merch. II, 6, 7. *k. fresh*, Tw. I, 1, 31. *k. dry*, I, 3, 79. *to k. in darkness*, V, 156. *well summered and warm kept*, H5 V, 2, 335. *opinion shall k. me on the side*, H6A II, 4, 54. *kept him a foreign man still*, H8 II, 2, 129. *we'll k. ourself till supper-time alone*, Mcb. III, 1, 43. *that great bond which —s me pale*, III, 2, 50. *k. you in the rear of your affection*, Hml. I, 3, 34 (Ff *k. within*). *—s himself in clouds*, IV, 5, 89. *k. yourself within yourself*, Ant. II, 5, 75. *you k. by land the legions and the horse whole*, III, 7, 71 etc.

7) *to continue, to pursue: k. your way*, Wiv. III, 2, 1; Ado I, 1, 143; H8 II, 4, 128. *k. a peaceful progress to the ocean*, John II, 339. *—s the roadway*, H4B II, 2, 62. *—s his course truly*, H5 V, 2, 173; H6C V, 3, 1; V, 4, 22; Ant. V, 2, 80. *k. my wonted calling*, H6A III, 1, 32. *no pulse shall k. his native progress*, Rom. IV, 1, 97. With *on: kept on his course*, R2 V, 2, 10. *k. on your way*, Cor. IV, 2, 10.

8) *to tend, to have the care of: I k. his house*, Wiv. I, 4, 100 (cf. *House*). *you will k. the house*, Meas. III, 2, 75 (quibbling). *I will forswear —ing house*, H4B II, 4, 220; cf. H5 II, 1, 37; Tim. III, 1, 24. *I have kept it* (a child) *myself*, Meas. III, 2, 214. *shall I k.*

your hogs, As I, 1, 40. *kept sheep*, John IV, 1, 17. *when thou didst k. my lambs*, H6A V, 4, 30.

9) to entertain, to maintain, to have in service or in the house: *she —s thee to this purpose*, Sonn. 126, 7. *kept hearts in liveries*, Compl. 195. *whom now I k. in service*, Tp. I, 2, 286. *if I can recover him and k. him tame*, II, 2, 79. *I will put off my hope and k. it no longer for my flatterer*, III, 3, 7. *I k. but three men*, Wiv. I, 1, 284. *I must k. her at the park*, LLL I, 2, 136. *thou wilt k. my tears for glasses*, IV, 3, 39. *my brother he —s at school*, As I, 1, 6. *he —s me rustically at home*, 7. *schoolmasters will I k.* Shr. I, 1, 94. *you will have Gremio to k. you fair*, II, 17. *whom thou —est command*, 259. *—s a good fire*, All's IV, 5, 51. *k. no fool*, Tw. III, 1, 37. *—s a school i 'the church*, III, 2, 81. *to k. you as a prisoner*, Wint. I, 2, 52. *k. ten thousand men*, R2 IV, 283. *k. lodgers*, H5 II, 1, 33. *he —s a Trojan drab*, Troil. V, 1, 104. *k. a dog*, Tim. IV, 3, 200. 317. *in his house I k. a servant fee'd*, Mcb. III, 4, 132. *k. a farm and carters*, Hml. II, 2, 167. *k. a schoolmaster*, Lr. I, 4, 195. *k. it as a cistern for foul toads*, Oth. IV, 2, 61 etc.

10) to observe, to practise, not to violate: *then can no horse with my desire k. pace*, Sonn. 51, 9; Ado III, 4, 93; Mids. III, 2, 445 (cf. *Pace*). *his prescriptions are not kept*, Sonn. 147, 6. *vowed chaste life to k.* 154, 3. *kept cold distance*, Compl. 237. *k. tune*, Gent. I, 2, 89. *I will k. the haviour of reputation*, Wiv. I, 3, 86. *unless they kept very good diet*, Meas. II, 1, 116; R3 I, 1, 139. *k. your instruction*, Meas. IV, 5, 3. *so he would k. fair quarter with his bed*, Err. II, 1, 108. *k. then fair league and truce with thy true bed*, II, 2, 147. *when I k. not hours*, III, 1, 2. *to k. those statutes*, LLL I, 1, 17. *barren tasks, too hard to k.* 47. *k. some state in thy exit*, V, 2, 598. *k. his day*, Merch. II, 8, 25. *k. no measure*, R2 III, 4, 7. *k. law and form*, 41. *he —s no mean*, H6A I, 2, 121. *you will not k. your hour*, H6B II, 1, 181. *k. your duties*, Cor. I, 7, 1. *k. decorum*, Ant. I, 2, 77. V, 2, 17. *k. the turn of tippling*, I, 4, 19. *which to the tune of flutes kept stroke*, II, 2, 200. *to k. an oath:* LLL I, 1, 23. II, 105. V, 2, 442. Merch. II, 7, 99. Tw. III, 4, 341 etc. (cf. *Oath*). *to k. peace:* Ado II, 3, 202. H6A III, 1, 87 etc. (cf. *Peace*). *to k. promise:* Mids. I, 1, 179. Tw. V, 106 etc. (cf. *Promise*). *—ing what is sworn*, LLL IV, 3, 356. *to k. time:* Lucr. 1127. Wiv. I, 3, 29. As V, 3, 38. Tw. II, 3, 100. R2 V, 5, 42 etc. (cf. *Time*). *to k. word:* Mids. I, 1, 222. III, 2, 266. H4A I, 2, 134. H6B III, 2, 293 etc. (cf. *Word*). *he knows the game: how true he —s the wind*, H6C III, 2, 14 (cf. *Wind*). *mine honour —s the weather of my fate*, Troil. V, 3, 26 (cf. *Weather*).

11) to hold or restrain in any manner, to detain: *'tis a foul thing when a cur cannot k. himself in all companies*, Gent. IV, 4, 11 (Launce's speech). *we'll k. him here*, R2 V, 2, 100; H6A IV, 7, 89; Ant. I, 3, 22. *to k. his tongue*, Shr. I, 1, 214. *kept him in captivity*, H6B II, 2, 42. *thou —est the stroke betwixt thy begging and my meditation*, R3 IV, 2, 117. *I will take order for her —ing close*, 53. Followed by *from* (= to withhold, or to prevent from): *that rich jewel he should k. unknown from thievish ears*, Lucr. 34. *a thousand crosses k. them from thy aid*, 912. *k. him from heart-easing words*, 1782. *you k. from me the rest o'the island*, Tp. I, 2, 343. *kept severely from resort of men*, Gent. III, 1, 108. *to k. them from uncivil outrages*, V,

4, 17. *k. a gamester from the dice*, Wiv. III, 1, 37. *k. it from my head*, H4B IV, 5, 175. *k. it from civil broils*, H6A I, 1, 53. *—s his men from mutiny*, 160. *—ing my house from me*, H6B I, 3, 20. *the means that —s me from it*, H6C III, 2, 141. *hath kept my eyes from rest*, R3 IV, 1, 82 (Ff *held*). *k. it not from me*, Mcb. IV, 3, 200. *k. her from her rest*, V, 3, 39. *I have kept me from the cup*, Ant. II, 7, 72. *the seven-fold shield of Ajax cannot k. the battery from my heart*, IV, 14, 38. By *out of:* *God k. him out of my sight*, Ado II, 1, 113. Joined with *asunder:* *k. them asunder*, Wiv. III, 1, 73. *kept asunder*, H6B I, 4, 55. With *away:* *that kept my rest away*, Pilgr. 182. *k. away the succours*, H6A IV, 4, 22. With *back:* *some k. back the clamorous owl*, Mids. II, 2, 5. *k. not back your powers*, H6A V, 2, 5. H6C IV, 7, 56. With *down:* *to k. down his heart*, LLL IV, 3, 136. With *in:* *k. in your weapon*, Wiv. III, 1, 75. *let her be secretly kept in*, Ado IV, 1, 205. *k. it in*, Tw. I, 5, 209 (do not recite it). *what I am willing to k. in*, II, 1, 14 (to hold secret). *could not all this flesh k. in a little life*, H4A V, 4, 103. *with thy lips k. in my soul awhile*, H6C V, 2, 35. *the flood kept in my soul*, R3 I, 4, 38 (Ff *stopped*). With *off:* *which* (displeasure) *I'll k. off*, All's V, 3, 236. *to k. the horsemen off from breaking in*, H6A I, 1, 119. *armour to k. off that word*, Rom. III, 3, 54. With *out:* *—est me out from the house*, Err. III, 1, 42. *k. him out*, All's I, 1, 125. *he will k. out water a great while*, Hml. V. 1, 187. With *together:* *kept together and put to use*, Tw. III, 1, 56. With *under:* *the wars have so kept you under*, All's I, 1, 209. With *up:* *k. up your swords*, Oth. I, 2, 59 (do not draw them). *k. up thy quillets*, III, 1, 25 (abstain from them).

12) to celebrate, to institute, to perform, to hold: *love —s his revels*, Ven. 123; Mids. II, 1, 18. *k. the obsequy so strict*, Phoen. 12. *we will our celebration k.* Tw. IV, 3, 30. *this day shall be kept festival*, John III, 1, 76. *shall our feast be kept with slaughtered men*, 302. *grief hath kept a tedious fast*, R2 II, 1, 75. *death —s his court*, III, 2, 162. *to k. our great Saint George's feast*, H6A I, 1, 154. *a holiday shall this be kept*, R3 II, 1, 73. *there are two councils kept*, III, 2, 12 (Qq *held*). *a brief span to k. your earthly audit*, H8 III, 2, 141. *as if we kept a fair here*, V, 4, 73. *to k. his state in Rome*, Caes. I, 2, 160. *k. leets and lawdays*, Oth. III, 3, 140. *Neptune's feast to k.* Per. V Prol. 17.

13) to perform, to do, to make: *to k. company*, Wiv. III, 2, 73; Err. V, 398; Mids. III, 1, 147; As I, 2, 287; Tw. V, 99: H4A II, 4, 457 etc. (cf. *Company*). *—s all this noise*, Err. III, 1, 61. *what a caterwauling do you k. here?* Tw. II, 3, 76; Tit. IV, 2, 57. *what stir —s good old York there?* R2 II, 3, 52. *what a brawling dost thou keep*, H4A II, 2, 6. *when thou —est not racket*, H4B II, 2, 23. *we'll k. no great ado*, Rom. III, 4, 23. *—s wassail*, Hml. I, 4, 9. *k. this dreadful pother*, Lr. III, 2, 50. *I would have kept such a jangling*, Per. II, 1, 45. *—s her guard in honestest defence*, All's III, 5, 76. *what watch the king —s to maintain the peace*, H5 IV, 1, 300. *care —s his watch*, Rom. II, 3, 35. *kept the watch*, Hml. I, 2, 208.

14) to hold, to have: *if of life you k. a care*, Tp. II, 1, 303. *k. a good tongue in your head*, III, 2, 39. 120. *k. good quarter and good care to-night*, John V, 5, 20. *two stars k. not their motion in one sphere*, H4A V, 4, 65. *the seal I k.* R3 II, 4, 71. *—s place with*

thought, Troil. III, 3, 199. *upon the right hand I, k. thou the left*, Caes. V, 1, 18. *k. eyes upon her*, Mcb. V, 1, 85. *—s them in the corner of his jaw*, Hml. IV, 2, 19. *to k. one's eyes of either side's nose*, Lr. I, 5, 22. Apparently quite = to hold, to manage: *kept his sword e'en like a dancer*, Ant. III, 11, 35 (but perhaps = kept his sword sheathed, which is expressed by *to keep up* in Oth. I, 2, 59).

II. intr. 1) to remain, to abide: *k. below*, Tp. I, 1, 12. *the image that hath kept with thy remembrance*, I, 2, 44. *k. in that mind*, Wiv. III, 3, 89. *to k. unwed*, Err. II, 1, 26. *you would k. from my heels*, III, 1, 18. *it —s on the windy side of care*, Ado II, 1, 327. *shall I always k. below stairs*, V, 2, 10. *k. not too long in one tune*, LLL III, 21. *still you k. o'the windy side of the law*, Tw. III, 4, 181. *kept loyal to possession*, H4A III, 2, 43. *k. aloof from strict arbitrement*, IV, 1, 70. *could not k. quiet in his conscience*, H5 I, 2, 79. *k. in one consent*, 181. *k. off aloof*, H6A IV, 4, 21. *k. in favour with the king*, R3 I, 1, 79. *I'll k. at home*, Cor. V, 1, 7. *why do you k. alone*, Mcb. III, 2, 8; Per. IV, 1, 22. *k. within the rear of your affection*, Hml. I, 3, 34 (Qq *k. you in*). *—s in the wonted pace*, II, 2, 353. *—s aloof*, III, 1, 8. *the rest shall k. as they are*, 156. *k. in-a-door*, Lr. I, 4, 138. *k. a week away*, Oth. III, 4, 173. *k. off them*, Ant. II, 7, 66. *we k. whole by land*, III, 7, 75. III, 8, 3. *her —ing close*, Cymb. III, 5, 46. *by his fall my honour must k. high*, Per. I, 1, 149.

2) to dwell, to live, to stay: *where earthdelving conies k.* Ven. 687. *k. in Tunis*, Tp. II, 1, 259. *assemblies, where youth and cost and witless bravery —s*, Meas. I, 3, 10. *this habitation where thou —est*, III, 1, 10. *outward courtesies would fain proclaim favours that k. within*, V, 16. *a Spaniard that —s here in court*, LLL IV, 1, 100. *the creatures of prey that k. upon't*, Wint. III, 3, 13. *'twas where the madcap duke his uncle kept*, H4A I, 3, 244. *as an outlaw in a castle —s*, H6A III, 1, 47. *he —s in the cold field*, H6C IV, 3, 14. *I will k. where there is wit stirring*, Troil. II, 1, 129. *in what place of the field doth Calchas k.?* IV, 5, 278. *knock at his study, where, they say, he —s*, Tit. V, 2, 5. *the confident tyrant —s still in Dunsinane*, Mcb. V, 4, 9. *where they k.* Hml. II, 1, 8. *it kept where I kept*, Per. II, 1, 136.

3) Followed by *with*, = to live, to converse with: *k. with thy hounds*, Ven. 678. *these banished men that I have kept withal*, Gent. V, 4, 152. *the most impenetrable cur that ever kept with men*, Merch. III, 3, 19. *k. with Bohemia*, Wint. I, 2, 344. *him k. with*, H4A II, 4, 473. *let pale-faced fear k. with the mean-born man*, H6B III, 1, 335. *noble minds k. ever with their likes*, Caes. I, 2, 315. *to k. with you at meals*, II, 1, 284. *I will k. still with my philosopher*, Lr. III, 4, 181. In the same sense with *together*: *treason and murder ever kept together*, H5 II, 2, 105. *we kept together in our chivalry*, IV, 6, 19.

4) With *on*, = to continue one's way, to proceed: *pray you, k. on*, Wiv. I, 1, 321 (enter the house); cf. Tim. II, 2, 34. *—s due on to the Propontic*, Oth. III, 3, 455.

Keep-down, name in Meas. III, 2, 211.

Keeper, one who has the care, custody, or possession of a thing or person: *give us kind —s, heavens*, Tp. III, 3, 20. *thy husband is thy lord, thy life, thy k.* Shr. V, 2, 146. *thou art his k.* John III, 3, 64.

k. of the king, H6C II, 1, 111. *thou'lt go, strong thief (viz gold) when gouty —s of thee cannot stand*, Tim. IV, 3, 46. Especially 1) one who has the care of a prison or a prisoner, a gaoler: LLL I, 1, 306. Wint. II, 2, 1. H6A II, 5, 17. 120. R3 I, 4, 66 (Ff *ah k., k.* Qq *O Brakenbury*). 73. Tim. I, 2, 69. IV, 3, 46 (quibbling). V, 1, 187. 2) an attendant on a patient: H4B I, 1, 143. H6A II, 5, 1. Rom. V, 3, 89. 3) one who has the care of a park: Wiv. I, 1, 116. IV, 4, 29. H6C III, 1, 22. Tit. II, 1, 94. 4) one who tends a beast: *the ape doth* (imitate) *his k.* LLL IV, 2, 131. *to make her come* (the hawk) *and know her —'s call*, Shr. IV, 1, 197. 5) the superintendent of a tennis-court: H4B II, 2, 21.

Keeper-back, one who prevents from going on: *a k. of death*, R2 II, 2, 70.

Keeping, 1) possession: *her mother's statue, which is in the k. of Paulina*, Wint. V, 2, 103. *never may that state or fortune fall into my k., which is not owed to you*, Tim. I, 1, 150.

2) maintenance, provision: *call you that k. for a gentleman of my birth*, As I, 1, 9.

Keisar, emperor: *thou'rt an emperor, Caesar, K., and Pheezar*, Wiv. I, 3, 9 (the host's speech).

Ken, subst. discerning by the eye, sight, eyeshot: *to drown in k. of shore*, Lucr. 1114. *within a k. our army lies*, H4B IV, 1, 151. *losing k. of Albion's wished coast*, H6B III, 2, 113. *thou wast within a k.* Cymb. III, 6, 6.

Ken, vb. 1) to discern, to descry: *as far as I could k. thy chalky cliffs*, H6B III, 2, 101. *'tis he, I k. the manner of his gait*, Troil. IV, 5, 14.

2) to know: *I k. the wight*, Wiv. I, 3, 40 (Pistol's speech).

Kendal, place in Westmoreland, famous for its clothing trade: *in K. green*, H4A II, 4, 246. 257.

Kenilworth, see *Killingworth*.

Kennel, subst. 1) a cot for dogs: *truth's a dog must to k.* Lr. I, 4, 124. Metaphorically: *from forth the k. of thy womb hath crept a hell-hound*, R3 IV, 4, 47. Used for a prison, in contempt: *go to k., Pompey*, Meas. III, 2, 89.

2) a pack of dogs: *a yelping k. of French curs*, H6A IV, 2, 47.

Kennel, subst. a sink, a gutter: *hop me over every k. home*, Shr. IV, 3, 98. *k., puddle, sink*, H6B IV, 1, 71.

Kennelled, lying as in a cot: *here k. in a brake she finds a hound*, Ven. 913.

Kent, 1) English county: John IV, 2, 200. V, 1, 30. H4A II, 1, 60. H6B IV, 1, 100. IV, 2, 130. IV, 7, 59. 60. 65 (*K. in the Commentaries Caesar writ is termed the civil'st place of all this isle*). IV, 10, 46. 78. V, 1, 75. H6C I, 1, 156. IV, 8, 12. R3 IV, 4, 505.

2) Earl of Kent: R2 V, 6, 8. Lr. I, 1, 27 and passim.

Kentish, native of Kent: H6B IV, 4, 42. 57.

Kentishman, a native of Kent: H6B III, 1, 356. H6C I, 2, 41.

Kerchief, a cloth to cover the head: Wiv. III, 3, 62. IV, 2, 74. Caes. II, 1, 315.

Kerne, an Irish soldier: R2 II, 1, 156. H5 III, 7, 56. H6B III, 1, 310. 361. 367. IV, 9, 26. Mcb. I, 2, 13. 30. V, 7, 17.

Kernel, 1) the edible substance of a nut: Shr. II, 257. All's II, 5, 47. Troil. II, 1, 112.

2) the seed of pulpy fruits: Tp. II, 1, 92. All's II, 3, 276.

3) Used to denote any thing diminutive: *how like I then was to this k.* Wint. I, 2, 159.

Kersey, coarse woollen cloth: *a list of an English k.* Meas. I, 2, 35. *in russet yeas and honest k. noes,* LLL V, 2, 413. *a k. boot-hose,* Shr. III, 2, 68.

Ketch, in *Tallow-catch,* q. v.

Ketly, name in H5 IV, 8, 109.

Kettle, = kettle-drum: Hml. V, 2, 286.

Kettle-drum, a drum made of a copper vessel: Hml. I, 4, 11.

Key, (rhyming to *survey:* Sonn. 52, 1. to *may:* Merch. II, 7, 59). 1) an instrument to shut and open a lock: Sonn. 52, 1. Gent. III, 1, 36. 111. Wiv. II, 2, 285. III, 3, 172. Meas. IV, 1, 31. V, 467. Err. IV, 1, 103. Ado V, 1, 318. LLL III, 5. Merch II, 5, 12. II, 7, 59. II, 9, 51. Wint. I, 2, 464. IV, 4, 624. H4B I, 2, 45. H6A II, 3, 2. H6C IV, 7, 37. R3 I, 4, 96. Rom. IV, 4, 1. Lr. I, 2, 186. Cymb. I, 1, 73. V, 4, 7. *to turn the k.* = a) to open the door: Meas. I, 4, 8. Mcb. II, 3, 2. Lr. II, 4, 53. III, 7, 64. Oth. IV, 2, 94. b) to shut the door: R2 V, 3, 36. Metaphorical use: *keep thy friend under thy own life's k.* All's I, 1, 76. *didst bear the k. of all my counsels,* H5 II, 2, 96. Hml. I, 3, 86. Oth. IV, 2, 22. *these counties were the —s of Normandy,* H6B I, 1, 114. *had he Duncan's sons under his k.* Mcb. III, 6, 18.

2) the fundamental note of a musical composition, the clef: Ado I, 1, 188. Mids. III, 2, 206. Metaphorically, = tone: *my feeble k. of untuned cares,* Err. V, 310. *I will wed thee in another k.* Mids. I, 1, 18. *in a bondman's k.* Merch. I, 3, 124. *an accent tuned in selfsame k.* Troil. I, 3, 53.

3) a tool for tuning stringed instruments, a tuning-key: *having both the key of officer and office, set all hearts i' the state to what tune pleased his ear,* Tp. I, 2, 83.

Key-cold, as cold as a key; used of dead bodies: Lucr. 1774. R3 I, 2, 5.

Keyhole, the aperture in a lock through which the key is put: As IV, 1, 164.

Khan, see *Cham.*

Kibe, a chap or sore in the heel: Tp. II, 1, 276. Wiv. I, 3, 35. Hml. V, 1, 153. Lr. I, 5, 9.

Kick, 1) tr. to strike with the foot: Err. III, 1, 17. Lr. III, 6, 50.

2) intr. to thrust out the feet: *she feels her young one k.* All's V, 3, 303. *his heels may k. at heaven,* Hml. III, 3, 93. Denoting contempt: *our spoils he —ed at,* Cor. II, 2, 128.

Kickshaws, a toy, a trifle: *any pretty little tiny k.* H4B V, 1, 29. Plur. *—es: art thou good at these —es?* Tw. I, 3, 122.

Kicky-wicky (F2.3.4 *kicksy-wicksy*) a ludicrous term for a wife: All's II, 3, 297.

Kid-fox, a young fox: Ado II, 3, 44.

Kidney (cf. *Fat-kidneyed*) the organ which separates the urine from the blood; used for constitution, temper: *a man of my k.* Wiv. III, 5, 116.

Kildáre, name in H8 II, 1, 41.*

Kill, to deprive of life, to put to death; absol.: Meas. III, 2, 282. Ado I, 1, 45. H5 III, 2, 36. H6B III, 2, 310. V, 1, 101. Troil. III, 1, 132 (*the wound to k.* = the mortal wound). Tim. III, 5, 54. Caes. III, 2, 209. Ant. V, 2, 244 etc. Used as a cry by troops

when they charged the enemy: *and in a peaceful hour doth cry K., k.!* Ven. 652. *k., k., k. him,* Cor. V, 6, 132. *then k., k., k.* Lr. IV, 6, 191. cf. *when I command them k.* H6B IV, 8, 5. Trans.: Ven. 464. 499. Lucr. 74. Tp. II, 2, 112. III, 2, 114. III, 3, 64. V, 78. Gent. I, 2, 107. IV, 1, 27. IV, 4, 36. Wiv. I, 4, 123. II, 3, 11. IV, 2, 198 etc. *care —ed a cat,* Ado V, 1, 133. *to k. a wife with kindness,* Shr. IV, 1, 211. *to k. a p. dead:* Mids. III, 2, 269. Tit. III, 1, 92. Hml. III, 2, 194. *to k. up* = to k. by wholesale: *to fright the animals and to k. them up,* As II, 1, 62. *to k. one's self:* Ado V, 1, 1. Mids. I, 2, 25. III, 1, 11. V, 67. R3 I, 2, 187. Caes. V, 5, 7 etc. *to k. a person's heart* = to distress, to grieve extremely: LLL V, 2, 149. As III, 2, 260 (quibbling). Wint. IV, 3, 88. R2 V, 1, 100; cf. Tit. III, 2, 15. H5 II, 1, 92. H6A V, 4, 2. Metaphorical use: *this blessed league to k.* Lucr. 383 (= to destroy). *to k. thine honour,* 516. *her lively colour —ed with deadly cares,* 1593. *and wretched minutes k.* Sonn. 126, 8. *that you might k. your stomach on your meat,* Gent. I, 2, 68 (= satiate). *will k. that grief,* III, 2, 15. *to k. care,* Ado V, 1, 134. *when truth —s truth,* Mids. III, 2, 129. *the first view shall k. all repetition,* All's V, 3, 21. *sleep k. those pretty eyes,* Troil. IV, 2, 4. *the great rage is —ed in him,* Lr. IV, 7, 79 (Qq *cured*). *to k. the marvel,* Cymb. III, 1, 10.

Used of slaying animals for food: 1) as a butcher; abs.: Ven. 618. H6B IV, 3, 8. Trans.: Meas. II, 2, 85. Err. IV, 3, 18. 2) as a huntsman; abs.: LLL IV, 1, 24. 29. Trans.: Wiv. I, 1, 84. 114. LLL IV, 1, 112. As II, 1, 21. III, 2, 260. IV, 2, 1. Cymb. III, 6, 39 etc.

Kill-courtesy, a rude fellow: Mids. II, 2, 77.

Killen, to kill: Per. II Prol. 20.

Killingworth (M. Edd. *Kenilworth*) place in England: H6B IV, 4, 39. 44.

Kiln, in *Lime-kiln,* q. v.

Kiln-hole, the opening of an oven: *creep into the k.* Wiv. IV, 2, 59. or *k., to whistle off these secrets,* Wint. IV, 4, 247.*

Kimbolton (O. Edd. *Kymmalton*) place in England: H8 IV, 1, 34. [= K. castle, Huntingdonshire].

Kin, subst. 1) kindred, race, relations: *one of thy k. has a most weak pia mater,* Tw. I, 5, 123. *my nearest of kin cry fie upon my grave,* Wint. III, 2, 54. *I will show thee to my k.* John I, 273. *bloody with the enemies of his k.* R2 II, 1, 183. *shall k. with k. and kind with kind confound,* IV, 141 (*with* = by). V, 2, 109. H6C I, 4, 169. R3 III, 7, 212 (Ff *kindred*). Troil. IV, 2, 104. Cor. V, 3, 37. Rom. I, 5, 60. Tim. I, 1, 121.

2) a person of the same race, a relation: *he is some k. to thee,* Merch. II, 9, 97. *what k. are you to me?* Tw. V, 237. *not our k.* Wint. IV, 4, 441. H4B II, 2, 171. Lr. I, 4, 199. Oth. IV, 2, 185. Cymb. V, 5, 111.

Kin, adj. (never before a subst.) of the same race, related: *lawful mercy is nothing k. to foul redemption,* Meas. II, 4, 113. *my sword and yours are k.* All's II, 1, 41. *k. to Jove's thunder,* Wint. III, 1, 10. *those that are k. to the king,* H4B II, 2, 120. 127. H5 III, 7, 72. Troil. I, 1, 76. I, 3, 25. III, 3, 175. IV, 5, 92. Tim. V, 4, 40. Hml. I, 2, 65. IV, 2, 6. Cymb. V, 5, 112.

Kind, subst. 1) generic class, race: *till mutual*

overthrow of mortal k. Ven. 1018. *myself, one of their k.* Tp. V, 23. *all the k. of the Launces have this fault,* Gent. II, 3, 2. *bred out of the Spartan k.* Mids. IV, 1, 124. *of what k. should this cock come of,* As II, 7, 90. *shall kin with kin and k. with k. confound,* R2 IV, 141. *the lazar kite of Cressid's k.* H5 II, 1, 80. *that dog of as bad a k.* Troil. V, 4, 15. *would, as his k., grow mischievous,* Caes. II, 1, 33. *came of a gentle k. and noble stock,* Per. V, 1, 68.

2) what is bred in the bone, quality, nature: *we will unfold to creatures stern sad tunes, to change their —s,* Lucr. 1147. *the impression of strange —s is formed in them,* 1242. *nature should bring forth, of its own k., all foison,* Tp. II, 1, 163 (plants growing wild, without culture). *my meaner ministers their several —s have done,* III, 3, 88 (have acted up to their respective characters). *in the doing of the deed of k.* Merch. I, 3, 86. *if the cat will after k.* As III, 2, 109 (Old proverb: *kit will to k.*). *whether that thy youth and k. will the faithful offer take,* IV, 3, 59. *your marriage comes by destiny, your cuckoo sings by k.* All's I, 3, 67. *fitted by k. for rape and villany,* Tit. II, 1, 116. *why birds and beasts from quality and k.* Caes. I, 3, 64. *the worm will do his k.* Ant. V, 2, 264.

3) Preceded by *in,* = way, particular manner: *dumb jewels often in their silent k. more than quick words do move,* Gent. III, 1, 90. *we dare trust you in this k.* III, 2, 56. *I would not ha' your distemper in this k.* Wiv. III, 3, 232. *still forfeit in the same k.* Meas. III, 2, 206. *if the prince do solicit you in that k.* Ado II, 1, 70. *they shall find, awaked in such a k., both strength of limb and policy of mind,* IV, 1, 199. *but in this k., wanting your father's voice, the other must be held the worthier,* Mids. I, 1, 54. *they can do nothing in this k.* V, 88. *the best in this k. are but shadows,* 213. *and, in that k., swears you do more usurp than doth your brother,* As II, 1, 27. *thine eyes see it so grossly shown in thy behaviours that in their k. they speak it,* All's I, 3, 185. R2 II, 3, 143. 146. H4A I, 3, 121. H8 I, 2, 53. Troil. I, 3, 285. II, 3, 137. Cor. III, 3, 81. Lr. IV, 6, 166. Oth. I, 3, 395. IV, 3, 63. Cymb. III, 2, 57. Per. IV Prol. 15. cf. Cor. II, 3, 169.

4) sort, species: *cannot dispraise but in a k. of praise,* Sonn. 95, 7. *all frailties that besiege all —s of blood,* 109, 10. Tp. II, 1, 148. 177. II, 2, 27. III, 1, 2. III, 3, 38. Gent. II, 4, 25. III, 1, 262. IV, 1, 40. Wiv. I, 1, 215. II, 1, 17. III, 5, 13. Meas. I, 1, 28. II, 2, 135. II, 3, 28. III, 1, 139. III, 2, 238. IV, 3, 189. Err. II, 2, 90. Mids. III, 2, 438. As I, 3, 114. Tw. I, 2, 45. 5, 159. II, 3, 151. H4A II, 1, 63. H4B IV, 5, 127 etc. *all k. of arguments,* Compl. 121 (= arguments of every k.). *use your manners discreetly in all k. of companies,* Shr. I, 1, 247. *all k. of natures,* Tim. I, 1, 65. *some k. of men,* As II, 3, 10. Tw. III, 4, 266. *such k. of men,* Ado III, 3, 55. Tit. V, 2, 63. *these set k. of fools,* Tw. I, 5, 95. *these k. of knaves,* Lr. II, 2, 107. *children of divers k.* Rom. II, 3, 11.

Kind, adj. 1) keeping to nature, natural: *conceit deceitful, so compact, so k.* Lucr. 1423. *a k. overflow of kindness,* Ado I, 1, 26.

2) not degenerate and corrupt, but such as a thing or person ought to be: *what mightst thou do, were all thy children k. and natural,* H5 II Chor. 19. *crown what I profess with k. event, if I speak true,* Tp. III, 1, 69 (corresponding). *set a fair fashion on our entertainment, which was not half so beautiful and k.* Tim.

I, 2, 153. *be, as thy presence is, gracious and k.* Sonn. 10, 11 (quibbling).

3) benevolent, gentle, friendly: Ven. 318. Sonn. 105, 5. 9. Tp. I, 2, 309. Gent. I, 2, 109. II, 7, 2. IV, 2, 44. IV, 3, 47. Wiv. I, 4, 10. III, 4, 106. Meas. I, 2, 181. V, 398. Mids. V, 89. Merch. I, 3, 143. II, 5, 46. John V, 1, 32. R3 IV, 4, 172. Cor. II, 2, 63. Mcb. II, 1, 24. Hml. I, 2, 65* etc.

4) full of tenderness, affectionate: *thou art covetous, and he is k.* Sonn. 134, 6. *where neither party is nor true nor k.* Compl. 186. *drew me from k. embracements of my spouse,* Err. I, 1, 44. Shr. Ind. I, 118. *I found you wondrous k.* All's V, 3, 311. *this hearty k. embrace,* H6A III, 3, 82. *this k. kiss,* H6B I, 1, 19. *do not slander him, for he is k.* R3 I, 4, 247.

Adverbially: *I take all and your several visitations so k. to heart,* Tim. I, 2, 225.

Kind-hearted, benevolent: Sonn. 10, 12.

Kindle, 1) tr. a) to set on fire, to make to burn: Lucr. 1475. Gent. II, 7, 19. Wiv. V, 5, 100. John V, 2, 83. H4A III, 2, 62. H6C II, 1, 83. H8 V, 4, 51. Cor. II, 1, 274. Per. III, 2, 83.

b) to inflame, to incite; absol.: *this is the way to k., not to quench,* Cor. III, 1, 197. trans.: *the warm effects she seeks to k.* Ven. 606. *his —d duty —d her mistrust,* Lucr. 1352. *nothing remains but that I k. the boy thither,* As I, 1, 179 (*thither* = to it). John I, 33. H8 II, 4, 25. Caes. II, 1, 121. Ant. V, 1, 46.

2) intr. to take fire, to be inflamed: *that from their coldest neglect my love should k. to inflamed respect,* Lr. I, 1, 258.

Kindle, to bring forth, to drop: *the cony that you see dwell where she is —d,* As III, 2, 358.

Kindless, degenerate, unnatural: Hml. II, 2, 609.

Kindly, adj. in keeping with the quality of a person or thing, natural: *by that fatherly and k. power that you have in her,* Ado IV, 1, 75. *my age is as a lusty winter, frosty, but k.* As II, 3, 53 (suited to the season). *washing with k. tears his gentle cheeks,* H4B IV, 5, 84 (not feigned). *the bishop hath a k. gird,* H6A III, 1, 131 (well suited to his character and calling). *'tis lack of k. warmth they are not kind,* Tim. II, 2, 226. *melt Egypt into Nile, and k. creatures turn all to serpents,* Ant. II, 5, 78 (such as the land naturally produces).

Kindly, adv. (compar. *—er,* Tp. V, 24), 1) naturally, in a manner suited to the character or occasion: *shall not myself, one of their kind, be —er moved than thou art,* Tp. V, 24. *this do, and do it k.* Shr. Ind. I, 66. *thou hast most k. hit it,* Rom. II, 4, 59 (pertinently). Quibbling: *thy other daughter will use thee k.* Lr. I, 5, 15.

2) in a benevolent and friendly manner, affectionately: Lucr. 253. Gent. II, 4, 39. IV, 4, 207. Meas. I, 4, 24. As I, 1, 144. IV, 3, 141. Shr. Ind. I, 15. II, 78. All's II, 4, 1. III, 5, 104. Tw. III, 4, 171. H5 Prol. 34. H6A II, 5, 40. H6B III, 1, 346. R3 II, 2, 24. 93. III, 2, 33. Troil. III, 1, 105. IV, 4, 62. Cor. I, 9, 83. II, 3, 81. Tit. IV, 3, 29. Tim. III, 2, 30. Mcb. IV, 1, 131. Ant. I, 5, 58. Cymb. I, 6, 14. Per. IV, 6, 63.

Kindness, 1) benevolence, good-will, goodness: Sonn. 36, 11. Tp. I, 2, 345. Gent. IV, 2, 45. Meas. IV, 2, 62. Merch. I, 3, 144. 154. As IV, 3, 129. H6A II, 2, 50. H6C IV, 6, 10. R3 III, 1, 198 (Qq *willingness*). Troil. IV, 5, 20. Cor. V, 1, 59. Caes. V, 4, 28 (*give him all k.*). Cymb. II, 3, 102. Per. I, 1, 67 etc.

2) affection, tenderness, love: *I have sworn deep oaths of thy deep k.* Sonn. 152, 9. *use her with more k.* Err. III, 2, 6. *a kind overflow of k.* Ado I, 1, 26. *my k. shall incite thee,* III, 1, 113. *to express the like k.* Shr. II, 77. *to kill a wife with k.* IV, 1, 211. *my bosom is full of k.* Tw. II, 1, 41. *I come in k.* H6C III, 3, 51. *thy k. freezeth,* R3 IV, 2, 22.

3) an act of benevolence, a good turn: *Padua affords this k.* Shr. V, 2, 13. *you shall have all k. at my hand,* H6C III, 3, 149. *I'll requite this k.* IV, 7, 78. *to do k.:* Tw. V, 69. H6B II, 4, 83. Tit. V, 3, 171. Per. IV, 6, 7. Plur. —*es:* Err. IV, 3, 5. Tw. III, 4, 385 *(do).* Tim. III, 2, 22. Cymb. I, 6, 23.

Kindred (O. Edd. sometimes *kinred*), 1) relations, race: Compl. 270. Meas. III, 2, 109. Ado II, 1, 68. As III, 2, 32. Wint. V, 2, 186. R2 I, 3, 138. H4A I, 1, 16. H4B II, 2, 30. R3 I, 1, 72. 95. I, 3, 67. II, 1, 135. II, 2, 150. III, 2, 50. III, 7, 212 (Qq *kin*). IV, 4, 223. Rom. V, 1, 20. V, 3, 254. Tim. IV, 3, 344. Oth. I, 1, 168. Cymb. V, 5, 429. The verb following in the sing.: Mids. III, 1, 199. Shr. Ind. 2, 30. H5 II, 4, 50. In the plural: H8 III, 1, 150. Troil. III, 2, 118. Rom. IV, 1, 112. Adjectively: *k. blood,* R2 II, 1, 182. *k. tears,* R3 II, 2, 63.

2) relationship: *disclaiming here the k. of the king,* R2 I, 1, 70. *whom conscience and my k. bids to right,* II, 2, 115. Metaphorically: *stirrups of no k.* Shr. III, 2, 50. Adjectively: *any k. action,* John III, 4, 14.

Kine, see *Cow.*

King, subst. monarch, sovereign: Tp. I, 1, 18. 57. 67. I, 2, 112. 121. 196. 212. 221 etc. etc. *Edward k.* for *K. Edward:* H6A II, 5, 66. *k. of Pont* for *the k.* Ant. III, 6, 72. Followed by *o'er: k. o'er him and all that he enjoys,* John II, 240. *who sought to be k. o'er her,* Lr. IV, 3, 17. *The* —*'s English,* Wiv. I, 4, 6. *in the* —*'s highway,* R2 III, 3, 155. *The ballad of the k. and the beggar,* LLL I, 2, 114. R2 V, 3, 80 (cf. *Cophetua*). *the k. of heaven* (God): R3 I, 2, 105. *the K. of* —*s:* H6A I, 1, 28. R3 I, 4, 200. II, 1, 13. *the* —*s' K.* IV, 4, 346. *the* —*s of* —*s =* supreme —*s,* Ant. III, 6, 13. *that dread K. that took our state upon him* (Christ) H6B III, 2, 154. Used of any chief or ruler; of Oberon, Mids. II, 1, 18. of a captain of robbers: Gent. IV, 1, 37. 67. *her lord, her governor, her k.* Merch. III, 2, 167. *to wound thy lord, thy k., thy governor,* Shr. V, 2, 138. *and filled her sweet perfections with one self king,* Tw. I, 1, 39. *all those beauties whereof now he's k.* Sonn. 63, 6. *thou art the k. of honour,* H4A IV, 1, 10. *her thoughts the k. of every virtue,* Per. I, 1, 13. *there spoke a k.* (= excellently well said) H4B V, 3, 73. Denoting a card with the picture of a king: H6C V, 1, 44. Confounded with emperor: Tit. I, 247. II, 3, 47. 85. 87. 206. 259. III, 1, 154. IV, 4, 81.

King, vb. see *Kinged.*

King-becoming, becoming a king, decorous in a king: Mcb. IV, 3, 91.

King-cardinal, a cardinal usurping royal power: H8 II, 2, 20.

Kingdom, 1) a country subject to a king: Lucr. Arg. 3. Tp. III, 2, 153. IV, 253. V, 174. Gent. II, 7, 10. As V, 4, 8. 10. Wint. I, 2, 338. V, 1, 10. 28. V, 3, 6. H4A II, 4, 151. H4B III, 1, 38. H6A IV, 7, 73. H6B I, 1, 154. II, 2, 47. H6C I, 2, 16. II, 1, 93. III, 3, 94 etc. *thy fairy k.* Mids. II, 1, 144. Used of heaven: *God knows whether those ... shall inherit his*

k. H4B II, 2, 28. Of hell: *hie thee to hell, thou cacodemon, there thy k. is,* R3 I, 3, 144. *sent from the infernal k.* Tit. V, 2, 30. Of the other world: *the k. of perpetual night.* R3 I, 4, 47. *his new k. of perpetual rest,* II, 2, 46. Of the elements: *the watery k.* Merch. II, 7, 44. *the k. of the shore,* Sonn. 64, 6. Of any sovereignty: —*s of hearts,* Sonn. 70, 14. Of the state of man: *this fleshly land, this k., this confine of blood and breath,* John IV, 2, 246. *this little k. man,* H4B IV, 3, 118. *the state of man, like to a little k., suffers then the nature of an insurrection,* Caes. II, 1, 68.

2) royalty: *I must be married to my brother's daughter, or else my k. stands on brittle glass,* R3 IV, 2, 62. Perhaps also in H6C I, 1, 175 *(enjoy the k. after my decease).*

Kingdomed, like a kingdom: *'twixt his mental and his active parts k. Achilles in commotion rages and batters down himself,* Troil. II, 3, 185; cf. John IV, 2, 246. H4B IV, 3, 118. Caes. II, 1, 68.

Kinged, 1) made a king: *then am I k. again,* R2 V, 5, 36. 2) furnished with a king: *she is so idly k.* H5 II, 4, 26. In John II, 371 most M. Edd. *k. of our fears;* O. Edd. *kings of our feare.*

King-killer, murderer of kings: Tim. IV, 3, 382 (Maginn: *kin-killer).*

Kinglike, in *Unkinglike,* q. v.

Kingly, adj. 1) royal, of royal rank, pertaining to a king: *k. poor flout,* LLL V, 2, 269 (poor mockery of a king). *thy k. hand,* All's II, 1, 196. Per. IV, 1, 55. *my k. guest,* Wint. III, 2, 167. *a k. eye,* John V, 1, 47. Hml. IV, 7, 45. *sway,* R2 IV, 206. *thy k. doom,* V, 6, 23. *the k. couch,* H4B III, 1, 16. *I give thee k. thanks,* H6A V, 3, 163. *my k. throne,* H6C I, 1, 124. *by your k. leave,* II, 2, 63. *k. sepulchres,* V, 2, 20. *the k. government,* R3 III, 7, 132. *title,* 239 (Ff *royal*). *glory,* IV, 4, 371. *dignity,* H8 II, 4, 227. *his k. ears,* Troil. I, 3, 219. *crown,* Caes. III, 2, 101. *seal,* Ant. III, 13, 125. *patient,* Per. V, 1, 71.

2) like a king, becoming a king: *flat treason 'gainst the k. state of youth,* LLL IV, 3, 293. *a king, woe's slave, shall k. woe obey,* R2 III, 2, 210. *her almost k. dukedoms,* H5 I, 2, 227. *more k. in my thoughts,* H6B V, 1, 29. *the k. lion,* H6C V, 7, 11. *the k. crowned head,* Cor. I, 1, 119.

Kingly, adv. with an air of royalty: *my great mind most k. drinks it up,* Sonn. 114, 10.

Kingly-poor, writing of M. Edd. in LLL V, 2, 269; not hyphened in O. Edd.

Kinsman, a male relation: Lucr. 237. Wiv. III, 4, 23. Meas. II, 2, 81. Ado V, 4, 112. Mids. V, 47 Merch. I, 1, 57. As II, 4, 67. All's III, 6, 10. Tw. I, 5, 113. II, 3, 104. II, 5, 61. 162. V, 216. Wint. IV, 3, 85. John III, 3, 18. IV, 2, 166. V, 3, 5. R2 I, 1, 59. I, 4, 22. II, 1, 262. II, 2, 114. H4A I, 3, 234. IV, 3, 93. V, 5, 5. H5 IV, 1, 59. IV, 3, 10. H6A V, 5, 45. H6B III, 1, 69. R3 III, 1, 109. Rom. I, 5, 62. II, 4, 6. III, 1, 150. 153. 181. III, 3, 105. III, 4, 3. III, 5, 96. V, 3, 75. Mcb. I, 4, 58. I, 7, 13. Cymb. III, 6, 61. *some great k.* Rom. IV, 3, 53 (= ancestor). Plur. *kinsmen:* Lucr. 521. All's II, 2, 68. R2 II, 2, 111. III, 3, 169. H6A IV, 1, 155. H6C I, 1, 96. H8 I, 1, 81. Tit. IV, 3, 1. 24. 31. 61. Rom. I, 1, 66. II, 2, 65. 69. V, 3, 295. Mcb. I, 4, 35. V, 7, 62. Oth. I, 1, 69. Cymb. V, 5, 71. Confusion of the genders: *melancholy, k. to grim despair, and at her heels a huge infectious troop,* Err. V, 80.

Kinswoman, female relation: Ado IV, 1, 305. H4B II, 2, 169. Troil. I, 1, 44.

Kirtle (cf. *Half-kirtle*) a jacket, with a petticoat attached to it: Pilgr. 363 (not Shakespearian). H4B II, 4, 297.

Kiss, subst. a touching with the lips, or joining lips in token of love: Ven. 18. 84 etc. Gent. I, 2, 116. II, 2, 7. II, 4, 160. II, 7, 29. Meas. IV, 1, 5. Ado II, 1, 322. LLL II, 249. IV, 3, 26. Merch. III, 2, 139. As III, 4, 10. IV, 1, 79 etc.

Kiss, vb. 1) to touch with the lips in love or respect; absol.: Ven. 47. As IV, 1, 75. Shr. V, 1, 151. All's IV, 3, 257. Wint. IV, 4, 163. Rom. I, 5, 112. Hml. II, 2, 182 (*a good —ing carrion,* i. e. a carrion good in point of kissing, worth kissing; cf. *too hard a keeping oath,* LLL I, 1, 65). Oth. II, 1, 176. III, 3, 425. Ant. IV, 15, 39. Per. I, 2, 79 etc. With an accus.: Ven. 59. 479. Tp. II, 2, 153. Gent. I, 2, 108. II, 3, 28. III, 1, 326. IV, 4, 204. Wiv. I, 1, 116. Ado IV, 1, 336. V, 2, 51. Mids. IV, 1, 4. Merch. II, 7, 40. As Epil. 19. Shr. II, 326. IV, 1, 155. V, 1, 148. V, 2, 25. 180 etc. *k. the book,* Tp. II, 2, 135. 145. *they kneel, they k. the earth,* Wint. V, 1, 199 (in sign of submission and repentance); cf. *to k. the ground before young Malcolm's feet,* Mcb. V, 8, 28. *k. the rod* (= to submit tamely to punishment) Gent. I, 2, 59. R2 V, 1, 32. Kissing one's own hand in token of respect to another: LLL IV, 1, 148. V, 2, 324. As III, 2, 50. Shr. IV, 1, 97. All's II, 2, 10. Tw. III, 4, 36. H6A V, 3, 48. H6B IV, 1, 53. Oth. II, 1, 174. An accus. denoting the effect: *—ed his hand away,* LLL V, 2, 324. *—ed away kingdoms,* Ant. III, 10, 7. *k. the honoured gashes whole,* IV, 8, 10. Reciprocally: *long may they k. each other,* Ven. 505; R3 V, 3, 13 (of the two lips of the same mouth). *let them k. one another,* H6B IV, 7, 138 (Cade's speech). Metaphorically: *—ing with golden face the meadows green,* Sonn. 33, 3. *the stairs, as he treads on them, k. his feet,* LLL V, 2, 330. *some there be that shadows k.* Merch. II, 9, 66. *when the sweet wind did gently k. the trees,* V, 2. *Fortune shall k. him with a glorious victory,* John II, 394. *k. the lips of unacquainted change,* III, 4, 166. *didst thou never see Titan k. a dish of butter,* H4A II, 4, 133. *the hearts of princes k. obedience, so much they love it,* H8 III, 1, 162. *these happy masks that k. fair ladies' brows,* Rom. I, 1, 236. *winds of all the corners —ed your sails,* Cymb. II, 4, 28.

2) to touch, to meet: *heaven to k. the turrets bowed,* Lucr. 1372. *beat the ground for —ing of their feet,* Tp. IV, 174. *by this virgin palm now —ing thine,* LLL V, 2, 816. *to k. her burial,* Merch. I, 1, 29. *when with his knees he —ed the Cretan strond,* Shr. I, 1, 175. *the stars will k. the valleys first,* Wint. V, 1, 206. *let heaven k. earth,* H4B I, 1, 153. *rub on, and k. the mistress,* Troil. III, 2, 52 (quibbling; cf. Cymb. II, 1, 2). *yond towers must k. their own feet,* IV, 5, 221. *till the lowest stream do k. the most exalted shores of all,* Caes. I, 1, 65. *darkness does the face of earth entomb, when living light should k. it,* Mcb. II, 4, 10. *when I —ed the jack,* Cymb. II, 1, 2*(cf. Jack 5.). the towers —ed the clouds,* Per. I, 4, 24.

3) to salute or caress each other by joining lips: *courtsied when you have and —ed,* Tp. I, 2, 378. *now k., embrace,* Gent. I, 2, 129. Wiv. III, 5, 75. Mids. III, 2, 140. Shr. IV, 2, 27. All's II, 5, 91. H6B III, 2, 354. IV, 7, 145. H6C II, 1, 29. Troil. IV, 4, 100. Tit. III, 1, 288.

4) to touch each other, to meet, to join (intr.): *the mightiest space in fortune nature brings to join like likes and k. like native things,* All's I, 1, 238. *I and greatness were compelled to k.* H4B III, 1, 74. *like fire and powder, which as they k. consume,* Rom. II, 6, 11. *solderest close impossibilities and makest them k.* Tim. IV, 3, 389. *here they might take two thieves —ing,* Ant. II, 6, 101.

Kissing-comfits, sugar-plums perfumed to make the breath sweet: Wiv. V, 5, 22.

Kitchen, a cook-room: Meas. II, 2, 84. H4B II, 4, 361. Oth. II, 1, 111. Compounds: *k. maid,* Err. IV, 4, 77. *k. malkin,* Cor. II, 1, 224. *k. trull,* Cymb. V, 5, 177. *k. vestal,* Err. IV, 4, 78. *k. wench,* III, 2, 96. Rom. II, 4, 42.

Kitchen, to regale in the cook-room: *a fat friend that —ed me for you,* Err. V, 415.

Kite, a bird of prey, Falco milvus: Shr. IV, 1, 198 (= hawk). Wint. II, 3, 186. IV, 3, 23. H6B III, 1, 249. III, 2, 193. 196. R3 I, 1, 133. Cor. IV, 5, 45. *carrion —s,* H6B V, 2, 11; cf. Caes. I, 85. Mcb. III, 4, 73. Hml. II, 2, 607. Term of reproach: H5 II, 1, 80. Lr. I, 4, 284. Ant. III, 13, 89.

Kitten, subst. a young cat: H4A III, 1, 129.

Kitten, vb. to bring forth young cats: H4A III, 1, 19.

Knack, a toy, a pretty trifle, a knick-knack: Mids. I, 1, 34. Shr. IV, 3, 67. Wint. IV, 4, 360. 439.

Knap, to bite off short, to knapple: *as lying a gossip as ever —ed ginger,* Merch. III, 1, 10.

Knap, to rap: *she —ed them o'the coxcombs with a stick,* Lr. II, 4, 125 (Qq rapt).

Knave, 1) a young fellow, a boy: *a young k. and begging!* H4B I, 2, 84. Often used in compellations, even as a term of endearment: *my good k.* Costard, LLL III, 144. *good my k.* 153. *the k. counterfeits well, a good k.* Tw. IV, 2, 22. *the k. will stick by thee,* H4B V, 3, 70 (= thou wilt ever be a sly rogue; quibbling). *poor k., I blame thee not,* Caes. IV, 3, 241. *gentle k., good night,* 269. *though this k. came something saucily into the world,* Lr. I, 1, 21. *where's my k., my fool?* I, 4, 46. *now, my friendly k., I thank thee,* 103. *my pretty k.* 107. *poor fool and k.* III, 2, 72. *my good k.* Eros, Ant. IV, 14, 12. *my k.* 14.

2) a menial: *a couple of Ford's —s, his hinds,* Wiv. III, 5, 99. *thou art the first k. that e'er madest a duke,* Meas. V, 361. *poor —s' caps and legs,* Cor. II, 1, 76. *my lady's father! my lord's k.* Lr. I, 4, 88. *being his k., I will,* II, 2, 144. *with a k. of common hire,* Oth. I, 1, 126. *not being Fortune, he's but Fortune's k.* Ant. V, 2, 3. Opposed to a knight: Tw. II, 3, 69. John I, 243.

3) rascal, villain: Tp. V, 268. Gent. III, 1, 263. Wiv. I, 1, 190. II, 1, 174. II, 2, 276. 281. 283. 296. III, 1, 14. 91. III, 3, 211. 256. 259. IV, 5, 122. Meas. V, 358. Err. I, 2, 72. 92. III, 1, 64. 74 etc. *bear the k. by the volume,* Cor. III, 3, 33 (= suffer to be called knave). *a crafty k. does need no broker,* H6B I, 2, 100 (proverb). *to play the k.* = to practise deceit: Merch. II, 3, 12. As III, 2, 315. All's V, 2, 32. Peculiar combination: *whores and — s,* Tp. II, 1, 166. *take order for the drabs and the —s,* Meas. II, 1, 247. *follow the k. and take this drab away,* H6B II, 1, 156. *that we may account thee a whoremaster and a k.* Tim. II, 2, 111. cf. also Troil. V, 4, 4 and 9.

Knavery, villany, roguery: Ado II, 3, 124. Mids.

III, 1, 115. 123. As I, 2, 80. Shr. I, 2 138. V, 1, 37. 142. Tw. IV, 2, 73. Wint. IV, 4, 697. H5 IV, 7, 3. H6B I, 2, 105. H8 V, 2, 33. Troil. II, 3, 78. Hml. III, 4, 205. V, 2, 19. Oth. I, 1, 100 (Qq *bravery*). I, 3, 400. II, 1, 321. Plur. —*ies* = roguish tricks: Wiv. IV, 4, 81. Mids. III, 2, 346. All's I, 3, 13. H5 IV, 7, 52. *amber bracelets, beads, and all this k.* Shr. IV, 3, 57 (= tricks, toys; for the sake of the rhyme).

Knavish, villanous, roguish: LLL V, 2, 97. Mids. II, 1, 33. III, 2, 440. Wint. IV, 3, 105. H5 IV, 2, 51. Hml. III, 2, 250. IV, 2, 25.

Knead, to work into dough: Troil. I, 1, 23. —*ing up the honey,* H5 I, 2, 199. *to become a* —*ed clod,* Meas. III, 1, 121. *I will k. him,* Troil. II, 3, 231 (beat him into a jelly).

Knee, subst. 1) the joint in which the leg and thigh meet: Lucr. 359. Wiv. V, 5, 76. LLL V, 2, 551. Shr. I, 1, 175. H4A II, 4, 361. III, 3, 173. H4B II, 4, 247. H5 II, 3, 26. H6A IV, 7, 5. Troil. I, 3, 50 etc. *bow my k. before his majesty,* R2 I, 3, 47. *had the tribute of his supple k.* I, 4, 33 (i. e. a courtesy). *the fearful bending of thy k.* III, 3, 73. *set your k. against my foot,* H6A III, 1, 169 (= kneel down). *on my k.* All's I, 3, 198. John I, 82. III, 1, 308. 309. V, 7, 103. H6A IV, 5, 32. H6B I, 1, 10. R3 I, 2, 179. II, 2, 105. Caes. II, 2, 54. 81 etc. *bended* —*s,* Gent. III, 1, 229. *go to your* —*s,* Meas. III, 1, 171. *raise me from my* —*s,* V, 231. *lend me your* —*s,* V, 436 (kneel down for my sake). *pursue we him on* —*s,* Troil. V, 3, 10. 54. *upon her* —*s,* Gent. III, 1, 226. Ado II, 1, 30. II, 3, 152. As III, 5, 57. Wint. II, 3, 149. R2 III, 3, 36. 114. H6A III, 3, 80. Mcb. IV, 3, 110 etc.

2) a genuflection, prostration: *show me thy humble heart and not thy k.* R2 II, 3, 83. *commandest the beggar's k.* H5 IV, 1, 273. *your k., sirrah,* Cor. V, 3, 75. *here's my k.* Cymb. V, 5, 325. *a thousand* —*s ten thousand years together,* Wint. III, 2, 212. *your* —*s to them, not arms, must help,* Cor. I, 1, 76. *your* —*s to me?* V, 3, 57. *let us shame him with our* —*s,* 169. *let her have your* —*s,* Oth. II, 1, 84. *her prayers, her* —*s,* Per. IV, 6, 9.

3) a courtesy (a sort of reverence anciently made by men): *came in with cap and k.* H4A IV, 3, 68. *cap and k. slaves,* Tim. III, 6, 107. *give them title, k. and approbation,* IV, 3, 36. cf. R2 I, 4, 33. Hml. III, 2, 66. Oth. I, 1, 45.

Knee, vb. to go on knees: *a mile before his tent fall down and k. the way into his mercy,* Cor. V, 1, 5 (F2.3.4 *kneel*). = to kneel to: *I could as well be brought to k. his throne,* Lr. II, 4, 217.

Knee-crooking, courtesying: Oth. I, 1, 45 (cf. Hml. III, 2, 66).

Knee-deep, very deep, thoroughly: *inch-thick, k., o'er head and ears a forked one,* Wint. I, 2, 186.

Kneel (impf. and part. —*ed*) to bend the knee: Lucr. 1830. Tp. III, 2, 46. Meas. I, 4, 81. V, 93. 442. Merch. V, 31. Shr. V, 2, 162. Wint. II, 3, 153. John III, 1, 310. H6B II, 2, 59. H8 IV, 2, 103 etc. *our knees shall k.* R2 V, 3, 106. *a* —*ing knee,* 132. *to k. down:* Ven. 350. Meas. V, 439. H6A V, 4, 25. H6B I, 1, 63. IV, 1, 57. V, 1, 78. H6C II, 2, 60. V, 1, 48 etc. *to k. at a person's feet:* H5 III, 6, 140. H6A V, 3, 194. R3 II, 1, 107. Tit. I, 161. *to k. before a p.:* Meas. V, 19. Cor. V, 1, 65. V, 3, 54. *to*

k. down before: Meas. II, 2, 44. H4B V, 5, 150. *tc k. to:* Tp. II, 1, 128. II, 2, 123. Err. V, 129. H4B IV, 5, 177. H6B I, 2, 39. H6C I, 1, 162. Ant. III, 13, 40. V, 2, 21. 28. Cymb. V, 5, 417 etc.

Knell, the sound of a bell rung at a funeral, a tolling: Lucr. 1495. Pilgr. 272. Tp. I, 2, 402. Merch. III, 2, 70. All's V, 3, 67. Wint. I, 2, 190. H8 II, 1, 32. IV, 2, 79. Cor. V, 4, 21. Tim. IV, 2, 26. Mcb. II, 1, 63. IV, 3, 170. V, 8, 50.

Knife (plur. *knives;* Saxon genit. *knives,* M. Edd. *knife's:* Ado II, 3, 264. Tit. V, 3, 63) 1) an instrument to cut anything: Sonn. 95, 14. Ado II, 3, 264. V, 1, 157. Merch. IV, 1, 121. 124. 245. V, 150. Wint. IV, 4, 610. H4B III, 2, 335. Tim. I, 2, 45. *a butcher's k.* H6B III, 2, 195. H6C V, 6, 9.

2) an offensive weapon, a dagger: Lucr. 1047. 1138. 1184. 1469. 1724. 1807. Sonn. 74, 11. Tp. II, 1, 161. III, 2, 99. Wiv. II, 2, 18. LLL II, 190. Tw. II, 5, 116. H4A I, 1, 17. H4B II, 4, 138. IV, 5, 87. H5 II, 1, 25. H6B III, 1, 174. R3 I, 3, 244. IV, 4, 226. H8 I, 2, 199 (*put his k. into him*). Troil. I, 1, 63. Tit. V, 3, 63. Rom. II, 4, 214 (*lay k. aboard* = to board, grapple). Mcb. I, 5, 53. I, 7, 16. III, 6, 35. Per. IV Prol. 14 etc. Denoting the scythe of Time: *confounding age's cruel k.* Sonn. 63, 10. *so thou preventest his scythe and cruel k.* 100, 14. cf. *set his murdering k. against the root,* H6C II, 6, 49.

Knight, subst. 1) a man-at-arms serving on horseback and admitted to a certain rank by certain ceremonies: Lucr. 1694. Pilgr. 216. 221. LLL I, 1, 173. As I, 2, 66. John I, 177. 244. R2 I, 3, 18. 26. 34. H4A I, 1, 68. III, 2, 140. V, 3, 20 etc. *rather go with sir priest than sir k.* Tw. III, 4, 299 (= rather in peace than at war). *a wandering k.* Mids. I, 2, 47. H4A I, 2, 17. *arise my* —*s o' the battle,* Cymb. V, 5, 20 (i. e. dubbed after a battle). *thou art the k. of the Burning Lamp,* H4A III, 3, 30.

2) a member of an order of chivalry: —*s of the garter,* H6A IV, 1, 34. *k. of the noble order of Saint George,* IV, 7, 68. Hence: *Oberon would have the child k. of his train,* Mids. II, 1, 25. And even applied to females as belonging to Dian's order of chastity: *those that slew thy virgin k.* Ado V, 3, 13. *Dian no queen of virgins, that would suffer her poor k. surprised,* All's I, 3, 120.

3) champion: *fashion's own k.* LLL I, 1, 179. *great is the rumour of this dreadful k.* H6A I, 3, 7. Particularly one devoted to the service of a lady, almost = lover: *in praise of ladies dead and lovely* —*s,* Sonn. 106, 4. *one k. loves both,* Pilgr. 116. *thine own true k.* Wiv. II, 1, 15. *to honour Helen and to be her k.* Mids. II, 2, 144. *mark, poor k., what dreadful dole is here,* V, 282. *like a wounded k.* As III, 2, 254. *am her k. by proof,* Troil. V, 5, 5. *give this ring to my true k.* Rom. III, 2, 142.

4) one of the rank of a baronet: Gent. I, 2, 10. Wiv. I, 1, 71. II, 1, 52. 112. III, 2, 21. IV, 2, 115 etc. etc. *sir k.* Tw. III, 4, 299. H5 II, 2, 67. Vocatively without *sir:* Wiv. I, 1, 114. IV, 5, 93. V, 5, 179. Tw. I, 3, 59 etc.

Knight, vb. 1) to make a knight, to dub: H5 IV, 8, 1. Cymb. III, 1, 70. —*ed in the field,* John I, 54. Tit. I, 196.

2) to promote to the rank of a baronet: Wiv. II, 1, 50. 55.

Knight-errant, a knight travelling in search of

adventures; ludicrously applied to Doll Tearsheet: *you she k.* H4B V, 4, 25.

Knighthood, 1) chivalry: *O shame to k.* Lucr. 197. *conjures him by k., gentry*, 569. 1697. R2 I, 1, 75. Lr. V, 3, 145.

2) the rank and dignity of a knight: *laid my k. on my shoulder*, R2 I, 1, 79. I, 3, 14. H6C II, 2, 58. Cymb. V, 2, 6.

3) the being one of an order of chivalry: *buckled below fair —'s bending knee*, Wiv. V, 5, 76. *this ornament of k.* H6A IV, 1, 29.

4) rank of a baronet: H4A III, 3, 137. H4B I, 2, 93. V, 3, 132.

Knightly, adj. pertaining to a knight, chivalrous: *my k. stomach*, John I, 191. *chivalrous design of k. trial*, R2 I, 1, 81. *my k. sword*, IV, 29. *the garter, blemished, pawned his k. virtue*, R3 IV, 4, 370.

Knightly, adv. in the manner of a knight: *thus k. clad in arms*, R2 I, 3, 12.

Knit, subst. texture: *their garters of an indifferent k.* Shr. IV, 1, 95.

Knit, vb. (imp. and part. *knit*), I. trans. 1) to twist, to make into a kind of network; absol.: *she can k.* (= make stockings) Gent. III, 1, 310. trans.: *to k. the cord*, Tit. II, 4, 10. With *up: sleep that —s up the ravelled sleave of care*, Mcb. II, 2, 37.

2) to tie, to make into a knot: *he shall not k. a knot in his fortunes with the finger of my substance*, Wiv. III, 2, 76. With *up: I'll k. it* (my hair) *up in silken strings*, Gent. II, 7, 45. *I'll have this knot k. up*, Rom. IV, 2, 24.

3) to tie, to bind, to join; properly and figuratively: *k. poisonous clouds about his golden head*, Lucr. 777. *I k. my handkercher about your brows*, John IV, 1, 42. *let the flames of the last day k. earth and heaven together*, H6B V, 2, 42. *to k. again this scattered corn into one mutual sheaf*, Tit. V, 3, 70. *that which —eth souls and prospers love*, Mids. I, 1, 172. *these couples shall eternally be k.* IV, 1, 186. *shall we k. our powers*, John II, 398. *this royal hand and mine are newly k.* III, 1, 226. *splintered, k. and joined together*, R3 II, 2, 118. *the amity that wisdom —s not*, Troil. II, 3, 110. *this yellow slave will k. and break religions*, Tim. IV, 3, 34. *to k. your hearts*, Ant. II, 2, 128. *for ever k. together*, II, 6, 122. *to k. their souls*, Cymb. II, 3, 122. *to k. in her their best perfections*, Per. I, 1, 11. With *up: mine enemies are all k. up in their distractions*, Tp. III, 3, 89. *thy stones with lime and hair k. up in thee*, Mids. V, 193. Followed by *to: to whom thy merit hath my duty strongly k.* Sonn. 26, 2. *my heart unto yours is k.* Mids. II, 2, 47. Ado IV, 1, 45. John V, 2, 63. H4B IV, 1, 177. H6A V, 1, 17. Troil. I, 3, 67. Mcb. III, 1, 18. Oth. I, 3, 342.

4) to contract: *k. brow*, Lucr. 709. *k. his brows*, H6B I, 2, 3. III, 1, 15. H6C II, 2, 20. III, 2, 82.

II. intr. to join: *our severed navy have k. again*, Ant. III, 13, 171. *when peers thus k., a kingdom ever stands*, Per. II, 4, 58.

Knitter, a woman that weaves or knits: Tw. II, 4, 45.

Knob, a protuberance: *his face is all bubukles, and whelks, and —s*, H5 III, 6, 108 (Fluellen's speech).

Knock, subst. a blow, a cuff: *gallows and k. are too powerful on the highway*, Wint. IV, 3, 29. *the —s are too hot*, H5 III, 2, 3. R3 V, 3, 5. Tit. V, 3, 71. Rom. I, 3, 54. Cymb. IV, 2, 74.

Knock, vb. 1) to strike, to beat; absol.: *as fire in a flint, which will not show without —ing*, Troil. III, 3, 258. With *against: the cry did k. against my very heart*, Tp. I, 2, 8. *to k. against the gates of Rome*, Cor. IV, 5, 147. With *at: make my seated heart k. at my ribs*, Mcb. I, 3, 136. With a superfluous *it: let the music k. it*, H8 I, 4, 108 (= play on). With an object: *'twere good you —ed him*, Gent. II, 4, 7. *k. the door hard. Let him k. till it ache*, Err. III, 1, 58. *whom should I k.* Shr. I, 2, 6. 9. 10. 12. 13. 30. 40. 41. *I have an humour to k. you*, H5 II, 1, 58. [Troil. IV, 2, 35. Hml. V, 1, 97. Oth. II, 3, 155. Reciprocally: *his knees —ing each other*, Hml. II, 1, 81. Joined with adverbs denoting the effect: *to the court I'll k. her back*, Cymb. III, 5, 148. *k. him down*, H6B IV, 6, 9. IV, 8, 2. H8 V, 4, 32. Tim. III, 4, 91. *k. off his manacles*, Cymb. V, 4, 199. *the brains of my Cupid's —ed out*, All's III, 2, 16. H6A III, 1, 83. Troil. II, 1, 110. III, 3, 303. Tim. I, 1, 192. Oth. IV, 2, 236. Cymb. IV, 2, 115.

2) to dash, to drive: *k. a nail into his head*, Tp. III, 2, 69. *I will k. his urinals about his costard*, Wiv. III, 1, 14. H5 IV, 1, 54. 57. *let us k. our prains together*, Wiv. III, 1, 122 (Evans' speech).

3) to rap for admittance: Wiv. IV, 5, 9. Meas. II, 2, 137. Err. III, 1, 121. Shr. I, 2, 5. 16. 19. V, 1, 16. H4B V, 3, 75. H6A I, 3, 5. III, 2, 12. H6C IV, 7, 16. R3 III, 7, 55. Troil. IV, 2, 41. Rom. I, 4, 33. III, 3, 71. 74. Caes. II, 1, 60. 304. 309. III, 2, 184. Mcb. II, 2, 57. 65. 69. 74. II, 3, 1. IV, 1, 47. Oth. IV, 3, 53. Cymb. II, 3, 82. With *at: another —s at the door*, Merch. I, 2, 147. All's IV, 1, 31. IV, 2, 54. H4B II, 4, 398. R3 III, 2, 2. *at door*, H4B II, 4, 381. *to k. at your ear and beseech listening*, Shr. IV, 1, 67. *at the gate*, Err. V, 165. Shr. I, 2, 11. 37. 39. 42. H4B I, 1, 5. Mcb. V, 1, 73. *jealousy —s at my heart*, Ven. 659. *k. at his study*, Tit. V, 2, 5. *at the taverns*, H4B II, 4, 388.

Knock, an exclamation in imitation of the sound of rapping: Mcb. II, 3, 3. 8. 14. 17.

Knoll, to ring, to toll: *where bells have —ed to church*, As II, 7, 114. *have with holy bell been —ed to church*, 121. *as a sullen bell, remembered —ing a departing friend*, H4B I, 1, 103 (Q *tolling*). *and so his knell is —ed*, Mcb. V, 8, 50.

Knot, subst. 1) a complication of a cord or string made by interweaving: Compl. 265. Gent. II, 7, 46. Shr. III, 2, 60. All's IV, 3, 163. 359. H5 I, 1, 46. Lr. II, 3, 10. Cymb. II, 2, 34. Metaphorical use: *knit a k. in his fortunes*, Wiv. III, 2, 76 (establish them surely). *it is too hard a k. for me to untie*, Tw. II, 2, 42. *unknit this churlish k. of war*, H4A V, 1, 16. *and not unknit himself the noble k. he made*, Cor. IV, 2, 32. *this k. intrinsicate of life at once untie*, Ant. V, 2, 307. *untied I still my virgin k. will keep*, Per. IV, 2, 160.

2) tie, bond of association: *and surer bind this k. of amity*, H6A V, 1, 16. *with another k.* Troil. V, 2, 157. *those strong —s of love*, Mcb. IV, 3, 27. *to knit your hearts with an unslipping k.* Ant. II, 2, 129. Especially marriage: *by this k. thou shalt so surely tie thy now unsured assurance to the crown*, John II, 470. H6C III, 3, 55. R3 IV, 3, 42. Rom. IV, 2, 24. Cymb. II, 3, 124.

3) folded arms: *his arms in this sad k.* Tp. I, 2, 224. *unknit that sorrow-wreathen k.* Tit. III, 2, 4.

4) a hard part in a tree: *as —s, by the conflux of meeting sap, infect the sound pine*, Troil. I, 3, 7. *blunt*

wedges rive hard —s, 316. Applied to the human body: *let grow thy sinews till their —s be strong*, Troil. V, 3, 33.

5) a company, association; in a good as well as in a bad sense: *a good k.* Wiv. III, 2, 52. *there's a k., a ging, a pack, a conspiracy against me*, IV, 2, 123. *his ancient k. of dangerous adversaries*, R3 III, 1, 182. *a k. you are of damned blood-suckers*, III, 3, 6. *you k. of mouth-friends*, Tim. III, 6, 99. *so often shall the k. of us be called the men that gave their country liberty*, Caes. III, 1, 117.

6) beds or plots in which a garden is laid out: *her —s disordered*, R2 III, 4, 46 (cf. *Curious-knotted*).

Knot, vb. to copulate; used of toads: Oth. IV, 2, 62.

Knot-grass, the plant polygonum aviculare; supposed to hinder growth: Mids. III, 2, 329.*

Knotted, 1) full of knots, hard: *k. oaks*, Troil. I, 3, 50. 2) interwoven: *would make thy k. and combined locks to part and each particular hair to stand an end*, Hml. I, 5, 18 (Ff *knotty*).

Knotty, 1) full of knots, hard: *k. oaks*, Tp. I, 2, 295. Caes. I, 3, 6. 2) interwoven: *thy k. and combined locks*, Hml. I, 5, 18 (Qq *knotted*).

Knotty-pated, blockheaded: H4A II, 4, 251. cf. *Not-pated*.

Know, vb. (impf. *knew*, part. *known*) 1) not to be ignorant, to be conscious, to have certain information about sth.; abs.: *thou must now k. farther*, Tp. I, 2, 33. *k. thus far forth*, 177 etc. *that I k. =* to my knowledge: Cor. II, 1, 168. *in my —ing*, in the same sense: Tim. III, 2, 74. With a dependent clause: Tp. I, 2, 18. 266. 286. II, 1, 224. 326 etc. *to learn to k. =* to learn: *let him learn to k., when maidens sue, men give like gods*, Meas. I, 4, 80 (Anacoluthon in II, 1, 8). *I k. not how.. =* it may well be that: Ant. II, 1, 41. *where then do you k. best we be affied =* where, for aught you know, may we best etc. Shr. IV, 4, 48. With an inf.: *I k. how to curse*, Tp. I, 2, 364 (cf. *How*). *I k. the gentleman to be of worth*, Gent. II, 4, 55. III, 1, 264. Wint. IV, 3, 91 etc. Inf. without *to:* *—ing thy heart torment me with disdain*, Sonn. 132, 2 (Ed. 1640 and M. Edd. *torments*). With a simple accus.: Tp. I, 2, 21. 356. II, 2, 83. Gent. I, 2, 32. 33. II, 5, 45. IV, 2, 88 etc. *this trick may chance to scathe you, I k. what*, Rom. I, 5, 86 (i. e. for me it may, for aught I care). With a double accus.: *she —s it cowardice*, Gent. V, 2, 21. *if you k. yourself clear*, Wiv. III, 3, 123. *I k. him a liar*, All's I, 1, 111. *a —n discreet man*, Tw. I, 5, 103 (= known to be discreet). *she —s them innocent*, Tit. III, 1, 115. *I knew it the most general way*, Tim. II, 2, 209. *to make —n =* to show, to tell, to betray: *I endowed thy purposes with words that made them —n*, Tp. I, 2, 358. *how well I like it, the execution of it shall make —n*, Gent. I, 3, 36. *make —n which way thou travellest*, Shr. IV, 5, 50. *I'll make thee —n*, Oth. V, 2, 165.

2) to be acquainted with: *I do not k. one of my sex*, Tp. III, 1, 48. *do you k. Madam Silvia?* Gent. II, 1, 14. *k. ye Don Antonio?* II, 4, 54 etc. *she knew her distance and did angle for me*, All's V, 3, 212. *I do beseech you, k. me*, Tim. III, 5, 90. *afraid to k. itself*, Mcb. IV, 3, 165. *to learn to know =* to make the acquaintance of: R2 II, 3, 40. With *for:* *thou shalt k. him for knave and cuckold*, Wiv. II, 2, 297. *knew me for a fool*, Meas. V, 505. *the duke —s him for no*

other but a poor officer of mine, All's IV, 3, 225. *he might have more diseases than he knew for*, H4B I, 2, 6 (i. e. than he knew for such). *k. us by these colours for thy foes*, H6A II, 4, 105. *I k. her for a spleeny Lutheran*, H8 III, 2, 98. *I k. thee well for our proud empress*, Tit. V, 2, 25. Caes. V, 4, 8. Tim. III, 2, 3. Partic. —*n: letters should not be —n*, Tp. II, 1, 150. *hate's —n injury*, Sonn. 40, 12. *the country proverb —n*, Mids. III, 2, 458. *a —n truth*, All's II, 5, 32. *though war nor no —n quarrel be in question*, H5 II, 4, 17. *of —n honour*, Hml. V, 2, 259. —*n to =* a) no stranger to; in a passive sense: *a man long —n to me*, Wiv. II, 2, 188. *well —n to the duke*, Meas. III, 2, 169. —*n unto these and to myself disguised*, Err. II, 2, 216 etc. b) no stranger to; in an active sense; acquainted with: *be ever —n to patience*, Ant. III, 6, 98. *be better —n to this gentleman*, Cymb. I, 4, 31. —*n alone, without to, =* acquainted: *to make us better friends, more —n*, Wint. IV, 4, 66. *better thus, and —n to be contemned, than still contemned and flattered*, Lr. IV, 1, 1 (= knowing). *be not you —n on't*, Oth. III, 3, 319 (Ff *be not acknown*).

3) to get acquainted with: *she shall thank you for't, if e'er you k. her*, Gent. IV, 4, 184. *let me make men k. more valour in me*, Cymb. V, 1, 29.

4) to be acquainted with each other: *you and I have —n*, Ant. II, 6, 86. *we have —n together in Orleans*, Cymb. I, 4, 36.

5) to recognize, to perceive to be: *in that* (thine eye) *I cannot k. thy change*, Sonn. 93, 6. *to k. him by his voice*, Gent. IV, 2, 89. *to be —n a reasonable creature*, Ado I, 1, 71. *I should k. the man by the Athenian garment*, Mids. III, 2, 248. *I have —n thee already*, All's II, 3, 107 (= I have seen what you are). *you k. me by my habit*, H5 III, 6, 121. *true ornaments to k. a holy man*, R3 III, 7, 99 etc.

6) to be informed, to have or receive information, to learn; a) with *of: my master —s not of your being here*, Wiv. III, 3, 29. *I knew of your purpose*, V, 5, 214. *who knew of your intent*, Meas. V, 124. —*ing aforehand of our merriment*, LLL V, 2, 461. *that you might the better arm you to the sudden time, than if you had at leisure —n of this*, John V, 6, 27. b) Trans.: *entreated me to call and k. her mind*, Gent. IV, 3, 2. *I come to k. your pleasure*, Meas. I, 1, 27. *come yourself alone to k. the reason of this strange restraint*, Err. III, 1, 97. *what would these strangers? k. their minds*, Boyet, LLL V, 2, 174. *shall I k. your answer?* Merch. I, 3, 8. *if your wife k. how well I have deserved the ring*, IV, 1, 446. *there shalt thou k. thy charge*, H4A III, 3, 225. *search, seek and k. how this foul murder comes*, Rom. V, 3, 198. *on the view and —ing of these contents*, Hml. V, 2, 44 etc. *as I am let to k. =* as I am informed: Hml. IV, 6, 11. With *from: as testy sick men no news but health from their physicians k.* Sonn. 140, 8. With *of: I would k. that of your honour*, Meas. II, 1, 166. *if you will k. of me what man I am*, As IV, 3, 96. *k. of me then, that...*, V, 2, 57. *what shall I k. of thee?* H5 III, 6, 122 etc. Hence *to k. of =* to ask: *turn you the key and k. his business of him*, Meas. I, 4, 8. *k. of your youth, examine well your blood, whether... you can endure*, Mids. I, 1, 68. *I beseech you to k. of the knight what my offence to him is*, Tw. III, 4, 278. *k. of the duke if his last purpose hold*, Lr. V, 1, 1. *go k. of Cassio where he supped tonight*, Oth. V, 1, 117.

7) to distinguish; with *from: to k. faithful friend from flattering foe*, Pilgr. 429. *to k. turtles from jays*, Wiv. III, 3, 44. All's III, 6, 25. Wint. IV, 4, 411. Troil. I, 3, 225. Cor. I, 6, 25. Hml. II, 2, 397. IV, 5, 23.

8) to experience, to see, to witness: *in having —n no travel in his youth*, Gent. I, 3, 16. *by the art of —n and feeling sorrows*, Lr. IV, 6, 226. *I will be —n your advocate*, Cymb. I, 1, 76. Followed by an inf.; a) with *to: he has been —n to commit outrages*, Tim. III, 5, 72. *stones have been —n to move*, Mcb. III, 4, 123. b) without *to: I never knew a woman so dote upon a man*, Wiv. II, 2, 106. *I never knew man hold vile stuff so dear*, LLL IV, 3, 276. *then k. the peril of our curses light on thee*, John III, 1, 294. H8 V, 3, 56. Caes. I, 3, 44. Mcb. V, 1, 33. Oth. IV, 1, 111. Followed by a dependent clause with *when: I have —n when there was no music with him but the drum and the fife*, Ado II, 3, 13. *I knew when seven justices could not take up a quarrel*, As V, 4, 103. *I have not known when his affections swayed*, Caes. II, 1, 20.

9) to have sexual commerce with: *before I k. myself, seek not to k. me*, Ven. 525. *I have —n my husband*, Meas. V, 186. *he ne'er knew my body*, 203. *he knew me as a wife*, 230. 426. *if I have —n her*, Ado IV, 1, 49. Merch. V, 229. All's V, 3, 288.

Know, subst. reading of Ff in Hml. V, 2, 44: *on the view and k. of these contents;* Qq *knowing.*

Knower, one who knows: Troil. II, 3, 51. 57.

Knowing, subst., 1) knowledge: *in my k. Timon has been this lord's father*, Tim. III, 2, 74. *on the view and k. of these contents*, Hml. V, 2, 44.

2) experience: *this sore night hath trifled former —s*, Mcb. II, 4, 4. *gentlemen of your k.* Cymb. I, 4, 30. *one of your great k. should learn forbearance*, II, 3, 102.

Knowing, adj. intelligent, experienced: *you have heard, and with a k. ear*, Hml. IV, 7, 3. *he's very k.* Ant. III, 3, 26.

Knowingly, by experience: *dost thou believe it? Ay, madam, k.* All's I, 3, 256. *did you but know the city's usuries and felt them k.* Cymb. III, 3, 46.

Knowledge, 1) the knowing a fact or truth, the having a clear perception or certain information of it: *being come to k. that there was complaint intended*, Meas. V, 153. *I speak it in the freedom of my k.* Wint. I, 1, 13. *which does behove my k. thereof to be informed*, I, 2, 395. *alack, for lesser k.* II, 1, 38 (would I knew less`. *his k. is not infected*, 41. *when you shall come to clearer k.* 97. *let him have k. who I am*, II, 2, 2. *something rare even then will rush to k.* III, 1, 21. *shall nothing benefit your k.* IV, 4, 514. *unthrifty to our k.* V, 2, 121. *hath by instinct k. from others' eyes that what he feared is chanced*, H4B I, 1, 86. *let us have k.* H6A II, 1, 4. *without the king's assent or k.* H8 III, 2, 310. 316. *call my thought a certain k.* Troil. IV, 1, 41. *I will not seal your k. with showing them*, Cor. II, 3, 115. *be innocent of the k.* Mcb. III, 2, 45. *from some k. and assurance*, Lr. III, 1, 41. *and to this hour no guess in k. which way they went*, Cymb. I, 1, 60. *thou shalt kneel and justify in k. she is thy very princess*, Per. V, 1, 219. With *of: let me the k. of my*

fault bear with me, As I, 3, 48. *if thou delay me not the k. of his chin*, III, 2, 222. *that upon k. of my parentage I may have welcome*, Shr. II, 96. *the certain k. of that truth*, John I, 1, 61. *has he had k. of it?* H8 V, 3, 4. *I shall ere long have k. of my success*, Cor. V, 1, 61.

2) the knowing a person, acquaintance: *if your k. be more*, Meas. III, 2, 156. *love talks with better k.*, and *k. with dearer love*, 159. 160. *I shall desire more love and k. of you*, As I, 2, 297. *I have a desire to hold my acquaintance with thee, or rather my k., that I may say in the default, he is a man I know*, All's II, 3, 241. *take you, as 'twere, some distant k. of him*, Hml. II, 1, 13. Euphemism for sexual commerce: *had I not brought the k. of your mistress home*, Cymb. II, 4, 51. *more particulars must justify my k.* 79. *k. of one's self* = either the knowing one's self, or consciousness: *I profit in the k. of myself*, Tw. V, 21. *would bear thee from the k. of thyself*, John V, 2, 35. *lose the k. of themselves*, Lr. IV, 6, 291. cf. *the k. of mine own desert*, Sonn. 49, 10. *K.* alone = consciousness: *to mope with his fat-brained followers so far out of his k.* H5 III, 7, 144 (so to lose all reason and reflection). *by the marks of sovereignty, k. and reason*, Lr. I, 4, 253. *poisoned hours had bound me up from mine own k.* Ant. II, 2, 91.

3) that which one knows, manner and degree of information: *from thine eyes my k. I derive*, Sonn. 14, 9. *some oracle must rectify our k.* Tp. V, 245. *shall you on your k. find this way?* Meas. IV, 1, 37. *a good opinion of my k.* As V, 2, 60. *say to the king the k. of the broil as thou didst leave it*, Mcb. I, 2, 6 (that which was known at that moment). *more than mortal k.* I, 5, 3. *dare not speak their k.* Ant. IV, 12, 6. *my k. touching her flight*, Cymb. III, 5, 99. *in my k.* = for aught I know: *that in your k. may by me be done*, Merch. I, 1, 159. *in mine own direct k. he is a most notable coward*, Alls III, 6, 9. *to my k. and on my k.*, in the same sense: R2 II, 3, 38; R3 I, 3, 109. All's IV, 3, 220. H4B V, 1, 46.

4) learning, mental accomplishment, skill, experience: *thou art as fair in k. as in hue*, Sonn. 82, 5. *if k. be the mark, to know thee shall suffice*, Pilgr. 63 and LLL IV, 2, 115. *less in your k. and your grace you show not than our earth's wonder*, Err. III, 2, 31. *that angel k.* LLL I, 1, 113. *where now his k. must prove ignorance*, II, 103. *how prove you that in the great heap of your k.?* As I, 2, 73. *O k. ill inhabited*, III, 3, 10. *if k. could be set up against mortality*, All's I, 1, 35. *ensconcing ourselves into seeming k.* II, 3, 5. *he is very great in k.* II, 5, 9. *feed your k. with viewing of the town*, Tw. III, 3, 41. *k. the wing wherewith we fly to heaven*, H6B IV, 7, 79. *be governed by your k.* Lr. IV, 7, 19. *I mine own gained k. should profane*, Oth. I, 3, 390. *being mature in k.* Ant. I, 4, 31. *leave unexecuted your own renowned k.* III, 7, 46. *which by my k. found*, Per. I, 2, 77. *your k.* III, 2, 46. With *in: he has no more k. in Hibocrates*, Wiv. III, 1, 66. *of great expedition and k. in the ancient wars*, H5 III, 2, 83. *the true k. he has in their disposition*, Cor. II, 2, 15. *her k. in killing creatures vile*, Cymb. V, 5, 251.

L.

L, the twelfth letter of the English alphabet: LLL IV, 2, 60.

L, the Latin figure denoting fifty: LLL IV, 2, 62.

La, an exclamation, 1) followed by *you,* = look, behold, there you have it: *la you, an you speak ill of the devil, how he takes it at heart,* Tw. III; 4, 111. *la you now, you hear: when she will take the rein, I let her run,* Wint. II, 3, 50.

2) iterated, = pooh: *La la la la! nothing doubting, says he?* Tim. III, 1, 22.

3) joined to terms of asseveration: *I thank you always with my heart, la, with my heart,* Wiv. I, 1, 86. *or else I would I might be hanged, la,* 266. *truly, I will not go first, truly, la,* 322. *you do yourself wrong, indeed, la,* 326. I, 4, 90. II, 2, 108. V, 5, 192. LLL V, 2, 414. H4B II, 1, 168. II, 4, 28. H5 III, 2, 93. 97. 121. IV, 7, 150. Troil. III, 1, 82. Cor. I, 3, 73. 100. Hml. IV, 5, 57. Ant. IV, 4, 8. Per. IV, 1, 77.

La, a musical note in Guido's scale: *ut, re, sol, la, mi, fa,* LLL IV, 2, 102. *E la mi,* Shr. III, 1, 78. *fa, sol, la, mi,* Lr. I, 2, 149.

Laban, the father-in-law of the patriarch Jacob: Merch. I, 3, 72. 79.

Label, a seal appended to a deed, as the custom was of old: *ere this hand, by thee to Romeo sealed, shall be the l. to another deed,* Rom. IV, 1, 57. Used for the deed itself: *I found this l. on my bosom,* Cymb. V, 5, 430.

Labelled, appended and annexed on a slip of paper: *l. to my will,* Tw. I, 5, 265.

Labeo (O. Edd. *Labio*) name in Caes. V, 3, 108.

Labienus, name in Ant. I, 2, 104.

Labour, subst. 1) toilsome work, painful exertion: *an unpractised swimmer with too much l. drowns for want of skill,* Lucr. 1099. *a charm joined to their suffered l.* Tp. I, 2, 231. *their l. delight in them sets off,* III, 1, 1. Meas. IV, 2, 69. Shr. V, 2, 149. Tw. III, 1, 73. Wint. IV, 4, 61. H4A IV, 3, 23. H4B IV, 4, 118. H5 II, 2, 37. H6C I, 4, 20. H8 I, 1, 25. Rom. IV, 5, 45. Mcb. I, 4, 44. II, 2, 38. Ant. I, 3, 93. II, 7, 105. IV, 14, 47. Cymb. III, 4, 107. III, 5, 168. Plur. *—s:* Tp. III, 1, 7. 14. H6B I, 1, 95. H6C V, 7, 20. Lr. I, 4, 7. *Hercules' —s:* Ado II, 1, 380. Shr. I, 2, 257. All's III, 4, 12 *(taken —s).* Cor. IV, 1, 18.

2) pains: *though I be o'er ears for my l.* Tp. IV, 214. *gave me nothing for my l.* Gent. I, 1, 104. *a mocker of my l.* As II, C, 14. R2 II, 3, 62. 64. Troil. I, 1, 70. 73. Tim. I, 1, 232. Mcb. II, 3, 55. Hml. II, 2, 83 *(well-took l.)* Lr. IV, 6, 274. Oth. IV, 1, 38. IV, 3, 81. Ant. IV, 14, 37. Per. I, 1, 66. *l. well bestowed,* Wiv. II, 1, 248. *ill bestowed,* Ado III, 2, 103. *to lose one's l.:* Wiv. II, 1, 247. Meas. V, 433. Err. V, 97. Merch. II, 7, 74. All's III, 5, 8. Wint. IV, 4, 787. Mcb. V, 8, 8. *to save l.:* Lucr. 1290. Err. IV, 1, 14. As II, 7, 8. H4A V, 4, 57. H5 IV, 3, 121. H8 II, 1, 3. Troil. III, 3, 241. Cor. I, 3, 90. Oth. V, 1, 101. *take it for your l.:* Gent. II, 1, 139. R2 V, 6, 41. H4A IV, 2, 7. Tim. I, 1, 213. Cymb. I, 5, 61. *there's for thy l.* H5 III, 6, 167.

3) any work: *till I have honoured you with some graver l.* Ven. Ded. 4. *you mar our l.* Tp. I, 1, 15.

shortly shall all my —s end, IV, 265. *bring this l. to an happy end,* John III, 2, 10. *I do not like that paying back, 'tis a double l.* H4A III, 3, 202. *with profitable l.* H5 IV, 1, 294. *a blessed l.* (peace-making) R3 II, 1, 52. Cor. I, 1, 104. Tim. I, 1, 152. Cymb. I, 6, 108. Per. II Prol. 19. II, 1, 56. 99.

4) the pangs of childbirth: *the queen's in l.* H8 V, 1, 18. *she'll with the l. end,* 20. *with news the time's with l.* Ant. III, 7, 81.

5) any pang or distress: *what labour is't to leave the thing we have not,* Compl. 239. *if lost, why then a grievous l. won,* Gent. I, 1, 33.

Labour, vb. 1) intr. a) to work hard, to toil, to make painful efforts: *our brains —ing for invention,* Sonn. 59, 3. *after you have —ed so hard,* H4B II, 2, 32. *I have —ed with all my wits,* H5 V, 2, 24. *all kind of natures that l. on the bosom of this sphere,* Tim. I, 1, 66. *—ed after him to the mountain's top,* I, 1, 86; cf. *you do climb up it now: look, how we l.* Lr. IV, 6, 2. Caes. V, 5, 42. Oth. II, 1, 189. Ant. II, 6, 14. *—ed* = fatigued, worn out: *whose —ed spirits crave harbourage,* John II, 232.

b) to endeavour, to take pains, to strive, to be intent: *the dire imagination she did follow this sound of hope doth l. to expel,* Ven. 976. *my sighs, like whirl-winds, l. hence to heave thee,* Lucr. 586. *in him the painter —ed with his skill to hide deceit,* 1506. *—ing in moe pleasures to bestow them,* Compl. 139. Meas. III, 1, 12. III, 2, 265. V, 396. Err. III, 2, 37. As I, 1, 146. V, 2, 62. All's II, 1, 121. IV, 4, 17. H6A II, 5, 80. H6B III, 1, 239. III, 2, 137. H8 V, 3, 33. Cor. II, 3, 235. Tim. III, 5, 26. Mcb. I, 3, 114 *(he —ed in his country's wreck,* = was intent on etc.). I, 4, 28. Hml. IV, 5, 211. V, 2, 34. Lr. III, 1, 16.

c) to work: *the —ing pioner,* Lucr. 1380. *l. in the quern,* Mids. II, 1, 36. *never —ed in their minds,* V, 73 (never did mental work). *to l. in his vocation,* H4A I, 2, 117. II, 1, 57. *l. for their own preferment,* H6B I, 1, 181. *the —ing spider,* III, 1, 339. *l. in thy vocation,* IV, 2, 17. *—ing men,* 19 (= workmen). *for your highness' good I ever —ed,* H8 III, 2, 191. *—ing for destiny,* Troil. IV, 5, 184. *a —ing day,* Caes. I, 1, 4. *there's no —ing in the winter,* Lr. II, 4, 69.

d) to suffer the pangs of childbirth: *when great things —ing perish in their birth,* LLL V, 2, 521. *in the birth of our own —ing breath,* Troil. IV, 4, 40. *what do you think the hour? —ing for nine,* Tim. III, 4, 8 (cf. *Nine). my Muse —s, and thus she is delivered,* Oth. II, 1, 128.

e) to suffer pain, to be in distress: *each passion —s so, that every present sorrow seemeth chief,* Ven. 969. *whom whilst I —ed of a love to see,* Err. I, 1, 131. *all descended to the —ing heart,* H6B III, 2, 163.

2) trans. to work, to strive to perform, to effect: *if your love can l. aught in sad invention,* Ado V, 1, 292. *to l. and effect one thing,* Shr. I, 1, 120. *—ed all I could to do him right,* R2 II, 3, 142. *he would l. my delivery,* R3 I, 4, 253. (Perhaps also Cor. II, 3, 235: *we —ed no impediment between,* = we strove to remove all impediments). *you are her —ed scholar,* Per. II, 3, 17 (a scholar formed by the hand of Art herself).

Labourer, 1) one who works and is not idle: *to give some —s room,* All's I, 2, 67. *make the night joint l. with the day,* Hml. I, 1, 78.

2) one who does service in the field: *I am a true l.* As III, 2, 77.

Laboursome, 1) (not in Ff) assiduous: *he hath wrung from me my leave by l. petition,* Hml. I, 2, 59.

2) elaborate, requiring much pains and industry: *your l. and dainty trims, wherein you made great Juno angry,* Cymb. III, 4, 167.

Labyrinth, a maze: Ven. 684. H6A V, 3, 188. Troil. II, 3, 2.

Lace, subst. 1) an ornament consisting of textures of thread: *l. for your cape,* Wint. IV, 4, 323. *sold many —s,* H6B IV, 2, 49. cf. *Tawdry-lace.*

2) a plaited string to fasten women's clothes: *cut my l.* Wint. III, 2, 174. R3 IV, 1, 34. Ant. I, 3, 71.

Lace, vb. 1) to fasten with a string through eyelet holes: *one* (boot) *buckled, another —d,* Shr. III, 2, 46.

2) to adorn with a texture sewed on; properly and metaphorically: *that sin should l. itself with his society,* Sonn. 67, 4. *—d with silver,* Ado III, 4, 20. *envious streaks do l. the severing clouds,* Rom. III, 5, 8. *his silver skin —d with his golden blood,* Mcb. II, 3, 118. *white and azure — d with blue of heaven's own tinct,* Cymb. II, 2, 22.

Laced mutton, according to glossarists and commentators a cant term for a prostitute; but probably only = woman's flesh, a petticoat, a smock: *she, a l., gave me, a lost mutton, nothing for my labour,* Gent. I, 1, 102.

Lacedaemon, another name for Sparta: Tim. II, 2, 160. III, 5, 60.

'Lack = alack, alas: Cymb. IV, 2, 374. V, 3, 59.

Lack, subst. the state of being without something, want: *our l. is nothing but our leave,* Mcb. IV, 3, 237. With *of:* Sonn. 30, 3. Meas. V, 68. 478. Merch. IV, 1, 162. As III, 2, 29. Wint. IV, 4, 365. H4B V, 5, 71. H8 I, 2, 35. Cor. V, 6, 29. Tim. II, 2, 226. IV, 3, 284. V, 1, 150. Hml. II, 2, 202. Cymb. II, 3, 114. II, 4, 22. *for l. of*: Mids. II, 1, 100. As II, 6, 17. IV, 1, 74. Shr. IV, 3, 9. All's I, 1, 23. H5 III, 1, 21. IV, 2, 23.

Lack, vb. 1) tr. a) to want, not to have; absol.: *all hearts which I by —ing have supposed dead,* Sonn. 31, 2. *thou shalt l.* Wiv. I, 3, 96 (= be in want; Pistol's speech). *and l. not to lose still,* All's I, 3, 210. Transitively: Ven. 136. 299. 600. Sonn. 52, 14. 86, 14. 106, 14. 127, 11. 132, 14. Phoen. 16. Tp. II, 1, 137. Gent. III, 1, 69. Wiv. IV, 6, 53. Meas. I, 2, 110. 152. Ado III, 4, 49. IV, 1, 182. 221. LLL IV, 3, 55. 251. Mids. II, 1, 223. Merch. I, 1, 37. III, 4, 62. IV, 1, 162. As I, 2, 259. I, 3, 98. III, 2, 337. 341. IV, 3, 165. All's I, 1, 11. I, 2, 59. II, 1, 20. III, 4, 19. V, 3, 193. Tw. I, 5, 38. III, 4, 332. Wint. II, 1, 157. H4A II, 4, 408. H4B IV, 1, 216. V, 3, 73. H6B III, 1, 345. Tim. II, 2, 124. 153. Hml. II, 1, 117. Lr. IV, 4, 13. Per. V Prol. 9 etc. *a hundred —ing one,* H6B IV, 3, 9 (= ninety nine).

b) to want, to need: *love —ed a dwelling and made him her place,* Compl. 82. *they l. no direction,* Wiv. III, 3, 19. *—s a helper,* Meas. IV, 2, 10. *you three fools —ed me fool to make up the mess,* LLL IV, 3, 206. *if a hart do l. a hind,* As III, 2, 107. Tw. I, 3, 85. I, 5, 304. Wint. IV, 4, 126. 229. H4B I, 2, 86. III, 2, 119. Rom. I, 3, 88. Lr. IV, 6, 119.

c) to perceive not to have, to feel the want of, to miss: *I cannot l. thee two hours,* As IV, 1, 182. *they that least lend it you shall l. you first,* All's I, 2, 68. *loved when I am —ed,* Cor. IV, 1, 15. *your noble friends do l. you,* Mcb. III, 4, 84. Oth. III, 3, 318. Ant. I, 4, 44. *what l. you?* = what ails you? John IV, 1, 48.

2) intr. to be wanting: *here —s but your mother for to say amen,* Tit. IV, 2, 44. *what so poor a man may do shall not l.* Hml. I, 5, 186. With *of: what hour now? I think it —s of twelve,* Hml. I, 4, 3 (= it is not yet twelve).

Lackbeard, one beardless: Ado V, 1, 195.

Lackbrain, a stupid fellow: H4A II, 3, 17.

Lackey, see *Lacquey.*

Lack-linen, having no shirt: H4B II, 4, 134.

Lack-love, one insensible to love: Mids. II, 2, 77.

Lack-lustre, wanting brightness: As II, 7, 21.

Lacquey or **Lackey,** subst. an attending servant, a footboy: Lucr. 967. As III, 2, 314. Shr. III, 2, 66. All's IV, 3, 323. H4A III, 1, 158. H5 III, 7, 121. IV, 1, 289. IV, 2, 26. IV, 4, 79. H8 V, 2, 18. Troil. V, 10, 33. Adjectively: *base l. peasants,* R3 V, 3, 317.

Lacquey or **Lackey,** vb. to follow like a servant: *goes to and back, —ing the varying tide,* Ant. I, 4, 46 (O. Edd. *lacking*).

Lacy, name in H6B IV, 2, 47.

Lad, 1) a boy, a stripling: Pilgr. 45. Mids. III, 2, 440. Tw. I, 4, 29. Wint. I, 2, 63. John IV, 1, 8. H6C IV, 6, 70. V, 4, 7. V, 5, 32. Cor. V, 6, 112. Cymb. IV, 2, 262. IV, 4, 52. V, 3, 19. V, 5, 101. 121.

2) fellow: Tp. V, 255. Mids. IV, 2, 25. Tw. IV, 2, 139. H4A II, 4, 13. 15. H4B V, 3, 21. H5 IV, 1, 45. Tit. IV, 2, 119. Oth. II, 3, 57. Used as a familiar compellation: Wiv. I, 3, 42. 82. III, 1, 113. Shr. I, 1, 168. IV, 1, 113. V, 2, 37. 181. Tw. III, 2, 58. Wint. IV, 4, 227. 231. H4A I, 2, 1. 44. 47. 112. 138. II, 4, 100. 304. 306. 400. III, 3, 102. 198. R3 I, 3, 355. Tit. II, 1, 132. IV, 2, 121. Hml. II, 2, 230. Lr. I, 4, 153. Oth. II, 1, 20. Ant. IV, 4, 25.

Ladder, an instrument by means of which one climbs, with steps of wood or cords: Gent. II, 4, 182. II, 6, 33. III, 1, 40. 117. 122. 126. 128. 152. R2 V, 1, 55. H4A I, 2, 42. I, 3, 166. H4B III, 1, 70. Troil. I, 3, 102. Cor. IV, 4, 22. Tit. V, 1, 53. Rom. II, 5, 75. Caes. II, 1, 22. 25.

Ladder-tackle, a rope-ladder in a ship: Per. IV, 1, 61.

Lade, vb. to draw, to drain: *he'll l. it* (the sea) *dry,* H6C III, 2, 139.

Laden, loaded: Ven. 1022. Tit. I, 36. Ant. III, 11, 5. V, 2, 123.

Lading, load, cargo: Merch. III, 1, 3. Tit. I, 72. Per. I, 2, 49.

Lady, fem. to *Lord,* 1) mistress, the woman who presides over an estate or family: *where their dear governess and l. lies,* Lucr. 443. *her —'s sorrow,* 1221. Mids. II, 2, 18. Tw. I, 5, 177. Cymb. III, 5, 84 etc. *she is the hopeful l. of my earth,* Rom. I, 2, 15. *of all these bounds we make thee l.* Lr. I, 1, 67. *My l.* = the mistress of the household: *my l. will hang thee,* Tw. I, 5, 3. 174. II, 3, 28. 80 etc. *my dear l.* and *my good l.* = my patroness: *Fortune, now my dear l.* Tp. I, 2, 179. *she's my good l. and will conceive the worst of me,* Cymb. III, 3, 158.

2) wife to a man of distinction: *I would make thee my l.* Wiv. III, 3, 54. 55. *I must be thy l.* Mids.

II, 1, 64. *I know his l.* All's III, 5, 58. *your l. is forth-coming,* H6B II, 1, 179. *a l. to the worthiest sir,* Cymb. I, 6, 160. *to fight against my —'s kingdom,* V, 1, 19 etc.

3) any woman of distinction: *I should be a pitiful l.* Wiv. III, 3, 56. *like my —'s eldest son,* Ado II, 1, 10. *so lords call —ies,* Shr. Ind. 2, 113. *some men must love my l. and some Joan,* LLL III, 207. *make me my l. thy wife,* H4B II, 1, 100 etc. Before names and titles: *dost thou know my l. Silvia?* Gent. II, 1, 44. *my L. Tongue,* Ado II, 1, 284 (Ff. *this l.*). *writ to my l. mother,* All's IV, 3, 102. *L. Marquess Dorset,* H8 V, 3, 169. *the l. widow of Vitruvio,* Rom. I, 2, 69. *your l. mother,* III, 5, 39. *dear l. daughter,* Cymb. I, 1, 154. *the l. abbess,* Err. V, 166. *the L. Beatrice,* Ado II, 1, 243. 382. *the L. Hero,* II, 3, 88. III, 3, 154. IV, 2, 51. V, 1, 243. Tw. III, 1, 36. John II, 540. H6B I, 1, 47. H6C II, 6, 90. III, 3, 128. 174. H8 III, 2, 403. Troil. IV, 2, 68. Cor. I, 3, 29 etc. In compellations: *no, l., no,* Ven. 785. *Ceres, most bounteous l.* Tp. IV, 60. *I know none of that name, l.* Ado I, 1, 32. 91. Merch. II, 1, 8. 31. III, 2, 266. Tw. I, 2, 2. Hml. III, 4, 115. 180. Ant. I, 2, 84. III, 4, 25. III, 6, 90. V, 2, 48 etc.

4) any woman, called so in complaisance and courtesy: Lucr. Arg. 10. Sonn. 106, 4. Tp. III, 1, 39. V, 196. Gent. III, 1, 81. IV, 1, 48. Meas. I, 2, 151. III, 1, 206. Err. V, 134. Ant. III, 4, 12 etc. *holiday and l. terms,* H4A I, 3, 46 (= becoming women). *that I some l. trifles have reserved,* Ant. V, 2, 165.

5) a woman beloved, mistress: *that I had my l. at this bay,* Pilgr. 155. *ringing in thy —'s ear,* 326. *thy former l.* Mids. III, 2, 457. Gent. II, 4, 125. 159. 205. III, 2, 83. IV, 2, 80. LLL IV, 3, 258. Tw. I, 4, 41. H5 III, 7, 101. Rom. II, 2, 10. II, 4, 42 etc.

6) the holy Virgin: *by 'r l.* Wiv. I, 1, 28. H8 I, 3, 46. *our L. help my lord,* LLL II, 98. *O well a day, L.* H5 II, 1, 39. *our L. gracious,* H6A I, 2, 74. *God's L. dear,* Rom. II, 5, 63. *Got's lords and his —ies,* Wiv. I, 1, 243 (Evans' speech). *Berlady,* or *birlady,* or *byrlady* = by our lady (M. Edd. *by'r lady*): Ado III, 3, 82. 89. III, 4, 82. H4A II, 4, 50. 329. 467. III, 1, 235. H4B V, 3, 93. R3 II, 3, 4. Tit. IV, 4, 48. Rom. I, 5, 35. Hml. II, 2, 445. III, 2, 140. Oth. III, 3, 74 (Ff *trust me*) etc.

7) the person performing the principal female part in a play: *to see the l. the epilogue,* As Epil. 1. *the l. shall say her mind freely,* Hml. II, 2, 338.

8) a name of dogs: *L., my brach,* H4A III, 1, 240. *L. the brach,* Lr. I, 4, 125.

9) the burden of a certain song: *there dwelt a man in Babylon, l., l.* Tw. II, 3, 84. Rom. II, 4, 151.

Lady-bird, a term of endearment used to Juliet by the nurse in Rom. I, 3, 3 [Cp. Germ. "Goldkäfer"].

Ladyship, the title given to a lady: Gent. I, 2, 66. 81. II, 1, 113. Ado I, 1, 134. LLL II, 101. IV, 2, 139. V, 2, 559. Merch. III, 4, 42. As I, 2, 120. All's I, 3, 19. Tw. I, 5, 89. John III, 1, 119. H6A II, 3, 12. 26. H6B I, 4, 4. H8 I, 4, 47. Rom. III, 5, 107. Hml. II, 2, 445. Oth. II, 1, 106. III, 4, 168 etc.

Lady-smocks, flowers of Cardamine pratensis: LLL V, 2, 905.

Laertes, name of 1) the father of Ulysses: Tit. I, 380. 2) the son of Polonius in Hml. I, 2, 42 etc.

Lafeu, name in All's II, 1, 90. III, 6, 112. IV, 3, 353. V, 2, 2. V, 3, 150.

Lag, subst. the lowest class; only by conjecture in Tim. III, 6, 90; O. Edd. *legge.*

Lag, late, tardy: *came too l. to see him buried,* R3 II, 1, 90. With *of,* = later than, behind: *some fourteen moonshines l. of a brother,* Lr. I, 2, 6.

Lag, vb. 1) to move slowly: *four —ing winters,* R2 I, 3, 214.

2) to stay behind, to straggle: *to hie as fast as —ing fowls before the northern blast,* Lucr. 1335. *makes him l. behind,* H6A III, 3, 34.

Lag-end, the latter end, the last part: *the l. of my life,* H4A V, 1, 24. *wear away the l. of their lewdness,* H8 I, 3, 35.

Lake, a large collection of inland water: Tp. IV, 183. V, 33. H4B II, 4, 170. H6B I, 4, 42. Tit. IV, 3, 43. Lr. III, 6, 8.

Lakin, the holy Virgin: *by'r l.* Tp. III, 3, 1. Mids. III, 1, 14 (O. Edd. *berlakin;* see *Berlady* sub *Lady*).

Lamb, the young of a sheep: Ven. 1098. Lucr. 677. 737. 878. Sonn. 96, 9. Gent. IV, 4, 97. Meas. V, 300. Ado I, 1, 15. III, 3, 75. LLL II, 220. IV, 1, 91. Merch. I, 3, 89. IV, 1, 74. As III, 2, 81. Shr. III, 2, 159. Tw. V, 133. Wint. I, 2, 67. John IV, 1, 80. R2 II, 1, 174. H5 III, 7, 35. H6A I, 2, 76. V, 4, 30. H6B III, 1, 55. 71. 77. IV, 2, 87. H6C I, 1, 242. I, 4, 5. II, 5, 75. IV, 8, 49. R3 IV, 2, 22. 50. 228. Troil III, 2, 200. Cor. II, 1, 9. 12. Tit. II, 3, 223. IV, 2 137. Rom. II, 5, 45. III, 2, 76. Tim. IV, 3, 331. Caes. IV, 3, 110. Mcb. IV, 3, 16. 54. Cymb. I, 6, 49. III, 4, 99. Used as a term of endearment: Troil. IV, 4, 25. Rom. I, 3, 3. IV, 5, 2.

Lambert, name of a saint: *upon Saint —'s day,* R2 I, 1, 199 (the seventeenth of September).

Lambkin, the diminutive of lamb; a term of endearment: H4B V, 3, 121. H5 II, 1, 133.

Lamb-skin, the skin of a lamb: Meas. III, 2, 9.

Lame, adj. 1) crippled, disabled in the feet: Lucr. 902. Tp. II, 2, 34. LLL V, 2, 291. John III, 1, 46. H6B II, 1, 95. 162. H8 I, 3, 11. Rom. II, 5, 4. Used of verses: *the feet were l.* As III, 2, 178. *on the l. feet of my rhyme,* Per. IV Prol. 48.

2) disabled in any manner, impaired in strength: *made l. by fortune's dearest spite,* Sonn. 37, 3. 9. *youth is nimble, age is l.* Pilgr. 162. *when service should in my old limbs lie l.* As II, 3, 41. *l. of sense,* Oth. I, 3, 63. *most l. and impotent conclusion,* II, 1, 162.

Lame, vb. to cripple, to disable: *when he hath —d me* (with blows) Err. IV, 4, 40 (cf. LLL V, 2, 291). *l. me with reasons,* As I, 3, 6. 8. *which —s report to follow it,* Wint. V, 2, 62. *I l. the foot of our design,* Cor. IV, 7, 7. *—ing the shrine of Venus;* or *straightpight Minerva,* Cymb. V, 5, 163 (making Venus and Minerva appear lame).

Lamely, in a halting manner, imperfectly: *l. writ,* Gent. II, 1, 97. *the feet stood l. in the verse,* As III, 2, 180. *so l. and unfashionable,* R3 I, 1, 22. *their limbs may halt as l. as their manners,* Tim. IV, 1, 25

Lameness, an impaired state of the limbs: Sonn. 89, 3. Lr. II, 4, 166.

Lament, subst. grief uttered in complaints, lamentation: Lucr. 1616. R2 IV, 296. H6A I, 1, 103. R3 II, 2, 67 (Ff *complaints*). Tit. III, 1, 219. III, 2, 46.

Lament, vb. 1) to bewail, to deplore; followed by an accus.: Lucr. 1500. Gent. III, 1, 242. Ado IV, 1, 218. Mids. III, 1, 205. As I, 2, 202. Wint. IV, 2,

28. V, 2, 93. V, 3, 135. R2 I, 3, 58. IV, 302. V, 6, 47. H4B II, 3, 47. H6B III, 2, 58. H6C I, 4, 85. V, 4, 38. R3 I, 2, 3. 32. II, 2, 9. Tit. II, 3, 205. Caes. I, 2, 55. Ant. I, 2, 174. V, 1, 29. V, 2, 366. Cymb. IV, 2, 193.

2) abs. to wail, to express grief: Lucr. 1079. 1465. Gent. III, 2, 82. H4B V, 3, 112. R3 I, 2, 262. II, 2, 43. Cor. IV, 2, 52. Tit. III, 1, 27. III, 2, 20. Rom. IV, 5, 82. Caes. II, 3, 13. Hml. III, 2, 208. Ant. V, 1, 40. Per. IV, 2, 72. Followed by *for*: Gent. III, 1, 241. Wiv. III, 5, 44. H6B IV, 4, 22. H8 II, 3, 12. By *at*: *the miserable change l. nor sorrow at,* Ant. IV, 15, 52.

Lamentable, 1) to be lamented, pitiful, causing pity or sorrow: Lucr. Arg. 17. 1373. Gent. IV, 4, 171. LLL V, 2, 273. Mids. I, 2, 11. R2 V, 1, 44. H5 II, 1, 125. H6B IV, 2, 86. Rom. II, 4, 32. IV, 5, 17. V, 3, 146. Lr. IV, 1, 5. Cymb. I, 4, 20. I, 6, 85.

2) pertaining to grief, expressing sorrow: *that l. rheum* (viz tears) John III, 1, 22.

Lamentably, pitifully: Wint. IV, 4, 190. Ant. III, 10, 26.

Lamentation, expression of sorrow, audible grief: Lucr. 1829. Meas. III, 1, 237. LLL V, 2, 819. All's I, 1, 64. H5 V Chor. 36. R3 I, 2, 9. II, 2, 66. 88. IV, 4, 14. Cor. IV, 6, 34. Rom. III, 2, 120. III, 3, 154.

Lamentings, lamentations: Mcb. II, 3, 61.

Lammas-eve, the day before Lammas-tide: Rom. I, 3, 17. 21.

Lammas-tide, the first of August: Rom. I, 3, 15.

Lamord (Qq) or **Lamound** (Ff), name in Hml. IV, 7, 93.

Lamp, 1) artificial light made with oil and a wick: Ven. 755. Err. III, 2, 98. H4A III, 3, 30. Rom. I, 4, 45. II, 2, 20. Ant. I, 4, 5. Per. III, 1, 63. Synonymous to torch: *Hymen's —s,* Tp. IV, 23. Used as the emblem of life: *my oil-dried l.* R2 I, 3, 221. *to feed for aye her l. and flames of love,* Troil. III, 2, 167. *our l. is spent, it's out,* Ant. IV, 15, 85.

2) any thing shining; a) a luminary: *from whom* (the sun) *each l. and shining star doth borrow,* Ven. 861. All's II, 1, 167. H6C II, 1, 31. Mcb. II, 4, 7. b) the eye: *four such —s,* Ven. 489. 1128. Err. V, 315. H6A II, 5, 8.

Lampass, a disease of horses, consisting in an excrescence of flesh above the teeth: Shr. III, 2, 52.*

Lancaster, English dukedom hereditary in the family of John of Gaunt: R2 I, 1, 1. 135. I, 3, 35. II, 1, 71. H4A III, 1, 8. III, 2, 171. H4B I, 1, 134.* H6A II, 5, 102. H6B I, 1, 244. 257. II, 2, 14. H6C I, 1, 23. V, 5, 24. R3 I, 2, 4 etc. etc.

Lance, subst. a spear: Ven. 103. Ado III, 1, 64. LLL V, 2, 650. 657. Shr. V, 2, 173. John V, 2, 157. R2 I, 1, 200. I, 3, 74. 101. 103. H4B IV, 1, 51. H6A I, 1, 122. III, 2, 50 (*break a l.*). 134 (*couched l.*). H6C II, 3, 16. R3 V, 3, 143. Troil. I, 3, 283. Cor. I, 1, 204. Lr. IV, 6, 170. V, 3, 50. Cymb. V, 3, 34. Per. II, 2, 51.

Lance, vb. to pierce, to cut: *whose hand soever —d their tender hearts,* R3 IV, 4, 224 (O. Edd. *lanched*). Lr. II, 1, 54 (Ff *latch'd*). = to cut in order to cure: *he bites, but —th not the sore,* R2 I, 3, 303. *we do l. diseases in our bodies,* Ant. V, 1, 36 (O. Edd. *launch*).

Lanch, see *Lance, vb.*

Land, subst. 1) the solid part of the surface of the earth, in distinction from the sea: Tp. II, 1, 122 Err. IV, 1, 91. LLL IV, 2, 7. Mids. II, 1, 132. Wint. V, 1, 144. R2 I, 3, 252. Cor. V, 4, 58. Mcb. I, 3, 33. Cymb. I, 6, 34 etc. As for *narrow —s* in Err. IV, 2, 38 see *Lane.* At *l.*: Tit. IV, 3, 9. Oth. II, 1, 5. Ant. II, 6, 25. III, 7, 54. IV, 5, 3. Cymb. III, 4, 193. *by l.:* Tp. V, 220. Ant. II, 2, 164. II, 6, 90. 93. 97. III, 7 43. 59. III, 8, 3. III, 13, 169. IV, 10, 2. Cymb. II, 4, 27. *by sea and l.:* Shr. V, 2, 149. Wint. III, 3, 85. Caes. I, 3, 87. Ant. I, 4, 78. III, 6, 54. *on l.:* Tp. III, 3, 10. V, 217. *o'er* and *over l.* LLL V, 2, 309. Cymb. III, 5, 8.

2) country (fem. in R2 II, 1, 57): Mids. II, 1, 90. Wint. III, 3, 11. IV, 4, 8. John II, 25. IV, 2, 7. 143. R2 II, 1, 57. H5 I, 2, 44. H6B I, 1, 77. 176. I, 3, 177. II, 4, 29. 43. H6C II, 6, 91. R3 II, 3, 11. 30. H8 III, 2, 284. Mcb. IV, 2, 1. Hml. I, 1, 72. 107 etc. cf. *Fairy-land. Holy Land:* R2 V, 6, 49. H4A I, 1, 48. H4B III, 1, 108. IV, 5, 211. Metaphorical use: *her bare breast, the heart of all her l.* Lucr. 439. *in this fleshly l.* John IV, 2, 245.

3) ground, soil: *ear so barren a l.* Ven. Ded. 6. *on this green l. answer your summons,* Tp. IV, 130. R2 III, 2, 212. H4A I, 3, 35. III, 1, 77. H4B IV, 3, 129. H8 I, 3, 56. Ant. III, 11, 1.

4) landed property, real estate: Compl. 138. Tp. II, 1, 152. Gent. II, 7, 87. Wiv. V, 5, 246. Merch. IV, 1, 310. As I, 1, 107. III, 1, 9. V, 2, 43. V, 4, 170. Shr. II, 118. 122. 126. 372. 374. 375. All's I, 3, 47. Tw. II, 4, 85. Wint. IV, 3, 104. John I, 70. H4A II, 4, 394. H4B III, 2, 352. H6A IV, 3, 53. H6B I, 3, 89. H6C IV, 6, 55. Lr. I, 4, 148 etc.

Land, vb. 1) tr. to set on shore: Tp. I, 2, 221. V, 161. John II, 59. H6C III, 3, 205. IV, 1, 132.

2) intr. to come to shore: Lucr. 336. R2 III, 3, 3. H5 V Chor. 13. Ant. II, 2, 224. Per. I, 3, 34. *we have —ed,* Wint. III, 3, 3. H8 I, 4, 54. *are —ed,* Wint. II, 3, 196. John IV, 2, 130. R3 IV, 4, 535. Lr. III, 7, 3. IV, 2, 4. Cymb. II, 4, 18. IV, 3, 25.

Land-carrack, the seaman Iago's term for a prize made by land: Oth. I, 2, 50.

Land-damn, a misprint of O. Edd. in Wint. II, 1, 143, which has been productive of much misinterpretation and many improbable conjectures. According to some, it means to banish from the land; to others, to stop one's urine; to others still, to set breast-deep in the earth and thus cause to die of hunger. Hanmer conjectured land-damn, Farmer laudanum, Collier lamback etc. Perhaps we ought to read: *would I knew the villain, I would — Lord, damn him!* *

Landed, having an estate in land: *well l.* Wiv. IV, 4, 86. *a l. squire,* John I, 177.

Landfish, a fish on land, one dumb like a fish: Troil. III, 3, 264.

Landless, having no estate, poor: John I, 177. Hml. I, 1, 98 (Qq *lawless*).

Landlord, the owner of an estate: *the true gouty l. which doth owe them,* Compl. 140. *l. of England art thou now, not king,* R2 II, 1, 113. *put yourself under his shrowd, the universal l.* Ant. III, 13, 72.

Landmen, land-soldiers: Ant. IV, 3, 11.

Land-rakers, vagabonds: H4A II, 1, 81 (Ff *footland-rakers,* Qq *footland rakers;* M. Edd. *foot land-rakers*).

Land-rat, a rat living on land: Merch. I, 3, 23.

Land-service, a word used improperly by the

clown in Wint. and by Falstaff: *and then for the l.* Wint. III, 3, 96 (the mischief happening on land). *my learned counsel in the laws of this l.* H4B I, 2, 154 (the annoyances attending a law-suit of this kind).

Land-thieves, thieves (or rather robbers) on land: Merch. I, 3, 24.

Lane, a narrow passage, in towns as well as in the country: *I'll go with thee to the —'s end,* Meas. IV, 3, 188. *attended him on bridges, stood in —s,* H4A IV, 3, 70. *three times did Richard mak⁴ a l. to me,* H6C I, 4, 9 (a way through the enemies). *the l. is guarded,* Cymb. V, 2, 12. V, 3, 7. 13. 18. 52. 57. Infested by thieves and robbers: *one that countermands the passages of alleys, creeks and narrow —s,* Err. IV, 2, 38 (O. Edd. *lans,* M. Edd. for the sake of the rhyme *lands,* which is perhaps an obsolete form of the word). *every —'s end yields a careful man work,* Wint. IV, 4, 701. *such as stand in narrow —s,* R2 V, 3, 8. *front them in the narrow l.* H4A II, 2, 63. In Caes. III, 1, 39 O. Edd. *lane,* M. Edd. *law* or *line.*

Langley: *Edmund L. Duke of York,* H6A II, 5, 85. H6B II, 2, 15. 46.

Langton: *Stephen L.,* chosen archbishop of Canterbury, John III, 1, 143.

Language, 1) expression of thoughts: *and kissing speaks, with lustful l. broken,* Ven. 47. *there was l. in their gesture,* Wint. V, 2, 15. *there's l. in her eye,* Troil. IV, 5, 55.

2) expression of thoughts by words: Tp. I, 2, 363. 365. II, 2, 86. Ado IV, 1, 98. All's II, 1, 20. IV, 1, 77. H8 V, 1, 158. Tim. V, 1, 223.

3) the peculiar tongue of a nation: Tp. I, 2, 428. II, 2, 69. Meas. I, 2, 23. LLL V, 1, 40. V, 2, 175. Shr. II, 82. All's II, 3, 197. IV, 1, 3. 18. Tw. I, 3, 27. R2 I, 3, 159. H4A II, 4, 21. III, 1, 208. H4B Ind. 7. IV, 4, 69. H8 III, 1, 44. Rom. I, 2, 64. Per. IV, 4, 6. *choughs' l.* All's IV, 1, 22.

4) style, manner of expression: Tp. II, 1, 211. Meas. II, 4, 140. Wint. II, 1, 85. III, 2, 81. H5 III, 6, 118. H6B IV, 9, 45. H8 I, 2, 27. III, 2, 22. Cor. III, 1, 322. Cymb. III, 3, 74. V, 5, 294.

Languageless, unable to speak, dumb: Troil. III, 3, 264.

Languish, subst. a lingering disease: *one desperate grief cures with another's l.* Rom. I, 2, 49. *death that rids our dogs of l.* Ant. V, 2, 42.

Languish, vb. 1) to sink and pine away: As II, 1, 35. Wint. II, 3, 17. Oth. III, 3, 43. Cymb. I, 1, 156. I, 5, 9. Per. I, 2, 31. With *of: what is it the king —es of?* All's I, 1, 37.

2) to long without gratification, to pine away for love: Ven. 603. Sonn. 145, 3. Mids. II, 2, 29. With *for: l. for assured bondage,* Cymb. I, 6, 72.

Languishings, lingering disease: *the desperate l. whereof the king is rendered lost,* All's I, 3, 235.

Languishment, state of pining; 1) in sorrow: Lucr. 1130. 1141. 2) in love: Tit. II, 1, 110.

Languor, state of pining: *my heart's deep l.* Tit. III, 1, 13.

Lank, adj. 1) lax and loose from emptiness, not filled up: *the clergy's bags are l. and lean with thy extortions,* H6B I, 3, 132.

2) shrunk, fallen away: *with l. and lean discoloured cheek,* Lucr. 708. *about her l. and all o'erteemed loins a blanket,* Hml. II, 2, 531.

Lank, vb. to shrink, to fall away: *thy cheek so much as —ed not,* Ant. I, 4, 71.

Lank-lean, shrunk, fallen away: *their gesture sad investing l. cheeks,* H5 IV Chor. 26.

Lanthorn (O. Edd.) or **Lantern** (some M. Edd.) 1) a transparent case for a candle: Wiv. V, 5, 82. Ado III, 3, 25. Mids. III, 1, 61. V, 136. 243. 248. 251. 262. 265. H4A II, 1, 38. III, 3, 29. H4B I, 2, 55 (quibbling with *horn*). H6B II, 3, 25 (*my guide and l. to my feet*).

2) a turret full of windows, by means of which cathedrals are illuminated: *a grave? O, no! a l., slaughtered youth,* Rom. V, 3, 84.

Lap, subst. the seat formed by a female body in sitting or lying down: Ado V, 2, 104. H4A III, 1, 215. 231. H4B V, 3, 110 (*lay thy head in Furies' l.*) cf. H6A V, 3, 26. H6B III, 2, 390. H6C III, 2, 148. Tit. IV, 3, 64. Rom. I, 1, 220. Tim. IV, 3, 387. Mcb. I, 3, 4. Hml. III, 2, 119. 121. Oth. IV, 3, 89. Ant. II, 1, 37. Used metaphorically of any delightful place: *or from their proud l. pluck them* (flowers) *where they grew,* Sonn. 98, 8. *frosts fall in the fresh l. of the crimson rose,* Mids. II, 1, 108. *the fresh green l. of fair King Richard's land,* R2 III, 3, 47. *the violets that strew the green l. of the new come spring,* V, 2, 47.

Lap, vb. to wrap up, to envelop: *all thy friends are —ed in lead,* Pilgr. 396. *he did l. me in his own garments,* R3 II, 1, 115. *—ed in proof,* Mcb. I, 2, 54. *—ed in a most curious mantle,* Cymb. V, 5, 360.

Lap, vb. to drink by licking, as a dog or cat: Tp. II, 1, 288. R3 IV, 4, 50. Tim. III, 6, 95.

Lapland, a country in the north of Europe: *L. sorcerers,* Err. IV, 3, 11.

Lapse, subst. moral decay: *I will throw thee from my care for ever into the staggers and the careless l. of youth and ignorance,* All's II, 3, 170.

Lapse, vb. to fall, to offend, to sin (in both passages used of the sin of lying): *all the size that verity would without —ing suffer,* Cor. V, 2, 19. *to l. in fulness is sorer than to lie for need,* Cymb. III, 6, 12.

Lapsed, surprised, taken in the act (cf. the Low German *belapsen*): *if I be l. in this place, I shall pay dear,* Tw. III, 3, 36. *do you not come your tardy son to chide, that, l. in time and passion, lets go by the important acting of your dread command?* Hml. III, 4, 107, i. e. who, surprised by you in a time and passion fit for the execution of your command, lets them go by.

Lapwing, the bird Vanellus, alias peewit: *'tis my familiar sin with maids to seem the l. and to jest, tongue far from heart,* Meas. I, 4, 32*; cf. *far from her nest the l. cries away,* Err. IV, 2, 27. *Beatrice like a l. runs close by the ground,* Ado III, 1, 24. *this l. runs away with the shell on his head,* Hml. V, 2, 193.

Lard, 1) to fatten: *Falstaff sweats to death and —s the lean earth,* H4A II, 2, 116. *it is the pasture —s the brother's sides,* Tim. IV, 3, 12. cf. *Enlard.*

2) to enrich, to garnish: *the mirth so —ed with my matter,* Wiv. IV, 6, 14. *in which array, brave soldier, doth he lie, —ing the plain,* H5 IV, 6, 8. *wit —ed with malice,* Troil. V, 1, 63. *—ed with sweet flowers,* Hml. IV, 5, 37. *an exact command, —ed with many several sorts of reasons,* V, 2, 20.

Larder, the room where meat and other articles of food are kept: H8 V, 4, 5.

Large, 1) of great size or dimensions: *whose will is l. and spacious,* Sonn. 135, 5 (quibbling). *my library* *was dukedom l. enough*, Tp. I, 2, 110. *the world's l. tongue*, LLL V, 2, 852 (= the l. world's tongue). *thy fair l. ears*, Mids. IV, 1, 4. *the l. composition of this man*, John I, 88. *this little abstract doth contain that l. which died in Geffrey*, II, 101. *here's a l. mouth*, II, 457. *my l. kingdom for a little grave*, R2 III, 3, 153. *l. proportion of his limbs*, H6A II, 3, 21. *the l. Achilles*, Troil. I, 3, 162. *the world's l. spaces*, II, 2, 162. *his l. and portly size*, IV, 5, 162. *our l. temples*, Cor. III, 3, 36. *l. cicatrices*, II, 1, 164; cf. *l. hurts*, Tim. III, 5, 109.

2) extensive, reaching far, going a great way, not confined within narrow bounds: *take heed of this l. privilege*, Sonn. 95, 13; cf. Meas. I, 4, 2. *whose will is l.* Sonn. 135, 5 (quibbling). *as l. a charter as the wind, to blow on whom I please*, As II, 7, 48. *your praises are too l.* Wint. IV, 4, 147. *make our peace upon such l. terms*, H4B IV, 1, 186. *ruling in l. and ample empery*, H5 I, 2, 226. *you sent a l. commission*, H8 III, 2, 320. *fair leave and l. security*, Troil. I, 3, 223. *fell to a l. confession*, III, 2, 161. *the mighty space of our l. honours*, Caes. IV, 3, 25. *with a —r tether may he walk*, Hml. I, 3, 125. *He that made us with such l. discourse*, IV, 4, 36. *your l. speeches*, Lr. I, 1, 187. *to —r reach*, Oth. III, 3, 219. *a restitution l. of gold and jewels*, V, 1, 15. *l. confusion* in Tim. IV, 3, 127 = wide-spreading ruin; cf. *not all the whips of heaven are l. enough*, V, 1, 64.

3) unrestrained, free, and in a bad sense = licentious: *be l. in mirth*, Mcb. III, 4, 11. *some l. jests he will make*, Ado II, 3, 206. *I never tempted her with word too large*, IV, 1, 53. *thou wouldst else have made thy tale l.* Rom. IV, 4, 102 (quibbling). *most l. in his abominations*, Ant. III, 6, 93.

4) great, considerable: *to leap l. lengths of miles*, Sonn. 44, 10; cf. John I, 105. *why so l. cost*, Sonn. 146, 5. *a dowry l. enough*, John II, 469; cf. H6A V, 1, 20. *thou dost consent in some l. measure*, R2 I, 2, 26. *l. sums of gold*, I, 4, 50; cf. H6B I, 1, 129. *it lends a —r dare to our great enterprise*, H4A IV, 1, 78. *l. fines*, H6A I, 3, 64. *whose l. style agrees not with the leanness of his purse*, H6B I, 1, 111. *l. gifts*, IV, 7, 76. *l. pay*, H6C IV, 7, 88. *l. fortune*, Tim. I, 1, 55; cf. Ant. II, 6, 34. *upon l. interest*, Tim. III, 5, 108. *a l. expense of time*, Mcb. V, 8, 60. *our —st bounty*, Lr. I, 1, 53. *the l. effects that troop with majesty*, 133. *a more —r list of sceptres*, Ant. III, 6, 76.

At l. = 1) by the scale, on a large scale: *a land itself at l., a potent dukedom*, As V, 4, 175. *there is seen the baby figure of the giant mass of things to come at l.* Troil. I, 3, 346. 2) without restriction: *so to the laws at l. I write my name*, LLL I, 1, 156. *in grant of all demands at l.* H5 II, 4, 121. *we shall meet and break our minds at l.* H6A I, 3, 81. 3) diffusely, not in a summary way, in detail, dwelling on particulars: Gent. III, 1, 253. III, 2, 61. Wiv. IV, 6, 18. Err. IV, 4, 146. V, 395. Mids. V, 152. R2 III, 1, 41. V, 6, 10. H4B IV, 4, 101. H5 I, 1, 78. Per. I, 1, 1. V, 1, 62. *more at l.* H6A I, 1, 109. II, 5, 59. H6B II, 1, 177. *so at l.* H6A V, 1, 42.

Large-handed, unrestrained, licentious: *l. robbers your great masters are*, Tim. IV, 1, 11.

Largely, 1) copiously, abundantly: *have given l. to many*, Wiv. II, 2, 207. *our supplies live l. in the hope of great Northumberland*, H4B I, 3, 12. *her prosperities so l. taste*, Per. I, 4, 53.

2) in detail, at large: *I'll tell you l. of fair Hero's death*, Ado V, 4, 69.

Largeness, bigness, great proportions: Compl. 91. Troil. I, 3, 5.

Largess, donation, present, bounty bestowed: Sonn. 4, 6. Shr. I, 2, 151. H5 IV Chor. 43. Unchanged in the plural: *our coffers, with too great a court and liberal l., are grown somewhat light*, R2 I, 4, 44. *sent forth great l. to your offices*, Mcb. II, 1, 14.

Lark, the bird Alauda: Ven. 853. Sonn. 29, 11. Pilgr. 198. LLL V, 2, 914. Mids. I, 1, 184. III, 1, 133. IV, 1, 99. Merch. V, 102. Shr. Ind. 2, 46. IV, 3, 177. All's II, 5, 7. Wint. IV, 3, 9. R2 III, 3, 183. H5 III, 7, 34. R3 V, 3, 56. H8 II, 3, 94. III, 2, 282 *(dare us with his cap like —s).* Troil. IV, 2, 9. Tit. II, 3, 149. III, 1, 158. Rom. III, 5, 2. 6. 21. 25. 27. 31 *(some say the l. and toad change eyes).* Lr. IV, 6, 58. Cymb. II, 3, 21. III, 6, 94.

Laroone, thief: Wiv. I, 4, 71 (from the French *larron*; Dr. Caius' speech).

Lartius, name in Cor. I, 1, 243 etc.

Larum (M. Edd. *'larum*), 1) alarm: *dwelling in a continual l. of jealousy*, Wiv. III, 5, 73. *a common l. bell*, H4B III, 1, 17.

2) loud noise: *have I not in a pitched battle heard loud —s*, Shr. I, 2, 207. *then shall we hear their l., and they ours*, Cor. I, 4, 9. *with loud —s welcome them to Rome*, Tit. I, 147.

'Las, alas: Oth. V, 1, 111 (Ff *alas*).

Lascivious, lewd, lustful: Sonn. 40, 13. 95, 6. Gent. II, 7, 41. Wiv. II, 1, 82. All's IV, 3, 248. 333. R2 II, 1, 19. H6A III, 1, 19. H6C V, 5, 34. R3 I, 1, 13. Tit. II, 3, 110. Tim. I, 1, 211. V, 4, 1. Oth. I, 1, 127. Ant. I, 4, 56.

Lash, subst. 1) the thong or cord of a whip: *the l. of film*, Rom. I, 4, 63.

2) a stroke with a whip: *how smart a l. that speech doth give my conscience*, Hml. III, 1, 50.

Lash, vb. to strike with a whip, to scourge: Err. II, 1, 15. R3 V, 3, 328. Lr. IV, 6, 165. Oth. IV, 2, 143.

Lass, a term of endearment for a girl, a sweetheart: Pilgr. 293. Tp. III, 2, 111. LLL V, 2, 558. As V, 3, 17. All's III, 6, 119. Wint. IV, 4, 156. 231. 363. Ant. V, 2, 319.

Lass-lorn, forsaken by his mistress, or made unhappy by her (cf. *Forlorn*): Tp. IV, 68.

Last, subst. the mould on which shoes are made: Rom. I, 2, 40.

Last, adj. 1) coming after all the others in time or place: *in that l. article*, Gent. III, 1, 365. *except it be the l. Err. V, 55. *the l. of December*, Ado I, 1, 194. *that l. is Biron*, LLL II, 215. *am I l. that knows it*, R2 III, 4, 94. *the seventh and l.* H6B II, 2, 17. *if for the l., say ay*, H6C II, 1, 165. *though l., not least in love*, Caes. III, 1, 189 and Lr. I, 1, 85 etc.

2) beyond which or whom there is no more: *till the l. step have brought me to my love*, Gent. II, 7, 36. *I am the l. that will keep l. his oath*, LLL I, 1, 161. *to the l. gasp*, As II, 3, 70; H6A I, 2, 127; Cymb. I, 5, 53. *l. scene of all*, As II, 7, 163. *her l. breath*, All's IV, 3, 62. *that l. hold*, John V, 7, 19. *try our fortunes to the l. man*, H4B IV, 2, 44. *the flames of the l. day*, H6B V, 2, 41. *to the l. penny*, H8 III, 2, 453. *his l. refuge*, Tim. III, 3, 11. *the l. of all the Romans*, Caes. V, 3, 99. *to the l. article*, Oth. III, 3, 22 etc. *the l.* =

the end: *hear the l. of our sea-sorrow*, Tp. I, 2, 170. *be patient till the l.* Caes. III, 2, 12. *and to the l. bended their light on me*, Hml. II, 1, 100. *bravest at the l., she levelled at our purposes*, Ant. V, 2, 338 (= at the close). *I will try the l.* Mcb. V, 8, 32 (I will run the hazard to the end). *one's l.* = for the last time, so as to do it never more: *it is thy l.* Compl. 168. *I will feed, although my l.* Tp. III, 3, 50. *that I may breathe my l. in wholesome counsel*, R2 II, 1, 1. *Montague hath breathed his l.* H6C V, 2, 40. *eyes, look your l.* Rom. V, 3, 112. *this is Timon's l.* Tim. III, 6, 100. *at first and l.* = throughout, uniformly, without alloy: *ay, grief, I fear me, both at first and l.* H6A V, 5, 102. *at first and l. the hearty welcome*, Mcb. III, 4, 2. *from first to l.* = from the beginning to the end: John II, 326. Lr. V, 3, 195. Oth. III, 3, 96. Per. V, 3, 61. *from the first to l.*: As IV, 3, 140.

3) next before the present, not followed by another till now: *l. morning*, Gent. II, 1, 86. *l. night*, 93. Ado IV, 1, 91. Merch. V, 262. All's V, 1, 23. Tw. II, 3, 23. II, 4, 3 etc. *the l. time*, Wiv. IV, 2, 32. *l. time*, 98. *l. year*, H4B V, 3, 2. *upon All-hallowmas l.* Wiv. I, 1, 211. *o' Wednesday l.* Err. I, 2, 55. Merch. I, 3, 127. II, 5, 25. *the tenth of August l.* H6A I, 1, 110. *before these l. times*, Sonn. 67, 14. *drowned in the l. rain*, Meas. III, 2, 52. *in our l. conflict*, Ado I, 1, 66. *this l. was broke across*, V, 1, 139. *your worship was the l. man in our mouths*, Merch. I, 3, 61. *the fall of the l. monarchy*, All's II, 1, 14. *my l. good deed*, Wint. I, 2, 97. *the l. king*, H5 I, 1, 2; Hml. I, 1, 80. *this l. old man*, Cor. V, 3, 8. *the l.* = the last time: *the l. that e'er I took her leave at court*, All's V, 3, 79.

4) *late, recent, lately happened: thou and thy meaner fellows your last service did worthily perform*, Tp. IV, 35. *when did you lose your daughter? In this l. tempest*, V, 153. *God 'ild you for your l. company*, As III, 3, 76. *after the l. enchantment you did here*, Tw. III, 1, 123. *the present consul and l. general*, Cor. II, 2, 47 (probably adv.).

At l. = 1) in the end, finally: *yields at l. to every light impression*, Ven. 566. *picks them all at l.* 576. Lucr. 1501. 1567. Tp. IV, 181. Ado V, 1, 173. Shr. IV, 2, 60. R2 IV, 286. H6A III, 1, 191. V, 4, 107. H6B I, 2, 104. I, 3, 102. H6C III, 3, 219. IV, 6, 14. V, 2, 45. R3 IV, 4, 164 etc. 2) at length: *at l. she thus begins*, Lucr. 1303. 1366. 1597. 1790. Merch. III, 2, 207. Shr. V, 2, 1. Tit. I, 36. IV, 1, 73. Hml. II, 1, 92 etc.

At the last, in the same sense: 1) *comes at the l. and bores through his castle wall*, R2 III, 2, 169. *am I guerdoned at the l. with shame?* H6C III, 3, 191. *till at the l. I seemed his follower*, Cor. V, 6, 38. *at the l., best*, Ant. I, 3, 61. 2) *I have arrived at the l. unto the wished haven*, Shr. V, 1, 130. *at the l. do as the heavens have done, forget your evil*, Wint. V, 1, 4.

In the l. = finally: Cor. V, 6, 42. *by the l.* = last, coming after the others, not followed by another: *nine husbands: Overdone by the l.* Meas. II, 1, 212 (Pompey's speech).

Last, adv. 1) after all the others: *if thou wilt leave me, do not leave me l.* Sonn. 90, 9. *my prime request, which I do l. pronounce*, Tp. I, 2, 426. *I am the l. that will keep l. his oath*, LLL I, 1, 161. *when I shall gust it l.* Wint. I, 2, 219. *to serve me l.* R2 III, 4, 95. *love thyself l.* H8 III, 2, 444. *and l. eat up himself*, Troil. I, 3, 124 etc.

2) lastly, in the last place: *first… next… and l.* Wiv. II, 2, 264. H4B V, 5, 116. H8 III, 2, 403.

3) next before the present: *Tuesday night l. gone he knew me as a wife*, Meas. V, 229.

4) for the last time, the next time before the present: *since I saw you l.* Tp. V, 283. Err. V, 297. Merch. II, 2, 105. Tw. V, 1, 55. *when l. the young Orlando parted from you*, As IV, 3, 99. *where left we l.?* Shr. III, 1, 26. R2 I, 1, 139. H6C II, 2, 103. R3 III, 2, 101. Mcb. V, 1, 3 etc.

5) lately: *and yet I was l. chidden for being too slow*, Gent. II, 1, 12. *when I from Thebes came l. a conqueror*, Mids. V, 51. *since l. I went to France to fetch his queen*, R2 I, 1, 131. *when I was l. in Holborn, I saw good strawberries*, R3 III, 4, 33. *when l. I was at Exeter*, IV, 2, 106. Cor. II, 2, 47.

Last, vb. 1) to continue, to endure, not to end: Ven. 507. Lucr. 894. 1765. Pilgr. 100. Err. IV, 1, 25. Shr. I, 2, 108. Wint. IV, 4, 486. V, 3, 8. R2 II, 1, 33. 35. H6B I, 1, 211. H6C II, 6, 2. III, 2, 114. R3 IV, 2, 6. IV, 4, 254. Oth. III, 3, 14. Cymb. IV, 2, 219. Per. IV, 1, 18. *to l. out* = to be longer than: *this will l. out a night in Russia*, Meas. II, 1, 139. Partic. *—ing* = eternal, everlasting: Lucr. 798. 1629. 1729. Sonn. 122, 2. Tp. V, 208. Tw. I, 1, 32. Wint. I, 2, 317. John III, 4, 27. V, 7, 24. R2 V, 2, 45. H6C V, 7, 46. H8 III, 1, 8. Tit. II, 3, 275. Rom. IV, 5, 45. Hml. III, 2, 232. Per. IV, 1, 20. *still —ing*, R3 IV, 4, 344.

2) to remain unimpaired, not to decay: *if I l. in this service*, Err. II, 1, 85. *if promise l.* Merch. III, 2, 207. *he —ed long*, All's I, 2, 28. *I cannot l. ever*, H4B I, 2, 240. *whilst this poor wealth —s*, Tim. IV, 3, 495. *sweet, not —ing*, Hml. I, 3, 8. *the houses that he makes l. till doomsday*, V, 1, 67. *he will l. some eight year*, 183.

3) to remain: *that it* (your love) *l. love*, LLL V, 2, 813.

Lastly, 1) in the last place: Wiv. I, 1, 142. Ado V, 1, 221. Merch. II, 9, 14. H6C III, 3, 54. Ant. III, 6, 27.

2) in the conclusion, finally, to boot: *l. hurried here to this place*, Wint. III, 2, 105. *l. myself unkindly banished*, Tit. V, 3, 104.

Latch, subst. a catch of a door moved by a string or handle: Lucr. 339. 358. Wint. IV, 4, 449.

Latch, vb. to catch, to fall in with: *it* (my eye) *no form delivers to the heart of bird, of flower, or shape, which it doth l.* Sonn. 113, 6. *but hast thou yet —ed the Athenian's eyes with the love-juice?* Mids. III, 2, 36 (according to some, = anointed, smeared over, for which meaning of the word no other instance has been pointed out). *I have words that would be howled out in the desert air, where hearing should not l. them*, Mcb. IV, 3, 195. In Lr. II, 1, 54 Ff *latched mine arm*, Qq *launcht*.

Late, adj. 1) far in the day or night: *your l. business*, H8 V, 1, 13 (performed in time of night). Mostly in the predicate: *'tis very l.* Ven. 531. Rom. III, 3, 172. III, 4, 5. 34. *though it were l. in the night*, Lucr. Arg. 10. *was it so l.* Mcb. II, 3, 24. *it grows l.* H4B II, 4, 299. Rom. III, 3, 164. *it waxes l.* Rom. I, 5, 128. Comp. *—r: 'tis —r*, Mcb. II, 1, 3.

2) coming or happening after due time; used only in the predicate and preceded by *too: be not too l.* Tp. IV, 133. Wiv. II, 2, 328. H8 I, 3, 65. V, 2, 1.

'tis too l. Meas. II, 2, 55. LLL I, 1, 108. As II, 3, 74. All's V, 2, 31. John V, 7, 1. H6A IV, 4, 1. Hml. V, 2, 303. Oth. V, 2, 84.

Compar. — *r* = done subsequently: *thy —r vows against thy first*, John III, 1, 288. Superl. —*st* always = last; a) coming behind all the others: *to leave that —st which concerns him first*, Oth. I, 3, 28. b) next before the present: *the —st breath was deep - sworn faith*, John III, 1, 230. *the —st news*, R2 V, 6, 1. *apply thy —st words*, Troil. I, 3, 33. c) beyond which there is no more: *at the —st minute of the hour*, LLL V, 2, 797. *the very —st counsel that ever I shall breathe*, H4B IV, 5, 183. *the —st parle we admit*, H5 III, 3, 2. H6A IV, 2, 33. H6C II, 1, 108. V, 2, 41. Cor. V, 3, 11. Tit. I, 83. 149. Caes. V, 5, 67. *the —st of my wealth*, Tim. IV, 2, 23.

3) recent, lately happened: *a loss as great to me as l.* Tp. V, 145. *our l. edict*, LLL I, 1, 11. *their l. escape*, Wint. II, 1, 95. *the boisterous l. appeal*, R2 I, 1, 4. *your l. tossing on the seas*, III, 2, 3. *the l. commissioners*, H5 II, 2, 61 (lately appointed); cf. *the l. ambassadors*, II, 4, 31 (lately sent). *l. examples*, II, 4, 12. *the l. overthrow*, H6A I, 2, 49. III, 1, 189. H6B I, 1, 196. I, 3, 100. H6C II, 1, 118. IV, 4, 3. IV, 6, 92. R3 I, 3, 91. IV, 2, 87. H8 I, 3, 6. IV, 1, 27. 31. III, 1, 64. Mcb. I, 6, 19. Hml. II, 2, 347. Lr. I, 2, 112. IV, 5, 24. *Of l. days* = recently: *did you not of l. days hear a buzzing of a separation?* H8 II, 1, 147. *as, of l. days, our neighbours can dearly witness*, V, 3, 29.

4) that was, former: *brake off his l. intent*, Ven. 469. *Archbishop l. of Canterbury*, R2 II, 1, 282. *the king hath wasted all his rods on l. offenders*, H4B IV, 1, 216. *the l. queen*, H8 III, 2, 94. *the l. marriage made of no effect*, IV, 1, 33. *our l. noble master*, Tim. V, 1, 58. *thy l. master*, Cymb. III, 5, 125. Hence = deceased: *our l. king*, H4B IV, 1, 58. H6A I, 3, 24. II, 4, 91. Hml. I, 2, 19.

Of l. = 1) a short time ago, lately: *which of you saw Sir Eglamour of l.?* Gent. V, 2, 32. *who called here of l.?* Meas. IV, 2, 77. *meeting her of l. behind the wood*, Mids. IV, 1, 53. Err. I, 1, 5. Tw. II, 5, 180. H6A II, 5, 42. III, 2, 113. Cor. III, 1, 42. Tim. I, 1, 78. Mcb. I, 7, 32. Lr. II, 4, 40. Per. I, 4, 34. = just now: *you seemed of l. to make the law a tyrant*, Meas. II, 4, 114. *a mess of Russians left us but of l.* LLL V, 2, 361. *this ring was his of l.* All's V, 3, 227.

2) in the last time, since some time: *you have of l. stood out against your brother*, Ado I, 3, 22. *losses have of l. so huddled on his back*, Merch. IV, 1, 28. *of l. this duke hath ta'en displeasure*, As I, 2, 289. *disgraces have of l. knocked at my door*, All's IV, 1, 31. *she is spread of l.* Wint. II, 1, 19. *he is of l. much retired from court*, IV, 2, 36. *how insolent of l. he is become*, H6B III, 1, 7. *now of l. she washes bucks*, IV, 2, 50. H8 III, 2, 338. V, 1, 98. Troil. III, 3, 74. 188. Cor. IV, 6, 11. Tim. IV, 3, 90. Caes. I, 2, 32. 40. II, 1, 195. Hml. I, 3, 91. 99. II, 1, 107. II, 2, 307. III, 2, 173. Lr. I, 4, 74. 208. 242. Cymb. III, 5, 52. IV, 2, 345.

3) formerly: *that was of l. an heretic*, Wiv. IV, 4, 9. *I was of l. as petty to his ends*, Ant. III, 12, 8. *of l., when I cried Ho! kings would start forth*, III, 13, 90.

Late, adv. 1) far in the day or night: *to be down l.* Wiv. I, 4, 108. *to be up l.* Tw. II, 3, 5. *sat in the council-house early and l.* H6B I, 1, 91. H8 V, 1, 6.

Troil. IV, 2, 55. Rom. III, 5, 67. Mcb. III, 6, 5. 7. Cymb. II, 3, 37. Per. II, 3, 113.

2) behind the due time: *bring thy news so l.* Cor. I, 6, 18. In all other passages preceded by *too:* Lucr. 1686. Pilgr. 313. Err. I, 2, 43. II, 2, 221. III, 1, 49. Merch. II, 8, 6. Shr. V, 1, 155. All's V, 3, 57. Wint. IV, 4, 238. R2 I, 3, 175. I, 4, 64. III, 2, 67. H6A IV, 4, 42. H8 II, 3, 84. IV, 2, 120. Cor. I, 6, 24. Tit. II, 3, 264. Rom. I, 4, 105. I, 5, 141. Tim. II, 2, 152. IV, 3, 519. V, 1, 45. Hml. V, 2, 379. Lr. II, 4, 279. Ant. IV, 14, 127. 128. With *of:* *you come too l. of our intents*, R3 III, 5, 69.

3) a short time ago, lately: *she leaps that was but l. forlorn*, Ven. 1026. *which she too early and too l. hath spilled*, Lucr. 1801. *which l. her noble suit in court did shun*, Compl. 234. *to abuse me, as l. I have been*, Tp. V, 113. *l. come from the See*, Meas. III, 2, 232. *l. deceased*, Mids. V, 53. *I was very l. more near her*, All's I, 3, 110. *was so very l.* Tw. I, 2, 30. *I saw thee l.*, 42. *but so l. ago*, V, 222. *that l. broke from the Duke of Exeter*, R2 II, 1, 281. H6A II, 5, 36. III, 1, 79. H6C II, 5, 93 (*too l.*).*III, 3, 63. R3 II, 2, 149. III, 1, 99 (*too l.*) Rom. III, 4, 24. V, 1, 38. Tim. II, 1, 1. Lr. I, 4, 226. II, 2, 123. III, 4, 173. III, 7, 42. 45. Ant. IV, 1, 13. Cymb. I, 1, 6. Per. IV, 4, 13. = just now: *his eye, which l. this mutiny restrains*, Lucr. 426. *that l. complained her wrongs to us*, 1839. *the pardon that I l. pronounced here*, Merch. IV, 1, 392. *bubbles in a l. disturbed stream*, H4A II, 3, 62. H5 II, 2, 79. H6C III, 3, 148. Rom. III, 1, 131. Cymb. II, 2, 44.

4) formerly, else, once: *whereat the impartial gazer l. did wonder*, Ven. 748. *their virtue lost, wherein they l. excelled*, 1131. *where l. to sweet birds sang*, Sonn. 73, 4. *where is the life that l. I led*, Shr. IV, 1, 143 and H4B V, 3, 146. *she, which l. was in my nobler thoughts most base, is now the praised of the king*, All's II, 3, 177. *who l. hath beat her husband, and now baits me*, Wint. II, 3, 91. *l. did he shine upon the English side*, H6A I, 2, 3. *whom you l. vanquished*, H6B IV, 8, 44. *a clout upon that head where l. the diadem stood*, Hml. II, 2, 530. *which l. on hopes depended*, Oth. I, 3, 203.

Late-betrayed, just now betrayed: H6A III, 2, 82. **Lated,** belated, benighted: Mcb. III, 3, 6. Ant. III, 11, 3.

Late-deceased, having lately died, late: H6A III, 2, 132. Tit. I, 184.

Late-disturbed, just now disturbed: H4A II, 3, 62.

Late-embarked, just now gone on shipboard: Ven. 818.

Lately, 1) a short time ago, recently: Wiv. V, 1, 28. Err. V, 293. Merch. IV, 1, 385. As II, 2, 14. All's I, 3, 33. I, 3, 224. II, 2, 52. John III, 1, 239. R2 III, 3, 3. V, 5, 101. H4A I, 1, 12. I, 3, 85. IV, 2, 37. H4B V, 4, 7. V, 5, 124. H5 I, 2, 247. H6C II, 1, 145. R3 III, 2, 118. H8 II, 1, 160. IV, 1, 98. Cor. I, 1, 231. Rom. III, 3, 136. Tim. II, 2, 231. Lr. III, 4, 173. Oth. III, 3, 413. Per. IV, 1, 87. = just now: *an islander that hath l. suffered by a thunderbolt*, Tp. II, 2, 38. *like eagles having l. bathed*, H4A IV, 1, 99. *who art thou that l. didst descend into this hollow?* Tit. II, 3, 248.

2) in the last time, since some time: *a tribute, which by thee l. is left untendered*, Cymb. III, 1, 9.

3) formerly: *to unfold, though l. we intended to*

keep in darkness, Tw. V, 155. *a righteous gentleman l. attendant on the Duke of Norfolk*, R3 II, 1, 101.

Late-sacked, lately pillaged: Lucr. 1740.

Late-walking, keeping late hours: Wiv. V, 5, 153.

Lath, a slip of wood: *dagger of l.* Tw. IV, 2, 136 and H4A II, 4, 151. *a sword, though made of a l.* H6B IV, 2, 2. *have your l. glued within your sheath*, Tit. II, 1, 41 (= sword, in contempt). *bow of l.* Rom. I, 4, 5.

Latin, 1) subst. the language of the ancient Romans: Wiv. I, 1, 185. LLL V, 1, 83. Merch. I, 2, 75. As III, 2, 337. Shr. I, 2, 29. II, 81. H6B IV, 7, 63. H8 III, 1, 42.

2) adj. written or used in the language of the ancient Romans: Wiv. IV, 1, 50. LLL III, 138. Shr. II, 101.

Latten, a compound of copper and calamine, too soft to make blades of: *I combat challenge of this l. bilbo*, Wiv. I, 1, 165.

Latter, last: *to find both or bring your l. hazard back again*, Merch. I, 1, 151. *'tis the rarest argument of wonder that hath shot out in our l. times*, All's II, 3, 8; cf. *to grace this l. age with noble deeds*, H4A V, 1, 92; *you, born in these l. times*, Per. Prol. 11. *farewell the l. spring*, H4A I, 2, 177 (= the end of the spring). *at the l. day*, H5 IV, 1, 143. *and in his bosom spend my l. gasp*, H6A II, 5, 38. *and in devotion spend my l. days*, H6C IV, 6, 43. *these well express in thee thy l. spirits*, Tim. V, 4, 74 (thy disposition at the end of life). *the foulest best fits my l. part of life*, Ant. IV, 6, 39. *the two l.* Per. III, 2, 29. *the l. end* = the end, the close: Tp. II, 1, 157. Wiv. I, 4, 9. LLL V, 2, 630. Mids. IV, 1, 223. All's II, 5, 31. H4A IV, 2, 85. H5 V, 2, 341.

Latter-born, last-born, younger: Err. I, 1, 79.

Lattice, bars crossing each other, used in windows: *some beauty peeped through l. of seared age*, Compl. 14. *my good window of l.* All's II, 3, 225. *through a red l.* H4B II, 2, 86.

Laud, subst. 1) praise, glory: Lucr. 622. 887. H4B IV, 5, 236. Troil. III, 3, 179.

2) a hymn: *she chanted snatches of old —s*, Hml. IV, 7, 178 (Ff *tunes*).

Laud, vb. to praise: H4A III, 3, 215. Cymb. V, 5, 476.

Laudable, praiseworthy: Tw. III, 2, 31. Mcb. IV, 2, 76.

Laugh, vb. 1) to express merriment by the features and certain sounds of the voice: Ven. 414. Sonn. 98, 4. Compl. 124. Gent. II, 1, 27. Wiv. I, 4, 162. IV, 2, 108. Err. III, 1, 50. LLL V, 2, 107 etc. etc. *interjections of —ing*, Ado IV, 1, 23. *they l. that win*, Oth. IV, 1, 126. Followed by an inf. denoting the cause: *we have —ed to see the sails conceive*, Mids. II, 1, 128. H6A II, 3, 45. H6B II, 1, 155. With *at:* Lucr. 1066. Tp. II, 1, 175. Wiv. I, 1, 122. II, 2, 326. V, 5, 181. Ado II, 1, 147. LLL IV, 3, 148. 170. Mids. II, 1, 39. Merch. I, 1, 53. III, 1, 57. As II, 2, 9. Wint. II, 3, 24. H5 IV, 2, 198. H6B IV, 4, 12. H8 I, 3, 35. III, 1, 107. Cor. IV, 1, 27. Rom. II, 2, 93. Cymb. IV, 2, 211 etc. With *upon* (= to laugh significatively in looking at one): LLL V, 2, 475. Shr. IV, 4, 76.

Followed by an accus. and an adv. or prepositional phrase, denoting the result: *Pompey doth l. away his fortune*, Ant. II, 6, 109. *l. this sport o'er by a country fire*, Wiv. V, 5, 256 (cf. *Over*). *—s out a loud ap-*

plause, Troil. I, 3, 163. *he denies it faintly, and —s it out*, Oth. IV, 1, 113 (seeks to hide it by laughing). *will you l. me asleep?* Tp. II, 1, 188. *I shall l. myself to death*, II, 2, 158. Ado III, 1, 75. Tw. III, 2, 72. Ant. II, 5, 19. 20. *to l. to scorn* = to deride: Ven. 4. Err. II, 2, 207. As IV, 2, 19. H6A IV, 7, 18. Mcb. IV, 1, 79. V, 5, 3. V, 7, 12. Double acc.: *l. themselves mortal*, Meas. II, 2, 123.

2) to be gay, to appear gay: *whom I have —ed with*, All's V, 3, 179. *the world may l. again*, H6B II, 4, 82.

Laughable, such as may properly excite laughter: Merch. I, 1, 56.

Laugher, one prone to laughing and jesting: Compl. 124. Caes. I, 2, 72 (OEdd. *laughter*).*

Laughing-stock, an object of ridicule: Wiv. III, 1, 88 (Evans' speech).

Laughter, expression of merriment by the features and certain sounds of the voice: Tp. II, 1, 33.* LLL III, 76. V, 2, 80. 116. 865. Mids. V, 70. Merch. I, 1, 80. Shr. Ind. 1, 134. All's II, 4, 38. III, 6, 36. Tw. II, 3, 49. V, 374. Wint. I, 2, 287. II, 1, 198. John III, 3, 45. H4A II, 2, 101. H4B I, 2, 10. V, 1, 89. Cor. III, 3, 52. Tit. V, 1, 113. Tim. III, 3, 20. IV, 3, 492. Caes. IV, 3, 49 (*I'll use you for my l.*). 114 (*to be but mirth and l. to his Brutus*). Lr. I, 4, 309. IV, 1, 6. Oth. IV, 1, 100. Cymb. I, 6, 74.

Launce, name of a servant in Gent. I, 3, 2. 36. I, 5, 1. III, 1, 257. 279. IV, 2, 75 etc.

Launcelot, Christian name of the servant L. Gobbo in Merch. II, 2, 4. II, 3, 5. III, 5, 29 etc.

Launch, vb. to cause to slide into the water, to push to sea: *whose price hath —ed above a thousand ships*, Troil. II, 2, 82.

Launch, vb. (M. Edd. *lance*) to pierce, to cut: *—eth not the sore*, R2 I, 3, 303 (Ff Q1 *lanceth*). *—ed their tender hearts*, R3 IV, 4, 224 (O. Edd. *lanched*, M. Edd. *lanced*). *—ed mine arm*, Lr. II, 1, 54 (Ff *latch'd*). *we do l. diseases in our bodies*, Ant. V, 1, 36.

Laund, a lawn, a glade: *through the dark l. runs*, Ven. 813.* *through this l. anon the deer will come*, H6C III, 1, 2.

Launder, to wash, to wet: *—ing the silken figures in the brine*, Compl. 17.

Laundress, a washerwoman: Wiv. III, 3, 157. 163.

Laundry, Evans' term for *laundress:* Wiv. I, 2, 5.

Laura, the celebrated mistress of Petrarca: Rom. II, 4, 41.

Laurel, the bay-tree, Laurus nobilis, the emblem of victory and glory: *crowns, sceptres, —s*, Troil. I, 3, 107 (= high distinctions). Adjectively: *l. crown.* H6C IV, 6, 34. *boughs*, Tit. I, 74. *l. victory*, Ant. I, 3, 100 (F 2. 3. 4 *laurell'd*).

Laurell'd, reading of F 2. 3. 4 in Ant. I, 3, 100; F 1 *laurel.*

Laurence, name of two friars in Gent. V, 2, 37 and Rom. II, 4, 193. II, 5, 70. III, 2, 141. III, 5, 232. IV, 2, 11. 20.

Lavatch, name in All's V, 2, 1 (some M. Edd. *Lavache*).

Lave, to wash, to bathe: Shr. II, 350. Tit. IV 2, 103. Metaphorically: *unsafe the while, that we must l. our honours in these flattering streams*, Mcb. III, 2, 33 (keep our honours clean and free from attaint by thus flattering others).

Lavender, the plant Lavendula Spica: Wint. IV, 4, 104.

Lavinia, name of the daughter of Titus Andronicus: Tit. I, 52 etc. etc.

Lavish, adj. 1) unrestrained, licentious: *when means and l. manners meet together,* H4B IV, 4, 64. *his l. tongue,* H6A II, 5, 47. *curbing his l. spirit,* Mcb. I, 2, 57.

2) profuse; used of things and persons: *let her have needful, but not l. means,* Meas. II, 2, 24. *had I so l. of my presence been,* H4A III, 2, 39.

Lavishly, licentiously, arbitrarily: *some about him have too l. wrested his meaning and authority,* H4B IV, 2, 57.

Lavolt, a dance consisting chiefly in high bounds: *heel the high l.* Troil. IV, 4, 88.

Lavolta, the same: *—s high,* H5 III, 5, 33.

Law, 1) a rule prescribed by the supreme power of a state: Lucr. 497. 571. Meas. I, 1, 66. I, 3, 19. I, 4, 63. II, 1, 1. 239. II, 4, 61. 94. III, 1, 109. Err. I, 1, 4. 143. Mids. I, 1, 44. 119. Merch. II, 8, 17 etc. *the strong l.* Hml. IV, 3, 3 (cf. *Strong*). *their aunt I am in l.* R3 IV, 1, 24 (i. e. by marriage; cf. *Father-in-law* etc.); cf. *and now by l., as well as reverend age, I may entitle thee my loving father,* Shr. IV, 5, 60. *by l.* = lawfully, legitimately: Err. I, 1, 26. Shr. IV, 5, 60. H6A V, 4, 61. H8 II, 2, 112. III. 2, 266. Tit. IV, 4, 54. Tim. IV, 1, 12. *by the l.:* Meas. III, 1, 195. Tim. I, 1, 196. *by the —s of Venice,* Merch. IV, 1, 311. *by course of l.* H6B III, 1, 237. R3 I, 4, 192. *by order of l.* Meas. III, 2, 8. Lr. I, 1, 9.

2) any rule of direction: *poor queen of love, in thine own l. forlorn,* Ven. 251; Sonn. 49, 13; H6C III, 2, 154. *by l. of nature thou art bound to breed,* Ven. 171; All's IV, 5, 65; Wint. II, 2, 60; H4B III, 2, 357; H5 II, 4, 80; Troil. II, 2, 176; 184; Lr. I, 2, 1; Cymb. V, 4, 38. *the l. of friendship,* Gent. III, 1, 5. *make their wills their l.* Gent. V, 4, 14. *so to the —s at large I write my name,* LLL I, 1, 156. *this bar in l.* Shr. I, 1, 140. *the l. of nations,* H5 II, 4, 80. Troil. II, 2, 184. *the l. of arms,* H5 IV, 7, 2. H6A III, 4, 38.* IV, 1, 100. Lr. V, 3, 152*). *martial l.* H5 IV, 8, 46. *—s of war,* H8 I, 4, 52. *the l. of writ and the liberty,* Hml. II, 2, 420 (see *Writ*). *) Ff of war.

3) the word of God: *charity itself fulfils the l.* LLL IV, 3, 364. *the canon of the l. is laid on him,* John II, 180. *in the tables of his l.* R3 I, 4, 201.

4) judicial proceeding: *in l., what plea so tainted,* Merch. III, 2, 75. *I'll answer him by l.* Shr. Ind. 1, 14. *as adversaries do in l.* I, 2, 278. *must I rob the l.?* John IV, 3, 78. *what shall we say to this in l.?* H6B I, 3, 207. *here's a fish hangs in the net, like a poor man's right in the l.* Per. II, 1, 124.

5) right, justice: *I shall have l. in Ephesus,* Err. IV, 1, 83. *I stand here for l.* Merch. IV, 1, 142 (cf. *for judgment* v. 103). *this is the l.* H6B I, 3, 214. *let us take the l. of our sides,* Rom. I, 1, 44 (*of* = on). *the —'s delay,* Hml. III, 1, 72.

6) jurisprudence: *I have been a truant in the l.* H6A II, 4, 7. *these quillets of the l.* 17. *a question in the l.* IV, 1, 95.

Law-breaker, one who violates the law: Cymb. IV, 2, 75.

Law-day, a court-day, a sitting of judges to administer justice: *keep leets and —s,* Oth. III, 3, 140.

Lawful, 1) rightful, legitimate: *spend the dowry of a l. bed,* Lucr. 938. *in the l. name of marrying,* Wiv. IV, 6, 50; cf. As III, 3, 71; All's III, 7, 45; H6C III, 3, 57; H8 II, 4, 53; 226; Lr. IV, 6, 118; Cymb. II, 5, 9; Per. I, 1, 82. *l. means,* Merch. IV, 1, 9. *a l. cause,* Shr. I, 2, 29. *claim,* John. I, 9. *king,* II, 95; 222; R2 III, 3, 74; H6A V, 4, 140; H6B V, 1, 4; H6C I, 1, 137; 150; II, 2, 86; III, 3, 29; V, 1, 88; R3 I, 3, 147. *l. power,* John III, 1, 172. *heir,* H6A II, 5, 65. *progeny,* III, 3, 61. *magistrate,* H6C I, 2, 23. *suit,* R3 III, 7, 203. *form,* Cor. III, 1, 325. *censure,* III, 3, 46. *ceremonies,* Caes. III, 1, 241. *race,* Ant. III, 13, 107.

Adverbially: *to link with him that were not l. chosen,* H6C III, 3, 115. *another's l. promised bride,* Tit. I, 298.

2) allowed, not forbidden, not contrary to law: *a l. kiss,* Lucr. 387. *a little harm done to a great good end for l. policy remains enacted,* 529. *be it l. I love thee,* Sonn. 142, 9. Meas. II, 1, 238. II, 4, 112. LLL IV, 3, 285. All's III, 7, 30. 38. Wint. II, 2, 11. V, 3, 105. 111. John III, 1, 180. H5 IV, 8, 122. R3 I, 2, 8. Troil. V, 3, 20. Hml. III, 1, 32. Lr. I, 1, 256. IV, 6, 266. Oth. I, 2, 51.

3) just, well-founded, acting on good authority: *to guard the l. reasons on thy part,* Sonn. 49, 12. *thy just and l. aid,* H6C III, 3, 32. *in session sit with meditations l.* Oth. III, 3, 141.

4) provided by law, concerning the administration of justice: *and 'gainst myself a l. plea commence,* Sonn. 35, 11 (a plea as in a law-suit). *a l. hangman,* Meas. IV, 2, 18. *what l. quest have given their verdict up,* R3 I, 4, 189. *set down by l. counsel,* Cymb. I, 4, 178 (i. e. by lawyers).

5) righteous, loyal, faithful, honorable: *rest thy unrest on England's l. earth, unlawfully made drunk,* R3 IV, 4, 29. *to use my l. sword,* Cor. V, 6, 131 (cf. *Lawless*).

Lawfully, legally, legitimately: Merch. IV, 1, 231. All's I, 3, 107. Per. II, 1, 120.

Lawless, 1) contrary to law, illegal: *no indirect nor l. course,* R3 I, 4, 224.

2) unruly, licentious: *our l. lives,* Gent. IV, 1, 54. *l. and incertain thought,* Meas. III, 1, 127. *this l. bloody book of rebellion,* H4B IV, 1, 91. *thy l. sons,* Tit. I, 312. *l. resolutes,* Hml. I, 1, 98 (Ff *landless*). *in his l. fit,* IV, 1, 8.

Lawlessly, in a manner contrary to law: *use a woman l.* Gent. V, 3, 14.

Lawn, fine linen: Ven. 590. Lucr. 258. 259. Wint. IV, 4, 220. Oth. IV, 3, 73. *—s,* Wint. IV, 4, 209.

Lawrence: *within the parish Saint L. Poultney,* H8 I, 2, 153.

Lawyer, a practitioner of law: As III, 2, 349. IV, 1, 13. Wint. IV, 4, 206. H6B IV, 2, 84. IV, 4, 36. Rom. I, 4, 73. Tim. II, 2, 116. IV, 3, 153. Hml. V, 1, 107. Lr. I, 4, 143. Cymb. II, 3, 79.

Lay, subst. a song: Sonn. 98, 5. 100, 7. 102, 6. Pilgr. 198. Phoen. 1. H6B I, 3, 93. Hml. IV, 7, 183. Per. V Prol. 4.

Lay, subst. stake, wager: *a dreadful l.* H6B V, 2, 27. *my fortunes against any l.* Oth. II, 3, 330. *I will have it no l.* Cymb. I, 4, 159.

Lay, adj. not clerical, pertaining to the laity: *had he been l.* Meas. V, 128. *my l. thoughts,* H8 I, 4, 11.

Lay, vb. (impf. and partic. *laid*) 1) to place along, to make to lie: *—d by his side his brand,* Sonn. 154, 2. *whom I can l. to bed for ever,* Tp. II, 1, 284; cf. Ant. II, 2, 232. *and l. my arms before the legs of this sweet lass,* LLL V, 2, 558. *it should here be —d,* Wint. III, 3, 44. H5 II, 3, 24. IV, 1, 284. Rom. IV, 3, 30.

Mcb. II, 2, 12. Hml. IV, 5, 69. V, 1, 261. Lr. III, 4, 54. III, 6, 97. Oth. IV, 2, 105. IV, 3, 22. V, 2, 237. V, 2, 59. Per. III, 1, 68. Used of a foundation: *—d great bases for eternity,* Sonn. 125, 3; *tyranny, l. thou thy basis sure,* Mcb. IV, 3, 32. Metaphorically: *and l. a sentence, which as a grise or step may help these lovers into your favour,* Oth. I, 3, 199. *l. him down,* Cymb. IV, 2, 282. to *l. low* = to bury: *I would that I were low —d in my grave,* John II, 164. *I saw her —d low in her kindred's vault,* Rom. V, 1, 20. And to *l.,* absolutely, = to place in the earth, to bury: *in sad cypress let me be —d,* Tw. II, 4, 53. *l. me where true lover never find my grave,* 65. *I desire to l. my bones there,* Wint. IV, 2, 6. *l. me where no priest shovels in dust,* IV, 4, 468. *we'll l. before this town our royal bones,* John II, 41. *therein —d,* R2 III, 3, 168. *l. these bones in an unworthy urn,* H5 I, 2, 228. *I'll blast his harvest, if your head were —d,* H6C V, 7, 21. to *l. his weary bones among ye,* H8 IV, 2, 22. to *l. them by their brethren,* Tit. I, 89. *not in a grave, to l. one in,* Rom. II, 3, 84. *l. me with Juliet,* V, 3, 73. *scarce hold the —ing in,* Hml. V, 1, 182. *where shall's l. him?* Cymb. IV, 2, 233. to *l. forth,* and to *l. out* = to dress in graveclothes and place in a decent posture: *embalm me, then l. me forth,* H8 IV, 2, 171. *she that —s thee out,* Troil. II, 3, 34.

Refl. = to lie down: *who —d him down,* As II, 7, 15. *bids you l. you down,* H4A III, 1, 214. *I l. me down to breathe,* H6C II, 3, 2. *l. thee all along,* Rom. V, 3, 3. *l. thee down and roar,* Oth. V, 2, 198.

2) to beat down, to turn upside down, to prostrate: *lay this Angiers even with the ground,* John II, 399. *who even with the earth shall l. your towers,* H6A IV, 2, 13. *mischance hath —d me on the ground,* H6C III, 3, 9. *when I have —d Athens on a heap,* Tim. IV, 3, 101. to *l. flat:* Cor. III, 1, 198. 204. Cymb. I, 4, 23. to *l. down: a speeding trick to l. down ladies,* H8 I, 3, 40. to *l. up* = to destroy: *there were too cousins — d up,* As I, 3, 7; cf. *Layer-up.*

3) to cause to sink, to prevent from rising: *l. the dust,* Gent. II, 3, 35. R2 III, 3, 43. Lr. IV, 6, 201. to *l. this wind,* Troil. IV, 4, 55. Of spirits, = to exorcise: *till she had —d it,* Rom. II, 1, 26 (quibbling); cf. *unlaid* in Cymb. IV, 2, 278.

4) to spread and set in order: *the carpets —d,* Shr. IV, 1, 52. *have you —d fair the bed?* H6B III, 2, 11. With *up: a wet cloak ill —d up,* H4B V, 1, 95. With *forth: l. forth the gown,* Shr. IV, 3, 62.

5) to put in confinement: *—d in some dark room,* Err. IV, 4, 97. *they have —d me here in hideous darkness,* Tw. IV, 2, 34. *Clarence whom I have —d in darkness,* R3 I, 3, 327 (Ff cast). *I'll l. ye all by the heels* H8 V, 4, 83 (i. e. in the stocks).

6) to place, to put in general: *roses that on lawn we l.* Lucr. 258. *other bars he —s before me,* Wiv. III, 4, 7. *have I —d my brain in the sun,* V, 5, 143. *l. it* (Carduus Benedictus) *to your heart,* Ado III, 4, 74. *never l. thy hand upon thy sword,* V, 1, 54; R2 I, 3, 179; Hml. I, 5, 158. *l. his wreathed arms athwart his bosom,* LLL IV, 3, 135. *the juice of it on sleeping eye-lids —d,* Mids. II, 1, 170. III, 2, 89. *how the young folks l. their heads together,* Shr. I, 2, 139; H6B III, 1, 165; IV, 8, 60. *more rags to l. on thee,* Wint. IV, 3, 58. *from forth thy reach he would have —d thy shame,* R2 II, 1, 106. *at his feet to l. my arms and power,* III, 3, 39; H4B III, 1, 63; Rom. II, 2, 147;

Hml. II, 2, 31; Ant. III, 13, 76. *l. thine ear close to the ground,* H4A II, 2, 33. *that I may l. my head in thy lap,* III, 1, 230; H4B V, 3, 110. *—d gifts before him,* H4A IV, 3, 71. *l. him in his father's arms,* H6A IV, 7, 29. *l. them* (my fingers) *gently on thy side,* V, 3, 49; H6B III, 2, 46; H8 III, 2, 115; Troil. I, 3, 240; Caes. I, 2, 243 *(off)*; Mcb. I, 3, 44; Oth. II, 1, 223. *is all my armour —d into my tent?* R3 V, 3, 51. *—ing manors on 'em,* H8 I, 1, 84. *—d any scruple in your way,* II, 4, 150. *this so dishonoured rub, —d falsely in the plain way of his merit,* Cor. III, 1, 60. *where we l. our scene,* Rom. Prol. 2. *l. hand on heart, advise,* III, 5, 192. *I had —d wormwood to my dug,* I, 3, 26. *—s her full mess before you,* Tim. IV, 3, 424. *l. it in the praetor's chair,* Caes. I, 3, 143. *your grace hath —d the odds o' the weaker side,* Hml. V, 2, 272. *—d his leg over my thigh,* Oth. III, 3, 424. *the poor last kiss I l. upon thy lips,* Ant. IV, 15, 21; cf. John II, 19. *we must l. his head to the east,* Cymb. IV, 2, 255. Peculiar phrases: *l. her a-hold,* Tp. I, 1, 52 (make the ship keep clear of the land); cf. *l. her off,* 53. *would fain l. knife aboard,* Rom. II, 4, 214 (= board); and hence: *—ing the prize aboard,* H6B IV, 1, 25 (= boarding it). *thou —est in every gash the knife that made it,* Troil. I, 1, 62. *then I will l. the serving creature's dagger on your pate,* Rom. IV, 5, 119. Metaphorically: *l. your heart at his dispose,* John I, 263. *l. it to thy heart* (= consider it) Mcb. I, 5, 14. *l. not that flattering unction to your soul,* Hml. III, 4, 145. *l. comforts to your bosom,* Lr. II, 1, 128. Refl.: *I will l. myself in hazard,* Meas. IV, 2, 165.

Joined with adverbs and adjectives: to *l. apart* = to put off, to renounce: *thy godhead —d apart,* As IV, 3, 44. *l. apart the borrowed glories,* H5 II, 4, 78. to *l. apart their particular functions,* III, 7, 41. to *l. his gay comparisons apart,* Ant. III, 13, 26. to *l. aside* = to put off, to discontinue, to renounce: *l. aside the thoughts of Sicilia,* Wint. IV, 2, 58. to *l. aside the sword,* John I, 12. to *l. aside life-harming heaviness,* R2 II, 2, 3. H4B I, 2, 99. H6C II, 2, 10. III, 3, 229. Cor. I, 1, 201. I, 3, 75. to *l. by* = a) to put at one's side: *Cupid —d by his brand,* Sonn. 153, 1. b) to put apart for a certain use: *l. it by,* Wint. IV, 4, 277. 290. *and l. it by,* Tit. IV, 1, 104. *l. by these,* Oth. IV, 3, 48. c) to take off, to put off, to set apart: *l. by all nicety,* Meas. II, 4, 162. to *l. my reverence by,* Ado V, 1, 64. *l. these glozes by,* LLL IV, 3, 370. *l. nice manners by,* All's V, 1, 15. *let them l. by their helmets,* R2 I, 3, 119. *got with swearing 'l. by',* H4A I, 2, 40 (i. e. throw off your load; according to others a nautical term, = to stop). *I have —d by my majesty,* H5 I, 2, 276. *his ceremonies —d by,* IV, 1, 109. *we l. by our appertainments,* Troil. II, 3, 86. *—ing by that nothing-gift of differing multitudes,* Cymb. III, 6, 85. to *l. down* = a) to place on the ground: *—ing them down,* Gent. I, 2, 135. b) to renounce, to quit, to give up: *l. down thy arms,* John II, 154. 345. V, 1, 24. V, 2, 126. H6C IV, 2, 131. *you must l. down the treasures of your body to this supposed,* Meas. II, 4, 96. *I dare my life l. down,* Wint. II, 1, 130. III, 2, 83. *l. down your head,* H6B IV, 1, 16. to *l.* = to ply, to apply eagerly: *l. to your fingers,* Tp. IV, 251. to *l. up* = to reposit, to store: *the gold is —d up safe at the Centaur,* Err. II, 2, 1. *ail comfort heaven ever —d up to make parents happy,* H8 V, 5, 8. to *l. bare* = to uncover: *l. bare your bosom,* Merch. IV, 1, 252.

to l. naked, in the same sense: R3 I, 2, 178. *to l. open* = to discover, to show, to display: Lucr. 747. 1248. Wiv. II, 2, 191. Err. III, 2, 34. Wint. III, 2, 19. John IV, 3, 38. H4A II, 3, 34. R3 III, 7, 15. Cymb.III, 2, 29.

Followed by prepositions; *to l. before* = to exhibit, to present to view: *those fell mischiefs our reasons —d before him*, H8 V, 1, 50. *wherefore had you not fully —d my state before me*, Tim. II, 2, 134. *I brought in my accounts, —d them before you*, 143. *to l. to the charge of* = to charge with, to impute: Ado V, 1, 228. As III, 2, 370. Wint. II, 3, 96 *(might we l. the old proverb to your charge).* V, 1, 195. John I, 256. R2 I, 1, 84. H6A III, 1, 4. H6B III, 1, 134. R3 I, 3, 326. Lr. I, 2, 138. *to l. to a person's answer*, and *to a p.* in the same sense: *this is not —d to thy answer*, Wint. III, 2, 200. *nor is't directly —d to thee*, 195. *it will be —d to us*, Hml. IV, 1, 17. *—ing defects of judgment to me*, Ant. II, 2, 55. *to l. to gage or to pawn* = to pawn: *pawned honest looks, but —d no words to gage*, Lucr. 1351. *you should l. my countenance to pawn*, Wiv. II, 2, 5. III, 1, 112. *to l. upon or on* = to bestow, to confer, to charge, to impose, to inflict: *l. bolts enough upon him*, Meas. V, 350. *this imposition which my love —s upon you*, Merch. III, 4, 35. *l. all the weight you can upon my patience*, H8 V, 3, 66. *—est thou thy leaden mace upon my boy*, Caes. IV, 3, 268. *these hard conditions as this time is like to l. upon us*, I, 2, 175. *for the command, I'll l. it upon you*, Oth. II, 1, 272. *a joint burden —d upon us all*, H4B V, 2, 55. *to whom as great a charge as little honour he meant to l. upon*, H8 I, 1, 78. *he has much worthy blame —d upon him*, All's IV, 3, 7; Mcb. III, 4, 44; IV, 3, 124; Lr. V, 3, 254. Oth. IV, 2, 46. *l. breath so bitter on your bitter foe*, Mids. III, 2, 44. *the canon of the law is —d on him*, John II, 180. *the care on thee I l.* Per. I, 2, 119. *l. on me this cross*, Sonn. 42, 12. *if you seek to l. on me a cruelty*, Ant. V, 2, 129. *the curse my noble father —d on thee*, R3 I, 3, 174. *have —d disgraces on my head*, H6B III, 1, 162. *to l. any of my evils on you*, Tw. II, 1, 7. *l. the fault on me*, H6A II, 1, 57; Cor. II, 3, 234; 242. *such griefs as you l. upon yourself*, Per. I, 2, 66. *—d their guilt upon my guiltless shoulders*, R3 I, 2, 98. *to l. a heavy and unequal hand upon our honours*, H4B IV, 1, 102. *the imputation —d on him*, Hml. V, 2, 149. *indignities you —d upon me*, H4B V, 2, 69. *wilt l. the leaven on all proper men*, Cymb. III, 4, 64. *the most loathed life that age can l. on nature*, Meas. III, 1, 131. *l. their murders on your neck*, Oth. V, 2, 170. *what penance your invention can l. upon my sin*, Ado V, 1, 283. *shall I l. perjury upon my soul?* Merch. IV, 1, 229. *what a scourge is —d upon your hate*, Rom. V, 3, 292. *if thou accountest it shame, l. it on me*, Shr. IV, 3, 183. *—d the sentence of banishment on yon man*, R2 III, 3, 134. *the sins of the father are to be —d upon the children*, Merch. III, 5, 2. H5 IV, 1, 249. *—ing these sullies on my son*, Hml. II, 1, 39. *could not have —d such terms upon his callat*, Oth. IV, 2, 121. *a torment to l. upon the damned*, Tp. I, 2, 290. *the wrong that thy unkindness —s upon my heart*, Sonn. 139, 2. *that still I l. upon my mother's head*, John I, 76. *l. on that shall make your shoulders crack*, II, 146. *all else this lord can l. upon my credit*, H8 III, 2, 265. In a good, or at least indifferent sense: *he hath —d courtesies upon me*, Ant. II, 2, 157. *on him I l. what you would l. on me*, R3 III, 7, 171 (i. e. the royal dignity). *to l. my*

duty on your hand (viz a kiss) Ant. III, 13, 81. *emblems —d nobly on her*, H8 IV, 1, 90. *the duke will l. upon him all the honour*, All's III, 2, 74; R3 I, 3, 97; Caes. IV, 1, 19. *upon thy cheek l. I this zealous kiss*, John II, 19; cf. Ant. IV, 15, 21. *we l. our best love and credence upon thy promising fortune*, All's III, 3, 2. *—d my knighthood on my shoulder*, R2 I, 1, 79. *l. negligent and loose regard upon him*, Troil. III, 3, 41. *—d good 'scuse upon your ecstasy*, Oth. IV, 1, 80. *l. a more noble thought upon mine honour*, All's V, 3, 180. *to l. so dear a trust on any soul*, H4A IV, 1, 34. *I will l. trust upon thee*, Lr. III, 5, 25. — *To l. violent hands on a person's life* = to kill or murder a p.: H6B III, 2, 138. 156. Tit. III, 2, 22. 25. *to l. hands on* = to use violence to, to seize: Ado III, 3, 58. As I, 1, 58. Shr. V, 1, 39. H6B I, 4, 44. H6C III, 1, 26. R3 I, 4, 196. Cor. III, 1, 222. Tit. V, 2, 159. Cymb. V, 3, 91. *to l. hand:* Lr. IV, 6, 192. *to l. hold on* = to seize: Meas. V, 364. Err. V, 91. Shr. V, 1, 91. Troil. V, 3, 59. Oth. I, 2, 80. *to l. hold of* (cf. *Of*): Cor. III, 1, 212. Rom. I, 5, 118.

7) to set, to place for the purpose of entrapping: *a bait on purpose —d*, Sonn. 129, 8. *the bait that we l. for it*, Ado III, 1, 33. *you must l. lime to tangle her desires*, Gent. III, 2, 68. *thou —dst a trap to take my life*, H6A III, 1, 22; H8 V, 1, 143. *l. an ambush for your life*, R2 I, 1, 137. *all the country is —d for me*, H6B IV, 10, 4 (= beset, filled with traps). Absol.: *I'll cheer up my discontented troops, and l. for hearts*, Tim. III, 5, 115 (strive to entrap, to captivate hearts).

8) to plan, to project, to contrive: *this plot of death when sadly she had —d*, Lucr. 1212; Wiv. III, 2, 39; III, 3, 202; John III, 4, 146; R2 IV, 333; H4A II, 1, 57; II, 3, 18; H6A II, 3, 4; R3 I, 1, 32. *to l. a complot*, Tit. V, 2, 147. *l. new platforms*, H6A II, 1, 77. *this is of purpose —d by some that hate me*, H8 V, 2, 14. *malice and lucre in them have —d this woe here*, Cymb. IV, 2, 325. With *down*, = to compute; to devise: *in better shape than I can l. it down in likelihood*, Ado IV, 1, 238. H4A I, 2, 168. H4B I, 3, 35. H5 I, 2, 137.

9) to institute, to apply, to bring to bear: *to l. a claim*, Lucr. 1794; Err. III, 2, 84; 86; 89; 144; As V, 1, 7; John I, 9; 72; R2 II, 3, 135; H6B II, 2, 40; H6C I, 1, 152. *to l. siege to sth.:* Wiv. II, 2, 243; Mids. I, 1, 142; H6B III, 3, 22; Tim. IV, 3, 7. *to l. down a siege*, All's III, 7, 18.

10) to stake, to wage; absol. with *on:* *—ing on my duty*, Shr. V, 2, 129. *he hath —d on twelve for nine*, Hml. V, 2, 174. Trans.: *I'll l. my head to any goodman's hat*, LLL I, 1, 310. *and on the wager l. two women*, Merch. III, 5, 85. *—d mine honour on't*, Tw. III, 4, 222 (M. Edd. *—d mine honour out*). *I dare l. any money*, 432. *I will l. odds*, H4B V, 5, 111. *l. twenty crowns to one*, H5 IV, 1, 242. *I'll l. my life*, Troil. III, 1, 95. Rom. I, 3, 12. Hml. V, 2, 172. Cymb. I, 1, 174. I, 4, 138. *l. down my soul at stake*, Oth. IV, 2, 13. *to l. a wager* = to bet: *he has —d a great wager on your head*, Hml. V, 2, 105. *the wager you have —d*, Cymb. II, 4, 95.

11) to spread on a surface, to apply as a colour (Germ. *auftragen*): *beauty needs no pencil, beauty's truth to l.* Sonn. 101, 7. *that was —d on with a trowel*, As I, 2, 112. *whose red and white nature's own cunning hand —d on*, Tw. I, 5, 258. *your sorrow was too sore —d on*, Wint. V, 3, 49 (Leontes' sorrow being

compared with the colouring of Hermione's statue). Hence perhaps = to paint, to colour: *l. them* (your hands) *in gore*, Mids. V, 346 (Thisbe's speech).

12) Joined with certain adverbs or prepositions, = to fall to work with might and main, to do one's best, especially in fighting: *I could l. on like a butcher*, H5 V, 2, 147. *he'll l. about him to-day*, Troil. I, 2, 58. *there's —ing on*, 224. *l. on, Macduff*, Mcb. V, 8, 33. *look you l. home to him*, Hml. III, 4, 1. *he —s it on* = he does his business well: Tp. III, 2, 160. *my father hath made her mistress of the feast, and she —s it on*, Wint. IV, 3, 43.

13) With *out*, = to expend: *they will l. out ten doits to see a dead Indian*, Tp. II, 2, 34. *honest fools l. out their wealth on courtsies*, Tim. I, 2, 241. *you l. out too much pains for purchasing but trouble*, Cymb. II, 3, 92. Absol. = to pay for another, to advance money: H4A IV, 2, 5.

14) Intr. = to lie: *and down I —d to list the sad-tuned tale*, Compl. 4 (some M. Edd. *lay*).

Layer-up (cf. *Lay*, vb. def. 2), destroyer: *old age, that ill l. of beauty*, H5 V, 2, 248.

Lazar, a person beggarly and thoroughly diseased, especially leperous: *to relief of —s and weak age*, H5 I, 1, 15. *the l. kite of Cressid's kind*, II, 1, 80. *she never shrouded any but —s*, Troil. II, 3, 36. *to be the louse of a l.* V, 1, 72.

Lazar-like, like a leper: *most l., with vile and loathsome crust*, Hml. I, 5, 72.

Lazarus, the beggar of the parable (S. Luke XVI, 20): H4A IV, 2, 27.

Lazy, idle, indolent, sluggish, slow: Ven. 181. Tp. III, 1, 28. Mids. V, 41. As III, 2, 322. H5 I, 2, 204. H6C II, 1, 130. H8 V, 4, 74. 84. Troil. I, 3, 147. 257. Rom. I, 4, 66.

Lazy-puffing, perhaps = slowly swelling (cf. *Puff*): *when he bestrides the l. clouds*, Rom. II, 2, 31. The spurious Q1 and M. Edd. *lazy-pacing*; Collier conjectures *lazy-passing*.

Le, the French article, used in *Harry le Roy*: H5 IV, 1, 49. 50.

Lea, a field of arable land: *thy rich —s of wheat, rye, barley*, Tp. IV, 60. *her fallow —s the darnel, hemlock and rank fumitory doth root upon*, H5 V, 2, 44. *plough-torn —s*, Tim. IV, 3, 193.

Lead, subst. the metal Plumbum: Wiv. IV, 2, 118. LLL III, 60. 62. V, 2, 621. Merch. I, 2, 33. II, 7, 8. 17. 21. 49. II, 9, 20. III, 2, 104. H4A V, 3, 34. Lr. IV, 7, 48. Used for bullets: LLL III, 58. 63. H4A V, 3, 35. for coffins: Pilgr. 396. Merch. II, 7, 50. H6A I, 1, 64. in a molten state, for torments: *boiling in —s or oils*, Wint. III, 2, 178. Emblem of heaviness: Ven. 1072. H4B I, 1, 118. R3 V, 3, 152. Cor. I, 1, 184. Rom. I, 1, 186. I, 4, 15. II, 5, 17. Mcb. II, 1, 6. Ant. III, 11, 72. Plur. *—s* = a flat roof covered with lead: R3 III, 7, 55. Cor. II, 1, 227. IV, 6, 82.

Lead, vb. (impf. and partic. *led*) 1) to guide or conduct by the hand, to aid and support in going, to make or enable to walk by any means: *led in the hand of her kind aunt*, R3 IV, 1, 2. *l. his apes into hell*, Ado II, 1, 43. *l. apes in hell*, Shr. II, 34 (to guide them by the hand like little children; cf. *Ape*). *we'll l. you thither*, As IV, 3, 162. *l. him to his tent*, H4A V, 4, 8. *the officers that led me*, H6A I, 4, 44. *thrice I led him off*, H6B V, 3, 9. *l. in your ladies*, H8 I, 4, 103. *l. me in*, III, 2, 451. IV, 2, 5. *I l. my bride along*, Tit. I,

328. *to l. him*, Lr. III, 7, 104. IV, 1, 10. 47. 48. 81. 82. IV, 6, 228. *l. him off*, Oth. II, 3, 254. *l. me from hence*, Ant. II, 5, 109. 119. IV, 4, 35. *I saw her led between her brother and Antony*, III, 3, 12. *—ing him prisoner in a red-rose chain*, Ven. 110. *led with manacles through our streets*, Cor. V, 3, 114. Used of the conduct given to ladies in dancing: *to l. her a coranto*, All's II, 3, 49. *a measure to l. 'em once again*, H8 I, 4, 107. Of animals: *the boy shall l. our horses*, H4A II, 2, 83. *bid Butler l. him forth*, II, 3, 75. *though authority be a stubborn bear, yet he is oft led by the nose with gold*, Wint. IV, 4, 832. *he will be led by the nose as asses are*, Oth. I, 3, 407. *led or driven*, Caes. IV, 1, 23.

2) to direct, to govern, to rule, to be guide of: *by reprobate desire thus madly led*, Lucr. 300. *the smallest twine may l. me*, Ado IV, 1, 252. *I am not solely led by nice direction of a maiden's eyes*, Merch. II, 1, 13. *blind fortune —ing me*, 36. *led by this priest*, John III, 1, 163. 168. *led by flatterers*, R2 II, 1, 241. *led by the impartial conduct of my soul*, H4B V, 2, 36. *the queen, that led calm Henry*, H6C II, 6, 34. *blind fear that seeing reason —s*, Troil. III, 2, 76. *what error —s must err*, V, 2, 111. *l. their successes as we wish our own*, Cor. I, 6, 7. *that god who —s him*, II, 1, 235. *a brain that —s my use of anger*, III, 2, 30. *if circumstances l. me, I will find where truth is hid*, Hml. II, 2, 157. *likelihood to l. it*, V, 1, 231. *their noses are led by their eyes*, Lr. II, 4, 70. *he —s himself*, 301. *the life that wants the means to l. it*, IV, 4, 20. *fortune l. you well*, V, 3, 41. *'tis not profit that does l. mine honour*, Ant. II, 7, 82. *our leader's led*, III, 7, 70. With *on*: *my election is led on in the conduct of my will*, Troil. II, 2, 62. Peculiar passage: *your son, that with a fearful soul —s discontented steps in foreign soil*, R3 IV, 4, 312, i. e. whose steps are guided, directed by fear.

3) to command, to conduct as a chief; absol.: *affection is my captain, and he —eth*, Lucr. 271. Trans.: *though the devil l. the measure*, All's II, 1, 57. *led by the Dauphin*, John V, 1, 65. *who —s his power*, H4A IV, 1, 18. H6A IV, 3, 7. R3 V, 3, 219. 323. Cor. IV, 6, 75. 90. Mcb. V, 6, 4. Oth. I, 1, 154. Ant. IV, 14, 139. With *off*: *l. their charges off*, Caes. IV, 2, 48. With *on*: *—s ancient lords and reverend bishops on*, H4A III, 2, 104. *led on by bloody youth*, H4B IV, 1, 34. *these three l. on their preparation*, Cor. I, 2, 15. *it sufficeth that Brutus —s me on*, Caes. II, 1, 334. *l. your battle softly on*, V, 1, 16. *led on by Malcolm*, Mcb. V, 2, 1. The destination added: *if they l. to any ill*, Ado II, 1, 159. *—ing the men of Herefordshire to fight*, H4A I, 1, 39. I, 3, 82. III, 2, 104. V, 3, 36. H4B I, 3, 32. 81. IV, 3, 72. IV, 4, 3. IV, 5, 211. H5 IV, 1, 152. H6B III, 1, 312. R3 V, 3, 291. Cor. IV, 6, 66. V, 6, 76. Tit. V, 1, 13. Ant. IV, 2, 42.

4) to draw, to bring on a way, to cause to go, to induce, to prevail on: *who l. thee there where thou art forced to break a twofold truth*, Sonn. 41, 11. *l. me in the dark out of my way*, Tp. II, 2, 6. *didst thou not l. him from Perigenia*, Mids. II, 1, 77. *I'll follow you, I'll l. you about a round*, III, 1, 109. *from each other look thou l. them thus*, III, 2, 363. 397. 399. *led hither by pure love*, All's III, 4, 38. *that same knave that —s him to these places*, III, 5, 86. *didst l. me forth of that sweet way*, R2 III, 2, 204. *let a rebel l. you to your deaths*, H6B IV, 8, 13. *will be led from himself*, Troil.

II, 3, 190. *if you should l. her into a fool's paradise,* Rom. II, 4, 175. *into what dangers would you l. me,* Caes. I, 2, 63. *yet something —s me forth,* III, 3, 4. *—s the will to desperate undertakings,* Hml. II, 1, 104. *partly led to diet my revenge,* Oth. II, 1, 303. *to what sport his addiction —s him,* II, 2, 6. *to l. astray:* Mids. III, 2, 358. *to l. away* = to seduce: *how many gazers mightst thou l. away,* Sonn. 96, 11. *to l. on* = to allure: *l. him on with a fine-baited delay,* Wiv. II, 1, 98. *you had my prayers to l. them on,* All's II, 4, 17. *to l. wrong* = to deceive: *how you were wrong led,* Ant. III, 6, 80.

5) to go at the head, to set the example of going; absol.: *l., monster, we'll follow,* Tp. III, 2, 159. *in God's name, l.* H6C III, 1, 99. Rom. V, 3, 168. Caes. III, 1, 120. *to l. first:* Err. V, 422. Cor. I, 1, 164. *l. away,* Wint. V, 3, 155. *l. on,* Cor. I, 1, 249. Oth. I, 1, 181. Trans.: *had you rather l. mine eyes,* Wiv. III, 2, 3. *l. us the way,* Per. V, 3, 84. Oftener only *l. the way:* Tp. II, 2, 177. 192. Wiv. I, 1, 318. Shr. IV. 4, 69. Tw. IV, 3, 34. H6B II, 4, 110. H6C V, 1, 112. Troil. III, 3, 54. H8 V, 5, 73. Metaphorically: *passion assays to l. the way,* Oth. II, 3, 207 (= to take the head).

Not seldom expressing a mere invitation to go along: *l. off this ground,* Tp. II, 1, 323 (= come). *l. away,* 325. *please it your grace l. on?* Ado I, 1, 160. *l. on, o' God's name,* H8 II, 1, 78. *why, then, l. on,* Caes. V, 1, 123. *about my galley I invite you all: will you l., lords?* Ant. II, 6, 83. *l., l.* Cymb. IV, 4, 53.

6) to take with one, to go along with, to conduct, to bring: *the heavens l. forth and bring you back in happiness,* Meas. I, 1, 75. *led by the provost to prison,* I, 2, 117. *art thou led in triumph?* III, 2, 47; cf. Caes. V, 1, 109 and Ant. V, 2, 109. *to l. you to our court,* LLL V, 2, 344. *—s me to your eyes,* Mids. II, 2, 121. *l. him to my bower,* III, 1, 202. Merch. II, 1, 23. As IV, 3, 143. 146. Shr. II, 109. All's III, 6, 118. Wint. III, 2, 243. V, 3, 152. John V, 4, 7. H4B III, 2, 322. IV, 3, 81. H6A IV, 4, 86. H6B II, 4, 30. H8 II, 1, 93. R3 III, 4, 108. IV, 4, 334. Troil. I, 3, 305. Caes. I, 1, 32. I, 3, 112. Mcb. III, 4, 63. Hml. I, 5, 1. Oth. I, 1, 159. Ant. II, 2, 171. III, 11, 51. With *on,* = a) to conduct away: *I led them on in this distracted fear,* Mids. III, 2, 31. *will l. thee on to gather from thee,* All's IV, 1, 90. *l. me on,* Tw. I, 2, 64. III, 4, 406. b) to bring to a certain point: *the path is smooth that —eth on to danger,* Ven. 788. *never-resting time —s summer on to hideous winter,* Sonn. 5, 5. *which must l. on to some foul issue,* Wint. II, 3, 153. *—s on to fortune,* Caes. IV, 3, 219.

7) to have a direction, to be the way, to conduct: *to shun the heaven that —s men to this hell,* Sonn. 129, 14. *upon the rising of the mountain-foot that —s towards Mantua,* Gent. V, 2, 47. *a little door that from the vineyard to the garden —s,* Meas. IV, 1, 33. All's IV, 5, 57. Oth. III, 3, 407. With an accus.: *the path which shall directly l. thy foot to England's throne,* John III, 4, 129.

8) to bear, to carry: *has led the drum before the English tragedians,* All's IV, 3, 298. *that thou but —est this fashion of thy malice to the last hour of act,* Merch. IV, 1, 18. *if you will l. these graces to the grave,* Tw. I, 5, 260.

9) to be attended with, to cause: *delay —s impotent and snail-paced beggary,* R3 IV, 3, 53. *whether love l. fortune, or else fortune love,* Hml. III, 2, 213.

10) to draw out, to pass, to spend: *she —s an ill life with him,* Wiv. II, 2, 92. 93. 122. *and with him l. my life,* Err. III, 2, 67. *where is the life that late I led,* Shr. IV, 1, 143 and H4B V, 3, 146. *ere I l. this life long,* H4A II, 4, 129. H4B II, 4, 310. H6C IV, 6, 42. Cor. V, 3, 96. *that we may l. on our days to age,* Caes. V, 1, 95.

Leaden, 1) made of lead: LLL V, 2, 481. Merch. II, 7, 15. All's III, 2, 111. H4A II, 4, 419. Cor. I, 5, 6. Caes. III, 1, 173.

2) Metaphorically, = a) heavy: *l. slumber,* Lucr. 124. R3 V, 3, 105. *sleep with l. legs,* Mids. III, 2, 365. *thy l. mace,* Caes. IV, 3, 268. *tie l. pounds to's heels,* Cor. III, 1, 314. b) dull, indolent: *with l. appetite,* Ven. 34. *in l. contemplation,* LLL IV, 3, 321. *l. age,* H6A IV, 6, 12. *if he be l., icy-cold,* R3 III, 1, 176. *l. servitor to dull delay,* IV, 3, 52. c) melancholy: *I have this while with l. thoughts been pressed,* Oth. III, 4, 177.

Leader, 1) one who leads, directs the steps, shows the way: *these mine eyes, true —s to their queen,* Ven. 503. *you were wont to be a follower, but now you are a l.* Wiv. III, 2, 3.

2) commander, captain: Lucr. 296. H4A V, 1, 118. H4B III, 2, 68. 178. IV, 1, 25. IV, 2, 99. H6A I, 1, 143. IV, 1, 32. IV, 3, 17. H6C IV, 2, 27. R3 V, 3, 25. Cor. I, 1, 232. Ant. III, 7, 70. Used of those who give directions in a dance: Ado II, 1, 157. of the queen-bee: H6B III, 2, 126.

Leading, 1) command, direction: *his eye commends the l. to his hand,* Lucr. 436. H5 IV, 3, 130. R3 V, 3, 297. *if thou wilt have the l. of thine own revenges,* Cor. IV, 5, 143.

2) generalship: *being men of such great l. as you are,* H4A IV, 3, 17.

Leaf (plur. *leaves*) 1) the part of plants called Folium and Petalum: Ven. 416. 798. 1055. Lucr. 1168. Sonn. 5, 7. 12, 5. 25, 5. 73, 2. 97, 14. Pilgr. 231. Ado II, 1, 247. LLL IV, 3, 44. All's IV, 4, 32. R2 I, 2, 20. III, 4, 50. H4A V, 1, 5. H4B II, 4, 117. H5 III, 2, 353. H6A IV, 1, 92. H6B III, 1, 90. V, 1, 206. H6C II, 6, 48. III, 3, 126. R3 II, 2, 42. II, 3, 33. H8 III, 2, 353. Tit. II, 3, 14. 200. II, 4, 45. Rom. I, 1, 158. I, 2, 52. Tim. IV, 3, 263. Hml. IV, 7, 168. Ant. III, 12, 9. Cymb. III, 3, 63. IV, 2, 223. The sing. collectively = leaves, foliage: *met with the fall of l.* R2 III, 4, 49. *fallen into the sear, the yellow l.* Mcb. V, 3, 23.

2) a part of a book containing two pages: Sonn. 77, 3. LLL V, 2, 8. Tit. IV, 1, 102 (*a l. of brass*). 105. Tim. IV, 3, 117 (*within the l. of pity writ*). *to turn the l. or the —ves* = to seek a passage in a book: Tit. IV, 1, 45. Mcb. I, 3, 152. *to fold down or to turn down the l.* = to mark a passage by folding the leaf: Caes. IV, 3, 273. Cymb. II, 2, 4. 45.

Leafy, see *Leavy.*

League, subst. a measure of the length of about three miles: Tp. I, 2, 145. II, 1, 247. III, 2, 17. Gent. V, 1, 11. Meas. IV, 3, 103. Err. I, 1, 63. 101. Ado I, 1, 4. Mids. I, 1, 159. 165. II, 1, 174. H4A III, 1, 227. H5 III, 2, 46. Caes. III, 1, 286. Per. IV, 4, 1.

League, subst. peace, amity, friendship: *now he vows a l., and now invasion,* Lucr. 287. *this blessed l. to kill,* 383. *this forced l. doth force a further strife,* 689. *betwixt mine eye and heart a l. is took,* Sonn. 47, 1 (peace is concluded). *there is such a l. between my good man and he,* Wiv. III, 2, 25. *keep then fair l. and* *truce with thy true bed*, Err. II, 2, 147. *back to Athens shall the lovers wend, with l. whose date till death shall never end*, Mids. III, 2, 373 (= mutual love). *I shall show you peace and fair-faced l.* John II, 417. 545. III, 1, 106. 228. IV, 2, 126. V, 1, 65. V, 2, 38. R2 V, 1, 22. H5 V, 2, 394. 400. H6A V, 4, 119. 148. H6B I, 1, 98. 127. H6C II, 1, 30. III, 3, 53. 74. R3 I, 3, 281. II, 1, 2. 29. H8 I, 1, 95. 182. II, 2, 25. III, 2, 323. Tit. IV, 1, 98. IV, 2, 136. V, 3, 23.

Leagued, 1) joined, folded together: *his arms thus l.* Cymb. IV, 2, 213.

2) connected by friendship: *partially affined, or l. in office*, Oth. II, 3, 218 (O. Edd. *league*).

Leaguer, camp: All's III, 6, 27.

Leah, name of the wife of Shylock: Merch. III, 1, 126.

Leak, subst. a fissure in a vessel that lets in water: Lr. III, 6, 28.

Leak, vb. 1) to get a fissure that lets in water: *that the united vessel of their blood shall never l.* H4B IV, 4, 47. *—ed is our bark*, Tim. IV, 2, 19.

2) to make water: *we l. in your chimney*, H4A II, 1, 22.

Leaky, letting in water: Tp. I, 1, 51. Ant. III, 13, 63.

Lean, vb. (impf. *—ed*: Lucr. 1415. Pilgr. 382. Troil. III, 3, 85. Cymb. I, 1, 78) 1) tr. to prop, to incline, to make to rest: *—ed her breast up-till a thorn*, Pilgr. 382. *—ing cheek to cheek*, Wint. I, 2, 285. *l. thine aged back against mine arm*, H6A II, 5, 43. *how she —s her cheek upon her hand*, Rom. II, 2, 23.

2) intr. a) to bend, to incline, to rest: *I'll but l.* Gent. II, 5, 31. *she —s me out of her mistress' chamber-window*, Ado III, 3, 155. Mostly with on: *—ing on their elbows*, Ven. 44. *these violets whereon we l.* 125. Lucr. 1415. LLL V, 1, 108. As III, 5, 22. John I, 194. H4A I, 3, 32. H6C II, 1, 68. 189. Troil. V, 3, 61. Cor. I, 1, 246. Ant. III, 13, 69.

b) to incline, to tend; with *to:* *howe'er you l. to the nayward*, Wint. II, 1, 64. *Northumberland did l. to him*, H4A IV, 3, 67. *l. to cutpurse*, H5 V, 1, 91 (Pistol's speech). *my lord —s to discontent*, Tim. III, 4, 70.

c) to depend: *the lives of all your loving complices l. on your health*, H4B I, 1, 164. *the love that —ed on them*, Troil. III, 3, 85. *every thing is sealed and done that else —s on the affair*, Hml. IV, 3, 59. Quibbling: *my name is Elbow; I do l. upon justice*, Meas. II, 1, 49.

d) to be in a bending posture, to be about to fall: *depender on a thing that —s*, Cymb. I, 5, 58.

e) to bow, to submit; with *to:* *'twere good you —ed unto his sentence with what patience your wisdom may inform you*, Cymb. I, 1, 78.

Lean, adj. 1) wanting flesh, meager, thin: Ven. 136. 931. As II, 7, 158. III, 2, 341. 392. Tw. IV, 2, 8. John IV, 2, 201. H4A II, 4, 358. 520. H4B III, 2, 294. H6A I, 2, 35. IV, 2, 11. Rom. V, 3, 104. Tim. IV, 3, 13. Caes. I, 2, 194. II, 2, 113. Hml. IV, 3, 25. Ant. III, 11, 37. *lank and l.* Lucr. 708. *the clergy's bags are lank and l.* H6B I, 3, 132.

2) not rich, barren, sterile: *lards the l. earth*, H4A II, 2, 116. H4B IV, 3, 129.

3) bare, stripped: *l., rent and beggared by the strumpet wind*, Merch. II, 6, 19. *the trees, though summer, yet forlorn and l.* Tit. II, 3, 94.

4) barren of thought: *l. penury within that pen doth dwell*, Sonn. 84, 5. *fat paunches have l. pates*, LLL I, 1, 26.

5) poor, insignificant: *I have but l. luck in the match*, Err. III, 2, 93. *out of my l. and low ability*, Tw. III, 4, 378. *whereof the hangman hath no l. wardrobe*, H4A I, 2, 82. *let not a —er action rend us*, Ant. II, 2, 19.

Leander, the lover of Hero: Gent. I, 1, 22. III, 1, 120. Ado V, 2, 30. As IV, 1, 100. Corrupted to *Limander* by the performer of Pyramus in Mids. V, 198.

Lean-faced, having an emaciated face: Err. V, 237. H6B III, 2, 315.

Lean-looked, having a miserable and hungry look: R2 II, 4, 11.

Leanness, 1) want of flesh, meagerness: R2 II, 1, 78. Cor. I, 1, 20.

2) poverty, emptiness: *the l. of his purse*, H6B I, 1, 112.

Lean-witted, stupid, foolish: R2 II, 1, 115.

Leap, subst. a spring, a bound: H4A I, 3, 201. H8 V, 1, 140.

Leap, vb. (impf. and partic. *leaped; leapt* in All's II, 5, 40, according to F1) 1) intr. a) to spring upwards, to rise from the ground with a bound: *l. upright*, Lr. IV, 6, 27. Used of one springing on a horse: H5 V, 2, 145. *the Moor hath —ed into my seat*, Oth. II, 1, 305. With over: *a hot temper —s over a cold decree*, Merch. I, 2, 20. H6A II, 2, 25. H6B II, 1, 144. = to skip, to pass over: *as the year had found some months asleep and —ed them over*, H4B IV, 4, 124. *our play —s o'er the firstlings of those broils*, Troil. Prol. 27.

b) to spring down: Lucr. 169. Tp. I, 2, 214. All's II, 5, 40. IV, 1, 60. John IV, 3, 1. H4B I, 3, 33. Tit. II, 3, 247. Rom. IV, 1, 77. Hml. V, 1, 301. Per. II, 4, 43. *to l. in:* Caes. I, 2, 103. V, 5, 24.

c) to skip, to bound: *imperiously he —s*, Ven. 265. *curvets and —s*, 279. *she —s that was but late forlorn*, 1026. Sonn. 98, 4. 128, 5. Pilgr. 377. LLL IV, 3, 148. V, 2, 291. Merch. I, 1, 49. R2 II, 4, 12.

d) to move in bounds: *to Windsor chimneys shalt thou l.* Wiv. V, 5, 47. *made the lame to l.* H6B II, 1, 162. *Romeo l. to these arms*, Rom. III, 2, 7. *l. thou to my heart*, Ant. IV, 8, 14. Hence = to be extremely desirous: *our master will l. to be his friend*, Ant. III, 13, 51. *my heart —s to be gone into my mother's bosom*, Per. V, 3, 45.

e) to rush, to start, to fly: *from their dark beds once more l. her eyes*, Ven. 1050 (or rather literally = spring from their beds, as in Lucr. 169). *ready to l. out of himself for joy*, Wint. V, 2, 54. *as if ruin —ed from his eyes*, H8 III, 2, 206.

2) trans. a) to spring over: *to l. large lengths of miles*, Sonn. 44, 10. *l. all civil bounds*, Tw. I, 4, 21. *—ed this orchard wall*, Rom. II, 1, 5. *dogs l. the hatch*, Lr. III, 6, 76.

b) to copulate with: *such strange bull —ed your father's cow*, Ado V, 4, 49.

Leap-frog, a play among boys in which one stoops down and another leaps over him: H5 V, 2, 142.

Leaping-house, a brothel: H4A I, 2, 9.

Leaping-time, time of swift motion, youth: *to have turned my l. into a crutch*, Cymb. IV, 2, 200.

Lear, name in Lr. I, 1, 141 etc.

Learn, 1) to gain knowledge or skill, to receive

instruction; absol.: *where subjects' eyes do l.* Lucr. 616. *though thou didst l.* Tp. I, 2, 359. *paid for my —ing,* Wiv. IV, 5, 63. Meas. II, 3, 23. IV, 2, 59. Merch. III, 2, 163. As I, 3, 76. Shr. II, 166. All's I, 1, 191. II, 2, 39. H4A V, 2, 65. Lr. II, 2, 134 etc. With *of: l. of the wise,* As III, 2, 68. *wilt thou l. of me?* R3 IV, 4, 270. Caes. IV, 3, 54. Oth. II, 1, 163.

Trans.; a simple accus. following: *where the devil should he l. our language?* Tp. II, 2, 69. Wiv. I, 3, 92. IV, 5, 61. Err. II, 1, 29. LLL III, 36 (*l. her by heart*). Merch. II, 9, 27. John IV, 2, 113. R3 I, 3, 261 etc. Accus. and *of: l. this of me,* As V, 1, 44. H4A IV, 2, 78. R3 IV, 4, 268. Tit. V, 1, 101. Rom. I, 5, 144. Cymb. V, 5, 421. *From* and *out of* following, to note the source of information: *the rudeness have I —ed from my entertainment,* Tw. I, 5, 231. *I —ed it out of women's faces,* Wint. II, 1, 12; cf. Meas. I, 2, 39. A subordinate clause following: *thence I l., drugs poison him,* Sonn. 118, 13. *they will l. you by rote where services are done,* H5 III, 6, 74. An inf.: *hath —ed to sport and dance,* Ven. 105. Sonn. 134, 7. Gent. II, 1, 19. Err. II, 2, 65 etc. *to l. to know:* Gent. IV, 2, 89. Meas. I, 4, 80. R2 II, 3, 40. H5 III, 6, 84. Tit. III, 2, 45. Inf. and *of: l. of him to take advantage,* Ven. 404. *if she l. not of her eye to look,* LLL IV, 3, 252. Ant. IV, 14, 103. Inf. and *out of: I will out of thine own confession l. to begin thy health,* Meas. I, 2, 39.

2) to be informed of, to be told, to hear; with an accus.: *let's go l. the truth of it,* Meas. I, 2, 82. Ado II, 2, 57. H8 II, 2, 135. Troil. II, 1, 142. Tit. III, 2, 39. Acc. and *of: —s news of him,* LLL II, 255. *to have —ed his health of you,* R2 II, 3, 24. H4B Ind. 39. Per. IV, 4, 8. A subord. clause: *we do l. by those... his givings-out were of an infinite distance,* Meas. I, 4, 52. *I l. in this letter that Don Peter comes,* Ado I, 1, 1. *what stuff 'tis made of, I am to l.* Merch. I, 1, 5. *l. how 'tis held,* Cor. I, 10, 28. John V, 2, 121. R2 III, 3, 1. 29. Mcb. V, 4, 8. Ant. II, 2, 29. *as I l.* R3 I, 1, 60. V, 2, 12. *as I can l.* I, 1, 53.

3) to teach (never abs.); with a double accus.: *—ing me your language,* Tp. I, 2, 365. *you l. me noble thankfulness,* Ado IV, 1, 31. *l. him forbearance,* R2 IV, 120. *do not l. her wrath,* Tit. II, 3, 143. Accus. and inf.: *to l. his wit to exchange the bad for better,* Gent. II, 6, 13. *have —ed me how to brook this,* V, 3, 4. *you must not l. me how to remember,* As I, 2, 6. *—s them to bear,* Rom. I, 4, 93. *—s me how to lose,* III, 2, 12. *l. me how to respect you,* Oth. I, 3, 183. *—ed me how to make perfumes,* Cymb. I, 5, 12. Subord. clause: *that should l. us there's a divinity,* Hml. V, 2, 9 (Ff *teach*).

4) to communicate, to tell: *l. me the proclamation,* Troil. II, 1, 22. *go l. me the tenour of the proclamation,* 99.

5) Refl. to be instructed, to receive a lesson: *where I have —ed me to repent the sin,* Rom. IV, 2, 17.

Learned, 1) versed in science; of persons: Pilgr. 64. 225. Meas. V, 475. Ado III, 5, 68. V, 1, 234. LLL V, 1, 5. 129. V, 2, 72. 895. Merch. IV, 1, 105. 144. 313. As V, 1, 42. All's II, 1, 119. H5 I, 2, 9. II, 2, 128. H6B I, 1, 89. IV, 7, 76. Cymb. III, 2, 27. *the l. ones* = scholars, H8 II, 2, 93. *the l.* = scholars: All's II, 2, 37. Rom. I, 2, 45. *added feathers to the —'s wing,* Sonn. 78, 7. With *in: my l. counsel in the laws,* H4B I, 2, 153. Of things: *l. books,* Lucr. 811. *l. prepara-*

tions, Wiv. II, 2, 237. *verses,* LLL IV, 2, 106. *by l. approbation,* H8 I, 2, 71.

2) skilful, wise, intelligent, clever: *well l. is that tongue that well can thee commend,* Pilgr. 64 and LLL IV, 2, 116. *never schooled and yet l.* As I, 1, 173. *free, l. and valiant,* Tw. I, 5, 279. *if you are l.,* be not as *common fools,* Cor. III, 1, 99. *the eyes of the ignorant are more l. than the ears,* III, 2, 77. *knows all qualities, with a l. spirit, of human dealings,* Oth. III, 3, 259.

Learnedly, with erudition, skilfully: Tp. II, 1, 44. Wint. IV, 4, 207. H8 II, 1, 28.*

Learning, 1) erudition, scholarship: Sonn. 78, 14. Pilgr. 224. Wiv. III, 1, 58. LLL IV, 2, 32. IV, 3, 314. 315. 317. V, 1, 54. Mids. V, 53. Merch. II, 2, 67. IV, 1, 158. As III, 2, 341. Shr. I, 1, 9. I, 2, 160. 169. H4B IV, 1, 44. IV, 3, 124. H8 II, 2, 139. II, 4, 59. III, 1, 73. IV, 2, 58. Troil. I, 2, 276. Rom. III, 3, 160. Tim. II, 2, 86. Cymb. IV, 2, 268.

2) instruction, acquirement: *of this book this l. mayst thou taste,* Sonn. 77, 4. *how to forget that l.* (viz to write fair) Hml. V, 2, 35. *puts to him all the —s that his time could make him the receiver of,* Cymb. I, 1, 43. *the court's a l. place,* Alls I, 1, 191.

3) information, intelligence: *and have my l. from some true reports,* Ant. II, 2, 47.

Lease, subst. 1) a temporary letting of an estate for a certain rent: *they are out by l.* Gent. V, 2, 29 (let, farmed out; a jest not quite intelligible. Perhaps Proteus hints that Silvia would like to see Thurio occupied with the cultivation of his land, instead of molesting her with his courtship). *my lands and —s,* Shr. II, 126. *to let this land by l.* R2 II, 1, 110.

2) any tenure or temporary possession: *so should that beauty which you hold in l. find no determination,* Sonn. 13, 5.

3) duration, time allotted, lifetime: *summer's l. hath all too short a date,* Sonn. 18, 4. *the l. of my true love,* 107, 3. *it fears not policy, that heretic, which works on —s of short-numbered hours,* 124, 10. *why so large cost, having so short a l., dost thou upon thy fading mansion spend?* 146, 5. *five year! a long l. for the clinking of pewter,* H4A II, 4, 50. *if I might have a l. of my life for a thousand years I could stay no longer,* H6B IV, 10, 6. *Macbeth shall live the l. of nature, pay his breath to time and mortal custom,* Mcb. IV, 1, 99.

Leased out, let, farmed out: R2 II, 1, 59.

Leash, a string or thong by which a greyhound is led: *not following my l. unwillingly,* Wint. IV, 4, 477. *like a fawning greyhound in the l.* Cor. I, 6, 38. Used in contempt of persons yoked together: *I am sworn brother to a l. of drawers, and can call them all by their Christen names, as Tom, Dick, and Francis,* H4A II, 4, 7 (three greyhounds making *a leash*).

Leashed in, bound and led in a string: *l. like hounds, should famine, sword and fire crouch for employment,* H5 Prol. 7 (three in number, as the *leash of drawers* in H4A II, 4, 7).

Leasing, a euphemism for lying, falsehoods: *now Mercury endue thee with l., for thou speakest well of fools,* Tw. I, 5, 105. *and in his praise have almost stamped the l.* Cor. V, 2, 22.

Least, adj. little beyond all others, most insignificant, most trifling: Ven. 745. Sonn. 92, 6. Gent. IV, 2, 13. Meas. III, 1, 111. LLL I, 1, 157. Tw. I, 5, 187. II, 1, 42. Wint. I, 2, 401. H4A III, 1, 186. H4B IV,

5, 173. H6A II, 3, 53. H6B I, 3, 73. III, 2, 178. R3 V, 3, 268. H8 II, 1, 129. II, 4, 153. III, 2, 7. Cor. II, 1, 245. Tit. I, 256. Tim. IV, 3, 521. Caes. III, 1, 189; cf. Lr. I, 1, 85. Mcb. III, 4, 27. Lr. II, 2, 25. Oth. IV, 2, 109. 179. Ant. I, 2, 145. II, 7, 2. III, 2, 35. Per. I, 4, 71. Substantively: *she as far surpasseth Sycorax as greatest does l.* Tp. III, 2, 111. *in l. speak most,* Mids. V, 105. *that is the l. of my fear,* Gent. II, 7, 68. *at the l. of thy sweet notice,* LLL I, 1, 278 (Armado's letter). *I have spoke the l.* Tim. V, 2, 2. *what in the l. will you require in present dower with her?* Lr. I, 1, 194 (= at least). *I cannot think my sister in the l. would fail her obligation,* II, 4, 143 (in the smallest degree).

At l. = to say no more, at the lowest degree, so much certainly if not more than: Lucr. 1053. Sonn. 10, 12. Tp. I, 2, 240. II, 1, 126. V, 170. Meas. I, 2, 21. V, 299. Ado I, 3, 9. Shr. I, 2, 72. 135. All's IV, 2, 31. Wint II, 3, 165. IV, 4, 366. V, 1, 154. John I, 69. V, 1, 75. R2 III, 3, 195. H4A III, 1, 156. H4B I, 3, 47. H6A I, 4, 73. II, 2, 9. H6C III, 1, 57. V, 1, 29. R3 V, 3, 37. H8 III, 2, 10. Mcb. V, 5, 52. Hml. I, 1, 80. Cymb. III, 4, 151. Per. I, 3, 21 etc.

At the l., in the same sense: Lucr. 1654. Sonn. 122, 5. Gent. IV, 2, 118. Wiv. II, 1, 11. IV, 6, 7. Ado I, 1, 150. LLL IV, 2, 9. Shr. IV, 1, 30. H6C III, 2, 113. IV, 7, 21. H8 I, 1, 81. Cor. II, 1, 34. Tit. V, 2, 79. Oth. III, 3, 364. Per. IV, 1, 46.

Least, adv. in the lowest degree: Sonn. 29, 8. 125, 14. Gent. I, 2, 32. Meas. IV, 3, 115. LLL II, 58. Merch. III, 2, 73. Shr. V, 2, 175. All's I, 2, 68. Tw. I, 4, 38. Wint. III, 2, 34. H4A I, 2, 241. Rom. V, 3, 223. Lr. I, 4, 154.

Leather, the dressed skin of an animal: Tp. II, 2, 73. Err. II, 1, 85. IV, 3, 23. Shr. III, 2, 58. H6B IV, 2, 26. Caes. I, 1, 29. Adjectively: As IV, 2, 12. H4B II, 2, 189 (Q *leathern*). H6B IV, 2, 13. H6C II, 5, 48. Troil. III, 3, 266. Caes. I, 1, 7.

Leather-coats, a kind of apples; brown russets: H4B V, 3, 44.

Leathern, made of leather: Ven. 392. Mids. II, 2, 4. As II, 1, 37. IV, 3, 24. H4A II, 4, 77. H4B II, 2, 189 (Ff *leather*).

Leave, subst. 1) permission, allowance, liberty granted: *I shall crave of you your l. that I may bear my evils alone,* Tw. II, 1, 6. *entering his fee-simple without l.* H6B IV, 10, 28. *without his l.* V, 1, 21. *fair l. and large security,* Troil. I, 3, 223. *as I had l. of means,* Tim. II, 2, 136 (= as my means allowed). *he hath wrung from me my slow l.* Hml. I, 2, 58. *woo for l. to do him good,* III, 4, 155 etc. *your l. and favour to return to France,* I, 2, 51. *by my father's love and l.* Shr. I, 1, 5. *to give l.:* Sonn. 39, 10. Wiv. I, 4, 128. Meas. I, 1, 61. 77. IV, 2, 156. V, 272. LLL V, 2, 342. Mids. II, 1, 206. As I, 1, 109 (*good l.*). I, 2, 167. H(A V, 3, 43 etc. Sometimes = to excuse, to pardon: *do you change colour? Give him l.; he is a kind of chameleon,* Gent. II, 4, 25. *I'll utter what my sorrow gives me l.* Err. I, 1, 36. *to have l.:* Merch. IV, 1, 364. Shr. I, 1, 54. I, 2, 136 etc. *to have good l.* Merch. III, 2, 326. H4A I, 3, 20. *by l.* = with permission: Caes. III, 1, 239. *by a person's l.* = with a p.'s permission: All's IV, 4, 13. Wint. V, 1, 70. H6C II, 2, 63. Cor. III, 1, 282. *under l. of Brutus* = with Brutus' permission, Caes. III, 2, 86. Used as a mere phrase of courtesy: *have at it then, by l.* Cymb. V, 5, 315. *by*

your l. = under your favour: Wiv. I, 1, 200. III, 5, 27. Meas. II, 1, 126. IV, 3, 115 (cf. Cymb. II, 3, 70). V, 367. Ado IV, 1, 24. Merch. III, 2, 140. 225. Shr. IV, 4, 24. V, 2, 189. Tw. II, 5, 103. III, 1, 117. H6B II, 1, 3. R3 IV, 1, 13. H8 I, 4, 85. Rom. II, 6, 36. Caes. V, 3, 89. Cymb. II, 3, 81. *L. alone,* = under your pardon: *l., gentle wax,* Lr. IV, 6, 264; Cymb. III, 2, 35; cf. Tw. II, 5, 103. *with l.,* in the same sense· Merch. III, 2, 251. *with your l. and favour,* H6C III, 3, 60.

Often used as a courteous form of bidding farewell: *by your l.* Wiv. III, 2, 28. Merch. II, 4, 15. *give us l. awhile* = leave us alone, Gent. III, 1, 1. Wiv. II, 2, 165. John I, 230. 231. H4A III, 2, 1. H6A I, 2, 70. H6C III, 2, 33. Rom. I, 3, 7 etc. *give me now l. to l. thee,* Tw. II, 4, 74 (= please to go). *my women, come; you have l.* Wint. II, 1, 124. *you have good l. to l. us,* H4A I, 3, 20; cf. H6C III, 2, 34.

2) liberty, license: *things out of hope are compassed oft with venturing, chiefly in love, whose l. exceeds commission,* Ven. 568. *you will have l., till youth take l.* H6C III, 2, 34.

3) ceremony of departure, farewell: *our lack is nothing but our l.* Mcb. IV, 3, 237. *occasion smiles upon a second l.* Hml. I, 3, 54. *to take l.* Tw. III, 4, 217. H6C III, 2, 35. *take ten thousand —s,* H6B III, 2, 354. *let us take our l.* Gent. I, 1, 56. *I'll take my l.* Meas. II, 1, 140. Ado I, 1, 102. LLL V, 2, 882. Merch. IV, 1, 420. H6A I, 1, 165. H6C II, 6, 42. H8 V, 1, 9. Troil. III, 2, 147. Ant. V, 2, 133 etc. *to take their l.* Merch. I, 2, 136. *we take our —s,* Per. II, 5, 13. *the last time that e'er I took her l. at court,* All's V, 3, 79 (bade her farewell). *to take l. of:* Tp. I, 1, 68. Merch. II, 2, 162 etc. *to take one's l. of:* Ven. 2. Gent. IV, 4, 38. Meas. I, 4, 90. Merch. II, 2, 176. H6A IV, 5, 52. R3 IV, 1, 91 etc. *taking their —s of me,* Cor. IV, 5, 139.

Leave, vb. (impf. and partic. *left*); 1) to part from, to quit: *to love that well which thou must l. ere long,* Sonn. 73, 14. *I will l. him,* Tp. II, 2, 103. III, 3, 91. IV, 72. 130. V, 9. Gent. I, 1, 64. II, 4, 119. III, 1, 165. Mids. II, 1, 215. Tw. II, 5, 211 etc. In a courteous style, = to dismiss: *give me now leave to l. thee,* Tw. II, 4, 74. Caes. I, 2, 31. *I'll l. you till night,* Hml. II, 2, 572. Peculiar passage: *a jewel that too casually hath left mine arm,* Cymb. II, 3, 147.

2) to forsake, to desert: *to l. my Julia,* Gent. II, 6, 1. *desolate and left,* IV, 4, 179. *did Angelo so l. her?* Meas. III, 1, 233. 234. *since night you left me,* Mids. III, 2, 275. Merch. V, 150. H6A III, 2, 107. III, 3, 20. Troil. III, 2, 156. Ant. III, 11, 19 etc.

3) to let remain in departing: *and left Adonis there,* Ven. 322. *whom I left cooling of the air,* Tp. I, 2, 322. *who I have left asleep,* 232. *and here was left by the sailors,* 270. *and left thee there,* 280. *I left them all in health,* Gent. II, 4, 124. *and l. no memory of what it was,* V, 4, 10. Err. I, 1, 43. Mids. III, 2, 32. John IV, 3, 104. R2 II, 3, 154. Ant. V, 2, 242 etc. With *behind:* Tp. III, 3, 41. IV, 156 etc. = to have remaining at death: *what acceptable audit canst thou l.?* Sonn. 4, 12. *thou no form of thee hast left behind,* 9, 6. *thou left'st me nothing,* Pilgr. 138. 139. Wiv. I, 1, 59. Merch. I, 1, 161. Hml. V, 2, 235 etc.

4) not to touch, not to take, to spare, to save; absol.: *here, there, and every where, he —s and takes,* Troil. V, 5, 26. Trans.: *as though I knew not what to*

l. and what to take, Shr. I, 1, 105. cf. Compl. 305 and Lr. I, 1, 208. *then l. her*, 210. *to l. the figure or disfigure it*, Mids. I, 1, 51. *you'll l. yourself hardly one subject*, Wint. II, 3, 111. *we will not l. one lord*, H6B IV, 2, 194 etc. *left* = untouched, unspent, remaining: *but the very smell were left me*, Ven. 441. *have no perfection of my summer left*, Lucr. 837. Gent. V, 4, 50. Err. II, 1, 115. V, 315. Ado I, 1, 71. IV, 1, 173. Mids. V, 355. Merch. IV, 1, 366. Wint. III, 3, 136. Mcb. I, 4, 20. Cymb. IV, 2, 304 etc. *endowed with all that Adam had left him, before he transgressed*, Ado II, 1, 259. *of all my lands is nothing left me*, H6C V, 2, 26. *hast the comfort of thy children left thee*, R3 II, 2, 56 (Ff om. *thee*).

Peculiar passage: *thou art left Marcius*, Cor. I, 4, 54; perhaps = whatever may be thy fate, thou art Marcius to the last. M. Edd. *thou art left, Marcius*, i. e. forsaken; Singer *lost*, Nicholson *reft*.

5) to desist, to discontinue, to cease; absol.: *where did I l.?* Ven. 715. *where left we last?* Shr. III, 1, 26. R2 V, 2, 4. *let us not l. till all our own be won*, H4A V, 5, 44. H6B III, 2, 333. H8 IV, 2, 94. Hml. II, 1, 51. Cymb. I, 4, 109. II, 2, 4. Per. II, 1, 46. Trans.; followed by an accus.: *to l. the battery*, Compl. 277. *l. me your snatches*, Meas. IV, 2, 6. *this fool-begged patience in thee will be left*, Err. II, 1, 41. *since you left it* (apprehension) Ado III, 4, 69. *l. this chat*, LLL IV, 3, 284. Mids. II, 1, 197. IV, 1, 21. John V, 7, 86. H4A V, 4, 168. H6A IV, J, 108. R3 I, 2, 115. III, 7, 108. H8 V, 4, 1. Cor. IV, 1, 1 etc. By a gerund: *bids them l. quaking*, Ven. 899. *l. thy peeping*, Lucr. 1089. *l. hollaing*, Merch. V, 43. Tw. I, 5, 29. Wint. IV, 4, 109. H4A II, 4, 34. H6A I, 4, 81. H6B II, 3, 80. Rom. I, 3, 44. Caes. IV, 3, 274 etc. By an inf.: *we l. to be the things we are*, Lucr. 148. *I cannot l. to love*, Gent. II, 6, 17. 18. III, 1, 182. H6B II, 1, 182. H6C II, 2, 168. Troil. III, 3, 133. Hml. III, 4, 66 etc. — *To l. off* = to cease: *l. off discourse of disability*, Gent. II, 4, 109. *l. off delays*, H6A I, 2, 146. *l. off to wonder*, H6C IV, 5, 2.

6) to part with, to give away, to renounce: *to l. for nothing all thy sum of good*, Sonn. 109, 12. *you loved not her, to l. her token*, Gent. IV, 4, 79. *l. her on such slight conditions*, V, 4, 138. *ere I will l. her*, Wiv. III, 5, 130. *he would not l. it* (the ring) Merch. V, 172. *how unwillingly I left the ring*, 196. *I may not l. it* (my office) *so*, R3 IV, 1, 27. *now you have left your voices, I have no further with you*, Cor. II, 3, 180. *will not l. their tinct*, Hml. III, 4, 91.

7) to abandon, to cede, to commit in departing, to confide, to surrender: *I l. it to your honourable survey*, Ven. Dedic. 6. *I l. him to your hand*, Meas. V, 491. *left the ship to us*, Err. I, 1, 78. *I'll l. him to the officer*, IV, 1, 61. Mids. II, 1, 228. V, 241. Merch. IV, 1, 164. V, 235. All's II, 5, 76. H4A III, 1, 259. H6A IV, 6, 3. H6B III, 2, 93. R3 I, 2, 211. Cor. IV, 7, 16. Hml. I, 5, 86 etc. *left me naked to mine enemies*, H8 III, 2, 458; cf. *left me bare to weather*, Cymb. III, 3, 64. *l. us to ourselves* = leave us alone, H6C V, 6, 6. Oth. III, 3, 85. *l. the world for me to bustle in*, R3 I, 1, 152. *pardon me for bringing these ill news, since you did l. it for my office*, Rom. V, 1, 23. With *off*: *the schools have left off the danger to itself*, All's I, 3, 247.

8) to commit, not to prevent from beginning or incurring, to give up; with *to: left me to a bootless*

inquisition, Tp. I, 2, 35. *to the hopeful execution do I l. you of your commissions*, Meas. I, 1, 60. *l. you to the hearing of the cause*, II, 1, 141. *but l. we him to his events*, III, 2, 252. *I will l. you to your humour*, Ado V, 1, 188. *and l. you to the crutch*, H6C III, 2, 35 etc. With an inf., almost = to let, to suffer: *you barely l. our thorns to prick ourselves*, All's IV, 2, 19. *England now is left to tug and scamble*, John IV, 3, 145. *him did you l. to look upon the hideous god of war*, H4B II, 3, 33. *and l. my followers here to fight and die*, H6A IV, 5, 45. *and l. your brothers to go speed elsewhere*, H6C IV, 1, 58. *l. us to cure this cause*, Cor. III, 1, 235. *how worthy he is I will l. to appear hereafter*, Cymb. I, 4, 33 etc.

9) to let be, to suffer to be: *to l. no rubs nor botches in the work*, Mcb. III, 1, 134. *where have you left the money?* Err. I, 2, 54; cf. Tp. IV, 170. 181. *all that is mine I l. at thy dispose*, Gent. II, 7, 86. *l. me not behind thee*, As III, 3, 103. *—ing the fear of God on the left hand*, Wiv. II, 2, 23. *the rank of osiers left on your right hand brings you to the place*, As IV, 3, 81. With a double accus.: *l. the faltering feeble souls alive*, Lucr. 1768. *thou art left the prey of every vulgar thief*, Sonn. 48, 8. *—s unswayed the likeness of a man*, 141, 11. *l. not the mansion so long tenantless*, Gent. V, 4, 8. Meas. I, 1, 55. III, 1, 73. Err. I, 1, 136. Mids. III, 1, 57. H4B I, 3, 60. 79. Cor. II, 2, 22. Cymb. III, 1, 10 etc. *to l. alone* = a) to quit: Ven. 382. Sonn. 66, 14. Meas. III, 1, 180. Ado III, 1, 13. Shr. Ind. 2, 118. John III, 1, 64 etc. b) to let be: *the fools are mad, if left alone*, Gent. III, 1, 99. *l. me alone to woo him*, As I, 3, 135. *to l. off* = not to put on, not to wear: *he goes in his doublet and hose and —s off his wit*, Ado V, 1, 203. *to l. out* = a) to omit, not to do, not to mention: *we must l. the killing out*, Mids. III, 1, 15. *left I his title out*, R2 III, 3, 11. R3 !, 3, 216. II, 2, 111. Cor. II, 2, 53. Caes. I, 2, 11. Ant. II, 5, 113. Cymb. V, 5, 244. b) to disregard, to neglect: *my verse, one thing expressing, —s out difference*, Sonn. 105, 8. *mannerly distinguishment l. out betwixt the prince and beggar*, Wint. II, 1, 86. *that I l. out ceremony*, IV, 4, 526. c) not to admit, not to make a partner, to exclude: *to bear your griefs yourself and l. me out*, As I, 3, 105. *each hath his place; I am left out*, H6A I, 1, 174. *l. me out on't*, H8 II, 3, 102. *let us not l. him out*, Caes. II, 1, 143. 152. *outwent her* (nature), *motion and breath left out*, Cymb. II, 4, 85 (= excepted).

10) to establish for future remembrance: *we'll l. a proof... wives may be merry*, Wiv. IV, 2, 106.

11) to depart, to die: *what is't to l. betimes?* Hml. V, 2, 235.

Leaven, subst. sour dough; used as a term of contempt and disgust: *thou vinewedst l.* Troil. II, 1, 15. Denoting what corrupts and depraves that with which it is mixed: *thou, Posthumus, wilt lay the l. on all proper men*, Cymb. III, 4, 64 (cf. *O'erleaven*).

Leavened, well fermented, ripened: *we have with a l. and prepared choice proceeded to you*, Meas. I, 1, 52.

Leavening, the admixing of sour dough: Troil. I, 1, 20. 22.

Leaver, in *Master-leaver*, q. v.

Leave-taking, bidding farewell, parting compliments: Troil. IV, 4, 36. Mcb. II, 3, 150. IV, 3, 28. Lr. I, 1, 306. Ant. V, 2, 301.

Leavy (most M. Edd. *leafy*) full of leaves: Ado II, 3, 75. Mcb. V, 6, 1. Per. V, 1, 51.

Le Beau, French name in As I, 2, 97. 104. 173.

Le Bon, French name in Merch. I, 2, 59.

Lecher, subst. a person given to lewdness: Lucr. 1637. Pilgr. 101. Wiv. III, 5, 147. Troil. IV, 1, 63. Lr. III, 4, 117. IV, 6, 282.

Lecher, vb. to indulge lust: Lr. IV, 6, 115.

Lecherous, lustful, lewd: Meas. III, 2, 186. H4B III, 2, 338. Hml. II, 2, 609. Lr. I, 2, 142.

Lechery, lewdness, indulgence of lust: Wiv. V, 3, 23. Meas. I, 2, 143. 148. III, 2, 103. Tw. I, 5, 133. H4B I, 2, 257. Troil. II, 3, 81. V, 1, 106. V, 2, 57. 195. V, 4, 37. Mcb. II, 3, 32. 35. Oth. II, 1, 263. Used in a wrong sense by the watch in Ado III, 3, 180.

Lecture, subst. lesson, discourse or reading for the purpose of instruction: *when in music we have spent an hour, your l. shall have leisure for as much,* Shr. III, 1, 8. *his l. will be done ere you have tuned,* 23. *you'll leave his l.* 24. *by my former l. and advice,* Hml. II, 1, 67. *to read —s* = 1) to give lessons for the instruction of others: *I have heard him read many —s against it,* As III, 2, 365. *read no other —s to her,* Shr. I, 2, 148. *say we read —s to you, how youngly he began to serve his country,* Cor. II, 3, 243. cf. *if thy offences were upon record, would it not shame thee in so fair a troop to read a l. of them?* R2 IV, 232. 2) to receive instruction: *wilt thou be the school where lust shall learn? must he in thee read —s of such shame?* Lucr. 618.

Leda, a mistress of Jove's, courted by him in the shape of a swan: Wiv. V, 5, 7. mother of Helen: Shr. I, 2, 244.

Lee, in *Be-lee,* q. v.

Leech (cf. *Horse-leech*) physician: Tim. V, 4, 84.

Leek, a plant of the genus Allium: H5 IV, 1, 54. IV, 7, 107. V, 1, 2. 10. 25. 39. 43. 49. 52. 65. Plur. *—s:* Mids. V, 342. H5 IV, 7, 103. V, 1, 58. 61.

Leer, subst. 1) an amorous and smiling look: *she gives the l. of invitation,* Wiv. I, 3, 50.

2) complexion: *he hath a Rosalind of a better l. than you,* As IV, 1, 67. *a young lad framed of another l.* Tit. IV, 2, 119.

Leer, vb. to look smilingly, to simper, to smile: *you l. upon me,* LLL V, 2, 480. *I will l. upon him,* H4B V, 5, 7. *I will no more trust him when he —s,* Troil. V, 1, 97.

Lees, dregs, sediment: Troil. IV, 1, 62. Mcb. II, 3, 100.

Leese, vb. to lose: *flowers distilled l. but their show,* Sonn. 5, 14.

Leet, 1) a manor court, court-leet, private jurisdiction: *you would present her at the l.* Shr. Ind. 2, 89. 2) a day on which such court is held: *keep —s and law-days,* Oth. III, 3, 140.

Left, on the side opposed to the right: Ven. 158. Gent. II, 3, 16. Err. III, 2, 148. LLL IV, 3, 25. Mids. V, 303. Merch. II, 2, 44. V, 177. Shr. IV, 1, 95. All's IV, 5, 102. H6C III, 1, 43. Cor. II, 1, 163. Caes. I, 3, 16. V, 1, 17. Oth. II, 3, 119. Cymb. II, 2, 37. *leaving the fear of God on the l. hand,* Wiv. II, 2, 24, i. e. disregarding it.

Leg, 1) the limb used in supporting the body and in walking: Ven. 297. 698. Lucr. 1427. Tp. II, 2, 62. 93. 108. 109. Gent. IV, 4, 41. V, 2, 4. Wiv. V, 5, 58. Ado II, 1, 15. 81. V, 2, 24. LLL IV, 3, 186.

V, 2. 217. 558. 644. Mids. III, 2, 343. 365. 445, Merch. II, 2, 6. As I, 2, 224. II, 4, 2. III, 5, 119. Shr. Ind. 2, 10. 60. III, 2, 68. H4B II, 3, 23. II, 4, 271. H6B II, 1, 133. IV, 10, 52. H6C V, 6, 71. Mcb. IV, 1, 17. Cymb. V, 3, 92 etc. *a capon's l.* Gent. IV, 4, 10. H4A I, 2, 129. *let them courtsy with their left —s,* Shr. IV, 1, 95. *I am there before my —s,* All's II, 2, 73. *we must have you find your --s,* H6B II, 1, 148 (i. e. learn to run). *he took up my - s,* Mcb. II, 3, 45. *overlusty at —s,* Lr. II, 4, 10.

2) a bow, an obeisance made by drawing one leg backward: *make a l.* All's II, 2, 10. R2 III, 3, 175. *here is my l.* H4A III, 4, 427. *ambitious for poor knaves' caps and —s,* Cor. II, 1, 77. *I doubt whether their —s be worth the sums that are given for 'em,* Tim. I, 2, 238.

Legacy, a bequest: Lucr. 1192. Sonn. 4, 2. Gent. III, 1, 343. All's I, 3, 251. III, 5, 13. Caes. III, 2, 141. IV, 1, 9.

Legate, an ambassador of the pope: John III, 1, 135. 139. V, 1, 62. V, 2, 65. 174. H6A V, 1, 51. H8 III, 2, 311.

Legatine, pertaining to a legate: *your power l.* H8 III, 2, 339.

Lege (M. Edd. *'lege*) to allege, to assert, to produce: *'tis no matter what he —s in Latin,* Shr. I, 2, 28 (Grumio's speech).

Legerity, lightness, alacrity: *with casted slough and fresh l.* H5 IV, 1, 23.

Legged, having legs: Tp. II, 2, 35.

Leggins, see *Liggens.*

Legion, 1) a body of infantry with the ancient Romans, consisting of about six thousand men: Caes. IV, 3, 76. 215. V, 2, 2. V, 3, 53. Ant. III, 7, 59. 72. III, 10, 34. III, 13, 22. Cymb. II, 4, 18. III, 7, 4. 12. IV, 2, 333. IV, 3, 24.

2) any military force: John II, 59. H6A IV, 4, 16.

3) any great number: *many —s of true hearts,* Sonn. 154, 6. *many —s of strange fantasies,* John V, 7, 18. Used, by eminence, of the hosts of hell: Tp. III, 3, 103. H5 II, 2, 124. R3 I, 4, 58. Mcb. IV, 3, 55. Hence, jocularly: *he hath a l.* (O. Edd. *legend*) *of angels,* Wiv. I, 3, 59 (quibbling). Treated as a noun proper, to denote a compound of all the devils of hell: *if all the devils of hell be drawn in little, and L. himself possessed him,* Tw. III, 4, 95 (Sir Toby's speech).

Legitimate, 1) lawfully begotten: John I, 116. H8 II, 4, 179. Lr. I, 2, 16. 18. 19. 21.

2) logically deduced, logical: *I will prove it l., sir, upon the oaths of judgment and reason,* Tw. III, 2, 15 (cf. *Illegitimate*).

Legitimation, legitimacy, lawful birth: *l., name and all is gone,* John I, 248.

Leicester, English town: R3 V, 2, 12. V, 5, 10. H8 IV, 2, 17.

Leicestershire, English county: H6C IV, 8, 15.

Leiger or **Leidger,** ambassador, messenger: *Lord Angelo, having affairs to heaven, intends you for his swift ambassador, where you shall be an everlasting l.* Meas. III, 1, 59. *which shall quite unpeople her of —s for her sweet,* Cymb. I, 5, 80.*

Leisure, 1) time of which one may freely dispose: *thy* (absence's) *sour l. gave sweet leave to entertain the time,* Sonn. 39, 10. *I have no l. taken to weigh how once I suffered,* 120, 7. *I have no superfluous l.*

Meas. III, 1, 158. *I hope I shall have l.* Err. V, 375. *I may have leave and l. to make love to her*, Shr. I, 2, 136. *your lecture shall have l. for as much*, III, 1, 8. *when thou hast l., say thy prayers*, All's I, 1, 227. *more l. shall express*, V, 3, 332. *ere further l. yield them further means*, R2 I, 4, 40. *how has he the l. to be sick?* H4A IV, 1, 17. *no l. had he to enrank his men*, H6A I, 1, 115. *had you such l. in the time of death to gaze upon the secrets of the deep?* R3 I, 4, 34. *which after hours give l. to repent*, IV, 4, 293. *God give us l. for these rites of love*, V, 3, 101. *I scarce have l. to salute you*, Troil. V, 2, 61. *I would not have you so slander any moment l.* Hml. I, 3, 133. *l. serves* = there is time for sth.: *debate where l. serves with dull debaters*, Lucr. 1019. *if your l. served, I would speak with you*, Ado III, 2, 84. *I am sorry that your l. serves you not*, Merch. IV, 1, 405. *my l. serves me now*, Rom. IV, 1, 39. *at l.* = having time: *are you at l. now?* Rom. IV, 1, 36. *come to me at your convenient l.* Wiv. III, 5, 137. *I will debate this matter at more l.* Err. IV, 1, 100. Shr. III, 2, 110. H4B IV, 4, 89. Hml. V, 2, 26. *more reasons for this action at our more l. shall I render you*, Meas. I, 3, 49.

2) convenient time, time fit for sth.: *might you dispense with your l., I would by and by have some speech with you*, Meas. III, 1, 154. *the boisterous late appeal, which then our l. would not let us hear*, R2 I, 1, 5, i. e. which then we had no l. to hear; cf. *the l. and the fearful time cuts off the ceremonious vows of love*, R3 V, 3, 97; *the l. and enforcement of the time forbids to dwell upon*, 238; *you have scarce time to steal from spiritual l. a brief span to keep your earthly audit*, H8 III, 2, 140; *on the supervise, no l. bated*, Hml. V, 2, 23. *pay them at thy l.* Ven. 518. *be better at thy l.* Lr. II, 4, 232. *at picked l. I'll resolve you*, Tp. V, 247. *at many —s*, Tim. II, 2, 137. *yet had he framed to himself many deceiving promises of life, which I by my good l. have discredited to him*, Meas. III, 2, 261, i. e. taking an opportunity of doing so.

3) freedom from hurry, the contrary to haste: *haste still pays haste, and l. answers l.* Meas. V, 415. *at l.* = leisurely, in no hurry, slowly: *who wooed in haste and means to wed at l.* Shr. III, 2, 11. *if you had at l. known of this*, John V, 6, 27. *by l.*, in the same sense: *I'll trust by l. him that mocks me once*, Tit. I, 301.

4) Used as a term of courtesy, almost = pleasure, liking: *let me have some patient l. to excuse myself*, R3 I, 2, 82 (i. e. please, vouchsafe to hear me with patience). *as Hector's l. and your bounties shall concur together, severally entreat him*, Troil. IV, 5, 273. cf. *not one whose flame ... any of my — s ever charmed*, Compl. 193 (i. e. my affections, inclinations). *to attend somebody's l.:* Sonn. 44, 12. Meas. IV, 1, 57. Mcb. III, 2, 3. Lr. II, 4, 37. *to attend on somebody's l.* = to be at somebody's service: *we'll make our —s to attend on yours*, Merch. I, 1, 68. *I will attend upon your lordship's l.* H6A V, 1, 55. *to stay somebody's l.:* Sonn. 58, 4. Shr. III, 2, 219. IV, 3, 59. John II, 58. H4A I, 3, 258. *to stay upon somebody's l.:* All's III, 5, 48. Mcb. I, 3, 148. *to wait for somebody's l.* Ado I, 3, 17. *at l.* = disposed, inclined: *since your ladyship is not at l., I'll sort some other time*, H6A II, 3, 26. *are you not at l.?* V, 3, 97. *if your lordship were at l., I should impart a thing to you*, Hml. V, 2, 91. *read it at your l.* Merch. V, 267. *nature and sickness*

debate it at their l. All's I, 2, 75. *at your best l.* Caes. III, 1, 5. *at your kindest l.* Mcb. II, 1, 24. *at thy sovereign l. read the garboils*, Ant. I, 3, 60.

Leisurely, adv. not in haste, deliberately, slowly: *promise more speed, but do it l.* Lucr. 1349. *where we may l. each one demand*, Wint. V, 3, 152. *so long a-growing and so l.* R3 II, 4, 19.

Leman, 1) masc. paramour, lover: *his wife's l.* Wiv. IV, 2, 172. 2) fem. mistress, sweetheart: Tw. II, 3, 26. H4B V, 3, 49.

Lemon, the fruit of the tree Citrus medica: LLL V, 2, 653.

Lena, Roman name: *Popilius L.* Caes. III, 1, 15. 23.

Lend (impf. and partic. *lent*), 1) to give for temporary use on condition of return; abs.: *nature's bequest gives nothing but doth l.* Sonn. 4, 3. *I neither l. nor borrow*, Merch. I, 3, 62. *take or l.* Cymb. III, 6, 24 (perhaps *take or leave*, i. e. destroy me or let me live; cf. Troil. V, 5, 26). Followed by a dative: *—s to bad debtors*, Lucr. 964. Sonn. 4, 4. Tim. III, 6, 83. By an accus.: *l. articles*, Wiv. IV, 1, 40. *men will l. nothing for God's sake*, Ado V, 1, 321. LLL II, 148. Merch. I, 3, 123. 133. III, 1, 51. R3 II, 2, 93. Tim. III, 1, 44. Lr. I, 4, 133. Cymb. I, 4, 154. By a dat. and accus.: *did you not l. it to Alice*, Wiv. I, 1, 210. *I will not l. thee a penny*, II, 2, 1. Ado II, 1, 287. Merch. I, 3, 130. 133. All's IV, 2, 40. V, 3, 274. 322. Tw. III, 4, 379. H4A II, 1, 38. III, 3, 85. V, 3, 41. H4B I, 2, 217. 250. H5 IV, 1, 24. H6B III, 1, 77. Cor. I, 4, 6. Tim. III, 6, 111. Oth. III, 4, 52. V, 1, 82. 88. With *out*: *he —s out money gratis*, Merch. I, 3, 45. III, 3, 2. The contrary of *to borrow*: Ven. 961. Lucr. 1083. 1498. Wiv. IV, 1, 40. Ado V, 1, 321. Merch. I, 3, 62.

2) to give in general: *l. me the letter*, Gent. I, 3, 55. *l. me your horn to make one*, LLL V, 1, 71. *I once did l. my body for his wealth*, Merch. V, 249. *l. me thy hand, I'll help thee*, Wint. IV, 3, 71. 72; cf. *l. me your arm*, Per. V, 1, 264 (lean on me). *what a madcap hath heaven lent us here*, John I, 84. *here I l. thee this sharp-pointed sword*, R3 I, 2, 175. *as I will l. you cause*, H8 III, 2, 151. *l. me a looking-glass*, Lr. V, 3, 261.

3) to afford, to grant, to admit to use for another's benefit: *you shall not grieve —ing me this acquaintance*, Lr. IV, 3, 56. *l. him aid*, H6A IV, 4, 23. R3 V, 3, 173. Ant. II, 2, 88. *Lucina lent not me her aid*, Cymb. V, 4, 43. *l. me an arm*, All's I, 2, 73. *to l. me arms and aid*, Ant. II, 2, 88. *l. my best attention*, Cymb. V, 5, 117. *—ing soft audience to my sweet design*, Compl. 278. *his (the sun's) golden beams to you here lent*, R2 I, 3, 146. *—ing your kind commiseration*, Tit. V, 3, 93. *l. thine ear*, Shr. IV, 1, 62 (= listen). R3 IV, 2, 80. Caes. III, 2, 78. *to my unfolding l. your prosperous ear*, Oth. I, 3, 245. *l. ear*, Cor. V, 3, 19. Per. V, 1, 82. *l. favourable ears*, R3 III, 7, 101. *l. no ear*, H4A I, 3, 217. *her arms do l. his neck a sweet embrace*, Ven. 539. *—s embracements unto every stranger*, 790. *l. to each man enough*, Tim. III, 6, 82. *till time l. friends*, R2 III, 3, 132. *some friendship will it l. you*, Lr. III, 2, 62. *her eyes their gazes l. to every place*, Compl. 26 (mark the difference from *glance* in Lucr. 1399). *l. thy hand*, Tp. I, 2, 23 (= assist me). H4A II, 4, 2. Tit. III, 1, 188. Caes. III, 1, 297. Per. III, 2, 108. *your gentle hands l. us*, All's V, 3, 340 (i.

e. clap, applaud). *l. thy serious hearing*, Hml. I, 5, 5. *the help that thou shalt l. me*, Lucr. 1685. *l. me your knees*, Meas. V, 436. *wilt thou not l. a knee?* 447. *I'll l. you all my life to do you service*, 437. *to l. the world his light*, Ven. 756. Lucr. 190. 1083. Sonn. 100, 4. Rom. V, 3, 125. Hml. II, 2, 482. *they that least l. it* (viz love) All's I, 2, 68. *he most narrow measure lent me*, Ant. III, 4, 8. *l. him your kind pains*, Meas. V, 246. *to l. your patience to us*, Hml. IV, 5, 210. *l. redress*, Rom. IV, 5, 146. *—s but weak relief*, Sonn. 34, 11. *his tail cool shadow to his buttock lent*, Ven. 315. *England has lent us good Siward and ten thousand men*, Mcb. IV, 3, 190. *until our stars that frown l. us a smile*, Per. I, 4, 108. *my heart can l. no succour to my head*, I, 1, 171. *you have lent him visitation*, Meas. III, 2, 255. Peculiarly = to cast: *the mild glance that sly Ulysses lent*, Lucr. 1399. *you, but one, can every shadow l.* Sonn. 53, 4 (forming the rhyme in both passages).

4) to bestow on, to endow with, to adorn, to arm with: *desire doth l. her force*, Ven. 29. *if love have lent you twenty thousand tongues*, 775. *what priceless wealth the heavens had him lent*, Lucr. 17. *thy sword was lent thee all that brood to kill*, 627. *—ing him wit*, 964. *the painter was no god to l. her those* (words) 1461. *she —s them words*, 1498. *that piteous looks to Phrygian shepherds lent*, 1502 (i. e. made the shepherds look compassionately). *thy sorrow to my sorrow —eth another power*, 1676. *he —s thee virtue*, Sonn. 79, 9. *what strained touches rhetoric can l.*, 82, 10. *the pen that to his subject —s not some small glory*, 84, 6. *lest sorrow l. me words*, 140, 3. *that they their passions likewise lent me*, Compl. 199. Gent. II, 6, 42. 43. IV, 2, 42. V, 4, 27. Meas. I, 1, 20. 37. Ado V, 4, 23. LLL IV, 3, 238. All's II, 1, 163. II, 2, 8. V, 3, 48. R2 I, 3, 228. H4A IV, 1, 77. V, 4, 24. H4B I, 1, 112. 122. H5 III, 1, 9. H6A I, 1, 87. H6B I, 1, 19. 20. Troil. II, 2, 101. Tit. V, 1, 29. Rom. I, 3, 84. II Prol. 13. II, 2, 81. III, 5, 166. Tim. V, 1, 160. Hml. I, 3, 117. III, 4, 166. Ant. V, 1, 23. Cymb. I, 6, 125. Per. Prol. 24.

Lender, one who lends money: Wiv. II, 2, 172. Hml. I, 3, 75. Lr. III, 4, 100.

Lendings, 1) advanced money (?): *that Mowbray hath received eight thousand nobles in name of l. for your highness' soldiers*, R2 I, 1, 89 (the expression is not very clear; nor does it receive light from what follows or from the Chronicles of Holinshed).

2) outward appurtenances not belonging to the essence of a thing: *off, off, you l.* Lr. III, 4, 113; cf. *to lend* in H6B iII, 1, 77.

Length, subst. 1) extent from end to end, contrary to breadth; used of space as well as time: Gent. III, 1, 130. 133. Ado II, 1, 276. Ado V, 1, 11. As III, 2, 334. All's IV, 3, 99. R2 III, 3, 14. H4B II, 3, 58. Hml. V, 1, 118. V, 2, 276. Ant. I, 2, 124 (*her l. of sickness* = the duration of her sickness). *to measure out my l.* = to lie down, Mids. III, 2, 429; cf. H6C V, 2, 26 and Lr. I, 4, 101. *within my sword's l.* Mcb. IV, 3, 234; Hml. I, 2, 204. *within my pistol's l.* Per. I, 1, 168 (i. e. within my pistol's shot). *then goes he to the l. of all his arm*, Hml. II, 1, 88.

2) great extent, contrary to shortness: *night doth nightly make grief's l. seem stronger*, Sonn. 28, 14 (M. Edd. *strength*, perhaps rightly, but cf. Ado V, 1, 11 and R2 V, 1, 94). *there is such l. in grief*, R2 V,

1, 94. *to draw it out in l.* Merch. III, 2, 23; cf. *my foreward shall be drawn out all in l.* R3 V, 3, 293. *through the l. of times*, Lucr. 718; *to leap large —s of miles*, Sonn. 44, 10; *large —s of seas and shores*, John I, 105. *this was of much l.* Meas. V, 95. *so it must be, for now all l. is torture*, Ant. IV, 14, 46 (= long duration, protraction; cf. the German proverb: die Länge trägt die Last). *of l.* = long: *is not my arm of l.* R2 IV, 11. *to end a tale of l.* Troil. I, 3, 136.

At l. = at last: Lucr. 1606. Pilgr. 319. Err. I, 1, 89. 113. R2 V, 5, 74. H8 III, 2, 362. IV, 1, 82. V, 4, 57. Cor. III, 3, 128. Tim. II, 2, 158. Per. II, 4, 24. *at the l.* Merch. II, 2, 85 (reading of Q1; the rest of O. Edd. *in the end*).

Length, vb. to lengthen, to make long: *short, night, to-night, and l. thyself to-morrow*, Pilgr. 210.

Lengthen, to draw out, to extend, to make longer in space or time: Lucr. Dedic. 6. Shr. Ind. 2, 138. R2 I, 4, 16. H6B I, 2, 12. R3 I, 3, 208. I, 4, 43. IV, 4, 353. Rom. I, 1, 169. Cymb. V, 3, 13. Per. I, 4, 46. *I shall short my word by —ing my return*, Cymb. I, 6, 201 (= delaying, retarding). With *out: to l. out the worst*, R2 III, 2, 199.

Lenity, mildness: H5 III, 2, 26. III, 6, 118 H6A V, 4, 125. H6C II, 2, 9. II, 6, 22. Cor. III, 1, 99. Rom. III, 1, 128. With *to: a little more l. to lechery*, Meas. III, 2, 103.

Lent, (cf. *Jack-a-lent*) the quadragesimal fast: H4B II, 4, 376. H6B IV, 3, 7. Rom. II, 4, 143.

Lenten, 1) used in Lent: *a hare in a l. pie*, Rom. II, 4, 139 (much quibbling).

2) much less than sufficient, spare, scanty, poor, answering very modest expectations: *a good l. answer*, Tw. I, 5, 9. *what l. entertainment the players shall receive from you*, Hml. II, 2, 329. Such is perhaps also the *l. pie* in Rom. II, 4, 139.

L'envoy, additional lines subjoined to a poem, '*an epilogue*, as Armado defines it, *or discourse, to make plain some obscure precedence*': LLL III, 72. 73. 75. 80. 81. 87. 88. 95. 100. 105. 108. 110. 116. 123.

Leonardo, name in Merch. II, 2, 178.

Leonato, name in Ado I, 1, 96. 114. 207. 278 etc.

Leonatus, name in Cymb. I, 1, 33. 41. I, 6, 12 etc. Plur. *Leonati:* V, 1, 31. *from Leonati seat*, V, 4, 60.

Leonine, name in Per. IV Prol. 52 etc.

Leontes, name in Wint. I, 2, 42. II, 1, 82. IV, 1, 17 etc.

Leopard (trisyll. in H6A, dissyll. in R2), the animal Felis leopardus: R2 I, 1, 174 (a golden l. was the Norfolk crest). H6A I, 5, 31. Tim. IV, 3, 343.

Leper, a person affected with leprosy: H6B III, 2, 75.

Leperous, causing leprosy: *the l. distilment*, Hml. I, 5, 64.

Lepidus, name of the third triumvir: Caes. III, 2, 269 etc. Ant. I, 4, 1. II, 1, 14 etc.

Leprosy, a loathsome cutaneous disease: Tim. IV, 1, 30. IV, 3, 35. 367. Ant. III, 10, 11.

Less, adj. 1) smaller, contrary to larger or bigger: *made more or l. by thy* (time's) *continual haste*, Sonn. 123, 12. *how to name the bigger light, and how the l.* Tp. I, 2, 335. *the greater hides the l.* Gent. III, 1, 372. *if I do grow great, I'll grow l.* H4A V, 4, 168. *make l. thy body*, H4B V, 5, 56. *no l. in space*, Lr. I, 1, 83.

2) of an inferior degree, contrary to greater: *the*

repetition cannot make it l. Lucr. 1285. *though l. the show appear,* Sonn. 102, 2. *shall we serve heaven with l. respect,* Meas. II, 2, 86. *l. in your knowledge and your grace you show not than our earth's wonder,* Err. III, 2, 31. *no l. likelihood,* Ado II, 2, 42. *of no l. weight,* LLL II, 7. *with no l. presence,* Merch. III, 2, 54. *make it l.* 114. *so doth the greater glory dim the l.* V, 93. As IV, 1, 201. V, 4, 154. H6A II, 3, 68. H6C II, 1, 85. H8 II, 2, 112. Troil. III, 3, 164. Rom. I, 3, 94. Mcb. I, 3, 138. Lr. V, 3, 167. Ant. II, 1, 31. Cymb. V, 5, 225 etc. *little l. in* = of nearly the same, *no l. in* = of as great: *hope to joy is little l. in joy than hope enjoyed,* R2 II, 3, 15. *a grandam's name is little l. in love than is the doting title of a mother,* R3 IV, 4, 299. *their story is no l. in pity than his glory,* Ant. V, 2, 365 (the compassion which their story excites is as great as the glory of their conqueror). *more or l.* = great or little, of what importance soever: *of that and all the progress, more or l., resolvedly more leisure shall express,* All's V, 3, 331. *without debatement further, more or l., he should the bearers put to death,* Hml. V, 2, 45. *so tell him, with the occurrents, more or l., which have solicited,* 368. cf. Aaron's jest in Tit. IV, 2, 53. Peculiar use after negatives: *wanted l. impudence,* Wint. III, 2, 57 (= had less impudence, or wanted impudence more). *a beggar without l. quality,* Cymb I, 4, 23 (= without more quality, or with less quality). cf. Cor. I, 4, 14. Substantively: *loved of more and l.* Sonn. 96, 3 (= loved by persons of any degree). *'tis wit in them* (great men), *but in the l. foul profanation,* Meas. II, 2, 128. *what great ones do the l. will prattle of,* Tw. I, 2, 33. *the more and l. came in with cap and knee,* H4A IV, 3, 68. *more and l. do flock to follow him,* H4B I, 1, 209. *both more and l. have given him the revolt,* Mcb. V, 4, 12. *No l.* = a) nothing of inferior weight or consequence: *he is no l. than what we say he is,* Shr. Ind. 1, 71. *look for no l. than death,* Wint. III, 2, 92. *thou deservest no l.* H6B IV, 3, 12. H6C IV, 7, 22. R3 III, 7, 68. Cor. I, 9, 22. Mcb. I, 3, 120. Ant. V, 2, 18 etc. b) nothing else: *those cheek-roses proclaim you are no l.* Meas. I, 4, 17 (= you are so). *you'll find good cause to whip them all. I think no l.* II, 1, 143 (= so I think too). *we did believe no l.* V, 142. *his incivility confirms no l.* Err. IV, 4, 49. *he is no l. than a stuffed man,* Ado I, 1, 58. *the letter is too long by half a mile. I think no l.* LLL V, 2, 55. As IV, 1, 188. Tw. III, 4, 206. V, 218. H4A IV, 4, 34. H5 II, 2, 39. H6C III, 2, 10. V, 4, 62. H8 I, 4, 68. Tim. III, 2, 3. Caes. I, 2, 278. Ant. I, 4, 40 etc. cf. *could he say l.?* Cor. V, 1, 22 (= what could he say else?).

3) not so much, opposed to more: *by hoping more they have but l.* Lucr. 137. *old men of l. truth than tongue,* Sonn. 17, 10. *l. than a pound shall serve me,* Gent. I, 1, 111. V, 4, 25. Meas. III, 2, 279. V, 58. Merch. III, 5, 45. IV, 1, 325. All's I, 1, 167. Tw. I, 4, 13. Lr. I, 4, 132 etc.

Less, adv. in a smaller or lower degree: *l. false* Sonn. 20, 5. *I love not l.* 102, 2; cf. H4B V, 2, 110. Tp. I, 1, 47. III, 1, 78. Gent. II, 7, 11. LLL II, 17. Wint. I, 2, 282. Cor. V, 1, 19 etc. *no l.:* As I, 1, 116. Wint. I, 2, 392. II, 1, 54. H5 II, 2, 92. H6B II, 3, 26. Mcb. III, 1, 136 etc. *nothing l.* = anything but: *'tis nothing but conceit. 'tis nothing l.* R2 II, 2, 34. *and yet, methinks, my father's execution was nothing l. than bloody tyranny,* H6A II, 5, 100. *ne'er the l.* = not

less on this account, or for this: *I will love thee ne'er the l.* Shr. I, 1, 77. *l. happier* = l. happy, R2 II, 1, 49. Peculiar use after a negative: *nor a man that fears you l. than he,* Cor. I, 4, 14 (instead of fears you more); cf. Wint. III, 2, 57 and Cymb. I, 4, 23.

Lessen, to diminish: Ado II, 1, 24. H5 III, 6, 155. R3 I, 3, 111. Rom. I, 2, 47. Ant. III, 12, 13. Cymb. III, 3, 13. *Buckingham shall l. this big look,* H8 I, 1, 119, = shall look less big.

Refl., = to become less, to be diminished: *the Roman eagle, from south to west on wing soaring aloft, —ed herself,* Cymb. V, 5, 472.

Lesser, adj. = less; 1) opposed to larger: *the l. thing should not the greater hide,* Lucr. 663. *the l. legs,* Tp. II, 2, 108. *l. linen,* Wint. IV, 3, 24. R2 II, 1, 95. H6B IV, 10, 50. Hml. III, 3, 19. Per. II, 3, 41.

2) opposed to greater: *l. noise,* Lucr. 1329. *'tis the l. sin,* Sonn. 114, 13; Gent. V, 4, 108. *with l. weight,* Err. I, 1, 109. *grace,* Mids. II, 2, 89. *knowledge,* Wint. II, 1, 38. *fear,* John IV, 2, 42. *waste,* R2 II, 1, 103. *l. than my name,* III, 3, 137. *cause,* Rom. IV, 4, 10 (reading of Q2). *the greater scorns the l.* Tim. IV, 3, 6. *l. than Macbeth,* Mcb. I, 3, 65. *malady,* Lr. III, 4, 9. *enmities,* Ant. II, 1, 43. *villain,* Cymb. V, 5, 219.

3) opposed to more: *more rage and l. pity,* Lucr. 468. *l. had been the thwartings of your dispositions,* Cor. III, 2, 20.

Lesser, adv. = less: *patience doth l. blench at sufferance,* Troil. I, 1, 28. *no man l. fears the Greeks,* II, 2, 8. Cor. I, 4, 15. I, 6, 70. Mcb. V, 2, 13. Cymb. V, 5, 187. R3 III, 4, 54 Ff *l.,* Qq *less.*

Lesson, subst. 1) something learned or to be learned: *O, learn to love: the l. is but plain,* Ven 407. *thence I learn, and find the l. true,* Sonn. 148, 13. *to learn any hard l.* Ado I, 1, 295. *learn my —s,* Shr. III, 1, 20. 60. H6C II, 2, 62. Tit. IV, 1, 106. Hml. I, 3, 45.

Lesson, vb. to teach, to instruct: *to l. me and tell me some good mean,* Gent. II, 7, 5. *as he —ed us to weep,* R3 I, 4, 246. *could you not have told him as you were —ed,* Cor. II, 3, 185. *well hast thou —ed us; this shall we do,* Tit. V, 2, 110.

Lest (O. Edd. usually *least*) for fear that, in order that not; followed by a subjunctive: *give it me, l. thy hard heart do steel it,* Ven. 375. *be wise, l. sorrow lend me words,* Sonn. 140, 3. *smooth not thy tongue, l. she some practice smell,* Pilgr. 307. Phoen. 16. Tp. I, 2, 451. Gent. V, 4, 9. Wiv. V, 5, 86. Meas. II, 3, 30. Err. II, 2, 63. 220. III, 1, 37. III, 2, 168. IV, 1, 41. Ado III, 1, 58. Mids. III, 2, 175. Merch. II, 2, 196. III, 1, 22. IV, 1, 258. Shr. Ind. 1, 95. V, 1, 101. H6A II, 4, 50. III, 1, 62. H6B V, 1, 160. H6C I, 3, 9. R3 II, 1, 13. V, 3, 186 etc. Followed by *should:* bid suspicion double-lock the door, l. jealousy should disturb the feast,* Ven. 449. *thy lips make modest Dian cloudy and forlorn, l. she should steal a kiss and die forsworn,* 726. 781. Lucr. 74. 1315. Sonn. 36, 10. 71, 13. 72, 1. 89, 11. 148, 14. Gent I, 3, 81. II, 4, 159. II, 7, 23. III, 2, 52. Wiv. III, 5, 150. V, 5, 39. Meas. III, 1, 75. Ado II, 1, 295. Mids. III, 2, 385 *(for fear l. day should look).* Merch. III, 2, 7. Wint. I, 2, 157. II, 1, 84. II, 2, 51. H5 III, 2, 40. R3 II, 2, 124 etc. Followed by *will* and *would: it were not good she knew his love, l. she'll make sport of it,* Ado III, 1, 58 (Ff *she make). I quaked for fear, l. the lunatic knave would* *have searched it*, Wiv. III, 5, 105. By *may* and *might:* *l. your true love may seem false in this*, *my name be buried*, Sonn. 72, 9. *I feared l. I might anger thee*, Tp. IV, 169. *fearing l. my jealous aim might err*, Gent. III, 1, 28. *why dost thou ask? l. I might be too rash*, Meas. II, 2, 9. Ado I, 1, 316. H6B III, 2, 262. Caes. II, 1, 28.

L. that = lest (cf. *That*): *l. that my mistress hear my song*, Pilgr. 348. Err. I, 2, 2. H6C I, 1, 98. Lr. IV, 6, 237. Per. I, 3, 22.

Lestrale, French name: H5 III, 5, 45. IV, 8, 105.

Let, subst. impediment, hindrance: *these —s attend the time*, Lucr. 330. *swells the higher by this l.* 646. *that I may know the l.* H5 V, 2, 65. In Rom. II, 2, 69 the surreptitious Q1 and most M. Edd. *let*, the authentic O. Edd. *stop*.

Let, vb. to hinder: *who with a lingering stay his course doth l.* Lucr. 328. *what —s but one may enter at her window?* Gent. III, 1, 113. *what —s it but he would be here?* Err. II, 1, 105. *if nothing —s to make us happy*, Tw. V, 256. *I'll make a ghost of him that —s me*, Hml. I, 4, 85. *that kings should l. their ears hear their faults hid*, Per. I, 2, 62 (but perhaps = to suffer. Dyce: *their faults chid*).

Let, vb. (impf. and partic. *let*), 1) to suffer, to allow: *how he mocks me! wilt thou l. him, my lord?* Tp. III, 2, 34. *thou —st thy fortune sleep*, II, 1, 216. *l. me see thy cloak*, Gent. III, 1, 132. Err. II, 2, 220. V, 59. All's III, 4, 20. Rom. II, 1, 25. Oth. II, 1, 72. Cymb. V, 4, 20 etc. *to l. go*, see *Go. l. me be* = cease your jesting, let me alone, Ado V, 1, 207. *to l. fall* = to drop, Gent. I, 2, 73. Wint. IV, 4, 117 etc. *l. me have* = tell me, Gent. II, 7, 57. *l. 's have the tongs and the bones*, Mids. IV, 1, 32 (= sing). *l. me have war*, Cor. IV, 5, 236 (= give me war, war is the word); cf. *l. me know*, Oth. IV, 1, 73 (= I am for knowing, I prefer knowing). Inf. omitted: *l. me to my fortune*, Merch. III, 2, 39 (= let me go to etc.). *to l. him there a month*, Wint. I, 2, 41 (= to l. him remain there). *l. him on*, H8 I, 2, 176. *I'ld whistle her off and l. her down the wind*, Oth. III, 3, 262. *to l. loose* = a) to give up, to abandon: *I do now let l. my opinion*, Tp. II, 2, 36. b) to quit one's hold: Mids. III, 2, 260. LLL III, 128. c) to turn loose upon the world: *their ragged curtains poorly are l. loose*, H5 IV, 2, 41. *that tyrant ... thy womb l. loose*, R3 IV, 4, 54 (cf. *Loose*). *to l. alone*, see *Alone*. *to l. forth: graves l. 'em* (their sleepers) *forth*, Tp. V, 49. Mids. V, 388. *would not l. it* (my soul) *forth*, R3 I, 4, 38. *to l. in* = to allow to enter: Meas. IV, 2, 94. Err. III, 1, 30. 49. Wint. I, 2, 205. John II, 232. H6A I, 3, 7, 21. H8 V, 4, 75. Hml. IV, 5, 54. *to l. out*, Tp. I, 2, 293. Wint. I, 2, 205. H6B IV, 3, 18.

Used imperatively, as a mere form of exhortation, or of concession: *l. 's assist them*, Tp. I, 1, 57. *l. 's all sink with the king*, 67. II, 1, 306. 322. 323. Gent. I, 1, 56. Merch. V, 297. H6B I, 3, 1. Troil. IV, 4, 146. 148. Lr. IV, 6, 263 etc. *l. me remember thee*, Tp. I, 2, 243 (= be reminded by me). *l. me not live* = I will not live, may I not live, Gent. III, 2, 21. *l. her go hang*, Tp. II, 2, 56. *all corners else o'the earth l. liberty make use of*, I, 2, 492. *l. Sebastian wake*, II, 1, 260. *l. them be hunted soundly*, IV, 263. *let no man take care for himself*, V, 256. *l. it lie on my head*, Wiv. II, 1, 191. *l. but your honour know*, Meas. II, 1, 8. *l. him be no kinsman to my liege*, R2 I, 1, 59 (supposing he were no kinsman). *a right good husband, l. him be*

a noble, H8 IV, 2, 146 (supposing even he were, though he were, a nobleman). *l. her know it*, Ant. III, 13, 16 etc. *l. be* = no matter: Wint. V, 3, 61. Hml. V, 2, 235 (Ff om.). Ant. IV, 4, 6. *l. it be so*, Lr. I, 1, 110. I, 4, 327. cf. H8 I, 1, 171. Ant. III, 5, 24 (cf. *Be*). Inf. omitted: *l. us about it*, H6C IV, 6, 102 (cf. *About*). *l. us into the city* = come with me into the city, Gent. III, 2, 91. *l. us to the Tiger*, Err. III, 1, 95. *l. us to the great supper*, Ado I, 3, 73. II, 1, 178. V, 4, 71. Tw. II, 3, 198. Wint. IV, 4, 727. John V, 1, 73. H4A V, 4, 164. H6A I, 1, 45. II, 4, 133. H6B I, 4, 15. III, 3, 33. H6C II, 3, 49. R3 III, 7, 246. V, 3, 312. Ant. II, 5, 3. *l. him from my thoughts*, H4A I, 1, 91. *l. us from it*, Cymb. IV, 4, 1. *l. us on our way*, H6C IV, 2, 28. *l. us away*, Wiv. V, 2, 16. As I, 3, 135. H6A I, 2, 149. H6B IV, 6, 18. H6C I, 1, 255. II, 1, 209. R3 III, 2, 96. *l. us hence*, Ado V, 3, 30. H6C IV, 1, 148. IV, 6, 87. *l. us in*, Merch. V, 49. H6B I, 1, 73. IV, 9, 48. R3 II, 1, 138. *l. us on*, H4B I, 3, 85. H6A III, 3, 90. *l. us thither*, Ado I, 3, 67. *l. him to field*, Troil. I, 1, 5. *l. it to the sea*, Cymb. IV, 2, 152.

2) to leave off, to forbear: *Collatine unwisely did not l. to praise*, Lucr. 10.

3) to cause, to make; followed by an inf. with *to:* *if your name be Horatio, as I am l. to know it is*, Hml. IV, 6, 11. *without to: l. this letter be read*, LLL IV, 3, 193. *thou still —'st slip*, H4A I, 3, 278. *four rogues in buckram l. drive at me*, II, 4, 217. 247 (cf. *Drive*). *not —ing it decline*, Troil. IV, 5, 189. *—ing "I dare not" wait upon "I would,"* Mcb. I, 7, 44. Without an inf.: *to l. forth my blood*, Lucr. 1029 (= to shed). *let him to the Tower*, H6B V, 1, 134 (i. e. be carried). *hath much blood l. forth*, All's III, 1, 3. *l. forth thy life*, R3 I, 2, 12. *l. the soul forth*, 177. *lest I l. forth your half-pint of blood*, Cor. V, 2, 60. *incision would l. her out in saucers*, LLL IV, 3, 98. *cursed the blood that l. this blood from hence*, R3 I, 2, 16. *l. it blood*, LLL II, 186. *without —ing blood*, R2 I, 1, 153. *his adversaries are l. blood*, R3 III, 1, 183. Troil. II, 3, 222. Caes. III, 1, 152. Cymb. IV, 2, 168.

4) to lease, to lend: *to l. this land by lease*, R2 II, 1, 110. With *out: l. out their coin upon large interest*, Tim. III, 5, 107.

Let-alone, subst. the not doing sth., forbearance, abstention: *the l. lies not in your good will*, Lr. V, 3, 79.

Lethargied, paralyzed, benumbed, dulled: *his discernings are l.* Lr. I, 4, 249.

Lethargy, unconsciousness, absence of thought and sensation; 1) = ecstasy, trance: *in this time of l. I picked and cut most of their festival purses*, Wint. IV, 4, 627. 2) drunkenness: *how came you so early by this l.?* Tw. I, 5, 132. 3) a diseased state, in which the mind is paralysed; as apoplexy and epilepsy: *this apoplexy is a kind of lethargy, a kind of sleeping in the blood*, H4B I, 2, 127 (Falstaff's speech). *—ies, cold palsies*, Troil. V, 1, 23. *peace is a very apoplexy, l.* Cor. IV, 5, 239. *the l. must have his quiet course*, Oth. IV, 1, 54.

Lethe, 1) the infernal river whose waters caused forgetfulness: *duller shouldst thou be than the fat weed that roots itself in ease on L. wharf, wouldst thou not stir in this*, Hml. I, 5, 33. Hence = oblivion: *steep my sense in L.* Tw. IV, 1, 66. *washed in L. and forgotten*, H4B V, 2, 72. *in the L. of thy angry soul drown the remembrance*, R3 IV, 4, 250. *till that the conquering* *wine hath steeped our sense in soft and delicate L.* Ant. II, 7, 114.

2) death (from the Latin *letum?*): *here thy hunters stand, signed in thy spoil, and crimsoned in thy l.* Caes. III, 1, 206 (O. Edd. *Lethee,* consequently dissyll.).*

Lethe'd (M. Edd.) or **Lethied** (O. Edd.), working like a draught from Lethe, oblivious, unconscious: *sleep and feeding may prorogue his honour even till a L. dulness,* Ant. II, 1, 27.

Letter, 1) a character in the alphabet: Gent. I, 2, 119. Ado I, 1, 267. III, 4, 56. LLL V, 2, 40. 44. John III, 1, 85. H4B IV, 4, 104. H6B IV, 2, 98. R3 I, 1, 55. Tit. V, 1, 139. Rom. I, 2, 64. II, 4, 220. Lr. IV, 6, 143 etc. *l. for l.* Wiv. II, 1, 71. *I will something affect the l.* LLL IV, 2, 56 (i. e. use alliteration). *I heard no l. from my master,* Cymb. IV, 3, 36 (not a jot?).

2) a written message, an epistle: Gent. I, 1, 57. 100. I, 2, 50. 119. I, 3, 51. II, 1, 110. 146. 156. III, 1, 248. Wiv. I, 2, 8 etc. etc. *whom I made lord of me and all I had, at your important —s,* Err. V, 138 (i. e. recommendations by letter); cf. *preferment goes by l. and affection,* Oth. I, 1, 36. *—s of commission,* H6A V, 4, 95. *—s patents* (writings by which some rights are granted) R2 II, 1, 202. II, 3, 130. H8 III, 2, 250.*

Plur. *—s,* as it seems, for the sing.: *are these your —s, knight?* Wiv. III, 3, 148. *now will I write —s to Angelo whose contents shall witness to him I am near at home,* Meas. IV, 3, 97. *I have delivered him —s,* Ado I, 1, 20. *a messenger with —s from the doctor,* Merch. IV, 1, 108. 110. All's II, 3, 293. IV, 5, 90. H6C IV, 1, 91. H4A IV, 1, 13 sq. R3 IV, 5, 19 (Qq *these —s,* Ff *my l.*). Tim. V, 3, 11. Mcb. I, 5, 57. Lr. I, 5, 2 (cf. v. 4). Caes. IV, 3, 5 etc.

3) literal meaning: *the bloody book of law you shall yourself read in the bitter l. after your own sense,* Oth. I, 3, 68. *answering the l. of the oracle,* Cymb. V, 5, 450.

4) Plur. *—s* = learning, erudition: *—s should not be known,* Tp. II, 1, 150. *whose learning and good —s peace hath tutored,* H4B IV, 1, 44. *trained in music's —s,* Per. IV Prol. 8 (M. Edd. *in music, letters*).

Lettered, learned, literate: LLL V, 1, 48 (Armado's speech).

Lettuce, the plant Lactuca: Oth. I, 3, 325.

Level, subst. 1) an instrument by which a line is ascertained to be horizontal: *we steal by line and l.* Tp. IV, 239. 243.*

2) the direction in which a missive weapon is aimed: *bring me within the l. of your frown,* Sonn. 117, 11. *not a heart which in his l. came,* Compl. 309. *proclaim myself against the l. of mine aim,* All's II, 1, 159. *out of the blank and l. of my brain,* plot-proof, Wint. II, 3, 6. *my life stands in the l. of your dreams,* III, 2, 82. *I stood in the l. of a full-charged confederacy,* H8 I, 2, 2. *shot from the deadly l. of a gun,* Rom. III, 3, 103.

3) equal elevation, state of equality: *hold their l. with thy princely heart,* H4A III, 2, 17.

Level, adj. 1) even, flat, not having one part higher than another: *make mountains l.* H4B III, 1, 47. *every thing lies l. to our wish,* IV, 4, 7.

2) equipoised, steady: *can thrust me from a l. consideration,* H4B II, 1, 124. Adverbially: *so sways she l. in her husband's heart,* Tw. II, 4, 32.

3) of the same height, equal: *where qualities were l.* All's I, 3, 118. *young boys and girls are l. now with men,* Ant. IV, 15, 66.

4) direct, straight, in a right line: *all is oblique; there's nothing l. in our cursed natures, but direct villany,* Tim. IV, 3, 19. Adverbially: *as l. as the cannon to his blank, transports his poisoned shot,* Hml. IV, 1, 42. *it shall as l. to your judgment pierce as day does to your eye,* IV, 5, 151.

Level, vb. 1) tr. to aim, to direct, to intend: *her —ed eyes,* Compl. 22. *whose sights were —ed on my face,* 282. *if all aim be —ed false,* Ado IV, 1, 239. *no —ed malice,* Tim. I, 1, 47.

2) intr. a) to aim: *l. not to hit their lives,* R3 IV, 4, 202. With *at:* Sonn. 121, 9. H4B III, 2, 286. H6B III, 1, 160. H6C II, 2, 19. Per. I, 1, 165. II, 3, 114.

b) to guess: *l. at my affection,* Merch. I, 2, 41. *she —ed at our purposes,* Ant. V, 2, 339.

c) to be equal, to be in keeping, to square: *such accommodation as —s with her breeding,* Oth. I, 3, 240.

Leven (M. Edd. *'leven*), eleven: *a l. pence farthing better,* LLL III, 172 (Costard's speech). *a l. widows,* Merch. II, 2, 171 (Launcelot's speech. Q1 *eleven*). *every l. wether tods,* Wint. IV, 3, 33 (the clown's speech).

Lever, an instrument to raise a great weight: H4A II, 2, 36.

Leviathan, a great whale: *huge —es forsake unsounded deeps to dance on sands,* Gent. III, 2, 80. *ere the l. can swim a league,* Mids. II, 1, 174. *as send precepts to the l. to come ashore,* H5 III, 3, 26.

Levity, lightness, thoughtlessness, inconsideration: Meas. V, 222. All's I, 2, 35. Troil. II, 2, 130. Tim. I, 1, 134. Ant. II, 7, 128. III, 7, 14.

Levy, subst. 1) the act of raising men for war: Mcb. III, 2, 25. Cymb. III, 7, 9. Plur. *—s:* Cor. V, 6, 67. Hml. I, 2, 31. II, 2, 62.

2) a force raised: Cymb. III, 7, 13.

Levy, vb. to collect, to raise; applied to soldiers: Tp. I, 2, 128. John IV, 2, 112. R2 II, 2, 124. II, 3, 34. H4A I, 1, 22 (where unnecessary emendations have been proposed, to set the anacoluthon right). H4B IV, 1, 12. H6A I, 5, 88. IV, 3, 11. IV, 4, 23. 31. H6C III, 3, 251. IV, 1, 131. IV, 8, 6. R3 IV, 4, 448. Caes. IV, 1, 42. Hml. II, 2, 75. Lr. V, 3, 104. Ant. III, 6, 67. Applied to money: Err. I, 1, 22. H5 IV, 3, 121. H6B III, 1, 61. H8 I, 2, 58. Singular passage: *never did thought of mine l. offence,* Per. II, 5, 52 (perhaps *level;* cf. Tim. I, 1, 47).

Lewd, 1) vile, mean, base: *how her acquaintance grew with this l. fellow,* Ado V, 1, 341. *a velvet dish: fie, fie! 'tis l. and filthy,* Shr. IV, 3, 65. *the which he hath detained for l. employments,* R2 I, 1, 90. *such poor, such bare, such l., such mean attempts,* H4A III, 2, 13. *so l. and so much engraffed to Falstaff,* H4B II, 2, 66. *thy l., pestiferous and dissentious pranks,* H6A III, 1, 15. *but you must trouble him with l. complaints,* R3 I, 3, 61.

2) dissolute, lustful: *admired of l. unhallowed eyes,* Lucr. 392. *let ghastly shadows his l. eyes affright,* 971. *wronged by this l. fellow,* Meas. V, 515. *a l. interpreter,* Merch. III, 4, 80. *not lolling on a l. day-bed,* R3 III, 7, 72. *l. minx,* Oth. III, 3, 475.

Lewdly, 1) wickedly, badly: *a sort of naughty persons, l. bent, have practised against your state,* H6B II, 1, 167.

2) lustfully, dissolutely: *if that man should be l. given*, H4A II, 4, 469. *her beauty* (shall) *stir up the l. inclined*, Per. IV, 2, 156.

Lewdness, 1) naughtiness, indecency: *wear away the lag end of their l. and be laughed at*, H8 I, 3, 35. 2) lustfulness, libertinism: *though l. court it in a shape of heaven*, Hml. I, 5, 54.

Lewdster, a lecher, a libertine: Wiv. V, 3, 23.

Lewd-tongued, using bad language, foul-spoken: Wint. II, 3, 172.

Lewis (monosyll.; dissyll. only in H6C III, 3, 169: *how L. stamps*. In John II, 149 O. Edd. *King L.*), name of 1) the son and successor of Charlemagne: H5 I, 2, 76. 2) the son of King Philip Augustus, afterwards King Lewis VIII: John II, 149 (read: *king, Lewis*). 425. III, 1, 3. 208. 316. V, 2, 62. V, 4, 30. 3) King Lewis the tenth of France: H5 I, 2, 77. 88. 4) L. the eleventh: H6C III, 1, 34. III, 3, 3. 23. 65. 74. 143. 159. 169. 181. 203. 224. IV, 1, 11. 15. 29. 34. 91. 94. 96. IV, 3, 56.

Liable, 1) allied, associated, compatible: *who else but I, and such as to my claim are l.* John V, 2, 101. *if my name were l. to fear*, Caes. I, 2, 199.

2) fit: *the posterior of the day is l., congruent and measurable for the afternoon*, LLL V, 1, 97. *apt, l. to be employed in danger*, John IV, 2, 226.

3) subject: *l. to our crown and dignity*, John II, 490. *reason to my love is l.* Caes. II, 2, 104. *to the choleric fisting of every rogue thy ear is l.* Per. IV, 6, 178.

Liar, one who knowingly utters falsehood: Wiv. I, 1, 69. Mids. V, 442. Shr. II, 246. All's I, 1, 111. III, 6, 11. Wint. II, 3, 145. R2 I, 1, 114. Cor. V, 2, 32. V, 6, 103. Rom. I, 2, 96. Mcb. IV, 2, 56. 57. V, 5, 35. Hml. II, 2, 118. Lr. I, 2, 134. Oth. V, 2, 129. Ant. I, 1, 60. I, 3, 39. *or there be —s* = people say: *he hath promised you more than that, or there be —s*, Wint. IV, 4, 240. *a great deal of your wit lies in your sinews, or else there be —s*, Troil. II, 1, 109.

Libbard, a leopard: *with —'s head on knee*, LLL V, 2, 551 (the knee-caps in old dresses and in plate-armour frequently represented a leopard's head. Dyce).

Libel, subst. a defamatory writing: *by drunken prophecies, —s and dreams*, R3 I, 1, 33.

Libelling, spreading defamation by writings: *what's this but l. against the senate*, Tit. IV, 4, 17.

Liberal, 1) free, frank: *my heart must break with silence, ere 't be disburdened with a l. tongue*, R2 II, 1, 229. *I'll be in speaking l. as the north*, Oth. V, 2, 220 (Ff adverbially: *I will speak as l. as the north*).

2) licentious, wanton: *who hath indeed, most like a l. villain, confessed the vile encounters*, Ado IV, 1, 93. *to excuse or hide the l. opposition of our spirits*, LLL V, 2, 743. *something too l.* Merch. II, 2, 194. *long purples that l. shepherds give a grosser name*, Hml. IV, 7, 171. *is he not a most profane and l. counsellor?* Oth. II, 1, 165.

3) such as a free man ought to be, humane, gentleman-like, accomplished in manners and intellectual improvement: *the people l., valiant, active, wealthy*, H6B IV, 7, 68. *witty, courteous, l., full of spirit*, H6C I, 2, 43.

4) becoming a gentleman, tending to improve the mind: *the l. arts*, Tp. I, 2, 73.

5) satisfactory to the judgment or the taste: *all l. reason I will yield unto*, LLL II, 168. *delicate carria-*

ges and of very l. conceit, Hml. V, 2, 160. Adverbially: *l. conceited carriages*, 169 (M. Edd. hyphened: *liberal-conceited*).

6) munificent, bounteous: Merch. IV, 1, 438. V, 226. H5 IV Chor. 44. R3 I, 3, 124. H8 I, 3, 61. Tim. III, 3, 41. Oth. III, 4, 46. With *of*: Gent. III, 1, 355. H8 II, 1, 126. With *to*: *l. to mine own children in good bringing up*, Shr. I, 1, 98. Used, in a bad sense, of women profuse of their favours: H6A V, 4, 82. Oth. III, 4, 38. cf. Merch. V, 226.

7) bounteously offered, large, ample: *with too great a court and l. largess*, R2 I, 4, 44. *the l. and kind offer of the king*, H4A V, 2, 2. *a l. dower*, H6A V, 5, 46. *well studied for a l. thanks*, Ant. II, 6, 48.

Liberal-conceited, see *Liberal* sub 5.

Liberality, bounty, munificence: Shr. I, 2, 150. Tit. II, 1, 92. Its meaning not quite discernible: Troil. I, 2, 277.

Libertine, one leading a dissolute life: Ado II, 1, 144. As II, 7, 65. H4A V, 2, 72 (Qq *so wild a libertie*. Ff *so wild at liberty*). H5 I, 1, 48. Hml. I, 3, 49. Ant. II, 1, 23.

Liberty, 1) freedom from restraint; opposed to confinement and imprisonment, or to dependance and slavery: Compl. 252. Tp. I, 2, 492. Wiv. III, 3, 31. As I, 3, 140. H6A V, 3, 140. H6C IV, 6, 3. 15. 63. R3 I, 4, 267. H8 I, 1, 205. Rom. I, 1, 233. III, 2, 58. Tim. I, 2, 8. Lr. I, 1, 57. Oth. III, 4, 40. Ant. V, 2, 236. Cymb. V, 4, 4. Often with the poss. pronoun: Sonn. 58, 6. Tp. I, 2, 245. Meas. IV, 2, 137. Err. IV, 3, 20. V, 340. Ado I, 3, 37. LLL III, 129. As V, 1, 59. Shr. IV, 2, 113. John III, 4, 72. 73. IV, 2, 63. 66. H6A II, 5, 81. V, 3, 32. R3 I, 1, 77. Rom. II, 2, 182. Hml. III, 2, 352. IV, 1, 14. *at l.* Tp. V, 235. R3 III, 6, 9. *to be at l.* = to be free: H6B V, 1, 87. R3 I, 3, 305. Cor. II, 3, 31. *to set at l.* LLL III, 125. John III, 3, 9. *prey at l.* R3 I, 1, 133. *so wild at l.* H4A V, 2, 72 (Qq *so wild a libertie*; most M. Edd. *a libertine*).

2) power of acting as one is inclined: *why should their l. than ours be more?* Err. II, 1, 10. 7. Wint. I, 2, 112. H5 V, 2, 297. H6C IV, 5, 6. *he hath evermore had the l. of the prison*, Meas. IV, 2, 156 (he was allowed to do within the prison whatever he pleased). Hence = leave, permission: *the l. of gazing*, Err. V, 53. *of flight*, H6A IV, 2, 24. *of feasting*, Oth. II, 2, 10. *l. to blow on whom I please*, As II, 7, 47. H6A III, 4, 42. *this l. is all that I request, that I may have welcome*, Shr. II, 95. Doubtful passage: *the law of writ and the l.* Hml. II, 2, 421 (interpreted by some as extemporal plays).

3) licentiousness: *those petty wrongs that l. commits*, Sonn. 41, 1. *too much l.* Meas. I, 2, 129. *l. plucks justice by the nose*, I, 3, 29. *to give fear to use and l.* I, 4, 62. *such like —s of sin*, Err. I, 2, 102 (the abstr. for the concr.). *headstrong l. is lashed with woe*, II, 1, 15. *in l. of bloody hand*, H5 III, 3, 12. *lust and l.* Tim. IV, 1, 25. *known to youth and l.* Hml. II, 1, 24. 32.

4) political freedom: H6B IV, 2, 193. Caes. III, 1, 78. 110. 118. Plur. —*s* = rights, immunities, privileges: Cor. II, 3, 188. 223. III, 1, 194. Caes. V, 1, 76. Cymb. III, 1, 75. *should he wrong my —s in my absence*, Per. I, 2, 112 (= royal rights, prerogatives).

Library, a collection of books: Tp. I, 2, 109. 167. Tit. IV, 1, 34.

Libya (O. Edd. *Libia* and *Lybia*) African country: Wint. V, 1, 157. 166. Troil. I, 3, 328. Ant. III, 6, 69.

License, subst. 1) leave, permission: *I come to thee for charitable l., that we may wander o'er this bloody field*, H5 IV, 7, 74. *that by his l. Fortinbras craves the conveyance of a promised march*, Hml. IV, 4, 2.

2) authorization, privilege: *your virtue hath a l. in't*, Meas. II, 4, 145. *thou shalt have a l. to kill for a hundred lacking one*, H6B IV, 3, 8.

3) unrestrained liberty, licentiousness: *a fellow of much l.* Meas. III, 2, 216. *headed evils that thou with l. of free foot hast caught*, As II, 7, 68. *taunt him with the l. of ink*, Tw. III, 2, 48. *Harry from curbed l. plucks the muzzle of restraint*, H4B IV, 5, 131. *did give ourself to barbarous l.* H5 I, 2, 271. *taunt my faults with such full l.* Ant. I, 2, 112.

License, vb. to permit: *we l. your departure with your son*, H4A I, 3, 123.

Licentious, 1) unrestrained by law or morality: *filled the time with all l. measure*, Tim. V, 4, 4 (= the whole measure of licentiousness).

2) dissolute, lustful: *shouldst thou but hear I were l.* Err. II, 2, 133. *what rein can hold l. wickedness*, H5 III, 3, 22. *my sanctity will to my sense bend no l. ear*, Per. V, 3, 30.

Lichas, name of the servant who brought Hercules the poisoned garment from Deianira and was thrown by him into the sea: Merch. II, 1, 32. Ant. IV, 12, 45.

Licio or **Litio,** name in Shr. II, 60. III, 1, 56. III, 2, 149. IV, 2, 1 etc.

Lick, to pass over with the tongue: Ven. 915. Tp. III, 2, 26. H4A IV, 2, 28. H6C II, 2, 13. Cor. III, 1, 156. Rom. IV, 2, 4. 7. 8. Hml. III, 2, 65. Lr. IV, 2, 42. *to l. up* = to consume: *may diseases l. up their false bloods*, Tim. IV, 3, 539.

Licker, in *Footlicker*, q. v.

Lictor, a beadle that attended the highest magistrates in ancient Rome: Ant. V, 2, 214.

Lid, the membrane that covers the eye, the eyelid: Tw. I, 5, 266. Wint. IV, 4, 121. Mcb. I, 3, 20. Hml. I, 2, 70. Cymb. II, 2, 20. *by God's l.* Troil. I, 2, 228 (Pandarus' oath).

Lie, subst. in *Chamber-lie*, q. v.

Lie, subst. falsehood uttered for the purpose of deception: Ven 804. Sonn. 72, 5. 138, 14. Compl. 52. Tp. I, 2, 102. Merch. V, 186. As IV, 1, 107. All's III, 6, 107. IV, 1, 26. Wint. IV, 4, 274. 744. R2 I, 1, 132. H4A II, 4, 249. V, 4, 161. H4B III, 2, 330. V, 1, 91. Cor. IV, 6, 161. Caes. II, 2, 65. Mcb. V, 7, 11. Lr. IV, 6, 107. Cymb. IV, 2, 32 etc. *a l. seven times removed*, As V, 4, 71. *the l. circumstantial and the l. direct*, 85. 86. 89. 90. *as cheap as —s*, Cor. V, 6, 47; cf. Hml. III, 2, 372. *that's a l. in thy throat*, H5 IV, 8, 17 (Fluellen's speech). *to thrust the l. unto him*, Cor. V, 6, 110. *to give the l.* = to charge with falsehood (cf. R2 I, 1, 132. IV, 53): Sonn. 150, 3. Tp. III, 2, 85. 86. Mids. III, 1, 138. As III, 2, 410. V, 4, 90. Wint. IV, 4, 746. 749. V, 2, 144. Cor. II, 2, 37. III, 2, 100. V, 6, 107. Mcb. II, 3, 40. *gives the l. in the throat*, Hml. II, 2, 601. *to tell a l.* or *—s:* Tp. I, 2, 248. III, 2, 32. Wiv. I, 1, 69. Ado IV, 1, 324. Merch. III, 4, 69. 74. H4A I, 2, 209. II, 4, 214. Cor. V, 2, 25. Playing on the word: Tw. III, 2, 49. R2 IV, 66. Mcb. II, 3, 40.

Lie, vb. (impf. and partic. *—d*) to utter falsehood intentionally: Sonn. 17, 7. 115, 1. 123, 11. 138, 2. Tp. I, 2, 257. II, 1, 66. III, 2, 28. 51. III, 3, 26. Gent. III, 1, 292. V, 2, 10. Wiv. I, 1, 167. II, 1, 51. 133. Meas. II, 1, 174. Err. II, 2, 165. Ado IV, 1, 154. 273. V, 1, 95. LLL I, 1, 176. II, 228. 253. IV, 3, 86. V, 2, 550. As III, 5, 19. Shr. IV, 3, 107. All's II, 3, 146. Tw. II, 3, 116 etc. *to l. to* = to tell a p. an untruth: Wiv. III, 5, 65. *to l. with*, in the same sense: *I l. with her and she with me*, Sonn. 138, 13 (but cf. Oth. IV, 1, 35). *he —s to the heart*, Oth. V, 2, 156. *I l. in my throat*, LLL IV, 3, 12. Shr. IV, 3, 133. Tw. III, 4, 172. H4B I, 2, 94. 97. R3 I, 2, 93. The two expressions joined: *as low as to thy heart, through the false passage of thy throat, thou —st*, R2 I, 1, 125. *—ing*, subst.: Tw. III, 4, 389. Wint. IV, 4, 745. H4A V, 4, 149. H4B III, 2, 326. Hml. III, 2, 372 (cf. Cor. V, 6, 47). Lr. I, 4, 201. Cymb. II, 5, 22. *—ing* = mendacious: Tp. I, 2, 344. Meas. V, 357. Ado V, 1, 224. Merch. III, 1, 9. Cor. III, 3, 72. Superl. *lyingest:* Shr. Ind. 2, 25. H6B II, 1, 125. Play on the word: Tp. III, 2, 22. Gent. I, 2, 76. 77. Mids. II, 2, 52. Rom. I, 4, 51. Hml. V, 1, 132. 133. Oth. III, 4, 2. 3.

Lie, vb. (impf. *lay*; partic. *lain* or *lien; lain:* Lucr. 233. Rom. III, 1, 28. IV, 5, 36. V, 3, 176. *lien:* John IV, 1, 50. In Hml. V, 1, 190 Qq *lien*, Ff *lain;* in Per. III, 2, 85 Qq *lien*, Ff *been*) 1) to be in a horizontal position, or nearly so: *panting he —s*, Ven. 62. *where they lay*, 176. 827. 1165. Sonn. 154, 1. Tp. II, 1, 280. 281. 300. II, 2, 11. Wiv. II, 1, 81. Meas. II, 2, 166. As II, 1, 30. III, 2, 253. Tw. II, 3, 147. Rom. III, 1, 28. Mcb. III, 2, 21. Per. III, 2, 85 etc. etc. *to l. down* = to lay the body on the ground, to go to rest: As II, 6, 2. H4A II, 2, 33. III, 1, 229. H4B III, 1, 30. Caes. IV, 3, 250. Lr. III, 6, 36. Ant. IV, 14, 47. Cymb. IV, 2, 294. *to l. by*, in the same sense: H8 III, 1, 11.

2) to be in bed, and, in general, to pass the time of night: *a stranger on that pillow lay*, Lucr. 1620. *in a cowslip's bell I l.* Tp. V, 89. *where they are —ing*, Gent. III, 1, 143. *l. in the woollen*, Ado II, 1, 33. *wheresoe'er she —s*, Mids. II, 2, 90. *where Cressid lay that night*, Merch. V, 6. 230. As II, 3, 23. H4A I, 2, 143. H4B IV, 2, 97. R3 I, 2, 112. II, 4, 1. V, 3, 7. Oth. III, 3, 413 etc. *to l. long* = to rise late, Troil. IV, 1, 3. *that you do l. so late*, Mcb. II, 3, 25. *to l. with* = to have carnal intercourse with: Wiv. II, 2, 295. V, 5, 259. Meas. III, 2, 292. Merch. V, 259. 262. 285. As I, 2, 213 (quibbling). All's IV, 2, 72. H6C III, 2, 69. R3 I, 2, 113. I, 4, 140. V, 3, 336. Rom. IV, 5, 36 etc. *to l. by*, in the same sense: H8 IV, 1, 70. cf. *not wholesome to our cause, that she should l. i' the bosom of our hard-ruled king*, H8 III, 2, 100. *in thy possession —s a lass unparalleled*, Ant. V, 2, 318.

3) to be buried, in the grave: *full fathom five thy father —s*, Tp. I, 2, 396. III, 3, 102. V, 152. Meas. III, 1, 119. Ado V, 1, 69. V, 3, 4. Wint. III, 2, 240. IV, 4, 467. R2 III, 3, 168. Rom. V, 3, 176 etc. *to l. low* = to be struck down, to be dead: *some of us would l. low*, Ado V, 1, 52. *and l. full low*, R2 III, 2, 140. *either we or they must lower l.* H4A III, 3, 228. *dost thou l. so low?* Caes. III, 1, 148.

4) to be confined; a) in prison: *without ransom to l. forfeited*, H4A IV, 3, 96. *I had rather l. in prison*, H6C III, 2, 70. *I will deliver you, or else l. for you*, R3 I, 1, 115. b) by illness: *the wretch that —s in woe,*

Mids. V, 384. *though you lay here in this chamber,* Shr. Ind. 2, 86. *—s he not bedrid,* Wint. IV, 4, 412. *to l. in* = to be in childbed: Cor. I, 3, 86.

5) to be placed in any manner implying want of motion: *her lily hand her rosy cheek —s under,* Lucr. 386. *l. there, my art,* Tp. I, 2, 25. *let it* (the letter) *l.* Gent. I, 2, 76. *in my chamber-window —s a book,* Ado II, 3, 3. Tw. II, 2, 16. II, 5, 24. III, 2, 49. John II, 143. III, 2, 3. H4B IV, 5, 21. 32. H5 IV, 2, 50. Tim. III, 6, 127. Mcb. I, 4, 50. Hml. V, 1, 190 etc.

6) to be situated: *where my land —s,* Wint. IV, 3, 105. *my fortunes do all l. there,* IV, 4, 602. *the remnant northward, —ing off from Trent,* H4A III, 1, 79. *here Southam —s,* H6C V, 1, 12. *in Troy there —s the scene,* Troil. Prol. 1. *the demesnes that here adjacent l.* Rom. II, 1, 20. *here —s the east,* Caes. II, 1, 101. Similarly: *the bath for my help —s where Cupid got new fire,* Sonn. 153, 13. *your conscience, where —s that?* Tp. II, 1, 276. *where —s thy grief?* LLL IV, 3, 171. 172. *what upward —s the street should see,* 280. John IV, 1, 48. *there —s your way,* Shr. III, 2, 212. Tw. I, 5, 215. III, 1, 145. Troil. IV, 1, 79. *large lengths of seas between my father and my mother lay,* John I, 106. *this way —s the game,* H6C IV, 5, 14. *if thy flight lay toward the sea,* Lr. III, 4, 10. *under her breast —s a mole,* Cymb. II, 4, 135.

7) to reside, to lodge, to dwell: *where —s Sir Proteus?* Gent. IV, 2, 137. *does he l. at the Garter?* Wiv. II, 1, 187. *when the court lay at Windsor,* II, 2, 63. *she must l. here on mere necessity,* LLL I, 1, 149. *there doth my father l.* Shr. IV, 4, 56. *she will l. at my house,* All's III, 5, 34. *the king —s by a beggar,* Tw. III, 1, 8. *when I lay at Clement's inn,* H4B III, 2, 299. *her poor castle where she —s,* H6A II, 2, 41. *there young Henry with his nobles l.* III, 2, 129. *I lay here in Corioli at a poor man's house,* Cor. I, 9, 82. *where great Aufidius —s,* IV, 4, 8. *where Cassio —s,* Oth. III, 4, 2. *his remembrance lay in Egypt with his joy,* Ant. I, 5, 57 etc.

8) to be posted in time of war, to be encamped, to be stationed: *the warlike band where her beloved Collatinus —s,* Lucr. 256. *how far off —s your power?* R2 III, 2, 63. 192. *the English l. within fifteen hundred paces,* H5 III, 7, 135. R3 V, 3, 37. Cor. I, 4, 8. Ant. II, 2, 162 etc. Similarly: *had Collatinus lain in ambush to betray my life,* Lucr. 233. *how —s their battle?* Cor. I, 6, 51.

9) to be contained, to be deposited: *look in mine eye-balls, there thy beauty —s,* Ven. 119. *who fears sinking where such treasure —s,* Lucr. 280. *the guiltless casket where it* (the jewel) *lay,* 1057. *if in the child the father's image —s,* 1753; cf. H4B V, 2, 74. *how long lay you there* (in the basket)? Wiv. III, 5, 95. *your goods that lay at host in the Centaur,* Err. V, 410. *whilst thou layest in thy unhallowed dam,* Merch. IV, 1, 136. *love-thoughts l. rich when canopied with bowers,* Tw. I, 1, 41. *where l. my maiden weeds,* V, 262. *my honesty that —s enclosed in this trunk,* Wint. I, 2, 435. *there —s such secrets in this fardel,* IV, 4, 783. *in my loyal bosom —s his power,* R2 II, 3, 98. *in the reproof of this —s the jest,* H4A I, 2, 213. *some lay in dead men's skulls,* R3 I, 4, 29 etc.

10) to rest, not to stir: *the wind is loud and will not l.* Per. III, 1, 49. *when our quick winds l. still,* Ant. I, 2, 114; cf. John IV, 1, 50.

11) to remain unsold: *'twas a commodity lay fret-* *ting by you,* Shr. II, 330. *'tis a commodity will lose the gloss with —ing,* All's I, 1, 167. *l. they upon thy hand,* Ant. II, 5, 105.

12) to be in a posture of defence: *here I lay, and thus I bore my point,* H4A II, 4, 216. *one knows not at what ward you l.; — at all these wards I l.* Troil. I, 2, 283. 288.

13) to be in a place or state, to be found: *making a famine where abundance —s,* Sonn. 1, 7. *being asked where all thy beauty —s,* 2, 5. *at this hour l. at my mercy all mine enemies,* Tp. IV, 264. *it* (labour) *—s starkly in the traveller's bones,* Meas. IV, 2, 70. *their business still —s out o' door,* Err. II, 1, 11. *where light in darkness —s,* LLL I, 1, 78. *in my heart l. there what hidden woman's fear there will,* As I, 3, 121. *fairer prove your honour than in my thought it —s,* All's V, 3, 184. *where —s your text?* Tw. I, 5, 240. *in delay there —s no plenty,* II, 3, 51. *the play so —s that I must play a part,* Wint. IV, 4, 669. *with me thy fortune —s,* John III, 1, 337. *if judgment l. in them,* R2 II, 2, 133. *every thing —s level to our wish,* H4B IV, 4, 7. *there —s a cooling card,* H6A V, 3, 84. *there the action —s in his true nature,* Hml. III, 3, 61. *here —s the point,* V, 1, 10. *thou —st in it,* 132. *that way madness —s,* Lr. III, 4, 21. *my acquaintance —s little amongst them,* Per. IV, 6, 206 etc. Joined with adjectives: *my mercy which —s dead,* John IV, 1, 26. *would thou mighst l. drowning the washing of ten tides,* Tp. I, 1, 60. *the shore that now —s foul and muddy,* V, 82. *griefs of mine l. heavy in my breast,* Rom. I, 1, 192. *in this life l. hid moe thousand deaths,* Meas. III, 1, 40. *when service should in my old limbs l. lame,* As II, 3, 41. *all ways do l. open,* Wiv. II, 2, 175. *I l. open to the law,* H6A I, 3, 159. H8 III, 2, 334. *l. all unlocked to your occasions,* Merch. I, 1, 139.

Followed by *in,* = to be in the power of, to depend on: *if thine honour lay in me,* Lucr. 834. *it —s in thee to make him much outlive a gilded tomb,* Sonn. 101, 10. *it —s much in your holding up,* Meas. III, 1, 273. *good luck —s in odd numbers,* Wiv. V, 1, 2. Ado II, 2, 21. LLL V, 2, 871. Mids. II, 1, 118. Merch. IV, 1, 355. As I, 1, 21. All's V, 2, 49. V, 3, 146. John II, 440. R2 I, 2, 4. II, 2, 130. Cor. III, 3, 94. Rom. I, 5, 4. Tim. IV, 3, 322. Ant. I, 2, 80 etc. Similarly *within:* *both our remedies within thy help and holy physic —s,* Rom. II, 3, 52. *that, opened, —s within our remedy,* Hml. II, 2, 18.

Followed by *on,* = a) to weigh, to press: *a heavy summons —s like lead upon me,* Mcb. II, 1, 6. With *heavy: this fever —s heavy on me,* John V, 3, 4. R2 IV, 66. H4A IV, 3, 80. Tim. III, 5, 10. b) to come on, to fall to the share of: *let it l. on my head,* Wiv. II, 1, 191. 194. *which fault —s on the hazards of all husbands,* John I, 119. *the penance —s on you,* H8 I, 4, 32. *his faults l. gently on him!* IV, 2, 31. c) to be a matter of obligation or duty: *now it —s you on to speak to the people,* Cor. III, 2, 52. d) to depend on: *my life on thy revolt doth l.* Sonn. 92, 10. *as if his life lay on it,* All's III, 7, 43. *would the quarrel lay upon our heads,* H4A V, 2, 48. *the glory of our Troy doth this day l. on his fair worth,* Troil. IV, 4, 149. *our fortune —s upon this jump,* Ant. III, 8, 5.

To lie heavy to = heavy on: *it would unclog my heart of what —s heavy to't.* Cor. IV, 2, 48. cf. Hml. I, 2, 124.

Followed by *under,* = to be subject to, to suffer from: *if this sweet lady l. not guiltless here under some biting error*, Ado IV, 1, 171. *let him, like an engine not portable, l. under this report*, Troil. II, 3, 144.

Lief or **Lieve** (both forms used by O. Edd., the first preferred by M. Edd.) dear, beloved: *stirred up my liefest liege to be mine enemy*, H6B III, 1, 164. *I had as l.* = I should like as much; followed by an inf. without *to: I had as l. bear so much lead*, Wiv. IV, 2, 117. *I had as l. be a list of an English kersey*, Meas. I, 2, 34. 137. As IV, 1, 52. Shr. I, 1, 135. Tw. III, 2, 33. R2 V, 2, 49. H4A IV, 2, 19. H4B III, 2, 238. H5 III, 7, 63. Cor. IV, 5, 186. Rom. II, 4, 215. Caes. I, 2, 95. Ant. II, 7, 13. With the inf. of the perf. = I should have liked as much: *I had as l. have heard the night-raven*, Ado II, 3, 84. *I had as l. have been alone*, As III, 2, 269. A subord. clause following: *I had as l. you would tell me*, Wiv. III, 1, 63. *I had as l. thou didst break his neck*, As I, 1, 152. *I had as l. they would put ratsbane in my mouth*, H4B I, 2, 47. *I had as l. Helen's golden tongue had commended Troilus*, Troil. I, 2, 114. *I had as l. the town-crier spoke my lines*, Hml. III, 2, 4.

Liege, lord paramount, sovereign: *l. of all loiterers*, LLL III, 185. *my sovereign l. was in my debt*, R2 I, 1, 129. *that misbecame my place, my person, or my —'s sovereignty*, H4B V, 2, 101. *stirred up my liefest l. to be mine enemy*, H6B III, 1, 164. *Humphrey, proved* (an enemy) *to my l.* 260. *I tender so the safety of my l.* 277. *Henry, our dread l.* V, 1, 17. *canst thou speak against thy l.* H6C III, 3, 95. Mostly in the vocative: Tp. V, 245. Meas. V, 433. Err. V, 214. 277. Ado I, 1, 292. LLL I, 1, 34. 50. 134. IV, 3, 152. 173. As I, 2, 234. I, 3, 66. Wint. II, 1, 170. H6A III, 4, 15. H6B III, 1, 94. H6C IV, 1, 86. H8 V, 1, 122. Mcb. I, 4, 2. Hml. II, 2, 43. Lr. I, 1, 36 etc. etc.

Liegeman, vassal, subject: *swore the devil his true l.* H4A II, 4, 372. With *to: as thou art l. to us*, Wint. II, 3, 174. *true liegemen to his crown*, H6A V, 4, 128. Hml. I, 1, 15.

Lieger, see *Leiger.*

Lie-giver, one who charges another with falsehood: R2 IV, 68.

Lieu (monosyll.); *in l. of* = in return for: *that he in l. o' the premises of homage should presently extirpate me*, Tp. I, 2, 123. *in l. thereof dispatch me hence*, Gent. II, 7, 88. LLL III, 130. Merch. IV, 1, 410. V, 262. As II, 3, 65. John V, 4, 44. H5 I, 2, 255.

Lieutenant, an officer who supplies the place of a superior in his absence: *thou shalt be my l., monster, or my standard*, Tp. III, 2, 18. 19. *like a —'s scarf*, Ado II, 1, 197. *my l.* Peto, H4A IV, 2, 9. *ancients, corporals, —s, gentlemen of companies*, 26. *l.* Pistol, H4B V, 5, 95. H5 II, 1, 2. *there is an aunchient l. there at the pridge*, III, 6, 13 (Fluellen's speech). H6A I, 3, 16. H6C IV, 6, 1. 9. R3 IV, 1, 12. Oth. I, 1, 9. 32 etc. Ant. III, 1, 18. III, 7, 78.

Lieutenantry, the office of a lieutenant, lieutenancy: *strip you out of your l.* Oth. II, 1, 173. *he alone dealt on l.* Ant. III, 11, 39 (acted by proxy, did not make war in his own person, but by those who commanded under him).

Lieve, see *Lief.*

Life, 1) the state in which the soul and body are united; opposed to death: *they would not take her l.* Tp. I, 2, 267. *every thing advantageous to l.* (= subsistence) II, 1, 49; cf. *competence of l.* H4B V, 5, 70. *if of l. you keep a care*, Tp. II, 1, 303. *a thrid of mine own life*, IV, 1, 3. *long l.* 24; cf. H4B V, 3, 54; Ant. I, 2, 32. *thy father hath his l.* Err. V, 390 (his life shall be spared). *God save your l.* LLL IV, 2, 150. *till thy l. end*, Mids. II, 2, 61. *there may as well be amity and l. 'tween snow and fire*, Merch. III, 2, 30 (snow and fire may as well be on terms of friendship and not destroy each other). *my l. upon't*, Tw. II, 4, 23. *doth sway my l.* II, 5, 118. *punish my l.* V, 141; cf. *upon pain of l.* R2 I, 3, 140 and 153. *the l. to come*, Wint. IV, 2, 30; Mcb. I, 7, 7. *I desire my l. once more to look on him*, Wint. V, 1, 137 (= in my l.). *the main chance of things as yet not come to l.* H4B III, 1, 84 (having begun to exist). *her l. in Rome would be eternal in our triumph*, Ant. V, 1, 65 (her being brought alive to Rome) etc. etc. *to give l.* = a) to beget: John IV, 1, 90. R2 II, 3, 155. H4B IV, 5, 117. H6A IV, 7, 6. H6C II, 5, 92. Tit. IV, 2, 123. b) to save: Merch. V, 286. Tw. V, 83. John II, 13. H6A IV, 6, 5. c) to spare: H5 II, 2, 50. Tit. II, 3, 159 etc. *for l.* = in order not to incur death: *from a bear a man would run for l.* Err. III, 2, 159. *I dare not for my l.* Shr. IV, 3, 1; John III, 1, 132; Caes. IV, 3, 62. *stir not, for your lives*, H6C II, 4, 18. *haste thee, for thy l.* Lr. V, 3, 251. *hold, for your lives*, Oth. II, 3, 164 etc. *l. and death!* Lr. I, 4, 318. *God's my l.* Ado IV, 2, 72 and Mids. IV, 1, 209 (Dogberry and Bottom speaking). *'od's my little l.* As III, 5, 43. *by my l.!* As IV, 1, 159. V, 2, 77. Tw. II, 5, 95. *for my l.* (= as sure as I live) Ado III, 2, 76. LLL V, 2, 728. Shr. III, 1, 49. Wint. IV, 3, 108. R3 IV, 1, 3. *on my l.!* Wiv. V, 5, 200. As I, 2, 294. Wint. V, 1, 43 (cf. Lr. II, 2, 52 and Tw. IV, 1, 49). *o' my l.!* Wiv. I, 1, 40. *a l.* = on my l. Wint. IV, 4, 264. — Plur. *lives:* Tp. I, 1, 50. Err. I, 1, 8. LLL I, 1, 1. Tw. II, 3, 10 (some M. Edd. *life*). II, 5, 15. John II, 277. 419. V, 4, 38. R2 I, 1, 198. II, 1, 245. III, 1, 4. III, 2, 151. H6A II, 5, 81 etc. Sing. for plur.: *they desire yet their l. to see him a man*, Wint. I, 1, 45. *from these a pair of lovers take their l.* Rom. Prol. 6. *all the voyage of their l. is bound in shallows*, Caes. IV, 3, 220. Singular use of the def. art.: *the aim of all is but to nurse the l. with honour, wealth and ease*, Lucr. 141. *that which we have fled during the l., let us not wrong it dead*, H6A IV, 7, 50. The abstr. for the concr.: *whilst I see lives, the gashes do better upon them*, Mcb. V, 8, 2 (= living creatures).

2) the time allotted for the existence of a man: *she that dwells ten leagues beyond man's l.* Tp. II, 1, 247 (at a greater distance than man is able to reach in his lifetime). *speak once in thy l.* III, 2, 24. *more wit than ever I learned before in my l.* Wiv. IV, 5, 62. *to live a barren sister all your l.* Mids. I, 1, 72. All's II, 3, 85. Tw. I, 3, 87. H4A V, 2, 8 etc.

3) course and manner of living: *a clear l.* Tp. III, 3, 82. *the story of my l.* V, 304; Err. I, 1, 138. *that l. is altered now*, Gent. II, 4, 128. *it is a l. that I have desired*, Wiv. I, 3, 21. *leads an ill l. with him*, II, 2, 92; 122; Err. III, 2, 67; Shr. IV, 1, 143; H4B II, 4, 310; V, 3, 146; Cor. V, 3, 95. *bid farewell to your good l.* Wiv. III, 3, 127. *I loved the l. removed*, Meas. I, 3, 8. *there is a kind of character in thy l.* I, 1, 28. *the idea of her l.* Ado IV, 1, 226. *a song of good l.* Tw. II, 3, 37. *I must give over this l.* H4A I, 2, 107. *I shall have such a l.* Troil. IV, 2, 22. *thinkest thou I'ld make a l. of jealousy*, Oth. III, 3, 177. *my desolation does begin to make a better l.* Ant. V, 2, 2 etc. Plur. *lives:*

Gent. IV, 1, 54. R2 II, 1, 11. V, 1, 24 etc. Sing. for plur.: *for some dishonest manners of their l.* H5 I, 2, 49.

4) vital energy, vivacity, animation, spirit: *the l. and feeling of her passion she hoards*, Lucr. 1317. *it was defect of spirit, l. and bold audacity*, 1346. *here's a simple line of l.* Merch. II, 2, 169 (a line in the palm of the hand promising good fortune); cf. Sonn. 16, 9. *these your unusual weeds to each part of you do give a l.* Wint. IV, 4, 2. *a lad of l.* H5 IV, 1, 45. *the tract of every thing would by a good discourser lose some l.* H8 I, 1, 41. *these looks infuse new l. in me*, Tit. I, 461. *high in name and power, higher than both in blood and l.* Ant. I, 2, 197. *she shows a body rather than a l.* III, 3, 23. *strikes l. into my speech*, Cymb. III, 3, 97 etc. *there's l. in it* = there are hopes still: Tw. I, 3, 118. Lr. IV, 6, 206. cf. *what l. is in that, to be the death of this marriage?* Ado II, 2, 19.

5) that which makes to live, the source of existence: *fly I hence, I fly away from l.* Gent. III, 1, 187. *thy husband is thy lord, thy l., thy keeper*, Shr. V, 2, 146. *behold our patroness, the l. of Rome*, Cor. V, 5, 1. *and die with looking on his l.* Ant. I, 5, 34. Used as a compellation of endearment: Gent. I, 3, 45. Mids. III, 2, 246. John III, 4, 104. H6A I, 4, 23. IV, 7, 1. Rom. IV, 5, 58. Cymb. V, 5, 226 etc.

6) the inmost part, essence, substance: *the l. of purity, the supreme fair* (viz the sun) Lucr. 780. *hear me breathe my l. before this ancient sir*, Wint. IV, 4, 371. *the l. of all his blood is touched corruptibly*, John V, 7, 1. *my l. itself, and the best part of it, thanks you for this great care*, H8 I, 2, 1. *our project's l. this shape of sense assumes*, Troil. I, 3, 385. *there you touched the l. of our design*, II, 2, 194.

7) reality, nature, naturalness: *when a painter would surpass the l.* Ven. 289. *a thousand objects art gave lifeless l.* Lucr. 1374. *with good l. and observation strange*, Tp. III, 3, 86. *never counterfeit of passion came so near the l. of passion*, Ado II, 3, 110. *the l. as lively mocked*, Wint. V, 3, 19. *with such l. of majesty, warm l., as now it coldly stands*, 35. *to demonstrate the l. of such a battle in l. so lifeless as it shows itself*, H5 IV, 2, 54. *things which cannot in their huge and proper l. be here presented*, V Chor. 5. *it is a pretty mocking of the l.* Tim. I, 1, 35. *livelier than l.* 38. *the true l. on't*, Cymb. II, 4, 76. *to the l.* = in exact keeping with nature and truth, naturally: *such a part which never I shall discharge to the l.* Cor. III, 2, 106. *give them repetition to the l.* Per. V, 1, 247.

Life-blood, vital blood, the blood with which life is lost: Merch. III, 2, 269. H4A IV, 1, 29. H6A IV, 6, 43. H6C I, 4, 138. H8 III, 2, 277. Tit. IV, 4, 37.

Life-harming, injurious to life: R2 II, 2, 3 (Ff *self-harming*).

Lifeless or rather **Liveless** (for such is the spelling of all O. Edd.) destitute of life, unanimated, dead: Ven. 211. Lucr. 1374. As I, 2, 263. H5 IV, 2, 55. H6B IV, 1, 142. *hopeless and helpless doth Aegeon wend, but to procrastinate his l. end*, Err. I, 1, 159, perhaps not the end brought on by death, but the end of his lifeless state, the end of his death-like life.

Lifelings; *'od's l.*, Sir Andrew's oath in Tw. V, 187.

Life-poisoning: Ven. 740.

Life-preserving: Err. V, 83.

Life-rendering, sacrificing one's life, ready to die for others: *and like the kind l. pelican repast them with my blood*, Hml. IV, 5, 146 (cf. Ant. IV, 14, 33).

Lifetime, the time which one has to live: H6C I, 1, 171.

Life-weary, tired of living: Rom. V, 1, 62.

Lift (impf. *—ed; lift* in H6A I, 1, 16) 1) tr. to heave, to raise; absol.: *l. there*, Per. III, 2, 49. With an accus.: *she —s the coffer-lids that close his eyes*, Ven. 1127. *l. the moon out of her sphere*, Tp. II, 1, 183. *she —ed the princess from the earth*, Wint. V, 2, 83. *l. their swords in such a just war*, John II, 35. *l. an angry arm against his minister*, R2 I, 2, 40; cf. III, 2. 59; III, 3, 89; Cor. I, 1, 70. *I will l. Mortimer as high*, H4A I, 3, 135. *his forward spirit would l. him where most trade of danger ranged*, H4B I, 1, 174 (cf. *Heave*). *we'll l. our heads to heaven*, H6B I, 2, 14. *l. my soul to heaven*, H8 II, 1, 78. *yet will he l. as much as his brother Hector*, Troil. I, 2, 126. *l. their bosoms higher*, I, 3, 112. *—s him from the earth*, IV, 5, 16; Rom. V, 1, 5. *—ing food to it*, Lr. III, 4, 16. *l. this arm*, Oth. II, 3, 208. With *up: when the gracious light —s up his burning head*, Sonn. 7, 2. *—ed up their noses*, Tp. IV, 177. *l. up your countenance*, Wint. IV, 4, 49. *l. up thy looks*, 490. *thy brow*, John V, 2, 54. *l. me up to reach at victory*, R2 I, 3, 71. *levers to l. me up*, H4A II, 2, 36. *can l. your blood up*, V, 2, 79. *l. up his hand*, H6A I, 1, 16. *shall l. up their privilege*, Cor. I, 10, 22. *I l. this one hand up to heaven*, Tit. III, 1, 207. *—s up her arms*, IV, 1, 37. *wilt thou l. up Olympus*, Caes. III, 1, 74. *it —ed up its head*, Hml. I, 2, 216. *did l. up eye*, Oth. V, 2, 200.

2) intr. to rise: *a summer bird which sings the —ing up of day*, H4B IV, 4, 93.

Lifter, a rook, a cheat, a plucker: Troil. I, 2, 129 (quibble).

Ligarius, name in Caes. II, 1, 215. 311 etc.

Liggens: *by God's l.*, Shallow's oath in H4B V, 3, 69.

Light (a word much played on by the poet) subst. 1) that by which it is possible to see, the agency of luminous matter which makes things visible; opposed to darkness: *to lend the world his l.* Ven. 756. *by the l. he spies Lucretia's glove*, Lucr. 316. *l. and lust are deadly enemies*, 674. *what l. is l., if Silvia be not seen?* Gent. III, 1, 174. *by day or night, or any kind of l.* Wiv. II, 1, 17. *l. and spirits will become it well*, V, 2, 13. *as there comes l. from heaven*, Meas. V, 225. *what obscured l. the heavens did grant*, Err. I, 1, 67. 91. *by her own l.* III, 2, 99. *a woman sometimes an you saw her in the l. Perchance l. in the l.* LLL II, 198. Mids. II, 2, 188. 386. 419. All's I, 1, 99. R2 I, 3, 176. III, 2, 43. V, 6, 44. H4A III, 3, 42. H4B II, 3, 19. H6B II, 4, 40. H6C II, 1, 37. II, 5, 2. R3 IV, 4, 401. Tit. V, 2, 33. Tim. V, 1, 48. Mcb. I, 4, 51. II, 4, 10. III, 2, 50. Cymb. III, 1, 45. Per. I, 2, 10. *to give l.* = to be luminous, to shine: Ven. 491. LLL IV, 3, 32. Mids. V, 398. Merch. V, 129. H4A V, 1, 18. H6B II, 1, 67. H6C II, 6, 2. Tim. IV, 3, 67. Caes. II, 1, 45. Ant. III, 2, 65. *by this l.*, used as an oath: Tp. II, 2, 154. III, 2, 17. Ado V, 1, 140. V, 4, 93. LLL IV, 3, 10. Shr. II, 275. John I, 259. H4B II, 2, 69. H8 V, 1, 173. *by this good l.* Tp. II, 2, 147. Wint. II, 3, 82. *by this day and this l.* H5 IV, 8, 66 (Fluellen's speech). *God's l.* H4A III, 3, 71 (the hostess' speech). *H4B II, 4, 142 (Doll's speech. Ff *what*). 159 (Ff om.).

2) any luminous body; the sun, a star, a torch, a taper etc.: Ven. 826. Lucr. 673. 1627. Sonn 7

Tp. I, 2, 335. Wiv. V, 2, 2. V, 3, 15. Meas. IV, 1, 4. LLL I, 1, 88. V, 2, 633. Mids. IV, 3, 231. Merch. V, 89. Tw. IV, 2, 113. 118. R2 I, 3, 221. H4A III, 3, 51. H6C II, 1, 31. R3 V, 3, 180. Troil. V, 1, 75. Rom. I, 4, 12. V, 3, 25. Tim. I, 2, 234. II, 2, 170. Mcb. III, 3, 9. 14. 19. V, 1, 25. Cymb. I, 6, 109 etc.

3) the brightness of the eye, power of seeing: *the eyes fly from their — s,* Lucr. 461. *dying eyes gleamed forth their ashy — s,* 1378. *O that your eyes had the —s they were wont to have,* Gent. II, 1, 77. *l. seeking l. doth l. of l. beguile,* LLL I, 1, 77. *by l. we lose l.* V, 2, 376. *bended their l. on me,* Hml. II, 1, 100. *to see the enclosed —s,* Cymb. II, 2, 21. cf. Meas. IV, 1, 4.

4) brightness, glory: *to lend base subjects l.* Sonn. 100, 4. *angels of l.* Err. IV, 3, 56. *spirits of l.* LLL IV, 3, 257. *thou keepest me from the l.* H6C V, 6, 84. *fair glass of l., I loved you,* Per. I, 1, 76. Applied to persons: *those suns of glory, those two —s of men,* H8 I, 1, 6.

5) illumination of mind, mental sight: *that hath dazzled my reason's l.* Gent. II, 4, 210. *the l. of truth,* LLL I, 1, 75. *l. seeking l. doth l. of l. beguile,* 77. *his small l. of discretion,* Mids. V, 257.

6) information, knowledge, notice given: *that I had any l. from thee of this,* Gent. III, 1, 49. *why you have given me such clear —s of favour,* Tw. V, 344. *we had a kind of light what would ensue,* John IV, 3, 61. *I'll give some l. unto you,* Per. I, 3, 18. *to bring to l. =* to make known: Lucr. 940. Meas. III, 2, 189. Ado V, 1, 240. H5 II, 2, 185. H6B III, 1, 65. *to come to l. =* to become known: Ado IV, 1, 112. Merch. II, 2, 83. H5 IV, 8, 23. H8 III, 2, 29. *to keep them from the l.* Per. I, 1, 136.

7) life: *brought to l.* and *come to l. =* born: R3 I, 2, 22. Tit. IV, 2, 125. cf. R2 I, 3, 221. Oth. I, 3, 410. V, 2, 7. 10.

Light, adj. bright, clear: *that, thou being dead, the day should yet be l.* Ven. 1134. *dark is l.* LLL IV, 3, 269. *before the sun rose he was harnessed l.* Troil. I, 2, 8. *earth-treading stars that make dark heaven l.* Rom. I, 2, 25. *more l. and l. it grows,* III, 5, 35. *made the night l. with drinking,* Ant. II, 2, 182. Play on the word: Lucr. 1434. Meas. V, 280. LLL V, 2, 19. Merch. II, 6, 42. Lr. IV, 6, 151.

Light, adj. 1) of little weight, opposed to heavy: Ven. 155. Gent. III, 1, 129. LLL V, 2, 26. Merch. IV, 1, 328. All's II, 5, 48. R2 I, 4, 44. H4B I, 2, 187. IV, 5, 33. R3 III, 1, 117. Troil. II, 3, 277. Tim. IV, 3, 379. Lr. III, 6, 115. IV, 6, 151. Cymb. V, 4, 168. Quibbling: Err. III, 2, 52. Mids. III, 2, 133. Merch. III, 2, 91. R2 III, 4, 86. H4A II, 3, 14. H4B IV, 1, 195. Troil. I, 3, 28. Cymb. V, 4, 25.

2) moving with ease, swift, nimble: *love is l. and will aspire,* Ven. 150. *in her l. chariot,* 1192. *too l. for such a swain as you to catch,* Shr. II, 205. *so l. of foot,* R2 III, 4, 92. *l. payment,* H4B V, 5, 135. *l. horsemen,* H6A IV, 2, 43. *his l. feathers,* Rom. I, 4, 20. *love's l. wings,* II, 2, 66. *so l. a foot,* II, 6, 16. *so l. is vanity,* 20.

3) not oppressive, not violent: *yields to every l. impression,* Ven. 566. *every l. occasion of the wind,* Compl. 86. *l. skirmishes,* H6A I, 4, 69. *thy love doth mince this matter, making it l. to Cassio,* Oth. II, 3, 248. *a tale whose —est word would harrow up thy soul,* Hml. I, 5, 15; cf. IV, 6, 26.

4) of no moment, of little value, slight, unimport-

ant (mostly with a play on the word): *make the prize l.* Tp. I, 2, 452. *my father's loss, the wreck of all my friends, are but l. to me,* 489. *as l. as tales,* Mids. III, 2, 133. *a heavy curse from Rome, or the l. loss of England,* John III, 1, 206. H4A II, 3, 14. H4B IV, 1, 195. V, 5, 135. H5 II, 2, 89. R3 III, 1, 118. Troil. I, 3, 28. Hml. II, 2, 268. Oth. III, 3, 322. Cymb. V, 4, 25. *to hold l. =* to treat as of little consequence, to estimate at a low rate: *he that stirs holds his soul l.* Oth. II, 3, 174. *to set l.,* in the same sense: *to set me l.* Sonn. 88, 1. *the man that mocks at it and sets it l.* R2 I, 3, 293. *to weigh l.,* in the same sense: *her worth that he doth weigh too l.* All's III, 4, 32. Applied to persons: *making them —est that wear most of it,* Merch. III, 2, 91. *to frown upon Sir Toby and the —er people,* Tw. V, 347 (meaner, inferior). *some few vanities that make him l.* R2 III, 4, 86.

5) easy, not difficult: *lest too l. winning make the prize l.* Tp. I, 2, 451.

6) in good spirits, cheerful, merry: *through their l. joy seemed to appear, like bright things stained, a kind of heavy fear,* Lucr. 1434. *so l. a tune,* Gent. I, 2, 84. *with a l. heart,* Meas. IV, 3, 152. *had she been l. like you, of such a merry spirit,* LLL V, 2, 15. *a l. heart lives long,* 18. *l. airs,* Tw. II, 4, 5. *I am passing l. in spirits,* H4B IV, 2, 85. *my heart is ten times — er than my looks,* R3 V, 3, 3. *I am l. and heavy,* Cor. II, 1, 201. *wantons l. of heart,* Rom. I, 4, 35. *my heart is wondrous l.* IV, 2, 46. *Seneca cannot be too heavy, nor Plautus too l.* Hml. II, 2, 420. *the l. and careless livery that youth wears,* IV, 7, 80. *smiles, gestures and l. behaviour,* Oth. IV, 1, 103.

7) full of levity, unsteady, frivolous, wanton: *women are l. at midnight,* Meas. V, 280. *a l. wench,* Err. V, 3, 52. 55. 77. LLL I, 2, 128. IV, 3, 385. V, 2, 25. *let love, being l., be drowned,* Err. III, 2, 52. Rom. II, 2, 105; cf. *the tune of L. o'love,* Gent. I, 2, 83. Ado III, 4, 44. *otherwise 'tis l.* (viz your heart) Ado III, 4, 37. *what's your dark meaning of this l. word? a l. condition in a beauty dark,* LLL V, 2, 19 20. *a woman ... perchance l. in the l.* II, 199. *they* (my shames) *are too too l.* Merch. II, 6, 42. *a l. wife doth make a heavy husband,* V, 130. *knowing thee to be but young and l.* Shr. II, 204. *in this my l. deliverance,* All's II, 1, 85. *l. vanity,* R2 II, 1, 38. *by this l. flesh,* H4B II, 4, 320. *thou mayst think my haviour l.* Rom. II, 2, 99. *false of heart, l. of ear,* Lr. III, 4, 95 (= forgetful, heedless?). *so l. so drunken, and so indiscreet an officer,* Oth. II, 3, 279 (Ff *slight*). *no more l. answers,* Ant. I, 2, 183.

8) not quite right, not in one's senses, deranged: *thereof comes it that his head is l.* Err. V, 72. *are his wits safe? is he not l. of brain?* Oth. IV, 1, 280. *the brain the heavier for being too l.* Cymb. V, 4, 167. cf. *lightness* in Hml. II, 2, 149.

Light, adv. nimbly, with an airy step: *the grass stoops not, she treads on it so l.* Ven. 1028. *hop as l. as bird from brier,* Mids. V, 401.

Light, vb. (part. *—ed*), 1) trans. a) to give light, to guide by light; absol.: *torches are made to l.* Ven 163. *l. to my chamber,* Rom. III, 4, 33. With an object: *as Hymen's lamps shall l. you,* Tp. IV, 23. *though he have his own lanthorn to l. him,* H4B I, 2, 55. *and l. thee on thy way,* Rom. III, 5, 15. *have —ed fools the way to death,* Mcb. V, 5, 22.

b) to illuminate, to make bright: *the eye of heaven*

that —s the lower world, R2 III, 2, 38. *—ed the little O, the earth*, Ant. V, 2, 80.

c) to kindle: *whereat a waxen torch he —eth*, Lucr. 178. 316. Tp. IV, 97. Meas. I, 1, 34. Mids. III, 1, 173. All's IV, 2, 5. Caes. II, 1, 8.

2) intr. to brighten, to shine, to break: *that shall be the day, whene'er it —s*, H4A III, 2, 138. *as when the sun doth l. a-scorn*, Troil. I, 1, 37 (i.e. in scorn; M. Edd. *a storm*).

Light, vb. (partic. *light* in Per. IV, 2, 77; everywhere else *—ed*) to descend; opposed to mount: *when I mount, alive may I not l.* R2 I, 1, 82. H4A I, 1, 63. H8 I, 1, 9. Caes. V, 3, 31. *she will l.* (like a bird) *to listen to the lays*, H6B I, 3, 93. Cymb. I, 4, 97. *this murderous shaft hath not yet —ed*, Mcb. II, 3, 148. *Mercury new —ed on a heaven-kissing hill*, Hml. III, 4, 59.

With *into*, = to fall: *you are l. into my hands*, Per. IV, 2, 77. With *on*, = 1) to fall, to come down on, to strike; in a bad sense: *let sin, alone committed, l. alone upon his head*, Lucr. 1480. *all the charms of Sycorax l. on you*, Tp. I, 2, 340. Merch. III, 1, 99. IV, 1, 38. John III, 1, 295. H4A II, 2, 31 (Qq om.). H6A V, 3, 39. H6B IV, 8, 33. R3 III, 4, 95. Cor. I, 4, 30. Tim. IV, 3, 357. Caes. I, 1, 60. III, 1, 262. Lr. III, 4, 70. Oth. I, 3, 178 (*if my bad blame l. on the man*). 2) to fall on, to fall to the share of; in a good sense: *a pack of blessings —s upon thy back*, Rom. III, 3, 141. *the election —s on Fortinbras*, Hml. V, 2, 366. 3) to fall in with, to meet, to find, to come by, to get: *you may l. on a husband, that hath no beard*, Ado II, 1, 34. *we'll l. upon some settled low content*, As II, 3, 68. *if I can l. upon a fit man*, Shr. I, 1, 112. 133. I, 2, 168. All's IV, 5, 15. *haply your eye shall l. upon some toy*, Tw. III, 3, 44. *if young Doricles do l. upon her*, Wint. IV, 4, 179. *then they l. on us*, H4A II, 2, 65.

Lighten, to make less heavy, to cheer: *—s my humour with his merry jests*, Err. I, 2, 21. *that we may l. our own hearts and our wives' heels*, Ado V, 4, 120.

Lighten, 1) to illuminate, to enlighten: *the Lord l. thee*, H4B II, 1, 208. *a gem to l. all this isle*, H8 II, 3, 79. *a precious ring that —s all the hole*, Tit. II, 3, 227.

2) to flash: *like the lightning, which doth cease to be ere one can say 'It —s,'* Rom. II, 2, 120. Caes. I, 3, 74. With an accus. denoting the effect: *his eye —s forth controlling majesty*, R2 III, 3, 69.

Lighter-heeled, nimbler in running: Mids. III, 2, 415.

Light-foot, nimble in running: *some l. friend post to the Duke of Norfolk*, R3 IV, 4, 440.

Lightless, dark: *the l. fire which, in pale embers hid, lurks to aspire*, Lucr. 4. *l. hell*, 1555.

Lightly, 1) with little weight, not heavily, nimbly: *could their master come and go as l.* (as thoughts) Gent. III, 1, 142. *was ever feather so l. blown to and fro*, H6B IV, 8, 57.

2) without oppression or dejection, cheerfully: *my bosom's lord sits l. in his throne*, Rom. V, 1, 3. *seeming to bear it l.* Ant. IV, 14, 138.

3) easily, readily: *will not l. trust*, Err. IV, 4, 5. *this man hath for a few light crowns l. conspired*, H5 II, 2, 89. *with tears not l. shed*, Tit. II, 3, 289.

4) slightly, indifferently, not highly: *they are but l. rewarded*, LLL I, 2, 157. *they love his grace but l.* R3 I, 3, 45. *I weigh it l.* III, 1, 121. *believe't not l.*

Cor. IV, 1, 29 (= believe it firmly, be firmly persuaded).

5) usually (cf. Nares' Glossary): *short summers l. have a forward spring*, R3 III, 1, 94.

Lightness, 1) want of weight: H4B I, 1, 122. Rom. I, 1, 185.

2) levity, wantonness: Meas. II, 2, 170. Shr. IV, 2, 24. H4B I, 2, 53. H6C III, 1, 89. Ant. I, 4, 25.

3) mental derangement: *thence to a l.* Hml. II, 2, 149 (cf. *light* in Err. V, 72 and Oth. IV, 1, 280).

Lightning, the flash of light that precedes thunder: Ven. 348. Pilgr. 67. Tp. I, 2, 201. III, 1, 16. LLL IV, 2, 119. Mids. I, 1, 145. John I, 24. R2 I, 3, 79. H6C II, 1, 129. R3 I, 2, 64. Rom. II, 2, 119. III, 1, 177. Caes. I, 3, 50. Mcb. I, 1, 2. Lr. II, 4, 167. IV, 7, 35. Ant. III, 13, 195. Cymb. V, 5, 394. *l. flash*, Tit. II, 1, 3. Cymb. IV, 2, 270. *a l. before death*, Rom. V, 3, 90 (a last blazing up of the flame of life).

Light o'love, 'an old tune of a dance, the name of which made it a proverbial expression of levity, especially in love matters' (Nares): Gent. I, 2, 83. Ado III, 4, 44.

Light-winged, volatile: *l. toys of feathered Cupid*, Oth. I, 3, 269.

Like, adj. (Comp. *—r:* Sonn. 16, 8. LLL V, 2, 846. John II, 126. Superl. *—st:* LLL IV, 2, 88. Merch. IV, 1, 196) 1) equal: *his case was l.* Err. I, 1, 128. Lr. IV, 3, 21. followed by a noun; with *to: wishing me l. to one more rich in hope*, Sonn. 29, 5. without *to: you l. none, none you, for constant heart*, Sonn. 53, 14. *be thou still l. thyself*, H6C III, 3, 15. *with honours l. himself*, Cor. II, 2, 52. IV, 1, 53. *he will be found l. Brutus*, Caes. V, 4, 25 etc. Peculiar expression: *her face nothing l. so clean kept*, Err. III, 2, 105 (i. e. nothing equals the cleanness with which her face is kept. Dromio's speech). Oftenest joined to a noun with the def. article, = the same: *when they in thee the l. offences prove*, Lucr. 613. *the l. loss*, Tp. V, 143. *give the l. notice to Valentinus*, Meas. IV, 5, 7. *to express the l. kindness*, Shr. II, 77. *I take the l. unfeigned oath*, IV, 2, 32. *all men have the l. oaths*, All's IV, 2, 71. *on the l. occasion*, Wint. I, 1, 2. *with the l. bold, just and impartial spirit*, H4B V, 2, 116. *they stoop with the l. wing*, H5 IV, 1, 112. *with hope to find the l. event in love*, H6A V, 5, 105. *have the l. success*, H6C I, 2, 76. *upon the l. devotion as yourselves*, R3 IV, 1, 9 etc. With the indef. art. (= the same): *there must be needs a l. proportion of lineaments, of manners and of spirit*, Merch. III, 4, 14. *should a l. language use to all degrees*, Wint. II, 1, 85. *nothing is at a l. goodness still*, Hml. IV, 7, 117. Without article: *aim at l. delight*, Ven. 400. *when with l. semblance it is sympathized*, Lucr. 1113. *such baseness had never l. executor*, Tp. III, 1, 13. *l. exhibition thou shalt have from me*, Gent. I, 3, 69. *with l. haste*, Meas. V, 420. *burdened with l. weight of pain*, Err. II, 1, 36. *to see l. right bereft*, 40. Wint. III, 3, 21. V, 3, 130. H4A III, 1, 109. H6A V, 4, 158. H6C III, 3, 10. IV, 1, 71. V, 4, 47. R3 I, 3, 201. IV, 4, 304. Troil. I, 3, 319. Cor. I, 1, 104. Tit. V, 3, 200. Tim. I, 1, 170. I, 2, 139. Mcb. IV, 3, 8. Oth. II, 1, 16. Cymb. V, 4, 75 etc. The noun in the plur.: *use l. loving charms*, Pilgr. 150. *l. offices of pity*, Wint. II, 3, 189. *this matched with other* (tidings) *l.* H4A I, 1, 49 (Qq *did*). *laden with l. frailties*, Ant. V, 2, 123. Followed by *as: in* *l. conditions as our argument,* Troil. Prol. 25. By *to: I must take l. seat unto my fortune,* H6B III, 3, 10. *make him of l. spirit to himself,* V, 4, 47.

2) similar, resembling: *much —r than your painted counterfeit,* Sonn. 16, 8. *these two so l.* Err. V, 357. *we are almost as l. as eggs,* Wint. I, 2, 130. *these hands are not more l.* Hml. I, 2, 212. *her smiles and tears were l. a better way,* Lr. IV, 3, 21 (i. e. her smiles and tears were similar, viz to sunshine and rain, but in a superior manner, still more beautiful). *With to: shadows l. to thee,* Sonn. 61, 4. *l. to the Garter's compass,* Wiv. V, 5, 70. *more l. to Claudio,* Meas. IV, 3, 80. *his actions show much l. to madness,* IV, 4, 4. *as l. almost to Claudio as himself,* V, 494. Ado V, 4, 51. LLL IV, 2, 88. Mids. I, 1, 9. III, 2, 209. As II, 4, 28. Shr. IV, 2, 105. John I, 83. II, 126. III, 4, 14. H4A III, 2, 100. H4B I, 1, 60. H6A II, 2, 30. II, 5, 11. H6B III, 2, 176. IV, 9, 32. Tit. IV, 2, 154 etc. *Without to: 'tis l. a dream,* Tp. I, 2, 45. *with hair, l. reeds, not hair,* 213. *make thyself l. a nymph,* 301. *if he were that which now he is l., that's dead,* II, 1, 282. Gent. III, 1, 124. V, 4, 26. Meas. V, 495. Err. I, 1, 52. Ado I, 1, 113. 116. LLL II, 256. V, 2, 846. Merch. III, 1, 70. IV, 1, 196. All's I, 1, 92. II, 1, 99. Tw. I, 5, 138. Wint. I, 2, 129. H5 V, 2, 110. R3 III, 5, 92. Cor. V, 3, 180. Hml. I, 1, 43. 44 etc. With the article: *of all mad matches never was the l.* Shr. III, 2, 244 (one resembling, coming near to this). *to warn false traitors from the l. attempts,* R3 III, 5, 49. *such l.* or *such-l.* = such, of that kind, more of that kind: *others, they think, delight in such l. circumstance, with such l. sport,* Ven. 844. *with such l. flattering,* Pilgr. 413. *with such l. valour,* Tp. III, 3, 59. *for such l. petty crimes as these,* Gent. IV, 1, 52. Err. I, 2, 102. R3 I, 1, 60. Troil. I, 2, 277 (Ff *and so forth*). Tim. III, 2, 23. Hml. V, 2, 43.

3) having a certain air, a look indicative of sth.: *in as l. a figure,* Cymb. III, 3, 96 (corresponding to, and expressive of, his thoughts). *by their show you shall know all that you are l. to know,* Mids. V, 117 (all that you know, to judge by appearances). *he is not l. to marry me well,* As III, 3, 93 (he does not look as if he would marry me well). *possessed with the glanders and l. to mose in the chine,* Shr. III, 2, 51. *'tis l. you'll prove a jolly surly groom,* 215. *lusty and l. to live,* Wint. II, 2, 27. *'tis l. to be loud weather,* III, 3, 11. *thou art l. enough to fight against me,* H4A III, 2, 124. *'tis l., my lord, you will not keep your hour,* H6B II, 1, 181. *'tis l. you would not feast him like a friend,* III, 2, 184. *'tis l. the commons, rude unpolished hinds, could send such message,* 271. *you are l. to do such business,* Cor. III, 1, 48. *more l. to run the country base,* Cymb. V, 3, 19.

4) likely, probable: *O that it were as l. as it is true!* Meas. V, 104. *which we, on l. conditions, will have counter-sealed,* Cor. V, 3, 205 (such as you may hope to obtain). *'tis l.* = it is probable; followed by a clause: *is't l. that lead contains her?* Merch. II, 7, 49. *then 'tis l. I should forget myself,* John III, 4, 49. *'tis l. that they will know us,* H4A I, 2, 195. II, 4, 396. H4B I, 3, 81. R3 III, 2, 122. Oth. V, 2, 92 etc. *'tis great l.* H6B III, 1, 379. *is it not very l.* Rom. IV, 3, 36. 45. Hml. I, 2, 237. Personal use, with an inf. following: *you are l. to lose your hair,* Tp. IV, 237. *we are l. to prove a goodly commodity,* Ado III, 3, 190. *here is l. to be a good presence of worthies,* LLL V,

2, 536. *nor none is l. to have,* As I, 2, 19. IV, 1, 69. Shr. IV, 4, 61. All's II, 1, 62. V, 1, 30. Tw. I, 3, 135. I, 4, 2. Wint. V, 1, 49. H4A V, 4, 39. H6A III, 2, 106. H6B IV, 7, 18. R3 IV, 2, 52. Troil. II, 3, 130 etc.

5) on the point, about, going, ready: *I was l. to be apprehended for the witch of Brainford,* Wiv. IV, 5, 119. *who is thus l. to be cozened with the semblance of a maid,* Ado II, 2, 39. *in that thou art l. to be my kinsman, live unbruised,* V, 4, 112. *I am as l. to call thee so again,* Merch. I, 3, 131.

Like, subst. 1) used of persons, = equal: *thy l. ne'er was,* Pilgr. 294. *that noble minds keep ever with their —s,* Caes. I, 2, 315. *I shall not look upon his l. again,* Hml. I, 2, 188. *to seek for one his l.* Cymb. I, 1, 21. *there never came her l. in Mytilene,* Per. IV, 6, 31. 2) a thing of the same quality or worth: *l. doth quit l.* Meas. V, 416. *to join like —s, and kiss like native things,* All's I, 1, 238. *the l.* = 1) things of that kind: *did you ever hear the l.?* Wiv. II, 1, 70. *for the encouragement of the l.* Meas. I, 2, 193. *who ever saw the l.?* H6A I, 2, 22. *'tis wondrous strange, the l. yet never heard of,* H6C II, 1, 33. 2) the same: *if the l. the snow-white swan desire,* Lucr. 1011. *do you the l.* Tp. II, 1, 295. *I must minister the l. to you,* Gent. II, 4, 150. *I do desire the l.* Meas. IV, 1, 52. Ado V, 1, 31. As I, 3, 115. Tw. I, 2, 21. H6A II, 3, 38. II, 5, 50. IV, 5, 50. H6C II, 4, 10. R3 II, 1, 11. Troil. IV, 6, 50. Tit. IV, 1, 111. Ant. V, 2, 353 etc.

3) a similar thing, that which resembles: *that every l. is not the same,* Caes. II, 2, 128. With *had,* it denotes probability, or a narrow escape: *we had l. to have had our two noses snapped off,* Ado V, 1, 115. *I have had four quarrels, and l. to have fought one,* As V, 4, 48. *your worship had l. to have given us one* (viz lie) Wint. IV, 4, 750.

Like, adv. 1) so as to resemble: *suit thy pity l. in every part,* Sonn. 132, 12. *he hath drawn my picture. Any thing l.?* LLL V, 2, 39.

2) in the same manner; before adjectives, = as: *l. invulnerable,* Tp. III, 3, 66. *l. heedful,* Err. I, 1, 83. *l. glorious,* H5 II, 2, 183. *l. warlike as the wolf,* Cymb. III, 3, 41. Followed by *as: l. as the waves make towards the pebbled shore,* Sonn. 60, 1. *l. as with eager compounds we our palate urge,* 118, 1. H6A V, 5, 5. Troil. I, 2, 7. Hml. I, 2, 217. With *to: l. to a mortal butcher,* Ven. 618. *l. to a new-killed bird,* Lucr. 457. 711. Sonn. 29, 11. Mids. I, 1, 5. III, 2, 360. Tw. V, 121. Wint. V, 1, 89. R2 IV, 280. H6A I, 5, 26. IV, 1, 23. H6B II, 1, 196. II, 4, 98. III, 1, 353. V, 1, 100. H6C II, 1, 129. II, 3, 18. II, 5, 1. III, 2, 161. IV, 8, 20. V, 7, 3 etc. The objects compared: *thou never shouldst love woman l. to me,* Tw. V, 275 (i. e. as thou lovedst me; cf. H6C III, 2, 161). Without *to: featured l. him, l. him with friends possessed,* Sonn. 29, 6. *my trust, l. a good parent, did beget of him a falsehood,* Tp. I, 2, 94. 99. 356. II, 1, 8. 10. 312. II, 2, 6. Gent. I, 2, 58. 133. Meas. I, 1, 39. Mids. III, 2, 362. H5 IV, 8, 53. H6C II, 1, 130. 131. III, 2, 35. III, 2, 162 etc. *l. he,* for *l. him:* Rom. III, 5, 84. Singular expression: *may I be bold to say so? Ay, sir, l. who more bold,* Wiv. IV, 5, 55 (= like the boldest). = as it becomes: *bear our hacked targets l. the men that owe them,* Ant. IV, 8, 31. *follow his chariot, l. the greatest spot of all thy sex,* IV, 12, 35. = as well as: *ghastly looks are at my service, l. enforced smiles,* R3 III, 5, 9.

3) probably: *and l. enough thou knowest thy estimate*, Sonn. 87, 2. Ado II, 3, 108. H4A IV, 4, 7. H4B III, 2, 139. Oth. III, 4, 190. *will money buy them? very l.* Tp. V, 265. *perchance, nay, and most l.* Ant. I, 1, 25. *most l. I did*, Cymb. V, 5, 259.

Like, conj. = as: *came pouring, l. the tide into a breach*, H5 I, 2, 149. *and l. an arrow shot from a well-experienced archer hits the mark*, Per. I, 1, 163 (Ff *as*). *l. goodly buildings left without a roof soon fall to ruin*, II, 4, 36. In Mids. IV, 1, 178 M. Edd. *l. in sickness*, O. Edd. *l. a sickness*. In Lucr. 506 there may be an anacoluthon (cf. Walker's Crit. Exam. II, 115).

Like, vb. 1) to compare, to liken: *the prince broke thy head for —ing his father to a singing-man of Windsor*, H4B II, 1, 97 (Ff *likening*). *l. me to the peasant boys of France*, H6A IV, 6, 48.

2) to be equal, to resemble? The two following passages admit also of another explanation: *in all external grace you have some part, but you l. none, none you, for constant heart*, Sonn. 53, 14. *weak shoulders, overborne with burthening grief, and pithless arms, l. to a withered vine that droops his sapless branches to the ground*, H6A II, 5, 11.

Like, vb. 1) to be pleased; a) absol.: *l. of hearsay well*, Sonn. 21, 13. *faults of his own —ing*, Meas. III, 2, 282. *I looked upon her with a soldier's eye, that —d, but had a rougher task in hand than to drive —ing to the name of love*, Ado I, 1, 301. 302. *if you please to l. no worse than I*, Shr. IV, 4, 32. *l. or find fault*, Troil. Prol. 30. Almost = to love: *if you l. elsewhere, do it by stealth*, Err. III, 2, 7. *longing and —ing*, As III, 2, 431. *if he see aught in you that makes him l.* John II, 511. 512. *I'll look to l., if looking —ing move*, Rom. I, 3, 97.

b) with an accus., = to be pleased with: Ven. 774. Tp. III, 1, 43. III, 2, 85. 117. Gent. I, 2, 90. I, 3, 34. II, 1, 127. II, 4, 174. II, 7, 52. V, 2, 15. Wiv. II, 1, 186. V, 5, 110. Meas. V, 128. Err. V, 144. Ado I, 1, 178. Merch. I, 2, 90. III, 5, 77. H6C III, 2, 82. 110. Troil. V, 2, 101. Cor. I, 1, 173 etc. = to love: *that on so little acquaintance you should l. her*, As V, 2, 2.

c) with *of*: —d *of her master*, Pilgr. 212. *a shape to l. of*, Tp. III, 1, 57. *if you l. of me*, Ado V, 4, 59. *I l. of each thing that in season grows*, LLL I, 1, 107. IV, 3, 158. Shr. II, 65. H6A V, 1, 43. H6C IV, 6, 89. R3 IV, 4, 354. Rom. I, 3, 96.

d) with an inf.: *I do not l. to stage me*, Meas. I, 1, 69.

2) to please: *the music —s you not*, Gent. IV, 2, 56. *complexions that —d me*, As Epil. 20. *it —s me well*, Shr. IV, 4, 62; John II, 533; R3 III, 4, 51; Hml. II, 2, 80. *the offer —s not*, H5 III Chor. 32. *this lodging —s me better*, IV, 1, 16; IV, 3, 77. *that that —s not you pleases me best*, Troil. V, 2, 102. *this —s me well*, Hml. V, 2, 276. *if all of it may fitly l. your grace*, Lr. I, 1, 203. *his countenance —s me not*, II, 2, 96. Used as a phrase of courtesy: *we steal by line and level, an't l. your grace*, Tp. IV, 240. Meas. II, 1, 169. V, 74. Shr. IV, 4, 55. Wint. IV, 4, 737. H4A II, 4, 462. H6B II, 1, 9. 30. 80. V, 1, 72 etc. *here, if it l. your honour*, Meas. II, 1, 33. *so l. you, sir, ambassadors from Rome*, Cymb. II, 3, 59. *l. it your grace, the state takes notice*, H8 I, 1, 100. *may it l. your grace to let my tongue excuse all*, V, 3, 148.

Like, vb. to be in a certain state concerning one's

body, to have an appearance, to look: *well —ing wits they have; gross, gross; fat, fat*, LLL V, 2, 268. *you l. well and bear your years very well*, H4B III, 2, 92 (Ff *look*). cf. *Liking* in Wiv. II, 1, 57 and H4A III, 3, 6.

Likelihood, 1) probability, chance: *what l. is in that?* Meas. IV, 2, 202. *in better shape than I can lay it down in l.* Ado IV, 1, 238. *a fellow of no mark nor l.* H4A III, 2, 45 (of no probability of success, of no chance). *to lay down —s and forms of hope*, H4B I, 3, 35. *by a lower but loving l.* H5 V Chor. 29 (on the probable occasion of an event of inferior importance, but fondly expected. Most commentators explain the word here as meaning 'similitude, parallel, comparison'). *what l. of his amendment*, R3 I, 3, 33. *to follow him thither with modesty enough, and l. to lead it*, Hml. V, 1, 230. *by all l.* = in all probability: Shr. V, 1, 14. Cymb. I, 4, 54.

2) that from which a conclusion may be drawn, appearances, sign, indication: *many —s informed me of this before*, All's I, 3, 128. *as by discharge of their artillery and shape of l. the news was told*, H4A I, 1, 58. *it should be put to no apparent l. of breach*, R3 II, 2, 136.*what of his heart perceive you in his face by any l. he showed to-day?* III, 4, 57 (Ff *livelihood*). Often = circumstantial evidence: *these —s confirm her flight from hence*, Gent. V, 2, 43. *offer them instances, which shall bear no less l. than to see me at her chamber-window*, Ado II, 2, 42. *your mistrust cannot make me a traitor: tell me whereon the l. depends*, As I, 3, 59. *these thin habits and poor —s of modern seeming*, Oth. I, 3, 108. *what place? what time? what form? what l.?* IV, 2, 138.

Likely, adj. 1) probable: *in l. thoughts the other kills thee quickly*, Ven. 990. *this is most l.* Meas. V, 103; H8 II, 1, 40; Cor. IV, 6, 68; Per. V, 1, 135. *I never thought it possible or l.* Shr. I, 1, 154. *l. peril*, H4B I, 1, 184. *a l. guess*, Tit. II, 3, 207. *l. wars*, Lr. II, 1, 11. *a l. piece of work*, Oth. IV, 1, 156. *it is l.*, followed by a clause: Rom. IV, 1, 73. Cymb. IV, 4, 16. Used personally, with an inf.: H4B I, 1, 171. H6A III, 1, 188. V, 5, 74. H6B IV, 5, 2. H6C III, 3, 209. IV, 6, 35. 74. Tim. V, 1, 16. Hml. V, 2, 408.

2) having a certain air, expressive: *never saw I figures so l. to report themselves*, Cymb. II, 4, 83.

Likely, adj. pleasing, well-looking: *I have not seen so l. an ambassador of love*, Merch. II, 9, 92. *a l. fellow*, H4B III, 2, 186. *they are your —est men*, 273.

Likely, adv. probably: H4B I, 3, 63. Cor. I, 2, 16. Hml. II, 2, 152 (Qq *like*). Per. III, 2, 78.

Liken, with *to*, = to compare with: H4B II, 1, 97 (Q *liking*). H6C V, 2, 20.

Likeness, semblance, resembling form: *thy l. is still left alive*, Ven. 174. *who leaves unswayed the l. of a man*, Sonn. 141, 11. *her dead l.* Wint. V, 3, 15. *thou, old Adam's l.* R2 III, 4, 73. *the Lord of Stafford dear to-day hath bought thy l.* H4A V, 3, 8. *thou l. of this railer here*, H6C V, 5, 38. *do not assume my l.* Tim. IV, 3, 218. *than the force of honesty can translate beauty into his l.* Hml. III, 1, 114. *I razed my l.* Lr. I, 4, 4. *in l. of* = in the shape of: Mids. II, 1, 46. 48. John III, 1, 209. Tit. III, 2, 78. *in the l. of:* Ado I, 1, 100. Merch. III, 1, 24. H4A II, 4, 493. Rom. II, 1, 8. *in thy l.* Tp. III, 2, 138. LLL IV, 3, 46. Rom. II, 1, 21. *in his true l.* H5 V, 2, 317. *in Tarquin's l.* Lucr. 596. *in this borrowed l. of shrunk* *death*, Rom. IV, 1, 104. — Corrupt passage: *how may l. made in crimes* etc. Meas. III, 2, 287.

Likewise, also, too: Lucr. 805. Compl. 199. Gent. I, 1, 60. IV, 2, 113. Wiv. IV, 4, 46. IV, 6, 29. 33. Meas. III, 1, 156. Err. I, 1, 28. Ado I, 1, 241. LLL IV, 3, 315. 317. V, 2, 782. Wint. IV, 2, 51. IV, 3, 26. H5 II, 1, 113. II, 2, 93. H6A I, 1, 147. II, 5, 31. R3 II, 2, 65. Rom. II, 2, 111. II, 3, 54. Tim. V, 1, 6. Hml. III, 4, 164. Oth. II, 1, 95. Cymb. II, 4, 86.

Liking, subst. 1) state of being pleased, contentedness: *bring him up to l.* Wint. IV, 4, 544. With a poss. pron., = inclination, pleasure: *bids them do their l.* Lucr. 434. *yoke thy l. to my will*, 1633. *kills for faults of his own l.* Meas. III, 2, 282. Ado I, 3, 38. V, 4, 32. Shr. I, 2, 183. III, 2, 131. All's I, 1, 164. III, 5, 57. Tw. II, 5, 183. Wint. V, 1, 212. H6B III, 2, 252. Plur. —*s:* Wiv. I, 1, 79. Oth. III, 1, 51.

2) love, favour: *to swallow Venus' l.* Ven. 243. *to drive l. to the name of love*, Ado I, 1, 302. *my l. might too sudden seem*, 316. *an ill word may empoison l.* III, 1, 86. *fall into so strong a l. with Sir Rowland's son*, As I, 3, 28. *in so true a flame of l.* All's I, 3, 217. John II, 512. H8 II, 4, 33. Cor. I, 1, 199 (*stand in their l.*). Rom. I, 3, 97. Lr. I, 1, 214. 236. Per. Prol. 25 (*with whom the father l. took*).

Liking, the condition of the body: *I shall think the worse of fat men, as long as I have an eye to make difference of men's l.* Wiv. I, 1, 57. *I'll repent, while I am in some l.* H4A III, 3, 6 (= while I have some flesh).

Lily, the flower Lilium candidum: Ven. 362. Lucr. 71. 478. Sonn. 94, 14. 98, 9. 99, 6. Pilgr. 89. Gent. II, 3, 22. LLL V, 2, 352. Wint. IV, 4, 126. John III, 1, 53. IV, 2, 11. H8 III, 1, 151. V, 5, 62. Tit. III, 1, 113. Cymb. II, 2, 15. IV, 2, 201. Adjectively, = delicately white: *l. fingers*, Ven. 228. *hand*, Lucr. 386. Tit. II, 4, 44. *lips*, Mids. V, 337 (Thisbe's speech). *tincture*, Gent. IV, 4, 160. *white*, Ven. 1053.

Lily-beds, delicate flowerbeds in Elysium: Troil. III, 2, 13.

Lily-livered, white-livered, cowardly: Mcb. V, 3, 15. Lr. II, 2, 18.

Lily-white, delicately white: Mids. III, 1, 95. cf. Ven. 1053.

Limander, Bottom's blunder for *Leander:* Mids. V, 198.

Limb, 1) an extremity of the human body, an arm, a leg: *each several l. is doubled*, Ven. 1067. *a breast, a waist, a leg, a l.* LLL IV, 3, 186. *some broken l.* As I, 1, 134. Tw. I, 5, 311. John IV, 3, 6. R2 III, 2, 187. IV, 165 (Qq *my —s*, Ff *my knee*). H4A IV, 1, 43. H4B IV, 1, 222. H6B II, 3, 42. IV, 10, 50. R3 III, 7, 125. H8 I, 1, 46. Troil. I, 3, 354. 356. IV, 5, 238. Cor. II, 2, 84. III, 1, 296. Tit. I, 143. V, 3, 72. Rom. V, 3, 36. Tim. IV, 1, 24. Caes. II, 1, 165. Plur. —*s* = body (pars pro toto): *repose for —s with travel tired*, Sonn. 27, 2. *by day my —s, by night my mind no quiet find*, 13. *let them keep their —s whole*, Wiv. III, 1, 79. Merch. II, 7, 71. As II, 3, 41. All's III, 2, 107. V, 1, 4. John I, 239. III, 1, 129. 131. 133. H4A V, 1, 13. H4B I, 1, 143. I, 2, 257. H5 III, 1, 26. IV, 7, 80. V, 1, 89. H6A II, 3, 21. II, 5, 4. IV, 4, 18. IV, 5, 4. H6C I, 3, 15. R3 II, 2, 58 (Ff *hands*). H8 II, 3, 38. Tit. I, 97. 129. II, 3, 64. Rom. II, 3, 38. Caes. I, 3, 81. II, 1, 163. III, 1, 262 (*a curse shall light upon the —s of men;* where various emendations have been tried). Hml. II, 2, 91. 537.

2) the frame of the body, with respect to its vigour: *thou hast neither heat, affection, l., nor beauty, to make thy riches pleasant*, Meas. III, 1, 37. *strength of l. and policy of mind*, Ado IV, 1, 200. *because of his great l. or joint*, LLL V, 1, 135. *care I for the l., the thews, the stature, bulk*, H4B III, 2, 276.

3) active member: *let us choose such —s of noble counsel that the great body of our state may go in equal rank*, H4B V, 2, 135. *these are the —s o'the plot*, H8 I, 1, 220. *the —s of Limehouse*, V, 4, 66.

Limbeck, an alembic, a still: Sonn. 119, 2. Mcb. I, 7, 67.

Limber, flexible, easily bent, strengthless: *you put me off with l. vows*, Wint. I, 2, 47.

Limb-meal, limb by limb, piecemeal: *to tear her l.* Cymb. II, 4, 147.

Limbo, the borders of hell, or hell itself: *talked of Satan and of L. and of Furies*, All's V, 3, 261. *as far from help as L. is from bliss*, Tit. III, 1, 149. Used for a prison: *he's in Tartar l.; worse than hell*, Err. IV, 2, 32. *I have some of 'em in L. Patrum*, H8 V, 4, 67 (Limbus Patrum, in the language of ecclesiastics, was the place bordering on hell, where the saints of the Old Testament remained till Christ's descent into hell).*

Lime, subst. 1) a viscous substance laid on twigs to catch birds; bird-lime: *lay l. to tangle her desires*, Gent. III, 2, 68. *poor bird, thou wouldst never fear the net nor l.* Mcb. IV, 2, 34. Hence: *put some l. upon your fingers*, Tp. IV, 246 (in order to steal the better).

2) the matter of which mortar is made: Mids. V, 132. 166. 193. John II, 219. R2 III, 3, 26. *here's l. in this sack*, H4A II, 4, 137. 140.*

Lime, vb. 1) to smear with birdlime: *have —d a bush for her*, H6B I, 3, 91. II, 4, 54.

2) to seek to catch with birdlime, to entangle, to ensnare: *birds never —d no secret bushes fear*, Lucr. 88. *she's —d*, Ado III, 1, 104. *they are —d with the twigs*, All's III, 5, 26. *I have —d her*, Tw. III, 4, 82. *—d in a bush*, H6C V, 6, 13. *my poor young was —d*, 17. *O —d soul, that, struggling to be free, art more engaged*, Hml. III, 3, 68.

3) to cement: *who gave his blood to l. the stones together*, H6C V, 1, 84.

4) to put lime into liquor; a meaning resting only on the authority of the spurious Qq in Wiv. I, 3, 15: *let me see thee froth and l.;* Ff not only intelligibly, but much more in accordance with the jocular pathos of the host: *let me see thee froth and live;* for frothing tankards make thriving tapsters.

Lime-grove, see *Line-grove.*

Limehouse, a locality in London: *these are the youths that thunder at a playhouse and fight for bitten apples; that no audience but the tribulation of Tower-hill, or the limbs of L., their dear brothers, are able to endure*, H8 V, 4, 66 (not yet satisfactorily explained).

Lime-kiln, a furnace in which stones are burned to lime: Wiv. III, 3, 86. —*s in the palm*, Troil. V, 1, 25 (= leprosy?).*

Lime-twig, a twig smeared with lime: H6B III, 3, 16.

Limit, subst. 1) bound, barrier: *grief dallied with nor law nor l. knows*, Lucr. 1120. *my trust, which had no l.* Tp. I, 2, 96. *beyond all l.* III, 1, 72. *without l.* Ado I, 3, 5. *within the l. of becoming mirth*, LLL II, 67. Tw. I, 3, 9. *above his —s*, R2 III, 2, 109. *within* *the —s of yon lime and stone*, III, 3, 26. *out of l. and true rule*, H4A IV, 3, 39. *give no —s to my tongue*, H6C II, 2, 119. R3 III, 7, 194. *a slave to l.* Troil. III, 2, 90. *into —s bind my woes*, Tit. III, 1, 221. *stony —s cannot hold out love*, Rom. II, 2, 67. *no end, no l.* III, 2, 125. *dares not to stride a l.* Cymb. III, 3, 35 (in prison).

2) fixed time: *between which time of the contract and l. of the solemnity*, Meas. III, 1, 224. *before I have got strength of l.* Wint. III, 2, 107 (the time of lying in before leaving childbed? or = the limited, prescribed strength? cf. *Of.* According to Nares, *limit* was sometimes used for *limb). the dateless l. of thy dear exile*, R3 I, 3, 151. *the l. of your lives is out*, R3 III, 3, 8.

3) extent, reach: *finding thy worth a l. past my praise*, Sonn. 82, 6. *take my king's defiance from my mouth, the farthest l. of my embassy*, John I, 22. *and many —s of the charge set down*, H4A I, 1, 35 (= amount).

4) district, confine: *within this l. is relief enough*, Ven. 235. *I would be brought from —s far remote*, Sonn. 44, 4. *buried in highways out of all sanctified l.* All's I, 1, 152. *divided it into three —s very equally*, H4A III, 1, 73. cf. R2 III, 3, 26.

Limit, vb. 1) to confine within bounds, to circumscribe: *there is boundless theft in —ed professions*, Tim. IV, 3, 431 (even in those which do not, like you, make of stealing a trade, but lay some restraints on those who follow them).

2) to fix, to appoint: *having the hour —ed*, Meas. IV, 2, 176. *I'll l. thee this day to seek thy help*, Err. I, 1, 151. *the scope and warrant —ed unto my tongue*, John V, 2, 123. *l. each leader to his several charge*, R3 V, 3, 25 (= appoint to every leader his command). *'tis my —ed service*, Mcb. II, 3, 56.

Limitation, 1) restriction, confinement from an indeterminate import: *am I yourself but, as it were, in sort or l.?* Caes. II, 1, 283.

2) appointed time: *you have stood your l.* Cor. II, 3, 146.

Limn (cf. *Dislimn*) to draw, to paint: As II, 7, 194. With *out:* Ven. 290.

Limoges, see *Lymoges.*

Limp, to walk lamely, to halt: Sonn. 66, 8. Merch. III, 2, 130. As II, 7, 131. Shr. II, 254. R2 II, 1, 23. H5 IV Chor. 21. Rom. I, 2, 28. Tim. IV, 1, 14.

Lincoln, English town: *L. Washes*, John V, 6, 41. *my Lord of L.* H8 II, 4, 207.*

Lincolnshire, English county: *a L. bagpipe*, H4A I, 2, 85.

Line, subst. 1) a slender cord, a string: *hang them on this l.* Tp. IV, 193.* *mistress l., is not this my jerkin?* 235. Used of the string that sustains the angler's hook: *hold hook and l.* H4B II, 4, 172 (cf. *Hold*). *you perceive me not how I give l.* Wint. I, 2, 181 (how I leave the fish free play with the bait). Hence metaphorically, = free scope, latitude: *give him l. and scope*, H4B IV, 4, 39. *with full l. of his authority*, Meas. I, 4, 56.

2) the string serving for a ruler; and metaphorically, rule, method, principle: *we steal by l. and level*, Tp. IV, 1, 239. 243. *his life is paralleled even with the stroke and l. of his great justice*, Meas. IV, 2, 83. *observe degree, priority and place .... in all l. of order,*

Troil. I, 3, 88. In a bad sense, *—s* = caprices: *your husband is in his old —s again*, Wiv. IV, 2, 22 (M. Edd. *lunes*; the spurious Qq *vein). his pettish —s, his ebbs, his flows*, Troil. II, 3, 139 (M. Edd. *lunes*; Q *his course and time*).

3) a mark which has length without breadth: *more —s than is in the new map*, Tw. III, 2, 84. *many —s close in the dial's centre*, H5 I, 2, 210. *yon grey —s that fret the clouds*, Caes. II, 1, 103. *of all these bounds, even from this l. to this*, Lr. I, 1, 64. *to meet in one l.* = to go the same way: *powers from home and discontents at home meet in one l.* John IV, 3, 152. *when in one l. two crafts directly meet*, Hml. III, 4, 210. Used of the work of a draughtsman: *so should the —s of life that life repair*, Sonn. 16, 9 (metaph.); cf. 19, 10. Of marks in the palm of the hand: *here's a simple l. of life*, Merch. II, 2, 169 (a good omen). Of wrinkles: *draw no —s there with thy antic pen*, Sonn. 19, 10. *filled his brow with —s and wrinkles*, 63, 4. *he does smile his face into more —s*, Tw. III, 2, 84.

4) lineament: *every l. and trick of his sweet favour*, All's I, 1, 107. *which warped the l. of every other favour*, V, 3, 49. *looking on the —s of my boy's face*, Wint. I, 2, 153. *those —s of favour which then he wore*, Cymb. IV, 2, 104. Used of the outline of the whole body: *the —s of my body are as well drawn as his*, Cymb. IV, 1, 10.

5) the equator: *under the l.* Tp. IV, 237. H8 V, 4, 44.

6) row, rank, file: *to show the l. and the predicament wherein you range*, H4A I, 3, 168. *in that very l. standest thou*, III, 2, 85.

7) lineage: *of the true l. and stock of Charles the Great*, H5 I, 2, 71. 84. *fourth of that heroic l.* H6A II, 5, 78. H6B II, 2, 34. H6C I, 1, 19. I, 3, 32. Mcb. III, 1, 60. IV, 1, 117. 153. Hence = pedigree: *he sends you this most memorable l.* H5 II, 4, 88; cf. 90.

8) the words which stand in one row between the two margins: *in one l. his name twice writ*, Gent. I, 2, 123. Hence = verse: *to attend each l.* Lucr. 818. *if you read this l.* Sonn. 71, 5. 74, 3. 86, 13. Gent. III, 2, 76. All's II, 1, 81. Hml. II, 2, 470. Plur. *—s* = a) anything written: *comest thou with deep premeditated —s*, H6A III, 1, 1. Tit. V, 2, 14. 22. b) verses: Ven. Dedic. 1. Lucr. Dedic. 3. Sonn. 18, 12. 32, 4. 63, 13. 103, 8. 115, 1. Gent. II, 1, 94. 128. LLL IV, 3, 55. 220. 348. H6A V, 5, 14. Tit. IV, 2, 27. Hml. II, 2, 462. 567. III, 2, 4. c) a letter: *in top of rage the —s she rents*, Compl. 55. Gent. I, 1, 160. I, 2, 42. I, 3, 45. IV, 4, 133. John IV, 3, 17. R3 V, 2, 6.

Line, vb. to delineate, to draw, to paint: *all the pictures fairest —d are but black to Rosalind*, As III, 2, 97.

Line, vb. 1) to cover on the inside: *winter garments must be —d*, As III, 2, 111. *we will not l. his thin bestained cloak with our pure honours*, John IV, 3, 24. *pluck the —d crutch from thy old limping sire*, Tim. IV, 1, 14 (stuffed, padded). *when they have —d their coats*, Oth. I, 1, 53.

2) to fill on the inside; used of money: *if I do l. one of their hands*, Cymb. II, 3, 72. *he will l. your apron with gold*, Per. IV, 6, 63. Of food, = to feed: *with good capon —d*, As II, 7, 154. *who —d himself with hope, eating the air*, H4B I, 3, 27.

3) to fortify, to strengthen: *now doth Death l.*

his dead chaps with steel, John II, 352. *to l. his enterprise*, H4A II, 3, 86. *to l. and new repair our towns of war*, H5 II, 4, 7. *did l. the rebel with hidden help*, Mcb. I, 3, 112.

Lineal, directly descending, hereditary: *put on the l. state and glory of the land*, John V, 7, 102. R2 III, 3, 113. H4B IV, 5, 46. *Queen Isabel was l. of the Lady Ermengare*, H5 I, 2, 82. *from whence you spring by l. descent*, H6A III, 1, 166. *the l. glory of your royal house*, R3 III, 7, 121. *unto a l. true-derived course*, 200. Peculiar usage: *if France in peace permit our just and l. entrance to our town*, John II, 85, i. e. due by right of birth.

Lineally, in a direct line: H6C III, 3, 87.

Lineament, feature: Ado V, 1, 14. Rom. I, 3, 83. Plur. —*s*: Merch. III, 4, 15. As I, 2, 44. III, 5, 56. R2 III, 1, 9. R3 III, 5, 91. III, 7, 12.

Line-grove, a grove of lime-trees: Tp. V, 10 (most M. Edd. *lime-grove*).

Linen (O. Edd. *linnen*) cloth made of hemp or flax: Lucr. 680.* Wiv. III, 3, 139. III, 5, 145. IV, 2, 83. 102. 156. LLL V, 2, 719. Mids. IV, 2, 40. Shr. II, 355. Wint. IV, 3, 24. H4A IV, 2, 52. H4B II, 2, 22. 27. V, 1, 38. Cymb. I, 3, 7. Per. III, 2, 109. Plur. —*s*, Tp. I, 2, 164. Adjectively: *a l. stock*, Shr. III, 2, 67. *l. cheeks*, Mcb. V, 3, 16 (white, pale).

Ling, the fish Gadus molva: All's III, 2, 14. 15. In Tp. I, 1, 70 O. Edd. *long heath*, some M. Edd. *ling, heath* (= broom, furze).

Lingare, daughter of Charlemain: H5 I, 2, 74.*

Linger, 1) tr. to protract, to draw out, not to bring to a speedy end; abs.: *a —ing dram*, Wint. I, 2, 320 (killing slowly). *smarting in —ing pickle*, Ant. II, 5, 66. *—ing poisons*, Cymb. I, 5, 34. With an accus.: *she —s my desires*, Mids. I, 1, 4. *who gently would dissolve the bands of life, which false hope —s*, R2 II, 2, 72. *unless his abode be —ed here*, Oth IV, 2, 231. With *on*: *l. your patience on*, H5 II Chor. 31. *l. not our sure destructions on*, Troil. V, 10, 9. With *out*: *to l. out a purposed overthrow*, Sonn. 90, 8. *borrowing only —s and —s it out*, H4B I, 2, 265.

2) intr. a) to tarry, to stay, to hesitate: *who with a —ing stay his course doth let*, Lucr. 328. *if thou l. in my territories*, Gent. III, 1, 163. *say that I —ed with you at your shop*, Err. III, 1, 3. Merch. II, 9, 74. H6B IV, 4, 54. H6C I, 1, 263. I, 2, 32. III, 1, 26.

b) to remain inactive in expectation of something, to wait: *we have —ed about a match between Anne Page and my cousin Slender*, Wiv. III, 2, 58. *and in advantage —ing, looks for rescue*, H6A IV, 4, 19.

c) to remain long in a state of languor and pain, to languish, or to be painfully protracted: *—ing perdition*, Tp. III, 3, 77. *—ing sufferance*, Meas. II, 4, 167. *—ing penance*, Merch. IV, 1, 271. *feed contention in a —ing act*, H4B I, 1, 156. *—ing wars*, H6A I, 1, 74. *—ing death*, H6B III, 2, 247. *pent to l.* Cor. III, 3, 89. *—ing languishment*, Tit. II, 1, 110. *l. in thy pain*, Oth. V, 2, 88. *—ing by inches*, Cymb. V, 5, 51.

Linguist, one who knows foreign languages: Gent. IV, 1, 57. All's IV, 3, 265.

Lining, 1) the inner covering of a garment: *as bombast and as l. to the time*, LLL V, 2, 791 (serving to stuff out and fill up the time).

2) that which is within: *the l. of his coffers shall make coats*, R2 I, 4, 61.

Link, subst. a torch of tow and pitch: *there was*

no *l. to colour Peter's hat*, Shr. IV, 1, 137 (by smoking it). *—s and torches*, H4A III, 3, 48.

Link, subst. a chain: *a new l. to the bucket must needs be had*, H4B V, 1, 23. *cracking ten thousand curbs of more strong l. asunder*, Cor. I, 1, 73. *strong —s of iron*, Caes. I, 3, 94.

Link, vb. (cf. *Enlink*). 1) tr. to chain, to tie, to join: *coupled and —ed together*, John III, 1, 228. *—ed in friendship*, H6C IV, 1, 116. With *to*: *to l. my friend to a stale*, Ado IV, 1, 66. Hml. I, 5, 55. Ant. I, 2, 193. With *with*: *—ed in love with a lady*, H6A V, 5, 76.

2) intr. to form a connexion, to be connected: *I were loath to l. with him that were not lawful chosen*, H6C III, 3, 115.

Linnen, see *Linen*.

Linsey-woolsey, galimatia: *what l. hast thou to speak to us again?* All's IV, 1, 13.

Linstock, a stick to hold the gunner's match: H5 III Chor. 33.

Lion, the animal Felis Leo: Ven. 628. 884. 1093. Lucr. 421. 956. Sonn. 19, 1. Tp. II, 1, 312. 316. Gent. II, 1, 29. V, 4, 33. Meas. I, 3, 22. I, 4, 64. Ado I, 1, 15. LLL IV, 1, 90. V, 2, 580. Mids. I, 2, 66. 68. II, 1, 180. III, 1, 29. IV, 2, 41. V, 140. 144. Merch. II, 1, 30. V, 8. As V, 2, 26. H6A I, 2, 27. H6B III, 1, 19. V, 3, 2. H6C II, 1, 14. II, 2, 11. V, 2, 13 etc. etc. *you are the hare of whom the proverb goes, whose valour plucks dead —s by the beard*, John II, 138. *the man that once did sell the —'s skin while the beast lived, was killed with hunting him*, H5 IV, 3, 93. Borne in the royal arms of England: R2 I, 1, 174. H6A I, 5, 28. H6C V, 2, 13. By Alexander the Great: LLL V, 2, 580.

Lionel, Duke of Clarence, second son of Edward III: H6A II, 4, 83. II, 5, 75. H6B II, 2, 13.

Lioness, the female of the lion kind: As IV, 3, 115. 127. 131. 148. John II, 291. Tit. IV, 2, '138. Caes. II, 2, 17.

Lion-mettled, having the disposition of a lion: *be l., proud*, Mcb. IV, 1, 90.

Lion-sick, 'sick of proud heart': Troil. II, 3, 93.

Lip, subst. the border of the mouth: Ven. 19. 504. Wiv. I, 1, 238. Meas. IV, 1, 1. LLL II, 220. IV, 1, 86. Mids. II, 1, 49. III, 2, 140. V, 192. 203. 337. Merch. III, 2, 118. As III, 2, 61. III, 4, 16. III, 5, 120. V, 1, 37. Shr. I, 1, 179. III, 2, 180. Tw. I, 4, 31. I, 5, 265. II, 5, 76. III, 1, 158. V, 161 etc. *to bite the l.*, a sign of anger: Shr. II, 250. R3 IV, 2, 27. Cor. V, 1, 48. Oth. V, 2, 43. *or of a mind absorbed in thought*: H8 III, 2, 113. Troil. III, 3, 254. *falling a l. of much contempt*, Wint. I, 2, 373; cf. *marked you his l. and eyes?* Cor. I, 1, 259. *he hangs the l. at something*, Troil. III, 1, 152. *I will make a l. at the physician*, Cor. II, 1, 127 (laugh at him, snap my fingers at him). *steeped me in poverty to the very —s*, Oth. IV, 2, 50. *kiss the —s of unacquainted change*, John III, 4, 166. *the murmuring —s of discontent*, IV, 2, 53. As organs of speech, —*s* almost = mouth: *she stops his —s*, Ven. 46. *mercy will breathe within your —s*, Meas. II, 2, 78. *I will open my —s*, III, 1, 199. Merch. I, 1, 94. As I, 3, 84. Tw. I, 5, 2. *locked within the teeth and the —s*, Meas. III, 2, 143. *—s, do not move*, Tw. II, 5, 109. Shr. I, 1, 179. *hold close thy —s*, H6C II, 2, 118. *his slanderous —s*, R2 IV, 24. *lay thy finger on thy —s* (be silent) Troil. I, 3, 240. Hml. I, 5, 187 etc.

Lip, vb. to kiss: *to l. a wanton*, Oth. IV, 1, 72. *a hand that kings have —ed*, Ant. II, 5, 30.

Lipsbury, name of a place nowhere else mentioned: *if I had thee in L. pinfold, I would make thee care for me*, Lr. II, 2, 9.*

Liquid, fluid, not solid: Sonn. 5, 10. Mids. I, 1, 211. H6B III, 2, 60. R3 IV, 4, 321. Troil. I, 3, 40. Rom. V, 1, 77. Tim. IV, 3, 442. Hml. I, 3, 41. Oth. V, 2, 280.

Liquor, subst. 1) any fluid: Mids. II, 1, 178. III, 2, 367. R2 I, 2, 19. H4B III, 1, 53. H8 I, 1, 144. Tit. V, 2, 200. Rom. IV, 1, 94.

2) a spirituous fluid: Tp. II, 2, 22. 122. 131. V, 280 (allusion to the grand elixir of the alchemists). Gent. III, 1, 351. 352. Wiv. II, 1, 197. II, 2, 158. As II, 3, 49. H5 II, 1, 113. Hml. V, 1, 68. V, 2, 353.

Liquor, vb. to grease with tallow, in order to keep out the water: Wiv. IV, 5, 100. H4A II, 1, 94.

Liquorish, spirituous: *l. draughts*, Tim. IV, 3, 194.

Lisbon, the capital of Portugal: Merch. III, 2, 272.

Lisp, to speak affectedly with a particular articulation: *these —ing hawthorn-buds*, Wiv. III, 3, 77. *a can carve and l.* LLL V, 2, 323. *look you l. and wear strange suits*, As IV, 1, 34. *antic, —ing, affecting fantasticoes*, Rom. II, 4, 29. *you amble and you l.* Hml. III, 1, 151. With *to: —ing to his master's old tables*, H4B II, 4, 289.

List, subst. 1) the outer edge or selvedge of cloth: Meas. I, 2, 31. 34. Shr. III, 2, 69.

2) boundary, limit, barrier: *your own science exceeds in that the —s of all advice my strength can give you*, Meas. I, 1, 6. *you have restrained yourself within the l. of too cold an adieu*, All's II, 1, 53. *the very l., the very utmost bound of all our fortunes*, H4A IV, 1, 51. *confined within the weak l. of a country's fashion*, H5 V, 2, 295. *the ocean, overpeering of his l.* Hml. IV, 5, 99. *confine yourself but in a patient l.* Oth. IV, 1, 76. Affectedly, = goal, end: *I am bound to your niece, I mean, she is the l. of my voyage*, Tw. III, 1, 86.

3) an enclosed ground in which combats are fought: *come fate into the l. and champion me*, Mcb. III, 1, 71. Mostly plur. *—s:* Ven. 595. R2 I, 2, 52. I, 3, 32. 38. 43. H6A V, 5, 32. H6B II, 3, 50. 54. Per. I, 1, 61.

List, subst. a catalogue: H8 IV, 1, 14. Hence = number: *a l. of lawless resolutes*, Hml. I, 1, 98. *the levies, the —s and full proportions*, I, 2, 32. *if any man of quality or degree within the —s of the army will maintain*, Lr. V, 3, 112 (Qq *in the host*). *a more larger l. of sceptres*, Ant. III, 6, 76.

List, subst. desire, inclination: *when I have l. to sleep*, Oth. II, 1, 105 (Ff *leave*).

List, vb. (impf. *listed:* R3 III, 5, 84; Ff *lusted: list:* Hml. I, 5, 177), to desire: *while she takes all she can, not all she —eth*, Ven. 564. *where his lustful eye —ed to make his prey*, R3 III, 5, 84 (Ff *lusted*). Mostly = to please, to choose: *conquers as she —s*, H6A I, 5, 22. Usually not inflected: *little stars may hide them when they l.* Lucr. 1008. *be where you l.* Sonn. 58, 9. *your lieutenant, if you l.* Tp. III, 2, 19. *take it as thou l.* 138. *go to bed when she l.* Wiv. II, 2, 124. *seize thee that l.* Shr. III, 1, 91. *take them up, if any l.* III, 2, 167. *what I l.* IV, 5, 7. *turns what he l.* H8 II, 2, 22. *do as thou l.* Cor. III, 2, 128. *what she l.* Tit. IV, 1, 100. Rom. I, 1, 47. Oth. II, 3, 352.

Followed by an inf.; with *io: even where I l. to sport me*, Ven. 154. Ado III, 4, 83. Hml. I, 5, 177. Lr. V, 3, 61. without *to: what of her ensues I l. not prophesy*, Wint. IV, 1, 26.

List, vb. to listen, to hearken; absol.: Troil. V, 2, 17. Caes. V, 5, 15. Hml. I, 5, 22. Ant. IV, 3, 12. Per. V, 1, 231. *l. if thou canst hear the tread of travellers*, H4A II, 2, 34. *l. what work he makes*, Cor. I, 4, 20. With an accus.: *to l. the sad-tuned tale*, Compl. 4. *l. your names*, Wiv. V, 5, 46. *to l. me with more heed*, Err. IV, 1, 101. H5 I, 1, 43. Hml. I, 3, 30. Lr. V, 3, 181. Oth. II, 1, 219. Ant. IV, 9, 6. With *to: l. to me*, Shr. II, 365. Wint. IV, 4, 552. H4A III, 3, 110. H6B I, 2, 35. I, 3, 95. *l. to this conjunction*, John II, 468. *l. to your tribunes*, Cor. III, 3, 40. With a subord. clause: *l. what we have done*, R2 I, 3, 124.

Listen, to hearken, to give attention, to prick the ears; 1) absol.: *with —ing ear*, Ven. 698. Lucr. 283. *all jointly —ing*, 1410. 1548. *l.* LLL IV, 3, 45. Shr. IV, 1, 68. H4B I, 2, 138. H8 I, 2, 120. Tit. II, 3, 139. Caes. II, 4, 17. Mcb. IV, 1, 89. Per. I, 2, 87. V, 1, 235.

2) with an accus.: *to l. our purpose*, Ado III, 1, 12. *he is —ed*, R2 II, 1, 9. *l. great things*, Caes. IV, 1, 41. *—ing their fear*, Mcb. II, 2, 29. cf. *l. what I say*, H6A V, 3, 103.

3) with *to:* Mids. V, 241 (Q2 Ff *hearken*). Shr. I, 2, 180. John III, 1, 198. R2 II, 1, 20. H4A II, 4, 235. H6B I, 3, 93. Per. IV, 2, 106.

4) with *after*, = to enquire about: *whom I sent to l. after news*, H4B I, 1, 29. *I will l. after Humphrey, how he proceeds*, H6B I, 3, 152.

Literatured, in the language of Fluellen, = learned: H5 IV, 7, 157.

Lither, soft, pliant: *two Talbots, winged through the l. sky*, H6A IV, 7, 21.

Litigious, precarious: *Tyrus stands in a l. peace*, Per. III, 3, 3.

Litter, subst. 1) a vehicle formed with shafts supporting a bed: John V, 3, 16. H6A III, 2, 95. Lr. III, 6, 97.

2) straw or hay used as a bed for animals: *to crouch in l. of your stable planks*, John V, 2, 140.

3) a brood of young: *fifteen i' the l.* Wiv. III, 5, 12. *hath overwhelmed all her l.* H4B I, 2, 14.

Litter, vb. to bring forth; used of beasts, and only in contempt of human beings: Tp. I, 2, 282. Wint. IV, 3, 25. Cor. III, 1, 239. Caes. II, 2, 46.

Little, adj. (comp. and superl. *less* or *lesser*, and *least*, q. v. *littlest:* Hml. III, 2, 181, only in Qq; Ff om.) 1) small in size or extent: *what says she to my l. jewel?* Gent. IV, 4, 51. *a l. wee face*, Wiv. I, 4, 22. *your l. page*, II, 2, 119. III, 2, 1. III, 3, 21. 27. IV, 4, 47. *a l. door*, Meas. IV, 1, 32. LLL I, 1, 109. All's IV, 5, 54. *if it* (the apparel) *be too l. for your thief*, Meas. IV, 2, 47. *she is too l. for a great praise*, Ado I, 1, 175. *with l. quill*, Mids. III, 1, 131. *though she be but l., she is fierce*, III, 2, 325. LLL I, 2, 22. 23. *that l. candle*, Merch. V, 1, 90. *a great reckoning in a l. room*, As III, 3, 15. *a l. pot and soon hot*, Shr. IV, 1, 6. *although the print be l.* Wint. II, 3, 98. *patches set upon a l. breach*, John IV, 2, 32. *attest in l. place a million*, H5 Prol. 16. *this house is l.* Lr. II, 4, 291. *as l. as a crow*, Cymb. I, 3, 15 etc. etc. *l. ones =* children: *come, l. ones*, R2 V, 5, 15. *hence with your l. ones*, Mcb. IV, 2, 69.

Substantively: *in l.* = a) in a small compass: *if all the devils of hell be drawn in l.* Tw. III, 4, 95. 2) in miniature: *on his visage was in l. drawn what ... in Paradise was sawn,* Compl. 90. *the quintessence of every sprite heaven would in l. show,* As III, 2, 148. *his picture in l.* Hml. II, 2, 384.

2) thin: *that my leg is too long? No, that it is too l. I'll wear a boot, to make it somewhat rounder,* Gent. V, 2, 5. *turned to one thread, one l. hair,* John V, 7, 54. Of the high sound of a voice (= small): *I'll speak in a monstrous l. voice,* Mids. I, 2, 54.

3) short in duration: *a l. time, a l. while,* Tp. III, 2, 93. Gent. III, 2, 9. 15. Meas. II, 2, 26. As II, 7, 127. R2 I, 1, 112 etc. *our l. life is rounded with a sleep,* Tp. IV, 157. *Od's my l. life,* As III, 5, 43 etc. Substantively, *a l.* = a short time: *for a l. follow,* Tp. IV, 266. *hear me a l.* Ado IV, 1, 157. *a l. ere the mightiest Julius fell,* Hml. I, 1, 114. *in a l.* = briefly: *I'll tell you in a l.* H8 II, 1, 11.

4) small in quantity, degree, or amount, not much, inconsiderable: *of as l. memory,* Tp. II, 1, 233. *dost me but l. hurt,* II, 2, 82. *his l. speaking,* Gent. I, 2, 29. *I have l. wealth to lose,* V, 1, 11. *not so l. grace,* Wiv. II, 2, 117. *with so l. preparation,* 162. *with as l. remorse,* III, 5, 10. *a l. chiding,* V, 3, 11. *a l. brief authority,* Meas. II, 2, 118. *l. honour,* II, 4, 149. *salt too l. which may season give,* Ado IV, 1, 144. *l. reason,* Mids. III, 1, 146. *how l. is the cost,* Merch. III, 4, 19. *to do a great right, do a l. wrong,* IV, 1, 216. *l. thanks,* 288. *the l. wit that fools have,* As I, 2, 95. *the l. strength that I have,* 206. *on so l. acquaintance,* V, 2, 1. *as l. beard,* All's II, 3, 67. *a l. thing would make me tell,* Tw. III, 4, 331. *the l. blood which I have left,* Wint. II, 3, 166. *I have a l. money,* IV, 3, 82. *a l. snow,* John III, 4, 176. *a l. water,* IV, 3, 131. Mcb. II, 2, 67. *a l. life,* H4A V, 4, 103. *of so l. regard,* H4B I, 2, 191. *a l. ratsbane,* H6A V, 4, 29. *a l. gale,* H6C V, 3, 10. *the blessedness of being l.* H8 V, 2, 66. *as l. is the wisdom,* Mcb. IV, 2, 13. *the —st doubts,* Hml. III, 2, 181 etc. etc. In general, *a l.* = some, though not much (see the above instances: Merch. IV, 1, 216. Wint. IV, 3, 82. John III, 4, 176. IV, 3, 131. Mcb. II, 2, 67. H6A V, 4, 29); *l.,* in a negative sense, = scarce any, no (see Tp. II, 2, 82. Gent. IV, 1, 11. Meas. II, 4, 149. Mids. III, 1, 146. Merch. IV, 1, 288); but sometimes *l.* = *a l.: hold l. faith, though thou hast too much fear,* Tw. V, 174. *restored with good advice and l. medicine,* H4B III, 1, 43.

Substantively, with the same difference between *l.* and *a l.* 1) *l.: of that there's none or l.* Tp. II, 1, 51. *'tis too l. for carrying a letter,* Gent. I, 1, 116. *set l. by such toys,* I, 2, 82. *I would l. or nothing with you,* Wiv. III, 4, 65. *l. have you to say,* Meas. IV, 1, 68. Merch. IV, 1, 264. *know l. but bowling,* Wint. IV, 4, 338 etc. With *of: we'll have very l. of it,* Meas. IV, 3, 189. *there's l. of the melancholy element in her,* Ado II, 1, 357. *l. of the marking,* LLL I, 1, 288. *it is not l. of his care to have them recompensed,* Wint. IV, 4, 530. *my heart weeps to see him so l. of his great self,* H8 III, 2, 336. *act l. of his will,* Hml. IV, 5, 125. 2) *a l.* = somewhat, in some degree: *hear a l. further,* Tp. I, 2, 135. *the painter flattered a l.* Gent. IV, 4, 192. *a l. nearer,* Wiv. II, 2, 47. *a l. further,* IV, 2, 210. *cut a l.* Meas. II, 1, 5. *to be a l. vain,* Err. III, 2, 27. *a l. worse,* Merch. I, 2, 94. Tw. II, 4, 25. II, 5, 152. John IV, 1, 29. Cymb. III, 4, 68 etc. or = some,

though not a great amount of a thing: *tarry a l.* Merch. IV, 1, 305. *an she stand him but a l.* Shr. I, 2, 113. All's II, 4, 27. Tw. III, 4, 393. H4A III, 2, 72. H4B IV, 5, 99 etc. But *a l.* = l.: *thou'ldst thank me but a l. for my counsel,* Shr. I, 2, 61. *have misdemeaned yourself, and not a l.* H8 V, 3, 14. *it is not a l. I have to say,* Lr. I, 1, 286 (Ff *not l.*). *for nothing or a l.* Ant. II, 2, 31. *a very l.* Cor. V, 3, 16.

Little, adv. not much, in a small degree: *our own doth l. advantage,* Tp. I, 1, 34. *has done l. better,* IV, 197. *I love him so l.* Gent. II, 4, 206. *recking as l. what betideth him,* IV, 3, 40. Meas. IV, 3, 166. Ado II, 1, 318. LLL I, 2, 23. II, 142. Mids. III, 1, 147. Merch. I, 2, 95. Tw. I, 5, 190. Wint. I, 1, 17. III, 1, 17. John III, 1, 116. R2 V, 1, 64. H6C I, 1, 36. H8 III, 2, 349 etc.

Live, vb. 1) to be alive, not to be dead: *give thanks that you have —d so long,* Tp. I, 1, 27. *he may l.* II, 1, 113. *to keep them —ing,* II, 1, 299. II, 2, 116. III, 3, 21. V, 108. 120. 149. Gent. III, 1, 23. IV, 4, 17. 80. Wiv. I, 1, 186. Meas. I, 2, 40. II, 2, 99. 104. Err. I, 1, 140. Ado II, 1, 257. Mids. III, 1, 34. As I, 1, 161 etc. etc. *made her thrall to —ing death,* Lucr. 726 (to death in life, to a life resembling death). *steal dead seeing of his —ing hue,* Sonn. 67, 6 (the hue which he has in life). *why not death rather than —ing torment,* Gent. III, 1, 170 (torment in life, a tormented life). *thy last —ing leave,* R2 V, 1, 39 (the last leave in thy life). *I drave my suitor from his mad humour of love to a —ing humour of madness,* As III, 2, 439 (a humour of madness concerning his life, his manner of living). *give me a —ing reason she's disloyal,* Oth. III, 3, 409 (a reason taken from life). *now they kill me with a —ing death,* R3 I, 2, 153. *no other speaker of my —ing actions,* H8 IV, 2, 70 (the actions of my life). *long l.,* used as a salutation, to express devotedness and attachment: *long l. Gonzalo!* Tp. II, 1, 169. *long l. Henry,* R2 IV, 112. H6B I, 1, 37. II, 2, 63. H6C I, 1, 202. IV, 7, 76. Tit. I, 169. 229. Caes. V, 1, 32. Hml. I, 1, 3. Cymb. III, 7, 10. Converted to a curse: *l. loathed and long,* Tim. III, 6, 103. *l.,* without *long,* in the same sense: *l. and flourish,* R3 V, 3, 130. *l. and beget a happy race of kings,* 157. *l., Brutus,* Caes. III, 2, 53. *l., noble Helicane!* Per. II, 4, 40. With an accus.: *to l. a second life,* Sonn. 68, 7. *l. an upright life,* Merch. III, 5, 79. And even: *he that shall see this day, and l. old age,* H5 IV, 3, 44 (M. Edd. *he that shall l. this day and see old age*). Not to mention such phrases as *l. a thousand years,* Rom. I, 3, 46; *l. the lease of nature,* Mcb. IV, 1, 99, which need no explanation. Followed by an inf., = a) to experience, to see the day, to have the good or ill fortune: *have I —d to be carried in a basket,* Wiv. III, 5, 4. *have I —d to stand to the taunt of one,* V, 5, 150. *I have —d to see inherited my very wishes,* Cor. II, 1, 214. *hath Cassius —d to be but mirth and laughter to his Brutus,* Caes. IV, 3, 113. *if you l. to see this come to pass,* Meas. II, 1, 256. *if thou l. to see like right bereft,* Err. II, 1, 40. *if I l. to be as old as Sibylla,* Merch. I, 2, 116. Wint. V, 2, 157. R2 IV, 218. H6B I, 3, 85. Oth. III, 3, 376 etc. *shall I l. on to see this bastard kneel,* Wint. II, 3, 155. *if we l. thus tamely to be thus jaded by a piece of scarlet,* H8 III, 2, 279. b) to get occasion by escaping death: *thou shalt not l. to brag what we have offered,* Gent. IV, 1, 69. *if I may l. to report you,* Meas. III, 2, 172. *let me in my present wildness die* *and never l. to show the incredulous world the noble change*, H4B IV, 5, 154. V, 2, 105. 107. H5 IV, 1, 233. H6B I, 3, 115. II, 2, 81. II, 4, 83. V, 1, 81. R3 I, 1, 127 etc. c) merely periphrastic: *let me not l. to look upon your grace*, Gent. III, 2, 21 (= let me not look). *'tis pity that thou —st to walk where honest men resort*, Err. V, 27. *I will l. to be thankful to thee*, Tw. IV, 2, 89. *I will not l. to be accounted Warwick*, H6A II, 4, 120. *ne'er may he l. to see a sunshine day*, H6C II, 1, 187. *we l. not to be griped by meaner persons*, H8 II, 2, 136. *which (benefits) l. to come in my behalf*, Troil. III, 3, 16. *Caesar cannot l. to be ungentle*, Ant. V, 1, 59 (O. Edd. *leave*).

2) to exist, to have being: *the sourest-natured dog that —s*, Gent. II, 3, 6. *the duke is marvellous little beholding to your reports, but the best is, he —s not in them*, Meas. IV, 3, 167 (in that character, in which you represent him, he has no existence). *who —d king, but I could dig his grave?* H6C V, 2, 21 (what king existed). *he —s that loves thee better*, R3 I, 2, 141. Very freely used of things (so that Walker, in his Critical Examination II, p. 209, was often tempted to change it to *lie*): *there —s more life in one of your fair eyes*, Sonn. 83, 13. *if shame l. in a disguise of love*, Gent. V, 4, 106. *mortality and mercy l. in thy tongue and heart*, Meas. I, 1, 46. *no glory —s behind the back of such*, Ado III, 1, 110. *the practice of it —s in John the bastard*, IV, 1, 190. *thine eyes, where all those pleasures l.* LLL IV, 2, 114. *in those freckles l. their savours*, Mids. II, 1, 13. *all affections else that l. in her*, Tw. I, 1, 37. *scarce any joy did ever so long l.* Wint. V, 3, 52. *the image of a wicked heinous fault —s in his eye*, John IV, 2, 72. *where no venom else but only they have privilege to l.* R2 II, 1, 158. *where nothing —s but crosses, cares and grief*, II, 2, 79. *my honour —s when his dishonour dies*, V, 3, 70. *to make misfortune l.* V, 5, 71. *in the reproof of this —s the jest*, H4A I, 2, 213 (reading of Q1; rest of Edd. *lies*). *a comfort of retirement —s in this*, IV, 1, 56. *all his offences l. upon my head and on his father's*, V, 2, 20. *our supplies l. large in the hope of great Northumberland*, H4B I, 3, 12. *his trespass yet —s guilty in thy blood*, H6A II, 4, 94. *peace —s again*, R3 V, 5, 40. *justice —s in Saturninus' health*, Tit. IV, 4, 23. *more courtship —s in carrion flies*, Rom. III, 3, 34. *confusion's cure —s not in these confusions*, IV, 5, 65. *artificial strife —s in these touches*, Tim. I, 1, 38. *if it l. in your memory*, Hml. II, 2, 470. *there —s within the very flame of love a kind of wick*, IV, 7, 115. *freedom —s hence*, Lr. I, 1, 184. *when slanders do not l. in tongues*, III, 2, 87. *the tears l. in an onion that should water this sorrow*, Ant. I, 2, 176.

3) to remain in life, not to die: *let her brother l.* Meas. II, 2, 175. *your brother cannot l.* II, 4, 33. 35. *I've hope to l.* III, 1, 4. 43. *he had —d*, IV, 3, 165. *would yet he had —d*, IV, 4, 35. Err. I, 1, 155. Merch. III, 2, 35. 61. Tw. II, 5, 69. Wint. II, 2, 27. H5 IV, I, 220. Tit. III, 1, 297. IV, 1, 112. IV, 4, 21. Caes. IV, 3, 265. Ant. IV, 2, 5 etc.

4) to continue to exist, to last, to remain, to hold out: *flowers distilled, though they with winter meet, leese but their show; their substance still —s sweet*, Sonn. 5, 14. *how is it that this —s in thy mind?* Tp. II, 1, 49. *to have his title l. in Aquitaine*, LLL II, 146. *it —s there unchecked that Antonio hath a ship wrecked*, Merch. III, 1, 2. *my fair name, despite of death that*

—s upon my grave, R2 I, 1, 168. *the truth should l. from age to age*, R3 III, 1, 76. *fame —s long*, 81. *to make his valour l.* 86. 88. *men's evil manners l. in brass*, H8 IV, 2, 45. *the evil that men do —s after them*, Caes. III, 2, 80. *—ing* = everlasting: *still and contemplative in —ing art*, LLL I, 1, 14. *this grave shall have a —ing monument*, Hml. V, 1, 320.

In the language of mariners, = not to sink, to float, to drive: *a strong mast that —d upon the sea*, Tw. I, 2, 14.

5) to pass life or time in a particular manner: *that for which I l.* Tp. IV, 1, 4. *merrily shall I l. now*, V, 93. *—ing dully sluggardized at home*, Gent. I, 1, 7. I, 3, 56. IV, 1, 63. Wiv. I, 1, 286. Meas. II, 4, 184. Err. II, 2, 148. Ado I, 1, 248. II, 1, 51. 265. V, 4, 112. Mids. I, 1, 72. Merch. III, 2, 25. III, 4, 28. All's I, 3, 223. Tw. I, 4, 39. IV, 3, 28. V, 127. H6A I, 2, 13. II, 2, 31. H6C I, 3, 43. R3 III, 1, 93 etc. Of things: *ere the crown he looks for l. in peace*, R2 III, 3, 95. *it (the crown) may with thee in true peace live*, H4B IV, 5, 220. Followed by *with*, = to be united, to have intercourse: *beauty —s with kindness*, Gent. IV, 2, 45. *will l. with you*, IV, 1, 70. *to l. with me my fellow-scholars*, LLL I, 1, 16. All's III, 4, 14. H6B III, 2, 153. R3 IV, 1, 43. Oth. I, 3, 249 etc.

6) to be full of life and animation: *by looking on thee in the —ing day*, Sonn. 43, 10; cf. *when —ing light should kiss it*, Mcb. II, 4, 10. *hath love in thy old blood no —ing fire?* R2 I, 2, 10. *no friend will rid me of this —ing fear*, V, 4, 2. *thy voluntary oath —s in this bosom, dearly cherished*, John III, 3, 24. *to undertake the death of all the world, so I might l. one hour in your sweet bosom*, R3 I, 2, 124 (lie? Qq *rest*). cf. *I will l. in thy heart*, Ado V, 2, 104. Hence = to thrive: *let me see thee froth and l.* Wiv. I, 3, 15 (the spurious Qq and M. Edd. *lime*). *l. and thrive*, Cor. IV, 6, 23. *you are light into my hands, where you are like to l.* Per. IV, 2, 78. cf. *well to l.* Merch. II, 2, 55 and Wint. III, 3, 125. *an you will have me l., play Heart's ease*, Rom. IV, 5, 103. And = to be valid, to be full of truth: *an old instance, that —d in the time of good neighbours*, Ado V, 2, 79. *so in approof —s not his epitaph as in your royal speech*, All's I, 2, 50. *I'll make my match to l.* Troil. IV, 5, 37.

7) to subsist, to be supported, to feed: *means to l.* Tp. II, 1, 50. *a poor fellow that would l.* Meas. II, 1, 235. III, 2, 22. 26. H4A II, 2, 96 etc. With *by*: *the means whereby I l.* Merch. IV, 1, 377. *as I do l. by food*, As II, 7, 14. *dies and —s by bloody drops*, III, 5, 7. *I can l. no longer by thinking*, V, 2, 55. *dost thou l. by thy tabor?* Tw. III, 1, 2. *l. by gazing*, Wint. IV, 4, 110. *l. honestly by the prick of their needles*, H5 II, 1, 36. *I'll l. by Nym, and Nym shall l. by me*, 115. *that competency whereby they l.* Cor. I, 1, 144. *all that I l. by*, Caes. I, 1, 24. With *on*: *—s upon his gains*, Sonn. 67, 12. *l. on thy confusion*, Err. II, 2, 182. *—d on the alms-basket of words*, LLL V, 1, 41. *a scattered smile, and that I'll l. upon*, As III, 5, 104. *the food which you do l. upon*, Cor. I, 1, 136. *that l. and feed upon your majesty*, Hml. III, 3, 10. *l. upon the vapour of a dungeon*, Oth. III, 3, 271. With *with*: *I l. with bread*, R2 III, 2, 175. *l. with cheese and garlic*, H4A III, 1, 161. *I l. with the awl*, Caes. I, 1, 24.

8) to abide, to dwell: *you 'mongst men being most unfit to l.* Tp. III, 3, 58. *where l. nibbling sheep*, IV, 62. *let me l. here ever*, 122. *I l. by the church*, Tw.

III, 1, 3. 5. Gent. II, 4, 28. Err. V, 7. LLL I, 1, 35. As I, 1, 119. II, 3, 72. R2 V, 5, 2. Tit. IV, 2, 152. Mcb. III, 6, 26. Per. V, 1, 114 etc.

Live, adj. living, not dead: *the next l. creature,* Mids. II, 1, 172.

Liveless, see *Lifeless.*

Livelihood, liveliness, animation, spirit: *the precedent of pith and l.* Ven. 26. *the tyranny of her sorrows takes all l. from her cheek,* All's I, 1, 58. In R3 III, 4, 57 Ff *l.,* Qq *likelihood.*

Livelong, long as it is, whole: *the l. day,* Troil. I, 3, 147. Caes. I, 1, 46. *clamoured the l. night,* Mcb. II, 3, 65.

Lively, adj. 1) living: *but now I lived, and life was death's annoy; but now I died, and death was l. joy,* Ven. 498 (pleasure of life). *beggared of blood to blush through l. veins,* Sonn. 67, 10. *a dateless l. heat,* 153, 6. *that record is l. in my soul,* Tw. V, 253. *now I behold thy l. body so,* Tit. III, 1, 105 (not only thy picture). *a pattern, precedent and l. warrant,* V, 3, 44 (taken from real life).

2) animated, sprightly: *her l. colour killed with deadly cares,* Lucr. 1593. *the l. Helena,* Rom. I, 2, 73. *l. lustre,* Tim. I, 2, 154 (F1 om.).

3) coming near to life, strongly resembling: *some l. touches of my daughter's favour,* As V, 4, 27. *—er than life,* Tim. I, 1, 38.

Lively, adv. to the life, very naturally: *her griefs, so l. shown,* Pilgr. 389. *which I so l. acted,* Gent. IV, 4, 174. *as l. painted as the deed was done,* Shr. Ind. 2, 58. *the life as l. mocked,* Wint. V, 3, 19. *thou counterfeitest most l.* Tim. V, 1, 85.

Liver, 1) one who lives, a man: *there's —s out of Britain,* Cymb. III, 4, 143.

2) one living in a particular manner: *humble —s,* H8 II, 3, 20. *the longer l. take all,* Rom. I, 5, 17. *prouder —s,* Cymb. III, 3, 9.

Liver, the viscus which secerns the bile: Wint. I, 2, 304. Troil. V, 1, 24. Mcb. IV, 1, 26. *more abhorred than spotted —s in the sacrifice,* Troil. V, 3, 18. Supposed to be the seat of passion: *you measure the heat of our —s with the bitterness of your galls,* H4B I, 2, 198. *I will inflame thy noble l. and make thee rage,* V, 5, 33. l., brain and heart constituting the range of mental functions: Tw. I, 1, 37. Cymb. V, 5, 14 (appetitive, intellectual, and sensitive faculty). Inspiring love: *the coal which in his l. glows,* Lucr. 47. *the ardour of my l.* Tp. IV, 56. *with l. burning hot,* Wiv. II, 1, 121. *if ever love had interest in his l.* Ado IV, 1, 233. *to wash your l. as clean as a sound sheep's heart,* As III, 2, 443. Tw. II, 4, 101. II, 5, 106. Heated with drinking: *let my l. rather heat with wine,* Merch. I, 1, 81; Ant. I, 2, 23. *hot —s and cold purses,* H4A II, 4, 355. The seat of courage: *to put fire in your heart, and brimstone in your l.* Tw. III, 2, 22. A white and bloodless l. a sign of cowardice: Merch. III, 2, 86. Tw. III, 2, 66. H4B IV, 3, 113. Troil. II, 2, 50 (cf. *Lily-livered, Milk-livered, Pigeon-livered, White-livered*).

Liver-vein, the style and manner of men in love: LLL IV, 3, 74.

Livery, subst. 1) delivery, the act of delivering a freehold into the possession of its heir: *to sue his l.* R2 II, 1, 204. II, 3, 129. H4A IV, 3, 62.*

2) a distinguishing dress of servants: Compl. 195. Gent. II, 4, 46. Merch. II, 2, 117. 124. 163. H4B V,

5, 11. R3 I, 1, 80. Rom. III, 1, 60. Tim. IV, 2, 17. Ant. V, 2, 90. Cymb. II, 3, 128.

3) any particular dress or garb: *never let their* (thy lips') *crimson —es wear,* Ven. 506. *putting on the destined l.* Meas. II, 4, 138. III, 1, 95. Mids. I, 1, 70. H6B IV, 2, 80. Per. II, 5, 10. III, 4, 10. V, 3, 7.

4) outward appearance, aspect: *the beauteous l. that he wore,* Ven. 1107. *I give a badge of fame to slander's l.* Lucr. 1054. *her face wore sorrow's l.* 1222. *thy youth's proud l.* Sonn. 2, 3. Mids. II, 1, 113. Merch. II, 1, 2. All's IV, 5, 106. H6B V, 2, 47. Rom. II, 2, 8. Hml. I, 4, 32.* III, 4, 164. IV, 7, 80.

Livery, vb. to dress: *did l. falseness in a pride of truth,* Compl. 105.

Livia, 1) the wife of Octavius Caesar: Ant. V, 2, 169. 2) name in Rom. I, 2, 72.

Living, subst. 1) life: *to spend her l. in eternal love,* Compl. 238. *my long sickness of health and l. now begins to mend,* Tim. V, 1, 190. cf. *Live,* vb.

2) livelihood, maintenance: *she can spin for her l.* Gent. III, 1, 318. *get your l. by reckoning,* LLL V, 2, 498. As II, 3, 33. III, 1, 8. III, 2, 84.

3) property, possession, fortune: *that I might in virtues, beauties, —s, friends, exceed account,* Merch. III, 2, 158. *you have given me life and l.* V, 286. *where my land and l. lies,* Wint. IV, 3, 104. Rom. IV, 5, 40. Tim. I, 2, 229. Lr. I, 4, 120.

Living-dead, writing of some M. Edd. in Err. V, 241: *a l. man;* perhaps rather *a living dead-man.* O. Edd. *a living dead man.*

Lizard, the animal Lacerta: Troil. V, 1, 67. Mcb. IV, 1, 17. Supposed to have a venomous sting: H6B III, 2, 325. H6C II, 2, 138.

Lo, look, behold; a word used to excite attention: *and, lo, I lie between that sun and thee,* Ven. 194. *but, lo, from forth a copse ...,* 259. *when, lo, the unbacked breeder doth forsake him,* 320. 853. 1128. 1135. 1185. Lucr. 653. 1082. 1485. 1660. Sonn. 7, 1. 27, 13. 143, 1. Compl. 218. 232. Tp. II, 2, 14. III, 2, 34. 38. Gent. I, 2, 123. Err. III, 2, 171. LLL IV, 2, 91. 483. Mids. III, 2, 192. As IV, 3, 103. Shr. III, 2, 19. Tw. III, 4, 101. John II, 50. 236. IV, 1, 104. R2 I, 2, 63. H4B II, 4, 35. IV, 1, 151. H6A I, 2, 76. IV, 2, 31. H6B V, 1, 66. R3 I, 2, 12. 175. IV, 1, 78. IV, 4, 215. V, 5, 4. Troil. II, 1, 74. IV, 5, 191. Cor. III, 3, 48. Rom. II, 3, 53. Mcb. V, 1, 22. Hml. II, 2, 499. V, 2, 329. Oth. III, 4, 108. Ant. I, 2, 80. Cymb. III, 2, 22 etc. *lo, behold these talents,* Compl. 204. Followed by *where: lo, where he comes,* H4B IV, 5, 90. H6A IV, 7, 17. H6C V, 1, 76. V, 5, 11. H8 I, 1, 113. Tit. V, 2, 45. Hml. I, 1, 126. The pronoun of the 2nd person added: *lo thee,* Ant. IV, 14, 87. *lo you now,* Wint. I, 2, 106. H8 I, 1, 202. An accus. following: *lo now my glory smeared in dust and blood,* H6C V, 2, 23.

In Troil. V, 2, 29 Q F1 *I will lo;* F2.3.4 *I will go;* M. Edd. *I will, la;* or *I will, lord.*

Loa, reduplication of the second syllable of *hilloa:* Wint. III, 3, 80.

Loach, the fish Cobitis: *chamber-lie breeds fleas like a l.* H4A II, 1, 23 (as for the speaker's knowledge of natural history, cf. v. 9.: *dank as a dog,* and v. 16: *stung like a tench*).

Load, subst. burden, grievous weight: Ven. 430. Lucr. 734. 1474. Ado V, 1, 28. H6B I, 2, 2. III, 1, 157. V, 2, 64. R3 I, 2, 1. 29. II, 2, 113. III, 7, 230.

H8 I, 2, 50. II, 3, 39. III, 2, 383. Troil. V, 1, 22. Caes. IV, 1, 20. 25. Hml. II, 2, 379. Pcr. I, 4, 91.

Load, vb. (impf. not used; partic. *laden:* Ven. 1022. Tit. I, 36. Ant. III, 11, 5. V, 2, 123. *loaden:* H4A I, 1, 37. H6A II, 1, 80. H8 IV, 2, 2. Cor. V, 3, 164. Tit. V, 2, 53. Tim. III, 5, 50) 1) to freight, to burden, to encumber: *like —en branches,* H8 IV, 2, 2 (F2.3.4 *—ed*). *to l. a falling man,* V, 3, 77. Followed by *with:* Ven. 1022. H4A I, 1, 37. H6A II, 1, 80. Tit. V, 2, 53. Tim. III, 5, 50. Ant. III, 11, 5. V, 2, 123.

2) to furnish or provide in abundance, to adorn, to reward: *to l. thy merit richly,* Cymb. I, 5, 74. Followed by *with: to l. my she with knacks,* Wint. IV, 4, 360. *to l. him with his desert* (with what he deserves) H5 III, 7, 85. *preferments, with which the time will l. him,* H8 V, 1, 37. *to l. me with precepts,* Cor. IV, 1, 9. *with honour,* V, 3, 164. Tit. I, 36. Tim. V, 1, 16. Mcb. I, 6, 18.

Loading, load, burden: *the tragic l. of this bed,* Oth. V, 2, 363.

Loaf, a mass of bread formed by the baker: Tit. II, 1, 87. Pl. *loaves:* H6B IV, 2, 71.

Loam, a species of earth, clay: Mids. III, 1, 70. V, 162. R2 I, 1, 179. Hml. V, 1, 233.

Loan, something lent: Sonn. 6, 6. Hml. I, 3, 76. In R3 IV, 4, 323 O. Edd. *love,* M. Edd. *loan.*

Loath, (comp. *—er,* H6B III, 2, 355) unwilling, not liking, disinclined: *although I seem so l., I am the last,* LLL I, 1, 160. *though l., yet must I be content,* H6C IV, 6, 48. Followed by an inf.: *that I shall be l. to do,* Gent. III, 2, 39. *I am very l. to be your idol,* IV, 2, 129. *I would be l. to turn them together,* Wiv. II, 1, 193. Meas. IV, 6, 1. Err. I, 1, 136. Mids. IV, 1, 16. Merch. II, 5, 16. As I, 1, 136. Shr. Ind. 2, 128. All's V, 3, 201. Tw. I, 5, 184. III, 1, 28. Wint. IV, 4, 583. John V, 5, 1. R2 II, 3, 169. H4A V, 1, 128. H4B I, 2, 166. II, 1, 167. H6A II, 4, 25. H6B III, 2, 355. H6C III, 3, 114. R3 II, 2, 10. III, 4, 88. III, 7, 209. Troil. III, 2, 50. Caes. I, 2, 243. Lr. I, 1, 273. Ant. V, 2, 107. Cymb. IV, 2, 86. Per. II, 5, 13.

Loathe, to hold in disgust, to abhor; absol.; *—ing* = disgust, abhorrence: Mids. II, 2, 138. Merch. IV, 1, 60. Per. II, 4, 10. Trans.: Lucr. 662. 742. 867. 984. Gent. V, 2, 7. Mids. III, 2, 264. IV, 1, 84. 178. Merch. IV, 1, 52. As III, 2, 436. All's IV, 4, 24. H4A III, 2, 72. R3 IV, 4, 356. Troil. III, 3, 218. V, 10, 40. Rom. I, 5, 143. Tim. III, 6, 103. V, 4, 33. Lr. IV, 6, 39. 272. Oth. III, 3, 268. III, 4, 62 (Q1 *lothely*). *—ed,* adjectively, = disgusting: Ven. 19. Meas. III, 1, 129. R3 I, 3, 232. III, 7, 189. Tit. IV, 2, 78. Rom. III, 5, 31. Per. I, 1, 147.

Loathly, adj. disgusting, nauseous: *weeds so l.* Tp. IV, 21. *l. births of nature,* H4B IV, 4, 122. In Oth. III, 4, 62 Q1 *l.,* Q2 Ff *loathed.*

Loathly, adv. with abhorrence: *how l. opposite I stood to his unnatural purpose,* Lr. II, 1, 51.

Loathness, unwillingness, reluctance: Tp. II, 1, 130. Ant. III, 11, 18. Cymb. I, 1, 108.

Loathsome: 1) disgusting, nauseous: Shr. Ind. 1, 35. 123. H4B III, 1, 16. H6B III, 2, 75. Troil. II, 1, 31 (*—st*). Tit. IV, 2, 68. Rom. II, 6, 12. IV, 3, 46. Hml, I, 5, 72.

2) hateful, odious, detestable: Ven. 637. Lucr. 184. 206. 812. 1636. Sonn. 35, 4. Err. IV, 4, 106.

H6A II, 5, 25. 57. H6B III, 2, 315. Tit. II, 3, 176. 193. Rom. V, 1, 81.

Loathsomeness, nauseousness: Wint. IV, 3, 59.

Lob, subst. a term of contempt, probably = lout, lubber: *thou l. of spirits,* Mids. II, 1, 16.*

Lob down, vb. to hang down languidly, to droop: *their poor jades l. down their heads,* H5 IV, 2, 47.

Lobby, a porch, an anteroom: H6B IV, 1, 61. Tim. I, 1, 80. Hml. II, 2, 161. IV, 3, 39.

Local, being in a particular place: *gives to airy nothing a l. habitation,* Mids. V, 17. *that I may give the l. wound a name,* Troil. IV, 5, 244.

Lock, subst. a tuft of hair, a ringlet: Ven. 1090. Compl. 85. Merch. I, 1, 169. III, 2, 92. H4A I, 3, 205. H6A II, 5, 5. Mcb. III, 4, 51. Hml. I, 5, 18. *a wears a l.* Ado III, 3, 183. *he wears a key in his ear and a l. hanging by it,* V, 1, 318 (a pendent lock of hair, often plaited and tied with riband, and hanging at the ear, was a prevalent fashion in the poet's time. Dogberry, having heard it mentioned, takes it for the fastening of a door to be opened with a key).

Lock, subst. an instrument to fasten doors or chests: Ven. 575. Lucr. 302. Mids. I, 2, 35. H5 I, 2, 176. Cor. III, 1, 138. Mcb. IV, 1, 46. Oth. IV, 2, 22. Cymb. III, 2, 36. V, 4, 1. 8. Metaphorically: *defile the —s of your shrill-shrieking daughters,* H5 III, 3, 35 (or = curls?); cf. *I have picked the l. and ta'en the treasure of her honour,* Cymb. II, 2, 41.

Lock, vb. 1) to fasten by turning the key: *the doors be —ed,* Gent. III, 1, 111. Err. III, 1, 30. IV, 4, 74. Hml. V, 2, 322. Oth. I, 1, 85. Cymb. III, 5, 43. 51. With *up:* were not my doors *—ed up,* Err. IV, 4, 73. Ado IV, 1, 106. Merch. II, 5, 29. Cymb. I, 1, 74. *her —ed up eyes,* Lucr. 446. With an accus. and adv. denoting the effect: *wherefore didst thou l. me forth,* Err. IV, 4, 98 (shut the door against me; shut me out by locking the door). *—ing me out of my doors,* Err. IV, 1, 18. *we were —ed out,* IV, 4, 102. V, 218. 255. Rom. I, 1, 145.

2) to shut up, to confine by turning the key; properly and figuratively: *safely —ed,* All's IV, 1, 104. *there l. yourself,* Ant. IV, 13, 4. The prep. *in* or *within* following: Meas. III, 2, 143. V, 10. Merch. III, 2, 40. John II, 369. H6A II, 5, 118. Troil. IV, 5, 195. Lr. III, 3, 11. Hml. I, 3, 85. Ant. IV, 14, 120. *Into* following: *a jewel —ed into the wofullest cask,* H6B III, 2, 409. With the adv. *in: that in gold clasps —s in the golden story,* Rom. I, 3, 92. With *up: thee have I not —ed up in any chest,* Sonn. 48, 9. *—ed up in sleep,* Meas. IV, 2, 69. *to l. up honesty from the access of visitors,* Wint. II, 2, 10. IV, 4, 369. John V, 2, 141. H4A V, 2, 10. H6B III, 2, 234. Cymb. I, 5, 41. *to l. from* = to detain, to keep back, to withhold: *I'll l. thy heaven from thee,* Tim. I, 2, 255. *to l. such rascal counters from his friends,* Caes. IV, 3, 80. *she should l. herself from his resort,* Hml. II, 2, 143. *sport and repose l. from me day and night,* III, 2, 227. *to l. it* (life) *from action,* Cymb. IV, 4, 2.

3) to enclose; to encircle: *his mistress did hold his eyes —ed in her crystal looks,* Gent. II, 4, 89. *all his senses were —ed in his eye,* LLL II, 242. *she —s her lily fingers one in one,* Ven. 228. *her hand, in my hand being —ed,* Lucr. 260. *l. hand in hand,* Wiv. V, 5, 81. *and so —s her in embracing,* Wint. V, 2, 83. *our —ed embrasures* (= close embraces) Troil. IV, 4, 39.

Locked-up, see *Lock,* vb.

Lockram, a cheap kind of linen: Cor. II, 1, 225.*

Locusts, mentioned as an aliment of a very sweet taste in Oth. I, 3, 354, perhaps from its being placed together with wild honey in St. Matthew III, 4. According to Beisly, the fruit of the Carob tree (Siliqua dulcis) was also called so.

Lode-star, the leading star, the pole-star: Lucr. 179. Mids. I, 1, 183.

Lodge, subst. a small house in a forest or park: Wiv. I, 1, 115. Ado II, 1, 222. LLL I, 2, 140. Tit. II, 3, 254.

Lodge, vb. 1) trans. a) to furnish with an habitation: Lucr. Arg. 15. Sonn. 10, 10. Compl. 84. Tp. I, 2, 346. Gent. III, 1, 35. LLL II, 85. 174. Shr. IV, 2, 107. All's III, 5, 44. Wint. II, 1, 135. R2 V, 1, 14. H5 II, 1, 35. Caes. IV, 3, 140. Mcb. II, 2, 26. Per. IV, 2, 124. *let me l. Lichas on the horns o' the moon,* Ant. IV, 12, 45.

b) to pen, to fold: *from the rising of the lark to the —ing of the lamb,* H5 III, 7, 34.

c) to harbour: *so fair a form —d not a mind so ill,* Lucr. 1530. *my bosom as a bed shall l. thee,* Gent. I, 2, 115. *I have that honourable grief —d here,* Wint. II, 1, 111. *I well might l. a fear,* H4B IV, 5, 208. *if ever any grudge were —d between us,* R3 II, 1, 65.

d) to fix, to settle: *a —d hate,* Merch. IV, 1, 60.

e) to lay flat, to beat down: *our sighs and they shall l. the summer corn,* R2 III, 3, 162. *the summer's corn by tempest —d,* H6B III, 2, 176. Mcb. IV, 1, 55.

2) intr. to reside, to dwell for a time: All's III, 5, 38. Tw. III, 3, 40. H6B I, 1, 80. H6C I, 1, 32. IV, 3, 13. H8 IV, 2, 18. Troil. IV, 1, 42. Lr. IV, 7, 68. Oth. III, 4, 7. 8. 11. Used of a lasting abode: Gent. III, 1, 143. Rom. III, 3, 107. Hml. V, 1, 252 (in a grave). Metaphorically: *where care —s, sleep will never lie,* Rom. II, 3, 36. *those thorns that in her bosom l.* Hml. I, 5, 87. *I l. in fear,* Cymb. II, 2, 49.

Lodger, one who lives in a hired room: Shr. IV, 4, 5. H5 II, 1, 33.

Lodging, 1) habitation, dwelling: Merch. II, 2, 125. 163. II, 4, 2. 27. Shr. I, 1, 44. IV, 4, 55. Tw. III, 3, 20. Rom. V, 1, 25. Oth. I, 2, 45. I, 3, 382. III, 3, 321. III, 4, 12. 172. Cymb. II, 4, 136. III, 5, 127. = house: *he means to burn the l. where you use to lie,* As II, 3, 23. *our —s, standing bleak upon the sea, shook as the earth did quake,* Per. III, 2, 14.

2) apartment, chamber: *burn sweet wood to make the l. sweet,* Shr. Ind. 1, 49. *empty —s and unfurnished walls,* R2 I, 2, 68. *doth any name particular belong unto the l. where I first did swoon?* H4B IV, 5, 234. *retire with me to my l.* Lr. I, 2, 184. Per. II, 3, 109.

3) a couch, a bed: *frosts and fasts, hard l. and thin weeds,* LLL V, 2, 811. *this l. likes me better,* H5 IV, 1, 16. *gallop apace, you fiery-footed steeds, towards Phoebus' l.* Rom. III, 2, 2. *take vantage, heavy eyes, not to behold this shameful l.* (the stocks) Lr. II, 2, 179.

Lodovico, name in Oth. IV, 1, 228. 233. IV, 3, 35. V, 1, 67.

Lodowick, name: Meas. V, 125. 126. 143. 262. All's IV, 3, 186.

Loffe, to laugh: Mids. II, 1, 55 (some M. Edd. *laugh*).

Lofty, 1) towering, high: *the l. pine,* Lucr. 1167. Sonn. 12, 5. R2 III, 4, 35. H6B II, 3, 45. Cymb. V, 5, 453. *l. towers,* Sonn. 64, 3. *the l. surge,* H5 III

Chor. 13. *of such a spacious l. pitch,* H6A II, 3, 55. Quibbling: *we are most l. runaways,* H5 III, 5, 35 (proud, and running away in high lavoltas).

2) proud, haughty; in a good sense: *they died in honour's l. bed,* Tit. III, 1, 11. In a bad sense: *l. proud encroaching tyranny,* H6B IV, 1, 96. *l. and sour to them that loved him not,* H8 IV, 2, 53.

3) sublime: *this was l.* Mids. I, 2, 41. *his humour is l.* LLL V, 1, 11. *shall this our l. scene be acted over,* Caes. III, 1, 112.

4) high-sounding: *sound all the l. instruments of war,* H4A V, 2, 98. *the cock doth with his l. and shrill-sounding throat awake the god of day,* Hml. I, 1, 151.

Lofty-plumed, decorated with a high plume: H6A V, 3, 25.

Log, a shapeless piece of wood: Tp. III, 1, 10. 17. 24. 2, 97. LLL V, 2, 924. Rom. IV, 4, 15. 17.

Loggats, a popular game, in which small logs are thrown at a stake fixed in the ground: *to play at l.* Hml. V, 1, 100.*

Loggerhead, a blockhead, a dolt: LLL IV, 3, 204. H4A II, 4, 4. Rom. IV, 4, 21.

Loggerheaded, blockheaded: Shr. IV, 1, 128.

Logic, the art of reasoning: Shr. I, 1, 34. cf. *Chop-logic.*

Log-man, one who carries logs: Tp. III, 1, 67.

Loins, the part of the body next to the genitals, the reins: Meas. III, 1, 30. Ado IV, 1, 137. H6C III, 2, 126. R3 I, 3, 232. Troil. IV, 1, 63. Cor. III, 3, 115. Rom. Prol. 5. Caes. II, 1, 322. Hml. II, 2, 531. Lr. II, 3, 10. II, 4, 9. Cymb. V, 5, 330.

Loiter, to lounge: Gent. IV, 4, 48. H4B II, 1, 198.

Loiterer, a lounger, idler: Gent. III, 1, 296. LLL III, 185.

Loll, 1) to thrust out (the tongue): *—ing the tongue with slaughtering,* Cymb. V, 3, 8. Obscene quibbling: *a great natural that runs —ing up and down to hide his bauble in a hole,* Rom. II, 4, 96.

2) to recline, to lean: *—ing on a lewd daybed,* R3 III, 7, 72 (O. Edd. *lulling*). *on his pressed bed —ing,* Troil. I, 3, 162. *hangs and —s and weeps upon me,* Oth. IV, 1, 143.

Lombard street in London, corrupted to *Lumbert street* by Mrs Quickly: H4B II, 1, 31.

Lombardy, the northern part of Italy: Shr. I, 1, 3.

London, the capital of England: John V, 1, 31. R2 III, 3, 208. III, 4, 90. 97. V, 2, 3. V, 3, 6. V, 6, 7 etc. Used as a fem. in H5 V Chor. 24. *Welcome to L., to your chamber,* R3 III, 1, 1. *through L. gates,* H6B IV, 8, 24. *in L. streets,* R2 V, 5, 77. H6B IV, 8, 47. *at L. bridge,* H6A III, 1, 23. H6B IV, 4, 49. *set L. bridge on fire,* IV, 6, 16 (it being, at that time, made of wood). *sitting upon L. stone,* H6B IV, 6, 2 (probably a monument called so).

Londoners, inhabitants of London: H8 I, 2, 154.

Lone, solitary, single, not assisted by a husband: *a poor l. woman,* H4B II, 1, 35.

Loneliness, retirement, seclusion from company: *show of such an exercise may colour your l.* Hml. III, 1, 46 (Qq *lowliness*). In All's I, 3, 177 O. Edd. *loveliness,* some M. Edd. *loneliness.*

Lonely, solitary: *a l. dragon,* Cor. IV, 1, 30. In Wint. V, 3, 18 O. Edd. *lovely,* most M. Edd. *lonely.*

Long, adj. opposed to short, extended; used of space: *fetlocks shag and l.* Ven. 295. *l. heath,* Tp. I,

1, 70. *I have no l. spoon*, II, 2, 103; cf. Err. IV, 3, 62. 64. *my l. nails*, Tp. II, 2, 172. *the way is l.* Gent. II, 7, 8. V, 2, 4. Wiv. II, 1, 236; cf. Rom. I, 1, 82. Err. IV, 4, 30. Mids. V, 63. H8 Prol. 16. IV, 2, 97. Ant. III, 3, 32 etc. As a relative term: *a cloak as l.* Gent. III, 1, 131. Preceded by an [accus. denoting a measure: *ten words l.* Mids. V, 61. *tricks eleven and twenty l.* Shr. IV, 2, 57. Substantively: *this l. 's the text*, Per. II Prol. 40 (i. e. so long, or thus l., is what I have to recite. Ff *thus l.*).

Used of time: *after l. sleep*, Tp. III, 2, 148. *l. continuance*, IV, 1, 107. *l. life*, IV, 1, 24. *the —est night*, Gent. IV, 2, 140. Wiv. IV, 5, 105. Meas. II, 1, 140. III, 1, 256. Err. I, 2, 15. Ado II, 1, 52; cf. John IV, 1, 18. Shr. I, 2, 193. Tw. III, 3, 21. Rom. I, 5, 16 etc. etc. *a l. time*, H8 I, 3, 45. *l. time* (without the article): R2 II, 1, 77. H6A II, 3, 36. Ant. II, 5, 25. *a hundred mark is a l. one for a poor lone woman*, H4B II, 1, 35 (see *One*). *to think l.* = to expect with impatience: *but l. she thinks till he return again*, Lucr. 1359. *have I thought l. to see this morning's face*, Rom. IV, 5, 41. *the short and the l.* = the whole in few words; in short, in a word: *he loves your wife; there's the short and the l.* Wiv. II, 1, 137. *this is the short and the l. of it*, II, 2, 60. *the short and the l. is, our play is preferred*, Mids. IV, 2, 39. Merch. II, 2, 135. Captain Jamy says *the breff and the l.* H5 III, 2, 126. *before it be long*, and *ere it be long*, = shortly: H6C IV, 6, 91. Meas. IV, 2, 70. H6A III, 2, 75. H6C III, 3, 232 (*ere l.*, see *Ere*). Uncertain, whether adj. or adv.: *to teach my tongue to be so l.* Pilgr. 350 (= so long talking; cf. *Long-tongued*). cf. *I'll not be l. before I call upon thee*, Wint. III, 3, 8. *though they be l. ere they are wooed*, Troil. III, 2, 118. *my lord is very l. in talk*, H6A I, 2, 118. *be not so l. to speak*, Rom. IV, 1, 66 (= be not so long silent); cf. *you're l. about it*, Cor. I, 1, 131. Substantively: *for l.* = a long time: Meas. I, 4, 63.

Long, adv. not for a short time: Tp. II, 1, 169. Gent. III, 1, 388. III, 2, 48. IV, 1, 20. V, 4, 8. 118. Wiv. II, 2, 188. Mids. I, 1, 6. R2 V, 2, 114. R3 I, 1, 139. Troil. IV, 1, 3. Lr. III, 6, 3 etc. etc. *l. ago:* Tw. I, 5, 282. Shr. III, 1, 71. R2 V, 1, 42. H8 III, 1, 120. Tit. IV, 2, 23. *not l. ago*, Tim. III, 2, 12. *l. agone:* Gent. III, 1, 85. *l. since:* Sonn. 30, 7. Wiv. V, 5, 236. H6A III, 4, 20. Tim. II, 2, 38. *at last, though l., our jarring notes agree*, Shr. V, 2, 1 (= late).

In a relative sense: Tp. I, 1, 27. II, 2, 37. III, 3, 8. Gent. II, 1, 70. II, 2, 15. III, 1, 164. III, 2, 20. Err. I, 1, 66. II, 2, 37. Mids. II, 1, 145. R2 III, 4, 95 etc. *how l. is't ago?* H4A II, 4, 360. Cymb. I, 1, 61. *no —er ago than Wednesday last*, H4B II, 4, 93; and in the same sense without *ago: no —er than yesterday*, Ant. V, 2, 251 (the clown's speech). *how l. is't since?* Cor. I, 6, 14; cf. Rom. I, 5, 34. Cymb. III, 5, 153. IV, 2, 103. *all the winter l.* = during all the winter, Wint. IV, 4, 75. *all day l.* Tit. V, 2, 55. *all night l.* Hml. I, 1, 160. *three days —er*, H6B III, 2, 288. Per. I, 1, 116. *as l. as:* Wiv. II, 1, 56. Tw. I, 3, 41. H5 IV, 7, 113. Oftener *so l. as:* Shr. V, 1, 25. Tw. I, 2, 17. Wint. III, 2, 241. H4A IV, 3, 39. H5 II, 1, 15. IV, 7, 119. H6B I, 1, 211. II, 4, 63. H6C IV, 1, 77. Lr. IV, 1, 30. Oth. I, 3, 211. Cymb. I, 3, 8. *l. live*, see *Live.*

Long (most M. Edd *'long*), adv., followed by *of*, = by the fault of, owing to: *you must not be so quick.*

'tis l. of you that spur me with such questions, LLL II, 119. *all this coil is l. of you*, Mids. III, 2, 339. *all l. of this vile traitor Somerset*, H6A IV, 3, 33. 46. *so 'twere not l. of him*, H6C IV, 7, 32. *all this is l. of you*, Cor. V, 4, 32. *l. of her it was that we meet here*, Cymb. V, 5, 271.

Long, vb. 1) to be desirous, to wish; absol.: *a bed that —ing have been sick for*, Meas. II, 4, 103. *quickly, sir; I l.* LLL V, 2, 244. *let me have it, I l.* Wint. I, 2, 101. *he did l. in vain*, H4B II, 3, 14. *vainly —ing*, H8 I, 2, 81. With *for: she —s for morrow*, Lucr. 1571; H5 III, 7, 98. 141. *like a child, that —s for every thing that he can come by*, Gent. III, 1, 125. *any —ed for change*, John IV, 2, 8. *—ing for what it had not*, Ant. III, 6, 48. With an inf.: *my heart —s not to groan*, Ven. 785. *I l. to know*, Err. IV, 4, 146; Troil. IV, 1, 31. *I l. to have some chat with her*, Shr. II, 163. *I l. to talk*, All's IV, 5, 109. *—s to enter in*, R2 I, 3, 2. *—ed to be a king*, H6B IV, 9, 5. 6. *I l. to have this young one made a Christian*, H8 V, 3, 179. *I l. to die*, Rom. IV, 1, 66. *I have —ed long to redeliver*, Hml. III, 1, 94. *l. to move*, Cymb. IV, 3, 32. Particularly with *to hear*, and *to see:* Lucr. 1610; 1698; Tp. V, 311; Shr. Ind. 1, 133; R2 V, 3, 115; H5 I, 1, 98; H6B II, 2, 6; R3 I, 4, 8; Troil. III, 1, 154. Hml. II, 2, 50; Per. V, 3, 56. Merch. II, 9, 99; As I, 2, 149; Wint. I, 2, 34; H6B II, 4, 110; R3 II, 4, 4; III, 4, 97; Troil. IV, 5, 153; Hml. II, 2, 2; Cymb. III, 2, 55; 56; III, 4, 2. With a subordinate clause: *I l. that we were safe and sound aboard*, Err. IV, 4, 154. *I l. till Edward fall by war's mischance*, H6C III, 3, 254.

The gerund as a subst.: *Cytherea a —ing tarriance for Adonis made*, Pilgr. 74 (a stay of yearning love); cf. *to furnish me upon my —ing journey*, Gent. II, 7, 85. *you have saved my —ing*, Tim. I, 1, 261. *I have immortal —ings in me*, Ant. V, 2, 284 (desire of immortality). *quenched of hope, not —ing*, Cymb. V, 5, 196. *we do our —ing stay*, Per. V, 3, 83.

2) to have an appetite for food: *by —ing for that food*, Gent. II, 7, 17. *I l. for grass*, Err. II, 2, 202. *come to my natural taste, now I do wish it, love it, l. for it*, Mids. IV, 1, 180. *he —s to eat the English*, H5 III, 7, 99. *—s for the garbage*, Cymb. I, 6, 50. cf. H8 I, 2, 81.

Especially, to have a preternatural appetite, as sick persons, or women with child: *my love is as a fever, —ing still for that which longer nurseth the disease*, Sonn. 147, 1. *—ing for stewed prunes*, Meas. II, 1, 92. 102. *she —ed to eat adders' heads*, Wint. IV, 4, 267. *for whose sight I have a woman's —ing*, 681. Troil. III, 3, 237.

3) to be capricious: *effeminate, changeable, —ing and liking*, As III, 2, 431. *our fancies are more giddy and unfirm, more —ing, wavering, sooner lost and worn than women's are*, Tw. II, 4, 35. *nice —ing, slanders, mutability*, Cymb. II, 5, 26.

Long, vb. to belong (q.v.): *no ceremony that to great ones —s*, Meas. II, 2, 59. *such grace as —eth to a lover's blessed case*, Shr. IV, 2, 45. *such austerity as —eth to a father*, IV, 4, 7. *it is an honour —ing to our house*, All's IV, 2, 42. *the child-bed privilege, which —s to women*, Wint. III, 2, 104. *the glories that l. to him*, H5 II, 4, 80. *to maintain the many to them —ing*, H8 I, 2, 32. *there —ed no more to the crown*, II, 3, 48. *to his surname —s more pride than pity to our prayers*, Cor. V, 3, 170.

Longaville, name in LLL I, 1, 15. II, 39. 43. IV, 3, 45. 172. V, 2, 278. 284. 662.*Rhyming to *ill:* IV, 3, 123. to *compile*, 133. to *mile*, V, 2, 53.

Long-boat, the largest boat belonging to a ship: H6B IV, 1, 68.

Long-continued, lasting a long time: Troil. I, 3, 262.

Long-during: *l. action*, LLL IV, 3, 307.

Longed-for, desired: John IV, 2, 8.

Long-engraffed (Qq *long-engrafted*) inveterate: Lr. I, 1, 301.

Long-experienced, tried by long experience: Lucr. 1820. Rom. IV, 1, 60.

Long-grown, old, inveterate: *the l. wounds of my intemperance*, H4A III, 2, 156.

Long-hid, concealed a long time: Lucr. 1816.

Long-imprisoned, kept a long time as in a prison: *thy l. thoughts*, H6B V, 1, 88.

Long-lane, name of a lane in Shr. IV, 3, 187.

Long-legged, having long legs: Mids. II, 2, 21.

Long-lived (not hyphened in O. Edd.) having a long life: *the l. phoenix*, Sonn. 19, 4.

Long-living, lasting long: *l. laud*, Lucr. 622.

Longly, longingly, fondly: *you looked so l. on the maid*, Shr. I, 1, 170.

Long-parted (not hyphened in O. Edd.) having been long separated, R2 III, 2, 8.

Long Purples, see *Purple*, subst. 2.

Long-since-due (not hyphened in O. Edd.): *l. debts*, Tim. II, 2, 39 (cf. *Long*, adv.).

Long-staff sixpenny strikers, fellows that infest the road with long staves and rob men of sixpence: H4A II, 1, 82.

Long-tail: *come cut and l.* Wiv. III, 4, 47; i. e. come dogs of all sorts, come what person will.

Long-tongued, prating: *l. Warwick*, H6C II, 2, 102. *a l. babbling gossip*, Tit. IV, 2, 150. cf. Pilgr. 350.

Long-vanished, long since past: *l. days*, H5 II, 4, 86.

Long-winded, long-breathed: H4A III, 3, 181.

Loo or **Low**, a cry to set dogs on: Troil. V, 7, 10. 11. Lr. III, 4, 79.

Loofed, luffed, brought close to the wind: *she once being l.* Ant. III, 10, 18.

Look, subst. 1) the act of looking, the casting or settling of the eye in a certain direction or on a certain object: *he borrows his wit from your ladyship's —s*, Gent. II, 4, 39. *his mistress did hold his eyes locked in her crystal —s*, 89. *too mean a servant to have a l. of such a worthy mistress*, 108. *his —s are my soul's food*, II, 7, 15. Err. III, 2, 18. LLL I, 1, 76. 85. Tw. III, 4, 215. Wint. IV, 4, 490. V, 1, 228 *(make).* R2 II, 1, 80. III, 2, 165 etc.

2) expression of the eye and countenance: *at his l. she flatly falleth down*, Ven. 463. *and sorts a sad l. to her lady's sorrow*, Lucr. 1221. *she lends them words, and she their —s doth borrow*, 1498. *did court the lad with many a lovely l.* Pilgr. 45. Tp. IV, 129. Gent. I, 1, 30. III, 1, 31. V, 4, 23. 42. Wiv. II, 2, 27. Meas. IV, 2, 35. Err. I, 1, 10. II, 1, 88. 99. II, 2, 33. IV, 4, 96. Ado IV, 2, 47. Mids. II, 2, 127. H4B I, 1, 71. H6A I, 2, 48. 62. III, 2, 72. H6C II, 2, 11. H8 I, 1, 119. Lr. II, 4, 37. Ant. I, 5, 56 etc.

3) appearance, aspect: *death's dim l. in life's mortality*, Lucr. 403. *kindness in women, not their beau-*

teous —s, shall win my love, Shr. IV, 2, 41. *had nature lent thee but thy mother's l.* Tit. V, 1, 29. *this l. of thine will hurl my soul from heaven*, Oth. V, 2, 274. *for her many a wight did die, as yon grim —s do testify*, Per. Prol. 40. Plur. for sing.: *how much more elder art thou than thy —s*, Merch. IV, 1, 251. *puts on his pretty —s*, John III, 4, 95. *when she seemed to shake and fear your —s, she loved them most*, Oth. III, 3, 207. *one that promised nought but beggary and poor —s*, Cymb. V, 5, 10.

Look, vb. 1) to use the eye, to set the organ of seeing to work: *she dares not l.* Lucr. 458. *the glass, the school, the book, where subjects' eyes do learn, do read, do l.* 616. *l. that way*, Wiv. III, 1, 9. *which way —s he?* Ado I, 3, 55 (who is she whom he has in view?). *you l. with your eyes as other women do*, III, 4, 92. *I would my father —ed but with my eyes*, Mids. I, 1, 56. *love —s not with the eyes, but with the mind*, 234. *the moon —s with a watery eye*, III, 1, 203. *the sternest eyes that l.* Merch. II, 1, 27. *my eyes can l. as swift as yours*, III, 2, 199. *every eye which in this forest —s*, As III, 2, 7. *I'll l. no more*, Lr. IV, 6, 22 etc. *such looks as none could l.* Pilgr. 46 (accus. denoting the effect). *eyes, l. your last*, Rom. V, 3, 112 (cf. *Last*). Hence often = to see: *l. who's at door there*, H4B V, 3, 74. *l. with thine ears*, Lr. IV, 6, 154. *I l. through thee*, All's II, 3, 226 (= I see through thee). *—s quite through the deeds of men*, Caes. I, 2, 202. Oftenest in the imperative: *l., he's winding up the watch*, Tp. II, 1, 12. *l. how well my garments sit upon me*, 272 (cf. *How).* *l. what a wardrobe here is for thee*, IV, 222. *O l., sir, l., sir*, V, 216. Gent. I, 2, 109. Mids. I, 1, 179. Hml. I, 4, 38 etc. *l. where he comes*, Meas. I, 1, 25. *l. where thy love comes*, Mids. III, 2, 176 (cf. *Where).* *l. who comes yonder*, Wiv. II, 1, 162. The personal pronoun joined to it: *l. thee here, boy*, Wint. III, 3, 116 (*thee* = thou). *l. you, sir, here is the hand and seal of the duke*, Meas. IV, 2, 207. *l. you, how cheerfully my mother —s*, Hml. III, 2, 132. Used to lay some stress on what one is going to say: *l., what is best, that best I wish in thee*, Sonn. 37, 13. *l., what thy memory cannot contain, commit to these waste blanks*, 77, 9. *l., what thou wantest, shall be sent after thee*, Gent. I, 3, 74. *l., what I will not, that I cannot do*, Meas. II, 2, 52. Err. II, 1, 12. Ado I, 1, 320. Merch. III, 4, 51. Shr. IV, 3, 194. All's I, 3, 182. R2 I, 1, 87. H4A I, 3, 253. R3 I, 3, 290. III, 1, 194. IV, 4, 291 etc. *l. thee*, used in the same manner: Gent. II, 5, 30. Cor. V, 2, 77. *l. you:* Tp. IV, 202. Gent. II, 3, 14. 22. III, 1, 261. 277. IV, 4, 2. Wiv. I, 1, 38. I, 4, 100. II, 2, 129. Meas. IV, 3, 44. LLL V, 2, 585. Merch. I, 3, 138. III, 5, 1. As III, 2, 20. V, 2, 18. Shr. I, 2, 77. H4A I, 3, 239. Cor. I, 1, 113. Rom. III, 4, 3. Hml. I, 5, 132 etc.

With adverbs or prepositions (never with *at;* cf. *Gaze*), = to use the eye in a particular direction, to cast the eye to or from an object; a) with adverbs; *after: —ing before and after*, Hml. IV, 4, 37 (= into the past). *go, l. after*, Cymb. III, 5, 55 (seek, inquire). *about: how it —s about*, Tp. I, 2, 410 (= in all directions). *l. about, Davy*, H4B V, 1, 59 (= take care, do your office). *be wary, l. about*, Rom. III, 5, 40 (be on your guard). *'tis time to l. about*, Lr. IV, 7, 93. *back: l. back, defend thee*, R3 III, 5, 19. *my thoughts shall ne'er l. back*, Oth. III, 3, 458. *—ing back what I have left behind*, Ant. III, 11, 53 (is this = bringing back by my look?). *before*, Hml. IV, 4, 37. *behind:* Oth. II, 1, 158. *down: l. down, you gods*, Tp. V, 201. *the gods l. down*, Cor. V, 3, 184. *in: l. in*, Tp. V, 167. *l. but in* (viz the brook) *and you shall see him*, As III, 2, 305. *let us l. in*, H6A I, 4, 62. *on: while idly I stood* —*ing on* (= was an idle spectator) Shr. I, 1, 155; cf. Troil. V, 4, 2. Rom. I, 4, 38. *the selfsame sun hides not his visage from our cottage but* —*s on alike*, Wint. IV, 4, 457 (regards both with the same eye). *out: l. out there, some of ye*, H8 I, 4, 50 (see what is the matter at the door). *l. out and speak to friends*, Tim. V, 1, 131. *thy crystal window ope, l. out*, Cymb. V, 4, 81. *up:* Gent. V, 4, 87. Ado IV, 1, 120. R2 V, 1, 8. Lr. IV, 6, 58. 59. = to take courage: *dear, l. up*, Wint. V, 1, 215. *cheer up yourself, l. up*, H4B IV, 4, 113. *only l. up clear*, Mcb. I, 5, 72. *then I'll l. up; my fault is past*, Hml. III, 3, 50. *upon* (= to be a spectator, a looker-on): *strike all that l. upon with marvel*, Wint. V, 3, 100. *all of you that stand and l. upon*, R2 IV, 237 (Ff *upon me*). *and l. upon, as if the tragedy were played in jest*, H6C II, 3, 27. *I will not l. upon*, Troil. V, 6, 10.

b) with prepositions; 1) *about; α)* = to cast the eye around: *master, l. about you*, Shr. I, 2, 141. *l. about you*, All's IV, 3, 348. *β)* to be on the watch: Caes. II, 3, 7. *l. with care about the town*, Oth. II, 3, 255. 2) *after; α)* to follow with the eye: *l. after him and cannot do him good*, H6B III, 1, 219. *β)* to take care of: *go, l. after him*, Tw. I, 5, 144. Mcb. V, 1, 83. *γ)* to care for: *will they yet l. after thee?* Wiv. II, 2, 146. *all those requisites that folly and green minds l. after*, Oth. II, 1, 251. *nobody l. after it*, Per. II, 1, 59. *δ)* to keep in the eye, to have an eye upon: *is lechery so* —*ed after?* Meas. I, 2, 148. 3) *against: she is too bright to be* —*ed against*, Wiv. II, 2, 254. 4) *beyond: you l. beyond him quite*, H4B IV, 4, 67 (you misjudge him). 5) *for; α)* to strive to see, to seek: *whose downward eye still* —*eth for a grave*, Ven. 1106. *which way have you* —*ed for Master Caius?* Wiv. III, 1, 3. *I* —*ed for the chalky cliffs*, Err. III, 2, 129. —*s for rescue*, H6A IV, 4, 19. *l. to heaven for grace*, I, 4, 83. *l. for thy reward among the nettles*, Tit. II, 3, 271. *β)* to expect with impatience, to wish for: *she hotter that did l. for his approach*, Pilgr. 77. *he in his speed* —*s for the morning light*, Lucr. 745. *she* —*s for night, and then she longs for morrow*, 1571. *telling the bushes that thou* —*est for wars*, Mids. III, 2, 408. *now is the day we long have* —*ed for*, Shr. II, 335. *if this be not that you l. for, I have no more to say*, IV, 4, 96. *to cross me from the golden time I l. for*, H6C III, 2, 127. *young bloods l. for a time of rest*, Caes. IV, 3, 262. *and waste the time which* —*s for other revels*, Per. II, 3, 93. *γ)* to expect in general: *I will proclaim thee, Angelo, l. for it*, Meas. II, 4, 151. *I l. for an earthquake, too, then*, Ado I, 1, 275. *l. you for any other issue?* II, 2, 30. *on this travail l. for greater birth*, IV, 1, 215. *we l. for you to-morrow*, V, 1, 338. Sonn. 23, 11. LLL I, 1, 281. As III, 5, 97. Shr. IV, 2, 116. IV, 4, 16. R2 IV, 161. H4A IV, 2, 63. IV, 3, 3. V, 4, 22. R3 I, 3, 237. II, 3, 34. III, 2, 65. III, 5, 50. 102. H8 III, 1, 75. V, 4, 10. Oth. III, 4, 149. Cymb. III, 1, 67 etc. 6) *from* (to turn the eye off): *Tyre, I now l. from thee*, Per. I, 2, 115. 7) *in: l. in thy glass*, Sonn. 3, 1; 103, 6; Meas. II, 2, 95; H5 V, 2, 154; H6B V, 1, 142. *l. in the almanac*, Mids. III, 1, 54. *l. in the calendar*, Caes. II, 1, 42. *l. in the chronicles*, Shr. Ind. 1, 4. *in*

the maps, H5 IV, 7, 24. *l. in thy last work*, Tim. I, 1, 228. *in the clouds*, Caes. II, 1, 26. *in the deep*, Lr. IV, 1, 77. *l. in mine eye-balls*, Ven. 119. —*ing in her eye*, LLL IV, 3, 243. *l. in this gentleman's face*, Meas. II, 1, 153. *l. in the lady's face*, John II, 495. *l. in my face*, Oth. IV, 2, 26. *I* —*ed her in the face*, Ant. III, 3, 12. *would gladly l. him in the face*, V, 2, 32. The last expression = to face, to meet boldly: *darest not stand nor l. me in the face*, Mids. III, 2, 424. *whom all France durst not presume to l. once in the face*, H6A I, 1, 140. *never after l. me in the face*, Rom. III, 5, 163. *an I tell you that, I'll never l. you i' the face again*, Caes. I, 2, 284. 8) *into*, = to inspect closely, to examine: *they l. into the beauty of thy mind, and that in guess they measure by thy deeds*, Sonn. 69, 9. *lest the wise world should l. into your moan*, 71, 13. *I will l. further into it*, Wiv. II, 1, 245. *to l. into the bottom of my place*, Meas. I, 1, 79. LLL V, 2, 779. As V, 2, 48. Shr. III, 2, 145. John II, 114. H4A II, 1, 80. H6B II, 1, 202. R3 IV, 2, 30. H8 II, 2, 41. Mcb. I, 3, 58. Hml. II, 2, 64. Lr. I, 4, 76. *he did l. far into the service of the time*, All's I, 2, 26. *into* for *unto*, Meas. II, 1, 126 (Pompey's speech). 9) *on; α)* to turn the eye on (the modern *to look at*): *he* —*s upon his love and neighs unto her*, Ven. 307. *not one of them that yet* —*s on me, or would know me*, Tp. V, 83. *worth the* —*ing on*, Meas. V, 208. *all that l. on him love him*, Tw. II, 3, 164. *l. on me with your welkin eye*, Wint. I, 2, 136. *what you l. on now*, V, 1, 227. *I will l. on both indifferently*, Caes. I, 2, 87. *we will not l. upon him*, Ant. I, 2, 91. *flesh which some did die to l. on*, I, 4, 68. *kills me to l. on't*, Cymb. II, 4, 108. *β)* to regard: *and l. upon myself and curse my fate*, Sonn. 29, 4. *when I l. on you, I can hardly think you my master*, Gent. II, 1, 33. *when I l. on her perfections*, II, 4, 211. *l. on Master Fenton*, Wiv. III, 4, 101. *l. upon the years of Lewis*, John II, 424. *γ)* to take notice of, to care for: *trowest thou that e'er I'll l. upon the world, or count them happy that enjoy the sun?* H6B II, 4, 38. *for yet I am not* —*ed on in the world*, H6C V, 7, 22. *one that* —*s on feeders*, Ant. III, 13, 109. *none would l. on her*, Per. IV, 3, 32. *δ)* to face, to meet: *durst thou have* —*ed upon him being awake*, Mids. III, 2, 69. *henceforth ne'er l. on me*, H4A II, 4, 491. —*s proudly on the crown*, R3 IV, 3, 42 (Qq *o'er*). *l. upon thy death*, Rom. I, 1, 74. *ε)* to read: *let me l. on that* (letter) *again*, Gent. IV, 4, 130. *I will not l. upon your master's lines*, 133. *let me l. upon the bond*, Merch. IV, 1, 225. *my books and instruments shall be my company, on them to l. and practise by myself*, Shr. I, 1, 83. *l. on this letter*, All's III, 2, 58. *give me the letter, I will l. on it*, Rom. V, 3, 278. *ζ)* to see: *who, being* —*ed on, ducks as quickly in*, Ven. 87. *in dreams they l. on thee*, Sonn. 43, 3. —*ing on an Englishman, the fairest that eye could see*, Pilgr. 213. *I am glad 'tis night, you do not l. on me*, Merch. II, 6, 34. Tp. I, 2, 310. V, 289. Gent. III, 1, 180. III, 2, 21. V, 2, 14. Meas. V, 375. 452. 474. Err. III, 2, 58. V, 210. Ado I, 1, 165. Mids. I, 1, 242. II, 1, 179. 212. III, 2, 385. Merch. I, 2, 130. As II, 7, 113. IV, 3, 159. R2 II, 3, 39. H6B III, 3, 13. R3 III, 4, 107. Cor. I, 3, 61. Mcb. II, 4, 20. Ant. V, 1, 39. Cymb. II, 1, 46. 10) *over, α)* to read over: *every man l. o'er his part*, Mids. IV, 2, 38. *β)* to look down on, to overtop: *and, by that knot,* —*s proudly o'er the crown*, R3 IV, 3, 42 (Ff *on*). *let Antony l. over Caesar's head*, Ant. II, 2, 5. 11) *through:* —*ed through the grate*, Wiv. II, 2, 8. *let her beauty l. through a casement*, Cymb. II, 4, 34. *a fog that I cannot l. through*, III, 2, 82. 12) *to; α*) to cast the eye towards: *l. not to the ground*, R2 III, 2, 87. *to l. to heaven for grace*, H6A I, 4, 83. *—s so many fathoms to the sea*, Hml. I, 4, 77. Costard says: *now will I l. to his remuneration*, LLL III, 137. *β*) to take care of, to guard, to be attentive to: *l. well to her heart*, Ven. 580. *l. to the boy*, Gent. V, 4, 85. *we'll l. to that anon*, Err. V, 412. *will you l. to those things I told you of?* Ado II, 1, 351. *you must be —ed to*, V, 1, 213. Mids. I, 2, 28. Merch. II, 5, 16. III, 1, 49. 51. 52. III, 3, 1. 3. Shr. Ind. I, 28. All's IV, 5, 62. Tw. I, 5, 146. III, 4, 67. 72. 186. Wint. IV, 3, 23. John I, 30. III, 1, 346. R2 V, 3, 39. H4A II, 4, 91. H6A II, 1, 62. H6B I, 1, 208. R3 III, 5, 15. Tit. IV, 1, 120. Oth. III, 4, 76. Ant. III, 2, 45 etc. With *narrowly* and *near*, = to watch, to inspect closely: *if my cousin do not l. narrowly to thee*, Ado V, 4, 118. *l. too near unto my state*, H4B IV, 5, 212. *l. to it* = be on your guard, take heed, take care: As III, 1, 4. H6A II, 4, 103. H6B I, 1, 156. I, 3, 147. R3 IV, 2, 90 etc. *we ought to l. to it*, Mids. III, 1, 34. *thou wert best l. to't*, As I, 1, 154.

c) Adverbs and prepositions joined: *l. back into your mighty ancestors*, H5 I, 2, 102 (cf. *Into*). *l. back with me unto the Tower*, R3 IV, 1, 98. *let me l. back upon thee*, Tim. IV, 1, 1. *l. down into the Pomgarnet*, H4A II, 4, 41. *l. down into this den*, Tit. II, 3, 215. *I l. down towards his feet*, Oth. V, 2, 286. *l. forward on the journey you shall go*, Meas. IV, 3, 61. *l. in upon me then and speak with me*, Oth. V, 2, 257 (= come in and look me in the face). *to l. out at her lady's chamber window*, Ado II, 2, 17. Merch. II, 5, 40. Shr. V, 1, 32. *he —s out of the window*, 57. *l. up to him*, H6A I, 4, 89. *how dare the plants l. up to heaven*, Per. I, 2, 55.

2) to show itself, to peep forth: *her business —s in her with an importing visage*, All's V, 3, 135. *what a deal of scorn —s beautiful in the contempt and anger of his lip*, Tw. III, 1, 157. With *through: my toes l. through the overleather*, Shr. Ind. 2, 12. *life —s through and will break out*, H4B IV, 4, 120. *what a haste —s through his eyes*, Mcb. I, 2, 46. *if our drift l. through our bad performance*, Hml. IV, 7, 152. With *out: the business of this man —s out of him*, Ant. V, 1, 50. *he tells her something that makes her blood l. out*, Wint. IV, 4, 160. *her wanton spirits l. out at every joint and motive of her body*, Troil. IV, 5, 56. *see the monstrousness of man when he —s out in an ungrateful shape*, Tim. III, 2, 80.

3) to have a particular air: *this ghastly —ing*, Tp. II, 1, 309. *you do l. in a moved sort*, IV, 146. *learn of her eye to l.* LLL IV, 3, 252. *teach me how to l.* Mids. I, 1, 192. *till the heavens l. with an aspect more favourable*, Wint. II, 1, 106. With an adjective: *those far-off eyes l. sad*, Lucr. 1386; LLL I, 2, 3; Mids. V, 294. *I will acquaintance strangle and l. strange*, Sonn. 89, 8; Err. II, 2, 112. *l. sweet, speak fair*, Err. III, 2, 11. *how fiery and how sharp he —s*, IV, 4, 53. *l. up clear*, Mcb. I, 5, 72. *l. big*, see *Big*. A preposition following: *why l. you strange on me*, Err. V, 295. *the pale-faced moon —s bloody on the earth*, R2 II, 4, 10. With adverbs: *—ing scornfully*, Lucr. 187. *you l. wearily*, Tp. III, 1, 32. *when you —ed sadly, it was for want of money*, Gent. II, 1, 30. *when he —s so merrily*, Wiv. II, 1, 198. *—ing wildly*,

III, 3, 94. *how tartly that gentleman —s*, Ado II, 1, 3. *walk softly and l. sweetly*, 91. *l. demurely*, Merch. II, 2, 201. *he —s successfully*, As I, 2, 162. *thou —est cheerly*, II, 6, 14. *you l. merrily*, II, 7, 11. *—s he as freshly as he did*, III, 2, 243. *the skies l. grimly*, Wint. III, 3, 3. *to l. so poorly*, R2 III, 3, 128. *he stares and —s so wildly*, V, 3, 24. *l. how we can, or sad or merrily*, H4A V, 2, 12. *I cannot l. greenly*, H5 V, 2, 149. *why —s your grace so heavily*, R3 I, 4, 1. II, 3, 40. *his grace —s cheerfully and smooth*, III, 4, 50. *l. fresh and merrily*, Caes. II, 1, 224. *—ed he frowningly*, Hml. I, 2, 231. *how cheerfully my mother —s*, III, 2, 133. *he —s sadly*, Oth. II, 1, 32. On following: *l. cheerfully upon me*, Shr. IV, 3, 38. *he —s well on't*, All's V, 3, 31 (= he is pleased with it). *you all l. strangely on me*, H4B V, 2, 63.

4) to appear, to have a particular exterior: *thou —est not like deceit*, Lucr. 585. *the rose —s fair*, Sonn. 54, 3. *my love —s fresh*, 107, 10. *how lush and lusty the grass —s* Tp. II, 1, 52. *yond cloud —s like a foul bombard*, II, 2, 21. Wiv. II, 1, 36. III, 4, 33. Err. IV, 2, 4. IV, 4, 111. Ado III, 2, 48. IV, 1, 69. LLL IV, 3, 266. Mids. III, 2, 57. Merch. V, 125. As II, 3, 47. H4B I, 1, 62 etc. *she —s us like a thing more made of malice than of duty*, Cymb. III, 5, 32 (= seems to us). With an accus. denoting the effect: *thou hast —ed thyself into my grace*, Cymb. V, 5, 94 (thou hast gained my grace by thy appearance). An inf. following: *that is there* (in his heart) *which —s with us to break his neck*, Cor. III, 3, 29 (= which is likely to break his neck).

5) to expect, (see above: *l. for*); with an accus.: *the gifts she —s from me*, Wint. IV, 4, 369. With a clause: *then l. I death my days should expiate*, Sonn. 22, 4. *I —ed when some of you should say I was too strict*, R2 I, 3, 243. *I —ed you would have given me your petition*, H8 V, 1, 118. With an inf.: *as you l. to have my pardon*, Tp. V, 292. *we l. to hear from you*, Gent. II, 4, 120. Meas. I, 1, 58. Mids. III, 2, 430. All's III, 6, 82. Tw. V, 298. H4A V, 4, 145. H4B IV, 2, 116. H6A I, 1, 38. H6C II, 6, 95. V, 5, 66. R3 II, 3, 9. III, 1, 198. Mcb. V, 3, 26 etc.

6) to take care (see above: *l. to*); followed by the subjunctive: *l. thou be true*, Tp. IV, 51. *l. you bring me in the names*, Meas. II, 1, 286. *and Helena of Athens l. thou find*, Mids. III, 2, 95. *l. thou lead them thus*, 363. Wiv. V, 5, 65. 69. Meas. V, 298. 531. Mids. I, 1, 117. II, 1, 267. Merch. II, 8, 25. As I, 3, 127. IV, 1, 33. John IV, 1, 1. H5 II, 4, 49. H6B II, 1, 189. R3 III, 7, 47. IV, 4, 497. H8 I, 1, 66. Oth. IV, 3, 9. Ant. III, 13, 140 etc. The subord. clause preceded by *that: l. that you love your wife*, Meas. V, 502. R3 III, 4, 80. V, 3, 65.

7) to seek, to search for; transitively: *I will l. some linen for your head*, Wiv. IV, 2, 83. *he hath been all this day to l. you*, As II, 5, 34. *I must go l. my twigs; he shall be caught*, All's III, 6, 115. *I will l. him and privily relieve him*, Lr. III, 3, 15 (Qq *seek*). In H5 IV, 7, 76 O. Edd. *book*, M. Edd. *to l. our dead*. With *out: I'll l. you out a good turn*, Tim. III, 2, 67.

Looked, adj. in *Lean-looked*, q. v.

Looker-on, 1) one who looks on an object, one who beholds: *so long could I stand by, a l.* (of Hermione's statue) Wint. V, 3, 85. *I'll salute your grace of York as mother and reverend l. of two fair queens*, R3 IV, 1, 31.

2) spectator: Meas. V, 319. Wint. V, 1, 29. H6C II, 1, 45.

Looking-glass, a mirror, a glass which shows forms reflected: Gent. IV, 4, 157. Wint. I, 2, 117. R2 IV, 268. R3 I, 1, 15. I, 2, 256. Lr. V, 3, 261.

Loon (cf. *Lown*) a sorry fellow, a brute: *thou cream-faced l.* Mcb. V, 3, 11.

Loop, hole, opening: *stop all sight-holes, every l. from whence the eye of reason may pry in upon us,* H4A IV, 1, 71. *that the probation bear no hinge nor l. to hang a doubt on,* Oth. III, 3, 365.

Looped, full of holes: *how shall your houseless heads and unfed sides, your l. and windowed raggedness defend you,* Lr. III, 4, 31.

Loophole, an aperture in the wall of a fortification: Lucr. 1383.

Loose, adj. 1) not tied, not held fast, not confined: *her hair, nor l. nor tied in formal plat,* Compl. 29. *slackly braided in l. negligence,* 35. *if you see the bear l.* Wiv. I, 1, 304. 307. *they are l. again,* Err. IV, 4, 147. *I will fast, being l.* LLL I, 2, 161. *had their faces been l.* H8 IV, 1, 75. *to break l.* Err. V, 169. Mids. III, 2, 258. H4B I, 1, 10. *to go l.* Wiv. IV, 2, 128. Hml. IV, 3, 2. *to let l.* Tp. II, 2, 36. LLL III, 128. Mids. III, 2, 260. *their ragged curtains poorly are let l.* H5 IV, 2, 41 (in contempt, = displayed). *to let l. = to uncouple, to set on: let l. on me the justice of the state,* Oth. I, 1, 140. cf. *that tyrant.... thy womb let l. to chase us to our graves,* R3 IV, 4, 54. *I would turn her l. to him,* Wiv. II, 1, 190. *fast and l.* (cf. *Fast*): LLL I, 2, 162. III, 104. John III, 1, 242. Ant. IV, 12, 28.

2) not dense, not compact: (the earth of the churchyard) *being l., unfirm, with digging up of graves,* Rom. V, 3, 6.

3) wide, not tight: *like an old lady's l. gown,* H4A III, 3, 4. Adverbially: *in green she shall be l. enrobed,* Wiv. IV, 6, 41. *now does he feel his title hang l. about him,* Mcb. V, 2, 21.

4) irregular, acting at random: *a file of boys behind 'em, l. shot, delivered such a shower of pebbles,* H8 V, 4, 59.

5) slight, negligent, superficial: *lay negligent and l. regard upon him,* Troil. III, 3, 41. *he fumbles up into a l. adieu,* IV, 4, 48.

6) too unrestrained, lax: *which parti-coated presence of l. love put on by us,* LLL V, 2, 776. *where you are liberal of your loves and counsels be sure you be not l.* H8 II, 1, 127. *men so l. of soul, that in their sleeps will mutter their affairs,* Oth. III, 3, 416.

7) wanton, dissolute: *the l. encounters of lascivious men,* Gent. II, 7, 41. *that l. grace which shallow laughing hearers give to fools,* LLL V, 2, 869. *these giddy l. suggestions,* John III, 1, 292. *unrestrained l. companions,* R2 V, 3, 7. H4A I, 2, 232. Tit. II, 1, 65. Oth. II, 1, 245.

Loose, vb. 1) to make or let loose; absol. = to quit hold: *thy hand once more; I will not l. again,* Tit. II, 3, 243. trans. = a) to untie: *I will l. his bonds,* Err. V, 339. Troil. V, 2, 156. b) to set at liberty, to set at large: *he that —d them* (the winds) *forth their brazen caves,* H6B III, 2, 89. *—d out of hell,* Hml. II, 1, 83. *both my revenge and hate —ing upon thee,* All's II, 3, 172. *I'll l. my daughter to him,* Hml. II, 2, 162.

2) to discharge; absol.: *l. when I bid,* Tit. IV, 3, 58. trans.: *—d his love-shaft smartly from his bow,*

Mids. II, 1, 159. *many arrows —d several ways, come to one mark,* H5 I, 2, 207. cf. As III, 5, 103.

3) to remit: *thou wilt not only l. the forfeiture,* Merch. IV, 1, 24 (F4 and some M. Edd. *lose;* cf. As III, 5, 103 and Oth. II, 3, 213, in which passages O. Edd. have *loose,* M. Edd. *lose*).

Loose, subst. the discharge of an arrow: (time) *sometimes at his very l. decides that which long process could not arbitrate,* LLL V, 2, 752 (i. e. at the critical moment).

Loose-bodied, loose, wide, not tight: *a l. gown,* Shr. IV, 3, 135. 136.

Loosely, wantonly: *a prince should not be so l. studied as to remember so weak a composition,* H4B II, 2, 9. *your most dreadful laws so l. slighted,* V, 2, 94.

Loosen, to unbind, to disjoin, to sever: *I had rather lose the battle than that sister should l. him and me,* Lr. V, 1, 19.

Loose-wived, having a wanton wife: Ant. I, 2, 75.

Lop, subst. that which is cut off trees: *we take from every tree l., bark and part o'the timber,* H8 I, 2, 96 (which to do was forbidden by statute 1. Jac. I cap. 22. sec. XXI).

Lop, vb. 1) to cut off, as branches from trees: H6C II, 6, 47. Cymb. V, 4, 141. V, 5, 454. Used of limbs: Tit. I, 143. *to l. that doubt,* Per. I, 2, 90. With *away:* R2 III, 4, 64. with *off:* H4A IV, 1, 43. H6A V, 3, 15. H6B II, 3, 42.

2) to shorten by cutting off the branches: *have —ed and hewed and made thy body bare of her two branches,* Tit. II, 4, 17.

Lóraine (M. Edd. *Lorraine*), country between France and Germany: H5 I, 2, 70. 83.

Lord, subst. 1) master, ruler, owner: *dear l. of that dear jewel I have lost,* Lucr. 1191. *l. of my love,* Sonn. 26, 1. *they are the —s and owners of their faces,* 94, 7. *the l. on't* (the island) Tp. I, 2, 456. *Prospero my l. shall know,* II, 1, 326. *thou shalt be l. of it,* III, 2, 65. V, 162. *Love's a mighty l.* Gent. II, 4, 136. *that they should harbour where their l. would be,* III, 1, 149. *—s of the wide world,* Err. II, 1, 21. *whom I made l. of me and all,* V, 137. *l. of folded arms* (Cupid) LLL III, 183. *I thought you l. of more true gentleness,* Mids. II, 2, 132. *my fairy l., this must be done,* III, 2, 378. *l. Love,* Merch. II, 9, 101. *thou shalt live as freely as thy l.* Tw. I, 4, 39. I, 5, 249. *our sovereign l. the king,* Wint. III, 2, 17. *l. of thy presence,* John I, 137. *l. of our presence,* II, 367. *gain, be my l.* 598. *were I but now the l. of such hot youth,* R2 II, 3, 99. *l. of such a spirit,* H4A V, 4, 18. *join in friendship, as your —s have done,* H6A III, 1, 145. *disdain to call us l.* H6B IV, 1, 88. *now is Mortimer l. of this city,* IV, 6, 1. *strength should be the l. of imbecility,* Troil. I, 3, 114. *no man is the l. of any thing,* III, 3, 115. *those chances which he was l. of,* Cor. IV, 7, 41. *my bosom's l. sits lightly in his throne,* Rom. V, 1, 3. *the rabble call him l.* Hml. IV, 5, 102. *you are the l. of duty,* Oth. I, 3, 184. *l. of his fortunes he salutes thee,* Ant. III, 12, 11. *would make his will l. of his reason,* III, 13, 4. *he that strikes the venison first shall be the l. o'the feast,* Cymb. III, 3, 75 (cf. *master of the feast,* III, 6, 29) etc. etc. *l. and master:* All's II, 3, 194. 257. 261. Tw. I, 5, 271. *l. of —s,* Ant. IV, 8, 16. *stand my good l. = be my patron,* H4B IV, 3, 89; *standing your friendly l.* Cor. II, 3, 198. Applied to women: *when they strive to be —s of their —s,* LLL IV, 1, 38; *but now I was the l. of* *this fair mansion,* Merch. III, 2, 169. *—s o' the field* = conquerors: Cor. I, 6, 47; cf. *if the French be —s of this loud day,* John V, 4, 14.

2) God: *I praise the L. for you,* LLL IV, 2, 75. *L. worshipped might he be,* Merch. II, 2, 98. *now L. be thanked,* Shr. Ind. 2, 99. *the deputy elected by the L.* R2 III, 2, 57. *the L. increase this business,* H8 III, 2, 161 etc. etc. *the L. of hosts,* H6A I, 1, 31. *by the L.!* Wiv. III, 3, 65. III, 5, 90. Tw. V, 299 etc. (Ff om. in H4A I, 2, 164. II, 3, 17. II, 4, 14. 160). *good L.!* Tp. II, 1, 80. Ado II, 1, 330. Shr. IV, 5, 2. H6A IV, 1, 111 etc. *goodly L.* Merch. III, 5, 55. *L., how mine eyes throw gazes to the east,* Pilgr. 193. Tp. I, 2, 410. Ado II, 1, 31. Mids. II, 2, 109 etc. *L., L., your worship's a wanton,* Wiv. II, 2, 56. Gent. I, 2, 15. LLL IV, 1, 143 etc. *O the L.* H4B V, 4, 13 (Mrs Quickly's speech). *O L., L.* As III, 2, 194. *O L.* Err. III, 1, 50. Tw. III, 4, 119. H6A I, 4, 70 etc. *O. L., sir,* LLL I, 2, 6. V, 2, 497; ridiculed as an unmeaning phrase then in fashion: All's II, 2, 43 sq. *write 'L. have mercy on us' on those three,* LLL V, 2, 419 (the inscription placed upon the doors of houses infected with the plague). *are now 'for the —'s sake',* Meas. IV, 3, 21 (the supplication of imprisoned debtors to the passers-by).

3) husband: *save of their l. no bearing yoke they (her breasts) knew,* Lucr. 409. *thou worthy l. of that unworthy wife,* 1303. *like widowed wombs after their —s' decease,* Sonn. 97, 8. Ado III, 1, 38. III, 4, 31. Mids. II, 1, 63. IV, 1, 104. Merch. III, 4, 4. As V, 4, 140. R2 III, 4, 85. R3 I, 2, 241. I, 3, 7. IV, 4, 338. Rom. III, 2, 66. III, 3, 82. Hml. III, 4, 98. Lr. I, 1, 103. Cymb. I, 5, 78 etc. *my l. and husband,* Shr. Ind. 2, 108. V, 2, 131. Ant. III, 4, 16.

4) a nobleman, a peer, a prince: *this false l.* Lucr. 50. *this lustful l.* 169. *all his —s,* Tp. I, 2, 437. *—s that can prate as amply,* II, 1, 263. *this l. of weak remembrance,* 232. *my brace of —s,* V, 126. *knights and —s,* Wiv. II, 2, 65. *I'll speak it before the best l.* Wiv. III, 3, 53. Ado I, 1, 55. LLL II, 52. Wint. II, 3, 113. H6B I, 1, 224. Tim. I, 1, 234. 241 etc. etc. *the L. Northumberland,* R2 II, 2, 53. III, 3, 7. *the L. Aumerle,* IV, 6. *the L. Scroop,* H4A I, 3, 271. Merch. III, 5, 77. 79. H6A III, 4, 13. H6B IV, 2, 169. IV, 7, 23. H6C III, 3, 102. IV, 1, 48. 57. R3 III, 2, 3. Tim. III, 2, 13. Hml. I, 3, 89. *the —s of York* etc. R2 II, 3, 55. *L. Angelo,* Meas. I, 1, 25. Merch. III, 4, 39. H5 IV, 8, 99 etc. *—s appealants,* R2 IV, 104 (cf. Lr. III, 7, 18). *l. governor* R2 II, 1, 220. *l. marquess,* H6B I, 1, 63. *l. consul,* Cor. III, 1, 6. *l. governor,* Per. I, 4, 85. *still so constant,* l. Tw. V, 114. *I can speak English,* l. H4A III, 1, 121. 180. IV, 1, 9. *old l., I cannot blame thee,* Tp. III, 3, 4. 34. *it is my l. the duke,* Gent. V, 4, 122. *my l. hath sent you this note,* Meas. IV, 2, 105. Merch. III, 4, 7. All's I, 1, 201. I, 3, 168. IV, 4, 13. IV, 5, 99. Mcb. III, 4, 53 etc. *my young l.* All's III, 2, 3. H4B I, 1, 52. *my l., it shall be done,* Tp. I, 2, 318. II, 1, 22. III, 2, 35. III, 3, 51. Ado IV, 1, 63. Tw. V, 104. H4A II, 3, 10. H4B IV, 3, 87 etc. *my l. Sebastian,* Tp. II, 1, 136. Merch. I, 1, 69. *my l. general,* Cor. I, 9, 81. *I thank my noble l.* Tp. III, 2, 43. *my loving —s,* LLL II, 37. *good morrow, my good —s,* Merch. I, 1, 65. R2 II, 3, 37. H4A I, 2, 179. *my holy l. of Milan,* John V, 2, 120. *good my l.* Tp. II, 1, 186. IV, 204. Gent. II, 7, 50. Meas. I, 1, 48. H4B III, 2, 188 etc. (cf. *Good*).

5) the principal actor in a play: *it is not the fashion to see the lady the epilogue; but it is no more unhandsome than to see the l. the prologue,* As Epil. 3. *A fair l. calf,* LLL V, 2, 248, = a male calf?

Lord, vb., with *it,* = to play the master: *I see them —ing it in London streets,* H6B IV, 8, 47.

Lorded, having become master, invested with power: *he being thus l.* Tp. I, 2, 97.

Lording, 1) little lord, lordling: *you were pretty —s then,* Wint. I, 2, 62. 2) lord: *it was a —'s daughter,* Pilgr. 211. *—s, farewell,* H6B I, 1, 145.

Lordliness, highness, majesty: *doing the honour of thy l. to one so meek,* Ant. V, 2, 161.

Lordly, high, proud; in a good as well as in a bad sense: *his l. crew,* Lucr. 1731. *ay, l. sir,* H6A III, 1, 43. *a l. nation,* III, 3, 62. *the l. monarch of the north,* V, 3, 6. *her l. peers,* H6B I, 1, 11. *your l. lord-protectorship,* II, 1, 30. *the George hath lost his l. honour,* R3 IV, 4, 369 (Qq *holy*).

Lord-protectorship (O. Edd. *Lords Protectorship*), dignity of lord protector: H6B II, 1, 30.

Lordship, 1) state of husband, conjugal right and duty: *ere I will yield my virgin patent up unto his l.* Mids. I, 1, 81. *you fly them* (wives) *as you swear them l.* All's V, 3, 156 (or in both passages = sway, sovereignty?)

2) the dignity of lord, seigniory: *be it a l., thou shalt have it,* H6B IV, 7, 5.

3) title of honor given to noblemen and persons of high rank: Ven. Ded. 1. Lucr. Ded. 1. 6. Gent. I, 3, 4. 25. Meas. II, 1, 143. Ado I, 3, 77. Merch. III, 2, 198. H4B I, 1, 4. H6A III, 1, 56. V, 1, 55. H6C IV, 8, 34. R3 I, 1, 125. III, 2, 8. 56. III, 5, 67 etc.

Lorenzo, name in Merch. I, 1, 58. 103. II, 2, 214. II, 3, 6. II, 6, 1 etc.

Lorraine, see *Loraine.*

Lose (impf. and partic. *lost*) 1) to keep no longer, to discontinue to have in consequence of want of care; opposed to find: *to l. our bottles,* Tp. IV, 208. *a lost mutton,* Gent. I, 1, 101. *a schoolboy that had lost his A B C,* II, 1, 23. *which* (ring) *when you l.* Merch. III, 2, 174. IV, 1, 443. H4A III, 3, 115. Oth. III, 3, 321. III, 4, 60. 80. Cymb. II, 4, 124 etc. etc.

2) to cease to have, in whatever manner; opposed to gain or win; absol.: *and lack not to l. still,* All's I, 3, 210. *where she is sure to l.* 221. *I break, and you l.* H4B V, 5, 129. *we l., they daily get,* H6A IV, 3, 32 etc. trans.: *having no fair to l.* Ven. 1083. *my son is lost,* Tp. II, 1, 109. 131. V, 137. 177. *to l. your hair,* IV, 237. *—ing his verdure,* Gent. I, 1, 49. *if the tied were lost,* II, 3, 41. *l. thy master,* 48. *thy service,* 49. *thy tongue,* 52. *doth l. his form,* III, 2, 8. *I have little wealth to l.* IV, 1, 11. *shall I l. my doctor?* Wiv. III, 1, 104. *this deceit —s the name of craft,* V, 5, 239. *if I do l. thee* (life) Meas. III, 1, 7. H6B IV, 7, 71. H6C III, 2, 7. *to l. his head,* Meas. V, 71; 493; R3 III, 4, 40. Err. II, 1, 110. IV, 3, 97. LLL I, 1, 147 *(so won, so lost).* Mids. III, 2, 27. Merch. I, 1, 140. III, 2, 304. Tw. II, 4, 35. III, 4, 116. V, 66. Wint. III, 2, 96 *(to give lost* = to have no more hope, to despair of). H6C I, 1, 140. H8 I, 1, 41. Hml. III, 2, 411. Ant. II, 6, 43 etc. *to l. one's breath:* Err. IV, 2, 30. Ant. II, 2, 235. *to l. hopes:* Merch. II, 2, 198. H6A IV, 5, 25. Mcb. IV, 3, 24. *to l. one's self:* loan oft *—s both itself and friend,* Hml. I, 3, 76. = to be no longer what one has been, to forfeit one's own nature, to perish:

if I keep them, I needs must l. myself, Gent. II, 6, 20. *we l. ourselves to keep our oaths*, LLL IV, 3, 362. *or l. myself in dotage*, Ant. I, 2, 121. *if I l. mine honour, I l. myself*, III, 4, 23.

3) to be deprived of, to be separated from: *he hath lost his fellows*, Tp. I, 2, 416. *I have played the sheep in —ing him*, Gent. I, 1, 73. *carouse together like friends long lost*, Ant. IV, 12, 13. In a moral sense = to alienate, to act so as to forfeit the favour of: *Julia I l. and Valentine I l.* Gent. II, 6, 19. *neglect me, l. me*, Mids. II, 1, 206. *lost their hearts*, R2 II, 1, 247. *the least of which haunting a noble man —th men's hearts*, H4A III, 1, 187. *l. not so noble a friend on vain suppose*, Tit. I, 440. *he that is approved in this offence, shall l. me*, Oth. II, 3, 213. *the way to l. him*, Ant. I, 3, 10.

4) to have the worst, to be the contrary to the gainer at a game, in a battle, or what is like it; absol.: *a captive victor that hath lost in gain*, Lucr. 730. *they have the wisdom by their wit to lose*, Merch. II, 9, 81. *if he l.* III, 2, 44. *thou shalt not l. by it*, Shr. Ind. 2, 101. John III, 1, 332. 335. R2 II, 2, 81. H6A IV, 3, 31. H6B III, 1, 183. H6C I, 1, 113. Ant. II, 3, 26. Lr. V, 2, 6. 3, 15. Cymb. II, 3, 4. *I follow thus a —ing suit against him*, Merch. IV, 1, 62 (a suit in which the loss is certain). *the first bringer of unwelcome news hath but a —ing office*, H4B I, 1, 101. *I shall have glory by this —ing day*, Caes. V, 5, 36. Trans.: Tp. I, 1, 54. Meas. I, 2, 196. All's I, 1, 137. III, 5, 91. R3 IV, 4, 538. Cor. I, 7, 4. Rom. III, 2, 12. Caes. V, 1, 98. Mcb. I, 1, 4. Hml. V, 2, 219. Lr. V, 1, 18. Ant. IV, 12, 9. Cymb. I, 6, 18 etc. With *to: rather l. her to an African*, Tp. II, 1, 125. *those lands lost by his father to our most valiant brother*, Hml. I, 2, 24.

5) to wander from, to miss: *l. my way among the thorns and dangers of this world*, John IV, 3, 140. Cor. V, 1, 60. Ant. III, 11, 4. *that which all the Parthian darts, though enemy, lost aim*, IV, 14, 71.

6) refl. to wander at random, to go astray: *so I, in quest of them, l. myself*, Err. I, 2, 40. *to l. itself in a fog*, Cor. II, 3, 34. *I have lost myself, I am not here*, Rom. I, 1, 203. *lost* = bewildered: *like one lost in a thorny wood*, H6C III, 2, 174. *lost in the labyrinth of thy fury*, Troil. II, 3, 1. *be not lost so poorly in your thoughts*, Mcb. II, 2, 71. *can you advise me? I am lost in it*, Hml. IV, 7, 55.

7) not to enjoy: *our doubts make us l. the good we oft might win by fearing to attempt*, Meas. I, 4, 78. *that her ear l. nothing of the false sweet bait*, Ado III, 1, 32. *you have lost much good sport*, As I, 2, 105. Alls III, 5, 2. Tw. II, 5, 2. Wint. V, 2, 46. H6B IV, 10, 66. H8 I, 1, 13. Mcb. I, 5, 13.

8) to throw away, not to profit by, to waste: *my pains... all lost*, Tp. IV, 190. All's V, 1, 24. *we shall l. our time*, Tp. IV, 248. Gent. I, 1, 67. All's V, 3, 39. 41. *if lost* (love), Gent. I, 1, 33. *you'll l. the tide*, II, 3, 39. 46. *l. thy voyage*, 47. *shall I not l. my suit?* Wiv. I, 4, 153. *I l. not my labour*, II, 1, 247. Meas. V, 433. Err. V, 97. Mcb. V, 8, 8. *the ploughman lost his sweat*, Mids. II, 1, 94. *I shall l. the grounds I work upon*, All's III, 7, 3. *that breath wilt thou l.* R2 II, 1, 30. *to l. thy youth in peace*, H6B V, 2, 46. *my shoot is lost*, H6C III, 1, 7. *l. no hour*, IV, 1, 148. *the virtues which our divines l. by them*, Cor. II, 3, 64 (*by* = on). *l. your voice*, Hml. I, 2, 45. *'tis a lost fear*, Oth. V, 2, 269 (groundless, vain). *so find we profit by —ing of*

our prayers, Ant. II, 1, 8. *the horse were merely lost*, III, 7, 9.

9) to suffer to vanish from the mind, to forget: *the lesson is but plain, and once made perfect, never lost again*, Ven. 408. *—ing her woes in shows of discontent*, Lucr. 1580. *l. an oath, to win a paradise*, LLL IV, 3, 73. *let us once l. our oaths*, 361. *my mind did l. it*, Mids. I, 1, 114. *l. and neglect the creeping hours of time*, As II, 7, 112. *hear what I say, and then go home and l. me*, H8 II, 1, 57. *what to ourselves in passion we propose, the passion ending, doth the purpose l.* Hml. III, 2, 205 (*forget* in v. 202). Perhaps also in Gent. II, 1, 23 and Mids. II, 1, 206. *I will go l. myself and wander up and down to view the city* Err. I, 2, 30 (i. e. I will try to forget my business and my cares; Germ. ich will mich zerstreuen).

10) to cause to be lost, to cause the loss of: *her eyes had lost her tongue*, Tw. II, 2, 21. *it shall l. thee nothing*, Lr. I, 2, 125 (perhaps also in H4A III, 1, 187; see sub 3). Hence = to ruin: *indent with fears, when they have lost and forfeited themselves*, H4A I, 3, 88. *a woman lost among ye*, H8 III, 1, 107 (= ruined by you). *though his bark cannot be lost*, Mcb. I, 3, 24. *not to have it hath lost me in your liking*, Lr. I, 1, 236. *the foul opinion you had of her pure honour gains or —s your sword or mine*, Cymb. II, 4, 59. *lost* = doomed to ruin: *thou wert but a lost monster*, Tp. IV, 203. *yourself and me cry lost*, Wint. I, 2, 411. *the languishings whereof the king is rendered lost*, All's I, 3, 236. = dead, gone: *lament till I am lost*, Wint. V, 3, 135. *since the cardinal fell, that title's lost*, H8 IV, 1, 96.

Losel, see *Lozel*.

Loser, 1) one who is deprived of what he had before: Oth. II, 3, 272.

2) one who has the worst at a game, in a battle etc.: Merch. II, 7, 77. H4A V, 1, 7. H4B IV, 2, 91. H6B III, 1, 182. 185. Tit. III, 1, 233. Hml. IV, 5, 143.

Loss, 1) privation, the ceasing of possession; absol.: *all —es are restored*, Sonn. 30, 14. *a l. in love that touches me*, 42, 4. *increasing store with l. and l. with store*, 64, 8. Tp. II, 1, 123. 135. IV, 210. V, 140. 143. Merch. III, 1, 96. III, 3, 32. Wint. II, 1, 169. R2 III, 2, 94. 96. H5 III, 6, 134. H6A I, 1, 59. IV, 3, 49. 53. H6C II, 2, 73. Troil. IV, 4, 10. Rom. III, 5, 75. 76. 77. Caes. IV, 3, 151. 193. Used of the slaughter made in battle: John II, 307. H5 IV, 8, 115. *to have a l. or —es*: Ado IV, 2, 87. Merch. III, 1, 45. John III, 4, 99. R3 II, 2, 78. IV, 4, 307. H8 I, 3, 37. *we are enow to do our country l.* H5 IV, 3, 21 (= to cause a great detriment to her). Preceded by the Saxon genit. a) in an obj. sense: *my father's l.* Tp. I, 2, 487. *his sweet life's l.* John IV, 3, 106. H4B I, 1, 121. H6B III, 1, 216. R3 I, 3, 193. 204. Tit. IV, 4, 31. b) in a subj. sense: *this war's l.* John II, 348. *the l. of mine*, Rom. III, 1, 196 (= my loss). *my l.* = a) the l. which I have suffered: Tp. II, 1, 3. Wiv. IV, 6, 5. Meas. IV, 4, 27. Merch. III, 1, 21. 58. IV, 1, 27. Shr. V, 2, 113. All's IV, 3, 77. H5 III, 6, 137. H6A II, 1, 53. H6C II, 3, 26. IV, 6, 15. V, 4, 1. R3 IV, 4, 66. 122. Tim. V, 1, 202. Cymb. I, 1, 120. b) the loss suffered in me: *thus find I by their l. for Valentine myself*, Gent. II, 6, 21. *your l. is great, no l. is known in me*, H6A IV, 5, 22. *Of* following, always objectively: *l. of thee*, Sonn. 90, 14; cf. Pilgr. 94; H6C II, 5, 119; Oth. III, 4, 102. *I hazarded the l. of whom I* *loved*, Err. I, 1, 132. *by the l. of a beard*, Ado III, 2, 49. All's I, 1, 138. III, 6, 59. Wint. V, 2, 81. John III, 1, 206. R2 IV, 196. H4A V, 4, 78. H6A I, 1, 63. V, 4, 112. H6C I, 1, 270. IV, 6, 15. R3 I, 3, 7. 8. Troil. IV, 1, 60. Tit. II, 4, 29. Cymb. V, 5, 70. Per. III Prol. 10. V, 1, 29. Two genitives: *whose l. of his queen*, Wint. IV, 2, 26; cf. H6C IV, 6, 15.

?) the having the worst, failure, defeat, as at ga-ming: *the most patient man in l.* Cymb. II, 3, 2. cf. II, 4, 49. With *of*: *l. of some battle*, H6C IV, 4, 4. *not what is dangerous present, but the l. of what is past,* Cor. III, 2, 71 (that which has already been done amiss). With a genitive: *soul, live thou upon thy ser-vant's l.* Sonn. 146, 9 (at the expense, to the detriment of thy servant, viz the body). *for their advantage and your highness' l.* R2 I, 4, 41. *wherefore grieve I at an hour's l.?* H6B III, 2, 381 (at the mischance of a fleeting moment). With a poss. pron.: *repeat and history his l. to new remembrance,* H4B IV, 1, 203. *their gain and l.* R3 II, 4, 59 (good and bad fortune).

Hence = disparagement, discomfiture, misfortune, overthrow, ruin: *the hopeless merchant of this l.* Lucr. 1660 (= wreck). *though thou repent, yet I have still the l.* Sonn. 34, 10. *one silly cross wrought all my l.* Pilgr. 258. *no l. shall touch her by my company,* Meas. III, 1, 181. *in the l. that may happen,* All's I, 3, 125. *that's the l. of men, though it be the getting of children,* III, 2, 44. *very envy and the tongue of l. cried fame and honour on him,* Tw. V, 61.* *why should that gentle-man give then such instances of l.?* H4B I, 1, 56. *we all that are engaged to this l.* 180. *that you shall read in your own —es,* H5 IV, 4, 139. *tidings were brought me of your l.* H6C II, 1, 110. *our hap is l.* II, 3, 9. *we might recover all our l. again,* V, 2, 30. *pitying my father's l. ... restored me to my honours,* H8 II, 1, 113. *success or l.* Troil. I, 3, 183. *and l. assume all reason,* V, 2, 145. *what l. your honour may sustain,* Hml. I, 3, 29. *to give —es their remedies,* Lr. II, 2, 177. *his life with thine stand in assured l.* III, 6, 102. *the Turkish l.* Oth. II, 1, 32. *rather makes choice of l. than gain which darkens him,* Ant. III, 1, 23. *beguiled me to the very heart of l.* IV, 12, 29. *your l. is as yourself, great,* V, 2, 101. *thou bid'st me to my l.* Cymb. III, 5, 163.

3) the state of not enjoying, not profiting by sth., waste: *but for l. of Nestor's golden words,* Lucr. 1420. *l. of time,* Gent. I, 3, 19. Troil. II, 2, 4. Cor. III, 1, 285.

4) the state of being cast off and discarded: *poor thing, condemned to l.* Wint. II, 3, 192. *that for thy mother's fault art thus exposed to l. and what may fol-low,* III, 3, 51. *he counsels a divorce, a l. of her that like a jewel has hung twenty years about his neck,* H8 II, 2, 31.

5) the state of being at fault, of having lost the trace and scent of the game: *he cried upon it at the merest l.* Shr. Ind. 1, 23 (cf. the modern phrase *to be at a l.*). Hence = embarrassment: *I subscribe not that, nor any other, but in the l. of question,* Meas. II, 4, 90 (as no better arguments present themselves to my mind, to make the point clear).

Lot, 1) a thing used in determining chances: *if we draw —s,* Ant. II, 3, 35. II, 6, 62. 63. Per. I, 4, 46. *as by l.* Hml. II, 2, 435. *it is —s to blanks* = it is very probable, Cor. V, 2, 10.

2) fate: *bequeath not to their l. the shame,* Lucr. 534. *however God or fortune cast my l.* R2 I, 3, 85.

3) a tax ('pars tributi sive solutionis alicujus,

quam inter alios quis tenetur praestare.' Spelman): *that hot termagant Scot had paid me scot and l. too,* H4A V, 4, 115.

Loth, see *Loath.*

Lottery, a game of chance in which lots are drawn: Merch. I, 2, 32. II, 1, 15. All's I, 3, 92. Troil. I, 3, 374. II, 1, 140. *let high-sighted tyranny range on, till each man drop by l.* Caes. II, 1, 119. *Octavia is a blessed l. to him,* Ant. II, 2, 248 (= prize, portion fallen to his share, allotment).

Loud, adj. high sounding, making a great noise, striking the ear with great force: *the l. pursuers* (dogs) Ven. 688. *their l. alarums,* 700. *the bird of —est lay,* Phoen. 1. *they are —er than the weather,* Tp. I, 1, 40. III, 3, 63. Wiv. I, 4, 96. Meas. I, 1, 71. Mids. V, 70. Shr. I, 1, 131. I, 2, 207. John III, 1, 303. H4A III, 2, 53. H4B Prol. 2. 1, 3, 91. IV, 1, 52. 122. H5 IV, 1, 76. H6A II, 2, 43. II, 4, 3. H6B I, 1, 160. H8 IV, 1, 73. Troil. I, 3, 163. 379. IV, 5, 3. 143. Cor. IV, 2, 12. Tit. I, 147. Mcb. V, 3, 27. Lr. II, 4, 43. IV, 7, 25. Ant. II, 7, 115. 139. Cymb. III, 5, 44 (O. Edd. *l. of noise,* M. Edd. *—est noise*). Per. II, 3, 97. III Prol. 3. = high, noisy, boisterous, turbulent: *my arrows, too slightly timbered for so l. a wind,* Hml. IV, 7, 22. *the wind is l.* Per. III, 1, 48. *'tis like to be l. weather,* Wint. III, 3, 11. *lords of this l. day,* John V, 4, 14. *in l. rebellion,* H8 I, 2, 29. *consort with me in l. and dear petition,* Troil. V, 3, 9. *had tongue at will and yet was never l.* Oth. II, 1, 150. *he's embarked with such l. reason to the Cyprus wars,* I, 1, 151. *to the —est* = speaking at the top of the voice: *to be her advocate, to the —est,* Wint. II, 2, 39.

Loud, adv. with a great sound or noise: Wiv. IV, 2, 17. Meas. V, 19. Mids. V, 383. Merch. IV, 1, 140. V, 73. Shr. I, 2, 95. III, 2, 162. V, 1, 16. All's II, 1, 17. Tw. I, 5, 290. III, 4, 4. Wint. III, 3, 103. John V, 2, 170. H4A I, 3, 192. H4B I, 2, 78. II, 4, 381. H6A I, 3, 72. H6B IV, 1, 3. H8 III, 2, 62. Troil. I, 2, 201. I, 3, 256. IV, 5, 275. Rom. V, 1, 57. Hml. I, 2, 218. III, 4, 52. Oth. II, 1, 275. Ant. II, 2, 6. II, 7, 117. III, 4, 17. Cymb. IV, 2, 215. Per. I, 4, 15. V, 1, 200. = in high words: *when we debate our tri-vial difference l.* Ant. II, 2, 21. = audibly, distinctly, urgently: *my griefs cry —er than advertisement,* Ado V, 1, 32. *your desert speaks l.* Meas. V, 9. *proclaim an enshield beauty ten times —er,* II, 4, 80. *such time that ... speaks as l. as his own state,* Ant. I, 4, 29.

Loudly, with a great sound: Hml. V, 2, 411.

Lour, see *Lower.*

Louse, subst. the insect Pediculus: Troil. V, 1, 72. Plur. *—s:* Wiv. I, 1, 19 (Evans' speech).

Louse, vb. to have lice: *the head and he shall l.* Lr. III, 2, 29.

Lousy, extremely low and contemptible: Wiv. III, 3, 256. All's IV, 3, 220. H5 IV, 8, 37. V, 1, 6. 19. 23. H6B IV, 1, 50 (Qq and M. Edd. *lowly*). H8 V, 3, 139.

Lout, subst. an awkward and foolish fellow, a bumpkin: Gent. IV, 4, 71. Wint. I, 2, 301. John II, 509. III, 1, 220. Cor. III, 2, 66. Cymb. V, 2, 9.

Louted, made a fool of: *I am l. by a traitor villain and cannot help the noble chevalier,* H6A IV, 3, 13.

Louvre, the palace of the French kings: H5 II, 4, 132. H8 I, 3, 23.

Love, subst. 1) strong liking, tender attachment,

particularly the passion between the sexes: Ven. 4. 38. 149. 158. 185. 202. 220 etc. etc. Lucr. Ded. 1. Compl. 238. Gent. I, 1, 21. II, 7, 2. Wiv. III, 4, 1. R2 III, 2, 135. R3 IV, 1, 4 etc. etc. *l. is blind,* Merch. II, 6, 36. H5 V, 2, 327 etc. (see below). Plur. *—s;* with reference to several persons, or to several attachments of the same person: *the story of your —s,* Gent. V, 4, 171. *met your —s in their own fashion,* LLL V, 2, 793. 798. Wint. I, 1, 10. John IV, 2, 168. H6C V, 7, 36. Cor. III, 2, 84. Tim. V, 4, 17. Caes. III, 2, 241. Mcb. III, 1, 122. with reference to two persons attached to each other: *our undivided —s are one,* Sonn. 36, 2. *our fathers would applaud our —s,* Gent. I, 3, 48. Ado III, 1, 114. Mids. I, 1, 172. As I, 2, 287. H8 IV, 2, 132. Oth. II, 1, 196. with reference to single persons: *make your —s to me,* Lr. V, 3, 88 (Qq *love). think on thy sins. They are —s I bear to you,* Oth. V, 2, 40 (the later Ff *love). dear l.* Wiv. IV, 6, 9 (cf. *Dear). true l.* (cf. *True)* Sonn. 40, 3. 72, 9. Tp. IV, 84. Gent. IV, 2, 126 etc. *to bear l.* (cf. *Bear):* Tp. I, 2, 141. Gent. III, 1, 166. Wiv. IV, 6, 9. As Epil. 13. 15. Oth. II, 1, 40. V, 2, 40 etc. *to give l.* As III, 5, 89. *to make l.* = to copulate: *making l. over the nasty sty,* Hml. III, 4, 93; with *to,* = to court, to woo: Gent. IV, 2, 126. Wiv. I, 3, 48. Mids. I, 1, 107. Shr. I, 2, 136. Lr. V, 3, 88. *that I to your assistance do make l.* Mcb. III, 1, 124. *they did make l. to this employment,* Hml. V, 2, 57. With *of:* Sonn. 10, 13. Gent. III, 1, 46. III, 2, 30. V, 2, 52. Wiv. V, 5, 7. Ado V, 1, 199. H6C IV, 1, 126. Cor. II, 1, 111. Ant. I, 1, 44 etc. With *to:* Ven. 412. 442. Sonn. 85, 11. Gent. II, 6, 28. III, 2, 48. LLL V, 2, 415. Mids. II, 1, 76. IV, 1, 170. As I, 1, 138. I, 2, 14. H6A II, 4, 121. Lr. I, 2, 17 (*my father's l. is to the bastard Edmund as to the legitimate;* perhaps *is to* = belongs to; see *Be)* etc. With an inf. (= inclination, propensity): *l. to disgrace it,* Ven. 412. *my l.* sometimes = the love borne to me, felt for me: *who shuns thy l. shuns all his l. in me,* All's II, 3, 79. *my l. and fear glued many friends to thee,* H6C II, 6, 5. *for l.* = impelled by kind attachment: *but l., for l., thus shall excuse my jade,* Sonn. 51, 12. *that you for l. speak well of me,* 72, 10. 136, 4. Mids. III, 2, 311. Merch. II, 5, 13. *for the l. of Silvia,* Gent. V, 2, 52. Wiv. V, 5, 7. Ado V, 1, 199. As Epil. 13. 15. H6C IV, 1, 126. *for l. of:* Sonn. 10, 13. *for my l.:* Sonn. 40, 5. Tw. II, 4, 93. III, 4, 347. = for the sake of: *for Collatine's dear l.* Lucr. 821. *for the fault's l. is the offender friended,* Meas. IV, 2, 116. *for your l. I'll take this ring from you,* Merch. IV, 1, 427. As I, 1, 136. Cor. II, 1, 111. Ant. I, 1, 44. *in l.* = a) out of love, moved by tender affection: *in l. of your brother's honour ... you have discovered thus,* Ado II, 2, 37. *in l. unto Demetrius, I told him,* Mids. III, 2, 309. Merch. IV, 1, 429. Troil. IV, 5, 84. b) enamoured: Ven. 438. Sonn. 47, 4. 138, 12. Gent I, 1, 24. II, 1, 17. 32. III, 1, 264. III, 2, 88. Meas. I, 2, 178. LLL I, 2, 60. Merch. I, 1, 46 etc. *in l. with:* Ven. 722. Gent. II, 1, 87. Wiv. I, 4, 110. Ado II, 3, 244. LLL I, 1, 62. Mids. II, 1, 260. III, 2, 6. Tw. II, 3, 180. Wint. IV, 4, 233. H4A V, 4, 106 etc. *to fall in l.* Gent. I, 2, 2. *to fall in l. with:* Ado II, 1, 397. V, 2, 61. Cor. I, 5, 22 etc. *my spirit grows heavy in l.* LLL I, 2, 127 (Armado's speech); cf. *my grief in l.* As III, 5, 88. *grew so in l. with the wenches' song,* Wint. IV, 4, 618. *sick in l. with Beatrice,* Ado III, 1, 21. *out of l.,* the con-

trary to it, = no more in l., disinclined to: *to make my master out of l. with thee,* Gent. IV, 4, 210. *I am so out of l. with life,* Meas. III, 1, 174. As IV, 1, 35. H4B II, 2, 14. *of all —s,* a kind adjuration: *Mistress Page would desire you to send her your little page, of all —s,* Wiv. II, 2, 119. *speak, of all —s,* Mids. II. 2, 154. *he desires you, of all —s, to make no more noise,* Oth. III, 1, 13 (Ff *for love's sake).* — Abstr. pro concr., = a person in love: *the prince and Monsieur L.* Ado II, 3, 38. As III, 2, 310. *like true, inseparable, faithful —s,* John III, 4, 66.

2) a kindness, a favour done: *what good l. may I perform to you?* John IV, 1, 49. *and get her l. to part,* Ant. I, 2, 186 (induce her to show me kindness at my departure. Most M. Edd. *leave). if I cannot win you to this l.* Per. II, 4, 49. [Meas. II, 3, 40*].

4) that which is cherished: *take all my —s,* Sonn. 40, 1. *his —s are brazen images of canonized saints,* H6B I, 3, 62. = a person beloved; a) masc. a lover, a paramour: *she hears no tidings of her l.* Ven. 867. *some l. of yours hath writ to you,* Gent. I, 2, 79. II, 7, 36. *to search his house for his wife's l.* Wiv. III, 5, 79. Lucr. 1193. Sonn. 144, 1. Wiv. V, 5, 122. Err. II, 2, 127. LLL I, 2, 126. V, 2, 134. John III, 4, 35. R3 IV, 4, 355 (Ff *low).* Rom. II, 4, 43. Hml. III, 2, 257. a friend: Sonn. 13, 1. 13. 19, 9. 40, 1. 63, 1. 66, 14. *whether Bassanio had not once a l.* Merch. IV, 1, 277. b) mistress: Ven. 287. 307. 317. 393. 397. Tp. V, 172. Gent. I, 1, 4. III, 1, 244. 250. IV, 2, 99. 105. IV, 3, 20. Mids. I, 1, 84 etc.

5) the god of love, Cupid: Ven. 123. 243. 947.* Sonn. 137, 1. 153, 9. Gent. I, 1, 39. II, 1, 76. II, 4, 95. 96. II, 7, 11. IV, 2, 46. IV, 4, 201. Mids. I, 1, 238. All's I, 3, 117. II, 3, 81. H5 V, 2, 320 etc. Hence the appellative sometimes used as a masc.: *herself hath taught her l. himself to write unto her lover,* Gent. II, 1, 174. *though l. use reason for his precisian, he admits him not for his counsellor,* Wiv. II, 1, 5. *if lusty l. should go in quest of beauty, where should he find it fairer,* John II, 426 (Usually neuter: Ven. 155. 409. 1136. Gent. IV, 2, 19 etc. etc.).

6) the goddess of love, Venus: *love-sick L.* Ven. 328. *she's L.* 610. *to which —'s eyes pay tributary gazes,* 632. *leaves L. upon her back,* 814. *your Dian was both herself and L.* All's I, 3, 219. *therefore do doves draw L.* Rom. II, 5, 7. Hence the appellative feminine: *l. lacked a dwelling and made him her place,* Compl. 82. *let l., being light, be drowned if she sink,* Err. III, 2, 52. *forerun fair l., strewing her way with flowers,* LLL IV, 3, 380. *I should not deal in her soft laws,* H6C III, 2, 154. *for the l. of l. and her soft hours,* Ant. I, 1, 44.

Love, vb. 1) to be tenderly affected towards a person; absol. = to be in love: *she cannot choose but l.* Ven. 79. 202. 407. 610. Gent. I, 1, 9. IV, 3, 18 etc. etc. Gerund: *tell my —ing tale,* Lucr. 480 (the tale of my love). R3 IV, 4, 359. *most friendship is feigning, most —ing mere folly,* As II, 7, 181. *thy —ing voyage is but for two months victualled,* V, 4, 197. Unintelligible passage: *who, as others do, —s for his own ends, not for you,* Mcb. III, 5, 13 (Halliwell *lives;* perhaps *looks).*

Partic. *—ing,* adjectively, = kind, affectionate, friendly: *there reigns love and all love's —ing parts,* Sonn. 31, 3. *did us but —ing wrong,* Tp. I, 2, 151. *my —ing Proteus,* Gent. I, 1, 1. II, 7, 7. *to tear such —ing* *words,* I, 2, 105. *my —ing lord,* LLL I, 1, 28. II, 37. *in —ing visitation,* Merch. IV, 1, 153 (not for business). *three or four —ing lords have put themselves into voluntary exile with him,* As I, 1, 106. *my —ing subjects,* John II, 203. *most —ing liege,* R2 I, 1, 21. *a —ing farewell,* l, 3, 51. *by a lower but —ing likelihood,* H5 V Chor. 29. *your —ing nephew now is come,* H6A II, 5, 33. *my friends and —ing countrymen,* III, 1, 137. *O —ing uncle,* 142. H6B III, 2, 268. 280. H6C II, 1, 47. 180. III, 2, 59. IV, 1, 53. IV, 8, 19. V, 7, 32. R3 III, 1, 96. III, 5, 54. V, 3, 6 (Qq *gracious*). H8 II, 1, 92. Troil. IV, 4, 77 (M. Edd. *they 're —ing;* Q om.; F1 *their —ing*). IV, 5, 155. Rom. I, 1, 198 (*—ing tears;* the spurious Q1 and M. Edd. *lovers' tears*). Caes. III, 1, 127. Lr. I, 1, 43. V, 1, 20. With *to: so —ing to my mother,* Hml. I, 2, 140.

Trans.: Ven. 77. 433. 610. 660. Tp. I, 1, 22. I, 2, 69. 336. II, 1, 294. II, 2, 50. III, 1, 67. 73. III, 3, 93. IV, 48 etc. etc. Peculiar expressions: *fortune l. you,* Lr. V, 1, 46 (cf. Cor. I, 5, 21). *—ing his own pride and purposes,* Oth. I, 1, 12. *for wisdom's sake, a word that all men love, or for love's sake, a word that —s all men,* LLL IV, 3, 358 (according to commentators, = is pleasing to all men; which is very improbable. Strained and obscure as the expression has become by the antithesis, it can only mean: a word for a thing that affects all men).

2) to like, to be pleased with: *hunting he —d,* Ven. 4. *his rider —d not speed,* Sonn. 50, 8. *'tis the lesser sin that mine eye —s it,* 114, 14. *whose shadow the dismissed bachelor —s,* Tp. IV, 67. *some book I l.* Gent. I, 1, 20. *I l. crusts,* III, 1, 346. Wiv. I, 1, 302. Err. II, 2, 8. Ado II, 1, 283. Merch. IV, 1, 47. As IV, 1, 4. Shr. Ind. 2, 51. IV, 1, 167. All's IV, 5, 50. John V, 4, 50. H6B II, 1, 101. Troil. I, 2, 146. Cor. II, 1, 52. Caes. V, 1, 28. Mcb. I, 6, 5 (*his —d mansionry*). Hml. II, 2, 467 etc. With an inf.: *I l. to hear her speak,* Sonn. 130, 9. *age in love —s not to have years told,* 138, 12. *a villain I do not l. to look on,* Tp. I, 2, 310. *I l. to walk by the Countergate,* Wiv. III, 3, 84. LLL I, 1, 176. As II, 1, 67. II, 5, 2. 41. Shr. IV, 3, 24. All's III, 4, 28. H6B II, 1, 11. Tim. I, 1, 232. Caes. II, 1, 203 etc.

3) to love each other, to be tenderly attached to each other: *never two ladies —d as they do,* As I, 1, 117. *they —d well when they were alive,* H6B IV, 7, 139. *l. and be friends,* Caes. IV, 3, 131. *you and I have —d,* Ant. I, 3, 88. *better might we have —d,* III, 2, 32 (cf. *Embrace, Greet, Hug, Kiss, Know, Kill, Look, See* etc.).

Love-affairs: Gent. III, 1, 254.

Love-bed, a bed for the indulgence of lust: *he is not lolling on a lewd l.* R3 III, 7, 72 (Qq *day-bed*).

Love-book, a book treating of love: Gent. I, 1, 19.

Love-broker, one who acts as agent between lovers, a procurer: *there is no l. in the world can more prevail with woman than report of valour,* Tw. III, 2, 39.

Love-cause, love-affair: *not any man died in his own person, videlicet, in a l.* As IV, 1, 97.

Love-day, a day appointed for the settlement of quarrels and differences: Tit. I, 491.

Love-devouring, making an end of love: *l. death,* Rom. II, 6, 7.

Love-discourse, a conversation about love: Gent. II, 4, 127.

Love-feat, exploit prompted by love: *and every one his l. will advance,* LLL V, 2, 123.

Love-god, the god of love, Cupid: Sonn. 154, 1. Ado II, 1, 402.

Love-in-idleness, the flower Viola tricolor: Mids. II, 1, 168. cf. Shr. I, 1, 156.

Love-juice, a juice producing love: Mids. III, 2, 37. 89.

Love-kindling, exciting love: Sonn. 153, 3.

Lovel, name of 1) a friend and assistant of Richard III: R3 III, 4, 80. III, 5, 21. 103. 2) Sir Thomas L.: R3 IV, 4, 520. H8 I, 2, 185. I, 3, 16. I, 4, 10. II, 1, 82. V, 1, 10. 30. 61. 171.

Love-lacking, void of love: Ven. 752.

Loveless, not loved: *to leave the master l.* Pilgr. 216.

Love-letters, letters of courtship: Gent. III, 1, 391. Wiv. II, 1, 1.

Love-line, a verse or letter of courtship: *write to her a l.* All's II, 1, 81.

Loveliness, a quality exciting love, attraction: *l. in favour,* Oth. II, 1, 232. Abstr. pro concr.: *unthrifty l., why dost thou spend upon thyself thy beauty's legacy?* Sonn. 4, 1. In All's I, 3, 177 O. Edd. *loveliness,* most M. Edd. *loneliness,* some *lowliness.*

Lovely (comp. *—er:* R3 I, 2, 243. Cor. I, 3, 44), 1) charming, attractive: Ven. 9. 247. Sonn. 3, 10. 5, 2. 18, 2. 54, 13. 79, 5. 95, 1. 106, 4 (*l. knights*). 126, 1. Pilgr. 44. Gent. I, 2, 19 (*l. gentlemen*). IV, 4, 191. Meas. V, 496. Ado IV, 1, 132. 228. LLL IV, 1, 62. Mids. I, 2, 89. II, 1, 22. II, 2, 18. III, 1, 97. III, 2, 211. V, 175. Merch. II, 6, 45. Shr. Ind. 2, 67. III, 2, 94. IV, 5, 33. 41. John II, 425. III, 4, 25. H4A I, 3, 175. H5 IV, 1, 48. V, 2, 37. H6A V, 5, 12. H6B I, 4, 77. IV, 4, 15. H6C II, 5, 41. V, 7, 26. R3 I, 2, 243. I, 3, 192. H8 V, 1, 166. Cor. I, 3, 44. Tit. I, 315. 334. II, 1, 113. II, 2, 4. II, 3, 10. 190. II, 4, 40. IV, 2, 7. IV, 4, 27 (*my l. Saturnine*). Rom. I, 2, 70. III, 5, 220 (*a l. gentleman*).

Adverbially: *I framed to the harp many an English ditty l. well,* H4A III, 1, 124. *so l. fair,* Oth. IV, 2, 68.

2) loving, tender: *a l. kiss,* Shr. III, 2, 125.

Love-monger, one who deals in affairs of love: LLL II, 254.

Love-news, a communication from a beloved person: Merch. II, 4, 14.

Love-performing, ministering to the works of love: *l. night,* Rom. III, 2, 5.

Love-prate, trifling talk about love: As IV, 1, 206.

Lover, 1) one loving, one kindly disposed: *I shall prove a l. of thy drum, hater of love,* All's III, 3, 11. *a true l. of the holy church,* H5 I, 1, 23. Hence = friend: *my —s gone,* Sonn. 31, 10. *thy deceased l.* 32, 4. *my —'s l.* 63, 12. *thy —'s withering,* 126, 4. *how dear a l. of my lord your husband,* Merch. III, 4, 7. *Antonio, the bosom l. of my lord,* 17. *they are the drops of thy —s,* H4B IV, 3, 14. *no great good l. of the archbishop's,* H8 IV, 1, 104. *I as your l. speak,* Troil. III, 3, 214. *thy general is my l.* Cor. V, 2, 14. *thy l. Artemidorus,* Caes. II, 3, 9. *Romans, countrymen, and —s,* III, 2, 13. *I slew my best l.* 49. *—s in peace,* V, 1, 95.

2) one enamoured, a person in love; absol.: *—s*

say, the heart hath treble wrong when it is barred the aidance of the tongue, Ven. 329. *like a lowly l. down she kneels,* 350. 573. Pilgr. 101. 233. Gent. II, 2, 21. II, 4, 97. II, 5, 44. III, 1, 41. 246. IV, 2, 13. V, 1, 4. Ado I, 1, 308. Mids. I, 1, 150. 223. III, 2, 452. Merch. II, 6, 4. As II, 4, 26. II, 7, 147. III, 2, 246. Troil. III, 1, 131. Cymb. III, 2, 36 etc. etc. *—s* = an amorous couple: Tp. IV, 86. Mids. V, 160. 165. Tw. II, 3, 44. Rom. Prol. 6. Oth. I, 3, 200. III, 4, 174. Used of the part of the amoroso in a play: *what is Pyramus? a l. or a tyrant?* Mids. I, 2, 24. *the l. shall not sigh gratis,* Hml. II, 2, 335. Relatively, a) one in love with: *and send you many —s,* LLL II, 126. *to mock our —s,* V, 2, 58. *thy l.* Mids. V, 197. *the l. of any other,* As III, 2, 403. *a l. of mine and a l. of hers,* V, 2, 82. *had she no l. there,* Troil. IV, 5, 288. b) one tied to another by love, one beloved; masc.: *to write unto her l.* Gent. II, 1, 174. Mids. I, 2, 55. III, 1, 206 (M. Edd. *love's*). V, 319. H5 II, 4, 108. Ant. V, 2, 298. fem. = mistress: *carrying a letter to your l.* Gent. I, 1, 116. *your brother and his l. have embraced,* Meas. I, 4, 40. *the heart of his l.* As III, 4, 46. *as to a —'s bed,* Ant. IV, 14, 101. *had a royal l.* Cymb. V, 5, 172.

Lovered: *so l.* = having such a lover, Compl. 320.

Love-rhymes, erotic poetry in rhymes: LLL III, 183.

Love-shaft, Cupid's arrow: Mids. II, 1, 159.

Love-shaked, shaken with an amorous fever: As III, 2, 385.

Love-sick, languishing with amorous desire: Ven. 175. 328. Tit. V, 2, 83. *so perfumed that the winds were l. with them,* Ant. II, 2, 199 (*with* = by).

Love-song, a song treating of love: Gent. II, 1, 20. As III, 2, 277. Tw. II, 3, 36. 38. Wint. IV, 4, 193. Rom. II, 4, 15.

Love-springs, the tender shoots and buds of love: *shall even in the spring of love thy l. rot?* Err. III, 2, 3.

Love-suit, courtship, a lover's solicitation: Sonn. 136, 4. H5 V, 2, 101. Cymb. III, 4, 136.

Love-thoughts, amorous fancies: Tw. I, 1, 41.

Love-tokens, presents given in token of love: Mids. I, 1, 29.

Love-wounded, wounded by Cupid's arrow: Gent. I, 2, 113.

Loving-jealous, fondly suspicious: *so l. of his liberty,* Rom. II, 2, 182.

Lovingly, kindly, affectionately: Tit. I, 165.

Low, adj. 1) depressed below some given or imagined station, deep: *the eyes converted are from his* (the sun's) *l. tract,* Sonn. 7, 12. *this —er world,* Tp. III, 3, 54, i. e. the earth; cf. R2 III, 2, 38. *a high hope for a l. heaven,* LLL I, 1, 196. *with a l. submissive reverence,* Shr. Ind. 1, 53; cf. H5 IV, 1, 272. *thou wert best set thy —er part where thy nose stands,* All's II, 3, 267. *in as l. an ebb,* H4A I, 2, 41; H4B II, 2, 22. *the valleys, whose l. vassal seat,* H5 III, 5, 51. *bear so l. a sail to strike to thee,* H6C V, 1, 52. *at the —er end of the hall,* R3 III, 7, 35. *you have gone slightly o'er l. steps,* H8 II, 4, 112. *in the —est hell,* Cor. III, 3, 68. *thy l. grave,* Tim. V, 4, 79. *till the —est stream kiss the most exalted shores,* Caes. I, 1, 64. *you petty spirits of region l.* Cymb. V, 4, 93. *the*

ground's the —est, Per. I, 4, 78. *l. Dutch,* All's IV, 1, 78. *thy l. countries,* H4B II, 2, 25. *—er Syria,* Ant. III, 6, 10.

2) not rising far upward, of little height or size, small, diminutive: *l. shrubs wither at the cedar's root,* Lucr. 665; cf. H6C V, 2, 15. *with foreheads villanous l.* Tp. IV, 250; cf. Gent. IV, 4, 198 and Ant. III, 3, 36. *sitting in a —er chair,* Meas. II, 1, 132 (there were such in every house for the ease of sick people). *she's too l. for a high praise,* Ado I, 1, 173; cf. III, 1, 65; Mids. III, 2, 295; 296; 297; 304; 305; As IV, 3, 88. *whose roof's as l. as ours,* Cymb. III, 3, 2.

3) not elevated in rank or station, mean: *l. vassals to thy state,* Lucr. 666. *too l. a mistress for so high a servant,* Gent. II, 4, 106. LLL I, 1, 194. Merch. II, 9, 46. As II, 3, 68. All's I, 2, 43. II, 1, 200. II, 3, 132. Wint. I, 2, 227. H4B III, 1, 30. H5 I, 2, 180. V, 1, 38. R3 I, 4, 82. Cor. I, 1, 161. Oth. II, 3, 97. Ant. III, 1, 12. Cymb. III, 5, 76 (*the l. Posthumus*). Per. II, 3, 26. Substantively: *too high to be enthralled to l.* Mids. I, 1, 136. Especially when joined with high: *high and l.* Wiv. I, 3, 95. II, 1, 117. Wint. V, 1, 207. Tim. IV, 1, 40. Mcb. IV, 1, 67. Cymb. IV, 2, 249. *from high to l.* Tim. V, 1, 212.

4) humble, mean, base (in a good and bad sense): *in l. simplicity he lends out money gratis,* Merch. I, 3, 44. *out of my lean and l. ability,* Tw. III, 4, 378. *l. desires,* H4A III, 2, 12. *a l. transformation,* H4B II, 2, 194. *by a —er, but loving likelihood,* H5 V Chor. 29. *I, her sovereign, am her subject l.* R3 IV, 4, 355 (Qq *love*). *your purposed l. correction,* Lr. II, 2, 149. *l. farms,* II, 3, 17. *thy mind to her is now as l. as were thy fortunes,* Cymb. III, 2, 10. *in simple and l. things to prince it,* III, 3, 85.

5) in reduced circumstances, brought down: *misery is trodden on by many, and being l. never relieved by any,* Ven. 708. *my creditors grow cruel, my estate is very l.* Merch. III, 2, 319. *this posting must wear your spirits l.* All's V, 1, 2. *journey-bated and brought l.* H4A IV, 3, 26 (or adv.?); cf. Tit. III, 2, 76 and Tim. IV, 2, 37. *sick in the world's regard, wretched and l.* H4A IV, 3, 57. *it is not so l. with him,* Tim. III, 6, 6. *the —est and most dejected thing of fortune,* Lr. IV, 1, 3. *if that ever my l. fortune's better,* Per. II, 1, 148.

6) of no high rate or amount: *falls under abatement and l. price,* Tw. I, 1, 13. *high and l. beguiles the rich and poor,* Wiv. I, 3, 95 (i. e. at dice).

7) of a deep and depressed sound: *in clamours of all size, both high and l.* Compl. 21. *you would sound me from my —est note to the top of my compass,* Hml. III, 2, 383.

8) not loud: *a lover's ear will hear the —est sound,* LLL IV, 3, 335. *with soft l. tongue,* Shr. Ind. 1, 114. *whose l. sound reverbs no hollowness,* Lr. I, 1, 155. *her voice was ever soft, gentle, and l.* V, 3, 273. *is she shrill-tongued or l.?* Ant. III, 3, 15 (perhaps adv., belonging to *tongued*).

Low, adv. 1) a great way down: *if those hills be dry, stray —er,* Ven. 234. *the homely villain courtsies to her l.* Lucr. 1338. *—er, —er!* Tp. I, 1, 37. *I did not look so l.* Err. III, 2, 143. *she is hit —er,* LLL IV, 1, 120. V, 2, 707. Merch. I, 1, 28. I, 3, 124. John V, 4, 55. R2 I, 1, 124. III, 3, 195. V, 2, 19. H4A II, 2, 63. H6B I, 2, 15. H6C I, 4, 94. H8 IV, 2, 76. Rom. III, 5, 55 (*so l.;* the spurious Q1 and M. Edd. *below*). Caes. III, 1, 56. Hml. II, 2, 519. Lr.

IV, 6, 12. Oth. II, 1, 190. Per. I, 2, 47. *to lay l.* = to lay in the grave, to bury: John II, 164. Rom. V, 1, 20. *to lie l.* = to be struck down: Ado V, 1, 52. R2 III, 2, 140. H4A III, 3, 228. Caes. III, 1, 148. *stooped his anointed head as l. as death*, H4B Ind. 32.

2) in or to a mean station and condition: *ne'er settled equally, but high or l.* Ven. 1139. *pardon me that I descend so l.* H4A I, 3, 167. *that I may conquer fortune's spite by living l.* H6C IV, 6, 20.

3) in a deep and depressed sound: *that can sing both high and l.* Tw. II, 3, 42.

4) not loudly: Meas. IV, 1, 69. Ado II, 1, 103. H4B II, 3, 26. IV, 4, 129. IV, 5, 15. H5 IV, 1, 66. 82.

Low, subst. the bellowing of a bull: *bull Jove had an amiable l.* Ado V, 4, 48.

Low, vb. to cry as an ox or cow, to bellow: Tp. IV, 179. H6B III, 1, 214.

Low, interj. see *Loo.*

Low-born, of mean birth: Wint. IV, 4, 156.

Low-crooked, bent, bowing deep: *l. courtesies,* Caes. III, 1, 43.

Low-declined, fallen, sunk deep: *my l. honour,* Lucr. 1705.

Lower, vb. to sink, to grow less: *the present pleasure, by revolution —ing,* Ant. I, 2, 129.

Lower or **Lour,** vb. to frown, to look sullen: Ven. 75. 183. Err. II, 1, 86. R2 I, 3, 187. H6B III, 1, 206. Rom. II, 5, 6. With *on* or *upon,* to mark the object: Sonn. 149, 7. R3 I, 1, 3. V, 3, 283. Rom. IV, 5, 94. With *at,* to mark the cause: *why at our justice seemest thou then to l.?* R2 I, 3, 235.

Low-laid, struck to the ground: *your l. son our godhead will uplift,* Cymb. V, 4, 103.

Lowliness, 1) mean condition: *thou the beggar; for so witnesseth thy l.* LLL IV, 1, 81. *witness the night, your garments, your l.* H5 IV, 8, 55.

2) freedom from pride, meekness, humility: *with as humble l. of mind,* H6A V, 5, 18. *l. is young ambition's ladder,* Caes. II, 1, 22. *the king-becoming graces, ... as mercy, l., devotion,* Mcb. IV, 3, 93.

Lowly, adj. 1) deep, declining: *thy sun sets weeping in the l. west,* R2 II, 4, 21.

2) brought down, enfeebled: *as looks the mother on her l. babe when death doth close his tender dying eyes,* H6A III, 3, 47 (see *Low* 5).

3) humble: *like a l. beggar down she kneels,* Ven. 350. *with soft low tongue and l. courtesy,* Shr. Ind. I, 114. *l. words were ransom for their fault,* H6B III, 1, 127.

4) mean, base: *banish these abject l. dreams,* Shr. Ind. 2, 34. *l. feigning was called compliment,* Tw. III, 1, 110. *poor l. maid,* Wint. IV, 4, 9. *obscure and l. swain,* H6B IV, 1, 50 (Ff *lousy*). 111. *l. factor for another's gain,* R3 III, 7, 134. *these l. courtesies,* Caes. III, 1, 36.

Lowly, adv. meanly, in a mean condition: *highly fed and l. taught,* All's II, 2, 3. *to be l. born,* H8 II, 3, 19.

Lown (cf. *Loon*), a base fellow: *he called the tailor l.* Oth. II, 3, 95. *we should have both lord and l.* Per. IV, 6, 19.

Lowness, 1) small elevation, the state of being below the ordinary level: *they know by the height, the l., or the mean, if dearth or foison follow,* Ant. II, 7, 22.

2) reduced circumstances, abject condition: *nothing could have subdued nature to such a l. but his unkind daughters,* Lr. III, 4, 73.

3) meanness: *dodge and palter in the shifts of l.* Ant. III, 11, 63.

Low-rated, despised: H5 IV Chor. 19.

Low-spirited, in the language of Armado, = base: LLL I, 1, 250.

Low-tongued, speaking not loudly: *shrill-tongued or low?* Ant. III, 3, 15 (i. e. shrill-tongued or low-tongued).

Low-voiced, the same: Ant. III, 3, 16.

Lowt and **Lowted,** see *Lout* and *Louted.*

Loyal, (superl. *loyallest,* Cymb. I, 1, 96) duteous, faithful to obligations; as a subject: Wiv. V, 5, 68. Wint. II, 3, 54. R2 I, 1, 148. 181. I, 3, 87. II, 3, 98. V, 3, 60. H5 I, 2, 127. H6A III, 1, 182. H6B II, 4, 63. III, 1, 96. H6C IV, 7, 44. R3 I, 4, 172. II, 1, 91. H8 III, 2, 180. 200. Cor. V, 6, 142. Mcb. II, 3, 115. IV, 3, 83. Cymb. IV, 3, 16. as a husband or wife, or lover: Lucr. 261. 1034. 1048. Phoen. 57. Tw. I, 5, 289. Oth. IV, 2, 35. Cymb. I, 1, 96. III, 4, 83. as a son: Lr. II, 1, 86. IV, 2, 7. With *to:* Tp. V, 69. Gent. III, 2, 20. John II, 271. H4A III, 2, 43. Cymb. III, 2, 47.

Loyally, dutifully, faithfully: Cymb. IV, 3, 19.

Loyalty, dutifulness, fidelity; in love: Gent. IV, 2, 7. Mids. II, 2, 63. Tit. II, 3, 125. Cymb. I, 6, 102. in the condition of a subject: R2 I, 1, 67. H4A IV, 1, 64. H5 II, 2, 5. H6A III, 4, 10. H6B III, 1, 203. III, 2, 250. V, 1, 166. H6C III, 3, 239. 240. R3 III, 3, 4. H8 I, 2, 28. III, 2, 177. Mcb. I, 4, 22. Lr. III, 5, 4. 23. Cymb. V, 5, 344. Per. V, 3, 92. of a servant: As II, 3, 70. Plur. —*s: flawed the heart of all their —s,* H8 I, 2, 22. With *to:* Gent. IV, 2, 7. R2 I, 3, 19. Ant. III, 13, 42. With *toward:* H8 III, 2, 272.

Lozel, a faint-hearted cowardly fellow: *l., thou art worthy to be hanged, that wilt not stay her tongue,* Wint. II, 3, 109.

Lubber, a heavy fellow, a looby: Gent. II, 5, 47. Tw. IV, 1, 14. Troil. III, 3, 139. Lr. I, 4, 101. Mrs. Quickly says —'*s head* for *Libbard's head* in H4B II, 1, 30.

Lubberly, clumsy, churlish: *a l. boy,* Wiv. V, 5, 195.

Luccicos (some M. Edd. *Lucchese*) name in Oth. I, 3, 44.

Luce, name of a female servant in Err. III, 1, 49. 53.

Luce, a pike, or = flower-de-luce? Wiv. I, 1, 16. 22. The commentators make no doubt to have here an allusion to the armorial bearings of the pretended old enemy of the poet, Sir Thomas Lucy, i. e. three, or, as others say, a dozen white pikes. But cf. Holinshed's continuation of the Chronicles of Ireland (quoted by Rushton): "Having lent the king his signet to seal a letter, who having powdered erinuts ingrailed in the seal; Why how now Wise (quoth the king) what, hast thou lice here? And if it like your majesty, quoth Sir William, a louse is a rich coat, for by giving the louse I part arms with the French king, in that he giveth the flower de lice. Whereat the king heartily laughed, to hear how prettily so biting a taunt was suddenly turned to so pleasant a conceit." It must be remembered that Sh. was a diligent reader of Holinshed).

Lucentio, name in Shr. I, 1, 221 and passim. Rom. I, 5, 37.

Lucetta, attendant of Julia in Gent. I, 2, 1. 60. II, 7, 1 etc.

Luciana, female name in Err. II, 1, 3. IV, 2, 1.

Lucianus, name in Hml. III, 2, 254.

Lucifer, Satan: Wiv. I, 3, 84. II, 2, 311. John IV, 3, 122. H4A II, 4, 371. H4B II, 4, 360. H5 IV, 7, 145. H8 III, 2, 371 (*he falls like L., never to hope again*).

Lucilius, name in Tim. I, 1, 111. 114. Caes. IV, 2, 3 and passim.

Lucina, the goddess who assisted women in labour: Cymb. V, 4, 43. Per. I, 1, 8. III, 1, 10.

Lucio, name: Meas. I, 2, 129 and passim. Rom. I, 2, 73.

Lucius, name of 1) L. Tarquinius: Lucr. Arg. 1. 2) a son of Titus Andronicus': Tit. I. 282 etc. 3) a lord in Tim. I, 2, 187 etc. (his servant assuming his name in III, 4, 2). 4) L. Pella: Caes. IV, 3, 2. 5) a servant of Brutus: Caes. II, 1, 1 etc. 6) the brother of Antony: Ant. I, 2, 94. 7) the Roman ambassador in Cymb. II, 3, 60 etc.

Luck, 1) fortune, good or bad: *good or evil l.* Sonn. 14, 3. *good l.* Wiv. III, 5, 84. V, 1, 2. V, 5, 61. Mids. I, 1, 221. II, 1, 41. Wint. III, 3, 69. H5 IV, 3, 11. R3 IV, 4, 402. *better l.* H8 V, 1, 136. *ill l.* Wiv. V, 5, 120. Merch. III, 1, 99. 102. 104. H4B I, 1, 51. *bad l.* H4B I, 1, 41. *worse l.* All's II, 2, 59. *hard l.* Wint. V, 2, 158. *lean l.* Err. III, 2, 93.

2) without an adj., good fortune: *if it be my l.* Wiv. III, 4, 67. *if we have unearned l. now to scape the serpent's tongue,* Mids. V, 439. *as if that l. bade him win all,* Troil. V, 5, 41. *of that natural l., he beats thee,* Ant. II, 3, 26. *mock the l. of Caesar,* V, 2, 289. *was there ever man had such l.!* Cymb. II, 1, 1 (Cloten is speaking of his adversary).

Luckily, fortunately: H4A V, 4, 33.

Luckless, unfortunate: H6C II, 6, 18. V, 6, 45.

Lucky, fortunate: *—er issue,* Ado V, 3, 32. *—est stars,* All's I, 3, 252. *we are l.* Wint. III, 3, 129. *a l. day,* 142. *l. joys,* H4B V, 3, 99 (Pistol's speech). *a l. war,* H5 II, 2, 184. *ruler,* H6B III, 1, 291. *when mine hours were nice and l.* Ant. III, 13, 180.

Lucre, avidity, thirst of gain: *'tis he and Cloten: malice and l. in them have laid this woe here,* Cymb. IV, 2, 324. With *of*: *shall I, for l. of the rest unvanquished, detract so much from that prerogative,* H6A V, 4, 141 (of avidity; cf. V 10).

Lucrece (in Lucr. 6. 512 and Tit. II, 1, 108 *Lucréce*. Genitive *Lucrece*), the wife of Collatine: Lucr. Arg. 12. Lucr. 7. 36. 64. 123. 182. 381 etc. Shr. II, 298. Tw. II, 5, 104. 116. Tit. II, 1, 108. IV, 1, 64. 91.

Lucretia, the same: Lucr. Arg. 7. Lucr. 317. 510. As III, 2, 156.

Lucretius, father of Lucrece: Lucr. 1751. 1773.

Lucullus, name in Tim. I, 2, 193. II, 2, 197 etc.

Lucy, name of 1) Sir William Lucy: H6A IV, 3, 43. IV, 4, 10. 2) Lady L.: R3 III, 7, 5. 179.

Lud's town, ancient name of London: Cymb. III, 1, 32. IV, 2, 99. 123. V, 5, 481.

Ludlow, town in England: R3 II, 2, 121. 142. 154.

Lug, to drag, to pull: *this will l. your priests and servants from your sides,* Tim. IV, 3, 31. *I'll l. the guts into the neighbour room,* Hml. III, 4, 212. *a —ed bear,* H4A I, 2, 83; cf. *Head-lugged.*

Luggage, any thing cumbersome to be carried: *to dote thus on such l.* Tp. IV, 231. *bestow your l. where you found it,* V, 298. *bring your l. on your back,* H4A V, 4, 160. = the baggage of an army: H5 IV, 4, 80. IV, 7, 1.

Luke, name of the third evangelist: *Saint —'s church,* Shr. IV, 4, 88. *to Saint —'s,* Meas. III, 1, 276. Shr. IV, 4, 103.

Lukewarm, tepid: H6C I, 2, 34. Tim. III, 6, 99.

Lull, to compose to sleep by pleasing sounds: Mids. II, 1, 254. H4B III, 1, 14. Cor. III, 2, 115. Tit. IV, 1, 99. In R3 III, 7, 72 O. Edd. *—ing,* M. Edd. *lolling.*

Lullaby, a word spoken or rather sung in composing babes to sleep: *Philomel, with melody sing in our sweet l.; lulla, lulla, lullaby,* Mids. II, 2, 14. 15. *so good night with l.* 19. *thou'rt like to have a l. too rough,* Wint. III, 3, 55. *be unto us as is a nurse's song of l.* Tit. II, 3, 29. Hence = good night: *then l., the learned man hath got the lady gay,* Pilgr. 225. *l. to your bounty till I come again,* Tw. V, 48.

Lumbert Street, Mrs Quickly's blunder for *Lombard Street:* H4B II, 1, 31.

Lump, a shapeless mass: *this counterfeit l. of ore,* All's III, 6, 40. *this l. of clay* (the body) H6A II, 5, 14. *foul indigested l.* H6B V, 1, 157. H6C V, 6, 51. R3 I, 2, 57. *all men's honours lie like one l. before him, to be fashioned into what pitch he please,* H8 II, 2, 49.

Lumpish, dull, spiritless: *she is l., heavy, melancholy,* Gent. III, 2, 62.

Luna, the moon: LLL IV, 2, 39 (Nathaniel's speech).

Lunacy, madness: As III, 2, 423. Shr. Ind. 2, 31. Tit. V, 2, 70. Hml. II, 2, 49. III, 1, 4. Plur. *—ies =* mad pranks: Hml. III, 3, 7 (Qq *browes*).

Lunatic, adj. mad: Wiv. III, 5, 105. IV, 1, 71. IV, 2, 130 (Evans *—s* for *lunacy*). Err. IV, 3, 94. LLL V, 1, 29. Shr. Ind. 1, 63. II, 289. V, 1, 74. R2 II, 1, 115. R3 I, 3, 254. Lr. II, 3, 19. III, 7, 46.

Lunatic, subst. madman: Mids. V, 7. Tw. IV, 2, 26.

Lunes, mad freaks: *these dangerous unsafe l. in the king,* Wint. II, 2, 30. Substituted by M. Edd. for *lines* in Wiv. IV, 2, 22 and Troil. II, 3, 139; for *lunacies* in Hml. III, 3, 7.

Lungs, the organs of respiration: Compl. 228. 326. Tp. II, 1, 47. 174. Wiv. IV, 5, 18. LLL III, 77. Merch. IV, 1, 140. As II, 7, 30. H4B IV, 5, 217. V, 3, 145. V, 5, 9. H5 II, 1, 52. Troil. IV, 5, 7. V, 1, 24. Cor. I, 1, 112. III, 1, 77. Hml. II, 2, 337. 602. Cymb. I, 6, 68. Per. IV, 6, 179.

Lupercal, a Roman festival in honour of the god Pan: Caes. I, 1, 72. III, 2, 100.

Lurch, vb. 1) to lurk: *am fain to shuffle, to hedge and to l.* Wiv. II, 2, 26.

2) to rob: *in the brunt of seventeen battles since he —ed all swords of the garland,* Cor. II, 2, 105.

Lure, subst. any thing to allure a hawk; a particular call or sound: *as falcon to the l. away she flies,*

Ven. 1027. perhaps the stuffed figure of a bird: *for then she never looks upon her l.* Shr. IV, 1, 195.*

Lure, vb. to call (a hawk), to allure: *O, for a falconer's voice, to l. this tassel-gentle back again,* Rom. II, 2, 160.

Lurk, to lie hidden and in wait: Ven. 644. 1086. Lucr. 5. 362. 851. 1535. Pilgr. 337. Mids. II, 1, 47. R2 III, 2, 20. H5 I, 1, 49. II, 2, 186. H6A V, 3, 189. H6C II, 2, 15. IV, 2, 15. IV, 7, 12. R3 IV, 4, 3. Troil. IV, 4, 92. Cor. V, 4, 49 (*where have you —ed, that you make doubt of it?*). Tit. I, 153. Rom. IV, 1, 79 (*bid me l. where serpents are*). Lr. III, 6, 122 (*l., l.!*).

Lurking-place, hiding place: Tit. V, 2, 35.

Luscious, sweet, delicious, delightful: *overcanopied with l. woodbine,* Mids. II, 1, 251. *the food that to him now is as l. as locusts, shall be to him shortly as bitter as coloquintida,* Oth. I, 3, 354.

Lush, juicy, succulent, fresh: *how l. and lusty the grass looks,* Tp. II, 1, 52.

Lust, subst. 1) pleasure, delight: *gazing upon the Greeks with little l.* Lucr. 1384. *whose eyes do never give but through l. and laughter,* Tim. IV, 3, 492.

2) desire: *I'll answer to my l.* Troil. IV, 4, 134 (I'll do at pleasure). Plur. *—s* = inordinate desires: *nor my —s burn hotter than my faith,* Wint. IV, 4, 34. *polluted with your —s,* H6A V, 4, 43. *there serve your —s,* Tit. II, 1, 130. *our unbitted —s,* Oth. I, 3, 335.

3) carnal appetite, indulgence of sensual desire: Ven. 42. 556. 792. 794. Lucr. 156. 168. 173. 560. 617. 1354. Sonn. 129, 2. Tp. IV, 28. Wiv. II, 1, 69. V, 5, 98. 99. 152. Meas. V, 98. Err. II, 2, 135. 143. All's III, 5, 21. IV, 4, 24. H5 III, 5, 30. H6C III, 3, 210. R3 III, 5, 81. Tit. II, 1, 130. II, 3, 130. 175. 180. IV, 2, 42. V, 1, 43. Tim. IV, 1, 25. IV, 3, 84. 257. Mcb. IV, 3, 63. 86. Hml. I, 5, 45. 55. Lr. I, 4, 265. III, 4, 89. 92. IV, 1, 62. Oth. I, 3, 339. II, 1, 264. 301. II, 3, 363. III, 3, 338. V, 1, 36. Ant. I, 1, 10. II, 1, 22. III, 6, 7. 61. Cymb. II, 5, 24. III, 5, 146. Per. I, 1, 138. V, 3, 86. Masc. in Ven. 794 and Lucr. 617.

Lust, vb. to desire carnally: *where his lustful eye or savage heart —ed to make his prey,* R3 III, 5, 84 (Qq listed). *thou hotly —est to use her in that kind for which thou whippest her,* Lr. IV, 6, 166.

Lust-breathed, animated by lust: *l. Tarquin,* Lucr. 3.

Lust-dieted, faring and feeding voluptuously: *the superfluous and l. man,* Lr. IV, 1, 70.*

Lustful, full of carnal desire, voluptuous: Ven. 47. Lucr. 169. 179. Shr. Ind. 2, 40. H6A III, 2, 53. H6C III, 2, 129. R3 III, 5, 83 (Ff *raging*). III, 7, 187 (Ff *wanton*). Tit. IV, 1, 79. Oth. II, 1, 304 (Ff *lusty*).

Lustihood, high animal spirits: *his May of youth and bloom of l.* Ado V, 1, 76. *reason and respect make livers pale and l. deject,* Troil. II, 2, 50.

Lustily, spiritedly: *she hears them chant it l.* Ven. 869. *let's tune, and to it l. awhile,* Gent. IV, 2, 25. *I determine to fight l. for him,* H5 IV, 1, 201. *you have rung it l.* Tit. II, 2, 14.

Lustre, brightness, splendour: LLL IV, 2, 89. Wint. III, 2, 206. H4A IV, 1, 77. H5 III, 1, 30. H8 I, 1, 29. II, 2, 33. Troil. I, 3, 361. IV, 4, 120. Tim. I, 2, 154. Caes. I, 2, 124. Lr. III, 7, 84. Ant. II, 3, 27. Cymb. I, 1, 143.

Lustrous, splendent, bright: *good sparks and l.* All's II, 1, 41. *as l. as ebony,* Tw. IV, 2, 42.

Lust-stained, polluted by lust: Oth. V, 1, 36.

Lust-wearied, sick and tired of lust: Ant. II, 1, 38.

Lusty, 1) full of animal life and spirits, lively and active: *under one arm the l. courser's rein,* Ven. 31. *a breeding jennet, l., young and proud,* 260. *the treasure of thy l. days,* Sonn. 2, 6 (thy youth). *l. Jove,* Ado V, 4, 46. *though I look old, yet I am strong and l.* As II, 3, 47. *my age is as a l. winter,* 52. *your dolphin is not —er,* All's II, 3, 31. *a goodly babe, l. and like to live,* Wint. II, 2, 27. *we will bear home that l. blood again,* John II, 255. 461. *if l. love should go in quest of beauty,* 426. *l., young and cheerly drawing breath,* R2 I, 3, 66. *such comfort as do l. young men feel when well-apparelled April....,* Rom. I, 2, 26. *I'll take him down, an a were —er than he is,* II, 4, 159. *who, in the l. stealth of nature, take more composition,* Lr. I, 2, 11.

Coming near the sense of gallant: *our l. English, all with purpled hands,* John II, 322. *what l. trumpet thus doth summon us?* V, 2, 117. *in the l. haviour of his son,* R2 I, 3, 77. *he would unhorse the —est challenger,* V, 3, 19. *with —er maintenance,* H4A V, 4, 22. *of l. earls, Grandpré and Roussi,* H5 IV, 8, 103. *who comes here, led by a l. Goth?* Tit. V, 1, 19. *many l. Romans came smiling,* Caes. II, 2, 78. *the l. Moor hath leaped into my seat,* Oth. II, 1, 304 (Qq *lustful*).

Almost = merry: *killed l. Pudding,* Meas. IV, 3, 17. *the l. horn,* As IV, 2, 18. *it is a l. wench,* Shr. II, 161. *he'll have a l. widow now,* IV, 2, 50. *when this same l. gentleman was got,* John I, 108. *you were called l. Shallow,* H4B III, 2, 17. *l. lads roam here and there,* V, 3, 21. *the l. George,* H6C I, 4, 74. *on, l. gentlemen,* Rom. I, 4, 113.

And = stout, vigorous: *oared himself in l. stroke to the shore,* Tp. II, 1, 119. *is't a l. yeoman? will a stand to it?* H4B II, 1, 4. *thou hast l. arms,* Troil. IV, 5, 136. *we did buffet it with l. sinews,* Caes. I, 2, 108.

2) full of sap, fresh, luxuriant: *sap checked with frost, and l. leaves quite gone,* Sonn. 5, 7. *how lush and l. the grass looks,* Tp. II, 1, 52. *a little riper and more l. red than that mixed in his cheek,* As III, 5, 121.

Lute, a stringed musical instrument: Pilgr. 108. 112. Gent. III, 2, 78. Ado II, 1, 98. LLL IV, 3, 343. Shr. II, 107. 147. 148. 149. 157. H4A I, 2, 84. III, 1, 211. H6A I, 4, 96. R3 I, 1, 13.* H8 III, 1, 1. 3. Tit. II, 4, 45. Per. IV Prol. 25.

Lute-case, a case for a lute: H5 III, 2, 45.

Lute-string, string of a lute: Ado III, 2, 61.

Lutheran, adherent of Luther: H8 III, 2, 99.

Luxurious, lustful, unchaste: *she knows the heat of a l. bed,* Ado IV, 1, 42. *thou damned and l. mountain goat,* H5 IV, 4, 20. *the dissembling l. drab,* Troil. V, 4, 9. *l. woman,* Tit. V, 1, 88. *bloody, l., avaricious,* Mcb. IV, 3, 58.

Luxuriously, lustfully, lasciviously: *what hotter hours you have l. picked out,* Ant. III, 13, 120.

Luxury, lust, lasciviousness: *when he most burned in heart-wished l., he preached pure maid,* Compl. 314. *fie on lust and l.* Wiv. V, 5, 98. *one all of l.* Meas. V, 506. *the emptying of our fathers' l.* H5 III, 5, 6. *urge his hateful l. and bestial appetite in change of lust,* R3 III, 5, 80. *how the devil l. tickles these together,*

Troil. V, 2, 55. *a couch for l. and damned incest,* Hml. I, 5, 83. *to it, l.* Lr. IV, 6, 119.

Lybia, see *Libya.*

Lycaonia, country in Asia Minor: Ant. III, 6, 75.

Lychorida, female name in Per. III Prol. 43. III, 1, 6 etc.

Lycurgus, the legislator of Sparta: *I cannot call you —es,* Cor. II, 1, 60 (O. Edd. *Licurgusses*).

Lydia, country in Asia Minor: Ant. I, 2, 107. III, 6, 10.

Lying, mendacious, see *Lie.*

Lym, bloodhound; conjecture of M. Edd. in Lr. III, 6, 72; Qq *him,* Ff *hym.**

Lymoges, a French county, whose proprietor was hostile to Richard Coeur-de-Lion. Confounded by the poet with another mortal enemy of the king, the Duke of Austria: *O L.! O Austria!* John III, 1, 114.

Lynn, place in England: H6C IV, 5, 20.

Lysander, name in Mids. I, 1, 26 etc.

Lysimachus, name in Per. IV, 6, 18 etc.

M.

M, the thirteenth letter of the alphabet: Tw. II, 5, 118. 121. 132. 136. 141. 151.

Mab, the queen of the fairies: Rom. I, 4, 53. 75. 88.*

Macbéth, name in Mcb. passim. Rhyming to *heath:* I, 1, 7. to *death:* I, 2, 65. III, 5, 4. to *breath:* IV, 1, 98.

Maccabaeus; *Judas M.,* the leader of the Jews against Antiochus of Syria; one of the Nine Worthies: LLL V, 1, 134. V, 2, 540. 602. 634.

Macdónwald (the later Ff *Macdonnell)* name in Mcb. I, 2, 9.

Macdúff (cf. *Duff*), name in Mcb. II, 4, 20 etc.

Mace, a spice, the second covering of the nutmeg: Wint. IV, 3, 49.

Mace, a club of metal used as an ensign of authority: *he that sets up his rest to do more exploits with his m. than a morris-pike,* Err. IV, 3, 28. *the sword, the m., the crown imperial,* H5 IV, 1, 278 (= sceptre). *with these borne before us instead of —s,* H6B IV, 7, 144. *O murderous slumber, layest thou thy leaden m. upon my boy?* Caes. IV, 3, 268 (to arrest him like a bailiff; cf. *Arrest*).*

Macedon, the kingdom of Alexander the Great: H5 IV, 7, 21. 22. 23. 26. 28. Per. II, 2, 24.

Machiavel, the famous Italian writer; proverbially for a crafty politician: *am I a M.?* Wiv. III, 1, 104. *Alençon, that notorious M.* H6A V, 4, 74. *set the murderous M. to school,* H6C III, 2, 193.

Machination, intrigue, plotting: *—s, hollowness, treachery,* Lr. I, 2, 122. *your business of the world hath so an end, and m. ceases,* V, 1, 46.

Machine, artificial structure; used of the body: *whilst this m. is to him,* Hml. II, 2, 124.*

Mackerel, the fish Scomber scomber: *buy land as cheap as stinking m.* H4A II, 4, 395.

Macmorris, name in H5 III, 2, 72. 91. 100.

Maculate, stained, impure: *m. thoughts,* LLL I, 2, 97.

Maculation, stain, impurity: *there's no m. in thy heart,* Troil. IV, 4, 66.

Mad, adj. 1) disordered in the mind, insane: Sonn. 129, 8. 140, 12. Tp. I, 2, 209. III, 3, 58. Meas. V, 60. Err. II, 2, 11. 215. IV, 3, 82. IV, 4, 131. Shr. I, 2, 18. III, 2, 19. Tw. I, 5, 145. 211. II, 3, 93 etc. etc. Used of dogs infected with the rabies canina: Wiv. IV, 2, 131. Err. V, 70. Ant. IV, 15, 80. *m. as a buck,* Err. III, 1, 72 (proverbial phrase). *stark m.* Err. II, 1, 59. V, 281. Shr. I, 1, 69. Wint. III, 2, 184. *very m.* H8 I, 4, 28. *to fall m.* Tit. II, 3, 104. *to grow*

m. Sonn. 140, 9. *to go m.* Troil. IV, 2, 78. Lr. II, 4, 289. Oth. IV, 1, 101. *to run m.* Lucr. 997. Ado I, 1, 88. 93. Tw. II, 5, 212. Wint. III, 2, 184. H4A III, 1, 145. 212. H8 II, 2, 130. Troil. V, 1, 54. Tit. IV, 1, 21. Rom. II, 4, 5. IV, 3, 48. IV, 5, 76. Oth. III, 3, 317. *to wax m.* Tit. III, 1, 223.

2) beside one's self, having lost all self-command: *at his own shadow let the thief run m.* Lucr. 997. *sometime her grief is dumb ... sometime 'tis mad and too much talk affords,* 1106. *m. that sorrow should his use control,* 1781. *the fools are m., if left alone,* Gent. III, 1, 99. Lucr. 1108. Wiv. I, 4, 69. III, 5, 154. IV, 1, 4. Mids. III, 2, 441. Merch. IV, 1, 48. V, 176. H4A I, 3, 53. Oth. III, 3, 317. IV, 1, 101 etc.

3) extravagant in any way; gay and frolicksome to wildness and wantonness: *a m. host,* Wiv. III, 1, 115. *do you hear, my m. wenches?* LLL II, 257. *how now, m. spirit?* Mids. III, 2, 4. *fetching m. bounds,* Merch. V, 73. *be m. and merry,* Shr. III, 2, 228. *like a m. lad,* Tw. IV, 2, 139. *how now, m. wag?* H4A I, 2, 50. IV, 2, 55. *m. Shallow,* H4B III, 2, 16. *the m. days that I have spent,* 37 etc. = furious, passionate: *her eyes are m. that they have wept till now,* Ven. 1062. *subject to the tyranny of m. mischances,* 738 (the later Qq *sad*). *the finest m. devil of jealousy,* Wiv. V, 1, 19. *m. ire,* H6A IV, 3, 28. *m. and fantastic execution,* Troil. V, 5, 38. *these hot days is the m. blood stirring,* Rom. III, 1, 4. = inflamed with desire: *he was m. for her,* All's V, 3, 260. *I am m. in Cressid's love,* Troil. I, 1, 51. = foolish, absurd: *a m. fantastical trick,* Meas. III, 2, 98. *his m. attire,* Shr. III, 2, 126. *a m. marriage,* 184. 244. *her m. and headstrong humour,* IV, 1, 212. *as m. in folly,* All's V, 3, 3. *m. world, m. kings,* John II, 561. *he she loved proved m. and did forsake her,* Oth. IV, 3, 27 (cf. All's V, 3, 3).

Mad, vb. 1) tr. to make mad, to madden: Sonn. 119, 8. Err. IV, 4, 129. V, 84. All's V, 3, 213. Tw. I, 5, 141. R2 V, 5, 61. Tit. III, 1, 104. Lr. IV, 2, 43. Cymb. II, 2, 37. IV, 2, 313.

2) to be mad: *when he to —ing Dido would unfold his father's acts,* H6B III, 2, 117.

Madam, title of honour given in speaking of or to ladies of rank: *what must I call her. Madam. Al'ce m., or Joan m.? M., and nothing else; so lords call ladies,* Shr. Ind. 2, 111; cf. Sly's blunders v. 145 and I, 1, 259. *ere long they should call me m.* H4B II, 1, 109. Lucr. 1277. Gent. I, 2, 3. 34. 77. 130. 138. IV, 2, 120. LLL II, 1, 1. 40 etc. etc. *m. my interpreter,* H5 V, 2, 282. *dear m.* Gent. I, 2, 17. *sweet m.* LLL V, 2, 339. *my dearest m.* All's I, 3, 213. *good m.* Tw.

III, 1, 173. *gracious m.* H6C III, 3, 59. *noble m.* H8 IV, 2, 44 etc. *M. Silvia*, Gent. II, 1, 6. 14. 152. II, 5, 12. IV, 3, 1. IV, 4, 39. 114. 116. Meas. I, 2, 45. 74 etc. *m. and mistress*, Gent. II, 1, 102. *m., and pretty mistresses, give ear*, LLL V, 2, 286. *our —s mock at us*, H5 III, 5, 28 (French ladies). *the —s too did almost sweat*, H8 I, 1, 23. *honest —'s issue*, Lr. I, 2, 9.

Mad-brain, adj. insane: Shr. III, 2, 10.

Mad-brained, the same: Shr. III, 2, 165. H6A I, 2, 15. Tim. V, 1, 177.

Mad-bred, produced by or in madness: *this m. flaw*, H6B III, 1, 354.

Madcap, a fellow of wild and eccentric habits: Gent. II, 5, 8. John I, 84. H4A I, 2, 160. Adjectively: *the merry m. lord*, LLL II, 215. *a m. ruffian*, Shr. II, 290. *the m. duke*, H4A I, 3, 244. *the m. Prince of Wales*, IV, 1, 95.

Madeira, a sort of wine: H4A I, 2, 128.

Made-up, complete, perfect: *a m. villain*, Tim. V, 1, 101.

Mad-headed, wild, foolish: H4A II, 3, 80.

Madly, 1) in a deranged mind, distractedly: *that's somewhat m. spoken*, Meas. V, 89. *wast thou mad, that thus so m. thou didst answer me?* Err. II, 2, 12. Mids. II, 1, 171. Shr. II, 329. III, 2, 246. Tw. V, 319. John III, 4, 58. Rom. IV, 3, 51.

2) wildly, without self-control: *which (fear) m. hurries her she knows not whither*, Ven. 904. *m. tossed between desire and dread*, Lucr. 171. *by reprobate desire thus m. led*, 300. Err. V, 152. Mids. II, 1, 153. III, 2, 23. H4B I, 1, 10. Troil. II, 2, 116. Cymb. V, 5, 31 (*m. dying*, = dying in a wild state of mind).

Madman, a man whose understanding is deranged: Meas. V, 506. Err. IV, 1, 93. V, 213. LLL V, 2, 338. Mids. V, 10. Shr. V, 1, 60. 76. Tw. I, 5, 139. 146. IV, 2, 46. 125. IV, 3, 221. V, 294. 299. 335. H6B III, 1, 347. Rom. I, 2, 55. II, 1, 7. V, 3, 67. Tim. III, 4, 103. Caes. IV, 3, 40. Lr. III, 6, 10. IV, 1, 32. V, 3, 187. *he speaks nothing but m.* Tw. I, 5, 115 (cf. H5 V, 2, 156). Plur. *madmen:* Sonn. 147, 11. Mids. V, 4. As III, 2, 422. Tw. III, 4, 154. R2 V, 5, 62. H4B I, 3, 32. Troil. V, 1, 56. Rom. III, 3, 61. Caes. III, 2, 274. Lr. III, 4, 81. IV, 1, 48. Cymb. V, 4, 146.

Madness, 1) insanity: Sonn. 140, 10. Tp. II, 2, 14. V, 116. Wiv. IV, 2, 27. Meas. IV, 4, 4. V, 51. 61. 63. Err. V, 76. Merch. I, 2, 69. As III, 2, 420. IV, 1, 218. Tw. III, 4, 16. 61. IV, 3, 4. 10. V, 302. Wint. IV, 4, 495 etc. etc. *in m.* = mad: Hml. III, 4, 187. Oth. I, 1, 98.

2) extreme folly: *of this m. cured*, H4B IV, 2, 41. *were't not m., to make the fox surveyor of the fold?* H6B III, 1, 252. *his flight was m.* Mcb. IV, 2, 2.

3) wild affection or emotion: *fetter strong m. in a silken thread*, Ado V, 1, 25. *such a hare is m. the youth*, Merch. I, 2, 21.

Madonna, the address used by the fool to Olivia in Tw. I, 5, 47. 64. 66. 68. 72. 74. 76. 120. 145. V, 306.

Madrigal, a pastoral song: Pilgr. 360. Wiv. III, 1, 18. 23.

Mad-woman, a woman deranged in her understanding: *if your wife be not a m.* Merch. IV, 1, 445.

Maecenas (O. Edd. *Mecenas*) friend of Octavius Caesar: Ant. II, 2, 17. 102. 175.

Maggot, a small grub, a fly-worm: LLL V, 2, 409. Hml. II, 2, 181. IV, 3, 24.

Maggot-pie or **Magot-pie**, magpie: Mcb. III, 4, 125.

Magic, subst. sorcery, enchantment: Tp. V, 50. Wint. V, 3, 39. 110. Tim. I, 1, 6. Hml. III, 2, 270. Oth. I, 2, 65. I, 3, 92. III, 4, 69. Ant. III, 10, 19.

Magic, adj. pertaining to sorcery: Tp. I, 2, 24. H6A I, 1, 27. Mcb. III, 5, 26.

Magical, the same: Ant. III, 1, 31.

Magician, sorcerer: As V, 2, 67. 78. V, 4, 33. H4A I, 3, 83. R3 I, 2, 34.

Magistrate, a public functionary: Tp. II, 1, 149. H5 I, 2, 191. H6A I, 3, 57. H6B IV, 2, 19. H6C I, 2, 23. Cor. II, 1, 47. III, 1, 104. 202.

Magnanimity, heroic bravery: *infuse his breast with m. and make him naked foil a man at arms*, H6C V, 4, 41.

Magnanimous, dauntless, heroic: *be m. in the enterprise*, All's III, 6, 70. *most m. mouse*, H4B III, 2, 171. *as m. as Agamemnon*, H5 III, 6, 6. IV, 7, 18. *valiant and m. deeds*, Troil. II, 2, 200. III, 3, 277. cf. Armado's letter in LLL IV, 1, 65.

Magnificence, pomp, splendour: Wint. I, 1, 13.

Magnificent, pompous, boastful: *a letter from the m. Armado*, LLL I, 1, 193. *than whom no mortal so m.* III, 180.

Magnifico, title given to Venetian grandees: Merch. III, 2, 282. Oth. I, 2, 12.

Magnify, to glorify, to exalt: *him that thou —est with all these titles*, H6A IV, 7, 75.

Magnus: *Saint M. Corner*, H6B IV, 8, 1.

Magot-pie, see *Maggot-pie*.

Mahomet, the Arabian prophet: H6A I, 2, 140.

Mahu, name of a devil: Lr. III, 4, 149. IV, 1, 63.

Maid, 1) virgin: *he preached pure m.* Compl. 315. *'tis not a m., for she hath had gossips*, Gent. III, 1, 269. *a wronged, I would fain have said a m.* Meas. V, 21. II, 2, 154. Ado II, 2, 40. IV, 1, 35. 86. Mids. II, 2, 59. Merch. III, 2, 312. As IV, 1, 148. All's IV, 2, 74. John II, 572. H4A IV, 1, 114. H5 V, 2, 323. H6A V, 4, 55. H6B IV, 7, 129. H6C I, 1, 216. Troil. IV, 5, 50. Rom. III, 2, 135. Hml. IV, 5, 54. Lr. I, 5, 54 etc. Used of a man who has not yet known woman: *you are betrothed both to a m. and man*, Tw. V, 270.

2) girl: *if you be m. or no*, Tp. I, 2, 427. 428 (not a goddess, but a mortal woman). *behold this m.* 491. IV, 95. V, 185. *knows I am a m. and would not force this letter to my view*, Gent. I, 2, 53. *can you love the m.?* Wiv. I, 1, 252. I, 4, 127. *is there a m. with child by him?* Meas. I, 2, 92. 94. I, 4, 32. II, 2, 20. III, 1, 180. V, 178. LLL I, 1, 137. 299. Mids. II, 2, 73. III, 2, 302. Tw. II, 4, 46. V, 268. 282. H4A III, 3, 130 (*M. Marian*). Rom. I, 4, 66 etc. Used as a compellation: *why went you not with master doctor, m.?* Wiv. V, 5, 232. *m.!* LLL I, 2, 138. *mates, m.!* Shr. I, 1, 59. *the gods to their dear shelter take thee*, m. Lr. I, 1, 185. *my —s*, LLL V, 2, 262. *good m., fair m.* etc. Wiv. II, 2, 38. Meas. II, 2, 79. Mids. I, 1, 46 etc. Proverb: *—s still answer nay, and take it*, R3 III, 7, 51; cf. *—s in modesty say no to that which they would have the profferer construe ay*, Gent. I, 2, 55.

3) female servant: *spinning amongst her —s*, Lucr. Arg. 10. *she hoarsely calls her m.* Lucr. 1214. *a m. of Dian's*, Sonn. 153, 2. Tp. III, 1, 84. Gent. I, 2, 69. II, 3, 8. III, 1, 269. Wiv. IV, 2, 77. V, 5, 49. Err.

V, 170. Merch. III, 2, 200. 311. V, 33. Shr. Ind. 2, 92. H8 III, 1, 75. Rom. II, 2, 6. Tim. IV, 1, 12. Oth. IV, 3, 26. Ant. III, 7, 15. IV, 15, 74 etc.

Maid-child, female child: Per. V, 3, 6.

Maiden, 1) virgin: *then are you no m.* Ado IV, 1, 88. All's II, 1, 175. H5 III, 3, 20. Oth. III, 4, 75. Oftenest adjectively: *the m. burning of his cheeks,* Ven. 50. *m. worlds,* Lucr. 408. *bud,* 848. Sonn. 16, 6. 66, 6. 154, 4. Meas. IV, 4, 27. Ado III, 1, 109. IV, 1, 166. 181. LLL V, 2, 351. 789. Mids. I, 1, 75. II, 1, 164. III, 2, 285. All's IV, 2, 57. John II, 98. H5 V, 2, 253. 349. 353. H6A II, 4, 47. V, 4, 52. H8 IV, 2, 169. V, 5, 41. Tit. II, 3, 232. Rom. II, 2, 86. Hml. I, 3, 121. V, 1, 256. Per. V, 1, 243. *a m. and an innocent hand,* John IV, 2, 252 (not yet stained with blood). *thy m. sword,* H4A V, 4, 134. *m. youth,* H6A IV, 7, 38.

2) girl: *—s' eyes stuck over all his face,* Compl. 81. Meas. I, 4, 80. LLL V, 2, 916. Mids. II, 1, 35. 168. II, 2, 74. III, 2, 66. Merch. II, 1, 14. III, 2, 8. As IV, 3, 41. Shr. IV, 5, 44. All's I, 1, 55. IV, 2, 6. Tw. I, 4, 33. Wint. IV, 4, 85. H5 II, 4, 107. Troil. III, 2, 219. Oth. I, 3, 94. Used as a compellation: Meas. II, 2, 48. All's I, 3, 155. II, 1, 117. Adjectively: *my m. weeds,* Tw. V, 262. *a m. lattle,* Troil. IV, 5, 87.*

Maidenhead, virginity: Shr. III, 2, 227. Tw. I, 5, 232. Wint. IV, 4, 116. H4A II, 4, 398. IV, 1, 59. H4B II, 2, 84. H6B IV, 7, 130. H8 II, 3, 23. 25. Troil. IV, 2, 23. Rom. I, 1, 31. I, 3, 2. III, 2, 137. Per. III Prol. 10. IV, 2, 64. IV, 6, 136.

Maidenhead, place in England: Wiv. IV, 5, 80.

Maidenhood, virginity: All's III, 5, 24. H6A IV, 6, 17. Rom. III, 2, 13.

Maidenly, 1) becoming a maid: *it is not friendly, 'tis not m.* Mids. III, 2, 217. 2) girlish: *what a m. man-at-arms are you become,* H4B II, 2, 82. 3) virginal, chaste: *the —est star,* Lr. I, 2, 143.

Maiden-tongued, speaking in a gentle and insinuating manner: Compl. 100.

Maiden-widowed, having become a widow, while yet a virgin: Rom. III, 2, 135.

Maidhood, girlhood: *by the roses of the spring, by m., honour, truth and every thing,* Tw. III, 1, 162. *is there not charms by which the property of youth and m. may be abused?* Oth. I, 1, 173.

Maid-pale (cf. *Pale*) having the white and tender complexion of a virgin: *change the complexion of her m. peace to scarlet indignation,* R2 III, 3, 98.

Mail, subst. armour: *a rusty m.* Troil. III, 3, 152 (O. Edd. *male*). Corrupt passage: *no egma, no riddle, no l'envoy; no salve in the m.* LLL III, 74 (Qq F1 *in thee male; m.* perhaps = budget, box).

Mailed, clad in armour: *the m. Mars,* H4A IV, 1, 116. *with his m. hand,* Cor. I, 3, 38 (gauntleted). *m. up* = completely covered and wrapped up: *I should not thus be led along, m. up in shame,* H6B II, 4, 31.

Maim, subst. a laming and crippling hurt, a deep injury: *so deep a m. as to be cast forth in the common air,* R2 I, 3, 156. *your father's sickness is a m. to us,* H4A IV, 1, 42. *that bears so shrewd a m.* H6B II, 3, 41. *stop those —s of shame seen through thy country,* Cor. IV, 5, 92 (*—s of shame* = shameful *—s*).

Maim, vb. to lame, to cripple: *you —ed the jurisdiction of all bishops,* H8 III, 2, 312. *with such —ed rites,* Hml. V, 1, 242 (defective). *a judgment —ed and*

most imperfect, Oth. I, 3, 99. *I am —ed for ever,* V, 1, 27. = to hurt in general: *did win whom he would m.* Pilgr. 312 (in the rhyme). *it —ed you two outright,* Shr. V, 2, 62. Cade says *mained* for *maimed,* H6B IV, 2, 172.

Main, subst. 1) with *of;* full might, the whole, the gross of a thing: *nativity, once in the m. of light, crawls to maturity,* Sonn. 60, 5. *empties itself, as doth an inland brook, into the main of waters,* Merch. V, 97. *to-morrow we must with all our m. of power stand fast,* Troil. II, 3, 273. *goes it against the m. of Poland, or for some frontier?* Hml. IV, 4, 15.

2) absol. a) the principal point, that which is first in question: *let's make haste away, and look unto the m.* H6B I, 1, 208. *I doubt it is no other than the m., his father's death and our o'erhasty marriage,* Hml. II, 2, 56.

b) the ocean, the great sea: Sonn. 64, 7. 80, 8. John II, 26. R3 I, 4, 20. Oth. II, 1, 3. 39.

c) the continent: *swell the curled waters 'bove the m.* Lr. III, 1, 6.

d) (probably from the French *main*) a stake at gaming: *to set so rich a m. on the nice hazard of one doubtful hour,* H4A IV, 1, 47.

Main, adj. 1) great, first in importance, principal, chief: *the m. flood,* Merch. IV, 1, 72 (the sea). *the man that the m. harvest reaps,* As III, 5, 103. *he might in a m. danger fail you,* All's III, 6, 17. *the m. consents are had,* V, 3, 69. *these m. parcels of dispatch,* IV, 3, 104. *our m. battle's front,* H6C I, 1, 8; R3 V, 3, 299. *m. end,* H8 II, 2, 41. III, 2, 215. Cor. II, 2, 43. IV, 3, 20. Mcb. IV, 3, 198. V, 4, 10. Hml. I, 1, 105. Lr. IV, 6, 217. Oth. I, 3, 11. II, 1, 269. Ant. I, 2, 198 (*the m. soldier*). Cymb. V, 4, 16. Per. V, 1, 29.

2) concerning the gross or whole; general: *a man may prophesy of the m. chance of things,* H4B III, 1, 83. *we do not mean the coursing snatchers only, but fear the m. intendment of the Scot,* H5 I, 2, 144. *m. chance, father you meant,* H6B I, 1, 212. *put your m. cause into the king's protection,* H8 III, 1, 93. *by the m. assent of all these learned men she was divorced,* H8 IV, 1, 31. *if he were foiled, we did our m. opinion crush in taint of our best man,* Troil. I, 3, 373. *quite from the m. opinion he held once,* Caes. II, 1, 196. *no farther than the m. voice of Denmark goes withal,* Hml. I, 3, 28.

3) superior, overruling: *which by m. force Warwick did win,* H6B I, 1, 210. *by commission and m. power,* H8 II, 2, 7.

Main-course, the main sail (cf. *Course,* 9): *bring her to try with m.* Tp. I, 1, 38 (i. e., according to Smith's Sea-Grammar: 'to hale the tacke aboord, the sheet close aft, the boling set up, and the helme tied close aboord').

Maine, French county: John I, 11. II, 152. 487. H6A IV, 3, 45. V, 3, 95. 154. H6B I, 1, 51. 209. 210. IV, 1, 86. IV, 2, 170. IV, 7, 70.

Mained, in the language of Cade, = maimed: H6B IV, 2, 172.

Mainly, forcibly, mightily: *these four came all a-front and m. thrust at me,* H4B II, 4, 222. *I do not call your faith in question so m. as my merit,* Troil. IV, 4, 87. *by your safety, wisdom, all things else, you m. were stirred up,* Hml. IV, 7, 9. *I am m. ignorant what place this is,* Lr. IV, 7, 65 (= perfectly).

Main-mast, the chief or middle mast: Wint. III, 3, 94.

Maintain (accentuated on the 2d syllable; on the first in H6A I, 1, 71. Tit. II, 1, 47. V, 2, 72). 1) to keep, to support, to sustain, to feed: *he will m. you like a gentlewoman,* Wiv. III, 4, 45. *sweat in this business and m. this war,* John V, 2, 102. *I have —ed that Salamander with fire,* H4A III, 3, 53. H5 I, 1, 12. II, 3, 45. H6B IV, 7, 75. IV, 10, 24. H6C III, 3, 126. 154. R3 I, 2, 260. H8 I, 2, 31. Hml. II, 2, 361. *to m. it* = to afford it: *I am able to m. it,* Shr. V, 1, 79. *so senseless of expense, that he will neither know how to m. it, nor cease his flow of riot,* Tim. II, 2, 2.

2) to support, to defend, to vindicate, to justify: *our country rights in Rome —ed,* Lucr. 1838. *if it be honest you have spoke, you have courage to m. it,* Meas. III, 2, 167. *never could m. his part,* Ado I, 1, 238. *a sceptre must be as boisterously —ed as gained,* John III, 4, 136. R2 I, 1, 62. 98. IV, 27. H4A IV, 3, 9. H4B III, 2, 82. IV, 1, 42. IV, 2, 67. IV, 5, 225. H5 III, 2, 85. III, 6, 95. IV, 1, 300. H6A II, 4, 32. 70. 73. 88. III, 1, 129. III, 4, 31. H6B I, 1, 161 (*Jesu m. your royal excellence!*). H6C I, 1, 88. Troil. II, 1, 138. II, 2, 129. Tit. V, 2, 72. Tim. IV, 3, 71. Lr. V, 3, 100. 112. Cymb. V, 4, 74.

3) to assert: *unless this general evil they m.* Sonn. 121, 13. *she dying, as it must be so —ed, upon the instant,* Ado IV, 1, 216. *say if I —ed the truth,* H6A II, 4, 5. *when the devout religion of mine eye —s such falsehood,* Rom. I, 2, 94. *heard him oft m. it to be fit,* Lr. I, 2, 77.

4) to keep, to entertain, to hold: *—ed the change of words with any creature,* Ado IV, 1, 185; *m. no words with him,* Tw. IV, 2, 107; *m. talk with the duke,* Lr. III, 3, 16. *m. a mourning ostentation,* Ado IV, 1, 207. *which —ed so politic a state of evil,* V, 2, 62. *it shall be so far forth friendly —ed till we set his youngest free,* Shr. I, 1, 141. *defences, musters, preparations, should be —ed, assembled and collected,* H5 II, 4, 19. *that here you m. several factions,* H6A I, 1, 71. *and m. such a quarrel openly,* Tit. II, 1, 47.

5) to represent: *the one —ed by the owl,* LLL V, 2, 902 (Armado's speech).

Maintenance, 1) sustenance: Gent. I, 3, 68. Shr. V, 2, 148.

2) deportment, carriage: *I saw him hold Lord Percy at the point with lustier m. than I did look for of such an ungrown warrior,* H4A V, 4, 22.•

Main-top, the top of the mainmast: Cymb. IV, 2, 320.

Majestic, grand, stately: Tp. IV, 118. Caes. I, 2, 130. Cymb. V, 5, 457.

Majestical, 1) pertaining to royalty, princely: *presence m. would put him out,* LLL V, 2, 102. *laid in bed m.* H5 IV, 1, 284.

2) grand, stately: LLL V, 1, 12. H5 III Chor. 16. H6A IV, 7, 39. R3 III, 7, 118. Hml. I, 1, 143. II, 2, 313.

Majestically, with princely dignity: H4A II, 4, 479.

Majesty, 1) grandeur, dignity of aspect and manner: *he trots with gentle m.* Ven. 278. *the sun ariseth in his m.* 856. *in great commanders grace and m. you might behold,* Lucr. 1387. Sonn. 7, 4. 78, 8. LLL I, 1, 137. IV, 3, 228. As III, 2, 154. Wint. V, 2, 39. V, 3, 35. 39. R2 III, 3, 70. H6A I, 2, 79. V, 3, 70. H6B I, 1, 33. III, 1, 6. III, 2, 50. H6C IV, 6, 71. R3 I, 1, 16. III, 1, 100. Ant. III, 3, 20. 45. 46 etc.

2) royalty: *hiding base sin in plaits of m.* Lucr.

93. *I sue for exiled —'s repeal; let him return,* 640; cf. *O fair return of banished m.* John III, 1, 321. *the sceptre, the attribute to awe and m.* Merch. IV, 1, 191. *to bless the bed of m.* Wint. V, 1, 33. John II, 350. III, 1, 98. 100. IV, 2, 213. IV, 3, 148. R2 II, 1, 120. 295. H6B I, 2, 36; R3 III, 7, 169. Hml. III, 3, 15. IV, 1, 31. Ant. V, 2, 17 etc. Masc. in Lucr. 640.

3) title given to kings and queens: Tp. II, 1, 168. LLL II, 141. V, 2, 311. 888. All's I, 1, 4. 13. I, 2, 10. 23. 76. H5 V, 2, 26. H6A III, 1, 96. 176. 179. H6B I, 1, 1. Hml. II, 2, 26. III, 1, 22 etc. *your high m.* All's II, 1, 113. *your sweet m.* R2 II, 2, 20. *my dear m. your queen,* Hml. II, 2, 135. *most royal m.* Lr. I, 1, 196. *good m.* Ant. III, 3, 2. *most gracious m.* 7 etc. *the m. of England,* John I, 3. *the double —s,* II, 480. *before my father's m.* H4A V, 1, 96. *the m. of buried Denmark,* Hml. I, 1, 48. *where is the beauteous m. of Denmark?* IV, 5, 21. *this old m.* Lr. V, 3, 299. Applied to the princess of France: LLL V, 2, 736 (probably as supposed to be heiress of her dead father).

Major, subst. the first proposition of a syllogism: *I deny your m.* H4A II, 4, 544 (perhaps quibbling with *mayor*).

Major, adj. greater: *my m. vow lies here,* Troil. V, 1, 49. *the m. part of your syllables,* Cor. II, 1, 64.

Majority, superiority, preeminence: *whose great name in arms holds from all soldiers chief m. and military title capital through all the kingdoms,* H4A III, 2, 109.

Make, vb. (impf. and partic. *made*). A. trans. 1) to create, to beget, to cause to exist, to form, to frame, to compose: *nature that made thee,* Ven. 11. 243. *bees that made 'em* (honey-combs) Tp. I, 2, 330. *thou art made like a goose,* II, 2, 136. *as if the garment had been made for me,* Gent. IV, 4, 168. *like man new made,* Meas. II, 2, 79 (new-created by salvation). *a man already made,* II, 4, 44. *a life true made,* 47. *to see the —ing of her carcanet,* Err. III, 1, 4. *by this I know 'tis made,* 115. *he were an excellent man that were made just in the midway between him and Benedick,* Ado II, 1, 8. *he speaks not like a man of God's —ing,* LLL V, 2, 529; As III, 2, 216. *God made him,* Merch. I, 2, 60. *put the liveries to —ing,* II, 2, 124. (the painter) *having made one* (eye) III, 2, 124. *Nathaniel's coat was not fully made,* Shr. IV, 1, 135. *He that made me,* R2 II, 1, 93; H6A II, 4, 88; H6C II, 2, 124; R3 I, 2, 62; Lr. I, 1, 210. *I was not made a horse,* R2 V, 5, 92; cf. *repent thou wast not made his daughter,* Ant. III, 13, 135. *I knew ye as well as he that made ye,* H4A II, 4, 296. *what I have to say is of mine own —ing,* H4B V, 5, 121. *his passport shall be made,* H5 IV, 3, 36. *you are weakly made,* H8 II, 3, 40. *my will shall here be made,* Troil. V, 10, 53; Wiv. III, 4, 60. *he sits in his state, as a thing made for Alexander,* Cor. V, 4, 23 (formed to represent A.). *he that made us with such large discourse,* Hml. IV, 4, 36. *there was good sport at his —ing,* Lr. I, 1, 24. *the issue that their lust hath made between them,* Ant. III, 6, 8. *made a law,* Per. Prol. 35 etc. etc. With *of*: *such stuff as dreams are made on,* Tp. IV, 157 (*on* = *of*). *the ladder made of cords,* Gent. II, 4, 182. III, 1, 117. *his guts are made of puddings,* Wiv. II, 1, 32. *what stuff 'tis made of,* Merch. I, 1, 4. *such as we are made of, such we be,* Tw. II, 2, 33. *the breath is gone whereof this praise is made,* Tim. II, 2, 179 etc. etc. Hence *made of* = consisting of: *if my breast had not been made* *of faith, and my heart of steel,* Err. III, 2, 150. *proud, idle, made of self-love,* All's I, 1, 157. Cor. I, 9, 44. *made of sterner stuff,* Caes. III, 2, 97. Without *of: were I not the better part made mercy,* As III, 1, 2; cf. *when he was less furnished than now he is with that which —s him both without and within,* Cymb. I, 4, 9 (= constitutes). *Made,* followed by an inf. or by *for,* = destined, and hence fit, well qualified: *nor made to court an amorous looking-glass,* R3 I, 1, 15. *a place by nature made for murders,* Tit. IV, 1, 58. The aux. vb. *to be* before it either in the present or impf. tense: *torches are made to light, beauty for the use,* Ven. 163. *we are made to be no stronger than faults may shake our frames,* Meas. II, 4, 132. *you are made rather to wonder at the things you hear than to work any,* Cymb. V, 3, 53. *if he'll do as he is made to do, I'll know he'll quickly fly my friendship too,* 61. *were not made to woo,* Mids. II, 1, 242. *this hand was made to handle nought but gold,* H6B V, 1, 7. *they were made for kissing,* R3 I, 2, 172. *meat was made for mouths,* Cor. I, 1, 211. *men's eyes were made to look,* Rom. III, 1, 57. *was this fair paper made to write whore upon?* Oth. IV, 2, 72.

Made up = finished, completed: *sent before my time into this breathing world, scarce half made up,* R3 I, 1, 21. *he's a made up villain,* Tim. V, 1, 101 (complete, perfect). *being scarce made up, I mean, to man, he had not apprehension of roaring terrors,* Cymb. IV, 2, 109 (full grown). *Made* without *up,* used in the same sense by Fluellen: H5 IV, 7, 45.

2) to effect, to produce, to cause, to perform: *to m. the breach,* Lucr. 469; H6A II, 1, 74; III, 2, 2; H6B V, 2, 82. *he does m. our fire,* Tp. I, 2, 311; Ado II, 1, 262; Shr. IV, 1, 4; Wint. II, 3, 115 etc. *widows of this business' —ing,* Tp. II, 1, 133. *to m. an earthquake,* 315. *m. flows and ebbs,* V, 270. *and m. rough winter everlastingly,* Gent. II, 4, 163. *m. water* (= to urine) Gent. IV, 4, 41; Meas. III, 2, 117; Tw. I, 3, 139. *to m. a hole,* Wiv. III, 5, 143; H4B II, 2, 88; Caes. V, 1, 31 etc. *m. the fairy oyes,* Wiv. V, 5, 45. *vice —s mercy,* Meas. V, 2, 115 (is the cause of mercy). *who —s that noise?* IV, 3, 27; Ado III, 3, 35; Mids. III, 2, 116; H4B IV, 5, 1; H8 IV, 1, 72; Lr. II, 1, 57 etc. *unquiet meals m. ill digestions,* Err. V, 74. *m. good room,* Ado II, 1, 88. *made a blot,* III, 1, 64. *your fair self should m. a yielding 'gainst some reason in my breast,* LLL II, 151. *—s sport to the prince,* IV, 1, 101; Wiv. IV, 4, 14; Mids. III, 2, 161. *the wound mine eye hath made,* As III, 5, 20; R2 IV, 279; Tit. III, 1, 247; Tim. III, 5, 66. *infirmity doth ever m. the better fool,* Tw. I, 5, 83; cf. *I'll m. a fat pair of gallows,* H4A II, 1, 74. *a solemn combination shall be made of our souls,* Tw. V, 392. *the need I have of thee thine own goodness hath made,* Wint. IV, 2, 14. *this league that we have made,* John II, 545; IV, 2, 126. *I have made a happy peace with him,* John V, 1, 63; V, 2, 91; R2 III, 2, 127; R3 I, 2, 198; II, 2, 132; Cor. V, 6, 79 etc. *made a divorce betwixt his queen and him,* R2 III, 1, 12; H5 V, 2, 394; Cymb. II, 1, 67. *m. fearful musters,* H4B Ind. 12. *his own merit —s his way,* H8 I, 1, 64; cf. H6B IV, 8, 62 and Oth. V, 2, 263. *this —s bold mouths,* H8 I, 2, 60. *this night he —s a supper* (= gives) H8 I, 3, 52; cf. *—s factious feasts,* Troil. I, 3, 191; *be every one officious to m. this banquet,* Tit. V, 2, 203. *all hoods m. not monks,* H8 III, 1, 23. *made this mischief,* II, 1, 22. *m. yourself*

mirth, II, 3, 101. *made emulous missions,* Troil. III, 3, 189 (caused). *made a shower and thunder with their caps and shouts,* Cor. II, 1, 282. *the noble knot he made,* Cor. IV, 2, 32. *m. a treaty,* V, 6, 68; Ant. II, 6, 85. *the harmony which that tongue has made,* Tit. II, 4, 48. *the sorrow that their sister —s* (= causes) III, 1, 119. *trenches made by grief,* V, 2, 23. *m. a mutual closure of our house,* 134. *let us m. a bay,* II, 2, 3. *the want whereof doth daily m. revolt in my penurious band,* Tim. IV, 3, 91 (mark the different meaning in Oth. I, 1, 135). *our old love made a particular force,* V, 2, 8. *abler than yourself to m. conditions,* Caes. IV, 3, 32. *it shall m. honour for you,* Mcb. II, 1, 26. *to m. mouths,* Hml. IV, 4, 50; cf. Mids. III, 2, 238 and Lr. III, 2, 35; *to m. faces,* LLL V, 2, 649; Cor. II, 1, 83; Mcb. III, 4, 67. *his quietus m.* Hml. III, 1, 75. *m. your own purpose, how in my strength you please,* Lr. II, 1, 113. *her garboils, made out of her impatience,* Ant. II, 2, 68. *made à gap,* 223. *made his will,* III, 4, 4. *my desolation does begin to m. a better life,* V, 2, 1 (is the beginning of the better life which is to come). *what —s your admiration?* Cymb. I, 6, 38. cf. Cor. III, 1, 27. Per. II Prol. 31 etc. etc. *to m. means* (cf. *Means*) = to take measures, to contrive, to practise: Gent. V, 4, 137. R3 V, 3, 40 (Qq *bear my good night to him*). 248. Cymb. II, 4, 3. (= to make possible, All's V, 1, 35). *to m. fair weather,* see *Weather.* With a double accus., to denote an effect or change produced: *m. the rope of his destiny our cable,* Tp. I, 1, 33. *words that made them* (thy purposes) *known,* I, 2, 358. *—s my labours pleasures,* III, 1, 7. *made wit with musing weak,* Gent. I, 1, 69. *one made privy to the plot,* III, 1, 12. *made me publisher of this pretence,* 47. *Silver made it good,* Shr. Ind. 1, 19 (cf. *Good*). *he'll be made an example,* Wint. IV, 4, 847 (cf. *Example*). *it made my imprisonment a pleasure,* H6C IV, 6, 11. *those you m. friends,* H8 II, 1, 127. *my boon I m. it that you know me not,* Lr. IV, 7, 10 etc. *to m. it strange* = to pretend to be shocked at what has been said or done: *she —s it strange, but she would be best pleased to be so angered with another letter,* Gent. I, 2, 102. *to achieve her? how? Why —st thou it so strange?* Tit. II, 1, 81. With *up,* to denote a complete effect: *what he with his oath and all probation will m. up full clear,* Meas. V, 157. Peculiar passage: *thou shouldst have made him as little as a crow, ere left to after-eye him,* Cymb. I, 3, 14 (= let him become). Reflexively: *m. yourself ready,* Tp. I, 1, 27. *m. thyself like a nymph,* I, 2, 301. *to m. myself acquainted with you,* Wiv. II, 2, 189 etc. etc. Sometimes *to m. one's self* = to become: *that, being a stranger in this city here, do m. myself a suitor to your daughter,* Shr. II, 91. *how sometimes nature will betray its folly and m. itself a pastime to harder bosoms,* Wint. I, 2, 152. *I dare not m. myself so guilty, to give up willingly that noble title,* H8 III, 1, 139. *Octavius with Mark Antony have made themselves so strong,* Caes. IV, 3, 154. *m. yourself my guest whilst you abide here,* Ant. II, 2, 249 (cf. Meas. III, 1, 205). Adverbial or prepositional expressions supplying the place of the second accusative: *till time had made them for us,* Meas. I, 2, 157 (= disposed them in our favour). *you have made the days and nights as one,* All's V, 1, 3. *that day that made my sister thirteen years,* Tw. V, 255. *what —s you in this sudden change?* H6C IV, 4, 1. *made of none effect,* H8 IV, 1, 33. *what —s* *that frontlet on?* Lr. I, 4, 207 (what causes that frontlet to be on your forehead?). *to m. away* = to m. away with, to destroy, to kill: Ven. 763. Sonn. 11, 8. As V, 1, 58. All's I, 1, 226. R2 I, 3, 244. H6B III, 1, 167. III, 2, 67. R3 IV, 4, 281. Tit. II, 3, 189. 208. IV, 2, 167. Tim. I, 2, 110. *to m. up* = to complete, to make full, to accomplish: Meas. V, 228. Err. I, 1, 154. LLL IV, 3, 207. Mids. III, 2, 438. Wint. II, 1, 179. John II, 541. III, 1, 106. H6C I, 4, 25. Troil. II, 2, 170. Cor. I, 1, 148. V, 3, 140. Rom. V, 1, 48. Mcb. I, 5, 38. I, 3, 36. Hml. V, 1, 294. Oth. IV, 2, 5. Per. III, 3, 5 (cf. *Up*). = to bring up, in the language of the fishermen in Per. II, 1, 155. The prepos. *of* supplying the place of the first accus.: *made such a sinner of his memory,* Tp. I, 2, 101. *to m. a wonder of a poor drunkard,* II, 2, 169. Wiv. I, 1, 2. Meas. I, 2, 57. II, 1, 1. LLL II, 252. Mids. II, 1, 243. III, 1, 123. Merch. I, 1, 6. Tw. III, 3, 2. H6A IV, 5, 15. R3 II, 1, 50. Rom. III, 1, 50. Oth. III, 4, 61 etc. *I'll m. a shaft or a bolt on't,* Wiv. III, 4, 24 (cf. *Bolt*). *m. your best of it,* Shr. IV, 3, 100; Cor. V, 6, 148 (cf. *Best*). *can anything be made of this?* Oth. III, 4, 10 (= is there any meaning in this?). *he will m. no deed at all of this,* All's III, 6, 102. *to m. much of* = to hold dear, to show love and respect to (cf. *Much*): Tp. I, 2, 333. All's I, 1, 87. H6C IV, 6, 75. R3 V, 5, 7. Cor. II, 3, 116. Tit. IV, 1, 10. Ant. IV, 2, 21. Cymb. IV, 2, 198. *Much* omitted: *he is so made on here within, as if he were son and heir to Mars,* Cor. IV, 5, 203 (*on* = of). *to m. more of: I'll m. more of thy old body than I have done,* Wiv. II, 2, 145. *to m. nothing of* = to treat with contempt: *his white hair, which the impetuous blasts catch in their fury and m. nothing of,* Lr. III, 1, 9.

Followed by an accus. and inf.; a) without *to: made thee more profit,* Tp. I, 2, 172. *m. his bold waves tremble,* 205. 288. 354. 370. 473. V, 303. Gent. III, 2, 29. Meas. I, 2, 124. Err. III, 2, 38. 173. III, 2, 151 etc. *I do m. myself believe,* Meas. III, 1, 205 (= I am inclined to believe). *a part to tear a cat in, to m. all split,* Mids. I, 2, 32 (a phrase expressing great violence of action). b) with *to: their ambition —s them still to fight,* Lucr. 68. Gent. III, 2, 19. V, 4, 163. Err. II, 1, 26. II, 2, 178. LLL V, 2, 556. Merch. I, 1, 68. Shr. I, 1, 174. All's I, 3, 238. V, 3, 114. Tw. III, 4, 369. Wint. IV, 4, 198. V, 3, 71. John IV, 2, 24. R2 I, 1, 72. H6A IV, 7, 12. V, 3, 168. H6B II, 1, 162. 164. IV, 8, 17. H6C I, 1, 108. 142. I, 2, 26. IV, 8, 54. R3 I, 3, 68. III, 2, 14. H8 II, 4, 183. Troil. IV, 4, 139. Cor. II, 3, 241. V, 3, 101. Tit. IV, 1, 21. 25. Hml. III, 4, 186. Oth. IV, 2, 147. Per. III. 2, 18 etc. *I am made to understand* = I am given to understand, Meas. III, 2, 254.

3) Joined, in a periphrastical way, to different substantives implying the idea of an action, to denote the performance of the respective action (cf. the resp. articles): *to m. abode,* Gent. IV, 3, 23. H6A V, 4, 88. Lr. I, 1, 137. *account,* Ado II, 1, 65. R3 III, 2, 71. *act,* R3 II, 2, 90. Ant. III, 1, 13. *ado,* Gent. IV, 4, 30. H4A II, 4, 223. H8 V, 3, 158. Tit. IV, 3, 102. *advantage,* Gent. II, 4, 68. *amends,* Tp. IV, 1, 2. Gent. III, 1, 331. IV, 2, 99. Wiv. II, 3, 70. III, 1, 90. III, 5, 48 etc. *answer,* Meas. III, 2, 165. Ado IV, 1, 18. Tw. III, 3, 14. John II, 121. 235. R2 IV, 20. H5 V, 2, 75. H6A V, 3, 150. Cor. I, 1, 110. Caes. I, 3, 114. Hml. I, 2, 215 etc. *apologies,* Lucr. 31. *appeal,* H8 V, 1, 153. *appear-*

ance, II, 4, 132. *appointment,* Meas. III, 1, 60. *approach,* H5 II, 4, 9. Ant. I, 3, 46. *article,* LLL I, 1, 140. *assault,* Meas. III, 1, 189. H6A II, 1, 38. Cymb. I, 4, 175. *assay,* Meas. III, 1, 163. Tim. IV, 3, 406. Hml. III, 3, 69. *assurance,* Shr. II, 389. 398. III, 2, 136. *atonement,* Wiv. I, 1, 33. H4B IV, 1, 221. R3 I, 3, 36. *audit,* Mcb. I, 6, 27. *bargain,* Ven. 512. LLL V, 2, 799. John III, 1, 93. Troil. III, 2, 204. Caes. I, 3, 120. *battery,* Ven. 426. H6A I, 4, 65. H6C III. 1, 36. Ant. II, 7, 115. Per. IV, 4, 43. V, 1, 47. *boast,* Ado III, 3, 20. As II, 5, 38. H5 III, 7, 66. Troil. III, 3, 98. Tit. II, 3, 11. *bond,* Merch. II, 6, 6. *boot,* H5 1, 2, 194. H6B IV, 1, 13. Ant. IV, 1, 9. *bout,* Hml. IV, 7, 159. *businesses,* Wint. IV, 2, 15. *care,* IV, 4, 366. *challenge,* LLL V, 2, 713. H8 II, 4, 77. *charter,* All's IV, 5, 97. *cheer,* H4B V, 3, 18. *choice,* Mids. V, 43. Merch. II, 7, 3. III, 2, 43. All's II, 1, 206. H6C IV, 1, 3. H8 I, 4, 85. Tit. II, 1, 73. Rom. II, 5, 38. Ant. III, 1, 23 etc. *cital,* H4A V, 2, 62. *claim,* John III, 4, 143. H5 I, 2, 68. H6C IV, 7, 59. *clamour,* Hml. II, 2, 538. *close,* Gent. V, 4, 117. *coil,* John II, 165. *collection,* Cymb. V, 5, 432. *comment,* Err. III, 1, 100. John IV, 2, 263. V, 7, 4. *commotion,* H6B III, 1, 29. 358. *compare,* Mids. III, 2, 290. Tw. II, 4, 104. *compromise,* Wiv. I, 1, 33. John V, 1, 67. *conclusion,* As V, 4, 132. Wint. I, 2, 81. *confession,* Rom. III, 5, 233. IV, 1, 22. Hml. IV, 7, 96. *conquest,* John III, 1, 290. R2 II, 1, 66. Per. I, 4, 69. *construction,* Wiv. II, 2, 232. *course,* R3 IV, 4, 529 (Qq *made away*). *courtesy,* Ado II, 1, 56. Meas. II, 4, 175. As Epil. 23. H4B II, 1, 135 (Ff om.). *covenant,* R2 II, 3, 50. *cry,* R2 V, 3, 75. Per. II, 1, 22. *defeat,* Ado IV, 1, 48. H5 I, 2, 107. Hml. II, 2, 598. *delay,* Mids. III, 2, 394. R3 V, 3, 17. *delivery,* Wint. V, 2, 10. *demand,* All's II, 1, 194. Troil. II, 3, 72. III, 3, 17. 272. Ant. V, 2, 305. Cymb. V, 5, 130. *denial,* Meas. III, 1, 166. Shr. II, 281. All's I, 2, 9. *descant,* R3 III, 7, 49 (Qq *build*). *diction,* Hml. V, 2, 123. *difference,* Wiv. II, 1, 57. *discord,* Oth. II, 1, 201. *disjunction,* Wint. IV, 4, 540. *dispatch,* Cor. I, 1, 281. *dispensation,* Lucr. 248. *distinction,* All's III, 4, 40. Tw. II, 3, 174. Cymb. IV, 2, 248. *division,* Tw. III, 4, 380. V, 229. *dole,* As I, 2, 138. *doubt,* Gent. V, 2, 20. LLL V, 2, 101. H8 V, 3, 67. Cor. I, 2, 18. V, 4, 49 etc. *election,* All's II, 3, 61. H6B I, 3, 165. Cymb. I, 2, 29. *end,* Wiv. I, 2, 12. Merch. III, 2, 44. Wint. III, 3, 99. H5 II, 3, 11. Tim. III, 4, 55. Hml. IV, 5, 186 etc. *entrance,* H6A II, 1, 30. *escape,* H6C IV, 6, 80. *exchange,* Gent. II, 2, 6. Wint. IV, 4, 647. Rom. II, 3, 62. *excuse,* Ven. 188. Lucr. 114. 225. Tw. I, 5, 33. R3 I, 2, 83. Troil. III, 1, 85. Rom. III, 5, 33 etc. *experiment,* Wiv. IV, 2, 35. All's II, 1, 157. *extent,* As III, 1, 17. *fault,* LLL V, 2, 562. Wint. III, 2, 218. R2 I, 2, 5. H5 IV, 1, 311. Cor. V, 6, 64. Cymb. III, 6, 58 etc. *feast,* Meas. I, 2, 57. Shr. III, 2, 16. *flight,* Gent. II, 7, 12. *fray,* Merch. III, 2, 62. *gambol,* Merch. III, 2, 93. *grapple,* Tw. V, 59. *greeting,* Meas. IV, 3, 92. *groan,* Per. IV, 2, 117. *guard,* Ant. IV, 1, 10. *hand,* H8 V, 4, 74. Cor. IV, 6, 117. *harm,* Lr. IV, 7, 29. *haste,* Gent. II, 4, 190. III, 1, 258. Meas. IV, 1, 57. IV, 5, 11. Merch. III, 2, 327 etc. *havoc,* Ado IV, 1, 197. Tw. V, 208. John II, 220. *hazard,* Lucr. 155. Merch. II, 1, 45. John II, 71. *holiday,* Tp. IV, 136. Caes. I, 1, 35. *impression,* R3 I, 4, 63. *impressure,* Troil. IV, 5, 131. *incision,* Merch. II, 1, 6. As III, 2, 75. H5 IV, 2, 9. *inquiry,* Meas. V, 5. Hml. II, 1, 4. *inroad,* Ant.

I, 4, 50. *intent*, Lr. IV, 7, 9 (*my made intent*). *jest*, Ado II, 3, 206. H6C V, 1, 30. *jointure*, H6C III, 3, 136. *journey*, Cymb. II, 4, 43. *joy*, John III, 4, 107 (or verb?). *leg*, All's II, 2, 10. *life*, Oth. III, 3, 177 (*m. a life of jealousy*, = lead a jealous life? or make jealousy my manner of living?). *lip*, Cor. II, 1, 126. *look*, Wint. V, 1, 228. Ant. I, 5, 56. *love*, Gent. IV, 2, 126. Wiv. I, 3, 48. Mids. I, 1, 107. Shr. I, 2, 136. Hml. III, 4, 93. Lr. V, 3, 86 etc. *manage*, R2 I, 4, 39. *mansion*, Tim. V, 1, 218. *march*, H6A IV, 3, 8. Mcb. V, 2, 31. Ant. IV, 8, 30. *marriage*, Ant. II, 3, 39. *match*, Ven. 586. Wiv. II, 2, 304. Ado II, 1, 314. II, 2, 38. Shr. IV, 4, 46. All's IV, 3, 254. H5 I, 2, 264 etc. *meal*, H4B IV, 3, 99. Cymb. III, 6, 52. *merchandise*, Merch. III, 1, 133. *mistakings*, Tp. I, 2, 248. *moan*, Gent. II, 3, 33. Mids. V, 341. Merch. I, 1, 126. III, 3, 23. R3 I, 2, 158. *mock*, Oth. V, 2, 151. *motion*, Err. I, 1, 60. Tw. III, 4, 316. H8 II, 4, 234. Cor. III, 2, 118. *note*, Ant. III, 3, 26. *oath*, R2 V, 1, 75. *observation*, Lr. I, 1, 292. *offence*, Meas. III, 2, 15. IV, 2, 199. As III, 5, 117. H5 IV, 8, 58. Lr. II, 4, 61 etc. *offer*, LLL V, 2, 810. Merch. IV, 1, 81. H5 I, 1, 75. IV, 1, 193. Ant. II, 6, 34 etc. *opening*, Meas. IV, 1, 31. *overture*, All's V, 3, 99. Lr. III, 7, 89. *pants*, Oth. II, 1, 80. *partition*, Cymb. I, 6, 37. *passage*, H8 II, 4, 165. *pastime*, Wint. II, 3, 24. Cymb. III, 1, 78. *pause*, Lucr. 541. John IV, 2, 231. H6C III, 2, 10. R3 I, 2, 162. Ant. V, 1, 3 etc. *period*, Mids. V, 96. H4B IV, 5, 231. R3 III, 1, 44. *pillage*, Tit. II, 3, 44. *play*, H8 I, 4, 46. *point*, H6B II, 1, 5. *practice*, Meas. III, 2, 288. *prayer*, Merch. IV, 1, 127. H6B IV, 7, 121. *preachment*, H6C I, 4, 72. *preparation*, Wiv. IV, 5, 89. Ado I, 1, 280. *prepare*, H6C IV, 1, 131. *pretence*, Per. I, 2, 91. *prey*, R3 I, 3, 71. III, 5, 84. Troil. I, 3, 123. *price*, Ado III, 3, 122. All's V, 3, 61. *prize*, R3 III, 7, 187. Ant. V, 2, 183. *probation*, Hml. I, 1, 156. *proclamation*, H6A I, 3, 71. H6C IV, 7, 70. V, 5, 9. R3 IV, 4, 519. *promise*, Wiv. IV, 6, 34. Meas. IV, 1, 34. Cor. III, 6, 86. Caes. IV, 2, 24. Hml. I, 3, 119 etc. *proof*, Ado II, 2, 27. Tw. I, 5, 67. H6A I, 2, 94. Caes. II, 1, 299. Oth. V, 1, 26. *provision*, Err. I, 1, 48. *purchase*, Ven. 515. R3 III, 7, 187. Oth. II, 3, 9. *pursuit*, R3 III, 2, 30. *push*, Ado V, 1, 38. *quarry*, Cor. I, 1, 202. *question*, Merch. I, 1, 156. 184. H4B IV, 1, 167. Troil. I, 2, 174. Cor. II, 1, 246. Lr. IV, 3, 26. Oth. III, 4, 17 etc. *ransom*, H6B IV, 1, 10. *recantation*, All's II, 3, 194. *reckoning*, H5 IV, 1, 141. Hml. I, 5, 78. *recompense*, Wiv. IV, 6, 55. *recordation*, Troil. V, 2, 116. *reference*, Ant. V, 2, 23, *remain*, Cor. I, 4, 62. *render*, Tim. V, 1, 152. *repair*, LLL II, 240. *repetition*, Ven. 831. R3 I, 3, 166. *replication*, Caes. I, 1, 52. Hml. IV, 2, 13. *reply*, John III, 3, 49. R2 II, 3, 73. Ant. III, 11, 18. *report*, Cor. IV, 5, 157. Lr. III, 1, 37. Ant. II, 5, 57. V, 2, 255. *request*, Cor. II, 3, 47. Tim. I, 1, 279. Caes. V, 5, 11. *rescue*, Err. IV, 4, 114. Ant. III, 11, 48. *reservation*, All's II, 3, 260. Cor. III, 3, 130. *rest*, Per. II Prol. 26. *restitution*, Wiv. V, 5, 32. *retire*, LLL II, 234. H5 IV, 3, 86. *retreat*, As III, 2, 169. H4B IV, 3, 78. *return*, Gent. II, 7, 14. Meas. III, 3, 107. Tw. I, 4, 22. H6B I, 2, 83. H6C IV, 1, 5. Lr. II, 4, 153 etc. *revolt*, Oth. I, 1, 135. *ring*, Caes. III, 2, 162. *road*, H5 I, 2, 138. Cor. III, 1, 5. *satisfaction*, Err. IV, 1, 5. V, 399. H5 IV, 8, 48. H6C V, 5, 14. Tit. V, 1, 8. *scruple*, H4B I, 2, 148. Troil. IV, 1, 56. Cymb. V, 5, 182. *search*, Tp. II, 1, 323. Per. III Prol. 19. *separation*, Wint.

I, 1, 28. *sermon*, Shr. IV, 1, 185. *set*, R3 V, 3, 19. *shift*, Merch. I, 2, 97. All's II, 5, 39. H4B II, 1, 169. II, 2, 25. H6B IV, 8, 32. Mcb. II, 3, 46. *shoot*, LLL IV, 1, 10. *shout*, Caes. I, 1, 49. *show*, Tp. I, 2, 470. Ado I, 3, 20. As I, 2, 96. H4A V, 4, 95. H6B I, 1, 241. Caes. IV, 2, 24. Cymb. I, 5, 40. Per. I, 4, 75 etc. *shrift*, R3 III, 4, 97. *sign*, Tit. III, 1, 121. III, 2, 43. *signal*, H6B III, 3, 28. *slander*, Ado III, 3, 170. *slaughter*, H6B III, 2, 190. Cymb. V, 3, 79. Per. IV, 4, 37. *smiles*, Wint. I, 2, 116. *sojourn*, Lr. I, 1, 48. *sound*, Shr. Ind. I, 51. Per. II, 3, 62. *spare*, H8 V, 4, 21. *speech*, Caes. III, 2, 64. *speed*, Gent. III, 1, 169. Meas. IV, 3, 109. Mids. II, 1, 233. Merch. II, 8, 37 etc. *spoil*, H6C V, 4, 80. *sport*, Wiv. III, 3, 160. Err. II, 2, 30. Ado III, 1, 58. Mids. III, 2, 389. As I, 2, 28. All's V, 3, 323. R2 II, 1, 85. Hml. II, 2, 536 etc. *stand*, Lucr. 438. Merch. II, 6, 2. V, 77. John IV, 2, 39. H4B II, 3, 64. H6C III, 1, 3. Cymb. V, 3, 1 etc. *start*, H6B IV, 8, 45. *stay*, Mids. III, 2, 87. V, 428. Tim. III, 6, 128. *step*, Troil. II, 3, 193. *strain*, Troil. I, 3, 326. *stray*, Lr. I, 1, 212. *stride*, R2 I, 3, 268. III, 3, 92. Cymb. V, 3, 43. *suit*, Tp. III, 2, 44. H8 I, 2, 197. Tit. I, 223. Cymb. V, 5, 71 etc. *summons*, H8 II, 4, 219. *supper*, H6C V, 5, 85 (or = to give?). *survey*, Cor. II, 1, 43. *tale*, H6C II, 1, 120. Hml. II, 2, 146. *taste*, H4B II, 3, 52. *tender*, Wiv. I, 1, 215. Ado II, 3, 185. LLL II, 171. Hml. I, 3, 99; in another sense: H4A V, 4, 49. *test*, Meas. I, 1, 49. *thought*, Oth. I, 3, 26. *thrust*, H4B II, 4, 228. H5 II, 1, 104. *title*, All's I, 3, 107. H5 I, 2, 68. *trespass*, H6C V, 1, 92. *trial*, Lucr. Arg. 9. Tp. I, 2, 467. Meas. III, 1, 203. Tw. IV, 2, 52. H6A V, 3, 76. Cor. V, 1, 40. *use*, Ven. 129. Tp. I, 2, 492. Gent. II, 4, 68. Ado I, 3, 40. All's IV, 4, 22. H5 I, 2, 268. Tim. III, 2, 89. Ant. III, 5, 7 etc. *vent*, All's II, 3, 212. *view*, Tw. II, 2, 20. *visitation*, H8 I, 1, 179. *vow*, LLL II, 22. Tw. V, 222. John III, 1, 266 etc. *voyage*, Ado I, 1, 82. R2 V, 5, 49. *wager*, Hml. IV, 7, 156. Cymb. I, 4, 120. *war*, H6A I, 2, 17. H6C II, 2, 31. Cor. I, 1, 238. Mcb. II, 4, 17. Ant. II, 2, 43. 95. III, 5, 4 etc. *waste*, Merch. I, 1, 157. H5 I, 2, 28. Rom. I, 1, 224. *way*, Shr. I, 1, 239. II, 155. Wint. V, 1, 233. R2 V, 2, 110. H6C IV, 5, 10 etc. *welcome*, Tim. I, 2, 135. *wing*, Mcb. III, 2, 51. *work*, John II, 302. 407. Cor. I, 4, 20. I, 8, 9. IV, 6, 80. 88. 95. 100. V, 1, 15. Rom. II, 6, 35 etc.

4) to put into the suitable form for use: *m. the beds*, Wiv. I, 4, 102. Merch. IV, 1, 96. Shr. IV, 1, 203. Rom. III, 5, 202. Of doors, = to close, to fasten, to bar: *the doors are made against you*, Err. III, 1, 93. *m. the doors upon a woman's wit and it will out at the casement*, As IV, 1, 162. Similarly: *there is no bar to m. against your highness' claim*, H5 I, 2, 36. With *up*: *ay, m. up that*, Tw. II, 5, 133 (= make it out, make it intelligible, solve the riddle).

5) to raise, to gather, to assemble, to bring together: *m. all the money thou canst*, Oth. I, 3, 361. 365. *the greatest strength and power he can m.* R3 IV, 4, 449. *m. friends with speed*, H4B I, 1, 214. *let our alliance be combined, our best friends made*, Caes. IV, 1, 44. *'tis fit you m. strong party*, Cor. III, 2, 94. *the army we can m.* I, 1, 37. *m. head*, H4A III, 1, 64. IV, 1, 80. Cor. II, 2, 92. III, 1, 1. Caes. IV, 1, 42. cf. *Head*. With *up*: *m. up no factious numbers for the matter*, H6B II, 1, 40. *he —s up the file of all the gentry*, H8 I, 1, 75. *the enemy by them shall m. a fuller number up*, Caes. IV, 3, 208.

6) to make the fortune of, to enrich, to make happy: *there would this monster m. a man*, Tp. II, 2, 31. *and m. and mar the foolish Fates*, Mids. I, 2, 39. *there's enough to m. us all*, H4A II, 2, 60. *it —s him and it mars him*, Mcb. II, 3, 35. *it — s us, or it mars us*, Oth. V, 1, 4 (cf. *Mar*). *that either —s me or fordoes me quite*, Oth. V, 1, 129. *Made* = fortunate, having one's fortune made: *we had all been made men*, Mids. IV, 2, 18. *thinks himself made in the unchaste composition*, All's IV, 3, 21. *go to, thou art made*, Tw. II, 5, 168. *you're a made old man*, Wint. III, 3, 124. *he's made for ever*, Oth. I, 2, 51.

7) to amount to: *this bottle —s an angel*, H4A IV, 2, 6 (= costs). *ten masts at each m. not the altitude*, Lr. IV, 6, 53.

8) to earn, to raise as a profit: *of whom I hope to m. much benefit*, Err. I, 2, 25. *of which he made five marks, ready money*, Meas. IV, 3, 7. *whether that thy youth and kind will the faithful offer take of me and all that I can m.* As IV, 3, 61.

9) to represent; to consider as, to pretend to be: *m. not impossible that which but seems unlike*, Meas. V, 51. *m. it no wonder*, Shr. III, 2, 193. *what place m. you special, when you put off that* (the court) *with such contempt?* All's II, 2, 5. *m. this haste as your own good proceeding*, II, 4, 50. *I beseech your majesty to m. it natural rebellion, done i' the blaze of youth*, V, 3, 5. *m. me not sighted like the basilisk*, Wint. I, 2, 388. *were it worse than the name of rebellion can tell how to m. it*, H4B I, 2, 90. *your virtue is to m. him worthy whose offence subdues him*, Cor. I, 1, 179.

10) to prove to be, to turn out, to become, to be (Germ. *abgeben*): *I myself could m. a chough of as deep chat*, Tp. II, 1, 265. *an old cloak —s a new jerkin*, Wiv. I, 3, 18. *thou wouldst m. an absolute courtier*, III, 3, 66. *he'll m. a proper man*, As III, 5, 115. *a would have made a good pantler*, H4B II, 4, 258. *I should m. four dozen of such*, V, 1, 70. *a far more glorious star thy soul will m. than Julius Caesar*, H6A I, 1, 55. *he would have made a noble knight*, IV, 7, 44. *thou wouldst m. a good fool*, Lr. I, 5, 41. *Jove knows what man thou mightst have made*, Cymb. IV, 2, 207. *to m. one* = to be of the party: Wiv. II, 3, 48. Shr. I, 2, 246. Tw. I, 5, 213. II, 5, 227. H4A I, 2, 112. Caes. V, 5, 72 (cf. *One*). *let the fool m. a third*, Tw. II, 3, 189. *the devil m. a third*, H6B III, 2, 303. Evans says: *I shall m. two*, Wiv. III, 3, 250.

11) to have to do, to be about, to do: *what they made there, I know not*, Wiv. II, 1, 244. *what m. you here?* IV, 2, 55. As I, 1, 31. II, 3, 4. *what —s treason here?* LLL IV, 3, 190. *what —s he here?* As III, 2, 234. Oth. I, 2, 49. *what doest thou m. here?* R2 V, 3, 89. *what —st thou in my sight?* R3 I, 3, 164. *what —s he upon the sea?* IV, 4, 474 (Qq *doth*). *what made your master in this place?* Rom. V, 3, 280. *what m. we abroad?* Tim. III, 5, 46. *what m. you from Wittenberg?* Hml. I, 2, 164. *what m. you at Elsinore*, II, 2, 277. *what m. you from home?* Oth. III, 4, 169. = to do, to operate: *this late complaint will m. but little for his benefit*, H6B I, 3, 101. *the policy of that purpose made more in the marriage than the love of the parties*, Ant. II, 6, 126. *she can m., unmake, do what she list*, Oth. II, 3, 352. Used, like *to do*, to supply the place of another verb: *if none appear to prove upon thy head thy heinous treasons, there is my pledge: I'll m. it on thy heart*, Lr. V, 3, 93 (Qq *prove*).

B) absol. and intr. 1) to do, to be active, to operate: *the less you meddle or m. with them*, Ado III, 3, 56. *I'll not meddle nor m. no further*, Troil. I, 1, 14. *I'll meddle nor m. no more in the matter*, 85. *to m. against* = to be contrary to, to oppose: *albeit considerations infinite do m. against it*, H4A V, 1, 103. *which —s much against my manhood*, H5 III, 2, 52. *what may m. against the house of Lancaster*, H6C II, 1, 176. *the time and place doth m. against me*, Rom. V, 3, 225 (speaks against me). With *up: election —s not up on such conditions*, Lr. I, 1, 209 (does not come to a decision).

2) Joined to adjectives, nearly = to be: *to m. bold*, Wiv. II, 2, 162. 262. Mids. III, 1, 187. H8 III, 2, 318. Rom. III, 1, 81. Mcb. II, 3, 56. Hml. V, 2, 16. Oth. III, 1, 35. Cymb. I, 6, 197. V, 5, 89 (cf. *Bold*). *she that —s dainty, she, I'll swear, hath corns*, Rom. I, 5, 21 (= plays the prude). *to m. merry*, Shr. V, 1, 23. H6B I, 2, 85. *he that stands upon a slippery place —s nice of no vile hold to stay him up*, John III, 4, 138 (is not over-scrupulous in laying hold of etc.). *m. ready* = m. yourself ready, Meas. III, 1, 172. Troil. IV, 4, 146. *'tis but wisdom to m. strong against him*, H4A IV, 4, 39. *that she m. friends to the strict deputy*, Meas. I, 2, 185 (= gain the friendship of).

3) to move, to go: *Venus —s amain to him*, Ven. 5. *as the waves m. towards the pebbled shore*, Sonn. 60, 1. *two ships —ing amain to us*, Err. I, 1, 93. *m. for Sicilia*, Wint. IV, 4, 554. R2 I, 4, 52. II, 1, 287. H6C II, 3, 56. IV, 5, 10. R3 IV, 4, 469. 529 (Qq *made away*, Ff *made his course*). H8 I, 4, 55. Tit. V, 1, 25. Rom. I, 1, 131. Caes. III, 1, 18. V, 3, 29. Lr. I, 1, 145 (*m. from the shaft*). Oth. I, 1, 68. I, 3, 14. 222. V, 1, 58. Per. I, 4, 61. III, 1, 78. IV, 4, 3. V, 1, 19. With *forth: the Dukes of Berry and of Bretagne shall m. forth*, H5 II, 4, 5. *m. forth: the generals would have some words*, Caes. V, 1, 25. With *out: seven of my people m. out for him*, Tw. II, 5, 65. With *up: Philip, m. up; my mother is assailed*, John III, 2, 5 (go to the place where my mother is). *m. up, lest your retirement do amaze your friends*, H4A V, 4, 5 (join our army). *m. up to Clifton*, 58.

Make, subst. mate, companion, husband or wife: *else one self mate and m. could not beget such different issues*, Lr. IV, 3, 36 (reading of Q2; the other O. Edd. mate and mate).

Makeless, mateless, widowed: *the world will wail thee, like a m. wife*, Sonn. 9, 4.

Make-peace, peacemaker: R2 I, 1, 160.

Maker, one who makes: *we are the —s of manners*, H5 V, 2, 296. *God, the best m. of marriages*, 387. *peace is a great m. of cuckolds*, Cor. IV, 5, 244. = creator: *man, the image of his M.* H8 III, 2, 443. *praise my M.* V, 5, 69.

Making, subst. (cf. *Make*, vb.) form, external appearance, show: *stigmatical in m., worse in mind*, Err. IV, 2, 22. *either I mistake your shape and m. quite*, Mids. II, 1, 32. *when by the Archbishop of Canterbury she had all the royal —s of a queen*, H8 IV, 1, 87 (ensigns of royalty).

Malady, disease: Ven. 745. Sonn. 118, 3. 153, 8. Gent. II, 1, 42. LLL IV, 3, 295. Shr. Ind. 2, 124. All's II, 1, 9. 124. Wint. IV, 4, 124. H4B I, 2, 139. H5 V, 1, 87. H6A III, 3, 49. Tim. III, 6, 108. Mcb. IV, 3, 142. Lr. III, 4, 8.

Malapert, pert, forward, saucy: Tw. IV, 1, 47. H6C V, 5, 32. R3 I, 3, 255

Malchus (O. Edd. *Mauchus*), king of Arabia: Ant. III, 6, 72.

Malcolm, name in Mcb. I, 4, 38 etc.

Malcontent, see *Malecontent*.

Male, adj. of the sex that begets, not bears young: Wiv. V, 5, 19 (quibbling). Err. I, 1, 56. John III, 4, 79. H4B IV, 3, 100. H5 I, 2, 70. H8 II, 4, 189. 191. Troil. V, 1, 17. Cor. V, 4, 30.

Male, subst. 1) one of the male sex, one whose office is to beget young: *the beasts are their —s' subjects*, Err. II, 1, 19. *you love the breeder better than the m.* H6C II, 1, 42. *compose nothing but —s*, Mcb. I, 7, 74.

2) male parent, father: *thy mother's son! like enough, and thy father's shadow: so the son of the female is the shadow of the m.* H4B III, 2, 141. *I, the hapless m. to one sweet bird*, H6C V, 6, 15.

Malecontent, adj. discontented, displeased: *that you stand pensive, as half m.* H6C IV, 1, 10. *is it for a wife that thou art m.?* 60.

Malecontent, subst. one who feels unhappy, because he has not what he wishes: *then, like a melancholy m., he vails his tail*, Ven. 313. *to wreathe your arms like a m.* Gent. II, 1, 20. *thou art the Mars of —s*, Wiv. I, 3, 113. *Cupid, liege of all loiterers and —s*, LLL III, 185.

Malediction, evil speaking: *menaces and —s against king and nobles*, Lr. I, 2, 160.

Malefaction, crime: Hml. II, 2, 621.

Malefactor, a criminal: Meas. II, 1, 52. Ado IV, 2, 3. Ant. II, 5, 53. Not understood by Elbow and Dogberry.

Malevolence, ill will, enmity: *the m. of fortune*, Mcb. III, 6, 28.

Malevolent, ill disposed, hostile: *m. to you in all aspects*, H4A I, 1, 97.

Malice, 1) malignity, disposition to injure others: Meas. III, 2, 157. Merch. IV, 1, 214. As II, 3, 36. All's III, 6, 9. Tw. I, 5, 196. V, 373. Wint. I, 1, 37. John IV, 1, 109. H4B I, 2, 195. H6A III, 1, 26. 75. B I, 3, 213. II, 1, 25. III, 1, 154. III, 2, 23. H8 I, 1, 105. II, 2, 69. III, 2, 237. 243. V, 1, 135. V, 2, 8. V, 3, 44. 145. 152. Troil. V, 1, 64. Cor. II, 1, 58. II, 2, 36. Tit. V, 3, 13. Tim. I, 1, 47. Mcb. II, 3, 138. III, 2, 25. Lr. II, 2, 137 (with *against*). Oth. II, 1, 148. V, 2, 343. Ant. I, 2, 112. Cymb. I, 5, 35. III, 5, 33. IV, 2, 324. Abstr. pro concr.: *shruggest thou, m.?* Tp. I, 2, 367.

2) hate, enmity, ill will: *our cannons' m.* John II, 251. *your sharpest deeds of m.* 380. *combine the blood of m. in a vein of league*, V, 2, 38. *I have heard you preach that m. was a great and grievous sin*, H6A III, 1, 128 (i. e. hatred). *I never sought their m.* H8 V, 2, 15. *translate his m. towards you into love*, Cor. II, 3, 197. *to affect the m. and displeasure of the people*, II, 2, 24. Merch. IV, 1, 18. As I, 2, 294. R2 I, 1, 9. 14. 155. H6A IV, 1, 108. H6C IV, 3, 46. IV, 6, 28. R3 I, 3, 29. II, 2, 125. H8 II, 1, 62. 80. 157. III, 2, 268. Cor. II, 1, 244. IV, 5, 78. 102. IV, 6, 41. Caes. III, 1, 174. Mcb. III, 2, 14. Oth. II, 3, 275. V, 1, 102. With *of*, to indicate the object of hate: *'tis in the m. of mankind that he thus advises us*, Tim. IV, 3, 456. With *towards*: *the m. towards you* (is) *to forgive you*, Cymb. V, 5, 419.

Malicious, 1) malignant, malevolent, prone to do mischief: H6A IV, 1, 7. H8 I, 2, 78. II, 4, 83.

IV, 2, 48. Cor. I, 1, 91. III, 3, 55. Mcb. IV, 3, 59. Hml. I, 1, 146. II, 2, 536. Lr. III, 5, 10. Oth. I, 1, 100.

2) full of hate: *commander of this hot m. day*, John II, 314.

Maliciously, 1) malignantly: Cor. I, 1, 35.

2) like one full of hate, with the strength of hate: *I will be treble-sinewed, hearted, breathed, and fight m.* Ant. III, 13, 179. Used of strong poison: *a lingering dram that should not work m. like poison*, Wint. I, 2, 321 (in an apparently pernicious manner).

Malign, vb. to regard with envy or malice: *as you m. our senators*, Cor. I, 1, 117. *wayward fortune did m. my state*, Per. V, 1, 90.

Malignancy, malevolence: *the m. of my fate*, Tw. II, 1, 4.

Malignant, 1) full of malice: *thou liest, m. thing*, Tp. I, 2, 257. *a m. and a turbaned Turk*, Oth. V, 2, 353.

2) injurious, pernicious, hostile: *unless the next word have some m. power upon my life*, Gent. III, 1, 238. *hearing your high majesty is touched with that m. cause*, All's II, 1, 114 (= disease). *O m. and ill-boding stars*, H6A IV, 5, 6. *cracked in pieces by m. death*, R3 II, 2, 52. *to your person his will is most m.* H8 I, 2, 141.

Malignantly, malevolently, maliciously: *if he should still m. remain fast foe to the plebeii*, Cor. II, 3, 191.

Malkin, a kitchen-wench: Cor. II, 1, 224. Per. IV, 3, 34.

Mall, diminutive of Mary: Tp. II, 2, 50. *are they like to take dust, like Mistress —'s picture?* Tw. I, 3, 135 (commonly supposed to allude to one Mall Cutpurse, but with little probability, as Mall Cutpurse was born in 1589 and died in 1659. Perhaps Sir Toby means only to say: like a picture intended for a beauty, but in fact representing Mall the kitchen-wench. In the poet's time it was the custom to hang curtains before pictures).

Mallard, a drake: Ant. III, 10, 20.

Malleable, capable of extension by the hammer: Per. IV, 6, 152.

Mallecho (O. Edd. *mallico* and *malicho*), probably from the Spanish *malhecho*, = mischief: *this is miching m.; it means mischief*, Hml. III, 2, 146.

Mallet, a wooden hammer: *there's no more conceit in him than is in a m.* H4B II, 4, 263 (or = mallard?).

Mallows, the plant Malva: Tp. II, 1, 144.

Malmsey, a kind of sweet wine: LLL V, 2, 233.

Malmsey-butt, a large cask of malmsey: R3 I, 4, 161. 277.

Malmsey-nose, red-nosed: *m. knave*, H4B II, 1, 42.

Malt, grain prepared for brewing: Lr. III, 2, 82.

Malt-horse, a brewer's horse; used as a term of contempt: Err. III, 1, 32. Shr. IV, 1, 132.

Malt-worm, a tippler of ale: H4A II, 1, 83. H4B II, 4, 361.

Malvolio, name in Tw. I, 5, 79 etc.

Mamillius, name in Wint. I, 1, 38. I, 2, 119. 211

Mammering, hesitating, Oth. III, 3, 70 (Q1 muttering).

Mammet, a doll, a puppet: *this is no world to play with —s*, H4A II, 3, 95. *a whining m.* Rom. III, 5, 186.

Mammock, to tear in pieces: *how he —ed it*, Cor. I, 3, 71.

Man, name of an island in the Irish sea: H6B II, 3, 13. II, 4, 78. 94.

Man, subst. (plur. *men*), 1) a human being: *this is the third m. that e'er I saw*, Tp. I, 2, 445. *a m. or a fish?* II, 2, 25. 35. II, 1, 154. III, 1, 51. H5 IV, 1, 106 etc. etc. *wilt thou be made a m. out of my vice?* Meas. III, 1, 138 (= wilt thou live etc.); cf. *am I dead? do I not breathe a m.?* H6C III, 1, 82; *since I was m.* Lr. III, 2, 45 (since my birth). The article omitted, to denote the whole human race: *beyond —'s life*, Tp. II, 1, 247. *where m. doth not inhabit*, III, 3, 57. Wiv. I, 1, 21. Meas. II, 2, 50. 79. Mids. IV, 1, 211. Wint. IV, 4, 829. 830. H4B IV, 3, 118. Tim. IV, 3, 194. 197 (*more. m.? plague, plague!*). Lr. III, 1, 10. Per. II Prol. 35. Plur.: *men hang and drown their proper selves*, Tp. III, 3, 59. V, 242. H6B III, 1, 301 etc. *a m.* = any person, one: *misery acquaints a m. with strange bedfellows*, Tp. II, 2, 41. *to sing at a —'s funeral*, 46. *as a 'nose on a —'s face*, Gent. II, 1, 142. II, 5, 5. III, 1, 311. V, 4, 1. Wiv. II, 1, 193. III, 2, 37. Ado II, 3, 247. H4B IV, 3, 95 etc. *not a m. of them* = none of them: LLL V, 2, 128. H4B Ind. 38. R3 II, 1, 119. *every m.* = everybody: Ado III, 2, 110. LLL I, 1, 152. Mids. I, 2, 4. IV, 2, 38 etc. *every m. of them*, H4A II, 4, 197. *no m.* = nobody: Tp. V, 213. 257. Gent. II, 1, 65. Wiv. V, 5, 52. Tw. II, 5, 110 etc.

2) a male of the human race: *more widows than we bring men to comfort them*, Tp. II, 1, 134. *kept from resort of men*, Gent. III, 1, 108. 109. *the putting down of men*, Wiv. II, 1, 30. *it is a —'s voice*, Meas. I, 4, 7. Tp. I, 2, 109. 214. 488. II, 2, 32 (cf. *Make*). III, 2, 114. Wiv. II, 1, 83. III, 3, 78. Meas. II, 1, 176. III, 2, 112. Err. II, 1, 7. Mids. I, 1, 66. Tw. III, 4, 333 etc. etc. Without the article, in a general sense: *were m. but constant, he were perfect*, Gent. V, 4, 110. *she could not love me, were m. as rare as phoenix*, As IV, 3, 17. *m. is enemy to virginity*, All's I, 1, 123. Tw. II, 2, 37. Lr. III, 4, 84. Oth. IV, 1, 111. Cymb. I, 6, 69 etc. *m. by m.* Mids. I, 2, 3. H4A III, 3, 65. *to the last m.* H4B IV, 2, 44. *man at arms* and *man of arms* = knight, warrior: LLL IV, 3, 290. H4B II, 2, 82. H6C V, 4, 42. H6A I, 4, 30. *m. of war* = warrior, soldier: *three thousand men of war*, R2 II, 1, 286. *with his men of war*, II, 3, 52. *doth the m. of war stay all night?* H4B V, 1, 31. *the nine men's morris*, Mids. II, 1, 98 (cf. *Morris*). Used as a familiar compellation: *no marrying? None*, *m.* Tp. II, 1, 166. II, 2, 133. 137. Gent. II, 3, 38. II, 4, 168. IV, 2, 55. Meas. I, 2, 97. Err. IV, 2, 41. LLL I, 2, 139. Merch. I, 3, 157. II, 8, 1. H6B I, 2, 85. Tit. II, 1, 85. Rom. I, 5, 36. Caes. I, 2, 135 etc. Used with some latitude; applied to boys: *bring my young m. here to school*, Wiv. IV, 1, 8. *go play, Mamillius, thou art an honest m.* Wint. I, 2, 211. to God: *God's a good m.* Ado III, 5, 40 (Dogberry's speech). to the devil: *no m. means evil but the devil*, Wiv. V, 2, 15. to flies: *they are free men*, Rom. III, 3, 42. Emphatically: *play the men*, Tp. I, 1, 11. H6A I, 6, 16. *to trial of a m.* Ado V, 1, 66. LLL V, 2, 697. H5 III, 2, 33. Mcb. I, 7, 46. 49. 51. Caes. I, 2, 153. 155. 157. Hml. I, 2, 187. III, 4, 62. Lr. II, 2, 127. II, 4, 42 etc. *my man of men*, Ant. I, 5, 72. Opposed to a boy: Compl. 92. Wiv. III, 2, 6. Tw. I, 5, 165. 169. V, 402 etc. *the m.* = the right

man, just the man wanted: *Ovidius Naso was the m.* LLL IV, 2, 127. *here comes the m.* Merch. II, 2, 119. *am I the m. yet?* As III, 3, 3. *soft, soft, unless the master were the m.* Tw. I, 5, 313. *I am the m.* II, 2, 26. *I will be point-devise the very m.* II, 5, 177. *Harry the Fifth's the m.* H4B V, 3, 122. *this is not the m.* V, 5, 149. *you'll be the m.* Rom. I, 5, 83. *'tis the m.* Ant. I, 5, 54. cf. *here comes my m.* Rom. III, 1, 59. *I was never mine own m. since*, H6B IV, 2, 91 (= I was not what I used to be). cf. *when no m. was his own*, Tp. V, 213 (in his senses).

Often joined, in O. Edd., by a hyphen to preceding monosyll. adjectives, or spelt as a compound, while M. Edd. prefer writing them in two words. Very often, too, the adjective is accentuated, so that in many such expressions a similar difference is discernible as between *madman, freshman, nobleman* and *mad man, fresh man, noble man*. Cf. *blind-man*, H6A II, 4, 24. H6B II, 1, 63. *deadman*, Err. V, 241. Wint. II, 1, 150. R2 IV, 144. H5 II, 4, 107. H6B IV, 1, 6. V, 2, 4. R3 I, 4, 29. Tit. II, 3, 229. Rom. IV, 1, 82. 85. V, 1, 7. V, 2, 30. Mcb. IV, 3, 170 etc. *dumb men*, Cor. II, 1, 278. *good m.* LLL I, 1, 310. As II, 7, 115. 122. R2 I, 1, 114. H5 IV, 3, 56. R3 II, 1, 61. H8 III, 1, 22. 64. Tit. IV, 1, 123. Oth. V, 1, 99 etc. (cf. *Goodman*). *great m.* Meas. II, 2, 110; cf. 128. H6B III, 1, 19. H8 II, 1, 67. III, 2, 375. Hml. III, 2, 214. *mean m.* R2 I, 2, 33. *old m.* Err. I, 1, 97. John II, 570. H6B V, 2, 51. H6C V, 6, 39. H8 IV, 2, 21. Rom. II, 3, 35. Caes. I, 3, 65. Lr. II, 1, 101. II, 4, 291. 298. Oth. I, 3, 78. Cymb. V, 3, 52. 57. 85. Per. Prol. 13. *plain m.* R3 I, 3, 51. *poor m.* John IV, 1, 50. H6B IV, 7, 93. Caes. I, 1, 62. Lr. IV, 6, 29. *prime m.* H8 III, 2, 162. *proud m.* Troil. III, 3, 49. *rich m.* Tim. I, 1, 2, 72. *rude m.* John I, 1, 64. *sick m.* R2 II, 1, 84. Cor. I, 1, 182. Caes. II, 1, 310. 327. *tame m.* Mids. III, 2, 259. *true m.* LLL IV, 3, 187. R2 V, 3, 73. H6C I, 4, 64. Cymb. II, 3, 76. *wise m.* Tw. II, 3, 45. III, 1, 73. 75. R2 I, 3, 276. V, 5, 63. H6C III, 1, 25. Rom. III, 3, 62. Lr. I, 4, 182. *young m.* Mids. I, 1, 6. Shr. II, 393. John II, 570. Troil. V, 2, 165. Tit. I, 484.

3) a servant: *one of my husband's men*, Lucr. 1291. *now they are my men*, Tp. II, 1, 274. *get a new m.* II, 2, 189. Gent. IV, 2, 75. Wiv. I, 1, 114. 136. 281. II, 1, 182. Meas. IV, 2, 103. Err. II, 1, 43. II, 2, 207. III, 2, 74. IV, 4, 8. Ado III, 2, 45. Merch. II, 2, 94. V, 183. Shr. Ind. 2, 107. John III, 3, 72. H5 III, 2, 32. R3 I, 1, 80. H8 IV, 2, 148. Rom. II, 4, 3. 200. III, 1, 59. Lr. II, 4, 201 etc.

4) *a m. of war* = a ship of war: Tit. IV, 3, 22.

Man, vb. 1) to furnish with men, to line, to guard: *the castle, —ed with three hundred men*, R2 II, 3, 54. *the castle royally is —ed*, III, 3, 21. *see how the surly Warwick —s the wall*, H6C V, 1, 17. *your ships are not well —ed*, Ant. III, 7, 35. *with the rest full-manned*, 52. *to m. his galleys*, IV, 11, 3.

2) to accustom to man, to tame: *to m. my haggard, to make her come and know her keeper's call*, Shr. IV, 1, 196. cf. *Unmanned*.

3) to furnish with a servant: *I was never —ed with an agate*, H4B I, 2, 18. *I were —ed, horsed and wived*, 60

4) Very singular use: *m. but a rush against O-thello's breast, and he retires*, Oth. V, 2, 270 (Johnson: to point, to aim. Perhaps = manage).

Manacle, subst. chain for the hands, shackles:

it is a m. of love, Cymb. I, 1, 122. Plur. —*s* = chains: Meas. II, 4, 93. Cor. I, 9, 57. V, 3, 115. Cymb. V, 4, 199.

Manacle, vb. to chain, to fetter: *I'll m. thy neck and feet together*, Tp. I, 2, 461. *m. the bear-herd in their chains*, H6B V, 1, 149.

Manage, subst. 1) training, government of a horse: *or he (became) his m. by the well doing steed,* Compl. 112. *they (his horses) are taught their m.* As I, 1, 13. *wanting the m. of unruly jades,* R2 III, 3, 179. *speak terms of m. to thy bounding steed,* H4A II, 3, 52. *spur them, till they obey the m.* H8 V, 3, 24. *she's not paced yet: you must take some pains to work her to your m.* Per. IV, 6, 69. By conjecture in LLL V, 2, 482: *merrily hath this brave m., this career, been run* (Q1 *nuage*, Q2 Ff *manager*).
2) administration, conduct: *and to him put the m. of my state,* Tp. I, 2, 70. *the husbandry and m. of my house,* Merch. III, 4, 25. *their negotiations all must slack, wanting his m.* Troil. III, 3, 25.
3) proceeding, taking of measures, contriving of means: *which now the m. of two kingdoms must with fearful bloody issue arbitrate,* John I, 37. *for the rebels which stand out in Ireland expedient m. must be made,* R2 I, 4, 39.
4) the bringing about, setting on foot: *I can discover all the unlucky m. of this brawl,* Rom. III, 1, 148.

Manage, vb. 1) to handle, to wield: *m. it (the staff of hope) against despairing thoughts,* Gent. III, 1, 247. *m. rusty bills against thy seat,* R2 III, 2, 118. *m. me your caliver,* H4B III, 2, 292. 301. *m. it (your sword) to part these men,* Rom. I, 1, 76. *that still would m. those authorities,* Lr. I, 3, 17.
2) to train, to break in (as a horse): *he will not m. her, although he mount her,* Ven. 598.
3) to administer, to control, to govern: *whose state so many had the —ing,* H5 Epil. 11. *the son (should) m. his revenue,* Lr. I, 2, 79. *Photinus and your maids m. this war,* Ant. III, 7, 16.
4) to handle, to treat with caution and address: *shame hath a bastard fame, well —d,* Err. III, 2, 19. *in the —ing of quarrels he is wise,* Ado II, 3, 197. Shr. Ind. 1, 45. Wint. IV, 2, 17. H4A I, 2, 181. H6A IV, 1, 181.
5) to bring about, to set on foot, to contrive: *to m. private and domestic quarrel,* Oth. II, 3, 215.

Manager, 1) one who wields: *rust, rapier! be still, drum! for your m. is in love,* LLL I, 2, 188.
2) one who sets on foot, a contriver: *where is our usual m. of mirth?* Mids. V, 35.

Manakin, little man; term of contempt: *this is a dear m. to you,* Tw. III, 2, 57.

Man-child, male child, boy: Cor. I, 3, 18. *men-children:* Mcb. I, 7, 72.

Mandate, order, authoritative command: Hml. III, 4, 204. Oth. I, 3, 72. IV, 1, 270. Ant. I, 1, 22.

Mandragora, mandrake; a soporific: Oth. III, 3, 330. Ant. I, 5, 4.

Mandrake, the plant Atropa mandragora, the root of which was thought to resemble the human figure, and to cause madness and even death, when torn from the ground: *thou whoreson m., thou art fitter to be worn in my cap,* H4B I, 2, 17. *the whores called him m.* III, 2, 339. *would curses kill, as doth the —'s groan,* H6B III, 2, 310. *shrieks like —s' torn out of the earth,* Rom. IV, 3, 47.

Mane, the hair growing on the necks of horses and lions: Ven. 271. 298. Troil. III, 3, 224. Rom. I, 4, 89. Used of the foaming crest of waves: Oth. II, 1, 13. In All's IV, 5, 41 O. Edd. *main,* M. Edd. *name.*

Man-entered, initiated in, introduced into manhood: *his pupil-age m. thus,* Cor. II, 2, 103.

Manfully, bravely: Gent. IV, 1, 28. Tit. I, 196.

Mangle, vb. to cut into pieces, to mutilate; absol.: *her sight dazzling makes the wound seem three, and then she reprehends her —ing eye,* Ven. 1065. trans.: As II, 7, 42. H4A V, 4, 96. H5 II, 4, 60. IV, 4, 41. H6C V, 2, 7. Troil. V, 5, 33. Tit. III, 1, 256. Rom. IV, 3, 52. Oth. V, 1, 79. Ant. IV, 2, 27. Metaphorically, = to take from, to impair, to reduce to nothing: *the naked, poor and —d peace,* H5 V, 2, 34. *—ing by starts the full course of their glory,* Epil. 4. *your dishonour —s true judgment,* Cor. III, 1, 158. *what tongue shall smooth thy name, when I have —d it?* Rom. III, 2, 99. *to m. me with that word 'banished',* III, 3, 51. *take up this —d matter at the best,* Oth. I, 3, 173. *our laws, whose use the sword of Caesar hath too oft —d,* Cymb. III, 1, 57.

Mangy, scabby: *a m. dog,* Tim. IV, 3, 371.

Manhood, 1) virility, opposed to womanhood: *fit you to your m.* Cymb. III, 4, 195.
2) virility, opposed to boyhood: *thy prime of m. daring,* R3 IV, 4, 170. *many unrough youths that even now protest their first of m.* Mcb. V, 2, 11.
3) qualities becoming a man, bravery, fortitude, honour: Ado IV, 1, 321. Mids. III, 2, 412. Tw. III, 4, 198. H4A I, 2, 155. II, 4, 141. 142. H5 II, 1, 103. III, 2, 53. IV, 3, 66. H6B V, 2, 75. H6C II, 2, 108. 125. IV, 2, 20. Troil. I, 2, 276. II, 2, 47. Cor. III, 1, 246. Tim. IV, 3, 14. Mcb. III, 1, 103. Lr. I, 4, 319. IV, 2, 68. Oth. III, 3, 153. Ant. III, 10, 23. Cymb. V, 2, 2. Mrs. Quickly and Fluellen agree in saying *saving your m.* for *saving your honour,* or *your reverence:* H4B II, 1, 29. H5 IV, 8, 36.

Manifest, adj. 1) obvious, evident, not doubtful: Meas. IV, 2, 145. Merch. IV, 1, 358. H6A I, 3, 33. III, 1, 21. Cor. III, 1, 172. Lr. V, 3, 92.
2) plain, open, notorious, public: *to retort your m. appeal,* Meas. V, 303. *his reading and m. experience,* All's I, 3, 229. *make't m. where she has lived,* Wint. V, 3, 114. *you are m. house-keepers,* Cor. I, 3, 54.

Manifest, vb. to make appear, to show plainly, to reveal: Wiv. IV, 6, 15. Meas. IV, 3, 94. V, 417. Ado III, 2, 100. Tw. II, 5, 181 *(she —s herself to my love).* H4B IV, 5, 105. Cor. II, 2, 14. Oth. I, 2, 32 *(my parts, my title and my perfect soul shall m. me rightly).* Partic. *—ed* adjectively: *to make you understand this in a —ed effect,* Meas. IV, 2, 169, i. e. so as to make the matter manifest, as to leave no doubt.

Manifold, multifarious: Compl. 216. Tp. I, 2, 264. H4A IV, 3, 47. Tim. I, 1, 5. Lr. II, 1, 49. *the m. linguist,* All's IV, 3, 265 (i. e. knowing many languages). *a m. traitor,* Lr. V, 3, 114.

Manifoldly, in many ways: All's II, 3, 214.

Manikin, see *Manakin.*

Mankind (accented mostly on the last syll. in Tim., on the first in the other plays) 1) the human race: *how beauteous m. is!* Tp. V, 183. Tw. III, 4, 108. Troil. II, 3, 30. Tim. III, 4, 84. IV, 1, 36. 40. IV, 3, 23. 42. 53. 456. 506. Mcb. II, 4, 18. Ant. IV, 8, 25.

2) the males of the human race: *so rails against all married m.* Wiv. IV, 2, 23. *should all despair that have revolted wives, the tenth of m. would hang themselves,* Wint. I, 2, 199. *what kind o' man is he? why, of m.* Tw. I, 5, 160. *thou art a woman, and disclaimest flinty m.* Tim. IV, 3, 491. Adjectively, = masculine: *a m. witch,* Wint. II, 3, 67. *are you m.?* Cor. IV, 2, 16 (quibbling).

Man-like, manly: *not more m. than Cleopatra,* Ant. I, 4, 5.

Manly, adj. 1) becoming a man, brave, full of fortitude, vigorous: Lucr. 109. 1486. 1777. Ado V, 2, 15. Mids. III, 2, 157. Merch. II, 3, 14. All's II, 3, 298. John V, 2, 49. H5 II, 3, 3. III, 2, 24. H6B IV, 8, 53. V, 2, 63. H6C II, 2, 40. R3 I, 2, 165. Troil. IV, 5, 104. Rom. III, 2, 53. Mcb. II, 3, 139. Cymb. IV, 2, 397. Per. III, 1, 22.

2) pertaining to a man, not like a woman or boy: *turn two mincing steps into a m. stride,* Merch. III, 4, 68. *his big m. voice,* As II, 7, 161.

Manly, adv. in the manner of a man, courageously: *this tune goes m.* Mcb. IV, 3, 235.

Man-monster, servant-monster, a monster in a person's service: Tp. III, 2, 14.

Manna, the food of the famished Israelites in the Arabian desert: *you drop m. in the way of starved people,* Merch. V, 294.

Manner, 1) form of executing and performing, way, mode: *mark the m. of his teaching,* Shr. IV, 2, 5. *the m. of his gait,* Tw. II, 3, 170. Troil. IV, 5, 14. *the m. of your bearing,* Wint. IV, 4, 569. *the pretty and sweet m. of it,* H5 IV, 6, 28. *the m. of his speech,* Ant. II, 2, 114 (opposed to *matter*). *sets down the m. how,* Tw. III, 4, 80. *the m. how he found it,* Wint. V, 2, 4. *the m. how she came to it,* 92. *unless I be obtained by the m. of my father's will,* Merch. I, 2, 118 (i. e. in the way prescribed by the testament of my father). *she is dead, and by strange m.* Caes. IV, 3, 189. *in this m.* Wiv. II, 1, 25. *in a most hideous and dreadful m.* IV, 4, 34. *in most uneven m.* Meas. IV, 4, 3. V, 196. Ado IV, 2, 64. 65. LLL I, 1, 206. 207. 211 (*in m. and form following*). Mids. II, 2, 130. As III, 2, 427. Tw. III, 4, 9. Wint. V, 2, 49. H6C III, 3, 178. H8 I, 2, 35. II, 4, 144. Troil. V, 7, 6. Cor. II, 3, 66. Tim. III, 6, 15. Lr. I, 4, 59. Per. I, 1, 147. *In a m.* and *in m.* = almost: *it is in a m. done already,* John V, 7, 89. *you have in m. with your sinful hours made a divorce betwixt his queen and him,* R2 III, 1, 11.

2) course, process: *I'll show you the m. of it,* Gent. II, 3, 15. *the cunning m. of our flight,* II, 4, 180. *the m. of it is, I was taken with the m.* LLL I, 1, 204. *tell us the m. of the wrestling,* As I, 2, 118. *the m. of their taking,* R2 V, 6, 9. *the m. how this action hath been borne,* H4B IV, 4, 88. *the m. and true order of the fight,* 100. *the treacherous m. of his death,* H6A II, 2, 16. *in writing I preferred the m. of thy vile outrageous crimes,* III, 1, 11. *tell us the m. of it,* Caes. I, 2, 234. 236. *to relate the m. were to add the death of you,* Mcb. IV, 3, 205. *he has done all this* .... *here's the m. of it,* Ant. III, 6, 2. *the m. of their deaths,* V, 2, 340.

3) custom, habit, fashion: *it was ever his m. to do so,* Meas. IV, 2, 138. *I'll view the —s of the town,* Err. I, 2, 12. *it is the m. of a man to speak to a woman,* LLL I, 1, 212. *my lady, to the m. of the days, in cour-*

tesy gives undeserving praise, V, 2, 365. *I am yet so near the —s of my mother,* Tw. II, 1, 41. *our country —s give our betters way,* John I, 156. *whose —s our apish nation limps after,* R2 II, 1, 22. *these external —s of laments,* IV, 296. *your m. of wrenching,* H4B II, 1, 120. *we are the makers of —s,* H5 V, 2, 296. *showing, as the m. is, his wounds to the people,* Cor. II, 1, 251. *as the m. of our country is,* Rom. IV, 1, 109. *I am native here and to the m. born,* Hml. I, 4, 15.

4) kind, sort: *and words express the m. of my pity-wanting pain,* Sonn. 140, 4. *the grosser m. of these world's delights he throws upon the gross world's baser slaves,* LLL I, 1, 29. *the m. and the purpose of his treason,* R3 III, 5, 58. *beyond all m. of so much I love you,* Lr. I, 1, 62 (i. e. beyond any 'so much', any comparison, of whatever kind it may be). *all m. of men assembled here,* H6A I, 3, 74. *that no m. of persons have recourse unto the princes,* R3 III, 5, 108 (Ff *no m. person*). *what m. of man?* As III, 2, 216. Tw. I, 5, 161. III, 4, 288. Wint. IV, 3, 89. H4A II, 4, 323. 462. H8 V, 1, 118. *what m. o' thing is your crocodile?* Ant. II, 7, 46. Evans: *Mistress Quickly, which is in the m. of his nurse,* Wiv. I, 2, 3.

5) *to be taken with the m.* (apparently from another root), a law-term, = to be taken in the fact: LLL I, 1, 205. H4A II, 4, 347. *if you had not taken yourself with the m.* Wint. IV, 4, 752.

6) Plur. —s = a) behaviour, carriage, bearing: *their —s are more gentle-kind,* Tp. III, 3, 32. *frame your —s to the time,* Shr. I, 1, 232. *I advise you use your —s discreetly in all kind of companies,* 247. *that changeth thus his —s,* Wint. I, 2, 375. *what foolish master taught you these —s?* H4B II, 1, 203. *thou dost affect my —s,* Tim. IV, 3, 199. *their —s are so apish,* Lr. I, 4, 184. *infected with their —s,* 264. *these bloody accidents must excuse my —s,* Oth. V, 1, 94. b) rules of good breeding and decency: *beshrew my —s and my pride,* Mids. II, 2, 54. *we stand upon our —s,* Wint. IV, 4, 164. *our griefs, and not our —s, reason now,* John IV, 3, 29. *whom our —s term the prince,* R3 III, 7, 191. *my —s tell me we have your wrong rebuke,* Oth. I, 1, 130. *I extend my —s,* II, 1, 99. *you put me to forget a lady's —s,* Cymb. II, 3, 110. *good —s* = good breeding, civility, decency: As II, 7, 92. III, 2, 42. 43. 47. V, 4, 95. H4A III, 1, 190. H8 V, 2, 29. Rom. I, 5, 4. *—s,* alone, in the same sense: *a million of —s,* Gent. II, 1, 105. *against all checks, rebukes and —s,* Wiv. III, 4, 84. *if you have any pity, grace, or —s,* Mids. III, 2, 241. *I lack —s,* As IV, 3, 15. *if God have lent a man any —s, he may easily put it off at court,* All's II, 2, 9. V, 1, 15. Tw. II, 3, 94. IV, 1, 53. Wint. IV, 4, 244. H4A III, 1, 184. H6A II, 2, 54. H8 III, 2, 308. V, 1, 161. Tit. II, 1, 27. Rom. V, 3, 214. Tim. II, 2, 147. IV, 1, 18. Hml. V, 2, 17. Lr. IV, 6, 264. V, 3, 234. Treated as a sing.: All's II, 2, 9. Wint. IV, 4, 244. Rom. V, 3, 214. Lr. V, 3, 234. as a plur.: Tw. IV, 1, 53. R3 III, 7, 191. *in —s, and with —s,* = decently: *my tongue-tied Muse in —s holds her still,* Sonn. 85, 1. *it charges me in —s to express myself,* Tw. II, 1, 15. *how thy worth with —s may I sing,* Sonn. 39, 1. *can we with —s ask what was the difference?* Cymb. I, 4, 56. *I was thinking with what —s I might safely be admitted,* All's IV, 5, 93 (= how I might decently be admitted). — c) cast of mind, morals, character: *their face their —s most expressly told,* Lucr. 1397. *public means*

which public —s breeds, Sonn. 111, 4. *as dispropor-tioned in his —s as in his shape*, Tp. V, 290. *though I am a daughter to his blood, I am not to his —s*, Merch. II, 3, 19. *a like proportion of lineaments, of —s and of spirit*, III, 4, 15. *neither his daughter, if we judge by —s*, As I, 2, 283. III, 2, 43. All's I, 1, 71. John II, 127. H4B IV, 4, 64. 123. H5 I, 2, 49. H6B V, 1, 158. R3 IV, 4, 206. H8 IV, 2, 45. Tim. IV, 1, 25. Hml. I, 4, 30. Oth. II, 1, 232.

Mannered, minded, affected, disposed: *he is one the truest m.* Cymb. I, 6, 166. *to give her princely training, that she may be m. as she is born*, Per. III, 3, 17.

Mannerly, adj. decent; civil: *let me have what thou thinkest meet and is most mannerly*, Gent. II, 7, 58. *m. distinguishment betwixt the prince and beggar*, Wint. II, 1, 86. *here is a m. forbearance*, H6A II, 4, 19. *which m. devotion shows in this*, Rom. I, 5, 100.

Mannerly, adv. decently; civilly: *the wedding m. modest*, Ado II, 1, 79. *Cupid's post that comes so m.* Merch. II, 9, 100. *we'll m. demand thee of thy story*, Cymb. III, 6, 92.

Manningtree, place in Essex, famous for its pastures and the size of its oxen: *that roasted M. ox with the pudding in his belly*, H4A II, 4, 498.

Mannish, 1) male: *we'll have a swashing and a martial outside, as many other m. cowards have that do outface it with their semblances*, As I, 3, 123. 2) pertaining to the age of manhood: *though now our voices have got the m. crack*, Cymb. IV, 2, 236. 3) masculine, bold in an unbecoming manner: *a woman impudent and m. grown*, Troil. III, 3, 217.

Man-of-war, see *Man.*

Manor, estate, land belonging to a nobleman: Wiv. II, 2, 19. All's III, 2, 10. R2 IV, 212. H6C V, 2, 24. H8 I, 1, 84.

Manor-house, house belonging to a manor: LLL I, 1, 208.

Man-queller, a slayer of men, murderer: H4B II, 1, 58.

Mansion, a lord's house: Lucr. 1171. Sonn. 95, 9. 146, 6. Compl. 138. Gent. V, 4, 8. Merch. III, 2, 170. H4B III, 2, 351. Rom. III, 2, 26. III, 3, 108. Tim. IV, 3, 191. V, 1, 218. Mcb. IV, 2, 7. Cymb. III, 4, 70. V, 4, 87. V, 5, 155.

Mansionry, abode in a place: *the martlet does approve, by his loved m., that the heaven's breath smells wooingly here*, Mcb. I, 6, 5 (O. Edd. *mansonry*, some M. Edd. *masonry*).

Manslaughter, unlawful killing of a man: Tim. III, 5, 27.

Mantle, subst. 1) cloak: Lucr. 170. Pilgr. 79. Mids. V, 143. 146. 287. Wint. V, 2, 36. Caes. III, 2, 174. 191. Ant. II, 5, 22. Cymb. V, 5, 361. Used of the darkness of night: H6A II, 2, 2. H6C IV, 2, 22. Rom. III, 2, 15. of the twilight of morning: *the morn, in russet m. clad*, Hml. I, 1, 166.

2) that which gathers on the surface of a pool: *the green m. of the standing pool*, Lr. III, 4, 139.

Mantle, vb. 1) trans. to cloak, to cover: *the ignorant fumes that m. their clearer reason*, Tp. V, 67. *if you come not in the blood of others, but —d in your own*, Cor. I, 6, 29. Applied to the filthy covering of a pool: *I left them in the filthy —d pool*, Tp. IV, 182.

2) intr. to gather a covering on the surface: *whose visages do cream and m. like a standing pool*, Merch. I, 1, 89.

Mantua, town in Italy: Gent. IV, 1, 50. IV, 3, 23. V, 2, 47. Shr. II, 60. IV, 2, 77. 81. Rom. I, 3, 28. III, 3, 149. 169. III, 5, 15. 89. IV, 1, 117. 124. V, 1, 51. 66. V, 2, 3. 12. 28. V, 3, 273.

Mantuan, a native of Mantua: LLL IV, 2, 97. 101 (the poet Baptista Spagnolus Mantuanus).

Manual seal, signet: *set thy seal manual on my wax-red lips*, Ven. 516. *my gage, the manual seal of death*, R2 IV, 25.

Manure, vb. 1) to cultivate, to till: *to have it sterile with idleness, or —d with industry*, Oth. I, 3, 328.

2) to fatten with composts, to dung: *the blood of English shall m. the ground*, R2 IV, 137. *the cold blood .... he hath, like lean, sterile and bare land, —d, husbanded and tilled with excellent endeavour of drinking fertile sherris*, H4B IV, 3, 129.

Many, subst. multitude: *O thou fond m., with what loud applause didst thou beat heaven*, H4B I, 3, 91.

Many, adj. 1) sing., used with the indef. art. behind it, = more than one, not few, more than one would suppose: *I sigh the lack of m. a thing I sought*, Sonn. 30, 3. *the expense of m. a vanished sight*, 8. *how m. a holy and obsequious tear hath dear religious love stolen from mine eye*, 31, 5. *the injury of m. a blasting hour*, Compl. 72. Err. I, 2, 17. II, 2, 83. LLL I, 1, 173. Merch. II, 7, 67. III, 1, 6. IV, 1, 221. As II, 7, 130. III, 3, 53. 54. IV, 1, 101. Wint. I, 2, 192. John II, 303. IV, 1, 50. H4B II, 3, 13. IV, 5, 25. H6A V, 4, 19. H6B III, 1, 115. H6C I, 2, 74. IV, 4, 21. Cymb. V, 5, 71. Per. Prol. 39 etc. etc. *of folded schedules had she m. a one*, Compl. 43. *though in this city he hath widowed and unchilded m. a one*, Cor. V, 6, 153. *these talents of their hair I have received from m. a several fair*, Compl. 206. *m. a thousand grains*, Meas. III, 1, 20. H6C V, 6, 37. *m. a time*, R2 IV, 92. Tit. V, 3, 162. *m. a time and oft*, Merch. I, 3, 107. H4A I, 2, 56. Caes. I, 1, 42. (Simpcox's wife says *m. time and oft*, H6B II, 1, 93). *m. a time and often*, Tim. III, 1, 25. *how does your honour for this m. a day?* Hml. III, 1, 91 (= the long time that I have not seen you). *I think your highness saw this m. a day*, H8 V, 2, 21 (i. e. it is a long time since you saw this). Reduplicated: *m. a m. foot of land the worse*, John I, 183; cf. Hml. III, 3, 9. Preceded by *full: full m. a glorious morning have I seen*, Sonn. 33, 1. Tp. III, 1, 39. Mids. III, 1, 135. *Many* and a separated by the verse: Wint. V, 3, 140. H8 II, 4, 49.

2) plur. a great number of: *burn in m. places*, Tp. I, 2, 199. II, 1, 60. III, 3, 34. V, 182. Gent. I, 2, 21. II, 7, 31. III, 1, 236 etc. etc. Saxon Genitive: *in —'s looks the false heart's history is writ*, Sonn. 93, 7. Seemingly for *much: one is one too m.* Err. III, 1, 35. *being one too m. by my weary self*, Rom. I, 1, 135 (not in Globe Ed., which here follows the spurious Q1). cf. *how m. is one thrice told?* LLL I, 2, 41. In the predicate: *your helps are m.* Cor. II, 1, 39. Various use of *so m.: this is a sleep that from this golden rigol hath divorced so m. English kings*, H4B IV, 5, 37 (= many an English king; German: *so manchen Koenig*). *they flock together like so m. wild-geese*, H4B V, 1, 79 (= as if they were wild geese). *fathers that, like so m. Alexanders, have fought*, H5 III, 1, 19. *those few almost no better than so m. French*, III, 6, 156. *he the cuts off twenty years of life cuts off so m. years of fearing death*, Caes. III, 1, 102. *we are but men, and what*

so m. may do, we have done, H8 V, 4, 79 (speaking of two only). *let him alone, or so m. so minded, wave thus*, Cor. I, 6, 73 (= all that are so minded). Preceding the poss. pron.: *an earnest inviting, which m. my near occasions did urge me to put off*, Tim. III, 6, 11 (= many motives which concerned myself very near). *the letters too of m. our contriving friends in Rome petition us at home*, Ant. I, 2, 189 (many friends who are busy in our interest). Preceded by the def. art.: *the m. will be too chill and tender*, All's IV, 5, 55 (the multitude; opposed to the elected few). *not able to maintain the m. to them longing*, H8 I, 2, 32. *the mutable, rank-scented m., let them regard me as I do not flatter*, Cor. III, 1, 66 (O. Edd. *Meyny*). Preceded by the indef. article: *I do know a m. fools*, Merch. III, 5, 73. *a m. merry men*, As I, 1, 121. *told of a m. thousand warlike French*, John IV, 2, 199. *you bear a m.* (stars) *superfluously*, H5 III, 7, 179. *a m. poor men's lives*, IV, 1, 127. *mother of a m. children*, R3 III, 7, 184. *with of: like a m. of these lisping hawthorn-buds*, Wiv. III, 3, 77. *a m. of our bodies*, H5 IV, 3, 95. *a m. of your horsemen*, IV, 7, 88. As for *this m. summers*, H8 III, 2, 360, see *This*.

Many-coloured: Tp. IV, 76. All's I, 3, 158.

Many-headed: Cor. II, 3, 18.

Map, subst. 1) a picture representing the surface of the earth or any part of it: Merch. I, 1, 19. Tw. III, 2, 85. H4A III, 1, 6. 70. H5 IV, 7, 25. Lr. I, 1, 38.

2) any picture or image: *showing life's triumph in the m. of death*, Lucr. 402. *the face, that m. which deep impression bears of hard misfortune*, 1712. *thus is his cheek the m. of days outworn*, Son. 68, 1. *and him as for a m. doth Nature store, to show false Art what beauty was of yore*, 13. *thou m. of honour*, R2 V, 1, 12. *in thy face I see the m. of honour*, H6B III, 1, 203. *if you see this in the m. of my microcosm*, Cor. II, 1, 68. *thou m. of woe, that thus dost talk in signs*, Tit. III, 2, 12 (cf. *Globe*). R3 II, 4, 54.

Map, vb. to delineate, to point out the situation of: *I am near to the place where they should meet, if Pisanio have —ed it truly*, Cymb. IV, 1, 2.

Mappery, study of maps, bookish theory: *they call this bed-work, m., closet war*, Troil. I, 3, 205.

Mar, to injure, to hurt, to spoil, to ruin: *m. not the thing that cannot be amended*, Lucr. 578. *striving to mend, to m. the subject*, Son. 103, 10. *you m. our labour*, Tp. I, 1, 14. *be mute, or else our spell is —ed*, IV, 127. *m. the concord*, Gent. I, 2, 94. *it is —ing, if he quarter it*, Wiv. I, 1, 26. Meas. II, 2, 148. II, 4, 127. Err. II, 1, 92. LLL IV, 3, 191. V, 2, 22. Mids. I, 2, 39. IV, 2, 5. Merch. V, 237. As I, 1, 34. III, 2, 276. 278. Shr. IV, 3, 97. 115. All's II, 3, 315. Wint. IV, 4, 490. V, 3, 82. H4B V, 5, 122. H6A V, 3, 84. H6C IV, 8, 61. R3 I, 3, 165. H8 III, 2, 21. Cor. II, 3, 64. III, 1, 254. Rom. I, 2, 13. II, 4, 122. Tim. IV, 2, 41. IV, 3, 153. Caes. III, 2, 201 (*—ed with traitors* = destroyed and disfigured by traitors). Mcb. V, 1, 50. Lr. I, 1, 97. I, 4, 35. III, 2, 82. III, 6, 64. Oth. V, 1, 4. V, 2, 357 (*all that's spoke is —ed* = has been spoken in vain). Ant. III, 11, 65. IV, 14, 48. V, 2, 279. Per. IV, 1, 27. Joined, in opposition, to *make*: LLL IV, 3, 191. Mids. I, 2, 39. As I, 1, 34. Shr. IV, 3, 97. H4B V, 5, 122. R3 I, 3, 165. Rom. I, 2, 13. II, 4, 122. Tim. IV, 2, 41. Mcb. II, 3, 36. Oth. V, 1, 4. Ant. III, 11, 65. V, 2, 279. to *mend*: Ven. 478. Lucr. 578. Son. 103, 10. Lr. I, 1, 97. Peculiar passage: *to mend*

the hurt that his unkindness —ed, Ven. 478 (the accus. denoting not the object, but the effect, = which his unkindness injuriously made. cf. *ruined* in Err. II, 1, 97).

Marble, the stone Marmor; used for monuments Son. 55, 1. H8 III, 2, 434. Adjectively: Meas. V 233. Hml. I, 4, 50. Emblem of hardness: Lucr. 560. 1241. Meas. III, 1, 238 (*a m. to her tears*). Err. II, 1, 93. H6C III, 2, 50. Tit. II, 3, 144. Adjectively: Lucr. 1240. Wint. V, 2, 98 (*who was most m. there changed colour*). H6C III, 1, 38. Used of the heavens (on account of their eternity?) Oth. III, 3, 460. Cymb. V, 4, 87. 120. cf. *Marbled. whole as the m.* Mcb. III, 4, 22; cf. Wint. II, 3, 90.

Marble-breasted, hard-hearted: Tw. V, 127.

Marble-constant, firm as marble: Ant. V, 2, 240.

Marbled, like marble (everlasting? cf. *Marble*): *the m. mansion all above*, Tim. IV, 3, 191.

Marble-hearted, hard-hearted: Lr. I, 4, 281.

Marcade (M. Edd. *Mercade*), name in LLL V, 2, 724.

Marcantant, from the Italian mercatante, merchant: Shr. IV, 2, 63 (M. Edd. *mercatante*).

Marcellus, name in Hml. I, 1, 12 etc. and in Ant. II, 6, 118.

March, the third month of the year: Wint. IV, 4, 120. H4A IV, 1, 111 (*the sun in M... doth nourish agues*). Caes. I, 2, 18. 19. 23. II, 1, 40. 59. III, 1, 1. IV, 3, 18. V, 1, 114.

March, subst. 1) military movement, journey of soldiers: John II, 60. 223. 242. V, 1, 7. H4A II, 4, 598. H5 I, 2, 195. III, 3, 58. III, 5, 57. III, 6, 115. H6C II, 6, 87. R3 I, 1, 8. V, 2, 13. Troil. V, 10, 30. Hml. IV, 4, 3. *to make a march:* H6A IV, 3, 8. Mcb. V, 2, 31. Ant. IV, 8, 30.

2) grave and solemn walk: *and with solemn m. goes slow and stately by them*, Hml. I, 2, 201.

March, vb. 1) intr. a) to move in a military manner: Lucr. 301. 782 (used of vapours compared with an army). 1430. Sonn. 32, 12. John II, 209. 315. 320. V, 2, 27. R2 II, 3, 92. III, 3, 49. 51. III, 6, 51. H4A I, 1, 15. III, 2, 174. III, 3, 103. IV, 1, 89. IV, 2, 2. 42. 43. V, 3, 25. H4B IV, 2, 94. H5 III, 6, 61. III, 5, 11. III, 6, 159. 179. 181. IV, 3, 111. H6A III, 1, 187. III, 3, 30. 39. IV, 1, 73. IV, 3. 4. 5. V, 2, 4. H6B IV, 2, 198. 200. IV, 3, 20. IV, 9, 27. IV, 10, 15. H6C I, 1, 92. II, 1, 114. 182. II, 2, 70. IV, 3, 61. IV, 7, 50. IV, 8, 4. V, 1, 3. 13. V, 3, 22. V, 5, 87. R3 V, 2, 4. 22. Troil. V, 9, 7. Cor. I, 4, 11. I, 6, 83. Tit. IV, 4, 63. Tim. V, 4, 29. Caes. IV, 3, 197. 207. Lr. IV, 4, 21. Cymb. V, 5, 481. *m. away* (as a word of command): H5 IV, 3, 131. Troil. V, 10, 21. Tit. V, 1, 165. *to m. on:* Lucr. 438. 1391. R2 III, 3, 61. H5 III, 6, 150. H6C V, 3, 9. R3 IV, 4, 530. V, 2, 4. V, 3, 312. Cor. I, 6, 85. Caes. IV, 2, 31. Mcb. V, 2, 25. *to m. up:* H4B II, 1, 187.

b) to walk, to go: *that thus he —eth with thee arm in arm*, H6B V, 1, 57. *that form in which the majesty of buried Denmark did sometimes m.* Hml. I, 1, 49. *come, m. to wakes and fairs*, Lr. III, 6, 77.

2) tr. to cause to move in a military manner: *on the marriage-bed of peace to m. a bloody host*, John III, 1, 246.

March, name of some earls (Edmund and Roger Mortimer) nearly related to the royal house of England: H4A I, 3, 84. IV, 3, 93. V, 5, 40. H6B II, 2, 36 37. IV, 2, 144. H6C I, 1, 106. II, 1, 179.

March-chick,a chicken hatched in March; used to denote precociousness: *a very forward M.* Ado I, 3, 58.

Marches, borders, border-country: H5 I, 2, 140. H6C II, 1, 140.

Marchioness, a woman having the rank of a marquis: H8 II, 3, 63. 94. III, 2, 90.

Marchpane, a sweet biscuit composed of sugar and almonds: Rom. I, 5, 9.

Marcians, name of a family of ancient Rome: Cor. II, 3, 246.

Marcius (O. Edd. *Martius*) the family name of Coriolanus: Cor. I, 1, 7 etc. etc. King Ancus M.: II, 3, 247.

Marcus, 1) Roman prenomen; a) of Cato, Caes. V, 4, 3. 5. b) of Brutus, III, 1, 185. IV, 3, 79. c) of Crassus, Ant. III, 1, 2. 5. d) of Antonius, Ant. II, 6, 119. e) of two officers of Antony, Ant. III, 7, 73. f) of the brother of Titus Andronicus, Tit. I, 47 etc. etc. g) of a Volscian, Cor. V, 6, 123. — 2) Christian name in Oth. I, 3, 44.

Mardian, name of a eunuch in Ant. I, 5, 8. II, 5, 4. IV, 13, 7. 9.

Mare, 1) the female of the horse: Ven. 384. H5 II, 1, 26. H4B II, 1, 84. Ant. III, 7, 8. 9. *to ride the wild m.* = to play at see-saw, H4B II, 4, 268. Proverbial phrases: *the man shall have his m. again* = all shall be right again, Mids. III, 2, 463. *whose m. is dead?* = what is the matter? what is amiss? H4B II, 1, 46.

2) the night-mare, incubus: *I will ride thee o'nights like the m.* H4B II, 1, 83.

Margarelon, name in Troil. V, 5, 7.*

Margaret, name of 1) Henry VI's queen: H6A V, 3, 51. 82 etc. H6B I, 1, 4. 16 etc. H6C I, 1, 228 etc. R3 I, 2, 93 etc. —'s *battle at Saint Albans,* I, 3, 130. 2) a waiting gentlewoman in Ado II, 2, 13 etc.

Marge, in *Sea-marge,* q. v.

Margent, margin, border, edge: *a river, upon whose weeping m. she was set,* Compl. 39. *in the beached m. of the sea,* Mids. II, 1, 85. *writ o' both sides the leaf, m. and all,* LLL V, 2, 8. Glosses or comments, in old books, usually printed on the margin of the leaf: *I knew you must be edified by the m. ere you had done,* Hml. V, 2, 162. The eyes, as interpreters of the mind, compared with the margin in books: *the subtle-shining secrecies writ in the glassy —s of such books,* Lucr. 102 (i. e. in the eyes). *his face's own m. did quote such amazes that all eyes saw his eyes enchanted with gazes,* LLL II, 246. *what obscured in this fair volume lies find written in the m. of his eyes,* Rom. I, 3, 86.

Margery, vulgar form of Margaret: Tp. II, 2, 50. Merch. II, 2, 95. 96. H6B I, 2, 75. Term of contempt: *Lady M., your midwife there,* Wint. II, 3, 159.

Maria, name of 1) the Holy Virgin: *Jesu M.!* Rom. II, 3, 69. 2) a lady attending on the princess in LLL IV, 3, 56. 133. V, 2, 843. 3) Olivia's chambermaid: Tw. II, 3, 129. II, 5, 27. III, 4, 67. V, 355. 370.

Marian, vulgar form of Mary or Maria: Tp. II, 2, 50. Err. III, 1, 31. LLL V, 2, 934. Shr. Ind. 2, 22. Tw. II, 3, 14. *Maid M.,* a personage in the morris dances, often a man dressed like a woman, and some-

times a strumpet: *for womanhood, Maid M. may be the deputy's wife of the ward to thee,* H4A III, 3, 129.

Mariana, female name in Meas. III, 1, 216. 265. IV, 1, 49. IV, 3, 145. V, 379 etc.

Marigold, the flower Calendula officinalis: *her eyes, like —s, had sheathed their light,* Lucr. 397. *great princes' favourites their fair leaves spread but as the m. at the sun's eye,* Sonn. 25, 6. *the m., that goes to bed with the sun,* Wint. IV, 4, 105. Per. IV, 1, 16.

Marina, female name in Per. III, 3, 12 etc.

Mariner, seaman, sailor: Tp. I, 1, 3. I, 2, 210. 225. 230. V, 98. Ant. III, 7, 36. Per. III, 1, 73. 75.

Maritime, pertaining to the sea: *the borders m.* Ant. I, 4, 51.

Marjoram, the plant Origanum Majorana: Sonn. 99, 7. Wint. IV, 4, 104. *sweet m.* All's IV, 5, 17. Lr. IV, 6, 94.

Mark, abbreviation of the Latin Marcus, used only before the name of Antony: H5 III, 6, 15. Caes. II, 1, 156. III, 1, 173. III, 2, 63. 143. Mcb. III, 1, 56. Ant. I, 5, 35 etc. etc.

Mark, subst. 1) a sign, trace, stain or impression made or left on a person or thing: *I have some —s of yours upon my pate,* Err. I, 2, 82. 83. *my tears shall wipe away these bloody —s,* H6C II, 5, 71. *he should have showed us his —s of merit, wounds received for his country,* Cor. II, 3, 172. *can show for Rome her enemies' —s upon me,* III, 3, 111. *hath more scars of sorrow in his heart than foemen's —s upon his battered shield,* Tit. IV, 1, 127. *I know it by this m.* Per. II, 1, 144. Especially any natural irregularity or deficiency by which a person is distinguished: *—s descried in men's nativity are nature's faults,* Lucr. 538. *told me what privy —s I had about me,* Err. III, 2, 146. *the m. of my shoulder, the mole in my neck,* 147. *never mole, hare-lip, nor scar, nor m. prodigious such as are despised in nativity,* Mids. V, 419. *foul moles and eye-offending —s,* John III, 1, 47. *some —s of secret on her person,* Cymb. V, 5, 205. *it was a m. of wonder,* 365. Such tokens being supposed to be ominous, the following expressions took rise: *he hath no drowning m. upon him,* Tp. I, 1, 31. *nor set a m. so bloody on the business,* I, 2, 142. *sin, death and hell have set their —s on him,* R3 I, 2, 293. *God bless the m.,* originally a phrase used to avert the evil omen, = saving your reverence, under your pardon: *who, God bless the m., is a kind of devil,* Merch. II, 2, 25. *and I, God bless the m., his Moorship's ancient,* Oth. I, 1, 33. *he had not been there — bless the m. — a pissing while,* Gent. IV, 4, 21. Similarly *God save the m.* = God have mercy: *talk so like a waiting gentlewoman of guns and drums and wounds — God save the m.!* H4A I, 3, 56.* *I saw the wound, I saw it with mine eyes — God save the m.! — here on his manly breast,* Rom. III, 2, 53.

Used in a good sense of any excellence: *this so darks in Philoten all graceful —s,* Per. IV Prol. 36.

2) a character made by a person who cannot write his name: *doest thou use to write thy name? or hast thou a m. to thyself, like an honest man?* H6B IV, 2, 110.

3) any sign of distinction, any token by which a thing is known: *with soft-slow tongue, true m. of modesty,* Lucr. 1220. *how know you that I am in love? Marry, by these special —s,* Gent. II, 1, 18. *I do spy some —s of love in her,* Ado II, 3, 255. *there is no vice so simple but assumes some m. of virtue on his*

outward parts, Merch. III, 2, 82. *there is none of my uncle's —s upon you*, As III, 2, 387. *in the official —s invested*, Cor. II, 3, 148. *by no means I may discover them by any m. of favour*, Caes. II, 1, 76. *—s of sovereignty*, Lr. I, 4, 252. *take you the —s of her, the colour of her hair, complexion, height*, Per. IV, 2, 61.

4) butt, target, aim: *thy m. is feeble age, but thy false dart mistakes that aim*, Ven. 941. *the scornful m. of every open eye*, Lucr. 520. *slander's m. was ever yet the fair*, Sonn. 70, 2. *if knowledge be the m., to know thee shall suffice*, Pilgr. 63 and LLL IV, 2, 115. *I stood like a man at a m., with a whole army shooting at me*, Ado II, 1, 254. LLL IV, 1, 132. All's III, 2, 110. H4B III, 2, 284. H5 I, 2, 208. H6B I, 1, 243. H8 II, 1, 165. Troil. V, 6, 27. Rom. I, 1, 213. II, 1, 33. Tim. V, 3, 10. Per. I, 1, 164. II, 3, 114. *beyond the m.* = beyond the reach, beyond the power: *he fought beyond the m. of others*, Cor. II, 2, 93. *you are abused beyond the m. of thought*, Ant. III, 6, 87.

5) an object looked to for guidance: *it* (love) *is an ever-fixed m. that looks on tempests and is never shaken*, Sonn. 116, 5. Hence = example, pattern: *your high self, the gracious m. of the land*, Wint. IV, 4, 8. *he was the m. and glass, copy and book, that fashioned others*, H4B II, 3, 31.

6) notice taken, observance, note: *the strong statutes stand like the forfeits in a barber's shop, as much in mock as m.* Meas. V, 324. *a fellow of no m. and likelihood*, H4A III, 2, 45. *he hath devoted and given up himself to the contemplation, m. and denotement of her parts and graces*, Oth. II, 3, 322.

7) a sum of thirteen shillings and four pence: *five —s*, Meas. IV, 3, 7. *a thousand —s*, Err. I, 1, 22. 25. I, 2, 81. 84. II, 1, 61. III, 1, 8. Shr. V, 2, 35. John II, 530. H4A II, 1, 61. II, 4, 569. III, 3, 48. H4B I, 2, 217. H6B V, 1, 79. H8 V, 1, 172. Uninflected: *forty m.* H4A III, 3, 95. H4B II, 1, 34.

Mark, vb. 1) to make a sign or incision on, to stain, to stamp: *his sword, death's stamp, where it did m., it took*, Cor. II, 2, 112. *when we have —ed with blood those sleepy two*, Mcb. I, 7, 75. *my body's —ed with Roman swords*, Cymb. III, 3, 56.

2) to set a mark on, to blemish, to brand: *a fellow by the hand of nature —ed, quoted and signed to do a deed of shame*, John IV, 2, 221. *—ed with a blot, damned in the book of heaven*, R2 IV, 236. *to m. the full-fraught man and best endued with some suspicion*, H5 II, 2, 139. *—ed by the destinies to be avoided*, H6C II, 2, 137. *that by their witchcraft thus have — ed me*, R3 III, 4, 74. *villains —ed with rape*, Tit. IV, 2, 9.

3) to point out, to designate, to elect; with a double accus.: *these signs have —ed me extraordinary*, H4A III, 1, 41. With *for: my will that —s thee for my earth's delight*, Lucr. 487. *that —s thee out for hell*, R2 IV, 26. *thou art only —ed for the hot vengeance and the rod of heaven*, H4A III, 2, 9. *—ed for the gallows*, H6B IV, 2, 131. *your brother Richard —ed him for the grave*, H6C II, 6, 40. *nor came any of his bounties over me, to m. me for his friend*, Tim. III, 2, 86. With *to: to this your son is —ed, and die he must*, Tit. I, 125. *God m. thee to his grace*, Rom. I, 3, 59. With an inf.: *whom the Fates have —ed to bear the extremity of dire mishap*, Err. I, 1, 141. *if we are —ed to die*, H5 IV, 3, 20. cf. *death-marked*, Rom. I Chor. 9.

4) to take notice of, to pay attention to, to heed, to observe; absol.: *attend and m.* Mids. IV, 1, 98. *m.*

a little while, Wint. V, 3, 118. *the disease of not listening, the malady of not —ing*, H4B I, 2, 139. *perpend my words and m.* H5 IV, 4, 8. *couch we awhile and m.* Hml. V, 1, 245. 247. Followed by an accus. or a clause: *did not I bid thee still m. me and do as I do?* Gent. IV, 4, 39. *m. it well*, Meas. II, 1, 158. *nobody —s you*, Ado I, 1, 118. *not —ed, or not laughed at*, II, 1, 153. *I do confess much of the hearing it, but little of the —ing of it*, LLL I, 1, 288. *they do not m. me, and that brings me out*, V, 2, 172. *I'll m. no words that smooth-faced wooers say*, 838. Merch. I, 3, 98. V, 88. 243. As II, 1, 41. Shr. I, 1, 171. IV, 2, 5. Tw. II, 4, 44. II, 5, 217. Wint. I, 2, 408. II, 1, 65. V, 1, 63. 233. John IV, 3, 85. R2 I, 1, 36. II, 1, 11. III, 3, 61. IV, 290. H4A I, 2, 96. II, 4, 234. III, 1, 159. H4B V, 5, 7. H5 IV, 3, 104. IV, 7, 33. R3 I, 3, 349. III, 6, 4. H8 III, 2, 440. Troil. I, 2, 204. 251. V, 7, 2. Cor. I, 1, 259. I, 4, 45. II, 3, 45. Tit. III, 1, 34. Rom. II, 4, 188. Caes. I, 2, 126. 236. II, 3, 3. III, 1, 18. III, 2, 122. Mcb. IV, 3, 169. Hml. I, 1, 43. II, 1, 15. II, 2, 164. 400. III, 2, 158. Lr. III, 6, 118. IV, 6, 142. Oth. II, 1, 224. IV, 1, 83. 87. 292. Per. V, 1, 81. Synonymous to *consider: if your grace m. every circumstance, you have great reason to do Richard right*, H6A III, 1, 153. *call we to mind, and m. but this for proof, was not the Duke of Orleans thy foe?* III, 3, 68. *do you but m. how this becomes the house*, Lr. II, 4, 155.

5) to be aware of, to perceive by the ear or eye, to listen to, to hear, so see: *she —ing them begins a wailing note*, Ven. 835. *—ing what he tells with trembling fear*, Lucr. 510. *m. how one string ... strikes each in each*, Sonn. 8, 9. *while Philomela sits and sings, I sit and m.* Pilgr. 197. Ven. 457. 643. 680. Lucr. 990. Sonn. 112, 12. Tp. I, 2, 67. 88. 117. II, 1, 169. V, 267. Gent. II, 3, 33. Wiv. III, 5, 108. IV, 1, 45. Meas. II, 1, 156. II, 4, 81. III, 1, 226. IV, 3, 130. Err. IV, 4, 54. Ado I, 1, 213. 215. LLL IV, 1, 133. IV, 3, 100. 138. Mids. II, 1, 127. 165. III, 1, 135. IV, 1, 115. V, 282. Merch. I, 3, 78. II, 2, 51. IV, 1, 313. 317. As III, 4, 59. III, 5, 124. IV, 3, 39. 104. Shr. I, 1, 176. Wint. II, 3, 170. IV, 4, 428. 442. John II, 475. III, 4, 130. R2 IV, 203. V, 4, 1. H4A III, 4, 278. 281. III, 1, 108. 139. H5 IV, 7, 3. H6A II, 5, 79. H6C III, 3, 169. R3 II, 1, 134. H8 II, 4, 169. IV, 2, 98. Cor. I, 1, 145. II, 2, 150. III, 1, 89. III, 3, 74. V, 3, 92. Tit. II, 3, 20. III, 1, 143. Rom. III, 4, 17. Tim. III, 4, 21. Caes. I, 2, 120. III, 2, 117. 182. Mcb. I, 2, 28. V, 1, 46. Hml. I, 5, 2. II, 1, 41. II, 2, 107. III, 2, 118. 214. IV, 5, 34. V, 1, 19. Lr. I, 4, 130. 333. IV, 6, 184. V, 3, 36. Oth. I, 1, 44. II, 1, 260. Ant. II, 5, 52. Cymb. I, 1, 58. Per. IV, 2, 127. Followed by an inf.; with *to: I have —ed a thousand blushing apparitions to start into her face*, Ado IV, 1, 160. without *to: who —s the waxing tide grow wave by wave*, Tit. III, 1, 95.

Market, 1) public place for buying and selling: *search the m.* Per. IV, 2, 3. 18. 99.

2) purchase and sale in a public place: *he ended the m.* LLL III, 111 (in allusion to the proverb: *three women and a goose make a market*). *meetings, —s, fairs*, V, 2, 318. *the right butter-women's rank to m.* As III, 2, 104. *you are not for all —s*, III, 5, 60. *I run before my horse to m.* R3 I, 1, 160 (= I count my chickens before they are hatched). *I can buy me twenty at any m.* Mcb. IV, 2, 40.

3) purchase, bargain: *your store is not for idle —s,* Tw. III, 3, 46. *what is a man, if his chief good and m. of his time be but to sleep and feed?* Hml. IV, 4, 34.

Marketable, likely to find a buyer: *one of them is a plain fish and no doubt m.* Tp. V, 266. *we shall be the more m.* As I, 2, 103.

Market-bell, a bell giving notice that trade may begin in the market: H6A III, 2, 16.

Market-cross, a cross in a market-place: H4A V, 1, 73.

Market-day, a day of public sale: H6B IV, 2, 62.

Market-folks, people going to market: H6A III, 2, 15.

Market-maid, a female servant coming to market: *you are come a m. to Rome,* Ant. III, 6, 51.

Market-men, men coming to market: H6A III, 2, 4. V, 5, 54.

Market-place, place of public sale: Gent. IV, 4, 60. Ado IV, 1, 309. Shr. V, 1, 10. John II, 42. H6A I, 4, 40. II, 2, 5. Cor. I, 5, 27. Ant. II, 2, 220. III, 6, 3. the Roman Forum: Cor. II, 1, 249. II, 2, 163. III, 1, 31. 112. 332. III, 2, 93. 104. 131. V, 6, 3. Caes. I, 2, 254. I, 3, 27. III, 1, 108. 228. 292. *on the m.:* Cor. II, 2, 163. III, 1, 332 (usually *in*).

Market-price, the current price of commodities: *at m.* All's V, 3, 219.

Market-town, a town that has the privilege of a stated market: H6B II, 1, 159. Lr. III, 6, 78.

Mark-man (F3. 4 *marks-man*) one skilful in shooting: Rom. I, 1, 212.

Marl, a kind of fat clay: *a clod of wayward m.* (viz man) Ado II, 1, 66.

Marle, French name in H5 IV, 8, 105.

Marmoset, a small monkey: Tp. II, 2, 174.

Marquess, a title of honour, next below that of duke: Merch. I, 2, 125. H6B I, 1, 15. 45. H6C III, 3, 164. R3 I, 3, 255. 261. IV, 2, 47. H8 IV, 1, 38. *lord m.* H6B I, 1, 63. R3 II, 1, 25. IV, 4, 520. Used as a fem.: *Lady M. Dorset,* H8 V, 3, 170.

Marriage (dissyll.; trisyll. in Lucr. 221, where it rhymes to *rage* and *sage;* in H6A V, 5, 55, and perhaps in V, 1, 21), 1) the act of marrying, of uniting a man and woman for life: *a m. between Master Abraham and Mistress Anne Page,* Wiv. I, 1, 57. *forced m.* V, 5, 243. *there was some speech of m.* Meas. V, 217. *he promised her m.* III, 2, 213. Err. III, 2, 94. Ado I, 3, 47. II, 2, 8. II, 3, 246. III, 2, 1 etc. *to make a m.* Ant. II, 3, 39. *to pass assurance of a dower in m. 'twixt me and one Baptista's daughter,* Shr. IV, 2, 117. *proffers his only daughter to your grace in m.* H6A V, 1, 20. *his daughter meanly have I matched in m.* R3 IV, 3, 37. *to speak for my master in the way of m.* Wiv. I, 4, 89. *never to speak to lady in way of m.* Merch. II, 1, 42. *to woo a maid in way of m.* II, 9, 13. *mocking him about the m. of the Lady Bona,* H6C IV, 1, 31.

2) the performance of the rites by which the union between a man and woman is sanctioned: *consenting to the safeguard of your honour, I thought your m. fit,* Meas. V, 425. *the plain form of m.* Ado IV, 1, 2. *incontinent before m.* As V, 2, 43. *the ceremonial rites of m.* Shr. III, 2, 6. John II, 539. *the vow I made to her in m.* Hml. I, 5, 50.

3) a feast made on occasion of marrying: *at the m. of the king's daughter to the king of Tunis,* Tp. II, 1, 70. *m. tables,* Hml. I, 2, 181. cf. Gent. V, 4, 172.

Ado II, 1, 312. II, 2, 58. Merch. III, 2, 53. Shr. III, 2, 15. H5 V, 2, 398.

4) state of perpetual union: *this siege that hath engirt his m.* Lucr. 221. *you violate a twofold m.* R2 V, 1, 72. *the bed of blessed m.* H5 V, 2, 392. Sonn. 116, 1. Ado III, 2, 6. As III, 3, 71. 87. V, 4, 59. Tw. I, 5, 21. H5 V, 2, 387. Oth. III, 3, 268 etc.

Compounds: *m. bed:* Err. II, 1, 27. John III, 1, 245. V, 2, 93. *m. blessing:* Tp. IV, 106. *m. day:* All's V, 3, 70. Rom. V, 3, 233. Per. V, 3, 76. *m. dowry:* Meas. III, 1, 230. *m. feast:* LLL II, 40. Per. III Prol. 4. *m. hour:* Gent. II, 4, 179. *m. joys:* R3 IV, 4, 330. *m. pleasures:* Per. Prol. 34. *m. vow:* Wiv. II, 2, 258. Hml. III, 4, 44.

Marrow, the substance contained in the cavities of animal bones: *my flesh is soft and plump, my m. burning,* Ven. 142. *spending his manly m. in her arms,* All's II, 3, 298. *would he were wasted, m., bones and all,* H6C III, 2, 125. *when crouching m. in the bearer strong cries of itself 'No more',* Tim. V, 4, 9. *the pith and m. of our attribute,* Hml. I, 4, 22. Plur. *—s: lust and liberty creep in the minds and —s of our youth,* Tim. IV, 1, 26. *dry up thy —s, vines, and plough-torn leas,* IV, 3, 193.

Marrow-eating, wasting the strength of the body: *m. sickness,* Ven. 741.

Marrowless, destitute of marrow: Mcb. III, 4, 94.

Marry, vb. 1) to take a husband or a wife; absol.: *no —ing 'mong his subjects,* Tp. II, 1, 165. *I will m. one day,* Err. II, 1, 42. Wiv. IV, 6, 50. Ado II, 3, 237. III, 4, 89. Hml. I, 2, 156 etc. trans.: *if you will m. me,* Tp. III, 1, 83. Gent. II, 5, 15. 17. IV, 3, 16. Wiv. I, 1, 232. V, 3, 9. V, 5, 182. Meas. I, 4, 49. III, 1, 221. V, 382. 518. Ado IV, 1, 4. Mids. I, 1, 25. 94. H6A II, 5, 86. H6B I, 1, 4. H6C III, 2, 111 etc. Intr., followed by *with: to m. with Nan Page,* Wiv. IV, 4, 85. *before he —ed with her,* Meas. II, 1, 179. *to m. with Demetrius,* Mids. I, 1, 40. Ado V, 4, 37. Shr. IV, 2, 33. R3 I, 3, 100. Rom. III, 5, 219. Hml. I, 2, 151. III, 4, 29. Oth. IV, 2, 90. *—ed =* having a husband or a wife: Wiv. III, 5, 144. IV, 2, 23. Meas. IV, 2, 4. V, 171. 184. Ado I, 1, 270. LLL V, 2, 912. 918. As III, 3, 61. Ant. I, 3, 20. II, 2, 125. Cymb. V, 2 etc. *my —ed wife,* R2 V, 1, 73. H6B II, 4, 28. *a —ed life,* Per. II, 5, 4. *—ed chastity,* Phoen. 61 (= a chaste matrimony).

The simple vb. for the refl.: *you two would m. =* m. each other, Wiv. III, 2, 15; cf. *Embrace, Greet, Hug, Kiss, Know, Kill, Look, Love, See.*

Used with reference to the ceremony performed by a priest; followed by *with: and with him at Eton immediately to m.* Wiv. IV, 6, 25. trans.: *thus, I trust, you will not m. her,* Shr. III, 2, 117. Wiv. IV, 4, 75. IV, 6, 32. Mids. I, 1, 161.

2) to join in matrimony; a) as disposing of a person: *would I had never —ed my daughter there,* Tp. II, 1, 108. *you would have —ed her most shamefully,* Wiv. V, 5, 234. I, 1, 256. All's III, 5, 56. Lr. I, 1, 131 etc. Followed by *with: to m. me with Octavius Caesar,* Ant. I, 2, 29. oftener by *to:* Wiv. III, 4, 87. V, 5, 204. Meas. II, 1, 184. IV, 3, 183. V, 520. Err. II, 2, 177. 184. Ado IV, 1, 7. 9. LLL III, 122. Merch. I, 2, 55. IV, 1, 94. H6C III, 2, 111. R3 IV, 2, 55 etc. b) as performing the rite (German *trauen*): Wiv. V, 5, 216. Ado III, 1, 100. IV, 1, 8. V, 4, 120. Mids. IV, 2, 17. As III, 3, 85. 92. 93. 94. IV, 1, 125.

Shr. II, 181. Rom. II, 3, 64. V, 3, 233. with *to: he —ed me before to Romeo*, Rom. IV, 3, 27.

3) Metaphorically, *—ed* = closely joined, and hence concordant, harmonious: *well-tuned sounds, by unions —ed*, Sonn. 8, 6. *thou wert not —ed to my Muse*, 82, 1. *our inward souls —ed in league*, John III, 1, 228. *their spirits are so —ed in conjunction*, H4B V, 1, 77. *the unity and —ed calm of states*, Troil. I, 3, 100. *speculation turns not to itself, till it hath travelled and is —ed there where it may see itself*, III, 3, 110 (some M. Edd. *mirrored*, but the verb *to mirror* is unknown to Sh.; cf., besides, John II, 501 etc.). *examine every —ed lineament and see how one another lends content*, Rom. I, 3, 83 (reading of Q2; the rest of O. Edd. *several*). *like a master —ed to your good service*, Ant. IV, 2, 31. *it must be —ed to that your diamond*, Cymb. II, 4, 97.

Marry, an exclamation supposed to have been derived from the name of the Holy Virgin, used 1) to express indignant surprise: *I'll ascend the regal throne. M., God forbid!* R2 IV, 114. *Gloster is dead. M., God forfend!* H6B III, 2, 30. *I fear we shall ne'er win him to it. M., God forbid!* R3 III, 7, 81.

2) to affirm a wish or imprecation, in which case it is joined to *amen: God be wi' you, good Sir Topas. M., amen!* Tw. IV, 2, 109. *the Lord forbid! M., amen!* H8 III, 2, 54. *a plague of all cowards I say, and a vengeance too! m., and amen!* H4A II, 4, 128. *God forgive me, m. and amen!* Rom. IV, 5, 8.

3) to affirm any thing, = indeed, to be sure: *to each of you one fair and virtuous mistress fall, when Love please! m., to each, but one*, All's II, 3, 64. *good counsel, m.* R3 I, 3, 261. *m., yet the fire of rage is in him*, Cymb. I, 1, 76. cf. Meas. II, 1, 191. 198. Err. III, 1, 15. Followed by *and*, by way of expressing a prompt and joyous assent: *you would all this time have proved there is no time for all things. M., and did, sir*, Err. II, 2, 103 (= and so indeed I did). *you bid me make it orderly and well. M., and did*, Shr. IV, 3, 96. *a virtue that was never seen in you. M., and I am glad of it*, H4A III, 1, 127. *go you and tell him so. M., and shall*, V, 2, 34. *I do beseech you send for some of them. M., and shall*, R3 III, 4, 36.

4) oftenest as an expletive particle, = why; imparting to the speech a slight tinge of contempt: *how do you bear with me? M., sir, the letter*, Gent. I, 1, 130. *how know you that I am in love? M., by these marks*, II, 1, 18. *how painted? M., so painted*, 64. II, 5, 13. III, 1, 295. IV, 2, 28. 138. IV, 4, 49. Meas. I, 2, 64. II, 1, 80. Err. II, 2, 52. LLL II, 84. Mids. I, 2, 11. V, 365. Merch. II, 2, 44. R2 I, 4, 16. H6A II, 3, 31. H6B II, 1, 39. R3 II, 2, 124. Rom. I, 3, 63. Hml. III, 2, 247. Lr. IV, 2, 68 etc. *m., come up* = you mistake your business! you will find your match! Rom. II, 5, 64. Per. IV, 6, 159. *m. trap* = you are caught (Nares): Wiv. I, 1, 170. Followed by an inversion of the subject in answers: *wilt thou be pleased? M., will I*, Tp. III, 2, 46. *you mean to whip the dog? Ay, m., do I*, Gent. IV, 4, 28. *were they his men? m., were they*, Wiv. II, 1, 185. *does he lie at the Garter? Ay, m., does he*, 188. IV, 5, 29. LLL I, 1, 126. Mids. III, 1, 92. As I, 1, 128. All's III, 5, 40. Wint. III, 3, 140. H4B III, 2, 104. R3 I, 3, 98. H8 I, 1, 97. Tit. IV, 1, 122. Caes. I, 2, 229. Hml. I, 4, 13. Oth. III, 1, 7.

Mars, 1) the Roman god of war: Sonn. 55, 7.

Pilgr. 145. Tp. IV, 98. Wiv. I, 3, 113. LLL V, 2, 650. 657. Merch. III, 2, 85. All's II, 1, 48. II, 3, 300. III, 3, 9. IV, 1, 33. R2 II, 1, 41. II, 3, 101. H4A III, 2, 112. IV, 1, 116. H5 Prol. 6. IV, 2, 43. H6A I, 2, 1. Troil. II, 1, 58. II, 3, 256. III, 3, 190. IV, 5, 177. 198. 255. V, 2, 164. V, 3, 52. Cor. I, 4, 10. IV, 5, 124. 204. V, 6, 100. Tim. IV, 3, 384. Hml. II, 2, 512. III, 4, 57. Ant. I, 1, 4. I, 5, 18. II, 2, 6. II, 5, 117. Cymb. V, 4, 32.

2) name of a planet: *you were born ... under M.* All's I, 1, 206. 207. 208. 210. *M. his true moving, even as in the heavens so in the earth, to this day is not known*, H6A I, 2, 1.

Marseilles, French town: Shr. II, 377. All's IV, 4, 9. IV, 5, 85.

Marsh, moorland: *the enemy is past the m.* R3 V, 3, 345.

Marshal, subst. 1) the chief officer of arms, who regulates combats in the lists and establishes rank and order at royal feasts and processions: *the —'s truncheon*, Meas. II, 2, 61. *lord m., command our officers at arms be ready to direct these home alarms*, R2 I, 1, 204. I, 3, 7. 26. 44. 46. 99. H4A IV, 4, 2. H4B I, 3, 4. II, 3, 42. III, 2, 348. IV, 1, 220. H8 IV, 1, 19 (*earl m.*).

2) in France, the highest military officer (apparently trisyll. in this sense): *the M. of France, Monsieur La Far*, Lr. IV, 3, 9. *Great m. to Henry the Sixth of all his wars within the realm of France*, H6A IV, 7, 70 (*marshal* as well as *Henry* trisyll.).

3) leader: *reason becomes the m. to my will*, Mids. II, 2, 120.

Marshal, vb. to direct, to lead: *thou —est me the way that I was going*, Mcb. II, 1, 42. *they must sweep my way and m. me to knavery*, Hml. III, 4, 205. *when these mutualities so m. the way, hard at hand comes the master and main exercise*, Oth. II, 1, 268. *m. the rest, as they deserve their grace*, Per. II, 3, 19.

Marshalsea, name of a prison: H8 V, 4, 90.

Mart, subst. 1) market-place: Err. I, 2, 74. II, 1, 5. II, 2, 6. III, 2, 155. 189. *you beat me at the m.* III, 1, 12. *I'll meet with you upon the m.* I, 2, 27. II, 2, 166. III, 1, 7. V, 261. *to come so smug upon the m.* Merch. III, 1, 49.

2) public purchase and sale: *at any Syracusian —s and fairs*, Err. I, 1, 18. *foreign m. for implements of war*, Hml. I, 1, 74. *we lost too much money this m.* Per. IV, 2, 5.

3) bargain: *venture on a desperate m.* Shr. II, 329 (cf. *Co-mart*).

Mart, vb. to traffic, to trade: *if he shall think it fit, a saucy stranger in his court to m. as in a Romish stew*, Cymb. I, 6, 151. trans. = to buy, or to sell: *you have let him go and nothing —ed with him*, Wint. IV, 4, 363. *to sell and m. your offices for gold to undeservers*, Caes. IV, 3, 11.

Mar-text, one who perverts the meaning of words; name in As III, 3, 43. 65. V, 1, 6.

Martial, 1) pertaining to war, opposed to civil: *m. law*, H5 IV, 8, 46. *a m. man* = a warrior, Lucr. 200. H6A I, 4, 74. *arts and m. exercises*, H4B IV, 5, 74.

2) warlike, becoming or like a true warrior: *a m. outside*, As I, 3, 122. *write it in a m. hand*, Tw. III, 2, 45. *a maid, and be so m.* H6A II, 1, 21. *warlike and m. Talbot*, III, 2, 118. *with a m. scorn*, Rom. III, 1, 166. *with m. stalk*, Hml. I, 1, 66.

3) resembling Mars: *his foot Mercurial, his M. thigh,* Cymb. IV, 2, 310.

Martin, name of a saint, whose feast falls on the eleventh of November: *expect Saint —'s summer, halcyon days,* H6A I, 2, 131 (fair weather after winter has set in, i. e. prosperity after misfortune).

Martino, name in Rom. I, 2, 67.

Martius, see *Marcius.*

Martlemas, the feast of Saint Martin; used of a person in the decline of life: *how doth the m., your master?* H4B II, 2, 110; cf. *All-hallown summer* in H4A I, 2, 178.

Martlet, the bird Hirundo urbica: Merch. II, 9, 28. In Mcb. I, 6, 4 O. Edd. *barlet,* M. Edd. *martlet.*

Martyr, subst. one who suffers for his faith or in defence of any cause: H4B IV, 1, 193. V, 5, 148. H8 III, 2, 450. Per. I, 1, 38.

Martyr, vb. to torture, to torment, to destroy in a savage manner: *that face which underneath thy black all-hiding cloak immodestly lies —ed with disgrace,* Lucr. 802. *speak, gentle sister, who hath —ed thee?* Tit. III, 1, 81. 107. *hark, wretches, how I mean to m. you,* V, 2, 181. *despised, distressed, hated, —ed, killed,* Rom. IV, 5, 59.

—ed, adjectively, = pertaining to a state of cruel suffering: *I can interpret all her —ed signs,* Tit. III, 2, 36.

Marullus (O. Edd. *Murrellus* and *Murellus*) name in Caes. I, 2, 288.

Marvel, subst. 1) astonishment: *I speak amazedly, and it becomes my m. and my message,* Wint. V, 1, 188. *strike all that look upon with m.* V, 3, 100. *and, to kill the m., shall be so ever,* Cymb. III, 1, 10.

2) wonder, something strange: *till I may deliver this m. to you,* Hml. I, 2, 195. Usually in the predicate: *it is m.* = it is strange, Shr. IV, 2, 86. *that's great m.* LLL I, 2, 128. *no m.* or *it is no m.* = it is not strange, H4B IV, 3, 96. Lr. II, 2, 58. Followed by a clause with the indic.: *it is m. he out-dwells his hour,* Merch. II, 6, 3. *'tis no m. he is so humorous,* H4A III, 1, 234. H6B II, 1, 9. *no m. though,* always followed by the subjunctive, = it is not strange that: *no m. though thy horse be gone,* Ven. 390. *no m., then, though I mistake my view,* Sonn. 148, 11. *no m. though she pause,* Err. II, 1, 32. *no m. though Demetrius do fly,* Mids. II, 2, 96. *no m. though it affrighted you,* R3 I, 4, 64. *no m. though you bite so sharp at reasons,* Troil. II, 2, 33. *no m., then, though he were ill affected,* Lr. II, 1, 100.

Marvel, vb. 1) to find something strange, to wonder; absol.: *you make me m.* Tim. II, 2, 133. with *at: you must not m. at my course,* All's II, 5, 63. Cor. V, 6, 42. Mcb. III, 2, 54. Usually followed by a clause: *I m. I hear not of Master Brook,* Wiv. III, 5, 58. *you may m. why I obscured myself,* Meas. V, 395. *I m. thy master hath not eaten thee,* LLL V, 1, 42. *I m. why I answered not,* As III, 5, 132. *I m. Cambio comes not,* Shr. V, 1, 8. *we m. much our cousin France ... would shut his bosom,* All's III, 1, 7. *I m. your ladyship takes delight,* Tw. I, 5, 89. *I do not only m. where thou spendest thy time,* H4A II, 4, 439. R3 II, 2, 111 (Qq *why,* Ff *that*). Troil. II, 2, 42. III, 3, 181. Lr. IV, 2, 1. Per. II, 1, 29. Followed by *should: I much m. that your lordship ... should shake off the golden slumber,* Per. III, 2, 21.

2) to wonder, to be curious to know: *I m. how he*

sped, H6A II, 1, 48 (= I should like to know). *I m. where Troilus is,* Troil. I, 2, 238. *I m. what kin thou and thy daughters are,* Lr. I, 4, 199.

Marvellous, adj. very great: *her husband has a m. infection to the little page,* Wiv. II, 2, 120 (Mrs. Quickly's speech).

Marvellous, adv. (joined only to adjectives and adverbs), very, extraordinarily: *m. sweet music,* Tp. III, 3, 19. *m. little beholding,* Meas. IV, 3, 166. *m. merry,* Err. IV, 3, 59. *a m. witty fellow,* Ado IV, 2, 27. *m. well shot,* LLL IV, 1, 132. IV, 2, 158. V, 2, 586. Mids. III, 1, 2. IV, 1, 26. Shr. II, 73. All's IV, 3, 179. H4B II, 4, 30. V, 1, 38. H5 III, 2, 81. R3 I, 2, 255. Troil. I, 2, 150. Cor. IV, 5, 30. Rom. III, 5, 230. Hml. II, 1, 3. III, 2, 312.

Marvellously, adv. (joined only to verbs) extraordinarily, very much: *you are m. changed,* Merch. I, 1, 76. *you may be m. mistook,* H5 III, 6, 85.

Mary, name 1) of the Holy Virgin: John II, 538. R2 II, 1, 56. H8 V, 2, 33. 2) a daughter of Henry VIII: H8 II, 4, 175. 3) of Olivia's woman: Tw. I, 3, 57. I, 5, 11. II, 3, 130 (cf. *Maria*).

Mary-buds, flowers of the marigold: *and winking m. begin to ope their golden eyes,* Cymb. II, 3, 25.

Masculine, male: *my m. usurped attire,* Tw. V, 257. *pray God she prove not m. ere long,* H6A II, 1, 22. *his m. whore,* Troil. V, 1, 20.

Masham, name in H5: *Henry Lord Scroop of M.* II Prol. 24. II, 2, 13. 67.

Mashed, see *Meshed.*

Mask, subst. 1) a cover for the face (used by the poet only in speaking of women; cf. *Vizard*); worn to preserve the complexion: *her sun-expelling m.* Gent. IV, 4, 158. *my m., to defend my beauty,* Troil. I, 2, 286. *with faces fit for —s, or rather fairer than those for preservation cased, or shame,* Cymb. V, 3, 21. cf. LLL II, 124. V, 2, 245. Wint. IV, 4, 223. Oth. IV, 2, 9. Black masks worn by ladies at the theatres: *as these black —s proclaim an enshield beauty,* Meas. II, 4, 79. *these happy —s that kiss fair ladies' brows being black put us in mind they hide the fair,* Rom. I, 1, 236. Masks worn by players performing a woman's part: *let not me play a woman; I have a beard coming. That's all one: you shall play it in a m.* Mids. I, 2, 52.

Metaphorically, applied to men as well as women: *stain my favours in a bloody m.* H4A III, 2, 136. *death put on his ugliest m.* H4B I, 1, 66. *thou knowest the m. of night is on my face,* Rom. II, 2, 85.

2) a diversion or procession in which the company wear masks, a masquerade: *revels, dances, —s,* LLL IV, 3, 379. *what —s, what dances,* Mids. V, 32. *will you prepare you for this m. to-night,* Merch. II, 4, 23. II, 5, 23. 28. II, 6, 64. Tw. I, 3, 121. John V, 2, 132. H8 I, 1, 26. Troil. I, 3, 84. Rom. I, 4, 48. I, 5, 35.

Mask, vb. 1) trans. to cover with a visor (applied to women): *being —ed,* Gent. V, 2, 40. *—ed and vizarded,* Wiv. IV, 6, 40 (girls and boys). Ado V, 4, 12. LLL V, 2, 127. 157. 295.

Metaphorically, applied to men as well as women: *to m. their brows and hide their infamy,* Lucr. 794. *when summer's breath their —ed buds discloses,* Sonn. 54, 8. *if some suspect of ill —ed not thy show,* 70, 13. LLL I, 2, 98. Cor. I, 8, 10. Caes. II, 1, 81. With *from* (= to conceal): *the region cloud hath —ed him* (the sun) *from me,* Sonn. 33, 12. *—ing the business from the common eye,* Mcb. III, 1, 125.

2) intr. to play a part in a masquerade: *and then we —ed*, Rom. I, 5, 39. *—ing* = pertaining to a masquerade: *our —ing mates*, Merch. II, 6, 59. *what —ing stuff is here*, Shr. IV, 3, 87.

Doubtful passage: *then give you up to the —ed Neptune and the gentlest winds of heaven*, Per. III, 3, 36 (perhaps = hiding his cruel nature).

Masker, one that takes part in a masquerade: *the —s come*, LLL V, 2, 157. *Lewis is sending over —s, to revel it with him*, H6C III, 3, 224. IV, 1, 94. *a m. and a reveller*, Caes. V, 1, 62.

Mason, a bricklayer: H5 I, 2, 198. Hml. V, 1, 47.

Masonry, 1) the art of a bricklayer: *root out the work of m.* Sonn. 55, 6. 2) the work of a bricklayer: *creaking my shoes on the plain m.* All's II, 1, 31 (= paved floor). cf. *Mansionry.*

Masque, orthography of some M. Edd. for *Mask* in its 2ᵈ signif.

Mass, 1) solid substance, bulk: *winnows the light away, and what hath m. or matter, by itself lies rich in virtue*, Troil. I, 3, 29. *in such indexes there is seen the baby figure of the giant m. of things to come at large*, 345. *not the dreadful spout which shipmen do the hurricano call, constringed in m. by the almighty sun*, V, 2, 173. *this solidity and compound m.* (the earth) Hml. III, 4, 49. *this army of such m. and charge*, IV, 4, 47.

2) great quantity: *hath —es of money*, Wiv. II, 2, 284. *have cost a m. of public treasure*, H6B I, 3, 134. Tim. IV, 3, 404. *let us pay betimes a moiety of that m. of moan to come*, Troil. II, 2, 107. *I remember a m. of things*, Oth. II, 3, 289. *to do the act not the world's m. of vanity could make me*, IV, 2, 164.

Mass, the service of the Romish church: *at evening m.* Rom. IV, 1, 38 (= vespers). *M. and by the m.* used as forms of asseveration; *m.:* Ado III, 3, 106. H6B II, 1, 101. IV, 7, 9. Rom. IV, 4, 19. Hml. V, 1, 62. *by the m.:* Wiv. IV, 2, 214. Ado IV, 2, 53 (Q *by m.*). H4A II, 4, 400. H5 IV, 3, 115. H6B V, 3, 16. Hml. III, 2, 395. Sometimes omitted in Ff, probably as indecent: H4A II, 1, 18. B II, 4, 4. 21. III, 2, 19. V, 3, 14. Hml. II, 1, 50. Sometimes changed: H4B II, 2, 73 (Ff *look*). Oth. II, 3, 384 (Ff *in troth*).

Massacre, subst. slaughter, carnage: H4A V, 4, 14. H6A I, 1, 135. II, 2, 18. V, 4, 160. R3 II, 4, 53. IV, 3, 2. Tit. V, 1, 63.

Massacre, vb. to slaughter, to butcher: Tit I, 450.

Massy, bulky, large, heavy: *your swords are now too m. for your strengths*, Tp. III, 3, 67. *his codpiece seems as m. as his club*, Ado III, 3, 147. *with m. staples*, Troil. Prol. 17. *drawing their m. irons and cutting the web*, II, 3, 18. *it is a m. wheel*, Hml. III, 3, 17.

Mast, the beam by which the sails and rigging of a vessel are supported: Tp. I, 2, 147. Err. I, 1, 80. 86. Tw. I, 2, 14. H4B III, 1, 18. H6C V, 4, 3. 17. R3 III, 4, 101. Lr. IV, 6, 53. Per. IV, 1, 56.

Mast, acorns, food for swine: *the oaks bear m., the briers scarlet hips*, Tim. IV, 3, 422.

Master, subst. (sometimes *maister* in O. Edd., f. i. Merch. II, 2, 34. H6B IV, 1, 12. Tit. V, 1, 15. Rom. II, 4, 11. Sometimes, before names or titles, abbreviated to *M.:* Wiv. II, 2, 48. II, 3, 39. 46. 49. 50. 76 etc. LLL V, 2, 84. 87. H8 V, 3, 1. 77. V, 4, 4. or to *Mr.:* Wiv. II, 3, 19. 20. Meas. II, 1, 223. IV, 3, 5. 9. 14. 23 etc. Err. III, 2, 170), 1) one who has possession and power of controlling and using;

owner, proprietor, ruler, governor: *m. of a full poor cell*, Tp. I, 2, 20. *the —s of some merchant*, II, 1, 5 (i. e. the owners of some trading ship). *a man is m. of his liberty*, Err. II, 1, 7. *he's m. of my state*, 95. *when thou didst make him m. of thy bed*, V, 163. *affections, —s of passion*, Merch. IV, 1, 51. *the cottage that the old carlot once was m. of*, As III, 5, 108. *lest it* (the dagger) *should bite its m.* Wint. I, 2, 157; cf. H4A I, 1, 18. *—s of their wealth*, II, 4, 280. *though most m. wear no breeches*, H6B I, 3, 149. *m. of his heart*, Troil. I, 1, 4. *—s of the field*, V, 10, 1. *—s of their fates*, Caes. I, 2, 139. *let every man be m. of his time*, Mcb. III, 1, 41. *the safer sense will ne'er accommodate his m. thus*, Lr. IV, 6, 82. *by sea he is an absolute m.* Ant. II, 2, 166. *I am the m. of my speeches*, Cymb. I, 4, 152. *you are m. of the feast*, III, 6, 29 etc. Applied to a female: *but now I was the lord of this fair mansion, m. of my servants*, Merch. III, 2, 170. Peculiar passage: *by whose aid, weak —s though ye be, I have bedimmed the noontide sun*, Tp. V, 41 (i. e. according to Blackstone: ye are powerful auxiliaries, but weak if left to yourselves).

2) the founder or chief of a sect or doctrine: *so Judas kissed his m.* H6C V, 7, 33. *ween you of better luck than your m.* (Christ) H8 V, 1, 137. cf. *tell me, love's m.* Ven. 585 (or = lord of the queen of love?).

3) one of perfect skill in an art or science: *that rare Italian m.* Wint. V, 2, 105. *he is not his craft's m.* H4B III, 2, 297. *each following day became the next day's m.* H8 I, 1, 17. *till by some elder —s, of known honour, I have a voice and precedent of peace*, Hml. V, 2, 259. *you are music's m.* Per. II, 5, 30. *a m. of fence*, Wiv. I, 1, 295 ("not merely a fencing-master, but a person who had taken his master's degree in the science. There were three degrees, a master's, a provost's, and a scholar's." Steevens). *he will answer the letters' m.* Rom. II, 4, 11 (or *letter's m.* = writer of the letter?).

4) chief, head, leader: *being then appointed m. of this design*, Tp. I, 2, 163. *the m. of the cross-bows*, H5 IV, 8, 99. *great m. of France*, 100 (grand maître de la maison du roi). *m. of the jewel house*, H8 IV, 1, 110. *m. o'the rolls*, V, 1, 34. *—s of the people* (viz the tribunes) Cor. II, 2, 55. 81. *bees led by their m.* Tit. V, 1, 15. Used of the commander of a merchant ship, and of a subordinate officer in ships of war: Tp. I, 1, 2. 8. 11. 13. II, 2, 48. V, 99. 237. H6B IV, 1, 12. 15. Mcb. I, 3, 7. Oth. II, 1, 211. Per. IV, 1, 65.

Adjectively, = chief, principal: *the m. cord on's heart*, H8 III, 2, 106. *choice and m. spirits*, Caes. III, 1, 163. *the m. and main exercise*, Oth. II, 1, 268. *she has me her quirks, her reasons, her m. reasons*, Per. IV, 6, 8.

5) a teacher: Pilgr. 212. 216. Wiv. IV, 1, 9. 20. H4B II, 1, 202. Per. II, 5, 38.

6) opposed to servant, one who has the command of another: Tp. I, 2, 189. 216. 293. 296. 299. II, 1, 297. II, 2, 182. 189. III, 2, 124. IV, 1, 34. V, 262. Gent. I, 1, 39. 70. 76. IV, 1, 39. Wiv. I, 1, 164. Err. II, 1, 20. 24. LLL I, 2, 26. 69. 97. Alls II, 3, 194. 196. 199. 261. IV, 5, 75. Tw. I, 5, 271. 313. Mcb. I, 3, 101 etc. etc.

7) a familiar title of respect: *mistress and m., you have oft inquired*, As III, 4, 50. *a plum-tree, m.* H6B II, 1, 97. *good m.* 102. *come on, young m.* Lr. II, 2, 49. *bless thee, m.* IV, 1, 41. *—s, let him go*, Err. IV, 4, 114.

well, —s, Ado III, 3, 90. 94. 113. 183. IV, 2, 18. V, 1, 232. V, 3, 24. 29. Mids. I, 2, 16. 101. III, 1, 30. 108. IV, 2, 15. 29. Shr. I, 2, 189. Cor. V, 6, 135. Caes. III, 2, 115. 126. Hml. II, 2, 440. Oth. II, 3, 176. V, 2, 188 etc. *my —s*, Shr. I, 2, 238. Tw. II, 3, 93. H4A II, 2, 80. II, 4, 550. H6A I, 1, 152. III, 1, 144. H6B I, 3, 1. I, 4, 1. II, 1, 72. 135. H6C IV, 3, 24. Tit. IV, 3, 35. *my noble — s*, Cor. V, 6, 133. *my very noble and approved good —s*, Oth. I, 3, 77. Placed, in courtesy, before names: Wiv. I, 1, 46. 112. II, 3, 39. Meas. II, 1, 104. 106. 126. 154. 271. IV, 3, 5. 9. 14. 23. Err. III, 2, 170. IV, 3, 45. LLL I, 2, 167. Mids. III, 1, 186. 191. 196. As III, 2, 12. H4A II, 1, 58. H4B II, 1, 191. H6A II, 4, 43. 128 etc. etc. Before titles: *m. parson*, Wiv. I, 1, 9. I, 4, 34. III, 1, 36. LLL IV, 2, 84. Tw. IV, 2, 13. *m. doctor*, Wiv. I, 4, 3. II, 2, 48. II, 3, 19. Err. IV, 4, 125. Cymb. I, 5, 4. *m. guest*, Wiv. II, 3, 76. *m. tapster*, Meas. II, 1, 223. *m. constable*, Meas. II, 1, 272. Ado III, 3, 17. 178. IV, 2, 8. 35. *m. schoolmaster*, LLL IV, 2, 87. *m. young-man*, Merch. II, 2, 34. *m. Jew*, 35. *m. sheriff*, H4A II, 4, 555. H6B II, 4, 74. *m. lieutenant*, H6C IV, 6, 1. R3 IV, 1, 13. *m. mayor*, H6C IV, 7, 20. *peace, m. marquess*, R3 I, 3, 255. *m. secretary*, H8 V, 3, 1. 77. *good m. porter*, V, 4, 4. *m. steward*, Tim. IV, 2, 1 etc. Dogberry and Verges strain their courtesy to saying: *m. gentleman Conrade; here comes m. Signior Leonato*, Ado IV, 2, 17. V, 1, 266.

Peculiar phrase: *we'll be thy good —s*, Wint. V, 2, 188; it being a common petitionary phrase to ask a superior to be *good lord* or *good master* to the supplicant. cf. *from my lord Biron, a good m. of mine*, LLL IV, 1, 106 (= wellwisher, patron).

Master, vb. 1) to be master of, to have as servant: *I will not say thou shalt be so well —ed*, Cymb. IV, 2, 383. *and rather father thee than m. thee*, 395.

2) to conquer, to subdue: *brag not of thy might, for —ing her that foiled the god of fight*, Ven. 114. *servilely —ed with a leathern rein*, 392. *—ing what not strives*, Compl. 240. *Love is your master, for he —s you*, Gent. I, 1, 39. *every one can m. a grief but he that has it*, Ado III, 2, 28. *affects ... not by might —ed*, LLL I, 1, 153. *they that m. so their blood*, Mids. I, 1, 74. *or Charles or something weaker —s thee*, As I, 2, 272. *not till now (I loved you) so much but I might m. it*, Troil. III, 2, 129. *m. the devil*, Hml. III, 4, 169 (reading of the later Qq). *to m. Caesar's sword*, Cymb. III, 1, 31.

3) to possess, to own: *leaves it (his gold) to be —ed by his young*, Lucr. 863. *such a beauty as you m. now*, Sonn. 106, 8. *for the wealth that the world —s*, Merch. V, 174. *as if he —ed there a double spirit*, H4A V, 2, 64. *the promise of his greener days and these he —s now*, H5 II, 4, 137.

Masterdom, dominion, supremacy: *which shall to all our nights and days to come give solely sovereign sway and m.* Mcb. I, 5, 71.

Master-gunner, an officer appointed to superintend the artillery: *chief m. am I of this town*, H6A I, 4, 6.

Master-leaver, one who forsakes his master: Ant. IV, 9, 22.

Masterless, having no owner: *what mean these m. and gory swords*, Rom. V, 3, 142. *gains or loses your sword or mine, or m. leaves both*, Cymb. II, 4, 60.

Masterly, adj.: *he made confession of you and gave you such a m. report for art and exercise in your defence*, Hml. IV, 7, 97; i. e. such a report of mastership, an account of your consummate skill.

Masterly, adv. like a master, most skilfully Tw. II, 4, 23. Wint. V, 3, 65. Oth. I, 1, 26.

Master-mistress (not hyphened in O. Edd.), a male mistress, one loved like a woman, but of male sex: *the m. of my passion*, Sonn. 20, 2.

Master-piece, capital performance: *confusion now hath done his m.* Mcb. II, 3, 71.

Mastership, 1) supreme skill: *when the sea was calm all boats alike showed m. in floating*, Cor. IV, 1, 7.

2) a title of respect used by low people: *what news with your m.?* Gent. III, 1, 280. *an't please your m.* Merch. II, 2, 61.

Mastick, probably but another form of *mastiff*: *when rank Thersites opes his m. jaws*, Troil. I, 3, 73 (many M. Edd. *mastiff*).*

Mastiff, a dog of the largest size: H5 III, 7, 151. 159. Troil. I, 3, 392. Lr. III, 6, 71.

Match, subst. a joining or meeting of two parties; 1) a marriage intended or made: *will it be a m.?* Gent. II, 5, 35. *the m. were rich and honourable*, III, 1, 63. 379. IV, 3, 30. Wiv. IV, 6, 27. Err. III, 2, 94. Ado II, 1, 384. As III, 2, 87. Shr. II, 321. 327. III, 2, 244. John II, 430. 447. 450. H6A V, 3, 96. R3 I, 3, 102. Tit. I, 244. Rom. III, 5, 224. Oth. III, 3, 229. IV, 2, 125. V, 2, 205. Cymb. I, 1, 12. With *between: I would effect the m. between Sir Thurio and my daughter*, Gent. III, 2, 23. *we have lingered about a m. between Anne Page and my cousin Slender*, Wiv. III, 2, 58. *to make a m.* = to effect, to bring about a marriage: *his grace hath made the m.* Ado II, 1, 315. II, 2, 38. Shr. IV, 4, 46. John II, 468. Ant. II, 5, 67. *to make up:* John II, 541.

2) a game played between two parties; joined with the verbs *to make* and *to play: half won is m. well made*, All's IV, 3, 254. *make some pretty m. with shedding tears*, R2 III, 3, 165. *what cunning m. have you made with this jest of the drawer?* H4A II, 4, 101. *he hath made a m. with such a wrangler*, H5 I, 2, 264. *if two gods should play some heavenly m.* Merch. III, 5, 84. *assured loss before the m. be played*, John III, 1, 336. V, 2, 106. Rom. III, 2, 12. Hence = wager: *I dare you to this m.* Cymb. I, 4, 158. *a m.!* = done! agreed! Tp. II, 1, 34. Shr. V, 2, 74. switch and spurs; *or I'll cry a m.* Rom. II, 4, 74 (?). And = bargain: *there I have another bad m.* Merch. III, 1, 46. *I'll make my m. to live; the kiss you take is better than you give; therefore no kiss*, Troil. IV, 5, 37 (= I'll make a reasonable and valid bargain).

3) a meeting of two in combat: *art thou for Hector's m.?* Troil. V, 4, 28 (the modern: a match for Hector). *unequal m.*, *Pyrrhus at Priam drives*, Hml. II, 2, 493 (Qq *matched*).

4) an agreement, appointment: *shall we (meet to-morrow)? wilt thou make the m.?* Ven. 586. *the hour is fixed, the m. is made*, Wiv. II, 2, 304. *this is the body that took away the m. from Isabel*, Meas. V, 211. *this is a m., and made between's by vows*, Wint. V, 3, 137. *now shall we know if Gadshill have set a m.* H4A I, 2, 119 (Ff *watch*). *the m. is made; she seals it with a courtsy*, H6C III, 2, 57. *thy hand upon that m.* Troil. IV, 5, 270. *you shall ha' it, worthy sir. A m., sir*, Cor. II, 3, 86. *Cadwal and I will play the cook and servant; 'tis our m.* Cymb. III, 6, 30.

5) equal, equality, equal measure: *she is no m. for you*, Wiv. III, 4, 77 (or = she is not fit to be your wife?). *the all-seeing sun ne'er saw her m.* Rom. I, 2, 98. *it were no m., your nail against his horn*, Troil. IV, 5, 46. *Clifford slew my steed, but m. to m. I have encountered him and made a prey for kites of the beast he loved so well*, H6B V, 2, 10 (= measure for measure). *that my integrity and truth to you might be affronted with the m. and weight of such a winnowed purity in love*, Troil. III, 2, 173.

Match, vb. 1) trans. a) to join, to sort, to pair in any way: *a sharp wit —ed with too blunt a will*, LLL II, 49. *God m. me with a good dancer*, Ado II, 1, 111. *—ed in mouth like bells*, Mids. IV, 1, 128. *I could m. this beginning with an old tale*, As I, 2, 127. *here comes another of the tribe: a third cannot be — ed, unless the devil himself turn Jew*, Merch. III, 1, 81. *this —ed with other*, H4A I, 1, 49. *such rude society as thou art —ed withal*, III, 2, 15. *when we have —ed our rackets to these balls*, H5 I, 2, 261. *his few bad words are —ed with as few good deeds*, III, 2, 41. Used of combatants meeting in fight: *the harder —ed, the greater victory*, H6C V, 1, 70. *unequal —ed Pyrrhus at Priam drives*, Hml. II, 2, 493 (Ff *match*).

b) to marry, to make husband or wife: *to have him —ed*, Shr. IV, 4, 32. *his daughter meanly have I —ed in marriage*, R3 IV, 3, 37. *to have her —ed*, Rom. III, 5, 180. *to m. you where I hate*, Lr. I, 1, 213. With *to*: *to m. Sir Thurio to my daughter*, Gent. III, 1, 62. With *with*: *whom should we m. with Henry*, H6A V, 5, 66.

c) to compare: *to m. us in comparisons with dirt*, Troil. I, 3, 194. *that fair ... with tender Juliet —ed, is now not fair*, Rom. II Prol. 4. *to m. you with her country forms*, Oth. III, 3, 237.

d) to equal, to rival: *all love's pleasure shall not m. his woe*, Ven. 1140. *thy odour —eth not thy show*, Sonn. 69, 13. As III, 2, 374. All's II, 1, 213. Wint. V, 3, 72. R3 IV, 2, 37. IV, 4, 66. Troil. IV, 5, 259. Tim. I, 1, 5. Lr. IV, 7, 2. Oth. III, 3, 183. III, 4, 68.

e) to cope with, to oppose as equal in combat: *that I can m. her*, Mids. III, 2, 305. *if you oppose yourselves to m. Lord Warwick*, H6B V, 1, 156. *I would my arms could m. thee in contention*, Troil. IV, 5, 205. *'twould be a sight indeed, if one could m. you*, Hml. IV, 7, 101. *I must go up and down like a cock that nobody can m.* Cymb. II, 1, 24.

2) intr. a) to marry, to take a husband or a wife: *I hold it a sin to m. in my kindred*, Ado II, 1, 68. *half won is match well meaning; m. and well make it*, All's IV, 3, 254. *she'll not m. above her degree*, Tw. I, 3, 116. *had he —ed according to his state*, H6C II, 2, 152. *—ing more for wanton lust than honour*, III, 3, 210. Followed by *with*: *to m. with her*, H6B I, 1, 131.

b) to cope, to meet in combat: *strength —ed with strength, and power confronted power*, John II, 330.

c) to suit, to tally: *as —ing to his youth and vanity, I did present him with the Paris balls*, H5 II, 4, 130.

Matchless, having no equal: LLL II, 7. Troil. IV, 5, 97.

Mate, subst. 1) companion, associate, fellow: *bestow thy fawning smiles on equal —s*, Gent. III, 1, 158. *these are my —s*, V, 4, 14. *our masking —s*, Merch. II, 6, 9. *if thou receive me* (Joan) *for thy warlike m.* H6A I, 2, 92. *we'll forward towards War-*

wick and his —s, H6C IV, 7, 82. *when grief hath —s* Lr. III, 6, 114. *my m. in empire*, Ant. V, 1, 43. *half-part, —s*, Per. IV, 1, 95. Especially used of seamen: *carousing to his —s after a storm*, Shr. III, 2, 173. *leaked is our bark, and we, poor —s, stand on the dying deck*, Tim. IV, 2, 20. = an officer in a ship who is subordinate to another: *the gunner and his m.* Tp. II, 2, 49. *thou that art his* (the master's) *m.* H6B IV, 1, 13.

2) husband or wife: *his beauteous m.* Lucr. 18. *thou hast no unkind m. to grieve thee*, Err. II, 1, 38. *no —s for you*, Shr. I, 1, 59. *one self m. and m. could not beget such different issues*, Lr. IV, 3, 36 (Q2 *mate and make*). Applied to animals: *I, an old turtle, will lament my m.* Wint. V, 3, 134. *as true as turtle to her m.* Troil. III, 2, 185.

3) fellow, as an appellation of contempt or familiarity: *to make a stale of me amongst these —s*, Shr. I, 1, 58. *you poor, base, lack-linen m.* H4B II, 4, 134. *disgraced by an inkhorn m.* H6A III, 1, 99. *how now, my hardy, stout resolved —s*, R3 I, 3, 340.

Mate, vb. 1) to marry: *mad herself, she's madly —d*, Shr. III, 2, 246. *the hind that would be —d by the lion*, All's I, 1, 102. *if she be —d with an equal husband*, Tim. I, 1, 140. Play on the word in Err. III, 2, 54.

2) to match, to cope with: *I ... that in the way of loyalty and truth ... dare m. a sounder man than Surrey can be*, H8 III, 2, 274.

Mate, vb. to confound, to paralyze, to disable: *her more than haste is —d with delays*, Ven. 909. *not mad, but —d*, Err. III, 2, 54 (double meaning). *I think you are all —d or stark mad*, V, 281. *that is good deceit which —s him first that first intends deceit*, H6B III, 1, 265. *my mind she has —d, and amazed my sight*, Mcb. V, 1, 86.

Material (cf. *Immaterial*), 1) full of matter, sensible: *a m. fool*, As III, 3, 32.

2) important: *made his business more m.* Wint. I, 2, 216. *whose absence is no less m. to me than is his father's*, Mcb. III, 1, 136. *which is m. to the tender of our present*, Cymb. I, 6, 207.*

3) substantial, constituting and forming the matter or substance: *she that herself will sliver and disbranch from her m. sap*, Lr. IV, 2, 35 (a passage omitted in Ff. Theobald *maternal*).

Mathematics, the science which treats of quantity: Shr. I, 1, 37. II, 56. 82.

Matin, morning: *the glow-worm shows the m. to be near*, Hml. I, 5, 89.

Matron, a respectable elderly lady: All's III, 5, 100. Cor. II, 1, 279. Rom. III, 2, 11. Tim. IV, 1, 3. IV, 3, 112. Mcb. IV, 3, 62. Hml. III, 4, 83. Cymb. III, 4, 40.

Matter, subst. 1) substance, materials: *dry combustious m.* Ven. 1162. *in him a plenitude of subtle m., applied to cautels, all strange forms receives*, Compl. 302. *have I laid my brain in the sun and dried it, that it wants m. to prevent so gross o'erreaching?* Wiv. V, 5, 144; cf. *I have almost m. enough in me for such an embassage*, Ado I, 1, 281 (German: *ich habe das Zeug dazu;* = capacity). *I do not know the m.: he's 'rested on the case*, Err. IV, 2, 42 (quibbling). *of this m. is Cupid's arrow made*, Ado III, 1, 21. *m. that should feed this fire*, John V, 2, 85. *what hath mass or m.* Troil. I, 3, 29. *when it serves for the base m. to illu-*

minate so vile a thing, Caes. I, 3, 110. More especially, substance excreted from animal bodies: *I have m. in my head against you,* Wiv. I, 1, 127. *till there be more m. in the shin,* LLL III, 120. *and quench his fiery indignation even in the m. of mine innocence* (i. e. my tears) John IV, 1, 64. *then would come some m. from him,* Troil. II, 1, 9 (quibbling).

2) contents, argument, meaning, sense: *what sayest thou to this tune, m. and method?* Meas. III, 2, 51. *that you swerve not from the smallest article of it, neither in time, m. or other circumstance,* IV, 2, 108. *how low soever the m., I hope for high words,* LLL I, 1, 194. *that for a tricksy word defy the m.* Merch. III, 5, 75. *the m. is in my head,* As III, 5, 137. *though there was no great m. in the ditty,* V, 3, 36. *although the print be little, the whole m. and copy of the father,* Wint. II, 3, 98. *doleful m. merrily set down,* IV, 4, 189. *I'll read you m. deep and dangerous,* H4A I, 3, 190. *both in word and m.* II, 4, 479. *mere words, no m. from the heart,* Troil. V, 3, 108. *conceit, more rich in m. than in words,* Rom. II, 6, 30. *was ever book containing such vile m. so fairly bound?* III, 2, 83. *a book where men may read strange —m.,* Mcb. I, 5, 64. *thy commandment all alone shall live within the book and volume of my brain, unmixed with baser m.* Hml. I, 5, 104. *what is the m.?* II, 2, 195. 197. *there were no sallets in the lines to make the m. savoury, nor no m. in the phrase that might indict the author of affectation,* 463. *there's m. in these sighs,* IV, 1, 1 (Ff —s). *this nothing is more than m.* IV, 5, 174. *the phrase would be more german to the m.* V, 2, 166. *I love you more than words can wield the m.* Lr. I, 1, 56. *when priests are more in word than m.* III, 2, 81 (Goethe: *wo Begriffe fehlen, da stellt ein Wort zur rechten Zeit sich ein*); cf. Merch. III, 5, 75. *the m. of the paper,* Lr. I, 2, 68. III, 5, 16. *thou speakest in better phrase and m. than thou didst,* IV, 6, 8. *nor curstness grow to the m.* Ant. II, 2, 25. *I do not much dislike the m., but the manner of his speech,* 113. *pour out the pack of m. to mine ear,* II, 5, 54.

Hence = good sense: *to speak all mirth and no m.* Ado II, 1, 344; cf. *he's all my exercise, my mirth, my m.* Wint. I, 2, 166 (quicum joca, quicum seria). *then he's full of m.* As II, 1, 68. *my words are as full of peace as m.* Tw. I, 5, 227. *then would come some m. from him,* Troil. II, 1, 9 (quibbling). *more m. with less art,* Hml. II, 2, 95. *O m. and impertinency mixed,* Lr. IV, 6, 178.

3) argument, theme, subject for conversation or thought: *when your countenance filled up his line, then lacked I m.* Sonn. 86, 14. *the setting of thine eye and cheek proclaim a m. from thee,* Tp. II, 1, 230. *her wit values itself so highly that to her all m. else seems weak,* Ado III, 1, 54. *gravelled for lack of m.* As IV, 1, 74. *more m. for a May morning,* Tw. III, 4, 156. *here is more m. for a hot brain,* Wint. IV, 4, 700. *like an old tale still, which will have m. to rehearse,* V, 2, 67. *I will devise m. enough out of this Shallow to keep Prince Harry in continual laughter,* H4B V, 1, 87. *many a m. hath he told to thee,* Tit. V, 3, 164 (= story). *wherein necessity, of m. beggared, will nothing stick our person to arraign,* Hml. IV, 5, 92. *we had much more monstrous m. of feast, which worthily deserved noting,* Ant. II, 2, 187. *new m. still?* Cymb. V, 5, 243. Hence = cause: *that is not the m. I challenge thee for,* Tw. III, 4, 172. *there is not in the world either malice*

or m. to alter it, Wint. I, 1, 37. *and pick strong m. of revolt and wrath out of the bloody finger's ends of John,* John III, 4, 167. See below.

4) subject of complaint: *I will make a Star-chamber m. of it,* Wiv. I, 1, 2. *what m. have you against me?* 125. *three umpires in this m.* 139. *you hear all these —s denied,* 193. *the m. being afoot, keep your instruction,* Meas. IV, 5, 3. *whom it concerns to hear this m. forth,* V, 255. *there were —s against you for your life,* H4B I, 2, 151. *I read in's looks m. against me,* H8 I, 1, 126. *the king hath found m. against him,* III, 2, 21. *if they shall chance, in charging you with —s, to commit you,* V, 1, 147. *we need not put new m. to his charge,* Cor. III, 3, 76. *m. whole you have not to make it* (a quarrel) *with,* Ant. II, 2, 53.

5) point in question, affair, business: *thy wretched wife mistook the m. so, to slay herself, that should have slain her foe,* Lucr. 1826. *open the m. in brief,* Gent. I, 1, 135. 138. *how stands the m. with them?* II, 5, 21. *there's some great m. she'ld employ me in,* IV, 3, 3. *I will description the m. to you,* Wiv. I, 1, 222. *the mirth whereof so larded with my m.* IV, 6, 14. *the m. will be known to-night or never,* V, 1, 11. *leaves unquestioned —s of needful value,* Meas. I, 1, 56. *few of any wit in such —s,* II, 1, 282. *well, the m.?* II, 2, 33. *as the m. now stands,* III, 1, 201. *the phrase is to the m.* V, 90. *I will debate this m. at more leisure,* Err. IV, 1, 100. *I will so fashion the m. that Hero shall be absent,* Ado II, 2, 47. *speaks a little off the m.* III, 5, 11; cf. *this m. of marrying his king's daughter ... words him a great deal from the m.* Cymb. I, 4, 17 (from the point, from that which must really be taken into account, in short from reality). *we will talk no more of this m.* LLL III, 119. *that is the very defect of the m.* Merch. II, 2, 152. *as the m. falls,* III, 2, 204. *I came to acquaint you with a m.* As I, 1, 129. *her m. was, she loved your son,* All's I, 3, 114. *trust him not in m. of heavy consequence,* II, 5, 49. *on a forgotten m. we can hardly make distinction of our hand,* Tw. II, 3, 174. *my m. hath no voice but to your own ear,* III, 1, 99. *do you know of this m.?* III, 4, 284. *heavy —s! —s!* Wint. III, 3, 115. *a million of beating may come to a great m.* IV, 3, 63 (the clown's speech). *to bring this m. to the wished end,* H6A III, 3, 28. *but to the m. that we have in hand,* H6B I, 3, 162; = let us come to the subject, to the question; cf. Hml. III, 2, 336 and Cymb. V, 5, 169. *I have great —s to impart to thee,* H6B III, 2, 299. *m. of marriage was the charge he gave me,* H6C III, 3, 258. *I'll hence to London on a serious m.* V, 5, 47; cf. Lr. IV, 5, 8. *in deep designs and —s of great moment,* R3 III, 7, 67. *never suffers m. of the world enter his thoughts,* Troil. II, 3, 196. *I scarce have leisure to salute you, my m. is so rash,* IV, 2, 62. *never trouble Peter for the m.* Rom. IV, 4, 18. *I meddle with no tradesmen's —s, nor women's —s,* Caes. I, 1, 25. *that m. is answered directly,* III, 3, 25. *and like a neutral to his will and m., did nothing,* Hml. II, 2, 503. *I meant country —s,* III, 2, 123. *of worldly —s and direction,* Oth. I, 3, 300 (Ff m.). *state —s,* III, 4, 155. *I could have given less m. a better ear,* Ant. II, 1, 31. *this m. of marrying his king's daughter,* Cymb. I, 4, 14. *I am amazed with m.* IV, 3, 28 etc.

6) weight, importance, consequence: *there may be m. in it,* Wint. IV, 4, 874 (= something may be made of it). *there's m. in't indeed, if he be angry,* Oth. III, 4, 139. Mostly with a negative; *no m.* = it is all

one, never mind: *no m. where*, Ven. 715. *no m. then,
although my foot did stand upon the farthest earth*,
Sonn. 44, 5. *no m., since they have left their viands behind*, Tp. III, 3, 40. 50. *no m. who's displeased*, Gent.
II, 7, 66. *nay then, no m.* III, 1, 58. Wiv. II, 2, 149.
Merch. V, 50. As II, 3, 30. All's IV, 1, 4. R2 V, 2, 58
etc. *it is no m.:* Gent. II, 3, 41. Wiv. I, 1, 131. 133.
V, 3, 10. Ado V, 1, 100. Tw. III, 2, 46. H6B III, 1,
263. Caes. I, 1, 73 etc. *that's no m.:* Ado V, 1, 81. As
III, 2, 176. IV, 3, 27 etc. With *for*, in the language
of the vulgar: *no m. for the dish*, Meas. II, 1, 98. *no
m. for your foins*, Lr. IV, 6, 251. *she doth talk in her
sleep. It's no m. for that, so she sleep not in her talk*,
Gent. III, 1, 334. *it is no m. ver dat*, Wiv. I, 4, 121
(Dr. Caius' speech). *though I struck him first, yet it's
no m. for that*, Tw. IV, 1, 38. *'tis no m. for his swellings*, H5 V, 1, 17. *who, my master? Nay, it's no m.
for that*, Cor. IV, 5, 173.

7) any thing that has happened and caused difficulty or disturbance; in the phrase *what is the m.?*
Tp. II, 1, 309. II, 2, 59. Gent. II, 3, 38. V, 4, 87. Wiv.
II, 1, 43. III, 3, 100. Meas. II, 1, 46. II, 2, 6. Err. IV,
2, 41. Merch. V, 146. As II, 3, 16. All's III, 2, 37.
R2 V, 2, 73. H4B II, 1, 47. Troil. IV, 2, 60. Hml. II,
2, 195 etc. etc. *the m.?* alone, in the same sense: Cor.
I, 1, 57. III, 1, 28. Ant. II, 7, 62. Cymb. IV, 2, 192.
what is the m. with thee? Tw. III, 4, 27. Oth. IV, 2,
98. With a clause following, = reason, cause: *what's
the m. that you have such a February face?* Ado V, 4,
40. All's I, 3, 156. Cor. III, 3, 58.

8) thing, in a very general sense: *what impossible
m. will he make easy next?* Tp. II, 1, 88. *most poor —s
point to rich ends*, III, 1, 3. *if —s grow to your likings*, Wiv. I, 1, 79. *an there be any m. of weight chances*, Ado III, 3, 91. *beg a greater m.* LLL V, 2, 207.
I think of as many —s as he, As II, 5, 37. *it is a hard
m. for friends to meet*, III, 2, 194. *to stop up the displeasure he hath conceived against your son, there is
no fitter m.* All's IV, 5, 81. *O, what better m. breeds
for you than I have named*, John III, 4, 170. *instinct
is a great m.* H4A II, 4, 301. *some eight-penny m.* III,
3, 119. *my thoughts aim at a farther m.* H6C IV, 1,
125. *he beseeched me to entreat your majesties to hear
and see the m.* Hml. III, 1, 23 (i. e. the piece). *though
thou deny me a m. of more weight*, Ant. I, 2, 71. *no
such m.* = a) nothing of the kind: *in sleep a king,
but waking no such m.* Sonn. 87, 14. *I see no such m.*
Ado I, 1, 192. b) it is not the case, not at all, by no
means: *the sport will be, when they hold one an opinion of another's dotage, and no such m.* Ado II, 3, 225.
*they swore that you were well-nigh dead for me. 'tis no
such m.* V, 4, 82. *art thou a churchman? No such m.*,
Tw. III, 1, 5. *the big year is thought with child . . . and no
such m.* H4B Ind. 15. *no such m., you are wide*, Troil.
III, 1, 97. *we'll wait upon you. No such m.* Hml. II, 2, 274.

Matthew, name in H6B IV, 5, 11.

Mattock, a kind of pickaxe: Tit. IV, 3, 11. Rom.
V, 3, 22. 185.

Mattress, a quilted bed: Ant. II, 6, 71.

Mature, (*máture* and *matúre*), perfected by time,
ripe: Wint. I, 1, 27. Troil. IV, 5, 97. Cor. IV, 3, 26.
Lr. IV, 6, 282. Ant. I, 4, 31. Cymb. I, 1, 48. V, 4, 52.

Maturity, ripeness: Sonn. 60, 6. Troil. I, 3, 317.

Mauchus, see *Malchus.*

Maud, diminutive of Magdalen; name of a female servant: Err. III, 1, 31.

Maudlin, Magdalen: All's V, 3, 68.

Maugre, in spite of: Tw. III, 1, 163. Tit. IV, 2,
110. Lr. V, 3, 131.

Maul, to hack: *I'll so m. you and your toasting-
iron*, John IV, 3, 99. *'tis sport to m. a runner*, Ant. IV,
7, 14.

Maund, a hand-basket: Compl. 36.

Mauritania, country in Africa: Oth. IV, 2, 229.

Maw, stomach; applied to animals: Ven. 602.
Mcb. III, 4, 73. IV, 1, 23. to human beings: Meas.
III, 2, 23. Err. I, 2, 66. John V, 7, 37. H5 II, 1, 52.
Tim. III, 4, 52. Metaphorically: *thou detestable m.*
(the grave) Rom. V, 3, 45.

Maxim, axiom, established truth: Troil. I, 2, 318.

May, subst. the fifth month of the year, the month
of vernal beauty: Sonn. 18, 3. Compl. 102. Pilgr.
228 and LLL IV, 3, 102. Pilgr. 374. Wiv. III, 2, 70.
Ado I, 1, 194. V, 1, 76. LLL I, 1, 106. Mids. I, 1, 167.
IV, 1, 138. As IV, 1, 148. Tw. III, 4, 156. R2 V, 1, 79.
H4A IV, 1, 101. H6B I, 1, 49. Troil. I, 2, 191. Hml.
III, 3, 81. IV, 5, 157.

May, vb. (impf. *might; mought* in H6C V, 2, 45),
1) denoting subjective ability, = can: *she hath assayed as much as may be proved*, Ven. 608. *whom
stripes may move, not kindness*, Tp. I, 2, 345. *means
much weaker than you may call to comfort you*, V, 147.
*nor have I seen more that I may call men than you and
my father*, III, 1, 51. *if any man may* (win her) *you
may as soon as any*, Wiv. II, 2, 245. *cutting a smaller
hair than may be seen*, LLL V, 2, 258. *it stands so
that I may hardly tarry so long*, Shr. Ind. 2, 127. *you,
cousin Nevil, as I may remember*, H4B III, 1, 66. *I
am coming on, to venge me as I may*, H5 I, 2, 292.
yet, as we may, we'll meet both thee and Warwick, H6C
IV, 7, 86. *with all the heed I may*, R3 III, 1, 187 (Ff
can). *with all the humbleness I may, I greet your honours from Andronicus*, Tit. IV, 2, 4. *your desire to
know what is between us, o'ermaster it as you may*,
Hml. I, 5, 140 etc. Likewise in negative and interrogative sentences: *may it be that thou shouldst think it
heavy?* Ven. 155. *what bargains may I make, still to
be sealing?* 512. *what may a heavy groan advantage
thee?* 950. *may my pure mind with the foul act dispense . . . . may any terms acquit me from this chance?*
Lucr. 1704. 1706. *may I not go out ere he come?* Wiv.
IV, 2, 51. *how may I do it?* Meas. IV, 2, 175. *and may
it be that you have quite forgot a husband's office?*
Err. III, 2, 1. *may this be so?* Ado III, 2, 120. *may
you stead me? will you pleasure me?* Merch. I, 3, 7.
*it is a surplus of your grace, which never my life may
last to answer*, Wint. V, 3, 8. *may this be possible? may
this be true?* John V, 4, 21. *such beastly transformation . . . as may not be without much shame retold*, H4A
I, 1, 45. *may it be possible?* H5 II, 2, 100 etc. *Can*
and *may* alternating: *can this cockpit hold the vasty
fields of France? or may we cram within this wooden
O the very casques*, H5 Prol. 12. The modern use of
can and *may* quite inverted: *whom may you else oppose, that can from Hector bring his honour off, if not
Achilles?* Troil. I, 3, 333.

Impf. *might* (not as a subjunctive, but as an indicative, = I was able): *not only with what my revenue
yielded, but what my power might else exact*, Tp. I, 2,
99. *when I might behold addrest the king*, LLL V, 2,
92. *but I might see young Cupid's fiery shaft quenched
in the chaste beams of the watery moon*, Mids. II, 1,

161. *from off our towers we might behold the onset and retire*, John II, 325. *but at last I well might hear*, H6C V, 2, 46. *when he might act the woman in the scene*, Cor. II, 2, 100. *what we did was mildly as we might*, Tit. I, 475 etc. Interrogative and negative sentences: *mightst thou perceive in his eye that he did plead in earnest?* Err. IV, 2, 2. *such a storm that mortal ears might hardly endure the din*, Shr. I, 1, 178. *might you not know she would do as she has done?* All's III, 4, 2. *and might by no suit gain our audience*, H4B IV, 1, 76. *like a clamour in a vault, that mought not be distinguished*, H6C V, 2, 45. *which till to-night I ne'er might see before*, Oth. II, 3, 236 etc.

2) denoting objective possibility, and synonymous to the adv. perhaps: *the season once more fits, that love-sick Love by pleading may be blest*, Ven. 328. *then happy I, that love and am beloved where I may not remove nor be removed*, Sonn. 25, 14. *I may be straight, though they themselves be bevel*, 121, 11. *if thou rememberest aught ere thou camest here, how thou camest here, thou mayst*, Tp. I, 2, 52. *he may live*, II, 1, 113. *to be your fellow you may deny me*, III, 1, 85. *hinder them from what this ecstasy may now provoke them to*, III, 3, 109. *as little as may be possible*, Gent. I, 2, 82. *I may make my case as Claudio's*, Meas. IV, 2, 178. *for which live long to thank both heaven and me. You may so in the end*, All's IV, 2, 68. *worst in this royal presence may I speak*, R2 IV, 115. *a score of ewes may be worth ten pounds*, H4B III, 2, 57. *happily met . . . . That may be, when I may be a wife. That may be must be*, Rom. IV, 1, 19. 20 etc. In negative and interrogative sentences: *why may not he be here again?* Wiv. IV, 2, 153. *and yet enough may not extend so far as to the lady*, Merch. II, 7, 28. *if you have any music that may not be heard*, Oth. III, 1, 16. *may you suspect who they should be that have thus mangled you?* V, 1, 78 etc. Similarly *might*: *who might be your mother, that you insult . . . over the wretched?* As III, 5, 35. *what I will not, that I cannot do. But might you do't and do the world no wrong, if so your heart were touched with that remorse as mine is to him?* Meas. II, 2, 53.

It may be and *may be* = possibly, perhaps: *it may be I shall raise you by and by*, Caes. IV, 3, 247. 251. *may be the knave bragged*, Wiv. III, 3, 211. *may be he tells you true*, III, 4, 11. *may be he will relent*, Meas. II, 2, 3. IV, 1, 23. All's III, 5, 72. John III, 4, 160. H4A IV, 3, 113. Cymb. II, 4, 104. Per. V, 1, 88.

Be it as it may = however it be: H6C I, 1, 194. *be it as it may be, I will marry thee*, As III, 3, 42. *that shall be as it may*, H5 II, 1, 7. *but come what may*, Tw. II, 1, 48. *come what come may*, Mcb. I, 3, 146. *chance it as it may*, Tim. V, 1, 129. *thrive I as I may*, Merch. II, 7, 60. *come again when you may*, Err. III, 1, 41. cf. *the jargon of Nym in H5 II, 1, 15. 17. 23. 25. 60. 62. 132.*

3) denoting opportunity or liberty offered: *so of concealed sorrow may be said*, Ven. 333. *yet mayst thou well be tasted*, 128. *where thou mayst knock a nail into his head*, Tp. III, 2, 69. *there thou mayst brain him*, 96. *to lesson me, how I may undertake a journey to my loving Proteus*, Gent. II, 7, 6. *then mightst thou pause*, Ven. 137. *might I but through my prison once a day behold this maid*, Tp. I, 2, 490. *your father might have kept this calf*, John I, 123. *that almost mightst have coined me into gold*, H5 II, 2, 98. Tp. I, 2, 415. 417.

II, 1, 204. 285. Gent. II, 1, 173. III, 2, 29. H4B III, 1, 45 (*might* always subjunctive). *you may, you may* = do, go on, divert yourself at my expense: Troil. III, 1, 118 and Cor. II, 3, 39 (cf. *you may thank yourself*, Tp. II, 1, 123, = the imper. thank yourself).

4) = to be allowed, to be authorized: *the poor fool prays her that he may depart*, Ven. 578. *if your maid may be so bold*, Lucr. 1282. *for that vast of night that they may work*, Tp. I, 2, 327. *and may I say to thee, this pride of hers hath drawn my love from her*, Gent. III, 1, 72. *thou dost but what thou mayst*, H6A I, 3, 86. Meas. I, 4, 9. Mids. I, 2, 53. Rom. IV, 1, 19 etc. *I may not* = I am not allowed, I must not: *I may not evermore acknowledge thee*, Sonn. 36, 9. *it may not be*, Gent. IV, 4, 131. *I may not go in without your worship*, Wiv. I, 1, 288. *my haste may not admit it*, Meas. I, 1, 63. *you may, I may not*, I, 4, 9. *you may not so extenuate his offence*, II, 1, 27. *such a one as a man may not speak of without he say Sir-reverence*, Err. III, 2, 92. *which princes, would they, may not disannul*, I, 1, 145. *passed sentence may not be recalled*, 148. *no woman may approach his silent court*, LLL II, 24. *you may not come in my gates*, 172. V, 2, 675. 712. Merch. I, 2, 24. Shr. III, 2, 200. Tw. V, 104. Wint. II, 2, 7. John III, 1, 66. R2 II, 3, 145. V, 2, 70. H4A IV, 3, 1. H6A I, 3, 7. 18. II, 2, 47. V, 3, 188. H6C I, 1, 263. IV, 6, 6. R3 IV, 1, 16. 27. V, 3, 94. Cor. V, 2, 5. Rom. III, 2, 31. V, 1, 82. Mcb. III, 1, 122. Hml. I, 3, 19. Lr. IV, 5, 17. III, 7, 24.

Might: no rightful plea might plead for justice there, Lucr. 1649. *a tailor might scratch her where'er she did itch*, Tp. II, 2, 55. *who mutually hath answered my affection, so far forth as herself might be her chooser*, Wiv. IV, 6, 11. *I might not be admitted*, Tw. I, 1, 24. *my brother might not claim him*, John I, 126. *in wholesome wisdom he might not but refuse you*, Oth. III, 1, 50.

5) sometimes denoting, quite as the German *moegen*, an inclination or desire, = to choose, to please: *may your grace speak of it*, Meas. I, 3, 6. *construe my speeches better, if you may. Then wish me better; I will give you leave*, LLL V, 2, 341. *I never may believe these antic fables*, Mids. V, 2. *'tis well for thee, that, being unseminared, thy freer thoughts may not fly forth of Egypt*, Ant. I, 5, 12. *since the cuckoo builds not for himself, remain in it as thou mayst*, II, 6, 29. *woe are we, sir, you may not live to wear all your true followers out*, IV, 14, 133. *and longer might have stayed, if crooked fortune had not thwarted me*, Gent. IV, 1, 21 (= would). *majesty might never yet endure the moody frontier of a servant brow*, H4A I, 3, 18. *who intercepts my expedition? O, she that might have intercepted thee, by strangling thee in her accursed womb*, R3 IV, 4, 137. *I might not this believe without the sensible and true avouch of mine own eyes*, Hml. I, 1, 56. *so loving that he might not beteem the winds of heaven visit her face too roughly*, I, 2, 141. 5, 177.

6) Used to supply the place of the subjunctive mood: *vouchsafe my prayer may know*, Tp. I, 2, 423. *and that you will some good instruction give how I may bear me here*, 425. *any villany that may not sully the chariness of our honesty*, Wiv. II, 1, 102. *give leave that we may bring you something on the way*, Meas. I, 1, 62. *I pray she may* (persuade) I, 2, 192. *God grant it may with thee in true peace live*, H4B IV, 5, 220. *any thing I have is his to use, so Somerset may die,*

H6B V, 1, 53. *beseech you, I may be consul*, Cor. II, 3, 110. *I do entreat that we may sup together*, Oth. IV, 1, 273. *if thou dost break her virgin knot before all sanctimonious ceremonies may be ministered*, Tp. IV, 1, 16. *he shall know you better if I may live to report you*, Meas. III, 2, 172. *if you may please to think I love the king*, Wint. IV, 4. 532; cf. *may it please you*, Gent. I, 3, 39; Meas. III, 2, 209; Err. V, 136. *one that will play the devil with you, an a may catch you and your hide alone*, John II, 136. *I'll never trouble you, if I may spy them*, H6A I, 4, 22. *lest your true love may seem false in this, my name be buried*, Sonn. 72, 9. *season your admiration for a while till I may deliver*, Hml. I, 2, 193 etc. *I had rather it would please you I might be whipped*, Meas. V, 512. *would they not wish the feast might ever last*, Ven. 447. *we will make it our suit that the wrestling may not go forward*, As I, 2, 193. *tell me if this might be a brother*, Tp. I, 2, 118. *his tongue had not offended so today, if Cassius might have ruled*, Caes. V, 1, 47. *I feared lest I might anger thee*, Tp. IV, 169. *fearing lest my jealous aim might err*, Gent. III, 1, 28. *why dost thou ask? lest I might be too rash*, Meas. II, 2, 9. Ado I, 1, 316. H4B IV, 5, 212. H6B III, 2, 263. *and canopied in darkness sweetly lay, till they might open to adorn the day*, Lucr. 399 etc.

Oftenest after *that*, to denote a purpose (= in order that): *thou art bound to breed, that thine may live when thou thyself art dead*, Ven. 172. *that the star-gazers may say, the plague is banished*, 510. *show me the strumpet, that with my nails her beauty I may tear*, Lucr. 1472. 1603. Sonn. 10, 9. 14. Tp. IV, 104. 194. Gent. I, 1, 138. I, 2, 49. I, 3, 35. III, 1, 33. IV, 1, 54. V, 4, 82. Wiv. II, 2, 194. Meas. I, 2, 165. Err. I, 1, 34. V, 40. 158. Merch. III, 2, 46. All's I, 3, 39. H6A II, 2, 14. H6B II, 1, 75. H6C IV, 1, 122 etc. *each trifle under truest bars to throw, that to my use it might unused stay*, Sonn. 48, 3. *and therefore from my face she turns my foes* (her eyes) *that they elsewhere might dart their injuries*, 139, 12. *that she might think me some untutored youth*, 138, 3. Tp. III, 1, 35. Gent. I, 2, 68. 80. IV, 2, 43. H6A II, 5, 32. H6C V, 5, 23 etc. *That* omitted: *Love made these hollows, if himself were slain, he might be buried in a tomb so simple*, Ven. 244. *direct mine arms I may embrace his neck*, H6A II, 5, 37.

Used to express a wish: *long may they kiss each other*, Ven. 505. *well may I get aboard!* Wint. III, 3, 57. *long mayst thou live*, R3 I, 3, 204. *prophet may you be*, Troil. III, 2, 190. *may you a better feast never behold*, Tim. III, 6, 98. *well may it sort that this portentous figure comes armed through our watch*, Hml. I, 1, 109 (see above *may it please you*). *Lord worshipped might he be!* Merch. II, 2, 98 (old Gobbo's speech). In subordinate clauses: *which I wish may always answer your own wish*, Ven. Ded. 7. *if ever the duke return, as our prayers are he may*, Meas. III, 2, 164. *were now the general of our gracious empress, as in good time he may, from Ireland coming*, H5 V Prol. 31. *who may I rather challenge for unkindness than pity for mischance*, Mcb. III, 4, 42. *O, that our night of woe might have remembered my deepest sense how hard true sorrow hits*, Sonn. 120, 9. *would thou mightst lie drowning*, Tp. I, 1, 60. *would I might but ever see that man*, I, 2, 168 etc.

7) Joined to adverbs denoting motion, = to have

opportunity or liberty to go: *shine comforts from the east, that I may back to Athens by day-light*, Mids. III, 2, 433. *you may away by night*, H4A III, 1, 142. cf. *Shall, Will* etc.

May-day, the first of May, a day of festivity in old England: All's II, 2, 25. H8 V, 4, 15.

May-morn, used as an image of fresh and promising youth: *in the very M. of his youth*, H5 I, 2, 120.

Mayor, the chief magistrate of a corporation: H5 V Chor. 25. H6A I, 3, 59. 86. H6B IV, 3, 16 *(the —'s sword)*. H6C IV, 7, 20. R3 III, 1, 17. III, 5, 13. 73. III, 7, 28. 44. 45. 66. IV, 2, 107. *lord m.* H6B IV, 5, 4. R3 III, 5, 14. 71. III, 7, 55. H8 II, 1, 151. V, 5, 70.

May-pole, a pole erected and danced round on the first of May: *thou painted m.* Mids. III, 2, 296.

Mazard (the later Ff *mazzard*) the head, contemptuously: *knocked about the m. with a sexton's spade*, Hml. V, 1, 97. *I'll knock you o'er the m.* Oth. II, 3, 155.

Maze, subst. a labyrinth: *one encompassed with a winding m.* Lucr. 1151. *here's a m. trod*, Tp. III, 3, 2. *as strange a m. as e'er men trod*, V, 242. *the quaint —s in the wanton green*, Mids. II, 1, 99. *I have thrust myself into this m.* Shr. I, 2, 55.

Mazed, perplexed, bewildered: *the m. world now knows not which is which*, Mids. II, 1, 113. *a little herd of England's timorous deer, m. with a yelping kennel of French curs*, H6A IV, 2, 47. *many m. considerings*, H8 II, 4, 185.

Mazzard, see *Mazard*.

Me, see *I*.

Meacock, spiritless, pusillanimous, hen-pecked: *how tame, when men and women are alone, a m. wretch can make the curstest shrew*, Shr. II, 315.

Mead, (rhyming to *dread* in Ven. 636); flat low land covered with grass: Ven. 636. Lucr. 1218. Tp. IV, 1, 63. Mids. II, 1, 83. Shr. V, 2, 139. H5 V, 2, 48. 54. Tit. II, 4, 54. Lr. I, 1, 66.

Meadow, the same: Sonn. 33, 3. LLL V, 2, 907. Tit. III, 1, 125. *m. fairies*, Wiv. V, 5, 69 (cf. Mids. II, 1, 9. 99).

Meagre, 1) thin, lean: Ven. 931. John III, 4, 85. H6B III, 2, 162. Rom. V, 1, 40.

2) poor, barren: *thou m. lead*, Merch. III, 2, 104. *turning the m. cloddy earth to glittering gold*, John III, 1, 80.

Meal, repast: Meas. IV, 3, 161. Err. V, 74. LLL I, 1, 40. H5 III, 7, 161. H6B IV, 10, 66. Troil. II, 3, 45. Cor. IV, 4, 14. Tim. I, 2, 51. Caes. II, 1, 284. Ant. IV, 2, 10. *we will eat our m. in fear*, Mcb. III, 2, 17. *hath made his m. on thee*, Tp. II, 1, 113. *I had made my m.* Cymb. III, 6, 52.

Meal, flour: *m. and bran*, Cor. III, 1, 322. Cymb. IV, 2, 27.

Meal, in *Inchmeal, Limb-meal*, q. v.

Mealed, sprinkled, tainted: *were he m. with that which he corrects, then were he tyrannous*, Meas. IV, 2, 86.

Mealy, covered as with meal: *men, like butterflies, show not their m. wings but to the summer*, Troil. III, 3, 79.

Mean, subst. 1) that which is between: *and so I chide the —s that keeps me from it*, H6C III, 2, 141. *let not the piece of virtue, which is set betwixt us as the cement of our love, to keep it builded, be the ram to batter the fortress of it; for better might we have loved* *without this m., if on both parts this be not cherished,* Ant. III, 2, 32. (cf. *Meantime*).

2) middle station, medium, mediocrity: *it is no mean happiness to be seated in the m.* Merch. I, 2, 8. *shall we disturb him, since he keeps no m.?* H6A I, 2, 121. *they know, by the height, the lowness, or the m., if dearth or foison follow,* Ant. II, 7, 22.

3) in music, the tenor or counter-tenor: *there wanteth but a m. to fill your song. The m. is drowned with your unruly base,* Gent. I, 2, 95. 96. *he can sing a m. most meanly,* LLL V, 2, 328. *they are most of them —s and bases,* Wint. IV, 3, 46.

4) that which is used to effect a purpose: *seek in vain some happy m. to end a hapless life,* Lucr. 1045. *they have devised a m. how he her chamber-window will ascend,* Gent. III, 1, 38. *that there were no earthly m. to save him,* Meas. II, 4, 95. *nature is made better by no m. but nature makes that m.* Wint. IV, 4, 89. *our sacks shall be a m. to sack the city,* H6A III, 2, 10. *we'll devise a m. to reconcile you all unto the king,* H6B IV, 8, 71. *that m. is cut from thee,* Tit. II, 4, 40. *sudden m. of death,* Rom. III, 3, 45. *devise some m. to rid her from this second marriage,* V, 3, 240 (reading of Q2). *I'll devise a m. to draw the Moor out of the way,* Oth. III, 1, 39. *a swifter m. shall outstrike thought,* Ant. IV, 6, 35. Used of persons: *be my m. to bring me where to speak with Madam Silvia,* Gent. IV, 4, 113. *make the Douglas' son your only m. for powers in Scotland,* H4A I, 3, 261. *you may deny that you were not the m. of my Lord Hastings' late imprisonment,* R3 I, 3, 90 (Qq cause). *no place will please me so, no m. of death, as here by Caesar, and by you cut off,* Caes. III, 1, 161.

Oftener used in the plur.: *these —s, as frets upon an instrument, shall tune our heart-strings,* Lucr. 1140. *fortify yourself in your decay with —s more blessed than my barren rhyme,* Sonn. 16, 4. *—s to live,* Tp. II, 1, 50. *supportable to make the dear loss have I —s much weaker,* V, 146. Gent. II, 4, 182. Meas. II, 4, 48 *(to put metal in restrained —s to make a false one).* III, 2, 22. Merch. IV, 1, 81. As II, 3, 25. 51. John IV, 2, 219. R2 I, 4, 40. III, 2, 29. 32. H6A V, 1, 8. Oth. IV, 2, 112 etc. etc. Used of medicaments: *till I have used the approved —s I have,* Err. V, 103. *healed by the same —s,* Merch. III, 1, 65. *with all appliances and —s,* H4B III, 1, 29. *use —s for her recovery,* H6C V, 5, 45. *by using —s, I lame the foot of our design,* Cor. IV, 7, 7. Used of persons: *being the superiors, or base second —s,* H4A I, 3, 165. *those that were the —s to help him,* R3 V, 3, 249 (= instruments).

The plural form used as a singular noun: *other —s was none,* Err. I, 1, 76. *who wins me by that —s I told you,* Merch. II, 1, 19. *by this —s,* Wint. IV, 4, 632. H6A I, 2, 63. *a —s,* Wint. IV, 4, 865. H6C III, 3, 39. *strain what other —s is left unto us,* Tim. V, 1, 230. *remove the —s that makes us strangers,* Mcb. IV, 3, 163 (but cf. Abbott's Grammar p. 235). *there is —s,* Lr. IV, 4, 11.

5) that which is at a person's disposal; resources, power, wealth, allowance: *would try him to the utmost, had ye m.* H8 V, 3, 146. With the exception of this single passage, only used in the plural: *that did not better for my life provide than public —s,* Sonn. 111, 4. *either in my mind or in my —s,* Wiv. II, 2, 211. *let her have needful, but not lavish —s,* Meas. II,

2, 24. *fortune made such havoc of my —s,* Ado IV, 1, 197. 201. Merch. I, 1, 125. 138. I, 3, 17. III, 2, 266. IV, 1, 377. As I, 2, 259. II, 7, 73. III, 2, 26. All's V, 1, 35. R2 II, 1, 39. H4B I, 2, 159. I, 3, 1. 7. IV, 4, 64. V, 5, 71. R3 IV, 2, 37. H8 IV, 2, 153. Tim. V, 4, 20 etc. *our —s secure us,* Lr. IV, 1, 22, i. e. our faculties, the advantages which we enjoy, make us secure and careless.*

6) opportunity; preparations made and measures taken to effect something: *tell me some good m. how I may undertake a journey,* Gent. II, 7, 5. *many a man would take you at your word and go indeed, having so good a m.* Err. I, 2, 18. Oftener plur. *—s: pausing for —s to mourn some newer way,* Lucr. 1365. *since they did plot the —s that dusky Dis my daughter got,* Tp. IV, 89. *I had never so good —s as desire to make myself acquainted with you,* Wiv. II, 2, 189. *he gains by death that has such —s to die,* Err. III, 2, 51. *I will come after you with what good speed our means will make us —s,* All's V, 1, 35. cf. *though time seem so adverse and —s unfit,* 26. *you would not give —s for this uncivil rule,* Tw. II, 3, 132. *let me have open —s to come to them,* R3 IV, 2, 77. *bid her devise some —s to come to shrift,* Rom. II, 4, 192. *his —s of death, his obscure burial,* Hml. IV, 5, 213. *give this fellow some —s to the king,* IV, 6, 13 (some opportunity to have access to him). *to make —s =* to contrive measures and opportunities: *to make such —s for her as thou hast done, and leave her on such slight conditions,* Gent. V, 4, 137. *make some good —s to speak with him,* R3 V, 3, 40 (Qq bear my good night to him). *what —s do you make to him?* Cymb. II, 4, 3 (= what steps do you take with respect to him? what have you done to gain his favour?). In a bad sense: *one that made —s to come by what he hath,* R3 V, 3, 248 (= laid plots, used indirect practices).

By —s, used 1) to denote instrumentality, = through, by: *by the woman's —s,* Meas. II, 1, 84. *murdered by Suffolk and the Cardinal Beaufort's —s,* H6B III, 2, 124. *mischance unto my state by Suffolk's —s,* 284. *our brother is imprisoned by your —s,* R3 I, 3, 78. *as if his sons have by my —s been butchered wrongfully,* Tit. IV, 4, 55. *either say thou'lt do't, or thrive by other —s,* Lr. V, 3, 34. *by your virtuous —s,* Oth. III, 4, 111.

2) to denote way and manner: *and have by underhand —s laboured to dissuade him,* As I, 1, 146. *till he hath ta'en thy life by some indirect —s or other,* 159. *hast thou by secret —s used intercession to obtain a league,* H6A V, 4, 147. *by wicked —s,* H6B III, 1, 52. *I have advertised him by secret —s,* H6C IV, 5, 9. *by fair or foul —s,* IV, 7, 14. *by what safe —s,* 52. *by vile —s,* Caes. IV, 3, 71. *by the worst —s,* Mcb. III, 4, 135. cf. *send me your prisoners with the speediest —s,* H4A I, 3, 120 (as soon as possible). *By all —s =* certainly, without fail: Wiv. IV, 2, 230. Tw. III, 2, 62. *by any —s =* anyhow: *if I can by any —s light on a fit man,* Shr. I, 1, 112. Wint. V, 2, 183. Rom. I, 1, 151. *by no —s =* not at all: Meas. III, 1, 15. Ado II, 1, 364. Mids. I, 1, 120. As III, 2, 326. Tim. I, 2, 8. Caes. II, 1, 75. 143. Hml. I, 3, 61. I, 4, 62. III, 1, 6. Lr. II, 1, 44. IV, 3, 42. *by some —s =* somehow or other: *but end it* (my life) *by some —s for Imogen,* Cymb. V, 3, 83. *by this —s =* thus: *my letters, by this —s being there so soon as you arrive,* Wint. IV, 4, 632. *by what —s and by which —s =*

in what or which manner: *by what —s gotst thou to be released?* H6A I, 4, 25. *by which —s I saw . . .*, Wint. IV, 4, 614.

3) to assign a cause: *we stand opposed by such —s as you yourself have forged against yourself by unkind usage,* H4A V, 1, 67 (= for such reasons, from such motives). *by this —s your lady is forthcoming yet at London,* H6B II, 1, 178 (= in consequence of this). *did he not levy great sums for soldiers' pay in France, and never sent it? by —s whereof the towns each day revolted,* H6B III, 1, 63. *stayed the soldiers' pay; by —s whereof his highness hath lost France,* 106. *I have much mistook your passion; by —s whereof this breast of mine hath buried thoughts of great value,* Caes. I, 2, 49. *By the —s,* in the same sense: *he is white-livered and red-faced; by the —s whereof a' faces it out, but fights not,* H5 III, 2, 34. *he hath a killing tongue and a quiet sword; by the —s whereof a' breaks words and keeps whole weapons,* 37. *their inhibition comes by the —s of the late innovation,* Hml. II, 2, 347.

Mean, adj. 1) common, vulgar, trivial, insignificant: *a very m. meaning,* Shr. V, 2, 31. *all in vain are these m. obsequies,* H6B III, 2, 146. *'tis a cause that hath no m. dependence upon our joint and several dignities,* Troil. II, 2, 192. *hadst thou no poison mixed, no sharp-ground knife, no sudden mean of death, though ne'er so m., but 'banished' to kill me?* Rom. III, 3, 45. *some natural notes about her body, above ten thousand —er moveables would testify,* Cymb. II, 2, 29. *if one of m. affairs may plod it in a week, why may not I glide thither in a day?* III, 2, 52.

2) low, humble, poor: *that —er men should vaunt that golden hap,* Lucr. 41. *this my m. task,* Tp. III, 1, 4. *my —er ministers their several kinds have done,* III, 3, 87. IV, 1, 35. *too m. a servant to have a look of such a worthy mistress,* Gent. II, 4, 107. Err. I, 1, 55. III, 1, 28. LLL II, 13. Merch. I, 2, 7. As I, 3, 113. Shr. I, 1, 210. IV, 3, 172. 176. 182. V, 2, 32. All's III, 5, 63. Wint. I, 2, 313. V, 1, 93. R2 I, 2, 33. H4A III, 2, 13. H5 III, 1, 29. IV Chor. 45. H6A II, 5, 123. IV, 6, 23. H6B II, 1, 185. IV, 8, 39. V, 1, 64. H6C I, 3, 19. III, 2, 97. IV, 1, 71. R3 V, 2, 24. H8 II, 2, 136. Troil. II, 2, 156. Cor. I, 6, 27. IV, 2, 40. Tit. II, 1, 73. IV, 4, 33. Lr. IV, 6, 208. Ant. II, 5, 83. IV, 15, 75. Cymb. II, 3, 121. 122. 138. IV, 2, 246. Per. II, 2, 59. IV, 6, 108.

Mean, vb. to moan, to lament: *and thus she —s, videlicet,* Mids. V, 330 (some M. Edd. *moans*).

Mean, vb. (impf. and partic. *meant*) 1) absol. to be minded, to be disposed; joined with an adverb (Germ. *es meinen*): *my cousin —t well,* Wiv. I, 1, 265. *Petruchio —s but well,* Shr. III, 2, 22. *if you m. well, now go with me and with this holy man into the chantry,* Tw. IV, 3, 22. *I cannot speak so well, nor m. better,* Wint. IV, 4, 392. *I do (perceive your mind) and m. accordingly,* H6A II, 2, 60. *if thou —est well, I greet thee well,* H6B V, 1, 14. *as if I —t naughtily,* Troil. IV, 2, 38. *we m. well in going to this mask,* Rom. I, 4, 48. *they that m. virtuously, and yet do so,* Oth. IV, 1, 7. Passively: *is it not —t damnable in us, to be trumpeters of our unlawful intents?* All's IV, 3, 31.

2) trans. a) to have in mind, to think of in speaking, to be saying (though not expressing directly); followed by an accus. or by a clause: *—t thereby thou shouldst print more,* Sonn. 11, 13 (cf. *by* in Gent. V,

4, 167. Err. III, 1, 10. Mids. III, 2, 236 etc.). *the miracle, I m. our preservation,* Tp. II, 1, 7. *I m., in a sort,* 103. *you mistake; I m. the pound,* Gent. I, 1, 113. II, 1, 49. 59. 127. II, 3, 46. II, 5, 51. III, 1, 101. 106. V, 4, 167. Wiv. III, 4, 63. Meas. II, 4, 118. Err. II, 1, 58. III, 1, 10. 111. IV, 2, 8. IV, 3, 15. Ado I, 1, 35. Mids. II, 2, 47. III, 2, 236. Merch. II, 9, 25 (*that 'many' may be —t by the fool multitude,* = of the fool multitude; cf. *By*). Shr. V, 2, 19. 27. 31. All's I, 3, 174. Wint. IV, 4, 197. Rom. I, 4, 44. Cymb. IV, 1, 9 etc. etc. With *how* and *so: how doest thou m. a fat marriage?* Err. III, 2, 95. *how m. you, sir?* LLL I, 2, 20. *how m. you that?* Shr. I, 1, 59. V, 2, 21. *how do you m.?* All's III, 5, 71. *m. you so?* Err. III, 1, 81. *I —t not so,* LLL IV, 1, 13. *What do you m. or what m. you?* used reproachfully, = do not so, or do not say so (Germ. *was denkst du dir dabei?*): *what dost thou m. to stifle beauty?* Ven. 933 (= in stifling beauty). *what do you m. to dote thus on such luggage?* Tp. IV, 230. *what m. you, sir? for God's sake, hold your hands,* Err. I, 2, 93. *what m. you, madam? I never swore such an oath,* LLL V, 2, 450. *what m. you? you will lose your reputation,* 708. *what doest thou m.? is it a world to hide virtues in?* Tw. I, 3, 140. *but what m. I to speak so true,* H4B Ind. 27. *what do you m.?* Lr. III, 7, 77. *what m. you, madam? I have made no fault,* Ant. II, 5, 74. *what m. you, sir, to give them this discomfort?* IV, 2, 33. Hence: *what —s the world to say it is not so?* Sonn. 148, 6 (= the world is mistaken). *what —s death in this rude assault? Villain, thy own hand yields thy death's instrument,* R2 V, 5, 106 (= death is mistaken and shall be disappointed). Jocularly: *what a plague —s my niece, to take the death of her brother thus?* Tw. I, 3, 1. *what a plague m. ye to colt me thus?* H4A II, 2, 39.

In speaking of things, = to signify, to indicate, to purport: *what —s this passion at his name?* Gent. I, 2, 16. *what —s this jest?* Err. II, 2, 21. *what —s this?* As III, 5, 41. H6A I, 3, 29. *we wot not what it (the word submission) —s,* IV, 7, 55 etc.

b) to have a mind, to intend, to purpose; with an accus.: *know not what we m.* Ven. 126. *I m. it not,* Wiv. III, 4, 88. *no man —s evil but the devil,* V, 2, 15. *nor I m. it not,* Meas. II, 1, 124. Merch. III, 5, 82. *if they m. a fray,* Mids. III, 2, 447. *do you m. good faith?* Merch. III, 2, 212. *what I did not well I —t well,* Wint. V, 3, 3. *he may m. more,* H6A I, 2, 122. *Talbot —s no goodness,* III, 2, 72. *things are often spoke and seldom —t,* H6B III, 1, 268. *he —t all harm,* H6C V, 7, 34. *where he did m. no chase,* R3 III, 2, 30. *where all faith was —t,* H8 III, 1, 53. *one that —s his proper harm,* Cor. I, 9, 57. *thankful even for hate, that is —t love,* Rom. III, 5, 149. *—s most deceit,* Per. I, 4, 75 etc. With accus. and dat.: *my hand —t nothing to my sword,* Ado V, 1, 57 (or can this be = my hand to my sword, i. e. put to my sword, meant nothing?). *the poor deer's blood, that my heart —s no ill,* LLL IV, 1, 35. *when fortune —s to men most good,* John III, 4, 119. *I never —t him any ill,* H6B II, 3, 91. *—ing treason to our royal person,* III, 1, 70. *you m. no good to him,* R3 III, 7, 87. Tit. V, 3, 10. Cymb. I, 5, 66. With an inf.: *their queen —s to immure herself,* Ven. 1194. *if thou m. to chide,* Lucr. 484. Gent. II, 1, 125. II, 4, 80. II, 6, 33. IV, 4, 27. Wiv. I, 3, 47. IV, 6, 46. Meas. II, 1, 242. IV, 2, 206. Err. III, 1, 108. IV, 3, 79. Ado II, 1, 370. III, 2, 91. Mids. I, 1, 250. II, 2, 55.

Merch. III, 2, 194. John I, 215. H6A II, 2, 58. H6B II, 1, 143. Cor. V, 1, 72. Rom. II, 1, 42. Caes. IV, 2, 28 etc. etc. With a clause: *you have taken it wiselier than I —t you should*, Tp. II, 1, 21. *her father —s she shall be all in white*, Wiv. IV, 6, 35. *as never I m. thou shalt*, Wint. IV, 4, 440.

Mean-apparelled, poorly dressed: Shr. III, 2, 76.

Mean-born, of low birth: H6B III, 1, 335. R3 IV, 2, 54 (Ff *mean poor*).

Meander, a winding way: *through forth-rights and —s*, Tp. III, 3, 3.

Meaning, subst. 1) sense; thought in any manner expressed or suggested: *his m. struck her ere his words begun*, Ven. 462. *could pick no m. from their parling looks*, Lucr. 100. *when thou didst not know thine own m.* Tp. I, 2, 356. *there's m. in thy snores*, II, 1, 218. Wiv. I, 1, 263. Err. II, 1, 51. III, 2, 36. Ado II, 3, 267. III, 4, 80. V, 1, 230. LLL III, 59. V, 2, 19. 21. Merch. I, 2, 34. I, 3, 15. III, 5, 64. Shr. IV, 4, 79. V, 2, 30. John IV, 2, 212. H5 I, 2, 240. III, 6, 53. V, 2, 334. H6A III, 2, 24. H6C IV, 5, 22. R3 I, 3, 74. I, 4, 95. IV, 4, 261. H8 IV, 2, 39. Tit. II, 3, 271. II, 4, 3. III, 2, 45. Hml. II, 1, 31. *to take the m.* = to understand what another means: *would not take her m. nor her pleasure*, Pilgr. 154. *love takes the m. in love's conference*, Mids. II, 2, 46. *take our good m.* Rom. I, 4, 46. Plur. *—s: speakest thou in sober —s?* As V, 2, 76. *two —s in one word*, R3 III, 1, 83. *I have fair —s*, Ant. II, 6, 67.

Used of the signification of a word: Tw. I, 3, 62. Of the solution of a riddle: *now behold the m.* All's V, 3, 305. Cymb. V, 5, 434. Per. I, 1, 109.

2) intention, purpose: *he hath some m. in his mad attire*, Shr. III, 2, 126. *my m. in't was very honest*, All's IV, 3, 246. *'tis not my m. to raze one title of your honour out*, R2 II, 3, 74. H4B IV, 2, 58. H6C IV, 7, 60. R3 III, 5, 55. Tim. V, 4, 59. Lr. V, 3, 4. *I am no honest man if there be any good m. towards you*, Lr. I, 2, 190.

= opinion, in the language of Sir Hugh: Wiv. I, 1, 263. cf. *mean* Tp. II, 1, 21 & Cymb. IV, 1, 9.

Meanly, 1) insignificantly, indifferently: *he can sing a mean most m.* LLL V, 2, 328.

2) not in a great degree, moderately: *not m. proud of two such boys*, Err. I, 1, 59.

3) lowly, poorly: *his daughter m. have I matched in marriage*, R3 IV, 3, 37. *trained up thus m.* Cymb. III, 3, 82.

Means, see *Mean* subst.

Meantime (*méantime* or *meantíme*), intervening time; *in the m.* (sometimes used to denote a contrast of opinion or design): Ado I, 1, 277. I, 3, 38. II, 2, 47. Mids. I, 2, 107. All's IV, 3, 44. John I, 103. H5 V, 1, 35. Rom. IV, 1, 113. Tim. III, 2, 44. Hml. III, 2, 47. Oth. III, 3, 252. *the m.* = in the m.: *the m. I'll raise the preparation of a war*, Ant. III, 4, 25. *m.*, alone, adverbially, in the same sense: Lucr. Ded. 5. Ado V, 4, 70. LLL II, 169. Merch. III, 2, 311. IV, 1, 149. As V, 4, 182. Tw. V, 393. John IV, 2, 43. R2 I, 1, 67. H6A I, 2, 117. II, 4, 62. 121. R3 I, 1, 111. 116. I, 3, 77. IV, 3, 33. Rom. V, 3, 220. 246. Hml. II, 2, 83. Lr. I, 1, 37. Ant. I, 4, 81. IV, 1, 5.

Meanwhile (*meanwhíle*), in the meantime, till then: H8 II, 4, 233. Tit. I, 408. II, 1, 43. IV, 3, 105.

Measles, leprosy: *so shall my lungs coin words*

against those m., which we disdain should tetter us, yet sought the very way to catch them, Cor. III, 1, 78.

Measurable, in the language of Holofernes, = well adapted, fit: *the posterior of the day is liable, congruent and m. for the afternoon*, LLL V, 1, 97 (cf. *measure* in Cor. II, 2, 127).

Measure, subst. 1) that by which extent or quantity is ascertained: (a tailor) *with his shears and m. in his hand*, John IV, 2, 196. Metaphorically: *these particulars are not my m.* Sonn. 91, 7 (i. e. to estimate human happiness). *their memory shall as a pattern or a m. live, by which his grace must mete the lives of others*, H4B IV, 4, 76. *know by m. of their observant toil the enemy's weight*, Troil. I, 3, 202. *my life will be too short, and every m. fail me*, Lr. IV, 7, 3. *this dotage o'erflows the m.* Ant. I, 1, 2.

2) a limited or ascertained extent or quantity; in a proper and a metaphorical sense: *the m. of one* (mile) *is easily told*, LLL V, 2, 190. *shrunk to this little m.* Caes. III, 1, 150. *—s of lawn*, Oth. IV, 3, 73. *send —s of wheat to Rome*, Ant. II, 6, 37. *there is no m. in the occasion that breeds*, Ado I, 3, 3. *more m. of this m.* LLL V, 2, 222 (= more of this dance). *according to the m. of their states*, As V, 4, 181. *fill up the m. of her will*, John II, 556. *a reasonable m. in strength*, H5 V, 2, 141. *to add more m. to your woes*, H6C II, 1, 105. *hath given me m. of revenge*, II, 3, 32. *the m. of his love*, III, 3, 120. *after the m. as you intended well*, Cor. V, 1, 46. *filled the time with all licentious m.* Tim. V, 4, 4 (= with all measure or degree of licence). *there is no end, no limit, m., bound, in that word's death*, Rom. III, 2, 125. *this . . . we will perform in m., time and place*, Mcb. V, 8, 73. *most narrow m. lent me*, Ant. III, 4, 8. *that he should dream, knowing all —s, the full Caesar will answer his emptiness*, III, 13, 35. *unfold his m. duly*, Cymb. I, 1, 26. *heaped m.* = great quantity, high degree: *with m. heaped in joy*, As V, 4, 185 (= joyful in the highest degree). *if the m. of thy joy be heaped like mine*, Rom. II, 6, 24. *to take m.* = to measure, to ascertain the extent or degree of a thing: *took m. of my body*, Err. IV, 3, 9. *taking the m. of an unmade grave*, Rom. III, 3, 70. *that he might take a m. of his own judgments*, All's IV, 3, 38. *m. for m.* = like for like: *like doth quit like, and m. still for m.* Meas. V, 416. *m. for m. must be answered*, H6C II, 6, 55. Hence used as a judicial term for dealing out justice: *justice always whirls in equal m.* LLL IV, 3, 384 (quibbling). *received no sinister m. from his judge*, Meas. III, 2, 257. *this is hard and undeserved m.* All's II, 3, 273 (= treatment). *Above m.* = immensely: Cymb. II, 4, 113. *loved me above the m. of a father*, Cor. V, 3, 10. *beyond all m.* Shr. I, 2, 90. *out of m.* = immoderately: Ado I, 3, 2. *in all fair m.* = in any fair degree, Troil. III, 1, 47. *in great m.* Ado I, 1, 25. *in some m.* Mids. I, 2, 30. John II, 557. H4B I, 1, 139. *in some large m.* R2 I, 2, 26. *in some little m.* As V, 2, 63. *in some slight m.* Mids. III, 2, 86. *with m.* = competently: *he cannot but with m. fit the honours which we devise him*, Cor. II, 2, 127. *come not within the m. of my wrath*, Gent. V, 4, 127 (= within the reach).

Used of a certain quantity of a beverage: *carouse full m. to her maidenhead*, Shr. III, 2, 227. *we'll drink a m. the table round*, Mcb. III, 4, 11. *would fain have a m. to the health of black Othello*, Oth. II, 3, 32.

3) moderation; just degree: *there is m. in every*

thing, Ado ll, 1, 74 (quibbling). *in m. rein thy joy*, Merch. lll, 2, 113. *my legs can keep no m. in delight when my poor heart no m. keeps in grief*, R2 III, 4, 7.

4) metre: *for the one* (verses) *I have neither words nor m.* H5 V, 2, 139.

5) music accompanying and regulating motion: *shall braying trumpets and loud churlich drums be —s to our pomp?* John lll, 1, 304.

6) a grave and solemn dance: *mannerly modest, as a m., full of state and ancientry*, Ado ll, 1, 80. *a delightful m. or a dance*, R2 l, 3, 291. Used of any dance: *to guide our m. round about the tree*, Wiv. V, 5, 83. *in our m. do vouchsafe one change*, LLL V, 2, 209. 221. *to the —s fall*, As V, 4, 185. *dancing —s*, 199. *the triplex is a good tripping m.* Tw. V, 41. H5 V, 2, 141. R3 I, 1, 8. Rom. I, 4, 10. I, 5, 52. Per. II, 3, 104. *to lead the m.* All's II, 1, 58. *a m. to lead 'em once again*, H8 I, 4, 106. *to tread the —s*, Ven. 1148. LLL V, 2, 185. As V, 4, 45. Play on the word: Ado ll, 1, 74. LLL IV, 3, 384. R2 III, 4, 7.

7) regulated and graceful motion in general: *the horse that doth untread again his tedious —s*, Merch. ll, 6, 11. *hath not my gait in it the m. of the court?* Wint. IV, 4, 757.

Measure, vb. 1) to ascertain the extent or degree of: Tp. V, 122. Wiv. I, 4, 124. II, 1, 215. Err. III, 2, 113. LLL V, 2, 189. 194. H5 III, 7, 137. *to m. one's length* = to lie down, or to be thrown down: *if you will m. your lubber's length again*, Lr. I, 4, 100. *to m. out my length on this cold bed*, Mids. lll, 2, 429. cf. *here lie I down and m. out my grave*, As ll, 6, 2. *till you had —d how long a fool you were*, Cymb. I, 2, 25. *to m. swords* = to fight: As V, 4, 91.

2) to make or suppose to be of a certain degree: *m. his woe the length and breadth of mine, and let it answer every strain for strain*, Ado V, 1, 11. *your cause of sorrow must not be —d by his worth*, Mcb. V, 8, 45 (= have the measure, the greatness of his worth).

3) to pass over: *thus far the miles are —d from my friend*, Sonn. 50, 4. *how shall that Claribel m. us* (cubits) *back to Naples?* Tp. II, 1, 259. *to m. kingdoms with his feeble steps*, Gent. II, 7, 10. LLL V, 2, 184. Merch. lll, 4, 84. Wint. V, 1, 145. John V, 5, 3. R2 III, 2, 125.

4) to consider, to judge: *not —ing what use we made of them*, H5 I, 2, 268. With an accus. (= to judge of): *with thoughts so qualified as your charities shall best instruct you, m. me*, Wint. II, 1, 114. *you do m. the heat of our livers with the bitterness of your galls*, H4B I, 2, 198. *if I be —d rightly, your majesty hath no just cause to hate me*, V, 2, 65. With *by*: *that* (thy mind) *they m. by thy deeds*, Sonn. 69, 10. *I m. him by my own spirit*, Ado II, 3, 149. Shr. V, 2, 29. Rom. I, 1, 133. I, 4, 9. Cymb. III, 6, 65. *With*, in the same sense: *m. my strangeness with my unripe years*, Ven. 524 (in judging of my strangeness, take my youth into account).

5) for a quibble's sake, = to dance: *we'll m. them a measure*, Rom. I, 4, 10 (or = to deal out, to allot, to grant? as perhaps in Ado V, 1, 11?).

Measureless, exceeding all bounds: *m. liar*, Cor. V, 6, 103. *m. content*, Mcb. II, 1, 17.

Meat, human food, particularly such as is prepared by cooking: *kill your stomach on your m.* Gent. I, 2, 68. *would fain have m.* II, 1, 181. *hot m.* Wiv. I, 1, 297. *the m. is cold*, Err. I, 2, 47. *your m. doth*

burn, II, 1, 63. *the m. wants basting*, II, 2, 57. *m. sweet-savoured*, 119. *good m.* lll, 1, 24. *his m. was sauced with thy upbraidings*, V, 73. *the boy that stole your m.* Ado ll, 1, 206. *a man loves the m. in his youth that he cannot endure in his age*, II, 3, 247. *he eats his m. without grudging*, III, 4, 90. Merch. lll, 5, 65. 68. As III, 3, 36. Shr. IV, 1, 164. 172. 200. 202. IV, 3, 9. 19. 32. 40. 46. All's II, 2, 49. R2 I, 1, 76. H4B V, 5, 143. H6B IV, 10, 41. Cor. I, 1, 211. IV, 2, 50. Rom. II, 4, 143. Tim. I, 1, 271. I, 2, 36. 38. 41. 46. 81. III, 1, 60. III, 4, 50. III, 6, 76. 85. IV, 3, 294. 419. Caes. I, 2, 149. Mcb. III, 4, 36. III, 6, 34. Oth. III, 3, 167. Cymb. III, 6, 38. 50. V, 4, 163. Per. III, 2, 3. Joined to *drink*: *dress m. and drink*, Wiv. I, 4, 102. H4B V, 3, 30. Ant. V, 2, 49. *that's m. and drink to me* = that is a treat to me: Wiv. I, 1, 306. As V, 1, 11. Used of the eatable interior of an egg: *as an egg is full of m.* Rom. III, 1, 25. *cut the egg and eat up the m.* Lr. I, 4, 174. Opposed to *porridge: porridge after m.* Troil. I, 2, 263 (*spoon-meat* in Err. IV, 3, 61 a non-entity?). = meal, repast: *the thanksgiving before m.* Meas. I, 2, 16. *the grace 'fore m.* Cor. IV, 7, 3. cf. Err. V, 73 and Oth. IV, 2, 170. Metaphorically: *I am m. for your master*, H4B II, 4, 135. *wishing him my m.* Per. II, 3, 32.

Plur. *—s: baked —s*, Rom. IV, 4, 5. Hml. I, 2, 180. *broken —s*, Lr. II, 2, 16.

Meazels, spelling of O. Edd. for *Measles*.

Mecaenas, see *Maecenas*.

Mechanic, subst. handicraftsman, workman; used in contempt: *capitulate with Rome's —s*, Cor. V, 3, 83.

Mechanic, adj. pertaining to the class of workmen, occupied in low drudgery, vulgar: *the poor m. porters crowding in*, H5 I, 2, 200. *m. slaves with greasy aprons*, Ant. V, 2, 209. *to stand on more m. compliment*, IV, 4, 32 (= such as becomes a journeyman).

Mechanical, subst. the same as mechanic, q. v.: *a crew of patches, rude —s*, Mids. III, 2, 9. *base dunghill villain and m.* H6B I, 3, 196.

Mechanical, adj. the same as mechanic, q. v.: *m. salt-butter rogue*, Wiv. II, 2, 290. *by most m. and dirty hand*, H4B V, 5, 38. *know you not, being m., you ought not walk upon a labouring day without the sign of your profession?* Caes. I, 1, 3.

Medal (O. Edd. *medull* or *medul*), a piece of metal stamped with a figure: *he that wears her like her m.*, hanging about his neck*, Wint. I, 2, 307 (like her portrait in a locket).

Meddle, 1) to mingle, to mix (cf. *Comeddle*): *more to know did never m. with my thoughts*, Tp. I, 2, 22 (= never entered my mind).

2) to have to do: *strip your sword stark naked, for m. you must, that's certain, or forswear to wear iron about you*, Tw. III, 4, 275 (you must not evade this business, you must fight.) Followed by *with: they are to m. with none but the prince's subjects*, Ado III, 3, 34. *m. not with her*, Shr. II, 25 (leave her alone). *we will not m. with him*, All's IV, 3, 41. Tw. III, 4, 308. *a mystery with whom relation durst never m.* Troil. III, 3, 202. *the shoemaker should m. with his yard*, Rom. I, 2, 40.

3) to intrude on the concerns of others; absol.: *a —ing friar*, Meas. V, 127. *do not you m.* Ado V, 1, 101. *—ing monkey*, Mids. II, 1, 181. *this —ing priest*, John III, 1, 163. *beat away the busy —ing fiend*, H6B III, 3, 21. *I'll not m.* Cor. V, 1, 38. Followed by *in:*

I'll not m. in it, Troil. I, 1, 66. By *with: m. with buck-washing*, Wiv. III, 3, 165. *I'll not m. with it*, R3 I, 4, 137. *do you m. with my master?* Cor. IV, 5, 50. *to m. with thy mistress*, 53. *I m. with no tradesman's matters*, Caes. I, 1, 25. Joined to *make*, in the same sense: *I will teach a scurvy priest to m. or make*, Wiv. I, 4, 116. *the less you m. or make with them*, Ado III, 3, 55. *I'll not m. nor make no further*, Troil. I, 1, 14. *I'll m. nor make no more in the matter*, 85.

Meddler, one who intrudes into the affairs of others, a busybody: Meas. V, 145. Tim. IV, 3, 309. *money's a m. that doth utter all men's ware-a*, Wint. IV, 4, 329 (O. Edd. *medler. =* interferes with, and is good at, anything).

Mede, Media: Ant. III, 6, 75.

Medea, the celebrated sorceress of antiquity: Merch. V, 13. H6B V, 2, 59.

Media, country in Asia: Ant. III, 1, 7. *Great M.* III, 6, 14.

Mediation, intercession in favour of another: *noble offices thou mayst effect of m. between his greatness and thy other brethren*, H4B IV, 4, 25. *some nobler token for Livia and Octavia, to induce their m.* Ant. V, 2, 170.

Mediator, one who intercedes and pleads for another: *to trembling clients be you —s*, Lucr. 1020. *nonsuits my —s*, Oth. I, 1, 16.

Medicinable (pronounced *méd'cinable*), medicinal, having the power of healing: *any impediment will be m. to me*, Ado II, 2, 5. *whose* (the sun's) *m. eye corrects the ill aspects of planets evil*, Troil. I, 3, 91. *I have derision m.* III, 3, 44. *drop tears as fast as the Arabian trees their m. gum*, Oth. V, 2, 351 (Qq *medicinal*). *some griefs are m.; that is one of them, for it doth physic love*, Cymb. III, 2, 33.

Medicinal (*méd'cinal* and *medicínal*) having the power of healing: *words as m. as true*, Wint. II, 3, 37. *m. gum*, Oth. V, 2, 351 (Ff *medicinable*).

Medicine, subst. 1) a substance administered to cure a disease; physic: Sonn. 118, 11. Wiv. III, 3, 204. Meas. II, 2, 135. III, 1, 2. Ado I, 3, 13. V, 1, 24. Mids. III, 2, 264. As II, 7, 61. All's I, 3, 239. John V, 1, 15. H4B III, 1, 43. Troil. V, 10, 35. Rom. II, 3, 24. Mcb. IV, 3, 214 (*—s*). Hml. V, 2, 325. Lr. IV, 7, 27 (*thy m. =* that which may cure thee). Cymb. V, 5, 29. *gold preserving life in m. potable*, H4B IV, 5, 163 (cf. *Gold*).

2) any thing particularly operating on the human body or mind; poison: *sick, sick! If not, I'll ne'er trust m.* Lr. V, 3, 96. *work on, my m., work!* Oth. IV, 1, 46. a philter: *if the rascal have not given me —s, to make me love him*, H4A II, 2, 19. *I have drunk —s*, 21. *by spells and —s bought of mountebanks*, Oth. I, 3, 61. the philosopher's stone: *Plutus that knows the tinct and multiplying m.* All's V, 3, 102. *coming from him, that great m. hath with his tinct gilded thee*, Ant. I, 5, 36.

3) physician: *I have seen a m. that's able to breathe life into a stone*, All's II, 1, 75. *Camillo, preserver of my father, now of me, the m. of our house*, Wint. IV, 4, 598. *meet we the m. of the sickly weal, and with him pour we ... each drop of us*, Mcb. V, 2, 27.

Medicine, vb. to restore by physic, to cure: *nor all the drowsy syrups of the world shall ever m. thee to that sweet sleep*, Oth. III, 3, 332. *great griefs m. the less*, Cymb. IV, 2, 243.

Meditate, 1) to contemplate, to muse, to revolve a subject in the mind: *—ing with two deep divines*, R3 III, 7, 75. *look, he —s*, Caes. V, 5, 12. With a clause: *with —ing that she must die once*, Caes. IV, 3, 191. With *on: are you —ing on virginity?* All's I, 1, 121. H8 IV, 2, 79.

2) to have in contemplation, to study, to plan; trans.: *—ing that shall dye your white rose in a bloody red*, H4A II, 4, 60 (i. e. that which shall dye etc. viz blood, combat). With *on: I will m. upon some horrid message*, Tw. III, 4, 219. *soldiers that nothing do but m. on blood*, H5 V, 2, 60.

Meditation, 1) thought: *O fearful m.* Sonn. 65, 9. *with wings as swift as m.* Hml. I, 5, 30. *uncleanly apprehensions ... in session sit with —s lawful*, Oth. III, 3, 141.

2) deep thought, contemplation: *in maiden m.* Mids. II, 1, 164. *thou keepest the stroke betwixt thy begging and my m.* R3 IV, 2, 118. *thrust yourselves into my private —s*, H8 II, 2, 66. III, 2, 345. Especially thought employed upon sacred objects: *let us all to m.* H6B III, 3, 33. *divinely bent to m.* R3 III, 7, 62. *on his knees at m.* 73. *continual —s, tears, and sorrows*, H8 IV, 2, 28.

Mediterranean, adj. concerning the sea between Europe and Africa: *the M. flote*, Tp. I, 2, 234.

Mediterraneum, the Mediterranean sea: LLL V, 1, 61 (Armado's speech).

Medlar, the tree Mespilus Germanica, and its fruit (quibblingly confounded with *meddler*): *they would else have married me to the rotten m.* Meas. IV, 3, 184.* *I'll graff it with you, and then I shall graff it with a m.* As III, 2, 125. *you'll be rotten ere you be half ripe, and that's the right virtue of the m.* 128. *now will we sit under a m. tree, and wish his mistress were that kind of fruit as maids call —s, when they laugh alone*, Rom. II, 1, 34 (i. e. open-arse). *there's a m. for thee, eat it. Dost hate a m.? Ay, though it look like thee. An thou hadst hated —s sooner, thou shouldst have loved thyself better now*, Tim. IV, 3, 305.

Meed, 1) reward, recompense, hire: *for thy m. a thousand honey secrets shalt thou know*, Ven. 15. *when great treasure is the m. proposed*, Lucr. 132. *duty never yet did want his m.* Gent. II, 4, 112. *for my m. V, 4, 23. *m. I have received none*, Wiv. II, 2, 211. *to receive the m. of punishment*, LLL I, 1, 270 (Armado's letter). *when service sweat for duty, not for m.* As II, 3, 58. *for his m. he is mewed up*, R3 I, 3, 139. *hired for m.* I, 4, 234. *when I have my m.* 289. *and for his m. was brow-bound with the oak*, Cor. II, 2, 101. *thanks to men of noble minds is honourable m.* Tit. I, 216. *there's m. for m., death for a deadly deed*, V, 3, 66. *labour be his m.* Cymb. III, 5, 168.

2) deserved praise, merit, worth: *that we, the sons of brave Plantagenet, each one already blazing by our —s, should join our lights*, H6C II, 1, 36. *my m. hath got me fame*, IV, 8, 38. *no m. but he repays sevenfold above itself*, Tim. I, 1, 288. *but in the imputation laid on him by them, in his m. he is unfellowed*, Hml. V, 2, 149.

Meek, 1) humble, spiritless, tame: *feeble desire, all recreant, poor and m., like to a bankrupt beggar wails his case*, Lucr. 710. *doing the honour of thy lordliness to one so m.* Ant. V, 2, 162.

2) indulgent, mild, gentle: *they can be m. that have no other cause*, Err. II, 1, 33. *hadst thou been m., our*

title still had slept, H6C II, 2, 160. *you're m. and humble-mouthed*, H8 II, 4, 107. *affable wolves, m. bears*, Tim. III, 6, 105. *that I am m. and gentle with these butchers*, Caes. III, 1, 255.

Adverbially: *this Duncan hath borne his faculties so m.* Mcb. I, 7, 17.

Meekly, gently, kindly: *to hear m. and to laugh moderately*, LLL I, 1, 199.

Meekness, gentleness, indulgent kindness: R3 II, 2, 107. H8 II, 4, 109. 138. V, 3, 62.

Meet, adj. 1) answering the purpose, proper, fit, good, decent: *let me have what thou thinkest m. and is most mannerly*, Gent. II, 7, 58. *we thought it m. to hide our love*, Meas. I, 2, 156. *I do confess it and repent it. 'tis m. so*, II, 3, 30. *if you think it m., compound with him by the year*, IV, 2, 25. *such m. food to feed it*, Ado I, 1, 122. *find me a m. hour to draw Don Pedro and the count alone*, II, 2, 33. LLL V, 2, 237. Shr. Ind. 2, 133. V, 2, 141. John V, 7, 94. H4A IV, 1, 33. H4B IV, 2, 117. R3 III, 5, 74. Troil. I, 3, 333. Cor. III, 1, 168. 170. Tit. V, 3, 165. Caes. I, 2, 170. Hml. I, 5, 171. V, 1, 72. Lr. I, 2, 200. IV, 7, 11. Oth. I, 1, 146. Ant. V, 1, 49. Per. III, 1, 55. With *for: for any or for all these exercises he said that Proteus was m.* Gent. I, 3, 12. *—est for death*, Merch. IV, 1, 115. Wint. II, 2, 46. R2 V, 3, 118. H5 I, 2, 254. Tit. III, 1, 179. Hml. V, 1, 105. With an inf.: *m. to be an emperor's counsellor*, Gent. II, 4, 77. *York is —est man to be your regent*, H6B I, 3, 163. *m. to be sent on errands*, Caes. IV, 1, 13. With a clause; either the subjunctive or *should* following: *it is not m. the council hear a riot*, Wiv. I, 1, 36. *it is very m. the Lord Bassanio live an upright life*, Merch. III, 5, 78. *it is m. I presently set forth*, IV, 1, 404. H5 II, 4, 15. 21. H6B III, 1, 237. 291. Troil. I, 3, 358. Caes. I, 2, 314. III, 2, 146. IV, 3, 125. Hml. I, 5, 107. Ant. II, 6, 2. Cymb. I, 5, 16. *it is not m. that I should be sad*, H4B II, 2, 42. *is it m. that we should also be an ass and a fool?* H5 IV, 1, 79. *it is not m. he should*, 104. *is't m. that he should leave the helm?* H6C V, 4, 6. R3 II, 2, 139. Troil. II, 2, 72. Caes. II, 1, 155. IV, 3, 7. Mcb. V, 1, 18. Hml. III, 3, 31. Oth. IV, 2, 107. — Comp. *—er:* H5 I, 2, 254. Ant. V, 1, 49. Superl. *—est:* Merch. IV, 1, 115. H6B I, 3, 163. R3 III, 5, 74.

Adverbially: *where we'll show what's yet behind, that m. you all should know* (the later Ff and M. Edd. *that's m.*) Meas. V, 545. *if it end so m., the bitter past, more welcome is the sweet*, All's V, 3, 333.

2) quit, even: *he'll be m. with you*, Ado I, 1, 47.

Meet, vb. (impf. and partic. met) 1) to encounter, to come face to face, by going in different directions; trans.: *I met her deity cutting the clouds*, Tp. IV, 92. *Friar Laurence met them both*, Gent. V, 2, 37. *I would my husband would m. him in this shape*, Wiv. IV, 2, 86. 97. Err. IV, 2, 56. IV, 3, 1. V, 152. Ado II, 1, 46. Mcb. V, 2, 6. Ant. I, 5, 61 etc. = to go the way by which another is coming, in order to salute and join him: *they are going to m. him*, Wiv. IV, 3, 3. *they are gone but to m. the duke*, IV, 5, 72. *him I'll desire to m. me at the consecrated fount*, Meas. IV, 3, 102. 136. IV, 4, 6. *his purpose —s you*, Troil. IV, 1, 36. *thou shalt be met with thanks*, Tim. V, 1, 164. Metaphorically: *met your loves in their own fashion*, LLL V, 2, 793. *have I with all my full affections still met the king?* H8 III, 1, 130. *let us m. them like necessities,*

H4B III, 1, 93; cf. *and m. the time as it seeks us,* Cymb. IV, 3, 33.

2) to encounter as an enemy; trans.: *breasted the surge that met him*, Tp. II, 1, 117. *I shall m. your wit in the career*, Ado V, 1, 135. *run to m. displeasure*, John V, 1, 60. *our party may well m. a prouder foe*, 79. *m. him*, R2 I, 1, 63. *I dare m. Surrey in a wilderness*, IV, 74. H4B IV, 1, 16. H6A III, 4, 43. IV, 2, 27 etc. etc. Intr.: *whose ridges with the —ing clouds contend*, Ven. 820. *he and I shall m.* Ado V, 1, 196. *where two raging fires m. together*, Shr. II, 133. *two desperate men which in the very —ing fall*, John III, 1, 33. R2 III, 3, 54. H4A I, 1, 12. H6A I, 3, 81. 82. IV, 1, 22. H6C II, 1, 120 etc. Followed by *with: we must prepare to m. with Caliban*, Tp. IV, 166. *the king with mighty and quick-raised power —s with Lord Harry*, H4A IV, 4, 13. *I must go and m. with danger there*, H4B II, 3, 48.

3) to join, to come in contact: *they all have met again and are upon the Mediterranean flote*, Tp. I, 2, 233. *is leaning cheek to cheek nothing? is —ing noses?* Wint. I, 2, 285 (O. Edd. *meating*); cf. *they met so near with their lips*, Oth. II, 1, 265. *powers from home and discontents at home m. in one line*, John IV, 3, 152. *many ways m. in one town*, H5 I, 2, 208. *by the conflux of —ing sap*, Troil. I, 3, 7. Hence = to concur, to operate together: *both our inventions m. and jump in one*, Shr. I, 1, 195. *when means and lavish manners m. together*, H4B IV, 4, 64. *patience perforce with wilful choler —ing makes my flesh tremble in their different greeting*, Rom. I, 5, 91. *all three do m. in thee at once*, III, 3, 120. *when these prodigies do so conjointly m.* Caes. I, 3, 29. *how rarely does it m. with this time's guise, when man was wished to love his enemies*, Tim. IV, 3, 472.

4) to find, to light on, and hence to get, to gain, to experience; trans.: *when thou dost m. good hap*, Gent. I, 1, 15. *should m. the blow of justice*, Meas. II, 2, 30. *when in the streets he —s such golden gifts*, Err. III, 2, 188. *you are come to m. your trouble*, Ado I, 1, 97. *I cannot m. my Hermia*, Mids. II, 1, 193. *if I could m. that fancy-monger*, As III, 2, 382. *I'll beat him, if I can m. him*, All's III, 3, 253. 256. *—ing the check of such another day*, H4A V, 5, 42. *by what by-paths I met this crown*, H4B IV, 5, 186. *how soon this mightiness —s misery*, H8 Prol. 30. *would I could m. that rogue Diomed*, Troil. V, 2, 190. *when we may profit m.* Tim. V, 1, 45. *m. the old course of death*, Lr. III, 7, 101. *he was met even now as mad as the vexed sea*, IV, 4, 1. *you'll never m. a more sufficient man*, Oth. III, 4, 91. *m. reproach*, IV, 1, 48. Intr., followed by *with: cry out for thee, but they ne'er m. with Opportunity*, Lucr. 903. *though they* (flowers) *with winter m.* Sonn. 5, 13. *if that flower with base infection m.* 94, 11. *—ing with Salerio by the way*, Merch. III, 2, 231. *—ing with an old religious man*, As V, 4, 166. *elsewhere they m. with charity*, Shr. IV, 3, 6. *thou mettest with things dying, I with things new-born*, Wint. III, 3, 117. *hath now himself met with the fall of leaf*, R2 III, 4, 49. *if they m. not with Saint Nicholas' clerks*, H4A II, 1, 67. *I muse we met not with the Dauphin's grace*, H6A II, 2, 19. *hast thou met with him?* Rom. II, 5, 19. *when Caesar's wife shall m. with better dreams*, Caes. II, 2, 99.

5) to come together: *the principal men of the army —ing one evening*, Lucr. Arg. 5. *would I flame dis-*

tinctly, *then m. and join*, Tp. I, 2, 201. *nor befitting this first —ing*, V, 165. *where m. we?* Gent. IV, 2, 84. *at the very instant of Falstaff's and our —ing*, Wiv. V, 3, 16. *ere the ships could m.* Err. I, 1, 101. Ado I, 1, 63. As V, 2, 121. All's IV, 5, 92. Tw. V, 172. Troil. IV, 2, 73. Tim. III, 4, 3. Mcb. I, 1, 1. Hml. II, 2, 216 etc. = to see each other after a long absence: *both stood, like old acquaintance in a trance, met far from home*, Lucr. 1596. *these are the parents to these children, which accidentally are met together*, Err. V, 361. *O my gentle brothers, have we thus met?* Cymb. V, 5, 375. = to have a rendezvous: *another embassy of —ing*, Wiv. III, 5, 132. *we could never m.* V, 5, 121. = to assemble in council: *therefore we m. not now*, H4A I, 1, 30. *are summoned to m. anon*, Cor. II, 3, 152. *and m. in the hall together*, Mcb. II, 3, 140. *to be met* = to be assembled: *as Falstaff, she and I are newly met*, Wiv. IV, 4, 52. *are we all met?* Mids. III, 1, 1. *a crew of patches were met together*, III, 2, 11. *when the parties were met*, As V, 4, 105. *wherefore we are met*, H5 V, 2, 1. R3 III, 4, 1. H8 V, 3, 2. Per. V, 1, 243. *many of the consuls, raised and met, are at the duke's*, Oth. I, 2, 43. — Having *with* after it: *and m. with me upon the rising ...*, Gent. V, 2, 45. *Falstaff at that oak shall m. with us*, Wiv. IV, 4, 42. *I'll m. with you upon the mart*, Err. I, 2, 27. *in the instant that I met with you*, IV, 1, 9. *to-morrow will I m. with thee*, Mids. I, 1, 178. *there to m. with Macbeth*, Mcb. I, 1, 7 etc.

Used in the partic., joined with an adverb, as a kind of salutation: *you are well met*, As III, 3, 65. Shr. I, 2, 164. Wint. V, 2, 139. H8 IV, 1, 1. Cor. IV, 2, 11. *you are very well met*, Wiv. I, 1, 200. As III, 3, 75. *you are fortunately met*, Mids. IV, 1, 182. *you are happily met*, Shr. IV, 4, 19. *you are kindly met*, Tim. III, 2, 30. Elliptically: *fairly met*, Meas. V, 1. H5 V, 2, 10. *happily met*, Shr. IV, 5, 59. Rom. IV, 1, 18. *ill met by moonlight, proud Titania*, Mids. II, 1, 60. *well met*, Wiv. III, 2, 9. Err. IV, 3, 45. As V, 3, 7. John II, 1. IV, 3, 21. R2 II, 2, 41. H5 II, 1, 1. R3 II, 3, 1. III, 2, 110. IV, 1, 5. H8 I, 1, 1. II, 2, 13. Tim. III, 4, 1. Oth. II, 1, 214. Ant. II, 6, 57. *exceedingly well met*, LLL III, 145. *heartily well met*, Cor. IV, 3, 53. *very well met*, Meas. IV, 1, 26.

Transitively, = to be with, to go to, to come together with: *how hast thou met us here?* Tp. V, 136. *bid him make haste and m. me at the North-gate*, Gent. III, 1, 258. *where shall I m. you?* IV, 3, 43. *the hour that Silvia should m. me*, V, 1, 3. *engrossed opportunities to m. her*, Wiv. II, 2, 204. *m. the senate*, Cor. II, 3, 149. *I shall not dine at home; I m. the captains at the citadel*, Oth. III, 3, 59. Wiv. IV, 4, 18. Meas. I, 2, 76. Err. III, 1, 7. 122. Ado V, 1, 152. Mids. I, 1, 166. John IV, 3, 11 etc. *go m. the French* = go to the French, John V, 1, 5. *I will go m. them*, Troil. IV, 2, 72. *I will go m. the ladies*, Cor. V, 4, 55. *I go to m. the noble Brutus*, Caes. V, 3, 73. *I will go m. him*, Oth. III, 4, 138 (= go to him, seek him).

6) to come to an assembly, to appear, to be present: *'tis past the hour that Sir Hugh promised to m.* Wiv. II, 3, 5. *much upon this time have I promised here to m.* Meas. IV, 1, 18. *as you love Rosalind, m., and as I love no woman, I'll m.* As V, 2, 129.

Meeting, subst. 1) a coming together, interview, assembly: Pilgr. 290. Wiv. II, 1, 97. III, 1, 92. IV, 4, 15. Ado I, 1, 335. LLL V, 2, 318. Wint. IV, 4, 4.

64. H5 V, 2, 1. H6C II, 2, 121. R3 I, 1, 7. Tit. IV, 4, 102. Mcb. III, 4, 37. 109.

2) place of coming together: *our m. is Bridge-north*, H4A III, 2, 174.

Meeting-place, place of coming together: Cymb. IV, 1, 26.

Meetly, in a proper manner, well: *you can do better yet, but this is m.* Ant. I, 3, 81.

Meetness, fitness, propriety: *found a kind of m. to be diseased ere that there was true needing*, Sonn. 118, 7.

Meg, diminutive of Margaret: Tp. II, 2, 50. Wiv. II, 1, 152. Ado III, 4, 8. 103. In H6B III, 2, 26 O. Edd. *Nell*, some M. Edd. *Meg*.

Meiny, followers, retinue: *they summoned up their m.* Lr. II, 4, 35 (Qq *men*). In Cor. III, 1, 66 O. Edd. *meyny* = multitude; M. Edd. *many*.

Meisen, a country in Germany: H5 I, 2, 53.

Melancholy, subst. gloomy temper, depression of spirits, sadness: Sonn. 45, 8. Err. I, 2, 20. V, 79 (80 masc.; 81 fem.). Ado II, 1, 14. 154. III, 2, 54. LLL I, 1, 234. I, 2, 8. III, 69. IV, 3, 15. Mids. I, 1, 14. As II, 5, 13. III, 2, 312. IV, 1, 10. 15. Shr. Ind. 2, 135. All's I, 2, 56. III, 2, 9. Tw. II, 4, 116. II, 5, 3. 222. Wint. IV, 4, 790. John III, 3, 42. R2 V, 6, 20. H4A I, 2, 88. II, 3, 49. H6B V, 1, 34. Troil. II, 3, 94. III, 1, 76. Tit. II, 3, 33. Tim. IV, 3, 203. 402. Caes. V, 3, 67. Hml. II, 2, 630. III, 1, 173. Lr. I, 2, 147. Ant. IV, 9, 12. Cymb. IV, 2, 203. 208. Per. I, 2, 2. II, 3, 91.

Melancholy, adj. depressed in spirits, sad: Ven. 313. Gent. III, 2, 62. Wiv. II, 1, 156. 157. Ado II, 1, 6. 221. 357. V, 1, 123. LLL I, 2, 2. IV, 3, 14. V, 2, 14. As II, 1, 26. 41. II, 5, 10. IV, 1, 3. All's III, 2, 4. III, 5, 89. Tw. II, 4, 75. H4A I, 2, 83. H6B IV, 1, 4. R3 I, 1, 136. III, 1, 3. V, 3, 68. Troil. I, 2, 27. Per. II, 3, 54. Used of things, = gloomy, dreary: Err. V, 120. Merch. I, 1, 101. As II, 7, 111. R3 I, 4, 45. IV, 4, 32. Rom. IV, 5, 86. Per. V, 1, 222. Applied blunderingly by Mrs Quickly: Wiv. I, 4, 96. Evans says: *how —ies I am*, III, 1, 13.

Meleager, the Greek hero, not named, but alluded to: H6B I, 1, 235.

Melford, place in England: H6B I, 3, 25.

Mell, to meddle, to have to do: *men are to m. with, boys are not to kiss*, All's IV, 3, 257.

Mellifluous, flowing with sweetness, honeysweet: *a m. voice*, Tw. II, 3, 54 (used by Sir Toby with intentional affectation).

Mellow, adj. soft with ripeness, full ripe: Ven. 527. Cor. IV, 6, 100. Hml. III, 2, 201. Cymb. III, 3, 63.

Mellow, vb. to ripen; intr.: LLL IV, 2, 72. Tw. I, 2, 43. R3 IV, 4, 1. *—ed* = ripened: H6C III, 3, 104. R3 III, 7, 168.

Melodious, full of harmony, delighting the ear: Ven. 431. Pilgr. 111. 360. Gent. I, 2, 86. Wiv. III, 1, 18. Tit. II, 3, 27. III, 1, 85. Hml. IV, 7, 183.

Melody, pleasing sounds, music: Lucr. 1108. Mids. I, 1, 189. II, 2, 13. H4B III, 1, 14. Troil. III, 1, 75. Tit. II, 3, 12. III, 2, 64. IV, 4, 86.

Melt (impf. and partic. *melted*; partic. *molten* only applied to metals, and placed before its subst.) 1) trans. a) to dissolve, to make liquid: *when sun doth m. their snow*, Lucr. 1218. Tit. III, 1, 20. *till the wicked fire of lust have —ed him in his own grease*, Wiv. II, 1, 69. *they would m. me out of my fat*, IV, 5,

99. to what metal this counterfeit lump of ore will be —ed, All's III, 6, 40. *the —ed snow,* H5 III, 5, 50. *to m. the city leads upon your pates,* Cor. IV, 6, 82. *the gold will I m.* Ant. II, 5, 34. *molten lead,* H4A V, 3, 34. Lr. IV, 7, 48. *molten coin,* Tim. III, 1, 55.

b) *to soften, to touch with pity: that which —eth fools,* Caes. III, 1, 42. *nor let pity m. thee,* Per. IV, 1, 7.

c) *to waste away, to reduce to nothing, to make away with* (cf. above: Wiv. II, 1, 69): *yet sometimes falls an orient drop* (i. e. a tear) *beside, which her cheek —s, as scorning it should pass,* Ven. 982 (= dries up, sucks in). *shall never m. mine honour into lust,* Tp. IV, 27 (destroy my honour by changing it to lust; destroy it by lust). *the morning ... —ing the darkness,* V, 66. *this weak impress of love is as a figure trenched in ice, which with an hour's heat dissolves to water and doth lose his form. A little time will m. her frozen thoughts, and worthless Valentine shall be forgot,* Gent. III, 2, 9 (will put an end to her love-thoughts which now seem firmly rooted). cf. *lest zeal, now — ed by the windy breath of soft petitions, pity and remorse, cool and congeal again to what is was,* John II, 477 (= lest zeal, now extinct, again gain life and form). *my love to Hermia, —ed as the snow,* Mids. IV, 1, 171. *the hearts ... do discandy, m. their sweets on blossoming Caesar,* Ant. IV, 12, 22 (= lose their sweets for me, and bestow or waste them on Caesar). *the opinion that fire cannot m. out of me,* Ado I, 1, 234. Reflexively: *and the continent ... m. itself into the sea,* H4B III, 1, 48. With *away: being three parts —ed away with rotten dews,* Cor. II, 3, 35. *tears will quickly m. thy life away,* Tit. III, 2, 51. *to m. myself away in water-drops,* R2 IV, 262. With *down: wouldst have —ed down thy youth in different beds of lust,* Tim. IV, 3, 256.

2) intr. a) *to dissolve, to become liquid: my smooth moist hand would seem to m.* Ven. 144. *snow —s with the sun,* 750. 1073. H6B III, 1, 223. H6C II, 6, 6. III, 2, 51. Applied to clouds beginning to rain: *when tempest of commotion doth begin to m. and drop upon our bare unarmed heads,* H4B II, 4, 393. *stain the sun with fog, as sometime clouds when they do hug him in their —ing bosoms,* Tit. III, 1, 214. cf. *what ribs of oak, when mountains m. on them, can hold the mortise,* Oth. II, 1, 8.

b) *to be softened to any gentle and tender passion: his tail cool shadow to his —ing buttock lent,* Ven. 315. *m. at my tears,* Lucr. 594. *my heart hath —ed at a lady's tears,* John V, 2, 47. *they must perforce have —ed,* R2 V, 2, 35. *—ed at the sweet tale of the sun's,* H4A II, 4, 134 *if you m., then will she run mad,* III, 1, 212. *open as day for —ing charity,* H4B IV, 4, 32 (Q *meeting*). *I should m. at an offender's tears,* H6B III, 1, 126. *steel thy —ing heart,* H6C II, 2, 41. H8 II, 3, 12. *I m. and am not of stronger earth than others,* Cor. V, 3, 28. *to steel with valour the —ing spirits of women,* Caes. II, 1, 122. Often applied to tears: *each flower moistened like a —ing eye,* Lucr. 1227. *appear to him all —ing,* Compl. 300. *a sea of —ing pearl, which some call tears,* Gent. III, 1, 224. *that will dry thy —ing tears,* H6C I, 4, 174. *I that did never weep now m. with woe,* II, 3, 46. *—ing with tenderness,* R3 IV, 3, 7. *learn of us to m. in showers,* Tit. V, 3, 161. *unused to the —ing mood,* Oth. V, 2, 349.

c) *to lose form and substance, to be reduced to nothing, to fade away, to vanish: the boy was —ed like a vapour from her sight,* Ven. 1166. *the morning's silver — ing dew against the golden splendour of the sun,* Lucr. 25 (i. e. melting against the sun. M. Edd. *silver-melting). candied be they* (twenty consciences) *and m. ere they molest,* Tp. II, 1, 280 (cf. above: Gent. III, 2, 9 & John II, 477). *are —ed into air,* Tp. IV, 150. *against whose charms faith —eth into blood,* Ado II, 1, 187. *manhood is —ed into courtesies,* IV, 1, 321. *and showers of oaths did m.* Mids. I, 1, 245. *she —ed into air,* Wint. III, 3, 37. *what seemed corporal —ed as breath into the wind,* Mcb. I, 3, 81. *O that this too too solid flesh would m.* Hml. I, 2, 129. *to flaming youth let virtue be as wax, and m. in her own fire,* III, 4, 85. *let Rome in Tiber m.* Ant. I, 1, 33. *m. Egypt into Nile,* II, 5, 78. *authority —s from me,* III, 13, 90. *the crown o'the earth doth m.* IV, 15, 63. *till he had —ed from the smallness of a gnat to air,* Cymb. I, 3, 20. *that on the touching of her lips I may m. and no more be seen,* Per. V, 3, 43. cf. H6C II, 6, 6.

Melun (O. Edd. *Meloone* or *Melloone*) French name: John IV, 3, 15. V, 2, 1. V, 4, 9. V, 5, 10.

Member, 1) limb: *festered —s rot but by degree,* H6A III, 1, 192. *I'll lop a m. off,* V, 3, 15. *thou shouldst not bear from me a Greekish m.* Troil. IV, 5, 130. Cor. I, 1, 99. 115. 153. Oth. III, 4, 147. Ant. I, 2, 171 (perhaps obscene quibbling. Hanmer *numbers*).

2) one of a community: Meas. IV, 2, 39. V, 237. LLL IV, 1, 41. IV, 2, 78. Merch. III, 5, 37. H5 V, 2, 5. Cor. II, 3, 13. In general, one belonging to, and partaking of, something: *all —s of our cause,* H4B IV, 1, 171. *the slave, a m. of the country's peace,* H5 IV, 1, 298. *count wisdom as no m. of the war,* Troil. I, 3, 198. *that I may be a m. of his love,* Oth. III, 4, 112.

Memorable, 1) kept in memory, remembered: *witness our too much m. shame when Cressy battle fatally was struck,* H5 II, 4, 53.

2) tending to preserve the remembrance of something, commemorative: *he sends you this most m. line, in every branch truly demonstrative,* H5 II, 4, 88. *I wear it for a m. honour,* IV, 7, 109. *worn as a m. trophy of predeceased valour,* V, 1, 76.

Memorandum, a note to help the memory: *—s of bawdy-houses,* H4A III, 3, 179.

Memorial, subst. something to preserve remembrance, a souvenir, a monument: *this line, which for m. still with thee shall stay,* Sonn. 74, 4. *let us satisfy our eyes with the —s and the things of fame that do renown this city,* Tw. III, 3, 23. *the primitive statue and oblique m. of cuckolds,* Troil. V, 1, 61.

Memorial, adj. given in memory of something: *takes my glove and gives m. dainty kisses to it,* Troil. V, 2, 80.

Memorize, to make memorable, to make glorious: *from her will fall some blessing to this land, which shall in it be — d,* H8 III, 2, 52. *or m. another Golgotha,* Mcb. I, 2, 40.

Memory, 1) the power of remembering things, recollection: Sonn. 77, 9. Tp. I, 2, 101. Wiv. IV, 1, 84. Err. V, 314. LLL IV, 1, 99. IV, 2, 71. V, 2, 150. Merch. I, 3, 55. III, 5, 71. H4B IV, 1, 202. H8 III, 2, 303. Cor. I, 9, 91. Rom. III, 2, 110. Mcb. I, 7, 65. V, 3, 41. Hml. I, 3, 58. 85. I, 5, 96. 98. II, 2, 470. V, 2, 119. Oth. IV, 1, 20. Cymb. II, 2, 44. III, 4, 97. *our great court made me to blame in m.* III, 5, 51 (= with respect to m.; made me forgetful). Plur. *—ies: toiled their unbreathed —ies,* Mids. V, 74. *freshly pitied in our —ies,* H8 V, 3, 31.

2) a retaining of past ideas, remembrance; absol.: *wear their state out of m.* Sonn. 15, 8. *he shall never cut from m. my sweet love's beauty,* 63, 11. *charactered with lasting m.* 122, 2. *shall be of little m.* Tp. II, 1, 233 (shall be soon forgotten). *many things of worthy m.* Shr. IV, 1, 84. *your grandfather of famous m.* H5 IV, 7, 95. *that ever-living man of m.* H6A IV, 3, 51 (= man of ever-living m.). *I'll note you in my book of m.* H6A II, 4, 101; cf. H6B I, 1, 100. *let m. upbraid my falsehood,* Troil. III, 2, 196. *he shall have a noble m.* Cor. V, 6, 155. *bare hateful m.* Ant. IV, 9, 9. *I have some rights of m. in this kingdom,* Hml. V, 2, 400 (rights living in the remembrance of men, traditional rights). With a genitive or a poss. pron.: *his tender heir might bear his m.* Sonn. I, 4. 55, 8. 81, 3. *the wrinkles … of mouthed graves will give thee m.* 77, 6. *leave no m. of what it was,* Gent. V, 4, 10. Wint. V, 1, 50. H4B IV, 1, 81. IV, 4, 75. IV, 5, 216. H6A I, 6, 23 (*in m. of her*). H8 III, 2, 418. Tim. V, 4, 80. Hml. I, 2, 2. III, 2, 139.

3) that which calls to remembrance, memorial: *O you m. of old Sir Rowland,* As II, 3, 3. *that surname, a good m. and witness of the malice and displeasure which thou shouldst bear me,* Cor. IV, 5, 77. *beg a hair of him for m.* Caes. III, 2, 139. *these weeds are —ies of those worser hours,* Lr. IV, 7, 7. *till by degrees the m. of my womb … lie graveless,* Ant. III, 13, 163. Perhaps also in Cor. V, 1, 17.

Memphis, town of ancient Egypt; thought by the poet to have been the name of a person: *a statelier pyramis to her I'll rear than Rhodope's or —'ever was,* H6A I, 6, 22.*

Menace, vb. to threaten; absol.: *who ever knew the heavens m. so?* Caes. I, 3, 44. trans.: *m. me,* R3 I, 4, 175. H8 I, 1, 183. Rom. V, 3, 133. *to whom by oath he —d revenge upon the cardinal,* H8 I, 2, 137.

Menaces, subst. threats: Lr. I, 2, 159.

Menaphon, name: Err. V, 368.

Menas, name in Ant. I, 4, 48. II, 1, 32. II, 6, 99 etc.

Mend, 1) trans. a) to repair from breach or decay: *like the —ing of highways,* Merch. V, 263. *let the botcher m. him,* Tw. I, 5, 51. 52. H4A II, 4, 130. H4B III, 2, 176. H5 IV, 8, 74. Tim. IV, 3, 285. Caes. I, 1, 18. 20. *like a chime a —ing,* Troil. I, 3, 159.

b) to make better, to improve: *in others' works thou dost but m. the style,* Sonn. 78, 11. *thus I m. it,* Err. II, 2, 107. *where fair is not, praise cannot m. the brow,* LLL IV, 1, 17. *we will m. thy wages,* As II, 4, 94. *God m. your voices,* V, 3, 42. *it would m. the lottery,* All's I, 3, 92. *would that have —ed my hair?* Tw. I, 3, 102. *this is an art which does m. nature,* Wint. IV, 4, 96. *to m. her kissing,* 163. *I will m. thy feast,* Tim. IV, 3, 282. 283. 284. *to m. it* (life) *or be rid on't,* Mcb. III, 1, 114. *m. his pace,* Hml. V, 1, 64. *m. your speech,* Lr. I, 1, 96. *upon my —ed judgment,* Cymb. I, 4, 49. = to add to, to increase the value of: *over and beside Signior Baptista's liberality, I'll m. it with a largess,* Shr. I, 2, 151. *you m. the jewel by the wearing it,* Tim. I, 1, 172. *to m. the petty present,* Ant. I, 5, 45. *I cannot m. it =* I cannot help it, it is not my fault: R2 II, 3, 153. III, 2, 100. cf. *will this gear ne'er be —ed?* Troil. I, 1, 6 (= will you ever lament thus?). Used of health to be restored: *God m. him,* H4B I, 2, 124. In a moral sense: *show now your —ed faiths,* John V, 7, 75. *hollow hearts*

I fear ye; m. 'em, H8 III, 1, 105. And reflexively: *bid the dishonest man m. himself,* Tw. I, 5, 50.

So God m. me, used as an oath: *by my troth, and in good earnest, and so God m. me, and by all pretty oaths that are not dangerous,* As IV, 1, 193. *in good sooth, and as true as I live, and as God shall m. me,* H4A III, 1, 255. *God shall m. my soul!* Rom. I, 5, 81. *God m. all!* an expression of acquiescence in a disagreeable truth: H8 I, 2, 201. Cymb. V, 5, 68. *our worser thoughts heaven m.* Ant. I, 2, 64.

c) to set right, to correct, to repair what is amiss: *to m. the hurt that his unkindness marred,* Ven. 478. *that fault may be —ed,* Gent. III, 1, 328. Err. III, 2, 107. *—ed again,* Meas. V, 91; cf. *very well —ed,* Shr. V, 2, 25. *think of this, and all is —ed,* Mids. V, 431. *I told him … of his oath-breaking, which he —ed thus, by now forswearing that he is forsworn,* H4A V, 2, 38. *you must return and m. it,* Cor. III, 2, 26. *what is amiss plague and infection m.* Tim. V, 1, 224. *m. it for your own good,* Oth. II, 3, 304. = to adjust: *he will m. the ruff and sing,* All's III, 2, 7. *your crown's awry; I'll m. it,* Ant. V, 2, 322.

d) to make in a better way, to perform better than before: *whether we are —ed, or whether better they,* Sonn. 59, 11. *those parts of thee that the world's eye doth view want nothing that the thought of hearts can m.* 69, 2. *were it not sinful then striving to m., to mar the subject?* 103, 9. *will you go with me? we'll m. our dinner here,* Err. IV, 3, 60; cf. *you have now a broken banquet, but we'll m. it,* H8 I, 4, 61. *he can sing, and in ushering m. him who can,* LLL V, 2, 329 (Germ. *mache es besser wer kann). m. the instance,* As III, 2, 70 (produce a better argument). *to-morrow it* (our dinner) *shall be —ed,* Shr. IV, 1, 179. *m. the plucking off the other* (boot) 151. *what here shall miss, our toil shall strive to m.* Rom. Prol. 14.

2) intr. a) to become better, to improve: *what think you of this fool? doth he not m.?* Tw. I, 5, 80. *they are people such that m. upon the world,* Cymb. II, 4, 26 (= get the upperhand of the world; cf. *grow in* As I, 1, 91). = to recover: *love me and m.* Ado V, 2, 95. *my long sickness of health and living now begins to m.* Tim. V, 1, 190. Used in a moral sense: *go m.* Meas. III, 2, 28. *if he m., he is no longer dishonest,* Tw. I, 5, 50. Ado II, 3, 239. Tim. V, 1, 92. Lr. II, 4, 232. Oth. IV, 3, 106.

b) to do better than before: *if you pardon, we will m.* Mids. V, 437. *m. and charge home,* Cor. I, 4, 38. *still he —s,* Ant. I, 3, 82.

Mender, one who mends or repairs: *a m. of bad soles,* Caes. I, 1, 15.

Mends, subst.: *if she be fair, 'tis the better for her; an she be not, she has the m. in her own hands,* Troil. I, 1, 68; according to Dyce, = she must make the best of it; according to Jervis, = remedy.

Menecrates, name in Ant. I, 4, 48.

Menelaus, the famous king of Sparta: Troil. Prol. 9 etc. Prototype of cuckoldom: H6C II, 2, 147 Troil. I, 1, 115. V, 1, 60.

Menenius (Agrippa) name in Cor. I, 1, 52 etc.

Menon, name in Troil. V, 5, 7.

Mental, pertaining to the mind, intellectual: *the still and m. parts,* Troil. I, 3, 200. *'twixt his m. and his active parts,* II, 3, 184. *what a m. power this eye shoots forth!* Tim. I, 1, 31.

Menteith, county in Scotland: H4A I, 1, 73.*

M

Mention, subst. incidental notice taken and expressed in words: *where no m. of me more must be heard of,* H8 III, 2, 434.

Mention, vb. to take and express occasional notice of, to alledge, to name: Wint. IV, 1, 22. Tit. V, 1, 107. Caes. III, 2, 140.

Mephostophilus, name of the evil spirit in the History of Faustus and in Marlowe's play; used by Pistol as a term of invective: Wiv. I, 1, 132.

Mercade, see *Marcade.*

Mercatante, see *Marcantant.*

Mercatio, name in Gent. I, 2, 12.

Mercenary, adj. venal, hired: *my mind was never yet more m.* Merch. IV, 1, 418. *soaked in m. blood,* H5 IV, 7, 79. *as if I had been m.* Cor. V, 6, 41.

Mercenary, subst. a hired soldier: *sixteen hundred —s,* H5 IV, 8, 93.

Mercer, a silk-merchant: Meas. IV, 3, 11.

Merchandize, subst. 1) goods bought or sold in trade, wares: Mids. II, 1, 134. Merch. I, 1, 40. H5 IV, 1, 155. Rom. II, 2, 84. Having the verb in the singular: *my m. makes me not sad,* Merch. I, 1, 45. in the plural: *the m. are all too dear for me,* Ant. II, 5, 104.

2) trade, commerce: *were he out of Venice, I can make what m. I will,* Merch. III, 1, 134.

Merchandized, treated like an article of trade, as a thing that may be bought and sold: *that love is m. whose rich esteeming the owner's tongue doth publish everywhere,* Sonn. 102, 3.

Merchant, 1) one who traffics to foreign countries: *huge rocks ... the m. fears ere rich at home he lands,* Lucr. 336. *the hopeless m. of this loss,* 1660. Tp. II, 1, 5. Err. I, 1, 3. 7. 151. I, 2, 3. 24. II, 1, 4. V, 124. Merch. I, 3, 50. III, 1, 26. III, 2, 281. IV, 1, 23. 156. 174. 205. 233. 263. 299. Shr. I, 1, 12. II, 328. IV, 2, 98. H5 I, 2, 192. H8 I, 1, 96. Troil. I, 1, 106. I, 3, 359. II, 2, 69. 83. Tim. I, 1, 7. 242. Ant. V, 2, 183. 184. *how doth that royal m., good Antonio?* Merch. III, 2, 242. *losses ... enow to press a royal m. down,* IV, 1, 29 (cf. Royal).

2) a ship of trade: *the masters of some m.* Tp. II, 1, 5. *a whole —'s venture,* H4B II, 4, 68.

3) a chap, fellow: *this is a riddling m.* H6A II, 3, 57. *what saucy m. was this, that was so full of his ropery?* Rom. II, 4, 153.

Merchant-like, like a merchant: H6B IV, 1, 41.

Merchant-marring, ruining merchants: *m. rocks,* Merch. III, 2, 274.

Merciful, disposed to pity, ready to forgive, compassionate: Ven. 1155. Tp. V, 178. Meas. II, 2, 114. III, 2, 203. Ado III, 3, 64. Merch. IV, 1, 182. 233. All's IV, 3, 144. Wint. II, 3, 185. H5 II, 2, 47. III, 2, 23. H6B IV, 2, 133. H8 V, 3, 61. Epil. 10. Tit. I, 118. Rom. III, 3, 12. V, 3, 72. Mcb. II, 1, 7. IV, 3, 207. Oth. V, 2, 87.

Mercifully, with compassion, mildly: *mock me m.* H5 V, 2, 214.

Merciless, pitiless, unfeeling: Ven. 821. Lucr. 1160. John II, 214. H6B IV, 4, 33. H6C II, 6, 25. R3 I, 3, 184. Mcb. I, 2, 9. With *to:* Err. I, 1, 100.

Mercurial, resembling Mercury: *his foot M.* Cymb. IV, 2, 310 (light and nimble like that of Mercury).

Mercury, 1) the ancient god, son and messenger of Jove: LLL V, 2, 940. John IV, 2, 174. H4A IV, 1, 106. H5 II Chor. 7. R3 II, 1, 88. IV, 3, 55. Troil.

II, 2, 45. IV, 3, 55. IV, 4, 14. Hml. III, 4, 58. Ant. IV, 15, 35. Patron of craftiness: *Mercury endue thee with leasing,* Tw. I, 5, 105. *littered under M.* Wint. IV, 3, 25. *M., lose all the serpentine craft of thy caduceus,* Troil. II, 3, 13. cf. Tit. IV, 1, 67.

2) name of a planet: Wint. IV, 3, 25. Tit. IV, 3, 55. IV, 4, 14.

Mercutio, name in Rom. I, 2, 70 (?). I, 4, 95. II, 1, 6 etc.

Mercy, 1) readiness to spare and forgive, grace, clemency, pity: Sonn. 145, 5. Tp. III, 2, 78. Epil. 18. Meas. I, 1, 45. II, 1, 297. II, 2, 50. 63. II, 4, 112. III, 1, 65. III, 2, 207. IV, 2, 115. V, 412. 481. 489. Ado IV, 1, 182. LLL IV, 1, 24. Merch. III, 3, 1. III, 5, 35. IV, 1, 6. 184. As III, 1, 2. Wint. II, 1, 73. John IV, 1, 26. H4A I, 3, 132. H5 II, 2, 44. H6B I, 3, 160. IV, 8, 12. H6C II, 6, 46. IV, 8, 43. R3 I, 1, 151. Hml. I, 5, 169 etc. Plur. *—ies,* H8 II, 1, 70. With *of: should she kneel down in m. of this fact,* Meas. V, 439; cf. Hml. IV, 5, 200. With *to: m. to thee would prove itself a bawd,* Meas. III, 1, 150. *to solicit him for m. to his country,* Cor. V, 1, 73. *in m.* = out of pity: Meas. V, 439. H5 IV, 3, 83. H6B I, 3, 160. *of his m.,* in the same sense: *God of his m. give you patience,* H5 II, 2, 179. *to have m.* = to take pity: As I, 3, 2. R3 V, 3, 178. Troil. I, 2, 133. Cor. IV, 6, 108. Oth. V, 2, 58. usually followed by *on* or *upon: Lord have m. on us,* LLL V, 2, 419. All's II, 3, 224. Tw. III, 4, 152. 184. H6A I, 4, 70. H6B I, 3, 219. H8 III, 2, 262. Hml. IV, 5, 199. Lr. III, 4, 75. Oth. V, 2, 35. Ant. V, 2, 175. *to render m.* = to show pity: Merch. IV, 1, 88. 378. *to take m. on* = to be merciful to: H5 II, 4, 103. H6A IV, 3, 34. *I cry you m.* = I beg your pardon: Wiv. III, 5, 27. Meas. IV, 1, 10. Ado I, 2, 27. II, 1, 353. H4A I, 3, 212. V, 2, 57. H6A V, 3, 109. H6B I, 3, 142. R3 I, 3, 235. II, 2, 104. IV, 1, 19. IV, 4, 515. Rom. IV, 5, 141. Oth. IV, 2, 88. V, 1, 69. *I cry your worships m.* Mids. III, 1, 182. *I cry your honour m.* H8 V, 3, 78. *I* omitted: *cry you m.* Gent. V, 4, 94. Lr. III, 6, 54. *cry m.* R3 V, 3, 224. Imperatively: *cry the man m.* As III, 5, 61. *By m.* in Tim. III, 5, 55, explained by some as = by your leave, under your pardon.

Often used as an exclamation of surprise or fear: *m., m., this is a devil,* Tp. II, 2, 101. *O m., God! what masking stuff is here!* Shr. IV, 3, 87. *God's m., maiden, does it curd thy blood,* All's I, 3, 155. *name of m., when was this?* Wint. III, 3, 105. *alack, for m.* Tp. I, 2, 436. *God, for thy m.* Err. IV, 4, 147. *God for his m.* R2 II, 2, 98. V, 2, 75. *m. on us,* Tp. I, 1, 64. III, 2, 141. Wint. III, 3, 70. *m. on me,* Wiv. III, 1, 22. John IV, 1, 12. H8 V, 4, 71.

2) power of acting at pleasure, discretion: *lies at the m. of his mortal sting,* Lucr. 364. Tp. IV, 264. *stand at m. of my sword,* Troil. IV, 4, 116. *the part that is at m.* Cor. I, 10, 7. *at thy m. shall they stoop,* Tit. V, 2, 118. *the offender's life lies in the m. of the duke,* Merch. IV, 1, 355. *hold our lives in m.* Lr. I, 4, 350. *all estates which lie within the m. of your wit,* LLL V, 2, 856. *leave thee to the m. of wild beasts,* Mids. II, 1, 228. *stoop unto the sovereign m. of the king,* R2 II, 3, 157. *to our best m. give yourselves,* H5 III, 3, 3. *left thee to the m. of the law,* H6B I, 3, 137. IV, 8, 12. 50. H6C I, 4, 30. H8 III, 2, 363. Plur. *—ies: what foolish boldness brought thee to their —ies,* Tw. V, 73. *I commit my body to your —ies,* H4B V, 5, 130.

Mercy-lacking, pitiless: John IV, 1, 121.

Mere, pure; 1) only; simply that which is designated, and nothing else: *the m. effusion of thy proper loins*, Meas. III, 1, 30. *upon his m. request came I hither*, V, 152 (his request was my only motive). *a m. anatomy*, Err. V, 238. *a quintain, a m. lifeless block*, As I, 2, 263. *we are m. usurpers*, II, 1, 61. *whose judgments are m. fathers of their garments*, All's I, 2, 62 (have no other business but to devise new fashions). *the m. word is a slave deboshed on every tomb*, II, 3, 144. *my determinate voyage is m. extravagancy*, Tw. II, 1, 12. *it is but weakness, m. weakness*, Wint. II, 3, 2. *the prince, with m. conceit and fear, is gone*, III, 2, 145. *wisdom, loyalty and m. dislike of our proceedings kept the earl from hence*, H4A IV, 1, 64. *honour is a m. scutcheon*, V, 1, 143. *this is m. digression*, H4B IV, 1, 140. *learning a m. hoard of gold*, IV, 3, 124. *submission! 'tis a m. French word*, H6A IV, 7, 54. *this is a m. distraction*, H8 III, 1, 112. *out of m. ambition*, III, 2, 324. *I am stifled with the m. rankness of their joy*, IV, 1, 59. *I with great truth catch m. simplicity*, Troil. IV, 4, 106. *m. words, no matter*, V, 3, 108. *in m. spite*, Cor. IV, 5, 88. *a m. satiety of commendations*, Tim. I, 1, 166. *answer m. nature*, IV, 3, 231. *love nought but even the m. necessities*, 377. *the m. want of gold* 401. *but a m. conceit*, V, 4, 14. *it was m. foolery*, Caes. I, 2, 236. *the m. lees is left*, Mcb. II, 3, 100. *to fill up your will, of your m. own*, IV, 3, 89. *m. implorators of unholy suits*, Hml. I, 3, 129. *pictures, or m. beasts*, IV, 5, 86. *this is m. madness*, V, 1, 307. *m. fetches*, Lr. II, 4, 90. *our m. defects prove our commodities*, IV, 1, 22. *this is m. practice*, V, 3, 151 (Qq *this is practice*). *m. prattle*, Oth. I, 1, 26. *for m. suspicion*, I, 3, 395. *putting on the m. form of civil seeming*, II, 1, 243. *make our faith m. folly*, Ant. III, 13, 43. *your pleasure was my m. offence*, Cymb. V, 5, 334 (which should be: your m. pleasure was my offence. But Ff *neer* and *near*).

2) unqualified, absolute: *cozenage, m. cozenage*, Wiv. IV, 5, 64. *she must lie here on m. necessity*, LLL I, 1, 149. *he speaks the m. contrary*, I, 2, 35. *engaged my friend to his m. enemy*, Merch. III, 2, 265. *second childishness and m. oblivion*, As II, 7, 165. *most loving (is) m. folly*, 181. *this is m. falsehood*, Wint. III, 2, 142. *of m. compassion and of lenity*, H6A V, 4, 125. *m. instinct of love and loyalty*, H6B III, 2, 250. *your m. enforcement shall acquittance me*, R3 III, 7, 233. *to the m. undoing of all the kingdom*, H8 III, 2, 329. *each thing meets in m. oppugnancy*, Troil. I, 3, 111. *may that soldier a m. recreant prove*, 287. *the m. despair of surgery*, Mcb. IV, 3, 152. *the m. perdition of the Turkish fleet*, Oth. II, 2, 3. *to thy further fear, nay, to thy m. confusion, thou shalt know*, Cymb. IV, 2, 92. *that pity begets you a good opinion, and that opinion a m. profit*, Per. IV, 2, 132. Superl. *—st: he cried upon it at the —st loss*, Shr. Ind. 1, 23.

Adverbially: *think you it is so? Ay, surely, m. the truth*, All's III, 5, 58.

Mered, sole, entire: *he being the m. question*, Ant. III, 13, 10 (he being the only cause and subject of the war).

Merely, 1) only: *thus m. with the garment of a Grace the naked and concealed fiend he covered*, Compl. 316. *m. thou (life) art death's fool*, Meas. III, 1, 11. *he shall have m. justice*, Merch. IV, 1, 339. As II, 7, 140. III, 2, 420. R2 IV, 297. H8 II, 1, 162. Hml. II, 2, 264.

Ant. III, 13, 62. *m. but:* Compl. 174. *but m.:* Meas. V, 459. H8 I, 3, 6. *not m. ... but:* Troil. II, 2, 146.

2) simply, absolutely, quite: *we are m. cheated of our lives by drunkards*, Tp. I, 1, 59. *that's the scene that I would see, which will be m. a dumb-show*, Ado II, 3, 226. *to live in a nook m. monastic*, As III, 2, 441. *m. our own traitors*, All's IV, 3, 25. *what they will inform, m. in hate, 'gainst any of us all*, R2 II, 1, 243. *this is clean kam; m. awry*, Cor. III, 1, 305. *their society may be m. poison*, Tim. IV, 1, 32. *that which I know is m. love*, IV, 3, 522. *I turn the trouble of my countenance m. upon myself*, Caes. I, 2, 39. *things rank and gross in nature possess it m.*, Hml. I, 2, 137. *it is m. a lust of the blood*, Oth. I, 3, 339. *the horse were m. lost*, Ant. III, 7, 9. *give up yourself m. to chance*, 48. *some falling m. through fear*, Cymb. V, 3, 11.

Meridian, the highest point, summit: *from that full m. of my glory I haste now to my setting*, H8 III, 2, 224.

Merit, subst. 1) that for which a person deserves honour or reward: *what a m. were it in death to take this poor maid from the world*, Meas. III, 1, 240. *my beauty will be saved by m.* LLL IV, 1, 21 (quibbling); cf. *if men were to be saved by m.* H4A I, 2, 120. *that clear honour were purchased by the m. of the wearer*, Merch. II, 9, 43. *the m. of service is seldom attributed to the true performer*, All's III, 6, 63. H5 II, 2, 34. Troil. III, 2, 99. Cor. II, 3, 172. Hml. II, 2, 558. Lr. I, 1, 54. Oth. II, 3, 270. III, 4, 117. Cymb. I, 4, 91. I, 5, 74. V, 4, 79. Per. II, 3, 12. = desert in a bad sense: *it was not altogether your brother's evil disposition made him seek his death, but a provoking m., set a-work by a reproveable badness in himself*, Lr. III, 5, 8. *so to use them as we shall find their —s and our safety may equally determine*, V, 3, 44. *when we fall we answer others' —s in our name*, Ant. V, 2, 178.

2) that which is deserved, reward, recompense: *my beauty will be saved by m.* LLL IV, 1, 21 (quibbling). *a dearer m., not so deep a maim, have I deserved*, R2 I, 3, 156.

3) worthiness, excellence, good quality: *to whom in vassalage thy m. hath my duty strongly knit*, Sonn. 26, 2. *what m. lived in me*, 72, 2. *place my m. in the eye of scorn*, 88, 2. *that may express my love or thy dear m.* 108, 4. *what m. do I in myself respect*, 149, 9. Gent. V, 4, 144. Wiv. III, 5, 52. Ado III, 1, 70. Mids. V, 92. Merch. II, 9, 39. All's I, 1, 242. II, 1, 151. R2 V, 6, 18. H4B II, 4, 405. H5 V, 1, 8. H8 I, 1, 64. Troil. I, 3, 349. II, 2, 60. II, 3, 202. III, 3, 83. IV, 1, 65. IV, 4, 87. Cor. III, 1, 61. IV, 7, 48. Rom. I, 2, 31. Tim. I, 2, 212. Hml. III, 1, 74. Oth. II, 1, 147. III, 3, 187. Per. II, 2, 9. Used of things, = worth, weight: *and by the m. of vile gold purchase corrupted pardon*, John III, 1, 165 (cf. above: *to be saved by m.*). *what m. is in that reason which denies the yielding of her up?* Troil. II, 2, 24. *if for the sake of m. thou wilt hear me, rise from thy stool*, Ant. II, 7, 61 (i. e. the importance of what I have to say).

Merit, vb. to deserve; trans.: Sonn. 142, 4. Pilgr. 325. Wiv. II, 2, 210. Meas. III, 1, 206. Ado III, 1, 19. As V, 4, 194. Shr. IV, 3, 41. All's II, 3, 291. Wint. V, 1, 175. John II, 520. H5 III, 6, 24. H6B V, 1, 81. Troil. IV, 1, 53. Tit. III, 1, 197. Rom. I, 1, 228. Lr. V, 3, 302. With *of:* *hath more of thee —ed than a band of Clotens had ever scar for*, Cymb. V, 5, 304 (*from* in Wint. V, 1, 175). With an inf.: *—ed to* *be so*, Wint. III, 2, 49. Troil. IV, 1, 55. Absol.: *all his faults to Marcius shall be honours, though indeed in aught he m. not*, Cor. I, 1, 280.

Meritorious, deserving honour or reward: *'tis a m. fair design*, Lucr. 1692. *m. service*, Wiv. IV, 2, 217. *m. shall that hand be called*, John III, 1, 176. *the deed is m.* H6B III, 1, 270.

Merlin, the famous sorcerer and prophet of ancient Britain: H4A III, 1, 150. Lr. III, 2, 95.

Mermaid, 1) a siren: *thy —'s voice hath done me double wrong*, Ven. 429. *bewitching like the wanton —'s song*, 777. *as if some m. did their ears entice*, Lucr. 1411. *train me not, sweet m., with thy note.* Err. III, 2, 45. *I'll stop mine ears against the —'s song*, 169. *a m. on a dolphin's back*, Mids. II, 1, 150. *I'll drown more sailors than the m.* H6C III, 2, 186.

2) water-nymph: Ant. II, 2, 212. 214.

Mermaid-like, like a water-nymph: *and m. a-while they bore her up*, Hml. IV, 7, 177.

Merops, father of Phaethon: Gent. III, 1, 153.

Merrily, with gayety, jovially: Tp. V, 92. Wiv. II, 1, 198. Err. IV, 2, 4. LLL V, 2, 477. 481. As II, 7, 11. III, 2, 340. All's II, 2, 63. Wint. IV, 3, 133. IV, 4, 189. H4A II, 2, 100. 111. IV, 1, 134. V, 2, 12. H4B V, 3, 22. 23. Troil. V, 10, 42. Cor. IV, 3, 41. Rom. II, 5, 22. Tim. II, 2, 107. Caes. II, 1, 224.

Merriman, name of a dog: Shr. Ind. 1, 17.

Merriment, diversion, amusement; mirth: *rather proved the sliding of your brother a m. than a vice*, Meas. 2, 4, 116. *they do it but in mocking m.* LLL V, 2, 139. *knowing aforehand of our m.* 461. *thou interruptest our m.* 725. *met your loves like a m.* 794. *stir up the Athenian youth to —s*, Mids. I, 1, 12. *for your m.* III, 2, 146. *friends that purpose m.* Merch. II, 2, 212. *frame your mind to mirth and m.* Shr. Ind. 2, 137. *our first m. hath made thee jealous*, IV, 5, 76. *strain their cheeks to idle m.* John III, 3, 46. *turn all to a m.* H4B II, 4, 324. *nature's tears are reason's m.* Rom. IV, 5, 83. *your flashes of m.* Hml. V, 1, 210.

Merriness, merry disposition, gayety: LLL I, 1, 202.

Merry, full of mirth, gay: Ven. 1025. Lucr. 989. 1110. Pilgr. 253. Tp. II, 1, 1. 177. III, 2, 125. IV, 135. Gent. IV, 2, 29. 30. Wiv. II, 1, 8. II, 1, 215. 227. IV, 2, 107. V, 5, 254. Meas. III, 2, 249. Err. I, 2, 21. 79. II, 1, 88. II, 2, 7. 20. III, 1, 26. 108. III, 2, 183. IV, 1, 90. LLL V, 2, 16. 638. Mids.I, 2, 15. II, 1, 43. 57. V, 58. Merch. V, 69. Shr. III, 2, 228 etc. etc. Compar. *—er:* Err. I, 2, 69. LLL III, 1, 66. Mids. II, 1, 57. As I, 2, 4. John IV, 1, 12. Cor. V, 4, 45. Cymb. V, 4, 175. Superl. *—est:* Meas. III, 2, 7. H5 I, 2, 272. H6A II, 4, 15. *she's a m. Greek*, Troil. I, 2, 118. *the m. Greeks*, IV, 4, 58 (cf. *Greek*). *a many m. men with him*, As I, 1, 121 (*m. men* being, in popular songs, a very common appellation given to the vassals of a lord). *three m. men be we* (scrap of a song), Tw. II, 3, 82. *the Hundred M. Tales*, Ado II, 1, 135. *there live we as m. as the day is long*, Ado II, 1, 52. *I should be as m. as the day is long*, John IV, 1, 18. *'twas never m. world since of two usuries the —est was put down*, Meas. III, 2, 6. *'twas never m. world since lowly feigning was called compliment*, Tw. III, 1, 109. *it was never m. world in England since gentlemen came up*, H6B IV, 2, 9. *'twas m. when . . .* Ant. II, 5, 15. *God rest you m.* (a parting compliment used by low people) As V, 1, 65. *rest you m.* Rom.

I, 2, 65. 86. *to make m.* = to enjoy one's self, to feast with mirth: Shr. V, 1, 23. H6B I, 2, 85. 87.

Followed by *at: m. at any thing*, Meas. III, 2, 250. *to be m. with* = to mock: *his lordship is but m. with me*, Tim. III, 2, 42. Followed by an infinitive denoting the occasion of gladness: *I am —er to die than thou art to live*, Cymb. V, 4, 175.

Mervailous, an unintelligible word used by Pistol in H5 II, 1, 50; the later Ff have *marvellous*, which is positively nonsensical.

Mesh, a net: *such a hare is madness the youth, to skip o'er the —es of good counsel the cripple*, Merch. I, 2, 22. *here in her hairs the painter plays the spider and hath woven a golden m. to entrap the hearts of men*, III, 2, 122. cf. *Enmesh.*

Meshed, mashed, brewed by mixing malt and water together: *she drinks no other drink but tears, brewed with her sorrow, m. upon her cheeks*, Tit. III, 2, 38.

Mesopotamia, country between the rivers Euphrates and Tigris: Ant. III, 1, 8.

Mess, mass: *by the m.* H5 III, 2, 122 (the Scotch Captain Jamy's speech).

Mess, 1) a dish: *I had as lief you would tell me of a m. of porridge*, Wiv. III, 1, 63. *one m. is like to be your cheer*, Shr. IV, 4, 70. *our feasts in every m. have folly, and the feeders digest it with a custom*, Wint. IV, 4, 11. *nature on each bush lays her full m. before you*, Tim. IV, 3, 424. *he that makes his generation —es to gorge his appetite*, Lr. I, 1, 119.

2) a small quantity, a small piece: *to borrow a m. of vinegar*, H4B II, 1, 103. *I will chop her into —es*, Oth. IV, 1, 211 (cf. gobbets in H6B V, 2, 58).

3) a party eating together, a dining-table: *he and his toothpick at my worship's m.* John I, 190. *let a beast be lord of beasts, and his crib shall stand at the king's m.* Hml. V, 2, 89. *lower —es* = persons of inferior rank (properly those who sat at the lower end of the table. Dyce): *lower —es perchance are to this business purblind*, Wint. I, 2, 227.

4) a set of four ('as at great dinners the company was usually arranged into fours'. Nares): *you three fools lacked me fool to make up the m.* LLL IV, 3, 207. *a m. of Russians left us but of late*, V, 2, 361. *where are your m. of sons to back you now?* H6C I, 4, 73.

Message, a communication from one party to another made by one sent for the purpose: Meas. V, 465. Ado II, 3, 262. LLL III, 52. Merch. I, 1, 164. Tw. I, 5, 203. III, 4, 220. Wint. V, 1, 188. R2 II, 3, 69. H5 I, 2, 298. II, 4, 110. H6A II, 3, 13. H6B III, 2, 272. 379. H8 V, 1, 64. 164. Troil. IV, 4, 132. Tit. IV, 2, 2. Tim. V, 4, 20. Mcb. I, 5, 38. III, 6, 47. Hml. I, 2, 22. Lr. I, 4, 36. Ant. II, 5, 86. Per. I, 3, 33. 36. *to do a m.:* Gent. IV, 4, 93. 95. Troil. I, 3, 219. Tit. IV, 1, 117. IV, 4, 104. Rom. II, 5, 66. *to be sent on a m.:* Gent. IV, 4, 117. H6A IV, 7, 53. *I go of m. from the queen to France*, H6B IV, 1, 113.

Messala, name in Caes. IV, 3, 141. 163. V, 1, 70 etc.

Messaline, name of a place (unknown in geography): Tw. II, 1, 18. V, 239.

Messenger, the bearer of a communication or errand: Lucr. Arg. 17. Lucr. 1583. Sonn. 45, 10. Tp. IV, 71. 76. Gent. I, 1, 159. II, 1, 173. II, 4, 53. II, 7, 77. III, 1, 52. IV, 4, 104. Wiv. II, 1, 163. Meas. V, 74. Err. I, 2, 67. II, 1, 77. IV, 4, 5. Mids. I, 1, 34.

III, 2, 4. Merch. IV, 1, 108. 110. 152. V, 117. As I, 2, 32. IV, 3, 12. All's I, 3, 157. III, 2, 111 (cf. John II, 260 and H6C I, 1, 99). III, 4, 34. 40. Tw. I, 5, 219. 319. II, 2, 24. John II, 51. 260 (cf. All's III, 2, 111). 554. H5 I, 2, 221. H6B III, 2, 48. V, 1, 16. H6C I, 1, 99. 272. III, 3, 222. IV, 1, 84. R3 II, 4, 38. III, 2, 3. Troil. II, 3, 86. Cor. IV, 6, 54. Tit. V, 1, 152. Rom. II, 2, 28. V, 2, 15. Tim. III, 6, 41. Caes. II, 1, 104. Mcb. III, 6, 41. Hml. II, 2, 144. IV, 3, 36. Lr. II, 1, 126. II, 2, 54. 139. 153. II, 4, 2. 38. Oth. I, 2, 41. 89. I, 3, 13. IV, 2, 170. Ant. I, 1, 29. 32. 52. I, 5, 62. III, 6, 31. III, 12, 5. III, 13, 37. 73. IV, 1, 2. IV, 6, 22. V, 2, 324.

Confounded with *message* by Mrs Quickly: Wiv. II, 2, 98.

Messina, town in Sicily: Ado I, 1, 2. 18. 39. 116. III, 5, 35. IV, 2, 85. V, 1, 193. 290. V, 4, 128.

Metal or **Mettle** (no distinction made in O. Edd. between the two words, either in spelling or in use); 1) heavy, hard and shining substance, not combustible, but fusible by heat: *no use of m.* Tp. II, 1, 153. *is not lead a m. heavy*, LLL III, 60. *no m. can bear half the keenness*, Merch. IV, 1, 124. *to what m. this counterfeit lump of ore will be melted*, All's III, 6, 39. *that I must draw this m. from my side*, John V, 2, 16. *the fineness of which m. is not found in fortune's love*, Troil. I, 3, 22. *m., steel to the very back*, Tit. IV, 3, 47. *touched and found base m.* Tim. III, 3, 6. *here's m. more attractive*, Hml. III, 2, 116. *a mineral of —s base*, IV, 1, 26. Par excellence = gold: *with twisted m. amorously impleached*, Compl. 205. *all the m. in your shop*, Err. IV, 1, 82. *a breed for barren m.* Merch. I, 3, 135. *my m. of India*, Tw. II, 5, 17 (= my jewel; Germ. *Goldmädchen*. The later Ff *nettle*). *like bright m. on a sullen ground*, H4A I, 2, 236. *the verge of golden m.* R3 IV, 1, 60. *the imperial m. circling now thy brow*, IV, 4, 382. Perhaps also in Tp. II, 1, 153.

2) the substance or material of which a thing is composed: *let there be some more test made of my m., before so noble and so great a figure be stamped upon it*, Meas. I, 1, 49; cf. *to put m. in restrained means to make a false one* (life) II, 4, 48 (in both passages the simile taken from minting). *not till God make men of some other m. than earth*, Ado II, 1, 63. *suits his folly to the m. of my speech*, As II, 7, 82 (= contents, purport). *that you were made of is m. to make virgins*, All's I, 1, 141. *that womb, that m., that self mould that fashioned thee*, R2 I, 2, 23. *show us here the m. of your pasture*, H5 III, 1, 27. *children even of your m., of your very blood*, R3 IV, 4, 302. *of what coarse m. ye are moulded*, H8 III, 2, 239. *whose self-same m. engenders the black toad*, Tim. IV, 3, 179. *I am made of the self-same m.* Lr. I, 1, 71.

3) constitutional disposition, character, temper: *I am one that had rather go with sir priest than sir knight: I care not who knows so much of my m.* Tw. III, 4, 300. *your service, so much against the m. of your sex*, V, 330. *if thou hast the m. of a king*, John II, 401. *whether their basest m. be not moved*, Caes. I, 1, 66. *thy honourable m. may be wrought from that it is disposed*, I, 2, 313. *thy undaunted m. should compose nothing but males*, Mcb. I, 7, 73. *gentlemen of brave m.* Tp. II, 1, 182. *good m.* H4A II, 4, 383.

4) a fiery temper, ardour, spirit of enterprise, high courage: *that horse his m. from his rider takes*, Compl. 107. *if you take it not patiently, why, your m. is the*

more, Meas. III, 2, 80. *thou hast m. enough in thee to kill care*, Ado V, 1, 133. *a lad of m.* H4A II, 4, 13. *their pride and m. is asleep*, IV, 3, 22. *this boy lends m. to us all*, V, 4, 24. *from his m. was his party steeled*, H4B I, 1, 116. *I did not think Master Silence had been a man of this m.* V, 3, 41. *where have they this m.?* H5 III, 5, 15. *our m. is bred out*, 29. *every Greek of m.* Troil. I, 3, 258. *the insuppressive m. of our spirits*, Caes. II, 1, 134. *make gallant show and promise of their m.* IV, 2, 24. *of unimproved m. hot and full*, Hml. I, 1, 96. *there's m. in thee*, Oth. IV, 2, 207. *I do think there is m. in death, which commits some loving act upon her*, Ant. I, 2, 147.

Abstr. pro concr.: *good sparks and lustrous, a word, good —s*, All's II, 1, 42. *he was quick m. when he went to school*, Caes. I, 2, 300.

Metamorphose, to change into a different form: Gent. I, 1, 66. II, 1, 32 (in evident allusion to the Metamorphoses of Ovid).

Metamorphosis (M. Edd. *Metamorphoses*), title of the principal work of the poet Ovid: Tit. IV, 1, 42.

Metaphor, a simile comprised in a word: All's V, 2, 12. 13. 14. Tw. I, 3, 76.

Metaphysical, supernatural: *the golden round, which fate and m. aid doth seem to have thee crowned withal*, Mcb. I, 5, 30.

Metaphysics, the science of mind: *the mathematics and the m., fall to them as you find your stomach serves you*, Shr. I, 1, 37.

Mete (cf. *Bemete*) to measure, to judge of: *their memory shall as a pattern or a measure live, by which his grace must m. the lives of others*, H4B IV, 4, 77. With *at*, = to measure or judge by in aiming, to aim at: *let the mark have a prick in't, to m. at*, LLL IV, 1, 134.

Metellus, name in Caes. I, 3, 134. 149. II, 1, 218 etc.

Meteor, a bright phenomenon, thought to be portentous, appearing in the atmosphere (cf. *Exhalation*): *it shall hang like a m. o'er the cuckold's horns*, Wiv. II, 2, 292. *his heart's — s tilting in his face*, Err. IV, 2, 6. *they will pluck away his natural cause and call them —s, prodigies and signs*, John III, 4, 157. *had I seen the vaulty top of heaven figured quite o'er with burning —s*, V, 2, 53. *—s fright the fixed stars of heaven*, R2 II, 4, 9. *like the —s of a troubled heaven*, H4A I, 1, 10. *do you see these —s? do you behold these exhalations? what think you they portend?* II, 4, 351. *and be no more an exhaled m., a prodigy of fear*, V, 1, 19. *it is some m. that the sun exhales*, Rom. III, 5, 13. *I missed the m. once*, H8 V, 4, 52.

Mete-yard, a measuring yard: Shr. IV, 3, 153.

Metheglin, a sweet beverage composed of various ingredients: Wiv. V, 5, 167 (—s; Evans' speech). LLL V, 2, 233.*

Methinks (cf. *Think*) it seems to me: Sonn. 14, 2. 62, 5. 104, 11. 112, 14. Pilgr. 168. Tp. I, 1, 31. II, 1, 68. 206. 269. Gent. I, 1, 41. I, 2, 90. II, 4, 203. IV, 2, 26. Wiv. II, 2, 249. IV, 4, 23. 24. Meas. IV, 2, 120. V, 500. Err. I, 2, 66. IV, 4, 157. V, 417. Ado I, 1, 173. III, 2, 16. III, 4, 43. 91. LLL I, 2, 67. 91. V, 2, 798. Mids. III, 1, 145. 203. IV, 1, 36. 194. V, 183. 322 etc. etc. Sometimes not parenthetical, but preceded by conjunctions: *because m. that she loved you as well*, Gent. IV, 4, 84. *for m. I am marvellous hairy*, Mids. IV, 1, 26. *and now m. I have* *a mind to it*, Merch. IV, 1, 433. *and since m. I would not grow so fast*, R3 II, 4, 14. cf. *but O, m., how slow this old moon wanes*, Mids. I, 1, 3. *how much m. I could despise this man*, H8 III, 2, 297. *so m.* Mids. IV, 1, 195.

Sometimes = it is just as if (Germ. *mir ist als ob*): *when a man thanks me heartily*, *m. I have given him a penny and he renders me the beggarly thanks*, As II, 5, 28. *m. it should be now a huge eclipse*, Oth. V, 2, 99.

Method, regulated proceeding, a manner of acting based on rules: *why with the time do I not glance aside to new-found — s and to compounds strange?* Sonn. 76, 4. *what sayest thou to this tune, matter and m.?* Meas. III, 2, 52. *I will beat this m. in your sconce*, Err. II, 2, 34. *to answer by the m.* Tw. I, 5, 244. *or am not able verbatim to rehearse the m. of my pen*, H6A III, 1, 13 (i. e. in the order in which I wrote it down). *and fall into a slower m.* R3 I, 2, 116. *though this be madness, yet there is m. in it*, Hml. II, 2, 208. *called it an honest m.* 465. *you do not hold the m. to enforce the like from him*, Ant. I, 3, 7.

Methought, it seemed to me: Tp. III, 3, 96. Wiv. IV, 2, 215. LLL II, 242. Merch. I, 3, 70. As V, 4, 29. All's V, 3, 199. Tw. I, 1, 20. II, 2, 21. II, 4, 4. III, 4, 396. Wint. I, 2, 159. V, 2, 7. John V, 5, 1. H4B II, 2, 88. II, 4, 227. H5 III, 7, 51. H6A IV, 1, 175. H6C II, 1, 13. H8 II, 4, 186. Cor. IV, 5, 164. Mcb. II, 2, 35. V, 5, 34. Hml. I, 2, 215. V, 1, 70. 72. V, 2, 5. Lr. IV, 6, 69. V, 3, 175. = it was as if: *when I said 'a mother', m. you saw a serpent*, All's I, 3, 147. = it seemed to me in sleep, I dreamt: Tp. III, 2, 150. Mids. II, 2, 149. IV, 1, 82. 213. 216. H6B I, 2, 25. 36. R3 I, 4, 18. 21. 24. 36. V, 3, 204. Cymb. V, 5, 426.

Methoughts = methought: Wint. I, 2, 154. R3 I, 4, 9. 24 (Qq *methought*). 58. Merch. I, 3, 70 (Ff Q2).

Metre, verse, numbers: *stretched m. of an antique song*, Sonn. 17, 12. *thou never wast where grace was said. No? a dozen times at least. What, in m.?* Meas. I, 2, 22 (which perhaps means: in a play, on the stage). *lascivious — s*, R2 II, 1, 19. *these same m. ballad-mongers*, H4A III, 1, 130.

Metropolis, mother city, seat of the head of the mother church: *stood out against the holy church, the great m. and see of Rome*, John V, 2, 72.

Mettle, see *Metal*.

Mew (cf. *Emmew*) to shut up, to confine: Mids. I, 1, 71. R3 I, 1, 132. With *up:* Shr. I, 1, 87. 188. John IV, 2, 57. R3 I, 1, 38. I, 3, 139. Rom. III, 4, 11 *(to-night she is — ed up to her heaviness).*

Mew, imitation of the cry of the cat: H4A III, 1, 129.

Mew, to cry as a cat: Mcb. IV, 1, 1. *the cat will m. and dog will have his day*, Hml. V, 1, 315.

Mewl, to cry like a cat, to squall: *the infant, —ing and puking in the nurse's arms*, As II, 7, 144.

Mexico, country in America: Merch. I, 3, 20. III, 2, 271.

Meyny, multitude: *the mutable, rank-scented m.* Cor. III, 1, 66 (M. Edd. *many*). cf. *Meiny*.

Mi, the third note in the musical scale between *re* and *fa:* LLL IV, 2, 102. Shr. III, 1, 75. 78. Lr. I, 2, 149.

Michael; 1) Saint M.: *knight of the noble order of Saint George, worthy Saint M. and the Golden Fleece*, H6A IV, 7, 69. 2) Sir M.: H4A IV, 4, 1. 8.

13. 35. 3) M. Hopkins: H8 I, 1, 221 (M. Edd. *Niciolas*). 4) M. Cassio: Oth. I, 1, 20. II, 1, 26 etc.

Michaelmas, the twenty ninth of September: Wiv. I, 1, 212. H4A II, 4, 60.

Micher, a truant: *shall the blessed sun of heaven prove a m. and eat blackberries?* H4A II, 4, 450.

Miching mallecho (Ff *miching Malicho*, Qq *munching Mallico*) probably = secret and insidious mischief (cf. *Mallecho*): *this is m.; it means mischief*, Hml. III, 2, 146 (Florio's Italian Dictionary, 1598, in v. Acciapinare: *to miche, to shrug or sneak in some corner*).

Mickle, much, great: *more m. was the pain*, Pilgr. 219. *the one ne'er got me credit, the other m. blame*, Err. III, 1, 45. *an oath of m. might*, H5 II, 1, 70. *I shall die with m. age*, H6A IV, 6, 35. *bows unto the grave with m. age*, H6B V, 1, 174. *m. is the powerful grace*, Rom. II, 3, 15.

Microcosm, little world; man considered as an epitome of the universe: *if you see this in the map of my m.* Cor. II, 1, 68.

Mid, subst. middle: *about the m. of night*, R3 V, 3, 77.

Mid, adj. middle: *past the m. season*, Tp. I, 2, 239 (noon). *m. age and wrinkled eld*, Troil. II, 2, 104 (i. e. the prime of life; cf. Sonn. 7, 6). In H6B IV, 8, 64 F1.2.3 *through the very middest of you;* F4 and most M. Edd. *midst*.

Midas, the Phrygian king who received from God Bacchus the gift of transforming every thing he touched into gold, and in consequence of it was near dying of hunger: Merch. III, 2, 102.

Midday, the time of the day when the sun is highest: *Titan, tired in the m. heat*, Ven. 177. *the m. sun*, Troil. H6A I, 1, 14. H6C V, 2, 17.

Middle, subst. the part equally distant from the extremities: *upon the heavy m. of the night*, Meas. IV, 1, 35. *sit i' the m.* As V, 3, 10. *now i' the m.* Wint. IV, 4, 59. *in the m. of a word*, R3 III, 5, 2. *beginning in the m.* Troil. Prol. 28. *cut i' the m.* Cor. IV, 5, 210. *the m. of humanity thou never knewest*, Tim. IV, 3, 300. *in the dead vast and m. of the night*, Hml. I, 2, 198. *in the m. of her favours*, II, 2, 237. *cut the egg i' the m.* Lr. I, 4, 174. 176. 205. *in the m. on's face*, I, 5, 20. *the very m. of my heart is warmed*, Cymb. I, 6, 27.

Middle, adj. equally distant from the extremes: *resembling strong youth in his m. age*, Sonn. 7, 6; i. e. in the prime of life; cf. *these are flowers of m. summer, and I think they are given to men of m. age*, Wint. IV, 4, 108. *since the m. summer's spring*, Mids. II, 1, 82 (= midsummer). *I smell a man of m. earth*, Wiv. V, 5, 84 (the terrestrial world as the middle habitation between heaven and hell). *the m. centre of this town*, H6A II, 2, 6.

Midnight, the middle of the night, twelve o' clock at night: Lucr. 1625. Tp. I, 2, 128. IV, 207. V, 39. Ado III, 2, 132. V, 3, 16. Mids. V, 370. As II, 4, 27. All's IV, 2, 54. IV, 3, 34. Tw. II, 3, 2. Wint. I, 2, 290. John III, 3, 37. H5 III, 7, 97. H8 V, 1, 72. Cor. III, 1, 85. Caes. I, 3, 163. Mcb. IV, 1, 48. Hml. III, 2, 268. Ant. III, 13, 185. Cymb. II, 2, 2. *dead m.* Meas. IV, 2, 67. H5 III Chor. 19. R3 V, 3, 180. *deep m.* Mids. I, 1, 223. *about m.* Wiv. V, 1, 12. Cymb. IV, 2, 283. *at m.* Tp. I, 2, 228. Wiv. IV, 4, 19. Meas. V, 281. John IV, 1, 45. H4A II, 4, 107. 325. H4B III, 2, 228. H8 V, 1, 14. Cymb. I, 3, 31. *at still m.* Wiv. IV, 4,

30. *by m.* All's III, 6, 82. Oth. IV, 1, 225. *and will
to-morrow m. solemnly dance,* Mids. IV, 1, 93.

Midriff, the diaphragm: *all filled up with guts
and m.* H4A III, 3, 175.

Midst, subst. middle: *our ship was splitted in the
m.* Err. I, 1, 104. *make periods in the m. of sentences,*
Mids. V, 96. *our archers shall be placed in the m.* R3
V, 3, 295. *it did remain in the m. of the body,* Cor. I,
1, 102. *unless our city cleave in the m.* III, 2, 28. *I'll
sit in the m.* Mcb. III, 4, 10. *in the m. of the fight,*
Ant. III, 10, 11. *then in the m. a tearing groan did
break the name of Antony,* IV, 14, 31. *in the m.,* used
to denote a contrast, by way of speaking of things
not expected under the circumstances: *but in the m.
of his unfruitful prayer ... even there he starts,* Lucr.
344. *in the m. of all her pure protestings she burned
with love,* Pilgr. 95. *first kiss me. What, in the m. of
the street?* Shr. V, 1, 149. *in the m. of this bright-shining day I spy a black cloud,* H6C V, 3, 3. — In H6B
IV, 8, 64 O. Edd. *middest.*

Midst, prep. in the middle of: *and m. the sentence
so her accent breaks,* Lucr. 566. *they left me m. my
enemies,* H6A I, 2, 24.

Midsummer, the summer solstice, the time of
the greatest heat: As IV, 1, 102. Tw. III, 4, 61 *(m.
madness).* *gorgeous as the sun at m.* H4A IV, 1, 102.

Midway, subst. 1) the middle way, the medium
between two extremes, the mean: *he were an excellent
man that were made just in the m. between him and
Benedick,* Ado II, 1, 8. *no m. 'twixt these extremes at
all,* Ant. III, 4, 19.

Adjectively, = being in the middle of the way:
*the crows and choughs that wing the m. air show scarce
so gross as beetles,* Lr. IV, 6, 13.

Midway, adv. in the middle of the way, half way:
m. between your tents and walls of Troy, Troil. I, 3,
278. *make a battery through his deafened parts, which
now are m. stopped,* Per. V, 1, 48 (= half?).

Midwife, a woman who assists other women in
childbirth: R2 II, 2, 62. H4B II, 2, 28. H6B IV, 2,
46. H6C V, 6, 74. Tit. IV, 2, 141. 167. Rom. I, 4,
54. Per. III, 1, 11. Term of contempt for an old
woman: *does it work upon him? Like aqua vitae with
a m.* Tw. II, 5, 215. *with Lady Margery, your m. there,*
Wint. II, 3, 160.

Mien, a word unknown to Sh., but inserted by
inexpert conjecturers in Gent. II, 4, 196 and Wiv. I,
3, 111.

Might, subst. 1) strength, force, efficiency: *brag
not of thy m., for mastering her,* Ven. 113. *which I to
conquer sought with all my m.* Lucr. 488. *o'ercharged
with burden of mine own love's m.* Sonn. 23, 8. (appetite) *sharpened in his former m.* 56, 4. *in the praise
thereof spends all his m.* 80, 3. *to speak of that which
gives thee all thy m.* 100, 2. *what needest thou wound
with cunning when thy m. is more than my o'erpressed
defence can bide?* 139, 7. *from what power hast thou
this powerful m. with insufficiency my heart to sway?*
150, 1. *makes her absence valiant, not her m.* Compl.
245. *with all his m. for thee to fight,* Wiv. II, 1, 18.
affects, not by m. mastered, but by special grace, LLL
I, 1, 153. *all my powers, address your love and m. to
honour Helen,* Mids. II, 2, 143. *to take from thence
all error with his m.* III, 2, 368. *what poor duty cannot
do, noble respect takes it in m., not merit,* V, 92 (accommodates its judgment to the abilities of the per-

formers, not to the worth of the performance). *to be
wise and love exceeds man's m.* Troil. III, 2, 164. *I
have a man's mind, but a woman's m.* Caes. II, 4, 8.
I should not urge thy duty past thy m. IV, 3, 261. =
validity, truth: *unless this miracle have m. that in black
ink my love may still shine bright,* Sonn. 65, 13. *now
I find thy saw of m.* As III, 5, 82.

2) power, dominion: *so shall I taste at first the
very worst of fortune's m.* Sonn. 90, 12. *thy pyramids
built up with newer m.* 123, 2. *no m. nor greatness can
censure 'scape,* Meas. III, 2, 196. *his* (Cupid's) *dreadful little m.* LLL III, 205. *I spread my conquering m.*
V, 2, 566. *Love was no god, that would not extend his
m.* All's I, 3, 118. *England shall give him office, honour,* m. H4B IV, 5, 130. *if any rebel spirit of mine
... did give entertainment to the m. of it* (the crown),
174. *that right should thus overcome m.* V, 4, 28 (Mrs
Quickly means to say the contrary). *your grace hath
cause and means and m.* H5 I, 2, 125. *with all his m.
to enforce it* (the law) *on,* Oth. I, 2, 16. *submits her
to thy m.* Ant. III, 12, 17,

Might, vb. see *May.*

Mightful, powerful: *the m. gods,* Tit. IV, 4, 5.

Mightily, very much, egregiously: *what could
he see but m. he noted?* Lucr. 414. *whose estimation
do you m. hold up,* Ado II, 2, 25. *the prince and Claudio m. abused,* V, 2, 100; Tit. II, 3, 87; Tim. V, 1, 97;
Lr.IV,7,53; Ant. I, 3, 25. *if he do not m. grace himself
on thee,* As I, 1, 155. *her benefits are m. misplaced,* I,
2, 37. *that have so m. persuaded him from the first,*
218. *strive m., but eat and drink as friends,* Shr. I, 2,
279. *how m. sometimes we make us comforts of our
losses,* All's IV, 3, 76. 78. *kindreds are m. strengthened,* H4B II, 2, 30. *thou wrongest thy children m.* H6C
III, 2, 74. *his physicians fear him m.* R3 I, 1, 137.

Mightiness, 1) high power, greatness: *let us fear
the native m. and fate of him,* H5 II, 4, 64. *how soon
this m. meets misery,* H8 Prol. 30.

2) Used as a title of dignity: *will't please your m.
to wash your hands?* Shr. Ind. 2, 78. *your m. on both
parts best can witness,* H5 V, 2, 28. *braves your m.*
Tit. II, 3, 126.

Mighty, 1) having great physical power, vigorous, strong: *thyself art m.; myself a weakling,* Sonn.
583. *he is in the m. hold of Bolingbroke,* R2 III, 4, 83.
Achilles hath the m. Hector slain, Troil. V, 8, 14. *a
man no — er than thyself or me in personal action,* Caes.
I, 3, 76. *mad as the sea and wind, when both contend
which is the — er,* Hml. IV, 1, 8.

2) very large, huge, vast: *never be forgot in m.
Rome,* Lucr. 1644; *two m. monarchies,* H5 Prol. 20;
the mistress-court of m. Europe, II, 4, 133; *m. states
characterless are grated to dusty nothing,* Troil. III, 2,
195; *m. kingdoms,* Tit. V, 3, 74. *the most m. Neptune*
(viz the sea) Tp. I, 2, 204; *like a m. sea forced by the
tide to combat with the wind,* H6C II, 5, 5. *a bark to
brook no m. sea,* R3 III, 7, 162. *a m. rock,* Err. I, 1,
102. *my brother Robert? Colbrand the giant, that same
m. man?* John I, 225. *the deep-mouthed sea, which like
a m. whiffler 'fore the king seems to prepare his way,*
H5 V Prol. 12. *provokes the — est hulk against the
tide,* H6A V, 5, 6. *a m. fire,* Caes. I, 3, 107. *on our
former ensign two m. eagles fell,* V, 1, 81.

3) great, considerable: *addressed a m. power,* As
V, 4, 162; *a m. and a fearful head they are,* H4A III,
2, 167; *with strong and m. preparation,* IV, 1, 93; IV,

4, 12; H6A IV, 3, 2. 7; H6B III, 1, 348; IV, 9, 25; R3 IV, 4, 535; V, 3, 38; Caes. IV, 3, 169; Oth. I, 3, 221; Ant. II, 1, 17. *you do yourself m. wrong*, Wiv. III, 3, 221. *the —est space in fortune nature brings to join like likes*, All's I, 1, 237. *stand off in differences so m.* II, 3, 128. *offence of m. note*, V, 3, 14. *the stripes I have received, which are m. ones and millions*, Wint. IV, 3, 61. *a —er task*, John II, 55. *the bloom that promises a m. fruit*, 473. *ripe for exploits and m. enterprises*, H5 I, 2, 121. *a m. sum*, 133; Tim. V, 1, 8. *—er crimes are laid unto your charge*, H6B III, 1, 134. *arguments of m. force*, H6C II, 2, 44; III, 1, 49. *so m. and so many my defects*, R3 III, 7, 160. *his promises were, as he then was, m.* H8 IV, 2, 41. *the m. space of our large honours*, Caes. IV, 3, 25.

4) important, weighty, forcible, efficacious: *the —er is the thing that makes him honoured or begets him hate*, Lucr. 1004. *wherefore do not you a —er way make war upon this bloody tyrant Time?* Sonn. 16, 1. *that I may example my digression by some m. precedent*, LLL I, 2, 122. *I had a m. cause to wish him dead*, John IV, 2, 205. *be not you spoke with, but by m. suit*, R3 III, 7, 46. *a state of m. moment*, H8 II, 4, 213. *a reason m., strong and effectual*, Tit. V, 3, 43. *m. business*, Lr. III, 5, 17.

5) powerful, having great command: *the —er man*, Lucr. 1004. *how m. then you are, O hear me tell*, Compl. 253. *Love's a m. lord*, Gent. II, 4, 136. *instruments of some more —er member*, Meas. V, 237. *'tis —est in the —est*, Merch. IV, 1, 188. *as his person's m.* Wint. I, 2, 453. II, 3, 20. *m. heaven*, John V, 6, 37. *m. magic*, Oth. I, 3, 92. cf. R2 V, 6, 32. H4A I, 3, 6. H5 II, 4, 44. H6A III, 2, 136. H6B III, 1, 220. R3 I, 1, 83. II, 1, 110. IV, 4, 347. Caes. I, 3, 55. II, 2, 27. II, 3, 9. V, 3, 94. Hml. V, 2, 62. Lr. IV, 6, 34. Cymb. IV, 2, 246. Per. II Prol. 1. V, 1, 92.

6) As an epithet of honour, applied to persons of high rank, = high, illustrious: *most m. duke, vouchsafe me speak a word*, Err. V, 282. 330. *here, m. Theseus*, Mids. V, 38. *he is nothing but a m. lord*, Shr. Ind. 1, 65. *O that a m. man of such descent should be infused with so foul a spirit*, 2, 15. *a m. man of Pisa*, Shr. II, 105. *most certain of one mother, m. king*, John I, 59. *welcome, high prince, the m. duke of York*, H6A III, 1, 177. *ere the —est Julius fell*, Hml. I, 1, 114. *most m. princess*, Cymb. I, 6, 172. cf. John II, 395. 421. R2 I, 3, 93. III, 3, 172. H5 I, 2, 102. 108. II, 4, 119. Epil. 3. H6B III, 2, 120. IV, 1, 80. H6C III, 2, 76. III, 3, 4. R3 II, 4, 44. III, 7, 201. IV, 4, 466. 479. 487. H8 V, 5, 3. 27. Troil. I, 3, 60. Tit. V, 2, 26. V, 3, 40. Caes. II, 2, 69. III, 1, 33. 127. 148. Hml. IV, 7, 43. Cymb. V, 5, 327.

7) Applied to heart, = magnanimous, heroic: *your hearts are m., your skins are whole*, Wiv. III, 1, 111. *little body with a m. heart*, H5 II Prol. 17. *then burst his m. heart*, Caes. III, 2, 190.

Milan, town and dukedom in Italy: Tp. I, 2, 54. 58. 115. 126. 130. 437. II, 1, 112. 279. 291. III, 3, 70. V, 107. Gent. I, 1, 57. 61. 71. II, 5, 2. IV, 1, 19. Ado III, 4, 16. John III, 1, 138. V, 2, 120.

= duke of Milan: *he needs will be absolute M.* Tp. I, 2, 109. *as I was sometime M.* V, 86. *was M. thrust from M.* 205.

Milch, giving milk: *like a m. doe whose swelling dugs do ache*, Ven. 875. *makes m. kine yield blood*, Wiv. IV, 4, 33. *I have a hundred m. kine to the pail*,

Shr. II, 359. *the instant burst of clamour that she made would have made m. the burning eyes of heaven*, Hml. II, 2, 540 (apparently = weeping, shedding milky tears).*

Mild, tender and gentle, not fierce or severe: Lucr. 979. 1096. 1268. 1399. 1505. 1520. 1542. Pilgr. 86. Gent. IV, 4, 185. V, 2, 2. V, 4, 56. Ado II, 3, 34. LLL IV, 3, 349. V, 2, 584. Mids. II, 1, 232. IV, 1, 63. As IV, 3, 53. Shr. I, 1, 60. 71. II, 50. All's III, 4, 18. R2 I, 3, 240. II, 1, 174. H6B II, 4, 48. III, 1, 9. 72. III, 2, 219. 392. H6C I, 4, 141. III, 1, 39. 91. IV, 1, 98. R3 I, 2, 104. III, 1, 40. IV, 3, 7 (Qq *kind*). IV, 4, 160. 172. Cor. III, 2, 14. Tit. I, 470. V, 1, 85. Lr. IV, 2, 1. Per. I, 1, 68. III, 1, 27. *testy wrath could never be her m. companion*, Per. I, 1, 18 (= the companion of her mildness; see Appendix).

Mildew, to taint with mildew, to blight, to blast: *like a —ed ear*, Hml. III, 4, 64 (cf. Genesis XLI, 6). *—s the white wheat*, Lr. III, 4, 123.

Mildly, gently: Err. V, 87. R2 II, 1, 69. V, 1, 32. Cor. III, 2, 139. 142. 144. Tit. I, 475.

Mildness, gentleness, clemency: Lucr. 979. Shr. II, 192. 252. H6C II, 1, 156. IV, 4, 20. IV, 8, 42. R3 III, 7, 123. Lr. I, 4, 367.

Mile, a measure of length, containing eight furlongs: Meas. III, 2, 38. LLL I, 1, 120. V, 2, 54. 187. 189. 193. 198. Mids. I, 2, 104. Wint. IV, 3, 86. 104. 135. H4B V, 3, 57. H5 III, 7, 87. R3 V, 3, 37. Cor. I, 4, 8. 34. I, 6, 16. 17. V, 1, 5. Tit. IV, 3, 65. Tim. IV, 3, 421. Mcb. III, 3, 12. Lr. IV, 1, 44. Plur. *mile*: Wiv. III, 2, 33. Ado II, 3, 17. H4B III, 2, 310. V, 5, 69. Cymb. IV, 2, 293. *within this three m.* Mcb. V, 5, 37. Plur. *miles*: Sonn. 44, 10. 50, 4. LLL V, 2, 184. 191. 197. Merch. III, 4, 31. 84. As I, 3, 46. R2 II, 3, 5. 93. H4A II, 2, 27. III, 3, 222. H6C II, 1, 144. H8 IV, 1, 27. Cor. I, 6, 20. Rom. III, 5, 82. Lr. II, 4, 304. Cymb. III, 2, 69. III, 4, 106. Ff *miles*, Qq *mile*: H4B II, 4, 179. R3 IV, 4, 461.

Mile-end or **Mile-end Green**, the usual exercise ground of the London trainbands: All's IV, 3, 302. H4B III, 2, 298.

Milford, sea-town in Wales: R3 IV, 4, 535. Cymb. III, 2, 61. 84. III, 6, 62. V, 5, 281. *Milford-Haven*: Cymb. III, 2, 44. 51. III, 4, 29. 145. III, 5, 8. IV, 2, 291. 335.

Militarist, soldier: *Parolles, the gallant m., — that was his own phrase*, All's IV, 3, 161.

Military, adj. 1) pertaining to the art or profession of war: *is there no m. policy, how virgins might blow up men?* All's I, 1, 132. *in m. rules*, H4B II, 3, 30. *troop in the throngs of m. men*, H4B IV, 1, 62. *he will maintain his argument as well as any m. man*, H5 III, 2, 86. *the direction of the m. discipline*, 107.

2) soldierly, martial: *speak from thy lungs m.* Wiv. IV, 5, 18. *most m. sir*, LLL V, 1, 38. *chief majority and m. title capital*, H4A III, 2, 110.

Milk, subst. the white fluid with which female animals feed their young: Ven. 902. Tp. II, 1, 288. LLL V, 2, 231. 925. Mids. II, 1, 36. V, 345. All's IV, 3, 124. Wint. III, 2, 101. H6A V, 4, 27. Cor. V, 4, 30. Tit. II, 3, 144. Hml. I, 5, 69. Lr. I, 1, 86. Applied, metaphorically, to things of a gentle influence: *adversity's sweet m., philosophy*, Rom. III, 3, 55. *too full of the m. of human kindness*, Mcb. I, 5, 18. *take my m. for gall*, 49. *I should pour the sweet m. of concord into hell*,

IV, 3, 98. Emblem of faintheartedness: *such a dish of skim m.* H4A II, 3, 36: cf. *livers white as m.* Merch. III, 2, 86. Of boyish greenness: *one would think his mother's m. were scarce out of him,* Tw. I, 5, 171.

Milk, vb. 1) to draw milk from the breast with the hand: Gent. III, 1, 277. 302. Ant. IV, 15, 74. Transitively: As II, 4, 51. Wint. IV, 4, 461.
2) to suck: *the babe that —s me,* Mcb. I, 7, 55.

Milking-time, the time of milking: Wint. IV, 4, 246.

Milk-livered, fainthearted, pusillanimous: Lr. IV, 2, 50; cf. Merch. III, 2, 86, and see *Liver.*

Milk-maid, a woman that milks or is employed in the dairy: Gent. III, 1, 268. Meas. I, 2, 177.

Milk-pap, a teat: Tim. IV, 3, 115.

Milksop, an effeminate and pusillanimous fellow: Ado V, 1, 91. R3 V, 3, 325.

Milk-white, white as milk: Pilgr. 119. Gent. III, 1, 250. Mids. II, 1, 167. H6B I, 1, 254. Tit. V, 1, 31. Tim. I, 2, 189.

Milky, weak: *has friendship such a faint and m. heart, it turns in less than two nights?* Tim. III, 1, 57. *his sword, which was declining on the m. head of reverend Priam,* Hml. II, 2, 500. *this m. gentleness and course of yours,* Lr. I, 4, 364.

Mill, a building in which corn is ground to meal: *more sacks to the m.* LLL IV, 3, 81. *more water glideth by the m. than wots the miller of,* Tit. II, 1, 85. Wint. IV, 4, 309. Cor. I, 10, 31. Lr. II, 3, 18.

Miller, one whose occupation is to grind corn to meal: Tit. II, 1, 86.
Name in Wiv. I, 1, 160.

Milliner, a man who deals in fancy articles: *no m. can so fit his customers with gloves,* Wint. IV, 4, 192. *he was perfumed like a m.* H4A I, 3, 36.

Million (ordinarily dissyll.; trisyll. in H5 Prol. 16 and Tit. II, 1, 49). 1) ten hundred thousand: *a crooked figure may attest in little place a m.* H5 Prol. 16. = a sum of ten hundred thousand pounds: Merch. III, 1, 57. H4A III, 3, 155. Tit. II, 1, 49. Cymb. I, 4, 147.
2) any very great number, an infinite number: Mids. III, 2, 93. Shr. III, 2, 241. Ant. I, 2, 39. IV, 14, 18. Cymb. II, 4, 143. With *of: a m. of manners,* Gent. II, 1, 105. *a m. of beating,* Wint. IV, 3, 62. *the m.* = the multitude: *the play pleased not the m.* Hml. II, 2, 457. Plur. —*s:* Tp. II, 1, 7. Wint. IV, 3, 61. Cor. III, 3, 71. Oth. IV, 1, 68. With *of:* Sonn. 53, 2. Meas. IV, 1, 60. Caes. IV, 1, 51. Hml. V, 1, 304.

Millioned, millionfold, innumerable: *time, whose m. accidents creep in 'twixt vows,* Sonn. 115, 5.

Mill-sixpence, an old English coin, milled in 1561, the earliest that was milled in this country: Wiv. I, 1, 158.

Millstone, used only in the proverbial expression *to weep —s* = not to weep at all, to remain hard and unfeeling as a stone: *your eyes drop —s, when fools' eyes drop tears,* R3 I, 3, 354. *he will weep. Ay, —s,* I, 4, 246. Applied to tears of laughter: *Queen Hecuba laughed that her eyes ran o'er. With —s,* Troil. I, 2, 158.

Mill-wheel, the wheel of a mill: *as fast as —s strike,* Tp. I, 2, 281.

Milo, the famous Greek athlete, who was able to bear an ox on his shoulders: Troil. II, 3, 258.

Mimic, subst. actor, player: *and forth my m. comes,* Mids. III, 2, 19 (i. e. Bottom with an ass's head. Q1 *minnick,* Q2 *minnock,* Ff. *mimmick*).

Mince, 1) to cut into pieces: *m. it* (the babe) *sans remorse,* Tim. IV, 3, 122. *—ing her husband's limbs,* Hml. II, 2, 537.
2) to make small, to extenuate, to palliate: *thy honesty and love doth m. this matter, making it light to Cassio,* Oth. II, 3, 247. *speak to me home, m. not the general tongue,* Ant. I, 2, 109.
3) to make small steps, to walk in a prim and affected manner: *hold up your head and m.* Wiv. V, 1, 9. *turn two —ing steps into a manly stride,* Merch. III, 4, 67. Metaphorically: *—ing poetry, 'tis like the forced gait of a shuffling nag,* H4A III, 1, 134. *I know no ways to m. it in love, but directly to say: I love you,* H5 V, 2, 130. And in general, = to speak or act with affectation: *which gifts, saving your —ing, the capacity of your soft cheveril conscience would receive,* H8 II, 3, 31. *—d* = affected: *is not birth, beauty, manhood, learning .... the spice and salt that season a man? Ay, a —d man,* Troil. I, 2, 279 (alluding, probably, to a minced pie). And transitively, = to affect, to make a parade of on the slightest occasion: *that —s virtue and does shake the head to hear of pleasure's name,* Lr. IV, 6, 122.

Mind, subst. (fem. in Lucr. 1656 and Per. I, 1, 153) 1) the soul, the mental power; opposed to the body: *the burden of a guilty m.* Lucr. 735. *let beasts bear gentle —s,* 1148. *unseen, save to the eye of m.* 1426; cf. Mids. I, 1, 234; Hml. I, 1, 112; I, 2, 185. *immaculate and spotless is my m.* Lucr. 1656. *since m. at first in character was done,* Sonn. 59, 8. *did his picture get, to serve their eyes, and in it put their m.* Compl. 135 (cf. Cymb. V, 5, 176). *the bettering of my m.* Tp. I, 2, 90. *to still my beating m.* IV, 163. *as his body uglier grows, so his m. cankers,* 192. *the affliction of my m. amends,* V, 115. *do not infest your m. with beating on the strangeness of this business,* 246. *complete in feature and in m.* Gent. II, 4, 73. *jewels move a woman's m.* III, 1, 91. *my m. is heavy,* Wiv. IV, 6, 2. *other sports are tasking of their —s,* 30. *the guiltiness of my m.* V, 5, 130. *profits of the m., study and fast,* Meas. I, 4, 61. *whose —s are dedicate to nothing temporal,* II, 2, 154. *fit his m. to death,* II, 4, 187. *did but convey unto our fearful —s a doubtful warrant of immediate death,* Err. I, 1, 68. *sorcerers that change the m.* I, 2, 99. *thou art* (transformed) *in m. Nay, both in m. and in my shape,* II, 2, 198. 199. *stigmatical in making, worse in m.* IV, 2, 22. *policy of m.* Ado IV, 1, 200. *the m. shall banquet, though the body pine,* LLL I, 1, 25. *nor hath love's m. of any judgment taste,* Mids. I, 1, 236. *which never laboured in their —s till now,* Mids. V, 73. *not sick, unless it be in m.* Merch. III, 2, 237. *if the quick fire of youth light not your m.,* you *are no maiden,* All's IV, 2, 5. *a m. that suits with this thy fair and outward character,* Tw. I, 2, 50. *I fear to find mine eye too great a flatterer for my m.* I, 5, 328. *she bore a m. that envy could not but call fair,* II, 1, 30. *thy m. is a very opal,* II, 4, 77. *not black in my m.* III, 4, 28. *admire not in thy m.* 166. *grapple your —s to sternage of this navy,* H5 III Chor. 18. *eke out our performance with your m.* 35. *in your fair —s let this acceptance take,* Epil. 14. *so* (a king) *I am, in m.* H6C III, 1, 60. *my m. exceeds the compass of her wheel. Then, for his m., be Edward England's king,*

IV, 3, 48. *men's —s mistrust ensuing danger*, R3 II, 3, 42. *I have considered in my m. the late demand*, IV, 2, 87. *the error of our eye directs our m.* Troil. V, 2, 110. *I'll ever serve his m. with my best will*, Tim. IV, 2, 49; cf. *duty and zeal to your unmatched m.* IV, 3, 523. *art thou but a dagger of the m.* Mcb. II, 1, 38. *I fear I am not in my perfect m.* Lr. IV, 7, 63. *which* (his mistress' picture) *by his tongue being made, and then a m. put in it*, Cymb. V, 5, 176. *our m. partakes her private actions to your secrecy*, Per. I, 1, 152 etc. etc. = a man, with regard to his intellectual capacity: *I have frequent been with unknown —s*, Sonn. 117, 5.

2) sentiments, disposition, cast of thought and feeling: *had thy mother borne so hard a m.* Ven. 203. *O that you bore the m. that I do*, Tp. II, 1, 267. *cannot soon revolt and change your m.* Gent. III, 2, 59. *he bears an honourable m.* V, 3, 13. *it is the lesser blots, modesty finds, women to change their shapes, than men their —s*, V, 4, 109. *whatsoever I have merited, either in my m. or in my means*. Wiv. II, 2, 211. *keep in that m.* III, 3, 89. *else I could not be in that m.* 91. *yet hath he in him such a m. of honour*, Meas. II, 4, 179 (= honourable mind; cf. *Of*). *my m. promises with my habit no loss shall touch her by my company*, III, 1, 181. *to transport him in the m. he is were damnable*, IV, 3, 72. *God keep your ladyship still in that m.* Ado I, 1, 135. *would the cook were of my m.* I, 3, 75. *a proverb never stale in thrifty m.* Merch. II, 5, 55. *my father loved Sir Rowland as his soul, and all the world was of my father's m.* As I, 2, 248. *I would not have my Rosalind of this m.* IV, 1, 110. *I am a fellow of the strangest m.* Tw. I, 3, 120. *I am not yet of Percy's m.* H4A II, 4, 114. *while Gloster bears this base and humble m.* H6B I, 2, 62. *I shall perceive the commons' m., how they affect the house and claim of York*, III, 1, 374. *continue still in this so good a m.* IV, 9, 17. *to make Lord Hastings of our m.* R3 III, 1, 162. *that's my m. too*, Troil. IV, 1, 6. *'tis pity bounty had not eyes behind, that man might ne'er be wretched for his m.* Tim. I, 2, 170. *I'ld rather than the worth of thrice the sum, had sent to me first, but for my —'s sake; I had such a courage to do him good*, III, 3, 23. *he bears too great a m.* Caes. V, 1, 113. *whose m. and mine in that are one*, Lr. I, 3, 15. *I would we were all of one m., and one m. good*, Cymb. V, 4, 212 etc.

3) reflection, thoughts: *your m. is tossing on the ocean*, Merch. I, 1, 9. *I have a m. presages me such thrift*, I, 1, 175 (= anticipation. cf. Caes. III, 1, 144). *this murder had not come into my m.* John IV, 2, 223. *those men you talk of came into my m.* R3 III, 2, 118. *my m. gave me ... ye blew the fire that burns ye*, H8 V, 3, 109 (= I suspected); cf. *my m. gave me his clothes made a false report of him*, Cor. IV, 5, 157. *have m. upon your health, tempt me no further*, Caes. IV, 3, 36 (= think of, take care of your health). *but yet have I a m. that fears him much, and my misgiving still falls shrewdly to the purpose*, III, 1, 144 (= suspicion; cf. Merch. I, 1, 175). *that song will not go from my m.* Oth. IV, 3, 31. *to put sth. in a person's m.* = to make him think of sth.: *that same groan doth put this in my m.* Sonn. 50, 13. *put it in the physician's m. to help him to his grave*, R2 I, 4, 59. *God put it in thy m. to take it hence*, H4B IV, 5, 179. And inversely, *to put a person in m.: the bells of Saint Bennet may put you in m.* Tw. V, 42. *these masks put us in m. they hide the fair*, Rom. I, 1, 237. *it were well the general were*

put in m. of it, Oth. II, 3, 137 (= were made aware of it).

4) recollection, memory: *keep by children's eyes her husband's shape in m.* Sonn. 9, 8. *that this lives in thy m.* Tp. I, 2, 49. *still 'tis beating in my m.* 176. *my m. did lose it*, Mids. I, 1, 114. *have in m. where we must meet*, Merch. I, 1, 71. *let no fair be kept in m.* As III, 2, 99. *this grief had wiped it from my m.* H4B I, 1, 211. *bearest thou her face in m.?* Ant. III, 3, 32. *to call to m.* = to remember: Lucr. 1366. Gent. III, 1, 6. H6A III, 3, 68. H8 II, 4, 34. *to put in a person's mind* = to remind him: *let me put in your —s, what you have been ere now*, R3 I, 3, 131. *to put it in my m.* II, 1, 120. *to put a person in m.*, in the same sense: *to put your grace in m. of what you promised me*, R3 IV, 2, 113. *will you be put in m. of his blind fortune?* Cor. V, 6, 118. *time out of m.* = since time immemorial: Meas. IV, 2, 17. Rom. I, 4, 69.

5) that which a man thinks; thoughts, opinion: *to me that brought your m.* Gent. I, 1, 147 (delivered your message). *I'll show my m.* I, 2, 7. *might her m. discover*, II, 1, 173. *being of an old father's m.* LLL IV, 2, 33. *he tells you flatly what his m. is*, Shr. I, 2, 78. *he and his physicians are of a m.* All's I, 3, 244 (of the same opinion). *be not of that m.* R2 V, 2, 107. *will resolve him of my m.* R3 IV, 5, 19. *with every minute you do change a m.* Cor. I, 1, 186. *by Jove, 'twould be my m. It is a m. that shall remain a poison where it is*, III, 1, 86. *she holds her virtue still and I my m.* Cymb. I, 4, 69 etc. *in the m.* = of opinion: *I am not in the m. but I were better to be married of him*, As III, 3, 91. *he was in the m. it was* (cut well) V, 4, 75. *in my m.* = in my opinion: *in my m. thy worst all best exceeds*, Sonn. 150, 8. Wiv. II, 1, 39. Ado II, 3, 192. Mids. III, 2, 135. Merch. II, 4, 7. IV, 1, 407. H6B III, 1, 238 etc. *to my m.*, in the same sense: Hml. I, 4, 14. *to break one's m.* = to make a disclosure of one's opinion: H6A I, 3, 81. *to know a person's m.:* Ven. 308. Gent. I, 2, 33. IV, 3, 2. Wiv. I, 4, 112. 135. III, 4, 80. IV, 4, 83. Err. II, 1, 47. Ado V, 1, 188. Tw. I, 5, 276. R2 V, 2, 104. H6B I, 1, 139. III, 2, 242. H6C III, 2, 17 etc. *to say one's m.:* Shr. IV, 3, 75. All's II, 1, 98. *to speak one's m.:* LLL V, 2, 589. As II, 7, 59. R2 II, 1, 230. H6B III, 1, 43. H8 V, 1, 41. *to tell one's m.:* Gent. I, 1, 148. Err. II, 1, 48 etc. *in a tedious sampler sewed her m.* Tit. II, 4, 39. *I'll call for pen and ink, and write my m.* H6A V, 3, 66. *write down thy m.* Tit. II, 4, 3. *if his m. be writ, give me his letter*, Rom. V, 2, 3. Sonn. 59, 8.

6) will, desire, intention, purpose: *all my m., my thought, my busy care is how to get my palfrey from the mare*, Ven. 383. *that you may know one another's m.* Wiv. II, 2, 132. *servants must their masters' —s fulfil*, Err. IV, 1, 113. *a time too brief to have all things answer my m.* Ado II, 1, 376. *it would better fit your honour to change your m.* III, 2, 119. *I'll hold my m., were she an Ethiope*, V, 4, 38. *what would these strangers? know their —s, Boyet*, LLL V, 2, 174. *my wooing m. shall be expressed in russet yeas*, 412. *to you our —s we will unfold*, Mids. I, 1, 208. *let it not enter in your m. of love*, Merch. II, 8, 42 (the same as wooing mind in LLL V, 2, 412). *already know my m.* Merch. III, 4, 37. *how far off from the m. of Bolingbroke it is*, R2 III, 3, 45. *the m. of Bolingbroke is changed*, V, 1, 51. *you perceive my m.?* H6A II, 2, 59. *my m. is changed*, R3 IV, 4, 456. *it is my father's m. that I*

repair to Rome, Tit. V, 3, 1. *if your m. hold*, Caes. I, 2, 295. *to be free and bounteous to her m.* Oth. I, 3, 266 etc. *to have a m.* = to be inclined: *have you a m. to sink?* Tp. I, 1, 42. Wint. IV, 4, 862. Ant. II, 5, 42. With *to: you have a month's m. to them*, Gent. I, 2, 137 (probably = a woman's longing, a morbid appetite).*I have a m. to it*, Merch. IV, 1, 433. cf. *command what cost your heart has m. to*, Ant. III, 4, 38. *hath more m. to feed on your blood*, Gent. II, 4, 27. *I have no m. of feasting forth*, Merch. II, 5, 37. *I had no m. to hunt*, Cymb. IV, 2, 147. *I have no m. to Isbel*, All's III, 2, 13.

Mind, vb. 1) to have in the mind, to think of, to mean: —*ing true things by what their mockeries be*, H5 IV Chor. 53.*

2) to attend to, to take notice of, to care for: *perchance he will not m. me*, Tp. II, 2, 17. *you do not m. the play*, Shr. I, 1, 254. *to stop the inundation of her tears, which, too much — ed by herself alone, may be put from her by society*, Rom. IV, 1, 13. *not —ing whether I dislike or no*, Per. II, 5, 20.

3) to remind, to make to think: *that have — ed you of what you should forget*, Wint. III, 2, 226. *I do thee wrong to m. thee of it*, H5 IV, 3, 13. *m. thy followers of repentance*, 84. *I —ed him how royal 'twas to pardon*, Cor. V, 1, 18.

4) to intend, to mean: *we do not come as — ing to content you*, Mids. V, 113. *I mind to tell him plainly what I think*, H6C IV, 1, 8. *I shortly m. to leave you*, 64. *she —s to play the Amazon*, 106. *if you m. to hold your true obedience*, 140. *the gods not —ing longer to withhold the vengeance*, Per. II, 4, 3.

Minded, adj. disposed, affected: Sonn. 11, 7. Tp. V, 126. H8 III, 1, 58. Cor. I, 6, 73. Lr. III, 1, 2. cf. *High-minded, Proud-minded.*

Mindful, careful: *but now the m. messenger, come back, brings home his lord*, Lucr. 1583.

Mindless, careless, regardless: *a m. slave*, Wint. I, 2, 301. *Athens, m. of thy worth*, Tim. IV, 3, 93.

Mine, subst. 1) an excavation in the earth, from which metallic ores or other mineral substances are taken by digging: *burn like the —s of sulphur*, Oth. III, 3, 329. Hence = a rich source of wealth: *either was the other's m.* Phoen. 36. *I would not wed her for a m. of gold*, Shr. I, 2, 92. H4A III, 1, 169. H8 I, 1, 22. Caes. IV, 3, 102. Ant. IV, 6, 32.

2) a subterraneous passage dug under a hostile fortification: H5 III, 2, 59. 61. 62. 63. 92. Hml. III, 4, 208.

3) any subterraneous cavity: *the wind is hushed within the hollow m. of earth*, Oth. IV, 2, 79.

Mine, vb. to undermine, to sap, to destroy by slow degrees: —*s my gentility with my education*, As I, 1, 21. *rank corruption, —ing all within, infects unseen*, Hml. III, 4, 148.

Mine, poss. pron. of the first pers. sing.; = belonging to me; 1) joined to nouns beginning with vowels, and used without any emphasis: *look in m. eye-balls*, Ven. 119. *m. eyes are grey*, 140. 503. Lucr. 228. *m. infamy*, 504. *m. only care*, Sonn. 48, 7. *m. art*, Tp. I, 2, 28 (v. 25 *my art*). *m. eyes*, 135. *m. enemies*, 179. *m. art*, 291. 435. 466. II, 1, 106. 111. 191. 313. 317. III, 1, 77. III, 2, 123. 147. III, 3, 89. IV, 28. 41. 120. 264. V, 53. 63. Gent. II, 1, 77. II, 4, 66. II, 5, 1. III, 1, 48. 74. 239. V, 4, 64. Meas. I, 1, 64. II, 1, 187. III, 1, 85. IV, 2, 119. 180. V, 59. 198.

Err. I, 2, 14. II, 1, 48. III, 1, 44. III, 2, 62. 169. V, 30. 106. 243. 331 etc. etc. Joined with *own: m. own love's might*, Sonn. 23, 8. *from m. own library*, Tp. I, 2, 167. 342. 347. II, 2, 128. III, 1, 50. IV, 1, 3. Epil. 2. Gent. I, 2, 120. I, 3, 82. II, 4, 135. 156. 168. IV, 4, 61. Wiv. I, 1, 157. II, 1, 88. Meas. I, 1, 65. II, 1, 30. 218. V, 377. Err. I, 2, 33. III, 1, 120. III, 2, 61 etc. etc.

Before *h: I am pale at m. heart*, Meas. IV, 3, 157. *m. host:* Gent. IV, 2, 28. Wiv. I, 1, 143. Err. II, 2, 4 etc. etc. (cf. *Host*). But *my ranting host*, Wiv. II, 1, 196.

Used for *my*, when separated from its noun: *the lady is dead upon m. and my master's false accusation*, Ado V, 1, 249. *mine and my father's death come not upon thee*, Hml. V, 2, 341. *m. and your mistress*, Cymb. V, 5, 230. *for m., if I may call offence*, Per. I, 2, 92. Even before a consonant: *his and m. loved darling*, Tp. III, 3, 93.

Placed after its noun: *brother m.* Tp. V, 75. *master m.* Wiv. I, 1, 164. Shr. I, 1, 25. *lady m.* H8 I, 2, 17. *pupil m.* Rom. II, 3, 82.

2) without a noun, but with reference to one preceding: *the creatures that were m.* Tp. I, 2, 82. *to no sight but thine and m.* 302. *this island's m.* 331. *here's my hand. And m.* III, 1, 90. IV, 201. V, 20. 189. 276. Gent. I, 1, 60. II, 1, 1. III, 1, 207. IV, 4, 142. Err. I, 2, 66 etc. etc. *to be m.* = to belong to me: *he never should be m.* Gent. I, 2, 11. III, 1, 365. V, 4, 83. Meas. V, 497 etc. *let that be m.* = let that be my care; *mind your own business*, Meas. II, 2, 12.

Of m., immediately following a subst., properly = one of those whom or which I have: *this fair child of m. shall sum my count*, Sonn. 2, 10. *there is a friend of m. come to town*, Wiv. IV, 5, 78. *he's a good friend of m.* LLL IV, 1, 54. *a good master of m.* 106. *kinsmen of m.* H8 I, 1, 81 etc. But as often = of me, my: *they have murdered this poor heart of m.* Ven. 502 (= this my poor heart). *clear from this attaint of m.* Lucr. 825. *in that sad hour of m.* 1179. *this face of m.* Gent. IV, 4, 190. *the revolt of m. is dangerous*, Wiv. I, 3, 111 (some M. Edd., quite preposterously, *of mien*). *to have it added to the faults of m.* Meas. II, 4, 72. *this finger of m.* V, 316. *your sister is no wife of m.* Err. III, 2, 42. *give me the ring of m.* IV, 3, 69. *a ring he hath of m. worth forty ducats*, 84. *these ears of m. did hear thee*, V, 26. 259. *this grained face of m.* 311. *what stuff of m. hast thou embarked?* 409. *time hath not yet so dried this blood of m.* Ado IV, 1, 195. *despise me, when I break this oath of m.* LLL V, 2, 441. *his folly is no fault of m.* Mids. I, 1, 200. *what wicked and dissembling glass of m. made me compare with Hermia's sphery eyne?* II, 2, 98. *this aspect of m. hath feared the valiant*, Merch. II, 1, 8. *the balls of m.* (= my eyeballs) III, 2, 118. *my loving greetings to those of m. in court*, All's I, 3, 259 (my friends or relations). *the youngest wren of m.* Tw. III, 2, 71 (M. Edd. *nine*). *those provinces these arms of m. did conquer*, H6B I, 1, 120. *whose natural gifts were poor to those of m.* Hml. I, 5, 52 etc. (cf. *the young whelp of Talbot's*, H6A IV, 7, 35. *the mantle of Queen Hermione's*, Wint. V, 2, 36. *the horn and noise o' the monster's*, Cor. III, 1, 95. *these quick blows of Fortune's*, Tim. I, 1, 91. *this dotage of our general's*, Ant. I, 1, 1. *the business of Cleopatra's*, I, 2, 182 etc.).

3) substantively, = a) my property: *myself I'll*

forfeit, so that other m. thou wilt restore, to be my comfort still, Sonn. 134, 3. *if you like me, she shall have me and m.* Shr. II, 385. *one that fixes no bourn 'twixt his and m.* Wint. I, 2, 134. b) the persons depending on me; my relations, my family: *should presently extirpate me and m.*, Tp. I, 2, 125. *this title honours me and m.* H6C IV, 1, 72. *so thrive I and m.* R3 II, 1, 24. *thy justice will take hold on me and you and m. and yours*, 132. = my servants: *how pomp is followed! m. will now be yours; and should we shift estates, yours would be m.* Ant. V, 2, 151.

Mineral, 1) a mine: *like some ore among a m. of metals base*, Hml. IV, 1, 26 (cf. Walker's Crit. Exam. II, 299 .

2) a fossile body used as a poisonous ingredient: *abused her delicate youth with drugs or —s that weaken motion*, Oth. I, 2, 74. *the thought whereof doth like a poisonous m. gnaw my inwards*, II, 1, 306. *she had for you a mortal m.* Cymb. V, 5, 50.

Minerva, the goddess of wisdom: *thou mayst hear M. speak*, Shr. I, 1, 84. *laming the shrine of Venus, or straight-pight M.* Cymb. V, 5, 164.

Mingle, subst. mixture, union: *O heavenly m.* Ant. I, 5, 59. *trumpeters, make m. with our rattling tabourines*, IV, 8, 37.

Mingle, vb. 1) trans. a) to mix: *there his smell with others being —d*, Ven. 691. *to m. beauty with infirmities*, 735. *milk and blood, being —d both together*, 902. *—ing my talk with tears*, Lucr. 797. *cheeks neither red nor pale, but —d so*, 1510. *my blood is —d with the crime of lust*, Err. II, 2, 143. *confess what treason there is —d with your love*, Merch. III, 2, 27. *the difference betwixt the constant red and —d damask*, As III, 5, 123. *the web of our life is of a —d yarn*, All's IV, 3, 83. *the united vessel of their blood, —d with venom of suggestion*, H4B IV, 4, 45. *make a quagmire of your —d brains*, H6A I, 4, 109. *m. tears with smiles*, Cor. I, 9, 3. *—ing them with us*, III, 1, 72. *when it* (love) *is —d with regards*, Lr. I, 1, 242. *m. eyes with one that ties his points*, Ant. III, 13, 156. *grief and patience ... m. their spurs together*, Cymb. IV, 2, 58. *we'll m. our bloods together in the earth*, Per. I, 2, 113.

b) to join: *to m. friendship far is —ing bloods*, Wint. I, 2, 109. *to m. faith with him*, IV, 4, 471. *part your —d colours*, John II, 389. *—d his royalty with capering fools*, H4A III, 2, 63. *beauty and honour in her are so —d*, H8 II, 3, 76. *those that m. reason with your passion*, Lr. II, 4, 237. *some dozen Romans have —d sums to buy a present for the emperor*, Cymb. I, 6, 186. *their discipline, now —d with their courage*, II, 4, 24 (F1 *wing-led*).

2) intr. to be mixed and joined: *m. with the state of floods*, H4B V, 2, 132. *ourself will m. with society*, Mcb. III, 4, 3. *fly and m. with the English epicures*, V, 3, 8. *though grey do something m. with our younger brown*, Ant. IV, 8, 20. *her fortunes —d with thine entirely*, IV, 14, 24.

Minikin, small and pretty: *for one blast of thy m. mouth*, Lr. III, 6, 45.

Minim, see *Minum*.

Minimus, any thing very small: *you m., of hindering knot-grass made*, Mids. III, 2, 329.

Minion, 1) favourite, darling: Sonn. 126, 9. Tp. IV, 98. Tw. V, 128. John II, 392. H4A I, 1, 83. I, 2, 30. Mcb. I, 2, 19. Cymb. II, 3, 46.

2) one generally loved and flattered: *is this the Athenian m., whom the world voiced so regardfully?* Tim. IV, 3, 80. *Duncan's horses, the —s of their race*, Mcb. II, 4, 15 (the pearls of their race; cf. *darling* in Oth. I, 2, 68).

3) Used with some contempt, a) of persons in whose company another finds pleasure: *his company must do his —s grace*, Err. II, 1, 87. *she vaunted 'mongst her —s t'other day*, H6B I, 3, 87. *go, rate thy —s, proud insulting boy*, H6C II, 2, 84. Perhaps also in Tp. IV, 98 and Cymb. II, 3, 46.

b) = a pert and saucy person (originally a spoiled favourite): *how now, m.!* Gent. I, 2, 88. *you, m., are too saucy*, 92. *do you hear, you m.?* Err. III, 1, 54. *you'll cry for this*, m. 59. *you m. you, are these your customers?* IV, 4, 63. *m., thou liest*, Shr. II, 13. *give me my fan: what, m., can you not?* H6B I, 3, 141. *this m. stood upon her chastity*, Tit. II, 3, 124. *mistress m. you, thank me no thankings*, Rom. III, 5, 152. *m., your dear lies dead*, Oth. V, 1, 33.

Minister, subst. 1) one employed to a certain end; instrument, executor: *the —s for the purpose*, Tp. I, 2, 131. *if they can find in their hearts the poor unvirtuous fat knight shall be any further afflicted, we two will still be the —s*, Wiv. IV, 2, 234. *he that of greatest works is finisher oft does them by the weakest m.* All's II, 1, 140. *in a weak and most debile m.* II, 3, 40. *who but to-day hammered of this design, but durst not tempt a m. of honour*, Wint. II, 2, 50 (i. e. one of high rank). *I chose Camillo for the m. to poison my friend Polixenes*, III, 2, 161. *for a m. of my attempt I have seduced a headstrong Kentishman*, H6B III, 1, 355. *thou son of hell, whom angry heavens do make their m.* V, 2, 34. R3 I, 2, 46. I, 3, 294. I, 4, 226. V, 3, 113. H8 I, 1, 108. Troil. Prol. 4. Cor. III, 3, 98. Tim. II, 2, 140. Mcb. I, 5, 49. V, 8, 68. Hml. III, 4, 175. Ant. III, 6, 88. III, 13, 23. V, 1, 20. V, 2, 4. Cymb. V, 3, 72.

2) a servant and messenger of God, an angel: *O you blessed —s above*, Meas. V, 115. *angels and —s of grace defend us*, Hml. I, 4, 39.

3) servant in general: *what me your m., for you obeys*, Compl. 229. *by help of her most potent —s*, Tp. I, 2, 275. III, 3, 61. 87. *I may never lift an angry arm against his m.* R2 I, 2, 41. *thou m. of hell*, H6A V, 4, 93. *your master* (Christ) *whose m. you are*, H8 V, 1, 138. Tit. V, 2, 60. 61. 133. Oth. V, 2, 8.

4) a parson: *send —s to me*, Tw. IV, 2, 100. *the m. is here*, 102. *Master Dumbe, our m.* H4B II, 4, 95.

Minister, vb. 1) to perform a function, to do service: *pluck the grave wrinkled senate from the bench, and m. in their steads*, Tim. IV, 1, 6. *a —ing angel shall my sister be, when thou liest howling*, Hml. V, 1, 264. With *to*, = to serve, to execute the orders and supply the wants of: *shall we serve heaven with less respect than we do m. to our gross selves?* Meas. II, 2, 86. *did m. unto the appetite and affection common of the whole body*, Cor. I, 1, 106. *to him the other two shall m.* Cymb. III, 3, 76. Used of spiritual advice: *make me know the nature of their crimes, that I may m. to them accordingly*, Meas. II, 3, 7. *how sweetly you do m. to love*, Ado I, 1, 314.

2) to perform, to execute: *before all sanctimonious ceremonies may with full and holy rite be —ed*, Tp. IV, 1, 17.

3) to suggest, to afford, to supply, to give: *to m.*

occasion to these gentlemen, Tp. II, 1, 173. *though sometimes you do blench from this to that, as cause doth m.* Meas. IV, 5, 6. *if you three will but m. such assistance as I shall give you direction,* Ado II, 1, 385. *what help we have that to your wanting may be —ed,* As II, 7, 126. *unless you laugh and m. occasion to him,* Tw. I, 5, 93. *how quickly should this arm ... chastise thee and m. correction to thy fault,* R2 II, 3, 105. *ruder terms, such as my wit affords and overjoy of heart doth m.* H6B I, 1, 31. *what did this vanity but m. communication of a most poor issue,* H8 I, 1, 86.* *or from what other course you please, which the time shall more favourably m.* Oth. II, 1, 277. *which* (learning) *he took, as we do air, fast as 'twas —ed,* Cymb. I, 1, 45.

4) to administer (medicines), to prescribe, to order: *you gave me bitter pills, and I must m. the like to you,* Gent. II, 4, 150. *thy physic I will try, that —s thine own death if I die,* All's II, 1, 189. *present medicine must be —ed,* John V, 1, 15. *may m. the potion of imprisonment to me,* H4B I, 2, 145. *a poison which the friar subtly hath —ed,* Rom. IV, 3, 25. *canst thou not m. to a mind diseased,* Mcb. V, 3, 40. 46. *—est a potion unto me,* Per. I, 2, 68. *there's nothing can be —ed to nature that can recover him,* III, 2, 8.

Ministration, service, the going through an incumbent function: *my course, which holds not colour with the time, nor does the m. and required office on my particular,* All's II, 5, 65.

Minnow, a very small fish; used as a term of contempt: *that low-spirited swain, that base m. of thy mirth,* LLL I, 1, 251 (Armado's letter). *hear you this Triton of the —s?* Cor. III, 1, 89.

Minola, name in Shr. I, 2, 97. 99. 165.

Minority, state of being under age: *his m. is put unto the trust of Richard Gloster,* R3 I, 3, 11. = childhood: *proving from world's m. their right,* Lucr. 67. *he shall present Hercules in m.* LLL V, 2, 141. *quoniam he seemeth in m.* V, 2, 596. *which, in the m. of them both, his majesty did first propose,* All's IV, 5, 77.

Minos, fabulous king of Crete: H6C V, 6, 22.

Minotaur, the monster dwelling in the labyrinth of Crete: H6A V, 3, 189.

Minstrel, one who sings and makes music for money: *feast-finding —s, tuning my defame,* Lucr. 817. *I will bid thee draw, as we do the —s,* Ado V, 1, 129. *none but —s like of sonneting,* LLL IV, 3, 158. *I hear the —s play,* Shr. III, 2, 185. *consort! what, dost thou make us —s? an thou make —s of us, look to hear nothing but discords,* Rom. III, 1, 49. 50. *no money, on my faith, but the gleek; I will give you the m.* IV, 5, 116.

Minstrelsy, 1) the place and office of a minstrel (which partly consisted in relating fabulous stories): *I love to hear him lie and I will use him for my m.* LLL I, 1, 177.

2) music: *when every room hath blazed with lights and brayed with m.* Tim. II, 2, 170. *m. and pretty din,* Per. V, 2, 7.

Mint, subst. the plant Mentha Piperita: LLL V, 2, 661. Wint. IV, 4, 104.

Mint, subst. the place where money is coined; metaphorically a place of invention and fabrication: LLL I, 1, 166. Tw. III, 2, 24. Troil. I, 3, 193.

Minum, the shortest note in music; a very short moment: *he rests his m., one, two, and the third in your*

bosom, Rom. II, 4, 22 (Q2 *he rests, his minum rests;* Q3.4.5 *he rests his minum rests;* the spurius Q1 and M. Edd. *rests me his minim rest*).

Minute, subst. the sixtieth part of an hour; a very short time: Ven. 746. 1187. Lucr. 213. 297. 329. 962. Sonn. 14, 5. 60, 2. 77, 2. 126, 8. Pilgr. 206. Tp. I, 2, 37. IV, 141. Wiv. II, 2, 328. V, 5, 2. LLL IV, 3, 182. Mids. II, 1, 176. II, 2, 2. 112. As III, 2, 321. IV, 1, 45. 47. 195. All's I, 2, 39. II, 1, 169. Tw. I, 1, 14. V, 98. Wint. I, 2, 290. John III, 4, 134. IV, 1, 46. R2 I, 3, 226. V, 5, 51. 58. H4A I, 2, 8. H4B I, 1. 7. IV, 1, 83. H6B III, 2, 338. H6C II, 5, 25. 38. H8 I, 2, 121. 149. Rom. II, 4, 156. II, 6, 5. III, 5, 45. V, 3, 257. Mcb. III, 1, 117. IV, 3, 176. Hml. I, 1, 27. I, 3, 9. Oth. II, 1, 41. III, 3, 169. Ant. I, 1, 46. III, 7, 82. Cymb. II, 5, 31. Per. I, 3, 25. II, 4, 44. V, 1, 160. 214. *every m. while,* H6A I, 4, 54. *to steal at a —'s rest,* Wiv. I, 3, 31 (in the shortest moment). *at the latest m. of the hour,* LLL V, 2, 797 (= at the last moment). *by the m.* = every minute, incessantly: Ant. III, 1, 20. Cymb. V, 5, 51. *with every m. you do change a mind,* Cor. I, 1, 186.

Minute-jacks, probably persons who change their minds every minute and are not to be trusted: *trencher-friends, time's flies, cap and knee slaves, vapours, and —s,* Tim. III, 6, 107 (generally interpreted to mean the same as *jacks of the clock,* q. v.).

Minutely, adj. happening every minute, continual: *now m. revolts upbraid his faith-breach,* Mcb. V, 2, 18.

Minx, a pert and wanton woman (cf. *Minion* 3 b): Tw. III, 4, 133. Oth. III, 3, 475. IV, 1, 159.

Mirable, admirable: *not Neoptolemus so m., on whose bright crest fame with her loudest Oyes cries This is he, could promise to himself a thought of added honour torn from Hector,* Troil. IV, 5, 142.

Miracle, 1) a supernatural event: Sonn. 65, 13. Tp. II, 1, 6. V, 177. Wiv. III, 5, 119. Ado V, 4, 91. All's II, 1, 144. II, 3, 1. Wint. IV, 4, 545. John II, 497. H5 I, 1, 67. H6B II, 1, 60. Troil. V, 4, 37. Lr. I, 1, 225. II, 2, 172. IV, 6, 55. Per. V, 3, 58. *by m.* Err. V, 264. H4A II, ?, 184. *to do a m.* H6B II, 1. 131. 161. 163. *to work a m.* Merch. III, 2, 90. Shr. V, 1, 127. H6A V, 4, 41. 66.

2) a wonder, something wonderful: *'tis that m. and queen of gems that nature pranks her in attracts my soul,* Tw. II, 4, 88. *O m. of men,* H4B II, 3, 33. *be not offended, nature's m.* H6A V, 3, 54.

Miracle, vb. refl., *to m. itself* = to make itself a miracle, to be incomprehensible: *who this should be, doth m. itself, loved before me,* Cymb. IV, 2, 29 (but perhaps subst.).

Miraculous, working miracles, supernatural: Tp. II, 1, 86. Mcb. IV, 3, 147. Hml. II, 2, 623.

Miranda, the daughter of Prospero: Tp. I, 2, 48. 53. III, 1, 36. 37. 60.

Mire, subst. mud, earth soaked with water: Lucr. 1009. Tp. II, 2, 5. Wiv. IV, 5, 69. Err. V, 173. LLL II, 121. Rom. I, 4, 41. Tim. I, 2, 60. Lr. II, 2, 5. Cymb. V, 5, 222.

Mire, vb. 1) to soil with mud: *smirched thus and —d with infamy,* Ado IV, 1, 135.

2) to sink in mud: *paint till a horse may m. upon your face,* Tim. IV, 3, 147.

Mirror, subst. 1) looking-glass: Lucr. 1760. Wint. I, 2, 381. R2 IV, 265. R3 II, 2, 51. Caes. I, 2,

56. Hml. III, 2, 24. V, 2, 124. Ant. V, 1, 34. Per. I, 1, 45.

2) pattern, exemplar: *the m. of all Christian kings,* H5 II Chor. 6. *m. of all martial men,* H6A I, 4, 74. *whose wisdom was a m. to the wisest,* H6C III, 3, 84. *the m. of all courtesy,* H8 II, 1, 53.

Mirth, 1) great gayety, jollity: Lucr. 213. 1109. Gent. I, 1, 30. V, 4, 161. Wiv. II, 1, 28. II, 2, 231. Meas. IV, 1, 13. Err. III, 1, 108 (cf. *Despite*). Ado III, 2, 10. LLL I, 1, 251. II, 67. V, 1, 121. V, 2, 79. 520. 867. Mids. I, 1, 13. II, 1, 56. V, 28. 35. Merch. I, 1, 80. II, 2, 211. As I, 2, 3. V, 4, 114. Shr. Ind. 2, 137. Tw. II, 3, 49. Wint. IV, 4, 42. 54. John V, 2, 59. H4B IV, 4, 38. H5 II, 2, 132. V, 2, 318. H6A I, 6, 15. II, 3, 44. H8 II, 3, 101 (*make yourself m.*). Troil. I, 1, 40. I, 3, 173. Cor. I, 3, 117. 123. Mcb. III, 4, 11. 109. Hml. I, 2, 12. II, 2, 307. Ant. I, 2, 86. I, 3, 4. Cymb. I, 6, 58. V, 4, 163. Per. II, 1, 99. II, 3, 7.

2) a subject of merriment: *the m. whereof so larded with my matter,* Wiv. IV, 6, 14. *to speak all m. and no matter,* Ado II, 1, 343. *very tragical m.* Mids. V, 57. *he's all my exercise, my m., my matter,* Wint. I, 2, 166. *I'll use you for my m.* Caes. IV, 3, 49. 114. *to give a kingdom for a m.* Ant. I, 4, 18.

Mirthful, merry: *m. comic shows,* H6C V, 7, 43.

Mirth-moving, causing merriness: *a m. jest,* LLL II, 71.

Miry, muddy: Shr. IV, 1, 77. Tit. III, 1, 126.

Misadventure, mischance, misfortune: *your looks are pale and wild, and do import some m.* Rom. V, 1, 29. *what m. is so early up,* V, 3, 188.

Misadventured, unfortunate: *whose m. piteous overthrows,* Rom. Prol. 7.

Misanthropos, a hater of mankind: *I am M.* Tim. IV, 3, 53.

Misapply, to use for bad purposes: Rom. II, 3, 21.

Misbecome (impf. *misbecame,* partic. *misbecomed*) to suit ill, not to befit, to be unseemly in: LLL V, 2, 778. H4B V, 2, 100. H5 II, 4, 118.

Misbegot, of a bad origin, and hence pernicious: *which indeed is valour m.* Tim. III, 5, 29.

Misbegotten, of a bad origin: *free from other m. hate,* R2 I, 1, 33. Hence = pernicious: *that m. devil Faulconbridge,* John V, 4, 4. *three m. knaves in Kendal green,* H4A II, 4, 246. *contaminated, base and m. blood I spill of thine,* H6A IV, 6, 22.

Misbehaved, conducting one's self improperly, ill-bred: *like a m. and sullen wench,* Rom. III, 3, 143.

Misbeliever, one who holds a false religion, an infidel: *you call me m.* Merch. I, 3, 112.

Misbelieving, holding a false religion, infidel: *that m. Moor,* Tit. V, 3, 143.

Miscall, to call by a wrong name, to name improperly: *simple truth —ed simplicity,* Sonn. 66, 11. *my heart will sigh when I m. it so,* R2 I, 3, 263. *thou dost m. retire,* Troil. V, 4, 21.

Miscarry, vb. intr. 1) to be carried wrongly, to come into wrong hands: *a letter which accidentally hath —ed,* LLL IV, 2, 144. *the cardinal's letters to the pope —ed,* H8 III, 2, 30.

2) to fail, not to succeed, to be lost, to perish, to die: *who —ed at sea,* Meas. III, 1, 217. *there —ed a vessel of our country,* Merch. II, 8, 29. *my ships have all —ed,* III, 2, 318. *which (my body), but for him, had quite —ed,* V, 251. *I would not have him m.* Tw. III, 4, 70. *if they* (the French) *m., we m. too,* John V,

4, 3. *all that by indictment and by dint of sword have since —ed under Bolingbroke,* H4B IV, 1, 129. *if they m., theirs shall second them,* IV, 2, 46. *if a son ... m. upon the sea,* H5 IV, 1, 155. *if he m., farewell wars in France,* H6A IV, 3, 16. *better ten thousand base-born Cades m.* H6B IV, 8, 49. *it must be, if the king m.* R3 I, 3, 16. *all that have —ed by underhand corrupted foul injustice,* V, 1, 5. *who —ing,* Troil. I, 3, 351. *what —es shall be the general's fault,* Cor. I, 1, 270. *if aught in this —ed by my fault,* Rom. V, 3, 267. *our sister's man is —ed,* Lr. V, 1, 5. *if you m.* 44. *I may m. in it,* Oth. V, 1, 6. Applied to failing fruits and abortions: *if horns that year m.* LLL IV, 1, 114. *an the child I now go with do m.* H4B V, 4, 10. 15.

Mischance, misfortune: Ven. 738. Lucr. 968. 976. Tp. I, 1, 28. IV, 206. Gent. II, 2, 11. V, 3, 3. R2 III, 4, 92. H4A I, 3, 232. IV, 1, 58. H6A I, 1, 89. IV, 6, 49. H6B III, 2, 284. 300. H6C III, 3, 8. 18. 254. IV, 3, 43. R3 IV, 4, 114. Rom. V, 3, 221. Mcb. III, 4, 43. Hml. III, 2, 238. V, 2, 405. Oth. V, 1, 38. Cymb. II, 3, 137.

Mischief, subst. 1) fatal event, calamity, misfortune: *so in thyself thyself art made away, a m. worse than civil home-bred strife,* Ven. 764. *invert what best is boded me to m.* Tp. III, 1, 71. *any extremity rather than a m.* Wiv. IV, 2, 76. *apply a moral medicine to a mortifying m.* Ado I, 3, 13. *I pray God his bad voice bode no m.* II, 3, 83. *O m. strangely thwarting,* III, 2, 135. *a portent of broached m. to the unborn times,* H4A V, 1, 21. *so success of m. shall be born,* H4B IV, 2, 47. *had your watch been good, this sudden m. never could have fallen,* H6A II, 1, 59. *a plaguing m. light on Charles,* V, 3, 39. *till m. and despair drive you to break your necks,* V, 4, 90. *m., thou art afoot,* Caes. III, 2, 265. *a m. that is past and gone,* Oth. I, 3, 204. 205.

Even in a subjective sense, = misery: *here they* (our griefs) *are felt and seen with —'s eyes,* Per. I, 4, 8 (Steevens *mistful,* Walker *misery's*).

2) evil done on purpose, harm, injury: *for —s manifold and sorceries,* Tp. I, 2, 264. *any model to build m. on,* Ado I, 3, 49. *my thoughts are ripe in m.* Tw. V, 132. *would mean m.* Wint. IV, 4, 197. John III, 2, 3. H4B IV, 2, 14. H5 IV, 3, 106. IV, 7, 186. H6A III, 1, 115. H6B IV, 8, 59. V, 2, 84. R3 I, 3, 325. H8 I, 1, 160. I, 2, 187. II, 1, 66. V, 1, 49. Tit. III, 1, 274. V, 1, 65. 110. Rom. V, 1, 35. Tim. IV, 3, 168. Caes. IV, 1, 51. Hml. III, 2, 148. Lr. III, 7, 82. With a genitive: *wherever you wait on nature's m.* Mcb. I, 5, 51 (i. e. on harm done to human life, on the destruction of life; cf. *Nature*). *with the m. of your person it* (his displeasure) *would scarcely allay,* Lr. I, 2, 178. *to do m.:* Tp. IV, 217. H4B II, 1, 16. Lr. IV, 2, 55. *to do a p. m.:* Mids. II, 1, 237. 239. Caes. III, 1, 93. *to do to a p. m.:* Cor. IV, 5, 73. *to make m.* H8 II, 1, 22. *to work m.* Lucr. 960. H6A III, 2, 39. H6B II, 1, 186.

Mischief, vb. to harm, to injure: *grant I may ever love, and rather woo those that would m. me than those that do,* Tim. IV, 3, 475.

Mischievous, injurious, harmful: *most m. foul sin,* As II, 7, 64. *which hatched would grow m.* Caes. II, 1, 33.

Misconceived, having a wrong conception, misjudging, erring: *no, m.! Joan of Arc hath been a virgin,* H6A V, 4, 49.

Misconstruction, wrong interpretation, misapprehension: Lr. II, 2, 124.

Misconstrue (O. Edd. mostly *misconster*), to interpret erroneously, misjudge, misunderstand: *lest I be —d,* Merch. II, 2, 197. *he —s all that you have done,* As I, 2, 277. H4A V, 2, 69. H6A II, 3, 73. R3 III, 5, 61. Caes. V, 3, 84.

Miscreant, a vile wretch: *thou art a traitor and a m.* R2 I, 1, 39. *well, m., I'll be there as soon as you,* H6A III, 4, 44. *curse, m., when thou comest to the stake,* V, 3, 44. *O vassal, m.!* Lr. I, 1, 163 (Qq *recreant*).

Miscreate, illegitimate: *opening titles m. whose right suits not in native colours with the truth,* H5 I, 2, 16.

Misdeed, a wicked action: Lucr. 609. 637. H6C III, 3, 183. R3 I, 4, 70.

Misdemean, vb. refl. to behave ill: *you have —ed yourself toward the king,* H8 V, 3, 14.

Misdemeanours, ill behaviour: Tw. II, 3, 106.

Misdoubt, subst. suspicion, diffidence, apprehension: *he cannot so precisely weed this land as his —s present occasion,* H4B IV, 1, 206. *steel thy fearful thoughts and change m. to resolution,* H6B III, 1, 332.

Misdoubt, vb. to mistrust: *I do not m. my wife,* Wiv. II, 1, 192. *let this letter be read: our parson —s it,* LLL IV, 3, 194. *I could neither believe nor m.* All's I, 3, 130. *if you m. me that I am not she,* III, 7, 1. *the bird —eth every bush,* H6C V, 6, 14. *this sudden stab of rancour I m.* R3 III, 2, 89. *do you m. this sword?* Ant. III, 7, 63.

Misdread, fear of evil: *the passions of the mind, that have their first conception by m., have after-nourishment and life by care; and what was first but fear what might be done, grows elder now and cares it be not done,* Per. I, 2, 12.

Misenum (O. Edd. *Mesena*) a promontory in ancient Campania: Ant. II, 2, 163.

Miser, 1) a miserable wretch. *decrepit m., base ignoble wretch,* H6A V, 4, 7.

2) a niggard: Sonn. 75, 4. As V, 4, 63. H5 II, 4, 47. Troil. III, 3, 143. Per. II, 1, 33.

Miserable, 1) unhappy, wretched: Tp. I, 1, 36. Gent. IV, 1, 35. V, 4, 28. Meas. III, 1, 2. Mids. III, 2, 234. As IV, 3, 133. Wint. I, 2, 351. H5 II, 2, 178. H6B III, 1, 201. H6C I, 4, 85. II, 5, 88. R3 I, 2, 27. I, 3, 258. I, 4, 2. III, 4, 105. IV, 1, 76. Tit. II, 3, 108. III, 2, 28. IV, 3, 18. Rom. III, 3, 145. IV, 5, 44. Tim. IV, 3, 248. 462. Mcb. IV, 3, 103. Lr. V, 3, 46. Ant. IV, 15, 51. Cymb. I, 6, 6.

2) worthless, despicable, wretched: *a m. world,* As II, 7, 13. *O m. age,* H6B IV, 2, 11. *gross and m. ignorance,* 178. *O m. thought,* H6C III, 2, 151. *we worldly men have m., mad, mistaking eyes,* Tit. V, 2, 66. *what m. praise hast thou for her,* Oth. II, 1, 140. Quibbling in Tim. IV, 3, 249.

Miserably, calamitously: *he be as m. slain as I,* H6C I, 3, 42.

Misery, 1) wretchedness, great distress, calamity: Ven. 707. 738. Pilgr. 404. Tp. II, 2, 41. Err. V, 322. Merch. III, 4, 21. IV, 1, 272. As II, 1, 51. III, 2, 296. Shr. IV, 3, 34. Tw. III, 4, 383. Wint. III, 2, 123. V, 1, 146. John III, 4, 35. R2 II, 1, 85. H6A III, 2, 137. H6B III, 1, 200. H6C III, 3, 264. R3 IV, 1, 53. H8 Prol. 30. Cor. I, 1, 21. IV, 5, 94. V, 2, 103. Tit. II, 5, 57. III, 1, 134. Rom. I, 2, 60. V, 1, 41. Tim. IV, 2, 32. IV, 3, 242. 531. Lr. II, 2, 173. IV, 1, 79. IV,

5, 12. IV, 6, 63. Oth. III, 3, 171. Cymb. I, 5, 55. Per. I, 4, 55. 66. *and the m. is, example cannot dissuade succession,* All's III, 5, 23; cf. *when we in our viciousness grow hard — O m. on't! — the wise gods seel our eyes,* Ant. III, 13, 112. *he covets less than m. itself would give,* Cor. II, 2, 131 (explained by most, but unnecessarily, as meaning avarice).

Plur. *—ies* = calamities, misfortunes: Merch. I, 2, 4. All's III, 2, 122. Wint. IV, 4, 579. 822. H6A I, 1, 88. II, 5, 29. H6B II, 4, 16. R3 IV, 4, 17. 129. H8 III, 1, 108. III, 2, 389. 430. Tit. III, 1, 226. 244. Tim. IV, 3, 76. Caes. IV, 3, 221. Lr. III, 6, 110. V, 3, 180. Cymb. V, 4, 86. 144. Per. I, 4, 88. V, 3, 41.

2) contemptibleness: *O noble m., to be i' the field, and ask 'what news',* Cymb. V, 3, 64 (= contemptibleness in a nobleman).

Misfortune, evil accident, calamity: Lucr. 1713. Ado V, 1, 17. Merch. I, 1, 21. II, 4, 36 (fem.). R2 I, 2, 49. V, 5, 71. H6C IV, 4, 3. 20. Rom. I, 4, 91. V, 3, 82. Per. II, 3, 88 (*by m. of the seas*). 90. Plur. *—s:* Err. I, 1, 120. R2 V, 5, 29 (Ff m.). H8 III, 2, 374.

Misgive, to have a presentiment of evil: *my —ing still falls shrewdly to the purpose,* Caes. III, 1, 145. *my mind —s,* Oth. III, 4, 89. Followed by a clause: *my mind —s some consequence yet hanging in the stars shall bitterly begin his fearful date,* Rom. I, 4, 106. With a dative: *my heart —s me,* Wiv. V, 5, 226. *so doth my heart m. me, in these conflicts what may befall him,* H6C IV, 6, 94.

Misgoverned, ill behaved, rude (cf. *Government*): *rude m. hands from windows' tops threw dust and rubbish on King Richard's head,* R2 V, 2, 5.

Misgoverning, want of self-control, bad conduct: *black lust, dishonour, shame, m., who seek to stain the ocean of thy blood,* Lucr. 654.

Misgovernment, the same: *thus, pretty lady, I am sorry for thy much m.* Ado IV, 1, 100.

Misgraffed, grafted amiss, ill placed: (love) *m. in respect of years,* Mids. I, 1, 137.

Misguide, to lead a wrong way: *her great charms m. thy opposers' swords,* Cor. I, 5, 23.

Mishap, subst. ill chance, misfortune: Err. I, 1, 142. H6A I, 1, 23. Plur. *—s:* Ven. 603. Err. I, 1, 121. Tit. I, 152.

Mishear, to mistake in hearing: *thou hast misspoke, misheard,* John III, 1, 4.

Misinterpret, to explain in a wrong sense: *your exposition —ing,* Per. I, 1, 112. Trans.: *you did make him m. me,* R2 III, 1, 18.

Mislead (impf. not used, partic. *misled*), to lead astray, to guide a wrong way: Lucr. 369. Meas. IV, 1, 4. Ado IV, 1, 189. Mids. II, 1, 39. All's IV, 5, 1. R2 III, 1, 8. H4A IV, 3, 51. V, 1, 105. H4B I, 2, 163. H6B III, 2, 8. H6C III, 3, 35. V, 1, 97.

Misleader, one who leads to ill: H4A II, 4, 508. H4B V, 5, 68. H6B V, 1, 163.

Mislike, subst. dislike, aversion: *setting your scorns and your m. aside,* H6C IV, 1, 24.

Mislike, vb. to dislike, to disapprove: *m. me not for my complexion,* Merch. II, 1, 1. *'tis not my speeches that you do m.* H6B I, 1, 140. *if he m. my speech and what is done,* Ant. III, 13, 147.

Misordered, out of order, deranged, irregular: *the time m.* H4B IV, 2, 33.

Misplace, to put in a wrong place; absol.: *do you hear how he —s?* Meas. II, 1, 90 (= misapplies the words). Trans.: *gilded honour shamefully —d*, Sonn. 66, 5. *her benefits are mightily —d*, As I, 2, 37. *the —d John*, John III, 4, 133. *the crown so foul —d*, R3 III, 2, 44.

Misprise or **Misprize**, to undervalue, to slight, to despise (Fr. *mépriser*): *—ing what they look on*, Ado III, 1, 52. *I am altogether —d*, As I, 1, 177. *your reputation shall not be —d*, I, 2, 192. *by the —ing of a maid too virtuous for the contempt of empire*, All's III, 2, 33. *—ing the knight opposed*, Troil. IV, 5, 74 (Ff *disprising*).

Misprised, mistaken: *you spend your passion on a m. mood*, Mids. III, 2, 74.

Misprision, 1) the taking one thing for another, mistake, error: *thyself thou gavest, thy own worth then not knowing, or me, to whom thou gavest it, else mistaking; so thy great gift, upon m. growing, comes home again, on better judgment making*, Sonn. 87, 11. *there is some strange m. in the princes*, Ado IV, 1, 187. *a fever in your blood! why, then incision would let her out in saucers: sweet m.* LLL IV, 3, 98. *of thy m. must perforce ensue some true love turned*, Mids. III, 2, 90. *m. in the highest degree*, Tw. I, 5, 61.*envy, therefore, or m. is guilty of this fault*, H4A I, 3, 27.

2) undervaluing, contempt: *proud scornful boy that dost in vile m. shackle up my love and her desert*, All's II, 3, 159.

Misproud, viciously proud: *m. York*, H6C II, 6, 7.

Misquote, to misinterpret, to misconstrue: *interpretation will m. our looks*, H4A V, 2, 13.

Misreport, vb. to speak ill of, to slander: *a man that never yet did m. your grace*, Meas. V, 148.

Miss, vb. 1) to fail in aiming at, not to hit: *he could not m. it*, Tp. II, 1, 40. *he —es not much*, 56. *you find not the apostraphas, and so m. the accent*, LLL IV, 2, 124. *you m. my sense*, Shr. V, 2, 18. *a health to all that shot and —ed*, 51. *I —ed my aim*, H6A I, 4, 4. *I —ed the meteor once*, H8 V, 4, 52. *hit or m.* Troil. I, 3, 384. *in that hit you m.* Rom. I, 1, 214. *may m. our name and hit the woundless air*, Hml. IV, 1, 43.

2) to fail of finding or obtaining: *so may I, blind fortune leading me, m. that which one unworthier may attain*, Merch. II, 1, 37. *so may you m. me*, III, 2, 12. *who ever strove to show her merit, that did m. her love?* All's I, 1, 242. *your free undertaking cannot m. a thriving issue*, Wint. II, 2, 44. *if misfortune m. the first career*, R2 I, 2, 49. *though thy master —ed it* (the way) H8 III, 2, 439. *he could not m. them* (the daggers) Mcb. II, 2, 13. *he that hath —ed the princess is a thing too bad for bad report*, Cymb. I, 1, 16. *I could not m. my way*, III, 6, 9. With an inf.: *if we m. to meet him handsomely*, Tit. II, 3, 268.

3) to be without, to want: *thy record never can be —ed*, Sonn. 122, 8. *we cannot m. him*, Tp. I, 2, 311. *what I can help thee to thou shalt not m.* All's I, 3, 262. *he would m. it rather than carry it but by the suit of the gentry to him*, Cor. II, 1, 253.

4) to perceive and feel the want of: *the moon being clouded presently is —ed*, Lucr. 1007. *I shall m. thee, but yet thou shalt have freedom*, Tp. V, 95. *when he shall m. me*, Wint. IV, 4, 505. *your Coriolanus is not much —ed*, Cor. IV, 6, 13. *our dear friend Banquo, whom we m.* Mcb. III, 4, 90. *the friends we m.* V, 8, 35. *you shall be —ed at court*, Cymb. III, 4, 129. 189. III, 5, 90.

5) to fail, to omit, not to observe, not to keep:

one that will not m. you morning nor evening prayer, Wiv. II, 2, 102. *for —ing your meetings and appointments*, III, 1, 92. *I will not m. her*, III, 5, 56 (= not fail her).

6) to be absent or deficient, to be wanting: *what here shall m., our toil shall strive to mend*, Rom. Prol. 14. Mostly in the partic. *—ing* = wanting: *the warm effects which she in him finds —ing*, Ven. 605. *there are yet —ing of our company some few odd lads*, Tp. V, 254. *the roynish clown is also —ing*, As II, 2, 9. *if in her marriage my consent be —ing*, Tim. I, 1, 136. *Macduff is —ing*, Mcb. V, 8, 38. *she was —ing*, Cymb. IV, 3, 17. *upon my lady's —ing*, V, 5, 275.

Miss, subst. 1) misbehaviour, offence: *he saith she is immodest, blames her m.* Ven. 53.*cf. *Amiss*.

2) state of missing, feeling the loss and want of sth.: *I should have a heavy m. of thee*, H4A V, 4, 105.

Misshaped, deformed: H6C III, 2, 170.

Misshapen, the same: Lucr. 925. Tp. V, 268. H6C II, 2, 136. V, 5, 35. R3 I, 2, 251 (Qq *unshapen*). Rom. I, 1, 185. III, 3, 131.

Missheathed, ill sheathed, ill scabbarded: *m. in my daughter's bosom*, Rom. V, 3, 205.

Missingly, so as to feel and regret the absence: *what his happier affairs may be, are to me unknown: but I have m. noted, he is of late much retired from court*, Wint. IV, 2, 35 (= with regret).

Mission, a sending, deputation: *whose glorious deeds made emulous —s 'mongst the gods themselves*, Troil. III, 3, 189 (moved the gods to depute some of their own number who were to emulate him).

Missive, messenger: *whiles I stood rapt in the wonder of it, came —s from the king, who all-hailed me "Thane of Cawdor"*, Mcb. I, 5, 7. *did gibe my m. out of audience*, Ant. II, 2, 74.

Misspeak, to mistake in speaking, to make a slip of the tongue: *thou hast misspoke, misheard*, John III, 1, 4.

Mist, subst. a thin cloud or vapours intercepting vision: Lucr. 548. 643. 773. Err. II, 2, 218. H4A I, 2, 226.

Mist, vb. to cloud, to cover with vapour: *if that her breath will m. or stain the stone, why, then she lives*, Lr. V, 3, 262.

Mistake, vb. (impf. *mistook*, partic. *mistook*, *mistaken* and *mista'en*) 1) to take wrongly, to commit an error or offence in taking: *I have mistook: this is the ring you sent to Silvia*, Gent. V, 4, 94 (Germ. *ich habe mich vergriffen*). *I have lost my edifice by —ing the place where I erected it*, Wiv. II, 2, 225 (= by choosing a wrong place). *I did but tell her she mistook her frets*, Shr. II, 150. *the better act of purposes mistook is to m. again*, John III, 1, 274. *purposes mistook fallen on the inventors' heads*, Hml. V, 2, 395. *so you m. your husbands*, III, 2, 262 (some M. Edd. *must take*). cf. the quibble in R2 III, 3, 17.

2) to take one person or thing for another: *their several counsels they unbosom shall to loves mistook*, LLL V, 2, 142. *for three-foot stool —th me*, Mids. II, 1, 52. cf. II, 1, 32. III, 2, 112. *it may be you have —n him*, All's II, 5, 43. *you do m. me*, Tw. III, 4, 362 (I am not he whom you mean). *you have mistook Polixenes for Leontes*, Wint. II, 1, 81. *unless I have mista'en his colours quite*, R3 V, 3, 35. *show duty, as —n all this while between the child and parent*, Cor. V, 3, 55 (= confounded). *your tributary drops belong*

to woe, which you —ing offer up to joy, Rom. III, 2, 104. *you did m. him sure*, Cymb. IV, 2, 102.

3) *to misjudge: or me, to whom thou gavest it, else —ing*, Sonn. 87, 10. *m. me not so much to think my poverty is treacherous*, As I, 3, 66. *you have mistook me all this while*, R2 III, 2, 174. *my father's purposes have been mistook*, H4B IV, 2, 56. *as you did m. the outward composition of his body*, H6A II, 3, 74. *thou —st me much to think I do*, H6B V, 1, 130. *I do m. my person all this while*, R3 I, 2, 253. *and could wish he were something —n in it*, H8 I, 1, 195. *your rage —s us*, III, 1, 101. *you m. my fortunes*, Tim. II, 2, 193. *you m. my love*, I, 2, 9. *I have much mistook your passion*, Caes. I, 2, 48. *— ing his purpose*, Lr. I, 2, 90.

4) *to misapprehend*, *to misunderstand; absol.: you m.* Gent. I, 1, 113. *you mistook*, 120. *or else I mistook*, II, 1, 10. IV, 2, 57. *your grace —s*, R2 III, 3, 10. *m. not, uncle*, 15. Trans.: *he doth but m. the truth*, Tp. II, 1, 57. *thou —st me*, Gent. II, 5, 49. *m. the word*, III, 1, 283. *they mistook their erection* (for direction) Wiv. III, 5, 41. *you must not m. my niece*, Ado I, 1, 61. *m. me not*, Shr. II, 66; Wint. III, 2, 110; R2 II, 3, 74; Cor. IV, 5, 86; Tim. IV, 3, 504. *it has an elder sister, or I m. you*, Wint. I, 2, 99. *you m. me*, H4B I, 2, 91; R3 II, 2, 8. *you will m. each other*, H5 III, 2, 146.

5) *to be wrong, to err, to blunder; absol.: oft the eye —s, the brain being troubled*, Ven. 1068; cf. *—ing eyes*, Shr. IV, 5, 45; Tit. V, 2, 66. *yet sinned I not but in —ing*, Ado V, 1, 284. *thou hast —n quite*, Mids. III, 2, 88; 345; 347. *the blind woman doth most m. in her gifts to women*, As I, 2, 38. *m. no more*, Shr. IV, 2, 16. *you m., sir*, V, 1, 82; Tw. I, 3, 59; III, 4, 247. *you, my lord, do but m.* Wint. II, 1, 81; 100. *if I m. in those foundations*, 100. *to m. again*, John III, 1, 274. *if I m. not*, H4A V, 4, 59. *for thy —ing so, we pardon thee*, H6B V, 1, 128. 129. *this dagger has mista'en*, Rom. V, 3, 203. — Trans., *to m. something,* = *to fail in, to err in, to be wrong with regard to sth.: to make the cunning hounds m. their smell*, Ven. 686. *thy false dart —s that aim and cleaves an infant's heart*, 942. *thy wretched wife mistook the matter so*, Lucr. 1826. *no marvel then though I m. my view*, Sonn. 148, 11. *this letter is mistook*, LLL IV, 1, 57 (=delivered into wrong hands). *thou hast —n his letter*, 108. *our sport shall be to take what they m.* Mids. V, 90. *you m. the matter*, R3 I, 3, 62. *what's he that hath so much thy place mistook to set thee here*, Lr. II, 4, 12. *you do m. your business*, Ant. II, 2, 45.

Reflexively: *had he mistook him and sent to me, I should ne'er have denied his occasion so many talents*, Tim. III, 3, 25 (= had he sent to me by mistake).

To be mistaken or *mistook* = *to be in an error, to be wrong: how am I mistook in you*, Wiv. III, 3, 111. *she, mistaken, seems to dote on me*, Tw. II, 2, 36. *you have been mistook*, V, 266. *you are too much mistaken in this king*, H5 II, 4, 30. *else you may be marvellously mistook*, III, 6, 85. *pardon me, if I be mistaken*, Lr. I, 4, 70. *you are mistaken*, Cymb. I, 4, 89.

Mistaking, subst. mistake, error, blunder: *made thee no —s*, Tp. I, 2, 248. *either this is envy in you, folly, or m.* Meas. III, 2, 150. *pardon for my mad m.* Shr. IV, 5, 49.

Mistempered, 1) compounded and hardened to an ill end: *throw your m. weapons to the ground*, Rom. I, 1, 94 (cf. *Temper*, subst. and vb.).

2) ill tempered, ill mixed, diseased, irritated (quibbling): *this inundation of m. humour rests by you only to be qualified*, John V, 1, 12.

Mistermed, called by a wrong name: *then banished, is death m.* Rom. III, 3, 21.

Mistership, corrupted from *mistressship* in Tit. IV, 4, 40.

Mistful, clouded, half blinded by tears: *I must perforce compound with m. eyes*, H5 IV, 6, 34.

Misthink, to misjudge: *how will the country m. the king*, H6C II, 5, 108. *we are misthought for things that others do*, Ant. V, 2, 176.

Mistletoe, the plant Viscum album: Tit. II, 3, 95.

Mist-like, like a mist, like a cloud: *unless the breath of heart-sick groans m. infold me from the search of eyes*, Rom. III, 3, 73.

Mistreadings, sins: *to punish my m.* H4A III, 2, 11.

Mistress, 1) a woman who has command and governs; opposed to servant: *I am the m. of my fate*, Lucr. 1069. *nature, sovereign m. over wrack*, Sonn. 126, 5. *m. of his heart*, Compl. 142; Shr. IV, 2, 10. *m. of the feast*, Wint. IV, 3, 42. IV, 4, 68. *m. of the field*, H8 III, 1, 152. *the m. of our charms*, Mcb. III, 5, 6. *m. of her choice*, Hml. III, 2, 68. *opinion, a sovereign m. of effects*, Oth. I, 3, 225. *O sovereign m. of true melancholy*, Ant. IV, 9, 12. *the m. which I serve*, Tp. III, 1, 6; Merch. III, 2, 200. *my m.* Tp. II, 2, 144. III, 1, 11. 21. 33. 86. Gent. IV, 4, 175. Err. I, 2, 46. Mids. II, 1, 59. III, 2, 6. LLL IV, 3, 230. *humbly called m.* All's V, 3, 19. *as full of quarrel and offence as my young —'dog*, Oth. II, 3, 53. *too low a m. for so high a servant*, Gent. II, 4, 106 etc. Used in adressing women: Gent. II, 1, 102. II, 4, 2. Err. IV, 2, 46 etc. etc. Adjectively: *the m. court of mighty Europe*, H5 II, 4, 133.

2) a female owner: *I'll use thee* (a picture) *kindly for thy —' sake*, Gent. IV, 4, 207. *more mirth than I am m. of*, As I, 2, 4. *more than m. of which comes to me in name of fault, I must not at all acknowledge*, Wint. III, 2, 60.

3) a woman beloved and courted: *my —' brows are raven black*, Sonn. 127, 9. 130, 1. *metamorphosed with a m.* Gent. II, 1, 32. *be not like your m.* 181. II, 4, 88. Err. II, 2, 113. LLL IV, 3, 270. 376. As I, 2, 257. II, 4, 38. Tw. II, 3, 40. H6B IV, 1, 143. Cor. IV, 5, 207 etc. etc.

4) a female teacher: *the art and practic part of life must be the m. to this theoric*, H5 I, 1, 52. *here she comes weeping for her only —' death*, Per. IV, 1, 11.*And = a woman well skilled in a thing: *she seems a m. to most that teach*, Wint. IV, 4, 593.

5) = lady: *from my two —es*, Wiv. III, 4, 115. *to meet some m. fine, when —es from common sense are hid*, LLL I, 1, 63. 64. *in praise of our country —es*, Cymb. I, 4, 62. = partner: *Mopsa must be your m.* Wint. IV, 4, 162.

6) a term of courtesy used in speaking of or to women (except those of high rank), indiscriminately whether they are married or not (comprising the modern Madam, Mrs., and Miss): Wiv. I, 1, 200. IV, 2, 138. Mids. I, 2, 106. III, 1, 145. Oth. II, 1, 97. IV, 1, 261. IV, 2, 27. V, 2, 183 etc. etc. Wiv. V, 5, 230. Meas. V, 282. Err. III, 2, 29. IV, 3, 81. LLL V, 2, 286 (*madam, and pretty —es; i. e. the princess and*

her attendants). 847. Mids. III, 2, 339. Merch. II, 5, 40. As I, 3, 43. III, 4, 50. Shr. III, 2, 245. Rom. I, 5, 20. IV, 5, 1. Hml. II, 2, 444 etc. etc. Before names: Wiv. I, 1, 85. 198. 199. I, 2, 3. IV, 2, 135. Meas. II, 1, 85. H4A III, 3, 106. H4B II, 2, 166. R3 I, 1, 73 etc. Gent. IV, 4, 8. 49. Wiv. I, 1, 48. 58. 197. 231. 268. Meas. III, 2, 211. Err. IV, 3, 49. Ado V, 2, 1. H4B II, 2, 167 etc. Before appellatives: *m. line*, Tp. IV, 235. *m. bride*, Shr. V, 2, 42. *m. minion*, Rom. III, 5, 152. Costard and Touchstone improperly addressing so princesses: LLL IV, 1, 49. As I, 2, 60. Thersites called in contempt *M. T.*: Troil. II, 1, 39.

Used with some unkindness or contempt of or to women, from whom the affections of the speaker have been estranged: *I suspect without cause, m., do I?* Wiv. IV, 2, 138. *now, m., how chance you went not with Master Slender?* V, 5, 230. *you, m., all this coil is 'long of you*, Mids. III, 2, 339. *m., dispatch you*, As I, 3, 43. *no, proud m., hope not after it*, III, 5, 45. *m., how mean you that?* Shr. V, 2, 21. *and my young m. thus I did bespeak*, Hml. II, 2, 140. *come hither, gentle m.* Oth. I, 3, 178. IV, 1, 261. IV, 2, 27. V, 2, 183. *'tis well, m.* Per. II, 5, 18. 73.

7) "the small ball at the game of bowls, now called the Jack, at which the players aim" (Nares): *so, so, rub on, and kiss the m.* Troil. III, 2, 52.

Once not inflected in the plural: *supposed them m. of his heart*, Compl. 142.

Mistressship, a term of courtesy in addressing women, corrupted to *mistership* by the clown: Tit. IV, 4, 40.

Mistrust, subst. 1) want of confidence: *your m. cannot make me a traitor*, As I, 3, 58. *he needs not our m., since he delivers our offices*, Mcb. III, 2, 2.

2) suspicion, apprehension, doubt: *full of foul hope and full of fond m.* Lucr. 284. *his kindled duty kindled her m.* 1352. *that ugly treason of m., which makes me fear the enjoying of my hope*, Merch. III, 2, 28. *we have but trivial argument, more than m., that shows him worthy death*, H6B III, 1, 242. *when care, m. and treason waits on him*, H6C II, 5, 54. With *of,* = doubt of: *m. of my success hath done this deed*, Caes. V, 3, 65. 66.

Mistrust, vb. 1) not to confide in, to be suspicious of: *I will never m. my wife again*, Wiv. V, 5, 141. *to m. any*, Ado I, 1, 246. *m. me not*, R3 IV, 4, 479. *—ing them*, 528. *to have —ed her*, Cymb. V, 5, 66. Absol.: *in time I may believe, yet I m.* Shr. III, 1, 51.

2) to suspect, to apprehend: *this is an accident of hourly proof, which I —ed not*, Ado II, 1, 189. *m. it not*, Shr. III, 1, 52 (= do not doubt it). *all's true that is —ed*, Wint. II, 1, 48. *many a thousand, which now m. no parcel of my fear*, H6C V, 6, 38. *men's minds m. ensuing dangers*, R3 II, 3, 42. With a clause: *jealousy itself could not m. false-creeping craft and perjury should thrust into so bright a day such black-faced storms*, Lucr. 1516. Absol.: *it shall not fear where it should most m.* Ven. 1154. *they had no cause to m.* R3 III, 2, 87.

Mistrustful, 1) wanting confidence, suspicious: *I hold it cowardice to rest m. where a noble heart hath pawned an open hand in sign of love*, H6C IV, 2, 8.

2) easily begetting suspicion and apprehension: *their light blown out in some m. wood*, Ven. 826.

Misty, overspread with mist; cloudy: *m. vapours when they blot the sky*, Ven. 184. Lucr. 782. *m. night covers the shame*, 356. *from their m. jaws breathe foul contagious darkness*, H6B IV, 1, 6. *Cocytus' m. mouth*, Tit. II, 3, 236. *m. vale*, V, 2, 36. *on the m. mountain tops*, Rom. III, 5, 10.

Misuse, subst. 1) ill treatment: *upon whose dead corpse there was such m. . . . by those Welshwomen done*, H4A I, 1, 43.

2) offence: *how have I been behaved, that he might stick the smallest opinion on my least m.?* Oth. IV, 2, 109 (Q1 *abuse*).

Misuse, vb. 1) to employ ill, to use to a wrong and bad purpose: *I have —d the king's press damnably*, H4A IV, 2, 13. *m. the tenour of thy kinsman's trust*, V, 5, 5. *he —s thy favours*, H4B II, 2, 138. *you m. the reverence of your place*, IV, 2, 23. *thyself thyself —st*, R3 IV, 4, 376 (Ff *thy self is self-misused*). *swear not by time to come, for that thou hast —d ere used, by time —d* (Ff *times ill-used*) *o'erpast*, 396.

2) to treat ill: *we cannot m. him enough*, Wiv. IV, 2, 105.

3) to speak falsely of, to misrepresent: *all my vows are oaths but to m. thee*, Sonn. 152, 7.

4) to speak ill of, to revile: *O, she —d me past the endurance of a block*, Ado II, 1, 246. *you have simply —d our sex in your love-prate*, As IV, 1, 205. *with twenty such vile terms, as had she studied to m. me so*, Shr. II, 160.

5) to deceive: *proof enough to m. the prince*, Ado II, 2, 28.

Mite, a small insect (Acarus) found in cheese: *virginity breeds —s, much like a cheese*, All's I, 1, 154. Used for any thing very small: *losing a m., a mountain gain*, Per. II Prol. 8.

Mithridates, king of Comagene: Ant. III, 6, 73.

Mitigate, 1) to soften, to make less severe: *I have spoke thus much to m. the justice of thy plea*, Merch. IV, 1, 203. *to m. the scorn*, R3 III, 1, 133.

2) to appease: *m. this strife*, H6A III, 1, 88.

Mitigation, alleviation, abatement of any thing painful and afflictive: *ye squeak out your coziers' catches without any m. or remorse of voice*, Tw. II, 3, 98. *how now for m. of this bill*, H5 I, 1, 70. — Lucio calls the bawd *Madam M.* Meas. I, 2, 45.

Mitylene, see *Mytilene*.

Mix, 1) to join and blend into one mass, to mingle: *were never four such lamps* (viz eyes) *together —ed*, Ven. 489. *her modest eloquence with sighs is —ed*, Lucr. 563. *take thou my oblation, poor but free, which is not —ed with seconds*, Sonn. 125, 11 (cf. *Second*). *solace —ed with sorrow*, Pilgr. 203. *you m. your sadness with some fear*, H4B V, 2, 46. *by fair persuasions — ed with sugared words*, H6A III, 3, 18. *this goodly summer with your winter —ed*, Tit. V, 2, 172. *the elements so —ed in him*, Caes. V, 5, 74. *matter and impertinency —ed*, Lr. IV, 6, 178.

2) to produce by mingling, by joining different ingredients: *a little riper and more lusty red than that —ed in his cheek*, As III, 5, 122. *hadst thou no poison —ed*, Rom. III, 3, 44.

Mixture, 1) a state of being mixed and confounded: *when the planets in evil m. to disorder wander*, Troil. I, 3, 95.

2) a powerful liquid composed of different ingredients: *if this m. do not work*, Rom. IV, 3, 21.

thou m. rank, Hml. III, 2, 268. *—s powerful o'er the blood*, Oth. I, 3, 104.

Mo or **Moe**, **more** (plurally): *the private pleasure of some one become the public plague of many moe*, Lucr. 1479. *in me moe woes than words are now depending*, 1615 (the later Qq *more*). *found yet moe letters sadly penned in blood*, Compl. 47. *in moe pleasures to bestow them*, 139. *in this life lie hid moe thousand deaths*, Meas. III, 1, 40. *sing no more ditties, sing no mo*, Ado II, 3, 72. *but two years mo*, Merch. I, 1, 108. *mar no mo of my verses*, As III, 2, 278. *many thousands moe*, Wint. I, 2, 8. *moe ballads*, IV, 4, 278. *I am past moe children*, V, 2, 137 (the later Ff *more*). *many moe with me*, John V, 4, 17 (F4 *more*). *many moe of noble blood*, R2 II, 1, 239. *many moe corrivals*, H4A IV, 4, 31. *many moe proud birds*, H6C II, 1, 170. *I have no moe sons*, R3 IV, 4, 199 (reading of Q1; the rest *more*). *with many moe confederates*, 504. *many moe of noble fame*, IV, 5, 13. (Ff. *other*). *moe thousands*, H8 II, 3, 97. *moe new disgraces*, III, 2, 5. *moe preferments*, V, 1, 36. *moe voices*, Cor. II, 3, 132. *moe noble blows*, IV, 2, 21 (the later Ff *more*). *mo suns than one*, Tit. V, 3, 17 (Ff *more*). *mo days*, Rom. III, 1, 124 (Q1 *more*). *look, moe*, Tim. I, 1, 41. *twenty moe*, II, 1, 7. *with two stones moe than's artificial one*, II, 2, 117 (later Ff *more*). *moe things like men*, IV, 3, 398. *he slays moe than you rob*, 436. *send out moe horses*, Mcb. V, 3, 35 (later Ff *more*). *there are moe with him*, Caes. II, 1, 72. *mo tears*, V, 3, 101. *if I court mo women, you'll couch with mo men*, Oth. IV, 3, 57. *there is no mo such Caesars*, Cymb. III, 1, 36 (later Ff *more*). *mo kings*, 64. *moe ministers*, V, 3, 72 (later Ff *more*). *a million moe*, Ant. IV, 14, 18 etc.

Moan, subst. lamentation: Lucr. 1363. Sonn. 44, 12. 71, 13. 149, 8. Pilgr. 295. 379. Ado V, 3, 16. H6A II, 3, 44. H6C V, 4, 10. R3 IV, 4, 58. Troil. II, 2, 107. Hml. IV, 5, 198. Cymb. IV, 2, 273. Per. IV Prol. 27. *to make m.* Compl. 217. Gent. II, 3, 33. Mids. V, 341. Merch. I, 1, 126. R3 I, 2, 158. *to make m. to* = to complain to: *I oft delivered from his forfeitures many that have at times made m. to me*, Merch. III, 3, 23. Plur. *—s:* Ven. 831. Lucr. 587. 977. 1108. Mids. V, 190. R2 V, 1, 90. R3 II, 2, 80 (Ff *griefs*). Rom. V, 3, 15. Oth. IV, 3, 45.

Passing into the sense of grief, sorrow: (*tears and groans*) *poor wasting monuments of lasting —s*, Lucr. 798. *the sad account of forebemoaned m.* Sonn. 30, 11. *thine being but a moiety of my m.* R3 II, 2, 60 (Qq *grief*). *that bear this mutual heavy load of m.* 113. cf. also Pilgr. 379 and Cymb. IV, 2, 273.

Moan, vb. to lament: *to make him m.* Lucr. 977. *m. the expense of many a vanished sight*, Sonn. 30, 8. Some M. Edd. *—s* for *means* in Mids. V, 330.

Moat, a ditch round a house for the purpose of defence: *as a m. defensive to a house*, R2 II, 1, 48.

Moated, surrounded with a ditch: *at the m. grange*, Meas. III, 1, 277.

Mobled, probably = having the head wrapped up or muffled: *who had seen the m. queen — The m. queen? — That's good; m. queen is good*, Hml. II, 2, 525—527 (F1 *inobled*).

Mock, subst. ridicule, derision, sneer: Meas. V, 324. LLL V, 2, 140. Wint. II, 1, 14. H5 I, 2, 281. 285. II, 4, 122. 125. Troil. III, 2, 104. IV, 5, 291. Tit. IV, 4, 58. Caes. II, 2, 96. Oth. I, 2, 69. Cymb. V, 4, 195. Plur. *—s:* Ado III, 1, 79. LLL V, 2, 251.

637. 853. As III, 5, 33. H4B III, 1, 51 (O. Edd. *chances*, i. e. *chance's, mocks and changes;* M. Edd. *chances mock*). H5 IV, 7, 52. Oth. V, 2, 151 (*villany hath made —s with thee*).

Mock, vb. 1) intr. to make contemptuous sport: *—ing birds*, Lucr. 1121. *m. not*, Ado I, 1, 287. *some merry —ing lord*, LLL II, 52. V, 2, 59. 139. 256. As III, 2, 226. Shr. V, 2, 132. H5 IV, 5, 5. Troil. IV, 2, 21. 26. Cor. II, 3, 215. Ant. IV, 6, 25. With a clause: *m. not, that I affect the untraded oath*, Troil. IV, 5, 178. With *at:* Lucr. 989. Merch. III, 1, 58. R2 I, 3, 293. III, 3, 171 (Qq *laugh*). H4B IV, 5, 119. H5 III, 5, 28. V, 1, 58. 74. V, 2, 102. H6C V, 4, 57. H8 I, 2, 86. Cor. III, 2, 127.

2) trans. a) to deride, to ridicule, to laugh to scorn: Lucr. 1090. Sonn. 107, 6. Tp. II, 1, 225. III, 2, 34. III, 3, 9. Wiv. III, 2, 49. III, 3, 245. V, 3, 20. 21. Meas. I, 3, 27. I, 4, 38. LLL V, 2, 58. 155. 156. 301. 909. 918. Mids. III, 2, 150. 156. 299. 426. As I, 2, 220. 221. Wint. III, 3, 101. 103. V, 3, 79. John V, 1, 72. R2 II, 1, 85. 87. III, 2, 23. 171. H4B II, 2, 156. V, 2, 90. H5 IV, 3, 92. V, 1, 39. V, 2, 214. H6C I, 4, 90. II, 6, 76. III, 2, 158. R3 I, 4, 33. III, 1, 129. IV, 4, 284. V, 1, 9. H8 II, 1, 101. Troil. I, 3, 146. IV, 2, 38. V, 2, 99. Cor. I, 9, 78. II, 3, 167. 169. III, 1, 42. IV, 6, 104. Tit. III, 1, 239. Tim. IV, 3, 303. Caes. I, 2, 206. Hml. I, 2, 177. V, 1, 211. V, 2, 268. Lr. III, 7, 71. IV, 7, 59. Oth. III, 3, 166 (Hanmer *make*, which may be right).*270. IV, 1, 61. Ant. III, 4, 15. V, 2, 288. Cymb. I, 6, 76. Per. V, 1, 143. 164. Followed by *with*, to note the cause of derision: *m. you with me, after I am gone*, Sonn. 71, 14. *m. us with our bareness*, All's IV, 2, 20. Followed by a prepositional expression, to denote an effect: *m. him home to Windsor*, Wiv. IV, 4, 64. *she would m. me into air*, Ado III, 1, 75. *she — s all her wooers out of suit*, II, 1, 364. *m. the good housewife Fortune from her wheel*, As I, 2, 33. *many widows shall this mock m. out of their dear husbands*, *m. mothers from their sons, m. castles down*, H5 I, 2, 285. 286.

b) to set at nought: *m. the lion when he roars for prey*, Merch. II, 1, 30. *such a headstrong potent fault it is that it but —s reproof*, Tw. III, 4, 225. *the surfeited grooms do m. their charge with snores*, Mcb. II, 2, 6. *let's m. the midnight bell*, Ant. III, 13, 185. cf. *to m. at:* R2 I, 3, 293. H4B IV, 5, 119. Cor. III, 2, 127.

c) to illude, to deceive, to beguile, to tantalize: *to m. the subtle in themselves beguiled*, Lucr. 957. *the scalps of many, almost hid behind, to jump up higher seemed, to m. the mind*, 1414. *shadows like to thee do m. my sight*, Sonn. 61, 4. *you will not m. me with a husband*, Meas. V, 422. 423. *their several counsels they unbosom shall to loves mistook, and so be —ed withal*, LLL V, 2, 142. *who would be so —ed with glory!* Tim. IV, 2, 33. *we are —ed with art*, Wint. V, 3, 68. *to m. the expectation of the world*, H4B V, 2, 126. *—ing him about the marriage*, H6C IV, 1, 30. *a mother only —ed with two sweet babes*, R3 IV, 4, 87. *how my achievements m. me*, Troil. IV, 2, 71. *I'll trust, by leisure, him that —s me once*, Tit. I, 301. *the babbling echo —s the hounds, replying shrilly to the well-tuned horns*, II, 3, 17. *m. the time with fairest show*, Mcb. I, 7, 81. *m. our eyes with air*, Ant. IV, 14, 7. *that villain hath —ed me*, Cymb. IV, 2, 63. *with marriage wherefore was he —ed*, V, 4, 58. *this is the* *rarest dream that e'er dull sleep did m. sad fools withal*, Per. V, 1, 164.

d) to mimic: *to see the life as lively —ed as ever still sleep —ed death*, Wint. V, 3, 19. 20. *another shall as loud as thine rattle the welkin's ear and m. the deep-mouthed thunder*, John V, 2, 173. *it is a pretty —ing of the life*, Tim. I, 1, 35.

e) to pretend or feign in a delusive manner: *for —ing marriage with a dame of France*, H6C III, 3, 255. *he —s the pauses that he makes*, Ant. V, 1, 2.

Mockable, ridiculous: *the behaviour of the country is most m. at the court*, As III, 2, 49.

Mocker, 1) scoffer: LLL V, 2, 552. Mids. III, 2, 168. Merch. I, 2, 62. Cor. II, 1, 93. Rom. II, 4, 223.

2) one who illudes and disappoints; with *of: if thou diest before I come, thou art a m. of my labour*, As II, 6, 13.

Mockery, 1) derision, ridicule: *on Hiems' crown an odorous chaplet ... is, as in m., set*, Mids. II, 1, 111. *this keen m.* II, 2, 123. *observe him, for the love of m.* Tw. II, 5, 22. *revenge on Edward's m.* H6C III, 3, 265. *was not this m.?* Cor. II, 3, 181. Plur. *—ies:* Wiv. III, 3, 260 (Evans' speech).

2) subject of laughter and derision: *what m. will it be to want the bridegroom*, Shr. III, 2, 4. *what a m. should it be to swear*, John III, 1, 285. *to hang like a rusty mail in monumental m.* Troil. III, 3, 153. *patience her injury a m. makes*, Oth. I, 3, 207. *will you rhyme upon't and vent it for a m.?* Cymb. V, 3, 56.

3) mimickry, counterfeit appearance, empty imitation: *a m. king of snow*, R2 IV, 260. *minding true things by what their —ies be*, H5 IV Chor. 53. *to trust the m. of unquiet slumbers*, R3 III, 2, 27. *unreal m., hence!* Mcb. III, 4, 107. *our vain blows are malicious m.* Hml. I, 1, 146 (a mere semblance of malice, i. e. of injury done).

Mock-water, "a jocular term of reproach used by the Host, in Wiv. II, 3, 60, to the French Doctor Caius. Considering the profession of the doctor, and the coarseness of the host, there can be no doubt, I think, that he means to allude to the mockery of judging of diseases by the water or urine, which was the practice of all doctors, regular and irregular, at that time, and the subject of much, not ill-placed, jocularity. Mock-water must mean, therefore, 'you pretending water-doctor.' A very few speeches before the same speaker calls Dr. Caius *King Urinal*, and, twice in the following scene, Sir Hugh threatens to *knock his urinals about his costard.*" Nares.

Mode, manner of being: *now my death changes the m.* H4B IV, 5, 200.

Model (cf. *Module*), 1) outline, pattern of something to be made, representation in little: *will it serve for any m. to build mischief on?* Ado I, 3, 48. *when we mean to build, we first survey the plot, then draw the m.* H4B I, 3, 42. *draw anew the m. in fewer offices*, 46. *the plot of situation and the m.* 51. *I'll draw the form and m. of our battle*, R3 V, 3, 24.

2) any thing shaped in imitation of something greater, a copy, image: *thy brother, who was the m. of thy father's life*, R2 I, 2, 28; cf. *the m. of our chaste love, his young daughter*, H8 IV, 2, 132; *princes are a m., which heaven makes like to itself*, Per. II, 2, 11. *that small m. of the barren earth which serves as paste and cover to our bones*, R2 III, 2, 153 (the grave,

which, to the dead, represents the whole earth. "According to Malone, the king means to say that the earth placed upon the body assumes its form; according to Douce, model seems to mean in this place a measure, portion, or quantity." Dyce. cf. besides *mould* in Edward III, A. V, Sc. 3: *the pillars of his herse shall be their bones; the mould that covers him, their cities' ashes*). *showing, as in a m., our firm estate*, R2 III, 4, 42. *thou, the m. where old Troy did stand*, V, 1, 11. *O England, m. to thy inward greatness, like little body with a mighty heart*, H5 II Chor. 16.*my father's signet, which was the m. of that Danish seal*, Hml. V, 2, 50.

Modena, (O. Edd. *Medena*), town in Italy: Ant. I, 4, 57.

Moderate, adj. temperate, not excessive, holding the mean: *O love, be m.* Merch. III, 2, 112. *m. lamentation*, All's I, 1, 64. *on a m. pace*, Tw. II, 2, 3. *be m.* Troil. IV, 4, 1. *a m. table*, Tim. III, 4, 117. *with m. haste*, Hml. I, 2, 238.

Moderate, vb. to restrain from excess, to temper: *how can I m. it* (my grief)? Troil. IV, 4, 5.

Moderately, in a middle degree, not excessively: *to laugh m.* LLL I, 1, 200. *love m.* Rom. II, 6, 14.

Moderation, forbearance of excess, equanimity: Troil. IV, 4, 2.

Modern, commonplace, common, trite: *how far a m. quill doth come too short, speaking of worth, what worth in you doth grow*, Sonn. 83, 7. *full of wise saws and m. instances*, As II, 7, 156. *betray themselves to every m. censure*, IV, 1, 7. *we have our philosophical persons, to make m. and familiar, things supernatural and causeless*, All's II, 3, 2. *her infinite cunning, with her m. grace, subdued me to her rate*, V, 3, 216.*that fell anatomy which cannot hear a lady's feeble voice, which scorns a m. invocation*, John III, 4, 42. *which m. lamentation might have moved*, Rom. III, 2, 120. *where violent sorrow seems a m. ecstasy*, Mcb. IV, 3, 170. *these thin habits and poor likelihoods of m. seeming*, Oth. I, 3, 109. *immoment toys, things of such dignity as we greet m. friends withal*, Ant. V, 2, 167.

Modest, 1) keeping just measure and proportion, acting with moderation: *sometime he trots, as if he told the steps, with gentle majesty and m. pride*, Ven. 278. *joy could not show itself m. enough without a badge of bitterness*, Ado I, 1, 22. *this is called the quip m.* As V, 4, 79. *you must confine yourself within the m. limits of order*, Tw. I, 3, 9. *I call thee by the most m. terms*, IV, 2, 36. *how m. in exception, and withal how terrible in constant resolution*, H5 II, 4, 34. *I could say more, but reverence to your calling makes me m.* H8 V, 3, 69. *the wound of peace is surety, surety secure; but m. doubt is called the beacon of the wise*, Troil. II, 2, 15 (i. e. moderate, sober apprehension); cf. *m. wisdom plucks me from over-credulous haste*, Mcb. IV, 3, 119 (= sober). *do not cry havoc, where you should but hunt with m. warrant*, Cor. III, 1, 276.

2) filling up the measure, neither going beyond nor falling short of what is required, corresponding, satisfactory, becoming: *give me m. assurance if you be the lady of the house*, Tw. I, 5, 192. *garnished and decked in m. complement*, H5 II, 2, 134. *resolve me with all m. haste*, Lr. II, 4, 25 (as much haste as may consist with telling the full truth). *all my reports go with the m. truth; nor more, nor clipped, but so*, IV, 7, 5.

3) not full of pretensions, not arrogant, unassu-

ming: *to silence that, which, to the spire and top of praises vouched, would seem but m.* Cor. I, 9, 25. *too m. are you,* 53. *further to boast were neither true nor m.* Cymb. V, 5, 18.

4) not bold or impudent, full of decency and propriety: *their* (the colts') *savage eyes turned to a m. gaze,* Merch. V, 78. *his will hath in it a more m. working* (than to lie with his mother earth) As I, 2, 215. *all are banished till their conversations appear more wise and m. to the world,* H4B V, 5, 107. *in peace there's nothing so becomes a man as m. stillness and humility,* H5 III, 1, 4. *bids them good morrow with a m. smile,* IV Chor. 33. *O, sir, I can be m.* Per. IV, 6, 41. *thou lookest m. as Justice,* V, 1, 122. Particularly, in speaking of women, = full of the decent and bashful reserve bespeaking a chaste mind: *m. Dian,* Ven. 725. *m. Lucrece,* Lucr. 123. *love's m. snow-white weed,* 196. *O m. wantons,* 401. *her m. eloquence,* 563. *m. eyes,* 683. *a civil m. wife,* Wiv. II, 2, 101. IV, 2, 136. *is she not a m. young lady?* Ado I, 1, 166. *I will do any m. office, to help my cousin to a good husband,* II, 1, 390. *comes not that blood as m. evidence to witness simple virtue?* IV, 1, 38. *this young m. girl,* Shr. I, 1, 161. II, 295. *humbly entreating from your royal thoughts a m. one,* All's II, 1, 131 (one acknowledging that I am m.).*H6C IV, 8, 21. H8 IV, 1, 82. IV, 2, 135. Troil. I, 3, 229. Cor. I, 1, 261. Oth. II, 3, 25. Ant. IV, 15, 27.

Modestly, 1) in the right measure, neither with exaggeration nor with extenuation: *I, your glass, will m. discover to yourself that of yourself which you yet know not of,* Caes. I, 2, 69.

2) without presumption: *I could wish he would m. examine himself, to see how much he is unworthy so good a lady,* Ado II, 3, 216. *I never in my life did hear a challenge urged more m.* H4A V, 2, 53. *there they stand yet, and m. I think, the fall of every Phrygian stone will cost a drop of Grecian blood,* Troil. IV, 5, 222.

3) with the decent reserve becoming a woman: *she m. prepares to let them know,* Lucr. 1607. *words sweetly placed and m. directed,* H6A V, 3, 179.

Modesty, 1) moderation, freedom from any exaggeration or excess: *it will be pastime passing excellent, if it be husbanded with m.* Shr. Ind. I, 68. *I am doubtful of your —ies,* 94. *deliver this with m. to the queen,* H8 II, 2, 137. *whom I most hated living, thou hast made me, with thy religious truth and m., now in his ashes honour,* IV, 2, 74. *win straying souls with m. again,* V, 3, 64. *the enemies of Caesar shall say this: then, in a friend, it is cold m.* Caes. III, 1, 213. *an excellent play, set down with as much m. as cunning,* Hml. II, 2, 461; cf. *o'erstep not the m. of nature,* III, 2, 21. *but to follow him thither with m. enough and likelihood to lead it,* V, 1, 230 (without exaggeration, which would impair the probability).

2) freedom from arrogance or obtrusive impudence: *I have laboured for the poor gentleman to the extremest shore of my m.* Meas. III, 2, 266. *in the m. of fearful duty I read as much as from the rattling tongue ...,* Mids. V, 101. *what man wanted the m. to urge the thing held as a ceremony,* Merch. V, 205. *for then we wound our m. and make foul the clearness of our deservings, when of ourselves we publish them,* All's I, 3, 6. *I perceive in you so excellent a touch of m. that you will not extort from me what I am willing to keep*

in, Tw. II, 1, 13. *with m. admiring thy renown,* H6A II, 2, 39 (= with becoming humility). *I have told more of you to myself than you can in m. speak in your own behalf,* Tim. I, 2, 97. *what gift beside thy m. can beg,* Ant. II, 5, 72.

4) sense of decency and propriety; bashful reserve: *to allay with some cold drops of m. thy skipping spirit,* Merch. II, 2, 195. *and tell me, in the m. of honour, why you have given me such clear lights of favour,* Tw. V, 343. *the sobriety of it* (war), *and the m. of it,* H5 IV, 1, 75 (Fluellen's speech). *there is a kind of confession in your looks which your —ies have not craft enough to colour,* Hml. II, 2, 289. *would to cinders burn up m.* Oth. IV, 2, 75. Especially used of the chaste demeanour of women: *O modest wantons, wanton m.* Lucr. 401. *with soft-slow tongue, true mark of m.* 1220. *effects of terror and dear m.* Compl. 202. *since maids, in m., say 'no' to that which they would have,* Gent. I, 2, 55. *and she, in m., could not again reply,* II, 1, 171. *it is the lesser blot, m. finds, women to change their shapes than men their minds,* V, 4, 108. Wiv. II, 1, 58. III, 2, 42. Meas. II, 2, 169. Err. III, 1, 90. V, 59. Ado IV, 1, 43. 181. Mids. I, 1, 60. II, 1, 214. II, 2, 57. III, 2, 285. As III, 2, 156. Shr. I, 2, 255. II, 49. H5 V, 2, 324. H6C III, 2, 84. Rom. III, 2, 16. III, 3, 38. IV, 2, 27. Hml. III, 4, 41. Ant. II, 2, 246. Cymb. III, 4, 155. Quite = chastity: *cold m., hot wrath, both fire from hence and chill extincture hath,* Compl. 293. *though there were no further danger known but the m. which is so lost,* All's III, 5, 30. cf. the oath *by my m.:* Tp. III, 1, 53. Gent. I, 2, 41.

Modicum, small quantity, pittance: *what —s of wit he utters,* Troil. II, 1, 74.

Modo, name of a fiend: Lr. III, 4, 149. IV, 1, 63.*

Module (cf. *Model*) empty representation, delusive image: *bring forth this counterfeit m.* All's IV, 3, 114 (viz seeming a soldier, and being a fool). *and then all this thou seest is but a clod and m. of confounded royalty,* John V, 7, 58.

Moe, see *Mo.*

Moiety, 1) one of two equal parts, a half: All's III, 2, 69. Wint. III, 2, 40. IV, 4, 842. H5 V, 2, 229. R3 I, 2, 250. II, 2, 60. H8 I, 2, 12. Ant. V, 1, 19. Cymb. I, 4, 118.

2) a portion, part in general: *the love I dedicate to your lordship is without end; whereof this pamphlet, without beginning, is but a superfluous m.* Lucr. Dedic. 2. *by their verdict is determined the clear eye's m. and the dear heart's part,* Sonn. 46, 12. *forgive a m. of the principal,* Merch. IV, 1, 26. *a m. of my rest might come to me again,* Wint. II, 3, 8. *my m. equals not one of yours,* H4A III, 1, 96. *pay betimes a m. of that mass of moan to come,* Troil. II, 2, 107. *a m. competent was gaged by our king,* Hml. I, 1, 90. *qualities are so weighed, that curiosity in neither can make choice of either's m.* Lr. I, 1, 7.

Moil, in *Bemoil,* q. v.

Moist, adj. moderately wet, damp: *my smooth m. hand,* Ven. 143. cf. Oth. III, 4, 36. 39. *his* (the lark's) *m. cabinet,* Ven. 854. *m. Hesperus,* All's II, 1, 167; cf. *the m. star* (the moon) Hml. I, 1, 118. *a m. eye* (a sign of old age) H4B I, 2, 203. *m. impediments* (tears) IV, 5, 140. *m. eyes,* H6A I, 1, 49. *the two m. elements* (water and air) Troil. I, 3, 41. *these m. trees,* Tim. IV, 3, 223 (many M. Edd. unnecessarily *mossed*).

Moist, vb. to wet: *write till your ink be dry, and*

with your tears m. it again, Gent. III, 2, 76. *no more the juice of Egypt's grape shall m. this lip*, Ant. V, 2, 285.

Moisten, to wet: *each flower —ed like a melting eye*, Lucr. 1227. *there she shook the holy water from her heavenly eyes, and clamour —ed her*, Lr. IV, 3, 33 (omitted in Ff. Most M. Edd. *and clamour —ed*).

Moisture, humidity: Ven. 64. 542. Compl. 323. H6C II, 1, 79.

Moldwarp, the mole: H4A III, 1, 149.

Mole, the animal Talpa: Tp. IV, 194. Wint. IV, 4, 868. Hml. I, 5, 162. Per. I, 1, 100.

Mole, a spot or mark on the body: Err. III, 2, 147. Mids. V, 418. Tw. V, 249. John III, 1, 47. Hml. I, 4, 24. Cymb. II, 2, 38. II, 4, 135. V, 5, 364.

Molehill, a hillock thrown up by a mole; used of any small hillock: H6C I, 4, 67. II, 5, 14. Cor. V, 3, 30.

Molest, to render uneasy, to trouble: Tp. II, 1, 280. Tit. V, 2, 9.

Molestation, disturbance, trouble: *I never did like m. view on the enchafed flood*, Oth. II, 1, 16.

Mollification, pacification, appeasement: *some m. for your giant*, Tw. I, 5, 218.

Molten, see *Melt.*

Mome, dolt, blockhead: *m., malt-horse, capon, coxcomb, idiot, patch*, Err. III, 1, 32.

Moment, 1) consequence, importance; preceded by of: *towns of any m.* H6A I, 2, 5. *an oath is of no m.* H6C I, 2, 22. *matters of great m.* R3 III, 7, 67. Hml. III, 1, 86. *of some m.* H8 I, 2, 163. *of mighty m.* II, 4, 213. *of more m.* V, 3, 51. *of m.* Oth. III, 4, 138. Cymb. I, 6, 182. Peculiar passage: *I have seen her die twenty times upon far poorer m.* Ant. I, 2, 147 (= a matter of less m.). cf. *Immoment.*

2) an instant: Sonn. 15, 2. Gent. I, 1, 30. Wiv. II, 1, 50. As III, 5, 24. Troil. IV, 5, 168. Mcb. III, 1, 131. IV, 1, 146. Lr. I, 1, 181. Oth. I, 3, 133. *any m. leisure*, Hml. I, 3, 133 (the later Qq and some M. Edd. *moment's*). *at this m.* Tw. III, 4, 260. *at that m.* H5 I, 1, 27. *in the m.* and *in that m.* = at the m.: *the sweets we wish for turn to loathed sours even in the m. that we call them ours*, Lucr. 868. *when in that m. Titania waked*, Mids. III, 2, 33. *in a m.* = a) on the spot, immediately: *which in a m. doth confound and kill all pure effects*, Lucr. 250. As I, 2, 135. John II, 391. H5 III, 3, 33. H6A II, 3, 66. IV, 2, 12. H8 Prol. 29. b) at the same time: *who can be wise, amazed, temperate and furious, loyal and neutral, in a m.?* Mcb. II, 3, 115. *On the m.* = immediately: *the accident which brought me to her eye upon the m. did her force subdue*, Compl. 248. *all those ... on the m. follow his strides*, Tim. I, 1, 79.

Momentany, lasting but a moment, very brief: *making it m. as a sound*, Mids. I, 1, 143 (Ff *momentary*).

Momentary, the same: Lucr. 690. Tp. I, 2, 202. Meas. III, 1, 114. Mids. I, 1, 143 (Qq *momentany*). R3 III, 4, 98. Mcb. III, 4, 55.

Momentary-swift (not hyphened in O. Edd.), passing with the swiftness of an instant: (night) *flies the grasps of love with wings more m. than thought*, Troil. IV, 2, 14.

Monarch, a prince on the throne, a king: Lucr. 611. Sonn. 114, 2. Compl. 41. LLL V, 2, 531. Merch. III, 2, 50. IV, 1, 189. All's I, 1, 118. Wint. IV, 4,

383. John V, 2, 148. H4B IV, 2, 11. H5 Prol. 4. I, 2, 122. II, 2, 25. III, 7, 30. V, 2, 306. H6A V, 3, 6. H6C I, 4, 124. III, 3, 122. H8 V, 3, 164. Rom. III, 2, 94. Caes. III, 1, 272. Hml. II, 2, 270. Oth. IV, 3, 77. Ant. I, 5, 31. II, 7, 120 (*m. of the vine*). Cymb. III, 3, 4. Per. I, 1, 94.

Monarchize, to play the king: *to m., be feared, and kill with looks*, R2 III, 2, 165.

Monarcho, nickname of a crack-brained Italian living in London shortly before the poet's time, who fancied to be the emperor of the world: *this Armado is a Spaniard, that keeps here in court; a phantasime, a m.* LLL IV, 1, 101.

Monarchy, kingdom, empire: Compl. 196. All's II, 1, 14. H5 Prol. 20. II, 4, 73. H6B IV, 10, 21. R3 I, 1, 83. I, 4, 51.

Monastery, a convent: Meas. IV, 2, 217. Merch. III, 4, 31. R3 I, 2, 215. Tit. V, 1, 21.

Monastic, monkish, secluded from society: *to forswear the full stream of the world and to live in a nook merely m.* As III, 2, 441.

Monday, the second day of the week: Ado II, 1, 374. V, 1, 169. H4A I, 2, 39. Rom. III, 4, 18. Hml. II, 2, 406.

Money, metal coined and used as the medium of commerce: Tp. V, 265. Gent. I, 1, 137. II, 1, 31. Wiv. I, 4, 167. II, 1, 198. II, 2, 147. 176. 177. V, 5, 118. Meas. II, 1, 284. Err. I, 2, 8. 54. 78. 105. II, 2, 98. III, 2, 180. Ado V, 1, 319. LLL II, 137. Merch. I, 1, 131. 178. I, 3, 45. III, 5, 28. As II, 4, 13. Shr. IV, 2, 89 etc. etc. *to make m.* = to procure m.: Oth. I, 3, 361. 365. *present m.* and *ready m.* = cash: Err. IV, 1, 34. Meas. IV, 3, 8. *sterling m.* H4B II, 1, 131. *to take eggs for m.* = to be easily duped, Wint. I, 2, 161. *a horn for my m.* = there is nothing like a horn; *a horn is the word*: Ado II, 3, 63. *the wars for my m.* Cor. IV, 5, 248.

Plur. *—s: importune him for my —s*, Tim. II, 1, 16. Used by Evans and Shylock and treated as a sing.: Wiv. I, 1, 52. Merch. I, 3, 109. 117 (Q1 *m.*). 120. 130.

Money-bag, a large purse: Merch. II, 5, 18. Wint. IV, 4, 267.

Moneyed, having money, rich: *the doctor is well m.* Wiv. IV, 4, 88.

'Mong = among, q. v.: *no marrying 'm. his subjects*, Tp. II, 1, 165. *'m. other things I shall digest it*, Merch. III, 5, 94. *'m. boys, grooms and lackeys*, H8 V, 2, 18. *'m. his friends*, Tim. II, 2, 240.

Monger, in *Ballad-monger, Barber-monger, Carpet-monger, Costermonger, Fancy-monger, Fashion-monger, Fish-monger, Flesh-monger, Love-monger, News-monger, Whore-monger*, q. v.

Mongrel, subst. a dog of a mixed breed: *hounds and greyhounds, —s, spaniels, curs*, Mcb. III, 1, 93. *mastiff, greyhound, m. grim*, Lr. III, 6, 71 (Ff *mongrel, grim*; Qq *mongrel, grim-hound*). Term of reproach: *where's that m.?* Lr. I, 4, 53.

Adjectively: *son and heir of a m. bitch*, Lr. II, 2, 24. Twice applied to Ajax by Thersites: Troil. II, 1, 14. V, 4, 14 (perhaps on account of his father being a Greek and his mother a Trojan).

'Mongst = amongst, q. v.: Phoen. 20. Tp. III, 3, 57. Gent. V, 4, 72. Shr. III, 97. Wint. II, 3, 106. R2 II, 1, 129. V, 3, 5. H6A I, 4, 50. H6B I, 3, 87. H8 I, 2, 119. V, 2, 24. Troil. II, 2, 19. III, 3, 189. IV, 4, 58. Tit. I, 316. Tim. I, 1, 258. I, 2, 230. III,

3, 21. Oth. II, 3, 61. Cymb. I, 6, 169. III, 6, 75. V, 4, 46.

Monied, see *Moneyed.*

Monk, one of a religious order: John V, 6, 23. 29. H8 I, 1, 221. I, 2, 160. II, 1, 21. III, 1, 23 (*all hoods make not —s;* cf. Meas. V, 263).

Monkey, an animal of the genus Simia: Merch. III, 1, 124. 128. H4B III, 2, 338. Tim. I, 1, 260. Lr. II, 4, 9. Oth. III, 3, 403. IV, 1, 274. Distinguished from the ape: *on meddling m. or on busy ape,* Mids. II, 1, 181. *more new-fangled than an ape, more giddy in my desires than a m.* As IV, 1, 154. *apes and —s,* Cymb. I, 6, 39. Used as a term of reproach: Tp. III, 2, 52. Oth. IV, 1, 131. Of endearment: *God help thee, poor m.* Mcb. IV, 2, 59.

Monmouth, birthplace of Henry V, who therefore bore the name of Henry M. before his accession: H4A V, 2, 50. V, 4, 59. H4B Ind. 29. I, 1, 19. II, 3, 45. H5 IV, 7, 12. 26. 29. 34. 49. H6A II, 5, 23. III, 1, 198. *M. caps:* H5 IV, 7, 104 (the place being formerly famous for the caps made there).

Monopoly, an exclusive privilege of selling something: *if I had a m. out, they would have part on't,* Lr. I, 4, 167.

Monsieur, French address used to gentlemen: *M. Monster,* Tp. III, 2, 21. *the prince and M. Love,* Ado II, 3, 38. *M., fare you well,* LLL II, 196. *a letter from M. Biron,* IV, 1, 53. IV, 2, 133. V, 1, 47. *m. the nice,* V, 2, 325. *M. Le Bon,* Merch. I, 2, 58. *M Le Beau,* As I, 2, 104. 142. 173. 175. *M. Jaques,* II, 5, 10. II, 7, 9. *M. Parolles,* All's I, 1, 201. II, 1, 39. II, 3, 191. II, 5, 36. III, 5, 61. III, 6, 46. 67. IV, 3, 161. *M. Malvolio,* Tw. II, 3, 144. *M. Remorse,* H4A I, 2, 125. *our —s,* H8 I, 3, 21. *M. La Far,* Lr. IV, 3, 9. *an eminent m.* Cymb. I, 6, 65. *M. Veroles,* Per. IV, 2, 115 (cf. *Mounseur* and *Mounsieur*).

Monster, subst. an unnatural and deformed creature: Sonn. 114, 5. Tp. II, 1, 314. II, 2, 31. 67. 94. 102. 148 etc. III, 2, 12. 21 etc. IV, 1, 196. 199 etc. Wiv. III, 2, 82. 93. LLL IV, 2, 24. Mids. II, 2, 97. III, 2, 6. 377. As I, 2, 23. Shr. III, 2, 71. All's V, 3, 155. Tw. II, 2, 35. Wint. IV, 4, 798 (*will break the back of man, the heart of m.*). John II, 293. III, 4, 33. H4B Ind. 18. Troil. III, 2, 81. 96. III, 3, 146. 265. Cor. II, 3, 11. III, 1, 95. Rom. V, 3, 104. Tim. IV, 3, 190. Mcb. V, 8, 25. Hml. III, 1, 144. III, 4, 161. Lr. I, 5, 43. IV, 2, 50. Oth. III, 3, 166. III, 4, 161. IV, 1, 63. 65. Cymb. IV, 2, 35. V, 3, 70. Per. IV Prol. 12. In a moral sense: H5 II, 2, 85. H8 II, 3, 11. Tit. III, 4, 44. Tim. IV, 3, 87. Lr. I, 2, 102. III, 6, 102. Cymb. III, 2, 2. Peculiar passage: *as if there were some m. in his thought too hideous to be shown,* Oth. III, 3, 107 (= something monstrous).

Monster, vb. to make monstrous, to put out of the common order of things: *to hear my nothings — ed,* Cor. II, 2, 81. *her offence must be of such unnatural degree, that —s it,* Lr. I, 1, 223.

Monster-like, like a monster: *most m. be shown for poorest diminutives,* Ant. IV, 12, 36.

Monstrosity, see *Monstruosity.*

Monstrous, 1) unnatural, against the ordinary course of things: *of a m. shape,* Tp. III, 3, 31. *m. to our human reason,* Wint. V, 1, 41. *this ingrateful seat of m. friends,* Tim. IV, 2, 46. (the fault) *is not m. in you,* V, 1, 91. *change their natures to m. quality,* Caes. I, 3, 68. *some m. state,* 71. *m. lust,* Per. V, 3, 86.

2) huge, enormous: *a m. lie,* Tp. III, 2, 32. *every one fault seeming m.* As III, 2, 373. *O m. arrogance,* Shr. IV, 3, 107. *an answer of most m. size,* All's II, 2, 34. *the sheriff with a most m. watch,* H4A II, 4, 530. *a huge half-moon, a m. cantle,* III, 1, 100. *curling their m. heads,* H4B III, 1, 23. *O m. coward,* H6B IV, 7, 88. *O m. fault,* H6C III, 2, 164. *with high and m. mane,* Oth. II, 1, 13. *more m. matter of feast,* Ant. II, 2, 187. *it's m. labour,* II, 7, 105.

3) shocking, horrible: Tp. III, 3, 95. Gent. III, 1, 374. Mids. III, 1, 107. V, 223. Shr. Ind. 1, 34. V, 1, 112. Wint. III, 2, 191. John II, 173. H4A II, 4, 243. 344. 591. H4B IV, 2, 34. H6A IV, 1, 61. H6B III, 3, 30. IV, 2, 94. IV, 10, 71. V, 1, 62. 106. R3 III, 2, 66. III, 4, 72. H8 I, 2, 122. Troil. III, 2, 82. Cor. II, 3, 10. 13. Tit. I, 308. IV, 4, 51. Tim. V, 1, 68. Caes. II, 1, 81. IV, 3, 277. Mcb. III, 6, 8. Lr. I, 1, 220. II, 2, 27. V, 3, 159. Oth. I, 3, 410. II, 3, 217. III, 3, 377. 427. V, 2, 190. Ant. II, 5, 53. In Hml. II, 2, 577: *is it not m. that this player here, but in a fiction, in a dream of passion, could force his soul so to his own conceit,* — it is not this faculty of the player that Hamlet means to call monstrous, but his own lethargy so different from it, which, however, by a kind of logical anacoluthon, he forgets to add.

Used as an adverb: *in a m. little voice,* Mids. I, 2, 54. *skill infinite or m. desperate,* All's II, 1, 187.

Monstrously, shockingly: *which he forswore most m. to have,* Err. V, 11.

Monstrousness, horribleness: *see the m. of man when he looks out in an ungrateful shape,* Tim. III, 2, 79.

Monstruosity (the later Ff *monstrosity*), shocking unnaturalness: *this is the m. in love, that the will is infinite and the execution confined,* Troil. III, 2, 87.

Montacute (O. Edd. *Mountacute*) name in H8 I, 1, 217.*

Montague (O Edd. sometimes *Mountague*) 1) name of Lord Warwick's brother: H6C I, 2, 55. II, 1, 167. III, 3, 164. IV, 1, 27. IV, 8, 14 etc.

2) name in Rom. I, 1, 9 etc. etc.

Montano, name in Oth. I, 3, 39. II, 3, 158. 190. 225.

Montant, an old fencing term, meaning "an upright blow or thrust" (Cotgrave): *to see thee pass thy punto, thy stock, thy reverse, thy distance, thy m.* Wiv. II, 3, 27.

Montanto (O. Edd. *Mountanto*), name given by Beatrice to Benedick, implying him to be a great fencer and bully: Ado I, 1, 30.

Montferrat, marquisate in Italy: Merch. I, 2, 126.

Montgomery (O. Edd. *Mountgomery*), name in H6C IV, 7, 40. 45.

Month (the Saxon gen. and the plur. monosyllabic; but dissyll. in Gent. I, 2, 137 and H6C II, 5, 38) the twelfth part of a year: Lucr. 690. Pilgr. 228. Tp. I, 2, 262. Gent. I, 3, 18. Ado I, 1, 72. 150. LLL I, 1, 304. IV, 2, 36. IV, 3, 102. V, 2, 679. Merch. I, 3, 2. 59. 182. As V, 4, 198. All's IV, 3, 99. H4B IV, 4, 124. H6B I, 3, 225. II, 4, 71. H6C II, 5, 38 etc. etc. *the m. of May,* Pilgr. 374. H4A IV, 1, 101. *this is no m. to bleed,* R2 I, 1, 157 (particular seasons were, in the almanacs of the time, pointed out as the most proper time for being bled. Ff *time*). *you have a —'s mind to them,* Gent. I, 2, 137 (i. e. a woman's longing?).* *two —s:* All's IV, 3, 56. Troil. IV, 10, 53.

Caes. II, 1, 109. Hml. I, 2, 138. III, 2, 138. IV, 7, 82. *twice two —s*, III, 2, 135. *three —s:* Merch. I, 3, 67. Tw. II, 5, 49. V, 97. 102. R2 V, 3, 2. R3 I, 2, 241. *for this three —s*, Per. V, 1, 24. *six —s:* Err. I, 1, 45. All's I, 2, 71. Tim. IV, 3, 143. *at nine —s old:* H6B IV, 9, 4. H6C I, 1, 112. III, 1, 76. R3 II, 3, 17. *my twelve —s are expired*, Per. III, 3, 2. *our purpose now is twelve m. old*, H4A I, 1, 28 (Ff *a twelvemonth*). *some sixteen —s*, Gent. IV, 1, 21. *for eighteen —s*, H6B I, 1, 42.

Monthly, adj. regulated by the duration of a month: *ourself*, *by m. course*, *shall our abode make with you by due turns*, Lr. I, 1, 134.

Monthly, adv. every month: *the moon*, *that m. changes*, Rom. II, 2, 110.

Montjoy, name of the French herald in H5 III, 5, 36. 61. III, 6, 147 etc.

Monument, 1) any thing by which something is remembered; memorial: *mingling my talk with tears*, *my grief with groans*, *poor wasting —s of lasting moans*, Lucr. 798. *if a man do not erect his own tomb ere he dies*, *he shall live no longer in m. than the bell rings and the widow weeps*, Ado V, 2, 81 (he shall leave nothing by which to remember him). *Burgundy enshrines thee in his heart and there erects thy noble deeds as valour's —s*, H6A III, 2, 120. *nor let the rain of heaven wet this place, to wash away my woful monuments* (viz my tears) H6B III, 2, 342. *this m. of the victory will I bear* (a brigandine) IV, 3, 12. *our bruised arms hung up for —s*, R3 I, 1, 6. *O m. and wonder of good deeds evilly bestowed*, Tim. IV, 3, 466.

2) any thing built or erected in memory of actions or persons: *to fill with worm-holes stately —s*, Lucr. 946. *wherefore gaze this goodly company, as if they saw some wondrous m., some comet or unusual prodigy?* Shr. III, 2, 97. *defacing —s of conquered France*, H6B I, 1, 102. Especially a memorial erected over a grave: *not marble, nor the gilded —s of princes shall outlive this powerful rhyme*, Sonn. 55, 1. *the earth can yield me but a common grave; .... your m. shall be my gentle verse*, 81, 9. 107, 13. *this grave shall have a living m.* Hml. V, 1, 320. *let their fathers lie without a m.* Cymb. IV, 2, 227. *for a m. upon thy bones*, Per. III, 1, 62. *her m. is almost finished*, Per. IV, 3, 42.

Allegorical figures a usual ornament of graves: *she sat like Patience on a m., smiling at grief*, Tw. II, 4, 117. Hence *m.* = a human figure, such as were seen on graves: *where like a virtuous m. she lies*, Lucr. 391 (a figure representing some virtue). *for ever be confixed here, a marble m.* Meas. V, 233. *you are no maiden, but a m.* All's IV, 2, 6. *be her sense but as a m., thus in a chapel lying*, Cymb. II, 2, 32.

3) a family-vault: *on your family's old m. hang mournful epitaphs*, Ado IV, 1, 208. *is this the m. of Leonato?* V, 3, 1. *this m. five hundred years hath stood*, Tit. I, 350. *which like a taper in some m., doth shine upon the dead man's earthy cheeks*, II, 3, 228. *in our household's m.* V, 3, 194. *make the bridal bed in that dim m. where Tybalt lies*, Rom. III, 5, 203. *her body sleeps in Capel's m.* V, 1, 18. V, 2, 24. V, 3, 127. 193. 274. *to the m.* Ant. IV, 13, 3. 6. 10. *locked in her m.* IV, 14, 120. IV, 15, 8. V, 1, 53. V, 2, 360.

4) a grave: *goodness and he fill up one m.* H8 II, 1, 94. *our —s shall be the maws of kites*, Mcb. III, 4, 72.

Monumental, 1) memorial: *he hath given her his m. ring*, All's IV, 3, 20. *like a rusty mail in m. mockery*, Troil. III, 3, 153.

2) pertaining to a human figure placed over a grave: *smooth as m. alablaster*, Oth. V, 2, 5.

Mood, 1) any temporary state of the mind with regard to passion or feelings; humour, disposition: *affection sways it* (passion) *to the m. of what it likes or loathes*, Merch. IV, 1, 51. *he must observe their m. on whom he jests*, Tw. III, 1, 69. *Fortune in her shift and change of m.* Tim. I, 1, 84. *Fortune is merry, and in this m. will give us any thing*, Caes. III, 2, 272. *in that m. the dove will peck the estridge*, Ant. III, 13, 196. *Fortune's m. varies again*, Per. III Prol. 46. Defined and restricted, but seldom so as to denote a kind or merry disposition: *who wayward once, his m. with nought agrees*, Lucr. 1095. *my wife is in a wayward m. to-day*, Err. IV, 4, 4. *you spend your passion on a misprised m.* Mids. III, 2, 74. *does show the m. of a much troubled breast*, John IV, 2, 73. *to break into this woman's m.* H4A I, 3, 237. *whom I stabbed in my angry m.* R3 I, 2, 242. *one on's father's —s*, Cor. I, 3, 72. *bring oil to fire, snow to their colder —s*, Lr. II, 2, 83. *when the rash m. is on*, II, 4, 172. *unused to the melting m.* Oth. V, 2, 349.

2) bad humour; either grief, distraction: *it small avails my m.* Lucr. 1273. *she is importunate, indeed distract: her m. will needs be pitied*, Hml. IV, 5, 3. Or anger, wrath: *who, in my m., I stabbed unto the heart*, Gent. IV, 1, 51. *to thwart me in my m.* Err. II, 2, 172. *I am now muddied in Fortune's m.* All's V, 2, 5. *his wraths, and his cholers, and his —s*, H5 IV, 7, 38 (Fluellen's speech). *thou art as hot a Jack in thy m. as any in Italy*, Rom. III, 1, 13. *you are but now cast in his m.* Oth. II, 3, 274.

3) external appearance, countenance expressive of disposition: *grief and blushes, aptly understood in bloodless white and the encrimsoned m.* (of rubies) Compl. 201. *in many's looks the false heart's history is writ in —s and frowns and wrinkles strange*, Sonn. 93, 8. *all forms, —s, shapes of grief*, Hml. I, 2, 82.

Moody, out of humour; 1) sullen, melancholy: *m. Pluto winks while Orpheus plays*, Lucr. 553. *unmask this m. heaviness*, 1602. *m. and dull melancholy*, Err. V, 79. *when after many m. thoughts they quite forget their loss of liberty*, H6C IV, 6, 13. *music, m. food of us that trade in love*, Ant. II, 5, 1.

2) discontented, peevish, angry: *how now, m.?* Tp. I, 2, 244. *majesty might never yet endure the m. frontier of a servant brow*, H4A I, 3, 19. *nor m. beggars, starving for a time of pellmell havoc*, V, 1, 81. *being m., give him line and scope*, H4B IV, 4, 39. *hath banished m. discontented fury*, H6A III, 1, 123. *m. mad and desperate stags*, IV, 2, 50 (most M. Edd. moody-mad). *your m. discontented souls*, R3 V, 1, 7. *he's m.* H8 III, 2, 75. *as soon moved to be m., and as soon m. to be moved*, Rom. III, 1, 14.

Moon (usually fem., f. i. Sonn. 107, 5. Tp. II, 1, 183. II, 2, 143. V, 271. LLL V, 2, 214. Mids. I, 1, 4. II, 1, 103. III, 1, 203. III, 2, 53. Rom. II, 2, 109. Mcb. II, 1, 2. Oth. V, 2, 109. Neuter in Mids. III, 1, 56. Seemingly masc. in Mids. V, 255, but here the person is meant that represents the moon): 1) the satellite which revolves round the earth: Ven. 492. Lucr. 371. 1007. Sonn. 21, 6. LLL IV, 2, 39. IV, 3, 30. 230. V, 2, 203. 205. Mids. I, 1, 9. III, 1, 52. 59.

IV, 1, 103. Merch. V, 1. Shr. IV, 5, 2 sq. Mcb. II, 1, 2. Ant. IV, 9, 7 etc. Plur. —s: John IV, 2, 182. R2 I, 3, 220. Lr. IV, 6, 70. *the full m.* H4B IV, 3, 57. Lr. IV, 6, 70. *the m. at full,* LLL V, 2, 214. *changing:* LLL V, 2, 212. Mids. V, 255. Shr. IV, 5, 20. Rom. II, 2, 110. *waning,* Mids. I, 1, 4. *a new m.* and *another m.* 3. 83. Hence image of change and inconstancy: Meas. III, 1, 25. LLL V, 2, 212. Rom. II, 2, 109. Lr. V, 3, 19. Oth. III, 3, 178. Ant. V, 2, 240. *'tis not that time of m.* with me to make one in so skipping a dialogue, Tw. I, 5, 213 (= I am not in that humour). Moving in a sphere: Tp. II, 1, 183. Mids. II, 1, 7. Having eclipses: Sonn. 107, 5. Mcb. IV, 1, 28. Lr. I, 2, 112. Oth. V, 2, 100. Ant. III, 13, 153. Governing the sea and causing ebb and flow: Tp. V, 270. Mids. II, 1, 103. Wint. I, 2, 427. H4A I, 2, 32. 35. Lr. V, 3, 19. *as true as plantage to the m.* Troil. III, 2, 184. Causing melancholy, and even madness: *O sovereign mistress of true melancholy,* Ant. IV, 9, 12. *she comes more nearer earth and makes men mad,* Oth. V, 2, 109. Conjured: Lr. II, 1, 41. Of a watery nature: Mids. II, 1, 162. III, 1, 203. R3 II, 2, 69. Rom. I, 4, 62. Peculiar theory: *the sea's a thief, whose liquid surge resolves the m. into salt tears,* Tim. IV, 3, 443. Behowled by wolves: Mids. V, 379. As V, 2, 119. Having horns: Mids. V, 243. Mcb. III, 5, 23. Cor. I, 1, 217. Ant. IV, 12, 45. The man in the m.: Tp. II, 1, 249. II, 2, 142. 149. LLL V, 2, 215. Mids. V, 249. 252. 262. With a dog and a bush: Tp. II, 2, 144. *To go by the m.* = to be a night-walker: H4A I, 2, 15; cf. *the —'s men,* 35. *Below,* or *beneath,* or *under the m.* = on the earth, earthly: *his thinkings are below the m.* H8 III, 2, 134. *all simples that have virtue under the m.* Hml. IV, 7, 146. *for all beneath the m.* Lr. IV, 6, 26. *there is nothing left remarkable beneath the visiting m.* Ant. IV, 15, 68. Used to express the idea of extreme height: *the ship boring the m. with her main-mast,* Wint. III, 3, 93. *York that reaches at the m.* H6B III, 1, 158. *scarred the m. with splinters,* Cor. IV, 5, 115. *you are smelt above the m.* V, 1, 32. *I aim a mile beyond the m.* Tit. IV, 3, 65. *I had rather be a dog and bay the m.* Caes. IV, 3, 27. *M. and stars!* Ant. III, 13, 95.

2) a month: *each minute seems a m.* Pilgr. 207. *thirty dozen —s with borrowed sheen about the world have times twelve thirties been,* Hml. III, 2, 167. *till now some nine —s wasted,* Oth. I, 3, 84. *not many — s gone by,* Ant. III, 12, 6. *one twelve —s more she'll wear Diana's livery,* Per. II, 5, 10. *in twice six —s,* III Prol. 13.

3) Dian: *the m. sleeps with Endymion,* Merch. V, 109. *bemock the modest m.* Cor. I, 1, 261. *the m., were she earthly, no nobler,* II, 1, 108. *the noble sister of Publicola, the m. of Rome,* V, 3, 65. *arise, fair sun, and kill the envious m., who is already sick and pale with grief that thou* (Juliet) *her maid art far more fair than she,* Rom. II, 2, 4. Hence the moon cold and chaste: Mids. I, 1, 73. II, 1, 156. 162. And sister of Phoebus: Mids. III, 2, 53.

Moonbeams, rays of lunar light: Mids. III, 1, 176.

Moon-calf, a deformed creature, abortion: Tp. II, 2, 111. 115. 139. III, 2, 24. 25.

Moonish, inconstant, capricious: *at which time would I, being but a m. youth, grieve, be effeminate, changeable, longing and liking,* etc. As III, 2, 430.

Moonlight, the light afforded by the moon: Mids. I, 1, 30. I, 2, 104. II, 1, 60. 141. III, 1, 49. 51. Merch. V, 54. Shr. IV, 5, 3.

Moonshine, the same: Tp. V, 37. Wiv. V, 5, 42. 106. LLL V, 2, 208 (*thou request'st but m. in the water;* i. e. a nothing). Mids. III, 1, 55. 62. V, 137. 138. 151. 318. 355. Rom. I, 4, 62. *I'll make a sop o'the m. of you,* Lr. II, 2, 35 (alluding, perhaps, to the dish called eggs in moonshine, i. e. poached eggs). = month: *for that I am some twelve or fourteen —s lag of a brother,* Lr. I, 2, 5.

Moor, a negro, a negress: *I shall answer that better to the commonwealth than you can the getting up of the negro's belly: the M. is with child by you,* Launcelot. *It is much that the M. should be more than reason,* Merch. III, 5, 42—44 (the same quibbling in Tit. IV, 2, 52). Tit. II, 3, 51. 68. 190. III, 2, 78 etc. etc. Oth. I, 1, 40 etc. etc.

Moor, a fen: *could you on this fair mountain leave to feed, and batten on this m.?* Hml. III, 4, 67.

Moorditch, "a large ditch in Moorfields, through which the waters of that once fenny situation were drained" (Nares): *what sayest thou to a hare, or the melancholy of M.?* H4A I, 2, 88.

Moorfields, a place of resort where the trainbands of the city used to be exercised: *is this M. to muster in?* H8 V, 4, 33.

Moorship, a title given in derision to Othello by Iago: *his —'s ancient,* Oth. I, 1, 33.

Mop, subst. a grimace; joined with *mow: each one, tripping on his toe, will be here with m. and mow,* Tp. IV, 47.

Mop, vb. to make grimaces; joined with *to mow: Flibbertigibbet,* (prince) *of —ing and mowing, who since possesses chambermaids and waiting-women,* Lr. IV, 1, 64.

Mope, to be in a state of unconsciousness, to move and act without the impulse and guidance of thought: *even in a dream were we divided from them and were brought —ing hither,* Tp. V, 240. *what a wretched and peevish fellow is this king of England, to m. with his fat-brained followers so far out of his knowledge,* H5 III, 7, 143. *eyes without feeling, feeling without sight, ears without hands or eyes, smelling sans all, or but a sickly part of one true sense could not so m.* Hml. III, 4, 81.

Mopsa, name of a shepherdess in Wint. IV, 4, 162. 233.

Moral, subst. 1) a truth proposed, a doctrine, a maxim: *the fox, the ape, the humble-bee, were still at odds, being but three. There's the m. Now the l'envoy,* LLL III, 87. 88. 93. *a good m., my lord: it is not enough to speak, but to speak true,* Mids. V, 120. *Fortune is an excellent m.* H5 III, 6, 40 (Fluellen's speech). *thus may we gather honey from the weed, and make a m. of the devil himself,* IV, 1, 12. *this m. ties me over to time and a hot summer,* V, 2, 339. *the m. of my wit is 'plain and true'; there's all the reach of it,* Troil. IV, 4, 109. *a pretty m.* Per. II, 1, 39. II, 2, 45.

2) a latent meaning: *you have some m. in this Benedictus,* Ado III, 4, 78. *to expound the meaning or m. of his signs and tokens,* Shr. IV, 4, 79. *mark, silent king, the m. of this sport,* R2 IV, 290. *she* (Fortune) *is painted also with a wheel, to signify to you, which is the m. of it, that she is turning,* H5 III, 6, 35.

Moral, adj. 1) relating to the principles of good

and evil: *to apply a m. medicine to a mortifying mischief*, Ado I, 3, 13. *I have no m. meaning*, III, 4, 80. *this virtue and this m. discipline*, Shr. I, 1, 30. *thy father's m. parts mayst thou inherit too*, All's I, 2, 21. *unfit to hear m. philosophy*, Troil. II, 2, 167. *these m. laws of nature and of nations*, 184.

2) moralizing, expounding the principles of good and evil: *to be so m. when he shall endure the like himself*, Ado V, 1, 30. *when I did hear the motley fool thus m. on the time*, As II, 7, 29. *whiles thou, a m. fool, sit'st still*, Lr. IV, 2, 58.

3) having a latent meaning: *a thousand m. paintings I can show that shall demonstrate these quick blows of Fortune's*, Tim. I, 1, 90.

Moral, vb. to moralize; perhaps in As II, 7, 29: *when I did hear the motley fool thus m. on the time;* but probably adj.

Moraler, one who moralizes: *you are too severe a m.* Oth. II, 3, 301.

Morality, the doctrine of the duties of life; ethics, philosophy: *I had as lief have the foppery of freedom as the m. of imprisonment*, Meas. I, 2, 138 (O. Edd. *mortality*).

Moralize, 1) to philosophize, to reason: *unlike myself thou hearest me m., applying this to that, and so to so; for love can comment upon every woe*, Ven. 712.

2) to comment upon, to interpret, to explain: *nor could she m. his wanton sight*, Lucr. 104. *did he not m. this spectacle?* As II, 1, 44. *m. them* (his signs and tokens) Shr. IV, 4, 81. *I m. two meanings in one word*, R3 III, 1, 83.

Mordake, name in H4A I, 1, 71. 95. II, 4, 391. IV, 4, 24.*

More, name of the famous lord chancellor of Henry VIII: H8 III, 2, 393.

More, adj. and adv. 1) greater: *her best is bettered with a m. delight*, Ven. 78. *to add a m. rejoicing to the prime*, Lucr. 332. *for m. it is* (my heaviness) *than I can well express*, 1286. *held back his sorrow's tide, to make it m.* 1789. *look for recompense m. than that tongue*, Sonn. 23, 12. *thy* (time's) *records and what we see doth lie, made m. or less by thy continual haste*, 123, 12. *to make thy large Will m.* 135, 12. *thy might is m. than my defence can bide*, 139, 8. *my rejoicing at nothing can be m.* Tp. III, 1, 94. *a thousand m. mischances than this one have learned me how to brook this patiently*, Gent. V, 3, 3. *your mettle is the m.* Meas. III, 2, 80. *if your knowledge be m. it is much darkened in your malice*, 156. *had I m. name for badness*, V, 59. *why should their liberty than ours be m.?* Err. II, 1, 10. *with a m. contempt*, II, 2, 174. *the m. my spite*, IV, 2, 8. *my love is m. than his*, Mids. I, 1, 100. *I desire your m. acquaintance*, III, 1, 200. *the m. my wrong, the m. his spite appears*, Shr. IV, 3, 2. *my reason haply m.* V, 2, 171. *of that and all the progress, m. or less, resolvedly m. leisure shall express*, All's V, 3, 331. *I hold it the m. knavery to conceal it*, Wint. IV, 4, 697. *so much the m. our carver's excellence*, V, 3, 30. *to make a m. requital to your love*, John II, 34. *make less thy body hence, and m. thy grace*, H4B V, 5, 56. *on his m. advice*, H5 II, 2, 43. *a proof of strength she could not publish m.* Troil. V, 2, 113. *for your voices I have done many things, some less, some m.* Cor. II, 3, 137. *it is my m. dishonour*, III, 2, 124. *the m. is my unrest*, Rom. I, 5, 122. *that thy skill be m. to blazon it*, II, 6, 25. *without debate-*

ment further, m. or less, Hml. V, 2, 45. *so tell him, with the occurrents, m. and less, which have solicited*, 368. *priests are m. in word than matter*, Lr. III, 2, 81. *I am no less in blood than thou; if m....* V, 3, 168. *give me a m. content*, Per. III, 2, 39. Substantively: *m. and less* = the great and small, high and low: *both grace and faults are loved of m. and less*, Sonn. 96, 3. *the m. and less came in with cap and knee*, H4A IV, 3, 68. *m. and less do flock to follow him*, H4B I, 1, 209. *both m. and less have given him the revolt*, Mcb. V, 4, 12.

2) a greater thing, a greater quantity, amount, or degree (the Lat. *plus*): *by hoping m. they have but less*, Lucr. 137. *that tongue that m. hath m. expressed*, Sonn. 23, 12. *what hast thou then m. than thou hadst before?* 40, 2. *m. to know did never meddle with my thoughts*, Tp. I, 2, 21. *here have I made thee m. profit than other princess can*, 172. *deserved m. than a prison*, 362. *that's m. to me than my wetting*, IV, 211. *three thousand dollars. Ay, and m.* Meas. I, 2, 51. *he's m.* V, 58. *these informal women are no m. but instruments*, 236. *it is no m., but that your daughter desires this ring*, All's III, 7, 30. *be prosperous in m. than this deed does require*, Wint. II, 3, 190. *I'll make it* (the gold) *as much m.* IV, 4, 838. *shall m. suffer*, Mcb. IV, 3, 48. *did these bones cost no m. the breeding, but to play at loggats with 'em?* Hml. V, 1, 100 etc. etc. *we are betrothed, nay, m., our marriage-hour determined of*, Gent. II, 4, 179. *to admit no traffic to our adverse towns, nay, m., if any....* Err. I, 1, 16 etc. *her m. than haste is mated with delays*, Ven. 909. *with m. than admiration he admired*, Lucr. 418. *at Ardea to my lord with m. than haste*, 1332. *speed m. than speed but dull and slow she deems*, 1336. Adjectively: *m. beauty*, Ven. 70. *m. rage*, 332. *there's m. work*, Tp. I, 2, 238. *is there m. toil?* 242. *at our m. leisure*, Meas. I, 3, 49. *at m. time*, Mcb. I, 3, 153 etc. etc.

3) a greater number (Lat. *plures*): *thou hadst, and m.* (than five women) Tp. I, 2, 48. *m. widows*, II, 1, 133. *nor have I seen m. that I may call men*, III, 1, 51. *here is m. of us*, V, 216. *m. reasons*, Meas. I, 3, 48. *charges she m. than me?* V, 200. *have m. vices*, Mcb. IV, 3, 47 etc.

4) something additional: *all mine was thine before thou hadst this m.* Sonn. 40, 4. *I'll no m. of you*, Tw. I, 5, 45. *we need no m. of your advice*, Wint. II, 1, 168. *what he gets m. of her than sharp words*, Wiv. II, 1, 190. *we have but trivial argument, m. than mistrust, that shows him worthy death*, H6B III, 1, 242. *m., Domitius: my lord desires you*, Ant. III, 5, 21 (German: *noch eins!*). *m. above* = moreover, Hml. II, 2, 126. *no m.* = enough! *no m. of love*, Ven. 185. *peace; no m.* John IV, 1, 127. *silence; no m.* 133. *no m. of stay!* to-morrow thou must go, Gent. I, 3, 75. Adjectively: = further: *no m. amazement*, Tp. I, 2, 14. *here cease m. questions*, 184. *we will not hand a rope m.* I, 1, 25. *there is no m. such shapes*, I, 2, 478. II, 2, 167. 184. *without any m. talking*, 178. *no m. evasion*, Meas. I, 1, 51. *no m. words*, III, 2, 218. *to trouble you with no m. suit*, Merch. I, 2, 112. *it is as easy for me to conquer the kingdom as to speak so much m. French*, H5 V, 2, 196. *I am all these three; and three times as much m.* LLL III, 48. *a French crown m.*, Meas. I, 2, 52 (= besides, moreover). After numerals: *once m.* Ven. 327. 367. Gent. I, 1, 53. II, 4, 118. III, 1, 366. Wiv. III, 5, 47. IV, 2, 172. Meas. I, 1, 73. Merch. II, 7, 36. II, 9, 35. As V, 4, 5. All's IV, 3, 276. Wint. IV, 4, 407.

H5 III, 1, 1. H6C II, 3, 48. R3 III, 7, 91. H8 I, 4, 62. Cor. V, 3, 13. Tim. III, 4, 119. Ant. III, 13, 173 etc. *one word m.* Tp. I, 2, 449. Hml. III, 4, 180. *two things provided m.* Merch. IV, 1, 386. *two or three lords and ladies m.* Mids. IV, 2, 17. *six scotches m.* Ant. IV, 7, 10. *ten m.* Merch. IV, 1, 399. *forty m.* Meas. IV, 3, 20. *a hundred thousand m.* LLL II, 135. *thousands m.* H6B III, 1, 152. *five m. Sir Johns,* H4B II, 4, 6. *let two m. summers wither,* Rom. I, 2, 10 etc. Adverbially, = again, further, in continuance: *what follows m. she murders with a kiss,* Ven. 54. *if thou m. murmurest,* Tp. I, 2, 294. Oftenest *no m.* = no longer, the contrary of *not yet:* Tp. I, 2, 388. II, 2, 44. 184. IV, 100. Gent. I, 3, 14. Err. I, 1, 3. LLL III, 119 etc.

5) to a greater degree (Lat. *magis*): *never did passenger m. thirst,* Ven. 92. *none that I m. love than myself,* Tp. I, 1, 22. Gent. I, 1, 24. 64. H6A IV, 1, 154. Cor. I, 6, 26. Mcb. IV, 3, 48 etc. etc. *m. and m.* Mids. III, 2, 128. *the m.: her woes the m. increasing,* Ven. 254. *the m. thou hast wronged me,* Lr. V, 3, 168. *by so much the m.* As V, 2, 49. *so much the m.* H8 II, 3, 12. *m.* = the m.: *m. villain thou,* As III, 1, 15. *no m.* = as little: *you are not young; no m. am I,* Wiv. II, 1, 7 etc. and = as much, where *no less* would have been expected: *know you not, master, to some kind of men their graces serve them but as enemies? No m. do yours,* As II, 3, 12. *or were you both our mothers, I care no m. for than I do for heaven, so I were not his sister,* All's I, 3, 170 (a passage much corrected by M. Edd.).

Used to form the comparative degree: Ven. 9. 332. Tp. I, 2, 202. 275. 329. II, 1, 219. III, 1, 8. III, 3, 32. IV, 53. 261. Gent. II, 1, 134. Meas. IV, 2, 149. Err. II, 1, 20 etc. Before monosyllables: *m. white,* Ven. 10. *bright,* Sonn. 20, 5. *rich,* 29, 5. *weak,* 102, 1. *fresh,* Gent. V, 4, 115. *strict,* Meas. I, 4, 4. *fit,* II, 3, 14. *near,* All's I, 3, 110. *soon,* Tw. III, 1, 159. *oft,* III, 4, 3. *fast,* John IV, 2, 269. *deep,* IV, 3, 122. *great* H4A IV, 1, 77. *near,* R3 IV, 3, 49. *long,* Cor. V, 2, 71. *deep,* Rom. I, 3, 98. *fair,* II, 2, 6. *rich,* II, 6, 30. *light,* III, 5, 35. *strong,* Caes. III, 2, 189. *fell,* Oth. V, 2, 362. *sharp,* Cymb. I, 1, 131. *strong,* IV, 1, 11. *with m. tame a tongue,* Meas. II, 2, 46 (cf. *A*). Superfluously before comparatives: *m. better,* Tp. I, 2, 19. *m. braver,* 439. *m. fitter,* Meas. II, 2, 17. *m. mightier,* V, 237. *m. fairer,* LLL IV, 1, 62. *m. better,* Mids. III, 1, 21. *m. elder,* Merch. IV, 1, 251. *m. sounder,* As III, 2, 62. *m. worthier,* III, 3, 60. *m. hotter,* All's IV, 5, 42. *m. fairer,* H4B IV, 5, 201. *m. sharper,* H5 III, 5, 39. *m. stronger,* H8 I, 1, 147. *m. softer,* Troil. II, 2, 11. *m. wider,* V, 2, 149. *m. worthier,* Cor. III, 1, 120. *m. proudlier,* IV, 7, 8. *m. kinder,* Tim. IV, 1, 36. *m. nearer,* Hml. II, 1, 11. *m. richer,* III, 2, 316. *m. rawer,* V, 2, 129. *m. richer,* Lr. I, 1, 80 (Ff *ponderous*). *m. worthier,* 214. *m. corrupter,* II, 2, 108. 155. *m. headier,* II, 4, 111. *m. harder,* III, 2, 64 (Qq. *hard*). *m. vilder,* Oth. I, 3, 107 (Qq *certain*). *m. safer,* 226. *m. nearer,* V, 2, 110. *m. larger,* Ant. III, 6, 76. *men become much m. the better for being a little bad,* Meas. V, 445. *I would have been much m. a fresher man,* Troil. V, 6, 20.

Used in two senses in juxtaposition: *that tongue that m. hath m. expressed,* Sonn. 23, 12. *and m. m. strong* (reasons) *I shall indue you with,* John IV, 2, 42. *and m. m. fearful is delivered,* Cor. VI, 6, 63. *if there be m. m. woeful, hold it in,* Lr. V, 3, 202. cf. *m., by all —s, than e'er I shall love wife,* Tw. V, 139.

More-having, subst. increase of property: *my m. would be as a sauce to make me hunger more,* Mcb. IV, 3, 81.

Moreo'er, by conjecture in Per. II, 1, 86 (O. Edd. *more, or*).

Moreover, besides, over and above: Wiv. II, 3 76. Ado V, 1, 181. 220. 313. V, 2, 105. LLL V, 2, 49. 446. Merch. I, 3, 19. Tw. I, 3, 38. II, 2, 7. R2 I, 1, 8. H4B I, 2, 122. H5 IV, 7, 28. H6B IV, 7, 47. R3 III, 5, 80. Caes. III, 1, 227. III, 2, 252. Lr. IV, 5, 13. Per. III, 4, 15. A clause depending: *m. that we much did long to see you, the need we have to use you did provoke our hasty sending,* Hml. II, 2, 2.

Morgan, name: All's IV, 3, 125. Cymb. III, 3, 106. V, 5, 332.

Morisco, a morris-dancer: *I have seen him caper upright like a wild M., shaking the bloody darts as he his bells,* H6B III, 1, 365.

Morn, the first part of the day; morning: Ven. 2 (= Aurora; cf. *Morning*). 154. 453. 484. 495. Lucr. 942. Sonn. 33, 9. 63, 4. Pilgr. 71. 159. Tp. V, 306. Gent. IV, 2, 134. Meas. IV, 1, 4. IV, 4, 18. V, 101. LLL V, 2, 660. Mids. I, 1, 167. V, 372. Shr. II, 296 (cf. Troil. I, 3, 229). H5 III, 1, 20. H6A V, 4, 24. H6B III, 1, 13. R3 IV, 4, 16. V, 3, 210. Troil. IV, 2, 1. Tit. II, 1, 5. II, 2, 1. Rom. II, 3, 1. III, 5, 6. 113. Mcb. IV, 3, 4. Hml. I, 1, 150 (Ff *day*). 166. I, 3, 41. Oth. III, 3, 60. Ant. II, 5, 20. IV, 4, 24. IV, 9, 4. Cymb. I, 3, 31. III, 6, 94. IV, 2, 30. Per. V, 3, 22. *m. prayer,* Meas. II, 4, 71. *m. dew,* Ant. III, 12, 9. Never in prose; therefore the speech of Angelo in Meas. IV, 4, 18, printed as prose in O. Edd. and some M. Edd., must be read as verse.

Morning, 1) the first part of the day: Ven. 855. Lucr. 24. Sonn. 33, 1. Tp. III, 1, 33. V, 65. Gent. II, 1, 86. Ado II, 1, 31. III, 3, 172. Mids. IV, 1, 187. Merch. V, 295. Shr. III, 2, 113. H5 III, 7, 6. IV Chor. 16. R3 I, 4, 77. Cor. V, 1, 52. Caes. II, 1, 221 etc. etc. *it is great m.* Troil. IV, 3, 1. Cymb. IV, 2, 61 (= late in the morning, broad day). *good m. to you,* Meas. IV, 3, 116. *when you have given good m. to your mistress,* Cymb. II, 3, 66. *this m.* Wiv. II, 2, 74. III, 5, 46. 130. Meas. IV, 3, 74. Ado III, 5, 51. H8 III, 2, 82. 120. Hml. I, 1, 174 etc. *this day m.* H4A II, 4, 176. *to-day m.* Tw. V, 294. *to-morrow m.* Wiv. III, 3, 246. Meas. II, 1, 34. IV, 2, 7. Ado V, 1, 295. Rom. IV, 2, 24 etc. *on Monday m.* H8 V, 4, 15. *a Monday m.* Hml. II, 2, 406. *on Tuesday m.* Ado V, 1, 170. H4A I, 2, 40. *a May m.* Tw. III, 4, 156. *at m. and at night,* Merch. III, 2, 279. *a brushes his hat a —s,* Ado III, 2, 42 (M. Edd. *o' —s*). *to give her music a —s,* Cymb. II, 3, 13 (M. Edd. *o' — s*). *ere m.* Meas. IV, 2, 98. Merch. V, 48. *in the m.* Gent. IV, 2, 132. Meas. IV, 3, 49. Merch. I, 2, 92. H4A II, 4, 595. 600 etc. *early in the m.* Lucr. Arg. 16. R3 V, 3, 88. Rom. V, 3, 23. *in the m. early,* Merch. IV, 1, 456. As II, 2, 6. *at six o' clock in the m.* Merch. II, 5, 26. *at eight in the m.* Merch. II, 5, 26. *at eight in the m.* Tw. V, 205. *by the second hour in the m.* R3 V, 3, 31. *their —'s joy,* Lucr. 1107. *a —'s draught of sack,* Wiv. II, 2, 153. *the —'s danger,* H5 IV Chor. 25. *my —'s dream,* H6B I, 2, 24. *like to the —'s war,* H6C II, 5, 1. *our —'s rest,* Rom. V, 3, 189. *—'s dew,* Tit. II, 3, 201. *a —'s holy office,* Cymb. III, 3, 4. *the m. air,* Lucr. 778. Hml. I, 5, 58. *the m. cock,* I, 2, 218. *m. dew,* Mids. IV, 1, 126. *m. drops,* LLL IV, 3, 27. *m.*

face, As II, 7, 146. *m. field*, H5 IV, 2, 40. *m. lark*, Mids. IV, 1, 99. Shr. Ind. 2, 46. *m. light*, Lucr. 745. *m. prayer*, Wiv. II, 2, 102. *m. rise*, Pilgr. 194. *m. roses*, Shr. II, 174. *his m. story*, Err. V, 356. *m. sun*, Sonn. 132, 5. H6C IV, 7, 80. *thy m. taste*, Tim. IV, 3, 226.

2) the goddess Aurora: *I with the* —'s *love have oft made sport*, Mids. III, 2, 389 (i. e. Cephalus). *see how the m. opes her golden gates, and takes her farewell of the glorious sun*, H6C II, 1, 21. *modest as m. when she coldly eyes the youthful Phoebus*, Troil. I, 3, 229. *a Grecian queen, whose youth and freshness wrinkles Apollo's, and makes stale the m.* II, 2, 79. *yon grey is not the* —'s *eye, 'tis but the pale reflex on Cynthia's brow*, Rom. III, 5, 19.

Morocco (O. Edd. *Moroco* and *Morocho*), country in Africa: Merch. I, 2, 137. = prince of M.: II, 7, 24.

Morris, 1) = morrisdance, q. v.: *as fit as a m. for Mayday*, All's II, 2, 25. 2) *the nine men's m.*, "a game called also the nine men's merrils, from merelles or mereaux, an ancient French word for the jettons or counters with which it was played" (Douce): Mids. II, 1, 98.*

Morris-dance, "a name given to dances used on festival occasions, and particularly on May-day, at which time they are not even now entirely disused in some parts of England. It appears that a certain set of personages were usually represented in the May-day morris-dance, who have been thus enumerated. 1. The Bavian, or fool. 2. Maid Marian, or the queen of May, the celebrated mistress of Robin Hood. 3. The friar, that is friar Tuck, chaplain to the same personage. 4. Her gentleman-usher, or paramour. 5. The hobby-horse. 6. The clown. 7. A gentleman. 8. The May-pole. 9. Tom Piper. 10, 11. Foreigners, perhaps Moriscos. 12. The domestic fool, or jester" (Nares): *with no more* (show of fear) *than if we heard that England were busied with a Whitsun m.* H5 II, 4, 25.

Morris-pike, a formidable weapon, supposed to be of Moorish origin: *to do more exploits with his mace than a m.* Err. IV, 3, 28 (O. Edd. *Moris pike*).

Morrow, 1) the day next after another (cf. *Tomorrow*): *we must starve our sight from lovers' food till m. deep midnight*, Mids. I, 1, 223. *shorten my days thou canst.... but not lend a m.* R2 I, 3, 228. *never shall sun that m. see*, Mcb. I, 5, 62. cf. the quibble in Troil. III, 3, 68. 69.

2) = morning; used only for the sake of the rhyme: *the blushing m. lends light to all fair eyes that light will borrow*, Lucr. 1082. *she looks for night, and then she longs for m.* 1571. *give not a windy night a rainy m.* Sonn. 90, 7. *I shall say good night till it be m.* Rom. II, 2, 186. But to express a kind wish at meeting and parting in the morning, *good morrow*, and not *good morning* (q. v.) is the ordinary form in any collocation: Ven. 859. Lucr. 1219. Gent. II, 1, 140. IV, 3, 6. 45. Wiv. III, 1, 36. Meas. II, 1, 143. IV, 2, 109. Ado III, 4, 39. 40. V, 3, 24. 29. V, 4, 34. 35. Mids. IV, 1, 144. Merch. I, 1, 65. As I, 1, 100. II, 7, 18. IV, 3, 76. Shr. II, 39. 40. All's IV, 3, 349. Tw. II, 4, 1. John IV, 1, 9. H6A III, 2, 41. R3 II, 1, 46. III, 2, 76. V, 3, 223. Troil. III, 3, 66. Caes. II, 4, 33 etc. etc. *to bid good m.* Shr. III, 2, 124. H5 IV Chor. 33. R3 III, 4, 52. Oth. III, 1, 2. *so soon to bid good*

m. to thy bed, Rom. II, 3, 34 (i. e. to part with it, to leave it). *do my good m. to them*, H5 IV, 1, 26 (= greet them from me). *give you good m.*, a salutation used only by common people: Wiv. II, 2, 35. II, 3, 21. III, 5, 28. R3 II, 3, 6. Lr. II, 2, 165. *God give you good m., master Parson*, LLL IV, 2, 84 (Jaquenetta's speech). *God ye good m.* Rom. II, 4, 116 (the nurse's speech). *many good* —s, a respectful form of salutation: H4B III, 1, 32. R3 III, 2, 35. Tit. II, 2, 11. cf. *a thousand times good m.* Gent. IV, 3, 6. ridiculed by Speed: *madam and mistress, a thousand good* —s! *O, give ye good even! here's a million of manners!* Gent. II, 1, 102.

Morsel, 1) a mouthful, a bit, a piece: *now comes in the sweetest m. of the night, and we must hence and leave it unpicked*, H4B II, 4, 396. *yet camest thou to a m. of this feast, having fully dined before*, Cor. I, 9, 10. *gorged with the dearest m. of the earth*, Rom. V, 3, 46. *liquorish draughts and* —s *unctuous*, Tim. IV, 3, 195. *I was a m. for a monarch*, Ant. I, 5, 31. *I found you as a m. cold upon dead Caesar's trencher*, III, 13, 116. *thou mayst cut a m. off the spit*, Per. IV, 2, 142.

2) piece in general, remnant: *whiles you, doing thus, to the perpetual wink for aye might put this ancient m., this Sir Prudence*, Tp. II, 1, 286. *how doth my dear m., thy mistress?* Meas. III, 2, 57. *this m. of dead royalty*, John IV, 3, 143.

Mort, a flourish blown at the death of the deer: *to sigh, as 'twere the m. o'the deer*, Wint. I, 2, 118.

Mortal, adj. 1) subject to death, sharing the common fate of mankind: Ven. 368. 996. Lucr. 13. 163. Sonn. 7, 7. 107, 5. Pilgr. 244 & LLL IV, 3, 120. Tp. V, 188. Meas. II, 2, 123. IV, 2, 153 (cf. *Desperately*). Ado I, 1, 60. LLL IV, 3, 85. V, 2, 161. Mids. II, 1, 135. III, 1, 163. As II, 4, 56. Shr. I, 1, 178. Tw. V, 254. John III, 1, 158. R2 III, 2, 161. IV, 48. H4A IV, 2, 73. H6B I, 2, 21. H6C II, 5, 29. R3 I, 2, 44. 45. 77. III, 4, 98. V, 3, 124. H8 II, 4, 228. III, 2, 148. Troil. III, 1, 34. Tit. II, 3, 103. Rom. III, 2, 82. Caes. II, 1, 66. Hml. IV, 4, 51. IV, 5, 160. Ant. V, 2, 51. Per. IV, 4, 30. V, 3, 62. *slave to m. rage*, Sonn. 64, 4 (= the rage of mortality, or of death). *put myself into my m. preparation*, All's III, 6, 81 (= prep. for death). *pay his breath to time and m. custom*, Mcb. IV, 1, 100. *this m. coil*, Hml. III, 1, 67 (= this coil of mortality, of mortal life).

Often = pertaining to mankind, human: *whose tushes never sheathed he* (the boar) *whetteth still, like to a m. butcher bent to kill*, Ven. 618. *must not die till mutual overthrow of m. kind*, 1018. *to write above a m. pitch*, Sonn. 86, 6. *this is no m. business*, Tp. I, 2, 406. *she excels each m. thing upon the dull earth dwelling*, Gent. IV, 2, 51. *the purest treasure m. times afford is spotless reputation*, R2 I, 1, 177 (m. times = human life). *m. griefs*, H5 IV, 1, 259. *m. knowledge*, Mcb. I, 5, 3. *know all m. consequences*, V, 3, 5. *things m. move them not*, Hml. II, 2, 539. *if m. eyes do see them bolster*, Oth. III, 3, 399. *more than a m. seeming*, Cymb. I, 6, 171. *no more show thy spite on m. flies*, V, 4, 31 (i. e. men). *be not with m. accidents opprest*, 99. Remarkable passage: *so is all nature in love m. in folly*, As II, 4, 56 (perhaps = human, resembling man in folly. Johnson: abounding in folly).

2) deadly, fatal: *now nature cares not for thy m. vigour*, Ven. 953. *his m. sting*, Lucr. 364. *their m.*

fault, 724. *at a m. war*, Sonn. 46, 1. *the m. and intestine jars*, Err. I, 1, 11. *if the living be enemy to the grief, the excess of it makes it soon m.* All's I, 1, 67 (cf. Lr. V, 3, 204: *this would have seemed a period to such as love not sorrow). even to a m. arbitrement*, Tw. III, 4, 286. *m. motion*, 304. *this news is m. to the queen*, Wint. III, 2, 149. *m. fury*, John II, 454. *m. paw*, III, 1, 259. *it ends a m. woe*, R2 II, 1, 152. *a m. touch*, III, 2, 21. *the m. worm*, H6B III, 2, 263. *m. sting*, H6C II, 2, 15. *the m. fortune of the field*, II, 2, 83. *m. foe*, III, 3, 257. V, 1, 94. *m. poison*, R3 I, 2, 146. *m. sword*, Troil. IV, 5, 134. cf. Cor. II, 2, 115. III, 1, 297. Tit. IV, 1, 93. Rom. III, 1, 115. V, 1, 66. Mcb. I, 5, 42. III, 4, 81. IV, 3, 3. Hml IV, 7, 143. Oth. II, 1, 72. III, 3, 355. III, 4, 115. V, 2, 205. Ant. I, 2, 138. V, 1, 64. V, 2, 306. Cymb. I, 4, 44. III, 4, 18. V, 3, 51. V, 5, 50. 236. Per. III, 2, 110. V, 1, 37.

Adverbially: *most dangerously you have with him prevailed, if not most m. to him*, Cor. V, 3, 189.

Mortal, subst. man, human being: LLL III, 180. IV, 3, 42. Mids. II, 1, 101 *(human —s)*. III, 1, 140. 178. III, 2, 115. IV, 1, 107. Troil. I, 3, 225. Rom. II, 2, 30. IV, 3, 48. Mcb. III, 5, 33.

Mortal-breathing (not hyphened in O. Edd.), endowed with human life: *to kiss this shrine, this m. saint*, Merch. II, 7, 40.

Mortal-living (not hyphened in O. Edd.) the same: *poor m. ghost*, R3 IV, 4, 26.

Mortality, 1) subjection to death, necessity of dying: *since brass, nor stone, nor earth, nor boundless sea, but sad m. o'ersways their power*, Sonn. 65, 2. *he was skilful enough to have lived still, if knowledge could be set up against m.* All's I, 1, 35. *two Talbots, winged through the lither sky, in thy (death's) despite shall 'scape m.* H6A IV, 7, 22. *it smells of m.* Lr. IV, 6, 136. *taught my frail m. to know itself*, Per. I, 1, 42.

2) human life; life: *showing life's triumph in the map of death, and death's dim look in life's m.* Lucr. 403 (= in mortal, human life). *no might nor greatness in m. can censure 'scape*, Meas. III, 2, 196. *his pure brain ... doth by the idle comments that it makes foretell the ending of m.* John V, 7, 5. *the swords that make such waste in brief m.* H5 I, 2, 28. *there's nothing serious in m.* Mcb. II, 3, 98. *what m. is!* Cymb. IV, 1, 16. *lest this great sea of joys rushing upon me o'erbear the shores of my m. and drown me with their sweetness*, Per. V, 1, 195.

3) death: *m. and mercy in Vienna live in thy tongue and heart*, Meas. I, 1, 45. *insensible of m.* IV, 2, 152. *we cannot hold —'s strong hand*, John IV, 2, 82. *here on my knee I beg m., rather than life preserved with infamy*, H6A IV, 5, 32.

4) deadliness: *that being dead, like to the bullet's grazing, break out into a second course of mischief, killing in relapse of m.* H5 IV, 3, 107.

Mortally, 1) in the manner of mortal men: *I was m. brought forth*, Per. V, 1, 105.

2) to death, irrecoverably: *some m., some lightly touched*, Cymb. V, 3, 10. *they hurt you m.* Per. III, 3, 6.

Mortal-staring (not hyphened in O. Edd.), having a deadly stare, grim-looking: *put thy fortune to the arbitrement of bloody strokes and m. war*, R3 V, 3, 90 (variously amended by M. Edd., but without urgent necessity).

Mortar, the cement used in bricklaying: *I will tread this unbolted villain into m. and daub the wall of a jakes with him*, Lr. II, 2, 71.

Mortar-piece, a short and wide piece of ordnance: H8 V, 4, 48.

Mortgage, vb. to put to pledge, to make over to a creditor: *I myself am —d to thy will*, Sonn. 134, 2.

Mortify (used only in the participles) to deprive of vital faculty, to make apathetic and insensible: *Dumain is —ed; to love, to wealth, to pomp, I pine and die*, LLL I, 1, 28. *thou, like an exorcist, hast conjured up my —ed spirit*, Caes. II, 1, 324. *their dear causes would to the bleeding and the grim alarm excite the —ed man*, Mcb. V, 2, 5.*strike in their numbed and —ed bare arms pins*, Lr. II, 3, 15.

Nearly = to kill: *to apply a moral medicine to a —ing mischief*, Ado I, 3, 13. *let my liver rather heat with wine than my heart cool with —ing groans*, Merch. I, 1, 82. *his wildness, —ed in him, seemed to die too*, H5 I, 1, 26.

Mortimer, name of a family allied to the royal house of England: H6A II, 5, 91. H6B IV, 2, 41 Edmund M. Earl of March, son-in-law of Lionel Duke of Clarence: H6B II, 2, 36. 49. IV, 2, 144. Roger M. Earl of March, his son: H6B II, 2, 37. H6C I, 1, 106. Edmund M., son of Roger, pretender to the crown under the reign of Henry IV: H4A I, 1, 38. I, 3, 80. 92. 93. 110. 156. II, 3, 84 etc. H6A II, 5, 2. 7. 122. H6B II, 2, 38. 39. Anne M., daughter of Roger, married to Richard of Cambridge: H6B II, 2, 38. 45. Eleanor M., her sister: H6B II, 2, 38. John M.: H6B III, 1, 359. 372. Sir John and Sir Hugh M. H6C I, 2, 62. Lord M. of Scotland, called so by mistake, Lord March of Scotland being meant: H4A III, 2, 164.

Mortise, subst. a hole made in timber to receive the tenon of another piece of timber: *what ribs of oak can hold the m.?* Oth. II, 1, 9.

Mortised, joined with a mortise: *to whose huge spokes ten thousand lesser things are m. and adjoined*, Hml. III, 3, 20.

Morton, name of 1) a retainer of the Earl of Northumberland: H4B I, 1, 64. 87. 2) John M. Bishop of Ely: R3 IV, 3, 46 (Qq *Ely*). IV, 4, 468 (Qq *Ely*).

Mose, vb. "*To m. in the chine*, a disorder in horses, by some called mourning in the chine" (Nares): Shr. III, 2, 51.*

Moss, plants of the genus Musci, growing on trees, stones, roofs etc.: Err. II, 2, 180. Tit. II, 3, 95. Cymb. IV, 2, 228.

Mossed, overgrown with moss: As IV, 3, 105. In Tim. IV, 3, 223 O. Edd. *moist*, M. Edd. *mossed*.

Moss-grown, the same: H4A III, 1, 33.

Most, adj. and adv. 1) greatest; with the article: *boys and women are for the m. part cattle of this colour*, As III, 2, 435. *I have for the m. part been aired abroad*, Wint. IV, 2, 5. *for the m. part such*, H8 I, 1, 76. *who for the m. part are capable of nothing but inexplicable dumb-shows*, Hml. III, 2, 12. *for the m. part they are foolish that are so*, Ant. III, 3, 34. *I have the m. cause to be glad of yours* (viz company) Cor. IV, 3, 56. Without the article: *m. part of all this night*, H6A II, 1, 67. *have we not lost m. part of all the towns*, V, 4, 108. *m. part of their fleet*, Oth. II, 1, 24. *is at m. odds with his own gravity*, Wiv. III, 1, 54. *with m. advantage*, H6A I, 4, 12. *resolute in m. extremes*, IV, 1, 38. *though in this place m. master wear no* *breeches*, H6B I, 3, 149 (i.e. the king). *'tis honour with m. lands to be at odds*, Tim. III, 5, 116. *I had m. need of blessing*, Mcb. II, 2, 32. *with m. gladness*, Ant. II, 2, 169. In the predicate: *the sense of death is m. in apprehension*, Meas. III, 1, 78. *whose right is m. in Helena*, Mids. III, 2, 337. *God's wrong is m. of all*, R3 IV, 4, 377. *whose merit m. shall be*, Rom. I, 2, 31. With the possessive pronoun: *my m. stay can be but brief*, Meas. IV, 1, 44. *enforced from our m. quiet*, H4B IV, 1, 71. *at your m. need*, Hml. I, 5, 180.

2) the greatest amount, the utmost in extent or effect: *and to the m. of praise add something more*, Sonn. 85, 10. *to you I owe the m.* Merch. I, 1, 131. *the m. you sought was her promotion*, Rom. IV, 5, 71. *that were the m., if he should husband you*, Lr. V, 3, 70. *who is it that says m.?* Sonn. 84, 1. *in least speak m.* Mids. V, 105. *making them lightest that wear m. of it*, Merch. III, 2, 91. *where m. it promises*, All's II, 1, 146. *he of these that can do m. of all*, H6B I, 3, 75. *At m.: within this hour at m. I will advise you*, Mcb. III, 1, 128 (= at the farthest, at the latest).

3) the greatest number: *to the m. of men this is a Caliban*, Tp. I, 2, 480. *men, for the m., become much more the better for being a little bad*, Meas. V, 445. *I had the m. of them out of prison*, H4A IV, 2, 45. *which m. of our city did*, Tw. III, 3, 35. *he has ampler strength than most have of his age*, Wint. IV, 4, 415. 594. 627. H6A I, 1, 147. Rom. I, 1, 134 (*where m. might not be found*). Oth. I, 1, 182 etc.

4) in the highest degree; in a very high degree; with the article: *of all be hated, but the m. of me*, Mids. II, 2, 142. *you speak of two the m. remarked i' the kingdom*, H8 V, 1, 33. Without the article: *where it should m. mistrust*, Ven. 1154. *joy in that I honour m.* Sonn. 25, 4. *when m. I wink, then do mine eyes best see*, 43, 1. *which shall be m. my glory*, 83, 10. *since his exile she hath despised me m.* Gent. III, 2, 3. *there is a vice that m. I do abhor*, Meas. II, 2, 29. II, 4, 168. *the thing it hunteth m.* LLL I, 1, 146. *wear the favours m. in sight*, V, 2, 136. Mids. II, 2, 140. Shr. V, 2, 175. Wint. IV, 3, 18. Rom. I, 1, 134. I, 2, 31. Lr. I, 1, 100 etc. *m. of all:* Gent. I, 2, 30. Meas. II, 2, 100. John III, 4, 115. *m. of all* = above all: *but, m. of all, agreeing with the proclamation*, Meas. I, 2, 80.

Used before adjectives and adverbs, 1) to denote a very high degree: Tp. I, 2, 78. 116. 138. 178. 182. 204. 241. 276. 344. 357. 421. 482. II, 1, 44. 46. 117. 140. 227. 313. II, 2, 93. 149. 154. 159. 169. III, 1, 3. 21. 75. III, 2, 28. 64. III, 3, 58. 80. IV, 60. V, 71. 77. 117. 130. 177. Epil. 3 etc. etc. 2) to form the superlative degree: Ven. 1156. 1157. Sonn. 113, 10. Tp. III, 1, 15. III, 2, 106. IV, 26. Gent. I, 1, 45. II, 7, 58. LLL I, 1, 72. All's I, 3, 122. R3 IV, 3, 2. H8 II, 3, 11 etc. Redundantly before a superlative: *the m. heaviest*, Gent. IV, 2, 141. *m. dearest*, Wint. I, 2, 137. *thy m. worst*, III, 2, 180. *m. stillest night*, H4B III, 1, 28. *m. despitefullest*, Troil. IV, 1, 32 (Q *m. despiteful*). *m. boldest*, Caes. III, 1, 121. *m. unkindest*, III, 2, 187. *O m. best*, Hml. II, 2, 122. *m. best, m. dearest*, Lr. I, 1, 219 (Ff *the best, the dearest*). *m. poorest*, II, 3, 7. *m. worthiest*, Cymb. I, 6, 162. *m. coldest*, II, 3, 2. *m. bravest*, IV, 2, 319.

Mot or **Mott**, motto, device: *reproach is stamped in Collatinus' face, and Tarquin's eye may read the m. afar, how he in peace is wounded, not in war*, Lucr.

Mote (frequently substituted by M. Edd. for *moth* of O. Edd.) 1) the smallest thing imaginable, an atom: *through crystal walls each little m. will peep*, Lucr. 1251.

2) any thing hovering in the air? *like —s and shadows see them move awhile; your ears unto your eyes I'll reconcile*, Per. IV, 4, 21 O. Edd. *moats* and *moates).*

Moth, 1) the insect Tinea: *thus hath the candle singed the m.* Merch. II, 9, 79. Figuratively, an idle eater, a parasite: *all the yarn she (Penelope) spun in Ulysses' absence did but fill Ithaca full of —s*, Cor. I, 3, 94.*if I be left behind, a m. of peace*, Oth. I, 3, 257.

2) the smallest thing imaginable, atom, mote (M. Edd. *mote*): *you found his m.; the king your m. did see; but I a beam do find in each of three*, LLL IV, 3, 161. *a m. will turn the balance*, Mids. V, 324. *that there were but a m. in yours (eye), a grain, a dust, a gnat, a wandering hair*, John IV, 1, 92. *therefore should every soldier wash every m. out of his conscience*, H5 IV, 1, 189. *a m. it is to trouble the mind's eye*, Hml. I, 1, 112.

Name of diminutive persons; of the page in LLL I, 2, 80. 167. III, 115. 134.* of a fairy: Mids. III, 1, 165.

Mother, 1) female parent: Ven. 202. Sonn. 3, 4. 9. Tp. I, 2, 56. 321. 331. V, 269. Gent. II, 3, 7. 17. 30. 32. Wiv. I, 1, 285. II, 2, 40. III, 4, 87. IV, 6, 27. 32. 38. 46. V, 5, 229. Meas. III, 1, 141. Err. I, 1, 51. I, 2, 39 etc. etc. *his queen m.* Hml. III, 1, 190. *by my m. I derived am from Lionel*, H6A II, 5, 74. *uncles, both by the father and m.* R3 II, 3, 23. *m. dead!* John IV, 2, 127. *were you both our —s*, All's I, 3, 169 (i. e. mother to both of us). *am I a m. to the birth of three?* Cymb. V, 5, 369. *that would hang us, every —'s son*, Mids. I, 2, 80. *sit down, every —'s son*, III, 1, 75. *ten thousand bloody crowns of —s' sons*, R2 III, 3, 96. *by my —'s son, and that's myself*, Shr. IV, 5, 6. *my —'s son (i. e. my brother)* John I, 128. *he is all the —'s, from the top to toe*, R3 III, 1, 156. *my father's wit, and my —'s tongue, assist me*, LLL I, 2, 100. *one would think his —'s milk were scarce out of him*, Tw. I, 5, 170. *that rash humour which my m. gave me*, Caes. IV, 3, 120 (= which is innate in me). *our father's minds are dead, and we are governed with our mothers' spirits*, I, 3, 83. *I am yet so near the manners of my m. that upon the least occasion more mine eyes will tell tales of me*, Tw. II, 1, 42. *all my m. came into mine eyes and gave me up to tears*, H5 IV, 6, 31. *let's leave the hermit pity with our —s*, Troil. V, 3, 45. *God's m.* H6A I, 2, 78. H6B II, 1, 51. H6C III, 2, 103. R3 I, 3, 306. III, 7, 2. H8 V, 1, 154. *the church, our holy m.* John III, 1, 141. *his m. earth*, As I, 2, 213. *your dear m. England*, John V, 2, 153. *it (Scotland) cannot be called our m., but our grave*, Mcb. IV, 3, 166. *I am the m. of these moans*, R3 II, 2, 80. *some jay of Italy whose m. was her painting*, Cymb. III, 4, 52 ("a creature, not of nature, but of painting," Johnson. cf. *Taylor*).

2) an appellation given to elderly women: *come, M. Prat*, Wiv. IV, 2, 191. *M. Jourdain*, H6B I, 4, 13. Applied to an abbess: *to give the m. notice of my affair*, Meas. I, 4, 86.

3) the hysterical passion: *how this m. swells up toward my heart*, Lr. II, 4, 56.

Mother-queen, the mother of the king: *the m.* John II, 62.

Mother-wit, natural wit: Shr. II, 265.

Mothy, full of moths, eaten by moths: *an old m. saddle,* Shr. III, 2, 49.

Motion, 1) the passing from one place to another, the state opposed to rest: *to soften it with their continual m.* Lucr. 591. *these present-absent with swift m. slide,* Sonn. 45, 4. *in winged speed no m. shall I know,* 51, 8. *so your sweet hue, which methinks still doth stand, hath m.* 104, 12 (i. e. change). *incite them to quick m.* Tp. IV, 39. *he gives me the potions and the —s,* Wiv. III, 1, 105. *m. and long-during action,* LLL IV, 3, 307. 329. All's II, 1, 78. John II, 453. 578. V, 7, 49. H4B I, 2, 247. III, 2, 281. H5 III Chor. 2. Troil. III, 3, 183. Cor. II, 2, 113. Rom. II, 5, 13. III, 2, 59. Tim. II, 1, 3. III, 6, 112. Caes. IV, 1, 33. Oth. II, 3, 174. Ant. I, 4, 47. Cymb. II, 4, 85. *to keep in m.* H4A I, 3, 226. *to put in m.* Cymb. IV, 3, 31. *to put to m.* Tw. III, 1, 87. *to set in continual m.* H5 I, 2, 185. Used of the turning of celestial bodies in their spheres: *not the smallest orb ... but in his m. like an angel sings,* Merch. V, 61. *the other four (moons) in wondrous m.* John IV, 2, 184. *two stars keep not their m. in one sphere,* H4A V, 4, 65. *unshaked of m.* Caes. III, 1, 70 (= of no m.; cf. *Of*). Of the changes in the direction and expression of the eye: *commanded by the m. of thine eyes,* Sonn. 149, 12. *seem they in m.?* Merch. III, 2, 118. *the fixure of her eye has m. in't,* Wint. V, 3, 67. *let not the world see fear and sad distrust govern the m. of a kingly eye,* John V, 1, 47. *this object, which takes prisoner the wild m. of mine eye, fixing it only here,* Cymb. I, 6, 103. Of the tongue as the organ of speaking: *O, never will I trust to speeches penned, nor to the m. of a schoolboy's tongue,* LLL V, 2, 403. *a beggar's tongue make m. through my lips,* Cor. III, 2, 118. Of the manner of walking, almost = gait: *would give an excellent m. to thy gait,* Wiv. III, 3, 68. *in what m. age will give me leave,* All's II, 3, 247. *have I in my poor and old m. the expedition of thought?* H4B IV, 3, 37. *if we shall stand still, in fear our m. will be mocked or carped at,* H8 I, 2, 86. *her m. and her station are as one,* Ant. III, 3, 22. Of attacks in fencing, opposed to guard or parrying: *he gives me the stuck in with such a mortal m.* Tw. III, 4, 304. *the scrimers ... had neither m., guard, nor eye,* Hml. IV, 7, 102. *when in your m. you are hot and dry,* 158.

2) any external act or change expressive of life or sentiment: *all that borrowed m. seeming owed,* Compl. 327. *in thy face strange —s have appeared,* H4A II, 3, 63. *nor our strong sorrow upon the foot of m.* Mcb. II, 3, 131 (apt to vent itself). *it lifted up its head and did address itself to m., like as it would speak,* Hml. I, 2, 217. *have you a working pulse? and are no fairy? m.! well, speak on,* Per. V, 1, 156 (= indeed, you have a pulse which I feel beating). Parolles even says, somewhat ludicrously: *I knew of their going to bed, and of other —s, as promising her marriage,* All's V, 3, 264.

3) the tuning of a musical instrument: *that blessed wood whose m. sounds with thy sweet fingers,* Sonn. 128, 2. *what occasion hath Cadwal now to give it m.?* Cymb. IV, 2, 188. Quibbling: *the music plays; vouchsafe some m. to it. Our ears vouch-safe it. But your legs should do it,* LLL V, 2, 216.

4) that which makes to move, motive, incitement: *he gives her folly m. and advantage,* Wiv. III, 2, 35. *we in your m. turn, and you may move us,* Err. III, 2, 24. *whom from the flow of gall I name not, but from sincere —s,* H8 I, 1, 153. *hasty and tinder-like upon too trivial m.* Cor. II, 1, 56.

5) movement of the soul, tendency of the mind, impulse (Germ. *Regung*): *the wanton stings and —s of the sense,* Meas. I, 4, 59. *full of forms, figures, shapes, objects, ideas, apprehensions, —s, revolutions,* LLL IV, 2, 69. *with what art you sway the m. of Demetrius' heart,* Mids. I, 1, 193. *the —s of his spirit are dull as night,* Merch. V, 86. *unstaid and skittish in all —s,* Tw. II, 4, 18. *their love may be called appetite, no m. of the liver, but the palate,* 101. *but from the inward m. to deliver sweet poison for the age's tooth,* John I, 212. *within this bosom never entered yet the dreadful m. of a murderous thought,* IV, 2, 255. *between the acting of a dreadful thing and the first m.* Caes. II, 1, 64. *sense, sure, you have, else could you not have m.* Hml. III, 4, 72. *in fell m.* Lr. II, 1, 52. *of spirit so still and quiet, that her m. blushed at herself,* Oth. I, 3, 95. *to cool our raging —s,* 335. *there's no m. that tends to vice in man,* Cymb. II, 5, 20.

5) sense, perceptivity, mental sight: *this sensible warm m. to become a kneaded clod,* Meas. III, 1, 120.* *an outward man, that the great figure of a council frames by self-unable m.* All's III, 1, 13. *drugs or minerals that weaken m.* Oth. I, 2, 75. *I see it in my m., have it not in my tongue,* Ant. II, 3, 14 (= intuitively).

6) proposal, offer, request: *it were a good m.* Wiv. I, 1, 55. 221. *your father and my uncle hath made —s,* III, 4, 67. *I have a m. much imports your good,* Meas. V, 541. *my wife made daily —s for our home return,* Err. I, 1, 60. *the m. 's good indeed,* Shr. I, 2, 280. 281. *I'll make the m.* Tw. III, 4, 316. *how doth your grace affect their m.?* H6A V, 1, 7. *thank you for your m.* H6C III, 3, 244. *meanwhile must be an earnest m. made to the queen, to call back her appeal,* H8 II, 4, 233. *we request your loving m. toward the common body, to yield what passes here,* Cor. II, 2, 57. *doth this m. please thee?* Tit. I, 243.

7) a puppet-show, and also a single puppet: *to see sad sights moves more than hear them told, for then the eye interprets to the ear the heavy m. that it doth behold,* Lucr. 1326. *he compassed a m. of the Prodigal Son,* Wint. IV, 3, 103. *O excellent m., O exceeding puppet,* Gent. II, 1, 100. *he is a m. generative,* Meas. III, 2, 119.

Motion, vb. to propose, to counsel: *one that still —s war and never peace,* H6A I, 3, 63.

Motionless, wanting motion: H5 IV, 2, 50.

Motive, 1) that which determines the choice and moves the will; cause, reason: *what m. may be stronger with thee than the name of wife?* John III, 1, 313. *if these be —s weak, break off betimes,* Caes. II, 1, 116. *why left you wife and child, those precious —s, those strong knots of love?* Mcb. IV, 3, 27. *the very place puts toys of desperation, without more m., into every brain,* Hml. I, 4, 76. *whose m. should stir me most,* V, 2, 256. *thy safety being the m.* Lr. I, 1, 159. With *of*: *the grounds and —s of her woe,* Compl. 63. *all impediments in fancy's course are —s of more fancy,* All's V, 3, 215. *this is the main m. of our preparations,* Hml. I, 1, 105. With *for*: *this was your m. for Paris?* All's I, 3, 236. *had he the m. and the cue for passion* *that I have*, Hml. II, 2, 587. *you had a m. for it*, Cymb. V, 5, 268. With *to: your three —s to the battle*, 388. With a clause: *the first m. that I wooed thee*, Wiv. III, 4, 14. *the other m. why to a public count I might not go*, Hml. IV, 7, 16.

Applied to persons, = author (cf. *Cause*): *nor are they living who are the —s that you first went out*, Tim. V, 4, 27. *am I the m. of these tears?* Oth. IV, 2, 43 (Qq *occasion*). *myself, the ignorant m., do so far ask pardon*, Ant. II, 2, 96.

2) instrument: *heaven hath fated her to be my m. and helper to a husband*, All's IV, 4, 20. *the slavish m. of recanting fear* (i. e. the tongue) R2 I, 1, 193. *for me, the gold of France did not seduce, although I did admit it as a m. the sooner to effect what I intended*, H5 II, 2, 156. *her wanton spirits look out at every joint and m. of her body*, Troil. IV, 5, 57.

Motley, 1) the particoloured dress of domestic fools or jesters: As II, 7, 34. 58. Tw. I, 5, 63. Lr. I, 4, 160. Adjectively: *a m. fool*, As II, 7, 13. 17. 29. *a m. coat*, 43. H8 Prol. 16.

2) a fool: *made myself a m. to the view*, Sonn. 110, 2. *will you be married, m.?* As III, 3, 79.

Motley-minded, having the habits, though not the dress, of a jester; foolish: As V, 4, 41.

Mott, see *Mot.*

Motto, a sentence added to a device: Per. II, 2, 38. 44.

Mought, see *May.*

Mould, subst. 1) the matrix in which any thing is cast and receives its form: Ven. 730. Cor. V, 3, 22. Hml. III, 1, 161. Lr. III, 2, 8. Used of the body as giving shape to the garments: *strange garments cleave not to their m. but with the aid of use*, Mcb. I, 3, 145.

2) cast, form, frame: *unless you were of gentler, milder m.* Shr. I, 1, 60. *the very m. and frame of hand, nail, finger*, Wint. II, 3, 103. *were there but this single plot to lose, this m. of Marcius, they to dust should grind it*, Cor. III, 2, 103. In Troil. I, 3, 293 Ff *m.*, Q and M. Edd. *host.*

3) In Pistol's language *men of m.* = men made of earth, earth-born, mortal: *be merciful, great duke, to men of m.* H5 III, 2, 23.

Mould, vb. to model, to form, to shape: Meas. V, 444. Mids. III, 2, 211. Shr. IV, 3, 64. John II, 100. H4A I, 1, 23. H8 III, 2, 239. Troil. III, 3, 177. V, 10, 29. Cymb. V, 4, 49. Per. III Prol. 11. *to m. up* = to compose: *all princely graces that m. up such a mighty piece as this is*, H8 V, 5, 27.

Mouldy, musty, fusty: *you m. rogue*, H4B II, 4, 134. *your m. chaps*, 139. *m. stewed prunes*, 158. *things that are m. lack use*, III, 2, 119. *whose wit was m.* Troil. II, 1, 115. Name in H4B III, 2, 109 etc.

Moult, to cast or shed as a feather, to lose: *so shall my anticipation prevent your discovery, and your secrecy to the king and queen m. no feather*, Hml. II, 2, 306.

Moulten, being in the state of casting feathers: *a clip-winged griffin and a m. raven*, H4A III, 1, 152.

Mounch, see *Munch.*

Mounseur, corruption from the French *Monsieur:* Wiv. II, 3, 59.

Mousieur, the same: Mids. IV, 1, 8. 10 etc. H6B IV, 7, 31.

Mount, subst. a high hill, a mountain; with a name:

M. Pelion, Wiv. II, 1, 81. *about the M. Misenum*, Ant. II, 2, 163. Without a name: *the base o'the m.* Tim. I, 1, 64. *the steepy m.* 74. *the highest m.* Hml. III, 3, 18. *be at the m. before you* (i. e. M. Misenum) Ant. II, 2, 4, 6. Metaphorically: *whose worth stood challenger on m. of all the age for her perfections*, Hml. IV, 7, 28, = at the highest place of, above, all the age (cf. *Top*).

Mount, vb. 1) tr. a) to raise aloft, to lift on high: *what power is it which —s my love so high?* All's I, 1, 235. *the fire that —s the liquor*, H8 I, 1, 144. *—ed* = high: *where castles —ed stand*, H6B I, 4, 40. *his affections are higher —ed than ours*, H5 IV, 1, 111.

b) to raise and place in readiness for annoyance: *like hedgehogs which lie tumbling in my barefoot way and m. their pricks at my footfall*, Tp. II, 2, 11. *encounters —ed are against your peace*, LLL V, 2, 82. *ready —ed are they* (cannons) John II, 211. *m. their battering cannon charged to the mouths*, 381. *he stretched him, and with one hand on his dagger, another spread on's breast, —ing his eyes, he did discharge a horrible oath*, H8 I, 2, 205 (looking in a threatening manner; cf. *Carriage*).

c) to climb, to ascend: *—ed the Trojan walls*, Merch. V, 4. *the stairs that m. the Capitol*, Cymb. I, 6, 106. Oftenest applied to horses, = to get on, to bestride, to ride: As III, 4, 49. H5 III, 7, 25. IV, 2, 9. R3 I, 1, 10. Caes. V, 3, 15. Ant. I, 5, 48. cf. *he will not manage her, although he m. her*, Ven. 598.

d) to make to ride, to place on or furnish with a horse: *I will m. myself upon a courser*, Per. II, 1, 163. *—ed* = riding, on horseback: Ven. 596. Sonn. 51, 7. As III, 2, 95. John V, 6, 42. R2 V, 2, 8. H4B IV, 1, 118. H6C I, 4, 127. And = seated in a carriage: *their mistress —ed ... in her light chariot is conveyed*, Ven. 1191.

2) intr. a) to ascend, to rise aloft; used of birds: Lucr. 508. R2 III, 3, 183. H6B I, 3, 94. II, 1, 14. R3 V, 3, 106. Cymb. V, 4, 113. Of high waves: Tp. I, 2, 4. Of a soul rising to heaven: R2 V, 5, 112. Of persons or thoughts occupied with the objects of worldly greatness: LLL IV, 1, 4. John I, 206. II, 82. R2 V, 1, 56. H4B IV, 3, 61. 62. H6B III, 1, 22. H6C V, 6, 62. H8 II, 4, 112. Tit. II, 1, 13. With an accus. denoting the result or amount: *to m. her pitch*, Tit. II, 1, 14. With *up:* Ven. 854. John III, 1, 215. R2 IV, 189.

b) to ascend, to climb; 1) in an assault: *here will Talbot m.* H6A II, 1, 34. 2) to get on horseback: Gent. V, 2, 45. Shr. IV, 3, 188. John II, 287. R2 I, 1, 82. H5 IV, 2, 35. H6C II, 5, 128. Cymb. II, 5, 17. With *on:* R2 V, 2, 111. H6A IV, 5, 9.

Mountacute, see *Montacute.*

Mountague, see *Montague.*

Mountain, a large hill: Ven. 232. Lucr. 548. Sonn. 113, 11. Pilgr. 356. Tp. IV, 62. LLL V, 1, 88. 90. Mids. IV, 1, 114. 193. Shr. II, 141. Tw. IV, 1, 52 (*fit for the —s and the barbarous caves*). Wint. III, 2, 213. John III, 4, 177. H4A I, 3, 89. II, 4, 250. III, 1, 39. H4B III, 1, 47. H5 II, 4, 57. IV, 2, 30. H6C I, 4, 68. III, 2, 157. Tim. I, 1, 86. Caes. II, 4, 7. Hml. III, 4, 66. IV, 1, 29. V, 1, 275. 303. Ant. IV, 14, 5. Cymb. III, 3, 73. IV, 4, 8. V, 5, 281. Per. I, 4, 6. *liquid —s* = waves, Troil. I, 3, 40; cf. Oth. II, 1, 8. Denoting any thing of great bulk or quantity: *I should have been a m. of mummy*, Wiv. III, 5, 18. *the m. of mad flesh*, Err. IV, 4, 158. *to bring Benedick and Beatrice into a m. of affection*, Ado II, 1, 382.

losing a mite, a m. gain, Per. II Prol. 8. cf. H4A II, 4, 250. Image of immovable fixedness: *—s and rocks more free from motion*, John II, 452. *stand as firm as rocky —s*, H4B IV, 1, 188. *like a m. not to be removed*, H6A II, 5, 103. The proverb *"friends may meet, but —s never greet"* alluded to: *it is a hard matter for friends to meet, but —s may be removed with earthquakes and so encounter*, As III, 2, 195.

Compounds: *a m. cedar*, H8 V, 5, 54. *m. foot*, Gent. V, 2, 46. *m. foreigner*, Wiv. I, 1, 164. *m. goat*, H5 IV, 4, 20. *m. lioness*, Tit. IV, 2, 138. *m. pines*, Merch. IV, 1, 75. Cymb. IV, 2, 175. *his m. sire*, H5 II, 4, 57. *m. snow*, Ven. 750. Hml. IV, 5, 34. *m. sport*, Cymb. III, 3, 10. *m. spring*, Lucr. 1077. *m. squire*, H5 V, 1, 37. *m. top*, Sonn. 33, 2. H6B III, 2, 336. V, 1, 205. H8 III, 1, 4. Rom. III, 5, 10. Cymb. III, 6, 5. *m. winds*, Tp. I, 2, 499.

Name of a dog: Tp. IV, 256.

Mountaineer, inhabitant of a mountain (supposed to be savage and barbarous): Tp. III, 3, 44. Cymb. IV, 2, 100. 120. 370 (the later Ff *mountainers*).

Mountainer, the same: Cymb. IV, 2, 71. Reading of the later Ff in v. 370.

Mountainous, huge, bulky: *and m. error be too highly heaped for truth to o'erpeer*, Cor. II, 3, 127.

Mountant, raised, high: *hold up, you sluts, your aprons m.* Tim. IV, 3, 135.

Mountanto, see *Montanto*.

Mountebank, subst. a quack: *disguised cheaters, prating —s, and many such-like liberties of sin*, Err. I, 2, 101. *a m., a thread-bare juggler and a fortune-teller*, V, 238. *I bought an unction of a m.* Hml. IV, 7, 142. *by spells and medicines bought of —s*, Oth. I, 3, 61.

Mountebank, vb. to gull in the manner of a quack: *I'll m. their loves, cog their hearts from them*, Cor. III, 2, 132.

Mountgomery, see *Montgomery*.

Mourn, 1) trans. to grieve for, to lament: H8 V, 5, 63. Caes. III, 2, 45. V, 3, 92. Oth. I, 3, 204. Per. II, 4, 32. V, 1, 246.

2) intr. to grieve, to show sorrow, to wear the habit of grief: Lucr. 1365. 1744. Sonn. 127, 13. 132, 9. Pilgr. 391. Err. I, 1, 74. Ado IV, 1, 232. V, 1, 339. LLL V, 2, 754. Shr. Ind. 2, 28. H5 I, 2, 158. H6A II, 5, 111. IV, 3, 32. H6C III, 1, 39. R3 IV, 4, 34. Tit. II, 4, 56. Caes. III, 1, 288. Hml. I, 2, 151. Per. IV, 3, 42. *to m. in black*, Pilgr. 263. H6A I, 1, 17. *in ashes*, R2 V, 1, 49. *in steel*, H6C I, 1, 58. With *at:* Shr. Ind. 1, 62. With *for:* Sonn. 71, 1. 132, 11. Mids. V, 52. All's IV, 3, 102. Tw. I, 5, 72. 76. Wint. IV, 3, 15. R2 V, 1, 49. V, 6, 47. H4B I, 1, 136. H6B III, 2, 383. IV, 4, 22. 24. 25. H6C II, 6, 19. R3 IV, 1, 89. Cor. V, 6, 144. Caes. III, 2, 108. Hml. II, 2, 151 (Ff *wail*). With *over:* Tp. V, 13. With a clause: LLL IV, 3, 259.

The gerund *mourning* as a subst.: Sonn. 132, 11. R2 V, 6, 51 (Ff *my m.* Qq *my —s*). Tit. II, 4, 57. Lr. IV, 4, 26. *m. black*, Lucr. 1585. *m. duties*, Hml. I, 2, 88. *black m. gowns*, H6C II, 1, 161. *in m. habit*, Lucr. Arg. 19. *m. house*, LLL V, 2, 818. *m. ostentation*, Ado IV, 1, 207. *m. weeds*, H6C III, 3, 229. IV, 1, 104. Tit. I, 70. V, 3, 196 (Q2 Ff *mournful*).

Mourner, one that grieves, one that wears the habit of grief: Ven. 920. Lucr. 1797. Sonn. 132, 3. Phoen. 20. R3 I, 2, 212. Rom. IV, 5, 150. With *at:* Sonn. 127, 10. With *for:* R3 III, 2, 51.

Mournful, 1) expressing sorrow: *her m. hymns*, Sonn. 102, 10. *m. epitaphs*, Ado IV, 1, 209. *the m. crocodile*, H6B III, 1, 226. *my m. tears*, III, 2, 340. *m. weeds*, Tit. V, 3, 196 (Q1 *mourning*). *m. bell*, 197.

2) causing sorrow: *his m. death*, H6A II, 2, 16.

Mournfully, in a manner expressive of grief: *beat thou the drum, that it speak m.* Cor. V, 6, 151.

Mourning, subst. see *Mourn*.

Mourningly, with sorrow: *the king spoke of him admiringly and m.* All's I, 1, 34.

Mouse, subst. the animal Mus: Lucr. 555. Mids. V, 223. 394. H4B III, 2, 171. H5 I, 2, 172. Cor. I, 6, 44. Rom. I, 4, 40 (cf. *Dun*). III, 1, 104. III, 3, 31. Hml. I, 1, 10 (*not a m. stirring*). Lr. IV, 6, 89. Per. III Prol. 6. IV, 1, 78. Used as a term of endearment: *what's your dark meaning, m.?* LLL V, 2, 19. *good my m. of virtue, answer me*, Tw. I, 5, 69. *call you his m.* Hml. III, 4, 183.

Plur. *mice:* Meas. I, 4, 64. H6A I, 2, 12. Lr. III, 4, 144. IV, 6, 18.

Mouse, vb. to hunt for mice: *a —ing owl*, Mcb. II, 4, 13. Jocularly applied to a lion: *well —d, lion*, Mids. V, 274 (O. Edd. *mouz'd*).* Trans., = to tear: (death) *—ing the flesh of men*, John II, 354 (in the ludicrous language of the Bastard).

Mouse-eaten, gnawed by mice: *that stale old m. dry cheese*, Troil. V, 4, 11.

Mouse-hunt, figuratively a petticoat-hunter: *you have been a m. in your time; but I will watch you from such watching now. A jealous-hood!* Rom. IV, 4, 11.

Mouse-trap, a snare or gin in which mice are caught: Hml. III, 2, 247.

Mouth, subst. 1) the aperture in the heads of men and animals, by which they receive food and utter their voices: Ven. 396. 542. 901. Tp. II, 2, 85. 87. 99. 101. III, 1, 63. V, 131. Gent. II, 3, 51. Wiv. I, 1, 237. Ado II, 1, 13. V, 2, 12. Mids. V, 144. Merch. I, 2, 56. As III, 2, 210. 213. All's II, 3, 66. Tw. II, 3, 127. H8 II, 3, 87 etc. etc. Plur. *—s:* Ven. 248. H4B IV, 5, 77. Cor. I, 1, 210 etc. *run winking into the m. of a Russian bear*, H5 III, 7, 154. *meet the bear i' the m.* Lr. III, 4, 11. *to foam at m.* Troil. V, 5, 36. Caes. I, 2, 255. Oth. IV, 1, 55. *foamed at the m.* Cymb. V, 5, 276. *if I had my m., I would bite*, Ado I, 3, 36 (= if I were not muzzled; cf. *Eye*). *she hath a sweet m.* Gent. III, 1, 330 (= a sweet or dainty tooth). *to make —s* = to make faces, to make grimaces: *she made —s in a glass*, Lr. III, 2, 36. *those that would make —s at him while my father lived*, Hml. II, 2, 381 (Ff *mows*). *makes —s at the invisible event*, IV, 4, 50. *make —s upon me when I turn my back*, Mids. III, 2, 238. *must our —s be cold?* Tp. I, 1, 56 (= must we die?). Metaphorically: *that boy from the rude sea's enraged and foamy m. did I redeem*, Tw. V, 81. *drop into the rotten m. of death*, R3 IV, 4, 2.

Almost = voice, speech; of dogs: *then do they spend their —s*, Ven. 695 (by barking). *coward dogs most spend their —s*, H5 II, 4, 70. *matched in m. like bells*, Mids. IV, 1, 128. *between two dogs, which hath the deeper m.* H6A II, 4, 12. Of a bell: *the midnight bell with his iron tongue and brazen m.* John III, 3, 38. Of men: *you shall live in the —s of men*, Sonn. 81, 14; *your worship was the last man in our — s*, Merch. I, 3, 61; *young Arthur's death is common in their —s*, John IV, 2, 187; *that fatal prophecy which was in the m. of every sucking babe*, H6A III, 1, 197; *your name is great in —s of wisest censure*, Oth. II, 3, 193 (Q1 *men*). *hast thou no m. by land?* Tp. V, 220. *to know that of your m.* Wiv. I, 1, 235. *heaven in my m.* Meas. II, 4, 4. *O perilous —s*, 172. *to speak as from his m.* V, 155. *put your trial in the villain's m.* 304. *in foul m. to call him villain*, 309. *I only made a m. of his eye*, LLL II, 252. *with his m. full of news*, As I, 2, 98. *till thou canst quit thee by thy brother's m.* III, 1, 11. *men's —s are full of it*, John IV, 2, 161. *no word like pardon for kings' —s so fit*, R2 V, 3, 118. *history shall with full m. speak of our acts*, H5 I, 2, 230. *to take occasion from their —s to raise a mutiny betwixt yourselves*, H6A IV, 1, 130 (from what they say). *I'll from a m. of honour quite cry down this Ipswich fellow's insolence*, H8 I, 1, 137. *he had a black m. that said other of him*, I, 3, 58. *this makes bold —s*, I, 2, 60. *his heart's his m.* Cor. III, 1, 257. *it is spoke freely out of many —s*, IV, 6, 64. *wounds...which, like dumb —s, do ope their ruby lips*, Caes. III, 1, 260. III, 2, 229. *if thou 'ldst rather hear it from our —s, or from our masters*, Mcb. IV, 1, 62. *I am now my father's m.* H6C V, 5, 18 (= I speak in my father's name, I am his representative); *you being their —s*, Cor. III, 1, 36; *the noble tribunes are the people's —s*, 271. *he will spend his m. and promise*, Troil. V, 1, 98. *to stop the m. of* = to put to silence: Gent. II, 3, 51. Ado II, 1, 322. V, 4, 98. R2 V, 1, 95 etc. etc. *what remains will hardly stop the m. of present dues*, Tim. II, 2, 156. Similarly: *to fill the m. of deep defiance up*, H4A III, 2, 116 (cf. H8 II, 3, 87). *seal up the m. of outrage for a while*, Rom. V, 3, 216. *By word of m.* = orally, personally, not by letter: Tw. II, 3, 141. III, 4, 209. Caes. III, 1, 280.

2) any aperture; as the opening of a piece of ordnance, by which the charge issues: As II, 7, 153. John II, 382. 403. H5 III Chor. 27. Any entrance: *these lovely caves* (viz dimples), *these round enchanting pits, opened their —s to swallow Venus' liking*, Ven. 248. *this is the m. of the cell*, Tp. IV, 216. *the m. of passage shall we fling wide open*, John II, 449. *our grave shall have a tongueless m., not worshipped with a waxen epitaph*, H5 I, 2, 232. *Henry's wounds open their congealed —s and bleed afresh*, R3 I, 2, 56. *what subtle hole is this, whose m. is covered with briers*, Tit. II, 3, 199. *this fell devouring receptacle, as hateful as Cocytus' misty·m.* 236. *the vault, to whose foul m. no healthsome air breathes in*, Rom. IV, 3, 34. *at the oven's m.* Per. III Prol. 7 etc.

Mouth, vb. 1) to join lips, to bill and coo: *he would m. with a beggar*, Meas. III, 2, 194.

2) to take into the mouth: *first —ed to be last swallowed*, Hml. IV, 2, 20.

3) to speak big: *an thou'lt m., I'll rant as well as thou*, Hml. V, 1, 306. trans., = to recite with a big and affected voice: *if you m. it, as many of your players do, I had as lief the town-crier spoke my lines*, Hml. III, 2, 3.

Mouthed, open, gaping: *the wrinkles ... of m. graves will give thee memory*, Sonn. 77, 6. *those m. wounds which valiantly he took*, H4A I, 3, 97.

Mouth-filling, making the mouth full: *a good m. oath*, H4A III, 1, 259.

Mouth-friend, one who professes friendship without entertaining it: Tim. III, 6, 99.

Mouthful, as much as the mouth contains at once, a morsel, a bit: *and at last devours them all at a m.* Per. II, 1, 35.

Mouth-honour, respect expressed without sincerity: Mcb. V, 3, 27.

Mouth-made, expressed without sincerity, hypocritical: *m. vows*, Ant. I, 3, 30.

Movable, see *Moveable*.

Move, I. trans. 1) to put in motion, to cause to change place, to stir, to propel, to carry: *we in your motion turn, and you may m. us*, Err. III, 2, 24. *we will not m. a foot*, LLL V, 2, 146. *a block —d with none* (viz wind) Ado III, 1, 67. *let him that —d you hither, remove you hence*, Shr. II, 196. *m. the still-peering air*, All's III, 2, 113. *then must my sea be —d with her sighs*, Tit. III, 1, 228. *to m. is to stir*, Rom. I, 1, 11. *do bravely, horse! for wot'st thou whom thou —st?* Ant. I, 5, 22. *from whence he —s his war for Britain*, Cymb. III, 5, 25. cf. the quibble in Tw. III, 4, 88. Reflexively: *my free drift halts not particularly, but —s itself in a wide sea of wax*, Tim. I, 1, 46.

2) to impel, to incite, to prevail on, to determine: *pity m. my father to be inclined my way*, Tp. I, 2, 446. *thy fair virtue's force doth m. me ... to swear, I love thee*, Mids. III, 1, 143. *see if you can m. him*, As I, 2, 172. *more than your force m. us to gentleness*, II, 7, 103. *myself am —d to woo thee for my wife*, Shr. II, 195. *what the devil should m. me to undertake the recovery of this drum?* All's IV, 1, 37. *I —d the king to speak in the behalf of my daughter*, IV, 5, 75. *thou perhaps mayst m. that heart, which now abhors, to like his love*, Tw. III, 1, 175. *without ripe —ing to it*, Wint. I, 2, 332. *could not m. the gods to look that way*, III, 2, 214. *what doth m. you to claim your brother's land?* John I, 91. *m. the murmuring lips of discontent to break into this argument*, IV, 2, 53. *should m. you to mew up your kinsman*, 57. *pity may m. thee pardon to rehearse*, R2 V, 3, 128. *the reason —d these warlike lords to this*, H6A II, 5, 70. *I —d him to those arms*, H6B III, 1, 378. R3 I, 1, 61. I, 3, 349. III, 7, 63. IV, 4, 279 (Qq *force*). H8 II, 4, 167. V, 1, 46. Troil. II, 3, 98. 118. Cor. V, 2, 78. Tit. IV, 3, 50. V, 3, 92. Rom. I, 1, 8. IV, 3, 4. Caes. I, 2, 207. I, 3, 121. III, 2, 233. Hml. IV, 5, 8. Ant. II, 1, 42. II, 6, 15. Cymb. I, 1, 103. I, 5, 70. V, 5, 342. With a clause: *have —d us and our council, that you shall this morning come before us*, H8 V, 1, 101.

3) to make impression, to rouse the feelings; a) absol.: *every tongue more —ing than your own*, Ven. 776. *to see sad sights —s more than hear them told*, Lucr. 1324. *the gentle spirit of —ing words*, Gent. V, 4, 55. *heaven give thee —ing graces*, Meas. II, 2, 36. *words that in an honest suit might m.* Err. IV, 2, 14. *more —ing delicate*, Ado IV, 1, 230. *these stubborn lines lack power to m.* LLL IV, 3, 55. *how then might your prayers m.* As IV, 3, 55. *thy —ing tongue*, R2 V, 1, 47. *what thou speakest may m.* H4A I, 2, 172. *soon won with —ing words*, H6C III, 1, 34. *how novelty may m.* Troil. IV, 4, 81. *if I could pray to m.* Caes. III, 1, 59. *it could not m. thus*, Hml. IV, 5, 169. *—ing accidents*, Oth. I, 3, 135. *thou —st no less with thy complaining*, Cymb. IV, 2, 375. b) with an object: = to make impression on, to affect: *thy outward parts would m. each part in me that were but sensible*, Ven. 435. *who, —ing others, are themselves as stone*, Sonn. 94, 3. *whom stripes may m., not kindness*, Tp. I, 2, 345. *jewels more than quick words do m. a woman's mind*, Gent. III, 1, 91. *a prone and speechless dialect, such as m. men*, Meas. I, 2, 189. *it hath not —d him*

at all, IV, 2, 161. *mirth cannot m. a soul in agony*, LLL V, 2, 867. *thy paleness —s me more than eloquence*, Merch. III, 2, 106. *not —d with concord of sweet sounds*, V, 84. *she —s me not*, Shr. I, 2, 72. *the bagpipe could not m. you*, Wint. IV, 4, 184. *the king is —d and answers not to this*, John III, 1, 217. *but that —s not him*, H4B II, 2, 113. *I shall never m. thee in French*, H5 V, 2, 197. *prayers and tears have —d me, gifts could never*, H6B IV, 7, 73. *none but myself could m. thee*, Cor. V, 2, 80. *ere he express himself or m. the people with what he would say*, V, 6, 55. *more to m. you, take my deserts to his*, Tim. III, 5, 78. *whether their basest metal be not —d*, Caes. I, 1, 66. *are not you —d, when all the sway of earth shakes*, I, 3, 3. *I could be well — d, if I were as you*, III, 1, 58. 59. *how much the people may be —d by that which he will utter*, 234. *how I had —d them*, III, 2, 276. *what is't that —s your highness?* Mcb. III, 4, 48. *virtue, as it never will be —d, though lewdness court it in a shape of heaven*, Hml. I, 5, 53. *things mortal m. them not at all*, II, 2, 539. *where he arrives he —s all hearts against us*, Lr. IV, 5, 10. *if I have any grace or power to m. you*, Oth. III, 3, 46. *'twould m. me sooner*, Cymb. IV, 2, 91.

Often = to make angry, to exasperate: *being —d, he strikes whate'er is in his way*, Ven. 623. *wherewith the people were so much —d*, Lucr. Arg. 24. *if men —d him, was he such a storm*, Compl. 101. *if he had been throughly —d*, Wiv. I, 4, 95. *Pompey is —d*, LLL V, 2, 694. *a woman —d is like a fountain troubled*, Shr. V, 2, 142. *do you not see you m. him?* Tw. III, 4, 121. *if this letter m. him not*, 188. *hath —d me so*, R2 IV, 32. *lest thou m. our patience*, R3 I, 3, 248. 249 (cf. *Peace*). *Hector was —d*, Troil. I, 2, 5. *be not —d*, IV, 4, 131. *you are —d*, V, 2, 36. *being —d, he will not spare to gird the gods*, Cor. I, 1, 260. *being —d*, Rom. I, 1, 7. *a dog of the house of Montague —s me*, 10. *hear the sentence of your —d prince*, 95. *as soon —d to be moody, and as soon moody to be —d*, III, 1, 13. 14. *m. them no more by crossing their high will*, IV, 5, 95. *he durst not thus have —d me*, Caes. IV, 3, 58. *ignorant of what hath —d you*, Lr. I, 4, 296. *the letter —d him*, Oth. IV, 1, 246. *if Caesar m. him*, Ant. II, 2, 4. *thou hast —d us*, Per. I, 2, 51. *do as I bid you, or you'll m. me else*, II, 3, 71. With *to: it did m. him to passion*, LLL IV, 3, 202. *highly —d to wrath*, Tit. I, 419. *—ing me to rage*, Ant. II, 5, 70.

= to trouble, to agitate: *you look in a —d sort, as if you were dismayed*, Tp. IV, 146. *are you —ed?* Wint. I, 2, 150. *I see you are —d*, Oth. III, 3, 217. 224.

= to affect with regret or compassion, to touch: *if ever man were —d with woman's moans*, Lucr. 587. *kindlier —d than thou art*, Tp. V, 24. *be —d, be —d*, Gent. II, 1, 181. *my poor mistress, —d therewithal, wept bitterly*, IV, 4, 175. *now shalt thou be —d*, H4A II, 4, 422. *in kind heart and pity —d*, IV, 3, 64. *—d with compassion of my country's wreck*, H6A IV, 1, 56. *—d with remorse*, V, 4, 97. *his passion —s me so*, H6C I, 4, 150. *would m. a monster*, H8 II, 3, 11. *—d with pity*, Tit. II, 3, 151. *the tender boy, in passion —d*, III, 2, 48. *then it —d her*, Lr. IV, 3, 17. *this speech hath —d me*, V, 3, 199.

4) to excite, to rouse, to awaken: *this —s in him more rage and lesser pity*, Lucr. 468. 1553. *to m. wild laughter*, LLL V, 2, 865. *O that my prayers could such affection m.* Mids. I, 1, 197. *I will m. storms*, I, 2, 29. *that which —s his liking*, John II, 512. *thy words m. rage and not remorse in me*, H6B IV, 1, 112. *this is he that —s both wind and tide*, H6C III, 3, 48. *scars to m. laughter only*, Cor. III, 3, 52. *if looking liking m.* Rom. I, 3, 97. *which modern lamentation might have —d*, III, 2, 120. *might m. more grief*, Hml. II, 1, 118. *m. anger*, Per. I, 2, 54.

5) to propose, to offer for consideration, to bring upon the carpet: *let me but m. one question to your daughter*, Ado IV, 1, 74. *we dare not m. the question of our place*, Troil. II, 3, 89. *in the cause against your city, in part for his sake —d*, Tim. V, 2, 13. *the instances that second marriage m.* Hml. III, 2, 192. *if I do find him fit, I'll m. your suit*, Oth. III, 4, 166.

6) to address one's self to, to call upon, to apply to, to speak to about an affair in question: *he hath never —d me*, Gent. I, 2, 27. *to me she speaks; she —s me for her theme*, Err. II, 2, 183. *the Florentine will m. us for speedy aid*, All's I, 2, 6. *I would he were the best in all this presence that hath —d me so*, R2 IV, 32 (?). *— ing such a dish of skim milk with so honourable an action*, H4A II, 3, 35. *in this just suit come I to m. your grace*, R3 III, 7, 140. *you remember how under my oppression I did reek, when I first —d you*, H8 II, 4, 209. *I then —d you, my Lord of Canterbury*, 217. *to this effect, Achilles, have I —d you*, Troil. III, 3, 216. *we have had no time to m. our daughter*, Rom. III, 4, 2. *I would not be any further —d*, Caes. I, 2, 167. *I have —d my lord on his behalf*, Oth. III, 4, 19. Without an accus., almost = to speak: *my wife must m. for Cassio to her mistress*, Oth. II, 3, 389.

II. intr. 1) to have motion, not to be fixed: *standing, speaking, —ing, and yet so fast asleep*, Tp. II, 1, 214. *m. these eyes?* Merch. III, 2, 116. *sedges which seem to m.* Shr. Ind. 2, 54. *I saw her coral lips to m.* I, 1, 179. *lips, do not m.* Tw. II, 5, 109. *m. still, still so*, Wint. IV, 4, 142. *it —s*, V, 3, 61. *I'll make the statue m.* 88. 94. *that weightless down perforce must m.* H4B IV, 5, 34. *saints do not m.* Rom. I, 5, 107. 108. *he —th not*, II, 1, 15. *stones have been known to m.* Mcb. III, 4, 123. *the wood began to m.* V, 5, 35. 38. *his slow and —ing finger*, Oth. IV, 2, 55 (= slowly moving. Qq *slow unmoving*). *no more —ing?* V, 2, 93. Used of celestial bodies: *you stars that m. in your right spheres*, John V, 7, 74. *m. in that obedient orb again*, H4A V, 1, 17. *by his light did all the chivalry of England m.* H4B II, 3, 20. *Mars his true —ing is not known*, H6A I, 2, 1. *doubt that the sun doth m.* Hml. II, 2, 117. *the star —s not but in his sphere*, IV, 7, 15. *to be called into a huge sphere, and not to be seen to m. in it*, Ant. II, 7, 17. *O sun, burn the great sphere thou —st in*, IV, 15, 10. cf. All's II, 1, 56 and Err. III, 2, 24. Metaphorically: *heaven still m. about her*, H8 V, 5, 18 (may she be, as it were, the centre of the world, the principal care of heaven). Used of ships tossed on the sea: *float upon a violent sea each way and m.* Mcb. IV, 2, 22. *his shipping . . . like egg-shells —d upon their surges*, Cymb. III, 1, 28.

2) to change place, to stir, to walk, to go, to proceed, to advance: *thou not farther than my thoughts canst m.* Sonn. 47, 11. *they perceive not how time —s*, As III, 2, 351. *and wish, ere I m., what my tongue speaks, my right drawn sword may prove*, R2 I, 1, 45.

not —ing from the casque to the cushion, Cor. IV, 7, 42. *he —s like an engine*, V, 4, 19. *—s like a ghost*, Mcb. II, 1, 56. *—s with its own organs*, Ant. II, 7, 49. *our faults can never be so equal, that your love can equally m. with them*, III, 4, 36. *like motes and shadows see them m. awhile*, Per. IV, 4, 21. Used of marching troops: *bid them m. away*, Caes. IV, 2, 45. *those he commands m. only in command*, Mcb. V, 2, 19. *her army is —d on*, Lr. IV, 6, 220. *those powers that long to m.* Cymb. IV, 3, 32.

3) to be alive and active: *the morning rise doth cite each —ing sense from idle rest*, Pilgr. 195. *there is no tongue that —s so soon as yours could win me*, Wint. I, 2, 20. *and newly m. with fresh legerity*, H5 IV, 1, 22. *how big imagination —s in this lip*, Tim. I, 1, 33. *observe how Antony becomes his flaw, and what thou thinkest his very action speaks in every power that —s*, Ant. III, 12, 36.

4) to conduct one's self, to live: *whatsoever star that guides my —ing*, Sonn. 26, 9. *eat, speak and m. under the influence of the most received star*, All's II, 1, 56 (cf. H4B II, 3, 20. H6A I, 2, 1. Ant. II, 7, 17). *in form and —ing how express and admirable*, Hml. II, 2, 317. *report should render him hourly to your ear as truly as he —s*, Cymb. III, 4, 154.

Moveable, subst. a piece of furniture, a property not fixed: *what's a m.? a joint-stool*, Shr. II, 198. Plur. *—s:* R2 II, 1, 161. H5 II, 3, 50. R3 III, 1, 195. IV, 2, 93. Cymb. II, 2, 29.

Mover, 1) he who gives motion: *O thou eternal m. of the heavens*, H6B III, 3, 19.

2) causer; that which causes: *these most poisonous compounds, which are the —s of a languishing death*, Cymb. I, 5, 9.

3) one that is alive and active: *O fairest m. on this mortal round*, Ven. 368. *see here these —s that do prize their hours at a cracked drachm*, Cor. I, 5, 5.

Moving-delicate (not hyphened in O. Edd.): Ado IV, 1, 230; see *Move*.

Movingly, in such a manner as to touch the heart: *I would have had them writ more m.* Gent. II, 1, 134.

Mow, subst. a wry face, a grimace: *will be here with mop and m.* Tp. IV, 47. *those that would make —s at him while my father lived*, Hml. II, 2, 381 (Qq *mouths*). *contemn with —s the other*, Cymb. I, 6, 41.

Mow, vb. to make faces: *apes that m. and chatter at me*, Tp. II, 2, 9. *mopping and —ing*, Lr. IV, 1, 64.

Mow, vb. (partic. *—ed*, H6C V, 7, 4) to cut down with a scythe: Sonn. 60, 12. H5 III, 3, 13. H6B III, 1, 67. H6C V, 7, 4. H8 V, 4, 23. Cor. I, 3, 39. IV, 5, 214.

Mowbray, name: R2 I, 1, 6 etc. H4B III, 2, 29. IV, 1, 103 etc.

Mower, one who cuts down corn: Troil. V, 5, 25.

Moy: *ayez pitié de moi! Moy shall not serve; I will have forty —s*, H5 IV, 4, 14. *O pardonnez moi! Say'st thou me so? is that a ton of —s?* 23. Douce: "Dr. Johnson says that *moy* is a piece of money, whence *moi d'or* or *moi of gold*. But where had the doctor made this discovery? His etymology of *moidor* is certainly incorrect. *Moidore* is an English corruption of the Portuguese *moeda d'ouro,* i. e. money of gold; but there were no moidores in the time of Shakespeare. We are therefore still to seek for Pistol's *moy*. Now a *moyos* or *moy* was a measure of

corn; in French *muy* or *muid,* Lat. *modius,* a bushel. It appears that 27 moys were equal to a last or two tons."

Moyses, name in Gent. V, 3, 8.

Mr., abbreviation of *Master* before names: As III, 3, 74 (M. Edd. *Master*). All's V, 2, 1 (M. Edd. *Monsieur*). H4B II, 1, 1 (Q *Master*).

Much, adj. and adv. 1) great in quantity or amount; before a subst.: *tamed with too m. handling*, Ven. 560. *with m. ado,* 694. *m. misery,* 738. *too m. wonder,* Lucr. 95. 1099. 1106. *not so m. perdition as an hair*, Tp. I, 2, 30. *how m. tribute,* 124. *m. vexation,* Gent. III, 1, 16. *m. attribute,* Troil. II, 3, 125. *I shall have so m. experience,* Oth. II, 3, 373 etc. *there's m. example for't,* Tim. I, 2, 47. *carry back to Italy m. tall youth,* Ant. II, 6, 7. *thanks for thy m. goodness,* Meas. V, 534. *I am sorry for thy m. misgovernment,* Ado IV, 1, 100. *m. fool may you find in you,* All's II, 4, 36. *is it not past two o'clock? and here m. Orlando!* As IV, 3, 2 (i. e. no Orlando). In the predicate: *yet would my love to thee be still as m.* Ven. 442. *thy love, though m., is not so great,* Sonn. 61, 9. *m. is the force of heaven-bred poesy,* Gent. III, 2, 72. *my inwardness and love is very m. unto the prince,* Ado IV, 1, 248. *his innocence, which seems m.* Wint. V, 2, 70. *our loss might be ten times so m.* H6A II, 1, 53. *m. is your sorrow, mine ten times so m.* H6C II, 5, 112. *so m. is my poverty of spirit,* R3 III, 7, 159. *m. the reason why we ascribe it to him,* Troil. II, 3, 125. *the hurt cannot be m.* Rom. III, 1, 98. *so m. was our love,* Hml. IV, 1, 19. *his fault is m.* Lr. II, 2, 148.

2) Substantively, = a great deal: *m. of love,* Rom. III, 5, 73. *m. of grief,* 74. *you want m. of meat,* Tim. IV, 3, 419. *she hath assayed as m. as may be proved,* Ven. 608. *cloyed with m., he pineth still for more,* Lucr. 98. *those that m. covet,* 134. *having m.* 151. *I will not take too m. for him,* Tp. II, 2, 80. *so m. shall you give,* H6B IV, 1, 17 etc. etc. *thinkest it m. to tread the ooze,* Tp. I, 2, 252 (= a great thing). *think you m. to pay two thousand crowns?* H6B IV, 1, 18. *to make m. of* = to hold dear, to show respect to: *thou strokedst me and madest m. of me,* Tp. I, 2, 333. *be comfortable to my mother and make m. of her,* All's I, 1, 87. *make m. of him,* H6C IV, 6, 75. *wear it, enjoy it, and make m. of it,* R3 V, 5, 7. *I will make m. of your voices,* Cor. II, 3, 116. *how m. she makes of thee,* Tit. IV, 1, 10. *make as m. of me as when mine empire was your fellow,* Ant. IV, 2, 21. *the bird is dead that we have made so m. on,* Cymb. IV, 2, 198. '*tis m.* = it is a hard thing, a sorry business: '*tis m. to borrow, and I will not owe it,* Ven. 411. '*tis m. when sceptres are in children's hands,* H6A IV, 1, 192. *when holy and devout religious men are at their beads, 'tis m. to draw them hence,* R3 III, 7, 93 (Qq *hard*). Merch. III, 5, 44. Lr. III, 4, 6. Oth. IV, 1, 254. *in himself, 'tis m.* Cymb. I, 6, 79. *m., alone, as an exclamation of ironical admiration: with two points on your shoulder? m.!* H4B II, 4, 143 (Germ. *das ist was Grosses, das ist was Rechtes!*) *you moved me m. M.!* Tim. I, 2, 119. *the son of the female is the shadow of the male: it is often so, indeed; but m. of the father's substance!* H4B III, 2, 142 (Ff *but not* of etc.). *That's as m. as to say* = that means in other words: Ado II, 3, 270. H4B II, 2, 142. *that's as much to say,* in the same sense: Err. IV, 3, 54. *that's as m. to say as:* Tw. I, 5, 62. *as m.* = just so, the same, this: *my friends told me

as m. As IV, 1, 188. *I thought as m.* H6B II, 1, 15. *I told your majesty as m. before*, H6C III, 3, 179. *I will tell her as m.* Rom. II, 4, 185. *I care not if thou dost for me as m.* Mcb. V, 5, 41. *I thought as m.* Per. I, 4, 62. *So m.*, in the same sense: *I would not have him know so m. by me*, LLL IV, 3, 150. *I must confess that I have heard so m.* Mids. I, 1, 111. *could not a worm, an adder, do so m.?* III, 2, 71. *'twere good you do so m. for charity*, Merch. IV, 1, 261. *she, hearing so m., will speed her foot again*, All's III, 4, 37. *he takes on him to understand so m.* Tw. I, 5, 149 (= to know it). *I have considered so m.* Wint. IV, 2, 39. *it serves you well, my lord, to say so m.* H6B III, 1, 119. *not resolute, except so m. were done*, 267. *you said so m. before, and yet you fled*, H6C II, 2, 106. Cor. II, 2, 35. Tim. III, 4, 38. *so m. my office* (= this it is that I have to say) H5 III, 6, 145. *even so m.* (= I have done) Troil. I, 3, 283. *so m. for him*, Hml. I, 2, 25. *thus m. the business is*, 27 (cf. *Thus*). *So m. as* = even, *not so m. as* = not even: *not one whose flame my heart so m. as warmed*, Compl. 191. *that cannot so m. as a blossom yield*, As II, 3, 64. *I would not so m. as make water but in a sinkapace*, Tw. I, 3, 138. *never shall so m. as frown on you*, John IV, 1, 58. *it must be great that can inherit us so m. as of a thought of ill in him*, R2 I, 1, 86. *every thing set off that might so m. as think you enemies*, H4B IV, 1, 146. (never have you) *been reguerdoned with so m. as thanks*, H6A III, 4, 23. *do thou so m. as dig the grave for him*, Tit. II, 3, 270. *thy cheek so m. as lanked not*, Ant. I, 4, 71. *who cannot be new built, nor has no friends, so m. as but to prop him*, Cymb. I, 5, 60. *for so m. as* = as far as: *for so m. as I have perused, I find it not fit*, Lr. I, 2, 39. *By how m., by so m. the more* = the more ... the more: *by so m. the more shall I be at the height of heart-heaviness, by how m. I shall think my brother happy*, As V, 2, 49. *which would be so m. the more dangerous, by how m. the estate is green*, R3 II, 2, 126. Similarly: *by how m. unexpected, by so m. we must awake endeavour*, John II, 80. *by how m. better than my word I am, by so m. shall I falsify men's hopes*, H4A I, 2, 234. Without an antecedent: *so m. the more our carver's excellence*, Wint. V, 3, 30. *so m. the worse, if your own rule by thee*, H4B IV, 2, 86. *and swell so m. the higher by their ebb*, H6C IV, 8, 56. *so m. the more must pity drop upon her*, H8 II, 3, 17. *you would be so m. more the man*, Mcb. I, 7, 51. Similarly: *by so m. is the wonder in extremes*, H6C III, 2, 115.

Before comparatives, = a great deal, by far: *m. feater than before*, Tp. II, 1, 273. *with m. more ease*, III, 1, 30. *dare m. less take what I shall die to want*, 78. *means m. weaker*, V, 146. *m. less shall she*, Gent. II, 7, 11 etc.

3) to a great degree; qualifying verbs: *the morning is so m. o'erworn*, Ven. 866. *how m. a fool was I*, 1015. *m. amazed*, Lucr. 446. *which since have steaded m.* Tp. I, 2, 165. *which throes thee m. to yield*, II, 1, 231. *so m. admire*, V, 154. *nor needst thou m. importune me*, Gent. I, 3, 17. *I love his lady too m.* II, 4, 205. *some men are m. to blame*, Cymb. I, 6, 77 etc. etc. Qualifying adjectives and adverbs, = very: *which I was m. unwilling to proceed in*, Gent. II, 1, 112. *m. different from the man he was*, Err. V, 46. *m. willing to be counted wise*, LLL II, 18. *I confess me m. guilty*, As I, 2, 196. *m. sea-sick*, Wint. V, 2, 128. *with m.*

expedient march, John II, 223. *I am m. ill*, H4B IV, 4, 111. *he is m. sorry*, Troil. II, 3, 116. *we shall be m. unwelcome*, IV, 1, 45. *so m. ungently tempered*, V, 3, 1. *'tis m. deep*, Tim. III, 4, 30. *I am m. forgetful*, Caes. IV, 3, 255. *seem m. unsinewed*, Hml. IV, 7, 10. *I take it m. unkindly*, Oth. I, 1, 1. *how m. unlike art thou Mark Antony*, Ant. I, 5, 35. *seems m. unequal*, II, 5, 101. *I am m. sorry*, Cymb. II, 3, 109. *as m., how m., so m., too m., very m.* = as, how, so etc.: *'tis as m. impossible*, H8 V, 4, 12. *how m. thou art degenerate*, H4A III, 2, 128. *so m. unreasonable*, Merch. V, 203. *too m. profane*, Sonn. 89, 11. *too m. sad*, R2 II, 2, 1. *our too m. memorable shame*, H5 II, 4, 53. *very m. glad of it*, Ado I, 1, 19. Qualifying prepositional expressions: *our escape is m. beyond our loss*, Tp. II, 1, 3. *I shall be m. in years*, Rom. III, 5, 46.

= pretty nearly, almost: *m. like a press of people at a door*, Lucr. 1301. *m. upon this riddle runs the wisdom of the world*, Meas. III, 2, 242. *m. upon th.. time have I promised here to meet*, IV, 1, 17. *to be m. at one*, H5 V, 2, 204 (pretty nearly of the same value). *m. about cock-shut time*, R3 V, 3, 70. *I was your mother m. upon these years*, Rom. I, 3, 72. *it was m. like an argument that fell out last night*, Cymb. I, 4, 60.

Muck, subst. filth: *and looked upon things precious as they were the common m. of the world*, Cor. II, 2, 130.

Muckwater, a needless emendation of M. Edd. for *Mockwater*, q. v.

Mud, subst. mire, slime: Lucr. 850. Sonn. 35, 2. Compl. 46. Mids. II, 1, 98. H6B III, 1, 101. H8 II, 3, 92. Tit. V, 2, 171. Ant. II, 7, 30. V, 2, 58.

Mud, vb. to make turbid, to pollute: *m. not the fountain*, Lucr. 577.

Mudded, buried in slime: *and with him there lie m.* Tp. III, 3, 102. *I wish myself were m. in that oozy bed*, V, 151.

Muddied, 1) soiled: *I have held familiarity with fresher clothes, but I am now m. in fortune's mood, and smell somewhat strong of her strong displeasure*, All's V, 2, 4. *has fallen into the unclean fishpond of her displeasure, and, as he says, is m. withal*, 23.

2) made turbid (like a fountain): *the people m., thick and unwholesome in their thoughts and whispers*, Hml. IV, 5, 81.

Muddy, adj. slimy, dirty, impure: *the reasonable shore that now lies foul and m.* Tp. V, 82. *the m. ditch*, Wiv. III, 3, 15. *crystal is m.* Mids. III, 2, 139. *this m. vesture of decay*, Merch. V, 64. *through m. passages*, R2 V, 3, 62. *you m. knave*, H4A II, 1, 106.*you m. rascal*, H4B II, 4, 43. *you m. conger*, 58. *pulled the poor wretch from her melodious lay to m. death*, Hml. IV, 7, 184.

Metaphorically, = disturbed, darkened in mind: *a woman moved is like a fountain troubled, m., ill-seeming, thick, bereft of beauty*, Shr. V, 2, 143. *dost think I am so m., so unsettled, to appoint myself in this vexation*, Wint. I, 2, 325.

Muddy-mettled, dull-spirited, heavy, irresolute: *yet I, a dull and m. rascal, peak like John-a-dreams, unpregnant of my cause*, Hml. II, 2, 594.

Muffins, see *Ragamuffins*.

Muffle, 1) to wrap, to cover by cloth or any garment: Lucr. 768. Meas. V, 491. Err. III, 2, 8. Wint. IV, 4, 665. Rom. V, 3, 21. Tim. III, 4, 41. With up: H6B IV, 1, 46. Caes. III, 2, 191.

2) to blindfold: *will keep him — d*, All's IV, 1, 100. IV, 3, 134. *love, whose view is — d still*, Rom. I, 1, 177.

Muffler, 1) a wrapper worn by women and covering the face: Wiv. IV, 2, 73. 81. 205.

2) a cloth with which a person is blindfolded: *Fortune is painted blind, with a m. afore her eyes*, H5 III, 6, 32.

Mugger, in *Hugger-mugger* q. v.

Mugs, name in H4A II, 1, 49.

Mulberry, 1) the tree Morus alba: *tarrying in m. shade*, Mids. V, 149 (in the play of Pyramus and Thisbe).

2) its fruit: Ven. 1103. Mids. III, 1, 170. Cor. III, 2, 79.

Mule, the animal Mulus: Merch. IV, 1, 91. All's IV, 1, 46. H6A I, 2, 10. H6B IV, 1, 54. H8 IV, 2, 16. Troil. V, 1, 67. Cor. II, 1, 263. Ant. IV, 6, 24.

Muleter (most M. Edd. *muleteer*) one who drives mules: *base —s of France*, H6A III, 2, 68. Ant. III, 7, 36.

Muliteus, name in Tit. IV, 2, 153 (most M. Edd. *Muli lives*).

Mulled, dispirited, blunted: *peace is a very apoplexy, lethargy; m., deaf, sleepy, insensible*, Cor. IV, 5, 239.

Mulmutius, name of an ancient king of Britain: Cymb. III, 1, 55. 59.

Multiply, 1) trans. a) to increase by the process of arithmetical multiplication: *like a cipher, yet standing in rich place*, *I m. with one 'We thank you' many thousands moe*, Wint. I, 2, 7.

b) to increase, to enlarge: *Plutus himself, that knows the tinct and —ing medicine*, All's V, 3, 102 (the philosopher's stone, which had the power to make a piece of gold larger). *your grace's title shall be —ed*, H6B I, 2, 73. *by his sight his sin is —ed*, II, 1, 71. Peculiar passage: *how shall this bosom —ed digest the senate's courtesy?* Cor. III, 1, 131 (i. e. this many-bosomed, many-hearted multitude. Some M. Edd. *this bisson multitude*).

2) intr. to increase in number, to be prolific, to breed: *your —ing spawn how can he flatter*, Cor. II, 2, 82. *take thou that too, with — ing bans*, Tim. IV, 1, 34. *the —ing villanies of nature do swarm upon him*, Mcb. I, 2, 11 (Qy.: —*ed* in Cor. and —*ing* = innumerable? cf. *Multipotent* and *Multitudinous*).

Multipotent, almighty: *by Jove m.* Troil. IV, 5, 129.

Multitude, 1) a great number: *what love I note in the fair m. of those her hairs*, John III, 4, 62. *every honour sitting on his helm, would they were —s*, H4A III, 2, 143. Especially a great number of people: *since they, so few, watch such a m.* H6A I, 1, 161. *his army is a ragged m. of hinds and peasants*, H6B IV, 4, 32. *not fit to govern and rule —s*, V, 1, 94. *why come you not? what, —s, and fear?* H6C I, 4, 39. *lest by a m. the new-healed wound of malice should break out*, R3 II, 2, 124. *what a m. are here*, H8 V, 4, 71. *advantageous care withdrew me from the odds of m.* Troil. V, 4, 23.

2) a crowd: *among the buzzing pleased m.* Merch. III, 2, 182. *followed him in golden —s*, H4A IV, 3, 73. *how the giddy m. do point*, H6B II, 4, 21. *stay with the rude m. till I return*, III, 2, 135. *was ever feather so lightly blown to and fro as this m.* IV, 8, 58.

3) the common people, the vulgar: *which the rude*

m. call the afternoon, LLL V, 1, 95. *that many may be meant by the fool m.* Merch. II, 9, 26. *rank me with the barbarous —s*, 33. *the still discordant wavering m.* H4B Ind. 19. *for the m. to be ingrateful, were to make a monster of the m.* Cor. II, 3, 11. 12. *the many-headed m.* 18. *the m., besides themselves with fear*, Caes. III, 1, 180. *he's loved of the distracted m.* Hml. IV, 3, 4. *that nothing-gift of differing —s*, Cymb. III, 6, 86.

Multitudinous, 1) belonging to the multitude: *at once pluck out the m. tongue; let them not lick the sweet which is their poison*, Cor. III, 1, 156.

2) innumerable, endless, immense (?): *this my hand will rather the m. seas incarnadine, making the green one red*, Mcb. II, 2, 62.

Mum, an expression implying or enjoining silence: *m., then, and no more*, Tp. III, 2, 59. *I come to her in white and cry m.; she cries budget*, Wiv. V, 2, 6. V, 5, 209. *speak not you to him till we call upon you. M.* Meas. V, 288. *go to, m., you are he*, Ado II, 1, 128. *peace, Tranio! m.* Shr. I, 1, 73. *Grumio, m.* I, 2, 163. *give no words but m.* H6B I, 2, 89. *the citizens are m. and speak not a word*, R3 III, 7, 3. *I will hold my tongue....m. m.* Lr. I, 4, 215.

Mumble, to speak between the teeth, to mutter: *—ing of wicked charms*, Lr. II, 1, 41. *you —ing fool*, Rom. III, 5, 174 (speaking inarticulately, as having lost the teeth and speaking only with the lips).

Mumble-news, a tell-tale, a prattler: LLL V, 2, 464.

Mummer, one masked: *you make faces like —s*, Cor. II, 1, 83.

Mummy, 1) a carcass; in the language of Falstaff: *I should have been a mountain of m.* Wiv. III, 5, 19.

2) a preparation for magical purposes, made from dead bodies: *witches' m.* Mcb. IV, 1, 23. *it was dyed in m. which the skilful conserved of maidens' hearts*, Oth. III, 4, 74.

Mun, a sound imitative of that of the wind: *says suum, mun, ha, no, nonny*, Lr. III, 4, 103 (Qq *hay no on ny*).

Munch, to chew with closed lips: *I could m. your good dry oats*, Mids. IV, 1, 36. *a sailor's wife had chestnuts in her lap, and —ed, and —ed, and —ed*, Mcb. I, 3, 5 (O. Edd. *mounch'd*). In Hml. III, 2, 146 Qq *munching*, Ff *miching*.

Mundane, worldly: *worth all our m. cost*, Per. III, 2, 71.

Muniments, expedients, instruments used as in war: *our steed the leg, the tongue our trumpeter, with other m. and petty helps in this our fabric*, Cor. I, 1, 122.

Munition, materials for war: *what penny hath Rome borne, what men provided, what m. sent, to underprop this action?* John V, 2, 98. *to view the artillery and m.* H6A I, 1, 168.

Mural, for *mure*, i. e. wall, Pope's conjecture, adopted by most M. Edd., in Mids. V, 208. Ff *now is the morall downe*; Qq *now is the moon used*: Hanmer: *now is the mure all down.*

Murder or **Murther** (the two forms used indiscriminately in O. Edd.) subst. the act of killing criminally: Ven. 906. Lucr. 168. 766. 909. 918. Wiv. IV, 2, 46. Meas. I, 2, 141. Merch. II, 2, 83. As III, 5, 10. Wint. III, 2, 102. R2 I, 2, 21. 32. III, 2, 40.

44. H6B III, 1, 131. III, 2, 200. 216. R3 I, 3, 198. V, 3, 197. Tit. II, 3, 287. V, 2, 34. 37 etc. *with twenty mortal—s on their crowns,* Mcb. III, 4, 81. *to do a m.:* Tp. IV, 232. R3 I, 4, 202. Rom. V, 1, 81. Hml. III, 2, 248. III, 3, 54. V, 1, 86. Oth. I, 2, 3. V, 2, 106. *to enact a m.* H6A III, 1, 115. *to perform a m.* Mcb. III, 4, 77. With a genitive: *a brother's m.* Hml. III, 3, 38. *by m. of a king,* H6B IV, 1, 95. Tit. IV, 4, 54. Hml. II, 2, 563. 624. Lr. II, 1, 46. *he m. cries,* Mids. III, 2, 26. H4B II, 1, 55. Used as a masc.: *m. as hating what himself hath done,* John IV, 3, 37.

Murder or **Murther,** vb. to kill criminally: abs.: H5 V, 2, 17. H6B III, 2, 324. H6C II, 5, 122. II, 6, 49. Mcb. I, 5, 49. II, 3, 91. trans.: Ven. 502. Lucr. Arg. 2. Lucr. 929. 1634. Err. IV, 4, 112. Mids. III, 2, 56. 58. Shr. V, 1, 61. 90. All's I, 1, 151. Tw. II, 1, 36. Wint. I, 2, 412. John IV, 2, 205. R2 V, 6, 40. H4B IV, 5, 168. H6A I, 3, 34. V, 4, 63. H6B II, 2, 27. II, 3, 107. III, 2, 123. 177. IV, 1, 136. IV, 7, 81. H6C I, 1, 260. I, 3, 8. V, 6, 32. R3 I, 4, 178. 260. Tit. V, 1, 91. Rom. III, 2, 109. V, 3, 50 etc. = to kill: *I'll m. all his wardrobe,* H4A V, 3, 27. *smilest upon the stroke that —s me,* Rom. III, 3, 23. *the repetition would m. as it fell,* Mcb III, 3, 91. Metaphorical use: *what follows more she —s with a kiss,* Ven. 54 (i. e. cuts short). *her eyes, as —ed with the view, like stars ashamed of day, themselves withdrew,* 1031. *thou smotherest honesty, thou —est troth,* Lucr. 885. *in my death I m. shameful scorn,* 1189. *I will m. your ruff for this,* H4B II, 4, 144 (Pistol's speech). *m. thy breath in the middle of a word,* R3 III, 5, 2. *—ing impossibility,* Cor. V, 3, 61 (explained in what follows: *to make what cannot be, slight work*). *to m. our solemnity,* Rom. IV, 5, 61.

Murderer or **Murtherer** (the two forms used indiscriminately; dissyll. and trisyll.) one who kills or has killed criminally: Meas. IV, 2, 65. V, 39. LLL IV, 1, 8. Mids. III, 2, 57. 60. As III, 5, 14. Tw. III, 2, 82. R2 V, 6, 40. H6B III, 1, 128. 254. III, 2, 92. 181. H6C V, 5, 52. R3 I, 1, 40. I, 2, 64. I, 4, 268. V, 3, 184. Tit. II, 3, 178. III, 2, 54. Rom. III, 1, 143. III, 3, 94. Mcb. II, 3, 120. Hml. III, 4, 96. Oth. V, 2, 294. Cymb. V, 5, 211 etc.

Murdering-piece, a piece of ordnance charged with grapeshot: *this, like to a m., in many places gives me superfluous death,* Hml. IV, 5, 95.

Murderous or **Murtherous** (dissyll.; only once, R3 IV, 1, 56, trisyll. at the end of the line) committing murder, sanguinary: Lucr. 1735. Sonn. 9, 14 (*m. shame* = shameful murder). 10, 5. 129, 3. Tw. III, 1, 159 (*m. guilt* = guilt of murder). John IV, 2, 255. H4A I, 3, 163. H6B III, 2, 49. 220. V, 1, 185. H6C III, 2, 193. R3 I, 2, 94. I, 3, 134. IV, 1, 56. IV, 4, 226. Tit. II, 3, 267. IV, 2, 88. Caes. IV, 3, 267. Mcb. II, 3, 147. Hml. V, 2, 336. Lr. II, 1, 64. IV, 6, 282. Oth. V, 1, 61. V, 2, 233. Cymb. IV, 2, 328 (*m. to the senses*).

Mure, a wall: *the incessant care and labour of his mind hath wrought the m. that should confine it in so thin that life looks through and will break out,* H4B IV, 4, 119.

Murk, darkness, gloom: *ere twice in m. and occidental damp moist Hesperus hath quenched his sleepy lamp,* All's II, 1, 166.

Murky, dark, gloomy: *hell is m.* Mcb. V, 1, 41. *the —est den,* Tp. IV, 25.

Murmur, subst. 1) a low and indistinct. noise: *each shadow makes him stop, each m. stay,* Ven. 706. *the current that with gentle m. glides,* Gent. II, 7, 25. *when creeping m. and the poring dark fills the wide vessel of the universe,* H5 IV Chor. 2.

2) rumour: *then 'twas fresh in m.* Tw. I, 2, 32.

Murmur, vb. 1) to give a low and indistinct sound: *the —ing stream,* As IV, 3, 80. *the —ing surge,* Lr. IV, 6, 20. trans.: *the fresh streams ran by her and —ed her moans,* Oth. IV, 3, 45.

2) to speak to one's self and indistinctly: *—ing 'Where's my serpent of old Nile'?* Ant. I, 5, 25. trans.: *I heard thee m. tales of iron wars,* H4A II, 3, 51.

3) to grumble: *if thou more —est,* Tp. I, 2, 294. *the —ing lips of discontent,* John IV, 2, 53.

Murmurer, grumbler: H8 II, 2, 131.

Murrain, an infectious disease among cattle; used as a curse: *a m. on your monster,* Tp. III, 2, 88. *a red m. o' thy jade's tricks,* Troil. II, 1, 20. *a m. on't,* Cor. I, 5, 3. In Mids II, 1, 97 some M. Edd. *m.,* O. Edd. *murrion.*

Murray, name in H4A I, 1, 73.*

Murrion, infected with the murrain: *crows are fatted with the m. flock,* Mids. II, 1, 97 (some M. Edd. *murrain*).

Murther, subst. and vb. see *Murder.*

Murtherer, see *Murderer.*

Murtherous, see *Murderous.*

Muscadel, a sweet sort of wine: Shr. III, 2, 174.

Muscat, the same: *fortune's cat, but not a m.* All's V, 2, 21 (M. Edd. *musk-cat,* perhaps rightly).

Muscle (O. Edd. *mussel*) a bivalvular shell-fish: Tp. I, 2, 463. *m. shell,* a name given by Falstaff to Simple, because he stands with his mouth open, Wiv. IV, 5, 29.

Muscovite, a Russian: LLL V, 2, 121. 265. 303.

Muscovy, Russia: LLL V, 2, 393.

Muse, 1) one of the nine goddesses presiding over the liberal arts; especially the goddess of poetry: Sonn. 38, 9. 78, 1. 85, 4. 100, 1. 5. 9. Mids. V, 52. H5 Prol. 1.

2) a particular power and practice of poetry: *so is it not with me as with that M. stirred by a painted beauty to his verse,* Sonn. 21, 1. *had my friend's M. grown with this growing age,* 32, 10. *how can my M. want subject to invent,* 38, 1. *my sick M. doth give another place,* 79, 4. *thou wert not married to my M.* 82, 1. *my tongue-tied M. in manners holds her still,* 85, 1. *my M. labours,* Oth. II, 1, 128.

Muse, vb. 1) to give one's self up to thought, particularly of a painful nature: *why m. you?* Gent. II, 1, 176. *I will m. no further,* Wiv. V, 5, 253 (I will no longer foster my grudge) *—ing and sighing,* Caes. II, 1, 240. With *of,* = to think, to dream of: *when he hath —d of taking kingdoms in,* Ant. III, 13, 83.

The gerund substantively: *made with —ing weak,* Gent. I, 1, 69. *given to allicholy and —ing,* Wiv. I, 4, 164. *thick-eyed —ing and cursed melancholy,* H4A II, 3, 49. Plur.: *he should still dwell in his —ings,* H8 III, 2, 133. *drew —ings into my mind,* Per. I, 2, 97.

2) to wonder; with *at: do not m. at me,* Mcb. III, 4, 85. With a clause: *—ing the morning is so much o'erworn,* Ven. 866. *m. not that I thus suddenly proceed,* Gent. I, 3, 64. *rather m. than ask why I entreat you,* All's II, 5, 70. *I m. your majesty doth seem so cold,* John III, 1, 317. *I m. you make so slight a*

question, H4B IV, 1, 167. *I m. we met not with the Dauphin's grace*, H6A II, 2, 19. *I m. my Lord of Gloster is not come*, H6B III, 1, 1. *you m. what chat we two have had*, H6C III, 2, 109. *I m. why she's at liberty*, R3 I, 3, 305 (Qq *wonder*). *I m. my mother does not approve me*, Cor. III, 2, 7.

Trans., = to wonder at: *I cannot too much m. such shapes*, Tp. III, 3, 36.

Muset, see *Musit*.

Mushroom, a plant of the order of Fungi: *to make midnight —s*, Tp. V, 39 (OEdd. *mushrumps*).

Music, 1) the art and science of harmonical sounds: *if m. and sweet poetry agree*, Pilgr. 103. 112. *skilled in m.* Gent. III, 2, 92. Merch. V, 83. Shr. I, 1, 36. I, 2, 134. II, 1, 56. III, 1, 7. 10. Per. II, 5, 30 (fem.). IV Prol. 8 (*trained in —'s letters; cf.* Letter; M. Edd. *in music, letters*).

2) vocal or instrumental harmony: Ven. 432. 1077. Sonn. 8, 1. 102, 11. 128, 1. 130, 10. Pilgr. 68. Phoen. 14. Tp. I, 2, 387. 391. III, 2, 154. III, 3, 19. IV, 178. V, 52. Gent. II, 7, 28. III, 1, 179. IV, 2, 17. 31. 35. 55. 66. 68. 86. Meas. IV, 1, 14. LLL I, 1, 167. Mids. II, 1, 154. IV, 1, 29. 86. 88. 111. V, 40. Merch. III, 2, 43. V, 68. 76. 79. 82. 88. 97. Tw. III, 1, 1. R2 V, 5, 61. H5 V, 2, 263 etc. etc. *give us some m.* As II, 7, 173. Tw. II, 4, 1. Ant. II, 5, 1. Cymb. II, 3, 13. *m. from the spheres*, Tw. III, 1, 121; cf. Merch. V, 60. *broken m.* As I, 2, 150. H5 V, 2, 263. Troil. III, 1, 52 (cf. *Break*). *m. in parts*, Shr. III, 1, 60. Troil. III, 1, 19 (cf. *Part*). Metaphorically: *m. to hear*, Sonn. 8, 1 (i. e. thou whom to hear speak is as delightful as to hear music). *thou, my m.* 128, 1. *never words were m. to thine ear*, Err. II, 2, 116. *it is my father's m. to speak your deeds*, Wint. IV, 4, 529. H6B II, 1, 56. Rom. II, 5, 23. II, 6, 27. Tim. I, 2, 252. Hml. III, 4, 141. Adjectively: *sucked the honey of his m. vows*, Hml. III, 1, 164 (Qq *musickt*).

3) a band of musicians: *wild m. burthens every bough*, Sonn. 102, 11. *play, m., then*, LLL V, 2, 211. *bring your m. forth*, Merch. V, 53. *your m. of the house*, 98. Ado I, 2, 2. V, 3, 11. V, 4, 123. As V, 4, 184. H4B II, 4, 245. H8 IV, 1, 91. IV, 2, 94. Rom. IV, 4, 21. Ant. II, 5, 2. Cymb. II, 3, 12. Per. III, 2, 91. Plur. *—s: every night he comes with —s of all sorts*, All's III, 7, 40. *I have assailed her with —s*, Cymb. II, 3, 44 (M. Edd. *m.*).

Musical, producing harmony, harmonious: *found me here so m.* Meas. IV, 1, 11. *as sweet and m. as bright Apollo's lute*, LLL IV, 3, 342. Mids. IV, 1, 115. 123. As II, 7, 5. H4A III, 1, 237. H5 III, 7, 18.

Musician, one skilled in music, or making music: Gent. IV, 2, 57. Ado II, 3, 36. Merch. V, 106. As IV, 1, 11. Shr. I, 2, 174. II, 145. III, 1, 63. III, 2, 149. IV, 2, 17. R2 I, 3, 288. H4A III, 1, 226. 235. H4B II, 4, 403. H8 IV, 2, 78. Troil. III, 1, 21. Rom. I, 5, 27. IV, 5, 102. 107. 136. 143. Oth. IV, 1, 199.

Musicked (?), musical: *his m. vows*, Hml. III, 1, 164 (Qq *musickt*, Ff *music*).

Musing, subst. see *Muse*, vb.

Musit, a hole for creeping through; "the opening in a fence or thicket through which a hare or other beast of sport is accustomed to pass" (Nares): *the many —s through the which he goes are like a labyrinth to amaze his foes*, Ven. 683.

Musk, an odorous substance: *smelling so sweetly, all m.* Wiv. II, 2, 68.

Musk-cat, emendation of M. Edd. for *muscat* of O. Edd. in All's V, 2, 21.

Musket, a hand-gun: All's III, 2, 111.

Muskos, name in All's IV, 1, 76 (*the M. regiment*).

Musk-rose, a very fragrant rose: Mids. II, 1, 252. II, 2, 3. IV, 1, 3.

Muss, "a scramble, when any small objects are thrown down, to be taken by those who can seize them" (Nares): *when I cried Ho, like boys unto a m., kings would start forth*, Ant. III, 13, 91.

Mussel, see *Muscle*.

Must, the verb expressing a necessity, whether physical, or moral, or fatal, or logical; 1) a physical necessity: *the sun doth burn my face; I m. remove*, Ven. 186. *so m. my soul* (decay), *her bark being peeled away* Lucr. 1169. *through the painter m. you see his skill*, Sonn. 24, 5. *the death-bed whereon it m. expire*, 73, 14. 75, 12. 81, 6. 126, 11. Tp. I, 2, 330. III, 3, 4. Gent. II, 2, 2. II, 4, 188. II, 6, 20 etc. etc. Impf.: *those palates who, not yet two summers younger, m. have inventions to delight the taste, would now be glad of bread*, Per. I, 4, 40.

2) Moral necessity: *affection is a coal that m. be cooled*, Ven. 387. *that posterity which by the rights of time thou needs m. have*, 759. *truth I m. confess*, 1001. 1117. Lucr. 486. 612. 1195. 1799. Sonn. 35, 13. 36, 1. 44, 12. 108, 6. 120, 3. 14. 136, 10. Tp. I, 2, 33. 241. 261. 372. II, 2, 4. Gent. I, 1, 159. I, 3, 75. II, 7, 53. Wiv. III, 4, 96. Meas. II, 2, 48. LLL V, 2, 552. Mids. I, 2, 90. Merch. II, 4, 30. III, 4, 14. IV, 1, 182. 205 etc. etc. *you m. know* = let me tell you, Meas. I, 1, 18. With a negative: *foul words and frowns m. not repel a lover*, Ven. 573. *we m. not be foes*, Son. 40, 14. *I m. ne'er love him whom thou dost hate*, 89, 14. 121, 12. H5 V, 2, 32 etc. *I m. not say so* = far be it from me to say so, R3 III, 1, 106. cf. *I m. not believe you*, Troil. V, 5, 221. *you m. in no way say he is covetous*, Cor. I, 1, 43. *I m. not think there are evils enow to darken all his goodness*, Ant. I, 4, 10.

3) a fatal necessity, one ordained by fate, or imposed by circumstances (often = to be to): *such hazard now m. doting Tarquin make, pawning his honour to obtain his lust, and for himself himself he m. forsake*, Lucr. 155. *whereat a waxen torch forthwith he lighteth, which m. be lodestar to his lustful eye*, 179. *as from this cold flint I enforced this fire, so Lucrece m. I force to my desire*, 182. *m. our mouths be cold?* Tp. I, 1, 56. *he m. fight singly to morrow with Hector*, Troil. III, 3, 247. *a charmed life, which m. not yield to one of woman born*, Mcb. V, 8, 12. Lucr. 348. 383. 385. 512. 513. 618. 703. 795. Sonn. 4, 13. 12, 10. 16, 14. 73, 11. 133, 4. Merch. II, 6, 40. R2 I, 1, 51 etc. etc. Impf.: *and I m. be from thence!* Mcb. IV, 3, 212.

4) a logical necessity: *then m. the love be great 'twixt thee and me, because thou lovest the one, and I the other*, Pilgr. 105. *it m. needs be of subtle, tender and delicate temperance*, Tp. II, 1, 41. *the story of your life, which m. take the ear strangely*, V, 312. Meas. II, 4, 30. V, 123. Mids. III, 2, 119. Merch. III, 4, 18 etc.

The verbs *to go, to get* or the like, omitted after it: *I m. after*, Gent. II, 4, 176. *I m. unto the road*, 187. *now m. we to her window*, IV, 2, 16. *I m. of another errand to Sir John Falstaff*, Wiv. III, 4, 113. *he m. before the deputy*, Meas. III, 2, 35. *thither I m.*

Err. IV, 1, 112. *I m. now to Oberon*, Mids. II, 2, 83. *I m. to the barber's*, IV, 1, 25. *I m. to Lorenzo*, Merch. II, 2, 114. *I m. away*, IV, 1, 403. *thus m. I from the smoke into the smother*, As I, 2, 299. *I m. away to-day*, Shr. III, 2, 192. *she m. with me*, 229. *thither m. I*, V, 1, 11. *we m. to horse again*, All's V, 1, 37. *we m. to the king*, Wint. IV, 4, 848. *m. I back*, John V, 2, 95. *I m. to Coventry*, R2 I, 2, 56. *you m. to the court*, H4A II, 4, 368. *we m. away all night*, IV, 2, 63. *we m. hence*, H4B II, 4, 397. *a' m. to the inns of court*, III, 2, 14. *I m. hence again*, H6B IV, 5, 13. *Edward needs m. down*, H6C IV, 3, 42. *King Edward's friends m. down*, IV, 4, 28. *I m. away*, R3 I, 4, 289 (Ff *will*). *I m. to bed*, H8 IV, 2, 166. *I m. to him*, V, 1, 8. *thou m. to thy father*, Troil. IV, 2, 97. *I m. then to the Grecians?* IV, 4, 57. *I m. to the learned*, Rom. I, 2, 45. *we m. out and talk*, Caes. V, 1, 22. *I m. to England*, Hml. III, 4, 200. *truth's a dog m. to kennel*, Lr. I, 4, 124. *I m. needs after him*, IV, 5, 15. *we m. to the watch*, Oth. II, 3, 12. *you m. to Parthia*, Ant. II, 3, 41. *to prepare this body, like to them, to what I m.* Per. I, 1, 44.

Mustachio, hair on the lip: *to lean upon my poor shoulder and dally with my m.* LLL V, 1, 110.

Mustachio-purple-hued, having red mustaches: *these mad m. malt-worms*, H4A II, 1, 83 (most M. Edd. *mustachio purple-hued*).

Mustard, the seed of Sinapis nigra, used to season meat: As I, 2, 68. 70. 85. Shr. IV, 3, 23. 25. 26. *his wit's as thick as Tewksbury m.* H4B II, 4, 262.

Mustard-seed, name of a fairy: Mids. III, 1, 165. 195. 196. 201. IV, 1, 18. 20.

Muster, subst. 1) a review of troops under arms: *let us take a m. speedily*, H4A IV, 1, 133.

2) a levy of troops: *make fearful —s and prepared defence*, H4B Ind. 12. *defences, —s, preparations should be maintained*, H5 II, 4, 18. *hasten his —s and conduct his powers*, Lr. IV, 2, 16.

3) troops under arms: *our present —s grow upon the file to five and twenty thousand men*, H4B I, 3, 10. *the m. of his kingdom too faint a number*, H5 III, 6, 139. *his eyes, that o'er the files and —s of the war have glowed like plated Mars*, Ant. I, 1, 3.

Muster, vb. 1) trans. to collect, to assemble (troops): Lucr. 773. LLL V, 2, 85. R2 II, 2, 108. III, 3, 86. H6A I, 1, 101. H6C II, 1, 112. R3 IV, 3, 56. IV, 4, 496. Cor. IV, 5, 134. Cymb. IV, 2, 344. IV, 4, 10 (*not —ed among the bands*, i. e. not entered on the muster-roll). With *up:* R2 II, 2, 118. H6C IV, 8, 11. 18. R3 IV, 4, 489. Dubious passage: *they wear themselves in the cap of the time, there do m. true gait*, All's II, 1, 55 (some M. Edd. *master*).

2) intr. to assemble (as troops): *is this Moorfields to m. in?* H8 V, 4, 33. With *to*, = to repair as to a meeting-place: *they, —ing to the quiet cabinet*, Lucr. 442. *to whose weak ruins m. troops of cares*, 720. *why does my blood thus m. to my heart?* Meas. II, 4, 20. *the commoners ... m. to their captain, the heart*, H4B IV, 3, 120.

Muster-book, a book in which the forces are registered: H4B III, 2, 146.

Muster-file, a register of forces: All's IV, 3, 189.

Musty, mouldy, stale: Ado I, 1, 50. I, 3, 61. Cor. I, 1, 230. V, 1, 26. Rom. V, 1, 46. Hml. III, 2, 359. Lr. IV, 7, 40.

Mutability, changeableness, inconstancy: Cymb. II, 5, 26. Used for *mutable* by Fluellen: H5 III, 6, 36.

Mutable, inconstant: *the m. rank-scented many*, Cor. III, 1, 66.

Mutation, change (as an effect of inconstancy): *O world! but that thy strange —s make us hate thee*, Lr. IV, 1, 11. *his humour was nothing but m., ay, and that from one bad thing to worse*, Cymb. IV, 2, 133.

Mute, adj. dumb, silent, not speaking: Ven. 208. 335. Lucr. 227. Sonn. 83, 11. 97, 12. Tp. IV, 126. LLL V, 2, 277. Shr. II, 175. All's II, 3, 83. Wint. I, 2, 271. H5 I, 1, 49. Tit. V, 3, 184. Cymb. I, 6, 116 (superl. *—st*). Per. IV Prol. 26. *m. and dumb:* Lucr. 1123. R3 IV, 4, 18 (Ff *still and m.*). Hml. II, 2, 137.

Mute, subst. one that is silent; a dumb spectator: *are but —s or audience to this act*, Hml. V, 2, 346. In Turkey a dumb officer acting as executioner: *be you his eunuch, and your m. I'll be: when my tongue blabs, then let mine eyes not see*, Tw. I, 2, 62. *or else our grave, like Turkish m., shall have a tongueless mouth*, H5 I, 2, 232. *that thou wilt be a voluntary m. to my design*, Cymb. III, 5, 158.

Mutine, subst. a rebel: *do like the —s of Jerusalem*, John II, 378 (like the factions in Jerusalem combining their strength against the Romans). *I lay worse than the —s in the bilboes*, Hml. V, 2, 6.

Mutine, vb. to rebel: *if thou canst m. in a matron's bones*, Hml. III, 4, 83.

Mutineer, rebel: Tp. III, 2, 40.

Mutiner, the same: Cor. I, 1, 254.

Mutinous, rebellious: Tp. V, 42. H6C II, 5, 90. IV, 8, 10. Cor. I, 1, 115. 153. I, 2, 11. V, 3, 59.

Mutiny, subst. 1) rebellion, insurrection: Ven. 1049. R2 IV, 142. H6A I, 1, 160. V, 1, 62. H6B III, 2, 128. H6C I, 4, 77. Troil. I, 3, 96. Cor. III, 1, 126. Tit. IV, 1, 85. Caes. III, 1, 86. III, 2, 127. 215. Lr. I, 2, 116. Oth. II, 3, 157. Per. III Prol. 29.

2) discord, strife, contention: *gives false alarms, suggesteth m.* Ven. 651. *his eye, which late this m. restrains, unto a greater uproar tempts his veins*, Lucr. 426. *with herself she is in m.* 1153. *whom right and wrong have chose as umpire of their m.* LLL I, 1, 170. *to raise a m. betwixt yourselves*, H6A IV, 1, 131. *there is a m. in's mind*, H8 III, 2, 120. *this m. were better put in hazard*, Cor. II, 3, 264. *from ancient grudge break to new m.* Rom. I Chor. 3. *you'll make a m. among my guests*, I, 5, 82.

Mutiny, vb. 1) to rebel: As I, 1, 24. R3 I, 4, 142. Caes. III, 2, 234. 235.

2) to be at odds, to fall out, to quarrel: *all too late comes counsel to be heard, where will doth m. with wit's regard*, R2 II, 1, 28. *out of that will I cause these of Cyprus to m.* Oth. II, 1, 282. *my very hairs do m., for the white reprove the brown for rashness, and they them for fear and doting*, Ant. III, 11, 13.

Mutius, name in Tit. I, 348. 363 etc.

Mutter, to utter with a low voice or with imperfect articulation: *what m. you?* H4A II, 4, 148. *amongst the soldiers this is —ed*, H6A I, 1, 70. *what m. you, or what conspire you, lords?* H6C I, 1, 165. *what does his cashiered worship m.?* Tim. III, 4, 61. *or stand so —ing on*, Oth. III, 3, 70 (reading of Q1; the rest of O. Edd. *mammering*). *there are a kind of men so loose of soul, that in their sleeps will m. their affairs*, 417.

Mutton, 1) a sheep: Gent. I, 1, 101. 106. Merch. I, 3, 168. As III, 2, 57.

2) the flesh of sheep dressed for food: LLL I, 1,

304. Shr. IV, 1, 163. Tw. I, 3, 130. H4B II, 4, 376. V, 1, 28.

2) woman's flesh: *the duke would eat m. on Fridays*, Meas. III, 2, 192; cf. H4B II, 4, 376. See *Laced mutton.*

Mutual, 1) taking place on both sides, pertaining to each of two (Germ. *beiderseitig*): *mark how one string, sweet husband to another, strikes each in each by m. ordering*, Sonn. 8, 10. *but m. render, only me for thee*, 125, 12. *confirmed by m. joinder of your hands*, Tw. V, 160. *there is division, although as yet the face of it be covered with m. cunning*, Lr. III, 1, 21. *when such a m. pair and such a twain can do't*, Ant. I, 1, 37.

2) intimate, cordial: *the stealth of our most m. entertainment*, Meas. I, 2, 158. *the m. conference that my mind hath had, by day, by night, waking and in my dreams, with you, my alderliefest sovereign*, H6B I, 1, 25.

3) common: *till m. overthrow of mortal kind*, Ven. 1018. *Phoenix and the turtle fled in a m. flame from hence*, Phoen. 24. *one feast, one house, one m. happiness*, Gent. V, 4, 173. *the skies, the fountains, every region near seemed all one m. cry*, Mids. IV, 1, 122. *you shall perceive them make a m. stand*, Merch. V, 77. *in m. well-beseeming ranks*, H4A I, 1, 14.* *that bear this m. heavy load of moan*, R3 II, 2, 113. *choice, being m. act of all our souls*, Troil. I, 3, 348. *to knit again this scattered corn into one m. sheaf*, Tit. V, 3, 71. *make a m. closure of our house*, 134.

Mutuality, intimacy, familiarity: *when these — es so marshal the way, hard at hand comes the master and main exercise, the incorporate conclusion*, Oth. II, 1, 267.

Mutually, 1) on both sides: *your most offenceful act was m. committed*, Meas. II, 3, 27.

2) in return: *who m. hath answered my affection*, Wiv. IV, 6, 10.

3) in common, all together: *pinch him, fairies, m.* Wiv. V, 5, 103. *the other instruments did see and hear, devise, instruct, walk, feel, and, m. participate, did minister unto the appetite*, Cor. I, 1, 106.

Muzzle, subst. a fastening for the mouth, which hinders from biting: Ado I, 3, 34. H4B IV, 5, 132.

Muzzle, vb. to restrain from biting by binding the mouth: Wint. I, 2, 156. John II, 249. H8 I, 1, 121.

My, poss. pron. of the first pers. sing.: Ven. 101. 105. 108. 112. 115. 139 etc. etc. Before vowels, 1) without emphasis: *answered my affection*, Wiv. IV, 6, 10. *this is the period of my ambition*, III, 3, 47. *my ancient skill beguiles me*, Meas. IV, 2, 164. *over my altars hath he hung his lance*, Ven. 103. *making my arms his field*, 108. *lie there, my art*, Tp. I, 2, 25. *my authority bears of a credent bulk*, Meas. IV, 4, 29. *gazed for tidings in my eager eyes*, Lucr. 254. *my expense*, Wiv. III, 4, 5. *show no colour for my extremity*, IV, 2, 169. *from the tempest of my eyes*, Mids. I, 1, 131 (Ff *mine*). *your kindred hath made my eyes water*, III, 1, 200. *to follow me and praise my eyes and face*, III, 2, 223. *go to my inn*, Err. I, 2, 23. *conceit, my comfort and my injury*, IV, 2, 66. *to feed my innocent people*, Tp. II, 1, 164. *I often did behold in thy sweet semblance my old age new born*, Lucr. 1759. *my old bones ache*, Tp. III, 3, 2. *that power which gave me first my oath*, Gent. II, 6, 4. *members of my occupation*, Meas. IV, 2, 40. *how, with my honour, I may

undertake*, Gent. II, 7, 6. *and, by my honour, depart untouched*, Caes. III, 1, 141. *I cannot put off my opinion*, Wiv. II, 1, 243. *my uncle can tell you*, III, 4, 38. 66. *measure my strangeness with my unripe years*, Ven. 524. *my untimely death*, Lucr. 1178. *remove your siege from my unyielding heart*, Ven. 423 etc. etc. 2) Emphatically: *I will not poison thee with my attaint*, Lucr. 1072. *they that level at my abuses reckon up their own*, Sonn. 121, 10. *the Percies, finding his usurpation most unjust, endeavoured my advancement to the throne*, H6A II, 5, 69. *my ear should catch your voice, my eye your eye*, Mids. I, 1, 188. *my eyes are oftener washed than hers*, II, 2, 93. *from thy cheeks my image thou hast torn*, Lucr. 1762. *his mother was a votaress of my order*, Mids. II, 1, 123 etc. Or expressing tenderness: *my Ariel*, Tp. I, 2, 188. III, 3, 84. IV, 1, 57. V, 316. *my eyas-musket*, Wiv. III, 3, 22. *O, my old master*, Err. V, 338. *my Oberon*, Mids. IV, 1, 81. *O my Antonio*, Merch. I, 1, 173. *my Icarus*, H6A IV, 7, 16 (cf. *my Lucio*, Meas. I, 2, 129).

Before *own*: Gent. IV, 2, 4. Err. V, 90. Mids. III, 2, 243 etc.

Superfluous: *I am one that am nourished by my victuals*, Gent. II, 1, 180. *if my gossip Report be an honest woman of her word*, Merch. III, 1, 7. *I am past my gamut long ago*, Shr. III, 1, 71. *my hostess of the tavern*, H4A I, 2, 45. 54. *as full of quarrel as my young mistress' dog*, Oth. II, 3, 53.

Transposed: *dear my liege*, R2 I, 1, 184. *dear my lord*, Ado IV, 1, 46. Caes. II, 1, 255. Hml. III, 3, 35. Ant. IV, 15, 22. *dear my brother*, Wint. V, 3, 53. *dear my sweet*, Tw. II, 5, 191. *dread my lord*, Hml. I, 2, 50 (Qq *my dread lord*). *gentle my lord*, Wint. II, 1, 98. Mcb. III, 2, 27. *good my brother*, Troil. IV, 3, 3. Hml. I, 3, 46. *good my complexion*, As III, 2, 204. *good my fellows*, Ant. IV, 14, 135. *good my friend*, Rom. V, 3, 124. *good my friends*, Cor. V, 2, 8. *good my girl*, H6A V, 4, 25. *good my glass*, LLL IV, 1, 18. *good my knave*, III, 153. *good my liege*, IV, 3, 152. As I, 3, 66. Cymb. IV, 3, 16. 28. *good my lord*, Ado II, 3, 46. As V, 4, 40. H6C II, 2, 75. Ant. III, 6, 55. *good my lords*, Wint. II, 3, 27. H6A IV, 1, 133. *good my mother*, John I, 249. II, 163. *good my mouse of virtue*, Tw. I, 5, 69. *gracious my lord*, Wint. IV, 4, 477. Mcb. V, 5, 30. Lr. III, 2, 61. *kind my lord*, Tim. I, 2, 177. *sweet my child*, LLL I, 2, 71. *sweet my coz*, As I, 2, 1. *sweet my mother*, Rom. III, 5, 200.

Myrmidon, one of the people of Achilles: *the great M.* (Achilles) Troil. I, 3, 378. Plur. *—s:* Tw. II, 3, 29 (O. Edd. *Mermidons*). Troil. V, 5, 33. V, 7, 1. V, 8, 13.

Myrtle, the tree Myrtus communis: Ven. 865. Pilgr. 144. 364. 376. Meas. II, 2, 117. *m. leaf*, Ant. III, 12, 9.

Myself (in two words in O. Edd.) 1) the same as I, another I: *Silvia is m.* Gent. III, 1, 172. *I would have daffed all other respects and made her half m.* Ado II, 3, 177 (i. e. my wife).

2) my own person, I or me in my own person; marking emphatically the distinction between the speaker and others: Tp. I, 1, 22. I, 2, 434. III, 3, 5. V, 22. 151. Gent. I, 1, 65. II, 3, 25. II, 4, 62. 64. II, 6, 20. 22. 23. III, 1, 12. 24. 147. 148. 171. IV, 1, 47. Meas. I, 4, 27. Err. I, 1, 70. As III, 2, 269. H4A I, 3, 157. R3 I, 2, 259. V, 3, 185. 186. 188. 190 etc. etc. Used as a subst.

and followed by the third person of the verb: *my self bewails good Gloster's case*, H6B III, 1, 217. *myself hath often overheard them say*, Tit. IV, 4, 74. *for praising myself, who ... is praiseworthy*, Ado V, 2, 89. With *I* (perhaps seldomer than without it): Tp. II, 1, 265. Gent. III, 1, 268. R3 V, 3, 188. Mcb. I, 3, 14 etc.

3) Refl. pron. of the first person: Tp. II, 1, 202. II, 2, 157. 158. V, 85. 144. Gent. IV, 2, 103 etc. etc.

Mystery, 1) a secret, any thing not easily comprehended: *to thy great comfort in this m. of ill opinions*, Wiv. II, 1, 73. *now I see the m. of your loneliness*, All's I, 3, 177. *Plutus ... hath not in nature's —es more science*, V, 3, 103. *this m. remained undiscovered*, Wint. V, 2, 130. *there is a m. in the soul of state*, Troil. III, 3, 201. *those —es which heaven will not have earth to know*, Cor. IV, 2, 35. *you would pluck out the heart of my m.* Hml. III, 2, 382. *take upon's the m. of things*, Lr. V, 3, 16. *—es* = mysterious rites: *the —es of Hecate*, Lr. I, 1, 112. Jocularly used of strange and incomprehensible fashions: *the spells of France should juggle men into such strange —es*, H8 I, 3, 2.

2) calling, trade, profession: *he will discredit our m.* Meas. IV, 2, 30. *do you call your occupation a m.?* 36. 37. *painting is a m.* 39. 41. 44. *instruction, manners, —es and trades*, Tim. IV, 1, 18. *not to have us (thieves) thrive in our m.* IV, 3, 458. *your m. (as a bawd)!* Oth. IV, 2, 30.

3) professional skill: *if you think your m. in stratagem can bring this instrument of honour again into his native quarter*, All's III, 6, 68.

Mytilene (some M. Edd. *Mitylene*) name of a town (in the island of Lesbos?): Per. IV, 2, 3. V, 1, 3 etc.